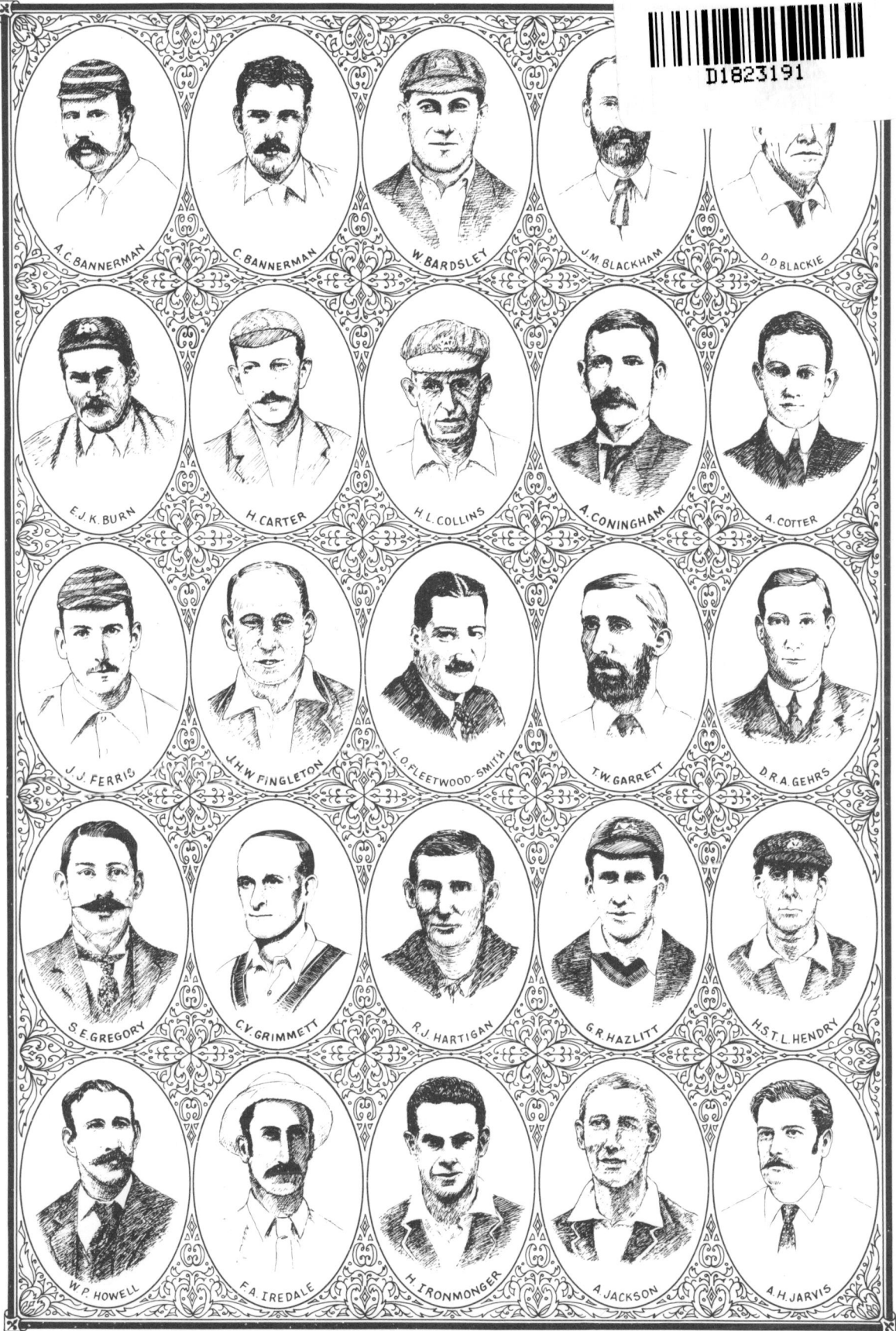

FIRST-CLASS

CRICKET

IN

AUSTRALIA

This edition is limited to 1500 numbered copies of which this is

No. 835

AWebster

FIRST-CLASS

CRICKET

IN

AUSTRALIA

VOL 1

1850-51 to 1941-42

Compiled by

RAY WEBSTER

EDITED BY
ALLAN MILLER

Published in 1991 by Ray Webster,
31 Driftwood Drive, Glen Waverley, Victoria 3150

National Library of Australia

Cataloguing-in-Publication Data

First-Class Cricket in Australia. Volume One, 1850-51 to 1941-42.

Includes index.
ISBN 0 7316 8570 9.
ISBN 0 7316 7453 7 (set).

1. Cricket - Australia - Records. I. Webster, Ray.
II. Miller, Allan, 1967-

796.35'8'09940-21

Typeset by Cricket Stats Publications ®

Endpapers by Vicki Foley.

Printed and bound in Australia by Globe Press, Melbourne.

INTRODUCTION

There has long been a need for a primary reference source providing accurate scorecards of all Australian first-class cricket matches. The major aim of this work is to fill that need. It is not necessarily intended to be a definitive history, although match reports and seasonal summaries are designed to put the scores themselves into an historical context.

Exhaustive attempts have been made to ensure the completeness and accuracy of all scores. Unfortunately, very few original scorebooks survive for the period covered in this first volume. Research has focused on contemporary publications and newspapers in an attempt to eliminate any errors which may have appeared in more recent publications. The names of all sources consulted are noted in the summary for each match, together with suggested corrections to errors which appear in the various publications.

An important example of repetitive error can be seen in the score for the Test match played at Sydney on February 10, 1888. The final dismissal in the match, that of Ferris, has been credited to Peel in *Wisden* and in all subsequent publications down the years. The scorebook and contemporary newspapers reveal, however, that Attewell was the successful bowler. Accepted career records, which have credited Peel with 102 wickets and Attewell with 27 wickets, now require amendment.

Matches included in this volume are in accord with the list of first-class games drawn up by the Association of Cricket Statisticians and published in November 1983. No doubt the status of some games will continue to be the subject of debate. However, the reasoning of the ACS in their consideration of doubtful matches is soundly based and it is most important that all statisticians work from a common base.

The matches have been numbered chronologically for ease of identification, with a secondary coding to denote the number of games between the participants, e.g. AFCM 37/22 indicates that it is the 37th Australian first-class match as well as the 22nd between the two teams. Sheffield Shield matches (SSM) are similarly coded in addition to the above. Tour matches (TM) indicate the match number in the visiting team's overall progress, followed by the total of first-class games within that number. Test Matches have been numbered as in The Wisden Book of Test Cricket for purposes of consistency.

It has not been possible to complete the scores for one or two matches from the sources available, and it could well prove that the passing of time will prevent their completion. Some minor details are lacking for other matches, and any suggestions or assistance forthcoming which would help complete them, would be greatly appreciated and acknowledged in future volumes in this series.

The authors have endeavoured to maintain a consistent style with regard to the treatment of players' names, which are listed in the index to this volume. Wherever possible, players are listed by their officially registered birth names, barring circumstances of religious changes or amendments made by deed poll. Whimsical spellings, adoptions of additional names and reversals in the order of initials which have been undertaken by players themselves, have not been followed. Hence, 'R.G.Beattie', 'A.A.Jackson', 'P.G.McShane' and 'E.R.Mayne' are listed in this volume under their given birth names, R.G.Beatty, A.Jackson, F.G.McShane and R.E.Mayne, and so on. Where a doubt exists as to the accuracy of the details given, the symbol '§' appears beside the player's name.

ACKNOWLEDGEMENTS

The following people have made invaluable contributions to the work:

Ric Finlay (Tasmania), Alf James (New South Wales), Bill Reynolds (Western Australia), Geoff Sando (South Australia) and Warwick Torrens (Queensland) are authorities in their respective States and have willingly given of their time in answering interminable queries over a period of several years. All are fellow members of the Association of Cricket Statisticians and their assistance is gratefully acknowledged. Charlie Bull (WACA honarary statistician) kindly provided copies of surviving WA scorebooks.

Rex Harcourt and Cliff Winning, custodians of the collections held by the Melbourne Cricket Club and New South Wales Cricket Association libraries respectively, gave authority to access invaluable source material such as original scorebooks and scrap-books. The assistance of Stephen Gibbs at the N.S.W.C.A. Library is also gratefully acknowledged.

Roger Page gave unlimited access to his own extensive library and has been a great source of encouragement. Lee Semmens and Ken Williams have freely rendered general assistance and advice throughout. Chris Harte supplied much invaluable information in respect of attendances at South Australian home matches. Philip Bailey, editor of *The Cricket Statistician*, journal of the Association of Cricket Statisticians, has given his support to the project and also willingly assisted where possible. A.C.S. publications in respect of Australian first-class cricket have been used as the base for determination of matches for inclusion. Vicki Foley has designed and drawn the portraits for the endpapers as well as other general design work. The co-operation of staff in the newspaper section of Melbourne's Latrobe Library in tolerating the presence of the compiler on virtually every Sunday over a period of several years is also acknowledged.

Finally, Charlie Wat generously undertook the entire typesetting of this book following the loss of 960 of the original pages in a fire at the editor's house in June 1990 - a painstaking task done quickly and cheerfully, for which we are indeed grateful. His general knowledge of the subject and advice has also been invaluable.

Ray Webster
Allan Miller
August 1991.

The laws of cricket underwent considerable change during the years covered. It may be of assistance if some of the changes relating to both laws and playing conditions are noted - particularly the differences between Marylebone Cricket Club and Australian interpretation.

THE OVER: The laws originally provided for the bowling of four balls to the over. The bowler was also permitted to change ends only twice during an innings. To achieve this, he was allowed to bowl *consecutive* overs, but no more than two in succession. A trial was conducted in England in 1862 with five balls to the over but this was not brought into being until 1889. The bowling of consecutive overs was also outlawed in 1889, and a bowler was permitted to change ends as often as he wished. In 1900 MCC amended the over to six balls.

The position in Australia has been as follows:

1850-51 to 1888-89:	4 balls, except	Victoria v Tasmania 1870-71 (6 balls)
		Tasmania v Victoria 1872-73 (6 balls)
		South Australia v Tasmania 1877-78 (6 balls)
		South Australia v Victoria 1883-84 (6 balls)
		Victoria v New South Wales 1887-88 (6 balls)
		South Australia v Victoria 1887-88 (6 balls)
		Victoria v South Australia 1888-89 (6 balls)
		Victoria v Tasmania 1888-89 (6 balls)
		New South Wales v Victoria 1888-89 (6 balls)
		Australia v The Rest 1888-89 (6 balls)
1889-90 to 1914-15:	6 balls, except	New South Wales v Lord Sheffield's XI 1891-92 (both games) (5 balls)
		New South Wales v Tasmania 1898-99 (5 balls)
		Tasmania v Victoria 1898-99 (5 balls)
1918-19 to 1941-42:	8 balls, except	All 13 MCC/England matches 1920-21 (6 balls)
		Victoria v MCC 1928-29 (2nd game) (6 balls)
		All 20 Tests played from 1928-29 to 1932-33 inclusive (6 balls)

DURATION OF MATCHES: The term 'timeless' has been used in this work to designate matches where the teams intended to play until a result was achieved. This was generally the case in Australia prior to 1927-28, when time restrictions were first brought into the Sheffield Shield competition. Test matches continued to be played out up until the Second World War, from which point they too were restricted. Those matches prior to 1927 which were set to strict time limits were usually done so because of travel arrangements or employment commitments, though in the years leading up to the late 1920s this continued to be less and less the case as the notion of limiting matches won wider favour.

From 1927-28, Sheffield Shield games were restricted to four days (11.30am to 6.00pm) and a portion of a fifth (11.00am to 1.30pm). The part-fifth day was abolished after the 1929-30 season and four-day matches were introduced for the first time. Many important matches in the period covered by this volume used times of play, 12 noon to 1.30pm, 2.15pm to 4.00pm and 4.15pm to 6.00pm on a regular basis.

It is interesting to note that many of the earliest first-class matches in Australia were conducted almost on a 'day to day basis', with the teams reaching agreement on such factors as hours of play and intervals as the game progressed. Advertised starting times were rarely adhered to. As the matches became more organised and steeped in tradition, so the conditions became more regimented.

DECLARATIONS: Provision was first made in the laws in 1889 but, due to matches generally being played out in Australia, declarations were rare until the restriction of Sheffield Shield matches in 1927-28, when an innings could be terminated at any time after the end of the second day's play. This was amended to 'after the end of the first day's play' from 1928-29 until 1954-55, when it became permissible to declare at any time.

In times when matches were generally played to a finish, many Australians considered declarations to be in fact unlawful - a reaction which P.F.Warner encountered first-hand when he closed the MCC innings against South Australia in the opening match of England's 1903-04 tour.

FOLLOW-ON: Australian cricket adhered to the law as laid down by Marylebone Cricket Club until 1897. From inception of Australian first-class cricket until 1854, this provided that the team batting second would immediately bat again if they were 100 runs or more in arrears. The situation did not arise in the three matches in the period covered. In 1854 the follow-on margin was reduced to 80 runs. It was amended again in 1894 to 120 runs. These developments were followed in Australia (although an experimental ruling which declined the right to follow-on was tried in 1893-94 but then discarded). However, an incident in the match between Victoria and South Australia at Melbourne in 1896-97, in which runs were deliberately conceded in order to avoid the follow-on, led Australian authorities to depart from MCC policy and increase the follow-on requirement (which remained compulsory) from 120 to 200 runs. The margin was modified to 150 runs for Stoddart's 1897-98 tour, but 200 was restored from 1898-99 until 1927-28, when it again reverted to 150 runs. Exceptions occured in matches which were laid down for three days or less, 150 runs usually being the follow-on figure in these.

MCC amended the law in 1900 to make the follow-on optional for the team leading by the required number of runs. However, it remained compulsory in Australia until probably the commencement of the 1907-08 season.

PITCHES: The law relating to pitches when Australian first-class cricket began in 1851 allowed for a new pitch to be used during a match if rain had fallen and both captains consented to the change. Until the 1880s, however, there seems to have been a number of instances where pitches were routinely changed during matches for no apparent reason. Although no precise documentation has been located it appears that, generally, matches played in Melbourne were always conducted on the same pitch, whereas those in Sydney frequently utilised two or more pitches - sometimes a fresh one for each of the four innings. Very few instances of multiple-pitch use have been located in other States, and the practice appears to have died out as preparation techniques improved.

Prior to 1934-35, the practice of covering pitches for protection from rain was left to the discretion of the local home association. Full covering of pitches, both overnight and during playing hours in the event of rain, was observed in all States for domestic matches from 1934-35.

TAKING OF THE NEW BALL: Until 1907, the law allowed either side the right to demand a new ball at the beginning of each innings. On June 20, 1907, MCC approved an amendment allowing a new ball to be taken after 200 runs had been scored with the old ball. This was not an amendment to the law as such, but was included under 'Instructions to Umpires' at the end of the laws of cricket. (It was not until 1947 that this provision was incorporated into the law relating to balls.) The English amendments above are believed to have been closely followed in Australia.

MISSING MATCH DETAILS

Although exhaustive attempts have been made to obtain complete scorecards for all matches in this work, some basic details have defied location. The following is a listing of the data that remains outstanding and the compiler would be most interested to hear from any reader who may be able to advise of the location of such data.

AFCM No.

1	Fall of some wickets, bowlers of all maidens.
2	Fall of some wickets, bowlers of all maidens.
3	Fall of all wickets, bowlers of all maidens.
4	Fall of all second innings wickets.
7	Fall of all wickets.
8	Fall of some wickets; overs bowled in Tas (2).
40	Bowler (or bowlers) of 3 no balls in NSW (1).
104	Fall of some wickets.
205	Breakdown of extras in all innings except Tas (1).
234	Breakdown of extras in both Qld innings.
236	Breakdown of extras in all innings.
242	Breakdown of extras in all innings.
259	Breakdown of extras in all innings.
309	Breakdown of extras in all innings.
362	Breakdown of extras in all innings.
369	Fall of some wickets.
385	Identity of all umpires.
497	Fall of second wicket in SA (1).
584	Identity of both umpires.

BIBLIOGRAPHY

Reference was made to the following primary sources:

16 Unpublished Australian Scores (Association of Cricket Statisticians).
Australian Cricket Annual (Ed: J.C.Davis) 1896, 1897, 1898.
Australian Cricket Record (Ed: J.Fitzpatrick) 1895.
Australian Cricket - A Weekly Record 1896-97.
Australian Cricketer 1930-31 to 1933-34.
Australian Cricketer's Guide (Ed: W.Fairfax) 1857, 1858, 1859.
Boyle & Scott's Australian Cricketer's Guide 1881, 1882, 1883, 1884.
Brisbane Cricketer 1892-93.
Cricket: A Weekly Record of the Game (various issues).
Cricket Quarterly (Ed. Rowland Bowen) Volume IV.
Cricket Scores & Biographies (Arthur Haygarth) - various volumes.
Guide to First Class Cricket Matches Played in Australia - Second Edition (Association of Cricket Statisticians).
History of South African Cricket (M.W.Luckin).
New South Wales Cricket Association Annual Reports (later Year Books) - various.
New Zealand Cricket (T.W.Reese) Volumes 1 and 2.
Queensland Cricketer 1893-94.
Queensland Cricket Association Annual Reports - various.
Sands & Kenny's Cricketer's Guide 1859 and 1861.
South Australian Cricket 1880 to 1930 (C.B.O'Reilly).
South Australian Cricket Association Annual Reports (later Year Books) - various.
Tasmanian Cricket Association (previously S.T.C.A.) Annual Reports - various.
The Cricketer (various issues).
Victorian Cricket Association Annual Reports - various.
Western Australian Cricket Association Annual Reports - various.
Who's Who of Cricketers (P.Bailey, P.Thorn & P.Wynne-Thomas).
Wisden Cricketers' Almanack - various editions.

Reference was also made to the note-books of R.H.Campbell, eminent Australian statistician between the two World Wars, held by Melbourne's Latrobe Library.

Extensive use was made of various editions of the following newspapers:

New South Wales - Bell's Life in Sydney, Daily Telegraph, Newcastle Herald, Sydney Mail, Sydney Morning Herald, Sydney Sun, The Referee, Town & Country Journal.

Queensland - Brisbane Courier, Daily Mail (later combined as The Courier-Mail), Daily Telegraph, Darling Downs Gazette, Maryborough Chronicle, Queensland Times, The Queenslander.

South Australia - Adelaide Advertiser, Adelaide Daily Herald, Adelaide Observer, South Australian Chronicle, South Australian Register, The News.

Tasmania - Cornwall Chronicle, Daily Telegraph, Hobart Mercury, Tasmanian Daily News, The Examiner, Weekly Courier.

Victoria - Ballarat Courier, Bell's Life in Victoria, Bendigo Advertiser, Geelong Advertiser, Sporting Globe, Sun News-Pictorial, The Age, The Argus, The Australasian, The Herald, The Leader, The Sportsman, Weekly Times.

Western Australia - Daily News, West Australian, Western Mail.

1850-51 to 1860-61 - THE BEGINNINGS (11 MATCHES)

First-Class Cricket in Australia began through a challenge issued by Melbourne Cricket Club to Launceston Cricket Club in March 1850. This challenge, which specified that representative teams be drawn from the colonies of Port Phillip (Victoria) and Van Diemen's Land (Tasmania), was accepted by Launceston, however their reply, indicating their eagerness to play and requesting that the match be staged in Launceston the very next month, failed to reach Melbourne in time for the match to take place in the 1849-50 season. In the event, the challenge was renewed, accepted, and arrangements completed by February 1851. The Victorians sailed across Bass Strait in *SS Shamrock* to be met by a lavish quayside reception, the local racecourse was selected as the match venue, and the home team took out a close contest by three wickets.

This inaugural match captured the imagination of the colonies, and negotiations immediately commenced for a return match in Melbourne the following year. This time the Victorians emerged winners, so a decider (or 'Conqueror') was played in Launceston in March 1854. The home side again won, Tasmania taking the series 2-1. Launceston attempted to arrange a further match the following year, but Melbourne declined, deciding instead to broaden the field of play by issuing a challenge to 'all comers'. This resulted in an acceptance from Sydney, in the process beginning the series between Victoria and New South Wales. Matches between Victoria and Tasmania did not resume again until 1858, and then only upon the initiative of Launceston. They quickly declined in importance.

The first Victoria-New South Wales match was played at the newly formed Melbourne Cricket Ground in March 1856. The new series soon grew to represent the ultimate in Australian domestic cricket. The rapid growth of the mainland colonies in the 1850s because of the gold rush saw to that. And, realising there was a need to arrange and control intercolonial matches properly, club secretaries in Sydney held a meeting on May 3, 1859 which led to the formation of the New South Wales Cricket Association later that year.

The cricket of the 1850s was a crude, barely recognisable version of the modern first-class game. There was no true overarm bowling, no all-white uniforms, scant protective equipment for players, and little preparation of pitch and outfield prior to the start of each match. Instead, underarm bowling was the norm in Tasmania and New South Wales (though Victoria boasted exclusively roundarm bowlers from the start of these games) and teams played in coloured uniforms; often blue or red silk shirts, with wicket-keepers being distinguished by additional colours. Pads (the only form of protection) were not always worn by batsmen, and keepers sometimes did their work bare-handed. In the inaugural Victoria-New South Wales match, fielders even discarded their footwear and patrolled the dusty, uneven outfield in their socks. It was commonplace for a level piece of turf to be selected to 'pitch the wickets' only after the players had assembled for the match. Hours of play were informal and games began unpunctually. Bowlers dominated, and in the 11 first-class matches in this decade, no batsman exceeded a score of 49 in an innings.

Despite these difficult-to-imagine features, the matches were keenly fought contests between reasonably representative teams. Unfailingly, they aroused great interest and intercolonial rivalry, and were treated as important social events by the pioneers who were, by virtue of the vast distances starved of contact with the outside world.

Leading Aggregates

Batsmen	M	I	NO	Runs	HS	Ave.	Bowlers	Runs	Wkts	Ave.
J.M.Bryant (V)	7	13	0	146	32	11.23	T.W.Wills (V)	290	56	5.17
T.W.Wills (V)	6	11	1	142	49*	14.20	G.Elliott (V)	236	48	4.91
T.F.Hamilton (V)	3	6	1	132	42	26.40	E.W.Ward (NSW)	143	25	5.72
G.H.B.Gilbert (NSW)	6	12	0	110	31	9.16	W.Henty (T)	179	19	9.42
G.Marshall (V)	7	13	1	96	32	8.00	W.Brown (T)	73	15	4.86
T.F.Morres (V)	6	11	0	87	47	7.90	R.M.McDowall (T)	89	15	5.93
W.J.S.Hammersley (V)	5	10	0	83	31	8.30	G.H.B.Gilbert (NSW)	122	15	8.13
J.L.B.Tabart (T)	5	9	2	80	20	11.42	G.B.Richardson (NSW)	105	15	7.00

TASMANIA v VICTORIA

Played at the Launceston Racecourse (later N.T.C.A. Ground), February 11, 12, 1851. (Timeless match)
Toss : Tasmania.   Result : TASMANIA WON BY THREE WICKETS.
Debuts: All players (f/c).
12th Men: No 12th men or emergency fieldsmen named.
Umpires: .Lyon and C J Weedon.
Attendances: 1000, 1500.   Total: About 2500.   Receipts: No admission charged.
Close of Play: 1st day Tas (2) 6/15 (Tabart 2, Arthur 0).

First-class cricket in Australia is generally acknowledged to have commenced at 11.00am on February 11, 1851 at the Launceston racecourse in Northern Tasmania with this fixture between an XI of Van Diemen's Land and an XI of Port Phillip. The teams were labelled in the Press as 'Tasmania' and 'Victoria', despite the titles not being adopted by the Colonies until the mid-1850s. Melburnians keenly followed the progress of the match in their morning newspaper under the banner of The Grand Cricket Match. The surface of the racecourse was of the roughest description and, "it was with considerable difficulty that the umpires could select a piece of ground for the occasion" (*Herald*). The Tasmanians, accustomed only to facing slow under-arm bowling, were not expected to be the equals of the visitors, who boasted a swift round-arm attack. Antill's record-making analysis of 13 for 52 for Victoria included the first three Tasmanian wickets in a four-ball spell (WW1W). Respective topscorers in the match were Hamilton (35 in 60 minutes, 3 fours) and Du Croz (27 in 93 minutes, 2 fours). All hits were run out, there being no boundaries to speak of. A ball used in the game was later donated to the Launceston museum by the family of C.J.Weedon, one of the umpires, where it still resides. *Cricket* debits extras to the bowling analyses. Sources: *Cricket, Launceston Examiner, Cornwall Chronicle, Melbourne Morning Herald.*

VICTORIA

Batsman	Dismissal	Runs	2nd inns	Runs
D.E.Cooper	b McDowall	4	(7) b Henty	0
*W.Philpott	c Maddox b McDowall	17	(6) run out (Tabart/Marshall)	3
T.F.Hamilton	b McDowall	10	(1) lbw b McDowall	35
C.Lister	run out (/Marshall)	10	c Maddox b Field	3
A.T.Thomson	b McDowall	1	b Henty	0
R.S.Philpott	b Henty	12	(8) c Westbrook b Henty	1
T.W.Antill	st Marshall b Henty	0	(11) not out	0
J.C.Brodie	c Henty b McDowall	17	(2) c Tabart b Henty	5
F.W.Marsden	b Henty	2	b McDowall	2
M.Hall	not out	6	(3) lbw b McDowall	6
M.Hervey	b Henty	0	(10) c McDowall b Henty	1
Extras	(b1, lb2)	3	(b1)	1
Total	(26.0 overs, 125 mins)	82	(17.0 overs, 80 mins)	57

TASMANIA

Batsman	Dismissal	Runs	2nd inns	Runs
G.B.Du Croz	b Antill	27	(2) b Antill	6
*†J.Marshall	c Lister b Antill	13	(7) c & b Antill	0
W.Field	b Antill	0	(5) c Thomson b Brodie	1
G.Maddox	b Antill	1		
G.Gibson	b Hamilton	8	(6) b Antill	1
W.H.Westbrook	b Antill	10	(3) c Cooper b Antill	4
C.Arthur	b Antill	1	(8) c Hervey b Antill	0
J.L.B.Tabart	b Hamilton	2	(4) not out	15
V.W.Giblin	not out	7	(1) b Antill	1
W.Henty	b Antill	0		
R.M.McDowall	c Antill b Hamilton	11	(9) not out	4
Extras	(b11, lb5, nb8)	24	(b3, lb2)	5
Total	(32.0 overs, 160 mins)	104	(13.0 overs, 74 mins) (7 wkts)	37

TASMANIA	O	M	R	W	w,nb		O	M	R	W	w,nb
Henty	13		52	4	-,-	9		26	5	-,-	
McDowall	13		27	5	-,-	5		21	3	-,-	
Field				3			9	1	-,-		

VICTORIA	O	M	R	W	w,nb			O	M	R	W	w,nb
Lister	12		23	0	-,6							
Hamilton	8		24	3	-,-							
Antill	12		33	7	-,2	(2)	6	19		6	-,-	
Brodie						(1)	7	13		1	-,-	

FALL OF WICKETS

Wkt	VIC 1st	TAS 1st	VIC 2nd	TAS 2nd
1st	14	40	12	1
2nd	21	40	18	4
3rd	34	41		11
4th	42			12
5th	42	44	28	12
6th	54			15
7th	71			-
8th	71			-
9th	79			-
10th	79	80	56	-

NOTE : All falls of wickets reported as "exclusive of byes throughout the score".

VICTORIA v TASMANIA

Played at South Yarra Ground, Melbourne, March 29, 30, 1852. (Timeless match)
Toss : See below.   Result : VICTORIA WON BY 61 RUNS.
Debuts: Victoria - E.F.a'Beckett, M.a'Beckett, H.B.Foot, F.A.Powlett, C.Sladen, J.W.Stevens (all f/c). Tasmania - H.Allison, J.Cox, A.Douglas, H.E.Lette, W.McEwan, A.J.Marriott, J.W.Watson (all f/c).
12th Men: No 12th men or emergency fieldsmen named.
Umpires: G.Living and W.A.Roles.
Attendances: 2000, 500.   Total: About 2,500.   Receipts: No admission charged.
Close of Play: 1st day Tas (2) 4/41 (McEwan 0, Cox 5).

Preliminary arrangements for this match were made in Launceston at the conclusion of the initial intercolonial in February 1851. Final arrangements were conducted by correspondence between committees of the Launceston and Melbourne Cricket Clubs. A party of nine (including W.A.Roles, Launceston C.C. secretary) travelled from Launceston, three Tasmanians then resident in Melbourne - Cox, McEwan and Watson - being recruited after arrival to complete the team. The match was played on the ground of the Melbourne C.C., then located on the South bank of the Yarra River opposite the present Queens Bridge. Acquisition of a portion of the ground as a right of way for the Melbourne-Sandridge railway in 1854 led to the loss of the ground and development of the present Melbourne Cricket Ground. There is some doubt as to the outcome of the toss; *The Herald* awards it to Tasmania who "put the Victorians in", whereas *The Argus* records the "Melbourne side". There is also no record of the identity of the Victorian captain, although it is most likely to have been either Hamilton or Powlett. E.F.a'Beckett, aged 15 years 349 days, and his brother Malwyn, aged 17 years 186 days were very young debutants for Victoria. The score is as from the original scorebook, held by the Melbourne Cricket Club, and differs from other sources in respect of Vic (1) M.a'Beckett's dismissal. No bowling figures, apart from number of overs, were recorded. *R.H.Campbell* has alternative bowling analyses to other sources as follows: Vic (1) Henty 5/39, Maddox 0/7, Lette 4/30; Vic (2) Henty 4/46, Lette 4/43, Marshall 0/5, Maddox 0/28, Tabart 0/3, Douglas 0/0; Tas (1) Hamilton 3/26, Brodie 0/0, Powlett 4/17, E.F.a'Beckett 1/12; Tas (2) Hamilton 5/39, Powlett 1/5, E.F.a'Beckett 1/6, Lister 2/11, Sladen 1/4. However, his source is unknown and is not confirmed elsewhere. Marriott is incorrectly given as Maryatt in some sources. Sources: *Cricket, Melbourne Morning Herald, The Argus, MCC Scorebook, R.H.Campbell*.

VICTORIA

Batsman	Dismissal 1		Runs 1	Dismissal 2	Runs 2
T.F.Hamilton	b Henty		42	(3) run out (Marshall)	42
H.B.Foot	run out (	/Marshall)	20	run out	2
J.W.Stevens	b Lette		0	(5) b Lette	5
C.Lister	b Henty		0	(1) b Henty	13
E.F.a'Beckett	b Lette		2	(6) b Lette	0
C.Sladen	b Lette		0	(7) b Henty	3
F.A.Powlett	lbw b Henty		1	(8) b Lette	33
J.C.Brodie	b Henty		0	(9) b Lette	8
F.W.Marsden	b Henty		8	(10) not out	10
M.a'Beckett	b Henty		3	(11) b Henty	7
M.Hervey	not out		0	(4) c Lette b Henty	2
Extras	(b3, w1)		4	(b2)	2
Total	(29.0 overs)		80	(42.0 overs)	127

TASMANIA

Batsman	Dismissal 1	Runs 1	Dismissal 2	Runs 2
*†J.Marshall	b Hamilton	1	b Hamilton	13
J.W.Watson	run out	0	b Lister	0
A.J.Marriott	b Powlett	2	(4) c & b Hamilton	7
H.Allison	run out	1	(9) lbw b Hamilton	2
A.Douglas	b Powlett	0	(8) c Hamilton b E.F.a'Beckett	6
J.L.B.Tabart	b E.F.a'Beckett	20	(7) b Sladen	18
G.Maddox	lbw b Hamilton	14	(3) b Lister	3
J.Cox	b Hamilton	15	(6) b Powlett	5
H.E.Lette	b Powlett	2	(11) b Hamilton	0
W.Henty	c & b Powlett	0	b Hamilton	1
W.McEwan	not out	0	(5) not out	10
Extras	(b10)	10	(b13, w3)	16
Total	(29.0 overs)	65	(34.0 overs)	81

TASMANIA	O	M	R	W	w,nb		O	M	R	W	w,nb
Henty	15		40	6	1,-		19		60	4	-,-
Maddox	2		5	0	-,-						
Lette	12		31	3	-,-	(2)	17		50	4	-,-
Marshall					-,-	(3)	3		8	0	-,-
Tabart					-,-	(4)	1		2	0	-,-
Douglas					-,-	(5)	2		5	0	-,-

VICTORIA	O	M	R	W	w,nb		O	M	R	W	w,nb
Hamilton	15		29	3	-,-		14		27	5	3,-
Brodie	1		2	0	-,-						
Powlett	7		13	4	-,-		4		7	1	-,-
E.F.a'Beckett	6		11	1	-,-	(5)	5		10	1	-,-
Lister						(2)	7		13	2	-,-
Sladen						(4)	4		8	1	-,-

FALL OF WICKETS				
Wkt	VIC 1st	TAS 1st	VIC 2nd	TAS 2nd
1st	44	1		
2nd	44	3		
3rd	48	3		
4th	53	4		36
5th	53	9		41
6th	59	34		
7th	62	43		
8th	62	50		
9th	73	51		
10th	76	55	125	65

NOTE : Falls of wickets are "exclusive of byes".

TASMANIA v VICTORIA

Played at Launceston Cricket Ground, March 3, 4, 1854. (Timeless match)
Toss : Tasmania.   Result : TASMANIA WON BY EIGHT WICKETS.
Debuts: Tasmania - R.Cox, A.M.Lochner, G.Matson, R.S.Still, J.M.Ware (all f/c). Victoria - R.S.Brodie, G.Cavenagh, jr, A.M.Dick,
    E.R.Rowlands, H.E.Stratford, R.B.Wilkinson (all f/c); J.Cox, G.B.Du Croz (both Vic only).
12th Men: No 12th men or emergency fieldsmen named.
Umpires: G.Cavenagh, sr and C.J.Weedon.
Attendances: No figures published.   Total: Not known   Receipts: No admission charged.
Close of Play: 1st day Tas 97 all out.

As the first two matches between the Colonies had resulted in a victory for each, this game was staged as a "Conqueror". The Victorian team which travelled across Bass Strait on board the *S.S.Clarence* was depleted by the last-minute withdrawals of three players ("Bennett, Ronsey and T.F.Wray") and consequently had only nine men, a scorer (H.E.Stratford) and an umpire G.Cavenagh, sr, who had replaced "Knox"). Their troubles were further compounded when one of the team ("Coles") was seriously hurt by a blow to the eye at practice the evening before the game began. Now desperately short of fit men, the Victorians called upon their scorer and co-opted Hall (a Melbourne cricketer and businessman who had played in the 1850-51 match and was for some reason in Tasmania at this time} and Launceston resident Du Croz, who had also played - for Tasmania - in the inaugural match, but is believed to have never lived in Victoria. The match got under way at 11.40am, the Tasmanian captain Marshall in his last match (allegedly 58 years old - he remains the oldest ever to play first-class cricket in Australia) again inviting the visitors to bat, who again scored 80, defending stoutly. Bowling throughout the match was predominantly underarm, Still (fast roundarm at times) being a possible exception. Westbrook received high praise for his long- stopping behind Marshall, "not a single ball going by him" (*Herald*). Remarkably, only one of the 32 dismissals involved a catch. Still, with 34 runs and seven wickets, was the chief architect in his side's win: Tasmania had to wait another 41 years for their next first-class victory. The Victorian captain is not known. *Cricket* incorrectly gives J.Watson instead of Matson in Tasmanian team and has incomplete dismissals for Cox and Marshall in the respective first innings. Bowling for Vic (2) remains 1 run short. *Scorebook* does not record runs conceded by each bowler (number of overs only). *R.H.Campbell* has Vic (1) J.Cox c Cox b Still. His bowling figures for Vic (1) Still 5/35, McDowall 2/19, Maddox 1/18, Cox 1/6; Vic (2) Still 3/25, McDowall 5/23; Tas (1) Cavenagh 5/35, Powlett 3/25, Dick 0/17, Brodie 0/12; Tas (2) Cavenagh 1/10, Powlett 0/10, Dick 1/14, must be considered doubtful; his source is unknown and the limited information from the scorebook disagrees with his version. All falls of wicket were unrecorded. Sources: *Cricket, Launceston Examiner, The Herald, MCC Scorebook, R.H.Campbell.*

VICTORIA

R.B.Wilkinson	b Still	4		b McDowall	17
A.M.Dick	b McDowall	3	(4)	b Still	1
G.Cavenagh, jr	b Still	35		b McDowall	10
†A.T.Thomson	b McDowall	0	(5)	b McDowall	0
M.Hall	run out	16	(2)	run out	1
G.B.Du Croz	b Still	4		b McDowall	8
F.A.Powlett	b Cox	0		b Still	3
J.Cox	c Cox b McDowall	7		run out	5
R.S.Brodie	b Maddox	6		b Still	1
E.R.Rowlands	b Still	1	(11)	not out	2
H.E.Stratford	not out	2	(10)	b McDowall	0
Extras	(w1, nb1)	2		(b2)	2
Total	(38.0 overs, 175 mins)	80		(18.0 overs, 80 mins)	50

TASMANIA

R.Cox	b Powlett	34			
*†J.Marshall	st Thomson b Cavenagh	10	(1)	b Cavenagh	9
J.L.B.Tabart	b Powlett	1			
J.M.Ware	b Cavenagh	9		not out	1
W.H.Westbrook	run out	1			
G.Gibson	b Cavenagh	0			
R.S.Still	run out	11	(3)	not out	23
A.M.Lochner	not out	19	(2)	b Dick	1
G.Matson	b Cavenagh	1			
G.Maddox	b Cavenagh	3			
R.M.McDowall	b Powlett	0			
Extras	(b7, lb1)	8		(b1)	1
Total	(29.0 overs, 110 mins)	97		(8.0 overs, 30 mins) (2 wkts)	35

TASMANIA	O	M	R	W	w,nb	O	M	R	W	w,nb		FALL OF WICKETS			
Still	11		23	4	1,1	9		24	3	-,-		VIC	TAS	VIC	TAS
McDowall	16		33	3	-,-	9		23	5	-,-	Wkt	1st	1st	2nd	2nd
Maddox	8		16	1	-,-						1st				
Cox	3		6	1	-,-						2nd				
											3rd				
VICTORIA	O	M	R	W	w,nb	O	M	R	W	w,nb	4th				
Cavenagh	15		46	5	-,-	4		17	1	-,-	5th				
Powlett	12		37	3	-,-						6th				
Wilkinson	2		6	0	-,-						7th				
Dick					(2)	4		17	1	-,-	8th				
											9th				
											10th				

VICTORIA v NEW SOUTH WALES

Played at Melbourne Cricket Ground March 26, 27, 1856. (Timeless match)

Toss : Victoria.   Result : NEW SOUTH WALES WON BY THREE WICKETS.

Debuts: Victoria - R.Coulstock, C.B.Cumberland, G.Elliott, A.T.Hotham, P.O.Kington, A.Lewis, F.Lowe, J.H.Mather, T.F.Morres, D.M.Serjeant (all f/c). New South Wales - J.C.Beal, J.S.Bradridge, R.Driver, H.Hilliard, G.Howell, J.J.McKone, R.Murray, E.Saddler, W.Tunks, R.Vaughan (all f/c); G.H.B.Gilbert (NSW only).

12th Men:No 12th men or emergency fieldsmen named.

Umpires: J.B.Bradshaw and C.F.Cameron.

Attendances: 5000, "a great number".   Total: Unknown.   Receipts: £60 (first day only).

Close of Play: 1st day NSW 76 all out.

The first match between these Colonies, and the first in which New South Wales played, was the result of a challenge to "all comers" issued by Melbourne Cricket Club in late 1855. It was the first big match staged at the M.C.G., and the first first-class match in Australia for which admission (1 shilling, ladies free) was charged. It was initially proposed to play for money - there was talk of a £500 stake - but the visitors had no way of raising betting money and the final agreement was that each side pay their own expenses. The New South Welshmen left Sydney on the *S.S.Telegraph* on March 19th, the journey to Port Phillip taking 48 hours. One of their principal bowlers, J.Rutter of Parramatta, was to have followed in the next steamer but he did not turn up so Driver, who had accompanied the team as umpire, played and Bradshaw, "a gentleman in Melbourne not long from Sydney", officiated for the visitors. The start of the match was delayed several days due to rain. A dispute arose after the umpires had tossed, Victoria winning. The New South Wales players insisted that, as the visiting team, they had the choice; Victoria eventually relented and were sent in. The prepared pitch was found to be unsuitable and the wickets were pitched alongside the strip instead. Mather, who topscored for Victoria, was run out attempting a fifth run after a hit to long-off, no boundaries being in operation. Gilbert (roundarm medium pace - previous matches for Middlesex and the Gentlemen), McKone and Murray (both fast underarm) shared the bowling. Elliott (fast roundarm) dismissed Murray with the first ball of the visitors' innings to claim a wicket with his first ball. Coulstock and Morres (both roundarm) and Lowe (roundarm with "a high delivery") were the other Victorian bowlers, Kington keeping wicket in the second innings. Driver's 18, which included 2 chances, believed to be his highest innings in all cricket. The visitors had no specialist keeper, various fielders back- stopping, minus protective equipment. Victoria's 28 remains their lowest total in this series, as does the match aggregate (183 runs) for all first-class matches in this country. The second day's play was poorly covered in the Press due to Easter; batting order and fall of wickets were unreported. McKone and Elliott both bowled consecutive overs. A ball used in the match was given to the NSWCA 50 years on by a niece of Driver. *S & B* gives NSW (1) Elliott 42, Coulstock 29, Morres 7 overs each and includes wides in the runs conceded. Sources: *Scores & Biographies, The Age, The Argus, The Herald, Australian Cricketers Guide.*

VICTORIA

Player	1st innings		2nd innings	
D.M.Serjeant	b McKone	7	b McKone	5
J.H.Mather	run out(/Hilliard)	16	b McKone	0
R.Coulstock	lbw b McKone	4	c McKone b Murray	2
T.F.Morres	b Gilbert	2	c Howell b Murray	1
A.T.Hotham	b McKone	0	b Murray	0
C.B.Cumberland	c Bradridge b Gilbert	2	run out	1
*W.Philpott	b McKone	5	run out	11
P.O.Kingston	not out	12	b McKone	0
†F.Lowe	b McKone	2	not out	1
A.Lewis	c & b Gilbert	8	b McKone	5
G.Elliott	b Gilbert	1	b McKone	1
Extras	(b4)	4	(b1)	1
Total	(34.0 overs)	63	(23.0 overs)	28

NEW SOUTH WALES

Player	1st innings		2nd innings	
R.Murray	c Morres b Elliott	0	b Elliott	5
W.Tunks	b Elliott	1	b Elliott	0
J.S.Bradridge	b Elliott	2	b Lowe	2
H.Hilliard	lbw b Elliott	0	not out	1
*G.H.B.Gilbert	c Morres b Coulstock	6	b Lowe	7
J.J.McKone	not out	18	b Lowe	0
R.Vaughan	b Elliott	0	not out	1
E.Saddler	b Coulstock	7		
J.C.Beal	st Lowe b Coulstock	0		
G.Howell	b Elliott	11	b Elliott	0
R.Driver	b Elliott	18	b Lowe	0
Extras	(b3, w9, nb1)	13		—
Total	(52.0 overs)	76	(20.0 overs) (7 wkts)	16

NEW SOUTH WALES	O	M	R	W	w,nb		O	M	R	W	w,nb
Gilbert	17	3	34	4	-,-						
McKone	17	3	25	5	-,-	(1)	13	4	11	5	-,-
Murray						(2)	10	2	16	3	-,-

VICTORIA	O	M	R	W	w,nb		O	M	R	W	w,nb
Elliott	26	16	25	7	3,1		11	4	7	3	-,-
Coulstock	20	9	30	3	1,-						
Morres	6	1	8	0	5,-						
Lowe						(2)	9	3	9	4	-,-

FALL OF WICKETS				
Wkt	VIC 1st	NSW 1st	VIC 2nd	NSW 2nd
1st	11	0		
2nd	23	0		
3rd	29	2		
4th	31	4		
5th	31	10		
6th	33	11		
7th	39	19		
8th	41	19		-
9th	55	40		-
10th	63	76	28	-

NEW SOUTH WALES v VICTORIA

Played at The Domain, Sydney, on January 14, 15, 1857. (Timeless match)
Toss : None - see below.   Result : NEW SOUTH WALES WON BY 65 RUNS.
Debuts: New South Wales - O.H.Lewis, T.H.Lewis, W.G.Rees, W.C.Still, E.W.Ward (all f/c). Victoria - B.Butterworth, G.Marshall,
    W.L.Rees (all f/c); J.M.Bryant, W.J.S.Hammersley, T.W.Wills (all Vic only).
12th Men: No 12th men or emergency fieldsmen named - see below.
Umpires: C.F.Cameron and R.Driver.
Attendances: 9000, 15000, 4000.   Total: About 28,000.   Receipts: No figures published.
Close of Play: 1st day Vic 63 all out; 2nd day Vic (2) 7/17 (Hammersley 2, Coulstock 4).

The first Intercolonial match to be played in Sydney. The ground in The Domain was specifically selected and prepared for the game under the supervision of R.Driver, W.Tunks and E.W.Ward. There was no time to provide any fencing to enclose the playing area and an appeal was made to spectators not to infringe. G.Howell and T.H.Lewis replaced J.Rutter and W.Tunks in the home side prior to the match. Rutter had also been selected for the game in Melbourne the previous year but had failed to arrive. Reasons for his second withdrawal were not announced but he was destined never to appear for his Colony, although considered a leading bowler of the time. M.a'Beckett accompanied the Victorian team and acted as a substitute for his brother (sprained ankle) in the second innings. There was no toss - New South Wales were allowed first innings by agreement. Coulstock was bowled by the second ball of the opening over of the Victorian first innings - also Ward's initial over in first-class cricket. There was criticism of the New South Wales policy of not using a wicket-keeper - "we consider it was throwing a chance away not playing a wicket-keeper" (*Bell's Life*). Bryant (Surrey), Hammersley (Cambridge University and Surrey) and Wills (Kent and Cambridge University) had previously played in England. Wills often appears with an additional Christian name, Spencer, which he did not possess. *Scores & Biographies* does not indicate Saddler c sub in NSW (2). Sources: *Scores & Biographies, Sydney Morning Herald, Bells Life in Sydney, Australian Cricketers Guide.*

NEW SOUTH WALES

G.Howell	c Bryant b Elliott	0		c Marshall b Wills	0
W.G.Rees	lbw b Wills	28		c Marshall b Hammersley	3
†H.Hilliard	b Wills	20	(5)	b Elliott	2
*G.H.B.Gilbert	b Wills	2	(7)	c Bryant b Wills	31
J.J.McKone	b Wills	1	(11)	not out	0
W.C.Still	run out (Rees/Marshall)	1	(4)	b Elliott	9
O.H.Lewis	c Bryant b Hammersley	3	(6)	c Elliott b Wills	2
R.Murray	b Wills	0	(9)	b Elliott	8
E.W.Ward	c Butterworth b Wills	1	(10)	c Coulstock b Hammersley	13
E.Saddler	not out	5	(3)	c sub (M.a'Beckett) b Wills	3
T.H.Lewis	c Wills b Hammersley	13	(8)	c sub (M.a'Beckett) b Elliott	8
Extras	(b1, lb3, w1, nb1)	6		(b3, lb3, nb1)	7
Total	(70.2 overs, in about 150 mins)	80		(89.1 overs, in about 195 mins)	86

VICTORIA

R.Coulstock	b Ward	0	(9)	b Ward	16
D.M.Serjeant	run out (Rees/)	7		b O.H.Lewis	6
W.L.Rees	b McKone	2	(5)	run out	0
E.F.a'Beckett	run out (Gilbert/)	3		c & b Ward	0
T.W.Wills	b McKone	0	(8)	c T.H.Lewis b Ward	1
J.M.Bryant	b Ward	23	(1)	c Murray b O.H.Lewis	0
†G.Marshall	c Saddler b O.H.Lewis	13	(3)	c McKone b O.H.Lewis	0
*W.J.S.Hammersley	b O.H.Lewis	10	(7)	b O.H.Lewis	10
C.B.Cumberland	c Still b O.H.Lewis	0	(10)	not out	0
B.Butterworth	c Ward b O.H.Lewis	0	(11)	b Ward	0
G.Elliott	not out	2	(6)	c Howell b Ward	2
Extras	(b1, lb1, w1)	3		(b2, lb1)	3
Total	(35.1 overs, in about 90 mins)	63		(52.3 overs, in about 115 mins)	38

VICTORIA	O	M	R	W	w,nb		O	M	R	W	w,nb
Elliott	20	7	32	1	-,-	(3)	24	10	19	4	-,1
Bryant	11	5	13	0	-,-	(4)	6	3	7	0	-,-
Wills	24	12	25	6	1,-	(1)	40	18	40	4	-,-
Hammersley	15.2	8	7	2	-,1	(2)	19.1	9	17	2	-,-

NEW SOUTH WALES	O	M	R	W	w,nb		O	M	R	W	w,nb
Ward	18	5	23	2	1,-		26.3	18	15	5	-,-
McKone	12	2	26	2	-,-						
O.H.Lewis	5.1	1	13	4	-,-	(2)	26	14	21	4	-,-

Note : All bowling figures appear to include leg byes

	FALL OF WICKETS			
	NSW	VIC	NSW	VIC
Wkt	1st	1st	2nd	2nd
1st	8	0	4	1
2nd	40	9	4	1
3rd	42	9	12	4
4th	51	9	16	4
5th	52	27	20	9
6th	59	41	23	12
7th	59	50	44	16
8th	59	60	60	38
9th	60	60	86	38
10th	80	63	86	38

VICTORIA v NEW SOUTH WALES

Played at Melbourne Cricket Ground on January 11, 12, 13, 1858. (Timeless match)
Toss : None - see below.   Result : VICTORIA WON BY 171 RUNS.
Debuts: Victoria - G.T.Pickering, T.F.Wray (both f/c). New South Wales - J.L.Beeston, J.Mills, N.Thompson (all f/c).
12th Men: No 12th men or emergency fieldsmen named.
Umpires: C.F.Cameron and W.Tunks.
Attendances: 5000, 7000, 3000.   Total: About 15,000.   Receipts: No figures published.
Close of Play: 1st day NSW 57 all out; 2nd day Vic (2) 238 all out

W.C.Still and E.W.Ward were unavailable for the New South Wales trip to Melbourne. Choice of innings was given to New South Wales, the visiting team. Gilbert took the first hat-trick in Australian first-class cricket, dismissing Wray, Elliott and Marshall with successive balls. Murray aggravated an old wrist injury while batting in the first innings and was forced to retire hurt at 4/17. He resumed his innings at 9/51. Wills (49 not out in about 135 minutes, 2 fives and 2 fours) and Morres (47 in about 70 minutes, 1 six, 1 five and 1 four) added valuable runs in the middle order of the Victorian second innings. Gilbert, when 7, became the second New South Wales batting casualty when he was struck by a ball from Wills at 2/30 in the second innings. Lunch was taken but Gilbert was unable to resume until the fall of the seventh wicket, and then only with the assistance of a runner, Vaughan. Faulty running by Vaughan led to Gilbert's dismissal. Vaughan had also been run out during his own innings earlier on. Pickering lost his life in a diving accident later in the year. *Scores & Biographies* does not include NSW bowling (2) Murray 0/15. Sources: *Scores & Biographies, Australian Cricketers Guide, Bells Life in Victoria, The Herald, The Argus.*

VICTORIA

J.M.Bryant	c Mills b Gilbert	11		run out (Gilbert/Hilliard)	18
T.F.Wray	lbw b Gilbert	12		c Mills b Gilbert	26
G.Elliott	c Mills b Gilbert	0	(10)	st Hilliard b Gilbert	10
†G.Marshall	c & b Gilbert	0	(6)	c Mills b Gilbert	8
W.J.S.Hammersley	lbw b O.H.Lewis	5		c McKone b Gilbert	31
G.T.Pickering	run out (O.H.Lewis/Hilliard)	4	(4)	c Mills b Beeston	26
*T.W.Wills	b O.H.Lewis	12		not out	49
W.L.Rees	c Thompson b Gilbert	1	(9)	b Hilliard	3
T.F.Morres	run out (Thompson/Hilliard)	10	(8)	c O.H.Lewis b Hilliard	47
T.F.Hamilton	not out	1	(3)	c & b Gilbert	2
B.Butterworth	b O.H.Lewis	0		hit wkt b Gilbert	0
Extras	(lb2, w1)	3		(b11, lb7)	18
Total	(20.0 overs, 87 mins)	59		(82.2 overs, in about 230 mins)	238

NEW SOUTH WALES

H.Hilliard	run out (Wills/Marshall)	1	(3)	c Hammersley b Elliott	1
J.L.Beeston	b Wills	6	(1)	b Elliott	5
G.Howell	c Elliott b Wills	0	(5)	b Wills	16
*G.H.B.Gilbert	b Wills	15		run out (Hamilton/Marshall)	12
J.J.McKone	b Elliott	0	(8)	b Elliott	1
R.Murray	b Bryant	8	(7)	b Wills	12
N.Thompson	b Morres	7	(2)	b Wills	10
O.H.Lewis	lbw b Wills	3	(9)	b Elliott	6
T.H.Lewis	b Wills	0	(11)	c Bryant b Elliott	0
R.Vaughan	not out	13	(6)	run out (Bryant/Marshall)	0
J.Mills	c & b Bryant	1	(10)	not out	0
Extras	(b1, w2)	3		(lb2, w2, nb2)	6
Total	(40.3 overs, 130 mins)	57		(56.1 overs, in about 170 mins)	69

NEW SOUTH WALES	O	M	R	W	w,nb		O	M	R	W	w,nb
McKone	2	0	15	0	1.-	(3)	7	3	16	0	-,-
O.H.Lewis	10	2	18	3	-,-		19	2	60	0	-,-
Gilbert	8	2	23	5	,	(1)	27.2	7	65	6	-,-
Murray							3	0	15	0	-,-
Beeston							5	0	16	1	-,-
Thompson							7	2	21	0	-,-
Hilliard							14	2	27	2	-,-

VICTORIA	O	M	R	W	w,nb		O	M	R	W	w,nb
Elliott	8	3	17	1	-,-		15.3	8	17	5	-,-
Wills	20	10	25	5	-,-		27	10	34	3	-,-
Morres	10	4	11	1	2,-	(4)	4.2	2	3	0	1,2
Bryant	2.3	2	1	2	-,-	(3)	9	2	9	0	1,-

FALL OF WICKETS

Wkt	VIC 1st	NSW 1st	VIC 2nd	NSW 2nd
1st	20	4	39	6
2nd	20	4	45	12
3rd	20	7	54	33
4th	28	7	98	33
5th	32	31	113	59
6th	47	37	135	60
7th	47	37	209	68
8th	53	52	221	69
9th	59	53	236	69
10th	59	57	238	69

TASMANIA v VICTORIA

Played at Launceston Cricket Ground on February 25, 26, 1858. (Timeless match)
Toss : See below.   Result : VICTORIA WON BY AN INNINGS AND 20 RUNS.
Debuts: Tasmania - N.G.Clayton, J.B.Dixon, C.F.Evans, W.A.B.Jamieson, T.Westbrook (all f/c). Victoria - A.A.Black, H.Box,
    F.Burchett, H.Creswick, R.Power (all f/c).
12th Men: No 12th men or emergency fieldsmen named.
Umpires: J.Marshall and (probably) various players of both sides.
Attendances & Receipts: No figures published.
Close of Play: 1st day Vic 115 all out.

Matches between these teams were resumed after a gap of four years at the instigation of the Launceston Cricket Club, who invited Wills to bring a team to Tasmania as soon as practicable after Victoria's match with New South Wales. Victoria were given choice of innings as the visiting team and sent Tasmania in. The result, the first victory by an innings margin in first-class cricket in Australia, was also Victoria's first win away from home at this level. Tasmania provided the first instance in this country of no batsman reaching double figures in a completed innings, while Still (roundarm) became the first bowler here to be no-balled for throwing when he raised his bowling arm above his shoulder in delivery. Tasmania's opening bowlers in Maddox and Jamieson both bowled under-arm. Elliott's scarcely-believable 9 for 2 - achieved with fast round-arm deliveries - remained the best innings analysis in Australia until George Giffen's 10 for 66 in 1883-84. Roundarm bowling had been outlawed for a time in Tasmania during their four-year isolation from outside competition and *Bell's Life* noted: "It is quite evident that until the Tasmanians can both bowl and play overhand bowling that they stand little chance of succeeding in the cricket field against any eleven comprising the names of Wills, Elliott, Bryant, Morres, Marshall, etc". There were only eleven men in the Victorian party and it is believed that they and the local players shared the umpiring duties with Marshall for this and the following match in Hobart. The match was given scant coverage in the Press, though Box's long-stopping was noted as a feature, "considering the state of the ground". The Tasmanian bowling is 2 runs short. *R.H.Campbell* gives Jamieson 5/65, which balances, but his source is not known and is not supported by contemporary records. Falls of wickets were not reported. Sources: *Cricket, Bells Life in Victoria, Launceston Examiner, Tasmanian Daily News, R.H.Campbell.*

TASMANIA

J.Cox	b Elliott	0	(11)	not out	0
N.G.Clayton	c Morres b Elliott	0	(1)	run out	2
W.A.B.Jamieson	b Elliott	0	(4)	b Morres	0
C.F.Evans	b Wills	3	(3)	b Wills	20
G.Maddox	lbw b Elliott	5	(8)	b Wills	3
*R.S.Still	b Elliott	3		c Morres b Bryant	12
†J.B.Dixon	c Burchett b Elliott	1	(10)	b Bryant	5
H.Allison	c Morres b Elliott	1	(5)	b Wills	0
T.Westbrook	b Elliott	0	(7)	b Wills	0
J.L.B.Tabart	not out	3	(2)	b Morres	8
G.Gibson	hit wkt b Elliott	3	(9)	b Wills	0
Extras	(b11, lb1, w2)	14		(b5, lb4, w2, nb1)	12
Total	(37.0 overs, in about 150 mins)	33		(51.3 overs, in about 210 mins)	62

VICTORIA

F.Burchett	b Jamieson	2
J.M.Bryant	run out	7
T.Butterworth	lbw b Jamieson	24
†G.Marshall	b Jamieson	20
*T.W.Wills	c Evans b Still	16
T.F.Morres	c Clayton b Jamieson	0
G.Elliott	c Allison b Maddox	28
H.Creswick	c Evans b Still	3
A.A.Black	b Still	0
R.Power	b Jamieson	2
H.Box	not out	4
Extras	(b5, lb3, nb1)	9
Total	(43.1 overs, in about 180 mins)	115

VICTORIA	O	M	R	W	w,nb		O	M	R	W	w,nb		FALL OF WICKETS		
													TAS	VIC	TAS
Elliott	19	17	2	9	2,-							Wkt	1st	1st	2nd
Wills	18	9	17	1	-,-		26	12	24	5	1,-	1st			
Morres						(1)	10.3	7	15	2	-,1	2nd			
Bryant						(3)	15	11	11	2	1,-	3rd			
												4th			
TASMANIA	O	M	R	W	w,nb							5th			
Maddox	8.1	0	20	1	-,-							6th			
Jamieson	22	1	63	5	-,-							7th			
Still	13	5	21	3	-,1							8th			
												9th			
												10th	33	115	62

TASMANIA v VICTORIA

Played at Lower Domain Ground (Government Paddock), Hobart, on March 4, 5, 1858. (Timeless match)
Toss : Victoria.   Result : VICTORIA WON BY 69 RUNS.
Debuts: Tasmania - G.W.Briant, W.Brown, J.C.Mace, G.Marshall, T.Patterson, T.Whitesides (all f/c).
12th Men: No 12th men or emergency fieldsmen named.
Umpires: J.Marshall and (probably) various players of both sides.
Attendances: 5000 1500, .   Total: About 6500.   Receipts: No figures published.
Close of Play: 1st day Vic (2) 67 all out.

The match was arranged at short notice, while the Victorians were in Launceston, and is the only match of first-class status to have been staged at this Hobart venue. A half-holiday was declared for business houses and retailers in the Southern capital in recognition of the first major match to be staged there. It was scheduled to start at 9.30am in an attempt to complete it in one day, but play did not eventually get under way until 11.00am. (The second day commenced at noon.) Only one umpire, John Marshall, was named prior to the match, players not directly involved (such as T.F.Morres who definitely stood at one time) probably accompanying him throughout. Tasmania uniquely had no innings of double figures by any batsman in either completed innings, and their aggregate (76 runs) is the lowest by any team in an Australian first-class match. Brown's combined figures of 15 for 73, achieved in his sole match, remained for more than 130 years the best by a bowler on first-class debut in Australia. Marshall's 32 for Victoria, the top score, consisted of 3 threes, 2 twos and 19 singles. Whitesides and Box both received high praise for their long-stopping for their respective teams. After the match a two-man foot race between Wills and a Tasmanian named Moran was run over 100 yards: Wills led out but was overtaken halfway and finished two or three yards behind Moran. The scorecard shown here is the generally accepted one. It is the only first-class match in Australia for which it has not been possible to determine all overs bowled; team overs for Tas (2) have been roughly estimated from team innings time. *Mercury* gives Tas (2) Patterson 2. Dixon 2. Some bowling figures have been estimated and *R.H.Campbell* gives the following variations in analyses: Vic (1) Brown 8/36, Patterson 1/41, Jamieson 0/0; Vic (2) Brown 8/30, Patterson 0/36; Tas (1) Elliott 3/20, Wills 6/24; Tas (2) Elliott 3/4, Wills 6/12. *R.H.Campbell* and *Cricket* both give Vic (1) Box c Whitesides b Brown, *Campbell's* source of analyses is not known and is not supported by contemporary newspapers. Most falls of wickets unreported. Sources: *Cricket, The Argus, Hobart Mercury, R.H.Campbell, Tasmanian Daily News.*

VICTORIA

J.M.Bryant	hit wkt b Brown	10	(5) st Marshall b Brown	2
F.Burchett	run out	8	(1) c & b Brown	14
H.Box	c Whitesides b Patterson	1	(11) not out	0
†G.Marshall	c & b Brown	32	(3) c & b Brown	0
T.Butterworth	c Brown b Patterson	0	(7) b Brown	6
*T.W.Wills	lbw b Brown	2	(4) run out	15
G.Elliott	b Brown	10	(8) b Brown	11
T.F.Morres	b Brown	0	(9) b Brown	0
H.Creswick	b Brown	0	(10) b Brown	13
A.A.Black	b Brown	13	(6) run out	5
R.Power	not out	1	(2) b Brown	0
Extras	(b1)	1	(b1)	1
Total	(26.0 overs, in about 105 mins)	78	(20.0 overs, in about 90 mins)	67

TASMANIA

T.F.Patterson	b Wills	6	(4) b Elliott	3
J.L.B.Tabart	b Wills	8	(6) b Wills	5
†G.Marshall	b Elliott	1	(8) b Elliott	0
W.A.B.Jamieson	b Wills	5	(2) b Wills	5
T.Westbrook	b Wills	0	(11) not out	0
G.W.Briant	c Box b Elliott	2	(7) b Wills	1
J.C.Mace	run out (Wills)	2	(3) run out	0
J.B.Dixon	b Wills	7	(5) c Butterworth b Wills	1
*W.Brown	c Burchett b Elliott	7	lbw b Wills	0
T.Whitesides	not out	0	(1) c Box b Wills	0
G.Matson	b Wills	6	(10) lbw b Elliott	1
Extras	(b5, lb1, w1)	7	(b6, lb1, w2)	9
Total	(32.0 overs, in about 115 mins)	51	(30 overs, in about 115 mins)	25

TASMANIA	O	M	R	W	w,nb		O	M	R	W	w,nb					
Brown	13	0	42	7	-,-		10	1	31	8	-,-					
Patterson	5	1	15	2	-,-											
Jamieson	8	1	20	0	-,-	(2)	10	0	35	0	-,-					

VICTORIA	O	M	R	W	w,nb	O	M	R	W	w,nb
Elliott	16	8	19	3	1,-		3	6	3	-,-
Wills	16	5	25	6	-,-		2	10	6	2,-

FALL OF WICKETS

Wkt	VIC 1st	TAS 1st	VIC 2nd	TAS 2nd
1st	16	12	0	
2nd	17	13	2	5
3rd	19	18		
4th	20	18		15
5th	25			
6th	48			
7th	48			20
8th	48			
9th	77			
10th	78	51	67	25

NEW SOUTH WALES v VICTORIA

Played at The Domain, Sydney, on January 20, 21, 22, 1859. (Timeless match)
Toss : None - see below.   Result : VICTORIA WON BY TWO WICKETS.
Debuts: New South Wales - F.Adams, J.Kinloch, J.H.Morris (all f/c). Victoria - A.Burchett, B.Grindrod, J.Thornton, E.H.Whitlow
  (all f/c).
12th Men: No 12th men or emergency fieldsmen named.
Umpires: J.Rhodes and W.Tunks.
Attendances: 8000, 8000, 10000.   Total: About 26,000.   Receipts: No figures published.
Close of Play: 1st day NSW 63 all out; 2nd day NSW (2) 3/60 (Lewis 40, Kinloch 0).

Rain delayed the start on the first day until 3.06pm and further rain overnight saturated the ground. Play on the second day began on time but the wet wicket and slow outfield reduced scoring opportunities. Victoria, having choice of innings as the visiting team, initially elected to bat but reconsidered and sent New South Wales in. Wills dislocated a finger on his left hand while attempting to catch Still on the first day but, being right-handed, he continued with no apparent inconvenience throughout the match. His match analysis of 11 for 49 included the crucial wicket of Lewis with the opening delivery of the last day. Bryant was out to the first ball of the Victorian first innings but atoned with the topscore in the second which saw his team well on the way to their victory target. Kinloch bowled unchanged throughout both Victorian innings. New South Wales elected not to use a wicket-keeper in the match, preferring a long-stop only, with a slip taking the stumps as required. There are several variations in the bowling for both second innings - NSW (2) Wills 6/24, Whitlow 1/15 (*SMH*), Morres 0/10 (*Bell's Life*); Vic (2) Ward 4/32, Kinloch 3/56 (*Bell's Life*). Those shown below are believed correct but NSW (2) figures include two leg-byes; it has not been possible to find in which bowler's analysis they have been added (they were scored as a double). *Scores & Biographies* has incorrect match dates. Sources: *Scores & Biographies, Victorian Cricketers Guide, Bells Life in Sydney, Sydney Morning Herald.*

NEW SOUTH WALES

E.W.Ward	c Bryant b Elliott	5	(2) c Burchett b Wills		0
G.Howell	b Wills	3	(1) b Whitlow		8
H.Hilliard	c Wills b Elliott	1	(8) c Burchett b Elliott		1
W.C.Still	b Wills	3	lbw b Hammersley		8
J.L.Beeston	b Bryant	18	(9) not out		7
*G.H.B.Gilbert	b Bryant	1	(7) b Wills		4
F.Adams	c Thornton b Bryant	14	(6) b Wills		4
O.H.Lewis	b Wills	13	(3) b Wills		40
N.Thompson	b Wills	0	(10) b Wills		0
J.H.Morris	b Wills	0	(11) run out (Morres/Marshall)		0
J.Kinloch	not out	0	(5) c Thornton b Wills		0
Extras	(lb1, nb1, w3)	5	(lb2, w3)		5
Total	(72.0 overs, in about 155 mins)	63	(78.0 overs, in about 175 mins)		77

VICTORIA

J.M.Bryant	c Hilliard b Ward	0	(6) c Gilbert b Ward		32
B.Grindrod	b Kinloch	5	b Ward		3
A.Burchett	c Hilliard b Ward	1	(1) c & b Ward		26
G.Elliott	b Kinloch	0	(8) not out		9
†G.Marshall	c Gilbert b Ward	1	run out (Thompson/Kinloch)		5
E.H.Whitlow	b Ward	3	(10) not out		3
W.J.S.Hammersley	lbw b Kinloch	0	(3) b Kinloch		9
T.F.Morres	c Thompson b Ward	13	(9) b Kinloch		3
*T.W.Wills	c Adams b Kinloch	15	(7) b Ward		8
T.F.Wray	c Lewis b Ward	0			
J.Thornton	not out	0	(4) b Kinloch		0
Extras		-	(b2, lb3)		5
Total	(39.3 overs, in about 90 mins)	38	(67.0 overs, in about 145 mins) (8 wkts)		103

VICTORIA	O	M	R	W	w,nb		O	M	R	W	w,nb		FALL OF WICKETS			
													NSW	VIC	NSW	VIC
Elliott	23	11	16	2	1,-	(4)	25	15	11	1	1,-	Wkt	1st	1st	2nd	2nd
Wills	30	17	24	5	-,-		24	10	25	6	-,-	1st	6	0	0	15
Bryant	13	6	11	3	2,-	(5)	6	2	12	0	1,-	2nd	7	6	31	41
Morres	6	2	7	0	-,1	(1)	9	3	9	0	-,-	3rd	10	6	60	41
Whitlow						(3)	9	2	14	1	-,-	4th	20	6	60	47
Hammersley							5	2	3	1	1,-	5th	23	9	62	49
												6th	39	10	67	77
NEW SOUTH WALES	O	M	R	W	w,nb		O	M	R	W	w,nb	7th	58	12	70	96
Ward	20	10	24	6	-,-		29	11	33	4	-,-	8th	58	38	70	100
Kinloch	19.3	11	14	4	-,-		33	11	51	3	-,-	9th	58	38	76	-
Lewis							2	0	7	0	-,-	10th	63	38	77	-
Thompson							3	1	7	0	-,-					

VICTORIA v NEW SOUTH WALES

Played at Melbourne Cricket Ground on February 2, 3, 4, 1860. (Timeless match)
Toss : None - see below.   Result : VICTORIA WON BY 69 RUNS.
Debuts: Victoria - J.Huddlestone, W.A.Ross (both f/c). New South Wales - E.Brown, J.Clarke, G.D.Dickson, J.L.Kettle, G.B.Richardson,
    E.Samuels (all f/c).
12th Men: No 12th men or emergency fieldsmen named - see below.
Umpires: C.F.Cameron and W.Tunks.
Attendances: 7000, 8000, 10000.   Total: About 25,000.   Receipts: "nearly £1300" (Age).
Close of Play: 1st day NSW 6/32 (Hilliard 13, Murray 1); 2nd day Vic (2) 6/67 (Wills 19, Hammersley 3).

F.Adams, J.Kinloch, O.H.Lewis and E.W.Ward all announced their unavailability for New South Wales for business reasons.
J.B.Thompson withdrew himself from the Victorian team shortly before the commencement of play, so that "unpleasantness might be
avoided by his adopting that course, and also that a blow from a cricket ball the previous day might prevent his fielding as well as he might
otherwise do" (Argus). T.F.Hamilton was sought as a replacement but declined and Ross was brought in for his sole first-class appearance.
Brown had the distinction of becoming the first player to gain selection for New South Wales in a first-class match as a wicket-keeper.
Previous selection policy in matches between the Colonies did not provide for the specialist position, a competent long-stop being
preferred. New South Wales were given choice of innings as the visiting team. The unevenness of bounce in the wicket made batting an
almost impossible exercise. "Undoubtedly, it is bad in soil and condition, and was as hard as a macadamised road; but the bouncings and
sudden rises of the ball were as bad for Victorians as for Sydneyites to play to, hindering both from scoring, and causing both to give
unusual chances away" (Bell's Life). Wills best utilised the conditions - to Victoria's advantage - bowling "with head as much as hand"
(Bell's Life) without a break in either New South Wales innings. W.Thompson substituted for Wray (recurrence of leg injury) on the last
day. Sources: Scores & Biographies, Bells Life in Victoria, The Age, The Argus, The Herald,.

VICTORIA

A.Burchett	c Brown b Thompson	1	(2) b Richardson	7
T.F.Wray	c Hilliard b Richardson	8	(1) c Murray b Richardson	12
J.Huddlestone	c & b Murray	13	(4) c Brown b Richardson	8
J.M.Bryant	c Hilliard b Murray	3	(3) c Brown b Murray	8
†G.Marshall	b Murray	4	(6) c Lewis b Richardson	0
*T.W.Wills	b Murray	4	(7) c Dickson b Richardson	20
W.J.S.Hammersley	b Murray	4	(8) c Dickson b Thompson	11
T.F.Morres	run out(Thompson/Brown)	1	(9) b Richardson	10
W.A.Ross	b Richardson	0	(5) b Thompson	3
J.Thornton	b Richardson	2	(11) run out (Dickson/Brown)	2
G.Elliott	not out	3	(10) not out	5
Extras	(b8, w3, nb2)	13	(b4, lb4, w5)	13
Total	(44.0 overs, 125 mins)	56	(85.2 overs, 256 mins)	99

NEW SOUTH WALES

E.Samuels	b Wills	5	b Wills	2
J.L.Kettle	b Elliott	6	(6) b Elliott	0
G.D.Dickson	b Wills	0	(8) b Elliott	0
H.Hilliard	c Thornton b Wills	15	c Hammersley b Elliott	0
N.Thompson	c Hammersley b Wills	0	(9) c Thornton b Elliott	3
*G.H.B.Gilbert	b Bryant	3	(7) b Elliott	13
J.Clarke	c Burchett b Bryant	0	(2) c Thornton b Wills	0
R.Murray	c Hammersley b Wills	10	(5) b Wills	4
T.H.Lewis	lbw b Wills	0	(3) c Bryant b Elliott	0
†E.Brown	b Elliott	1	not out	9
G.B.Richardson	not out	0	run out (Marshall/Bryant)	8
Extras	(b2, lb1, w1)	4	(lb1, w2)	3
Total	(52.1 overs, 154 mins)	44	(39.3 overs, 137 mins)	42

NEW SOUTH WALES	O	M	R	W	w,nb		O	M	R	W	w,nb
Thompson	6	1	18	1	-,-	(3)	17	10	19	2	1,-
Richardson	22	12	12	3	-,2	(1)	38.2	21	42	6	3,-
Murray	16	6	13	5	3,-	(2)	30	15	25	1	1,-

VICTORIA	O	M	R	W	w,nb		O	M	R	W	w,nb
Elliott	21.1	13	13	2	-,-		20	8	23	6	2,-
Wills	26	14	23	6	1,-		19.3	10	16	3	-,-
Bryant	5	3	4	2	-,-						

FALL OF WICKETS

Wkt	VIC 1st	NSW 1st	VIC 2nd	NSW 2nd
1st	10	9	20	2
2nd	27	10	29	3
3rd	29	14	31	3
4th	35	14	41	8
5th	42	23	41	8
6th	45	31	47	8
7th	46	37	72	13
8th	50	37	81	19
9th	52	44	94	26
10th	56	44	99	42

NEW SOUTH WALES v VICTORIA

Played at The Domain, Sydney, on February 14, 15, 16, 1861. (Timeless match)
Toss : None - see below.　　　　Result : VICTORIA WON BY 21 RUNS.
Debuts: New South Wales - H.C.E.Newcombe, F.Rowley (both f/c). - S.Cosstick, S.Hopkinson, J.N.Jacomb, J.Mace, C.Makinson
(all f/c).
12th Men: A.L.Park (NSW) and R.Ryder (Vic).
Umpires: V.Marshall and W.Tunks.
Attendances: 8000, 8000, 10000.　　　Total: About 26,000.　　　Receipts: No figures published.
Close of Play: 1st day NSW 6/36 (Newcombe 4, Lewis 2); 2nd day Vic (2) 4/26 (Cosstick 7, Makinson 0).

Originally intended to be played on February 12, 13 & 14, the match dates were changed to avoid playing on the 13th, Ash Wednesday.
G.Howell stood down from the New South Wales team to allow Kinloch to play. T.W.Wills was unavailable for Victoria due to family
business in Queensland. Choice of innings was given to Victoria, the visiting team. Kettle received a blow on the inside of his knee from
the bowling of Cosstick and retired hurt at 8/42 in the first innings. Richardson was then dismissed first ball, forcing Kettle to resume
again, with Gilbert as runner. Later, as Gilbert completed a run for him, Kettle wandered out of his crease and Marshall removed a bail,
claiming that the ball was not dead. Umpire Marshall (nephew of the Victorian keeper) agreed and ruled the batsman out, but after strong
protests from Ward and his team - as well as the loss of half an hour's play while the matter was debated - Kettle was reluctantly allowed to
continue by the Victorians. Cosstick made a most impressive debut, his bowling "being for the most part dead on the wicket" (*Victorian
Cricketer's Guide*) and he operated unchanged throughout both New South Wales innings. Sources: *Scores & Biographies, Victorian
Cricketers Guide, Bells Life in Victoria, Sydney Morning Herald.*

VICTORIA

J.C.Brodie	c Clarke b Richardson	13		c Ward b Richardson	0
J.Mace	run out (Gilbert)	2	(8)	run out (Gilbert/Thompson)	5
J.M.Bryant	c Kinloch b Richardson	22	(4)	c Richardson b Kinloch	10
J.Huddlestone	b Richardson	7	(5)	b Kinloch	4
C.Makinson	c Gilbert b Richardson	2	(6)	c Lewis b Ward	23
*†G.Marshall	not out	12	(7)	b Kinloch	1
W.J.S.Hammersley	b Ward	0	(9)	b Ward	3
J.N.Jacomb	lbw b Ward	0	(2)	run out (Newcombe/Thompson)	0
G.Elliott	b Ward	5	(10)	b Ward	1
S.Cosstick	b Ward	0	(3)	c Kinloch b Richardson	12
S.Hopkinson	st Thompson b Ward	0		not out	0
Extras	(b1, lb2, w2)	5		(b1, lb5, w6)	12
Total	(53.2 overs, in about 125 mins)	68		(72.3 overs, in about 165 mins)	71

NEW SOUTH WALES

*E.W.Ward	b Elliott	1	(8)	c Bryant b Cosstick	0
J.Clarke	c Jacomb b Cosstick	4		c Jacomb b Cosstick	1
J.Kinloch	run out (Hammersley/Marshall)	3	(9)	run out (Makinson/Marshall)	1
G.H.B.Gilbert	b Bryant	15	(6)	c Marshall b Cosstick	1
†N.Thompson	b Bryant	7	(7)	c Mace b Bryant	12
J.L.Beeston	b Cosstick	0	(3)	c Bryant b Cosstick	4
H.C.E.Newcombe	not out	23	(5)	c Hammersley b Bryant	2
O.H.Lewis	b Cosstick	2	(4)	b Cosstick	2
F.Rowley	c Hammersley b Bryant	0	(1)	c Makinson b Cosstick	5
J.L.Kettle	lbw b Cosstick	9		not out	13
G.B.Richardson	b Cosstick	0		run out (Jacomb/Marshall)	0
Extras	(b1, lb4, w5)	10		(b1, lb1, w1)	3
Total	(90.1 overs, in about 195 mins)	74		(52.1 overs, in about 110 mins)	44

NEW SOUTH WALES	O	M	R	W	w,nb		O	M	R	W	w,nb
Ward	21.2	7	31	5	-,-		16.3	7	18	3	-,-
Kinloch	13	8	9	0	-,-	(3)	25	16	13	3	-,-
Richardson	19	7	23	4	2,-	(2)	31	12	28	2	6,-

VICTORIA	O	M	R	W	w,nb		O	M	R	W	w,nb
Elliott	26	13	27	1	2,-						
Cosstick	45.1	23	25	5	1,-		26	14	23	6	-,-
Bryant	19	10	12	3	2,-	(1)	26.1	16	18	2	1,-

FALL OF WICKETS

Wkt	VIC 1st	NSW 1st	VIC 2nd	NSW 2nd
1st	10	4	0	1
2nd	23	8	0	9
3rd	39	15	20	11
4th	48	29	24	14
5th	51	30	34	16
6th	51	32	39	16
7th	54	38	49	16
8th	66	39	59	19
9th	66	42	70	37
10th	68	74	71	44

1861-62 to 1869-70 - THE FIRST INTERNATIONAL INFLUENCE (10 MATCHES)

Australia received its first touring teams in the early 1860s and these played crucial roles in raising the standard of cricket in the country. Spiers & Ponds, a leading Melbourne catering firm, sent W.B.Mallam to England in 1861 to act as their agent in attracting the leading cricketers on a tour of Australia. Mallam succeeded only in signing a team of mainly Surrey players under the leadership of H.H.Stephenson. Other leading English professionals deemed the offer of £150 per player to be insufficient. Stephenson's band of 12 arrived in Australia in December 1861 to a tumultuous reception. The tour was a huge financial success and Stephenson's XI played 12 matches against sides from Victoria, New South Wales and Tasmania. (Some of the games were actually referred to as 'Test matches' in W.J.S.Hammersley's *Victorian Cricketer's Guide* for 1861-62 - the first known use of these words.) But as the local teams contained odds of 18 or 22 men, none of these ranked as first-class. The only game to receive this recognition was the 'Surrey v The World' fixture played at Melbourne in March 1862.

One of the tourists, Charles Lawrence, stayed on and was hired to coach Sydney's Albert Club. Through this he made an outstanding contribution to Australian cricket. He also represented New South Wales and captained the first Australian team to tour England, the Aboriginal side of 1868.

George Marshall, assisted by the Melbourne Cricket Club, organised the second English team to tour Australia, that led by George Parr in 1863-64. Matches were played in New South Wales and Victoria (several were also played in New Zealand), but again the local sides fielded odds, and the matches could not now be considered first-class. Only the match between Parr's XI and Anderson's XI in March 1864 was played on even terms. Profits from the tour exceeded those of 1861-62, and again one of the tourists, William Caffyn, remained in Australia as a highly successful coach.

The annual clash between Victoria and New South Wales, which had begun in 1855-56 and had been staged alternatively in Melbourne and Sydney every year since, was halted after a match in Sydney in February 1863 because of an umpiring dispute. Matches between the colonies did not resume until December 1865, though links were maintained in the intervening 2-1/2 years with matches between Sydney's Albert Club and Melbourne Cricket Club. These matches cannot be considered first-class because they were not fully representative of the colonies. By the time intercolonial games resumed, the last of the New South Wales's underarm bowlers had given way to roundarm exponents.

Administrative bodies were formed in Victoria and Tasmania in the 1860s. T.W.Wills convened a meeting at the Freemasons Hotel in Melbourne in February 1864 which resulted in the formation of the Victorian Cricketers Council - forerunner to the Victorian Cricketers' Association which came into being that October. Years later the title was changed to the Victorian Cricket Association. Despite this, Melbourne Cricket Club continued to be a dominating influence.

A meeting in Hobart on February 1, 1866 saw the formation of the Southern Tasmanian Cricket Association. It continued until 1906, when it was reconstituted as the Tasmanian Cricket Association. But cricket in Tasmania had now fallen behind the game on the mainland - partly because of the persistence with underarm bowling and the North-South rivalry on the island. The match against Victoria in Melbourne in 1869 was Tasmania's first on even terms for 11 years.

Leading Aggregates

Batsmen	M	I	NO	Runs	HS	Ave.	Bowlers	Runs	Wkts	Ave.
R.W.Wardill (V)	8	15	2	327	110	25.15	T.W.Wills (V)	507	45	11.26
W.Caffyn (NSW, etc)	6	11	1	261	75*	26.10	S.Cosstick (V, NSW)	383	41	9.34
N.Thompson (NSW)	7	13	0	187	60	14.38	J.Conway (V)	323	29	11.13
J.Phillips (V)	5	8	1	178	115	25.42	C.Lawrence (NSW, etc)	305	26	11.73
E.J.Gregory (NSW)	5	9	0	166	64	18.44	D.W.Gregory (NSW)	221	17	13.00
T.W.Wills (V)	7	10	3	157	58	22.42	F.E.Allan (V)	149	16	9.31
S.Cosstick (V, NSW)	9	15	0	157	27	10.46	N.Thompson (NSW)	306	15	20.40

VICTORIA v NEW SOUTH WALES

Played at Melbourne Cricket Ground on January 9, 10, 11, 1862. (Timeless match)

Toss : Victoria.   Result : VICTORIA WON BY TEN WICKETS.

Debuts: Victoria - J.Conway, C.Mace, W.Stewart, J.B.Thompson, R.W.Wardill (all f/c). New South Wales - G.T.Curtis, J.Moore, A.L.Park (all f/c).

12th Men: H.Deane (NSW). G.Elliott, S.Hopkinson & G.J.P.O'Mullane named as Victorian emergencies.

Umpires: P.C.Curtis (NSW) and J.A.Smith (Vic).

Attendances: 500, 1000, 2000.   Total: About 3500.   Receipts: No figures published.

Close of Play: 1st day Vic 182 all out; 2nd day NSW (2) 5/52 (Moore 8, Gilbert 4).

Poor attendances were blamed on the staging of a match between Victoria and H.H.Stephenson's English Touring Team in Melbourne the previous week. Both sides dispensed with their wicket-keeper at various times throughout the match. New South Wales do not appear to have used a keeper while Thompson bowled, and Victoria lost the services of Marshall when he injured a finger early in the New South Wales first innings. Makinson, and later Bryant, took the gloves for the remainder of the innings but no one was used behind the stumps in the New South Wales second innings. Huddlestone (44 in about 90 minutes, 4 fours) was run out by the bowler at the non-striker's end while backing up before the ball had been bowled "amidst much laughter" (*Victorian Cricketer's Guide*). Kinloch's action was complimented in *The Argus* as a "prettily played dodge". The follow-on by New South Wales was the first recorded in first-class matches in Australia. *The Argus* gives NSW (1) Kettle c Cosstick, other sources as shown here. Sources: *Scores & Biographies, Victorian Cricketers Guide, Bells Life in Victoria, The Age, The Argus, The Herald.*

VICTORIA

*†G.Marshall	b Thompson	35		
C.Mace	b Ward	1		
J.M.Bryant	lbw b Kinloch	3		
S.Cosstick	b Ward	10		
J.Huddlestone	run out (Kinloch)	44		
R.W.Wardill	lbw b Gilbert	36	(1) not out	3
J.B.Thompson	b Moore	16		
C.Makinson	b Moore	19		
J.Conway	run out (Gilbert/Thompson)	0		
W.Stewart	b Kinloch	2		
B.Butterworth	not out	2	(2) not out	2
Extras	(b7, lb5, w2)	14		-
Total	(79.1 overs, in about 195 mins)	182	(4.0 overs, in about 8 mins) (0 wkts)	5

NEW SOUTH WALES

*E.W.Ward	b Conway	0	(8) b Conway	7
A.L.Park	c Bryant b Cosstick	13	(5) b Cosstick	0
E.Saddler	b Stewart	1	(10) hit wkt b Bryant	1
H.C.E.Newcombe	run out (Cosstick/Stewart)	0	(1) c Butterworth b Cosstick	9
J.L.Kettle	c Conway b Stewart	7	(3) c Cosstick b Bryant	6
†N.Thompson	b Conway	15	(2) b Cosstick	12
G.H.B.Gilbert	b Conway	6	b Bryant	26
G.T.Curtis	b Stewart	14	(9) not out	0
F.Rowley	run out (Stewart)	1	(4) c Conway b Cosstick	4
J.Moore	b Stewart	9	(6) b Bryant	21
J.Kinloch	not out	0	b Conway	1
Extras	(b7, w3)	10	(b10, lb6, w6)	22
Total	(65.1 overs, in about 140 mins)	76	(75.0 overs, in about 165 mins)	109

NEW SOUTH WALES	O	M	R	W	w,nb		O	M	R	W	w,nb
Ward	21	2	63	2	-,-						
Kinloch	27	8	46	2	-,-	(1)	2	1	1	0	-,-
Moore	15.1	7	20	2	-,-	(2)	2	0	4	0	-,-
Thompson	8	2	20	1	2,-						
Gilbert	8	0	19	1	-,-						

VICTORIA	O	M	R	W	w,nb		O	M	R	W	w,nb
Conway	23	10	17	3	-,-		22.1	9	22	2	-,-
Stewart	24.1	9	31	4	3,-		10.3	6	8	0	5,-
Bryant	10	7	7	0	-,-	(4)	18	6	29	3	-,-
Cosstick	8	4	11	1	-,-	(3)	21	9	22	5	1,-
Makinson							3	0	6	0	-,-

FALL OF WICKETS

Wkt	VIC 1st	NSW 1st	NSW 2nd	VIC 2nd
1st	5	3	25	-
2nd	22	16	28	-
3rd	41	16	34	-
4th	62	20	38	-
5th	124	37	38	-
6th	148	48	73	-
7th	170	57	107	-
8th	170	58	107	-
9th	174	73	108	-
10th	182	76	109	-

SURREY v THE WORLD

Played at Melbourne Cricket Ground on March 1, 3, 4, 1862. (Timeless match)
Toss : The World.   Result : THE WORLD WON BY SIX WICKETS.
Debuts: Surrey - C.O.Blanchard, F.C.Christy (both f/c).
12th Men: No 12th men or emergency fieldsmen named.
Umpires: J.C.Brodie and J.A.Smith.
Attendances: 4500, 2500, 1000.   Total: About 8000.   Receipts: No figures published.
Close of Play: 1st day World 211 all out; 2nd day Surrey (2) 6/110 (Caffyn 33, Bryant 18).

"When the programme of matches to be played by the English Eleven was being arranged, it was deemed advisable to introduce one in which the Britishers should be divided amongst themselves, and as one-half of them were Surrey men, it was decided on playing that famous cricketing county against all comers, more especially as two or three of our own best men are also Surrey players" (*Bell's Life*). W.J.S.Hammersley was invited to appear for the Surrey XI but declined through lack of practice and his place went to Blanchard. The game was referred to as Surrey v All Comers in *Bell's Life*, but as shown in other sources, and was substituted for the England XI v Victoria XXII match in the original itinerary. Wells (48 in about 120 minutes, 1 five and 4 fours), Bennett (72 in about 210 minutes, 4 fours) and Marshall (45 in about 75 minutes, 6 fours) led the scoring for The World XI. Bennett (14 for 115) completed a fine all-round performance but "the feature of the third day's play was the brilliant innings played by Caffyn" (*Age*), an unbeaten 75 (in about 165 minutes, 11 fours). The World XI used two wicket-keepers - Stephenson in the first innings and Marshall in the second. Griffith took the gloves for the Surrey XI when H.H.Stephenson bowled. F.C.Christy is believed to be the player 'Christy' (or Christie) in the Surrey XI but some doubt exists. Several variations to the bowling analyses exist, those shown are from *Victorian Cricketer's Guide*, the others not adding up. *Scores & Biographies* incorrectly gives Surrey (2) Mudie c Marshall b Bennett, Iddison 1/65, Bennett 8/85. Sources: *Scores & Biographies, Victorian Cricketers Guide, Bell's Life in Victoria, The Age, The Argus, The Herald.*

THE WORLD

G.Wells	b Caffyn	48	(5)	not out	27
R.W.Wardill	c Mudie b Caffyn	7	(4)	b Griffith	12
†E.Stephenson	b Griffith	4		st Stephenson b Griffith	2
G.Bennett	c Cosstick b Griffith	72			
G.Marshall	c Mudie b Stephenson	45			
R.Iddison	c Stephenson b Griffith	28			
C.Lawrence	c Elliott b Griffith	0	(2)	run out (/Stephenson)	15
*T.Hearne	b Bryant	1	(1)	b Bryant	5
J.Huddlestone	b Bryant	0	(6)	not out	17
J.Moore	b Griffith	0			
J.Conway	not out	0			
Extras	(b1, lb3, w1, nb1)	6		(b6, lb2)	8
Total	(98.0 overs, in about 235 mins)	211		(42.1 overs, in about 105 mins) (4 wkts)	86

SURREY

*†H.H.Stephenson	c Iddison b Lawrence	4	(7)	c Bennett b Iddison	3
W.Mortlock	b Iddison	15	(5)	b Bennett	4
G.Griffith	c Wardill b Bennett	39	(6)	b Bennett	13
W.Caffyn	c & b Bennett	13		not out	75
S.Cosstick	lbw b Bennett	22	(3)	b Bennett	15
J.M.Bryant	c & b Bennett	1	(8)	b Conway	24
W.Mudie	c Stephenson b Bennett	14	(1)	c Marshall b Iddison	13
T.Sewell, jr	st Stephenson b Bennett	4	(2)	c & b Bennett	10
C.O.Blanchard	c Lawrence b Bennett	0	(10)	c Wardill b Bennett	11
G.Elliott	not out	0	(9)	c Huddlestone b Bennett	7
F.C.Christy	run out (Iddison/Stephenson)	0		b Bennett	0
Extras	(b2, w1)	3		(b2, lb1, w1)	4
Total	(61.2 overs, in about 145 mins)	115		(91.2 overs, in about 205 mins)	179

SURREY	O	M	R	W	w,nb		O	M	R	W	w,nb
Caffyn	26	6	63	2	1,-	(4)	3	1	11	0	-,-
Griffith	35	15	52	5	-,-	(1)	16.1	4	37	2	-,-
Bryant	13	6	22	2	-,-	(2)	18	8	17	1	-,-
Sewell	3	0	12	0	-,-	(3)	5	3	13	0	-,-
Mudie	1	0	3	0	-,-						
Mortlock	5	0	13	0	-,-						
Cosstick	6	0	8	0	-,-						
Stephenson	9	0	32	1	-,1						

THE WORLD	O	M	R	W	w,nb		O	M	R	W	w,nb
Iddison	30	10	53	1	1,-		36	13	65	2	-,-
Lawrence	14	3	29	1	-,-	(4)	5	3	5	0	-,-
Bennett	17.2	7	30	7	-,-	(2)	40.2	10	85	7	1,-
Wells						(3)	4	0	10	0	-,-
Conway							6	2	10	1	-,-

FALL OF WICKETS

Wkt	WOR 1st	SUR 1st	WOR 2nd	SUR 2nd
1st	18	16	20	15
2nd	22	28	40	24
3rd	90	55	40	24
4th	162	85	48	25
5th	209	94	67	-
6th	209	100	70	-
7th	210	113	133	-
8th	210	113	144	-
9th	211	115	179	-
10th	211	115	179	-

15

NEW SOUTH WALES v VICTORIA

Played at The Domain, Sydney, February 5, 6, 7, 1863. (Timeless match)
Toss : Victoria.   Result : NEW SOUTH WALES WON BY 84 RUNS.
Debuts: New South Wales - D.D'Arcy, E.B.Docker, F.O.Gorman, E.J.Gregory, S.Jones, W.G.MacNish (all f/c); C.Lawrence (NSW only).
   Victoria - V.L.Cameron, W.H.Greaves, A.Hope, J.Redfearn (all f/c).
12th Men: J.Boak (NSW) and J.Bennett (Vic).
Umpires: R.Driver and J.A.Smith. See below.
Attendances: 5000, 6000, 8000.   Total: About 19,000   Receipts: No figures published.
Close of Play: 1st day Vic 8/51 (Wills 11, Hopkinson 3); 2nd day NSW (2) 4/15 (Jones 7, Gorman 3). See below.

The match was dominated by the umpiring dispute after lunch on the second day during the New South Wales second innings. Jones, the batsman on strike, left his crease at the end of the over and while the field was changing over Marshall, the Victorian keeper, took off the bails and appealed for a run out. Smith, the Victorian umpire, promptly gave the batsman out but Driver, at the bowler's end, stated that he had called over. Discussions took place on the ground for 20 minutes without resolution before both teams left the field and play was abandoned for the day. A meeting of the Victorians that evening decided that Jones would be allowed to continue on the following day. Marshall and Greaves however refused to play further, Bennett and G.T.Curtis substituting in the field on the following day. Both umpires also withdrew from the match and were replaced by W.Fairfax and E.W.Ward for the final day. There was some uncertainty as to whether the game was over when Victoria reached 8/45 on the last day. "After a delay of about ten minutes, and no other batsman being forthcoming on the side of Victoria, the match was given in by Wills" (*SMH*). Huddlestone was out first ball in each innings. New South Wales did not use a wicket-keeper at any stage of the game. Lawrence had previously appeared for Surrey and Middlesex. *Scores & Biographies* incorrectly gives NSW (2) Conway 4/31; Vic (2) Conway 7, extras 1. Sources: *Scores & Biographies, Bells Life in Sydney , Sydney Morning Herald.*

NEW SOUTH WALES

N.Thompson	c Marshall b Conway	6	(7) c sub (G.T.Curtis) b Wills	16
J.Clarke	c Hope b Conway	8	b Conway	1
S.Jones	b Conway	0	(4) b Wills	15
F.O.Gorman	c & b Greaves	19	(6) c Redfearn b Wills	5
G.H.B.Gilbert	st Marshall b Conway	22	c Conway b Wills	0
*C.Lawrence	c Conway b Cosstick	1	(3) c & b Wills	5
H.C.E.Newcombe	c Hopkinson b Wills	13	(8) b Conway	0
E.J.Gregory	c Marshall b Wills	3	(11) c Hope b Conway	13
D.D'Arcy	c Hope b Wills	17	not out	34
W.G.MacNish	b Conway	12	b Cosstick	1
E.B.Docker	not out	0	(1) c Redfearn b Conway	1
Extras	(b2, lb3, w2)	7	(lb4, w2)	6
Total	(84.0 overs, in about 185 mins)	108	(81.0 overs, in about 175 mins)	97

VICTORIA

S.Cosstick	b Thompson	4	(4) lbw b Lawrence	6
R.W.Wardill	c MacNish b Lawrence	3	(1) c Thompson b Lawrence	4
J.Huddlestone	lbw b Lawrence	0	c Thompson b Lawrence	0
J.Redfearn	c Gilbert b Lawrence	5	(5) b Thompson	0
W.H.Greaves	b Thompson	11	absent	-
†G.Marshall	b Lawrence	5	absent	-
*T.W.Wills	not out	25	(6) not out	17
J.Conway	b Thompson	1	(9) c & b Lawrence	1
V.L.Cameron	lbw b Lawrence	4	(2) lbw b Lawrence	9
S.Hopkinson	c & b Lawrence	5	(7) c Gilbert b Lawrence	4
A.Hope	b Lawrence	8	(8) c & b Lawrence	2
Extras	(b3, w2)	5	(b2)	2
Total	(54.1 overs, in about 125 mins)	76	(33.0 overs, in about 75 mins)	45

VICTORIA	O	M	R	W	w,nb	O	M	R	W	w,nb
Conway	27	6	35	5	1,-	29	14	30	4	1,-
Wills	32	12	45	3	1,-	40	13	51	5	1,-
Cosstick	21	10	17	1	-,-	12	7	10	1	-,-
Greaves	4	0	4	1	-,-					

NEW SOUTH WALES	O	M	R	W	w,nb	O	M	R	W	w,nb
Lawrence	24.1	4	48	7	-,-	16	8	25	7	-,-
Thompson	27	13	21	3	1,-	16	8	17	1	-,-
Docker	3	2	2	0	1,-	1	0	1	0	-,-

FALL OF WICKETS

Wkt	NSW 1st	VIC 1st	NSW 2nd	VIC 2nd
1st	12	3	3	8
2nd	12	3	7	8
3rd	17	7	11	20
4th	50	13	11	21
5th	52	28	17	21
6th	67	32	37	25
7th	70	34	40	41
8th	81	39	60	45
9th	101	57	65	-
10th	108	76	97	-

G.ANDERSON'S XI v G.PARR'S XI

Played at Melbourne Cricket Ground on March 5, 7, 8, 1864. (Timeless match)
Toss : G.Parr's XI.   Result : G ANDERSON'S XI WON BY FOUR WICKETS.
Debuts: G.Parr's XI - T.J.D.Kelly, J.P.McPherson, G.Tait (all f/c). G.Anderson's XI - M.E.O'Brien, W.Simmonds (both f/c).
12th Men: No 12th men or emergency fieldsmen named.
Umpires: T.Butterworth and G.Elliott.
Attendances: 5000, 4000, 4000.   Total: About 13,000   Receipts: No figures published.
Close of Play: 1st day Parr's XI 153 all out; 2nd day Parr's XI (2) 3/30 (Tarrant 10, Caffyn 7).

The origins of this match were attributed to criticism from local followers of the game "that no opportunity had as yet been offered of thoroughly testing the skill of the English champions" (*Bell's Life*). The English tourists were divided and leading Victorian players selected to complete the two XI's. The start of the match was delayed 90 minutes because of a dispute over match payments. Five of the Australian professionals selected - J.M.Bryant, R.C.Hewitt, J.Huddlestone (Parr's XI); S.Cosstick and W.H.Greaves (Anderson's XI) - contended that the three-guinea allowance per player was insufficient and demanded an increase. *The Age* reported that the five finally agreed to play but George Parr then objected and threatened to withdraw from the game with the English players if the five played. The situation was resolved with the substitution of Hope, Kelly, McPherson, O'Brien and Tait for the professionals, a move which lowered the standard of what was effectively an exhibition match. Wills took three wickets in four balls - Kelly, ball, Caesar, Carpenter - in the second innings. *Scores & Biographies* has incorrect match dates, also Anderson (1) Hayward c Cameron instead of Wardill (substitute for Cameron, absent); Anderson (2) Caffyn 2/21. Sources: *Scores & Biographies, Bells Life in Victoria, The Age, The Argus, The Herald.*

G.PARR'S XI

J.Caesar	st Lockyer b Grace	9	(3) b Wills	0
R.C.Tinley	c Simmonds b Hayward	24	(11) b Hayward	13
G.F.Tarrant	b Jackson	9	(1) c Hayward b Jackson	17
R.P.Carpenter	b Hayward	22	b Wills	0
W.Caffyn	b Grace	34	c Wills b Grace	40
†G.Marshall	st Lockyer b Jackson	1	(8) c & b Grace	9
*G.Parr	not out	26	(6) c Wills b Grace	4
V.L.Cameron	c & b Grace	1	(10) not out	20
T.J.D.Kelly	b Grace	0	(2) b Wills	13
G.Tait	c Anderson b Grace	4	(7) b Wills	3
J.P.McPherson	c Clarke b Hayward	12	(9) lbw b Grace	7
Extras	(b2, lb9)	11	(b1, lb2)	3
Total	(93.0 overs, in about 200 mins)	153	(106.0 overs, in about 215 mins)	129

G.ANDERSON'S XI

E.M.Grace	b Tarrant	21	b Caffyn	0
R.W.Wardill	c & b Tinley	9	b Tarrant	7
T.W.Wills	b Tinley	4		
T.Hayward	c sub (R.W.Wardill) b Tinley	17	c Carpenter b Tarrant	1
*G.Anderson	st Marshall b Tinley	5	c Tait b Caffyn	38
M.E.O'Brien	st Marshall b Tinley	0	b Tarrant	6
†T.Lockyer	b Caffyn	44	not out	40
A.Clarke	b Caffyn	40	not out	6
J.Jackson	c Kelly b Tinley	12	(3) b Tarrant	12
W.Simmonds	b Tinley	3		
A.Hope	not out	2		
Extras	(b3, lb8)	11	(b4, lb1)	5
Total	(109.3 overs, in about 215 mins)	168	(75.1 overs, in about 155 mins) (6 wkts)	115

G.ANDERSON'S XI	O	M	R	W	w,nb		O	M	R	W	w,nb
Wills	6	1	11	0	-,-		35	19	34	4	-,-
Jackson	46	23	60	2	-,-	(4)	18	11	17	1	-,-
Grace	16	4	33	5	-,-		25	9	36	4	-,-
Hayward	25	11	38	3	-,-	(2)	28	11	39	1	-,-

G.PARR'S XI	O	M	R	W	w,nb		O	M	R	W	w,nb
Tarrant	44.1	20	50	1	-,-	(2)	33	13	63	4	-,-
Tinley	46.2	11	76	7	-,-	(3)	14	4	21	0	-,-
Caffyn	15	5	14	2	-,-	(1)	28.1	17	26	2	-,-
McPherson	4	0	17	0	-,-						

FALL OF WICKETS

Wkt	PAR 1st	AND 1st	PAR 2nd	AND 2nd
1st	24	30	13	0
2nd	39	34	13	13
3rd	42	46	13	17
4th	78	56	48	25
5th	79	56	67	40
6th	111	67	74	100
7th	117	135	80	-
8th	117	154	94	-
9th	127	166	95	-
10th	153	168	129	-

VICTORIA v NEW SOUTH WALES

Played at Melbourne Cricket Ground on December 26, 27, 28, 1865. (Timeless match)
Toss : New South Wales.   Result : VICTORIA WON BY AN INNINGS AND 20 RUNS.
Debuts: Victoria - E.Fowler, G.W.H.Gibson, G.J.P.O'Mullane, J.Phillips, J.B.Turner, D.Wilkie (all f/c). New South Wales - R.C.Hewitt,
   C.M.Kellick, J.N.Oatley, C.N.J.Oliver (all f/c); W.Caffyn, S.Cosstick (both NSW only).
12th Men: S.W.G.Campbell (Vic) and C.Readett (NSW).
Umpires: R.Driver and G.Wisden.
Attendances: 5000, 2000, 3000.   Total: About 10,000.   Receipts: No figures published.
Close of Play: 1st day Vic 5/121 (Greaves 5); 2nd day NSW (2) 2/55 (Kellick 23, Gregory 2).

Competition between the two Colonies resumed after a two-season abandonment brought on by the dispute in the match in Sydney in 1863. Contact had been maintained with a match in each of the intervening seasons between Sydney's Albert Club and the Melbourne Cricket Club. These games were privately arranged and could not be considered truly representative. George Marshall, a key figure in the 1863 dispute, was unavailable for Victoria. Gregory (43 in about 105 minutes, 5 fours) scored invaluable runs for the visitors on the opening day. The Victorian batsmen also struggled until the advent of Wills to the crease. His 58 (in about 125 minutes, 1 five and 3 fours) "was undoubtedly the best innings he has played for many years" (*Age*) and, with the support of Rees and O'Mullane, he saw the addition of 132 for the last two wickets to put Victoria in a strong position. Tight bowling in both innings (6 for 58 from 71.1 overs) completed a fine all-round match for him, despite murmurings about the legality of his action. An unidentified member of the New South Wales team was quoted in *The Age* - "We were beaten on our merits, sir; there is no doubt of that, except the 'shying'". Cosstick, a former Victorian player, bowled tirelessly in what was to be his only match for New South Wales. Caffyn, who had remained in Australia after the 1863-64 tour, had previously appeared with Surrey (1849-63); Kelly's previous appearance was for Parr's XI two years before. Sources: *Scores & Biographies, Bells Life in Victoria, The Age, The Argus, The Herald*.

NEW SOUTH WALES

C.M.Kellick	c Kelly b Wills	11		c O'Mullane b Wills	23
W.Caffyn	run out (O'Mullane)	2	(5)	c O'Mullane b Conway	5
N.Thompson	c Conway b Wills	2	(7)	b Conway	2
S.Cosstick	b Wills	2	(8)	run out (Rees/O'Mullane)	21
†R.C.Hewitt	c Conway b Turner	12	(6)	b Conway	3
E.J.Gregory	c Rees b Wilkie	43	(4)	c Kelly b Conway	18
*C.Lawrence	b Conway	3	(2)	run out (Wills/Turner)	23
S.Jones	c Wills b Conway	11	(3)	lbw b Wills	3
G.T.Curtis	c & b Wilkie	13		b Conway	0
J.N.Oatley	b Wills	2	(11)	not out	3
C.N.J.Oliver	not out	6	(10)	c Fowler b Conway	29
Extras	(b5, lb10)	15		(b1, lb10, w1, nb1)	13
Total	(80.1 overs, in about 185 mins)	122		(87.0 overs, in about 190 mins)	143

VICTORIA

J.B.Turner	c Gregory b Cosstick	12
G.W.H.Gibson	b Cosstick	17
J.Conway	c Gregory b Cosstick	33
T.J.D.Kelly	c & b Cosstick	4
E.Fowler	c & b Cosstick	37
W.H.Greaves	c Thompson b Cosstick	25
J.Phillips	c Lawrence b Cosstick	2
W.L.Rees	c Caffyn b Cosstick	37
D.Wilkie	b Lawrence	3
*T.W.Wills	lbw b Lawrence	58
†G.J.P.O'Mullane	not out	33
Extras	(b14, lb9, w1)	24
Total	(123.3 overs, in about 265 mins)	285

VICTORIA	O	M	R	W	w,nb		O	M	R	W	w,nb		FALL OF WICKETS			
Conway	30	11	47	2	-,-		36	12	68	6	1,-			NSW	VIC	NSW
Wills	37.1	17	33	4	-,-	(5)	34	18	25	2	-,-	Wkt	1st	1st	2nd
Turner	5	3	7	1	-,-	(4)	8	2	17	0	-,1	1st	15	34	46
Greaves	2	0	8	0	-,-	(3)	4	2	7	0	-,-	2nd	15	39	53
Wilkie	6	2	12	2	-,-	(2)	5	0	13	0	-,-	3rd	19	45	56
												4th	28	116	69
NEW SOUTH WALES	O	M	R	W	w,nb							5th	42	121	73
Cosstick	50	6	109	8	-,-							6th	69	127	77
Thompson	30	8	43	0	1,-							7th	87	148	102
Lawrence	23.3	2	57	2	-,-							8th	114	153	104
Caffyn	15	4	44	0	-,-							9th	114	231	130
Hewitt	3	0	7	0	-,-							10th	122	285	143
Gregory	2	1	1	0	-,-										

NEW SOUTH WALES v VICTORIA

Played at The Domain, Sydney, on December 26, 27, 1866. (Timeless match)
Toss : New South Wales.   Result : NEW SOUTH WALES WON BY AN INNINGS AND 13 RUNS.
Debuts: New South Wales - S.H.Belcher, G.H.Gordon, D.W.Gregory, G.B.Stack (all f/c). Victoria - S.W.G.Campbell, B.J.Wardill
   (both f/c); J.P.McPherson, G.P.Robertson (both Vic only).
12th Men: E.O.Sheridan (NSW) and G.R.Rippon (Vic).
Umpires: G.T.Curtis and J.C.Stewart.
Attendances: 5000, 3000.   Total: About 8000.   Receipts: No figures published.
Close of Play: 1st day NSW 4/93 (Caffyn 17, Gordon 6).
The Victorians were weakened by the unavailability of V.L.Cameron, E.Fowler, T.J.D.Kelly, G.J.P.O'Mullane, W.Simmonds,
R.W.Wardill and T.W.Wills for various reasons. All were considered worthy of inclusion. Turner was a late addition to the Victorian
team, causing Rippon to be relegated to 12th man. Richard Driver, secretary to the New South Wales Cricket Association, was appointed
as the home umpire for the match but stood down in favour of Curtis following criticism of a possible conflict of interests. Hot, sultry
weather prevailed throughout the two days required to complete the match and bowlers dictated the terms. D.W.Gregory bowled unchanged
through both Victorian innings and Conway operated without a break during the New South Wales innings. The game produced another
instance of a bowler (Thompson) running out the non-striker (Campbell) for backing up before the delivery. "Thompson feinted a delivery
and finding Campbell advanced beyond the crease, stumped him" (*SMH*). The lack of comment in contemporary reports however indicates
that this form of dismissal was considered fair play at the time. Victoria employed the use of two wicket-keepers, Gibson on the first day
and Phillips on the second. McPherson and Robertson had previously represented G.Parr's XI in 1863-64 and Oxford University in 1866
respectively. Sources: *Scores & Biographies, Bells Life in Sydney, Sydney Morning Herald.*

VICTORIA

J.B.Turner	b Thompson	4		b D.W.Gregory		0
J.Phillips	b Thompson	1	(6)	st Hewitt b Lawrence		6
J.Conway	c Lawrence b D.W.Gregory	6	(7)	run out (	/D.W.Gregory)	1
G.P.Robertson	run out (Gordon)	9		b Thompson		1
*†G.W.H.Gibson	run out (Thompson/Hewitt)	22	(2)	b D.W.Gregory		1
W.H.Greaves	b D.W.Gregory	3	(8)	c Gilbert b Lawrence		15
S.W.G.Campbell	run out (Thompson)	1	(3)	b Thompson		1
S.Cosstick	c E.J.Gregory b Thompson	11	(9)	c Belcher b Thompson		18
J.P.McPherson	b D.W.Gregory	0	(11)	not out		0
D.Wilkie	run out (Gilbert/Thompson)	12	(5)	st Hewitt b D.W.Gregory		8
B.J.Wardill	not out	0	(10)	lbw b D.W.Gregory		4
Extras	(b1, lb3, nb1)	5		(w2, nb1)		3
Total	(48.1 overs, in about 100 mins)	74		(45.2 overs, in about 95 mins)		58

NEW SOUTH WALES

G.H.B.Gilbert	c Cosstick b Conway	16
S.H.Belcher	b Conway	9
N.Thompson	c Phillips b Cosstick	16
†R.C.Hewitt	c Campbell b Conway	19
W.Caffyn	c & b Cosstick	24
G.H.Gordon	b Conway	19
*C.Lawrence	run out (McPherson)	14
E.J.Gregory	c Wilkie b Cosstick	8
G.B.Stack	not out	4
A.L.Park	c Wardill b Conway	0
D.W.Gregory	b Conway	0
Extras	(b5, lb6, w5)	16
Total	(99.2 overs, in about 225 mins)	145

NEW SOUTH WALES	O	M	R	W	w,nb	O	M	R	W	w,nb
D.W.Gregory	24.1	9	36	3	,1	23	6	31	4	1,2
Thompson	24	10	33	3	-,-	16.2	9	13	3	-,-
Lawrence						6	1	11	2	-,-

VICTORIA	O	M	R	W	w,nb
Conway	50.2	25	42	6	3,-
Greaves	11	5	16	0	-,-
Cosstick	27	8	48	3	2,-
Wilkie	11	1	23	0	-,-

FALL OF WICKETS

	VIC	NSW	VIC
Wkt	1st	1st	2nd
1st	4	11	1
2nd	5	31	2
3rd	18	58	4
4th	24	73	4
5th	30	113	13
6th	40	115	16
7th	55	133	34
8th	55	145	43
9th	73	145	52
10th	74	145	58

VICTORIA v NEW SOUTH WALES

Played at Melbourne Cricket Ground on December 26, 27, 28, 30, 1867. (Timeless match)
Toss : New South Wales.   Result : VICTORIA WON BY SEVEN WICKETS.
Debuts: Victoria - F.E.Allan, J.Bennett (both f/c). New South Wales - J.Coates, E.O.Sheridan, A.Sinclair (all f/c).
12th Men: C.Blair (NSW). None named for Victoria.
Umpires: S.A.Neale and J.A.Smith.
Attendances: 4000, 400, 4000, 600.   Total: About 9000.   Receipts: No figures published.
Close of Play: 1st day Vic 252 all out; 2nd day NSW 5/85 (Caffyn 15, Lawrence 5); 3rd day NSW (2) 173 all out.

Gilbert replaced S.H.Belcher (unavailable) in the New South Wales team before its departure from Sydney. Richard Driver, the appointed New South Wales umpire, was also unavailable at the last moment and was replaced by S.A.Neale, a member of the New South Wales Legislative Assembly. Lawrence surprisingly sent Victoria in to bat on "a splendid wicket, which looked for all the world like a first class billiard-table" (*Age*). Wardill (110 in about 260 minutes, 9 fours, chance at 47) compiled the first century in Australian first-class cricket. When dismissed at 235 his score was shown as 107, but was altered later when it was discovered that a three had been incorrectly credited as byes. His fourth wicket stand of 113 with Robertson (53 in about 105 minutes, 7 fours) was also the first century partnership at this level. After the match, he was presented with a bat and a silver cup in recognition of his effort. A dust-storm, followed by heavy rain, caused the abandonment of the second day's play in mid-afternoon, with New South Wales precariously placed. Thompson (35 in about 60 minutes, 4 fours and 60 in about 115 minutes, 6 fours) topscored in each innings but Allan (8 for 102) and Wills (9 for 149) bowled Victoria to victory. W.J.S.Hammersley, writing as 'Longstop' in *The Australasian*, considered Allan's performance on debut to have been the major factor in Victoria's win and that "he bowled with extraordinary precision". Ned Gregory and Thompson alternated as wicket-keeper while Hewitt bowled.   Sources: *Scores & Biographies, The Age, The Argus, The Herald, The Australasian*.

VICTORIA

R.W.Wardill	c Caffyn b E.J.Gregory	110	not out	45
†G.W.H.Gibson	c Thompson b Lawrence	21	c Sinclair b Coates	1
J.Conway	st Hewitt b Lawrence	8	c Sinclair b E.J.Gregory	23
T.J.D.Kelly	c Coates b Lawrence	0	hit wkt b E.J.Gregory	2
G.P.Robertson	c Thompson b Hewitt	53	not out	2
S.W.G.Campbell	c Thompson b Caffyn	0		
S.Cosstick	c Hewitt b Caffyn	6		
*T.W.Wills	c E.J.Gregory b Hewitt	23		
W.H.Greaves	run out	8		
J.Bennett	b Hewitt	0		
F.E.Allan	not out	1		
Extras	(b10, lb7, w5)	22	(b4, lb3, w2)	9
Total	(120.2 overs, in about 280 mins)	252	(39.2 overs, in about 95 mins) (3 wkts)	82

NEW SOUTH WALES

N.Thompson	c Gibson b Wills	35	c Bennett b Wills	60
E.O.Sheridan	b Wills	13	(3) run out	1
†R.C.Hewitt	b Allan	4	(7) b Wills	14
E.J.Gregory	b Allan	6	b Allan	4
W.Caffyn	c Greaves b Wills	24	c Kelly b Allan	38
G.H.Gordon	c Kelly b Wills	1	(9) run out (Robertson/Gibson)	31
*C.Lawrence	c Kelly b Allan	15	(8) c Wills b Allan	1
A.Sinclair	c Wills b Allan	7	(10) c Greaves b Wills	12
D.W.Gregory	c Gibson b Wills	0	(11) not out	2
G.H.B.Gilbert	b Allan	22	(6) run out (Gibson)	2
J.Coates	not out	18	(2) st Gibson b Wills	3
Extras	(b2, lb9, w2)	13	(lb5)	5
Total	(142.3 overs, in about 275 mins)	158	(98.3 overs, in about 210 mins)	173

NEW SOUTH WALES	O	M	R	W	w,nb		O	M	R	W	w,nb
Thompson	17	5	27	0	-,-	(3)	12.2	0	26	0	-,-
Coates	20	6	44	0	2,-		7	1	15	1	-,-
Lawrence	13	3	31	3	-,-	(4)	4	1	10	0	-,-
D.W.Gregory	10	0	34	0	-,-	(1)	7	3	8	0	2,-
Gilbert	5	0	19	0	-,-						
Caffyn	19	3	33	2	-,-						
Hewitt	23.2	8	28	3	2,-						
E.J.Gregory	13	5	14	1	1,-	(5)	9	3	14	2	-,-

VICTORIA	O	M	R	W	w,nb		O	M	R	W	w,nb
Conway	17	6	25	0	2,-	(3)	5	0	21	0	-,-
Allan	62.3	32	59	5	-,-	(1)	40.3	21	43	3	-,-
Wills	58	31	55	5	-,-	(2)	44	11	94	4	-,-
Cosstick	5	2	6	0	-,-		9	4	10	0	-,-

FALL OF WICKETS

Wkt	VIC 1st	NSW 1st	NSW 2nd	VIC 2nd
1st	45	43	8	3
2nd	54	54	9	55
3rd	60	54	27	73
4th	173	62	103	-
5th	174	65	111	-
6th	186	98	111	-
7th	236	108	112	-
8th	250	112	136	-
9th	250	112	164	-
10th	252	158	173	-

VICTORIA v TASMANIA

Played at Melbourne Cricket Ground on February 12, 13, 1869. (Two-day match)
Toss : Victoria. Result : VICTORIA WON BY AN INNINGS AND 260 RUNS.
Debuts: Victoria - D.Campbell, J.W.Egglestone, W.W.Gaggin, L.Goldsmith (all f/c). Tasmania - G.H.Arthur, J.L.A.Arthur, W.T.Birch, J.H.Burn, D.C.Cuthbert, T.Daly, H.R.G.Dumaresq, H.Evans, J.Hamilton (all f/c).
12th Men: No 12th men or emergency fieldsmen named. Only 11 men in Tasmanian party.
Umpires: H.E.Lette and J.A.Smith.
Attendances: 1000, 2000. Total: About 3000. Receipts: No figures published.
Close of Play: 1st day Vic 6/265 (Phillips 70, Egglestone 75).

This was the first eleven-a-side encounter between Victoria and Tasmania since 1858. Intervening matches saw Tasmanian XVI's in the field against Victorian XI's, the last three games resulting in Tasmanian victories. This prompted Tasmanian requests that future matches be contested on even terms. A secondary request that no "professional assistance" (*STCA Report*) be included in the Victorian team was refused by the Melbourne Cricket Club. The Tasmanian team was further weakened by the inability of leading players, D.Barclay, W.T.Glynn, T.Hogg, J.C.Lord and W.H.Walker to make the trip to Melbourne. Wills and Cosstick swept away the Tasmanian first innings in under 90 minutes, Cosstick conceding only a single run and that not until his twentieth over. Evans bowled Gibson with his first ball in his only first-class match and quickly picked up the wickets of Wardill and Campbell to have 3 for 8 after three overs. However, Phillips (chanceless 115 in about 310 minutes, 4 fours) "played a fine steady innings throughout" (*Argus*) to guide Victoria to the highest total yet recorded (it remained so until February 1882). He had partnerships of 102 with Kelly (63 in about 95 minutes, 8 fours) for the fourth wicket, 136 with Egglestone (90 in about 75 minutes, 1 five and 10 fours) for the seventh wicket and 94 with Campbell (52 in about 80 minutes, 7 fours) for the ninth wicket. The brothers G.H. and J.L.A.Arthur "exhibited some excellent cricket" (*Argus*) in a half-century fourth wicket stand in the second innings but there the Tasmanian resistance ended. Sources: *Scores & Biographies, STCA Report, The Age, The Argus, The Herald, The Australasian*.

TASMANIA

*†J.L.A.Arthur	b Wills	0	(5)	c Egglestone b Cosstick	43
H.R.G.Dumaresq	c D.Campbell b Wills	1	(6)	b Wills	0
T.Whitesides	c Gaggin b Cosstick	2	(1)	b Wardill	14
C.T.H.Perry	run out (S.W.G.Campbell)	0	(2)	b Wardill	13
W.T.Birch	b Cosstick	2	(4)	b Wardill	0
T.Daly	b Wills	1	(8)	b Cosstick	2
D.C.Cuthbert	b Cosstick	0	(9)	not out	10
H.Evans	b Cosstick	1	(10)	c & b Wills	12
J.H.Burn	b Cosstick	0	(11)	c D.Campbell b Wills	1
G.H.Arthur	not out	4	(3)	b Wills	26
J.Hamilton	c Wills b Cosstick	6	(7)	c Kelly b Wills	2
Extras	(lb1)	1		(b4, lb4)	8
Total	(43.1 overs, in about 85 mins)	18		(88.3 overs, in about 165 mins)	131

VICTORIA

†G.W.H.Gibson	b Evans	1
*R.W.Wardill	c & b Evans	9
J.Phillips	c Daly b Evans	115
S.W.G.Campbell	c Daly b Evans	2
T.J.D.Kelly	b J.L.A.Arthur	63
W.W.Gaggin	b J.L.A.Arthur	21
S.Cosstick	b J.L.A.Arthur	3
J.W.Egglestone	c Dumaresq b Daly	90
L.Goldsmith	b J.L.A.Arthur	12
D.Campbell	c & b Evans	52
T.W.Wills	not out	0
Extras	(b19, lb1, w21)	41
Total	(150.1 overs, in about 315 mins)	409

VICTORIA	O	M	R	W	w,nb		O	M	R	W	w,nb		FALL OF WICKETS		
													TAS	VIC	TAS
Wills	22	12	16	3	-,-	(4)	22.3	9	31	5	-,-	Wkt	1st	1st	2nd
Cosstick	21.1	20	1	6	-,-	(3)	27	16	24	2	-,-	1st	0	3	24
Wardill						(1)	22	6	39	3	-,-	2nd	3	12	27
Gaggin						(2)	17	3	29	0	-,-	3rd	3	14	30
												4th	5	116	86
TASMANIA	O	M	R	W	w,nb							5th	5	155	95
Daly	37	11	78	1	1,-							6th	5	159	101
Evans	27.1	4	87	5	9,-							7th	7	295	105
Hamilton	25	5	52	0	3,-							8th	7	315	107
Perry	17	4	33	0	1,-							9th	11	409	128
J.L.A.Arthur	37	2	100	4	7,-							10th	18	409	131
Whitesides	7	0	18	0	-,-										

NEW SOUTH WALES v VICTORIA

Played at The Domain, Sydney, on March 4, 5, 6, 1869. (Three-day match)
Toss : Victoria.   Result : VICTORIA WON BY 78 RUNS.
Debuts: New South Wales - R.J.Fairweather, J.Kellick (both f/c). Victoria - A.W.F.Noyes (f/c); E.S.Carter (Vic only).
12th Men: No 12th men or emergency fieldsmen named.
Umpires: G.T.Curtis and J.A.Smith.
Attendances: 10000, 12000, 12000.   Total: About 34,000.   Receipts: No figures published.
Close of Play: 1st day Vic (2) 1/4 (Phillips 4); 2nd day NSW (2) 0/21 (Sheridan 8, Gregory 13).

Fairweather and Kellick replaced G.H.B.Gilbert and J.Moore (both unavailable) in a squad of thirteen named for New South Wales, from which C.S. and E.J.Gregory were finally omitted. Wardill was out to the first ball of the match and runs were at a premium thereafter. Thompson kept wickets while Hewitt bowled, an interchange of roles that was a common occurrence of the times. Allan captured the wickets of Fairweather and Stack with his second and third deliveries, his career-best 8 for 20 destroying the New South Wales first innings. Carter (63 in about 150 minutes, 11 twos and 41 singles) was missed three times, "but played with an ability that surprised his confreres as much as it baffled his opponents" (*SMH*). His grafting innings proved to be the difference between the teams in the final analysis. He had previously appeared for Oxford University (1865-68) and was in Australia on holiday, recovering from pleurisy. It was his only match for Victoria, as he returned home and later played for Yorkshire (1876-78). Wills (career-best 7 for 44) bowled unchanged throughout the New South Wales second innings to wrap up the match for his team. This was the last of six first-class matches played at Sydney's Domain ground. *Scores & Biographies* incorrectly gives NSW (2) Oatley b Cosstick. Sources: *Scores & Biographies, Bells Life in Sydney, Sydney Morning Herald.*

VICTORIA

Player	Dismissal	Runs		2nd innings	Runs
*R.W.Wardill	c & b Thompson	0	(6)	c Hewitt b Thompson	3
J.Phillips	st Thompson b Hewitt	14	(1)	c Caffyn b Hewitt	4
†G.W.H.Gibson	c & b Gregory	3		c & b Thompson	29
T.J.D.Kelly	lbw b Thompson	1		c & b Coates	3
E.S.Carter	b Coates	16		b Kellick	63
J.W.Egglestone	b Coates	2	(2)	b Hewitt	0
S.Cosstick	c Caffyn b Hewitt	5		c Thompson b Gregory	27
A.W.F.Noyes	c Thompson b Coates	7		c Hewitt b Gregory	13
T.W.Wills	lbw b Hewitt	7		c Hewitt b Gregory	1
L.Goldsmith	b Coates	0	(11)	c Caffyn b Gregory	0
F.E.Allan	not out	3	(10)	not out	4
Extras	(b3)	3		(lb1, nb1)	2
Total	(52.2 overs, in about 105 mins)	61		(97.3 overs, in about 195 mins)	149

NEW SOUTH WALES

Player	Dismissal	Runs		2nd innings	Runs
E.O.Sheridan	lbw b Allan	2		lbw b Wills	37
R.J.Fairweather	b Allan	0	(9)	c Gibson b Cosstick	1
G.B.Stack	c Cosstick b Allan	0	(7)	c Kelly b Wills	0
W.Caffyn	c Egglestone b Cosstick	0	(5)	c Wills b Cosstick	6
N.Thompson	run out (/Gibson)	1	(4)	b Wills	8
*†R.C.Hewitt	c Carter b Allan	7		c & b Wills	0
D.W.Gregory	c Goldsmith b Allan	9	(2)	c sub (Christie) b Wills	15
J.Coates	c Carter b Allan	15	(3)	b Wills	8
A.L.Park	c Egglestone b Allan	2	(8)	b Cosstick	15
J.N.Oatley	not out	1		b Wills	4
J.Kellick	b Allan	0		not out	0
Extras		-		(lb1)	1
Total	(45.2 overs, in about 90 mins)	37		(105.2 overs, in about 200 mins)	95

NEW SOUTH WALES	O	M	R	W	w,nb		O	M	R	W	w,nb
Thompson	15	5	24	2	-,-	(4)	17	3	25	2	-,-,1
Gregory	10	4	10	1	-,-	(3)	20.3	4	34	4	-,-
Coates	16	4	19	4	-,-	(1)	23	7	30	1	-,-
Hewitt	11.2	6	5	3	-,-	(2)	24	5	38	2	-,-
Sheridan							6	1	10	0	-,-
Kellick							7	2	10	1	-,-

VICTORIA	O	M	R	W	w,nb		O	M	R	W	w,nb
Cosstick	23	14	17	1	-,-	(3)	28.2	14	23	3	-,-
Allan	22.2	9	20	8	-,-		24	12	27	0	-,-
Wills						(1)	53	31	44	7	-,-

FALL OF WICKETS

Wkt	VIC 1st	NSW 1st	VIC 2nd	NSW 2nd
1st	0	0	4	27
2nd	7	0	11	53
3rd	8	1	20	64
4th	29	2	50	73
5th	33	4	57	73
6th	40	11	104	75
7th	43	21	138	75
8th	53	27	143	78
9th	53	36	149	91
10th	61	37	149	95

VICTORIA v NEW SOUTH WALES

Played at Melbourne Cricket Ground on February 24, 25, 26, 28, 1870. (Timeless match)
Toss : Victoria.　　　　　　　　　Result : VICTORIA WON BY 265 RUNS.
Debuts: Victoria - C.S.Gordon, C.A.Reid (both f/c). New South Wales - C.D.Thompson, Twopenny (both f/c).
12th Men: B.J.Figgis (Vic) and A.L.Park (NSW).
Umpires: J.A.Smith and R.Teece.
Attendances: 800, 1000, 6000, 200.　　　　Total: About 8000.　　　Receipts: No figures published.
Close of Play: 1st day NSW 2/40 (E.J.Gregory 28, Sheridan 5); 2nd day Vic (2) 1/96 (Wardill 45, Gordon 19); 3rd day NSW (2) 3/60
　　(N.Thompson 6, Sheridan 3).

W.Caffyn (business commitments) was unavailable for New South Wales and Twopenny was a late replacement for G.H.B.Gilbert. Campbell came into the Victorian team to replace G.W.H.Gibson, who also had business to attend to. F.E.Allan and J.Mullagh had earlier indicated their unavailability to the Victorian match committee. Twopenny (Murrumgunarriman) and Mullagh (Unaarrimin) were members of the 1868 Aboriginal team to England, and a third member of that team, Cuzens (Zellanach), fielded as a substitute for Victoria on the last day of the match. Figgis was brought from Ballarat for the match and the inclusion of Reid at his expense "created the greatest surprise" (*Age*). Lieutenant C.S.Gordon, stationed temporarily in Melbourne with his English regiment, recorded a century (chanceless 121 in about 255 minutes, 8 fours) in his only first-class match in Australia. He returned to England a few days after this match and later appeared for Gloucestershire (1870-75). Kelly (53 in about 90 minutes, 4 fours), Wardill (55 in about 130 minutes, 2 fives and 3 fours) and E.J.Gregory (64 in about 130 minutes, 6 fours) hit half-centuries. Sources: *Scores & Biographies, The Age, The Argus, The Australasian.*

VICTORIA

C.S.Gordon	b Jones	22	(3) lbw b Jones	121
R.W.Wardill	run out (　　　/Hewitt)	24	(1) b D.W.Gregory	55
S.W.G.Campbell	c E.J.Gregory b Lawrence	13	(6) b D.W.Gregory	10
D.Campbell	run out (Oliver/Hewitt)	4	(7) b D.W.Gregory	49
G.P.Robertson	b Coates	32	c Hewitt b Lawrence	28
T.J.D.Kelly	run out (Oliver/Sheridan)	53	(4) b Sheridan	17
S.Cosstick	b Sheridan	0	(8) b Coates	7
†J.Phillips	not out	14	(2) b Coates	22
J.Conway	b Sheridan	1	(10) b D.W.Gregory	0
*T.W.Wills	lbw b Lawrence	13	(9) b D.W.Gregory	9
C.A.Reid	c N.Thompson b Lawrence	0	not out	0
Extras	(b2, lb3)	5	(b14, lb5)	19
Total	(101.2 overs, in about 210 mins)	181	(141.2 overs, in about 325 mins)	337

NEW SOUTH WALES

N.Thompson	c Gordon b Cosstick	3	(4) b Cosstick	11
E.J.Gregory	c Cosstick b Wardill	64	(6) b Cosstick	7
C.N.J.Oliver	b Cosstick	3	(9) b Cosstick	0
E.O.Sheridan	b Wardill	43	(5) run out (Kelly)	18
J.Coates	c Gordon b Wills	4	(7) b Cosstick	0
†R.C.Hewitt	b Wardill	0	(8) c sub (Cuzens) b Cosstick	1
*C.Lawrence	c Wardill b Gordon	6	(1) b Gordon	24
D.W.Gregory	b Cosstick	14	(3) b Gordon	2
S.Jones	b Wills	5	(2) b Cosstick	20
Twopenny	b Cosstick	8	(11) b Wills	0
C.D.Thompson	not out	3	(10) not out	0
Extras	(b1, lb2, w8)	11	(b4, lb2)	6
Total	(90.2 overs, in about 190 mins)	164	(72.1 overs, in about 140 mins)	89

NEW SOUTH WALES	O	M	R	W	w,nb		O	M	R	W	w,nb
Twopenny	21	10	41	0	-,-		9	2	15	0	-,-
Coates	14	3	27	1	-,-	(4)	17	1	57	2	-,-
N.Thompson	11	3	18	0	-,-		20	4	39	0	-,-
Jones	17	9	16	1	-,-	(8)	11	2	32	1	-,-
D.W.Gregory	6	0	13	0	-,-	(7)	38.2	14	55	5	-,-
Lawrence	16.2	3	32	3	-,-		15	1	47	1	-,-
Hewitt	4	0	13	0	-,-	(2)	5	0	20	0	-,-
Sheridan	10	4	12	2	-,-	(5)	12	4	27	1	-,-
E.J.Gregory	2	0	4	0	-,-		14	6	26	0	-,-

VICTORIA	O	M	R	W	w,nb		O	M	R	W	w,nb
Cosstick	22.2	9	37	4	1,-		36	13	40	6	-,-
Wills	34	13	48	2	-,-	(3)	24.1	14	20	1	-,-
Reid	11	5	16	0	-,-	(2)	4	0	7	0	-,-
Gordon	11	4	24	1	-,-		8	1	16	2	-,-
Conway	3	0	5	0	6,-						
Wardill	9	1	23	3	1,-						

FALL OF WICKETS

	VIC	NSW	VIC	NSW
Wkt	1st	1st	2nd	2nd
1st	44	8	46	44
2nd	54	23	117	50
3rd	62	117	159	56
4th	65	122	221	71
5th	147	122	237	85
6th	147	130	301	87
7th	155	137	314	87
8th	158	151	334	88
9th	181	161	334	89
10th	181	164	337	89

1870-71 to 1880-81 - TEST MATCHES BEGIN (29 MATCHES)

After an unsuccessful attempt the previous year, Melbourne Cricket Club persuaded W.G.Grace to lead an English team to Australia in 1873-74. The tourists were again opposed by teams containing odds, with the result that none of the 15 matches played were accorded first-class status. However, such was the increased calibre of the opposition that losses were inflicted upon the Englishmen by 18s of both Victoria and New South Wales. It was evident that Australian cricket would have to be taken more seriously.

The all-professional side of 1876-77 led by James Lillywhite again began with matches against odds, but losses to 15s of New South Wales (twice) and Victoria brought forth a challenge from New South Wales to meet on level terms. England agreed, and the result was the first first-class match by an England XI in Australia. It was also the first match in this country to be played to a time limit, being restricted to two days because of the visitor's imminent departure to New Zealand. It commenced on January 15, 1877 and the Englishmen gained the upper hand in the little playing time that was available. They returned in March without their specialist wicket-keeper, E.Pooley (who was in prison in New Zealand following a gambling trick he had tried on the locals during the brief tour) and met a combined Australian team in what subsequently became recognised as the first Test match. Australia recorded an unexpected victory thanks to a glorious unbeaten 165 from Charles Bannerman and fine bowling from Tom Kendall on the final day. A return match saw the Englishmen triumph, but history had been made and the Australians no longer felt inferior.

Lord Harris led the fifth English team to Australia in 1878-79. Melbourne Cricket Club had asked that an all-amateur side be invited, but most of the leading amateurs could not be drawn. Two professionals, Emmett and Ulyett, made up the numbers, leaving a below-strength team which was not truly representative. This was reflected in the team's record: five matches (including a Test) ranked as first-class, and of these two were won and three lost. Fred Spofforth (13 for 110) destroyed England's batting in the Test match, leading to a 10-wicket defeat. Ulyett and Emmett were easily the most successful men on tour, leading the batting and bowling averages respectively in the five matches.

Victoria and New South Wales continued their annual matches and expanded them to two per season from 1874-75 (one match on home turf each). Of the 26 matches between the colonies from 1855-56 to 1880-81, Victoria won 15 and New South Wales 11. Their clash in February 1878 was the initial first-class match at the Association Ground (now the Sydney Cricket Ground).

Cricket in South Australia progressed rapidly in the 1870s. A meeting of club secretaries at the Prince Alfred Hotel in Adelaide on May 31, 1871 saw the birth of the South Australian Cricket Association. Their early priority was the development of an association ground - the Adelaide Oval. Entry into first-class cricket came in November 1877 when South Australia met Tasmania at home. Eleven-a-side matches against Victoria began in 1880-81, though odds matches had been played between the teams from 1874-75.

Tasmania's first-class appearances were restricted to three in the 1870s: two against Victoria - in 1870-71 and 1872-73 - and one against South Australia in 1877-78.

The Queensland Cricket Association was formed on April 5, 1876 but another 17 years passed before a match involving Queensland was accorded first-class status.

Leading Aggregates

Batsmen	M	I	NO	Runs	HS	Ave.	Bowlers	Runs	Wkts	Ave.
C.Bannerman (NSW)	18	35	4	801	165*	25.83	E.Evans (NSW)	1082	99	10.92
T.P.Horan (V)	15	28	1	667	113	24.70	F.R.Spofforth (NSW)	1134	69	16.43
D.W.Gregory (NSW)	17	32	5	579	85	21.44	J.Coates (NSW)	679	66	10.28
G.Ulyett (E)	8	14	0	549	94	39.21	F.E.Allan (V)	603	59	10.22
H.H.Massie (NSW)	9	18	1	519	80	30.52	S.Costick (V)	567	54	10.50
N.Thompson (NSW)	16	30	1	479	73	16.51	T.Emmett (E)	564	44	12.81
W.L.Murdoch (NSW)	11	21	3	466	82*	25.88	W.E.Midwinter (V)	629	41	15.34
H.F.Boyle (V)	14	25	0	381	108	15.24	H.F.Boyle (V)	643	39	16.48
A.C.Bannerman (NSW)	9	16	0	373	73	23.31	W.H.Cooper (V)	705	39	18.07

VICTORIA v TASMANIA

Played at Melbourne Cricket Ground on February 24, 25, 1871. (Timeless match)
Toss : Tasmania.   Result : VICTORIA WON BY TEN WICKETS.
Debuts: Victoria - A.R.Loughnan, B.McGan, N.M.Osborne (all f/c); B.B.Cooper (Vic only). Tasmania - R.T.B.Barnes, H.Barrett,
    H.V.Bayly, E.H.Butler, M.C.Coverdale, J.G.Davies, J.A.Ferguson, W.T.Glynn, F.G.Haymes, J.O.Thomas (all f/c).
12th Men: V.L.Cameron (Vic). Only 11 men in Tasmanian party.
Umpires: T.E.Hewitt and T.W.Wills.
Attendances: 200, 1600.   Total: About 1800.   Receipts: No figures published.
Close of Play: 1st day Vic 4/71 (Phillips 14, Loughnan 8).

Tasmania again requested that the match - conducted on level terms, as it was in 1869 - be restricted to amateurs only. Victoria relented this time and professionals, such as Wills (who umpired) and Sam Cosstick, were not selected. In March 1870, a Victorian XI (including Wills and Cosstick) had defeated a Tasmanian XVI by an innings at Launceston, although the home team was not truly representative and really only a Northern side. *The Australasian* referred to the Melbourne match as The Gentlemen of Victoria versus The Gentlemen of Tasmania. Loughnan replaced S.W.G.Campbell (unavailable) in the selected Victorian team. Six-ball overs were tried for the first time in Australian first-class cricket. The experiment was repeated on several other occasions until it was generally adopted in the 1889/90 season. Curtis Reid, one of the umpires in the first-ever Test, captured 12 wickets for 69 in the second of his three-match playing career and precipitated a collapse in the Tasmanian second innings that saw the last eight wickets fall for only 4 runs. Allan was struck by a ball from Glynn and the Victorian innings closed with his retirement. He was unable to take the field for the Tasmanian second innings, W.Simmonds substituting. Cooper's previous games were with Middlesex (1863-67) and Kent (1868-69). *Scores & Biographies* has incorrect match dates and modes of dismissal for Davies and Arthur in Tas (1); also Vic (1) Butler 0/22. Sources: *Scores & Biographies, The Age, The Argus, The Australasian.*

TASMANIA

*†J.G.Davies	lbw b Reid	11	(2) c Goldsmith b Reid	15
J.L.A.Arthur	b Reid	3	(4) b McGan	3
J.O.Thomas	b Reid	15	b Reid	6
M.C.Coverdale	b Allan	0	(7) b Reid	2
W.T.Glynn	c Kelly b Reid	3	(6) st Cooper b McGan	0
R.T.B.Barnes	b Reid	36	(5) c Wardill b Reid	1
H.Barrett	st Cooper b Reid	1	(8) hit wkt b McGan	0
E.H.Butler	c Reid b Allan	1	(10) not out	0
F.G.Haymes	b Allan	1	c sub (W.Simmonds) b Reid	0
J.A.Ferguson	not out	25	(1) c Kelly b Wardill	7
H.V.Bayly	c Cooper b Allan	3	b Reid	0
Extras	(lb3, w1)	4	(b1, w1)	2
Total	(60.4 overs, in about 115 mins)	103	(30.2 overs, in about 65 mins)	36

VICTORIA

*R.W.Wardill	b Barnes	15		
G.W.H.Gibson	b Barnes	5		
J.Phillips	b Barrett	22		
T.J.D.Kelly	c Ferguson b Barnes	3		
†B.B.Cooper	c Butler b Barnes	22	(1) not out	8
A.R.Loughnan	c & b Barrett	24	(2) not out	2
L.Goldsmith	c Glynn b Barrett	2		
B.McGan	c Barnes b Barrett	8		
F.E.Allan	retired hurt	7		
C.A.Reid	lbw b Barrett	3		
N.M.Osborne	not out	4		
Extras	(b3, w10, nb1)	14	(nb1)	1
Total	(79.2 overs, in about 165 mins)	129	(6.1 overs, in about 15 mins) (0 wkts)	11

VICTORIA	O	M	R	W	w,nb		O	M	R	W	w,nb		FALL OF WICKETS			
														TAS	VIC	TAS	VIC
Allan	30.4	17	31	4	-,-							Wkt	1st	1st	2nd	2nd
Reid	28	5	64	6	1,-	(3)	6.2	4	5	6	1,-	1st	8	18	18	-
Osborne	2	1	4	0	-,-							2nd	29	21	26	-
Wardill						(1)	9	0	14	1	-,-	3rd	30	25	32	-
McGan						(2)	15	5	15	3	-,-	4th	33	58	34	-
												5th	36	101	34	-
TASMANIA	O	M	R	W	w,nb		O	M	R	W	w,nb	6th	38	104	36	-
Bayly	18	7	27	0	2,-		3.1	1	3	0	-,-	7th	39	112	36	-
Barnes	29.2	12	45	4	6,-		3	0	7	0	-,1	8th	43	117	36	-
Glynn	11	2	15	0	-,-							9th	80	121	36	-
Butler	11	2	20	0	1,1							10th	103	-	36	-
Barrett	10	4	8	5	1,-											

NEW SOUTH WALES v VICTORIA

Played at Albert Ground, Sydney on March 9, 10, 11, 13, 1871. (Timeless match)
Toss : Victoria.   Result : VICTORIA WON BY 48 RUNS
Debuts: New South Wales - C.Bannerman, H.M.Faithfull, C.S.Gregory, G.Moore (all f/c). Victoria - W.F.Darke, E.D.Heather,
    R.McFarland, O.C.Williams (all f/c).
12th Men: C.N.J.Oliver (NSW). Only 11 men in Victorian party.
Umpires: G.Howell and F.P.Miller.
Attendances: 4000, 4000, 8000, 2000.   Total: About 18,000.   Receipts: No figures published.
Close of Play: 1st day Vic 8/171 (Wills 16, Reid 1); 2nd day Vic (2) 1/33 (Campbell 12, Cooper 7); 3rd day NSW (2) 8/56 (Coates 1,
    Faithfull 0).

This was the first first-class match staged at the Albert Ground in Redfern. C.S.Gregory and Moore were selected for New South Wales ahead of C.M.Kellick and A.L.Park after a reconsideration by the selectors two days before the start of the match. Moore, aged 49 years 326 days, remains the second-oldest debutant in Australian first-class cricket to this day. Hewitt and Thompson alternated as the New South Wales wicket-keeper throughout the match. Park, after being omitted, was appointed to umpire but was replaced on the day of the match by Howell. Miller, the other umpire, was a former Surrey player in Australia for health reasons. D.W.Gregory (51 in about 90 minutes, 4 fours) and Hewitt (60 in about 90 minutes, 9 fours) hit half-centuries for New South Wales. Bannerman (32 in about 45 minutes, 6 fours) on debut, established himself "as a premier bat" (*T & C*). Heavy overnight rain after the second day saturated the wicket and the New South Wales second innings was begun on the drying pitch. Cosstick fully exploited the conditions to bowl his team to victory. *Scores & Biographies* incorrectly gives Vic (1) extras 11, Coates 3/28, Hewitt 0/8; Vic (2) Loughnan c Coates b Moore, Sheridan 1/11, Faithfull 0/11. *SMH* has minor differences with some falls of wicket but those shown here appear in *The Australasian* and *Town & Country Journal* and are believed correct. *T & C* does however give NSW (2) Moore 5, Reid 2/63, total 85, won by 47 runs. Sources: *Scores & Biographies, The Australasian, Sydney Morning Herald, Town & Country Journal*.

VICTORIA

L.Goldsmith	c D.W.Gregory b Moore	12	run out (Moore/Thompson)		13
S.W.G.Campbell	c Hewitt b Coates	26	lbw b Sheridan		37
†B.B.Cooper	c Moore b Coates	11	run out (C.S.Gregory/Hewitt)		27
A.R.Loughnan	c D.W.Gregory b Thompson	36	c Moore b Coates		11
O.C.Williams	c & b D.W.Gregory	19	c Thompson b Coates		20
E.D.Heather	c & b Thompson	9	b Coates	(9)	0
S.Costick	b Faithfull	30	c E.J.Gregory b Moore	(6)	4
*T.W.Wills	not out	39	b Moore	(7)	11
R.McFarland	st Hewitt b Moore	0	c Faithfull b Moore	(10)	1
C.A.Reid	run out (Hewitt)	4	lbw b Coates	(8)	5
W.F.Darke	b Coates	0	not out		0
Extras	(b3, lb7, nb2)	12	(b2, w2, nb1)		5
Total	(131.3 overs, in about 275 mins)	198	(81.0 overs, in about 170 mins)		134

NEW SOUTH WALES

D.W.Gregory	c Cooper b Darke	51	c Williams b Cosstick		10
E.J.Gregory	lbw b Darke	13	b Cosstick	(6)	15
E.O.Sheridan	b Cosstick	6	c Williams b Cosstick	(4)	3
W.Caffyn	b Darke	5	c Goldsmith b Cosstick	(7)	10
†R.C.Hewitt	b Reid	60	b Cosstick		0
C.S.Gregory	c Goldsmith b Darke	5	b Reid	(8)	9
*†N.Thompson	c Williams b Cosstick	6	b Reid	(2)	4
C.Bannerman	b Wills	32	b Cosstick	(3)	3
J.Coates	c Williams b Cosstick	1	lbw b Cosstick		1
H.M.Faithfull	b Reid	5	c Williams b Cosstick		24
G.Moore	not out	8	not out		4
Extras	(b3, lb4, nb1)	8	(w1)		1
Total	(88.0 overs, in about 185 mins)	200	(59.1 overs, in about 125 mins)		84

NEW SOUTH WALES	O	M	R	W	w,nb		O	M	R	W	w,nb		FALL OF WICKETS			
														VIC	NSW	VIC	NSW
D.W.Gregory	28	11	42	1	-,-	(2)	12	4	19	0	-,-	Wkt	1st	1st	2nd	2nd
Moore	30.3	12	47	2	-,2	(1)	24	10	39	3	-,1	1st	16	38	14	10
Coates	22	9	30	3	-,-	(7)	20	10	18	4	-,-	2nd	53	47	75	13
Sheridan	10	5	9	0	-,-	(6)	3	1	9	1	2,-	3rd	53	66	91	16
Hewitt	7	4	5	0	-,-	(3)	5	0	11	0	-,-	4th	89	94	92	16
Faithfull	25	15	32	1	-,-	(4)	8	1	14	0	-,-	5th	115	104	104	23
Thompson	9	1	21	2	-,-	(5)	8	2	19	0	-,-	6th	120	149	128	38
												7th	166	159	133	55
VICTORIA	O	M	R	W	w,nb		O	M	R	W	w,nb	8th	171	160	133	55
Cosstick	39	20	43	3	-,-		30	21	21	8	-,-	9th	191	167	134	62
Reid	12	4	20	2	-,-		29.1	10	62	2	1,-	10th	198	200	134	84
Darke	28	4	89	4	-,-											
Wills	9	5	40	1	-,1											

VICTORIA v NEW SOUTH WALES

Played at Melbourne Cricket Ground on March 30, April 1, 1872. (Timeless match)
Toss : Victoria.   Result : VICTORIA WON BY AN INNINGS AND 26 RUNS.
Debuts: Victoria - H.F.Boyle (f/c). New South Wales - H.A.Allan, A.R.Docker, W.C.Hand (all f/c).
12th Men: W.F.Darke (Vic) and J.N.Oatley (NSW).
Umpires: A.Sellars and J.A.Smith.
Attendances: 4000, 4000.   Total: About 8000.   Receipts: No figures published.
Close of Play: 1st day Vic 6/95 (Robertson 2, Boyle 2).

Heavy rain on the days leading up to the match left the ground "disgustingly heavy" (*Age*) and, by the second day, the "wicket was a good deal cut up by the two innings played on it" (*Argus*). Consequently, it was agreed that a fresh wicket be selected for the second innings but the New South Wales batting again failed. Allan relished the conditions and bowled unchanged throughout both innings of the visitors. He bowled Dickson with the second ball of the match and was never mastered at any stage. Wills was no-balled for throwing on three occasions by umpire Sellars - once in his first over and twice in his second. The local Press was adamant that Sellars, the New South Wales umpire, had set out to call Wills before the match and accused him of inconsistency in respect of the action of D.W.Gregory. "It is no doubt time that the practice of throwing was put down with a firm hand, but it is by no means clear that the best way of accomplishing this is to 'no-ball' the opponent's bowler for high delivery and allow one's own bowler to indulge in a deliberate throw" (*Argus*). C.S.Gregory broke a bone in his left hand when he fell against the fence while attempting to save a boundary early in the Victorian innings. He was only able to bat one-handed in the second innings, his injured arm held in a sling. D.W.Gregory and Thompson alternated behind the stumps during their opening bowling spell. Sources: *Scores & Biographies, The Age, The Argus, The Australasian.*

NEW SOUTH WALES

G.D.Dickson	b Allan	0	(7) not out		0
†N.Thompson	c Kelly b Costick	31	run out (Robertson/Gibson)		15
D.W.Gregory	b Allan	11	b Allan		7
H.A.Allan	b Allan	0	(5) st Gibson b Allan		3
*E.J.Gregory	lbw Allan	16	(6) c & b Costick		17
C.Bannerman	st Gibson b Allan	0	(4) b Allan		5
E.O.Sheridan	not out	8	(1) c Allan b Costick		1
W.C.Hand	b Allan	0	c Kelly b Costick		1
C.S.Gregory	c Kelly b Allan	0	(11) b Allan		0
A.R.Docker	c Campbell b Costick	5	(9) run out		0
G.Moore	st Gibson b Allan	5	(10) st Gibson b Allan		0
Extras	(w1, nb3)	4	(b6)		6
Total	(53.0 overs, in about 95 mins)	80	(44.3 overs, in about 85 mins)		55

VICTORIA

L.Goldsmith	b Moore	12
S.W.G.Campbell	b Moore	4
†G.W.H.Gibson	b Docker	41
B.B.Cooper	c Moore b Docker	2
T.J.D.Kelly	c D.W.Gregory b Moore	25
G.P.Robertson	b Moore	23
S.Costick	lbw b Moore	5
H.F.Boyle	c Sheridan b Moore	27
O.C.Williams	c & b E.J.Gregory	1
*T.W.Wills	b E.J.Gregory	7
F.E.Allan	not out	11
Extras	(b1, lb1, w1)	3
Total	(110.0 overs, in about 225 mins)	161

VICTORIA	O	M	R	W	w,nb	O	M	R	W	w,nb
Allan	27	13	35	8	-,-	22.3	13	25	5	-,-
Costick	24	11	37	2	-,-	22	12	24	3	-,-
Wills	2	0	4	0	1,3					

NEW SOUTH WALES	O	M	R	W	w,nb
D.W.Gregory	22	11	24	0	-,-
Thompson	11	5	12	0	-,-
Moore	26	6	56	6	-,-
Docker	18	10	24	2	-,-
Sheridan	4	1	13	0	1,-
E.J.Gregory	25	13	27	2	-,-
Bannerman	4	2	2	0	-,-

FALL OF WICKETS

Wkt	NSW 1st	VIC 1st	NSW 2nd
1st	0	14	1
2nd	34	21	20
3rd	46	32	26
4th	46	86	32
5th	50	86	48
6th	65	93	53
7th	65	138	55
8th	65	139	55
9th	70	145	55
10th	80	161	55

VICTORIA v XIII OF NEW SOUTH WALES, TASMANIA AND SOUTH AUSTRALIA

Played at Melbourne Cricket Ground on December 26, 27, 28, 1872. (Timeless match)
Toss : XIII of NSW, Tas and SA.   Result : XIII OF NSW, TAS AND SA WON BY FIVE WICKETS.
Debuts: Victoria - T.R.Hepburn (f/c). Com XIII - J.E.Gooden, T.Hogg, J.F.King, S.Morcom, R.Teece (all f/c).
12th Men: No 12th men or emergency fieldsmen named. Only 13 men with Combined team.
Umpires: G.T.Curtis and J.A.Smith.
Attendances: 4000, 2000, 2000.   Total: About 8000.   Receipts: No figures published.
Close of Play: 1st day Com XIII 1/28 (D.W.Gregory 12); 2nd day Vic (2) 6/69 (McGan 9).

Victoria had not been defeated since December 1866 and it was felt in Melbourne that their dominance over opponents would only be evened out by playing against odds. It was determined that a composite thirteen be selected from the best available players in New South Wales, Tasmania and South Australia. Although the controlling bodies in these three Colonies were not consulted about the staging of the match, no objections were raised. Known as the Combination Match, the game was promoted by Melbourne theatrical entrepreneur G.S.Coppin and it is the only odds match in Australia accepted as first-class. J.G.Davies of Tasmania "ran against the iron roller" (*Australasian*) at practice on the day before the match began, sustaining cuts and severe bruising to his arms, legs and body. He was replaced by Teece, who had been named to umpire. Curtis (Teece's replacement) twice no-balled D.W.Gregory for throwing (the second of which was scored from) on the first day. Gregory did not bowl again due to the "determination on the part of the umpire to allow nothing but perfectly fair bowling" (*Argus*). Curtis later "stepped back a few paces" to closely study the action of Wills and twice called him in his second over when he delivered "less simply" (*Argus*). Cosstick and Coates returned career-best analyses, bowling unchanged through the respective innings in the process. Thompson kept wickets while Hewitt bowled. *Scores & Biographies* omits lbw from dismissal of Kelly in Vic (2). Sources: *Scores & Biographies, The Age, The Argus, The Herald, The Australasian.*

VICTORIA

†G.W.H.Gibson	b Coates	2	b Coates		24
S.W.G.Campbell	c Gooden b Hogg	12	b Coates		5
B.B.Cooper	run out (/Hewitt)	29	b Barnes		1
W.W.Gaggin	c Teece b Coates	27	b Hogg		11
T.J.D.Kelly	b Barnes	0	lbw b Coates		12
J.Conway	st Hewitt b Barnes	2	(8) not out		17
S.Cosstick	b Hogg	36	(6) b Coates		4
T.R.Hepburn	run out (Coates)	5	(10) lbw b Coates		0
B.McGan	b Coates	7	(7) b Coates		10
H.F.Boyle	b Barnes	7	(9) b Coates		2
*T.W.Wills	not out	0	run out		0
Extras	(b6, lb2, nb1)	9	(b2, nb1)		3
Total	(128.3 overs, in about 245 mins)	136	(90.3 overs, in about 175 mins)		89

XIII OF NEW SOUTH WALES, TASMANIA AND SOUTH AUSTRALIA

J.L.A.Arthur	b Conway	15	not out		34
D.W.Gregory	b Cosstick	12	c & b Cosstick		6
J.F.King	b Cosstick	1			
R.Teece	b Cosstick	0			
C.Bannerman	b Cosstick	11	(7) run out (McGan/Gibson/Conway)		22
N.Thompson	b Cosstick	9	(5) b Cosstick		8
*E.J.Gregory	c Gaggin b Boyle	23	(6) c Cooper b Conway		27
J.Coates	b Cosstick	6	(9) not out		3
†R.C.Hewitt	b Cosstick	6	(8) c Kelly b Conway		3
S.Morcom	b Cosstick	4	(3) b Cosstick		0
R.T.B.Barnes	not out	20	(4) b Boyle		7
J.E.Gooden	b McGan	3			
T.Hogg	b Cosstick	0			
Extras	(b1, lb2)	3	(w1, nb2)		3
Total	(59.0 overs, in about 115 mins)	113	(62.3 overs, in about 135 mins) (7 wkts)		113

COMBINED XIII	O	M	R	W	w,nb		O	M	R	W	w,nb		FALL OF WICKETS			
Coates	50.2	28	48	3	-,-		45	22	39	7	-,-			VIC	XIII	VIC	XIII
D.W.Gregory	3	1	5	0	-,1								Wkt	1st	1st	2nd	2nd
Hogg	39	23	27	2	-,-		19	10	13	1	-,-		1st	7	28	12	9
E.J.Gregory	4	1	6	0	-,-		2	1	1	0	-,-		2nd	23	28	13	9
Thompson	4	3	2	0	-,-								3rd	73	29	35	18
Hewitt	3	0	9	0	-,-								4th	73	38	54	31
Barnes	22	10	26	3	-,-	(2)	24.3	11	33	1	-,1		5th	75	47	58	77
King	3	0	4	0	-,-								6th	79	50	69	105
													7th	112	80	77	108
VICTORIA	O	M	R	W	w,nb		O	M	R	W	w,nb		8th	122	81	79	-
Cosstick	30	6	61	9	-,-		27	11	38	3	-,-		9th	136	86	87	-
McGan	5	1	10	1	-,-	(5)	6	1	11	0	1,-		10th	136	98	89	-
Conway	22	9	34	1	-,-		11.3	1	24	2	-,-		11th	-	111	-	-
Boyle	2	1	5	1	-,-	(2)	16	5	25	1	-,-		12th	-	113	-	-
Wills						(4)	2	0	12	0	-,2						

NEW SOUTH WALES v VICTORIA

Played at Albert Ground, Sydney, on February 28, March 1, 2 - 6 (no play), 7, 8, 1873. (Timeless match)
Toss : New South Wales.   Result : VICTORIA WON BY 24 RUNS.
Debuts: New South Wales - W.J.Pocock, T.Powell (both f/c); A.F.Jeffreys (NSW only). Victoria - C.G.Allee, C.S.Carr, E.H.Elliott, E.Fanning (all f/c).
12th Men: C.S.Gregory (NSW) and W.E.Midwinter (Vic).
Umpires: H.C.E.Newcombe and J.A.Smith.
Attendances: 2000, 7000, 4000, 8000.   Total: About 21,000.   Receipts: "over £1100" (*Sydney Mail*).
Close of Play: 1st day Vic 9/111 (Elliott 5, Loughnan 3); 2nd day Vic (2) 2/32 (Gibson 8, Elliott 1); 3rd day NSW (2) 3/61 (Powell 24, Kellick 18).

The match was intended to start on February 27th but was delayed by the weather. Rain brought further interruptions on the first and second days and washed out the the scheduled third day. As there was no prospect of an immediate improvement in the conditions, the N.S.W.C.A., with the agreement of the two captains, postponed continuation of the match until play was again possible. A new wicket was selected for each innings. The heavy turf, outfield as well as wickets, made the scoring of runs an almost impossible task and bowlers dictated the terms throughout. Cosstick bowled unchanged throughout both New South Wales innings to return an amazing 11 for 51 from 78.2 overs. His pinpoint accuracy denied easy runs and he was able to extract maximum assistance from the wickets. D.W.Gregory injured a hand at practice prior to the second Victorian innings and left the field after bowling only two overs, his brother Charles substituting. Coates bowled unchanged through the innings to limit the visitors' advantage and off-set Gregory's absence from the attack. Jeffreys had played with MCC the previous year and later appeared for Hampshire. *Scores & Biographies* incorrectly gives Vic (2) E.Gregory 0/5 instead of D.Gregory and match dates. Sources: *Scores & Biographies, The Australasian, The Leader, Sydney Morning Herald, Town & Country Journal, Sydney Mail.*

VICTORIA

W.W.Gaggin	c Kellick b Coates	13		b Pocock	7
S.W.G.Campbell	b Coates	0	(9)	lbw b Coates	1
B.B.Cooper	c Pocock b D.W.Gregory	30	(2)	c E.J.Gregory b Moore	16
*G.W.H.Gibson	c Hewitt b D.W.Gregory	32	(3)	not out	15
S.Cosstick	c Jeffreys b Moore	14	(7)	b Moore	2
E.Fanning	c D.W.Gregory b Pocock	11		b Coates	0
H.F.Boyle	c & b D.W.Gregory	0	(8)	c & b Moore	6
†E.H.Elliott	b Coates	5	(4)	c Moore b Coates	2
C.S.Carr	c Kellick b Pocock	0	(11)	b Coates	0
C.G.Allee	c Bannerman b Pocock	2		b Coates	0
A.R.Loughnan	not out	5	(5)	b Coates	6
Extras	(w1)	1		(lb1)	1
Total	(109.3 overs, in about 210 mins)	113		(81.1 overs, in about 165 mins)	56

NEW SOUTH WALES

D.W.Gregory	b Allee	13	(3)	run out (Carr/Elliott)	5
A.F.Jeffreys	c Allee b Cosstick	4	(4)	b Cosstick	3
C.M.Kellick	c Elliott b Cosstick	0	(1)	c Allee b Boyle	18
E.J.Gregory	run out (Elliott)	2	(6)	c Gibson b Boyle	4
T.Powell	b Cosstick	3		lbw b Allee	29
C.Bannerman	b Allee	1	(8)	b Cosstick	0
C.N.J.Oliver	b Allee	6	(2)	c Elliott b Allee	10
†R.C.Hewitt	b Cosstick	6	(7)	b Cosstick	7
W.J.Pocock	b Cosstick	6		c Elliott b Cosstick	0
*J.Coates	b Cosstick	1		not out	19
G.Moore	not out	0		b Cosstick	5
Extras	(b2)	2		(lb1)	1
Total	(34.1 overs, in about 70 mins)	44		(122.1 overs, in about 235 mins)	101

NEW SOUTH WALES	O	M	R	W	w,nb		O	M	R	W	w,nb
Coates	32	13	40	3	-,-		40.1	31	19	6	-,-
D.W.Gregory	36.3	18	24	3	-,-		2	0	5	0	-,-
Moore	20	7	24	1	-,-	(4)	26	16	17	3	-,-
Pocock	12	7	10	3	-,-	(3)	13	6	14	1	-,-
Bannerman	5	0	6	0	1,-						
E.J.Gregory	4	1	8	0	-,-						

VICTORIA	O	M	R	W	w,nb		O	M	R	W	w,nb
Cosstick	17.1	9	15	6	-,-		61.1	43	36	5	-,-
Boyle	8	0	17	0	-,-	(3)	35	20	36	2	-,-
Allee	9	4	10	3	-,-	(2)	26	10	28	2	-,-

FALL OF WICKETS

Wkt	VIC 1st	NSW 1st	VIC 2nd	NSW 2nd
1st	3	7	17	12
2nd	26	11	31	17
3rd	62	15	34	31
4th	87	24	44	61
5th	96	24	44	65
6th	96	25	49	72
7th	98	32	55	72
8th	101	40	56	72
9th	103	43	56	80
10th	113	44	56	101

TASMANIA v VICTORIA

Played at Launceston Cricket Ground on March 14, 15, 1873. (Timeless match)
Toss : Tasmania. Result : VICTORIA WON BY SEVEN WICKETS.
Debuts: Tasmania - G.H.Bailey, C.W.Butler, W.A.Collins, E.J.Freeman, J.M.Martin, W.H.Walker, J.H.Walshe (all f/c); J.C.Lord (Tas only). Victoria - H.S.Bishop, H.J.Jennings, J.Stewart (all f/c); E.H.Butler (Vic only).
12th Men: None named.
Umpires: D.C.Cuthbert, B.James and W.Sidebottom.
Attendances & Receipts: No figures published.
Close of Play: 1st day Vic 150 all out.

The composition of both teams was restricted to players of amateur status, as it had been for the contest in Melbourne in 1871. The match was again reported in *The Australasian* as being between Eleven Gentlemen of Tasmania and Eleven Gentlemen of Victoria. *Hobart Mercury*, on the other hand, reflected Tasmanian North-South rivalry by titling it Victoria v United North and South XI. Six-ball overs were used throughout the match. R.T.B.Barnes and E.J.C.Whitesides were unable to travel to Launceston to represent Tasmania and T.Hogg was unavailable. James was selected to play for Victoria but was prevented from doing so by the after affects of the voyage and a hand injury sustained at pre-match practice. He umpired on the first day but was replaced by Cuthbert for the second day's play due to illness. Wardill was no-balled for throwing three times on the first day by umpire Sidebottom. Players on both sides were reportedly shocked by the umpire's action "and what surprised the Victorians was that he was able to discern any distinction between one ball and another" (*Leader*). Hepburn began the match as the Victorian wicket-keeper but the position was shared amongst his teammates later on. The identity of all the replacement keepers used is not known. Heavy rain overnight saturated the wicket after the first day and it was agreed that the second day be played on a new wicket. E.H.Butler and Lord had previously played for Tasmania and Hampshire respectively. Some minor variations are recorded in falls of wickets. Sources: *STCA Report, The Australasian, The Leader, Launceston Examiner, Hobart Mercury*.

TASMANIA

J.L.A.Arthur	b Allee	4		b Allee	33
J.G.Davies	lbw b Allee	4		c Stewart b Allee	10
G.H.Bailey	c Williams b Wardill	0	(4)	b Butler	7
C.W.Butler	c Williams b Wilkie	14	(3)	b Butler	0
E.J.Freeman	b Allee	13		b Butler	19
J.C.Lord	c Allee b Wilkie	11		c Hepburn b Allee	3
J.M.Martin	run out (Wardill)	5	(10)	b Butler	8
W.A.Collins	c Goldsmith b Wilkie	2	(7)	b Butler	14
*†W.H.Walker	b Butler	27	(8)	c Bishop b Hepburn	16
F.G.Haymes	c Williams b Allee	30	(9)	c Williams b Butler	20
J.H.Walshe	not out	7		not out	0
Extras	(lb4, nb3)	7		(b3, lb2, w1)	6
Total	(59.0 overs, in about 150 mins)	124		(62.1 overs, in about 180 mins)	136

VICTORIA

L.Goldsmith	c Bailey b Walshe	19		run out (Butler)	20
J.Stewart	c Bailey b Davies	5	(4)	st Arthur b Walker	1
†T.R.Hepburn	c Walker b Walshe	24	(2)	not out	52
O.C.Williams	b Bailey	4	(3)	c Walshe b Bailey	19
A.R.Loughnan	b Walshe	3		not out	11
D.Wilkie	c Collins b Haymes	22			
*R.W.Wardill	b Freeman	39			
C.G.Allee	b Walker	15			
H.S.Bishop	b Walker	8			
H.J.Jennings	c Lord b Walker	2			
E.H.Butler	not out	2			
Extras	(lb1, w6)	7		(b2, lb1, w5)	8
Total	(62.3 overs, in about 195 mins)	150		(41.4 overs, in about 120 mins) (3 wkts)	111

VICTORIA	O	M	R	W	w,nb		O	M	R	W	w,nb					
Allee	29	13	46	4	-,-	(2)	20	8	39	3	-,-					
Wardill	4	0	8	1	-,3											
Stewart	4	1	8	0	-,-											
Wilkie	12	1	40	3	-,-	(3)	5	1	16	0	-,-					
Butler	10	4	15	1	-,-	(1)	32.1	8	62	6	-,-					
Hepburn						(4)	4	0	11	1	-,-					
Loughnan						(5)	1	0	2	0	1,-					

	FALL OF WICKETS			
	TAS	VIC	TAS	VIC
Wkt	1st	1st	2nd	2nd
1st	6	11	10	40
2nd	7	38	10	82
3rd	13	43	22	84
4th	33	57	59	-
5th	39	60	75	-
6th	48	119	76	-
7th	54	131	103	-
8th	56	143	111	-
9th	114	145	131	-
10th	124	150	136	-

TASMANIA	O	M	R	W	w,nb		O	M	R	W	w,nb
Bailey	23	8	44	1	-,-		21	6	36	1	-,-
Davies	4	1	16	1	1,-	(6)	0.4	0	3	0	1,-
Walshe	14	1	34	3	4,-	(2)	2	0	8	0	4,-
Walker	11.3	1	20	3	-,-		7	0	27	1	-,-
Haymes	8	2	18	1	1,-	(3)	7	1	22	0	-,-
Freeman	2	0	11	1	-,-	(5)	4	1	7	0	-,-

VICTORIA v NEW SOUTH WALES

Played at Melbourne Cricket Ground on December 26, 28, 29, 30, 1874. (Timeless match)
Toss : New South Wales.   Result : NEW SOUTH WALES WON BY SIX WICKETS.
Debuts: Victoria - J.M.Blackham, T.P.Horan, M.A.Murphy, J.Slight (all f/c). New South Wales - G.Morgan, F.R.Spofforth, E.Tindall, W.Woods (all f/c).
12th Men: E.P.Hastings (Vic) and R.Fancourt (NSW).
Umpires: E.Barton and J.Thornton.
Attendances: 8000, 4000, 4000, 400.   Total: About 16,400.   Receipts: No figures published.
Close of Play: 1st day NSW 2/40 (Sheridan 11, Bannerman 0); 2nd day Vic (2) 3/70 (Kelly 37, Horan 12); 3rd day NSW (2) 4/86 (Bannerman 22, Gregory 1).

D.W.Gregory, who had been invited to lead the side, H.M.Faithfull, E.Evans and H.H.Massie were unavailable for New South Wales and F.E.Allan was unable to play for Victoria. Overnight rain softened the ground "and an arrangement was consequently made by the two captains that a fresh wicket should be provided for each innings" (*Argus*). Slight, on debut, was bowled by the last ball of the opening over, which was also Spofforth's first in first-class cricket. Cooper (45 in about 115 minutes, 6 fours) and Kelly (career-best 86 in about 145 minutes, 9 fours) headed the scoring for Victoria, Cooper also hitting his highest score in eleven matches for the Colony. However, the outstanding batting in the match was provided by Charles Bannerman (81 in about 140 minutes, 1 seven, 1 five and 7 fours and 32 not out in about 75 minutes, 4 fours). His 81, in particular, was put together "in fine cricketing style" (*Argus*), featuring strong driving and a sound defence. Murphy was absent on the second and third days owing to the sudden death of his brother. Edmund Barton, the New South Wales umpire, was elected to the New South Wales Legislative Assembly in 1879 and, in 1901, became Australia's first Prime Minister.
Sources: *Scores & Biographies, The Age, The Argus, The Herald, The Australasian.*

VICTORIA

J.Slight	b Spofforth	0	(9)	not out	7
*B.B.Cooper	c Woods b Spofforth	45		b Coates	4
T.J.D.Kelly	c Spofforth b Coates	14		b Coates	86
T.P.Horan	b Coates	3	(5)	b Coates	22
H.F.Boyle	run out (Morgan/Tindill)	17	(4)	c Sheridan b Spofforth	3
L.Goldsmith	c Thompson b Tindall	3	(1)	b Spofforth	14
S.Cosstick	c Gilbert b Tindall	6		b Spofforth	33
B.McGan	b Tindall	0	(10)	b Coates	2
S.W.G.Campbell	b Spofforth	25	(8)	c Tindall b Coates	6
†J.M.Blackham	b Thompson	32	(6)	c Gregory b Thompson	5
M.A.Murphy	not out	0		absent	-
Extras	(b3, lb1)	4		(lb2, w1)	3
Total	(107.1 overs, in about 210 mins)	149		(113.1 overs, in about 220 mins)	185

NEW SOUTH WALES

G.H.B.Gilbert	st Blackham b Murphy	11	(2)	c sub (E.P.Hastings) b Boyle	3
†N.Thompson	c Murphy b Cosstick	17	(1)	c Blackham b Slight	35
E.O.Sheridan	lbw b Boyle	25		c Blackham b Cosstick	18
C.Bannerman	c Cosstick b Horan	81		not out	32
T.Powell	c Horan b Boyle	6			
E.J.Gregory	c Blackham b Boyle	0		not out	24
*J.Coates	c Cosstick b Boyle	0			
F.R.Spofforth	b Cosstick	21			
E.Tindall	not out	26	(5)	run out (Blackham)	6
G.Morgan	b Cosstick	0			
W.Woods	c Horan b Boyle	9			
Extras	(b4, lb15, w1)	20		(lb1)	1
Total	(138.2 overs, in about 250 mins)	216		(73.1 overs, in about 135 mins) (4 wkts)	119

NEW SOUTH WALES	O	M	R	W	w,nb		O	M	R	W	w,nb			
Spofforth	37	19	56	3	,		24.1	4	67	3	1,-			
Coates	29.1	9	57	2	-,-		45	25	46	5	-,-			
Tindall	34	18	27	3	-,-		15	2	43	0	-,-			
Thompson	7	5	5	1	-,-		29	17	26	1	-,-			

VICTORIA	O	M	R	W	w,nb		O	M	R	W	w,nb
Cosstick	43	22	73	3	1,-		32	12	54	1	-,-
Murphy	12	2	17	1	-,-	(5)	5	1	12	0	-,-
Boyle	42.2	17	63	5	-,-	(2)	25.1	14	26	1	-,-
Horan	41	20	43	1	-,-	(3)	6	3	13	0	-,-
Slight						(4)	5	1	13	1	-,-

FALL OF WICKETS

Wkt	VIC 1st	NSW 1st	VIC 2nd	NSW 2nd
1st	0	23	10	6
2nd	21	40	22	57
3rd	43	111	36	61
4th	77	125	90	71
5th	82	125	97	-
6th	87	135	157	-
7th	91	165	171	-
8th	96	180	177	-
9th	149	194	185	-
10th	149	216	-	-

NEW SOUTH WALES v VICTORIA

Played at Albert Ground, Sydney, on March 5, 6, 8, 1875. (Timeless match)
Toss : New South Wales.   Result : NEW SOUTH WALES WON BY 77 RUNS.
Debuts: New South Wales - E.Evans (f/c). Victoria - E.P.Hastings, W.E.Midwinter (both f/c).
12th Men: H.H.Massie (NSW) and W.W.Gaggin (Vic).
Umpires: E.Barton and W.W.Gaggin.
Attendances: 7000, 10000, 10000.   Total: About 27,000.   Receipts: No figures published.
Close of Play: 1st day Vic 7/44 (Blackham 14, Midwinter 0); 2nd day NSW (2) 7/77 (Evans 21, Powell 7).

T.J.D.Kelly was unavailable for Victoria's trip North and Powell (originally 12th man) was a late replacement for Charles Bannerman (hand injury). Umpire Barton arrived late on the second day and former New South Wales player George Moore stood for the opening overs. Gaggin, 12th man in the Victorian party, stood throughout the match as the other umpire. "It was decided that a fresh wicket should be prepared within a defined space for every innings, so as to secure a true pitch throughout" (*SMH*). "Ned" Gregory (career-best 65 not out in about 155 minutes, 4 fours) scored the only half-century of a low-scoring match and received "half a hatful of current coin of the realm subscribed by the public" (*SMH*) in recognition of his effort. When 45, a ball from Midwinter lifted and glanced from his bat, striking him on his right cheek bone and leaving a cut below the eye. He was able to continue after treatment but his vision was impaired to the extent that he did not field in either Victorian innings, J.A.Tooher substituting due to the non-attendance of 12th man Massie at the game. The "dead wickets" (*SMH*) and slow outfield contributed in no small way to the low scoring but the sustained accuracy of Cosstick and Midwinter (Victoria) and Coates, Evans and Faithfull (New South Wales) should not be overlooked. Cosstick's figures in the second innings - though bearing in mind that the overs were of four balls - are remarkable and are not likely to be emulated. Evans (31 not out in about 255 minutes, 2 fours) gave "a display of patient defence and fine safe play" (*T & C Journal*) in addition to his fine medium-pace bowling. *Scores & Biographies* incorrectly gives NSW (1) Gilbert 10, NSW substitute as Tooker and incorrect match dates. Sources: *Scores & Biographies, Sydney Morning Herald, Town & Country Journal, Sydney Mail.*

NEW SOUTH WALES

D.W.Gregory	c Cooper b Cosstick	1	(3)	c Cooper b Cosstick		1
†N.Thompson	run out (Loughnan/Blackham)	3	(1)	c & b Midwinter		13
G.H.B.Gilbert	b Midwinter	1	(2)	b Cosstick		1
E.O.Sheridan	b Cosstick	0		c Blackham b Cosstick		0
E.Evans	c Cosstick b Midwinter	11		not out		31
E.J.Gregory	not out	65		c Midwinter b Cosstick		18
F.R.Spofforth	c Cooper b Midwinter	2	(8)	b Cosstick		13
T.Powell	c Conway b Midwinter	1	(9)	c Cooper b Horan		20
*J.Coates	st Blackham b Midwinter	14	(7)	b Midwinter		0
H.M.Faithfull	run out (/Blackham)	3		b Horan		0
W.Woods	c & b Midwinter	9		c Conway b Horan		0
Extras	(b2, lb3, nb1)	6		(lb2, nb3)		5
Total	(82.2 overs, in about 165 mins)	116		(163.0 overs, in about 290 mins)		102

VICTORIA

B.B.Cooper	run out (Thompson)	2	(4)	c Woods b Faithfull		8
S.W.G.Campbell	c Thompson b Coates	3	(1)	b Evans		18
T.P.Horan	c & b Spofforth	3		c Woods b Faithfull		16
H.F.Boyle	b Coates	6	(6)	b Evans		2
J.Slight	c Spofforth b Coates	10	(8)	c sub (J.A.Tooher) b Evans		5
E.P.Hastings	b Coates	0	(10)	b Evans		0
S.Cosstick	lbw b Coates	1	(9)	c Sheridan b Evans		7
†J.M.Blackham	c Powell b Spofforth	15	(7)	b Evans		0
W.E.Midwinter	not out	15	(5)	c sub (J.A.Tooher) b Faithfull		8
*J.Conway	b Coates	0	(11)	not out		0
A.R.Loughnan	c Spofforth b Coates	10	(2)	st Thompson b Coates		4
Extras	(b1, lb4, nb1)	6		(b2)		2
Total	(53.2 overs, in about 105 mins)	71		(77.0 overs, in about 150 mins)		70

VICTORIA	O	M	R	W	w,nb	O	M	R	W	w,nb
Cosstick	35	14	36	2	-,-	83	66	25	5	-,-
Midwinter	41.2	13	61	6	-,1	58	27	61	2	-,3
Boyle	6	2	13	0	-,-	14	7	10	0	-,-
Horan						8	7	1	3	-,-

NEW SOUTH WALES	O	M	R	W	w,nb	O	M	R	W	w,nb
Spofforth	27	12	25	2	-,-	9	4	10	0	-,-
Coates	26.2	14	40	7	-,1	11	1	17	1	-,-
Evans						30	16	25	6	-,-
Faithfull						27	18	16	3	-,-

FALL OF WICKETS

Wkt	NSW 1st	VIC 1st	NSW 2nd	VIC 2nd
1st	4	6	6	4
2nd	5	10	12	38
3rd	5	10	12	38
4th	5	20	16	53
5th	39	20	46	56
6th	63	22	47	58
7th	65	38	69	58
8th	92	54	100	70
9th	97	55	100	70
10th	116	71	102	70

VICTORIA v NEW SOUTH WALES

Played at Melbourne Cricket Ground on December 27, 28 (no play), 29, 1875. (Timeless match)
Toss : New South Wales.   Result : NEW SOUTH WALES WON BY AN INNINGS AND 1 RUN.
Debuts: Victoria - G.Alexander (f/c). New South Wales - W.L.Murdoch, J.A.Tooher (both f/c).
12th Men: E.O.Sheridan (NSW). W.W.Gaggin and T.K.Kendall named as Vic emergencies.
Umpires: E.Barton and C.A.Reid.
Attendances: 12000, 500, 5000.   Total: About 17,500.   Receipts: No figures published.
Close of Play: 1st day NSW 6/87 (C.Bannerman 43, Powell 0); 2nd day no play.

L.Goldsmith and E.P.Hastings were originally selected for Victoria but were replaced by Alexander and Allee by virtue of their better form. "The wicket was not as good as is usually to be found on the Melbourne ground" (*Argus*) due to heavy rain earlier in the day. Spofforth and Evans each took a wicket with their first ball. Campbell falling to the first ball of the match and Allan to the first ball of the second over. Kelly survived a confident lbw appeal first ball to score 71 (in about 100 minutes, 6 fours) out of 92 while he was at the crease. Bannerman (83 in about 165 minutes, 6 fours) dominated the New South Wales innings in similar fashion. Thompson began as the New South Wales wicket-keeper but handed over to Murdoch at about 4/50 after he injured a hand while attempting to catch Cooper. Heavy rain prevented any play on the second day and those who attended were given a refund. The wicket "had been carefully covered with a tarpaulin in order to preserve it" (*Argus*) and was not considered responsible for the Victorian second innings capitulation. Evans (career-best 7 for 16) bowled with immaculate control on the drying wicket. He conceded 12 runs from his initial overs before obtaining his first wicket and proceeded to capture a further six (all without assistance from the field) at a further personal cost of only 4 runs. *Scores & Biographies* incorrectly gives Vic (2) Kelly c & b Evans, omits bowling of Tindall and misspells Tooher. Sources: *Scores & Biographies, The Age, The Argus, The Herald, The Australasian.*

VICTORIA

S.W.G.Campbell	b Spofforth	0	(7)	b Coates	3
F.E.Allan	lbw b Evans	0	(9)	c & b Evans	0
T.J.D.Kelly	b Evans	71	(5)	b Evans	2
T.P.Horan	b Spofforth	1	(6)	b Evans	7
J.Slight	b Spofforth	2	(3)	b Evans	2
B.B.Cooper	c Tindall b Evans	36	(1)	run out (Tindall/Murdoch)	4
C.G.Allee	c Coates b Evans	9	(4)	b Coates	1
†J.M.Blackham	c Murdoch b Coates	5	(10)	not out	0
*H.F.Boyle	b Coates	1	(8)	b Evans	0
G.Alexander	not out	8	(2)	c & b Evans	11
S.Cosstick	b Coates	0		b Evans	2
Extras	(b1, lb2)	3		(b2)	2
Total	(69.3 overs, in about 145 mins)	136		(34.3 overs, in about 90 mins)	34

NEW SOUTH WALES

D.W.Gregory	b Allan	6
†N.Thompson	b Allan	12
E.Evans	b Allan	12
C.Bannerman	c Boyle b Alexander	83
E.Tindall	c Kelly b Boyle	5
E.J.Gregory	b Allan	2
F.R.Spofforth	b Allee	3
T.Powell	hit wkt b Allan	29
W.L.Murdoch	c Kelly b Allan	6
*J.Coates	b Alexander	5
J.A.Tooher	not out	0
Extras	(b1, lb6, nb1)	8
Total	(134.2 overs, in about 225 mins)	171

NEW SOUTH WALES	O	M	R	W	w,nb		O	M	R	W	w,nb
Spofforth	21	7	39	3	-,-						
Evans	30	13	50	4	-,-	(1)	17.3	13	16	7	-,-
Coates	12.3	4	25	3	-,-	(2)	17	9	16	2	-,-
Tindall	6	0	19	0	-,-						

VICTORIA	O	M	R	W	w,nb
Allan	68.2	32	66	6	-,1
Horan	31	15	35	0	-,-
Boyle	12	5	19	1	-,-
Alexander	11	7	12	2	-,-
Allee	3	1	3	1	-,-
Cosstick	9	1	28	0	-,

FALL OF WICKETS	VIC	NSW	VIC
Wkt	1st	1st	2nd
1st	0	21	15
2nd	0	22	17
3rd	1	51	17
4th	37	60	19
5th	92	75	23
6th	118	81	30
7th	127	156	30
8th	127	164	30
9th	130	171	32
10th	136	171	34

NEW SOUTH WALES v VICTORIA

Played at Albert Ground, Sydney, on February 25, 26, 28, 1876. (Timeless match)
Toss : New South Wales.   Result : NEW SOUTH WALES WON BY 195 RUNS.
Debuts: New South Wales - J.Humphreys (f/c). Victoria - J.S.Swift (f/c).
12th Men: A.R.Docker & T.Onus (NSW emergencies). No 12th named for Vic.
Umpires: W.C.Goddard and E.J.Prevot.
Attendances: 8000, 13000, 8000.   Total: About 29,000.   Receipts: No figures published.
Close of Play: 1st day Vic 37 all out; 2nd day NSW (2) 6/208 (Murdoch 0, Humphreys 2).

J.M.Blackham and T.J.D.Kelly were unavailable for Victoria and L.Goldsmith declined the selector's invitation. Allee, Allan and Alexander were later brought in as replacements for the unavailable F.A.McEvoy, W.Newing and R.B.Terry. It was agreed that a fresh wicket would be selected for each innings "in order to render the contest as fairly equal as possible for both teams competing" (*T & C Journal*). Actually the first innings of each team was played "upon anything but a good wicket" (*Sydney Mail*), although those for the second innings "played well" (*Sydney Mail*). Spofforth and Evans provided the second instance in Australian first-class cricket of two bowlers operating unchanged throughout both innings of a game, Spofforth's "pace was something not likely to be forgotten by those who had to stand up against it", while Evans "was as puzzling as ever" (*Sydney Mail*). Evans strained a leg soon after starting his second innings (46 in about 255 minutes, 4 fours) and used five different runners (Bannerman, Powell, Ned Gregory, Murdoch and Spofforth) but the injury did not prevent him bowling on the final day. Dave Gregory (36 in about 75 minutes, 2 fours and 74 in about 115 minutes, 4 fours) batted well in both innings and his brother Ned (40 in about 90 minutes, 4 fours) "played vigorously and safely" (*Sydney Mail*) in the second innings. New South Wales achieved their fourth consecutive victory over Victoria. *Scores & Biographies* incorrectly gives NSW (1) Powell b Cosstick, Coates c Alexander b Horan; Vic (1) bowling omitted; Vic (2) dismissal of Wills omitted. Sources: *Scores & Biographies, The Australasian, Sydney Morning Herald, Town & Country Journal, Sydney Mail*.

NEW SOUTH WALES

D.W.Gregory	c Swift b Midwinter	36		c Elliott b Cosstick	74
N.Thompson	c Cosstick b Allan	6		run out (/Elliott)	10
E.Evans	run out (Alexander/Elliott)	10		b Allan	46
C.Bannerman	b Cosstick	3		c Allan b Cosstick	0
T.Powell	run out (Cooper/Midwinter)	11		c Allan b Allee	31
E.J.Gregory	b Allan	14		c & b Midwinter	40
†W.L.Murdoch	b Allan	9		b Allan	1
F.R.Spofforth	b Allan	0	(9)	c Elliott b Allan	0
E.Tindall	c Williams b Horan	4	(10)	c & b Alexander	8
J.Humphreys	not out	1	(8)	b Cosstick	4
*J.Coates	c Alexander b Horan	1		not out	8
Extras	(b2, lb2)	4		(lb6)	6
Total	(80.3 overs, in about 160 mins)	99		(173.2 overs, in about 320 mins)	228

VICTORIA

B.B.Cooper	b Spofforth	0		b Spofforth	11
G.Alexander	b Evans	1	(6)	b Spofforth	23
T.P.Horan	b Spofforth	1	(4)	c Tindall b Evans	12
F.E.Allan	c Evans b Spofforth	6	(3)	st Murdoch b Evans	11
W.E.Midwinter	c Tindall b Evans	9	(2)	c Murdoch b Spofforth	9
O.C.Williams	run out	3	(5)	b Spofforth	1
†E.H.Elliott	b Spofforth	3	(8)	c Tindall b Spofforth	16
S.Cosstick	b Evans	2	(7)	b Evans	0
J.S.Swift	b Evans	2	(10)	not out	3
C.G.Allee	c E.J.Gregory b Evans	7	(9)	b Evans	0
*T.W.Wills	not out	0		b Evans	4
Extras	(b3)	3		(b5)	5
Total	(31.2 overs, in about 70 mins)	37		(40.2 overs, in about 90 mins)	95

VICTORIA	O	M	R	W	w,nb		O	M	R	W	w,nb			
Allan	21.3	12	23	5	-,-	(2)	36	18	29	3	-,-			
Cosstick	31	19	37	1	-,-	(4)	34	18	39	3	-,-			
Midwinter	19	8	24	1	-,-	(7)	18	9	21	1	-,-			
Horan	9	5	11	1	-,-	(1)	10	1	14	0	-,-			
Allee						(6)	12	4	32	1	-,-			
Alexander						(3)	14.2	6	22	1	-,-			
Wills						(5)	49	18	65	0	-,-			

NEW SOUTH WALES	O	M	R	W	w,nb		O	M	R	W	w,nb
Spofforth	16	4	22	4	-,-		21	7	50	5	-,-
Evans	15.2	7	12	5	-,-		19.2	5	40	5	-,-

FALL OF WICKETS

Wkt	NSW 1st	VIC 1st	NSW 2nd	VIC 2nd
1st	17	3	21	20
2nd	50	3	112	32
3rd	53	5	112	40
4th	55	16	158	47
5th	75	22	206	55
6th	92	22	206	55
7th	92	25	209	81
8th	96	27	211	84
9th	97	37	211	88
10th	99	37	228	95

NEW SOUTH WALES v J.LILLYWHITE'S ENGLAND XI

Played at Albert Ground, Sydney, on January 15, 16, 1877. (Two-day match)
Toss : New South Wales.   Result : MATCH DRAWN.
Debuts: New South Wales - A.C.Bannerman, W.Dummett, T.W.Garrett (all f/c).
12th Men: W.Woods (NSW). No 12th available for England team (Jupp ill).
Umpires: G.T.Curtis and R.Driver.
Attendances: 4500, 3500.   Total: About 8000.   Receipts: No figures published.
Close of Play: 1st day NSW 2/6 D.W.Gregory 3).

The first contest between an England team and an eleven-a-side in Australia was hurriedly arranged following the success of a New South Wales Fifteen against the tourists two days previously. The duration was restricted to two days because of the scheduled departure of the English team to New Zealand. The tourists were unable to select H.Jupp through illness and New South Wales brought in Dummett as a late replacement for E.J.Seale, who was also ill. J.A.Tooher fielded as a substitute in the early part of the English innings, in the absence of 12th man Woods, until Dummett arrived. Murdoch began as the New South Wales keeper but handed the gloves to Thompson at 6/185. Some scores incorrectly credit England with winning the toss. Ulyett (94 in about 150 minutes, 8 fours) "played a free hitting innings" (*SMH*) on the first day to hold the England innings together. The New South Wales batsman made heavy work of the sustained accuracy of the Englishmen, Shaw leading the way with 9 for 54 from 97 overs in the match. Gregory (53 not out in about 135 minutes, 6 fours) "played all the bowlers right well" (*T & C Journal*) in the second innings. Sources: *Scores & Biographies, Sydney Morning Herald, Town & Country Journal, Sydney Mail.*

J.LILLYWHITE'S ENGLAND XI

A.Shaw	b Spofforth	23
H.R.J.Charlwood	c Gregory b Evans	18
A.Greenwood	b Evans	9
T.Armitage	c Thompson b Evans	0
G.Ulyett	b Garrett	94
J.Selby	c Murdoch b Garrett	31
T.Emmett	b Garrett	18
†E.Pooley	b Garrett	36
*J.Lillywhite	st Thompson b Evans	13
A.Hill	c C.Bannerman b Evans	2
J.Southerton	not out	16
Extras	(b10)	10
Total	(141.3 overs, in about 250 mins)	270

NEW SOUTH WALES

C.Bannerman	b Shaw	2	(3) b Shaw		32
D.W.Gregory	c Southerton b Shaw	3	(4) not out		53
T.Powell	lbw b Lillywhite	1	(7) st Pooley b Armitage		19
T.W.Garrett	b Shaw	6	(5) b Shaw		0
*E.Evans	b Hill	30	(1) b Hill		4
F.R.Spofforth	b Lillywhite	5	lbw b Shaw		7
N.Thompson	b Hill	19	(8) not out		17
†W.L.Murdoch	not out	7	(2) b Shaw		5
A C.Bannerman	c Emmett b Shaw	3			
W.Dummett	b Hill	3			
E.Tindall	b Hill	1			
Extras	(b1, lb1)	2	(lb3)		3
Total	(105.0 overs, in about 165 mins)	82	(104.0 overs, in about 170 mins) (6 wkts)		140

NEW SOUTH WALES	O	M	R	W	w,nb
Spofforth	35	8	79	1	-,-
Evans	53	12	96	5	,
Garrett	38.3	12	69	4	-,-
Tindall	12	5	16	0	-,-
Thompson	3	3	0	0	-,-

ENGLISH XI	O	M	R	W	w,nb		O	M	R	W	w,nb
Lillywhite	30	10	34	2	-,-	(3)	10	3	16	0	-,-
Shaw	53	34	19	5	-,-	(1)	44	23	35	4	-,-
Armitage	3	0	16	0	-,-	(6)	6	3	11	1	-,-
Hill	19	10	11	3	-,-	(2)	31	16	49	1	-,-
Emmett						(4)	4	2	16	0	-,-
Ulyett						(5)	9	5	10	0	-,-

FALL OF WICKETS				
		ENG	NSW	NSW
Wkt		1st	1st	2nd
1st		32	5	7
2nd		44	6	11
3rd		44	6	61
4th		62	21	61
5th		127	28	69
6th		197	66	115
7th		204	71	-
8th		238	74	-
9th		244	79	-
10th		270	82	-

AUSTRALIA v ENGLAND (1st Test)

Played at Melbourne Cricket Ground on March 15, 16, 17, 19, 1877. (Timeless match)
Toss : Australia.   Result : AUSTRALIA WON BY 45 RUNS.
Debuts: All (Test). Australia - J.Hodges, T.K.Kendall (both f/c).
12th Men: None named.
Umpires: C.A.Reid and R.B.Terry.
Attendances: 4500, 4000, 10000, 2000.   Total: About 20,500.   Receipts: No figures published.
Close of Play: 1st day Aust 6/166 (Bannerman 126, Blackham 3); 2nd day Eng 4/109 (Jupp 54); 3rd day Aust (2) 9/83 (Kendall 5, Hodges 3).

Now recognised as the inaugural Test match, this game was arranged at short notice following successful odds matches between Lillywhite's English Team and New South Wales and Victorian sides. It was intended that the home team would comprise six players from New South Wales and five from Victoria but the balance was altered by the unavailability of E.Evans and the withdrawal of F.R.Spofforth (both New South Welshmen), the latter refusing to take part because W.L.Murdoch had been overlooked for the position of wicket-keeper. The local bowling was further depleted by the last-minute withdrawal of F.E.Allan, who said he could not spare the time to play, Hodges being brought in. Before 1500 spectators (numbers swelled to 4500 by mid-afternoon) Bannerman faced the first ball at 1.05pm, bowled by Shaw, and began the scoring with a cut past point for a single off the second ball. Hill claimed the first Test wicket, clean bowling Thompson in the fourth over. Lunch was taken from 2.00pm to 2.40pm and stumps were drawn at 5.00pm (there was no tea break). Bannerman's historic innings (165 in about 290 minutes, 18 fours), which included an ankle-high chance to Shaw at mid-off in the nineties, ended at 3.00pm on the second day when a fast ball by Ulyett badly split the index finger on his right hand. He had been wearing gloves but the padding had gone from the affected finger and he retired at 7/240, his innings forming 67.3 per cent of the eventual total. W.Newing, a Melbourne CC professional, substituted for Bannerman in the field. Jupp (63 in about 190 minutes, 2 fours), England's highest scorer, survived an appeal for hit wicket in the first over when he dislodged a bail leg-glancing. Southerton (49 years 119 days) remains Test cricket's oldest debutant. Sources: *Scores & Biographies, The Age, The Argus, The Herald, The Australasian.*

AUSTRALIA

C.Bannerman	retired hurt	165		b Ulyett	4
N.Thompson	b Hill	1		c Emmett b Shaw	7
T.P.Horan	c Hill b Shaw	12		c Selby b Hill	20
*D.W.Gregory	run out (Jupp)	1	(9)	b Shaw	3
B.B.Cooper	b Southerton	15		b Shaw	3
W.E.Midwinter	c Ulyett b Southerton	5		c Southerton b Ulyett	17
E.J.Gregory	c Greenwood b Lillywhite	0		c Emmett b Ulyett	11
†J.M.Blackham	b Southerton	17		lbw b Shaw	6
T.W.Garrett	not out	18	(4)	c Emmett b Shaw	0
T.K.Kendall	c Southerton b Shaw	3		not out	17
J.Hodges	b Shaw	0		b Lillywhite	8
Extras	(b4, lb2, w2)	8		(b5, lb3)	8
Total	(169.3 overs, in about 300 mins)	245		(68.0 overs, in about 135 mins)	104

ENGLAND

H.Jupp	lbw b Garrett	63	(3)	lbw b Midwinter	4
†J.Selby	c Cooper b Hodges	7	(5)	c Horan b Hodges	38
H.R.J.Charlwood	c Blackham b Midwinter	36	(4)	b Kendall	13
G.Ulyett	lbw b Thompson	10	(6)	b Kendall	24
A.Greenwood	c E.J.Gregory b Midwinter	1	(2)	c Midwinter b Kendall	5
T.Armitage	c Blackham b Midwinter	9	(8)	c Blackham b Kendall	3
A.Shaw	b Midwinter	10		st Blackham b Kendall	2
T.Emmett	b Midwinter	8	(9)	b Kendall	9
A.Hill	not out	35	(1)	c Thompson b Kendall	0
*J.Lillywhite	c & b Kendall	10		b Hodges	4
J.Southerton	c Cooper b Garrett	6		not out	1
Extras	(lb1)	1		(b4, lb1)	5
Total	(136.1 overs, in about 250 mins)	196		(66.1 overs, in about 130 mins)	108

ENGLAND	O	M	R	W	w,nb		O	M	R	W	w,nb
Shaw	55.3	34	51	3	-,-		34	16	38	5	-,-
Hill	23	10	42	1	-,-	(3)	14	6	18	1	-,-
Ulyett	25	12	36	0	-,-	(2)	19	7	39	3	-,-
Southerton	37	17	61	3	-,-						
Armitage	3	0	15	0	2,-						
Lillywhite	14	5	19	1	-,-	(4)	1	0	1	1	-,-
Emmett	12	7	13	0	-,-						

AUSTRALIA	O	M	R	W	w,nb		O	M	R	W	w,nb
Hodges	9	0	27	1	-,-	(5)	7	5	7	2	-,-
Garrett	18.1	10	22	2	-,-	(4)	2	0	9	0	-,-
Kendall	38	16	54	1	-,-	(1)	33.1	12	55	7	-,-
Midwinter	54	23	78	5	-,-	(2)	19	7	23	1	-,-
Thompson	17	10	14	1	-,-						
D.W.Gregory						(3)	5	1	9	0	-,-

FALL OF WICKETS

	AUST	ENG	AUST	ENG
Wkt	1st	1st	2nd	2nd
1st	2	23	7	0
2nd	40	79	27	7
3rd	41	98	31	20
4th	118	109	31	22
5th	142	121	35	62
6th	143	135	58	68
7th	197	145	71	92
8th	243	145	75	93
9th	245	168	75	100
10th	-	196	104	108

AUSTRALIA v ENGLAND (2nd Test)

Played at Melbourne Cricket Ground on March 31, April 2, 3, 4, 1877. (Timeless match)
Toss : Australia.   Result : ENGLAND WON BY FOUR WICKETS.
Debuts: Australia - T.J.D.Kelly, W.L.Murdoch, F.R.Spofforth (all Test).
12th Men: None named.
Umpires: S.Cosstick and R.B.Terry.
Attendances: 4500, 6500, 2000, 1500.   Total: About 14,500.   Receipts: No figures published.
Close of Play: 1st day Eng 2/7 (Greenwood 4, Charlwood 2); 2nd day Eng 261 all out; 3rd day Aust (2) 7/207 (Spofforth 3, Kendall 4).

Australia's victory in the first match, allied with a healthy financial profit from the game, led to the impromptu staging of this return match, which was intended to benefit the touring professionals. Evans and Pooley continued to be unavailable for their respective teams, the Englishmen again having only eleven men available to play. T.P.Horan (in Adelaide on business) was a further absentee from the Australian line-up. Although no reserve was named, E.J.Gregory fielded as substitute for the first 20 minutes on the second day after Kelly had missed his train to the ground. Selby began as England's wicket-keeper but was replaced by Jupp after lunch on the first day (at 4/60) and he kept that role for the rest of the match. Murdoch similarly took over from Blackham (slight sunstroke) for the final day, W.Newing making up the numbers in the field. Kendall continued his success from the First Test (in which he made his first-class debut) by bowling Jupp with the fourth ball of the England first innings. Ulyett (52 in about 95 minutes, 5 fours and 63 in about 90 minutes, 1 five and 5 fours) hit a half-century in each innings. Bannerman's 30 in 15 minutes included the first score of five in Test cricket, a drive off Lillywhite which soared "over the heads of spectators". Hill had earlier hit Spofforth clean out of the arena, being "very well caught by one of the spectators" (*Argus*), but he was awarded only four for the stroke. Recent sources incorrectly give Aust (1) 2/29. Sources: *Scores & Biographies, The Age, The Argus, The Herald, The Australasian.*

AUSTRALIA

N.Thompson	lbw b Hill	18		b Lillywhite	41
C.Bannerman	b Hill	10	(3)	c Jupp b Ulyett	30
†J.M.Blackham	c Lillywhite b Hill	5	(10)	lbw b Southerton	26
T.W.Garrett	b Hill	12	(7)	c Jupp b Lillywhite	18
T.J.D.Kelly	b Ulyett	19	(4)	b Southerton	35
W.E.Midwinter	c Emmett b Lillywhite	31		c Greenwood b Lillywhite	12
F.R.Spofforth	b Ulyett	0	(8)	b Hill	17
W.L.Murdoch	run out (Selby/Jupp)	3	(5)	c Shaw b Southerton	8
T.K.Kendall	b Lillywhite	7		b Southerton	12
*D.W.Gregory	not out	1	(2)	c Ulyett b Lillywhite	43
J.Hodges	run out (Lillywhite)	2		not out	0
Extras	(b8, lb5, w1)	14		(b10, lb7)	17
Total	(112.1 overs, in about 200 mins)	122		(154.3 overs, in about 287 mins)	259

ENGLAND

H.Jupp	b Kendall	0		b Kendall	1
A.Shaw	st Blackham b Spofforth	1	(8)	not out	0
A.Greenwood	b Hodges	49		c Murdoch b Hodges	22
H.R.J.Charlwood	c Kelly b Kendall	14		b Kendall	0
†J.Selby	b Kendall	7	(2)	b Spofforth	2
G.Ulyett	b Spofforth	52	(5)	c Spofforth b Hodges	63
T.Emmett	c Kendall b Spofforth	48	(6)	b Midwinter	8
A.Hill	run out (Thompson/Midwinter)	49	(7)	not out	17
T.Armitage	c Thompson b Midwinter	21			
*J.Lillywhite	not out	2			
J.Southerton	c Thompson b Kendall	0			
Extras	(b5, lb12, nb1)	18		(b8, lb1)	9
Total	(130.2 overs, in about 250 mins)	261		(52.1 overs, in about 100 mins) (6 wkts)	122

ENGLAND	O	M	R	W	w,nb		O	M	R	W	w,nb
Shaw	42	27	30	0	-,-	(4)	32	19	27	0	-,-
Lillywhite	29	17	36	2	-,-	(3)	41	15	70	4	-,-
Hill	27	12	27	4	1,-	(1)	21	9	43	1	-,-
Ulyett	14.1	6	15	2	-,-	(2)	19	9	33	1	-,-
Emmett							13	6	23	0	-,-
Southerton							28.3	13	46	4	-,-

AUSTRALIA	O	M	R	W	w,nb		O	M	R	W	w,nb
Kendall	52.2	21	82	4	-,-		17	7	24	2	-,-
Spofforth	29	6	67	3	-,1		15	3	44	1	-,-
Midwinter	21	8	30	1	-,-	(5)	13.1	6	25	1	-,-
Hodges	12	2	37	1	-,-		6	2	13	2	-,-
Garrett	5	2	10	0	-,-	(3)	1	0	7	0	-,-
Thompson	11	6	17	0	-,-						

FALL OF WICKETS

Wkt	AUST 1st	ENG 1st	AUST 2nd	ENG 2nd
1st	29	0	88	2
2nd	30	4	112	8
3rd	50	55	135	9
4th	60	72	164	54
5th	96	88	169	76
6th	104	162	196	112
7th	108	196	203	-
8th	114	255	221	-
9th	119	259	259	-
10th	122	261	259	-

SOUTH AUSTRALIA v TASMANIA

Played at Adelaide Oval on November 10, 12, 1877. (Timeless match)
Toss : South Australia.   Result : SOUTH AUSTRALIA WON BY AN INNINGS AND 13 RUNS.
Debuts: South Australia - J.L.Bevan, R.D.Botten, C.H.Gibbs, G.Giffen, H.A.Gooden, A.H.Jarvis, T.T.Lucas, W.D.Moffat, E.G.Phillips, S.Rigaud (all f/c); J.F.King (SA only). Tasmania - J.E.Bennison, H.C.Lovett, E.Lucas, W.Martin (all f/c).
12th Men: J.Noel (SA emergency) and J.A.Ferguson (Tas - see below).
Umpires: H.D.O'Halloran and S.Toms.
Attendances: 1450, 400.   Total: 1870.   Receipts: £89.
Close of Play: 1st day Tas 72 all out

This was the first eleven-a-side match involving South Australia as well as the first first-class match on South Australian soil. It came about indirectly, following an invitation from the Queen and Albert Association of Port Adelaide to the Launceston Cricket Club for a match to inaugurate their new ground at Alberton. After the game, the S.A.C.A. arranged for a match against a South Australian team, resulting in this contest. Leading players from both Colonies - J.E.Gooden, J.E.Goodfellow and W.O.Whitridge (South Australia) and G.H.Bailey, E.H.Butler and E.J.C.Whitesides (Tasmania) - were unavailable. Ferguson was relegated to 12th man after a dispute with the captain, Walker. He was later permitted by the South Australians to bat instead of Birch, who had badly damaged his hand while attempting to catch Phillips from his own bowling. The match is ruled first-class despite this highly irregular occurrence. The captains selected a new wicket for the second day's play, even though that used on the first day "had played well until late in the afternoon. The change was anything but an improvement" (*Register*). Bevan (14 for 59) bowled unchanged throughout both Tasmanian innings in his only first-class match. Davies kept wicket while Walker bowled and later, when called upon to bowl himself, began with two wides and then captured two wickets with his only legitimate deliveries. Six-ball overs were bowled. King had previously appeared in the 'Combination Match' in 1872-73. *O'Reilly* omits c Walker from the dismissal of Gibbs. Sources: *C.B.O'Reilly, Adelaide Advertiser, South Australian Register, Adelaide Observer, South Australian Chronicle.*

SOUTH AUSTRALIA

J.F.King	b Bayly	0
T.T.Lucas	b Bayly	43
G.Giffen	c Davies b Birch	27
†A.H.Jarvis	st Walker b Birch	0
H.A.Gooden	c Bayly b Birch	6
*C.H.Gibbs	c Walker b Davies	47
E.G.Phillips	run out	16
W.Moffat	c Davies b Martin	3
R.D.Botten	c & b Walker	17
S.Rigaud	not out	8
J.L.Bevan	b Davies	0
Extras	(b9, lb4, w2)	15
Total	(57.2 overs, in about 185 mins)	182

TASMANIA

J.G.Davies	b Bevan	0	(2) b Bevan		19
G.H.Arthur	c Gibbs b Bevan	1	(5) c Moffat b Bevan		2
*†W.H.Walker	lbw b Bevan	26	(1) st Jarvis b Giffen		4
J.E.Bennison	st Jarvis b Bevan	6	(3) c Moffat b Bevan		11
C.W.Butler	c Botten b Giffen	17	(4) c & b Bevan		31
W.Martin	c Rigaud b Bevan	0	(8) hit wkt b Bevan		3
J.A.Ferguson	st Jarvis b Giffen	0	(6) b Bevan		8
E.Lucas	b Giffen	13	(7) b Giffen		8
H.C.Lovett	c Rigaud b Bevan	0	b Bevan		7
D.C.Cuthbert	not out	0	not out		0
H.V.Bayly	c King b Giffen	1	st Jarvis b Bevan		0
W.T.Birch	absent hurt	-	absent hurt		-
Extras	(b7, w1)	8	(b4)		4
Total	(35.3 overs, in about 105 mins)	72	(47.3 overs, in about 135 mins)		97

TASMANIA	O	M	R	W	w,nb
Bayly	22	5	54	2	-,-
Martin	11	1	35	1	-,-
Lucas	2	0	21	0	-,-
Birch	5	0	13	3	-,-
Walker	17	3	44	1	-,-
Davies	0.2	0	0	2	2,-

SOUTH AUSTRALIA	O	M	R	W	w,nb		O	M	R	W	w,nb
Bevan	18	6	23	6	-,-		24.3	5	36	8	-,-
Rigaud	8	1	13	0	-,-	(4)	2	0	8	0	-,-
King	2	0	12	0	1,-						
Giffen	7.3	2	16	4	-,-	(2)	18	4	40	2	-,-
Phillips						(3)	3	0	9	0	-,-

FALL OF WICKETS

Wkt	SA 1st	TAS 1st	TAS 2nd
1st	0	0	7
2nd	58	3	31
3rd	61	22	40
4th	77	58	42
5th	82	58	67
6th	112	58	81
7th	124	58	84
8th	159	71	87
9th	182	71	97
10th	182	72	97

VICTORIA v NEW SOUTH WALES

Played at Melbourne Cricket Ground on December 26, 27, 1877. (Timeless match)
Toss : Victoria.   Result : NEW SOUTH WALES WON BY AN INNINGS AND 6 RUNS.
Debuts: Victoria - F.Baker, F.A.McEvoy, W.McEvoy, W.Slight, G.E.Smith, R.B.Terry (all f/c); J.Hodges (Vic only). New South Wales -
       J.Burrows, A.Geary, T.H.Iceton, E.Scanlan (all f/c).
12th Men: S.English (Vic) and J.Humphreys (NSW).
Umpires: H.H.Budd and L.J.K.Park.
Attendances: 3500, 600.   Total: About 4100.   Receipts: No figures published.
Close of Play: 1st day NSW 7/144 (Powell 23, Coates 4).

Both teams were below full strength because the players selected for the 1878 tour of England were involved in a program of matches around the country to raise funds for the trip. The bowling of Evans (9 for 92) and Coates (9 for 71) proved too much for the Victorian batsmen on a wicket that was "fast" on the first day and with "a strong inclination to bump" (*Argus*) on the second. They bowled unchanged throughout the first innings and for the greater majority of the second. Thompson (career-best 73 in about 170 minutes, 5 fours) "played a long, steady, patient innings", although "at times very stiffly" (*Argus*), to put New South Wales in a winning position. Cooper relieved Smith of the wicket-keeping duties after lunch on the second day for the final half-hour or so of the New South Wales innings. Two sets of brothers, the McEvoys and the Slights, represented Victoria. Hodges and Terry had participated in both Test matches of 1876-77, as player and umpire respectively. *Scores & Biographies* gives NSW (1) Allee 1/33. Sources: *Scores & Biographies, The Age, The Argus, The Herald, The Australasian.*

VICTORIA

Batsman	Dismissal	Runs		Dismissal	Runs
F.Baker	b Coates	12	(4)	b Geary	22
F.A.McEvoy	b Coates	5	(7)	c & b Evans	16
E.P.Hastings	c Scanlan b Evans	5	(5)	hit wkt b Coates	4
B.B.Cooper	b Evans	2	(2)	b Evans	16
R.B.Terry	run out (/Thompson)	14	(11)	not out	3
J.Slight	st Thompson b Coates	5	(1)	b Coates	8
W.McEvoy	c Dummett b Evans	3	(3)	lbw b Coates	4
†G.E.Smith	b Coates	3	(10)	c Dummett b Evans	5
W.Slight	lbw b Coates	6	(8)	b Evans	5
*C.G.Allee	b Coates	2	(6)	b Evans	7
J.Hodges	not out	13	(9)	c Scanlan b Evans	22
Extras	(b4, lb5)	9		(b5, lb8)	13
Total	(52.0 overs, in about 105 mins)	79		(88.1 overs, in about 150 mins)	125

NEW SOUTH WALES

Batsman	Dismissal	Runs
E.O.Sheridan	c Allee b W.McEvoy	14
†N.Thompson	c Cooper b Allee	73
E.Evans	b Terry	0
W.Dummett	c Hodges b Terry	3
E.J.Gregory	b Terry	4
A.Geary	c Allee b Hodges	15
T.Powell	b Baker	27
J.Burrows	b W.McEvoy	0
*J.Coates	not out	36
T.H.Iceton	run out (Hastings/Smith)	1
E.Scanlan	b W.McEvoy	25
Extras	(b10, lb1, nb1)	12
Total	(138.3 overs, in about 270 mins)	210

NEW SOUTH WALES	O	M	R	W	w,nb	O	M	R	W	w,nb
Evans	26	12	35	3	-,-	39.1	12	57	6	-,-
Coates	26	12	35	6	-,-	36	18	36	3	-,-
Geary						6	4	9	1	-,-
Iceton						7	3	10	0	-,-

VICTORIA	O	M	R	W	w,nb
Hodges	30	11	42	1	-,-
Baker	39	17	52	1	-,1
W.McEvoy	27.3	13	41	3	-,-
Terry	17	5	23	3	-,-
W.Slight	7	4	6	0	-,-
Allee	16	6	27	1	-,-
J.Slight	2	0	7	0	-,-

FALL OF WICKETS

	VIC	NSW	VIC
Wkt	1st	1st	2nd
1st	6	36	21
2nd	25	37	27
3rd	29	42	31
4th	29	47	59
5th	36	80	61
6th	43	140	79
7th	54	140	92
8th	54	148	97
9th	56	153	110
10th	79	210	125

NEW SOUTH WALES v VICTORIA

Played at Sydney Cricket Ground on February 22, 23, 25, 1878. (Timeless match)
Toss : Victoria.   Result : NEW SOUTH WALES WON BY ONE WICKET.
Debuts: New South Wales - H.H.Massie, E.J.Seale (both f/c). Victoria - P.S.McDonnell, H.J.H.Scott, J.P.Tennent, L.S.Woolf (all f/c).
12th Men: E.Scanlan (NSW) and F.G.McShane (Vic).
Umpires: H.H.Budd and W.C.Goddard.
Attendances: 3000, 8000, 3000.   Total: About 14,000.   Receipts: No figures published.
Close of Play: 1st day NSW 4/40 (Powell 0); 2nd day NSW (2) 5/31 (Evans 4, Sheridan 9).

This was the first match played at the Sydney Cricket Ground, then known as the Association Ground. It did not officially become the Sydney Cricket Ground until 1894 but is referred to as such throughout this volume for purposes of continuity. Both teams were again without the services of their leading players because of Australian XI commitments. A new wicket was selected for each innings, all being as "good and true as can be conceived" (*T & C Journal*). Despite this, bowlers of both sides dominated proceedings throughout the two and a half days. Scott captured the wicket of Coates with his first ball in first-class cricket on his way to a career-best analysis. He was to take only another 12 wickets in an 85 match career, becoming better known for skill as a batsman. Allee and Tindall also recorded career-best returns. Tindall was involved in the last wicket stand of 16 with Dummett that won the match for New South Wales by the narrowest of margins. The runs were obtained amidst great excitement, neither giving a chance, and the "ground was immediately rushed by the spectators" (*SMH*) when Dummett hit Allee to leg for the final 2. Unusually, there were no extras in either Victorian innings. The match marked the end of a meteororic four-match career (including 2 Tests) for Hodges. Sources: *Scores & Biographies, Sydney Morning Herald, Town & Country Journal, Sydney Mail.*

VICTORIA

B.B.Cooper	run out (Dummett)	3	(7)	c Tindall b Geary	1
J.Slight	b Evans	29	(1)	b Evans	0
J.P.Tennent	b Evans	25		c Evans b Tindall	27
†E.H.Elliott	c Tindall b Coates	5	(6)	c Dummett b Tindall	8
F.Baker	b Tindall	22	(4)	b Tindall	6
R.B.Terry	st Thompson b Tindall	13	(5)	b Tindall	0
H.J.H.Scott	c Dummett b Evans	2	(10)	c Seale b Evans	0
*C.G.Allee	st Thompson b Evans	9	(9)	b Tindall	10
P.S.McDonnell	b Evans	0	(11)	not out	0
J.Hodges	b Evans	13	(8)	b Tindall	17
L.S.Woolf	not out	10	(2)	c Tindall b Evans	7
Extras		-			-
Total	(108.3 overs, in about 205 mins)	131		(70.1 overs, in about 145 mins)	76

NEW SOUTH WALES

†N.Thompson	c & b Allee	16		b Scott	12
E.J.Gregory	b Terry	0	(8)	c Slight b Hodges	9
E.O.Sheridan	c Allee b Hodges	6	(7)	c Woolf b Scott	35
H.H.Massie	b Allee	17	(3)	c Elliott b Hodges	1
T.Powell	not out	25		b Scott	1
E.J.Seale	c & b Allee	3	(9)	c Allee b Scott	19
*J.Coates	b Allee	3	(2)	c sub (McShane) b Scott	1
A.Geary	b Allee	7	(4)	lbw b Scott	3
E.Tindall	c & b Allee	4	(10)	not out	15
E.Evans	c Elliott b Hodges	2	(6)	run out (Cooper/Hodges)	15
W.Dummett	c Elliott b Hodges	2		not out	6
Extras	(b3, lb1)	4		(b3)	3
Total	(45.1 overs, in about 95 mins)	89		(79.3 overs, in about 160 mins) (9 wkts)	120

NEW SOUTH WALES	O	M	R	W	w,nb		O	M	R	W	w,nb		FALL OF WICKETS			
														VIC	NSW	VIC	NSW
Evans	55.3	22	75	6	-,-		28.1	18	26	3	-,-	Wkt	1st	1st	2nd	2nd
Coates	28	13	31	1	-,-		8	4	9	0	-,-	1st	9	4	0	4
Tindall	25	10	25	2	-,-		27	12	31	6	-,-	2nd	53	17	23	5
Geary							7	2	10	1	-,-	3rd	62	37	32	16
												4th	62	40	32	17
VICTORIA	O	M	R	W	w,nb		O	M	R	W	w,nb	5th	96	46	44	18
Hodges	15.1	7	11	3	-,-		35	11	61	2	-,-	6th	97	50	49	51
Terry	17	4	35	1	-,-	(4)	5	3	2	0	-,-	7th	108	64	51	64
Baker	2	0	4	0	-,-							8th	108	74	73	95
Allee	11	1	35	6	-,-	(3)	8.3	1	21	0	-,-	9th	111	81	76	104
Scott						(2)	31	12	33	6	-,-	10th	131	89	76	-

AUSTRALIA v ENGLAND (Only Test)

Played at Melbourne Cricket Ground on January 2, 3, 4, 1879. (Timeless match)
Toss : England.   Result : AUSTRALIA WON BY TEN WICKETS.
Debuts: Australia - F.E.Allan, A.C.Bannerman, H.F.Boyle (all Test). England - C.A.Absolom, Lord Harris, L.Hone, A.N.Hornby,
    A.P.Lucas, F.A.MacKinnon, V.P.F.A.Royle, S.S.Schultz, A.J.Webbe (all Test).
12th Men: None named.
Umpires: P.Coady and G.Coulthard.
Attendances: 7000, 6500, 1000.   Total: About 14,500.   Receipts: No figures published.
Close of Play: 1st day Aust 3/95 (A.C.Bannerman 23, Spofforth 35); 2nd day Eng (2) 6/103 (MacKinnon 5).

It was originally intended that the English touring team would be an all-amateur contingent, but when it was found that a side of sufficient strength could not be mustered, two professionals, Emmett and Ulyett, were added. Consequently the team was often promoted as "Gentlemen of England (with Ulyett and Emmett)" and as the home team comprised ten members of the 1878 side that toured England, plus Kelly, the newspapers of the day reported the match as "Gentlemen of England v Australian XI". It is now recognised as the third Test match between the two countries. A violent rain-squall on the morning the match began softened the wicket, but did not dissuade Lord Harris from deciding to bat first. Ulyett played on to the second ball, by Spofforth, who later dismissed Royle, MacKinnon and Emmett (a drinks break intervening before Emmett faced) to record the first Test hat-trick. Lord Harris (33 with 3 fours) and Absolom (52 with 5 fours) retrieved England from a dire 7/26 to 113 all out. Alec Bannerman's 73 on debut (7 fours) included no chances but was complied in very slow time (about 235 minutes). He was the last man out, playing on to Schultz, "a fast roundarm bowler with a very high delivery, which some people call a throw" (*Argus*). Hornby bowled seven overs of fast underhand grubbers and was not scored off. Gregory, captaining Australia for the third and last time in Tests, put himself in last as he was suffering with a cold. Lord Harris (36 with 4 fours) led the scoring in England's second innings, Spofforth (match figures of 13 for 110) bettering his first-innings analysis and becoming the first bowler to capture ten or more wickets in a Test. Charles Bannerman - who like Gregory played just the first three Tests - hit the winning shot, a three to the on-side, all of which were included in the score though two were enough to win the game. Later that same afternoon, at 3.00pm, a second match was started at the ground: Melbourne Cricket Club v Canterbury (of New Zealand). Sources: *Wisden, The Age, The Argus, The Herald, The Australasian.*

ENGLAND

G.Ulyett	b Spofforth	0	b Spofforth	14
A.P.Lucas	b Allan	6	c Boyle b Allan	13
A.J.Webbe	b Allan	4	lbw b Allan	0
A.N.Hornby	b Spofforth	2	b Spofforth	4
*Lord Harris	b Garrett	33	c Horan b Spofforth	36
V.P.F.A.Royle	b Spofforth	3	c Spofforth b Boyle	18
F.A.MacKinnon	b Spofforth	0	b Spofforth	5
T.Emmett	c Horan b Spofforth	0	(9) not out	24
C.A.Absolom	c A.C.Bannerman b Boyle	52	(8) c & b Spofforth	6
†L.Hone	c Blackham b Spofforth	7	b Spofforth	6
S.S.Schultz	not out	0	c & b Spofforth	20
Extras	(b4, lb2)	6	(b10, lb4)	14
Total	(54.0 overs, in about 110 mins)	113	(83.0 overs, in about 170 mins)	160

AUSTRALIA

C.Bannerman	b Emmett	15	not out	15
W.L.Murdoch	c Webbe b Ulyett	4	not out	4
T.P.Horan	c Hone b Emmett	10		
A.C.Bannerman	b Schultz	73		
F.R.Spofforth	c Royle b Emmett	39		
T.W.Garrett	c Hone b Emmett	26		
F.E.Allan	b Hornby	5		
H.F.Boyle	c Royle b Emmett	28		
†J.M.Blackham	b Emmett	6		
T.J.D.Kelly	c Webbe b Emmett	10		
*D.W.Gregory	not out	12		
Extras	(b19, lb2, w7)	28		—
Total	(159.3 overs, in about 275 mins)	256	(2.3 overs, in about 10 mins) (0 wkts)	19

AUSTRALIA	O	M	R	W	w,nb	O	M	R	W	w,nb		FALL OF WICKETS			
Spofforth	25	9	48	6	-,-	35	16	62	7	-,-		ENG	AUST	ENG	AUST
Allan	17	4	30	2	-,-	28	11	50	2	-,-	Wkt	1st	1st	2nd	2nd
Garrett	5	0	18	1	-,-	10	6	18	0	-,-	1st	0	16	26	-
Boyle	7	1	11	1	-,-	10	4	16	1	-,-	2nd	7	30	28	-
											3rd	10	37	28	-
ENGLAND	O	M	R	W	w,nb	O	M	R	W	w,nb	4th	14	101	34	-
Emmett	59	31	68	7	7,-						5th	26	131	78	-
Ulyett	62	24	93	1	-,-	1	0	9	0	-,-	6th	26	158	103	-
Lucas	18	6	31	0	-,-						7th	26	215	103	-
Schultz	6.3	3	16	1	-,-	(1) 1.3	0	10	0	-,-	8th	89	224	118	-
Hornby	7	7	0	1	-,-						9th	113	234	128	-
Royle	4	1	6	0	-,-						10th	113	256	160	-
Harris	3	0	14	0	-,-										

NEW SOUTH WALES v LORD HARRIS'S ENGLAND XI

Played at Sydney Cricket Ground on January 24, 25, 27, 28, 1879. (Timeless match)
Toss : New South Wales.   Result : NEW SOUTH WALES WON BY FIVE WICKETS.
Debuts: New South Wales - R.C.Allen (f/c).
12th Men: T.Powell (NSW) and F.A.MacKinnon (Eng).
Umpires: G.Coulthard and W.C.Goddard.
Attendances: 4000, 10000, 15000, 5000.   Total: About 34,000.   Receipts: No figures published.
Close of Play: 1st day NSW 0/16 (A.C.Bannerman 9, Garrett 7); 2nd day Eng (2) 0/29 (Ulyett 7, Absolom 17); 3rd day NSW (2) 2/83
     (Murdoch 43, Massie 13).

The omission of D.W.Gregory, captain of the Australian XI, from the New South Wales team brought a lot of criticism and did not meet with "the approval of the public" (*SMH*). No reasons were given, and he was returned to lead the team for the return match. Coates was a late replacement for F.R.Spofforth (injured wrist). Ulyett (51 in about 75 minutes, 8 fours), Lord Harris (50 in about 105 minutes, 5 fours) and Penn (56 in about 105 minutes, 3 fours) hit half-centuries on the opening day after being sent in. Murdoch (70 in about 190 minutes, 8 fours) and Thompson (50 in about 125 minutes, 4 fours) replied in kind for the home team. Consistent scoring by the Englishmen in the second innings set New South Wales 226 to win. Massie (78 not out in about 220 minutes, 8 fours) and Charles Bannerman (60 not out in about 130 minutes, 1 five and 5 fours) combined to add 110 runs for the sixth wicket without being separated to see their side home from an uncomfortable 5/116. Bannerman had suffered an injury to the fingers of one hand in the field but his batting was of such quality that there was no apparent inconvenience. A collection amounting to £140 was raised from the spectators in recognition of his effort. Webbe took over the wicket-keeping duties from Hone for the final day. *Wisden* incorrectly gives Eng (1) Royle 12, Absolom 17. Sources: *Wisden, The Australasian, Sydney Morning Herald, Town & Country Journal, Sydney Mail*.

LORD HARRIS'S ENGLAND XI

Batsman	Dismissal 1	Runs		Dismissal 2	Runs
G.Ulyett	c Thompson b Tindall	51		st Murdoch b Evans	20
A.P.Lucas	c & b Tindall	7	(3)	b Coates	15
†A.J.Webbe	c Allen b Coates	1	(7)	b Coates	27
A.N.Hornby	c A.C.Bannerman b Evans	12		b Evans	20
*Lord Harris	b Evans	50		c A.C.Bannerman b Tindall	22
F.Penn	c Garrett b Coates	56		c Garrett b Evans	18
T.Emmett	c Garrett b Tindall	9	(9)	not out	16
V.P.F.A.Royle	c A.C.Bannerman b Tindall	13		b Coates	29
C.A.Absolom	c Seale b Tindall	16	(2)	c Allen b Evans	22
S.S.Schultz	not out	13		b Coates	1
†L.Hone	c Garrett b Tindall	16		c Thompson b Evans	0
Extras	(b1, lb2, w1)	4		(b18, lb8, w1)	27
Total	(135.3 overs, in about 255 mins)	248		(143.1 overs, in about 270 mins)	217

NEW SOUTH WALES

Batsman	Dismissal 1	Runs		Dismissal 2	Runs
A.C.Bannerman	c Lucas b Emmett	28		b Lucas	15
T.W.Garrett	c Absolom b Emmett	12			
C.Bannerman	b Ulyett	0	(7)	not out	60
*†W.L.Murdoch	c Webbe b Ulyett	70	(2)	b Lucas	49
E.Evans	lbw b Lucas	21	(6)	c Emmett b Lucas	1
N.Thompson	b Emmett	50	(3)	c Hornby b Ulyett	9
R.C.Allen	b Lucas	0	(5)	c Webbe b Ulyett	5
H.H.Massie	run out (Webbe/Emmett)	30	(4)	not out	78
E.J.Seale	st Hone b Emmett	0			
E.Tindall	not out	9			
J.Coates	st Hone b Lucas	2			
Extras	(b6, lb5, w7)	18		(b2, lb6, w 1)	9
Total	(158.1 overs, in about 290 mins)	240		(152.0 overs, in about 280 mins) (5 wkts)	226

NEW SOUTH WALES	O	M	R	W	w,nb		O	M	R	W	w,nb					
Tindall	60.3	26	89	6	-,-		31	13	44	1	-,-					
Evans	41	16	68	2	-,-		67.1	34	82	5	-,-					
Coates	22	5	52	2	1,-		25	14	38	4	1,-					
Garrett	12	2	35	0	-,-		20	6	26	0	-,-					

		FALL OF WICKETS

Wkt	ENG 1st	NSW 1st	ENG 2nd	NSW 2nd
1st	21	25	46	33
2nd	30	25	47	58
3rd	54	62	85	98
4th	85	108	87	113
5th	151	188	124	116
6th	174	194	127	-
7th	194	204	180	-
8th	215	210	207	-
9th	227	235	216	-
10th	248	240	217	-

ENGLAND XI	O	M	R	W	w,nb			O	M	R	W	w,nb
Emmett	64	32	70	4	7,-	(2)		43	22	51	0	1,-
Ulyett	31	16	51	2	-,-	(3)		33	18	57	2	-,-
Lucas	35.1	16	53	3	-,-	(1)		54	24	76	3	-,-
Schultz	21	8	43	0	-,-	(5)		9	2	18	0	-,-
Hornby	4	3	2	0	-,-	(4)		13	8	15	0	-,-
Penn	3	1	3	0	-,-							

NEW SOUTH WALES v LORD HARRIS'S ENGLAND XI

Played at Sydney Cricket Ground on February 7, 8, 10, 1879. (Timeless match)
Toss : England XI.   Result : LORD HARRIS'S ENGLAND XI WON BY AN INNINGS AND 41 RUNS.
Debuts: Nil.
12th Men: E.J.Gregory (NSW) and F.A.MacKinnon (Eng).
Umpires: E.Barton and G.Coulthard.
Attendances: 4000, 10000, 1500.   Total: About 15,500.   Receipts: No figures published.
Close of Play: 1st day NSW 2/53 (Murdoch 28, Massie 3); 2nd day NSW (2) 1/19 (A.C.Bannerman 6, Thompson 0).

This match became famous for an invasion of the ground by the crowd on the second day. After following on, New South Wales were fighting to recover their position when Murdoch, the hero of the first innings, was adjudged run out. Coulthard, who gave the decision, had been invited to Sydney by Lord Harris to act on behalf of the Englishmen and this fact, combined with heavy batting on the event and Gregory's refusal to send another man to the wicket in protest, led to the unrest. When Lord Harris moved towards the pavilion to plead with the New South Wales captain to continue the match, riled spectators jumped the fence en masse and attacked Harris, Hornby and Ulyett, the Englishmen being forced to flee the ground. Coulthard was also set upon by the mob. Attempts to clear the ground proved unsuccessful, so the remaining 90 minutes of play on the day were abandoned. The match continued on Monday without further incident but overnight rain had turned the pitch into a batsman's nightmare and the last six wickets fell without addition. Record books traditionally credit Ulyett with four wickets in four balls with the score at 49, but lack of specific comment in the Press indicates that this may not have happened. Murdoch (82 not out in 220 minutes, 11 fours) became the first batsman to carry his bat in a first-class match in Australia. The Englishmen owed their total to half-centuries from Hornby (67 in about 110 minutes, 7 fours), Lucas (51 in about 100 minutes, 4 fours) and Ulyett (55 in about 80 minutes, 7 fours). It is not known which bowler, or bowlers, is responsible for the no-balls in NSW (1).
Sources: *Wisden, The Australasian, Sydney Morning Herald, Town & Country Journal, Sydney Mail.*

LORD HARRIS'S ENGLAND XI

A.N.Hornby	b Spofforth	67
A.P.Lucas	b Spofforth	51
G.Ulyett	c Evans b Spofforth	55
*Lord Harris	b Evans	41
F.Penn	c Massie b Spofforth	13
†A.J.Webbe	b Evans	0
T.Emmett	c Evans b Spofforth	0
V.P.F.A.Royle	c & b Evans	6
C.A.Absolom	b Evans	6
S.S.Schultz	c & b Evans	5
L.Hone	not out	4
Extras	(b14, lb3, nb2)	19
Total	(120.0 overs, in about 225 mins)	267

NEW SOUTH WALES

†W.L.Murdoch	not out	82	run out (/Webbe)		10
A.C.Bannerman	c Royle b Ulyett	16	c Webbe b Emmett		20
N.Thompson	c Lucas b Emmett	3	c Penn b Emmett		0
H.H.Massie	b Hornby	38	b Emmett		8
C.Bannerman	c Penn b Emmett	9	c Hornby b Emmett		4
E.Evans	b Emmett	5	c Emmett b Ulyett		1
*D.W.Gregory	c Ulyett b Emmett	4	(8) c Webbe b Ulyett		0
E.O.Sheridan	c Schultz b Emmett	0	(11) b Emmett		0
F.R.Spofforth	b Emmett	0	c Webbe b Ulyett		0
T.Powell	c Hone b Emmett	5	not out		0
E.Tindall	lbw b Emmett	0	(7) c & b Ulyett		0
Extras	(b9, w3, nb3)	15	(b1, lb2, w2, nb1)		6
Total	(117.3 overs, in about 220 mins)	177	(55.0 overs, in about 85 mins)		49

NEW SOUTH WALES	O	M	R	W	w,nb
Spofforth	44	12	93	5	-,2
Evans	38	13	62	5	-,-
Tindall	27	6	79	0	-,-
Thompson	11	4	14	0	-,-

ENGLAND XI	O	M	R	W	w,nb		O	M	R	W	w,nb
Lucas	12	4	20	0	-,-						
Schultz	15	3	27	0	-,-						
Emmett	51.3	27	47	8	3,-	(1)	28	23	21	5	2,-
Ulyett	17	4	44	1	-,-	(2)	22	15	13	4	-,-
Hornby	22	13	24	1	-,-	(3)	5	2	9	0	-,1

FALL OF WICKETS

	ENG	NSW	NSW
Wkt	1st	1st	2nd
1st	125	34	19
2nd	132	37	19
3rd	217	107	30
4th	234	130	38
5th	234	135	49
6th	235	147	49
7th	247	152	49
8th	255	158	49
9th	262	177	49
10th	267	177	49

VICTORIA v LORD HARRIS'S ENGLAND XI

Played at Melbourne Cricket Ground on February 21, 22, 24, 25, 1879. (Timeless match)
Toss : England XI.   Result : VICTORIA WON BY TWO WICKETS.
Debuts: Victoria - W.H.Cooper, T.U.Groube, A.G.Major, W.H.Moule (all f/c).
12th Men: No 12th men or emergency fieldsmen named.
Umpires: G.Coulthard and R.B.Terry.
Attendances: 1500, 4000, 4000, 1000.   Total: About 10,500.   Receipts: No figures published.
Close of Play: 1st day Vic 1/2 (Groube 2, Cooper 0); 2nd day Eng (2) 3/59 (Ulyett 24, Webbe 8); 3rd day Vic (2) 7/178 (Boyle 15, Major 0).

This was the first match between Victoria and an English team to be played on even terms. F.Penn severely dislocated a knee in the tourists' previous match, against the Bohemian Club, and was unable to play again on the tour. Lucas had a minor hand injury as a result of a fielding mishap but was forced to play as the Englishmen had no reserves. Hornby (50 in about 75 minutes, 4 fours), Ulyett (71 in about 95 minutes, 8 fours) and Royle (57 in about 85 minutes, 8 fours) took advantage of a good wicket and fast outfield on the first day to hit half-centuries. Blackham's five stumpings in the innings remains unsurpassed (although since equalled) in Australian first-class cricket. Campbell (51 in about 135 minutes, 4 fours) and Horan (69 in about 175 minutes, 2 fives and 5 fours) reached half-centuries for Victoria, who won a close contest amidst intense excitement. Hone missed a run out opportunity when 26 were still required by the home team and eight wickets down. Hornby was brought on to bowl underarm "grubbers" (*Argus*) but Major and Allan saw their team home. Cooper bowled well on debut but Emmett had 9 wickets for 146 from 138 overs to take out the bowling honours. Sources: *Wisden, The Age, The Argus, The Herald, The Australasian, The Leader.*

LORD HARRIS'S ENGLAND XI

A.P.Lucas	b Cooper	38	c Baker b Allan	1
A.N.Hornby	b Alexander	50	c Allan b Cooper	8
*Lord Harris	st Blackham b Cooper	26	c Blackham b Cooper	8
G.Ulyett	b Horan	71	b Alexander	48
A.J.Webbe	b Allan	3	c Campbell b Boyle	20
T.Emmett	c Boyle b Moule	41	run out (Boyle/Blackham)	20
V.P.F.A.Royle	st Blackham b Cooper	57	b Alexander	13
C.A.Absolom	st Blackham b Cooper	20	b Alexander	2
S.S.Schultz	st Blackham b Cooper	2	b Allan	5
F.A.MacKinnon	not out	5	not out	10
†L.Hone	st Blackham b Boyle	2	b Boyle	22
Extras	(b5, lb4, nb1)	10	(b8, lb6)	14
Total	(144.3 overs, in about 275 mins)	325	(99.0 overs, in about 185 mins)	171

VICTORIA

F.E.Allan	b Emmett	0	(10) not out	14
T.U.Groube	c Absolom b Emmett	2	b Emmett	12
W.H.Cooper	b Lucas	0		
T.P.Horan	c Absolom b Lucas	26	lbw b Absolom	69
F.Baker	c Royle b Ulyett	31	(6) c Royle b Absolom	2
D.Campbell	c Ulyett b Lucas	51	(5) b Emmett	37
G.Alexander	b Emmett	24	(1) b Emmett	17
*H.F.Boyle	c Royle b Emmett	3	b Emmett	26
†J.M.Blackham	run out	46	(7) c Hone b Lucas	6
A.G.Major	lbw b Emmett	24	(9) not out	27
W.H.Moule	not out	17	(3) c & b Lucas	6
Extras	(b27, lb8, w1, nb1)	37	(b10, lb7, w3)	20
Total	(161.0 overs, in about 295 mins)	261	(165.0 overs, in about 290 mins) (8 wkts)	236

VICTORIA	O	M	R	W	w,nb		O	M	R	W	w,nb
Allan	34	13	63	1	-,-		37	17	57	2	-,-
Boyle	22.3	8	48	1	-,-	(3)	13	8	20	2	-,-
Cooper	29	3	79	5	-,-	(2)	27	8	46	2	-,-
Major	7	1	18	0	-,1	(5)	5	1	12	0	-,-
Alexander	29	8	50	1	-,-	(4)	17	8	22	3	-,-
Campbell	7	5	8	0	-,-						
Horan	5	1	15	1	-,-						
Moule	8	0	24	1	-,-						
Baker	3	2	10	0	-,-						

ENGLAND XI	O	M	R	W	w,nb		O	M	R	W	w,nb
Emmett	63	34	93	5	1,-		75	46	53	4	3,-
Lucas	43	21	43	3	-,-	(4)	43	20	72	2	-,-
Ulyett	26	7	56	1	-,1	(2)	11	4	18	0	-,-
Absolom	18	9	21	0	-,-	(6)	21	10	37	2	-,-
Hornby	6	3	5	0	-,-	(3)	7	1	15	0	-,-
Schultz	5	3	6	0	-,-	(5)	8	3	21	0	-,-

FALL OF WICKETS

Wkt	ENG 1st	VIC 1st	ENG 2nd	VIC 2nd
1st	89	0	13	25
2nd	115	3	19	34
3rd	131	9	44	42
4th	134	42	82	133
5th	220	80	116	137
6th	268	136	118	147
7th	305	154	126	178
8th	313	170	135	208
9th	318	209	139	-
10th	325	261	171	-

VICTORIA v LORD HARRIS'S ENGLAND XI

Played at Melbourne Cricket Ground on March 7, 8, 10, 1879. (Timeless match)
Toss : England XI.   Result : LORD HARRIS'S ENGLAND XI WON BY SIX WICKETS.
Debuts: Victoria - J.Mullagh, G.E.Palmer (both f/c).
12th Men: H.J.H.Scott (Vic). No reserve available for England XI.
Umpires: G.Coulthard and R.B.Terry.
Attendances: 5000, 9000, 500.   Total: About 14,500.   Receipts: No figures published.
Close of Play: 1st day Vic 6/112 (Boyle 4, Moule 2); 2nd day Eng (2) 4/31 (Lucas 15, Webbe 5).

Mullagh was selected for his sole first-class appearance "on the strength of certain performances in the Western District lately" (*Age*). He had been the outstanding player on the 1868 Aboriginal tour of England but previous attempts to get him into the Victorian team had always failed. He had preferred to remain in western Victoria rather than travel to and remain in Melbourne. His second innings created such an impression that a subscription amounting to £50 was soon collected from the spectators. Palmer was brought in as a last minute replacement for F.E.Allan, who had cabled that he had missed his train at Colac (also in western Victoria). Scott fielded as substitute on the first day until Palmer arrived. Consequently, he was the seventh bowler used but made an immediate impression with nine wickets (all bowled) on debut. Emmett's "wily bowling" (*Age*) brought him 11 wickets for 109 from 98 overs in the match, bowling almost unchanged through the second innings. Although it was noted that the Englishmen had the better of the conditions for their innings, the wicket was not held to account for the failure of the Victorians. At the conclusion of the Victorian second innings just before 5.00pm on the second day, Lord Harris "expressed a desire to play on until half past six o'clock, so that the game might be concluded" (*Age*) but bad light brought a minor collapse. Harris then came onto the field to object to Boyle about the light and an argument ensued in front of the crowd before play was suspended at 5.52pm. Less than 20 minutes were required to finish the match on the following day. Sources: *Wisden, The Age, The Argus, The Herald, The Australasian.*

LORD HARRIS'S ENGLAND XI

A.P.Lucas	c Mullagh b Alexander	6		not out	21
A.N.Hornby	c Cooper b Alexander	2		b Alexander	2
*Lord Harris	b Palmer	67	(5)	b Palmer	6
†A.J.Webbe	c Palmer b Boyle	24	(6)	not out	22
G.Ulyett	b Palmer	47	(4)	b Palmer	0
T.Emmett	b Palmer	0			
V.P.F.A.Royle	b Palmer	75			
F.A.MacKinnon	not out	15	(3)	b Palmer	2
C.A.Absolom	b Palmer	4			
L.Hone	b Palmer	1			
S.S.Schultz	b Boyle	0			
Extras	(b3, lb3, nb1)	7		(lb1)	1
Total	(140.2 overs, in about 235 mins)	248		(39.0 overs, in about 65 mins) (4 wkts)	54

VICTORIA

J.Slight	b Emmett	1		c Royle b Emmett	8
G.Alexander	c Webbe b Emmett	0	(7)	b Hornby	31
T.P.Horan	b Schultz	46		c Royle b Emmett	31
D.Campbell	c Hone b Lucas	5		c Royle b Emmett	2
†J.M.Blackham	c Harris b Emmett	39		lbw b Absolom	4
F.Baker	c Royle b Emmett	10	(2)	c Royle b Emmett	17
*H.F.Boyle	b Lucas	17	(8)	b Hornby	2
W.H.Moule	b Lucas	13	(10)	b Schultz	2
J.Mullagh	b Emmett	4	(6)	b Schultz	36
G.E.Palmer	not out	0	(9)	c Harris b Emmett	0
W.H.Cooper	b Emmett	0		not out	1
Extras	(b4, lb3, w4)	11		(b10, lb7, w4)	21
Total	(112.2 overs, in about 165 mins)	146		(108.1 overs, in about 160 mins)	155

VICTORIA	O	M	R	W	w,nb		O	M	R	W	w,nb					
Alexander	31	14	52	2	-,-	(2)	19	8	23	1	-,-					
Cooper	19	4	48	0	-,-											
Boyle	45.2	7	44	2	-,-											
Horan	4	1	9	0	-,-											
Moule	4	2	16	0	-,-											
Mullagh	3	0	8	0	-,-											
Palmer	34	13	64	6	-,1	(1)	20	8	30	3	-,-					

ENGLAND XI	O	M	R	W	w,nb		O	M	R	W	w,nb
Emmett	46.2	27	41	6	4,-		52	23	68	5	4,-
Ulyett	22	13	20	0	-,-	(4)	5	3	6	0	-,-
Lucas	25	11	32	3	-,-		9	3	20	0	-,-
Schultz	9	1	25	1	-,-	(6)	5.1	2	8	2	-,-
Absolom	10	3	17	0	-,-	(2)	22	8	23	1	-,-
Hornby						(5)	15	11	9	2	-,-

FALL OF WICKETS

Wkt	ENG 1st	VIC 1st	VIC 2nd	ENG 2nd
1st	3	0	19	10
2nd	8	5	42	15
3rd	100	15	63	15
4th	100	84	67	23
5th	100	101	67	-
6th	199	110	122	-
7th	236	127	126	-
8th	240	143	131	-
9th	242	144	142	-
10th	248	146	155	-

NEW SOUTH WALES v VICTORIA

Played at Sydney Cricket Ground on November 21, 22, 24, 1879. (Timeless match)
Toss : New South Wales.   Result : NEW SOUTH WALES WON BY 32 RUNS.
Debuts: Nil.
12th Men: T.Powell (NSW). No 12th man or emergency fieldsman named for Victoria.
Umpires: A.R.Docker and R.B.Terry.
Attendances: 3000, 10000, 2000.   Total: About 15,000.   Receipts: No figures published.
Close of Play: 1st day Vic 2/78 (McDonnell 41, Allan 5); 2nd day Vic (2) 3/62 (Allan 25, Horan 15).

J.Coates (business) was unavailable for New South Wales and there was surprise expressed in Melbourne at the omission of T.K.Kendall from the Victorian team. It was agreed beforehand that the game would be played out on the one wicket despite heavy rain on the preceding days. Alec Bannerman (52 in about 80 minutes, 9 fours) compiled an uncharacteristically fluent half-century on the first day, the only one of the match, and his second wicket stand of 82 with his brother Charles was also the only half-century partnership. McDonnell (48 in about 90 minutes, 6 fours) topscored for the visitors. Rungetting became more and more difficult the further the match progressed, Cooper's leg-breaks finding such response on the second day that the New South Wales second innings collapsed completely on his introduction to the attack soon after 50 was passed. Spofforth used the worn turf to his advantage on the third day to bowl his team to victory, "being better equal to the occasion than on either of the preceding days" (*T & C Journal*). *T & C Journal* gives NSW (2) A.C.Bannerman 18, Alexander 2/39, total 114; Vic (2) Allan 33, extras 2, Spofforth 5/32; also minor differences with some falls of wickets. However, although claiming to be correct, they noted that they "differ from the officials". Sources: *Australian Cricketers Guide, The Australasian, Sydney Morning Herald, Town & Country Journal.*

NEW SOUTH WALES

†W.L.Murdoch	c & b Boyle	21	st Blackham b Palmer		16
C.Bannerman	c Cooper b Alexander	36	b Alexander		29
A.C.Bannerman	c Cooper b Alexander	52	b Cooper		17
N.Thompson	lbw b Allan	25	b Alexander		13
E.Evans	st Blackham b Cooper	8	c Horan b Cooper		3
H.H.Massie	b Palmer	13	c McDonnell b Cooper		8
F.R.Spofforth	b Palmer	1	st Blackham b Cooper		0
*D.W.Gregory	not out	19	b Cooper		6
T.W.Garrett	c Campbell b Boyle	17	not out		6
A.Geary	c McDonnell b Palmer	0	c Slight b Cooper		0
E.Tindall	b Boyle	4	c Horan b Cooper		10
Extras	(b1, lb4, nb3)	8	(b4, nb1)		5
Total	(125.1 overs, in about 205 mins)	204	(72.0 overs, in about 125 mins)		113

VICTORIA

J.Slight	c Massie b Spofforth	15	(2) run out (A.C.Bannerman/Murdoch)		3
P.S.McDonnell	c C.Bannerman b Tindall	48	(1) b Evans		5
T.P.Horan	c Geary b Tindall	13	(5) b Evans		14
F.E.Allan	c Gregory b Tindall	28	(3) b Tindall		29
D.Campbell	c Massie b Evans	6	(7) b Spofforth		16
G.Alexander	c & b Evans	8	(9) b Spofforth		0
†J.M.Blackham	b Tindall	1	(4) c Garrett b Spofforth		10
*H.F.Boyle	c Massie b Spofforth	26	b Spofforth		25
J.P.Tennent	c Spofforth b Evans	10	(6) c & b Tindall		2
G.E.Palmer	c A.C.Bannerman b Spofforth	3	not out		6
W.H.Cooper	not out	1	c & b Spofforth		1
Extras	(b2, lb4, nb3)	9	(b4, lb1, nb1)		6
Total	(100.3 overs, in about 165 mins)	168	(66.3 overs, in about 110 mins)		117

VICTORIA	O	M	R	W	w,nb		O	M	R	W	w,nb			FALL OF WICKETS		
														NSW	VIC NSW	VIC
Palmer	37	13	67	3	-,2	(3)	11	2	22	1	-,1	Wkt	1st	1st	2nd	2nd
Boyle	29.1	14	39	3	-,-		9	4	11	0	-,-	1st	25	34	35	9
Alexander	26	15	29	2	-,-	(1)	36	19	38	2	-,-	2nd	107	69	67	9
Cooper	20	7	39	1	-,-		16	3	37	7	-,-	3rd	111	99	67	33
Allan	13	5	22	1	-,1							4th	132	115	78	62
												5th	155	119	88	66
NEW SOUTH WALES	O	M	R	W	w,nb		O	M	R	W	w,nb	6th	158	125	91	69
Spofforth	23	10	57	3	-,2	(2)	19.3	10	28	5	-,1	7th	167	127	91	104
Evans	37.3	18	36	3	-,-	(1)	29	11	42	2	-,-	8th	188	160	99	106
Garrett	13	6	18	0	-,-	(4)	2	1	4	0	-,-	9th	195	166	99	111
Tindall	26	6	48	4	-,1	(3)	16	5	37	2	-,-	10th	204	168	113	117
Geary	1	1	0	0	-,-											

VICTORIA v NEW SOUTH WALES

Played at Melbourne Cricket Ground on December 26, 27, 1879. (Timeless match)
Toss : Victoria.   Result : VICTORIA WON BY AN INNINGS AND 96 RUNS.
Debuts: Victoria - T.K.Kendall (Vic only). New South Wales - J.Davis (f/c).
12th Men: T.U.Groube (Vic) and A.Geary (NSW).
Umpires: J.Swift and R.B.Terry.
Attendances: 9000, 10000.   Total: About 19,000.   Receipts: No figures published.
Close of Play: 1st day NSW 0/12 (Murdoch 5, Davis 5).

E.Evans and D.W.Gregory were unavailable for New South Wales. Alexander (career-best 75 in about 105 minutes, 8 fours) "played dashing cricket" (*Age*) on the opening day and his second wicket partnership of 92 with Horan (43 in about 75 minutes, 8 fours) established the Victorian innings. Consistent scoring down the order, culminated in a last wicket stand of 61 between Blackham and Kendall. Light rain on the second morning, apart from slowing the outfield, was not a factor in the double failure of the New South Wales batting. Tindall (52 in about 55 minutes, 6 fours) hit defiantly in the first innings but was unable to bat in the second innings when he had to return to Sydney on hearing of the serious illness of his father. New South Wales were further handicapped by an ankle injury to Thompson sustained in the field which required him to bat with a runner in each innings. Garrett (47 in about 75 minutes, 4 fours) played a lone hand in the second innings and the match was over inside two days. Kendall had played in the two Test Matches of 1876-77 and this was his only appearance for Victoria. Sources: *Australian Cricketers Guide, The Age, The Argus, The Herald, The Australasian*.

VICTORIA

G.Alexander	c A.C.Bannerman b Coates	75
P.S.McDonnell	b Spofforth	12
T.P.Horan	lbw b Coates	43
J.Slight	run out (/Spofforth)	10
D.Campbell	b Spofforth	8
*H.F.Boyle	c A.C.Bannerman b Coates	36
F.E.Allan	c Massie b Garrett	34
†J.M.Blackham	not out	41
G.E.Palmer	c Spofforth b Coates	4
W.H.Cooper	lbw b Spofforth	13
T.K.Kendall	b A.C.Bannerman	43
Extras	(b10, lb9)	19
Total	(137.1 overs, in about 260 mins)	338

NEW SOUTH WALES

†W.L.Murdoch	c Kendall b Alexander	27	b Alexander	2
J.Davis	b Boyle	5	(7) c Alexander b Allan	4
A.C.Bannerman	c Blackham b Boyle	18	run out (Slight/Alexander)	16
C.Bannerman	c Allan b Alexander	0	(2) c Slight b Kendall	6
E.Tindall	st Blackham b Cooper	52	absent	-
N.Thompson	st Blackham b Cooper	5	b Cooper	1
H.H.Massie	c Cooper b Alexander	19	(5) st Blackham b Cooper	8
T.W.Garrett	run out (Palmer/Alexander)	0	(4) c Kendall b Alexander	47
T.Powell	b Allan	7	(8) c Palmer b Allan	9
F.R.Spofforth	c Kendall b Allan	1	(9) not out	4
*J.Coates	not out	1	(10) b Allan	0
Extras	(lb4)	4	(b4, lb2)	6
Total	(63.3 overs, in about 125 mins)	139	(57.3 overs, in about 115 mins)	103

NEW SOUTH WALES	O	M	R	W	w,nb
Spofforth	45	9	121	3	-,-
Coates	40	10	85	4	-,-
Tindall	20	5	58	0	-,-
Garrett	18	6	26	1	-,-
Thompson	4	0	11	0	-,-
A.C.Bannerman	10.1	5	18	1	-,-

VICTORIA	O	M	R	W	w,nb		O	M	R	W	w,nb
Palmer	14	6	27	0	-,-						
Boyle	14	5	41	2	-,-						
Kendall	6	1	10	0	-,-	(2)	13	7	21	1	-,-
Alexander	19	8	34	3	-,-	(1)	29	15	30	2	-,-
Cooper	7	0	18	2	-,-	(3)	10	1	35	2	-,-
Allan	3.3	2	5	2	-,-	(4)	5.3	3	11	3	-,-

FALL OF WICKETS

Wkt	VIC 1st	NSW 1st	NSW 2nd
1st	39	14	4
2nd	131	45	14
3rd	140	45	42
4th	153	84	53
5th	157	108	67
6th	213	115	89
7th	238	115	99
8th	245	137	99
9th	277	137	103
10th	338	139	-

VICTORIA v SOUTH AUSTRALIA

Played at East Melbourne Cricket Ground on November 12, 13, 15, 1880. (Timeless match)
Toss : Victoria.   Result : VICTORIA WON BY SEVEN WICKETS.
Debuts: Victoria - G.Coulthard, G.Mackay, F.G.McShane, R.Pateman, W.A.Tobin, T.Trinnick (all f/c). South Australia - W.Bullough,
  J.E.Goodfellow, J.Noel, A.M.Pettinger, T.O.Richards (all f/c); J.E.Gooden, J.B.Hide, W.Slight (all SA only).
12th Men: L.S.Woolf (Vic) and A.F.Slight (SA).
Umpires: J.Chittleborough and R.B.Terry.
Attendances: 500, 1000, 250.   Total: About 1750.   Receipts: No figures published.
Close of Play: 1st day Vic 6/304 (Horan 97); 2nd day SA (2) 2/134 (Slight 55).

This was the first eleven-a-side encounter between Victoria and South Australia as well as the first of four first-class matches to be staged at the East Melbourne ground in the 1880's. It was demolished when the Jolimont railway yards were extended in 1922. Horan (113 in about 305 minutes, 2 fives and 10 fours) survived a chance when 25 to anchor the Victorian innings. Campbell (55 in about 75 minutes, 7 fours) and Baker (83 in about 125 minutes, 8 fours) batted fluently in support. Pateman batted "in his every-day attire" (*Australasian*) when he came in late on the first day. The South Australians collapsed before "the puzzling deliveries" (*Australasian*) of Cooper but performed much better after being forced to follow on. Giffen (63 in about 105 minutes, 7 fours) and Slight (70 in about 150 minutes, 7 fours) established the innings with a second wicket partnership of 125 and Hide (48 in about 65 minutes, 4 fours) and H.A.Gooden (49 in about 90 minutes, 6 fours) also played well, forcing the home team to bat again. J.E.Gooden had appeared in the so-called 'Combination Match' in 1872-73, while Hide and Slight had previously played with Sussex and Victoria respectively. Coulthard had umpired several matches, including the 1878-79 Test Match, prior to his playing debut in this match. *O'Reilly* omits c Tobin from dismissal of Bullough in SA (2) and, in common with *The Argus*, credits the wicket of Baker to H.A.Gooden, also reversing his bowling analysis with that of J.E.Gooden.
Sources: *Australian Cricketers Guide, C.B.O'Reilly, The Age, The Argus, The Herald, The Australasian, The Leader.*

VICTORIA

†E.H.Elliott	c Goodfellow b Hide	5	c Pettinger b Bullough		18
W.A.Tobin	b King	15	b Bullough		2
T.P.Horan	c Slight b Giffen	113	not out		18
G.Coulthard	c Richards b Giffen	31	b Goodfellow		0
*D.Campbell	c & b Slight	55	not out		24
F.Baker	c Richards b J.E.Gooden	83			
R.Pateman	b Bullough	4			
G.Mackay	run out (Bullough)	4			
J.Trinnick	b Bullough	3			
W.H.Cooper	b Bullough	0			
F.G.McShane	not out	0			
Extras	(b11, lb5)	16	(b2)		2
Total	(190.2 overs, in about 325 mins)	329	(36.0 overs, in about 60 mins) (3 wkts)		64

SOUTH AUSTRALIA

†J.Noel	b Cooper	9	(6) b Cooper		10
H.A.Gooden	c McShane b Coulthard	6	(7) run out		49
W.Slight	c Horan b Cooper	11	run out (Trinnick/Elliott)		70
G.Giffen	b Coulthard	3	(2) lbw b McShane		63
J.B.Hide	c Mackay b Cooper	10	b Cooper		48
T.O.Richards	c Horan b Cooper	0	(10) c Cooper b Mackay		3
J.F.King	run out (Pateman/Cooper)	1	(9) not out		28
A.M.Pettinger	b Coulthard	0	c Horan b Cooper		12
*J.E.Gooden	st Elliott b Cooper	1	(4) b McShane		3
W.Bullough	not out	26	(1) c Tobin b Coulthard		9
J.E.Goodfellow	run out	6	b Mackay		1
Extras	(b2, lb2)	4	(b11, lb7)		18
Total	(56.0 overs, in about 105 mins)	77	(195.3 overs, in about 305 mins)		314

SOUTH AUSTRALIA	O	M	R	W	w,nb		O	M	R	W	w,nb
Goodfellow	32	20	37	0	-,-	(3)	11	5	14	1	-,-
Hide	27	8	45	1	-,-						
King	13	0	30	1	-,-	(4)	2	0	16	0	-,-
Giffen	35	16	47	2	-,-	(1)	5	1	14	0	-,-
Bullough	40.2	21	54	3	-,-	(2)	18	11	18	2	-,-
J.E.Gooden	12	3	24	1	-,-						
H.A.Gooden	11	4	25	0	-,-						
Slight	15	3	34	1	-,-						
Richards	5	0	17	0	-,-						

VICTORIA	O	M	R	W	w,nb	O	M	R	W	w,nb
Cooper	28	15	44	5	-,-	48	17	84	3	-,-
Coulthard	28	16	29	3	-,-	27	9	49	1	-,-
McShane						48	18	79	2	-,-
Mackay						33.3	17	35	2	-,-
Baker						7	2	12	0	-,-
Campbell						15	12	4	0	-,-
Horan						3	1	11	0	-,-
Tobin						14	6	22	0	-,-

FALL OF WICKETS

Wkt	VIC 1st	SA 1st	SA 2nd	VIC 2nd
1st	11	10	9	17
2nd	33	23	134	26
3rd	79	26	140	26
4th	160	34	193	-
5th	296	34	210	-
6th	304	41	223	-
7th	313	42	240	-
8th	329	43	301	-
9th	329	45	308	-
10th	329	77	314	-

VICTORIA v NEW SOUTH WALES

Played at Melbourne Cricket Ground on December 27, 28, 29, 1880. (Timeless match)
Toss : Victoria. Result : VICTORIA WON BY TWO WICKETS.
Debuts: Victoria - J.D.Edwards (f/c). New South Wales - A.H.Gregory, R.Hall, H.C.S.Hiddleston, S.P.Jones, W.S.Wearne (all f/c).
12th Men: H.A.Musgrove (Vic). R.C.Allen & E.J.Seale named as NSW emergencies.
Umpires: J.Swift and R.B.Terry.
Attendances: 7000, 4000, 3000. Total: About 14,000. Receipts: No figures published.
Close of Play: 1st day NSW 7/61 (D.W.Gregory 8, Wearne 0); 2nd day NSW (2) 8/247 (Hiddleston 11, Jones 9).

Both teams were without their Australian XI representatives, who were engaged in a series of matches before disbanding. A tight, hard-fought contest ensued in which bowlers of both sides generally held the upper hand. Allan bowled unchanged throughout the New South Wales first innings, demonstrating "all his old precision of pitch, and breaking both ways" (*Age*). Cooper's "peculiars" commanded respect during both innings. However, it was the form of Evans that impressed all and "justified his claim to be considered the premier bowler of Australia" (*Age*). He bowled unchanged throughout the Victorian second innings to almost snatch victory for his team. Only a stubborn ninth wicket stand of 45 in an hour by Allan and Elliott saw Victoria home. Midwinter (76 in about 125 minutes, 7 fours), Dave Gregory (85 in about 210 minutes, 4 fours) and Evans (51 in about 105 minutes, 5 fours) recorded the only half-centuries in the match - Gregory and Evans adding 87 for the fifth wicket in the New South Wales second innings. Sources: *Australian Cricketers Guide, The Age, The Argus, The Herald, The Australasian, The Leader, Town & Country Journal.*

VICTORIA

W.E.Midwinter	c D.W.Gregory b Evans	76		b Garrett	4
G.Mackay	b Tindall	26		b Evans	3
T.P.Horan	run out (Hiddleston/Garrett)	27		b Jones	36
G.Coulthard	b Evans	1		c Hall b Evans	1
W.A.Tobin	b Garrett	4		lbw b Evans	0
*D.Campbell	c Hall b Evans	4	(7)	c Garrett b Evans	5
J.D.Edwards	not out	28	(6)	b Jones	14
F.E.Allan	run out (/Hall)	0		not out	35
F.G.McShane	b Evans	27		c Wearne b Evans	4
†E.H.Elliott	c & b Evans	0		not out	20
W.H.Cooper	c Tindall b Wearne	7			
Extras	(b6, lb1)	7		(b5)	5
Total	(150.0 overs, in about 210 mins)	207		(100.2 overs, in about 165 mins) (8 wkts)	127

NEW SOUTH WALES

H.H.Massie	hit wkt b Allan	29		c Horan b Cooper	42
A.H.Gregory	b Allan	9	(4)	b Midwinter	8
C.Bannerman	b Cooper	7		b Allan	5
E.Tindall	hit wkt b Allan	0	(8)	b Cooper	2
E.Evans	c Tobin b Allan	1	(6)	c & b Cooper	51
*D.W.Gregory	not out	14	(2)	lbw b Midwinter	85
H.C.S.Hiddleston	b Allan	2		not out	11
S.P.Jones	st Elliott b Cooper	0	(10)	run out	13
W.S.Wearne	b Cooper	4		b Midwinter	0
T.W.Garrett	c Campbell b Cooper	2	(5)	c McShane b Cooper	23
†R.Hall	b Allan	6		b Midwinter	0
Extras	(b4, lb1)	5		(b9, lb2)	11
Total	(65.0 overs, in about 105 mins)	79		(157.3 overs, in about 260 mins)	251

NEW SOUTH WALES	O	M	R	W	w,nb		O	M	R	W	w,nb			FALL OF WICKETS			
														VIC	NSW	NSW	VIC
Evans	61	29	71	5	-,-		51.2	35	34	5	-,-		Wkt	1st	1st	2nd	2nd
Wearne	20	9	35	1	-,-	(3)	2	0	7	0	-,-		1st	55	39	54	5
Tindall	24	8	47	1	-,-	(5)	3	1	4	0	-,-		2nd	129	50	70	13
Garrett	35	17	33	1	-,-	(2)	36	10	58	1	-,-		3rd	131	50	79	31
Jones	10	3	14	0	-,-	(4)	8	3	19	2	-,-		4th	136	50	125	35
													5th	136	56	212	57
VICTORIA	O	M	R	W	w,nb		O	M	R	W	w,nb		6th	141	58	224	58
Cooper	20	7	42	4	-,-		55	18	96	4	-,-		7th	146	61	230	74
Allan	33	23	27	6	-,-		18	7	30	1	-,-		8th	188	65	235	82
Edwards	12	9	5	0	-,-		19	7	33	0	-,-		9th	192	71	251	-
McShane							18	7	24	0	-,-		10th	207	79	251	-
Midwinter							35.3	19	39	4	-,-						
Coulthard							8	1	11	0	-,-						
Tobin							4	0	7	0	-,-						

COMBINED NEW SOUTH WALES-VICTORIA XI v AUSTRALIAN XI

Played at Melbourne Cricket Ground on January 1, 3, 4, 1881. (Timeless match)
Toss : Australian XI.   Result : AUSTRALIAN XI WON BY 178 RUNS.
Debuts: Nil.
12th Men: T.Powell (Comb XI). A.H.Jarvis & W.H.Moule named as Aust XI emergencies.
Umpires: J.Swift and R.B.Terry.
Attendances: 9000, 7000, 400.   Total: About 16,400.   Receipts: No figures published.
Close of Play: 1st day Comb XI 8/84 (Midwinter 9, Garrett 3); 2nd day Comb XI (2) 4/40 (Campbell 4).

The Australian XI was comprised of the members of the 1880 team that had toured England. D.Campbell and D.W.Gregory, captains of their respective teams in the just completed New South Wales - Victoria match, were charged with the task of selecting the Combined XI. Contemporary reports indicate that there was not enough time to invite leading players from interstate and consequently their team was chosen from those that appeared in the NSW v Vic match. They were further handicapped by the unavailability of F.E.Allan, who declined to play, and were forced to substitute A.H.Gregory for W.H.Cooper (work commitments) at the last moment. The wicket "played very indifferently" on the first day and then overnight rain had further effect, "it being most bumpy and treacherous" (*Age*) on the second day. Bonnor (55 in 43 minutes, 1 five and 6 fours) was the only batsman to exceed fifty in the match, his runs dominating a sixth wicket stand of 57 with Bannerman. Spofforth and Palmer provided the second instance in Australia of a pair of bowlers completing both innings unchanged. *The Argus* gives Aust XI (1) Bonnor 54, extras 15, other sources as shown here. Sources: *Australian Cricketers Guide, The Age, The Argus, The Herald, The Australasian, The Leader, Weekly Times.*

AUSTRALIAN XI

A.C.Bannerman	c Elliott b Evans	29		c A.H.Gregory b Evans	11
*W.L.Murdoch	c Elliott b Midwinter	7	(3)	b Midwinter	39
T.U.Groube	lbw b Midwinter	6	(10)	b Evans	19
P.S.McDonnell	b Midwinter	0		c Horan b Evans	37
J.Slight	st Elliott b Midwinter	12	(6)	run out	4
†J.M.Blackham	c D.W.Gregory b Midwinter	5	(2)	lbw b Evans	6
G.J.Bonnor	c Mackay b Midwinter	55		b Midwinter	13
H.F.Boyle	c Campbell b Midwinter	6		c Mackay b Evans	4
G.Alexander	b Evans	3	(11)	not out	42
G.E.Palmer	b Garrett	10	(9)	lbw b Midwinter	2
F.R.Spofforth	not out	25	(5)	c Massie b Midwinter	4
Extras	(b13, lb1)	14		(b3, lb1)	4
Total	(115.1 overs, in about 195 mins)	172		(115.2 overs, in about 200 mins)	185

COMBINED XI

H.H.Massie	b Spofforth	12		b Spofforth	8
T.P.Horan	b Palmer	9		b Palmer	7
E.Evans	b Spofforth	33		b Palmer	11
D.Campbell	b Palmer	7		c Alexander b Spofforth	6
†E.H.Elliott	c Bonnor b Spofforth	8		b Spofforth	4
G.Mackay	b Palmer	0	(9)	b Palmer	7
W.E.Midwinter	c & b Spofforth	11	(6)	c Palmer b Spofforth	0
*D.W.Gregory	c Boyle b Spofforth	3	(7)	run out (Groube)	34
A.H.Gregory	c Boyle b Spofforth	0	(10)	b Palmer	0
T.W.Garrett	b Spofforth	7	(11)	not out	1
E.Tindall	not out	1	(8)	c Alexander b Spofforth	1
Extras	(b3)	3		(b4, lb2)	6
Total	(56.0 overs, in about 100 mins)	94		(62.3 overs, in about 110 mins)	85

COMBINED XI	O	M	R	W	w,nb		O	M	R	W	w,nb
Evans	50	33	31	2	-,-		49.2	26	38	5	-,-
Midwinter	58	27	107	7	-,-		52	20	104	4	-,-
Garrett	7.1	2	20	1	-,-						
Tindall						(3)	4	1	10	0	-,-
Mackay						(4)	6	1	16	0	-,-
D.W.Gregory						(5)	4	0	13	0	-,-

AUSTRALIAN XI	O	M	R	W	w,nb		O	M	R	W	w,nb
Spofforth	29	9	55	7	-,-		31.3	14	50	5	-,-
Palmer	27	10	36	3	-,-		31	17	29	4	-,-

FALL OF WICKETS

Wkt	AUST 1st	COM 1st	AUST 2nd	COM 2nd
1st	18	12	11	12
2nd	26	42	32	28
3rd	26	56	78	29
4th	42	65	88	40
5th	48	65	102	40
6th	105	77	115	45
7th	116	80	117	53
8th	120	80	121	76
9th	133	93	126	78
10th	172	94	185	85

NEW SOUTH WALES v VICTORIA

Played at Sydney Cricket Ground on February 18, 19, 21, 1881. (Timeless match)
Toss : Victoria.   Result : VICTORIA WON BY 30 RUNS.
Debuts: New South Wales - T.Nunn, W.Roberts (both f/c). Victoria - J.J.Healy, E.Turner (both f/c).
12th Men: H.C.S.Hiddleston (NSW) and F.H.Walters (Vic).
Umpires: J.Swift and R.B.Terry.
Attendances: 4000, 10000, 7000.   Total: About 21,000.   Receipts: No figures published.
Close of Play: 1st day NSW 1/34 (Massie 22, C.Bannerman 10); 2nd day Vic (2) 6/89 (Midwinter 23, Kelly 13).

E.H.Elliott (ill) was unavailable for Victoria. The visitors began badly, losing the wickets of Mackay, from Garrett's first ball, and Midwinter, from the first ball of the following over. Wickets continued to fall at regular intervals until McShane (61 in about 105 minutes, 10 fours) led a revival. Massie (70 in about 105 minutes, 7 fours) similarly dominated the New South Wales first innings after Alec Bannerman had been caught from the second ball of the opening over. The Victorian top-order again failed as the struggle continued. Kelly (50 in about 90 minutes, 4 fours) and Midwinter (42 not out in about 135 minutes, 2 fours) then added an invaluable 73 for the seventh wicket to set the home team a competitive target. Poor light, intermittent rain and the bowling of Allan, who operated unchanged, combined to thwart New South Wales hopes of victory, only Alec Bannerman (52 in about 135 minutes, 7 fours) mounting any challenge. The bowling of both teams held sway over all three days with Allan, Midwinter and Evans continuing on from where they had left off in the previous encounter of the two teams in Melbourne. Evans bowled unchanged throughout both Victorian innings. A new wicket was used for each innings of the match. Sources: *Australian Cricketers Guide, The Australasian, Sydney Morning Herald, Town & Country Journal, Sydney Mail.*

VICTORIA

W.E.Midwinter	b Evans	0	(7) not out		42
G.Mackay	b Garrett	0	(1) b Evans		1
T.P.Horan	b Garrett	26	c Gregory b Evans		28
F.E.Allan	c A.C.Bannerman b Evans	26	(6) b Jones		2
†E.Turner	c & b Garrett	3	(9) c & b Gregory		10
G.Coulthard	b Garrett	5	(10) c Massie b Gregory		6
T.J.D.Kelly	b Evans	12	(8) st Roberts b Gregory		50
F.G.McShane	c Jones b Evans	61	(4) b Gregory		12
J.D.Edwards	not out	31	(2) c Massie b Garrett		2
J.J.Healy	c Roberts b Evans	12	(5) c & b Evans		4
*W.H.Cooper	b Gregory	1	b Evans		1
Extras	(b10, lb6)	16	(b4, lb6)		10
Total	(161.3 overs, in about 260 mins)	193	(129.0 overs, in about 200 mins)		168

NEW SOUTH WALES

H.H.Massie	run out (Edwards/Turner)	70	c Edwards b Allan		8
A.C.Bannerman	c Edwards b Allan	0	b Allan		52
C.Bannerman	c Kelly b Midwinter	24	b Allan		0
†W.Roberts	c Kelly b Cooper	0	c Healy b Cooper		10
*D.W.Gregory	c Turner b Midwinter	16	c Turner b Cooper		9
E.Evans	c Kelly b Allan	8	b Allan		18
S.P.Jones	b Midwinter	6	b Allan		7
T.W.Garrett	not out	35	b Edwards		13
A.Geary	c & b Midwinter	5	(10) b Edwards		0
T.Powell	c Allan b Midwinter	18	(9) b Allan		4
T.Nunn	b Edwards	11	not out		3
Extras	(lb7)	7	(b7)		7
Total	(111.2 overs, in about 195 mins)	200	(88.3 overs, in about 155 mins)		131

NEW SOUTH WALES	O	M	R	W	w,nb		O	M	R	W	w,nb		FALL OF WICKETS			
													VIC	NSW	VIC	NSW
Evans	81	45	62	5	-,-		66	37	49	4	-,-		Wkt	1st	1st	2nd	2nd
Garrett	41	20	50	4	,		23	8	33	1	-,-		1st	0	3	2	17
Jones	18	10	20	0	-,-	(4)	12	6	17	1	-,-		2nd	0	72	4	17
Geary	11	4	16	0	-,-	(5)	3	1	6	0	-,-		3rd	52	84	35	42
Nunn	4	1	17	0	-,-								4th	56	116	49	60
Powell	2	0	8	0	-,-								5th	58	116	52	95
Gregory	4.3	2	4	1	-,-	(3)	25	3	53	4	-,-		6th	62	130	68	109
													7th	122	134	141	120
VICTORIA	O	M	R	W	w,nb		O	M	R	W	w,nb		8th	153	139	157	128
Allan	41	18	62	2	-,-	(2)	44	29	37	6	-,-		9th	188	173	165	128
Cooper	17	4	49	1	-,-	(1)	15	3	41	2	-,-		10th	193	200	168	131
McShane	16	5	36	0	-,-		21	13	31	0	-,-						
Midwinter	27	15	27	5	-,-												
Edwards	7.2	2	15	1	-,-		5.3	3	6	2	-,-						
Coulthard	3	0	4	0	-,-	(4)	3	1	9	0	-,-						

COMBINED NEW SOUTH WALES-VICTORIA XI v AUSTRALIAN XI

Played at Sydney Cricket Ground on March 4, 5, 7, 8, 1881. (Timeless match)
Toss : Combined XI.   Result : COMBINED XI WON BY 246 RUNS.
Debuts: Nil.
12th Men: S.P.Jones (Comb XI). No 12th man or emergency fieldsman named for Australian XI.
Umpires: J.McWhirter and J.Swift.
Attendances: 3000, 10000, 5000, 300.   Total: About 18,300.   Receipts: "over £1200" (*T & C Journal*).
Close of Play: 1st day Aust 1/59 (Bannerman 21, Murdoch 31); 2nd day Comb XI (2) 2/74 (Horan 11, Evans 1); 3rd day Aust (2) 3/10
   (Slight 3, Murdoch 0).

Following a month-long tour of New Zealand, the 1880 Australians faced a stronger New South Wales-Victoria combined side than the
team they had played in Melbourne in January. Heavy rain shortened play on the second day, and further rain and hail interrupted the last
day. The Australian XI had the misfortune to be batting on both occasions and the wicket was affected. McShane's figures in the second
innings had been bettered only by G.Elliott's 9 for 2 in Launceston in 1857-58 among matches in Australia. Massie (80 in about 105
minutes, 1 five and 11 fours and 50 in about 80 minutes, 5 fours), Charles Bannerman (64 in about 160 minutes, 4 fours) and Murdoch (65
in about 155 minutes, 8 fours) scored half-centuries, Massie and Bannerman opening the game with a stand of 118. A new wicket was used
for each innings. *The Australasian* and *Australian Cricketers Guide* give Comb XI (2) Edwards run out, other sources as shown here.
Town & Country Journal on the incident states: "Blackham appealed for a catch off the first of Alexander's over put up by Edwards; the
batsman thinking he was out stepped out of his crease, and the bails were off in an instant". *The Australasian* also incorrectly gives Aust
XI (1) Palmer c & b Evans. Sources: *Australian Cricketers Guide, The Australasian, The Leader, Sydney Morning Herald, Town &
Country Journal.*

COMBINED XI

*H.H.Massie	b Spofforth	80		b Alexander	50
C.Bannerman	c Alexander b Spofforth	64		b Boyle	11
T.P.Horan	c Blackham b Alexander	5		b Alexander	49
W.E.Midwinter	b Alexander	0	(6)	c & b Alexander	45
E.Evans	c Blackham b Boyle	4	(4)	c & b Boyle	9
F.G.McShane	b Boyle	11	(7)	st Blackham b Palmer	22
D.W.Gregory	b Boyle	15	(9)	c Murdoch b Alexander	25
J.D.Edwards	st Blackham b Boyle	0		st Blackham b Alexander	17
T.W.Garrett	st Blackham b Boyle	13	(5)	b Alexander	34
†E.H.Elliott	b Spofforth	1		not out	13
W.H.Cooper	not out	0		c Murdoch b Boyle	5
Extras	(b4)	4		(b4, lb5)	9
Total	(109.0 overs, in about 205 mins)	197		(163.2 overs, in about 325 mins)	289

AUSTRALIAN XI

A.C.Bannerman	b Midwinter	21		c Elliott b McShane	2
F.R.Spofforth	b Midwinter	3		c Massie b McShane	1
*W.L.Murdoch	b Evans	65	(5)	not out	31
P.S.McDonnell	c & b Midwinter	0	(6)	c & b Evans	18
J.Slight	b Evans	1	(4)	b McShane	4
T.U.Groube	c Gregory b Evans	7	(3)	c Garrett b McShane	0
†J.M.Blackham	b McShane	36		c Evans b McShane	2
A.H.Jarvis	b Evans	11		b McShane	8
H.F.Boyle	c Elliott b McShane	0	(10)	b McShane	6
G.E.Palmer	c Elliott b Evans	1	(11)	c Gregory b McShane	0
G.Alexander	not out	6	(9)	c Gregory b McShane	4
Extras	(b4)	4		(b9)	9
Total	(115.1 overs, in about 195 mins)	155		(58.1 overs, in about 105 mins)	85

AUSTRALIAN XI	O	M	R	W	w,nb		O	M	R	W	w,nb
Spofforth	46	20	69	3	-,-		43	10	92	0	-,-
Palmer	17	7	36	0	-,-	(3)	27	12	52	1	-,-
Boyle	30	9	60	5	-,-	(2)	52.2	15	79	3	-,-
Alexander	16	5	28	2	-,-		41	22	57	6	-,-

COMBINED XI	O	M	R	W	w,nb		O	M	R	W	w,nb
Midwinter	24	11	29	3	-,-						
Evans	49.1	32	44	5	-,-		29	14	31	1	-,-
Cooper	9	2	27	0	-,-						
Garrett	11	4	15	0	-,-						
Edwards	10	7	12	0	-,-						
McShane	9	4	11	2	-,-	(1)	29.1	15	45	9	-,-
Gregory	3	0	13	0	-,-						

FALL OF WICKETS

Wkt	COM 1st	AUST 1st	COM 2nd	AUST 2nd
1st	118	3	30	3
2nd	127	60	69	3
3rd	129	60	113	8
4th	150	65	137	11
5th	156	83	166	40
6th	178	135	202	45
7th	178	143	240	67
8th	192	143	251	79
9th	197	146	277	85
10th	197	155	289	85

SOUTH AUSTRALIA v VICTORIA

Played at Adelaide Oval on April 1, 2 , 4, 1881. (Timeless match)
Toss : Victoria.   Result : VICTORIA WON BY 151 RUNS.
Debuts: South Australia - H.Blinman, W.Knill (both f/c). Victoria - G.B.Gordon, V.B.Trapp, F.H.Walters, (all f/c); W.Rickman
     (Vic only).
12th Men: A.F.Slight (SA) and C.Manion (Vic).
Umpires: B.McGan and P.Samson.
Attendances: 2500, 5000, 200.   Total: About 7700.   Receipts: No figures published.
Close of Play: 1st day SA 1/42 (Noel 15, Giffen 0); 2nd day Vic (2) 3/71 (McShane 28, Turner 0).

The match was the first between the two Colonies to be played in South Australia. A new wicket was selected for each innings, that used by the home team on the final day "played very badly, although the utter failure of the team cannot be excused on this account" (*Register*). Giffen did not arrive at the ground until just after the luncheon adjournment on the first day and J.L.Sellars acted as substitute. Boyle's sole first-class century (108 in about 185 minutes, 1 seven, 2 fives and 10 fours, chances at 16 and 28) was also the first in such matches at the Adelaide Oval. Noel (52 in about 135 minutes, no fours) and McShane (58 in about 115 minutes, 1 seven and 6 fours) were the only other players to exceed 31 on either side in a low-scoring game. McShane's seven came from a straight drive off Giffen that stopped "by the chains" (*Register*) without the benefit of overthrows, an incredible feat. Many catches were missed during the match and the fielding of both sides, particularly in each first innings, was described as "simply execrable" (*Register*). Boyle and McShane completed fine all-round performances by bowling unchanged throughout the South Australian second innings. Jarvis, who had suffered a strain while keeping wickets on the first day, complained of chest pain shortly after coming in to bat and retired at 3/89. First A.F.Slight, and later H.Arthur, acted as substitute in the Victorian second innings with King, and later Noel, keeping wickets. Rickman had played a match with Lancashire in 1876. Sources: *Australian Cricketers Guide, C.B.O'Reilly, Adelaide Advertiser, South Australian Register*.

VICTORIA

V.B.Trapp	b Hide	7	(2)	c Knill b Hide	19
F.G.McShane	c Hide b Noel	4	(4)	c Giffen b Bullough	58
*H.F.Boyle	b Slight	108		b Hide	23
E.Turner	run out (sub J.L.Sellars/Jarvis)	0	(5)	c Hide b Giffen	6
R.B.Terry	b King	30	(1)	b Giffen	0
W.Rickman	c Hide b Bullough	5	(8)	c Bullough J.E.Gooden	19
G.B.Gordon	c Jarvis b King	4		c Hide b Giffen	0
G.Coulthard	b Bullough	5	(9)	not out	27
†E.H.Elliott	run out (Blinman/Jarvis)	7	(6)	c Knill b Giffen	2
F.H.Walters	b Giffen	8		c J.E.Gooden b Giffen	8
W.H.Cooper	not out	11		st Noel b Hide	9
Extras	(b2)	2		(b1, lb2)	3
Total	(100.2 overs, in about 190 mins)	191		(107.3 overs, in about 210 mins)	174

SOUTH AUSTRALIA

J.Noel	c Cooper b Boyle	52		b McShane	3
W.Knill	c & b Terry	26		c Coulthard b Boyle	4
G.Giffen	c Gordon b Boyle	10	(6)	c Boyle b McShane	10
†A.H.Jarvis	retired ill	0		absent ill	-
*W.Slight	b Coulthard	31	(7)	c Coulthard b Boyle	13
J.B.Hide	c McShane b Terry	0	(3)	st Elliott b Boyle	5
J.F.King	run out (McShane)	0	(4)	c & b Boyle	1
H.Blinman	st Elliott b Cooper	13		not out	0
J.E.Gooden	c Cooper b Boyle	18		st Elliott b McShane	1
H.A.Gooden	not out	2	(5)	c Rickman b McShane	3
W.Bullough	st Elliott b Boyle	2	(10)	st Elliott b McShane	6
Extras	(b8, lb1)	9		(lb5)	5
Total	(121.2 overs, in about 235 mins)	163		(41.3 overs, in about 75 mins)	51

SOUTH AUSTRALIA	O	M	R	W	w,nb		O	M	R	W	w,nb
Hide	16	7	33	1	-,-	(3)	27.3	14	37	3	-,-
Noel	25	13	22	1	-,-	(4)	5	3	8	0	-,-
Bullough	24	8	65	2	-,-	(2)	26	9	39	1	-,-
Giffen	11	2	29	1	-,-	(1)	34	12	59	5	-,-
King	23	10	40	2	-,-	(6)	4	1	10	0	-,-
Slight	1.2	1	0	1	-,-	(5)	4	2	7	0	-,-
J.E.Gooden							7	3	11	1	-,-

VICTORIA	O	M	R	W	w,nb		O	M	R	W	w,nb
McShane	34	16	42	0	-,-	(2)	20.3	14	19	5	-,-
Boyle	31.2	16	33	4	-,-	(1)	21	10	27	4	-,-
Rickman	4	1	7	0	-,-						
Cooper	8	1	20	1	-,-						
Terry	28	16	34	2	-,-						
Trapp	10	5	12	0	-,-						
Coulthard	6	2	6	1	-,-						

FALL OF WICKETS

	VIC	SA	VIC	SA
Wkt	1st	1st	2nd	2nd
1st	4	42	0	7
2nd	18	83	33	9
3rd	19	89	70	13
4th	99	89	87	20
5th	116	93	91	20
6th	127	130	96	43
7th	132	151	126	43
8th	147	159	138	45
9th	159	163	149	51
10th	191	-	174	-

1881-82 SEASON (10 MATCHES)

The 1881-82 season saw the modern cricket itinerary start to take shape. A total of 10 first-class matches were played - almost doubling the number staged in any previous season. For the first time in Australia, intercolonial matches were played in addition to first-class matches by tourists. The season also saw new records for the highest individual score and highest team total.

An English touring team, organised by J.Lillywhite, A.Shrewsbury and A.Shaw (captain), left home in September 1881 for America where five matches were played against teams comprising odds. They then continued on to Australia, arriving in mid-November, and played seven matches which are now considered first-class, winning three, losing two and drawing two. Their stay in Australia was interrupted by a four-week tour of New Zealand in January-February. (The Englishmen had originally intended to play these fixtures in November prior to arriving in Australia.)

Four of the seven first-class matches involving Shaw's XI in Australia were subsequently given Test status. The first two were staged, respectively, after the annual Victoria v New South Wales clashes in Melbourne and Sydney, the home captains, Boyle (Victoria) and Murdoch (New South Wales), having the honour of selecting the Australian XI on each occasion. The Australian sides for the third and fourth matches were drawn from a squad of 13 which had been named to tour England at the end of the season.

Australia had the best of the four-match 'series' against England, winning two matches and drawing two. Local critics had predicted that the Australian bowling, in the expected absence of Evans, Allan and Spofforth, would struggle against the Englishmen. (As matters would have it, Evans appeared in two of the matches and Spofforth one.) The real heroes were Garrett (18 wickets) and Palmer (24 wickets), who exceeded all expectations by bowling Australia to victory in the second and third games at Sydney. McDonnell and Horan, with a century apiece combined with Murdoch and Alec Bannerman to form the mainstays of the batting. Ulyett (438 runs at 54.75) had an outstanding series for the Englishmen, while Barnes, Selby, Shrewsbury, Barlow and Scotton all showed their abilities at times. Bates completed a fine series by capturing 16 wickets and leading the averages for his side. Midwinter, a member of Australia's team in the first-ever Test, now represented England.

The annual intercolonial fixtures between Victoria and New South Wales saw the home team triumph on each occasion. New South Wales's total at Sydney (775) was the highest recorded to date in any first-class match, and Murdoch's 321 - curiously the first three-figure score ever made for New South Wales - was the highest individual innings thus far in Australian first-class cricket. Only W.G.Grace (344 for MCC v Kent in 1876) had scored higher.

South Australia recorded their first win against Victoria at first-class level at the third attempt, winning a low-scoring encounter at Adelaide in March 1882 by 31 runs.

The selection of the Third Australian XI to England in 1882, following previous tours in 1878 and 1880, created much interest. Edwin Evans, originally named in the side, withdrew through 'family reasons'. (It was also reported that he had a fear of sea voyages.) S.P.Jones replaced him. The selection in the team of Bonnor at the expense of F.G.McShane, whose left-handed bowling would have been 'a decided acquisition' (*Town & Country Journal*), came under some criticism. But the side was one of the strongest ever taken to England, and in August defeated an England XI on home soil for the first time.

Leading Aggregates

Batsmen	M	I	NO	Runs	HS	Ave.	Bowlers	Runs	Wkts	Ave.
W.L.Murdoch (NSW)	7	12	1	679	321	61.72	G.E.Palmer (V)	1013	47	21.55
G.Ulyett (E)	7	14	0	549	149	39.21	T.W.Garrett (NSW)	718	35	20.51
P.S.McDonnell (V)	8	15	1	496	147	35.42	W.Bates (E)	520	30	17.33
T.P.Horan (V)	8	15	1	477	124	34.07	E.Peate (E)	553	30	18.43
R.G.Barlow (E)	7	14	1	391	75	30.07	E.Evans (NSW)	662	24	27.58
A.Shrewsbury (E)	7	12	2	382	82	38.20	W.H.Cooper (V)	460	16	28.75
W.Bates (E)	7	13	1	349	84	29.08	F.G.McShane (V)	268	14	19.14
J.M.Blackham (V)	8	14	0	340	96	24.28	W.E.Midwinter (E)	435	13	33.46

NEW SOUTH WALES v A.SHAW'S ENGLAND XI

Played at Sydney Cricket Ground on December 9, 10, 12, 13, 1881. (Four-day match)
Toss : England XI.   Result : A.SHAW'S ENGLAND XI WON BY 68 RUNS.
Debuts: New South Wales - H.Moses (f/c).
12th Men: W.S.Wearne (NSW). No 12th named for England XI; Lillywhite umpired.
Umpires: J.Lillywhite and J.Swift.
Attendances: 7000, 18000, 10000, 5000.   Total: About 40,000.   Receipts: No figures published.
Close of Play: 1st day Eng 5/235 (Barlow 71, Scotton 25); 2nd day NSW 3/164 (Murdoch 52, Gregory 9); 3rd day Eng (2) 6/143
(Midwinter 45).

Three days were allocated for completion of the match but it was agreed at the end of the third day to continue for one more day to obtain a result. It was further agreed that should no result be obtained then, the match would be left drawn so that the English team's travel arrangements to Cootamundra for their next fixture would not be altered. A new wicket was used for each innings. Barlow (75 in about 345 minutes, 5 fours) "played a splendid defensive innings" (*T & C Journal*) to anchor the England XI's first innings. Jones took a wicket with his first ball but later on the first day sprained an ankle while fielding and took no further part in the match. Massie (56 in about 80 minutes, 9 fours and 76 in about 135 minutes, 8 fours) batted with his customary aggression for the locals. Shaw bowled in miserly fashion in both innings, operating unchanged from 2/110 in the second innings and allowing only four scoring strokes in 29 overs. *Wisden* omits Eng (1) Midwinter c C.Bannerman, and incorrectly shows Massie as caught, instead of stumped, in NSW (2). There are some variations in numbers of maidens and overs bowled but these are believed correct. Sources: *Wisden, The Australasian, Sydney Morning Herald, Town & Country Journal*.

A.SHAW'S ENGLAND XI

R.G.Barlow	c Davis b Garrett	75	b Evans	23
G.Ulyett	b Jones	47	b Evans	17
J.Selby	c & b Hiddleston	56	c Murdoch b Evans	24
W.Bates	c & b Hiddleston	0	c Murdoch b Evans	12
W.E.Midwinter	c C.Bannerman b Hiddleston	10	c Massie b A.C.Bannerman	48
A.Shrewsbury	c Davis b Garrett	23	b Garrett	12
W.H.Scotton	b Garrett	25	c C.Bannerman b A.C.Bannerman	7
T.Emmett	b Evans	13	b Evans	0
*A.Shaw	c Davis b Garrett	5	c Murdoch b Evans	0
†R.Pilling	not out	5	not out	7
E.Peate	c Garrett b Evans	2	c Evans b A.C.Bannerman	6
Extras	(b7, lb4)	11	(b3, lb3)	6
Total	(235.1 overs, in about 370 mins)	272	(122.0 overs, in about 195 mins)	162

NEW SOUTH WALES

H.H.Massie	c Midwinter b Barlow	56	st Pilling b Emmett	76
C.Bannerman	b Bates	23	b Peate	11
*†W.L.Murdoch	b Peate	58	b Emmett	21
A.C.Bannerman	c Pilling b Bates	15	not out	30
D.W.Gregory	c Pilling b Bates	15	b Shaw	0
H.Moses	c & b Bates	5	(8) c Pilling b Peate	0
T.W.Garrett	run out	6	(6) c Emmett b Midwinter	2
J.Davis	not out	18	(7) c Midwinter b Peate	6
E.Evans	c Emmett b Peate	2	b Shaw	4
H.C.S.Hiddleston	b Peate	3	st Pilling b Shaw	0
S.P.Jones	absent hurt	-	absent hurt	-
Extras	(b2, lb7)	9	(b5, w1)	6
Total	(186.1 overs, in about 305 mins)	210	(119.1 overs, in about 190 mins)	156

NEW SOUTH WALES	O	M	R	W	w,nb		O	M	R	W	w,nb
Evans	90.1	58	77	2	-,-		61	34	60	6	-,-
Garrett	78	40	86	4	-,-		41	13	65	1	-,-
Gregory	10	0	27	0	-,-						
Jones	15	7	21	1	-,-						
Hiddleston	27	12	39	3	-,-	(4)	9	3	19	0	-,-
A.C.Bannerman	7	4	8	0	-,-	(3)	11	5	12	3	-,-
Massie	8	6	3	0	-,-						

ENGLAND XI	O	M	R	W	w,nb		O	M	R	W	w,nb
Peate	66.1	33	64	3	-,-		43	14	36	3	-,-
Midwinter	22	10	33	0	-,-	(4)	8	1	23	1	-,-
Shaw	26	16	24	0	-,-	(6)	29	25	5	3	-,-
Barlow	10	3	19	1	-,-	(3)	9	2	31	0	-,-
Ulyett	5	0	10	0	-,-						
Bates	57	36	51	4	-,-	(2)	13.1	4	25	0	-,-
Emmett						(5)	17	6	30	2	1,-

FALL OF WICKETS				
Wkt	ENG 1st	NSW 1st	ENG 2nd	NSW 2nd
1st	71	73	26	35
2nd	143	109	65	87
3rd	143	147	79	127
4th	159	174	80	132
5th	199	178	109	137
6th	239	183	143	147
7th	260	201	146	147
8th	260	206	148	152
9th	265	210	152	156
10th	272	-	162	-

VICTORIA v A.SHAW'S ENGLAND XI

Played at Melbourne Cricket Ground on December 16, 17, 19, 20, 1881. (Timeless match)
Toss : Victoria.   Result : A.SHAW'S ENGLAND XI WON BY 18 RUNS.
Debuts: Victoria - G.J.Bonnor (Vic only).
12th Men: W.H.Moule (Vic). No 12th named for England XI; Lillywhite umpired.
Umpires: G.Coulthard and J.Lillywhite.
Attendances: 6000, 12000, 4000, 3000.   Total: About 25,000.   Receipts: No figures published.
Close of Play: 1st day Vic 8/249 (Edwards 64, Allan 2); 2nd day Eng (2) 2/47 (Barlow 18, Bates 0); 3rd day Eng (2) 7/167
   (Shrewsbury 61, Shaw 1).

The England team agreed prior to the match that it should be played out to a finish. McDonnell (51 in about 72 minutes, 1 five and 5 fours), Blackham (66 in about 165 minutes, 4 fours) and Edwards (career-best 65 in about 165 minutes, 5 fours) reached half-centuries on the opening day. Rain on the third and fourth days reduced playing time considerably on each day. Arrangements to travel to Adelaide on the 20th were delayed in order to meet the pre-match commitment. Shrewsbury (80 in about 195 minutes, 6 fours) gave a masterly display in difficult conditions. The wicket became more difficult on the last day as it dried, conditions used to the full by Peate in bowling the visitors to victory. This was the first time in Australian matches - and only the third time overall - that a team followed on and managed to win. Bonnor had toured England in 1880 without having previously played at first-class level. *Wisden* and *Argus* give Eng (2) McShane 1/42, Boyle 0/39, other sources as shown here are believed correct. Sources: *Wisden, Australian Cricketers Guide, VCA Report, The Age, The Argus, The Australasian, The Leader.*

VICTORIA

P.S.McDonnell	b Barlow	51	st Pilling b Peate		0
T.U.Groube	st Pilling b Peate	3	c Shrewsbury b Peate		1
T.P.Horan	c Scotton b Peate	1	c Shrewsbury b Peate		0
†J.M.Blackham	b Ulyett	66	st Pilling b Bates		4
G.J.Bonnor	c Pilling b Emmett	26	b Peate		0
*H.F.Boyle	c Shrewsbury b Emmett	0	c Selby b Peate		43
J.D.Edwards	c Emmett b Peate	65	b Bates		0
G.E.Palmer	b Bates	4	(9) c Shaw b Emmett		14
F.G.McShane	c Peate b Shaw	22	(8) c Shrewsbury b Peate		4
F.E.Allan	c Shaw b Bates	2	b Barlow		8
W.H.Cooper	not out	0	not out		0
Extras	(b5, lb5, w1)	11	(b1)		1
Total	(160.2 overs, in about 290 mins)	251	(71.2 overs, in about 135 mins)		75

A.SHAW'S ENGLAND XI

G.Ulyett	b Palmer	2	b Palmer	4
R.G.Barlow	c Bonnor b Allan	12	run out (Groube/Blackham)	42
J.Selby	b Palmer	6	c Boyle b Palmer	23
W.Bates	c McDonnell b Cooper	42	c Groube b McShane	19
W.E.Midwinter	c Edwards b Palmer	1	c Cooper b Palmer	0
A.Shrewsbury	c Blackham b Allan	9	not out	80
T.Emmett	b Allan	11	b Edwards	9
W.H.Scotton	b Palmer	28	b Palmer	2
*A.Shaw	c Edwards b McShane	23	c McShane b Palmer	5
†R.Pilling	b McShane	1	b Palmer	3
E.Peate	not out	3	c Boyle b Palmer	2
Extras	(b4, lb2, nb2)	8	(b3, lb4, nb2)	9
Total	(79.3 overs, in about 150 mins)	146	(174.2 overs, in about 295 mins)	198

ENGLAND XI	O	M	R	W	w,nb		O	M	R	W	w,nb		FALL OF WICKETS			
Peate	51.2	21	80	3	-,-		31	17	30	6	-,-			VIC	ENG	ENG	VIC
Midwinter	21	9	39	0	-,-							Wkt	1st	1st	2nd	2nd
Barlow	13	3	26	1	-,-	(5)	3.2	1	4	1	-,-	1st	26	4	4	0
Emmett	20	8	29	2	1,-		5	2	8	1	-,-	2nd	34	19	46	0
Shaw	21	12	23	1	-,-	(3)	15	9	10	0	-,-	3rd	67	27	73	3
Bates	25	13	25	2	-,-	(2)	17	10	22	2	-,-	4th	104	30	73	3
Ulyett	9	4	18	1	-,-							5th	104	52	132	5
												6th	186	82	156	7
VICTORIA	O	M	R	W	w,nb		O	M	R	W	w,nb	7th	199	94	161	20
Palmer	33	15	53	4	-,2		58.2	28	46	7	-,2	8th	247	133	183	58
Allan	32	15	52	3	-,-	(5)	31	19	23	0	-,-	9th	251	143	194	75
Cooper	7	0	21	1	-,-		3	0	13	0	-,-	10th	251	146	198	75
McShane	7.3	4	12	2	-,-	(2)	29	15	41	1	-,-					
Boyle						(4)	34	18	40	0	-,-					
McDonnell							4	2	10	0	-,-					
Edwards							15	6	16	1	-,-					

VICTORIA v NEW SOUTH WALES

Played at Melbourne Cricket Ground on December 24, 26, 27, 1881. (Timeless match)
Toss : Victoria. Result : VICTORIA WON BY TWO WICKETS.
Debuts: New South Wales - F.Downes (f/c).
12th Men: W.H.Cooper (Vic) and H.Moses (NSW).
Umpires: E.H.Elliott and J.Swift.
Attendances: 7000, 10000, 10000. Total: About 27,000. Receipts:"more than £1000" (*Australasian*).
Close of Play: 1st day NSW 1/21 (C.Bannerman 2, Murdoch 14); 2nd day NSW (2) 5/101 (C.Bannerman 4).

S.P.Jones and F.R.Spofforth were both unavailable for New South Wales due to injury. The selectors then omitted A.Geary and W.S.Wearne from their original squad before the team left Sydney. Palmer is recorded as bowling 57 overs out of 109 in the New South Wales first innings which, if correct, means that he must have delivered consecutive overs on more than one occasion. Massie was dismissed in the first over of each New South Wales innings. Tom Horan (95 in about 195 minutes, 7 fours), under his pen-name of 'Felix' in *The Australasian*, claimed that he had been deprived of four runs (recorded as byes) in the first innings by a misunderstanding between the umpires and scorers. He further stated that several unofficial scorers made him 103. Sources: *Australian Cricketers Guide, The Age, The Argus, The Herald, The Australasian, The Leader*.

VICTORIA

Batsman	Dismissal 1	Score 1		Dismissal 2	Score 2
P.S.McDonnell	c Hiddleston b Downes	17		c Massie b Garrett	37
†J.M.Blackham	run out (C.Bannerman/Downes)	16	(4)	b Evans	19
T.P.Horan	c Murdoch b A.C.Bannerman	95		st Murdoch b Evans	23
*H.F.Boyle	c Gregory b Downes	9	(7)	c Murdoch b Garrett	0
G.J.Bonnor	c A.C.Bannerman b Evans	17		b Evans	3
J.D.Edwards	b Garrett	43		c Gregory b Garrett	3
G.E.Palmer	b Garrett	5	(8)	not out	17
W.H.Moule	c Gregory b A.C.Bannerman	0	(9)	b Garrett	18
F.G.McShane	b Garrett	0			
G.Coulthard	b A.C.Bannerman	4		not out	6
F.E.Allan	not out	3	(2)	run out (Garrett/Murdoch)	0
Extras	(b21, lb2)	23		(b2, lb2, nb1)	5
Total	(141.2 overs, in about 260 mins)	232		(91.3 overs, in about 155 mins) (8 wkts)	131

NEW SOUTH WALES

Batsman	Dismissal 1	Score 1		Dismissal 2	Score 2
H.H.Massie	b Palmer	0		c Palmer b Allan	0
C.Bannerman	b Palmer	25	(6)	b Palmer	5
*†W.L.Murdoch	b Palmer	21	(2)	c Moule b Boyle	43
A.C.Bannerman	b Allan	27	(3)	c Moule b Boyle	18
R.C.Allen	c McShane b Allan	13	(4)	c Moule b Allan	3
D.W.Gregory	b Palmer	1	(7)	c McShane b Allan	6
J.Davis	run out (McShane/Blackham)	11	(9)	b Palmer	53
E.Evans	b Palmer	8	(10)	run out (Edwards/Blackham)	10
T.W.Garrett	b Allan	12	(8)	c Coulthard b Boyle	39
H.C.S.Hiddleston	not out	9	(5)	b Palmer	30
F.Downes	b Allan	1		not out	4
Extras	(b12, lb3, nb3)	18		(lb2, nb2)	4
Total	(109.1 overs, in about 175 mins)	146		(115.2 overs, in about 185 mins)	215

NEW SOUTH WALES	O	M	R	W	w,nb		O	M	R	W	w,nb
Evans	49	19	64	1	-,-		46	22	54	2	-,-
Downes	50	22	75	2	-,-		10	1	26	0	-,1
Garrett	28	15	28	3	-,-		35.3	14	46	5	-,-
A.C.Bannerman	14.2	1	42	3	-,-						

VICTORIA	O	M	R	W	w,nb		O	M	R	W	w,nb
Palmer	57	28	64	5	-,3	(2)	43	21	62	3	-,2
Allan	33.1	16	38	4	-,-	(1)	39.2	14	82	3	-,-
McShane	19	6	26	0	-,-	(4)	5	1	14	0	-,-
Boyle						(3)	20	5	36	3	-,-
Coulthard							8	2	17	0	-,-

FALL OF WICKETS

Wkt	VIC 1st	NSW 1st	NSW 2nd	VIC 2nd
1st	19	4	0	1
2nd	57	31	62	60
3rd	70	75	63	65
4th	97	85	82	70
5th	202	91	101	78
6th	216	114	106	82
7th	221	118	112	86
8th	221	126	166	115
9th	221	140	202	-
10th	232	146	215	-

AUSTRALIA v ENGLAND (1st Test)

Played at Melbourne Cricket Ground on December 31, 1881, January 2, 3, 4, 1882. (Timeless match)
Toss : England.   Result : MATCH DRAWN.
Debuts: Australia - W.H.Cooper, E.Evans, G.Giffen, H.H.Massie (all Test). England - R.G.Barlow, W.Bates, E.Peate, R.Pilling,
    A.Shrewsbury, W.H.Scotton (all Test); W.E.Midwinter Eng only).
12th Men: J.D.Edwards (Aust). No 12th named for Eng.
Umpires: J.Lillywhite and J.Swift.
Attendances: 16500, 20000, 10000, 1500.   Total: About 50,000.   Receipts: No figures published.
Close of Play: 1st day Eng 294 all out; 2nd day Aust 6/277 (Horan 106, Palmer 23); 3rd day Eng (2) 7/238 (Scotton 13, Shaw 14).

This was the first first-class match in Australia in which 1000 runs were scored. Three days were allocated for the match in the tour itinerary so that the all-professional English party could depart on January 4th for New Zealand, where they played seven non-first-class matches before returning to Australia. Play was however extended into the day of their departure in an attempt to reach a result, the match being called off only at the last possible moment, 3.45pm, so that the players could catch their boat. T.W.Garrett withdrew from the Australian side named for the match and returned to Sydney due to the death of his father. Cooper was brought in as the replacement and Edwards remained 12th man as originally named. F.R.Spofforth and S.P.Jones (both injured) could not be considered. Midwinter, who had previously represented Australia (and would do so again), became the only cricketer to play for Australia against England and vice versa. Ulyett (87 in about 135 minutes, 1 five and 6 fours) who scored 80 out of 126 before lunch on the first day, added 137 with Selby (the best Test-partnership yet) after Barlow had been caught at mid-off in the third over of the match without scoring. Selby (55 in about 140 minutes, 2 fours and 70 in about 165 minutes, 5 fours) hit a half-century in each innings. Giffen, the first South Australian to play Test cricket, took 50 minutes to score his first run and added 107 for the fifth wicket with Horan - Australia's first century partnership at the highest level. Horan's chanceless 124 (in about 250 minutes, 7 fours); his sole Test century, was the second scored in Tests by an Australian. Cooper, who took his best first-class figures in England's second innings, captured the first five-wicket analysis by a bowler of legbreaks in Tests. The game was called off shortly after McDonnell hit Bates over the boundary on the full to register the only five of the match. Sources: *Wisden, The Age, The Argus, The Herald, The Australasian, The Leader.*

ENGLAND

G.Ulyett	c McDonnell b Cooper	87	st Blackham b Cooper		23
R.G.Barlow	c Bannerman b Palmer	0	st Blackham b Palmer		33
J.Selby	run out (Massie/Cooper)	55	c Boyle b Cooper		70
W.Bates	c Giffen b Boyle	58	c Bannerman b Cooper		47
A.Shrewsbury	c Blackham b Evans	11	b Cooper		16
W.E.Midwinter	b Evans	36	c Massie b Cooper		4
T.Emmett	b Evans	5	b Cooper		6
W.H.Scotton	run out (Horan/Blackham)	21	not out		50
*A.Shaw	c Boyle b Cooper	5	c Cooper b Boyle		40
†R.Pilling	c Giffen b Cooper	5	b Palmer		3
E.Peate	not out	4	run out (Palmer/Blackham)		2
Extras	(lb6, nb1)	7	(b7, lb2, nb5)		14
Total	(170.2 overs, in about 310 mins)	294	(229.3 overs, in about 380 mins)		308

AUSTRALIA

H.H.Massie	st Pilling b Midwinter	2			
A.C.Bannerman	b Ulyett	38	b Ulyett		8
*W.L.Murdoch	b Ulyett	39	(4) not out		22
P.S.McDonnell	b Midwinter	19	(5) not out		33
T.P.Horan	run out (Selby/Peate)	124	(3) c Emmett b Bates		26
G.Giffen	b Emmett	30			
†J.M.Blackham	b Emmett	2	(1) b Bates		25
G.E.Palmer	c Pilling b Bates	34			
E.Evans	b Bates	3			
H.F.Boyle	not out	4			
W.H.Cooper	st Pilling b Peate	7			
Extras	(b4, lb11, w3)	18	(b9, lb3, w1)		13
Total	(237.0 overs, in about 405 mins)	320	(55.0 overs, in about 110 mins) (3 wkts)		127

AUSTRALIA	O	M	R	W	w,nb		O	M	R	W	w,nb			FALL OF WICKETS			
Palmer	36	9	73	1	-,1		77	19	77	2	-,4			ENG	AUST	ENG	AUST
Evans	71	35	81	3	-,-		73	45	63	0	-,-	Wkt		1st	1st	2nd	2nd
Cooper	32.2	8	80	3	-,-		61	19	120	6	-,1	1st		5	9	37	35
Boyle	18	9	18	1	-,-		14.3	6	19	1	-,-	2nd		142	82	96	70
Giffen	3	0	12	0	-,-							3rd		151	97	179	72
Bannerman	10	3	23	0	-,-							4th		187	113	183	-
McDonnell						(5)	4	1	15	0	-,-	5th		227	220	188	-
												6th		232	226	197	-
ENGLAND	O	M	R	W	w,nb		O	M	R	W	w,nb	7th		277	305	217	-
Peate	59	24	64	1	1,-	(4)	11	5	22	0	-,-	8th		284	309	300	-
Midwinter	39	21	50	2	-,-							9th		289	309	304	-
Bates	41	20	43	2	-,-		13	2	43	2	-,-	10th		294	320	308	-
Emmett	35	12	61	2	-,-	(2)	16	11	19	0	-,-						
Ulyett	20	5	41	2	2,-	(1)	15	3	30	1	1,-						
Barlow	23	13	22	0	-,-												
Shaw	20	11	21	0	-,-												

NEW SOUTH WALES v VICTORIA

Played at Sydney Cricket Ground on February 10, 11, 13, 14, 15, 1882. (Timeless match)
Toss : New South Wales.   Result : NEW SOUTH WALES WON BY AN INNINGS AND 138 RUNS.
Debuts: Nil.
12th Men: F.Downes (NSW) and G.Coulthard (Vic).
Umpires: C.A.Reid and J.Swift.
Attendances: 4000, 17000, 7000, 2000, 600.   Total: About 30,600.   Receipts: No figures published.
Close of Play: 1st day NSW 3/350 (Murdoch 183, Jones 91); 2nd day NSW 6/640 (Garrett 75, Gregory 21); 3rd day Vic 6/206
    (Bonnor 38, Palmer 12); 4th day Vic (2) 2/193 (Blackham 96, Horan 61).

The mammoth New South Wales total produced several records. It was the highest yet in all first-class cricket, Murdoch's innings (321 in 495 minutes, 38 fours) provided the first century for New South Wales and, with those of Jones (109 in 220 minutes, 11 fours) and Garrett (career-best 163 in 322 minutes, 23 fours), the first instance of three individual centuries in an innings. Murdoch's innings remained the highest in Australia until Clem Hill's 365 not out in 1900-01 and was recognised by a collection which totalled £200, the presentation of a gold watch, and a trophy in the form of a Maltese cross. He shared century partnerships of 245 for the fourth wicket with Jones, and 149 for the sixth wicket with Garrett. Palmer (76 not out in about 150 minutes, 1 six and 6 fours) headed the scoring in the Victorian first innings and Horan (102 in about 305 minutes, 9 fours) and Blackham (96 in about 140 minutes, 12 fours) added 169 for the third wicket in the follow-on, all to no avail. Murdoch was absent on the fourth day, having travelled home to Cootamundra on business. Downes substituted in the field and first Alec Bannerman, then Massie, Spofforth and Evans, in turn, kept wickets during the day. Spofforth had at first declined to play in the match because of doubts about his fitness and it was not until the second day that he finally agreed to take part.
Sources: *Australian Cricketers Guide, The Argus, The Australasian, Sydney Morning Herald, Town & Country Journal, Sydney Mail.*

NEW SOUTH WALES

A.C.Bannerman	c Palmer b Turner	30	
H.H.Massie	b Palmer	17	
*†W.L.Murdoch	c Blackham b Horan	321	
C.Bannerman	lbw b Baker	3	
S.P.Jones	c Boyle b Baker	109	
J.Davis	c Boyle b Baker	4	
T.W.Garrett	b McShane	163	
D.W.Gregory	c McDonnell b Palmer	28	
H.C.S.Hiddleston	st Blackham b Cooper	27	
E.Evans	not out	2	
F.R.Spofforth	b McShane	8	
Extras	(b34, lb26, nb3)	63	
Total	(398.0 overs, 698 mins)	775	

VICTORIA

†J.M.Blackham	c Gregory b Spofforth	8	(4)	b Garrett	96
P.S.McDonnell	b Spofforth	48	(1)	c Massie b Evans	11
T.P.Horan	c Evans b Spofforth	0		c Murdoch b Spofforth	102
J.Slight	b Garrett	26	(6)	c Evans b Garrett	0
F.Baker	b Spofforth	50		c & b Garrett	18
G.J.Bonnor	b Evans	44	(7)	c Jones b Evans	7
*H.F.Doyle	c Gregory b Evans	1	(8)	c Jones b Evans	0
G.E.Palmer	not out	76	(2)	run out (Jones/A.C.Bannerman)	6
E.Turner	b Spofforth	0		not out	41
F.G.McShane	b Spofforth	0	(11)	b Jones	2
W.H.Cooper	b Evans	29	(10)	b Jones	7
Extras	(b27, lb5, nb1)	33		(b28, lb3, nb1)	32
Total	(142.2 overs, 283 mins)	315		(177.0 overs, 338 mins)	322

VICTORIA	O	M	R	W	w,nb
Palmer	80	28	161	2	-,2
McShane	43	13	91	2	-,-
Boyle	67	31	115	0	-,-
Cooper	70	26	120	1	-,-
Turner	30	10	66	1	-,-
Baker	69	26	109	3	-,1
Horan	23	15	23	1	-,-
Slight	2	0	8	0	-,-
Blackham	12	8	11	0	-,-
Bonnor	2	0	8	0	-,-

FALL OF WICKETS

Wkt	NSW 1st	VIC 1st	VIC 2nd
1st	21	35	11
2nd	149	35	24
3rd	156	68	193
4th	401	136	217
5th	423	164	217
6th	572	165	224
7th	652	212	225
8th	749	215	298
9th	765	215	320
10th	775	315	322

NEW SOUTH WALES	O	M	R	W	w,nb		O	M	R	W	w,nb
Spofforth	68	25	122	6	-,-		42	14	94	1	-,-
Evans	41.2	16	78	3	-,-		66	39	72	3	-,-
Garrett	20	5	63	1	-,-		45	21	63	3	-,-
Jones	10	7	10	0	-,-	(6)	9	3	23	2	-,1
Hiddleston	3	0	9	0	-,1	(7)	5	1	8	0	-,-
A.C.Bannerman						(4)	3	0	13	0	-,-
Gregory						(5)	7	1	17	0	-,-

AUSTRALIA v ENGLAND (2nd Test)

Played at Sydney Cricket Ground on February 17, 18, 20, 21, 1882. (Timeless match)
Toss : England.   Result : AUSTRALIA WON BY FIVE WICKETS.
Debuts: Australia - G.Coulthard, S.P.Jones (both Test).
12th Men: G.J.Bonnor (Aust). No 12th named for Eng.
Umpires: J.Lillywhite and J.Swift.
Attendances: 5000, 16000, 8000, 5000.   Total: About 34,000.   Receipts: No figures published.
Close of Play: 1st day Aust 1/86 (Blackham 30, Evans 5); 2nd day Eng (2) 0/8 (Barlow 1, Ulyett 7); 3rd day Aust (2) 2/35 (Murdoch 2, Horan 6).

The match was promoted as All England v Combined New South Wales and Victoria, only subsequently being recognised as a Test; the first to be played at Sydney. A.C.Bannerman (injured hand) and F.R.Spofforth (strained arm muscles) withdrew after selection and were replaced by Coulthard (who had umpired the 1878-79 Test) and Garrett. Palmer and Evans toiled for over three hours to become the first pair of bowlers to operate unchanged throughout a completed Test innings. England had elected to bat on a pitch which had not fully recovered from being excessively watered at the conclusion of the intercolonial match between New South Wales and Victoria. Ulyett and Barlow were both missed several times in the course of recording the first century partnership for the first wicket in Tests. Ulyett began by hitting the first ball he faced, Garrett's first of the match, clean over the fence for five. He was dropped when 10 by Coulthard (a simple catch) and gave two stumping chances to Murdoch , who, having kept wicket throughout the first innings while Blackham fielded at mid-off (excellently), swapped places with the Victorian after lunch on the third day at 0/114 in the second innings. Blackham kept for the rest of the match, catching Selby "splendidly" (*SMH*) off the second ball the batsman faced. Barlow was "in the opinion of many" caught-and-bowled by Jones on 30, "but our umpire (Swift) decided that the batsman was not out" (*SMH*). *Wisden* incorrectly gives Eng (1) Bates st Murdoch and gives incorrect match dates. *T & C Journal* incorrectly gives Aust (2) McDonnell st Pilling b Shaw. Sources: *Wisden, The Australasian, Sydney Morning Herald, Town & Country Journal*.

ENGLAND

G.Ulyett	c Murdoch b Evans	25	(2)	lbw b Palmer	67
R.G.Barlow	b Palmer	31	(1)	c Boyle b Garrett	62
J.Selby	c & b Evans	6		c Blackham b Palmer	2
W.Bates	c Murdoch b Palmer	4		b Palmer	5
A.Shrewsbury	b Palmer	7		c McDonnell b Garrett	22
W.E.Midwinter	c Blackham b Palmer	4		b Palmer	8
W.H.Scotton	b Palmer	30		lbw b Garrett	12
T.Emmett	b Evans	10		c McDonnell b Garrett	9
*A.Shaw	c Massie b Palmer	11		b Evans	30
†R.Pilling	b Palmer	3		b Jones	9
E.Peate	not out	1		not out	1
Extras	(lb1)	1		(b3, lb2)	5
Total	(115.0 overs, 190 mins)	133		(153.1 overs, 254 mins)	232

AUSTRALIA

H.H.Massie	c Shrewsbury b Bates	49	(2)	b Ulyett	22
J.M.Blackham	c Shaw b Midwinter	40	(1)	c & b Bates	4
E.Evans	run out (Bates/Pilling)	11			
*†W.L.Murdoch	c Emmett b Bates	10	(3)	c Barlow b Midwinter	49
T.P.Horan	run out (/Pilling)	4	(4)	b Ulyett	21
P.S.McDonnell	b Bates	14	(5)	b Shaw	25
S.P.Jones	c Emmett b Ulyett	37	(6)	not out	13
T.W.Garrett	c Shrewsbury b Peate	4	(7)	not out	31
G.E.Palmer	b Bates	16			
H.F.Boyle	c Shrewsbury b Ulyett	0			
G.Coulthard	not out	6			
Extras	(b1, lb2, w2, nb1)	6		(b3, lb1)	4
Total	(194.2 overs, 297 mins)	197		(107.1 overs, 195 mins) (5 wkts)	169

AUSTRALIA	O	M	R	W	w,nb		O	M	R	W	w,nb
Palmer	58	36	68	7	-,-		66	29	97	4	-,-
Evans	57	32	64	3	-,-	(3)	40.1	19	49	1	-,-
Garrett						(2)	36	12	62	4	-,-
Jones							11	4	19	1	-,-

ENGLAND	O	M	R	W	w,nb		O	M	R	W	w,nb
Peate	52	28	53	1	-,-	(3)	20	12	22	0	-,-
Midwinter	34	16	43	1	-,1	(5)	18	8	23	1	-,-
Emmett	6	2	24	0	2,-	(4)	6	3	17	0	-,-
Ulyett	22.2	16	11	2	-,-	(2)	15	4	48	2	-,-
Bates	72	43	52	4	-,-	(1)	24	11	37	1	-,-
Barlow	8	4	8	0	-,-	(7)	4	1	6	0	-,-
Shaw						(6)	20.1	15	12	1	-,-

FALL OF WICKETS

Wkt	ENG 1st	AUST 1st	ENG 2nd	AUST 2nd
1st	39	78	122	10
2nd	47	102	124	28
3rd	64	103	130	67
4th	73	111	156	113
5th	77	132	165	127
6th	90	133	175	-
7th	115	140	183	-
8th	123	167	204	-
9th	132	168	230	-
10th	133	197	232	-

VICTORIA v A.SHAW'S ENGLAND XI

Played at Melbourne Cricket Ground on February 24, 25, 27, 28, 1882. (Timeless match)
Toss : Victoria.   Result : A.SHAW'S ENGLAND XI WON BY EIGHT WICKETS.
Debuts: Victoria - J.M.Minchin (f/c).
12th Men: T.J.D.Kelly (Vic). No 12th named for England XI; Lillywhite umpired
Umpires: J.Lillywhite and C.A.Reid.
Attendances: 4000, 6000, 2500, 200.   Total: About 12,700.   Receipts: No figures published.
Close of Play: 1st day Vic 8/209 (Boyle 25, Cooper 3); 2nd day Eng 5/201 (Shrewsbury 35, Scotton 2); 3rd day Eng (2) 0/3 (Peate 0, Pilling 3).

F.G.McShane (ill), F.E.Allan and J.D.Edwards were all unavailable for Victoria. The team was further handicapped when Slight was hit in the left eye when the ball bounced awkwardly as he attempted to gather it early in the England first innings. He left the field and took no further part in the match. The substitute, Kelly, an outstanding point specialist, took two superb catches in that position soon after and Shaw insisted that he be moved elsewhere. Bates (84 in about 125 minutes, 7 fours) "batted with freedom and vigour that was admirable" (*Age*) on the second day. In the second innings the Victorians collapsed on a wicket freshened by overnight rain; though Shrewsbury (72 not out in about 210 minutes, 5 fours) had batted in masterly fashion on the same wicket earlier in the day. *Wisden* has incorrect match dates. Sources: *Wisden, Australian Cricketers Guide, VCA Report, The Age, The Argus, The Australasian, The Leader.*

VICTORIA

P.S.McDonnell	c Emmett b Midwinter	21		b Midwinter	12
J.Slight	b Peate	36		absent hurt	-
T.P.Horan	c Pilling b Shaw	21		c Ulyett b Bates	23
F.Baker	run out (Peate/Shaw)	15		lbw b Peate	14
G.E.Palmer	c Pilling b Shaw	5	(8)	b Bates	2
*†J.M.Blackham	c Shaw b Emmett	25	(2)	c Shrewsbury b Peate	25
G.J.Bonnor	c Barlow b Emmett	30	(5)	c Shaw b Peate	0
E.Turner	b Bates	21	(7)	not out	11
H.F.Boyle	c Midwinter b Emmett	37	(6)	b Bates	4
W.H.Cooper	not out	22	(9)	c Ulyett b Bates	0
J.M.Minchin	b Ulyett	8	(10)	b Bates	0
Extras	(b7, lb1)	8		(lb1)	1
Total	(188.3 overs, in about 330 mins)	249		(75.3 overs, in about 135 mins)	92

A.SHAW'S ENGLAND XI

G.Ulyett	st Blackham b Cooper	38	(3)	b Minchin	3
R.G.Barlow	c sub (T.J.D.Kelly) b Cooper	19	(4)	not out	10
J.Selby	c sub (T.J.D.Kelly) b Cooper	1			
W.Bates	b Boyle	84			
A.Shrewsbury	not out	72			
W.E.Midwinter	c & b Cooper	12			
W.H.Scotton	c Blackham b Boyle	8			
T.Emmett	b Palmer	13			
*A.Shaw	c Palmer b Boyle	6			
†R.Pilling	b Palmer	0	(2)	c Boyle b Cooper	10
E.Peate	c sub (T.J.D.Kelly) b Minchin	18	(1)	not out	33
Extras	(b 9 lb5)	14		(lb1)	1
Total	(160.3 overs, in about 295 mins)	285		(41.0 overs, in about 78 mins) (2 wkts)	57

ENGLAND XI	O	M	R	W	w,nb		O	M	R	W	w,nb			FALL OF	WICKETS	
														VIC	ENG	VIC	ENG
Bates	31	13	46	1	-,-	(3)	18.3	10	17	5	-,-	Wkt	1st	1st	2nd	2nd
Midwinter	37	20	38	1	-,-		19	7	30	1	-,-	1st	29	58	23	19
Ulyett	24.3	4	49	1	-,-							2nd	58	60	39	43
Shaw	34	22	33	2	-,-							3rd	86	81	67	-
Peate	33	15	42	1	-,-	(1)	38	17	44	3	-,-	4th	96	173	67	-
Emmett	22	10	27	3	-,-							5th	102	190	79	-
Barlow	7	5	6	0	-,-							6th	155	217	84	-
												7th	160	245	92	-
VICTORIA	O	M	R	W	w,nb		O	M	R	W	w,nb	8th	202	252	92	-
Cooper	36	9	84	4	-,-	(3)	9	1	22	1	-,-	9th	230	253	92	-
Minchin	7.3	0	28	1	-,-	(4)	11	6	12	1	-,-	10th	249	285	-	-
Palmer	60	20	92	2	-,-	(1)	11	3	13	0	-,-					
Baker	5	1	16	0	-,-											
Boyle	52	29	51	3	-,-	(2)	10	6	9	0	-,-					

AUSTRALIA v ENGLAND (3rd Test)

Played at Sydney Cricket Ground on March 3, 4, 6, 7, 1882. (Timeless match)
Toss : England.   Result : AUSTRALIA WON BY SIX WICKETS.
Debuts: - Nil.
12th Men: G.J.Bonnor (Aust) No 12th named for England.
Umpires: J.Lillywhite and J.Swift.
Attendances: 2000, 7000, 4000, 1000.   Total: About 15,000.   Receipts: No figures published.
Close of Play: 1st day Aust 3/24 (Bannerman 15, McDonnell 0); 2nd day Aust 3/146 (Bannerman 59, McDonnell 72); 3rd day Eng (2)
    9/121 (Shrewsbury 39, Peate 4).

F.R.Spofforth (in Melbourne) and E.Evans were unavailable for Australia. A new pitch was selected for at least the first innings of each side. McDonnell's first-innings century (147 in 250 minutes, 1 five and 16 fours) was the highlight of the match, despite his offering chances on 22, 53, 97 and 134. Australia were a shaky 3/16 when he began, but with Bannerman (70 in about 240 minutes, 11 fours) he added 199 for the fourth wicket and turned the game in Australia's favour. McDonnell's five was a magnificent hit, "the ball going over the northern end of the pavilion and lodging near the caretaker's cottage in the north-western corner" (*SMH*). He was sixth out at 235. Shrewsbury (82 in about 170 minutes, 12 fours and 47 in about 115 minutes, 4 fours) was the first batsman to topscore in both completed innings of a Test. *The Herald*, and most recent publications incorrectly give Aust (1) 14 extras (wides omitted), total 260; Aust (2) McDonnell 4, Jones 10*, extras 9 (b2, lb5, w2, nb 1), total 4/66. All sources incorrectly give Aust (2) Peate 3/14, which does not balance with the score below. However, *SMH* match commentary describes all 64 runs, Peate conceding 15 . Sources: *Wisden, The Herald, The Australasian, Sydney Morning Herald, Town & Country Journal*.

ENGLAND

G.Ulyett	b Palmer	0	(2) b Garrett		23
R.G.Barlow	c Blackham b Garrett	4	(1) c & b Garrett		8
J.Selby	c Massie b Palmer	13	b Palmer		1
W.Bates	c & b Palmer	1	c Bannerman b Garrett		2
A.Shrewsbury	c & b Boyle	82	c Boyle b Garrett		47
W.E.Midwinter	b Palmer	12	b Palmer		10
W.H.Scotton	c Jones b Garrett	18	b Palmer		1
T.Emmett	b Garrett	4	b Garrett		2
*A.Shaw	b Boyle	3	b Garrett		6
†R.Pilling	b Palmer	12	b Palmer		23
E.Peate	not out	11	not out		8
Extras	(b22, lb6)	28	(b2, nb1)		3
Total	(140.2 overs, 230 mins)	188	(80.1 overs, 145 mins)		134

AUSTRALIA

A.C.Bannerman	b Midwinter	70	(2) c Pilling b Peate		14
H.H.Massie	b Bates	0	(1) c Midwinter b Peate		9
*W.L.Murdoch	c Ulyett b Bates	6	c Midwinter b Bates		4
T.P.Horan	c & b Bates	1	not out		16
P.S.McDonnell	c Midwinter b Peate	147	c Emmett b Peate		9
G.Giffen	c Pilling b Peate	2			
†J.M.Blackham	b Peate	4			
S.P.Jones	not out	7	(6) not out		6
T.W.Garrett	b Peate	0			
G.E.Palmer	b Midwinter	6			
H.F.Boyle	c Pilling b Peate	3			
Extras	(b6, lb8, w2)	16	(b2, lb3, w1)		6
Total	(172.0 overs, 290 mins)	262	(49.3 overs, 80 mins) (4 wkts)		64

AUSTRALIA	O	M	R	W	w,nb		O	M	R	W	w,nb					
Palmer	45.2	23	46	5	-,-		40	19	44	4	-,1				FALL OF WICKETS	
Garrett	60	24	85	3	-,-		36.1	10	78	6	-,-			ENG	AUST	ENG	AUST
Jones	8	5	11	0	-,-								Wkt	1st	1st	2nd	2nd
Boyle	27	18	18	2	-,-	(3)	4	1	9	0	-,-		1st	2	0	28	14
													2nd	8	10	29	21
													3rd	17	16	33	39
ENGLAND	O	M	R	W	w,nb		O	M	R	W	w,nb		4th	35	215	42	49
Peate	45	24	43	5	-,-		25	18	15	3	1,-		5th	56	228	60	-
Bates	38	17	67	3	-,-		24.3	13	43	1	-,-		6th	148	235	70	-
Ulyett	3	1	10	0	-,-								7th	154	244	73	-
Midwinter	62	25	75	2	-,-								8th	159	245	79	-
Shaw	8	4	14	0	-,-								9th	164	252	113	-
Emmett	16	6	37	0	2,-								10th	188	262	134	-

AUSTRALIA v ENGLAND (4th Test)

Played at Melbourne Cricket Ground on March 10, 11, 13, 14 (no play), 1882. (Timeless match)
Toss : England.   Result : MATCH DRAWN.
Debuts: Nil.
12th Men: G.J.Bonnor (Aust). No 12th named for England.
Umpires: G.Coulthard and J.Lillywhite.
Attendances: 2000, 8000, 3000, no play.   Total: About 13,000.   Receipts: No figures published.
Close of Play: 1st day Eng 7/282 (Emmett 27, Shaw 1); 2nd day Aust 5/228 (McDonnell 41, Blackham 0); 3rd day Eng (2) 2/234
    (Selby 48, Bates 52).

This was the last drawn Test in Australia until 1946-47. It was advertised as a match that would be played out, but in truth it was limited to four days (the last was washed out) because the Englishmen were destined to play XXII of Dunolly on March 15th and 16th (a match they won by an innings and 13 runs, 141 to 79 & 49) and XX of Ballarat on March 17th and 18th before returning to England on March 22nd aboard the Orient boat *Chimborazo*. The Australians sailed from Williamstown on March 17th on board *R.M.S.S.Assam*; their side for this and the previous Test was the same as that which had been selected to tour England. 'Felix' (Tom Horan) suggested in *The Australasian* after this match that "it would be well in future if the public be not misled by advertisements to the effect that such and such a match will positively be played out". Extremely hot weather prevailed over the first two days of the game. Bannerman suffered sunstroke while fielding on the first day but had recovered sufficiently by the second to post with Murdoch (85 in about 165 minutes, 6 fours) Australia's first century opening partnership. Ulyett (149 in about 240 minutes, 13 fours) gave a chance when 132 before being sixth out at 239. He was fortunate to survive an appeal for a catch at the wicket off Garrett when 6, Coulthard adjudicating. Three hits during the match carried the boundary on the full, each worth five runs, the batsmen being Emmett, McDonnell, and in the second innings Ulyett, who lifted Boyle into the Pavilion reserve on the third day. A score of 6 by Massie off Shaw included 3 overthrows. Some recent publications incorrectly give Aust 6/237. Sources: *Wisden, The Age, The Argus, The Herald, The Australasian, The Leader*.

ENGLAND

G.Ulyett	c Blackham b Garrett	149	c Palmer b Boyle	64
R.G.Barlow	c Blackham b Garrett	16	run out (Murdoch)	56
J.Selby	b Spofforth	7	not out	48
W.Bates	st Blackham b Garrett	23	not out	52
A.Shrewsbury	lbw b Palmer	1		
W.E.Midwinter	c Palmer b Boyle	21		
W.H.Scotton	st Blackham b Giffen	26		
T.Emmett	b Giffen	27		
*A.Shaw	c Murdoch b Garrett	3		
†R.Pilling	not out	6		
E.Peate	c & b Garrett	13		
Extras	(b10, lb7)	17	(b12, lb2)	14
Total	(159.2 overs, in about 305 mins)	309	(97.3 overs, in about 200 mins (2 wkts)	234

AUSTRALIA

*W.L.Murdoch	b Midwinter	85
A.C.Bannerman	c & b Midwinter	37
T.P.Horan	c & b Midwinter	20
P.S.McDonnell	c Barlow b Ulyett	52
H.H.Massie	c Emmett b Shaw	19
G.Giffen	c Scotton b Peate	14
†J.M.Blackham	c Pilling b Midwinter	6
T.W.Garrett	c Ulyett b Bates	10
G.E.Palmer	c Ulyett b Bates	32
H.F.Boyle	c Shrewsbury b Bates	6
F.R.Spofforth	not out	3
Extras	(b2, lb7, w6, nb1)	16
Total	(163.1 overs, in about 315 mins)	300

AUSTRALIA	O	M	R	W	w,nb		O	M	R	W	w,nb		FALL OF WICKETS			
Spofforth	51	14	92	1	-,-	(4)	15	3	36	0	-,-			ENG	AUST	ENG
Garrett	54.2	23	80	5	-,-		27	6	62	0	-,-	Wkt		1st	1st	2nd
Palmer	23	5	70	1	-,-	(1)	20	5	47	0	-,-	1st		32	110	98
Boyle	18	4	33	1	-,-	(3)	25	9	38	1	-,-	2nd		49	149	152
Giffen	13	6	17	2	-,-		8.3	1	25	0	-,-	3rd		98	153	-
Bannerman							2	0	12	0	-,-	4th		109	189	-
												5th		177	228	-
ENGLAND	O	M	R	W	w,nb							6th		239	247	-
Bates	28.1	14	49	3	-,-							7th		281	247	-
Peate	20	6	38	1	-,-							8th		284	280	-
Emmett	19	14	22	0	-,-							9th		288	297	-
Ulyett	24	8	40	1	5,-							10th		309	300	-
Midwinter	41	9	81	4	-,1											
Barlow	15	6	25	0	1,-											
Shaw	16	6	29	1	-,-											

SOUTH AUSTRALIA v VICTORIA

Played at Adelaide Oval on March 10, 11, 13, 1882. (Timeless match)
Toss : South Australia.   Result : SOUTH AUSTRALIA WON BY 31 RUNS.
Debuts: South Australia - W.G.Jones, W.Knill, J.Quilty, A.E.Waldron (all f/c). Victoria - C.F.Foot, J.Lawlor, S.Morris, H.A.Musgrove,
    G.W.Stokes (all f/c).
12th Men: A.M.Pettinger (SA) and H.S.Freeman (Vic).
Umpires: E.H.Elliott and W.Travers (see below).
Attendances: 600, 1000, 300.   Total: About 1900.   Receipts: £93.
Close of Play: 1st day Vic 7/63 (Turner 17, Morris 13); 2nd day SA (2) 200 all out.

South Australia's victory was their first against Victoria in eleven-a-side matches. Quilty took the first seven wickets in Victoria's first innings; his analysis of 9 for 55 remains the best for a bowler on debut in Australia. Despite this introduction he played in only one further first-class match. Another to have a limited career was Stokes, whose innings of 58 (in about 90 minutes, 7 fours) came in his only match. Turner kept wickets throughout the first innings and until the score was 0/49 in the second innings, when he handed over to Foot for the rest of the innings. Noel (career-best 61 in about 105 minutes, 2 fours) made his runs out of 94 added for the first wicket in the South Australian second innings. R.Bruce umpired on the second day in the absence of Elliott, who was ill, and came under criticism for two decisions he made, namely the dismissals of Slight and Quilty. *O'Reilly* incorrectly gives SA (1) Waldron 8, extras 5, Scott 0/17.
Sources: *Australian Cricketers Guide, C.B.O'Reilly, The Australasian, Adelaide Advertiser, South Australian Register.*

SOUTH AUSTRALIA

J.Noel	c Musgrove b McShane	5		st Foot b Turner	61
†A.H.Jarvis	b Mackay	33	(3)	b Scott	33
J.B.Hide	b Trapp	5	(8)	c Stokes b McShane	13
W.Knill	b Trapp	7	(6)	b Mackay	1
T.O.Richards	b McShane	24		c & b Mackay	7
W.Slight	c Turner b McShane	5	(4)	lbw b Scott	4
*J.E.Gooden	c Morris b McShane	19		not out	27
A.E.Waldron	b McShane	0	(9)	c Lawlor b McShane	6
J.F.King	not out	8	(2)	st Foot b Turner	34
J.Quilty	st Turner b McShane	0		c & b McShane	2
W.G.Jones	c & b Trapp	0		c & b Turner	2
Extras	(b6, lb7)	13		(b8, lb2)	10
Total	(85.0 overs, in about 165 mins)	119		(122.2 overs, in about 225 mins)	200

VICTORIA

H.J.H.Scott	b Quilty	9	(4)	b Waldron	10
H.A.Musgrove	b Quilty	0	(8)	c Hide b Noel	2
G.W.Stokes	c King b Quilty	12	(7)	c Jarvis b Waldron	58
J.Lawlor	b Quilty	6	(6)	b Noel	4
V.B.Trapp	b Quilty	2	(2)	c Noel b Waldron	32
*†E.Turner	st Jarvis b Quilty	34	(3)	c Jarvis b King	0
F.G.McShane	b Quilty	0	(9)	run out (Jarvis)	13
G.Mackay	b Quilty	1	(10)	st Jarvis b Quilty	0
S.Morris	c Gooden b Noel	28	(5)	b Jones	14
R.Pateman	not out	8	(1)	c Quilty b Jones	32
C.F.Foot	st Jarvis b Quilty	3		not out	4
Extras	(b3)	3		(b7, lb5, nb 1)	13
Total	(78.1 overs, in about 125 mins)	106		(138.1 overs, in about 235 mins)	182

VICTORIA	O	M	R	W	w,nb		O	M	R	W	w,nb
McShane	36	18	43	6	-,-		33	11	41	3	-,-
Trapp	36	17	37	3	-,-	(3)	20	10	24	0	-,-
Mackay	6	2	17	1	-,-	(6)	15	9	19	2	-,-
Scott	7	2	9	0	-,-	(2)	28	10	44	2	-,-
Morris						(4)	9	3	11	0	-,-
Turner						(5)	17.2	2	51	3	-,-

SOUTH AUSTRALIA	O	M	R	W	w,nb		O	M	R	W	w,nb
Jones	27	13	28	0	-,-		33	14	48	2	-,-
Quilty	37.1	8	55	9	-,-		18	4	42	1	-,1
Hide	7	5	5	0	-,-	(4)	6	3	3	0	-,-
Noel	7	0	15	1	-,-	(3)	30	13	33	2	-,-
King							21	15	14	1	-,-
Waldron							23.1	13	18	3	-,-
Slight							7	2	11	0	-,-

FALL OF WICKETS

Wkt	SA 1st	VIC 1st	SA 2nd	VIC 2nd
1st	10	4	94	63
2nd	38	15	117	63
3rd	54	24	122	80
4th	62	32	143	98
5th	78	33	147	103
6th	97	33	147	103
7th	97	35	170	113
8th	114	90	189	153
9th	114	100	197	167
10th	119	106	200	182

1882-83 SEASON (10 MATCHES)

The Hon. Ivo Bligh led the seventh English team to Australia in 1882-83 at the invitation of Melbourne Cricket Club. Bligh pledged to bring home 'the ashes of English cricket' - his reference to a joke obituary notice which had appeared in the London Press after Australia's historic win at The Oval in August 1882. Bligh's team played four Tests in Australia, the first three against the returning 1882 Australians and the fourth against a 'United Australian XI' (*Sydney Morning Herald*). Australia won the first and last matches and England the middle two. But because the 'Ashes' were to be determined by the results of the three matches against the 1882 Australians, Bligh was able to keep his pledge to English cricket. Some Melbourne ladies took the joke a step further by presenting Bligh with a real urn containing the remains of (what is traditionally accepted to be) a burnt pair of bails. The Ashes were no longer mythical, and over the years the legend gained widespread acceptance among cricket followers. The Ashes remain on display at Lord's as the perpetual trophy for Test matches between England and Australia.

The leading run-getters in the four Tests were A.C.Bannerman (255), G.J.Bonnor (217) and J.M.Blackham (204) for Australia, and A.G.Steel (274) and W.W.Read (228) for England. Steel recorded the only century of the series. The leading wicket-takers were G.E.Palmer (21) and F.R.Spofforth (18) for Australia, and Billy Bates (19) and R.G.Barlow (15) for England. Palmer (10 for 126) and Bates (14 for 102, including a hat-trick) decided the first and second matches respectively on their bowling feats.

Following the series which had been squared 2-all, a fifth Test was proposed by Melbourne Cricket Club after a request from W.L.Murdoch. However 'insuperable difficulties' (*The Age*) prevented it taking place. The Englishmen played 13 matches in addition to the four Tests, but of these only three ranked as first-class, the other 10 involving odds.

As was the case the previous year, three domestic first-class matches were played in addition to the English touring program. The New South Wales v Victoria clashes resulted in a win to each colony, the visiting team being successful on each occasion. T.P.Horan (33 and 129) and A.C.Bannerman (78 and 101*) topscored for their respective teams in each innings of the match at Melbourne. H.F.Boyle (4 for 14 and 4 for 32) and Palmer (4 for 32 and 5 for 29) bowled unchanged through each innings of the return match in Sydney, in which New South Wales had the misfortune to be caught on a rain-affected wicket.

In the remaining first-class match of 1882-83, South Australia met Victoria at the East Melbourne Ground and were bowled out for 23 in the best batting conditions of the game.

Leading Aggregates

Batsmen	M	I	NO	Runs	HS	Ave.	Bowlers	Runs	Wkts	Ave.
A.C.Bannerman (NSW)	6	10	2	434	101*	54.25	G.E.Palmer (V)	588	51	11.52
A.G.Steel (E)	7	11	1	415	135*	41.50	A.G.Steel (E)	401	25	16.04
G.J.Bonnor (V)	7	11	0	353	87	32.09	H.F.Boyle (V)	264	24	11.00
C.F.H.Leslie (E)	7	11	1	310	144	31.00	W.Bates (E)	429	24	17.87
W.L.Murdoch (NSW)	6	12	1	310	71	28.18	R.G.Barlow (E)	473	23	20.56
T.P.Horan (V)	8	12	0	300	129	25.00	F.R.Spofforth (NSW)	597	23	25.95

VICTORIA v Hon. I.F.W.BLIGH'S ENGLISH XI

Played at Melbourne Cricket Ground on November 17, 18, 20, 1882. (Timeless match)
Toss : England XI.   Result : Hon. I.F.W.BLIGH'S ENGLISH XI WON BY TEN WICKETS.
Debuts: Victoria - W.Bruce, W.Logan, J.Rosser (all f/c)
Umpires: E.H.Elliott and J.A.Smith.
Attendances: 5000, 10000, 400.   Total: About 15,400.   Receipts: No figures published.
Close of Play: 1st day Vic 2/16 (Swift 8, Rosser 4); 2nd day Vic (2) 7/121 (McShane 8, Bruce 8).

Victoria were weakened by the absence of nine players, J.M.Blackham, G.J.Bonnor, H.F.Boyle, T.P.Horan, P.S.McDonnell and G.E.Palmer had not yet returned from the 1882 tour of England, F.E.Allan and J.Slight were unavailable and in addition, T.U.Groube withdrew after being selected, citing poor recent form. He was replaced by Rosser. England also had selection problems. Bligh (hand injury) and Morley (injury to ribs) were hurt on the voyage out, but as there were only 12 players in the party one - Morley - had to play. However, he was unable to field in either innings, George Alexander, the Australian player engaged as the England Manager, acted as substitute throughout and distinguished himself by throwing down Kelly's wicket and taking a fine catch to dismiss McShane. Bates (48 in about 50 minutes, 5 fours), C.T.Studd (56 in about 135 minutes, 4 fours) and Leslie (51 not out in about 65 minutes, 6 fours) were the major contributors to the English total. The Victorian batting twice failed on "a perfect wicket" (*Age*) to the steady English bowling. Byes from the first ball (a bouncer that cleared batsman and wicket-keeper) of the English second innings settled the match. Sources: *Wisden, VCA Report, Australian Cricketers Guide, The Age, The Argus, The Herald, The Australasian, The Leader.*

Hon. I.F.W.BLIGH'S ENGLISH XI

Batsman	Dismissal	Score	2nd Dismissal	Score
R.G.Barlow	b Cooper	44	not out	0
G.B.Studd	b Cooper	1	not out	0
W.Bates	c Swift b McShane	48		
C.T.Studd	b McShane	56		
A.G.Steel	b Cooper	2		
W.W.Read	b Edwards	1		
W.Barnes	c & b Cooper	1		
*†E.F.S.Tylecote	st Turner b Cooper	37		
C.F.H.Leslie	not out	51		
G.F.Vernon	b Scott	17		
F.Morley	b Bruce	3		
Extras	(b10, lb2)	12	(b4)	4
Total	(126.2 overs, in about 250 mins)	273	(0.1 overs, 1 min) (0 wkts)	4

VICTORIA

Batsman	Dismissal	Score	2nd Dismissal	Score
J.S.Swift	c Barnes b Steel	8	(4) hit wkt b Steel	18
H.J.H.Scott	run out (Barlow/Tylecote)	0	b Barnes	26
J.D.Edwards	lbw b Steel	3	b Barlow	2
J.Rosser	c Tylecote b Read	22	(5) b Steel	11
†E.Turner	b Read	25	(6) b Steel	17
F.Baker	c Tylecote b Read	5	(7) b Bates	5
T.J.D.Kelly	run out (sub G.Alexander)	20	(1) c Leslie b Barlow	14
W.Bruce	b Read	2	(9) c G.B.Studd b C.T.Studd	40
F.G.McShane	b Bates	14	(8) c sub (G.Alexander) b Bates	15
*W.H.Cooper	b Steel	0	c Tylecote b Barlow	8
W.Logan	not out	2	not out	0
Extras	(b1, lb1, nb1)	3	(b10, lb3)	13
Total	(95.1 overs, in about 170 mins)	104	(96.1 overs, in about 175 mins)	169

VICTORIA	O	M	R	W	w,nb	O	M	R	W	w,nb
Cooper	35	9	89	5	-,-					
Edwards	28	12	39	1	-,-					
Bruce	15.2	1	42	1	-,-					
McShane	25	12	37	2	-,-	0.1	0	0	0	-,-
Scott	11	4	21	1	-,-					
Logan	12	2	33	0	-,-					

ENGLAND XI	O	M	R	W	w,nb		O	M	R	W	w,nb
Steel	26	15	15	3	-,-		21	4	54	3	-,-
Barnes	19	4	32	0	-,-	(3)	12	4	19	1	-,-
Barlow	11	8	6	0	-,-	(2)	16	7	31	3	-,-
C.T.Studd	11	6	6	0	-,-		23.1	16	19	1	-,-
Bates	16.1	8	14	1	-,-	(6)	20	10	27	2	-,-
Read	12	3	28	4	-,1	(5)	4	0	6	0	-,-

FALL OF WICKETS				
	ENG	VIC	VIC	ENG
Wkt	1st	1st	2nd	2nd
1st	7	0	31	-
2nd	72	7	37	-
3rd	134	16	52	-
4th	138	55	78	-
5th	139	65	86	-
6th	142	68	101	-
7th	178	74	101	-
8th	200	102	131	-
9th	257	102	169	-
10th	273	104	169	-

NEW SOUTH WALES v Hon. I.F.W.BLIGH'S ENGLISH XI

Played at Sydney Cricket Ground on December 1, 2, 4, 1882. (Timeless match)
Toss : New South Wales.   Result : Hon. I.F.W.BLIGH'S ENGLISH XI WON BY AN INNINGS AND 144 RUNS.
Debuts: New South Wales - J.J.C.Callachor, A.P.Marr, C.T.B.Turner (all f/c).
12th Men: T.Nunn (NSW). No reserve available for England.
Umpires: W.C.Goddard and J.Swift.
Attendances: 3000, 10000, 2000.   Total: About 15,000.   Receipts: No figures published.
Close of Play: 1st day Eng 1/39 (Barlow 17, Leslie 15); 2nd day Eng 8/442 (Barnes 6, Vernon 13).

New South Wales were without their returning Australian XI representatives, A.C.Bannerman, T.W.Garrett, S.P.Jones, H.H.Massie, W.L.Murdoch and F.R.Spofforth. Bligh was again unavailable, his hand not yet fully healed. The below-strength New South Wales team proved no match for the visitors in cool but fine conditions. Leslie (144 in 155 minutes, 1 five and 21 fours) "played a superb innings" (*SMH*), despite a chance at 15 and two others after reaching his century. He took his score from 15 to 108 in the 85-minute pre-lunch session on the second day and his 144 came from the second wicket stand of 224 with Barlow (80 in about 180 minutes, 7 fours). Consistent scoring thereafter took the visitors to an unassailable position. Evans toiled manfully but the "rest of the bowling on the New South Wales side was of an inferior description" (*SMH*). Davis (career-best 85 in about 210 minutes, 9 fours, 2 chances) put up a stubborn resistance in the second innings but to no avail. A new wicket was used for each innings. *Wisden* incorrectly gives NSW (1) Allen c Tylecote and debits the wide and no-ball to C.T.Studd and Steel respectively; NSW (2) Allen c & b C.T.Studd. Sources: *Wisden, Sydney Morning Herald, Town & Country Journal, Sydney Mail, Sydney Daily Telegraph.*

NEW SOUTH WALES

J.Davis	st Tylecote b Steel	18	(2) b Barlow		85
A.Geary	run out (Bates/C.T.Studd)	6	(1) c Tylecote Read		22
H.Moses	c Bates b Steel	21	c Vernon b C.T.Studd		2
R.C.Allen	st Tylecote b Steel	6	c & b Steel		9
H.C.S.Hiddleston	c Tylecote b C.T.Studd	8	run out (/Tylecote)		0
*T.Powell	b Barlow	22	not out		32
A.P.Marr	c Barnes b Steel	34	b Barlow		0
C.T.B.Turner	b Bates	4	(10) c Steel b C.T.Studd		2
E.Evans	c Tylecote b Steel	10	run out (/Tylecote)		2
W.S.Wearne	c Steel b C.T.Studd	6	(11) c G.B.Studd b C.T.Studd		1
†J.J.C.Callachor	not out	11	(8) b Barlow		0
Extras	(b4, w1, nb1)	6	(b7, lb2, nb1)		10
Total	(140.1 overs, in about 235 mins)	152	(148.0 overs, in about 245 mins)		165

Hon. I.F.W.BLIGH'S ENGLISH XI

R.G.Barlow	b Evans	80
G.B.Studd	b Wearne	6
C.F.H.Leslie	c Moses b Evans	144
C.T.Studd	b Marr	23
W.Bates	c & b Evans	30
W.W.Read	c & b Evans	46
A.G.Steel	b Evans	52
*†E.F.S.Tylecote	b Powell	26
W.Barnes	c & b Evans	12
G.F.Vernon	b Turner	24
F.Morley	not out	2
Extras	(b16)	16
Total	(221.0 overs, in about 390 mins)	461

ENGLAND XI	O	M	R	W	w,nb		O	M	R	W	w,nb
Morley	20	10	32	0	-,1	(2)	17	10	15	0	-,-
Barlow	54	34	41	1	1,-	(3)	26	19	18	3	-,-
Steel	28	17	32	5	-,-	(1)	23	13	26	1	-,1
C.T.Studd	22.1	12	19	2	-,-	(6)	20	9	28	3	-,-
Barnes	2	1	3	0	-,-	(7)	7	3	12	0	-,-
Bates	14	7	19	1	-,-	(4)	32	17	31	0	-,-
Read						(5)	23	10	25	1	-,-

NEW SOUTH WALES	O	M	R	W	w,nb
Evans	85	33	146	6	-,-
Wearne	14	1	52	1	-,-
Turner	45	16	76	1	-,-
Marr	29	15	46	1	-,-
Geary	19	7	45	0	-,-
Allen	14	1	32	0	-,-
Powell	13	5	32	1	-,-
Moses	2	0	16	0	-,-

	FALL OF WICKETS		
	NSW	ENG	NSW
Wkt	1st	1st	2nd
1st	24	14	54
2nd	26	238	60
3rd	37	240	86
4th	54	280	86
5th	67	314	149
6th	103	355	149
7th	115	417	149
8th	134	429	156
9th	135	455	160
10th	152	461	165

VICTORIA v NEW SOUTH WALES

Played at Melbourne Cricket Ground on December 23, 26, 27, 28, 29, 1882. (Timeless match)
Toss : Victoria.   Result : NEW SOUTH WALES WON BY SEVEN WICKETS.
Debuts: New South Wales - J.O.Cleeve (f/c).
12th Men: J.Slight (Vic) and T.Powell (NSW).
Umpires: B.McGan and J.Swift.
Attendances: 6000, 10000, 5000, 3000, 500.   Total: About 24,500.   Receipts: No figures published.
Close of Play: 1st day NSW 1/76 (Bannerman 43, Murdoch 33); 2nd day Vic (2) 1/60 (McDonnell 32); 3rd day Vic (2) 6/333 (Rosser 17, Allan 0); 4th day NSW (2) 1/165 (Bannerman 51, Murdoch 55).

E.H.Elliott was appointed to umpire, but was replaced at the last moment by McGan after a protest from the New South Wales team. Elliott recorded his disappointment over the decision in a letter to the Editor of *The Age*. W.H.Cooper (hand injury) and G.E.Palmer (rested for Test match) were unavailable for Victoria. Bannerman (78 in about 235 minutes, 2 fours and 101 not out in about 355 minutes, 11 fours) and Murdoch (71 in about 195 minutes, 6 fours and 67 in about 150 minutes, 5 fours) batted soundly in both innings to ensure victory for their side. They shared a century second wicket stand in each innings, 136 in the first and 123 in the second. Massie was out to the first ball of the New South Wales first innings but redeemed himself with a half-century (51 in about 100 minutes, 8 fours) in the second innings. Victoria's best batting came from McDonnell (70 in about 90 minutes, 2 fives and 7 fours) and Horan (129 in about 285 minutes, 1 five and 13 fours). Cleeve bowled well on debut but his career was to prove fleeting as he was to make only two further first-class appearances. Jones was bowled by Scott before scoring in the first innings but was adjudged to have been drawing away from taking strike and therefore ruled not out. Sources: *Australian Cricketers Guide, VCA Report, The Age, The Argus, The Herald, The Australasian, The Leader*.

VICTORIA

P.S.McDonnell	run out (/Murdoch)	12	(2)	b Cleeve	70
W.E.Midwinter	b Gregory	17	(6)	c Spofforth b Cleeve	38
T.P.Horan	c Bannerman b Garrett	33		c Bannerman b Gregory	129
H.J.H.Scott	b Spofforth	11		c Spofforth b Cleeve	15
G.J.Bonnor	c Hiddleston b Garrett	27		c Hiddleston b Cleeve	13
J.Rosser	b Spofforth	19	(7)	not out	33
*†J.M.Blackham	b Spofforth	0	(1)	lbw b Gregory	27
T.J.D.Kelly	c & b Garrett	2	(10)	b Evans	4
H.F.Boyle	c Gregory b Garrett	5		c & b Cleeve	13
W.Bruce	b Garrett	1	(11)	b Evans	0
F.E.Allan	not out	6	(8)	c Spofforth b Cleeve	3
Extras	(b13, lb1, nb1)	15		(b18, lb5, w2, nb1)	26
Total	(70.2 overs, in about 165 mins)	148		(199.2 overs, in about 405 mins)	371

NEW SOUTH WALES

H.H.Massie	c Scott b Midwinter	0	(2)	c & b Boyle	51
A.C.Bannerman	run out (Midwinter/Scott)	78	(1)	not out	101
*†W.L.Murdoch	c Blackham b Allan	71		c Boyle b Bruce	67
J.Davis	b Scott	5		b Scott	15
S.P.Jones	b Allan	15		not out	25
T.W.Garrett	c & b Scott	10			
D.W.Gregory	lbw b Scott	4			
H.C.S.Hiddleston	b Scott	0			
E.Evans	not out	22			
F.R.Spofforth	c Bruce b Boyle	31			
J.O.Cleeve	run out (sub J.Slight/Blackham)	6			
Extras	(b4, lb1)	5		(b12, nb2)	14
Total	(220.0 overs, in about 345 mins)	247		(213.0 overs, in about 355 mins) (3 wkts)	273

NEW SOUTH WALES	O	M	R	W	w,nb		O	M	R	W	w,nb		FALL OF WICKETS			
Evans	10	6	15	0	-,-	(3)	28.2	11	47	2	-,-			VIC	NSW	VIC	NSW
Cleeve	10	2	28	0	-,-	(5)	72	33	95	6	2,-	Wkt	1st	1st	2nd	2nd
Garrett	24.2	9	45	5	-,-	(1)	14	7	28	0	-,-	1st	18	0	60	67
Gregory	7	3	10	1	-,-		31	8	72	2	-,-	2nd	65	136	118	190
Spofforth	19	6	35	3	-,1	(2)	44	17	79	0	-,1	3rd	79	151	158	231
Jones							4	1	11	0	-,-	4th	79	168	186	-
Bannerman							6	3	13	0	-,-	5th	116	183	281	-
												6th	116	187	330	-
VICTORIA	O	M	R	W	w,nb		O	M	R	W	w,nb	7th	123	187	342	-
Midwinter	47	27	31	1	-,-		60	40	50	0	-,1	8th	135	189	362	-
Allan	69	38	84	2	-,-		25	9	44	0	-,1	9th	140	241	367	-
Boyle	27	14	37	1	-,-	(5)	39	23	28	1	-,-	10th	148	247	371	-
Bruce	25	14	24	0	-,-		51	22	69	1	-,-					
Kelly	4	2	2	0	-,-											
McDonnell	3	0	7	0	-,-											
Scott	45	22	57	4	-,-	(3)	27	10	56	1	-,-					
Horan						(6)	11	6	12	0	-,-					

AUSTRALIA v ENGLAND (1st Test)

Played at Melbourne Cricket Ground on December 30, 1882, January 1, 2, 1883. (Timeless match)
Toss : Australia.   Result : AUSTRALIA WON BY NINE WICKETS.
Debuts: England - Hon. I.F.W.Bligh, C.F.H.Leslie, W.W.Read, G.B.Studd, E.F.S.Tylecote, G.F.Vernon (all Test).
12th Men: H.F.Boyle (Aust) and G.Alexander (Eng manager).
Umpires: E.H.Elliott and J.Swift.
Attendances: 15000, 23000, 16000.   Total: About 54,000.   Receipts: No figures published.
Close of Play: 1st day Aust 7/258 (Bonnor 60, Spofforth 1); 2nd day Eng (2) 0/11 (Barlow 8, Tylecote 3).

F.Morley was still handicapped by the injury he sustained on the voyage out and could not be considered for selection. Alexander, the team manager, again acted as 12th man and fielded as substitute for Leslie (ill) on the final day. The Australian side for this and the following two matches against Bligh's Team, all of which were later catalogued as Tests, was drawn from the successful 1882 touring team to England. It was at first thought that the English umpire would be G.Coulthard but the tourists eventually plumped for Elliott, who had been rejected for the Vic v NSW clash prior to this game. He was to retain their confidence throughout the season. Bonnor, whose selection at the expense of Boyle by Messrs. Murdoch, Blackham and Bannerman was considered a shock, topscored with 85 (in about 135 minutes, 5 fours and 4 fives - one of which just missed the curator's cottage and struck against the outer fence). Overnight rain after the first day softened the pitch in favour of the bowlers, though "it is treating Palmer very unfairly to put forward the false plan that it was a very bad wicket, and not Palmer's bowling, which caused the unexpected downfall of the Englishmen" (*The Australasian*). Blackham retrieved a wayward return and ran the length of the wicket to effect a run out at the bowler's end when both G.B.Studd and Tylecote contrived to finish at the other end. Recent publications differ in some falls of wickets. Sources: *Wisden, Australian Cricketers Guide, The Age, The Argus, The Herald, The Australasian, The Leader.*

AUSTRALIA

A.C.Bannerman	st Tylecote b Leslie	30		not out	25
H.H.Massie	c & b C.T.Studd	4		c & b Barnes	0
*W.L.Murdoch	b Leslie	48		not out	33
T.P.Horan	c Barlow b Leslie	0			
P.S.McDonnell	b Bates	43			
G.Giffen	st Tylecote b Steel	36			
G.J.Bonnor	c Barlow b Barnes	85			
†J.M.Blackham	c Tylecote b C.T.Studd	25			
F.R.Spofforth	c Steel b Barnes	9			
T.W.Garrett	c C.T.Studd b Steel	0			
G.E.Palmer	not out	0			
Extras	(b4, lb2, w2, nb3)	11			-
Total	(169.0 overs, in about 330 mins)	291		(53.1 overs, in about 95 mins) (1 wkt)	58

ENGLAND

R.G.Barlow	st Blackham b Palmer	10		b Spofforth	28
*Hon. I.F.W.Bligh	b Palmer	0	(5)	b Spofforth	3
C.F.H.Leslie	c Garrett b Palmer	4	(7)	b Giffen	4
C.T.Studd	b Spofforth	0	(3)	b Palmer	21
A.G.Steel	b Palmer	27	(4)	lbw b Giffen	29
W.W.Read	b Palmer	19		b Giffen	29
W.Bates	c Bannerman b Garrett	28	(8)	c Massie b Palmer	11
†E.F.S.Tylecote	b Palmer	33	(2)	b Spofforth	38
G.B.Studd	run out (Giffen/Blackham)	7		c Palmer b Giffen	0
W.Barnes	b Palmer	26		not out	2
G.F.Vernon	not out	11		lbw b Palmer	3
Extras	(b8, lb1, nb3)	12		(lb1)	1
Total	(107.2 overs, in about 195 mins)	177		(99.1 overs, in about 185 mins)	169

ENGLAND	O	M	R	W	w,nb		O	M	R	W	w,nb			
C.T.Studd	46	30	35	2	-,-		14	11	7	0	-,-			
Barnes	30	11	51	2	-,-		13	8	6	1	-,-			
Steel	33	16	68	2	-,-		9	4	17	0	-,-			
Barlow	20	6	37	0	1,-	(5)	4	2	6	0	-,-			
Read	8	2	27	0	-,3									
Bates	21	7	31	1	-,-	(4)	13.1	7	22	0	-,-			
Leslie	11	1	31	3	1,-									

	FALL OF WICKETS				
		AUST	ENG	AUST	ENG
	Wkt	1st	1st	2nd	2nd
	1st	5	2	64	0
	2nd	81	7	75	-
	3rd	81	8	105	-
	4th	96	36	108	-
	5th	162	45	132	-
	6th	190	96	150	-
	7th	251	100	164	-
	8th	287	117	164	-
	9th	287	156	164	-
	10th	291	177	169	-

AUSTRALIA	O	M	R	W	w,nb		O	M	R	W	w,nb
Spofforth	28	11	56	1	-,-	(3)	41	15	65	3	-,-
Palmer	52.2	25	65	7	-,3	(1)	36.1	11	61	3	-,-
Garrett	27	6	44	1	-,-	(2)	2	1	4	0	-,-
Giffen							20	7	38	4	-,-

AUSTRALIA v ENGLAND (2nd Test)

Played at Melbourne Cricket Ground on January 19, 20, 22, 1883. (Timeless match)
Toss : England.   Result : ENGLAND WON BY AN INNINGS AND 27 RUNS.
Debuts: Nil.
12th Men: H.F.Boyle (Aust) and G.F.Vernon (Eng).
Umpires: E.H.Elliott and J.Swift.
Attendances: 4000, 12000, 4000.   Total: About 20,000.   Receipts: No figures published.
Close of Play: 1st day Eng 7/248 (Read 51, Bates 35); 2nd day Aust (2) 1/28 (Bannerman 5, Blackham 6).

Billy Bates became the first England bowler to perform the hat-trick in Tests when he dismissed McDonnell, Giffen and Bonnor in the first innings. A quirk of Bates's feat involved the taking of drinks between the dismissals of Giffen and Bonnor. He went on to become the first bowler to take 14 wickets in a Test in Australia. Fielding lapses proved costly for Australia for Bates (55 in about 95 minutes, 4 fours), who put on a vital 88 for England's eighth wicket with Read (75 in about 190 minutes, 7 fours), was missed before he had scored. Read was also let off on more than one occasion. Massie's first innings was a typically brilliant affair which included 7 fours: he struck fours from the first two deliveries of the innings and was first out at 56. However, the scoring slowed immediately after he departed and 14 maidens were bowled in succession at one stage when Murdoch (19 not out in about 150 minutes) came to join Bannerman (14 in 105 minutes). Bonnor's 34 included three blows over the fence, worth five each, all off Bates. The margin of victory - by an innings - was a first for Test cricket. *Wisden* incorrectly gives Aust (2) Garrett c Barnes b Barlow, Barlow 4/67, Bates 6/74. Sources: *Wisden, Australian Cricketers Guide, The Age, The Argus, The Australasian, The Leader.*

ENGLAND

R.G.Barlow	b Palmer	14
C.T.Studd	b Palmer	14
C.F.H.Leslie	run out (Spofforth)	54
A.G.Steel	c McDonnell b Giffen	39
W.W.Read	c & b Palmer	75
W.Barnes	b Giffen	32
†E.F.S.Tylecote	b Giffen	0
*Hon. I.F.W.Bligh	b Giffen	0
W.Bates	c Horan b Palmer	55
G.B.Studd	b Palmer	1
F.Morley	not out	0
Extras	(b3, lb3, nb4)	10
Total	(183.3 overs, in about 340 mins)	294

AUSTRALIA

H.H.Massie	b Barlow	43	(7) c C.T.Studd b Barlow	10
A.C.Bannerman	b Bates	14	(1) c Bligh b Bates	14
*W.L.Murdoch	not out	19	(2) b Bates	17
T.P.Horan	c & b Barnes	3	(5) c Morley b Bates	15
P.S.McDonnell	b Bates	3	(6) b Bates	13
G.Giffen	c & b Bates	0	(8) c Bligh b Bates	19
G.J.Bonnor	c Read b Bates	0	(4) c Morley b Barlow	34
†J.M.Blackham	b Barnes	5	(3) b Barlow	6
T.W.Garrett	b Bates	10	c Barnes b Bates	6
G.E.Palmer	b Bates	7	c G.B.Studd b Bates	4
F.R.Spofforth	b Bates	0	not out	14
Extras	(b6, lb3, nb1)	10	(b1)	1
Total	(98.2 overs, in about 190 mins)	114	(69.0 overs, in about 135 mins)	153

AUSTRALIA	O	M	R	W	w,nb
Spofforth	34	11	57	0	-,1
Palmer	66.3	25	103	5	-,3
Giffen	49	13	89	4	-,-
Garrett	34	16	35	0	-,-

ENGLAND	O	M	R	W	w,nb		O	M	R	W	w,nb
C.T.Studd	4	1	22	0	-,-						
Morley	23	16	13	0	-,1	(4)	2	0	7	0	-,-
Barnes	23	7	32	2	-,-		3	1	4	0	-,-
Barlow	22	18	9	1	-,-	(2)	31	6	67	3	-,-
Bates	26.2	14	28	7	-,-	(1)	33	14	74	7	-,-

FALL OF WICKETS

Wkt	ENG 1st	AUST 1st	AUST 2nd
1st	28	56	21
2nd	35	72	28
3rd	106	75	66
4th	131	78	72
5th	195	78	93
6th	199	78	104
7th	199	85	113
8th	287	104	132
9th	293	114	139
10th	294	114	153

AUSTRALIA v ENGLAND (3rd Test)

Played at Sydney Cricket Ground on January 26, 27, 29, 30, 1883. (Timeless match)
Toss :England.   Result : ENGLAND WON BY 69 RUNS.
Debuts: Nil.
12th Men: S.P.Jones (Aust) and G.F.Vernon (Eng).
Umpires: E.H.Elliott and J.Swift.
Attendances: 20000, 14000, 13000, 6000.   Total: About 54,000.   Receipts: No figures published.
Close of Play: 1st day Aust 0/8 (Giffen 6, Bannerman 1); 2nd day Aust 1/133 (Bannerman 68, Murdoch 17); 3rd day Aust (2) 0/0
    (Giffen 0, Bannerman 0).

Two pitches, one for the batsmen of each side, were used in this Test. Prior to the commencement, Murdoch protested to Bligh about spikes in Barlow's boots causing extreme damage to the wickets in previous matches. "Mr. Bligh, with great courtesy, had the offending plates removed" (*SMH*). It got under way in ideal conditions, however showers on the second day reduced the playing time to three hours and further rain on the Sunday created a treacherous pitch for the resumption of the match on Monday. Bannerman's steadfast 94, compiled in about 245 minutes, mostly in dull light and frequently interrupted by the elements, included 13 fours. The last day commenced at 11.00am, an hour early, so that the Englishmen could keep travel arrangements to Queensland for the next stage of their tour. After the match some Melbourne ladies presented the English captain with an embroidered bag and urn containing the burnt remains of a bail, stump or ball as a memento of the tour. When Bligh died in 1927 the Ashes found their way to Lord's, where they now remain as an eternal symbol of supremacy in England v Australia Test matches. Sources: *Wisden, Australian Cricketers Guide, Sydney Morning Herald, Town & Country Journal*.

ENGLAND

R.G.Barlow	c Murdoch b Spofforth	28	(3)	c Palmer b Horan	24
C.T.Studd	c Blackham b Garrett	21	(1)	b Spofforth	25
C.F.H.Leslie	b Spofforth	0	(2)	b Spofforth	8
A.G.Steel	b Garrett	17		lbw b Spofforth	6
W.W.Read	c Massie b Bannerman	66		b Horan	21
W.Barnes	b Spofforth	2		lbw b Spofforth	3
†E.F.S.Tylecote	run out (Horan/Blackham)	66		c Bonnor b Spofforth	0
W.Bates	c McDonnell b Spofforth	17		c Murdoch b Horan	4
G.B.Studd	b Palmer	3	(10)	c Garrett b Spofforth	8
*Hon. I.F.W.Bligh	b Palmer	13	(9)	not out	17
F.Morley	not out	2		b Spofforth	0
Extras	(b8, lb3, nb1)	12		(b5, lb2)	7
Total	(143.0 overs, in about 270 mins)	247		(80.1 overs, in about 165 mins)	123

AUSTRALIA

G.Giffen	st Tylecote b Bates	41		b Barlow	7
A.C.Bannerman	c Bates b Morley	94		c Bligh b Barlow	5
*W.L.Murdoch	lbw b Steel	19		c G.B.Studd b Morley	0
P.S.McDonnell	b Steel	0	(5)	c Bligh b Morley	0
T.P.Horan	c Steel b Morley	19	(4)	run out (G.B.Studd/Tylecote)	8
H.H.Massie	c Bligh b Steel	1		c C.T.Studd b Barlow	11
G.J.Bonnor	c G.B.Studd b Morley	0		b Barlow	8
†J.M.Blackham	b Barlow	27		b Barlow	26
T.W.Garrett	c Barlow b Morley	0	(11)	b Barlow	0
G.E.Palmer	c G.B.Studd b Barnes	7		not out	2
F.R.Spofforth	not out	0	(9)	c Steel b Barlow	7
Extras	(b6, lb2, w1, nb1)	10		(b6, lb2, w1)	9
Total	(179.1 overs, in about 310 mins)	218		(69.2 overs, in about 140 mins)	83

AUSTRALIA	O	M	R	W	w,nb		O	M	R	W	w,nb					
Giffen	12	3	37	0	-,-											
Palmer	38	21	38	2	-,1	(3)	9	3	19	0	-,-					
Spofforth	51	19	73	4	-,-	(1)	41.1	23	44	7	-,-					
Garrett	27	8	54	2	-,-	(2)	13	3	31	0	-,-					
Bannerman	11	2	17	1	-,-											
McDonnell	4	0	16	0	-,-											
Horan						(4)	17	10	22	3	-,-					

FALL OF WICKETS

	ENG	AUST	ENG	AUST
Wkt	1st	1st	2nd	2nd
1st	41	76	13	11
2nd	44	140	45	12
3rd	67	140	55	18
4th	69	176	87	18
5th	76	177	94	30
6th	191	178	94	33
7th	223	196	97	56
8th	224	196	98	72
9th	244	218	115	80
10th	247	218	123	83

ENGLAND	O	M	R	W	w,nb		O	M	R	W	w,nb
Bates	45	20	55	1	-,-						
Morley	34	16	47	4	-,1	(1)	35	19	34	2	-,-
Steel	26	14	27	3	-,-						
Barlow	47.1	31	52	1	-,-	(2)	34.2	20	40	7	1,-
Barnes	13	6	22	1	-,-						
C.T.Studd	14	11	5	0	1,-						

NEW SOUTH WALES v VICTORIA

Played at Sydney Cricket Ground on February 9, 10, 1883. (Timeless match)
Toss : Victoria.   Result : VICTORIA WON BY AN INNINGS AND 166 RUNS.
Debuts: New South Wales - R.Bryant (f/c).
12th Men: F.Downes (NSW) and J.Duffy (Vic).
Umpires: E.H.Elliott and J.Swift.
Attendances: 2000, 10000.   Total: About 12,000.   Receipts: No figures published.
Close of Play: 1st day Vic 8/274 (Scott 21, Boyle 21).

Victoria won the toss in hot, oppressive conditions with every possibility of a thunderstorm. Bonnor (42 in about 65 minutes, 1 five and 5 fours) and McDonnell (61 in about 75 minutes, 2 fives and 9 fours) hit hard to head the scoring. The anticipated storm ended play at 5.30pm and affected the wicket to such a degree that the match was over before the scheduled end of the second day. "The turf played very treacherously . . . and the finest batting team in the world would do well to make a score of 100 runs on it" (*SMH*). New South Wales were further handicapped by the inability of Alec Bannerman to bat in either innings due to injury. The exact nature of the injury was not reported but it occurred when attempting to catch "a hot one" from Bonnor before lunch on the first day. Boyle and Palmer provided the fourth instance in Australia of bowlers operating unchanged throughout both innings, Palmer being "quite unplayable" (*SMH*) in the second innings. Sources: *Australian Cricketers Guide, VCA Report, Sydney Morning Herald, Town & Country Journal.*

VICTORIA

G.J.Bonnor	run out (Massie/Bryant)	42
J.Rosser	c Bryant b Garrett	19
T.P.Horan	c C.Bannerman b Cleeve	21
W.E.Midwinter	c Evans b Garrett	10
P.S.McDonnell	c Jones b Garrett	61
†J.M.Blackham	c Massie b Garrett	37
G.E.Palmer	b Jones	34
F.G.McShane	b Jones	0
H.J.H.Scott	c Cleeve b Spofforth	28
H.F.Boyle	b Spofforth	21
*W.H.Cooper	not out	0
Extras	(b3, lb2, w2, nb1)	8
Total	(151.1 overs, in about 265 mins)	281

NEW SOUTH WALES

H.H.Massie	b Palmer	2		c McShane b Boyle	0
S.P.Jones	c Blackham b Boyle	7	(4)	c Horan b Boyle	13
*W.L.Murdoch	b Palmer	16		b Palmer	3
C.Bannerman	c Palmer b Boyle	4	(2)	b Palmer	1
A.H.Gregory	b Palmer	0	(6)	c Cooper b Palmer	8
E.Evans	run out	10	(5)	b Palmer	7
T.W.Garrett	st Blackham b Boyle	4		c Midwinter b Boyle	3
F.R.Spofforth	st Blackham b Boyle	0		b Palmer	26
†R.Bryant	b Palmer	2	(10)	not out	0
J.O.Cleeve	not out	1	(9)	c Scott b Boyle	0
A.C.Bannerman	absent hurt	-		absent hurt	-
Extras	(nb3)	3		(b2, lb2, nb1)	5
Total	(41.1 overs, in about 87 mins)	49		(48.0 overs, in about 100 mins)	66

NEW SOUTH WALES	O	M	R	W	w,nb
Spofforth	32.1	9	75	2	-,-
Cleeve	21	7	59	1	2,-
Evans	40	26	56	0	-,1
Garrett	51	26	59	4	-,-
Jones	7	2	24	2	-,-

VICTORIA	O	M	R	W	w,nb	O	M	R	W	w,nb
Boyle	21	13	14	4	-,-	24	9	32	4	-,-
Palmer	20.1	10	32	4	-,3	24	11	29	5	-,1

FALL OF WICKETS

Wkt	VIC 1st	NSW 1st	NSW 2nd
1st	52	3	0
2nd	67	18	3
3rd	86	28	8
4th	123	30	20
5th	178	31	28
6th	224	43	38
7th	229	45	52
8th	230	46	57
9th	274	49	66
10th	281	-	-

AUSTRALIA v ENGLAND (4th Test)

Played at Sydney Cricket Ground on February 17, 19, 20, 21, 1883. (Timeless match)
Toss : England.   Result : AUSTRALIA WON BY FOUR WICKETS.
Debuts: Nil.
12th Men: S.P.Jones (Aust) and G.F.Vernon (Eng).
Umpires: E.H.Elliott and J.Swift.
Attendances: 17000, 12000, 8000, 10000.   Total: About 47,000.   Receipts: No figures published.
Close of Play: 1st day Eng 9/263 (Steel 135); 2nd day Aust 9/248 (Evans 20, Boyle 20); 3rd day Eng (2) 197 all out.

Having completed a three-match series against the 1882 Australian touring team, Bligh's Team played this fixture (which formed part of the original tour itinerary) against a combined side. In keeping with many first-class matches in Sydney at this time, the captains agreed to use a fresh pitch for each of the four innings. It was scheduled to commence on February 16th but was delayed until the following day at the request of the Englishmen. Giffen twisted his knee at practice on the day before the match but retained his place in the Australian team. He attempted to field on the first day but was unable to continue after the luncheon adjournment and Jones was allowed to substitute. Giffen batted with Murdoch as a runner in both innings; he was unable to bowl. Steel (135 not out in about 238 minutes, 16 fours) survived chances at 4, 37 and 103. Bonnor's 87 (in about 165 minutes, 7 fours) included numerous chances - five to Steel alone. Blackham (57 in about 110 minutes, 6 fours and 58 not out in about 115 minutes, 1 six and 4 fours) and Bannerman (63 in about 175 minutes, 1 five and 5 fours) scored invaluable half-centuries. Sources: *Wisden, The Age, The Australasian, Sydney Morning Herald, Town & Country Journal.*

ENGLAND

R.G.Barlow	c Murdoch b Midwinter	2		c Bonnor b Midwinter	20
C.T.Studd	run out (Midwinter/Horan)	48		c Murdoch b Midwinter	31
C.F.H.Leslie	c Bonnor b Boyle	17		b Horan	19
A.G.Steel	not out	135		b Spofforth	21
W.W.Read	c Bonnor b Boyle	11		b Spofforth	7
†E.F.S.Tylecote	b Boyle	5		b Palmer	0
W.Barnes	b Spofforth	2	(9)	c & b Boyle	20
W.Bates	c Bonnor b Midwinter	9	(7)	not out	48
*Hon. I.F.W.Bligh	b Palmer	19	(8)	c Murdoch b Horan	10
G.B.Studd	run out (Bannerman/Spofforth)	3		c Murdoch b Boyle	9
F.Morley	b Palmer	0		c Blackham b Palmer	2
Extras	(b4, lb7, nb1)	12		(b8, lb1, nb1)	10
Total	(155.0 overs, in about 288 mins)	263		(126.3 overs, in about 250 mins)	197

AUSTRALIA

A.C.Bannerman	c Barlow b Morley	10		c Bligh b C.T.Studd	63
G.J.Bonnor	c Barlow b Steel	87	(3)	c G.B.Studd b Steel	3
*W.L.Murdoch	b Barlow	0	(2)	c Barlow b Bates	17
T.P.Horan	c G.B.Studd b Morley	4		c & b Bates	0
G.Giffen	c G.B.Studd b Leslie	27		st Tylecote b Steel	32
W.E.Midwinter	b Barlow	10	(8)	not out	8
†J.M.Blackham	b Bates	57	(6)	not out	58
G.E.Palmer	c Bligh b Steel	0			
E.Evans	not out	22	(7)	c Leslie b Steel	0
F.R.Spofforth	c Bates b Steel	1			
H.F.Boyle	c G.B.Studd b Barlow	29			
Extras	(b10, lb3, w2)	15		(b10, lb4, w4)	18
Total	(146.0 overs, in about 280 mins)	262		(163.1 overs, in about 290 mins) (6 wkts)	199

AUSTRALIA	O	M	R	W	w,nb		O	M	R	W	w,nb
Palmer	24	9	52	2	-,1	(3)	43.3	19	59	2	-,1
Midwinter	47	24	50	2	-,-	(4)	23	13	21	2	-,-
Spofforth	21	8	56	1	-,-	(1)	28	6	57	2	-,-
Boyle	40	19	52	3	-,-	(2)	23	6	35	2	-,-
Horan	12	4	26	0	-,-		9	2	15	2	-,-
Evans	11	3	15	0	-,-						

ENGLAND	O	M	R	W	w,nb		O	M	R	W	w,nb
Barlow	48	21	88	3	-,-	(2)	37.1	20	44	0	-,-
Morley	44	25	45	2	-,-	(3)	12	9	4	0	-,-
Barnes	10	2	33	0	-,-	(7)	16	5	22	0	-,-
Bates	15	6	24	1	-,-	(1)	39	19	52	2	-,-
Leslie	5	2	11	1	2,-	(4)	8	7	2	0	4,-
Steel	18	6	34	3	-,-	(5)	43	9	49	3	-,-
C.T.Studd	6	2	12	0	-,-	(6)	8	4	8	1	-,-

		FALL OF WICKETS			
		ENG	AUST	ENG	AUST
Wkt		1st	1st	2nd	2nd
1st		13	31	54	44
2nd		37	34	55	51
3rd		110	39	77	51
4th		150	113	99	107
5th		156	128	100	162
6th		159	160	112	164
7th		199	164	137	-
8th		236	220	178	-
9th		263	221	192	-
10th		263	262	197	-

VICTORIA v Hon. I.F.W.BLIGH'S ENGLISH XI

Played at Melbourne Cricket Ground on March 9, 10, 12, 1883. (Timeless match)
Toss : Victoria.   Result : VICTORIA WON BY AN INNINGS AND 73 RUNS.
Debuts: Nil.
12th Men: W.Bruce (Vic) and F.Morley (Eng).
Umpires: E.H.Elliott and A.Hope.
Attendances: 7000, 10000, 5000.   Total: About 22,000.   Receipts: No figures published.
Close of Play: 1st day Vic 7/213 (Midwinter 57, Boyle 2); 2nd day Eng 7/47 (Barlow 1).

J.Slight was unavailable for Victoria as his mother was seriously ill, and McShane was a late replacement for J.Rosser (business). Morley was unable to appear for the Englishmen due to recurring pain from the injury suffered on the voyage out. Charles Bannerman was originally engaged to umpire but was replaced by Hope "as the English captain demurred" (*Australasian*). It was alleged that his liking for a bet could affect his adjudication. Midwinter (92 not out in about 250 minutes, 8 fours) hit his highest score in his 13 matches for Victoria and Bonnor (54 in about 128 minutes, 1 five and 5 fours) also exceeded the half-century "on a perfect wicket" (*Australasian*). Cooper and Palmer then swept away the early English batting before rain ended play on the second day at 4.20pm. It continued intermittently through the following day (Sunday) and had "played sad havoc with the turf" (*Age*) by the time play resumed on Monday. Palmer used the conditions to the optimum and bowled virtually unchanged through both innings to finish with 11 wickets for 86. Steel (76 in about 125 minutes, 5 fours) gave "one of the very finest displays ever witnessed in the colony . . . on one of the worst wickets ever seen" (*Age*) but was unable to prevent an innings defeat for his team. *VCA Report* incorrectly gives Eng (1) Bligh 2. Sources: *Wisden, VCA Report, The Age, The Argus, The Herald, The Australasian, The Leader.*

VICTORIA

P.S.McDonnell	c Bates b Barnes	6
†J.M.Blackham	run out (Barlow/Barnes)	1
G.J.Bonnor	c Tylecote b Barnes	54
H.J.H.Scott	c Tylecote b Barlow	29
T.P.Horan	b Barnes	37
W.E.Midwinter	not out	92
G.E.Palmer	c Steel b Barnes	2
E.Turner	c Barlow b Steel	18
H.F.Boyle	c Tylecote b Steel	4
F.G.McShane	b Bates	27
*W.H.Cooper	lbw b Barnes	1
Extras	(b9, lb4)	13
Total	(219.2 overs, in about 380 mins)	284

Hon. I.F.W.BLIGH'S ENGLISH XI

C.T.Studd	b Cooper	11	(2)	c Blackham b Palmer	3
†E.F.S.Tylecote	b Cooper	4	(7)	b Palmer	0
W.Bates	b Palmer	0		b Palmer	21
C.F.H.Leslie	lbw b Palmer	0		c Horan b Midwinter	9
A.G.Steel	b Cooper	11		b Palmer	76
W.W.Read	c Midwinter b Cooper	7		b Palmer	9
R.G.Barlow	not out	4	(1)	c McDonnell b Palmer	27
W.Barnes	run out (Boyle/Blackham)	11		c Blackham b Turner	2
G.F.Vernon	b Boyle	3		c & b Palmer	2
G.B.Studd	b Palmer	2		not out	0
*Hon. I.F.W.Bligh	b Palmer	0		st Blackham b Turner	2
Extras	(lb1, nb1)	2		(b4, nb1)	5
Total	(31.1 overs, in about 65 mins)	55		(109.0 overs, in about 185 mins)	156

ENGLAND XI	O	M	R	W	w,nb
Bates	37	21	52	1	-,-
Barnes	51.2	23	70	5	-,-
Steel	55	25	79	2	-,-
Barlow	25	11	34	1	-,-
Leslie	19	9	17	0	-,-
C.T.Studd	26	16	13	0	-,-
Read	6	3	6	0	-,-

VICTORIA	O	M	R	W	w,nb		O	M	R	W	w,nb
Cooper	13	5	29	4	-,1	(5)	9	3	11	0	-,-
Palmer	15.1	6	21	4	-,-		48	19	65	7	-,1
Boyle	3	1	3	1	-,-	(1)	21	7	29	0	-,-
McShane							4	2	8	0	-,-
Midwinter						(3)	15	5	17	1	-,-
Horan							3	2	3	0	-,-
Turner							9	1	18	2	-,-

FALL OF WICKETS

Wkt	VIC 1st	ENG 1st	ENG 2nd
1st	7	5	6
2nd	7	8	32
3rd	60	8	41
4th	113	25	133
5th	160	34	147
6th	166	34	147
7th	207	47	152
8th	221	50	154
9th	283	55	154
10th	284	55	156

VICTORIA v SOUTH AUSTRALIA

Played at East Melbourne Cricket Ground on March 24, 26, 27, 1883. (Timeless match)
Toss : South Australia. Result : VICTORIA WON BY AN INNINGS AND 98 RUNS.
Debuts: South Australia - W.F.Giffen, G.Watsford (both f/c).
12th Men: W.Bruce (Vic) and G.E.Craigie (SA).
Umpires: J.H.Denby and E.H.Elliott.
Attendances: 2500, 3000, 200.   Total: About 5700.   Receipts: £273.
Close of Play: 1st day Vic 2/13 (Horan 3, Blackham 0); 2nd day Vic 7/189 (Slight 44, Palmer 9).

Despite batting under the best conditions of the match on the first day, South Australia were dismissed for what remains their lowest first-class total. Drizzling rain set in at the start of the Victorian innings and shortened the first day's play. Heavier rain on the second day prevented play after 4.00pm and created favourable conditions for the bowlers on the final day. Palmer bowled unchanged throughout both South Australian innings, taking three wickets in four balls in the first innings (not a hat-trick as some sources reported). His victims, all in one over, were Jarvis, Richards and Hide, with a ball between the dismissals of Jarvis and Richards. George Craigie, South Australia's 12th man was destined never to make a first-class appearance; however his brother J.E.Craigie, represented the State in 1887-88. Some minor variations in the falls of wickets are recorded in other sources. Sources: *C.B.O'Reilly, Australian Cricketers Guide, VCA Report, The Age, The Argus, The Herald, The Australasian, The Leader.*

SOUTH AUSTRALIA

G.Giffen	b Palmer	1		b Boyle	19
J.Noel	b Boyle	18		run out (/Cooper)	12
†A.H.Jarvis	b Palmer	0		c Blackham b Palmer	6
T.O.Richards	b Palmer	0	(6)	lbw b Boyle	2
J.B.Hide	b Palmer	0	(4)	b Boyle	2
W.F.Giffen	c Palmer b Boyle	0	(7)	st Blackham b Palmer	8
J.F.King	run out (Palmer)	0	(5)	b Palmer	15
G.Watsford	c & b Boyle	2	(10)	b Palmer	0
*J.E.Gooden	b Boyle	0	(8)	c Horan b Boyle	9
W.Knill	b Palmer	1	(9)	not out	0
J.Quilty	not out	0		b Palmer	0
Extras	(nb1)	1		(b2, lb2, nb2)	6
Total	(42.1 overs, in about 85 mins)	23		(89.3 overs, in about 175 mins)	79

VICTORIA

P.S.McDonnell	b Hide	4
J.Rosser	b G.Giffen	4
T.P.Horan	run out (/Jarvis)	31
†J.M.Blackham	c Knill b G.Giffen	5
W.E.Midwinter	b G.Giffen	40
J.Slight	b Noel	44
H.J.H.Scott	c Jarvis b Quilty	26
H.F.Boyle	c Jarvis b King	10
G.E.Palmer	b G.Giffen	9
F.G.McShane	c Noel b G.Giffen	7
*W.H.Cooper	not out	4
Extras	(b8, lb7, nb1)	16
Total	(117.1 overs, in about 220 mins)	200

VICTORIA	O	M	R	W	w,nb	O	M	R	W	w,nb
Boyle	21.1	16	6	4	-,-	31	17	28	4	-,2
Palmer	21	16	16	5	-,1	44.3	26	28	5	-,-
Cooper						6	2	7	0	-,-
Scott						8	2	10	0	-,-

SOUTH AUSTRALIA	O	M	R	W	w,nb
G.Giffen	39.1	17	61	5	-,-
Hide	21	5	30	1	-,1
Noel	32	14	41	1	-,-
Quilty	13	0	33	1	-,-
King	12	6	19	1	-,-

	FALL OF WICKETS		
Wkt	SA 1st	VIC 1st	SA 2nd
1st	1	7	29
2nd	1	9	37
3rd	1	32	41
4th	1	75	43
5th	6	109	50
6th	20	157	64
7th	20	173	79
8th	20	189	79
9th	23	189	79
10th	23	200	79

1883-84 SEASON (5 MATCHES)

With no visiting team in Australia in 1883-84, the chief interest centred on the composition of the Fourth Australian team to tour England the following winter. Twelve players and a player-manager would be taken on the tour. The nucleus of the team - 10 players and the player-manager, George Alexander - had already been chosen by the time an Australian XI appeared against a Combined XI at Melbourne on January 1, 1884. The Australian captain W.L.Murdoch's score of 279 not out in this match was only the second score of over 200 in first-class cricket in Australia. Murdoch had also made the first, in 1881-82. Edwin Evans and F.R.Spofforth were both sought by the selectors to complete the Australian 12, however both men, and Evans in particular, were reluctant to announce their availability to tour. H.J.H.Scott, who became the 11th member, appeared in the second encounter for the Australian XI against a Combined XI at Sydney on February 15. George Giffen took all 10 wickets in the second innings of this match for the Australians - one of only two instances of 'all ten' in this country prior to the Second World War. Spofforth played for the Combined XI, and he finally agreed to join the party just before its departure.

Victoria defeated New South Wales by three wickets in the opening intercolonial match of the 1883-84 season. Tom Horan, who hit a chanceless century for Victoria, said in *The Australasian* that the side was 'perhaps the best Victorian team ever sent into the field'. H.J.H.Scott also hit a century for the home team and W.E.Midwinter captured 7 for 53 in the second innings on a deteriorating surface. Murdoch led the way for New South Wales by scoring 158 on the opening day.

New South Wales turned the tables in the return match at Sydney, in which the batting of A.C.Bannerman and Harry Moses in the second innings proved decisive. G.E.Palmer (11 for 140) for Victoria, and Evans (10 for 92) and T.W.Garrett (7 for 69) for New South Wales were outstanding with the ball.

Victoria met South Australia in Adelaide in the final first-class match of the season, and won a high-scoring affair after trailing on the first innings. Jim Trinnick, who scored 109 and 89, came within a whisker of becoming the first batsman to record a century in each innings in Australia. The feat was not performed until 1894-95.

Tasmania became the first Australian Colony to tour overseas when they arranged a tour of the South Island of New Zealand in early 1884. This was the first tour of New Zealand by an Australian team wherein first-class matches were played (the 1878 and 1880 Australian touring teams to England had previously played a series of non-first-class matches on their way to and from England respectively). Tasmania played seven matches, of which four are deemed to be first-class, drawing one and losing the other three. The team was comprised of : J.G.Davies (captain), E.J.K.Burn, E.H.Butler, G.H.Gatehouse, H.Hale, H.V.P.Harris, T.K.Kendall, R.G.Kirby, J.Mansfield, G.F.Read, R.H.Sams and W.L.Sidebottom. Burn, Gatehouse, Hale, Harris, Kirby, Mansfield, Sams and Sidebottom all made their first-class debuts, while Kendall (Victoria and Australia) made his Tasmanian debut. Kirby, Mansfield and Sams played their only first-class cricket on this tour.

Leading Aggregates

Batsmen	M	I	NO	Runs	HS	Ave.	Bowlers	Runs	Wkts	Ave.
W.L.Murdoch (NSW)	4	6	1	567	279*	113.40	G.E.Palmer (V)	508	29	17.51
P.S.McDonnell (V)	4	6	0	255	111	42.50	E.Evans (NSW)	306	18	17.00
T.P.Horan (V)	3	5	0	214	126	42.80	G.Giffen (A)	168	17	9.88
S.P.Jones (NSW)	4	7	0	206	88	29.42	T.W.Garrett (NSW)	313	16	19.56
J.Trinnick (V)	1	2	0	198	109	99.00	W.E.Midwinter (V)	212	11	19.27
H.J.H.Scott (V)	4	7	2	171	114*	34.20				

VICTORIA v NEW SOUTH WALES

Played at Melbourne Cricket Ground on December 26, 27, 28, 29, 31, 1883. (Timeless match)
Toss : New South Wales.   Result : VICTORIA WON BY THREE WICKETS.
Debuts: Victoria - P.M.Lewis (f/c).
12th Men: E.Turner (Vic) and   Armstrong (NSW).
Umpires: E.H.Elliott and J.Swift (see below).
Attendances: 12000, 7000, 5000, 5000, 4000.   Total: About 33,000.   Receipts: £1600.
Close of Play: 1st day NSW 4/278 (Evans 25, Garrett 3); 2nd day Vic 2/107 (Horan 37, Lewis 8); 3rd day Vic 5/352 (Scott 97,
     Walters 21); 4th day Vic (2) 0/1 (Boyle 0, McShane 0).

Armstrong was brought to Melbourne direct from the Cootamundra district of New South Wales on the recommendation of Murdoch. All his cricket had been played in that area where he had established a considerable reputation as a bowler. However he did not impress in the nets before the match, was excluded, and immediately returned to from whence he came, never to receive another call. Edwin Evans was absent after lunch on the second day due to receiving news of the death of his brother and did not bowl until the third day. J.J.C.Callachor, who was in Melbourne, substituted in his absence. J.W.Fletcher stood as umpire on the second day in the absence of Swift through illness. Victoria narrowly won a close-fought contest, batsmen of both sides dictating terms over the first three days and bowlers then gaining the ascendancy as the wicket crumbled over the last two days. Murdoch (158 in about 230 minutes, 8 fours), Horan (126 in about 330 minutes, 6 fours) and Scott (114 not out in about 325 minutes, 9 fours) hit centuries, Horan and Scott adding 161 for the fifth wicket in the Victorian first innings. Garrett (64 in about 120 minutes, 3 fours) batted well in the first innings, and in partnership with Evans, then performed the bulk of the bowling for his team in both innings. Palmer and Midwinter fulfilled a similar function for Victoria. Some sources incorrectly give NSW (2) Boyle 0/5. Some variations also appear in falls of wickets. Sources: *Cricket, Australian Cricketers Guide, The Age, The Argus, The Australasian.*

NEW SOUTH WALES

A.C.Bannerman	b Palmer	12		c & b Midwinter	34
*W.L.Murdoch	c & b Midwinter	158		b Palmer	22
S.P.Jones	c Walters b Horan	52		b Midwinter	4
H.Moses	b Palmer	18		c & b Midwinter	0
E.Evans	b Midwinter	33		c & b Midwinter	11
T.W.Garrett	c & Bonnor	64		st Blackham b Palmer	4
R.C.Allen	b Bonnor	27		b Palmer	0
T.Nunn	b Palmer	24		b Midwinter	24
A.P.Marr	c Walters b Palmer	0		c Bonnor b Midwinter	29
J.O.Cleeve	not out	8		b Midwinter	2
†R.Hall	b Palmer	0		not out	2
Extras	(b7, lb4, nb5)	16		(b5, lb1, w2, nb3)	11
Total	(260.2 overs, in about 430 mins)	412		(111.3 overs, in about 205 mins)	143

VICTORIA

P.S.McDonnell	c Cleeve b Garrett	15	(4)	c & b Evans	42
G.J.Bonnor	c Garrett b Jones	41	(7)	c Evans b Garrett	5
T.P.Horan	b Garrett	126		lbw b Garrett	21
P.M.Lewis	b Garrett	15	(9)	not out	7
W.E.Midwinter	c Murdoch b Evans	16	(8)	c Bannerman b Evans	10
H.J.H.Scott	not out	114	(5)	run out (Hall/Garrett)	12
F.H.Walters	b Evans	25			
*†J.M.Blackham	b Garrett	3	(6)	not out	12
G.E.Palmer	run out (Bannerman/Evans/Hall)	10			
F.G.McShane	lbw b Garrett	25	(2)	c Murdoch b Evans	17
H.F.Boyle	hit wkt b Garrett	1	(1)	c Nunn b Garrett	4
Extras	(b20, lb3, w1, nb5)	29		(b5, lb1)	6
Total	(302.0 overs, in about 505 mins)	420		(103.0 overs, in about 190 mins) (7 wkts)	136

VICTORIA	O	M	R	W	w,nb		O	M	R	W	w,nb				FALL OF WICKETS	
McShane	28	12	48	0	-,-	(6)	2	1	1	0	-,-			NSW	VIC	NSW	VIC
Palmer	90.2	32	130	5	-,3	(4)	49	21	56	3	-,2	Wkt	1st	1st	2nd	2nd
Boyle	23	16	38	0	-,-	(2)	3	2	3	0	-,-	1st	30	42	38	8
Horan	26	14	33	1	-,-	(3)	2	1	1	0	-,-	2nd	168	74	45	36
Scott	19	4	39	0	-,1							3rd	231	125	47	43
Midwinter	49	15	70	2	-,-	(5)	50.3	27	53	7	-,1	4th	260	148	62	97
Lewis	6	3	10	0	-,-							5th	299	309	70	98
Bonnor	19	5	28	2	-,1	(1)	5	0	18	0	2,-	6th	381	356	72	107
												7th	385	359	92	122
NEW SOUTH WALES	O	M	R	W	w,nb		O	M	R	W	w,nb	8th	386	376	123	-
Marr	24	12	21	0	-,-							9th	412	412	136	-
Cleeve	28	7	56	0	-,-							10th	412	420	143	-
Garrett	113.1	63	126	6	1,1	(1)	52	24	76	3	-,-					
Jones	35	13	67	1	-,2	(3)	1	0	6	0	-,-					
Nunn	4	2	2	0	-,-											
Allen	9	1	15	0	-,1											
Evans	77	38	83	2	-,1	(2)	50	28	48	3	-,-					
Bannerman	9	1	17	0	-,-											
Moses	3	1	4	0	-,-											

AUSTRALIAN XI v COMBINED XI

Played at Melbourne Cricket Ground on January 1, 2, 3, 1884. (Three-day match)
Toss : Australian XI.   Result : MATCH DRAWN.
Debuts: Nil.
12th Men: W.A.Tobin (Comb XI). No 12th man or emergency fieldsman named for Australian XI.
Umpires: E.H.Elliott and J.Phillips.
Attendances: 5000, 1500, 500.   Total: About 7000.   Receipts: No figures published.
Close of Play: 1st day Aust 3/328 (Murdoch 145, Bonnor 2); 2nd day Aust 9/619 (Murdoch 279, Boyle 40).

This match was the first in a program of nine (seven of which were against odds) played by the 1884 Australian XI prior to their departure for England in March. The Australian team comprised the ten players already chosen to tour, together with Alexander, who had been appointed manager. The Combined XI was weakened by the inability of E.Evans (death of brother) and T.W.Garrett to play. The game was originally scheduled for four days, to immediately follow the Victoria-New South Wales match. However, complications arose when the first match went into a fifth day, leaving the majority of the 15 players involved in both games unable to obtain further leave from their employers. Murdoch (279 not out in about 550 minutes, 17 fours) gave an early stumping chance off Noel but then proceeded to give "an exhibition of true, scientific cricket, elegant and vigorous in attack, graceful and impregnable in defence" (Tom Horan in *The Australasian*). His stands of 199 for the second wicket with McDonnell (111 in about 170 minutes, 2 fives and 5 fours), 105 for the third wicket with George Giffen (53 in about 95 minutes, 4 fours) and 93 for the seventh wicket with Alexander (50 in about 85 minutes, 6 fours) put the match beyond the reach of the Combined XI. W.Bruce and J.Lawlor fielded as substitutes for Bonnor and Cooper (both ill with dysentery). Turner kept wickets while Jarvis bowled on the first day. Sources: *Cricket, The Age, The Argus, The Herald, The Australasian, The Leader.*

AUSTRALIAN XI

P.S.McDonnell	c Giffen b Walters	111
A.C.Bannerman	c Jarvis b Bruce	11
*W.L.Murdoch	not out	279
G.Giffen	b McShane	53
G.J.Bonnor	run out (Scott/Jarvis)	2
W.E.Midwinter	lbw b Turner	19
†J.M.Blackham	b Turner	0
G.Alexander	b McShane	50
G.E.Palmer	b McShane	5
W.H.Cooper	b Jones	33
H.F.Boyle	b McShane	40
Extras	(b5, lb8, nb3)	16
Total	(339.1 overs, in about 569 mins)	619

COMBINED XI

J.Noel	c & b Midwinter	2
S.P.Jones	c Boyle b Palmer	30
*T.P.Horan	b Palmer	22
H.J.H.Scott	b Palmer	26
W.F.Giffen	b Palmer	15
†A.H.Jarvis	c Boyle b Giffen	19
P.M.Lewis	b Giffen	23
F.G.McShane	c Murdoch b Giffen	12
F.H.Walters	not out	13
E.Turner	b Giffen	0
W.Bruce	did not bat	
Extras	(b18, nb1)	19
Total	(157.0 overs, in about 265 mins) (9 wkts)	181

COMBINED XI	O	M	R	W	w,nb
Bruce	61	18	104	1	-,-
Noel	53	25	61	0	-,-
Turner	61	15	141	2	-,-
McShane	55.1	28	60	4	-,-
Jones	50	15	113	1	-,-
Scott	19	7	33	0	-,2
Horan	25	9	57	0	-,-
Walters	9	2	17	1	-,-
Jarvis	6	0	17	0	-,1

AUSTRALIAN XI	O	M	R	W	w,nb
Palmer	74	36	80	4	-,1
Midwinter	43	23	39	1	-,-
Giffen	36	24	40	4	-,-
Boyle	4	1	3	0	-,-

FALL OF WICKETS

	AUST	COMB
Wkt	1st	1st
1st	15	3
2nd	214	36
3rd	319	84
4th	329	95
5th	372	104
6th	374	147
7th	467	150
8th	489	181
9th	552	181
10th	619	-

NEW SOUTH WALES v VICTORIA

Played at Sydney Cricket Ground on February 8, 9, 11, 12, 1884. (Timeless match)
Toss : New South Wales.   Result : NEW SOUTH WALES WON BY 202 RUNS.
Debuts: Victoria - J.W.Trumble (f/c).
12th Men: H.C.S.Hiddleston (NSW) and W.H.Cooper (Vic).
Umpires: E.H.Elliott and J.Swift.
Attendances: 3000, 10000, 3000, 500.   Total: About 16,500.   Receipts: No figures published.
Close of Play: 1st day Vic 2/23 (Horan 8, Scott 3); 2nd day NSW (2) 3/168 (Moses 58, Bannerman 61); 3rd day Vic (2) 5/108
(Trumble 15, Palmer 4).

F.R.Spofforth was named in the New South Wales squad of thirteen and was expected to play, although C.T.B.Turner was asked to stand
by. When Spofforth did not appear and "no one had heard from him" (*SMH*), curiously Turner was also omitted. R.Bryant (the chosen
wicket-keeper) and Hiddleston were also left out, Nunn and Powell (a selector along with A.H.Gregory and H.H.Massie) were then
surprisingly included after not being in the original squad, with Murdoch to keep wickets. F.G.McShane was unavailable for Victoria and
Trapp was a late replacement for W.E.Midwinter, whose wife was ill. It was agreed beforehand "to play the match out on one wicket"
(*T & C Journal*). Bannerman (91 in about 215 minutes, 15 fours) and Moses (85 in about 190 minutes, 11 fours) added 165 for the fourth
wicket in the second innings to set up the New South Wales win. Palmer (11 for 140) and Evans (10 for 92) were the outstanding bowlers
for their respective teams in conditions that favoured batting for most of the game. Evans bowled unchanged throughout both Victorian
innings. Murdoch had the unusual experience (for him) of a first-ball dismissal in the second innings. *Cricket* has incorrect match dates,
NSW (1) omits c Lewis from Murdoch's dismissal; Vic (2) Evans 4/51. *VCA Report* incorrectly gives Vic (2) McDonnell 21, Scott 0.
Sources: *Cricket, VCA Report, Sydney Morning Herald, Town & Country Journal, Sydney Daily Telegraph*.

NEW SOUTH WALES

A.C.Bannerman	b Palmer	3	(2)	b Palmer	91
H.H.Massie	b Palmer	7	(1)	c Horan b Trumble	21
*†W.L.Murdoch	c Lewis b Trumble	25		b Trumble	0
S.P.Jones	b Palmer	6		c Blackham b Palmer	16
H.Moses	c Trumble b Palmer	43		c Trumble b Palmer	85
E.Evans	run out (/Blackham)	28		lbw b Palmer	23
A.H.Gregory	b Palmer	0	(9)	b Boyle	6
A.P.Marr	st Blackham b Horan	29	(7)	b Boyle	1
T.W.Garrett	c Bonnor b Trumble	6	(11)	b Palmer	1
T.Powell	not out	14	(8)	not out	9
T.Nunn	c Trumble b Palmer	1	(10)	c Palmer b Boyle	9
Extras	(b1, lb1, w2, nb3)	7		(b8, lb11, w1, nb7)	27
Total	(134.2 overs, in about 245 mins)	169		(159.3 overs, in about 315 mins)	289

VICTORIA

P.S.McDonnell	c & b Evans	6		st Murdoch b Evans	20
*†J.M.Blackham	c Bannerman b Evans	2	(8)	b Evans	5
T.P.Horan	c Marr b Evans	16		c Marr b Garrett	29
H.J.H.Scott	c Powell b Marr	9	(2)	c Gregory b Evans	1
G.J.Bonnor	c Murdoch b Garrett	29		b Garrett	15
V.B.Trapp	b Marr	8	(9)	not out	8
P.M.Lewis	b Evans	13	(6)	run out (/Murdoch)	7
H.F.Boyle	c Bannerman b Evans	1	(10)	c & b Garrett	13
G.E.Palmer	lbw b Garrett	9	(7)	b Evans	20
J.W.Trumble	not out	0	(4)	c Bannerman b Garrett	16
E.Turner	c Garrett b Evans	1		c Moses b Garrett	0
Extras	(b8)	8		(b17, lb3)	20
Total	(111.0 overs, in about 175 mins)	102		(98.0 overs, in about 165 mins)	154

VICTORIA	O	M	R	W	w,nb		O	M	R	W	w,nb		FALL OF WICKETS			
Palmer	61.2	28	72	6	-,3	(2)	54.3	30	68	5	-,3					
Trumble	53	28	64	2	2,-	(1)	31	10	81	2	1,-	Wkt	NSW	VIC	NSW	VIC
Turner	5	1	9	0	-,-	(6)	6	3	18	0	-,-		1st	1st	2nd	2nd
Horan	15	8	17	1	-,-		8	2	23	0	-,-	1st	10	7	30	1
Boyle							44	25	46	3	-,-	2nd	13	18	30	39
Scott						(3)	5	4	2	0	-,1	3rd	26	37	57	65
Bonnor							10	3	23	0	-,3	4th	61	37	222	92
Trapp							1	0	1	0	-,-	5th	93	58	252	99
												6th	93	79	253	111
												7th	141	80	258	124
NEW SOUTH WALES	O	M	R	W	w,nb		O	M	R	W	w,nb	8th	151	97	273	135
Evans	56	39	40	6	-,-		49	28	52	4	-,-	9th	157	101	288	154
Marr	36	19	45	2	-,-		10	4	22	0	-,-	10th	169	102	289	154
Garrett	19	13	9	2	-,-		39	21	60	5	-,-					

AUSTRALIAN XI v COMBINED XI

Played at Sydney Cricket Ground on February 15, 16, 18, 1884. (Four-day match)
Toss : Australian XI.   Result : AUSTRALIAN XI WON BY 9 WICKETS.
Debuts: Nil.
12th Men: G.Alexander (Aust XI). No 12th man or emergency named for Combined XI.
Umpires: J.W.Fletcher and J.Swift.
Attendances: 2000, 5000, 1000.   Total: About 8000.   Receipts: No figures published.
Close of Play: 1st day Aust 318 all out; 2nd day Comb (2) 4/52 (Moses 0).

Powell, Allen and Nunn replaced A.H.Gregory, H.C.S.Hiddleston and T.P.Horan (all unavailable) in the Combined team which comprised 10 players from New South Wales and one, Lewis, from Victoria. South Australians W.F.Giffen, A.H.Jarvis and J.Noel, who had appeared in the corresponding match in Melbourne in January, elected to remain in Adelaide to prepare for the forthcoming match against Victoria. McDonnell (61 out of 82 in about 75 minutes, 11 fours), Murdoch (83 in about 195 minutes, 14 fours) and Bonnor (67 in about 90 minutes, 2 fives and 9 fours) hit half-centuries on an opening day wicket that "was in grand order for batting" (*SMH*). On the second day, Jones (88 in about 165 minutes, 11 fours) fashioned an innings that was "perhaps the best seen on the ground for several seasons" (*T & C Journal*) but was unable to avert the follow-on. In the second innings, George Giffen became the first bowler to take all ten wickets in an innings in a first-class match in Australia. He bowled two consecutive overs by delivering the last over on the second day and the first over of the third. The same wicket was used throughout the game despite wear caused by the bowlers' foot marks. *Cricket* omits Comb (1) Allen c Boyle, and (2) Moses c sub. Sources: *Cricket, The Argus, The Leader, Sydney Morning Herald, Town & Country Journal*.

AUSTRALIAN XI

P.S.McDonnell	c Evans b Spofforth	61			
A.C.Bannerman	b Marr	1		not out	10
*W.L.Murdoch	c Allen b Spofforth	83			
G.Giffen	c Powell b Evans	1	(1)	b Spofforth	2
G.J.Bonnor	b Spofforth	67			
W.E.Midwinter	c Moses b Evans	46			
H.J.H.Scott	lbw b Marr	1	(3)	not out	8
†J.M.Blackham	b Marr	15			
G.E.Palmer	not out	24			
H.F.Boyle	c Lewis b Spofforth	0			
W.H.Cooper	c Massie b Evans	6			
Extras	(b11, lb1, nb1)	13			-
Total	(156.2 overs, in about 285 mins)	318	(8.3 overs, in about 12 mins) (1 wkt)		20

COMBINED XI

*H.H.Massie	c Scott b Palmer	20		c McDonnell b Giffen	29
R.C.Allen	c Boyle b Palmer	1	(5)	c Palmer b Giffen	0
S.P.Jones	b Palmer	88		c & b Giffen	10
H.Moses	b Midwinter	0		c sub (Alexander) b Giffen	14
†P.M.Lewis	c Boyle b Giffen	20	(7)	not out	19
E.Evans	c Boyle b Giffen	12		lbw b Giffen	2
A.P.Marr	c Palmer b Giffen	0	(8)	b Giffen	5
T.Powell	b Palmer	0	(10)	b Giffen	3
T.W.Garrett	not out	26	(2)	c Scott b Giffen	3
F.R.Spofforth	c Midwinter b Palmer	29	(9)	c Bannerman b Giffen	14
T.Nunn	b Palmer	10		c Blackham b Giffen	0
Extras	(b13, lb1, nb2)	16		(b9, w2, nb3)	14
Total	(118.3 overs, in about 225 mins)	222	(50.0 overs, in about 105 mins)		113

COMBINED XI	O	M	R	W	w,nb		O	M	R	W	w,nb
Evans	39.2	16	73	3	-,-	(2)	4	1	10	0	-,-
Marr	35	19	50	3	-,-						
Spofforth	53	18	101	4	-,1	(1)	4.3	2	10	1	-,-
Garrett	17	6	42	0	-,-						
Jones	10	4	21	0	-,-						
Allen	2	0	18	0	-,-						

AUSTRALIAN XI	O	M	R	W	w,nb		O	M	R	W	w,nb
Palmer	56.3	25	75	6	-,2		16	8	27	0	2,3
Midwinter	24	7	50	1	-,-						
Boyle	13	7	19	0	-,-		8	3	6	0	-,-
Giffen	25	8	62	3	-,-	(2)	26	16	66	10	-,-

FALL OF WICKETS

Wkt	AUST 1st	COM 1st	COM 2nd	AUST 2nd
1st	8	9	42	2
2nd	81	26	42	-
3rd	82	26	52	-
4th	180	105	52	-
5th	234	137	59	-
6th	235	145	80	-
7th	261	150	93	-
8th	299	157	107	-
9th	303	205	113	-
10th	318	222	113	-

SOUTH AUSTRALIA v VICTORIA

Played at Adelaide Oval on February 22, 23, 25, 26, 27, 1884. (Timeless match)
Toss : South Australia.   Result : VICTORIA WON BY FOUR WICKETS.
Debuts: South Australia - J.Brideson, H.C.Chittleborough, W.D.H.Claxton, W.G.Jones, J.U.Rundell, W.H.Watling (all f/c). Victoria -
    G.R.Browning, P.J.Deely, J.Harry, R.Hosie, J.Worrall (all f/c).
12th Men: A.W.Hogg (Vic manager). H.Blinman and J.Quilty named as SA emergencies.
Umpires: G.J.Hodges and I.A.Fisher.
Attendances: 2000, 3500, 1500, 1000, 1500.   Total: 9665.   Receipts: No figures published.
Close of Play: 1st day SA 6/122 (Jarvis 41, King 0); 2nd day Vic 1/125 (Trinnick 68, McShane 0); 3rd day SA (2) 2/169 (Giffen 76,
    Watling 48); 4th day Vic (2) 3/208 (Trinnick 87, Deely 38).

J.M.Blackham, H.F.Boyle, G.J.Bonnor, W.H.Cooper, P.S.McDonnell, W.E.Midwinter, G.E.Palmer and H.J.H.Scott (Victoria), and
G.Giffen (South Australia) were all unavailable as they were playing in a series of matches arranged as a prelude to the tour of England.
Chittleborough was a late replacement for J.Noel (work) in the South Australian team who had only eight players present when the game
began, W.F.Giffen, Jarvis and a third unidentified player arriving late. Rain on the first day allowed little more than an hour's play after the
luncheon adjournment but the wicket was unaffected and a high-scoring game ensued. Return travel arrangements for the Victorians
provided for them to leave on the evening of the fourth scheduled day but, as the game was undecided at that stage, only Browning, Slight
and E.D.Heather (VCA Secretary) left as planned. Trinnick (109 in about 205 minutes, 15 fours and 89 in about 225 minutes, 7 fours)
narrowly missed being the first player to score a century in each innings in first-class cricket in Australia. Jarvis (91 in about 160 minutes,
1 five and 9 fours), Claxton (72 in about 75 minutes, 4 fours and 73 in about 105 minutes, 1 five and 4 fours), Giffen (career-best 89 in
about 190 minutes, 1 six, 1 five and 5 fours), Harry (57 in about 105 minutes, 3 fours and 60 in about 135 minutes, 6 fours), Deely (69 in
about 105 minutes, 8 fours) and Morris (career-best 64 not out in about 115 minutes, 1 five and 4 fours) also batted well. Six-ball overs
were bowled. Sources: *C.B.O'Reilly, Adelaide Advertiser, Adelaide Observer, South Australian Register, South Australian Chronicle.*

SOUTH AUSTRALIA

T.O.Richards	run out (Browning/Harry)	4	(2)	lbw b Trinnick	0
J.U.Rundell	c McShane b Morris	15	(6)	b McShane	7
W.H.Watling	b McShane	24	(4)	b Worrall	54
*J.E.Gooden	b Morris	1	(7)	b Hosie	17
H.C.Chittleborough	b Morris	9		c & b McShane	7
†A.H.Jarvis	c & b Browning	91	(1)	b Worrall	40
W.F.Giffen	c Trinnick b Mackay	20	(3)	b Worrall	89
J.F.King	run out (Slight/Harry)	29	(10)	c & b Morris	0
J.Brideson	c Hosie b Morris	52	(8)	b McShane	0
W.D.H.Claxton	b Browning	72	(9)	st Harry b Worrall	73
W.G.Jones	not out	3		not out	26
Extras	(b9, lb5)	14		(b4, lb2)	6
Total	(127.0 overs, in about 320 mins)	334		(119.0 overs, in about 315 mins)	319

VICTORIA

J.Slight	run out (/King)	53		b Claxton	37
J.Trinnick	c Chittleborough b Claxton	109		c Giffen b Claxton	89
*F.G.McShane	run out (Chittleborough/Jarvis)	9	(4)	c Richards b Claxton	26
S.Morris	b Jones	4	(7)	not out	64
P.J.Deely	run out (Watling/Jarvis)	9		st Jarvis b Jones	69
J.Lawlor	c King b Rundell	0			
†J.Harry	b King	57	(6)	b Claxton	60
J.Worrall	b Rundell	11			
G.R.Browning	lbw b Jones	5	(3)	c Richards b Claxton	13
G.Mackay	c Jarvis b Richards	10			
R.Hosie	not out	5	(8)	not out	1
Extras	(b4, lb9)	13		(b9, nb1)	10
Total	(108.5 overs, in about 280 mins)	285		(133.3 overs, in about 350 mins) (6 wkts)	369

VICTORIA	O	M	R	W	w,nb		O	M	R	W	w,nb
McShane	28	8	68	1	-,-	(5)	28	8	61	3	-,-
Morris	40	11	82	4	-,-	(1)	17	1	54	1	-,-
Worrall	25	6	63	0	-,-		37	7	93	4	-,-
Lawlor	4	1	13	0	-,-	(9)	2	0	13	0	-,-
Browning	13	2	48	2	-,-	(6)	7	0	20	0	-,-
Mackay	13	6	32	1	-,-	(7)	8	3	6	0	-,-
Hosie	4	1	14	0	-,-	(4)	13	3	37	1	-,-
Trinnick						(2)	4	1	18	1	-,-
Deely						(8)	3	0	6	0	-,-
Slight							3	1	5	0	-,-

SOUTH AUSTRALIA	O	M	R	W	w,nb	O	M	R	W	w,nb
Jones	38	8	106	2	-,-	23	6	66	1	-,-
Brideson	17	6	39	0	-,-	11	2	36	0	-,-
Rundell	26	13	39	2	-,-	16	6	40	0	-,1
Claxton	12	0	55	1	-,-	51.3	10	116	5	-,-
Richards	11	4	28	1	-,-	10	5	38	0	-,-
King	4.5	2	5	1	-,-	11	1	23	0	-,-
Jarvis						6	1	17	0	-,-
Giffen						3	0	15	0	-,-
Chittleborough						2	0	8	0	-,-

	FALL OF WICKETS			
	SA	VIC	SA	VIC
Wkt	1st	1st	2nd	2nd
1st	4	123	8	72
2nd	23	138	58	90
3rd	27	154	187	136
4th	55	170	192	222
5th	55	172	201	247
6th	114	208	206	364
7th	205	221	206	-
8th	205	230	253	-
9th	320	256	256	-
10th	334	285	319	-

81

1884-85 SEASON (11 MATCHES)

Ill-feeling between Australian and English cricketers over the issue of gatemoney led to a season of turmoil in 1884-85. The Australians had returned from their tour of England embittered at the actions of three English professionals, Shrewsbury, Barnes and Flowers, who had refused to play for the Players against the Australians at Sheffield. These players were included in the English touring party to Australia. Worse, Shrewsbury was captain and co-organiser of the tour. The Australians, with the exception of Spofforth who was injured, took their revenge by refusing to represent their Colonies in the tour matches against the Englishmen prior to the internationals. The Australians followed up by demanding 50 percent of the gatemoney from the First Test of the series - the first to be played at Adelaide. This was knocked back, but the SACA guaranteed both teams a flat £450. The Test went ahead and the SACA lost heavily. In Melbourne, the VCA took a tougher stance and refused the Australians' financial demands. The Test XI resigned and a completely new team was chosen for the Second Test. The VCA banned the 1884 Australians from appearing in any matches controlled by the association. This was not supported by the NSWCA. The Press sided against the Australians and accused them of 'putting money before nation'. Murdoch announced his retirement and turned to his law practice, and although some of the rebels relented as the season wore on, the Australian XI was never fully representative after the First Test.

The English team - the eighth to visit Australia and the second to be privately promoted by Shaw, Shrewsbury and Lillywhite - won the First, Second and Fifth Tests. The presence of Spofforth, returning from injury, saw Australia win the third and fourth matches. England chose the same XI for all five Tests, whereas Australia used no fewer than 28 players. The Englishmen contested 33 matches during their five-month tour, of which only eight were given first-class status, the remainder involving odds. Of these, six were won and two lost.

New South Wales met Victoria twice, as had been the tradition since 1874-75, and each team won their home match. George Bonnor created a unique record by appearing for both sides in the one season. His suspension by the VCA over his part in the 1884 Australians' dispute led him to move north, and the New South Wales selectors did not hesitate to include him against Victoria upon the late withdrawal of Edwin Evans. He was on the winning side in both matches.

South Australia defeated a seriously undermanned Victorian XI at Melbourne in the remaining first-class fixture in January. George Giffen was out to the first ball of the match but left his usual mark by taking 10 wickets and scoring 73 in the second innings.

Summing up the season in *The Australasian* 'Felix' commented that the game had come under 'a deep and lasting shadow, which cast a universal gloom upon our manly game' - a reflection of the general community feeling.

Leading Aggregates

Batsmen	M	I	NO	Runs	HS	Ave.	Bowlers	Runs	Wkts	Ave.
W.Barnes (E)	8	13	1	520	134	43.33	R.Peel (E)	673	35	19.22
A.Shrewsbury (E)	8	14	3	440	105*	40.00	W.Attewell (E)	428	28	15.28
W.Bates (E)	8	12	0	363	68	30.25	W.Barnes (E)	344	26	13.23
S.P.Jones (NSW)	8	16	1	357	72	23.80	F.R.Spofforth (NSW)	469	25	18.76
J.W.Trumble (V)	7	12	1	340	87	30.90	W.Flowers (E)	332	22	15.09
P.S.McDonnell (V)	3	5	0	311	124	62.20	G.E.Palmer (V)	298	21	14.19
T.P.Horan (V)	7	13	1	295	63	24.58	G.Giffen (SA)	484	21	23.04
G.J.Bonnor (V, NSW)	5	8	0	274	128	34.25	G.Ulyett (E)	361	20	18.05
A.C.Bannerman (NSW)	6	11	1	260	96*	26.00	W.Bruce (V)	507	20	25.35

VICTORIA v A.SHAW'S ENGLAND XI

Played at Melbourne Cricket Ground on November 14, 15, 17, 18, 1884. (Timeless match)
Toss : England XI.   Result : A.SHAW'S ENGLAND XI WON BY 118 RUNS.
Debuts: Victoria - J.McIlwraith, W.R.Robertson (both f/c).
12th Men: J.S.Swift (Vic). No 12th named for England XI; Lillywhite umpired.
Umpires: E.H.Elliott and J.Lillywhite.
Attendances: 1500, 5000, 2000, 1500.   Total: About 10,000.   Receipts: No figures published.
Close of Play: 1st day Eng 6/168 (Barnes 61, Briggs 8); 2nd day Vic 6/118 (Walters 26, Smith 2); 3rd day Eng (2) 9/130 (Barnes 37).

Victoria were without J.Slight (unavailable) and their Australian XI representatives, J.M.Blackham, G.J.Bonnor, H.F.Boyle, W.H.Cooper, P.S.McDonnell, G.E.Palmer and H.J.H.Scott who all declined to play. In addition McIlwraith was brought in as a late replacement for T.U.Groube (business commitments). Unsettled weather caused several interruptions through rain and bad light on each of the first three days. The wicket was affected to various degrees during this time but "was in first-class condition" (*Australasian*) on the final day when sunny conditions prevailed and it was not held responsible for the Victorian second innings capitulation. Shrewsbury (80 in about 160 minutes, 6 fours) and Barnes (61 in about 165 minutes, 4 fours and 46 in about 135 minutes, 3 fours) "showed capital cricket" (*Australasian*) when the wicket was at its most difficult. They added 129 for the third wicket on the opening day after Scotton had been bowled in the third over of the game. Flowers gave a fine exhibition of accurate offspin on the last day to bowl the visitors to a comfortable win. *VCA Report* incorrectly gives Eng (1) Shrewsbury 0, Bruce 49.2 overs, omits Horan 0/0; Vic (1) Peel 34 maidens. Sources: *Wisden, VCA Report, The Age, The Argus, The Herald, The Australasian, The Leader.*

A.SHAW'S ENGLAND XI

W.H.Scotton	b Bruce	0	c Bruce b Robertson		19
*A.Shrewsbury	st Lewis b Robertson	80	b Robertson		26
G.Ulyett	c Trinnick b Bruce	7	c McShane b Bruce		21
W.Barnes	b Trumble	61	run out (Robertson/Lewis)		46
W.Flowers	c Morris b Bruce	0	b Robertson		1
W.Bates	c Smith b Robertson	6	st Lewis b Bruce		2
J.M.Read	b Robertson	3	st Lewis b Robertson		10
J.Briggs	c Lewis b Trumble	33	c Bruce b Horan		5
W.Attewell	c & b Bruce	0	c McIlwraith b Horan		6
R.Peel	b Trumble	6	not out		9
†J.Hunter	not out	1	c & b Robertson		1
Extras	(b2, lb3)	5	(b2, lb2)		4
Total	(118.1 overs, in about 235 mins)	202	(97.1 overs, in about 200 mins)		150

VICTORIA

W.Bruce	b Ulyett	7	(6) c Shrewsbury b Flowers	5
J.Trinnick	b Barnes	5	(4) c Peel b Flowers	0
*T.P.Horan	b Peel	37	c Shrewsbury b Flowers	5
†P.M.Lewis	b Ulyett	0	(9) b Flowers	7
J.W.Trumble	b Peel	20	(7) b Flowers	18
F.H.Walters	st Hunter b Attewell	32	(5) b Flowers	0
F.G.McShane	c Barnes b Attewell	21	(8) b Flowers	7
G.E.Smith	b Peel	18	(10) b Flowers	3
J.McIlwraith	c Shrewsbury b Peel	2	(1) run out (Briggs/Peel)	0
S.Morris	c Peel b Attewell	3	(11) not out	2
W.R.Robertson	not out	0	(2) st Hunter b Peel	33
Extras	(b1)	1	(b4, lb3, nb1)	8
Total	(181.1 overs, in about 260 mins)	146	(131.3 overs, in about 195 mins)	88

VICTORIA	O	M	R	W	w,nb		O	M	R	W	w,nb
Bruce	48	15	88	4	-,-	(2)	22	6	43	2	-,-
Trumble	25.1	9	37	3	,	(1)	22	13	22	0	-,-
Horan	3	3	0	0	-,-	(5)	5	1	11	2	-,-
Morris	6	0	12	0	-,-	(6)	7	1	13	0	-,-
McShane	18	9	24	0	-,-	(4)	7	2	11	0	-,-
Robertson	18	9	36	3	-,-	(3)	34.1	13	46	5	-,-

ENGLAND XI	O	M	R	W	w,nb		O	M	R	W	w,nb
Attewell	51	35	32	3	-,-	(4)	18	13	9	0	-,-
Peel	59.3	31	46	4	-,-		30	16	26	1	-,-
Ulyett	27.2	11	40	2	-,-	(1)	22	16	10	0	-,-
Barnes	20	13	14	1	-,-	(5)	17	14	4	0	-,1
Bates	23	16	13	0	-,-						
Flowers						(3)	44.3	26	31	8	-,-

FALL OF WICKETS				
	ENG	VIC	ENG	VIC
Wkt	1st	1st	2nd	2nd
1st	0	12	41	4
2nd	12	12	56	13
3rd	141	12	80	15
4th	142	67	85	15
5th	149	72	92	25
6th	152	110	117	61
7th	176	137	122	69
8th	177	141	130	78
9th	197	144	149	83
10th	202	146	150	88

NEW SOUTH WALES v A.SHAW'S ENGLAND XI

Played at Sydney Cricket Ground on November 21, 22, 24, 1884. (Timeless match)
Toss : New South Wales.   Result : A.SHAW'S ENGLAND XI WON BY FOUR WICKETS.
Debuts: Nil.
12th Men: A.P.Marr (NSW). No 12th named for England XI.
Umpires: A.Shaw and J.Swift.
Attendances: 5000, 15000, 7000.   Total: About 27,000.   Receipts: No figures published.
Close of Play: 1st day NSW 5/154 (Allen 6, Hiddleston 0); 2nd day NSW (2) 3/27 (Evans 3).

New South Wales were without F.R.Spofforth, not yet returned from the Australian tour of England, as well as A.C.Bannerman and W.L.Murdoch, who had both refused to play because of an on-going dispute over distribution and share of gate money with the English team. It was agreed beforehand that the match would be played on two wickets, "in order that too much advantage should not be gained by the side winning the toss" (*SMH*). Massie was dismissed in the third over before Jones (72 in about 195 minutes, 10 fours) and Moses (49 in about 185 minutes, 4 fours) added 121 for the second wicket, the only time in the match that the bat had supremacy over the ball. Heavy overnight rain "had saturated the turf considerably, and consequently the ball hung somewhat" (*SMH*). Thereafter batting became progressively more difficult. Shrewsbury was out to the second ball of the English first innings and both Barnes and Read suffered first ball dismissals. New South Wales lost Jones, Moses (first ball) and Allen in their second innings in poor light late on the second day. Hiddleston (0) also dislocated a finger at this time when struck by a ball from Attewell and was forced to retire at 2/9. He resumed on the following day at 9/43. Attewell (8/37) and Barnes (6/34) utilised the conditions to the full, although the wicket was not considered to blame for the meagre New South Wales second innings. Sources: *Wisden, The Australasian, Sydney Morning Herald, Town & Country Journal, Sydney Daily Telegraph.*

NEW SOUTH WALES

*H.H.Massie	c Scotton b Flowers	0	(6)	b Attewell	5
S.P.Jones	c Hunter b Peel	72	(1)	b Ulyett	22
H.Moses	c Barnes b Bates	49		lbw b Attewell	0
R.C.Allen	c & b Attewell	24	(2)	c Barnes b Attewell	1
C.T.B.Turner	c Bates b Peel	1	(9)	b Barnes	0
C.Bannerman	c Barnes b Flowers	25	(7)	b Barnes	9
H.C.S.Hiddleston	c Shrewsbury b Attewell	10	(4)	not out	0
E.Evans	c Scotton b Barnes	0	(5)	b Attewell	3
T.W.Garrett	c Ulyett b Attewell	2	(8)	b Attewell	0
†R.Bryant	not out	0		c Shrewsbury b Barnes	0
F.Downes	b Briggs b Barnes	0		c Hunter b Barnes	0
Extras	(w1)	1		(b3, lb1)	4
Total	(228.2 overs, in about 340 mins)	184		(59.1 overs, in about 105 mins)	44

A.SHAW'S ENGLAND XI

*A.Shrewsbury	c Evans b Downes	0	b Garrett	25
W.H.Scotton	c Evans b Downes	13	b Garrett	19
G.Ulyett	b Garrett	5	b Downes	5
W.Barnes	b Garrett	0	run out (Bannerman/Bryant)	11
W.Flowers	c Turner b Garrett	19	c Turner b Evans	15
W.Bates	b Garrett	32	c & b Evans	33
J.M.Read	c & b Downes	0	not out	4
J.Briggs	b Downes	0	not out	0
W.Attewell	run out (Garrett)	17		
R.Peel	not out	21		
†J.Hunter	b Evans	2		
Extras	(b1)	1	(b6, w1)	7
Total	(63.0 overs, in about 105 mins)	110	(95.0 overs, in about 135 mins) (6 wkts)	119

ENGLAND XI	O	M	R	W	w,nb		O	M	R	W	w,nb
Flowers	56	39	37	2	-,-						
Peel	76	46	70	2	1,-		21	10	20	0	-,-
Ulyett	11	7	9	0	-,-		2	2	0	1	-,-
Attewell	31	22	18	3	-,-	(1)	30	19	19	5	-,-
Barnes	32.2	19	33	2	-,-	(4)	6.1	5	1	4	-,-
Bates	22	13	16	1	-,-						

NEW SOUTH WALES	O	M	R	W	w,nb		O	M	R	W	w,nb
Downes	26	9	49	4	-,-		26	10	46	1	1,-
Garrett	31	12	50	4	-,-		48	30	30	2	-,-
Evans	6	2	10	1	-,-		21	8	36	2	-,-

FALL OF WICKETS

Wkt	NSW 1st	ENG 1st	NSW 2nd	ENG 2nd
1st	0	0	9	42
2nd	121	9	9	49
3rd	121	9	27	56
4th	122	33	27	74
5th	154	43	40	112
6th	178	43	40	118
7th	181	44	41	-
8th	183	81	43	-
9th	184	99	43	-
10th	184	110	44	-

AUSTRALIA v ENGLAND (1st Test)

Played at Adelaide Oval on December 12, 13, 15, 16, 1884. (Timeless match)
Toss : Australia.   Result : ENGLAND WON BY EIGHT WICKETS.
Debuts: England - W.Attewell, J.Briggs, W.Flowers, J.Hunter, R.Peel (all Test).
12th Men: None named.
Umpires: N.Cole and I.A.Fisher.
Attendances: 7000, 8000+, 2500, 1000.   Total: About 19,000.   Receipts: £792.
Close of Play: 1st day Aust 243 all out; 2nd day Eng 2/233 (Scotton 71, Barnes 86); 3rd day Aust (2) 4/152 (Giffen 43, Cooper 3).

Adelaide's first Test match was organised by the secretary of the SACA, John Creswell, notwithstanding several difficulties. Firstly, the Englishmen only agreed when the Association offered to stand any losses and guaranteed a return on the match. Secondly, the Australian XI - which had not yet disbanded following the tour of England - were in dispute with the Englishmen over their share of the gate money. The sides finally settled on £450 each. Further problems arose with the appointment of umpires. Murdoch objected to J.Lillywhite standing for the Englishmen and two locals, I.A.Fisher and W.Travers were named. However, Travers was replaced before the match by Cole - a fact which has not been noted in previous reference works. Two local players acted as substitute for Bannerman, who badly split a finger early on the second day in fielding a drive by Ulyett. T.O.Richards fielded at first but F.Cornish replaced him for the third day. Shrewsbury substituted early on the third day until Cornish arrived. F.R.Spofforth (family bereavement) was unavailable for Australia, and Midwinter (congestion of the lungs) was replaced in the eleven by Alexander. McDonnell topscored in each innings for Australia with 124 (in about 210 minutes, 9 fours) and 83 (in about 150 minutes, 6 fours); had Giffen paid more attention to his call for an easy run, McDonnell may well have become the first batsman to score centuries in each innings of an Australian first-class match. Scotton (82 in about 360 minutes, 2 fours) and Barnes (134 in about 300 minutes, 7 fours) endured a tricky pitch early on the third day to take their stand to 175 for England's third wicket, which proved decisive. A dust-storm held up play for a while on the second afternoon. More recent sources incorrectly give Aust (2) 6/171, 7/182, 8/191. Sources: *Wisden, The Australasian, Adelaide Advertiser, South Australian Register.*

AUSTRALIA

A.C.Bannerman	lbw b Peel	2		absent hurt	-
P.S.McDonnell	b Attewell	124		run out	83
*W.L.Murdoch	c Hunter b Peel	5		b Peel	7
H.J.H.Scott	b Peel	19	(5)	lbw b Peel	1
†J.M.Blackham	c Attewell b Bates	66	(1)	b Peel	11
G.Giffen	b Bates	4	(4)	c Shrewsbury b Peel	47
G.J.Bonnor	c Read b Bates	4		c Peel b Barnes	19
G.E.Palmer	c Shrewsbury b Bates	6		b Barnes	0
H.F.Boyle	c Hunter b Bates	1	(10)	not out	0
G.Alexander	run out (Flowers/Hunter)	3	(9)	st Hunter b Peel	10
W.H.Cooper	not out	0	(6)	c Shrewsbury b Barnes	6
Extras	(b7, w2)	9		(b7)	7
Total	(149.1 overs, in about 280 mins)	243		(116.1 overs, in about 220 mins)	191

ENGLAND

W.H.Scotton	st Blackham b Giffen	82	(2)	c Scott b Boyle	2
*A.Shrewsbury	b Boyle	0	(3)	not out	26
G.Ulyett	c Alexander b Boyle	68			
W.Barnes	b Palmer	134		not out	28
W.Bates	c Giffen b Palmer	18			
W.Flowers	lbw b Palmer	15	(1)	c Scott b Palmer	7
J.M.Read	c & b Giffen	14			
J.Briggs	c Blackham b Palmer	1			
W.Attewell	not out	12			
R.Peel	b Palmer	4			
†J.Hunter	run out (sub F.Cornish/Blackham)	1			
Extras	(b18, lb1, nb1)	20		(b4)	4
Total	(243.2 overs, in about 450 mins)	369		(31.0 overs, in about 60 mins) (2 wkts)	67

ENGLAND	O	M	R	W	w,nb		O	M	R	W	w,nb
Attewell	50	23	48	1	-,-	(4)	18	10	26	0	-,-
Peel	41	15	68	3	-,-	(1)	40.1	15	51	5	-,-
Ulyett	10	3	23	0	-,-	(6)	2	1	3	0	-,-
Flowers	10	1	27	0	-,-	(5)	16	4	27	0	-,-
Barnes	14	2	37	0	-,-	(3)	31	10	51	3	,
Bates	24.1	10	31	5	2,-	(2)	9	3	26	0	-,-

AUSTRALIA	O	M	R	W	w,nb		O	M	R	W	w,nb
Boyle	63	25	95	2	-,-	(2)	9	3	21	1	-,-
Giffen	56.2	26	80	2	-,-	(3)	6	0	19	0	-,-
Cooper	18	4	26	0	-,-						
Bonnor	16	10	23	0	-,-						
Palmer	73	37	81	5	-,1	(1)	16	5	23	1	-,-
McDonnell	3	0	11	0	-,-						
Scott	4	1	9	0	-,-						
Alexander	10	3	24	0	-,-						

FALL OF WICKETS

	AUST	ENG	AUST	ENG
Wkt	1st	1st	2nd	2nd
1st	33	11	28	8
2nd	47	107	56	14
3rd	95	282	125	-
4th	190	306	139	-
5th	224	325	160	-
6th	227	344	160	-
7th	233	349	171	-
8th	239	349	182	-
9th	242	361	191	-
10th	243	369	-	-

VICTORIA v NEW SOUTH WALES

Played at Melbourne Cricket Ground on December 26, 27, 29, 30, 1884. (Timeless match)
Toss : New South Wales.   Result : VICTORIA WON BY AN INNINGS AND 5 RUNS.
Debuts: New South Wales - W.J.O'Hanlon, R.J.Pope (both f/c).
12th Men: S.Morris (Vic). R.C.Allen and J.Baxter were omitted from the NSW 13 before the match.
Umpires: E.H.Elliott and J.Swift (see below).
Attendances: 7000, 9000, 5000, 1500.   Total: About 22,500.   Receipts: £1053.
Close of Play: 1st day NSW 5/277 (C.Bannerman 6); 2nd day Vic 1/143 (Scott 53, Trumble 6); 3rd day Vic 7/423 (Bruce 29, Palmer 6).

E.Evans and F.R.Spofforth (injured foot) were both unavailable for New South Wales. Victoria included McShane in place of Midwinter, who was also unavailable. J.W.Fletcher umpired with Elliott for the first few overs of the match due to the late arrival of Swift. A.C.Bannerman (51 in about 145 minutes, 2 fours) and Jones (59 in about 135 minutes, 5 fours) gave New South Wales a sound start with a century opening stand. Murdoch (97 in about 145 minutes, 8 fours) "played that masterly, scientific game for which he has for years been noted" (*Australasian*) and Marr (69 in about 135 minutes, 7 fours) added valuable runs in the late order. Scott (58 in about 160 minutes, 5 fours) and McDonnell (81 in about 105 minutes, 8 fours) led the Victorian reply with an opening partnership of 134, on which Trumble (87 in about 225 minutes, 1 four) and Blackham built. Blackham scored his only first-class century in a career spanning 21 seasons; his innings included 6 fours, 7 threes, 18 twos and 28 singles. His wicket was also the only one captured by Moses at first-class level in a lengthy career. The New South Wales collapse in the second innings came as a surprise, Palmer and Bruce exploiting the worn pitch. *Cricket* incorrectly gives NSW (1) Murdoch 98, Hiddleston 7, Downes 10, extra 19, Bonnor 0/28. Sources: *Cricket, VCA Report, The Age, The Argus, The Herald, The Australasian, The Leader.*

NEW SOUTH WALES

A.C.Bannerman	c Scott b Palmer	51		b Palmer	12
S.P.Jones	c Bonnor b Palmer	59		b Palmer	6
*W.L.Murdoch	c Blackham b Palmer	97		b Bruce	11
H.Moses	c Scott b Palmer	2		b Palmer	10
R.J.Pope	st Blackham b Bruce	47		b Palmer	8
C.Bannerman	c Palmer b Trumble	37		c & b Palmer	2
T.W.Garrett	c Palmer b Bruce	3	(9)	c Horan b Bruce	0
H.C.S.Hiddleston	lbw b Bruce	1		c Palmer b Bruce	5
A.P.Marr	c Bonnor b Palmer	69	(7)	c Walters b Palmer	12
†W.J.O'Hanlon	c Bonnor b Trumble	1	(11)	b Bruce	0
F.Downes	not out	9	(10)	not out	4
Extras	(b17, lb4, w1, nb5)	27		(b4)	4
Total	(265.0 overs, 423 mins)	403		(54.1 overs, 97 mins)	74

VICTORIA

H.J.H.Scott	b Downes	58
P.S.McDonnell	c Hiddleston b Marr	81
J.W.Trumble	run out (/O'Hanlon)	87
T.P.Horan	b Garrett	24
G.J.Bonnor	c Jones b Downes	12
*†J.M.Blackham	b Moses	109
F.H.Walters	run out (Pope/O'Hanlon)	5
W.Bruce	b Marr	41
G.E.Palmer	b Marr	24
F.G.McShane	b Downes	20
W.R.Robertson	not out	1
Extras	(b9, lb8, w1, nb2)	20
Total	(282.1 overs, 490 mins)	482

VICTORIA	O	M	R	W	w,nb		O	M	R	W	w,nb
Bruce	60	25	90	3	-,-	(3)	18.1	10	30	4	-,-
Palmer	83	49	101	5	-,4		27	15	26	6	-,-
Trumble	37	20	37	2	1,-						
Robertson	34	17	46	0	-,-	(1)	9	4	14	0	-,-
Bonnor	13	4	20	0	-,1						
McShane	17	4	43	0	-,-						
Horan	16	5	30	0	-,-						
Scott	5	1	9	0	-,-						

NEW SOUTH WALES	O	M	R	W	w,nb
Garrett	74.2	32	122	1	-,-
Downes	78.3	32	138	3	1,1
Moses	11	3	19	1	-,-
C.Bannerman	25	8	36	0	-,-
Jones	19	8	38	0	-,-
Marr	58	28	75	3	-,1
Hiddleston	4	0	10	0	-,-
A.C.Bannerman	12	4	24	0	-,-

FALL OF WICKETS

Wkt	NSW 1st	VIC 1st	NSW 2nd
1st	113	134	10
2nd	120	160	29
3rd	126	205	39
4th	237	218	40
5th	277	348	48
6th	282	371	53
7th	285	399	70
8th	340	454	70
9th	342	461	70
10th	403	482	74

AUSTRALIA v ENGLAND (2nd Test)

Played at Melbourne Cricket Ground on January 1, 2, 3, 5, 1885. (Timeless match)
Toss : England.   Result : ENGLAND WON BY TEN WICKETS.
Debuts: Australia - W.Bruce, A.H.Jarvis, A.P.Marr, S.Morris, H.A.Musgrove, R.J.Pope, W.R.Robertson. J.W.Trumble, J.Worrall
   (all Test).
12th Men: J.E.Barrett, T.U.Groube & J.Slight (Aust emergencies) and A.Shaw (Eng).
Umpires: E.H.Elliott and J.Lillywhite.
Attendances: 11000, 5000, 6000, 400.   Total: About 22,400.   Receipts: No figures published.
Close of Play: 1st day Eng 9/303 (Briggs 65); 2nd day Aust 3/151 (Trumble 41, Jarvis 15); 3rd day Aust (2) 2/66 (Bruce 41).

The dispute over distribution of gate receipts between the Englishmen and Murdoch's Australians peaked in the lead-up to this match. The Australians refused to play en masse when their demand for a 50 percent share of the gate was denied. The VCA gave A.G.Major, selector of Victorian teams, the onerous task of picking a completely new Australian side. His job was made doubly difficult with the unavailability of F.R.Spofforth (injured), H.Moses and F.H.Walters (both for business reasons) and W.F.Giffen, who declined to travel from Adelaide, probably under pressure from his brother, George, one of the rebels. The eventual side included no fewer than nine debutants, five of whom - Marr, Morris, Musgrove, Pope and Robertson - were never chosen again. Morris was the first Tasmanian, and also the first black man (he was born in Hobart of West Indian parents) to play Test cricket. Shrewsbury (72 in about 180 minutes, 6 fours) and Barnes (58 in about 125 minutes, 3 fours) added 116 for the second wicket on the opening day. Briggs registered his sole Test century, 121 in about 150 minutes, which was comprised of 16 fours, 8 threes, 11 twos and 11 singles. He added 98 with Hunter for the tenth wicket. Horan (63 in about 165 minutes, 3 fours), Trumble (59 in about 210 minutes, 2 fours) and Jarvis (82 in about 220 minutes, 2 fours) fought hard to keep Australia in the game but lacked support. Forced to follow on with the wicket worn, their fate was sealed.
Sources: *Wisden, The Age, The Argus, The Herald, The Australasian, The Leader.*

ENGLAND

W.H.Scotton	b Bruce	13	not out	7
*A.Shrewsbury	c Worrall b Morris	72	not out	0
W.Barnes	b Morris	58		
W.Bates	b Bruce	35		
W.Flowers	c Worrall b Bruce	5		
J.M.Read	b Jones	3		
J.Briggs	c Horan b Jones	121		
G.Ulyett	b Jones	0		
W.Attewell	c Jones b Worrall	30		
R.Peel	b Jones	5		
†J.Hunter	not out	39		
Extras	(b7, lb12, nb1)	20		-
Total	(216.2 overs, 346 mins)	401	(1.1 overs, 5 mins) (0 wkts)	7

AUSTRALIA

S.P.Jones	lbw b Peel	19		b Ulyett	9
S.Morris	lbw b Attewell	4	(10)	not out	10
*T.P.Horan	c Shrewsbury b Peel	63		c Hunter b Barnes	16
J.W.Trumble	c & b Barnes	59		c & b Barnes	11
†A.H.Jarvis	c Briggs b Flowers	82		lbw b Peel	10
R.J.Pope	c Flowers b Attewell	0		b Peel	3
A.P.Marr	b Barnes	0		c & b Barnes	5
H.A.Musgrove	c Read b Barnes	4		c Bates b Peel	9
J.Worrall	b Flowers	34		c & b Barnes	6
W.Bruce	not out	3	(2)	c Hunter b Barnes	45
W.R.Robertson	c Barnes b Peel	0		b Barnes	2
Extras	(b3, lb4, w2, nb2)	11			-
Total	(274.1 overs, in about 400 mins)	279	(114.3 overs, in about 180 mins)		126

AUSTRALIA	O	M	R	W	w,nb		O	M	R	W	w,nb
Bruce	55	22	88	3	-,-	(2)	0.1	0	4	0	-,-
Worrall	56	28	97	1	-,-						
Marr	11	6	11	0	-,-	(1)	1	0	3	0	-,-
Trumble	23	9	41	0	-,-						
Robertson	11	3	24	0	-,-						
Morris	34	14	73	2	-,1						
Jones	25.2	9	47	4	-,-						
Horan	1	1	0	0	-,-						

ENGLAND	O	M	R	W	w,nb		O	M	R	W	w,nb
Peel	102.1	56	78	3	-,-	(2)	44	26	45	3	-,-
Attewell	61	35	54	2	-,-	(5)	5	2	7	0	-,-
Barnes	50	27	50	3	-,1	(6)	38.3	26	31	6	-,-
Flowers	29	12	46	2	-,-	(1)	11	6	11	0	-,-
Ulyett	15	7	23	0	-,1	(3)	8	3	19	1	-,-
Bates	17	11	17	0	2,-						
Briggs						(4)	8	3	13	0	-,-

FALL OF WICKETS

Wkt	ENG 1st	AUST 1st	AUST 2nd	ENG 2nd
1st	28	4	29	-
2nd	144	46	66	-
3rd	161	124	80	-
4th	191	190	83	-
5th	194	193	86	-
6th	204	193	95	-
7th	204	203	99	-
8th	254	276	108	-
9th	303	278	116	-
10th	401	279	126	-

VICTORIA v SOUTH AUSTRALIA

Played at Melbourne Cricket Ground on January 23, 24, 26, 1885. (Timeless match)
Toss : South Australia.   Result : SOUTH AUSTRALIA WON BY 53 RUNS.
Debuts: Victoria - J.E.Barrett, R.S.Houston, W.Vint (all f/c). South Australia - T.A.Caterer, B.C.E.Kemp, J.J.Lyons, J.McKenzie (all f/c).
12th Men: D.F.Cotter (Vic) and J.H.Brideson (SA).
Umpires: G.J.Hodges and F.Mitchell.
Attendances: 400, 2000, 200.   Total: About 2600.   Receipts: No figures published.
Close of Play: 1st day Vic 2/62 (Bruce 43, McShane 9); 2nd day SA (2) 7/146 (Kemp 38, Gooden 4).

Victoria had numerous selection problems. The Victorian members of Murdoch's 1884 Australian touring team - J.M.Blackham, G.J.Bonnor, H.F.Boyle, P.S.McDonnell, G.E.Palmer and H.J.H.Scott - had all been suspended by the Victorian Cricketers' Association. T.U.Groube, T.P.Horan, W.R.Robertson, J.Slight, J.W.Trumble and F.H.Walters all announced their unavailability, making a total of twelve Australian representatives unable to appear. In addition, Browning, Houston and Vint had to be brought in as late replacements for H.A.Musgrove, J.S.Swift and J.Worrall, resulting in Victoria fielding a virtual second eleven. Watling (58 in about 140 minutes, 1 five and 5 fours), Bruce (63 in about 105 minutes, 5 fours) and Lewis (65 in about 100 minutes, 10 fours) hit half-centuries in the respective first innings of each team. George Giffen was out to the first ball of the match but still made the most significant contribution with 73 (in about 105 minutes, 9 fours) and 10 wickets. Cotter substituted for Lawlor (injured hand) in the South Australian second innings. Umpire Mitchell was also the South Australian manager. *Cricket* incorrectly gives SA (1) Bruce 1/37; SA (2) omits sub from dismissal of Rundell; Vic (2) Lawlor 8, Tobin 0. Sources: *Cricket, C.B.O'Reilly, The Age, The Argus, The Herald, The Australasian.*

SOUTH AUSTRALIA

G.Giffen	c Morris b Bruce	0	(4)	c Bruce b Barrett	73
J.Noel	b Morris	13	(3)	c McShane b Barrett	1
J.J.Lyons	b Tobin	21	(1)	b Tobin	21
W.H.Watling	c Browning b Barrett	58	(2)	b Barrett	4
H.C.Chittleborough	b Tobin	0	(7)	c Bruce b Barrett	3
J.F.King	st Lewis b Morris	28		c Browning b Barrett	1
†J.McKenzie	c Vint b Barrett	32	(8)	b McShane	0
*J.E.Gooden	c McShane b Barrett	0	(9)	b McShane	4
J.U.Rundell	b Barrett	0	(10)	c sub (D.F.Cotter) b Barrett	5
B.C.E.Kemp	not out	11	(5)	b McShane	38
T.A.Caterer	b Barrett	0		not out	0
Extras	(b5, lb1, nb1)	7		(lb2, nb2)	4
Total	(116.0 overs, in about 210 mins)	170		(82.0 overs, in about 160 mins)	154

VICTORIA

W.Bruce	c McKenzie b Lyons	63		b Rundell	2
J.Trinnick	run out (/McKenzie)	0	(5)	b Rundell	18
R.S.Houston	run out (Gooden/McKenzie)	7	(6)	b Giffen	0
*F.G.McShane	lbw b Caterer	32	(2)	b Rundell	22
†P.M.Lewis	c Watling b Giffen	65	(4)	b Rundell	13
S.Morris	c King b Giffen	7	(7)	c Chittleborough b Giffen	2
W.Vint	b Giffen	0	(9)	b Giffen	4
J.Lawlor	c & b Giffen	0	(11)	not out	0
W.A.Tobin	c Lyons b Giffen	2	(8)	b Rundell	8
G.R.Browning	c McKenzie b Rundell	2		c Chittleborough b Giffen	1
J.E.Barrett	not out	6	(3)	c Noel b Giffen	10
Extras	(b2, lb3)	5		(lb1, nb1)	2
Total	(117.0 overs, in about 205 mins)	189		(62.3 overs, in about 115 mins)	82

VICTORIA	O	M	R	W	w,nb		O	M	R	W	w,nb		FALL OF WICKETS			
														SA	VIC	SA	VIC
Bruce	28	18	27	1	-,-		19	7	38	0	-,-			1st	1st	2nd	2nd
Morris	32	7	66	2	-,-	(4)	6	2	19	0	-,1	Wkt				
Barrett	22	10	31	5	-,-	(2)	32	16	49	6	-,1	1st	0	11	10	9
Tobin	18	10	17	2	-,-	(3)	10	3	20	1	-,-	2nd	18	39	18	28
Browning	8	3	9	0	-,1		7	1	15	0	-,-	3rd	48	102	48	47
McShane	8	2	13	0	-,-		8	4	9	3	-,-	4th	48	116	125	55
												5th	109	143	129	61
SOUTH AUSTRALIA	O	M	R	W	w,nb		O	M	R	W	w,nb	6th	149	149	133	63
Giffen	50	16	87	5	-,-		31.3	10	49	5	-,-	7th	151	149	133	74
Caterer	31	15	42	1	-,-							8th	151	155	147	77
Kemp	2	0	9	0	-,-							9th	170	167	152	78
Noel	8	1	17	0	-,-							10th	170	189	154	82
Rundell	17	11	10	1	-,-	(2)	31	13	31	5	-,1					
Lyons	9	4	19	1	-,-											

NEW SOUTH WALES v A.SHAW'S ENGLAND XI

Played at Sydney Cricket Ground on January 24, 26, 27, 1885. (Timeless match)
Toss : England XI.   Result : A.SHAW'S ENGLAND XI WON BY AN INNINGS AND 37 RUNS.
Debuts: Nil.
12th Men: R.C.Allen (NSW). No 12th named for England XI; Lillywhite umpired.
Umpires: J.Lillywhite and J.W.Payne.
Attendances: 7000, 8000, 500.   Total: About 15,500.   Receipts: No figures published.
Close of Play: 1st day NSW 2/21 (Bannerman 7, Nunn 3); 2nd day NSW (2) 1/42 (Jones 32, Bannerman 8).

J.Swift was originally appointed as the New South Wales umpire but was unable to accept and was replaced by Payne. A new wicket was selected for each innings. Australian XI representatives W.L.Murdoch, A.C.Bannerman and G.J.Bonnor (who had recently moved from Victoria because of his suspension by the VCA) again refused to play against the English team. H.H.Massie was invited but declined, and F.R.Spofforth was still sidelined with his injured foot. H.Moses (business) and J.R.Wood also declined invitations to play. The late inclusions were Hiddleston (the original choice as 12th man), Nunn and Powell. Rain, poor light and gale-force winds affected play at various stages on all three days. Although both teams struggled under the conditions, the Englishmen conceded that the home team had the worst for their two innings. Bates (68 in about 90 minutes, 8 four) defied the elements on the opening day to score the only half-century in the match. *SMH* and *Daily Telegraph* give NSW (2) extras 12 (b9, lb2, w1), total 107. All other sources as shown here. Sources: *Wisden, Cricket, Sydney Morning Herald, Town & Country Journal, Sydney Daily Telegraph.*

A.SHAW'S ENGLAND XI

*A.Shrewsbury	b Jones	8
W.H.Scotton	b Jones	14
G.Ulyett	c Nunn b Garrett	11
W.Barnes	c O'Hanlon b Jones	33
W.Bates	b Evans	68
J.Briggs	b Jones	1
W.Flowers	b Jones	10
J.M.Read	c Garrett b Evans	18
W.Attewell	c Downes b Evans	27
R.Peel	c Marr b Evans	11
†J.Hunter	not out	0
Extras	(b3, lb1)	4
Total	(112.1 overs, in about 185 mins)	205

NEW SOUTH WALES

S.P.Jones	c Briggs b Attewell	1		c Barnes b Bates	32
C.Bannerman	c Read b Peel	7	(3)	run out (Read/Hunter)	37
A.P.Marr	b Peel	8	(5)	c Barnes b Bates	7
T.Nunn	st Hunter b Peel	9	(8)	lbw b Ulyett	0
R.J.Pope	c Hunter b Attewell	7	(4)	c Scotton b Bates	0
H.C.S.Hiddleston	c Barnes b Peel	2	(10)	b Ulyett	0
E.Evans	c Shrewsbury b Attewell	0	(6)	b Flowers	9
T.Powell	b Peel	5	(9)	b Ulyett	4
*T.W.Garrett	b Peel	13	(2)	b Attewell	0
F.Downes	b Peel	0	(11)	not out	0
†W.J.O'Hanlon	not out	4	(7)	run out (/Hunter)	6
Extras	(lb4)	4		(b8, lb4, w1)	13
Total	(100.1 overs, in about 170 mins)	60		(122.0 overs, in about 195 mins)	108

NEW SOUTH WALES	O	M	R	W	w,nb
Downes	18	11	26	0	-,-
Evans	40.1	17	67	4	-,-
Garrett	17	9	29	1	-,-
Jones	32	11	54	5	-,-
Marr	5	0	25	0	-,-

ENGLAND XI	O	M	R	W	w,nb	O	M	R	W	w,nb
Peel	50.1	27	27	7	-,-	36	23	33	0	-,-
Attewell	50	37	29	3	-,-	22	16	11	1	-,-
Bates						38	26	29	3	1,-
Flowers						18	12	15	1	-,-
Ulyett						8	4	7	3	-,-

FALL OF WICKETS

Wkt	ENG 1st	NSW 1st	NSW 2nd
1st	25	1	13
2nd	32	14	43
3rd	38	21	47
4th	128	30	54
5th	138	36	76
6th	138	36	98
7th	153	38	99
8th	185	45	99
9th	204	47	106
10th	205	60	108

NEW SOUTH WALES v VICTORIA

Played at Sydney Cricket Ground on February 13, 14, 16, 17, 1885. (Timeless match)
Toss : New South Wales.   Result : NEW SOUTH WALES WON BY THREE WICKETS.
Debuts: New South Wales - G.J.Bonnor (NSW only).
12th Men: F.Downes (NSW) and J.Trinnick (Vic).
Umpires: E.H.Elliott and J.Swift.
Attendances: 2000, 4000, 2000, 500.   Total: About 8500.   Receipts: No figures published.
Close of Play: 1st day NSW 1/10 (Spofforth 4); 2nd day Vic (2) 1/22 (Swift 5); 3rd day NSW (2) 2/59 (A.C.Bannerman 24, Bonnor 9).

The NSWCA did not endorse the action of the VCA in banning Australian representatives who had refused to play against the England touring team and included A.C.Bannerman and Bonnor in their twelve for the match. Bonnor, who was in the Victorian team against New South Wales in Melbourne last December, was named as 12th man and fielded as substitute initially, pending the expected arrival of Edwin Evans. Bonnor was brought into the team later in the day when Evans failed to appear. Evans later claimed that he had not been asked to play. Bonnor's inclusion led to a call from Tom Horan ('Felix' in *The Australasian*) for a residential qualification in future. W.Bruce was unavailable for Victoria who selected a squad of thirteen for the trip to Sydney. J.McIlwraith was omitted after arrival and the 12th man was determined by drawing one name out of Harry, Swift and Trinnick from a hat. Pre-match rain prompted Massie to send Victoria in but the wicket played much better than expected despite no visiting batsman exceeding 50 in the match. The batting of the Bannerman brothers ultimately decided a close fought contest in favour of the home team. Charles (79 not out in about 195 minutes, 9 fours) held the first innings together while Alec (96 not out in about 175 minutes, 9 fours) anchored the second on a wearing wicket softened by rain on the last morning. His third wicket stand with the aggressive Bonnor (58 in about 75 minutes, 1 five and 4 fours) proved crucial. *VCA Report* incorrectly gives Vic (1) Worrall 13. *Cricket* has incorrect extras in Vic (2) and NSW (2). Sources: *Cricket, VCA Report, The Australasian, Sydney Morning Herald, Town & Country Journal, Sydney Daily Telegraph.*

VICTORIA

F.H.Walters	c A.C.Bannerman b Garrett	28	(4) b Marr	26
J.S.Swift	b Spofforth	6	(1) c Bonnor b Spofforth	28
*T.P.Horan	b Marr	45	b Spofforth	21
J.W.Trumble	c Pope b Garrett	16	(5) b Spofforth	35
†P.M.Lewis	c Bonnor b Marr	16	(7) b Spofforth	1
J.Worrall	c O'Hanlon b Garrett	2	(8) b Jones	27
H.A.Musgrove	c & b Garrett	13	(9) lbw b Jones	0
F.G.McShane	not out	48	(2) run out (A.C.Bannerman/O'Hanlon)	11
S.Morris	run out	0	(10) not out	22
J.Harry	c Jones b Garrett	26	(6) b Marr	6
J.E.Barrett	b Garrett	3	c O'Hanlon b Spofforth	6
Extras	(b10, lb5, nb5)	20	(b11, lb7, nb5)	23
Total	(150.1 overs, in about 275 mins)	223	(142.3 overs, in about 265 mins)	206

NEW SOUTH WALES

G.J.Bonnor	c & b Worrall	6	(4) b Horan	58
F.R.Spofforth	b Trumble	36	(7) c Morris b Horan	5
A.C.Bannerman	c Walters b Trumble	4	(1) not out	96
S.P.Jones	b Worrall	3	(2) b McShane	12
H.Moses	c Walters b Worrall	7	(3) b McShane	11
C.Bannerman	not out	79	b McShane	1
*H.H.Massie	b McShane	25	(5) b Horan	17
R.J.Pope	b Trumble	5	b Horan	0
A.P.Marr	c Morris b Trumble	0		
T.W.Garrett	c Walters b Trumble	38	(9) not out	3
†W.J.O'Hanlon	lbw b Trumble	3		
Extras	(b10, w3, nb2)	15	(b3, lb5)	8
Total	(129.2 overs, in about 250 mins)	221	(81.3 overs, in about 175 mins) (7 wkts)	211

NEW SOUTH WALES	O	M	R	W	w,nb		O	M	R	W	w,nb					
Spofforth	47	22	68	1	-,4		62.3	25	95	5	-,5			VIC	NSW	VIC	NSW
Jones	17	1	42	0	-,1	(3)	21	15	13	2	-,-	Wkt	1st	1st	2nd	2nd
Garrett	64.1	34	65	6	-,-	(2)	37	21	38	0	-,-	1st	29	10	22	27
Marr	22	10	28	2	-,-	(5)	21	8	33	2	-,-	2nd	50	27	48	43
Bonnor						(4)	1	0	4	0	-,-	3rd	77	31	95	126
												4th	113	57	101	175
VICTORIA	O	M	R	W	w,nb		O	M	R	W	w,nb	5th	115	63	110	188
Worrall	27	11	47	3	-,-	(3)	9	2	25	0	-,-	6th	133	119	115	193
Barrett	18	11	22	0	-,1	(5)	2	0	10	0	-,-	7th	139	131	155	193
Trumble	51.2	20	84	6	3,-	(2)	17.3	4	51	0	-,-	8th	140	131	155	-
McShane	21	9	33	1	-,-	(1)	37	13	81	3	-,-	9th	207	198	187	-
Horan	9	4	14	0	-,-	(4)	14	5	29	4	-,-	10th	223	221	206	-
Morris	3	1	6	0	-,1		2	0	7	0	-,-					

FALL OF WICKETS

AUSTRALIA v ENGLAND (3rd Test)

Played at Sydney Cricket Ground on February 20, 21, 23, 24, 1885. (Timeless match)
Toss : Australia.   Result : AUSTRALIA WON BY 6 RUNS.
Debuts: Nil.
12th Men: F.H.Walters (Aust). No 12th named for Eng.
Umpires: E.H.Elliott and J.W.Payne (J.Bryant deputised).
Attendances: 2000, 10000, 6000, 2000.   Total: About 20,000.   Receipts: No figures published.
Close of Play: 1st day Aust 8/97 (Spofforth 3, Garrett 2); 2nd day Eng 133 all out; 3rd day Eng (2) 2/29 (Shrewsbury 12, Barnes 5).

Although not at full strength, Australia were a more powerful combination than in the previous Test with the inclusion of Bannerman, Bonnor, Scott and Spofforth. They won a tight contest through the fine bowling of Spofforth, who began by taking the first three England wickets in four balls (spread over two overs) and went on to bowl unchanged throughout the first innings. Only Read and Flowers were able to hold him out for any length of time in the second innings. A severe hailstorm during the lunch break on the first day held up play for more than two hours: "The ground was speedily covered inches deep in some places, and it had the appearance of being wrapped in a coating of snow" (*T & C Journal*). Bowlers held sway from then on, and only a tenth-wicket stand of 80 between Garrett and Evans saved the Australian first innings. Horan recorded a career-best bowling analysis. Jarvis, Barnes and Attewell sustained first-ball dismissals, Barnes being displaced when the ball rebounded from Jarvis's pads on to the stumps. Barnes refused to bowl in the second innings in protest at not being given an opportunity with the ball in the first. Bryant stood for umpire Elliott for part of the first day. A fresh pitch was selected for each innings. More recent publications vary with some falls of wickets. Sources: *Wisden, Sydney Morning Herald, Town & Country Journal, Sydney Daily Telegraph.*

AUSTRALIA

A.C.Bannerman	c Peel b Flowers	13		c Shrewsbury b Ulyett	16
S.P.Jones	st Hunter b Flowers	28	(4)	b Attewell	22
T.P.Horan	c Hunter b Attewell	7		b Bates	36
H.J.H.Scott	c Ulyett b Attewell	5	(5)	c Barnes b Attewell	4
G.J.Bonnor	c Barnes b Flowers	18	(2)	b Ulyett	29
J.W.Trumble	c Read b Attewell	13		c Ulyett b Bates	32
*H.H.Massie	c Scotton b Flowers	2		b Bates	21
†A.H.Jarvis	b Attewell	0		c & b Peel	2
F.R.Spofforth	st Hunter b Flowers	3	(11)	c Attewell b Bates	0
T.W.Garrett	not out	51		not out	0
E.Evans	c Hunter b Ulyett	33	(9)	b Bates	1
Extras	(b3, lb5)	8		(b1, lb1)	2
Total	(167.2 overs, in about 270 mins)	181		(157.0 overs, in about 240 mins)	165

ENGLAND

W.H.Scotton	c Jarvis b Horan	22		b Spofforth	2
*A.Shrewsbury	c & b Spofforth	18		b Spofforth	24
G.Ulyett	b Spofforth	2		run out (Bannerman)	4
W.Barnes	st Jarvis b Spofforth	0		c Jarvis b Trumble	5
W.Bates	c Evans b Horan	12		c Jarvis b Spofforth	31
J.Briggs	c Scott b Horan	3		b Spofforth	1
W.Flowers	c Jarvis b Spofforth	24		c Evans b Spofforth	56
J.M.Read	c Evans b Horan	4		b Spofforth	56
W.Attewell	b Horan	14		run out (Jarvis)	0
R.Peel	not out	8		c Jarvis b Trumble	3
†J.Hunter	b Horan	13		not out	5
Extras	(b8, lb3, nb2)	13		(b7, lb9, w3, nb1)	20
Total	(95.1 overs, in about 160 mins)	133		(111.1 overs, in about 215 mins)	207

ENGLAND	O	M	R	W	w,nb		O	M	R	W	w,nb			FALL OF WICKETS		
Peel	32	13	51	0	-,-	(2)	20	10	24	1	-,-			AUST	ENG AUST	ENG
Attewell	71	47	53	4	-,-	(3)	58	36	54	2	-,-	Wkt	1st	1st 2nd	2nd
Ulyett	12.2	8	17	1	-,-	(1)	39	25	42	2	-,-	1st	45	31 37	14
Flowers	46	24	46	5	-,-		20	14	19	0	-,-	2nd	46	33 56	18
Bates	6	2	6	0	-,-		20	10	24	5	-,-	3rd	56	33 91	29
												4th	73	46 95	59
AUSTRALIA	O	M	R	W	w,nb		O	M	R	W	w,nb	5th	77	56 119	61
Spofforth	48	23	54	4	-,2		48.1	22	90	6	-,1	6th	83	70 151	92
Garrett	6	2	17	0	-,-		21	8	31	0	-,-	7th	83	82 161	194
Horan	37.1	22	40	6	-,-	(4)	9	4	23	0	-,-	8th	92	111 165	194
Evans	4	1	9	0	-,-	(5)	4	1	8	0	3,-	9th	101	111 165	199
Trumble						(3)	26	13	26	2	-,-	10th	181	133 165	207
Jones							3	0	9	0	-,-				

AUSTRALIA v ENGLAND (4th Test)

Played at Sydney Cricket Ground on March 14, 16, 17, 1885. (Timeless match)
Toss : England.   Result : AUSTRALIA WON BY EIGHT WICKETS.
Debuts: Nil.
12th Men: E.Evans & F.G.McShane (Aust emergencies). No 12th named for Eng.
Umpires: E.H.Elliott and F.G.McShane (H.H.Massie deputised).
Attendances: 13000, 5000, 6000 .   Total: About 24,000.   Receipts: No figures published.
Close of Play: 1st day Aust 1/11 (Garrett 9, Trumble 2); 2nd day Aust 8/308 (Jones 40, Blackham 11).

J.W.Payne was appointed to umpire with Elliott but was unavailable. J.Swift, who had been passed over, then refused and, finally C.Bannerman was rejected by the Englishmen just before play was due to begin. McShane, the Australian 12th man, then stepped into the breach and acted throughout the match. Elliott was late on the first day, Massie standing for a few overs. The option of chosing a fresh pitch before each innings was agreed upon, but in the event each team opted to play their second innings on the other's first-innings track. Bonnor rescued Australia by recording one of the most famous of all Test centuries on the second afternoon. He began half an hour prior to tea and was 15* at the interval. After tea, with Jones in support, he took his score to 128 (115 minutes, 4 fives, 14 fours, 4 threes, 13 twos and 14 singles) before losing his wicket 20 minutes before stumps. He hit 120 out of his 154-run stand with Jones in 100 minutes - the time it took him to reach his hundred, then the Test-record fastest. England's poor showing in their second innings "may be put down to the rain which fell on Tuesday morning " (*T & C Journal*). Jones ran himself out to the first ball of the day's play. Palmer had been dismissed by the fourth ball of Australia's first innings. Some recent publications give Aust (2) McDonnell c Flowers, and vary with some falls of wickets. An alternative version of Australia's second innings is 2/40, with 2 byes, however the target was 38 and the match was won by a double scored by Jones. Sources: *Wisden, The Australasian, Sydney Morning Herald, Town & Country Journal, Sydney Daily Telegraph.*

ENGLAND

*A.Shrewsbury	b Giffen	40	(2) c Bonnor b Spofforth	16
G.Ulyett	b Giffen	10	(1) c Garrett b Palmer	2
W.H.Scotton	c Blackham b Giffen	4	c Jones b Spofforth	0
W.Barnes	b Giffen	50	c Bannerman b Spofforth	20
W.Bates	c & b Jones	64	c Blackham b Palmer	1
J.M.Read	b Giffen	47	c Bannerman b Spofforth	6
W.Flowers	b Giffen	14	c Jones b Palmer	7
J.Briggs	c Palmer b Spofforth	3	run out (McDonnell/Blackham)	5
W.Attewell	b Giffen	1	not out	1
R.Peel	not out	17	c & b Spofforth	0
†J.Hunter	b Spofforth	13	b Palmer	4
Extras	(b5, nb1)	6	(b14, nb1)	15
Total	(126.0 overs, in about 250 mins)	269	(39.1 overs, in about 75 mins)	77

AUSTRALIA

G.E.Palmer	b Ulyett	0		
T.W.Garrett	b Barnes	32		
J.W.Trumble	b Peel	5		
P.S.McDonnell	c Attewell b Ulyett	20	(1) c Ulyett b Peel	3
A.C.Bannerman	c Shrewsbury b Flowers	51	(2) b Barnes	8
G.Giffen	c Attewell b Barnes	1		
T.P.Horan	c Barnes b Ulyett	9	(3) not out	12
G.J.Bonnor	c Bates b Barnes	128		
S.P.Jones	run out (Peel/Hunter)	40	(4) not out	15
*†J.M.Blackham	not out	11		
F.R.Spofforth	c Read b Barnes	1		
Extras	(b5, lb1, w2, nb3)	11		—
Total	(169.3 overs, in about 300 mins)	309	(24.3 overs, in about 40 mins) (2 wkts)	38

AUSTRALIA	O	M	R	W	w,nb		O	M	R	W	w,nb		FALL OF WICKETS			
														ENG	AUST	ENG	AUST
Giffen	52	14	117	7	-,-								Wkt	1st	1st	2nd	2nd
Palmer	16	5	35	0	-,-		19.1	7	32	4	-,-		1st	19	0	3	7
Spofforth	29	10	61	2	-,1	(1)	20	8	30	5	-,1		2nd	52	15	16	16
Garrett	2	1	5	0	-,-								3rd	76	40	19	-
Trumble	12	5	16	0	-,-								4th	159	98	20	-
Horan	5	2	12	0	-,-								5th	186	108	27	-
Jones	10	5	17	1	-,-								6th	219	119	46	-
													7th	222	134	66	-
ENGLAND	O	M	R	W	w,nb		O	M	R	W	w,nb		8th	229	288	69	-
Ulyett	54	25	91	3	-,2								9th	252	308	69	-
Peel	31	12	53	1	-,-		9	4	16	1	-,-		10th	269	309	77	-
Attewell	18	13	22	0	-,-		3	1	4	0	-,-						
Bates	17	5	44	0	2,-												
Barnes	35.3	17	61	4	-,1	(1)	9	3	15	1	-,-						
Flowers	14	5	27	1	-,-	(4)	3.3	2	3	0	-,-						

AUSTRALIA v ENGLAND (5th Test)

Played at Melbourne Cricket Ground on March 21, 23, 24, 25, 1885. (Timeless match)
Toss : Australia.   Result : ENGLAND WON BY AN INNINGS AND 98 RUNS.
Debuts: Australia - F.G.McShane, F.H.Walters (both Test).
12th Men: J.Worrall (Aust). No 12th named for Eng.
Umpires: G.J.Hodges and J.Phillips (J.C.Allen, T.W.Garrett and J.Lillywhite deputised).
Attendances: 8000, 3000, 1000, 1000.   Total: About 13,000.   Receipts: No figures published.
Close of Play: 1st day Eng 0/44 (Barnes 19, Scotton 21); 2nd day Eng 5/270 (Shrewsbury 54, Briggs 11); 3rd day Aust (2) 7/105
     (Bruce 28, Jarvis 1).

E.H.Elliott, one of the appointed umpires, died suddenly on March 19th and Hodges was called upon to replace him. Flags were flown at
half-mast and black armbands were worn by the players in memory of Elliott on the first day. Further umpiring problems occured when
Lillywhite, the English appointee, decided to concentrate on his managerial duties, forcing Phillips to take over on the day of the match.
Hodges refused to stand after tea on the third day as a result of remarks passed by some of the English players (notably Peel) over his
decisions; Garrett deputised for the last session and Lillywhite took over on the last day. Allen, of Melbourne Cricket Club, stood for
umpire Phillips for the last two days when the latter was taken ill. On a pitch that was still damp from watering, Australia collapsed to
9/99 before Spofforth (50 in about 70 minutes, 1 five and 4 fours), the first No.11 batsman to score a half-century in Australian first-class
cricket, added 64 with Trumble. Barnes (74 in about 175 minutes, 8 fours) batted soundly in the English reply. Shrewsbury, the first
England captain to score a Test century (105 not out in 320 minutes, 10 fours), gave his sole chance on 24 - a very easy catch to McShane
off Spofforth. Bates (54) retired ill at 4/214 and resumed next day at 7/324. G.F.Vernon substituted in the field for him on the third day,
catching Bannerman, while Australians McShane and Jarvis alternated as replacements for Barnes (hit by Spofforth while batting) on the
last day. Recent publications vary with some falls of wickets. Sources: *Wisden, The Age, The Argus, The Australasian, The Leader.*

AUSTRALIA

A.C.Bannerman	c Peel b Ulyett	5		c sub (G.F.Vernon) b Ulyett	2
W.Bruce	c Briggs b Peel	15	(6)	c Bates b Attewell	35
G.Giffen	b Ulyett	13		c Peel b Ulyett	12
*T.P.Horan	lbw b Ulyett	0	(5)	b Attewell	20
S.P.Jones	lbw b Peel	0	(4)	b Peel	17
F.H.Walters	b Ulyett	7	(8)	c Attewell b Flowers	5
†A.H.Jarvis	c Hunter b Peel	15	(9)	c Peel b Flowers	1
J.W.Trumble	not out	34	(7)	lbw b Attewell	10
F.G.McShane	c Hunter b Barnes	9	(11)	not out	12
T.W.Garrett	c Briggs b Barnes	6	(2)	b Ulyett	5
F.R.Spofforth	b Attewell	50	(10)	c sub (A.H.Jarvis) b Flowers	1
Extras	(b5, lb1, nb3)	9		(b5)	5
Total	(106.0 overs, in about 190 mins)	163		(102.1 overs, in about 180 mins)	125

ENGLAND

W.Barnes	c Horan b Bruce	74
W.H.Scotton	b Bruce	27
J.M.Read	b Giffen	13
G.Ulyett	b Spofforth	1
*A.Shrewsbury	not out	105
W.Bates	c Walters b Bruce	61
W.Flowers	b Spofforth	16
J.Briggs	c Walters b Trumble	43
W.Attewell	c Bannerman b Trumble	0
R.Peel	b Trumble	0
†J.Hunter	b Giffen	18
Extras	(b10, lb14, nb4)	28
Total	(221.3 overs, in about 425 mins)	386

ENGLAND	O	M	R	W	w,nb		O	M	R	W	w,nb			FALL OF WICKETS		
Peel	41	26	28	3	-,-	(2)	30	16	37	1	-,-			AUST	ENG	AUST
Ulyett	23	7	52	4	-,-	(1)	15	7	25	3	-,-	Wkt	1st	1st	2nd
Barnes	28	12	47	2	-,3							1st	21	61	4
Flowers	9	6	9	0	-,-		21	7	34	3	-,-	2nd	21	96	17
Attewell	5	1	18	1	-,-	(3)	36.1	22	24	3	-,-	3rd	21	97	26
												4th	34	141	60
AUSTRALIA	O	M	R	W	w,nb							5th	34	256	60
Giffen	74.3	31	132	2	-,4							6th	45	324	91
Bruce	51	13	99	3	-,-							7th	67	324	100
Spofforth	49	21	71	2	-,-							8th	89	335	106
Trumble	28	14	29	3	-,-							9th	99	337	108
Garrett	8	6	12	0	-,-							10th	163	396	125
McShane	3	2	3	0	-,-										
Jones	5	2	7	0	-,-										
Horan	3	0	5	0	-,-										

1885-86 SEASON (4 MATCHES)

Only four first-class matches were staged in a purely domestic 1885-86 season: Australian XI v Victorian XI, South Australia v Victoria, and the two New South Wales-Victoria fixtures. The South Australia-Victoria match, scheduled to start on January 22, was postponed until March 11 following a request from the NSWCA to the VCA for the match at Sydney between New South Wales and Victoria to start on January 23. The VCA complied and, anxious to field their strongest possible XI against South Australia - especially in light of the previous season's defeat - postponed the match at Adelaide by seven weeks.

Major interest centred on the selection of the Australian team to tour England in 1886. Melbourne Cricket Club organised the tour and proposed a series of trial matches in the lead-up to aid selection of the touring party. The first of these trials was intended to pit an Australian XI already chosen to tour against a Combined XI from remaining Victorian and New South Wales cricketers. No New South Wales players were ultimately available and the game proceeded on January 1 between the Australian XI and a purely Victorian XI. The imbalance between the sides became evident. The second trial proposed by Melbourne Cricket Club was intended to take place at Sydney following the New South Wales-Victoria match in late January. Again the plan involved the Australians playing a Combined XI and, with all players available, it promised much. The match was eventually cancelled because the Melbourne club refused to agree to the ground rental charges demanded by the SCG trustees.

Of the 13 players to tour England in 1886, 10 were nominated in January - T.P.Horan, J.M.Blackham, W.Bruce, F.R.Spofforth, G.E.Palmer, G.J.Bonnor, J.McIlwraith, H.J.H.Scott, A.H.Jarvis and George Giffen. Horan however announced his unavailability, and the remaining four places were eventually filled by Edwin Evans, T.W.Garrett, S.P.Jones and J.W.Trumble. Evans had knocked back previous invitations to tour England in 1882 and 1884. 'Felix' reported in *The Australasian* in early January that, before accepting a tour spot, Evans had 'written to his better-half, soliciting her consent'.

New South Wales were weakened in 1885-86 by the unavailability of former leading players W.L.Murdoch (retired), A.C.Bannerman (in dispute with the NSWCA), H.H.Massie (not considered due to 'lack of practice') and F.R.Spofforth (moved to Melbourne). Bannerman had demanded a £15 match fee to play Victoria, which the NSWCA refused to meet. New South Wales were soundly beaten in Melbourne by a full-strength Victorian side. Spofforth, in his first match for Victoria, captured 10 wickets. The return match at Sydney saw New South Wales get up in rain-affected conditions.

South Australia won their match against Victoria for the second successive year. George Giffen, who returned analyses of 9 for 91 and 8 for 110, captured match figures of 17 for 201 - the best by any bowler covered in this volume.

The Western Australian Cricket Association was formed in November 1885 but the colony did not commence first-class cricket until 1892-93.

Leading Aggregates

Batsmen	M	I	NO	Runs	HS	Ave.	Bowlers	Runs	Wkts	Ave.
J.McIlwraith (V)	3	4	0	315	133	78.75	F.R.Spofforth (V)	274	18	15.22
H.J.H.Scott (V)	3	4	0	201	111	50.25	G.Giffen (SA)	201	17	11.82
S.P.Jones (NSW)	2	4	1	178	77*	59.33	T.W.Garrett (NSW)	232	17	13.64
G.J.Bonnor (NSW)	3	6	1	169	84	33.80	G.E.Palmer (V)	357	14	25.50
W.Bruce (V)	4	6	0	164	71	27.33	W.Bruce (V)	338	12	28.16
R.S.Houston (V)	3	6	1	131	31	26.20	E.Evans (NSW)	170	11	15.45

VICTORIA v NEW SOUTH WALES

Played at Melbourne Cricket Ground on December 26, 28, 29, 30, 1885. (Timeless match)
Toss : Victoria.　　　　　　　　Result : VICTORIA WON BY AN INNINGS AND 69 RUNS.
Debuts: Victoria - F.R.Spofforth (Vic only). New South Wales - F.J.Burton, W.W.McGlinchey, A.Mather, D.S.Ogilvy (all f/c);
　　P.S.McDonnell (NSW only).
12th Men: W.R.Robertson & G.H.S.Trott (Vic emergencies) and H.C.S.Hiddleston (NSW).
Umpires: J.W.Payne and J.Phillips.
Attendances: 7000, 10000, 3000, 1000.　　　　Total: About 21,000.　　　Receipts: £884.
Close of Play: 1st day Vic 3/294 (McIlwraith 66, Palmer 30); 2nd day NSW 4/106 (Mather 18, Garrett 12); 3rd day NSW (2) 5/179
　　(Jones 60, Garrett 46).

A.C.Bannerman declared his unavailability after the NSWCA refused to meet his demand for a match payment of £15. W.L.Murdoch was also unavailable for New South Wales, whose selectors omitted C.Bannerman, J.Davis, J.J.Ferris and Hiddleston from the fifteen originally named. New records were established for the Victorian first and fourth wickets. Scott (111 in about 225 minutes, 6 fours) and Bruce (71 in about 135 minutes, 3 fours) began with 136 while McIlwraith (career-best 133 in about 235 minutes, 8 fours) and Palmer (71 in about 160 minutes, 0 fours) put on 170 for the fourth wicket. Mather's 49 on debut for New South Wales included 3 fours. Jones (77 not out in about 210 minutes, 1 four) and Garrett (50 in about 95 minutes, 2 fours) scored second-innings fifties. Spofforth (10 for 138) had a fine debut with Victoria against his former team-mates. Similarly, McDonnell's first match for New South Wales was against his old team. *VCA Report* incorrectly gives NSW (2) Ogilvy c Bruce. Sources: *Cricket, VCA Report, The Age, The Argus, The Australasian, The Leader.*

VICTORIA

H.J.H.Scott	b Marr	111
W.Bruce	c Jones b Garrett	71
T.P.Horan	c Marr b Garrett	4
J.McIlwraith	c Turner b Evans	133
G.E.Palmer	c Burton b Garrett	71
J.W.Trumble	b Evans	19
*†J.M.Blackham	b Evans	3
F.H.Walters	lbw b Garrett	10
W.H.Moule	b Evans	8
J.Worrall	not out	7
F.R.Spofforth	c Jones b Garrett	11
Extras	(b9, lb10, w1, nb3)	23
Total	(319.2 overs, 482 mins)	471

NEW SOUTH WALES

G.J.Bonnor	c Worrall b Spofforth	15		c Walters b Spofforth	29
P.S.McDonnell	c Bruce b Spofforth	26		c Scott b Spofforth	7
C.T.B.Turner	b Palmer	0	(9)	c Spofforth b Worrall	13
S.P.Jones	b Bruce	25	(3)	not out	77
A.Mather	b Spofforth	49	(4)	b Spofforth	7
*T.W.Garrett	b Trumble	17	(7)	b Spofforth	50
A.P.Marr	c Trumble b Spofforth	15	(8)	c Blackham b Worrall	5
E.Evans	b Bruce	2	(10)	run out (Bruce/Blackham)	4
W.W.McGlinchey	not out	2	(6)	b Bruce	0
†F.J.Burton	b Spofforth	2	(11)	b Worrall	7
D.S.Ogilvy	b Bruce	3	(5)	c Scott b Spofforth	19
Extras	(b1, lb6, nb5)	12		(b5, lb7, w1, nb3)	16
Total	(114.2 overs, in about 190 mins)	168		(126.2 overs, in about 230 mins)	234

NEW SOUTH WALES	O	M	R	W	w,nb
Turner	38	14	44	0	-,-
McGlinchey	17	4	40	0	-,-
Garrett	92.2	37	121	5	-,-
Jones	33	15	69	0	-,-
Evans	77	41	69	4	-,-
Bonnor	9	1	28	0	1,3
Ogilvy	15	5	32	0	-,-
Marr	33	17	34	1	-,-
Mather	5	1	11	0	-,-

VICTORIA	O	M	R	W	w,nb		O	M	R	W	w,nb
Spofforth	43	17	43	5	-,2	(2)	51	16	95	5	-,3
Palmer	36	10	63	1	-,3	(4)	10	2	21	0	-,-
Bruce	17.2	6	31	3	-,-	(1)	19	5	46	1	-,-
Trumble	18	7	19	1	-,-	(3)	14	3	27	0	-,-
Worrall							29.2	14	26	3	-,-
Scott							3	1	3	0	1,-

FALL OF WICKETS

Wkt	VIC 1st	NSW 1st	NSW 2nd
1st	136	34	20
2nd	154	37	48
3rd	224	50	62
4th	394	92	92
5th	420	121	96
6th	430	154	193
7th	435	161	200
8th	451	163	218
9th	453	165	225
10th	471	168	234

VICTORIAN XI v AUSTRALIAN XI

Played at Melbourne Cricket Ground on January 1, 2, 4, 1886. (Four-day match)
Toss : Victorian XI. Result : AUSTRALIAN XI WON BY TEN WICKETS.
Debuts: Victorian XI - G.H.S.Trott, F.W.Wingrove (both f/c); G.Watsford (Vic only).
12th Men: None named.
Umpires: J.Duffy and J.Phillips.
Attendances: 2000, 1500, 200. Total: About 3700 Receipts: No figures published.
Close of Play: 1st day Aust 2/69 (Scott 26, McIlwraith 40); 2nd day Aust 375 all out.

The match organisers (Melbourne Cricket Club) had intended the contest to be between a team of Australians already chosen to tour England and a "Combined Colonies" side representing the rest. However, four New South Welshmen (E.Evans, T.W.Garrett, A.P.Marr and A.Mather) and two Victorians (W.E.Midwinter and F.R.Spofforth) declined invitations to play, which left a purely Victorian side to play the tourists. G.Giffen withdrew from the Australian XI at the last moment due to work commitments, leaving Blackham with only ten men when the coin was tossed. Boyle refused to part with any of his team (Trott, Wingrove or Worrall were requested) so Blackham settled for Healy (who had been present at the ground only to score and was not highly regarded as a player) as a substitute in the hope that Giffen would arrive before his side had to bat. Healy was brought into the side as a full member on the second day when Giffen failed to front. McIlwraith (125 in about 165 minutes, 13 fours) became the first to score hundreds in successive innings in Australia and shared a double-century stand with Scott (74 in about 185 minutes, 5 fours) for the third wicket. Wingrove captured the wicket of Bruce with his first ball in his only first-class match. Jarvis (77 in about 150 minutes, 2 fours) batted well after providing Australia's first instance of a wicket-keeper completing six dismissals in an innings. McShane (79 in about 165 minutes, 6 fours) was the only Victorian to exceed 34 in the match. Watsford, a sole South Australian representative three years past, now played his only match with Victoria. Sources: *Cricket, The Age, The Argus, The Australasian, The Leader, The Sportsman.*

VICTORIAN XI

†P.M.Lewis	c Trumble b Bruce	20		c Healy b Bruce	34
G.Watsford	c Jarvis b Palmer	10		c Palmer b Trumble	10
J.D.Edwards	st Jarvis b Palmer	25	(4)	st Jarvis b Palmer	7
R.S.Houston	st Jarvis b Palmer	27	(3)	b Palmer	31
J.Trinnick	c Jarvis b Palmer	9	(6)	lbw b Bonnor	20
G.H.S.Trott	b Palmer	4	(9)	not out	18
*H.F.Boyle	c McIlwraith b Palmer	2	(11)	c Walters b Trumble	3
W.R.Robertson	c Jarvis b Trumble	9	(7)	b Bruce	12
F.G.McShane	b Palmer	13	(5)	c Blackham b Bruce	79
J.Worrall	not out	5	(8)	c Bonnor b Bruce	11
F.W.Wingrove	st Jarvis b Palmer	0	(10)	b Trumble	20
Extras	(b1, lb4, w2, nb4)	11		(b6, lb7, w1, nb1)	15
Total	(126.2 overs, in about 210 mins)	135		(149.0 overs, in about 255 mins)	260

AUSTRALIAN XI

H.J.H.Scott	c Worrall b Boyle	74			
W.Bruce	c Robertson b Wingrove	1			
T.P.Horan	b Wingrove	2			
J.McIlwraith	st Lewis b Boyle	125			
G.E.Palmer	c Wingrove b Boyle	0			
G.J.Bonnor	c Edwards b McShane	20	(1)	not out	11
†A.H.Jarvis	not out	77			
J.W.Trumble	c Boyle b Robertson	40			
*J.M.Blackham	c Houston b Boyle	12			
F.H.Walters	lbw b Robertson	3	(2)	not out	8
J.J.Healy	run out (Lewis)	8			
Extras	(b4, lb4, nb5)	13		(b1, lb1)	2
Total	(199.0 overs, in about 345 mins)	375		(5.1 overs, 13 mins) (0 wkts)	21

AUSTRALIAN XI	O	M	R	W	w,nb		O	M	R	W	w,nb
Bruce	42	18	58	1	2,-	(3)	48	18	86	4	1,-
Palmer	54.2	41	59	8	-,4		60	27	86	2	-,1
Trumble	30	25	7	1		(1)	30	9	56	3	-,-
Bonnor							8	2	7	1	-,-
Walters							3	0	10	0	-,-

VICTORIA	O	M	R	W	w,nb		O	M	R	W	w,nb
Worrall	27	12	37	0	-,-	(2)	2.1	0	7	0	-,-
Wingrove	29	6	58	2	-,3						
Houston	4	1	13	0	-,-						
Robertson	26	5	47	2	-,2	(1)	3	0	12	0	-,-
Trott	18	1	39	0	-,-						
Edwards	9	5	19	0	-,-						
McShane	32	14	37	1	-,-						
Boyle	38	13	59	4	-,-						
Watsford	4	1	23	0	-,-						
Trinnick	12	4	30	0	-,-						

FALL OF WICKETS

Wkt	VIC 1st	AUST 1st	VIC 2nd	AUST 2nd
1st	27	2	31	-
2nd	31	7	56	-
3rd	80	207	63	-
4th	95	207	98	-
5th	102	207	147	-
6th	106	231	197	-
7th	106	325	219	-
8th	130	347	224	-
9th	131	350	250	-
10th	135	375	260	-

NEW SOUTH WALES v VICTORIA

Played at Sydney Cricket Ground on January 23, 25, 26, 27, 28, 1886. (Timeless match)
Toss : New South Wales.   Result : NEW SOUTH WALES WON BY 150 RUNS.
Debuts: Nil.
12th Men: D.S.Ogilvy (NSW) and G.H.S.Trott (Vic).
Umpires: J.W.Fletcher and J.Phillips.
Attendances: 8000, 1500, 10000, 3000, "poor".   Total: About 23,000.   Receipts: No figures published.
Close of Play: 1st day Vic 1/51 (Scott 16, Horan 0); 2nd day Vic 6/160 (Walters 35); 3rd day NSW (2) 5/196 (Jones 53, Bonnor 78);
    4th day Vic (2) 4/35 (Palmer 6, Trumble 0).

Two pitches were used during the match, each exclusively used by one team. A.C.Bannerman declined an offer to play for the home team and J.McIlwraith was unavailable for Victoria. Moses (74 in about 190 minutes, 3 fours) batted soundly on the opening day. Rain severely shortened playing time on the second and fourth days. "The condition of the turf precluded any chance of a display of first-class cricket" (*SMH*) after the third day. Bonnor (84 in about 120 minutes, 1 five and 4 fours) and Jones (67 in about 235 minutes, 1 five and 3 fours) added an unfinished stand of 114 for the New South Wales sixth wicket; Bonnor (78) was unable to resume immediately on the fourth day due to a knock he received on the wrist just before stumps the previous evening. He came in at 7/216, able to use only one hand on the bat, and added a further 6 runs. Ogilvy substituted for him throughout the Victorian second innings. Garrett (12 for 111) returned his best figures for New South Wales. Sources: *Cricket, VCA Report, Sydney Morning Herald, Town & Country Journal, Sydney Daily Telegraph.*

NEW SOUTH WALES

P.S.McDonnell	run out (/Spofforth)	6	(4) b Spofforth	1
S.P.Jones	b Spofforth	9	(5) lbw b McShane	67
H.Moses	c Trumble b Bruce	74	(6) st Blackham b Palmer	5
G.J.Bonnor	b Palmer	10	(7) run out (/Blackham)	84
A.Mather	run out (Blackham)	0	(8) c Worrall b Spofforth	0
C.Bannerman	b Spofforth	14	(1) b Spofforth	4
*T.W.Garrett	run out (Bruce)	45	(9) c Trumble b Spofforth	4
C.T.B.Turner	b Spofforth	7	(2) c Bruce b Palmer	22
E.Evans	lbw b Spofforth	22	(10) not out	2
A.P.Marr	c Palmer b Bruce	5	(3) run out (Horan/Blackham)	24
†F.J.Burton	not out	5	c Walters b McShane	0
Extras	(b6, lb4, w1, nb7)	18	(b6, lb5, nb8)	19
Total	(108.3 overs, 215 mins)	215	(140.2 overs, 282 mins)	232

VICTORIA

H.J.H.Scott	b Evans	16	c Burton b Evans	0
W.Bruce	c McDonnell b Garrett	28	c McDonnell b Garrett	2
T.P.Horan	c McDonnell b Garrett	8	(8) c Garrett b Evans	2
*†J.M.Blackham	b Garrett	20	(3) b Garrett	23
F.H.Walters	b Garrett	36	(4) c Marr b Evans	4
G.E.Palmer	c & b Evans	28	(5) b Garrett	21
J.W.Trumble	b Garrett	3	(6) b Jones	30
F.G.McShane	c Bonnor b Evans	11	(9) c Jones b Garrett	0
R.S.Houston	not out	4	(7) c Marr b Garrett	24
F.R.Spofforth	c Garrett b Evans	0	(11) not out	0
J.Worrall	b Garrett	10	(10) c Mather b Garrett	0
Extras	(b11, lb12)	23	(b4)	4
Total	(110.1 overs, 228 mins)	187	(89.1 overs, in about 150 mins)	110

VICTORIA	O	M	R	W	w,nb		O	M	R	W	w,nb		FALL OF WICKETS			
														NSW	VIC	NSW	VIC
Spofforth	45.3	17	66	4	-,6		45	23	70	4	-,3	Wkt	1st	1st	2nd	2nd
Palmer	21	11	42	1	-,1		53	21	86	2	-,5	1st	7	49	19	0
Bruce	18	2	44	2	1,		15	8	26	0	-,-	2nd	30	55	30	2
Trumble	5	1	15	0	-,-	(5)	16	8	16	0	-,-	3rd	47	77	33	29
McShane	9	5	15	0	-,-	(6)	11.2	5	12	2	-,-	4th	49	88	69	35
Worrall	10	6	15	0	-,-							5th	71	151	82	57
Horan						(4)	5	3	3	0	-,-	6th	154	160	196	108

NEW SOUTH WALES	O	M	R	W	w,nb		O	M	R	W	w,nb					
												7th	161	173	216	108
Jones	12	4	21	0	-,-	(4)	3	1	5	1	-,-	8th	194	173	227	108
Evans	50	21	70	4	-,-	(1)	37.1	21	31	3	-,-	9th	205	173	229	108
Garrett	41.1	20	55	6	-,-	(2)	37	17	56	6	-,-	10th	215	187	232	110
Marr	5	2	8	0	-,-	(3)	5	1	6	0	-,-					
Turner	2	0	10	0	-,-		7	3	8	0	-,-					

SOUTH AUSTRALIA v VICTORIA

Played at Adelaide Oval on March 11, 12, 13, 15, 1886. (Timeless match)
Toss : South Australia.   Result : SOUTH AUSTRALIA WON BY 40 RUNS.
Debuts: South Australia - L.W.Evan, C.G.Godfrey, T.Turner, A.Wilkinson (all f/c). Victoria - F.G.A.Barnard, J.Phillips, C.H.Ross (all f/c).
12th Men: R.Bruce (Vic). No 12th named for SA.
Umpires: D.F.Cotter and I.A.Fisher.
Attendances: 1500, 1500, 4000, 700.   Total: About 7700.   Receipts: No figures published.
Close of Play: 1st day Vic 1/36 (Slight 23); 2nd day SA (2) 3/74 (Giffen 25, Godfrey 11); 3rd day Vic (2) 0/75 (Bruce 46, McIlwraith 25).

W.F.Giffen and A.F.Slight were unavailable for South Australia and Evan and E.G.Phillips were late replacements for J.Noel and W.H.Watling. Victoria were seriously undermanned due to the unavailability of H.F.Boyle, J.D.Edwards, T.P.Horan, F.G.McShane, S.Morris, G.E.Palmer, W.R.Robertson, H.J.H.Scott, F.R.Spofforth, J.S.Swift, J.Trinnick, F.H.Walters and J.Worrall. Jim Phillips, originally named to umpire, was brought into the team, reversing intended roles with Cotter. Before play began, Jarvis requested that six-ball overs be bowled but Blackham refused and insisted that the standard four-ball over be adhered to. George Giffen (102 runs and a career-best 17 wickets for 201) became the first to complete the 100 runs/10 wickets double in a first-class match in Australia. It was also the first of nine such match doubles for South Australia, seven of them against Victoria. His second innings occupied about 160 minutes (11 fours) and he shared a South Australian record fourth wicket stand of 139 with Godfrey (80 in about 180 minutes, 6 fours). Trott (54 not out in about 120 minutes, 1 five and 3 fours), Bruce (49 in about 58 minutes, 5 fours) and McIlwraith (50 in about 105 minutes, 5 fours) led the scoring for Victoria. Trott substituted for Wilkinson (late arrival) early on the last day in the absence of a South Australia reserve.
Sources: *Cricket, C.B.O'Reilly, VCA Report, The Australasian, Adelaide Advertiser, South Australian Register, Adelaide Observer, South Australian Chronicle.*

SOUTH AUSTRALIA

Batsman	Dismissal 1		R	Dismissal 2		R
G.Giffen	b Phillips		20	(4) b Phillips		82
J.J.Lyons	c Ross b Trumble		29	c Bruce b Phillips		23
*†A.H.Jarvis	c Blackham b Phillips		0	(1) c Trott b Phillips		13
H.Blinman	run out (Lewis/Blackham)		14	(3) b Trumble		1
C.G.Godfrey	run out (/Blackham)		38	b Phillips		80
W.Knill	b Trott		22	c Barnard b Trott		14
L.W.Evan	b Trott		2	(8) run out (/Phillips)		0
B.C.E.Kemp	c Blackham b Bruce		25	(7) c Bruce b Trott		11
A.Wilkinson	b Trott		10	c McIlwraith b Trott		21
E.G.Phillips	c Barnard b Trott		9	c Houston b Phillips		18
T.Turner	not out		0	not out		5
Extras	(w3)		3	(b1, lb2, w3)		6
Total	(133.0 overs, 220 mins)		172	(169.2 overs, 285 mins)		274

VICTORIA

Batsman	Dismissal 1	R	Dismissal 2	R
W.Bruce	b Giffen	13	c sub (G.H.S.Trott) b Giffen	49
J.Slight	c Wilkinson b Giffen	42	(8) c Blinman b Giffen	2
R.S.Houston	c Turner b Giffen	28	(4) b Giffen	17
J.McIlwraith	c & b Giffen	7	(2) st Jarvis b Giffen	50
G.H.S.Trott	not out	54	c & b Giffen	21
J.W.Trumble	b Phillips	8	b Giffen	0
*†J.M.Blackham	lbw b Giffen	23	run out (Kemp/Giffen)	27
P.M.Lewis	c Godfrey b Giffen	2	(3) c Jarvis b Kemp	32
C.H.Ross	c Kemp b Giffen	2	c Knill b Giffen	1
F.G.A.Barnard	c Godfrey b Giffen	1	(11) b Giffen	4
J.Phillips	c Blinman b Giffen	5	(10) not out	4
Extras	(lb1, w1)	2	(b8, lb3, w1)	12
Total	(138.2 overs, 230 mins)	187	(103.0 overs, 165 mins)	219

VICTORIA	O	M	R	W	w,nb		O	M	R	W	w,nb
Trumble	47	23	66	1	-,-		29	10	50	1	-,-
Bruce	14	7	21	1	3,-	(4)	9	2	26	0	2,-
Phillips	46	19	56	2	-,-	(2)	63	28	84	5	-,-
Trott	26	10	26	4	-,-	(3)	59.2	24	95	3	1,-
Houston							4	2	3	0	-,-
Blackham							5	0	10	0	-,-

SOUTH AUSTRALIA	O	M	R	W	w,nb		O	M	R	W	w,nb
Giffen	69.2	29	91	9	-,-		47	12	110	8	-,-
Wilkinson	8	1	14	0	-,-	(4)	5	1	9	0	-,-
Turner	32	15	35	0	1,-	(2)	14	5	25	0	1,-
Phillips	29	13	45	1	-,-	(3)	17	7	19	0	-,-
Kemp							20	3	44	1	-,-

FALL OF WICKETS

Wkt	SA 1st	VIC 1st	SA 2nd	VIC 2nd
1st	49	36	21	78
2nd	49	70	30	128
3rd	49	92	45	136
4th	74	95	184	163
5th	111	117	219	163
6th	117	148	219	196
7th	147	164	226	210
8th	154	168	235	210
9th	171	171	266	212
10th	172	187	274	219

1886-87 SEASON (14 MATCHES)

Rain affected most matches in the Australian summer of 1886-87. A total of 14 first-class fixtures were played, including 10 by the English touring team whose bowlers revelled in the damp conditions.

The English party was the 9th to visit Australia and the third to be promoted by Lillywhite, Shaw and Shrewsbury. They played 29 matches in all including two Tests - both of which they won narrowly. In addition, the tourists participated in the Smokers v Non Smokers combination match at East Melbourne in mid-March, a match which was remarkable for the highest total (803) yet compiled in an Australian first-class match. The Englishmen, who still played under the label of 'Shaw's XI' despite the fact that Shaw was manager and not captain, lost only two matches on the tour, both to New South Wales. Much of their success in the first-class games was attributed to the batting of Arthur Shrewsbury (721 runs at 48.06) and the bowling of George Lohmann (59 wickets at 17.42). In the minor matches, Read, Barlow and Bates also scored heavily with the bat, while Briggs, Bates and Flowers joined Lohmann with the ball in exceeding 100 wickets.

Relations between the Test teams boiled over at times - as they had done on the previous tour in 1884-85. English allrounder Billy Barnes clashed heatedly with McDonnell, the Australian captain, in an off-field incident after the First Test which left Barnes nursing a severe hand injury. England were forced to co-opt Reginald Wood - who had migrated to Australia - as a replacement for the injured Barnes. Wood had already played for Victoria this season, and he made history by appearing both for and against a touring team in one summer. Wood also played for and against Victoria this year.

From an Australian viewpoint, the highlight of the season was the emergence of the Turner-Ferris bowling combination. Operating in tandem for most of the season, they captured 117 wickets for New South Wales and Australia in just seven first-class matches. Charlie 'Terror' Turner (right-arm medium-fast) and Jack Ferris (left-arm medium pace) both had natural control and the ability to break the ball sharply off the pitch. They bowled into each other's footmarks and complimented one another perfectly.

New South Wales won both their domestic encounters against Victoria this season by comfortable margins. Percy McDonnell hit a superb 239 out of 310 runs made while he was at the wicket in the first match between the teams at Melbourne, when batting conditions were far from easy. The return match at Sydney was badly influenced by rain, so much so that neither side totalled 100 in an innings. The remaining intercolonial match at Melbourne saw Victoria defeat South Australia for the first time since February 1884.

Further developments in cricket administration in the colonies led to the formation of the Northern Tasmanian Cricket Association on December 1, 1886.

Leading Aggregates

Batsmen	M	I	NO	Runs	HS	Ave.	Bowlers	Runs	Wkts	Ave.
A.Shrewsbury (E)	11	19	4	721	236	48.06	C.T.B.Turner (NSW)	538	70	7.68
W.Gunn (E)	11	17	1	473	150	29.56	G.A.Lohmann (E)	1028	59	17.42
W.Bruce (V)	7	13	0	448	131	34.46	J.J.Ferris (NSW)	689	47	14.65
P.S.McDonnell (NSW)	7	14	0	447	239	31.92	J.Briggs (E)	808	34	23.76
W.Bates (E)	11	18	0	383	86	21.27	W.Bates (E)	558	28	19.92
H.Moses (NSW)	7	13	2	357	73	32.45	W.Barnes (E)	352	25	14.08
R.G.Barlow (E)	11	19	3	339	86	21.18	W.Flowers (E)	438	24	18.25
W.Barnes (E)	8	12	1	319	109	29.00	T.W.Garrett (NSW)	281	20	14.05
J.Briggs (E)	11	17	0	319	86	18.76				
G.E.Palmer (V)	5	10	0	317	113	31.70				
S.P.Jones (NSW)	7	14	0	314	48	22.42				

VICTORIA v A.SHAW'S ENGLAND XI

Played at Melbourne Cricket Ground on November 6, 8, 9, 10, 1886. (Four-day match)
Toss : Victoria.   Result : MATCH DRAWN.
Debuts: Victoria - R.Wood (Vic only).
12th Men: None named.
Umpires: D.F.Cotter and J.Lillywhite.
Attendances: 3500, 3000, 8000, 600.   Total: About 15,100.   Receipts: No figures published.
Close of Play: 1st day Vic 4/204 (Horan 46, McShane 63); 2nd day Eng 1/73 (Barnes 41, Barlow 27); 3rd day Eng 7/333 (Flowers 51, Lohmann 6).

The Victorian members of the 1886 Australian team (there were six) had not returned yet from England and in addition J.D.Edwards, W.E.Midwinter, J.Slight and F.H.Walters were all unavailable, significantly depleting the strength of the home side. Lohmann (14 for 195) dismissed Lewis with the first ball of the match to secure a wicket with his first ball in Australian first-class cricket. Houston (68 in about 135 minutes, 6 fours), Horan (117 not out in about 330 minutes, 5 fours), McShane (65 in about 135 minutes, 6 fours) and Morris (54 not out in about 120 minutes, 3 fours) surpassed 50 for Victoria, who had two tenth-wicket partnerships of 77, Horan/Boyle and Morris/Phillips (unbroken), each occupying about 90 minutes. Shrewsbury, attempting to stop a hot drive near the end of the first innings, split the webbing on his right hand and took no further part in the match; Barlow deputised in his absence and H.Wilson (local player) and R.Wood (opposition) alternately fielded for him in the second innings. Wood (Lancashire 1880-1884) was playing the first of two matches for Victoria before he was co-opted into the England team later in the season. The match was restricted to four days in order to adhere to the tourists' travel arrangements. Barnes (109 in about 180 minutes, 9 fours) and Barlow (86 in almost 4 hours, 0 fours) added 193 for the second wicket. *Wisden* incorrectly gives Vic (2) Lewis 4, Phillips 30. Sources: *Wisden, VCA Report, The Age, The Argus, The Australasian, The Leader.*

VICTORIA

Batsman	Dismissal		R		Dismissal	R
†P.M.Lewis	c Sherwin b Lohmann		0	(2)	c Barlow b Bates	3
J.Trinnick	b Lohmann		2	(8)	c Bates b Lohmann	2
R.S.Houston	b Barnes		68	(1)	b Lohmann	23
G.H.S.Trott	b Bates		20	(5)	b Lohmann	0
T.P.Horan	not out		117	(4)	c & b Lohmann	12
F.G.McShane	c Shrewsbury b Lohmann		65	(3)	b Lohmann	42
R.Wood	c Sherwin b Lohmann		0		c Bates b Lohmann	19
J.Worrall	b Lohmann		4	(6)	c Bates b Lohmann	8
S.Morris	c Shrewsbury b Lohmann		0		not out	54
J.Phillips	c Sherwin b Bates		10	(11)	not out	31
*H.F.Boyle	run out (Barnes/Sherwin)		30	(10)	c Briggs b Lohmann	5
Extras	(b3, lb4, w6)		13		(b4, lb4)	8
Total	(299.2 overs, 460 mins)		329		(174.0 overs, 275 mins) (9 wkts)	207

A.SHAW'S ENGLAND XI

Batsman	Dismissal	R
W.H.Scotton	b McShane	4
W.Barnes	c Trott b McShane	109
R.G.Barlow	b McShane	86
J.M.Read	b Trott	18
W.Gunn	b McShane	47
W.Bates	b Trott	3
J.Briggs	b Trott	0
W.Flowers	run out (Wood/Lewis)	52
G.A.Lohmann	st Lewis b Trott	18
†M.Sherwin	not out	6
*A.Shrewsbury	absent hurt	-
Extras	(b5, lb4)	9
Total	(244.2 overs, 427 mins)	352

ENGLAND XI	O	M	R	W	w,nb		O	M	R	W	w,nb
Lohmann	86.1	34	115	6	2,-		62	24	80	8	-,-
Briggs	27	14	36	0	1,-	(3)	23	12	43	0	-,-
Bates	51	31	45	2	2,-	(2)	48	24	47	1	-,-
Barlow	32.1	15	32	0	1,-	(5)	8	5	7	0	-,-
Barnes	63	37	59	1	-,-	(4)	15	9	9	0	-,-
Flowers	34	21	25	0	-,-		12	7	6	0	-,-
Read	6	3	4	0	-,-		6	3	7	0	-,-

VICTORIA	O	M	R	W	w,nb
Phillips	43	23	44	0	-,-
McShane	66	31	90	4	-,-
Trott	78.2	31	125	4	-,-
Worrall	20	6	32	0	-,-
Morris	8	6	6	0	-,-
Horan	7	1	12	0	-,-
Boyle	5	1	8	0	-,-
Wood	10	4	18	0	-,-
Houston	7	4	8	0	-,-

FALL OF WICKETS

Wkt	VIC 1st	ENG 1st	VIC 2nd
1st	0	11	6
2nd	9	204	60
3rd	72	211	83
4th	111	229	85
5th	211	235	93
6th	211	235	98
7th	219	325	100
8th	223	337	125
9th	252	352	130
10th	329	-	-

NEW SOUTH WALES v A.SHAW'S ENGLAND XI

Played at Sydney Cricket Ground on November 19, 20, 1886. (Four-day match)
Toss : England XI.   Result : NEW SOUTH WALES WON BY SIX WICKETS.
Debuts: New South Wales - J.J.Ferris, A.W.H.Whiting (both f/c).
12th Men: C.A.Richardson (NSW). No 12th named for Eng XI.
Umpires: J.Lillywhite and T.Nunn.
Attendances: 5000, 12000.   Total: About 17,000.   Receipts: No figures published.
Close of Play: 1st day Eng (2) 0/4 (Shrewsbury 0, Barlow 4).

Early morning rain on the first day created a treacherous pitch that was exploited by the bowlers on both sides, the same pitch being used for the duration of the match. Play continued after 6.00pm on the second day to enable New South Wales to score the 7 runs still required for victory. The light was very poor and Moses objected, but the umpires overruled in order to complete the match that evening. New South Wales lost a further two wickets in the gloom before the runs were scored. Turner (13 for 54) proved virtually unplayable in the conditions, bowling unchanged in the first innings and for all but three overs from one end in the second. His opening partner Ferris gave an indication of events to come. Ogilvy and Briggs sustained first-ball dismissals. Sources: *Wisden, The Australasian, Sydney Morning Herald, Town & Country Journal, Sydney Daily Telegraph.*

A.SHAW'S ENGLAND XI

*A.Shrewsbury	c Mather b Ferris	6		c McDonnell b Turner	4
W.H.Scotton	b Turner	2	(5)	c Gregory b Turner	21
W.Barnes	b Turner	4		lbw b Ferris	7
R.G.Barlow	c & b Ferris	11	(2)	c McDonnell b Turner	16
J.M.Read	c McDonnell b Turner	13	(4)	b Ferris	24
W.Gunn	c McDonnell b Turner	18		b Turner	8
W.Bates	b Ferris	2		b Turner	0
W.Flowers	b Ferris	11		not out	12
J.Briggs	b Turner	2		b Turner	0
G.A.Lohmann	b Turner	0		st Burton b Ferris	1
†M.Sherwin	not out	2		b Turner	1
Extras	(b3)	3		(b2, lb2)	4
Total	(53.2 overs, 135 mins)	74		(83.1 overs, in about 160 mins)	98

NEW SOUTH WALES

*P.S.McDonnell	b Barnes	32	(7)	c Gunn b Lohmann	0
A.C.Bannerman	c Barlow b Barnes	7	(1)	c Sherwin b Flowers	26
H.Moses	not out	31		not out	30
A.Mather	st Sherwin b Briggs	14		c Lohmann b Flowers	1
C.T.B.Turner	c Lohmann b Briggs	4	(6)	not out	4
A.H.Gregory	b Barlow	2			
A.P.Marr	c Sherwin b Barlow	9	(5)	b Lohmann	0
A.W.H.Whiting	run out	5			
†F.J.Burton	c Barnes b Flowers	0			
D.S.Ogilvy	c Barlow b Flowers	0			
J.J.Ferris	b Flowers	0			
Extras	(b7)	7		(lb1)	1
Total	(66.2 overs, in about 145 mins)	111		(93.1 overs, in about 135 mins) (4 wkts)	62

NEW SOUTH WALES	O	M	R	W	w,nb		O	M	R	W	w,nb					
Ferris	25	7	50	4	-,-		39	22	49	3	-,-					
Turner	26.2	14	20	6	-,-		38.1	23	34	7	-,-					
Ogilvy	2	1	1	0	-,-	(4)	3	1	9	0	-,-					
Marr						(3)	3	2	2	0	-,-					

													FALL OF WICKETS			
													ENG	NSW	ENG	NSW
												Wkt	1st	1st	2nd	2nd
												1st	8	39	22	1
												2nd	11	40	29	51
												3rd	26	62	29	55
ENGLAND XI	O	M	R	W	w,nb		O	M	R	W	w,nb	4th	28	66	74	57
Lohmann	16	7	32	0	-,-		29.1	15	30	2	-,-	5th	49	69	74	-
Barnes	17	9	26	2	-,-		14	11	4	0	-,-	6th	52	83	81	-
Barlow	14	6	23	2	-,-	(5)	5	4	4	0	-,-	7th	64	93	90	-
Briggs	14.2	10	20	2	-,-		11	9	5	0	-,-	8th	72	110	90	-
Flowers	5	4	3	3	-,-	(6)	17	12	8	2	-,-	9th	72	110	95	-
Bates						(3)	17	10	10	0	-,-	10th	74	111	98	-

NEW SOUTH WALES v A.SHAW'S ENGLAND XI

Played at Sydney Cricket Ground on December 10, 11, 13, 1886. (Four-day match)
Toss : England XI.   Result : A.SHAW'S ENGLAND XI WON BY NINE WICKETS.
Debuts: New South Wales - C.A.Richardson (f/c).
12th Men: None named.
Umpires: T.Nunn and H.Smith.
Attendances: 2500, 10000, 1500.   Total: About 14,000.   Receipts: No figures published.
Close of Play: 1st day Eng 2/20 (Shrewsbury 11); 2nd day NSW (2) 0/14 (Marr 4, Allen 6).

Rain, which had marked the first encounter between the teams, returned to influence the return match in favour of the visitors. New South Wales were sent in on a pitch softened by rain the previous day and were forced to play their second innings in similar conditions when further rain fell on Sunday, December 12th. Moses (44 with 3 fours) batted almost 3 hours in the first innings while Marr and Allen opened well in the second innings before the wicket cut up. Shrewsbury, who selected a new pitch for his side to bat on, gave a fine exhibition of wet-wicket technique for about 210 minutes to compile 64 (7 fours), the only fifty of the match. Lohmann (40 not out with 1 five and 4 fours) and Sherwin added 48 for the last wicket. Turner with eight wickets continued his fine bowling form. After the match, the pitch "looked more like a harrowed field than a cricket ground" (*SMH*). Sources: *Wisden, The Australasian, Sydney Morning Herald, Town & Country Journal, Sydney Daily Telegraph.*

NEW SOUTH WALES

A.C.Bannerman	c Barlow b Flowers	14	(6)	c Shrewsbury b Flowers	0
*P.S.McDonnell	b Briggs	0	(5)	c Lohmann b Flowers	25
H.Moses	b Briggs	44	(4)	b Lohmann	5
H.H.Massie	b Barnes	8	(3)	c Bates b Lohmann	9
C.A.Richardson	b Briggs	19	(8)	not out	3
R.C.Allen	b Briggs	0	(2)	c Barlow b Lohmann	30
C.T.B.Turner	b Barlow	15		b Lohmann	4
A.P.Marr	c Gunn b Barlow	4	(1)	c Lohmann b Flowers	23
W.W.McGlinchey	b Briggs	4	(10)	c Barlow b Flowers	1
†F.J.Burton	b Barlow	0	(9)	c Sherwin b Lohmann	0
J.J.Ferris	not out	0		b Flowers	3
Extras	(b8, nb1)	9		(b4)	4
Total	(156.1 overs, in about 240 mins)	117		(95.0 overs, in about 160 mins)	107

A.SHAW'S ENGLAND XI

*A.Shrewsbury	c Marr b Turner	64	(2)	not out	2
R.G.Barlow	c Burton b Ferris	4	(3)	not out	1
W.Barnes	b Turner	2			
J.M.Read	b Ferris	35			
W.H.Scotton	b Ferris	1			
W.Gunn	b Turner	34			
J.Briggs	b Turner	0			
W.Bates	b Turner	12			
W.Flowers	b Turner	0			
G.A.Lohmann	not out	40			
†M.Sherwin	b Turner	20	(1)	b Turner	1
Extras	(b4, lb4)	8		(lb1)	1
Total	(159.1 overs, in about 250 mins)	220		(3.3 overs, 6 mins) (1 wkt)	5

ENGLAND XI	O	M	R	W	w,nb		O	M	R	W	w,nb
Briggs	48.1	28	45	5	-,-		17	12	11	0	-,-
Lohmann	20	16	13	0	-,-	(3)	31	12	47	5	-,-
Flowers	36	27	16	1	-,-	(4)	29	18	21	5	-,-
Barnes	31	20	18	1	-,1						
Barlow	21	14	16	3	-,-	(2)	18	8	24	0	-,-

NEW SOUTH WALES	O	M	R	W	w,nb		O	M	R	W	w,nb
Ferris	59	31	81	3	-,-		2	1	1	0	-,-
Turner	70.1	39	77	7	-,-		1.3	0	3	1	-,-
McGlinchey	7	1	14	0	-,-						
Marr	12	3	24	0	-,-						
Allen	11	5	16	0	-,-						

FALL OF WICKETS

Wkt	NSW 1st	ENG 1st	NSW 2nd	ENG 2nd
1st	7	11	52	1
2nd	52	20	62	-
3rd	61	87	69	-
4th	74	89	81	-
5th	76	125	89	-
6th	95	125	98	-
7th	109	149	102	-
8th	116	149	102	-
9th	117	172	104	-
10th	117	220	107	-

AUSTRALIAN XI v A.SHAW'S ENGLAND XI

Played at Melbourne Cricket Ground on December 17, 18, 20, 21, 22, 1886. (Timeless match)
Toss : Australian XI.   Result : A.SHAW'S ENGLAND XI WON BY 57 RUNS.
Debuts: Nil.
12th Men: None named.
Umpires: D.F.Cotter and J.Phillips.
Attendances: 1500, 1000, 2500, 1500, 1000.   Total: About 7500.   Receipts: No figures published.
Close of Play: 1st day Aust 5/206 (Bruce 33, Blackham 24); 2nd day Aust 8/283 (Garrett 21); 3rd day Eng 8/191 (Scotton 39, Lohmann 7); 4th day Eng (2) 9/227 (Lohmann 19, Sherwin 3).

This was the first of three matches between the 1886 Australians and Shaw's England Team to be organised by the Melbourne Cricket Club. H.J.H.Scott and G.J.Bonnor had not yet returned from England and G.Giffen was unable to play because of illness; Trott was brought into the Australian team to make up the numbers and Garrett made captain in Scott's absence. Shrewsbury (62 in about 145 minutes, 3 fours) was the only batsman to exceed 50 in the match. A storm followed by several showers allowed little play on the second day but the pitch did not seem affected on the following days and was not considered a factor in the Australians' second-innings collapse. Poor judgement in running between wickets accounted for six Australian dismissals, Trott being twice a victim. The match provided the second instance in Australia of a victory after following on; Shaw's Team had also beaten Victoria in 1881-82 similarly. Phillips complained after the match that the Englishmen had questioned the impartiality of some of his decisions, citing an incident with the captain, Shrewsbury. The local Press supported Phillips, Tom Horan in *The Australasian* noting that "the Englishmen in their calmer moments will doubtless acknowledge that they were decidedly in the wrong". Sources: *Wisden, The Age, The Argus, The Australasian, The Leader, The Sportsman.*

AUSTRALIAN XI

S.P.Jones	c Scotton b Lohmann	46	(2)	b Briggs	0
G.E.Palmer	b Briggs	14	(1)	run out (Flowers)	1
J.W.Trumble	b Flowers	26		c Sherwin b Briggs	4
†A.H.Jarvis	c & b Bates	37		b Briggs	3
W.Bruce	c Sherwin b Briggs	48		c Barnes b Briggs	32
G.H.S.Trott	run out (/Lohmann)	14	(8)	run out (Lohmann/Sherwin)	13
J.M.Blackham	run out (Barnes/Sherwin)	32	(6)	st Sherwin b Briggs	2
J.McIlwraith	lbw b Lohmann	27	(9)	run out (Barlow/Flowers)	12
*T.W.Garrett	not out	24	(10)	c Shrewsbury b Barnes	12
E.Evans	b Briggs	6	(11)	not out	1
F.R.Spofforth	run out (Sherwin/Briggs)	2	(7)	c Lohmann b Barlow	25
Extras	(b10, lb8)	18		(b5, lb4)	9
Total	(262.0 overs, 435 mins)	294		(124.0 overs, 195 mins)	114

A.SHAW'S ENGLAND XI

*A.Shrewsbury	lbw b Trott	38		c Jones b Garrett	62
R.G.Barlow	c Jarvis b Garrett	19		b Palmer	12
W.Barnes	c Jarvis b Garrett	9		c Evans b Trott	13
J.M.Read	c Garrett b Trott	0		c Jones b Spofforth	38
W.Gunn	b Palmer	26		st Jarvis b Trott	25
W.H.Scotton	b Trott	39		run out (Trumble/Spofforth)	3
W.Bates	c Palmer b Evans	36		b Trumble	21
J.Briggs	c Bruce b Evans	7		c Bruce b Trumble	7
W.Flowers	b Spofforth	6		c Bruce b Trott	7
G.A.Lohmann	c McIlwraith b Evans	16		not out	32
†M.Sherwin	not out	1		c Spofforth b Garrett	25
Extras	(b1, lb1, w1, nb1)	4		(b12, lb5, nb2)	19
Total	(178.2 overs, 285 mins)	201		(189.2 overs, 315 mins)	264

ENGLAND XI	O	M	R	W	w,nb		O	M	R	W	w,nb
Lohmann	94	48	105	2	-,-	(3)	11	3	21	0	-,-
Briggs	83	46	64	3	-,-	(1)	62	42	42	5	-,-
Flowers	26	3	34	1	-,-	(4)	13	5	19	0	-,-
Barnes	25	14	29	0	-,-	(5)	4	2	3	1	-,-
Barlow	13	4	17	0	-,-	(2)	34	22	20	1	-,-
Bates	21	11	27	1	-,-						

AUSTRALIAN XI	O	M	R	W	w,nb		O	M	R	W	w,nb
Spofforth	20	10	24	1	-,-	(3)	42	19	59	1	-,-
Palmer	32	14	34	1	-,1	(4)	32	17	35	1	-,1
Garrett	41	25	41	2	-,-	(5)	15.2	7	21	2	-,-
Trott	51	28	55	3	-,-	(2)	41	10	73	3	-,-
Bruce	9	4	17	0	1,-	(7)	7	4	7	0	-,-
Evans	25.2	16	26	3	-,-	(1)	30	19	19	0	-,-
Trumble						(6)	22	10	31	2	-,1

FALL OF WICKETS

Wkt	AUST 1st	ENG 1st	ENG 2nd	AUST 2nd
1st	24	38	40	1
2nd	78	58	87	1
3rd	131	59	111	4
4th	131	82	143	21
5th	162	108	154	25
6th	230	159	180	69
7th	234	169	196	75
8th	283	178	196	100
9th	290	191	213	110
10th	294	201	264	114

VICTORIA v NEW SOUTH WALES

Played at Melbourne Cricket Ground on December 27, 28, 29, 30, 1886. (Timeless match)
Toss : New South Wales.   Result : NEW SOUTH WALES WON BY 184 RUNS.
Debuts: Nil.
12th Men: J.McIlwraith (Vic) and R.C.Allen (NSW).
Umpires: T.Nunn and J.Phillips.
Attendances: 5000, 3000, 2000, 2000.   Total: About 12,000.   Receipts: No figures published.
Close of Play: 1st day NSW 226 all out; 2nd day Vic 3/213 (Trumble 30, Midwinter 33); 3rd day NSW (2) 3/217 (McDonnell 158, Richardson 1).

Morris was a late replacement for F.R.Spofforth (groin strain) in the Victorian side. Little separated the teams after completion of the first innings, Turner (57 in about 75 minutes, 8 fours) and Palmer (77 in about 195 minutes, 6 fours) topscoring for their respective teams. McDonnell (239 in 260 minutes, 3 fives and 19 fours, chances at 28, 139 and 173) then took complete command. "The bowlers knew not where to pitch the ball to avoid his resolute and powerful strokes...and never once played in a faltering or hesitating style" (T.P.Horan, writing in *The Australasian*). He made 77% of the 310 runs scored while he was at the wicket, dominating century stands for the third wicket with Moses and the fourth wicket with Richardson in a career-best performance. This performance, on a wicket offering the bowlers some encouragement, ultimately proved to be the difference between the teams. Turner continued his wicket-taking with another ten-wicket haul which included the hat-trick (Palmer, Horan, Trumble) in the second innings. *Cricket* incorrectly gives NSW (2) Jones b Palmer. *VCA Report* incorrectly gives NSW (2) Jones 12, Palmer 2/91, omits Horan 0/10. Sources: *Cricket, VCA Report, The Age, The Argus, The Australasian, The Leader*.

NEW SOUTH WALES

A.C.Bannerman	c Trumble b Midwinter	16	(2)	b Trumble	7
*P.S.McDonnell	c Midwinter b McShane	30	(1)	c McShane b Morris	239
S.P.Jones	b Trott	46		c Walters b Palmer	10
H.Moses	b McShane	10		b Palmer	29
C.T.B.Turner	c Bruce b Trumble	57	(6)	b Morris	9
C.A.Richardson	b Morris	7	(5)	st Blackham b Trumble	20
T.W.Garrett	lbw b Trott	0		c Houston b Trumble	5
A.P.Marr	c Blackham b Trumble	9		c Horan b Morris	7
E.Evans	lbw b Morris	4		b Morris	9
†F.J.Burton	not out	5	(11)	not out	9
J.J.Ferris	b Palmer	36	(10)	c McShane b Trumble	5
Extras	(b3, lb2, w1)	6		(b2, lb11, w1)	14
Total	(149.0 overs, 285 mins)	226		(143.3 overs, 287 mins)	363

VICTORIA

W.Bruce	b Evans	39		c Burton b Turner	44
G.E.Palmer	b Turner	77		b Turner	15
T.P.Horan	b Ferris	22		b Turner	0
J.W.Trumble	c Marr b Turner	42		b Turner	0
W.E.Midwinter	b Turner	45	(6)	c Evans b Ferris	9
R.S.Houston	run out (Jones/Burton)	0	(8)	not out	29
F.H.Walters	run out (Bannerman/Burton)	5	(10)	c McDonnell b Ferris	10
F.G.McShane	b Garrett	7	(9)	b Ferris	0
*†J.M.Blackham	c Evans b Ferris	12	(5)	lbw b Turner	5
S.Morris	b Turner	2	(11)	lbw b Turner	5
G.H.S.Trott	not out	4	(7)	b Ferris	5
Extras	(b5, lb6, nb1)	12		(b15, lb1)	16
Total	(230.3 overs, 380 mins)	267		(88.0 overs, 150 mins)	138

VICTORIA	O	M	R	W	w,nb		O	M	R	W	w,nb
Trott	35	17	65	2	-,-	(2)	21	7	39	0	-,-
Palmer	16	8	25	1	-,-	(1)	37	15	81	2	‹-,-
McShane	26	10	42	2	-,-	(4)	12	3	31	0	-,-
Midwinter	37	24	36	1	-,-	(3)	11	2	26	0	-,-
Bruce	6	3	10	0	1,-	(7)	12	2	38	0	1,-
Trumble	17	7	26	2	-,-	(5)	26	9	58	4	-,-
Morris	12	6	16	2	-,-	(6)	18.3	3	66	4	-,-
Horan							6	3	10	0	-,-

NEW SOUTH WALES	O	M	R	W	w,nb		O	M	R	W	w,nb
Ferris	68.3	35	73	2	-,-	(5)	23	10	42	4	-,-
Turner	80	37	93	4	-,-		36	18	42	6	-,-
Jones	14	2	18	0	-,1		8	4	11	0	-,-
Garrett	35	17	41	1	-,-	(1)	13	6	15	0	-,-
Evans	28	17	20	1	-,-	(4)	8	2	12	0	-,-
Marr	5	2	10	0	-,-						

FALL OF WICKETS

Wkt	NSW 1st	VIC 1st	NSW 2nd	VIC 2nd
1st	46	66	63	50
2nd	46	147	109	50
3rd	77	149	209	50
4th	157	226	310	63
5th	171	232	327	76
6th	171	239	327	90
7th	181	248	333	101
8th	181	260	339	101
9th	188	263	348	127
10th	226	267	363	138

AUSTRALIAN XI v A.SHAW'S ENGLAND XI

Played at Melbourne Cricket Ground on January 1, 3, 4, 5, 1887. (Four-day match)
Toss : Australian XI   Result : MATCH DRAWN.
Debuts: Nil.
12th Men: None named.
Umpires: W.E.Midwinter and J.Phillips.
Attendances: 5000, 6000, 2000, 1000.   Total: About 14,000.   Receipts: No figures published.
Close of Play: 1st day Aust 8/223 (Blackham 50, Spofforth 0); 2nd day Eng 9/272 (Shrewsbury 29, Sherwin 20); 3rd day Aust (2) 9/223 (Trott 14).

Current Victorian player W.E.Midwinter, who was in the unique position of having represented both England and Australia in Tests, was requested to officiate in the match by the Englishmen due to some "unpleasantness" over recent decisions against them, according to *The Leader*. The tourists further objected to the appointment of Phillips but the Melbourne Cricket Club stood firm. G.Giffen (ill) was still unavailable and C.T.B.Turner was invited but could not obtain leave from his bank employers, so Trott was retained in the Australian team. The pre-match publicity announced that the game would be played out, but during the game it was agreed that play would cease at 4.00pm on Wednesday, January 5th. In the event, stumps were drawn at 3.45 on that day to allow the players to catch their train to Sydney for the third match in the series. Shrewsbury badly bruised a finger while fielding on the first day and held himself back in the first-innings order for that reason. Scotton was run out attempting a run off a no-ball. Barnes (93 in about 210 minutes, 4 fours) "showed fine driving power, impregnable defence and sound judgement in timing and placing" (*Australasian*). Blackham (63 in about 130 minutes, 2 fours) topped the scoring for the home team. Sources: *Wisden, The Age, The Argus, The Australasian, The Leader, The Sportsman*.

AUSTRALIAN XI

W.Bruce	c & b Bates	15	lbw b Bates		20
G.E.Palmer	c Barnes b Bates	1	b Barlow		25
S.P.Jones	c Lohmann b Flowers	48	c Scotton b Briggs		45
J.W.Trumble	run out (Read/Sherwin)	28	c Scotton b Lohmann		4
†A.H.Jarvis	b Bates	8	b Bates		42
J.McIlwraith	run out (Lohmann/Sherwin)	35	c Read b Lohmann		35
J.M.Blackham	c Barnes b Bates	63	b Barnes		21
G.H.S.Trott	c Lohmann b Barlow	0	not out		29
*T.W.Garrett	run out (Read/Sherwin)	31	lbw b Briggs		8
F.R.Spofforth	b Bates	6	b Briggs		5
E.Evans	not out	4	c Sherwin b Barlow		11
Extras	(lb6, w1)	7	(b2, lb2)		4
Total	(183.3 overs, 298 mins)	246	(234.1 overs, 390 mins)		249

A.SHAW'S ENGLAND XI

W.Barnes	c Palmer b Bruce	93	(2) b Spofforth		4
R.G.Barlow	b Spofforth	2			
J.M.Read	b Spofforth	7	(1) c & b Evans		5
W.H.Scotton	run out (Evans/Jarvis)	13	(5) b Bruce		22
W.Gunn	b Bruce	48	(4) not out		61
W.Bates	c Garrett b Bruce	14	(3) b Spofforth		6
G.A.Lohmann	lbw b Bruce	24			
J.Briggs	b Palmer	4			
W.Flowers	b Bruce	0			
*A.Shrewsbury	b Evans	31	(6) not out		15
†M.Sherwin	not out	22			
Extras	(b9, lb3, w1, nb5)	18	(b7, lb4, nb1)		12
Total	(172.0 overs, 310 mins)	276	(123.0 overs, 205 mins) (4 wkts)		125

ENGLAND XI	O	M	R	W	w,nb		O	M	R	W	w,nb		FALL OF WICKETS			
Briggs	42	20	51	0	-,-		59	31	67	3	-,-			AUST	ENG	AUST	ENG
Bates	43.3	16	72	5	-,-		37	12	69	2	-,-		Wkt	1st	1st	2nd	2nd
Lohmann	22	11	24	0	1,-	(5)	50	34	40	2	-,-		1st	6	7	31	9
Barlow	33	17	39	1	-,-		39.1	18	42	2	-,-		2nd	21	23	68	9
Flowers	25	9	41	1	-,-	(3)	21	15	8	0	-,-		3rd	93	56	87	21
Barnes	18	11	12	0	-,-		28	18	19	1	-,-		4th	98	157	119	84
													5th	120	180	153	-
AUSTRALIAN XI	O	M	R	W	w,nb		O	M	R	W	w,nb		6th	166	206	186	-
Spofforth	32	10	56	2	1,4		20	7	33	2	-,1		7th	166	221	201	-
Trott	20	7	40	0	-,-	(7)	4	2	7	0	-,-		8th	223	221	215	-
Garrett	17	7	22	0	-,-	(5)	12	8	8	0	-,-		9th	239	227	223	-
Trumble	13	7	12	0	-,-	(6)	4	2	6	0	-,-		10th	246	276	249	-
Bruce	35	17	56	5	-,-	(3)	28	20	19	1	-,-						
Palmer	36	12	60	1	-,-	(4)	22	15	13	0	-,-						
Jones	5	2	3	0	-,1	(8)	12	4	14	0	-,-						
Evans	14	8	9	1	-,-	(2)	21	13	13	1	-,-						

AUSTRALIAN XI v A.SHAW'S ENGLAND XI

Played at Sydney Cricket Ground on January 7, 8, 10, 11, 1887. (Four-day match)
Toss : England XI. Result : A.SHAW'S ENGLAND XI WON BY NINE WICKETS.
Debuts: Nil.
12th Men: None named.
Umpires; C.Bannerman and H.Rawlinson.
Attendances: 3500, 10000, 1500, 500. Total: About 15,500. Receipts: No figures published.
Close of Play: 1st day Eng 7/258 (Scotton 27, Briggs 68); 2nd day Aust 132 all out; 3rd day Eng (2) 0/4 (Barlow 1, Shrewsbury 0).

C.T.B.Turner was unable to obtain leave from his employers and Allen was called up to replace him. McIlwraith was absent on the second day through illness and W.Gunn substituted for him in the field. The Englishmen came under criticism for insisting that the Australian first innings be completed on the second day upon the fall of the ninth wicket at 5.55pm, rather than allowing stumps to be drawn so McIlwraith could bat on the following day's play. (As Sunday play was almost 80 years in the future, this would have given him an extra day to recover.) Although each innings was played on a new pitch, steep and unpredictable bounce made batting extremely hazardous. Barlow was repeatedly struck by Spofforth during a fiery opening spell on the first day and batsmen on both sides suffered. Read (53 out of 61 in about 60 minutes, 8 fours), Briggs (69 in about 105 minutes, 1 five and 6 fours) and Trumble (60 out of 75 in about 90 minutes, 1 five and 6 fours) hit the only half-centuries in the match. *Wisden* incorrectly gives Eng (1) Shrewsbury c Palmer. Sources: *Wisden, Sydney Referee, Sydney Morning Herald, Town & Country Journal, Sydney Mail, Sydney Daily Telegraph.*

A.SHAW'S ENGLAND XI

*A.Shrewsbury	c & b Garrett	28	(2) not out		16
R.G.Barlow	c Evans b Garrett	23	(1) c Evans b Garrett		3
W.Barnes	c Garrett b Trumble	13	not out		33
J.M.Read	run out (Allen/Blackham)	53			
W.Gunn	b Palmer	0			
W.H.Scotton	not out	43			
W.Bates	run out (Garrett/Blackham)	40			
G.A.Lohmann	c Trumble b Garrett	1			
J.Briggs	c & b Garrett	69			
W.Flowers	hit wkt b Garrett	5			
†M.Sherwin	c Trumble b Garrett	0			
Extras	(lb4, nb1)	5	(b1, lb4)		5
Total	(156.3 overs, in about 280 mins)	280	(20.1 overs, in about 40 mins) (1 wkt)		57

AUSTRALIAN XI

W.Bruce	c Sherwin b Barnes	22	c Lohmann b Barnes		12
G.E.Palmer	st Sherwin b Barnes	27	c Flowers b Lohmann		20
S.P.Jones	c & b Barnes	29	run out (Briggs/Barlow)		18
J.W.Trumble	c Sherwin b Barnes	6	c Gunn b Barlow		60
A.H.Jarvis	c Barnes b Lohmann	7	(7) c Sherwin b Barlow		11
R.C.Allen	c Gunn b Barnes	18	(8) c Sherwin b Barnes		30
†J.M.Blackham	c Shrewsbury b Barnes	14	(6) b Barnes		33
*T.W.Garrett	c Barlow b Barnes	7	(9) c Barnes b Barlow		0
F.R.Spofforth	c Sherwin b Barlow	0	(5) c Gunn b Barlow		1
E.Evans	not out	0	(11) b Barnes		2
J.McIlwraith	absent ill	-	(10) not out		4
Extras	(lb2)	2	(b9, lb3)		12
Total	(115.1 overs, in about 210 mins)	132	(142.1 overs, in about 250 mins)		203

AUSTRALIAN XI	O	M	R	W	w,nb		O	M	R	W	w,nb
Spofforth	33	13	67	0	-,1	(3)	2.1	0	14	0	-,-
Bruce	15	4	40	0	-,-						
Evans	19	12	16	0	-,-						
Trumble	28	14	34	1	-,-	(2)	10	4	16	0	-,-
Garrett	40.3	22	53	6	-,-	(1)	8	2	22	1	-,-
Jones	6	1	15	0	-,-						
Palmer	15	2	50	1	-,-						

ENGLAND XI	O	M	R	W	w,nb		O	M	R	W	w,nb
Briggs	8	3	21	0	-,-	(3)	13	6	22	0	-,-
Bates	5	2	4	0	-,-						
Lohmann	44	28	39	1	-,-	(2)	46	26	51	1	-,-
Barnes	50	28	51	7	-,-	(1)	41.1	21	61	4	-,-
Barlow	8.1	5	15	1	-,-	(4)	33	11	43	4	-,-
Flowers						(5)	9	6	14	0	-,-

FALL OF WICKETS

Wkt	ENG 1st	AUST 1st	ENG 2nd	AUST 2nd
1st	53	30	28	6
2nd	58	72	34	-
3rd	119	82	109	-
4th	122	91	110	-
5th	123	91	116	-
6th	166	113	133	-
7th	169	130	184	-
8th	264	132	191	-
9th	280	132	195	-
10th	280	-	203	-

NEW SOUTH WALES v VICTORIA

Played at Sydney Cricket Ground on January 22 (no play), 24, 25, 26 - 27 (no play), 28, 1887. (Timeless match)
Toss : New South Wales.   Result : NEW SOUTH WALES WON BY SIX WICKETS.
Debuts: Nil.
12th Men: J.T.Cottam (NSW) and S.Morris (Vic).
Umpires: C.Bannerman and J.Phillips.
Attendances & Receipts: No figures published.
Close of Play: 1st day no play; 2nd day NSW 6/84 (Richardson 3); 3rd day NSW (2) 2/19 (Jones 2, Turner 9); 4th day no play;
     5th day no play.

The New South Wales selectors omitted J.T.Cottam, J.Donoghue and A.P.Marr from their practice squad of 14. J.D.Edwards, J.McIlwraith, J.S.Swift and J.Trinnick were all unavailable for Victoria and G.E.Palmer withdrew after being selected. Evans was absent after the first actual day's play due to "domestic trouble" (*Sydney Telegraph*). T.Nunn was originally appointed as the home umpire but was replaced by Bannerman prior to the match getting under way. Rain severely disrupted the game, preventing play on the first, fourth and fifth days and interrupting proceedings on the intervening days. The wicket was in "deplorable condition" (*SMH*) and batting was a nightmare throughout, Garrett (28) topscoring in a match which saw 33 wickets fall for 260 runs in probably less than six hours of actual play. The sides argued over whether to start on the fourth and fifth days, the home team wishing to play, Phillips (visiting umpire) disagreeing. The *Town & Country Journal* reported that play would probably have got under way on the fourth day had not "Spofforth, Trumble and Bruce left the ground at about noon on Wednesday and did not return". Sources: *Cricket, VCA Report, Sydney Morning Herald, Town & Country Journal, Sydney Mail, Sydney Daily Telegraph.*

VICTORIA

W.Bruce	lbw b Garrett	5	(2) c Richardson b Turner		0
F.H.Walters	c Allen b Turner	0	(1) st Burton b Ferris		1
T.P.Horan	c Allen b Garrett	3	(11) not out		4
J.W.Trumble	c Burton b Ferris	27	(3) c Garrett b Ferris		3
*W.E.Midwinter	c Jones b Turner	0	(4) c Burton b Turner		0
F.G.McShane	b Ferris	8	(5) b Garrett		19
R.S.Houston	c Jones b Ferris	3	(6) b Ferris		0
J.Worrall	c Bannerman b Ferris	3	(9) c Richardson b Ferris		14
†J.M.Blackham	c McDonnell b Turner	1	(7) lbw b Ferris		0
G.H.S.Trott	b Turner	3	b Turner		7
F.R.Spofforth	not out	0	(8) b Turner		9
Extras	(b6, lb2)	8	(b9, lb2)		11
Total	(39.1 overs, in about 80 mins)	61	(55.3 overs, in about 100 mins)		68

NEW SOUTH WALES

A.C.Bannerman	b Spofforth	4	b Spofforth		0
*P.S.McDonnell	b Spofforth	25	c Bruce b Midwinter		6
S.P.Jones	b Spofforth	3	c Blackham b McShane		7
H.Moses	c Midwinter b Spofforth	10			
R.C.Allen	c McShane b Midwinter	6	(6) not out		0
T.W.Garrett	b Trumble	28	(5) b McShane		0
C.A.Richardson	not out	3			
C.T.B.Turner	b Trumble	2	(4) not out		26
J.J.Ferris	b Spofforth	3			
†F.J.Burton	b Spofforth	0			
E.Evans	absent	-			
Extras	(b4, nb1)	5	(b1, lb2)		3
Total	(64.0 overs, in about 120 mins)	89	(19.2 overs, in about 40 mins) (4 wkts)		42

NEW SOUTH WALES	O	M	R	W	w,nb		O	M	R	W	w,nb
Turner	20	10	24	4	-,-		20.3	6	25	4	-,-
Garrett	11	5	12	2	-,-	(3)	10	7	4	1	-,-
Ferris	8.1	2	17	4	-,-	(2)	25	12	28	5	-,-

VICTORIA	O	M	R	W	w,nb		O	M	R	W	w,nb
Spofforth	30	11	47	6	-,1		7	3	14	1	-,-
Midwinter	28	18	24	1	-,-		6.2	3	12	1	-,-
Trumble	5	1	10	2	-,-	(4)	2	1	1	0	-,-
Horan	1	0	3	0	-,-						
McShane						(3)	4	2	12	2	,

FALL OF WICKETS

Wkt	VIC 1st	NSW 1st	VIC 2nd	NSW 2nd
1st	9	4	1	6
2nd	9	8	4	9
3rd	14	40	4	35
4th	14	53	4	35
5th	34	53	5	-
6th	40	84	11	-
7th	43	86	20	-
8th	53	89	54	-
9th	59	89	58	-
10th	61	-	68	-

AUSTRALIA v ENGLAND (1st Test)

Played at Sydney Cricket Ground on January 28, 29, 31, 1887. (Timeless match)
Toss : Australia.   Result : ENGLAND WON BY 13 RUNS.
Debuts: Australia - J.J.Ferris, H.Moses, C.T.B.Turner (all Test). England - W.Gunn, M.Sherwin (both Test).
12th Men: R.C.Allen (Aust). No 12th named for Eng.
Umpires: C.Bannerman and H.Rawlinson.
Attendances: 1000, 6500, 2000.   Total: About 9500.   Receipts: £637.
Close of Play: 1st day Aust 4/76 (Moses 21, Bannerman 2); 2nd day Eng (2) 7/103 (Briggs 0).

This match began at 1.45pm, following the conclusion that morning to the intercolonial match between New South Wales and Victoria. It provided Australian first-class cricket with its only instance of two matches being played at the same ground on the same day. Rain before and during the intercolonial had left the ground in very poor shape and McDonnell became the first captain in Test cricket to send the opposition in to bat on winning the toss. Despite the choice of a fresh pitch for each innings, batsmen struggled throughout and scored very slowly. It was the first Test in Australia in which no one reached 50. Turner and Ferris bowled unchanged on their international debut, firming their first-class partnership by dismissing England for their lowest total in any Test. Two outstanding catches by Spofforth at point, and one by McShane at square-leg - who dived up to deflect the ball and leaped at it again to catch Shrewsbury - assisted the cause. Despite gaining a handy start on the first innings, Australia failed to peg back the England lead of 110 runs, Bannerman taking 50 minutes to score his first run and batting an hour for 4. Barnes, who on the second day was accused by The *Sydney Morning Herald* of "impertinence" when, after being dismissed for 32, "he walked away from his wicket a few yards and then, going back to the pitch, began to pat down the ground with his bat, implying by his action that the ground was not in a proper condition to play on", took his best analysis in 21 Tests for England to lead the tourists to victory. Spofforth finished his 18-match Test career with 94 wickets, a record number to this time. McShane was a last-minute replacement for G.E.Palmer (ill) in the Australian side, G.Giffen (also ill), W.Bruce and J.W.Trumble being unavailable in addition. Allen, the nominated 12th man, did not attend the match at any stage due to business. Sources: *Wisden, Sydney Referee, Sydney Morning Herald, Town & Country Journal, Sydney Daily Telegraph.*

ENGLAND

W.Bates	c Midwinter b Ferris	8		b Ferris	24
*A.Shrewsbury	c McShane b Ferris	2		b Ferris	29
W.Barnes	c Spofforth b Turner	0		c Moses b Garrett	32
R.G.Barlow	b Turner	2		c Jones b Ferris	4
J.M.Read	c Spofforth b Ferris	5		b Ferris	0
W.Gunn	b Turner	0		b Turner	4
W.H.Scotton	c Jones b Turner	1	(9)	c Spofforth b Garrett	6
J.Briggs	c Midwinter b Turner	5		b Spofforth	33
G.A.Lohmann	c Garrett b Ferris	17	(7)	lbw b Ferris	3
W.Flowers	b Turner	2		c McDonnell b Turner	14
†M.Sherwin	not out	0		not out	21
Extras	(b2, lb1)	3		(b7, lb7)	14
Total	(35.3 overs, in about 70 mins)	45		(136.2 overs, in about 270 mins)	184

AUSTRALIA

*P.S.McDonnell	b Barnes	14	(2)	lbw b Barnes	0
†J.M.Blackham	c Sherwin b Lohmann	4	(1)	b Barnes	5
H.Moses	b Barlow	31		c Shrewsbury b Barnes	24
S.P.Jones	c Shrewsbury b Bates	31		c Read b Barnes	18
C.T.B.Turner	b Barlow	3		c & b Barnes	7
A.C.Bannerman	not out	15		b Lohmann	4
F.G.McShane	lbw b Briggs	5		b Briggs	0
W.E.Midwinter	c Shrewsbury b Barlow	0		lbw b Barnes	10
T.W.Garrett	b Lohmann	12		c Gunn b Lohmann	10
F.R.Spofforth	b Lohmann	2		b Lohmann	5
J.J.Ferris	c Barlow b Barnes	1		not out	0
Extras	(b1)	1		(b12, lb2)	14
Total	(113.1 overs, in about 230 mins)	119		(107.0 overs, in about 220 mins)	97

AUSTRALIA	O	M	R	W	w,nb		O	M	R	W	w,nb		FALL OF WICKETS			
														ENG	AUST	ENG	AUST
Turner	18	11	15	6	-,-		44.2	22	53	2	-,-		Wkt	1st	1st	2nd	2nd
Ferris	17.3	7	27	4	-,-		61	30	76	5	-,-		1st	11	8	31	4
Spofforth							12	3	17	1	-,-		2nd	11	18	80	5
Midwinter							4	1	10	0	-,-		3rd	13	64	92	29
Garrett							12	7	8	2	-,-		4th	13	67	92	38
McShane							3	0	6	0	-,-		5th	13	86	98	58
													6th	17	95	99	61
ENGLAND	O	M	R	W	w,nb		O	M	R	W	w,nb		7th	21	96	103	80
Barnes	22.1	16	19	2	-,-	(2)	46	29	28	6	-,-		8th	29	116	128	83
Lohmann	21	12	30	3	-,-	(4)	24	11	20	3	-,-		9th	41	118	153	95
Briggs	14	5	25	1	-,-	(5)	7	5	7	1	-,-		10th	45	119	184	97
Barlow	35	23	25	3	-,-	(1)	13	6	20	0	-,-						
Bates	21	9	19	1	-,-	(3)	17	11	8	0	-,-						

VICTORIA v SOUTH AUSTRALIA

Played at Melbourne Cricket Ground on February 11, 12, 14, 1887. (Timeless match)
Toss : Victoria.   Result : VICTORIA WON BY 144 RUNS.
Debuts: Victoria - W.Over (f/c). South Australia - H.Haldane, A.F.Slight (both f/c).
12th Men: H.C.Chittleborough & J.E.Gooden (SA emergencies). No 12th named for Vic.
Umpires: J.Duffy and I.A.Fisher.
Attendances: 400, 1000, 200.   Total: About 1600.   Receipts: No figures published.
Close of Play: 1st day SA 4/98 (Godfrey 34, W.F.Giffen 8); 2nd day Vic (2) 5/188 (Midwinter 29, Wood 0).

W.Bruce, T.P.Horan, G.E.Palmer, F.R.Spofforth, J.W.Trumble and F.H.Walters were unavailable and Lewis, Over and Wood replaced J.M.Blackham (fishing trip), J.D.Edwards (unable to obtain leave) and J.Slight (death of father) in the selected Victorian team. J.Trinnick was refused leave at the last moment; Phillips, who had been appointed to umpire, was co-opted, with Duffy taking over the umpiring duties. South Australia omitted Chittleborough and Gooden from their party of thirteen. Trott strained a groin muscle just before lunch on the second day and took no further part in the match, C.F.Foot acting as substitute during the second innings. The VCA made efforts to have the six-ball over used in the match but G.Giffen objected and the matter was not pursued further. McIlwraith (72 out of 104 in about 80 minutes, 1 five and 10 fours) gave "a first-class exhibition of dashing and powerful cricket" (*Australasian*) in the second innings. McShane (49 in about 120 minutes, 6 fours) and Midwinter (52 not out in about 90 minutes, 1 five and 5 fours) built on his beginning to set the visitors a formidable task that proved way beyond their capabilities. G.Giffen (12 for 187) bowled unchanged through the Victorian first innings. Sources: *Cricket, C.B.O'Reilly, The Age, The Argus, The Australasian, The Leader, The Sportsman.*

VICTORIA

R.S.Houston	b G.Giffen	16	(2) b G.Giffen		4
J.McIlwraith	lbw b G.Giffen	0	(1) c W.F.Giffen b Haldane		72
F.G.McShane	c Lyons b G.Giffen	39	b G.Giffen		49
S.Morris	b G.Giffen	24	b McKenzie		25
*W.E.Midwinter	c Noel b G.Giffen	7	not out		52
G.H.S.Trott	c McKenzie b G.Giffen	21	absent hurt		-
†P.M.Lewis	b Lyons	13	(8) b G.Giffen		3
R.Wood	not out	11	(7) b Noel		4
J.Worrall	b G.Giffen	3	c Kemp b G.Giffen		6
W.Over	b G.Giffen	0	c & b Noel		6
J.Phillips	run out (Noel/Jarvis)	2	(6) lbw b Noel		0
Extras	(b2)	2	(b6, lb3)		9
Total	(84.2 overs, 170 mins)	138	(102.3 overs, 195 mins)		230

SOUTH AUSTRALIA

C.G.Godfrey	b Morris	40	(7) c & b Midwinter		13
W.Knill	c Worrall b Midwinter	24	(1) c McShane b Midwinter		6
J.J.Lyons	c Midwinter b Morris	24	(2) c Lewis b Midwinter		10
*G.Giffen	c & b Morris	4	(3) b Morris		0
†A.H.Jarvis	c & b Worrall	4	(4) st Lewis b Midwinter		3
W.F.Giffen	c Trott b Over	25	(5) c McShane b Morris		4
J.Noel	b Worrall	0	(8) c & b Morris		2
A.F.Slight	not out	16	(6) c & b Midwinter		1
J.McKenzie	c Houston b Morris	6	c McIlwraith b Morris		4
H.Haldane	b Phillips	25	b Morris		4
B.C.E.Kemp	c Over b Worrall	2	not out		6
Extras		-	(b1)		1
Total	(129.3 overs, 225 mins)	170	(50.0 overs, 110 mins)		54

SOUTH AUSTRALIA	O	M	R	W	w,nb		O	M	R	W	w,nb
Noel	16	8	24	0	-,-	(3)	29.3	11	43	3	-,-
G.Giffen	42	14	83	8	-,-		39	9	104	4	-,-
Lyons	26.2	16	29	1	-,-	(1)	15	5	29	0	-,-
Haldane							6	1	21	1	-,-
Kemp							7	1	16	0	-,-
McKenzie							6	3	8	1	-,-

VICTORIA	O	M	R	W	w,nb		O	M	R	W	w,nb
Trott	9	3	17	0	-,-						
McShane	7	3	13	0	-,-						
Over	18	12	11	1	-,-						
Midwinter	20	9	26	1	-,-	(3)	22	12	22	5	-,-
Morris	26	8	59	4	-,-	(1)	25	13	21	5	-,-
Phillips	18	10	15	1	-,-	(2)	3	1	10	0	-,-
Worrall	31.3	16	29	3	-,-						

FALL OF WICKETS

Wkt	VIC 1st	SA 1st	VIC 2nd	SA 2nd
1st	8	40	32	13
2nd	35	81	104	16
3rd	70	85	149	17
4th	80	90	182	21
5th	107	104	185	23
6th	107	105	196	27
7th	121	123	199	30
8th	130	131	210	38
9th	130	163	230	42
10th	138	170	-	54

NEW SOUTH WALES v A.SHAW'S ENGLAND XI

Played at Sydney Cricket Ground on February 18, 19, 21, 1887. (Four-day match)
Toss : England XI.   Result : NEW SOUTH WALES WON BY 122 RUNS
Debuts: New South Wales - J.T.Cottam, I.F.Wales (both f/c).
12th Men: S.Deane (NSW). No 12th named for Eng XI.
Umpires: C.Bannerman and J.Swift (see below).
Attendances: 800, 7000, 2000.   Total: About 9800   Receipts: No figures published.
Close of Play: 1st day NSW 8/134 (Richardson 3); 2nd day NSW (2) 1/87 (Moses 46, Bannerman 5).

This match was not on the original itinerary of the English team but replaced one against a combined side from Melbourne and Sydney universities at the same ground. The Englishmen co-opted Wood, a former Lancashire player currently residing in (and playing for) Victoria, as a replacement for W.Barnes who had injured his hand in a fight with P.S.McDonnell after the Sydney Test; his punch had missed and connected with a brick wall instead. Cottam (originally 12th man) and R.Bryant were selected in the New South Wales team to replace F.J.Burton and E.Evans (both unavailable) but Bryant did not arrive on time and Wales was sent for and included in his place. When Bryant eventually turned up, after the match had begun, he stood aside in fairness to Wales. Bannerman had Lillywhite as his umpiring partner on the first day due to the late arrival of Swift. Swift was late again on the third day and Wallington and Lillywhite deputised in turn until he arrived. All four innings were played on a different pitch. Moses (73 in about 165 minutes, 8 fours) compiled the only half-century in the match. Turner's match figures of 14 for 59 included 8 for 32, his best for New South Wales, achieved without assistance from the field. Inclement weather again caused interruptions and created favourable bowling conditions. *Wisden* incorrectly gives NSW (1) Ferris b Lohmann. Sources: *Wisden, The Australasian, Sydney Morning Herald, Town & Country Journal, Sydney Daily Telegraph.*

NEW SOUTH WALES

*P.S.McDonnell	c Shrewsbury b Lohmann	15	(7)	c Shrewsbury b Briggs	16
A.C.Bannerman	b Lohmann	3	(3)	c Shrewsbury b Lohmann	24
R.C.Allen	c Gunn b Bates	41	(4)	c & b Lohmann	0
S.P.Jones	c Shrewsbury b Bates	12	(5)	c Read b Flowers	1
J.T.Cottam	b Briggs	29	(8)	not out	14
T.W.Garrett	c Sherwin b Briggs	8	(9)	lbw b Lohmann	4
C.T.B.Turner	c Wood b Lohmann	12	(6)	c Shrewsbury b Flowers	12
C.A.Richardson	not out	6	(1)	run out (/Sherwin)	25
H.Moses	b Briggs	9	(2)	b Lohmann	73
J.J.Ferris	c Wood b Lohmann	3		c Briggs b Lohmann	0
†I.F.Wales	b Lohmann	1		b Lohmann	0
Extras	(b2)	2		(b10, nb1)	11
Total	(96.0 overs, in about 170 mins)	141		(123.0 overs, in about 220 mins)	180

A.SHAW'S ENGLAND XI

W.Bates	c & b Turner	48		c Moses b Ferris	40
*A.Shrewsbury	b Turner	0		b Turner	0
R.G.Barlow	b Turner	0	(5)	b Turner	4
W.H.Scotton	b Turner	0	(7)	c Bannerman b Turner	4
J.M.Read	b Turner	0	(3)	c Bannerman b Ferris	2
W.Gunn	b Ferris	13	(4)	c Cottam b Ferris	2
G.A.Lohmann	b Turner	4	(8)	b Turner	26
J.Briggs	lbw b Garrett	10	(6)	b Turner	5
W.Flowers	b Turner	2		c McDonnell b Turner	0
R.Wood	not out	10		c & b Garrett	9
†M.Sherwin	b Turner	0		not out	0
Extras	(b11, lb1)	12		(b8)	8
Total	(68.2 overs, in about 120 mins)	99		(59.1 overs, in about 100 mins)	100

ENGLAND XI	O	M	R	W	w,nb		O	M	R	W	w,nb		FALL OF WICKETS			
Briggs	35	14	43	3	-,-		30	13	34	1	-,-			NSW	ENG	NSW	ENG
Lohmann	34	11	56	5	-,-	(3)	33	13	41	6	-,-	Wkt	1st	1st	2nd	2nd
Barlow	13	3	24	0	-,-	(2)	13	4	25	0	-,1	1st	16	2	75	4
Bates	14	7	16	2	-,-	(5)	15	6	21	0	-,-	2nd	19	49	129	7
Flowers						(4)	14	4	32	2	-,-	3rd	66	51	129	19
Read							10	6	8	0	-,-	4th	74	51	134	48
Wood							8	5	8	0	-,-	5th	91	62	134	49
												6th	122	72	151	54
NEW SOUTH WALES	O	M	R	W	w,nb		O	M	R	W	w,nb	7th	122	80	165	71
Ferris	30	11	43	1	-,-		29	7	62	3	-,-	8th	134	84	176	79
Turner	33.2	14	32	8	-,-		29.1	13	27	6	-,-	9th	137	92	180	100
Garrett	5	2	12	1	-,-		1	0	3	1	-,-	10th	141	99	180	100

AUSTRALIA v ENGLAND (2nd Test)

Played at Sydney Cricket Ground on February 25, 26, 28, March 1, 1887. (Timeless match)
Toss : England.   Result : ENGLAND WON BY 71 RUNS.
Debuts: Australia - R.C.Allen, F.J.Burton, J.T.Cottam, W.F.Giffen, J.J.Lyons (all Test). England - R.Wood (Test).
12th Men: None named.
Umpires: C.Bannerman and J.Swift (W.Gunn deputised).
Attendances: 1000, 6000, 2000, 500.   Total: About 9500.   Receipts: £557.
Close of Play: 1st day Eng 7/128 (Barlow 24, Flowers 37); 2nd day Eng (2) 5/73 (Barlow 10, Scotton 0); 3rd day Aust (2) 5/101
    (Allen 19, Midwinter 4).

The Australian team was undermanned and was not truly representative. Attempts were made to obtain George Giffen (South Australia), J.M.Blackham, W.Bruce, G.E.Palmer and J.W.Trumble (all Victoria) but for various reasons none could be enticed to Sydney. The selectors chose to ignore A.C.Bannerman and F.R.Spofforth. S.P.Jones, named in the Australian side, was absent when the match began and Cottam was promoted from 12th man, his Test debut being only his second first-class appearance. England, unable to select W.Barnes (injured hand), co-opted Wood, who had been resident in Victoria for two years. In the absence of an England reserve, first Ferris and then Turner substituted for William Gunn while he stood on the final day for umpire Swift (absent). Overnight rain and early drizzle prevented play on the first day before 3.00pm and virtually sealed the fate of batsmen for the match although Barlow (34 in about 165 minutes, 2 fours, and 42 not out in about 210 minutes, 1 fours) was able to demonstrate his renowned defensive skills. Turner and Ferris accounted for 18 of the 20 English wickets, bowling almost without a break in the two innings. Lohmann bowled unchanged throughout the Australian first innings to record the first eight-wicket analysis in a Test match innings. He learnt the following day that his mother had died. Giffen was out to the first ball he faced in the second innings. *Wisden* incorrectly gives Aust (1) Cottam hit wkt b Lohmann; Eng (2) Wood hit wkt b Midwinter. Sources: *Wisden, Sydney Referee, Sydney Morning Herald, Town & Country Journal, Sydney Mail, Sydney Daily Telegraph.*

ENGLAND

W.Bates	c Ferris b Turner	8		b Turner		30
*A.Shrewsbury	b Turner	9		b Turner		6
J.M.Read	b Turner	11	(4)	st Burton b Ferris		2
W.Gunn	b Turner	9	(5)	c Cottam b Ferris		10
R.G.Barlow	c Allen b Ferris	34	(3)	not out		42
G.A.Lohmann	b Ferris	2		b Ferris		6
W.H.Scotton	b Turner	0		b Ferris		2
J.Briggs	b Ferris	17		b Garrett		16
W.Flowers	c Allen b Ferris	37		b Turner		18
R.Wood	lbw b Ferris	6		b Midwinter		0
†M.Sherwin	not out	4		b Turner		5
Extras	(b9, lb3, nb2)	14		(b12, lb5)		17
Total	(109.0 overs, in about 220 mins)	151		(140.1 overs, in about 245 mins)		154

AUSTRALIA

J.J.Lyons	b Lohmann	11	(4)	c Gunn b Bates		0
W.F.Giffen	b Lohmann	2	(6)	b Briggs		0
R.C.Allen	b Lohmann	14		c sub (C.T.B.Turner) b Bates		30
H.Moses	b Flowers	28	(2)	st Sherwin b Bates		33
*P.S.McDonnell	c Gunn b Lohmann	10	(1)	c Gunn b Lohmann		35
W.E.Midwinter	b Lohmann	1	(7)	c Sherwin b Lohmann		4
J.T.Cottam	b Lohmann	1	(5)	st Sherwin b Briggs		3
C.T.B.Turner	c & b Flowers	9		c Briggs b Bates		9
T.W.Garrett	b Lohmann	1		c Sherwin b Briggs		20
J.J.Ferris	b Lohmann	1		run out (Briggs/Sherwin)		2
†F.J.Burton	not out	0		not out		2
Extras	(b5, lb1)	6		(b9, lb3)		12
Total	(55.1 overs, in about 110 mins)	84		(110.0 overs, in about 210 mins)		150

AUSTRALIA	O	M	R	W	w,nb		O	M	R	W	w,nb			FALL OF WICKETS		
Ferris	45	16	71	5	-,-	(2)	60	33	69	4	-,-		ENG	AUST	ENG	AUST
Turner	53	29	41	5	-,1	(1)	64.1	33	52	4	-,-	Wkt	1st	1st	2nd	2nd
Garrett	6	2	12	0	-,-		10	6	7	1	-,-	1st	14	12	21	51
Midwinter	3	1	2	0	-,1		6	3	9	1	-,-	2nd	19	15	42	86
Lyons	2	0	11	0	,							3rd	35	40	47	86
												4th	38	56	59	95
ENGLAND	O	M	R	W	w,nb		O	M	R	W	w,nb	5th	43	59	73	95
Briggs	20	6	34	0	-,-	(2)	22	9	31	3	-,-	6th	50	65	77	106
Lohmann	27.1	12	35	8	-,-	(1)	40	16	52	2	-,-	7th	73	82	98	121
Flowers	8	3	9	2	-,-		13	5	17	0	-,-	8th	130	83	136	129
Barlow							9	2	12	0	-,-	9th	145	83	137	135
Bates							26	13	26	4	-,-	10th	151	84	154	150

VICTORIA v A.SHAW'S ENGLAND XI

Played at Melbourne Cricket Ground on March 4, 5, 7 (no play), 8, 9, 1887. (Timeless match)
Toss : Victoria.   Result : A.SHAW'S ENGLAND XI WON BY NINE WICKETS.
Debuts: Victoria - D.F.Cotter (f/c).
12th Men: None named.
Umpires: J.Duffy and J.Taylor.
Attendances: 500, 2000, no play, 1000, 200.   Total: About 3700.   Receipts: No figures published.
Close of Play: 1st day Vic 9/245 (Horan 23, Cotter 27); 2nd day Eng 3/220 (Shrewsbury 123, Gunn 15); 3rd day no play; 4th day Vic (2)
    5/137 (Horan 42, Morris 8).

G.H.S.Trott (ill), J.M.Blackham, G.E.Palmer and F.R.Spofforth were all unavailable for Victoria. Shaw's Team were again unable to play W.Barnes because of his hand injury so Wood, who was on the Victorian side in their earlier clash, again appeared. They were also without Gunn (ill) on the first day, several Victorians alternating as substitutes in the field. Lillywhite had been expected to act as the English umpire but was replaced at the last moment by Joe Taylor, a long-serving Victorian scorer. Bruce (62 out of 82 in 70 minutes, 8 fours) and McIlwraith (64 in about 210 minutes, 3 fours) recorded contrasting half-centuries but the remainder of the Victorian batting disappointed on "a billiard-table-like pitch" (*Australasian*). Shrewsbury (144 in about 315 minutes, 16 fours, 2 chances) "played admirable cricket from first to last" (*Australasian*) and, with the stolid support of Barlow (43 in about 195 minutes, 2 fours) put the visitors in a strong position. Rain prevented any play on the scheduled third day and "had an effect on the wicket" (*Age*) for a time on the following day that assisted Bruce to capture a career-best 7 for 72. The Victorian batting failed for a second time, despite improving conditions, and Bates (86 in about 105 minutes, 8 fours) hit the visitors to a comfortable victory. Sources: *Wisden, VCA Report, The Age, The Argus, The Herald, The Australasian, The Leader.*

VICTORIA

W.Bruce	c Flowers b Briggs	62		c Gunn b Lohmann	18
J.McIlwraith	c Shrewsbury b Flowers	64		c Sherwin b Briggs	23
J.W.Trumble	c Sherwin b Flowers	4	(5)	c Gunn b Barlow	2
F.G.McShane	c Briggs b Read	45		c Lohmann b Briggs	2
T.P.Horan	not out	23	(3)	b Lohmann	47
*W.E.Midwinter	c Shrewsbury b Flowers	7		b Lohmann	35
S.Morris	c Sherwin b Flowers	4		c Sherwin b Flowers	8
R.S.Houston	c Shrewsbury b Flowers	2		c & b Lohmann	10
J.Worrall	c Shrewsbury b Bates	2		st Sherwin b Lohmann	0
J.Phillips	c Barlow b Bates	0		not out	2
†D.F.Cotter	b Bates	27		c Gunn b Flowers	1
Extras	(b4, lb1)	5		(b2, lb4, w1, nb1)	8
Total	(161.1 overs, 270 mins)	245		(154.2 overs, 245 mins)	156

A.SHAW'S ENGLAND XI

*A.Shrewsbury	b Bruce	144	(2)	not out	29
W.Bates	b Midwinter	1	(1)	c & b Worrall	86
R.G.Barlow	lbw b Morris	43		not out	4
J.M.Read	c McShane b Bruce	23			
W.Gunn	b Bruce	18			
W.H.Scotton	c Bruce b Trumble	2			
G.A.Lohmann	b Bruce	1			
J.Briggs	b Bruce	4			
W.Flowers	not out	26			
R.Wood	lbw b Bruce	1			
†M.Sherwin	c McIlwraith b Bruce	0			
Extras	(b14, nb6)	20			–
Total	(195.0 overs, 350 mins)	283		(65.0 overs, 115 mins) (1 wkt)	119

ENGLAND XI	O	M	R	W	w,nb		O	M	R	W	w,nb
Lohmann	23	11	40	0	-,-	(2)	52	29	44	5	-,-
Bates	41.1	18	66	3	-,-	(5)	10	2	15	0	-,-
Barlow	17	7	33	0	-,-	(4)	16	8	18	1	-,-
Briggs	26	13	37	1	-,-	(3)	21	7	29	2	1,1
Flowers	48	27	50	5	-,-	(1)	55.2	31	42	2	-,-
Read	6	1	14	1	-,-						

VICTORIA	O	M	R	W	w,nb		O	M	R	W	w,nb
Midwinter	39	25	26	1	-,6		13	3	32	0	-,-
Morris	20	5	43	1	-,-	(3)	8	3	19	0	-,-
Bruce	50	18	72	7	-,-	(2)	10	1	21	0	-,-
Worrall	13	2	30	0	-,-	(7)	6	5	1	1	-,-
Trumble	41	23	46	1	-,-		7	1	16	0	-,-
McShane	24	11	35	0	-,-	(4)	13	3	22	0	-,-
Phillips	5	2	3	0	-,-	(6)	8	4	8	0	-,-
Horan	1	1	0	0	-,-						
Houston	2	0	8	0	-,-						

FALL OF WICKETS

	VIC	ENG	VIC	ENG
Wkt	1st	1st	2nd	2nd
1st	82	6	31	111
2nd	87	148	47	-
3rd	163	196	56	-
4th	186	228	62	-
5th	202	237	116	-
6th	206	244	138	-
7th	212	248	146	-
8th	215	259	146	-
9th	215	275	155	-
10th	245	283	156	-

SMOKERS v NON-SMOKERS

Played at East Melbourne Cricket Ground on March 17, 18, 19, 21, 1887. (Four-day match)
Toss : Non-Smokers.   Result : MATCH DRAWN.
Debuts: Smokers - W.V.Duffy (f/c).
12th Men: None named.
Umpires: J.Phillips and R.Wood.
Attendances: 400, 500, 600, 100.   Total: About 1600.   Receipts: No figures published.
Close of Play: 1st day Non- Smokers 2/423 (Shrewsbury 183, Gunn 104); 2nd day Non-Smokers 8/792 (Cooper 40, Sherwin 1);
     3rd day Smokers 3/302 (Flowers 48, Lohmann 16).

Initial arrangements for the English tour were that all Melbourne games would be played at the East Melbourne ground, home of East Melbourne Cricket Club, but upon their arrival in Australia the tourists successfully negotiated with Melbourne Cricket Club to have the venue switched to the M.C.G. As compensation for E.M.C.C., a match was then scheduled between Shaw's Team and a Combined XI of Australia, but the unavailability of many leading players from Melbourne and Sydney led to the staging of this match instead. Duffy was a last-minute replacement for W.E.Midwinter (unavailable). Boyle led the Smokers into the field, "each blowing a cloud from a cigar of colonial manufacture; but immediately the business of the day commenced 'butts' were thrown away" (*Age*). On a perfect batting wicket, Non-Smokers compiled the highest total in first-class cricket to date. Shrewsbury (236 in about 345 minutes, 40 fours, 3 chances) and Bruce (131 in about 135 minutes, 1 six and 17 fours, 2 chances) added 196 for the first wicket. Shrewsbury's third-wicket stand of 310 with Gunn (150 in about 195 minutes, 1 five and 21 fours, 1 chance) was the highest partnership so far recorded for any wicket in Australia. Barnes did not bat due to his long-standing hand injury. Palmer's 113 for Smokers included 11 fours. A thunderstorm on the last day ruled out play before lunch and completely changed the character of the wicket. Scotton defended the last ball of the match and picked it up as a souvenir, putting it in his pocket, only to be given out "handled the ball" - the first batsman so dismissed in Australia. Wood, who had previously played for and against the Englishmen during the season, now appeared as umpire. Most falls of wickets for Smokers were not recorded in any source. Sources: *Wisden, The Age, The Argus, The Herald, The Australasian, The Leader, The Sportsman*.

NON-SMOKERS

*A.Shrewsbury	c Duffy b Briggs	236
W.Bruce	lbw b Palmer	131
W.Bates	b Palmer	4
W.Gunn	b Boyle	150
R.G.Barlow	b Palmer	29
R.S.Houston	c & b Briggs	57
H.A.Musgrove	st Lewis b Briggs	62
J.Worrall	b Read	78
W.H.Cooper	c & b Briggs	46
†M.Sherwin	not out	5
W.Barnes	absent hurt	-
Extras	(b3, lb1, w1)	5
Total	(302.1 overs, in about 550 mins)	803

SMOKERS

J.M.Read	st Sherwin b Cooper	30			
G.E.Palmer	c Worrall b Bruce	113	(1) c Houston b Worrall	24
J.Briggs	c Shrewsbury b Bates	86	(2) st Sherwin b Bates	54
W.Flowers	run out (/Sherwin)	69	(3) b Houston	25
G.A.Lohmann	c sub (J.Briggs) b Bates	19	(4) lbw b Gunn	2
W.H.Scotton	c Bruce b Bates	11	(5) handled the ball	18
*H.F.Boyle	b Bruce	7	(6) not out	0
G.R.Browning	b Bates	1		
F.H.Walters	st Sherwin b Bates	0		
†P.M.Lewis	c Houston b Bates	2		
W.V.Duffy	not out	0		
Extras	(b12, lb2, w2, nb2)	18	(b9, lb2, nb1)	12
Total	(150.3 overs, in about 270 mins)	356	(71.0 overs, in about 130 mins) (5 wkts)	135

SMOKERS	O	M	R	W	w,nb
Briggs	55.1	11	141	4	1,-
Palmer	54	10	189	3	-,-
Boyle	31	14	60	1	-,-
Lohmann	48	18	113	0	-,-
Flowers	38	12	93	0	,
Scotton	26	4	82	0	-,-
Duffy	15	2	52	0	-,-
Read	26	10	43	1	-,-
Walters	9	4	25	0	-,-

NON-SMOKERS	O	M	R	W	w,nb		O	M	R	W	w,nb
Bates	49	18	73	6	-,-		21	8	40	1	-,-
Cooper	29	5	85	1	-,-	(5)	4	0	18	0	-,-
Bruce	36.3	10	92	2	2,-		14	7	15	0	-,-
Worrall	15	7	30	0	-,-		12	5	22	1	-,-
Gunn	12	4	27	0	-,2	(6)	6	5	1	1	-,-
Houston	9	2	31	0	-,-	(7)	5	1	13	1	-,-
Barnes						(2)	8	3	14	0	-,-
Shrewsbury							1	1	0	0	-,1

FALL OF WICKETS

	N	S	S
Wkt	1st	1st	2nd
1st	196	44	
2nd	204	204	
3rd	514	267	
4th	524		
5th	575		135
6th	656		-
7th	686		-
8th	788		-
9th	803		-
10th	-	356	-

113

1887-88 SEASON (19 MATCHES)

The frequency of English trips to Australia came to a head in 1887-88 when two parties undertook simultaneous tours. One (G.F.Vernon's Team) was sponsored by Melbourne Cricket Club while the other (Shrewsbury's Team) was sponsored by the firm of Lillywhite, Shaw and Shrewsbury in conjunction with the NSWCA. Both ventures proved to be financial disasters.

Vernon's Team, the first organised of the two, came about after an announcement by Major B.J.Wardill, the Australian manager, at the end of Australia's 1886 tour of England. Melbourne CC would invite a team to Australia for the 1887-88 season. Six months later Lillywhite and Co., promoters of three previous tours to Australia, announced that they would also tour that season. Appeals by Melbourne CC to the NSWCA for Lillywhite to withdraw were rejected and both tours went ahead; in fact, they arrived in Australia on the same boat, SS Iberia, on October 25.

Vernon's Team was led at first by Hon. M.B. (later Lord) Hawke, who had to return to England in December upon the death of his father. Vernon succeeded him as captain. C.A.Smith (later a famous Hollywood actor) led the other team. A total of 48 matches were played, 26 by Vernon's Team and 22 by the Lillywhite-Shrewsbury combination, of which 15 ranked as first-class. In addition, a combined side drawn from both teams met Australia at Sydney in the only Test of the summer. Neither Smith or Vernon played in the Test, the England team being led by W.W.Read. Spectators, who had had their fill of touring teams of late (four English teams had visited in the past six years), generally stayed away from the matches. Both touring teams insisted on four-ball overs being used for all games despite requests from Australian administrators for six-ball overs.

Many administrators had by now seen the need for a body to control and administer Australian cricket. A meeting in Melbourne on December 23, 1887 attracted representatives from New South Wales, Victoria, South Australia and even Western Australia, and although no specific attempt was made to form a controlling body as such, several resolutions were passed, including no further visits from English teams for three years and no Australian team to tour England for four years. The first part of this resolution was kept, but shortly after this meeting an Australian team was selected by C.W.Beal (manager and promoter), J.M.Blackham, P.S.McDonnell and P.Sheridan to tour England in 1888. Both Beal and Sheridan had attended the Melbourne conference, as New South Wales delegates, and had obviously disagreed with the majority. McDonnell (captain), Blackham, H.F.Boyle, J.D.Edwards, J.J.Ferris, A.H.Jarvis, J.J.Lyons, S.P.Jones and C.T.B.Turner were the first players to make up the 6th Australians. G.Giffen, T.P.Horan, H.Moses and J.W.Trumble were sought to complete the party but announced their unavailability. A.C.Bannerman was invited in March, and finally G.J.Bonnor, G.H.S.Trott and J.Worrall were added to complete the 13 required.

Interest was maintained in the annual New South Wales-Victoria encounters this season with higher attendances than those found at the tour matches. New South Wales won both fixtures, the second emphatically thanks to an unbeaten 297 from Harry Moses. George Giffen (166, 8 for 65 and 6 for 60) ensured success for South Australia over Victoria. C.T.B.Turner became the first bowler to capture 100 first-class wickets in an Australian season - a feat rendered most remarkable by the passage of time.

Leading Aggregates

Batsmen	M	I	NO	Runs	HS	Ave.	Bowlers	Runs	Wkts	Ave.
H.Moses (NSW)	9	16	3	815	297*	62.69	C.T.B.Turner (NSW)	1441	106	13.59
A.Shrewsbury (E)	8	14	1	766	232	58.92	G.A.Lohmann (E)	755	63	11.98
W.W.Read (E)	8	13	2	610	183	55.45	W.Attewell (E)	590	55	10.72
P.S.McDonnell (NSW)	12	23	1	495	112	22.50	R.Peel (E)	822	49	16.77
G.Giffen (SA)	3	5	1	493	203	123.25	J.J.Ferris (NSW)	937	47	19.93
A.E.Stoddart (E)	9	15	0	450	94	30.00	J.Briggs (E)	434	30	14.46
R.Peel (E)	9	15	2	449	55	34.53	G.Giffen (SA)	466	27	17.25
S.P.Jones (NSW)	9	16	1	374	134*	24.93	G.H.S.Trott (V)	687	26	26.42
T.P.Horan (V)	7	14	2	364	68	30.33	J.Beaumont (E)	668	22	30.36
J.M.Blackham (V)	8	16	1	360	97	24.00				

SOUTH AUSTRALIA v G.F.VERNON'S ENGLAND XI

Played at Adelaide Oval on October 28, 29, 31, November 1, 1887. (Timeless match)
Toss : England XI.   Result : G.F.VERNON'S ENGLAND XI WON BY 71 RUNS.
Debuts: South Australia - J.E.Craigie, G.G.Liston, J.Musgrove, A.E.Weeks (all f/c).
12th Men: None named.
Umpires: I.A.Fisher and J.F.King.
Attendances: 1200, 1600, "wretched", "wretched".   Total: 4297.   Receipts: No figures published.
Close of Play: 1st day SA 2/64 (Lyons 39, G.Giffen 4); 2nd day Eng (2) 2/136 (Abel 51, O'Brien 15); 3rd day SA (2) 1/93 (G.Giffen 47).

South Australia's first match on even terms against a touring side was delayed a day due to the late arrival of the ship carrying the Englishmen. W.W.Read and G.F.Vernon (both injured) were unable to play for the visitors, while C.G.Godfrey and E.G.Phillips were unavailable for south Australia. Play was held up for half an hour on the final day while argument raged over which of the Giffen brothers was run out. The bails were removed from the wicket to which Walter was running and he immediately headed for the pavilion. The Englishmen, particularly Read who was an observer, contended that the batsmen had not crossed and therefore George was out. The umpires finally decided that Walter was out. George went on to score 81 in about 270 minutes, fitting 4 fours, to add to his unbeaten 37 and, earlier, a hat-trick (Newton, Attewell, Beaumont) to finish off the visitors' first innings. Stoddart (64 in 90 minutes, 7 fours) and Abel (95 in about 240 minutes, 3 fours) hit fifties. *Wisden* incorrectly gives Eng (1) Hawke c Liston, Rawlin c & b Lyons. Sources: *Wisden, C.B.O'Reilly, The Australasian, Adelaide Advertiser, South Australian Register, Adelaide Observer, South Australian Chronicle.*

G.F.VERNON'S ENGLAND XI

A.E.Stoddart	b Musgrove	25	(2)	b Lyons	64
R.Abel	c Lyons b Musgrove	3	(1)	b G.Giffen	95
W.Bates	b G.Giffen	2	(7)	b G.Giffen	5
T.C.O'Brien	c Knill b Musgrove	4		b Lyons	15
R.Peel	b Lyons	28		b Musgrove	26
*Hon.M.B.Hawke	c W.F.Giffen b G.Giffen	6	(3)	b Lyons	0
J.T.Rawlin	c Kemp b Lyons	33	(6)	b G.Giffen	0
M.P.Bowden	not out	0		c G.Giffen b Musgrove	5
†A.E.Newton	b G.Giffen	0		not out	41
W.Attewell	b G.Giffen	0		b Lyons	28
J.Beaumont	b G.Giffen	0		c W.F.Giffen b Lyons	1
Extras	(b3)	3		(b4, lb5, w2)	11
Total	(75.1 overs, 135 mins)	104		(176.3 overs, 305 mins)	291

SOUTH AUSTRALIA

†A.H.Jarvis	c Abel b Peel	0	(2)	run out (Stoddart/Rawlin)	45
W.F.Giffen	run out (/Newton)	19	(4)	run out (Peel/Newton)	1
J.J.Lyons	b Peel	39		run out (/Newton)	20
*G.Giffen	not out	37	(1)	c Stoddart b Bates	81
J.E.Craigie	st Newton b Peel	7		b Attewell	1
A.E.Weeks	c Peel b Bates	5	(9)	c Bates b Beaumont	21
H.Haldane	b Peel	3		c Beaumont b Attewell	8
W.Knill	b Peel	0		c Peel b Abel	1
B.C.E.Kemp	c Attewell b Bates	0	(6)	c Peel b Attewell	3
G.G.Liston	b Attewell	6		not out	8
J.Musgrove	c O'Brien b Attewell	0		c Peel b Bates	15
Extras	(b1, nb1)	2		(b2)	2
Total	(172.3 overs, 265 mins)	118		(188.0 overs, 310 mins)	206

SOUTH AUSTRALIA	O	M	R	W	w,nb		O	M	R	W	w,nb
Musgrove	30	9	50	3	w,nb	(3)	46	21	60	2	2,-
Lyons	17	6	19	2	-,-	(1)	46.3	19	75	5	-,-
G.Giffen	28.1	13	32	5	-,-	(2)	79	29	124	3	-,-
Kemp							5	0	21	0	-,-

ENGLAND XI	O	M	R	W	w,nb		O	M	R	W	w,nb
Peel	53	33	31	5	-,-	(2)	39	18	38	0	-,-
Beaumont	38	26	24	0	-,1	(1)	26	14	34	1	-,-
Attewell	35.3	22	24	2	-,-		69	38	47	3	-,-
Rawlin	28	17	14	0	-,-	(6)	16	8	18	0	-,-
Abel	4	0	11	0	-,-		17	6	23	1	-,-
Bates	14	7	12	2	-,-	(4)	20	7	41	2	-,-
Stoddart							1	0	3	0	-,-

FALL OF WICKETS				
	ENG	SA	ENG	SA
Wkt	1st	1st	2nd	2nd
1st	21	1	105	93
2nd	30	44	105	116
3rd	36	68	136	121
4th	36	78	196	128
5th	45	99	199	136
6th	93	102	205	153
7th	104	102	212	157
8th	104	103	226	168
9th	104	118	279	186
10th	104	118	291	206

VICTORIA v G.F.VERNON'S ENGLAND XI

Played at Melbourne Cricket Ground on November 9, 10, 11, 1887. (Timeless match)
Toss : Victoria.   Result : G.F.VERNON'S ENGLAND XI WON BY AN INNINGS AND 18 RUNS.
Debuts: Victoria - H.Trumble (f/c).
12th Men: W.R.Robertson (Vic) and M.P.Bowden (Eng).
Umpires: D.F.Cotter and J.Phillips.
Attendances: 5000, 1500, 500.   Total: About 7000.   Receipts: No figures published.
Close of Play: 1st day Eng 1/23 (Stoddart 13, Peel 1); 2nd day Eng 296 all out.

W.Bruce (exams), J.D.Edwards, W.L.Murdoch (business), G.H.S.Trott (work) and J.Slight all announced their unavailability for the home team before selection. Several unsuccessful attempts to coax Murdoch out of retirement had been made since 1884/85, all from Melbourne which was closer geographically than Sydney to his residence in the southern New South Wales town of Cootamundra. Worrall was a late replacement for W.E.Midwinter (also unavailable). This is believed to be the first match in Australia in which both umpires wore white coats as their distinguishing garb. Rain caused interruptions on the second and fourth days but was not considered an important factor in the outcome, the wicket not being "materially affected" (*Australasian*). McIlwraith (60 in about 120 minutes, 1 four) and Blackham (68 in about 135 minutes, 2 four) were the only Victorians to exceed 21 in either innings against the persistent and accurate English bowlers. Stoddart (94 in about 150 minutes, 4 fours) and Peel (55 in about 135 minutes, 2 fours) added 136 for the second wicket in a decisive stand for the visitors. Sources: *Wisden, VCA Report, The Age, The Argus, The Herald, The Australasian, The Leader, The Sportsman.*

VICTORIA

J.McIlwraith	c Stoddart b Beaumont	60		c Newton b Beaumont	1
R.S.Houston	c O'Brien b Peel	17		b Beaumont	1
T.P.Horan	c Stoddart b Peel	15	(4)	b Beaumont	0
J.W.Trumble	c Attewell b Bates	19	(3)	c Attewell b Bates	10
†J.M.Blackham	run out (Peel/Bates)	14		c Abel b Attewell	68
H.A.Musgrove	c Attewell b Beaumont	0	(7)	lbw b Attewell	5
F.G.McShane	b Bates	15	(6)	c O'Brien b Bates	3
*H.F.Boyle	run out (Peel/Bates)	0		b Peel	6
H.Trumble	run out (Attewell/Newton)	2	(10)	not out	4
J.Worrall	c Newton b Bates	6	(9)	c Stoddart b Peel	21
F.R.Spofforth	not out	0		c Hawke b Peel	4
Extras	(b2, lb2)	4		(b1, nb2)	3
Total	(146.3 overs, 243 mins)	152		(84.3 overs, 147 mins)	126

G.F.VERNON'S ENGLAND XI

R.Abel	b H.Trumble	6
A.E.Stoddart	c H.Trumble b J.W.Trumble	94
R.Peel	b J.W.Trumble	55
W.W.Read	b Boyle	12
W.Bates	b J.W.Trumble	24
*Hon.M.B.Hawke	c Blackham b Spofforth	20
T.C.O'Brien	b Spofforth	27
J.T.Rawlin	b J.W.Trumble	9
†A.E.Newton	c Houston b Spofforth	17
W.Attewell	run out (H.Trumble)	20
J.Beaumont	not out	4
Extras	(b1, lb4, nb3)	8
Total	(143.0 overs, 268 mins)	296

ENGLAND XI	O	M	R	W	w,nb		O	M	R	W	w,nb
Peel	38	13	49	2	-,-		24.3	9	28	3	-,-
Beaumont	43	29	34	2	-,-		16	3	34	3	-,2
Attewell	28	18	16	0	-,-	(4)	26	9	40	2	-,-
Rawlin	5	1	12	0	-,-						
Bates	30.3	14	36	3	-,-	(3)	18	8	21	2	-,-
Abel	2	1	1	0	-,-						

VICTORIA	O	M	R	W	w,nb
Spofforth	29	8	67	3	-,1
H.Trumble	18	4	40	1	-,2
Boyle	15	3	42	1	-,-
J.W.Trumble	43	17	68	4	-,-
Worrall	7	1	15	0	-,-
Horan	5	3	2	0	-,-
McShane	26	8	54	0	-,-

	FALL OF WICKETS		
Wkt	VIC	ENG	VIC
	1st	1st	2nd
1st	69	7	2
2nd	95	143	5
3rd	95	161	5
4th	129	197	31
5th	129	197	48
6th	129	241	55
7th	129	248	78
8th	142	256	114
9th	149	291	119
10th	152	296	126

NEW SOUTH WALES v A.SHREWSBURY'S ENGLAND XI

Played at Sydney Cricket Ground on November 10 (no play), 11, 12, 1887. (Timeless match)
Toss : New South Wales.   Result : NEW SOUTH WALES WON BY TEN WICKETS.
Debuts: Nil.
12th Men: J.Davis (NSW - see below). No 12th named for Eng XI.
Umpires: C.Bannerman and J.Swift.
Attendances: no play, 2500, 6000.   Total: About 8500.   Receipts: No figures published.
Close of Play: 1st day no play; 2nd day NSW 7/80 (Hiddleston 3, Davis 5).

Rain washed out the first day and caused several interruptions on each of the succeeding days, rendering the pitch completely useless for batting. So soft was the turf that the toss had to be done three times before the coin would lie flat; it stuck sideways in the ground on the first two attempts. S.P.Jones did not turn up for New South Wales when play finally got underway (it was learnt that he had a neck problem, later diagnosed as a carbuncle) and because the nominated 12th man Davis was also absent, Brann fielded as substitute against his own team. Davis was sent for and eventually arrived to take Jones's place in the side. C.A.Smith, captain of Shrewsbury's Team, stood down because of an ear infection. Turner (10 for 45) and Ferris (9 for 59) took full advantage of the conditions to further enhance their reputation against English teams. Ferris was twice on a hat-trick in the first innings, Ulyett and Docker falling to successive balls and later Preston and Pougher. Allen was dismissed with the third ball of the New South Wales first innings. *Wisden* incorrectly gives NSW (1) Turner c & b Pougher; NSW (2) Briggs 0/2 instead of Preston, extras 4, total 25. Sources: *Wisden, The Australasian, Sydney Morning Herald, Sydney Mail, Sydney Daily Telegraph.*

A.SHREWSBURY'S ENGLAND XI

A.Shrewsbury	c sub (G.Brann) b Ferris	20		lbw b Turner	3
G.Ulyett	st Burton b Ferris	9	(3)	b Turner	9
W.Newham	b Turner	2	(4)	b Turner	2
*L.C.Docker	b Ferris	0	(6)	c Bannerman b Ferris	7
J.M.Read	st Burton b Ferris	2		c Garrett b Turner	4
G.A.Lohmann	b Turner	4	(2)	b Allen	20
J.Briggs	b Turner	5		b Turner	2
J.M.Preston	b Ferris	0	(9)	not out	3
A.D.Pougher	b Ferris	0	(8)	b Ferris	6
G.Brann	not out	4		b Turner	3
†R.Pilling	b Turner	0		c Richardson b Ferris	3
Extras	(nb3)	3		(b2, lb2)	4
Total	(37.0 overs, 70 mins)	49		(75.1 overs, 150 mins)	66

NEW SOUTH WALES

R.C.Allen	c Docker b Lohmann	0	(2)	not out	6
A.C.Bannerman	c Pilling b Lohmann	21			
H.Moses	st Pilling b Briggs	0			
C.A.Richardson	b Pougher	2			
C.T.B.Turner	b Pougher	13			
*P.S.McDonnell	c Pougher b Lohmann	27	(1)	not out	15
T.W.Garrett	b Briggs	7			
H.C.S.Hiddleston	b Lohmann	3			
J.Davis	lbw b Lohmann	8			
†F.J.Burton	not out	4			
J.J.Ferris	b Briggs	5			
Extras	(b2, lb1, w1)	4		(lb2)	2
Total	(91.0 overs, 175 mins)	94		(10.1 overs, 20 mins) (0 wkts)	23

NEW SOUTH WALES	O	M	R	W	w,nb		O	M	R	W	w,nb
Turner	19	10	22	4	-,-		37	23	23	6	-,-
Ferris	18	7	24	6	-,3		35.1	21	35	3	-,-
Allen							2	1	4	1	-,-
Garrett							1	1	0	0	-,-

ENGLAND XI	O	M	R	W	w,nb		O	M	R	W	w,nb
Lohmann	46	34	26	5	-,-		5.1	1	12	0	-,-
Briggs	33	22	35	3	1,-						
Pougher	12	5	29	2	-,-	(2)	4	1	7	0	-,-
Preston						(3)	1	0	2	0	-,-

FALL OF WICKETS

Wkt	ENG 1st	NSW 1st	ENG 2nd	NSW 2nd
1st	30	0	10	-
2nd	34	1	36	-
3rd	34	17	36	-
4th	36	37	42	-
5th	36	47	49	-
6th	42	70	51	-
7th	45	73	52	-
8th	45	80	59	-
9th	45	83	62	-
10th	49	94	66	-

NEW SOUTH WALES v G.F.VERNON'S ENGLAND XI

Played at Sydney Cricket Ground on November 25, 26, 28, 29, 30, 1887. (Timeless match)
Toss : England XI.   Result : NEW SOUTH WALES WON BY NINE WICKETS.
Debuts: Nil.
12th Men: C.A.Richardson (NSW) and M.P.Bowden (Eng).
Umpires: C.Bannerman and J.Phillips.
Attendances: 4000, 1000, 3000, 4000, 2000.   Total: About 14,000.   Receipts: No figures published.
Close of Play: 1st day Eng 4/263 (Abel 87, Peel 31); 2nd day Eng 5/286 (Peel 46, Newton 6); 3rd day NSW 2/186 (Moses 47, Allen 17);
    4th day NSW 9/408 (Burton 13, Ferris 12).

Play on the second day was restricted to only 30 minutes from 4.20pm because of rain. In keeping with the majority of Sydney first-class matches at the time, each innings was played on a separate pitch. Abel batted about 300 minutes, scoring 88 with 8 fours, to anchor the English innings after Stoddart (55 in 65 minutes, 3 fours) had dominated their opening stand. Hawke (48 in about 80 minutes, 1 five and 5 fours) and Peel (54 in about 115 minutes, 5 fours) also played the leading roles in their stands with the 5ft 4ins Surrey professional. Turner and Ferris with 9 apiece again captured the lion's share of wickets. McDonnell (112 in 135 minutes, 11 fours) scored his runs out of 151 while at the crease, while Moses (77 in about 195 minutes, 5 fours) and Jones (60 in about 135 minutes, 2 fours) registered sound half-centuries for New South Wales. Sources: *Wisden, The Australasian, Sydney Morning Herald, Town & Country Journal, Sydney Daily Telegraph.*

G.F.VERNON'S ENGLAND XI

A.E.Stoddart	b Turner	55		b Turner	16
R.Abel	c Bannerman b Ferris	88		c Bannerman b Ferris	5
W.Bates	b Garrett	28		c Hiddleston b Ferris	0
W.W.Read	lbw b Turner	8		st Burton b Ferris	14
*Hon.M.B.Hawke	b Turner	48		c Evans b Ferris	2
R.Peel	c & b Turner	54		not out	34
†A.E.Newton	b Turner	30		c Allen b Ferris	5
G.F.Vernon	c Moses b Ferris	3	(9)	c Evans b Ferris	4
J.T.Rawlin	b Turner	4	(10)	b Turner	5
W.Attewell	not out	13	(8)	c Burton b Jones	17
J.Beaumont	b Turner	2		b Ferris	1
Extras	(b5, lb2)	7		(b3)	3
Total	(205.3 overs, 370 mins)	340		(73.1 overs, 140 mins)	106

NEW SOUTH WALES

*P.S.McDonnell	c Vernon b Attewell	112	(2)	c Attewell b Peel	2
A.C.Bannerman	b Peel	8			
H.Moses	b Stoddart	77		not out	15
R.C.Allen	run out (Attewell/Newton)	34	(1)	not out	22
S.P.Jones	b Peel	60			
H.C.S.Hiddleston	st Newton b Rawlin	37			
C.T.B.Turner	c Read b Attewell	32			
T.W.Garrett	c Abel b Peel	13			
E.Evans	b Peel	0			
†F.J.Burton	not out	13			
J.J.Ferris	b Attewell	12			
Extras	(lb7, w2, nb1)	10		(lb1)	1
Total	(298.1 overs, 475 mins)	408		(46.0 overs, 70 mins) (1 wkt)	40

NEW SOUTH WALES	O	M	R	W	w,nb		O	M	R	W	w,nb		FALL OF WICKETS			
														ENG	NSW	ENG	NSW
Turner	77.3	36	106	7	-,-		31	12	40	2	-,-	Wkt	1st	1st	2nd	2nd
Ferris	70	24	135	2	-,-		33.1	15	49	7	-,-	1st	74	62	24	5
Garrett	24	8	40	1	-,-		6	2	7	0	-,-	2nd	122	151	24	-
Evans	15	6	24	0	-,-							3rd	130	224	24	-
Allen	6	3	10	0	-,-							4th	198	245	30	-
Jones	13	7	18	0	-,-	(4)	3	0	7	1	-,-	5th	272	330	45	-
												6th	308	332	59	-
ENGLAND XI	O	M	R	W	w,nb		O	M	R	W	w,nb	7th	315	355	96	-
Beaumont	46	22	88	0	-,1	(3)	9	8	4	0	-,-	8th	321	379	100	-
Peel	80	44	98	4	1,-	(1)	15	6	17	1	-,-	9th	338	381	105	-
Bates	46	15	75	0	-,-	(4)	9	4	9	0	-,-	10th	340	408	106	-
Attewell	81.1	49	64	3	-,-	(2)	13	7	9	0	-,-					
Rawlin	30	10	53	1	-,-											
Stoddart	15	8	20	1	1,-											

NEW SOUTH WALES v A.SHREWSBURY'S ENGLAND XI

Played at Sydney Cricket Ground on December 9, 10, 12, 1887. (Timeless match)
Toss : New South Wales.   Result : A.SHREWSBURY'S ENGLAND XI WON BY TEN WICKETS.
Debuts: Nil.
12th Men: W.J.O'Hanlon (NSW). No 12th named for Eng XI.
Umpires: C.Bannerman and G.Brann.
Attendances & Receipts: No figures published.
Close of Play: 1st day Eng 2/53 (Shrewsbury 21, Read 0); 2nd day NSW (2) 3/49 (Moses 12, Bannerman 8).

Richardson (the nominated 12th man) was a late replacement for S.P.Jones, who was still suffering some soreness from a carbuncle on his neck. In good batting conditions (the same wicket was used throughout), the home batsmen had no answer to the English bowling in either innings with one notable exception. Moses (78 not out in 195 minutes, 5 fours and 68 in about 150 minutes, 8 fours) demonstrated an almost faultless technique based on a "remarkably sure defence" (*SMH*) to be the most outstanding batsman on either side during the match. An eighth wicket stand of 83 by Briggs (4 fours) and Smith (8 fours) in even time gave the Englishmen the advantage that virtually ensured victory. Briggs had earlier finished the local first innings with the wickets of Evans and Ferris with successive balls. Brann was the first of three Shrewsbury tourists to umpire a first-class match during the season, Ulyett and Pougher following suit in later games. Sources: *Wisden, Sydney Morning Herald, Town & Country Journal, Sydney Mail, Sydney Daily Telegraph.*

NEW SOUTH WALES

*P.S.McDonnell	run out (Briggs/Pilling)	13		c Read b Lohmann	14
A.C.Bannerman	b Briggs	4	(5)	c Briggs Pougher	25
H.Moses	not out	78	(4)	b Pougher	68
R.C.Allen	b Preston	12	(2)	b Preston	13
H.C.S.Hiddleston	b Pougher	3	(6)	c Pilling Pougher	11
C.T.B.Turner	c Docker b Lohmann	13	(3)	c Preston b Lohmann	2
C.A.Richardson	c Pilling b Lohmann	2		c Briggs b Preston	2
T.W.Garrett	b Smith	7	(9)	c Pilling Pougher	3
†F.J.Burton	run out (Preston/Lohmann)	9	(8)	not out	18
E.Evans	lbw b Briggs	0		run out (Pougher/Pilling)	0
J.J.Ferris	b Briggs	0		b Briggs	4
Extras	(b3, lb4, w1)	8		(b5)	5
Total	(124.3 overs, 215 mins)	149		(121.3 overs, 210 mins)	165

A.SHREWSBURY'S ENGLAND XI

G.Ulyett	b Turner	19	not out	20
A.Shrewsbury	c Turner b Allen	48	not out	19
L.C.Docker	lbw b Ferris	12		
J.M.Read	c & b Turner	35		
G.A.Lohmann	c & b Ferris	7		
W.Newham	c Burton b Turner	2		
J.Briggs	c Burton b Turner	46		
J.M.Preston	b Turner	1		
*C.A.Smith	b Turner	68		
A.D.Pougher	not out	25		
†R.Pilling	c Burton b Turner	10		
Extras	(b6)	6		—
Total	(152.3 overs, 280 mins)	279	(16.1 overs, 30 mins) (0 wkts)	39

ENGLAND XI	O	M	R	W	w,nb		O	M	R	W	w,nb
Lohmann	39	15	49	2	-,-		45	25	60	2	-,-
Briggs	25.3	14	24	3	1,-	(3)	2.3	1	2	1	-,-
Pougher	25	14	21	1	-,-	(5)	39	21	40	4	-,-
Preston	26	10	32	1	-,-	(2)	29	9	40	2	-,-
Ulyett	3	0	7	0	-,-	(6)	5	1	10	0	-,-
Smith	6	2	8	1	-,-	(4)	1	0	8	0	-,-

NEW SOUTH WALES	O	M	R	W	w,nb		O	M	R	W	w,nb
Turner	67.3	28	117	7	-,-		8.1	3	21	0	-,-
Ferris	61	21	107	2	-,-		8	1	18	0	-,-
Garrett	13	3	27	0	-,-						
Allen	11	3	22	1	-,-						

FALL OF WICKETS

Wkt	NSW 1st	ENG 1st	NSW 2nd	ENG 2nd
1st	15	32	22	-
2nd	24	49	29	-
3rd	62	118	29	-
4th	73	120	93	-
5th	92	122	113	-
6th	101	140	136	-
7th	116	141	136	-
8th	149	224	145	-
9th	149	257	149	-
10th	149	279	165	-

VICTORIA v A.SHREWSBURY'S ENGLAND XI

Played at Melbourne Cricket Ground on December 16, 17, 19, 1887. (Timeless match)
Toss : Victoria.   Result : A.SHREWSBURY'S ENGLAND XI WON BY AN INNINGS AND 456 RUNS.
Debuts: Victoria - H.S.Freeman, T.J.Hastings (both f/c); T.Turner (Vic only).
12th Men: G.H.Freeman (Vic) and W.Newham (Eng).
Umpires: C.Bannerman and D.F.Cotter.
Attendances: 500, 1000, 700.   Total: About 2200.   Receipts: No figures published.
Close of Play: 1st day Eng 2/178 (Shrewsbury 86, Lohmann 13); 2nd day Eng 4/500 (Shrewsbury 221, Briggs 38).

Victoria, severely undermanned by the unavailability of J.M.Blackham, W.Bruce, R.S.Houston, J.McIlwraith, W.E.Midwinter, S.Morris, F.R.Spofforth and G.H.S.Trott, suffered the heaviest defeat by an innings margin in all first-class cricket to date; it remains Victoria's worst loss on record. The team was further depleted on the second day with the absence of Hastings (ill) and McShane (who elected to play for his club side Fitzroy during the afternoon before returning to the match next day!). Read and Smith substituted against their own side until the arrival of W.H.Cooper and F.H.Walters, Harry replacing Hastings as wicket-keeper. Shrewsbury, who scored his second double hundred in Australia within nine months (232 in 445 minutes, 18 fours), outscored the entire opposition and added 217 for the fourth wicket with Brann (118 in about 150 minutes, 1 five and 16 fours) and 111 for the fifth wicket with Briggs (75 in about 120 minutes, 3 fours). Preston was unluckily dismissed when his straight drive struck the bat of his partner Pilling and deflected to McShane at mid-on. The visitors' total was the highest by a touring side in Australia until A.C.MacLaren's XI scored 769 against New South Wales in 1901-02. Turner made his debut for Victoria after a handful of games with South Australia. *VCA Report* incorrectly gives Eng; Brann c Turner.
Sources: *Wisden, VCA Report, The Age, The Argus, The Herald, The Australasian, The Leader, The Sportsman.*

VICTORIA

J.W.Trumble	run out (/Pilling)	6		b Briggs	2
J.Harry	b Briggs	5	(6)	b Smith	8
F.G.McShane	run out (Preston)	20	(2)	b Briggs	0
T.P.Horan	c Pilling b Preston	12	(3)	not out	49
*H.F.Boyle	c Smith b Pougher	12		c Ulyett b Lohmann	4
J.Worrall	b Preston	1	(4)	b Lohmann	11
†T.J.Hastings	st Pilling b Preston	4	(9)	b Briggs	10
T.Turner	c Brann b Pougher	1	(7)	b Smith	0
H.S.Freeman	lbw b Preston	2	(10)	c Shrewsbury b Briggs	6
W.R.Robertson	not out	1	(8)	c Lohmann b Smith	0
W.Logan	c Read b Pougher	0		run out	0
Extras	(b2, w1, nb1)	4		(b8, lb2)	10
Total	(77.3 overs, 135 mins)	68		(90.0 overs, 155 mins)	100

A.SHREWSBURY'S ENGLAND XI

A.Shrewsbury	b Trumble	232
G.Ulyett	c Robertson b Trumble	29
J.M.Read	c Hastings b Trumble	38
G.A.Lohmann	b Turner	25
G.Brann	c Boyle b McShane	118
J.Briggs	b Robertson	75
L.C.Docker	c Harry b Worrall	48
*C.A.Smith	b Worrall	0
J.M.Preston	c McShane b Worrall	22
A.D.Pougher	b Robertson	0
†R.Pilling	not out	1
Extras	(b22, lb10, w1, nb3)	36
Total	(301.2 overs, 550 mins)	624

ENGLAND XI	O	M	R	W	w,nb		O	M	R	W	w,nb
Lohmann	23	16	17	0	-,1		24	16	18	2	-,-
Briggs	20	11	20	1	1,-		30	15	32	4	-,-
Pougher	18.3	11	11	3	-,-	(5)	9	4	6	0	-,-
Preston	16	8	16	4	-,-		12	4	23	0	-,-
Smith						(3)	15	7	11	3	-,-

VICTORIA	O	M	R	W	w,nb
Trumble	73	40	91	3	-,3
Logan	29	8	73	0	-,-
Turner	41	17	72	1	-,-
Boyle	22	7	50	0	-,-
Worrall	32.2	11	73	3	-,-
McShane	33	8	93	1	-,-
Robertson	49	14	93	2	1,-
Horan	22	5	43	0	-,-

FALL OF WICKETS

Wkt	VIC 1st	ENG 1st	VIC 2nd
1st	8	47	0
2nd	21	136	5
3rd	36	197	22
4th	53	414	34
5th	54	525	61
6th	60	566	63
7th	63	569	67
8th	63	622	88
9th	67	622	100
10th	68	624	100

VICTORIA v NEW SOUTH WALES

Played at Melbourne Cricket Ground on December 24, 26, 27, 1887. (Timeless match)
Toss : New South Wales.   Result : NEW SOUTH WALES WON BY TWO WICKETS.
Debuts: New South Wales - H.Donnan, W.A.Richardson (both f/c).
12th Men: F.G.McShane & W.R.Robertson (Vic emergencies) and A.H.Gregory & J.C.Rice (NSW emergencies).
Umpires: C.Bannerman and D.F.Cotter.
Attendances: 3000, 6000, 1500.   Total: About 10,500.   Receipts: £475.
Close of Play: 1st day Vic (2) 4/101 (J.W.Trumble 19, Trott 0); 2nd day NSW (2) 3/105 (Burton 1, Garrett 11).

Sent in on a rain-affected pitch, Victoria lost Bruce to the first ball of the match and were all out on the hour for 35 to Turner and Ferris who were virtually unplayable in the conditions. In his second match Hugh Trumble then captured 7 for 52 to dismiss New South Wales cheaply as the wicket dried, 24 wickets in all falling on the opening day. Moses was bowled by a no-ball from Trumble early in his innings. "The turf was firm, hard and true" (*Australasian*) on the second day and fifties from J.W.Trumble (57 in about 140 minutes, 0 fours) and Horan (54 not out in about 165 minutes, 2 fours) gave Victoria a chance. A sound opening from Bannerman and McDonnell together with 52 (in about 110 minutes, 0 fours) from Garrett took New South Wales to victory, though Turner, Allen and Donnan all fell without addition at 194. Six-ball overs were bowled. W.E.Midwinter (work) was unavailable for Victoria while S.P.Jones, still troubled by a neck carbuncle, was unfit for New South Wales. *Wisden* incorrectly gives Vic (2) Trott b Turner, H.Trumble lbw b Ferris. Sources: *Wisden, The Age, The Argus, The Herald, The Australasian, The Leader, The Sportsman.*

VICTORIA

W.Bruce	c McDonnell b Turner	0	(2)	c Garrett b Donnan	38
J.McIlwraith	b Ferris	20	(1)	b Turner	31
T.P.Horan	run out (Bannerman)	5	(7)	not out	54
J.W.Trumble	b Turner	0	(3)	b Ferris	57
†J.M.Blackham	b Turner	0	(4)	b Turner	5
G.H.S.Trott	b Turner	0		lbw b Ferris	0
J.Worrall	c Moses b Turner	1	(8)	c Garrett b Ferris	26
*H.F.Boyle	c & b Ferris	1	(9)	c Burton b Donnan	23
S.Morris	c Bannerman b Ferris	0	(5)	b Turner	4
H.Trumble	st Burton b Ferris	2		lbw b Turner	3
F.R.Spofforth	not out	5		c Garrett b Ferris	6
Extras	(lb1)	1		(b8, lb8, w1, nb2)	19
Total	(17.3 overs, 61 mins)	35		(117.2 overs, 270 mins)	266

NEW SOUTH WALES

A.C.Bannerman	c & b H.Trumble	5		c Blackham b Bruce	38
*P.S.McDonnell	c Boyle b Spofforth	22		c H.Trumble b Worrall	35
H.Moses	b H.Trumble	29		lbw b Bruce	12
R.C.Allen	b H.Trumble	0	(6)	c & b Trott	11
J.Davis	c Boyle b H.Trumble	1	(8)	not out	1
C.T.B.Turner	c Blackham b H.Trumble	6	(7)	c Blackham b J.W.Trumble	12
†F.J.Burton	c Boyle b H.Trumble	12	(4)	st Blackham b Trott	21
T.W.Garrett	st Blackham b Trott	6	(5)	b Trott	52
H.Donnan	b Trott	6		b Trott	0
W.A.Richardson	not out	4		not out	5
J.J.Ferris	c & b H.Trumble	0			
Extras	(b5, lb1, nb5)	11		(b4, lb5, w3, nb1)	13
Total	(34.0 overs, 105 mins)	102		(90.3 overs, 232 mins) (8 wkts)	200

NEW SOUTH WALES	O	M	R	W	w,nb		O	M	R	W	w,nb
Turner	9	3	17	5	-,-		48	13	97	4	-,-
Ferris	8.3	2	17	4	-,-		39.2	9	90	4	1,-
Garrett							13	4	23	0	-,-
Donnan							14	4	28	2	-,2
Richardson							3	0	9	0	-,-

VICTORIA	O	M	R	W	w,nb		O	M	R	W	w,nb
Spofforth	11	3	29	1	-,4		10	2	21	0	-,1
H.Trumble	17	1	52	7	-,4		14	2	37	0	-,-
Trott	6	2	10	2	-,-	(4)	27.3	13	50	4	-,-
J.W.Trumble						(3)	11	4	24	1	-,-
Worrall							12	4	14	1	-,-
Bruce							16	4	41	2	3,-

FALL OF WICKETS

Wkt	VIC 1st	NSW 1st	VIC 2nd	NSW 2nd
1st	0	11	68	72
2nd	8	42	79	89
3rd	8	48	91	93
4th	8	65	101	155
5th	10	66	102	173
6th	16	71	178	194
7th	18	83	206	194
8th	22	96	249	194
9th	30	102	255	-
10th	35	102	266	-

SOUTH AUSTRALIA v G.F.VERNON'S ENGLAND XI

Played at Adelaide Oval on December 24, 26, 27, 28, 29, 1887. (Five-day match)
Toss : England XI.   Result : MATCH DRAWN.
Debuts: Nil.
12th Men: None named.
Umpires: I.A.Fisher and J.Phillips.
Attendances: 1000, 2000, 500, 1500, 200.   Total: 4903.   Receipts: No figures published.
Close of Play: 1st day Eng 4/282 (Read 166, O'Brien 33); 2nd day SA (2) 0/11 (Godfrey 8, Craigie 0); 3rd day SA (2) 1/249 (Godfrey 113, G.Giffen 89); 4th day SA (2) 8/450 (Waldron 0).

Vernon took over the captaincy of this English team for this and the remaining matches as The Hon.M.B.Hawke had returned to England, due to his father's death, to become the seventh Lord Hawke. The tourists were also without W.Bates, who had received a severe blow in the eye during net practice at Melbourne and remained there for treatment: his sight was permanently affected and it ended his career. So that their travel plans to Melbourne for the next match would not be disrupted, it was agreed before play started that the maximum duration would be four days plus the pre-lunch session on the fifth day. The pitch was vandalised on the night following the second day's play when unknown pranksters flooded it at each end and dragged the big iron roller along its length, lifting turf and leaving footprints embedded. Groundsman Charlie Checkett reported the incident at 7.00am to Vernon at his hotel, who supervised the rolling and general repairs. George Giffen, whose suggestion to continue on a new pitch had been rejected by Vernon, then went out and compiled the first double century against a touring team in Australia (203 in 530 minutes, 14 fours), giving chances along the way at 2, 95 and 180. Godfrey (119 in 340 minutes, 4 fours) was missed in the fifties. Read (183 in 250 minutes, 20 fours) topscored for his side while Jarvis (75 in 150 minutes, 6 fours) registered the only fifty. Bowden replaced Newton as wicket-keeper after tea on the fourth day, stumping Noel. Waldron was absent on the final day due to the sudden death of his child overnight and was ruled, somewhat harshly, "out". A.E.Weeks substituted for him in the field. *Wisden* incorrectly gives SA (2) W.F.Giffen 20, Noel 10, Blinman 9, Craigie 20, Waldron absent. Sources: *Wisden, C.B.O'Reilly, The Australasian, Adelaide Advertiser, South Australian Register.*

G.F.VERNON'S ENGLAND XI

W.W.Read	c Musgrove b G.Giffen	183		
A.E.Stoddart	b G.Giffen	38		
R.Abel	c Musgrove b G.Giffen	4	(2) not out	23
R.Peel	c Godfrey b Lyons	31		
†A.E.Newton	c & b G.Giffen	5		
T.C.O'Brien	run out (Musgrove)	43		
*G.F.Vernon	b G.Giffen	27		
M.P.Bowden	c & b Lyons	21	(1) not out	35
J.T.Rawlin	c Waldron b Lyons	14		
W.Attewell	c Waldron b Lyons	5		
J.Beaumont	not out	5		
Extras	(b3, lb3)	6	(lb1)	1
Total	(163.1 overs, 285 mins)	382	(23.0 overs, 45 mins) (0 wkts)	59

SOUTH AUSTRALIA

*G.Giffen	b Peel	6	(3) b Attewell	203
†A.H.Jarvis	c Vernon b Beaumont	75	(4) c & b Peel	12
J.J.Lyons	b Peel	0	(5) c Abel b Rawlin	33
W.F.Giffen	b Attewell	21	(6) b Attewell	33
C.G.Godfrey	b Attewell	4	(1) c Newton b Peel	119
J.Noel	b Rawlin	0	(8) st Bowden b Attewell	0
H.Blinman	c Attewell b Beaumont	12	c & b Attewell	0
J.E.Craigie	not out	12	(2) c Read b Stoddart	36
A.E.Waldron	b Beaumont	2	retired out	0
E.G.Phillips	b Attewell	4	b Rawlin	14
J.Musgrove	b Attewell	3	not out	29
Extras	(b2, lb1, nb1)	4	(b6, lb2, w2, nb4)	14
Total	(126.3 overs, 225 mins)	143	(411.1 overs, 630 mins)	493

SOUTH AUSTRALIA	O	M	R	W	w,nb		O	M	R	W	w,nb
Musgrove	9	1	37	0	-,-	(3)	5	2	11	0	-,-
Lyons	27.1	6	72	4	-,-		6	0	25	0	-,-
Noel	47	15	94	0	-,-						
G.Giffen	78	24	163	5	-,-	(1)	12	4	22	0	-,-
Phillips	2	0	10	0	-,-						

ENGLAND XI	O	M	R	W	w,nb		O	M	R	W	w,nb
Peel	26	12	34	2	-,-	(4)	102	41	138	2	1,2
Beaumont	41	21	48	3	-,1		38	14	73	0	1,2
Attewell	40.3	26	32	4	-,-	(1)	107	58	103	4	-,-
Rawlin	19	9	25	1	-,-	(3)	122.1	81	87	2	-,-
Stoddart							31	12	51	1	-,-
Read							5	1	16	0	-,-
Abel							6	2	11	0	-,-

FALL OF WICKETS

Wkt	ENG 1st	SA 1st	SA 2nd	ENG 2nd
1st	91	12	65	-
2nd	99	12	257	-
3rd	204	61	283	-
4th	214	73	345	-
5th	296	82	445	-
6th	325	114	445	-
7th	338	128	445	-
8th	365	130	450	-
9th	370	137	450	-
10th	382	143	493	-

AUSTRALIAN XI v G.F.VERNON'S ENGLAND XI

Played at Melbourne Cricket Ground on December 31, 1887, January 2, 3, 1888. (Timeless match)
Toss : England XI.   Result : G.F.VERNON'S ENGLAND XI WON BY AN INNINGS AND 78 RUNS.
Debuts: Australian XI - H.Thorpe (f/c).
12th Men: F.G.McShane (Aust XI). No 12th named for Eng XI.
Umpires: D.F.Cotter and J.Phillips.
Attendances: 5000, 6000, 1000.   Total: About 12,000.   Receipts: No figures published.
Close of Play: 1st day Aust 3/21 (H.Trumble 0, Garrett 2); 2nd day Aust (2) 0/1 (Lyons 0, Bruce 1).

The Australian XI was not truly representative owing to the unavailability of G.Giffen, A.H.Jarvis, H.Moses, P.S.McDonnell and C.T.B.Turner. Thorpe, who had played all his cricket in the Parramatta district, had never been seriously considered for the New South Wales team but was brought into the Australian side after a good performance for Parramatta XXII against Vernon's Team. It proved to be his only first-class appearance. The Englishmen recovered from 4/16 and 6/51 to reach 292 through some fine batting from the middle and late order, Newton (77 in 105 minutes, 12 fours), Vernon (50 in 75 minutes, 4 fours), Rawlin (78 not out in 105 minutes, 5 fours), and Attewell (43 in 45 minutes, 5 fours) all recording their highest scores for the tour. Umpire Cotter instructed the scorers to add 2 runs to Rawlin's total at the end of the innings, the double having been incorrectly signalled as byes earlier in the day. The Australians batted poorly in their first innings in good conditions. Rain came overnight, after two overs in the follow-on, and thoroughly soaked the wicket which cut up badly on the third day. Attewell began his unchanged second innings spell with ten successive maidens and finished with match figures of 8 for 55 from his 69.3 overs. "His fine length and varied pace made him exceedingly difficult, especially in the second innings" (*Australasian*). Sources: *Wisden, The Age, The Argus, The Herald, The Australasian, The Leader, The Sportsman.*

G.F.VERNON'S ENGLAND XI

Batsman	Dismissal	Runs
A.E.Stoddart	st Blackham b Trott	10
W.W.Read	st Blackham b J.W.Trumble	10
R.Abel	b Trott	0
R.Peel	b Trott	0
T.C.O'Brien	b Trott	2
A.E.Newton	run out (Lyons/Blackham)	77
†M.P.Bowden	run out (Bruce/J.W.Trumble)	0
*G.F.Vernon	c Bruce b J.W.Trumble	50
J.T.Rawlin	not out	78
W.Attewell	b Bruce	43
J.Beaumont	b Bruce	16
Extras	(b1, lb5)	6
Total	(119.2 overs, 230 mins)	292

AUSTRALIAN XI

Batsman	Dismissal	Runs		2nd Innings	Runs
J.J.Lyons	c Attewell b Peel	12		c Newton b Beaumont	0
W.Bruce	c Read b Peel	7		c Bowden b Beaumont	18
J.W.Trumble	b Attewell	0		c O'Brien b Attewell	8
H.Trumble	c Read b Beaumont	7	(10)	c Abel b Attewell	1
*T.W.Garrett	b Stoddart	26	(4)	b Attewell	18
T.P.Horan	c Bowden b Beaumont	20	(5)	c Read b Peel	2
†J.M.Blackham	b Attewell	42	(6)	st Bowden b Peel	13
G.H.S.Trott	lbw b Attewell	1		c Abel b Attewell	2
J.Worrall	b Attewell	4	(7)	c Rawlin b Peel	6
H.Thorpe	c Read b Beaumont	8	(11)	not out	0
J.J.Ferris	not out	4	(9)	c Newton b Peel	7
Extras	(b2, lb1, w1, nb1)	5		(b2, lb1)	3
Total	(88.3 overs, 155 mins)	136		(64.0 overs, 122 mins)	78

AUSTRALIAN XI	O	M	R	W	w,nb
Trott	29	5	78	4	-,-
Thorpe	18	7	36	0	-,-
J.W.Trumble	26	8	48	2	-,-
Ferris	20	4	38	0	-,-
Lyons	2	0	20	0	-,-
H.Trumble	4	0	20	0	-,-
Garrett	4.2	1	11	0	-,-
Bruce	11	3	20	2	-,-
Worrall	5	1	15	0	-,-

ENGLAND XI	O	M	R	W	w,nb		O	M	R	W	w,nb
Attewell	36.3	18	34	4	-,-		33	21	21	4	-,-
Peel	23	12	26	2	-,-	(3)	16	9	15	4	-,-
Beaumont	22	7	52	3	1,1	(2)	15	7	39	2	-,-
Stoddart	7	1	19	1	-,-						

FALL OF WICKETS

Wkt	ENG 1st	AUST 1st	AUST 2nd
1st	12	18	1
2nd	12	19	28
3rd	12	19	29
4th	16	51	47
5th	50	59	53
6th	51	88	60
7th	146	97	66
8th	151	110	77
9th	227	127	78
10th	292	136	78

NEW SOUTH WALES v A.SHREWSBURY'S ENGLAND XI

Played at Sydney Cricket Ground on January 13, 14, 16, 17, 1888. (Timeless match)
Toss : New South Wales.   Result : NEW SOUTH WALES WON BY 153 RUNS.
Debuts: Nil.
12th Men: W.A.Richardson (NSW). No reserve named for England XI.
Umpires: C.Bannerman and G.Ulyett.
Attendances: 3500 (1st day), no other figures published.   Total & Receipts: No figures published.
Close of Play: 1st day NSW 6/99 (Turner 7, Burton 9); 2nd day NSW (2) 0/6 (Garrett 6, Hiddleston 0); 3rd day NSW (2) 216 all out.

G.Ulyett (hand injury) was unable to play for the tourists and agreed to stand as umpire, emulating Brann who had done so in the previous match between the teams. Ulyett's umpiring raised the ire of the spectators on the third day when he adjudged McDonnell to be caught from a ball that "got up in the slips" but appeared to have "touched the ground after leaving the bat" (*Sydney Mail*). It was further alleged that he then gave Jones not out when caught at the wicket soon after "to make amends" (*Sydney Mail*). Pilling (ill) was unable to take the field on the first day, Newham keeping wickets while the New South Wales players alternated as substitute fielder. Moses again showed outstanding form, scoring 58 (in about 150 minutes, 9 fours) and 109 (in about 270 minutes, 13 fours); his batting proved to be the difference between the teams. Turner's 16 for 79 with the ball (he bowled unchanged throughout) remains the best match analysis for New South Wales; only G.Giffen's 17 for 201 for South Australia against Victoria in 1885-86 has surpassed it in Australia. Lohmann's accuracy similarly reaped 14 for 165 for the visitors. Ideal conditions for the medium-pacers had been produced by the rain which ended the first day at 4.00pm. Pilling showed scant regard for his own safety by batting without pads or gloves in the first innings. Four pitches were again used: a new one for each innings. Sources: *Wisden, The Australasian, Sydney Morning Herald, Town & Country Journal, Sydney Mail, Sydney Daily Telegraph.*

NEW SOUTH WALES

*P.S.McDonnell	b Lohmann	6	(7)	c Pougher b Lohmann	16
A.C.Bannerman	c Newham b Lohmann	16	(5)	c Pougher b Smith	7
H.Moses	run out (Preston)	58		c Briggs b Lohmann	109
S.P.Jones	c Newham b Lohmann	0	(8)	b Lohmann	3
R.C.Allen	c & b Lohmann	0	(9)	c Briggs b Lohmann	14
H.C.S.Hiddleston	c Shrewsbury b Lohmann	2	(2)	c Newham b Lohmann	4
C.T.B.Turner	c Newham b Lohmann	19	(10)	c Smith b Lohmann	1
†F.J.Burton	c Lohmann b Preston	30	(4)	b Smith	12
T.W.Garrett	c Read b Lohmann	2	(1)	c Pilling b Lohmann	18
H.Donnan	not out	18	(6)	lbw b Smith	5
J.J.Ferris	b Preston	0		not out	18
Extras	(b1, lb1)	2		(b8, w1)	9
Total	(182.2 overs, 305 mins)	153		(164.3 overs, 285 mins)	216

A.SHREWSBURY'S ENGLAND XI

J.M.Read	c & b Turner	11		b Turner	5
A.Shrewsbury	c McDonnell b Ferris	9		c Donnan b Turner	56
W.Newham	b Turner	16		lbw b Garrett	32
G.A.Lohmann	c McDonnell b Ferris	17		c Bannerman b Turner	5
L.C.Docker	b Turner	4	(6)	b Turner	0
J.Briggs	b Turner	10	(7)	b Turner	0
*C.A.Smith	c & b Turner	3	(5)	b Turner	0
G.Brann	b Turner	0	(9)	c Moses b Turner	3
J.M.Preston	b Turner	3	(8)	c Bannerman b Garrett	6
A.D.Pougher	b Turner	6		c Burton b Turner	17
†R.Pilling	not out	5		not out	1
Extras	(b3)	3		(b4)	4
Total	(66.3 overs, 140 mins)	87		(90.0 overs, 165 mins)	129

ENGLAND XI	O	M	R	W	w,nb		O	M	R	W	w,nb
Lohmann	78	47	68	7	-,-		70.3	34	97	7	-,-
Briggs	55	34	41	0	-,-	(4)	13	8	11	0	1,-
Pougher	17	9	18	0	-,-	(2)	24	12	35	0	-,-
Smith	18	11	9	0	-,-	(5)	34	18	38	3	-,-
Preston	14.2	6	15	2	-,-	(3)	23	11	26	0	-,-

NEW SOUTH WALES	O	M	R	W	w,nb		O	M	R	W	w,nb
Turner	33.3	19	39	8	-,-		46	26	40	8	-,-
Ferris	33	15	45	2	-,-		1	0	12	0	-,-
Donnan							13	6	26	0	-,-
Garrett							25	11	39	2	-,-
Jones							5	1	8	0	-,-

FALL OF WICKETS				
	NSW	ENG	NSW	ENG
Wkt	1st	1st	2nd	2nd
1st	6	12	22	18
2nd	49	36	23	86
3rd	51	36	61	91
4th	63	55	79	93
5th	79	61	89	93
6th	87	71	124	95
7th	114	71	153	108
8th	118	75	187	108
9th	153	82	188	127
10th	153	87	216	129

NEW SOUTH WALES v VICTORIA

Played at Sydney Cricket Ground on January 26, 27, 28, 30, 31, 1888. (Timeless match)
Toss : Victoria.   Result : NEW SOUTH WALES WON BY AN INNINGS AND 35 RUNS.
Debuts: New South Wales - J.R.Wood (f/c).
12th Men: H.C.S.Hiddleston (NSW) and E.E.Bean (Vic).
Umpires: C.Bannerman and D.F.Cotter.
Attendances & Receipts: No figures published.
Close of Play: 1st day Vic 267 all out; 2nd day NSW 3/269 (Moses 146, Burton 47); 3rd day NSW 7/507 (Moses 262, Wood 77); 4th day Vic (2) 4/157 (Horan 65, Walters 5).

Fine weather prevailed for most of the match which was played on a wicket "as true as a billiard table" (*Sydney Mail*). Victoria failed to take full advantage from the winning of the toss, despite fifties from Bruce (55 in 50 minutes, 7 fours), Horan (63 in about 195 minutes, 3 fours) and Blackham (54 in about 105 minutes, 5 fours). A marathon innings of 297 not out (in about 615 minutes, 1 five and 24 fours, 4 chances) by Moses transcended all else in the game. He was perhaps fortunate to survive a difficult chance to McShane at third man off Trott before scoring but "did much as he liked with the bowling" (*SMH*) thereafter. He achieved his dominance by the calm measured approach that was the hallmark of all his innings. Burton (47 in about 195 minutes, 5 fours) and Wood (81 in about 165 minutes, 1 five and 5 fours, chances at 7 and 8) assisted him in stands of 185 and 170 for the fourth and eighth wickets respectively. Wood also added 4 wickets to his invaluable innings but it was destined to be his sole first-class appearance for New South Wales. Garrett was caught by Blackham in consecutive overs from Trumble, the first from a delivery belatedly called as a no-ball by Cotter. Another half-century from Horan (68 in about 195 minutes, 4 fours) failed to prevent an innings victory to the home team. Four-ball overs were bowled, by mutual agreement of the captains, despite both colonial associations agreeing that six balls should apply. Sources: *Wisden, Sydney Morning Herald, Town & Country Journal, Sydney Mail, Sydney Daily Telegraph.*

VICTORIA

W.Bruce	c Garrett b Wood	55		b Garrett	24
F.H.Walters	c Jones b Wood	18	(6)	b Turner	44
T.P.Horan	c Burton b Garrett	63		b Turner	68
R.S.Houston	c & Wood	31		lbw b Richardson	36
F.G.McShane	b Turner	0		c Richardson b Turner	2
*†J.M.Blackham	b Richardson	54	(2)	b Richardson	17
J.Worrall	b Richardson	31		c McDonnell b Turner	2
G.H.S.Trott	b Richardson	0		b Turner	16
W.R.Robertson	b Richardson	0		not out	32
H.F.Boyle	c Burton b Garrett	4		b Wood	3
H.Trumble	not out	0		run out (Jones/Richardson)	12
Extras	(b1, lb7, w2, nb1)	11		(b12, lb6)	18
Total	(159.2 overs, 280 mins)	267		(192.0 overs, 340 mins)	274

NEW SOUTH WALES

*P.S.McDonnell	c Bruce b Robertson	42
A.C.Bannerman	st Blackham b Trott	19
H.Moses	not out	297
H.H.Massie	b Bruce	1
†F.J.Burton	b Trott	47
S.P.Jones	lbw b McShane	27
C.T.B.Turner	c Boyle b McShane	5
H.Donnan	b McShane	2
J.R.Wood	b Trott	81
T.W.Garrett	c Blackham b Trumble	21
W.A.Richardson	st Blackham b Bruce	5
Extras	(b15, lb9, nb5)	29
Total	(380.2 overs, 650 mins)	576

NEW SOUTH WALES	O	M	R	W	w,nb		O	M	R	W	w,nb
Turner	46	19	79	1	-,-		71	25	102	5	-,-
Donnan	10	2	28	0	-,-	(5)	6	2	8	0	-,-
Garrett	41	18	54	2	1,-		53	35	41	1	-,-
Jones	3	0	7	0	-,-						
Wood	44	17	65	3	-,-	(4)	32	17	32	1	-,-
Moses	3	0	5	0	-,-						
Richardson	12.2	4	18	4	-,-	(2)	30	7	73	2	-,-

VICTORIA	O	M	R	W	w,nb
Trumble	53	32	49	1	-,5
Trott	74	49	124	3	-,-
Bruce	56.2	29	82	2	-,-
Robertson	38	14	64	1	-,-
Horan	15	6	28	0	-,-
McShane	30	12	64	3	-,-
Boyle	46	23	47	0	-,-
Worrall	53	20	66	0	-,-
Walters	11	5	16	0	-,-
Houston	4	1	7	0	-,-

FALL OF WICKETS

Wkt	VIC 1st	NSW 1st	VIC 2nd
1st	79	39	32
2nd	80	89	58
3rd	129	90	136
4th	130	275	146
5th	218	329	161
6th	252	343	163
7th	259	346	181
8th	259	516	233
9th	266	548	236
10th	267	576	274

COMBINED XI v A.SHREWSBURY'S ENGLAND XI

Played at Sydney Cricket Ground on February 3, 4, 6, 7, 1888. (Timeless match)
Toss : Combined XI.   Result : A.SHREWSBURY'S ENGLAND XI WON BY FIVE WICKETS.
Debuts: Nil.
12th Men: None named.
Umpires: C.Bannerman and A.D.Pougher.
Attendances: 1000, 2000, 1200, 300.   Total: About 4500.   Receipts: No figures published.
Close of Play: 1st day Comb 8/232 (Turner 17, Worrall 1); 2nd day Eng 5/218 (Newham 28, Docker 13); 3rd day Comb (2) 7/78
   (Bannerman 45).

The match was intended to be between Shrewsbury's Team and a representative Australian XI. However, G.Giffen, A.H.Jarvis and J.J.Lyons (South Australia) as well as J.M.Blackham, W.Bruce and T.P.Horan (Victoria) all declined to play and H.H.Massie (New South Wales) withdrew at the last moment. McShane, Walters and Worrall - the only Victorians remaining in Sydney after the just-finished intercolonial match - were the only non-New South Wales players included in the eventual line-up, hardly representative of Australia. The Englishmen chose a fresh pitch for their innings; the second innings of both teams was played on the same pitch. Ulyett (72 in 90 minutes) and Newham (53 in about 180 minutes) scored half-centuries for the tourists. Bannerman was the second opener after W.L.Murdoch (NSW v Lord Harris's XI at Sydney 1878-79) to bat undefeated through an innings in Australia. Smith was run out while backing up at the non-striker's end when a straight drive by Newham was deflected by the bowler into the stumps. Sources: *Wisden, Sydney Referee, Sydney Morning Herald, Town & Country Journal, Sydney Mail, Sydney Daily Telegraph.*

COMBINED XI

A.C.Bannerman	c Lohmann b Briggs	5	not out		45
S.P.Jones	st Pilling b Preston	17	c & b Lohmann		10
H.Moses	c Newham b Lohmann	46	lbw b Lohmann		2
†F.J.Burton	b Lohmann	20	c Pilling b Lohmann		4
F.H.Walters	b Ulyett	29	b Lohmann		1
*P.S.McDonnell	c Docker b Preston	54	c Pilling b Lohmann		5
T.W.Garrett	c Briggs b Lohmann	18	c Shrewsbury b Briggs		7
F.G.McShane	c Brann b Briggs	23	st Pilling b Lohmann		2
C.T.B.Turner	b Lohmann	23	c & b Lohmann		0
J.Worrall	c Shrewsbury b Lohmann	19	c Smith b Briggs		3
H.Donnan	not out	6	c Shrewsbury b Briggs		0
Extras	(b2)	2	(b4)		4
Total	(191.0 overs, 315 mins)	262	(87.3 overs, 155 mins)		83

A.SHREWSBURY'S ENGLAND XI

A.Shrewsbury	lbw b McShane	39	(2) lbw b Turner		14
J.M.Read	b McShane	39	(1) c Moses b Turner		2
G.Ulyett	c Donnan b McShane	72	c Worrall b Garrett		15
W.Newham	c Worrall b Garrett	53	c Bannerman b McShane		3
G.A.Lohmann	b McShane	17	c Garrett b Turner		4
J.Briggs	lbw b McShane	9	not out		6
L.C.Docker	c Turner b Garrett	21	not out		4
*C.A.Smith	run out (Garrett)	17			
J.M.Preston	c McDonnell b Turner	3			
G.Brann	not out	14			
†R.Pilling	c Burton b Garrett	6			
Extras	(b2, w3)	5	(b3)		3
Total	(184.1 overs, 310 mins)	295	(34.0 overs, 70 mins) (5 wkts)		51

ENGLAND XI	O	M	R	W	w,nb		O	M	R	W	w,nb		FALL OF WICKETS			
Lohmann	82	44	83	5	-,-		44	21	43	7	-,-		COMB	ENG	COMB	ENG
Briggs	48	25	67	2	-,-		22.3	16	18	3	-,-	Wkt	1st	1st	2nd	2nd
Preston	35	17	62	2	-,-	(4)	10	6	7	0	-,-	1st	9	52	31	14
Smith	12	6	16	0	-,-	(3)	11	7	11	0	-,-	2nd	56	152	39	19
Ulyett	14	4	32	1	-,-							3rd	80	154	51	29
												4th	103	174	55	34
COMBINED XI	O	M	R	W	w,nb		O	M	R	W	w,nb	5th	173	192	64	40
Turner	49	18	80	1	1,-		17	6	19	3	-,-	6th	173	245	75	-
McShane	68	24	103	5	1,-		7	3	20	1	-,-	7th	207	272	78	-
Jones	5	1	13	0	1,-							8th	217	274	78	-
Garrett	53.1	25	74	3	-,-	(3)	10	5	9	1	-,-	9th	249	278	81	-
Worrall	4	1	8	0	-,-							10th	262	295	83	-
Donnan	5	1	12	0	-,-											

AUSTRALIA v ENGLAND (Only Test)

Played at Sydney Cricket Ground on February 10, 11 - 13 (no play), 14, 15, 1888. (Timeless match)
Toss : Australia.   Result : ENGLAND WON BY 126 RUNS.
Debuts: England - W.Newham, A.E.Stoddart (both Test).
12th Men: None named.
Umpires: C.Bannerman and J.Phillips.
Attendances: 1173, no play, no play, 700, 100.   Total: 1973.   Receipts: £117.
Close of Play: 1st day Aust 8/35 (Garrett 9, Turner 3); 2nd day no play; 3rd day no play; 4th day Aust (2)5/47 (Jones 13, Garrett 1).

The two English touring teams pooled their resources to field a Combined England Team against All Australia in an attempt to manufacture a match truly representative of the two countries. However, the Australians were without W.Bruce, G.Giffen and A.H.Jarvis, who all declined invitations, and T.P.Horan and J.R.Wood later withdrew from the nominated squad of thirteen. The final team could in no way be considered indicative of the country's strength. Nevertheless, this match was the only match of the season to be later awarded Test status. Heavy rain before and during the match ruined the pitch as a true contest between bat and ball, bowlers of both sides being able to extract unexpected bounce and prodigious turn to make batting a nightmare. Australia's first-innings total was their lowest in any Test in Australia; it remained until 1902 their lowest in all Test cricket. The batting of Shrewsbury (44 in about 120 minutes, 3 fours) and Read (39 in about 60 minutes, 1 five and 4 fours), allied to the greater accuracy of the English attack, proved to be the deciding factor. Attracting a bare 2000 people, it was the poorest ever attended Test in Australia. *Wisden* incorrectly gives Aust (2) Ferris c Shrewsbury b Peel, Attewell 0/4. All publications down the years have also incorrectly credited Peel with the wicket of Ferris in Aust (2) and given Peel 5/40, Attewell 1/4. After examining all contemporary reports, and the official scorebook kept by the NSWCA, there can be absolutely no doubt that Attewell captured the final wicket. Sources: *Wisden, The Australasian, Sydney Morning Herald, Town & Country Journal, NSWCA Scorebook, Sydney Mail, Sydney Daily Telegraph.*

ENGLAND

A.Shrewsbury	c Turner b Ferris	44	b Ferris	1
A.E.Stoddart	c McShane b Turner	16	c Blackham b Turner	17
G.Ulyett	c Burton b Turner	5	b Ferris	5
*W.W.Read	b Turner	10	b Turner	8
J.M.Read	c & b Turner	0	c Bannerman b Turner	39
R.Peel	hit wkt b Ferris	3	st Blackham b Turner	9
W.Newham	c Worrall b Ferris	9	(8) lbw b Turner	17
G.A.Lohmann	c Jones b Ferris	12	(7) c Blackham b Turner	0
J.Briggs	b Turner	0	c Worrall b McShane	14
W.Attewell	not out	7	not out	10
†R.Pilling	run out (Bannerman/Blackham)	3	b Turner	5
Extras	(b4)	4	(b7, lb5)	12
Total	(100.0 overs, 185 mins)	113	(75.0 overs, 145 mins)	137

AUSTRALIA

A.C.Bannerman	c Ulyett b Lohmann	2	c Attewell b Lohmann	2
S.P.Jones	c Shrewsbury b Peel	0	(4) c Shrewsbury b Lohmann	15
H.Moses	c W.W.Read b Lohmann	3	c Briggs b Lohmann	11
F.J.Burton	c Stoddart b Lohmann	1	(5) c Pilling b Peel	1
J.Worrall	st Pilling b Peel	6	(10) b Lohmann	1
F.G.McShane	c Shrewsbury b Peel	0	(9) b Peel	0
*P.S.McDonnell	b Lohmann	3	(2) b Peel	6
†J.M.Blackham	c Shrewsbury b Peel	2	not out	25
T.W.Garrett	c Pilling b Lohmann	10	(7) c Shrewsbury b Peel	1
C.T.B.Turner	not out	8	(6) lbw b Attewell	12
J.J.Ferris	c W.W.Read b Peel	0	c Shrewsbury b Attewell	5
Extras	(b6, w1)	7	(b2, lb1)	3
Total	(37.3 overs, 70 mins)	42	(69.2 overs, 130 mins)	82

AUSTRALIA	O	M	R	W	w,nb		O	M	R	W	w,nb		FALL OF WICKETS			
Turner	50	27	44	5	-,-		38	23	43	7	-,-			ENG	AUST	ENG	AUST
Ferris	47	25	60	4	-,-		16	4	43	2	-,-		Wkt	1st	1st	2nd	2nd
Garrett	3	1	5	0	-,-								1st	27	2	9	8
McShane						(3)	21	7	39	1	-,-		2nd	36	2	15	8
													3rd	54	10	27	20
ENGLAND	O	M	R	W	w,nb		O	M	R	W	w,nb		4th	54	16	54	21
Lohmann	19	13	17	5	1,-		32	18	35	4	-,-		5th	57	18	82	44
Peel	18.3	9	18	5	-,-		33	14	40	4	-,-		6th	86	21	82	47
Attewell							4.2	2	4	2	-,-		7th	102	23	84	53
													8th	103	26	111	60
													9th	103	37	131	61
													10th	113	42	137	82

NEW SOUTH WALES v G.F.VERNON'S ENGLAND XI

Played at Sydney Cricket Ground on February 17, 18, 20, 21, 1888. (Timeless match)
Toss : England XI.   Result : G.F.VERNON'S ENGLAND XI WON BY EIGHT WICKETS.
Debuts: Nil.
12th Men: None named.
Umpires: J.Phillips and D.S.Ogilvy (J.M.Blackham and W.B.Fairfax deputised).
Attendances & Receipts: No figures published.
Close of Play: 1st day Eng 7/297 (Rawlin 21, Attewell 12); 2nd day NSW 7/144 (Hiddleston 20, Garrett 17); 3rd day NSW (2) 4/135 (Jones 39, Burton 9).

New South Wales had only nine players present when the match began, H.Donnan, J.J.Ferris and J.R.Wood all withdrawing from the twelve at the last moment. Members of Vernon's Team alternated as substitutes until the arrival of Hiddleston (a nominated emergency) and Wearne. H.Moses had indicated his unavailability for New South Wales before the team was announced. Ogilvy was absent on the third day and J.M.Blackham (who was still in Sydney after the Test) and W.B.Fairfax deputised in turn as Phillips's partner. After dispatching the opening delivery of the match to the fence, Stoddart lost his wicket off the next ball to Turner, who bowled him again in the third over of the second innings before he had scored. Read, who gave a straightforward caught-and-bowled chance to Turner on 0, went on to make 119 in 210 minutes. Charles Bannerman, scorer of Test cricket's first run and first hundred - and at this stage also a first-class umpire - played his last match. Sources: *Wisden, Sydney Referee, Sydney Morning Herald, Town & Country Journal, Sydney Mail, Sydney Daily Telegraph.*

G.F.VERNON'S ENGLAND XI

A.E.Stoddart	b Turner	4	b Turner		0
R.Abel	c Burton b Turner	34	run out (Richardson/Burton)		0
R.Peel	b Turner	27	not out		52
W.W.Read	run out (Allen)	119	not out		53
T.C.O'Brien	c Burton b Jones	45			
A.E.Newton	b Wearne	17			
J.T.Rawlin	c Allen b Garrett	39			
*G.F.Vernon	c McDonnell b Turner	6			
W.Attewell	b Garrett	25			
†M.P.Bowden	lbw b Turner	4			
J.Beaumont	not out	2			
Extras	(b10, lb5)	15	(b4)		4
Total	(189.3 overs, 310 mins)	337	(60.1 overs, 100 mins) (2 wkts)		109

NEW SOUTH WALES

C.Bannerman	c & b Peel	6	(5) c Bowden b Rawlin		0
A.C.Bannerman	c Peel b Stoddart	33	(1) c Rawlin b Peel		15
*P.S.McDonnell	c Rawlin b Beaumont	4	lbw b Beaumont		56
S.P.Jones	run out (Beaumont)	0	lbw b Attewell		40
R.C.Allen	b Peel	8	(9) c Rawlin b Stoddart		4
C.T.B.Turner	c O'Brien b Stoddart	27	(7) c Peel b Stoddart		45
†F.J.Burton	c Stoddart b Peel	16	(6) c Abel b Beaumont		22
H.C.S.Hiddleston	b Attewell	36	(2) b Peel		14
T.W.Garrett	c Newton b Attewell	45	(8) c Bowden b Beaumont		12
W.A.Richardson	lbw b Attewell	0	not out		30
W.S.Wearne	not out	2	c Beaumont b Peel		11
Extras	(b12, lb4)	16	(lb3)		3
Total	(150.2 overs, 250 mins)	193	(227.2 overs, 380 mins)		252

NEW SOUTH WALES	O	M	R	W	w,nb		O	M	R	W	w,nb
Turner	81	35	128	5	-,-		24.1	10	34	1	-,-
Garrett	73.3	35	91	2	-,-		26	6	41	0	-,-
Richardson	7	0	26	0	-,-						
Wearne	11	3	39	1	-,-	(3)	5	1	17	0	-,-
Jones	17	4	38	1	-,-	(4)	5	2	13	0	-,-

ENGLAND XI	O	M	R	W	w,nb		O	M	R	W	w,nb
Beaumont	47	27	53	1	-,-	(4)	41	24	61	3	-,-
Peel	54	26	61	3	-,-		78.2	43	83	3	-,-
Attewell	28.2	14	32	3	-,-	(1)	69	45	58	1	-,-
Stoddart	21	10	31	2	-,-	(3)	25	11	35	2	-,-
Rawlin							14	8	12	1	-,-

FALL OF WICKETS				
	ENG	NSW	ENG	NSW
Wkt	1st	1st	2nd	2nd
1st	4	14	24	0
2nd	56	19	41	1
3rd	75	19	110	-
4th	173	39	113	-
5th	248	82	139	-
6th	262	89	183	-
7th	271	120	197	-
8th	324	184	207	-
9th	331	188	210	-
10th	337	193	252	-

SOUTH AUSTRALIA v VICTORIA

Played at Adelaide Oval on February 17, 18, 20, 1888. (Timeless match)
Toss : Victoria   Result : SOUTH AUSTRALIA WON BY AN INNINGS AND 113 RUNS.
Debuts: South Australia - E.H.Coombe, J.C.Reedman (both f/c). Victoria - E.E.Bean, J.Duffy, R.Mitchell (all f/c).
12th Men: J.H.Stuckey (Vic). No 12th named for SA.
Umpires: T.Flynn and J.F.King.
Attendances: 1000, 2000, 300.   Total: About 3300   Receipts: £64.
Close of Play: 1st day SA 3/116 (G.Giffen 49, Godfrey 6); 2nd day SA 407 all out.

George Giffen, who scored 166 in 335 minutes and hit 12 fours - offering a half-chance to the keeper when 87 as his only blemish - became the first to score a century and take ten or more wickets in an Australian first-class match, a feat he repeated five times for his State before it could be achieved by anyone else in the country. His match bowling analysis of 14 for 125 (he bowled himself unchanged in both innings) included the wickets of all eleven batsmen. Slight finished off the South Australian innings with successive deliveries after Giffen had added 104 for the fourth wicket with Godfrey and 108 for the sixth wicket with Noel. McIlwraith (88 in 145 minutes, 2 fours, 2 chances) recorded the only notable score for Victoria. Six-ball overs were agreed by the captains before the start. Cotter kept wicket while Lewis bowled. J.D.Edwards, J.M.Blackham (in Sydney), R.S.Houston and J.W.Trumble were all unavailable for Victoria, Duffy and Stuckey replacing W.E.Midwinter and W.R.Robertson when they withdrew from the selected team. Reedman was a late replacement for J.E.Craigie (unavailable) in the local line-up. Sources: *Cricket, C.B.O'Reilly, The Australasian, Adelaide Advertiser, South Australian Register.*

VICTORIA

J.McIlwraith	b G.Giffen	88		b Noel	27
J.Slight	b G.Giffen	6		b G.Giffen	2
F.H.Walters	run out (Lyons/Jarvis)	0	(4)	b G.Giffen	0
†P.M.Lewis	b Lyons	12	(5)	b G.Giffen	9
G.H.S.Trott	c & b G.Giffen	30	(3)	run out (Musgrove/G.Giffen)	1
T.Turner	b G.Giffen	3	(10)	not out	2
*H.F.Boyle	lbw b G.Giffen	0	(8)	c Musgrove b Noel	18
E.E.Bean	not out	7	(7)	c Haldane b G.Giffen	7
J.Duffy	c Noel b G.Giffen	12		c Godfrey b Noel	39
R.Mitchell	c Godfrey b G.Giffen	3	(6)	st Jarvis b G.Giffen	10
D.F.Cotter	b G.Giffen	2		b G.Giffen	1
Extras	(b5)	5		(b9, lb1)	10
Total	(67.3 overs, 170 mins)	168		(48.5 overs, 135 mins)	126

SOUTH AUSTRALIA

†A.H.Jarvis	b Trott	4
J.J.Lyons	b Turner	27
*G.Giffen	b Trott	166
W.F.Giffen	st Lewis b Trott	30
C.G.Godfrey	b Trott	52
W.H.Watling	c Lewis b Trott	0
J.Noel	c & b Trott	47
E.H.Coombe	st Lewis b Trott	10
H.Haldane	not out	33
J.Musgrove	c Mitchell b Slight	35
J.C.Reedman	b Slight	0
Extras	(b3)	3
Total	(163.3 overs, 415 mins)	407

SOUTH AUSTRALIA	O	M	R	W	w,nb		O	M	R	W	w,nb
Musgrove	7	0	22	0	-,-						
G.Giffen	33.3	13	65	8	-,-	(1)	24.5	5	60	6	-,-
Lyons	12	1	47	1	-,-						
Noel	15	4	29	0	-,-	(2)	24	6	56	3	-,-

VICTORIA	O	M	R	W	w,nb
Trott	62	7	216	7	-,-
Turner	45	19	62	1	-,-
Cotter	31	11	60	0	-,-
Duffy	12	2	32	0	-,-
Boyle	8	2	15	0	-,-
Bean	1	0	2	0	-,-
Lewis	4	1	13	0	-,-
Slight	0.3	0	4	2	-,-

FALL OF WICKETS

Wkt	VIC 1st	SA 1st	VIC 2nd
1st	20	4	8
2nd	20	38	22
3rd	55	107	27
4th	126	211	39
5th	138	211	47
6th	138	319	65
7th	145	331	68
8th	159	350	114
9th	162	407	124
10th	168	407	126

AUSTRALIAN XI v A.SHREWSBURY'S ENGLAND XI

Played at Sydney Cricket Ground on February 24, 25, 1888. (Timeless match)
Toss : Australian XI.   Result : A.SHREWSBURY'S ENGLAND XI WON BY AN INNINGS AND 42 RUNS.
Debuts: Nil.
12th Men: None named.
Umpires: C.Bannerman and J.Swift.
Attendances & Receipts: No figures published.
Close of Play: 1st day Aust 3/21 (Jones 10, Lyons 4).

Final selection of the Australian team to tour England later in the year had not been completed at the time of this match. Nine of those already chosen to tour appeared and G.Giffen and H.Moses were eagerly sought to play but had not yet confirmed their availability to tour; in any event Moses played here but like Giffen eventually declined to tour. Burn was included as a trial, as he had scored 99 in Tasmania against Vernon's Team in a non-first-class fixture earlier in the season. T.P.Horan and J.W.Trumble turned down invitations to play in the match because of work commitments. McDonnell won the toss and sent the Englishmen in on a pitch softened by pre-match rain, even though it had been covered overnight. Outstanding batting by Shrewsbury, combined with hitting from the tail, produced a good total in the conditions. Further overnight rain on the (now uncovered) pitch produced an impossible surface for batting and Lohmann and Briggs exploited the conditions to the fullest. They provided the fifth and final instance in Australia of two bowlers operating unchanged through both innings of a first-class match. *Wisden* incorrectly gives Aust (1) Lyons 7, McDonnell 8, Burn c Pilling; Aust (2) Jarvis hit wkt.
Sources: *Wisden, Sydney Referee, Sydney Morning Herald, Town & Country Journal, Sydney Mail, Sydney Daily Telegraph.*

A.SHREWSBURY'S ENGLAND XI

A.Shrewsbury	b Turner	51
J.M.Read	c Jarvis b Turner	10
W.Newham	b Turner	5
G.Ulyett	st Jarvis b Ferris	18
J.Briggs	b Turner	1
G.A.Lohmann	b Turner	7
L.C.Docker	lbw b Trott	8
*C.A.Smith	c Jarvis b Trott	10
J.M.Preston	c Jarvis b Trott	27
A.D.Pougher	b Ferris	22
†R.Pilling	not out	3
Extras	(b8, lb1, w2)	11
Total	(112.3 overs, about 200 mins)	173

AUSTRALIAN XI

†A.H.Jarvis	st Pilling b Briggs	3	(8)	b Briggs	5
S.P.Jones	c Lohmann b Briggs	27		c Pilling b Briggs	6
H.Moses	c Smith b Lohmann	2		b Lohmann	8
C.T.B.Turner	b Briggs	1	(7)	c Preston b Lohmann	29
J.J.Lyons	lbw b Briggs	8	(6)	c Pougher b Lohmann	0
*P.S.McDonnell	c Ulyett b Lohmann	7	(1)	c Newham b Briggs	2
J.M.Blackham	lbw b Lohmann	5	(5)	c Shrewsbury b Lohmann	2
J.D.Edwards	b Lohmann	4	(9)	c & b Lohmann	1
E.J.K.Burn	st Pilling b Briggs	13	(4)	c Shrewsbury b Briggs	0
G.H.S.Trott	c Pilling b Briggs	0		c Shrewsbury b Briggs	2
J.J.Ferris	not out	0		not out	0
Extras	(b1, lb4)	5		(b1)	1
Total	(85.3 overs, about 150 mins)	75		(35.1 overs, about 70 mins)	56

AUSTRALIAN XI	O	M	R	W	w,nb
Trott	32	9	76	3	1,-
Turner	53	31	64	5	-,-
Ferris	24.3	13	21	2	-,-
Jones	3	2	1	0	1,-

ENGLAND XI	O	M	R	W	w,nb	O	M	R	W	w,nb
Lohmann	43	27	30	4	-,-	18	8	37	5	-,-
Briggs	42.3	26	40	6	-,-	17.1	8	18	5	-,-

FALL OF WICKETS

Wkt	ENG 1st	AUST 1st	AUST 2nd
1st	14	5	7
2nd	24	12	17
3rd	61	17	17
4th	70	27	17
5th	96	42	19
6th	107	52	19
7th	111	58	44
8th	133	74	54
9th	152	74	56
10th	173	75	56

AUSTRALIAN XI v G.F.VERNON'S ENGLAND XI

Played at Melbourne Cricket Ground on March 2, 3, 5, 1888. (Timeless match)
Toss : England XI.   Result : G.F.VERNON'S ENGLAND XI WON BY 87 RUNS.
Debuts: Nil.
12th Men: None named.
Umpires: D.F.Cotter and J.Phillips.
Attendances: 500, 3000, 300.   Total: About 3800.   Receipts: No figures published.
Close of Play: 1st day Aust 2/43 (Horan 16, Lyons 14); 2nd day Aust 219 all out.

Horan replaced A.H.Jarvis (ill) in the Australian line-up. Only 2 runs separated the teams after the first innings, Peel (45 in 135 minutes, 4 fours) and Newton (54 in 105 minutes, 9 fours) and Horan (67 in 195 minutes, 4 fours) and Lyons (42 in 105 minutes, 6 fours) batting well for their respective sides. Heavy rain fell on the Sunday, saturating the pitch and outfield. Vernon's Team had the best use of the sodden wicket before it cut up too badly. Peel (38 in 150 minutes, 1 four) again making a worthwhile contribution. As the wicket dried after lunch batting became almost impossible. The Englishmen lost their last 8 wickets for 36 and then Peel (3 for 17) and Attewell (7 for 15) were virtually unplayable on the severely scarred surface, bundling out the Australians for 32 in a little over an hour. The dismissal of Jones was controversial (the batsman maintained he had hit his stumps after completing his stroke), Cotter at square-leg ruling otherwise.
Sources: *Wisden, The Age, The Argus, The Herald, The Australasian, The Leader, The Sportsman.*

G.F.VERNON'S ENGLAND XI

A.E.Stoddart	c Blackham b Ferris	28		c Edwards b Turner	6
R.Abel	lbw b Ferris	32	(7)	c & b Turner	0
R.Peel	b Boyle	45		c Horan b Turner	38
W.W.Read	c Burn b Turner	2	(2)	c McDonnell b Boyle	25
T.C.O'Brien	c McDonnell b Ferris	7	(4)	c Ferris b Turner	23
A.E.Newton	c Blackham b Boyle	54	(5)	c & b Ferris	3
J.T.Rawlin	b Turner	3	(9)	b Turner	0
W.Attewell	b Turner	19	(6)	b Turner	2
*G.F.Vernon	c Blackham b Turner	12	(8)	c McDonnell b Ferris	11
†M.P.Bowden	b Ferris	0		not out	0
J.Beaumont	not out	2		b Turner	2
Extras	(b13, lb3, nb1)	17		(b7)	7
Total	(109.1 overs, 220 mins)	221		(81.1 overs, 165 mins)	117

AUSTRALIAN XI

*P.S.McDonnell	c O'Brien b Peel	6		c Peel b Attewell	4
S.P.Jones	c Bowden b Beaumont	0		hit wkt b Peel	0
T.P.Horan	b Attewell	67		st Bowden b Attewell	1
J.J.Lyons	c Peel b Read	42		c Abel b Peel	0
†J.M.Blackham	b Attewell	4		c Read b Attewell	11
C.T.B.Turner	b Attewell	10		not out	11
E.J.K.Burn	b Attewell	6		c Read b Attewell	2
J.D.Edwards	b Attewell	13		c Read b Attewell	0
G.H.S.Trott	b Peel	30		c Read b Attewell	0
H.F.Boyle	b Beaumont	0	(11)	c Bowden b Peel	0
J.J.Ferris	not out	22	(10)	c Stoddart b Attewell	3
Extras	(b9, lb9, w1)	19			–
Total	(190.3 overs, 330 mins)	219		(41.1 overs, 70 mins)	32

AUSTRALIAN XI	O	M	R	W	w,nb		O	M	R	W	w,nb		FALL OF WICKETS			
														ENG	AUST	ENG	AUST
Trott	11	0	26	0	-,-							Wkt	1st	1st	2nd	2nd
Turner	46.1	19	71	4	-,-		40.1	17	48	7	-,-	1st	60	5	15	4
Jones	8	1	26	0	-,1							2nd	67	13	39	5
Ferris	30	10	63	4	-,-	(1)	32	13	47	2	-,-	3rd	72	91	81	5
Boyle	14	9	18	2	-,-	(3)	9	3	15	1	-,-	4th	79	103	84	9
												5th	178	115	95	20
ENGLAND XI	O	M	R	W	w,nb		O	M	R	W	w,nb	6th	187	141	99	22
Beaumont	48	18	73	2	-,-							7th	193	144	110	24
Peel	72.3	45	54	2	1,-		20.1	11	17	3	-,-	8th	216	183	113	24
Attewell	53	21	33	5	-,-	(1)	21	14	15	7	-,-	9th	217	184	113	30
Stoddart	10	3	24	0	-,-							10th	221	219	117	32
Read	7	1	16	1	-,-											

AUSTRALIAN XI v A.SHREWSBURY'S ENGLAND XI

Played at Sydney Cricket Ground on March 9, 10, 12, 13, 1888. (Timeless match)
Toss : England XI.   Result : A.SHREWSBURY'S ENGLAND XI WON BY 158 RUNS.
Debuts: Nil.
12th Men: None named.
Umpires: C.Bannerman and J.Swift.
Attendances: 2nd day 3000, other days no figures published.   Total & Receipts: No figures published.
Close of Play: 1st day Aust 0/55 (Blackham 38, Jones 17); 2nd day Eng (2) 1/101 (Shrewsbury 53, Briggs 46); 3rd day Eng (2) 8/355
    (Shrewsbury 183, Pougher 7).

The Australian XI only had ten players when the game commenced, as Burn and Horan did not travel north after the match at Melbourne. Shrewsbury's XI provided one of their number as a substitute until the arrival of Richardson, who had been urgently summoned to the ground. Once again the match was evenly poised after the completion of an innings apiece. Blackham (97 in about 135 minutes), who was fifth out at 149, provided more than half of the first-innings runs for the Australians and completed seven dismissals in the match. Shrewsbury's masterly knock of 206 in 437 minutes, compiled over three days, tipped the scales in favour of the Englishmen. He shared century partnerships with Briggs for the second wicket and Smith for the seventh, setting the Australians 425 for victory. Jones (134 not out in 205 minutes, 3 fives and 10 fours) fought hard against a varied attack but it was never likely that the Australians would reach their target. The game was continued until 6.25pm on the fourth day in order to achieve a result that evening. Turner took his season's tally of first-class wickets to a record 106 (average 13.59) from just 12 matches. Sources: *Wisden, The Australasian, Sydney Morning Herald, Town & Country Journal, Sydney Mail, Sydney Daily Telegraph.*

A.SHREWSBURY'S ENGLAND XI

A.Shrewsbury	c Jones b Turner	24	c Trott b Turner	206
J.M.Read	b Turner	33	b Turner	0
J.Briggs	b Turner	7	c Blackham b Turner	54
J.M.Preston	c Richardson b Turner	7	(7) c Blackham b Jones	9
W.Newham	lbw b Turner	4	(4) lbw b Ferris	1
G.A.Lohmann	c Blackham b Ferris	16	(5) c & b Trott	39
L.C.Docker	st Blackham b Turner	33	(6) c Richardson b Trott	1
*C.A.Smith	c & b Turner	59	c Blackham b Edwards	40
G.Brann	b Trott	13	st Blackham b Turner	3
A.D.Pougher	not out	7	c Blackham b Jones	24
†R.Pilling	c Boyle b Ferris	3	not out	8
Extras	(b6)	6	(b11, lb4, w2)	17
Total	(120.1 overs, 225 mins)	212	(255.3 overs, 460 mins)	402

AUSTRALIAN XI

†J.M.Blackham	c Docker b Preston	97	c Docker b Preston	1
S.P.Jones	b Briggs	35	(4) not out	134
J.D.Edwards	c Brann b Preston	8	(7) c Preston b Briggs	24
C.T.B.Turner	c Pilling b Lohmann	7	(6) c & b Lohmann	17
J.J.Lyons	b Preston	1	lbw b Lohmann	0
*P.S.McDonnell	c Pilling b Lohmann	15	(2) c Briggs b Lohmann	29
J.R.Wood	b Preston	2	(8) b Preston	4
W.A.Richardson	b Lohmann	8	(9) c & b Lohmann	14
G.H.S.Trott	not out	9	(3) run out (Brann/Smith)	15
J.J.Ferris	run out (Briggs/Preston)	2	b Pougher	13
H.F.Boyle	c Briggs b Lohmann	6	c Docker b Pougher	8
Extras		-	(b7)	7
Total	(109.3 overs, 200 mins)	190	(129.2 overs, 230 mins)	266

AUSTRALIAN XI	O	M	R	W	w,nb		O	M	R	W	w,nb
Turner	54	27	72	7	-,-	(2)	91	43	135	4	-,-
Trott	14	3	30	1	-,-	(1)	39	20	77	2	-,-
Ferris	25.1	8	59	2	-,-		66	40	74	1	-,-
Wood	21	9	32	0	-,-		16	10	21	0	-,-
Lyons	6	1	13	0	-,-		3	0	13	0	-,-
Jones							35.3	13	57	2	2,-
Boyle							3	1	8	0	-,-
Edwards							2	2	0	1	-,-

ENGLAND XI	O	M	R	W	w,nb		O	M	R	W	w,nb
Lohmann	44.3	20	93	4	-,-		53	25	70	4	-,-
Briggs	22	10	34	1	-,-	(3)	39	15	92	1	-,-
Pougher	3	1	12	0	-,-	(5)	5.2	1	10	2	-,-
Preston	30	13	38	4	-,-	(2)	20	8	48	2	-,-
Smith	10	4	13	0	-,-	(4)	12	2	39	0	-,-

FALL OF WICKETS

Wkt	ENG 1st	AUST 1st	ENG 2nd	AUST 2nd
1st	45	87	4	1
2nd	63	134	115	37
3rd	75	141	116	77
4th	75	146	184	79
5th	90	149	200	116
6th	98	165	211	173
7th	175	165	317	189
8th	201	174	333	225
9th	201	176	386	252
10th	212	190	402	266

VICTORIA v G.F.VERNON'S ENGLAND XI

Played at Melbourne Cricket Ground on March 9, 10, 12, 13, 1888. (Timeless match)
Toss : England XI.   Result : G.F.VERNON'S ENGLAND XI WON BY 282 RUNS.
Debuts: Victoria - C.Letcher (f/c).
12th Men: W.H.Cooper (Vic emergency). No 12th named for Eng XI.
Umpires: D.F.Cotter and J.Phillips.
Attendances: 100, 9000, 300, 200.   Total: About 9600.   Receipts: No figures published.
Close of Play: 1st day Eng 8/96 (Vernon 31, Bowden 2); 2nd day Eng (2) 0/31 (Bowden 14, Abel 11); 3rd day Eng (2) 8/367 (Read 142, Attewell 16).

Rain prevented a start until 3.20pm and was blamed for the low scoring, the pitch and outfield being very soft. In view of the conditions, W.H.Cooper, Victoria's sole selector, left himself out of the final eleven in favour of Letcher, a left-arm pace bowler. By prior agreement, play ceased at 5.00pm on the second day so that an exhibition Australian Rules football match between the Melbourne and Geelong clubs could be staged for the Englishmen on the ground. The local Press attributed the big crowd on that day to the football match rather than the cricket; certainly attendances on the other days was very poor. Stoddart (75 in 105 minutes, 8 fours) and Read (142 not out in about 270 minutes, 1 five and 12 fours) in the second innings provided Vernon's Team with an insurmountable lead of 417 runs. Letcher was unluckily run out at the non-striker's end when a straight drive by Hugh Trumble was deflected onto the wicket via the bowler's hand. For the second match running, Attewell captured more than half the wickets for his side. *Wisden* incorrectly gives Vic (1) Bruce 31, McIlwraith b Attewell, Walters 7, Robertson 0, extras 3, Beaumont 1/20; Eng (2) Peel b Trumble. Sources: *Wisden, VCA Report, The Age, The Argus, The Herald, The Australasian, The Leader.*

G.F.VERNON'S ENGLAND XI

Batsman	1st innings	R	2nd innings	R
A.E.Stoddart	c McIlwraith b H.Trumble	2	(3) b Robertson	75
W.W.Read	c Worrall b J.W.Trumble	24	(4) not out	142
R.Peel	run out (Worrall)	4	(5) st Lewis b H.Trumble	43
T.C.O'Brien	c H.Trumble b J.W.Trumble	2	(6) b Robertson	18
A.E.Newton	c Worrall b H.Trumble	14	(7) c J.W.Trumble b Worrall	1
W.Attewell	run out (Bruce/Lewis)	6	(10) c Lewis b Worrall	17
R.Abel	c H.Trumble b J.W.Trumble	0	(2) c & b McShane	30
*G.F.Vernon	c McIlwraith b J.W.Trumble	39	(9) b Worrall	3
J.T.Rawlin	c Letcher b H.Trumble	6	(8) b Worrall	2
†M.P.Bowden	c McIlwraith b Letcher	20	(1) b H.Trumble	14
J.Beaumont	not out	5	c McShane b Worrall	0
Extras	(b4, lb2, nb2)	8	(b11, lb5, w1, nb6)	23
Total	(91.2 overs, 180 mins)	130	(183.3 overs, 330 mins)	368

VICTORIA

Batsman	1st innings	R	2nd innings	R
W.Bruce	b Beaumont	30	run out (Peel/Bowden)	14
J.McIlwraith	c & b Attewell	15	b Attewell	21
J.W.Trumble	c Newton b Peel	13	lbw b Attewell	25
*T.P.Horan	c Read b Attewell	7	lbw b Attewell	1
F.H.Walters	c Vernon b Peel	8	b Attewell	24
F.G.McShane	st Bowden b Attewell	0	b Attewell	2
J.Worrall	c Beaumont b Attewell	0	c O'Brien b Beaumont	1
W.R.Robertson	not out	1	c Peel b Read	18
†P.M.Lewis	c Rawlin b Peel	0	b Peel	6
C.Letcher	st Bowden b Attewell	3	run out (Attewell)	7
H.Trumble	c Stoddart b Attewell	2	not out	10
Extras	(b1, nb1)	2	(b4, lb2)	6
Total	(64.3 overs, 125 mins)	81	(145.3 overs, 235 mins)	135

VICTORIA	O	M	R	W	w,nb		O	M	R	W	w,nb
J.W.Trumble	42	17	47	4	-,-	(3)	28	14	40	0	-,-
H.Trumble	32	12	55	3	-,2		26	8	56	2	-,4
Bruce	4	1	4	0	-,-	(4)	24	8	61	0	-,-
Robertson	2	0	5	0	-,-	(6)	37	10	79	2	-,2
McShane	4	1	4	0	-,-		13	3	36	1	-,-
Letcher	7.2	3	7	1	-,-	(1)	27	12	40	0	-,-
Worrall							28.3	13	33	5	1,-

FALL OF WICKETS				
Wkt	ENG 1st	VIC 1st	ENG 2nd	VIC 2nd
1st	6	35	36	31
2nd	11	52	104	35
3rd	15	67	156	37
4th	43	67	267	74
5th	47	67	304	76
6th	48	73	305	81
7th	62	76	320	105
8th	77	76	334	113
9th	110	79	368	120
10th	130	81	368	135

ENGLAND XI	O	M	R	W	w,nb		O	M	R	W	w,nb
Attewell	32.3	18	30	6	-,-	(3)	65.3	45	28	5	-,-
Peel	18	11	28	3	-,-		33	15	47	1	-,-
Beaumont	14	6	21	1	-,1	(1)	35	22	30	1	-,-
Stoddart							3	0	4	0	-,-
Read							9	3	20	1	-,-

Conflict broke out this season between the Victorian Cricketers' Association and Melbourne Cricket Club over the right to organise intercolonial matches between Victoria and New South Wales. There was no touring team to distract from the issue. A resolution passed by the VCA the previous year - that there should only be one match per season between Victoria and New South Wales - was ignored by Melbourne CC, whose administrators went ahead and arranged two games with NSWCA officials for January 1889. Two matches had been the custom for years and the Melbourne club saw no reason to change the arrangements.

The VCA's stance on the matter was ridiculed in the Press and public opinion was firmly on the side of Melbourne. Melbourne had already offered a compromise by moving their own Victoria-Tasmania match from the Melbourne Cricket Ground to the East Melbourne ground in order to give the VCA the main venue for the Victoria-South Australia clash, starting on Boxing Day. Not satisfied, the VCA made a bid to overpower Melbourne CC by approaching Victorian players and asking them to boycott matches organised by the latter. But the players refused and the VCA were forced to back down. The dispute formed part of an on-going campaign, which had been developing in Australian cricket for years, over who should control and administer major matches. The problem festered for another quarter of a century.

What was a domestic season began in an innocent enough way with a match between South Australia and the returning Sixth Australians at Adelaide. South Australia got up in a surprise result, their victory coming about after Giffen had won the toss and inserted the Australians on an underprepared wicket. The Australians performed much better in follow-up matches against Victoria and New South Wales, winning the contest in Melbourne by an innings and finishing strongly in a drawn game at Sydney.

The intercolonial series began with South Australia meeting Victoria at the Melbourne Cricket Ground. George Giffen (154 runs and 13 wickets) made his usual contributions to give the visitors the whip hand, only to see South Australia's position deteriorate in a heart-stopping collapse in the second innings. Three days later, Victoria met Tasmania on level terms for the first time since March 1873, in the process beginning an annual series which continued almost uninterrupted until 1915. The Tasmanians, in their first first-class match for 11 years, were unable to come to terms with the difficult conditions at the East Melbourne ground and were heavily defeated despite a fine second-innings century from C.W.Rock.

Victoria ended a sequence of six consecutive losses to New South Wales in the match at Sydney starting on Anniversary Day. New South Wales had won the earlier contest at Melbourne by six wickets. Bowlers dictated terms in both games.

The season finished with a match at Sydney between the Sixth Australians (who then disbanded) and a Combined XI selected from remaining players in New South Wales and Victorian teams. The Australians took command of the game from the opening session and never relinquished their grip.

Leading Aggregates

Batsmen	M	I	NO	Runs	HS	Ave.	Bowlers	Runs	Wkts	Ave.
G.H.S.Trott (V)	7	13	0	507	172	39.00	J.J.Ferris (NSW)	570	36	15.83
A.C.Bannerman (NSW)	6	11	1	311	134	31.10	C.T.B.Turner (NSW)	583	29	20.10
C.T.B.Turner (NSW)	6	10	0	265	102	26.50	G.H.S.Trott (V)	436	25	17.44
S.P.Jones (NSW)	6	11	0	230	46	20.90	G.Giffen (SA)	285	22	12.95
J.J.Lyons (Aust)	4	7	1	227	101	37.83	P.C.Charlton (NSW)	312	17	18.35
H.Donnan (NSW)	4	6	3	192	87*	64.00	J.Worrall (V)	228	16	14.25
G.Giffen (SA)	2	4	1	192	135	64.00	J.W.Trumble (V)	260	15	17.33
J.E.Barrett (V)	5	9	2	191	40*	27.28				

SOUTH AUSTRALIA v AUSTRALIAN XI

Played at Adelaide Oval on November 23, 24, 26, 1888. (Timeless match)
Toss : South Australia.   Result : SOUTH AUSTRALIA WON BY EIGHT WICKETS.
Debuts: South Australia - W.Delaney, R.S.Wigley (both f/c).
12th Men: None named.
Umpires: I.A.Fisher and W.Travers.
Attendances: 500, 1200, "poor".   Total: 1971.   Receipts: No figures published.
Close of Play: 1st day SA 0/81 (Wigley 37, Reedman 44); 2nd day SA 248 all out.

This was the first of four first-class matches played by the Australian team on their return from England. The overall attendance was surprisingly poor, in view of the fact that more than 2000 people had attended a reception and concert in honour of the Australian XI at the ground in extremely hot weather the day before the match began. (Conditions during the game itself were much more pleasant). Giffen sent the Australians in on a pitch still damp from preparation, which he utilised to the full. Wigley (44 in 75 minutes, 6 fours) and Reedman (63 in 150 minutes, 6 fours) then gave the home side a fine start to set up a first-innings advantage. Watling's 5 runs occupied an hour and a half, the last 45 minutes of which did not yield a single run. In the Australian's second innings, Lyons (58 with 1 five and 8 fours) and Turner (41 with 1 five and 4 fours) got a start but the rest failed, Giffen finishing with nine wickets and scoring most of the victory runs off his own bat. *Cricket* and *Advertiser* give Aust (2) Lyons 59, Edwards 14. Sources: *Cricket, C.B.O'Reilly, Adelaide Advertiser, South Australian Register.*

AUSTRALIAN XI

A.C.Bannerman	c Phillips b G.Giffen	4	(8)	not out	1
G.H.S.Trott	c McKenzie b G.Giffen	11	(3)	c McKenzie b Reedman	4
S.P.Jones	c McKenzie b G.Giffen	45	(4)	st McKenzie b Delaney	16
J.J.Lyons	run out (G.Giffen/Reedman)	4	(5)	c G.Giffen b Delaney	58
†A.H.Jarvis	run out (Phillips/McKenzie)	8	(6)	c W.F.Giffen b G.Giffen	8
*P.S.McDonnell	c Blinman b Reedman	10	(2)	c & b Reedman	7
C.T.B.Turner	b G.Giffen	5		c McKenzie b Delaney	41
J.M.Blackham	b Reedman	1	(10)	c Phillips b Delaney	1
J.Worrall	c Watling b G.Giffen	31		c Phillips b G.Giffen	6
J.D.Edwards	not out	9	(1)	c Wigley b G.Giffen	13
J.J.Ferris	c & b Delaney	0		c Blinman b G.Giffen	4
Extras	(b4, lb2)	6		(b2, lb2)	4
Total	(72.0 overs, 180 mins)	134		(60.3 overs, 150 mins)	163

SOUTH AUSTRALIA

R.S.Wigley	b Ferris	44			
J.C.Reedman	b Ferris	63		c Jones b Trott	8
W.F.Giffen	b Ferris	16		c Lyons b Ferris	0
*G.Giffen	c Jarvis b Turner	3	(1)	not out	35
W.H.Watling	b Trott	5			
H.Haldane	c & b Worrall	30			
H.Blinman	st Jarvis b Trott	24			
W.Delaney	b Turner	4			
†J.McKenzie	st Jarvis b Worrall	32	(4)	not out	5
T.Turner	not out	11			
F.G.Phillips	st Jarvis b Trott	11			
Extras	(lb5)	5		(b3, lb1)	4
Total	(157.0 overs, 330 mins)	248		(35.0 overs, 70 mins) (2 wkts)	52

SOUTH AUSTRALIA	O	M	R	W	w,nb		O	M	R	W	w,nb		FALL OF WICKETS			
Reedman	26	7	54	2	-,-	(2)	21	7	58	2	-,-			AUST	SA	AUST	SA
G.Giffen	34	15	54	5	-,-	(1)	29.3	12	72	4	-,-		Wkt	1st	1st	2nd	2nd
Turner	8	2	8	0	-,-								1st	14	88	10	36
Delaney	4	1	12	1	-,-	(3)	10	3	29	4	-,-		2nd	15	120	26	40
													3rd	19	123	38	-
AUSTRALIAN XI	O	M	R	W	w,nb		O	M	R	W	w,nb		4th	31	129	71	-
Turner	57	33	74	2	-,-		7	3	16	0	-,-		5th	47	166	91	-
Ferris	49	15	87	3	-,-		17	8	17	1	-,-		6th	62	166	145	-
Trott	16	6	22	3	-,-		11	6	15	1	-,-		7th	63	176	150	-
Jones	8	2	18	0	-,-								8th	114	224	156	-
Lyons	6	2	16	0	-,-								9th	134	226	159	-
Worrall	19	5	20	2	-,-								10th	134	248	163	-
Blackham	2	0	6	0	-,-												

VICTORIA v AUSTRALIAN XI

Played at Melbourne Cricket Ground on December 7, 8, 10, 1888. (Timeless match)
Toss : Victoria.   Result : AUSTRALIAN XI WON BY AN INNINGS AND 22 RUNS.
Debuts: Victoria - J.Drysdale, M.A.Morris (both f/c); F.J.Burton (Vic only).
12th Men: None named.
Umpires: D.F.Cotter and J.Taylor.
Attendances: 400, 1800, "sparse".   Total: About 2500.   Receipts: No figures published.
Close of Play: 1st day Aust 0/14 (Jarvis 4, Edwards 10); 2nd day Vic (2) 2/7 (Morris 2, Phillips 3).

J.M.Blackham (split finger) was unable to appear for the Australians while Freeman, selected as Victoria's 12th man, was a late replacement for T.P.Horan (work commitments). W.Over and V.B.Trapp earlier withdrew from the Victorian team, with Letcher and Lewis the chosen replacements. Lewis took over as wicket-keeper late in the Australian innings after Burton, a former New South Wales player, took a severe blow on the body from an awkwardly bouncing ball. Turner's second-innings analysis included a sequence of ten successive maidens. The match was played under perfect conditions on a true pitch, the Victorians unable to counter the talents of Turner and Ferris, who took seven wickets apiece. Sources: *Cricket, VCA Report, The Age, The Argus, The Australasian, The Leader.*

VICTORIA

*W.Bruce	b Ferris	18		b Turner	0
M.A.Morris	b Turner	3		lbw b Ferris	4
J.McIlwraith	lbw b Ferris	2	(5)	b Turner	41
J.W.Trumble	b Ferris	2	(6)	st Jarvis b Jones	20
P.M.Lewis	c Jarvis b Ferris	3	(10)	run out (Jones/Jarvis)	0
J.Drysdale	b Jones	33	(7)	c Bannerman b Turner	11
J.E.Barrett	not out	40	(3)	b Turner	2
†F.J.Burton	c Bannerman b Turner	10	(9)	run out (Boyle/Ferris)	2
H.S.Freeman	c Trott b Ferris	10	(8)	b Ferris	17
C.Letcher	run out (Bannerman)	7	(11)	not out	0
J.Phillips	c Jones b Lyons	11	(4)	c Trott b Turner	4
Extras	(b4, lb5, nb1)	10		(b1, nb1)	2
Total	(134.1 overs, 245 mins)	149		(113.3 overs, 205 mins)	103

AUSTRALIAN XI

†A.H.Jarvis	b Phillips	6
J.D.Edwards	c & b Trumble	52
*P.S.McDonnell	c Freeman b Drysdale	39
G.H.S.Trott	b Bruce	59
S.P.Jones	c Lewis b Bruce	36
A.C.Bannerman	c McIlwraith b Bruce	4
J.J.Lyons	not out	44
C.T.B.Turner	b Bruce	3
J.Worrall	b Trumble	17
J.J.Ferris	b Bruce	4
H.F.Boyle	b Bruce	0
Extras	(b2, lb4, w1, nb3)	10
Total	(149.1 overs, 265 mins)	274

AUSTRALIAN XI	O	M	R	W	w,nb		O	M	R	W	w,nb
Turner	48	25	38	2	-,-		56	32	50	5	-,-
Ferris	44	17	52	5	-,1		41.3	23	28	2	-,1
Worrall	9	4	13	0	-,-						
Lyons	19.1	7	22	1	-,-	(3)	1	1	0	0	-,-
Jones	14	8	14	1	-,-		10	6	11	1	-,-
Trott						(4)	5	1	12	0	-,-

VICTORIA	O	M	R	W	w,nb
Trumble	38	5	94	2	-,-
Phillips	32	14	52	1	-,-
Barrett	12	0	15	0	-,2
Drysdale	12	2	32	1	-,-
Letcher	12	8	9	0	-,-
Morris	5	1	15	0	-,1
Bruce	38.1	7	47	6	1,-

FALL OF WICKETS

Wkt	VIC 1st	AUST 1st	VIC 2nd
1st	21	23	0
2nd	21	75	2
3rd	25	122	11
4th	29	191	11
5th	34	202	71
6th	83	204	75
7th	103	210	92
8th	119	243	98
9th	137	258	101
10th	149	274	103

NEW SOUTH WALES v AUSTRALIAN XI

Played at Sydney Cricket Ground on December 21, 22, 24, 26, 1888. (Timeless match)
Toss : New South Wales.   Result : MATCH DRAWN.
Debuts: New South Wales - S.T.Callaway, P.C.Charlton, G.Cowper, F.A.Iredale, A.C.K.Mackenzie, J.Searle (all f/c).
12th Men: None named.
Umpires: C.Bannerman, E.J.Briscoe, T.Nunn, J.W.Payne and J.Swift.
Attendances & Receipts: No figures published.
Close of Play: 1st day NSW 5/133 (C.A.Richardson 49, Charlton 17); 2nd day Aust 1/61 (Trott 26, Turner 31); 3rd day Aust (2) 1/128 (Bannerman 29, Trott 81).

It was intended that the match would be played to a finish, but at the end of the fourth day the players abruptly decided not to continue further. For reasons not known, several umpires partnered Bannerman during the course of the match; Nunn and later Swift on the first day, Briscoe on the second and third days, and Payne on the last day. Rain caused several interruptions on the first day, reducing playing time to three and a half hours. Richardson (73 in about 270 minutes, 7 fours) and Donnan (87 not out in about 150 minutes, 9 fours) topscored for New South Wales. Trott's maiden century (172 in about 210 minutes, 20 fours, out of 261 scored) was reported as having been compiled "in a fine masterly style, his cricket being not perhaps showy, but full of sound play" (*SMH*). He dominated a stand of 243 for the second wicket with Bannerman. Lyons (101 in about 135 minutes, 14 fours) also reached the century; his "hitting was hard, but his play in general could not be compared to Trott's" (*SMH*). *Cricket* incorrectly gives Aust (1) Bannerman c Edwards. Sources: *Cricket, Sydney Morning Herald, Town & Country Journal, Sydney Daily Telegraph.*

NEW SOUTH WALES

C.A.Richardson	c Edwards b Jones	73			
G.Cowper	c Blackham b Turner	11			
*H.C.S.Hiddleston	c & b Ferris	2			
W.A.Richardson	c Trott b Ferris	2			
A.H.Gregory	b Ferris	12			
A.C.K.Mackenzie	b Ferris	34			
P.C.Charlton	c Blackham b Trott	50			
S.T.Callaway	c Blackham b Turner	14			
H.Donnan	not out	87			
F.A.Iredale	b Ferris	13			
†J.Searle	b Worrall	36			
Extras	(b6, lb1, nb1)	8			
Total	(258.1 overs, 460 mins)	342			

AUSTRALIAN XI

A.C.Bannerman	c Gregory b Charlton	3	(2) c Callaway b W.A.Richardson	54
C.T.B.Turner	c Charlton b W.A.Richardson	64	(5) c Searle b Charlton	22
G.H.S.Trott	c Searle b W.A.Richardson	57	c C.A.Richardson b Callaway	172
S.P.Jones	c C.A.Richardson b Charlton	46	b Callaway	16
J.D.Edwards	c & b Charlton	10	(6) c Mackenzie b Callaway	1
*P.S.McDonnell	c W.A.Richardson b Callaway	13	(1) c Mackenzie b Charlton	9
J.J.Lyons	b Callaway	5	b Donnan	101
J.Worrall	c & b W.A.Richardson	14	(9) c Callaway b Donnan	27
†J.M.Blackham	b Callaway	0	(11) not out	1
J.J.Ferris	c Hiddleston b Charlton	13	not out	32
A.H.Jarvis	not out	10	(8) c Searle b Callaway	5
Extras	(b14, lb4, nb1)	19	(b25, lb6, nb1)	32
Total	(116.2 overs, 210 mins)	254	(198.0 overs, 390 mins) (9 wkts)	472

AUSTRALIAN XI	O	M	R	W	w,nb
Turner	86	57	77	2	-,-
Ferris	86	43	92	5	-,1
Trott	33	11	62	1	-,-
Jones	23	13	46	1	-,-
Lyons	23	12	43	0	-,-
Bannerman	5	1	10	0	-,-
Worrall	2.1	1	4	1	-,-

NEW SOUTH WALES	O	M	R	W	w,nb		O	M	R	W	w,nb
Charlton	40.2	13	82	4	-,1		46	13	102	2	-,-
Callaway	50	20	89	3	-,-		57	22	92	4	,
W.A.Richardson	17	6	35	3	-,-	(4)	34	8	108	1	-,-
Donnan	5	0	26	0	-,-	(5)	33	12	58	2	-,-
Gregory	4	2	3	0	-,-	(6)	8	1	21	0	-,-
Iredale						(3)	15	3	41	0	-,1
C.A.Richardson							5	1	18	0	-,-

FALL OF WICKETS

	NSW	AUST	AUST
Wkt	1st	1st	2nd
1st	23	14	18
2nd	34	120	261
3rd	36	143	267
4th	40	186	287
5th	104	197	299
6th	189	201	311
7th	191	214	317
8th	223	214	394
9th	256	232	467
10th	342	254	-

VICTORIA v SOUTH AUSTRALIA

Played at Melbourne Cricket Ground on December 26, 27, 28, 29, 1888. (Timeless match)
Toss : Victoria.   Result : VICTORIA WON BY 15 RUNS.
Debuts: Nil.
12th Men: R.P.Dickson (Vic). No 12th named for SA; only 11 men in party.
Umpires: D.F.Cotter and W.Travers.
Attendances: 3000, 2500, 1000, 500.   Total: About 7000.   Receipts: No figures published.
Close of Play: 1st day SA 3/81 (G.Giffen 39, Reedman 16); 2nd day Vic (2) 4/49 (Phillips 3, Lewis 0); 3rd day SA (2) 5/56 (Wigley 1, G.Giffen 7).

Victoria staged a remarkable recovery after their eighth wicket in the second innings had fallen with the scores level. Horan (53 not out in about 135 minutes, 4 fours) and Barrett (39) added 92 for the ninth wicket and the Victorians then successfully defended a 103-run lead. Play continued well past 6.00pm on the third day after Bruce suggested that an attempt be made to complete the game that evening; stumps were drawn after the visitors lost five quick wickets in failing light. George Giffen provided the highlights, bowling unchanged through both Victorian innings to capture 13 out of the 16 wickets that fell to his side's bowlers and scoring 135 in about 300 minutes (11 fours), surviving stumping chances at 46 and 131. Tom Horan writing in *The Australasian*, was critical of Giffen's captaincy but admitted that as a player "he has no superior in the world as an allround man". Gordon kept wickets when Lewis bowled. Six-ball overs were bowled. *Cricket* incorrectly gives Vic (2) McIlwraith 20, extras 15; SA (1) Reedman 43, Watling 8, Turner 14; SA (2) Drysdale 3/18. Sources: *Cricket, C.B.O'Reilly, VCA Report, The Age, The Argus, The Herald, The Australasian, The Leader, The Sportsman.*

VICTORIA

*W.Bruce	st McKenzie b G.Giffen	24		b G.Giffen	4
J.McIlwraith	run out (/McKenzie)	15		lbw b Delaney	18
T.P.Horan	b G.Giffen	0	(7)	not out	53
J.W.Trumble	lbw b Reedman	0	(8)	c & b G.Giffen	7
J.Drysdale	run out (Phillips/G.Giffen)	52	(4)	b G.Giffen	6
J.E.Barrett	c & b G.Giffen	7	(10)	b Phillips	39
H.S.Freeman	b G.Giffen	1	(11)	c Wigley b G.Giffen	8
M.A.Morris	run out (/McKenzie)	30	(9)	lbw b G.Giffen	0
†P.M.Lewis	c Phillips b G.Giffen	42	(6)	c W.F.Giffen b G.Giffen	21
G.B.Gordon	not out	7	(3)	run out (/McKenzie)	15
J.Phillips	c & b G.Giffen	2	(5)	c Blinman b G.Giffen	4
Extras	(lb1)	1		(b10, lb6, w1)	17
Total	(57.4 overs, 165 mins)	181		(107.4 overs, 270 mins)	192

SOUTH AUSTRALIA

R.S.Wigley	b Trumble	0	(6)	b Bruce	10
W.F.Giffen	c Lewis b Trumble	13		c Bruce b Drysdale	12
*G.Giffen	c Freeman b Horan	135	(7)	b Trumble	19
C.G.Godfrey	b Bruce	8	(5)	c sub (R.P.Dickson) b Phillips	2
J.C.Reedman	c Barrett b Lewis	48	(1)	b Drysdale	17
W.H.Watling	lbw b Phillips	5	(3)	c sub (R.P.Dickson) b Drysdale	10
H.Blinman	c Lewis b Trumble	14	(4)	b Phillips	4
†J.McKenzie	c Lewis b Bruce	13		b Bruce	5
T.Turner	c Bruce b Phillips	12		not out	3
W.Delaney	b Drysdale	5	(11)	run out (Drysdale/Lewis)	0
E.G.Phillips	not out	0	(10)	b Bruce	2
Extras	(b10, lb4, w2, nb1)	17		(b3, lb1)	4
Total	(129.2 overs, 330 mins)	270		(61.4 overs, 185 mins)	88

SOUTH AUSTRALIA	O	M	R	W	w,nb		O	M	R	W	w,nb
Reedman	15	3	57	1	-,-	(3)	14	5	23	0	-,-
G.Giffen	28.4	9	82	6	-,-		53.4	25	77	7	-,-
Turner	9	0	25	0	-,-	(4)	10	2	15	0	-,-
Delaney	5	0	16	0	-,-	(1)	20	3	55	1	1,-
Phillips							10	5	5	1	-,-

VICTORIA	O	M	R	W	w,nb		O	M	R	W	w,nb
Trumble	43	17	58	3	-,-		16	6	17	1	-,-
Phillips	29	9	67	2	-,-	(4)	15	5	28	2	-,-
Bruce	31	9	63	2	2,-	(2)	12.4	5	22	3	-,-
Drysdale	3.2	1	5	1	-,-	(3)	18	10	17	3	-,-
Morris	2	0	5	0	-,-						
Lewis	8	2	26	1	-,1						
Barrett	7	2	13	0	-,-						
Horan	6	1	16	1	-,-						

FALL OF WICKETS

Wkt	VIC 1st	SA 1st	VIC 2nd	SA 2nd
1st	39	0	7	32
2nd	39	19	38	33
3rd	39	36	39	44
4th	39	167	49	48
5th	70	185	60	48
6th	74	219	74	68
7th	120	239	89	73
8th	172	246	89	86
9th	179	268	181	88
10th	181	270	192	88

VICTORIA v TASMANIA

Played at East Melbourne Cricket Ground on January 1, 2 (no play), 3 (no play), 4, 5, 1889. (Timeless match)
Toss : Tasmania.   Result : VICTORIA WON BY NINE WICKETS.
Debuts: Tasmania - E.Maxwell, T.P.Ryan, J.H.Savigny, W.H.Savigny, C.E.Vautin (all f/c); C.W.Rock (Tas only).
12th Men: A.P.Haddrick (Vic) and H.Wilson (Tas).
Umpires: T.Flynn and J.Phillips.
Attendances: 2500, no play, no play, 200, 300.   Total: About 3000.   Receipts: £123.
Close of Play: 1st day Tas 4/41 (W.H.Savigny 18); 2nd day no play; 3rd day no play; 4th day Tas 4/52 (W.H.Savigny 21, Sidebottom 7).

Rain before and during the match marred Tasmania's first encounter with Victoria for 16 years; the island colony had not played on even terms at all since 1877-78 against South Australia. This was the last of four games now accepted as first-class to be staged at the East Melbourne ground. Six-ball overs were bowled throughout the match. Sidebottom sent the Victorians in on a soft pitch, but batting conditions worsened further when steady rain prevented any play on the scheduled second and third days and permitted only 15 minutes on the fourth. Play, scheduled to begin at 12.00 on all days, was begun at 10.30 on the final day (Saturday) in an attempt to obtain a result before the departure of the Tasmanians for home on Monday. Rock (102 in 280 minutes, 3 fours), an ex-Cambridge University allrounder making his debut for his native province, "was warmly and deservedly applauded for his sterling and patient play" (*Australasian*) after Tasmania followed on, taking 70 minutes to reach double figures. Gordon deputised as wicket-keeper when Lewis put himself on to bowl and returned his best figures of 3 for 10. Sources: *Cricket, VCA Report, The Age, The Argus, The Herald, The Australasian, The Leader, The Sportsman.*

VICTORIA

G.H.S.Trott	st Vautin b Ryan	38	c Rock b Maxwell	24
J.Worrall	c Ryan b Rock	16	not out	4
T.P.Horan	c Gatehouse b Ryan	12		
J.Drysdale	c W.H.Savigny b Maxwell	20		
G.B.Gordon	c Rock b Maxwell	20		
J.E.Barrett	run out (Ryan/Vautin)	18		
*†P.M.Lewis	b Ryan	0		
W.Over	c & b W.H.Savigny	38		
M.A.Morris	c J.H.Savigny b W.H.Savigny	48	(3) not out	4
H.S.Freeman	b W.H.Savigny	2		
R.Mitchell	not out	4		
Extras	(b13, lb1)	14	(nb1)	1
Total	(72.3 overs, 175 mins)	230	(7.1 overs, 20 mins) (1 wkt)	33

TASMANIA

G.H.Gatehouse	b Over	7	(2) c & b Trott	5
C.W.Rock	b Trott	3	(1) c Horan b Lewis	102
J.H.Savigny	b Trott	1	(4) b Over	7
W.H.Savigny	b Trott	23	(3) c Trott b Over	35
E.J.K.Burn	run out (Over/Lewis/Worrall)	8	c Over b Trott	11
*W.L.Sidebottom	b Worrall	7	b Lewis	2
T.P.Ryan	b Worrall	4	c Lewis b Trott	5
C.W.Butler	b Worrall	0	st Gordon b Trott	0
†C.E.Vautin	c Lewis b Worrall	5	lbw b Lewis	9
E.Maxwell	not out	3	b Trott	0
T.K.Kendall	b Trott	1	not out	4
Extras	(b3, lb2)	5	(b11, lb2, w1, nb1)	15
Total	(42.3 overs, 95 mins)	67	(130.5 overs, 290 mins)	195

TASMANIA	O	M	R	W	w,nb		O	M	R	W	w,nb
Kendall	26	5	66	0	-,-	(2)	3.1	1	14	0	-,-
Rock	18	2	63	1	-,-						
Ryan	17	1	57	3	-,-						
Maxwell	6	4	4	2	-,-	(1)	4	0	18	1	-,1
Sidebottom	2	0	7	0	-,-						
W.H.Savigny	3.3	0	19	3	-,-						

VICTORIA	O	M	R	W	w,nb		O	M	R	W	w,nb
Trott	21.3	9	20	4	-,-	(2)	38	15	67	5	-,-
Over	10	4	17	1	-,-	(6)	25	10	37	2	-,-
Worrall	11	2	25	4	-,-	(1)	17	6	23	0	-,-
Drysdale						(3)	8	6	2	0	-,1
Barrett						(4)	12	4	12	0	-,-
Mitchell						(5)	3	2	1	0	-,-
Horan							6	2	10	0	-,-
Morris							7	2	11	0	-,-
Gordon							4	2	7	0	-,-
Lewis							10.5	3	10	3	1,-

FALL OF WICKETS

Wkt	VIC 1st	TAS 1st	VIC 2nd	TAS 2nd
1st	22	7	6	29
2nd	57	8	83	-
3rd	68	19	101	-
4th	107	41	153	-
5th	114	52	162	-
6th	114	58	172	-
7th	160	58	172	-
8th	192	60	186	-
9th	205	66	187	-
10th	230	67	195	-

VICTORIA v NEW SOUTH WALES

Played at Melbourne Cricket Ground on January 11, 12, 14, 15, 1889. (Timeless match)
Toss : Victoria.   Result : NEW SOUTH WALES WON BY SIX WICKETS.
Debuts: Nil.
12th Men: M.A.Morris (Vic) and J.Davis (NSW).
Umpires: C.Bannerman and D.F.Cotter.
Attendances: 2500, 10000, 3000, 2000.   Total: About 17,500.   Receipts: No figures published.
Close of Play: 1st day NSW 0/16 (Richardson 10, Bannerman 2); 2nd day Vic (2) 1/17 (Blackham 10, Burton 4); 3rd day NSW (2) 1/34
  (Moses 22, Richardson 7).

With this win, their sixth in succession against Victoria, New South Wales took a 21-20 lead in the series; it was the first time in 30 years that Victoria had fallen behind. The match was organised by Melbourne Cricket Club after the VCA had failed to make arrangements. "The muddling policy" of the VCA "prevented the time honoured match being commenced as usual on Boxing Day" (*Age*). The visitors omitted Davis and A.C.K.Mackenzie from their party of thirteen. J.W.Trumble (honeymoon) was unavailable for Victoria. Garrett took no further part after tearing back muscles while fielding on the first day. Bruce, who had been expected to captain Victoria, was late due to his business and Burton was elected leader after several other senior players declined the position. Lewis dismissed Ferris and Searle with consecutive balls to finish the New South Wales first innings. A score of four all-run by Edwards, partnering Barrett on the third day, was halved by Charles Bannerman (the NSW umpire) who ruled two of the runs short, "which induced a number of thoughtless spectators to jeer and chaff" (*Age*). Later in the day, he adjudged Barrett run out in a very close decision and "was howled at in a manner which said very little for the manliness of the offenders" (*Age*). In bowling the last over of the match, Worrall brought to a close the era of four-ball overs in first-class cricket in Australia. Sources: *Cricket, The Age, The Argus, The Herald, The Australasian, The Leader, Sydney Mail*.

VICTORIA

J.McIlwraith	run out (Charlton/Searle)	5	(10)	not out	7
J.D.Edwards	c Moses b Charlton	50	(5)	c McDonnell b Ferris	20
T.P.Horan	c sub (J.Davis) b Charlton	36	(7)	b Turner	7
G.H.S.Trott	c Ferris b Charlton	0		c sub (J.Davis) b Charlton	22
J.Drysdale	b Charlton	3	(8)	lbw b Charlton	10
J.Worrall	c McDonnell b Ferris	10	(9)	b Ferris	11
W.Bruce	c Charlton b Turner	23	(1)	c Bannerman b Ferris	1
J.E.Barrett	not out	2	(6)	run out (Moses/Ferris)	36
P.M.Lewis	b Ferris	2	(11)	lbw b Ferris	0
*F.J.Burton	c Bannerman b Turner	9	(3)	b Ferris	17
†J.M.Blackham	c Searle b Ferris	1	(2)	b Ferris	19
Extras	(b8, lb2, nb1)	11		(b8, lb5)	13
Total	(140.0 overs, 255 mins)	152		(180.0 overs, 305 mins)	163

NEW SOUTH WALES

C.A.Richardson	c McIlwraith b Trott	41	(3)	b Trott	14
A.C.Bannerman	b Trott	39	(1)	b Bruce	1
H.Moses	c Worrall b Trott	4	(2)	lbw b Worrall	43
S.P.Jones	lbw b Drysdale	41		c Blackham b Worrall	9
H.Donnan	not out	48		not out	1
*P.S.McDonnell	c Edwards b Worrall	27		not out	4
C.T.B.Turner	b Worrall	5			
P.C.Charlton	b Lewis	8			
J.J.Ferris	c Horan b Lewis	13			
†J.Searle	b Lewis	0			
T.W.Garrett	absent hurt	-			
Extras	(b3, lb6, w2, nb1)	12		(b1, lb2, w3)	6
Total	(191.0 overs, 310 mins)	238		(80.0 overs, 159 mins) (4 wkts)	78

NEW SOUTH WALES	O	M	R	W	w,nb		O	M	R	W	w,nb
Turner	46	30	44	2	-,-		51	31	35	1	-,-
Ferris	56	36	46	3	-,1		66	37	62	6	-,-
Garrett	8	5	9	0	-,-						
Charlton	18	9	30	4	-,-	(3)	39	26	28	2	-,-
Donnan	12	7	12	0	-,-	(4)	17	8	19	0	-,-
Jones						(5)	7	4	6	0	-,-

VICTORIA	O	M	R	W	w,nb		O	M	R	W	w,nb
Bruce	19	8	25	0	1,-		25	14	22	1	1,-
Trott	65	30	93	3	1,-	(3)	16	8	17	1	1,-
Worrall	54	30	46	2	-,-	(2)	33	21	26	2	-,-
Drysdale	30	16	33	1	-,-	(5)	2	1	1	0	-,-
Edwards	6	3	9	0	-,-						
Barrett	8	4	8	0	-,-						
Lewis	9	2	12	3	-,1	(4)	4	2	6	0	1,-

FALL OF WICKETS

Wkt	VIC 1st	NSW 1st	VIC 2nd	NSW 2nd
1st	16	85	1	6
2nd	94	91	34	62
3rd	94	112	51	73
4th	99	138	71	74
5th	102	184	102	-
6th	138	190	109	-
7th	138	217	127	-
8th	140	238	153	-
9th	151	238	159	-
10th	152	-	163	-

NEW SOUTH WALES v VICTORIA

Played at Sydney Cricket Ground on January 26, 28, 29, 30, 1889. (Timeless match)
Toss : New South Wales.   Result : VICTORIA WON BY 12 RUNS.
Debuts: Nil.
12th Men: None named.
Umpires: E.J.Briscoe and D.F.Cotter.
Attendances & Receipts: No figures published.
Close of Play: 1st day NSW 240 all out; 2nd day Vic (2) 0/9 (Bruce 8, Trumble 1); 3rd day Vic (2) 178 all out.

Victoria won a rain-affected match after being forced to follow-on; the third side to do so in Australia, they defended a lead of just 75 runs. Trumble (6 for 33) dismissed McDonnell with the first ball of the New South Wales second innings and only Bannerman (12) and Turner (16) reached double figures, all ten wickets falling to catches. New South Wales had batted in perfect conditions on the first day before steady rain fell on Sunday and further showers followed on subsequent days to make batting increasingly more difficult. One casualty of the rough and uneven-wearing wicket, O'Hanlon, was struck in the face attempting to take a ball from Charlton early on the third day. Bannerman deputised for the rest of the session, catching both Horan and Walters with the gloves on while Gordon substituted against his own side. O'Hanlon was able to resume as wicket-keeper after lunch. Six-ball overs were used for the first time in New South Wales.
Sources: *Cricket, Sydney Referee, Sydney Morning Herald, Town & Country Journal, Sydney Daily Telegraph.*

NEW SOUTH WALES

*P.S.McDonnell	c & b Trott	65		c Walters b Trumble	0
A.C.Bannerman	lbw b Trott	4		c Edwards b Trumble	12
H.Moses	lbw b Bruce	31		c Bruce b Trumble	9
S.P.Jones	c & b Worrall	16		c Edwards b Trumble	2
C.A.Richardson	c Blackham b Trumble	5	(9)	c Bruce b Worrall	0
H.Donnan	c Barrett b Trumble	45		c Trumble b Worrall	5
C.T.B.Turner	c Blackham b Trumble	0	(5)	c Morris b Worrall	16
W.A.Richardson	not out	59	(7)	c Blackham b Worrall	3
†W.J.O'Hanlon	b Trott	11	(11)	c & b Trumble	0
P.C.Charlton	c Barrett b Trott	0		not out	0
J.J.Ferris	c Worrall b Trott	0	(8)	c Horan b Trumble	7
Extras	(b1, lb1, w1, nb1)	4		(b8, w1)	9
Total	(104.5 overs, 260 mins)	240		(38.5 overs, 125 mins)	63

VICTORIA

†J.M.Blackham	c Donnan b Ferris	1	(11)	b Turner	8
G.B.Gordon	b Turner	19	(10)	not out	21
G.H.S.Trott	b Turner	44		c McDonnell b Charlton	36
F.H.Walters	b Turner	2	(6)	c Bannerman b Ferris	7
T.P.Horan	c Moses b Turner	9	(4)	c Bannerman b Turner	26
J.E.Barrett	c & b Charlton	15	(5)	c & b Ferris	32
*W.Bruce	c & b Charlton	18	(1)	lbw b W.A.Richardson	29
J.D.Edwards	c W.A.Richardson b Charlton	4	(7)	b Ferris	4
J.Worrall	b Turner	3	(8)	b Ferris	2
J.W.Trumble	not out	5	(2)	lbw b Turner	3
M.A.Morris	c McDonnell b Charlton	11	(9)	b Ferris	0
Extras	(b5, lb1)	6		(b6, lb4)	10
Total	(79.3 overs, 200 mins)	137		(118.5 overs, 305 mins)	178

VICTORIA	O	M	R	W	w,nb		O	M	R	W	w,nb			FALL OF WICKETS			
														NSW	VIC	NSW	VIC
Trott	28.5	8	72	5	-,-							Wkt	1st	1st	2nd	2nd
Trumble	33	16	58	3	-,-	(1)	19.5	6	33	6	1,-	1st	9	1	13	0
Worrall	22	9	41	1	-,1	(2)	17	8	19	4	-,-	2nd	83	43	56	23
Bruce	13	2	49	1	1,-	(3)	2	1	2	0	-,-	3rd	100	45	86	25
Horan	1	0	9	0	-,-							4th	119	76	102	48
Barrett	7	4	7	0	-,-							5th	141	79	117	49
												6th	141	100	124	54
NEW SOUTH WALES	O	M	R	W	w,nb		O	M	R	W	w,nb	7th	209	112	130	57
Turner	40	20	58	5	-,-		45.5	19	62	3	-,-	8th	232	117	138	63
Ferris	25	8	57	1	-,-	(4)	32	16	45	5	-,-	9th	240	117	161	63
Charlton	14.3	7	16	4	-,-	(2)	38	16	54	1	-,-	10th	240	137	178	63
W.A.Richardson						(3)	3	0	7	1	-,-					

COMBINED NEW SOUTH WALES-VICTORIA v AUSTRALIAN XI

Played at Sydney Cricket Ground on February 1, 2, 4, 5, 1889. (Timeless match)
Toss : Australian XI.   Result : AUSTRALIAN XI WON BY 214 RUNS.
Debuts: Nil.
12th Men: None named.
Umpires: J.E.Barrett and J.C.Davis.
Attendances: No figures published, but "meagre".   Total & Receipts: No figures published.
Close of Play: 1st day Aust 7/275 (Bannerman 84, Ferris 33); 2nd day Comb 6/189 (Walters 96, Morris 19); 3rd day Aust (2) 173 all out.

The 1888 Australians had returned to Sydney from Brisbane, where they had played a non-first-class match against Queensland, so that the New South Wales and Victorian members of the squad could participate in the intercolonial match. This game was then played before the side disbanded, the Combined XI comprising other players from New South Wales and Victoria who had gathered in Sydney for the intercolonial. Cotter, who had umpired in the intercolonial, played in this match, the last of his three first-class appearances. The game was poorly attended, "no doubt owing to the great interest taken by the general public in the Parliamentary elections" (*T&C Journal*). Turner hit his century in 105 minutes (14 fours), 95 of his runs coming in the pre-lunch session. With Bannerman - who by contrast took 390 minutes (10 fours) over his 134 and was last man out - he posted the first 100 runs of the match in just 63 minutes. Walters emulated Turner's brilliance with a chanceless display of hitting for the Combined XI. He began his innings at the resumption of play after tea on the second day and was 96 at stumps, batting about 135 minutes in all (18 fours) for his 122. Trumble, who was ill, scored 39 while Moses ran for him. With Donnan and Morris both absent for "business reasons" on the last day, the Combined XI collapsed on a badly rain-affected wicket, "the ball cutting peculiar capers" (*T & C Journal*). Moses fell to the second ball of the innings and a bowling change was not required. *Cricket* incorrectly gives Comb (1) Moses b Turner; S.Morris instead of M.A.Morris in Comb side, and omits Comb (2) Callaway b Turner. Sources: *Cricket, Sydney Referee, Sydney Morning Herald, Town & Country Journal, Sydney Mail, Sydney Daily Telegraph.*

AUSTRALIAN XI

C.T.B.Turner	b Pope b Trumble	102	c Trumble b Callaway	7
A.C.Bannerman	c Cotter b Garrett	134	c Gordon b Garrett	55
G.H.S.Trott	run out (Callaway/Houston)	2	c Trumble b Callaway	38
S.P.Jones	c Trumble b Cotter	3	b Callaway	0
J.D.Edwards	b Cotter	18	lbw b Trumble	4
J.J.Lyons	b Garrett	15	b Trumble	0
*P.S.McDonnell	b Garrett	0	c & b Trumble	6
J.Worrall	b Garrett	5	(9) c Moses b Callaway	5
J.J.Ferris	c Garrett b Trumble	57	(8) c Gordon b Trumble	12
†J.M.Blackham	b Trumble	0	b Callaway	31
H.F.Boyle	not out	21	not out	13
Extras	(b15, lb2, nb3)	20	(b2)	2
Total	(136.5 overs, 390 mins)	377	(60.4 overs, 180 mins)	173

COMBINED XI

G.B.Gordon	b Turner	9	(2) c Worrall b Ferris	8
H.Donnan	c Blackham b Ferris	6	absent	-
*H.Moses	c Edwards b Turner	37	(1) c McDonnell b Turner	0
R.J.Pope	b Ferris	7	(7) run out	1
F.H.Walters	b Lyons	122	(3) lbw b Turner	14
T.W.Garrett	c Jones b Trott	6	(4) c Blackham b Turner	13
†R.S.Houston	st Blackham b Trott	8	(5) st Blackham b Ferris	2
M.A.Morris	b Ferris	32	absent	-
S.T.Callaway	c Worrall b Jones	13	(8) b Turner	0
H.Trumble	hit wkt b Jones	39	(6) st Blackham b Turner	0
D.F.Cotter	not out	12	(9) not out	0
Extras	(b5, lb2)	7		-
Total	(112.3 overs, 285 mins)	298	(17.4 overs, 75 mins)	38

COMBINED XI	O	M	R	W	w,nb		O	M	R	W	w,nb
Garrett	42.5	12	94	4	-,-		15	6	33	1	-,-
Trumble	20	4	70	3	-,-	(3)	20	4	49	4	-,-
Callaway	32	10	85	0	-,-	(2)	25.4	2	89	5	-,-
Moses	3	1	8	0	-,-						
Cotter	21	6	63	2	-,3						
Donnan	18	4	37	0	-,-						

AUSTRALIAN XI	O	M	R	W	w,nb		O	M	R	W	w,nb
Turner	40	13	109	2	-,-		9	2	20	5	-,-
Ferris	36	10	66	3	-,-		8.4	2	18	2	-,-
Worrall	8	3	11	0	-,-						
Trott	11	1	56	2	-,-						
Jones	7.3	1	22	2	-,-						
Boyle	3	0	15	0	-,-						
Lyons	7	2	12	1	-,-						

FALL OF WICKETS

	AUST	COMB	AUST	COMB
Wkt	1st	1st	2nd	2nd
1st	144	9	8	0
2nd	148	29	76	20
3rd	154	40	76	23
4th	188	75	81	26
5th	211	93	81	33
6th	211	107	89	38
7th	217	207	111	38
8th	314	229	119	38
9th	314	265	141	-
10th	377	298	173	-

Speculation over the makeup of the side to tour England in 1890 dominated this Australian season in which only five first-class matches were played - all of a domestic nature. New South Wales played Victoria at home and away, South Australia played Victoria at Adelaide and New South Wales at Sydney, and Victoria travelled to Hobart to play Tasmania.

The fact that New South Wales and Victoria were again able to play twice came about despite the continued efforts of the Victorian Cricketers' Association to restrict the encounters to one per season. Frustrated at their inability to wrest control of intercolonial matches from Melbourne Cricket Club, the VCA placed a ban on players who appeared in matches organised by the Melbourne club. Its effect on first-class cricket was minimal.

A remarkable century from Jack Lyons on a worn last-day track nearly enabled South Australia to snatch a win over Victoria in Adelaide. In February 1890 the South Australians created history when at Sydney they met New South Wales for the first time. The game was played in difficult conditions for batting and New South Wales recorded an easy win, by nine wickets.

Victoria made the boat journey to Hobart for their game against Tasmania early in the New Year and inflicted a heavy defeat on the home side. The late arrival to the ground on the second day of two Tasmanians, including the captain, did not help the islanders' situation. It was the first match of first-class status to be staged in Hobart since March 1858.

J.C.Davis, later better known as the long-serving critic "Not Out" of *The Referee* sporting newspaper, arranged, selected and managed a team of New South Wales players on a tour of New Zealand at the end of January. He sought the official sanction of the N.S.W.C.A. but was informed that his team "could not be recognised as the representative team of the colony" (*Sydney Mail*). Despite this ruling, the team was promoted throughout the five-week tour as New South Wales and has retained that title in most subsequent references although, not N.S.W.C.A. records. Davis is often mistakenly credited as captaining the team. His namesake, Joe Davis, a previous New South Wales representative, led the side with J.C.Davis acting as the team's umpire. They filled identical roles in 1893-94 when J.C.Davis arranged a second tour of the "Shaky Isles". The full side was: J.Davis (captain), S.T.Callaway, A.E.Clarke, J.T.Cottam, G.Cowper, J.Joseph, W.W.McGlinchey, A.L.Newell, H.J.W.Robinson, J.Shepherd and G.J.Youill. The tour provided Joseph and Shepherd with their only opportunities at first-class level. S.E.Gregory had also been invited too tour but was unavailable and subsequently selected for the Australian team to England.

H.F.Boyle was appointed to manage the 1890 Australian team - historically the 7th to tour England - and he, together with J.M.Blackham and C.T.B.Turner, was responsible for selection of the party. W.L.Murdoch was persuaded to come out of retirement to captain the side, but A.C.Bannerman, W.Bruce, P.S.McDonnell and H.Moses all declined invitations to go. George Giffen also announced his unavailability, after agreeing earlier in the season to tour if Murdoch, Turner and Ferris were available. After some time, 12 of the 13 players became known. The remaining place in the side was to be filled by a second wicket-keeper, and interest centred on a choice between J.Harry (Victoria) and S.Deane (New South Wales), each of whom had his loyal supporters. There was general surprise when the announcement came that the E.J.K.Burn, of Tasmania, had been chosen to fill the berth. Apparently he was Blackham's choice. 'Felix' (T.P.Horan) of *The Australasian* obviously agreed with the choice when, shortly after the team was announced, he commented, "That last notion of sending for Kenny Burn I like very well." It was only after the team assembled in Adelaide for the trip to England that it became known that Burn had never kept wicket in his life. 'Felix' later reported that, 'Blackham had seen in print that "Burn" had stumped men in Tasmania - but that Burn was Kenny's brother, and quite an inferior player'. Despite the selection blunder - the tale of which is often repeated in cricketing circles - Ken Burn played many matches on the 1890 tour, as a batsman if not a keeper. At Lord's he became only the second native-born Tasmanian to play Test cricket for Australia.

The Seventh Australians, a generally unsuccessful crew, were W.L.Murdoch (captain), J.E.Barrett, J.M.Blackham, E.J.K.Burn, P.C.Charlton, J.J.Ferris, S.E.Gregory, S.P.Jones, J.J.Lyons, G.H.S.Trott, H.Trumble, C.T.B.Turner and F.H.Walters.

Leading Aggregates

Batsmen	M	I	NO	Runs	HS	Ave.	Bowlers	Runs	Wkts	Ave.
J.J.Lyons (SA)	2	4	0	254	134	63.50	H.Trumble (V)	412	29	14.20
J.M.Blackham (V)	4	6	0	243	66	40.50	G.H.S.Trott (V)	379	18	21.05
J.E.Barrett (V)	4	7	1	230	69	38.33	R.W.McLeod (V)	284	16	17.75
G.H.S.Trott (V)	4	7	1	228	72	38.00	P.C.Charlton (NSW)	230	15	15.33
A.C.Bannerman (NSW)	3	6	1	227	117	45.40	C.T.B.Turner (NSW)	263	14	18.78
S.P.Jones (NSW)	2	4	0	193	100	48.25	G.Giffen (SA)	352	12	29.33
H.Moses (NSW)	3	6	2	187	52*	46.75	J.C.Reedman (SA)	173	10	17.30
G.Giffen (SA)	2	4	0	178	85	44.50				

SOUTH AUSTRALIA v VICTORIA

Played at Adelaide Oval on December 13, 14, 16, 17, 1889. (Timeless match)
Toss : Victoria.   Result : VICTORIA WON BY 18 RUNS.
Debuts: South Australia - A.Jarvis, G.T.Parkin (both f/c). Victoria - E.A.Barrett, R.W.McLeod (both f/c).
12th Men: J.Phillips (Vic). No 12th named for SA.
Umpires: I.A.Fisher and T.Flynn.
Attendances: No daily figures published.   Total: About 15,000.   Receipts: No figures published.
Close of Play: 1st day Vic 7/278 (Harry 16); 2nd day SA 6/235 (W.F.Giffen 6, Reedman 3); 3rd day Vic (2) 8/176 (Morris 30, McLeod 3).

On a badly worn fourth-day wicket tailor-made for Trumble's offbreaks, Lyons scored a dashing 134 in 150 minutes, hitting 2 fives and 17 fours. Difficult chances at 24 and 27 were his only major mistakes. Trumble's match figures of 15 for 199 remained his best for Victoria. Play was held up for half an hour soon after lunch on the second day following an appeal against George Giffen on 9. Trumble had appealed unsuccessfully for lbw before his team-mates noticed that a bail was off, and a further appeal for hit wicket was tried, which Flynn at the bowler's end upheld. However, Giffen refused to leave his crease because Fisher at square leg had not given him out. The players argued heatedly, the laws were produced, and Blackham threatened to walk out of the match but "after consultation with his comrades and the Manager, Mr Greig, it was decided for the sake of the public, and to save friction, to play on under protest" (*Register*). Giffen was allowed to carry on batting, adding a further 76 runs. *Cricket* incorrectly gives SA (1) Phillips 10*. Sources: *Cricket, C.B.O'Reilly, The Australasian, Adelaide Advertiser, South Australian Register.*

VICTORIA

J.McIlwraith	c Reedman b G.Giffen	8	(2) b G.Giffen		0
E.A.Barrett	c & b Lyons	3	(1) b G.Giffen		3
G.H.S.Trott	lbw b Lyons	36	b G.Giffen		72
J.E.Barrett	b Parkin	41	c A.H.Jarvis b G.Giffen		27
*J.M.Blackham	b Reedman	48	c & b Lyons		20
J.Drysdale	c & b Haldane	66	c A.H.Jarvis b Reedman		9
S.Morris	c Haldane b Reedman	50	c Phillips b G.Giffen		36
J.Harry	b Reedman	28	b G.Giffen		7
†P.M.Lewis	st A.H.Jarvis b Reedman	24	b Reedman		1
R.W.McLeod	not out	1	not out		29
H.Trumble	c Phillips b Reedman	4	b G.Giffen		12
Extras	(b5, lb5, nb1)	11	(b1, lb4)		5
Total	(109.5 overs, 305 mins)	320	(91.1 overs, 245 mins)		221

SOUTH AUSTRALIA

†A.H.Jarvis	c Blackham b Trumble	7	(3) c J.E.Barrett b Trumble		6
J.J.Lyons	b McLeod	38	(1) c & b Trumble		134
*G.Giffen	b Trumble	85	(4) c Drysdale b Trumble		9
R.S.Wigley	b McLeod	6	(2) c Trott b Trumble		6
H.Haldane	c & b Trumble	70	c Lewis b Trott		0
H.Blinman	b Trott	10	(8) b Morris		6
W.F.Giffen	b Trumble	12	(6) c Drysdale b Trumble		10
J.C.Reedman	c Trott b Trumble	15	(7) b Trumble		0
G.T.Parkin	st Lewis b Trumble	11	(10) b Trumble		18
A.Jarvis	c Trott b Trumble	15	(9) b Trumble		32
E.G.Phillips	not out	2	not out		6
Extras	(b7, lb4)	11	(b11, lb3)		14
Total	(106.5 overs, 285 mins)	282	(66.3 overs, 210 mins)		241

SOUTH AUSTRALIA	O	M	R	W	w,nb		O	M	R	W	w,nb
Lyons	26	4	79	2	-,-	(4)	8	1	31	1	-,-
G.Giffen	47	19	108	1	-,1		45.1	15	104	7	-,-
Reedman	16.5	6	50	5	-,-	(1)	30	8	66	2	-,-
Parkin	6	2	23	1	-,-						
A.Jarvis	4	1	10	0	-,-	(3)	4	1	9	0	-,-
Phillips	6	0	24	0	-,-	(5)	4	0	6	0	-,-
Haldane	4	1	15	1	-,-						

VICTORIA	O	M	R	W	w,nb		O	M	R	W	w,nb
Morris	12	2	35	0	-,-	(4)	10	2	24	1	-,-
Trumble	37.5	11	89	7	-,-	(1)	30.3	4	110	8	-,-
Trott	36	13	85	1	-,-	(2)	17	3	59	1	-,-
McLeod	17	3	48	2	-,-	(3)	9	0	34	0	-,-
Drysdale	4	1	14	0	-,-						

FALL OF WICKETS

Wkt	VIC 1st	SA 1st	VIC 2nd	SA 2nd
1st	8	17	2	25
2nd	26	67	3	39
3rd	53	89	45	77
4th	123	197	78	82
5th	162	222	110	93
6th	240	228	142	97
7th	278	244	152	143
8th	313	262	157	203
9th	316	279	189	218
10th	320	282	221	241

VICTORIA v NEW SOUTH WALES

Played at Melbourne Cricket Ground on December 26, 27, 28, 30, 1889. (Timeless match)
Toss : Victoria.   Result : VICTORIA WON BY EIGHT WICKETS.
Debuts: Nil.
12th Men: S.P.Jones (NSW). No 12th for Vic.
Umpires: E.J.Briscoe and J.Phillips.
Attendances: 7500, 6000, 8000, 5000.   Total: About 26,500.   Receipts: £977.
Close of Play: 1st day Vic 9/239 (J.W.Trumble 2, H.Trumble 2); 2nd day NSW (2) 1/91 (Bannerman 57, Moses 27); 3rd day NSW (2)
    7/259 (Donnan 33, Ferris 9).

Edwards, originally named as Victoria's 12th man but included in the side as a replacement for T.P.Horan (injured ankle), was missed by
Charlton in the slips off the first ball of the match. Half-centuries by Bruce (61 in 125 minutes, 4 fours), Barrett (69 in about 200
minutes, 9 fours) and Blackham (63 in about 140 minutes, 1 five and 5 fours) were the only double-figure scores of the innings.
Following on, Bannerman held the New South Wales second innings together, contributing a typically stubborn 117 in 355 minutes
including 9 fours, his only chance at 96 to J.W.Trumble at slip of McLeod. Hugh Trumble finished off the innings by dismissing
Charlton and Wales with successive balls. Needing 120 runs, Victoria lost Harry to the last ball of the opening over but a fine 71 not out
from Trott guided the team home. Sources: *Wisden, VCA Report, The Age, The Argus, The Herald, The Australasian, The Leader.*

VICTORIA

J.D.Edwards	c Wales b Ferris	2			
W.Bruce	c Moses b Charlton	61	lbw b Turner		17
G.H.S.Trott	c Wales b Ferris	2	not out		71
J.E.Barrett	c Charlton b Garrett	69	not out		29
*†J.M.Blackham	b Charlton	63			
J.Drysdale	b Garrett	0			
S.Morris	c Richardson b Garrett	7			
R.W.McLeod	b Charlton	7			
J.Harry	c Turner b Garrett	0	(1) c Charlton b Turner		0
J.W.Trumble	b Turner	9			
H.Trumble	not out	6			
Extras	(b24, lb1)	25	(b4)		4
Total	(116.0 overs, 295 mins)	251	(68.5 overs, 165 mins) (2 wkts)		121

NEW SOUTH WALES

A.C.Bannerman	c Blackham b H.Trumble	12	(2) run out (J.W.Trumble/Blackham)		117
A.C.K.Mackenzie	c McLeod b H.Trumble	4	(4) c & b H.Trumble		8
*H.Moses	b McLeod	20	b McLeod		27
C.T.B.Turner	c Trott b Bruce	14	(5) b Bruce		26
H.Donnan	b H.Trumble	6	(7) not out		34
G.J.Bonnor	b H.Trumble	16	(1) st Blackham b McLeod		5
W.A.Richardson	c Blackham b H.Trumble	3	(8) b McLeod		6
J.J.Ferris	b McLeod	0	(9) c Bruce b H.Trumble		9
T.W.Garrett	b McLeod	10	(6) c Blackham b McLeod		24
P.C.Charlton	st Blackham b H.Trumble	3	c J.W.Trumble b H.Trumble		1
†I.F.Wales	not out	6	b H.Trumble		0
Extras	(b9, lb5, nb1)	15	(b1, lb2, w1)		4
Total	(62.0 overs, 155 mins)	109	(170.1 overs, 405 mins)		261

NEW SOUTH WALES	O	M	R	W	w,nb		O	M	R	W	w,nb		FALL OF WICKETS			
Turner	26	9	54	1	-,-		29	15	41	2	-,-			VIC	NSW	VIC	NSW
Ferris	30	8	68	2	-,-	(3)	7	1	18	0	-,-	Wkt	1st	1st	2nd	2nd
Garrett	27	13	44	4	-,-	(4)	15.5	7	27	0	-,-	1st	11	16	13	0
Charlton	27	9	37	3	-,-	(2)	17	5	31	0	-,-	2nd	15	17	93	33
Richardson	5	0	17	0	-,-							3rd	109	44	110	-
Donnan	1	0	6	0	-,-							4th	200	61	139	-
												5th	202	61	186	-
VICTORIA	O	M	R	W	w,nb		O	M	R	W	w,nb	6th	214	83	239	-
H.Trumble	31	12	40	6	-,1	(2)	53.1	25	67	4	-,-	7th	232	84	248	-
Trott	4	1	10	0	-,-	(5)	12	4	26	0	1,-	8th	235	86	259	-
Bruce	14	7	20	1	-,-		18	6	38	1	-,-	9th	235	97	261	-
McLeod	13	7	24	3	-,-	(1)	45	20	81	4	-,-	10th	251	109	261	-
J.W.Trumble						(4)	19	12	18	0	-,-					
Morris							5	1	10	0	-,-					
Drysdale							18	11	17	0	-,-					

TASMANIA v VICTORIA

Played at S.T.C.A. Ground, Hobart, on January 8, 9, 1890. (Three-day match)

Toss : Victoria.   Result : VICTORIA WON BY AN INNINGS AND 147 RUNS.

Debuts: Tasmania - C.J.Eady, C.McAllen, G.S.Pennefather, G.J.P.Vautin, H.Wilson, J.T.Wilson (all f/c). Victoria - W.G.Ingleton, F.L.Richards, R.T.Smith, W.A.Tarrant (all f/c).

12th Men: J.H.Stuckey (Vic). No 12th named for Tas.

Umpires: D.F.Cotter and J.G.Davies.

Attendances: 2000, 500.   Total: About 2500.   Receipts: No figures published.

Close of Play: 1st day Tas 2/30 (Gatehouse 18).

Tasmania hosted their first first-class match since 1872-73, a break of 17 years. E.A.Barrett replaced J.D.Edwards (unavailable) in the Victorian team prior to departure from Melbourne. A stand of 129 in 105 minutes between J.E.Barrett (39 in 110 minutes, 3 fours) and Over (91 in 125 minutes, 12 fours) assisted by an unbeaten 60 in even time from McLeod (10 fours) saw Victoria total 338 on the first day. Sidebottom severely strained his back attempting to catch Over in the lunch-tea session and took no further part, E.A.Barrett substituting in the absence of a local reserve. An early start on the second day at 11.20am (the first began at 11.55am) heralded a dramatic collapse as Tasmania lost 5 for 9 in half an hour, all to Trott. Two of the local debutants, McAllen and Vautin, were caught napping by the early start and failed to get to the ground in time to bat. McAllen's lax attitude as captain earned him a severe rebuke in the Press. Trott's 6 for 10 included 3 for 0 in 4 balls and 4 for 0 in 6 balls (Eady, ball, Gatehouse, ball, Burn, Butler), the first two falling to catches at deep square-leg (batsmen crossing) and Butler to the first ball of a new over. It remained the lowest total at this ground (hosting its first match - it was known as the TCA Ground after 1906) until first-class cricket ceased there in 1987. Following on, Trott bowled Gatehouse with the last ball of Tasmania's first over and finished with 12 for 91 in the match as Victoria won with a day and a session in hand. *Cricket* incorrectly gives Tas (2) Gatehouse 6, J.Wilson 20, H.Wilson 25. Sources: *Cricket, VCA Report, Launceston Examiner, Hobart Mercury.*

VICTORIA

E.A.Barrett	b Pennefather	34
W.A.Tarrant	b Eady	25
G.H.S.Trott	c Eady b Pennefather	7
J.E.Barrett	c McAllen b Sidebottom	39
*†J.M.Blackham	st McAllen b Pennefather	0
W.Over	c Butler b Pennefather	91
G.E.Palmer	b Pennefather	35
R.W.McLeod	not out	60
R.T.Smith	b Pennefather	9
F.L.Richards	c McAllen b Burn	0
W.G.Ingleton	c H.Wilson b J.T.Wilson	11
Extras	(b16, lb10, w1)	27
Total	(111.3 overs, 235 mins)	338

TASMANIA

G.H.Gatehouse	c Richards b Trott	22		b Trott	0
G.S.Pennefather	c Smith b McLeod	0	(7)	lbw b Trott	14
J.T.Wilson	c Richards b Trott	9	(4)	lbw b Trott	25
C.J.Eady	c Richards b Trott	0	(6)	c McLeod b Smith	37
E.J.K.Burn	b Trott	0		c Blackham b Smith	26
T.P.Ryan	b Trott	5	(3)	st Blackham b Trott	16
C.W.Butler	c & b Trott	0	(9)	not out	6
H.Wilson	not out	0	(2)	c Blackham b Trott	20
G.J.P.Vautin	absent	-	(8)	b Smith	7
*†C.McAllen	absent	-		lbw b Trott	0
W.L.Sidebottom	absent hurt	-		absent hurt	-
Extras	(b1, lb1, nb1)	3		(b1)	1
Total	(19.4 overs, 55 mins)	39		(48.3 overs, 130 mins)	152

TASMANIA	O	M	R	W	w,nb		O	M	R	W	w,nb		FALL OF WICKETS		
													VIC	TAS	TAS
Ryan	7	0	22	0	-,-							Wkt	1st	1st	2nd
Eady	30	8	74	1	-,-							1st	42	1	0
Pennefather	33	10	86	6	-,-							2nd	67	30	28
Burn	19	5	64	1	-,-							3rd	71	34	60
J.T.Wilson	9.3	2	24	1	-,-							4th	72	34	69
Sidebottom	5	1	15	1	-,-							5th	201	34	99
H.Wilson	8	2	26	0	1,-							6th	222	34	134
												7th	256	39	142
VICTORIA	O	M	R	W	w,nb		O	M	R	W	w,nb	8th	277	-	150
McLeod	10	4	14	1	-,1							9th	290	-	152
Palmer	4	1	12	0	-,-							10th	338	-	-
Trott	5.4	3	10	6	-,-	(1)	22.3	4	81	6	-,-				
Over						(2)	16	4	44	0	-,-				
Smith						(3)	10	3	26	3	-,-				

NEW SOUTH WALES v VICTORIA

Played at Sydney Cricket Ground on January 25, 27, 28, 29, 30, 1890. (Timeless match)
Toss : New South Wales.   Result : NEW SOUTH WALES WON BY FOUR WICKETS.
Debuts: New South Wales - S.Deane, S.E.Gregory (both f/c).
12th Men: No 12th men named.
Umpires: E.J.Briscoe and J.Phillips.
Attendances: 7000, 8000, ? , ? , ? .   Total & Receipts: No figures published.
Close of Play: 1st day NSW 4/232 (Moses 44, Gregory 4); 2nd day Vic 4/101 (J.E.Barrett 11, McLeod 1); 3rd day Vic (2) 4/126
    (Blackham 22, McLeod 10); 4th day NSW (2) 6/92 (Moses 45, Garrett 3).

Jones batted 195 minutes for his century, going from 96 to 100 with his tenth four but falling to the next ball. He scored his runs out of the opening 156-run partnership with Bannerman. McLeod took three wickets in four balls (Turner, Gregory, ball, Iredale) late on the fourth day, rain and bad light ending play soon after (just before 6.00pm); 15 minutes on the fifth morning were sufficient to finish the match. When Turner (11 for 168 in the match) bowled Morris in the second innings, the bails carried halfway to the fence; Deane later complained of sore hands as a result of taking his faster than normal deliveries. Iredale was a late replacement for W.A.Richardson (unavailable) in the New South Wales side. *Wisden* and *VCA Report* incorrectly give Vic (2) Barrett b Ferris. *VCA Report* incorrectly gives NSW (2) Jones 20, Moses 54, Donnan 2, Turner 9, Gregory 8. Sources: *Wisden, VCA Report, Sydney Referee, Sydney Morning Herald, Town & Country Journal, Sydney Daily Telegraph.*

NEW SOUTH WALES

A.C.Bannerman	c J.E.Barrett b Trott	49	c Over b Drysdale	0
S.P.Jones	c McLeod b Trott	100	lbw b McLeod	24
*H.Moses	c Trott b Trumble	48	not out	52
H.Donnan	b Trott	6	c & b McLeod	9
C.T.B.Turner	c Morris b Trott	17	b McLeod	8
S.E.Gregory	c Trott b Trumble	27	lbw b McLeod	0
F.A.Iredale	lbw b Trumble	53	b McLeod	0
T.W.Garrett	c & b Morris	20	not out	8
J.J.Ferris	not out	10		
P.C.Charlton	c Morris b Trumble	0		
†S.Deane	lbw b McLeod	3		
Extras	(b5, lb6, w4, nb1)	16	(b2, lb2, nb1)	5
Total	(185.5 overs, 470 mins)	349	(29.4 overs, 130 mins) (6 wkts)	106

VICTORIA

E.A.Barrett	lbw b Turner	1	(10)	c & b Charlton	0
W.Bruce	c Ferris b Charlton	12	(1)	c Deane b Turner	45
G.H.S.Trott	c Deane b Turner	6		c Jones b Turner	34
J.E.Barrett	c Ferris b Charlton	22		b Garrett	3
*†J.M.Blackham	c Charlton b Garrett	66		b Turner	46
R.W.McLeod	c Deane b Turner	19		c Deane b Turner	10
J.Drysdale	b Garrett	26		c Moses b Turner	17
W.Over	c Deane b Turner	15	(9)	run out (Iredale/Bannerman)	12
S.Morris	run out (Gregory/Deane)	17	(2)	b Turner	0
J.Worrall	not out	6	(8)	c Deane b Charlton	59
H.Trumble	b Turner	4		not out	2
Extras	(b19, lb1, nb2)	22		(b9)	9
Total	(130.3 overs, 315 mins)	216		(88.3 overs, 220 mins)	237

VICTORIA	O	M	R	W	w,nb		O	M	R	W	w,nb		FALL OF WICKETS			
Trumble	48	21	80	4	-,1	(2)	7	2	26	0	-,1		NSW	VIC	VIC	NSW
McLeod	37.5	12	53	1	-,-	(4)	8	2	30	5	-,-	Wkt	1st	1st	2nd	2nd
Trott	46	17	108	4	-,-							1st	156	3	1	0
Bruce	18	7	26	0	4,-	(5)	0.4	0	4	0	-,-	2nd	183	17	80	54
Over	24	11	38	0	-,-							3rd	199	19	89	72
Worrall	4	2	8	0	-,-	(3)	8	3	20	0	-,-	4th	228	92	89	82
Morris	8	2	20	1	-,-							5th	258	136	133	82
Drysdale						(1)	6	1	21	1	-,-	6th	265	138	154	82
												7th	307	178	181	-
NEW SOUTH WALES	O	M	R	W	w,nb		O	M	R	W	w,nb	8th	339	195	228	-
Charlton	29	10	58	2	-,-	(3)	7.3	1	31	2	-,-	9th	344	208	230	-
Turner	59.3	27	71	5	-,2	(1)	39	12	97	6	-,-	10th	349	216	237	-
Ferris	9	3	31	0	-,-	(5)	18	6	35	0	-,-					
Donnan	3	0	11	0	-,-		3	0	14	0	-,-					
Garrett	30	21	23	2	-,-	(2)	21	6	51	1	-,-					

NEW SOUTH WALES v SOUTH AUSTRALIA

Played at Sydney Cricket Ground on February 14, 15, 17 (no play), 18, 1890. (Timeless match)
Toss : South Australia.   Result : NEW SOUTH WALES WON BY NINE WICKETS.
Debuts: South Australia - D.M.Ballans, A.Hill, J.H.Tardif (all f/c).
12th Men: F.A.Iredale (NSW) and N.Richards (SA).
Umpires: C.Bannerman and G.H.G.Searcy.
Attendances: 3000, 6000, no play, 2000.   Total: About 11,000.   Receipts: No figures published.
Close of Play: 1st day NSW 8/228 (Deane 14, Ferris 2); 2nd day SA (2) 1/59 (Lyons 44); 3rd day no play.

The inaugural match between these colonies, agreed to by the NSWCA largely on Giffen's feats for South Australia in recent seasons, was preceded by rain and enough sunshine to produce a tricky batting surface, which persuaded Giffen to insert the New South Welshmen. Their first-innings total of 240 was accumulated despite the ball moving about prodigiously, Jones (68 in about 180 minutes, 5 fours) and Donnan (51 in about 95 minutes, 5 fours) scoring notable half-centuries. The visitors, with the notable exception of George Giffen himself and Jack Lyons, were unable to handle the conditions quite as well. Rain prevented any play on the third day but New South Wales were untroubled in recording a nine-wicket win when the match resumed, Charlton's medium-pacers returning his best figures of 7 for 44. Reedman kept wicket on the final day during McKenzie's stint as an opening bowler, before the two reverted to their normal roles. Due to bronchitis, C.T.B.Turner was unable to represent New South Wales. Arthur Hill was the first of six brothers to play first-class cricket, all for South Australia, an unrivalled contribution by Australian siblings to the game. *Cricket* incorrectly gives NSW (2) G.Giffen 1/27, McKenzie 0/15. Sources: *Cricket, C.B.O'Reilly, Sydney Referee, Sydney Morning Herald, Town & Country Journal, Sydney Mail, Sydney Daily Telegraph.*

NEW SOUTH WALES

A.C.Bannerman	b Jarvis	21	not out		28
S.P.Jones	c & b Jarvis	68	c Jarvis b G.Giffen		1
H.Moses	c & b Jarvis	10	not out		30
*W.L.Murdoch	c Tardif b Jarvis	13			
S.E.Gregory	b G.Giffen	25			
T.W.Garrett	c McKenzie b G.Giffen	5			
H.Donnan	st McKenzie b G.Giffen	51			
W.A.Richardson	b Reedman	1			
†S.Deane	not out	23			
J.J.Ferris	c Jarvis b Reedman	2			
P.C.Charlton	c Haldane b Reedman	3			
Extras	(b14, lb4)	18	(b6, lb1)		7
Total	(102.4 overs, 250 mins)	240	(48.0 overs, 120 mins) (1 wkt)		66

SOUTH AUSTRALIA

J.J.Lyons	b Richardson	19	c Moses b Charlton		63
W.F.Giffen	c Moses b Charlton	0	(8) run out (Bannerman/Charlton)		14
*G.Giffen	c Deane b Garrett	52	c & b Ferris		32
H.Haldane	b Richardson	4	c Ferris b Charlton		2
H.Blinman	b Richardson	0	c Ferris b Charlton		8
J.H.Tardif	b Richardson	6	(7) c Murdoch b Charlton		0
A.Hill	c & b Ferris	1	(11) not out		0
D.M.Ballans	c Murdoch b Garrett	15	(10) c Moses b Charlton		0
†J.McKenzie	run out (Bannerman/Garrett)	23	(6) b Charlton		5
J.C.Reedman	not out	24	(2) c Moses b Charlton		15
A.Jarvis	c Gregory b Garrett	7	(9) b Ferris		3
Extras	(b3, lb1)	4	(b4, lb1, nb1)		6
Total	(70.2 overs, 170 mins)	155	(68.0 overs, 160 mins)		148

SOUTH AUSTRALIA	O	M	R	W	w,nb		O	M	R	W	w,nb			FALL OF WICKETS			
														NSW	SA	SA	NSW
Reedman	27.4	10	47	3	-,-	(3)	6	1	10	0	-,-	Wkt	1st	1st	2nd	2nd
G.Giffen	47	12	110	3	-,-		23	9	30	1	-,-	1st	58	2	59	8
Jarvis	28	7	65	4	-,-	(4)	8	3	7	0	-,-	2nd	78	45	82	-
McKenzie						(1)	11	4	12	0	-,-	3rd	112	53	84	-
												4th	126	53	106	-
NEW SOUTH WALES	O	M	R	W	w,nb		O	M	R	W	w,nb	5th	131	71	114	-
Ferris	13	1	38	1	-,-	(5)	15	6	22	2	-,1	6th	178	86	114	-
Charlton	11	1	29	1	-,-	(4)	23	4	44	7	-,-	7th	203	95	142	-
Richardson	18	4	43	4	-,-		8	2	17	0	-,-	8th	218	105	147	-
Garrett	28.2	11	41	3	-,-	(1)	19	5	48	0	-,-	9th	228	136	148	-
Donnan						(2)	3	0	11	0	-,-	10th	240	155	148	-

1890-91 SEASON (5 MATCHES)

For the second consecutive season only five first-class matches were played. Fixtures were identical to the past year. Little controversy surrounded the games and the season was overall a quiet one.

New South Wales made their inaugural trip to Adelaide in December 1890 to play South Australia. Superb bowling by Jack Ferris (8 for 84 and 6 for 108) supported by solid batting gave the visitors a comfortable six-wicket victory.

Returning via Melbourne, New South Wales met Victoria in the first of their annual two encounters. Batsmen on both sides struggled on a wicket which gave assistance to the bowlers. On this occasion, Ferris's bowling played a support role to Percie Charlton (5 for 84 and 6 for 45). Although requiring only 99 to win when they batted a second time, the New South Welshmen were dismissed for a mere 62. Jim Phillips, later a famous umpire, followed up his 7 for 20 in the first innings with 3 for 24 in the second. Hugh Trumble (6 for 33) inflicted the most damage on the final day.

One week later, South Australia visited Melbourne to play the Victorians in the match starting on New Year's day. George Giffen demonstrated his virtuoso allround ability with an innings of 237 and followed up with analyses of 5 for 89 and 7 for 103. Victoria's defeat by an innings was almost completely due to his efforts.

Three weeks later, the Victorians suffered their second consecutive innings defeat, this time at the hands of New South Wales in Sydney. F.H.Walters hit a rapid-fire century on the first day but thereafter little went right for the visitors. Their bugbear this time was C.T.B.Turner, who captured 8 for 74 and 7 for 100 in his only first-class appearance of the summer.

Rain had a severe effect on the final match of the season in Melbourne between Victoria and Tasmania. The commencement of the match, on the scheduled second day of play, saw three innings virtually completed in dreadful conditions in six hours' play. The Victorians proved the steadier. John Carlton, in only his second appearance for Victoria, had match figures of 12 for 79.

Leading Aggregates

Batsmen	M	I	NO	Runs	HS	Ave.	Bowlers	Runs	Wkts	Ave.
G.Giffen (SA)	2	3	0	275	237	91.66	J.Phillips (V)	250	25	10.00
H.Moses (NSW)	3	5	0	232	147	46.40	J.J.Ferris (NSW)	272	20	13.60
F.H.Walters (V)	2	4	1	172	106	57.33	G.Giffen (SA)	352	19	18.52
W.Bruce (V)	3	6	0	167	58	27.83	P.C.Charlton (NSW)	357	18	19.83
G.H.S.Trott (V)	4	8	1	161	81	23.00	C.T.B.Turner (NSW)	174	15	11.60
A.C.Bannerman (NSW)	3	5	1	141	45*	35.25	J.Carlton (V)	192	13	14.76

SOUTH AUSTRALIA v NEW SOUTH WALES

Played at Adelaide Oval on December 19, 20, 22, 23, 1890. (Timeless match)
Toss : South Australia.   Result : NEW SOUTH WALES WON BY SIX WICKETS.
Debuts: South Australia - W.Amos, W.A.Magarey (both f/c).
12th Men: A.E.Clarke (NSW). No 12th named for SA.
Umpires: E.J.Briscoe and I.A.Fisher.
Attendances: No daily figures published.   Total: About 20,500.   Receipts: No figures published.
Close of Play: 1st day NSW 0/6 (Richardson 2, Bannerman 4); 2nd day NSW 7/341 (Charlton 6); 3rd day SA (2) 191 all out.

Ferris returned his best figures for New South Wales of 8 for 84; this was the only time he captured ten or more wickets in 19 matches for the State. The pitch was still slightly damp from preparation when the game began which assisted him, and further light showers on the third day interrupted the play and freshened the pitch, again to his advantage. His usual opening partner C.T.B.Turner had announced himself unavailable for New South Wales's first trip to Adelaide; the team travelled on to Melbourne afterwards to play Victoria. Play went past 6.00pm on the third day in an attempt to finish the match but the last South Australian pair remained at the wicket until 6.20pm, when stumps were drawn. Alfred Jarvis took 3 for 0 in two overs the following day before the required runs were scored by the visitors; he was twice on a hat-trick in the match, dismissing Ferris and Callaway in succession in the first innings and Moses and Donnan in the second innings. Sources: *Wisden, C.B.O'Reilly, The Australasian, Adelaide Advertiser, South Australian Register.*

SOUTH AUSTRALIA

J.J.Lyons	c Callaway b Ferris	10	(3) c Bannerman b Ferris	0
†A.H.Jarvis	b Ferris	13	(4) c & b Ferris	33
*G.Giffen	lbw b Charlton	21	(5) b Charlton	17
J.E.Gooden	b Ferris	28	(6) lbw b Ferris	39
J.C.Reedman	b Ferris	12	(9) c Wales b Ferris	60
W.A.Magarey	b Charlton	0	(10) c Wales b Callaway	7
H.Blinman	not out	73	c Moses b Ferris	4
W.F.Giffen	c Iredale b Ferris	55	c Wales b Charlton	2
A.Hill	b Ferris	6	(1) c Wales b Charlton	5
A.Jarvis	b Ferris	7	(11) not out	14
W.Amos	lbw b Ferris	9	(2) c Wales b Ferris	6
Extras	(b3, lb4)	7	(b3, lb1)	4
Total	(133.1 overs, 315 mins)	241	(87.5 overs, 235 mins)	191

NEW SOUTH WALES

C.A.Richardson	b G.Giffen	56	(2) not out	2
A.C.Bannerman	lbw b Lyons	44	(1) lbw b G.Giffen	17
*H.Moses	c & b G.Giffen	67	c A.H.Jarvis b A.Jarvis	3
H.Donnan	b G.Giffen	58	c Blinman b A.Jarvis	0
F.A.Iredale	b G.Giffen	67		
A.P.Marr	c W.F.Giffen b G.Giffen	4	(5) c A.H.Jarvis b A.Jarvis	0
S.E.Gregory	c Blinman b Amos	32	(6) not out	5
P.C.Charlton	st A.H.Jarvis b G.Giffen	34		
J.J.Ferris	b A.Jarvis	33		
S.T.Callaway	b A.Jarvis	0		
†I.F.Wales	not out	0		
Extras	(b2, lb9)	11		-
Total	(185.3 overs, 435 mins)	406	(18.5 overs, 50 mins) (4 wkts)	27

NEW SOUTH WALES	O	M	R	W	w,nb		O	M	R	W	w,nb
Ferris	65.1	30	84	8	-,-		44	13	108	6	-,-
Charlton	45	19	74	2	-,-		35	13	63	3	-,-
Callaway	16	5	44	0	-,-		8.5	3	16	1	-,-
Marr	2	0	11	0	-,-						
Richardson	5	0	21	0	-,-						

SOUTH AUSTRALIA	O	M	R	W	w,nb		O	M	R	W	w,nb
Amos	20	3	87	1	-,-						
G.Giffen	83.3	35	150	6	-,-		9	3	10	1	-,-
Reedman	24	9	54	0	-,-						
Lyons	28	13	59	1	-,-						
A.Jarvis	30	9	45	2	-,-	(1)	9.5	4	17	3	-,-

FALL OF WICKETS

Wkt	SA 1st	NSW 1st	SA 2nd	NSW 2nd
1st	14	72	9	17
2nd	31	138	11	20
3rd	65	226	25	20
4th	83	239	49	20
5th	86	245	65	-
6th	86	325	69	-
7th	205	341	74	-
8th	211	406	160	-
9th	231	406	170	-
10th	241	406	191	-

VICTORIA v NEW SOUTH WALES

Played at Melbourne Cricket Ground on December 26, 27, 29, 1890. (Timeless match)
Toss : Victoria.   Result : VICTORIA WON BY 36 RUNS.
Debuts: Victoria - S.J.Donahoo (f/c).
12th Men: C.H.Ross (Vic) & R.S.Houston (Vic emergencies) and A.E.Clarke (NSW).
Umpires: E.J.Briscoe and D.F.Cotter.
Attendances: 8000, 8000, 4000.   Total: About 20,000.   Receipts: £850.
Close of Play: 1st day NSW 1/32 (Bannerman 12, Moses 9); 2nd day Vic (2) 1/12 (Donahoo 7, Trumble 2).

Downes and Garrett arrived from Sydney to join the New South Wales team and were included at the expense of S.T.Callaway and A.P.Marr who had played in Adelaide. The first two days were played in fine weather; a damp patch gave some assistance to the bowlers on the first day but conditions were ideal for the second and player-umpire Jim Phillips recorded remarkable figures of 7 for 20 from 41.5 overs on a true pitch, runs coming from only 15 balls of the 251 that he delivered. Bannerman (45 not out in 310 minutes, 4 fours) carried his bat in typical style while Gregory (50 in 75 minutes, 4 fours) attacked. Heavy rain on the Sunday made conditions more treacherous as the final day progressed, handicapping New South Wales. Trumble captured the wickets of Bannerman and Richardson with the third and fifth balls of the opening over and the rest followed within 90 minutes. Bannerman was "manifestly displeased" (*Age*) with his decision (given by Cotter) and was reluctant to leave the crease. Felix commented in *The Australasian* that "some men require to be told half-a-dozen times that they are out before they will move away". Ferris (first innings) and Blackham (second innings) were dismissed first ball. Sources: *Wisden, VCA Report, The Age, The Argus, The Herald, The Australasian, The Leader.*

VICTORIA

W.Bruce	c Downes b Charlton	6	(4) c Moses b Charlton	10
G.E.Palmer	c Downes b Charlton	17	b Ferris	2
T.P.Horan	c Richardson b Charlton	5	(6) lbw b Charlton	12
G.H.S.Trott	c Wales b Charlton	7	(5) c Charlton b Ferris	18
R.W.McLeod	st Wales b Ferris	7	(8) b Ferris	1
S.Morris	b Ferris	39	(7) c Donnan b Ferris	5
J.Worrall	b Charlton	9	(9) b Charlton	1
*†J.M.Blackham	c Donnan b Downes	23	(10) lbw b Charlton	0
S.J.Donahoo	c Garrett b Downes	0	(1) c Bannerman b Charlton	7
J.Phillips	run out (Wales)	22	(11) not out	2
H.Trumble	not out	21	(3) c Wales b Charlton	27
Extras	(b1, lb2, nb2)	5	(b2, w1)	3
Total	(80.3 overs, 210 mins)	161	(55.2 overs, 150 mins)	88

NEW SOUTH WALES

A.C.Bannerman	not out	45	c Blackham b Trumble	0
C.A.Richardson	b McLeod	6	(3) c Palmer b Trumble	0
*H.Moses	c Blackham b Phillips	9	(4) c Trumble b Phillips	6
H.Donnan	c & b Phillips	2	(2) c Horan b Trumble	4
F.A.Iredale	c Phillips b Bruce	13	run out (Worrall/Blackham)	5
S.E.Gregory	c Trumble b Morris	50	st Blackham b Phillips	3
P.C.Charlton	lbw b Phillips	10	c Donahoo b Trumble	12
J.J.Ferris	lbw b Phillips	0	b Trumble	6
T.W.Garrett	c Horan b Phillips	0	not out	12
F.Downes	c Blackham b Phillips	3	c Palmer b Trumble	7
†I.F.Wales	c Horan b Phillips	0	c McLeod b Phillips	2
Extras	(b4, lb8, w1)	13	(b3, lb2)	5
Total	(140.5 overs, 310 mins)	151	(23.1 overs, 90 mins)	62

NEW SOUTH WALES	O	M	R	W	w,nb		O	M	R	W	w,nb
Ferris	40.3	16	53	2	-,2		24.2	12	27	4	-,-
Charlton	30	11	84	5	-,-		19	7	45	6	1,-
Downes	10	3	19	2	-,-		12	5	13	0	-,-

VICTORIA	O	M	R	W	w,nb		O	M	R	W	w,nb
McLeod	42	24	60	1	-,-						
Trumble	20	13	13	0	-,-	(1)	12	2	33	6	-,-
Worrall	12	6	14	0	1,-						
Phillips	41.5	28	20	7	-,-	(2)	11.1	2	24	3	-,-
Palmer	10	8	8	0	-,-						
Bruce	4	2	8	1	-,-						
Morris	11	3	15	1	-,-						

FALL OF WICKETS

Wkt	VIC 1st	NSW 1st	VIC 2nd	NSW 2nd
1st	11	9	5	0
2nd	30	33	21	0
3rd	34	35	39	7
4th	43	49	56	16
5th	45	113	72	19
6th	69	137	82	25
7th	101	137	82	33
8th	101	139	86	39
9th	132	151	86	51
10th	161	151	88	62

VICTORIA v SOUTH AUSTRALIA

Played at Melbourne Cricket Ground on January 1, 2, 3, 5, 1891. (Timeless match)
Toss : South Australia.   Result : SOUTH AUSTRALIA WON BY AN INNINGS AND 62 RUNS.
Debuts: South Australia - E.J.Hiscock, B.V.Scrymgour (both f/c).
12th Men: W.Smith (SA). No 12th named for Vic.
Umpires: D.F.Cotter and G.H.G.Searcy.
Attendances: 7000, 3000, 10000, 1500.   Total: About 21,500.   Receipts: About £900.
Close of Play: 1st day SA 5/275 (Giffen 119, Hiscock 10); 2nd day Vic 0/48 (Houston 18, Bruce 25); 3rd day Vic (2) 0/15 (Bruce 9, Ross 6).

Scoring more runs and taking more wickets than all his team-mates combined, Giffen single-handedly led South Australia to victory, becoming the first cricketer to register a double-century and capture ten or more wickets in an Australian match. He notched 237 in 445 minutes (1 five and 23 fours) and followed it with 12 for 192; he bowled unchanged for all but a single over from one end. Lyons (53 in 40 minutes, 2 fives and 7 fours) and Blinman (50 in 100 minutes, 5 fours) compiled contrasting fifties in support. Houston took over from Blackham as wicket-keeper mid-afternoon on the second day and both Blackham's catches were taken at mid-off. Houston (54 in about 210 minutes, 1 four) and Bruce (58 in 105 minutes, 1 five and 5 fours) hit half-centuries in the Victorian first innings. Heavy rain on Sunday and Monday morning delayed the start of the fourth day until 2.40pm. Batting on a wet wicket, Trott (81 in 115 minutes, 8 fours) and Trumble (48 in about 60 minutes, 6 fours) both survived early chances to topscore in the second innings. *O'Reilly* and *VCA Report* give Vic (2) A.Jarvis 1/55, Reedman 1/5. Sources: *Wisden, C.B.O'Reilly, VCA Report, The Age, The Argus, The Australasian, The Leader.*

SOUTH AUSTRALIA

J.J.Lyons	b McLeod	53
†A.H.Jarvis	c Houston b Phillips	29
*G.Giffen	c Blackham b Phillips	237
J.E.Gooden	c McLeod b Phillips	1
J.C.Reedman	b Trumble	7
H.Blinman	c McLeod b Phillips	50
E.J.Hiscock	c Trumble b Phillips	11
J.Noel	b Morris	49
L.W.Evan	c Morris b Trott	3
A.Jarvis	c Blackham b Phillips	9
B.V.Scrymgour	not out	0
Extras	(b11, w12)	23
Total	(195.4 overs, 450 mins)	472

VICTORIA

R.S.Houston	run out (/A.H.Jarvis)	54	(7) c Evan b Giffen	8
W.Bruce	c & b Giffen	58	(1) b Giffen	13
G.H.S.Trott	c Blinman b Lyons	0	c Gooden b Giffen	81
S.Morris	lbw b Giffen	3	(6) b A.Jarvis	0
R.W.McLeod	b Giffen	24	(8) st A.H.Jarvis b Giffen	14
C.H.Ross	not out	29	(2) c Scrymgour b Giffen	6
*†J.M.Blackham	b A.Jarvis	0	(5) c Hiscock b Giffen	0
J.Worrall	c Scrymgour b A.Jarvis	20	(4) run out (/A.H.Jarvis)	1
H.Trumble	b Giffen	20	st A.H.Jarvis b Reedman	48
S.J.Donahoo	run out (Lyons/A.H.Jarvis)	0	st A.H.Jarvis b Giffen	0
J.Phillips	c Scrymgour b Giffen	0	not out	17
Extras	(b5, lb7)	12	(lb1, nb1)	2
Total	(105.2 overs, 285 mins)	220	(50.3 overs, 165 mins)	190

VICTORIA	O	M	R	W	w,nb
Trumble	39	13	104	1	1,-
Phillips	55.4	20	91	6	-,-
McLeod	26	7	66	1	-,-
Trott	10	2	38	1	-,-
Bruce	27	9	58	0	8,-
Ross	7	1	18	0	2,-
Morris	12	4	39	1	-,-
Worrall	19	5	35	0	1,-

SOUTH AUSTRALIA	O	M	R	W	w,nb	O	M	R	W	w,nb
A.Jarvis	30	10	74	2	-,-	18	2	54	1	-,-
Giffen	51.2	21	89	5	-,-	25	5	103	7	-,-
Lyons	23	10	42	1	-,-	6	0	25	0	-,-
Reedman	1	0	3	0	-,-	1.3	0	6	1	-,1

FALL OF WICKETS

	SA	VIC	VIC
Wkt	1st	1st	2nd
1st	64	96	18
2nd	119	101	19
3rd	129	108	25
4th	152	144	25
5th	249	158	25
6th	287	159	38
7th	416	187	101
8th	442	217	140
9th	471	217	140
10th	472	220	190

NEW SOUTH WALES v VICTORIA

Played at Sydney Cricket Ground on January 24, 26, 27, 28, 29, 1891. (Timeless match)
Toss : Victoria.　　　　Result : NEW SOUTH WALES WON BY AN INNINGS AND 94 RUNS.
Debuts: Victoria - J.Carlton (f/c).
12th Men: A.E.Clarke (NSW) and R.W.McLeod (Vic).
Umpires: E.J.Briscoe and T.Flynn.
Attendances: 6000, 7000, "limited", "very small".　　　Total: About 16,000.　　　Receipts: £730.
Close of Play: 1st day Vic 181 all out; 2nd day NSW 6/262 (Moses 80, Charlton 2); 3rd day Vic (2) 0/5 (Houston 0, Blackham 5);
　　　　4th day Vic (2) 7/170 (Morris 25, Tarrant 13).

Victoria were disadvantaged by rain during both innings. The match began in "very close and sultry" conditions on "a prefect wicket" (*SMH*) but the rain began soon after and most of the pre-lunch session was lost. Walters (106 in 110 minutes, 13 fours) played "a free hard-hitting innings" (*SMH*), his runs coming from 139 added while he was at the wicket. New South Wales began their innings in fine weather on the following day. Turner (70 in 75 minutes, 8 fours) gave them a flying start, after which Moses (147 in 425 minutes, 10 fours), Iredale (46 in about 90 minutes, 6 fours) and Garrett (76 in about 135 minutes, 9 fours) ensured that a substantial first innings advantage was gained. Moses's innings was "a mixture of cautious batting and genuine hard hitting" (*SMH*). Blackham (50 in 65 minutes, 5 fours) began the Victorian second innings aggressively but the return of rain and associated poor light halted the momentum, conditions again favouring the bowlers thereafter. Turner returned the best match figures (15 for 174) thus far in matches between the two teams, his great skill utilizing the rain-affected wicket to the optimum. Sources: *Wisden, VCA Report, Sydney Referee, Sydney Morning Herald, Town & Country Journal.*

VICTORIA

F.H.Walters	c Wales b Turner	106	(4) c Charlton b Turner	20
G.H.S.Trott	c Charlton b Turner	19	(3) c Wales b Turner	4
S.Morris	b Turner	0	(8) c Moses b Turner	29
T.P.Horan	c Moses b Turner	20	(5) lbw b Turner	2
R.S.Houston	run out (Garrett/Donnan)	1	(1) b Charlton	24
H.Trumble	b Turner	4	(7) c Garrett b Turner	10
W.A.Tarrant	b Turner	1	(9) run out (Donnan/Wales)	14
J.Worrall	not out	22	(6) c Bonnor b Turner	19
*†J.M.Blackham	c Garrett b Downes	3	(2) c Charlton b Turner	50
J.Phillips	lbw b Turner	2	c Bonnor b Charlton	10
J.Carlton	c Downes b Turner	1	not out	5
Extras	(lb2)	2	(b3)	3
Total	(74.5 overs, 235 mins)	181	(101.5 overs, 250 mins)	190

NEW SOUTH WALES

A.C.Bannerman	lbw b Carlton	35
C.T.B.Turner	c Carlton b Phillips	70
*H.Moses	c Tarrant b Phillips	147
H.Donnan	c Houston b Phillips	7
S.E.Gregory	c Tarrant b Phillips	1
F.A.Iredale	c Morris b Worrall	46
G.J.Bonnor	run out (Worrall/Blackham)	12
P.C.Charlton	b Worrall	28
T.W.Garrett	c Trott b Phillips	76
F.Downes	st Blackham b Trott	12
†I.F.Wales	not out	12
Extras	(b6, lb3, w6, nb4)	19
Total	(207.0 overs, 530 mins)	465

NEW SOUTH WALES	O	M	R	W	w,nb	O	M	R	W	w,nb
Turner	31.5	9	74	8	-,-	49	21	100	7	-,-
Downes	8	2	30	1	-,-	14	7	25	0	-,-
Charlton	14	4	33	0	-,-	36.5	15	58	2	-,-
Garrett	21	6	42	0	-,-	2	1	4	0	-,-

VICTORIA	O	M	R	W	w,nb
Phillips	56	24	88	5	2,4
Trumble	23	7	66	0	1,-
Carlton	42	12	113	1	3,-
Horan	9	4	21	0	-,-
Morris	16	4	33	0	-,-
Worrall	44	18	63	2	-,-
Trott	15	2	60	1	-,-
Walters	2	0	2	0	-,-

FALL OF WICKETS

Wkt	VIC 1st	NSW 1st	VIC 2nd
1st	65	92	57
2nd	65	125	65
3rd	139	142	91
4th	146	145	101
5th	150	240	101
6th	150	256	120
7th	151	317	140
8th	170	433	172
9th	179	446	180
10th	181	465	190

VICTORIA v TASMANIA

Played at Melbourne Cricket Ground on March 30 (no play), 31, April 1, 1891. (Timeless match)
Toss : Tasmania.   Result : VICTORIA WON BY NINE WICKETS.
Debuts: Victoria - H.McLean, J.E.Rogers - see below - (both f/c). Tasmania - N.V.Rock, E.A.C.Windsor (both f/c).
12th Men: None named.
Umpires: D.F.Cotter and W.L.Sidebottom.
Attendances: no play, 2500, 500.   Total: About 3000.   Receipts: No figures published.
Close of Play: 1st day no play; 2nd day Tas (2) 9/149 (McAllen 13, N.V.Rock 0).

After the first day had been abandoned due to rain, 29 wickets fell in rapid succession when the match began on an ill-suited pitch on the second day. Carlton (5 for 26) and Phillips (3 for 13) destroyed the visitor's first innings within 90 minutes, Carlton taking 12 for 79 in the match. Bruce (48 in 55 minutes, 3 fours) and Gatehouse (40 in 110 minutes, 1 four) recorded the highest scores for the respective teams. Norman Rock captured 5 for 21 on debut for Tasmania. Both teams were forced to alter their original sides before the game, J.Watt (family bereavement), W.H.Ewart and G.J.P.Vautin withdrawing from the Tasmanian twelve with McAllen, W.L.Sidebottom and N.V.Rock taking their places. Sidebottom acted as the visiting team's umpire after his omission from the final XI. Carlton, Harry and Rogers replaced S.Morris, C.H.Ross and H.Trumble (all unavailable) after the original Victorian selection. R.W.McLeod named to replace W.A.Tarrant (minor injury) in the Victorian line-up, withdrew because of a prior commitment and was replaced by Donahoo. McLean was brought in for J.M.Blackham (unavailable); Harry kept wickets throughout the first innings but gave way to Houston at 2/83 in the second innings, accepting his two catches in the deep field. Tasmania's keeper, McAllen, was struck in the face at 0/36 in Victoria's second innings. McLean fielded as substitute against his own team while Gatehouse, and later Eady, took the gloves. Rogers played his two first-class matches under the assumed name of "Jack Marshall". Sources: *VCA Report, STCA Report, The Age, The Argus, The Herald, The Australasian, The Leader.*

TASMANIA

*C.W.Rock	c Trott b Phillips	14		c Trott b Bruce	13
G.H.Gatehouse	run out (Bruce)	0		c Harry b Carlton	40
E.J.K.Burn	c Worrall b Carlton	0	(4)	b Carlton	26
J.H.Savigny	c Worrall b Carlton	2	(7)	c & b Carlton	3
C.J.Eady	c Carlton b Phillips	0		b Carlton	15
E.Maxwell	c McLean b Phillips	2	(9)	c & b Carlton	6
W.H.Savigny	b Carlton	7	(3)	b Worrall	1
E.A.C.Windsor	not out	14		c Harry b Carlton	4
H.Wilson	hit wkt b Rogers	2	(6)	hit wkt b Carlton	10
†C.McAllen	c Phillips b Carlton	3		c McLean b Phillips	13
N.V.Rock	c & b Carlton	3		not out	0
Extras	(b3)	3		(b15, lb3)	18
Total	(30.5 overs, 85 mins)	50		(71.3 overs, 185 mins)	149

VICTORIA

*W.Bruce	c Gatehouse b N.V.Rock	48		c Eady b N.V.Rock	32
F.H.Walters	b Windsor	12		not out	34
G.H.S.Trott	c C.W.Rock b Maxwell	4		not out	28
R.S.Houston	c Gatehouse b Windsor	11			
J.Worrall	b N.V.Rock	5			
H.McLean	c C.W.Rock b Windsor	3			
†J.Harry	b N.V.Rock	2			
J.Carlton	run out (/McAllen)	0			
S.J.Donahoo	b N.V.Rock	0			
J.Phillips	not out	6			
J.E.Rogers	b N.V.Rock	6			
Extras	(b6, lb2, w1)	9		(b2)	2
Total	(35.5 overs, 98 mins)	106		(24.4 overs, 70 mins) (1 wkt)	96

VICTORIA	O	M	R	W	w,nb		O	M	R	W	w,nb
Carlton	15.5	2	26	5	-,-		25	9	53	7	-,-
Phillips	12	4	13	3	-,-		9.3	3	14	1	-,-
Rogers	3	0	8	1	-,-	(5)	13	4	18	0	-,-
Worrall						(3)	11	3	27	1	-,-
Bruce						(4)	13	5	19	1	-,-

TASMANIA	O	M	R	W	w,nb		O	M	R	W	w,nb
Windsor	18	3	44	3	1,-		7	0	30	0	-,-
Maxwell	6	0	32	1	-,-						
N.V.Rock	11.5	5	21	5	-,-	(2)	6.4	1	34	1	-,-
Wilson						(3)	6	1	17	0	-,-
Eady						(4)	5	1	13	0	-,-

FALL OF WICKETS				
Wkt	TAS 1st	VIC 1st	TAS 2nd	VIC 2nd
1st	11	17	45	45
2nd	15	36	46	-
3rd	17	80	83	-
4th	17	82	95	-
5th	17	85	110	-
6th	23	91	120	-
7th	32	91	123	-
8th	35	91	126	-
9th	42	91	135	-
10th	50	106	149	-

1891-92 SEASON (12 MATCHES)

Lord Sheffield, a benefactor of Sussex cricket, arranged for an England touring team to visit Australia in the 1891-92 season. It was the first England tour in four years and Lord Sheffield's aim, in part, was to restore the popularity of cricket in Australia which had been on the wane. To do this, he brought to the country a combined team of professionals and amateurs and arranged for W.G.Grace (now 43) to captain the side. Grace's only previous tour of Australia had been a non-first-class one in 1873-74, and he was paid £3000 plus expenses in order to make the trip a second time. His presence was a major drawcard.

Beginning in Adelaide, as they had done in 1887-88, the Englishmen undertook a tour of 27 matches, of which eight were first-class including three Tests. The only defeats sustained on the tour occurred in the first two Tests. Grace headed the batting averages in first-class games, as he did in all matches, but he did not produce an innings of real note in the Tests and at times his heart did not seem to be in the tour. W.Attewell, J.Briggs and G.A.Lohmann led the bowling, each bettering 100 wickets in all matches. Interest in the games exceeded all expectations and attendances were high; Lord Sheffield was successful in that respect. But overall he made a loss on the tour.

Before arriving in Australia, Lord Sheffield had decided to offer the cricket associations of Victoria, New South Wales and South Australia a purse of £150 for the creation of a perpetual trophy for intercolonial cricket. Lord Sheffield announced his plan to Major B.J.Wardill, Melbourne Cricket Club secretary, in November 1891, not long after the tourists landed. He agreed that if the associations rejected the idea for a trophy, they could instead split the money evenly between themselves. Officials were slow to warm to Lord Sheffield's offer but, following nearly twelve months of procrastination and debate, representatives of Victoria, New South Wales and South Australia met on September 13, 1892 and voted by the slender margin of 6-5 to dedicate Lord Sheffield's money to the purchase of a premiership Shield. Four Victorian delegates and one from South Australia had preferred the alternative - that each association receive £50, to do with as they wished. And so began the history of the Sheffield Shield competition.

Another major development to spring from the season involved the creation of a controlling body for Australian cricket. A meeting on March 25, 1892 attracted five delegates from each of New South Wales, Victoria and South Australia, and a motion to form the Australasian Cricket Council was unanimously passed. It was reported in the *South Australian Register* that Tasmanian officials had apologised for being unable to attend the meeting, while Queensland administrators had not answered an offer to take part. The Australasian Cricket Council was to survive less than eight years, failing to win either the support of the players or a measure of financial independence.

On-field domestic events in 1891-92 were restricted to the annual meetings between New South Wales, Victoria and South Australia. George Giffen reached the pinnacle of his allround powers in South Australia's clash with Victoria when he scored 271 and followed up with 9 for 96 and 7 for 70. Again he single-handedly won a match for his side. Jack Lyons was also in great form for South Australia, scoring centuries against both Victoria and New South Wales as well as a third in the Second Test at Sydney.

Leading Aggregates

Batsmen	M	I	NO	Runs	HS	Ave.	Bowlers	Runs	Wkts	Ave.
J.J.Lyons (SA)	6	10	0	557	145	55.70	G.Giffen (SA)	865	50	17.30
G.Giffen (SA)	6	10	0	509	271	50.90	W.Attewell (E)	573	44	13.02
A.E.Stoddart (E)	8	12	0	450	134	37.50	C.T.B.Turner (NSW)	979	43	22.76
W.G.Grace (E)	8	11	1	448	159*	44.80	G.A.Lohmann (E)	640	40	16.00
W.Bruce (V)	7	13	0	421	72	32.38	J.Briggs (E)	420	32	13.12
A.C.Bannerman (NSW)	8	16	0	393	91	24.56	R.W.McLeod (V)	591	27	21.88
R.Abel (E)	8	12	2	388	132*	38.80	S.T.Callaway (NSW)	503	22	22.86
C.T.B.Turner (NSW)	8	16	1	351	66	23.40				
J.M.Read (E)	8	11	0	326	106	29.63				
S.E.Gregory (NSW)	6	12	1	308	93*	28.00				
R.W.McLeod (V)	7	13	1	304	87	25.33				

SOUTH AUSTRALIA v VICTORIA

Played at Adelaide Oval on November 7, 9, 10, 11, 1891. (Timeless match)
Toss : South Australia.   Result : SOUTH AUSTRALIA WON BY AN INNINGS AND 164 RUNS.
Debuts: South Australia - C.W.Hayward, H.T.Moore (both f/c). Victoria - A.N.A.Bowman, F.J.Laver, J.H.Stuckey (all f/c).
12th Men: B.V.Scrymgour (SA) and H.C.Maplestone (Vic).
Umpires: D.F.Cotter and I.A.Fisher.
Attendances: 3000, 4000, ? , ? .   Total & Receipts: No figures published.
Close of Play: 1st day SA 3/256 (G.Giffen 105, Blinman 29); 2nd day SA 7/519 (Hayward 6, Moore 0); 3rd day Vic 4/166 (Stuckey 5, Blackham 10).

George Giffen recorded the greatest allround performance in any first-class cricket match, scoring a career-best 271 and capturing 16 wickets for 166. Both his innings and the team total (562) set new South Australian records. He survived chances at 90 and 155 to bat for 425 minutes and hit 1 five and 17 fours, sharing stands of 167 with Lyons (104 in 130 minutes, 13 fours) and an unbroken 161 with brother Walter (65 in about 165 minutes, an all-run five and 4 fours), who retired at 4/441 when as the non-striker his hand was crushed against the bat handle by one of George's searing drives. Shortly after Giffen passed 200 the *Register* reported that the bowlers "now resorted to all sorts of wiles" to get him out, Harry occasionally bowling with his left hand (without warning) and McLean "now and then bowling a fast underhand grubber". Wicket-keeper Blackham also bowled two overs of underhand daisy-cutters. Giffen's combined bowling figures (which included all eleven batsmen) were the best in matches between these teams and included a sequence of 4 for 1 in 7 balls; Phillips with the last ball of the first innings and Bowman, McLeod and Walters with the first, fourth and sixth balls of the opening over in the follow-on. A.H.Jarvis, attempting to gather a return from the outfield on the third day, sustained a split thumb and was replaced by Haldane. A local player, Holbrook, acted as substitute because Scrymgour was already standing for W.F.Giffen and J.J.Woods (another local) for Reedman, who had to work. Reedman returned on the final day but Scrymgour and Woods continued in the absence of the other two. Victoria were significantly undermanned by the inability of J.E.Barrett, W.Bruce, G.H.S.Trott and H.Trumble to make the trip to Adelaide. Sources: *Wisden, C.B.O'Reilly, Adelaide Advertiser, South Australian Register.*

SOUTH AUSTRALIA

J.J.Lyons	c Laver b Phillips	104
†A.H.Jarvis	b McLeod	2
*G.Giffen	c McLean b Phillips	271
H.Haldane	c Harry b Phillips	9
H.Blinman	c Harry b Phillips	32
W.F.Giffen	retired hurt	65
J.C.Reedman	c McLeod b Rogers	11
J.Noel	c Harry b Phillips	10
C.W.Hayward	lbw b Rogers	27
H.T.Moore	c McLeod b Phillips	0
A.Jarvis	not out	19
Extras	(b8, lb4)	12
Total	(206.3 overs, 495 mins)	562

VICTORIA

F.H.Walters	b G.Giffen	50	(2) c & b G.Giffen	0
A.N.A.Bowman	lbw b G.Giffen	52	(1) b G.Giffen	0
R.W.McLeod	c Noel b G.Giffen	27	b G.Giffen	0
J.Harry	c & b Lyons	17	b G.Giffen	19
J.H.Stuckey	b G.Giffen	7	(8) st Haldane b G.Giffen	22
*†J.M.Blackham	b G.Giffen	22	b Lyons	31
H.McLean	b G.Giffen	12	(5) st Haldane b Lyons	33
J.Carlton	c Reedman b G.Giffen	16	(7) c & b G.Giffen	16
F.J.Laver	c Reedman b G.Giffen	5	(10) c sub (B.V.Scrymgour) b Moore	1
J.Phillips	c Hayward b G.Giffen	13	(9) not out	39
J.E.Rogers	not out	5	c Noel b G.Giffen	0
Extras	(b7, w1, nb1)	9	(lb2)	2
Total	(131.1 overs, 330 mins)	235	(50.5 overs, 135 mins)	163

VICTORIA	O	M	R	W	w,nb
McLeod	40	11	116	1	-,-
Laver	28	4	64	0	-,-
Rogers	37.3	6	96	2	-,-
Phillips	60	7	156	6	-,-
Carlton	22	1	72	0	-,-
Blackham	2	1	4	0	-,-
Harry	13	5	31	0	-,-
McLean	4	0	11	0	-,-

SOUTH AUSTRALIA	O	M	R	W	w,nb		O	M	R	W	w,nb
A.Jarvis	22	11	30	0	-,-	(2)	13	3	29	0	-,-
Lyons	33	12	59	1	-,-	(3)	8	0	51	2	-,-
G.Giffen	50.1	12	96	9	-,-	(1)	25.5	4	70	7	-,-
Noel	16	4	26	0	1,-						
Moore	6	2	13	0	-,-	(4)	4	1	11	1	-,-
Reedman	4	3	2	0	-,1						

FALL OF WICKETS			
	SA	VIC	VIC
Wkt	1st	1st	2nd
1st	5	74	0
2nd	172	116	0
3rd	184	151	1
4th	280	151	34
5th	460	176	76
6th	501	179	98
7th	506	194	98
8th	520	204	157
9th	562	223	162
10th	-	235	163

SOUTH AUSTRALIA v LORD SHEFFIELD'S ENGLAND XI

Played at Adelaide Oval on November 20, 21, 23, 1891. (Timeless match)
Toss : England XI   Result : LORD SHEFFIELD'S ENGLAND XI WON BY AN INNINGS AND 62 RUNS.
Debuts: - Nil.
12th Men: None named.
Umpires: I.A.Fisher and G.H.G.Searcy.
Attendances: 4000, 9000, 3000.   Total: 16,349.   Receipts: No figures published.
Close of Play: 1st day Eng 0/2 (Bean 2, Briggs 0); 2nd day Eng 323 all out.

Sent in by Grace on a pitch still damp from persistent rain on the days preceding the match, George Giffen attempted to buy time by opening with his rabbits, Scrymgour and Delaney, followed by Alfred Jarvis. Both openers registered their highest scores for South Australia and Jarvis also did his job, but the recognised batsmen were unable to take advantage. The second innings was played in perfect conditions, Attewell bowling unchanged to complete a match haul of 11 for 81, continuing his form from the 1887-88 tour with Vernon's Team. Briggs (91 in 135 minutes, 13 fours), Stoddart (78 in 95 minutes, 10 fours) and Read (60 in 95 minutes, 2 fives and 4 fours) hit fifties for the visitors. Fisher replaced W.Slight (business) after the original umpiring appointments were made. Scrymgour had replaced J.Noel (unavailable) in the local team. The match finished at 3.30pm and the Englishmen played an exhibition innings to appease the crowd. The scores: W.G.Grace c A.Jarvis b Haldane 48, O.G.Radcliffe lbw b A.Jarvis 59, H.Philipson not out 17, G.MacGregor not out 3, byes 2, total 2/129; bowling, Jarvis 1/2, Haldane 1/45, Delaney, Reedman and Lyons no details. Sources: *Wisden, C.B.O'Reilly, Adelaide Advertiser, South Australian Register.*

SOUTH AUSTRALIA

B.V.Scrymgour	b Attewell	37	(8)	b Attewell	0
W.Delaney	c Abel b Lohmann	20	(10)	b Briggs	0
A.Jarvis	b Lohmann	28	(9)	c Grace b Briggs	0
J.J.Lyons	c Stoddart b Attewell	13	(1)	b Peel	8
*G.Giffen	c Grace b Peel	27	(3)	b Attewell	1
H.Haldane	b Attewell	0	(4)	c & b Attewell	1
W.F.Giffen	b Attewell	0	(6)	not out	42
†A.H.Jarvis	c Abel b Sharpe	15	(2)	b Attewell	17
H.Blinman	run out (MacGregor)	1	(5)	c Grace b Attewell	7
J.C.Reedman	not out	13	(7)	b Attewell	15
C.W.Hayward	b Attewell	0		c & b Briggs	1
Extras	(b6, lb1, nb2)	9		(b6)	6
Total	(120.4 overs, 267 mins)	163		(78.3 overs, 195 mins)	98

LORD SHEFFIELD'S ENGLAND XI

G.Bean	b G.Giffen	15
J.Briggs	c & b G.Giffen	91
*W.G.Grace	c Reedman b G.Giffen	2
A.E.Stoddart	c Haldane b G.Giffen	78
R.Abel	c A.H.Jarvis b Haldane	23
J.M.Read	c A.Jarvis b Haldane	60
R.Peel	lbw b G.Giffen	19
G.A.Lohmann	c Blinman b G.Giffen	9
W.Attewell	c Blinman b Haldane	17
†G.MacGregor	c Scrymgour b G.Giffen	8
J.W.Sharpe	not out	0
Extras	(w1)	1
Total	(98.1 overs, 285 mins)	323

ENGLAND XI	O	M	R	W	w,nb		O	M	R	W	w,nb
Lohmann	44	20	74	2	-,2	(4)	2	1	5	0	-,-
Briggs	5	1	10	0	-,-	(5)	7.3	1	19	3	-,-
Sharpe	17	7	18	1	-,-		9	8	3	0	-,-
Attewell	44.4	17	47	5	-,-	(1)	39	20	34	6	-,-
Grace	6	3	4	0	-,-						
Peel	4	3	1	1	-,-	(2)	21	7	31	1	-,-

SOUTH AUSTRALIA	O	M	R	W	w,nb
G.Giffen	41	5	152	7	-,-
Delaney	16	3	47	0	-,-
A.Jarvis	12	2	34	0	-,-
Reedman	5	0	29	0	-,-
Lyons	10	2	34	0	-,-
Haldane	14.1	4	26	3	1,-

FALL OF WICKETS

	SA	ENG	SA
Wkt	1st	1st	2nd
1st	63	40	9
2nd	63	42	10
3rd	90	182	12
4th	107	187	33
5th	108	247	42
6th	112	289	91
7th	139	291	91
8th	140	305	92
9th	162	323	94
10th	163	323	98

VICTORIA v LORD SHEFFIELD'S ENGLAND XI

Played at Melbourne Cricket Ground on November 27, 28, 1891. (Timeless match)
Toss : Victoria.   Result : LORD SHEFFIELD'S ENGLAND XI WON BY AN INNINGS AND 107 RUNS.
Debuts: Victoria - B.C.E.Kemp (Vic only).
12th Men: F.H.Walters (Vic) and H.Philipson (Eng).
Umpires: D.F.Cotter and J.Phillips.
Attendances: 5000, 14000.   Total: About 19,000.   Receipts: No figures published.
Close of Play: 1st day Eng 4/185 (Grace 102, Read 1).

Phillips, the Victorian professional, was chosen to play with the home team but asked the VCA to increase his payment from £5 to £10 to match the fee offered by Lord Sheffield's Team for his umpiring services. This was refused, so he withdrew and acted as the visitors' official instead of the appointed R.M.Crockett. A "smart shower" preceded the opening and the wicket "played less easily than had been anticipated" but was "in excellent order" (*Age*) on the following day. Attewell bowled unchanged throughout both innings, with excellent support from Sharpe and Lohmann alternately. Grace (159 not out in 265 minutes, 1 five and 13 fours), who was badly missed by Morris at third man off Kemp when 14, became the first touring player to carry his bat through an innings in Australia. As there was no tea break - the visitors began batting at 3.30pm and after 35 minutes "the bell rang for an adjournment but the players wisely declined to accept the invitation" (*Age*) - Grace technically scored a century in the last session. Kemp (ex-South Australia) played his first match for Victoria. R.Peel (pleurisy) could not be considered for the tourists. *VCA Report* incorrectly gives Grace 156, Stoddart 19, Read 0, Briggs 15, Radcliffe 16, Attewell 3, MacGregor 6, Sharpe 0. Sources: *Wisden, VCA Report, The Age, The Argus, The Herald, The Australasian, The Leader*.

VICTORIA

Batsman	1st innings		2nd innings	
R.S.Houston	b Sharpe	6	b Attewell	4
W.Bruce	b Attewell	5	lbw b Attewell	25
G.H.S.Trott	c Lohmann b Sharpe	15	b Attewell	9
J.E.Barrett	c Attewell b Sharpe	6	c MacGregor b Attewell	1
C.H.Ross	b Sharpe	1	c Briggs b Lohmann	25
S.Morris	c Grace b Sharpe	7	b Lohmann	0
H.Trumble	c Briggs b Attewell	8	st MacGregor b Lohmann	6
J.Worrall	b Sharpe	0	lbw b Attewell	0
*†J.M.Blackham	c & b Attewell	5	not out	20
J.Carlton	not out	17	c Sharpe b Lohmann	10
B.C.E.Kemp	c MacGregor b Attewell	2	b Lohmann	0
Extras	(b1)	1	(lb3, nb1)	4
Total	(54.1 overs, 135 mins)	73	(41.2 overs, 119 mins)	104

LORD SHEFFIELD'S ENGLAND XI

*W.G.Grace	not out	159
R.Abel	b Worrall	29
G.A.Lohmann	c Worrall b Bruce	39
A.E.Stoddart	c Trumble b Barrett	10
G.Bean	c Trott b Barrett	0
J.M.Read	c Worrall b Trumble	5
J.Briggs	b Barrett	16
O.G.Radcliffe	c Trumble b Worrall	13
W.Attewell	b Trott	6
†G.MacGregor	b Trott	0
J.W.Sharpe	c Houston b Barrett	1
Extras	(b4, nb2)	6
Total	(103.0 overs, 265 mins)	284

ENGLAND XI	O	M	R	W	w,nb		O	M	R	W	w,nb
Attewell	27.1	17	26	4	-,-		21	6	41	5	-,1
Sharpe	25	9	40	6	-,-		6	2	18	0	-,-
Briggs	2	0	6	0	-,-						
Lohmann						(3)	14.2	1	41	5	-,-

VICTORIA	O	M	R	W	w,nb
Trumble	19	6	51	1	-,2
Kemp	5	0	28	0	-,-
Carlton	5	0	20	0	-,-
Worrall	19	6	41	2	-,-
Morris	10	1	24	0	-,-
Ross	5	0	19	0	-,-
Barrett	27	8	51	4	-,-
Bruce	5	0	29	1	-,-
Trott	8	2	15	2	-,-

FALL OF WICKETS

Wkt	VIC 1st	ENG 1st	VIC 2nd
1st	9	91	24
2nd	11	161	38
3rd	17	176	41
4th	23	180	54
5th	35	193	61
6th	44	222	72
7th	44	258	72
8th	51	279	82
9th	58	279	100
10th	73	284	104

NEW SOUTH WALES v LORD SHEFFIELD'S ENGLAND XI

Played at Sydney Cricket Ground on December 4, 5, 7, 1891. (Timeless match)
Toss : England XI.   Result : LORD SHEFFIELD'S ENGLAND XI WON BY FOUR WICKETS.
Debuts: - Nil.
12th Men: W.A.Richardson (NSW) and O.G.Radcliffe (Eng).
Umpires: E.J.Briscoe and A.Shaw.
Attendances: 6000, 20000, 12000.   Total: About 38,000.   Receipts: About £1800.
Close of Play: 1st day Eng 4/47 (Read 16, Bean 2); 2nd day NSW (2) 5/132 (Moses 30, Gregory 11).

The start of the match was delayed 50 minutes because Moses objected to the Englishmen appointing D.F.Cotter, a Victorian, as their umpire. The New South Wales players were still peeved over Cotter's decision against A.C.Bannerman in the previous season's match at Melbourne, when the batsman was given out to a catch at the wicket before he had scored. Alfred Shaw, the England Manager, finally replaced Cotter to avoid any dissent over decisions. Several showers on the first day caused brief interruptions and livened up the pitch, which led to the low scores. Moses (51 in about 180 minutes, 6 fours) compiled the only half-century and Jones, Newell and Briggs all recorded pairs of spectacles. Turner (11 for 122) bowled unchanged in the first innings and went one better in the second, sending down 44 out of 85 overs - he must have bowled consecutive overs at some stage. *Wisden* incorrectly gives NSW (2) Bannerman 9, Moses 55, Gregory 19, extras 3, Grace 0/7. Sources: *Wisden, The Australasian, Sydney Referee, Sydney Morning Herald, Town & Country Journal, Sydney Mail.*

NEW SOUTH WALES

Batsman	Dismissal (1st)	Score		Dismissal (2nd)	Score
S.P.Jones	c & b Lohmann	0		c MacGregor b Attewell	0
A.C.Bannerman	c Grace b Briggs	25		st MacGregor b Attewell	7
C.T.B.Turner	c Stoddart b Lohmann	2	(4)	c Abel b Peel	40
H.Donnan	c MacGregor b Briggs	11	(3)	b Sharpe	32
*H.Moses	c Attewell b Lohmann	0		c Sharpe b Lohmann	51
F.A.Iredale	c Read b Lohmann	4		c & b Lohmann	9
S.E.Gregory	c Grace b Attewell	15		c MacGregor b Attewell	21
P.C.Charlton	c & b Briggs	3		lbw b Attewell	0
S.T.Callaway	not out	12		b Attewell	3
A.L.Newell	c Sharpe b Briggs	0		b Attewell	0
†I.F.Wales	c Peel b Briggs	0		not out	2
Extras	(b1, lb1)	2		(b5, lb2)	7
Total	(74.4 overs, 170 mins)	74		(135.4 overs, 295 mins)	172

LORD SHEFFIELD'S ENGLAND XI

Batsman	Dismissal (1st)	Score	Dismissal (2nd)	Score
R.Abel	c Bannerman b Turner	7	c Wales b Charlton	31
*W.G.Grace	c Turner b Callaway	15	c & b Turner	19
A.E.Stoddart	c Donnan b Turner	4	b Turner	28
J.M.Read	run out (Wales)	20	c Bannerman b Turner	6
J.Briggs	b Turner	0	c Wales b Turner	0
G.Bean	c Charlton b Turner	17	c Gregory b Turner	4
G.A.Lohmann	c Charlton b Turner	7	not out	34
R.Peel	c Jones b Turner	0	not out	26
W.Attewell	c Callaway b Charlton	0		
†G.MacGregor	not out	12		
J.W.Sharpe	c Callaway b Charlton	7		
Extras	(b2, lb3)	5	(b5, lb2)	7
Total	(37.2 overs, 105 mins)	94	(85.4 overs, 205 mins) (6 wkts)	155

ENGLAND XI	O	M	R	W	w,nb		O	M	R	W	w,nb
Attewell	18	10	18	1	-,-		34	15	49	6	-,-
Lohmann	33	13	44	4	-,-	(4)	32.4	17	35	2	-,-
Briggs	23.4	16	10	5	-,-	(2)	8	3	12	0	-,-
Sharpe						(3)	38	20	53	1	-,-
Peel							19	13	13	1	-,-
Grace							4	1	3	0	-,-

NEW SOUTH WALES	O	M	R	W	w,nb	O	M	R	W	w,nb
Turner	19	6	45	6	-,-	44	16	77	5	-,-
Callaway	11	2	31	1	-,-	21	10	25	0	-,-
Charlton	7.2	2	13	2	-,-	16	7	29	1	-,-
Newell						3	0	10	0	-,-
Donnan						1.4	0	7	0	-,-

FALL OF WICKETS

Wkt	NSW 1st	ENG 1st	NSW 2nd	ENG 2nd
1st	5	22	0	36
2nd	10	27	26	56
3rd	36	38	77	69
4th	37	38	85	69
5th	41	55	106	85
6th	43	66	162	88
7th	49	74	162	-
8th	71	75	170	-
9th	74	77	170	-
10th	74	94	172	-

VICTORIA v NEW SOUTH WALES

Played at Melbourne Cricket Ground on December 26, 28, 29, 30, 1891. (Timeless match)
Toss : New South Wales.   Result : VICTORIA WON BY SIX WICKETS.
Debuts: Victoria - S.A.McMichael (f/c).
12th Men: G.Beacham (Vic) and A.C.K.Mackenzie (NSW).
Umpires: E.J.Briscoe and T.Flynn.
Attendances: 12000, 9000, 5000, 1000.   Total: About 27,000.   Receipts: £1070.
Close of Play: 1st day NSW 8/191 (Richardson 12, Callaway 6); 2nd day Vic 5/220 (McLeod 85, Phillips 60); 3rd day NSW (2) 7/121
     (Callaway 27, Garrett 4).

South Melbourne district players J.E.Barrett, G.H.S.Trott and A.N.A.Bowman (emergency) withdrew from the Victorian team in protest at the selection committee's omission of fellow club cricketers B.C.E.Kemp and S.Morris. (Both had played in Victoria's last match against Lord Sheffield's Team.) J.Carlton and Tarrant were named as replacements for Barrett and Trott but Carlton was unavailable and McMichael was brought in. McLeod (87 in about 210 minutes, 6 fours) shared a decisive stand of 135 with Phillips (85 in about 225 minutes, 5 fours, several chances) for the Victorian sixth wicket and captured seven wickets in a fine allround performance. Callaway took the wickets of Blackham and McMichael with successive deliveries (McMichael out first ball on debut) and came close to a hat-trick when Turner in the slips missed Tarrant from the next ball. Donnan (54 in about 150 minutes, 1 five and 2 fours) was the only New South Wales batsman to exceed fifty in the match. Last first-class appearance by T.P.Horan. *Wisden* incorrectly gives NSW (2) Donnan 9, extras 5; Vic (2) Worrall c Iredale b Callaway, Turner 0/25, Callaway 3/34. Sources: *Wisden, VCA Report, The Age, The Argus, The Herald, The Australasian, The Leader.*

NEW SOUTH WALES

A.C.Bannerman	b Phillips	23		c Blackham b McLeod	14
H.Donnan	c Blackham b McLeod	54		b McLeod	10
*H.Moses	c Blackham b Phillips	25		b Worrall	37
C.T.B.Turner	c Phillips b McLeod	11	(6)	b Bruce	3
F.A.Iredale	c Horan b Trumble	32		b Bruce	0
S.E.Gregory	run out (Worrall/McLeod)	5	(4)	run out (Bruce/Blackham)	22
P.C.Charlton	b Worrall	5	(11)	not out	3
W.A.Richardson	b McLeod	15		run out (Ross)	0
T.W.Garrett	c Trumble b McLeod	10		run out (Bruce/Blackham)	12
S.T.Callaway	not out	17	(7)	c McMichael b Trumble	34
†I.F.Wales	b Trumble	13	(10)	lbw b McLeod	4
Extras	(b8)	8		(b2, w2)	4
Total	(119.3 overs, 297 mins)	218		(84.0 overs, 212 mins)	143

VICTORIA

F.H.Walters	lbw b Callaway	6	(2)	c Wales b Garrett	34
W.Bruce	b Turner	17	(1)	c Garrett b Callaway	11
T.P.Horan	b Callaway	7		b Callaway	1
J.Worrall	c Iredale b Turner	13		c Iredale b Turner	11
R.W.McLeod	b Callaway	87		not out	6
C.H.Ross	c Wales b Charlton	28		not out	1
J.Phillips	lbw b Callaway	85			
*†J.M.Blackham	b Callaway	0			
S.A.McMichael	b Callaway	0			
W.A.Tarrant	c Callaway b Garrett	26			
H.Trumble	not out	11			
Extras	(b7, lb1, w1, nb1)	10		(b7, lb1)	8
Total	(133.5 overs, 335 mins)	290		(36.4 overs, 98 mins) (4 wkts)	72

VICTORIA	O	M	R	W	w,nb		O	M	R	W	w,nb
McLeod	37	17	54	4	-,-		29	10	53	3	-,-
Trumble	31.3	10	63	2	-,-		18	6	32	1	-,-
Ross	3	0	8	0	-,-						
Phillips	31	17	38	2	-,-		11	4	20	0	-,-
Worrall	10	3	22	1	-,-		5	3	11	1	-,-
Bruce	7	2	25	0	-,-	(3)	21	10	23	2	2,-

NEW SOUTH WALES	O	M	R	W	w,nb		O	M	R	W	w,nb
Turner	51	20	95	2	-,1	(2)	17	7	25	1	-,-
Callaway	38.5	10	85	6	-,-	(1)	14	3	34	2	-,-
Richardson	5	0	15	0	-,-						
Charlton	9	2	19	1	-,-						
Garrett	22	4	47	1	1,-	(3)	5.4	3	5	1	-,-
Donnan	6	3	15	0	-,-						
Gregory	2	0	4	0	-,-						

FALL OF WICKETS

	NSW	VIC	NSW	VIC
Wkt	1st	1st	2nd	2nd
1st	65	13	18	22
2nd	87	27	27	36
3rd	113	31	65	65
4th	115	48	68	68
5th	123	91	72	-
6th	147	226	107	-
7th	163	226	107	-
8th	182	226	131	-
9th	194	274	140	-
10th	218	290	143	-

AUSTRALIA v ENGLAND (1st Test)

Played at Melbourne Cricket Ground on January 1, 2, 4, 5, 6, 1892. (Timeless match)
Toss : Australia.   Result : AUSTRALIA WON BY 54 RUNS.
Debuts: Australia - S.T.Callaway, H.Donnan, R.W.McLeod (all Test). England - G.Bean (Test).
12th Men: S.E.Gregory (Aust). No 12th named for Eng.
Umpires: T.Flynn and J.Phillips.
Attendances: 20110, 20101, 10441, 10000, 3000.   Total: 63,652.   Receipts: £3091.
Close of Play: 1st day Aust 7/191 (Moses 23, Callaway 11); 2nd day Eng 7/248 (Briggs 41, Attewell 7); 3rd day Aust (2) 5/152 (Moses 0, Trott 0); 4th day Eng (2) 7/104 (Abel 16, MacGregor 3).

This match, the first Test to reach a fifth playing day and Australia's first to be played in what became known as The Golden Age, saw a remarkable revival of interest in international cricket fixtures in this country. The attendance of 63,652 - 46,908 of whom paid, the balance being members - was easily a record for any game in Australia up to this time. It was also the first Test in Australia in which the six-ball over was used. Bean made an impressive Test debut in batting 65 minutes (50 with 5 fours) on the second day. Grace (50 in 75 minutes, 1 five and 3 fours), Bruce (57 in 115 minutes, 4 fours) and Lyons (51 in 90 minutes, 1 four) also recorded half-centuries in excellent batting conditions. McLeod took his first three Test wickets (Abel, Grace and Stoddart) in a five-ball spell (WW00W) spread over two overs on the second day. Bannerman (45 in 195 minutes, 4 fours and 41 in 230 minutes, 1 four) occupied the crease for more than seven hours for 86 runs. He scored just 7 runs, progressing from 12 to 19, in the 100-minute lunch-tea session on the third day. Moses "wrenched his leg badly" (*Age*) early in his first innings and had Giffen to run for him; he was out to the third ball of the second day. Giffen again acted as his runner in the early part of the second innings but Blackham took over for the fourth day's play. Moses was unable to field at all, Gregory substituting throughout both England innings. *Wisden* gives Eng (1) Read 38, extras 12, McLeod 5/55. Sources: *Wisden, The Age, The Argus, The Herald, The Australasian, The Leader.*

AUSTRALIA

A.C.Bannerman	c Read b Sharpe	45	c Grace b Sharpe		41
J.J.Lyons	c Grace b Peel	19	c Abel b Briggs		51
G.Giffen	lbw b Peel	2	b Attewell		1
W.Bruce	b Sharpe	57	c Lohmann b Sharpe		40
H.Donnan	b Sharpe	9	c & b Lohmann	(9)	2
H.Moses	c Lohmann b Sharpe	23	run out (Sharpe)		15
G.H.S.Trott	c MacGregor b Sharpe	6	lbw b Attewell		23
R.W.McLeod	b Sharpe	14	b Peel		31
S.T.Callaway	b Attewell	21	not out	(10)	13
C.T.B.Turner	b Peel	29	c Peel b Lohmann	(5)	19
*†J.M.Blackham	not out	4	c MacGregor b Peel		0
Extras	(b5, lb6)	11			-
Total	(151.1 overs, 335 mins)	240	(191.5 overs, 350 mins)		236

ENGLAND

*W.G.Grace	b McLeod	50	c Bannerman b Turner		25
R.Abel	b McLeod	32	c Blackham b Turner	(5)	28
G.Bean	c Bruce b Giffen	50	c McLeod b Trott		3
A.E.Stoddart	c Giffen b McLeod	0	b Callaway	(2)	35
J.M.Read	c & b Giffen	36	b Trott	(4)	11
R.Peel	b McLeod	19	b Turner		6
G.A.Lohmann	lbw b Giffen	3	c Bannerman b Turner		0
J.Briggs	c Bruce b Turner	41	c Trott b McLeod		4
W.Attewell	c Bannerman b Turner	8	c Donnan b Turner	(10)	24
†G.MacGregor	not out	9	c sub (S.E.Gregory) b Trott	(9)	16
J.W.Sharpe	c Blackham b McLeod	2	not out		5
Extras	(b9, lb2, nb3)	14	(lb1)		1
Total	(91.4 overs, 245 mins)	264	(82.2 overs, 210 mins)		158

ENGLAND	O	M	R	W	w,nb		O	M	R	W	w,nb		FALL OF WICKETS			
Sharpe	51	20	84	6	-,-		54	25	81	2	-,-			AUST	ENG	AUST	ENG
Peel	43	23	54	3	-,-		16.5	7	25	2	-,-		Wkt	1st	1st	2nd	2nd
Attewell	21.1	11	28	1	-,-	(4)	61	32	51	2	-,-		1st	32	84	66	60
Lohmann	28	14	40	0	-,-	(3)	39	15	53	2	-,-		2nd	36	85	67	60
Briggs	3	1	13	0	-,-		21	9	26	1	-,-		3rd	123	85	120	71
Stoddart	5	2	10	0	-,-								4th	136	171	152	75
													5th	136	179	152	93
AUSTRALIA	O	M	R	W	w,nb		O	M	R	W	w,nb		6th	148	187	182	93
Trott	10	2	25	0	-,-	(3)	19	2	52	3	-,-		7th	168	232	197	98
Giffen	20	3	75	3	-,3	(5)	3	0	8	0	-,-		8th	191	249	210	125
Turner	16	3	40	2	-,-	(2)	33.2	14	51	5	-,-		9th	232	256	236	139
McLeod	28.4	12	53	5	-,-	(1)	23	8	39	1	-,-		10th	240	264	236	158
Callaway	14	2	39	0	-,-	(4)	4	1	7	1	-,-						
Bruce	3	0	18	0	-,-												

NEW SOUTH WALES v SOUTH AUSTRALIA

Played at Sydney Cricket Ground on January 8, 9, 11, 12 (no play), 13, 1892. (Timeless match)
Toss : New South Wales.   Result : SOUTH AUSTRALIA WON BY AN INNINGS AND 53 RUNS.
Debuts: New South Wales - J.C.Wilson (f/c).
12th Men: W.W.McGlinchey (NSW) and W.Delaney (SA).
Umpires: A.Chizlett and W.Slight.
Attendances & Receipts: No figures published.
Close of Play: 1st day NSW 215 all out; 2nd day SA 2/249 (G.Giffen 95, W.F.Giffen 1); 3rd day SA 2/289 (G.Giffen 120,
     W.F.Giffen 14); 4th day no play.

South Australia defeated New South Wales for the first time in the third meeting between the teams. Rain caused severe delays, restricting play to 3 hours on the second day, 1 hour on the third and preventing play at all on the fourth. Batting became almost impossible as the wicket dried on the fifth day and the fate of the home team was sealed. Giffen recorded his fourth instance in Australia of a century and ten wickets in the same match. He bowled unchanged through both New South Wales innings, capturing seven wickets on the first day when conditions favoured batting and another five on the last day when they did not. With the bat he partnered Lyons in a second-wicket stand of 234, a new South Australian record for any wicket, scoring 120 in 235 minutes (243 balls, 13 fours) including two chances after he reached three figures. Lyons, who had been missed by Mackenzie at long-on in the first over of the innings, plundered the bowling to score 145 in 170 minutes (140 balls, 21 fours); "his great punishing powers were highly appreciated by the spectators" (*SMH*). E.J.Briscoe, nominated as the home umpire, was unavailable and Chizlett replaced him. P.C.Charlton (cut hand) and H.Moses (injured leg) were unavailable for New South Wales. Donnan was out first ball in the second innings. Sources: *Wisden, C.B.O'Reilly, Sydney Referee, Sydney Morning Herald, Town & Country Journal, Sydney Daily Telegraph.*

NEW SOUTH WALES

A.C.Bannerman	c & b G.Giffen	36	c W.F.Giffen b A.Jarvis	4
S.P.Jones	lbw b A.Jarvis	27	c Reedman b A.Jarvis	12
H.Donnan	c A.H.Jarvis b Noel	30	c Reedman b A.Jarvis	0
F.A.Iredale	c Noel b G.Giffen	1	c Noel b G.Giffen	1
*C.T.B.Turner	c Hayward b G.Giffen	16	c & b A.Jarvis	3
S.E.Gregory	c Blinman b G.Giffen	11	c Blinman b G.Giffen	13
S.T.Callaway	run out (Wilkinson/Noel)	8	st A.H.Jarvis b G.Giffen	7
A.E.Clarke	c A.H.Jarvis b G.Giffen	14	c Reedman b G.Giffen	18
A.C.K.Mackenzie	c A.Jarvis b G.Giffen	25	st A.H.Jarvis b G.Giffen	0
J.C.Wilson	not out	15	c W.F.Giffen b A.Jarvis	2
†I.F.Wales	c Reedman b G.Giffen	21	not out	1
Extras	(b10, w1)	11	(lb1)	1
Total	(109.3 overs, 285 mins)	215	(24.0 overs, 95 mins)	62

SOUTH AUSTRALIA

J.J.Lyons	c Gregory b Callaway	145
†A.H.Jarvis	c & b Callaway	5
*G.Giffen	c Clarke b Callaway	120
W.F.Giffen	c Jones b Callaway	25
H.Haldane	c Wilson b Callaway	10
J.C.Reedman	b Callaway	0
A.Jarvis	c Wilson b Turner	11
A.Wilkinson	lbw b Turner	4
J.Noel	b Turner	0
H.Blinman	not out	0
C.W.Hayward	c Iredale b Turner	2
Extras	(b7, w1)	8
Total	(110.1 overs, 290 mins)	330

SOUTH AUSTRALIA	O	M	R	W	w,nb		O	M	R	W	w,nb
A.Jarvis	29	13	47	1	-,-		12	6	33	5	-,-
G.Giffen	54.3	19	122	7	-,-		12	3	28	5	-,-
Noel	19	8	29	1	-,-						
Haldane	7	4	6	0	1,-						

NEW SOUTH WALES	O	M	R	W	w,nb
Turner	41.1	13	132	4	-,-
Callaway	48	17	95	6	-,-
Donnan	6	0	15	0	-,-
Wilson	4	0	21	0	-,-
Bannerman	7	0	34	0	1,-
Clarke	1	0	13	0	-,-
Jones	3	0	12	0	-,-

FALL OF WICKETS

Wkt	NSW 1st	SA 1st	NSW 2nd
1st	41	10	8
2nd	91	244	8
3rd	102	291	13
4th	103	307	17
5th	128	307	34
6th	136	322	39
7th	137	327	41
8th	169	327	53
9th	184	328	58
10th	215	330	62

NEW SOUTH WALES v VICTORIA

Played at Sydney Cricket Ground on January 23, 25, 26, 27, 1892. (Timeless match)
Toss : New South Wales.　　　　　Result : VICTORIA WON BY AN INNINGS AND 15 RUNS.
Debuts: Victoria - E.H.Hutton (f/c).
12th Men: W.W.McGlinchey (NSW) and J.Carlton (Vic).
Umpires: T.Flynn and D.W.Gregory.
Attendances & Receipts: No figures published.
Close of Play: 1st day NSW 6/171 (Callaway 9); 2nd day Vic 3/194 (Walters 101, Worrall 23); 3rd day NSW (2) 8/136 (Callaway 21, Charlton 2).

Hutton was included in the Victorian team before its departure from Melbourne to replace J.Phillips, who withdrew because of another dispute with the VCA over his match fees. Their offer of £5 fell well short of his demand of £10. H.Moses was still unavailable for New South Wales because of his leg injury sustained in the First Test. Turner (66 in about 135 minutes, 6 fours and 45 in 75 minutes, 7 fours) topscored in each innings for the home side whose batsmen struggled. Victoria by contrast took the lead after two days, batting only 160 minutes to reach 3/194. Walters (112 in about 180 minutes, 19 fours) gave a difficult chance to Callaway at slip in the eighties and another at 107. "He played a fine defensive game, without being slow" (*SMH*). Tarrant (82 in about 165 minutes, 8 fours) "played an excellent game..., combining good defence with plenty of punishing capacity, especially on the off side" (*SMH*). New South Wales lost Bannerman and Garrett to the second and fourth balls of their second innings, and Mackenzie fell to his first ball in the later stages. *VCA Report* incorrectly gives NSW (2) Worrall 0/15. Sources: *Wisden, VCA Report, Sydney Referee, Sydney Morning Herald, Town & Country Journal, Sydney Mail, Sydney Daily Telegraph*.

NEW SOUTH WALES

A.C.Bannerman	c Tarrant b Trumble	4		c Trumble b McLeod	0
H.Donnan	b Trumble	24	(6)	run out (Hutton/Blackham)	0
A.E.Clarke	c Trumble b McLeod	0	(7)	c Houston b McLeod	4
C.A.Richardson	lbw b Hutton	31	(5)	b Trumble	12
C.T.B.Turner	c Ross b McLeod	66	(4)	lbw b McLeod	45
S.E.Gregory	lbw b Worrall	28	(2)	st Blackham b Trott	44
S.T.Callaway	b Worrall	14	(8)	run out (Hutton)	23
A.C.K.Mackenzie	b Worrall	1	(9)	b Trumble	0
P.C.Charlton	c Blackham b McLeod	4	(10)	not out	18
*T.W.Garrett	not out	7	(3)	c Trumble b McLeod	0
†I.F.Wales	lbw b Worrall	5		c & b Trumble	8
Extras	(b5, lb3, w1)	9		(b4, lb1, w3)	8
Total	(110.2 overs, 255 mins)	193		(61.1 overs, 135 mins)	162

VICTORIA

W.Bruce	b Charlton	33
F.H.Walters	b Donnan	112
G.H.S.Trott	b Turner	5
R.W.McLeod	c Donnan b Turner	25
J.Worrall	b Turner	23
C.H.Ross	c Wales b Turner	18
W.A.Tarrant	b Donnan	82
R.S.Houston	b Donnan	17
E.H.Hutton	c Callaway b Turner	2
*†J.M.Blackham	b Callaway	33
H.Trumble	not out	11
Extras	(b6, lb3)	9
Total	(146.0 overs, 345 mins)	370

VICTORIA	O	M	R	W	w,nb		O	M	R	W	w,nb
Trumble	31	14	37	2	-,-	(2)	16.1	7	42	3	-,-
McLeod	40	21	58	3	-,-	(1)	23	11	46	4	-,-
Trott	8	1	30	0	-,-	(5)	6	1	26	1	-,-
Bruce	3	0	11	0	1,-		10	4	15	0	3,-
Hutton	10	3	20	1	-,-						
Ross	4	0	7	0	-,-						
Worrall	14.2	8	21	4	-,-	(3)	6	0	25	0	-,-

NEW SOUTH WALES	O	M	R	W	w,nb
Garrett	10	3	25	0	-,-
Callaway	19	7	41	1	-,-
Turner	58	27	146	5	-,-
Charlton	32	11	89	1	-,-
Donnan	27	11	60	3	-,-

FALL OF WICKETS

Wkt	NSW 1st	VIC 1st	NSW 2nd
1st	18	63	0
2nd	19	68	0
3rd	29	150	66
4th	117	194	103
5th	157	206	108
6th	171	244	112
7th	175	285	125
8th	180	300	125
9th	182	342	140
10th	193	370	162

AUSTRALIA v ENGLAND (2nd Test)

Played at Sydney Cricket Ground on January 29, 30, February 1, 2, 3, 1892. (Timeless match)
Toss : Australia.   Result : AUSTRALIA WON BY 72 RUNS.
Debuts: - Nil.
12th Men: S.E.Gregory (Aust). No 12th named for Eng.
Umpires: T.Flynn and J.A.Tooher.
Attendances: 7184, 20169, 8704, 9949, 6972.   Total: 52,978.   Receipts: £2828.
Close of Play: 1st day Eng 0/38 (Grace 23, Abel 15); 2nd day Aust (2) 1/1 (Bannerman 0); 3rd day Aust (2) 3/263 (Bannerman 67,
   Bruce 5); 4th day Eng (2) 3/11 (Stoddart 1).

With this victory Australia could lay claim to the real Ashes for the first time. However, the legend of the urn did not gain popular acceptance until the early years of the 20th Century. Abel (132 not out in 314 minutes, 11 fours, chance at 77) was the first Englishman to carry his bat through a completed Test Innings. Bannerman (a tedious 91 in 421 minutes, 3 fours) and Lyons (134 in 185 minutes, 16 fours, 2 chances at 49) got Australia back into the game on the third day with innings of contrast, Lyons scoring his sole Test century. Bruce (72 in 108 minutes, 8 fours) also batted well. Briggs took the wickets of Walter Giffen, Blackham and Callaway in succession to end Australia's second innings with a hat-trick. Attewell suffered a king pair. Stoddart (69 in 137 minutes, 5 fours) played a lone hand in the second innings to no avail. Moses, who had elected to play despite his leg injury from the previous Test not having fully recovered, severely aggravated the injury while running a sharp single on the first day and was lame for the rest of the match. Grace, who had made it known prior to the match that, should Moses break down, he would not allow either a runner or a substitute fieldsman to do his workload, kept his word on the first day (Moses hobbled about at slip while England batted) but relented on the second and allowed T.W.Garrett to field in Moses's place. McLeod, who received news of the death of a brother, was absent from the tea adjournment on the fourth day onwards; he threw away his wicket just before the break so he could catch the train to Melbourne that afternoon. H.Donnan fielded for him and the Australians wore black armbands on the last two days in memory of McLeod's brother. Lyons's 41 (56 minutes) on the first day included two fives off Lohmann's bowling, one of which "dropped with a crash on to the roof of the Ladies' Stand" (*SMH*). *Wisden* incorrectly gives Aust (1) extras 7, total 145. Sources: *Wisden, Sydney Referee, Sydney Morning Herald, Town & Country Journal, NSWCA Scorebook, Sydney Mail.*

AUSTRALIA

A.C.Bannerman	c Abel b Lohmann	12		c Grace b Briggs	91
J.J.Lyons	c Grace b Lohmann	41	(3)	c Grace b Lohmann	134
G.Giffen	c Abel b Lohmann	6	(4)	lbw b Attewell	49
H.Moses	c Grace b Lohmann	29		absent hurt	-
C.T.B.Turner	c MacGregor b Lohmann	15	(7)	not out	14
W.Bruce	c Bean b Attewell	15	(5)	c Briggs b Sharpe	72
G.H.S.Trott	b Lohmann	2	(2)	c Sharpe b Lohmann	1
R.W.McLeod	c Attewell b Lohmann	13	(6)	c Read b Peel	18
W.F.Giffen	c & b Lohmann	1	(8)	b Briggs	3
S.T.Callaway	run out (Read/Lohmann)	1		c Grace b Briggs	0
*†J.M.Blackham	not out	3	(9)	lbw b Briggs	0
Extras	(b3, lb3)	6		(b6, lb2, w1)	9
Total	(94.2 overs, 219 mins)	144		(219.4 overs, 478 mins)	391

ENGLAND

*W.G.Grace	b Turner	26	c Blackham b Turner	5
R.Abel	not out	132	c W.F.Giffen b G.Giffen	1
G.Bean	b G.Giffen	19	c Lyons b Turner	4
A.E.Stoddart	c Blackham b McLeod	27	b Turner	69
J.M.Read	c Turner b G.Giffen	3	c & b G.Giffen	22
R.Peel	c G.Giffen b Turner	20	st Blackham b G.Giffen	6
G.A.Lohmann	b G.Giffen	10	c Bruce b G.Giffen	15
†G.MacGregor	lbw b McLeod	3	c & b G.Giffen	12
J.Briggs	lbw b Trott	28	c Trott b Turner	12
W.Attewell	b Trott	0	c & b G.Giffen	0
J.W.Sharpe	c Bannerman b G.Giffen	26	not out	4
Extras	(b10, lb2, w1)	13	(b4, lb2)	6
Total	(114.2 overs, 314 mins)	307	(66.2 overs, 177 mins)	156

ENGLAND	O	M	R	W	w,nb		O	M	R	W	w,nb
Briggs	10	2	24	0	-,-	(2)	32.4	8	69	4	-,-
Sharpe	10	1	31	0	-,-	(4)	35	7	91	1	-,-
Lohmann	43.2	18	58	8	-,-	(1)	51	14	84	2	1,-
Attewell	31	20	25	1	-,-	(3)	46	24	43	1	-,-
Peel							35	13	49	1	-,-
Grace							16	2	34	0	-,-
Stoddart							4	1	12	0	-,-

AUSTRALIA	O	M	R	W	w,nb		O	M	R	W	w,nb
Turner	37	11	90	2	1,-		23.2	7	46	4	-,-
McLeod	18	6	55	2	-,-						
G.Giffen	28.2	5	88	4	-,-	(2)	28	10	72	6	-,-
Trott	14	3	42	2	-,-	(3)	5	0	11	0	-,-
Callaway	17	10	19	0	-,-	(4)	10	6	21	0	-,-

FALL OF WICKETS

Wkt	AUST 1st	ENG 1st	AUST 2nd	ENG 2nd
1st	31	50	1	2
2nd	57	79	175	6
3rd	62	123	254	11
4th	90	127	347	64
5th	117	152	364	83
6th	123	167	376	116
7th	126	178	391	134
8th	132	235	391	140
9th	141	235	391	140
10th	144	307	-	156

NEW SOUTH WALES v LORD SHEFFIELD'S ENGLAND XI

Played at Sydney Cricket Ground on February 19, 20, 22, 23, 1892. (Timeless match)
Toss : England XI.   Result : LORD SHEFFIELD'S ENGLAND XI WON BY SEVEN WICKETS.
Debuts: New South Wales - J.W.Gould (f/c).
12th Men: W.Driver (NSW). No 12th named for Eng.
Umpires: E.J.Briscoe and J.Swift (C.Bannerman deputised).
Attendances: ? , 12000, ? , ? .   Total & Receipts: No figures published.
Close of Play: 1st day Eng 5/270 (Read 101, Lohmann 27); 2nd day NSW 2/58 (Bannerman 27, Donnan 19); 3rd day NSW (2) 4/55
(Bannerman 28, Charlton 1).

M.Pierce, C.A.Richardson and H.J.H.Scott withdrew from an invited squad of thirteen and Gould was included to make up the numbers. It had been hoped that Scott, now living at Scone in northern New South Wales, could have been coaxed out of retirement. McDonnell, after a three-year lay-off, returned to play his final match for New South Wales. G.Bean (leg strain) was unavailable for the visitors. J.W.Payne and J.A.Tooher were invited to umpire but, when unavailable, were replaced by Briscoe and Swift. Briscoe refused to continue after receiving abuse from Grace when an appeal for a catch behind against Charlton off Lohmann was turned down on the third day. There was a 45-minute delay before the New South Wales follow-on while a replacement umpire (C.Bannerman) was found, who officiated with Swift for the rest of the match. Read (106 in about 300 minutes, 10 fours) and Lohmann (102 in 155 minutes, 8 fours) put their side in a winning position. Gregory's unbeaten 93 forced the Englishmen to bat again, his batting considered "by far the best cricket of the match" (*SMH*). As in the previous match between the teams in December, five-ball overs were bowled. Sources: *Wisden, The Australasian, Sydney Referee, Sydney Morning Herald, Town & Country Journal, Sydney Mail, Sydney Daily Telegraph.*

LORD SHEFFIELD'S ENGLAND XI

*W.G.Grace	b Callaway	45			
R.Abel	b Callaway	48	(5) not out	0	
J.M.Read	c Callaway b Turner	106			
A.E.Stoddart	b Gould	16	(1) lbw b Turner	17	
R.Peel	b Callaway	29			
O.G.Radcliffe	run out (Clarke/Wales)	0	(2) c Gregory b Turner	18	
G.A.Lohmann	c Gregory b Turner	102			
J.Briggs	c Wales b Gould	6	(3) c Charlton b Callaway	1	
†G.MacGregor	st Wales b Gould	10			
W.Attewell	not out	22	(4) not out	6	
J.W.Sharpe	b Callaway	16			
Extras	(b9, lb2, nb3)	14		–	
Total	(194.4 overs, 450 mins)	414	(17.1 overs, 45 mins) (3 wkts)	42	

NEW SOUTH WALES

*P.S.McDonnell	c Briggs b Lohmann	5		c Sharpe b Lohmann	2
A.C.Bannerman	c Abel b Grace	29		c Grace b Briggs	49
S.P.Jones	b Attewell	5		c Grace b Lohmann	13
H.Donnan	b Grace	19		b Grace	11
C.T.B.Turner	run out (Stoddart/MacGregor)	66	(7)	b Attewell	7
A.E.Clarke	c Briggs b Attewell	33	(9)	c Attewell b Peel	6
S.E.Gregory	c Abel b Lohmann	46	(8)	not out	93
J.W.Gould	lbw b Peel	6	(10)	c Lohmann b Briggs	2
S.T.Callaway	not out	19	(11)	b Attewell	14
P.C.Charlton	c Stoddart b Lohmann	0	(6)	c MacGregor b Lohmann	10
†I.F.Wales	lbw b Grace	11	(5)	c MacGregor b Grace	0
Extras	(b2, lb3)	5		(b3)	3
Total	(173.3 overs, 430 mins)	244		(119.0 overs, 300 mins)	210

NEW SOUTH WALES	O	M	R	W	w,nb		O	M	R	W	w,nb
Turner	53	19	98	2	-,-		8.1	1	23	2	-,-
Gould	36	5	120	3	-,1						
Callaway	62.4	31	92	4	-,2	(2)	7	2	14	1	-,-
Charlton	39	8	77	0	-,-	(3)	2	0	5	0	-,-
Donnan	4	1	13	0	-,-						

ENGLAND XI	O	M	R	W	w,nb		O	M	R	W	w,nb
Attewell	54	31	46	2	-,-	(4)	24	10	38	2	-,-
Lohmann	33	18	46	3	-,-	(1)	40	22	48	3	-,-
Briggs	16	9	17	0	-,-	(5)	17	4	45	?	-,-
Sharpe	22	7	36	0	-,-	(2)	17	7	34	0	-,-
Grace	31.3	9	64	3	-,-	(3)	16	6	29	2	-,-
Peel	17	6	30	1	-,-		5	0	13	1	-,-

FALL OF WICKETS

Wkt	ENG 1st	NSW 1st	NSW 2nd	ENG 2nd
1st	52	9	2	27
2nd	142	18	21	36
3rd	185	60	51	38
4th	224	71	51	-
5th	231	156	71	-
6th	314	174	84	-
7th	336	200	139	-
8th	374	219	158	-
9th	387	223	161	-
10th	414	244	210	-

VICTORIA v LORD SHEFFIELD'S ENGLAND XI

Played at Melbourne Cricket Ground on March 17, 18, 19, 1892. (Timeless match)
Toss : England XI.   Result : LORD SHEFFIELD'S ENGLAND XI WON BY NINE WICKETS.
Debuts: - Nil.
12th Men: H.Graham (Vic) and O.G.Radcliffe (Eng).
Umpires: R.M.Crockett and T.Flynn.
Attendances: 4000, 2500, "a few".   Total: About 6550.   Receipts: No figures published.
Close of Play: 1st day Eng 2/72 (Grace 34, Bean 4); 2nd day Vic (2) 100 all out.

J.M.Blackham stood out of the Victorian team to rest for the Adelaide Test. Pre-match rain prompted Grace to insert the Victorians on a pitch which, though reported to be in a surprisingly good condition, offered sharp spin to the bowlers of both sides. Bruce hit the only half-centuries, 54 (54 minutes, 7 fours) and 50 (55 minutes, 1 five and 2 fours), and scored his runs out of 61 and 72 respectively while he was at the crease. Grace (44 in 160 minutes, 2 fours) survived a chance to Letcher off Trott when 1 but otherwise batted soundly. Only an hour's play was needed on the third day to finish the game and the Englishmen travelled on to Caulfield racecourse for the afternoon. Walters (severe cold) did not field on the final morning, Graham substituting and catching Briggs. *VCA Report* incorrectly gives Vic (2) Trott c & b Briggs. Sources: *Wisden, VCA Report, The Age, The Argus, The Herald, The Australasian, The Leader.*

VICTORIA

Batsman	Dismissal 1		1st	Dismissal 2		2nd
W.Bruce	c & b Peel		54	(2) c Philipson b Attewell		50
A.N.A.Bowman	c Bean b Attewell		3	(1) b Attewell		7
G.H.S.Trott	st Philipson b Peel		4	c Philipson b Briggs		4
F.H.Walters	c Stoddart b Peel		4	(10) not out		15
R.W.McLeod	c Abel b Lohmann		33	c & b Briggs		0
W.A.Tarrant	lbw b Lohmann		7	st Philipson b Briggs		7
C.H.Ross	c & b Peel		5	(4) b Briggs		3
J.Worrall	b Lohmann		9	(9) c Attewell b Lohmann		4
*†R.S.Houston	run out (/Philipson)		11	(8) b Briggs		4
H.Trumble	not out		6	(7) b Attewell		5
C.Letcher	c Peel b Lohmann		0	b Attewell		0
Extras	(lb1)		1	(b1)		1
Total	(79.0 overs, 199 mins)		137	(49.5 overs, 135 mins)		100

LORD SHEFFIELD'S ENGLAND XI

Batsman	Dismissal 1	1st	Dismissal 2	2nd
*W.G.Grace	b Trumble	44		
R.Abel	b McLeod	33		
J.M.Read	c Trott b McLeod	0		
G.Bean	b Trott	11	(2) not out	39
A.E.Stoddart	c Walters b Worrall	32		
R.Peel	b Worrall	7	(3) not out	14
G.A.Lohmann	b Trumble	3		
J.Briggs	lbw b Worrall	21	(1) c sub (H.Graham) b Trott	3
†H.Philipson	not out	15		
W.Attewell	c Walters b Worrall	0		
J.W.Sharpe	c Ross b Worrall	2		
Extras	(b13, lb3)	16	(lb1)	1
Total	(85.4 overs, 217 mins)	184	(17.0 overs, 60 mins) (3 wkts)	57

ENGLAND XI	O	M	R	W	w,nb		O	M	R	W	w,nb
Lohmann	26	12	43	4	-,-		8	3	15	1	-,-
Attewell	21	11	24	1	-,-	(3)	21.5	7	34	4	-,-
Sharpe	3	0	19	0	-,-						
Peel	29	11	50	4	-,-	(2)	3	0	17	0	-,-
Briggs						(4)	17	6	33	5	-,-

VICTORIA	O	M	R	W	w,nb		O	M	R	W	w,nb
Trumble	22	8	28	2	-,-	(4)	3	0	8	0	-,-
Trott	17	3	49	1	-,-	(1)	6	1	29	1	-,-
Letcher	4	0	22	0	-,-						
McLeod	21	10	34	2	-,-	(2)	5	2	5	0	-,-
Worrall	20.4	5	34	5	-,-	(3)	3	0	14	0	-,-
Bruce	1	0	1	0	-,-						

FALL OF WICKETS				
Wkt	VIC	ENG	VIC	ENG
	1st	1st	2nd	2nd
1st	36	65	35	6
2nd	61	65	44	-
3rd	65	80	54	-
4th	71	122	54	-
5th	102	131	72	-
6th	107	134	72	-
7th	111	139	81	-
8th	130	173	81	-
9th	137	173	99	-
10th	137	184	100	-

AUSTRALIA v ENGLAND (3rd Test)

Played at Adelaide Oval on March 24, 25, 26, 28, 1892. (Timeless match)
Toss : England.   Result : ENGLAND WON BY AN INNINGS AND 230 RUNS.
Debuts: England - H.Philipson (Test).
12th Men: None named.
Umpires: G.E.Downs and W.O.Whitridge.
Attendances: 10000, 5000, 12000, 1000.   Total: About 28,000.   Receipts: £1221.
Close of Play: 1st day Eng 4/313 (Stoddart 129, Peel 24); 2nd day Eng 9/490 (MacGregor 29, Attewell 36); 3rd day Aust (2) 8/124
    (McLeod 8).

Donnan, the intended 12th man, came into the Australian side when S.T.Callaway returned to Sydney before the match on learning that his
father was gravely ill. England batted in ideal conditions to register their highest total in a Test so far. Stoddart (134 in 230 minutes, 2
fives and 15 fours) was missed at the wicket off Turner when 1 but gave no further chance until he was 116. Grace (58 in about 120
minutes, 8 fours), Read (57 in about 75 minutes, 10 fours) and Peel (83 in about 150 minutes, 8 fours) hit half-centuries while MacGregor
and Attewell added 74 for the last wicket. Heavy rain ended play on the second day at 3.30pm and continued during the night to turn
conditions totally in favour of the bowlers. Briggs took 12 of the 18 Australian wickets to fall on the third day; a little over an hour was
needed on the fourth day to complete the game. Sources: *Wisden, The Australasian, Adelaide Advertiser, South Australian Register.*

ENGLAND

R.Abel	st Blackham b Trott	24
*W.G.Grace	b McLeod	58
A.E.Stoddart	lbw b G.Giffen	134
J.M.Read	c Gregory b Turner	57
G.Bean	c McLeod b Lyons	16
R.Peel	c G.Giffen b Turner	83
G.A.Lohmann	lbw b G.Giffen	0
J.Briggs	b Turner	39
†H.Philipson	c Blackham b McLeod	1
G.MacGregor	run out (Bruce/Blackham)	31
W.Attewell	not out	43
Extras	(b5, lb7, w1)	13
Total	(173.1 overs, 430 mins)	499

AUSTRALIA

J.J.Lyons	c Peel b Briggs	23	c Stoddart b Briggs	19
A.C.Bannerman	c Bean b Lohmann	12	b Briggs	1
G.Giffen	run out (Philipson)	5	c Bean b Attewell	27
W.Bruce	lbw b Lohmann	5	lbw b Attewell	37
C.T.B.Turner	c Lohmann b Briggs	10	c Grace b Briggs	5
S.E.Gregory	c Abel b Briggs	3	c Peel b Briggs	7
R.W.McLeod	b Briggs	20	c Grace b Lohmann	30
G.H.S.Trott	b Briggs	0	st Philipson b Briggs	16
W.F.Giffen	b Lohmann	3	c Peel b Briggs	2
H.Donnan	c Bean b Briggs	7	not out	11
*†J.M.Blackham	not out	7	b Attewell	9
Extras	(b5)	5	(b3, lb2)	5
Total	(42.5 overs, 110 mins)	100	(68.0 overs, 180 mins)	169

AUSTRALIA	O	M	R	W	w,nb
G.Giffen	51.1	17	154	2	1,-
McLeod	41	11	78	2	-,-
Trott	12	0	80	1	,
Turner	46	17	111	3	-,-
Donnan	9	2	22	0	-,-
Lyons	5	0	22	1	-,-
Bruce	9	3	19	0	-,-

ENGLAND	O	M	R	W	w,nb		O	M	R	W	w,nb
Briggs	21.5	4	49	6	-,-		28	7	87	6	-,-
Lohmann	21	8	46	3	-,-	(3)	6	2	8	1	-,-
Attewell						(2)	34	10	69	3	-,-

FALL OF WICKETS

	ENG	AUST	AUST
Wkt	1st	1st	2nd
1st	47	30	1
2nd	121	38	42
3rd	218	48	51
4th	272	48	85
5th	327	51	91
6th	333	66	99
7th	412	66	120
8th	425	73	124
9th	425	90	157
10th	499	100	169

1892-93 SEASON (10 MATCHES)

Competition for the Sheffield Shield began this season between teams representing New South Wales, Victoria and South Australia. A meeting of the Australasian Cricket Council in Sydney on September 14, 1892 had agreed - following the inaugural meeting of the Council the previous night - that the Shield would be conducted on a challenge basis. It would be immediately awarded to the winners of the first match in the competition, and that team would hold the Shield until they suffered a defeat. The Shield would then be passed to the victors of that match, and so on. No decision was taken to correct the imbalance of fixtures that had existed up to that time - that New South Wales would meet Victoria twice, whereas South Australia would only play one match against each of the other two. The South Australians drew the Council's attention to the unfairness of this, and on November 8 the matter was ironed out when Victoria joined New South Wales in agreeing to play South Australia twice each season.

New South Wales visited Adelaide to meet South Australia in the inaugural Sheffield Shield match in December and the home team won, despite having to follow-on. Thus, on December 21, 1892, South Australia became the first winners of the Sheffield Shield. Their success was to be shortlived, however, as Victoria, after accounting for New South Wales in the interim, defeated South Australia by six wickets in Melbourne on January 4 to take the title from them. An anomaly in the rules determining the winners of the Sheffield Shield now became apparent. The Shield could be won in the last match of the season by the team that did not necessarily have the most overall wins. Action was taken, and on January 30, 1893 - 40 days after the Sheffield Shield had been first awarded - the title was suspended, pending the outcome of the remaining matches in the season. In the event, Victoria won both their remaining away games to New South Wales and South Australia to maintain an unblemished 4-0 record and become deserving winners of the Shield overall for 1892-93. A curiosity was that Victoria was led by four different captains in the campaign.

Further history was made this season with the introduction of Queensland and Western Australia to first-class cricket. Western Australia negotiated at the start of the season for a tour east to include matches against South Australia, Victoria and New South Wales. Ultimately a program of eight matches was settled on - two in South Australia and six in Victoria - but only two of these could be considered first-class. The westerners were heavily defeated in both encounters.

Queensland entered the first-class scene on the right note when they met New South Wales at Brisbane in April. The two colonies had met on eight previous occasions, starting in 1864, but because odds were involved none of these matches could be considered first-class.

Victoria also played Tasmania at Launceston in January 1893 and won a close-fought encounter by four wickets. This match was played at the same time as Victoria's Sheffield Shield fixture against New South Wales in Sydney, beginning a practice that continued in most succeeding seasons up until the First World War. The matches were considered first-class despite Victoria fielding virtual second XIs against Tasmania.

Another priority of the fledgling Australasian Cricket Council - in addition to overseeing the start of Sheffield Shield cricket - was the selection and organisation of the 1893 tour of England. A.C.Bannerman and C.T.B.Turner (New South Wales), J.M.Blackham and G.H.S.Trott (Victoria), and G.Giffen and J.J.Lyons (South Australia) were charged with selecting the team, and they began by including themselves. W.Bruce, S.E.Gregory and Hugh Trumble were considered certainties and Harry Graham, W.F.Giffen, R.W.McLeod, A.H.Jarvis and Arthur Coningham made up the required party of 14. There was general agreement with 12 of the names, but the selection of Walter Giffen was known to be a concession to persuade brother George to tour, and Coningham was included on instructions from the ACC. The Council failed to persuade the players to hand over control of the tour finances and profits.

Leading Aggregates

Batsmen	M	I	NO	Runs	HS	Ave.	Bowlers	Runs	Wkts	Ave.
G.Giffen (SA)	4	8	0	468	181	58.50	G.Giffen (SA)	759	33	23.00
J.J.Lyons (SA)	4	8	0	342	124	42.75	M.Pierce (NSW)	662	28	23.64
G.H.S.Trott (Vic)	4	8	1	304	70*	43.42	E.Jones (SA)	533	24	22.20
W.Bruce (V)	3	6	0	283	128	47.16	H.Trumble (V)	298	22	13.54
F.A.Iredale (NSW)	4	7	0	282	101	40.28	R.W.McLeod (V)	448	22	20.36
H.Graham (V)	4	7	2	262	86*	52.40				
J.Harry (V)	3	5	1	249	114	62.25				
H.Moses (NSW)	2	4	0	242	99	60.50				

SHEFFIELD SHIELD TABLE

	P	W	L	D	Runs Scored	Wkts Lost	Runs Conceded	Wkts Taken
VICTORIA	4	4	-	-	2181	61	1946	80
SOUTH AUSTRALIA	4	1	3	-	1842	80	1847	59
NEW SOUTH WALES	4	1	3	-	1741	70	1971	72
TOTAL	6	6	6	-	5764	211	5764	211

SOUTH AUSTRALIA v NEW SOUTH WALES (Shield Match 1)

Played at Adelaide Oval on December 16, 17, 19, 20, 21, 1892. (Timeless match)
Toss : New South Wales.   Result : SOUTH AUSTRALIA WON BY 57 RUNS.
Debuts: South Australia - E.Jones (f/c). New South Wales - M.Pierce (f/c).
12th Men: W.J.Camphin (NSW). No 12th named for SA.
Umpires: C.Bannerman and G.H.G.Searcy.
Attendances: 2000, 7000, 4000, 1500, 500.   Total: About 15,000.   Receipts: No figures published.
Close of Play: 1st day NSW 4/243 (Donnan 97, Iredale 18); 2nd day SA 4/142 (Giffen 53, Hill 46); 3rd day SA (2) 4/195 (Reedman 0);
     4th day NSW (2) 5/86 (Bannerman 26, Iredale 4).

The first Sheffield Shield match of all resulted in South Australia's first win at home against New South Wales. It was the fourth time a side had won in Australia after following on. Giffen captured the first wicket in the Competition - Jones with the third ball of the match - and went on to complete the first five- and ten-wicket analyses. Moses scored the first run and narrowly missed registering the first century (99 in 270 minutes, 6 fours), an honour which befell Donnan (120 in 305 minutes, 10 fours). Pierce (13 for 265) returned the best match figures by a New South Wales bowler on debut. Lyons scored 124 in only 117 minutes late on the third day and hit 15 fours. Delaney was unable to bowl due to a strained arm. P.C.Charlton, A.Coningham and C.T.B.Turner were unavailable for the trip to Adelaide. *Wisden* incorrectly gives NSW (2) Iredale out to Jones, Jones 4/49, Giffen 5/58. Sources: *Wisden, C.B.O'Reilly, The Australasian, Adelaide Advertiser, South Australian Register*

NEW SOUTH WALES

S.P.Jones	c Reedman b Giffen	0	(2) st A.H.Jarvis b Jones	6
A.C.Bannerman	c Delaney b A.Jarvis	16	(1) c & b Jones	30
*H.Moses	b Giffen	99	b Jones	5
S.E.Gregory	run out (Jones/A.H.Jarvis)	2	c & b Giffen	13
H.Donnan	b Jones	120	c & b Giffen	20
F.A.Iredale	lbw b Giffen	22	(7) c & b Giffen	36
S.T.Callaway	b Jones	19	(8) b Giffen	10
G.J.Youill	not out	36	(6) b A.Jarvis	6
A.L.Newell	c A.H.Jarvis b Giffen	5	not out	3
M.Pierce	b Giffen	3	b Giffen	0
†I.F.Wales	b Giffen	2	c A.Jarvis b Giffen	5
Extras	(b7, lb6)	13	(b12, lb2)	14
Total	(164.1 overs, 410 mins)	337	(82.4 overs, 210 mins)	148

SOUTH AUSTRALIA

J.J.Lyons	b Pierce	16	c Wales b Iredale	124
†A.H.Jarvis	c Wales b Callaway	1	(3) c Jones b Pierce	40
A.Wilkinson	c Gregory b Pierce	9	(10) c Donnan b Pierce	3
*G.Giffen	c Moses b Pierce	75	(2) b Pierce	10
J.C.Reedman	c & b Pierce	11	b Donnan	73
A.Hill	b Pierce	60	(4) b Newell	9
A.Jarvis	c Wales b Pierce	0	(8) c Jones b Pierce	13
G.T.Parkin	b Callaway	0	(9) not out	3
H.Blinman	b Pierce	23	(6) c & b Donnan	30
W.Delaney	not out	2	(7) b Donnan	3
E.Jones	b Pierce	0	c Bannerman b Pierce	6
Extras	(b11, lb4)	15	(b10, lb5, w1)	16
Total	(97.3 overs, 250 mins)	212	(107.2 overs, 270 mins)	330

SOUTH AUSTRALIA	O	M	R	W	w,nb		O	M	R	W	w,nb
Giffen	74.1	33	133	6	-,-		41.4	18	58	6	-,-
Jones	36	8	93	2	-,-		25	4	49	3	-,-
A.Jarvis	22	6	45	1	,		16	6	27	1	-,-
Lyons	6	2	11	0	-,-						
Parkin	22	6	40	0	-,-						
Reedman	4	2	2	0	-,-						

NSW SOUTH WALES	O	M	R	W	w,nb		O	M	R	W	w,nb
Callaway	32	7	65	2	-,-	(3)	14	5	30	0	-,-
Pierce	46.3	13	111	8	-,-		39.2	2	154	5	-,-
Newell	16	8	20	0	-,-	(1)	27	11	59	1	1,-
Jones	3	2	1	0	-,-		7	0	23	0	-,-
Gregory							8	2	19	0	-,-
Iredale							3	2	3	1	-,-
Donnan							9	2	26	3	-,-

FALL OF WICKETS

Wkt	NSW 1st	SA 1st	SA 2nd	NSW 2nd
1st	0	7	66	10
2nd	39	27	173	20
3rd	48	38	195	39
4th	199	66	195	63
5th	252	166	288	80
6th	287	170	294	117
7th	292	171	313	133
8th	325	195	321	142
9th	333	212	324	142
10th	337	212	330	148

VICTORIA v NEW SOUTH WALES (Shield Match 2)

Played at Melbourne Cricket Ground on December 24, 26, 27, 28, 29, 1892. (Timeless match)
Toss : New South Wales.   Result : VICTORIA WON BY EIGHT WICKETS.
Debuts: Victoria - H.Graham (f/c). New South Wales - A.Coningham (f/c).
12th Men: F.J.Laver & J.H.Stuckey (Vic emergencies) and W.J.Camphin (NSW).
Umpires: C.Bannerman and T.Flynn.
Attendances: 9000, 15618, 11633, 5816, 6000.   Total: About 48,067.   Receipts: £1970.
Close of Play: 1st day NSW 9/191 (Callaway 58); 2nd day Vic 5/325 (Phillips 4, McLeod 12); 3rd day NSW (2) 2/142 (Moses 56,
    Jones 44); 4th day NSW (2) 5/301 (Donnan 50, Iredale 79).

J.M.Blackham (injured finger) was replaced by C.H.Ross in the Victorian team, only for Ross to withdraw with a similar injury on the day
of the match. P.M.Lewis was sought as a replacement but could not be contacted so Houston, who was present at the ground, was co-
opted. Coningham was brought down from Sydney to reinforce the visitors and Camphin and A.L.Newell were omitted. Bruce (128 in
155 minutes, 15 fours) scored Victoria's maiden Shield hundred and with backup from Barrett (44 in about 120 minutes, 4 fours and 56 in
about 120 minutes, 4 fours) and Trott (63 in 135 minutes, 7 fours and 70 not out in 135 minutes, 6 fours) in the top order led the side to
the first of five victories in competition matches before encountering defeat. For New South Wales, Moses made 77 (254 minutes, 5 fours)
and 61 (195 minutes, 1 four), Callaway 61 not out (125 minutes, 5 fours), Donnan 58 (270 minutes, 1 four) and Iredale 101 (265 minutes,
4 fours). Sources: *Wisden, The Age, The Argus, The Herald, The Australasian, The Leader, Sydney Referee.*

NEW SOUTH WALES

S.P.Jones	c Trott b Trumble	3	(4) run out (Trott/Houston)		45
A.C.Bannerman	c Houston b McLeod	7	(1) b McLeod		18
*H.Moses	b Bruce	77	c & b McLeod		61
S.E.Gregory	c Carlton b McLeod	1	(5) c Trott b McLeod		17
H.Donnan	c Trott b McLeod	0	(6) b Trumble		58
F.A.Iredale	lbw b McLeod	14	(7) b Trumble		101
G.J.Youill	c Bruce b Trott	18	(8) b McLeod		11
A.Coningham	c Worrall b Trott	0	(9) c & b Trumble		17
S.T.Callaway	not out	61	(2) c Trott b McLeod		10
M.Pierce	lbw b McLeod	8	not out		1
†I.F.Wales	c Houston b McLeod	0	c & b Trumble		3
Extras	(b6, lb1, w1)	8	(b18, lb3, nb1)		22
Total	(120.5 overs, 294 mins)	197	(254.1 overs, 575 mins)		364

VICTORIA

W.Bruce	c Wales b Pierce	128	(2) b Pierce		16
J.E.Barrett	c Donnan b Coningham	44	(1) run out (Youill/Callaway)		56
G.H.S.Trott	b Coningham	63	not out		70
*J.Worrall	c Youill b Pierce	31			
H.Graham	hit wkt b Pierce	30			
J.Phillips	b Iredale	12			
R.W.McLeod	b Pierce	14			
†R.S.Houston	c Youill b Pierce	19			
J.Carlton	c Jones b Pierce	4			
R.Mitchell	not out	7			
H.Trumble	run out (Iredale/Wales)	7	(4) not out		34
Extras	(b8, lb5, w1, nb2)	16	(b3, lb4, w4)		11
Total	(136.5 overs, 345 mins)	375	(64.3 overs, 167 mins) (2 wkts)		187

VICTORIA	O	M	R	W	w,nb		O	M	R	W	w,nb		FALL OF WICKETS			
														NSW	VIC NSW	VIC
Trumble	36	18	38	1	-,-	(4)	53	23	63	4	-,-	Wkt	1st	1st	2nd	2nd
McLeod	37.5	16	54	6	-,-	(1)	82.1	42	98	5	-,-	1st	4	138	19	30
Carlton	9	3	19	0	-,-	(5)	40	13	42	0	-,-	2nd	12	203	49	130
Trott	12	1	31	2	-,-	(6)	21	3	52	0	-,-	3rd	16	259	146	-
Mitchell	5	1	16	0	-,-	(7)	4	0	20	0	-,-	4th	16	296	156	-
Phillips	11	5	12	0	-,-	(2)	22	12	22	0	-,-	5th	50	310	173	-
Bruce	7	5	10	1	1,-	(3)	12	4	25	0	-,-	6th	91	328	323	-
Worrall	3	0	9	0	-,-		9	5	6	0	-,-	7th	92	346	341	-
Barrett							11	3	14	0	-,1	8th	170	353	353	-
												9th	191	365	361	-
NEW SOUTH WALES	O	M	R	W	w,nb		O	M	R	W	w,nb	10th	197	375	364	-
Coningham	15	2	62	2	1,-	(7)	9	5	14	0	4,-					
Callaway	26	5	71	0	-,-	(1)	16.3	3	44	0						
Pierce	42.5	4	100	6	-,2	(2)	19	4	63	1	-,-					
Jones	13	4	31	0	-,-	(6)	4	1	20	0	-,-					
Gregory	2	0	8	0	-,-		6	1	9	0	-,-					
Donnan	10	1	26	0	-,-	(4)	3	1	4	0	-,-					
Iredale	28	9	61	1	-,-	(3)	7	2	22	0	-,-					

VICTORIA v SOUTH AUSTRALIA (Shield Match 3)

Played at Melbourne Cricket Ground on December 31, 1892, January 2, 3, 4, 1893. (Timeless match)

Toss : Victoria.　　　　　　　　　Result : VICTORIA WON BY SIX WICKETS.

Debuts: Nil.

12th Men: R.Mitchell (Vic) and W.Delaney (SA).

Umpires: G.E.Downs and T.Flynn.

Attendances: 9500, 13000, 6500, 1000.　　　Total: About 30,000.　　　Receipts: £1330.

Close of Play: 1st day SA (2) 0/27 (Hiscock 14, Blinman 12); 2nd day SA (2) 6/296 (A.H.Jarvis 30, Tardif 14); 3rd day Vic (2) 4/176 (Barrett 44, Graham 52).

W.F.Giffen and A.Hill were both unavailable for South Australia's trip east. Early morning rain on the first day produced a lively wicket which bowlers on both sides exploited. A masterly innings by Lewis (85 in 126 minutes, 9 fours) gave Victoria a decisive first-innings lead. However, the wicket-keeper-batsman sustained a split finger during the pre-lunch session on the second day and took no further part in the match. First Graham and later Worrall kept wicket for the rest of the day, Mitchell substituting in the field, and Carlton took the gloves on the third day. Giffen put in a fine allround performance, topscoring in both South Australia innings with 32 (75 minutes, 2 fours) and 92 (195 minutes, 6 fours) and bowling himself unchanged, apart from an over on the first day to change ends, to secure eight wickets. Reedman (50 in about 90 minutes, 4 fours) and A.H.Jarvis (66 not out in about 150 minutes, 5 fours) also hit half-centuries in the second innings. Barrett, whose nomination as captain over Worrall was considered surprising by the Press of the day, scored an unbeaten 68 (225 minutes, 4 fours) and Graham an unbeaten 86 (150 minutes, 8 fours) to get Victoria home with an unbroken stand of 133. Sources: *Wisden, C.B.O'Reilly, The Age, The Argus, The Herald, The Australasian, The Leader.*

SOUTH AUSTRALIA

J.J.Lyons	b Bruce	0	(3) c McLeod b Trumble	30
*G.Giffen	c Graham b Carlton	32	(4) c Trott b Laver	92
J.C.Reedman	b Trumble	3	(5) run out	50
A.Jarvis	hit wkt b Bruce	5	(7) c Trott b Trumble	13
†A.H.Jarvis	c Trott b Trumble	10	(6) not out	66
E.J.Hiscock	c Trott b Trumble	2	(1) c Trumble b Carlton	39
J.H.Tardif	c Bruce b Trumble	1	(8) b Trumble	16
G.T.Parkin	c Bruce b Trumble	1	(9) b Trumble	3
J.Noel	c Trott b Carlton	1	(10) run out (Bruce/Carlton)	0
H.Blinman	b Carlton	4	(2) c Lewis b Trumble	12
E.Jones	not out	13	b Laver	3
Extras	(w1)	1	(b14, lb7, nb2)	23
Total	(25.2 overs, 88 mins)	73	(157.0 overs, 375 mins)	347

VICTORIA

G.H.S.Trott	c Parkin b Jones	29	c Reedman b Giffen	13
*J.E.Barrett	c Hiscock b Jones	5	(5) not out	68
J.Worrall	b Giffen	1	b Giffen	39
†P.M.Lewis	b Giffen	85		
W.Bruce	c Tardif b Giffen	9	(2) b Giffen	20
H.Graham	c A.H.Jarvis b Jones	7	not out	86
H.Trumble	b Jones	0	(4) b Jones	0
R.W.McLeod	c A.H.Jarvis b Jones	6		
J.H.Stuckey	c A.Jarvis b Giffen	14		
F.J.Laver	c & b Giffen	8		
J.Carlton	not out	7		
Extras	(b8, lb1)	9	(b9, lb2, nb4)	15
Total	(48.3 overs, 143 mins)	180	(100.0 overs, 270 mins) (4 wkts)	241

VICTORIA	O	M	R	W	w,nb		O	M	R	W	w,nb
Trumble	13	4	27	5	-,-	(2)	57	24	93	5	-,1
Bruce	5	0	17	2	1,-	(5)	5	0	17	0	-,-
Carlton	7.2	1	28	3	-,-	(4)	8	1	22	1	-,-
Trott						(1)	16	3	51	0	-,-
McLeod						(3)	49	19	83	0	-,-
Laver							17	7	38	2	-,1
Worrall							5	0	20	0	-,-

SOUTH AUSTRALIA	O	M	R	W	w,nb		O	M	R	W	w,nb
Jones	15	2	60	5	-,-	(2)	27	5	56	1	-,-
Giffen	23.3	3	80	5	-,-	(1)	50	11	126	3	-,4
A.Jarvis	7	1	20	0	-,-		21	10	39	0	-,-
Parkin	3	0	11	0	-,-						
Lyons						(4)	2	0	5	0	-,-

FALL OF WICKETS

Wkt	SA	VIC	SA	VIC
1st	4	15	30	27
2nd	13	16	64	42
3rd	22	54	133	46
4th	36	69	220	108
5th	44	86	246	-
6th	48	86	263	-
7th	50	96	303	-
8th	53	145	315	-
9th	60	165	336	-
10th	73	180	347	-

NEW SOUTH WALES v SOUTH AUSTRALIA (Shield Match 4)

Played at Sydney Cricket Ground on January 7, 9, 10, 1893. (Timeless match)
Toss : New South Wales.   Result : NEW SOUTH WALES WON BY AN INNINGS AND 60 RUNS.
Debuts: New South Wales - L.Moore (f/c).
12th Men: H.Blinman (SA). No 12th named for NSW.
Umpires: C.Bannerman and G.E.Downs.
Attendances: 9703, 6579, 3540.   Total: 19,822.   Receipts: £1181.
Close of Play: 1st day NSW 6/229 (Richardson 28, Callaway 19); 2nd day SA 8/155 (Noel 0).

Scheduled for January 6th, the start of the match was put forward a day when wet weather in the preceding week delayed preparation of the pitch. Richardson, originally named as 12th man, made the top score (75 not out in about 240 minutes, 4 fours) after replacing S.P.Jones (ill) on the morning of the match. Earlier, Gregory (41 in 75 minutes, 4 fours) and Turner (62 in 105 minutes, 1 five and 4 fours) had exhibited some fine stroke play. To his fifty, Turner added bowling figures of 10 for 106. Giffen attempted to optimise his side's batting conditions by personally sweeping the wicket after the New South Wales innings had finished, only for South Australia to be bowled out cheaply and lose wickets in each of the opening two overs of the follow-on. His experimentation with the batting order, which had had mixed results on previous tries, failed this time. Conditions throughout the match were good and the wicket pronounced as "in perfect condition from first to last" (*SMH*). Sources: *Wisden, C.B.O'Reilly, Sydney Referee, Sydney Morning Herald, Town & Country Journal.*

NEW SOUTH WALES

*A.C.Bannerman	b Giffen	16
S.E.Gregory	c Tardif b A.Jarvis	41
L.Moore	b Jones	14
C.T.B.Turner	c Lyons b Jones	62
H.Donnan	c A.H.Jarvis b Jones	8
C.A.Richardson	not out	75
F.A.Iredale	c Giffen b Parkin	36
S.T.Callaway	c & b Giffen	39
G.J.Youill	c A.H.Jarvis b Jones	0
M.Pierce	c Lyons b Reedman	32
†I.F.Wales	c A.Jarvis b Reedman	4
Extras	(b7, w1)	8
Total	(161.5 overs, 435 mins)	335

SOUTH AUSTRALIA

J.J.Lyons	c Wales b Donnan	28	(6)	c Bannerman b Turner	10
†A.H.Jarvis	run out (Donnan/Wales/Turner)	1	(9)	c Wales b Callaway	28
*G.Giffen	c Pierce b Turner	31	(7)	c Bannerman b Turner	4
J.C.Reedman	c Bannerman b Donnan	36	(8)	st Wales b Pierce	10
E.J.Hiscock	c Wales b Turner	4	(1)	c Iredale b Turner	0
A.Jarvis	c Gregory b Turner	10	(4)	b Callaway	6
J.H.Tardif	c Youill b Turner	41	(10)	c Gregory b Turner	11
W.Delaney	b Donnan	0	(3)	b Turner	18
J.Noel	c Wales b Pierce	3	(11)	not out	3
G.T.Parkin	not out	6	(2)	b Callaway	0
E.Jones	b Callaway	16	(5)	b Turner	0
Extras	(b5, w1, nb1)	7		(b1, nb1)	2
Total	(71.3 overs, 175 mins)	183		(42.5 overs, 105 mins)	92

SOUTH AUSTRALIA	O	M	R	W	w,nb
Jones	44	12	98	4	1,-
Giffen	72	26	127	2	-,-
A.Jarvis	22	4	44	1	-,-
Parkin	13	4	34	1	-,-
Reedman	8.5	3	22	2	-,-
Lyons	2	1	2	0	-,-

NEW SOUTH WALES	O	M	R	W	w,nb		O	M	R	W	w,nb
Turner	33	11	65	4	1,1		21	9	41	6	-,1
Pierce	17	3	54	1	-,-	(3)	6	1	21	1	-,-
Callaway	14.3	3	43	1	-,-	(2)	15.5	7	28	3	-,-
Donnan	7	3	14	3	-,-						

FALL OF WICKETS

Wkt	NSW 1st	SA 1st	SA 2nd
1st	50	2	0
2nd	62	61	0
3rd	127	69	9
4th	142	74	10
5th	149	98	24
6th	198	142	33
7th	260	144	50
8th	261	155	50
9th	331	164	76
10th	335	183	92

NEW SOUTH WALES v VICTORIA (Shield Match 5)

Played at Sydney Cricket Ground on January 26, 27, 28, 30, 31, 1893. (Timeless match)
Toss : Victoria.   Result : VICTORIA WON BY 232 RUNS.
Debuts: Nil.
12th Men: None named.
Umpires: C.Bannerman and T.Flynn.
Attendances: 14531, 5502, 10311, 3826, negligible.   Total: 34,170.   Receipts: £2056.
Close of Play: 1st day Vic 9/291 (Graham 37, Blackham 31); 2nd day NSW 7/177 (Iredale 29, Youill 3); 3rd day Vic (2) 4/163 (Barrett 4);
    4th day NSW (2) 9/99 (Pierce 6).

Under the now-accepted rules, this win ensured Victoria were the first winners of the Sheffield Shield. (The competition had been held on a challenge basis until January 30th 1893 and the trophy itself was not manufactured until the following year.) J.H.Stuckey and W.A.Tarrant were left out of the visitor's squad of thirteen for the match. Blackham's unbeaten 64 at No. 11 (49 minutes, 9 fours) helped Victoria reach 331 early on the second day after sharing a tenth-wicket stand of 82 with Graham. Barrett (55 in 150 minutes, 7 fours) in the first innings and Bruce (86 in 105 minutes, 12 fours) and Graham (65 in 120 minutes, 6 fours) in the second also scored half-centuries for Victoria. Bannerman (52 in about 150 minutes, 3 fours and 46 in about 120 minutes, 6 fours) and Iredale (55 in about 120 minutes, 4 fours) batted best for New South Wales. Turner (1) retired at 1/22 after he was hit on the hand by a lifter from Trumble. He returned at the start of the fifth day's play (Blackham had sportingly allowed stumps to be drawn a minute or two before 6.00pm the previous evening at the fall of the ninth wicket so he could return) but only three balls were needed to dismiss him without further addition to the score. Trumble and McLeod were assisted in their task by a wearing wicket. Sources: *Wisden, The Leader, Sydney Referee, Sydney Morning Herald, Town & Country Journal.*

VICTORIA

P.M.Lewis	c Gregory b Pierce	35		b Coningham	2
J.E.Barrett	c & b Coningham	55	(5)	b Coningham	4
G.H.S.Trott	c Wales b Donnan	19		b Callaway	38
J.Worrall	b Pierce	38		c Youill b Coningham	12
W.Bruce	b Coningham	24	(2)	c & b Coningham	86
H.Graham	run out (Donnan/Turner)	39		lbw b Callaway	65
J.Phillips	b Coningham	5	(10)	not out	17
R.W.McLeod	b Coningham	4	(9)	b Turner	9
H.Trumble	b Callaway	21	(8)	b Turner	4
J.Carlton	lbw b Pierce	15	(11)	lbw b Callaway	0
*†J.M.Blackham	not out	64	(7)	b Coningham	0
Extras	(b9, lb1, nb2)	12		(b20, lb3, w1)	24
Total	(128.4 overs, 315 mins)	331		(107.3 overs, 270 mins)	261

NEW SOUTH WALES

*A.C.Bannerman	c & b McLeod	52	(2)	c Trott b Trumble	46
S.E.Gregory	c Carlton b McLeod	31	(1)	c Barrett b McLeod	9
C.A.Richardson	b McLeod	16	(6)	c Worrall b Trumble	0
C.T.B.Turner	c Carlton b Phillips	9	(3)	c Trumble b McLeod	1
H.Donnan	run out (Lewis/Bruce)	1	(4)	b Trumble	6
F.A.Iredale	c Trott b Phillips	55	(5)	st Blackham b McLeod	18
A.Coningham	c Blackham b Trumble	30		st Blackham b Trumble	8
S.T.Callaway	c Carlton b Phillips	1		run out (Bruce/Blackham)	3
G.J.Youill	st Blackham b Trumble	39		b Trumble	0
M.Pierce	c Carlton b McLeod	6		not out	6
†I.F.Wales	not out	2		b McLeod	1
Extras	(b11, lb2, w1, nb5)	19		(b1)	1
Total	(158.0 overs, 350 mins)	261		(66.0 overs, 160 mins)	99

NEW SOUTH WALES	O	M	R	W	w,nb		O	M	R	W	w,nb
Turner	22.4	11	49	0	-,1		38	12	75	2	-,-
Callaway	19	10	32	1	-,-	(3)	20.3	6	36	3	-,-
Donnan	26	11	56	1	-,-	(5)	5	2	20	0	-,-
Pierce	28	1	92	3	-,-		8	0	27	0	-,-
Coningham	33	10	90	4	-,1	(2)	36	12	79	5	1,-

VICTORIA	O	M	R	W	w,nb		O	M	R	W	w,nb
Trumble	44	29	44	2	-,4		26	11	33	5	-,-
McLeod	51	24	76	4	-,-		26	12	46	4	-,-
Carlton	17	4	30	0	-,-	(4)	4	3	1	0	-,-
Bruce	15	7	29	0	1,-						
Trott	3	0	15	0	-,-		3	0	8	0	-,-
Worrall	2	0	4	0	-,1						
Phillips	26	9	44	3	-,-	(3)	7	4	10	0	-,-

FALL OF WICKETS

Wkt	VIC 1st	NSW 1st	VIC 2nd	NSW 2nd
1st	65	62	11	17
2nd	95	103	125	38
3rd	135	107	149	81
4th	168	111	163	81
5th	182	124	168	81
6th	188	165	168	85
7th	196	168	174	85
8th	225	234	195	92
9th	249	255	261	99
10th	331	261	261	99

TASMANIA v VICTORIA

Played at N.T.C.A. Ground, Launceston, on January 28, 30, 31, February 1, 1893. (Timeless match)
Toss : Tasmania.   Result : VICTORIA WON BY FOUR WICKETS.
Debuts: Tasmania - J.E.Bingham (f/c). Victoria - A.R.Carlton, A.P.Haddrick, D.H.McLeod, H.C.Maplestone (all f/c).
12th Men: E.E.Bean (Vic) and A.J.Douglas & N.R.Westbrook (Tas).
Umpires: P.Boland and D.F.Cotter.
Attendances: No figures published, but "very few" attended.   Receipts: No figures published.
Close of Play: 1st day Tas 8/265 (Eady 64, Sidebottom 8); 2nd day Vic 378 all out; 3rd day Vic (2) 3/101 (Harry 51).

For the first time in Australia eleven batsmen reached double figures in an innings, batsmen on both sides scoring freely in a close-fought contest. Eady (88 not out in about 195 minutes, 16 fours) and Bailey (57 not out in about 120 minutes, 6 fours) hit half-centuries for the home team, Donahoo (57 in about 45 minutes, 2 fives and 7 fours), McShane (88 in about 150 minutes, 2 fives and 12 fours), Morris (58 in about 120 minutes, 1 five and 9 fours) and Harry (67 in about 105 minutes, 1 five and 7 fours) replying in kind for the visitors. Both Bailey and McShane hit their career-best scores in their final appearance; Bailey using a runner for the duration of his unbeaten fifty after he strained a leg while batting on the first day. He did not field at all, Westbrook (first innings) and Douglas (second) substituting, each taking a catch. Carlton, one of three brothers to appear for Victoria, captured 6 for 93 on debut. Houston sustained a broken bone in his wrist at 7/160 on the third day when he was struck by Maplestone's first ball of the innings; he took no further part in the match, Harry deputising as wicket-keeper and H.Wilson fielding against his own team. *STCA Report* incorrectly gives Vic (2) Haddrick b Wilson, Windsor 3/26, Wilson 1/13, Sidebottom 0/33. *VCA Report* gives Tas (1) Bingham 13, total 311 and incorrectly gives Vic (1) Maplestone b Burn. Sources: *VCA Report, STCA Report, The Leader, Launceston Examiner, Hobart Mercury.*

TASMANIA

†G.H.Gatehouse	b Laver	32		b Carlton	27
*C.W.Rock	c Houston b Mitchell	18		run out (Haddrick/Laver)	4
E.J.K.Burn	b Carlton	23		b Carlton	34
W.H.Savigny	c Houston b Laver	24		b Carlton	4
G.H.Bailey	c Mitchell b Laver	25	(9)	not out	57
J.H.Savigny	b McLeod	25		b Morris	11
C.J.Eady	not out	88	(5)	c Houston b Harry	3
E.A.C.Windsor	b McLeod	19	(7)	c Carlton b Maplestone	40
H.Wilson	c Laver b Maplestone	21	(8)	c Laver b Carlton	16
W.L.Sidebottom	c McLeod b Haddrick	12		c Haddrick b Carlton	14
J.E.Bingham	b Morris	11		st Harry b Carlton	23
Extras	(b5, lb3, nb3)	11		(lb3)	3
Total	(147.3 overs, 340 mins)	309		(94.3 overs, 240 mins)	236

VICTORIA

J.Harry	b Bingham	4		c sub (A.J.Douglas) b Bingham	67
R.Mitchell	b Windsor	11		c Eady b Bingham	18
S.J.Donahoo	c sub (N.R.Westbrook) b Windsor	57		c Gatehouse b Windsor	1
F.J.Laver	c Gatehouse b Windsor	26		b Sidebottom	27
*†R.S.Houston	b Burn	47			
A.P.Haddrick	run out (Windsor)	43	(5)	b Windsor	20
H.C.Maplestone	c Windsor b Burn	25	(8)	not out	21
S.Morris	c Eady b Wilson	58	(6)	b Windsor	2
F.G.McShane	b Eady	88	(7)	not out	4
D.H.McLeod	c Gatehouse b Wilson	8			
A.R.Carlton	not out	2			
Extras	(b5, lb2, w2)	9		(b9, w1)	10
Total	(117.0 overs, 270 mins)	378		(52.2 overs, 130 mins) (6 wkts)	170

VICTORIA	O	M	R	W	w,nb		O	M	R	W	w,nb
Mitchell	22	6	44	1	-,-	(4)	5	3	6	0	-,-
Maplestone	21	9	33	1	-,-	(8)	5	4	6	1	-,-
McLeod	30	12	54	2	-,2	(2)	12	5	30	0	;,-
Carlton	14	2	43	1	-,-	(3)	32.3	8	93	6	-,-
Laver	26	7	53	3	-,1	(1)	13	4	34	0	-,-
McShane	6	3	10	0	-,-	(9)	10	3	33	0	-,-
Morris	9.3	2	28	1	-,-	(6)	6	4	8	1	-,-
Haddrick	17	8	29	1	-,-	(7)	6	3	11	0	-,-
Harry	2	1	4	0	-,-	(5)	5	1	12	1	-,-

TASMANIA	O	M	R	W	w,nb		O	M	R	W	w,nb
Windsor	29	3	104	3	2,-		17.2	6	56	3	1,-
Bingham	18	1	79	1	-,-		16	2	45	2	-,-
Eady	29	13	52	1	-,-		5	1	11	0	-,-
W.H.Savigny	4	0	28	0	-,-						
Wilson	25	6	83	2	-,-	(4)	3	0	13	0	-,-
Burn	12	2	23	2	-,-		4	2	2	0	-,-
Sidebottom						(5)	7	1	33	1	-,-

FALL OF WICKETS

Wkt	TAS 1st	VIC 1st	TAS 2nd	VIC 2nd
1st	25	11	7	31
2nd	73	15	54	32
3rd	77	98	58	101
4th	113	101	63	138
5th	131	190	83	142
6th	159	208	87	146
7th	209	219	116	-
8th	249	363	164	-
9th	283	373	196	-
10th	309	378	236	-

SOUTH AUSTRALIA v VICTORIA (Shield Match 6)

Played at Adelaide Oval on March 16, 17, 18, 20, 21, 1893. (Timeless match)
Toss : South Australia. Result : VICTORIA WON BY FIVE WICKETS.
Debuts: Nil.
12th Men: S.Morris (Vic). No 12th named for SA.
Umpires: G.E.Downs and T.Flynn.
Attendances: 2000, 4000, 6000, 3000, 2000. Total: About 17,000. Receipts: No figures published.
Close of Play: 1st day SA 242 all out; 2nd day Vic 7/255 (McLeod 43, Laver 55); 3rd day SA (2) 3/153 (G.Giffen 54); 4th day SA (2)
  9/358 (A.Jarvis 20).

J.M.Blackham (injured finger), W.Bruce, H.Trumble and J.Worrall were all unavailable for Victoria and Stuckey was a late replacement for
J.E.Barrett just before the team departed. George Giffen recorded his almost obligatory allround impact on the game with over 200 runs and
eleven wickets. It was his fourth (and last) return of nine or more wickets in an innings in Australia; only L.O.Fleetwood-Smith and
W.J.O'Reilly (twice each) did it more than once in the following 100 years. Giffen's 181 occupied about 375 minutes (11 fours) and he
gave a caught-and-bowled chance to Carlton when 20. Lyons (72 in 85 minutes, 1 five and 12 fours and 62 in about 60 minutes, 8 fours)
hammered the Victorian bowling in both innings. The Victorians struggled against Giffen's bowling in the first innings until McLeod
(career-best 101 in about 180 minutes, 6 fours) and Laver (104 in about 180 minutes, 1 five and 14 fours) combined in an eighth-wicket
stand of 198, a new record for that wicket in Australia. Walter Giffen was out to the last ball of the opening over in South Australia's
second innings. Harry (50 in 71 minutes, 6 fours) and Stuckey (56 in 95 minutes, 8 fours) opened Victoria's second run quest with a
century stand. At the conclusion of the first Sheffield Shield season, Victoria remained unbeaten from four matches. Sources: *Wisden*,
C.B.O'Reilly, The Australasian, Adelaide Advertiser, South Australian Register.

SOUTH AUSTRALIA

J.J.Lyons	c Carlton b Phillips	72		c Bean b McLeod	62
W.F.Giffen	c Lewis b Carlton	21		c & b Phillips	0
*G.Giffen	c Trott b Phillips	43		b Carlton	181
†A.H.Jarvis	c Bean b Phillips	6	(5)	c & b Phillips	10
J.C.Reedman	c Harry b Phillips	4	(4)	run out (Graham/Laver)	32
H.Blinman	b Harry	41		b Harry	18
A.Hill	c Trott b Harry	13		b Phillips	19
J.H.Tardif	b McLeod	25		c Tarrant b Phillips	2
A.Jarvis	c Graham b Phillips	8		not out	22
W.Amos	c Carlton b Phillips	0	(11)	lbw b Carlton	3
E.Jones	not out	0	(10)	b McLeod	3
Extras	(b4, lb1, nb4)	9		(b2, lb6, w1, nb2)	11
Total	(94.3 overs, 270 mins)	242		(144.5 overs, 390 mins)	363

VICTORIA

†P.M.Lewis	b G.Giffen	18	(3)	c & b Reedman	23
J.H.Stuckey	b G.Giffen	37		c Lyons b Reedman	56
*G.H.S.Trott	c Lyons b G.Giffen	52	(4)	c Blinman b G.Giffen	20
H.Graham	c & b G.Giffen	14	(5)	not out	21
W.A.Tarrant	run out (Reedman/A.H.Jarvis)	12			
J.Carlton	c Reedman b G.Giffen	2			
J.Phillips	b G.Giffen	0			
R.W.McLeod	c W.F.Giffen b G.Giffen	101	(6)	b G.Giffen	15
F.J.Laver	c A.Jarvis b G.Giffen	104	(7)	not out	9
J.Harry	not out	14	(1)	c A.Jarvis b Reedman	50
E.E.Bean	c Reedman b G.Giffen	19			
Extras	(b6, lb18, w5, nb1)	30		(b7, lb1, nb1)	9
Total	(146.0 overs, 420 mins)	403		(59.0 overs, 170 mins) (5 wkts)	203

VICTORIA	O	M	R	W	w,nb		O	M	R	W	w,nb		FALL OF WICKETS			
														SA	VIC	SA	VIC
McLeod	18	5	34	1	-,-	(6)	34	16	57	2	-,-	Wkt	1st	1st	2nd	2nd
Carlton	20	2	77	1	-,-	(5)	23.5	2	68	2	-,-	1st	101	46	1	103
Harry	18	5	47	2	-,4	(4)	11	0	35	1	1,-	2nd	102	99	89	132
Bean	3	0	18	0	-,-	(3)	9	2	42	0	-,-	3rd	111	128	153	157
Laver	12	6	18	0	-,-	(7)	18	7	28	0	-,1	4th	115	139	172	157
Phillips	23.3	7	39	6	-,-	(1)	44	15	100	4	-,1	5th	178	148	227	183
Trott						(2)	5	0	22	0	-,-	6th	194	148	304	-
												7th	224	163	316	-
SOUTH AUSTRALIA	O	M	R	W	w,nb		O	M	R	W	w,nb	8th	240	361	352	-
Amos	11	2	35	0	-,-	(4)	4	1	7	0	-,-	9th	242	370	359	-
Jones	21	9	43	0	4,-	(1)	4	1	26	0	-,-	10th	242	403	363	-
G.Giffen	64	25	147	9	-,1	(2)	25	7	88	2	-,1					
Reedman	17	3	68	0	-,-	(5)	16	4	46	3	-,-					
A.Jarvis	30	11	64	0	1,-	(3)	10	2	27	0	-,-					
Lyons	3	1	16	0	-,-											

SOUTH AUSTRALIA v WESTERN AUSTRALIA

Played at Adelaide Oval on March 27, 28, 1893. (Four-day match)
Toss : South Australia.   Result : SOUTH AUSTRALIA WON BY TEN WICKETS.
Debuts: South Australia - A.C.Edwards, R.Evans, C.Hill, P.Hill, W.Reid (all f/c). Western Australia - W.Back, W.A.Bateman, F.Bennett,
    E.G.Bishop, T.Cullinan, P.L.Hussey, A.A.Moffatt, F.D.North, E.A.Randell (all f/c); W.V.Duffy, H.R.Orr (both WA only).
12th Men: J.W.C.Bird (WA). No 12th named for SA.
Umpires: J.Creswell and H.Wilson.
Attendances: No daily figures published.   Total: 1631.   Receipts: No figures published.
Close of Play: 1st day WA 5/92 (Bateman 17, Cullinan 7).

This match marked Western Australia's introduction to first-class cricket, and for most of the team it was their first encounter with a turf wicket. South Australia were without their England tourists, G.Giffen, W.F.Giffen, A.H.Jarvis and J.J.Lyons, and fielded virtually a second eleven. The visitors were handicapped by the loss of their wicket-keeper H.Wilson, who had damaged a knee in a heavy fall during the sea voyage from Perth. Wilson stood as umpire with the SACA secretary John Creswell. However, they began well and had the locals tottering at 5/20 before missing two or three vital chances which allowed Reid, Edwards and Jarvis to record half-centuries. The Westerners' inexperience on turf saw them undone against the pace of Jones and Jarvis, only forties from the more experienced Duffy (Smokers 1886-87) and Orr (Cambridge University 1886) averting an innings defeat. Clem Hill, who had been born during the progress of the very First Test in 1877 and was introduced to first-class cricket as a wicket-keeper-batsman aged 16 years 9 days, had a miserable debut; he was bowled first ball and did not take a catch, missing a chance off Jones in the opening over of Western Australia's first innings. Gooden played his last match at the age of 47 years 95 days. Sources: *C.B.O'Reilly, Adelaide Advertiser, South Australian Register, Adelaide Observer, South Australian Chronicle.*

SOUTH AUSTRALIA

A.Wilkinson	b Bateman	12			
D.M.Ballans	c Bateman b Duffy	1			
*J.E.Gooden	b Bishop	4			
W.Delaney	b Duffy	0	(1) not out		11
W.Reid	b Bishop	50			
†C.Hill	b Bateman	0	(2) not out		0
A.C.Edwards	c Bateman b Duffy	60			
A.Jarvis	not out	69			
P.Hill	b Bishop	2			
R.Evans	b Bishop	32			
E.Jones	b Bishop	4			
Extras	(b2)	2			-
Total	(69.0 overs, 200 mins)	236	(1.3 overs, 5 mins) (0 wkts)		11

WESTERN AUSTRALIA

W.Back	c Gooden b Delaney	4	(2) run out (Jarvis)		7
P.L.Hussey	b Jones	8	(7) run out (Evans)		14
W.V.Duffy	c Edwards b Jarvis	14	(6) b Jones		42
F.D.North	b Jarvis	25	(3) c Jarvis b Delaney		5
*H.R.Orr	b Jones	9	b Jarvis		44
W.A.Bateman	lbw b Jones	20	(4) b Jarvis		1
T.Cullinan	b Jones	8	(8) b Jarvis		1
†F.Bennett	c Edwards b Jones	0	(1) b Jones		10
E.A.Randell	b Jones	0	b Jarvis		1
A.A.Moffatt	b Jarvis	2	(11) not out		1
E.G.Bishop	not out	3	(10) c Delaney b Jones		0
Extras	(b14, lb4)	18	(b3, lb2)		5
Total	(42.3 overs, 120 mins)	111	(40.5 overs, 120 mins)		131

WESTERN AUSTRALIA	O	M	R	W	w,nb		O	M	R	W	w,nb			FALL OF WICKETS			
Bishop	23	3	60	5	-,-		1	0	5	0	-,-			SA	WA	WA	SA
Duffy	19	5	53	3	-,-		0.3	0	6	0	-,-	Wkt		1st	1st	2nd	2nd
Bateman	9	1	38	2	-,-							1st		2	9	17	-
Randell	8	2	20	0	-,-							2nd		7	17	18	-
Moffatt	5	0	17	0	-,-							3rd		8	51	19	-
Cullinan	2	0	19	0	-,-							4th		20	55	42	-
Orr	3	0	27	0	-,-							5th		20	78	110	-
												6th		125	94	110	-
SOUTH AUSTRALIA	O	M	R	W	w,nb		O	M	R	W	w,nb	7th		143	102	111	-
Jones	16	5	53	6	-,-		16	1	55	3	-,-	8th		152	102	115	-
Delaney	13	7	13	1	-,-	(3)	5	1	12	1	-,-	9th		232	108	120	-
Jarvis	13.3	2	27	3	-,-	(2)	16.5	5	44	4	-,-	10th		236	111	131	-
Ballans							3	0	15	0	-,-						

VICTORIA v WESTERN AUSTRALIA

Played at Melbourne Cricket Ground on April 1, 3, 4, 1893. (Timeless match)
Toss : Western Australia.　　　　Result : VICTORIA WON BY AN INNINGS AND 243 RUNS.
Debuts: Victoria - A.E.Trott (f/c). Western Australia - H.Wilson (f/c).
12th Men: H.C.Maplestone (Vic) and T.Cullinan (WA).
Umpires: H.J.Alessio and R.E.Bush (E.D.Heather deputised).
Attendances: 600, 1500, 100.　　　Total: About 2200.　　　Receipts: £91.
Close of Play: 1st day Vic 1/213 (Harry 102, Lewis 54); 2nd day WA 38 all out.

Victoria were unable to consider F.J.Laver and J.Worrall (both had club commitments) for their first match against Western Australia as well as representatives in England: J.M.Blackham, W.Bruce, H.Graham, R.W.McLeod, G.H.S.Trott and H.Trumble. Wilson, picked as wicket-keeper despite a knee injury sustained in the boat trip from Perth to Adelaide, conceded a record number of byes in an Australian innings and was forced to bat with a runner on the last day. Pre-match rain prompted Orr to insert the Victorians but further showers, which limited the first day's play to just 150 minutes, were considered to actually improve conditions for batting. Harry (114 in about 150 minutes, 12 fours) survived two chances in the fifties to compile his career-best score, "on a wicket which certainly did not favour him" (*Australasian*). More rain on the Sunday worsened the pitch as the second day progressed, to the disadvantage of the visitors who recorded their lowest-ever total, beginning with the wicket of Back with the last ball of the first over. North (77 in 145 minutes, 10 fours) scored Western Australia's maiden half-century in the second innings; his "cutting, off-driving and leg-hitting showed beyond question that he is an able batsman" (*Australian*). Aitken took his catches while substituting for Morris, who had injured his back on the second day. Heather stood for umpire Bush after lunch on the final day. Sources: *VCA Report, The Age, The Argus, The Herald, The Australasian, The Leader, The Sportsman*.

VICTORIA

J.Harry	c North b Bishop	114		
J.H.Stuckey	lbw b Moffatt	28		
†P.M.Lewis	b Duffy	63		
R.Mitchell	st Wilson b Duffy	52		
W.A.Tarrant	c Bennett b Duffy	7		
S.Morris	c Wilson b North	52		
*C.H.Ross	c Bishop b Duffy	10		
J.Carlton	c Bateman b North	2		
A.P.Haddrick	not out	20		
A.E.Trott	c Wilson b Bishop	4		
E.E.Bean	st Wilson b Duffy	5		
Extras	(b45, lb5, w3, nb1)	54		
Total	(100.0 overs, 295 mins)	411		

WESTERN AUSTRALIA

W.Back	b Carlton	0	c Harry b Trott	1
E.A.Randell	run out	8	c sub (A.A.Aitken) b Trott	15
F.D.North	run out	2	c & b Carlton	77
*H.R.Orr	b Carlton	6	c sub (A.A.Aitken) b Carlton	18
W.V.Duffy	st Lewis b Haddrick	0	b Mitchell	6
P.L.Hussey	b Haddrick	0	(7) b Carlton	5
W.A.Bateman	b Carlton	0	absent ill	
F.Bennett	st Lewis b Haddrick	3	b Mitchell	0
†H.Wilson	not out	10	(6) b Mitchell	3
A.A.Moffatt	c Carlton b Haddrick	0	not out	0
E.G.Bishop	run out (Harry)	6	(9) b Mitchell	1
Extras	(b3)	3	(b1, lb2, w1)	4
Total	(21.2 overs, 70 mins)	38	(62.0 overs, 150 mins)	130

WESTERN AUSTRALIA	O	M	R	W	w,nb	O	M	R	W	w,nb
Bishop	35	9	101	2	-,1					
Duffy	31	2	124	5	1,-					
Randell	3	0	26	0	-,-					
Bateman	9	1	33	0	-,-					
Moffatt	6	0	30	1	-,-					
Orr	10	2	29	0	1,-					
North	6	1	14	2	1,-					

VICTORIA	O	M	R	W	w,nb		O	M	R	W	w,nb
Carlton	11	4	25	3	-,-	(4)	17	7	28	3	-,-
Haddrick	10.2	7	10	4	-,-						
Bean						(1)	9	4	25	0	-,-
Trott						(2)	14	4	35	2	-,-
Mitchell						(3)	22	12	38	4	1,-

FALL OF WICKETS

Wkt	VIC 1st	WA 1st	WA 2nd
1st	84	0	8
2nd	234	7	26
3rd	234	12	77
4th	245	16	98
5th	362	18	110
6th	364	18	119
7th	373	18	120
8th	381	21	126
9th	400	21	130
10th	411	38	-

QUEENSLAND v NEW SOUTH WALES

Played at Exhibition Ground, Brisbane, on April 1 (no play), 3. 4. 1893. (Timeless match)
Toss : Queensland. Result : QUEENSLAND WON BY 14 RUNS.
Debuts: Queensland - All (all f/c). New South Wales - S.W.Austin, W.J.Camphin, S.R.Walford (all f/c).
12th Men: None named.
Umpires: C.W.Patrick and E.O.Sheridan.
Attendances: no play, 3500, 1000. Total: About 4500 Receipts: No figures published.
Close of Play: 1st day no play; 2nd day Qld (2) 5/48 (Grew 0).

Queensland's inaugural first-class match got off to a hectic start after the first day had been lost to rain, 25 wickets tumbling when play finally started on a sodden wicket and outfield. The pitch cut up badly during the Queensland first innings and made orthodox batting impossible for the remainder of the game. The match aggregate of 342 runs included a mere 10 boundaries - 1 five and 9 fours - only two of which were struck by New South Wales, Pierce and Austin the scorers. Martin (42 not out with 1 five and 2 fours) was the only batsman to pass the twenties; he had been given a reprieve when 1 by Newell in the deep. New South Wales were without many of their leading players, importantly A.C.Bannerman, A.Coningham, S.E.Gregory and C.T.B.Turner, en route to England with the Australian team. Patrick, who had been omitted from the visitor's twelve stood as umpire. Goldman and Spry (the nominated 12th man) replaced A.C.Byrne and E.H.Hutton (both unavailable) in the Queensland side, which had been solely selected by J.V.Francis. By winning their first match Queensland emulated Tasmania (v Victoria 1850-51), New South Wales (v Victoria 1855-56) and South Australia (v Tasmania 1877-78), however they had to wait a further 15 years for their second victory on Australian soil. Prior to their first-class initiation, Queensland had played odds matches against first-class opposition as far back as 1864, as well as a match on even terms against a private New South Wales side in 1884. *Cricket Quarterly* incorrectly gives Qld (1) Munro b Newell, some fall of wickets. *Queensland Times* incorrectly gives Qld (2) Goldman c Wales. Sources: *Cricket Quarterly, NSWCA Scorebook, Brisbane Courier, Queensland Times, The Queenslander.*

QUEENSLAND

W.T.Fisher	lbw b Newell	11	(4)	lbw b Austin	11
E.S.Grew	b Pierce	3	(6)	c & b Callaway	0
W.Munro	c & b Newell	0	(9)	not out	4
M.F.Ramsay	b Newell	21	(3)	c Moore b Newell	16
*†W.F.Bradley	b Newell	0	(2)	c Newell b Callaway	13
W.Hoare	b Pierce	6	(5)	b Newell	2
E.R.Crouch	lbw b Pierce	0		c & b Callaway	4
C.Martin	not out	42	(1)	c McGlinchey b Callaway	1
R.O'Brien	b Newell	10	(8)	b Newell	12
R.Spry	run out (Callaway)	0		c Austin b Callaway	0
A.E.A.Goldman	lbw b Newell	1		st Wales b Newell	10
Extras	(b5, lb1)	6		(b2, lb3)	5
Total	(58.2 overs, 170 mins)	100		(51.1 overs, 150 mins)	78

NEW SOUTH WALES

G.J.Youill	b Hoare	3	(3)	c Bradley b Grew	27
S.T.Callaway	b Hoare	5	(5)	b Hoare	5
W.J.Camphin	b O'Brien	1	(4)	b Hoare	3
L.Moore	b O'Brien	9	(2)	st Bradley b Hoare	2
W.W.McGlinchey	c Martin b Hoare	5	(1)	c Fisher b O'Brien	1
H.J.W.Robinson	c & b O'Brien	0	(8)	not out	7
*S.R.Walford	b Hoare	1	(6)	b Ramsay	26
S.W.Austin	c & b Hoare	0	(7)	c & b Munro	13
A.L.Newell	b Hoare	4	(10)	c Grew b Munro	2
M.Pierce	not out	17	(9)	lbw b Munro	0
†I.F.Wales	c Hoare b Grew	11		b Ramsay	7
Extras	(b4, lb4)	8		(b4, lb3)	7
Total	(38.0 overs, 110 mins)	64		(66.3 overs, 190 mins)	100

NEW SOUTH WALES	O	M	R	W	w,nb		O	M	R	W	w,nb
Callaway	13	7	17	0	-,-		18	7	25	5	-,-
Newell	22.2	11	25	6	-,-	(3)	18.1	7	27	4	-,-
Pierce	18	5	30	3	-,-	(2)	6	2	10	0	-,-
McGlinchey	5	0	22	0	-,-	(5)	3	0	3	0	-,-
Austin						(4)	6	2	8	1	-,-

QUEENSLAND	O	M	R	W	w,nb		O	M	R	W	w,nb
Hoare	19	12	12	6	-,-		24	8	33	3	-,-
O'Brien	18	4	40	3	-,-		21	9	24	1	-,-
Grew	1	0	4	1	-,-	(4)	7	3	13	1	-,-
Ramsay						(3)	6.3	3	10	2	-,-
Munro							8	3	13	3	-,-

FALL OF WICKETS

Wkt	QLD 1st	NSW 1st	QLD 2nd	NSW 2nd
1st	15	4	2	1
2nd	15	11	27	7
3rd	21	11	46	13
4th	21	17	48	21
5th	36	18	48	65
6th	36	23	51	81
7th	71	23	58	83
8th	83	31	64	83
9th	84	31	65	87
10th	100	64	78	100

1893-94 SEASON (8 MATCHES)

The Australasian Cricket Council slightly amended the method of determining the winner of the Sheffield Shield prior to the commencement of the 1893-94 season. It was decided that, in the event of two teams attaining an equal number of wins during the course of the season, places would be determined by 'percentages' (overall batting average/bowling average). The Shield would not be shared in the event of two teams finishing level. This method of separating teams tied on wins or points remained in use and became known in later years as the 'quotient'.

The fixtures for the Shield were drawn up along precisely the same lines as the previous season, with New South Wales, South Australia and Victoria each touring in that order and playing their away matches in quick succession before returning home. South Australia opened the season well with an emphatic win over New South Wales at Adelaide, a double-century from George Giffen proving to be the difference between the teams. Returning via Melbourne, as became the custom, New South Wales went down again in a low-scoring encounter with Victoria, who made the highest total of the match to win by three wickets.

South Australia travelled to Melbourne to meet Victoria in the first of their away games in the New Year and won well, George Giffen again playing a pivotal role. Again, Victoria put up the highest innings of the match on the last day - but this time to no avail. Moving on to Sydney, the South Australians failed to come to terms with a rain-softened pitch and lost to New South Wales by an innings and 158 runs.

Similar pitch conditions prevailed at Sydney during Victoria's visit a fortnight later, but this match was a much closer affair and New South Wales won by 19 runs. Yet again, Victoria managed to make the highest total of the match in the fourth innings. One match now remained in the competition - South Australia versus Victoria at Adelaide - and any one of the three teams could theoretically still win the Shield. A win for Victoria at Adelaide would force a Shield result based on percentages, whereas a win for South Australia would be more clear-cut. The outcome remained in doubt almost to the end. Victoria, chasing 371 to win, looked on target at 3 for 230, before losing their last seven wickets for 82 to lose by 58 runs. But in order to win the Shield - on quotient - Victoria would had to have won the match by 10 wickets. Had they attained the 371 run-target set by South Australia and lost any wickets in doing so, New South Wales would have taken out the Shield. So Victoria had virtually no chance of retaining the title they won the previous year.

South Australia were well served throughout this successful season by the batting of Lyons, Darling and Reedman allied to the bowling of Jones and "Fred" Jarvis and, as usual, the allround skills of George Giffen.

Two other first-class matches were played. Tasmania met Victoria at Melbourne and were convincingly beaten by seven wickets, A.E.Trott - younger brother of G.H.S. - creating a fine impression with 4 for 53 and 7 for 85 in only his second match for Victoria. Queensland journeyed to Sydney to meet New South Wales in late March and rain - a problem in both Sheffield Shield matches there earlier in the season - again created awkward conditions early in the piece. The visitors hung on doggedly despite this, finally going down by a two-wicket margin. Arthur Coningham, who represented Queensland in this match, had played in the two previous Shield matches at Sydney this season for New South Wales.

In January, a New South Wales team toured New Zealand, again promoted and managed by J.C.Davis as in 1889-90, and again without N.S.W.C.A. endorsement. Under the leadership of Joe Davis, as in 1889-90, the other members of the side were S.W.Austin, O.W.Cowley, J.W.Gould, A.C.K.Mackenzie, D.L.Miller, L.Moore, E.G.Noble, M.A.Noble, J.Searle and S.R.Walford. This tour thus launched the outstanding career of M.A.Noble, one of Australia's all-time greats, but his brother was less fortunate. Ted Noble, along with Cowley and Miller, played his only matches for New South Wales on this trip.

Leading Aggregates

Batsmen	M	I	NO	Runs	HS	Ave.	Bowlers	Runs	Wkts	Ave.
G.Giffen (SA)	4	8	1	526	205	75.14	C.T.B.Turner (NSW)	369	30	12.30
J.J.Lyons (SA)	4	8	0	319	101	39.87	C.E.McLeod (V)	421	27	15.59
S.T.Callaway (NSW)	5	9	1	285	71	35.62	A.L.Newell (NSW)	489	25	19.56
H.Moses (NSW)	4	7	1	272	104	45.33	A.Coningham (NSW & Q)	263	19	13.84
J.C.Reedman (SA)	4	8	0	251	113	31.37	E.Jones (SA)	389	19	20.47
J.Harry (V)	4	8	1	223	82	31.85	G.H.S.Trott (V)	395	18	21.94
J.Darling (SA)	4	8	1	216	87	30.85	G.Giffen (SA)	519	17	30.52

SHEFFIELD SHIELD TABLE

	P	W	L	D	Quotient	Runs Scored	Wkts Lost	Runs Conceded	Wkts Taken
SOUTH AUSTRALIA	4	3	1	-	0.952	1969	80	1758	68
NEW SOUTH WALES	4	2	2	-	1.083	1352	68	1413	77
VICTORIA	4	1	3	-	0.950	1602	77	1752	80
TOTAL	6	6	6	-	1.000	4923	225	4923	225

SOUTH AUSTRALIA v NEW SOUTH WALES (Shield Match 1)

Played at Adelaide Oval on December 15, 16, 18, 19, 1893. (Timeless match)
Toss : South Australia.   Result : SOUTH AUSTRALIA WON BY 237 RUNS.
Debuts: South Australia - J.Darling (f/c). New South Wales - W.H.Moore (f/c).
12th Men: A.E.Green (SA emergency) and J.Cupitt (NSW).
Umpires: G.E.Downs and J.A.Tooher.
Attendances: 2000, 3500, 3000, 1000.   Total: About 9500.   Receipts: No figures published.
Close of Play: 1st day NSW 2/27 (Mackenzie 11, Donnan 10); 2nd day SA (2) 3/211 (G.Giffen 66, W.F.Giffen 8); 3rd day SA (2) 483 all out.

H.Moses, A.Coningham, W.L.Murdoch and C.T.B.Turner all declared themselves unavailable for the rail trip to Adelaide. Cupitt, picked in the New South Wales twelve purely on his performances in country cricket at Bowral, was destined never to make it into the team. Rain on the first morning prevented any play before lunch and softened the pitch, giving the bowlers some encouragement. Newell's ten wickets included those of A.H.Jarvis (second ball) and Blinman (first ball) for first-innings ducks. Bannerman was out to the last ball of the opening over in New South Wales first innings. Lyons (82 in 95 minutes, 9 fours) launched the South Australian second innings with a typical display of hard hitting. George Giffen scored the first Sheffield Shield double-century (205 in about 390 minutes, 10 fours), improving on his earlier 181 as the highest score in the competition. He gave only one chance, to the wicket-keeper when 104, and also topscored in the first innings (47 in about 150 minutes, 2 fours). New South Wales lost Donnan (old hand wound reopened) and Pierce (sprained foot) in fielding mishaps in the second innings, Cupitt and several members of the local side substituting in their places. Callaway (71 in 110 minutes, 6 fours) was the only visiting batsman to exceed 50 to complete a fine allround performance. Sources: *Wisden, C.B.O'Reilly, Sydney Referee, Sydney Morning Herald, Adelaide Advertiser, South Australian Register.*

SOUTH AUSTRALIA

J.J.Lyons	c Mackenzie b Callaway	33	c Callaway b Newell		82
J.C.Reedman	c Pierce b Callaway	2	c Pierce b Newell		23
*G.Giffen	c Bannerman b Callaway	47	c sub (J.Cupitt) b Bannerman		205
†A.H.Jarvis	c Iredale b Newell	0	c Callaway b Garrett		25
W.F.Giffen	c Garrett b Callaway	11	b Newell		12
A.Jarvis	b Newell	1	c Callaway b Garrett		30
H.Haldane	run out	0	b Newell		21
J.Darling	run out (Mackenzie/Moore)	5	lbw b Newell		32
H.Blinman	b Newell	0	not out		28
G.T.Parkin	not out	4	b Newell		10
E.Jones	c Youill b Callaway	0	b Newell		0
Extras	(b3)	3	(b8, lb4, w2, nb1)		15
Total	(52.3 overs, 155 mins)	106	(181.1 overs, 465 mins)		483

NEW SOUTH WALES

A.C.Bannerman	c G.Giffen b Jones	0		b A.Jarvis	1
A.C.K.Mackenzie	c Jones b Reedman	24	(4)	c Jones b Reedman	21
F.A.Iredale	c Parkin b A.Jarvis	2		c Reedman b G.Giffen	41
H.Donnan	b Jones	26		absent hurt	-
S.E.Gregory	c A.H.Jarvis b Reedman	12	(2)	b Jones	4
G.J.Youill	c A.H.Jarvis b Jones	6	(5)	st A.H.Jarvis b G.Giffen	16
S.T.Callaway	b Jones	1	(6)	b Parkin	71
*T.W.Garrett	b Jones	13	(7)	c Blinman b A.Jarvis	24
G.M.Pierce	lbw b Reedman	0		absent hurt	-
†W.H.Moore	c G.Giffen b Reedman	16	(8)	not out	31
A.L.Newell	not out	9	(9)	c A.Jarvis b Haldane	10
Extras	(b3, lb3, w3)	9		(b10, lb5)	15
Total	(40.2 overs, 130 mins)	118		(70.3 overs, 230 mins)	234

NEW SOUTH WALES	O	M	R	W	w,nb		O	M	R	W	w,nb			FALL OF WICKETS		
														SA	NSW	SA	NSW
Callaway	23.3	6	55	5	-,-	(2)	31	10	67	0	-,-		Wkt	1st	1st	2nd	2nd
Newell	26	10	43	3	-,-	(4)	75.1	16	190	7	'2,-		1st	4	1	60	3
Garrett	3	1	5	0	-,-		39	6	98	2	-,-		2nd	53	9	136	13
Pierce						(1)	19	3	57	0	-,1		3rd	53	56	191	61
Iredale							6	0	16	0	-,-		4th	84	62	224	76
Youill							3	0	15	0	-,-		5th	87	74	279	110
Bannerman							8	1	25	1	-,-		6th	93	80	314	151
													7th	98	80	366	221
SOUTH AUSTRALIA	O	M	R	W	w,nb		O	M	R	W	w,nb		8th	98	80	470	234
Jones	18.2	4	50	5	2,-		15	1	39	1	-,-		9th	106	108	481	-
A.Jarvis	9	0	32	1	1,-		18	2	63	2	-,-		10th	106	118	483	-
G.Giffen	2	1	2	0	-,-	(4)	21	4	63	2	-,-						
Reedman	11	3	25	4	-,-	(3)	10	2	34	1	-,-						
Parkin							5	1	13	1	-,-						
Haldane							1.3	0	7	1	-,-						

VICTORIA v NEW SOUTH WALES (Shield Match 2)

Played at Melbourne Cricket Ground on December 23, 26, 27, 28 - 29 (no play), 30, 1893. (Timeless match)
Toss : New South Wales.　　　Result : VICTORIA WON BY THREE WICKETS
Debuts: Victoria - C.E.McLeod (f/c).
12th Men: P.M.Lewis & C.H.Ross (Vic emergencies) and G.J.Youill (NSW).
Umpires: J.Phillips and J.A.Tooher.
Attendances: 7000, 13000, 6000, no play, no play, 3000.　　　Total: About 29,000.　　　Receipts: £1283.
Close of Play: 1st day Vic 0/13 (Harry 3, Stuckey 10); 2nd day NSW (2) 4/106 (Murdoch 39, Iredale 22); 3rd day Vic (2) 3/71 (Trott 44, Graham 5); 4th day no play; 5th day no play.

Laver replaced R.W.McLeod who withdrew, "on account of feeling that he was not in sufficiently good form" (*Age*). H.Donnan (injured hand) and S.E.Gregory (ill) returned to Sydney after the match in Adelaide and Moses, Murdoch and Turner joined the team from Sydney. J.Cupitt and G.J.Youill were then omitted from the thirteen players assembled for the game. Turner was run out in the first over of the match without having faced a ball. Bannerman (6 in 85 minutes) batted typically in his last first-class appearance while Moses (71 in 200 minutes, 2 fours) scored New South Wales's only half-century in perfect conditions on the first day. Rain during the Christmas two-day break freshened the wicket and made batting more difficult from the second day onwards. Turner captured the first match analysis of ten wickets or more for New South Wales in a Shield match at Melbourne. Murdoch (64 not out in about 195 minutes, 2 fours) batted solidly on his return to Australian first-class cricket. He had been living in England (and had even played a Test match for that country) since his last appearance in Australia, in 1889-90. Set 204 for victory on an improving pitch, Victoria had reached 3/71 when a fierce storm washed out play at 5.10pm on the third day. Steady rain then prevented any play on the scheduled fourth and fifth days. Graham (68 in about 135 minutes, 4 fours) gave a masterly display in difficult conditions on the final day as Victoria achieved their fifth win in succession over New South Wales. Sources: *Wisden, VCA Report, The Age, The Argus, The Herald, The Australasian, The Leader.*

NEW SOUTH WALES

A.C.Bannerman	c Laver b Trumble	6		c Blackham b Trumble	4
C.T.B.Turner	run out (Graham/Trumble)	0	(7)	c Trott b McLeod	3
*H.Moses	c McLeod b Trott	71	(4)	c & b Trumble	4
W.L.Murdoch	run out (Harry/Blackham/McLeod)	0	(5)	not out	64
F.A.Iredale	c Blackham b Carlton	27	(6)	c Trumble b Carlton	37
S.T.Callaway	run out (Graham/Blackham)	0	(8)	c Trott b Carlton	0
T.W.Garrett	c Carlton b Trott	16	(3)	c Trott b Trumble	3
A.C.K.Mackenzie	b Trott	0	(2)	c Blackham b Carlton	33
†W.H.Moore	c & b Trott	19	(10)	c Worrall b Trott	12
A.L.Newell	not out	9	(9)	c Trumble b McLeod	4
G.M.Pierce	c & b Trott	3		st Blackham b Trott	4
Extras	(b4)	4		(b3, lb3)	6
Total	(95.2 overs, 235 mins)	155		(112.2 overs, 255 mins)	174

VICTORIA

J.Harry	c Moore b Newell	5	(7)	not out	22
J.H.Stuckey	c & b Turner	29	(6)	c Mackenzie b Turner	29
G.H.S.Trott	c Turner b Newell	0		c Bannerman b Garrett	54
J.Worrall	c Iredale b Newell	21		b Turner	10
H.Graham	run out (Callaway/Moore)	6		c Newell b Turner	68
W.Bruce	c Iredale b Turner	26	(2)	c Moore b Turner	0
H.Trumble	b Turner	5	(8)	c Iredale b Turner	0
F.J.Laver	b Newell	1			
C.E.McLeod	c Pierce b Turner	0			
J.Carlton	b Turner	17	(9)	not out	0
*†J.M.Blackham	not out	11	(1)	b Newell	12
Extras	(b4, lb1)	5		(b7, lb2)	9
Total	(60.5 overs, 165 mins)	126		(79.4 overs, 220 mins) (7 wkts)	204

VICTORIA	O	M	R	W	w,nb		O	M	R	W	w,nb		
Trumble	27	12	33	1	-,-	(2)	19	8	28	3	-,-		
McLeod	24	8	33	0	-,-	(4)	28	14	25	2	-,-		
Carlton	21	9	32	1	-,-		42	16	60	3	-,-		
Harry	3	0	9	0	-,-								
Trott	20.2	6	44	5	-,-	(1)	19.2	2	41	2	-,-		
Bruce						(5)	2	0	12	0	-,-		
Laver						(6)	2	0	2	0	-,-		

NEW SOUTH WALES	O	M	R	W	w,nb		O	M	R	W	w,nb	
Turner	29.5	9	58	5	-,-		31.1	6	84	5	-,-	
Newell	25	10	48	4	-,-	(3)	16	4	30	1	-,-	
Garrett	1	0	10	0	-,-	(5)	14	5	33	1	-,-	
Callaway	5	1	5	0	-,-		16.3	2	38	0	-,-	
Pierce						(2)	2	0	10	0	-,-	

FALL OF WICKETS

Wkt	NSW 1st	VIC 1st	NSW 2nd	VIC 2nd
1st	0	15	7	6
2nd	45	21	22	22
3rd	45	45	40	61
4th	96	54	52	100
5th	96	68	127	165
6th	117	87	132	196
7th	117	94	135	201
8th	128	95	144	-
9th	149	101	166	-
10th	155	126	174	-

VICTORIA v SOUTH AUSTRALIA (Shield Match 3)

Played at Melbourne Cricket Ground on January 1, 2, 3, 4, 1894. (Timeless match)
Toss : South Australia.   Result : SOUTH AUSTRALIA WON BY 74 RUNS.
Debuts: Nil.
12th Men: C.H.Ross (Vic) and A.Hill (SA).
Umpires: P.Argall and T.Flynn.
Attendances: 12000, 8000, 4500, 3000.   Total: About 27,500.   Receipts: £1002.
Close of Play: 1st day SA 272 all out; 2nd day SA (2) 1/69 (A.H.Jarvis 26, G.Giffen 26); 3rd day Vic (2) 1/18 (Walters 8, Worrall 1).

This match was scheduled to commence on December 31st but was postponed owing to the late finish of the Vic v NSW game. Maplestone replaced J.Phillips (arm injury) after the Victorian side had been selected. J.M.Blackham, H.Graham (strained groin) and H.Trumble had previously requested that they be rested; consequently they were not considered. George Giffen (103 in 230 minutes, 4 fours) recorded his sixth and last century against Victoria. Affie Jarvis (51 in about 120 minutes, 3 fours and 64 in about 180 minutes, 1 four) and Darling (63 not out in about 150 minutes, 4 fours) hit half-centuries for South Australia. Walters for Victoria (95 in about 210 minutes, 1 five and 6 fours) was twice run out. Bruce (56 in 105 minutes, 5 fours) and Worrall (58 in about 150 minutes, 1 five and 2 fours) also hit fifties for Victoria. The umpires drew stumps at 5.47pm on the fourth day due to failing light with Victoria 9/268, but Trott generously suggested that the game be continued to a finish that evening. A flurry of big hitting took place before the last wicket fell at 6.05pm. It brought to an end Victoria's unbeaten five-match run in the Sheffield Shield competition. *Wisden* and *O'Reilly* incorrectly give SA (1) Haldane c & b McLeod; Vic (1) McLeod b Giffen, Maplestone not out. Sources: *Wisden, C.B.O'Reilly, The Age, The Argus, The Herald, The Australasian, The Leader, The Sportsman.*

SOUTH AUSTRALIA

J.J.Lyons	c Stuckey b McLeod	31	b McLeod		15
†A.H.Jarvis	c Harry b Carlton	51	c Carlton b Trott		64
*G.Giffen	b Carlton	24	b Harry		103
J.C.Reedman	st Lewis b Trott	17	c Bruce b Carlton		26
J.Darling	not out	63	c Trott b Carlton		0
W.F.Giffen	c Worrall b McLeod	18	c Maplestone b McLeod		10
A.Jarvis	b Trott	7	b Harry		5
H.Blinman	b Carlton	3	not out		15
H.Haldane	b McLeod	14	c Bruce b Trott		16
G.T.Parkin	b McLeod	0	c Maplestone b Harry		5
E.Jones	c Lewis b McLeod	42	b Harry		14
Extras	(b1, nb1)	2	(b1, lb5, w1, nb1)		8
Total	(105.5 overs, 265 mins)	272	(136.3 overs, 324 mins)		281

VICTORIA

J.Harry	run out (Reedman)	24	(6) b Jones		11
J.H.Stuckey	lbw b G.Giffen	10	b Jones		8
*G.H.S.Trott	c A.Jarvis b G.Giffen	2	(4) c Reedman b G.Giffen		21
J.Worrall	run out (W.F.Giffen)	43	(3) c Reedman b A.Jarvis		58
F.H.Walters	run out (W.F.Giffen/A.H.Jarvis)	19	(1) run out (/G.Giffen)		95
W.Bruce	c Lyons b Jones	56	(5) c Lyons b G.Giffen		0
†P.M.Lewis	b A.Jarvis	10	b G.Giffen		5
F.J.Laver	b Jones	4	st A.H.Jarvis b A.Jarvis		42
J.Carlton	b G.Giffen	0	(10) lbw b A.Jarvis		2
C.E.McLeod	not out	2	(9) not out		28
H.C.Maplestone	b G.Giffen	0	c Jones b A.Jarvis		9
Extras	(b5, lb5, nb1)	11	(b9, lb9, w1)		19
Total	(64.5 overs, 185 mins)	181	(115.4 overs, 317 mins)		298

VICTORIA	O	M	R	W	w,nb		O	M	R	W	w,nb	
McLeod	30.5	6	58	5	-,-		39	19	46	2	-,-	
Trott	28	5	81	2	-,-	(3)	35	2	111	2	-,-	
Maplestone	5	0	24	0	-,-	(4)	2	0	7	0	1,-	
Carlton	34	5	85	3	-,-	(2)	28	5	64	2	-,-	
Harry	4	3	5	0	-,1	(6)	12.3	7	20	4	-,1	
Laver	4	1	17	0	-,-	(8)	9	4	7	0	-,-	
Worrall						(5)	7	2	13	0	-,-	
Bruce						(7)	4	2	5	0	-,-	

SOUTH AUSTRALIA	O	M	R	W	w,nb		O	M	R	W	w,nb	
Jones	20	6	36	2	-,-		24	8	54	2	-,-	
A.Jarvis	16	2	45	1	-,-		31.4	9	62	4	-,-	
G.Giffen	17.5	3	56	4	-,-		37	8	104	3	-,-	
Reedman	8	3	28	0	-,-	(5)	9	4	17	0	-,-	
Parkin	3	1	5	0	-,1	(4)	4	2	11	0	-,-	
Haldane							6	1	19	0	1,-	
Lyons							4	1	12	0	-,-	

FALL OF WICKETS

Wkt	SA 1st	VIC 1st	SA 2nd	VIC 2nd
1st	46	23	16	17
2nd	93	27	154	154
3rd	116	38	200	192
4th	126	137	203	192
5th	173	142	218	205
6th	183	157	226	210
7th	188	172	227	234
8th	224	177	258	262
9th	224	179	263	268
10th	272	181	281	298

NEW SOUTH WALES v SOUTH AUSTRALIA (Shield Match 4)

Played at Sydney Cricket Ground on January 6, 8, 9, 1894. (Timeless match)
Toss : South Australia.   Result : NEW SOUTH WALES WON BY AN INNINGS AND 158 RUNS.
Debuts: New South Wales - H.J.K.Macpherson (f/c).
12th Men: S.R.Walford (NSW) and H.Haldane (SA).
Umpires: P.Argall and J.A.Tooher.
Attendances: 10079, 8441, 3209.   Total: 21,729.   Receipts: £1014.
Close of Play: 1st day NSW 3/38 (W.H.Moore 9, Newell 8); 2nd day NSW 393 all out.

It was originally intended that this match would start on January 5th, but the postponement of the Victoria-South Australia game led to a similar adjustment in Sydney. As the South Australians did not arrive from Melbourne until the morning of the 6th, the start was delayed until 2.30pm rather than forego the usual Saturday gate. Rain during the week had produced a soft pitch lacking the normal preparation, but despite this Giffen elected to bat in order to rest his men after their journey. Conditions suited Turner, who bowled unchanged throughout both innings, with Coningham and Newell offering admirable support. Moses held his leading batsmen back until the second day in the hope of easier conditions and his tactics were vindicated. He scored his only Shield century (104 in 195 minutes, 10 fours) and was aided by half-centuries from Newell (60 in 105 minutes, 1 five and 6 fours), Iredale (64 in about 120 minutes, 6 fours) and Callaway (60 not out in about 60 minutes, 10 fours). Moses and Iredale added 152 for the seventh wicket in just over two hours while Callaway and Macpherson (32 with 4 fours) put on 98 for the last wicket in 57 minutes. Rain on the second night and next morning sealed the fate of the visitors with conditions again tailor-made for Turner and Coningham. Sources: *Wisden, C.B.O'Reilly, Sydney Referee, Sydney Morning Herald, Town & Country Journal, Sydney Mail, Sydney Daily Telegraph.*

SOUTH AUSTRALIA

J.J.Lyons	c Newell b Coningham	20	c Callaway b Coningham		16
†A.H.Jarvis	c W.H.Moore b Coningham	9	c Mackenzie b Coningham		22
*G.Giffen	c & b Coningham	7	c & b Turner		22
J.C.Reedman	b Turner	6	c Moses b Coningham		37
J.Darling	c Murdoch b Turner	4	c Mackenzie b Turner		1
W.F.Giffen	c Murdoch b Newell	13	c Iredale b Coningham		0
H.Blinman	c & b Turner	25	c L.Moore b Turner		5
A.Jarvis	st W.H.Moore b Newell	13	c Mackenzie b Turner		5
A.Hill	b Turner	2	c L.Moore b Turner		6
G.T.Parkin	not out	0	b Coningham		0
E.Jones	c Mackenzie b Newell	4	not out		2
Extras	(b8, lb4, w1, nb1)	14	(lb1, w1)		2
Total	(45.4 overs, 127 mins)	117	(38.5 overs, 125 mins)		118

NEW SOUTH WALES

L.Moore	c G.Giffen b Jones	8
A.C.K.Mackenzie	c W.F.Giffen b G.Giffen	4
A.Coningham	c Jones b G.Giffen	8
†W.H.Moore	b A.Jarvis	9
A.L.Newell	c G.Giffen b A.Jarvis	60
W.L.Murdoch	b Jones	19
*H.Moses	c A.H.Jarvis b Jones	104
F.A.Iredale	c A.H.Jarvis b A.Jarvis	64
C.T.B.Turner	b A.Jarvis	0
S.T.Callaway	not out	60
H.J.K.Macpherson	run out (Blinman)	32
Extras	(b8, lb11, w6)	25
Total	(120.2 overs, 325 mins)	393

NEW SOUTH WALES	O	M	R	W	w,nb	O	M	R	W	w,nb
Turner	23	3	47	4	-,1	19.5	3	70	5	1,-
Coningham	18	2	43	3	1,-	19	5	46	5	-,-
Newell	4.4	2	13	3	-,-					

SOUTH AUSTRALIA	O	M	R	W	w,nb
Jones	32.2	5	86	3	5,-
G.Giffen	34	2	117	2	-,-
A.Jarvis	31	3	95	4	-,-
Reedman	10	1	39	0	-,-
Lyons	7	0	28	0	-,-
Parkin	6	4	3	0	1,-

FALL OF WICKETS

Wkt	SA 1st	NSW 1st	SA 2nd
1st	28	8	21
2nd	39	21	56
3rd	40	21	77
4th	53	46	79
5th	56	86	79
6th	91	139	103
7th	107	291	109
8th	111	295	110
9th	113	295	114
10th	117	393	118

NEW SOUTH WALES v VICTORIA (Shield Match 5)

Played at Sydney Cricket Ground on January 26, 27 (no play), 29, 30, 1894. (Timeless match)
Toss : Victoria.   Result : NEW SOUTH WALES WON BY 19 RUNS.
Debuts: Nil.
12th Men: J.Carlton (Vic). No 12th named for NSW.
Umpires: T.Flynn and J.A.Tooher.
Attendances: 13726, no play, 5798, 1853.   Total: 21,377.   Receipts: £976.
Close of Play: 1st day NSW (2) 3/45 (Newell 8, Turner 6); 2nd day no play; 3rd day Vic (2) 5/106 (Graham 16, McLeod 7).

Overnight rain completely ruined the pitch for batsmen on the first day. Callaway (38 in 55 minutes, 4 fours) was sent in to hit before it dried and easily made top score. Though the morning was "dull and muggy" (*Referee*), the sun emerged after lunch (NSW 2/72) and Moses was out straight away, the first of 21 wickets to fall in the afternoon on the now-damaged and sticky wicket. McLeod took three wickets in four balls (WWOW): Macpherson and Turner with the last two balls of an over and Newell, after an intervening maiden by Trumble, with the second ball of his next over. Walters was run out in the opening over of the Victorian innings. Intermittent rain saw the eventual abandonment of the second day's play without a ball bowled. Callaway (50 in 105 minutes, 5 fours) again topscored for New South Wales and Victoria were set 191 for victory on a difficult wicket. Further overnight showers softened the wicket even more and the umpires disagreed about the prospects of play. Tooher (New South Wales) did not want play to start whereas Flynn (Victoria) did. Play eventually began 50 minutes after the scheduled time and the visitors lost their last five wickets for 65. Edwin Evans was co-opted to substitute for Murdoch, who had left for Melbourne on business after the third day. (It was Murdoch's last first-class match in Australia; he returned to England and played there a further ten years.) Blackham was critical of the umpires after the match, claiming that his team had not received fair treatment. Tooher took some exception to his remarks and vowed never to umpire again, a decision he soon revoked. *Wisden* incorrectly gives L.Moore instead of W.H.Moore in NSW team. Sources: *Wisden, VCA Report, Sydney Referee, Sydney Morning Herald, Town & Country Journal, Sydney Mail, Sydney Daily Telegraph.*

NEW SOUTH WALES

W.L.Murdoch	b McLeod	2	c Worrall b Trumble	9
S.T.Callaway	c Trott b Phillips	38	(7) b Phillips	50
*H.Moses	c Trumble b McLeod	24	(6) lbw b McLeod	11
F.A.Iredale	c Walters b Trumble	8	(8) b Trumble	3
H.Donnan	c Trott b McLeod	6	(9) not out	13
S.E.Gregory	not out	20	(2) lbw b Trumble	10
H.J.K.Macpherson	st Blackham b McLeod	16	(3) b McLeod	7
C.T.B.Turner	c Trott b McLeod	0	(5) c Phillips b Trott	26
A.L.Newell	c Trott b McLeod	0	(4) b Trott	8
A.Coningham	run out (/Blackham)	10	b McLeod	1
†W.H.Moore	c Worrall b Trumble	0	c Trott b Phillips	4
Extras	(b1, nb2)	3	(b8, w1)	9
Total	(48.4 overs, 145 mins)	127	(67.1 overs, 175 mins)	151

VICTORIA

F.H.Walters	run out (Gregory/Moore)	0	c Callaway b Coningham	34
J.Harry	c Murdoch b Newell	4	b Turner	25
G.H.S.Trott	c Iredale b Turner	20	c Macpherson b Turner	19
F.J.Laver	b Turner	2	(10) b Turner	6
J.Worrall	c Turner b Newell	4	c Iredale b Turner	1
J.H.Stuckey	st Moore b Turner	1	(11) b Coningham	2
H.Graham	c Moses b Newell	10	(4) c Gregory b Coningham	45
H.Trumble	c Iredale b Turner	26	(9) c sub (E.Evans) b Coningham	1
*†J.M.Blackham	st Moore b Turner	12	(8) not out	9
J.Phillips	b Turner	3	(6) b Newell	0
C.E.McLeod	not out	0	(7) b Turner	23
Extras	(b6)	6	(b3, lb1, w1, nb1)	6
Total	(27.0 overs, 83 mins)	88	(87.1 overs, 235 mins)	171

VICTORIA	O	M	R	W	w,nb		O	M	R	W	w,nb
Trumble	20.4	7	46	2	-,2	(2)	28	11	45	3	-,-
McLeod	21	5	64	6	-,-	(1)	22	5	67	3	-,-
Phillips	4	2	11	1	-,-	(4)	5.1	1	4	2	-,-
Worrall	3	1	3	0	-,-						
Trott						(3)	12	3	26	2	1,-

NEW SOUTH WALES	O	M	R	W	w,nb		O	M	R	W	w,nb
Turner	14	2	51	6	-,-		39	12	59	5	-,1
Newell	13	2	31	3	-,-		24	8	46	1	-,-
Coningham							24.1	8	60	4	1,-

FALL OF WICKETS

Wkt	NSW 1st	VIC 1st	NSW 2nd	VIC 2nd
1st	32	0	20	60
2nd	54	12	29	64
3rd	72	27	35	83
4th	74	29	55	88
5th	82	35	68	91
6th	106	37	93	148
7th	106	48	112	153
8th	106	75	143	159
9th	123	88	144	168
10th	127	88	151	171

VICTORIA v TASMANIA

Played at Melbourne Cricket Ground on January 26, 27, 29, 1894. (Timeless match)
Toss : Tasmania.   Result : VICTORIA WON BY SEVEN WICKETS.
Debuts: Victoria - I.S.Drape, T.Tatchell (both f/c). Tasmania - A.J.Douglas, R.H.Sams, J.Watt, N.R.Westbrook (all f/c).
12th Men: C.H.Ross (Vic) and E.Maxwell (Tas).
Umpires: D.F.Cotter and R.M.Crockett.
Attendances: 2500, 2000, 200.   Total: About 4700.   Receipts: £180.
Close of Play: 1st day Vic 1/20 (Barrett 13, Tarrant 2); 2nd day Vic 9/327 (Bean 103).

Ingleton (originally 12th man) replaced R.Mitchell (family bereavement) in the Victorian team selected for the game. C.W.Rock and W.H.Savigny were unavailable for Tasmania. Letcher suffered a badly-split webbing on his left hand while attempting to catch Eady off his own bowling on the first day and took no further part in the match. Ross fielded for him for the rest of the innings and A.S.Carter did so on the last day. Bean's sole first-class century (103 not out in about 195 minutes, 4 fours) included a chance to Rock off Windsor at 37. His sixth-wicket stand of 144 with Houston (72 in about 120 minutes) swung the match Victoria's way. Tom Horan ('Felix' in *The Australasian*) wrote that Houston played "the best innings of the match" whereas Bean's century "was a meritorious essay, but not faultless". The innings concluded on Monday when it was found Letcher's hand injury had not healed sufficiently for him to bat. Tatchell was run out in the second innings attempting a fifth run off a hit by Barrett. Albert Trott, in his second match for Victoria, hinted at future deeds. *Cricket* and *VCA Report* incorrectly give Vic (1) Trott b Rock. *Age* and *Leader* incorrectly give Vic (1) Carlton c McAllen. Sources: *Cricket, VCA Report, The Age, The Argus, The Herald, The Australasian, The Leader, The Sportsman.*

TASMANIA

C.J.Eady	c Carlton b Trott	20	(5)	c Ingleton b Trott	55
†G.H.Gatehouse	c Barrett b Carlton	1	(6)	b Trott	0
J.H.Savigny	c Carlton b Trott	33	(1)	b Trott	20
*E.J.K.Burn	c Trott b Ingleton	35	(7)	b Trott	30
A.J.Douglas	c Barrett b Ingleton	2	(2)	lbw b Ingleton	3
E.A.C.Windsor	c Lewis b Bean	14	(4)	b Trott	3
N.R.Westbrook	c Lewis b Bean	24	(3)	b Ingleton	12
J.Watt	b Carlton	22		b Trott	0
R.H.Sams	c & b Trott	6	(10)	not out	28
C.McAllen	not out	16	(9)	c Barrett b Trott	26
N.V.Rock	b Trott	8		st Lewis b Carlton	8
Extras	(b10, lb2, w1, nb2)	15		(b5, nb1)	6
Total	(103.3 overs, 245 mins)	196		(85.5 overs, 195 mins)	191

VICTORIA

E.A.Barrett	c Eady b Sams	42		not out	28
T.Tatchell	b Eady	2		run out	3
W.A.Tarrant	b Eady	16		c Rock b Watt	17
I.S.Drape	lbw b Rock	32	(5)	not out	5
†P.M.Lewis	b Windsor	25			
*R.S.Houston	b Eady	72			
E.E.Bean	not out	103			
W.G.Ingleton	b Eady	4			
A.R.Carlton	c Gatehouse b Eady	3			
A.E.Trott	b Windsor	7	(4)	c Rock b Watt	5
C.Letcher	absent hurt	-			
Extras	(b7, lb7, w7)	21		(b4)	4
Total	(130.0 overs, 315 mins)	327		(20.0 overs, 45 mins) (3 wkts)	62

VICTORIA	O	M	R	W	w,nb		O	M	R	W	w,nb
Letcher	8.2	4	16	0	-,-						
Carlton	19.5	4	44	2	-,-	(4)	10.5	3	25	1	-,1
Ingleton	24	10	43	2	1,-	(2)	24	7	47	2	-,-
Trott	33.2	12	53	4	-,2	(1)	40	8	85	7	-,-
Bean	17	7	25	2	-,-	(3)	10	1	24	0	-,-
Drape	1	1	0	0	-,-						
Barrett						(5)	1	0	4	0	-,-

TASMANIA	O	M	R	W	w,nb		O	M	R	W	w,nb
Windsor	28	7	56	2	-,-		7	2	19	0	-,-
Eady	41	13	94	5	3,-		6	0	14	0	-,-
Sams	18	3	43	1	-,-		4	0	15	0	-,-
Rock	25	6	64	1	-,-						
Watt	8	2	15	0	3,-	(4)	3	0	10	2	-,-
Burn	6	2	16	0	-,-						
Douglas	4	1	18	0	-,-						

FALL OF WICKETS

Wkt	TAS 1st	VIC 1st	TAS 2nd	VIC 2nd
1st	4	8	4	9
2nd	49	58	20	46
3rd	68	70	29	53
4th	71	122	46	-
5th	105	126	46	-
6th	116	270	122	-
7th	157	284	122	-
8th	157	290	138	-
9th	179	327	166	-
10th	196	-	191	-

SOUTH AUSTRALIA v VICTORIA (Shield Match 6)

Played at Adelaide Oval on March 2, 3, 5, 6, 7, 1894. (Timeless match)
Toss : South Australia.   Result : SOUTH AUSTRALIA WON BY 58 RUNS.
Debuts: South Australia - R.H.Dyer, R.J.Hill (both f/c).
12th Men: J.McKenzie (SA) and W.A.Tarrant (Vic).
Umpires: G.E.Downs and J.Phillips.
Attendances: 5000, 7000, 4000, 2000, 1500.   Total: About 19,500.   Receipts: No figures published.
Close of Play: 1st day SA 5/290 (Darling 81, Dyer 28); 2nd day Vic 7/200 (R.W.McLeod 6, Mitchell 10); 3rd day SA (2) 4/244
    (Giffen 69); 4th day Vic (2) 3/229 (R.W.McLeod 44, Laver 43).

This win gave South Australia the Shield for the 1893-94 season and the trophy (which had still not been finished, two years after the competition's inception) was presented for the first time on July 14th 1894 during the half-time interval of an Australian Rules football match (Norwood v Port Adelaide) at the Adelaide Oval. Hill (no relation to the famous brotherhood) replaced A.H.Jarvis (unavailable) in the South Australian team and his sole first-class match became a personal nightmare. A delivery from Jones "split his left hand" (*Register*) in the opening over of the Victorian first innings and, although he continued in the position, his performance "was not first class" (*Register*). He was finally forced from the field in the final session of the fourth day when "a warm return from Hiscock put out" (*Register*) one of his fingers. First Reedman, and later Noel, took the gloves for the rest of the second innings while McKenzie substituted in the field. South Australia owed their victory firstly to batting contributions from Reedman (113 in 185 minutes, 16 fours) and Darling (87 in about 180 minutes, 9 fours), and later Lyons (101 in 125 minutes, 9 fours) and Giffen (89 not out in about 210 minutes), before Jones (5 for 73 - all bowled) took three wickets in four balls (Laver, C.E.McLeod, ball, Walters) in the first over of the last day to severely impair the Victorians' challenge. Lyons had scored his 101 out of 132 either side of the lunch break on the fourth day while Jones - who played a part in the dismissal of eight men - later removed Lewis and Carlton with successive deliveries to follow his near-hat-trick. Harry topscored in both innings for the visitors, his 82 occupying 115 minutes (1 five and 13 fours). Sources: *Wisden, C.B.O'Reilly, The Australasian, Adelaide Advertiser, South Australian Register.*

SOUTH AUSTRALIA

J.J.Lyons	b C.E.McLeod	21		c R.W.McLeod b Carlton	101
J.Noel	run out (/C.E.McLeod)	3		st Lewis b Carlton	17
*G.Giffen	c & b C.E.McLeod	29		not out	89
J.C.Reedman	c Lewis b C.E.McLeod	113		c & b A.E.Trott	27
J.Darling	b C.E.McLeod	87		b R.W.McLeod	24
A.Jarvis	c Laver b Carlton	2		c Carlton b G.H.S.Trott	7
R.H.Dyer	c Mitchell b G.H.S.Trott	40		b G.H.S.Trott	0
B.V.Scrymgour	st Lewis b G.H.S.Trott	4		st Lewis b C.E.McLeod	4
E.J.Hiscock	c G.H.S.Trott b C.E.McLeod	1		b C.E.McLeod	1
†R.J.Hill	not out	3		c A.E.Trott b C.E.McLeod	0
E.Jones	b G.H.S.Trott	0		c & b C.E.McLeod	0
Extras	(b7, lb6)	13		(b3, lb3)	6
Total	(128.5 overs, 320 mins)	316		(114.0 overs, 295 mins)	276

VICTORIA

F.H.Walters	lbw b Giffen	24	(7)	b Jones	0
J.H.Stuckey	b Giffen	37		b Noel	27
*G.H.S.Trott	run out (Scrymgour)	5		b Noel	11
J.Harry	c Jones b Jarvis	50	(1)	c & b Giffen	82
F.J.Laver	c Dyer b Jarvis	42		b Jones	44
C.E.McLeod	c Reedman b Jarvis	4		b Jones	0
†P.M.Lewis	b Jarvis	14	(8)	b Jones	41
R.W.McLeod	b Giffen	16	(4)	c Jones b Giffen	70
R.Mitchell	b Jones	15	(10)	run out (Giffen)	4
A.E.Trott	c & b Giffen	0	(11)	not out	0
J.Carlton	not out	6	(9)	b Jones	0
Extras	(b6, lb2, w1)	9		(b20, lb12, w1)	33
Total	(82.0 overs, 245 mins)	222		(110.4 overs, 320 mins)	312

VICTORIA	O	M	R	W	w,nb		O	M	R	W	w,nb
C.E.McLeod	38	17	77	5	-,-		34	16	51	4	-,-
Mitchell	18	5	40	0	-,-		11	2	34	0	-,-
G.H.S.Trott	19.5	6	45	3	-,-		15	4	47	2	-,-
A.E.Trott	9	2	32	0	-,-	(6)	8	3	24	1	-,-
Carlton	14	6	40	1	-,-		24	11	56	2	-,-
R.W.McLeod	20	9	43	0	-,-	(4)	15	2	36	1	-,-
Harry	8	3	18	0	-,-		2	0	7	0	-,-
Laver	2	0	8	0	-,-		5	1	15	0	-,-

SOUTH AUSTRALIA	O	M	R	W	w,nb		O	M	R	W	w,nb
Jarvis	27	7	56	4	-,-	(2)	27	4	64	0	-,-
Jones	16	7	51	1	-,-	(1)	23	5	73	5	-,-
Giffen	27	5	76	4	-,-		36.4	8	101	2	-,-
Reedman	5	0	13	0	-,-	(6)	5	4	3	0	-,-
Noel	7	1	17	0	1,-	(4)	13	4	26	2	1,-
Lyons						(5)	6	1	12	0	-,-

	FALL OF WICKETS			
	SA	VIC	SA	VIC
Wkt	1st	1st	2nd	2nd
1st	15	51	111	93
2nd	25	62	132	121
3rd	117	83	172	129
4th	236	165	244	230
5th	243	167	251	230
6th	304	184	251	230
7th	312	185	260	308
8th	313	206	270	308
9th	313	209	276	312
10th	316	222	276	312

NEW SOUTH WALES v QUEENSLAND

Played at Sydney Cricket Ground on March 24, 26, 27, 28, 1894. (Timeless match)
Toss : New South Wales.   Result : NEW SOUTH WALES WON BY TWO WICKETS.
Debuts: New South Wales - R.C.Brewster, C.W.Patrick, W.C.Robison (all f/c). Queensland - S.H.Bowden, R.Macdonald (both f/c);
A.Coningham, H.S.Freeman, E.H.Hutton, W.W.McGlinchey (all Qld only).
12th Men: W.Fraser (NSW). No 12th for Qld.
Umpires: C.Bannerman and J.A.Tooher.
Attendances: 1000, 3000, 500, 100.   Total: About 4600.   Receipts: No figures published.
Close of Play: 1st day Qld 2/25 (Macdonald 5, Freeman 2); 2nd day NSW 8/156 (Moses 41, Newell 1); 3rd day Qld (2) 6/182 (Freeman 55, Fisher 0).

Rain restricted play on the first day to 45 minutes (all before lunch) after Moses had invited Queensland to bat. Fine weather prevailed on the second and third days, however the wicket "began to get very difficult" (*SMH*) about an hour into the second day. The batting of Moses (43 not out with 1 four), although lacking his normal timing, held the New South Wales first innings together when the pitch was at its most difficult. Freeman (65 in about 180 minutes, 4 fours) and Callaway (60 in about 75 minutes) recorded half-centuries later in the match, the wicket being "in first class order" on the third day. Gould was out first ball in the second innings. Garrett and Newell got New South Wales home to their first win over Queensland with an unbroken stand of 35 for the ninth wicket. J.C.Davis, writing in the *Sydney Referee*, reported that the bowling action of Ramsay "was open to suspicion" when he delivered "with a little extra pace" and "at times threw the ball". However, umpires obviously did not share this view as he was not called in any of his first-class appearances. Bannerman replaced W.B.Fairfax, who had been originally appointed by the NSWCA to umpire with Tooher, while Brewster and Gould were late replacements for A.J.Hanigan and C.T.B.Turner (both unavailable) in the New South Wales team. Coningham and McGlinchey (both from New South Wales) and Freeman and Hutton (both from Victoria) all played their first match for Queensland, who had only eleven players in their party to Sydney. Coningham had actually played for New South Wales earlier this same season, and he returned there in 1895-96. There is some confusion over the dismissal of Ramsay in Qld (2). All sources give Ramsay c Callaway b Garrett in scorecards, but give Garrett 5/78 and Donnan 2/17. As Ramsay was last out, and Donnan is credited with the incomplete over, it seems likely Donnan was the successful bowler. Commentary in *SMH* also gives Donnan two wickets (no commentary in other sources). *Cricket* incorrectly gives NSW (1) Moses 44, total 161; Qld (2) Macdonald 27, Fisher 12. Sources: *Cricket, Sydney Referee, Sydney Morning Herald, Town & Country Journal, Sydney Mail, Sydney Daily Telegraph.*

QUEENSLAND

A.Coningham	c Gould b Garrett	7	c Patrick b Garrett		7
R.Macdonald	c Donnan b Garrett	5	c Wales b Callaway		28
W.W.McGlinchey	c Patrick b Newell	10	c Robison b Gould		40
H.S.Freeman	c Wales b Donnan	19	c Gregory b Gould		65
E.H.Hutton	lbw b Newell	31	b Garrett		4
C.Martin	b Callaway	2	c Newell b Garrett		5
†W.F.Bradley	c Wales b Garrett	11	lbw b Donnan		35
W.T.Fisher	run out (Brewster/Newell)	7	c Gould b Garrett		11
*M.F.Ramsay	c Newell b Garrett	5	c Callaway b Donnan		27
W.Hoare	b Newell	7	b Garrett		13
S.H.Bowden	not out	1	not out		1
Extras	(b7, lb1)	8	(b8, lb2)		10
Total	(60.5 overs, 160 mins)	113	(155.1 overs, 350 mins)		246

NEW SOUTH WALES

H.Donnan	c Ramsay b Hoare	12	st Bradley b Ramsay		47
S.T.Callaway	b Coningham	5	c Freeman b Coningham		60
*H.Moses	not out	43	c Macdonald b Coningham		15
S.E.Gregory	c Bradley b Bowden	28	c Hutton b Coningham		21
J.W.Gould	c Bowden b McGlinchey	23	b Coningham		0
R.C.Brewster	c Hoare b McGlinchey	7	(7) c Hoare b Ramsay		0
T.W.Garrett	c Macdonald b McGlinchey	0	(6) not out		35
W.C.Robison	st Bradley b Hoare	15	b Ramsay		0
C.W.Patrick	b Ramsay	12	c & b Ramsay		1
A.L.Newell	b Coningham	3	not out		16
†I.F.Wales	b Coningham	0			
Extras	(b10, lb1, w1)	12	(b5)		5
Total	(83.5 overs, 190 mins)	160	(84.5 overs, 195 mins) (8 wkts)		200

NEW SOUTH WALES	O	M	R	W	w,nb		O	M	R	W	w,nb						
Newell	19.5	6	44	3	-,-	(2)	25	12	44	0	-,-						
Garrett	21	6	37	4	-,-	(1)	49	20	78	5	-,-						
Donnan	11	5	15	1	-,-	(4)	16.1	9	17	2	-,-						
Callaway	9	5	9	1	-,-	(3)	35	19	34	1	-,-						
Gould							24	9	44	2	-,-						
Robison							3	1	8	0	-,-						
Brewster							3	0	11	0	-,-						

FALL OF WICKETS

Wkt	QLD 1st	NSW 1st	QLD 2nd	NSW 2nd
1st	9	9	14	99
2nd	20	21	70	111
3rd	26	63	91	142
4th	58	92	103	142
5th	71	104	111	149
6th	81	104	174	159
7th	95	128	204	159
8th	99	153	204	165
9th	105	160	245	-
10th	113	160	246	-

QUEENSLAND	O	M	R	W	w,nb		O	M	R	W	w,nb
Coningham	31.5	7	40	3	1,-		35	3	74	4	-,-
Hoare	12	0	38	2	-,-	(4)	6	0	26	0	-,-
Bowden	14	3	26	1	-,-		4	1	14	0	-,-
Ramsay	12	6	18	1	-,-	(5)	35.5	6	61	4	-,-
McGlinchey	14	4	26	3	-,-	(2)	4	0	20	0	-,-

1894-95 SEASON (20 MATCHES)

I mprovements in the preparation of Australian pitches were becoming evident by now and the 1894-95 season saw the staging of 20 first-class matches - a number not exceeded for a further nine years. In comparison with 1887-88 - admittedly an unusually wet summer - there was almost twice as many runs scored from a similar number of games: around 12,000 runs (an average of 598 per match) as against 7000 (366 per match). The better pitches immediately led to a higher standard of play in the colonies.

For the first time, an English team was brought to Australia under the joint patronage of the Melbourne Cricket Club and Sydney Cricket Ground trustees. A.E.Stoddart's team, the 13th English team to visit Australia, played 23 matches in all, including five Tests and seven other matches which are now considered first-class. Four games were lost - two Tests and one match each to South Australia and Victoria. The Test series created extraordinary interest, not only in this country, with the tourists clinching a 3-2 result in the deciding Fifth Test at Melbourne. The England batting gave a good account of itself throughout the tour with Stoddart, MacLaren, Ward and Brown each exceeding 1000 runs in all matches. The bowling, however, relied heavily on Richardson, Peel and Briggs to do the work in the important matches. Humphreys, the underhand lob bowler, captured 79 wickets in all matches, but 73 of those were in non-first-class games and he was not considered for the Tests. Stoddart was acclaimed as a competent and popular leader.

George Giffen had a remarkable season. He inherited the Australian captaincy from Blackham after the First Test and, as he was wont to do, led from the front. He dominated the Australian Test batting and bowling aggregates, scoring 475 runs (average 52.77) and taking 34 wickets (average 24.11). He enjoyed the captaincy which allowed him to deliver nearly twice as many balls as the next Australian. In all first-class matches in the season, Giffen had unparalleled figures: 902 runs at 50.11 and 93 wickets at 22.54.

Victoria regained the Sheffield Shield, losing only one of their four matches to the title-holders South Australia. Victoria fielded a well-balanced team throughout the campaign and the influence of Bruce, Graham and the McLeod and Trott brothers was readily evident. South Australia began well by winning both their home games but then lost comprehensively to New South Wales and Victoria away. Giffen, as his figures indicated, was a colossus who virtually carried the side alone. South Australia's batting looked good on paper, with Lyons, Reedman, Darling and the emerging Clem Hill to support Giffen, but it proved inconsistent. New South Wales - potentially another very good side - had similar problems of inconsistency. Iredale, Donnan and Syd Gregory batted well and McKibbin enjoyed some prolific returns late in the season to earn a Test berth.

The two remaining first-class matches were now also accepted as annual affairs. Victoria journeyed to Hobart to meet Tasmania and were defeated by eight wickets in a match which saw Charles Eady become the first batsman in Australian first-class cricket to compile a century in each innings. New South Wales visited Brisbane in February and defeated Queensland by six wickets in a low-scoring rain-affected game, McKibbin revelling with 14 for 87 in the match.

Leading Aggregates

Batsmen	M	I	NO	Runs	HS	Ave.	Bowlers	Runs	Wkts	Ave.
A.Ward (E)	12	22	0	916	219	41.63	G.Giffen (SA)	2097	93	22.54
G.Giffen (SA)	11	20	2	902	161	50.11	T.Richardson (E)	1616	68	23.76
F.A.Iredale (NSW)	12	23	3	882	140	44.10	R.Peel (E)	1441	57	25.28
A.E.Stoddart (E)	10	18	1	870	173	51.17	T.R.McKibbin (NSW)	733	44	16.65
S.E.Gregory (NSW)	12	23	1	849	201	38.59	C.T.B.Turner (NSW)	916	44	20.81
J.T.Brown (E)	12	21	2	825	140	43.42	J.Briggs (E)	1058	44	24.04
A.C.MacLaren (E)	11	20	3	803	228	47.23	G.H.S.Trott (V)	806	41	19.65
J.Darling (SA)	11	20	2	709	117	39.38	A.E.Trott (V)	773	35	22.08
G.H.S.Trott (V)	11	21	1	630	152	31.50				
F.G.J.Ford (E)	11	20	1	508	106	26.73				
W.Brockwell (E)	12	22	1	504	81	24.00				

SHEFFIELD SHIELD TABLE

	P	W	L	D	Quotient	Runs Scored	Wkts Lost	Runs Conceded	Wkts Taken
VICTORIA	4	3	1	-	1.156	1599	70	1383	70
SOUTH AUSTRALIA	4	2	2	-	0.994	1654	66	1764	70
NEW SOUTH WALES	4	1	3	-	0.893	1647	80	1753	76
TOTAL	6	6	6	-	1.000	4900	216	4900	216

SOUTH AUSTRALIA v A.E.STODDART'S ENGLAND XI

Played at Adelaide Oval on November 9, 10, 12, 13, 14, 1894. (Timeless match)
Toss : England XI.   Result : SOUTH AUSTRALIA WON BY SIX WICKETS.
Debuts: Nil.
12th Men: A.E.Green (SA). No 12th named for Eng XI.
Umpires: J.Phillips and G.H.G.Searcy.
Attendances: 5000, 8000, 8000, 3500, 1000.   Total: About 25,500.   Receipts: About £730.
Close of Play: 1st day Eng 5/342 (Brown 92, Ford 47); 2nd day SA 4/155 (G.Giffen 28, Darling 33); 3rd day Eng (2) 1/16 (Briggs 5);
    4th day SA (2) 3/164 (Reedman 76, G.Giffen 42).

South Australia defeated an English XI for the first time, largely due to the performance of their captain George Giffen who became the first allrounder in Australia to score at least 50 runs or take at least five wickets in all four innings of a first-class match. Darling hit his maiden century at this level (117 in 198 minutes, 1 five and 12 fours) and was missed by Brown off Humphreys when past 100; his stand of 173 with Giffen was a new South Australian fifth-wicket record. Reedman's steadying 83 (115 minutes, 9 fours) took the home team to victory and earned him a berth with Darling in the First Test the following month. Stoddart (66 in 75 minutes, 6 fours) and Brown added 110 for the third English wicket on the opening day in just over an hour. Brown's 115 (210 minutes, 1 five and 5 fours) included a solitary chance to Lyons off Jones when 64. Of the first nine English batsmen only Peel, who was out first ball, failed to reach 38. Sources: *Wisden, C.B.O'Reilly, The Australasian, Adelaide Advertiser, South Australian Register.*

A.E.STODDART'S ENGLAND XI

W.H.Lockwood	c A.H.Jarvis b G.Giffen	39	(8)	b G.Giffen	14
A.Ward	b G.Giffen	41	(1)	b Jones	11
*A.E.Stoddart	c Hill b Lyons	66		c W.F.Giffen b G.Giffen	9
J.T.Brown	c A.Jarvis b G.Giffen	115		c Dyer b G.Giffen	20
W.Brockwell	c Darling b A.Jarvis	45		c A.H.Jarvis b G.Giffen	1
R.Peel	b G.Giffen	0		lbw b A.Jarvis	15
F.G.J.Ford	c A.H.Jarvis b Jones	66		b G.Giffen	16
J.Briggs	c Dyer b G.Giffen	38	(2)	lbw b G.Giffen	8
†L.H.Gay	not out	39		st A.H.Jarvis b A.Jarvis	29
W.A.Humphreys	c A.H.Jarvis b A.Jarvis	0		c Blinman b A.Jarvis	4
T.Richardson	b A.Jarvis	15		not out	2
Extras	(b6, lb6, nb1)	13		(w1)	1
Total	(135.0 overs, 365 mins)	477		(47.0 overs, 135 mins)	130

SOUTH AUSTRALIA

J.J.Lyons	c Ford b Peel	29		c Lockwood b Peel	32
W.F.Giffen	b Peel	14		b Richardson	3
†A.H.Jarvis	b Peel	10		st Gay b Peel	9
J.C.Reedman	c Peel b Humphreys	29		c & b Humphreys	83
*G.Giffen	c Stoddart b Humphreys	64		not out	58
J.Darling	b Richardson	117		not out	37
R.H.Dyer	b Briggs	23			
A.Jarvis	st Gay b Briggs	35			
H.Blinman	not out	19			
C.Hill	b Peel	20			
E.Jones	c Humphreys b Peel	0			
Extras	(b7, lb7, nb9)	23		(b2, lb2)	4
Total	(138.5 overs, 375 mins)	383		(79.2 overs, 205 mins) (4 wkts)	226

SOUTH AUSTRALIA	O	M	R	W	w,nb		O	M	R	W	w,nb					
Jones	35	5	109	1	-,-		11	2	42	1	-,-					
A.Jarvis	33	8	118	3	-,-	(3)	13	1	38	3	1,-					
G.Giffen	53	7	175	5	-,-	(2)	23	7	49	6	-,-					
Reedman	5	1	22	0	-,-											
Lyons	9	1	40	1	-,1											

						FALL OF WICKETS
			ENG	SA	ENG	SA
Wkt	1st	1st	2nd	2nd		
1st	86	46	16	17		
2nd	96	49	26	44		
3rd	206	79	30	44		
4th	277	103	31	172		
5th	277	276	62	-		
6th	369	287	68	-		
7th	403	340	91	-		
8th	438	342	94	-		
9th	439	383	119	-		
10th	477	383	130	-		

ENGLISH XI	O	M	R	W	w,nb		O	M	R	W	w,nb
Richardson	33	9	85	1	-,-		13	4	41	1	-,-
Peel	36.5	14	69	5	-,-		27.2	6	62	2	-,-
Lockwood	22	3	70	0	-,9	(5)	7	0	32	0	-,-
Humphreys	22	3	62	2	-,-	(3)	18	3	54	1	-,-
Briggs	25	8	74	2	-,-	(4)	8	2	23	0	-,-
Brockwell							6	0	10	0	-,-

VICTORIA v A.E.STODDART'S ENGLAND XI

Played at Melbourne Cricket Ground on November 16, 17, 19, 20, 21, 1894. (Timeless match)
Toss : England XI.   Result : A.E.STODDART'S ENGLAND XI WON BY 145 RUNS.
Debuts: Nil.
12th Men: W.H.Lockwood (Eng). No 12th named for Vic.
Umpires: T.Flynn and J.Phillips.
Attendances: 3000, 11000, 7000, 5000, 2000.   Total: About 28,000.   Receipts: £1037.
Close of Play: 1st day Eng 4/379 (MacLaren 220, Peel 48); 2nd day Vic 7/201 (Harry 35, R.W.McLeod 20); 3rd day Eng (2) 4/191
    (Stoddart 78, Peel 51); 4th day Vic (2) 6/160 (C.E.McLeod 12, R.W.McLeod 30).

W.Bruce (work) and J.Worrall (hand injury) withdrew from the Victorian side named for the match. It had been expected that F.H.Walters, one of the emergencies, would replace Worrall but he declined, "taking umbrage at being left out of the original eleven" (*Age*). Palmer and Stuckey were the replacements. MacLaren (228 in 300 minutes, 22 fours) emulated his team-mate Brown's feat in the previous match to become the second England batsman to score a hundred on debut in Australia. He was the first batsman to compile a double-century in his maiden first-class appearance in this country and gave two chances, at 158 (Blackham off C.E.McLeod) and 168 (Mitchell off A.E.Trott). His second-wicket stand of 181 with Stoddart (77 with 8 fours) took only 145 minutes, the England captain completing a fine double with another half-century (78 in 210 minutes), in the second innings. Peel (48 in 110 minutes, 2 fours and 65 in 90 minutes, 3 fours) also batted well for the tourists. Victoria's best scorers were Harry (70 in 135 minutes), Harry Trott (63 in 90 minutes, 8 fours) and Bob McLeod (62 in 135 minutes, 5 fours). Stuckey was out first ball in the first innings. The game was played in ideal conditions. Sources: *Wisden, VCA Report, The Age, The Argus, The Herald, The Australasian, The Leader.*

A.E.STODDART'S ENGLAND XI

A.C.MacLaren	c G.H.S.Trott b C.E.McLeod	228	c A.E.Trott b R.W.McLeod	25
A.Ward	c G.H.S.Trott b A.E.Trott	4	b A.E.Trott	4
*A.E.Stoddart	b G.H.S.Trott	77	c Palmer b C.E.McLeod	78
J.T.Brown	c Laver b A.E.Trott	15	c Blackham b G.H.S.Trott	11
W.Brockwell	c A.E.Trott b G.H.S.Trott	4	c Graham b C.E.McLeod	20
R.Peel	b A.E.Trott	48	b C.E.McLeod	65
J.Briggs	c R.W.McLeod b A.E.Trott	0	c A.E.Trott b R.W.McLeod	43
†L.H.Gay	c C.E.McLeod b A.E.Trott	17	b C.E.McLeod	3
H.Philipson	c Harry b A.E.Trott	4	c & b A.E.Trott	12
W.A.Humphreys	c Blackham b C.E.McLeod	1	not out	18
T.Richardson	not out	0	c C.E.McLeod b G.H.S.Trott	3
Extras	(b6, lb9, w1, nb2)	18	(lb6)	6
Total	(138.1 overs, 315 mins)	416	(139.2 overs, 330 mins)	288

VICTORIA

R.Mitchell	c Gay b Briggs	25	(4) b Briggs	10
G.E.Palmer	c Peel b Briggs	6	(9) c Brown b Humphreys	36
G.H.S.Trott	c Brockwell b Briggs	16	(1) run out (Briggs)	63
F.J.Laver	c Brockwell b Humphreys	40	(3) c Humphreys b Peel	26
H.Graham	c Gay b Peel	29	b Briggs	0
J.H.Stuckey	b Peel	0	(2) lbw b Peel	17
C.E.McLeod	b Richardson	19	b Briggs	25
J.Harry	c Ward b Briggs	70	(6) lbw b Peel	1
R.W.McLeod	c Stoddart b Briggs	36	(8) b Peel	62
*†J.M.Blackham	not out	28	(11) st Gay b Peel	0
A.E.Trott	c Gay b Peel	25	(10) not out	11
Extras	(b3, lb9)	12	(b1, w1)	2
Total	(124.0 overs, 285 mins)	306	(105.5 overs, 265 mins)	253

VICTORIA	O	M	R	W	w,nb		O	M	R	W	w,nb			FALL OF WICKETS		
														ENG	VIC	ENG	VIC
C.E.McLeod	42.1	13	89	2	-,-	(2)	52	25	71	4	-,-	Wkt	1st	1st	2nd	2nd
A.E.Trott	42	13	103	6	1,-	(1)	45	14	110	2	-,-	1st	12	33	7	41
G.H.S.Trott	16	1	60	2	-,-		10.2	0	39	2	-,-	2nd	193	34	54	102
Mitchell	2	0	14	0	-,-							3rd	223	61	75	109
Palmer	8	2	36	0	-,1	(7)	1	1	0	0	-,-	4th	248	111	109	109
R.W.McLeod	11	1	48	0	-,-	(4)	24	8	40	2	-,-	5th	383	111	191	118
Harry	10	1	29	0	-,1	(5)	3	0	13	0	-,-	6th	383	133	244	118
Laver	7	3	19	0	-,-	(6)	4	2	9	0	-,-	7th	392	152	250	186
												8th	415	238	254	230
ENGLISH XI	O	M	R	W	w,nb		O	M	R	W	w,nb	9th	416	261	277	253
Richardson	32	6	92	1	-,-	(2)	17	2	45	0	-,-	10th	416	306	288	253
Briggs	38	4	97	5	-,-	(4)	36	6	95	3	-,-					
Humphreys	34.2	3	71	1	-,-		9	0	38	1	-,-					
Peel	17.4	4	27	3	-,-	(1)	43.5	15	73	5	1,-					
Brockwell	2	0	7	0	-,-											

NEW SOUTH WALES v A.E.STODDART'S ENGLAND XI

Played at Sydney Cricket Ground on November 23, 24, 26, 27, 1894. (Timeless match)
Toss : New South Wales.   Result : A.E.STODDART'S ENGLAND XI WON BY EIGHT WICKETS.
Debuts: New South Wales - B.W.Farquhar, W.P.Howell, J.J.Kelly, T.R.McKibbin (all f/c).
12th Men: A.C.K.Mackenzie (NSW) and H.Philipson (Eng).
Umpires: C.Bannerman and J.Phillips,
Attendances: 9729, 21548, 8537, 4592.   Total: 44,406.   Receipts: £2316.
Close of Play: 1st day NSW 5/244 (Donnan 29, Howell 9); 2nd day Eng 3/208 (Brown 83, Brockwell 5); 3rd day NSW (2) 3/56
     (Gregory 27, Donnan 13).

The match was notable for the first appearance of Howell, Kelly and McKibbin, all destined to play important roles in Test cricket over the next decade. Howell had been included in the team primarily as a hard-hitting batsman, but made an immediate impression as a right-arm fast-medium bowler when he was given the ball mid-innings, taking five wickets (all clean bowled), the last two with successive deliveries to wrap up the England innings. Iredale survived a difficult chance to Gay off Lockwood at 16 and went on to compile a highly-impressive 133 in 245 minutes with 20 fours. Richardson (48 with 3 fours) put up stoic resistance for 3 hours. Brown's 117 (190 minutes, 15 fours), his second hundred in three matches on tour, included chances at 26 (to Farquhar) and 92 (Donnan), both off Turner's bowling. Stoddart (79 in 168 minutes, 7 fours) and Brockwell (81 in 180 minutes, 10 fours) scored half-centuries for the tourists. Both Iredale and Farquhar suffered first-ball dismissals to Peel in the second innings. Gregory's 87 occupied 120 minutes with 12 fours. *Wisden* incorrectly gives NSW (2) Newell c & b Briggs; Eng (1) MacLaren 5, Extras 7, Newell 0/80, Gregory 0/7. Sources: *Wisden, Sydney Referee, Sydney Morning Herald, Town & Country Journal, Sydney Daily Telegraph.*

NEW SOUTH WALES

*C.A.Richardson	b Brockwell	48		b Peel	5
S.T.Callaway	b Lockwood	8		b Peel	10
S.E.Gregory	b Lockwood	6		b Briggs	87
F.A.Iredale	run out (Ford/Peel)	133		c Gay b Peel	0
H.Donnan	b Peel	37		b Humphreys	39
B.W.Farquhar	b Lockwood	1	(7)	lbw b Peel	0
W.P.Howell	b Lockwood	16	(9)	b Lockwood	6
C.T.B.Turner	run out (Stoddart/Gay)	12	(6)	b Peel	1
A.L.Newell	c Stoddart b Peel	2	(10)	c Ward b Briggs	5
†J.J.Kelly	not out	5	(8)	c Lockwood b Briggs	24
T.R.McKibbin	c Gay b Peel	12		not out	0
Extras	(b3, lb5, w1, nb4)	13		(b1, nb2)	3
Total	(133.3 overs, 350 mins)	293		(59.2 overs, 160 mins)	180

A.E.STODDART'S ENGLAND XI

A.C.MacLaren	c Richardson b Turner	4	(3)	not out	12
A.Ward	c Richardson b Callaway	36	(1)	c Callaway b Turner	18
*A.E.Stoddart	b Howell	79			
J.T.Brown	b Howell	117			
W.Brockwell	run out (Kelly)	81			
W.H.Lockwood	b Howell	21			
R.Peel	c Richardson b Donnan	8			
F.G.J.Ford	b Donnan	0	(2)	c Farquhar b Callaway	39
J.Briggs	b Howell	24			
†L.H.Gay	not out	16	(4)	not out	12
W.A.Humphreys	b Howell	0			
Extras	(b6, lb1, nb1)	8			-
Total	(166.5 overs, 390 mins)	394		(28.1 overs, 75 mins) (2 wkts)	81

ENGLAND XI	O	M	R	W	w,nb		O	M	R	W	w,nb
Lockwood	39	10	90	4	1,4		21	7	59	1	-,2
Peel	47.3	19	75	3	-,-		25	5	64	5	-,-
Briggs	15	3	39	0	-,-	(4)	4.2	2	9	3	-,-
Humphreys	12	1	32	0	-,-	(3)	9	0	45	1	-,-
Brockwell	16	5	33	1	-,-						
Ford	4	1	11	0	-,-						

NEW SOUTH WALES	O	M	R	W	w,nb		O	M	R	W	w,nb
Turner	41	14	100	1	-,1	(4)	7.1	4	17	1	-,-
Newell	40	10	83	0	-,-	(3)	5	1	19	0	-,-
McKibbin	19	3	68	0	-,-						
Callaway	22	6	44	1	-,-	(5)	5	0	16	1	-,-
Donnan	16	6	44	2	-,-	(2)	4	1	12	0	-,-
Howell	25.5	9	44	5	-,-	(1)	7	2	17	0	-,-
Gregory	3	2	3	0	-,-						

FALL OF WICKETS				
	NSW	ENG	NSW	ENG
Wkt	1st	1st	2nd	2nd
1st	11	10	15	40
2nd	25	72	34	62
3rd	151	179	34	-
4th	229	295	108	-
5th	231	339	109	-
6th	256	350	109	-
7th	262	350	166	-
8th	268	350	173	-
9th	274	394	180	-
10th	293	394	180	-

SOUTH AUSTRALIA v VICTORIA (Shield Match 1)

Played at Adelaide Oval on November 30, December 1, 3, 1894. (Timeless match)
Toss : Victoria.   Result : SOUTH AUSTRALIA WON BY TEN WICKETS.
Debuts: Victoria - C.J.Alsop (all f/c).
12th Men: J.H.Stuckey (Vic). No 12th named for SA.
Umpires: T.Flynn and G.H.G.Searcy.
Attendances: 3000, 6000, 3500.   Total: About 12,500.   Receipts: No figures published.
Close of Play: 1st day SA 1/15 (Reedman 9, Darling 4); 2nd day SA 6/281 (G.Giffen 74, Jarvis 15).

W.Bruce (work) and H.Trumble (ill) were unavailable for Victoria's trip to Adelaide. A.H.Jarvis was unable to be considered for the home team due to the aggravation of a long-standing hand injury in the game against England. Dyer survived four chances (25, 43, 56, 75) during his 170-minute stay at the crease. His 102 (his sole first-class century) included 10 fours and was scored out of 171 while he was at the wicket, including 118 for the third wicket in partnership with Darling. George Giffen made another match-winning allround contribution with 12 wickets for 147 and an unbeaten 94 in 4 hours. Several Victorian batsmen started promisingly but none went on to reach fifty. This was Victoria's fourth consecutive loss in their nine Shield matches to date, somewhat tempering their bright start of five straight wins. *Wisden* incorrectly gives Vic (1) Jones 2/72, Lyons 1/13. *O'Reilly* incorrectly gives Vic (2) G.H.S.Trott 12, Laver 21. Sources: *Wisden, C.B.O'Reilly, The Australasian, Adelaide Advertiser, South Australian Register.*

VICTORIA

H.Graham	c G.Giffen b Jarvis	6	(5) b G.Giffen		2
G.H.S.Trott	b Jones	15	(1) c G.Giffen b Lyons		21
F.J.Laver	b Jones	2	b G.Giffen		12
J.Worrall	c Blinman b G.Giffen	47	c Hill b G.Giffen		2
J.Harry	c Lyons b G.Giffen	35	(2) c & b G.Giffen		45
R.W.McLeod	b G.Giffen	46	b G.Giffen		0
C.E.McLeod	b G.Giffen	14	(9) not out		14
C.J.Alsop	c & b G.Giffen	1	(10) c Reedman b Lyons		13
A.E.Trott	c McKenzie b Lyons	38	(8) b Lyons		5
R.Mitchell	c Jarvis b G.Giffen	5	(11) c Reedman b G.Giffen		2
*†J.M.Blackham	not out	35	(7) c Jarvis b Lyons		10
Extras	(b4, lb1, w3)	8	(b6, lb2)		8
Total	(88.1 overs, 250 mins)	252	(56.5 overs, 150 mins)		134

SOUTH AUSTRALIA

J.J.Lyons	b C.E.McLeod	2	not out	19
J.C.Reedman	c & b Worrall	9	not out	10
J.Darling	c Mitchell b R.W.McLeod	46		
R.H.Dyer	run out (C.E.McLeod/Blackham)	102		
W.F.Giffen	b R.W.McLeod	5		
*G.Giffen	not out	94		
H.Blinman	run out (Graham/Blackham)	22		
A.Jarvis	c & b R.W.McLeod	20		
C.Hill	c A.E.Trott b Worrall	21		
†J.McKenzie	c Laver b C.E.McLeod	2		
E.Jones	c G.H.S.Trott b C.E.McLeod	26		
Extras	(b4, lb3, w2)	9		-
Total	(160.2 overs, 405 mins)	358	(5.5 overs, 15 mins) (0 wkts)	29

SOUTH AUSTRALIA	O	M	R	W	w,nb		O	M	R	W	w,nb
Jarvis	31	6	72	1	-,-	(2)	9	2	20	0	-,-
Jones	21	2	79	2	3,-	(1)	9	3	21	0	-,-
G.Giffen	34	9	87	6	-,-		25.5	7	60	6	-,-
Lyons	2.1	0	6	1	-,-		13	3	25	4	-,-

VICTORIA	O	M	R	W	w,nb		O	M	R	W	w,nb
C.E.McLeod	48.2	16	81	3	-,-		3	0	12	0	-,-
G.H.S.Trott	28	4	68	0	-,-	(3)	1.5	1	8	0	-,-
Worrall	9	2	33	2	-,-						
A.E.Trott	31	5	76	0	-,-	(2)	1	0	9	0	-,-
R.W.McLeod	38	13	82	3	1,-						
Harry	6	2	9	0	1,-						

FALL OF WICKETS

Wkt	VIC 1st	SA 1st	VIC 2nd	SA 2nd
1st	14	2	49	-
2nd	21	16	81	-
3rd	26	134	82	-
4th	101	144	86	-
5th	111	187	86	-
6th	151	246	87	-
7th	165	293	94	-
8th	174	321	103	-
9th	182	330	132	-
10th	252	358	134	-

QUEENSLAND v A.E.STODDART'S ENGLAND XI

Played at Exhibition Ground, Brisbane on December 7, 8, 10, 1894. (Timeless match)
Toss : England XI.   Result : A.E.STODDART'S ENGLAND XI WON BY AN INNINGS AND 274 RUNS.
Debuts: Queensland - O.C.Hitchcock (f/c); J.Carlton, I.S.Drape, P.S.McDonnell, M.Pierce (all Qld only).
12th Men: E.A.Cresswick & R.O'Brien (Qld emergencies) and W.A.Humphreys (Eng).
Umpires: J.Phillips and J.T.Wallace.
Attendances: 5000, 13000, 3500.   Total: About 21,500.   Receipts: About £700.
Close of Play: 1st day Eng 4/364 (Brockwell 31, MacLaren 14); 2nd day Qld (2) 2/29 (Macdonald 3).

The first first-class meeting between these teams produced the largest margin of victory by an innings at the Exhibition Ground. Ward (107 in 185 minutes, 1 five and 8 fours) and Stoddart (149 in 160 minutes, 1 six, 3 fives and 19 fours) shared a second-wicket partnership of 255 in 160 minutes, which remained for 15 years the highest stand against a Queensland side. Stoddart's chanceless innings was the first first-class century scored off the northern attack. Ward was missed twice, at 38 by McGlinchey off his own bowling, and at 65 by Macdonald off Carlton. MacLaren (74 not out in 135 minutes, 10 fours) added 102 in 90 minutes with Philipson (59 with 8 fours) for the ninth wicket. Pierce dismissed Philipson and Richardson in three balls to close the innings. The pitch was still in excellent condition and it was expected that the home batsmen would give a good account of themselves. However, after the opening stand had been broken only Coningham (43 in 75 minutes, 1 five and 7 fours) showed any capacity to handle the pace of Richardson, whose eleven wickets (ten bowled) were achieved without the help of fielders. Queensland failed again in the follow-on despite Stoddart resting his opening bowlers. Bradley sustained a king pair (clean bowled twice). Queensland's first innings had provided the sixth instance in Australia (the first since 1872-73) of no catches being held in a completed innings. Carlton and Drape (both ex-Victorians), McDonnell (ex-Victoria and New South Wales) and Pierce (ex-New South Wales) all had prior intercolonial experience prior to their Queensland debuts in this match. Sources: *Wisden, Brisbane Courier, Queensland Times, The Queenslander, R.H.Campbell.*

A.E.STODDART'S ENGLAND XI

A.Ward	lbw b McGlinchey	107
W.H.Lockwood	c Carlton b Coningham	14
*A.E.Stoddart	c Pierce b McGlinchey	149
J.T.Brown	c McDonnell b McGlinchey	34
W.Brockwell	b Coningham	33
A.C.MacLaren	not out	74
R.Peel	lbw b Coningham	3
F.G.J.Ford	b Coningham	1
J.Briggs	b Coningham	5
†H.Philipson	c McDonnell b Pierce	59
T.Richardson	c & b Pierce	0
Extras	(b9, lb5, w1)	15
Total	(150.4 overs, 385 mins)	494

QUEENSLAND

*P.S.McDonnell	b Richardson	21		c Ward b Lockwood	22
A.Coningham	b Peel	43	(5)	b Lockwood	19
W.F.Bradley	b Richardson	0	(6)	b Lockwood	0
R.Macdonald	b Richardson	18	(3)	b Richardson	20
W.W.McGlinchey	b Richardson	15	(4)	c & b Briggs	5
H.S.Freeman	b Richardson	8	(7)	run out	7
I.S.Drape	b Peel	0	(8)	b Richardson	2
W.Hoare	lbw b Richardson	0	(9)	b Richardson	6
J.Carlton	b Richardson	13	(2)	c Stoddart b Briggs	3
M.Pierce	b Richardson	0		not out	7
†O.C.Hitchcock	not out	1		b Lockwood	0
Extras	(lb2)	2		(b7, lb1)	8
Total	(37.1 overs, 120 mins)	121		(50.0 overs, 137 mins)	99

QUEENSLAND	O	M	R	W	w,nb
Coningham	51	11	152	5	-,-
Carlton	25	6	86	0	-,-
Pierce	24.4	1	109	2	1,-
McGlinchey	36	11	97	3	-,-
Hoare	14	3	35	0	-,-

ENGLAND XI	O	M	R	W	w,nb		O	M	R	W	w,nb
Peel	19	5	67	2	-,-						
Richardson	18.1	5	52	8	-,-	(3)	8	2	11	3	-,-
Briggs						(1)	17	8	26	2	-,-
Lockwood						(2)	25	7	54	4	-,-

FALL OF WICKETS

	ENG	QLD	QLD
Wkt	1st	1st	2nd
1st	25	49	5
2nd	280	49	29
3rd	287	77	35
4th	336	87	62
5th	368	97	62
6th	372	98	81
7th	378	99	82
8th	392	120	91
9th	494	120	98
10th	494	121	99

AUSTRALIA v ENGLAND (1st Test)

Played at Sydney Cricket Ground on December 14, 15, 17, 18, 19, 20, 1894. (Timeless match)
Toss : Australia.   Result : ENGLAND WON BY 10 RUNS.
Debuts: Australia - J.Darling, F.A.Iredale, E.Jones, C.E.McLeod, J.C.Reedman (all Test). England - J.T.Brown, F.G.J.Ford, L.H.Gay,
   A.C.MacLaren (all Test).
12th Men: H.Graham (Aust) and H.Philipson (Eng).
Umpires: C.Bannerman and J.Phillips.
Attendances: 10917, 24120, 11606, 8034, 6168, 1268.   Total: 62,113.   Receipts: £2832.
Close of Play: 1st day Aust 5/346 (Gregory 85, Reedman 4); 2nd day Eng 3/130 (Ward 67, Brockwell 18); 3rd day Eng 325 all out; 4th day
   Eng (2) 4/268 (Brockwell 20, Peel 9); 5th day Aust (2) 2/113 (Giffen 30, Darling 44).

This remarkable match produced many records and a surprising, weather-affected, result. After Richardson had taken three early wickets -
including that of Darling to his first ball in Test cricket - Australia rallied to their highest total so far, Gregory (career-best 201 in 243
minutes, 28 fours, 3 chances) and Blackham, in his final Test, (career-best 74 in 86 minutes, 8 fours) establishing the longest-standing of
all Australian wicket-partnership records, 154 in 76 minutes for the ninth wicket. Gregory's was the first Test double-century in Australia;
a public collection raised £103 for him on the second afternoon. Giffen (161 in 254 minutes, 1 five and 22 fours, 3 chances - his sole Test
hundred) and Iredale (81 in 146 minutes, 12 fours) also shared a big stand. Ward (75 in 166 minutes, 10 fours and a Test-best 117 in 224
minutes, 11 fours, chance at 28) registered a fine double for the Englishmen, who followed on. Blackham (badly cut thumb) was replaced
by McLeod at 8/313 in the first innings; the wicket-keeping alternated in the second innings between McLeod (start - 2/183, 4/268 - 6/313)
and Reedman (2/183 - 4/268, 6/313 - 10/437). Australia seemed certainties when stumps were drawn after five days, needing just 64 more
runs, but it rained heavily that night and next morning "the sun shone out bright and hot, making the wicket sticky and very difficult"
(*SMH*). Peel and Briggs caused Australia to lose their last 8 for 36. It was the first instance in Tests that a side had won after following
on. The match aggregate (1514 runs) and duration (six playing days) were new first-class records. *Wisden* incorrectly gives Eng (2) extras
21, Jones 1/58. Sources: *Wisden, The Leader, Sydney Referee, Sydney Morning Herald, NSWCA Scorebook, Sydney Telegraph.*

AUSTRALIA

J.J.Lyons	b Richardson	1		b Richardson	25
G.H.S.Trott	b Richardson	12		c Gay b Peel	8
G.Giffen	c Ford b Brockwell	161		lbw b Briggs	41
J.Darling	b Richardson	0		c Brockwell b Peel	53
F.A.Iredale	c Stoddart b Ford	81	(6)	c & b Briggs	5
S.E.Gregory	c Peel b Stoddart	201	(5)	c Gay b Peel	16
J.C.Reedman	c Ford b Peel	17		st Gay b Peel	4
C.E.McLeod	b Richardson	15		not out	2
C.T.B.Turner	c Gay b Peel	1		c Briggs b Peel	2
*†J.M.Blackham	b Richardson	74	(11)	c & b Peel	2
E.Jones	not out	11	(10)	c MacLaren b Briggs	1
Extras	(b8, lb3, w1)	12		(b2, lb1, nb4)	7
Total	(172.3 overs, 431 mins)	586		(68.0 overs, 198 mins)	166

ENGLAND

A.C.MacLaren	c Reedman b Turner	4	b Giffen	20
A.Ward	c Iredale b Turner	75	b Giffen	117
*A.E.Stoddart	c Jones b Giffen	12	c Giffen b Turner	36
J.T.Brown	run out (Lyons/Blackham)	22	c Jones b Giffen	53
W.Brockwell	c Blackham b Jones	49	b Jones	37
R.Peel	c Gregory b Giffen	4	b Giffen	17
F.G.J.Ford	st Blackham b Giffen	30	c & b McLeod	48
J.Briggs	b Giffen	57	b McLeod	42
W.H.Lockwood	c Giffen b Trott	18	b Trott	29
†L.H.Gay	c Gregory b Reedman	33	b Trott	4
T.Richardson	not out	0	not out	12
Extras	(b17, lb3, w1)	21	(b14, lb8)	22
Total	(140.3 overs, 344 mins)	325	(181.4 overs, 412 mins)	437

ENGLAND	O	M	R	W	w,nb		O	M	R	W	w,nb					
Richardson	55.3	13	181	5	-,-		11	3	27	1	-,-				FALL OF WICKETS	
Peel	53	14	140	2	-,-		30	9	67	6	-,-			AUST	ENG	ENG	AUST
Briggs	25	4	96	0	-,-	(4)	11	2	25	3	-,-	Wkt	1st	1st	2nd	2nd
Brockwell	22	7	78	1	-,-							1st	10	14	44	26
Ford	11	2	47	1	1,-							2nd	21	43	115	45
Stoddart	3	0	31	1	-,-							3rd	21	78	217	130
Lockwood	3	2	1	0	-,-	(3)	16	3	40	0	-,4	4th	192	149	245	135
												5th	331	155	290	147
												6th	379	211	296	158
AUSTRALIA	O	M	R	W	w,nb		O	M	R	W	w,nb	7th	400	211	385	159
Jones	19	7	44	1	1,-		19	0	57	1	-,-	8th	409	252	398	161
Turner	44	16	89	2	-,-		35	14	78	1	-,-	9th	563	325	420	162
Giffen	43	17	75	4	-,-		75	25	164	4	-,-	10th	586	325	437	166
Trott	15	4	59	1	-,-		12.4	2	22	2	-,-					
McLeod	14	2	25	0	-,-		30	7	67	2	-,-					
Reedman	3.3	1	12	1	-,-		6	1	12	0	-,-					
Lyons	2	2	0	0	-,-		2	0	12	0	-,-					
Iredale							2	1	3	0	-,-					

VICTORIA v NEW SOUTH WALES (Shield Match 2)

Played at Melbourne Cricket Ground on December 22, 24, 26, 27, 1894. (Timeless match)
Toss : Victoria.   Result : VICTORIA WON BY 161 RUNS.
Debuts: Nil.
12th Men: C.J.Alsop & R.Mitchell (Vic emergencies) and B.W.Farquhar (NSW).
Umpires: E.J.Briscoe and T.Flynn.
Attendances: 5000, 9000, 4000, 2500.   Total: About 20,500.   Receipts: £719.
Close of Play: 1st day Vic 9/175 (C.E.McLeod 21, A.E.Trott 24); 2nd day Vic (2) 1/54 (Worrall 34, Trumble 2); 3rd day NSW (2) 1/7 (Kelly 5).

Rain caused substantial delays on each of the first three days, resulting in a soft wicket and saturated outfield. Hot humid weather on the last day manufactured a "sticky" to further compound batting problems. Gregory gave a dazzling display in the circumstances, hitting 101 in about 90 minutes (1 five and 9 fours) including 20 off an over from G.H.S.Trott. He made his runs out of 142 and gave a solitary chance to Harry off Charlie McLeod at 75. Either or both of the Trott brothers featured in all ten second-innings dismissals. The Victorians had batted manfully for their first-innings runs before being dismissed with the second ball of the second day's play. Bob McLeod's best figures for Victoria (6 for 20) accounted for New South Wales's lowest total in the Sheffield Shield. Worrall, promoted to open the second innings, scored 96 in 210 minutes and hit 1 five and 10 fours. Sources: *Wisden, VCA Report, The Age, The Argus, The Herald, The Australasian, The Leader, Town & Country Journal.*

VICTORIA

*G.H.S.Trott	c Iredale b Turner	12	(5) b Turner	38
W.Bruce	c & b Turner	19	(4) c Howell b Callaway	13
F.J.Laver	b Howell	24	(7) c Garrett b Howell	18
H.Graham	b Howell	16	(9) c Kelly b Turner	4
J.Harry	c Donnan b Callaway	29	(6) c & b Howell	10
J.Worrall	c Turner b Callaway	11	(1) c Gregory b Howell	96
H.Trumble	c Donnan b Callaway	4	(3) b Newell	12
R.W.McLeod	c Kelly b Callaway	0	(11) st Kelly b Turner	1
†P.M.Lewis	c Donnan b Turner	10	(10) not out	4
C.E.McLeod	not out	21	(2) c Macpherson b Newell	15
A.E.Trott	b Turner	24	(8) b Turner	9
Extras	(b2, lb3)	5	(b13, lb13)	26
Total	(84.2 overs, 206 mins)	175	(107.3 overs, 257 mins)	246

NEW SOUTH WALES

H.Donnan	c A.E.Trott b C.E.McLeod	2	(3) c A.E.Trott b G.H.S.Trott	0
C.T.B.Turner	b R.W.McLeod	12	(9) b A.E.Trott	6
S.E.Gregory	c Laver b R.W.McLeod	2	(5) c A.E.Trott b C.E.McLeod	101
F.A.Iredale	b Trumble	24	b A.E.Trott	9
W.J.Camphin	c Laver b R.W.McLeod	5	(8) b G.H.S.Trott	13
S.T.Callaway	c Lewis b R.W.McLeod	2	(7) run out (A.E.Trott)	23
*T.W.Garrett	c Worrall b Trumble	7	(10) not out	11
†J.J.Kelly	run out	1	(1) b A.E.Trott	16
H.J.K.Macpherson	not out	8	(6) b A.E.Trott	6
W.P.Howell	c Trumble b R.W.McLeod	0	(11) c G.H.S.Trott b A.E.Trott	0
A.L.Newell	c Harry b R.W.McLeod	0	(2) c A.E.Trott b G.H.S.Trott	2
Extras	(b3)	3	(b4, lb2, nb1)	7
Total	(33.5 overs, 95 mins)	66	(82.1 overs, 195 mins)	194

NEW SOUTH WALES	O	M	R	W	w,nb		O	M	R	W	w,nb					
Turner	31.2	15	64	4	-,-		40.3	15	65	4	-,-					
Howell	26	12	49	2	-,-	(3)	27	5	66	3	-,-					
Callaway	21	5	46	4	-,-	(2)	18	3	39	1	-,-					
Donnan	5	2	9	0	-,-	(6)	3	1	7	0	-,-					
Garrett	1	0	2	0	-,-		4	2	8	0	-,-					
Newell						(4)	15	8	35	2	-,-					

FALL OF WICKETS

Wkt	VIC 1st	NSW 1st	VIC 2nd	NSW 2nd
1st	33	4	48	7
2nd	46	7	83	7
3rd	71	27	119	27
4th	76	47	184	32
5th	95	50	188	46
6th	101	51	208	125
7th	109	57	229	169
8th	128	64	237	175
9th	130	66	239	192
10th	175	66	246	194

VICTORIA	O	M	R	W	w,nb		O	M	R	W	w,nb
C.E.McLeod	7	1	16	1	-,-	(6)	15	4	35	1	-,-
R.W.McLeod	16.5	6	20	6	-,-	(4)	10	5	17	0	-,-
Trumble	10	1	27	2	-,-	(1)	10	3	28	0	-,1
A.E.Trott						(2)	32.1	14	55	5	-,-
G.H.S.Trott						(3)	13	3	47	3	-,-
Bruce						(5)	2	0	5	0	-,-

AUSTRALIA v ENGLAND (2nd Test)

Played at Melbourne Cricket Ground on December 29, 31, 1894, January 1, 2, 3, 1895. (Timeless match)
Toss : Australia.   Result : ENGLAND WON BY 94 RUNS.
Debuts: Australia - A.Coningham (Test).
12th Men: J.Harry (Aust). No 12th named for England.
Umpires: T.Flynn and J.Phillips.
Attendances: 14000, 15000, 21000, 14000, few.   Total: About 65,000.   Receipts: £2879.
Close of Play: 1st day Aust 123 all out; 2nd day Eng (2) 4/287 (Stoddart 151, Peel 18); 3rd day Aust (2) 0/86 (Bruce 43, Trott 43); 4th day Aust (2) 9/328 (Iredale 63, Turner 26).

Heavy rain before the match saturated the pitch and Giffen, on winning the toss (which was conducted 20 minutes late due to the players electing their new captain), delayed putting England in until a further inspection with Bruce and Trott. Arthur Coningham - the 43rd Australian and 101st player overall to bowl in a Test - became the first to secure a wicket with his first ball, MacLaren popping a dolly catch to Trott at point. It was the first time a wicket had fallen to the first ball of a Test. Coningham, playing in his only Test, was the first to represent Australia while playing for Queensland. England were bowled out inside two hours for 75, the pitch being particularly bad at one end. However, it "improved wonderfully" (*The Age*) when subjected to the heavy roller, and in the circumstances Australia should have greatly exceeded their 123 in reply; they were dismissed at 5.58pm mainly due to the efforts of Richardson, 20 wickets falling on the first day. By mutual consent, the pitch was given an extended rolling before play commenced on Monday. Stoddart's 173 (320 minutes, 3 fives and 14 fours) was the highest Test innings by an Englishman so far and remained until 1974-75 the best by an England captain in Australia. Peel (53 in 168 minutes, 0 fours) was the only other batsman to surpass 50 in the innings, but for the first time in a Test all eleven men reached double figures. Bruce (54 in 85 minutes) and Trott (95 in 220 minutes, 6 fours) began the chase promisingly, but Australia, after being 1/191 at one stage, lost 8 for 77, Brockwell taking three vital wickets; and seven balls sufficed on the fifth day to finish the match. Late on the fourth day Turner had survived a vociferous appeal for "obstructing the field" when Lockwood (mid-on) had taken a shot at his wicket, Turner intercepting it with his bat. *Wisden* incorrectly gives Aust (2) Trumble 3. Sources: *Wisden, The Age, The Argus, The Herald, The Australasian, The Leader, The Sportsman*.

ENGLAND

A.C.MacLaren	c Trott b Coningham	0	b Turner		15
A.Ward	c Darling b Trumble	30	b Turner		41
*A.E.Stoddart	b Turner	10	b Giffen		173
J.T.Brown	c Trumble b Turner	0	c Jarvis b Bruce		37
W.Brockwell	c Iredale b Coningham	0	b Turner		21
R.Peel	c Trumble b Turner	6	st Jarvis b Giffen		53
F.G.J.Ford	c Giffen b Trumble	9	c Trott b Giffen		24
W.H.Lockwood	not out	3	(9) not out		33
J.Briggs	c Bruce b Turner	5	(8) lbw b Giffen		31
†H.Philipson	c Darling b Turner	1	b Giffen		30
T.Richardson	c Iredale b Trumble	0	c Gregory b Giffen		11
Extras	(lb9, nb2)	11	(b1, lb2, nb3)		6
Total	(40.1 overs, 115 mins)	75	(202.2 overs, 477 mins)		475

AUSTRALIA

J.J.Lyons	b Richardson	2	(7) b Peel		14
W.Bruce	c Ford b Peel	4	(1) c Stoddart b Peel		54
*G.Giffen	c Philipson b Briggs	32	c Brown b Brockwell		43
S.E.Gregory	c Ward b Richardson	2	b Richardson		12
J.Darling	b Lockwood	32	b Brockwell		5
F.A.Iredale	b Richardson	10	b Peel		68
G.H.S.Trott	run out (Peel/Richardson)	16	(2) c & b Brockwell		95
A.Coningham	c Philipson b Richardson	10	(9) b Peel		3
H.Trumble	b Richardson	1	(10) run out (Briggs/Philipson)		2
†A.H.Jarvis	c Brown b Briggs	11	(8) b Richardson		4
C.T.B.Turner	not out	1	not out		26
Extras	(w2)	2	(b5, lb1, nb1)		7
Total	(55.5 overs, 150 mins)	123	(136.1 overs, 366 mins)		333

AUSTRALIA	O	M	R	W	w,nb		O	M	R	W	w,nb
Coningham	11	5	17	2	-,-		20	4	59	0	-,-
Turner	20	9	32	5	-,-	(3)	55	21	99	3	-,-
Trumble	9.1	4	15	3	-,2	(5)	26	6	72	0	-,3
Giffen						(2)	78.2	21	155	6	-,-
Trott						(4)	17	0	60	0	-,-
Bruce							4	0	21	1	-,-
Lyons							2	1	3	0	-,-

ENGLAND	O	M	R	W	w,nb		O	M	R	W	w,nb
Richardson	23	6	57	5	1,-		40	10	100	2	-,-
Peel	14	4	21	1	-,-		40.1	9	77	4	-,-
Lockwood	5	0	17	1	1,-		25	5	60	0	-,1
Briggs	13.5	2	26	2	-,-		12	0	49	0	-,-
Ford							5	2	7	0	-,-
Brockwell							14	3	33	3	-,-

FALL OF WICKETS

Wkt	ENG 1st	AUST 1st	ENG 2nd	AUST 2nd
1st	0	4	24	98
2nd	19	12	101	191
3rd	23	15	191	206
4th	26	53	222	214
5th	44	80	320	216
6th	58	86	362	241
7th	60	108	383	254
8th	70	110	402	263
9th	71	116	455	268
10th	75	123	475	333

SOUTH AUSTRALIA v NEW SOUTH WALES (Shield Match 3)

Played at Adelaide Oval on January 5, 7, 8, 9, 1895. (Timeless match)
Toss : New South Wales.   Result : SOUTH AUSTRALIA WON BY FOUR WICKETS.
Debuts: New South Wales - V.T.Trumper (f/c).
12th Men: None named.
Umpires: E.J.Briscoe and G.E.Downs.
Attendances: 6000, 4000, 3000, 1500.   Total: About 14,500.   Receipts: No figures published.
Close of Play: 1st day SA 1/6 (Hill 1); 2nd day NSW (2) 0/13 (Kelly 6, Newell 7); 3rd day SA (2) 3/24 (A.Jarvis 5, Blinman 1).

George Giffen - already the title-holder to the highest innings in the Sheffield Shield (205) and the best innings bowling figures (9 for 147) - now took a match analysis of 16 for 186 which, to the time of writing, still remains the best in the competition's history. Mr.J.Portus (NSW Manager) said of Giffen after the match that the performance "stamped him as the best bowler on a good wicket the world had seen for many a day" (*Register*). A.H.Jarvis (career-best 98 not out in 165 minutes, 9 fours) shared a new South Australian ninth-wicket record of 128 with Blinman, whose undefeated 67 on the last day (188 minutes, 7 fours) guided the South Australians to victory. Moses batted 3 hours to score 77 (5 fours), the only half-century for New South Wales. Trumper made his debut, a quiet one, at the age of 17 years 64 days. Sources: *Wisden, C.B.O'Reilly, Sydney Morning Herald, Sydney Daily Telegraph, Adelaide Advertiser, South Australian Register.*

NEW SOUTH WALES

Batsman	First Innings	Runs	Second Innings	Runs
F.A.Iredale	c A.Jarvis b G.Giffen	25	(4) c Jones b G.Giffen	25
*T.W.Garrett	b G.Giffen	48	(7) c Reedman b Lyons	4
H.Moses	b G.Giffen	13	b G.Giffen	77
H.Donnan	b Jones	24	(6) not out	48
S.E.Gregory	c & b G.Giffen	2	c Jones b G.Giffen	42
V.T.Trumper	run out (Reedman/A.H.Jarvis)	11	(9) c Jones b G.Giffen	0
S.T.Callaway	c Lyons b G.Giffen	23	(10) b G.Giffen	15
C.T.B.Turner	b G.Giffen	3	(11) c W.F.Giffen b G.Giffen	9
W.P.Howell	c Reedman b G.Giffen	24	(8) c Hill b Lyons	2
†J.J.Kelly	b G.Giffen	13	(1) b G.Giffen	9
A.L.Newell	not out	0	(2) c A.H.Jarvis b G.Giffen	12
Extras	(b6)	6	(b3, lb1)	4
Total	(93.2 overs, 235 mins)	192	(96.1 overs, 255 mins)	247

SOUTH AUSTRALIA

Batsman	First Innings	Runs	Second Innings	Runs
W.F.Giffen	b Howell	4		
C.Hill	b Callaway	9		
J.J.Lyons	b Callaway	47	(2) b Callaway	8
*G.Giffen	c & b Callaway	3	(7) b Howell	26
J.Darling	b Callaway	14	(8) not out	26
J.C.Reedman	c Gregory b Newell	20	(1) b Callaway	4
R.H.Dyer	b Newell	26	(3) b Howell	4
A.Jarvis	b Turner	2	(4) b Howell	24
†A.H.Jarvis	not out	98	(6) b Howell	5
H.Blinman	lbw b Turner	37	(5) not out	67
E.Jones	b Callaway	6		
Extras	(b1, lb3)	4	(b4, lb2)	6
Total	(120.3 overs, 285 mins)	270	(76.4 overs, 208 mins) (6 wkts)'	170

SOUTH AUSTRALIA	O	M	R	W	w,nb		O	M	R	W	w,nb
Jones	17	4	53	1	-,-	(2)	11	0	59	0	-,-
A.Jarvis	33	10	56	0	-,-	(3)	17	3	33	0	-,-
G.Giffen	43.2	10	77	8	-,-	(1)	48.1	9	109	8	-,-
Reedman							1	0	3	0	-,-
Lyons							19	2	39	2	-,-

NEW SOUTH WALES	O	M	R	W	w,nb		O	M	R	W	w,nb
Newell	18	9	24	2	-,-	(5)	11	4	29	0	-,-
Callaway	43.3	9	108	5	-,-	(1)	22	11	38	2	-,-
Howell	28	7	83	1	-,-	(2)	24	7	55	4	-,-
Garrett	5	2	7	0	-,-	(6)	6.4	5	7	0	-,-
Turner	15	2	32	2	-,-	(3)	8	3	13	0	-,-
Donnan	8	6	6	0	-,-	(4)	5	0	22	0	-,-
Gregory	3	1	6	0	-,-						

FALL OF WICKETS

Wkt	NSW 1st	SA 1st	NSW 2nd	SA 2nd
1st	60	6	18	12
2nd	90	22	29	17
3rd	94	32	87	17
4th	99	75	153	70
5th	123	90	183	76
6th	134	125	194	125
7th	141	126	201	-
8th	162	129	203	-
9th	187	257	233	-
10th	192	270	247	-

AUSTRALIA v ENGLAND (3rd Test)

Played at Adelaide Oval on January 11, 12, 14, 15, 1895. (Timeless match)
Toss : Australia.   Result : AUSTRALIA WON BY 382 RUNS.
Debuts: Australia - J.Harry, A.E.Trott (both Test).
12th Men: C.T.B.Turner (Aust) and L.H.Gay (Eng).
Umpires: J.Phillips and G.H.G.Searcy.
Attendances: 5000, 12000, 9000, 1500.   Total: About 27,500.   Receipts: £1154.
Close of Play: 1st day Eng 0/5 (MacLaren 1, Briggs 4); 2nd day Aust (2) 4/145 (Iredale 31); 3rd day Eng (2) 3/56 (Stoddart 1, Brown 2).

Australia gained the first Test victory by a margin exceeding 300 runs with this performance, in which the 21-year-old Albert Trott, making his debut, played a big part. Temperatures soared well above 100ºF on the first two days, an unimaginable 155ºF (68.3ºC) prevailing at one stage. England's poor showing in the first innings was attributed to the heat; doubts had been expressed before the match about the pitch, a new one, but it generally played well. For the Australians, who had gone into the match without H.Moses (business commitments) and C.T.B.Turner (ill), Giffen (58 in 155 minutes, 4 fours), Bruce (80 in 110 minutes, 11 fours) and most of all Iredale (a Test-best 140 in 304 minutes, 17 fours, chances at 40 and 49) found the strength to exceed 50 in the top order. Albert Trott, batting at No. 10, shared last-wicket stands with Callaway of 81 and 64, scoring 110 runs without being dismissed (including 72 in 90 minutes, 11 fours), and captured the best innings-analysis (8 for 43) by a debutant in all Test cricket. He and his captain, who combined to take the last wicket - Giffen bowled himself virtually unchanged throughout both innings - were chaired off shoulder-high at the finish. Peel's pair included a first-ball dismissal in the second innings. *Wisden* incorrectly gives Aust (2) Briggs 2/57, Lockwood 1/71; Eng (2) Ford b A.E.Trott. Sources: *Wisden, Australian Cricket Record, The Australasian, Adelaide Advertiser, South Australian Register.*

AUSTRALIA

W.Bruce	b Richardson	11	(2) c Brockwell b Briggs	80
G.H.S.Trott	run out (/Peel)	48	(1) b Peel	0
*G.Giffen	c Lockwood b Brockwell	58	c Ford b Peel	24
F.A.Iredale	b Richardson	7	c & b Peel	140
J.Darling	c Philipson b Briggs	10	c Philipson b Lockwood	3
S.E.Gregory	c Brown b Richardson	6	b Richardson	20
J.Harry	b Richardson	2	b Richardson	6
J.Worrall	run out (Richardson/Philipson)	0	c Peel b Briggs	11
†A.H.Jarvis	c & b Lockwood	13	c Brown b Peel	29
A.E.Trott	not out	38	not out	72
S.T.Callaway	b Richardson	41	b Richardson	11
Extras	(b2, w1, nb1)	4	(b7, lb7, nb1)	15
Total	(81.1 overs, 250 mins)	238	(115.2 overs, 330 mins)	411

ENGLAND

A.C.MacLaren	b Callaway	25	c Iredale b A.E.Trott	35
J.Briggs	b Callaway	12	(9) b A.E.Trott	0
W.Brockwell	c Harry b Callaway	12	(6) c & b A.E.Trott	24
A.Ward	c Bruce b Giffen	5	(2) b A.E.Trott	13
*A.E.Stoddart	b Giffen	1	(3) not out	34
J.T.Brown	not out	39	(5) b A.E.Trott	2
R.Peel	b Callaway	0	c & b A.E.Trott	0
F.G.J.Ford	c Worrall b Giffen	21	c G.H.S.Trott b A.E.Trott	14
W.H.Lockwood	c Worrall b Giffen	0	(10) c Iredale b A.E.Trott	1
†H.Philipson	c Gregory b Giffen	7	(4) b Giffen	1
T.Richardson	c Worrall b Callaway	0	c A.E.Trott b Giffen	12
Extras	(b2)	2	(b5, lb2)	7
Total	(57.3 overs, 165 mins)	124	(67.1 overs, 175 mins)	143

ENGLAND	O	M	R	W	w,nb		O	M	R	W	w,nb		FALL OF WICKETS			
Richardson	21.1	4	75	5	-,-	(2)	31.2	8	89	3	-,-	Wkt	AUST	ENG	AUST	ENG
Peel	16	1	43	0	-,-	(1)	34	6	96	4	-,-		1st	1st	2nd	2nd
Brockwell	20	13	30	1	1,-	(4)	10	1	50	0	-,-	1st	31	14	0	52
Ford	8	2	19	0	-,-	(6)	6	0	33	0	-,-	2nd	69	30	44	52
Briggs	8	2	34	1	-,-		19	3	58	2	-,-	3rd	84	49	142	53
Lockwood	8	2	33	1	-,1	(3)	15	2	70	1	-,1	4th	103	50	145	64
												5th	120	56	197	102
AUSTRALIA	O	M	R	W	w,nb		O	M	R	W	w,nb	6th	124	64	215	102
A.E.Trott	3	1	9	0	-,-	(3)	27	10	43	8	-,-	7th	137	111	238	128
Giffen	28	11	76	5	-,-		33.1	12	74	2	-,-	8th	157	111	283	128
Callaway	26.3	13	37	5	-,-	(1)	7	1	19	0	-,-	9th	157	124	347	130
												10th	238	124	411	143

NEW SOUTH WALES v VICTORIA (Shield Match 4)

Played at Sydney Cricket Ground on January 25, 26, 28, 29, 30, 31, 1895. (Timeless match)
Toss : Victoria.   Result : VICTORIA WON BY 55 RUNS.
Debuts: Nil.
12th Men: V.T.Trumper (NSW) and R.Mitchell (Vic).
Umpires: C.Bannerman and R.M.Crockett.
Attendances: 4306, 6966, 3055, 2570, 2832, 1095.   Total: 20,824.   Receipts: £635.
Close of Play: 1st day NSW 0/54 (Garrett 26, Iredale 28); 2nd day NSW 3/159 (Donnan 30, Gregory 3); 3rd day NSW 5/242 (Gregory 52, Callaway 18); 4th day Vic (2) 0/16 (Trumble 11, C.E.McLeod 4); 5th day Vic (2) 247 all out.

The first Sheffield Shield match to involve six playing days was dogged by rain on the first four. However, the pitch rolled out well and was not held accountable for the home team's collapse on the last day. Blackham badly injured his thumb when taking a ball from Bob McLeod just after tea on the fourth day, reopening the wound sustained in the First Test. The injury forced his retirement not only from the match but from first-class cricket altogether. Harry took over as wicket-keeper (catching McKibbin in the position) and Mitchell substituted in the field for the rest of the game with Harry Trott assuming the captaincy. Bowlers of both sides generally kept the batsmen in check. Laver (65 in 145 minutes, 1 five and 8 fours) and Graham (61 in 100 minutes, 7 fours) for Victoria and Iredale (86 in 160 minutes, 7 fours) and Gregory (69 in 120 minutes, 5 fours) for New South Wales scored fifties. Sources: *Wisden, VCA Report, Sydney Referee, Sydney Morning Herald, Town & Country Journal, Sydney Daily Telegraph*.

VICTORIA

G.H.S.Trott	c Turner b Callaway	18	(4)	b McKibbin	11
J.H.Stuckey	c Howell b McKibbin	28	(9)	c Howell b Turner	0
J.Worrall	b McKibbin	12	(7)	b Turner	0
H.Graham	st Kelly b Turner	23	(6)	b Howell	61
A.E.Trott	c McKibbin b Turner	0	(3)	b Turner	24
F.J.Laver	run out (Gregory/McKibbin)	1	(5)	c & b Turner	65
C.E.McLeod	c Kelly b McKibbin	31	(2)	c & b McKibbin	35
J.Harry	b Turner	27		c Callaway b Howell	9
*†J.M.Blackham	b McKibbin	23	(11)	not out	0
R.W.McLeod	b McKibbin	0		b Howell	0
H.Trumble	not out	10	(1)	b McKibbin	30
Extras	(b1, lb6, nb1)	8		(b3, lb7, nb2)	12
Total	(68.3 overs, 195 mins)	181		(105.0 overs, 285 mins)	247

NEW SOUTH WALES

*T.W.Garrett	c Trumble b A.E.Trott	36		b G.H.S.Trott	6
F.A.Iredale	c Laver b A.E.Trott	86		c R.W.McLeod b G.H.S.Trott	22
H.Moses	b C.E.McLeod	1		st Harry b A.E.Trott	16
H.Donnan	c & b C.E.McLeod	40		b A.E.Trott	3
S.E.Gregory	c sub (R.Mitchell) b R.W.McLeod	69		c sub (R.Mitchell) b G.H.S.Trott	24
M.A.Noble	c G.H.S.Trott b C.E.McLeod	5		c Trumble b A.E.Trott	7
S.T.Callaway	c Trumble b R.W.McLeod	22	(8)	c Trumble b G.H.S.Trott	11
C.T.B.Turner	b Worrall	3	(9)	c Trumble b G.H.S.Trott	0
†J.J.Kelly	c A.E.Trott b R.W.McLeod	3	(10)	run out (Stuckey/A.E.Trott/C.E.McLeod)	0
T.R.McKibbin	c Harry b R.W.McLeod	0	(11)	not out	0
W.P.Howell	not out	3	(7)	c & b A.E.Trott	5
Extras	(b5, lb1)	6		(lb5)	5
Total	(107.1 overs, 290 mins)	274		(48.3 overs, 130 mins)	99

NEW SOUTH WALES	O	M	R	W	w,nb		O	M	R	W	w,nb
Howell	16	8	35	0	-,-	(2)	17	8	25	3	-,-
Callaway	15	3	35	1	-,-	(3)	10	1	30	0	-,-
Turner	19	6	48	3	-,1	(1)	36	13	56	4	-,2
McKibbin	13.3	2	36	5	-,-		28	6	86	3	-,-
Noble	2	0	9	0	-,-	(7)	4	0	13	0	-,-
Garrett	3	0	10	0	-,-		1	0	5	0	-,-
Donnan						(5)	9	2	20	0	-,-

VICTORIA	O	M	R	W	w,nb		O	M	R	W	w,nb
A.E.Trott	31	5	74	2	-,-		20.3	9	39	4	-,-
C.E.McLeod	38	8	88	3	-,-	(3)	10	4	12	0	-,-
G.H.S.Trott	3	0	9	0	-,-	(2)	14	3	31	5	-,-
R.W.McLeod	15.1	3	50	4	-,-		4	1	12	0	-,-
Trumble	9	0	30	0	-,-						
Worrall	11	3	17	1	-,-						

FALL OF WICKETS				
	VIC	NSW	VIC	NSW
Wkt	1st	1st	2nd	2nd
1st	37	78	62	7
2nd	54	79	96	30
3rd	83	151	96	34
4th	87	185	107	70
5th	88	209	230	73
6th	88	251	231	82
7th	133	256	246	97
8th	166	265	246	97
9th	170	267	246	99
10th	181	274	247	99

TASMANIA v VICTORIA

Played at S.T.C.A. Ground, Hobart, on January 26, 28, 29, 30, 1895. (Timeless match)
Toss : Tasmania.   Result : TASMANIA WON BY EIGHT WICKETS.
Debuts: Tasmania - F.B.Campbell, J.S.Howe (both f/c). Victoria - A.J.W.Philpott, W.Roche, G.Stuckey, T.S.Warne, C.G.Wilson
    (all f/c); G.J.P.Vautin (Vic only).
12th Men: None named.
Umpires: C.McAllen and S.Morris.
Attendances & Receipts: No figures published.
Close of Play: 1st day Vic 0/24 (Philpott 13, Stuckey 11); 2nd day Vic (2) 1/178 (McLeod 94, Stuckey 1); 3rd day Tas (2) 1/153 (Eady 69,
    Douglas 52).

Tasmania owed their first victory since 1853-54 (ending a sequence of 11 first-class losses) to Charles Eady, who became the first batsman to record a century in each innings of an Australian first-class match. A slight shoulder injury, which he carried into the game, prevented his bowling more than 1 over; however, he scored 116 (195 minutes, 1 five and 7 fours) and an unbeaten 112 (185 minutes, 5 fours), only the second and third centuries for Tasmania in their 15 matches thus far. Eady's feat was not matched for Tasmania until 1987-88. Tasmania's first innings (330) was their highest yet, and the Eady/Douglas second-wicket partnership of 163 was the island's first three-figure stand for any wicket. Dan McLeod, the youngest and least-known of three brothers to play for Victoria, captured his best figures (6 for 95) and scored his sole hundred (107 - no details) in his second and last first-class match, establishing a new Victorian first-wicket record of 169 with Roche. The pair had added 58 for the last wicket in the first innings and were sent straight back when the follow-on was enforced. This was Vautin's only match for Victoria after a sole appearance for the opposition in 1889-90. Brothers J.H. and W.H.Savigny were selected for Tasmania but opted not to travel down to Hobart and were replaced by Maxwell and Sidebottom. *VCA Report* incorrectly gives Vic (2) Ingleton b Bingham. Sources: *VCA Report, TCA Report, Australian Cricket Record, Hobart Mercury*.

TASMANIA

C.J.Eady	c McLeod b Bean	116	not out		112
†G.H.Gatehouse	c Warne b McLeod	45	c Philpot b Warne		19
A.J.Douglas	c & b McLeod	2	c Warne b Roche		64
*E.J.K.Burn	c Vautin b Bean	48	not out		28
J.S.Howe	b Roche	1			
E.A.C.Windsor	c Lewis b Bean	23			
F.B.Campbell	c Tatchell b McLeod	1			
W.L.Sidebottom	b McLeod	0			
E.Maxwell	c & b McLeod	55			
J.Watt	c Lewis b McLeod	16			
J.E.Bingham	not out	9			
Extras	(b10, lb4)	14	(b18, lb8, w1)		27
Total	(96.0 overs, 260 mins)	330	(68.3 overs, 185 mins) (2 wkts)		250

VICTORIA

A.J.W.Philpott	c Watt b Windsor	16	(9) lbw b Burn		31
G.Stuckey	b Windsor	51	(3) b Bingham		5
T.S.Warne	b Windsor	2	(4) b Bingham		69
W.G.Ingleton	b Windsor	0	(6) c Gatehouse b Bingham		17
*†P.M.Lewis	b Watt	46	(7) b Bingham		8
T.Tatchell	c Burn b Watt	3	(5) b Bingham		24
G.J.P.Vautin	c Burn b Watt	4	(8) c Douglas b Burn		44
C.G.Wilson	c Windsor b Watt	0	(11) c Eady b Maxwell		1
E.E.Bean	b Windsor	1	(10) not out		2
D.H.McLeod	not out	27	(1) c Douglas b Windsor		107
W.Roche	c Maxwell b Howe	25	(2) b Sidebottom		77
Extras	(b4, lb5, nb2)	11	(b2, lb4, w1, nb1)		8
Total	(68.4 overs, 180 mins)	186	(127.3 overs, 315 mins)		393

VICTORIA	O	M	R	W	w,nb		O	M	R	W	w,nb		FALL OF WICKETS			
Roche	31	7	95	1	-,-	(2)	23.3	8	63	1	-,-			TAS	VIC	TAS	VIC
McLeod	35	6	95	6	-,-	(1)	8	0	34	0	-,-	Wkt	1st	1st	2nd	2nd
Ingleton	3	0	16	0	-,-	(7)	6	1	16	0	1,-	1st	83	169	-	31
Philpott	4	2	12	0	-,-	(5)	7	2	11	0	-,+	2nd	97	32	191	194
Warne	4	0	26	0	-,-	(3)	8	0	48	1	-,-	3rd	181	32	195	-
Bean	19	1	72	3	-,-	(4)	15	6	44	0	-,-	4th	198	107	230	-
Wilson						(6)	1	0	7	0	-,-	5th	249	110	254	-
												6th	250	125	276	-
TASMANIA	O	M	R	W	w,nb		O	M	R	W	w,nb	7th	250	125	339	-
Eady	1	0	5	0	-,-							8th	250	128	388	-
Bingham	17	8	37	0	-,-	(7)	37	8	105	5	-,1	9th	303	128	388	-
Windsor	29	9	72	5	-,-		19	6	57	1	-,-	10th	330	186	393	-
Douglas	5	2	21	0	-,-	(5)	16	6	41	0	-,-					
Watt	10	5	24	4	-,1	(8)	13	2	63	0	1,-					
Burn	5	0	16	0	-,-	(4)	9	3	22	2	-,-					
Howe	1.4	1	0	1	-,1	(1)	18	6	36	0	-,-					
Maxwell						(2)	8.3	2	25	1	-,-					
Sidebottom						(6)	7	1	36	1	-,-					

AUSTRALIA v ENGLAND (4th Test)

Played at Sydney Cricket Ground on February 1, 2 (no play), 4, 1895. (Timeless match)
Toss : England.   Result : AUSTRALIA WON BY AN INNINGS AND 147 RUNS.
Debuts: Nil.
12th Men: C.E.McLeod (Aust) and L.H.Gay (Eng).
Umpires: C.Bannerman and J.Phillips.
Attendances: 8277, no play (4158), 15953.   Total: 24,230 (excluding second day).   Receipts: £1178.
Close of Play: 1st day Eng 1/11 (Ward 5, Briggs 4); 2nd day no play.

Stoddart won the toss and after some deliberation sent Australia in (the first England captain to do so) on a badly rain-damaged wicket. Conditions improved in the afternoon and Australia recovered from 6/51 (which included the wickets of Harry Trott to the fifth ball of the match and Gregory and Iredale to successive balls from Briggs) mainly due to an eighth-wicket stand of 112 in 65 minutes between Graham (105 in 145 minutes, 14 fours, chances at 25, 37, 53 and 87) and Albert Trott (85 not out in 120 minutes, 9 fours), the latter taking his Test batting aggregate to 195 runs from two matches without being dismissed. Graham's hundred came in his first Test in Australia and followed his maiden hundred on debut in England in 1893; a rare double. Darling's 31 included a 110-yard drive out of the ground (worth five runs) off Briggs, the ball landing in the tennis courts at the northern end (later the site of the M.A.Noble stand). Heavy rain after the first day, accompanied by a howling gale, continued through the second day; more than 4000 people were given free passes for the Monday when play was abandoned mid-afternoon. When the game resumed on that day, the waterlogged pitch was very slow to mend with the result that 17 England wickets fell in three hours, the match finishing at 4.25pm on the second playing day. Lockwood, who sustained a cut right hand before the match when a drink bottle burst, could not bat; he aggravated the injury by bowling during the late stages of the Australian Innings. Peel became the first batsman to register four consecutive Test ducks and two pairs in the one series. Turner, playing in his 17th and final Test, became the first Australian to take 100 Test wickets when he had Brockwell caught in the second innings at deep mid-wicket; his co-selectors J.M.Blackham and G.Giffen voted him out of the side for the Fifth Test. *Wisden* incorrectly gives Aust, Moses 0, A.E.Trott 86*. Sources: *Wisden, Australian Cricket Record, Sydney Referee, Sydney Morning Herald, Town & Country Journal.*

AUSTRALIA

G.H.S.Trott	c Brown b Peel	1			
W.Bruce	c Brockwell b Peel	15			
*G.Giffen	b Peel	8			
H.Moses	b Richardson	1			
H.Graham	st Philipson b Briggs	105			
S.E.Gregory	st Philipson b Briggs	5			
F.A.Iredale	c & b Briggs	0			
J.Darling	b Richardson	31			
A.E.Trott	not out	85			
†A.H.Jarvis	c Philipson b Briggs	5			
C.T.B.Turner	c Richardson b Lockwood	22			
Extras	(b3, lb1, w1, nb1)	6			
Total	(83.5 overs, 245 mins)	284			

ENGLAND

A.C.MacLaren	st Jarvis b G.H.S.Trott	1	(4) c Bruce b Giffen	0
A.Ward	c & b Turner	7	c Darling b Giffen	6
J.Briggs	b G.H.S.Trott	11	(8) c Bruce b Giffen	6
*A.E.Stoddart	st Jarvis b G.H.S.Trott	7	(3) c Iredale b Turner	0
J.T.Brown	not out	20	(1) b Giffen	0
W.Brockwell	c Darling b Turner	1	(5) c Bruce b Turner	17
F.G.J.Ford	c G.H.S.Trott b Giffen	0	c Darling b Giffen	11
R.Peel	st Jarvis b Turner	0	(6) st Jarvis b Turner	0
†H.Philipson	c Graham b Giffen	4	c & b Turner	9
T.Richardson	c & b Giffen	2	not out	10
W.H.Lockwood	absent hurt	-	absent hurt	-
Extras	(b7, lb3, nb2)	12	(b5, lb7, nb1)	13
Total	(38.5 overs, 115 mins)	65	(29.1 overs, 94 mins)	72

ENGLAND	O	M	R	W	w,nb
Peel	24	5	74	3	-,-
Richardson	22	5	78	2	-,-
Briggs	22	4	65	4	1,-
Brockwell	5	1	25	0	-,-
Ford	2	0	14	0	-,-
Lockwood	8.5	3	22	1	-,1

AUSTRALIA	O	M	R	W	w,nb		O	M	R	W	w,nb
G.H.S.Trott	14	5	21	3	-,-						
Turner	19	10	18	3	-,2		14.1	6	33	4	-,1
Giffen	5.5	1	14	3	-,-	(1)	15	7	26	5	-,-

FALL OF WICKETS

	AUST	ENG	ENG
Wkt	1st	1st	2nd
1st	2	2	0
2nd	20	20	5
3rd	26	24	5
4th	26	31	12
5th	51	40	14
6th	51	43	29
7th	119	56	47
8th	231	63	52
9th	239	65	72
10th	284	-	-

QUEENSLAND v NEW SOUTH WALES

Played at Exhibition Ground, Brisbane on February 9, 11, 12, 1895. (Timeless match)
Toss : Queensland.   Result : NEW SOUTH WALES WON BY SIX WICKETS.
Debuts: Queensland - E.A.Cresswick, J.W.Lewis, E.J.Metcalfe (all f/c); S.W.Austin (Qld only).
12th Men: B.W.Farquhar (NSW). No 12th named for Qld.
Umpires: C.Bannerman and R.Thompson.
Attendances: 5000, 2000, 200.   Total: About 7200.   Receipts: No figures published.
Close of Play: 1st day NSW 1/66 (Mackenzie 31); 2nd day NSW (2) 2/17 (Gregory 6).

In his third first-class match McKibbin (medium-paced offbreaks) returned the best innings and match figures of his career. Both analyses remained records at this ground. Rain during the week had left a heavy outfield but the starting pitch was "all that could be desired" (*Courier*). Bradley (44 in 135 minutes, 5 fours) made the match topscore before a dramatic Queensland collapse claimed 8 for 13, the last 6 for 4 in 4.3 overs to McKibbin (3 for 3) and Iredale (3 for 1). More rain on the Sunday softened the wicket and left the outfield even heavier. The visitors began their innings well but some fine bowling from New South Wales turncoats Coningham and Austin (playing his first match for Queensland) inflicted another collapse (6 for 9), Austin dismissing Donnan and Callaway with successive deliveries. Metcalfe bowled Jones with his first ball in first-class cricket - the first Queenslander to do so. O'Brien's pair included a first-ball duck in the second innings. McDonnell (22 in 23 minutes, 1 six and 3 fours) attempted to hit McKibbin out of the attack on the second day, on which 21 wickets fell. Sources: *Cricket, Sydney Referee, NSWCA Scorebook, Sydney Daily Telegraph, Brisbane Courier, Queensland Times, The Queenslander.*

QUEENSLAND

A.Coningham	b Turner	5		c Iredale b McKibbin	6
*P.S.McDonnell	c McKibbin b Turner	15		b McKibbin	22
†W.F.Bradley	b McKibbin	44		b McKibbin	21
R.Macdonald	c Howell b Iredale	30		c Howell b Turner	6
W.W.McGlinchey	c Gregory b McKibbin	0		c Turner b McKibbin	4
H.S.Freeman	c Howell b Iredale	7		lbw b McKibbin	16
J.W.Lewis	b McKibbin	1	(8)	c Donnan b McKibbin	3
E.J.Metcalfe	c Kelly b Iredale	0	(7)	c Mackenzie b McKibbin	13
E.A.Cresswick	b McKibbin	0	(10)	st Kelly b McKibbin	4
S.W.Austin	not out	1	(9)	not out	10
R.O'Brien	b McKibbin	0		b McKibbin	0
Extras	(lb2, nb1)	3		(b1, lb1)	2
Total	(76.3 overs, 221 mins)	106		(43.0 overs, 125 mins)	107

NEW SOUTH WALES

S.P.Jones	b Metcalfe	32		run out (Freeman)	1
A.C.K.Mackenzie	c Bradley b Coningham	37		c Coningham b Austin	10
F.A.Iredale	c McDonnell b Coningham	20	(5)	not out	14
H.Donnan	b Austin	35		c McDonnell b Austin	14
*S.E.Gregory	b Austin	17	(3)	c Austin b Coningham	7
V.T.Trumper	c Austin b Coningham	6		not out	5
C.T.B.Turner	c & b Coningham	7			
S.T.Callaway	b Austin	0			
†J.J.Kelly	b Coningham	1			
W.P.Howell	run out	0			
T.R.McKibbin	not out	0			
Extras	(b6, nb2)	8		(b1)	1
Total	(68.2 overs, 172 mins)	163		(27.5 overs, 75 mins) (4 wkts)	52

NEW SOUTH WALES	O	M	R	W	w,nb		O	M	R	W	w,nb			FALL OF WICKETS		
Turner	21	7	36	2	-,-	(2)	14	3	32	1	-,-		QLD	NSW	QLD	NSW
Howell	14	3	28	0	-,-							Wkt	1st	1st	2nd	2nd
Callaway	17	10	18	0	-,-	(4)	1	0	1	0	-,-	1st	10	66	8	2
McKibbin	19.3	11	19	5	-,1	(1)	22	2	68	9	-,-	2nd	30	81	45	17
Donnan	1	0	1	0	-,-							3rd	93	107	56	19
Iredale	4	3	1	3	-,-	(3)	6	3	4	0	-,-	4th	93	140	56	41
												5th	102	154	62	-
QUEENSLAND	O	M	R	W	w,nb		O	M	R	W	w,nb	6th	105	160	86	-
Coningham	32.2	6	68	5	-,2		14	4	20	1	-,-	7th	105	160	92	-
O'Brien	5	1	27	0	-,-							8th	105	161	101	-
McGlinchey	14	2	32	0	-,-							9th	105	163	107	-
Austin	13	2	23	3	-,-	(2)	13.5	2	31	2	-,-	10th	106	163	107	-
Cresswick	2	0	3	0	-,-											
Metcalfe	2	1	2	1	-,-											

COMBINED NEW SOUTH WALES & QUEENSLAND XI v A.E.STODDART'S ENGLAND XI

Played at Exhibition Ground, Brisbane on February 15, 16, 18, 19, 1895. (Timeless match)
Toss : England XI.   Result : A.E.STODDART'S ENGLAND XI WON BY 278 RUNS.
Debuts: Nil.
12th Men: W.W.McGlinchey (Comb) and L.H.Gay (Eng).
Umpires: C.Bannerman and J.Phillips.
Attendances: 6000, 11000, 2000, 1000.   Total: About 20,000.   Receipts: No figures published.
Close of Play: 1st day Eng 192 all out; 2nd day Eng (2) 1/33 (Ward 4, Briggs 2); 3rd day Eng (2) 279 all out.

The Combined XI had the worst of the wicket in both innings. Heavy rain fell 10 minutes into the second day's play and lasted for an hour, soaking the ground. Immediate sunshine afterwards made the pitch more difficult to bat on as the day progressed, Richardson's pace proving particularly unpleasant for the batsmen. Bradley was twice struck painfully on the hand before his dismissal and Jones was felled by a sickening crack on the knee soon after. Play was held up for some time in each instance before the batsman could continue, but the injuries ruled both Bradley and Jones out of action for the rest of the match. McGlinchey and E.A.Cresswick substituted in the field in England's second innings, while first Austin and finally Iredale kept wicket. Overnight rain after the third day re-softened the wicket for the English bowlers on the final day. MacLaren (106 in 123 minutes, 11 fours), the only batsman to exceed 50 in the match, was missed twice by Iredale behind the wicket (at 16 off McKibbin and at 99 off Callaway) and was also let off at 69, by Callaway off Coningham. Richardson, McDonnell and McKibbin all sustained first-ball dismissals. On the opening day the volatile Coningham, annoyed at being no-balled by Bannerman for over-stepping, had deliberately thrown the next-ball from behind the umpire at the batsman, Stoddart, who remonstrated. After apologising to Stoddart and the umpire (the delivery was not called), Coningham dismissed the batsman with the next ball. Sources: *Wisden, Sydney Referee, Brisbane Courier, Queensland Times, The Queenslander.*

A.E.STODDART'S ENGLAND XI

W.Brockwell	run out (Gregory)	14		c & b Turner	15
A.Ward	b Turner	9		b McKibbin	47
*A.E.Stoddart	b Coningham	40	(4)	c McKibbin b Callaway	20
J.T.Brown	b Coningham	4	(5)	b McKibbin	24
A.C.MacLaren	lbw b Coningham	37	(6)	c Gregory b Callaway	106
R.Peel	c Callaway b Turner	30	(7)	c Gregory b McKibbin	23
F.G.J.Ford	c Bradley b Turner	4	(8)	c Iredale b McKibbin	4
J.Briggs	b McKibbin	13	(3)	c McKibbin b Coningham	2
†H.Philipson	c Iredale b Austin	21		b McKibbin	5
W.A.Humphreys	not out	9		not out	10
T.Richardson	c Gregory b Austin	0		b Callaway	1
Extras	(b7, w3, nb1)	11		(b17, lb4, w1)	22
Total	(99.4 overs, 265 mins)	192		(101.2 overs, 280 mins)	279

COMBINED XI

A.Coningham	c Ward b Richardson	20		c Brown b Richardson	3
*P.S.McDonnell	c Humphreys b Richardson	18	(3)	b Richardson	0
F.A.Iredale	not out	37	(4)	not out	33
S.E.Gregory	b Richardson	15	(5)	c MacLaren b Richardson	16
†W.F.Bradley	c Philipson b Richardson	11		absent hurt	-
C.T.B.Turner	b Richardson	2		c Brockwell b Briggs	20
S.P.Jones	c Philipson b Briggs	0		absent hurt	-
S.T.Callaway	c & b Briggs	0	(7)	b Briggs	0
R.Macdonald	c Stoddart b Briggs	1	(2)	c Philipson b Peel	12
S.W.Austin	st Philipson b Briggs	0	(8)	c Ward b Briggs	1
T.R.McKibbin	run out (Ward/Philipson)	1	(9)	b Richardson	0
Extras	(lb1, w1)	2		(lb1)	1
Total	(49.3 overs, 160 mins)	107		(56.3 overs, 149 mins)	86

COMBINED XI	O	M	R	W	w,nb		O	M	R	W	w,nb			FALL OF WICKETS			
Turner	42	18	69	3	-,-		25	8	37	1	-,-			ENG	COM	ENG	COM
Coningham	27	10	36	3	1,1		31	9	65	1	-,-		Wkt	1st	1st	2nd	2nd
McKibbin	19	4	49	1	2,-	(4)	26	1	98	5	-,-		1st	23	39	30	12
Austin	6.4	1	17	2	-,-	(5)	5	0	18	0	1,-		2nd	24	40	33	12
Callaway	5	2	10	0	-,-	(3)	14.2	3	39	3	-,-		3rd	43	63	82	18
													4th	112	89	118	37
ENGLAND XI	O	M	R	W	w,nb		O	M	R	W	w,nb		5th	130	93	129	83
Peel	18	4	47	0	-,-	(2)	14	5	21	1	-,-		6th	137	96	215	84
Richardson	24	8	42	5	1,-	(1)	24.3	11	35	4	-,-		7th	160	96	227	86
Brockwell	1	0	1	0	-,-	(4)	4	2	3	0	-,-		8th	164	100	243	86
Briggs	6.3	1	15	4	-,-	(5)	6	1	14	3	-,-		9th	192	104	271	-
Humphreys						(3)	8	2	12	0	-,-		10th	192	107	279	-

VICTORIA v SOUTH AUSTRALIA (Shield Match 5)

Played at Melbourne Cricket Ground on February 15, 16, 18 (no play), 19, 1895. (Timeless match)
Toss : Victoria.   Result : VICTORIA WON BY TEN WICKETS.
Debuts: South Australia - A.E.Green (f/c).
12th Men: None named.
Umpires: I.A.Fisher and T.Flynn.
Attendances: 3000, 6000, no play, 1000.   Total: About 10,000.   Receipts: £296.
Close of Play: 1st day Vic 9/336 (Trumble 5, R.W.McLeod 5); 2nd day SA (2) 2/159 (Lyons 100, Darling 43); 3rd day no play.

South Australia omitted T.Bennett and J.Noel from their touring party of thirteen. Harry Trott (152 in 195 minutes, 16 fours) and Laver (78 in 155 minutes, 1 five and 6 fours) added 195 on the first day, a new Victorian third-wicket record, Trott compiling his best score for the side in a career which spanned 22 years. Worrall had been out to the fourth ball of the match. South Australia failed unaccountably in their first innings and followed on. Beginning immediately after the tea adjournment, Lyons (135 in 145 minutes, 18 fours) flayed the bowling to reach his century just on stumps. He scored his runs out of 218 and gave two difficult chances (80, 126) and put on 98 for the third wicket with Darling. Rain washed out the third day's play and its effect on the wicket sealed South Australia's fate. Jones became the first batsman to be given out "handled the ball" in Sheffield Shield matches - the second in first-class cricket in Australia after W.H.Scotton (Smokers v Non-Smokers at East Melbourne 1886-87) - when he removed a ball that had lodged in his shirt pocket, from a defensive stroke, and lobbed it back to the bowler, Trumble. The law was amended in 1899 to rule such a ball was "dead" once it had lodged in a batsman's clothing. *Wisden* incorrectly gives SA (1) Lyons 6, W.F.Giffen 0; SA (2) Trumble 3/52, Laver 0/10. Sources: *Wisden, VCA Report, The Age, The Argus, The Herald, The Australasian, The Leader*.

VICTORIA

Batsman	Dismissal	Score		2nd innings	Score
J.Worrall	b Jones	5			
W.Bruce	c A.Jarvis b Jones	8		not out	12
*G.H.S.Trott	c Reedman b G.Giffen	152	(1)	not out	3
F.J.Laver	c & b G.Giffen	78			
A.E.Trott	b Jones	41			
†P.M.Lewis	lbw b G.Giffen	10			
C.E.McLeod	c Lyons b G.Giffen	23			
J.Harry	b G.Giffen	0			
E.A.Barrett	b Jones	5			
H.Trumble	not out	13			
R.W.McLeod	b Jones	9			
Extras	(b2, lb1, nb1)	4		(b1)	1
Total	(105.1 overs, 295 mins)	348		(4.5 overs, 10 mins) (0 wkts)	16

SOUTH AUSTRALIA

Batsman	Dismissal	Score		2nd innings	Score
J.J.Lyons	c Trumble b G.H.S.Trott	5		c Trumble b G.H.S.Trott	135
J.C.Reedman	b C.E.McLeod	3	(5)	st Lewis b G.H.S.Trott	8
*G.Giffen	b A.E.Trott	15		run out (R.W.McLeod/Lewis)	9
J.Darling	c Lewis b A.E.Trott	6		c Barrett b A.E.Trott	45
†A.H.Jarvis	b A.E.Trott	0	(2)	c A.E.Trott b G.H.S.Trott	5
R.H.Dyer	c G.H.S.Trott b C.E.McLeod	2		c Barrett b Trumble	7
C.Hill	c Harry b G.H.S.Trott	33		c Barrett b G.H.S.Trott	1
W.F.Giffen	b C.E.McLeod	1		c & b Trumble	3
A.Jarvis	c Worrall b G.H.S.Trott	22		not out	14
A.E.Green	not out	11		c & Trumble	0
E.Jones	b A.E.Trott	15		handled the ball	9
Extras	(lb5)	5		(b6, lb3)	9
Total	(57.1 overs, 160 mins)	118		(54.0 overs, 165 mins)	245

SOUTH AUSTRALIA	O	M	R	W	w,nb		O	M	R	W	w,nb
Jones	23.1	3	71	5	-,-		2.5	0	10	0	-,-
A.Jarvis	25	6	70	0	-,-						
G.Giffen	47	6	147	5	-,-	(2)	2	0	5	0	-,-
Reedman	3	0	22	0	-,-						
Lyons	6	0	28	0	-,1						
Green	1	0	6	0	-,-						

VICTORIA	O	M	R	W	w,nb		O	M	R	W	w,nb
C.E.McLeod	24	13	31	3	-,-	(2)	6	0	30	0	-,-
G.H.S.Trott	15	2	41	3	-,-	(1)	17	0	70	4	-,-
A.E.Trott	13.1	4	24	4	-,-		10	1	40	1	-,-
R.W.McLeod	5	1	17	0	-,-	(7)	2	0	10	0	-,-
Bruce						(4)	5	0	24	0	-,-
Trumble						(5)	12	4	50	3	-,-
Laver						(6)	2	0	12	0	-,-

FALL OF WICKETS

Wkt	VIC 1st	SA 1st	SA 2nd	VIC 2nd
1st	6	6	43	-
2nd	31	12	72	-
3rd	226	31	170	-
4th	263	31	190	-
5th	279	32	217	-
6th	307	34	218	-
7th	320	38	221	-
8th	321	84	221	-
9th	328	90	230	-
10th	348	118	245	-

NEW SOUTH WALES v SOUTH AUSTRALIA (Shield Match 6)

Played at Sydney Cricket Ground on February 22, 23, 25, 26, 1895. (Timeless match)
Toss : New South Wales.   Result : NEW SOUTH WALES WON BY 111 RUNS.
Debuts: South Australia - T.Bennett (f/c).
12th Men: M.A.Noble (NSW) and A.E.Green (SA).
Umpires: C.Bannerman and I.A.Fisher.
Attendances: 2685, 4763, 4152, 1443.   Total: 13,043.   Receipts: £577.
Close of Play: 1st day SA 1/14 (Dyer 9); 2nd day NSW (2) 1/22 (Garrett 6, Howell 10); 3rd day SA (2) 1/52 (G.Giffen 26, Darling 20).

McKibbin's 14 for 189, which emulated his performance at Brisbane earlier in the month, boosted his career aggregate to 42 wickets from five matches and earned him Test selection in his debut season of first-class cricket. He captured three wickets (Jarvis, W.F.Giffen and Bennett) within the space of five balls in South Australia's second innings and was almost solely responsible for the collapse which took place. Donnan (58 in 120 minutes, 1 five and 8 fours), Garrett (82 in 105 minutes, 7 fours), Howell (62 in 80 minutes, 1 five and 8 fours), Iredale (91 in 195 minutes, 7 fours) and Gregory (66 not out in 90 minutes, 9 fours) hit half-centuries for New South Wales while Dyer (71 in 150 minutes, 11 fours), Darling (70 in 115 minutes, 2 fives and 10 fours) and G.Giffen (65 in 140 minutes, 7 fours) replied in kind for the visitors. Giffen also returned 10 wickets to finish the Sheffield Shield season with 43 wickets, a new record. Howell's five, off the bowling of Jarvis, "sailed right out of the ground and over the roof of the temporary smoking stand - one of the biggest hits in the history of the ground" (*Town & Country Journal*). Kelly, the local wicket-keeper, split his hand in stopping a hot return from Gregory on the second day and at 5/200 he surrendered the gloves to Howell, who retained them for the rest of the innings. Howell ran out Hill shortly afterwards by cleverly gathering an edge and throwing down the stumps with Hill still out of his ground. Hill himself had been chosen to keep wicket for South Australia because A.H.Jarvis, who was travelling with the team, was resting for the upcoming Test match. Last first-class appearance by H.Moses. C.T.B.Turner (work) was unavailable for New South Wales. His place went to Callaway, Noble being unable to obtain leave from his bank. Sources: *Wisden, C.B.O'Reilly, Sydney Referee, Sydney Morning Herald, Town & Country Journal, Sydney Daily Telegraph.*

NEW SOUTH WALES

F.A.Iredale	b Jarvis	26	(4)	c Darling b G.Giffen	91
A.C.K.Mackenzie	c G.Giffen b Jarvis	14	(8)	c Darling b G.Giffen	7
H.Moses	c Jarvis b G.Giffen	1	(5)	b Jones	34
S.E.Gregory	b Jones	33	(7)	not out	66
H.Donnan	c Lyons b Jarvis	58	(6)	c Hill b Jones	16
L.Moore	b Jones	0	(2)	b Jones	5
*T.W.Garrett	c W.F.Giffen b G.Giffen	82	(1)	b G.Giffen	27
S.T.Callaway	b G.Giffen	5	(10)	run out (W.F.Giffen/Jarvis)	0
T.R.McKibbin	b Jarvis	12		b G.Giffen	8
†J.J.Kelly	not out	2	(11)	b G.Giffen	4
W.P.Howell	b G.Giffen	1	(3)	c Reedman b G.Giffen	62
Extras	(b2, lb3)	5		(b8, lb8)	16
Total	(76.5 overs, 230 mins)	239		(100.2 overs, 295 mins)	336

SOUTH AUSTRALIA

T.Bennett	b McKibbin	5	(9)	b McKibbin	0
R.H.Dyer	c Kelly b Donnan	71	(5)	b Howell	3
J.J.Lyons	b Howell	22	(1)	b McKibbin	6
*G.Giffen	b McKibbin	15	(2)	st Kelly b McKibbin	65
J.Darling	b McKibbin	70	(3)	run out (Moore/Howell)	39
J.C.Reedman	c Iredale b Callaway	30	(4)	lbw b McKibbin	10
A.Jarvis	c Callaway b McKibbin	21	(6)	b McKibbin	3
†C.Hill	run out (Howell)	30	(7)	not out	15
W.F.Giffen	not out	20	(8)	st Kelly b McKibbin	0
J.Noel	b McKibbin	0		b McKibbin	5
E.Jones	lbw b McKibbin	2		c Garrett b McKibbin	10
Extras	(b15, lb1, w2)	18		(b3, lb1)	4
Total	(96.4 overs, 285 mins)	304		(62.5 overs, 183 mins)	160

SOUTH AUSTRALIA	O	M	R	W	w,nb		O	M	R	W	w,nb
Jones	12	0	36	2	-,-	(2)	27	5	95	3	-,-
G.Giffen	37.5	7	114	4	-,-	(1)	50.2	12	132	6	-,-
Jarvis	27	4	84	4	-,-		18	6	75	0	-,-
Noel							5	0	18	0	-,-

NEW SOUTH WALES	O	M	R	W	w,nb		O	M	R	W	w,nb
McKibbin	36.4	6	123	6	2,-		28.5	7	66	8	-,-
Howell	14	2	50	1	-,-		19	5	46	1	-,-
Callaway	24	10	39	1	-,-		4	1	13	0	-,-
Garrett	9	5	18	0	-,-		2	0	11	0	-,-
Iredale	3	0	16	0	-,-						
Donnan	10	3	40	1	-,-	(5)	9	3	20	0	-,-

	FALL OF WICKETS			
	NSW	SA	NSW	SA
Wkt	1st	1st	2nd	2nd
1st	34	14	6	10
2nd	43	42	62	107
3rd	47	68	107	122
4th	103	172	183	125
5th	103	200	209	127
6th	192	228	273	132
7th	210	256	299	132
8th	233	294	318	132
9th	238	294	322	148
10th	239	304	336	160

AUSTRALIA v ENGLAND (5th Test)

Played at Melbourne Cricket Ground on March 1, 2, 4, 5, 6, 1895. (Timeless match)
Toss : Australia.   Result : ENGLAND WON BY SIX WICKETS.
Debuts: Australia - T.R.McKibbin (Test).
12th Men: C.T.B.Turner (Aust). No 12th named for Eng.
Umpires: T.Flynn and J.Phillips.
Attendances: 18000, 29123, 19200, 13500, 14259.   Total: 103,636.   Receipts: £4004.
Close of Play: 1st day Aust 4/282 (Gregory 70, Darling 72); 2nd day Eng 4/200 (MacLaren 40, Peel 18); 3rd day Aust (2) 1/69
(G.H.S.Trott 37, Giffen 14); 4th day Eng (2) 1/28 (Ward 6, Stoddart 11).

For the first time in Australia more than 100,000 people attended a cricket match; the second-day figure of 29,123 was similarly the biggest yet for one day's play in this country. McKibbin, a Bathurst-born bowler of break-backs, was chosen for his Test debut, at the expense of Turner, after just five first-class matches. The fate of the series, deadlocked at 2-2, depended on the result of this match and fittingly it was played on a pitch which remained true and impartial to the very end. Australia exceeded 400 for the first time at Melbourne with contributions right down the order, Darling (74 in 115 minutes, 9 fours) and Gregory (70 in 135 minutes, 8 fours) adding 142 for the fifth wicket. England's reply included a fine stand of 162 for the fifth wicket between MacLaren (120 in 220 minutes, 12 fours, chances at 69 and 114) and Peel (73 in 160 minutes, 7 fours). Stoddart (68 in 95 minutes, 7 fours) also batted well. Excellent bowling by Richardson and Peel restricted the Australians in their second innings, though Giffen and Darling again scored half-centuries, Giffen finishing the series with a remarkable 475 runs/34 wickets double. When Stoddart fell to the first ball on the fifth day, leaving England 2/28 and chasing 297, Australia were heavily favoured to win. However, Brown attacked immediately he came to the crease and played an immortal innings: 140 in 145 minutes (16 fours, difficult chances at 47 and 88) to set up a historic win for the Englishmen. His fifty arrived in 28 minutes, the fastest in Test cricket, and his hundred in 95 minutes was also, briefly, a Test record. With Ward (93 in 180 minutes, 1 five and 5 fours) he added 210 in 145 minutes for the third wicket, the Test record partnership until 1896. Albert Trott finished his three-match Test career for Australia (he played two Tests for England v South Africa in 1898-99) with a batting average of 102.50, which is unsurpassed among Australians. Sources: *Wisden, The Age, The Argus, The Herald, The Australasian, The Leader, The Sportsman.*

AUSTRALIA

G.H.S.Trott	b Briggs	42	b Peel		42
W.Bruce	c MacLaren b Peel	22	c & b Peel		11
*G.Giffen	b Peel	57	b Richardson		51
F.A.Iredale	b Richardson	8	b Richardson		18
S.E.Gregory	c Philipson b Richardson	70	b Richardson		30
J.Darling	c Ford b Peel	74	b Peel		50
J.J.Lyons	c Philipson b Lockwood	55	b Briggs		15
H.Graham	b Richardson	6	lbw b Richardson		10
A.E.Trott	c Lockwood b Peel	10	b Richardson		0
†A.H.Jarvis	not out	34	not out		14
T.R.McKibbin	c Peel b Briggs	23	c Philipson b Richardson		13
Extras	(b3, lb10)	13	(b5, lb6, nb2)		13
Total	(128.4 overs, 390 mins)	414	(123.2 overs, 345 mins)		267

ENGLAND

A.Ward	b McKibbin	32	(2) b G.H.S.Trott		93
W.Brockwell	st Jarvis b G.H.S.Trott	5	(1) c & b Giffen		5
*A.E.Stoddart	st Jarvis b G.H.S.Trott	68	lbw b G.H.S.Trott		11
J.T.Brown	b A.E.Trott	30	c Giffen b McKibbin		140
A.C.MacLaren	hit wkt b G.H.S.Trott	120	not out		20
R.Peel	c Gregory b Giffen	73	not out		15
W.H.Lockwood	c G.H.S.Trott b Giffen	5			
F.G.J.Ford	c A.E.Trott b Giffen	11			
J.Briggs	c G.H.S.Trott b Giffen	0			
†H.Philipson	not out	10			
T.Richardson	lbw b G.H.S.Trott	11			
Extras	(b8, lb8, w4)	20	(b6, lb5, w2, nb1)		14
Total	(133.0 overs, 350 mins)	385	(88.1 overs, 215 mins) (4 wkts)		298

ENGLAND	O	M	R	W	w,nb		O	M	R	W	w,nb		FALL OF WICKETS			
Richardson	42	7	138	3	-,-		45.2	7	104	6	-,-			AUST	ENG	AUST	ENG
Peel	48	13	114	4	-,-		46	16	89	3	-,-		Wkt	1st	1st	2nd	2nd
Lockwood	27	7	72	1	-,-		16	7	24	0	-,2		1st	40	6	32	5
Briggs	23.4	5	46	2	-,-		16	3	37	1	-,-		2nd	101	110	75	28
Brockwell	6	1	22	0	-,-								3rd	126	112	125	238
Ford	2	0	9	0	-,-								4th	142	166	148	278
													5th	284	328	179	-
AUSTRALIA	O	M	R	W	w,nb		O	M	R	W	w,nb		6th	286	342	200	-
Giffen	45	13	130	4	-,-	(2)	31	4	106	1	-,-		7th	304	364	219	-
G.H.S.Trott	24	5	71	4	-,-	(1)	20.1	1	63	2	-,1		8th	335	364	219	-
A.E.Trott	30	4	84	1	4,-		19	2	56	0	-,-		9th	367	366	248	-
McKibbin	29	6	73	1	-,-		14	2	47	1	2,-		10th	414	385	267	-
Bruce	5	1	7	0	-,-		3	1	10	0	-,-						
Lyons							1	0	2	0	-,-						

VICTORIA v A.E.STODDART'S ENGLAND XI

Played at Melbourne Cricket Ground on March 21, 22, 25, 1895. (Three-day match)
Toss : Victoria.   Result : VICTORIA WON BY SEVEN WICKETS.
Debuts: Victoria - A.E.Johns, C.H.Peryman (both f/c).
12th Men: E.A.Barrett & W.G.Ingleton (Vic emergencies) and W.A.Humphreys (Eng).
Umpires: R.M.Crockett and T.Flynn.
Attendances: 2600, 2700, 1000.   Total: About 6300.   Receipts: £176.
Close of Play: 1st day Vic 5/160 (C.E.McLeod 19, Peryman 5); 2nd day Eng (2) 6/188 (Ford 60, Briggs 22).

Victoria achieved their first win over an English team in 10 first-class matches since 1882-83. This match was not on the original tour itinerary but was arranged by the VCA in an attempt to recoup financial losses on the season. It was limited to three days so that the final tour match, against South Australia, would not be affected. The players further agreed to abide with a VRC request not to play on Saturday (23rd) so as not to detract from a farewell race meeting at Flemington to Lord Hopetoun, the retiring Governor of Victoria (later to become Australia's first Governor-General). Without the normal Saturday gate, the VCA however failed in its objective. A.E.Stoddart (severe cold) was unable to lead the England XI and Trott sent the visitors in on a slightly soft wicket mainly, it was reported, to avoid what Richardson might do on it had he batted. Harry Trott then proceeded to run through the Englishmen with his medium-paced legbreaks. Bruce (42 in 53 minutes, 6 fours and 72 not out in 105 minutes, 7 fours, several chances) and Ford (85 in 135 minutes, 1 five and 8 fours) topscored for their teams. Ward was dismissed in the first over of the England second innings. J.Phillips (on holiday) was replaced by Crockett after the umpires were appointed. *Wisden* incorrectly gives Vic (2) Brockwell 0/17. Sources: *Wisden, VCA Report, The Age, The Argus, The Herald, The Australasian, The Leader.*

A.E.STODDART'S ENGLAND XI

W.Brockwell	c C.E.McLeod b Trumble	25	b R.W.McLeod	36
A.Ward	c Trumble b G.H.S.Trott	1	b C.E.McLeod	0
J.T.Brown	c Johns b G.H.S.Trott	4	st Johns b G.H.S.Trott	37
A.C.MacLaren	c & b G.H.S.Trott	43	c Trumble b C.E.McLeod	16
R.Peel	c Peryman b G.H.S.Trott	3	st Johns b C.E.McLeod	1
F.G.J.Ford	run out (Trumble/Johns)	1	b A.E.Trott	85
W.H.Lockwood	st Johns b G.H.S.Trott	9	c Warne b Trumble	15
J.Briggs	c Trumble b G.H.S.Trott	3	c Warne b A.E.Trott	33
†L.H.Gay	not out	8	not out	24
*H.Philipson	c A.E.Trott b G.H.S.Trott	10	c Laver b R.W.McLeod	5
T.Richardson	c Warne b G.H.S.Trott	20	c A.E.Trott b G.H.S.Trott	15
Extras	(b3, lb1)	4	(lb2, w1)	3
Total	(49.5 overs, 135 mins)	131	(91.5 overs, 235 mins)	270

VICTORIA

*G.H.S.Trott	c Brockwell b Peel	12	run out (Brown/Gay)	5
W.Bruce	c Brown b Peel	42	not out	72
F.J.Laver	c Brockwell b Lockwood	25	c Brown b Richardson	4
A.E.Trott	b Richardson	46	b Lockwood	44
J.H.Stuckey	c Gay b Richardson	5	not out	6
C.E.McLeod	b Richardson	52		
C.H.Peryman	c Brockwell b Briggs	40		
T.S.Warne	not out	15		
H.Trumble	st Gay b Briggs	3		
R.W.McLeod	run out (Brockwell/Gay)	5		
†A.E.Johns	c Brockwell b Briggs	10		
Extras	(b4, lb7, w1, nb2)	14	(b4, nb1)	5
Total	(93.5 overs, 230 mins)	269	(37.1 overs, 105 mins) (3 wkts)	136

VICTORIA	O	M	R	W	w,nb		O	M	R	W	w,nb		FALL OF WICKETS			
Trumble	13	3	30	1	-,-	(5)	4	0	23	1	-,-		ENG	VIC	ENG	VIC
G.H.S.Trott	24.5	7	63	8	-,-		19.5	1	74	2	-,-	Wkt	1st	1st	2nd	2nd
A.E.Trott	6	1	20	0	-,-	(4)	13	6	31	2	1,-	1st	4	13	1	22
C.E.McLeod	6	1	14	0	-,-	(1)	38	10	94	3	-,-	2nd	24	71	52	36
R.W.McLeod						(3)	17	6	45	2	-,-	3rd	36	112	78	116
												4th	43	134	79	-
ENGLAND XI	O	M	R	W	w,nb		O	M	R	W	w,nb	5th	44	139	92	-
Richardson	37	10	88	3	-,1		13	3	37	1	-,1	6th	72	219	148	-
Peel	21	4	63	2	1,-		11	3	28	0	-,-	7th	93	239	216	-
Briggs	18.5	2	59	3	-,-		2	0	25	0	-,-	8th	94	250	230	-
Lockwood	17	5	45	1	-,1		6	1	22	1	-,-	9th	106	257	239	-
Brockwell							5.1	2	19	0	-,-	10th	131	269	270	-

SOUTH AUSTRALIA v A.E.STODDART'S ENGLAND XI

Played at Adelaide Oval on March 28, 29, 30, April 1, 2, 1895. (Timeless match)
Toss : South Australia.   Result : A.E.STODDART'S ENGLAND XI WON BY TEN WICKETS.
Debuts: Nil.
12th Men: B.V.Scrymgour (SA) and W.A.Humphreys (Eng).
Umpires: G.E.Downs and J.Phillips.
Attendances: 2000, 4000, 7000, 3000, 1900.   Total: About 17,900.   Receipts: £656.
Close of Play: 1st day SA 7/230 (Hill 63, W.F.Giffen 35); 2nd day Eng 1/82 (Ward 31, Brown 14); 3rd day Eng 4/452 (Ward 181, Peel 3); 4th day SA (2) 2/66 (G.Giffen 19, Darling 10).

A.E.Stoddart (recovering from illness) was unable to appear for the Englishmen in their final match on this historic tour. A.H.Jarvis sustained cuts and bruises in an accident with his horse-drawn carriage on his way home after the first day and was unable to take any further part in the match. Scrymgour substituted in the field and Hill kept wicket throughout. Hill's maiden first-class century (150 not out in 245 minutes, 1 five and 10 fours) - brought up at the age of 18 years 11 days - included a solitary chance at 122. His stand of 192 for the eighth wicket with W.F.Giffen (81 in 165 minutes, 7 fours) was a South Australian record. Ward (career-best 219 in 395 minutes, 21 fours) hit the first double-century against South Australia and his side the first total over 600 against that team; he gave chances when 128, 132 and 202, and featured in stands of 174 with Brown (101 in 165 minutes, 11 fours) and 181 with Ford (106 in 105 minutes, 15 fours). George Giffen, who as usual could not bear to take himself off, became the first bowler to concede 300 runs in any first-class innings. The match finished with only 3 minutes left on the fifth day. *Wisden* incorrectly gives Eng (1) Philipson 2. Sources: *Wisden, C.B.O'Reilly, Sydney Referee, Adelaide Advertiser, South Australian Register.*

SOUTH AUSTRALIA

J.J.Lyons	c Peel b Richardson	6	c Philipson b Peel	32
†A.H.Jarvis	b Richardson	5	absent hurt	-
*G.Giffen	c MacLaren b Briggs	51	c Brown b Richardson	27
J.Darling	b Richardson	15	b Briggs	36
J.C.Reedman	run out (MacLaren/Richardson)	46	(2) b Peel	1
R.H.Dyer	b Briggs	0	(8) not out	40
H.Blinman	c Peel b Richardson	3	c Philipson b Richardson	17
C.Hill	not out	150	(5) c Philipson b Richardson	56
W.F.Giffen	b Lockwood	81	(6) c Philipson b Richardson	4
A.Jarvis	b Richardson	31	(9) b Briggs	27
E.Jones	c Ward b Brockwell	1	(10) b Lockwood	3
Extras	(lb4, w3, nb1)	8	(b5, lb4, w2, nb1)	12
Total	(123.4 overs, 350 mins)	397	(101.5 overs, 305 mins)	255

A.E.STODDART'S ENGLAND XI

W.Brockwell	lbw b G.Giffen	35	not out	24
A.Ward	lbw b G.Giffen	219		
J.T.Brown	b G.Giffen	101		
A.C.MacLaren	c & b G.Giffen	18		
F.G.J.Ford	run out (Reedman)	106	(2) not out	18
R.Peel	b Lyons	57		
W.H.Lockwood	run out (A.Jarvis/W.F.Giffen)	23		
J.Briggs	not out	27		
L.H.Gay	c Hill b Lyons	1		
*†H.Philipson	c Reedman b G.Giffen	9		
T.Richardson	c & b Lyons	0		
Extras	(b9, lb4)	13	(b3)	3
Total	(180.4 overs, 460 mins)	609	(7.4 overs, 22 mins) (0 wkts)	45

ENGLAND XI	O	M	R	W	w,nb		O	M	R	W	w,nb
Richardson	37	8	148	5	-,1	(2)	44	17	91	4	-,1
Peel	26	7	62	0	-,-	(1)	29	7	62	2	-,-
Briggs	32	6	92	2	1,-	(4)	17	3	54	2	-,-
Lockwood	12	1	43	1	2,-	(3)	11.5	1	36	1	2,-
Brockwell	10.4	3	25	1	-,-						
Ford	6	1	19	0	-,-						

SOUTH AUSTRALIA	O	M	R	W	w,nb		O	M	R	W	w,nb
Jones	37	10	84	0	-,-	(2)	2	0	19	0	-,-
A.Jarvis	21	2	85	0	-,-	(3)	1.4	0	10	0	-,-
G.Giffen	87	12	309	5	-,-	(1)	4	0	13	0	-,-
Lyons	20.4	6	80	3	-,-						
Reedman	15	5	38	0	-,-						

FALL OF WICKETS

Wkt	SA 1st	ENG 1st	SA 2nd	ENG 2nd
1st	6	62	7	-
2nd	23	236	46	-
3rd	45	262	87	-
4th	113	443	125	-
5th	113	536	141	-
6th	124	558	181	-
7th	137	591	184	-
8th	329	594	249	-
9th	388	609	255	-
10th	397	609	-	-

Chief interest centred on the battle for the Sheffield Shield and the selection of the 9th Australian team to tour England in 1896. The Shield, contested over a four-month period, was deservedly won by New South Wales for the first time. It heralded the start of their domination of the crown - a trend that continued well into the 20th century. The New South Welshmen began the season confidently by defeating a strong Victorian team at Melbourne, and followed up with an equally meritorious performance against South Australia - their first win at Adelaide in four attempts. The only setback for the eventual champions came against victoria in the return match at Sydney, a game which saw fortunes fluctuate over five days. New South Wales finished their campaign with a nine-wicket win against South Australia in a high-scoring encounter at Sydney. Their batting was led by Donnan, Iredale, Mackenzie, Walters and Gregory, while McKibbin and Howell were consistent performers with the ball.

Victoria fielded virtually the same team as that which had won the Shield the previous year. The Trott brothers and Harry Graham were the best members of the side this time, though Bruce, Laver, Harry and the McLeod brothers all had brief moments of success.

George Giffen had an indifferent year by his standards and South Australia struggled as a consequence. Strangely, they showed their best form away from home, winning convincingly at Melbourne and putting up some tall scoring in a losing cause at Sydney. The young Clem Hill hit a double-century at Sydney to confirm the promise he had demonstrated against Stoddart's English team in the final match of their last tour. Darling also hit a century at Sydney and generally performed well, but the outstanding player in the team was bowler Ernie Jones. His pace and stamina made him a daunting proposition for any batsman, well-set or not.

Arthur Coningham repeated his achievement of 1893-94 by appearing for both Queensland and New South Wales. He hit 151 for Queensland against New South Wales in December and then played for New South Wales in their final Shield encounter at the end of February, capturing five wickets. He finished the season by representing Rest of Australia against the 9th Australians.

Tasmania won their annual match against Victoria by an innings, Eady and Windsor bowling virtually unchanged throughout both innings and taking all the wickets to fall to the bowlers. Queensland went down to New South Wales by nine wickets, despite Coningham's century.

W.Bruce, T.W.Garrett and G.Giffen were appointed to select the 9th Australian team to tour England, and their side had its share of controversies. The omission of A.E.Trott, 'one of the finest young cricketers that Australia has ever produced,' ('Felix' in *The Australasian*) brought a public outcry. The party of 13 initially released by the Australasian Cricket Council read: H.Donnan, S.E.Gregory, F.A.Iredale, T.R.McKibbin (New South Wales), H.Graham, J.Harry, A.E.Johns, G.H.S.Trott, H.Trumble (Victoria), J.Darling, G.Giffen, E.Jones (South Australia) and C.J.Eady (Tasmania). Jack Harry, who was forced to miss Victoria's final Shield match because of knee trouble, did not travel to Sydney for the 9th Australians' match against The Rest. After the completion of that game, the Council announced that Harry would be replaced in the touring party by J.J.Kelly, and that Clem Hill would be added to the team as a 14th man. Harry protested strongly at his omission, pronouncing himself fit. He demanded compensation, and was paid.

In December, an official New South Wales team toured New Zealand for the first time, previous visits being privately promoted. The leading players remained at home to conduct the Sheffield Shield campaign and the following team was announced: L.T.Cobcroft (captain), S.W.Austin, F.J.Burton, S.T.Callaway, R.Lyndsay, D.J.Noonan, L.O.S.Poidevin, D.G.Pryor, M.Shea, F.H.Wade, S.R.Walford and Wilson. A.J.Furness, A.E.Hume and F.M.Ridge later replaced Austin, Lyndsay and Wilson, who were unable to accept their invitations. The tour provided the sole first-class experience for Furness, Hume, Noonan, Pryor, Ridge, Shea and Wade, none of them subsequently able to force their way into the strong New South Wales teams of the next decade. Cobcroft played his only matches for New South Wales on this tour. He moved to New Zealand in 1897 and led the first New Zealand team to Australia in 1898-99. Callaway also subsequently moved to New Zealand and gained national representation.

Leading Aggregates

Batsmen	M	I	NO	Runs	HS	Ave.	Bowlers	Runs	Wkts	Ave.
H.Donnan (NSW)	6	11	2	626	160	69.55	T.R.McKibbin (NSW)	1098	46	23.86
F.A.Iredale (NSW)	6	10	1	528	187	58.66	E.Jones (SA)	548	31	17.67
C.Hill (SA)	5	9	1	451	206*	56.37	W.P.Howell (NSW)	612	24	25.50
A.C.K.Mackenzie (NSW)	5	9	0	376	97	41.77	G.Giffen (SA)	726	20	36.30
F.H.Walters (NSW)	5	8	2	336	150	56.00	A.E.Trott (V)	441	17	25.94
J.Darling (SA)	5	9	0	327	121	36.33	A.Coningham (Q & NSW)	411	15	27.40
G.H.S.Trott (V)	5	10	0	306	66	30.60	C.T.B.Turner (NSW)	413	15	27.53
H.Graham (V)	5	10	0	300	103	30.00				

SHEFFIELD SHIELD TABLE

	P	W	L	D	Quotient	Runs Scored	Wkts Lost	Runs Conceded	Wkts Taken
NEW SOUTH WALES	4	3	1	-	1.341	2181	61	2027	76
VICTORIA	4	2	2	-	0.896	1898	76	1952	70
SOUTH AUSTRALIA	4	1	3	-	0.819	1578	70	1678	61
TOTAL	6	6	6	-	1.000	5657	207	5657	207

SOUTH AUSTRALIA v VICTORIA (Shield Match 1)

Played at Adelaide Oval on November 9, 11, 12, 13, 1895. (Timeless match)
Toss : Victoria.   Result : VICTORIA WON BY 66 RUNS.
Debuts: Nil.
Twelfth Men: B.V.Scrymgour (SA) and W.A.Tarrant (Vic).
Umpires: R.M.Crockett and G.E.Downs.
Attendances: 5000, 5000, 2000, 500.   Total: About 12,500.   Receipts: No figures published.
Close of Play: 1st day SA 3/47 (Giffen 18); 2nd day Vic (2) 1/210 (Harry 106, G.H.S.Trott 34); 3rd day SA (2) 8/205 (A.Jarvis 29, Claxton 3).

The ambidextrous Harry (right-arm offbreaks this time) cleaned up the South Australian tail, taking his best figures and then scoring 107 (150 minutes, 12 fours, chance at 78), putting on 151 for the first wicket with Graham (68 in 110 minutes) to consolidate Victoria's position. Lyons opened South Australia's second innings with 2 fours and a two off the first five balls before falling to the last ball of the opening over. Alfred Jarvis and Ernie Jones added 91 in an hour for the last wicket. When he dismissed Carlton in the second innings, Giffen became the first bowler to attain 100 Sheffield Shield wickets. *Wisden* incorrectly gives SA (1) G.H.S.Trott 0/25, Roche 4/60, Harry 4/18, Phillips 0/10. *O'Reilly* incorrectly gives SA (1) Roche 4/60. Sources: *Wisden, C.B.O'Reilly, VCA Report, SACA Report, Adelaide Advertiser, South Australian Register.*

VICTORIA

J.Harry	b Jones	15	c Darling b Giffen	107
H.Graham	c Darling b Giffen	50	st A.H.Jarvis b Reedman	68
*G.H.S.Trott	c Lyons b Giffen	6	c & b Giffen	56
A.E.Trott	b Jones	3	b Giffen	10
F.J.Laver	c A.H.Jarvis b A.Jarvis	42	b Jones	4
C.H.Peryman	b A.Jarvis	34	b Jones	5
†P.M.Lewis	c Giffen b A.Jarvis	12	b A.Jarvis	34
R.W.McLeod	run out (Jones)	17	not out	35
J.Carlton	lbw b Giffen	9	b Giffen	1
W.Roche	c Dyer b Jones	13	c Darling b A.Jarvis	2
J.Phillips	not out	9	b Giffen	0
Extras	(b7, lb1, w2)	10	(b4, lb3)	7
Total	(74.2 overs, 225 mins)	220	(99.5 overs, 260 mins)	329

SOUTH AUSTRALIA

J.J.Lyons	c A.E.Trott b Roche	15	c Graham b G.H.S.Trott	10
J.C.Reedman	c A.E.Trott b Roche	8	(5) c Lewis b Harry	5
*G.Giffen	c McLeod b Roche	36	b Harry	6
J.Darling	b A.E.Trott	6	c Laver b A.E.Trott	50
C.Hill	c Lewis b Roche	60	(2) c Peryman b Carlton	41
†A.H.Jarvis	st Lewis b A.E.Trott	0	c A.E.Trott b G.H.S.Trott	32
H.Blinman	b Harry	15	c & b Carlton	6
R.H.Dyer	b Harry	10	st Lewis b G.H.S.Trott	17
A.Jarvis	lbw b Harry	10	b Carlton	68
W.D.H.Claxton	st Lewis b Harry	0	b Roche	9
E.Jones	not out	2	not out	66
Extras	(nb1)	1	(b6, lb4)	10
Total	(58.3 overs, 185 mins)	163	(77.5 overs, 235 mins)	320

SOUTH AUSTRALIA	O	M	R	W	w,nb		O	M	R	W	w,nb		FALL OF WICKETS			
														VIC	SA	VIC	SA
Jones	21.2	5	51	3	-,-		24	2	66	2	-,-	Wkt	1st	1st	2nd	2nd
Giffen	37	5	108	3	-,-		41.5	8	141	5	-,-	1st	34	23	151	10
A.Jarvis	16	0	51	3	2,-	(4)	17	2	51	2	-,-	2nd	53	24	213	19
Claxton					-,-	(3)	6	0	21	0	-,-	3rd	60	47	233	90
Lyons					-,-		3	0	21	0	-,-	4th	106	82	238	110
Reedman					-,-		8	2	22	1	-,-	5th	149	83	248	118
												6th	170	126	252	154
VICTORIA	O	M	R	W	w,nb		O	M	R	W	w,nb	7th	175	145	317	154
G.H.S.Trott	5	0	23	0	-,-		8	0	63	3	-,-	8th	190	157	324	176
Roche	25.3	9	59	4	-,1		18	2	75	1	-,-	9th	196	161	328	229
A.E.Trott	13	1	45	2	-,-	(4)	12	2	32	1	-,-	10th	220	163	329	320
McLeod	1	0	4	0	-,-	(8)	2	0	12	0	-,-					
Phillips	7	0	16	0	-,-		2	0	16	0	-,-					
Harry	7	1	15	4	-,-	(3)	22	7	58	2	-,-					
Carlton						(6)	10.5	2	39	3	-,-					
Laver						(7)	3	0	15	0	-,-					

NEW SOUTH WALES v QUEENSLAND

Played at Sydney Cricket Ground on December, 13, 14, 16, 17, 1895. (Timeless match)
Toss : New South Wales.   Result : NEW SOUTH WALES WON BY NINE WICKETS.
Debuts: New South Wales - F.H.Walters (NSW only). Queensland - A.A.Atkins, H.W.Chapman (both f/c).
Twelfth Men: None named.
Umpires: T.Arundel and J.A.Tooher.
Attendances: 1000, 3000, 1000, 100.   Total: About 5100.   Receipts: £198.
Close of Play: 1st day NSW 5/340 (Walters 91, Gould 31); 2nd day Qld 6/214 (Coningham 119, Hoare 4); 3rd day Qld (2) 7/159
    (Macdonald 40, Hoare 11).

Coningham's sole first-class century - a chanceless 151 in 215 minutes with 15 fours - was also the first for Queensland, and with McDonnell (65 in 55 minutes, 2 fives and 10 fours) he recorded that team's first century partnership in quick time. Selected in the original team, Coningham had at first withdrawn (his place going to Hoare) when the QCA had refused to meet the £10 which he assessed as his losses for the two weeks he would be away. He was promised the fee by the NSWCA, who wanted him as a drawcard, and he left on the Wednesday to join the team. Of the thirteen players in Sydney, H.F.Boyle (the ex-Victorian, destined never to play for Queensland) and A.H.V.Hewitt were omitted. Bradley kept wicket in the first innings only until 4.00pm ob the first day, when sore hands forced him to hand the job over to Chapman. However, Chapman's performance on debut was unimpressive (he managed to fluke a stumping when the ball rebounded from his pads on to the wicket with McKibbin out of his ground) and he also failed to score in either innings, registering third-ball and first-ball ducks respectively. Bradley resumed as wicket-keeper for the second innings. Walters became the first batsman to score a hundred on debut for New South Wales (he had previously represented Victoria), compiling a career-best 150 in 325 minutes with 16 fours (chances at 32 and 91). Mackenzie (76 in 150 minutes, 12 fours) and Gould (53 in 105 minutes, 5 fours) scored half-centuries for New South Wales. Macdonald, who sustained a first-ball duck, returned to topscore in the Queensland second innings with an unbeaten 77 in 255 minutes (8 fours). C.T.B.Turner had been selected in the home team but was forced out, having hurt his hand in a club match the previous Saturday. *Cricket* incorrectly gives NSW (1) Newell 2*, McGlinchey 3/93. Sources: *Cricket, Sydney Referee, Sydney Morning Herald, Town & Country Journal, Sydney Daily Telegraph.*

NEW SOUTH WALES

A.C.K.Mackenzie	run out (Macdonald)	76	st Bradley b Coningham		21
H.Donnan	c McDonnell b Coningham	40	not out		30
F.A.Iredale	c Cresswick b Coningham	9			
*S.E.Gregory	c O'Brien b McGlinchey	43			
F.H.Walters	c McDonnell b McGlinchey	150	(3) not out		0
G.J.Youill	c McGlinchey b Hoare	40			
J.W.Gould	c McGlinchey b O'Brien	53			
T.R.McKibbin	st Chapman b Coningham	17			
W.P.Howell	b Coningham	12			
A.L.Newell	not out	12			
†J.J.Kelly	c & b McGlinchey	9			
Extras	(b17, lb3, w4)	24			-
Total	(154.0 overs, 405 mins)	485	(24.1 overs, 60 mins) (1 wkt)		51

QUEENSLAND

A.Coningham	c Newell b McKibbin	151	c Mackenzie b Gould		51
*P.S.McDonnell	c Donnan b Newell	65	c Howell b McKibbin		3
R.Macdonald	lbw b Howell	0	(4) not out		77
†W.F.Bradley	run out (McKibbin/Kelly)	2	(3) b Howell		18
J.W.Lewis	b Howell	0	(6) b Howell		8
W.W.McGlinchey	run out (Gregory/McKibbin)	12	(5) lbw b McKibbin		12
A.A.Atkins	c Kelly b Gould	11	c Iredale b Howell		8
W.Hoare	b McKibbin	6	(9) c Kelly b Newell		18
†H.W.Chapman	run out (Gould/Kelly)	0	(8) b Howell		0
E.A.Cresswick	c McKibbin b Donnan	6	c Kelly b McKibbin		21
R.O'Brien	not out	4	c & b Gould		48
Extras	(lb4, nb1)	5	(b1, lb3, nb4)		8
Total	(89.3 overs, 225 mins)	262	(99.0 overs, 290 mins)		272

QUEENSLAND	O	M	R	W	w,nb		O	M	R	W	w,nb
Coningham	42	6	175	4	3,-	(2)	12	4	19	1	-,-
Cresswick	26	4	89	0	-,-						
McGlinchey	37	4	94	3	-,-		7.1	2	17	0	-,-
O'Brien	35	13	64	1	1,-	(1)	5	1	15	0	-,-
Hoare	11	3	29	1	-,-						
Lewis	3	0	10	0	-,-						

NEW SOUTH WALES	O	M	R	W	w,nb		O	M	R	W	w,nb
McKibbin	20	1	89	2	-,1		40	11	94	3	-,4
Newell	31	13	74	1	-,-	(4)	13	5	25	1	-,-
Howell	19	4	58	2	-,-	(2)	27	9	75	4	-,-
Gould	15	4	28	1	-,-	(3)	16	1	61	2	-,-
Donnan	4.3	2	8	1	-,-		3	1	9	0	-,-

FALL OF WICKETS

	NSW	QLD	QLD	NSW
Wkt	1st	1st	2nd	2nd
1st	81	107	8	48
2nd	97	107	41	-
3rd	169	129	94	
4th	177	129	113	-
5th	265	168	130	-
6th	384	201	142	-
7th	436	246	142	-
8th	452	246	178	-
9th	467	253	207	-
10th	485	262	272	

VICTORIA v NEW SOUTH WALES (Shield Match 2)

Played at Melbourne Cricket Ground on December 26, 27, 28, 30, 31, 1895. (Timeless match)
Toss : New South Wales.   Result : NEW SOUTH WALES WON BY 123 RUNS.
Debuts: Nil.
Twelfth Men: S J Donahoo (Vic) and A L Newell (NSW).
Umpires: J.Phillips and J.A.Tooher.
Attendances: 11000, 6000, 8000, 5000, 5500.   Total: About 35,500.   Receipts: £1188.
Close of Play: 1st day NSW 2/266 (Donnan 124, Richardson 59); 2nd day Vic 3/105 (G.H.S.Trott 35, Graham 12); 3rd day NSW (2) 0/22
    (Donnan 13, Mackenzie 8); 4th day NSW (2) 8/319 (Kelly 53, McKibbin 4).

A patient century by Donnan, who compiled his best score for the team over 13 seasons (160 in 410 minutes, 15 fours, chances at 61 and
91), led New South Wales to their first win in a Shield match away from home (their seventh such game). Mackenzie (46 in 115 minutes,
4 fours), Richardson (76 in 150 minutes, 1 five and 7 fours), Walters (69 in 105 minutes, 9 fours), Garrett (69 in 105 minutes, 4 fours) and
Kelly (58 not out in 130 minutes, 4 fours) also batted well. Harry Trott made no fewer than 17 bowling changes on the first day in an
attempt to shift the resolute cornstalks; his brother Albert, surprisingly the seventh bowler to be tried, eventually proved most successful.
Graham's maiden hundred for Victoria (103 in 190 minutes, 8 fours) followed his two Test centuries (107 and 105) for Australia. He was
supported by G.H.S.Trott (66 in 105 minutes, 4 fours) and R.W.McLeod (56 not out in 105 minutes,4 fours) but Bruce (90 in 150
minutes,6 fours) played a lone hand in the second innings. McKibbin took his tally of wickets in the Sheffield Shield to 34 from 3
matches. The match aggregate of 1353 runs, a new Shield record, was not surpassed until 1905-06. S.E.Gregory (disagreement over match
fees) and C.T.B.Turner (thumb injury) were unavailable for New South Wales. *Wisden* incorrectly gives Vic (2) R.W.McLeod 19, Lewis
12. Sources: *Wisden, VCA Report, The Age, The Argus, The Herald, The Australasian, The Leader, Sydney Referee.*

NEW SOUTH WALES

Batsman	1st innings	Runs	2nd innings	Runs
H.Donnan	b Harry	160	st Lewis b A.E.Trott	46
A.C.K.Mackenzie	c G.H.S.Trott b A.E.Trott	46	b A.E.Trott	19
F.A.Iredale	c A.E.Trott b Trumble	31	c G.H.S.Trott b Roche	21
W.A.Richardson	c G.H.S.Trott b C.E.McLeod	76	b C.E.McLeod	5
F.H.Walters	c Trumble b C.E.McLeod	2	c Trumble b R.W.McLeod	69
G.J.Youill	hit wkt b A.E.Trott	34	run out (Harry)	3
J.W.Gould	c C.E.McLeod b A.E.Trott	14	c Lewis b R.W.McLeod	16
*T.W.Garrett	c Laver b A.E.Trott	5	(9) c Bruce b A.E.Trott	70
T.R.McKibbin	run out (Harry)	0	(10) c Harry b R.W.McLeod	10
†J.J.Kelly	not out	7	(8) not out	58
W.P.Howell	c Bruce b A.E.Trott	20	b A.E.Trott	1
Extras	(b7, lb2, w3)	12	(b11, nb2)	13
Total	(202.2 overs, 470 mins)	407	(142.2 overs, 335 mins)	331

VICTORIA

Batsman	1st innings	Runs	2nd innings	Runs
W.Bruce	b McKibbin	26	st Kelly b McKibbin	90
J.Harry	b Howell	16	b McKibbin	3
*G.H.S.Trott	b Richardson	66	b McKibbin	27
A.E.Trott	c Richardson b Gould	13	(5) c Mackenzie b McKibbin	11
H.Graham	c Gould b McKibbin	103	(4) lbw b McKibbin	16
F.J.Laver	c Richardson b McKibbin	22	c & b McKibbin	29
H.Trumble	b McKibbin	6	c Mackenzie b McKibbin	26
C.E.McLeod	run out (McKibbin)	12	b Howell	6
R.W.McLeod	not out	56	b Howell	12
†P.M.Lewis	c McKibbin b Howell	17	b McKibbin	19
W.Roche	b Howell	11	not out	6
Extras	(b5, lb1, nb3)	9	(b8, lb4, w1)	13
Total	(135.3 overs, 345 mins)	357	(98.3 overs, 255 mins)	258

VICTORIA	O	M	R	W	w,nb		O	M	R	W	w,nb
Roche	19	3	54	0	-,-	(6)	13	2	38	1	-,-
G.H.S.Trott	35	12	75	0	-,-	(3)	13	3	35	0	-,-
C.E.McLeod	42	20	55	2	1,-	(5)	28	11	50	1	-,-
Harry	19.2	8	45	1	-,-	(7)	2	0	10	0	-,-
Bruce	7	0	21	0	-,-	(8)	3	1	16	0	-,-
Trumble	32	15	36	1	2,-	(4)	16	3	38	0	-,2
A.E.Trott	35	11	77	5	-,-	(1)	39.2	8	94	4	-,-
R.W.McLeod	6	1	23	0	-,-	(2)	28	9	37	3	-,-
Laver	7	3	9	0	-,-						

NEW SOUTH WALES	O	M	R	W	w,nb		O	M	R	W	w,nb
McKibbin	52	15	127	4	-,3		39.3	10	93	8	-,-
Richardson	21	2	64	1	-,-		6	0	25	0	1,-
Howell	39.3	8	87	3	-,-		37	7	84	2	-,-
Gould	9	2	21	1	-,-	(6)	2	0	10	0	-,-
Garrett	7	0	31	0	-,-		6	1	14	0	-,-
Donnan	5	2	9	0	-,-	(4)	8	1	19	0	-,-
Youill	2	0	9	0	-,-						

FALL OF WICKETS

Wkt	NSW 1st	VIC 1st	NSW 2nd	VIC 2nd
1st	108	34	55	8
2nd	169	54	80	102
3rd	295	86	97	138
4th	301	157	103	141
5th	340	222	130	154
6th	374	238	191	205
7th	374	257	194	212
8th	375	299	315	220
9th	387	329	330	234
10th	407	357	331	258

SOUTH AUSTRALIA v NEW SOUTH WALES (Shield Match 3)

Played at Adelaide Oval on January 3, 4, 6, 1896. (Timeless match)
Toss : New South Wales.   Result : NEW SOUTH WALES WON BY AN INNINGS AND 34 RUNS.
Debuts: South Australia - A.E.Evans, C.Martin (both f/c).
12th Men: J.W.Gould (NSW. No 12th named for SA.
Umpires: I.A.Fisher and J.A.Tooher.
Attendances: 4000, 9000, 1000.   Total: About 14,000.   Receipts: £403.
Close of Play: 1st day NSW 8/231 (Garrett 7); 2nd day SA (2) 2/8 (Scrymgour 0).

Having beaten Victoria in Melbourne for the first time in the competition, New South Wales now proceeded to win their first Shield match in Adelaide with a fine display of bowling and fielding. They were given a good start by the in-form Donnan (93 in 210 minutes, 6 fours), Mackenzie (52 in 115 minutes, 3 fours) and Iredale (51 in 90 minutes, 4 fours) before the pace of Jones (7 for 103) upset the middle-order after tea. Garrett (61 in 90 minutes, 2 fives and 4 fours) and Howell (33 not out in 55 minutes, 5 fours) added 84 for the last wicket. Reedman's four catches were all held at mid-off. Giffen (74 in 135 minutes, 5 fours) scored South Australia's only half-century, the rest failing to the pace of Richardson and the medium-paced offbreaks of McKibbin and Howell. Following on they fared no better, losing Reedman to the second ball of the innings and Martin immediately after he had hit 2 fours. Giffen went to his second ball on the third morning and Howell bowled unchanged through the innings. *Wisden* incorrectly gives SA (1) McKibbin 4/62, Newell 0/19. Sources: *Wisden, C.B.O'Reilly, SACA Report, Sydney Morning Herald, Adelaide Advertiser, South Australian Register.*

NEW SOUTH WALES

H.Donnan	c Reedman b Giffen	93
A.C.K.Mackenzie	b Jones	52
F.A.Iredale	lbw b Jones	51
W.A.Richardson	lbw b Jones	0
F.H.Walters	lbw b Jones	13
G.J.Youill	b Jones	2
†J.J.Kelly	c & b Jones	0
A.L.Newell	c Reedman b Giffen	12
*T.W.Garrett	c Reedman b Giffen	61
T.R.McKibbin	c Reedman b Jones	1
W.P.Howell	not out	33
Extras	(lb2)	2
Total	(127.5 overs, 320 mins)	320

SOUTH AUSTRALIA

C.Martin	c Kelly b Richardson	1	(2)	b McKibbin	8
A.E.Evans	b Richardson	6	(9)	b Howell	2
J.J.Lyons	b Howell	28	(4)	c Iredale b Howell	29
*G.Giffen	c & b McKibbin	74	(5)	b McKibbin	0
J.Darling	c Newell b McKibbin	7	(6)	c Iredale b McKibbin	33
C.Hill	c Newell b McKibbin	5	(7)	b Howell	2
J.C.Reedman	not out	19	(1)	c McKibbin b Howell	0
A.Jarvis	b McKibbin	0	(10)	not out	12
†A.H.Jarvis	st Kelly b Howell	5	(8)	c McKibbin b Richardson	27
B.V.Scrymgour	b Howell	2	(3)	lbw b McKibbin	7
E.Jones	run out (Youill/Howell)	1		c McKibbin b Howell	9
Extras	(b2, lb1, nb1)	4		(b3, lb1, nb1)	5
Total	(60.3 overs, 175 mins)	152		(44.1 overs, 130 mins)	134

SOUTH AUSTRALIA	O	M	R	W	w,nb
Jones	43	13	103	7	-,-
Giffen	41.5	11	140	3	-,-
A.Jarvis	11	4	30	0	-,-
Reedman	11	5	19	0	-,-
Lyons	11	2	26	0	-,-

NEW SOUTH WALES	O	M	R	W	w,nb		O	M	R	W	w,nb
McKibbin	23	7	61	4	-,1	(2)	18	2	72	4	-,1
Richardson	12	4	28	2	-,-	(3)	4	1	8	1	-,-
Howell	21.3	8	39	3	-,-	(1)	22.1	9	49	5	-,-
Newell	4	0	20	0	-,-						

FALL OF WICKETS			
Wkt	NSW 1st	SA 1st	SA 2nd
1st	99	5	0
2nd	193	8	8
3rd	195	60	35
4th	197	91	35
5th	204	114	45
6th	204	125	47
7th	217	129	92
8th	231	136	99
9th	236	151	120
10th	320	152	134

NEW SOUTH WALES v VICTORIA (Shield Match 4)

Played at Sydney Cricket Ground on January 25, 27, 28, 29, 30, 1896. (Timeless match)
Toss : Victoria.　　　　　　　　Result : VICTORIA WON BY FOUR WICKETS.
Debuts: Nil.
12th Men: G.J.Youill (NSW) and J.Carlton (Vic).
Umpires: J.Phillips and J.A.Tooher.
Attendances: 5002, 22807, 5318, 3083, 3000.　　　Total: 39,210.　　　Receipts: £1658.
Close of Play: 1st day NSW 1/33 (Donnan 16, Iredale 16); 2nd day Vic 1/94 (C.E.McLeod 29, G.H.S.Trott 40); 3rd day NSW (2) 0/22
　　(Donnan 11, Mackenzie 10); 4th day NSW (2) 9/307 (Walters 45, McKibbin 5).

The NSWCA rescheduled the start of the match from January 24th to take advantage of the anticipated attendance on the Anniversary Day (now Australia Day) weekend, and although rain restricted play on the first day to just 52 minutes prior to lunch, a great crowd turned out on the second day to compensate for the loss. In fact, it remained the biggest single-day attendance for a Sheffield Shield match at Sydney until the 1927-28 season. Sent in, New South Wales were bowled out on a soft wicket, Iredale (56 in 120 minutes, 5 fours) and Garrett (53 in 135 minutes, 3 fours) being the top scorers. Charlie McLeod (100 in 265 minutes, 12 fours) consolidated Victoria's position with a maiden first-class century. Harry Trott (63 in 105 minutes, 4 fours) and Donahoo (33 in 25 minutes, 1 five and 5 fours), who hit McKibbin (49 wickets in five Shield games so far) into the Smokers' reserve, provided other highlights. Mackenzie (97 in 250 minutes, 1 five and 8 fours) and Walters (68 not out in 130 minutes, 10 fours) scored half-centuries for New South Wales in reply while Turner (30 in 15 minutes, 2 fives and 4 fours) cracked two skyscraping hits off Harry, the first landing near the tennis courts (northern end) and the second rocketing into the pavilion. C.E.McLeod (50 in 125 minutes, 3 fours) led Victoria to victory. Laver hit a four to finish the match, but it was not reported why the match continued after the score had reached 203, the required target. Perhaps the scoreboard lapsed behind. Most sources incorrectly add wides and no-balls into the bowling analyses, viz NSW (1) Harry 1/24; NSW (2) G.H.S.Trott 1/43, C.E.McLeod 1/56. Sources: *Wisden, VCA Report, Sydney Referee, Sydney Morning Herald, Town & Country Journal, Sydney Daily Telegraph.*

NEW SOUTH WALES

H.Donnan	c Trumble b G.H.S.Trott	19		b Harry	26
A.C.K.Mackenzie	c A.E.Trott b Trumble	0		c R.W.McLeod b Harry	97
F.A.Iredale	c R.W.McLeod b Trumble	56		c Johns b G.H.S.Trott	43
*T.W.Garrett	b Trumble	53	(6)	b Harry	0
S.E.Gregory	c Trumble b Harry	3	(4)	c Harry b Laver	36
F.H.Walters	run out (Donahoo/R.W.McLeod)	28	(5)	not out	68
W.A.Richardson	b Trumble	1		b Harry	0
†J.J.Kelly	not out	5		c R.W.McLeod b Trumble	0
C.T.B.Turner	c Trumble b R.W.McLeod	9		c Trumble b R.W.McLeod	30
W.P.Howell	st Johns b Trumble	5		c Graham b C.E.McLeod	7
T.R.McKibbin	c G.H.S.Trott b A.E.Trott	3		c Graham b A.E.Trott	7
Extras	(lb4, w1)	5		(b15, lb4, w1, nb1)	21
Total	(96.3 overs, 245 mins)	187		(138.1 overs, 325 mins)	335

VICTORIA

W.Bruce	c Kelly b Turner	23	(2)	c McKibbin b Turner	11
C.E.McLeod	c & b Turner	100	(1)	c Richardson b McKibbin	50
*G.H.S.Trott	c McKibbin b Richardson	63		c Kelly b McKibbin	27
H.Graham	b Howell	1		b Richardson	15
A.E.Trott	c Richardson b Howell	18		c Kelly b Turner	24
S.J.Donahoo	c Iredale b Richardson	33		c Kelly b McKibbin	2
F.J.Laver	b McKibbin	38		not out	38
J.Harry	c Richardson b McKibbin	31		not out	39
H.Trumble	b McKibbin	1			
R.W.McLeod	not out	5			
†A.E.Johns	c Richardson b McKibbin	3			
Extras	(b2, lb1)	3		(lb1)	1
Total	(133.0 overs, 355 mins)	319		(70.2 overs, 200 mins) (6 wkts)	207

VICTORIA	O	M	R	W	w,nb		O	M	R	W	w,nb	FALL OF WICKETS				
													NSW	VIC	NSW	VIC
Trumble	43	17	61	5	-,-	(3)	38	18	74	1	-,-	Wkt	1st	1st	2nd	2nd
R.W.McLeod	20	4	46	1	-,-		13	5	22	1	-,-	1st	9	27	48	13
A.E.Trott	9.3	1	23	1	-,-	(4)	18.1	6	41	1	-,-	2nd	37	145	138	62
G.H.S.Trott	12	2	29	1	-,-	(1)	10	2	42	1	1,-	3rd	106	146	195	97
Harry	12	3	23	1	1,-		21	8	53	4	-,-	4th	109	190	240	111
C.E.McLeod							27	6	55	1	-,1	5th	159	239	248	121
Laver							9	4	16	1	-,-	6th	165	245	248	135
Bruce							2	0	11	0	-,-	7th	166	286	249	-
												8th	175	304	287	-
NEW SOUTH WALES	O	M	R	W	w,nb		O	M	R	W	w,nb	9th	182	313	298	-
Richardson	21	2	50	2	-,-		7	1	34	1	-,-	10th	187	319	335	-
Turner	45	15	91	2	-,-		28	8	54	2	-,-					
McKibbin	35	9	114	4	-,-	(5)	22.2	4	85	3	-,-					
Howell	32	13	61	2	-,-	(3)	11	4	22	0	-,-					
Donnan						(4)	2	0	11	0	-,-					

VICTORIA v TASMANIA

Played at Melbourne Cricket Ground on January 25, 27, 1896. (Timeless match)
Toss : Tasmania.   Result : TASMANIA WON BY AN INNINGS AND 58 RUNS.
Debuts: Victoria - A.H.Fenton, J.A.O'Connor (both f/c).
12th Men: J.Beulke, E.Herring & T.Tatchell (Vic emergencies) and C.W.Butler (Tas).
Umpires: R.M.Crockett and C.E.Over.
Attendances: 2000, 1750.   Total: About 3750.   Receipts: £153.
Close of Play: 1st day Tas 9/178 (Windsor 16).

This was Tasmania's first first-class win away from home. Heavy rain on the day preceding the match had left the wicket sodden, underprepared and spiteful, and the batsmen of both sides struggled. Lewis (11) was struck by a lifter from Eady and retired at 3/45 to receive stitches in a gash on his chin; he resumed after lunch at 4/53. Eady's best-ever 8 for 34 had been shaded only by W.Brown's 8 for 31 (1857-58) among Tasmanians. Burn scored the only half-century in the match (66 in 105 minutes, 7 fours) after being dropped at 12 and 61. Windsor, batting at No. 9, scored 45 in an hour with 5 fours. The pitch rolled out well on the second day and the Victorians were expected to make a better showing in their second innings, but Eady (who operated unchanged throughout the match) and Windsor bowled superbly to shoot the home side out in under 90 minutes. Windsor's figures at one stage read 4 for 0, while Eady's 12 wickets helped him win a spot in the Australian team to England. The balls used were presented to Eady (first innings) and Windsor (second) after the match, in recognition of their efforts in giving Tasmania their first innings-victory at first-class level. Sources: *VCA Report, The Age, The Argus, The Herald, The Australasian, The Leader, The Sportsman.*

VICTORIA

T.S.Warne	c Windsor b Eady	14	(2)	b Windsor	0
J.H.Stuckey	c Westbrook b Windsor	2	(4)	lbw b Windsor	9
*J.Worrall	c Burn b Eady	12		c Burn b Windsor	0
C.G.Wilson	c J.H.Savigny b Eady	2	(7)	lbw b Eady	3
†P.M.Lewis	c Vautin b Eady	11	(6)	b Eady	5
R.Mitchell	c Burn b Eady	17	(1)	b Windsor	9
C.H.Peryman	c & b Eady	6	(5)	b Windsor	0
W.G.Ingleton	c Maxwell b Eady	19		c Maxwell b Windsor	6
W.Roche	not out	8		not out	19
J.A.O'Connor	c W.H.Savigny b Eady	0	(11)	b Eady	11
A.H.Fenton	run out (W.H.Savigny/Vautin)	0	(10)	b Eady	3
Extras	(b10)	10			-
Total	(46.0 overs, 135 mins)	101		(38.1 overs, 85 mins)	65

TASMANIA

J.H.Savigny	b Fenton	37
W.H.Savigny	c Roche b O'Connor	4
*E.J.K.Burn	b Worrall	66
C.J.Eady	c Mitchell b Worrall	18
E.Maxwell	st Lewis b Worrall	3
A.J.Douglas	c Roche b Mitchell	5
N.R.Westbrook	c Roche b Mitchell	0
†C.E.Vautin	st Lewis b Mitchell	1
E.A.C.Windsor	c Worrall b Roche	45
J.E.Bingham	c Ingleton b Worrall	16
J.Watt	not out	13
Extras	(b12, lb4)	16
Total	(58.3 overs, 165 mins)	224

TASMANIA	O	M	R	W	w,nb	O	M	R	W	w,nb
Eady	23	13	34	8	-,-	19.1	8	29	4	-,-
Windsor	17	3	37	1	-,-	19	8	36	6	-,-
Bingham	6	1	20	0	-,-					

VICTORIA	O	M	R	W	w,nb
Roche	13.3	1	51	1	-,-
O'Connor	5	0	25	1	-,-
Fenton	8	1	36	1	-,-
Worrall	14	1	46	4	-,-
Mitchell	10	1	40	3	-,-
Ingleton	8	3	10	0	-,-

FALL OF WICKETS

Wkt	VIC 1st	TAS 1st	VIC 2nd
1st	2	6	9
2nd	21	67	9
3rd	29	130	9
4th	53	133	9
5th	59	138	20
6th	67	140	24
7th	72	140	26
8th	97	151	37
9th	97	178	43
10th	101	224	65

VICTORIA v SOUTH AUSTRALIA (Shield Match 5)

Played at Melbourne Cricket Ground on February 21, 22, 24, 1896. (Timeless match)
Toss : South Australia.   Result : SOUTH AUSTRALIA WON BY TEN WICKETS.
Debuts: South Australia - E.H.Leak, J.P.F.Travers (both f/c); J.J.Ferris (SA only).
12th Men: S.J.Donahoo (Vic) and J.J.Lyons (SA).
Umpires: R.M.Crockett and T.A.Reeves.
Attendances: 4000, 3500, 1000.   Total: About 8500.   Receipts: £179.
Close of Play: 1st day SA 4/134 (Hill 41, Reedman 34); 2nd day Vic (2) 1/0 (Trumble 0).

J.Harry (knee injury) was unable to be considered for Victoria and A.H.Jarvis was unavailable for South Australia's trip east. Recent heavy rains produced a soft wicket which prompted Giffen to send the Victorians in, and Jones demonstrated from the first over that the ball would rise sharply and unpredictably. Laver's half-century (50 in 75 minutes, 7 fours) was a fine innings under the conditions. Trumble was simultaneously caught and stumped off Giffen's bowling. Ferris was out to the first ball of the South Australian reply in the only match that he was to play for the croweaters. Two further wickets fell almost immediately, but the pitch was improving as the day wore on, and Giffen (43), Hill (43) and Reedman (60) all got starts. Rain returned on the second day to prevent any play before 4.00pm, the wicket and the outfield well and truly soaked, and South Australia lost their last six wickets for 65 runs. Victoria began their second innings very late in the day, opening with tail-enders, and when Johns was out to' the fourth ball of the second over stumps were drawn. On Monday, Trumble succumbed to the first ball of Jones's opening over on a wicket which was "like glue" (*The Age*), and the Victorians were routed for their lowest score against South Australia in unplayable conditions; this stood as the lowest total in the Sheffield Shield until 1906-07. Jones had bowled unchanged throughout both innings. Lyons (heat exhaustion) was made 12th man. *Wisden* omits SA (2) Carlton 0/2, A.E.Trott 0/6. Sources: *Wisden, C.B.O'Reilly, VCA Report, The Age, The Argus, The Herald, The Australasian, The Leader.*

VICTORIA

C.E.McLeod	c Darling b Jones	2	(3) b Jarvis	1
W.Bruce	st McKenzie b Giffen	13	(4) c Travers b Jarvis	1
*G.H.S.Trott	run out (Hill/Giffen)	18	(5) c Martin b Jones	13
H.Graham	c Ferris b Jones	6	(6) b Jones	4
J.Worrall	c McKenzie b Jones	3	(8) not out	10
A.E.Trott	b Giffen	22	(9) b Jones	0
F.J.Laver	run out (McKenzie)	50	c Darling b Jones	13
H.Trumble	c McKenzie b Giffen	19	(1) c McKenzie b Jones	0
R.W.McLeod	c Hill b Giffen	4	(10) c Darling b Jones	0
J.Carlton	not out	17	(11) c Hill b Jarvis	0
†A.E.Johns	run out (Reedman/McKenzie)	0	(2) c Travers b Jarvis	0
Extras	(b4, lb7)	11	(lb1)	1
Total	(36.0 overs, 125 mins)	165	(23.4 overs, 78 mins)	43

SOUTH AUSTRALIA

J.J.Ferris	c Trumble b Carlton	0		
E.H.Leak	st Johns b G.H.S.Trott	8	(1) not out	1
*G.Giffen	c G.H.S.Trott b Carlton	43		
J.Darling	c Johns b Carlton	1		
C.Hill	b C.E.McLeod	43		
J.C.Reedman	run out (Graham/Johns)	60		
A.Jarvis	c Johns b R.W.McLeod	6		
C.Martin	b R.W.McLeod	9		
E.Jones	b C.E.McLeod	4	(2) not out	7
†J.McKenzie	not out	12		
J.P.F.Travers	c Trumble b Carlton	2		
Extras	(b7, lb4)	11	(b2)	2
Total	(79.0 overs, 235 mins)	199	(3.5 overs, 12 mins) (0 wkts)	10

SOUTH AUSTRALIA	O	M	R	W	w,nb		O	M	R	W	w,nb
Jones	18	2	57	3	-,-		12	7	15	6	-,-
Giffen	17	0	94	4	-,-						
Ferris	1	0	3	0	-,-						
Jarvis						(2)	11.4	6	27	4	-,-

VICTORIA	O	M	R	W	w,nb		O	M	R	W	w,nb
Carlton	26	7	44	4	-,-	(2)	1.5	0	2	0	-,-
G.H.S.Trott	9	1	30	1	-,-						
A.E.Trott	11	2	36	0	-,-	(1)	2	1	6	0	-,-
Trumble	3	0	10	0	-,-						
C.E.McLeod	18	3	42	2	-,-						
R.W.McLeod	12	3	26	2	-,-						

FALL OF WICKETS

Wkt	VIC 1st	SA 1st	VIC 2nd	SA 2nd
1st	14	0	0	-
2nd	24	28	0	-
3rd	38	37	2	-
4th	41	82	15	-
5th	57	136	15	-
6th	73	155	23	-
7th	125	169	38	-
8th	139	176	38	-
9th	159	185	38	-
10th	165	199	43	-

NEW SOUTH WALES v SOUTH AUSTRALIA (Shield Match 6)

Played at Sydney Cricket Ground on February 28, 29, March 2, 3, 4, 1896. (Timeless match)
Toss : South Australia.   Result : NEW SOUTH WALES WON BY NINE WICKETS.
Debuts: Nil.
12th Men: A.L.Newell (NSW) and J.J.Ferris (NSW).
Umpires: T.A.Reeves and J.A.Tooher.
Attendances: 4227, 12994, 5692, 4019, 573.   Total: 27,505.   Receipts: £1056.
Close of Play: 1st day SA 7/326 (Hill 166); 2nd day NSW 5/206 (Iredale 69, Kelly 3); 3rd day SA (2) 3/99 (Giffen 6, Hill 2); 4th day
    NSW (2) 1/103 (Donnan 33, Iredale 44).

A fine double by the lanky, stylish Iredale (187 in 285 minutes, 1 five and 24 fours and 80 not out in 120 minutes, 10 fours) - who on the second day became the second batsman after George Giffen to reach 1000 runs in the Sheffield Shield - guided New South Wales to both victory in the match and the competition for the first time. Superb, economical bowling by Turner on a batsman's track restricted the South Australians in the second innings to 200, of which Giffen scored 55 (255 minutes, 2 fours) under the handicap of an attack of sciatica. Giffen was unable to take the field on the last two days, Ferris substituting (he had been left out due to a bout of sunstroke after the Melbourne match) and Reedman deputising as captain. Lyons (13) joined Giffen and Iredale with 1000 Shield runs, his 46 coming in only 25 minutes (8 fours). Darling (121 in 169 minutes, 2 fives and 15 fours) and Hill (206 not out in 304 minutes, 14 fours) dominated the first innings after the loss of Lyons to the second ball of the match and Leak in Turner's second over. Hill carried his score from 71 to 166 (out of 123 added) in the final session of the first day and went on to beat by a single run the previous highest Shield innings - established by his captain in 1893-94. At 18 years 348 days he was the youngest to compile a double-hundred in Australia. He also kept wicket for all but the first few overs in the fourth innings, McKenzie being rested in the field. Donnan's unbeaten 67 included 5 fours. Coningham returned to New South Wales after a two-year four-match stint with Queensland. Sources: *Wisden, C.B.O'Reilly, Sydney Referee, Sydney Morning Herald, Town & Country Journal, Sydney Daily Telegraph.*

SOUTH AUSTRALIA

J.J.Lyons	c Coningham b McKibbin	0		c Donnan b Coningham	46
E.H.Leak	b Turner	0	(7)	c Coningham b Turner	17
*G.Giffen	c Coningham b McKibbin	11		b Turner	55
J.Darling	b Garrett	121		c Mackenzie b McKibbin	32
C.Hill	not out	206		b Turner	14
J.C.Reedman	b Coningham	17		b Coningham	3
A.Jarvis	c & b Coningham	0	(2)	run out (Callaway/McKibbin)	11
C.Martin	b Coningham	9		b Turner	13
†J.McKenzie	b McKibbin	19		c Garrett b Turner	0
E.Jones	run out (Donnan)	5		b Turner	2
J.P.F.Travers	c Turner b Garrett	10		not out	1
Extras	(lb2)	2		(b4, lb1, w1)	6
Total	(130.2 overs, 345 mins)	400		(106.3 overs, 285 mins)	200

NEW SOUTH WALES

H.Donnan	b Jones	48		not out	67
A.C.K.Mackenzie	c Martin b Reedman	45		run out (McKenzie/Travers/Jarvis)	20
F.A.Iredale	c McKenzie b Jones	187		not out	80
S.E.Gregory	st McKenzie b Travers	22			
F.H.Walters	lbw b Giffen	6			
A.Coningham	st McKenzie b Giffen	6			
†J.J.Kelly	c Darling b Reedman	37			
C.T.B.Turner	b Jones	40			
*T.W.Garrett	c Jarvis b Giffen	21			
S.T.Callaway	b Jones	4			
T.R.McKibbin	not out	1			
Extras	(b9, lb1, w1)	11		(b2, lb3, w1)	6
Total	(135.2 overs, 360 mins)	428		(75.4 overs, 165 mins) (1 wkt)	173

NEW SOUTH WALES	O	M	R	W	w,nb		O	M	R	W	w,nb			FALL OF WICKETS		
														SA	NSW	SA	NSW
McKibbin	42	9	124	3	-,-		27	9	75	1	-,-		Wkt	1st	1st	2nd	2nd
Turner	42	10	120	1	-,-	(3)	43.3	25	35	6	-,-		1st	0	81	52	30
Callaway	9	1	33	0	-,-	(5)	1	1	0	0	-,-		2nd	0	108	57	-
Coningham	22	9	65	3	-,-	(2)	26	6	68	2	-,-		3rd	34	152	95	-
Iredale	3	1	15	0	-,-								4th	203	175	117	-
Walters	1	0	11	0	-,-								5th	292	191	126	-
Garrett	11.2	1	30	2	-,-	(4)	9	4	16	0	1,-		6th	292	311	160	-
													7th	326	391	193	-
SOUTH AUSTRALIA	O	M	R	W	w,nb		O	M	R	W	w,nb		8th	358	412	195	-
Jones	47	15	110	4	-,-		25	10	49	0	-,-		9th	371	420	197	-
Jarvis	11	0	59	0	-,-		23	6	54	0	1,-		10th	400	428	200	-
Giffen	52.2	9	166	3	1,-												
Reedman	14	4	48	2	-,-		9	3	15	0	-,-						
Travers	11	0	34	1	-,-	(3)	18.4	4	49	0	-,-						

AUSTRALIAN XI v THE REST

Played at Sydney Cricket Ground on March 6, 7, 9, 10, 1896. (Timeless match)
Toss : The Rest. Result : AUSTRALIAN XI WON BY TWO WICKETS.
Debuts: Nil.
12th Men: H.Trumble (Aust) and F.H.Walters (Rest).
Umpires: T.Arundel and J.Thompson.
Attendances: 9000, 25000, 9000, 2000. Total: About 45,000. Receipts: £1673.
Close of Play: 1st day Aust 4/166 (Donnan 71, Gregory 18); 2nd day Rest (2) 3/196 (McLeod 64); 3rd day Aust (2) 2/112 (Darling 74, Iredale 1).

An overnight thunderstorm left the nature of the wicket in doubt, but after consulting Bruce and Turner, McDonnell in what was to be his last match, elected to bat. (Heart disease ended the life of the 35-year-old ex-Australian captain before the start of the next season.) McKibbin was battered out of the attack by Lyons and Bruce, who took 30 from his opening two overs, but he returned after a short break to partner Jones in the quickfire dismissal of The Rest. Donnan (88 in 210 minutes, 5 fours) held out while the drying pitch improved, but his team-mates did not take full advantage. Consistent batting led by McLeod (64 in 140 minutes, 7 fours) and Hill (74 in 110 minutes, 8 fours) set the Australians 244 for victory. Darling (75 in 135 minutes, 8 fours) launched the chase and they were well-placed at stumps on the third day at 2/112, but another thunderstorm that night, followed by a sunny morning, manufactured a difficult surface and wickets began to tumble. With Giffen unlikely to bat due to a recurrence of sciatica, 60 were still required when Jones joined Gregory 7 minutes before lunch. Against expectations they got the runs; though with 18 needed Gregory (75 not out in 105 minutes, 8 fours) was badly missed by McLeod at mid-off off Trott, which cost The Rest the game. Hill was subsequently added to the touring party on the strength of his past two matches but A.E.Trott - against public outcry at his omission - was not. *Cricket* incorrectly gives Rest (2) Jones 1/69, Giffen 2/75; Aust (1) Coningham 2/48, McLeod 0/24; Aust (2) Jones 22, extras 4, Howell 2/94. Sources: *Cricket, Sydney Referee, Sydney Morning Herald, Town & Country Journal, Sydney Daily Telegraph.*

THE REST

J.J.Lyons	c Darling b Jones	23		b McKibbin	9
W.Bruce	b McKibbin	36		c Giffen b McKibbin	38
C.E.McLeod	b Eady	3		c Giffen b McKibbin	64
C.Hill	c Iredale b Jones	6		b McKibbin	74
A.Coningham	c Jones b McKibbin	3	(6)	c Darling b Giffen	20
J.Worrall	c Donnan b McKibbin	10	(7)	lbw b McKibbin	36
C.T.B.Turner	c Giffen b Jones	13	(8)	c Trott b McKibbin	31
*P.S.McDonnell	c Johns b Jones	1	(5)	c Darling b Giffen	17
A.E.Trott	b Jones	10		st Jones b Trott	23
†J.J.Kelly	c & b McKibbin	2		not out	15
W.P.Howell	not out	0		b Jones	10
Extras	(b8, lb2)	10		(b10, lb8)	18
Total	(31.3 overs, 95 mins)	117		(93.3 overs, 300 mins)	355

AUSTRALIAN XI

J.Darling	b Howell	2		st Kelly b Howell	75
H.Donnan	b Coningham	88		b Turner	9
G.Giffen	run out (Howell/Kelly)	0			
F.A.Iredale	c & b Trott	40		run out (McLeod/Kelly)	10
*G.H.S.Trott	st Kelly b Coningham	30		b Howell	0
S.E.Gregory	st Kelly b Turner	40		not out	75
H.Graham	c Kelly b Turner	10	(3)	run out (Howell/Kelly)	27
C.J.Eady	b Turner	4		b Coningham	0
E.Jones	b Trott	3	(7)	b Coningham	21
T.R.McKibbin	not out	1	(9)	c Worrall b Coningham	8
†A.E.Johns	c Howell b Trott	0	(10)	not out	15
Extras	(b8, w3, nb1)	12		(b3, lb2)	5
Total	(115.2 overs, 255 mins)	230		(92.1 overs, 235 mins) (8 wkts)	245

AUSTRALIAN XI	O	M	R	W	w,nb		O	M	R	W	w,nb
Jones	16	5	30	5	-,-		19.3	4	67	1	-,-
McKibbin	10.3	0	60	4	-,-	(3)	33	7	104	6	-,-
Eady	5	2	17	1	-,-	(2)	11	1	43	0	-,-
Giffen							18	5	77	2	-,-
Trott							12	1	46	1	-,-

THE REST	O	M	R	W	w,nb		O	M	R	W	w,nb
Howell	14	2	44	1	-,-	(3)	30	5	93	2	-,-
Turner	31	11	48	3	-,-	(1)	31	6	65	1	-,-
Coningham	22	7	45	2	3,-	(5)	13.1	3	39	3	-,-
Trott	29.2	9	58	3	-,-	(2)	13	3	29	0	-,-
McLeod	19	7	23	0	-,1	(4)	5	1	14	0	-,-

FALL OF WICKETS

Wkt	REST 1st	AUST 1st	REST 2nd	AUST 2nd
1st	35	2	34	29
2nd	45	3	57	106
3rd	73	68	196	115
4th	76	140	197	115
5th	76	198	230	132
6th	88	220	242	164
7th	91	226	291	164
8th	114	229	320	184
9th	116	229	334	-
10th	117	230	355	-

1896-97 SEASON (8 MATCHES)

New South Wales won all four of their Sheffield Shield fixtures to take out the competition for the second successive season. They fielded an unchanged XI throughout their campaign, choosing eight Australian representatives plus Bill Howell and Monty Noble (both to be capped by Australia the following year) and Alex Mackenzie. Mackenzie, the odd man out, never played Test cricket despite being highly regarded by his contemporaries.

The Shield program followed the now established formula, and New South Wales began by visiting Adelaide and Melbourne to play their away games. They won at Adelaide after a hard battle, conceding a small first-innings advantage to the South Australians. The bowling of McKibbin (7 for 51 and 8 for 74) was the decisive factor. New South Wales were favoured by the weather in their match at Melbourne and managed to catch the Victorians on a rain-affected wicket. The Victorians were unable to cope with the deliveries of McKibbin, Howell and Coningham. Comment abounded in the Press over the umpiring of J.W.Evers, who travelled with New South Wales to adjudicate in both their away matches. The *South Australian Register* reported that Evers gave 'a couple of bad decisions' against South Australia and the Melbourne Press reacted similarly over his performance in the match against Victoria. It was not the first time that a visiting umpire had come under fire from local critics, but there was more vehemence than normal in the comments. Whatever the merits of the incidents, Evers was never called on again to umpire at first-class level. One of his brothers, Harold, debuted as a player for New South Wales later in the season.

New South Wales won both their Shield matches at home by convincing margins. Kelly, Garrett and Noble all hit centuries and the bowling of McKibbin, Howell and Coningham subdued the visiting batsmen despite some resistance from George Giffen, Harry Trott and Frank Laver.

Honours were shared in the two Victoria-South Australia encounters, each team winning at home. Jack Lyons struck centuries in both games. Events in the match at Melbourne stirred debate over the 120-run compulsory follow-on law, then in vogue in all first-class cricket. The Victorians, not wanting South Australia to immediately bat again and leave themselves last use of the wicket, bowled deliberate no-balls to boost the South Australian total. They were severely criticised for their ethics by 'Mid-On' of the Melbourne *Age*. However, the incident directly led the Australasian Cricket Council to amend the follow-on requirement in Australia to specify '200 runs in arrears'. The obvious solution to the issue - to make the follow-on optional for the team in charge - was not tackled until 1900, by Marylebone Cricket Club.

The first-class program was completed by the staging of the annual Tasmania-Victoria and New South Wales-Queensland fixtures. The Victorians won by eight wickets at Launceston, while New South Wales overwhelmed Queensland by an innings at Brisbane.

George Giffen led an Australian XI on a visit to Western Australia in April for a series of matches. Two matches against a full-strength Western Australian team were included in the itinerary, and had they gone ahead as planned they would have been the first first-class matches played in Western Australia. But in the end the Western Australians fielded odds of 18 men, relegating both games to the non-first-class bin.

A Queensland team toured New Zealand in December and January in response to the endeavours of the infant New Zealand Cricket Council to encourage visits from abroad. The team was: O.C.Hitchcock (captain), W.F.Bradley, T.Byrne, O.W.Cowley, S.J.Donahoo, W.Hoare, S.P.Jones, J.W.Lewis, R.Macdonald, W.W.McGlinchey, D.L.Miller and R.Wilson. Cowley (1893-94), McGlinchey (1889-90) and Miller (1893-94) had previously visited New Zealand with New South Wales teams. Curiously Cowley's entire first-class career was confined to his two tours.

Leading Aggregates

Batsmen	M	I	NO	Runs	HS	Ave.	Bowlers	Runs	Wkts	Ave.
J.J.Lyons (SA)	4	7	0	404	113	57.71	T.R.McKibbin (NSW)	655	44	14.88
M.A.Noble (NSW)	4	6	1	344	153*	68.80	E.Jones (SA)	575	32	17.96
G.H.S.Trott (V)	4	8	0	323	104	40.37	W.P.Howell (NSW)	450	27	16.66
T.W.Garrett (NSW)	4	6	0	252	131	42.00	H.Trumble (V)	396	17	23.29
C.Hill (SA)	4	7	0	245	95	35.00	W.Roche (V)	444	16	27.75
G.Giffen (SA)	4	7	1	240	104*	40.00	A.Coningham (NSW)	349	15	23.26
J.J.Kelly (NSW)	4	6	0	223	108	37.16				

SHEFFIELD SHIELD TABLE

	P	W	L	D	Quotient	Runs Scored	Wkts Lost	Runs Conceded	Wkts Taken
NEW SOUTH WALES	4	4	-	-	1.519	1868	61	1613	80
SOUTH AUSTRALIA	4	1	3	-	0.991	1719	69	1760	70
VICTORIA	4	1	3	-	0.670	1797	80	2011	60
TOTAL	6	6	6	-	1.000	5384	210	5384	210

SOUTH AUSTRALIA v NEW SOUTH WALES (Shield Match 1)

Played at Adelaide Oval on December, 19, 21, 22, 23, 1896. (Timeless match)
Toss : New South Wales. Result : NEW SOUTH WALES WON BY 51 RUNS.
Debuts: South Australia - B.T.Bailey (f/c).
12th Men: F.H.Walters (NSW). No 12th named for SA.
Umpires: J.W.Evers and I.A.Fisher.
Attendances: 7000, 3500, 2000, 200. Total: About 12,700. Receipts: £515.
Close of Play: 1st day SA 1/47 (Darling 19, Lyons 21); 2nd day NSW (2) 7/136 (Garrett 7, Turner 4); 3rd day SA (2) 8/148 (Jarvis 0).

Despite ideal batting conditions prevailing throughout the match, bowlers dominated from the outset. Jones dismissed Iredale with the opening delivery and later captured the wickets of Donnan and Coningham with successive balls. Evans caused a sensation by dismissing Mackenzie and Gregory in his first over in first-class cricket. It was not reported clearly which deliveries of Evans's first over claimed wickets, except that a single to Kelly (50 in 90 minutes, 7 fours) intervened between the two; Mackenzie may well have been out to the opening ball. McKibbin bowled New South Wales back into the game on the second day despite the efforts of Lyons (78 in 90 minutes, 8 fours) and Hill. Noble (69 in 100 minutes, 7 fours) played a fine innings after New South Wales again lost early wickets, and a crucial eighth-wicket partnership of 93 between Garrett and Turner gave the visitors a chance. Set 213 for victory, South Australia again wilted before the prodigious medium-paced offbreaks of McKibbin who became the first New South Wales bowler to capture 15 wickets in a Sheffield Shield match. After 13 first-class matches in Australia this controversial bowler had amassed 105 wickets (68 in 7 Shield games). Hill (51 in 120 minutes, 3 fours) and Bailey (45 in 60 minutes, 1 five and 5 fours) added 73 for South Australia's fourth wicket. Giffen, troubled by a knee injury, failed to take a wicket in a match for his colony for the first time since his debut 19 years previously. *Wisden* incorrectly gives NSW (1) Evans 4/47; SA (1) Turner 1/68. Sources: *Wisden, C.B.O'Reilly, The Australasian, Adelaide Advertiser, South Australian Register.*

NEW SOUTH WALES

F.A.Iredale	b Jones	0	(3)	c Darling b Travers	21
A.C.K.Mackenzie	c Reedman b Evans	34		c A.H.Jarvis b Jones	14
H.Donnan	b Jones	35	(1)	c & b Evans	6
A.Coningham	b Jones	0	(7)	c Hill b Jones	1
S.E.Gregory	b Evans	0	(4)	c Giffen b Evans	3
†J.J.Kelly	c A.Jarvis b Jones	50	(5)	run out (Bailey/Evans)	3
M.A.Noble	c Darling b Evans	5	(6)	c & b Evans	69
C.T.B.Turner	c Darling b Evans	9	(9)	b Reedman	48
*T.W.Garrett	run out (Evans)	13	(8)	c Jones b Reedman	49
T.R.McKibbin	not out	7		not out	8
W.P.Howell	b Jones	3		b Reedman	0
Extras	(b2, lb3, nb1)	6		(b8, lb7)	15
Total	(60.1 overs, 190 mins)	162		(73.4 overs, 235 mins)	237

SOUTH AUSTRALIA

J.Darling	c Donnan b McKibbin	19	(2)	lbw b McKibbin	0
A.Jarvis	b McKibbin	7	(9)	b McKibbin	0
J.J.Lyons	b Howell	78	(1)	b McKibbin	1
C.Hill	c & b McKibbin	49		c Coningham b McKibbin	51
B.T.Bailey	c McKibbin b Turner	5		c Kelly b Turner	45
*G.Giffen	c Kelly b McKibbin	3	(3)	c Howell b McKibbin	12
J.C.Reedman	b McKibbin	0	(6)	b McKibbin	26
A.E.Evans	c Kelly b McKibbin	11		c Mackenzie b McKibbin	4
†A.H.Jarvis	c & b McKibbin	8	(7)	b Howell	0
E.Jones	b Howell	4		not out	13
J.P.F.Travers	not out	0		st Kelly b McKibbin	0
Extras	(lb1, w2)	3		(b2, lb6, w1)	9
Total	(71.1 overs, 205 mins)	187		(53.3 overs, 171 mins)	161

SOUTH AUSTRALIA	O	M	R	W	w,nb		O	M	R	W	w,nb
Jones	25.1	6	49	5	-,-		24	3	76	2	-,-
A.Jarvis	17	2	54	0	-,-	(5)	3	2	1	0	-,-
Giffen	1	1	0	0	-,-		13	1	47	0	-,-
Evans	12	2	46	4	-,1	(2)	20	1	59	3	-,-
Travers	5	3	7	0	-,-	(4)	9	1	24	1	-,-
Reedman							4.4	0	15	3	-,-

NEW SOUTH WALES	O	M	R	W	w,nb		O	M	R	W	w,nb
Howell	25	6	60	2	-,-		23	5	53	1	-,-
McKibbin	24.1	6	51	7	-,-		23.3	5	74	8	-,-
Coningham	4	0	7	0	-,-		3	0	15	0	-,-
Turner	18	2	66	1	2,-	(5)	3	1	5	1	-,-
Garrett						(4)	1	0	5	0	1,-

FALL OF WICKETS

Wkt	NSW 1st	SA 1st	NSW 2nd	SA 2nd
1st	0	16	23	1
2nd	70	49	25	4
3rd	70	112	30	33
4th	70	132	37	106
5th	71	135	115	123
6th	87	137	119	124
7th	103	171	129	129
8th	150	182	222	148
9th	155	187	237	161
10th	162	187	237	161

VICTORIA v NEW SOUTH WALES (Shield Match 2)

Played at the Melbourne Cricket Ground on December 26, 28, 29, 30, 1896. (Timeless match)
Toss : New South Wales.   Result : NEW SOUTH WALES WON BY NINE WICKETS.
Debuts: Nil.
12th Men: W.Roche (Vic) and F.H.Walters (NSW).
Umpires: J.W.Evers and J.Phillips.
Attendances: 10000, 7500, 3000, 200.   Total: About 20,700.   Receipts: £815.
Close of Play: 1st day NSW 5/277 (Kelly 51, Coningham 17); 2nd day Vic 3/58 (Graham 20, Bruce 4); 3rd day Vic (2) 8/191 (McLeod 75, Stuckey 1)

New South Wales owed their easy victory to drenching overnight rain after the first day's play. Conditions for the visiting batsmen had been perfect after they won the toss and batted - apart from some smoke from nearby bushfires - with Donnan (50 in 175 minutes, 3 fours), Iredale (54 in 80 minutes, 7 fours), Gregory (68 in 105 minutes, 2 fours) and Kelly (51 in 105 minutes, 5 fours) all hitting half-centuries. However, only 90 minutes was possible on the second day, in two periods either side of lunch, and although a full day's play was possible on the third the pitch was still soft and it became progressively more difficult to bat on as it dried. McLeod's 78 (150 minutes, 4 fours), compiled in the worst conditions, was remarkable although he had a stroke of luck before reaching 20. Gregory threw the stumps down with McLeod "feet short of the crease" (*Argus*) attempting a run. As the bails "were off previously" (*Argus* - no explanation) umpire Evers adjudged him not out. Noble suffered a leg strain in the field on the third day and Walters replaced him, catching Trumble. Stuckey had been a last-minute replacement for A.E.Trott (severe leg strain) in the Victorian side. *Wisden* incorrectly gives NSW (2) Donnan 4, Iredale 2. Sources: *Wisden, VCA Report, The Age, The Argus, The Herald, The Australasian, The Leader*.

NEW SOUTH WALES

H.Donnan	c Johns b Harry	50	st Johns b Trott	2
A.C.K.Mackenzie	c Graham b Carlton	19	not out	2
F.A.Iredale	c Worrall b Trumble	54	not out	4
M.A.Noble	c Trott b McLeod	8		
S.E.Gregory	c Carlton b Trott	68		
†J.J.Kelly	b Trumble	51		
A.Coningham	st Johns b Trumble	38		
*T.W.Garrett	c Graham b Carlton	7		
C.T.B.Turner	c McLeod b Trumble	0		
T.R.McKibbin	c Graham b Trumble	3		
W.P.Howell	not out	1		
Extras	(b5, lb5, w3)	13		-
Total	(124.0 overs, 305 mins)	312	(7.3 overs, 15 mins) (1 wkt)	8

VICTORIA

C.E.McLeod	st Kelly b McKibbin	4	(4) c Kelly b Coningham	78
J.Worrall	c Noble b Howell	21	(1) c McKibbin b Howell	27
H.Graham	c Garrett b McKibbin	34	c & b Coningham	33
*G.H.S.Trott	c Donnan b Howell	8	(5) c Howell b Coningham	0
W.Bruce	c Iredale b McKibbin	12	(6) c Coningham b McKibbin	13
F.J.Laver	c Gregory b Howell	2	(7) b Coningham	5
J.H.Stuckey	c Iredale b McKibbin	4	(10) not out	19
J.Harry	b Howell	3	c Turner b Coningham	18
H.Trumble	not out	5	c sub (F.H.Walters) b Coningham	4
J.Carlton	lbw b Howell	2	(2) b McKibbin	7
†A.E.Johns	c & b McKibbin	2	c Gregory b McKibbin	7
Extras	(lb2)	2	(b6, lb2, w1)	9
Total	(33.1 overs, 115 mins)	99	(89.4 overs, 225 mins)	220

VICTORIA	O	M	R	W	w,nb		O	M	R	W	w,nb
Trumble	34	4	89	5	2,-	(2)	3.3	2	4	0	-,-
Carlton	38	12	83	2	-,-						
Trott	15	4	34	1	-,-	(1)	4	2	4	1	-,-
Bruce	10	3	20	0	1,-						
McLeod	14	5	31	1	-,-						
Harry	8	0	27	1	-,-						
Worrall	4	0	13	0	-,-						
Laver	1	0	2	0	-,-						

NEW SOUTH WALES	O	M	R	W	w,nb		O	M	R	W	w,nb
McKibbin	17.1	4	47	5	-,-	(2)	31.4	6	80	3	-,-
Coningham	3	0	13	0	-,-	(4)	22	8	38	6	1,-
Howell	13	3	37	5	-,-	(1)	21	3	55	1	-,-
Turner						(3)	15	1	38	0	-,-

FALL OF WICKETS

Wkt	NSW 1st	VIC 1st	NSW 2nd	VIC 2nd
1st	24	8	18	4
2nd	112	32	48	-
3rd	125	41	87	-
4th	156	69	87	-
5th	230	73	109	-
6th	277	85	120	-
7th	294	88	177	-
8th	296	90	189	-
9th	311	96	204	-
10th	312	99	220	-

VICTORIA v SOUTH AUSTRALIA (Shield Match 3)

Played at the Melbourne Cricket Ground on January 1, 2, 4, 5, 1897. (Timeless match)
Toss : Victoria.   Result : VICTORIA WON BY 49 RUNS.
Debuts: Victoria - J.P.O'Halloran (f/c). South Australia - R.O.Homburg (f/c).
12th Men: J.H.Stuckey (Vic) and A.J.Carracher (SA).
Umpires: P.Argall and J.Phillips.
Attendances: 8000, 11185, 3000, 3500.   Total: 25,685.   Receipts: £984.
Close of Play: 1st day Vic 9/335 (O'Halloran 117, Johns 50); 2nd day Vic (2) 0/8 (Worrall 7, Bruce 0); 3rd day SA (2) 0/19 (Darling 6, Lyons 12).

G.E.Downs, the SACA-appointed umpire for matches in the Eastern States, withdrew when the SACA would not agree to reimburse him for the time lost. I.A.Fisher was then sought but Argall was the one who eventually made the trip. Jones bowled Bruce with the fifth ball of the match and Graham with the first ball of his next over. One of Jones's thunderbolts struck Jarvis on the chest in the first session; Hill kept wicket for the rest of the game while Carracher substituted in the field. O'Halloran, a late replacement for J.Carlton (whose mother had died), scored a century on debut - the first to do so in a Sheffield Shield match - (128 not out in 225 minutes, 1 five and 12 fours, chances at 35 and 57). He added 77 with Roche (75 minutes) for the ninth wicket and 136 with Johns (57 in 120 minutes, 6 fours) for the tenth, the highest stand for the last wicket yet in Australian first-class cricket. Lyons (70 in 65 minutes, 11 fours and 110 in 118 minutes, 9 fours, chances at 16 and 37) played two typically hard-hitting innings for South Australia. Late on the second day, when South Australia were 8/225 with the last pair (Evans and Travers) at the wicket, Trumble, under instructions, deliberately bowled three consecutive no-balls so that the follow-on - then compulsory for a team 120 runs in arrears - would be avoided. The first two were allowed through to the fence by Johns and the third was cut for two by Evans. Trott (63 in 105 minutes, 6 fours) and Trumble (82 in 120 minutes, 10 fours) scored half-centuries on the third day, which was interrupted several times by light rain. Darling (65 in 210 minutes, 1 five and 4 fours) added 143 with Lyons, a new South Australian first-wicket record (beaten later in the season). *Wisden* incorrectly gives Vic (1) extras 23, total 357, Evans 0/63; Vic (2) Harry 8, Roche 14; SA (1) Trumble 3/67, Trott 0/53; SA (2) Hill 4, Bailey 5, Reedman 20. Sources: *Wisden, C.B.O'Reilly, VCA Report, The Age, The Argus, The Herald, The Australasian, The Leader, South Australian Register.*

VICTORIA

W.Bruce	b Jones	0	(2) b Jones	8
C.E.McLeod	b Jones	32	(4) b Jones	0
H.Graham	b Jones	0	run out (Homburg)	9
J.Worrall	run out (Travers/Jarvis)	4	(1) b Giffen	14
*G.H.S.Trott	b Jones	42	b Jones	63
F.J.Laver	c Bailey b Giffen	27	(7) lbw b Giffen	2
J.Harry	c Giffen b Jones	14	(8) b Jones	14
H.Trumble	b Giffen	1	(9) b Giffen	82
J.P.O'Halloran	not out	128	(6) c Reedman b Jones	2
W.Roche	c Giffen b Jones	29	b Jones	8
†A.E.Johns	run out (Jones)	57	not out	13
Extras	(b13, lb6, nb1)	20	(b8, lb7)	15
Total	(111.4 overs, 305 mins)	354	(68.5 overs, 185 mins)	230

SOUTH AUSTRALIA

J.Darling	b Roche	25	c Graham b Trott	65
J.J.Lyons	c Worrall b Trumble	70	c Johns b Trumble	110
*G.Giffen	c Laver b O'Halloran	40	b Roche	17
C.Hill	b Roche	3	b Roche	0
B.T.Bailey	c Graham b Trumble	2	c Johns b Roche	4
J.C.Reedman	b Harry	22	c Roche b Trott	25
A.E.Evans	run out (/Trumble)	39	c & b Trumble	18
E.Jones	b O'Halloran	5	c & b McLeod	34
R.O.Homburg	c Harry b Trumble	10	b Trumble	4
J.P.F.Travers	not out	10	(11) not out	2
†A.H.Jarvis	absent injured	-	(10) c Roche b Trumble	0
Extras	(b4, lb1, nb8)	13	(b6, lb9, w1, nb1)	17
Total	(86.4 overs, 220 mins)	239	(103.3 overs, 275 mins)	296

SOUTH AUSTRALIA	O	M	R	W	w,nb		O	M	R	W	w,nb		FALL OF WICKETS			
														VIC	SA	VIC	SA
Jones	51	12	122	6	-,-		34	11	84	6	-,-	Wkt	1st	1st	2nd	2nd
Evans	13	3	62	0	-,1	(3)	3	0	23	0	-,-	1st	0	91	17	143
Reedman	14.4	4	42	0	-,-							2nd	0	99	33	166
Giffen	22	5	71	2	-,-	(2)	31.5	3	108	3	-,-	3rd	20	107	33	166
Homburg	3	1	8	0	-,-							4th	69	112	47	177
Travers	6	0	24	0	-,-							5th	96	165	54	231
Lyons	2	0	5	0	-,-							6th	132	167	63	231
												7th	132	179	92	286
SOUTH AUSTRALIA	O	M	R	W	w,nb		O	M	R	W	w,nb	8th	141	213	141	291
Roche	23	7	72	2	-,-	(3)	31	10	82	3	-,1	9th	218	239	188	291
Trumble	27.4	6	59	3	-,8	(1)	34.3	12	83	4	-,-	10th	354	-	230	296
Trott	15	1	52	0	-,-	(2)	15	1	55	2	-,-					
Harry	6	0	22	1	-,-											
O'Halloran	15	7	21	2	-,-		9	4	29	0	-,-					
McLeod						(4)	11	3	23	1	-,-					
Laver						(6)	1	1	0	0	-,-					
Bruce						(7)	2	1	7	0	1,-					

NEW SOUTH WALES v SOUTH AUSTRALIA (Shield Match 4)

Played at Sydney Cricket Ground on January 8, 9, 11, 1897. (Timeless match)
Toss : South Australia.　　　　Result : NEW SOUTH WALES WON BY AN INNINGS AND 11 RUNS.
Debuts: South Australia - A.J.Carracher (f/c).
12th Men: V.T.Trumper (NSW). No 12th named for SA.
Umpires: P.Argall and J.Thompson.
Attendances: 8546, 15810, 6452.　　　Total: 30,808.　　　Receipts: £1199.
Close of Play: 1st day NSW 4/108 (Kelly 61, Noble 24); 2nd day NSW 420 all out.

With this innings victory, New South Wales became the first team to successfully defend the Sheffield Shield. South Australia made three changes to the side that met Victoria. McKenzie, the first-selected wicket-keeper for the trip east (he had withdrawn citing work commitments), now joined the team as a replacement for the injured A.H.Jarvis, and Carracher and Scrymgour, the team manager, were included in addition, R.O.Homburg and J.P.F.Travers being omitted from the thirteen. Howell and McKibbin dismissed the visitors cheaply on a flat first-day wicket. Donnan, who was off the field for most of the innings following a mishap before lunch in which an Iredale return had hit him in the groin, took his second battering when he went out to open the New South Wales innings: Jones's first ball struck him on the body and dropped onto his wicket. "Jonah" captured 4 for 10 in his first five overs before Kelly (career-best 108 in 175 minutes, 11 fours) and Noble (batting without gloves) saw him off with a 111-run stand for the fifth wicket, Kelly having offered a chance to Lyons off his bowling when only 7. Jones's eventual 8 for 157 was his best analysis for South Australia and it remained the best by a South Australian at Sydney until T.W.Wall's 10 for 36 in 1932-33. Garrett (131 in 180 minutes, 17 fours, chances at 21, 66 and 122) and McKibbin (career-best 75 in 105 minutes) added 170 runs together, a new ninth-wicket record in Australian first-class cricket. Garrett went from 21 to 111 in the 100-minute lunch-tea session (out of 156 added) on the second day. He and Giffen (104 not out in 243 minutes, 5 fours), whose bowling had been restricted by an attack of sciatica, became the first pair of captains to score centuries in the same first-class match in Australia. *Wisden* incorrectly gives SA (1) extras 4, total 160; NSW won by an innings and 10 runs. Sources: *Wisden, C.B.O'Reilly, Sydney Referee, Sydney Morning Herald, Town & Country Journal.*

SOUTH AUSTRALIA

J.Darling	c Iredale b Howell	24	run out (Gregory/Kelly)		4
J.J.Lyons	b Howell	18	b McKibbin		14
*G.Giffen	c & b McKibbin	17	not out		104
C.Hill	c Kelly b Howell	42	c Coningham b McKibbin		5
J.C.Reedman	c sub (V.T.Trumper) b Howell	11	c Turner b Coningham		32
B.T.Bailey	c Iredale b Howell	8	c Donnan b Coningham		45
A.E.Evans	c Kelly b McKibbin	9	c Coningham b McKibbin		13
B.V.Scrymgour	c Kelly b McKibbin	8	c McKibbin b Coningham		3
E.Jones	b McKibbin	0	c Iredale b Coningham		10
†J.McKenzie	b Howell	7	c Iredale b McKibbin		0
A.J.Carracher	not out	12	c Garrett b Howell		14
Extras	(lb2, w1)	3	(b5, w1)		6
Total	(56.5 overs, 170 mins)	159	(93.3 overs, 250 mins)		250

NEW SOUTH WALES

H.Donnan	b Jones	0
A.C.K.Mackenzie	c McKenzie b Jones	1
F.A.Iredale	c McKenzie b Jones	10
†J.J.Kelly	run out (Jones/McKenzie)	108
S.E.Gregory	b Jones	4
M.A.Noble	c McKenzie b Jones	38
A.Coningham	b Jones	10
*T.W.Garrett	c Giffen b Reedman	131
C.T.B.Turner	c Carracher b Jones	23
T.R.McKibbin	c McKenzie b Jones	75
W.P.Howell	not out	4
Extras	(b9, lb4, w3)	16
Total	(117.4 overs, 345 mins)	420

NEW SOUTH WALES	O	M	R	W	w,nb		O	M	R	W	w,nb
Howell	20	9	40	6	-,-	(2)	21.3	6	43	1	-,-
Coningham	5	0	26	0	1,-	(3)	27	6	69	4	-,-
Turner	12	2	28	0	-,-	(4)	10	2	31	0	-,-
McKibbin	19.5	0	62	4	-,-	(1)	35	6	101	4	1,-

SOUTH AUSTRALIA	O	M	R	W	w,nb
Jones	51	11	157	8	1,-
Evans	19	2	93	0	2,-
Giffen	10	4	21	0	-,-
Reedman	14.4	3	68	1	-,-
Carracher	18	0	51	0	-,-
Lyons	5	1	14	0	-,-

FALL OF WICKETS

Wkt	SA 1st	NSW 1st	SA 2nd
1st	36	0	9
2nd	47	11	19
3rd	85	12	25
4th	107	28	77
5th	114	139	152
6th	123	155	175
7th	140	205	186
8th	140	246	210
9th	147	416	212
10th	159	420	250

TASMANIA v VICTORIA

Played at N.T.C.A. Ground, Launceston, on January 20, 21, 22, 1897. (Timeless match)
Toss : Tasmania.   Result : VICTORIA WON BY EIGHT WICKETS.
Debuts: Tasmania - C.M.Campbell, T.A.Tabart (both f/c); G.E.Palmer (Tas only). Victoria - H.J.Fry, J.F.Giller, R.T.B.Kelly, E.R.Rush, D.Sutherland (all f/c).
12th Men: C.P.Hammond (Tas) and L.McLelland (Vic).
Umpires: F.C.Hobkirk and S.Morris.
Attendances: "fair", less than 1st day, "limited".   Total & Receipts: No figures published.
Close of Play: 1st day Vic 2/74 (Warne 20, Sutherland 13); 2nd day Tas (2) 6/104 (Palmer 19).

Tabart replaced G.H.Gatehouse (unavailable) in the selected Tasmanian team. Kelly led Victoria in his sole first-class appearance. Windsor (career-best 90 in 145 minutes, 13 fours and 83 not out in 110 minutes, 8 fours) batted brilliantly for the locals but had little support. Giller (unbeaten 65 in 120 minutes, 10 fours and 9 wickets) made a fine allround debut. He shared a Victorian record ninth-wicket stand of 95 with Ingleton (64 with 11 fours) in 90 minutes. McMichael (55 in 90 minutes, 6 fours) recorded the only other half-century, "a nice free innings" according to the *Daily Telegraph* correspondent. Ingleton, McMichael and Sutherland had replaced W.A.Tarrant, T.Tatchell and G.L.Wilson (all unavailable) in the Victorian team before its departure from Melbourne. Palmer (ex-Victoria) made his sole appearance for Tasmania. It was his last first-class match. *Cricket* and *VCA Report* incorrectly give Tas (1) McAllen b Giller. *VCA Report* also incorrectly gives Vic (1) Palmer 2/40, Savigny 1/9. Sources: *Cricket, VCA Report, Launceston Daily Telegraph, Launceston Examiner*.

TASMANIA

J.H.Savigny	b Giller	16		b O'Connor	13
C.J.Eady	b Giller	22	(6)	b Harry	4
C.M.Campbell	st Hastings b Giller	0	(7)	c Sutherland b Giller	17
*E.J.K.Burn	b Giller	6	(2)	c Ingleton b Harry	23
N.R.Westbrook	b O'Connor	32	(9)	b Kelly	13
G.E.Palmer	b Giller	0	(5)	lbw b O'Connor	25
E.A.C.Windsor	b Giller	90	(8)	not out	83
J.E.Bingham	b O'Connor	0	(10)	c Warne b Harry	0
T.A.Tabart	run out (Giller/Hastings)	16	(3)	b O'Connor	4
†C.McAllen	st Hastings b Giller	0	(11)	b Giller	13
G.S.Pennefather	not out	5	(4)	c Hastings b O'Connor	17
Extras	(b3, nb1)	4			15
Total	(79.5 overs, 200 mins)	191		(79.5 overs, 215 mins)	227

VICTORIA

E.R.Rush	b Eady	6		b Eady	5
T.S.Warne	c McAllen b Eady	22		not out	32
J.Harry	b Pennefather	34			
D.Sutherland	b Windsor	27			
S.A.McMichael	b Palmer	55	(4)	not out	34
H.J.Fry	b Pennefather	23			
*R.T.B.Kelly	b Pennefather	3			
J.F.Giller	not out	65	(3)	st McAllen b Pennefather	11
†T.J.Hastings	b Palmer	12			
W.G.Ingleton	run out	64			
J.A.O'Connor	c Campbell b Savigny	0			
Extras		22			6
Total	(92.5 overs, 270 mins)	333		(25.0 overs, 60 mins) (2 wkts)	88

VICTORIA	O	M	R	W	w,nb		O	M	R	W	w,nb
O'Connor	22	6	59	2	-,1		35	13	77	4	-,1
Giller	31.5	7	67	7	-,-	(4)	16.5	3	35	2	-,-
Ingleton	11	3	18	0	-,-						
Harry	8	0	19	0	-,-	(3)	18	2	62	3	-,-
Kelly	7	1	24	0	-,-	(2)	10	0	38	1	-,-

TASMANIA	O	M	R	W	w,nb		O	M	R	W	w,nb
Windsor	27	3	81	1	-,-		7	2	20	0	-,-
Eady	28	5	64	2	-,-		8	2	21	1	-,-
Pennefather	17	1	76	3	-,-		6	1	21	1	-,-
Bingham	4	0	27	0	-,-						
Palmer	11	0	49	2	-,-	(4)	4	1	20	0	-,-
Burn	3	0	14	0	-,-						
Savigny	2.5	2	0	1	-,-						

FALL OF WICKETS

Wkt	TAS 1st	VIC 1st	TAS 2nd	VIC 2nd
1st	40	7	18	15
2nd	41	58	26	32
3rd	42	80	48	-
4th	63	102	62	-
5th	63	168	73	-
6th	129	174	104	-
7th	129	200	120	-
8th	164	232	166	-
9th	164	327	167	-
10th	191	333	227	-

NEW SOUTH WALES v VICTORIA (Shield Match 5)

Played at Sydney Cricket Ground on January 23, 25, 26, 27, 28, 1897. (Timeless match)
Toss : New South Wales.   Result : NEW SOUTH WALES WON BY 192 RUNS.
Debuts: Nil.
12th Men: V.T.Trumper (NSW) and J.H.Stuckey (Vic).
Umpires: J.Phillips and J.Thompson.
Attendances: 14902, 8370, 18557, 6625, 1501.   Total: 49,955.   Receipts: £1911.
Close of Play: 1st day Vic 4/111 (Trott 24, Laver 31); 2nd day NSW (2) 2/135 (Donnan 43, Garrett 17); 3rd day NSW (2) 8/404
    (Noble 74); 4th day Vic (2) 4/94 (Roche 2, Trott 4).

After failing unaccountably in their first innings, New South Wales posted the first 500-run total in the Sheffield Shield competition.
Noble (153 not out in 315 minutes, 1 five and 13 fours, chance at 71) scored his maiden first-class hundred and shared with Howell New
South Wales's first three-figure stand for the tenth wicket. Gregory (58 in 75 minutes, 7 fours), Donnan (84 in 165 minutes, 9 fours),
Iredale (62 in 90 minutes, 7 fours) and Mackenzie (50 in 75 minutes, 2 fives and 6 fours) all hit half-centuries. Noble (71 in 129 minutes,
9 fours) had also topscored in the first innings. Trott (104 in 180 minutes, 13 fours, 3 chances) and Laver (81 in 165 minutes, 1 five and
15 fours) established a new Victorian fifth-wicket record. Trumble (58 in 90 minutes, 9 fours) topscored in the second innings. Several
showers on the third and fourth days briefly interrupted play but served only to bind the wicket together. McKibbin (13 for 240) continued
his prolific run of wicket-taking in Australian first-class cricket: 134 wickets from 16 matches. His 44 wickets from four matches in the
1896-97 season was not surpassed by a bowler in the Sheffield Shield until 1934-35 (under an expanded program). *Wisden* incorrectly gives
NSW (1) Donnan 9, McKibbin 20; NSW (2) Iredale 63, Coningham 12. Sources: *Wisden, VCA Report, Sydney Referee, Sydney Morning
Herald, Town & Country Journal, Sydney Mail.*

NEW SOUTH WALES

H.Donnan	b Trumble	7	(3)	b Trumble	84
A.C.K.Mackenzie	b Roche	6	(8)	c McLeod b Worrall	50
F.A.Iredale	b Roche	22	(5)	c McLeod b Trott	62
†J.J.Kelly	c Carlton b Roche	0	(7)	run out (Graham/Johns)	11
S.E.Gregory	run out (Trott/Roche)	0	(2)	c Johns b Roche	58
M.A.Noble	c Johns b Roche	71		not out	153
A.Coningham	c Johns b Trumble	6	(1)	c Johns b Trumble	13
*T.W.Garrett	c Trott b Trumble	10	(4)	run out (Johns)	42
C.T.B.Turner	c McLeod b Roche	10		b Worrall	4
T.R.McKibbin	not out	22		c McLeod b Carlton	37
W.P.Howell	c Trumble b Roche	4		c Worrall b Roche	48
Extras	(nb1)	1		(b5, lb1, w1, nb1)	8
Total	(64.1 overs, 175 mins)	159		(203.1 overs, 450 mins)	570

VICTORIA

W.Bruce	c Coningham b McKibbin	16	(7)	b McKibbin	36
C.E.McLeod	b McKibbin	6	(1)	b McKibbin	38
H.Graham	c & b McKibbin	17		lbw b McKibbin	1
J.Worrall	b McKibbin	15	(2)	run out (Noble/Kelly)	31
*G.H.S.Trott	c Gregory b McKibbin	104	(6)	c Turner b McKibbin	40
F.J.Laver	b Coningham	81	(4)	c Coningham b Howell	13
J.P.O'Halloran	st Kelly b McKibbin	2	(9)	not out	28
H.Trumble	c Kelly b Howell	13		lbw b Howell	58
†A.E.Johns	c Turner b McKibbin	10	(11)	c Coningham b Turner	13
J.Carlton	lbw b McKibbin	0		b Howell	0
W.Roche	not out	0	(5)	c Coningham b McKibbin	3
Extras	(b3, lb2)	5		(b5, lb1, w1)	7
Total	(109.2 overs, 270 mins)	269		(91.3 overs, 255 mins)	268

VICTORIA	O	M	R	W	w,nb		O	M	R	W	w,nb
Roche	28.1	10	63	6	-,1		34.1	5	122	2	-,-
Trumble	28	4	63	3	-,-		43	18	98	2	-,-
Carlton	4	0	22	0	-,-	(6)	33	9	87	1	-,-
McLeod	4	0	10	0	-,-	(8)	24	8	53	0	-,-
Trott						(3)	23	2	84	1	-,-
Laver						(4)	14	2	27	0	-,1
O'Halloran						(5)	18	6	51	0	1,-
Bruce						(7)	3	0	7	0	-,-
Worrall							11	1	33	2	-,-

NEW SOUTH WALES	O	M	R	W	w,nb		O	M	R	W	w,nb
McKibbin	38	11	111	8	-,-		41	7	129	5	1,-
Howell	26.2	6	45	1	-,-	(3)	13	6	29	3	-,-
Coningham	32	10	73	1	-,-	(2)	22	2	60	0	-,-
Turner	7	1	22	0	-,-	(5)	8.3	3	26	1	-,-
Noble	6	3	13	0	-,-	(4)	7	3	17	0	-,-

FALL OF WICKETS

Wkt	NSW 1st	VIC 1st	NSW 2nd	VIC 2nd
1st	7	9	39	56
2nd	21	36	99	57
3rd	21	45	176	88
4th	23	68	246	88
5th	51	243	283	104
6th	62	243	305	154
7th	76	245	400	172
8th	99	265	404	247
9th	153	269	459	249
10th	159	269	570	268

SOUTH AUSTRALIA v VICTORIA (Shield Match 6)

Played at Adelaide Oval on February, 26, 27, March 1, 1897. (Timeless match)
Toss : Victoria.   Result : SOUTH AUSTRALIA WON BY AN INNINGS AND 70 RUNS.
Debuts: Nil.
12th Men: G.L.Wilson (Vic). No 12th named for SA.
Umpires: G.E.Downs and J.Phillips.
Attendances: 2000, 5000, 2500.   Total: About 9500.   Receipts: £278.
Close of Play: 1st day Vic 8/277 (McMichael 27); 2nd day SA 3/343 (Hill 74, Giffen 26).

The match began on a good wicket, in ideal conditions which the Victorian batsmen failed to fully utilise. Trott (61 in 80 minutes, 8 fours) scored the only half-century for his side. By dismissing Worrall, Jones became the second bowler after George Giffen to take 100 Sheffield Shield wickets. Darling (75 in 130 minutes, 1 five and 6 fours) and Lyons (113 in 140 minutes, 12 fours) shared a record first-wicket stand for South Australia, surpassing that which they had established in Melbourne earlier in the season. A running catch by Laver on the asphalt bicycle track ended the partnership in controversial circumstances. Darling was given out despite the crowd thinking otherwise, but "the arrangement is that though the edge of the grass is the boundary for hits along the sward, a fieldsman may stand on the track to catch a batsman" (*Register*). Hill (95 in 180 minutes) scored the first of his many nineties in Australian first-class cricket. Substantial rain on Sunday followed by sunshine on Monday morning rendered the pitch "sodden and stodgy, just as the bowler likes" (*Register*) and Worrall disposed of the South Australians rather too quickly for his own team's benefit, the wicket being at its stickiest when Victoria commenced batting a second time. Jones captured a wicket (McLeod - third ball) in the opening over of an innings for the fourth successive match, another "first" for the Sheffield Shield. *Wisden* incorrectly gives Vic (2) Jones 4/26; SA (1) Roche 3/106, Laver 0/26, O'Halloran 1/47, Harry 0/16. Sources: *Wisden, C.B.O'Reilly, VCA Report, Adelaide Advertiser, South Australian Register.*

VICTORIA

C.E.McLeod	b Evans	48	c Giffen b Jones		0
J.H.Stuckey	b Giffen	5	(7) c Darling b Jones		1
J.Worrall	b Jones	26	c Reedman b Carracher		5
*G.H.S.Trott	c Darling b Reedman	61	c Bailey b Carracher		5
F.J.Laver	b Giffen	27	st McKenzie b Carracher		7
J.P.O'Halloran	c & b Giffen	5	c Hill b Carracher		0
J.Harry	b Giffen	20	(2) c Jones b Carracher		4
J.F.Giller	run out (McKenzie)	42	not out		24
S.A.McMichael	b Carracher	28	b Evans		22
†T.J.Hastings	not out	0	c McKenzie b Jones		0
W.Roche	b Carracher	0	b Jones		0
Extras	(b5, lb11, nb1)	17	(b5, lb4, nb1)		10
Total	(109.5 overs, 295 mins)	279	(53.2 overs, 130 mins)		78

SOUTH AUSTRALIA

J.Darling	c Laver b Worrall	75
J.J.Lyons	c Trott b O'Halloran	113
C.Hill	c Hastings b Worrall	95
J.C.Reedman	b Trott	49
*G.Giffen	c & b Worrall	47
B.T.Bailey	c Laver b Worrall	2
E.H.Leak	c Giller b Roche	0
A.E.Evans	not out	2
A.J.Carracher	b Worrall	4
E.Jones	c Hastings b Roche	11
†J.McKenzie	c Trott b Roche	18
Extras	(b3, lb5, nb3)	11
Total	(122.5 overs, 345 mins)	427

SOUTH AUSTRALIA	O	M	R	W	w,nb		O	M	R	W	w,nb
Jones	32	7	59	1	-,-		24.2	14	28	4	-,-
Giffen	31	7	71	4	-,-	(4)	2	0	8	0	-,-
Evans	15	0	63	1	-,1		3	1	6	1	-,1
Carracher	12.5	3	27	2	-,-	(2)	21	11	24	5	-,-
Reedman	15	0	33	1	-,-		3	2	2	0	-,-
Leak	4	1	9	0	-,-						

VICTORIA	O	M	R	W	w,nb
Roche	31.5	7	105	3	-,2
Trott	8	0	56	1	-,-
Giller	21	3	54	0	-,-
McLeod	14	4	40	0	-,-
Laver	6	1	28	0	-,-
O'Halloran	12	2	46	1	-,1
Worrall	24	5	68	5	-,-
Harry	6	0	19	0	-,-

FALL OF WICKETS

Wkt	VIC 1st	SA 1st	VIC 2nd
1st	14	184	0
2nd	66	194	6
3rd	110	294	15
4th	163	386	25
5th	175	389	25
6th	188	389	29
7th	221	389	33
8th	277	398	76
9th	279	409	76
10th	279	427	78

QUEENSLAND v NEW SOUTH WALES

Played at Exhibition Ground, Brisbane, on April 16, 17, 19, 1897. (Timeless match)
Toss : Queensland.   Result : NEW SOUTH WALES WON BY AN INNINGS AND 101 RUNS.
Debuts: Queensland - J.M.Blackstock, A.H.Jones, T.T.T.Long (all f/c). New South Wales - T.C.Connell, H.A.Evers, A.J.Y.Hopkins,
   L.W.Pye, E.L.Waddy (all f/c); A.A.Atkins (NSW only).
12th Men: T.E.Green (Qld) and V.T.Trumper (NSW).
Umpires: J.W.Roberts and J.Thompson.
Attendances: 2000, 3000, 3000.   Total: About 8000.   Receipts: Not known.
Close of Play: 1st day Qld 6/160 (Hoare 46, Blackstock 5); NSW 4/289 (Pye 140, Evers 59).

The New South Wales side was greatly weakened by the absence of S.E.Gregory, J.J.Kelly and T.R.McKibbin (all with George Giffen's XI in Perth for non-first-class matches), H.Donnan, T.W.Garrett, A.C.K.Mackenzie, M.A.Noble and C.T.B.Turner all being unavailable in addition. T.Byrne and R.McGraw (the first emergency) withdrew from the Queensland team and A.H.Jones (the second emergency) came in. The first day was "an ideal one for cricket" (*Courier*) but play did not begin until 2.10pm. Other starting times were noon (second day) and 11.00am (third day). Hoare (56 in 155 minutes, 4 fours) and S.P.Jones (46 in 90 minutes, 4 fours) made the top scores for Queensland, who had first use of a good wicket. Pye (166 in 275 minutes, 1 five and 13 fours) survived three chances to score a century in his first first-class match. He was the first New South Wales player to perform this feat although F.H.Walters, a former Victorian, had also done so in his first match for the side (NSW v Qld at Sydney 1895-96). Evers (66 in 40 minutes, 3 fives and 5 fours) dominated his fifth-wicket stand with Pye in which 98 runs were added in 40 minutes. Atkins (ex-Queensland) was out first ball in his sole match for New South Wales. Evers sustained a split thumb at 4/20 in the Queensland second innings and was replaced as wicket-keeper for the rest of the match by Waddy, who held a sharp chance to dismiss O'Brien soon after. Coningham, the turncoat, finished the match by dismissing Hoare and Long with successive balls. This was the last first-class match to be held at the Exhibition ground until the 1919-20 season. *ACA* incorrectly gives Qld (2) McGlinchey b Howell. *Qld Times* gives Qld (2) Wilson c Atkins. Sources: *Australian Cricket Annual, Sydney Referee, Brisbane Courier, The Queenslander, Queensland Times.*

QUEENSLAND

Batsman	Dismissal	Runs		Dismissal	Runs
*S.J.Donahoo	run out (Connell/Coningham)	11		c Hopkins b Newell	3
R.Macdonald	c Pye b Howell	1		st Evers b Newell	7
†W.F.Bradley	run out	15		b Howell	0
W.W.McGlinchey	b Howell	30		lbw b Howell	3
R.O'Brien	c Howell b Coningham	2	(6)	c Waddy b Howell	4
W.Hoare	b Newell	56	(5)	b Coningham	27
S.P.Jones	c Coningham b Howell	46		c Poidevin b Newell	12
J.M.Blackstock	b Newell	12		c Howell b Newell	0
R.Wilson	b Howell	1		c Poidevin b Coningham	3
A.H.Jones	b Howell	0		not out	5
T.T.T.Long	not out	0		b Coningham	0
Extras	(b1, lb5)	6		(b9)	9
Total	(96.5 overs, 245 mins)	180		(44.4 overs, 105 mins)	73

NEW SOUTH WALES

Batsman	Dismissal	Runs
L.W.Pye	c Bradley b McGlinchey	166
A.Coningham	run out (/Bradley)	1
*F.A.Iredale	b Long	36
L.O.S.Poidevin	c & b Wilson	37
A.J.Y.Hopkins	c O'Brien b Wilson	10
†H.A.Evers	c Blackstock b McGlinchey	66
A.A.Atkins	b McGlinchey	0
E.L.Waddy	c Bradley b Long	1
A.L.Newell	c Donahoo b McGlinchey	15
W.P.Howell	not out	13
T.C.Connell	b Long	2
Extras	(b6, nb1)	7
Total	(100.3 overs, 290 mins)	354

NEW SOUTH WALES	O	M	R	W	w,nb		O	M	R	W	w,nb
Coningham	15	4	40	1	-,-	(3)	4.4	2	8	3	-,-
Howell	33	13	55	4	-,-	(1)	18	6	33	3	-,-
Pye	10	2	21	0	-,-						
Connell	15	7	24	0	-,-						
Newell	23.5	10	34	3	-,-	(2)	22	14	23	4	-,-

QUEENSLAND	O	M	R	W	w,nb
Wilson	22	5	78	2	-,-
McGlinchey	26	2	84	4	-,-
Long	23.3	4	67	3	-,-
O'Brien	19	4	54	0	-,1
A.H.Jones	6	0	28	0	-,-
Hoare	4	0	36	0	-,-

FALL OF WICKETS

Wkt	QLD 1st	NSW 1st	QLD 2nd
1st	12	5	7
2nd	12	90	9
3rd	42	174	13
4th	49	207	13
5th	81	305	34
6th	152	305	65
7th	179	309	65
8th	180	337	68
9th	180	352	73
10th	180	354	73

1897-98 SEASON (19 MATCHES)

The Melbourne Cricket Club and Sydney Cricket Ground trustees co-operated again to bring an English team to Australia. They asked A.E.Stoddart, captain of the highly popular 1894-95 team, to arrange selection of the players and to lead the side. The tour began at Adelaide, as had become the custom, and 22 matches in all were played, including five Tests and seven other games ranked as first-class. The Western Australian Cricket Association attempted to arrange a further first-class match at Perth to close the tour, but the Englishmen were unable (or unwilling) to change their schedule to incorporate such a game.

The 14th English team were unable to repeat the success of the previous visit under Stoddart. Stoddart was initially dogged by illness and then suffered the death of his mother -a combination which reduced his appearances and weakened his effectiveness. The tourists began well by winning the First Test but then fell away markedly and lost the last four internationals by conclusive margins. The batting relied heavily on MacLaren and Ranjitsinhji, while the bowling - apart from Richardson and Hearne - was almost innocuous. The Australians, on the other hand, formed a strong allround combination and were shrewdly led by Harry Trott. Darling (three), Hill and McLeod all hit centuries, while others made useful contributions when the need arose. The majority of the wickets were shared by Jones, Noble and Trumble. It was initially thought that George Giffen - unavailable due to a disagreement over match finances - would be sorely missed, but this was not the case. Giffen also failed to come to terms with the SACA and appeared in only two games during the season.

Victoria won the Sheffield Shield for the third time. They began badly with a nine-wicket defeat at the hands of South Australia at Adelaide but then went on to win their remaining three matches, two of them narrowly on rain-affected pitches. Roche, who consistently took wickets, was their most important player. New South Wales, unbeaten last season, managed a solitary win against South Australia at Adelaide. They were unfortunate to suffer extremes in conditions in their matches against Victoria - extreme heat at Melbourne and rain at Sydney - but their batting proved most disappointing given the lineup. The South Australians missed Giffen in two matches but held up reasonably well despite his absence. They managed a win against New South Wales at Sydney after their early success at home against Victoria.

Tasmania met Victoria at Melbourne and inflicted defeat on the mainland colony, for only the second time at Melbourne. Their international representatives, Burn and Eady, played leading roles. The annual New South Wales-Queensland match was not played owing to the visit of the English team.

The annual meeting of the Australasian Cricket Council, at Melbourne on January 3, brought forward a surprise motion. C.F.W.Lloyd (New South Wales) proposed that the body be disbanded, 'for having failed to carry out the objects for which it was formed'. Lloyd was hinting at the Council's inability to win control of the finances and tour arrangements from the various associations. But his move received no support from other delegates and the Council continued its meanderings for a further year or two, eventually winding up early in 1900.

Leading Aggregates

Batsmen	M	I	NO	Runs	HS	Ave.	Bowlers	Runs	Wkts	Ave.
C.Hill (SA)	11	19	1	1196	200	66.44	E.Jones (SA)	1653	76	21.75
K.S.Ranjitsinhji (E)	12	22	3	1157	189	60.89	M.A.Noble (NSW)	1333	58	22.98
A.C.MacLaren (E)	11	20	1	1037	142	54.57	T.Richardson (E)	1593	54	29.50
J.Darling (SA)	11	19	0	978	178	51.47	J.T.Hearne (E)	1307	44	29.70
S.E.Gregory (NSW)	10	18	2	738	171	46.12	H.Trumble (V)	1108	39	28.41
T.W.Hayward (E)	12	21	3	695	96	38.61	W.Roche (V)	684	33	20.72
W.Storer (E)	11	17	1	604	84	37.75	T.R.McKibbin (NSW)	1171	32	36.59
C.E.McLeod (V)	10	18	2	592	112	37.00	G.H.S.Trott (V)	786	29	27.10
J.Worrall (V)	7	14	0	563	103	40.21				

SHEFFIELD SHIELD TABLE

	P	W	L	D	Quotient	Runs Scored	Wkts Lost	Runs Conceded	Wkts Taken
VICTORIA	4	3	1	-	0.993	1798	77	1623	69
SOUTH AUSTRALIA	4	2	2	-	1.160	1964	71	1908	80
NEW SOUTH WALES	4	1	3	-	0.869	1698	78	1929	77
TOTAL	6	6	6	-	1.000	5460	226	5460	226

SOUTH AUSTRALIA v A.E.STODDART'S ENGLISH XI

Played at Adelaide Oval on October 28, 29, 30, November 1, 1897. (Four-day match)
Toss : South Australia.   Result : MATCH DRAWN.
Debuts: South Australia - T.M.Drew (f/c).
12th men: A.E.Peters (SA) and J.H.Board (Eng).
Umpires: I.A.Fisher and J.Phillips.
Attendances: 7000, 10000, 14000, 5000.   Total: About 36000.   Receipts: £1250.
Close of Play: 1st day SA 5/361 (Hill 200, Jarvis 66); 2nd day Eng 3/263 (Ranjitsinhji 137, Wainwright 27); 3rd day SA (2) 3/124 (Reedman 15).

The tour organisers restricted this match to four days to ensure that the tourists would be in Victoria for the running of the Melbourne Cup on November 2nd. Frequent rain showers on the final day limited play to an hour in total. Influenza kept N.F.Druce out of the England line-up and debilitated Stoddart; he took no part further after the first day, MacLaren deputising as captain. George Giffen was unable to agree terms and declared himself unavailable for South Australia. Richardson dismissed Darling with the second ball of the match. Fine innings by Hill (200 in 272 minutes, 21 fours) and Ranjitsinhji (189 in 270 minutes, 23 fours), who became the third Englishman to score a hundred on debut in Australia, dominated the high-scoring game. Hill did not give a chance whereas Ranji was missed six times, all off Jones, the first when he was 1 but the others after he had reached three figures. He was finally out to "the catch of the season" (*Register*) from a shoulder high full toss. Jones (7 for 189) bowled at great pace and was once no-balled for throwing by Phillips, just before lunch on the third day. He at once slowed down and "his bowling lost its suspicious character" (*Register*). Half-centuries were scored by Jarvis (79 in 115 minutes, 13 fours), Lyons (56 in 90 minutes), Mason (79 in 94 minutes, 9 fours) and Storer (84 in 115 minutes, 16 fours).
Sources: *Wisden, C.B.O'Reilly, The Australasian, Adelaide Advertiser, South Australian Register.*

SOUTH AUSTRALIA

J.Darling	c & b Richardson	0	b Hirst		1
*J.J.Lyons	c Briggs b Hirst	36	b Richardson		56
C.Hill	b Hayward	200	c Storer b Richardson		45
J.C.Reedman	c Hirst b Hearne	22	c Hirst b Hayward		37
W.F.Giffen	b Richardson	13	not out		28
A.E.Evans	b Hearne	20	c MacLaren b Hearne		9
A.Jarvis	c Mason b Richardson	79	not out		0
A.E.Green	b Richardson	4			
T.M.Drew	not out	5			
E.Jones	c Ranjitsinhji b Hearne	12			
†J.McKenzie	c Mason b Richardson	11			
Extras	(b2, w1, nb3)	6	(b10, nb1)		11
Total	(110.1 overs, 310 mins)	408	(54.1 overs, 155 mins) (5 wkts)		187

A.E.STODDART'S ENGLAND XI

A.C.MacLaren	b Evans	0
J.R.Mason	lbw b Jones	79
K.S.Ranjitsinhji	c Drew b Green	189
T.W.Hayward	c Jarvis b Jones	6
E.Wainwright	b Jones	36
G.H.Hirst	b Jones	16
†W.Storer	b Jones	84
J.Briggs	b Jones	1
J.T.Hearne	not out	31
T.Richardson	b Jones	0
*A.E.Stoddart	absent ill	-
Extras	(b17, lb12, nb4)	33
Total	(131.2 overs, 388 mins)	475

ENGLAND XI	O	M	R	W	w,nb		O	M	R	W	w,nb
Richardson	33.1	7	117	5	1,1	(2)	19	0	80	2	-,-
Briggs	15	0	90	0	-,-	(4)	2	0	5	0	-,-
Hirst	20	6	63	1	-,-	(1)	11	4	37	1	-,1
Hearne	28	3	86	3	-,-	(3)	15.1	5	32	1	-,-
Wainwright	8	2	26	0	-,-						
Hayward	6	0	20	1	-,2		6	1	22	1	-,-
Ranjitsinhji						(6)	1	1	0	0	-,-

SOUTH AUSTRALIA	O	M	R	W	w,nb
Jones	54.2	11	189	7	-,1
Evans	24	3	90	1	-,3
Reedman	14	2	50	0	-,-
Jarvis	21	8	52	0	-,-
Lyons	10	4	29	0	-,-
Green	8	0	32	1	-,-

FALL OF WICKETS			
	SA	ENG	SA
Wkt	1st	1st	2nd
1st	0	9	4
2nd	74	137	89
3rd	125	193	124
4th	169	291	174
5th	217	311	184
6th	365	372	-
7th	380	373	-
8th	381	475	-
9th	396	475	-
10th	408	-	-

VICTORIA v A.E.STODDART'S ENGLAND XI

Played at the Melbourne Cricket Ground on November 6, 8, 9, 10, 1897. (Timeless match)
Toss : Victoria.   Result : A.E.STODDART'S ENGLAND XI WON BY TWO WICKETS.
Debuts: Nil.
12th men: R.Mitchell (Vic) and J.H.Board (Eng).
Umpires: R.M.Crockett and J.Phillips.
Attendances: 16994, 12146, 19037, 9040.   Total: 57,217.   Receipts: £2222.
Close of play: 1st day Vic 6/272 (Harry 13, McMichael 1); 2nd day Eng 7/213 (Storer 47, Hirst 30); 3rd day Vic (2) 9/242 (McMichael 20, Johns 17).

McLeod (63 in 110 minutes, 6 fours) and Bruce (88 in 121 minutes, 11 fours) saw Victoria to a respectable first-innings total despite an economical 5 for 61 by Hearne. MacLaren, missed by Trott at point off the first ball of the England innings, did not go on, and the Englishmen struggled until Storer hit a fluent fifty (71 not out in 110 minutes, 6 fours). Worrall (83 in 255 minutes, 7 fours) added 104 for the sixth wicket with Harry (50 in 95 minutes, 3 fours) in Victoria's second innings to set the visitors a challenging target. The result remained uncertain to the end, Mason (128 not out in 267 minutes, 6 fours) eventually getting his side home, supported by Ranji (64 in 75 minutes, 5 fours) and Storer (47 in 105 minutes, 2 fours). J.Briggs, the latest influenza victim, was unable to be considered for the tourists. Sources: *Wisden, VCA Report, The Age, The Argus, The Herald, The Australasian, The Leader.*

VICTORIA

Batsman		Runs			Runs
C.E.McLeod	c Stoddart b Hearne	63		c Storer b Hearne	14
J.Worrall	c Wainwright b Hearne	25		b Richardson	83
*G.H.S.Trott	c Hirst b Richardson	25		c Storer b Hayward	12
W.Bruce	c Mason b Richardson	88		c Mason b Hayward	5
H.Graham	c Richardson b Hayward	33		b Hayward	25
J.F.Giller	c Mason b Hearne	22		b Hayward	2
J.Harry	b Hearne	18		c Wainwright b Richardson	50
S.A.McMichael	lbw b Richardson	1		not out	25
H.Trumble	c Druce b Richardson	23		run out(Mason/Storer)	3
†A.E.Johns	c Richardson b Hearne	0	(11)	lbw b Richardson	17
W.Roche	not out	6	(10)	c Richardson b Hayward	0
Extras	(lb2)	2		(b2, lb4, nb5)	11
Total	(118.4 overs, 318 mins)	306		(108.2 overs, 297 mins)	247

A.E.STODDART'S ENGLAND XI

Batsman		Runs			Runs
A.C.MacLaren	b Roche	26		b Trott	10
J.R.Mason	c Trumble b Roche	36		not out	128
K.S.Ranjitsinhji	c Trumble b Trott	13		lbw b Trumble	64
T.W.Hayward	c McMichael b Trumble	7		st Johns b Trott	5
N.F.Druce	c Johns b Trott	13		c Johns b Giller	26
*A.E.Stoddart	c Trumble b Trott	26		c Trott b Giller	0
E.Wainwright	run out (Bruce)	13		c Johns b McLeod	6
†W.Storer	not out	71		run out (Harry/Roche)	47
G.H.Hirst	c Worrall b Trumble	36		c Graham b Roche	7
J.T.Hearne	b Trumble	2		not out	4
T.Richardson	b Trumble	4			
Extras	(b1, lb1, w1)	3		(b6, w2)	8
Total	(114.4 overs, 275 mins)	250		(106.4 overs, 267 mins) (8 wkts)	305

ENGLAND XI	O	M	R	W	w,nb		O	M	R	W	w,nb
Richardson	42.4	7	127	4	-,-		33.2	10	71	3	-,1
Hirst	16	7	38	0	-,-	(3)	17	5	31	0	-,1
Hearne	40	20	61	5	-,-	(2)	28	14	44	1	-,-
Wainwright	11	2	47	0	-,-	(5)	5	0	24	0	-,-
Hayward	9	2	31	1	-,-	(4)	25	5	66	5	-,3

VICTORIA	O	M	R	W	w,nb		O	M	R	W	w,nb
Trumble	43.4	10	80	4	-,-		29	3	95	1	1,-
Roche	33	15	60	2	-,-	(3)	19.4	5	55	1	-,-
Trott	19	3	52	3	1,-	(2)	25	6	66	2	-,-
Giller	14	0	34	0	-,-		15	2	52	2	1,-
McLeod	4	0	17	0	-,-		17	7	27	1	-,-
Bruce	1	0	4	0	-,-						
Harry						(6)	1	0	2	0	-,-

FALL OF WICKETS

Wkt	VIC 1st	ENG 1st	VIC 2nd	ENG 2nd
1st	50	57	34	15
2nd	106	62	50	116
3rd	118	79	59	124
4th	177	82	93	163
5th	243	116	95	165
6th	263	124	199	178
7th	277	161	200	288
8th	277	221	203	301
9th	285	240	206	-
10th	306	250	247	-

NEW SOUTH WALES v A.E.STODDART'S ENGLAND XI

Played at Sydney Cricket Ground on November 12, 13, 15, 16, 1897. (Timeless match)
Toss : New South Wales.   Result : A.E.STODDART'S ENGLAND XI.WON BY EIGHT WICKETS.
Debuts: Nil.
12th men: L.W.Pye (NSW) and J.H.Board (Eng).
Umpires: J.Phillips and J.Thompson.
Attendances: 10673, 32253, 13949, 12290.   Total: 69,165.   Receipts: £2730.
Close of play: 1st day NSW 5/303 (Mackenzie 80, Kelly 4); 2nd day Eng 7/324 (Stoddart 27, Hirst 12); 3rd day NSW (2) 9/259 (Kelly 2).

MacLaren became the first Englishman - in fact only the second batsman so far - to score a century in each innings in Australia. His 142 (175 minutes, 21 fours) was chanceless, while his second-innings 100 (123 minutes, 14 fours) included a difficult chance to McKibbin off Trumper in the nineties. He and Ranjitsinhji (112 not out in 142 minutes, 20 fours) gave a dazzling exhibition of strokeplay in adding 180 in 115 minutes on the last day. Storer (81 in 180 minutes, 12 fours) continued his good form with the bat, Ranji keeping wicket when he bowled. New South Wales lost early wickets on the opening day until a fine knock by Iredale (90 in 105 minutes, 19 fours), supported by Donnan (104 in 255 minutes, 1 five and 17 fours) and Mackenzie (80 in 150 minutes, 9 fours), retrieved the situation. Mackenzie again batted well in the second innings (59 in 141 minutes, 6 fours) and shared a seventh-wicket partnership of 117 with Garrett (71 in 83 minutes, 11 fours). *Wisden* incorrectly has NSW (1) Iredale 89, McKibbin 3; NSW (2) Howell 1, extras 13, Richardson 5/80. Sources: *Wisden, Sydney Referee, Sydney Morning Herald, Town & Country Journal, Sydney Daily Telegraph.*

NEW SOUTH WALES

Batsman	Dismissal (1st)	Score		Dismissal (2nd)	Score
H.Donnan	run out (Hayward)	104		b Hirst	29
V.T.Trumper	c Ranjitsinhji b Hirst	5	(4)	b Richardson	0
S.E.Gregory	run out (Druce)	14	(2)	c Storer b Richardson	44
M.A.Noble	b Richardson	4	(5)	c Storer b Richardson	15
F.A.Iredale	lbw b Hayward	90	(3)	c Hearne b Richardson	19
A.C.K.Mackenzie	b Richardson	80		c & b Hirst	59
†J.J.Kelly	c Storer b Richardson	5	(9)	not out	2
A.Coningham	c & b Richardson	0	(10)	b Hirst	0
*T.W.Garrett	c Ranjitsinhji b Hearne	5	(8)	c Storer b Hirst	71
T.R.McKibbin	not out	2	(7)	b Hearne	7
W.P.Howell	c Druce b Hearne	0		b Richardson	0
Extras	(b2)	2		(b5, lb7, w1, nb1)	14
Total	(113.5 overs, 303 mins)	311		(90.2 overs, 255 mins)	260

A.E.STODDART'S ENGLAND XI

Batsman	Dismissal (1st)	Score	Dismissal (2nd)	Score
A.C.MacLaren	c Iredale b Noble	142	b Noble	100
J.R.Mason	b McKibbin	1	b Noble	4
K.S.Ranjitsinhji	c Kelly b Noble	10	not out	112
T.W.Hayward	c Trumper b Noble	9	not out	18
N.F.Druce	c Donnan b McKibbin	16		
†W.Storer	c Kelly b Noble	81		
E.Wainwright	c Mackenzie b McKibbin	24		
*A.E.Stoddart	b Noble	32		
G.H.Hirst	lbw b McKibbin	16		
J.T.Hearne	not out	2		
T.Richardson	b McKibbin	0		
Extras	(b2)	2	(b1, lb2)	3
Total	(90.1 overs, 265 mins)	335	(51.1 overs, 155 mins) (2 wkts)	237

ENGLAND XI	O	M	R	W	w,nb		O	M	R	W	w,nb
Richardson	33	9	105	4	-,-		38.2	12	79	5	-,-
Hirst	22	11	55	1	-,-		24	6	66	4	-,-
Hearne	27.5	9	55	2	-,-	(4)	18	5	41	1	1,-
Hayward	16	6	48	1	-,-	(3)	6	0	39	0	-,1
Storer	9	1	27	0	-,-		4	0	21	0	-,-
Wainwright	6	1	19	0	-,-						

NEW SOUTH WALES	O	M	R	W	w,nb		O	M	R	W	w,nb
McKibbin	37.1	7	139	5	-,-		13	2	64	0	-,-
Coningham	11	3	48	0	-,-	(4)	9.1	2	31	0	-,-
Noble	29	4	111	5	-,-	(2)	21	2	92	2	-,-
Howell	13	4	35	0	-,-	(3)	5	1	22	0	-,-
Trumper							3	0	25	0	-,-

FALL OF WICKETS

Wkt	NSW 1st	ENG 1st	NSW 2nd	ENG 2nd
1st	8	6	69	12
2nd	22	32	79	192
3rd	26	64	84	-
4th	157	100	100	-
5th	284	250	114	-
6th	304	277	131	-
7th	304	292	248	-
8th	309	333	251	-
9th	309	333	259	-
10th	311	335	260	-

SOUTH AUSTRALIA v VICTORIA (Shield Match 1)

Played at Adelaide Oval on November 13, 15, 16, 17, 1897. (Timeless match)

Toss : Victoria. Result : SOUTH AUSTRALIA WON BY NINE WICKETS.

Debuts: Nil.

12th men: A.E.Peters (SA) and G.Beacham (Vic).

Umpires: R.M.Crockett and G.E.Downs.

Attendances: 4000, 6000, 1500, 200. Total: About 11,700. Receipts: £293.

Close of play: 1st day SA 0/88 (Lyons 52, Darling 29); 2nd day Vic (2) 0/0 (Giller 0, McMichael 0); 3rd day SA (2) 0/8 (Reedman 6, Green 2).

H.Trumble (work) was unavailable for Victoria and J.P.O'Halloran, who had accepted a coaching offer in South Africa, was replaced in the team by Bruce. Beacham was Trumble's replacement. Jarvis was absent on the third day due to the illness of a close friend, and with no 12th man present, B.V.Scrymgour was called on to substitute. The Victorian batting twice failed on a good wicket. Jones reported a strained side on the first morning and the match did not start until 12.25pm while he was bound up. However, he showed no discomfort or loss of pace as, with the assistance of George Giffen, he ran through the Victorian first innings. Giller (81 in 235 minutes, 5 fours) and McMichael (46 in 93 minutes, 3 fours) began the second innings soundly but thereafter only McLeod (44 in 115 minutes, 3 fours) offered any serious resistance. George Giffen was troubled by a rheumatic shoulder on the third day which prevented him bowling after lunch. Lyons (65 in 90 minutes, 5 fours), Walter Giffen (63 in 175 minutes, 4 fours) and Jarvis (92 in 170 minutes, 12 fours) put South Australia in a strong position on the second day, George Giffen sustaining a first-ball dismissal. The required runs were knocked off in an hour on the fourth day, ahead of a storm. Sources: *Wisden, C.B.O'Reilly, VCA Report, The Argus, Adelaide Advertiser, South Australian Register.*

VICTORIA

W.Bruce	b G.Giffen	1	(6) c Jones b Lyons		5
J.Worrall	b Jones	30	(3) run out (Reedman/Lyons)		7
C.E.McLeod	b Jones	6	(4) c sub (B.V.Scrymgour) b Evans		44
H.Graham	c Lyons b G.Giffen	0	(8) not out		22
*G.H.S.Trott	c Evans b G.Giffen	27	c Evans b Lyons		0
J.F.Giller	c McKenzie b G.Giffen	12	(1) c McKenzie b Lyons		81
J.Harry	lbw b Jones	16	c Jones b Evans		14
F.J.Laver	b Jones	9	(9) lbw b Evans		1
S.A.McMichael	not out	35	(2) c Evans b Lyons		46
W.Roche	b Jones	1	st McKenzie b Evans		3
†A.E.Johns	c Hill b G.Giffen	11	c sub (B.V.Scrymgour) b Evans		0
Extras	(lb9)	9	(b2, lb2, nb4)		8
Total	(65.4 overs, 190 mins)	157	(104.4 overs, 270 mins)		231

SOUTH AUSTRALIA

J.J.Lyons	c Worrall b Giller	65	(3) not out	14
J.Darling	run out (/Johns)	33		
C.Hill	c Roche b Trott	11		
J.C.Reedman	c Harry b Giller	22	(1) c McMichael b Giller	31
W.F.Giffen	c Giller b Roche	63		
*G.Giffen	c Trott b Giller	0		
A.E.Evans	b Giller	9		
A.Jarvis	c Trott b Roche	92		
A.E.Green	not out	3	(2) not out	33
†J.McKenzie	c Harry b Roche	0		
E.Jones	c Graham b Roche	1		
Extras	(b8, lb3, w1, nb2)	14		-
Total	(123.1 overs, 320 mins)	313	(30.0 overs, 75 mins) (3 wkts)	78

SOUTH AUSTRALIA	O	M	R	W	w,nb		O	M	R	W	w,nb
Jones	33	7	79	5	-,-		31	10	71	0	-,-
G.Giffen	32.4	17	69	5	-,-		10	3	17	0	-,-
Reedman							11	3	29	0	-,-
Evans							17.4	5	33	5	-,3
Lyons							31	7	70	4	-,1
Green							4	2	3	0	-,-

VICTORIA	O	M	R	W	w,nb		O	M	R	W	w,nb
Roche	29.1	10	59	4	-,2		10	5	21	0	-,-
McLeod	33	11	64	0	-,-	(3)	5	1	17	0	-,-
Giller	31	8	70	4	1,-	(4)	5	2	8	1	-,-
Trott	19	0	70	1	-,-	(2)	8	0	25	0	-,-
Worrall	6	2	15	0	-,-						
Harry	5	1	21	0	-,-						
Bruce						(5)	2	0	7	0	-,-

FALL OF WICKETS

Wkt	VIC 1st	SA 1st	VIC 2nd	SA 2nd
1st	1	103	81	50
2nd	16	105	91	-
3rd	21	131	179	-
4th	69	139	180	-
5th	73	139	190	-
6th	94	155	199	-
7th	102	304	218	-
8th	114	311	226	-
9th	116	311	231	-
10th	157	313	231	-

AUSTRALIA v ENGLAND (1st Test)

Played at Sydney Cricket Ground on December 13, 14, 15, 16, 17, 1897. (Timeless match)
Toss : England.   Result : ENGLAND WON BY NINE WICKETS.
Debuts: England - N.F.Druce, G.H.Hirst, J.R.Mason, W.Storer (all Test).
12th men: H.Donnan (Aust) and J.H.Board (Eng).
Umpires: C.Bannerman and J.Phillips.
Attendances: 22620, 19303, 10450, 9403, 1515.   Total: 63,291.   Receipts: £2446.
Close of play: 1st day Eng 5/337 (Hirst 37, Ranjitsinhji 39); 2nd day Aust 5/86 (Gregory 18); 3rd day Aust (2) 1/126 (Darling 80,
    McLeod 20); 4th day Eng (2) 0/30 (MacLaren 16, Mason 13).

The game was scheduled to commence on Friday, December 10th, but poor weather put the start back several days. McLeod (originally
12th man) replaced G.Giffen (who declined an invitation for financial reasons) in the selected Australian team. A.E.Stoddart (mourning the
death of his mother) was unable to lead the Englishmen. MacLaren, his deputy, scored a century in his first Test as captain (a chanceless
109 in 189 minutes, 15 fours) to become the first batsman to score three hundreds in successive first-class innings in Australia.
Ranjitsinhji (who was held back in the order due to a bout of quinsy - the rain-delayed start had enabled his condition to improve) emulated
H.Graham in scoring a century in his first Test in Australia having also done so in England. His chanceless 175 (223 minutes, 26 fours)
remained the highest Test innings by an Englishman in Australia until R.E.Foster's 287 in 1903-04. Similarly this commanding total, in
which Hayward (72 in 116 minutes, 10 fours) and Hirst (62 in 100 minutes, 1 five and 8 fours) scored steady half-centuries, remained
England's best in Tests in Australia until the corresponding match two tours later. Kelly became the first wicket-keeper to prevent any
byes in a total of more than 500 in a first-class match in Australia; a highest byeless total was not attained here until 1935-36. Darling
(101 in 194 minutes, 19 fours) scored the first Test century by a left-hander. Hill (96 in 143 minutes, 11 fours) made the first of five
personal scores between 96 and 99 in Test matches in Australia. Trumble (70 in 138 minutes, 13 fours) and McLeod (50 not out in 105
minutes, 5 fours) hit fifties. McLeod, who was slightly deaf, was bowled by a no-ball in the second innings but left his crease not having
heard the call and was run out. *Wisden* incorrectly gives Aust (2) Iredale 19, Hill 86. Sources: *Wisden, The Australasian, Sydney Referee,
Sydney Morning Herald, Town & Country Journal.*

ENGLAND

J.R.Mason	b Jones	6	(2) b McKibbin		32
*A.C.MacLaren	c Kelly b McLeod	109	(1) not out		50
T.W.Hayward	c Trott b Trumble	72			
†W.Storer	c & b Trott	43			
N.F.Druce	c Gregory b McLeod	20			
G.H.Hirst	b Jones	62			
K.S.Ranjitsinhji	c Gregory b McKibbin	175	(3) not out		8
E.Wainwright	b Jones	10			
J.T.Hearne	c & b McLeod	17			
J.Briggs	run out (Kelly)	1			
T.Richardson	not out	24			
Extras	(lb11, w1)	12	(b5, nb1)		6
Total	(175.0 overs, 433 mins)	551	(28.0 overs, 68 mins) (1 wkt)		96

AUSTRALIA

J.Darling	c Druce b Richardson	7	(2) c Druce b Briggs		101
J.J.Lyons	b Richardson	3	(7) c Hayward b Hearne		25
F.A.Iredale	c Druce b Hearne	25	(1) b Briggs		18
C.Hill	b Hearne	19	b Hearne		96
S.E.Gregory	c Mason b Hearne	46	run out (Hearne)		31
*G.H.S.Trott	b Briggs	10	(8) b Richardson		27
†J.J.Kelly	b Richardson	1	(9) not out		46
H.Trumble	c Storer b Mason	70	(6) c Druce b Hearne		2
C.E.McLeod	not out	50	(3) run out (Druce/Storer)		26
T.R.McKibbin	b Hearne	0	(11) b Hearne		6
E.Jones	c Richardson b Hearne	0	(10) lbw b Richardson		3
Extras	(b1, lb1, nb4)	6	(b12, lb1, w4, nb10)		27
Total	(100.1 overs, 280 mins)	237	(121.0 overs, 360 mins)		408

AUSTRALIA	O	M	R	W	w,nb		O	M	R	W	w,nb
McKibbin	34	5	113	1	-,-	(3)	5	1	22	1	-,-
Jones	50	8	130	3	-,-	(1)	9	1	28	0	-,1
McLeod	28	12	80	3	-,-						
Trumble	40	7	138	1	-,-	(2)	14	4	40	0	-,-
Trott	23	2	78	1	1,-						

ENGLAND	O	M	R	W	w,nb		O	M	R	W	w,nb
Richardson	27	8	71	3	-,1		41	9	121	2	4,7
Hirst	28	7	57	0	-,3	(5)	13	3	49	0	-,2
Hearne	20.1	7	42	5	-,-	(2)	38	8	99	4	-,-
Briggs	20	7	42	1	-,-	(3)	22	3	86	2	-,-
Hayward	3	1	11	0	-,-	(4)	5	1	16	0	-,1
Mason	2	1	8	1	-,-		2	0	10	0	-,-

FALL OF WICKETS

Wkt	ENG 1st	AUST 1st	AUST 2nd	ENG 2nd
1st	26	8	37	80
2nd	162	24	135	-
3rd	224	56	191	-
4th	256	57	269	-
5th	258	86	271	-
6th	382	87	318	-
7th	422	138	321	-
8th	471	228	382	-
9th	477	237	390	-
10th	551	237	408	-

VICTORIA v NEW SOUTH WALES (Shield Match 2)

Played at the Melbourne Cricket Ground on December 27, 28, 29, 30, 1897. (Timeless match)
Toss : Victoria.   Result : VICTORIA WON BY 149 RUNS.
Debuts: Victoria - A.W.Murray (f/c).
12th men: D.Sutherland (Vic) and V.T.Trumper (NSW).
Umpires: R.M.Crockett and J.A.Tooher.
Attendances: 7000, 6000, 1500, 750.   Total: About 15,250.   Receipts: £634.
Close of play: 1st day Vic 7/276 (McMichael 28, Murray 16); 2nd day NSW 6/241 (Noble 16, Garrett 3); 3rd day NSW (2) 1/2 (Garrett 1).
Warne (originally 12th man) was a late replacement for C.E.McLeod, who had decided to rest an injured finger for the Second Test. Century temperatures prevailed throughout all four days of the match and the oppressive heat took its toll on the players. Kelly (sunstroke) took no part after Victoria's first innings, Noble keeping wicket before lunch on the third day and Iredale afterwards. Trumper and W.P.Howell, who were left out of the New South Wales thirteen, were both required to field from the first day, for Gregory (split finger) and Noble (heat-affected) in the first innings and for Gregory and Kelly in the second. Graham (53 in 85 minutes, 4 fours) and McMichael (53 not out in 113 minutes, 3 fours) for Victoria and Pye (80 in 177 minutes, 4 fours) and Mackenzie (88 in 147 minutes, 1 five and 8 fours) for New South Wales surpassed 50 in the first innings, while McKibbin was out to the first ball he faced. Trott (61) did not continue batting directly after the tea break on the third day with Victoria 7/141; he had been unwell before the match and now had sunstroke and needed to rest. However, the quick exit of Johns and Roche saw him resume (with Worrall as his runner) at 9/148, and he added 31 out of the last-wicket stand of 36 with Warne: his final 92 occupied 194 minutes (9 fours). Sutherland fielded for him in the second innings, Worrall deputising as captain. Sources: *Wisden, VCA Report, The Age, The Argus, The Herald, The Australasian, The Leader, The Sportsman.*

VICTORIA

W.Bruce	c Garrett b McKibbin	13	(5) run out (sub W.P.Howell/McKibbin)		21
T.S.Warne	c Kelly b McKibbin	6	(9) not out		5
J.Worrall	lbw b Noble	49	b Pye		0
H.Trumble	c Kelly b McKibbin	40	b McKibbin		7
J.F.Giller	c Garrett b Donnan	45	(7) c Iredale b Ferris		16
*G.H.S.Trott	run out (sub V.T.Trumper/Noble)	14	b Noble		92
H.Graham	b Ferris	53	(1) lbw b McKibbin		2
S.A.McMichael	not out	53	(2) b Pye		4
A.W.Murray	b Pye	18	(8) c Noble b McKibbin		19
W.Roche	c sub (W.P.Howell) b McKibbin	4	(11) b McKibbin		4
†A.E.Johns	b Pye	11	(10) run out		3
Extras	(b1, lb5, w7, nb1)	14	(b7, lb4)		11
Total	(130.0 overs, 324 mins)	320	(80.4 overs, 242 mins)		184

NEW SOUTH WALES

H.Donnan	b Trumble	11	(4) st Johns b Roche		14
J.J.Ferris	c Trumble b Roche	4	(9) c Johns b Trumble		7
F.A.Iredale	b Trott	13	(7) c Worrall b Roche		4
L.W.Pye	c McMichael b Bruce	80	(5) c McMichael b Roche		15
S.E.Gregory	c Giller b Trumble	22	(3) c & b Trumble		17
A.C.K.Mackenzie	c Murray b Bruce	88	st Johns b Giller		8
M.A.Noble	b Trott	22	(8) not out		16
*T.W.Garrett	st Johns b Trott	10	(1) c Trumble b Roche		5
P.C.Charlton	not out	5	(2) run out (McMichael/Trumble)		1
T.R.McKibbin	b Trott	0	c Graham b Roche		1
†J.J.Kelly	absent injured	-	absent injured		-
Extras	(b3, lb2, w3)	8	(b2, w2)		4
Total	(115.3 overs, 280 mins)	263	(74.0 overs, 188 mins)		92

NEW SOUTH WALES	O	M	R	W	w,nb		O	M	R	W	w,nb					
McKibbin	42	8	108	4	1,1		32	8	79	4	-,-					
Noble	20	6	59	1	1,-	(4)	2.4	0	4	1	-,-					
Charlton	15	4	34	0	2,-											
Ferris	24	9	47	1	3,-	(3)	18	4	36	1	-,-					
Pye	20	6	42	2	-,-	(2)	28	11	54	2	-,-					
Donnan	9	3	16	1	-,-											

						FALL OF WICKETS			
							VIC	NSW	VIC	NSW

VICTORIA	O	M	R	W	w,nb		O	M	R	W	w,nb		Wkt	1st	1st	2nd	2nd
													1st	21	4	2	2
													2nd	34	28	5	21
													3rd	106	28	16	32
													4th	120	60	26	51
													5th	136	219	49	56
Trumble	44	16	74	2	2,-	(2)	17	8	20	2	2,-		6th	218	222	76	64
Roche	23	7	57	1	-,-	(1)	37	13	51	5	-,-		7th	240	254	128	70
Trott	24.3	10	44	4	1,-								8th	278	263	144	91
Giller	8	2	26	0	-,-	(3)	20	10	17	1	-,-		9th	287	263	148	92
Murray	5	0	13	0	-,-								10th	320	-	184	-
Bruce	9	1	30	2	-,-												
Worrall	2	0	11	0	-,-												

AUSTRALIA v ENGLAND (2nd Test)

Played at the Melbourne Cricket Ground on January 1, 3, 4, 5, 1898. (Timeless match)
Toss : Australia.   Result : AUSTRALIA WON BY AN INNINGS AND 55 RUNS.
Debuts: Australia - M.A.Noble (Test).
12th men: H.Donnan (Aust) and J.H.Board (Eng).
Umpires: C.Bannerman and J.Phillips.
Attendances: 24744, 26858, 20116, 12192.   Total: 83,910.   Receipts: £3838.
Close of play: 1st day Aust 3/283 (Gregory 54, Iredale 12); 2nd day Eng 1/22 (MacLaren 9, Wainwright 3); 3rd day Eng 8/311 (Druce 44, Briggs 45).

Prior to the start it was thought that Ranjitsinhji (persistent throat infection) would be unfit to play and that A.E.Stoddart would take his place. However, the Australians agreed to let Board field for Ranji while he received treatment in the pavilion and on this basis he was included in the English side and took his place in the field later on the opening day. McLeod (career-best 112 in 244 minutes, 4 fours) scored his second and last first-class century - it was Australia's first in nine Melbourne Tests since the 1881-82 season. Hill (58 in 115 minutes, 1 four), Gregory (71 in 133 minutes, 3 fours), Iredale (89 in 166 minutes, 6 fours) and Trott (79 in 193 minutes, 11 fours) hit half-centuries. Only Ranjitsinhji (71 in 140 minutes, 4 fours) and Storer (51 in 85 minutes, 6 fours) exceeded 50 for the Englishmen. Noble (6 for 49) bowled a fine spell on a wearing last-day wicket in his first match for Australia. Jones was the first bowler to be no-balled for throwing in a Test, umpire Phillips calling him once in the pre-lunch session on the third day. Sources: *Wisden, The Age, The Argus, The Herald, The Australasian, The Leader, The Sportsman.*

AUSTRALIA

C.E.McLeod	b Storer	112
J.Darling	c Hirst b Briggs	36
C.Hill	c Storer b Hayward	58
S.E.Gregory	b Briggs	71
F.A.Iredale	c Ranjitsinhji b Hirst	89
*G.H.S.Trott	c Wainwright b Briggs	79
M.A.Noble	b Richardson	17
H.Trumble	c Hirst b Mason	14
†J.J.Kelly	c Richardson b Hearne	19
E.Jones	run out (Wainwright/Storer)	7
T.R.McKibbin	not out	2
Extras	(b14, w1, nb1)	16
Total	(185.0 overs, 532 mins)	520

ENGLAND

*A.C.MacLaren	c Trumble b McKibbin	35		c Trott b Trumble	38
J.R.Mason	b McKibbin	3		b Trumble	3
E.Wainwright	c Jones b Noble	21	(8)	b Noble	11
K.S.Ranjitsinhji	b Trumble	71	(3)	b Noble	27
T.W.Hayward	c Jones b Trott	23	(4)	c Trumble b Noble	33
†W.Storer	c Kelly b Trumble	51	(5)	c Trumble b Noble	1
G.H.Hirst	b Jones	0	(6)	lbw b Trumble	3
N.F.Druce	lbw b Trumble	44	(7)	c McLeod b Noble	15
J.T.Hearne	b Jones	1	(10)	c Jones b Noble	0
J.Briggs	not out	46	(9)	c Trott b Trumble	12
T.Richardson	b Trumble	3		not out	2
Extras	(b10, lb3, nb4)	17		(b3, lb1, w1)	5
Total	(119.5 overs, 323 mins)	315		(65.4 overs, 190 mins)	150

ENGLAND	O	M	R	W	w,nb						
Richardson	48	12	114	1	,						
Hirst	25	1	89	1	-,1						
Briggs	40	10	96	3	1,-						
Hearne	36	6	94	1	-,-						
Mason	11	1	33	1	-,-						
Hayward	9	4	23	1	-,-						
Storer	16	4	55	1	-,-						

AUSTRALIA	O	M	R	W	w,nb		O	M	R	W	w,nb
McKibbin	28	7	66	2	-,3	(3)	4	0	13	0	-,-
Trumble	26.5	5	54	4	-,-	(1)	30.4	12	53	4	1,-
Jones	22	5	54	2	-,1						
Trott	17	3	49	1	-,-		7	0	17	0	-,-
Noble	12	3	31	1	-,-		17	1	49	6	-,-
McLeod	14	2	44	0	-,-	(2)	7	2	13	0	-,-

FALL OF WICKETS

	AUST	ENG	ENG
Wkt	1st	1st	2nd
1st	43	13	10
2nd	167	60	65
3rd	244	74	71
4th	310	133	75
5th	434	203	80
6th	453	208	115
7th	478	223	128
8th	509	224	144
9th	515	311	148
10th	520	315	150

SOUTH AUSTRALIA v NEW SOUTH WALES (Shield Match 3)

Played at Adelaide Oval on January 8, 10, 11, 12, 1898. (Timeless match)
Toss : New South Wales.   Result : NEW SOUTH WALES WON BY 216 RUNS.
Debuts: New South Wales - H.Carter (f/c).
12th men: A.E.Peters (SA). No 12th for NSW.
Umpires: P.Argall and J.A.Tooher.
Attendances: 4000, 2000, 300, 250.   Total: About 6550.   Receipts: £264.
Close of play: 1st day NSW 228 all out; 2nd day NSW (2) 0/65 (Donnan 26, Iredale 37); 3rd day NSW (2) 316 all out.

J.J.Kelly and S.E.Gregory were rested for the ensuing Test at their request. In addition, P.C.Charlton had returned to Sydney after the match against Victoria, leaving New South Wales with no 12th man. H.A.Evers was sought as Kelly's replacement to keep wickets but was unable to make the journey and Carter was chosen for the first time. Temperatures hovered around 100°F throughout the game. The tea break was extended to 40 minutes on some days to provide some respite, while fielders were issued with a selection of cold drinks and wore damp cabbage leaves under their hats to combat the heat. Despite the trying conditions, fast bowler Jones (11 for 125) was the best of the local bowlers and his team's heavy defeat was no fault of his. He dismissed Donnan with the third ball of the third over, following two maidens, to open the match. Darling (74 in 225 minutes, 4 fours) was the only South Australian to record a half-century. The greater depth of the New South Wales batting stood out in comparison with Donnan (81 in 225 minutes, 6 fours), Noble (80 in 140 minutes, 9 fours), Iredale (51 in 105 minutes, 5 fours), Mackenzie (50 in 100 minutes, 3 fours) and Ferris (51 in 90 minutes, 5 fours) all scoring fifties. Noble continued the fine form with the ball that he had shown in Melbourne against the Englishmen a few days earlier. Mackenzie was run out in the most unfortunate manner at the non-striker's end when a drive by Trumper crashed into the stumps after being deflected by the bowler. Sources: *Wisden, C.B.O'Reilly, SACA Report, Sydney Morning Herald, Adelaide Advertiser, South Australian Register.*

NEW SOUTH WALES

Batsman	Dismissal 1	Runs 1		Dismissal 2	Runs 2
H.Donnan	b Jones	0		c McKenzie b Reedman	81
M.A.Noble	c Jarvis b G.Giffen	40	(4)	c & b Jones	80
F.A.Iredale	c Hill b Jones	2	(2)	c McKenzie b Reedman	51
L.W.Pye	c Jones b Evans	11	(3)	b Evans	0
A.C.K.Mackenzie	run out (Jarvis)	50		b Jones	14
V.T.Trumper	c & b G.Giffen	48		b Jones	13
*T.W.Garrett	c Jarvis b G.Giffen	9	(8)	b Jones	8
J.J.Ferris	b Jones	51	(7)	b Jones	0
W.P.Howell	b Jones	3	(11)	not out	21
T.R.McKibbin	b Jones	3	(9)	b Jones	25
†H.Carter	not out	6	(10)	c & b Evans	15
Extras	(lb5)	5		(b1, lb6, w1)	8
Total	(86.5 overs, 260 mins)	228		(109.4 overs, 315 mins)	316

SOUTH AUSTRALIA

Batsman	Dismissal 1	Runs 1	Dismissal 2	Runs 2
J.Darling	b Noble	8	c Carter b Howell	74
J.J.Lyons	c Trumper b Howell	14	b Howell	5
C.Hill	lbw b Pye	20	b Noble	2
J.C.Reedman	b Howell	6	c Howell b McKibbin	25
*G.Giffen	b Howell	49	c Garrett b Noble	12
A.Jarvis	b Howell	6	b Noble	0
W.F.Giffen	b Howell	11	b Noble	2
T.M.Drew	c Ferris b Noble	9	not out	33
A.E.Evans	b Noble	0	b Howell	9
†J.McKenzie	not out	7	c Carter b McKibbin	3
E.Jones	c Trumper b Noble	0	c Iredale b McKibbin	8
Extras	(b2, lb6, nb1)	9	(b10, lb5, w1)	16
Total	(65.4 overs, 200 mins)	139	(78.1 overs, 245 mins)	189

SOUTH AUSTRALIA	O	M	R	W	w,nb		O	M	R	W	w,nb
Jones	26.5	6	54	5	-,-		28	7	71	6	-,-
Evans	17	5	43	1	-,-		19.4	4	50	2	1,-
G.Giffen	30	2	93	3	-,-		34	4	116	0	-,-
Jarvis	13	1	33	0	-,-	(7)	9	2	36	0	-,-
Reedman						(4)	8	2	11	2	-,-
Lyons						(5)	6	1	14	0	-,-
Drew						(6)	5	1	10	0	-,-

NEW SOUTH WALES	O	M	R	W	w,nb		O	M	R	W	w,nb
Howell	29	10	60	5	-,-		20	3	50	3	-,-
Noble	19.4	8	32	4	-,1		29	6	63	4	1,-
Pye	13	4	22	1	-,-	(4)	4	2	9	0	-,-
McKibbin	4	0	16	0	-,-	(3)	25.1	5	51	3	-,-

FALL OF WICKETS

Wkt	NSW 1st	SA 1st	NSW 2nd	SA 2nd
1st	0	17	103	9
2nd	4	30	106	14
3rd	33	37	191	59
4th	94	65	225	80
5th	125	72	242	80
6th	141	117	242	101
7th	200	120	252	160
8th	205	125	273	174
9th	213	135	292	181
10th	228	139	316	189

AUSTRALIA v ENGLAND (3rd Test)

Played at Adelaide Oval on January 14, 15, 17, 18, 19, 1898. (Timeless match)
Toss : Australia.   Result : AUSTRALIA WON BY AN INNINGS AND 13 RUNS.
Debuts: Australia - W.P.Howell (Test).
12th men: H.Donnan (Aust) and E.Wainwright (Eng). J.H.Board substitute when required.
Umpires: C.Bannerman and J.Phillips.
Attendances: 10000, 17000, 11000, 5000, 3000.   Total: 46,366.   Receipts: £2163.
Close of play: 1st day Aust 2/309 (Darling 178, Gregory 16); 2nd day Aust 9/552 (Trumble 32); 3rd day Eng 6/197 (Hirst 50, Stoddart 11);
    4th day Eng (2) 4/161 (MacLaren 70, Druce 0).

Darling became the first batsman to score more than one century in a Test series. He batted through the first day, only to fall to the fifth ball of the next after making 178 in 285 minutes with 1 six, 2 fives and 26 fours. He went from 98 to 104 with his six off Briggs, "a hit to square leg which sent the ball sailing out of the Oval" (*Register*). He had been dropped in the previous over when 98 by Ranji at point, cutting Richardson. He also gave a chance when 86. His first five was hit off Briggs, "a mighty stroke over the heads of the crowd near the entrance gate" in the first session, the second, also off Briggs, coming after lunch, "a fine hit, though not quite as big as the former one" (*Register*). He added 148 in 98 minutes for the second wicket with Hill (81 with 7 fours), while Gregory (52 in 145 minutes, 5 fours) and Iredale (84 in 197 minutes, 8 fours) also hit half-centuries as Australia became the first side to score 500 in successive Test innings. Druce kept wickets when Storer was called on to bowl. Hayward (70 in 165 minutes, 7 fours) and Hirst (85 in 200 minutes, 11 fours) were unable to prevent the follow-on. Hirst had earlier strained abdominal muscles while bowling his 25th over. MacLaren (124 in 317 minutes, 10 fours) completed his second century of the series, emulating the feat of Darling. His second-wicket stand of 142 with Ranji (77 in 147 minutes, 8 fours) was the only highlight of the second innings. Noble took the wickets of Hearne and Richardson with successive balls to finish the match. A dust storm had marked the fourth day's play, The *Register* describing it as "a regular brickfielder" and noting "that the twin towers of King William Street could not be seen from the Oval". Sources: *Wisden, The Australasian, The Leader, Adelaide Advertiser, South Australian Register*.

AUSTRALIA

C.E.McLeod	b Briggs	31
J.Darling	c Storer b Richardson	178
C.Hill	c Storer b Richardson	81
S.E.Gregory	c Storer b Hirst	52
F.A.Iredale	b Richardson	84
*G.H.S.Trott	b Hearne	3
M.A.Noble	b Richardson	39
H.Trumble	not out	37
†J.J.Kelly	b Stoddart	22
E.Jones	run out (/Storer)	8
W.P.Howell	b Hearne	16
Extras	(b16, lb5, nb1)	22
Total	(214.2 overs, 565 mins)	573

ENGLAND

A.C.MacLaren	b Howell	14	c Kelly b Noble	124
J.R.Mason	b Jones	11	c Jones b Noble	0
K.S.Ranjitsinhji	c Noble b Trumble	6	c Trumble b McLeod	77
T.W.Hayward	b Jones	70	c & b McLeod	1
†W.Storer	b Howell	4	c Hill b McLeod	6
N.F.Druce	c Darling b Noble	24	b Noble	27
G.H.Hirst	c Trumble b Noble	85	lbw b McLeod	6
*A.E.Stoddart	c Jones b Howell	15	c Jones b McLeod	24
J.Briggs	c Kelly b Noble	14	not out	0
J.T.Hearne	b Howell	0	c & b Noble	4
T.Richardson	not out	25	c Jones b Noble	0
Extras	(b2, lb6, w2)	10	(b2, lb6, w3, nb2)	13
Total	(126.5 overs, 325 mins)	278	(144.0 overs, 345 mins)	282

ENGLAND	O	M	R	W	w,nb
Richardson	56	11	164	4	-,-
Briggs	63	27	128	1	-,-
Hearne	44.1	15	94	2	-,-
Hirst	24.1	6	62	1	-,1
Hayward	9	1	36	0	-,-
Mason	11	2	41	0	-,-
Storer	3	0	16	0	-,-
Stoddart	4	1	10	1	-,-

AUSTRALIA	O	M	R	W	w,nb		O	M	R	W	w,nb
Howell	54	23	70	4	-,-		40	18	60	0	-,-
Jones	27	3	67	2	1,-	(6)	1	0	5	0	-,-
Trumble	17	3	39	1	1,-		16	5	37	0	-,-
Noble	24.5	5	78	3	-,-	(2)	33	7	84	5	3,1
Trott	4	0	14	0	-,-		6	0	18	0	-,-
McLeod						(4)	48	24	65	5	-,1

FALL OF WICKETS

	AUST	ENG	ENG
Wkt	1st	1st	2nd
1st	97	24	10
2nd	245	30	152
3rd	310	34	154
4th	374	42	160
5th	389	106	212
6th	474	172	235
7th	493	206	262
8th	537	223	278
9th	552	224	282
10th	573	278	282

NEW SOUTH WALES v VICTORIA (Shield Match 4)

Played at Sydney Cricket Ground on January 22, 24 (no play), 25, 26, 27, 1898. (Timeless match)
Toss : New South Wales.   Result : VICTORIA WON BY THREE WICKETS
Debuts: Nil.
12th men: J.Marsh (NSW) and A.W.Murray (Vic).
Umpires: C.Bannerman and R.M.Crockett.
Attendances: 6850, no play (171), 1173, 5351, 42.   Total: 13,416.   Receipts: £670.
Close of play: 1st day NSW 4/177 (Gregory 44); 2nd day no play; 3rd day Vic 7/153 (Worrall 91, Stuckey 9); 4th day Vic (2) 6/150
(Bruce 33, Giller 4).

There were doubts over the final composition of the New South Wales team right up until the last moment. W.P.Howell was nursing a thigh muscle strain from the Adelaide Test, J.J.Kelly reported ill after the Test and T.R.McKibbin was reluctant to play. The selectors named H.A.Evers, J.Marsh and A.L.Newell as standbyes and invited S.W.Austin to replace McKibbin. Ultimately Newell replaced Howell, Kelly was fit to play and McKibbin made himself available. Victoria were forced to omit Murray from their twelve due to a lacerated leg sustained at a seaside accident on the morning of the match. The match did not get under way until 2.00pm, owing to the arrival only that morning of those who played in the Adelaide Test. Donnan (56 in 173 minutes, 6 fours), Noble (56 in 87 minutes, 8 fours) and Gregory (72 in 135 minutes, 8 fours) hit half-centuries in the first innings. Frequent showers prevented any play on the second day and further rain that night made the pitch difficult to bat on for the remainder of the game. Worrall's fine century (103 in 160 minutes, 14 fours) included a chance at 43 to Trumper off Newell; he was last out having batted through the innings. Newell, brought in to replace J.J.Ferris who had remained in Adelaide, captured a career-best 8 for 56 including the wickets of McMichael, Trumble and Trott in a five-ball spell within one over (WW00W). *Wisden* incorrectly gives NSW (1) McKibbin 12, extras 3, Trumble 0/22; Vic (2) Bruce 38, Noble 2/39, total 7/180, bowling of Donnan omitted. Last first-class appearance by T.W.Garrett. *SMH* and *T&C* give NSW (1) Donnan b McLeod (off pads), other sources st Johns (off wk pads). Sources: *Wisden, VCA Report, Sydney Referee, Sydney Morning Herald, Town & Country Journal, Sydney Daily Telegraph.*

NEW SOUTH WALES

F.A.Iredale	c Trumble b Roche	13	c Bruce b Trumble	10
H.Donnan	st Johns b McLeod	56	st Johns b Roche	19
M.A.Noble	b Trott	56	c Worrall b Trumble	1
S.E.Gregory	c Graham b Roche	72	st Johns b Trott	15
A.C.K.Mackenzie	run out (Giller/Johns)	6	c Giller b Trott	0
V.T.Trumper	c & b McLeod	12	c Roche b Trott	12
L.W.Pye	c Trumble b Roche	9	lbw b Trott	9
†J.J.Kelly	c Trumble b Roche	12	c McMichael b Roche	5
*T.W.Garrett	c Trumble b Roche	3	c Stuckey b Trott	2
A.L.Newell	c Graham b Roche	19	not out	1
T.R.McKibbin	not out	13	c Graham b Roche	0
Extras	(w2)	2	(b10, lb6)	16
Total	(124.0 overs, 320 mins)	273	(25.2 overs, 80 mins)	90

VICTORIA

C.E.McLeod	c & b Newell	31	b Newell	4
J.Worrall	c Kelly b McKibbin	103	c Trumper b McKibbin	33
H.Graham	c Mackenzie b McKibbin	3	c Mackenzie b McKibbin	14
S.A.McMichael	b Newell	1	c Kelly b Noble	30
H.Trumble	b Newell	0	b McKibbin	4
*G.H.S.Trott	c Kelly b Newell	0	c Garrett b Noble	24
W.Bruce	c Trumper b Newell	9	c Gregory b McKibbin	37
J.F.Giller	c Pye b Newell	0	not out	11
J.H.Stuckey	c Kelly b Newell	31	not out	14
†A.E.Johns	st Kelly b Newell	0		
W.Roche	not out	0		
Extras	(b6, lb2, nb1)	9	(b7, nb1)	8
Total	(50.3 overs, 160 mins)	187	(55.0 overs, 165 mins) (7 wkts)	179

VICTORIA	O	M	R	W	w,nb		O	M	R	W	w,nb
McLeod	39	12	88	2	-,-						
Giller	30	13	48	0	2,-						
Roche	32	8	88	6	-,-	(1)	13.2	2	29	3	-,-
Trott	12	1	24	1	-,-	(3)	8	0	21	5	-,-
Trumble	11	3	23	0	-,-	(2)	4	0	24	2	-,-

NEW SOUTH WALES	O	M	R	W	w,nb		O	M	R	W	w,nb
Noble	10	1	42	0	-,-	(4)	13	3	38	2	-,-
McKibbin	15.3	1	68	2	-,-	(3)	18	1	64	4	-,-
Newell	19	4	56	8	-,1	(1)	17	5	45	1	-,-
Pye	6	3	12	0	-,-						
Donnan						(2)	7	2	24	0	-,1

FALL OF WICKETS

Wkt	NSW 1st	VIC 1st	NSW 2nd	VIC 2nd
1st	27	72	13	15
2nd	109	75	26	44
3rd	148	92	48	63
4th	177	92	48	69
5th	210	92	72	106
6th	220	126	72	114
7th	230	128	83	159
8th	234	187	89	-
9th	247	187	90	-
10th	273	187	90	-

VICTORIA v TASMANIA

Played at the Melbourne Cricket Ground on January 22, 24, 25, 1898. (Timeless match)
Toss : Victoria.   Result : TASMANIA WON BY 72 RUNS.
Debuts: Victoria - G.Beacham, F.J.Wright (both f/c). Tasmania - F.S.Pictet, J.Ramsay, W.G.Ward (all f/c).
12th men: P.A.McAlister (Vic) and R.J.Hawson (Tas).
Umpires: E.Barrass and C.E.Over.
Attendances: 2200, 200, 200.   Total: About 2600.   Receipts: No figures published.
Close of play: 1st day Vic 107 all out; 2nd day Vic (2) 0/13 (Wilson 10, Sutherland 1).

Tasmania were unable to consider J.E.Bingham, G.E.Palmer, G.S.Pennefather and E.A.C.Windsor (all unavailable for various reasons). Rain on the day before the match saturated the pitch and prompted Houston to insert the visitors; the wicket improved as the game progressed. Tasmania's Test men, Eady and Burn, played leading roles in their side's victory. Burn topscored in each innings with 45 (83 minutes, 2 fours) and 88 (175 minutes, 11 fours), while Eady (12 for 161) bowled unchanged throughout. Gatehouse (46 in 105 minutes, 4 fours) and McAllen (53 not out in 130 minutes, 5 fours) also batted well for Tasmania and shared the wicket-keeping (Gatehouse kept in the first and McAllen in second innings). Rush (59 in 83 minutes, 4 fours) scored Victoria's only half-century. Pictet's first-class career was fleeting: playing in his only match he fell and fractured a wrist attempting to field a ball midway through Victoria's innings on the first day. Maplestone substituted for the rest of the first innings (catching a team-mate) and Hawson did so in the second innings. The fall of the first four wickets in Vic (1) were not reported in any source, but newspaper commentary suggests they could well have fallen at 1, 7, 7, 13. Sources: *VCA Report, STCA Report, The Age, The Argus, The Herald, The Australasian, The Leader, The Sportsman.*

TASMANIA

Batsman	Dismissal	Runs		Dismissal	Runs
C.J.Eady	c Kemp b Maplestone	26		c Wilson b Kemp	7
G.H.Gatehouse	c Beacham b Kemp	20		c Hastings b Maplestone	46
J.H.Savigny	c & b Wright	0	(6)	st Hastings b Beacham	21
E.Maxwell	c Houston b Kemp	0	(3)	b Maplestone	0
*E.J.K.Burn	c Beacham b Maplestone	45		lbw b Maplestone	88
T.A.Tabart	lbw b Kemp	13	(4)	b Maplestone	12
J.Ramsay	b Kemp	0	(9)	run out	0
W.G.Ward	c Hastings b Kemp	2	(7)	st Hastings b Houston	17
†C.McAllen	c Stuckey b Maplestone	0	(8)	not out	53
F.S.Pictet	lbw b Beacham	17		absent injured	-
C.W.Butler	not out	14	(10)	c Stuckey b Beacham	5
Extras	(b13, lb4)	17		(b6, lb3)	9
Total	(65.3 overs, 175 mins)	154		(95.4 overs, 250 mins)	258

VICTORIA

Batsman	Dismissal	Runs		Dismissal	Runs
C.G.Wilson	run out	8		lbw b Burn	45
D.Sutherland	b Eady	0		b Eady	29
E.R.Rush	b Eady	5		c & b Eady	59
H.C.Maplestone	b Eady	0	(8)	c Burn b Savigny	18
W.A.Tarrant	c Savigny b Eady	12		run out (Ramsay/McAllen)	7
*R.S.Houston	c Ward b Eady	25		c Burn b Eady	14
G.Stuckey	b Eady	17		c Savigny b Eady	6
F.J.Wright	c Burn b Eady	11	(4)	lbw b Burn	0
G.Beacham	b Ward	0	(10)	not out	9
†T.J.Hastings	not out	19	(9)	lbw b Savigny	2
B.C.E.Kemp	c sub (H.C.Maplestone) b Ward	9		c Burn b Eady	33
Extras	(b1)	1		(b5, lb5, w1)	11
Total	(31.5 overs, 90 mins)	107		(74.4 overs, 205 mins)	233

VICTORIA	O	M	R	W	w,nb		O	M	R	W	w,nb		FALL OF WICKETS				
														TAS	VIC	TAS	VIC
Kemp	27	6	53	5	-,-	(2)	21	4	79	1	-,-	Wkt	1st	1st	1st	2nd	2nd
Beacham	5.3	0	29	1	-,-	(3)	19.4	4	45	2	-,-	1st	33	1*	15	70
Wright	14	3	28	1	-,-	(4)	14	3	29	0	-,-	2nd	33	7*	16	98
Maplestone	19	9	27	3	-,-	(1)	31	11	64	4	-,-	3rd	34	7*	46	98
Houston							10	0	32	1	-,-	4th	89	13*	94	112
												5th	116	25	131	148
TASMANIA	O	M	R	W	w,nb		O	M	R	W	w,nb	6th	118	54	165	151
Eady	16	2	57	7	-,-		37.4	7	104	5	-,-	7th	118	74	232	178
Maxwell	9	4	28	0	-,-		5	0	21	0	-,-	8th	120	79	234	183
Ward	6.5	1	21	2	-,-		9	1	22	0	1,-	9th	120	79	258	192
Burn							17	3	50	2	-,-	10th	154	107	-	233
Savigny							6	0	25	2	-,-					

AUSTRALIA v ENGLAND (4th Test)

Played at the Melbourne Cricket Ground on January 29, 31, February 1, 2, 1898. (Timeless match)
Toss : Australia.   Result : AUSTRALIA WON BY EIGHT WICKETS.
Debuts: Nil.
12th men: J.Worrall (Aust) and J.H.Board (Eng).
Umpires: C.Bannerman and J.Phillips.
Attendances: 19600, 15569, 11979, 6900.   Total: 54,048.   Receipts: £2282.
Close of play: 1st day Aust 7/275 (Hill 182, Kelly 22); 2nd day Eng (2) 1/7 (Briggs 4); 3rd day Eng (2) 7/254 (Mason 25, Storer 24).

England were unable to consider G.H.Hirst (strained side). Richardson, whose only wickets resulted from successive deliveries, combined with Hearne to make early inroads into the Australian first innings before a record seventh-wicket stand of 165 between the 20-year-old Hill (188 in 305 minutes, 1 five and 21 fours) and Trumble (46 in 152 minutes, 4 fours) retrieved the situation. Hill's sole chance, a difficult one, was to Storer off Hearne when 65. Druce kept wicket while Storer bowled, and it was later found that Storer had broken a finger while keeping on the first day. Druce kept for all but the first four overs in the second innings. Hot, sultry weather produced most oppressive conditions which greatly affected the Englishmen. Smoke from nearby bushfires mingled with the heat haze to make batting more difficult and only Ranjitsinhji (55 in 97 minutes, 2 fours) exceeded 50. MacLaren, the next highest scorer, claimed that a fly in his eye caused his dismissal (he was caught at short leg). McLeod (64 not out in 99 minutes, 1 six and 5 fours) guided his team to victory on the final day. Richardson strained muscles in his side during the first innings and was not risked with the ball in the second, though he did field. Sources: *Wisden, The Age, The Argus, The Herald, The Australasian, The Leader, The Sportsman.*

AUSTRALIA

C.E.McLeod	b Hearne	1	not out		64
J.Darling	c Hearne b Richardson	12	c Druce b Hayward		29
C.Hill	c Stoddart b Hearne	188	lbw b Hayward		0
S.E.Gregory	b Richardson	0	not out		21
F.A.Iredale	c Storer b Hearne	0			
M.A.Noble	c & b Hearne	4			
*G.H.S.Trott	c Storer b Hearne	7			
H.Trumble	c Mason b Storer	46			
†J.J.Kelly	c Storer b Briggs	32			
E.Jones	c Hayward b Hearne	20			
W.P.Howell	not out	9			
Extras	(b3, w1)	4	(nb1)		1
Total	(101.4 overs, 341 mins)	323	(39.4 overs, 99 mins) (2 wkts)		115

ENGLAND

A.C.MacLaren	b Howell	8	(3) c Iredale b Trumble		45
E.Wainwright	c Howell b Trott	6	(1) c McLeod b Jones		2
K.S.Ranjitsinhji	c Iredale b Trumble	24	(4) b Noble		55
T.W.Hayward	c Gregory b Noble	22	(5) c & b Trumble		25
N.F.Druce	lbw b Jones	24	(7) c Howell b Trott		16
†W.Storer	c & b Trumble	2	(9) c Darling b McLeod		26
J.R.Mason	b Jones	30	(8) b Howell		26
*A.E.Stoddart	c Darling b Jones	17	(6) b Jones		25
J.Briggs	not out	21	(2) c Darling b Howell		23
J.T.Hearne	c Trott b Jones	0	not out		4
T.Richardson	b Trott	20	c Trumble b McLeod		2
Extras		-	(b1, lb11, w1, nb1)		14
Total	(61.1 overs, 195 mins)	174	(114.2 overs, 318 mins)		263

ENGLAND	O	M	R	W	w,nb		O	M	R	W	w,nb
Richardson	26	2	102	2	-,-						
Hearne	35.4	13	98	6	-,-	(1)	7	3	19	0	-,-
Hayward	10	4	24	0	-,-		10	4	24	2	-,-
Briggs	17	4	38	1	-,-	(2)	6	1	31	0	-,-
Stoddart	6	1	22	0	1,-						
Storer	4	0	24	1	-,-						
Wainwright	3	1	11	0	-,-	(4)	9	2	21	0	-,-
Mason						(5)	4	1	10	0	-,1
Ranjitsinhji						(6)	3.4	1	9	0	-,-

AUSTRALIA	O	M	R	W	w,nb		O	M	R	W	w,nb
Howell	16	7	34	1	-,-		30	12	58	2	-,-
Trott	11.1	1	33	2	-,-	(3)	12	2	39	1	-,-
Noble	7	1	21	1	-,-	(5)	16	6	31	1	-,1
Trumble	15	4	30	2	-,-		23	6	40	2	-,-
Jones	12	2	56	4	-,-	(2)	25	7	70	2	1,-
McLeod							8.2	4	11	2	-,-

FALL OF WICKETS

	AUST	ENG	AUST	ENG
Wkt	1st	1st	2nd	2nd
1st	1	14	7	50
2nd	25	16	63	56
3rd	25	60	91	-
4th	26	60	147	-
5th	32	67	157	-
6th	58	103	192	-
7th	223	121	209	-
8th	283	148	257	-
9th	303	148	257	-
10th	323	174	263	-

NEW SOUTH WALES v A.E.STODDART'S ENGLAND XI

Played at Sydney Cricket Ground on February, 5, 7, 8, 9, 10, 11, 1898. (Timeless match)
Toss : New South Wales.   Result : NEW SOUTH WALES WON BY 239 RUNS.
Debuts: Nil.
12th men: A.Coningham (NSW). No 12th available for Eng XI.
Umpires: C.Bannerman and J.Phillips.
Attendances:11382, 7796, 4949, 3640, 3361, 2933.   Total: 34,061.   Receipts: £1427.
Close of play: 1st day NSW 7/297 (Pye 40); 2nd day Eng (1) 6/227 (Druce 47, Briggs 6); 3rd day NSW (2) 2/140 (Donnan 55, Pye 23);
    4th day NSW (2) 8/452 (Newell 54, McKibbin 31); 5th day Eng (2) 1/258 (MacLaren 135, Ranjitsinhji 42).

The Englishmen had difficulty fielding eleven players. T.Richardson (strained side) and W.Storer (broken finger) could not be considered while MacLaren ("slight indisposition") and Hirst (strained side) had to play, Hirst not being able to bowl. MacLaren batted down the order in the first innings and Coningham fielded for him in the New South Wales second innings. Batsmen dominated, 14 innings of 50 or more being recorded, and the match aggregate of 1739 runs was a new record for all first-class cricket. Howell, batting at No. 11, scored 48 (44 minutes, 1 five and 7 fours) and a remarkable 95 (59 minutes, 4 fives and 14 fours), sharing his second century partnership for the New South Wales tenth wicket in two seasons. Other notable efforts were: Mackenzie (sole first-class century - 130 in 145 minutes, 21 fours and 52 in 55 minutes, 11 fours), Pye (80 not out in 150 minutes, 14 fours), Donnan (59 in 175 minutes), Gregory (171 in 227 minutes, 23 fours), Newell (career-best 68 not out in 210 minutes) and Noble (12 wickets for 248) for New South Wales and Wainwright (50 in 68 minutes and 68 in 119 minutes, 11 fours), Hayward (63 in 110 minutes, 9 fours and 64 in 112 minutes, 9 fours), Druce (109 in 205 minutes, 19 fours) and MacLaren (61 in 85 minutes, 10 fours and 140 in 212 minutes, 1 five and 20 fours) for England. *Wisden* incorrectly gives Eng (2) Mason 8, Wainwright 64, Hayward 62, Hirst 5, Druce 11, Stoddart 6, Howell 3/64, Newell 0/20. Sources: *Wisden, Sydney Referee, Sydney Morning Herald, Town & Country Journal, Sydney Mail, Sydney Daily Telegraph.*

NEW SOUTH WALES

Batsman	Dismissal 1	Runs		Dismissal 2	Runs
H.Donnan	c Board b Wainwright	41		c Hirst b Hearne	59
F.A.Iredale	c Stoddart b Briggs	2		b Hearne	7
M.A.Noble	c MacLaren b Hayward	34	(6)	b Hearne	8
A.C.K.Mackenzie	c Hayward b Hearne	130	(3)	c sub (A.Coningham) b Mason	52
*S.E.Gregory	c & b Mason	25		c Hayward b Briggs	171
V.T.Trumper	b Mason	4	(7)	b Hearne	23
L.W.Pye	not out	80	(4)	b Hearne	31
†J.J.Kelly	b Stoddart	14		c Hirst b Mason	4
A.L.Newell	c Hirst b Stoddart	6		not out	68
T.R.McKibbin	c Druce b Briggs	20		b Hearne	39
W.P.Howell	b Mason	48		c Wainwright b Mason	95
Extras	(b4, lb2, w3, nb2)	11		(b10, lb2, w1, nb4)	17
Total	(130.2 overs, 355 mins)	415		(188.0 overs, 495 mins)	574

A.E.STODDART'S ENGLAND XI

Batsman	Dismissal 1	Runs		Dismissal 2	Runs
J.R.Mason	c Howell b Noble	11	(7)	c Gregory b Noble	6
E.Wainwright	c Howell b Noble	50		b McKibbin	68
K.S.Ranjitsinhji	c Gregory b Noble	37		c McKibbin b Howell	44
T.W.Hayward	c Howell b Noble	63		not out	64
G.H.Hirst	c Newell b Noble	4		c Gregory b Noble	1
N.F.Druce	c Noble b Trumper	109		c Kelly b Noble	12
*A.E.Stoddart	c Iredale b McKibbin	5	(8)	b Noble	5
J.Briggs	c Mackenzie b McKibbin	18	(9)	c & b Noble	0
A.C.MacLaren	b Noble	61	(1)	b Howell	140
†J.H.Board	c Mackenzie b McKibbin	14		b Noble	9
J.T.Hearne	not out	6		b Howell	1
Extras	(b4, w3, nb2)	9		(b11, lb1, nb1)	13
Total	(128.4 overs, 350 mins)	387		(118.1 overs, 320 mins)	363

ENGLAND XI	O	M	R	W	w,nb		O	M	R	W	w,nb
Hearne	32	13	96	1	-,-		54	18	126	6	-,-
Briggs	39	13	98	2	1,-	(3)	36	10	101	1	-,-
Hayward	15	3	58	1	-,-	(5)	34	4	106	0	-,1
Wainwright	14	4	32	1	1,-	(7)	11	2	49	0	-,-
Mason	12.2	0	53	3	-,1	(4)	34	10	120	3	1,-
Ranjitsinhji	5	1	17	0	1,1	(2)	10	2	32	0	-,3
Stoddart	13	4	50	2	-,-	(6)	8	1	22	0	-,-
Druce							1	0	1	0	-,-

NEW SOUTH WALES	O	M	R	W	w,nb		O	M	R	W	w,nb
Noble	57	15	131	6	1,1		37	13	117	6	-,1
Howell	12	2	45	0	-,-	(5)	24.1	4	61	3	-,-
McKibbin	27.4	4	108	3	1,-	(2)	25	5	99	1	-,-
Newell	11	1	36	0	1,1	(6)	4	1	23	0	-,-
Pye	11	2	28	0	-,-	(3)	16	6	37	0	-,-
Donnan	3	1	9	0	-,-	(7)	7	3	9	0	-,-
Trumper	7	3	21	1	-,-	(4)	5	4	4	0	-,-

FALL OF WICKETS

Wkt	NSW 1st	ENG 1st	NSW 2nd	ENG 2nd
1st	14	28	19	172
2nd	73	94	106	262
3rd	97	99	151	271
4th	178	112	156	278
5th	204	205	167	312
6th	264	212	229	320
7th	297	247	242	344
8th	311	344	411	344
9th	334	372	465	354
10th	415	387	574	363

VICTORIA v SOUTH AUSTRALIA (Shield Match 5)

Played at the Melbourne Cricket Ground on February 11, 12, 14, 15, 1898. (Timeless match)
Toss : Victoria.   Result : VICTORIA WON BY 26 RUNS.
Debuts: South Australia - V.Hugo (f/c).
12th men: F.J.Laver (Vic) and A.E.Green (SA).
Umpires: R.M.Crockett and G.E.Downs.
Attendances: 1000, 4212, 1000, 500.   Total: About 6712.   Receipts: £178.
Close of play: 1st day Vic 5/320 (McMichael 72, Bruce 24); 2nd day SA 6/216 (Hill 54, Evans 9); 3rd day SA (2) 1/3 (Drew 1).

A narrow victory ensured Victoria won their third Sheffield Shield title. For the first time in the six years of competition George Giffen was absent from the South Australian side. He made himself unavailable for the trip after the SACA refused to meet his terms. Victoria chose to bat despite the pitch being damp in the pre-lunch session of the first day because of a burst water pipe, "hot weather without rain" (*Age*) preceding the match. Half-centuries by Worrall (79 in 100 minutes, 13 fours), McMichael (career-best 97 in 166 minutes, 1 five and 10 fours), Trott (68 in 84 minutes, 9 fours) and Stuckey (52 not out in 128 minutes, 3 fours) gave Victoria - briefly - their biggest Shield score. Graham was the victim of a freak first-ball dismissal by Jones who struck him on the foot: as he flexed his leg in pain, the ball shot high into the air and landed on the popping crease before spinning back onto his stumps. Hill (135 in 198 minutes, 11 fours) replied for South Australia with a century which, with rapid half-centuries from Lyons (64 in 66 minutes, 2 fives and 5 fours) and Jones (66 in 63 minutes, 1 five and 7 fours), kept the visitors in contention. The second-innings collapse of both teams was a complete surprise and could not be attributed to any deterioration in the wicket, which the *Age* correspondent considered to be still "perfect". Jones dismissed McLeod, Trumble, Graham and McMichael to claim 4 for 6 in a four-over spell. *O'Reilly* incorrectly gives SA (2) Hill c McLeod. Sources: *Wisden, C.B.O'Reilly, VCA Report, The Age, The Argus, The Herald, The Australasian, The Leader.*

VICTORIA

C.E.McLeod	st McKenzie b Evans	32	b Jones		4
J.Worrall	b Jones	79	lbw b Evans		12
H.Trumble	c Darling b Evans	43	b Jones		8
S.A.McMichael	b Reedman	97	c McKenzie b Jones		7
H.Graham	b Jones	0	b Jones		1
*G.H.S.Trott	lbw b Lyons	68	c Lyons b Evans		11
W.Bruce	c Darling b Evans	25	c Reedman b Hugo		20
J.H.Stuckey	not out	52	c Jarvis b Lyons		28
J.F.Giller	c Darling b Reedman	8	c McKenzie b Hugo		6
†A.E.Johns	c Drew b Jarvis	7	not out		3
W.Roche	run out (Darling/McKenzie)	9	c Hill b Hugo		8
Extras	(b5, lb1, w2)	8	(b1, nb3)		4
Total	(128.5 overs, 395 mins)	428	(40.4 overs, 130 mins)		112

SOUTH AUSTRALIA

J.Darling	c Worrall b Trumble	34	(3) b Trumble	16
*J.J.Lyons	c McLeod b Trott	64	(5) c Johns b Roche	4
C.Hill	b Trumble	135	(4) c McMichael b Roche	29
J.C.Reedman	c Worrall b Trott	19	(1) c Giller b Trott	2
A.Jarvis	b Roche	10	(6) b Roche	31
W.F.Giffen	c McLeod b Giller	11	(7) c Trumble b Roche	6
T.M.Drew	c Giller b Trumble	2	(2) c Giller b Trumble	9
A.E.Evans	run out (Giller)	28	b Trumble	0
E.Jones	b Giller	66	lbw b Trumble	4
V.Hugo	b McLeod	9	st Johns b Roche	10
†J.McKenzie	not out	0	not out	6
Extras	(b11, lb3, w2)	16	(b2, w1)	3
Total	(104.1 overs, 297 mins)	394	(60.0 overs, 171 mins)	120

SOUTH AUSTRALIA	O	M	R	W	w,nb		O	M	R	W	w,nb
Jones	56.5	12	154	2	-,-		15	2	43	4	-,-
Hugo	10	2	41	0	-,-	(4)	5.4	1	11	3	-,2
Evans	28	3	110	3	1,-	(2)	14	4	40	2	-,-
Drew	1	0	2	0	-,-						
Jarvis	10	2	39	1	1,-						
Reedman	16	2	54	2	-,-						
Lyons	7	0	20	1	-,-	(3)	6	1	14	1	-,1

VICTORIA	O	M	R	W	w,nb		O	M	R	W	w,nb
Roche	30	6	86	1	-,-	(3)	29	10	58	5	1,-
McLeod	18.1	4	75	1	1,-						
Trumble	28	4	120	3	-,-	(4)	26	11	39	4	-,-
Trott	11	0	59	2	-,-	(1)	4	0	20	1	-,-
Giller	17	5	38	2	1,-	(2)	1	1	0	0	-,-

FALL OF WICKETS

Wkt	VIC 1st	SA 1st	VIC 2nd	SA 2nd
1st	81	101	15	3
2nd	138	111	21	25
3rd	158	145	24	32
4th	158	164	26	39
5th	287	194	39	79
6th	322	201	47	87
7th	359	278	87	90
8th	373	357	99	102
9th	401	394	99	104
10th	428	394	112	120

NEW SOUTH WALES v SOUTH AUSTRALIA (Shield Match 6)

Played at Sydney Cricket Ground on February 18, 19, 21, 22, 1898. (Timeless match)
Toss : South Australia.   Result : SOUTH AUSTRALIA WON BY 295 RUNS.
Debuts: Nil.
12th Men: G.J.Youill (NSW) and T.M.Drew (SA).
Umpires: C.Bannerman and G.E.Downs.
Attendances: 1078, 4020, 1240, 951.   Total: 7289.   Receipts: £342.
Close of Play: 1st day SA 289 all out; 2nd day SA (2) 2/48 (Hill 16, Reedman 6); 3rd day SA (2) 6/387 (Jarvis 142, Evans 8).

South Australia defeated New South Wales at home for the first time in the Sheffield Shield competition at their sixth try. Hill (116) became the first batsman to aggregate 1000 first-class runs in an Australian season and was followed three weeks later by two members of the touring team in MacLaren and Ranjitsinhji. Hill's chanceless 170 (205 minutes, 25 fours) combined with Jarvis's sole first-class hundred (154 in 250 minutes, 23 fours - difficult chance at 45 to Kelly off Coningham) to put South Australia in a winning position on the third day, the pair adding 193 for the fourth wicket. New South Wales, whose half-centuries were scored by Trumper (68 in 130 minutes, 7 fours), Gregory (83 in 95 minutes, 9 fours) and Coningham (51 in 66 minutes, 5 fours), collapsed on a still-perfect wicket on the fourth day to the unchanged Jones and Evans, the former bowling with great pace (11 wickets for 202). Youill fielded for Coningham, who arrived at the ground late, in the pre-lunch session on the last day and Kelly handed the gloves to Evers during the same session to rest in the field. On the first day Darling (75 in 150 minutes, 11 fours) and Reedman (67 in 106 minutes, 11 fours) had hit fifties for South Australia. Coningham (originally 12th man) was brought in to replace W.P.Howell (injured leg), F.A.Iredale earlier indicating that he wished to be rested from the New South Wales side. Sources: *Wisden, C.B.O'Reilly, Sydney Referee, Sydney Morning Herald, Town & Country Journal, Sydney Daily Telegraph*.

SOUTH AUSTRALIA

J.Darling	c Pye b Noble	75		b Noble	16
*J.J.Lyons	c Gregory b Noble	28		c McKibbin b Noble	5
C.Hill	c Noble b McKibbin	0		b Donnan	170
J.C.Reedman	c Gregory b Noble	67		b Trumper	21
A.Jarvis	c Evers b Noble	20		c & b Noble	154
W.F.Giffen	b Trumper	38		b Newell	1
A.E.Evans	run out (Donnan/Kelly)	1	(8)	c sub (G.J.Youill) b McKibbin	32
A.E.Green	not out	35	(7)	b Newell	8
E.Jones	b Trumper	5		c & b Noble	19
V.Hugo	b Trumper	1		run out (Newell/Evers)	0
†J.McKenzie	c Newell b Trumper	4		not out	0
Extras	(b4, lb2, w5, nb4)	_15_		(b1, lb5, w7, nb3)	_16_
Total	(88.5 overs, 252 mins)	289		(125.0 overs, 365 mins)	442

NEW SOUTH WALES

M.A.Noble	b Jones	27	(5)	c & b Evans	38
V.T.Trumper	run out (Hill/Jones)	68		st McKenzie b Evans	7
*S.E.Gregory	c Evans b Jones	83		b Jones	11
A.C.K.Mackenzie	b Evans	6	(6)	b Jones	9
H.Donnan	c & b Reedman	34	(1)	b Jones	8
L.W.Pye	b Jones	9	(4)	c & b Evans	2
H.A.Evers	c McKenzie b Jones	4	(9)	b Jones	10
A.L.Newell	b Jones	4	(7)	c Lyons b Jones	0
A.Coningham	b Jones	51	(8)	run out (Evans)	24
†J.J.Kelly	not out	9		not out	7
T.R.McKibbin	c Giffen b Hugo	1		c Darling b Evans	8
Extras	(b5, lb6, nb3)	_14_		(b1, w1)	_2_
Total	(80.2 overs, 220 mins)	310		(37.5 overs, 115 mins)	126

NEW SOUTH WALES	O	M	R	W	w,nb		O	M	R	W	w,nb					
Noble	36	10	95	4	4,-		42	8	164	4	6,-				FALL OF WICKETS	
McKibbin	23	5	89	1	1,3		19	3	72	1	1,-	Wkt	1st	1st	2nd	2nd
Coningham	10	4	31	0	-,-	(4)	9	2	40	0	-,-		SA	NSW	SA	NSW
Pye	6	0	22	0	-,-	(5)	5	1	19	0	-,-	1st	41	32	9	14
Newell	7	5	5	0	-,1	(6)	23	12	37	2	-,1	2nd	46	175	40	22
Trumper	6.5	1	32	4	-,-	(3)	16	3	53	1	-,-	3rd	173	191	108	24
Donnan							11	2	41	1	-,2	4th	186	197	301	28
												5th	212	208	303	51
												6th	213	212	353	51
SOUTH AUSTRALIA	O	M	R	W	w,nb		O	M	R	W	w,nb	7th	254	218	408	99
Jones	35	6	140	6	-,-		19	4	62	5	1,-	8th	260	276	438	102
Evans	24	4	73	1	-,-		18.5	3	62	4	-,-	9th	263	309	442	117
Hugo	7.2	0	36	1	-,-							10th	289	310	442	126
Reedman	14	3	47	1	-,3											

COMBINED QUEENSLAND & VICTORIA v A.E.STODDART'S ENGLAND XI

Played at Brisbane Cricket Ground (Woolloongabba) on February 19, 21 - 22 (no play), 1898. (Timeless match)
Toss : England XI   Result : MATCH DRAWN.
Debuts: Combined XI - A.H.V.Hewitt (f/c).
12th Men: None named.
Umpires: D.L.Miller and J.Phillips.
Attendances: 5000, no play, no play.   Total: About 5000.   Receipts: £270.
Close of Play: 1st day Eng 5/133 (Druce 5, Hirst 3); 2nd day no play.

Persistent rain before the match left the wicket soft and the outfield sodden. Play did not get under way until after the scheduled luncheon adjournment and drizzle held up the game after about an hour's cricket, preventing a resumption until 4.30pm. The slow outfield militated against quick scoring and Ranjitsinhji found the boundary only twice in 95 minutes at the crease. The batsmen were handicapped late in the day by poor light but pressed on. After no play at all on the second and third days it was decided to abandon the game and allow the Englishmen and the Victorians to return to Sydney on Wednesday, February 23rd. The match had been originally scheduled to be played to a finish. A.E.Johns (Victoria) had been invited to play but was unable to make the trip because of business commitments. W.Roche (Victoria) and T.Byrne (Queensland) withdrew through illness and were replaced by Hewitt and Long respectively. Sources: *Wisden, The Leader, Sydney Morning Herald, Brisbane Courier, Queensland Times, The Queenslander.*

A.E.STODDART'S ENGLAND XI

*A.C.MacLaren	c Giller b Hewitt	20
J.R.Mason	c Trott b Giller	27
K.S.Ranjitsinhji	c Hewitt b Giller	33
T.W.Hayward	b Hewitt	8
W.Storer	c Donahoo b Worrall	32
N.F.Druce	not out	5
G.H.Hirst	not out	3
J.Briggs	)	
J.T.Hearne	) did not bat	
T.Richardson	)	
†J.H.Board	)	
Extras	(lb5)	5
Total	(57.0 overs, 153 mins) (5 wkts)	133

COMBINED XI

*G.H.S.Trott
W.Bruce
J.F.Giller
H.Graham
J.Worrall
†W.F.Bradley
S.J.Donahoo
A.H.V.Hewitt
W.Hoare
S.P.Jones
T.T.T.Long

COMBINED XI	O	M	R	W	w,nb
Hewitt	22	2	54	2	-,-
Giller	28	5	56	2	-,-
Worrall	7	1	18	1	-,-

FALL OF WICKETS	
	ENG
Wkt	1st
1st	22
2nd	58
3rd	75
4th	113
5th	127
6th	-
7th	-
8th	-
9th	-
10th	-

AUSTRALIA v ENGLAND (5th Test)

Played at Sydney Cricket Ground on February 26, 28, March 1, 2, 1898. (Timeless match)
Toss : England.   Result : AUSTRALIA WON BY SIX WICKETS.
Debuts: Nil.

12th men: F.A.Iredale (Aust) and J.H.Board (Eng).
Umpires: C.Bannerman and J.Phillips.
Attendances: 36222, 19435, 15647, 13070.   Total: 84,374.   Receipts: £3291.
Close of play: 1st day Eng 5/301 (Druce 43, Hirst 43); 2nd day Aust 5/184 (Noble 31, Trott 14); 3rd day Eng (2) 9/172 (Hearne 3)

Iredale was omitted from the Australian team at his own request, stating lack of current fitness as his reason. Stoddart stood down from the England XI. He had had a miserable tour, beginning with illness and followed soon after by the news of the death of his mother. He was never able to run into any sort of form. Even batting from the English top order, including fifties from MacLaren (65 in 113 minutes, 8 fours) and Druce (64 in 114 minutes, 10 fours), and some inspired fast bowling from Richardson saw them with a first-innings advantage of 96. McLeod (64 in 163 minutes, 8 fours) topscored for Australia. However, the loss of MacLaren to the first ball of the second innings initiated a collapse from which the visitors never really recovered. Set 275 to win, the Australians lost McLeod and Hill early. Darling then proceeded to dominate the English attack. He scored 160 in 171 minutes (30 fours) and gave two chances (17 and 58). He brought up his hundred in 91 minutes - the fastest yet in Test cricket - and hit 80 of those runs in boundaries. He was well supported by Worrall (62 in 121 minutes, 9 fours) in a third-wicket stand of 193. Druce kept wicket while Storer bowled in the first innings. Sources: *Wisden, The Leader, Sydney Referee, Sydney Morning Herald, Town & Country Journal.*

ENGLAND

*A.C.MacLaren	b Trott	65	c Darling b Jones	0
E.Wainwright	c Hill b Trumble	49	b Noble	6
K.S.Ranjitsinhji	c Gregory b Trott	2	lbw b Jones	12
T.W.Hayward	b Jones	47	c Worrall b Trumble	43
†W.Storer	b Jones	44	c Gregory b Trumble	31
N.F.Druce	lbw b Noble	64	c Howell b Trumble	18
G.H.Hirst	b Jones	44	c Trott b Jones	7
J.R.Mason	c Howell b Jones	7	b Trumble	11
J.Briggs	b Jones	0	b Howell	29
J.T.Hearne	not out	2	not out	3
T.Richardson	b Jones	1	b Howell	6
Extras	(b2, lb5, w2, nb1)	10	(lb12)	12
Total	(129.2 overs, 333 mins)	335	(78.1 overs, 215 mins)	178

AUSTRALIA

C.E.McLeod	b Richardson	64	b Hearne	4
J.Darling	c Mason b Briggs	14	c Wainwright b Richardson	160
C.Hill	b Richardson	8	b Richardson	2
J.Worrall	c Ranjitsinhji b Richardson	26	c Hirst b Hayward	62
S.E.Gregory	c Storer b Richardson	21	not out	22
M.A.Noble	c Storer b Richardson	31	not out	15
*G.H.S.Trott	c Ranjitsinhji b Hearne	18		
H.Trumble	b Richardson	12		
†J.J.Kelly	not out	27		
W.P.Howell	c MacLaren b Richardson	10		
E.Jones	c Storer b Richardson	1		
Extras	(b5, w1, nb1)	7	(b6, w1, nb4)	11
Total	(100.1 overs, 280 mins)	239	(62.4 overs, 189 mins) (4 wkts)	276

AUSTRALIA	O	M	R	W	w,nb		O	M	R	W	w,nb		FALL OF WICKETS			
Noble	26	6	57	1	1,1	(2)	15	4	34	1	-,-		ENG	AUST	ENG	AUST
Howell	17	6	40	0	-,-	(3)	6.1	0	22	2	-,-	Wkt	1st	1st	2nd	2nd
Trumble	26	4	67	1	-,-	(5)	24	7	37	4	-,-	1st	111	36	0	23
Jones	26.2	3	82	6	-,-	(1)	26	3	61	3	-,-	2nd	117	45	16	40
Trott	23	6	56	2	1,-	(4)	7	1	12	0	-,-	3rd	119	99	30	233
McLeod	11	4	23	0	-,-							4th	197	132	99	252
												5th	230	137	104	-
ENGLAND	O	M	R	W	w,nb		O	M	R	W	w,nb	6th	308	188	121	-
Richardson	36.1	7	94	8	-,-		21.4	1	110	2	-,-	7th	318	188	137	-
Briggs	17	4	39	1	-,-	(4)	5	1	25	0	-,-	8th	324	221	148	-
Hearne	21	9	40	1	1,-	(2)	15	5	52	1	-,-	9th	334	232	172	-
Storer	5	1	13	0	-,-							10th	335	239	178	-
Mason	13	7	20	0	-,1		11	1	27	0	-,-					
Hayward	4	0	12	0	-,-		3	0	18	1	-,2					
Hirst	4	1	14	0	-,-	(3)	7	0	33	0	1,2					

VICTORIA v A.E.STODDART'S ENGLAND XI

Played at the Melbourne Cricket Ground on March 11, 12, 14, 15, 1898. (Timeless match)
Toss : Victoria.   Result : A.E.STODDART'S ENGLAND XI WON BY SEVEN WICKETS
Debuts: Nil.
12th men: J.Briggs (Eng). No 12th for Vic.
Umpires: R.M.Crockett and J.Phillips.
Attendances: 4580, 11078, 2000, 2400.   Total: 20,058.   Receipts: £662.
Close of play: 1st day Vic 9/283 (Johns 9, Roche 1); 2nd day Eng (1) 7/238 (Storer 24, Board 20); 3rd day Vic (2) 6/99 (Trott 7, Bruce 6).
S.A.McMichael (injured hand) was replaced in the Victorian team by Rush, who had been named 12th man. Briggs fielded during the pre-lunch session on the first day pending the arrival of Ranjitsinhji from Sydney, where he had remained after the Test for treatment for his persistent throat infection. A.E.Stoddart again left himself out of the side. Trumble (career-best 107 in 123 minutes, 14 fours) scored his only first-class century for Victoria and shared a third-wicket stand of 116 with Stuckey (59 in 130 minutes, 7 fours). In the England first innings MacLaren (13) and Ranjitsinhji (41) became the second and third batsmen respectively - and the first touring players - after C.Hill to attain 1000 runs in an Australian first-class season. Hayward (96 in 158 minutes, 2 fives and 8 fours) and Ranji (61 in 122 minutes, 7 fours and 61 not out in 90 minutes) passed 50 for the Englishmen. Rain shortly before the start of play on the third day made batting awkward and showers returned that afternoon to cause interruptions and further liven up the wicket. Bruce retired at 7/116 after being struck on the hand by a ball from Richardson, who made the most of the conditions. *Wisden* incorrectly gives Vic (2) Worrall 14. Sources: *Wisden, VCA Report, The Age, The Argus, The Herald, The Australasian, The Leader.*

VICTORIA

C.E.McLeod	c Board b Mason	16		c Mason b Richardson	26
J.Worrall	st Board b Storer	13		b Richardson	41
H.Trumble	c Hearne b Storer	107	(6)	b Richardson	7
J.H.Stuckey	b Mason	59		c Board b Richardson	2
E.R.Rush	st Board b Storer	0		run out (Board)	0
J.F.Giller	c & b Mason	17	(3)	c Storer b Richardson	1
*G.H.S.Trott	c Hirst b Richardson	39		c MacLaren b Hayward	7
W.Bruce	b Mason	0		retired hurt	12
F.J.Laver	b Richardson	15		not out	19
†A.E.Johns	not out	31		c Board b Mason	4
W.Roche	c & b Storer	24		c Hearne b Mason	4
Extras	(b3, w3, nb1)	7		(b8, lb1)	9
Total	(114.3 overs, 334 mins)	328		(59.5 overs, 165 mins)	132

A.E.STODDART'S ENGLAND XI

*A.C.MacLaren	c Johns b Trott	29	(3)	c Rush b Trumble	21
E.Wainwright	c Trumble b Trott	8		c Laver b Trott	36
K.S.Ranjitsinhji	c Johns b Giller	61	(4)	not out	61
T.W.Hayward	c & b Roche	96	(5)	not out	39
W.Storer	c Bruce b Giller	31			
N.F.Druce	c & b McLeod	0			
G.H.Hirst	c Trumble b Roche	0			
J.R.Mason	b Roche	0			
†J.H.Board	c Johns b Roche	36	(1)	c Laver b Trumble	15
J.T.Hearne	not out	2			
T.Richardson	c Bruce b Roche	10			
Extras	(b4, lb1)	5		(b3, lb8)	11
Total	(107.1 overs, 257 mins)	278		(59.0 overs, 145 mins) (3 wkts)	183

ENGLAND XI	O	M	R	W	w,nb		O	M	R	W	w,nb
Richardson	31	3	104	2	3,-	(4)	18	7	35	5	-,-
Storer	23.3	2	79	4	-,-						
Mason	25	8	53	4	-,-	(2)	6.5	1	12	2	-,-
Hearne	30	14	56	0	-,-	(1)	23	8	42	0	-,-
Hirst	5	0	29	0	-,1						
Wainwright						(3)	5	0	20	0	-,-
Hayward						(5)	7	2	14	1	-,-

VICTORIA	O	M	R	W	w,nb		O	M	R	W	w,nb
Trumble	26	10	54	0	-,-	(2)	18	5	44	2	-,-
Trott	23	4	55	2	-,-	(3)	16	2	51	1	-,-
McLeod	11	3	36	1	-,-	(5)	2	0	5	0	-,-
Roche	22.1	5	77	5	-,-	(1)	5	0	43	0	-,-
Giller	25	11	51	2	-,-	(4)	12	5	19	0	-,-
Laver							6	3	10	0	-,-

FALL OF WICKETS				
	VIC	ENG	VIC	ENG
Wkt	1st	1st	2nd	2nd
1st	25	24	67	35
2nd	60	41	72	63
3rd	176	155	73	82
4th	176	203	77	-
5th	199	206	80	-
6th	218	209	89	-
7th	218	217	99	-
8th	257	265	126	-
9th	274	267	132	-
10th	328	278	-	-

SOUTH AUSTRALIA v A.E.STODDART'S ENGLAND XI

Played at Adelaide Oval on March 19, 21, 22, 23, 1898. (Four-day match)
Toss : England XI.   Result : MATCH DRAWN.
Debuts: Nil.
12th men: H.G.W.Chinner & E.H.Leak (SA emergencies) and J.Briggs (Eng).
Umpires: J.Phillips and T.A.Reeves.
Attendances: 5000, 2500, 2000, 1500.   Total: About 11,000.   Receipts: £414.
Close of play: 1st day SA 0/54 (Darling 28, Lyons 21); 2nd day Eng (2) 0/32 (Wainwright 21, Mason 11); 3rd day Eng (2) 5/350
     (Druce 27, Hirst 29).

The match was restricted to four days to enable the Englishmen to sail for home on March 24th. Stoddart indicated after the third day's play that he would close his innings at lunch on the last day but his team was bowled out before then and Australian first-class cricket had to wait another four years before the first declaration was made. Jones (14 for 237) toiled manfully for the locals to capture the best combined figures in matches between these teams; he bowled almost without a break in the second innings. Darling (88 in 103 minutes, 3 fives and 8 fours and 96 in 183 minutes, 10 fours) scored a fine double for South Australia, Lyons (79 in 128 minutes, 8 fours) and Hill (124 not out in 189 minutes, 18 fours) also batted well. Wainwright (105 in 147 minutes, 9 fours) and Mason (84 in 162 minutes, 5 fours) put on 187 for the England first wicket, Wainwright giving a chance when 69. Storer, who caught Jarvis in the field, kept wicket from the tea interval on the second day after Board received a knock on the fingers; he also kept wickets in the second innings and caught Darling at the wicket. Sources: *Wisden, C.B.O'Reilly, The Age, The Leader, Adelaide Advertiser, South Australian Register.*

A.E.STODDART'S ENGLAND XI

E.Wainwright	b Jones	9	c Hugo b Jones		105
J.R.Mason	b Jones	9	c & b Jones		84
K.S.Ranjitsinhji	b Jones	40	b Hugo		36
T.W.Hayward	b Jones	4	c McKenzie b Jones		40
W.Storer	c Evans b Jones	32	c Reedman b Hugo		18
N.F.Druce	c & b Jones	8	b Jones		33
G.H.Hirst	c McKenzie b Evans	7	c & b Jones		41
*A.E.Stoddart	c Jarvis b Hugo	40	c Giffen b Evans	(9)	16
†J.H.Board	b Jones	59	b Jones	(8)	7
J.T.Hearne	not out	4	not out		4
T.Richardson	c Green b Hugo	4	c Giffen b Jones		4
Extras	(b1, lb5)	6	(b6, lb1, w1, nb3)		11
Total	(83.3 overs, 225 mins)	222	(142.3 overs, 345 mins)		399

SOUTH AUSTRALIA

J.Darling	b Mason	88	c Storer b Mason	(2)	96
*J.J.Lyons	c Board b Mason	79	b Hearne	(1)	27
C.Hill	lbw b Hearne	8	not out		124
J.C.Reedman	c & b Mason	1	not out		15
A.Jarvis	c Storer b Hearne	17			
W.F.Giffen	b Richardson	24			
A.E.Green	c Ranjitsinhji b Richardson	31			
A.E.Evans	b Mason	2			
E.Jones	not out	17			
†J.McKenzie	b Mason	0			
V.Hugo	b Hearne	0			
Extras	(b12, lb1, w6, nb1)	20	(b2, nb3)		5
Total	(88.0 overs, 270 mins)	287	(71.0 overs, 215 mins) (2 wkts)		267

SOUTH AUSTRALIA	O	M	R	W	w,nb		O	M	R	W	w,nb
Jones	35	9	80	7	-,-		67.3	16	157	7	-,-
Evans	30	6	79	1	-,-		18	4	67	1	1,-
Hugo	10.3	3	31	2	-,-		28	6	87	2	-,-
Reedman	7	1	22	0	-,-		11	3	36	0	-,-
Lyons	1	0	4	0	-,-	(6)	9	4	15	0	-,3
Jarvis						(5)	9	1	26	0	-,-

ENGLAND XI	O	M	R	W	w,nb		O	M	R	W	w,nb
Richardson	9	1	48	2	3,-		11	1	51	0	-,-
Hearne	30	10	87	3	-,-		16	2	43	1	-,-
Hirst	10	4	25	0	3,1	(4)	6	0	34	0	-,1
Storer	9	0	49	0	-,-						
Mason	25	10	41	5	-,-	(3)	24	6	74	1	-,2
Hayward	5	1	17	0	-,-	(5)	13	1	60	0	-,-
Board						(6)	1	1	0	0	-,-

FALL OF WICKETS

Wkt	ENG 1st	SA 1st	ENG 2nd	SA 2nd
1st	12	166	187	34
2nd	19	177	193	221
3rd	27	180	245	-
4th	93	185	289	-
5th	105	209	291	-
6th	106	264	366	-
7th	124	270	374	-
8th	201	270	375	-
9th	217	270	392	-
10th	222	287	399	-

An official New Zealand team visited Australia for the first time this season, playing four matches. Only two of these games are considered first-class - those against Victoria and New South Wales. Both ended in heavy defeats for the visitors and only New South Wales fielded a full-strength XI against them.

Victoria retained the Sheffield Shield. They won their first three matches by wide margins to take an unassailable lead on the table, before unexpectedly going down to New South Wales at Sydney in their final game. The pairing of Trumble and McLeod to open the bowling played a major part in Victoria's success. The pair captured 55 of the team's 72 wickets and restricted the opposition scoring to a remarkable extent. New South Wales put themselves out of contention for the Shield by losing both their road matches in December. South Australia had the basis of a strong side - Hill and Darling as batsmen, Jones to head the bowling and Giffen as allrounder - but the support players this season were weak and the side had little depth.

Fresh ground was broken during the summer with the staging of three inaugural meetings. Tasmania visited New South Wales for the first time in December but were completely outclassed. New South Wales had paid the islanders a compliment prior to the match by fielding a full-strength side. Victor Trumper (21) announced himself to the Australian cricket follower with an unforgettable double-century in the mammoth New South Wales total of 839. Queensland played host to South Australia for the first time in January when the Shield side continued on to Brisbane after their engagement in Sydney. Darling and Giffen hit centuries for the visitors and Queensland succumbed by an innings. A South Australian team also visited Western Australia for the first time in April, and the resulting encounter at Perth was the first match of first-class status to be played on Western Australian soil. The locals were unable to mark the occasion with a victory, but nevertheless gave a good account of themselves in losing by four wickets.

A Victorian XI which journeyed to Hobart in January for the annual intercolonial match against Tasmania was soundly beaten by 365 runs. Charles Eady (123 runs and 12 wickets) made an outstanding contribution for the Tasmanians while Burn, the captain, hit a century.

Great interest surrounded the selection of the 10th Australian team to tour England in 1899. There was debate not only on the names, but also on the number of players that should be taken. J.C.Davis ('Not Out' in *The Referee*) was a leading advocate for 14 players to be taken, rather than the traditional 13. As late as March - when three trial matches were staged - the numbers were still uncertain. Eleven players already selected made up the Australian XI in the trials, with the remaining tourists to come from The Rest. At the conclusion of the second trial match at Melbourne, selectors Joe Darling, Syd Gregory and Hugh Trumble announced the addition of Laver and Johns to the touring party, with Trumper as a reserve - should one of the 13 be unable to go at the last moment. Newspaper critics, with J.C.Davis at the helm, urged Trumper's inclusion irrespective of any withdrawal, and the selectors were forced to act when Trumper batted brilliantly in the first innings of the final trial at Adelaide. They included him as a 14th member of the team, and it is now history that that was the launching of a memorable career.

Leading Aggregates

Batsmen	M	I	NO	Runs	HS	Ave.	Bowlers	Runs	Wkts	Ave.
V.T.Trumper (NSW)	9	15	1	873	292*	62.35	E.Jones (SA)	1239	45	27.53
C.Hill (SA)	8	14	1	841	159	64.69	T.R.McKibbin (NSW)	1061	44	24.11
F.A.Iredale (NSW)	9	15	1	781	196	55.78	W.P.Howell (NSW)	891	41	21.73
J.Darling (SA)	7	12	0	675	210	56.25	H.Trumble (V)	743	40	18.57
F.J.Laver (V)	8	14	2	612	137*	51.00	M.A.Noble (NSW)	1058	39	27.12
M.A.Noble (NSW)	9	13	1	552	111	46.00	G.Giffen (SA)	1132	38	29.78
J.Worrall (V)	8	13	2	494	109	44.90	C.E.McLeod (V)	643	36	17.86
J.F.Giller (V)	7	13	0	463	116	35.61	A.Jarvis (SA)	498	22	22.63
G.Giffen (SA)	8	15	1	425	115	30.35				
J.J.Kelly (NSW)	8	11	4	424	102*	60.57				
S.E.Gregory (NSW)	8	15	0	418	89	27.86				

SHEFFIELD SHIELD TABLE

	P	W	L	D	Quotient	Runs Scored	Wkts Lost	Runs Conceded	Wkts Taken
VICTORIA	4	3	1	-	1.512	2198	70	1495	72
NEW SOUTH WALES	4	2	2	-	1.033	2011	69	2255	79
SOUTH AUSTRALIA	4	1	3	-	0.674	1901	80	2360	67
TOTAL	6	6	6	-	1.000	6110	219	6110	219

SOUTH AUSTRALIA v VICTORIA (Shield Match 1)

Played at Adelaide Oval on November 12, 14, 15, 16, 17, 1898. (Timeless match)
Toss : Victoria.   Result : VICTORIA WON BY 296 RUNS.
Debuts: South Australia - H.G.W.Chinner, A.E.Peters (both f/c). Victoria - P.A.McAlister (f/c); G.L.Wilson (Vic only).
12th Men : T.M.Drew (SA) and D.Sutherland (Vic).
Umpires : P.Argall and R.M.Crockett.
Attendances: 4500, 6000, 2000, 2000, 1000.   Total: About 15,500.   Receipts: £420.
Close of play : 1st day Vic 3/274 (Giller 100, Stuckey 4); 2nd day SA 1/54 (Jarvis 13); 3rd day Vic (2) 1/11 (Bruce 5, Wilson 6); 4th day
    SA (2) 0/18 (Chinner 9, Jarvis 9).

Chinner replaced J.Darling (death of infant son) at the last moment and the South Australians wore black armbands as a mark of respect.
Giller was struck in the chest by a ball from Jones early on the second day and although he completed his innings (116 in 345 minutes, 8
fours, chances at 49 and 91), he was unable to field during the South Australian first innings. He had recovered by the fourth day and
bowled his team to victory on the last, taking a career-best 7 for 51. Worrall (104 in 167 minutes, 2 fives and 12 fours, chances at 37 and
91) and Stuckey (134 in 225 minutes, 12 fours, chances at 12 and 74) completed the first instance of three batsmen scoring centuries in the
same Sheffield Shield innings. Stuckey (113) was awarded a four from a cut which was intercepted "by a small dog which got in the way"
(*Register*). Victoria's total remained their highest in the Shield competition until 1905-06. Graham (51 in 80 minutes, 6 fours) and Bruce
(73 in 120 minutes) also hit half-centuries for the visitors, while Hill (86 in 170 minutes, 7 fours) was South Australia's top scorer. Jones
(1 five and 6 fours) hit 42 in only 25 minutes on the third day. Conditions were fine throughout and the wicket was not to blame for
South Australia's demise. Wilson (previous matches for Oxford University, Sussex, and MCC) played the first of his two matches for
Victoria. *Wisden* and *VCA Report* give SA (1) Chinner 38, total 331, Bruce 2/65. Sources: *Wisden, C.B.O'Reilly, VCA Report,
Adelaide Advertiser, South Australian Register.*

VICTORIA

J.F.Giller	c Hill b Jones	116	(4)	c Evans b Hugo	14
S.A.McMichael	b Jones	10	(5)	c McKenzie b Jarvis	12
*J.Worrall	b Hugo	104	(6)	c Chinner b Hugo	15
H.Graham	c Reedman b Jarvis	51	(8)	b Jarvis	4
J.H.Stuckey	b Giffen	134	(7)	c McKenzie b Jones	7
F.J.Laver	c & b Lyons	36	(9)	c & b Jones	36
H.Trumble	b Jones	9	(10)	not out	26
W.Bruce	b Jones	6	(1)	b Jones	73
G.L.Wilson	b Jones	9	(3)	st McKenzie b Hugo	25
P.A.McAlister	c Hill b Jarvis	21	(2)	lbw b Giffen	0
†A.E.Johns	not out	0		b Jones	2
Extras	(b7, lb4)	11		(lb3)	3
Total	(197.1 overs, 485 mins)	507		(92.0 overs, 225 mins)	217

SOUTH AUSTRALIA

*J.J.Lyons	c McAlister b Bruce	38	(3)	c Worrall b Giller	22
A.Jarvis	c Laver b Trumble	19		c Trumble b Giller	11
C.Hill	c Bruce b Trumble	86	(4)	b Giller	3
G.Giffen	c McAlister b Trumble	2	(5)	c Worrall b Giller	0
J.C.Reedman	b Trumble	38	(6)	b Giller	5
A.E.Peters	c Worrall b Trumble	18	(7)	c Johns b Giller	6
H.G.W.Chinner	not out	37	(1)	c Giller b Trumble	11
E.Jones	b Bruce	42		b Trumble	4
A.E.Evans	b Trumble	21		c Graham b Giller	0
V.Hugo	c Johns b Trumble	0	(11)	c & b Trumble	11
†J.McKenzie	c McAlister b Trumble	18	(10)	not out	25
Extras	(b5, lb4, w2)	11			—
Total	(113.0 overs, 305 mins)	330		(47.2 overs, 135 mins)	98

SOUTH AUSTRALIA	O	M	R	W	w,nb		O	M	R	W	w,nb		FALL OF WICKETS			
														VIC	SA	VIC	SA
Jones	70	12	192	5	-,-		32	4	67	4	-,-	Wkt	1st	1st	2nd	2nd
Giffen	44	6	128	1	-,-		15	2	49	1	-,-	1st	12	54	2	21
Evans	15	4	40	0	-,-	(4)	3	0	16	0	-,-	2nd	178	78	61	29
Hugo	30	13	54	1	-,-	(3)	31	10	56	3	-,-	3rd	261	80	111	34
Jarvis	18.1	5	39	2	-,-	(6)	9	2	24	2	-,-	4th	317	160	113	34
Reedman	8	2	16	0	-,-							5th	385	198	136	49
Lyons	12	4	27	1	-,-	(5)	2	0	2	0	-,-	6th	400	217	146	57
												7th	424	271	153	62
VICTORIA	O	M	R	W	w,nb		O	M	R	W	w,nb	8th	444	304	154	62
Wilson	12	0	40	0	-,-							9th	507	304	213	77
Trumble	49	4	129	8	1,-	(1)	22.2	8	36	3	-,-	10th	507	330	217	98
Laver	35	11	85	0	-,-	(2)	2	1	1	0	-,-					
Bruce	16	2	64	2	1,-	(5)	1	0	5	0	-,-					
Worrall	1	0	1	0	-,-											
Giller						(3)	21	6	51	7	-,-					
Graham						(4)	1	0	5	0	-,-					

NEW SOUTH WALES v TASMANIA

Played at Sydney Cricket Ground on December 9, 10, 12, 1898. (Three-day match)
Toss : Tasmania.   Result : NEW SOUTH WALES WON BY AN INNINGS AND 487 RUNS.
Debuts: New South Wales - R.A.Duff (f/c). Tasmania - O.H.Douglas, C.P.Hammond, W.B.Richardson (all f/c).
12th Men : A.Coningham (NSW). No 12th for Tas; R.J.Hawson (emergency) did not leave Tasmania.
Umpires : C.Bannerman and J.Thompson.
Attendances: 1500, 5000, 500.   Total: About 7000.   Receipts: No figures published.
Close of play : 1st day NSW 4/293 (Iredale 66, Pye 56); 2nd day Tas (2) 0/18 (McAllen 12, Douglas 2).

The first match between these teams set records, all since beaten, for the highest total, highest sixth wicket stand, most runs scored in a day's play (by both a player and by teams) and biggest margin of victory in Australian first-class cricket. The game was set to a strict time limit, the local players having to leave on Tuesday for Adelaide to play a Shield match. Hours of play (for all days) were set at 11.00 to 1.15, 2.00 to 4.00 and 4.15 to 6.00 but, as with most 19th-Century matches there was little punctuality, the second day starting at 11.15 and the last being brought forward to 10.30. Noble and Coningham were absent at the start, Tabart (Tasmania) substituting. Noble's bank employer, had refused him leave and he was not expected to play so Coningham was sent away to collect his gear, but before he returned Noble had arrived and took the field, capturing a hat-trick (Douglas, Hammond, Butler) in his first over (2nd, 3rd and 4th balls). Burn (77 not out in 165 minutes, 8 fours) scored Tasmania's sole half-century. Mackenzie (56 in 45 minutes, 10 fours), Iredale (career-best 196 in 236 minutes, 26 fours), Pye (68 in 75 minutes, 11 fours), Trumper (292 not out in 275 minutes, 39 fours) and Kelly (60 in 90 minutes, 6 fours) led the home scoring. Trumper began at 11.25 and brought up his maiden first-class century in 94 minutes, being the first man to score a hundred in Australia before lunch (NSW 5/510, Iredale 160, Trumper 103 - 217 in 2-hour session). He gave his sole chance at 155 (a hot return catch to Windsor) and reached 200 in 3 hours (tea NSW 7/750, Trumper 247, Kelly 28 - 240 in 2-hour session). He was still undefeated when the innings closed at 5.23, having "made every sort of stroke, both off and on, before and behind the wicket, with the grace and power of a master hand" (*Referee*). His 258-run stand with Iredale (who survived an appeal for a catch behind at 11 and was recalled at 147 when Bannerman decreed that a ball had not carried to Windsor at cover-point) remained the State sixth-wicket record until 1958-59. In all 564 runs were plundered in 330 minutes on the day. New South Wales began the last day with three substitute fieldsmen, including two of the visitors, Noble, Iredale and Mackenzie all being absent. Five-ball overs were bowled. *Wisden* incorrectly gives Tas (1) Eady c & b McKibbin; Tas (2) Burn st Kelly b McKibbin, Richardson not out. Some sources give Tas (2) McKibbin 61 overs, 16 mdns. Sources: *Wisden, Sydney Referee, Sydney Morning Herald, Sydney Daily Telegraph, Newcastle Herald.*

TASMANIA

C.J.Eady	c sub (T.A.Tabart) b McKibbin	10	(3) c Howell b Noble		10
†G.H.Gatehouse	b McKibbin	1	(7) b McKibbin		5
J.E.Bingham	c Duff b McKibbin	19	(4) b Howell		4
*E.J.K.Burn	st Kelly b McKibbin	5	(6) not out		77
E.A.C.Windsor	c Gregory b Noble	43	c Mackenzie b McKibbin		34
O.H.Douglas	c & b Noble	3	(2) run out		39
C.P.Hammond	b Noble	0	(9) c Duff b McKibbin		22
C.W.Butler	c Gregory b Noble	0	(10) c Kelly b Howell		0
T.A.Tabart	b McKibbin	5	(8) b McKibbin		0
C.McAllen	not out	23	(1) b Howell		17
W.B.Richardson	st Kelly b Noble	11	st Kelly b McKibbin		2
Extras	(b1, lb1, w4, nb4)	10	(b5, lb4, nb3)		12
Total	(53.2 overs, 180 mins)	130	(113.3 overs, 300 mins)		222

NEW SOUTH WALES

A.C.K.Mackenzie	st Gatehouse b Bingham	56
H.Donnan	b Bingham	24
M.A.Noble	b Richardson	38
*S.E.Gregory	c Gatehouse b Eady	43
F.A.Iredale	c & b Windsor	196
L.W.Pye	b Eady	68
V.T.Trumper	not out	292
R.A.Duff	b Windsor	27
†J.J.Kelly	c McAllen b Eady	60
W.P.Howell	c Douglas b Bingham	2
T.R.McKibbin	b Bingham	10
Extras	(b12, lb9, nb2)	23
Total	(178.0 overs, 480 mins)	839

NEW SOUTH WALES	O	M	R	W	w,nb		O	M	R	W	w,nb
McKibbin	27	8	64	5	4,4	(2)	41.3	10	93	5	-,3
Howell	10	4	19	0	-,-	(3)	35	16	42	3	-,-
Pye	4	1	12	0							
Noble	12.2	5	25	5	-,-	(1)	32	15	63	1	-,-
Trumper						(4)	5	1	12	0	-,-

TASMANIA	O	M	R	W	w,nb
Eady	56	7	232	3	-,1
Windsor	45	6	202	2	-,1
Bingham	39	4	148	4	-,-
Richardson	16	0	109	1	-,-
Hammond	11	1	53	0	-,-
Butler	5	0	23	0	-,-
Burn	3	0	28	0	-,-
Tabart	3	0	21	0	-,-

FALL OF WICKETS

	TAS	NSW	TAS
Wkt	1st	1st	2nd
1st	1	69	36
2nd	17	96	74
3rd	39	150	79
4th	45	209	83
5th	59	313	137
6th	59	571	163
7th	59	639	167
8th	71	811	209
9th	101	814	213
10th	130	839	222

SOUTH AUSTRALIA v NEW SOUTH WALES (Shield Match 2)

Played at Adelaide Oval on December 16, 17, 19, 20, 21, 1898. (Timeless match)
Toss : South Australia.　　　　　Result : SOUTH AUSTRALIA WON BY 57 RUNS.
Debuts: - Nil.
12th Men : A.E.Peters (SA) and A.Coningham (NSW).
Umpires: C.Bannerman and G.E.Downs.
Attendances: 4000, 5000, 2500, 2000, 500.　　　Total: About 14,000.　　　Receipts: No figures published.
Close of play : 1st day SA 334 all out; 2nd day NSW 7/260 (Donnan 102); 3rd day SA (2) 1/138 (Hill 68, Darling 57); 4th day NSW (2)
　　7/105 (Iredale 39, Kelly 1).

The match began in warm, pleasant conditions that became hotter as each day passed, the last being played in "sultry, oppressive weather, with the thermometer standing over 100 degrees in the shade" (*Register*). Hill (73 in 130 minutes, 7 fours and a chanceless 109 in 210 minutes, 14 fours), Jones (career-best 82 in 65 minutes, 1 six, 1 five and 9 fours) and Darling (70 in 130 minutes, 8 fours) led the scoring for South Australia. Jones's six included 4 overthrows and his five was all-run, from a snick down the long Adelaide Oval. Donnan (160 not out in 445 minutes, 15 fours, chance at 14), who compiled his equal-best score for New South Wales, was the first batsman to carry his bat through a completed innings in a Sheffield Shield match. He was out to the third ball he faced in the second innings. Trumper (68 in 95 minutes, 1 five and 4 fours) suffered a nose bleed just before he was dismissed while Kelly (53 in 145 minutes, 2 fours) fainted in the dressing room with heat exhaustion shortly after he was out. Coningham substituted in the field for the South Australian innings that day while Duff kept wicket, conceding 10 byes. Kelly was back behind the stumps at the start of the last day. Iredale (55 in 120 minutes, 3 fours) topscored in the visitors' second innings, Giffen, in his 40th year, finishing with 10 wickets. Jones became the first bowler to take 150 Sheffield Shield wickets. *Wisden* incorrectly gives SA (1) Hugo st Kelly b Howell, Howell 3/70, McKibbin 1/99. Sources: *Wisden, C.B.O'Reilly, Sydney Referee, Sydney Morning Herald, Adelaide Advertiser, South Australian Register.*

SOUTH AUSTRALIA

J.J.Lyons	c Gregory b Noble	6	b Noble	1
*J.Darling	b Noble	27	c Gregory b Howell	70
C.Hill	c Kelly b Howell	73	b Howell	109
G.Giffen	c & b Noble	15	b Howell	3
J.C.Reedman	c & b Noble	38	b Pye	25
A.Jarvis	b McKibbin	21	b McKibbin	27
H.G.W.Chinner	c Howell b Noble	3	c Mackenzie b McKibbin	0
E.Jones	c Noble b Howell	82	c Gregory b Howell	3
A.E.Evans	b Noble	0	not out	4
†J.McKenzie	not out	33	c Noble b Howell	7
V.Hugo	st Kelly b McKibbin	25	b Howell	0
Extras	(w1, nb10)	11	(b13, lb1, w4, nb2)	20
Total	(87.5 overs, 275 mins)	334	(83.3 overs, 260 mins)	269

NEW SOUTH WALES

A.C.K.Mackenzie	b Hugo	35	st McKenzie b Giffen	10
H.Donnan	not out	160	c Reedman b Giffen	0
M.A.Noble	run out (Hill/McKenzie)	1	c & b Giffen	30
*S.E.Gregory	b Jones	3	b Jones	1
F.A.Iredale	c Darling b Jones	6	c Darling b Giffen	55
V.T.Trumper	c Jones b Jarvis	68	c Jarvis b Lyons	0
L.W.Pye	lbw b Giffen	16	c Hugo b Giffen	9
R.A.Duff	b Jones	25	c Jarvis b Giffen	7
†J.J.Kelly	c & b Giffen	53	not out	27
W.P.Howell	c Jarvis b Giffen	0	b Jones	1
T.R.McKibbin	c Hugo b Giffen	0	b Jones	23
Extras	(b1, lb4, w1, nb1)	7	(lb6, w1, nb2)	9
Total	(154.4 overs, 445 mins)	374	(66.4 overs, 210 mins)	172

SOUTH AUSTRALIA	O	M	R	W	w,nb		O	M	R	W	w,nb	
Noble	37	8	129	6	1,2		9	3	27	1	1,1	
Howell	18	2	73	2	-,-		39.3	10	116	6	-,-	
McKibbin	20.5	1	96	2	-,4	(4)	11	1	46	2	1,1	
Pye	8	2	19	0	-,1	(5)	23	5	52	1	2,-	
Trumper	4	1	6	0	-,3	(3)	1	0	8	0	-,-	

SOUTH AUSTRALIA	O	M	R	W	w,nb		O	M	R	W	w,nb	
Jones	50	16	121	3	1,-		23.4	8	62	3	1,1	
Giffen	39.4	6	111	4	-,-		33	8	83	6	-,-	
Hugo	19	5	41	1	-,-							
Evans	10	2	25	0	-,1							
Jarvis	20	6	40	1	-,-	(4)	5	3	5	0	-,-	
Reedman	8	2	15	0	-,-							
Lyons	8	4	14	0	-,-	(3)	5	0	13	1	-,1	

FALL OF WICKETS

Wkt	SA 1st	NSW 1st	SA 2nd	NSW 2nd
1st	14	58	2	0
2nd	65	61	152	28
3rd	95	67	163	31
4th	140	91	209	61
5th	179	189	242	66
6th	182	218	250	77
7th	193	260	253	93
8th	193	373	257	138
9th	304	373	269	139
10th	334	374	269	172

VICTORIA v NEW SOUTH WALES (Shield Match 3)

Played at Melbourne Cricket Ground on December 24, 26, 27, 1898. (Timeless match)
Toss : New South Wales.   Result : VICTORIA WON BY 190 RUNS.
Debuts: - Nil.
12th Men: P.A.McAlister (Vic) and R.A.Duff (NSW).
Umpires: C.Bannerman and R.M.Crockett.
Attendances: 5161, 9490, 8500.   Total: 23,151.   Receipts: £947.
Close of Play: 1st day NSW 8/35 (Coningham 0); 2nd day Vic (2) 3/120 (Giller 29, Graham 45).

Heavy rain on the day prior to the match ruined the wicket and it was expected that the loser of the toss would be expected to bat first.
Worrall (109 in 115 minutes, 4 fives and 11 fours, chances at 16, 65, 81, 94) hit out in attempt to score as many runs as possible before
the wicket cut up. He made his runs out of 142 while he was at the crease - an outstanding effort on a day when 18 wickets fell for 224
with 17 the next-best contribution. As the preparation of the wicket had been badly affected by the weather, it was agreed beforehand that
the pitch would be rolled after each day's play in addition to before each innings commenced. Set 310 to win, New South Wales lost
Donnan to the second ball and Noble to the fifth of Trumble's opening over. Gregory (51 in 115 minutes, 0 fours) alone offered serious
resistance as Trumble took full advantage of the badly scarred wicket to capture his second eight-wicket-analysis in as many Shield games.
Mackenzie required stitches in a hand which was split when he attempted to catch Worrall (94) on the opening day. Duff substituted for the
rest of the innings and the injury led Gregory to hold him back in the batting order. *VCA Report* incorrectly gives NSW (2) Pye 9.
Sources: *Wisden, VCA Report, The Age, The Argus, The Herald, The Australasian, Town & Country Journal, The Sportsman, The
Leader.*

VICTORIA

Batsman	1st innings		2nd innings	
C.E.McLeod	c Howell b Coningham	9	run out (Mackenzie/Howell)	18
*J.Worrall	b Howell	109	c Iredale b Pye	23
H.Graham	c Howell b Coningham	6	(5) b Pye	45
S.A.McMichael	c Coningham b Howell	17	(3) st Kelly b Pye	2
J.H.Stuckey	b Howell	11	(6) lbw b Noble	35
F.J.Laver	b Howell	6	(8) not out	22
H.Trumble	b Howell	0	(9) c & b McKibbin	3
J.F.Giller	c Mackenzie b Donnan	10	(4) run out (Gregory/Kelly)	37
W.Bruce	run out (Noble/Donnan)	13	(10) c Noble b McKibbin	15
T.S.Warne	not out	0	(7) b McKibbin	8
†A.E.Johns	run out (/Kelly)	3	b Noble	1
Extras	(b2, lb3)	5	(b2, lb4, w2, nb2)	10
Total	(65.4 overs, 205 mins)	189	(123.0 overs, 299 mins)	219

NEW SOUTH WALES

Batsman	1st innings		2nd innings	
H.Donnan	c Johns b McLeod	2	b Trumble	0
†J.J.Kelly	c Bruce b Trumble	13	(7) lbw b Trumble	2
V.T.Trumper	c Graham b McLeod	4	(6) c Johns b Trumble	19
*S.E.Gregory	c Johns b Trumble	5	lbw b Trumble	51
F.A.Iredale	b McLeod	5	c Trumble b McLeod	23
L.W.Pye	c Worrall b McLeod	2	(9) b Trumble	0
T.R.McKibbin	c Laver b Trumble	0	(11) c Warne b Trumble	15
W.P.Howell	c Trumble b McLeod	2	(10) not out	2
A.Coningham	c Trumble b McLeod	7	(8) c Johns b Giller	4
M.A.Noble	not out	34	(3) c Giller b Trumble	0
A.C.K.Mackenzie	b Warne	23	(2) b Trumble	3
Extras	(b1, lb1)	2		—
Total	(56.3 overs, 155 mins)	99	(51.1 overs, 142 mins)	119

NEW SOUTH WALES	O	M	R	W	w,nb		O	M	R	W	w,nb
Noble	8	2	19	0	-,-		30	7	65	2	1,-
Howell	25.4	6	75	5	-,-		24	13	33	0	-,-
Coningham	13	3	31	2	-,-	(5)	11	5	17	0	1,-
McKibbin	7	1	42	0	-,-		24	13	29	3	-,2
Donnan	12	3	17	1	-,-						
Pye						(3)	29	9	54	3	-,-
Trumper						(6)	5	1	11	0	-,-

VICTORIA	O	M	R	W	w,nb	O	M	R	W	w,nb
Trumble	26	10	45	3	-,-	25.1	5	58	8	-,-
McLeod	25	11	42	6	-,-	20	3	46	1	-,-
Giller	3	1	6	0	-,-	6	1	15	1	-,-
Warne	2.3	0	4	1	-,-					

FALL OF WICKETS

Wkt	VIC 1st	NSW 1st	VIC 2nd	NSW 2nd
1st	40	11	38	0
2nd	52	15	40	0
3rd	142	22	48	9
4th	147	30	120	42
5th	157	33	139	75
6th	157	33	165	87
7th	170	33	185	100
8th	186	35	188	100
9th	186	56	212	102
10th	189	99	219	119

VICTORIA v SOUTH AUSTRALIA (Shield Match 4)

Played at Melbourne Cricket Ground on December 31 1898, January 2, 3, 1899. (Timeless match)
Toss : Victoria.   Result : VICTORIA WON BY AN INNINGS AND 218 RUNS.
Debuts: South Australia - F.T.Hack (f/c).
12th Men: P.A.McAlister (Vic) and A.E.Peters (SA).
Umpires: P.Argall and R.M.Crockett.
Attendances: 5994, 10719, 7287.   Total: 24,000.   Receipts: £909.
Close of Play: 1st day Vic 7/273 (Laver 64, Warne 44); 2nd day SA 3/113 (Darling 55, Giffen 18).

With this rain-affected win Victoria retained the Sheffield Shield; it was their fourth title in the first seven seasons of the competition. The game began in intense heat before rain arrived on the day of rest. The wicket played well on Monday but further rain that night turned it into a batsman's nightmare and the South Australians lost 17 wickets for 124 when play resumed next morning. Trumble (11 for 96) and McLeod (8 for 73) exploited the gluey wicket, Trumble taking his best innings figures for Victoria. South Australia had started very well on the opening day, but the heat affected Jones in particular, who had to be assisted from the field late in the day suffering from sunstroke. He had recovered sufficiently to resume next day. Laver (137 not out in 303 minutes, 16 fours), Bruce (52 in 63 minutes, 6 fours), Warne (63 in 117 minutes, 7 fours) and Trumble (70 in 90 minutes, 10 fours) took advantage of the tired attack, taking Victoria from a precarious 6/112 to 455 all out. Stuckey (43 in 93 minutes, 4 fours) had been the best of the top-order. Darling (62 in 140 minutes, 1 five and 1 four) scored a half-century for the visitors before the wicket was at its worst. Giffen was twice out first ball on the last day: resuming his innings and again in the follow-on. Sources: *Wisden, VCA Report, The Age, The Argus, The Herald, The Australasian, The Leader.*

VICTORIA

J.F.Giller	b Giffen	6
*J.Worrall	c Hill b Jones	13
C.E.McLeod	b Giffen	0
J.H.Stuckey	c A.H.Jarvis b A.Jarvis	43
H.Graham	b Jones	22
S.A.McMichael	b A.Jarvis	25
F.J.Laver	not out	137
W.Bruce	c Lyons b Jones	52
T.S.Warne	c Hill b Giffen	63
H.Trumble	c & b Jones	70
†A.E.Johns	b A.Jarvis	11
Extras	(b3, lb8, w2)	13
Total	(133.3 overs, 415 mins)	455

SOUTH AUSTRALIA

*J.Darling	c Johns b McLeod	62		b Trumble	1
J.J.Lyons	c Bruce b McLeod	10	(6)	c Warne b Trumble	3
C.Hill	c & b Giller	27		c Giller b Trumble	33
J.C.Reedman	c Laver b McLeod	2		c McMichael b Trumble	8
G.Giffen	c Warne b McLeod	18		b Trumble	0
A.Jarvis	c Worrall b Trumble	0	(7)	c Johns b McLeod	22
F.T.Hack	c Worrall b Trumble	0	(2)	b Trumble	22
E.Jones	not out	7		c Stuckey b Trumble	5
A.E.Green	st Johns b McLeod	0		c Giller b Trumble	0
†A.H.Jarvis	c Johns b Trumble	2		not out	1
V.Hugo	st Johns b McLeod	0		b McLeod	5
Extras	(b7, lb1)	8		(lb1)	1
Total	(65.1 overs, 188 mins)	136		(51.1 overs, 147 mins)	101

SOUTH AUSTRALIA	O	M	R	W	w,nb
Jones	49	13	138	4	1,-
Giffen	44	7	145	3	-,-
Jarvis	23.3	4	77	3	1,-
Hugo	9	1	34	0	-,-
Lyons	2	0	6	0	-,-
Reedman	6	0	42	0	-,-

VICTORIA	O	M	R	W	w,nb		O	M	R	W	w,nb
Trumble	23	3	57	3	-,-		26	8	39	8	-,-
McLeod	30.1	14	37	6	-,-		15.1	4	36	2	-,-
Giller	10	1	32	1	-,-						
Laver	2	1	2	0	-,-	(3)	3	1	5	0	-,-
Warne						(4)	7	0	20	0	-,-

FALL OF WICKETS

Wkt	VIC 1st	SA 1st	SA 2nd
1st	19	14	2
2nd	19	54	48
3rd	23	59	60
4th	71	113	60
5th	103	120	64
6th	112	123	75
7th	191	126	83
8th	308	131	87
9th	430	134	95
10th	455	136	101

NEW SOUTH WALES v SOUTH AUSTRALIA (Shield Match 5)

Played at Sydney Cricket Ground on January 6, 7, 9, 10, 11, 1899. (Timeless match)
Toss : New South Wales.   Result : NEW SOUTH WALES WON BY THREE WICKETS.
Debuts: - Nil.
12th Men: A.Coningham (NSW) and V.Hugo (SA).
Umpires: P.Argall and C.Bannerman.
Attendances: 7486, 15735, 7283, 5245, 16.   Total: 35,765.   Receipts: £1320.
Close of Play: 1st day NSW 9/378 (Pye 51, Howell 17); 2nd day SA (2) 1/105 (Hack 35, Hill 27); 3rd day SA (2) 8/434 (Reedman 51,
     Green 15); 4th day NSW (2) 7/247 (Kelly 8).

Trumper was out to the first ball of the match, caught off the fingers (he wore no gloves). Gregory (89 in 112 minutes, 13 fours) Kelly (66 in 133 minutes, 7 fours) and Pye (51 in 66 minutes, 6 fours) hit half-centuries for New South Wales in the first innings while Noble (101 in 195 minutes, 11 fours) and Iredale (77 in 104 minutes, 11 fours) saw them home to a three-wicket victory. Lyons (41 in 41 minutes, 8 fours) led the South Australian first innings scoring. In the follow-on, Hill (159 in 242 minutes, 22 fours, chances at 60, 110 and 112), Giffen (68 in 110 minutes, 10 fours) and Reedman (68 not out in 123 minutes, 8 fours) topscored, Giffen being bowled by a McKibbin no-ball during his innings. Half an hour was lost on the fourth day when a brief and violent thunderstorm broke during the luncheon interval. The pitch was not significantly affected. Sources: *Wisden, C.B.O'Reilly, Sydney Referee, Sydney Morning Herald, Town & Country Journal.*

NEW SOUTH WALES

Player	Dismissal	Score	Dismissal	Score
V.T.Trumper	c A.H.Jarvis b Jones	0	c Darling b Jones	15
H.Donnan	b Jones	5	b Giffen	1
M.A.Noble	c A.H.Jarvis b Giffen	30	c Hack b Giffen	101
*S.E.Gregory	c Darling b Jones	89	c Darling b Jones	14
F.A.Iredale	b Jones	20	c Darling b Reedman	77
R.A.Duff	c Giffen b A.Jarvis	42	c Giffen b Reedman	2
A.L.Newell	c Reedman b Peters	48	b Jones	19
†J.J.Kelly	c Hack b Jones	66	not out	9
L.W.Pye	b Jones	51	not out	8
T.R.McKibbin	b Giffen	0		
W.P.Howell	not out	18		
Extras	(lb10)	10	(b6, lb4)	10
Total	(90.5 overs, 280 mins)	379	(66.3 overs, 208 mins) (7 wkts)	256

SOUTH AUSTRALIA

Player	Dismissal	Score		Dismissal	Score
*J.Darling	c McKibbin b Howell	10		b Pye	34
F.T.Hack	c & b Noble	14		b McKibbin	35
C.Hill	c Kelly b Howell	12		c McKibbin b Pye	159
G.Giffen	b McKibbin	8		b Pye	68
J.J.Lyons	b McKibbin	41		b Pye	2
A.Jarvis	st Kelly b McKibbin	4		b McKibbin	15
J.C.Reedman	c Noble b McKibbin	30		not out	68
A.E.Green	b McKibbin	0	(10)	b McKibbin	16
A.E.Peters	not out	17	(8)	c Kelly b McKibbin	4
E.Jones	c Kelly b Newell	24	(9)	c Trumper b Noble	33
†A.H.Jarvis	c Kelly b Newell	0		b McKibbin	13
Extras	(b2, lb1, w1)	4		(b5, lb10, w2, nb5)	22
Total	(55.5 overs, 160 mins)	164		(158.4 overs, 419 mins)	469

SOUTH AUSTRALIA	O	M	R	W	w,nb		O	M	R	W	w,nb
Jones	36.5	4	154	6	-,-		30.3	13	69	3	-,-
Giffen	33	4	133	2	-,-		15	0	79	2	-,-
A.Jarvis	12	3	52	1	-,-		10	2	40	0	-,-
Peters	6	1	20	1	-,-		2	0	17	0	-,-
Lyons	3	0	10	0	-,-						
Reedman						(5)	9	0	41	2	-,-

NEW SOUTH WALES	O	M	R	W	w,nb		O	M	R	W	w,nb
Howell	11	2	28	2	-,-	(3)	20	5	66	0	-,-
Noble	15	2	51	1	1,-	(1)	39	11	79	1	1,-
McKibbin	17	3	54	5	-,-	(5)	44.4	10	168	5	-,5
Pye	10	4	25	0	-,-		38	15	87	4	1,-
Newell	2.5	0	2	2	-,-	(2)	14	5	40	0	-,-
Trumper							2	1	6	0	-,-
Donnan							1	0	1	0	-,-

FALL OF WICKETS

Wkt	NSW 1st	SA 1st	SA 2nd	NSW 2nd
1st	0	18	65	8
2nd	21	28	105	22
3rd	51	40	248	40
4th	112	61	252	183
5th	179	93	313	186
6th	191	98	329	229
7th	285	106	346	247
8th	359	125	400	-
9th	360	156	437	-
10th	379	164	469	-

QUEENSLAND v SOUTH AUSTRALIA

Played at Brisbane Cricket Ground (Woolloongabba) on January 14, 16, 17, 1899. (Timeless match)
Toss : Queensland.   Result : SOUTH AUSTRALIA WON BY AN INNINGS AND 284 RUNS.
Debuts: Queensland - T.Allen, J.Carew, J.P.Clark, W.T.Evans, N.K.Foster, J.Higgins, J.D.Leary, S.A.Schreiber (all f/c).
12th Men: A.E.Green (SA). No 12th named for Qld.
Umpires: P.Argall and F.A.Narracott.
Attendances: 10000, 4000, 1500.   Total: About 15,500.   Receipts: £587.
Close of Play: 1st day SA 2/230 (Darling 101, Giffen 24); 2nd day SA 7/555 (Peters 9).

The first-ever meeting between these teams, and the first match to be staged at the Woolloongabba Ground, aroused great local interest. Government offices and many businesses in Brisbane closed on Monday afternoon (January 16th) to encourage people to attend the match. Queensland had selection problems from the beginning. C.T.B.Turner (ex-New South Wales, now living at Gympie) and S.J.Donahoo (ex-Victorian, living at Rockhampton) were invited to play but were unable to. The appointed captain, S.P.Jones, learned of his father's death in Sydney the day before the match, A.H.V.Hewitt injured his hand the previous night, and Dr. R.Macdonald had professional duties to attend to. Carew, Evans and Leary were the replacements and Bradley was elected to the captaincy by the players. Darling (career-best 210 in 265 minutes, 36 fours, chance at 35), Giffen (chanceless 115 in 180 minutes, 12 fours), Hill (78 in 65 minutes, 2 fives and 9 fours) and Hack (63 in 150 minutes, 3 fours) led South Australia to their highest first-class total so far. Darling advanced his score from 101 to 201 in the pre-lunch session (90 minutes) on the second day. Allen, in his only first-class match, was denied a wicket with his first ball when Lyons was missed by Byrne. Schreiber (67 in 71 minutes, 7 fours) and Bradley (51 in 90 minutes, 5 fours) scored half-centuries for Queensland. Evans on debut (later to become a wicket-keeper) captured seven of his eight first-class wickets in 30 matches spread over 15 years. The final margin remained the record by an innings in matches between these teams for more than 90 years. *Cricket* incorrectly gives Qld (1) Carew c Hill. Sources: *Cricket, C.B.O'Reilly, Sydney Referee, Brisbane Courier, Queensland Times, The Queenslander.*

QUEENSLAND

*†W.F.Bradley	c Hack b Jones	2	(5) c & b Giffen	51
J.P.Clark	c Peters b Jones	8	(3) b Hugo	6
N.K.Foster	c A.H.Jarvis b Giffen	9	(2) lbw b Hugo	4
J.Carew	c Reedman b Giffen	4	(7) c Jones b Giffen	38
S.A.Schreiber	b Jones	0	(4) c Hugo b Giffen	67
E.J.Metcalfe	not out	26	(1) b Hugo	14
W.T.Evans	b Jones	23	(6) c Hugo b Giffen	2
T.Allen	b A.Jarvis	6	(9) c Jones b Giffen	0
T.Byrne	b A.Jarvis	0	(10) b Giffen	5
J.Higgins	c A.H.Jarvis b A.Jarvis	10	(8) b Giffen	6
J.D.Leary	b A.Jarvis	0	not out	2
Extras		12		3
Total	(36.0 overs, 130 mins)	100	(55.2 overs, 165 mins)	198

SOUTH AUSTRALIA

*J.Darling	c Clark b Leary	210
J.J.Lyons	b Byrne	24
C.Hill	run out (Carew/Bradley)	78
G.Giffen	st Bradley b Evans	115
F.T.Hack	c & b Evans	63
J.C.Reedman	b Evans	1
A.Jarvis	c Schreiber b Evans	42
A.E.Peters	c Schreiber b Evans	16
E.Jones	b Evans	17
V.Hugo	b Evans	1
†A.H.Jarvis	not out	1
Extras	(b12, nb2)	14
Total	(153.5 overs, 435 mins)	582

SOUTH AUSTRALIA	O	M	R	W	w,nb		O	M	R	W	w,nb
Jones	18	7	33	4		(5)	6	1	23	0	
Giffen	15	1	45	2		(6)	13.2	1	56	7	
A.Jarvis	3	1	10	4		(1)	11	0	45	0	
Hugo						(2)	14	3	28	3	
Hack						(3)	1	0	8	0	
Reedman						(4)	6	1	25	0	
Peters							4	0	10	0	

QUEENSLAND	O	M	R	W	w,nb
Byrne	42	9	176	1	-,1
Allen	20	1	117	0	-,-
Carew	14	2	52	0	-,-
Higgins	14	0	53	0	-,-
Leary	24	7	45	1	-,1
Schreiber	12	3	36	0	-,-
Metcalfe	6	1	19	0	-,-
Evans	21.5	2	70	7	-,-

FALL OF WICKETS			
	QLD	SA	QLD
Wkt	1st	1st	2nd
1st	8	41	8
2nd	23	182	18
3rd	27	384	45
4th	27	460	136
5th	29	462	139
6th	79	546	178
7th	86	555	190
8th	86	577	190
9th	100	580	191
10th	100	582	198

NEW SOUTH WALES v VICTORIA (Shield Match 6)

Played at Sydney Cricket Ground on January 26, 27, 28, 30, 1899. (Timeless match)
Toss : New South Wales.　　　　　Result : NEW SOUTH WALES WON BY EIGHT WICKETS.
Debuts: - Nil.
12th Men: R.A.Duff (NSW) and P.A.McAlister (Vic).
Umpires: C.Bannerman and R.M.Crockett.
Attendances: 16887, 7954, 13232, 5565.　　　　Total: 43,638.　　　Receipts: £1501.
Close of Play: 1st day NSW 6/345 (Donnan 33, Pye 20); 2nd day Vic 7/154 (Giller 62, Trumble 12); 3rd day Vic (2) 5/271 (Giller 0).

A looping beamer by Worrall (called wide by umpire Crockett) conceded the match for Victoria at 6.05pm on the fourth day; their first loss in seven Shield games. Play had been continued past the scheduled 6.00pm stumps to obtain a result that evening. Noble (100 in 175 minutes, 12 fours) and Iredale (98 in 140 minutes, 13 fours) added 164 for the New South Wales third wicket on the first day, Donnan (60 in 136 minutes, 7 fours) also passing 50. Giller (87 in 210 minutes, 13 fours) topscored in Victoria's first innings, while in the follow-on Worrall (68 in 53 minutes, 14 fours), Graham (career-best 124 in 200 minutes, 19 fours), Laver (55 in 90 minutes) and Giller again (55 in 160 minutes) all batted well. Mackenzie (62 not out in 120 minutes, 4 fours) and Iredale (49 not out in 75 minutes, 6 fours) took New South Wales to victory with an unfinished stand of 98. Newell was run out off a no-ball. *Wisden* incorrectly gives Vic (1) Laver 17, McMichael 18, Noble 2 wickets. Sources: *Wisden, Sydney Referee, Sydney Morning Herald, Town & Country Journal, Sydney Daily Telegraph.*

NEW SOUTH WALES

*S.E.Gregory	c Johns b Trumble	45	b Laver		46
A.L.Newell	c Johns b Giller	6	run out (Trumble/McLeod)		6
M.A.Noble	c Johns b McLeod	100			
F.A.Iredale	c Laver b McLeod	98	not out		49
H.Donnan	b Giller	60			
A.C.K.Mackenzie	b McLeod	12	(3) not out		62
V.T.Trumper	c Trumble b McLeod	23			
L.W.Pye	c Johns b McLeod	20			
†J.J.Kelly	not out	43			
T.R.McKibbin	b Giller	6			
W.P.Howell	b McLeod	20			
Extras	(b5, lb1, w2, nb1)	9	(b5, w1, nb1)		7
Total	(151.2 overs, 370 mins)	442	(57.0 overs, 145 mins) (2 wkts)		170

VICTORIA

C.E.McLeod	b McKibbin	1	(7) b Noble		1
F.J.Laver	b Noble	16	(5) b Noble		55
*J.Worrall	b McKibbin	9	(1) c Iredale b Howell		68
J.F.Giller	c Gregory b Pye	87	(6) b Howell		55
H.Graham	c Pye b Noble	11	(3) st Kelly b McKibbin		124
J.H.Stuckey	c Kelly b Howell	28	(4) c Howell b Noble		5
T.S.Warne	b Howell	9	(10) not out		28
W.Bruce	b Noble	5	(9) c Kelly b McKibbin		7
H.Trumble	c Kelly b Pye	24	(8) c Pye b Noble		19
S.A.McMichael	c Noble b Howell	19	(2) c Noble b Pye		11
†A.E.Johns	not out	4	b Noble		12
Extras	(lb2)	2	(b4, lb2, w3, nb2)		11
Total	(90.5 overs, 245 mins)	215	(139.5 overs, 345 mins)		396

VICTORIA	O	M	R	W	w,nb		O	M	R	W	w,nb					
Trumble	43	11	120	1	-,-		18	2	40	0	-,-					
McLeod	53.2	15	138	6	-,1		20	2	64	0	-,1					
Giller	21	5	46	3	-,-	(4)	5	0	18	0	-,-					
Warne	12	0	50	0	-,-											
Laver	17	7	61	0	-,-	(3)	14	2	41	1	-,-					
Bruce	5	0	18	0	2,-											
Worrall						(5)	0.0	0	0	0	1,-					

		FALL OF WICKETS			
	Wkt	NSW	VIC	VIC	NSW
		1st	1st	2nd	2nd
	1st	28	1	27	18
	2nd	81	25	93	72
	3rd	245	27	106	-
	4th	262	51	250	-
	5th	280	100	271	-
	6th	322	126	276	-
	7th	346	137	304	-
	8th	393	187	318	-
	9th	415	194	376	-
	10th	442	215	396	-

NEW SOUTH WALES	O	M	R	W	w,nb		O	M	R	W	w,nb
Noble	32	12	77	3	-,-	(2)	41.5	13	128	5	1,-
McKibbin	26	5	65	2	-,-	(5)	29	3	91	2	-,2
Howell	19.5	10	23	3	-,-		40	15	73	2	2,
Pye	13	3	48	2	-,-	(1)	21	6	70	1	-,-
Newell						(4)	3	0	8	0	-,-
Trumper							4	0	15	0	-,-
Donnan							1	1	0	0	-,-

TASMANIA v VICTORIA

Played at S.T.C.A. Ground, Hobart, on January 26, 27, 28, 30, 1899. (Timeless match)
Toss : Tasmania.   Result : TASMANIA WON BY 365 RUNS.
Debuts: Tasmania - N.Dodds, R.J.Hawson, G.D.Paton (all f/c). Victoria - W.W.Armstrong, A.S.Carter, W.Carlton, A.Fox,
H.F.Hetherington, D.Mailer, F.A.Tarrant (all f/c).
12th Men: None named.
Umpires: C.W.Butler and S.Morris.
Attendances & Receipts: No figures published.
Close of Play: 1st day Vic 0/7 (Carter 3, Carlton 2); 2nd day Tas (2) 0/89 (Savigny 40, Burn 45); 3rd day Vic (2) 4/66 (Sutherland 15).

The Victorian selectors were forced to replace W.M.Morgan and G.L.Wilson (both unavailable) with Carlton and Hetherington before the team left Melbourne. Paton was a late replacement for W.B.Richardson (unavailable) in the Tasmanian side. This was the last first-class match in Australia in which the five-ball over was used. Tasmania atoned for their heavy defeat in Sydney six weeks earlier by recording what was easily their biggest victory by a runs margin yet. It was their fourth win out of five recent matches between the teams. Carlton (73 not out in 195 minutes, 6 fours) was the first Victorian batsman to carry his bat through a completed innings; he was also the first to carry his bat in Australian first-class cricket. Eady (92 in 135 minutes, 1 five and 12 fours and 12 wickets for 129) was the first allrounder other than George Giffen (eight times so far) to do the 100 runs/10 wickets double in a first-class match in Australia. Burn (119 in 195 minutes) and Savigny (145 for the first wicket) and Ward and Dodds (122 for the tenth wicket in just 75 minutes) established new Tasmanian wicket-partnership records. Tasmania fielded a substitute on the last day but it is not known who was absent; it may have been Gatehouse as Dodds kept wickets throughout the Victorians' second innings. Gatehouse had missed Carter from the first ball of Victoria's first innings. *VCA Report* gives Tas (2) Eady c Mailer, Murray 4/80, Armstrong 4/79; Vic (2) Maplestone c Hawson (omits sub), Murray b Windsor, Hastings st Dodds b Eady. Tasmanian sources as shown, which is believed correct. The identity of the substitute catcher in Vic (2) remains doubtful; it is thought to have been E.S.Hawson. Sources: *VCA Report, STCA Report, The Australasian, The Leader, Hobart Mercury, Launceston Examiner.*

TASMANIA

J.H.Savigny	b Maplestone	4		c Hetherington b Armstrong	60
C.J.Eady	b Murray	92	(3)	st Hastings b Murray	31
R.J.Hawson	c Hastings b Maplestone	40	(4)	c Sutherland b Murray	9
E.A.C.Windsor	lbw b Murray	27	(5)	c & b Tarrant	69
*E.J.K.Burn	c Tarrant b Murray	5	(2)	c Tarrant b Murray	119
†G.H.Gatehouse	b Tarrant	1	(8)	lbw b Armstrong	0
N.R.Westbrook	c Fox b Murray	47	(6)	lbw b Armstrong	11
C.McAllen	b Murray	18	(9)	not out	20
G.D.Paton	c & b Murray	7	(11)	b Murray	10
W.G.Ward	not out	97	(7)	c Mailer b Fox	15
N.Dodds	c Hetherington b Carter	36	(10)	lbw b Armstrong	0
Extras		10			25
Total	(94.3 overs, 260 mins)	384		(110.0 overs, 300 mins)	369

VICTORIA

A.S.Carter	c Savigny b Windsor	28		c Dodds b Eady	15
W.Carlton	not out	73		run out (Windsor)	14
D.Mailer	b Windsor	0		b Eady	11
H.C.Maplestone	b Eady	1	(9)	c sub (E.S.Hawson*) b Eady	12
D.Sutherland	b Eady	20		c Dodds b Windsor	54
A.W.Murray	b Eady	13		c Ward b Eady	5
H.F.Hetherington	c Ward b Eady	12	(8)	c & b Eady	5
W.W.Armstrong	b Eady	6	(7)	b Ward	33
A.Fox	b Ward	34	(4)	b Ward	7
*†T.J.Hastings	b Eady	3		st Dodds b Windsor	9
F.A.Tarrant	b Eady	7		not out	0
Extras		14			12
Total	(65.2 overs, 195 mins)	211		(46.0 overs, 135 mins)	177

VICTORIA	O	M	R	W	w,nb		O	M	R	W	w,nb
Tarrant	32	7	81	1	-,-	(3)	21	1	60	1	-,-
Maplestone	15	3	56	2	-,-	(1)	15	4	49	0	-,-
Fox	13	2	52	0	-,-	(4)	23	4	69	1	-,-
Carter	2.3	0	9	1	-,-	(5)	5	2	7	0	-,-
Murray	27	1	145	6	-,-	(2)	19	2	81	4	-,-
Carlton	3	0	17	0	-,-						
Mailer	2	0	14	0	-,-						
Armstrong						(6)	27	7	78	4	-,-

TASMANIA	O	M	R	W	w,nb		O	M	R	W	w,nb
Eady	32.2	7	66	7	-,-		22	5	63	5	-,2
Windsor	26	2	99	2	-,-		22	1	98	2	-,-
Dodds	4	2	10	0	-,-						
Ward	3	0	22	1	-,-	(3)	2	1	4	2	-,-

FALL OF WICKETS

Wkt	TAS 1st	VIC 1st	TAS 2nd	VIC 2nd
1st	5	45	145	20
2nd	98	51	216	39
3rd	167	52	228	44
4th	173	76	236	66
5th	174	96	267	73
6th	176	120	315	146
7th	220	130	323	148
8th	230	196	343	158
9th	262	199	354	168
10th	384	211	369	177

VICTORIA v NEW ZEALAND XI

Played at Melbourne Cricket Ground on February 17, 18, 20, 21, 1899. (Timeless match)
Toss : New Zealand XI.   Result : VICTORIA WON BY AN INNINGS AND 132 RUNS.
Debuts: Victoria - G.A.Honeybone (f/c).
12th Men: G.Mills (NZ). No 12th named for Vic.
Umpires: R.M.Crockett and H.J.Fry.
Attendances: 500, 1300, 300, 100.   Total: About 2200.   Receipts: £89.
Close of Play: 1st day NZ 7/264 (Ashbolt 23, Boxshall 17); 2nd day Vic 6/291 (McAlister 71, Murray 39); 3rd day NZ (2) 0/15
    (Ashbolt 9, Sims 6).

New Zealand's inaugural match in Australia was played to a finish at their request. The VCA agreed to meet all expenses in staging the match and all gate receipts went to the New Zealanders. McAlister (224 in 385 minutes, 25 fours, 2 chances) recorded his career-best score in only his second first-class match and led Victoria to their highest total in this level of cricket yet. McAlister also compiled the highest innings by a Victorian to this time and shared stands of 87 with Stuckey (60 in 75 minutes, 6 fours, 3 chances), 187 with Murray (92 in 150 minutes, 4 fours, chance at 76), 95 with Wilson (68 in 55 minutes, 8 fours) and 103 in 90 minutes with Tarrant for the tenth wicket. New Zealand had started the match with an opening stand of 135 between Baker (56 in 160 minutes, 3 fours) and Reese (88 in 110 minutes, 7 fours), but only Cobcroft (59 not out in 135 minutes, 1 four) exceeded 50 in either innings that followed. Downe's pair included a first-ball dismissal in the first innings. Boxshall received a knock on the thumb late in the Victorian innings and was replaced as wicket-keeper by Cobcroft for the remainder; he was unable to bat in the second innings. J.F.Giller, T.J.Hastings, A.E.Johns, C.E.McLeod and H.Trumble were all unavailable for Victoria. Victoria's scorer in this match, 16-year-old Percy Heather (son of VCA secretary Edward Heather). played his only match for Victoria against New Zealand on their next visit to Australia in 1913-14. Sources: *T.W.Reese, VCA, Report, The Age, The Argus, The Herald, The Australasian, The Leader, The Sportsman.*

NEW ZEALAND XI

J.C.Baker	c Laver b Murray	56	(3)	c & b Laver	7
D.Reese	st Honeybone b Worrall	88	(4)	b Laver	10
H.B.Lusk	c & b Worrall	12	(5)	c & b Worrall	7
*L.T.Cobcroft	c Graham b Murray	5	(6)	not out	59
I.Mills	lbw b Laver	31	(7)	c Honeybone b Tarrant	19
A.Sims	c McMichael b Murray	18	(2)	b Laver	6
A.D.Downes	c Graham b Murray	0	(8)	c McMichael b Tarrant	0
F.L.Ashbolt	c Laver b Murray	31	(1)	st Honeybone b Worrall	14
†C.Boxshall	c Worrall b Laver	38		absent hurt	-
F.S.Frankish	b Worrall	6		lbw b Armstrong	26
E.F.Upham	not out	11	(9)	run out	2
Extras	(b18, lb2, w1)	21		(b1, lb2)	3
Total	(122.5 overs, 330 mins)	317		(75.5 overs, 190 mins)	153

VICTORIA

*J.Worrall	b Frankish	36
S.A.McMichael	b Frankish	12
H.Graham	c Downes b Upham	31
F.J.Laver	c Baker b Reese	30
J.H.Stuckey	c Boxshall b Downes	60
W.W.Armstrong	c Downes b Reese	6
P.A.McAlister	c & b Downes	224
A.W.Murray	c Upham b Downes	92
G.L.Wilson	b Downes	68
†G.A.Honeybone	b Upham	0
F.A.Tarrant	not out	30
Extras	(b10, lb3)	13
Total	(184.0 overs, 450 mins)	602

VICTORIA	O	M	R	W	w,nb		O	M	R	W	w,nb
Laver	28	16	61	2	-,-	(2)	28	11	50	3	-,-
Murray	24	2	71	5	1,-	(1)	16	1	41	0	-,-
Tarrant	12	3	33	0	-,-	(4)	16	8	21	2	-,-
Wilson	17	6	46	0	-,-	(5)	2	0	7	0	-,-
Worrall	35.5	11	60	3	-,-	(3)	11	2	23	2	-,-
Armstrong	3	0	12	0	-,-		2.5	0	8	1	-,-
Graham	3	0	13	0	-,-						

NEW ZEALAND XI	O	M	R	W	w,nb
Downes	47	13	127	4	-,-
Upham	46	9	135	2	-,-
Frankish	37	7	127	2	-,-
Reese	32	6	113	2	-,-
Ashbolt	14	1	53	0	-,-
Cobcroft	3	1	5	0	-,-
Baker	3	0	16	0	-,-
Sims	2	0	13	0	-,-

FALL OF WICKETS

Wkt	NZ 1st	VIC 1st	NZ 2nd
1st	135	41	17
2nd	157	50	27
3rd	162	105	37
4th	178	113	39
5th	204	129	46
6th	204	216	83
7th	236	403	83
8th	287	498	85
9th	301	499	153
10th	317	602	-

NEW SOUTH WALES v NEW ZEALAND XI

Played at Sydney Cricket Ground on February 24, 25, 27, 1899. (Timeless match)
Toss : New Zealand XI.   Result : NEW SOUTH WALES WON BY AN INNINGS AND 384 RUNS.
Debuts: New South Wales - C.W.Gregory (f/c).
12th Men: A.J.Y.Hopkins (NSW) and I.Mills (NZ).
Umpires: C.Bannerman and J.Thompson.
Attendances: 903, 1415, 297.   Total: 2615.   Receipts: £116.
Close of Play: 1st day NSW 2/151 (Trumper 81, Farquhar 61); 2nd day NSW 7/546 (Gregory 24).

The New Zealanders were outclassed in all departments of the game by a New South Wales team that included their normal complement of bowlers but gave opportunities to some promising young batsmen. Trumper's batting transcended all else in the match. He began at the dismissal of Duff in the first over of the innings and survived two difficult caught-and-bowled chances to Frankish early on from hard-hit drives, but gave no further chance until he was 249. He batted in all for 315 minutes, scoring 253 with 31 fours and displaying an ease of strokeplay that was to characterise his innings throughout his career. He shared century stands of 224 for the third wicket with Farquhar (110 in 150 minutes, 13 fours), 101 for the fourth wicket with Noble and 124 for the fifth wicket with Poidevin. Boxshall (sore hands) was of the field for the final session of the second day, Mills substituting in the field while Lusk kept wicket. Downes captured his two wickets with successive deliveries. The New Zealanders were unable to cope with the sharp offbreaks of Howell and in the second innings McKibbin, who bowled in splendid style, "whipping back and making pace from the pitch" (*Referee*). Cobcroft had earlier batted 100 minutes for 10 runs while Frankish and Upham added 62 for the tenth wicket in an hour. Sources: *T.W.Reese, Sydney Referee, Sydney Morning Herald, Town & Country Journal, Sydney Mail, Sydney Daily Telegraph.*

NEW ZEALAND XI

J.C.Baker	b Howell	29	(2)	b Howell	17
D.Reese	c & b Noble	1	(3)	c & b McKibbin	3
H.B.Lusk	b Howell	15	(4)	st Evers b McKibbin	15
*L.T.Cobcroft	b Howell	10	(1)	b McKibbin	7
G.Mills	run out (Trumper/Evers)	0		c Iredale b McKibbin	0
A.D.Downes	b Howell	5	(7)	c Farquhar b McKibbin	1
F.L.Ashbolt	c Farquhar b Pye	2	(6)	b McKibbin	1
A.H.Fisher	lbw b Howell	3		run out (Iredale)	5
†C.Boxshall	run out (Trumper)	5	(11)	not out	0
F.S.Frankish	b Noble	19		b Pye	0
E.F.Upham	not out	31	(9)	st Evers b McKibbin	6
Extras	(b16, w2, nb2)	20		(b2, lb1, nb6)	9
Total	(62.1 overs, 165 mins)	140		(34.2 overs, 90 mins)	64

NEW SOUTH WALES

R.A.Duff	c Ashbolt b Frankish	0
L.W.Pye	c Frankish b Upham	4
V.T.Trumper	lbw b Cobcroft	253
B.W.Farquhar	c Fisher b Reese	110
M.A.Noble	c Boxshall b Frankish	37
L.O.S.Poidevin	b Reese	69
C.W.Gregory	not out	40
*F.A.Iredale	c Ashbolt b Mills	31
†H.A.Evers	b Downes	15
T.R.McKibbin	lbw b Downes	0
W.P.Howell	run out (Baker/Boxshall)	7
Extras	(b13, lb7, w2)	22
Total	(150.3 overs, 405 mins)	588

NEW SOUTH WALES	O	M	R	W	w,nb		O	M	R	W	w,nb			FALL OF WICKETS		
McKibbin	13	2	32	0	-,2		17.2	3	30	7	-,6			NZ	NSW	NZ
Noble	16.1	3	40	2	2,-							Wkt	1st	1st	2nd
Howell	18	12	22	5	-,-	(2)	13	4	20	1	-,-	1st	4	0	17
Pye	15	9	26	1	-,-	(3)	4	2	5	1	-,-	2nd	48	13	29
												3rd	54	237	29
NEW ZEALAND XI	O	M	R	W	w,nb							4th	56	338	30
Frankish	34	3	127	2	-,-							5th	61	462	41
Upham	30	2	114	1	-,-							6th	68	500	47
Fisher	16	0	62	0	1,-							7th	71	546	51
Downes	27.3	7	103	2	-,-							8th	78	570	62
Reese	30	4	112	2	-,-							9th	78	570	64
Ashbolt	4	0	19	0	-,-							10th	140	588	64
Cobcroft	7	0	24	1	1,-										
Mills	2	0	5	1	-,-										

AUSTRALIAN XI v THE REST

Played at Sydney Cricket Ground on March 3, 4, 6, 7, 8, 1899. (Timeless match)
Toss : Australian XI.　　　　　Result : AUSTRALIAN XI WON BY SEVEN WICKETS.
Debuts: - Nil.
12th Men: A.C.K.Mackenzie (both sides).
Umpires: C.Bannerman and R.M.Crockett.
Attendances: 6000, 12000, 6000, 4000, 1000.　　　Total: About 29,000.　　　Receipts: £950.
Close of Play: 1st day Aust 6/354 (Noble 60, Kelly 14); 2nd day Rest 3/138 (Laver 28, Donnan 19); 3rd day Rest (2) 1/145 (Reedman 74, Trumper 22); 4th day Rest (2) 8/478 (Coningham 1).

The Australian party to tour England had not been finalised for this match, the first in a series of three before the players caught the boat. The Australian XI comprised the nine already selected plus Howell and Iredale (both were eventually included in the fourteen). Batsmen dominated proceedings, those exceeding 50 as follows, Iredale (85 in 135 minutes, 13 fours), Hill (76 in 108 minutes, 13 fours and 101 not out in 165 minutes, 12 fours), Noble (111 in 150 minutes, 16 fours), Kelly (102 not out in 142 minutes, 18 fours) and Darling (104 in 150 minutes, 17 fours) for the Australian XI and Reedman (51 in 90 minutes, 7 fours and 108 in 187 minutes, 12 fours), Giffen (67 in 120 minutes, 10 fours and 59 in 125 minutes, 6 fours) and Laver (136 in 193 minutes, 23 fours) for The Rest. *Wisden* gives incorrect match dates and venue; Aust (1) Noble c Graham, Trumble c Graham; Aust (2) Trumper 0/23 instead of Graham; Rest (2) Giller c Gregory b Noble, Jones 1/110, Noble 1/99, Howell 4/143, McLeod 3/94. Sources: *Wisden, Aust XI Scorebook, Sydney Morning Herald, Town & Country Journal, Sydney Daily Telegraph.*

AUSTRALIAN XI

Batsman	Dismissal		Dismissal (2)	
F.A.Iredale	run out (Giller/Johns)	85	(2) c Laver b McKibbin	14
*J.Darling	c Graham b Coningham	36	(1) c Pye b Laver	104
C.Hill	c Pye b Coningham	76	not out	101
S.E.Gregory	c Johns b Laver	22	c Johns b Reedman	10
J.Worrall	c Trumper b McKibbin	32	not out	16
M.A.Noble	c McKibbin b Coningham	111		
C.E.McLeod	c Johns b Giffen	17		
†J.J.Kelly	not out	102		
H.Trumble	c Giller b McKibbin	24		
E.Jones	c Coningham b McKibbin	2		
W.P.Howell	c Coningham b McKibbin	5		
Extras	(b1, lb10, w2, nb2)	15	(b4, lb1, nb1)	6
Total	(139.1 overs, 405 mins)	527	(61.5 overs, 195 mins) (3 wkts)	251

THE REST

Batsman	Dismissal		Dismissal (2)	
J.C.Reedman	c Kelly b Trumble	51	c & b Howell	108
J.F.Giller	c Gregory b Noble	28	c Gregory b McLeod	43
V.T.Trumper	c Kelly b Noble	6	run out (Jones/Kelly)	46
F.J.Laver	c Trumble b McLeod	30	c Kelly b Howell	136
H.Donnan	b Jones	28	c Trumble b McLeod	22
H.Graham	b Jones	3	b Howell	21
*G.Giffen	b Howell	67	b Howell	59
L.W.Pye	b Jones	4	b McLeod	28
A.Coningham	b Howell	21	b Jones	23
†A.E.Johns	c Kelly b Trumble	1	not out	24
T.R.McKibbin	not out	0	b McLeod	1
Extras	(b2, lb2, w2, nb3)	9	(b4, lb8, w1, nb3)	16
Total	(117.3 overs, 295 mins)	248	(172.2 overs, 450 mins)	527

THE REST	O	M	R	W	w,nb		O	M	R	W	w,nb
McKibbin	22.1	0	68	4	1,-		14	1	66	1	-,1
Pye	23	4	93	0	-,-	(6)	3	0	11	0	-,-
Coningham	26	3	113	3	-,-	(4)	5	1	7	0	-,-
Giller	20	3	65	0	1,-	(3)	5	1	15	0	-,-
Giffen	22	2	83	1	-,-	(2)	9	0	37	0	-,-
Laver	18	2	61	1	-,-	(5)	13.5	3	63	1	-,-
Reedman	6	0	20	0	-,2	(8)	9	2	23	1	-,-
Trumper	2	0	9	0	-,-						
Graham						(7)	3	0	23	0	-,-

AUSTRALIAN XI	O	M	R	W	w,nb		O	M	R	W	w,nb
Jones	28	5	62	3	-,-		31	3	111	1	-,-
Noble	29	7	58	2	1,-	(4)	28	0	99	0	1,1
Howell	16.3	7	26	2	-,-	(2)	49	11	142	4	-,-
McLeod	24	7	52	1	-,3	(5)	40.2	10	94	4	-,-
Trumble	20	10	41	2	1,-	(3)	24	6	65	0	-,2

FALL OF WICKETS

Wkt	AUST 1st	REST 1st	REST 2nd	AUST 2nd
1st	68	82	91	39
2nd	188	89	193	195
3rd	215	90	207	216
4th	247	144	256	-
5th	275	147	286	-
6th	321	181	435	-
7th	442	195	468	-
8th	519	235	478	-
9th	521	248	526	-
10th	527	248	527	-

AUSTRALIAN XI v THE REST

Played at Melbourne Cricket Ground on March 10, 11, 13, 1899. (Timeless match)
Toss : The Rest.   Result : AUSTRALIAN XI WON BY NINE WICKETS.
Debuts: - Nil.
12th Men: L.W.Pye (both sides).
Umpires: C.Bannerman and R.M.Crockett.
Attendances: 3000, 7652, 2000.   Total: About 12,652.   Receipts: £424.
Close of Play: 1st day Aust 1/8 (Darling 0, Trumble 7); 2nd day Rest (2) 1/28 (Reedman 9, McKibbin 15).

Eady replaced H.Donnan (unavailable) in The Rest line-up. Pye (ill) swapped places with Mackenzie as the nominated reserve. Jones extracted life from an even first-day pitch, Trumper (46 in 70 minutes, 5 fours) and Giffen (57 not out in 110 minutes, 3 fours) topscoring for The Rest. Darling (49 in 100 minutes, 6 fours), Hill (51 in 63 minutes, 1 five and 5 fours) and Kelly (48 in 81 minutes, 3 fours) led the reply for the Australian XI, all batsmen except Nos 1 and 11 passing 20. The Rest lost Giller to the third ball of their second innings, Laver (44 in 80 minutes, 5 fours) cementing his place in the touring party. Noble's swerve and offspin returned 6 for 45. *Wisden* gives incorrect dates and venue. Sources: *Wisden, Aust XI Scorebook, The Age, The Argus, The Herald, The Australasian, The Leader.*

THE REST

J.F.Giller	c Iredale b Jones	10		c Howell b Jones	4
J.C.Reedman	c Kelly b Jones	4		b Jones	10
V.T.Trumper	b McLeod	46	(4)	c & b Noble	26
F.J.Laver	c & b Jones	33	(5)	b Noble	44
A.C.K.Mackenzie	b Trumble	23	(6)	b Howell	0
H.Graham	c Trumble b McLeod	10	(7)	c McLeod b Noble	19
*G.Giffen	not out	57	(8)	b Noble	1
A.Coningham	c Hill b Noble	8	(9)	c Jones b Noble	9
C.J.Eady	b Jones	3	(10)	not out	23
†A.E.Johns	c & b Howell	17	(11)	b Noble	3
T.R.McKibbin	c Trumble b Howell	5	(3)	c & b Trumble	20
Extras	(b5, lb5, w1)	11		(b3, lb4, w1, nb3)	11
Total	(83.2 overs, 227 mins)	227		(50.1 overs, 150 mins)	170

AUSTRALIAN XI

F.A.Iredale	c Eady b Giller	1			
*J.Darling	c McKibbin b Giffen	49			
H.Trumble	b McKibbin	28			
C.Hill	b Eady	51			
S.E.Gregory	c Giller b Laver	36	(1)	b Giffen	20
J.Worrall	c Mackenzie b Coningham	33			
M.A.Noble	c Eady b Laver	30			
†J.J.Kelly	c Coningham b Laver	48			
C.E.McLeod	c McKibbin b Coningham	32	(2)	not out	20
E.Jones	c Reedman b Eady	22			
W.P.Howell	not out	0	(3)	not out	20
Extras	(b3, lb1, w1, nb3)	8			-
Total	(89.2 overs, 275 mins)	338		(13.2 overs, 40 mins) (1 wkt)	60

AUSTRALIAN XI	O	M	R	W	w,nb		O	M	R	W	w,nb		FALL OF WICKETS				
														REST	AUST	REST	AUST
Jones	27	7	68	4	-,-		19	2	71	2	1,-			1st	1st	2nd	2nd
Noble	16	2	52	1	1,-		15.1	4	45	6	-,-		Wkt				
Howell	11.2	2	27	2	-,-		7	2	22	1	-,-		1st	9	1	4	27
Trumble	15	4	29	1	-,-		9	3	21	1	-,3		2nd	28	52	34	-
McLeod	14	2	40	2	-,-								3rd	86	104	36	-
													4th	102	150	83	-
THE REST	O	M	R	W	w,nb		O	M	R	W	w,nb		5th	117	197	90	-
Eady	27.2	6	104	2	-,-		6	0	33	0	-,-		6th	145	225	118	-
Giller	10	4	32	1	-,-								7th	165	231	122	-
Laver	17	7	49	3	-,-								8th	175	305	137	-
McKibbin	12	1	66	1	-,3	(3)	1	0	7	0	-,-		9th	210	336	163	-
Giffen	8	0	33	1	-,-	(2)	6.2	3	20	1	-,-		10th	227	338	170	-
Coningham	12	3	40	2	1,-												
Reedman	3	1	6	0	-,-												

AUSTRALIAN XI v THE REST

Played at Adelaide Oval on March 17, 18, 20, 21, 22, 1899. (Five-day match)
Toss : The Rest.　　　　　　　　Result : AUSTRALIAN XI WON BY BY FOUR WICKETS.
Debuts: - Nil.
12th Men: V.Hugo (both sides).
Umpires: P.Argall and G.E.Downs.
Attendances: 2000, 5000, 1000, 200, 100.　　　Total: About 8300.　　　Receipts: £265.
Close of Play: 1st day Aust 2/31 (Howell 13, Jones 10); 2nd day Aust 9/316 (McLeod 8, Trumble 1); 3rd day Rest (2) 4/82 (Giller 43); 4th day Aust (2) 5/58 (Worrall 14, McLeod 3).

The match was restricted to five days because of the tour arrangements to England, the *Ormuz* sailing on March 23rd (4.00pm) from Largs Bay, Adelaide. Trumper (75 in 145 minutes, 6 fours) was named as the 14th and last member of the Australian team after his innings on the opening day, consequently he had less than a week's advice that he would be leaving the country. Lyons (42 in 60 minutes, 5 fours and 42 in 60 minutes, 1 five and 4 fours) hit hard in both innings, breaking a bat during his first innings effort. Fred Jarvis (75 not out in 105 minutes, 7 fours) and McKibbin added 77 for the last wicket in the first innings. Giffen dismissed Kelly with his first ball. Darling (69 in 105 minutes, 1 five and 8 fours) and Iredale (87 in 140 minutes, 1 five and 8 fours) provided the batting highlights for the Australian XI. The match began in perfect weather but rain arrived on the third day and caused several interruptions to play on that and the fourth day. Batting became more difficult on the wicket as it cut up. Kelly had severe earache on the fourth day and did not take the field, Hugo substituting and Hill keeping wicket. The scorebook consulted for this and the previous two matches between the teams was the Australian tour book taken to England. *Wisden* gives incorrect match dates and venue. Sources: *Wisden, Aust XI Scorebook, SACA Report, Adelaide Advertiser, South Australian Register.*

THE REST

J.F.Giller	c Hill b Jones	10		c Noble b Howell	43
J.C.Reedman	b Jones	5	(5)	c Hill b Howell	3
V.T.Trumper	c Hill b McLeod	75		b Trumble	0
F.J.Laver	b Noble	5		b Noble	26
F.T.Hack	b Noble	3	(2)	run out (Hill/Kelly)	6
J.J.Lyons	c Hill b Jones	42		c sub (V.Hugo) b McLeod	42
*G.Giffen	c & b McLeod	11		b Howell	1
C.J.Eady	c Iredale b McLeod	4		c Darling b McLeod	16
A.Jarvis	not out	75		not out	9
†A.H.Jarvis	c Hill b Trumble	2		c Noble b McLeod	5
T.R.McKibbin	c Jones b McLeod	27		c sub (V.Hugo) b McLeod	0
Extras	(b5, lb1, nb1)	7		(b4, lb4, w1, nb1)	10
Total	(79.5 overs, 250 mins)	266		(70.3 overs, 210 mins)	161

AUSTRALIAN XI

J.Worrall	lbw b Giffen	7	(5)	not out	29
†J.J.Kelly	b Giffen	1			
W.P.Howell	c A.H.Jarvis b A.Jarvis	26			
E.Jones	b Giffen	11			
*J.Darling	c A.Jarvis b Laver	69	(2)	c Hack b Giffen	3
C.Hill	b Laver	33	(3)	b Laver	0
F.A.Iredale	c A.Jarvis b Giffen	87	(1)	c Hack b Giffen	34
S.E.Gregory	lbw b Reedman	30	(4)	c Giffen b Laver	3
M.A.Noble	c Giller b Eady	39	(6)	b Giffen	1
C.E.McLeod	not out	30	(7)	c Lyons b Eady	9
H.Trumble	c A.H.Jarvis b Giller	15	(8)	not out	0
Extras	(b3, nb1)	4			-
Total	(126.5 overs, 360 mins)	352		(33.3 overs, 90 mins) (6 wkts)	79

AUSTRALIAN XI	O	M	R	W	w,nb		O	M	R	W	w,nb
Jones	21	3	68	3	-,-						
Noble	19	1	81	2	-,-	(4)	11	5	20	1	-,-
Howell	13	2	42	0	-,-		13	1	42	3	-,-
McLeod	17.5	5	48	4	-,-	(1)	24.3	7	46	4	-,-
Trumble	9	4	20	1	-,1	(2)	22	6	43	1	1,1

THE REST	O	M	R	W	w,nb		O	M	R	W	w,nb
Eady	30	5	79	1	-,-	(3)	3	1	6	1	-,-
Giffen	27	2	99	4	-,-	(1)	14	2	31	3	-,-
A.Jarvis	15	2	31	1	-,-						
Laver	16	3	44	2	-,-	(2)	14	7	27	2	-,-
Giller	14.5	2	28	1	-,-						
Reedman	9	0	24	1	-,-						
Lyons	4	0	14	0	-,-						
McKibbin	11	3	29	0	-,1	(4)	2.3	0	15	0	-,-

FALL OF WICKETS

Wkt	REST 1st	AUST 1st	REST 2nd	AUST 2nd
1st	9	2	24	15
2nd	26	21	26	22
3rd	31	35	73	40
4th	37	79	82	40
5th	108	146	91	42
6th	135	153	101	64
7th	149	228	139	-
8th	167	303	150	-
9th	189	314	159	-
10th	266	352	161	-

WESTERN AUSTRALIA v SOUTH AUSTRALIA

Played at W.A.C.A. Ground, Perth, on April 3, 4, 5, 6, 1899. (Timeless match)

Toss : South Australia.   Result : SOUTH AUSTRALIA WON BY FOUR WICKETS.

Debuts: Western Australia - L.L.Herring, A.W.Hoskings, A.E.Jackson, E.J.Keogh, W.T.Lockwood, R.A.Selk, F.Devenish-Meares - (all f/c); H.V.P.Harris, W.H.Moore (WA only). South Australia - N.Claxton, H.J.Day, W.A.Hewer, A.V.Rosman, A.C.Thomas (all f/c).

12th Men: C.W.Caldwell and F.L.Richards named as emergencies for WA. Only 11 players in SA party.

Umpires: S.Greenwood and A.Marshall.

Attendances: 2000, 900, 1000, 500.   Total: About 4400.   Receipts: No figures published.

Close of Play: 1st day SA 7/151 (Hewer 19, Travers 8); 2nd day WA (2) 7/227 (Jackson 23, Moore 8); 3rd day SA (2) 5/143 (Rosman 25).

The first intercolonial match to be played on even terms in Western Australia is now accepted as that State's inaugural first-class match on home soil. It was scheduled to start on April 1, but the *S.S.Paroo* carrying the South Australians was delayed in departure from Port Adelaide and by heavy weather in transit. The journey via Albany took six days. The home batsmen appeared overawed by the occasion on the first day to be all out soon after the luncheon adjournment. The South Australians fared little better, only "Fred" Jarvis (48 in 76 minutes, 3 fours) showing any capacity for scoring. Hoskings (53 in 95 minutes, 7 fours) gave the Western Australians a sound beginning in the second innings and consistent batting down the order set the scene for an interesting finish. Hack (69 in 185 minutes, 5 fours) laid the foundations for the visitors and Rosman (63 in 200 minutes, 4 fours) and Hewer (46 not out in 130 minutes, 3 fours) methodically completed the task. Thomas (the second wicket-keeper in the South Australian party) took the gloves for the pre-lunch session of the second day but A.H.Jarvis resumed the duties thereafter. Three days had been allocated for the match but a fourth (which commenced at 2.45pm) was added in order to obtain a result. The wicket was "an excellent one" and "ideal cricket weather" (*West Australian*) prevailed. Harris had previously appeared for Tasmania in New Zealand (4 matches) in 1883-84 and Moore for New South Wales (4 matches) in 1893-94. Sources: *C.B.O'Reilly, The West Australian, Daily News.*

WESTERN AUSTRALIA

A.W.Hoskings	c Day b A.Jarvis	26	b A.Jarvis		53
W.T.Lockwood	c Hack b Travers	0	b Hugo		21
F.Devenish-Meares	lbw b Travers	16	c Hugo b A.Jarvis		16
L.L.Herring	run out (A.H.Jarvis)	7	lbw b Hugo		34
H.V.P.Harris	c A.H.Jarvis b Homburg	22	b A.Jarvis		32
E.J.Keogh	c & b A.Jarvis	13	lbw b A.Jarvis		1
A.E.Jackson	b Hugo	4	c Claxton b A.Jarvis		43
R.A.Selk	b Homburg	4	b Hugo		6
*†W.H.Moore	b Hugo	4	b Hugo		14
E.A.Randell	b Homburg	0	c Travers b A.Jarvis		36
E.G.Bishop	not out	1	not out		0
Extras		3			37
Total	(37.0 overs, 115 mins)	100	(106.0 overs, 280 mins)		293

SOUTH AUSTRALIA

F.T.Hack	run out (Bishop/Moore)	13	b Selk		69
H.J.Day	st Moore b Keogh	14	c Moore b Selk		14
*A.Jarvis	c Randell b Selk	48	c Devenish-Meares b Selk		13
†A.H.Jarvis	run out (Devenish-Meares/Moore)	8	b Randell		11
N.Claxton	b Bishop	0	c Harris b Randell		0
R.O.Homburg	lbw b Selk	4	(8) not out		3
V.Hugo	c Harris b Randell	19			
W.A.Hewer	b Selk	19	(7) not out		46
J.P.F.Travers	b Selk	13			
A.V.Rosman	not out	3	(6) b Keogh		63
A.C.Thomas	b Randell	0			
Extras		18			16
Total	(69.0 overs, 200 mins)	159	(124.0 overs, 315 mins) (6 wkts)		235

SOUTH AUSTRALIA	O	M	R	W	w,nb		O	M	R	W	w,nb
Travers	14	0	50	2		(2)	9	3	26	0	
Homburg	10	2	18	3		(1)	14	4	23	0	
A.Jarvis	7	1	21	2		(4)	43	9	114	6	
Hugo	6	2	8	2		(3)	28	9	69	4	
Claxton							3	0	11	0	
Rosman							9	2	13	0	

WESTERN AUSTRALIA	O	M	R	W	w,nb		O	M	R	W	w,nb
Randell	15	5	37	2		(3)	28	13	31	2	
Selk	21	7	48	4		(1)	40	12	86	3	2,-
Bishop	20	10	23	1		(2)	26	6	40	0	
Keogh	9	1	27	1			16	2	41	1	
Hoskings	4	1	6	0			9	3	12	0	
Devenish-Meares							5	1	9	0	

FALL OF WICKETS

Wkt	WA 1st	SA 1st	WA 2nd	SA 2nd
1st	1	26	39	30
2nd	37	70	68	49
3rd	49	94	98	73
4th	51	94	150	81
5th	72	102	154	143
6th	87	109	185	226
7th	92	129	195	-
8th	99	151	235	-
9th	99	158	291	-
10th	100	159	293	-

1899-1900 SEASON (11 MATCHES)

A totally domestic season saw in the 20th century. Eleven first-class matches in all were staged, culminating in a patriotic event to raise funds for the Australian commitment to the Boer War in South Africa. It was a season of particularly high run-scoring, especially in the Sheffield Shield, and several new records were established.

The winner of the Sheffield Shield boiled down to the result of the final match at Sydney between New South Wales and Victoria. Both teams had won two of their three matches going into the game. It remained evenly poised until a fine century from Noble (155) in the second innings gave New South Wales the upper hand. Victoria were presented with a difficult task of scoring 375 to win, and Noble ensured victory for New South Wales by shooting out the first six batsmen. It was a fitting climax to the season.

The battle for the Shield began in late November with the visits to Adelaide of Victoria and then New South Wales. Both visiting teams scored heavily, New South Wales exceeding 800, and South Australia were completely outplayed on both occasions. New South Wales accounted for Victoria by an innings at Melbourne on their return journey to establish themselves as favourites for the title. South Australia met Victoria at Melbourne a week later and suffered their third heavy defeat in succession, despite an unbeaten century from Clem Hill. Moving on to Sydney, they caused a big upset by beating the in-form New South Welshmen - despite the loss of George Giffen through injury after the first innings. South Australia's otherwise disappointing season had had an encouraging conclusion, thanks to a fine show of bowling from Jones and an unbeaten 158 from Fred Hack, and it set up the fascinating Shield decider between New South Wales and Victoria.

New South Wales this season were able to boast one of the strongest batting lineups in the history of Australian domestic cricket. Trumper, Noble, Gregory, Donnan, Iredale and Kelly were all Australian representatives, while emerging players Hopkins and Duff were to join the Test ranks within a year or two. New South Wales scored 2541 runs at an average of 42.35 in the four Sheffield Shield matches, and Noble completed an outstanding allround season by finishing with more wickets than any other player and more runs than anyone else, other than Trumper who was at his brilliant best.

In other matches, Queensland met New South Wales both at home and away. It was the first time they had played twice in one season, and New South Wales fielded strong XIs to win both encounters by an innings. New South Wales also sent their first team to Tasmania, though it was virtually a Second XI owing to Sheffield Shield commitments.

The 1899 Australians, who had defeated England 1-0 in a five-Test series the previous winter, overcame an XI comprising the Rest of Australia at Sydney in early February 1900 to bring the first-class season to a close.

On the administrative front, the Australasian Cricket Council was disbanded. New South Wales had withdrawn from the council in May 1899, and at a meeting in January 1900 the remaining delegates from South Australia and Victoria bowed to the inevitable. The ACC had failed to gain control of the off-field affairs from powerful local bodies such as Melbourne Cricket Club, and they had also failed to win the confidence of players, who feared the loss of their share of profits from overseas tours. Four years passed before a second, and ultimately more successful, attempt was made to form a controlling body.

Leading Aggregates

Batsmen	M	I	NO	Runs	HS	Ave.	Bowlers	Runs	Wkts	Ave.
V.T.Trumper (NSW)	7	10	0	721	208	72.10	M.A.Noble (NSW)	764	37	20.64
M.A.Noble (NSW)	7	10	0	694	200	69.40	H.Trumble (V)	688	28	24.57
H.Graham (V)	5	10	0	487	118	48.70	G.Giffen (SA)	654	24	27.25
F.T.Hack (SA)	3	6	1	441	158*	88.20	J.V.Saunders (V)	538	21	25.61
C.Hill (SA)	5	10	1	423	126*	47.00	E.Jones (SA)	913	20	45.65
S.E.Gregory (NSW)	5	8	0	381	176	47.62				
J.H.Stuckey (V)	5	10	0	374	94	37.40				
A.J.Y.Hopkins (NSW)	7	10	1	370	86	41.11				
H.Donnan (NSW)	6	8	0	352	113	44.00				

SHEFFIELD SHIELD TABLE

	P	W	L	D	Quotient	Runs Scored	Wkts Lost	Runs Conceded	Wkts Taken
NEW SOUTH WALES	4	3	1	-	1.751	2541	60	1765	73
VICTORIA	4	2	2	-	0.879	2237	80	2195	69
SOUTH AUSTRALIA	4	1	3	-	0.683	1939	72	2757	70
TOTAL	6	6	6	-	1.000	6717	212	6717	212

NEW SOUTH WALES v QUEENSLAND

Played at Sydney Cricket Ground on November 17 (no play), 18, 20, 21, 1899. (Timeless Match)
Toss : New South Wales.   Result : NEW SOUTH WALES WON BY AN INNINGS AND 315 RUNS.
Debuts: New South Wales - A.J.Bowden, T.H.Howard, E.W.Jansan (all f/c). Queensland - M.M.Campbell, P.Carew, E.W.Currie,
    C.F.Morgan (all f/c).
12th Men: R.A.Duff (NSW) and W.Richardson (Qld).
Umpires : R.Callaway and A.Lucas.
Attendances: no play, 2000, 800, 100.   Total: About 2900.   Receipts: No figures published.
Close of Play : 1st day no play; 2nd day NSW 6/462 (Farquhar 18, Kelly 10); 3rd day Qld 9/149 (Crouch 8, Currie 5)

Queensland conceded their highest total and suffered their biggest defeat by an innings margin yet. Rain prevented play on the first day but good drying conditions and much rolling produced a better wicket than had been expected. Trumper (208 in 185 minutes, 1 five and 25 fours) gave two chances, both off McGlinchey, the first to Morgan when 47 and the second to Macdonald when 49. He reached his century in 120 minutes, brought up 150 in 150 minutes, and scored his last 182 runs in 143 minutes (26* - 151* in lunch-tea session). With Donnan (113 in 165 minutes, 8 fours) he put on 243 for the second wicket. Farquhar (57 in 75 minutes, 2 fives and 7 fours) also batted well, while Pye (61 in 60 minutes, 7 fours) and Bowden (45 not out in 60 minutes, 4 fours) added 105 for the tenth wicket. James Carew (52 in 75 minutes, 9 fours) topscored for Queensland. Howard (offbreaks) took his best first-class figures at the earliest opportunity. Patrick Carew was out to the first and third balls he faced respectively on debut. S.E.Gregory (flu), F.A.Iredale (flu) and W.P.Howell (leg injury) were unavailable for New South Wales. T.Byrne, J.A.Cuffe, A.H.V.Hewitt, W.Hoare and E.J.Metcalfe all withdrew from the Queensland side for a variety of reasons. *Cricket* incorrectly gives Qld (1) Clark c Mackenzie b Noble, omits Pye 0/21; Qld (2) Noble 2/24, omits Pye 0/14 and Hopkins 0/21; NSW innings, omits Macdonald 0/18 and Jones 0/20. *Sydney Telegraph* gives NSW innings, P.Carew 2/153, J.Carew 2/104; Qld (2) extras 8 total 170, NSW winning by an innings & 316 runs. Sources: *Cricket, Sydney Referee, Sydney Morning Herald, Town & Country Journal, Sydney Mail, Sydney Daily Telegraph*.

NEW SOUTH WALES

H.Donnan	c Atkins b McGlinchey	113
M.A.Noble	lbw b McGlinchey	15
V.T.Trumper	c Campbell b Crouch	208
E.W.Jansan	b P.Carew	22
A.C.K.Mackenzie	c Atkins b McGlinchey	33
A.J.Y.Hopkins	c J.Carew b Campbell	35
B.W.Farquhar	b J.Carew	57
*†J.J.Kelly	b J.Carew	35
L.W.Pye	b McGlinchey	61
T.H.Howard	c Jones b P.Carew	1
A.J.Bowden	not out	45
Extras	(b11, lb1, nb3)	15
Total	(159.0 overs, 385 mins)	640

QUEENSLAND

*S.P.Jones	b Bowden	8	c Farquhar b Bowden		33
J.Carew	c Pye b Howard	52	b Howard		2
R.Macdonald	st Kelly b Howard	3	b Howard		26
W.W.McGlinchey	c Donnan b Howard	12	run out (Howard/Noble)		23
A.A.Atkins	lbw b Noble	33	b Trumper		30
M.M.Campbell	b Howard	3	c Mackenzie b Noble		7
C.F.Morgan	c Pye b Howard	21	run out (Donnan/Kelly)		0
J.P.Clark	c Mackenzie b Howard	0	b Noble		0
E.R.Crouch	not out	10	not out		35
P.Carew	c Mackenzie b Noble	0	b Trumper		0
†E.W.Currie	b Bowden	8	c Pye b Bowden		6
Extras	(b4)	4	(b7, nb2)		9
Total	(62.0 overs, 170 mins)	154	(68.0 overs, 195 mins)		171

QUEENSLAND	O	M	R	W	w,nb
McGlinchey	46	5	180	4	-,-
P.Carew	36	5	152	2	-,-
Campbell	23	5	83	1	-,-
J.Carew	29	2	105	2	-,3
Crouch	19	2	67	1	-,-
Macdonald	3	0	18	0	-,-
Jones	3	0	20	0	-,-

NEW SOUTH WALES	O	M	R	W	w,nb		O	M	R	W	w,nb
Noble	19	9	33	2	-,-	(3)	11	4	21	2	-,-
Bowden	16	5	37	2	-,-		19	4	42	1	-,-
Howard	20	5	59	6	-,-	(1)	20	5	52	3	-,1
Pye	7	1	21	0	-,-		5	2	14	0	-,1
Hopkins							6	1	21	0	-,-
Trumper							7	2	12	2	-,-

FALL OF WICKETS

	NSW	QLD	QLD
Wkt	1st	1st	2nd
1st	32	19	13
2nd	275	57	42
3rd	318	68	89
4th	375	82	95
5th	418	85	102
6th	443	121	103
7th	531	125	106
8th	534	140	150
9th	535	140	150
10th	640	154	171

SOUTH AUSTRALIA v VICTORIA (Shield Match 1)

Played at Adelaide Oval on November 24, 25, 27, 28, 29, 30, 1899. (Timeless match).
Toss : Victoria   Result : VICTORIA WON BY 246 RUNS.
Debuts: South Australia - P.M.Newland (f/c). Victoria - F.B.Collins (f/c).
12th Men: T.S.Warne (Vic). No 12th named for SA.
Umpires : R.M.Crockett and T.A.Reeves.
Attendances: 2000, 5000, 1500, 1000, 1000, 100.   Total: About 10,600.   Receipts: No figures published.
Close of Play : 1st day Vic 5/277 (Graham 106, Bruce 0); 2nd day SA 5/131 (Giffen 20);3rd day Vic (2) 5/161 (Stuckey 43, Collins 4);
   4th day Vic (2) 408 all out; 5th day SA (2) 7/301 (Hack 112, Travers 13)

J.F.Giller, F.J.Laver (influenza), C.E.McLeod (work) and J.Worrall (injured knee) were unavailable for the trip to Adelaide and Victoria were forced to leave out Warne (influenza) after their arrival. He returned to Melbourne on the first day, R.W.McLeod, the Victorian manager, having taken his place in the team for his last first-class match. McAlister (52 in 125 minutes, 3 fours), Graham (118 in 170 minutes, 8 fours, 3 chances) and Trumble (50 in 90 minutes, 4 fours) batted well on the first day. Collins (6 for 81) made a most impressive debut with the ball. Stuckey (94 in 250 minutes, 7 fours) held the second innings together before a last-wicket stand of 132 by Ross and No. 11 batsman McLeod (91 in 120 minutes, 6 fours) put the match out of South Australia's reach. It was the second-highest tenth-wicket partnership recorded thus far in Australian first-class matches (136 by J.P.O'Halloran/A.E.Johns, Vic v SA at Melbourne 1896-97 being higher). Hack, who had ended the stand by dismissing McLeod with his seventh ball in first-class cricket, scored his maiden first-class hundred (115 in 260 minutes, 4 fours) in South Australia's second innings. Hill (54 in 90 minutes, 1 four) made an uncertain half-century. Giffen, who had injured a finger attempting to catch Ross on the fourth day, elected to bat only if victory was a possibility for South Australia. *Wisden* incorrectly gives Vic (1) McAlister 54. Sources: *Wisden, C.B.O'Reilly, The Australasian, Adelaide Advertiser, South Australian Register.*

VICTORIA

P.A.McAlister	b Giffen	52	c Jones b Lyons		18
S.A.McMichael	c Newland b Jarvis	27	st Newland b Giffen		40
H.Graham	b Giffen	118	c Leak b Travers		42
J.H.Stuckey	b Lyons	32	c Jarvis b Giffen		94
*H.Trumble	c & b Reedman	50	b Jarvis		2
D.Sutherland	b Jarvis	1	lbw b Giffen	(8)	49
W.Bruce	lbw b Giffen	24	b Giffen	(9)	2
W.W.Armstrong	not out	32	b Jones	(6)	8
R.W.McLeod	c Hill b Jones	14	c Giffen b Hack	(11)	91
†C.H.Ross	run out (Jones)	0	not out		39
F.B.Collins	b Giffen	0	b Giffen	(7)	9
Extras	(b6, lb4)	10	(b12, lb2)		14
Total	(153.4 overs, 390 mins)	360	(157.1 overs, 405 mins)		408

SOUTH AUSTRALIA

J.J.Lyons	c McMichael b Collins	20	c Stuckey b Collins		35
*J.Darling	c McLeod b Collins	9	lbw b Trumble		5
C.Hill	lbw b Collins	1	b Trumble		54
F.T.Hack	c McAlister b Trumble	33	c McLeod b Trumble		115
J.C.Reedman	b McLeod	44	c Armstrong b Trumble		16
G.Giffen	c McAlister b Collins	39	absent injured		-
A.Jarvis	c McAlister b Trumble	29	b Armstrong	(6)	13
E.H.Leak	c McLeod b Trumble	6	b Bruce	(7)	33
E.Jones	b Collins	0	c Armstrong b Bruce	(8)	8
J.P.F.Travers	not out	14	c & b Collins	(9)	14
†P.M.Newland	b Collins	0	not out	(10)	0
Extras	(b4, lb5)	9	(b10, lb1, w1)		12
Total	(102.3 overs, 285 mins)	204	(111.1 overs, 300 mins)		318

SOUTH AUSTRALIA	O	M	R	W	w,nb		O	M	R	W	w,nb			FALL OF WICKETS			
														VIC	SA	VIC	SA
Jones	43	17	97	1	-,-		36	12	97	1	-,-		Wkt	1st	1st	2nd	2nd
Giffen	51.4	16	101	4	-,-		57	14	145	5	-,-		1st	68	28	42	23
Travers	14	4	40	0	-,-		19	4	47	1	-,-		2nd	108	31	65	52
Lyons	9	1	29	1	-,-	(5)	10	1	24	1	-,-		3rd	171	36	125	130
Jarvis	24	4	54	2	-,-	(4)	26	6	59	1	-,-		4th	273	100	134	153
Reedman	12	4	29	1	-,-		9	2	22	0	-,-		5th	276	131	150	185
Hack							0.1	0	0	1	-,-		6th	310	163	171	250
													7th	315	174	265	260
VICTORIA	O	M	R	W	w,nb		O	M	R	W	w,nb		8th	358	175	271	304
Collins	42.3	8	81	6	-,-		30.1	4	105	2	-,-		9th	359	203	276	318
Trumble	32	4	69	3	-,-		42	12	101	4	-,-		10th	360	204	408	-
Bruce	17	6	24	0	-,-	(4)	15	6	31	2	1,-						
McLeod	11	5	21	1	-,-	(3)	7	0	22	0	-,-						
Armstrong							12	5	20	1	-,-						
Graham							2	0	21	0	-,-						
McAlister							3	1	6	0	-,-						

QUEENSLAND v NEW SOUTH WALES

Played at Brisbane Cricket Ground (Woolloongabba) on November 25, 27, 28, 1899. (Timeless Match)
Toss : New South Wales.   Result : NEW SOUTH WALES WON BY AN INNINGS AND 85 RUNS.
Debuts: Queensland - C.Y.Adamson (f/c); A.H.V.Hewitt (Qld only).
12th Men : J.A.Cuffe & C.F.Morgan (Qld emergencies) and E.W.Jansan (NSW).
Umpires : R.Callaway and G.F.J.Hewitt.
Attendances: 4000, 500, 100.   Total: About 4600.   Receipts: No figures published.
Close of Play : 1st day NSW 8/346 (Hopkins 33, Bowden 19); 2nd day Qld (2) 3/62 Atkins 4, Jones 2)

This was Queensland's sixth loss in a row against New South Wales, the last three being by innings margins. Adamson replaced J.P.Clark (unavailable) in the selected Queensland team as neither Cuffe nor Morgan, the nominated emergencies, were available when invited. Hewitt had previously appeared for the Combined Queensland-Victoria XI against Stoddart's England XI in 1897-98. Half-centuries by Trumper (77 in 75 minutes, 10 fours), Farquhar (85 in 90 minutes, 1 five and 5 fours) and an unbeaten 48 by Hopkins (75 minutes, 5 fours) gave the visitors a respectable score on an initially soft wicket. The *Courier* correspondent reported that Adamson ran "fully 40 yards" to dismiss Iredale and that "better has never been seen in Brisbane". Despite the pitch playing fast and true on the second day only Macdonald (50 not out in 150 minutes, 6 fours) reached the half-century for Queensland. Pye's career-best 5 for 29 included the wicket of Adamson, out first ball on debut. Bowden and Howard were the only bowlers used by Kelly on a wearing last-day wicket. *Cricket* incorrectly gives NSW Pye b Jones; Qld (1) Bradley c & b Noble, Noble 4/54, Pye 4/29. *Cricket* and *Referee* give Qld (1) McGlinchey 4, extras 11. Other sources give McGlinchey 5, extras 10, Hopkins 1/16 (does not tally). There is much confusion in Qld (2). *Courier, Qld Times* and *Queenslander* all give extras 9, total 129, while *SMH, Telegraph* and *Mail* all give Crouch 1, extras 9, total 130. The score of Qld (2) given here is from *Referee*. All sources except *Cricket, Referee* and *Telegraph* incorrectly give Qld (2) Pye 2/34. Sources: *Cricket, Sydney Referee, Sydney Morning Herald, Town & Country Journal, Sydney Daily Telegraph, Sydney Mail, Brisbane Courier, Queensland Times, The Queenslander.*

NEW SOUTH WALES

*†J.J.Kelly	c Ramsay b Byrne	0
R.A.Duff	run out (Crouch)	26
H.Donnan	b McGlinchey	37
M.A.Noble	b Hewitt	12
V.T.Trumper	c Byrne b Ramsay	77
F.A.Iredale	c Adamson b McGlinchey	10
B.W.Farquhar	c Byrne b Jones	85
L.W.Pye	lbw b Jones	40
A.J.Y.Hopkins	not out	48
A.J.Bowden	c & b Jones	27
T.H.Howard	b Hewitt	2
Extras	(b4, lb2, w1)	7
Total	(95.0 overs, 307 mins)	371

QUEENSLAND

†W.F.Bradley	c & b Pye	40		b Pye	20
J.Carew	b Noble	1	(3)	c Trumper b Pye	29
R.Macdonald	not out	50	(2)	c Kelly b Noble	1
A.A.Atkins	b Pye	0		st Kelly b Bowden	13
*S.P.Jones	b Noble	19		c Hopkins b Bowden	26
M.F.Ramsay	lbw b Hopkins	17		c Iredale b Howard	9
W.W.McGlinchey	b Pye	5		c Hopkins b Howard	7
C.Y.Adamson	st Kelly b Pye	0		b Howard	10
E.R.Crouch	b Farquhar	3		b Bowden	0
A.H.V.Hewitt	b Noble	11		not out	5
T.Byrne	lbw b Pye	0		b Howard	0
Extras	(b5, lb4, w1)	10		(b6, lb2, w1, nb1)	10
Total	(62.0 overs, 178 mins)	156		(53.0 overs, 149 mins)	130

QUEENSLAND	O	M	R	W	w,nb
Byrne	10	1	40	1	-,-
McGlinchey	16	1	72	2	-,-
Hewitt	24	3	85	2	1,-
Adamson	12	0	67	0	-,-
Ramsay	16	1	53	1	-,-
Carew	5	1	19	0	-,-
Jones	12	4	28	3	-,-

NEW SOUTH WALES	O	M	R	W	w,nb		O	M	R	W	w,nb
Noble	19	7	54	3	-,-	(2)	10	1	22	1	1,-
Howard	6	1	24	0	-,-	(4)	14	4	40	4	-,-
Bowden	5	0	8	0	-,-	(5)	13	4	24	3	-,-
Trumper	6	1	12	0	-,-						
Pye	18	9	29	5	-,-	(1)	13	2	33	2	-,1
Hopkins	6	1	15	1	1,-						
Farquhar	2	1	4	1	-,-	(3)	3	2	1	0	-,-

FALL OF WICKETS

		NSW	QLD	QLD
	Wkt	1st	1st	2nd
	1st	10	9	5
	2nd	42	57	49
	3rd	58	57	56
	4th	104	88	79
	5th	116	121	100
	6th	197	126	110
	7th	287	126	114
	8th	296	140	125
	9th	364	151	125
	10th	371	156	130

SOUTH AUSTRALIA v NEW SOUTH WALES (Shield Match 2)

Played at Adelaide Oval on December 16, 18, 19, 20, 1899. (Timeless Match)
Toss : South Australia.   Result : NEW SOUTH WALES WON BY AN INNINGS AND 392 RUNS.
Debuts: Nil
12th Men : E.L.Walkley (SA) and A.J.Bowden (NSW).
Umpires : P.Argall and R.Callaway.
Attendances : 3000, 1000, 500, 200.   Total: About 4700.   Receipts: £137.
Close of Play : 1st day NSW 1/69 (Donnan 22, Trumper 38); 2nd day NSW 4/446 (Noble 134, Gregory 57); 3rd day SA (2) 0/12 (Leak 4,
   Chinner 6)

South Australia won the toss but lost Lyons to the second ball of the match but never recovered. Only Hill (53 in 125 minutes, 6 fours)
and Reedman (83 in 145 minutes, 10 fours) scored half-centuries for the home side. New South Wales's total was easily the highest yet in
a Sheffield Shield match (previously 570, NSW v Vic at Sydney 1896-97) and contained centuries by Trumper (165 in 195 minutes, 1 five
and 16 fours), Noble (200 in 285 minutes, 18 fours) and Gregory (176 in 305 minutes, 14 fours) and half-centuries by Donnan (72 in 140
minutes, 5 fours) and Hopkins (86 in 120 minutes). Noble, who scored his third century in a row in Shield matches, and Gregory added
286, the highest partnership yet for the fifth wicket in Australian first-class cricket and the highest in a Shield match for any wicket.
Giffen conceded the record number of runs by a bowler in a Shield innings until 1926-27. South Australia played without Darling
(influenza) after the second day. Reedman led the side in his absence and Walkley fielded as substitute. The match had been scheduled to
commence on December 15th but was delayed due to uncertainty about the time of arrival of the New South Wales team. F.T.Hack and
J.P.F.Travers were unavailable for South Australia. Last first-class appearance by J.J.Lyons. *Wisden* incorrectly gives SA (2) Reedman
88. Sources: *Wisden, C.B.O'Reilly, Sydney Referee, Sydney Morning Herald, Adelaide Advertiser, South Australian Register.*

SOUTH AUSTRALIA

J.J.Lyons	c & b Noble	0	(4)	b Pye	11
A.Jarvis	b Howell	6	(7)	b Hopkins	2
C.Hill	c & b Howell	16		b Pye	53
*J.Darling	b Noble	4		absent ill	-
G.Giffen	b Howell	9	(6)	c Pye b Hopkins	18
J.C.Reedman	c Pye b Howell	32	(5)	b Trumper	83
E.H.Leak	not out	40	(1)	b Howell	4
N.Claxton	b Pye	11		c Kelly b Pye	1
H.G.W.Chinner	run out (Noble/Kelly)	26	(2)	c Iredale b Pye	37
†A.H.Jarvis	run out	4	(9)	c Noble b Trumper	32
E.Jones	b Howell	6	(10)	not out	1
Extras	(lb1)	1		(b8, lb8, nb2)	18
Total	(77.5 overs, 225 mins)	155		(105.0 overs, 285 mins)	260

NEW SOUTH WALES

A.C.K.Mackenzie	run out (Leak/A.H.Jarvis)	9
H.Donnan	b Giffen	72
V.T.Trumper	lbw b Giffen	165
B.W.Farquhar	b Giffen	0
M.A.Noble	lbw b Giffen	200
*S.E.Gregory	c sub (E.L.Walkley) b Jones	176
F.A.Iredale	c & b Giffen	12
A.J.Y.Hopkins	c & b Giffen	86
†J.J.Kelly	b Giffen	23
L.W.Pye	lbw b Giffen	27
W.P.Howell	not out	24
Extras	(b5, lb5, w3)	13
Total	(217.1 overs, 585 mins)	807

NEW SOUTH WALES	O	M	R	W	w,nb		O	M	R	W	w,nb
Noble	26	8	71	2	-,-		24	7	50	0	-,-
Howell	32.5	14	52	5	-,-		25	16	66	1	-,-
Pye	12	5	17	1	-,-	(5)	34	8	71	4	-,-
Trumper	7	4	14	0	-,-	(6)	1	0	1	2	-,-
Farquhar						(3)	4	0	9	0	-,-
Hopkins						(4)	17	3	45	2	-,2

SOUTH AUSTRALIA	O	M	R	W	w,nb
Jones	50	6	210	1	-,-
Giffen	77.1	7	287	8	-,-
Reedman	24	3	75	0	1,-
Lyons	26	4	78	0	-,-
A.Jarvis	24	2	84	0	-,-
Claxton	5	0	19	0	-,-
Leak	2	0	12	0	-,-
Hill	9	1	29	0	2,-

FALL OF WICKETS

Wkt	SA 1st	NSW 1st	SA 2nd
1st	0	10	15
2nd	8	201	85
3rd	17	201	105
4th	32	278	114
5th	55	564	149
6th	82	588	155
7th	97	694	156
8th	144	744	259
9th	149	763	260
10th	155	807	-

VICTORIA v NEW SOUTH WALES (SHIELD MATCH 3)

Played at the Melbourne Cricket Ground on December 23, 26, 27, 28, 1899. (Timeless Match)
Toss : New South Wales.   Result : NEW SOUTH WALES WON BY AN INNINGS AND 274 RUNS.
Debuts: Nil
12th Men : W.W.Armstrong (Vic) and A.J.Bowden (NSW).
Umpires : R.Callaway and R.M.Crockett.
Attendances: 4000, 6000, 4000, 1500.   Total: About 15,500.   Receipts: £571.
Close of Play : 1st day NSW 3/321 (Mackenzie 52, Gregory 13); 2nd day NSW 5/469 (Iredale 67, Hopkins 44); 3rd day Vic (2) 0/35
    (Worrall 29, Warne 5)

New South Wales continued their exceptional form of late by recording their fifth successive victory by an innings against first-class opposition; the margin here was a new record for New South Wales against Victoria. Noble (122 in 192 minutes, 1 five and 9 fours) scored his fourth hundred in consecutive Sheffield Shield innings. Half-centuries were scored for New South Wales by Trumper (57 in 61 minutes, 6 fours), Donnan (74 in 175 minutes, 6 fours), Mackenzie (65 in 148 minutes, 4 fours) and Iredale (91 in 152 minutes, 7 fours). Light rain fell during the luncheon interval on the second day and further showers of increasing intensity prevailed throughout the afternoon, at first interrupting play and finally causing an abandonment at 4.45pm. The following day the pitch became more treacherous as it cut up; Victoria were heavily disadvantaged by having to bat on it at its worst. Further rain overnight delayed the start of the fourth day's play until after the scheduled lunch break. The last two wickets, Bruce (run out) and Collins (out first ball), fell to successive deliveries by Hopkins. C.E.McLeod was unavailable for Victoria. *Wisden* incorrectly gives NSW (1) Howell 9. Sources: *Wisden, VCA Report, The Age, The Argus, The Herald, The Australasian, The Leader.*

NEW SOUTH WALES

V.T.Trumper	c & b Trumble	57
H.Donnan	c Ross b Bruce	74
M.A.Noble	c Laver b Worrall	122
A.C.K.Mackenzie	c McAlister b Trumble	65
*S.E.Gregory	c Worrall b Collins	28
F.A.Iredale	c McMichael b Trumble	91
A.J.Y.Hopkins	lbw b Laver	44
B.W.Farquhar	c & b Trumble	10
†J.J.Kelly	not out	14
L.W.Pye	c Worrall b Laver	0
W.P.Howell	c Stuckey b Trumble	0
Extras	(b9, lb3, w3)	15
Total	(189.3 overs, 502 mins)	520

VICTORIA

S.A.McMichael	c Hopkins b Howell	3	(3)	b Noble	1
J.Worrall	c Iredale b Howell	19	(1)	c Howell b Noble	45
H.Graham	c Iredale b Hopkins	39	(4)	c Iredale b Hopkins	14
F.J.Laver	c & b Howell	1	(5)	c & b Hopkins	1
P.A.McAlister	c Hopkins b Howell	8	(6)	lbw b Noble	5
*H.Trumble	c Gregory b Noble	12	(7)	c Iredale b Hopkins	1
J.II.Stuckey	c Farquhar b Hopkins	18	(8)	c Mackenzie b Hopkins	5
W.Bruce	b Noble	0	(9)	run out (Trumper/Kelly)	6
T.S.Warne	not out	12	(2)	c Kelly b Noble	28
†C.H.Ross	c Kelly b Noble	8		not out	5
F.B.Collins	b Noble	2		c Farquhar b Hopkins	0
Extras	(b4, lb5)	9		(b3, nb1)	4
Total	(58.2 overs, 154 mins)	131		(50.5 overs, 145 mins)	115

VICTORIA	O	M	R	W	w,nb
Collins	34	3	104	1	1,-
Trumble	63.3	17	149	5	2,-
Laver	54	11	135	2	-,-
Warne	12	1	51	0	-,-
Bruce	21	3	56	1	-,-
Worrall	5	1	10	1	-,-

NEW SOUTH WALES	O	M	R	W	w,nb		O	M	R	W	w,nb
Pye	17	7	23	0	-,-	(5)	1	1	0	0	-,-
Howell	21	6	53	4	-,-	(1)	15	6	19	0	-,-
Noble	12.2	5	27	4	-,-	(2)	24	8	51	4	-,1
Hopkins	8	1	19	2	-,-	(3)	6.5	1	24	5	-,-
Trumper						(4)	4	1	17	0	-,-

FALL OF WICKETS

Wkt	NSW 1st	VIC 1st	VIC 2nd
1st	89	3	56
2nd	198	39	60
3rd	303	40	91
4th	345	48	93
5th	361	73	93
6th	477	102	99
7th	496	102	99
8th	511	112	109
9th	515	127	115
10th	520	131	115

VICTORIA v SOUTH AUSTRALIA (Shield Match 4)

Played at the Melbourne Cricket Ground on December 30, 1899, January 1, 2, 3, 4, 1900. (Timeless Match)
Toss : Victoria.   Result : VICTORIA WON BY 181 RUNS.
Debuts: Victoria - J.V.Saunders (f/c). South Australia - E.H.Kekwick, W.P.Stuart (both f/c).
12th Men: S.J.Donahoo (Vic) and J.J.Lyons (SA).
Umpires : P.Argall and R.M.Crockett.
Attendances: 5000, 4000, 2000, 1500, 500.   Total: About 13,000.   Receipts: £384.
Close of Play : 1st day Vic 7/243 (Trumble 36, Ross 3); 2nd day SA 5/140 (A.Jarvis 17); 3rd day Vic (2) 4/161 (Stuckey 1); 4th day
    SA (2) 2/149 (Hill 80, Darling 10)

Kekwick and Stuart replaced N.Claxton and E.H.Leak (both unavailable) before the South Australian team left Adelaide. Lyons fell ill before the match began and a replacement was sent for so he could return home. V.Hugo arrived on the third day of the match, just in time to field in the second innings for Giffen, who had strained his left side while bowling his 20th over in the first innings. Trumble split the webbing on his bowling hand in his 29th over and a strained back prevented Collins from bowling more than one over in the second innings. Donahoo, who had previously represented Victoria but was now playing with Queensland and was down in Melbourne on holiday, was engaged as the home side's 12th man. McAlister (63 in 124 minutes, 8 fours), Trumble (95 in 175 minutes, 11 fours), Graham (77 in 108 minutes, 6 fours) and McMichael (63 in 158 minutes, 1 five and 4 fours) for Victoria and Hack (54 in 145 minutes, 3 fours) and Alfred Jarvis (66 in 117 minutes, 7 fours) for South Australia all hit half-centuries with Hill (126 not out in 208 minutes, 12 fours) being the sole centurion. Kekwick's pair on debut included a first-ball dismissal in the second innings. Jones was out first ball in the first innings. *Wisden* incorrectly gives SA (2) Reedman 16. Sources: *Wisden, C.B.O'Reilly, The Age, The Argus, The Herald, The Australasian, The Leader.*

VICTORIA

J.Worrall	c A.H.Jarvis b Jones	35		c A.Jarvis b Reedman	44
T.S.Warne	c Giffen b Jones	22	(7)	b Travers	10
H.Graham	run out (Kekwick/Giffen)	22		c A.H.Jarvis b Reedman	77
S.A.McAlister	c Jones b Giffen	10	(8)	b A.Jarvis	63
F.J.Laver	c A.H.Jarvis b Reedman	44	(4)	st A.H.Jarvis b Travers	21
J.H.Stuckey	c Jones b Giffen	6	(5)	c A.Jarvis b Reedman	10
P.A.McAlister	c A.H.Jarvis b Travers	63	(2)	b Reedman	14
*H.Trumble	c Hill b Reedman	95	(6)	b Reedman	0
†C.H.Ross	b A.Jarvis	33		b Jones	9
J.V.Saunders	b Jones	8		not out	29
F.B.Collins	not out	6		b Jones	6
Extras	(b6, lb1, w2)	9		(b15)	15
Total	(141.0 overs, 382 mins)	353		(116.3 overs, 314 mins)	298

SOUTH AUSTRALIA

J.C.Reedman	st Ross b Trumble	10	(5)	c Ross b Trumble	1
F.T.Hack	c Saunders b Laver	54	(1)	c Laver b Saunders	37
C.Hill	b Trumble	8		not out	126
*J.Darling	b Collins	40		c Ross b Trumble	16
A.Jarvis	c Ross b Collins	66	(6)	c McAlister b Trumble	0
E.H.Kekwick	c Laver b Warne	0	(8)	c Ross b Saunders	0
G.Giffen	c & b Laver	15		b Saunders	6
W.P.Stuart	not out	22	(9)	b Trumble	2
†A.H.Jarvis	b Collins	9	(10)	c Trumble b Saunders	5
E.Jones	c McAlister b Collins	0	(11)	c Laver b Saunders	4
J.P.F.Travers	b Saunders	6	(2)	c McMichael b Saunders	14
Extras	(b16, lb2, w2)	20		(b5, lb4)	9
Total	(104.1 overs, 293 mins)	250		(78.3 overs, 224 mins)	220

SOUTH AUSTRALIA	O	M	R	W	w,nb		O	M	R	W	w,nb
Jones	49	18	119	3	1,-		34	10	98	2	-,-
Giffen	19.1	6	62	2	-,-						
Travers	37	17	50	1	-,-	(2)	23	7	42	2	-,-
A.Jarvis	17	3	56	1	1,-		13.3	1	33	1	-,-
Reedman	18.5	4	57	2	-,-	(3)	37	12	92	5	-,-
Hill						(5)	9	1	18	0	-,-

VICTORIA	O	M	R	W	w,nb		O	M	R	W	w,nb
Saunders	23.4	7	61	1	-,-		24.3	5	71	6	-,-
Trumble	28.3	9	52	2	-,-	(3)	24	7	51	4	-,-
Collins	22	4	46	4	2,-	(5)	1	0	3	0	-,-
Laver	23	8	49	2	-,-	(2)	12	2	37	0	-,-
Warne	7	1	22	1	-,-	(4)	4	1	16	0	-,-
Worrall							13	2	33	0	-,-

FALL OF WICKETS

Wkt	VIC 1st	SA 1st	VIC 2nd	SA 2nd
1st	50	11	29	21
2nd	65	31	80	132
3rd	86	105	151	158
4th	94	137	161	172
5th	104	140	161	174
6th	181	199	173	195
7th	229	215	193	195
8th	295	232	219	197
9th	308	232	245	208
10th	353	250	298	220

TASMANIA v NEW SOUTH WALES

Played at S.T.C.A. Ground, Hobart, on December 30, 1899, January 1, 2, 1900. (Timeless Match)
Toss : Tasmania.   Result : NEW SOUTH WALES WON BY FOUR WICKETS.
Debuts: Tasmania - A.W.Pickett (f/c). New South Wales - G.R.C.Clarke, B.X.Colreavy, A.Diamond, E.W.Jansan, A.McBeath, K.H.Quist
  (all f/c).
12th Men :D.J.Noonan (NSW). No 12th named for Tas.
Umpires: J.E.Bingham and A.Lucas.
Attendances & Receipts: No figures published.
Close of Play : 1st day Tas 5/341 (Gatehouse 52); 2nd day Tas (2) 0/1 (Wilson 1, Pickett 0)

This was New South Wales's first match in Tasmania. The NSWCA had envisaged it starting on either March 3rd or 10th when it drew up
the fixtures pre-season, however the game was brought to the New Year at the request of the STCA. Tasmania batted well on the first day
and recorded their highest first-class total yet. The Savigny/Burn and Windsor/Gatehouse partnerships set new Tasmanian third- and fifth-
wicket records. Gatehouse's sole first-class hundred, the first to be attained in the 20th Century, occured in his final first-class appearance.
Batsmen ushered in the 1900s by scoring 528 runs on January 1st, a record number (subsequently beaten) for a day's play in Australia. The
Tasmanians missed several chances, those of Evers (twice before he reached 20) and Jansan (early) proving costly: both registered their sole
centuries in first-class cricket. The absence of Eady (ill) on the final day greatly depleted the strength of the Tasmanian attack. No details
on any individual innings were published. *Mercury* incorrectly gives NSW (1) Jansan c Hawson b Wilson. Sources: *NSWCA Report,
STCA Report, Sydney Referee, Hobart Mercury, Launceston Examiner.*

TASMANIA

J.H.Savigny	c Duff b Newell	77	(3)	c Newell b McBeath	4
C.J.Eady	c Evers b Colreavy	8		absent ill	-
H.Hale	b Clarke	19	(7)	c Evers b Colreavy	44
*E.J.K.Burn	lbw b Newell	86		b McBeath	10
E.A.C.Windsor	c Duff b Newell	89		c Colreavy b Clarke	18
†G.H.Gatehouse	c Clarke b McBeath	105		lbw b McBeath	0
R.J.Hawson	b Newell	4	(8)	not out	11
H.Wilson	c Diamond b Colreavy	5	(1)	c Newell b Clarke	10
C.McAllen	c Evers b McBeath	11		c & b Clarke	0
C.P.Hammond	b Colreavy	2		b Clarke	0
A.W.Pickett	not out	2	(2)	c Evers b McBeath	30
Extras	(b1, lb11)	12		(b4, lb9)	13
Total	(158.3 overs, 435 mins)	420		(72.0 overs, 200 mins)	140

NEW SOUTH WALES

R.A.Duff	c McAllen b Savigny	49		c Gatehouse b Pickett	6
C.W.Gregory	b Windsor	10		b Windsor	12
†H.A.Evers	c Gatehouse b Eady	138		lbw b Windsor	6
L.O.S.Poidevin	b Eady	34		b Windsor	55
E.W.Jansan	c Hawson b Windsor	105		b Windsor	0
*A.L.Newell	b Eady	21	(7)	not out	10
K.H.Quist	c & b Eady	25	(8)	not out	3
A.Diamond	not out	46	(6)	b Windsor	15
B.X.Colreavy	c Gatehouse b Pickett	0			
G.R.C.Clarke	b Pickett	4			
A.McBeath	b Eady	6			
Extras	(b1, lb9)	10		(b2, lb4)	6
Total	(90.1 overs, 270 mins)	448		(33.0 overs, 90 mins) (6 wkts)	113

NEW SOUTH WALES	O	M	R	W	w,nb		O	M	R	W	w,nb
McBeath	31.3	11	75	2	-,-		25	13	45	4	-,-
Colreavy	40	12	93	3	-,-	(4)	12	4	32	1	-,-
Clarke	37	5	113	1	,	(2)	15	8	30	4	,
Newell	40	13	82	4	-,-	(3)	20	3	20	0	-,-
Gregory	2	0	13	0	-,-						
Jansan	3	1	6	0	-,-						
Evers	1	0	8	0	-,-						
Quist	4	1	18	0	-,-						

TASMANIA	O	M	R	W	w,nb		O	M	R	W	w,nb
Eady	34.1	3	144	5	-,-						
Windsor	27	4	119	2	-,-	(1)	17	2	60	5	-,-
Pickett	10	1	54	2	-,-	(2)	16	3	47	1	-,-
Savigny	4	0	35	1	-,-						
Hale	6	0	35	0	-,-						
Wilson	6	0	28	0	-,-						
Burn	3	0	23	0	-,-						

FALL OF WICKETS				
	TAS	NSW	TAS	NSW
Wkt	1st	1st	2nd	2nd
1st	22	23	44	9
2nd	51	143	48	26
3rd	185	244	52	31
4th	208	245	61	31
5th	341	306	61	75
6th	351	342	127	110
7th	382	410	140	-
8th	407	410	140	-
9th	418	418	140	-
10th	420	448	-	-

NEW SOUTH WALES v SOUTH AUSTRALIA (Shield Match 5)

Played at Sydney Cricket Ground on January 6 (no play), 8 (no play), 9, 10, 11, 12, 1900. (Timeless Match)
Toss : South Australia.   Result : SOUTH AUSTRALIA WON BY SIX WICKETS.
Debuts: Nil
12th Men: A.J.Bowden (NSW) and W.Gunn (SA).
Umpires: P.Argall and C.Bannerman
Attendances: no play, no play, 2564, 2727, 2014, 1096.   Total: 8401.   Receipts: £481.
Close of Play: 1st day no play; 2nd day no play; 3rd day SA 1/14 (Hack 6); 4th day NSW (2) 1/22 (Iredale 2, Howell 9); 5th day
     SA (2) 0/11 (Hack 8, Stuart 1).

J.P.F.Travers (illness in family) returned to Adelaide after the match against Victoria and Hugo, who had been summoned to Melbourne because of J.J.Lyons's illness, was now brought into the team. Gunn, the South Australian manager, was forced to field for some of the first innings and for all of the second when Giffen aggravated a recent side-strain while bowling. Rain had prevented any play on the first two scheduled days and left doubts about the quality of the wicket, but apart from a few inconsistencies on the first day it played well. Hill (67 in 106 minutes, 5 fours) hit the only half-century on either side in the first innings. Iredale (75 in 135 minutes, 9 fours), Hopkins (54 in 54 minutes, 9 fours) and Kelly (52 in 70 minutes, 7 fours) led the scoring in the New South Wales second innings. Hack (career-best 158 not out in 302 minutes, 18 fours) survived four chances to steer South Australia to victory with assistance from Darling (55 in 72 minutes, 9 fours) and Reedman (55 in 83 minutes, 9 fours). It ended a run of five consecutive Shield-match losses for the South Australians. *Wisden* incorrectly gives SA (2) Pye 1/19 and omits Hopkins 0/53. Sources: *Wisden, C.B.O'Reilly, Sydney Referee, Sydney Morning Herald, Town & Country Journal, Sydney Daily Telegraph.*

NEW SOUTH WALES

V.T.Trumper	lbw b Giffen	45	c Hugo b Jones	7
F.A.Iredale	run out (Kekwick/Jones)	31	b A.Jarvis	75
M.A.Noble	c A.H.Jarvis b Giffen	13	(6) c A.H.Jarvis b Jones	12
*S.E.Gregory	c Giffen b Jones	5	(5) c A.H.Jarvis b Jones	24
A.J.Y.Hopkins	b Jones	13	(7) c Stuart b Jones	54
H.Donnan	c Hill b Giffen	9	(4) c Darling b Hugo	18
A.C.K.Mackenzie	st A.H.Jarvis b Giffen	0	(8) c Darling b Jones	16
B.W.Farquhar	c Hugo b Giffen	7	(9) b Hill	36
†J.J.Kelly	c Stuart b A.Jarvis	40	(10) b Hill	52
L.W.Pye	c sub (W.Gunn) b Jones	23	(11) not out	0
W.P.Howell	not out	2	(3) b Jones	14
Extras	(b14, lb8, w1, nb3)	26	(b8, w1)	9
Total	(69.3 overs, 207 mins)	214	(100.0 overs, 277 mins)	317

SOUTH AUSTRALIA

F.T.Hack	lbw b Trumper	44	not out	158
A.Jarvis	b Howell	8	(6) not out	19
*J.Darling	c Noble b Hopkins	47	(4) c Mackenzie b Howell	55
C.Hill	b Noble	67	(3) c Mackenzie b Pye	22
J.C.Reedman	b Trumper	1	c Farquhar b Trumper	55
W.P.Stuart	c Kelly b Trumper	11	(2) c Mackenzie b Noble	13
G.Giffen	b Noble	4		
E.H.Kekwick	run out (Hopkins)	2		
†A.H.Jarvis	b Noble	0		
E.Jones	c Howell b Noble	3		
V.Hugo	not out	0		
Extras	(b4, lb2, w4)	10	(b10, lb2, w1)	13
Total	(78.4 overs, 209 mins)	197	(113.4 overs, 302 mins) (4 wkts)	335

SOUTH AUSTRALIA	O	M	R	W	w,nb		O	M	R	W	w,nb
Jones	22	8	49	3	1,-		37	11	88	6	-,-
Reedman	5	0	35	0	-,-	(3)	14	0	65	0	-,-
Giffen	17	2	59	5	-,-						
Hugo	9	2	18	0	-,3		17	2	65	1	-,-
A.Jarvis	16.3	6	27	1	-,-	(2)	23	6	71	1	-,-
Hack						(5)	5	1	13	0	1,-
Hill						(6)	4	1	6	2	-,-

NEW SOUTH WALES	O	M	R	W	w,nb		O	M	R	W	w,nb
Noble	25.4	9	68	4	-,-		29.4	7	106	1	-,-
Howell	16	7	47	1	-,-	(3)	26	8	57	1	-,-
Hopkins	12	2	25	1	1,-	(5)	12	2	53	0	-,-
Trumper	15	6	26	3	2,-	(2)	21	9	47	1	-,-
Pye	10	3	21	0	1,-	(4)	21	5	49	1	-,-
Farquhar							4	1	10	0	1,-

FALL OF WICKETS

Wkt	NSW 1st	SA 1st	NSW 2nd	SA 2nd
1st	81	14	12	38
2nd	81	99	31	91
3rd	90	105	74	192
4th	114	113	134	299
5th	136	139	152	-
6th	136	159	174	-
7th	137	174	227	-
8th	168	174	234	-
9th	212	187	310	-
10th	214	197	317	-

NEW SOUTH WALES v VICTORIA (Shield Match 6)

Played at Sydney Cricket Ground on January 26, 27, 29, 30, 31, 1900. (Timeless Match)
Toss : New South Wales.   Result : NEW SOUTH WALES WON BY 111 RUNS.
Debuts: Nil
12th Men : A.Diamond (NSW) and R.W.McLeod (Vic Manager).
Umpires : C.Bannerman and R.M.Crockett.
Attendances: 7949, 5596, 2175, 913, 182.   Total: 16,825.   Receipts: £1102.
Close of Play : 1st day Vic 4/33 (Trumble 6); 2nd day NSW (2) 1/0 (Kelly 0); 3rd day NSW (2) 6/252 (Noble 97, Duff 7); 4th day Vic (2)
    4/98 (Stuckey 34, Warne 11).

Another fine all-round performance from Noble inspired New South Wales to victory and their third Sheffield Shield title. He compiled a chanceless 155 in 320 minutes (19 fours) over the third and fourth days to swing the match, also capturing nine wickets including the first six to fall in Victoria's second innings. His century was his third in the competition for the season. The visitors had travelled to Sydney without C.E.McLeod (unavailable) and F.B.Collins (back injury), who was replaced by Armstrong. Gregory (66 in 102 minutes, 1 five and 8 fours) and Duff (75 in 103 minutes, 10 fours) rescued the New South Wales first innings with a century partnership. Trumble (87 in 116 minutes, 17 fours), Laver (80 in 163 minutes, 9 fours) and Stuckey (55 in 97 minutes, 8 fours) performed a similar task when Victoria batted. McBeath, in his first Shield match, captured 6 for 94 including the first three wickets for 8 runs. New South Wales lost Pye to the third ball of their second innings, but Iredale (54 in 115 minutes, 7 fours) and Duff (76 in 189 minutes, 8 fours) dug in to partner Noble and build a big lead. Set 375 to win, Victoria steadily lost wickets and never looked likely to reach their target, only Stuckey (53 in 75 minutes, 6 fours) and Armstrong (45 in 90 minutes, 4 fours) challenging the bowlers. *Wisden* incorrectly gives NSW (2) Hopkins 8. *VCA Report* incorrectly gives NSW (1) Howell 32, extras 8, Armstrong 2/20; Vic (1) Pye 0/26, Trumper 1/40. Sources: *Wisden, VCA Report, Sydney Referee, Sydney Morning Herald, Town & Country Journal, Sydney Daily Telegraph.*

NEW SOUTH WALES

V.T.Trumper	b Saunders	31	(4) b Trumble		41
F.A.Iredale	b Saunders	18	(6) c Worrall b Trumble		54
M.A.Noble	c McAlister b Trumble	13	(5) st Ross b Warne		155
H.Donnan	c Saunders b Trumble	13	(3) c Graham b Saunders		16
*S.E.Gregory	b Armstrong	66	(7) b Laver		14
A.J.Y.Hopkins	b Saunders	4	(9) b Warne		7
†J.J.Kelly	run out (Graham/Ross)	1	(2) b Trumble		12
R.A.Duff	c Saunders b Armstrong	75	b Laver		76
L.W.Pye	run out (Saunders/Worrall)	0	(1) c Trumble b Saunders		0
W.P.Howell	not out	31	c Stuckey b Trumble		22
A.McBeath	run out (Worrall/Ross)	10	not out		0
Extras	(b6, lb2, w1)	9	(b4, lb4, w2, nb5)		15
Total	(85.5 overs, 245 mins)	271	(181.0 overs, 456 mins)		412

VICTORIA

T.S.Warne	b Noble	9	(6) b Noble		11
J.Worrall	c Kelly b McBeath	4	(1) b Noble		5
S.A.McMichael	b McBeath	1	(7) b Hopkins		33
P.A.McAlister	c Hopkins b McBeath	4	(8) c & b Hopkins		20
*H.Trumble	b Trumper	87	(2) c McBeath b Noble		15
H.Graham	b McBeath	41	(3) c & b Noble		23
F.J.Laver	c Hopkins b Noble	80	(4) c Kelly b Noble		8
J.H.Stuckey	c Kelly b McBeath	55	(5) b Noble		53
W.W.Armstrong	c & b Noble	1	b Pye		45
†C.H.Ross	not out	14	not out		39
J.V.Saunders	b McBeath	0	b Trumper		2
Extras	(b4, lb6, w1, nb2)	13	(lb6, nb3)		9
Total	(118.3 overs, 295 mins)	309	(106.5 overs, 275 mins)		263

VICTORIA	O	M	R	W	w,nb		O	M	R	W	w,nb		FALL OF WICKETS			
														NSW	VIC	NSW	VIC
Saunders	25	6	85	3	-,-		57	15	135	2	-,-	Wkt	1st	1st	2nd	2nd
Trumble	38.5	9	85	2	1,-		61	24	112	4	2,2	1st	35	4	0	10
Warne	4	0	30	0	-,-	(5)	19	7	45	2	-,1	2nd	58	10	27	35
Laver	5	0	27	0	-,-	(3)	24	5	53	2	-,-	3rd	64	14	38	48
Worrall	4	0	11	0	-,-							4th	98	33	86	62
Armstrong	9	1	24	2	-,-	(4)	20	6	52	0	-,2	5th	105	146	193	107
												6th	106	168	230	128
NEW SOUTH WALES	O	M	R	W	w,nb		O	M	R	W	w,nb	7th	219	268	356	168
Noble	32	11	66	3	1,2		39	9	91	6	-,2	8th	219	288	368	181
McBeath	41.3	15	94	6	-,-		31	13	70	0	-,1	9th	242	307	408	260
Howell	17	6	37	0	-,-		10	7	13	0	-,-	10th	271	309	412	263
Pye	7	0	25	0	-,-	(6)	5	1	6	1	-,-					
Trumper	17	2	49	1	-,-	(4)	8.5	3	26	1	-,-					
Hopkins	4	0	25	0	-,-	(5)	13	1	48	2	-,-					

VICTORIA v TASMANIA

Played at Melbourne Cricket Ground on January 26, 27, 29, 30, 1900. (Timeless Match)
Toss : Victoria.   Result : VICTORIA WON BY 185 RUNS.
Debuts: Victoria - J.Ainslie, J.L.Drew, W.M.Morgan, W.T.C.Perraton (all f/c). Tasmania - E.S.Hawson (f/c).
12th Men: None named.
Umpires : E.Barrass and C.E.Over.
Attendances: 1600, 2000,   ? ,   ? .   Total: About 5000.   Receipts: No figures published.
Close of Play : 1st day Tas 4/122 (Eady 39, Windsor 11); 2nd day Vic (2) 2/258 (Murray 100, Carter 32); 3rd day Vic (2) 9/375
    (Hastings 22, Drew 11).

The Victorian selectors gave country players ,Morgan (Ballarat), Perraton (Maryborough) and Drew (Bendigo), an opportunity at a higher level. Each played his sole first-class match. Murray, who had previously represented Victoria, was also a Bendigo man without experience in Melbourne District cricket. E.J.K.Burn, who would have captained Tasmania, was unable to make the trip to Melbourne due to the illness of his sister. In his absence Eady (81 in 120 minutes, 10 fours and 7 for 229) and Windsor (62 in 130 minutes, 6 fours and 8 for 189) played major roles for the visitors. Mitchell (career-best 92 in 78 minutes, 9 fours) and Carlton (42 not out in 73 minutes, 5 fours) rescued the Victorian first innings with an eighth-wicket stand of 113 in just an hour. Sutherland (94 in 145 minutes, 5 fours) and Murray (104 in 136 minutes, 11 fours - his sole first-class century) added 161 for the second wicket in the second innings. Carter (63 in 58 minutes, 7 fours) batted well in his second and last match for Victoria. Ward (legbreaks) returned his best figures for Tasmania. Victoria's leading scorers, Mitchell (twice), Sutherland (twice) and Murray (three times), were all given reprieves in the field. McAllen handed the wicket-keeping duties to Dodds for the rest of the match at 5/80 on the first day, Dodds having already taken two catches in the field. Hastings, who injured a thumb while keeping wicket in Tasmania's first innings, kept only briefly in the second, Mitchell at first and then Sutherland taking over behind the stumps while various Tasmanian players took turns to substitute. Play on the third day was restricted to the pre-lunch session due to rain, which created favourable conditions for the bowlers on the fourth day. Sources: *VCA Report, STCA Report, The Age, The Argus, The Herald, The Australasian, The Leader.*

VICTORIA

D.Sutherland	c Savigny b Eady	18		c E.S.Hawson b Ward	94
A.W.Murray	c Dodds b Windsor	16	(3)	c Eady b Windsor	104
A.S.Carter	c Dodds b Eady	0	(4)	lbw b Eady	63
J.Ainslie	c & b Eady	7	(5)	b Ward	16
W.M.Morgan	c Eady b Windsor	28	(7)	b Ward	1
W.T.C.Perraton	b Windsor	8	(8)	b Eady	1
*W.Bruce	c Wilson b Windsor	38	(9)	b Ward	16
R.Mitchell	c Wilson b Savigny	92	(6)	c R.J.Hawson b Eady	6
W.Carlton	not out	42	(2)	c Savigny b Windsor	21
†T.J.Hastings	b Eady	1		b Windsor	23
J.L.Drew	b Windsor	1		not out	11
Extras	(b11, lb1)	12		(b15, lb4, w1)	20
Total	(67.5 overs, 199 mins)	263		(101.1 overs, 275 mins)	376

TASMANIA

J.H.Savigny	b Carlton	44		c Carter b Bruce	28
R.J.Hawson	c Carlton b Mitchell	16	(4)	c Mitchell b Bruce	7
H.Hale	c & b Carlton	2		b Bruce	32
C.J.Eady	hit wkt b Carter	81	(5)	c Carlton b Bruce	0
H.Wilson	c Murray b Carlton	1	(2)	c Morgan b Mitchell	12
E.A.C.Windsor	b Murray	62		lbw b Murray	24
W.G.Ward	c Hastings b Carter	4	(8)	st Sutherland b Carlton	27
*†C.McAllen	lbw b Carter	7	(9)	c Bruce b Carlton	19
E.S.Hawson	not out	5	(10)	not out	23
N.Dodds	c Hastings b Murray	0	(7)	b Murray	27
A.W.Pickett	c Carter b Murray	5		c Carlton b Bruce	11
Extras	(b5, lb3, w4)	12		(b4, w1)	5
Total	(105.0 overs, 237 mins)	239		(82.3 overs, 190 mins)	215

TASMANIA	O	M	R	W	w,nb		O	M	R	W	w,nb					
Eady	28	0	98	4	-,-		39	5	131	3	-,-					
Windsor	28.5	4	90	5	-,-		27.1	7	99	3	-,-					
Pickett	6	0	41	0	-,-		3	0	24	0	-,-					
Savigny	5	0	22	1	-,-	(5)	9	0	20	0	-,-					
Wilson						(4)	5	0	34	0	-,-					
Ward							18	2	48	4	1,-					

	Wkt	VIC 1st	TAS 1st	VIC 2nd	TAS 2nd
	1st	28	61	47	42
	2nd	28	64	208	42
	3rd	48	83	262	57
	4th	48	97	310	57
	5th	59	191	316	89
	6th	114	197	320	130
	7th	145	229	321	143
	8th	258	229	326	169
	9th	262	229	347	190
	10th	263	239	376	215

FALL OF WICKETS

VICTORIA	O	M	R	W	w,nb		O	M	R	W	w,nb
Murray	17	5	35	3	1,-	(6)	15	3	46	2	-,-
Drew	4	0	15	0	-,-	(5)	5	0	20	0	1,-
Mitchell	32	16	32	1	-,-	(1)	21	6	56	1	-,-
Carlton	22	1	96	3	-,-	(7)	10	3	29	2	-,-
Bruce	3	1	5	0	3,-	(4)	16.3	10	25	5	-,-
Morgan	12	5	24	0	-,-	(3)	3	0	6	0	-,-
Carter	15	6	20	3	-,-	(2)	12	4	28	0	-,-

AUSTRALIAN XI v THE REST

Played at Sydney Cricket Ground on February 2, 3, 5, 6, 1900. (Timeless Match)
Toss : Australian XI.　　　　　Result : AN AUSTRALIAN XI WON BY 151 RUNS.
Debuts: Nil
12th Men : W.P.Howell (Aust) and P.A.McAlister (Rest).
Umpires : R.Callaway and R.M.Crockett.
Attendances: 2000, 9000, 2000, 500.　　　Total: About 13,500.　　　Receipts: £512.
Close of Play : 1st day Rest 2/59 (Graham 19, Stuckey 25); 2nd day Aust (2) 1/80 (Kelly 17, Hill 10); 3rd day Rest (2) 2/19 (Graham 2, Reedman 2)

This match was staged for the benefit of the Australian Bushmen's Contingent and New South Wales Patriotic Funds for the Boer War. Jarvis replaced R.A.Duff (work) for The Rest and Callaway umpired as a replacement for C.Bannerman (injured foot) The SCG Trustees agreed to meet all expenses. The funds raised, £512 at the gate, were boosted by contributions to a total of £640. Eady and Saunders accounted for the Australian XI on a good first-day wicket, only Trumper (41 in 50 minutes) and Noble (94 in 153 minutes, 12 fours) showing any real form. Despite the absence of Worrall (severe cold) in the second innings the Test men fared much better, Trumper (49 in 42 minutes, 8 fours, scored out of 59), Hill (69 in 120 minutes), Noble (58 in 90 minutes), Darling (72 in 76 minutes, 13 fours) and Gregory (68 in 110 minutes, 1 five and 10 fours) all scoring well. Iredale however was out to the first ball he faced. Graham (73 in 161 minutes, 1 six and 9 fours) and Stuckey (88 in 158 minutes, 1 five and 16 fours) added 145 for the third wicket in The Rest's first innings and Hopkins (62 in 100 minutes) batted well in the second innings against a sustained, accurate Australian attack. *Wisden* incorrectly gives Aust (1) Saunders 6/91; Aust (2) Laver 48. Sources: *Wisden, Sydney Referee, Sydney Morning Herald, Town & Country Journal, Sydney Daily Telegraph.*

AUSTRALIAN XI

J.Worrall	c Stuckey b Saunders	8		absent ill	-
V.T.Trumper	c Jarvis b Windsor	41	(1)	c Stuckey b Windsor	49
C.Hill	c Windsor b Saunders	7		c Windsor b McBeath	69
M.A.Noble	c Evers b Saunders	94		c & b Reedman	58
*J.Darling	c Stuckey b Eady	4		c McBeath b Hopkins	72
S.E.Gregory	c Evers b Eady	0		c Evers b Jarvis	68
H.Trumble	b Saunders	5		c Hopkins b Saunders	0
F.A.Iredale	b McBeath	38		c Hopkins b Saunders	0
F.J.Laver	c Eady b Saunders	25		c Mackenzie b Jarvis	46
†J.J.Kelly	not out	7	(2)	c Graham b Saunders	29
E.Jones	c Graham b Saunders	0	(10)	not out	0
Extras	(b4, lb2, w1, nb1)	8		(b6, lb3)	9
Total	(70.0 overs, 205 mins)	237		(106.0 overs, 300 mins)	400

THE REST

A.Jarvis	b Noble	4		c Laver b Noble	12
A.C.K.Mackenzie	c Worrall b Noble	9		b Noble	3
H.Graham	c Jones b Noble	73		lbw b Laver	38
J.H.Stuckey	st Kelly b Trumble	88	(5)	b Jones	13
*J.C.Reedman	b Laver	40	(4)	c Darling b Trumper	28
A.J.Y.Hopkins	b Trumper	17		b Trumble	62
E.A.C.Windsor	c & b Laver	35	(8)	lbw b Laver	6
C.J.Eady	b Jones	4	(9)	b Trumble	29
†H.A.Evers	not out	1	(7)	b Jones	1
A.McBeath	c & b Laver	0		c Iredale b Trumble	0
J.V.Saunders	lbw b Laver	0		not out	3
Extras	(b4, lb2, w1, nb3)	10		(b8, lb2)	10
Total	(95.0 overs, 262 mins)	281		(67.0 overs, 185 mins)	205

THE REST	O	M	R	W	w,nb		O	M	R	W	w,nb
Eady	24	8	71	2	,1		25	1	100	0	-,-
Saunders	24	5	90	6	1,-		28	8	96	3	-,-
Windsor	3	0	17	1	-,-	(4)	15	0	77	1	-,-
Hopkins	7	0	29	0	-,-	(6)	4	0	20	1	-,-
McBeath	9	3	11	1	-,-	(3)	24	10	51	1	-,-
A.Jarvis	3	2	11	0	-,-	(7)	3	0	14	2	-,-
Reedman						(5)	7	0	33	1	-,-

AUSTRALIAN XI	O	M	R	W	w,nb		O	M	R	W	w,nb
Jones	25	3	98	1	-,-		20	3	57	2	-,-
Noble	28	10	72	3	-,3		18	8	32	2	-,-
Trumble	24	10	50	1	-,-		9	3	19	3	-,-
Laver	10	4	30	4	1,-		15	2	64	2	-,-
Trumper	9	3	21	1	-,-		1	1	0	1	-,-
Hill							4	0	23	0	-,-

FALL OF WICKETS

	AUST	REST	AUST	REST
Wkt	1st	1st	2nd	2nd
1st	17	7	59	14
2nd	30	18	117	15
3rd	68	163	197	86
4th	88	181	231	88
5th	94	213	323	108
6th	100	269	324	122
7th	189	276	324	131
8th	223	280	396	200
9th	237	281	400	200
10th	237	281	-	205

1900-01 SEASON (7 MATCHES)

Australian Federation coincided with the briefest first-class program in 10 years. The usual six Sheffield Shield matches were contested, together with the annual encounter between Tasmania and Victoria, this year in Launceston. There was no match between New South Wales and Queensland due to a disagreement among the associations over expenses. It was the last time New South Wales and Queensland failed to meet in a full Australian season.

Victoria regained the Sheffield Shield by winning all their matches. Their team remained unchanged through the campaign with one exception, Hugh Trumble (ill) being replaced by Collins for the opening match at Adelaide. Victoria's bowlers, Trumble, McLeod and Saunders, who shared in 62 wickets, virtually decided the title.

The season saw two remarkable encounters between South Australia and New South Wales. Each team thrashed the other at home, New South Wales doing it by the resounding margin of an innings and 605 runs at Sydney in early January. New South Wales's total of 918 was then a record in all first-class cricket, while Clem Hill's unbeaten 365 for South Australia, in the earlier match between the sides at Adelaide, surpassed Billy Murdoch's 321 in 1881-82 as the highest innings scored in Australia.

The two Shield matches at Melbourne were low-scoring affairs and Victoria emerged successful on each occasion. The first, against New South Wales, was played in hot, blustery weather on a good wicket, while the second against South Australia was rain-affected in the first half. Improved conditions from the second day onwards brought forth centuries from Graham and Armstrong who, with the support of McMichael and McAlister, set up victory for their side. The results ensured the destiny of the Shield for another season.

A sparkling double-century from Trumper almost brought victory to New South Wales in the final match of the summer against Victoria at Sydney. The visitors required 244 runs to win and snatched victory by a solitary wicket.

It was remarkable that the powerful New South Wales team won only one of their four matches. Their batting lineup of Trumper, Noble, Duff, Syd Gregory, Iredale, Hopkins, Donnan, Poidevin and Kelly was without precedent and the bowling appeared to be more than adequate. Jack Marsh's bowling made an immediate impact but his action came under immediate criticism, and it persisted throughout his short career.

George Giffen had an abysmal season for South Australia who consequently struggled. Their batting was totally dependent on the scoring ability of Clem Hill and this lack of depth was always evident. Travers had his best season to date with the ball, but apart from Matthews he lacked the support necessary to maintain pressure on opposing batsmen.

The NSWCA invited Tasmania to play a match in Sydney over Christmas as part of the celebrations for the Federation of the Australian colonies. However, the Tasmanians were unable to accept, so New South Wales extended their invitation to Queensland instead. QCA delegates indicated their willingness to send a team to Sydney, but the QCA executive insisted they would only travel if the NSWCA agreed to meet all expenses. The NSWCA refused and the match did not proceed.

Leading Aggregates

Batsmen	M	I	NO	Runs	HS	Ave.	Bowlers	Runs	Wkts	Ave.
C.Hill (SA)	4	7	1	620	365*	103.33	J.V.Saunders (V)	497	29	17.13
V.T.Trumper (NSW)	4	7	0	458	230	65.42	J.P.F.Travers (SA)	602	29	20.75
S.E.Gregory (NSW)	4	7	1	430	168	71.66	J.Marsh (NSW)	537	24	22.37
M.A.Noble (NSW)	4	7	0	352	153	50.28	H.Trumble (V)	413	18	22.94
W.W.Armstrong (V)	4	7	0	316	118	45.14	C.E.McLeod (V)	362	15	24.13
H.Graham (V)	4	8	1	283	120	40.42				
R.A.Duff (NSW)	4	7	0	268	119	38.28				

SHEFFIELD SHIELD TABLE

	P	W	L	D	Quotient	Runs Scored	Wkts Lost	Runs Conceded	Wkts Taken
VICTORIA	4	4	-	-	1.388	1899	66	1658	80
NEW SOUTH WALES	4	1	3	-	1.183	2368	70	1801	63
SOUTH AUSTRALIA	4	1	3	-	0.601	1637	69	2445	62
TOTAL	6	6	6	-	1.000	5904	205	5904	205

SOUTH AUSTRALIA v VICTORIA (Shield Match 1)

Played at Adelaide Oval on November 10, 12, 13, 14, 1900. (Timeless match)
Toss : South Australia.   Result : VICTORIA WON BY EIGHT WICKETS.
Debuts: South Australia - J.G.F.Matthews, A.H.Pellew (both f/c).
12th Men: W.Bruce (Vic). No 12th man or emergency fieldsman named for South Australia.
Umpires: R.M.Crockett and G.S.Downs.
Attendances: 4000, 4000, 1000, 500.   Total: About 9500.   Receipts: No figures published.
Close of Play: 1st day SA 8/244 (Matthews 75, Jarvis 57); 2nd day Vic 6/245 (Armstrong 42, McLeod 38); 3rd day SA (2) 2/122
     (Leak 37, Stuart 0).

J.J.Lyons (ill) could not be considered for South Australia and Jarvis replaced J.McKenzie (unavailable). Collins replaced H.Trumble (ill) in the Victorian team. Matthews (79 in about 190 minutes, 7 fours), on debut, and Jarvis combined to add 121 for the ninth wicket in the South Australian first innings. It was Matthews' first half-century in any grade of cricket. Armstrong (118 in 165 minutes, 13 fours) hit the first of his 23 centuries for Victoria. His century partnerships with McLeod (52 in 75 minutes, 6 fours) and Ross (67 in 90 minutes, 1 five and 7 fours) for the seventh and eighth wickets put the visitors in a strong position. Clem Hill (70 in 115 minutes, 7 fours) and Leak (46 in 180 minutes, 3 fours) began the second innings soundly but the remaining batsmen gave the Victorian bowlers little trouble on a last day wicket of variable bounce. Sources: *Wisden, C.B.O'Reilly, Adelaide Advertiser, South Australian Register.*

SOUTH AUSTRALIA

F.T.Hack	c Ross b McLeod	16		c Worrall b Saunders	10
E.H.Leak	b Saunders	5		c Saunders b McLeod	46
C.Hill	b McLeod	24		c McAlister b Armstrong	70
G.Giffen	st Ross b McLeod	24	(5)	c Saunders b Laver	5
*J.C.Reedman	b McLeod	0	(6)	run out	7
W.P.Stuart	c McAlister b McLeod	9	(4)	c McAlister b Collins	23
A.H.Pellew	c & b Saunders	0		c Armstrong b Collins	11
J.G.F.Matthews	c Armstrong b Saunders	79		c Collins b Saunders	6
E.Jones	b Collins	20		b Collins	2
†A.H.Jarvis	c Armstrong b McLeod	67		c Armstrong b Saunders	2
J.P.F.Travers	not out	8		not out	4
Extras	(b7, w4, nb4)	15		(b7, lb1, w1, nb2)	11
Total	(106.3 overs, 290 mins)	267		(101.1 overs, 280 mins)	197

VICTORIA

*J.Worrall	c Jarvis b Jones	6			
P.A.McAlister	c Pellew b Giffen	62	(1)	b Jones	13
H.Graham	b Travers	47		not out	17
S.A.McMichael	lbw b Travers	34		not out	10
J.H.Stuckey	c & b Travers	11			
F.J.Laver	c Pellew b Giffen	1			
W.W.Armstrong	c Reedman b Jones	118			
C.E.McLeod	st Jarvis b Travers	52			
†C.H.Ross	not out	67	(2)	run out	22
J.V.Saunders	b Matthews	1			
F.B.Collins	c Hill b Matthews	0			
Extras	(b1, lb3)	4			-
Total	(125.4 overs, 370 mins)	403		(28.0 overs, 75 mins) (3 wkts)	62

VICTORIA	O	M	R	W	w,nb		O	M	R	W	w,nb		
McLeod	44.3	12	100	6	3,-		24	8	55	1	-,-		
Saunders	31	7	54	3	1,4		34.1	11	56	3	1,-		
Collins	15	3	32	1	-,-		18	7	37	3	-,-		
Laver	11	0	45	0	-,-		20	6	26	1	-,-		
Armstrong	3	0	12	0	-,-		5	0	12	1	-,2		
Worrall	2	0	9	0	-,-								

												FALL OF WICKETS	
											Wkt	SA 1st	VIC 1st	SA 2nd	VIC 2nd

SOUTH AUSTRALIA	O	M	R	W	w,nb		O	M	R	W	w,nb				
Jones	29	4	97	2	-,-		11	4	11	1	-,-	1st	19	16	13	30
Giffen	34	5	146	2	-,-	(3)	2	0	9	0	-,-	2nd	32	108	115	43
Travers	42	8	93	4	-,-	(2)	10	2	26	0	-,-	3rd	51	140	143	-
Matthews	17.4	5	42	2	-,-		3	0	7	0	-,-	4th	51	154	161	-
Reedman	3	0	21	0	-,-							5th	61	155	167	-
Hack						(5)	2	0	9	0	-,-	6th	65	172	175	-
												7th	96	272	188	-
												8th	132	402	188	-
												9th	253	403	191	-
												10th	267	403	197	-

SOUTH AUSTRALIA v NEW SOUTH WALES (Shield Match 2)

Played at Adelaide Oval on December 15, 17, 18, 19, 1900. (Timeless match)
Toss : New South Wales.　　　　　Result : SOUTH AUSTRALIA WON BY AN INNINGS AND 36 RUNS.
Debuts: South Australia - E.Walkley (f/c). New South Wales - J.Marsh (f/c).
12th Men: A.H.Pellew (SA) and A.McBeath (NSW).
Umpires: R.Callaway and T.A.Reeves.
Attendances: No daily figures published.　　　　Total: 9239.　　　Receipts: No figures published.
Close of Play: 1st day NSW 279 all out; 2nd day SA 6/311 (Hill 176, Matthews 4); 3rd day NSW (2) 2/22 (S.E.Gregory 4).

Hill's 365 not out (515 minutes, 1 eight, 1 all-run five and 35 fours) remained the highest first-class innings in Australia until 1906-07 and the highest by a South Australian until 1935-36. A chance when 19 (snicked between Howell and Marsh in the slips off Noble's bowling) was Hill's only mistake as he shared new South Australian wicket-partnership records with Reedman (206 in 140 minutes for the fifth wicket) and Walkley (232 in 180 minutes for the ninth wicket), that with Walkley also being the highest in Australian first-class cricket. Walkley had been a replacement for Ernie Jones (hip injury) in the South Australian side named for the match and he was awarded a gold medal by the SACA for his effort in supporting Hill. It was the first of South Australia's 34 Shield Matches since 1892-93 in which Jones did not play. Hill started his landmark innings as 12.20pm on the second day (lunch SA 3/72, Hill 34). He reached 50 in 120 minutes and moved to his century in a further 50 minutes with a flurry of shots (tea SA 4/189 Hill 106, Reedman 35). In the last session Hill reached 150 in 225 minutes and at stumps was 176. Next morning he progressed to 200 in 315 minutes (lunch SA 8/404, Hill 243, Walkley 12). He went from 292 to 300 via his "eight", Iredale's inaccurate return from a straight drive (off which four had already been run) finding the boundary at the opposite end (tea SA 8/531, Hill 328, Walkley 45). When the last home wicket fell shortly after 5.00pm Hill had scored 63.4 per cent of his side's innings, both Stuart and Affie Jarvis having suffered first-ball dismissals. The visitors gave Hill three cheers as he left the ground to a magnificent ovation; he later received a trophy worth £25. Half-centuries were scored for New South Wales by Hopkins (65 in 95 minutes, 1 five and 5 fours) and Syd Gregory (51 in 90 minutes, 4 fours) in the first innings and by Trumper and Syd Gregory again (no details) in the second. Noble (injured foot) had been unable to bowl for much of Hill's innings. *Wisden* incorrectly gives SA Reedman 71, total 575, Noble 0/57. Sources: *Wisden, C.B.O'Reilly, Adelaide Advertiser, South Australian Register.*

NEW SOUTH WALES

Batsman	Dismissal	Runs		Dismissal	Runs
V.T.Trumper	b A.Jarvis	32	(4)	lbw b Travers	53
H.Donnan	c Matthews b Giffen	19	(1)	b Travers	13
M.A.Noble	b Travers	28	(5)	b Travers	46
F.A.Iredale	c Leak b A.Jarvis	37	(6)	b Matthews	9
A.J.Y.Hopkins	st A.H.Jarvis b Travers	65	(7)	not out	17
*S.E.Gregory	st A.H.Jarvis b Reedman	51	(3)	lbw b Matthews	81
R.A.Duff	c Stuart b Reedman	5	(8)	b Matthews	16
C.W.Gregory	b Travers	16	(2)	c Hill b Travers	4
†J.J.Kelly	c & b Reedman	11		b Travers	0
W.P.Howell	b Reedman	5		c Leak b Matthews	19
J.Marsh	not out	3		c Reedman b Travers	1
Extras	(b5, lb2)	7		(lb2)	2
Total	(93.3 overs, 290 mins)	279		(93.1 overs, 270 mins)	261

SOUTH AUSTRALIA

Batsman	Dismissal	Runs
F.T.Hack	b Marsh	12
E.H.Leak	b Marsh	4
C.Hill	not out	365
G.Giffen	c & b Howell	7
A.Jarvis	c Howell b Hopkins	9
*J.C.Reedman	c Howell b Hopkins	72
W.P.Stuart	b Hopkins	0
J.G.F.Matthews	b Marsh	12
†A.H.Jarvis	b Marsh	0
E.Walkley	b Marsh	53
J.P.F.Travers	b Howell	0
Extras	(b23, lb10, w9)	42
Total	(164.0 overs, 520 mins)	576

SOUTH AUSTRALIA	O	M	R	W	w,nb		O	M	R	W	w,nb
Travers	35	7	85	3	-,-		31.1	10	74	6	-,-
Matthews	9	1	29	0	-,-	(3)	24	6	61	4	-,-
A.Jarvis	18	2	50	2	-,-	(4)	11	1	29	0	-,-
Giffen	12	0	49	1	-,-	(2)	18	1	67	0	-,-
Walkley	7	0	27	0	-,-	(6)	5	0	18	0	-,-
Reedman	12.3	3	32	4	-,-	(5)	4	1	10	0	-,-

NEW SOUTH WALES	O	M	R	W	w,nb
Noble	26	7	58	0	5,-
Marsh	53	12	181	5	2,-
Howell	34	3	100	2	-,-
Hopkins	34	8	116	3	2,-
Trumper	15	1	67	0	-,-
S.E.Gregory	2	0	12	0	-,-

FALL OF WICKETS			
	NSW	SA	NSW
Wkt	1st	1st	2nd
1st	50	8	9
2nd	54	43	22
3rd	111	65	130
4th	123	88	176
5th	226	294	194
6th	242	294	208
7th	249	341	229
8th	261	341	236
9th	270	573	259
10th	279	576	261

VICTORIA v NEW SOUTH WALES (Shield Match 3)

Played at Melbourne Cricket Ground on December 24, 26, 27, 1900. (Timeless match)
Toss : New South Wales.   Result : VICTORIA WON BY FIVE WICKETS.
Debuts: Nil.
12th Men: C.W.Gregory (NSW). No 12th man or emergency fieldsman named for Victoria.
Umpires: R.Callaway and R.M.Crockett.
Attendances: 5000, 6000, 1500.   Total: About 12,500.   Receipts: £415.
Close of Play: 1st day Vic 6/104 (McLeod 30, McMichael 7); 2nd day Vic (2) 5/45 (Stuckey 3).

Bowlers of both sides were on top throughout the match in what were considered to be favourable batting conditions. Gregory (66 not out in 94 minutes, 9 fours) held the New South Wales first innings together and Noble (55 in 117 minutes, 6 fours) performed a similar function in the second. The bowling styles of Trumble (right-arm offbreaks) and Saunders (left-arm medium) complimented each other perfectly as they operated in tandem for most of the time. Armstrong (50 in 94 minutes, 8 fours) scored Victoria's sole half-century in the match but it was the unfinished sixth wicket stand of 90 between Stuckey and Trumble that ultimately decided the game. Worrall was out to the third ball of the Victorian first innings and Marsh took early wickets in each innings. Marsh was no-balled twice for throwing by umpire Crockett (bowler's end) during Victoria's second innings on the last day, one of these actually bowling Stuckey. After the match, Crockett at first "declined to say whether it was for questionable delivery or going over the line" (*Age*) but later confirmed that it was for illegal delivery. Further controversy over his bowling action occurred in the return match in Sydney and was to continue for the remainder of his short career. *Wisden* omits Vic (1) Trumper 0/1; NSW (2) Marsh c McAlister. Sources: *Wisden, VCA Report, The Age, The Argus, The Australasian, The Leader, Town & Country Journal.*

NEW SOUTH WALES

Batsman	1st innings	Runs	2nd innings	Runs
H.Donnan	b Trumble	1	c Trumble b Saunders	2
V.T.Trumper	c Graham b Saunders	26	run out (Saunders/McLeod)	26
M.A.Noble	c Trumble b Saunders	0	c Stuckey b Trumble	55
F.A.Iredale	c Graham b Saunders	10	lbw b Trumble	5
A.J.Y.Hopkins	b Saunders	20	b Trumble	1
*S.E.Gregory	not out	66	c Laver b Saunders	9
R.A.Duff	c McLeod b Trumble	14	b Trumble	10
†J.J.Kelly	c Armstrong b Saunders	0	b Trumble	7
W.P.Howell	c Worrall b Saunders	0	c Laver b Trumble	13
A.McBeath	lbw b Laver	12	not out	5
J.Marsh	c Laver b McLeod	0	c McAlister b Trumble	0
Extras	(b1, lb3)	4	(b2)	2
Total	(52.0 overs, 151 mins)	153	(52.0 overs, 154 mins)	135

VICTORIA

Batsman	1st innings	Runs	2nd innings	Runs
*J.Worrall	c Gregory b Marsh	0	(2) c Gregory b Marsh	9
P.A.McAlister	c Kelly b McBeath	8	(1) c Hopkins b Marsh	2
H.Graham	lbw b McBeath	0	b Noble	14
H.Trumble	c Kelly b McBeath	0	(7) not out	45
W.W.Armstrong	b Hopkins	50	(4) b Marsh	8
C.E.McLeod	c McBeath b Hopkins	46	(5) c Howell b Noble	8
F.J.Laver	b Marsh	0		
S.A.McMichael	c Howell b Hopkins	7		
J.H.Stuckey	not out	26	(6) not out	32
†C.H.Ross	b Hopkins	0		
J.V.Saunders	b Marsh	2		
Extras	(b4, lb8, w2, nb1)	15	(b7, lb2, w4, nb4)	17
Total	(70.0 overs, 177 mins)	154	(41.3 overs, 128 mins) (5 wkts)	135

VICTORIA	O	M	R	W	w,nb		O	M	R	W	w,nb
Trumble	23	5	65	2	-,-	(2)	26	9	54	7	-,-
Saunders	23	5	70	6	-,-	(1)	15	1	50	2	-,-
Laver	3	2	4	1	-,-						
McLeod	3	1	10	1	-,-	(3)	11	4	29	0	-,-

NEW SOUTH WALES	O	M	R	W	w,nb		O	M	R	W	w,nb
Marsh	15	6	39	3	1,1		17	3	52	3	4,3
McBeath	23	13	38	3	1,-		8	2	22	0	-,-
Howell	15	6	24	0	-,-	(5)	8.3	1	24	0	-,-
Hopkins	16	4	37	4	-,-						
Trumper	1	0	1	0	-,-	(4)	1	0	9	0	-,-
Noble						(3)	7	2	11	2	-,1

FALL OF WICKETS

Wkt	NSW 1st	VIC 1st	NSW 2nd	VIC 2nd
1st	10	1	4	2
2nd	15	2	51	19
3rd	25	2	59	34
4th	52	28	65	34
5th	65	86	84	45
6th	88	91	99	-
7th	88	105	112	-
8th	88	126	126	-
9th	152	138	135	-
10th	153	154	135	-

VICTORIA v SOUTH AUSTRALIA (Shield Match 4)

Played at Melbourne Cricket Ground on December 31, 1900, January 1, 2, 3, 1901. (Timeless match)
Toss : Victoria.   Result : VICTORIA WON BY 238 RUNS.
Debuts: Nil.
12th Men: A.H.Pellew (SA). No 12th man or emergency fieldsman named for Victoria.
Umpires: P.Argall and R.M.Crockett.
Attendances: 6500, 8000, 2000, 200.   Total: About 16,700.   Receipts: £556.
Close of Play: 1st day Vic (2) 0/4 (Graham 4, McMichael 0); 2nd day Vic (2) 3/377 (McAlister 65, Trumble 11); 3rd day SA (2) 5/139
      (Walkley 3).

Rain on the previous day saturated the wicket and, as the first day progressed, it "became more and more treacherous" (*Age*). The Victorians batted first to take advantage before the wicket cut up but Travers bowled unchanged to take 9 for 30, an analysis bettered for South Australia only by Tim Wall's 10 for 36 in 1932-33. The South Australians fared little better against McLeod and Laver to be all out before stumps - 20 wickets having fallen in the day. Graham (120 in 168 minutes, 11 fours, 2 chances) and McMichael (76 in 123 minutes, 4 fours) added 157 for the first wicket on the following day on a drier pitch much improved by the roller. Armstrong (102 in 149 minutes, 11 fours, 2 chances) and McAlister (74 in 156 minutes, 3 fours) extended Victoria's advantage. Overnight rain again softened the wicket and wickets tumbled on the third and fourth days. Victoria had the ideal bowlers for the conditions in the persons of Trumble and Saunders. Bailey (43 in 42 minutes, 5 fours) "played good, skilful and lively cricket" (*Age*) in a brave attempt to wrest the initiative. *Wisden* incorrectly gives Vic (2) Trumble c Reedman b Matthews; SA (1) Bailey c Trumble; SA (2) Matthews 16 and omits A.Jarvis c Graham b Trumble 16. *O'Reilly* incorrectly gives Vic (2) Travers 2/97, Matthews 6/95. Sources: *Wisden, C.B.O'Reilly, VCA Report, The Age, The Argus, The Australasian, The Leader.*

VICTORIA

*J.Worrall	c Bailey b Travers	8	(6)	c Reedman b Matthews	23
H.Graham	c Giffen b Travers	22	(1)	lbw b Matthews	120
H.Trumble	c Hill b Travers	4	(5)	c Reedman b Travers	18
W.W.Armstrong	st A.H.Jarvis b Travers	1	(3)	c Matthews b Walkley	102
J.H.Stuckey	b Travers	18	(7)	b Matthews	2
P.A.McAlister	st A.H.Jarvis b Travers	11	(4)	b Matthews	74
†C.H.Ross	st A.H.Jarvis b Travers	3	(10)	c Reedman b Matthews	0
C.E.McLeod	c A.H.Jarvis b Travers	0		b Travers	10
F.J.Laver	c Stuart b A.Jarvis	7		b Travers	12
S.A.McMichael	not out	1	(2)	c Stuart b Giffen	76
J.V.Saunders	c Hill b Travers	0		not out	2
Extras	(lb1)	1		(b4, lb3)	7
Total	(44.4 overs, 136 mins)	76		(148.5 overs, 415 mins)	446

SOUTH AUSTRALIA

F.T.Hack	lbw b McLeod	14		b Trumble	25
E.Walkley	c Trumble b Saunders	8	(6)	b Saunders	20
C.Hill	lbw b McLeod	46		b Saunders	40
G.Giffen	c Worrall b Laver	1		c Graham b Saunders	22
A.Jarvis	run out	2	(7)	c Graham b Trumble	16
*J.C.Reedman	c Trumble b McLeod	4	(5)	c & b Saunders	1
B.T.Bailey	c Graham b Laver	6	(2)	c McAlister b Laver	43
W.P.Stuart	c Trumble b Laver	4		c & b Trumble	0
J.G.F.Matthews	c Trumble b McLeod	0		not out	1
†A.H.Jarvis	not out	3		c Trumble b Saunders	4
J.P.F.Travers	c Ross b Laver	4		b Trumble	0
Extras	(b13, lb2)	15		(b4, lb1)	5
Total	(50.4 overs, 145 mins)	107		(69.4 overs, 195 mins)	177

SOUTH AUSTRALIA	O	M	R	W	w,nb		O	M	R	W	w,nb		FALL OF WICKETS			
Travers	22.4	9	30	9	-,-		45	10	97	3	-,-			VIC	SA	VIC	SA
Matthews	15	6	30	0	-,-	(4)	26.5	5	95	5	-,-	Wkt	1st	1st	2nd	2nd
A.Jarvis	7	3	15	1	-,-	(2)	23	6	55	0	-,-	1st	16	20	157	60
Reedman						(3)	10	0	39	0	-,-	2nd	34	78	234	109
Hill							4	3	6	0	-,-	3rd	35	79	333	125
Giffen							24	1	104	1	-,-	4th	38	79	393	126
Walkley							14	3	35	1	-,-	5th	65	85	393	139
Bailey							2	0	8	0	-,-	6th	68	87	396	172
												7th	68	91	421	172
VICTORIA	O	M	R	W	w,nb		O	M	R	W	w,nb	8th	69	91	439	172
Trumble	14	2	33	0	-,-		26.4	7	65	4	-,-	9th	75	103	444	176
Saunders	9	3	24	1	-,-	(4)	20	6	38	5	-,-	10th	76	107	446	177
McLeod	16	5	25	4	-,-		10	2	31	0	-,-					
Laver	11.4	5	10	4	-,-	(2)	13	1	38	1	-,-					

NEW SOUTH WALES v SOUTH AUSTRALIA (Shield Match 5)

Played at Sydney Cricket Ground on January 5, 7, 8, 9, 1901.   (Timeless match)
Toss : South Australia.   Result : NEW SOUTH WALES WON BY AN INNINGS AND 605 RUNS.
Debuts: Nil.
12th Men: J.S.Redgrave (NSW) and W.P.Stuart (SA).
Umpires: P.Argall and R.Callaway.
Attendances: 8590, 5317, 2127, 12.   Total: 16,046.   Receipts: £1034.
Close of Play: 1st day NSW 1/224 (Iredale 107, Noble 43); 2nd day NSW 6/723 (Poidevin 33, Howard 25); 3rd day SA (2) 7/144
    (Matthews 23).

The capitulation of the South Australian batting to the pace of Marsh on the first day gave no indication of what was to follow. Trumper (70 in 88 minutes, 11 fours) and Iredale (118 in 135 minutes, 17 fours) opened with a stand of 148, Iredale scoring 107 in the tea-stumps session elongated by an earlier tea adjournment. Noble (153 in 163 minutes, 19 fours), Gregory (168 in 170 minutes, 2 fives and 23 fours) and Duff (119 in 130 minutes, 16 fours) continued the New South Wales dominance to assist in the addition of a further 499 runs in the day. The third day saw Poidevin (140 not out in 210 minutes, 20 fours) and Howard (64 in 68 minutes, 11 fours) chiefly responsible for carrying the total to a final 918 - the highest in all first-class cricket to date and still the highest for New South Wales. An unprecedented five centuries (as well as five century partnerships) were recorded in the innings. The margin of victory (after a second South Australian collapse) was also a record in first-class cricket at the time. In South Australia's first innings, Reedman appeared to be caught by Trumper but, when given out, strongly disputed the decision. Umpire Callaway later ruled that the dismissal was in fact lbw. Giffen aggravated a strained muscle while fielding on the second day and took no further part in the match. Last first-class appearance by A.H.Jarvis (debut in South Australia's initial match in 1877-78). *Wisden* and *O'Reilly* incorrectly give McBeath c Matthews; SA (2) A.Jarvis 9. Sources: *Wisden, C.B.O'Reilly, Sydney Referee, Sydney Morning Herald, Town & Country Journal, Sydney Daily Telegraph*.

SOUTH AUSTRALIA

F.T.Hack	c Kelly b Noble	2		c Kelly b Trumper	12
B.T.Bailey	b Marsh	57		b Marsh	0
C.Hill	c Howard b Marsh	55		c Noble b Marsh	20
G.Giffen	b Marsh	6		absent hurt	-
A.Jarvis	b Trumper	7	(4)	c Duff b Marsh	49
*J.C.Reedman	lbw b Marsh	1	(5)	b Marsh	6
E.Walkley	b Trumper	0	(6)	b Marsh	17
J.G.F.Matthews	b Hopkins	12	(7)	not out	24
A.H.Pellew	b Marsh	7	(8)	c Kelly b Hopkins	14
†A.H.Jarvis	c Gregory b Hopkins	3	(9)	b Noble	0
J.P.F.Travers	not out	0	(10)	lbw b Noble	11
Extras	(lb3, w4)	7		(lb3)	3
Total	(46.1 overs, 135 mins)	157		(47.2 overs, 140 mins)	156

NEW SOUTH WALES

V.T.Trumper	b A.Jarvis	70
F.A.Iredale	c A.H.Jarvis b Travers	118
M.A.Noble	c Giffen b Matthews	153
A.J.Y.Hopkins	c A.H.Jarvis b Travers	27
*S.E.Gregory	b A.Jarvis	168
R.A.Duff	st A.H.Jarvis b Travers	119
L.O.S.Poidevin	not out	140
T.H.Howard	c Bailey b Matthews	64
†J.J.Kelly	c Hill b Hack	34
A.McBeath	c Walkley b Bailey	7
J.Marsh	lbw b Travers	1
Extras	(b9, lb8)	17
Total	(208.0 overs, 560 mins)	918

NEW SOUTH WALES	O	M	R	W	w,nb		O	M	R	W	w,nb			FALL OF WICKETS	
Noble	4	1	7	1	-,-		6.2	1	7	2	-,-			SA	NSW	SA
McBeath	6	0	36	0	-,-		1	1	0	0	-,-	Wkt	1st	1st	2nd
Marsh	16	8	34	5	4,-		20	3	59	5	-,-	1st	20	148	3
Howard	2	0	5	0	-,-		9	1	38	0	-,-	2nd	86	238	29
Trumper	8	2	23	2	-,-		8	1	39	1	-,-	3rd	94	306	41
Hopkins	10.1	0	45	2	-,-		3	1	10	1	-,-	4th	118	414	47
												5th	132	628	85
SOUTH AUSTRALIA	O	M	R	W	w,nb							6th	135	679	114
Travers	69	15	197	4	-,-							7th	135	784	144
Matthews	27	2	162	2	-,-							8th	151	900	144
Giffen	23	0	119	0	-,-							9th	157	911	156
A.Jarvis	49	7	225	2	-,-							10th	157	918	-
Reedman	17	1	70	0	-,-										
Walkley	6	0	43	0	-,-										
Hack	10	1	44	1	-,-										
Hill	1	0	18	0	-,-										
Bailey	6	1	23	1	-,-										

TASMANIA v VICTORIA

Played at N.T.C.A. Ground, Launceston, on January 24, 25, 26, 1901. (Three-day match)
Toss : Victoria.   Result : VICTORIA WON BY FIVE WICKETS.
Debuts: Victoria - M.Ellis, J.F.Horan, W.H.McCormack, D.F.Noonan, H.L.Wright (all f/c).
12th Men: No 12th men or emergency fieldsmen named. Only 11 men in Victorian party.
Umpires: E.Barrass and J.Conway.
Attendances: No figures published, but considered "only moderate" (*Daily Telegraph*)   Receipts: No figures published.
Close of Play: 1st day Vic 375 all out; 2nd day Tas (2) 3/144 (Eady 36, Dodds 17).

The match was scheduled to start on January 23rd but was postponed due to the death of Queen Victoria. It was determined beforehand that the captains would decide each day's starting and finishing times "according to the exigencies of the game" (*Mercury*) The Victorians intended to keep to their original travel arrangements and leave for home on January 26th; this led to the Tasmanians following on, by mutual agreement, in an attempt to reach a decision as soon as possible, despite the follow-on law in Australia at the time requiring a mandatory deficit of 200 runs. Ultimately, the ship delayed its sailing time in order that the Victorians could catch it. Murray, Wright and J.A.O'Connor replaced F.B.Collins, D.Mailer and J.McDonald (all unavailable) before the Victorians left Melbourne. It is believed that O'Connor then also withdrew before the team left. E.J.K.Burn and G.H.Gatehouse were both unavailable for Tasmania. McCormack (99 in 195 minutes, 10 fours) and Sutherland (180 in 245 minutes, 2 fives and 23 fours) added 206 for the Victorian second wicket on the opening day. Neither gave a chance. Tasmania were best served by Savigny (63 in 110 minutes, 8 fours), R.J.Hawson (56 in 80 minutes, 1 five and 7 fours) and Eady (104 in 155 minutes, 4 fives and 14 fours). *Cricket* gives Vic (1) Hale 0/10, Paton 0/35 whereas *VCA Report* has Hale 0/20, Paton 0/1. Sources: *Cricket, VCA Report, Launceston Examiner, Launceston Daily Telegraph, Hobart Mercury.*

VICTORIA

M.Ellis	b Windsor	5	c Savigny b Windsor		12
W.H.McCormack	c McAllen b Dodds	99	c E.S.Hawson b Eady		12
D.Sutherland	c R.J.Hawson b Eady	180	c sub (J.Ramsay) b Eady		43
J.F.Horan	b Windsor	46	b Windsor		15
*G.H.S.Trott	b Eady	17	c & b Eady		22
R.Mitchell	c Savigny b Eady	2	not out		19
D.F.Noonan	not out	6	not out		1
A.W.Murray	b Eady	0			
F.A.Tarrant	c Dodds b Eady	0			
A.R.Carlton	b Windsor	3			
†H.L.Wright	c R.J.Hawson b Eady	7			
Extras		10			10
Total	(120.0 overs, 340 mins)	375	(53.4 overs, 130 mins) (5 wkts)		134

TASMANIA

J.H.Savigny	run out (/Wright)	63	b Carlton		15
H.Wilson	lbw b Tarrant	3	(9) not out		7
J.E.Bingham	c Tarrant b Carlton	47	st Wright b Carlton		16
E.A.C.Windsor	c Tarrant b Trott	43	(6) c Ellis b Carlton		5
C.J.Eady	b Trott	9	(4) c Ellis b Trott		104
H.Hale	c Wright b Trott	9	(7) b Carlton		12
N.Dodds	st Wright b Trott	30	(5) b Ellis		29
R.J.Hawson	not out	12	(2) c Murray b Ellis		56
E.S.Hawson	c & b Mitchell	5	(8) c Tarrant b Carlton		10
G.D.Paton	b Trott	1	c Ellis b Trott		4
*†C.McAllen	c McCormack b Mitchell	4	b Trott		5
Extras		6			12
Total	(83.0 overs, 230 mins)	232	(76.2 overs, 220 mins)		275

TASMANIA	O	M	R	W	w,nb		O	M	R	W	w,nb		FALL OF WICKETS			
														VIC	TAS	TAS	VIC
Windsor	48	9	152	3			27	9	61	2		Wkt	1st	1st	2nd	2nd
Eady	32	10	74	6			26.4	4	63	3		1st	16	11	59	18
Bingham	7	2	21	0								2nd	222	102	77	36
Wilson	5	1	17	0								3rd	321	132	111	75
Hale	6	0	20	0								4th	341	143	166	102
Dodds	10	2	34	1								5th	359	169	187	119
Savigny	5	1	22	0								6th	359	198	210	-
Paton	7	1	25	0								7th	359	211	224	-
												8th	363	220	260	-
VICTORIA	O	M	R	W	w,nb		O	M	R	W	w,nb	9th	366	227	265	-
Tarrant	27	12	43	1	(4)		13	6	23	0		10th	375	232	275	-
Carlton	17	2	60	1	(3)		19	2	94	5						
Trott	24	2	101	5	(2)		16.2	2	76	3						
Mitchell	15	9	22	2	(1)		7	2	15	0						
Ellis							19	7	50	2						
McCormack							2	0	5	0						

NEW SOUTH WALES v VICTORIA (Shield Match 6)

Played at Sydney Cricket Ground on February 1, 4, 5, 6, 1901. (Timeless match)
Toss : New South Wales.   Result : VICTORIA WON BY ONE WICKET.
Debuts: Nil.
12th Men: J.S.Redgrave (NSW) and C.E.Jones (Vic).
Umpires: R.M.Crockett and S.P.Jones.
Attendances: 1831, 2104, 1376, 855.   Total: 6166.   Receipts: £393.
Close of Play: 1st day Vic 5/67 (Stuckey 23, McLeod 3); 2nd day NSW (2) 4/150 (Trumper 67, Noble 15); 3rd day Vic (2) 1/47
    (Graham 35, Laver 1).

Jones, the former Australian representative, was a late umpiring replacement for R.Callaway (ill). Play on February 2nd, a Saturday was cancelled due to the funeral of Queen Victoria. The visitors won a close fought match by the narrowest of margins but should have lost - McBeath fumbling a return at the bowler's wicket that would have run out Saunders when 9 runs were still required. Trumper (230 in 290 minutes, 31 fours) "exhibited superb cricket from start to finish" (*Referee*) in a faultless innings to give his team a chance of victory after a first innings deficit. Duff (75 in 117 minutes, 9 fours) assisted him in a sixth wicket stand of 173. Stuckey (130 not out in 218 minutes, 26 fours, 3 chances) batted for all but 20 minutes of the Victorian first innings. Crockett no-balled Marsh for throwing three times in his first over, twice in his second, and 17 times in all in the first innings. Crockett was the only umpire to call Marsh in his six-match first-class career. Graham (58 in 72 minutes, 1 five and 9 fours), Trumble (63 in 100 minutes, 9 fours) and Worrall (90 in 150 minutes, 1 five and 16 fours) scored half-centuries in Victoria's second innings run chase. *Wisden* incorrectly gives Vic (1) Marsh 2/67, Howard 0/32; Vic (2) McAlister 22, Marsh 1/105, Howard 0/0; NSW (1) Laver 0/5. Sources: *Wisden, Sydney Referee, Sydney Morning Herald, Town & Country Journal.*

NEW SOUTH WALES

V.T.Trumper	c Saunders b Trumble	21		c Ross b Saunders	230
F.A.Iredale	lbw b Saunders	10		lbw b Trumble	8
M.A.Noble	c & b Saunders	43	(6)	st Ross b Saunders	27
A.J.Y.Hopkins	b Saunders	3		st Ross b Trumble	0
*S.E.Gregory	c Ross b Saunders	6		c Worrall b McLeod	49
R.A.Duff	b Trumble	29	(7)	b Saunders	75
L.O.S.Poidevin	b Saunders	4	(3)	c Graham b Trumble	11
T.H.Howard	c McMichael b McLeod	25		c Graham b Saunders	0
†J.J.Kelly	b Laver	17		not out	28
A.McBeath	not out	0		c McLeod b Laver	12
J.Marsh	c Trumble b McLeod	5		b Laver	8
Extras	(b5, lb2)	7		(b2, lb1, nb1)	4
Total	(69.1 overs, 190 mins)	170		(129.2 overs, 330 mins)	452

VICTORIA

*J.Worrall	c Poidevin b Noble	2	(7)	st Kelly b McBeath	90
W.W.Armstrong	b Marsh	5	(5)	b Trumper	32
H.Graham	run out (Hopkins/Kelly)	5	(2)	c Trumper b Noble	58
J.H.Stuckey	not out	130		c Trumper b McBeath	16
P.A.McAlister	b Marsh	0	(9)	not out	29
S.A.McMichael	lbw b Noble	17	(8)	c Kelly b Noble	18
C.E.McLeod	c Iredale b Hopkins	23	(1)	b Marsh	6
F.J.Laver	c Marsh b McBeath	56	(3)	c Kelly b Trumper	8
H.Trumble	lbw b McBeath	2	(6)	c Marsh b Trumper	63
†C.H.Ross	run out (/Kelly)	1		lbw b McBeath	2
J.V.Saunders	b McBeath	1		not out	3
Extras	(b8, lb5, w1, nb23)	37		(b12, lb3, w4)	19
Total	(77.5 overs, 238 mins)	279		(122.3 overs, 343 mins) (9 wkts)	344

VICTORIA	O	M	R	W	w,nb		O	M	R	W	w,nb		FALL OF WICKETS			
Trumble	32	12	71	2	-,-		34	5	125	3	-,1			NSW	VIC	NSW	VIC
Saunders	30	6	78	5	-,-		39	5	127	4	-,-		Wkt	1st	1st	2nd	2nd
McLeod	4.1	1	9	2	-,-		32	8	103	1	-,-		1st	10	12	29	26
Laver	3	1	5	1	-,-		21.2	1	81	2	-,-		2nd	52	17	45	70
Armstrong							3	1	12	0	-,-		3rd	55	24	47	89
													4th	67	26	128	101
NEW SOUTH WALES	O	M	R	W	w,nb		O	M	R	W	w,nb		5th	118	50	186	187
Noble	28	8	72	2	-,3		40	18	69	2	1,-		6th	118	124	359	217
Marsh	18	3	68	2	1,17		23	3	104	1	2,-		7th	122	266	361	286
Howard	8	2	31	0	-,3	(5)	1	0	1	0	-,-		8th	162	268	410	332
Trumper	5	0	23	0	-,-	(3)	25.3	7	71	3	1,-		9th	164	278	444	334
McBeath	12.5	3	26	3	-,-	(4)	26	7	57	3	-,-		10th	170	279	452	-
Hopkins	6	3	22	1	-,-		7	3	23	0	-,-						

1901-02 SEASON (17 MATCHES)

The visit of the 15th English team to Australia held centre stage. Melbourne Cricket Club had invited England to come in 1900-01, but the tour was abandoned due to the Boer War in South Africa. Marylebone Cricket Club were then asked to visit Australia the following summer and accepted the offer - only to withdraw when several leading players became unavailable. Melbourne Cricket Club finally persuaded A.C.MacLaren to get a touring team together. But the inability of Ranjitsinhji, Fry and Palairet to make the trip - together with the subsequent withdrawal of Hirst and Rhodes at the direction of their county, Yorkshire - severely weakened the team.

The Englishmen undertook a program of 22 matches, 11 of which were first-class including five Tests. The Western Australian Cricket Association attempted to arrange a match at Perth to close the tour, but were advised by Melbourne CC that the tourist's itinerary was inflexible and that the players had to leave Australia on March 20. The Englishmen encountered strong opposition throughout their stay and lost the Test series 4-1, as well as going down to both South Australia and New South Wales early on. They were not always favoured by the weather. MacLaren, Hayward and Tyldesley were the outstanding batsmen, each exceeding 1000 in all matches. Braund headed the bowling aggregates but the outstanding bowler was Barnes, a little-known player recruited by MacLaren, and his loss through injury during the Third Test was a real body blow to the tourists. He was unable to play again on the tour. The Australians, despite a heavy loss in the First Test, were definitely the stronger team in the series. Clem Hill shone with the bat, scoring over 500 runs in the Tests and 1000 runs in all first-class matches in the season. The Australian attack was effectively spearheaded by Noble and Trumble.

New South Wales won all their Sheffield Shield matches to easily regain the trophy from Victoria. For the first time, a match in the program of six was missed. Prior to the season, fixtures had been finalised for all games bar the last, South Australia's home match against Victoria. The SACA and VCA delayed setting a firm date because of uncertainty over the duration of matches involving the English team. The match was finally cancelled when it became obvious it would have no bearing on the outcome of the Shield, which had already been won by New South Wales.

The annual Victoria-Tasmania fixture was another casualty of the heavy first-class program in the New Year. The match was tentatively scheduled to start on January 26 at Melbourne, but when this became impractical Easter was suggested. This idea, too, went by the board and the match eventually lapsed. The WACA, who had failed to attract the Englishmen to Perth, also sought a match against South Australia this season, but again their efforts came to no end.

The final first-class match was played at Brisbane over Easter, between Queensland and New South Wales, and it saw the first declaration in first-class cricket in Australia.

The selection of the 11th Australian team to England in 1902 was carried out by Clem Hill, M.A.Noble and Hugh Trumble. The side virtually picked itself and the inclusion of Carter instead of Jack McKenzie as second keeper was considered the only real surprise. The party of 14 comprised J.Darling (captain), W.W.Armstrong, H.Carter, R.A.Duff, S.E.Gregory, C.Hill, A.J.Y.Hopkins, W.P.Howell, E.Jones, J.J.Kelly, M.A.Noble, J.V.Saunders, H.Trumble and V.T.Trumper.

Leading Aggregates

Batsmen	M	I	NO	Runs	HS	Ave.	Bowlers	Runs	Wkts	Ave.
C.Hill (SA)	10	20	0	1035	107	51.75	L.C.Braund (E)	1779	62	28.69
A.C.MacLaren (E)	10	16	0	929	167	58.06	M.A.Noble (NSW)	848	47	18.04
S.E.Gregory (NSW)	10	18	1	777	182	45.70	S.F.Barnes (E)	676	41	16.48
T.W.Hayward (E)	11	19	1	701	174	38.94	H.Trumble (V)	702	34	20.64
J.T.Tyldesley (E)	11	19	0	696	142	36.63	C.Blythe (E)	711	34	20.91
R.A.Duff (NSW)	9	16	1	488	104	32.53	J.R.Gunn (E)	769	29	26.51
V.T.Trumper (NSW)	10	18	0	486	73	27.00	J.V.Saunders (V)	691	28	24.67
W.Quaife (E)	11	19	1	440	68	24.44	A.McBeath (NSW)	641	27	23.74
M.A.Noble (NSW)	10	17	0	430	74	25.29				

SHEFFIELD SHIELD TABLE

	P	W	L	D	Quotient	Runs Scored	Wkts Lost	Runs Conceded	Wkts Taken
NEW SOUTH WALES	4	4	-	-	1.498	1888	60	1680	80
VICTORIA	3	1	2	-	1.032	1559	55	1647	60
SOUTH AUSTRALIA	3	-	3	-	0.539	1462	60	1582	35
TOTAL	5	5	5	-	1.000	4909	175	4909	175

SOUTH AUSTRALIA v A.C.McLAREN'S ENGLAND XI

Played at Adelaide Oval on November 9, 11, 12, 1901. (Timeless match)
Toss : South Australia.   Result : SOUTH AUSTRALIA WON BY 233 RUNS.
Debuts: Nil.
12th Men: H.P.Kirkwood (SA). No 12th named for England XI.
Umpires: P.Argall and R.M.Crockett.
Attendances: 8000, 9000, 6000.   Total: About 23,000.   Receipts: £902.
Close of Play: 1st day Eng XI 0/7 (Braund 7, Gunn 0); 2nd day SA (2) 4/170 (Reedman 25, Giffen 3).

Having arrived in Australia only five days previously, the tourists were short of practice and still recovering from the effects of the voyage out. The pitch was also a little under-prepared and overnight rain after the second day made batting difficult on the third day "on a wicket that was like a gluepot" (*Register*). Clem Hill (107 in 205 minutes, 11 fours and 80 in 105 minutes, 9 fours) "played himself into splendid form" (*Register*) and was the only batsman to exceed fifty in the match. George Giffen (13 for 93) took full advantage of the conditions to record his best match analysis for South Australia against an English team. His 7 for 46 in the first innings remains the best return for South Australia against an English team. Jarvis was out to the last ball of the opening over of the match. Play on the last day was not possible until 2.15pm due to the effects of the overnight rain referred to earlier. Sources: *Wisden, C.B.O'Reilly, Town & Country Journal, Adelaide Advertiser, South Australian Register.*

SOUTH AUSTRALIA

A.Jarvis	c Lilley b Gunn	0		c Barnes b Braund	7
F.T.Hack	b Braund	2		run out (Quaife/Lilley)	41
C.Hill	b Barnes	107		c Blythe b Barnes	80
G.Giffen	b Gunn	7	(6)	c Lilley b Blythe	19
*J.C.Reedman	c Quaife b Braund	4		c Jessop b Blythe	31
E.H.Leak	st Lilley b Blythe	39	(4)	run out (Hayward/Lilley)	11
B.T.Bailey	c Jessop b Barnes	15		c Quaife b Blythe	2
J.G.F.Matthews	c MacLaren b Blythe	11		c Jones b Blythe	6
†J.McKenzie	not out	37		c Gunn b Blythe	0
E.Jones	c Lilley b Barnes	2		c MacLaren b Gunn	0
J.P.F.Travers	c MacLaren b Barnes	0		not out	4
Extras	(b4, nb2)	6		(b1, lb1, nb4)	6
Total	(70.2 overs, 230 mins)	230		(87.5 overs, 260 mins)	207

A.C.MacLAREN'S ENGLAND XI

L.C.Braund	b Jones	7	(9)	c Jones b Giffen	4
J.R.Gunn	c Hill b Giffen	21	(6)	c & b Giffen	5
*A.C.MacLaren	b Jones	3	(1)	st McKenzie b Travers	6
W.Quaife	c Bailey b Giffen	28	(5)	c Matthews b Travers	9
T.W.Hayward	b Giffen	1	(4)	b Giffen	12
J.T.Tyldesley	c Travers b Giffen	4	(3)	b Travers	14
G.L.Jessop	b Giffen	38		c Travers b Giffen	0
A.O.Jones	b Giffen	0	(2)	c Hill b Giffen	5
†A.F.A.Lilley	c Leak b Giffen	2	(8)	c Matthews b Giffen	23
S.F.Barnes	not out	8		st McKenzie b Travers	1
C.Blythe	b Travers	0		not out	5
Extras	(b3, lb3)	6		(b1, lb1)	2
Total	(47.2 overs, 160 mins)	118		(31.4 overs, 101 mins)	86

ENGLAND XI	O	M	R	W	w,nb		O	M	R	W	w,nb
Gunn	14	5	30	2	-,1	(3)	24	6	36	1	-,4
Braund	17	3	69	2	-,-	(1)	16	1	58	1	-,-
Blythe	21	2	64	2	-,-	(4)	24.5	10	45	5	-,-
Barnes	11.2	0	32	4	-,1	(2)	14	2	34	1	-,-
Jones	5	1	17	0	-,-		5	0	18	0	-,-
Jessop	2	0	12	0	-,-						
Quaife						(6)	2	0	6	0	-,-
Hayward						(7)	2	0	4	0	-,-

SOUTH AUSTRALIA	O	M	R	W	w,nb		O	M	R	W	w,nb
Jones	14	4	41	2	-,-						
Travers	18.2	10	25	1	-,-	(1)	16	3	37	4	-,-
Giffen	15	3	46	7	-,-	(2)	15.4	2	47	6	-,-

FALL OF WICKETS				
Wkt	SA	ENG	SA	ENG
	1st	1st	2nd	2nd
1st	0	10	13	10
2nd	2	20	125	12
3rd	15	43	141	27
4th	20	45	141	43
5th	111	49	186	47
6th	139	107	188	49
7th	152	108	198	55
8th	222	109	198	59
9th	225	114	198	66
10th	230	118	207	86

VICTORIA v A.C.MacLAREN'S ENGLAND XI

Played at Melbourne Cricket Ground on November 15, 16, 18, 1901. (Timeless match)
Toss : Victoria.   Result : ENGLAND WON BY 118 RUNS.
Debuts: Nil.
12th Men: W.Carlton (Vic) and J.R.Gunn (Eng).
Umpires: R.M.Crockett and W.A.Young.
Attendances: 5899, 15240, 6517.   Total: 27,656.   Receipts: No figures published.
Close of Play: 1st day Eng XI 166 all out; 2nd day Eng XI (2) 1/107 (Hayward 38, Braund 3).

MacLaren (rheumatism) was unable to lead the Englishmen and Hugh Trumble (ill) was unavailable for Victoria. Rain prevented any play before lunch on the opening day and returned to delay the start of the third day. The pitch favoured bowlers throughout and by the third day, "at no time was the wicket easy to play on" (*Age*). Barnes (12 for 99), McLeod (10 for 132) and Collins (5 for 58) used the conditions to best advantage. Garnett was missed behind the wicket from the first ball of the match while Worrall was out to the last ball of the opening over of the Victorian first innings and McLeod to the first ball of the second innings. McGahey (57 in 102 minutes, 3 fours) recorded the sole half-century in the match but was missed when only 2. Sources: *Wisden, VCA Report, The Age, The Argus, The Herald, The Australasian, The Leader*.

A.C.MacLAREN'S ENGLAND XI

H.G.Garnett	b McLeod	17	(6)	c Graham b Collins	3
G.L.Jessop	c Fry b Saunders	26	(4)	b McLeod	0
J.T.Tyldesley	c Saunders b McLeod	10	(5)	c Graham b Collins	9
T.W.Hayward	c Collins b Saunders	12	(1)	c Collins b McLeod	38
W.Quaife	not out	36	(7)	b Collins	11
†A.F.A.Lilley	b Saunders	6	(8)	c McMichael b McLeod	19
*A.O.Jones	c Stuckey b McLeod	18	(9)	lbw b McLeod	5
C.P.McGahey	c McAlister b McLeod	15	(2)	c Stuckey b Collins	57
L.C.Braund	c McAlister b McLeod	2	(3)	c Armstrong b Collins	9
S.F.Barnes	c Laver b Armstrong	19		c Graham b McLeod	6
C.Blythe	st Fry b Armstrong	1		not out	3
Extras	(b2, lb1, w1)	4		(b7, lb4, w1, nb2)	14
Total	(70.5 overs, 190 mins)	166		(75.2 overs, 210 mins)	174

VICTORIA

C.E.McLeod	b Barnes	29		c Braund b Barnes	0
*J.Worrall	c Jones b Barnes	0		b Barnes	8
H.Graham	b Barnes	26		b Barnes	26
W.W.Armstrong	c & b Barnes	6		c Braund b Barnes	1
S.A.McMichael	lbw b Barnes	14		c Garnett b Blythe	4
J.H.Stuckey	c Braund b Blythe	9		c Lilley b Hayward	17
P.A.McAlister	c Barnes b Braund	22		b Barnes	5
F.J.Laver	c & b Blythe	10		c Garnett b Barnes	6
†H.J.Fry	not out	6		b Hayward	8
F.B.Collins	b Braund	1		b Barnes	3
J.V.Saunders	b Blythe	1		not out	0
Extras	(b5, lb3, nb1)	9		(b6, lb3, nb2)	11
Total	(65.5 overs, 166 mins)	133		(31.1 overs, 99 mins)	89

VICTORIA	O	M	R	W	w,nb		O	M	R	W	w,nb					
Saunders	22	6	61	3	1,-		14	3	27	0	1,-					
McLeod	34	10	75	5	-,-		26.2	8	57	5	-,2					
Laver	11	4	18	0	-,-	(5)	5	3	3	0	-,-					
Armstrong	3.5	0	8	2	-,-		7	3	15	0	-,-					
Collins						(3)	23	5	58	5	-,-					

	FALL OF WICKETS			
Wkt	ENG 1st	VIC 1st	ENG 2nd	VIC 2nd
1st	39	1	95	0
2nd	49	50	107	30
3rd	60	65	107	38
4th	68	83	120	44
5th	77	86	122	45
6th	105	96	133	61
7th	131	124	147	73
8th	133	125	161	78
9th	160	126	167	89
10th	166	133	174	89

ENGLAND XI	O	M	R	W	w,nb		O	M	R	W	w,nb
Barnes	29	5	61	5	-,1		16	5	38	7	-,2
Blythe	27.5	12	37	3	-,-		11	2	25	1	-,-
Braund	9	3	26	2	-,-						
Hayward						(3)	4.1	1	15	2	-,-

NEW SOUTH WALES v A.C.MacLAREN'S XI

Played at Sydney Cricket Ground on November 22, 23, 25, 26, 27, 1901. (Timeless match)
Toss : New South Wales.   Result : NEW SOUTH WALES WON BY 53 RUNS.
Debuts: Nil.
12th Men: B.W.Farquhar (NSW) and H.G.Garnett (Eng).
Umpires: R.Callaway and R.M.Crockett.
Attendances: 9303, 27891, 12710, 8724, 3986.   Total: 62,614.   Receipts: £2774.
Close of Play: 1st day Eng XI 0/25 (MacLaren 17, McGahey 7); 2nd day NSW (2) 0/18 (Howell 12, Kelly 0); 3rd day NSW (2) 8/310
     (Poidevin 95, Iredale 21); 4th day Eng XI (2) 4/160 (Tyldesley 22, Jones 6).

The NSWCA appointed Callaway and J.J.Giltinan to umpire the match. However MacLaren insisted that "the right of appointing one umpire is mine entirely and I must request that your association allow me to make one appointment". The Melbourne Cricket Club, the tour organizer, had appointed an umpire to tour with the team and the NSWCA relented to MacLaren's request under protest. MacLaren (145 in 255 minutes, 22 fours and 73 in 165 minutes, 9 fours) led the scoring in both innings for his team and Lilley (80 in 105 minutes, 11 fours, 2 chances) made a gallant but unsuccessful bid for victory on the final day. Poidevin (151 not out in 260 minutes, 19 fours, 3 chances), Trumper (67 in 79 minutes, 9 fours), Noble (74 in 165 minutes, 9 fours) and Iredale (67 in 105 minutes, 6 fours) batted well for New South Wales. Legspinners, Braund (12 for 239) and Clarke (career-best 10 for 231) proved the most successful bowlers for their respective teams. Sources: *Wisden, NSWCA Report, Sydney Referee, Sydney Morning Herald, Town & Country Journal, Sydney Daily Telegraph.*

NEW SOUTH WALES

V.T.Trumper	b Braund	67	(3)	b Braund	12
M.A.Noble	b Braund	22	(6)	b Barnes	74
C.W.Gregory	lbw b Braund	0	(7)	lbw b Braund	3
*S.E.Gregory	c Braund b Barnes	14	(5)	b Barnes	26
A.J.Y.Hopkins	c Lilley b Jessop	36	(4)	c Tyldesley b Braund	4
F.A.Iredale	c Lilley b Braund	15	(10)	c McGahey b Jones	67
R.A.Duff	c MacLaren b Barnes	1	(8)	c & b Braund	0
L.O.S.Poidevin	c & b Braund	30	(9)	not out	151
†J.J.Kelly	not out	33	(2)	c MacLaren b Braund	26
G.R.C.Clarke	c MacLaren b Braund	17	(11)	lbw b Braund	10
W.P.Howell	run out (Jessop)	34	(1)	b Barnes	27
Extras	(b9, lb1, nb9)	19		(b10, lb5, nb7)	22
Total	(90.4 overs, 250 mins)	288		(156.0 overs, 410 mins)	422

A.C.MacLAREN'S ENGLAND XI

*A.C.MacLaren	c C.W.Gregory b Hopkins	145		c & b Clarke	73
C.P.McGahey	c & b Clarke	7		c S.E.Gregory b Clarke	2
T.W.Hayward	lbw b Noble	0		b Clarke	53
W.Quaife	lbw b Howell	11		c Kelly b Howell	1
J.T.Tyldesley	c S.E.Gregory b Clarke	10		c Trumper b Clarke	57
A.O.Jones	b Clarke	44		lbw b Clarke	9
G.L.Jessop	b Clarke	15		c Kelly b Clarke	0
†A.F.A.Lilley	b Hopkins	34		c & b Trumper	80
J.R.Gunn	b Howell	30	(10)	b Howell	0
S.F.Barnes	st Kelly b Trumper	11	(11)	b Howell	13
L.C.Braund	not out	23	(9)	not out	29
Extras	(nb2)	2		(b3, lb1, w1, nb3)	8
Total	(113.3 overs, 285 mins)	332		(146.4 overs, 340 mins)	325

ENGLAND XI	O	M	R	W	w,nb		O	M	R	W	w,nb
Gunn	8	2	36	0	-,5	(5)	11	4	21	0	-,6
Barnes	28	2	83	2	-,4		45	8	105	3	-,1
Braund	40	11	109	6	-,-		56	18	130	6	-,-
Jessop	14.4	3	41	1	-,-	(1)	18	2	57	0	-,-
Jones						(4)	9	3	24	1	-,-
Hayward							9	1	41	0	-,-
McGahey							5	1	10	0	-,-
Quaife							3	0	12	0	-,-

NEW SOUTH WALES	O	M	R	W	w,nb		O	M	R	W	w,nb
Hopkins	20	1	80	2	-,-	(3)	17	7	42	0	-,-
Trumper	19.3	3	68	1	-,1	(4)	21	5	51	1	1,1
Clarke	34	7	98	4	-,-	(2)	51	16	133	6	-,2
Howell	32	9	62	2	-,-	(1)	57.4	18	91	3	-,-
Noble	8	3	22	1	-,1						

		FALL OF WICKETS		
Wkt	NSW 1st	ENG 1st	NSW 2nd	ENG 2nd
1st	85	25	35	8
2nd	87	26	63	116
3rd	101	50	69	127
4th	112	75	101	141
5th	145	141	106	164
6th	146	160	115	164
7th	177	233	115	253
8th	205	298	264	297
9th	227	298	399	298
10th	288	332	422	325

VICTORIA v SOUTH AUSTRALIA (Shield Match 1)

Played at Melbourne Cricket Ground on November 22, 23, 25, 26, 27, 1901. (Timeless match)
Toss : South Australia.   Result : VICTORIA WON BY FIVE WICKETS.
Debuts: South Australia - H.P.Kirkwood (f/c).
12th Men: W.Carlton (Vic) and E.Walkley (SA).
Umpires: G.A.Watson and W.A.Young.
Attendances: 2500, 4500, 2500, 2500, 1500.   Total: About 13,500.   Receipts: £332.
Close of Play: 1st day SA 4/287 (Leak 44, Jarvis 18); 2nd day Vic 3/134 (Armstrong 24, McAlister 10); 3rd day Vic 9/449 (Laver 98, Saunders 18); 4th day SA (2) 259 all out.

George Giffen was unavailable for South Australia. C.E.McLeod was absent for the last two days of the match due to the death of his brother Dan, a fellow Victorian representative. Flags at the ground were flown at half-mast and players of both teams wore black arm-bands as a mark of respect. Four centuries were scored in the match: Hack 110 in 259 minutes with 2 fours, Stuckey 130 in 192 minutes with 14 fours and a chance at 1, Laver 105 not out in 205 minutes with 7 fours and McAlister - who scored the winning runs with a four to bring up his century - 100 not out in 193 minutes with 1 five and 9 fours. Other high scorers in the match were Hill (95 in 130 minutes, 10 fours) and Jarvis (80 in 85 minutes, 1 five and 9 fours). *Wisden* incorrectly gives SA (2) Leak 11, Jarvis 8, Matthews 11, Kirkwood 10, McKenzie 29, Jones 13, Travers 5; all other sources as printed here. Sources: *Wisden, C.B.O'Reilly, The Age, The Argus, The Australasian.*

SOUTH AUSTRALIA

F.T.Hack	b Fry	110	b Worrall	60
B.T.Bailey	c Worrall b McLeod	4	c McAlister b Laver	9
C.Hill	c Stuckey b McLeod	95	c McAlister b Worrall	43
*J.C.Reedman	c Armstrong b Saunders	6	c McAlister b Laver	53
E.H.Leak	st Fry b Laver	68	c Worrall b Collins	19
A.Jarvis	c & b Armstrong	80	c & b Saunders	5
J.G.F.Matthews	c Stuckey b McLeod	3	c & b Collins	13
H.P.Kirkwood	c Armstrong b Laver	11	c McAlister b Collins	11
†J.McKenzie	b McLeod	11	c McAlister b Saunders	20
E.Jones	c McMichael b McLeod	4	b Saunders	18
J.P.F.Travers	not out	2	not out	1
Extras	(b9, lb5, nb2)	16	(b6, nb1)	7
Total	(162.2 overs, 412 mins)	410	(90.0 overs, 245 mins)	259

VICTORIA

*J.Worrall	c Kirkwood b Travers	7	c Jarvis b Travers	35
S.A.McMichael	b Matthews	53	b Jones	9
H.Graham	c Travers b Jones	37	c McKenzie b Jones	14
W.W.Armstrong	c Travers b Jones	36	b Travers	4
P.A.McAlister	b Jones	11	not out	100
J.H.Stuckey	c McKenzie b Jones	130	c Kirkwood b Jones	1
C.E.McLeod	b Jones	21		
F.J.Laver	not out	105	(7) not out	40
†H.J.Fry	b Kirkwood	27		
F.B.Collins	c Hill b Kirkwood	5		
J.V.Saunders	b Travers	22		
Extras	(b1, lb8, w1)	10	(b4, lb1)	5
Total	(156.5 overs, 458 mins)	464	(93.3 overs, 243 mins) (5 wkts)	208

VICTORIA	O	M	R	W	w,nb		O	M	R	W	w,nb
Saunders	31	8	63	1	-,1		28	7	71	3	-,-
McLeod	50	11	126	5	-,-						
Collins	28	6	78	0	-,1		14	3	43	3	-,1
Laver	30.2	6	67	2	-,-	(2)	29	4	86	2	-,-
Armstrong	9	2	24	1	-,-		4	1	10	0	-,-
Fry	7	1	24	1	-,-						
Worrall	7	3	12	0	-,-	(4)	15	3	42	2	-,-

SOUTH AUSTRALIA	O	M	R	W	w,nb		O	M	R	W	w,nb
Jones	55	13	148	5	1,-		26	5	74	3	-,-
Travers	36.5	12	84	2	-,-		38.3	15	58	2	-,-
Kirkwood	19	1	80	2	-,-		4	0	14	0	-,-
Matthews	21	1	64	1	-,-		5	0	19	0	-,-
Bailey	3	0	14	0	-,-						
Jarvis	17	2	53	0	-,-		15	7	25	0	-,-
Reedman	5	1	11	0	-,-		5	2	13	0	-,-

FALL OF WICKETS

Wkt	SA 1st	VIC 1st	SA 2nd	VIC 2nd
1st	6	25	14	14
2nd	162	91	106	32
3rd	191	103	140	36
4th	263	137	180	75
5th	358	156	186	82
6th	375	196	203	-
7th	386	346	215	-
8th	403	395	222	-
9th	407	411	258	-
10th	410	464	259	-

NEW SOUTH WALES v SOUTH AUSTRALIA (Shield Match 2)

Played at Sydney Cricket Ground on November 30, December 2, 3, 1901. (Timeless match)
Toss : New South Wales.　　　　Result : NEW SOUTH WALES WON BY AN INNINGS AND 98 RUNS.
Debuts: Nil.
12th Men: B.T.Bailey (SA). No 12th man or emergency fieldsman named for NSW (see below).
Umpires: R.Callaway and G.A.Watson.
Attendances: 5000, 3500, 1000.　　　　Total: About 9500.　　　　Receipts: £411.
Close of Play: 1st day NSW 3/219 (Noble 47, S.E.Gregory 20); 2nd day SA 6/86 (Jarvis 9, Walkley 2).

G.R.C.Clarke, who had university exams, was unavailable for New South Wales. Farquhar, originally named 12th man, was a late replacement for Poidevin who was suffering from a leg strain. No replacement 12th man was announced. A dispute arose at the conclusion of South Australia's first innings over which team should have next innings, as both sides wanted to avoid batting last on a deteriorating pitch. South Australia claimed the right to follow on under an Australasian Cricket Council rule which stated that a team 200 runs behind must bat again. New South Wales argued that under a new rule introduced by Marylebone Cricket Club, a team which led by 150 runs had the option of next innings. A 45-minute delay was resolved when John Cresswell, secretary of the SACA and also of the now defunct Cricket Council, cabled from Adelaide that the Council rule was still in force. Top scorers in the match were C.W.Gregory (87 in 95 minutes, 14 fours) and Kelly (77 in 83 minutes, 1 five and 13 fours) for New South Wales, Hill (50 in 60 minutes, 6 fours and 40 in 70 minutes, 3 fours) and Kirkwood (46 in 38 minutes, 8 fours) for South Australia. Howell scored 44 in 20 minutes, with 3 fives and 6 fours. Uncertainty exists over the identity of two fielders involved in dismissals in the New South Wales innings. *Wisden, O'Reilly* and the *NSWCA Report* all give Iredale "c Travers", whereas all newspaper reports independently report that Walkley, at mid-off, was the fieldsman responsible. Similarly, *Wisden* and *NSWCA* give Howell "c Kirkwood", and *Wisden* even awards the wicket to Travers. *O'Reilly* incorrectly gives C.W.Gregory c Kirkwood b Travers, Travers 4/129, Jarvis 1/78; SA (2) Leak 0, extras 10, Howell 1/71, McBeath 4/82. *Wisden* incorrectly gives SA (1) Howell 3/66, McBeath 6/30. Sources: *Wisden, C.B.O'Reilly, Sydney Referee, Sydney Morning Herald, Town & Country Journal, Sydney Daily Telegraph.*

NEW SOUTH WALES

V.T.Trumper	c Hill b Jones	21
†J.J.Kelly	c Hill b Kirkwood	77
F.A.Iredale	c Walkley b Jones	45
M.A.Noble	c Matthews b Jones	55
*S.E.Gregory	b Jones	30
A.J.Y.Hopkins	b Travers	16
R.A.Duff	c McKenzie b Travers	30
C.W.Gregory	c Kirkwood b Jarvis	87
B.W.Farquhar	lbw b Travers	19
W.P.Howell	c Walkley b Jarvis	44
A.McBeath	not out	12
Extras	(b6, lb6)	12
Total	(141.0 overs, 385 mins)	438

SOUTH AUSTRALIA

F.T.Hack	b Howell	1	(2) b McBeath		0
†J.McKenzie	b Hopkins	4	(9) b Trumper		31
C.Hill	b Howell	50	b Hopkins		40
*J.C.Reedman	b McBeath	14	b Howell		45
E.H.Leak	b Howell	1	c McBeath b Trumper		1
A.Jarvis	c Kelly b McBeath	24	(1) b McBeath		23
H.P.Kirkwood	b McBeath	5	(8) c Farquhar b Hopkins		46
E.Walkley	b McBeath	9	(7) st Kelly b McBeath		0
J.G.F.Matthews	b McBeath	5	(6) c C.W.Gregory b McBeath		7
E.Jones	c Trumper b McBeath	6	(11) not out		2
J.P.F.Travers	not out	0	(10) c Trumper b Hopkins		17
Extras		-	(b4, lb5)		9
Total	(48.4 overs, 135 mins)	119	(69.1 overs, 180 mins)		221

SOUTH AUSTRALIA	O	M	R	W	w,nb
Jones	48	15	121	4	-,-
Matthews	8	1	35	0	-,-
Travers	46	13	129	3	-,-
Kirkwood	11	1	49	1	-,-
Jarvis	22	3	78	2	-,-
Reedman	6	1	14	0	-,-

NEW SOUTH WALES	O	M	R	W	w,nb		O	M	R	W	w,nb
Hopkins	9	2	23	1	-,-	(2)	11	2	35	3	-,-
Howell	24	4	60	3	-,-	(4)	24	6	70	1	-,-
McBeath	15.4	7	36	6	-,-	(1)	27	4	84	4	-,-
Trumper						(3)	7.1	3	23	2	-,-

FALL OF WICKETS

	NSW	SA	SA
Wkt	1st	1st	2nd
1st	30	5	1
2nd	135	5	28
3rd	166	69	90
4th	237	69	91
5th	238	70	113
6th	272	83	118
7th	319	95	132
8th	380	103	189
9th	400	119	219
10th	438	119	221

AUSTRALIA v ENGLAND (1st Test)

Played at Sydney Cricket Ground on December 13, 14, 16, 1901. (Timeless match)
Toss : England.   Result : ENGLAND WON BY AN INNINGS AND 124 RUNS.
Debuts: England - S.F.Barnes, C.Blythe, L.C.Braund, J.R.Gunn (all Test).
12th Men: L.O.S.Poidevin (Aust) and C.P.McGahey (Eng).
Umpires: R.Callaway and R.M.Crockett.
Attendances: 15471, 34167, 17472.   Total: 67,110.   Receipts: £3064.
Close of Play: 1st day Eng 6/272 (Lilley 22); 2nd day Aust 3/103 (Hill 42, Howell 4).

Darling was called on to lead Australia after an absence of two years from the first-class scene. His only first-class cricket this season was to be the first three Tests, but his leadership was held in such esteem that at the end of the summer he was elected to captain the Australian side to England. The Australian XI in this match, drawn from Darling's successful 1899 team to England, came to grief against a completely inexperienced Test attack comprising Barnes (right-arm fast-medium), Braund (legbreaks) and Blythe (slow left-arm). Gregory (48 in 76 minutes, 6 fours and 43 in 85 minutes, 4 fours) and Hill (46 in 105 minutes, 3 fours) were the best of Australia's batsmen. MacLaren (116 in 207 minutes, 20 fours, chance when 46) and Hayward (69 in 156 minutes, 11 fours) started the game with a stand of 154, compiled in even time, and Lilley (84 in 143 minutes, 13 fours) and Braund (58 in 128 minutes, 10 fours) led off on the second day with another century stand - 124 for the seventh wicket. Sources: *Wisden, Sydney Morning Herald, Town & Country Journal, Sydney Daily Telegraph.*

ENGLAND

*A.C.MacLaren	lbw b McLeod	116
T.W.Hayward	c Hill b Trumble	69
J.T.Tyldesley	c McLeod b Laver	1
W.Quaife	b Howell	21
G.L.Jessop	b McLeod	24
A.O.Jones	c Kelly b Noble	9
†A.F.A.Lilley	c Laver b McLeod	84
L.C.Braund	c Jones b McLeod	58
J.R.Gunn	c & b Jones	21
S.F.Barnes	not out	26
C.Blythe	c Trumble b Laver	20
Extras	(b6, lb7, w1, nb1)	15
Total	(186.0 overs, 465 mins)	464

AUSTRALIA

S.E.Gregory	c Braund b Blythe	48	(5)	c MacLaren b Braund	43
V.T.Trumper	c & b Barnes	2		c Lilley b Blythe	34
C.Hill	b Barnes	46		b Braund	0
M.A.Noble	st Lilley b Braund	2		c Lilley b Blythe	14
W.P.Howell	c Braund b Blythe	9	(10)	not out	31
C.E.McLeod	b Barnes	0		b Blythe	0
†J.J.Kelly	b Blythe	0		c Barnes b Blythe	12
*J.Darling	c Quaife b Barnes	39	(1)	c Jessop b Braund	3
F.J.Laver	c Quaife b Braund	6		st Lilley b Braund	0
H.Trumble	not out	5	(8)	c Lilley b Barnes	26
E.Jones	c Jessop b Barnes	5		c Jones b Braund	2
Extras	(b1, lb3, nb2)	6		(b5, lb2)	7
Total	(72.1 overs, 205 mins)	168		(57.4 overs, 155 mins)	172

AUSTRALIA	O	M	R	W	w,nb
Jones	36	8	98	1	-,-
Noble	33	17	91	1	1,-
Howell	21	8	52	1	-,-
McLeod	44	17	84	4	-,-
Trumble	34	12	85	1	-,1
Laver	17	6	39	2	-,-
Trumper	1	1	0	0	-,-

ENGLAND	O	M	R	W	w,nb		O	M	R	W	w,nb
Barnes	35.1	9	65	5	-,2		16	2	74	1	-,-
Braund	15	4	40	2	-,-		28.4	8	61	5	-,-
Gunn	5	0	27	0	-,-						
Blythe	16	8	26	3	-,-	(3)	13	5	30	4	-,-
Jessop	1	0	4	0	-,-						

FALL OF WICKETS

		ENG	AUST	AUST
Wkt		1st	1st	2nd
1st		154	3	12
2nd		162	89	12
3rd		193	97	52
4th		220	112	59
5th		236	112	59
6th		272	112	89
7th		396	112	129
8th		405	142	136
9th		425	163	147
10th		464	168	172

VICTORIA v NEW SOUTH WALES (Shield Match 3)

Played at Melbourne Cricket Ground on December 26, 27, 28, 30, 1901. (Timeless match)
Toss : New South Wales.   Result : NEW SOUTH WALES WON BY 42 RUNS.
Debuts: Nil.
12th Men: T.S.Warne (Vic) and L.O.S.Poidevin (NSW).
Umpires: R.Callaway and R.M.Crockett.
Attendances: 8000, 5000, 5000, 2500.   Total: About 20,500.   Receipts: £745.
Close of Play: 1st day Vic 2/29 (McAlister 16); 2nd day Vic 9/291 (Armstrong 135); 3rd day NSW 231 all out.

Harry Graham was unavailable for Victoria. Poidevin was relegated to the position of 12th man for New South Wales because of a finger injury. Wickets tumbled throughout the match in hot, but otherwise, good conditions. Trumper (73 in 93 minutes, 10 fours) and Kelly began the game with a century partnership before the Victorian bowlers settled into their task. McAlister (89 in 177 minutes, 11 fours) and Armstrong (137 in 275 minutes, 18 fours) put their team into a good position before a "magnificent bowling performance by Noble" (*Age*) - 7 for 44 from 33 overs - restricted the first innings lead. Duff (51 in 100 minutes, 5 fours) and Hopkins (42 in 93 minutes, 4 fours) batted well in the second innings but the home team needed only 153 for victory at the close of the third day. However, the Victorian batting meekly surrendered to the sustained accuracy of Howell and Noble, who completed a ten-wicket match. Laver's bowling (8 for 63 in the match) was also highly praised. *The Age* reported that umpire Callaway inadvertently allowed Noble an extra delivery in the final over of the second day's play, and Hastings was bowled by it. Sources: *Wisden, NSWCA Report, The Age, The Argus, The Australasian.*

NEW SOUTH WALES

V.T.Trumper	b Armstrong	73		b Trumble	19
†J.J.Kelly	c McAlister b McLeod	24	(9)	b Laver	4
M.A.Noble	c Saunders b Trumble	24	(6)	b Laver	26
C.W.Gregory	c Trumble b Armstrong	0		b Trumble	0
*S.E.Gregory	c Laver b Trumble	24	(7)	b Laver	10
R.A.Duff	b Laver	28	(5)	st Hastings b Laver	51
F.A.Iredale	b Trumble	8	(2)	c & b Saunders	13
A.J.Y.Hopkins	c Hastings b Laver	5		c McMichael b Laver	42
W.P.Howell	not out	18	(3)	b McLeod	27
G.R.C.Clarke	c McAlister b Laver	1		run out (Stuckey/McLeod)	24
A.McBeath	b Trumble	0		not out	6
Extras	(b11, lb1, nb4)	16		(lb6, nb3)	9
Total	(80.0 overs, 215 mins)	221		(91.4 overs, 261 mins)	231

VICTORIA

C.E.McLeod	c Howell b McBeath	11	(6)	run out (S.E.Gregory/Kelly)	16
W.Carlton	run out (S.E.Gregory)	0	(8)	b Noble	0
P.A.McAlister	c Duff b Noble	89	(2)	c Clarke b Howell	5
J.H.Stuckey	b McBeath	1	(7)	b Noble	8
W.W.Armstrong	b Noble	137	(3)	b Howell	12
*J.Worrall	lbw b Noble	0	(1)	c & b McBeath	4
H.Trumble	b Noble	4	(4)	b Howell	28
F.J.Laver	c Howell b Noble	21	(5)	c Noble b Howell	0
S.A.McMichael	c Iredale b Noble	20		not out	12
†T.J.Hastings	b Noble	0		c S.E.Gregory b Clarke	12
J.V.Saunders	not out	3		c Howell b Noble	0
Extras	(b6, lb7, nb1)	14		(b4, lb8, nb1)	13
Total	(130.0 overs, 330 mins)	300		(73.1 overs, 188 mins)	110

VICTORIA	O	M	R	W	w,nb		O	M	R	W	w,nb		FALL OF WICKETS			
Trumble	27	6	66	4	-,1		32	10	75	2	-,2	Wkt	NSW	VIC	NSW	VIC
Saunders	17	4	56	0	-,-		15	4	48	1	-,1		1st	1st	2nd	2nd
McLeod	13	2	47	1	-,-		16	1	41	1	-,-	1st	106	1	32	16
Armstrong	11	4	14	2	-,3		6	1	17	0	-,-	2nd	120	29	32	20
Laver	12	4	22	3	-,-		22.4	6	41	5	-,-	3rd	124	39	32	34
												4th	144	183	72	34
NEW SOUTH WALES	O	M	R	W	w,nb		O	M	R	W	w,nb	5th	169	186	131	75
Howell	31	14	53	0	-,-	(2)	33	14	40	4	-,-	6th	187	192	148	80
Clarke	25	6	83	0	-,-	(4)	3	1	3	1	-,-	7th	201	252	159	80
Noble	33	17	44	7	-,1		28.1	12	38	3	-,1	8th	210	290	169	89
McBeath	32	9	69	2	-,-	(1)	9	3	16	1	-,-	9th	220	291	217	108
Trumper	5	0	17	0	-,-							10th	221	300	231	110
Hopkins	4	1	20	0	-,-											

AUSTRALIA v ENGLAND (2nd Test)

Played at Melbourne Cricket Ground on January 1, 2, 3, 4, 1902. (Timeless match)
Toss : England.   Result : AUSTRALIA WON BY 229 RUNS.
Debuts: Australia - W.W.Armstrong, R.A.Duff (both Test).
12th Men: F.J.Laver (Aust) and H.G.Garnett (Eng).
Umpires: R.Callaway and R.M.Crockett.
Attendances: 28133, 24500, 16831, 3500.   Total: 72,464.   Receipts: No figures published.
Close of Play: 1st day Aust (2) 5/48 (Gregory 0); 2nd day Aust (2) 9/300 (Duff 71, Armstrong 25); 3rd day Eng (2) 5/147 (Tyldesley 60, Braund 13).

Rain on the day before the match and again on the first morning saturated the pitch and prompted MacLaren to send Australia in. *The Age* reported that "the wicket proved to be unplayable". Both teams had completed an innings by 4.16pm and 25 wickets fell in 265 minutes of play on the first day. Trumper was out to the second ball of the match, Duff (32 in 42 minutes, 5 fours) and Jessop (27 in 20 minutes, 1 five and 2 fours) making the most of things. The second day brought perfect weather, *The Age* noting that "the wicket had completely changed in character under the process of cutting and rolling. The conditions were as opposite as possible to those of the opening day". Hill, held back by Darling, responded by scoring Test cricket's first innings of 99 (196 minutes, 7 fours) and Duff, in at No. 10, grafted a chanceless debut century (104 in 206 minutes, 11 fours) and shared with Armstrong (45 not out in 148 minutes, 4 fours) the first three-figure stand for the tenth wicket in Tests. The perfect wicket held for the third day but heavy rain overnight delayed the start of the fourth day until after lunch. Only 34 minutes were required to finish the match on a sodden wicket, Trumble wrapping it up with a hat-trick (Jones, Gunn and Barnes). Tyldesley (66 in 210 minutes, 8 fours) was England's top scorer while the stern-faced Barnes, in his second Test, captured 13 wickets. Sources: *Wisden, The Age, The Argus, The Australasian.*

AUSTRALIA

V.T.Trumper	c Tyldesley b Barnes	0	(8)	c Lilley b Barnes	16
*J.Darling	c Lilley b Blythe	19		c Tyldesley b Barnes	23
C.Hill	b Barnes	15	(7)	c Jones b Barnes	99
H.Trumble	c Braund b Blythe	16	(1)	c Braund b Barnes	16
M.A.Noble	c Lilley b Blythe	0	(9)	lbw b Blythe	16
S.E.Gregory	st Lilley b Blythe	0	(5)	c Jones b Barnes	17
R.A.Duff	c Braund b Barnes	32	(10)	b Braund	104
†J.J.Kelly	c Quaife b Barnes	5	(3)	run out (Quaife/Braund)	3
W.W.Armstrong	not out	4	(11)	not out	45
W.P.Howell	b Barnes	1	(4)	c Hayward b Barnes	0
E.Jones	c MacLaren b Barnes	14	(6)	c MacLaren b Barnes	5
Extras	(b6)	6		(b7, lb1, nb1)	9
Total	(32.1 overs, 114 mins)	112		(156.2 overs, 426 mins)	353

ENGLAND

*A.C.MacLaren	c Jones b Trumble	13	(2)	c Trumble b Noble	1
T.W.Hayward	c Darling b Trumble	0	(1)	st Kelly b Trumble	12
J.T.Tyldesley	c Gregory b Trumble	2		c Trumble b Noble	66
W.Quaife	b Noble	0		b Noble	25
G.L.Jessop	st Kelly b Noble	27		c Gregory b Noble	32
J.R.Gunn	st Kelly b Noble	0	(9)	c Jones b Trumble	2
†A.F.A.Lilley	c Trumper b Noble	6	(6)	c Darling b Noble	0
A.O.Jones	c Kelly b Noble	0		c Darling b Trumble	6
L.C.Braund	not out	2	(7)	c Darling b Noble	25
S.F.Barnes	c & b Noble	1		c & b Trumble	0
C.Blythe	c Trumper b Noble	4		not out	0
Extras	(b6)	6		(b1, lb1, nb4)	6
Total	(15.4 overs, 65 mins)	61		(79.5 overs, 230 mins)	175

ENGLAND	O	M	R	W	w,nb		O	M	R	W	w,nb		FALL OF WICKETS				
Barnes	16.1	5	42	6	-,-		64	17	121	7	-,1			AUST	ENG	AUST	ENG
Blythe	16	2	64	4	-,-		31	7	85	1	-,-		Wkt	1st	1st	2nd	2nd
Braund							53.2	17	114	1	-,-		1st	0	5	32	2
Jessop							1	0	9	0	-,-		2nd	32	16	42	29
Gunn							6	1	13	0	-,-		3rd	34	16	42	80
Jones							1	0	2	0	-,-		4th	34	24	42	123
													5th	38	36	48	123
AUSTRALIA	O	M	R	W	w,nb		O	M	R	W	w,nb		6th	81	51	98	156
Trumble	8	1	38	3	-,-	(3)	22.5	10	49	4	-,2		7th	85	51	128	173
Noble	7.4	2	17	7	-,-		26	5	60	6	-,2		8th	90	56	167	175
Jones						(1)	12	2	33	0	-,-		9th	94	57	233	175
Howell							15	6	23	0	-,-		10th	112	61	353	175
Armstrong							2	1	3	0	-,-						
Trumper							2	1	1	0	-,-						

SOUTH AUSTRALIA v NEW SOUTH WALES (Shield Match 4)

Played at Adelaide Oval on January 10, 11, 13, 14, 1902. (Timeless match)
Toss : New South Wales.   Result : NEW SOUTH WALES WON BY AN INNINGS AND 19 RUNS.
Debuts: Nil.
12th Men: R.W.Waters (SA) and L.O.S.Poidevin (NSW).
Umpires: R.Callaway and G.S.Downs.
Attendances: 4000, 6000, 1500, 500.   Total: About 12,000.   Receipts: No figures published.
Close of Play: 1st day NSW 5/269 (S.E.Gregory 103, C.W.Gregory 48); 2nd day SA 3/123 (Hack 42); 3rd day SA (2) 8/105
  (Kirkwood 23, Travers 16).

Poidevin was again left out of the New South Wales side because of his finger injury. S.E.Gregory, who scored 182 in 275 minutes with 22 fours, strained a leg muscle while batting and did not field at any stage of the match. S.E.Gregory, on 27, played a ball from Jarvis on to his wicket without removing a bail. T.Duggan, captain of Glebe Cricket Club and a prominent Rugby League footballer, substituted in his absence in both innings, while Noble captained the team. Duggan was in Adelaide on a private visit. Iredale, in his last first-class appearance (83 in 165 minutes, 9 fours), C.W.Gregory (74 in 160 minutes, 8 fours) and Howell (67 in 60 minutes, 1 five and 9 fours) also compiled notable innings for New South Wales. Trumper took the wickets of Hack and Jarvis with consecutive balls in South Australia's first innings, while Kirkwood (66 in 110 minutes, 7 fours) and Travers combined for a ninth-wicket stand of 109 in the second innings. Kelly strained a leg muscle while wicket-keeping on the third day and left the field early on the fourth day when the injury stiffened up. Duff kept wickets and Poidevin was forced to substitute for the remainder of the game. *Wisden* incorrectly gives SA (2) Giffen 20, Jarvis c sub b Howell, Kirkwood 67, extras 16, Howell 4/71, Noble 3/27, McBeath 0/22. *O'Reilly* incorrectly gives SA (1) extras 14, total 261; SA (2) Kirkwood 67, extras 14, Hopkins 1/23; result NSW by an innings and 20 runs. Sources: *Wisden, C.B.O'Reilly, NSWCA Report, Adelaide Advertiser, South Australian Register.*

NEW SOUTH WALES

V.T.Trumper	c McKenzie b Travers	5
F.A.Iredale	c Hill b Jarvis	83
M.A.Noble	st McKenzie b Travers	0
R.A.Duff	lbw b Jarvis	17
*S.E.Gregory	b Travers	182
A.J.Y.Hopkins	b Jones	0
C.W.Gregory	c G.Giffen b Reedman	74
†J.J.Kelly	c Reedman b Travers	11
W.P.Howell	c Travers b G.Giffen	67
G.R.C.Clarke	not out	10
A.McBeath	b Travers	1
Extras	(b4, lb18)	22
Total	(141.4 overs, 415 mins)	472

SOUTH AUSTRALIA

F.T.Hack	b Trumper	42	b Noble		0
W.F.Giffen	run out (McBeath)	7	c Duff b Noble		3
*C.Hill	b Howell	26	b Howell		10
J.C.Reedman	c Clarke b Hopkins	45	b Noble		9
G.Giffen	b Howell	50	b Howell		22
A.Jarvis	b Trumper	0	c sub (T.Duggan) b Noble		11
H.P.Kirkwood	c Kelly b McBeath	33	b Clarke		66
N.Claxton	b Howell	39	run out		4
†J.McKenzie	b Howell	0	b Howell		2
E.Jones	b Hopkins	4	(11) not out		9
J.P.F.Travers	not out	1	(10) c Trumper b Hopkins		40
Extras	(b3, lb10, nb2)	15	(b7, lb6, w1, nb1)		15
Total	(109.4 overs, 285 mins)	262	(51.5 overs, 165 mins)		191

SOUTH AUSTRALIA	O	M	R	W	w,nb
Jones	38	9	130	1	-,-
Travers	43.4	15	105	5	-,-
G.Giffen	27	3	112	1	-,-
Jarvis	24	6	56	2	-,-
Kirkwood	2	0	17	0	-,-
Reedman	7	1	30	1	-,-

NEW SOUTH WALES	O	M	R	W	w,nb		O	M	R	W	w,nb
Clarke	20	2	56	0	-,1	(5)	4.5	0	22	1	-,1
McBeath	26	7	55	1	-,-	(4)	6	0	23	0	1,-
Howell	21.4	3	54	4	-,-	(2)	21	1	71	3	-,-
Noble	19	3	34	0	-,1	(1)	10	2	27	4	-,-
Hopkins	15	5	29	2	-,-	(3)	6	0	22	1	-,-
Trumper	8	2	19	2	-,-		4	2	11	0	-,-

FALL OF WICKETS

Wkt	NSW 1st	SA 1st	SA 2nd
1st	7	16	0
2nd	7	57	9
3rd	39	123	13
4th	143	123	27
5th	145	123	49
6th	359	172	59
7th	380	250	66
8th	445	250	68
9th	465	260	177
10th	472	262	191

AUSTRALIA v ENGLAND (3rd Test)

Played at Adelaide Oval on January 17, 18, 20, 21, 22, 23, 1902. (Timeless match)
Toss : England.   Result : AUSTRALIA WON BY FOUR WICKETS.
Debuts: Nil.
12th Men: E.Jones (Aust) and C.P.McGahey (Eng).
Umpires: P.Argall and R.M.Crockett.
Attendances: 8500, 15000, 10000, 5000, 6000, 3000.   Total: 48,105.   Receipts: £2258.
Close of Play: 1st day Eng 5/266 (Quaife 51, Braund 35); 2nd day Aust 2/173 (Hill 83, Duff 22); 3rd day Eng (2) 1/98 (Hayward 44,
    Tyldesley 4); 4th day Eng (2) 5/204 (Quaife 27, Lilley 21); 5th day Aust (2) 4/201 (Darling 40, Trumble 4).

Barnes, who had taken 19 wickets in his first two Tests, badly twisted a knee while bowling on the second day and took no further part in the match or the tour. The England attack was further depleted with the loss of Blythe (split finger) for much of the first innings. Hayward (90 in 170 minutes, 11 fours) and Braund (103 not out in 222 minutes, 1 five and 12 fours, chances at 44 and 62) topscored for England while Hill, who had scored 99 in his previous innings for Australia, completed an extraordinary sequence with scores of 98 (159 minutes, 11 fours) and 97 (172 minutes, 1 five and 7 fours). A dust storm severely curtailed play on the fourth day. McLeod had been in doubt because of illness and J.P.F.Travers was called to the ground on the first day. He was not needed. *Wisden* incorrectly gives Aust (2) Braund 14 overs, Blythe 23 overs, Gunn 22 overs, Jessop 13 overs, Hayward 4 overs; Eng (2) extras as all byes. Sources: *Wisden, The Australasian, Sydney Morning Herald, Adelaide Advertiser, South Australian Register.*

ENGLAND

*A.C.MacLaren	run out (Trumper/Trumble)	67	b Trumble	44
T.W.Hayward	run out (Kelly)	90	b Trumble	47
J.T.Tyldesley	c & b Trumble	0	run out (Trumper/Kelly)	25
G.L.Jessop	c Trumper b Trumble	1	(5) b Trumble	16
†A.F.A.Lilley	lbw b Trumble	10	(7) b McLeod	21
W.Quaife	c Kelly b Howell	68	(4) lbw b Trumble	44
L.C.Braund	not out	103	(6) b Howell	17
A.O.Jones	run out (Hill/Kelly)	5	c & b Trumble	11
J.R.Gunn	b Noble	24	lbw b Trumble	5
S.F.Barnes	c Hill b Noble	5	absent hurt	-
C.Blythe	c Hill b Noble	2	(10) not out	10
Extras	(b9, w1, nb3)	13	(b6, w1)	7
Total	(170.0 overs, 395 mins)	388	(111.0 overs, 283 mins)	247

AUSTRALIA

*J.Darling	c MacLaren b Blythe	1	(5) c Hayward b Jessop	69
V.T.Trumper	run out (sub H.G.Garnett/Jessop)	65	b Gunn	25
C.Hill	c Tyldesley b Braund	98	b Jessop	97
R.A.Duff	lbw b Braund	43	(1) hit wkt b Gunn	4
S.E.Gregory	c Blythe b Braund	55	(4) c Braund b Gunn	23
W.W.Armstrong	c & b Gunn	9	(8) not out	9
H.Trumble	b Gunn	13	(6) not out	62
W.P.Howell	c Braund b Gunn	3		
M.A.Noble	b Gunn	14	(7) run out (Jessop/Lilley)	13
†J.J.Kelly	not out	5		
C.E.McLeod	b Gunn	7		
Extras	(b2, lb6)	8	(b9, lb3, nb1)	13
Total	(113.0 overs, 315 mins)	321	(134.0 overs, 366 mins) (6 wkts)	315

AUSTRALIA	O	M	R	W	w,nb		O	M	R	W	w,nb
Trumble	65	23	124	3	-,-	(3)	44	18	74	6	-,-
Noble	26	10	58	3	-,2	(1)	21	7	72	0	1,-
Howell	36	10	82	1	-,-	(2)	27	9	54	1	-,-
Armstrong	18	5	45	0	-,1		5	0	9	0	-,-
Trumper	6	3	17	0	1,-						
McLeod	19	5	49	0	-,-	(5)	14	3	31	1	-,-

ENGLAND	O	M	R	W	w,nb		O	M	R	W	w,nb
Braund	46	9	143	3	-,-	(2)	25	5	79	0	-,-
Blythe	11	3	54	1	-,-	(3)	41	16	66	0	-,-
Barnes	7	0	21	0	-,-						
Gunn	42	14	76	5	-,-	(1)	38	14	88	3	-,-
Jessop	7	0	19	0	-,-		23	9	41	2	-,1
Hayward						(4)	7	0	28	0	-,-

FALL OF WICKETS

Wkt	ENG 1st	AUST 1st	ENG 2nd	AUST 2nd
1st	149	1	80	5
2nd	160	138	113	50
3rd	164	197	126	98
4th	171	229	144	194
5th	186	260	165	255
6th	294	288	204	287
7th	302	289	218	-
8th	371	302	224	-
9th	384	309	247	-
10th	388	321	-	-

NEW SOUTH WALES v VICTORIA (Shield Match 5)

Played at Sydney Cricket Ground on January 25, 27, 28, 29, 1902. (Timeless match)
Toss : New South Wales.   Result : NEW SOUTH WALES WON BY 49 RUNS.
Debuts: New South Wales - A.Cotter, A.Kermode, W.E.Pite (all f/c); F.Devenish-Meares (NSW only).
12th Men: A.Diamond (NSW) and W.Bruce (Vic).
Umpires: R.Callaway and R.M.Crockett.
Attendances: 8000, 2500, 1000, 200.   Total: About 11,700.   Receipts: £686.
Close of Play: 1st day Vic 0/13 (Worrall 2, McAlister 11); 2nd day NSW 5/116 (Devenish-Meares 11, Kermode 4); 3rd day Vic (2) 3/239
     (Warne 69, McCormack 27).

Both teams requested a late start on the first day to enable players from the just-completed Adelaide Test to participate. However, the authorities refused and consequently four replacements were required - Farquhar, Devenish-Meares and Pite (New South Wales) and McCormack (Victoria). F.A.Iredale was unavailable for New South Wales. Hopkins (117 in 128 minutes, 23 fours) and Gregory (60 in 90 minutes, 11 fours) began the match for New South Wales with a "vigorous" (*SMH*) opening stand of 165. Of these, 158 were compiled in the 85 minutes before lunch (Hopkins 88). After their departure, only Poidevin (82 in 110 minutes, 10 fours) made any impression, Saunders finishing the innings with a final spell of 6 for 13. Overnight rain produced conditions more conducive to the bowlers and batsmen of both sides struggled until it improved by the third day. Set 375, Worrall (106 in 112 minutes, 1 five and 19 fours) and Warne (89 in 220 minutes, 10 fours) gave the Victorians second innings a great start of 154, but the batting fell away thereafter and the home team triumphed. As the Victorian second innings began at 2.45 on the third day a five minutes drinks break was substituted for the normal 4 o'clock tea adjournment. Devenish-Meares (previously one match for Western Australia) recorded a half-century (55 in 103 minutes, 9 fours) on debut for his State of birth. *Wisden* incorrectly gives Vic (1) Hastings 10, total 151, Hopkins 0/30; NSW (2) Collins 5 overs.
Sources: *Wisden, Sydney Referee, Sydney Morning Herald, Town & Country Journal, Sydney Daily Telegraph.*

NEW SOUTH WALES

*A.J.Y.Hopkins	c Carlton b Warne	117	(2)	b Saunders	0
C.W.Gregory	c & b Warne	60	(1)	c Hastings b Saunders	27
L.O.S.Poidevin	c Hastings b Saunders	82		b Saunders	9
B.W.Farquhar	c Collins b Saunders	35		c & b McAlister	40
W.E.Pite	b Laver	13		b Saunders	8
F.Devenish-Meares	b Saunders	0		c Collins b Warne	55
G.R.C.Clarke	c Worrall b Saunders	0	(8)	c McMichael b Saunders	23
†H.Carter	st Hastings b Saunders	0	(9)	not out	6
A.McBeath	c Collins b Saunders	0	(11)	b Collins	6
A.Cotter	b Laver	0		b Collins	0
A.Kermode	not out	7	(7)	st Hastings b Collins	4
Extras	(b7, lb4, w1, nb1)	13		(b8, lb12, nb1)	21
Total	(98.2 overs, 243 mins)	327		(73.0 overs, 213 mins)	199

VICTORIA

*J.Worrall	st Carter b McBeath	24		c & b Clarke	106
S.A.McMichael	c Cotter b Kermode	13	(6)	run out (Pite/Carter)	3
P.A.McAlister	c Clarke b McBeath	5		b Kermode	7
J.H.Stuckey	b Kermode	11		b Hopkins	15
F.J.Laver	b Kermode	27	(8)	not out	34
T.S.Warne	c Carter b McBeath	7	(2)	c Carter b McBeath	89
W.H.McCormack	not out	33	(5)	c Hopkins b Clarke	37
W.Carlton	run out (Devenish-Meares)	0	(7)	c Carter b McBeath	0
†T.J.Hastings	lbw b Clarke	11		c & b McBeath	5
F.B.Collins	b Kermode	3		b Clarke	9
J.V.Saunders	b Clarke	9		c & b Clarke	3
Extras	(b1, lb3, w5)	9		(b6, lb8, nb3)	17
Total	(56.1 overs, 160 mins)	152		(120.4 overs, 305 mins)	325

VICTORIA	O	M	R	W	w,nb		O	M	R	W	w,nb		FALL OF WICKETS			
													NSW	VIC	NSW	VIC
Saunders	24	9	57	6	-,1	(2)	31	9	73	5	-,-	Wkt	1st	1st	2nd	2nd
Laver	35.2	11	88	2	-,-	(1)	7	3	9	0	-,-	1st	165	26	2	154
Collins	12	1	62	0	1,-		25	9	62	3	-,1	2nd	220	43	24	178
Warne	23	2	88	2	-,-	(5)	5	0	25	1	-,-	3rd	293	43	47	200
Worrall	4	0	19	0	-,-							4th	310	81	67	261
McAlister						(4)	5	1	9	1	-,-	5th	312	84	108	265
												6th	314	90	116	265
NEW SOUTH WALES	O	M	R	W	w,nb		O	M	R	W	w,nb	7th	314	93	174	283
Cotter	5	0	10	0	-,-		7	0	15	0	-,-	8th	320	115	193	288
Clarke	6.1	2	14	2	1,-		30.4	6	110	4	-,3	9th	320	138	193	315
McBeath	19	9	39	3	3,-		39	18	73	3	-,-	10th	327	152	199	325
Kermode	20	2	49	4	1,-		20	4	50	1	-,-					
Hopkins	6	0	31	0	-,-		24	11	60	1	-,-					

NEW SOUTH WALES v A.C.MacLAREN'S XI

Played at Sydney Cricket Ground on January 31, February 1, 3, 4, 5, 1902. (Timeless match)
Toss : New South Wales.   Result : ENGLAND XI WON BY AN INNINGS AND 128 RUNS.
Debuts: Nil.
12th Men: F.Devenish-Meares (NSW) and C.Robson (Eng).
Umpires: C.Bannerman and R.Callaway.
Attendances: 7878, 18962, 11091, 4877, 319.   Total: 43,127.   Receipts: £1563.
Close of Play: 1st day NSW 5/337 (S.E.Gregory 106, Noble 52); 2nd day Eng XI 0/255 (MacLaren 136, Hayward 115); 3rd day Eng XI
    4/650 (Quaife 52, Garnett 0); 4th day NSW (2) 5/79 (S.E.Gregory 24, Noble 0).

R.M.Crockett was originally engaged to umpire but was replaced by Bannerman after an objection from MacLaren. The England total of
769 remains the highest ever by a touring team in Australia. MacLaren (167 in 237 minutes, 19 fours) and Hayward (174 in 291 minutes,
1 five and 30 fours) began the innings with a stand of 314, since surpassed only by Hobbs and Rhodes with 323 at Melbourne in the
Fourth Test 1911-12. Tyldesley (142 in 175 minutes, 21 fours), Jessop (87 in 57 minutes, 1 five and 15 fours) and Quaife (62 in 237
minutes, 8 fours) took full advantage of the situation. New South Wales creditable first innings total paled into insignificance as a result.
Heavy rain delayed the start of the fourth day's play and enlivened the wicket to the delight of the England bowlers. The fate of New South
Wales was sealed. Syd Gregory (147 in 228 minutes, 15 fours and 75 in 110 minutes, 8 fours) gave "one of his best exhibitions", his
second innings in particular "was very meritorious" (*Town & Country Journal*) given the conditions. In the second innings, Poidevin edged
a ball from Braund which was retrieved by Lilley who then removed the bails. Although Poidevin was initially presumed to have been run
out, the umpires later directed that the dismissal be recorded as stumped and the wicket therefore credited to Braund. *Wisden* incorrectly
gives NSW (1) Jessop 14 overs; NSW (2) Poidevin run out. Sources: *Wisden, Sydney Referee, Sydney Morning Herald, Town & Country
Journal, Sydney Daily Telegraph.*

NEW SOUTH WALES

C.W.Gregory	b Braund	45	c MacLaren b Gunn	7
A.J.Y.Hopkins	c Jones b Jessop	40	b Braund	0
V.T.Trumper	lbw b Braund	35	c Lilley b Jessop	35
L.O.S.Poidevin	b Gunn	1	st Lilley b Braund	9
*S.E.Gregory	run out (Quaife/Gunn)	147	c MacLaren b Jones	75
R.A.Duff	b Jessop	50	c MacLaren b Jessop	0
M.A.Noble	c Lilley b Jessop	56	st Garnett b Braund	35
†H.Carter	run out (Quaife/Braund)	19	c Hayward b Braund	4
G.R.C.Clarke	lbw b Braund	25	b Braund	15
A.Kermode	not out	5	c Gunn b Braund	2
A.McBeath	run out (Garnett/Lilley)	0	not out	15
Extras	(b2, lb4, w1, nb2)	9	(b7, lb2, w2, nb1)	12
Total	(156.0 overs, 365 mins)	432	(80.1 overs, 200 mins)	209

A.C.MacLAREN'S ENGLAND XI

*A.C.MacLaren	b Kermode	167
T.W.Hayward	c Clarke b Trumper	174
J.T.Tyldesley	b Hopkins	142
W.Quaife	c Clarke b Kermode	62
G.L.Jessop	b McBeath	87
H.G.Garnett	c Poidevin b McBeath	8
L.C.Braund	c S.E.Gregory b Kermode	20
†A.F.A.Lilley	c Trumper b McBeath	27
A.O.Jones	c Carter b Kermode	13
C.P.McGahey	not out	32
J.R.Gunn	c Trumper b Clarke	0
Extras	(b20, lb7, w4, nb6)	37
Total	(247.0 overs, 610 mins)	769

ENGLAND XI	O	M	R	W	w,nb		O	M	R	W	w,nb
Gunn	40	10	98	1	-,1		15	2	36	1	-,-
Braund	62	14	162	3	-,-		33.1	6	90	6	-,-
McGahey	21	9	49	0	-,-						
Jessop	24	6	78	3	1,-	(3)	15	5	32	2	1,1
Jones	5	0	19	0	-,-	(4)	17	3	39	1	1,-
Hayward	4	0	17	0	-,1						

NEW SOUTH WALES	O	M	R	W	w,nb
McBeath	63	20	166	3	-,-
Clarke	46	11	134	1	-,1
Kermode	49	13	162	4	4,-
Hopkins	24	5	84	1	-,1
Noble	25	7	75	0	-,1
Trumper	40	8	111	1	-,3

FALL OF WICKETS

Wkt	NSW 1st	ENG 1st	NSW 2nd
1st	73	314	2
2nd	117	390	10
3rd	124	546	25
4th	124	649	67
5th	251	659	75
6th	345	690	159
7th	391	695	171
8th	417	719	179
9th	432	769	181
10th	432	769	209

AUSTRALIA v ENGLAND (4th Test)

Played at Sydney Cricket Ground on February 14, 15, 17, 18, 1902. (Timeless match)
Toss : England.   Result : AUSTRALIA WON BY SEVEN WICKETS.
Debuts: Australia - A.J.Y.Hopkins, J.V.Saunders (both Test). England - C.P.McGahey (Test).
12th Men: C.J.Eady (Aust) and H.G.Garnett (Eng).
Umpires: C.Bannerman and R.Callaway.
Attendances: 17324, 37997, 20794, 8183.   Total: 84,298.   Receipts: £3822.
Close of Play: 1st day Eng 6/266 (McGahey 18, Lilley 10); 2nd day Aust 5/148 (Noble 51, Armstrong 11); 3rd day Eng (2) 7/77
    (McGahey 12, Jones 6).

The Australian selectors named a squad of thirteen for this Test, Eady and C.W.Gregory being omitted on the morning of the match. The captaincy fell to Trumble due to the unavailability of Darling, who remained at his property in Tasmania, duties there requiring his attention. MacLaren (92 in 190 minutes, 15 fours) and Tyldesley (79 in 174 minutes, 1 five and 14 fours) took England to 179 before their second wicket fell and, although a mammoth score did not eventuate, Jessop appeared to consolidate England's hold on the match by taking Australia's first four wickets cheaply. However, half-centuries by Noble (56 in 165 minutes, 6 fours) and Armstrong (55 in 115 minutes, 7 fours) got Australia back into the game together with a quickfire innings by Howell (35 in 14 minutes, 15 balls, 1 five and 6 fours), who hit 23 from his first eight balls including 18 off one over by Gunn. England's collapse in the second innings occurred in fine weather while the wicket was still good, and Duff (51 not out in 97 minutes, 6 fours) steered Australia to victory and retention of the Ashes. Saunders (left-arm fast-medium) secured nine wickets on debut, while Kelly became the first wicket-keeper to complete eight dismissals in a Test. Sources: *Wisden, Sydney Morning Herald, Town & Country Journal, Sydney Daily Telegraph.*

ENGLAND

*A.C.MacLaren	c Duff b Saunders	92	c Kelly b Noble	5
T.W.Hayward	b Saunders	41	b Noble	12
J.T.Tyldesley	c Kelly b Noble	79	c Trumble b Saunders	10
W.Quaife	c Kelly b Saunders	4	lbw b Noble	15
G.L.Jessop	c Noble b Saunders	0	b Saunders	15
L.C.Braund	lbw b Trumble	17	b Saunders	0
C.P.McGahey	b Trumble	18	c Kelly b Saunders	13
†A.F.A.Lilley	c Kelly b Noble	40	c Trumble b Noble	0
A.O.Jones	c Kelly b Trumble	15	c Kelly b Noble	6
J.R.Gunn	not out	0	not out	13
C.Blythe	b Noble	4	c Kelly b Saunders	8
Extras	(b5, nb2)	7	(lb2)	2
Total	(138.2 overs, 348 mins)	317	(48.1 overs, 143 mins)	99

AUSTRALIA

*H.Trumble	c MacLaren b Jessop	6		
V.T.Trumper	c Braund b Jessop	7	(1) lbw b Blythe	25
C.Hill	c Jones b Jessop	21	c Lilley b Gunn	30
S.E.Gregory	c Braund b Jessop	5	(5) not out	12
M.A.Noble	lbw b Braund	56		
R.A.Duff	c Lilley b Blythe	39	(2) not out	51
W.W.Armstrong	b Braund	55		
A.J.Y.Hopkins	c Lilley b Braund	43		
†J.J.Kelly	not out	24		
W.P.Howell	c MacLaren b Gunn	35	(4) c sub (H.G.Garnett) b Gunn	0
J.V.Saunders	b Braund	0		
Extras	(b7, nb1)	8	(lb1, nb2)	3
Total	(139.0 overs, 336 mins)	299	(36.3 overs, 97 mins) (3 wkts)	121

AUSTRALIA	O	M	R	W	w,nb		O	M	R	W	w,nb		FALL OF WICKETS			
Noble	33.2	12	78	3	-,1	(2)	24	7	54	5	-,-		ENG	AUST	ENG	AUST
Saunders	43	11	119	4	-,1	(1)	24.1	8	43	5	-,-	Wkt	1st	1st	2nd	2nd
Howell	22	10	40	0	-,-							1st	73	7	5	50
Trumble	38	18	65	3	-,-							2nd	179	18	24	105
Armstrong	2	1	8	0	-,-							3rd	188	30	36	105
												4th	188	48	57	-
ENGLAND	O	M	R	W	w,nb		O	M	R	W	w,nb	5th	225	119	57	-
Braund	60	25	118	4	-,-	(2)	15	2	55	0	-,-	6th	245	160	57	-
Jessop	26	5	68	4	-,1	(1)	7	0	23	0	-,-	7th	267	205	60	-
Gunn	16	5	48	1	-,-	(4)	8.3	1	17	2	-,1	8th	312	252	78	-
Blythe	37	17	57	1	-,-	(3)	6	0	23	1	-,-	9th	312	288	88	-
												10th	317	299	99	-

VICTORIA v A.C.MacLAREN'S XI

Played at Melbourne Cricket Ground on February 22, 24, 25, 1902. (Timeless match)
Toss : Victoria. Result : ENGLAND XI WON BY EIGHT WICKETS.
Debuts: Victoria - J.R.H.Woodford (f/c).
12th Men: W.H.McCormack (Vic) and J.R.Gunn (Eng).
Umpires: C.Bannerman and R.M.Crockett.
Attendances: 7500, "few", "sparse". Total: About 9000. Receipts: No figures published.
Close of Play: 1st day Eng XI 2/160 (Quaife 29); 2nd day Eng XI 5/232 (McGahey 17, Tyldesley 21).

Collins and Woodford replaced H.Trumble and T.J.Hastings (both unavailable) in the selected Victorian team. The match began in fine weather on a wicket that provided some assistance to the England bowlers, Braund bowling unchanged throughout both Victorian innings. Rain arrived to prevent any play on the second day until 4.36pm. The England innings was completed before the wicket dried and the Victorians had the misfortune to be caught on it when it "was very bad" (*Age*) during their second innings. The view was expressed that the bowlers at MacLaren's command were not suited to its character and that "Trumble and Barnes would have been almost unplayable on it (*Age*). As it was, the visitors won easily. MacLaren (100 in 136 minutes, 8 fours) gave chances when 5, 71 and 78 but rode his luck to put his team in a winning position. Warne (6 fours) carried his bat through the Victorian first innings during which Laver (13) retired at 3/31 after being struck by a ball from Braund. He resumed at 6/53. Out first ball in the first innings, Stuckey (54 in 78 minutes, 3 fives and 2 fours) topscored in the second. Saunders fractured his right collarbone when he fell heavily while attempting to catch Robson in the pre-lunch session on the final day. He took no further part in the match. Sources: *Wisden, VCA Report, The Age, The Argus, The Australasian*.

VICTORIA

*J.Worrall	c Garnett b Blythe	15	lbw b Braund		8
T.S.Warne	not out	61	c Braund b McGahey		13
W.W.Armstrong	st Robson b Braund	0	c Jones b McGahey		28
P.A.McAlister	lbw b Braund	0	c MacLaren b McGahey		16
F.J.Laver	c Hayward b Braund	35	c Jones b Braund		23
J.H.Stuckey	b Braund	0	c Braund b Blythe		54
C.E.McLeod	run out (Quaife)	6	c MacLaren b Blythe		17
S.A.McMichael	c Jones b Blythe	4	st Robson b Blythe		0
†J.R.H.Woodford	st Robson b McGahey	3	b Braund		15
F.B.Collins	c & b Braund	1	not out		4
J.V.Saunders	b McGahey	2	absent hurt		-
Extras	(b1, lb1)	2	(b3, lb1)		4
Total	(55.4 overs, 149 mins)	129	(59.1 overs, 153 mins)		182

A.C.MacLAREN'S ENGLAND XI

*A.C.MacLaren	c & b Collins	100			
A.O.Jones	c Worrall b Laver	22	(4) not out		0
W.Quaife	lbw b Collins	45			
T.W.Hayward	c Woodford b Collins	16			
H.G.Garnett	lbw b McLeod	0	(1) run out (Stuckey)		3
C.P.McGahey	c Armstrong b Laver	34	(3) not out		4
J.T.Tyldesley	c Woodford b Laver	45			
L.C.Braund	c McMichael b Collins	3			
A.F.A.Lilley	c & b Collins	1			
†C.Robson	not out	17	(2) c sub (W.H.McCormack) b Warne		7
C.Blythe	st Woodford b Laver	0			
Extras	(b10, lb3, nb2)	15			-
Total	(98.0 overs, 267 mins)	298	(3.0 overs, 10 mins) (2 wkts)		14

ENGLAND XI	O	M	R	W	w,nb		O	M	R	W	w,nb					
Braund	28	8	67	5	-,-		30	5	97	3	-,-					
Blythe	23	10	47	2	-,-		16.1	4	23	3	-,-					
McGahey	4.4	0	13	2	-,-		13	0	58	3	-,-					

	FALL OF WICKETS			
Wkt	VIC 1st	ENG 1st	VIC 2nd	ENG 2nd
1st	17	42	8	9
2nd	17	160	36	10
3rd	17	191	55	-
4th	31	192	80	-
5th	49	192	92	-
6th	53	262	135	-
7th	106	269	135	-
8th	123	278	174	-
9th	124	293	182	-
10th	129	298	-	-

VICTORIA	O	M	R	W	w,nb		O	M	R	W	w,nb
Saunders	21	3	73	0	-,-						
Laver	23	3	82	4	-,-						
McLeod	24	8	48	1	-,-						
Warne	8	1	26	0	-,-	(1)	2	0	11	1	-,-
Collins	21	4	52	5	-,2						
Armstrong	1	0	2	0	-,-						
Worrall						(2)	1	0	3	0	-,-

AUSTRALIA v ENGLAND (5th Test)

Played at Melbourne Cricket Ground on February 28, March 1, 3, 4, 1902. (Timeless match)
Toss : Australia.   Result : AUSTRALIA WON BY 32 RUNS.
Debuts: Australia - J.P.F.Travers (Test).
12th Men: W.P.Howell (Aust) and H.G.Garnett (Eng).
Umpires: C.Bannerman and R.M.Crockett.
Attendances: 9000, 19000, 9700, 2300.   Total: About 40,000.   Receipts: No figures published.
Close of Play: 1st day Eng 5/133 (Braund 26, Lilley 10); 2nd day Aust (2) 6/226 (Trumble 10, Kelly 2); 3rd day Eng (2) 3/87 (Jessop 16, Tyldesley 0).

J.V.Saunders, unavailable due to the injury which he sustained in Victoria's return match against England, was replaced in the Australian line-up by Travers, who arrived from Adelaide on the morning of the match. S.F.Barnes tested his injured knee in the nets before play began, but it was felt that it would not stand up for the duration of the game, and he was left out. Pre-match rain badly softened the wicket for the start but it gradually improved over the first two days. MacLaren (25 in 40 minutes, 2 fours) and Jessop (35 in 21 minutes, 1 five and 5 fours) raised England's first 50 runs in just 20 minutes, Jessop hitting Noble for 4 fours in one over alone. Hill (87 in 157 minutes, 8 fours) survived two chances to score the sole half-century of the match. He became the first batsman to score 500 runs in a Test series without making one century. Gregory (41 in 71 minutes, 3 fours) also batted well for Australia. MacLaren (49 in 99 minutes, 2 fours) topscored in England's second innings, through which Noble and Trumble bowled virtually unchanged. Some rain fell on Sunday, and again on Monday, causing two interruptions to play that day. The afternoon rain "had considerably affected the wicket" (*Age*) for the final day and, although no further rain fell, the damage was done. Jessop was out to the first ball and the game was over in less than an hour and a half. Sources: *Wisden, The Age, The Argus, The Herald, The Australasian, The Leader*.

AUSTRALIA

V.T.Trumper	b Blythe	27		c McGahey b Braund	18
R.A.Duff	b Braund	10		c & b Braund	28
C.Hill	c Jones b Gunn	28		c Lilley b Hayward	87
S.E.Gregory	c Jones b Gunn	25		b Gunn	41
M.A.Noble	lbw b Hayward	7		c MacLaren b Gunn	16
*H.Trumble	c Quaife b Hayward	3	(7)	b Blythe	22
W.W.Armstrong	not out	17	(6)	lbw b Braund	20
A.J.Y.Hopkins	c Lilley b Hayward	4	(9)	c MacLaren b Blythe	0
†J.J.Kelly	c Gunn b Hayward	0	(8)	not out	11
C.J.Eady	b Gunn	5		c Gunn b Braund	3
J.P.F.Travers	c Braund b Gunn	9		c & b Braund	1
Extras	(b7, w1, nb1)	9		(b3, lb1, nb4)	8
Total	(53.0 overs, 143 mins)	144		(89.1 overs, 261 mins)	255

ENGLAND

*A.C.MacLaren	c & b Trumble	25		run out (Hill/Kelly)	49
G.L.Jessop	c Hopkins b Trumble	35	(4)	c Trumper b Trumble	16
W.Quaife	c Trumble b Noble	3		lbw b Noble	4
J.T.Tyldesley	c Kelly b Eady	13	(5)	c Eady b Trumble	36
T.W.Hayward	c Trumper b Travers	19	(2)	c Travers b Trumble	15
L.C.Braund	c Hopkins b Trumble	32		c Hill b Noble	2
†A.F.A.Lilley	c Eady b Trumble	41		c Duff b Noble	9
C.P.McGahey	b Trumble	0		c Hill b Noble	7
A.O.Jones	c Kelly b Eady	10		c & b Noble	28
J.R.Gunn	lbw b Eady	8		c Hill b Noble	4
C.Blythe	not out	0		not out	5
Extras	(b1, lb2)	3		(lb2, nb1)	3
Total	(67.3 overs, 185 mins)	189		(65.3 overs, 191 mins)	178

ENGLAND	O	M	R	W	w,nb		O	M	R	W	w,nb
Jessop	1	0	13	0	-,-						
Braund	10	2	33	1	-,-		26.1	4	95	5	-,-
Blythe	9	2	29	1	-,-	(4)	13	3	36	2	-,-
Hayward	16	9	22	4	1,-	(1)	22	4	63	1	-,4
Gunn	17	6	38	4	-,1	(3)	28	11	53	2	-,-

AUSTRALIA	O	M	R	W	w,nb		O	M	R	W	w,nb
Noble	26	4	80	1	-,-		33	4	98	6	-,-
Trumble	25	4	62	5	-,-		30.3	7	64	3	-,1
Travers	8	2	14	1	-,-						
Eady	8.3	2	30	3	-,-	(3)	2	0	13	0	-,-

FALL OF WICKETS

	AUST	ENG	AUST	ENG
Wkt	1st	1st	2nd	2nd
1st	16	50	30	40
2nd	54	62	52	64
3rd	81	64	131	87
4th	98	91	149	87
5th	104	96	208	93
6th	108	164	224	104
7th	112	168	249	120
8th	112	173	249	157
9th	125	186	252	161
10th	144	189	255	178

SOUTH AUSTRALIA v A.C.MacLAREN'S XI

Played at Adelaide Oval on March 14, 15, 17, 18, 1902. (Timeless match)
Toss : South Australia.   Result : ENGLAND XI WON BY SIX WICKETS.
Debuts: South Australia - R.W.Waters (f/c).
12th Men: C.Blythe (Eng). No 12th man or emergency fieldsman named for SA.
Umpires: C.Bannerman and T.A.Reeves.
Attendances: Individual days not published.   Total: About 9000.   Receipts: No figures published.
Close of Play: 1st day Eng XI 0/53 (MacLaren 20, Hayward 33); 2nd day SA (2) 0/21 (Reedman 5, Jarvis 9); 3rd day Eng XI (2) 0/21 (Gunn 14, Quaife 5).

Jarvis and Newland replaced F.T.Hack (unavailable) and J.McKenzie (retired) in the selected South Australian side. McKenzie's retirement from first-class cricket was in response to his being overlooked for the Australian team selected to tour England later in the year. Claxton (61 in 105 minutes, 7 fours and 83 in 109 minutes, 12 fours) "gave a splendid exhibition of dashing cricket" (*Register*), particularly in the second innings. Clem Hill (61 in 112 minutes, 6 fours) also batted well in the second innings. Braund bowled unchanged throughout the first South Australian innings. Tyldesley (126 in 203 minutes, 21 fours, chance at 93 and 47 in 57 minutes, 7 fours) batted in his very best form, his century being described as "one of his finest performances" (*Register*). MacLaren ("bad ankle") did not take the field during the short period of batting of the South Australians at the end of the second day, the Englishmen having only ten players. No reason was given as to why no substitute was requested. MacLaren resumed in the field from the start of the next day. Sources: *Wisden, C.B.O'Reilly, Adelaide Advertiser, South Australian Register*.

SOUTH AUSTRALIA

J.C.Reedman	st Lilley b Braund	19		b Gunn	24
A.Jarvis	c Jessop b Gunn	37		c Braund b Gunn	19
*C.Hill	b Braund	2		c Hayward b McGahey	61
G.Giffen	b Gunn	17		lbw b Jones	30
H.P.Kirkwood	b Braund	5		c McGahey	23
N.Claxton	c & b Braund	61		b Braund	83
A.E.Evans	c Lilley b Gunn	30		c Jones b Braund	7
R.W.Waters	lbw b Gunn	1		c Gunn b Hayward	23
†P.M.Newland	c McGahey b Braund	27		not out	7
J.P.F.Travers	c Braund b Gunn	1	(11)	c Tyldesley b Hayward	0
E.Jones	not out	0	(10)	b Hayward	3
Extras	(b3, lb3, nb1)	7		(b12, lb10, nb4)	26
Total	(66.3 overs, 197 mins)	207		(80.5 overs, 250 mins)	306

A.C.MacLAREN'S ENGLAND XI

*A.C.MacLaren	b Travers	23			
T.W.Hayward	c & b Giffen	57	(4)	not out	33
J.T.Tyldesley	b Travers	126		b Jarvis	47
W.Quaife	b Travers	12	(2)	c Travers b Evans	41
G.L.Jessop	b Travers	2		c Claxton b Evans	25
L.C.Braund	c Giffen b Jones	32		not out	19
†A.F.A.Lilley	b Jones	3			
C.P.McGahey	c Reedman b Giffen	21			
A.O.Jones	b Jarvis	23			
H.G.Garnett	not out	10			
J.R.Gunn	b Jarvis	0	(1)	c Travers b Giffen	21
Extras	(b3, lb5, w1)	9		(b6, lb1, w2, nb1)	10
Total	(105.2 overs, 298 mins)	318		(61.1 overs, 177 mins) (4 wkts)	196

ENGLAND XI	O	M	R	W	w,nb		O	M	R	W	w,nb
Braund	33.3	2	116	5	-,-		31	0	117	2	-,-
Gunn	29	9	73	5	-,1		22	4	79	2	-,4
Hayward	3	2	6	0	-,-	(5)	7	1	12	3	-,-
Jones	1	0	5	0	-,-		3	1	37	1	-,-
McGahey						(3)	17.5	3	35	2	-,-

	FALL OF WICKETS			
	SA	ENG	SA	ENG
Wkt	1st	1st	2nd	2nd
1st	48	57	32	40
2nd	51	99	65	107
3rd	66	136	119	122
4th	82	142	171	154
5th	82	199	184	-
6th	116	211	191	-
7th	118	260	287	-
8th	198	304	303	-
9th	207	316	306	-
10th	207	318	306	-

SOUTH AUSTRALIA	O	M	R	W	w,nb		O	M	R	W	w,nb
Jones	24	3	71	2	-,-		10	1	25	0	2,1
Travers	39	9	109	4	-,-		19	7	42	0	-,-
Giffen	30	5	83	2	-,-		10.1	2	39	1	-,-
Reedman	5	1	24	0	-,-						
Jarvis	7.2	2	22	2	1,-		9	1	34	1	-,-
Evans						(4)	10	1	32	2	-,-
Waters						(6)	3	0	14	0	-,-

NEW SOUTH WALES v QUEENSLAND

Played at Brisbane Cricket Ground (Woolloongabba) on March 29, 31, April 1, 1902. (Three-day match)
Toss : New South Wales.   Result : MATCH DRAWN.
Debuts: Queensland - A.Henry (f/c); C.W.Patrick (Qld only). New South Wales - T.H.Hogue (f/c).
12th Men: W.S.Duff (NSW) and L.J.Evans (Qld).
Umpires: T.Muir and J.P.Orr.
Attendances: 3500, 4000, 700.   Total: About 8200.   Receipts: No figures published.
Close of Play: 1st day NSW 9/245 (Hogue 74, Marsh 9); 2nd day NSW (2) 2/53 (Pye 6, Mackenzie 0).

Evers became the first captain to declare an innings closed in Australia; he set Queensland 223 runs in 195 minutes on the last day. New South Wales were depleted by the absence of B.W.Farquhar, F.A.Iredale (the nominated captain), W.D.Loveridge and A.L.Newell who withdrew from the twelve and were replaced by Duff, Evers, Hogue and Howard. Hogue on debut (75 not out in 154 minutes, 3 fours) topscored in the match and ran out Clarke with a straight drive which was deflected by the bowler, Henry, into the non-striker's stumps. J.Carew deputised for Chapman (sore hands) at 8/196 in the New South Wales first innings and kept for the rest of the match, taking both his catches in that role. McBeath dismissed Morgan and Hoare with successive deliveries in the Queensland first innings, which provided a rare instance of no catches being held. Patrick had previously played once for New South Wales in 1893-94 prior to his Queensland debut here. Queensland newspapers give NSW (2) Devenish-Meares 3, extras 14. Sources: *NSWCA Report, Sydney Morning Herald, Brisbane Courier, Queensland Times, The Queenslander.*

NEW SOUTH WALES

C.W.Gregory	c Chapman b Hoare	30	(2)	c J.Carew b Hoare	19
L.W.Pye	b Henry	2	(3)	c Patrick b P.Carew	41
A.C.K.Mackenzie	c Lewis b Hoare	20	(4)	b Hoare	7
F.Devenish-Meares	c Henry b Hoare	12	(5)	b Henry	2
A.Diamond	c Henry b Hoare	3	(7)	lbw b P.Carew	4
*†H.A.Evers	c Atkins b Hoare	33		c & b Crouch	35
T.H.Hogue	not out	75	(1)	b Byrnes	21
G.R.C.Clarke	run out (Henry)	7		c Morgan b Crouch	4
T.H.Howard	b Crouch	24		not out	0
A.McBeath	c J.Carew b Hoare	9			
J.Marsh	b Henry	9			
Extras	(b15, lb4, nb5)	24		(b10, lb3, nb2)	15
Total	(93.2 overs, 260 mins)	248		(43.1 overs, 135 mins) (8 wkts dec)	148

QUEENSLAND

*C.W.Patrick	b Marsh	3	(6)	c Gregory b Clarke	37
J.W.Lewis	st Evers b McBeath	0	(7)	c Howard b Clarke	3
E.R.Crouch	b McBeath	15	(2)	b Marsh	10
P.Carew	lbw b Clarke	28		c Devenish-Meares b Howard	25
A.A.Atkins	not out	59	(3)	run out (Devenish-Meares/Evers)	12
C.F.Morgan	b McBeath	3	(5)	c Diamond b Marsh	42
W.Hoare	b McBeath	0	(8)	c & b Clarke	5
J.Carew	run out	28	(1)	c Clarke b Marsh	7
†H.W.Chapman	b Howard	16		not out	22
T.Byrnes	run out (/Evers)	0		not out	20
A.Henry	b Marsh	9			
Extras	(b10, lb2, nb1)	13		(b11, lb10, nb2)	23
Total	(64.2 overs, 200 mins)	174		(62.0 overs, 195 mins) (8 wkts)	206

QUEENSLAND	O	M	R	W	w,nb		O	M	R	W	w,nb
Byrnes	15	2	41	0	-,1	(3)	7	0	19	1	-,-
Henry	27.2	5	59	2	-,4		11	0	38	1	-,2
Hoare	27	8	58	6	-,-	(1)	16	0	57	2	-,-
P.Carew	11	3	28	0	-,-	(5)	4	0	8	2	-,-
Crouch	7	0	19	1	-,-	(4)	5.1	0	11	2	-,-
Lewis	6	0	19	0	-,-						

NEW SOUTH WALES	O	M	R	W	w,nb		O	M	R	W	w,nb
Marsh	22.2	4	64	2	-,1		20	1	67	3	-,-
McBeath	27	10	40	4	-,-		21	2	40	0	-,-
Howard	7	0	21	1	-,-	(4)	8	1	27	1	-,-
Clarke	8	0	36	1	-,-	(5)	7	0	42	3	-,2
Pye						(3)	6	2	7	0	-,-

FALL OF WICKETS

Wkt	NSW 1st	QLD 1st	NSW 2nd	QLD 2nd
1st	16	3	40	12
2nd	48	9	42	23
3rd	59	33	69	48
4th	63	47	72	69
5th	87	54	131	151
6th	118	54	143	151
7th	134	118	146	154
8th	182	153	148	159
9th	224	157	-	-
10th	248	174	-	-

1902-03 SEASON (13 MATCHES)

New South Wales retained the Sheffield Shield by winning all their fixtures for the second consecutive season. They were rarely troubled, the strong batting lineup headed by Trumper and Duff providing a platform from which the New South Wales bowlers could operate with confidence. Duff enjoyed almost uninterrupted success with the bat, scoring four centuries and two half-centuries in his nine innings. He added consecutive double-century opening stands with Trumper within a fortnight in January. Noble and Hopkins also hit centuries during the season, while McBeath, Howell and Pye had their share of success with the ball.

Victoria won both matches against South Australia but were unable to challenge the powerful New South Wales combination. Their batting lacked consistency despite the best efforts of Armstrong, Graham, McAlister and Laver - as well as a record-breaking double-century stand for the tenth wicket between Ellis and Hastings against South Australia at Melbourne. Armstrong, Collins, Laver and Saunders had fine seasons as bowlers and formed a well-balanced and varied attack.

The South Australians were again no match for the Eastern States, too much being left to too few. Hack batted soundly throughout the summer but Clem Hill had a poor season by his own standards. George Giffen, who was available only for home matches, recorded his last great allround performance for South Australia, some years after his previous herculean efforts. Against Victoria he scored 81 and 97 not out and returned match figures of 15 for 185. Travers, South Australia's stock bowler, was always accurate but he lacked penetration. More importantly he lacked adequate support.

An English team played a match against each of the Sheffield Shield States after touring New Zealand in early 1903. The team was organised by Lord Hawke and, although he was subsequently unable to tour, it retained his name. The matches in Australia were undertaken at short notice, upon the initiative of the New South Wales Cricket Association, with the Englishmen receiving their invitation to tour during their stay in New Zealand. Arrangements for the matches at Melbourne and Sydney were concluded in January, but the decision for the tourists to play at Adelaide was not communicated to the South Australian Cricket Association until late February - a month prior to the match taking place. The fact that the Adelaide Oval had already been booked, for a non-cricket event, resulted in the staging of the first first-class match at a South Australian venue other than the Adelaide Oval.

New South Wales played Queensland twice this season, winning both home and away games. The NSWCA and QCA agreed that the teams would continue to meet each other twice per season from now on. Queensland and Victoria met for the first time at first-class level in January 1903, at the initiative of the QCA. The Victorians made the journey to Brisbane after their Shield engagement against New South Wales at Sydney, and completely outplayed the Queenslanders. Tasmania resumed their annual fixture against Victoria after a one-year break and emerged victorious. The Western Australian Cricket Association continued unsuccessful attempts to draw a South Australian team to Perth.

Jack Worrall, the former Test player and Victorian captain over the past two seasons, finished his first-class playing career in controversy, He had written a series of articles for the London *Sportsman* prior to the 1902 tour of England in which he assessed the chances of the Australian players. In the articles he questioned the legality of the bowling actions of Saunders and Noble. The Australian players, not surprisingly, resented Worrall's comments, and when he was selected for Victoria's opening match of 1902-03, Worrall was confronted by the refusal of Saunders, Trumble and Armstrong to appear in any team of which he was a member. The VCA convened an emergency interview with Worrall, at which he stated his regret at having made the assertions. Worrall repeated the apology he had already made to the accused players, and then resigned as Victorian selector, withdrawing from the team. There the matter rested.

Leading Aggregates

Batsmen	M	I	NO	Runs	HS	Ave.	Bowlers	Runs	Wkts	Ave.
R.A.Duff (NSW)	5	9	0	786	194	87.33	J.V.Saunders (V)	666	32	20.81
W.W.Armstrong (V)	6	11	1	580	145	58.00	F.B.Collins (V)	634	31	20.45
H.Graham (V)	6	11	0	456	101	41.45	A.McBeath (NSW)	568	29	19.58
V.T.Trumper (NSW)	5	9	0	446	178	49.55	W.P.Howell (NSW)	527	26	20.26
F.T.Hack (SA)	5	10	0	417	90	41.70	L.W.Pye (NSW)	444	23	19.30
P.A.McAlister (V)	6	11	0	390	84	35.45	W.W.Armstrong (V)	448	23	19.47

SHEFFIELD SHIELD TABLE

	P	W	L	D	Quotient	Runs Scored	Wkts Lost	Runs Conceded	Wkts Taken
NEW SOUTH WALES	4	4	-	-	1.476	2109	65	1758	80
VICTORIA	4	2	2	-	0.973	2079	80	2003	75
SOUTH AUSTRALIA	4	-	4	-	0.707	1807	80	2234	70
TOTAL	6	6	6	-	1.000	5995	225	5995	225

QUEENSLAND v NEW SOUTH WALES

Played at Brisbane Cricket Ground (Woolloongabba) on November 8, 10, 11, 1902. (Timeless match)
Toss : New South Wales.   Result : NEW SOUTH WALES WON BY 77 RUNS.
Debuts: Queensland - J.J.Fitzgerald, H.B.Griffith, (both f/c). New South Wales - W.S.Duff, N.Ebsworth, W.D.Loveridge (all f/c).
12th Men: N.K.Foster (Qld) and R.N.Hickson (NSW).
Umpires: E.Beard and J.P.Orr.
Attendances: 2500, 2500, 1000.   Total: About 6000.   Receipts: No figures published.
Close of Play: 1st day Qld 7/51 (Fitzgerald 7, Evans 3); 2nd day Qld (2) 1/33 (J.Carew 25, Morgan 3).

C.W.Patrick withdrew from the selected Queensland team because of business commitments and was replaced by Atkins, who was then named captain. The nominated Queensland reserve, J.L.Halpin, also withdrew for business reasons. Foster was called up and acted as substitute when Byrnes left the field after bowling three overs in the New South Wales second innings. The tenth-wicket partnership of 67 between Atkins and Byrnes (44 in 50 minutes, 5 fours) was a new Queensland record for the last wicket. Henry was no-balled once in the first innings by umpire Beard for "a deliberate throw" (*Queensland Times*). He was no-balled twice in the second innings for overstepping the crease. The home team went to lunch on the final day requiring a further 86 runs for victory with five wickets in hand. However, 18 minutes and 8 runs later, Marsh (3 for 0) and McBeath (2 for 4) had ensured a New South Wales victory. Loveridge captained New South Wales in his only first-class appearance. *Queensland Times* gives NSW (2) Henry 5/37, Hoare 0/36. Sources: *NSWCA Report, Sydney Morning Herald, Brisbane Courier, Queensland Times, The Queenslander.*

NEW SOUTH WALES

A.C.K.Mackenzie	c Crouch b Byrnes	18		b Henry	7
T.H.Hogue	c Evans b Byrnes	11	(5)	b Henry	17
N.Ebsworth	c J.Carew b Byrnes	16		c Atkins b Henry	7
L.W.Pye	b Fitzgerald	45		b P.Carew	10
C.W.Gregory	b Fitzgerald	33	(2)	lbw b P.Carew	30
A.Diamond	st Evans b Hoare	7		c J.Carew b P.Carew	0
W.S.Duff	c Crouch b P.Carew	35		b Griffith	30
*†W.D.Loveridge	c Atkins b Hoare	0		b Henry	10
T.H.Howard	c Griffith b Hoare	2		b Henry	1
A.McBeath	c J.Carew b Hoare	7		not out	7
J.Marsh	not out	9		c Fitzgerald b Griffith	4
Extras	(b5, nb3)	8		(b14, w1, nb2)	17
Total	(59.2 overs, 195 mins)	191		(48.0 overs, 155 mins)	140

QUEENSLAND

J.Carew	run out (Loveridge)	1		c Loveridge b Pye	42
E.R.Crouch	b McBeath	5		c McBeath b Pye	4
H.B.Griffith	c Loveridge b Marsh	0	(6)	c Duff b Marsh	28
P.Carew	b Pye	11	(5)	run out (Diamond/Loveridge)	5
W.Hoare	b McBeath	4	(9)	c Duff b Marsh	0
C.F.Morgan	b Pye	11	(3)	b Pye	11
J.J.Fitzgerald	c Loveridge b Marsh	11	(8)	c Mackenzie b Marsh	0
A.Henry	b Pye	2	(11)	not out	4
†W.T.Evans	b McBeath	7	(7)	b McBeath	15
*A.A.Atkins	not out	26	(4)	b Pye	1
T.Byrnes	b Pye	44	(10)	b McBeath	0
Extras	(b4, lb5)	9		(lb10, nb3)	13
Total	(36.2 overs, 125 mins)	131		(42.0 overs, 136 mins)	123

QUEENSLAND	O	M	R	W	w,nb		O	M	R	W	w,nb
Henry	10	2	39	0	-,1	(2)	17	6	40	5	1,2
Griffith	12	3	35	0	-,-	(5)	6	1	15	2	-,-
Byrnes	15	2	51	3	-,-	(1)	3	0	18	0	-,-
Hoare	16	7	40	4	-,2		16	4	33	0	-,-
Fitzgerald	6	0	18	2	-,-						
P.Carew	0.2	0	0	1	-,-	(3)	6	0	17	3	-,-

NEW SOUTH WALES	O	M	R	W	w,nb		O	M	R	W	w,nb
Marsh	12	3	39	2	-,-		12	4	23	3	-,1
McBeath	15	3	36	3	-,-		14	5	30	2	-,-
Pye	6.2	0	32	4	-,-		10	1	36	4	-,2
Howard	3	0	15	0	-,-		6	1	21	0	-,-

FALL OF WICKETS

Wkt	NSW 1st	QLD 1st	NSW 2nd	QLD 2nd
1st	27	2	32	30
2nd	48	4	43	57
3rd	51	12	68	60
4th	123	22	77	66
5th	130	39	79	79
6th	146	44	95	115
7th	147	48	109	115
8th	155	59	111	115
9th	169	64	136	115
10th	191	131	140	123

SOUTH AUSTRALIA v NEW SOUTH WALES (Shield Match 1)

Played at Adelaide Oval on December 19, 20, 22, 23, 1902. (Timeless match)
Toss : New South Wales.   Result : NEW SOUTH WALES WON BY 210 RUNS.
Debuts: South Australia - D.R.A.Gehrs, C.F.W.Thamm (both f/c).
12th Men: E.H.Leak (SA) and J.Marsh (NSW).
Umpires: P.Argall and J.Quilty.
Attendances: No individual days published.   Total: 6850.   Receipts: No figures published.
Close of Play: 1st day NSW 6/277 (Gregory 4, McBeath 1); 2nd day SA 140 all out; 3rd day SA (2) 0/57 (Hack 25, Reedman 28).

Overnight rain delayed the start until 2.00pm on the first day. Wicket covering of "galvanised iron and tarpaulin "(*NSWCA Report*) offered pre-match protection but low scoring occurred throughout the game. The second wicket partnership of 181 on the first day between Duff (94 in 195 minutes, 13 fours) and Noble (108 in 160 minutes, 1 five and 10 fours, 3 chances) proved decisive in the final result. Reedman was bowled by the first ball of the South Australian first innings and the local batsmen struggled thereafter. Hack (48 in 165 minutes, 5 fours) displayed his well-known defensive skills to record his team's highest individual score for the match. Mackenzie (77 in 120 minutes, 9 fours) and Noble (52 not out in 80 minutes, 6 fours) hit half-centuries in the second innings. Spin was to the fore, the most successful bowler being Howell (medium-paced offspin) and Pye (legbreaks) for New South Wales, and Travers (orthodox left-arm) and Kirkwood (legbreaks) for South Australia. Thamm was a late replacement for P.M.Newland (injured hand). *Wisden* incorrectly gives NSW (1) Claxton 2/6; SA (1) Kirkwood 6; SA (2) Hack 28. Sources: *Wisden, C.B.O'Reilly, NSWCA Report, Adelaide Advertiser, South Australian Register.*

NEW SOUTH WALES

R.A.Duff	b Kirkwood	94	(7) b Kirkwood	18
V.T.Trumper	c Waters b Travers	10	(6) hit wkt b Claxton	2
*M.A.Noble	c Claxton b Kirkwood	108	(8) not out	52
N.Ebsworth	c Travers b Kirkwood	1	(9) c & b Kirkwood	4
W.P.Howell	c Waters b Claxton	0	(10) c Reedman b Kirkwood	10
†J.J.Kelly	c Reedman b Claxton	1	(2) b Travers	0
C.W.Gregory	lbw b Jones	7	(5) b Travers	33
A.McBeath	c Reedman b Jones	10	(11) b Travers	2
A.J.Y.Hopkins	c Waters b Jones	8	(4) lbw b Giffen	10
A.C.K.Mackenzie	c Claxton b Travers	13	(1) c Kirkwood b Travers	77
L.W.Pye	not out	25	(3) c Kirkwood b Travers	17
Extras	(b3, lb4, w1)	8	(lb4)	4
Total	(99.4 overs, 295 mins)	285	(69.3 overs, 205 mins)	229

SOUTH AUSTRALIA

J.C.Reedman	b Howell	0	(2) st Kelly b Pye	40
F.T.Hack	c Mackenzie b Noble	48	(1) b Howell	29
*C.Hill	b Howell	10	c & b Howell	0
G.Giffen	c & b Pye	27	st Kelly b Pye	19
H.P.Kirkwood	b Pye	0	c Noble b Trumper	3
N.Claxton	b Pye	6	lbw b Pye	7
D.R.A.Gehrs	b Pye	8	b Trumper	3
R.W.Waters	c Duff b Howell	14	c Kelly b Howell	4
E.Jones	lbw b Noble	11	b Howell	34
J.P.F.Travers	c Kelly b Noble	2	not out	11
†C.F.W.Thamm	not out	8	c Trumper b McBeath	9
Extras	(lb6)	6	(b3, lb1, nb1)	5
Total	(71.5 overs, 195 mins)	140	(80.5 overs, 225 mins)	164

SOUTH AUSTRALIA	O	M	R	W	w,nb		O	M	R	W	w,nb
Jones	25	10	68	3	-,-		9	1	47	0	-,-
Travers	26.4	5	68	2	-,-		25.3	10	54	5	-,-
Waters	20	8	49	0	-,-	(4)	7	1	16	0	-,-
Reedman	3	0	10	0	-,-						
Giffen	12	1	38	0	-,-	(3)	14	2	52	1	-,-
Claxton	6	1	16	2	1,-	(5)	5	0	23	1	-,-
Kirkwood	7	0	28	3	-,-	(6)	9	0	33	3	-,-

NEW SOUTH WALES	O	M	R	W	w,nb		O	M	R	W	w,nb
Howell	26	7	51	3	-,-		28	9	59	4	-,-
Noble	18.5	8	34	3	-,-	(5)	11	5	10	0	-,1
Pye	17	2	31	4	-,-	(4)	17	2	28	3	-,-
McBeath	10	4	18	0	-,-	(2)	10.5	2	29	1	-,-
Trumper						(3)	14	2	33	2	-,-

	FALL OF WICKETS			
Wkt	NSW 1st	SA 1st	NSW 2nd	SA 2nd
1st	16	0	2	61
2nd	197	14	54	61
3rd	211	49	74	89
4th	215	49	138	96
5th	221	67	140	96
6th	226	85	140	106
7th	233	114	181	106
8th	246	120	187	138
9th	249	131	215	151
10th	285	140	229	164

VICTORIA v NEW SOUTH WALES (Shield Match 2)

Played at Melbourne Cricket Ground on December 26, 27, 29, 1902. (Timeless match)
Toss : New South Wales.   Result : NEW SOUTH WALES WON BY 136 RUNS.
Debuts: Nil.
12th Men: W.Bruce (Vic) and J.Marsh (NSW).
Umpires: R.M.Crockett and W.A.Young.
Attendances: 10000, 7000, 5000.   Total: About 22,000.   Receipts: £724.
Close of Play: 1st day Vic 9/81 (Noonan 4); 2nd day Vic (2) 0/57 (Graham 30, McAlister 25).

J.Worrall, one of the selection committee, withdrew from the Victorian team when Armstrong and Saunders refused to play alongside him. The conflict arose from Worrall's criticism of the legality of the bowling actions of Saunders and M.A.Noble, published in the London *Sportsman* prior to the 1902 tour of England. Worrall was called upon by the VCA for an explanation of his criticism and, although no action was taken against him, the incident ended his first-class playing career. "The wicket was perfect" (*Argus*) but batsmen of both sides were unable to combat the quality of the bowling for much of the time. Duff (102 in 176 minutes, 11 fours and 66 in 116 minutes, 3 fours) was the notable exception, his stands with Trumper (51 in 64 minutes, 5 fours) in the first innings and Noble (60 in 86 minutes, 8 fours) in the second innings being the sole batting highlights. Armstrong performed the hat-trick in the New South Wales first innings in dismissing Mackenzie, Hopkins and Gregory. Howell's second innings analysis of 9 for 52 has been bettered only twice by a bowler for New South Wales, both times by W.J.O'Reilly. The last seven of his wickets were obtained at a cost of only 17 runs. Sources: *Wisden, NSWCA Report, VCA Report, The Age, The Argus, The Herald, The Australasian, The Leader.*

NEW SOUTH WALES

R.A.Duff	c Laver b Saunders	102	lbw b Collins	66
V.T.Trumper	c Noonan b Laver	51	c Stuckey b Laver	22
*M.A.Noble	c McAlister b Laver	0	lbw b Armstrong	60
A.C.K.Mackenzie	lbw b Armstrong	21	b Collins	1
A.J.Y.Hopkins	lbw b Armstrong	0	c Warne b Armstrong	2
C.W.Gregory	b Armstrong	0	c Armstrong b Collins	10
L.W.Pye	c Hastings b Laver	3	c Saunders b Collins	12
N.Ebsworth	b Saunders	19	b Collins	1
†J.J.Kelly	c McAlister b Collins	1	c Saunders b Armstrong	9
W.P.Howell	b Collins	0	c Hastings b Collins	13
A.McBeath	not out	0	not out	1
Extras	(b1)	1	(b8, lb7)	15
Total	(65.1 overs, 176 mins)	198	(63.3 overs, 190 mins)	212

VICTORIA

H.Graham	st Kelly b McBeath	32		b Howell	36
P.A.McAlister	c Kelly b Noble	0		b Howell	37
T.S.Warne	b Noble	0		c Kelly b Howell	20
J.H.Stuckey	b Howell	9		b Pye	22
W.W.Armstrong	b McBeath	22		b Howell	36
*F.J.Laver	c Pye b McBeath	3	(7)	b Howell	14
D.Mailer	st Kelly b Pye	8	(8)	not out	3
D.F.Noonan	not out	10	(6)	b Howell	0
†T.J.Hastings	c Trumper b Pye	0		lbw b Howell	0
F.B.Collins	run out (/Noble)	3		b Howell	7
J.V.Saunders	c Duff b McBeath	5		b Howell	0
Extras	(lb1)	1		(b6)	6
Total	(33.4 overs, 95 mins)	93		(111.3 overs, 255 mins)	181

VICTORIA	O	M	R	W	w,nb		O	M	R	W	w,nb
Saunders	10.1	1	37	2	-,-		8	0	40	0	-,-
Collins	5	0	27	2	-,-	(4)	19	2	54	6	-,-
Laver	23	6	63	3	-,-	(2)	15	3	43	1	-,-
Warne	6	0	25	0	-,-	(5)	2	0	9	0	-,-
Armstrong	21	6	45	3	-,-	(3)	19.3	5	51	3	-,-

NEW SOUTH WALES	O	M	R	W	w,nb		O	M	R	W	w,nb
Noble	10	0	42	2	-,-		24	8	45	0	-,-
Howell	7	1	27	1	-,-		30.3	15	52	9	-,-
McBeath	9.4	5	9	4	-,-		28	19	20	0	-,-
Pye	7	1	14	2	-,-		22	8	44	1	-,-
Trumper							7	2	14	0	-,-

FALL OF WICKETS

	NSW	VIC	NSW	VIC
Wkt	1st	1st	2nd	2nd
1st	102	1	42	67
2nd	107	1	159	76
3rd	146	16	161	117
4th	146	57	164	149
5th	146	63	164	153
6th	149	72	185	160
7th	185	74	187	173
8th	198	74	190	173
9th	198	81	208	181
10th	198	93	212	181

NEW SOUTH WALES v QUEENSLAND

Played at Sydney Cricket Ground on December 26, 27, 29, 30, 1902. (Timeless match)
Toss : Queensland.   Result : NEW SOUTH WALES WON BY TWO WICKETS
Debuts: New South Wales - J.A.Cuffe, N.Y.Deane, R.N.Hickson, J.R.M.Mackay, E.F.Waddy (all f/c). Queensland - W.M.Abell (f/c).
12th Men: T.H.Hogue (NSW) and S.J.Donahoo (Qld).
Umpires: R.Callaway and A.C.Jones.
Attendances: 2000, 4000, 400, 200.   Total: About 6600.   Receipts: £155.
Close of Play: 1st day Qld 9/275 (Hoare 25, Henry 0); 2nd day Qld (2) 1/75 (Crouch 43, Fitzgerald 11); 3rd day NSW (2) 1/74
    (Hickson 37, Duff 32).

W.T.Evans and J.L.Halpin (both unavailable) withdrew from a Queensland squad of fifteen from which the final selection for Sydney was to
be made. Abell replaced Evans, with H.B.Griffith and C.F.Morgan being omitted. S.E.Gregory declined the New South Wales captaincy
(no reasons reported) and Diamond was elected to the leadership. The match was closely fought throughout all four days before being
finally decided by the narrowest of margins. Howard finished off the Queensland second innings with four wickets in five balls, including
the hat-trick (Hoare, ball, Byrnes, Abell, Henry). Batting statistics were poorly reported but the following can be noted. Macdonald (51 in
155 minutes and 61 in 215 minutes) anchored the Queensland innings but the most attractive batting for the Northern State came from
Atkins (82 in 125 minutes and 60 in about 105 minutes). They added 104 for the fifth wicket in the second innings. *Cricket* incorrectly
gives Qld (1) Hoare 25, extras 16, Cuffe 0/23, Howard 2/89, Bowden 3/94; Qld (2) Cuffe 1/38, Howard 5/78; NSW (1) Henry 3/82;
Macdonald 0/19 in first innings instead of second innings. Most sources confirm the *Cricket* version of the bowling figures for Qld (1) but
those below are believed correct. Sources: *Cricket, NSWCA Report, Sydney Referee, Sydney Morning Herald, Town & Country Journal,
Sydney Mail, Sydney Telegraph, Brisbane Courier.*

QUEENSLAND

C.W.Patrick	c Cuffe b Deane	61		c Carter b Cuffe	20
J.Carew	c Gregory b Bowden	15	(5)	c Gregory b Bowden	0
P.Carew	b Deane	2	(7)	c Hickson b Deane	32
R.Macdonald	b Bowden	51		not out	61
E.R.Crouch	c Bowden b Deane	0	(2)	c Carter b Bowden	56
J.J.Fitzgerald	run out (Hickson/Deane)	14	(3)	b Howard	17
*A.A.Atkins	run out (Gregory/Carter)	82	(6)	run out (Cuffe/Carter)	60
W.Hoare	not out	28		b Howard	1
T.Byrnes	lbw b Howard	3		lbw b Howard	0
†W.M.Abell	b Howard	8		c Diamond b Howard	0
A.Henry	st Carter b Bowden	7		b Howard	0
Extras	(b6, lb5, w1, nb1)	13		(b9, lb1)	10
Total	(118.0 overs, 290 mins)	284		(101.2 overs, 265 mins)	257

NEW SOUTH WALES

J.R.M.Mackay	b Henry	8		b Byrnes	1
R.N.Hickson	b Henry	39		c Atkins b Byrnes	50
W.S.Duff	c J.Carew b Byrnes	62		b Hoare	67
S.E.Gregory	c P.Carew b Byrnes	49		run out (/Hoare)	13
*A.Diamond	b Byrnes	4		not out	54
E.F.Waddy	c Abell b Henry	6		c & b Hoare	9
J.A.Cuffe	b Byrnes	5	(9)	c Atkins b Hoare	25
N.Y.Deane	c & b Hoare	54	(7)	b Byrnes	1
A.J.Bowden	b Byrnes	24	(8)	c & b Byrnes	20
†H.Carter	b Hoare	0			
T.H.Howard	not out	2	(10)	not out	8
Extras	(b13, lb8, w2, nb4)	27		(b12, lb5)	17
Total	(69.0 overs, 205 mins)	280		(72.0 overs, 220 mins) (8 wkts)	265

NEW SOUTH WALES	O	M	R	W	w,nb		O	M	R	W	w,nb			FALL OF WICKETS			
Cuffe	22	11	28	0	1,-	(4)	11	2	39	1	-,-			QLD	NSW	QLD	NSW
Howard	32	6	88	2	-,1	(3)	35.2	13	77	5	-,-	Wkt	1st	1st	2nd	2nd
Bowden	36	6	93	3	-,-	(1)	37	16	82	2	-,-	1st	37	23	56	10
Deane	25	5	58	3	-,-	(2)	15	3	35	1	-,-	2nd	42	91	81	101
Gregory	3	2	4	0	-,-		3	1	14	0	-,-	3rd	98	162	103	136
												4th	102	169	107	142
QUEENSLAND	O	M	R	W	w,nb		O	M	R	W	w,nb	5th	119	174	211	157
Henry	33	0	86	3	1,-		20	2	70	0	-,-	6th	199	181	245	162
Byrnes	23	2	100	5	1,2		31	4	99	4	-,-	7th	245	189	257	200
P.Carew	1	0	8	0	-,-		1	0	5	0	-,-	8th	261	266	257	253
Hoare	9	1	44	2	-,2	(5)	15	1	55	3	-,-	9th	269	266	257	-
Fitzgerald	3	0	15	0	-,-							10th	284	280	257	-
Macdonald						(4)	5	0	19	0	-,-					

VICTORIA v SOUTH AUSTRALIA (Shield Match 3)

Played at Melbourne Cricket Ground on January 1, 2, 3, 5, 1903. (Timeless match)
Toss : Victoria.   Result : VICTORIA WON BY 179 RUNS.
Debuts: Nil.
12th Men: C.B.Jennings (SA). No 12th man or emergency fieldsman named for Victoria (see below).
Umpires: R.M.Crockett and E.J.Harvey.
Attendances: 7000, 6000, 7000, 2000.   Total: About 22,000.   Receipts: £680.
Close of Play: 1st day Vic 9/348 (Ellis 60, Hastings 40); 2nd day SA 4/222 (Hill 110, Gehrs 23); 3rd day Vic (2) 3/102 (Mailer 49, Graham 10).

McAlister (68 in 105 minutes, 12 fours) and Noonan (54 in 79 minutes, 5 fours) hit half-centuries as South Australia restricted Victoria to 9/261 soon after tea on a good wicket on the first day. Ellis (118 in 185 minutes, 9 fours) and Hastings (106 not out in 157 minutes, 9 fours, chance at 14) then added 211 for the last wicket, only once surpassed in Australian first-class cricket and still the Victorian record for that wicket. Ellis (originally named as 12th man) was a late replacement for J.V.Saunders (ill). Hastings became the first batsman in all first-class cricket, and to date the only Australian, to score a century at number eleven. Hastings had never reached three figures before in any cricket and neither scored another at first-class level. Clem Hill (124 in 205 minutes, 11 fours) demonstrated his renowned skills in a chanceless century. Light rain caused brief interruptions late on the third day but no affect on the wicket was reported. Kirkwood's hitting (44 in 37 minutes, 6 fours) and Armstrong's bowling were the features of the last day. Jennings substituted for Hewer (leg injury) in the Victorian second innings. Sources: *Wisden, C.B.O'Reilly, VCA Report, The Age, The Argus, The Herald, The Australasian, The Leader, South Australian Register.*

VICTORIA

H.Graham	b Jones	4	(5)	b Jones	23
P.A.McAlister	b Jones	68	(4)	c Hill b Kirkwood	4
W.W.Armstrong	c Kirkwood b Claxton	40	(7)	b Travers	10
J.H.Stuckey	b Claxton	14	(6)	c Waters b Travers	2
D.Mailer	b Travers	13	(1)	c & b Jones	49
D.F.Noonan	b Jones	54	(3)	c sub (C.B.Jennings) b Travers	22
*F.J.Laver	c Hack b Jones	46	(9)	not out	28
T.S.Warne	b Travers	2		b Travers	0
M.Ellis	st Newland b Reedman	118	(2)	b Reedman	14
F.B.Collins	b Travers	1	(11)	b Reedman	0
†T.J.Hastings	not out	106	(10)	c Gehrs b Reedman	9
Extras	(lb3, w3)	6		(b2, lb1)	3
Total	(140.2 overs, 385 mins)	472		(66.3 overs, 188 mins)	164

SOUTH AUSTRALIA

F.T.Hack	c Collins b Armstrong	10		b Collins	21
J.C.Reedman	b Armstrong	13		b Laver	6
*C.Hill	b Collins	124		b Collins	20
H.P.Kirkwood	c Ellis b Laver	19		c Graham b Armstrong	44
N.Claxton	c Armstrong b Laver	37		lbw b Armstrong	26
D.R.A.Gehrs	run out (Collins/Warne)	45		b Armstrong	0
†P.M.Newland	run out (McAlister)	22		c Collins b Ellis	3
R.W.Waters	c Graham b Warne	5	(9)	c Laver b Armstrong	0
W.A.Hewer	run out (/Warne)	3	(8)	b Armstrong	1
E.Jones	run out (/Hastings)	13		c Noonan b Ellis	15
J.P.F.Travers	not out	6		not out	1
Extras	(b13, lb3, w4)	20		(b3)	3
Total	(98.0 overs, 275 mins)	317		(50.5 overs, 140 mins)	140

SOUTH AUSTRALIA	O	M	R	W	w,nb		O	M	R	W	w,nb
Jones	43	11	134	4	-,-		22	4	69	2	-,-
Travers	45	6	129	3	2,-		28	5	57	4	-,-
Waters	15	3	42	0	-,-						
Kirkwood	7	0	42	0	-,-		4	0	12	1	-,-
Claxton	18	2	72	2	1,-						
Hewer	3	0	21	0	-,-						
Reedman	9.2	2	26	1	-,-	(3)	12.3	3	23	3	-,-

VICTORIA	O	M	R	W	w,nb		O	M	R	W	w,nb
Collins	30	1	90	1	3,-		14	1	51	2	-,-
Armstrong	30	5	71	2	-,-	(3)	11.5	4	20	5	-,-
Laver	26	2	71	2	-,-	(2)	14	3	45	1	-,-
Warne	6	0	42	1	1,-						
Ellis	6	1	23	0	-,-	(4)	11	7	21	2	-,-

FALL OF WICKETS

Wkt	VIC 1st	SA 1st	VIC 2nd	SA 2nd
1st	6	19	40	12
2nd	96	54	71	46
3rd	128	83	78	57
4th	128	184	102	100
5th	151	251	107	101
6th	233	289	123	120
7th	244	295	123	124
8th	248	297	137	124
9th	261	303	163	139
10th	472	317	164	140

NEW SOUTH WALES v SOUTH AUSTRALIA (Shield Match 4)

Played at Sydney Cricket Ground on January 9, 10, 12, 13, 1903. (Timeless match)
Toss : South Australia.   Result : NEW SOUTH WALES WON BY TEN WICKETS.
Debuts: South Australia - C.B.Jennings (f/c).
12th Men: C.W.Gregory (NSW - see below) and W.A.Hewer (SA).
Umpires: R.Callaway and E.J.Harvey.
Attendances: 3979, 9374, 4912, 1377.   Total: 19,642.   Receipts: £674.
Close of Play: 1st day SA 6/278 (Newland 19, Gehrs 30); 2nd day NSW 2/329 (Hopkins 7); 3rd day SA (2) 0/60 (Reedman 40, Hack 19).

S.E.Gregory severely strained a leg muscle while fielding soon after lunch on the first day. C.W.Gregory substituted and it was later determined that S.E.Gregory would be unable to take any further part in the match. Before play started on the third day, Hill, the South Australian captain, generously offered that C.W.Gregory could replace his brother as a full member of the New South Wales side. Noble accepted the offer after some initial reluctance. Trumper and Duff set a New South Wales first-wicket partnership record, subsequently broken, by adding 298 runs in 133 minutes. Trumper (29 fours) was first out and Duff (17 fours) followed 15 minutes later. Neither batsman gave a chance in brilliant exhibitions of strokeplay. Hopkins (69 in 142 minutes, 5 fours) and Mackenzie (50 in 111 minutes, 3 fours) also batted well. Hack (84 in 246 minutes, 6 fours), Claxton (80 in 102 minutes, 15 fours) and Gehrs (63 in 122 minutes, 11 fours) hit half-centuries in the South Australian first innings. Heavy rain during the night of the third day soaked the wicket and left the visitors no chance, seven wickets falling in the pre-lunch session of the final day. The only delivery sent down in the New South Wales innings was a wide bowled by Hack which went to the boundary. *Wisden* incorrectly gives SA (2) Waters 6; NSW (1) Noble 117. Sources: *Wisden, C.B.O'Reilly, NSWCA Report, Sydney Morning Herald, Town & Country Journal.*

SOUTH AUSTRALIA

J.C.Reedman	st Kelly b Howell	23		c Kelly b Howell	42
F.T.Hack	st Kelly b McBeath	84		b Hopkins	41
*C.Hill	c Kelly b Howell	31		st Kelly b Howell	6
H.P.Kirkwood	c Mackenzie b McBeath	7	(6)	st Kelly b McBeath	0
N.Claxton	c Kelly b Noble	80		c Noble b McBeath	7
D.R.A.Gehrs	c & b McBeath	63	(4)	b Howell	0
E.Jones	b McBeath	0	(10)	b Hopkins	6
†P.M.Newland	b McBeath	31	(7)	b Howell	2
C.B.Jennings	lbw b Hopkins	20	(8)	not out	19
R.W.Waters	not out	39	(9)	c Noble Hopkins	0
J.P.F.Travers	run out (Hopkins/Howell)	30		c Trumper b Howell	6
Extras	(b3, w1)	4		(b3, lb1, nb1)	5
Total	(170.5 overs, 405 mins)	412		(65.5 overs, 165 mins)	134

NEW SOUTH WALES

R.A.Duff	c Travers b Kirkwood	178			
V.T.Trumper	c Kirkwood b Reedman	132			
A.J.Y.Hopkins	c Hill b Jones	69			
*M.A.Noble	c Jones b Travers	17			
A.C.K.Mackenzie	c Newland b Waters	50			
R.N.Hickson	c Reedman b Waters	18			
C.W.Gregory	b Waters	32			
L.W.Pye	c Gehrs b Claxton	6			
†J.J.Kelly	c Newland b Travers	8	(2)	not out	0
W.P.Howell	not out	11	(1)	not out	0
A.McBeath	run out (Jones)	0			
S.E.Gregory	absent hurt	-			
Extras	(b20, lb4)	24		(w4)	4
Total	(134.5 overs, 371 mins)	545		(0.0 overs, 1 min) (0 wkts)	4

NEW SOUTH WALES	O	M	R	W	w,nb		O	M	R	W	w,nb		FALL OF WICKETS			
														SA	NSW	SA	NSW
Howell	43.5	15	109	2	-,-		21.5	10	40	5	-,-	Wkt	1st	1st	2nd	2nd
Noble	30	9	69	1	-,-	(3)	11	5	13	0	-,1	1st	32	298	68	-
Pye	30	9	59	0	1,-	(6)	4	1	10	0	-,-	2nd	88	329	78	-
McBeath	46	15	110	5	-,-	(2)	21	4	54	2	-,-	3rd	97	361	78	-
Trumper	8	3	25	0	-,-	(4)	2	1	3	0	-,-	4th	221	446	85	-
Hopkins	13	3	36	1	-,-	(5)	6	2	9	3	-,-	5th	237	480	91	-
												6th	237	489	94	-
SOUTH AUSTRALIA	O	M	R	W	w,nb		O	M	R	W	w,nb	7th	302	496	105	-
Jones	35	6	118	1	-,-							8th	337	532	109	-
Travers	38	5	130	2	-,-							9th	347	538	123	-
Claxton	19	3	74	1	-,-							10th	412	545	134	-
Reedman	12	1	55	1	-,-											
Kirkwood	13	1	65	1	-,-											
Waters	14.5	4	53	3	-,-											
Hill	14.5	4	53	3	-,-											
Hack						(1)	0.0	0	0	0	4,-					

NEW SOUTH WALES v VICTORIA (Shield Match 5)

Played at Sydney Cricket Ground on January 24, 26, 27, 28, 29, 1903. (Timeless match)
Toss : Victoria.   Result : NEW SOUTH WALES WON BY FIVE WICKETS.
Debuts: Nil.
12th Men: W.S.Duff (NSW) and B.J.Tuckwell (Vic).
Umpires: R.Callaway and R.M.Crockett.
Attendances: 9604, 5770, 4888, 1351, 1409.   Total: 23,022.   Receipts: £884.
Close of Play: 1st day NSW 0/141 (Duff 61, Trumper 77); 2nd day NSW 0/265 (Duff 130, Trumper 130); 3rd day Vic (2) 2/85
    (McAlister 34); 4th day Vic (2) 427 all out.

Duff (132 in 152 minutes, 17 fours) and Trumper (130 in 137 minutes, 18 fours) shared an opening stand of 267, their second big partnership for New South Wales within a month. Rain considerably reduced playing time on the second day. Hastings, while keeping on the third day. was struck on the head by a ball from Collins and left the field a short time afterwards. Tuckwell substituted and Armstrong took over as wicket-keeper for the rest of the innings, conceding a number of byes. Hastings resumed in his position in the second innings. Armstrong (118 in 175 minutes, 15 fours), McAlister (84 in 170 minutes), Noble (103 not out in 213 minutes, 15 fours) and Hickson (89 not out in 107 minutes, 1 five and 11 fours) all compiled noteworthy innings, the last two sharing an unbroken partnership of 152 to finish the match. *Wisden* gives incorrect match dates. Sources: *Wisden, NSWCA Report, Sydney Morning Herald, Town & Country Journal, Sydney Daily Telegraph.*

VICTORIA

W.Bruce	run out (Mackenzie)	38		c Howell b McBeath	48
P.A.McAlister	b Howell	37		st Kelly b McBeath	84
H.Graham	st Kelly b Pye	25	(4)	b Howell	1
W.W.Armstrong	b Pye	26	(5)	c Howell b McBeath	118
*F.J.Laver	c McBeath b Pye	5	(6)	c Mackenzie b McBeath	34
D.F.Noonan	c Noble b McBeath	29	(7)	st Kelly b McBeath	18
D.Mailer	b Pye	0	(8)	b Noble	24
M.Ellis	c Kelly b McBeath	23	(9)	run out (R.A.Duff/Kelly)	53
†T.J.Hastings	c & b McBeath	1	(10)	c & b Trumper	25
F.B.Collins	c Trumper b McBeath	17	(11)	not out	12
J.V.Saunders	not out	0	(3)	lbw b Pye	2
Extras	(b4, nb2)	6		(b2, lb4, nb2)	8
Total	(86.1 overs, 195 mins)	207		(155.2 overs, 350 mins)	427

NEW SOUTH WALES

R.A.Duff	b Collins	132		c Graham b Saunders	39
V.T.Trumper	c Hastings b Collins	130		c Hastings b Collins	0
C.W.Gregory	c McAlister b Laver	37	(5)	run out (Mailer)	0
R.N.Hickson	st Hastings b Saunders	1	(7)	not out	89
*M.A.Noble	c sub (B.J.Tuckwell) b Collins	3	(3)	not out	103
A.C.K.Mackenzie	c & b Saunders	2	(4)	c Armstrong b Saunders	2
A.J.Y.Hopkins	lbw b Laver	11	(6)	b Saunders	17
L.W.Pye	c Laver b Collins	6			
†J.J.Kelly	not out	3			
W.P.Howell	b Laver	2			
A.McBeath	c Mailer b Collins	1			
Extras	(b32, lb2, nb5)	39		(b16, lb3)	19
Total	(87.3 overs, 234 mins)	367		(76.3 overs, 219 mins) (5 wkts)	269

NEW SOUTH WALES	O	M	R	W	w,nb		O	M	R	W	w,nb
Howell	24	11	45	1	-,-	(1)	32	10	84	1	-,-
McBeath	27.1	6	70	4	-,-	(2)	41	14	111	5	-,-
Hopkins	12	1	33	0	-,1	(4)	13	0	54	0	-,1
Pye	23	7	53	4	-,1	(5)	40	9	96	1	-,1
Noble						(3)	22	5	60	1	-,-
Trumper							7.2	1	14	1	-,-

VICTORIA	O	M	R	W	w,nb		O	M	R	W	w,nb
Saunders	19	2	93	2	-,-		30	7	94	3	-,-
Collins	30.3	6	85	5	-,4		10	1	48	1	-,-
Armstrong	16	1	50	0	-,1	(4)	13	4	33	0	-,-
Laver	17	1	72	3	-,-	(3)	18	8	37	0	-,-
Bruce	2	0	10	0	-,-	(6)	1.3	0	16	0	-,-
Ellis	3	1	18	0	-,-	(5)	3	0	17	0	-,-
Graham							1	0	5	0	-,-

FALL OF WICKETS

Wkt	VIC 1st	NSW 1st	VIC 2nd	NSW 2nd
1st	72	267	74	2
2nd	90	270	85	66
3rd	118	279	86	78
4th	131	292	188	79
5th	144	296	280	117
6th	148	331	303	-
7th	184	346	314	-
8th	189	348	384	-
9th	194	355	399	-
10th	207	367	427	-

VICTORIA v TASMANIA

Played at Melbourne Cricket Ground on January 24, 26, 27, 28, 1903. (Timeless match)
Toss : Tasmania.   Result : TASMANIA WON BY 57 RUNS.
Debuts: Victoria - W.W.Blundell, B.Grant, I.Hopkins, H.Howson, L.N.Rainey (all f/c). Tasmania - A.J.Betts, F.E.Chancellor,
    E.W.Harrison, F.W.Richardson (all f/c).
12th Men: H.J.Fry (Vic). No 12th named for Tasmania; only 11 men in party.
Umpires: C.E.Over and W.A.Young.
Attendances: 2000, 1000, 500, 300.   Total: About 3800.   Receipts: £71.
Close of Play: 1st day Vic 1/20 (Stuckey 13, Grant 6); 2nd day Tas (2) 3/78 (Burn 22); 3rd day Vic (2) 7/157 (Hopkins 23, Grant 35).

L.A.Cuff, N.Dodds, H.P.Kissling, J.H.Savigny, D.R.Smith and E.A.C.Windsor were all unavailable for Tasmania. Hawson (74 in 107 minutes, 8 fours and 35 in 83 minutes, 2 fours) batted "with that easy, graceful style suggestive of the first-class public school player in England" (*Australasian*) to be the best batsman on view in the match. With the assistance of Douglas, he twice gave the visitors a great start. Paton (41 not out in 84 minutes, 5 fours and 9 for 112) also made a major contribution to the Tasmanian win. Bean (81 in 173 minutes, 7 fours) and Howson (40 in 122 minutes, 5 fours) added 104 for the ninth wicket in the first innings to keep Victoria in contention. Warne (46 in 75 minutes, 4 fours and 8 for 174) also fought hard for the home side. Rainey finished off the Tasmanian second innings with the wickets of Chancellor and Betts with successive deliveries. *VCA Report* incorrectly gives Bean 2/25 and omits Grant 0/10 in Tas (1). Sources: *VCA Report, STCA Report, The Age, The Argus, The Herald, The Australasian, The Leader.*

TASMANIA

R.J.Hawson	st Hopkins b Warne	74		c Hopkins b Bean	35
O.H.Douglas	c Howson b Bean	31		lbw b Warne	11
C.J.Eady	c Rainey b Warne	2	(4)	c Bean b Blundell	7
H.Hale	b Bean	13	(5)	c & b Blundell	16
E.W.Harrison	c Howson b Warne	26	(8)	c Hopkins b Howson	9
T.A.Tabart	c & b Warne	13		c Warne b Howson	43
*E.J.K.Burn	c Warne b Blundell	36	(3)	c Horan b Warne	32
G.D.Paton	run out (/Hopkins)	17	(9)	not out	41
F.W.Richardson	not out	18	(7)	c Horan b Warne	4
F.E.Chancellor	c Grant b Warne	0		b Rainey	13
†A.J.Betts	b Blundell	0		b Rainey	0
Extras	(b7, nb1)	8		(b4, lb2, nb2)	8
Total	(108.4 overs, 265 mins)	238		(133.5 overs, 285 mins)	219

VICTORIA

J.H.Stuckey	c Betts b Paton	30		c Betts b Eady	5
J.F.Horan	c Tabart b Paton	1	(4)	c Eady b Paton	21
B.Grant	b Paton	7	(9)	c Harrison b Paton	44
L.N.Rainey	c Betts b Eady	7	(6)	c & b Hale	7
T.S.Warne	b Eady	3	(2)	b Chancellor	46
*E.E.Bean	c Richardson b Hale	81	(5)	c Betts b Chancellor	16
G.Stuckey	c Betts b Paton	9		c Eady b Hale	1
†I.Hopkins	b Eady	26		c Betts b Paton	25
R.Mitchell	b Paton	3	(3)	run out	1
H.Howson	c Eady b Tabart	40		not out	2
W.W.Blundell	not out	4		lbw b Paton	0
Extras	(b7, lb2)	9		(b9, lb3)	12
Total	(95.0 overs, 234 mins)	220		(65.5 overs, 165 mins)	180

VICTORIA	O	M	R	W	w,nb		O	M	R	W	w,nb		FALL OF WICKETS			
													TAS	VIC	TAS	VIC
Howson	15	2	43	0	-,-	(2)	34	16	43	2	-,-	Wkt	1st	1st	2nd	2nd
Mitchell	10	4	16	0	-,-	(5)	14	4	26	0	-,-	1st	111	10	47	6
Blundell	23.4	11	41	2	-,-		18	8	26	2	-,-	2nd	113	32	47	7
Rainey	13	4	25	0	-,1	(6)	6.5	4	9	2	-,2	3rd	115	39	78	42
Warne	34	10	80	5	-,-	(1)	47	14	94	3	-,-	4th	138	48	102	81
Bean	10	3	15	2	-,-	(4)	14	7	13	1	-,-	5th	156	49	105	94
Grant	3	1	10	0	-,-							6th	173	66	118	95
												7th	212	101	142	99
TASMANIA	O	M	R	W	w,nb		O	M	R	W	w,nb	8th	226	108	198	161
Eady	38	7	95	3	-,-		22	6	43	1	-,-	9th	231	212	219	180
Paton	36	10	66	5	-,-		22.5	7	46	4	-,-	10th	238	220	219	180
Chancellor	11	2	23	0	-,-	(4)	8	0	39	2	-,-					
Tabart	4	1	10	1	-,-	(5)	1	0	6	0	-,-					
Hale	6	1	17	1	-,-	(3)	11	4	28	2	-,-					
Richardson							1	0	6	0	-,-					

QUEENSLAND v VICTORIA

Played at Brisbane Cricket Ground (Woolloongabba) on January 31, February 2, 1903. (Timeless match)
Toss : Queensland.   Result : VICTORIA WON BY AN INNINGS AND 327 RUNS.
Debuts: Victoria - B.J.Tuckwell (f/c).
12th Men: D.Mailer (Vic). G.S.Crouch and J.W.Lewis named as Queensland emergencies.
Umpires: E.Beard and T.Muir.
Attendances: 5000, 1000.   Total: About 6000.   Receipts: No figures published.
Close of Play: 1st day Vic 5/374 (Armstrong 109, Tuckwell 46).

The first eleven-a-side match between the two States. In their only previous encounter Victoria had drawn with a Queensland fifteen in Brisbane in April 1889. Two pitches were prepared for the match but it was agreed that only one would be used, to be determined by the weather conditions on the first day. Morgan replaced R.Macdonald (unavailable) in the Queensland team. Graham (101 in 107 minutes, 5 fives and 4 fours), Armstrong (145 in 195 minutes, 2 fives and 13 fours) and Tuckwell, on debut, (93 not out in 166 minutes, 2 fives and 8 fours) were the main contributors to Victoria's innings. Noonan was given out in circumstances now disallowed; advancing down the pitch to a ball from Byrnes, which had been called a no-ball, he missed and Evans removed the bails. Not having heard the umpire's call, Noonan left thinking he was stumped. Evans then pulled out a stump and Noonan was ruled "run out". Queensland's second-innings total remains their lowest in all first-class cricket. *Queensland Times* incorrectly gives Vic: Hastings c J.Carew b P.Carew; Byrnes 0/111, P.Carew 2/104. Sources: *VCA Report, Brisbane Courier, Queensland Times, The Queenslander.*

VICTORIA

W.Bruce	c P.Carew b Henry	15
P.A.McAlister	run out (Henry/Byrnes/Evans)	67
H.Graham	b Griffith	101
W.W.Armstrong	run out (Atkins)	145
M.Ellis	b Griffith	6
D.F.Noonan	run out (Evans)	13
B.J.Tuckwell	not out	93
*F.J.Laver	b P.Carew	25
†T.J.Hastings	c J.Carew b Byrnes	1
F.B.Collins	b Henry	3
J.V.Saunders	b Henry	1
Extras	(b10, lb9, nb1)	20
Total	(123.0 overs, 359 mins)	490

QUEENSLAND

C.W.Patrick	c Armstrong b Saunders	11	(2) c Laver b Armstrong	3
J.Carew	b Collins	30	(1) lbw b Armstrong	2
P.Carew	c Noonan b Saunders	15	b Laver	7
E.R.Crouch	b Collins	1	b Laver	5
*A.A.Atkins	c McAlister b Saunders	0	c & b Armstrong	2
C.F.Morgan	c Armstrong b Saunders	3	b Laver	0
J.J.Fitzgerald	b Collins	1	b Laver	10
H.B.Griffith	lbw b Collins	21	b Laver	0
†W.T.Evans	not out	25	lbw b Laver	0
T.Byrnes	c Tuckwell b Saunders	1	c Graham b Armstrong	0
A.Henry	b Saunders	4	not out	1
Extras	(b11)	11	(b8, lb2)	10
Total	(32.3 overs, 108 mins)	123	(11.1 overs, 47 mins)	40

QUEENSLAND	O	M	R	W	w,nb
Henry	36	10	76	3	-,-
Byrnes	34	3	111	1	-,1
P.Carew	21	0	104	1	-,-
Griffith	26	2	131	2	-,-
Fitzgerald	3	0	28	0	-,-
Crouch	3	0	20	0	-,-

VICTORIA	O	M	R	W	w,nb		O	M	R	W	w,nb
Saunders	16.3	3	57	6	-,-						
Collins	16	3	55	4	-,-						
Armstrong						(1)	6	0	13	4	-,-
Laver						(2)	5.1	1	17	6	-,-

FALL OF WICKETS

Wkt	VIC 1st	QLD 1st	QLD 2nd
1st	25	15	6
2nd	177	37	16
3rd	202	46	20
4th	214	57	21
5th	264	65	21
6th	431	66	38
7th	474	88	38
8th	475	95	38
9th	484	104	38
10th	490	123	40

SOUTH AUSTRALIA v VICTORIA (Shield Match 6)

Played at Adelaide Oval on February 27, 28, March 2, 3, 4, 1903. (Timeless match)
Toss : Victoria.   Result : VICTORIA WON BY 35 RUNS.
Debuts: Victoria - J.E.Monfries (f/c).
12th Men: A.E.Evans (SA) and D.Mailer (Vic).
Umpires: R.M.Crockett and G.S.Downs.
Attendances: 1200, 3000, other days not published.   Total: About 6000.   Receipts: £173.
Close of Play: 1st day Vic 4/227 (Stuckey 53, Laver 32); 2nd day SA 4/216 (Giffen 68, Claxton 6); 3rd day Vic (2) 5/190 (Laver 40, Bean 5); 4th day SA (2) 3/33 (Giffen 7, Gehrs 9).

George Giffen, aged 43, completed an outstanding match double of 178 runs and 15 wickets, the ninth occasion on which he performed the 100 runs/10 wickets "double" and the sixth time that he took 15 or more wickets in a first-class match; no other Australian has performed the feat more than three times. Saunders, with 13 wickets, almost emulated Giffen's bowling performance and included a sequence of three wickets in four balls (Jennings, Jarvis, ball, Kirkwood) in his second innings analysis. Armstrong "opened his shoulders and hit Travers beautifully over the smokers' stand - one of the finest strokes seen on Adelaide Oval" (*Register*) during his 66 in 65 minutes (1 five and 9 fours). A thunderstorm on the morning of the fourth day saturated the ground and delayed the start of play until 3.30pm. Both Giffen and Saunders utilized the extra life that was injected into the wicket during the 150 minutes play. Conditions gradually improved as the final day progressed but Saunders continued to make inroads to the South Australian batting, at one stage having a personal 8 for 56. Giffen and Travers then added 101 for the last wicket, a new State record, which almost achieved victory for the home team. *Wisden* incorrectly gives SA (1) Gehrs st Monfries b Collins; Vic (2) Claxton 0/4, Jarvis 0/14. Sources: *Wisden, C.B.O'Reilly, SACA Report, Adelaide Advertiser, South Australian Register.*

VICTORIA

H.Graham	c Giffen b Reedman	59		b Giffen	45
P.A.McAlister	b Travers	39		lbw b Giffen	6
J.H.Stuckey	b Giffen	63		st Newland b Travers	8
W.W.Armstrong	c Hill b Giffen	40		b Giffen	66
M.Ellis	lbw b Giffen	0	(6)	c & b Giffen	14
*F.J.Laver	c Hack b Reedman	50	(5)	c & b Travers	61
E.E.Bean	b Giffen	0		not out	30
B.J.Tuckwell	b Giffen	27		c Jennings b Giffen	1
†J.E.Monfries	not out	0		c Hill b Giffen	0
F.B.Collins	c Kirkwood b Giffen	0		st Newland b Giffen	1
J.V.Saunders	b Giffen	5		c Gehrs b Giffen	2
Extras	(b5, lb3)	8		(b3, lb5, w1, nb1)	10
Total	(123.5 overs, 340 mins)	291		(84.2 overs, 220 mins)	244

SOUTH AUSTRALIA

F.T.Hack	c Armstrong b Saunders	88	(2)	c Saunders b Laver	3
J.C.Reedman	c & b Laver	40	(1)	c & b Saunders	8
*C.Hill	b Collins	8		b Saunders	2
G.Giffen	c Stuckey b Armstrong	81	(5)	not out	97
D.R.A.Gehrs	st Monfries b Saunders	0	(4)	b Saunders	9
N.Claxton	c & b Saunders	7		b Saunders	29
C.B.Jennings	run out (Collins/Monfries)	6		b Saunders	8
A.Jarvis	c Monfries b Saunders	12		b Saunders	0
H.P.Kirkwood	c Monfries b Armstrong	12		b Saunders	0
†P.M.Newland	not out	5		c Stuckey b Saunders	2
J.P.F.Travers	c Tuckwell b Saunders	8		lbw b Collins	41
Extras	(b5, lb1, w1, nb4)	11		(b9, lb5, nb9)	23
Total	(109.1 overs, 305 mins)	278		(118.3 overs, 320 mins)	222

SOUTH AUSTRALIA	O	M	R	W	w,nb		O	M	R	W	w,nb
Travers	35	7	80	1	-,-	(2)	30	10	69	2	-,-
Claxton	7	0	30	0	-,-	(5)	2	0	3	0	1,-
Jarvis	17	3	47	0	-,-	(4)	6	1	13	0	-,1
Giffen	37.5	10	75	7	-,-	(1)	38.2	7	110	8	-,-
Kirkwood	14	5	20	0	-,-	(6)	5	0	22	0	-,-
Reedman	13	3	31	2	-,-	(3)	3	0	17	0	-,-

VICTORIA	O	M	R	W	w,nb		O	M	R	W	w,nb
Collins	11	1	61	1	-,2	(3)	19.3	10	22	1	-,7
Saunders	34.1	5	88	5	1,-		50	9	106	8	-,-
Armstrong	38	11	58	2	-,1	(4)	17	6	22	0	-,1
Laver	22	8	41	1	-,1	(1)	20	3	27	1	-,-
Bean	4	0	19	0	-,-	(7)	4	1	9	0	-,-
Ellis						(5)	6	2	10	0	-,1
Graham						(6)	2	1	3	0	-,-

FALL OF WICKETS

Wkt	VIC 1st	SA 1st	VIC 2nd	SA 2nd
1st	89	97	13	12
2nd	117	108	30	16
3rd	169	194	109	16
4th	169	194	130	37
5th	240	221	170	101
6th	240	232	217	118
7th	286	242	224	118
8th	286	265	228	118
9th	286	267	234	121
10th	291	278	244	222

VICTORIA v LORD HAWKE'S ENGLAND XI

Played at Melbourne Cricket Ground on March 13, 14, 16, 1903. (Four-day match)
Toss : England XI   Result : VICTORIA WON BY SEVEN WICKETS.
Debuts: Nil.
12th Men: E.E.Bean (Vic) and A.E.Leatham (Eng XI).
Umpires: R.M.Crockett and C.E.Over.
Attendances: 1500, 7000, 1500.   Total: About 10,000.   Receipts: No figures published.
Close of Play: 1st day Eng XI 350 all out; 2nd day Eng XI (2) 2/85 (Burnup 36, Stanning 7).

Taylor (59 in 95 minutes, 6 fours), Dowson (51 in 68 minutes, 5 fours) and Bosanquet (51 in 56 minutes, 6 fours) hit half-centuries in an even batting display by the Englishmen on the first day. Bowlers appreciated the "good fast wicket" (*Argus*) that was in evidence from the second day and thereafter kept the batsmen of both sides in check. Collins (career-best 7 for 61), in particular, surprised the visitors with his pace from the pitch. Harry Graham (92 in 128 minutes, 5 fours) steered Victoria to a win with a fine display in his last first-class appearance for the State - he emigrated to New Zealand where he represented Otago and New Zealand 1903-04 to 1906-07. Armstrong kept wickets on the second day in the absence of Monfries, who had suffered a hand injury while batting without gloves. He was able to resume in his chosen role, "though considerably handicapped" (*Argus*), on the following day. Stanning kept wickets after the tea adjournment on the final day to rest Taylor. *VCA Report* incorrectly gives Vic (1) Burnup 0/32. Sources: *Wisden, VCA Report, The Age, The Argus, The Herald, The Australasian, The Leader.*

LORD HAWKE'S ENGLAND XI

*P.F.Warner	st Monfries b Saunders	30		lbw b Collins	12
C.J.Burnup	c Armstrong b Saunders	21		c Armstrong b Collins	40
F.L.Fane	c Monfries b Collins	19		b Collins	24
†T.L.Taylor	lbw b Armstrong	59	(5)	c Laver b Armstrong	0
E.M.Dowson	c McAlister b Laver	51	(6)	c McAlister b Armstrong	23
B.J.T.Bosanquet	c Monfries b Saunders	51	(7)	c Armstrong b Collins	8
G.J.Thompson	st Monfries b Saunders	38	(8)	b Collins	0
A.E.Trott	c Graham b Saunders	17	(9)	c & b Collins	0
P.R.Johnson	not out	37	(10)	not out	8
J.Stanning	c Monfries b Saunders	11	(4)	c Armstrong b Collins	11
S.Hargreave	b Ellis	5		b Armstrong	2
Extras	(b11)	11		(b6)	6
Total	(115.4 overs, 296 mins)	350		(54.2 overs, 152 mins)	134

VICTORIA

P.A.McAlister	c Bosanquet b Trott	28		c Stanning b Dowson	20
W.Bruce	c Bosanquet b Hargreave	19		c Trott b Dowson	36
H.Graham	c Burnup b Trott	38		c Warner b Burnup	92
W.W.Armstrong	c Johnson b Dowson	29		not out	48
J.H.Stuckey	b Trott	7		not out	6
*F.J.Laver	c Taylor b Thompson	44			
M.Ellis	c Burnup b Trott	11			
D.Mailer	b Dowson	16			
†J.E.Monfries	not out	33			
F.B.Collins	run out (Bosanquet/Taylor)	4			
J.V.Saunders	c Taylor b Thompson	18			
Extras	(b20, lb3, w1)	24		(b7, lb2, w6)	15
Total	(86.4 overs, 230 mins)	271		(73.1 overs, 185 mins) (3 wkts)	217

VICTORIA	O	M	R	W	w,nb		O	M	R	W	w,nb			FALL OF WICKETS			
Collins	21	4	80	1	-,-		27	2	61	7	-,-			ENG	VIC	ENG	VIC
Saunders	39	6	118	6	-,-		11	2	33	0	-,-	Wkt	1st	1st	2nd	2nd
Armstrong	30	9	63	1	-,-		11.2	3	22	3	-,-	1st	55	36	21	54
Laver	19	8	38	1	-,-		5	1	12	0	-,-	2nd	56	86	67	75
Ellis	6.4	0	40	1	-,-							3rd	105	87	92	204
												4th	185	111	93	-
ENGLAND XI	O	M	R	W	w,nb		O	M	R	W	w,nb	5th	185	142	95	-
Burnup	7	2	30	0	-,-	(5)	4	1	15	1	-,-	6th	259	164	112	-
Hargreave	22	4	47	1	-,-	(3)	12.1	3	23	0	-,-	7th	282	198	112	-
Bosanquet	5	0	18	0	-,-	(4)	4	0	20	0	2,-	8th	315	216	112	-
Trott	23	6	88	4	1,-	(6)	17	3	51	0	-,-	9th	341	236	128	-
Thompson	16.4	3	45	2	-,-	(1)	18	5	42	0	4,-	10th	350	271	134	-
Dowson	13	2	19	2	-,-	(2)	18	4	51	2	-,-					

NEW SOUTH WALES v LORD HAWKE'S ENGLAND XI

Played at Sydney Cricket Ground on March 20, 21, 23, 24 (no play), 1903. (Four-day match)
Toss : England XI.   Result : MATCH DRAWN.
Debuts: Nil.
12th Men: C.W.Gregory (NSW). No 12th named for England XI.
Umpires: R.Callaway and A.C.Jones.
Attendances: 3487, 10696, 2663, no play.   Total: 16,846.   Receipts: £594.
Close of Play: 1st day Eng XI 3/66 (Fane 28, Dowson 7); 2nd day NSW (2) 3/120 (Duff 60, McBeath 0); 3rd day Eng XI (2) 0/32
    (Burnup 13, Warner 19).

Rain delayed the start of the match until 2.00pm and the wicket consequently favoured the bowlers early on. Trott "mixed his pace with excellent judgment' (*T & C Journal*) to take advantage of the conditions. Batting became easier from the second day as Fane (41 in 92 minutes, 5 fours), Dowson (86 in 140 minutes, 10 fours) and Bosanquet (52 in 48 minutes, 8 fours) took the Englishmen to a 138 run advantage on the first innings. Victory for the visitors seemed assured as New South Wales slumped to 7/175 in their second innings. It was then that R.A.Duff (194 in 275 minutes, 20 fours) and Hopkins (133 in 130 minutes, 21 fours) intervened to add 236 for the eighth wicket, a new Australian record, "by most brilliant batting" (*SMH*). The rain returned to prevent any play at all on the final day when an interesting finish was in prospect. Play was to have started and finished earlier than usual (11.30am to 5.30pm) to enable the England players to leave by train for their next match in Adelaide. Sources: *Wisden, NSWCA Report, Sydney Morning Herald, Town & Country Journal*.

NEW SOUTH WALES

V.T.Trumper	c Dowson b Trott	16		b Bosanquet	37
R.A.Duff	c Bosanquet b Trott	9		b Bosanquet	194
*M.A.Noble	c Trott b Hargreave	4	(7)	c Taylor b Thompson	9
W.S.Duff	c Johnson b Trott	1	(3)	b Bosanquet	9
S.E.Gregory	lbw b Trott	21	(6)	c Taylor b Thompson	1
R.N.Hickson	b Trott	0	(8)	b Thompson	14
A.J.Y.Hopkins	c Johnson b Trott	23	(9)	lbw b Burnup	133
L.W.Pye	not out	29	(10)	not out	13
†J.J.Kelly	b Thompson	12	(4)	c Hargreave b Bosanquet	10
W.P.Howell	c Bosanquet b Dowson	20	(11)	b Bosanquet	24
A.McBeath	c Johnson b Thompson	4	(5)	c Hargreave b Bosanquet	1
Extras	(b4, nb1)	5		(b12, lb4, nb2)	18
Total	(45.5 overs, 125 mins)	144		(103.1 overs, 290 mins)	463

LORD HAWKE'S ENGLAND XI

C.J.Burnup	b McBeath	8	not out	13
*P.F.Warner	lbw b Noble	23	not out	19
F.L.Fane	c Pye b Noble	41		
†T.L.Taylor	st Kelly b McBeath	0		
E.M.Dowson	c R.A.Duff b Noble	86		
B.J.T.Bosanquet	c Hickson b Noble	52		
P.R.Johnson	c Noble b McBeath	12		
G.J.Thompson	not out	30		
A.E.Trott	c Pye b Noble	5		
J.Stanning	c Trumper b Hopkins	20		
S.Hargreave	c Kelly b Hopkins	3		
Extras	(b1, nb1)	2		—
Total	(113.3 overs, 350 mins)	282	(22.0 overs, 50 mins) (0 wkts)	32

ENGLAND XI	O	M	R	W	w,nb		O	M	R	W	w,nb
Trott	20	2	88	6	-,-	(3)	9	0	76	0	-,-
Hargreave	15	3	32	1	-,-	(4)	10	2	23	0	-,-
Thompson	7.5	2	16	2	-,1	(5)	32	5	105	3	-,1
Dowson	3	1	3	1	-,-	(1)	12	0	49	0	-,1
Bosanquet						(6)	30.1	1	153	6	-,-
Burnup						(2)	10	0	39	1	-,-

		FALL OF WICKETS		
Wkt	NSW	ENG	NSW	ENG
	1st	1st	2nd	2nd
1st	28	13	72	-
2nd	33	44	100	-
3rd	33	45	116	-
4th	37	119	130	-
5th	38	204	131	-
6th	73	212	150	-
7th	80	224	175	-
8th	104	229	411	-
9th	139	265	436	-
10th	144	282	463	-

NEW SOUTH WALES	O	M	R	W	w,nb		O	M	R	W	w,nb
Howell	23	7	54	0	-,-	(3)	3	0	6	0	-,-
McBeath	33	8	73	3	-,-	(1)	8	5	8	0	-,-
Noble	27	5	78	5	-,1	(2)	7	3	15	0	-,-
Hopkins	8.3	2	37	2	-,-	(5)	1	1	0	0	-,-
Pye	22	7	38	0	-,-	(4)	3	1	3	0	-,-

SOUTH AUSTRALIA v LORD HAWKE'S ENGLAND XI

Played at Unley Oval, Adelaide, on March 27, 28, 30, 31, 1903. (Four-day match)
Toss : England XI.   Result : SOUTH AUSTRALIA WON BY 97 RUNS.
Debuts: South Australia - H.Hay (f/c).
12th Men: E.H.Leak (SA). No 12th named for England XI.
Umpires: P.Argall and J.Quilty.
Attendances: ? , 2000, ? , ? .   Total: 6660.   Receipts: £215.
Close of Play: 1st day Eng XI 4/380 (Dowson 57, Bosanquet 12); 2nd day SA 5/227 (Claxton 72, Jennings 44); 3rd day SA (2) 4/260
    (Reedman 30, Gehrs 22).

Due to the staging of a bicycle meeting organised by the League of Wheelmen, the Adelaide Oval was unavailable for the final match of
Lord Hawke's team's tour of New Zealand and Australia. Sturt Cricket Club, in offering their ground as a replacement, provided the venue
for the only first-class match in South Australia played away from Adelaide Oval. Harry Hay, a right-arm fast-medium trundler called up to
replace H.P.Kirkwood who withdrew through injury, captured 9 for 67 on debut including a hat-trick (Burnup, Fane, Taylor) for his initial
wickets. He remains the only player to perform the hat-trick on debut in Australia - later he dismissed Warner and Bosanquet with
consecutive balls. J.Quilty, the only other bowler to this day to take nine wickets in an innings on debut in Australia, was coincidentally
one of the umpires. Thompson's analysis of 9 for 85 remains the best by an Englishman in Australia. Burnup (103 in 140 minutes, 13
fours), Taylor (105 in 118 minutes, 1 five and 14 fours), Dowson (66 in 93 minutes, 1 five and 10 fours) and Bosanquet (57 in 53 minutes,
8 fours) led the visitors to a seemingly impregnable position. Hill (58 in 65 minutes, 9 fours), Claxton (88 in 85 minutes, 16 fours) and
Jennings (52 in 89 minutes, 5 fours) hit half-centuries in reply. South Australia, forced to follow on under contemporary Australian law,
rallied to take advantage of a weary field. Hack (90 in 130 minutes, 1 five and 6 fours), Hill (73 in 85 minutes, 11 fours) and Gehrs (100
in 155 minutes, 8 fours) topscored, the wicket being disturbed in every dismissal. On the last day A.Richardson of Sturt substituted in the
field for Giffen (leg injury). Sources: *Wisden, C.B.O'Reilly, Adelaide Advertiser, South Australian Register, South Australian Chronicle.*

LORD HAWKE'S ENGLAND XI

*P.F.Warner	b Giffen	47		lbw b Hay	25
C.J.Burnup	c & b Giffen	103		b Hay	3
F.L.Fane	c Newland b Travers	47		b Hay	0
†T.L.Taylor	c & b Claxton	105		b Hay	0
E.M.Dowson	lbw b Travers	66		run out (Hill/Newland)	46
B.J.T.Bosanquet	c Claxton b Giffen	57		b Hay	0
G.J.Thompson	b Travers	18		not out	15
J.Stanning	c Gehrs b Reedman	38	(10)	b Hay	2
A.E.Trott	b Giffen	4		b Hay	8
P.R.Johnson	c Travers b Reedman	54	(8)	c & b Hay	4
S.Hargreave	not out	2		c Newland b Hay	4
Extras	(lb11, w1)	12		(b1)	1
Total	(146.5 overs, 405 mins)	553		(42.2 overs, 115 mins)	108

SOUTH AUSTRALIA

F.T.Hack	c Taylor b Thompson	3	(2)	b Dowson	90
A.E.Evans	b Thompson	15	(1)	b Thompson	1
*C.Hill	b Thompson	58		st Taylor b Bosanquet	73
J.C.Reedman	b Thompson	18	(5)	b Thompson	41
D.R.A.Gehrs	c Fane b Bosanquet	6	(6)	run out	100
N.Claxton	b Thompson	88	(7)	b Trott	32
C.B.Jennings	b Thompson	52	(8)	b Trott	0
G.Giffen	b Thompson	14	(4)	b Thompson	37
†P.M.Newland	b Thompson	0		b Dowson	48
H.Hay	not out	14		b Dowson	0
J.P.F.Travers	c Bosanquet b Thompson	15		not out	14
Extras	(b13, lb4, w3, nb1)	21		(b13, lb4, nb1)	18
Total	(70.3 overs, 208 mins)	304		(122.5 overs, 325 mins)	454

SOUTH AUSTRALIA	O	M	R	W	w,nb		O	M	R	W	w,nb
Giffen	55	9	218	4	-,-						
Travers	47	8	145	3	-,-		21	10	40	0	-,-
Hay	19	3	70	0	1,-	(1)	21.2	4	67	9	-,-
Reedman	13.5	3	47	2	-,-						
Evans	7	0	29	0	-,-						
Claxton	5	1	32	1	-,-						

ENGLAND XI	O	M	R	W	w,nb		O	M	R	W	w,nb
Thompson	28.3	6	85	9	-,1	(2)	39	5	113	3	-,-
Bosanquet	9	0	69	1	-,-	(5)	22	0	82	1	-,-
Trott	21	3	78	0	1,-		24.5	1	101	2	-,-
Dowson	3	0	14	0	-,-	(6)	20	3	62	3	-,-
Hargreave	6	0	30	0	1,-	(4)	9	1	37	0	-,-
Burnup	3	0	7	0	1,-	(1)	8	1	41	0	-,1

FALL OF WICKETS				
	ENG	SA	SA	ENG
Wkt	1st	1st	2nd	2nd
1st	106	6	1	16
2nd	170	21	138	16
3rd	269	75	209	16
4th	341	96	214	49
5th	421	115	275	49
6th	437	250	316	82
7th	455	261	316	92
8th	460	267	407	100
9th	550	272	415	104
10th	553	304	454	108

1903-04 SEASON (22 MATCHES)

The busiest first-class season yet was highlighted by the visit of the 16th English team. It was the first to tour under the banner of Marylebone Cricket Club, hence it became England's first official visit to Australia. In all, 20 matches were played on the tour, including five Tests and nine other first-class matches. The visitors took the Test series 3-2 and won six of the contests against the States, the remaining three being unfinished. For the first time the Englishmen played Tasmania on even terms.

R.E. 'Tip' Foster and Tom Hayward headed the batting aggregates in both Tests and first-class matches. Both exceeded 1000 runs in all games and a number of others gave good support - Tyldesley and Warner among them. But it was the varied attack of Rhodes, Hirst, Braund, Arnold and Bosanquet that gave the Englishmen the edge over Australia. Bosanquet created a sensation with his introduction of the googly, the offbreak with the legbreak action. It confused most of the opposition, despite being waywardly delivered at times.

Victor Trumper and Hugh Trumble enjoyed fine series for Australia in their respective departments, as did M.A.Noble, the premier allrounder. Trumble finished off the Test series and his own career with a hat-trick. Albert 'Tibby' Cotter, displaying extreme pace, emerged as a fine prospect.

New South Wales continued to dominate the Sheffield Shield competition, easily retaining the trophy for the third successive season. Points were allocated for each match for the first time, based on the simple formula of one point for a win and the deduction of one point for a loss. South Australia's home match against Victoria was again not played - as in 1901-02 - because of the heavy touring program. It would not have affected the outcome of the competition.

New South Wales fielded under-strength teams to win both their matches against Queensland. Christmas had by now become the customary time for the meeting between the teams at Sydney - coinciding with the New South Wales-Victoria Sheffield Shield fixture at Melbourne. The match between New South Wales and Queensland at Brisbane, however, was subject to change every season, and this year it was scheduled for February, only to take place at Easter. The QCA asked New South Wales to send a full-strength team to Brisbane in a bid to have players such as Trumper, Duff, Noble, etcetera as drawcards. They were partially appeased with the inclusion of Duff, Noble, Cotter, Carter and Hopkins in an otherwise inexperienced team. Two made first-class debuts - Warren Bardsley and Roger Hartigan.

Victoria won the remaining first-class fixture against Tasmania in early March. The Western Australian Cricket Association repeated recent attempts to draw either the MCC team or the South Australians to Perth for a first-class match, but both declined invitations.

Umpires this season were provided by the home association in all matches except Tests. The policy had been partially introduced the previous year, South Australia being the only State to reject the proposal. Prior to 1902, each visiting team brought their own umpire.

Leading Aggregates

Batsmen	M	I	NO	Runs	HS	Ave.	Bowlers	Runs	Wkts	Ave.
V.T.Trumper (NSW)	11	21	3	990	185*	55.00	W.Rhodes (MCC)	1055	65	16.23
M.A.Noble (NSW)	12	20	3	961	230	56.52	E.G.Arnold (MCC)	884	46	19.21
R.A.Duff (NSW)	11	20	1	938	271	49.36	A.J.Y.Hopkins (NSW)	935	39	23.97
R.E.Foster (MCC)	13	22	4	821	287	45.61	L.C.Braund (MCC)	729	37	19.70
C.Hill (SA)	10	20	0	794	147	39.70	M.A.Noble (NSW)	809	37	21.86
T.W.Hayward (MCC)	11	17	0	785	157	46.17	B.J.T.Bosanquet (MCC)	1009	37	27.27
P.F.Warner (MCC)	14	24	1	694	79	30.17	G.H.Hirst (MCC)	882	36	24.50
J.T.Tyldesley (MCC)	13	22	2	670	97	33.50	W.P.Howell (NSW)	854	31	27.54
B.J.T.Bosanquet (MCC)	12	19	3	587	124*	36.68	A.Cotter (NSW)	404	30	13.46
G.H.Hirst (MCC)	12	18	1	569	92	33.47	H.Trumble (V)	528	28	18.85
S.E.Gregory (NSW)	10	17	0	564	152	33.17				

SHEFFIELD SHIELD TABLE

	P	W	L	D Pts	Quotient	Runs Scored	Wkts Lost	Runs Conceded	Wkts Taken
NEW SOUTH WALES	4	3	1	- 2	1.637	2279	52	2141	80
VICTORIA	3	1	2	- -1	0.915	1586	60	1443	50
SOUTH AUSTRALIA	3	1	2	- -1	0.595	1600	60	1881	42
TOTAL	5	5	5	- 0	1.000	5465	172	5465	172

SOUTH AUSTRALIA v M.C.C.

Played at Adelaide Oval on November 7, 9, 10, 11, 1903. (Four-day match)
Toss : M.C.C.   Result : MATCH DRAWN.
Debuts: Nil.
12th Men: R.B.C.Rees (SA) and H.Strudwick (MCC).
Umpires: P.Argall and G.S.Downs.
Attendances: 6000, 7000, 4000, 2000.   Total: About 19,000.   Receipts: No figures published.
Close of Play: 1st day MCC 3/247 (Hayward 126, Braund 47); 2nd day SA 3/93 (Giffen 15, Travers 4); 3rd day SA (2) 2/191 (Hill 102,
    Giffen 16).

Warner's declaration of the MCC first innings at the tea adjournment on the second day caused a great deal of discussion. Although not without precedent in Australia (see Qld v NSW 1901-02 match 277), it had not occurred before in a match of such importance. It was considered illegal by most Australians, even though the match was one of a number of early games subjected to time restrictions. Warner (65 in 145 minutes, 7 fours) and Hayward (157 in 368 minutes, 19 fours) gave MCC a sound start which Braund (58 in 112 minutes, 5 fours) and Lilley (91 not out in 105 minutes, 11 fours) capitalized on. South Australia followed on after a disappointing display in the first innings. Clem Hill (116 in 190 minutes, 12 fours) returned to form and, with the assistance of Hack (54 in 158 minutes, 3 fours) and Jennings (77 not out in 95 minutes, 5 fours), avoided the humiliation of an innings defeat. Stumps were drawn at 3.00pm on the final day by mutual consent of the captains so that travel arrangements could be adhered to. Sources: *Wisden, C.B.O'Reilly, Sydney Morning Herald, Adelaide Advertiser, South Australian Register.*

M.C.C.

*P.F.Warner	c Jennings b Claxton	65
T.W.Hayward	c Hill b Travers	157
J.T.Tyldesley	c Giffen b Claxton	1
R.E.Foster	run out (Gehrs/Newland)	2
L.C.Braund	b Giffen	58
G.H.Hirst	c Evans b Claxton	37
B.J.T.Bosanquet	b Hay	19
†A.F.A.Lilley	not out	91
A.E.Relf	c Travers b Claxton	30
E.G.Arnold	not out	7
W.Rhodes	did not bat	
Extras	(b8, lb7, w1)	16
Total	(182.0 overs, 477 mins) (8 wkts dec)	483

SOUTH AUSTRALIA

F.T.Hack	b Rhodes	16		c Hayward b Rhodes	54
D.R.A.Gehrs	run out (Warner)	31		b Arnold	7
*C.Hill	st Lilley b Bosanquet	18		c Braund b Relf	116
G.Giffen	c Lilley b Arnold	22		c Braund b Relf	18
J.P.F.Travers	b Hirst	18	(5)	lbw b Relf	14
N.Claxton	b Arnold	11	(6)	not out	77
C.B.Jennings	not out	26		c Hirst b Braund	22
A.E.Evans	lbw b Hirst	0	(7)	c Braund b Rhodes	1
J.C.Reedman	c Lilley b Arnold	1	(9)	not out	13
†P.M.Newland	c Rhodes b Braund	10			
H.Hay	b Braund	0			
Extras	(b6, lb8, nb5)	19		(b10, lb5, w1, nb5)	21
Total	(72.0 overs, 178 mins)	172		(140.0 overs, 315 mins) (7 wkts)	343

SOUTH AUSTRALIA	O	M	R	W	w,nb
Travers	50	20	95	1	-,-
Giffen	46	7	129	1	-,-
Hay	30	11	67	1	1,-
Reedman	13	1	41	0	-,-
Claxton	26	2	76	4	-,-
Evans	10	2	37	0	-,-
Hack	6	1	13	0	-,-
Hill	1	0	9	0	-,-

M.C.C.	O	M	R	W	w,nb		O	M	R	W	w,nb
Hirst	17	8	19	2	-,-		17	5	32	0	1,2
Arnold	20	6	49	3	-,5		22	4	63	1	-,1
Braund	9	2	15	2	-,-	(6)	12	1	39	1	-,-
Bosanquet	13	0	38	1	-,-	(3)	21	4	62	0	-,-
Rhodes	11	2	27	1	-,-	(4)	41	11	78	2	-,1
Relf	2	1	5	0	-,-	(5)	27	10	48	3	-,1

FALL OF WICKETS

Wkt	MCC 1st	SA 1st	SA 2nd
1st	122	37	14
2nd	134	66	156
3rd	149	85	207
4th	266	104	208
5th	322	123	242
6th	336	133	244
7th	367	144	288
8th	446	147	-
9th	-	171	-
10th	-	172	-

VICTORIA v M.C.C.

Played at Melbourne Cricket Ground on November 13, 14, 16, 1903. (Four-day match)
Toss : Victoria.   Result : M.C.C. WON BY AN INNINGS AND 71 RUNS.
Debuts: Nil.
12th Men: C.M.Baker (Vic) and L.C.Braund (MCC).
Umpires: E.Barrass and R.M.Crockett.
Attendances: 5500, 13000, 5000.   Total: About 23,500.   Receipts: No figures published.
Close of Play: 1st day MCC 1/32 (Warner 18, Tyldesley 7); 2nd day MCC 5/376 (Hirst 81, Bosanquet 36).

P.Argall accompanied the MCC team from Adelaide, at Warner's invitation, to act as umpire for the visiting side. Warner had to withdraw the offer when told of the current MCC policy to allow local authorities to appoint the umpires. Horan replaced Giller (unavailable) in the Victorian team. Hirst dismissed McAlister with the fourth ball of the match and the home side never recovered. Tyldesley (90 in 210 minutes, 9 fours), Foster (71 in 155 minutes, 5 fours), Hirst (92 in 152 minutes, 7 fours) and Bosanquet (79 in 98 minutes, 1 five and 8 fours) combined to put MCC 281 runs ahead before Warner declared. Bruce (51 in 125 minutes, 2 fours) and McAlister (45 in 160 minutes, 4 fours) began the Victorian second innings soundly but there was little resistance after their departure. Rhodes (8 for 84) bowled well throughout the match. *Wisden* incorrectly gives Vic (1) Collins 3, extras 2. Sources: *Wisden, VCA Report, The Age, The Argus, The Herald, The Australasian, The Leader.*

VICTORIA

P.A.McAlister	b Hirst	0	(2)	b Bosanquet	45
W.Bruce	c Bosanquet b Relf	4	(1)	c Bosanquet b Rhodes	51
G.H.S.Trott	st Strudwick b Rhodes	20		c & b Rhodes	16
W.W.Armstrong	b Rhodes	28		c Hayward b Rhodes	35
M.Ellis	c Relf b Hirst	1	(6)	run out (Strudwick/Rhodes)	8
*F.J.Laver	b Fielder	26	(5)	c Relf b Fielder	23
J.F.Horan	c Strudwick b Fielder	25		c Strudwick b Fielder	1
B.J.Tuckwell	c Bosanquet b Rhodes	3	(9)	c Foster b Relf	11
F.B.Collins	lbw b Rhodes	0	(10)	not out	0
†J.E.Monfries	not out	41	(8)	c Relf b Fielder	4
J.V.Saunders	c Bosanquet b Rhodes	9		b Relf	2
Extras	(lb3, w2)	5		(b5, lb4, w1, nb4)	14
Total	(86.2 overs, 220 mins)	162		(111.4 overs, 256 mins)	210

M.C.C.

T.W.Hayward	c Armstrong b Saunders	6
*P.F.Warner	c Armstrong b Saunders	22
J.T.Tyldesley	c Laver b Armstrong	90
R.E.Foster	c Collins b Laver	71
A.E.Knight	c Trott b Ellis	47
G.H.Hirst	c Armstrong b Saunders	92
B.J.T.Bosanquet	b Laver	79
A.E.Relf	c Collins b Laver	8
W.Rhodes	not out	2
A.Fielder	) did not bat	
†H.Strudwick	)	
Extras	(b11, lb10, nb5)	26
Total	(143.0 overs, 388 mins) (8 wkts dec)	443

M.C.C.	O	M	R	W	w,nb		O	M	R	W	w,nb			FALL OF WICKETS	
Hirst	17	7	33	2	-,-		17	4	34	0	-,-			VIC	MCC	VIC
Relf	22	8	39	1	-,-	(3)	18.4	6	26	2	-,-	Wkt	1st	1st	2nd
Rhodes	20.2	8	26	5	1,-	(2)	40	15	58	3	-,-	1st	0	11	88
Bosanquet	7	0	31	0	-,-	(5)	13	1	43	1	-,-	2nd	10	36	116
Fielder	20	5	28	2	1,-	(4)	23	9	35	3	1,4	3rd	33	196	116
												4th	34	196	172
VICTORIA	O	M	R	W	w,nb							5th	81	292	188
Saunders	45	13	126	3	-,-							6th	81	396	188
Armstrong	44	11	73	1	-,-							7th	84	441	191
Collins	18	2	58	0	-,5							8th	84	443	204
Laver	21	3	76	3	-,-							9th	145	-	208
Trott	8	0	46	0	-,-							10th	162	-	210
Ellis	6	0	33	1	-,-										
Bruce	1	0	5	0	-,-										

NEW SOUTH WALES v M.C.C.

Played at Sydney Cricket Ground on November 20, 21, 23, 1903. (Four-day match)
Toss : M.C.C.　　　　　　　Result : NEW SOUTH WALES WON BY AN INNINGS AND 10 RUNS.
Debuts: New South Wales - A.D.W.Fisher (f/c).
12th Men: J.R.M.Mackay (NSW). No 12th named for MCC.
Umpires: R.Callaway and A.C.Jones.
Attendances: 11310, 26656, 2623.　　　Total: 40,589.　　　Receipts: £1699.
Close of Play: 1st day MCC 3/172 (Tyldesley 76, Braund 1); 2nd day NSW (2) 6/114 (Hickson 6).

Rain on the day preceding the match influenced Warner's decision to send New South Wales in to bat. Rhodes and Arnold used the conditions and ensured that "his action was adequately justified by the result" (*SMH*). Trumper (46 in 55 minutes, 5 fours) alone showed any fluency, to score his runs out of 67 added while he was at the wicket. Warner (46 in 102 minutes, 6 fours), Tyldesley (80 in 131 minutes, 13 fours) and Hirst (66 in 90 minutes, 12 fours) demonstrated greater skill as the wicket dried and conditions improved to put MCC in an unassailable position. New South Wales batted a second time on a now "perfect wicket" (*SMH*) but again were unable to cope with the MCC attack, particularly the legbreaks and googlies of Bosanquet. Only a second wicket stand from Duff (44 in 73 minutes, 6 fours) and C.W.Gregory threatened the English supremacy. Fisher, on debut, captured the wicket of Hayward with his 11th delivery and before conceding a run. Sources: *Wisden, NSWCA Report, Sydney Referee, Sydney Morning Herald, Town & Country Journal, Sydney Mail.*

NEW SOUTH WALES

V.T.Trumper	st Lilley b Rhodes	46		c Braund b Hirst	11
R.A.Duff	c Lilley b Arnold	14		c Lilley b Bosanquet	44
*M.A.Noble	c Lilley b Arnold	3	(8)	b Hirst	16
A.J.Y.Hopkins	c Braund b Rhodes	4	(9)	st Lilley b Braund	23
S.E.Gregory	lbw b Rhodes	25	(4)	c Arnold b Bosanquet	8
†J.J.Kelly	c Tyldesley b Rhodes	2	(10)	lbw b Bosanquet	12
W.P.Howell	c Arnold b Rhodes	9	(6)	c Relf b Arnold	8
C.W.Gregory	st Lilley b Rhodes	4	(3)	c Warner b Arnold	36
R.N.Hickson	c Rhodes b Arnold	0	(5)	c Warner b Braund	30
A.D.W.Fisher	c Foster b Arnold	0	(7)	lbw b Bosanquet	0
A.McBeath	not out	0		not out	0
Extras	(b1)	1		(b9, lb1, w1, nb2)	13
Total	(37.2 overs, 110 mins)	108		(74.4 overs, 215 mins)	201

M.C.C.

*P.F.Warner	run out (C.W.Gregory)	46
T.W.Hayward	c & b Fisher	13
J.T.Tyldesley	b Noble	80
R.E.Foster	c Howell b McBeath	35
L.C.Braund	c Trumper b McBeath	36
G.H.Hirst	b Howell	66
B.J.T.Bosanquet	c Howell b Noble	8
†A.F.A.Lilley	b Noble	3
E.G.Arnold	c Duff b Hopkins	14
A.E.Relf	b McBeath	12
W.Rhodes	not out	0
Extras	(b4, nb2)	6
Total	(137.4 overs, 348 mins)	319

M.C.C.	O	M	R	W	w,nb		O	M	R	W	w,nb
Hirst	7	2	22	0	-,-	(2)	18	6	36	2	-,2
Rhodes	17	2	55	6	-,-	(4)	7	2	17	0	-,-
Arnold	13.2	3	30	4	-,-	(1)	19	2	62	2	1,-
Bosanquet						(3)	19	1	60	4	-,-
Braund							11.4	2	13	2	-,-

NEW SOUTH WALES	O	M	R	W	w,nb
McBeath	37.4	14	72	3	-,-
Howell	26	10	48	1	-,-
Noble	34	8	81	3	-,1
Fisher	11	2	35	1	-,-
Trumper	8	0	34	0	-,1
Hopkins	21	10	43	1	-,-

FALL OF WICKETS

Wkt	NSW 1st	MCC 1st	NSW 2nd
1st	35	28	12
2nd	55	80	83
3rd	67	162	99
4th	68	176	101
5th	74	265	114
6th	86	276	114
7th	107	280	152
8th	108	297	164
9th	108	319	197
10th	108	319	201

AFCM No. 294/35
SSM No. 66/24

VICTORIA v SOUTH AUSTRALIA (Shield Match 1)

Played at Melbourne Cricket Ground on November 20, 21, 23, 24, 25, 1903. (Timeless match)
Toss : South Australia. Result : SOUTH AUSTRALIA WON BY 17 RUNS.
Debuts: Victoria - C.M.Baker (f/c). South Australia - R.B.C.Rees (f/c).
12th Men: R.M.Osborne (Vic) and J.H.Pellew (SA).
Umpires: R.M.Crockett and C.E.Over.
Attendances: 3000, 5000, 3000, 2500, "handful". Total: About 13,500. Receipts: £215.
Close of Play: 1st day SA 7/294 (Newland 6, Travers 1); 2nd day Vic 6/189 (Laver 38, Baker 3); 3rd day SA (2) 9/166 (Travers 18, Hay 10); 4th day Vic (2) 7/213 (Ellis 8).

Baker replaced D.F.Noonan (unavailable) in the selected Victorian side. Hill (chanceless 147 in 204 minutes, 17 fours) "played a superb innings" (*Age*) on the first day as wickets fell at regular intervals at the other end. Laver (79 not out in 178 minutes, 8 fours) virtually played a lone hand for Victoria after a steady beginning from his earlier batsmen. Trott (47 in 71 minutes, 7 fours and 59 in 126 minutes, 6 fours) "batted quite in his old form" (*Age*) in both innings but the batting of both sides was disappointing overall. Trott (7 for 76) also bowled well to complete a fine match. Rees, on debut, contributed ten wickets to his team's narrow victory and it was fitting that he captured the final wicket. *Wisden* incorrectly gives SA (2) Gehrs 47, Rees 8, Hay 12, extras 12, Trott 5/38. Sources: *Wisden, C.B.O'Reilly, The Age, The Argus, The Australasian.*

SOUTH AUSTRALIA

D.R.A.Gehrs	b Laver	34		c Laver b Trott	48
F.T.Hack	c Trott b Saunders	22		st Monfries b Saunders	15
*C.Hill	st Monfries b Laver	147		b Saunders	2
C.B.Jennings	c Monfries b Saunders	37		b Laver	23
N.Claxton	b Trott	12	(6)	c Bruce b Trott	7
A.E.Evans	run out (Trott/Monfries)	12	(7)	b Trott	11
J.C.Reedman	c Armstrong b Laver	6	(5)	c McAlister b Trott	20
†P.M.Newland	c Monfries b Saunders	8	(9)	c & b Collins	1
J.P.F.Travers	not out	40	(8)	c & b Trott	31
R.B.C.Rees	c Laver b Saunders	0		b Collins	2
H.Hay	lbw b Trott	5		not out	18
Extras	(b4, lb9, w5, nb1)	19		(b7, lb3, w1)	11
Total	(128.0 overs, 337 mins)	342		(78.1 overs, 215 mins)	189

VICTORIA

P.A.McAlister	st Newland b Rees	40	c Hill b Rees	30
W.Bruce	lbw b Hay	31	c Hill b Travers	38
G.H.S.Trott	c Jennings b Rees	47	c Reedman b Rees	59
W.W.Armstrong	b Rees	9	st Newland b Reedman	39
*F.J.Laver	not out	79	b Travers	5
M.Ellis	st Newland b Travers	7	b Hay	27
J.F.Horan	c Newland b Claxton	13	b Rees	1
C.M.Baker	lbw b Hay	4	b Reedman	16
†J.E.Monfries	c Jennings b Rees	36	not out	7
F.B.Collins	b Rees	1	b Hay	1
J.V.Saunders	b Rees	0	lbw b Rees	0
Extras	(w1)	1	(b13, lb4, w6)	23
Total	(117.5 overs, 293 mins)	268	(100.4 overs, 254 mins)	246

VICTORIA	O	M	R	W	w,nb		O	M	R	W	w,nb
Collins	26	7	52	0	-,1	(3)	15	6	35	2	-,-
Armstrong	15	5	21	0	-,-		13	2	28	0	-,-
Saunders	37	10	110	4	4,-	(1)	17	4	40	2	1,-
Laver	30	8	72	3	-,-		17	4	36	1	-,-
Ellis	9	0	31	0	1,-						
Trott	11	2	37	2	-,-	(5)	16.1	4	39	5	-,-

SOUTH AUSTRALIA	O	M	R	W	w,nb		O	M	R	W	w,nb
Hay	20	3	70	2	1,-		12	5	20	2	2,-
Claxton	19	6	43	1	-,-	(3)	7	1	20	0	3,-
Travers	33	9	56	1	-,-	(2)	29	7	74	2	-,-
Rees	33.5	6	80	6	-,-		35.4	7	61	4	-,-
Evans	2	1	1	0	-,-	(6)	4	1	20	0	1,-
Reedman	10	5	17	0	-,-	(5)	13	3	28	2	-,-

FALL OF WICKETS

Wkt	SA 1st	VIC 1st	SA 2nd	VIC 2nd
1st	43	55	27	75
2nd	101	97	33	81
3rd	186	122	76	175
4th	229	128	108	187
5th	258	144	117	188
6th	286	174	130	195
7th	287	194	138	213
8th	299	261	147	243
9th	303	268	149	245
10th	342	268	189	246

QUEENSLAND v M.C.C.

Played at Brisbane Cricket Ground (Woolloongabba) on November 27, 28, 30, 1903. (Three-day match)
Toss : Queensland.   Result : M.C.C. WON BY SIX WICKETS.
Debuts: Nil.
12th Men: C.F.Morgan (Qld). No 12th available for MCC.
Umpires: T.Muir and J.P.Orr.
Attendances: 4000, 13000, 2000.   Total: About 19,000.   Receipts: No figures published.
Close of Play: 1st day MCC 1/21 (Warner 11, Arnold 3); 2nd day Qld (2) 9/90 (Crouch 13).

Wisden states that this match was not considered first-class in Australia and excludes the figures from its first-class tour averages. However, the Queensland team was fully representative and, since the State had been accorded first-class status from 1893, there is no valid reason to exclude this match. The tourists took only eleven men to Brisbane - Hayward, Hirst and Tyldesley remaining in Sydney. Patrick was caught from the first ball of the match and he was fortunate to escape the ignominy of a "king pair" when missed by Arnold off Braund from his first ball in the second innings. Macdonald (59 in 222 minutes, 5 fours) and Evans (72 in 66 minutes, 2 fives and 10 fours) added 96 for the fourth wicket, the only substantial partnership in the match. Braund was caught from the last ball of the first over of the MCC innings. Knight (46 in 70 minutes, 5 fours) recorded the highest score for his team as MCC failed to reach the Queensland total. Braund and Arnold bowled them back into the match in the final session of the second day and a comfortable victory eventuated. The quality of the bowling accounted for the low scoring in the match as the weather was fine throughout and the pitch "played as fast and true in the last innings as in the first" (*Courier*). Sources: *Wisden, Brisbane Courier, Queensland Times, The Queenslander.*

QUEENSLAND

Batsman		Runs			Runs
C.W.Patrick	c Braund b Fielder	0	(2)	b Arnold	12
J.Carew	b Bosanquet	28	(1)	run out (Warner/Braund)	0
*A.A.Atkins	b Arnold	30		st Strudwick b Braund	3
R.Macdonald	lbw b Arnold	59		lbw b Braund	6
†W.T.Evans	c Foster b Rhodes	72		c Arnold b Fielder	27
J.J.Fitzgerald	c & b Braund	12		b Braund	2
E.R.Crouch	c Bosanquet b Braund	0		b Arnold	13
H.B.Griffith	lbw b Braund	8		c Relf b Braund	4
N.K.Foster	c Foster b Arnold	18		b Arnold	20
T.Byrnes	c Foster b Fielder	8		c Rhodes b Braund	0
A.Henry	not out	0		not out	0
Extras	(b1, nb6)	7		(lb3, nb1)	4
Total	(97.1 overs, 260 mins)	242		(48.4 overs, 139 mins)	91

M.C.C.

Batsman		Runs			Runs
L.C.Braund	c Foster b Henry	2			
*P.F.Warner	c Macdonald b Griffith	37	(1)	c Fitzgerald b Byrnes	4
E.G.Arnold	b Henry	34	(5)	c Atkins b Griffith	8
R.E.Foster	c & b Fitzgerald	21		not out	34
A.E.Knight	c Evans b Byrnes	46	(3)	b Griffith	25
B.J.T.Bosanquet	c Crouch b Byrnes	37		not out	20
A.F.A.Lilley	c Crouch b Byrnes	2			
A.E.Relf	b Byrnes	0	(2)	c Foster b Griffith	24
W.Rhodes	c Macdonald b Byrnes	6			
†H.Strudwick	c Macdonald b Griffith	17			
A.Fielder	not out	5			
Extras	(b4, lb1, nb3)	8		(b1, lb1, nb2)	4
Total	(53.0 overs, 167 mins)	215		(33.0 overs, 100 mins) (4 wkts)	119

M.C.C.	O	M	R	W	w,nb		O	M	R	W	w,nb
Fielder	14	4	30	2	-,4	(3)	7	1	15	1	-,1
Braund	25	8	54	3	-,-		19	4	50	5	-,-
Bosanquet	17	2	65	1	-,-						
Relf	8	5	10	0	-,2						
Arnold	23.1	11	38	3	-,-	(1)	17.4	12	16	3	-,-
Rhodes	10	0	38	1	-,-	(4)	5	1	6	0	-,-

QUEENSLAND	O	M	R	W	w,nb		O	M	R	W	w,nb
Henry	12	0	60	2	-,-		5	1	21	0	-,-
Byrnes	24	6	74	5	-,-		16	3	60	1	-,-
Griffith	15	1	59	2	-,1		12	5	34	3	-,2
Fitzgerald	2	0	14	1	-,2						

FALL OF WICKETS

Wkt	QLD 1st	MCC 1st	QLD 2nd	MCC 2nd
1st	0	6	7	12
2nd	46	65	12	47
3rd	70	99	16	66
4th	166	101	25	90
5th	178	162	29	-
6th	178	174	59	-
7th	188	191	63	-
8th	229	191	89	-
9th	241	194	90	-
10th	242	215	91	-

NEW SOUTH WALES v SOUTH AUSTRALIA (Shield Match 2)

Played at Sydney Cricket Ground on December 4, 5, 7, 8, 1903. (Timeless match)
Toss : New South Wales.   Result : NEW SOUTH WALES WON BY AN INNINGS AND 297 RUNS.
Debuts: New South Wales - F.B.Johnson (f/c). South Australia - J.H.Pellew (f/c).
12th Men: J.R.M.Mackay (NSW) and A.E.Evans (SA).
Umpires: A.C.Jones and J.Laing.
Attendances: 4404, 10747, 3175, 50.   Total: 18,376.   Receipts: £574.
Close of Play: 1st day NSW 4/472 (Noble 126); 2nd day SA 1/115 (Hack 31, Hill 83); 3rd day SA (2) 7/115 (Claxton 23).

Duff (271 in 280 minutes, 39 fours) and Noble (230 in 302 minutes, 32 fours) were involved in a fourth-wicket partnership of 293 for New South Wales, the highest first-class stand at the time for the fourth wicket outside England. Jennings kept wickets for South Australia from just before tea until stumps on the first day, due to an injury sustained by Newland. Evans substituted in the field. Pellew took over as wicket-keeper for the start of play on the second day. Gehrs was run out while attempting a second run from the second ball of the South Australian first innings. Hill (85 in 96 minutes) batted brilliantly late on the second day. Overnight rain led to South Australia's collapse. Hopkins did the hat-trick to wrap up the first innings, dismissing Newland, Rees and Hay. *Wisden* incorrectly gives SA team A.H.Pellew; NSW Kelly 12, extras 22, Rees 3/159, Travers 0/115, Claxton 4/127, Hack 0/30, Pellew 0/25; SA (2) Gehrs 3, Hack 14. *O'Reilly* incorrectly gives five days duration. Sources: *Wisden, C.B.O'Reilly, NSWCA Report, Sydney Morning Herald, Town & Country Journal.*

NEW SOUTH WALES

V.T.Trumper	c Newland b Reedman	26
R.A.Duff	c Hack b Gehrs	271
C.W.Gregory	c Newland b Claxton	24
A.J.Y.Hopkins	lbw b Hay	13
*M.A.Noble	b Rees	230
S.E.Gregory	c Travers b Claxton	57
R.N.Hickson	b Rees	6
†J.J.Kelly	c Gehrs b Claxton	14
W.P.Howell	not out	18
F.B.Johnson	b Claxton	1
A.McBeath	lbw b Rees	1
Extras	(b10, lb8, w2)	20
Total	(170.0 overs, 470 mins)	681

SOUTH AUSTRALIA

F.T.Hack	st Kelly b McBeath	49		b McBeath	13
D.R.A.Gehrs	run out (S.E.Gregory/Kelly)	1	(4)	b Hopkins	4
*C.Hill	c Howell b McBeath	85		c C.W.Gregory b McBeath	9
C.B.Jennings	b Howell	1	(5)	b Howell	26
N.Claxton	b McBeath	2	(6)	b Hopkins	54
J.C.Reedman	b Howell	24	(7)	c Kelly b McBeath	29
J.P.F.Travers	lbw b Johnson	11	(8)	c S.E.Gregory b Hopkins	4
J.H.Pellew	not out	30	(2)	c Noble b Hopkins	5
†P.M.Newland	b Hopkins	3		b Hopkins	12
R.B.C.Rees	c & b Hopkins	0		b Johnson	8
H.Hay	c Kelly b Hopkins	0		not out	8
Extras	(b1, lb1, w1)	3		(b2, lb1)	3
Total	(90.3 overs, 230 mins)	209		(61.5 overs, 170 mins)	175

SOUTH AUSTRALIA	O	M	R	W	w,nb
Rees	47	6	160	3	-,-
Hay	14	0	68	1	-,-
Travers	31	3	117	0	-,-
Reedman	15	0	91	1	1,-
Claxton	42	5	115	4	-,-
Hack	10	1	40	0	1,-
Pellew	4	0	26	0	-,-
Gehrs	5	0	28	1	-,-
Hill	2	0	16	0	-,-

NEW SOUTH WALES	O	M	R	W	w,nb		O	M	R	W	w,nb
Howell	30	5	64	2	-,-	(3)	10	3	28	1	-,-
McBeath	24	7	42	3	1,-		17	3	40	3	-,-
Johnson	20	4	44	1	-,-	(4)	13	1	48	1	-,-
Hopkins	5.3	0	28	3	-,-	(1)	20.5	6	49	5	-,-
Trumper	4	2	7	0	-,-		1	0	7	0	-,-
Noble	7	1	21	0	-,-						

FALL OF WICKETS

	NSW	SA	SA
Wkt	1st	1st	2nd
1st	64	2	18
2nd	141	119	18
3rd	179	120	20
4th	472	127	33
5th	608	164	62
6th	629	166	109
7th	656	202	115
8th	660	209	129
9th	678	209	149
10th	681	209	175

AUSTRALIA v ENGLAND (1st Test)

Played at Sydney Cricket Ground on December 11, 12, 14, 15, 16, 17, 1903. (Timeless match)
Toss : Australia.   Result : ENGLAND WON BY FIVE WICKETS.
Debuts: England - E.G.Arnold, B.J.T.Bosanquet, R.E.Foster, A.E.Relf (all Test).
12th Men: C.B.Jennings (Aust) and A.E.Knight (Eng).
Umpires: R.M.Crockett and A.C.Jones.
Attendances: 17351, 35499, 13628, 11451, 17335, 1075.   Total: 96,339.   Receipts: £4274.
Close of Play: 1st day Aust 7/259 (Noble 131); 2nd day Eng 4/243 (Foster 73, Braund 67); 3rd day Aust (2) 0/16 (Gregory 6, Kelly 5);
    4th day Aust (2) 5/367 (Trumper 119, Armstrong 14); 5th day Eng (2) 4/122 (Hayward 60, Hirst 21).

Arnold captured the wicket of Trumper with his first ball in Test cricket. Noble, in his first match as Australian captain, rescued his side from a perilous position by scoring his sole Test century, a chanceless 133 in 287 minutes with 16 fours. With Armstrong (48 in 122 minutes, 4 fours) he added 106. Foster's 287 on debut (419 minutes, 37 fours) remained the highest Test innings in Australia until 1931-32. He gave two chances - on 51, when Gregory got one hand to a drive off Saunders, and on 134, to Hill at short leg off Saunders - and progressed from 109* to 203* in the lunch-tea session on the third day. He shared century century partnerships with Braund (102 in 171 minutes, 15 fours) and Relf (31 in 86 minutes, 2 fours) before adding a record 130 in 66 minutes for the tenth wicket with Rhodes. Tyldesley (53 in 66 minutes, 8 fours) also batted well. Trumper (chanceless 185 not out in 230 minutes, 26 fours) "gave an exhibition impossible to describe in too high terms" (*SMH*). He brought up his 1000th Test run when 14 and reached his century in a mere 94 minutes. Duff (84 in 130 minutes, 7 fours) and Hill (51 in 105 minutes) scored half-centuries. The dismissal of Hill, who was given out by umpire Crockett while attempting a fifth run from an overthrow, caused an immediate uproar among the crowd and howls of "Crock, Crock, Crock!". Hill was adamant that he had made his ground and Warner came close to taking his men from the field as the disturbance continued. Hayward (91 in 240 minutes, 6 fours) and Hirst (60 not out in 135 minutes, 9 fours) saw England to victory on the sixth morning, adding 99. Sources: *Wisden, The Age, Sydney Morning Herald.*

AUSTRALIA

R.A.Duff	c Lilley b Arnold	3	(3)	c Relf b Rhodes	84
V.T.Trumper	c Foster b Arnold	1	(5)	not out	185
C.Hill	c Lilley b Hirst	5	(4)	run out (Relf/Lilley)	51
*M.A.Noble	c Foster b Arnold	133	(6)	st Lilley b Bosanquet	22
W.W.Armstrong	b Bosanquet	48	(7)	c Bosanquet b Rhodes	27
A.J.Y.Hopkins	b Hirst	39	(8)	c Arnold b Rhodes	20
W.P.Howell	c Relf b Arnold	5	(10)	c Lilley Arnold	4
S.E.Gregory	b Bosanquet	23	(1)	c Lilley b Rhodes	43
F.J.Laver	lbw b Rhodes	4		c Relf b Rhodes	6
†J.J.Kelly	c Braund b Rhodes	10	(2)	b Arnold	13
J.V.Saunders	not out	11		run out (Hirst/Rhodes/Lilley)	2
Extras	(nb3)	3		(b10, lb15, w2, nb1)	28
Total	(118.2 overs, 309 mins)	285		(145.2 overs, 415 mins)	485

ENGLAND

T.W.Hayward	b Howell	15		st Kelly b Saunders	91
*P.F.Warner	c Kelly b Laver	0		b Howell	8
J.T.Tyldesley	b Noble	53		c Noble b Saunders	9
E.G.Arnold	c Laver b Armstrong	27			
R.E.Foster	c Noble b Saunders	287	(4)	st Kelly b Armstrong	19
L.C.Braund	b Howell	102	(5)	c Noble b Howell	0
G.H.Hirst	b Howell	0	(6)	not out	60
B.J.T.Bosanquet	c Howell b Noble	2	(7)	not out	1
†A.F.A.Lilley	c Hill b Noble	4			
A.E.Relf	c Armstrong b Saunders	31			
W.Rhodes	not out	40			
Extras	(b6, lb7, w1, nb2)	16		(b3, lb1, w2)	6
Total	(181.2 overs, 482 mins)	577		(95.5 overs, 255 mins) (5 wkts)	194

ENGLAND	O	M	R	W	w,nb		O	M	R	W	w,nb
Hirst	24	8	47	2	-,2		29	1	79	0	1,-
Arnold	32	7	76	4	-,-		28	2	93	2	-,1
Braund	26	9	39	0	-,-	(5)	12	2	56	0	-,-
Bosanquet	13	0	52	2	-,-		23	1	100	1	1,-
Rhodes	17.2	3	41	2	-,-	(3)	40.2	10	94	5	-,-
Relf	6	1	27	0	-,1		13	5	35	0	-,-

AUSTRALIA	O	M	R	W	w,nb		O	M	R	W	w,nb
Saunders	36.2	8	125	2	-,-	(3)	18.5	3	51	2	2,-
Laver	37	12	119	1	-,-	(4)	16	4	37	0	-,-
Howell	31	7	111	3	-,-	(2)	31	18	35	2	-,-
Noble	34	8	99	3	1,2	(1)	12	2	37	0	-,-
Armstrong	23	3	47	1	-,-		18	6	28	1	-,-
Hopkins	11	1	40	0	-,-						
Trumper	7	2	12	0	-,-						
Gregory	2	0	8	0	-,-						

FALL OF WICKETS

Wkt	AUST 1st	ENG 1st	AUST 2nd	ENG 2nd
1st	2	0	36	21
2nd	9	49	108	39
3rd	12	73	191	81
4th	118	117	254	82
5th	200	309	334	181
6th	207	311	393	-
7th	259	318	441	-
8th	263	332	468	-
9th	271	447	473	-
10th	285	577	485	-

SOUTH AUSTRALIA v NEW SOUTH WALES (Shield Match 3)

Played at Adelaide Oval on December 19, 21, 22, 23, 1903. (Timeless match)
Toss : New South Wales.   Result : NEW SOUTH WALES WON BY EIGHT WICKETS.
Debuts: Nil.
12th Men: J.H.Pellew (SA) and R.A.Duff (NSW).
Umpires: P.Argall and T.A.Reeves.
Attendances: 3000, 1000, 1000, 500.   Total: About 5500.   Receipts: No figures published.
Close of Play: 1st day NSW 3/272 (Trumper 47, Noble 39); 2nd day SA 1/34 (Gehrs 18, Travers 3); 3rd day SA (2) 2/62 (Gehrs 22, Travers 4).

The match began at 2.00pm and only two sessions were played on the first day to allow Test players, Duff, S.E.Gregory, Hill, Hopkins, Kelly, Noble and Trumper, to rest after arriving in Adelaide on the morning of December 19th. Duff was made 12th man due to a sore heel. C.W.Gregory (97 in 162 minutes, 1 five and 10 fours), Trumper (61 in 60 minutes, 6 fours), Noble (147 in 202 minutes, 1 five and 18 fours) and S.E.Gregory (152 in 180 minutes, 24 fours) stood out for the visitors, Noble and S.E.Gregory adding 202 for the sixth wicket in 180 minutes. Mackay was out to the sixth and last ball of the opening over in the second innings. Hill (89 in 115 minutes, 9 fours), Newland (77 in 90 minutes, 1 five and 10 fours), Travers (77 in 160 minutes, 7 fours) and Gehrs (159 in 247 minutes, 1 five and 19 fours) topscored for South Australia. Last appearance in first-class cricket by George Giffen. He made his debut in South Australia's first-ever match in 1877-78. *Wisden* incorrectly gives SA (2) Giffen 6, Newland 21. Sources: *Wisden, C.B.O'Reilly, NSWCA Report, Sydney Morning Herald, South Australian Register.*

NEW SOUTH WALES

C.W.Gregory	c Rees b Claxton	97	(3) st Newland b Travers		27
B.W.Farquhar	c Newland b Claxton	31	not out		29
J.R.M.Mackay	c Hack b Claxton	56	(1) b Hay		0
V.T.Trumper	c Hack b Claxton	61	not out		6
*M.A.Noble	c Hay b Gehrs	147			
A.J.Y.Hopkins	c Claxton b Travers	19			
S.E.Gregory	c Newland b Travers	152			
†J.J.Kelly	c Newland b Claxton	4			
W.P.Howell	c Newland b Hack	39			
A.McBeath	not out	0			
F.B.Johnson	lbw b Hack	2			
Extras	(b6, lb9, w1)	16			—
Total	(151.4 overs, 415 mins)	624	(18.0 overs, 45 mins) (2 wkts)		62

SOUTH AUSTRALIA

F.T.Hack	c & b Johnson	10	c Hopkins b Trumper		13
D.R.A.Gehrs	c Hopkins b Howell	35	(3) b McBeath		159
J.P.F.Travers	b McBeath	23	(4) lbw b Noble		77
*C.Hill	c Trumper b Johnson	89	(5) b McBeath		23
C.B.Jennings	c Kelly b Noble	15	(6) lbw b McBeath		2
G.Giffen	b Hopkins	1	(8) b Howell		5
N.Claxton	b Noble	19	lbw b Howell		23
J.C.Reedman	c Kelly b Noble	10	(9) not out		9
†P.M.Newland	c Hopkins b Noble	77	(2) c Noble b Johnson		22
R.B.C.Rees	b Noble	45	b Howell		0
H.Hay	not out	5	b Howell		4
Extras	(b4, lb3, w2)	9	(b7, lb3)		10
Total	(107.4 overs, 295 mins)	338	(118.2 overs, 320 mins)		347

SOUTH AUSTRALIA	O	M	R	W	w,nb		O	M	R	W	w,nb		FALL OF WICKETS			
Rees	17	2	70	0	-,-	(4)	3	0	24	0	-,-		NSW	SA	SA	NSW
Hay	11	0	65	0	-,-	(1)	5	2	10	1	-,-	Wkt	1st	1st	2nd	2nd
Travers	30	4	93	2	1,-		4	3	2	1	-,-	1st	83	26	19	0
Giffen	29	2	134	0	-,-							2nd	177	61	48	46
Claxton	36	5	129	5	-,-	(2)	5	2	18	0	-,-	3rd	192	71	243	-
Reedman	15	0	60	0	-,-							4th	290	120	286	-
Hack	10.4	1	39	2	-,-							5th	332	121	292	-
Gehrs	3	0	18	1	-,-							6th	534	187	327	-
Jennings						(5)	1	0	8	0	-,-	7th	543	205	333	-
												8th	622	205	343	-
NEW SOUTH WALES	O	M	R	W	w,nb		O	M	R	W	w,nb	9th	622	311	343	-
Howell	22	4	80	1	-,-	(6)	21.2	3	64	4	-,-	10th	624	338	347	-
Johnson	18	4	52	2	-,-	(3)	14	0	35	1	-,-					
McBeath	28	5	70	1	1,-	(4)	28	10	77	3	-,-					
Hopkins	9	1	27	1	1,-	(1)	27	5	62	0	-,-					
Noble	23.4	3	67	5	-,-		18	3	54	1	-,-					
Trumper	5	0	21	0	-,-	(2)	8	0	38	1	-,-					
Farquhar	2	0	12	0	-,-		2	0	7	0	-,-					

VICTORIA v NEW SOUTH WALES (Shield Match 4)

Played at Melbourne Cricket Ground on December 26, 28, 29, 30, 31, 1903. (Timeless match)
Toss : Victoria.   Result : VICTORIA WON BY 161 RUNS.
Debuts: Nil.
12th Men: F.B.Johnson (NSW). No 12th man or emergency named for Victoria (see below).
Umpires: E.Barrass and R.M.Crockett.
Attendances: 7000, 14000, 4000, 4000, 1000.   Total: About 30,000.   Receipts: £768.
Close of Play: 1st day Vic 7/276 (Trumble 63, McLeod 13); 2nd day Vic 7/287 (Trumble 68, McLeod 17); 3rd day Vic (2) 0/29
  (McAlister 16, Giller 10); 4th day NSW (2) 5/82 (Noble 2).

Hugh Trumble returned to first-class cricket for his first match since returning from the 1902 England tour. He had announced his retirement from the game after that tour but had been persuaded to return to oppose the visiting English team. He held the Victorian first innings together (80 in 176 minutes, 9 fours) after Bruce had been bowled by the first ball of the match. Stuckey (81 not out in 105 minutes, 9 fours), in the second innings, was the only other local player to exceed 50. Steady rainfall restricted the second day's play to 20 minutes. McLeod utilised the "bowler's wicket" (*Age*) to destroy the New South Wales first innings and give his team the advantage that ensured victory. Duff (41 in 41 minutes, 4 fours and 51 in 76 minutes, 4 fours) and Trumper (43 in 50 minutes, 1 five and 2 fours and 68 in 63 minutes, 8 fours) showed their skill in both innings. Clem Hill, in Melbourne for the Second Test, fielded as substitute for Stuckey, who arrived late, during the early overs of the final day. *Wisden* incorrectly gives NSW (2) McBeath c & b Trumper. Sources: *Wisden, NSWCA Report, The Age, The Argus, The Herald, The Australasian, The Leader.*

VICTORIA

W.Bruce	b McBeath	0	(4)	b Hopkins	26
P.A.McAlister	b Noble	34	(1)	b Howell	39
W.W.Armstrong	c Kelly b Noble	44		b Howell	1
G.H.S.Trott	c Noble b Hopkins	38	(5)	c Noble b Hopkins	35
J.F.Giller	c S.E.Gregory b Hopkins	14	(2)	c Hopkins b Howell	12
*H.Trumble	c Duff b Noble	80		st Kelly b Hopkins	9
F.J.Laver	b Farquhar	49		b Hopkins	0
J.H.Stuckey	b Howell	14	(9)	not out	81
C.E.McLeod	not out	30	(8)	st Kelly b McBeath	26
†J.E.Monfries	c Kelly b Noble	0		c Howell b Hopkins	9
J.V.Saunders	lbw b Howell	0		c & b Howell	6
Extras	(b3, lb2, w2, nb2)	9		(b1, lb4, w4)	9
Total	(132.1 overs, 350 mins)	312		(112.4 overs, 286 mins)	253

NEW SOUTH WALES

R.A.Duff	lbw b Trumble	41		c Monfries b Trumble	51
†J.J.Kelly	c Bruce b Trumble	31	(11)	c McLeod b Trott	2
V.T.Trumper	b Laver	43	(7)	st Monfries b Trott	68
*M.A.Noble	b McLeod	8	(6)	lbw b Laver	23
S.E.Gregory	c & b McLeod	2	(8)	c Monfries b Trott	6
A.J.Y.Hopkins	c Trumble b McLeod	7	(9)	not out	26
C.W.Gregory	b McLeod	18	(10)	b Trott	15
J.R.M.Mackay	c Trumble b McLeod	?	(3)	c Monfries b Laver	25
B.W.Farquhar	c Armstrong b McLeod	3	(2)	c Laver b Saunders	3
W.P.Howell	c Saunders b McLeod	18	(4)	c Monfries b Laver	0
A.McBeath	not out	0	(5)	c & b Trumble	0
Extras	(b10)	10		(lb2)	2
Total	(50.5 overs, 152 mins)	183		(66.0 overs, 191 mins)	221

NEW SOUTH WALES	O	M	R	W	w,nb		O	M	R	W	w,nb
McBeath	36	14	63	1	1,-		21	9	37	1	1,-
Noble	35	12	68	4	-,2		22	9	41	0	-,-
Hopkins	22	6	57	2	-,-	(4)	30	13	70	5	3,-
Howell	27.1	5	67	2	-,-	(3)	39.4	12	94	4	-,-
Farquhar	10	1	40	1	1,-						
Trumper	2	0	8	0	-,-	(5)	1	0	2	0	-,-

VICTORIA	O	M	R	W	w,nb		O	M	R	W	w,nb
Laver	16	5	44	1	-,-	(5)	12	3	31	3	-,-
Trumble	15	1	67	2	-,-	(3)	15	2	63	2	-,-
Saunders	8	1	28	0	-,-	(1)	17	4	54	1	-,-
McLeod	11.5	2	34	7	-,-	(2)	9	0	27	0	-,-
Armstrong						(4)	3	1	10	0	-,-
Trott							10	1	34	4	-,-

FALL OF WICKETS

Wkt	VIC 1st	NSW 1st	VIC 2nd	NSW 2nd
1st	0	61	37	11
2nd	66	84	49	80
3rd	97	113	69	80
4th	129	129	103	80
5th	132	131	127	82
6th	216	148	128	163
7th	237	154	131	176
8th	305	163	190	181
9th	309	183	220	215
10th	312	183	253	221

NEW SOUTH WALES v QUEENSLAND

Played at Sydney Cricket Ground on December 26, 28, 29, 30, 1903. (Timeless match)
Toss : New South Wales.　　　　Result : NEW SOUTH WALES WON BY 2 RUNS.
Debuts: New South Wales - M.H.Blaxland, T.H.Foster, D.A.Gee (all f/c), G.G.Black (NSW only).
12th Men: A.Haddon (NSW) and G.S.Crouch (Qld).
Umpires: R.Callaway and W.G.Curran.
Attendances: 3000, 1000, 250, 50.　　　　Total: About 4300.　　　　Receipts: £51.
Close of Play: 1st day Qld 0/6 (Byrnes 2, Miller 2); 2nd day NSW (2) 3/23 (Carter 7, Diamond 5); 3rd day Qld (2) 2/172 (Foster 69, Macdonald 10).

Queensland omitted J.W.Lewis and relegated Crouch to the position of 12th man from their selected squad of thirteen. Top scorers for New South Wales were Black, playing his only match for New South Wales, (72 in 81 minutes, 12 fours) and Bowden (57 in 78 minutes, 9 fours). For Queensland, Macdonald (62 not out in 204 minutes, 8 fours) and Evans (78 in 78 minutes, 1 five and 12 fours) established a new State fourth-wicket record partnership of 122. In the second innings, Foster made 131 in 270 minutes with 13 fours and Patrick 56 in 95 minutes with 7 fours. Apart from the players themselves, hardly a soul was present at the ground on the fourth day to witness the close finish. Black had appeared once for London County in 1903. *Cricket* gives incorrect details for Qld (2) Carew, Macdonald, Evans, Bowden bowling; dismissal of Bowden (1) and Hickson (2). Sources: *Cricket, NSWCA Report, Sydney Referee, Sydney Morning Herald, Town & Country Journal.*

NEW SOUTH WALES

M.H.Blaxland	c Miller b Byrnes	15	(8)	lbw b Fitzgerald	9
R.N.Hickson	c Griffith b Byrnes	50	(1)	c Evans b Henry	4
T.H.Foster	b Byrnes	8	(10)	c & b Fitzgerald	0
L.W.Pye	c & b Griffith	4	(7)	b Fitzgerald	32
*A.Diamond	b Miller	21		b Byrnes	39
N.Y.Deane	c Foster b Byrnes	11	(3)	c Fitzgerald b Byrnes	0
D.A.Gee	c Griffith b Miller	43	(2)	b Henry	7
G.G.Black	b Fitzgerald	72	(6)	b Henry	31
A.J.Bowden	c Evans b Byrnes	57		not out	6
A.D.W.Fisher	b Griffith	23	(11)	b Henry	5
†H.Carter	not out	16	(4)	c sub (G.S.Crouch) b Miller	38
Extras	(b8, lb2, w3, nb1)	14		(b5, lb1, w3)	9
Total	(84.2 overs, 250 mins)	334		(57.4 overs, 172 mins)	180

QUEENSLAND

T.Byrnes	st Carter b Pye	7	(9)	c & b Deane	0
D.L.Miller	c Black b Pye	9	(8)	c Pye b Bowden	6
J.Carew	c Carter b Deane	15		c Gee b Pye	16
R.Macdonald	not out	62		b Deane	22
†W.T.Evans	c Blaxland b Pye	78		st Carter b Bowden	15
C.W.Patrick	c & b Bowden	0	(1)	b Fisher	56
*A.A.Atkins	st Carter b Black	6		b Bowden	1
J.J.Fitzgerald	st Carter b Black	5	(6)	c Carter b Fisher	14
N.K.Foster	b Bowden	21	(2)	c Fisher b Bowden	131
H.B.Griffith	lbw b Bowden	6		b Bowden	0
A.Henry	c Diamond b Bowden	0		not out	0
Extras	(b2, lb3, nb8)	13		(b18, lb5, w1, nb5)	29
Total	(102.4 overs, 265 mins)	222		(110.0 overs, 285 mins)	290

QUEENSLAND	O	M	R	W	w,nb		O	M	R	W	w,nb		FALL OF WICKETS			
Henry	18	3	57	0	1,-	(2)	19.4	5	49	4	3,-			NSW	QLD	NSW	QLD
Byrnes	29	6	112	5	-,-	(1)	14	5	20	2	-,-	Wkt	1st	1st	2nd	2nd
Griffith	15.2	2	70	2	-,1							1st	48	16	10	115
Miller	14	2	49	2	2,-	(3)	10	2	50	1	-,-	2nd	66	30	11	149
Fitzgerald	8	1	32	1	-,-	(4)	14	3	52	3	-,-	3rd	71	36	13	207
												4th	87	158	68	230
NEW SOUTH WALES	O	M	R	W	w,nb		O	M	R	W	w,nb	5th	105	158	97	253
Fisher	18	8	32	0	-,6	(3)	17	4	41	2	1,3	6th	144	173	151	274
Pye	28	9	49	3	-,-	(4)	20	4	35	1	-,-	7th	169	183	167	287
Deane	26	13	39	1	-,-	(2)	34	8	66	2	-,1	8th	277	216	167	290
Black	13	5	41	2	-,2	(5)	7	1	32	0	-,1	9th	294	222	167	290
Bowden	13.4	2	38	4	-,-	(1)	29	6	70	5	-,-	10th	334	222	180	290
Gee	4	1	10	0	-,-		3	0	17	0	-,-					

AUSTRALIA v ENGLAND (2nd Test)

Played at Melbourne Cricket Ground on January 1, 2, 4, 5, 1904. (Timeless match)
Toss : England.   Result : ENGLAND WON BY 185 RUNS.
Debuts: England - A.Fielder, A.E.Knight (both Test).
12th Men: D.R.A.Gehrs (Aust) and H.Strudwick (Eng).
Umpires: P.Argall and R.M.Crockett.
Attendances: 32000, 20500, 12500, 9500.   Total: About 74,500.   Receipts: £3359.
Close of Play: 1st day Eng 2/221 (Tyldesley 46, Foster 49); 2nd day Eng 6/306 (Tyldesley 97); 3rd day Eng (2) 5/74 (Tyldesley 48).

E.G.Arnold and B.J.T.Bosanquet were unable to play due to injury. Fielder, selected solely for his bowling, was not called upon in either innings. Foster woke up on the second day with a severe chill and was unable to take any further part in the game. Despite the pitch on the first day being "all that could be desired" (*Age*), England progressed slowly, scoring 2/221, Warner (68 in 170 minutes, 8 fours), Hayward (58 in 155 minutes, 2 fours) and Tyldesley (97 in 225 minutes, 8 fours) compiling half-centuries. Showers restricted play to the lunch-tea session on the second day and conditions began to get difficult by the close of play. There was no play before 1.20pm on the third day, by which time the wicket was sticky, and Trumper's 74 in 112 minutes (1 five and 5 fours) was of the highest calibre considering the state of the ground. He was, however, let off at 3 (by Lilley), 50 (Hayward at long-on), 59 (Warner at point) and 73 (substitute Strudwick in the long field): all of Rhodes who bowled unchanged throughout both Australian innings and returned magnificent figures of 15 for 124, which remained the best in a Test match in Australia until 1985-86. Heavy overnight rain and morning showers prevented play before 3.30pm on the fourth day, and the remaining 14 wickets fell before the day was out. Tyldesley (62 in 78 minutes, 2 fives and 6 fours), who batted on all four days, and Trumper (35 in 52 minutes, 1 five and 4 fours) were the respective top scorers. Some recent publications incorrectly give Aust (1) 7/97; Eng (2) 1/5. Sources: *Wisden, The Age, The Argus, The Australasian*.

ENGLAND

*P.F.Warner	c Duff b Trumble	68		c Trumper b Saunders	3
T.W.Hayward	c Gregory b Hopkins	58		c Trumper b Trumble	0
J.T.Tyldesley	c Trumble b Howell	97		c Trumble b Howell	62
R.E.Foster	retired ill	49		absent ill	-
L.C.Braund	c Howell b Trumble	20	(4)	b Saunders	3
A.E.Knight	b Howell	2	(7)	lbw b Trumble	0
G.H.Hirst	c Noble b Howell	7	(5)	c Gregory b Howell	4
W.Rhodes	lbw b Trumble	2	(6)	lbw b Trumble	9
†A.F.A.Lilley	c Howell b Trumble	4	(8)	st Kelly b Trumble	0
A.E.Relf	not out	3	(9)	not out	10
A.Fielder	b Howell	1	(10)	c Hill b Trumble	4
Extras	(lb3, w1)	4		(b7, lb1)	8
Total	(152.5 overs, 405 mins)	315		(28.5 overs, 91 mins)	103

AUSTRALIA

R.A.Duff	st Lilley b Rhodes	10		c Braund b Rhodes	8
V.T.Trumper	c Tyldesley b Rhodes	74		c Relf b Rhodes	35
C.Hill	c Rhodes b Hirst	5		c Relf b Rhodes	20
*M.A.Noble	c sub (H.Strudwick) b Rhodes	0		not out	31
S.E.Gregory	c Hirst b Rhodes	1		c Rhodes b Hirst	0
A.J.Y.Hopkins	c sub (H.Strudwick) Relf	18		c & b Rhodes	7
H.Trumble	c sub (H.Strudwick) b Rhodes	2		c Braund b Rhodes	0
W.W.Armstrong	c Braund b Rhodes	1		c Hayward b Rhodes	0
†J.J.Kelly	run out (Lilley)	8		c Lilley b Rhodes	7
W.P.Howell	c Fielder b Rhodes	0		c Hirst b Rhodes	3
J.V.Saunders	not out	2		c Fielder b Hirst	0
Extras	(lb1)	1			-
Total	(30.2 overs, 112 mins)	122		(29.4 overs, 115 mins)	111

AUSTRALIA	O	M	R	W	w,nb		O	M	R	W	w,nb
Trumble	50	10	107	4	-,-		10.5	2	34	5	-,-
Noble	6	3	4	0	-,-						
Saunders	16	3	60	0	-,-	(2)	8	0	33	2	-,-
Howell	34.5	14	43	4	-,-	(3)	8	3	25	2	-,-
Armstrong	25	6	43	0	-,-						
Hopkins	20	2	50	1	1,-	(4)	2	1	3	0	-,-
Trumper	1	0	4	0	-,-						

ENGLAND	O	M	R	W	w,nb		O	M	R	W	w,nb
Rhodes	15.2	3	56	7	-,-		15	0	68	8	-,-
Hirst	8	1	33	1	-,-		13.4	4	38	2	-,-
Relf	2	0	12	1	-,-		1	0	5	0	-,-
Braund	5	0	20	0	-,-						

FALL OF WICKETS

Wkt	ENG 1st	AUST 1st	ENG 2nd	AUST 2nd
1st	122	14	3	14
2nd	132	23	7	59
3rd	277	23	27	73
4th	279	33	40	77
5th	297	67	74	86
6th	306	73	74	90
7th	306	79	74	90
8th	314	105	90	102
9th	315	116	103	105
10th	-	122	-	111

AUSTRALIA v ENGLAND (3rd Test)

Played at Adelaide Oval on January 15, 16, 18, 19, 20, 1904. (Timeless match)
Toss : Australia.   Result : AUSTRALIA WON BY 216 RUNS.
Debuts: Nil.
12th Men: D.R.A.Gehrs (Aust) and A.E.Knight (Eng).
Umpires: P.Argall and R.M.Crockett.
Attendances: 10000, 18000, 7000, 4500, 3500.   Total: 42,962.   Receipts: £2023.
Close of Play: 1st day Aust 6/355 (Noble 38, Trumble 4); 2nd day Eng 8/199 (Arnold 11); 3rd day Aust (2) 4/263 (Noble 52); 4th day
    Eng (2) 2/150 (Warner 79).

Partnerships of 129 in 88 minutes and 143 in 101 minutes for the first two wickets, involving Duff (79 in 88 minutes, 13 fours), Trumper
(chanceless 113 in 189 minutes, 12 fours) and Hill (88 in 125 minutes, 7 fours), gave Australia an ideal start. During his innings Hill
became the first batsman to score 2000 Test runs, while Trumper and later Gregory (chanceless 112 in 122 minutes, 17 fours) were the first
Australians to make four Test centuries. Half-hundreds by Trumper (59 in 75 minutes, 7 fours) and Noble (65 in 180 minutes, 4 fours) in
the second innings appeared to put the match out of England's reach, although Warner (79 in 182 minutes) and Hayward (67 in 162
minutes, 3 fours) began the quest to score 495 with an impressive opening stand. The chief scorers in England's first innings had been
Warner (48 in 105 minutes, 6 fours) and Hirst (58 in 105 minutes, 8 fours). *Wisden* incorrectly gives Aust (2) Gregory c Fielder. Sources:
Wisden, The Australasian, Adelaide Advertiser, South Australian Register.

AUSTRALIA

R.A.Duff	b Hirst	79	c Braund b Hirst		14
V.T.Trumper	b Hirst	113	lbw b Rhodes		59
C.Hill	c Lilley b Arnold	88	b Fielder		16
*M.A.Noble	st Lilley b Arnold	59	c Bosanquet b Braund		65
S.E.Gregory	c Tyldesley b Arnold	8	c Rhodes b Braund		112
A.J.Y.Hopkins	b Bosanquet	0	(7) run out (Rhodes)		7
W.W.Armstrong	lbw b Rhodes	10	(6) c Hirst b Bosanquet		39
H.Trumble	b Bosanquet	4	c & b Bosanquet		9
C.E.McLeod	run out (Rhodes/Lilley)	8	b Bosanquet		2
†J.J.Kelly	lbw b Bosanquet	1	st Lilley b Bosanquet		13
W.P.Howell	not out	3	not out		1
Extras	(b7, lb5, w3)	15	(b8, lb2, w3, nb1)		14
Total	(106.1 overs, 332 mins)	388	(114.5 overs, 325 mins)		351

ENGLAND

T.W.Hayward	b Howell	20	(2) lbw b Hopkins		67
*P.F.Warner	c McLeod b Trumble	48	(1) c & b Trumble		79
J.T.Tyldesley	c Kelly b Hopkins	0	(4) c Noble b Hopkins		10
R.E.Foster	c Howell b Noble	21	(5) b McLeod		16
L.C.Braund	c Duff b Hopkins	13	(6) b Howell		25
G.H.Hirst	c Trumper b Trumble	58	(7) b Trumble		44
B.J.T.Bosanquet	c Duff b Hopkins	10	(9) c Trumper b Hopkins		10
W.Rhodes	c Armstrong b McLeod	9	(10) run out (Armstrong/Hopkins)		8
E.G.Arnold	not out	23	(3) b Hopkins		1
†A.F.A.Lilley	run out (Armstrong/Kelly)	28	(8) c & b Howell		0
A.Fielder	b Trumble	6	not out		14
Extras	(b4, lb1, w4)	9	(lb2, w2)		4
Total	(102.0 overs, 270 mins)	245	(117.1 overs, 303 mins)		278

ENGLAND	O	M	R	W	w,nb		O	M	R	W	w,nb		FALL OF WICKETS			
Fielder	7	0	33	0	1,-	(5)	25	11	51	1	1,1		AUST	ENG	AUST	ENG
Arnold	27	4	93	3	-,-		19	3	74	0	1,-	Wkt	1st	1st	2nd	2nd
Rhodes	14	3	45	1	1,-	(4)	21	4	46	1	1,-	1st	129	47	48	148
Bosanquet	30.1	4	95	3	-,-	(3)	15.5	0	73	4	-,-	2nd	272	48	81	150
Braund	13	1	49	0	-,-	(6)	21	6	57	2	-,-	3rd	296	88	101	160
Hirst	15	1	58	2	1,-	(1)	13	1	36	1	-,-	4th	308	99	263	160
												5th	310	116	289	195
AUSTRALIA	O	M	R	W	w,nb		O	M	R	W	w,nb	6th	343	146	320	231
McLeod	24	6	56	1	-,-	(2)	25	4	46	1	-,-	7th	360	173	324	231
Trumble	28	9	49	3	2,-	(3)	33	8	73	2	-,-	8th	384	199	326	256
Howell	13	4	28	1	-,-	(1)	20	5	52	2	-,-	9th	384	234	350	256
Hopkins	24	5	68	3	1,-		28.1	9	81	4	1,-	10th	388	245	351	278
Armstrong	10	3	25	0	-,-		7	2	15	0	-,-					
Noble	3	0	10	1	1,-											
Trumper						(6)	4	0	7	0	1,-					

TASMANIA v M.C.C.

Played at S.T.C.A. Ground, Hobart, on January 25, 26, 1904. (Two-day match)
Toss : M.C.C.   Result : MATCH DRAWN.
Debuts: Tasmania - G.K.B.Bailey, D.R.Smith (both f/c); L.A.Cuff (Tas only).
12th Men: None named.
Umpires: C.McAllen and J.Watt.
Attendances: No figures published, but "exceeded expectations".   Total: Not known   Receipts: No figures published.
Close of Play: 1st day Tas 4/116 (Douglas 38, Eady 13).

Tasmania's first match on even terms against an English XI was restricted to two days (it had been scheduled for three) due to the length of the Third Test at Adelaide. The S.T.C.A. had originally arranged an odds match along the same lines as previous contests between Tasmania and England, but when it was discovered that Warner would permit only eleven fieldsmen on the ground at any one time they reduced their side from fifteen to eleven. *Wisden* - and even Warner himself - did not consider the eventual match first-class, but it has generally been accepted as such despite the two-day limit. The Tasmanian side was fully representative, although J.Darling (who was living on the island at the time) was unavailable and Bailey and Hale were called up to replace F.E.Chancellor (injured at practice) and J.H.Savigny (unavailable) in the team after it had been named. The bowling of Fielder (ill) and Relf (bruised heel) was restricted. Bosanquet (124 not out) dominated an unbroken fifth-wicket stand of 166 with Knight before Warner's token declaration - the fourth in first-class cricket in Australia (and Warner's third on this tour alone). Cuff (Canterbury 1886-87 to 1896-97), who had recently emigrated from New Zealand, joined Bailey and Smith in playing his first match for Tasmania. Sources: *Wisden, Hobart Mercury, Launceston Examiner*.

M.C.C.

*P.F.Warner	c Cuff b Smith	26	c Paton b Smith	64
R.E.Foster	c Cuff b Smith	43	b Windsor	23
J.T.Tyldesley	b Eady	4	st Dodds b Windsor	85
E.G.Arnold	c Cuff b Smith	4	b Windsor	8
A.E.Knight	c Smith b Windsor	19	not out	45
B.J.T.Bosanquet	b Eady	35	not out	124
A.F.A.Lilley	c Cuff b Windsor	11		
A.E.Relf	run out (Douglas)	24		
W.Rhodes	not out	6		
A.Fielder	c Eady b Windsor	1		
†H.Strudwick	b Eady	1		
Extras	(b6, lb4, nb1)	11	(b4, lb1)	5
Total	(55.2 overs, 150 mins)	185	(73.0 overs, 200 mins) (4 wkts dec)	354

TASMANIA

R.J.Hawson	c Arnold b Bosanquet	29	(2) not out	37
L.A.Cuff	c Tyldesley b Relf	9		
O.H.Douglas	c Foster b Arnold	38		
†N.Dodds	c Rhodes b Arnold	24	(3) not out	2
E.A.C.Windsor	c Arnold b Rhodes	2		
C.J.Eady	b Rhodes	16		
*E.J.K.Burn	not out	28	(1) c Strudwick b Foster	24
H.Hale	b Arnold	9		
D.R.Smith	c Relf b Arnold	13		
G.D.Paton	run out (Warner)	18		
G.K.B.Bailey	b Fielder	3		
Extras	(b1, nb1)	2		—
Total	(88.1 overs, 240 mins)	191	(17.0 overs, 50 mins) (1 wkt)	63

TASMANIA	O	M	R	W	w,nb		O	M	R	W	w,nb
Paton	5	1	24	0	-,-	(4)	4	0	25	0	-,-
Windsor	16	3	68	3	-,-		24	2	96	3	-,-
Eady	22.2	5	40	3	-,1	(1)	19	4	80	0	-,-
Smith	12	1	42	3	-,-	(3)	20	0	97	1	-,-
Bailey							3	1	13	0	-,-
Hale							3	0	38	0	-,-

M.C.C.	O	M	R	W	w,nb		O	M	R	W	w,nb
Fielder	4.1	0	18	1	-,-						
Relf	8	2	20	1	-,1						
Arnold	34	15	44	4	-,-						
Bosanquet	11	2	55	1	-,-						
Rhodes	31	13	52	2	-,-						
Foster						(1)	7	2	34	1	-,-
Warner						(2)	6	3	16	0	-,-
Knight						(3)	2	0	9	0	-,-
Lilley						(4)	2	0	4	0	-,-

FALL OF WICKETS

	MCC	TAS	MCC	TAS
Wkt	1st	1st	2nd	2nd
1st	72	11	57	60
2nd	78	53	158	-
3rd	78	90	175	-
4th	82	97	188	-
5th	127	119	-	-
6th	139	121	-	-
7th	163	131	-	-
8th	182	153	-	-
9th	184	186	-	-
10th	185	191	-	-

NEW SOUTH WALES v VICTORIA (Shield Match 5)

Played at Sydney Cricket Ground on January 25, 26, 27, 1904. (Timeless match)
Toss : Victoria.   Result : NEW SOUTH WALES WON BY TEN WICKETS.
Debuts: Nil.
12th Men: B.W.Farquhar (NSW) and E.E.Bean (Vic).
Umpires: R.Callaway and A.C.Jones.
Attendances: 4183, 10063, 1779.   Total: 16,025.   Receipts: £524.
Close of Play: 1st day NSW 3/207 (Noble 43, S.E.Gregory 31); 2nd day Vic (2) 3/139 (McAlister 72, Stuckey 59).

Duff (67 in 65 minutes, 12 fours and 62 not out in 55 minutes, 9 fours) and Trumper (53 in 58 minutes, 9 fours and 53 not out in 55 minutes, 7 fours) became the first opening pair in Australia to register a century stand in each innings of a first-class match. McAlister (104 in 196 minutes, 16 fours), Stuckey (64 in 91 minutes, 9 fours) and McLeod (77 in 111 minutes, 10 fours) batted well in the Victorian second innings, while for New South Wales S.E.Gregory made 81 in 96 minutes with 10 fours in the first innings. Cotter was brought into the New South Wales team as a last-minute replacement for W.P.Howell. Saunders was unable to take the field for the New South Wales second innings due to an injured foot. Bean substituted in his place. Last first-class appearance by W.Bruce (debut in 1882-83).
Sources: *Wisden, NSWCA Report, Sydney Referee, Sydney Morning Herald, Town & Country Journal.*

VICTORIA

Batsman	Dismissal 1	Score 1	Dismissal 2	Score 2
P.A.McAlister	c Trumper b McBeath	7	c Kelly b McBeath	104
W.Bruce	b Cotter	26	lbw b Hopkins	1
G.H.S.Trott	b Cotter	25	b Hopkins	6
J.H.Stuckey	b Cotter	4	(5) c Bowden b Cotter	64
W.W.Armstrong	b Cotter	11	(4) b Hopkins	11
*F.J.Laver	c Kelly b Bowden	21	c Trumper b Hopkins	5
C.E.McLeod	st Kelly b Bowden	46	c & b Bowden	77
J.F.Giller	c Kelly b McBeath	9	b Cotter	29
H.J.Fry	not out	1	st Kelly b Bowden	22
†J.E.Monfries	c Trumper b Bowden	3	b Hopkins	3
J.V.Saunders	st Kelly b Bowden	0	not out	6
Extras	(b5, lb3, w1, nb1)	10	(b9, lb4, w3)	16
Total	(50.4 overs, 135 mins)	163	(117.5 overs, 295 mins)	344

NEW SOUTH WALES

Batsman	Dismissal 1	Score 1	Dismissal 2	Score 2
R.A.Duff	c Bruce b Giller	67	(2) not out	62
V.T.Trumper	c Fry b Trott	53	(1) not out	53
A.J.Y.Hopkins	lbw b Giller	11		
*M.A.Noble	b Trott	58		
S.E.Gregory	b Saunders	81		
C.W.Gregory	b Laver	44		
J.R.M.Mackay	c & b Armstrong	56		
†J.J.Kelly	c Stuckey b Armstrong	5		
A.J.Bowden	not out	6		
A.Cotter	c Stuckey b Armstrong	3		
A.McBeath	run out (Stuckey/Monfries)	0		
Extras	(b1, lb4)	5	(b4)	4
Total	(102.3 overs, 260 mins)	389	(22.3 overs, 55 mins) (0 wkts)	119

NEW SOUTH WALES	O	M	R	W	w,nb		O	M	R	W	w,nb
Hopkins	9	2	30	0	-,-	(2)	34	7	96	5	1,-
McBeath	12	3	40	2	-,-	(3)	30	12	57	1	2,-
Cotter	13	1	50	4	1,1	(1)	20	4	75	2	-,-
Bowden	16.4	2	33	4	-,-		30.5	7	88	2	-,-
Trumper							3	0	12	0	-,-

VICTORIA	O	M	R	W	w,nb		O	M	R	W	w,nb
Trott	31	1	131	2	-,-	(5)	1.3	0	4	0	-,-
McLeod	11	5	50	0	-,-						
Laver	16	4	49	1	-,-		2	0	19	0	-,-
Saunders	18	3	70	1	-,-						
Giller	19	3	59	2	-,-	(2)	6	0	37	0	-,-
Fry	1	0	15	0	-,-	(4)	3	0	28	0	-,-
Armstrong	6.3	3	10	3	-,-	(1)	10	4	27	0	-,-

FALL OF WICKETS

Wkt	VIC 1st	NSW 1st	VIC 2nd	NSW 2nd
1st	8	113	16	-
2nd	64	129	44	-
3rd	77	141	60	-
4th	81	223	172	-
5th	82	296	183	-
6th	132	344	214	-
7th	155	361	290	-
8th	159	367	319	-
9th	163	389	326	-
10th	163	389	344	-

TASMANIA v M.C.C.

Played at N.T.C.A. Ground, Launceston, on January 29, 30, 1904. (Two-day match)
Toss : Tasmania.   Result : MATCH DRAWN.
Debuts: Tasmania - A.G.Addison, E.L.James (both f/c). M.C.C. - G.H.Drummond (f/c).
12th Men: None named.
Umpires: W.Lawrence and J.Masterton.
Attendances: 3000, 2000.   Total: About 5000.   Receipts: £202.
Close of Play: 1st day MCC 8/321 (Lilley 32, Fielder 19).

This match was scheduled to be between Northern Tasmania and MCC, but a week before it began the N.T.C.A. decided to invite five men - F.E.Chancellor, N.Dodds, C.J.Eady, R.J.Hawson and either of O.H.Douglas or H.Hale - from the south of the island to form a fully representative Tasmanian side. Eady (work) was not available and Chancellor (hampered by the leg injury he sustained before the Hobart match) withdrew from the selected side, Harrison replacing him. Thus the team, labelled "Tasmania" in the press, contained three southerners (Dodds, Douglas and Hawson) and would have had five had Eady and Chancellor been able to play. It was not, as *Wisden* and many reference books say, "Northern Tasmania". MCC were without L.C.Braund, who remained in Melbourne instead of travelling to Tasmania, and B.J.T.Bosanquet and R.E.Foster, both of whom had stayed in southern Tasmania on a fishing trip. Drummond, later with Northamptonshire, a Harrow-educated 20-year-old who was travelling with the Englishmen, made his first-class debut as an emergency replacement for A.E.Relf (bruised heel). Hayward's 134 took 135 minutes and included 4 fives and 17 fours. Savigny (164 not out in 295 minutes, 21 fours) scored his sole hundred in his last first-class appearance. He was missed when 33 (a simple catch to Lilley) and shared an opening partnership of 202 with Douglas, a Tasmanian first-wicket record. The tourists provided the first instance in Australia of all eleven players bowling in the same innings. *Cricket* incorrectly gives MCC Hirst 4, Fielder 28, E.Jones instead of James in Tasmanian team. Sources: *Wisden, Cricket, Hobart Mercury, Launceston Examiner.*

TASMANIA

J.H.Savigny	c Hirst b Fielder	0		not out	164
R.J.Hawson	b Hirst	0	(5)	not out	1
O.H.Douglas	b Fielder	1	(2)	c Rhodes b Hirst	59
L.A.Cuff	b Hirst	6	(3)	b Knight	15
†N.Dodds	c Strudwick b Fielder	48	(4)	st Strudwick b Knight	2
E.L.James	b Hirst	4			
*E.A.C.Windsor	c Strudwick b Hirst	33			
N.R.Westbrook	st Strudwick b Arnold	26			
A.G.Addison	b Arnold	0			
D.R.Smith	b Hirst	5			
E.W.Harrison	not out	7			
Extras	(b4, lb6, nb1)	11		(b16, lb1, nb1)	18
Total	(48.2 overs, 150 mins)	141		(103.0 overs, 295 mins) (3 wkts)	259

M.C.C.

*P.F.Warner	b Windsor	4
T.W.Hayward	c Douglas b Smith	134
J.T.Tyldesley	b Smith	1
A.E.Knight	b Addison	30
G.H.Hirst	c Cuff b Windsor	51
W.Rhodes	run out (Addison/Dodds)	39
A.F.A.Lilley	not out	37
E.G.Arnold	lbw b Smith	5
G.H.Drummond	b Smith	1
A.Fielder	b Windsor	23
†H.Strudwick	b Windsor	21
Extras	(b4, lb3)	7
Total	(77.0 overs, 210 mins)	353

M.C.C.	O	M	R	W	w,nb	O	M	R	W	w,nb
Hirst	16.2	7	37	5	-,1	19	8	32	1	-,-
Fielder	12	3	44	3	-,-	16	6	29	0	-,1
Rhodes	9	2	33	0	-,-	11	4	21	0	-,-
Arnold	11	4	16	2	-,-	8	3	22	0	-,-
Hayward						10	4	17	0	-,-
Warner						4	0	12	0	-,-
Drummond						5	0	21	0	-,-
Tyldesley						8	1	28	0	-,-
Lilley						5	1	19	0	-,-
Strudwick						5	2	6	0	-,-
Knight						12	2	34	2	-,-

FALL OF WICKETS	TAS	MCC	TAS
Wkt	1st	1st	2nd
1st	7	16	202
2nd	7	19	254
3rd	14	71	256
4th	14	181	-
5th	30	261	-
6th	92	270	-
7th	121	276	-
8th	129	282	-
9th	129	325	-
10th	141	353	-

TASMANIA	O	M	R	W	w,nb
Smith	28	5	111	4	-,-.
Windsor	30	4	106	4	-,-
Addison	10	0	64	1	-,-
James	7	0	36	0	-,-
Savigny	2	0	29	0	-,-

VICTORIA v M.C.C.

Played at Melbourne Cricket Ground on February 5, 6 (no play), 8, 9, 1904. (Timeless match)
Toss : Victoria.   Result : M.C.C. WON BY EIGHT WICKETS.
Debuts: Victoria - W.Carkeek, V.S.Ransford, W.J.Scott (all f/c).
12th Men: J.H.Stuckey (Vic). No 12th named for MCC.
Umpires: E.Barrass and R.M.Crockett.
Attendances: 3000, no play, 2500, 600.   Total: About 6100.   Receipts: No figures published.
Close of Play: 1st day Vic 4/269 (McAlister 133, Laver 28); 2nd day no play; 3rd day MCC 248 all out.

Victoria's second-innings total remains to this day the lowest ever scored in first-class cricket in Australia. Rhodes dismissed McAlister and Armstrong with consecutive balls in the first over and had Trott put down by Bosanquet next ball. Arnold then took the wickets of McLeod and Ransford with his first two balls, making four wickets in eight balls for the innings without a run on the board. Collins, named in the side for Victoria, came down with influenza on the rained-off second day. As he had not yet participated in the match, Fry was permitted to replace him in the team when the match resumed on the third day, as Stuckey, the nominated emergency, had injured his leg. The following season Fry was brought into the Victorian team on similar grounds in a match against South Australia. McAlister (139 in 290 minutes, 1 six and 7 fours) hit a century on the first day before rain soaked the wicket. Hayward (77 in 113 minutes, 1 five and 6 fours) however, "played a fine skilful innings under difficult conditions" (*Age*). *Wisden* omits MCC (2) extras. Sources: *Wisden, The Age, The Argus, The Herald, The Australasian.*

VICTORIA

P.A.McAlister	b Rhodes	139	st Strudwick b Rhodes	0
C.E.McLeod	st Strudwick b Bosanquet	23	c & b Arnold	0
W.W.Armstrong	lbw b Rhodes	31	c Strudwick b Rhodes	0
*G.H.S.Trott	c Arnold b Bosanquet	13	c Arnold b Rhodes	9
V.S.Ransford	b Arnold	26	c Rhodes b Arnold	0
F.J.Laver	c Foster b Rhodes	34	b Rhodes	1
C.M.Baker	st Strudwick b Arnold	14	st Strudwick b Arnold	3
W.J.Scott	c Arnold b Rhodes	2	not out	1
†W.Carkeek	c Hirst b Rhodes	2	c Bosanquet b Arnold	0
H.J.Fry	c Warner b Rhodes	0	c Bosanquet b Rhodes	0
J.V.Saunders	not out	0	absent ill	-
F.B.Collins	absent ill	-	absent ill	-
Extras	(b3, lb9, w3)	15	(b1)	1
Total	(117.3 overs, 312 mins)	299	(12.1 overs, 45 mins)	15

M.C.C.

*P.F.Warner	c Saunders b McLeod	49	c Trott b Fry	16
J.T.Tyldesley	b Saunders	2	(3) not out	23
L.C.Braund	run out (Laver/Carkeek)	6		
R.E.Foster	st Carkeek b Laver	7	not out	1
T.W.Hayward	c McAlister b Laver	77	(2) run out (Scott/Carkeek)	26
A.E.Knight	c McAlister b Saunders	6		
G.H.Hirst	c Laver b Saunders	21		
B.J.T.Bosanquet	c Baker b Armstrong	13		
E.G.Arnold	not out	17		
W.Rhodes	b Laver	5		
†H.Strudwick	c Ransford b Armstrong	13	(w2)	2
Extras	(b22, lb9, w1)	32		
Total	(62.2 overs, 180 mins)	248	(27.0 overs, 70 mins) (2 wkts)	68

M.C.C.	O	M	R	W	w,nb		O	M	R	W	w,nb		FALL OF WICKETS			
													VIC	MCC	VIC	MCC
Hirst	10	2	26	0	2,-							Wkt	1st	1st	2nd	2nd
Arnold	26.3	9	61	2	1,-		6	2	8	4	-,-	1st	65	6	0	26
Braund	22	6	50	0	-,-							2nd	122	33	0	60
Rhodes	30	6	62	6	-,-	(1)	6.1	3	6	5	-,-	3rd	147	49	0	-
Bosanquet	25	3	75	2	-,-							4th	205	102	0	-
Hayward	4	1	10	0	-,-							5th	281	114	5	-
												6th	282	149	12	-
VICTORIA	O	M	R	W	w,nb		O	M	R	W	w,nb	7th	290	185	14	-
Saunders	15	3	39	3	1,-							8th	297	214	15	-
Laver	16	1	64	3	-,-	(3)	6	2	9	0	-,-	9th	297	227	15	-
Trott	3	0	15	0	-,-							10th	299	248	-	-
McLeod	9	0	35	1	-,-	(1)	8	0	21	0	-,-					
Ransford	2	0	5	0	-,-	(4)	3	0	12	0	-,-					
Fry	5	1	23	0	-,-	(2)	10	1	24	1	2,-					
Armstrong	12.2	3	35	2	-,-											

NEW SOUTH WALES v M.C.C.

Played at Sydney Cricket Ground on February 12, 13, 15, 1904. (Four-day match)
Toss : M.C.C.   Result : M.C.C. WON BY 278 RUNS.
Debuts: Nil.
12th Men: B.W.Farquhar (NSW - see below) and A.Fielder (MCC).
Umpires: W.G.Curran and J.J.Giltinan.
Attendances: 7406, 14046, 6844.   Total: 28,296.   Receipts: £969.
Close of Play: 1st day NSW 6/152 (Hopkins 25, Kelly 8); 2nd day MCC (2) 6/255 (Knight 75, Bosanquet 17).

Farquhar, the nominated New South Wales 12th man, was unable to obtain leave from his employer and was not at the match at any stage. Consequently, Relf acted as a substitute when Cotter sustained a shoulder injury during MCC's second innings. J.E.B.B.P.Q.C.Dwyer of the Glebe club (and Sussex 1904/09) took over from Relf from the start of the final day. Cotter's pace accounted for the MCC top order on the first day, only a late stand by Hirst (44 in 67 minutes, 5 fours) and Bosanquet (54 in 68 minutes, 1 five and 7 fours) preventing a rout. Trumper (44 in 35 minutes, 7 fours) began the New South Wales reply fluently but wickets fell at regular intervals. Knight (104 in 214 minutes, 11 fours) and Bosanquet (114 in 87 minutes, 1 five and 17 fours) hit contrasting centuries to put their side in a strong position. Bosanquet took his score from 17 to 114 in the pre-lunch session of the final day. He then capped off a fine match by bowling his team to victory. Hopkins (52 in 70 minutes, 9 fours and 56 in 62 minutes, 8 fours) topped the New South Wales scoring in each innings. *Wisden* incorrectly gives MCC (1) Relf c Trumper; NSW (1) S.E.Gregory c Lilley. Sources: *Wisden, NSWCA Report, Sydney Referee, Sydney Morning Herald, Town & Country Journal, Sydney Mail.*

M.C.C.

T.W.Hayward	c Kelly b Cotter	5		b Cotter	46
*P.F.Warner	c Noble b Cotter	0		b Bowden	8
J.T.Tyldesley	c Trumper b Cotter	17		lbw b Cotter	28
R.E.Foster	lbw b Bowden	19	(5)	c Bowden b Cotter	4
L.C.Braund	b Hopkins	5	(6)	c S.E.Gregory b Noble	32
A.E.Knight	b Howell	23	(4)	c Bowden b Howell	104
G.H.Hirst	c Noble b Cotter	44		c Noble b Hopkins	40
B.J.T.Bosanquet	c Howell b Hopkins	54		c Howell b Noble	114
†A.F.A.Lilley	run out (Bowden/Kelly)	8		b Bowden	2
A.E.Relf	c Kelly b Cotter	1	(11)	c Noble b Hopkins	21
W.Rhodes	not out	2	(10)	not out	49
Extras	(b10, lb1, w1)	12		(b7, lb2, w3, nb1)	13
Total	(52.0 overs, 154 mins)	190		(120.1 overs, 335 mins)	461

NEW SOUTH WALES

V.T.Trumper	c Hayward b Hirst	44		b Braund	5
C.W.Gregory	b Hirst	1	(7)	c Rhodes b Bosanquet	8
*M.A.Noble	c Lilley b Bosanquet	36		c Lilley b Hirst	11
J.R.M.Mackay	b Braund	2	(6)	b Bosanquet	9
S.E.Gregory	st Lilley b Bosanquet	20		c Rhodes b Bosanquet	24
R.A.Duff	run out (Hayward/Rhodes)	10	(2)	c Relf b Hirst	18
A.J.Y.Hopkins	b Rhodes	52	(4)	b Bosanquet	56
†J.J.Kelly	not out	33		c & b Bosanquet	1
A.J.Bowden	b Rhodes	0	(10)	run out (Hirst)	5
A.Cotter	b Rhodes	16	(9)	c Knight b Bosanquet	3
W.P.Howell	c Tyldesley b Hirst	8		not out	0
Extras	(b4, lb3, w3)	10		(b1)	1
Total	(63.3 overs, 190 mins)	232		(40.4 overs, 131 mins)	141

NEW SOUTH WALES	O	M	R	W	w,nb		O	M	R	W	w,nb
Cotter	14	3	44	5	-,-		11	0	56	3	-,-
Hopkins	18	4	65	2	1,-	(4)	26.1	5	85	2	2,-
Bowden	12	0	34	1	-,-	(2)	39	6	135	2	-,-
Howell	8	2	35	1	-,-	(3)	23	3	80	1	-,-
Noble							21	1	82	2	1,1

M.C.C.	O	M	R	W	w,nb		O	M	R	W	w,nb
Hirst	16.3	3	61	3	-,-		11	0	37	2	-,-
Relf	4	0	30	0	-,-						
Bosanquet	14	2	51	2	1,-	(4)	9.4	0	45	6	-,-
Braund	10	0	30	1	-,-	(2)	10	2	38	1	-,-
Rhodes	19	7	50	3	2,-	(3)	10	3	20	0	-,-

FALL OF WICKETS

Wkt	MCC 1st	NSW 1st	MCC 2nd	NSW 2nd
1st	1	2	38	12
2nd	26	55	76	32
3rd	29	57	86	40
4th	34	95	104	113
5th	68	113	165	117
6th	92	114	235	128
7th	147	204	378	130
8th	169	204	383	137
9th	174	222	395	141
10th	190	232	461	141

AFCM No. 308/41
Test No. 81/70
TM No. 18/12

AUSTRALIA v ENGLAND (4th Test)

Played at Sydney Cricket Ground on February 26, 27, 29 (no play), March 1, 2, 3, 1904. (Timeless match)
Toss : England.   Result : ENGLAND WON BY 157 RUNS.
Debuts: Australia - A.Cotter, P.A.McAlister (both Test).
12th Men: W.W.Armstrong (Aust) and A.E.Relf (Eng).
Umpires: P.Argall and R.M.Crockett.
Attendances: 16952, 34606, no play, 5867, 7252, 11667.   Total: 76,344.   Receipts: £3256.
Close of Play: 1st day Eng 7/207 (Knight 64); 2nd day Aust 5/114 (McLeod 12, Kelly 3); 3rd day no play; 4th day Eng (2) 1/50
    (Hayward 23, Arnold 0); 5th day Eng (2) 9/155 (Warner 6).

Australia named a squad of thirteen from which Armstrong and W.P.Howell were omitted on the morning of the match. Cotter, the 19-year-old express bowler from Sydney, was included for his first Test. Rain had fallen on all four days prior to the match which began in "fine, but muggy, weather" (*T&C Journal*), the wicket good but slow. Showers caused a loss of 10 minutes on the first day, most of the lunch-tea session on the second, all of the third (the pitch was aflood) and all play before tea on the fourth, and allowed only 45 minutes prior to tea on the fifth. The wicket remained "slow and easy" (*SMH*) throughout and never became unplayable. The slow outfield accounted in part for the low as well as slow scoring. The crowd became impatient on the second day over the frequent interruptions to play. Pieces of watermelons were thrown as a "few youths amused themselves" (*SMH*), there was some "hooting", but when ground staff began to remove the debris this "incited the crowd to further misbehaviour" (*T&C Journal*) and bottles were thrown, some breaking on the cycle track. Knight (70 not out in 255 minutes, 6 fours) made the highest score of the match while Hayward (52 in 157 minutes, 4 fours), Duff (47 in 65 minutes, 4 fours) and Noble (53 not out in 128 minutes, 5 fours) stood out in the other innings. Bosanquet took 5 for 12 and later had 6 for 32 - all his bowling was done in one spell either side of the tea adjournment - as England regained the Ashes on the sixth afternoon. Some publications incorrectly give Eng (2) Cotter 17.3 overs; Aust (2) Hirst 12.5 overs. Sources: *Wisden, Sydney Morning Herald, Town & Country Journal, Sydney Daily Telegraph.*

ENGLAND

T.W.Hayward	c McAlister b Trumble	18		lbw b Trumble	52
*P.F.Warner	b Noble	0	(9)	not out	31
J.T.Tyldesley	c Gregory b Noble	16	(4)	b Cotter	5
R.E.Foster	c McAlister b Noble	19	(2)	c Noble b Hopkins	27
A.E.Knight	not out	70		c McAlister b Cotter	9
L.C.Braund	c Trumble b Noble	39		c McLeod b Hopkins	19
G.H.Hirst	b Noble	25		c Kelly b McLeod	18
B.J.T.Bosanquet	b Hopkins	12		c Hill b McLeod	7
E.G.Arnold	lbw b Noble	0	(3)	c Kelly b Noble	0
†A.F.A.Lilley	c Hopkins b Trumble	24		b McLeod	6
W.Rhodes	st Kelly b Noble	10		c McAlister b Cotter	29
Extras	(b6, lb7, w2, nb1)	16		(b1, lb6)	7
Total	(114.1 overs, 320 mins)	249		(99.3 overs, 268 mins)	210

AUSTRALIA

R.A.Duff	b Arnold	47		b Arnold	19
V.T.Trumper	b Braund	7	(4)	lbw b Arnold	12
C.Hill	c Braund b Arnold	33		st Lilley b Bosanquet	26
P.A.McAlister	c Arnold b Rhodes	2	(2)	b Hirst	1
A.J.Y.Hopkins	b Braund	9	(7)	st Lilley b Bosanquet	0
C.E.McLeod	b Rhodes	18	(8)	c Lilley b Bosanquet	6
†J.J.Kelly	c Foster b Arnold	5	(10)	c Foster b Bosanquet	10
*M.A.Noble	not out	6	(5)	not out	53
S.E.Gregory	c Foster b Rhodes	2	(6)	lbw Bosanquet	0
H.Trumble	c Lilley b Rhodes	0	(9)	st Lilley b Bosanquet	0
A.Cotter	c Tyldesley b Arnold	0		b Hirst	34
Extras	(b1, w1)	2		(b10)	10
Total	(51.3 overs, 180 mins)	131		(72.5 overs, 206 mins)	171

AUSTRALIA	O	M	R	W	w,nb		O	M	R	W	w,nb					
Cotter	14	1	44	0	1,-	(5)	18.3	3	41	3	-,-					
Noble	41.1	10	100	7	-,1		19	8	40	1	-,-					
Trumble	43	20	58	2	-,-	(1)	28	10	49	1	-,-					
Hopkins	8	3	22	1	1,-		14	5	31	2	-,-					
McLeod	8	5	9	0	-,-	(3)	20	5	42	3	-,-					

												FALL OF WICKETS			
													ENG	AUST	ENG	AUST
ENGLAND	O	M	R	W	w,nb		O	M	R	W	w,nb	Wkt	1st	1st	2nd	2nd
Hirst	13	1	36	0	-,-		18.5	2	32	2	-,-	1st	4	28	49	7
Braund	11	2	27	2	-,-		16	3	24	0	-,-	2nd	34	61	50	35
Rhodes	11	3	33	4	-,-	(4)	11	7	12	0	-,-	3rd	42	72	57	59
Arnold	14.3	5	28	4	1,-	(3)	12	3	42	2	-,-	4th	66	97	73	76
Bosanquet	2	1	5	0	-,-		15	1	51	6	-,-	5th	155	101	106	76
												6th	185	116	120	76
												7th	207	124	138	86
												8th	208	126	141	90
												9th	237	130	155	114
												10th	249	131	210	171

TASMANIA v VICTORIA

Played at S.T.C.A. Ground, Hobart, on March 4, 5, 7 (no play), 8, 9, 1904. (Timeless match)
Toss : Tasmania.   Result : VICTORIA WON BY FIVE WICKETS.
Debuts: Victoria - A.H.Christian, J.T.Howlett, R.M.Osborne (all f/c).
12th Men: None named.
Umpires: T.K.Kendall and C.McAllen.
Attendances & Receipts: no figures published.
Close of Play: 1st day Tas 9/338 (Harrison 19); 2nd day Vic 6/266 (Horan 26, Howlett 25); 3rd day no play; 4th day Vic (2) 0/15
     (Horan 3, Baker 6).

Eady, suffering from lumbago, took no part on the opening day but was expected to bat at No. 11 when play resumed. Next day however he was still unwell and permission was granted for Bailey to replace him as a full member of the side. Rain prevented any play on the scheduled third day and delayed the start of the fourth until mid-afternoon. R.J.Hawson (79 in 110 minutes, 12 fours) and Windsor (76 in 108 minutes, 10 fours) for Tasmania, Ellis (70 in 80 minutes, 8 fours) and Warne (60 in 165 minutes, 4 fours) for Victoria made the highest individual scores. Osborne (legbreaks) and Christian (left-arm medium) each achieved their best bowling figures for Victoria while Chancellor (right-arm fast-medium) did so for Tasmania. Two northern Tasmanians D.R.Smith and N.R.Westbrook were invited to take part but announced their unavailability and Harrison and E.S.Hawson replaced them. *Cricket* incorrectly gives Vic (1) extras 14, total 317, omits bowling for Paton and Tabart, Vic (2) incorrectly gives Chancellor's figures. Sources: *Cricket, The Age, Hobart Mercury*.

TASMANIA

Batsman	Dismissal	Score	Dismissal	Score
R.J.Hawson	lbw b Warne	79	lbw b Osborne	6
T.A.Tabart	c McMichael b Warne	42	b Christian	8
†N.Dodds	b Christian	1	st Carkeek b Osborne	16
E.A.C.Windsor	c Christian b Warne	76	b Christian	2
O.H.Douglas	run out (Osborne/Carkeek)	45	c Osborne b Christian	2
*E.J.K.Burn	st Carkeek b Osborne	48	c Warne b Christian	6
E.W.Harrison	lbw b Osborne	36	c Horan b Osborne	13
G.D.Paton	b Osborne	2	c McMichael b Osborne	7
E.S.Hawson	b Osborne	2	c Baker b Osborne	1
F.E.Chancellor	c Scott b Christian	11	st Carkeek b Christian	0
G.K.B.Bailey	not out	7	not out	0
C.J.Eady	absent ill	-	absent ill	-
Extras		13		3
Total	(123.3 overs, 310 mins)	362	(30.3 overs, 80 mins)	64

VICTORIA

Batsman	Dismissal	Score		Dismissal	Score
T.S.Warne	c Dodds b Windsor	60			
C.M.Baker	b Chancellor	42		b R.J.Hawson b Windsor	42
M.Ellis	c Douglas b Chancellor	70		c Harrison b Windsor	20
V.S.Ransford	c R.J.Hawson b Chancellor	11			
J.F.Horan	c Chancellor b Windsor	34	(1)	lbw b Paton	24
*S.A.McMichael	c Dodds b Windsor	10	(7)	not out	3
W.J.Scott	c Harrison b Chancellor	12	(4)	lbw b Chancellor	4
J.T.Howlett	c Harrison b Chancellor	33	(6)	not out	0
A.H.Christian	c Bailey b Chancellor	17			
†W.Carkeek	c Tabart b Windsor	14	(5)	c Tabart b Chancellor	5
R.M.Osborne	not out	0			
Extras		15			11
Total	(105.5 overs, 275 mins)	318		(52.5 overs, 135 mins) (5 wkts)	109

VICTORIA	O	M	R	W	w,nb		O	M	R	W	w,nb
Osborne	30.3	10	60	4	-,-	(2)	15	2	37	5	-,-
Ellis	14	7	23	0	-,-						
Christian	37	9	113	2	-,-	(1)	15.3	5	24	5	-,-
Howlett	20	7	62	0	-,-						
Warne	22	2	91	3	-,-						

TASMANIA	O	M	R	W	w,nb		O	M	R	W	w,nb
Windsor	42	10	120	4	-,-		23	9	40	2	-,-
Paton	20	3	49	0	-,-	(3)	13	6	21	1	-,-
Chancellor	37.5	8	117	6	-,1	(2)	12.5	3	22	2	-,-
Tabart	6	1	17	0	-,-	(5)	2	0	7	0	-,-
Bailey						(4)	2	0	8	0	-,-

FALL OF WICKETS

Wkt	TAS 1st	VIC 1st	TAS 2nd	VIC 2nd
1st	112	71	7	51
2nd	118	166	29	94
3rd	152	187	33	97
4th	241	187	33	106
5th	262	211	41	106
6th	313	224	41	-
7th	321	282	52	-
8th	323	285	60	-
9th	338	309	64	-
10th	362	318	64	-

AUSTRALIA v ENGLAND (5th Test)

Played at Melbourne Cricket Ground on March 5, 7, 8, 1904. (Timeless match)
Toss : Australia.   Result : AUSTRALIA WON BY 218 RUNS.
Debuts: Australia - D.R.A.Gehrs (Test).
12th Men: S.E.Gregory (Aust) and A.E.Relf (Eng).
Umpires: P.Argall and R.M.Crockett.
Attendances: 17839, 3000, 3000.   Total: 23,839.   Receipts: No figures published.
Close of Play: 1st day Eng 2/4 (Rhodes 3, Warner 1); 2nd day Aust (2) 3/13 (Kelly 4).

Trumper's 88 occupied 110 minutes and included 11 fours. Braund's analysis, achieved on a steady wicket, remained the best by a wrist-spinner in a Test match in this country until 1920-21. Noble dismissed Hayward and the night-watchman, Arnold, with the final two deliveries of his opening over in the English innings. Rain overnight and on Sunday brought about a dramatic change in the character of the wicket and when play resumed on the second day at 3.45pm wickets began to fall immediately, Rhodes going to the very first ball. The wicket deteriorated further as it dried and, with the ball "cutting through" the surface, Cotter was able to extract dangerous bounce. Braund was dismissed by the first ball of the second innings and Hugh Trumble, in his final first-class match, snared his second Test hat-trick: Bosanquet, Warner and Lilley. Tonsillitis prevented Hayward from batting a second time. This was the first Test in Australia in which as many as 11 ducks were recorded. *Wisden* incorrectly gives Aust (1) Braund 21.3 overs. Sources: *Wisden, The Age, The Argus, The Herald, The Australasian.*

AUSTRALIA

R.A.Duff	b Braund	9	(7) c Warner b Rhodes		31
V.T.Trumper	c & b Braund	88	(5) b Hirst		0
C.Hill	c Braund b Rhodes	16	(6) c Warner b Hirst		16
*M.A.Noble	c Foster b Arnold	29	(8) st Lilley b Rhodes		19
P.A.McAlister	st Lilley b Braund	36	(1) c Foster b Arnold		9
D.R.A.Gehrs	c & b Braund	3	(10) c & b Hirst		5
A.J.Y.Hopkins	c Knight b Braund	32	(9) not out		25
C.E.McLeod	c Rhodes b Braund	8	(2) c Bosanquet b Braund		0
H.Trumble	c Foster b Braund	6	(11) c Arnold b Hirst		0
†J.J.Kelly	not out	6	(3) c & Arnold		24
A.Cotter	b Braund	6	(4) b Hirst		0
Extras	(b4, lb4)	8	(b1, lb3)		4
Total	(82.1 overs, 231 mins)	247	(43.5 overs, 135 mins)		133

ENGLAND

T.W.Hayward	b Noble	0	absent ill		
W.Rhodes	c Gehrs b Cotter	3	(8) not out		16
E.G.Arnold	c Kelly b Noble	0	(10) c Duff b Trumble		19
*P.F.Warner	c McAlister b Cotter	1	(5) c & b Trumble		11
J.T.Tyldesley	c Gehrs b Noble	10	(3) c Hopkins b Cotter		15
R.E.Foster	b Cotter	18	(2) c Trumper b Trumble		30
G.H.Hirst	c Trumper b Cotter	0	(6) c McAlister b Trumble		1
L.C.Braund	c Hopkins b Noble	5	(1) c McAlister b Cotter		0
A.E.Knight	b Cotter	0	(4) c Kelly b Trumble		0
B.J.T.Bosanquet	c Noble b Cotter	16	(7) c Gehrs b Trumble		4
†A.F.A.Lilley	not out	6	(9) lbw b Trumble		0
Extras	(b1, nb1)	2	(b1, lb4)		5
Total	(31.2 overs, 102 mins)	61	(22.5 overs, 84 mins)		101

ENGLAND	O	M	R	W	w,nb		O	M	R	W	w,nb					
Hirst	19	6	44	0	-,-	(4)	16.5	4	48	5	-,-					
Braund	29.1	6	81	8	-,-	(3)	4	1	6	1	-,-	Wkt	1st	1st	2nd	2nd
Rhodes	12	1	41	1	-,-	(1)	15	2	52	2	-,-	1st	13	0	9	0
Arnold	18	4	46	1	-,-	(2)	8	3	23	2	-,-	2nd	67	0	9	24
Bosanquet	4	0	27	0	-,-							3rd	142	4	13	38
												4th	144	5	13	47
AUSTRALIA	O	M	R	W	w,nb		O	M	R	W	w,nb	5th	159	23	43	54
Noble	15	8	19	4	-,1	(2)	6	2	19	0	-,-	6th	218	26	49	61
Cotter	15.2	2	40	6	-,-	(1)	5	0	25	2	-,-	7th	221	36	92	61
McLeod	1	1	0	0	-,-	(4)	5	0	24	0	-,-	8th	231	36	115	61
Trumble						(3)	6.5	0	28	7	-,-	9th	235	48	133	101
												10th	247	61	133	-

FALL OF WICKETS — AUST 1st, ENG 1st, AUST 2nd, ENG 2nd

SOUTH AUSTRALIA v M.C.C.

Played at Adelaide Oval on March 12, 14, 15, 1904. (Timeless match)
Toss : South Australia.   Result : M.C.C. WON BY NINE WICKETS.
Debuts: South Australia - P.H.Coombe, H.J.Hill (both f/c).
12th Men: F.J.Dickenson (SA). No 12th named for MCC.
Umpires: P.Argall and G.A.Watson (see below).
Attendances: 5000, 2000, 500.   Total: About 7500.   Receipts: No figures published.
Close of Play: 1st day MCC 1/9 (Warner 2, Bosanquet 5); 2nd day SA 77 (2) all out.

Umpire Argall became ill on the last day and was replaced after lunch by T.A.Reeves. Gehrs (63 in 118 minutes, 7 fours) and Newland (50 in 55 minutes, 7 fours) led the scoring for South Australia. H.J.Hill, making his only first-class appearance, was out second ball in the first innings. Braund bowled unchanged through the second innings. Foster (73 in 110 minutes, 9 fours) and Tyldesley (50 in 25 minutes, 8 fours) finished the match with a quick partnership. Warner (50 in 119 minutes, 4 fours and 54 in 85 minutes, 5 fours) hit a half-century in each innings. *Wisden* and some newspapers give SA (1) Jennings 31, extras 7 (lb7, nb2), Relf 2/45, MCC bowling not tallying. *O'Reilly* as shown here except MCC (2) Bosanquet incorrectly given 50 not out instead of Tyldesley. Sources: *Wisden, C.B.O'Reilly, The Age, Sydney Morning Herald, Adelaide Advertiser, South Australian Register.*

SOUTH AUSTRALIA

D.R.A.Gehrs	b Hirst	63	st Strudwick b Braund		30
F.T.Hack	b Bosanquet	13	c Relf b Hirst		5
*C.Hill	c Strudwick b Hirst	22	c Fielder b Braund		7
C.B.Jennings	c Strudwick b Relf	32	lbw b Braund		0
N.Claxton	c Strudwick b Bosanquet	40	b Hirst		1
J.H.Pellew	b Relf	4	b Braund		13
A.E.Evans	c & b Braund	29	b Braund		0
H.J.Hill	b Bosanquet	0	c Strudwick b Braund		10
†P.M.Newland	b Fielder	50	c Tyldesley b Braund		8
J.P.F.Travers	run out	0	not out		1
P.H.Coombe	not out	0	b Braund		1
Extras	(lb5, nb1)	6	(lb1)		1
Total	(77.2 overs, 252 mins)	259	(29.4 overs, 105 mins)		77

M.C.C.

R.E.Foster	c Hack b Claxton	2	not out		73
*P.F.Warner	c H.J.Hill b Pellew	50	c Evans b Claxton		54
B.J.T.Bosanquet	c C.Hill b Coombe	22			
J.T.Tyldesley	b H.J.Hill	12	(3) not out		50
A.E.Knight	c Jennings b Claxton	18			
L.C.Braund	c Travers b Claxton	30			
G.H.Hirst	c Evans b Claxton	1			
A.E.Relf	c Newland b Claxton	3			
W.Rhodes	b H.J.Hill	4			
A.Fielder	not out	5			
†H.Strudwick	c Pellew b H.J.Hill	1			
Extras	(b6)	6	(b7)		7
Total	(69.4 overs, 195 mins)	154	(36.3 overs, 110 mins) (1 wkt)		184

M.C.C.	O	M	R	W	w,nb		O	M	R	W	w,nb
Hirst	18	3	40	2	-,1		11	4	22	2	-,-
Fielder	11	3	40	1	-,-						
Bosanquet	17	1	70	3	-,-		4	0	11	0	-,-
Rhodes	5	0	18	0	-,-						
Braund	9.2	1	38	1	-,-	(2)	14.4	2	43	8	-,-
Relf	17	6	47	2	-,-						

FALL OF WICKETS				
	SA	MCC	SA	MCC
Wkt	1st	1st	2nd	2nd
1st	36	2	15	117
2nd	79	52	30	-
3rd	116	75	30	-
4th	143	106	31	-
5th	149	122	43	-
6th	191	124	43	-
7th	191	130	63	-
8th	256	135	75	-
9th	257	151	75	-
10th	259	154	77	-

SOUTH AUSTRALIA	O	M	R	W	w,nb		O	M	R	W	w,nb
Claxton	27	7	56	5	-,-		12	1	58	1	-,-
Travers	9	4	20	0	-,-		7	1	34	0	-,-
Coombe	6	1	22	1	-,-	(4)	5	1	23	0	-,-
H.J.Hill	19.4	8	27	3	-,-	(3)	6	0	18	0	-,-
Evans	2	0	4	0	-,-		2	0	10	0	-,-
Pellew	6	1	19	1	-,-		1	0	8	0	-,-
Gehrs							2	0	16	0	-,-
Hack							1.3	0	10	0	-,-

QUEENSLAND v NEW SOUTH WALES

Played at Brisbane Cricket Ground (Woolloongabba) on April 2, 4, 1904. (Timeless match)
Toss : Queensland.   Result : NEW SOUTH WALES WON BY NINE WICKETS.
Debuts: Queensland - G.S.Crouch, A.Marshal, R.D.Pyke (all f/c). New South Wales - W.Bardsley, W.T.Grounds, R.J.Hartigan (all f/c).
12th Men: M.F.McCaffrey (Qld). No 12th named for NSW; only 11 men in party.
Umpires: F.Holland and T.Muir.
Attendances: 3000, 4000.   Total: About 7000.   Receipts: No figures published.
Close of Play: 1st day NSW 1/93 (Jansan 30).

New South Wales had numerous troubles in selecting a team. S.E.Gregory was unavailable and V.T.Trumper (on holiday), A.J.Bowden, B.W.Farquhar, C.W.Gregory and J.J.Kelly all withdrew from the named side. Bardsley, Carter, Hartigan, Jansan and Johnson were called in as replacements. The selection of Grounds was considered surprising but he gave a fine display of accurate medium-paced bowling to silence his critics. H.B.Griffith withdrew from the Queensland squad of thirteen. Pre-match rain hampered preparation of the wicket which "gave the bowlers a good deal of help" (*Courier*). Duff (56 in 55 minutes, 7 fours) and Jansan (40 in 68 minutes, 3 fours) provided the only instances of bat dominating ball in the match during their opening stand of 93. The match was concluded shortly after tea on the second day. New South Wales were then asked to continue batting to entertain the spectators; Noble consented, and play went on for at least another 30 minutes. Hartigan was run out (Marshal) for 21, Mackay c Foster b Miller 43, Carter not out 19. Play was halted at 5.20pm on the dismissal of Mackay, with the New South Wales total 3/111. Only the score at the point of decision (shown here) was officially recorded. Marshal was dismissed first ball in Queensland's second innings, in which the last seven wickets fell for four runs. *Cricket* gives incorrect match dates and dismissals for Qld (1) Lewis and Marshal. Sources: *Cricket, NSWCA Report, Brisbane Courier, Queensland Times, The Queenslander.*

QUEENSLAND

J.W.Lewis	c Cotter b Grounds	9	b Hopkins		14
G.S.Crouch	b Grounds	26	c Carter b Noble		9
N.K.Foster	b Noble	2	c Bardsley b Noble		0
J.Carew	c Bardsley b Noble	3	c Carter b Grounds		12
†W.T.Evans	b Grounds	16	b Cotter		17
*A.A.Atkins	c Bardsley b Hopkins	11	c Carter b Cotter		0
A.Marshal	b Noble	22	c Noble b Cotter		0
J.J.Fitzgerald	run out (Jansan/Hopkins)	8	not out		2
R.D.Pyke	c Jansan b Noble	18	c Bardsley b Grounds		0
D.L.Miller	b Cotter	0	b Grounds		0
T.Byrnes	not out	1	b Cotter		1
Extras	(b9, lb7)	16	(b1, lb2, nb1)		4
Total	(55.4 overs, 175 mins)	132	(28.0 overs, 95 mins)		59

NEW SOUTH WALES

R.A.Duff	hit wkt b Fitzgerald	56			
E.W.Jansan	c Marshal b Miller	40			
J.R.M.Mackay	run out (Lewis/Evans)	1	not out		5
*M.A.Noble	c Marshal b Miller	12			
A.J.Y.Hopkins	c Pyke b Byrnes	8	(1) b Byrnes		25
W.Bardsley	c Miller b Lewis	19			
R.J.Hartigan	c Pyke b Miller	4	(2) not out		9
A.Cotter	c Foster b Lewis	4			
†H.Carter	c Lewis b Miller	0			
W.T.Grounds	not out	0			
F.B.Johnson	c Foster b Miller	0			
Extras	(b4, lb4, nb1)	9			
Total	(35.0 overs, 123 mins)	153	(6.0 overs, 20 mins) (1 wkt)		39

NEW SOUTH WALES	O	M	R	W	w,nb		O	M	R	W	w,nb
Cotter	8	2	24	1	-,-	(4)	4	3	5	4	-,-
Johnson	13	2	49	0	-,-						
Grounds	14	8	7	3	-,-		5	4	1	3	-,-
Noble	13.4	7	19	4	-,-	(1)	10	2	38	2	-,1
Hopkins	7	2	17	1	-,-	(2)	9	5	11	1	-,-

QUEENSLAND	O	M	R	W	w,nb		O	M	R	W	w,nb
Byrnes	13	1	52	1	-,1	(3)	2	0	16	1	-,-
Lewis	4	0	24	2	-,-		1	0	13	0	-,-
Fitzgerald	6	1	22	1	-,-	(4)	1	0	1	0	-,-
Miller	12	3	46	5	-,-	(1)	2	0	9	0	-,-

FALL OF WICKETS

	QLD	NSW	QLD	NSW
Wkt	1st	1st	2nd	2nd
1st	38	93	21	29
2nd	43	101	23	-
3rd	43	104	25	-
4th	49	118	55	-
5th	77	126	55	-
6th	77	139	55	-
7th	95	153	55	-
8th	125	153	55	-
9th	126	153	58	-
10th	132	153	59	-

1904-05 SEASON (11 MATCHES)

In the first purely domestic season since 1900-01, New South Wales reigned supreme. They retained the Sheffield Shield for the fourth successive year, having lost only one match of their 16 in that time, to Victoria in Melbourne in December 1903. The strength of New South Wales lay with the likes of Noble, Trumper, Duff, Kelly, Syd Gregory, Howell and Hopkins - all once household names in Australia. New South Wales had a far greater depth of talent in their reserves also, and the current season saw E.F.Waddy and F.B.Johnson give notice that, together with 'Tibby' Cotter, they were likely to remain a force for years to come.

Victoria began their Shield campaign well with a convincing nine-wicket win over South Australia at Adelaide. However, this proved to be Victoria's only success of the summer, their defeats being equally convincing. Armstrong, Collins, Laver, Ransford and Saunders, at times, all had fine individual returns.

South Australia's sole success, an innings defeat inflicted on Victoria at Melbourne for the first time, in the leadup to their match against New South Wales, was inspired by 170 from Gehrs and a 13-wicket haul from Reedman. Both players led the team's end-of-season aggregates but, as with Victoria, there was a lack of consistency in overall performance.

Away from the Shield, Queensland met Victoria at Melbourne for the first time, in the leadup to their match against New South Wales at Sydney. Queensland were defeated by an innings despite a century on debut from H.G.S.Morton. A double-century from Armstrong, 152 from Ransford and 98 from Laver swamped the visitors.

New South Wales won both their matches against Queensland by innings margins to illustrate their depth; both sides were virtual Second XIs. Mackay, Poidevin, Pye and Carter all hit centuries and Jack O'Connor secured a 10-wicket haul in the second match.

Tasmania fielded a weak team for their match against Victoria at Melbourne in January - Eady, Burn and Windsor were missing - and not surprisingly they were beaten by an innings. Tasmania had actually asked Victoria to include a full-strength XI for this match, which would have necessitated a change in the match dates. The VCA were unwilling to accommodate such a change. The Tasmanians bounced back two months after this loss to register their first victory against a New South Wales team, at the third attempt. Eady (11 for 99) and Windsor (6 for 122) were the architects of the victory in a low-scoring game at Hobart.

Interest in the New Year centred on the selection of the 12th Australian team to tour England. Joe Darling, R.W.McLeod and M.A.Noble, the appointed selectors, named an experienced side, P.M.Newland being the only surprise inclusion. For the first time, 15 players were taken. But supporters of J.V.Saunders and E.A.C.Windsor, who had been overlooked, rallied to force a meeting of the Australian team at Sydney prior to their departure for England. The original names were re-endorsed - despite an offer by the supporters to subsidise the fares of Saunders and Windsor - and the selectors stated that the two would only be considered should any of the original members be incapacitated. The touring party comprised J.Darling (captain), W.W.Armstrong, A.Cotter, R.A.Duff, D.R.A.Gehrs, S.E.Gregory, C.Hill, A.J.Y.Hopkins, W.P.Howell, J.J.Kelly, F.J.Laver, C.E.McLeod, P.M.Newland, M.A.Noble and V.T.Trumper.

Moves for the establishment of a Board of Control were initiated by the VCA, together with NSWCA representatives who met at Sydney on January 6, 1905 to draft a constitution. Delegates from the associations of New South Wales, Queensland, South Australia and Victoria attended a meeting in Melbourne on May 6 to vote on the formation of a Board. The SACA, although in favour of the principle, refused to join until the Board defined what it meant by 'financial control'. The vote nevertheless went ahead and was carried, and the Board came into being, consisting only of representatives from New South Wales and Victoria.

Leading Aggregates

Batsmen	M	I	NO	Runs	HS	Ave.	Bowlers	Runs	Wkts	Ave.
W.W.Armstrong (V)	5	8	0	460	200	57.50	F.B.Collins (V)	631	27	23.37
V.S.Ransford (V)	5	8	1	427	152	61.00	F.B.Johnson (NSW)	484	20	24.20
E.F.Waddy (NSW)	6	10	2	407	129*	50.87	J.C.Reedman (SA)	391	19	20.57
M.A.Noble (NSW)	4	6	0	373	112	62.16	A.Cotter (NSW)	427	18	23.72
W.P.Howell (NSW)	4	7	1	333	128	55.50	J.V.Saunders (V)	482	18	26.77
F.J.Laver (V)	5	8	0	330	164	41.25	A.J.Y.Hopkins (NSW)	279	17	16.41
D.R.A.Gehrs (SA)	4	7	0	304	170	43.42	J.D.A.O'Connor (NSW)	147	15	9.80

SHEFFIELD SHIELD TABLE

	P	W	L	D	Pts	Quotient	Runs Scored	Wkts Lost	Runs Conceded	Wkts Taken
NEW SOUTH WALES	4	4	-	-	4	1.584	2303	63	1846	80
VICTORIA	4	1	3	-	-2	0.808	1841	71	2246	70
SOUTH AUSTRALIA	4	1	3	-	-2	0.748	1688	70	1740	54
TOTAL	6	6	6	-	0	1.000	5832	204	5832	204

AFCM No. 313/36
SSM No. 71/23

SOUTH AUSTRALIA v VICTORIA (Shield Match 1)

Played at Adelaide Oval on November 12, 14, 15, 16, 1904. (Timeless match)
Toss : South Australia.   Result : VICTORIA WON BY NINE WICKETS.
Debuts: South Australia - H.W.Short (f/c).
12th Men: A.E.Evans (SA) and R.M.Osborne (Vic).
Umpires: P.Argall and T.A.Reeves.
Attendances: 3500, 3500, 500, 250.   Total: About 7750.   Receipts: No figures published.
Close of Play: 1st day SA 7/230 (Hill 98, Travers 2); 2nd day Vic 6/250 (Laver 106, Ransford 4); 3rd day SA(2) 3/105 (Hill 53, Darling 6).

H.Trumble (retired) and J.F.Giller (unavailable) were replaced in the Victorian team by Osborne and Ransford. Hill (111 not out in 220 minutes, 1 five and 11 fours, 3 chances and 67 in 75 minutes, 11 fours) was the only South Australian batsman to effectively counter the Victorian bowlers in either innings. Claxton bowled McAlister and Stuckey with successive deliveries and captured the first four wickets at a personal cost of 28 before Laver (career-best 164 in 285 minutes, 20 fours) and McLeod (65 in 124 minutes, 7 fours) steadied the innings with a fifth wicket partnership of 154. Laver and Ransford (80 not out in 235 minutes, 6 fours) put on a further 129 for the seventh wicket after the loss of McLeod and Scott to consecutive balls from Travers. *O'Reilly* incorrectly gives SA (2) Collins 0/24, Armstrong 1/32.
Sources: *Wisden, C.B.O'Reilly, The Australasian, Adelaide Advertiser, South Australian Register.*

SOUTH AUSTRALIA

D.R.A.Gehrs	b Armstrong	23	(2) b Laver		19
F.T.Hack	c Armstrong b Saunders	18	(1) st Wright b Saunders		27
*C.Hill	not out	111	b Saunders		67
C.B.Jennings	c Collins b Saunders	1	b McLeod		0
J.Darling	c McAlister b Collins	16	b McLeod		19
N.Claxton	b Armstrong	43	c Trott b Laver		32
J.H.Pellew	c Wright b Collins	12	c Laver b Saunders		3
†P.M.Newland	c Saunders b Collins	8	c Armstrong b Laver		37
J.P.F.Travers	c McLeod b Saunders	6	b Armstrong		4
P.H.Coombe	st Wright b Collins	0	c McAlister b Laver		0
H.W.Short	b Collins	0	not out		1
Extras	(b4, lb4, nb1)	9	(w1)		1
Total	(101.3 overs, 285 mins)	247	(66.2 overs, 195 mins)		210

VICTORIA

P.A.McAlister	b Claxton	8	(3) not out		5
G.H.S.Trott	b Claxton	26			
J.H.Stuckey	b Claxton	0			
W.W.Armstrong	b Claxton	24			
*F.J.Laver	c Newland b Claxton	164			
C.E.McLeod	b Travers	65			
W.J.Scott	b Travers	0	(2) not out		13
V.S.Ransford	not out	80			
F.B.Collins	b Short	20	(1) b Hill		1
†H.L.Wright	c Travers b Pellew	14			
J.V.Saunders	b Travers	10			
Extras	(b16, lb7, w3)	26	(w2)		2
Total	(162.5 overs, 450 mins)	437	(5.0 overs, 15 mins) (1 wkts)		21

VICTORIA	O	M	R	W	w,nb		O	M	R	W	w,nb
Saunders	29	10	58	3	-,-		18	6	72	3	-,-
Collins	24.3	8	50	5	-,-		12	2	44	0	-,-
Trott	6	1	17	0	-,-		2	0	10	0	-,-
McLeod	19	3	48	0	-,1	(5)	15	3	40	2	1,-
Armstrong	15	3	36	2	-,-	(6)	7.2	3	12	1	-,-
Laver	8	2	29	0	-,-	(4)	12	2	31	4	-,-

SOUTH AUSTRALIA	O	M	R	W	w,nb		O	M	R	W	w,nb
Claxton	60	21	130	5	3,-						
Coombe	36	13	81	0	-,-						
Travers	33.5	8	88	3	-,-						
Short	14	0	57	1	-,-						
Pellew	11	1	35	1	-,-						
Hack	7	3	13	0	-,-						
Gehrs	1	0	7	0	-,-						
Jennings						(1)	2	0	9	0	1,-
Hill						(2)	2	1	3	1	-,-
Darling						(3)	1	0	7	0	1,-

FALL OF WICKETS

Wkt	SA 1st	VIC 1st	SA 2nd	VIC 2nd
1st	45	12	42	3
2nd	59	12	77	-
3rd	61	59	78	-
4th	88	66	133	-
5th	178	220	133	-
6th	207	220	140	-
7th	223	349	191	-
8th	242	393	208	-
9th	247	416	208	-
10th	247	437	210	-

VICTORIA v QUEENSLAND

Played at Melbourne Cricket Ground on December 16, 17, 19, 1904. (Timeless match)
Toss : Queensland.   Result : VICTORIA WON BY AN INNINGS AND 181 RUNS.
Debuts: Queensland - H.G.S.Morton, F.R.V.Timbury (both f/c).
12th Men: J.F.Horan (Vic) and W.B.Hayes (Qld).
Umpires: R.M.Crockett and H.S.Freeman.
Attendances: 1300, 2500, 500.   Total: About 4300.   Receipts: £81.
Close of Play: 1st day Vic 0/21 (McAlister 4, Stuckey 17); 2nd day Vic 4/481 (Ransford 103, Scott 28).

Queensland were soundly beaten in their first match in Victoria. Morton (135 not out in 228 minutes, 15 fours) "played well all round the wicket" (*Age*) to score a century on debut; from Maryborough, it was only his second match on a turf wicket. Armstrong (200 in 217 minutes, 29 fours) went from 44 to 140 between lunch and tea on the second day, which saw Victoria score 460 runs. With Laver (98 in 120 minutes, 15 fours) and Ransford (152 in 250 minutes, 19 fours), Armstrong established new State records for the third wicket (197 in 110 minutes) and fourth wicket (206 in 100 minutes). Collins and Saunders both suffered first-ball dismissals late in the innings. Illness prevented McLeod from taking part after the first day. *Cricket* incorrectly gives Vic Wright 0*, Saunders 28, extras, total, Qld bowling figures.   Sources: *Cricket, VCA Report, The Age, The Argus, The Herald, The Australasian.*

QUEENSLAND

J.W.Lewis	c McAlister b Saunders	13		c Laver b Collins	14
*J.Carew	c Wright b Osborne	36		b Collins	11
N.K.Foster	c Osborne b Collins	11		lbw b Collins	2
A.Marshal	st Wright b Saunders	1	(7)	not out	21
H.G.S.Morton	not out	135		b Saunders	4
C.F.Morgan	c Armstrong b Saunders	35		c Osborne b Collins	6
†W.T.Evans	lbw b Armstrong	0	(4)	lbw b Saunders	15
J.J.Fitzgerald	b Armstrong	8		c sub (J.F.Horan) b Saunders	20
T.T.T.Long	c Armstrong b Osborne	14		c McAlister b Saunders	1
F.R.V.Timbury	lbw b Collins	9		b Collins	7
T.Byrnes	c Armstrong b Collins	2		b Collins	7
Extras	(b5, lb8, w2, nb1)	16		(b2, lb2)	4
Total	(99.1 overs, 257 mins)	280		(33.1 overs, 115 mins)	112

VICTORIA

J.H.Stuckey	c Marshal b Byrnes	18
P.A.McAlister	b Fitzgerald	11
*F.J.Laver	c Marshal b Lewis	98
W.W.Armstrong	c Carew b Byrnes	200
V.S.Ransford	b Long	152
W.J.Scott	b Byrnes	28
R.M.Osborne	b Marshal	11
F.B.Collins	b Marshal	0
†H.L.Wright	not out	28
J.V.Saunders	b Long	0
C.E.McLeod	absent ill	-
Extras	(b23, lb1, w3)	27
Total	(131.4 overs, 395 mins)	573

VICTORIA	O	M	R	W	w,nb	O	M	R	W	w,nb
Saunders	25	11	66	3	1,-	17	6	44	4	-,-
Collins	13.1	3	41	3	1,-	16.1	0	64	6	-,-
Armstrong	24	7	52	2	-,1					
McLeod	18	4	46	0	-,-					
Osborne	14	1	37	2	-,-					
Laver	5	0	22	0	-,-					

QUEENSLAND	O	M	R	W	w,nb
Byrnes	36	8	137	3	2,-
Marshal	20	2	83	2	-,-
Fitzgerald	23	1	110	1	-,-
Timbury	17	2	74	0	-,-
Long	15.4	1	57	2	-,-
Lewis	20	3	85	1	1,-

FALL OF WICKETS

Wkt	QLD 1st	VIC 1st	QLD 2nd
1st	14	25	23
2nd	25	29	28
3rd	26	226	37
4th	84	432	44
5th	176	481	55
6th	177	496	55
7th	194	496	85
8th	239	573	93
9th	278	573	100
10th	280	-	112

SOUTH AUSTRALIA v NEW SOUTH WALES (Shield Match 2)

Played at Adelaide Oval on December 17, 19, 20, 1904. (Timeless match)
Toss : New South Wales.   Result : NEW SOUTH WALES WON BY AN INNINGS AND 120 RUNS.
Debuts: South Australia - R.F.Cowan (f/c).
12th Men: J.H.Pellew (SA) and G.L.Garnsey (NSW).
Umpires: P.Argall and G.A.Watson.
Attendances: 2750, 1500, 250.   Total: About 4500.   Receipts: No figures published.
Close of Play: 1st day NSW 8/351 (Waddy 85, Howell 59); 2nd day SA 177 all out.

Cowan, chosen by South Australia in place of H.Hay who was unable to obtain leave from work, dismissed C.W.Gregory with his first ball in first-class cricket. S.E.Gregory was run out while backing up at the non-striker's end when a powerful drive by Hopkins was deflected by Reedman into the stumps. Waddy (129 in 210 minutes, 10 fours) and Howell (128 in 141 minutes, 20 fours) put on 221 in 141 minutes for the New South Wales ninth wicket, a new State record. Earlier, Duff (61 in 100 minutes, 1 five and 7 fours) had hit an attractive half-century. V.T.Trumper who had recently opened a sports store in Sydney in partnership with H.Carter, was unavailable for New South Wales's southern tour and his place in the New South Wales team went to Garnsey. *Wisden* incorrectly gives SA (1) bowling for Johnson, Noble. *O'Reilly* incorrectly gives SA (2) extras 0, total 163, NSW innings and 125 runs. Sources: *Wisden, C.B.O'Reilly, NSWCA Report, Adelaide Advertiser, South Australian Register.*

NEW SOUTH WALES

J.R.M.Mackay	b Claxton	1
R.A.Duff	c Travers b Cowan	61
*M.A.Noble	b Reedman	23
C.W.Gregory	c & b Cowan	2
S.E.Gregory	run out (Reedman)	46
A.J.Y.Hopkins	b Reedman	32
E.F.Waddy	not out	129
†J.J.Kelly	c Newland b Cowan	34
A.Cotter	c Hack b Cowan	2
W.P.Howell	c Hill b Claxton	128
F.B.Johnson	b Coombe	1
Extras	(b4, lb2)	6
Total	(133.4 overs, 370 mins)	465

SOUTH AUSTRALIA

F.T.Hack	b Johnson	1	c Cotter b Johnson		3
D.R.A.Gehrs	b Johnson	1	st Kelly b Hopkins		37
*C.Hill	c Kelly b Cotter	5	b Hopkins		37
J.Darling	c Howell b Noble	67	b Hopkins		0
C.B.Jennings	lbw b Noble	14	b Howell		10
N.Claxton	b Noble	0	c Hopkins b Cotter		26
†P.M.Newland	c Hopkins b Johnson	20	c S.E.Gregory b Hopkins		5
J.C.Reedman	b Johnson	39	b Cotter		37
R.F.Cowan	b Noble	0	c Waddy b Noble		8
J.P.F.Travers	not out	15	not out		0
P.H.Coombe	c Kelly b Noble	6	c Howell b Noble		0
Extras	(b3, lb4, nb2)	9	(b3, lb2)		5
Total	(62.1 overs, 180 mins)	177	(60.3 overs, 170 mins)		168

SOUTH AUSTRALIA	O	M	R	W	w,nb
Claxton	31	8	85	2	-,-
Coombe	23.4	5	81	1	-,-
Reedman	26	3	102	2	-,-
Cowan	24	1	104	4	-,-
Travers	25	5	69	0	-,-
Gehrs	4	0	18	0	-,-

NEW SOUTH WALES	O	M	R	W	w,nb		O	M	R	W	w,nb
Cotter	13	1	43	1	-,2		15	3	47	2	-,-
Johnson	24	2	68	4	-,-		8	0	25	1	-,-
Noble	22.1	5	51	5	-,-	(5)	2.3	0	8	2	-,-
Howell	3	1	6	0	-,-		13	2	49	1	-,-
Hopkins						(3)	22	10	34	4	-,-

FALL OF WICKETS

	NSW	SA	SA
Wkt	1st	1st	2nd
1st	17	2	6
2nd	64	5	76
3rd	76	12	76
4th	101	39	88
5th	169	39	90
6th	169	104	103
7th	238	130	139
8th	242	130	168
9th	463	168	168
10th	465	177	168

VICTORIA v NEW SOUTH WALES (Shield Match 3)

Played at Melbourne Cricket Ground on December 24, 26, 27, 28, 1904. (Timeless match)
Toss : New South Wales.　　　　　Result : NEW SOUTH WALES WON BY 135 RUNS.
Debuts: New South Wales - G.L.Garnsey (f/c).
12th Men: C.W.Gregory (NSW). No 12th man or emergency fieldsman for Victoria.
Umpires: E.Barrass and R.M.Crockett.
Attendances: 6000, 8600, 8500, 5000.　　　Total: About 28,100.　　　Receipts: £872.
Close of Play: 1st day Vic 3/83 (Stuckey 35, Osborne 7); 2nd day NSW (2) 3/206 (Noble 43, Howell 57); 3rd day Vic (2) 0/71
　　(Stuckey 39, McAlister 30).

Stuckey (originally 12th man) was a late replacement for J.F.Giller (unavailable) in the Victorian team and headed the scoring for his side
in each innings (73 in 130 minutes, 10 fours and 75 in 143 minutes, 8 fours). Noble (85 in 141 minutes, 9 fours and 70 in 160 minutes,
6 fours) did New South Wales a similar service. Consistent scoring from Duff(60 in 77 minutes, 5 fours), Waddy (63 in 101 minutes, 6
fours) and Kelly (56 in 83 minutes) allied with some strong hitting from Howell (64 in 70 minutes, 1 five and 8 fours) and Cotter (56 not
out in 37 minutes, 7 fours) put the visitors in a strong position after a tied first innings. Set 481 for victory, Stuckey and McAlister (59
in 125 minutes, 2 fours) led off with a century opening stand. McLeod (57 in 147 minutes, 3 fours) and Ransford (43 in 80 minutes, 4
fours) took over in the middle order but the task proved too great and New South Wales ran out comfortable winners. *NSWCA Report*
incorrectly gives NSW (2) Duff c McAlister. Sources: *Wisden, NSWCA Report, VCA Report, The Age, The Argus, The Herald, The
Australasian, The Leader.*

NEW SOUTH WALES

R.A.Duff	c McAlister b Collins	5		b Collins	60
†J.J.Kelly	b Collins	14	(9)	lbw b Armstrong	56
*M.A.Noble	c McAlister b McLeod	85		c Ransford b Laver	70
E.F.Waddy	b Collins	7	(7)	lbw b Laver	63
S.E.Gregory	c Scott b Saunders	31	(6)	c Carkeek b Collins	49
A.J.Y.Hopkins	c Ransford b McLeod	14	(2)	c Armstrong b Laver	30
J.R.M.Mackay	c Carkeek b McLeod	13	(4)	lbw b Collins	15
G.L.Garnsey	run out (Scott/Carkeek)	3		c Carkeek b Collins	5
W.P.Howell	c McAlister b Laver	27	(5)	run out (Scott)	64
A.Cotter	c Scott b McLeod	5		not out	56
F.B.Johnson	not out	0		b Collins	0
Extras	(b8, lb1)	9		(b8, lb2, w1, nb1)	12
Total	(66.1 overs, 201 mins)	213		(131.3 overs, 327 mins)	480

VICTORIA

J.H.Stuckey	st Kelly b Johnson	73		b Cotter	75
P.A.McAlister	c Kelly b Cotter	12		st Kelly b Johnson	59
V.S.Ransford	c Kelly b Howell	23	(7)	b Hopkins	43
F.B.Collins	c Johnson b Hopkins	5	(10)	b Garnsey	1
R.M.Osborne	lbw b Howell	7	(9)	not out	9
W.W.Armstrong	b Johnson	46	(4)	c Garnsey b Johnson	37
*F.J.Laver	c Kelly b Garnsey	0	(5)	b Johnson	0
C.E.McLeod	b Garnsey	7	(6)	c Garnsey b Howell	57
W.J.Scott	b Johnson	19	(3)	c Duff b Garnsey	24
†W.Carkeek	b Johnson	16	(8)	b Cotter	24
J.V.Saunders	not out	1		b Garnsey	4
Extras	(b2, lb2)	4		(b6, lb6)	12
Total	(64.4 overs, 182 mins)	213		(121.2 overs, 358 mins)	345

VICTORIA	O	M	R	W	w,nb		O	M	R	W	w,nb
Saunders	17	5	41	1	-,-		27	6	93	0	-,-
Collins	22	3	98	3	-,-	(5)	27.3	2	103	5	-,1
McLeod	17	4	42	4	-,-	(2)	14	1	66	0	-,-
Laver	1.1	0	10	1	-,-		27	4	97	3	-,-
Osborne	1	0	3	0	-,-	(3)	12	0	41	0	-,-
Armstrong	8	3	10	0	-,-		21	5	56	1	-,-
Ransford							3	0	12	0	1,-

NEW SOUTH WALES	O	M	R	W	w,nb		O	M	R	W	w,nb
Noble	8	2	28	0	-,-						
Cotter	14	3	39	1	-,-	(1)	21	2	59	2	-,-
Johnson	20.4	3	70	4	-,-	(5)	27	1	64	3	-,-
Hopkins	3	0	14	1	-,-	(2)	28	5	79	1	-,-
Howell	12	4	38	2	-,-	(3)	29	7	64	1	-,-
Garnsey	7	2	20	2	-,-	(4)	16.2	2	67	3	-,-

FALL OF WICKETS

Wkt	NSW 1st	VIC 1st	NSW 2nd	VIC 2nd
1st	5	15	68	130
2nd	38	69	102	141
3rd	56	76	124	195
4th	109	83	225	203
5th	159	155	266	206
6th	178	168	312	281
7th	178	168	318	330
8th	189	195	405	330
9th	212	195	469	331
10th	213	213	480	345

NEW SOUTH WALES v QUEENSLAND

Played at Sydney Cricket Ground on December 24, 26, 27, 1904. (Timeless match)
Toss : Queensland.　　　　　　　　　Result : NEW SOUTH WALES WON BY AN INNINGS AND 272 RUNS.
Debuts: New South Wales - A.E.Johnston, K.McPhillamy, A.P.Penman (all f/c). Queensland - W.B.Hayes (f/c).
12th Men: A.Single (NSW) and F.R.V.Timbury (Qld).
Umpires: W.G.Curran and A.C.Jones.
Attendances: 1000, 2000, 2000.　　　　Total: About 5000.　　　Receipts: £147.
Close of Play: 1st day NSW 3/118 (Poidevin 28, Diamond 9); 2nd day NSW 8/597 (Carter 91, McPhillamy 3).

Centuries by Poidevin (179 in 246 minutes, 24 fours), Pye (117 in 117 minutes, 16 fours) and Carter at No. 9 (149 in only 119 minutes, 27 fours) enabled New South Wales to register their highest total yet against Queensland; 479 runs were scored off the northern attack on the second day alone. Both Poidevin and Carter achieved their highest scores in lengthy first-class careers, Carter (strong cutting and hooking) being especially severe on anything short. Pye, whose hundred was his second and last in first-class cricket, had been a late replacement in the New South Wales side for B.W.Farquhar (thumb injury at practice) after withdrawing himself from the original selection for business reasons. Lewis was out to the third ball of Queensland's second innings and Marshal fell attempting to steal a fourth run from a hit into the deep. Morton (52 in 87 minutes, 7 fours) recorded the only Queensland half-century of the match. *Cricket* gives incorrect details for Qld (1) Hayes, Morgan and extras. Sources: *Cricket, NSWCA Report, Sydney Referee, Sydney Morning Herald, Town & Country Journal, Sydney Mail.*

QUEENSLAND

*J.Carew	b Penman	43	(2) c Diamond b Deane	34
J.W.Lewis	c Poidevin b Bowden	39	(1) c Poidevin b Penman	0
A.Marshal	b Bowden	4	(6) run out (Deane/Penman)	5
H.G.S.Morton	b Penman	1	(3) c Poidevin b Bowden	52
N.K.Foster	b Pye	10	b Bowden	35
†W.T.Evans	b Pye	14	(7) b Bowden	25
C.F.Morgan	b McPhillamy	1	(8) c Carter b Penman	17
J.J.Fitzgerald	c Carter b McPhillamy	24	(4) c Bardsley b Bowden	0
W.B.Hayes	c Diamond b McPhillamy	6	not out	25
T.T.T.Long	not out	3	b Penman	1
T.Byrnes	lbw b Pye	7	b Hickson	27
Extras	(b11, lb9, w2)	22	(b9, lb6, w1, nb3)	19
Total	(70.1 overs, 185 mins)	174	(71.1 overs, 210 mins)	240

NEW SOUTH WALES

R.N.Hickson	c Marshal b Byrnes	42
W.Bardsley	c Evans b Hayes	21
A.E.Johnston	c Byrnes b Long	9
L.O.S.Poidevin	c Long b Byrnes	179
*A.Diamond	c Morton b Lewis	64
L.W.Pye	c Lewis b Byrnes	117
N.Y.Deane	c Foster b Byrnes	31
A.J.Bowden	b Byrnes	13
†H.Carter	c Marshal b Long	149
K.McPhillamy	c Evans b Lewis	11
A.P.Penman	not out	15
Extras	(b23, lb7, nb5)	35
Total	(165.2 overs, 435 mins)	686

NEW SOUTH WALES	O	M	R	W	w,nb		O	M	R	W	w,nb
Penman	17	9	18	2	-,-		14	2	51	3	-,1
McPhillamy	16	2	51	3	1,-		18	1	65	0	1,1
Pye	12.1	1	26	3	-,-						
Deane	10	4	22	0	1,-		15	6	43	1	-,1
Bowden	15	7	35	2	-,-	(3)	21	3	52	4	-,-
Hickson						(5)	3.1	1	10	1	-,-

QUEENSLAND	O	M	R	W	w,nb
Byrnes	53	13	169	5	-,-
Fitzgerald	16	0	91	0	-,-
Hayes	20	3	95	1	-,2
Long	28.2	7	76	2	-,-
Lewis	30	3	145	2	-,-
Marshal	18	2	75	0	-,3

FALL OF WICKETS

Wkt	QLD 1st	NSW 1st	QLD 2nd
1st	73	62	0
2nd	84	77	76
3rd	103	82	77
4th	107	207	109
5th	132	444	123
6th	133	477	151
7th	133	488	162
8th	147	545	187
9th	164	632	201
10th	174	686	240

VICTORIA v SOUTH AUSTRALIA (Shield Match 4)

Played at Melbourne Cricket Ground on December 31, 1904, January 2, 3, 4, 1905. (Timeless match)
Toss : South Australia.   Result : SOUTH AUSTRALIA WON BY AN INNINGS AND 72 RUNS.
Debuts: Nil.
12th Men: H.J.Fry (Vic - see below) and R.F.Cowan (SA).
Umpires: W.J.Bruton and R.M.Crockett.
Attendances: 6000, 6000, 4000, 1500.   Total: About 17,500.   Receipts: £483.
Close of Play: 1st day SA 7/364 (Claxton 40); 2nd day Vic 0/6 (McAlister 4, Ransford 2); 3rd day Vic (2) 4/162 (Armstrong 70, Carkeek 5).

Stuckey, in fielding a ball at third man early on the first day, sustained a fractured kneecap and took no further part in the match. An offer from Hill to permit Victoria's 12th man, Fry, to replace Stuckey as a full member of the team was then taken up. Gehrs (chanceless 170 in 245 minutes, 19 fours) and Hack (67 in 139 minutes, 3 fours) put on 168 for the first wicket. Claxton (58 in 100 minutes, 7 fours) also batted well. Although Carkeek injured a finger while wicket-keeping and was forced to give the gloves to Fry late on the first day, he remained in the field throughout the South Australian innings, which ended right on lunch on the second day. Rain then curtailed playing time for the rest of the day and badly affected the conditions of the pitch for both innings of Victoria. Reedman took full advantage to return his best match figures in 76 games for South Australia. Armstrong scored 85 in 131 minutes and hit 9 fours. Ransford, who was struck by a ball from Claxton just before his dismissal in the first innings, batted with a runner in the second innings. *O'Reilly* incorrectly gives Vic (1) extras 6, total 130, South Australia by an innings and 71 runs. Sources: *Wisden, C.B.O'Reilly, VCA Report, The Age, The Argus, The Australasian.*

SOUTH AUSTRALIA

D.R.A.Gehrs	c McLeod b Saunders	170
F.T.Hack	c Osborne b Laver	67
*C.Hill	b McLeod	28
J.Darling	b Collins	35
N.Claxton	c Collins b Armstrong	58
C.B.Jennings	c Laver b Saunders	5
J.H.Pellew	b Saunders	0
†P.M.Newland	lbw b Armstrong	4
J.C.Reedman	c Osborne b Saunders	5
J.P.F.Travers	not out	27
P.H.Coombe	st Fry b McLeod	4
Extras	(b8, lb8, nb1)	17
Total	(133.2 overs, 360 mins)	420

VICTORIA

P.A.McAlister	b Reedman	34	(2) c Newland b Travers		13
V.S.Ransford	c Hill b Reedman	18	(7) b Coombe		31
C.E.McLeod	c Newland b Reedman	3	c Travers b Reedman		0
W.W.Armstrong	c Jennings b Reedman	13	b Reedman		85
*F.J.Laver	c & b Reedman	41	(1) c Newland b Claxton		20
W.J.Scott	st Newland b Travers	3	(5) c Reedman b Claxton		45
†W.Carkeek	c Claxton b Reedman	3	(6) b Reedman		7
H.J.Fry	c Darling b Reedman	0	b Reedman		9
R.M.Osborne	st Newland b Travers	0	c Newland b Reedman		0
F.B.Collins	b Travers	4	c & b Reedman		0
J.V.Saunders	not out	5	not out		0
J.H.Stuckey	absent hurt	-	absent hurt		-
Extras	(b4, lb1)	5	(b6, lb1, w2)		9
Total	(59.2 overs, 145 mins)	129	(76.4 overs, 207 mins)		219

VICTORIA	O	M	R	W	w,nb					
Saunders	37	8	108	4	-,-					
Collins	24	1	85	1	-,1					
Armstrong	32	11	46	2	-,-					
McLeod	12.2	0	60	2	-,-					
Laver	16	2	62	1	-,-					
Osborne	7	0	20	0	-,-					
Fry	5	0	22	0	-,-					

FALL OF WICKETS			
	SA	VIC	VIC
Wkt	1st	1st	2nd
1st	168	40	19
2nd	215	51	20
3rd	290	64	49
4th	323	71	150
5th	339	97	166
6th	339	102	187
7th	364	102	215
8th	377	103	215
9th	391	107	219
10th	420	129	219

SOUTH AUSTRALIA	O	M	R	W	w,nb		O	M	R	W	w,nb
Claxton	9	1	20	0	-,-	(3)	18	4	43	2	-,-
Reedman	30.2	13	54	7	-,-	(1)	29.4	3	95	6	-,-
Travers	20	3	50	3	-,-	(2)	21	3	50	1	-,-
Hack							5	1	17	0	2,-
Coombe							3	1	5	1	-,-

AFCM No. 319/29
SSM No. 75/26

NEW SOUTH WALES v SOUTH AUSTRALIA (Shield Match 5)

Played at Sydney Cricket Ground on January 6, 7, 9, 1905. (Timeless match)
Toss : South Australia.   Result : NEW SOUTH WALES WON BY SEVEN WICKETS.
Debuts: Nil.
12th Men: A.Diamond (NSW) and P.H.Coombe (SA).
Umpires: W.G.Curran and J.Laing.
Attendances: 5490, 10740, 3006.   Total: 19,236.   Receipts: £645.
Close of Play: 1st day NSW 1/89 (Duff 60); 2nd day SA (2) 6/107 (Pellew 24, Travers 8).

Carter was brought into the New South Wales side to replace J.J.Kelly, who had not recovered from the illness contracted during the match against Victoria in Melbourne. Gehrs (48 in 60 minutes, 1 five and 8 fours) began the match in dazzling style but the loss of Hill to the first ball that he received slowed proceedings. Pellew (68 in 110 minutes, 9 fours and 53 in 99 minutes, 8 fours) topscored in each South Australian innings and was assisted in a ninth wicket stand in the first by Travers (58 in 60 minutes, 12 fours). Cotter "making the ball fly", (*Sydney Morning Herald*), captured the first seven wickets to fall in the second innings. Duff (80 in 85 minutes, 11 fours) and Trumper (76 in 65 minutes, 13 fours) began the first and second innings respectively, in characteristically brilliant fashion and Howell (62 in 61 minutes, 11 fours) hit strongly. Waddy (57 in 133 minutes, 4 fours and 43 not out in 79 minutes, 3 fours) played valuable supporting innings. *Wisden* incorrectly gives NSW (2) extras 8, total 174. Sources: *Wisden, C.B.O'Reilly, NSWCA Report, Sydney Referee, Sydney Morning Herald, Town & Country Journal.*

SOUTH AUSTRALIA

Batsman	Dismissal 1	Score 1	Dismissal 2	Score 2
D.R.A.Gehrs	c & b Hopkins	48	(2) b Cotter	6
F.T.Hack	c Noble b Johnson	24	(1) c Garnsey b Cotter	5
*C.Hill	b Johnson	0	b Cotter	41
J.Darling	c Carter b Hopkins	17	b Cotter	5
N.Claxton	b Howell	22	c Carter b Cotter	7
C.B.Jennings	st Carter b Johnson	22	lbw b Cotter	1
J.H.Pellew	c Waddy b Hopkins	68	c Noble b Hopkins	53
†P.M.Newland	b Howell	4	(10) not out	7
J.C.Reedman	c Noble b Howell	12	b Hopkins	18
J.P.F.Travers	c Cotter b Hopkins	58	(8) c Howell b Cotter	12
R.F.Cowan	not out	0	run out (Gregory/Carter)	19
Extras	(b4, lb2)	6	(b5, lb3, w2, nb1)	11
Total	(77.3 overs, 206 mins)	281	(54.4 overs, 155 mins)	185

NEW SOUTH WALES

Batsman	Dismissal 1	Score 1	Dismissal 2	Score 2
V.T.Trumper	c Hill b Travers	28	c Newland b Pellew	76
R.A.Duff	c Hill b Reedman	80	b Reedman	13
*M.A.Noble	b Reedman	18		
E.F.Waddy	c Hill b Travers	57	(3) not out	43
S.E.Gregory	st Newland b Travers	3		
A.J.Y.Hopkins	b Reedman	5	(4) b Cowan	20
W.P.Howell	b Hack	62	(5) not out	14
†H.Carter	lbw b Travers	22		
G.L.Garnsey	not out	5		
A.Cotter	c Reedman b Travers	12		
F.B.Johnson	st Newland b Travers	3		
Extras	(lb2, w2)	4	(b1, lb3)	4
Total	(87.4 overs, 235 mins)	299	(39.5 overs, 105 mins) (3 wkts)	170

NEW SOUTH WALES	O	M	R	W	w,nb		O	M	R	W	w,nb
Cotter	11	0	51	0	-,-		19	0	77	7	-,1
Garnsey	9	0	35	0	-,-		1	0	4	0	-,-
Johnson	23	2	73	3	-,-	(4)	8.4	3	21	0	-,-
Hopkins	18.3	2	58	4	-,-	(5)	16	8	35	2	2,-
Howell	15	4	52	3	-,-	(3)	10	4	37	0	-,-
Trumper	1	0	6	0	-,-						

SOUTH AUSTRALIA	O	M	R	W	w,nb		O	M	R	W	w,nb
Claxton	18	1	66	0	-,-						
Reedman	26	3	79	3	-,-		11	2	61	1	-,-
Travers	32.4	9	102	6	-,-	(1)	14	2	33	0	-,-
Pellew	4	0	18	0	1,-		8.5	1	44	1	-,-
Hack	3	1	17	1	-,-						
Cowan	4	0	13	0	1,-	(3)	6	0	28	1	-,-

FALL OF WICKETS

Wkt	SA 1st	NSW 1st	SA 2nd	NSW 2nd
1st	67	89	11	55
2nd	67	125	12	108
3rd	79	133	24	149
4th	96	136	52	-
5th	131	145	62	-
6th	135	233	76	-
7th	144	270	112	-
8th	159	280	157	-
9th	254	296	160	-
10th	281	299	185	-

NEW SOUTH WALES v VICTORIA (Shield Match 6)

Played at Sydney Cricket Ground on January 27, 28, 30, 31, February 1, 1905. (Timeless match)
Toss : New South Wales.   Result : NEW SOUTH WALES WON BY 199 RUNS.
Debuts: Nil.
12th Men: A.Diamond (NSW) and J.V.Saunders (Vic).
Umpires: W.G.Curran and J.Laing.
Attendances: 3492, 10381, 7867, 3610, 882.   Total: 26,232.   Receipts: £830.
Close of Play: 1st day NSW 4/240 (Gregory 13, Johnson 2); 2nd day Vic 2/126 (Giller 45, Carkeek 7); 3rd day Vic 6/310 (Giller 113, McLeod 21); 4th day Vic (2) 3/50 (Carkeek 1, Scott 4).

Giller, in his last first-class match, batted for 343 minutes, spread over three days, to compile 125 with 15 fours. He sustained bruising during his innings and used Carlton as a runner on the third day. Carlton wore no pads for the first eight overs of play until Noble objected and requested he pad up. Giller was unable to field in the second innings; J.S.Redgrave substituted throughout. Trumper (81 in 88 minutes, 1 five and 9 fours) and Noble (65 in 97 minutes, 7 fours and 112 in 116 minutes, 2 fives and 16 fours) made notable scores for New South Wales. Collins dismissed Noble, Howell and Garnsey in two overs in the second innings to take three wickets in four balls. McAlister was dismissed first ball in the second innings and Ransford, who was hit on the head by a ball from Cotter, retired hurt when 8 with the score at 3/45, resuming next day at 7/115. Carkeek top scored with 46 in 108 minutes, hitting 7 fours. Saunders was made 12th man due to strained side muscles. Last first-class appearance by C.E.McLeod. Sources: *Wisden, NSWCA Report, Sydney Referee, Sydney Morning Herald, Town & Country Journal.*

NEW SOUTH WALES

A.J.Y.Hopkins	c Ransford b Armstrong	37	(7)	b Armstrong	30
V.T.Trumper	st Carkeek b Giller	81	(1)	run out (Carlton/Laver/Carkeek)	13
*M.A.Noble	c Armstrong b Laver	65	(4)	b Collins	112
W.P.Howell	b McLeod	34	(8)	c Scott b Collins	4
S.E.Gregory	c Laver b Armstrong	40		c McAlister b Warne	10
F.B.Johnson	run out (Scott/Carkeek)	12	(11)	not out	11
E.F.Waddy	c Carkeek b Giller	35	(6)	b Armstrong	17
R.A.Duff	b Collins	8	(2)	b Warne	26
†J.J.Kelly	c Scott b Laver	50	(3)	b Armstrong	22
G.L.Garnsey	b McLeod	16	(9)	c Warne b Collins	0
A.Cotter	not out	21	(10)	b Armstrong	1
Extras	(b6, lb13, w1, nb2)	22		(b2, lb6, nb1)	9
Total	(107.5 overs, 310 mins)	421		(74.2 overs, 203 mins)	255

VICTORIA

P.A.McAlister	b Cotter	8	(2)	b Garnsey	0
J.F.Giller	run out (Waddy/Noble)	125	(9)	b Hopkins	1
V.S.Ransford	b Cotter	62	(4)	c Noble b Howell	18
†W.Carkeek	c Gregory b Howell	25	(5)	b Hopkins	46
W.W.Armstrong	c Duff b Cotter	55	(8)	b Hopkins	0
*F.J.Laver	b Cotter	4	(7)	c Trumper b Howell	3
W.J.Scott	c Trumper b Hopkins	9	(6)	c Duff b Johnson	21
C.E.McLeod	c Howell b Noble	22	(1)	c Duff b Noble	18
T.S.Warne	c & b Cotter	11	(10)	not out	8
W.Carlton	not out	2	(3)	b Garnsey	12
F.B.Collins	b Noble	1		lbw b Hopkins	0
Extras	(b9, lb8, w2, nb2)	21		(b2, lb3)	5
Total	(118.1 overs, 350 mins)	345		(46.3 overs, 118 mins)	132

VICTORIA	O	M	R	W	w,nb		O	M	R	W	w,nb
Collins	22	6	89	1	-,1		9	0	57	3	-,1
Giller	25	5	96	2	1,-						
Armstrong	33	8	95	2	-,1	(2)	26.2	7	57	4	-,-
McLeod	14.5	1	69	2	-,-	(5)	6	1	31	0	-,-
Warne	3	0	15	0	-,-	(3)	11	1	50	2	-,-
Laver	10	2	35	2	-,-	(4)	14	4	28	0	-,-
Ransford						(6)	8	3	23	0	-,-

NEW SOUTH WALES	O	M	R	W	w,nb		O	M	R	W	w,nb
Cotter	29	4	83	5	1,1		16	4	28	0	-,-
Noble	32.1	10	70	2	-,1	(3)	2	0	5	1	-,-
Johnson	16	3	48	0	-,-	(4)	7	0	32	1	-,-
Hopkins	20	7	45	1	-,-	(6)	7.3	2	14	4	-,-
Howell	19	2	59	1	-,-		8	3	23	2	-,-
Garnsey	2	0	19	0	1,-	(2)	6	1	25	2	-,-

FALL OF WICKETS

Wkt	NSW 1st	VIC 1st	NSW 2nd	VIC 2nd
1st	102	8	26	4
2nd	150	115	45	24
3rd	199	152	114	45
4th	237	233	164	84
5th	264	241	206	108
6th	280	268	206	113
7th	295	315	210	115
8th	345	342	210	122
9th	398	344	213	132
10th	421	345	255	132

VICTORIA v TASMANIA

Played at Melbourne Cricket Ground on January 28, 30 (no play), 31, February 1, 1905. (Timeless match)
Toss : Victoria.   Result : VICTORIA WON BY AN INNINGS AND 137 RUNS.
Debuts: Victoria - J.G.M.Garland, E.A.Goss, W.M.McPetrie, F.Vaughan (all f/c). Tasmania - A.E.Frost, J.C.Watt (both f/c).
12th Men: J.T.Howlett (Vic). No 12th named for Tasmania; only 11 men in party.
Umpires: R.M.Crockett and C.E.Over.
Attendances: 500 1st day, no figures other days but assessed as "very small".   Total: About 700.   Receipts: £18.
Close of Play: 1st day Vic 9/429 (Goss 20); 2nd day no play; 3rd day Tas (2) 7/140 (Watt 29, Chancellor 54).

Tasmania were severely undermanned through the absence of C.J.Eady, T.A.Tabart and E.A.C.Windsor (all unavailable) and the late withdrawal of E.J.K.Burn (the nominated captain) due to the illness of his brother. Frost was brought into the side and E.S.Hawson made captain. McPetrie's innings on debut (123 in 155 minutes, 3 fives and 15 fours) was interrupted when struck a severe blow on the knee by a ball from Smith with his score on 90 and the total at 2/194. He retired hurt but was able to resume at 3/320. Baker (58 in 60 minutes, 1 five and 8 fours) and Grant (79 in 62 minutes, 12 fours) scored almost at will. Rainey (60 not out in 140 minutes, 5 fours) became the second casualty of the innings when hit a "nasty blow" (*Australasian*) by a ball from Frost with his score at 60 (total, 4/374). He was assisted to the pavilion where he collapsed and the attending doctor "had to use artificial means to restore respiration" (*Australasian*). He quickly recovered and was able to resume at 9/429. Heavy rain prevented any play on the scheduled second day and Tasmania had the misfortune to be caught on the softened wicket. Cuff was caught from the first ball of the innings (also Goss's first in first-class cricket) and the steady fall of wickets thereafter saw the follow-on enforced. The second innings was a repeat of the first until Watt and Chancellor (92 in 135 minutes, 9 fours) added 127 for the eighth wicket. E.S.Hawson (5) was the third batsman in the match to retire hurt when he was struck by a ball from Fry at 4/35. He resumed next day at 9/188. *Cricket* incorrectly gives Baker 38. Sources: *Cricket, The Age, The Herald, The Australasian*.

VICTORIA

W.M.McPetrie	c Smith b Frost	123
J.F.Horan	c R.J.Hawson b Frost	37
*C.M.Baker	b Paton	58
L.N.Rainey	not out	60
B.Grant	b Smith	79
F.Vaughan	c E.S.Hawson b Frost	12
H.J.Fry	lbw b Paton	10
A.H.Christian	c Paton b Frost	4
E.A.Goss	c R.J.Hawson b Chancellor	21
J.G.M.Garland	c R.J.Hawson b Frost	9
†J.R.H.Woodford	lbw b Smith	3
Extras	(b9, lb4, w1)	14
Total	(94.4 overs, 290 mins)	430

TASMANIA

L.A.Cuff	c McPetrie b Goss	0	(3)	c McPetrie b Rainey	1
†N.Dodds	run out	0	(5)	b Rainey	1
O.H.Douglas	c Woodford b Garland	21	(1)	c Grant b Rainey	5
R.J.Hawson	c Horan b Christian	4	(2)	c Baker b Rainey	9
G.D.Paton	b Garland	19	(4)	c Horan b Fry	15
*E.S.Hawson	c McPetrie b Goss	24		c McPetrie b Christian	16
E.W.Harrison	c Christian b Fry	3	(8)	c Grant b Rainey	7
D.R.Smith	c McPetrie b Christian	13	(7)	c Woodford b Rainey	9
F.E.Chancellor	lbw b Christian	1	(10)	c Grant b Garland	92
A.E.Frost	c Woodford b Goss	0	(11)	not out	1
J.C.Watt	not out	1	(9)	c Garland b Christian	36
Extras	(b5, w1, nb1)	7		(b3, w5)	8
Total	(54.4 overs, 142 mins)	93		(85.3 overs, 225 mins)	200

TASMANIA	O	M	R	W	w,nb						
Chancellor	13.4	1	68	1	1,-						
Paton	28	4	121	2	-,-						
Smith	25	4	84	2	-,-						
Frost	19	3	69	5	-,-						
Cuff	3	0	29	0	-,-						
Watt	3	0	24	0	-,-						
Harrison	1	0	9	0	-,-						
E.S.Hawson	2	0	12	0	-,-						

VICTORIA	O	M	R	W	w,nb		O	M	R	W	w,nb
Goss	17.4	8	21	3	-,1	(2)	8	1	25	0	-,-
Christian	14	8	18	3	1,-	(6)	22.3	10	31	2	-,-
Garland	13	4	21	2	-,-	(5)	14	5	38	1	-,-
Fry	10	2	26	1	-,-	(3)	12	1	33	1	-,-
Rainey						(1)	26	12	46	6	5,-
Grant						(4)	3	0	19	0	-,-

FALL OF WICKETS

		VIC	TAS	TAS
Wkt		1st	1st	2nd
1st		63	0	13
2nd		186	0	14
3rd		320	5	22
4th		370	35	26
5th		389	56	43
6th		397	69	51
7th		399	90	59
8th		426	91	186
9th		429	92	188
10th		430	93	200

TASMANIA v NEW SOUTH WALES

Played at S.T.C.A. Ground, Hobart, on March 24, 25, 27, 1905. (Timeless match)
Toss : Tasmania.   Result : TASMANIA WON BY 68 RUNS.
Debuts: New South Wales - J.D.A.O'Connor, J.S.Redgrave (both f/c).
12th Men: No 12th men or emergency fieldsmen named; only 11 men in NSW party.
Umpires: C.McAllen and G.L.Nettlefold.
Attendances: "satisfactory", 1800, "moderate".   Total: About 3000.   Receipts: No figures published.
Close of Play: 1st day NSW 5/103 (Mackay 33); 2nd day Tas (2) 4/124 (Windsor 26, Paton 5).

Redgrave replaced L.W.Pye (unavailable) in the New South Wales team before departure from Sydney. R.J.Hawson was unavailable for the home team. Paton was caught from the third ball of the match and wickets fell at a steady rate for the remainder of the game on a wicket that was reported to be in "capital condition" (*Mercury*) throughout. Windsor (41 in 100 minutes, 6 fours) and Tabart (48 in 105 minutes, 4 fours) were the only Tasmanian batsmen to exceed 40 in either innings. Mackay (67 in 114 minutes, 6 fours) recorded the sole half-century for the match, the bowlers of both sides holding sway. Redgrave's three wickets were all obtained in his second over in first-class cricket at the cost of a single run (Douglas, Windsor, Chancellor). Eady and Windsor bowled Tasmania to victory in an unchanged spell in the post-lunch session on the third day. Their performances - Eady 11 for 99, Windsor 41, 26 and 6 for 122 - provided Tasmania with their first win against New South Wales. *NSWCA Report* incorrectly gives Tas (2) Hawson b Garnsey. Sources: *NSWCA Report, Sydney Morning Herald, Hobart Mercury, Launceston Examiner.*

TASMANIA

G.D.Paton	c Carter b Penman	0	(6) not out		37
E.S.Hawson	c Redgrave b Penman	5	(9) c & b Garnsey		2
C.J.Eady	c Johnston b Johnson	3	(5) c Waddy b O'Connor		0
E.A.C.Windsor	lbw b Redgrave	41	b Johnson		26
*E.J.K.Burn	b O'Connor	29	(3) lbw b O'Connor		9
T.A.Tabart	c O'Connor b Penman	8	(1) b O'Connor		48
O.H.Douglas	c Johnson b Redgrave	13	(2) c Waddy b Garnsey		31
†N.Dodds	c Carter b Johnson	24	c Johnson b Penman		14
F.E.Chancellor	b Redgrave	0	(10) c Diamond b Garnsey		4
A.E.Frost	not out	26	(7) run out		1
R.H.Sams	c Diamond b Johnson	24	b O'Connor		1
Extras	(b1, lb5, nb4)	10	(b6, lb2, nb2)		10
Total	(59.3 overs, 175 mins)	183	(82.0 overs, 238 mins)		183

NEW SOUTH WALES

R.N.Hickson	lbw b Eady	5	lbw b Windsor		10
J.R.M.Mackay	c Sams b Frost	67	c Dodds b Windsor		15
E.F.Waddy	lbw b Eady	33	b Eady		17
A.E.Johnston	c Dodds b Eady	0	c Tabart b Eady		0
*A.Diamond	c Dodds b Windsor	3	b Eady		4
†H.Carter	b Eady	23	c Eady Windsor		15
J.S.Redgrave	c Chancellor b Eady	12	c Dodds b Eady		4
G.L.Garnsey	c Hawson b Eady	0	b Windsor		0
J.D.A.O'Connor	b Chancellor	16	c Tabart b Windsor		4
F.B.Johnson	not out	19	b Eady		14
A.P.Penman	c Tabart b Chancellor	1	not out		11
Extras	(b14, lb1, nb2)	17	(b7, w1)		8
Total	(54.5 overs, 160 mins)	196	(24.1 overs, 78 mins)		102

NEW SOUTH WALES	O	M	R	W	w,nb		O	M	R	W	w,nb
Penman	11	3	16	3	-,4	(3)	11	4	26	1	-,2
Johnson	20.3	4	64	3	-,-	(5)	10	2	19	1	-,-
O'Connor	8	1	25	1	-,-	(1)	24	7	43	4	-,-
Garnsey	9	1	35	0	-,-		17	4	39	3	-,-
Redgrave	11	3	33	3	-,-	(2)	20	6	46	0	-,-

TASMANIA	O	M	R	W	w,nb	O	M	R	W	w,nb
Eady	27	10	58	6	-,2	12.1	4	41	5	-,-
Windsor	13	1	69	1	-,-	12	0	53	5	1,-
Chancellor	10.5	1	35	2	-,-					
Frost	4	0	17	1	-,-					

	FALL OF WICKETS			
Wkt	TAS 1st	NSW 1st	TAS 2nd	NSW 2nd
1st	0	6	83	20
2nd	7	64	83	42
3rd	11	64	103	50
4th	66	67	103	54
5th	79	103	124	58
6th	104	121	132	73
7th	105	121	156	73
8th	105	155	174	73
9th	131	177	182	77
10th	183	196	183	102

QUEENSLAND v NEW SOUTH WALES

Played at Brisbane Cricket Ground (Woolloongabba) on April 22, 24, 25, 1905. (Timeless match)
Toss : Queensland.   Result : NEW SOUTH WALES WON BY AN INNINGS AND 12 RUNS.
Debuts: Queensland - J.Whalley (f/c). New South Wales - J.C.Barnes, A.E.Sullivan (both f/c).
12th Men: C.F.Morgan (Qld) and E.R.Bubb (NSW).
Umpires: A.L.Cossart and J.P.Orr.
Attendances: 2000, 1500, 500.   Total: About 4000.   Receipts: No figures published.
Close of Play: 1st day NSW 4/176 (Mackay 82, Redgrave 28); 2nd day Qld (2) 3/89 (G.S.Crouch 12, Hayes 7).

B.W.Farquhar, R.N.Hickson and L.W.Pye all announced their unavailability and New South Wales were further weakened by the late withdrawal of C.W.Gregory and F.B.Johnson, who were replaced by Bubb and Sullivan. Whalley was a late replacement in the Queensland team for J.Carew, quarantined at Goodna Asylum (his place of employment) due to an outbreak of dengue fever. E.R.Crouch (49 in 90 minutes, 7 fours) topscored for Queensland on a wicket described as "somewhat soft" (*Courier*) which the accurate O'Connor used to advantage. Mackay (131 in 155 minutes, 19 fours) played an innings described as "faultless" and "masterly" (*Courier*) to put New South Wales in a commanding position. O'Connor (54 in 53 minutes, 7 fours) hit well late in the order. G.S.Crouch (48 in 94 minutes, 4 fours) and Lewis (40 in 45 minutes, 2 fives and 4 fours) fought hard in the second innings but could not avert the innings defeat. O'Connor completed a ten-wicket haul to cap a fine all-round performance. Sources: *NSWCA Report, Brisbane Courier, Queensland Times, The Queenslander.*

QUEENSLAND

Batsman	Dismissal (1st)	R		Dismissal (2nd)	R
J.W.Lewis	c Waddy b Penman	9	(8)	run out (Waddy/Carter)	40
E.R.Crouch	st Carter b Sullivan	49		c Carter b O'Connor	17
G.S.Crouch	b Penman	0	(4)	b Sullivan	48
N.K.Foster	c Garnsey b O'Connor	15	(1)	b Garnsey	34
H.G.S.Morton	b O'Connor	0	(7)	c Carter b O'Connor	0
*†W.T.Evans	c Carter b O'Connor	4		c & b O'Connor	4
H.B.Griffith	c Mackay b O'Connor	0	(9)	c Carter b Sullivan	2
W.B.Hayes	c Carter b O'Connor	38	(5)	c Garnsey b O'Connor	10
J.Whalley	c Mackay b Sullivan	0	(3)	c & b Sullivan	16
T.Byrnes	c Sullivan b Garnsey	24		b O'Connor	15
A.Henry	not out	4		not out	5
Extras	(lb3, nb2)	5		(b1, lb1, nb2)	4
Total	(44.0 overs, 135 mins)	148		(59.0 overs, 170 mins)	195

NEW SOUTH WALES

Batsman	Dismissal	R
E.F.Waddy	c E.R.Crouch b Byrnes	6
J.R.M.Mackay	c Henry b Lewis	131
W.Bardsley	c Evans b Byrnes	4
†H.Carter	b Henry	5
*A.Diamond	c Hayes b Griffith	46
J.S.Redgrave	b Byrnes	44
J.C.Barnes	c E.R.Crouch b Hayes	20
G.L.Garnsey	c Evans b Hayes	26
J.D.A.O'Connor	c G.S.Crouch b E.R.Crouch	54
A.E.Sullivan	st Evans b E.R.Crouch	10
A.P.Penman	not out	1
Extras	(b5, lb3)	8
Total	(79.1 overs, 220 mins)	355

NEW SOUTH WALES	O	M	R	W	w,nb	O	M	R	W	w,nb
Penman	11	3	22	2	-,2	10	2	37	0	-,1
Sullivan	11	1	53	2	-,-	18	5	67	3	-,1
O'Connor	11	2	27	5	-,-	20	4	52	5	-,-
Garnsey	7	1	29	1	-,-	11	2	35	1	-,-
Redgrave	4	0	12	0	-,-					

QUEENSLAND	O	M	R	W	w,nb
Henry	17	2	78	1	-,-
Byrnes	21	1	102	3	-,-
Griffith	10	0	72	1	-,-
Lewis	14	5	27	1	-,-
Hayes	14	2	65	2	-,-
E.R.Crouch	3.1	2	3	2	-,-

FALL OF WICKETS

Wkt	QLD 1st	NSW 1st	QLD 2nd
1st	14	7	45
2nd	14	15	53
3rd	49	20	80
4th	49	112	110
5th	57	207	119
6th	57	255	123
7th	92	265	153
8th	92	309	167
9th	144	354	181
10th	148	355	195

1905-06 SEASON (12 MATCHES)

New South Wales again retained the Sheffield Shield, stretching their winning sequence of titles to five. They remained undefeated for the second year in succession, and began by recording innings victories in both their away games to assert their authority. They finished with comfortable wins in their two home fixtures. Noble had a fine season, but it was the efforts of the younger players, such as E.F.Waddy, Diamond, O'Connor, Garnsey and Mackay, that caught the eye. 'Sunny Jim' Mackay had a golden season. He began with 203 against Queensland and followed up with scores of 90, 194, 105, 102*, 4, 136, 18 and 50 in his remaining eight innings. Some critics had considered him unlucky to miss the tour of England the previous winter, and it seemed that a brilliant career had begun.

Victoria began the season with an innings victory at South Australia's expense at Adelaide, only to lose their remaining three matches by resounding margins to repeat their experience of the previous season. Armstrong, Collins, McAlister, Saunders and Warne did well for them this year.

South Australia continued to wallow at the foot of the Shield table. They finished last for the eighth successive season, by virtue of poor percentages. Clem Hill, Gehrs, Claxton, Travers and Wright were their main performers.

Below-strength New South Wales teams again easily accounted for Queensland this season. Herbert 'Ranji' Hordern (11 for 164) had a fine debut in the second of the matches. Victoria travelled on to Brisbane after their Shield encounter with New South Wales at Sydney to inflict a third heavy defeat on Queensland.

A match between the 1905 Australians and New South Wales was staged in January 1906 for the benefit of J.J.Kelly, who had announced his retirement after the English tour. The Australians won, despite a spirited bid for victory by the Shield-holders who scored 472 in the fourth innings.

Western Australia's persistent invitations to South Australia over many years at last resulted in a second visit from their nearest neighbours. The results encouraged the home State even more, with a win and a well-placed draw to show for their efforts.

Tasmania were the only State not to play a first-class match. Victoria were scheduled to visit Hobart for the annual interstate fixture, but the VCA advised that they were unable to send a team because of financial reasons. Arrangements for Tasmania to meet New South Wales at Sydney on December 8 fell through when the NSWCA announced a postponement of the match to January 1. This was not acceptable to the TCA, who then made attempts to invite a South Australian team to Hobart, again without success.

The Queensland Cricket Association formally joined the Board of Control on September 22, 1905. They applied as a result of a Board promise to stage a Test match at Brisbane during the next England tour - a promise which was not honoured for many years. The Tasmanian Cricket Association were also anxious to join the Board, but did not have the support of the Northern Tasmanian Cricket Association. The Board advised the TCA they would only consider admitting a body which was totally representative of Tasmanian interests.

Leading Aggregates

Batsmen	M	I	NO	Runs	HS	Ave.	Bowlers	Runs	Wkts	Ave.
J.R.M.Mackay (NSW)	6	9	1	902	203	112.75	G.L.Garnsey (NSW)	772	36	21.44
M.A.Noble (NSW)	5	8	1	631	281	90.14	J.V.Saunders (V)	793	34	23.32
P.A.McAlister (V)	5	9	0	610	157	67.77	A.Cotter (NSW)	760	32	23.75
D.R.A.Gehrs (SA)	5	10	4	583	148	97.16	J.D.A.O'Connor (NSW)	673	31	21.70
N.Claxton (SA)	6	12	1	401	199*	36.45	F.B.Collins (V)	564	22	25.63
E.F.Waddy (NSW)	6	8	0	354	95	44.25				
A.Diamond (NSW)	5	7	1	348	164*	58.00				
T.S.Warne (V)	5	8	0	305	115	38.12				

SHEFFIELD SHIELD TABLE

	P	W	L	D	Pts	Quotient	Runs Scored	Wkts Lost	Runs Conceded	Wkts Taken
NEW SOUTH WALES	4	4	-	-	4	1.924	2464	51	1983	79
VICTORIA	4	1	3	-	-2	0.858	2029	69	2399	70
SOUTH AUSTRALIA	4	1	3	-	-2	0.597	1856	79	1967	50
TOTAL	6	6	6	-	0	1.000	6349	199	6349	199

QUEENSLAND v NEW SOUTH WALES

Played at Brisbane Cricket Ground (Woolloongabba) on November 11, 13, 14, 1905. (Timeless match)
Toss : New South Wales.   Result : NEW SOUTH WALES WON BY AN INNINGS AND 262 RUNS.
Debuts: Queensland - E.K.Armstrong, T.B.Faunce, J.S.Hutcheon, M.F.McCaffrey (all f/c); R.J.Hartigan (Qld only). New South Wales -
C.G.Macartney (f/c).
12th Men: C.F.Morgan (Qld). Only 11 men in NSW party.
Umpires: T.Muir and J.P.Orr.
Attendances: 2500, 2000, 300.   Total: About 4800.   Receipts: No figures published.
Close of Play: 1st day NSW 5/465 (Redgrave 37, Barnes 20); 2nd day Qld (2) 0/6 (McCaffrey 4, Miller 0).

Faunce was a last-minute replacement in the Queensland team for J.W.Lewis (leg injury). A.L.Cossart, who was appointed by the
Queensland Cricket Association to umpire with Orr, withdrew several days before the match and was replaced by Muir. Mackay's 203 took
167 minutes and included 32 fours, coming to an end with a magnificent catch by Morgan, who was substituting for Hartigan at the time.
Gregory batted for 168 minutes and hit 14 fours. Hartigan, in his first match for Queensland, made 98 in 96 minutes with 20 fours and
shared in a new State fourth-wicket partnership record of 152 with Crouch. Hartigan had previously appeared once for NSW v Queensland
in 1903-04. Foster kept wickets while Evans bowled in the New South Wales innings. *Cricket* incorrectly gives NSW Bardsley 26,
Macartney 57, extras 18; Qld (1) Crouch 45, total 132; Qld (2) Hutcheon 10, extras 1. Newspaper reports vary in some details; the
Brisbane Courier version shown here is believed correct. Sources: *Cricket, Brisbane Courier, Queensland Times, The Queenslander.*

NEW SOUTH WALES

J.R.M.Mackay	c sub (C.F.Morgan) b McCaffrey	203
W.Bardsley	run out (Foster/McCaffrey)	25
E.F.Waddy	run out (Hartigan/Miller)	43
C.W.Gregory	c Crouch b McCaffrey	102
*A.Diamond	c sub (C.F.Morgan) b McCaffrey	22
J.S.Redgrave	c McCaffrey b Hayes	94
J.C.Barnes	c McCaffrey b Hayes	77
C.G.Macartney	c Hutcheon b McCaffrey	56
†H.Carter	b Hayes	12
G.L.Garnsey	c Faunce b McCaffrey	37
J.D.A.O'Connor	not out	1
Extras	(b9, lb8, nb2)	19
Total	(163.1 overs, 426 mins)	691

QUEENSLAND

R.J.Hartigan	c & b O'Connor	10	(4) c & b Garnsey		98
W.B.Hayes	c Diamond b Garnsey	23	(3) b O'Connor		5
G.S.Crouch	c Diamond b Garnsey	44	(5) c Carter b Macartney		68
N.K.Foster	lbw b O'Connor	7	(8) b Garnsey		13
*A.A.Atkins	b O'Connor	6	(7) c Diamond b Garnsey		4
J.S.Hutcheon	st Carter b Garnsey	4	(10) st Carter b Garnsey		14
†W.T.Evans	b Garnsey	13	(9) b Macartney		1
T.B.Faunce	not out	21	(6) c Macartney b Garnsey		25
M.F.McCaffrey	c Carter b O'Connor	0	(1) b O'Connor		31
D.L.Miller	c Bardsley b Garnsey	0	(2) b Macartney		21
E.K.Armstrong	c Bardsley b Garnsey	0	not out		1
Extras	(b2, lb1)	3	(b10, lb7)		17
Total	(36.4 overs, 100 mins)	131	(79.5 overs, 205 mins)		298

QUEENSLAND	O	M	R	W	w,nb
McCaffrey	63.1	8	204	5	-,-
Armstrong	21	3	104	0	-,2
Hayes	33	5	153	3	-,-
Hutcheon	9	1	40	0	-,-
Miller	22	2	101	0	-,-
Hartigan	5	0	24	0	-,-
Faunce	4	0	23	0	-,-
Evans	6	0	23	0	-,-

NEW SOUTH WALES	O	M	R	W	w,nb		O	M	R	W	w,nb
Garnsey	18.4	2	77	6	-,-	(4)	22.5	2	95	5	-,-
O'Connor	18	4	51	4	-,-	(3)	17	4	69	2	-,-
Redgrave						(1)	14	4	37	0	-,-
Macartney						(2)	26	8	80	3	-,-

FALL OF WICKETS

	NSW	QLD	QLD
Wkt	1st	1st	2nd
1st	44	33	54
2nd	158	33	54
3rd	314	60	67
4th	358	66	219
5th	430	79	259
6th	570	100	263
7th	591	115	267
8th	630	120	270
9th	687	121	297
10th	691	131	298

SOUTH AUSTRALIA v VICTORIA (Shield Match 1)

Played at Adelaide Oval on November 11, 13, 14, 15, 1905. (Timeless match)
Toss : South Australia.　　　　　Result : VICTORIA WON BY AN INNINGS AND 148 RUNS.
Debuts: South Australia - L.R.Hill (f/c). Victoria - E.V.Carroll (f/c).
12th Men: R.F.Cowan (SA) and W.J.Scott (Vic).
Umpires: P.Argall and T.A.Reeves.
Attendances: 1000, 2500, 400, 100.　　　Total: About 4000.　　　Receipts: No figures published.
Close of Play: 1st day SA 9/244 (Newland 10, Coombe 2); 2nd day Vic 3/292 (McAlister 135, Armstrong 65); 3rd day SA (2) 4/62
　　(Travers 1).

The first match in Australia in which six runs were awarded for every hit over the boundary on the full. Previously five runs had been the standard, with the batsman losing the strike; to score six the ball had to be clean out of the ground. F.J.Laver and C.E.McLeod (Victoria) and D.R.A.Gehrs (South Australia) had not returned from the tour of England. Pellew (87 in 130 minutes, 10 fours) was the only South Australian to reach 50 in the match but Hack (43 in 168 minutes, 2 fours) and Claxton (48 in 60 minutes, 5 fours) also batted well. McAlister (157 in 310 minutes, 1 six and 23 fours) gave three chances during his innings, while Armstrong (165 in 240 minutes, 12 fours) gave four chances after passing 100. The pair added 191 for Victoria's fourth wicket. Earlier McAlister and Warne (62 in 160 minutes, 4 fours) had put on 146 for the second wicket. Saunders bowled throughout the second innings as the South Australians collapsed on the wearing wicket. Sources: *Wisden, C.B.O'Reilly, The Australasian, Adelaide Advertiser, South Australian Register.*

SOUTH AUSTRALIA

C.B.Jennings	c & b Saunders	5		c Horan b Collins	29
F.T.Hack	c Horan b Collins	43		c Ransford b Saunders	3
C.Hill	c Saunders b Collins	22		c Christian b Collins	23
J.H.Pellew	c Armstrong b Collins	87		b Collins	4
*J.Darling	c McAlister b Saunders	11	(6)	c & b Armstrong	36
N.Claxton	b Armstrong	48	(7)	b Saunders	18
J.P.F.Travers	b Collins	6	(5)	c McAlister b Saunders	3
J.C.Reedman	c Collins b Saunders	0		b Armstrong	7
L.R.Hill	b Saunders	2		c Armstrong b Saunders	1
†P.M.Newland	not out	10		not out	2
P.H.Coombe	c Armstrong b Saunders	2		c Saunders b Armstrong	3
Extras	(b3, lb5)	8		(b2, lb1, nb2)	5
Total	(85.2 overs, 265 mins)	244		(37.3 overs, 126 mins)	134

VICTORIA

A.H.Christian	run out (Pellew/Newland)	14
T.S.Warne	b L.R.Hill	62
*P.A.McAlister	c L.R.Hill b Claxton	157
V.S.Ransford	b L.R.Hill	2
W.W.Armstrong	b Reedman	165
J.F.Horan	c Claxton b Travers	16
W.M.McPetrie	c Travers b Reedman	2
E.V.Carroll	c & b Reedman	31
†W.Carkeek	b Reedman	45
F.B.Collins	b Coombe	14
J.V.Saunders	not out	1
Extras	(b12, lb4, nb1)	17
Total	(184.1 overs, 488 mins)	526

VICTORIA	O	M	R	W	w,nb		O	M	R	W	w,nb			FALL OF WICKETS		
														SA	VIC	SA
Armstrong	17	5	29	1	-,-	(3)	6.3	0	20	3	-,-	Wkt		1st	1st	2nd
Saunders	29.2	7	76	5	-,-	(1)	19	7	46	4	-,1	1st		19	18	10
Collins	26	5	89	4	-,-	(2)	12	1	63	3	-,1	2nd		51	164	56
Christian	9	2	28	0	-,-							3rd		137	166	61
Warne	3	0	14	0	-,-							4th		172	357	62
Ransford	1	1	0	0	-,-							5th		177	402	66
												6th		194	422	119
SOUTH AUSTRALIA	O	M	R	W	w,nb							7th		195	439	123
L.R.Hill	34	5	93	2	-,-							8th		207	482	129
Coombe	28	8	84	1	-,1							9th		239	518	131
Reedman	46.1	15	111	4	-,-							10th		244	526	134
Claxton	28	6	72	1	-,-											
Travers	32	7	99	1	-,-											
Pellew	10	3	34	0	-,-											
Hack	6	1	16	0	-,-											

NEW SOUTH WALES v QUEENSLAND

Played at Sydney Cricket Ground on December 15, 16, 18, 1905. (Timeless match)
Toss : Queensland.   Result : NEW SOUTH WALES WON BY FOUR WICKETS.
Debuts: New South Wales - E.R.Bubb, H.Goddard, H.V.Hordern, W.R.McIntyre, F.S.Middleton, A.B.S.White, W.C.Whitting (all f/c).
    Queensland - J.Thomson (f/c).
12th Men: G.G.Black (NSW). No 12th named for Queensland.
Umpires: W.G.Curran and J.Laing.
Attendances: 1000, 2000, 200.   Total: About 3200.   Receipts: No figures published.
Close of Play: 1st day NSW 3/66 (Bubb 22, White 12); 2nd day Qld (2) 9/122 (Byrnes 7).

Heavy rain during the preceding night left the outfield sodden for the start of play although, surprisingly, the wicket "was in splendid order" (*Town & Country Journal*). Further showers during the first day and overnight limited the value of scoring shots and led to the low scoring throughout the match. Carew (43 in 80 minutes, 6 fours) was the only Queensland batsman to exceed 40 but Bubb (57 in 118 minutes, 3 fours), Bardsley (64 in 135 minutes, 4 fours), Pye (51 in 75 minutes) and Barnes (55 in 65 minutes) all recorded half-centuries for New South Wales. Hordern (11 for 164) made a fine impression on debut. *Cricket* gives NSW match bowling analysis instead of individual innings, NSW (1) Timbury 4/43, NSW (2) Whitting batting and Hayes bowling omitted. Sources: *Cricket, Sydney Referee, Sydney Morning Herald, Town & Country Journal, Sydney Mail, Brisbane Courier.*

QUEENSLAND

J.Carew	b Hordern	43	c Goddard b Hordern		21
W.B.Hayes	b Penman	1	c White b Hordern		17
G.S.Crouch	c McIntyre b Penman	36	c Middleton b Hordern		11
N.K.Foster	st McIntyre b Hordern	1	b Hordern		8
C.F.Morgan	c Pye b Penman	37	b Hordern		0
T.B.Faunce	c Barnes b Hordern	4	c Bardsley b Hordern		16
J.Thomson	b Penman	13	c McIntyre b Hordern		24
*†W.T.Evans	b Middleton	28	b Penman		7
F.R.V.Timbury	c Pye b Penman	10	c White b Hordern		6
M.F.McCaffrey	b Middleton	7	(11) b Penman		13
T.Byrnes	not out	2	(10) not out		22
Extras	(b4, lb4, nb2)	10	(b3, lb2, nb1)		6
Total	(56.4 overs, 190 mins)	192	(55.3 overs, 160 mins)		151

NEW SOUTH WALES

*L.W.Pye	st Evans b Byrnes	3	(4) c McCaffrey b Byrnes		51
F.S.Middleton	c Evans b Timbury	22	(8) not out		9
J.C.Barnes	b Timbury	6	(5) c Thomson b Timbury		55
E.R.Bubb	c Hayes b McCaffrey	57	(2) b Timbury		9
A.B.S.White	c Carew b Byrnes	19	(3) b McCaffrey		3
W.C.Whitting	b Timbury	1	(7) b Timbury		0
W.Bardsley	c Morgan b McCaffrey	64	(1) run out		1
H.Goddard	c Thomson b McCaffrey	1	(6) not out		7
†W.R.McIntyre	c Hayes b Byrnes	12			
A.P.Penman	not out	9			
H.V.Hordern	c Foster b Timbury	0			
Extras	(b8, lb3, w1, nb2)	14	(b3)		3
Total	(83.0 overs, 220 mins)	208	(39.2 overs, 110 mins) (6 wkts)		138

NEW SOUTH WALES	O	M	R	W	w,nb		O	M	R	W	w,nb					
Penman	18	4	48	5	-,2		16.3	4	34	2	-,-					
Hordern	17	0	83	3	-,-	(3)	24	3	81	8	-,-					
Middleton	10.4	3	24	2	-,-	(4)	6	1	16	0	-,1					
Pye	5	3	12	0	-,-											
Barnes	2	0	8	0	-,-											
Whitting	4	1	7	0	-,-	(2)	9	4	14	0	-,-					

FALL OF WICKETS

	QLD 1st	NSW 1st	QLD 2nd	NSW 2nd
Wkt				
1st	3	9	37	4
2nd	79	29	48	13
3rd	84	40	52	15
4th	85	74	52	118
5th	91	77	64	126
6th	120	131	79	127
7th	169	136	94	-
8th	182	154	113	-
9th	183	206	122	-
10th	192	208	151	-

QUEENSLAND	O	M	R	W	w,nb		O	M	R	W	w,nb
Timbury	28	11	46	4	-,-		17	2	47	3	-,-
Byrnes	26	6	59	3	1,2	(3)	10.2	1	27	1	-,-
McCaffrey	19	5	42	3	-,-	(2)	9	1	37	1	-,-
Hayes	5	0	27	0	-,-		3	0	24	0	-,-
Thomson	5	0	20	0	-,-						

SOUTH AUSTRALIA v NEW SOUTH WALES (Shield Match 2)

Played at Adelaide Oval on December 15, 16, 18, 1905. (Timeless match)
Toss : South Australia.   Result : NEW SOUTH WALES WON BY AN INNINGS AND 82 RUNS.
Debuts: South Australia - L.H.Hanson, W.F.P.Hutton, A.W.Wright (all f/c).
12th Men: J.P.F.Travers (SA) and W.T.Grounds (NSW).
Umpires: P.Argall and T.A.Reeves.
Attendances & Receipts: No figures published.
Close of Play: 1st day SA 9/325 (Hutton 0); 2nd day NSW 2/357 (Diamond 164, Waddy 52).

L.R.Hill replaced J.C.Reedman (unavailable) in the South Australian team originally selected. R.A.Duff, F.B.Johnson and V.T.Trumper were unavailable for New South Wales for business reasons and A.J.Y.Hopkins could not be considered due to illness. Clem Hill (146 in 185 minutes, 18 fours) and J.H.Pellew (72 in 130 minutes, 10 fours) put the home team in a sound position on the opening day with a third wicket stand of 169. Diamond (164 in 253 minutes, 24 fours, chance at 29) and Mackay (90 in 100 minutes, 12 fours) began the New South Wales reply with a century stand and Waddy (65 in 90 minutes, 6 fours), Gregory (54 in 115 minutes, 5 fours) and Macartney (70 not out in 90 minutes, 7 fours) followed up with half-centuries. Diamond learned of the death of his brother in an accident in Sydney on his return to the pavilion at stumps on the second day and decided "to take no further part in the match" (*Register*). Gehrs took over as wicket-keeper at 4/387 when Hutton "tore" a finger nail attempting to catch Redgrave and was forced from the field. Garnsey "bowled exceedingly well" (*Register*) throughout the South Australian second innings on a wicket beginning to turn. O'Reilly has incorrect match dates. Sources: *Wisden, C.B.O'Reilly, Adelaide Advertiser, South Australian Register.*

SOUTH AUSTRALIA

D.R.A.Gehrs	b O'Connor	34	(7) not out		33
F.T.Hack	run out (Macartney/Garnsey)	14	run out		19
C.Hill	b Noble	146	c O'Connor b Garnsey		0
J.H.Pellew	b Noble	72	c Carter b Cotter		24
*J.Darling	b Cotter	26	c Carter b Garnsey		1
N.Claxton	run out (/Carter)	0	b Garnsey		9
C.B.Jennings	b Garnsey	26	(1) b Garnsey		1
L.R.Hill	b Cotter	0	b Garnsey		0
†W.F.P.Hutton	not out	22	c Redgrave b O'Connor		8
A.W.Wright	b Garnsey	0	b O'Connor		0
L.H.Hanson	b Noble	10	c Mackay b Garnsey		12
Extras	(b7, lb1, nb1)	9	(b6, lb2)		8
Total	(99.1 overs, 309 mins)	359	(31.2 overs, 103 mins)		115

NEW SOUTH WALES

J.R.M.Mackay	c Pellew b Claxton	90
A.Diamond	retired	164
*M.A.Noble	c Hack b Claxton	27
E.F.Waddy	b Hanson	65
C.W.Gregory	st Gehrs b Wright	54
J.S.Redgrave	lbw b Wright	24
C.G.Macartney	not out	70
†H.Carter	b Hanson	1
A.Cotter	c sub (J.P.F.Travers) b Wright	10
G.L.Garnsey	b Wright	7
J.D.A.O'Connor	b Wright	11
Extras	(b26, lb4, w1, nb2)	33
Total	(143.2 overs, 435 mins)	556

NEW SOUTH WALES	O	M	R	W	w,nb	O	M	R	W	w,nb
Cotter	26	1	105	2	-,1	10	2	27	1	-,-
Garnsey	14	2	56	2	-,-	15.2	3	48	6	-,-
O'Connor	20	3	67	1	-,-	6	1	32	2	-,-
Macartney	17	3	57	0	-,-					
Noble	22.1	5	65	3	-,-					

SOUTH AUSTRALIA	O	M	R	W	w,nb
Hanson	29	5	102	2	-,1
Claxton	36	9	123	2	-,-
L.R.Hill	22	2	90	0	-,1
Wright	40.2	7	150	5	-,-
Pellew	3	0	10	0	-,-
Hack	7	3	15	0	1,-
Gehrs	4	0	21	0	-,-
C.Hill	2	0	12	0	-,-

FALL OF WICKETS			
	SA	NSW	SA
Wkt	1st	1st	2nd
1st	34	139	1
2nd	73	237	1
3rd	242	357	32
4th	275	384	37
5th	275	437	52
6th	323	487	70
7th	323	497	70
8th	325	521	98
9th	325	534	98
10th	359	556	115

VICTORIA v NEW SOUTH WALES (Shield Match 3)

Played at Melbourne Cricket Ground on December 23, 26, 27, 28, 1905. (Timeless match)
Toss : Victoria.   Result : NEW SOUTH WALES WON BY AN INNINGS AND 253 RUNS.
Debuts: Nil.
12th Men: No 12th men or emergency fieldsmen named. Only 11 men in NSW party (see below).
Umpires: R.M.Crockett and W.Hannah.
Attendances: 5500, 9000, 6000, 3000.   Total: About 23,500.   Receipts: £601.
Close of Play: 1st day Vic 6/345 (Laver 20, Ransford 8); 2nd day NSW 2/370 (Noble 123, Gregory 6); 3rd day NSW 8/796 (Carter 67,
    O'Connor 5).

Mackay (194 in 221 minutes, 26 fours) and Noble (281 in 369 minutes, 21 fours, chances at 123 and 193) were involved in a partnership
of 268, a new Australian record for the second wicket. Gregory (73 in 200 minutes, 4 fours) then assisted Noble to add 225 for the third
wicket. Redgrave (41 in 67 minutes, 7 fours), Waddy (50 in 54 minutes, 6 fours) and Carter (67 in 72 minutes, 10 fours) scored freely
while Cotter hit 68 in 35 minutes (2 sixes and 7 fours) including 26 (6,4,6,4,4,2) in one over from Saunders. Macartney was the only
recognised batsman not to enjoy the run feast; he was out to the first ball he faced. Warne topscored in each innings for Victoria with 115
(236 minutes, 16 fours, chances at 18 and 111) and 56 (128 minutes, 5 fours). Christian, brought into the team to replace J.F.Giller, who
had announced his retirement, also contributed for Victoria with 98 (91 minutes, 16 fours, chance at 83). New South Wales had only
eleven players due to the fact that A.Diamond had returned to Sydney during the team's previous match in Adelaide. *Wisden* incorrectly
gives Vic (2) Warne b Macartney. Sources: *Wisden, VCA Report, The Age, The Argus, The Herald, The Australasian.*

VICTORIA

T.S.Warne	c Macartney b Garnsey	115	b O'Connor	56
A.H.Christian	c Carter b Redgrave	98	b Garnsey	6
*P.A.McAlister	c Grounds b Macartney	40	hit wkt b Cotter	3
W.W.Armstrong	c Redgrave b O'Connor	43	b Cotter	3
F.J.Laver	b Cotter	24	(6) c Waddy b Cotter	17
J.F.Horan	c Gregory b Garnsey	0	(7) run out (Waddy/Carter)	2
E.V.Carroll	c Noble b Garnsey	5	(8) c Cotter b Macartney	48
V.S.Ransford	not out	22	(5) st Carter b Garnsey	0
†W.Carkeek	b Cotter	0	b Macartney	30
F.B.Collins	b Macartney	0	c Carter b O'Connor	6
J.V.Saunders	c Waddy b Cotter	2	not out	0
Extras	(b8, lb4, w2, nb4)	18	(b9, lb1, w1, nb3)	14
Total	(111.0 overs, 314 mins)	367	(49.2 overs, 153 mins)	185

NEW SOUTH WALES

J.R.M.Mackay	c McAlister b Saunders	194
J.S.Redgrave	b Armstrong	41
*M.A.Noble	b Christian	281
C.W.Gregory	c McAlister b Collins	73
E.F.Waddy	b Saunders	50
C.G.Macartney	c Armstrong b Christian	0
†H.Carter	b Warne	67
A.Cotter	c Ransford b Laver	68
G.L.Garnsey	c Collins b Warne	2
J.D.A.O'Connor	c Armstrong b Laver	9
W.T.Grounds	not out	5
Extras	(b8, lb5, w2)	15
Total	(215.3 overs, 548 mins)	805

NEW SOUTH WALES	O	M	R	W	w,nb		O	M	R	W	w,nb
Cotter	29	4	78	3	-,4		17	4	56	3	1,3
Garnsey	22	3	78	3	-,-		17	2	51	2	-,-
Noble	9	2	42	0	-,-						
Grounds	9	3	23	0	-,-						
O'Connor	18	5	57	1	-,-	(4)	7	1	28	2	-,-
Redgrave	12	1	45	1	2,-						
Macartney	12	3	26	2	-,-	(3)	8.2	1	36	2	-,-

VICTORIA	O	M	R	W	w,nb
Saunders	37	5	146	2	-,-
Armstrong	56	16	125	1	-,-
Laver	52.3	12	184	2	1,-
Collins	27	2	138	1	1,-
Christian	21	1	103	2	-,-
Warne	21	2	92	2	-,-
Ransford	1	0	2	0	-,-

FALL OF WICKETS			
	VIC	NSW	VIC
Wkt	1st	1st	2nd
1st	144	78	12
2nd	217	346	17
3rd	307	571	25
4th	309	643	26
5th	309	643	58
6th	319	657	65
7th	357	754	141
8th	357	756	151
9th	358	797	183
10th	367	805	185

VICTORIA v SOUTH AUSTRALIA (Shield Match 4)

Played at Melbourne Cricket Ground on December 30 1905, January 1, 2, 3, 4, 1906. (Timeless match)
Toss : South Australia.   Result : SOUTH AUSTRALIA WON BY 120 RUNS.
Debuts: Victoria - G.R.Hazlitt (f/c). South Australia - C.E.Dolling, H.G.Hutton, H.S.C.Jarvis (all f/c).
12th Men: W.M.McPetrie (Vic - see below) and D.R.A.Gehrs (SA).
Umpires: W.J.Bruton and R.M.Crockett.
Attendances: 4000, 7000, 5000, 2000, 200.   Total: About 18,200.   Receipts: £458.
Close of Play: 1st day SA 3/127 (Claxton 46, Dolling 0); 2nd day Vic 9/166 (Horan 42); 3rd day SA (2) 4/254 (Claxton 137,
      Reedman 44); 4th day Vic (2) 3/173 (Armstrong 63, Horan 11).

South Australia were forced to omit Gehrs (hand injury) from their eleven. Bad light and rain prevented any play on the first day after 3.20pm. Saunders was denied a hat-trick on the second day when he dismissed Claxton and Travers with consecutive balls and then saw Carkeek fumble a stumping chance from Jarvis next ball. Jarvis was however dismissed first ball in the second innings. Warne sustained a split finger while bowling on the third day and took no further part in the match. Victoria's 12th man, McPetrie, was not at the ground so Darling was forced to act as substitute against his own side until W.Carlton, a Victorian player not engaged for this match, arrived to replace him. McPetrie fielded in Warne's absence on the fourth day. Claxton top-scored in each innings for South Australia with 67 (189 minutes, 6 fours) and 199 not out (366 minutes, 21 fours, 2 chances), carrying his bat in the second innings. Horan (50 not out in 123 minutes, 6 fours) and Carkeek (52 in 77 minutes, 4 fours) scored fifties for Victoria under trying conditions on the second day. *O'Reilly* gives Vic (2) Armstrong 65, Carkeek 14, but the scores shown here are believed correct; also incorrectly gives Vic (1) Reedman 1/30, Cowan 0/12. Sources: *Wisden, C.B.O'Reilly, VCA Report, The Age, The Argus, The Herald, The Australasian.*

SOUTH AUSTRALIA

F.T.Hack	b Hazlitt	0	(2)	run out (Christian/Carkeek)	0
N.Claxton	c Laver b Saunders	67	(1)	not out	199
*J.Darling	st Carkeek b Laver	48		c Warne b Saunders	10
J.H.Pellew	run out (Horan/Carkeek)	33		run out (Horan/Armstrong)	25
C.E.Dolling	c Carkeek b Armstrong	15		lbw b Armstrong	30
J.C.Reedman	b Armstrong	0		c Carroll b Armstrong	64
R.F.Cowan	c Laver b Armstrong	12		b Christian	25
J.P.F.Travers	b Saunders	0		c Christian b Armstrong	11
†H.S.C.Jarvis	b Saunders	2		b Armstrong	0
H.G.Hutton	not out	2		b Christian	0
A.W.Wright	b Armstrong	0		run out (/Carkeek)	0
Extras	(b2)	2		(b8, lb6)	14
Total	(79.5 overs, 212 mins)	181		(150.3 overs, 366 mins)	378

VICTORIA

A.H.Christian	b Wright	0	(2)	c Pellew b Reedman	15
T.S.Warne	b Reedman	0		absent hurt	-
P.A.McAlister	c Claxton b Wright	13	(1)	c & b Reedman	56
W.W.Armstrong	c Darling b Wright	0		b Wright	64
V.S.Ransford	b Wright	17	(3)	c Darling b Travers	24
E.V.Carroll	c Dolling b Wright	15		c & b Reedman	2
*F.J.Laver	c Hack b Wright	17		c Claxton b Travers	27
J.F.Horan	not out	50	(5)	c Jarvis b Cowan	37
†W.Carkeek	b Dolling	52	(8)	c Reedman b Hutton	15
G.R.Hazlitt	lbw b Travers	4	(9)	c Dolling b Travers	2
J.V.Saunders	c Claxton b Wright	8	(10)	not out	10
Extras	(b4, lb3)	7		(b2, lb2)	4
Total	(77.2 overs, 191 mins)	183		(87.4 overs, 210 mins)	256

VICTORIA	O	M	R	W	w,nb		O	M	R	W	w,nb
Hazlitt	16	2	62	1	-,-		19	4	63	0	-,-
Saunders	27	9	65	3	-,-		29	7	92	1	-,-
Armstrong	23.5	13	26	4	-,-		49	12	82	4	-,-
Laver	13	3	26	1	-,-	(6)	22	6	50	0	-,-
Warne						(4)	3.1	2	4	0	-,-
Christian						(5)	25.2	8	57	2	-,-
Carroll							3	0	16	0	-,-

SOUTH AUSTRALIA	O	M	R	W	w,nb		O	M	R	W	w,nb
Wright	24.2	7	66	7	-,-		31	5	90	1	-,-
Reedman	25	8	40	1	-,-		24	7	78	3	-,-
Claxton	7	2	17	0	-,-						
Hutton	5	0	20	0	-,-	(3)	8	1	20	1	-,-
Travers	11	4	16	1	-,-	(4)	12.4	2	34	3	-,-
Dolling	4	0	15	1	-,-						
Cowan	1	0	2	0	-,-	(5)	12	4	30	1	-,-

FALL OF WICKETS

Wkt	SA 1st	VIC 1st	SA 2nd	VIC 2nd
1st	0	0	0	20
2nd	67	4	20	82
3rd	127	4	65	129
4th	164	21	145	177
5th	166	38	300	182
6th	170	49	349	211
7th	170	70	374	242
8th	176	155	374	245
9th	179	166	375	256
10th	181	183	378	-

NEW SOUTH WALES v SOUTH AUSTRALIA (Shield Match 5)

Played at Sydney Cricket Ground on January 6, 8, 9, 10, 1906. (Timeless match)
Toss : South Australia.   Result : NEW SOUTH WALES WON BY NINE WICKETS.
Debuts: Nil.
12th Men: C.W.Gregory (NSW) and H.G.Hutton (SA).
Umpires: W.G.Curran and J.Laing.
Attendances: 8926, 1809, 2038, 1811.   Total: 14,584.   Receipts: £541.
Close of Play: 1st day NSW 0/55 (Mackay 39, Trumper 16); 2nd day NSW 8/201 (Carter 6, Garnsey 0); 3rd day SA (2) 7/161
    (Dolling 68, Travers 10).

Mackay became the first batsman to score a century in each innings for New South Wales, making 105 (137 minutes, 7 fours) and 102 not out (114 minutes, 11 fours). In the second innings his partner, Noble, refused a number of easy runs for himself to give Mackay a chance to register his second century before the target was reached. Jarvis sustained a hand injury when attempting to catch Noble in the first innings and took no further part in the match and never reappeared for South Australia again. Gehrs kept wickets for the rest of the first innings and until 1/120 in the second innings, when Pellew took over. Rain restricted playing time on the second day to 160 minutes. Gehrs (101 in 141 minutes, 1 five and 9 fours) and Dolling (83 not out in 202 minutes, 7 fours) batted well for South Australia. Sources: *Wisden, C.B.O'Reilly, NSWCA Report, Sydney Referee, Sydney Morning Herald, Town & Country Journal, Sydney Daily Telegraph.*

SOUTH AUSTRALIA

F.T.Hack	b Garnsey	32		c Carter b Cotter	41
N.Claxton	c Waddy b Cotter	5	(4)	b Cotter	1
*J.Darling	b Cotter	14	(2)	c Waddy b Noble	2
J.H.Pellew	c Noble b Garnsey	36	(3)	b Macartney	9
D.R.A.Gehrs	c Diamond b O'Connor	101		c Macartney b Cotter	10
C.E.Dolling	st Carter b O'Connor	13		not out	83
J.C.Reedman	c Carter b Cotter	31		c Garnsey b O'Connor	8
R.F.Cowan	c Trumper b Macartney	3		b O'Connor	2
J.P.F.Travers	not out	6		lbw b Garnsey	16
†H.S.C.Jarvis	c Cotter b Garnsey	3		absent hurt	-
A.W.Wright	c & b Garnsey	0	(10)	b Garnsey	0
Extras	(lb10, w1, nb2)	13		(b4, lb8, w1, nb3)	16
Total	(81.5 overs, 217 mins)	257		(96.2 overs, 251 mins)	188

NEW SOUTH WALES

V.T.Trumper	c Jarvis b Reedman	16	c Hack b Reedman	35
J.R.M.Mackay	c Darling b Claxton	105	not out	102
*M.A.Noble	c Claxton b Reedman	43	not out	37
A.Diamond	c Gehrs b Claxton	15		
A.Cotter	c Cowan b Claxton	0		
E.F.Waddy	c Pellew b Claxton	4		
C.G.Macartney	c Gehrs b Reedman	1		
J.S.Redgrave	c Reedman b Travers	8		
†H.Carter	b Wright	40		
G.L.Garnsey	not out	32		
J.D.A.O'Connor	c Gehrs b Wright	2		
Extras	(lb2, w1)	3	(b1, nb2)	3
Total	(87.1 overs, 249 mins)	269	(38.0 overs, 114 mins) (1 wkt)	177

NEW SOUTH WALES	O	M	R	W	w,nb		O	M	R	W	w,nb
Cotter	24	4	97	3	-,2		29	12	47	3	1,3
Garnsey	20.5	1	70	4	-,-	(3)	19.2	6	46	2	-,-
Macartney	14	2	25	1	-,-	(4)	22	13	21	1	-,-
Redgrave	5	0	15	0	1,-	(6)	2	1	3	0	-,-
O'Connor	12	3	25	2	-,-		16	4	35	2	-,-
Noble	6	2	12	0	-,-	(2)	8	3	20	1	-,-

SOUTH AUSTRALIA	O	M	R	W	w,nb		O	M	R	W	w,nb
Wright	14.1	2	61	2	-,-	(2)	7	0	32	0	-,-
Reedman	26	0	98	3	-,-	(3)	9	1	48	1	-,-
Claxton	20	4	44	4	-,-	(4)	9	1	34	0	-,-
Cowan	2	0	6	0	-,-	(5)	3	1	16	0	-,-
Travers	25	6	57	1	1,-	(1)	6	0	26	0	-,-
Dolling							4	0	18	0	-,2

FALL OF WICKETS

	SA	NSW	SA	NSW
Wkt	1st	1st	2nd	2nd
1st	8	56	4	60
2nd	31	164	16	-
3rd	87	167	17	-
4th	98	171	33	-
5th	149	175	102	-
6th	217	176	119	-
7th	232	194	127	-
8th	254	194	178	-
9th	257	267	188	-
10th	257	269	-	-

NEW SOUTH WALES v AUSTRALIAN XI

Played at Sydney Cricket Ground on January 12, 13, 15, 16, 1906. (Timeless match)
Toss : Australian XI.   Result : AUSTRALIAN XI WON BY 79 RUNS.
Debuts: Nil.
12th Men: J.S.Redgrave (NSW) and S.E.Gregory (Aust).
Umpires: W.G.Curran and J.Laing (see below).
Attendances: 6000, 15000, 3000, 4000.   Total: About 28,000.   Receipts: £1154 (gate only).
Close of Play: 1st day NSW 5/53 (E.L.Waddy 27, Macartney 11); 2nd day Aust (2) 4/256 (Noble 54, Armstrong 0); 3rd day NSW (2) 0/154 (Mackay 88, Diamond 59).

The match was arranged as a benefit for J.J.Kelly and raised £1400 in his favour. Noble topscored for the representative side that had toured England the previous year with 100 in 171 minutes (12 fours). The second innings total of 472 by New South Wales was a new record for the fourth innings in Australia and included contributions from Mackay (136 in 207 minutes, 16 fours), Diamond (97 in 217 minutes, 13 fours), E.F.Waddy (95 in 135 minutes, 8 fours) and his elder brother E.L.Waddy (74 in 76 minutes, 8 fours). Cotter dismissed O'Connor and Penman with successive balls. Reports in *Sydney Morning Herald* and *Town & Country Journal* contain references to umpire P.Caswell on the first two days but the above names are given in both *NSWCA Report* and *Sydney Referee* and are believed more likely correct. Sources: *Wisden, NSWCA Report, Sydney Referee, Sydney Morning Herald, Town & Country Journal, Sydney Daily Telegraph, Newcastle Herald.*

AUSTRALIAN XI

V.T.Trumper	b Macartney	15		c E.F.Waddy b O'Connor	60
R.A.Duff	c Diamond b Macartney	58		lbw b O'Connor	38
C.Hill	b O'Connor	12		c Gregory b Johnson	76
M.A.Noble	c Johnson b O'Connor	20		c Garnsey b Macartney	100
W.W.Armstrong	st Carter b O'Connor	0	(6)	c & b O'Connor	17
*J.Darling	c Diamond b O'Connor	66	(7)	c Diamond b Macartney	73
D.R.A.Gehrs	c Garnsey b Johnson	30	(8)	not out	36
A.Cotter	lbw b Johnson	0	(9)	st Carter b O'Connor	20
F.J.Laver	st Carter b O'Connor	12	(10)	c Johnson b O'Connor	2
†J.J.Kelly	not out	1	(5)	b Garnsey	22
W.P.Howell	c Gregory b O'Connor	2		b Macartney	6
Extras	(b6, w3, nb1)	10		(b10, lb3, w1, nb1)	15
Total	(62.2 overs, 203 mins)	226		(109.0 overs, 327 mins)	465

NEW SOUTH WALES

J.R.M.Mackay	b Cotter	4		c Kelly b Cotter	136
*A.Diamond	lbw b Cotter	0		c Cotter b Laver	97
C.W.Gregory	st Kelly b Armstrong	2		b Cotter	9
E.F.Waddy	b Armstrong	0		b Armstrong	95
E.L.Waddy	b Howell	60		c & b Laver	74
†H.Carter	c Laver b Armstrong	6		lbw b Cotter	6
C.G.Macartney	run out (Noble/Kelly)	24		run out (Armstrong/Noble)	25
G.L.Garnsey	c Cotter b Laver	22		b Cotter	11
A.P.Penman	b Laver	8	(10)	b Cotter	0
J.D.A.O'Connor	c Noble b Laver	1	(9)	b Cotter	0
F.B.Johnson	not out	3		not out	1
Extras	(b8, w1, nb1)	10		(b7, lb1, w6, nb4)	18
Total	(49.5 overs, 140 mins)	140		(144.1 overs, 380 mins)	472

NEW SOUTH WALES	O	M	R	W	w,nb		O	M	R	W	w,nb
Penman	6	2	22	0	-,1		22	1	121	0	-,1
Macartney	24	3	83	2	-,-	(4)	21	7	40	3	-,-
O'Connor	18.2	4	50	6	-,-		34	6	138	5	1,-
Garnsey	7	1	33	0	3,-	(2)	15	1	77	1	-,-
Johnson	7	0	28	2	-,-		17	2	74	1	-,-

AUSTRALIAN XI	O	M	R	W	w,nb		O	M	R	W	w,nb
Cotter	17	4	40	2	1,1		46.1	8	163	6	4,3
Armstrong	18	3	59	3	-,-		29	4	68	1	-,-
Howell	7	3	12	1	-,-		8	2	26	0	-,-
Noble	2	0	3	0	-,-		29	8	78	0	-,1
Laver	5.5	2	16	3	-,-		28	5	99	2	2,-
Duff							4	0	20	0	-,-

FALL OF WICKETS

Wkt	AUST 1st	NSW 1st	AUST 2nd	NSW 2nd
1st	47	3	83	244
2nd	70	4	106	254
3rd	108	5	223	254
4th	109	15	256	399
5th	109	21	295	412
6th	205	79	358	443
7th	205	116	419	456
8th	218	128	444	460
9th	224	129	450	460
10th	226	140	465	472

NEW SOUTH WALES v VICTORIA (Shield Match 6)

Played at Sydney Cricket Ground on January 26, 27, 29, 30, 1906. (Timeless match)
Toss : New South Wales.   Result : NEW SOUTH WALES WON BY 145 RUNS.
Debuts: Victoria - C.F.Jones (f/c).
12th Men: E.L.Waddy (NSW) and J.Ainslie (Vic).
Umpires: R.Callaway and W.G.Curran.
Attendances: 8929, 8231, 3277, 815.   Total: 21,252.   Receipts: £710.
Close of Play: 1st day Vic 2/115 (McAlister 51, Collins 10); 2nd day NSW (2) 4/274 (Noble 107, Waddy 66); 3rd day Vic (2) 3/202
    (McAlister 92, Carroll 0).

The game was promoted as "The Jubilee Match" as almost 50 years had elapsed since the first meeting of the two teams. Ainslie was a late replacement in the Victorian side for W.W.Armstrong, who became unavailable after the team was named. Trumper's 101 took just 60 minutes and included 1 six and 18 fours. Noble (123 in 169 minutes, 11 fours) and Waddy (82 in 100 minutes, 12 fours) were the chief scorers in the New South Wales second innings. Jones, the new Victorian 'keeper, sustained a hand injury late in the second innings and was unable to continue. He never represented his State again. Ainslie fielded as substitute and Warne kept wickets for the short remainder of the innings. McAlister (53 in 94 minutes, 5 fours and 128 in 194 minutes, 1 six and 12 fours) topped Victoria's scoring in each innings. Sources: *Wisden, VCA Report, Sydney Referee, Sydney Morning Herald, Town & Country Journal, Sydney Daily Telegraph.*

NEW SOUTH WALES

J.R.M.Mackay	c Collins b Saunders	18	c Collins b Christian		50
A.Diamond	c Warne b Saunders	27	lbw b Collins		23
*M.A.Noble	c Laver b Saunders	0	st Jones b Saunders		123
V.T.Trumper	b Saunders	101	b Christian		23
R.A.Duff	b Saunders	27	b Saunders		0
E.F.Waddy	c Collins b Saunders	15	b Collins		82
C.G.Macartney	b Saunders	1	c Laver b Saunders		8
†H.Carter	c Jones b Collins	13	c Laver b Saunders		14
A.Cotter	b Collins	35	c Ellis b Saunders		30
G.L.Garnsey	c Christian b Collins	13	b Collins		25
J.D.A.O'Connor	not out	6	not out		5
Extras	(b2, lb4, nb1)	7	(b6, lb5)		11
Total	(51.4 overs, 168 mins)	263	(92.0 overs, 266 mins)		394

VICTORIA

T.S.Warne	c Carter Cotter	7	c Garnsey b Macartney		53
M.Ellis	Cotter	40	st Carter b O'Connor		46
P.A.McAlister	c Carter Cotter	35	b Garnsey		128
F.B.Collins	c Waddy b Cotter	19	(9) not out		6
V.S.Ransford	b O'Connor	14	(7) c & b Garnsey		4
J.F.Horan	lbw b Noble	5	b Garnsey		0
A.H.Christian	Cotter	38	(4) b Cotter		4
E.V.Carroll	c Carter b O'Connor	7	(5) c Carter Cotter		13
*F.J.Laver	b O'Connor	7	(8) c Garnsey Cotter		24
†C.F.Jones	not out	6	c Duff b Garnsey		6
J.V.Saunders	b Garnsey	9	b Cotter		0
Extras	(b5, lb1, nb4)	10	(b6, lb3, nb4)		13
Total	(81.3 overs, 222 mins)	215	(101.2 overs, 280 mins)		297

VICTORIA	O	M	R	W	w,nb		O	M	R	W	w,nb
Saunders	25	5	122	7	-,-		32	2	140	5	-,-
Collins	11.4	1	65	3	-,1		27	3	131	3	-,-
Laver	4	0	26	0	-,-	(5)	11	2	25	0	-,-
Christian	10	1	37	0	-,-	(3)	18	3	59	2	-,-
Warne	1	0	6	0	-,-	(4)	4	0	28	0	-,-

NEW SOUTH WALES	O	M	R	W	w,nb		O	M	R	W	w,nb
Cotter	27	6	83	5	-,3		28.2	9	64	4	-,4
Garnsey	16.3	4	40	1	-,-		26	1	101	4	-,-
O'Connor	25	9	57	3	-,-	(4)	22	5	64	1	-,-
Macartney	8	1	14	0	-,1	(3)	13	1	41	1	-,-
Noble	5	2	11	1	-,-		12	6	14	0	-,-

FALL OF WICKETS

Wkt	NSW 1st	VIC 1st	NSW 2nd	VIC 2nd
1st	40	16	60	63
2nd	40	98	99	170
3rd	71	123	147	192
4th	171	140	148	244
5th	180	144	305	245
6th	195	158	307	249
7th	204	167	323	270
8th	236	199	334	288
9th	243	199	369	296
10th	263	215	394	297

WESTERN AUSTRALIA v SOUTH AUSTRALIA

Played at W.A.C.A. Ground, Perth, on January 27, 29, 30, 1906. (Three-day match)
Toss : Western Australia. Result : WESTERN AUSTRALIA WON BY 103 RUNS.
Debuts: Western Australia - H.C.Howard, E.F.Parker, S.H.D.Rowe, T.M.Coombe, L.Gouly, T.H.Coyne, H.W.Edmondson, W.H.Kelly
(all f/c). South Australia - J.N.S.Rees, J.Richardson, C.T.Chamberlain (all f/c).
12th Men: T.McNamara and A.Richardson named as emergencies for WA. No 12th named for SA.
Umpires: G.Berry and J.C.Brickhill.
Attendances: 3000, 2500, 800. Total: About 6300. Receipts: £415.
Close of Play: 1st day SA 1/0 (Rees 0); 2nd day WA (2) 9/185 (Gouly 69, Coyne 21).

J.J.Lyons, captain of the South Australian team, took ill on the voyage from Adelaide and was unable to appear in either first-class match of their tour. Quist (47 in 115 minutes, 4 fours) led the scoring on the first day. Selk bowled unchanged on the second day as South Australia unaccountably collapsed on a wicket that "was not to blame" (*West Australian*). Rees, on debut, batted throughout to become the first South Australian to carry his bat. Fellow debutant, Gouly, (70 not out in 140 minutes, 5 fours) held the Western Australian second innings together. Rees replaced Richardson as wicket-keeper during the final session of the second day. Gehrs (84 in 130 minutes, 7 fours) and Hack (60 in 135 minutes, 3 fours) made a determined bid for a South Australian victory on the last day but, after they were separated, Selk proved too much for the remaining batsmen. *Cricket* incorrectly gives WA (1) Coyne; WA (2) Gouly, Coyne, extras, total; SA (2) bowling for Coombe and Reedman. Sources: *Cricket, C.B.O'Reilly, The West Australian, Daily News, Western Mail*.

WESTERN AUSTRALIA

H.C.Howard	lbw b Claxton	34		c Claxton b Travers	9
E.F.Parker	b Jarvis	30		b Travers	4
S.H.D.Rowe	c Gehrs b Coombe	38		b Coombe	0
*K.H.Quist	st Richardson b Travers	47		lbw b Travers	6
T.M.Coombe	c & b Gehrs	0		c Claxton b Travers	15
L.Gouly	b Claxton	9		not out	70
†H.A.Evers	b Travers	15		b Coombe	12
T.H.Coyne	c Gehrs b Travers	2	(11)	b Coombe	24
H.P.D.Edmondson	lbw b Claxton	0	(8)	b Coombe	5
W.H.Kelly	not out	0	(9)	b Hanson	9
R.A.Selk	b Claxton	5	(10)	st Rees b Reedman	17
Extras	(b16, lb2)	18		(b17, w1,)	18
Total	(92.3 overs, 250 mins)	198		(75.3 overs, 210 mins)	189

SOUTH AUSTRALIA

J.N.S.Rees	not out	21	(4)	b Selk	0
J.P.F.Travers	st Evers b Coyne	0	(7)	c Quist b Kelly	4
D.R.A.Gehrs	lbw b Selk	7	(2)	c Evers b Selk	84
N.Claxton	c Kelly b Selk	9	(1)	b Coyne	1
F.T.Hack	b Coyne	0	(3)	st Evers b Selk	60
*J.C.Reedman	b Selk	4		b Selk	22
A.Jarvis	b Coyne	2	(5)	c Rowe b Selk	4
P.H.Coombe	c Rowe b Coyne	0		st Evers b Selk	1
†J.Richardson	c & b Coyne	0		c Coyne b Selk	25
C.T.Chamberlain	c & b Selk	1		c Parker b Kelly	3
L.H.Hanson	b Selk	3		not out	4
Extras	(b5, lb1, nb1)	7		(b18, lb4)	22
Total	(26.1 overs, 70 mins)	54		(65.2 overs, 200 mins)	230

SOUTH AUSTRALIA	O	M	R	W	w,nb		O	M	R	W	w,nb		FALL OF WICKETS			
Hanson	14	1	41	0	-,-	(3)	5	0	20	1	-,-		WA	SA	WA	SA
Coombe	29	9	46	1	-,-		25.3	9	49	4	-,-	Wkt	1st	1st	2nd	2nd
Jarvis	9	4	19	1	-,-	(6)	7	2	21	0	-,-	1st	60	0	9	3
Reedman	7	4	6	0	-,-	(5)	8	2	13	1	-,-	2nd	104	15	14	161
Claxton	14.3	5	19	4	-,-	(4)	5	1	19	0	1,-	3rd	110	30	23	161
Travers	11	1	29	3	-,-	(1)	22	10	34	4	-,-	4th	111	31	24	162
Gehrs	8	1	20	1	-,-							5th	133	42	42	169
Chamberlain						(7)	3	0	15	0	-,-	6th	180	49	63	189
												7th	182	49	69	190
WESTERN AUSTRALIA	O	M	R	W	w,nb		O	M	R	W	w,nb	8th	185	49	103	220
Selk	13.1	5	19	5	-,1		27	1	108	7	-,-	9th	193	50	128	226
Coyne	12	0	27	5	-,-		11	2	30	1	-,-	10th	198	54	189	230
Kelly	1	0	1	0	-,-	(5)	19.2	3	41	2	-,-					
Rowe							3	0	8	0	-,-					
Quist						(3)	1	0	5	0	-,-					
Edmondson							4	0	16	0	-,-					

QUEENSLAND v VICTORIA

Played at Brisbane Cricket Ground (Woolloongabba) on February 3 (no play), 5, 6, 7, 1906. (Timeless match)
Toss : Queensland.   Result : VICTORIA WON BY 178 RUNS.
Debuts: Queensland - M.M.F.Dunn (f/c).
12th Men: J.S.Hutcheon (Qld). No 12th named for Vic.
Umpires: W.H.Carvosso and A.L.Cossart.
Attendances: no play, 1500, 1500,   ? .   Total: About 3500.   Receipts: No figures published.
Close of Play: 1st day no play; 2nd day Qld 4/88 (Hartigan 54); 3rd day Qld (2) 2/35 (Hayes 7).

Rain washed out the opening day and prompted an agreement between the captains early in the game to play both second innings on a new pitch; an especially rare occurrence in Queensland cricket and probably the last time more than one pitch was used during the course of a first-class match in Australia. Victoria had selection problems following their match against New South Wales. V.S.Ransford had returned to Melbourne to join the Melbourne Cricket Club's tour of New Zealand, and wicket-keeper C.F.Jones had not recovered from the hand injury he sustained in the Sydney match. Ainslie (12th man in Sydney) and Bean (the team manager) made up the numbers and the wicket-keeping was shared between four men, in order, Ellis on the first day of play, Ainslie when play resumed next day at 4/88, and McAlister later in the day due to increasing byes and finally Warne, who kept throughout the second innings after not being called upon at all in the first. McAlister topscored in the match with 141 (177 minutes, 15 fours), which included a chance at 119. Collins (6 for 52) bowled unchanged throughout the Queensland second innings. T.B.Faunce (knee injury) was unavailable for Queensland. *Cricket* incorrectly gives Qld (1) E.R.Crouch c Carroll b Christian 1, G.S.Crouch b Christian 7, extras 44, Laver 0/12; Vic (1) Hartigan 0/10, Thomson 1/22; Vic (2) Bean c Evans. Sources: *Cricket, The Age, Sydney Morning Herald, Brisbane Courier, Queensland Times, The Queenslander.*

VICTORIA

†M.Ellis	c E.R.Crouch b Timbury	9	st Evans b McCaffrey	32
T.S.Warne	c McCaffrey b Lewis	6	c G.S.Crouch b Timbury	6
P.A.McAlister	c & b Hayes	19	lbw b Thomson	141
A.H.Christian	b Lewis	5	b McCaffrey	2
E.V.Carroll	c G.S.Crouch b E.R.Crouch	22	c Hayes b Lewis	6
J.Ainslie	c Evans b McCaffrey	39	c Evans b McCaffrey	2
J.F.Horan	c Dunn b McCaffrey	44	c G.S.Crouch b Thomson	34
*F.J.Laver	c & b McCaffrey	5	b Hayes	26
E.E.Bean	st Evans b McCaffrey	1	b Timbury	10
F.B.Collins	not out	0	not out	37
J.V.Saunders	b Thomson	2	b Thomson	1
Extras	(b9, nb1)	10	(b7, lb2)	9
Total	(40.4 overs, 110 mins)	162	(75.3 overs, 205 mins)	306

QUEENSLAND

R.J.Hartigan	b Saunders	65	b Christian	12
W.B.Hayes	b Collins	4	(3) c Collins b Saunders	27
J.W.Lewis	c Christian b Collins	2	(2) c Christian b Collins	14
E.R.Crouch	b Christian	7	(7) b Christian	33
G.S.Crouch	c Warne b Christian	1	(8) c Christian b Collins	15
J.Thomson	b Saunders	1	c Collins b Saunders	1
H.G.S.Morton	c Christian b Saunders	12	(4) c Ainslie b Collins	11
M.M.F.Dunn	lbw b Saunders	6	(5) b Collins	0
*†W.T.Evans	c Horan b Saunders	0	b Collins	12
M.F.McCaffrey	lbw b Christian	6	b Collins	10
F.R.V.Timbury	not out	0	not out	1
Extras	(b32, lb8, nb1)	41	(b8, lb1)	9
Total	(35.2 overs, 105 mins)	145	(40.4 overs, 115 mins)	145

QUEENSLAND	O	M	R	W	w,nb		O	M	R	W	w,nb			FALL OF WICKETS		
Timbury	8	0	24	1	-,1		20	3	58	2	-,-	Wkt	VIC	QLD	VIC	QLD
McCaffrey	14	1	45	4	-,-		23	1	115	3	-,-		1st	1st	2nd	2nd
Hayes	5	0	19	1	-,-	(5)	7	0	30	1	-,-	1st	10	9	17	14
Lewis	3	0	18	2	-,-	(3)	10	0	45	1	-,-	2nd	37	17	56	35
E.R.Crouch	3	0	14	1	-,-	(6)	4	0	14	0	-,-	3rd	37	64	58	56
Hartigan	3	0	20	0	-,-							4th	42	88	79	56
Thomson	4.4	1	12	1	-,-	(4)	11.3	1	35	3	-,-	5th	82	101	92	68
												6th	136	112	158	72
VICTORIA	O	M	R	W	w,nb		O	M	R	W	w,nb	7th	146	128	196	87
Saunders	13	3	42	5	-,-		15	4	64	2	-,-	8th	149	128	223	109
Collins	6	0	26	2	-,1		20	6	52	6	-,-	9th	160	141	298	135
Laver	5	1	15	0	-,-							10th	162	145	306	145
Christian	11.2	4	21	3	-,-	(3)	5.4	1	20	2	-,-					

WESTERN AUSTRALIA v SOUTH AUSTRALIA

Played at Fremantle Oval on February 3, 5, 6, 1906. (Three-day match)
Toss : South Australia. Result : MATCH DRAWN.
Debuts: Western Australia - W.J.Dunstan, E.Harvey, V.Jones, C.Munro (all f/c). South Australia - G.C.Gurr (f/c).
12th Men: H.Booth and Dr. Deravin named as emergencies for WA.
Umpires: G.Berry and J.C.Brickhill.
Attendances: 1000, 1000, 400. Total: About 2400. Receipts: No figures published.
Close of Play: 1st day WA 1/59 (Howard 14, Rowe 29); 2nd day SA (2) 3/105 (Gehrs 23).

This was the first of five interstate matches played at Fremantle - still the only venue apart from the W.A.C.A.Ground to have staged first-class cricket in WA. H.A.Evers (unavailable) was replaced by Dunstan. Gurr, who had accompanied the team as scorer, was brought into the South Australian side in the absence of J.J.Lyons and J.N.S.Rees. He was bowled by the only ball he faced in first-class cricket and replaced as wicket-keeper by Gehrs at 2/119 in WA (1). Gehrs became the first to score a century in each innings for South Australia. He hit 12 fours and carried his bat in the first innings and hit 8 fours in 120 minutes in the second innings. Howard for WA also carried his bat; his knock was described by a journalist as "one long-drawn poke - a remarkably patient and chanceless innings, but it was not cricket." Parker took 145 minutes for his 116 and hit 9 fours. He dominated an opening stand of 172 in 130 minutes with Quist. Travers' only 6 overs on the first day were all maidens. Last first-class appearance by A.Jarvis. *Cricket* incorrectly gives Harvey (1) and omits SA (2) and WA (2) bowling. Sources: *Cricket, C.B.O'Reilly, The West Australian, Daily News.*

SOUTH AUSTRALIA

D.R.A.Gehrs	not out	148	(4) not out		100
F.T.Hack	lbw b Munro	6	(3) b Kelly		31
N.Claxton	b Munro	0	(1) run out (Parker/Dunstan)		44
*J.C.Reedman	c Munro b Selk	0	(6) not out		58
A.Jarvis	st Dunstan b Selk	7	(2) c Munro b Selk		5
J.P.F.Travers	c Quist b Selk	22	(5) c Jones b Munro		15
C.T.Chamberlain	b Selk	3			
J.Richardson	run out (Parker)	29			
P.H.Coombe	c Parker b Selk	2			
L.H.Hanson	b Munro	3			
†G.C.Gurr	b Munro	0			
Extras	(b8, lb6, w1)	15	(b1, lb4, nb1)		6
Total	(69.5 overs, 195 mins)	235	(72.0 overs, 195 mins) (4 wkts dec)		259

WESTERN AUSTRALIA

H.C.Howard	not out	47	(7) not out		6
L.Gouly	b Coombe	6			
S.H.D.Rowe	c Travers b Hanson	32	b Travers		21
E.F.Parker	c Travers b Coombe	76	(2) b Claxton		116
*K.H.Quist	c Coombe b Jarvis	2	(1) c Gehrs b Travers		56
V.C.Jones	b Coombe	1	(4) b Coombe		15
E.Harvey	run out (/Gehrs)	0	(5) not out		14
W.H.Kelly	b Coombe	1			
C.Munro	c Claxton b Coombe	0			
R.A.Selk	b Travers	19	(6) c Jarvis b Claxton		2
†W.J.Dunstan	b Coombe	0			
Extras	(b17, lb1)	18	(b11, lb1)		12
Total	(85.0 overs, 215 mins)	202	(81.0 overs, 205 mins) (5 wkts)		242

WESTERN AUSTRALIA	O	M	R	W	w,nb		O	M	R	W	w,nb					
Selk	30	2	103	5	1,-		27	1	77	1	-,1					
Munro	28.5	7	63	4	-,-		21	3	67	1	-,-					
Kelly	6	0	26	0	-,-	(4)	12	0	44	1	-,-					
Jones	5	1	28	0	-,-	(5)	4	0	24	0	,					
Quist						(3)	4	1	17	0	-,-					
Harvey							3	0	17	0	-,-					
Parker							1	0	7	0	-,-					

FALL OF WICKETS

Wkt	1st SA	1st WA	2nd SA	2nd WA
1st	18	12	9	172
2nd	18	70	60	194
3rd	18	162	105	216
4th	29	169	129	227
5th	89	172	-	230
6th	107	174	-	-
7th	198	175	-	-
8th	209	175	-	-
9th	235	199	-	-
10th	235	202	-	-

SOUTH AUSTRALIA	O	M	R	W	w,nb		O	M	R	W	w,nb
Hanson	14	1	40	1	-,-		3	0	23	0	-,-
Coombe	27	6	59	6	-,-		22	3	78	1	-,-
Travers	13	8	12	1	-,-		30	6	63	2	-,-
Claxton	12	3	32	0	-,-		19	2	48	2	-,-
Jarvis	16	5	37	1	-,-		7	2	18	0	-,-
Gehrs	1	0	3	0	-,-						
Reedman	2	1	1	0	-,-						

Again 12 first-class matches were played in a virtual carbon-copy of the previous season. New South Wales continued to dominate the Sheffield Shield and South Australia fought out last place. And as they had done the previous year, New South Wales won both their matches against Queensland by comprehensive margins.

Not only did New South Wales win the Sheffield Shield for a sixth successive season, which was unprecedented, they did it in a more resounding fashion than ever before. The team's end-of-season quotient of 2.330 - a batting average of 39.85 as against a bowling average of 17.10 - had never been remotely matched in the past. Victoria pressed them in a hard-fought match at Melbourne before going down by two wickets, but New South Wales's superiority was demonstrated with emphatic innings victories in each of their other three Shield fixtures. The leadership and allround skills of Noble continued to play a vital role and there seemed to be no end to the number of talented young players staking their claims. Diamond, Garnsey, Macartney and E.L.Waddy all consolidated their places alongside the likes of Hopkins and Cotter, who both had fine seasons. Charlie Macartney had started out the previous season as a slow left-arm bowler and lower-order right-hand batsman. This season he finished high in both batting and bowling averages, and his performances soon stamped him as a player of very rare talent.

At Brisbane in the opening match of the first-class season, Charles Gregory scored 383 to establish a new record for the highest individual score in Australian first-class cricket. It was a record that remained unsurpassed until the advent of Ponsford and Bradman in the 1920s. Curiously, Gregory managed a total of only 17 runs in his other four innings for New South Wales this season.

New South Wales broke new ground in March 1907 by visiting Western Australia for the first time. Two first-class matches were played, resulting in a win to each team. Both were achieved by narrow margins. The NSWCA reported that the trip 'had proved a great success from every point of view', and the WACA shared that view.

Tasmania and Victoria resumed their annual fixture after a one-year absence. Charles Eady (13 for 185) inspired a five-wicket victory for the islanders despite a fighting 168 from Peter McAlister in the Victorian second innings.

The NSWCA staged a match between New South Wales and The Rest as a benefit for S.E.Gregory. Gregory appeared for The Rest and scored 94 and 4 in a winning effort. It was his only first-class match this season.

A series of off-field developments took place in the winter leadup to the season. The South Australian Cricket Association gained admittance to the Board of Control on July 28, 1906, their reservations over financial control having been resolved to their satisfaction. But the Board continued to be at odds with the players, and bodies such as Melbourne Cricket Club, over the issue of touring teams to and from Australia. In early 1906 Melbourne CC had entered into agreements securing a number of Australian cricketers, with the intention of inviting an English team for the 1906-07 season. The Board had previously attempted to arrange a similar tour for the same season, but Marylebone Cricket Club had declined the invitation on the grounds that the Board was not yet fully representative of Australian cricket, only New South Wales, Victoria and Queensland being members. In May, the NSWCA suspended the 11 New South Wales players who were party to Melbourne CC's plans for an English tour (Carter, Cotter, Diamond, Duff, Garnsey, Hopkins, Mackay, Noble, O'Connor, Trumper and E.F.Waddy), but the suspensions were lifted in August, following the SACA's admission to the Board. The Board's constitution was amended, ensuring that profits from tours would be evenly divided amongst players in future. A settlement had now been reached - that the Board would continue to conduct tours in future - but the mid-year resolution left no time to organise an English tour for 1906-07.

Leading Aggregates

Batsmen	M	I	NO	Runs	HS	Ave.	Bowlers	Runs	Wkts	Ave.
A.J.Y.Hopkins (NSW)	8	12	1	617	171	56.09	G.L.Garnsey (NSW)	702	32	21.93
A.Diamond (NSW)	5	7	1	502	210*	83.66	C.G.Macartney (NSW)	546	30	18.20
E.L.Waddy (NSW)	9	13	0	495	129	38.07	A.W.Wright (SA)	616	29	21.24
C.G.Macartney (NSW)	9	12	2	405	122	40.50	M.A.Noble (NSW)	334	24	13.91
C.W.Gregory (NSW)	4	5	0	400	383	80.00	A.Cotter (NSW)	629	24	26.20
P.A.McAlister (V)	5	10	0	360	168	36.00	J.V.Saunders (V)	593	20	29.65

SHEFFIELD SHIELD TABLE

	P	W	L	D	Pts	Quotient	Runs Scored	Wkts Lost	Runs Conceded	Wkts Taken
NEW SOUTH WALES	4	4	-	-	4	2.330	1913	48	1368	80
SOUTH AUSTRALIA	4	1	3	-	-2	0.713	1740	80	1768	58
VICTORIA	4	1	3	-	-2	0.655	1569	78	2086	68
TOTAL	6	6	6	-	0	1.000	5222	206	5222	206

QUEENSLAND v NEW SOUTH WALES

Played at Brisbane Cricket Ground (Woolloongabba) on November 10, 12, 13, 1906. (Timeless match)
Toss : Queensland.　　　　　　　　Result : NEW SOUTH WALES WON BY AN INNINGS AND 302 RUNS.
Debuts: Queensland - C.B.Barstow, G.A.L.Brown, C.E.Simpson (all f/c).
12th Men: J.W.McLaren (Qld). No 12th named for NSW.
Umpires: G.A.Carter and W.H.Carvosso (see below).
Attendances: 1500, 1000, 300.　　　　Total: About 2800.　　　　Receipts: £130.
Close of Play: 1st day NSW 1/109 (Gregory 48, Hickson 42); 2nd day NSW 5/654 (Gregory 366, Blaxland 72).

On the second day of the match, Charles William Gregory, aged 28, became the first batsman in the world to score 300 first-class runs in one day's play. He progressed from 48 to 366, contributing a big portion of the 545 runs scored by New South Wales in 104.4 overs on the day. Gregory batted for 345 minutes in all, scoring 383 - a new record individual score in Australia and surpassed by A.C.MacLaren's 424 in 1895. He gave chances at 1, 42, 142, 175 and 325 and hit 55 fours, 12 threes, 26 twos and 75 singles. He shared partnerships of 230 for the fourth wicket with Waddy (100 in 114 minutes, 15 fours) and 220 for the sixth wicket with Blaxland (94 in 130 minutes, 12 fours). Gregory was actually in the twilight of his first-class career - he played in only four more matches, scoring just 31 in five innings. Queensland named a squad of thirteen for the match, from which J.L.Halpin withdrew and McLaren was omitted. E.Beard, appointed by the Queensland Cricket Association to umpire with Carter, withdrew before the start and was replaced by Carvosso, who became ill during the match and was replaced by W.Busby on the final day. Simpson acted as wicket-keeper when Evans bowled late in the New South Wales innings. *Wisden* incorrectly gives Qld (1) Hayes c & b Cotter; Qld (2) extras 15, total 317, NSW by an innings and 301 runs. Sources: *Wisden, NSWCA Report, Brisbane Courier, Queensland Times, The Queenslander.*

QUEENSLAND

R.J.Hartigan	c Waddy b Garnsey	50		c Bardsley b Barnes	61
G.A.L.Brown	st Carter b Macartney	30		c Redgrave b Barnes	32
T.B.Faunce	b Cotter	11		c Redgrave b Garnsey	17
C.E.Simpson	b Macartney	8		st Carter b Barnes	59
M.M.F.Dunn	b Macartney	3		c & b Garnsey	19
W.B.Hayes	b Cotter	4		run out	21
*†W.T.Evans	run out	19		c Garnsey b Barnes	43
J.Thomson	c Cotter b Garnsey	3		c Blaxland b Garnsey	43
F.R.V.Timbury	c Waddy b Garnsey	5	(10)	not out	2
M.F.McCaffrey	c Waddy b Garnsey	0	(11)	lbw b Barnes	5
C.B.Barstow	not out	0	(9)	c Bardsley b Garnsey	0
Extras	(b4, lb8)	12		(b9, lb4, nb1)	14
Total	(38.0 overs, 127 mins)	145		(62.5 overs, 190 mins)	316

NEW SOUTH WALES

C.W.Gregory	c & b Hayes	383
W.Bardsley	b Barstow	12
R.N.Hickson	run out (Dunn/Evans)	48
J.S.Redgrave	run out (Brown/　　　　　)	32
E.L.Waddy	c Hartigan b McCaffrey	100
J.C.Barnes	c Thomson b Timbury	13
M.H.Blaxland	b Barstow	94
C.G.Macartney	not out	21
A.Cotter	c Hartigan b Hayes	34
*†H.Carter	c Simpson b Hayes	1
G.L.Garnsey	c Faunce b Hayes	10
Extras	(b10, lb4, w1)	15
Total	(165.3 overs, 396 mins)	763

NEW SOUTH WALES	O	M	R	W	w,nb	O	M	R	W	w,nb
Cotter	14	1	53	2	-,-	11	3	40	0	-,1
Garnsey	17	3	64	4	-,-	21	1	94	4	-,-
Macartney	5	2	14	3	-,-	10	0	31	0	-,-
Redgrave	2	1	2	0	-,-	8	2	32	0	-,-
Barnes						12.5	0	105	5	-,-

QUEENSLAND	O	M	R	W	w,nb
Timbury	29	6	123	1	1,-
McCaffrey	28	2	132	1	-,-
Barstow	27	2	115	2	-,-
Hayes	28.3	0	120	4	-,-
Thomson	10	3	37	0	-,-
Dunn	10	0	59	0	-,-
Hartigan	17	3	65	0	-,-
Simpson	11	1	59	0	-,-
Evans	3	0	28	0	-,-
Brown	2	0	10	0	-,-

FALL OF WICKETS

Wkt	QLD 1st	NSW 1st	QLD 2nd
1st	63	45	96
2nd	86	119	105
3rd	94	188	136
4th	100	418	176
5th	111	471	206
6th	112	691	233
7th	125	697	299
8th	145	752	299
9th	145	753	308
10th	145	763	316

SOUTH AUSTRALIA v VICTORIA (Shield Match 1)

Played at Adelaide Oval on November 10, 12, 13, 14, 1906. (Timeless match)
Toss : Victoria.   Result : VICTORIA WON BY 70 RUNS.
Debuts: South Australia - E.A.Bailey (f/c) A.McBeath, J.D.A.O'Connor (both SA only). Victoria - T.R.Rush (f/c).
12th Men: J.N.S.Rees (SA) and G.R.Hazlitt (Vic).
Umpires: P.Argall and T.A.Reeves.
Attendances: 2000, 3000, 1000, 200.   Total: About 6200.   Receipts: No figures published.
Close of Play: 1st day SA 3/169 (Pellew 27, Claxton 18); 2nd day Vic (2) 4/176 (Ransford 35, Carroll 35); 3rd day SA (2) 7/156
    (Jennings 23, O'Connor 13).

C.E.Dolling was unavailable for South Australia due to university exams. Goss and Vaughan replaced W.W.Armstrong (injured knee) and M.Ellis (ill) in the Victorian team. Bailey was brought in at the last minute by South Australia to replace R.B.C.Rees, who was unable to get leave from work. Carroll (112 in 160 minutes, 16 fours) shared in a decisive seventh-wicket partnership of 118 with Rush (62 in 65 minutes, 7 fours) in the Victorian second innings. The two South Australians to reach 50 were Darling (77 in 86 minutes, 8 fours) and C.Hill (71 in 102 minutes, 8 fours). Bailey undefeated in his first innings at first-class level, was out first ball in the second innings. McBeath and O'Connor had previously both represented New South Wales. Sources: *Wisden, C.B.O'Reilly, The Age, Sydney Morning Herald, Adelaide Advertiser, South Australian Register.*

VICTORIA

†W.Carkeek	b O'Connor	0	b O'Connor		3
F.Vaughan	c Jennings b Wright	11	c Jennings b McBeath		65
P.A.McAlister	b L.R.Hill	39	c C.Hill b McBeath		15
J.Ainslie	c McBeath b Wright	29	b O'Connor		17
V.S.Ransford	b McBeath	8	b O'Connor		46
E.V.Carroll	c Claxton b Wright	13	c Pellew b McBeath		112
*F.J.Laver	b McBeath	4	c Gehrs b O'Connor		6
T.R.Rush	b McBeath	8	run out (Gehrs/Jennings)		62
E.A.Goss	st Jennings b McBeath	1	not out		9
F.B.Collins	not out	2	c C.Hill b O'Connor		1
J.V.Saunders	c C.Hill b Wright	0	b McBeath		1
Extras	(b3, lb4, nb3)	10	(b5, lb4, w2, nb4)		15
Total	(60.0 overs, 160 mins)	125	(115.0 overs, 298 mins)		352

SOUTH AUSTRALIA

*J.Darling	c Carroll b Collins	77	b Saunders		14
D.R.A.Gehrs	b Goss	4	c & b Saunders		2
C.Hill	b Saunders	40	c sub (G.R.Hazlitt) b Goss		71
J.H.Pellew	b Goss	32	c & b Saunders		25
N.Claxton	b Saunders	20	lbw b Laver		3
†C.B.Jennings	c Carroll b Saunders	3	b Saunders		24
E.A.Bailey	not out	23	b Goss		0
L.R.Hill	b Saunders	8	c Ransford b Laver		2
J.D.A.O'Connor	c McAlister b Goss	3	b Saunders		15
A.McBeath	c & b Saunders	1	not out		10
A.W.Wright	b Goss	5	b Collins		10
Extras	(lb3, nb2)	5	(b4, lb4, nb2)		10
Total	(60.2 overs, 191 mins)	221	(59.5 overs, 175 mins)		186

SOUTH AUSTRALIA	O	M	R	W	w,nb	O	M	R	W	w,nb
McBeath	27	12	41	4	-,-	40	9	136	4	1,1
O'Connor	9	1	28	1	-,2	37	7	93	5	-,1
Wright	21	11	42	4	-,-	20	4	54	0	-,-
L.R.Hill	3	1	4	1	-,1	7	0	23	0	-,2
Claxton						11	2	31	0	1,-

VICTORIA	O	M	R	W	w,nb	O	M	R	W	w,nb
Goss	14.2	2	60	4	-,1	15	0	53	2	-,-
Saunders	23	3	83	5	-,-	21	3	60	5	-,-
Collins	12	3	42	1	-,1	11.5	0	28	1	-,2
Laver	9	3	22	0	-,-	12	1	35	2	-,-
McAlister	2	1	9	0	-,-					

FALL OF WICKETS

Wkt	VIC 1st	SA 1st	VIC 2nd	SA 2nd
1st	3	6	3	7
2nd	46	92	28	28
3rd	60	125	73	89
4th	91	176	119	108
5th	97	176	209	127
6th	105	186	222	127
7th	113	206	340	130
8th	117	209	340	161
9th	125	210	346	162
10th	125	221	352	186

NEW SOUTH WALES v QUEENSLAND

Played at Sydney Cricket Ground on December 7, 8, 10, 1906. (Timeless match)
Toss : New South Wales. Result : NEW SOUTH WALES WON BY AN INNINGS AND 154 RUNS.
Debuts: Queensland - J.W.McLaren, G.F.Martin (both f/c).
12th Men: J.S.Redgrave (NSW). No 12th named for Queensland.
Umpires: P.Caswell and J.Laing.
Attendances: 1000, 1000, 200. Total: About 2200. Receipts: £69.
Close of Play: 1st day NSW 9/465 (Hopkins 126, McIntyre 6); 2nd day Qld 2/161 (Simpson 19).

H.Carter and A.Cotter (New South Wales) and A.A.Atkins and J.L.Halpin (Queensland) were all unavailable. Hopkins (171 in 152 minutes, 25 fours) survived a chance when 130 and was involved in a tenth-wicket partnership of 120 with McIntyre, a new State record for that wicket. White (77 in 110 minutes, 7 fours), Blaxland (93 in 105 minutes, 16 fours, chance at 77) and Macartney (122 in 131 minutes, 13 fours) were chiefly responsible for the New South Wales total. Hopkins took his score from 22 to 126 in the final session of the first day. Heavy rain during the luncheon adjournment on the second day prevented any play until after the tea break. Despite a wicket that "seemed very wet on parts" (*Newcastle Herald*), Hartigan (68 in 97 minutes, 9 fours) and Brown (70 in 143 minutes, 5 fours) began Queensland's reply with a century stand. Good conditions returned for the final day and Garnsey, who began with figures of 0 for 36, bowled New South Wales to an innings victory with 12 for 70 during the day. Sources: *Cricket, NSWCA Report, Sydney Referee, Sydney Morning Herald, Newcastle Herald*.

NEW SOUTH WALES

C.W.Gregory	c Hartigan b Timbury	3
A.B.S.White	c Evans b Armstrong	77
E.F.Waddy	c Evans b Hayes	9
R.N.Hickson	c Hartigan b Timbury	11
M.H.Blaxland	c Hartigan b Simpson	93
E.L.Waddy	run out (/Timbury)	5
C.G.Macartney	b McLaren	122
*A.J.Y.Hopkins	c & b McLaren	171
G.L.Garnsey	b McLaren	0
A.J.Bowden	c Hartigan b McLaren	1
†W.R.McIntyre	not out	36
Extras	(b16, lb1, w3)	20
Total	(110.5 overs, 332 mins)	548

QUEENSLAND

R.J.Hartigan	b Bowden	68		c E.L.Waddy b Macartney	13
G.A.L.Brown	c E.F.Waddy b Macartney	70		b Macartney	11
C.E.Simpson	c Bowden b Garnsey	27		c & b Garnsey	58
W.B.Hayes	c Hickson b Garnsey	0	(7)	c & b Garnsey	2
E.R.Crouch	lbw b Garnsey	3	(4)	c McIntyre b Hopkins	17
T.B.Faunce	b Garnsey	10		b Garnsey	37
G.F.Martin	b Garnsey	10	(5)	b Hopkins	0
*†W.T.Evans	b Macartney	1		c Blaxland b Garnsey	13
E.K.Armstrong	run out (Garnsey/McIntyre)	2		c Bowden b Garnsey	3
J.W.McLaren	not out	15		not out	5
F.R.V.Timbury	b Garnsey	9		c & b Garnsey	4
Extras	(w1, nb3)	4		(b2, lb8, w2)	12
Total	(76.4 overs, 223 mins)	219		(54.1 overs, 155 mins)	175

QUEENSLAND	O	M	R	W	w,nb
Timbury	35	1	139	2	1,-
Hayes	19	0	120	1	-,-
Armstrong	18	0	85	1	-,-
McLaren	15	0	74	3	1,-
Simpson	9	1	42	1	-,-
Hartigan	9	1	37	0	-,-
Martin	3.5	0	25	1	1,-
Crouch	2	0	6	0	-,-

NEW SOUTH WALES	O	M	R	W	w,nb		O	M	R	W	w,nb
Garnsey	20.4	2	71	6	1,-	(4)	9.1	1	35	6	2,-
Macartney	29	12	55	2	-,-		22	8	37	2	-,-
Hopkins	8	1	25	0	-,2		7	1	41	2	-,-
Hickson	6	1	21	0	-,1						
Bowden	13	0	43	1	-,-	(1)	16	2	50	0	-,-

FALL OF WICKETS

	NSW	QLD	QLD
Wkt	1st	1st	2nd
1st	8	113	22
2nd	19	161	27
3rd	48	169	82
4th	170	170	86
5th	180	178	130
6th	214	183	132
7th	422	188	157
8th	422	194	158
9th	428	198	163
10th	548	219	175

SOUTH AUSTRALIA v NEW SOUTH WALES (Shield Match 2)

Played at Adelaide Oval on December 15, 17, 18, 1906. (Timeless match)
Toss : New South Wales.   Result : NEW SOUTH WALES WON BY AN INNINGS AND 109 RUNS.
Debuts: South Australia - D.McRae, R.E.Mayne (both f/c).
12th Men: R.J.B.Townsend (SA) and R.N.Hickson (NSW).
Umpires: P.Argall and G.A.Watson.
Attendances: 1000, 300, 500.   Total: About 1800.   Receipts: No figures published.
Close of Play: 1st day NSW 349 all out; 2nd day SA (2) 3/6 (Travers 1).

Hickson replaced V.T.Trumper (business) in the New South Wales team for their southern tour. Hopkins (120 not out in 197 minutes, 1 six and 14 fours) and E.L.Waddy (63 in 68 minutes, 9 fours) consolidated the New South Wales innings on the first day with a sixth wicket stand of 119 in only 68 minutes. Thunderstorms on the rest day (Sunday) thoroughly soaked the wicket and the home team had the misfortune to be caught on a wicket described as a "gluepot" (*Register*). Play was not possible until 3.26pm on the second day. Macartney and Noble utilised the conditions to the full to account for the locals in less than two hours. Following on, three further wickets were lost before stumps. Clem Hill (65 in 84 minutes, 7 fours) "stood a long way ahead of his comrades" (*Register*) on an improving wicket on the final day but the visitors ran out comfortable winners before tea on the third day. *NSWCA Report* gives SA (2) Cotter 3/59, Garnsey 2/49.
Sources: *Wisden, C.B.O'Reilly, NSWCA Report, Adelaide Advertiser, South Australian Register.*

NEW SOUTH WALES

R.A.Duff	b O'Connor	26
A.Diamond	c McBeath b Wright	26
*M.A.Noble	b Wright	20
E.F.Waddy	lbw b O'Connor	21
C.W.Gregory	st Gehrs b Wright	3
A.J.Y.Hopkins	not out	120
E.L.Waddy	b Wright	63
C.G.Macartney	lbw b Wright	0
A.Cotter	c McBeath b Wright	32
†H.Carter	c Gehrs b O'Connor	0
G.L.Garnsey	c O'Connor b McBeath	36
Extras	(lb2)	2
Total	(99.3 overs, 284 mins)	349

SOUTH AUSTRALIA

†D.R.A.Gehrs	c Garnsey b Macartney	4	(5)	run out (Carter)	22
J.H.Pellew	c Hopkins b Macartney	21	(7)	b Garnsey	4
*C.Hill	c Gregory b Macartney	10	(6)	c Duff b Macartney	65
N.Claxton	c Diamond b Macartney	8	(11)	not out	16
D.McRae	c E.F.Waddy b Hopkins	2	(8)	b Cotter	1
C.E.Dolling	b Noble	0	(10)	c sub (R.N.Hickson) b Garnsey	2
J.D.A.O'Connor	c & b Noble	3	(3)	c Cotter b Hopkins	4
R.E.Mayne	c Gregory b Macartney	1	(9)	c Macartney b Cotter	24
J.P.F.Travers	run out	0	(2)	b Cotter	27
A.McBeath	b Noble	5	(1)	b Macartney	1
A.W.Wright	not out	2	(4)	b Hopkins	0
Extras	(b4, nb1)	5		(b5, lb5, nb3)	13
Total	(33.1 overs, 109 mins)	61		(61.0 overs, 185 mins)	179

SOUTH AUSTRALIA	O	M	R	W	w,nb							
O'Connor	31	8	119	3	-,-							
McBeath	25.3	8	69	1	-,-							
Travers	12	2	50	0	-,-							
Wright	25	4	91	6	-,-							
Claxton	5	0	16	0	-,-							
Pellew	1	0	2	0	-,-							

FALL OF WICKETS

		NSW	SA	SA
Wkt		1st	1st	2nd
1st		36	16	2
2nd		70	33	6
3rd		75	41	6
4th		79	48	44
5th		123	49	68
6th		242	49	89
7th		242	51	99
8th		286	52	141
9th		289	57	154
10th		349	61	179

NEW SOUTH WALES	O	M	R	W	w,nb		O	M	R	W	w,nb
Hopkins	12	1	28	1	-,1	(3)	6	2	17	2	-,-
Macartney	16	8	18	5	-,-		7	2	17	2	-,-
Noble	5.1	1	10	3	-,-	(1)	15	7	24	0	-,-
Cotter							19	2	57	3	-,2
Garnsey							14	4	51	2	-,1

VICTORIA v NEW SOUTH WALES (Shield Match 3)

Played at Melbourne Cricket Ground on December 24, 26, 27, 1906. (Timeless match)
Toss : Victoria.   Result : NEW SOUTH WALES WON BY TWO WICKETS.
Debuts: Nil.
12th Men: E.A.Goss (Vic) and C.W.Gregory (NSW).
Umpires: R.M.Crockett and D.A.Elder.
Attendances: 5600, 7546, 4000.   Total: About 17,146.   Receipts: £548.
Close of Play: 1st day NSW 2/129 (Hopkins 55, Macartney 8); 2nd day Vic (2) 4/164 (Armstrong 55, Rush 12).

Ransford was a late replacement for M.Ellis (injured knee) in the Victorian side. Carkeek was unable to keep wickets on the first day due to a hand injury; Warne took over in his absence and the New South Wales 12th man, C.W.Gregory, fielded as substitute because Goss was not at the ground. Carkeek resumed as wicket-keeper on the second and third days. Armstrong kept Victoria in contention with a fine all-round performance. His sustained accuracy restricted the New South Wales reply to the home team's mediocre first innings and he then held the Victorian second innings together with an unbeaten century (168 not out in 230 minutes, 1 six and 18 fours). Hopkins (63 in 85 minutes, 9 fours and 51 in 70 minutes, 5 fours), E.L.Waddy (51 in 68 minutes, 8 fours) and Diamond (62 in 102 minutes, 5 fours) hit half-centuries for New South Wales. Warne's leg-breaks almost took out the match on the final day with the visiting batsmen anxious to finish the game that evening. *Wisden* has incorrect match dates and *The Age* incorrectly gives Vic (2) Carroll c E.F.Waddy. Sources: *Wisden, NSWCA Report, VCA Report, The Age, The Argus, The Herald, The Australasian.*

VICTORIA

Batsman	Dismissal	Score		Dismissal	Score
P.A.McAlister	c & b Noble	15		c & b Garnsey	36
F.Vaughan	c Garnsey b Noble	34		b Cotter	9
T.S.Warne	c Cotter b Macartney	10		run out (Duff/Macartney)	27
*W.W.Armstrong	c E.F.Waddy b Cotter	27	(5)	not out	168
E.V.Carroll	b Noble	18	(4)	c E.L.Waddy b Hopkins	17
T.R.Rush	c Carter b Cotter	30		run out (Diamond)	12
V.S.Ransford	c & b Noble	4		b Hopkins	13
F.J.Laver	run out (/Cotter)	3		b Noble	26
†W.Carkeek	not out	8		c Diamond b Garnsey	21
G.R.Hazlitt	c Carter b Cotter	0		c Noble b Garnsey	0
J.V.Saunders	b Garnsey	3		b Noble	1
Extras	(b2, lb3, nb2)	7		(b3, lb4, w1, nb1)	9
Total	(51.1 overs, 170 mins)	159		(104.4 overs, 315 mins)	339

NEW SOUTH WALES

Batsman	Dismissal	Score		Dismissal	Score
R.A.Duff	c Rush b Armstrong	47		c Saunders b Hazlitt	18
A.Diamond	b Hazlitt	15		st Carkeek b Warne	62
A.J.Y.Hopkins	c Ransford b Hazlitt	63		b Warne	51
C.G.Macartney	c Warne b Armstrong	42		st Carkeek b Warne	6
*M.A.Noble	c McAlister b Hazlitt	9	(10)	not out	0
E.L.Waddy	c Carkeek b Armstrong	51	(5)	b Saunders	17
R.N.Hickson	b Armstrong	2	(6)	not out	27
E.F.Waddy	lbw b Armstrong	6	(7)	b Warne	1
†H.Carter	b Armstrong	18			
A.Cotter	c Laver b Hazlitt	47	(9)	c McAlister b Warne	0
G.L.Garnsey	not out	7	(8)	st Carkeek b Warne	0
Extras	(b2, lb2, nb2)	6		(b3, lb2)	5
Total	(91.3 overs, 255 mins)	313		(44.0 overs, 135 mins) (8 wkts)	187

NEW SOUTH WALES	O	M	R	W	w,nb		O	M	R	W	w,nb
Noble	18	4	55	4	-,-	(2)	26.4	12	46	2	-,-
Cotter	21	3	65	3	-,2	(1)	29	3	109	1	1,-
Macartney	5	2	8	1	-,-		17	3	48	0	-,-
Garnsey	7.1	2	24	1	-,-		20	0	87	3	-,1
Hopkins							12	2	40	2	-,-

VICTORIA	O	M	R	W	w,nb		O	M	R	W	w,nb
Hazlitt	27	1	114	4	-,-		8	1	34	1	-,-
Saunders	23	3	79	0	-,-		13	4	46	1	-,-
Laver	13	2	48	0	-,-	(5)	8	1	26	0	-,-
Armstrong	28.3	10	66	6	-,2	(3)	6	1	26	0	-,-
Warne						(4)	9	1	50	6	-,-

FALL OF WICKETS

Wkt	VIC 1st	NSW 1st	VIC 2nd	NSW 2nd
1st	30	37	15	26
2nd	57	104	75	125
3rd	75	141	76	133
4th	104	163	123	148
5th	118	215	164	172
6th	144	217	202	177
7th	146	240	282	177
8th	147	245	317	183
9th	148	303	323	-
10th	159	313	339	-

VICTORIA v SOUTH AUSTRALIA (Shield Match 4)

Played at Melbourne Cricket Ground on December 29, 31, 1906, January 1, 2, 1907. (Timeless match)
Toss : South Australia. Result : SOUTH AUSTRALIA WON BY 319 RUNS.
Debuts: Victoria - T.I.B.Horan (f/c).
12th Men: R.J.B.Townsend (SA). No 12th named for Vic.
Umpires: R.M.Crockett and W.Hannah.
Attendances: 5000, 4000, 5500, 500. Total: About 15,000. Receipts: £420.
Close of Play: 1st day Vic 3/58 (Carroll 13); 2nd day SA (2) 4/217 (McRae 63, Jennings 29); 3rd day Vic (2) 3/148 (Carroll 75, Goss 7).

Victoria were weakened by the withdrawal of W.W.Armstrong (work commitments) and T.S.Warne (sprained wrist) on the morning of the match. J.Darling and C.Hill - the first- and second-choice captains - were unavailable for South Australia's trip east. Dolling (93 in 143 minutes, 12 fours), Gehrs (75 in 90 minutes, 9 fours), McRae (49 in 80 minutes, 6 fours and 70 in 105 minutes, 1 six and 6 fours), Claxton (74 in 85 minutes, 7 fours), Mayne (65 in 100 minutes, 1 five and 5 fours) and Carroll (64 in 74 minutes, 7 fours and 85 in 130 minutes, 10 fours) compiled the highest scores. Victoria lost five wickets for 22 when play recommenced on the last day, and with Collins and Saunders both absent the game thus concluded. The V.C.A. conducted a hearing afterwards into their absences; Collins maintained that he had been required to work that day in his clerical job with A.M.P., however, Saunders admitted that he had not expected to be needed to bat before lunch, so instead of attending the match he had gone to his work as a caretaker with Carlton Cricket Club for the morning. *Wisden* incorrectly gives SA (2) Jennings c Rush. *O'Reilly* incorrectly gives J.F.Horan instead of T.I.B.Horan in Victorian side. Sources: *Wisden, C.B.O'Reilly, The Age, The Argus, The Herald, The Australasian.*

SOUTH AUSTRALIA

D.R.A.Gehrs	b Saunders	75		b Hazlitt	3
J.H.Pellew	b Hazlitt	3	(3)	b Hazlitt	10
*N.Claxton	b Saunders	10	(4)	c McAlister b Hazlitt	74
D.McRae	st Carkeek b Saunders	49	(5)	b Hazlitt	70
R.E.Mayne	b Goss	65	(2)	b Saunders	28
C.E.Dolling	c & b Saunders	4	(7)	c Rush b Horan	93
†C.B.Jennings	b Hazlitt	41	(6)	c Hazlitt b Saunders	31
L.R.Hill	c Saunders b Goss	21		b Collins	31
J.D.A.O'Connor	b Saunders	1		c McAlister b Collins	4
A.McBeath	c Carroll b Goss	6		lbw b McAlister	36
A.W.Wright	not out	4		not out	2
Extras	(b5, lb4, nb2)	11		(b7, lb5, nb4)	16
Total	(77.3 overs, 223 mins)	290		(109.4 overs, 315 mins)	398

VICTORIA

*P.A.McAlister	b McBeath	12		b McBeath	9
F.Vaughan	c Mayne b Hill	20		c O'Connor b Wright	17
T.R.Rush	c Wright b O'Connor	11	(6)	b Wright	4
E.V.Carroll	b O'Connor	64	(3)	st Jennings b Wright	85
T.I.B.Horan	c & b Wright	46	(4)	b Wright	29
J.Ainslie	b O'Connor	0	(7)	b McBeath	0
†W.Carkeek	c Jennings b O'Connor	5	(8)	c McRae b McBeath	3
G.R.Hazlitt	lbw b Wright	12	(9)	not out	0
E.A.Goss	not out	20	(5)	c Mayne b Wright	7
F.B.Collins	b Wright	0		absent	-
J.V.Saunders	c Mayne b Wright	2		absent	-
Extras	(b6, nb1)	7		(b8, lb7, nb1)	16
Total	(65.3 overs, 190 mins)	199		(55.5 overs, 155 mins)	170

VICTORIA	O	M	R	W	w,nb		O	M	R	W	w,nb	
Saunders	26	5	97	5	-,-		30	10	83	2	-,-	
Hazlitt	14	1	58	2	-,-		37	4	149	4	-,-	
Goss	9.3	1	43	3	-,-		12	0	71	0	-,2	
Collins	14	1	47	0	-,2	(5)	21	4	51	2	-,2	
Horan	14	0	34	0	-,-	(4)	5.4	1	26	1	-,-	
McAlister							4	2	2	1	-,-	

SOUTH AUSTRALIA	O	M	R	W	w,nb		O	M	R	W	w,nb	
O'Connor	24	8	72	4	-,-		13	4	34	0	-,-	
McBeath	19	6	50	1	-,-		20.5	5	39	3	-,1	
Wright	13.3	2	54	4	-,-		13	1	42	5	-,-	
Hill	5	1	11	1	-,1	(6)	2	0	14	0	-,-	
Claxton	4	1	5	0	-,-	(4)	4	1	12	0	-,-	
Gehrs						(5)	3	0	13	0	-,-	

FALL OF WICKETS

Wkt	SA 1st	VIC 1st	SA 2nd	VIC 2nd
1st	6	17	3	11
2nd	25	32	31	43
3rd	136	58	67	129
4th	145	123	151	149
5th	155	123	229	159
6th	234	149	229	163
7th	279	166	284	163
8th	280	183	296	170
9th	280	183	391	-
10th	290	199	398	-

NEW SOUTH WALES v SOUTH AUSTRALIA (Shield Match 5)

Played at Sydney Cricket Ground on January 4, 5, 7, 1907. (Timeless match)
Toss : South Australia.   Result : NEW SOUTH WALES WON BY AN INNINGS AND 168 RUNS.
Debuts: Nil.
12th Men: A.B.S.White (NSW) and R.J.B.Townsend (SA).
Umpires: J.Laing and A.Lucas.
Attendances: 3005, 6068, 1670.   Total: 10,743.   Receipts: £406.
Close of Play: 1st day NSW 1/133 (Diamond 64, Hopkins 30); 2nd day NSW 8/538 (Cotter 7).

Hickson and Blaxland replaced Duff and Trumper, who had business commitments, for New South Wales. The match was played on a good wicket with fine weather throughout but the South Australians were completely outplayed in every department of the game. Jennings, who began the match as the South Australian wicket-keeper, was replaced by Gehrs at the start of the second day because of his poor form on the first day. He had missed Hopkins early on and had failed to impress in general. Chief run-getters for New South Wales were Diamond (138 in 217 minutes, 1 six and 13 fours), Hopkins (108 in 130 minutes, 15 fours), Noble (99 in 135 minutes, 16 fours) and Blaxland (75 in 120 minutes, 9 fours). *Wisden* incorrectly gives SA (1) Noble 5/35. Sources: *Wisden, C.B.O'Reilly, NSWCA Report, Sydney Morning Herald, Town & Country Journal.*

SOUTH AUSTRALIA

†D.R.A.Gehrs	b Cotter	7	c Carter b Cotter		25
R.E.Mayne	c & b Noble	17	b Cotter		38
J.H.Pellew	b Cotter	7	(4) b Hopkins		22
C.E.Dolling	c Cotter b Garnsey	37	(3) c Noble b Cotter		34
*N.Claxton	c Carter b Noble	2	(6) b Macartney		31
D.McRae	c Carter b Cotter	3	(5) b Cotter		9
†C.B.Jennings	c Garnsey b Noble	42	c Carter b Noble		45
L.R.Hill	run out (E.F.Waddy/Carter)	23	b Noble		10
J.D.A.O'Connor	st Carter b Noble	3	b Macartney		12
A.McBeath	b Garnsey	8	not out		9
A.W.Wright	not out	1	b Noble		1
Extras	(b1, lb5, nb1)	7	(b2, lb7, w2, nb1)		12
Total	(55.2 overs, 173 mins)	157	(79.0 overs, 231 mins)		248

NEW SOUTH WALES

R.N.Hickson	b Wright	32
A.Diamond	c McRae b McBeath	138
A.J.Y.Hopkins	st Gehrs b Wright	108
E.F.Waddy	b Wright	9
*M.A.Noble	b Hill	99
M.H.Blaxland	c Pellew b Hill	75
C.G.Macartney	c O'Connor b Wright	25
E.L.Waddy	b Wright	29
A.Cotter	b O'Connor	8
†H.Carter	not out	18
G.L.Garnsey	st Gehrs b Wright	16
Extras	(b13, lb3)	16
Total	(154.5 overs, 405 mins)	573

NEW SOUTH WALES	O	M	R	W	w,nb		O	M	R	W	w,nb
Cotter	17	5	50	3	-,1		20	2	76	4	2,1
Garnsey	17	2	43	2	-,-		19	0	61	0	-,-
Noble	11.2	2	35	4	-,-	(5)	6	1	13	3	-,-
Macartney	10	7	22	0	-,-	(3)	19	4	38	2	-,-
Hopkins						(4)	15	2	48	1	-,-

SOUTH AUSTRALIA	O	M	R	W	w,nb
O'Connor	49	10	137	1	-,-
McBeath	29	4	105	1	-,-
Hill	16	2	53	2	-,-
Wright	46.5	6	209	6	-,-
Claxton	12	1	43	0	-,-
Pellew	2	0	10	0	-,-

FALL OF WICKETS

Wkt	SA 1st	NSW 1st	SA 2nd
1st	8	64	63
2nd	22	257	85
3rd	43	277	126
4th	50	307	136
5th	55	470	142
6th	86	477	199
7th	145	523	226
8th	146	538	227
9th	155	548	247
10th	157	573	248

NEW SOUTH WALES v VICTORIA (Shield Match 6)

Played at Sydney Cricket Ground on January 25, 26, 28, 1907. (Timeless match)
Toss : New South Wales.   Result : NEW SOUTH WALES WON BY AN INNINGS AND 266 RUNS.
Debuts: Victoria - L.P.Vernon (f/c).
12th Men: R.N.Hickson (NSW) and V.S.Ransford (Vic).
Umpires: W.J.Bruton and J.Laing.
Attendances: 4358, 9561, 1186.   Total: 15,105.   Receipts: £578.
Close of Play: 1st day NSW 5/334 (Diamond 148, Macartney 48); 2nd day Vic 9/177 (Armstrong 103).

Victoria collapsed on a virtually unplayable pitch on the third day, following heavy rain on Sunday, January 27th, with no batsman reaching double figures in the second innings. Four Victorians were dismissed first ball in the match, Carroll and Vaughan in the first innings and Rush and Hazlitt in the second. Armstrong (111 in 158 minutes, 1 six and 8 fours, chance at 20) compiled more than half of his team's runs in the match. Diamond (210 not out in 317 minutes, 1 six and 19 fours) shared a sixth-wicket stand of 219 in 151 minutes with Macartney (9 fours) for New South Wales. Ransford was brought into the Victorian twelve in place of T.S.Warne, who had not recovered from a wrist injury sustained in the previous match. Sources: *Wisden, NSWCA Report, Sydney Referee, Sydney Morning Herald, Town & Country Journal.*

NEW SOUTH WALES

R.A.Duff	b Armstrong	38
V.T.Trumper	c McAlister b Saunders	11
*M.A.Noble	c Horan b Hazlitt	68
A.J.Y.Hopkins	b Armstrong	7
A.Diamond	not out	210
E.L.Waddy	c McAlister b Hazlitt	9
C.G.Macartney	c Carkeek b Vernon	72
M.H.Blaxland	b Vernon	12
A.Cotter	c Rush b Armstrong	34
†H.Carter	c Carkeek b Saunders	9
G.L.Garnsey	c Vaughan b Armstrong	4
Extras	(b11, lb5, nb1)	17
Total	(129.5 overs, 378 mins)	491

VICTORIA

M.Ellis	c & b Garnsey	1	b Macartney	1
P.A.McAlister	c Noble b Macartney	51	b Noble	0
E.V.Carroll	c Cotter b Garnsey	0	b Macartney	8
*W.W.Armstrong	b Noble	111	b Noble	6
F.Vaughan	b Macartney	0	c Carter b Macartney	0
T.R.Rush	run out (Duff/Hopkins)	7	b Macartney	0
T.I.B.Horan	b Cotter	2	b Noble	1
L.P.Vernon	b Hopkins	0	c Hopkins b Noble	5
†W.Carkeek	b Cotter	0	not out	6
G.R.Hazlitt	b Cotter	2	b Noble	0
J.V.Saunders	not out	5	c Diamond b Noble	0
Extras	(b6, lb4, w2, nb3)	15	(b2, lb2)	4
Total	(58.1 overs, 178 mins)	194	(20.5 overs, 77 mins)	31

VICTORIA	O	M	R	W	w,nb
Vernon	28	3	100	2	-,-
Saunders	34	6	145	2	-,-
Armstrong	36.5	6	116	4	-,1
Hazlitt	28	6	99	2	-,-
Ellis	3	0	14	0	-,-

NEW SOUTH WALES	O	M	R	W	w,nb		O	M	R	W	w,nb
Cotter	15	2	37	3	2,3						
Garnsey	12	1	47	2	-,-						
Macartney	16	3	43	2	-,-	(2)	10	7	6	4	-,-
Noble	8.1	1	32	1	-,-	(1)	10.5	2	21	6	-,-
Hopkins	7	1	20	1	-,-						

	FALL OF WICKETS		
Wkt	NSW 1st	VIC 1st	VIC 2nd
1st	50	7	1
2nd	50	7	3
3rd	63	135	10
4th	159	135	14
5th	181	151	14
6th	400	165	17
7th	412	170	20
8th	474	173	31
9th	486	177	31
10th	491	194	31

NEW SOUTH WALES v THE REST

Played at Sydney Cricket Ground on February 15, 16, 18, 19, 1907. (Timeless match)
Toss : New South Wales.   Result : THE REST WON BY EIGHT WICKETS.
Debuts: Nil.
12th Men: A.B.S.White (NSW). No 12th named for The Rest.
Umpires: P.Caswell and R.M.Wallace.
Attendances: 3000, 9500, 2000, 500.   Total: About 15,000.   Receipts: £603 (£788 incl donations).
Close of Play: 1st day Rest 2/34 (Ransford 22, Bowden 4); 2nd day Rest 6/356 (Hill 37, Kelly 0); 3rd day NSW (2) 5/92 (Blaxland 4, Garnsey 1).

The match was arranged for the benefit of S.E.Gregory and he finally received £630. Ransford batted 221 minutes and hit 16 fours, giving his only chance at 111. His bat slipped in the execution of a pull shot and hit him in the head before it fell on his wicket. Gregory (94 in 137 minutes, 10 fours) and Hill (92 in 161 minutes, 9 fours) provided Duff with his only wickets in 38 matches for New South Wales. Macartney left the field with cramp on the second afternoon and returned on the third day, only to be struck in the mouth while attempting to field an awkwardly bouncing ball. He suffered a split lip and several loosened teeth and took no further part in the match. White substituted on both occasions. Waddy scored 129 in 115 minutes and hit 14 fours. Hazlitt and O'Connor shared a ninth-wicket partnership of 100 in 72 minutes. Last first-class appearance by J.J.Kelly. All pre-match publicity declared that J.Laing and C.Nicholls were the appointed umpires but the *Sydney Morning Herald* named Caswell and Wallace on the day and this has been accepted. Sources: *Wisden, NSWCA Report, Sydney Morning Herald, Town & Country Journal, Sydney Mail.*

NEW SOUTH WALES

R.A.Duff	b Hazlitt	5	(4) b Armstrong		12
V.T.Trumper	c Bowden b Wright	9	(5) c Bowden b Hazlitt		3
*M.A.Noble	c Hartigan b O'Connor	67	b Armstrong		6
A.J.Y.Hopkins	c Bowden b Wright	16	(2) st Kelly b Armstrong		40
A.Diamond	c Kelly b Wright	25	(1) run out (Hartigan/Armstrong)		26
E.L.Waddy	c Hartigan b O'Connor	6	(8) b Bowden		129
C.G.Macartney	run out (Hill/Kelly)	0	absent hurt		-
M.H.Blaxland	b Armstrong	18	(6) b O'Connor		43
A.Cotter	c & b Wright	3	c C.W.Gregory b O'Connor		8
†H.Carter	not out	63	not out		32
G.L.Garnsey	c & b Bowden	33	(7) c Kelly b Hazlitt		9
Extras	(b10, lb1)	11	(b4)		4
Total	(79.3 overs, 223 mins)	256	(88.0 overs, 247 mins)		312

THE REST

C.W.Gregory	b Cotter	4	b Cotter		7
R.J.Hartigan	b Garnsey	4	not out		7
V.S.Ransford	hit wkt b Cotter	136			
A.J.Bowden	b Macartney	34			
W.W.Armstrong	b Noble	31			
S.E.Gregory	b Duff	94	(3) c Waddy b Cotter		4
*C.Hill	b Duff	92			
†J.J.Kelly	b Macartney	17			
J.D.A.O'Connor	not out	50	(4) not out		7
G.R.Hazlitt	c Cotter b Garnsey	52			
A.W.Wright	b Cotter	7			
Extras	(b9, lb10, nb4)	23			-
Total	(155.5 overs, 480 mins)	544	(6.4 overs, 18 mins) (2 wkts)		25

THE REST	O	M	R	W	w,nb		O	M	R	W	w,nb
O'Connor	27	6	82	2	-,-		24	4	85	2	-,-
Hazlitt	17	3	52	1	-,-	(4)	24	5	92	2	-,-
Wright	24	4	81	4	-,-	(2)	15	0	43	0	-,-
Bowden	4.3	1	13	1	-,-	(3)	10	0	44	1	-,-
Armstrong	7	0	17	1	-,-		15	2	44	3	-,-

NEW SOUTH WALES	O	M	R	W	w,nb		O	M	R	W	w,nb
Cotter	37.5	2	129	3	-,4		3	0	13	2	-,-
Garnsey	28	4	118	2	-,-		2	0	7	0	-,-
Macartney	17	5	48	2	-,-						
Hopkins	33	10	99	0	-,-						
Noble	29	4	98	1	-,-						
Duff	11	5	29	2	-,-						
Waddy						(3)	1	1	0	0	-,-
Blaxland						(4)	0.4	0	5	0	-,-

	FALL OF WICKETS			
	NSW	REST	NSW	REST
Wkt	1st	1st	2nd	2nd
1st	13	6	66	8
2nd	26	8	66	12
3rd	52	102	78	-
4th	120	172	87	-
5th	131	261	87	-
6th	131	355	102	-
7th	133	389	204	-
8th	137	437	212	-
9th	173	537	312	-
10th	256	544	-	-

TASMANIA v VICTORIA

Played at T.C.A. Ground, Hobart, on February 22, 23, 25, 1907. (Timeless match)
Toss : Victoria.   Result : TASMANIA WON BY FIVE WICKETS.
Debuts: Tasmania - F.J.Hanson, J.L.Hudson, J.R.Meech (all f/c). Victoria - P.C.Desmazeures, T.C.Grant, T.J.Matthews, W.H.Reeves
    (all f/c).
12th Men: G.K.B.Bailey (Tas) and R.G.Johnstone (Vic).
Umpires: R.Bartlett and N.Paul.
Attendances: No figures published, but described as "satisfactory".   Receipts: £38.
Close of Play: 1st day Tas 4/164 (Eady 59, Paton 4); 2nd day Vic (2) 8/260 (McAlister 166, Collins 6).

The Tasmanian side was comprised of only southern players. The Northern Tasmanian Cricket Association, refusing to recognise the newly-constituted Tasmanian Cricket Association as the ruling body for the game in Tasmania, declined to take any part in the match. W.M.Bradshaw was appointed to umpire but became unavailable before the match started and was replaced by Paul. Ward was a late replacement for T.A.Tabart in the Tasmanian side. Eady dismissed Ellis with the first ball of the match and it was his bowling (7 for 72 and 6 for 113) that ultimately won the match for the home team. McAlister (168 in 204 minutes, 22 fours, chances at 17 and 154) was the only Victorian batsman to seriously challenge Eady's dominance. Eady (61 in 92 minutes, 8 fours) also led the scoring in Tasmania's first innings to complete a fine all-round performance. Hawson (45 in 85 minutes, 6 fours and 90 not out in 192 minutes, 12 fours) and Dodds (43 in 42 minutes, 6 fours) also batted well. The professional competence of umpire Bartlett was questioned in the press, he "frequently made the error of allowing seven, instead of six, balls to the over" (*Mercury*). It was further reported that there were 13 such overs. Sources: *Cricket, TCA Report, Hobart Mercury, Launceston Examiner.*

VICTORIA

M.Ellis	c Paton b Eady	0	c Eady b Paton		3
F.Vaughan	c Burn b Paton	31	b Eady		26
*P.A.McAlister	c Dodds b Paton	15	b Eady		168
T.I.B.Horan	b Eady	13	c Dodds b Eady		2
T.R.Rush	c Dodds b Eady	11	c Burn b Meech		9
P.C.Desmazeures	run out	5	b Chancellor		18
T.C.Grant	c Paton b Eady	15	c Burn b Eady		5
T.J.Matthews	b Eady	20	c Dodds b Eady		20
E.A.Goss	not out	11	c Burn b Eady		0
F.B.Collins	b Eady	0	not out		17
†W.H.Reeves	b Eady	0	b Paton		4
Extras	(b4, lb3)	7	(b1, lb4)		5
Total	(36.5 overs, 112 mins)	128	(81.3 overs, 224 mins)		277

TASMANIA

*E.J.K.Burn	c Matthews b Ellis	25	(2) b Matthews		8
R.J.Hawson	b Matthews	45	(1) not out		90
H.Hale	b Ellis	8	(5) st Reeves b Ellis		8
C.J.Eady	b Matthews	61	c Collins b Ellis		26
†N.Dodds	st Reeves b Collins	19	(6) c Reeves b Grant		43
G.D.Paton	not out	28	(3) b Collins		2
J.L.Hudson	b Collins	0	not out		8
F.J.Hanson	b Matthews	0			
W.G.Ward	b Collins	3			
F.E.Chancellor	b Collins	6			
J.R.Meech	c & b Matthews	1			
Extras	(b3, lb1)	4	(b16, lb4, w1)		21
Total	(74.4 overs, 227 mins)	200	(69.3 overs, 192 mins) (5 wkts)		206

TASMANIA	O	M	R	W	w,nb		O	M	R	W	w,nb
Eady	18.5	3	72	7	-,-		35	5	113	6	-,-
Paton	18	3	49	2	-,-		22.3	2	66	2	-,-
Meech							8	0	28	1	-,-
Hanson							6	0	23	0	-,-
Chancellor							10	2	42	1	-,-

VICTORIA	O	M	R	W	w,nb		O	M	R	W	w,nb
Collins	23	5	58	4	-,-		19	5	61	1	1,-
Goss	16	3	43	0	-,-	(3)	11	1	21	0	-,-
Matthews	21.4	5	50	4	-,-	(2)	19.3	6	43	1	-,-
Ellis	10	0	36	2	-,-		13	4	38	2	-,-
Desmazeures	4	2	9	0	-,-						
Horan						(5)	3	0	12	0	-,-
Grant						(6)	4	2	10	1	-,-

FALL OF WICKETS

Wkt	VIC 1st	TAS 1st	VIC 2nd	TAS 2nd
1st	0	61	11	34
2nd	43	71	57	43
3rd	50	95	67	94
4th	70	142	82	126
5th	79	170	132	192
6th	84	179	153	-
7th	105	180	217	-
8th	124	187	217	-
9th	124	199	266	-
10th	128	200	277	-

WESTERN AUSTRALIA v NEW SOUTH WALES

Played at W.A.C.A. Ground, Perth, on March 16, 18, 19, 1907. (Timeless match)
Toss : Western Australia.   Result : NEW SOUTH WALES WON BY TWO WICKETS.
Debuts: Western Australia - J.A.Chamberlain, R.M.Evans, O.H.Kelly, C.W.Wellington (all f/c); A.H.Christian, T.H.Hogue, E.Jones (all WA only). New South Wales - R.B.Minnett (f/c).
12th Men: No 12th men or emergency fieldsmen named.
Umpires: G.Berry and J.C.Brickhill.
Attendances: 4500, 1500, 800.   Total: About 6800.   Receipts: No figures published.
Close of Play: 1st day NSW 2/28 (Sullivan 15, Johnson 2); 2nd day WA (2) 6/183 (Jones 18, Evans 0).

The first visit to Western Australia by New South Wales included two matches now recognised as first-class. Trumper "could not see his way clear to make the trip" (*Sydney Mail*) and Johnson replaced A.L.Newell (unavailable) in the New South Wales team before it left Sydney. T.H.Howard set out with the visitors as an emergency fieldsman but became ill during the voyage and left the ship at Hobart to return home, leaving New South Wales with only 11 men. T.H.Coyne was unavailable for WA due to work commitments. The home team overcame a shaky start due to the third wicket stand of 118 by Hogue (67 in about 130 minutes, 8 fours) and Rowe (81 in 100 minutes, 10 fours). Jones (48 in 20 minutes, 2 sixes and 7 fours) smashed 43 (10, 15, 18) from 3 successive overs from Macartney. Barnes and Macartney took the visitors into a narrow lead with an eighth wicket stand of 145 in about 105 minutes. Parker (69 in 39 minutes, 11 fours) reportedly bore comparison with Trumper, such was his brilliance on the second afternoon. Mackenzie fell heavily running between wickets and retired at 2/90; his shoulder was injured seriously enough to prevent a resumption of his innings, despite the closeness of the match. Bubb (53 not out in about 105 minutes, 7 fours) made :an invaluable contribution at a critical time" and Johnson "rose above expectations" (*West Australian*) to thwart Western Australian hopes of victory. Christian, Hogue and Jones had previously played for Victoria, New South Wales and South Australia respectively. Sources: *Cricket, Sydney Morning Herald, Sydney Mail, The West Australian, Daily News, Sunday Times, Western Mail.*

WESTERN AUSTRALIA

T.H.Hogue	run out (Mackenzie/McIntyre)	67	b Barnes	27
E.F.Parker	b Johnson	26	b Barnes	69
C.W.Wellington	b Barnes	5	(6) b Johnson	4
S.H.D.Rowe	c Bubb b Minnett	81	(3) st McIntyre b Barnes	37
O.H.Kelly	b Johnson	23	(4) run out (Macartney/McIntyre)	0
A.H.Christian	c Sullivan b Johnson	1	(5) b Johnson	15
*†H.A.Evers	b Macartney	15	(9) not out	31
J.A.Chamberlain	b Minnett	0	(10) b Barnes	11
R.M.Evans	b Barnes	27	(8) c Sullivan b Barnes	5
E.Jones	c Johnson b Hopkins	48	(7) b Minnett	23
R.A.Selk	not out	2	c Minnett b Johnson	2
Extras	(b10, lb1, w1)	12	(b12, lb2)	14
Total	(73.2 overs, 220 mins)	307	(51.1 overs, 155 mins)	238

NEW SOUTH WALES

E.R.Bubb	c & b Jones	2	(7) not out	53
W.Bardsley	lbw b Jones	9	(6) c Evans b Selk	31
A.E.Sullivan	c Christian Jones	38	(10) lbw b Christian	2
F.B.Johnson	c Parker b Christian	29	(11) not out	20
*A.J.Y.Hopkins	c Evers b Evans	26	st Evers b Christian	0
E.L.Waddy	b Selk	33	(2) b Christian	15
A.C.K.Mackenzie	c Kelly b Selk	0	(1) retired hurt	51
J.C.Barnes	c Evers b Christian	82	(4) c Chamberlain b Selk	22
C.G.Macartney	not out	80	(3) run out (Rowe/Evers)	22
R.B.Minnett	b Hogue	1	(9) run out (Hogue)	1
†W.R.McIntyre	run out	4	(8) c & b Christian	9
Extras	(b5, lb1)	6	(b6, lb5, w1)	12
Total	(82.3 overs, in about 235 mins)	310	(61.3 overs, 220 mins) (8 wkts)	238

NEW SOUTH WALES	O	M	R	W	w,nb		O	M	R	W	w,nb
Minnett	15	4	39	2	-,-		15	2	65	1	-,-
Macartney	16	4	79	1	-,-	(5)	3	2	4	0	-,-
Johnson	16	5	55	3	-,-		9.1	2	27	3	-,-
Barnes	11.2	0	64	2	1,-		18	2	91	5	-,-
Hopkins	11	7	28	1	-,-	(2)	6	0	37	0	-,-
Sullivan	4	1	30	0	-,-						

WESTERN AUSTRALIA	O	M	R	W	w,nb		O	M	R	W	w,nb
Selk	26	4	89	2	-,-		22.3	1	85	2	1,-
Jones	25	4	81	3	-,-	(3)	11	2	31	0	-,-
Christian	16.3	1	60	2	-,-	(2)	21	3	77	4	-,-
Evans	6	0	33	1	-,-	(5)	5	0	26	0	-,-
Chamberlain	1	0	17	0	-,-						
Hogue	8	0	24	1	-,-	(4)	2	0	7	0	-,-

FALL OF WICKETS

Wkt	WA 1st	NSW 1st	WA 2nd	NSW 2nd
1st	43	5	95	22
2nd	48	26	106	71
3rd	166	81	106	99
4th	195	82	129	130
5th	201	138	135	151
6th	209	142	177	172
7th	213	148	193	173
8th	242	293	193	199
9th	304	300	221	-
10th	307	310	238	-

WESTERN AUSTRALIA v NEW SOUTH WALES

Played at Fremantle Oval on March 23, 25, 26, 27, 28, 1907. (Timeless match)
Toss : Western Australia.   Result : WESTERN AUSTRALIA WON BY 5 RUNS.
Debuts: New South Wales - W.D.Lough (f/c).
12th Men: No 12th men or emergency fieldsmen named.
Umpires: J.F.Dwyer and V.Gray.
Attendances: 4000, 1200, 800, 800, 400.   Total: About 7200.   Receipts: £300.
Close of Play: 1st day WA 9/255 (Evans 26, Selk 34); 2nd day NSW 8/248 (Bardsley 107, Johnson 7); 3rd day WA (2) 5/172
     (Howard 14, Evers 23); 4th day NSW (2) 8/176 (Sullivan 21).

Mackenzie, still recovering from his shoulder injury, was replaced in the NSW team by Lough, a Sydney player appearing with Kings Park in Perth cricket. Coyne was again not permitted leave from his work to represent WA; Howard took his place. In the WA first innings, 10 of Macartney's first 15 overs were maidens. McIntyre was ill for a time on the third day; WA players Howard and Rowe took turns to field as substitute while Bubb kept wickets. Johnson fielded in place of Kelly in part of the NSW second innings and, standing at point, caught Waddy. At the tea adjournment on the fourth day Jones refused to play any further, saying he had to catch the Goldfields train that night; Bubb took his place in the field. The captains agreed on the fourth evening to extend the match to a fifth day. Sources: *Cricket, Sydney Morning Herald, The West Australian, Daily News.*

WESTERN AUSTRALIA

T.H.Hogue	c & b Macartney	20	(3) c Lough b Hopkins	23
E.F.Parker	c Bardsley b Johnson	5	(1) c Waddy b Hopkins	67
S.H.D.Rowe	c Hopkins b Barnes	50	(2) b Macartney	17
O.H.Kelly	c Waddy b Barnes	13	c Barnes b Hopkins	4
H.C.Howard	b Barnes	17	(6) run out (Macartney)	15
*†H.A.Evers	c Minnett b Johnson	29	(7) b Hopkins	31
A.H.Christian	b Minnett	28	(5) c McIntyre b Minnett	11
R.M.Evans	not out	26	c & b Macartney	0
E.Jones	c Sullivan b Barnes	3	c Macartney b Hopkins	3
C.Munro	c McIntyre b Hopkins	24	c Waddy b Macartney	0
R.A.Selk	b Johnson	34	not out	0
Extras	(lb1, w2, nb3)	6	(b9, lb5)	14
Total	(91.3 overs, 270 mins)	255	(87.2 overs, 245 mins)	185

NEW SOUTH WALES

*A.J.Y.Hopkins	c Evans b Selk	11	c Jones b Christian	4
E.L.Waddy	lbw b Christian	35	c sub (F.B.Johnson) b Jones	3
C.G.Macartney	b Christian	5	b Jones	10
E.R.Bubb	b Jones	6	b Christian	18
W.Bardsley	c Parker b Christian	107	lbw b Jones	2
J.C.Barnes	c Munro b Christian	15	run out (Parker/Evers)	50
R.B.Minnett	run out (Parker/Rowe)	14	b Jones	3
†W.R.McIntyre	c Christian b Selk	7	c Hogue b Christian	55
A.E.Sullivan	run out (Parker)	31	not out	22
F.B.Johnson	b Jones	7	b Selk	5
W.D.Lough	not out	3	b Selk	2
Extras	(b6, lb3, nb1)	10	(b9, lb1)	10
Total	(89.0 overs, 250 mins)	251	(92.0 overs, 260 mins)	184

NEW SOUTH WALES	O	M	R	W	w,nb		O	M	R	W	w,nb
Barnes	22	2	103	4	2,1	(3)	12	0	40	0	-,-
Johnson	20.3	4	34	3	-,-	(1)	19	3	33	0	-,-
Macartney	21	11	35	1	-,1	(2)	24.2	6	43	3	-,-
Minnett	22	9	45	1	-,1	(5)	5	0	16	1	-,-
Hopkins	4	0	16	1	-,-	(4)	27	10	39	5	-,-
Sullivan	2	0	16	0	-,-						

WESTERN AUSTRALIA	O	M	R	W	w,nb		O	M	R	W	w,nb
Selk	16	0	60	2	-,1	(3)	24	12	36	2	-,-
Jones	21	3	63	2	-,-	(1)	19	5	40	4	-,-
Christian	25	5	49	4	-,-	(2)	34	12	69	3	-,-
Evans	4	1	11	0	-,-						
Hogue	12	0	31	0	-,-		5	0	10	0	-,-
Munro	11	1	27	0	-,-	(4)	10	3	19	0	-,-

FALL OF WICKETS

Wkt	WA 1st	NSW 1st	WA 2nd	NSW 2nd
1st	8	36	53	5
2nd	41	44	104	9
3rd	75	59	108	29
4th	106	61	125	31
5th	112	97	131	39
6th	157	121	177	44
7th	168	134	178	127
8th	171	234	182	176
9th	211	248	185	182
10th	255	251	185	184

Teams from both England and Fiji toured Australia this season, although Fiji's matches against the States were ruled not first-class by the Board of Control. A total of 26 first-class matches were contested, making this the busiest season yet.

The 17th English team to Australia played 19 matches in all, only one of which is excluded from this volume. The number of first-class matches undertaken, 18, remains a record for any touring team to Australia. It included England's first matches in Western Australia - one at either end of the tour.

England were no match for Australia in the Test series, the home side running out 4-1 victors. However, no other games were lost by the tourists. George Gunn, who was co-opted into the team following several illnesses and injuries (a severe cold affected the captain, A.O.Jones), led the batting averages in both Tests and all tour matches. The batting lineup generally failed in the Tests, where only the bowling efforts of Barnes, Crawford and Fielder kept England in contention. The Australians were stronger everywhere and possessed the capacity to fight back from periods of crisis, should they arise. Noble, Armstrong, Saunders and Hill played key roles while Trumper, Hartigan and Carter produced some fine innings.

The Sheffield Shield program was cut from six matches to four because of the busy touring itinerary of the Englishmen. South Australia's two matches at home were cancelled. Victoria ended the protracted run of New South Wales as Shield holders with a decisive win in Sydney in the final match. Up to that stage, all three States had won one game each. New South Wales, having not lost a home game since February 1901, now lost both their matches at Sydney. Batsmen dominated the competition, and the return of Frank Tarrant from England greatly bolstered the Victorian side. But before allowing him to play, the VCA took the precaution of canvassing interstate for any objections. None were forthcoming.

New South Wales won the first of their matches against Queensland, at Sydney, but the northern State turned the tables in the return match at Brisbane, their first victory since the inaugural meeting in April 1893. Despite their overall lack of success against New South Wales and Victoria, Queensland pushed hard for inclusion in the Sheffield Shield competition. Their application (with the support of New South Wales) was dealt with at a Board of Control meeting in Melbourne on May 29, 1908, but was rejected in a 7-5 vote - presumably due to opposition from South Australian and Victorian delegates. The SACA had refused a request from the QCA in March for return matches to be regularly played between the States each season.

Tasmania were admitted to the Board of Control in August 1907. Matches against the touring MCC team were followed by a visit to Melbourne, which resulted in a comprehensive defeat from Victoria. The VCA invited both the TCA and the NTCA to send delegates to a conference at the end of this match, to discuss the staging of future matches between Victoria and Tasmania. At the conference it was agreed that matches would be played alternately in the States as before, but that two matches would now be played on each visit to Tasmania, one each at Hobart and Launceston.

Leading Aggregates

Batsmen	M	I	NO	Runs	HS	Ave.	Bowlers	Runs	Wkts	Ave.
J.Hardstaff (MCC)	17	28	2	1360	135	52.30	J.V.Saunders (V)	1587	66	24.04
M.A.Noble (NSW)	10	19	1	1071	176	59.50	J.N.Crawford (MCC)	1663	66	25.19
W.W.Armstrong (V)	10	16	2	1033	231	73.78	S.F.Barnes (MCC)	1185	54	21.94
K.L.Hutchings (MCC)	17	28	0	953	126	34.03	A.Fielder (MCC)	1208	50	24.16
W.Rhodes (MCC)	17	27	8	929	119	48.89	L.C.Braund (MCC)	1644	50	32.88
J.B.Hobbs (MCC)	13	22	1	876	115	41.71	C.Blythe (MCC)	935	41	22.80
V.S.Ransford (V)	11	19	1	821	129	45.61	W.Rhodes (MCC)	1069	31	34.48
G.Gunn (MCC)	11	18	3	817	122*	54.46	A.Cotter (NSW)	797	28	28.46
V.T.Trumper (NSW)	10	19	0	797	166	41.94	J.D.A.O'Connor (SA)	1024	28	36.57
C.Hill (SA)	9	16	0	796	160	49.75	C.G.Macartney (NSW)	719	26	27.65
L.C.Braund (MCC)	16	25	3	783	160	35.59	W.W.Armstrong (V)	734	26	28.23
F.L.Fane (MCC)	16	24	1	774	133	33.65	M.A.Noble (NSW)	739	23	32.13
F.A.Tarrant (V)	6	10	0	762	206	76.20				

SHEFFIELD SHIELD TABLE

	P	W	L	D	Pts	Quotient	Runs Scored	Wkts Lost	Runs Conceded	Wkts Taken
VICTORIA	3	2	1	-	1	1.281	1985	50	1611	52
SOUTH AUSTRALIA	2	1	1	-	0	0.679	1402	40	1547	30
NEW SOUTH WALES	3	1	2	-	-1	1.031	1925	52	2154	60
TOTAL	4	4	4	-	0	1.000	5312	142	5312	142

WESTERN AUSTRALIA v M.C.C.

Played at W.A.C.A. Ground, Perth, on October 26, 28, 29, 1907. (Three-day match)
Toss : M.C.C.   Result : M.C.C. WON BY AN INNINGS AND 134 RUNS.
Debuts: Western Australia - W.W.Hogue, A.Robinson (both f/c).
12th Men: No 12th men or emergency fieldsmen named.
Umpires: J.C.Brickhill and J.F.Dwyer.
Attendances: 6000, 2500, 500.   Total: About 9000.   Receipts: £561.
Close of Play: 1st day MCC 7/350 (Rhodes 6, Barnes 4); 2nd day WA (2) 0/12 (Christian 9, Rowe 3).

The first visit to Western Australia by an international touring team created great interest in the State. A new pressbox and scoreboard were erected at the ground prior to the match; the board being described by Ernie Jones, who was making his final first-class appearance, as "bettered by only Sydney and Melbourne in the world." Selk strained a leg muscle in his 28th over and took no further part in the match. Fane scored the first century by an Englishman in WA, reaching 100 in 150 minutes with 11 fours, and batting in all for 200 minutes with 13 fours. Tom Hogue (60 not out in 195 minutes, 5 fours) batted "with the utmost caution" (*West Australian*) throughout the Western Australian first innings. The *Daily News* noted on October 25: "In the English matches this season the follow-on rule will be optional to the side leading by 200 runs. In interstate cricket it is compulsory. On principle, the optional clause should be universally recognised."
Sources: *Wisden, Cricket, The West Australian, Western Mail, Daily News.*

M.C.C.

F.L.Fane	run out (T.H.Hogue/Evers)	133
*A.O.Jones	b Selk	45
E.G.Hayes	lbw b Selk	0
R.A.Young	lbw b Christian	9
L.C.Braund	c W.W.Hogue b Selk	59
J.Hardstaff, sr	lbw b Christian	46
J.N.Crawford	run out	43
W.Rhodes	not out	32
S.F.Barnes	b Christian	14
†J.Humphries	c Jones b Christian	7
C.Blythe	c Parker b Christian	8
Extras	(b4, lb1, w1)	6
Total	(127.1 overs, 315 mins)	402

WESTERN AUSTRALIA

T.H.Hogue	not out	60	(5)	c & b Blythe	11
E.F.Parker	lbw b Blythe	22	(3)	b Barnes	11
S.H.D.Rowe	c Jones b Barnes	1	(2)	b Crawford	11
A.Robinson	b Crawford	23		c Braund b Crawford	1
A.H.Christian	b Rhodes	3	(1)	c Humphries b Crawford	13
L.Gouly	b Crawford	1		not out	22
*†H.A.Evers	b Crawford	2		hit wkt b Hayes	24
R.M.Evans	c Hayes b Crawford	5		c Humphries b Blythe	0
W.W.Hogue	c Blythe b Barnes	11		c Humphries b Rhodes	16
E.Jones	c Crawford b Barnes	17		b Rhodes	4
R.A.Selk	absent hurt	-		absent hurt	-
Extras	(b4, lb3)	7		(b3)	3
Total	(77.3 overs, 195 mins)	152		(39.4 overs, 110 mins)	116

WESTERN AUSTRALIA	O	M	R	W	w,nb
Jones	23	3	64	0	1,-
Christian	46.3	11	132	5	-,-
Selk	27.4	5	108	3	-,-
W.W.Hogue	24	7	80	0	-,-
Evans	6	1	12	0	-,-

M.C.C.	O	M	R	W	w,nb		O	M	R	W	w,nb
Blythe	15	6	28	1	-,-	(3)	10	3	17	2	-,-
Barnes	21.3	3	53	3	-,-		12	4	27	1	-,-
Braund	8	1	20	0	-,-						
Rhodes	17	9	16	1	-,-	(5)	0.4	0	4	2	-,-
Crawford	16	8	28	4	-,-	(1)	10	4	31	3	-,-
Hayes						(4)	7	0	34	1	-,-

FALL OF WICKETS

	MCC	WA	WA
Wkt	1st	1st	2nd
1st	91	25	16
2nd	95	26	31
3rd	110	81	35
4th	251	88	36
5th	262	89	51
6th	318	91	82
7th	340	103	85
8th	366	130	112
9th	390	152	116
10th	402	-	-

SOUTH AUSTRALIA v M.C.C.

Played at Adelaide Oval on November 9, 11, 12, 13, 1907. (Four-day match)
Toss : South Australia.   Result : M.C.C. WON BY AN INNINGS AND 183 RUNS.
Debuts: South Australia - W.L.Chamberlain (f/c).
12th Men: J.B.Hobbs (MCC). No 12th for SA.
Umpires: P.Argall and G.A.Watson.
Attendances: 4500, 6000, 2000, 1000.   Total: About 13,500.   Receipts: No figures published.
Close of Play: 1st day SA 5/274 (Jennings 68, Claxton 31); 2nd day MCC 4/233 (Hardstaff 16, Braund 14); 3rd day MCC 8/660
(Rhodes 11).

MCC's highest total so far included hundreds from Jones (119 in 150 minutes, 11 fours), Hardstaff (135 in 200 minutes, 17 fours), Braund (160 in 255 minutes, 19 fours) and Crawford (114 in just 58 minutes, 3 sixes and 18 fours). It was the first time in Australia that four hundreds were scored in an innings (five had been scored for NSW v SA at Sydney 1900-01). Crawford's century in 54 minutes, the fastest yet in Australian first-class cricket, remained the record for five years until beaten by D.R.A.Gehrs on the same ground; his 114 included 90 (78.95 per cent) in boundaries. C.Hill (104 in 185 minutes, 9 fours) and Jennings (79 in 156 minutes, 6 fours) topscored for South Australia. Chamberlain, who had been named as 12th man, was a late replacement for D.R.A.Gehrs (influenza) in the local side. Jennings deputised as keeper in Gehrs's absence but sustained badly-bruised hands and gave the gloves to Pellew at the start of the third day. Mayne became the third wicket-keeper in the innings when Pellew bowled. The match was scheduled to finish at 3.45pm on the fourth day so the Englishmen could comfortably catch their train to Melbourne; Crawford's off-breaks returned 5 for 40 to finish the game early. C.E.Dolling (university exams) and R.B.C.Rees (business) were unavailable for South Australia. Last first-class appearance by J.Darling.
Sources: *Wisden, C.B.O'Reilly, The Australasian, Adelaide Advertiser, South Australian Register.*

SOUTH AUSTRALIA

*J.Darling	c Jones b Barnes	11	b Barnes		2
R.E.Mayne	lbw b Barnes	22	c Humphries b Blythe		0
C.Hill	c Humphries b Rhodes	104	c Jones b Crawford		61
J.H.Pellew	b Braund	35	b Crawford		32
†C.B.Jennings	c Crawford b Blythe	79	c & b Braund		0
L.R.Hill	b Barnes	2	b Crawford		4
N.Claxton	st Humphries b Blythe	57	c Fane b Braund		19
W.L.Chamberlain	b Barnes	4	b Crawford		2
J.D.A.O'Connor	b Braund	15	b Braund		1
A.McBeath	not out	10	b Crawford		4
A.W.Wright	b Crawford	1	not out		8
Extras	(b1, nb2)	3	(nb1)		1
Total	(136.4 overs, 375 mins)	343	(46.4 overs, 150 mins)		134

M.C.C.

*A.O.Jones	c O'Connor b Wright	119
F.L.Fane	c Claxton b Wright	32
E.G.Hayes	c Chamberlain b L.R.Hill	8
K.L.Hutchings	c Pellew b Wright	26
J.Hardstaff, sr	c Darling b Claxton	135
L.C.Braund	c O'Connor b Claxton	160
J.N.Crawford	c & b Chamberlain	114
W.Rhodes	not out	11
S.F.Barnes	c L.R.Hill b Wright	11
†J.Humphries	) did not bat	
C.Blythe	)	
Extras	(b35, lb6, w1, nb2)	44
Total	(169.0 overs, 465 mins) (8 wkts dec)	660

M.C.C.	O	M	R	W	w,nb		O	M	R	W	w,nb
Barnes	39	6	107	4	-,2		9	1	27	1	-,-
Blythe	38	7	75	2	-,-		7	1	19	1	-,1
Crawford	25.4	5	64	1	-,-	(4)	14.4	2	40	5	-,-
Rhodes	16	4	44	1	-,-						
Hayes	3	0	16	0	-,-						
Braund	15	6	34	2	-,-	(3)	16	4	47	3	-,-

SOUTH AUSTRALIA	O	M	R	W	w,nb
O'Connor	34	6	108	0	-,1
L.R.Hill	26	6	90	1	-,-
Wright	52	8	171	4	-,-
McBeath	27	4	98	0	-,1
Claxton	23	3	106	2	1,-
Pellew	4	0	20	0	-,-
Chamberlain	3	0	23	1	-,-

FALL OF WICKETS

	SA	MCC	SA
Wkt	1st	1st	2nd
1st	24	122	2
2nd	43	151	2
3rd	137	183	83
4th	194	202	83
5th	205	472	89
6th	289	581	108
7th	295	643	116
8th	321	660	117
9th	342	-	122
10th	343	-	134

VICTORIA v M.C.C.

Played at Melbourne Cricket Ground on November 15, 16, 18, 19, 20, 1907. (Five-day match)
Toss : Victoria.　　　　　　　　Result : MATCH DRAWN.
Debuts: Victoria - C.McKenzie (f/c).
12th Men: F.B.Collins and F.Vaughan were named as Victorian emergencies. No 12th named for MCC.
Umpires: E.Barrass and R.M.Crockett.
Attendances: 6800, 14000, 7200, 7800, 4500.　　　Total: About 40,300.　　　Receipts: £1182.
Close of Play: 1st day MCC 3/42 (Young 15, Braund 2); 2nd day Vic (2) 0/5 (McKenzie 5, Warne 0); 3rd day Vic (2) 5/287 (Ransford 48);
　　4th day MCC (2) 1/105 (Jones 52, Young 16).

Scheduled to be played over four days, the match was extended into a fifth in order to obtain a result. As it eventuated, play was called off at 4.15pm on the fifth day so that travel arrangements to Sydney could be kept, with MCC on the brink of defeat. Tarrant, in his first match for Victoria in seven seasons, scored 65 in 121 minutes with 7 fours and 81 in 171 minutes with 5 fours. Ransford, 51 in 114 minutes with 1 six and 5 fours, and 102 in 192 minutes with 10 fours was Victoria's other chief contributor. Vernon's 62 occupied 150 minutes and included 7 fours. MCC were saved with innings from Jones (82 in 197 minutes, 5 fours), Hutchings (91 in 78 minutes, 1 six and 16 fours) and Hardstaff (95 not out in 198 minutes, 9 fours). Due to an eye infection, W.W.Armstrong was unavailable to play for Victoria. *Wisden* incorrectly gives Vic (1) Rush c Hayes. Sources: *Wisden, The Age, The Argus, The Herald, The Australasian, Sydney Morning Herald.*

VICTORIA

C.McKenzie	c Crawford b Fielder	7	(2) c Crawford b Fielder	54
T.S.Warne	c Crawford b Fielder	7	(1) c Hayes b Fielder	7
*P.A.McAlister	c Young b Barnes	1	c Young b Crawford	43
F.A.Tarrant	c & b Braund	65	c Hutchings b Rhodes	81
E.V.Carroll	c Young b Crawford	7	c Young b Fielder	43
V.S.Ransford	c Hutchings b Braund	51	c Rhodes b Braund	102
G.R.Hazlitt	b Fielder	28	c Crawford b Fielder	4
T.R.Rush	c Hobbs b Fielder	29	b Fielder	0
L.P.Vernon	not out	25	c & b Braund	62
†W.Carkeek	c Braund b Barnes	5	c Hutchings b Braund	35
J.V.Saunders	b Fielder	4	not out	12
Extras	(b1, lb1, nb2)	4	(b11, lb6, nb3)	20
Total	(73.0 overs, 237 mins)	233	(157.5 overs, 458 mins)	463

M.C.C.

*A.O.Jones	c Saunders b Hazlitt	18	c Carkeek b Hazlitt	82
J.B.Hobbs	c McAlister b Saunders	3	b Tarrant	26
J.Hardstaff, sr	c McAlister b Hazlitt	0	(7) not out	95
†R.A.Young	lbw b Hazlitt	26	(3) b Saunders	25
L.C.Braund	c Ransford b Warne	62	(4) c Vernon b Hazlitt	4
K.L.Hutchings	b Vernon	31	c Ransford b Saunders	91
J.N.Crawford	c Rush b Saunders	13	(9) lbw b Saunders	10
E.G.Hayes	b Vernon	4	b Hazlitt	4
W.Rhodes	not out	27	(5) c Tarrant b Saunders	40
S.F.Barnes	c Tarrant b Warne	0	c McAlister b Hazlitt	26
A.Fielder	st Carkeek b Warne	4	not out	1
Extras	(b3, lb4, w3)	10	(b11, lb3, w3, nb1)	18
Total	(67.0 overs, 209 mins)	198	(147.0 overs, 448 mins) (9 wkts)	422

M.C.C.	O	M	R	W	w,nb		O	M	R	W	w,nb
Fielder	22	6	71	5	-,-		43	13	98	5	-,3
Barnes	27	3	69	2	-,2		36	9	81	0	-,-
Crawford	11	3	27	1	-,-	(5)	32	5	98	1	-,-
Braund	13	0	62	2	-,-		24.5	5	86	3	-,-
Rhodes						(3)	20	0	78	1	-,-
Hobbs							2	1	2	0	-,-

VICTORIA	O	M	R	W	w,nb		O	M	R	W	w,nb
Saunders	20	4	63	2	2,-		44	10	138	4	-,-
Hazlitt	21	6	39	3	-,-		38	11	88	4	-,-
Tarrant	5	0	17	0	-,-		27	10	57	1	-,-
Vernon	14	2	43	2	1,-	(5)	17	3	53	0	2,1
McKenzie	2	1	8	0	-,-						
Warne	5	1	18	3	-,-	(4)	21	6	68	0	1,-

FALL OF WICKETS

Wkt	VIC 1st	MCC 1st	VIC 2nd	MCC 2nd
1st	10	8	21	65
2nd	15	9	99	125
3rd	15	40	119	142
4th	45	63	203	157
5th	125	107	287	264
6th	146	141	293	295
7th	180	152	293	302
8th	202	189	399	315
9th	212	189	425	414
10th	233	198	463	-

NEW SOUTH WALES v M.C.C.

Played at Sydney Cricket Ground on November 22, 23, 25, 1907. (Four-day match)
Toss : M.C.C.   Result : M.C.C. WON BY 408 RUNS.
Debuts: Nil.
12th Men: R.N.Hickson (NSW) and J.B.Hobbs (MCC).
Umpires: W.J.Bruton and J.Laing.
Attendances: 9796, 23142, 8510.   Total: 41,448.   Receipts: £1842.
Close of Play: 1st day MCC 9/289 (Blythe 22, Fielder 5); 2nd day MCC (2) 4/130 (Rhodes 19, Humphries 1).

G.L.Garnsey was unavailable for New South Wales, who named a squad of thirteen for the match from which Hickson and C.Kelleway were omitted. Hardstaff (53 in 75 minutes, 8 fours and 71 in 94 minutes, 10 fours) top scored in each innings for MCC. All batsmen reached double figures in the first innings. New South Wales failed twice on a good pitch, with Cotter (49 in 33 minutes, 7 fours) providing the only innings of note. Barnes bowled unchanged through the first innings. Fielder ended the match with the wickets of Carter and Johnson with successive deliveries. *SMH* gives MCC (1) extras as shown in first day report, but the following day gives breakdown as b17, w2, nb 4. *Wisden* incorrectly gives NSW (2) Cotter c Fane b Fielder. Sources: *Wisden, NSWCA Report, Sydney Morning Herald, Town & Country Journal*.

M.C.C.

*A.O.Jones	c Blaxland b Johnson	16	(2)	c Blaxland b Cotter	0
F.L.Fane	lbw b Johnson	30	(1)	run out (Noble/Carter)	38
L.C.Braund	c Trumper b Johnson	28		lbw b Noble	24
K.L.Hutchings	c Hopkins b Cotter	35		b Johnson	42
J.Hardstaff, sr	b Cotter	53	(7)	c Waddy b Macartney	71
W.Rhodes	c Hopkins b Cotter	28	(5)	b Johnson	50
J.N.Crawford	c & b Hopkins	17	(8)	c Waddy b Cotter	10
S.F.Barnes	c Noble b Blaxland	22	(9)	not out	33
†J.Humphries	lbw b Cotter	10	(6)	c Waddy b Cotter	3
C.Blythe	not out	27		c Trumper b Cotter	23
A.Fielder	b Cotter	15		hit wkt b Johnson	0
Extras	(b9, lb7, w3, nb4)	23		(b2, lb2, w3)	7
Total	(104.3 overs, 295 mins)	304		(89.3 overs, 258 mins)	301

NEW SOUTH WALES

V.T.Trumper	c Braund b Blythe	38		c Braund b Fielder	6
A.Diamond	c Hutchings b Barnes	0	(5)	c Humphries b Fielder	4
*M.A.Noble	c Hutchings b Fielder	1		c Jones b Barnes	2
E.L.Waddy	b Barnes	4		c Hutchings b Fielder	8
R.A.Duff	c Blythe b Barnes	11	(2)	b Crawford	11
A.J.Y.Hopkins	c Hutchings b Barnes	13		c & b Fielder	2
C.G.Macartney	not out	9		not out	13
M.H.Blaxland	c & b Blythe	7		c Braund b Crawford	0
A.Cotter	c & b Barnes	0		c Fane b Blythe	49
†H.Carter	run out (sub J.B.Hobbs/Humphries)	3		c Fane b Fielder	0
F.B.Johnson	b Barnes	5		c Humphries b Fielder	0
Extras	(b7, lb2, w1)	10		(w1)	1
Total	(41.2 overs, 133 mins)	101		(29.2 overs, 90 mins)	96

NEW SOUTH WALES	O	M	R	W	w,nb		O	M	R	W	w,nb
Cotter	27.3	6	113	4	1,4		24	1	98	4	2,-
Noble	19	7	35	0	-,-	(3)	18	4	45	1	1,-
Macartney	8	3	8	0	-,-	(4)	21	5	55	1	-,-
Johnson	30	7	62	4	-,-	(2)	25.3	3	84	3	-,-
Duff	4	1	21	0	1,-						
Hopkins	15	2	38	1	-,-	(5)	1	0	12	0	-,-
Blaxland	1	0	4	1	1,-						

M.C.C.	O	M	R	W	w,nb		O	M	R	W	w,nb
Fielder	10	0	43	1	-,-		12.2	2	27	6	1,-
Barnes	20.2	7	24	6	-,-		8	3	12	1	-,-
Blythe	11	3	24	2	1,-	(5)	1	0	4	1	-,-
Crawford						(3)	6	1	29	2	-,-
Braund						(4)	2	0	23	0	-,-

FALL OF WICKETS

Wkt	MCC 1st	NSW 1st	MCC 2nd	NSW 2nd
1st	49	6	7	6
2nd	59	9	56	12
3rd	116	14	84	16
4th	118	32	121	27
5th	206	71	148	29
6th	206	71	193	35
7th	232	84	220	35
8th	248	85	256	96
9th	282	92	300	96
10th	304	101	301	96

VICTORIA v SOUTH AUSTRALIA (Shield Match 1)

Played at Melbourne Cricket Ground on November 29, 30, December 2, 3, 1907. (Timeless match)
Toss : Victoria.   Result : VICTORIA WON BY AN INNINGS AND 165 RUNS.
Debuts: South Australia - R.J.B.Townsend (f/c).
12th Men: W.D.Shew (Vic). No 12th named for South Australia.
Umpires: R.M.Crockett and W.Hannah.
Attendances: 2000, 7000, 2000, 1000.   Total: About 12,000.   Receipts: £303.
Close of Play: 1st day Vic 3/339 (Tarrant 56, Armstrong 36); 2nd day Vic 699 all out; 3rd day SA(2) 1/15 (Mayne 13, Dolling 2).

L.P.Vernon, a bowler, made himself unavailable after being selected in the Victorian side and was replaced by Rush, a batsman. Victoria's total of 699 set a new State record, as did the fourth-wicket partnership of 224 between Tarrant (105 in 235 minutes, 7 fours) and Armstrong (231 in 316 minutes, 1 six and 25 fours). Warne (82 in 172 minutes, 8 fours) and Ransford (109 in 152 minutes, 8 fours) also combined for a second-wicket partnership of 149. Mayne (75 in 75 minutes, 1 five and 8 fours) scored quickly for South Australia but could not prevent his team from following on. Hill (58 in 86 minutes, 5 fours) topped the scoring in the second innings. Sources: *Wisden, C.B.O'Reilly, The Age, The Argus, The Herald, The Australasian.*

VICTORIA

C.McKenzie	c & b Claxton	51
T.S.Warne	b O'Connor	82
V.S.Ransford	b Hill	109
F.A.Tarrant	c Dolling b O'Connor	105
*W.W.Armstrong	b O'Connor	231
P.A.McAlister	c Claxton b O'Connor	24
E.V.Carroll	c Claxton b O'Connor	29
G.R.Hazlitt	b O'Connor	21
T.R.Rush	c Mayne b Hill	5
†W.Carkeek	b Wright	22
J.V.Saunders	not out	6
Extras	(b5, lb2, w6, nb1)	14
Total	(218.5 overs, 533 mins)	699

SOUTH AUSTRALIA

R.E.Mayne	c Armstrong b Saunders	75	(2)	c sub (W.D.Shew) b Saunders	26
†D.R.A.Gehrs	b Armstrong	9	(4)	st Carkeek b Saunders	9
C.E.Dolling	run out (Armstrong/Carkeek)	62		st Carkeek b Armstrong	25
J.H.Pellew	c Tarrant b Armstrong	41	(5)	b Hazlitt	12
C.B.Jennings	c & b Warne	52	(1)	c Carkeek b Armstrong	0
*N.Claxton	c McAlister b Saunders	65		c McKenzie b Hazlitt	7
L.R.Hill	c Tarrant b Saunders	32		c & b Hazlitt	58
W.L.Chamberlain	b Hazlitt	4		b Tarrant	34
R.J.B.Townsend	c & b Saunders	0		c Carkeek b Saunders	1
J.D.A.O'Connor	not out	2		not out	5
A.W.Wright	b Hazlitt	0		b Hazlitt	0
Extras	(b9, lb4, nb2)	15			-
Total	(113.2 overs, 304 mins)	357		(63.2 overs, 180 mins)	177

SOUTH AUSTRALIA	O	M	R	W	w,nb
O'Connor	83	17	249	6	1,-
Hill	36	6	106	2	4,1
Wright	66.5	7	222	1	-,-
Claxton	22	5	57	1	1,-
Chamberlain	3	0	10	0	-,-
Pellew	8	0	41	0	-,-

VICTORIA	O	M	R	W	w,nb		O	M	R	W	w,nb
Hazlitt	24.2	6	80	2	-,-	(5)	15.2	2	54	4	-,-
Saunders	36	4	92	4	-,1		21	5	60	3	-,-
Armstrong	30	8	61	2	-,1	(1)	13	3	31	2	-,-
Tarrant	13	1	54	0	-,-		13	2	31	1	-,-
Warne	8	0	42	1	-,-	(3)	1	0	1	0	-,-
McKenzie	2	0	13	0	-,-						

FALL OF WICKETS

Wkt	VIC 1st	SA 1st	SA 2nd
1st	80	55	0
2nd	229	111	31
3rd	277	181	43
4th	501	226	66
5th	577	285	79
6th	635	340	80
7th	656	355	142
8th	661	355	147
9th	685	357	177
10th	699	357	177

QUEENSLAND v M.C.C.

Played at Brisbane Cricket Ground (Woolloongabba) on November 30, December 2, 1907. (Timeless match)
Toss : Queensland.   Result : M.C.C. WON BY AN INNINGS AND 44 RUNS.
Debuts: Queensland - J.S.Redgrave (Qld only).
12th Men: W.Armstrong (Qld) and S.F.Barnes (MCC).
Umpires: T.Muir and J.W.Roberts.
Attendances: 7000, 1500.   Total: About 8500.   Receipts: £323.
Close of Play: 1st day MCC 7/251 (Rhodes 34, Jones 53).

Three days were allocated for the match but it was agreed before the start that the game be played out to a finish. Pre-match rain hampered the wicket preparation and enabled "the ball to grip and turn" (*Courier*) for Braund and Blythe on the first day. Hartigan was bowled by Blythe's first ball and the team never recovered thereafter. Hutchings (67 in 75 minutes, 3 sixes and 5 fours), Young (40 in 36 minutes, 5 fours), Rhodes (70 not out in 103 minutes, 8 fours) and Jones (69 in 65 minutes, 7 fours) batted briskly on the improving wicket. Hartigan (59 in 93 minutes, 4 fours) began the Queensland second innings well but Blythe again bowled well and took his team to an innings victory at 4.39pm on the second day. It was during this match that Jones, the MCC captain, contracted a chill which nearly developed into pneumonia, and kept him out of the game until the beginning of February. Redgrave had previously appeared for New South Wales. Sources: *Wisden, Brisbane Courier, Queensland Times, The Queenslander.*

QUEENSLAND

R.J.Hartigan	b Blythe	2		c Hutchings b Blythe	59
G.A.L.Brown	c Humphries b Blythe	9		c Hayes b Crawford	16
J.S.Redgrave	b Braund	11		lbw b Rhodes	18
W.B.Hayes	b Braund	8		c Rhodes b Blythe	15
J.S.Hutcheon	st Humphries b Blythe	19		c Hobbs b Blythe	10
G.F.Martin	c & b Blythe	7		c Rhodes b Blythe	2
M.M.F.Dunn	c Jones b Braund	6		b Rhodes	0
*†W.T.Evans	c Humphries b Braund	10	(9)	b Rhodes	12
J.Thomson	b Blythe	5	(8)	not out	33
J.W.McLaren	run out (Humphries)	0		c Hobbs b Blythe	5
F.R.V.Timbury	not out	1		c Hutchings b Blythe	5
Extras		-		(b8, lb3)	11
Total	(24.0 overs, 75 mins)	78		(61.3 overs, 152 mins)	186

M.C.C.

J.B.Hobbs	lbw b McLaren	21
F.L.Fane	c Timbury b McLaren	8
E.G.Hayes	c Hutcheon b Timbury	12
K.L.Hutchings	c Hutcheon b Hayes	67
L.C.Braund	b McLaren	8
R.A.Young	b Redgrave	40
W.Rhodes	not out	70
J.N.Crawford	b McLaren	3
*A.O.Jones	lbw b Hayes	69
†J.Humphries	b McLaren	5
C.Blythe	st Evans b Hayes	0
Extras	(b4, lb1)	5
Total	(77.5 overs, 240 mins)	308

M.C.C.	O	M	R	W	w,nb	O	M	R	W	w,nb
Braund	12	0	43	4	-,-	9	0	45	0	-,-
Blythe	12	3	35	5	-,-	19.3	4	48	6	-,-
Crawford						12	4	24	1	-,-
Rhodes						21	5	58	3	-,-

QUEENSLAND	O	M	R	W	w,nb
Timbury	10	3	27	1	-,-
Hayes	15.5	1	59	3	-,-
McLaren	29	9	104	5	-,-
Redgrave	16	1	79	1	-,-
Thomson	3	0	9	0	-,-
Dunn	4	0	25	0	-,-

	FALL OF WICKETS		
	QLD	MCC	QLD
Wkt	1st	1st	2nd
1st	3	27	44
2nd	22	40	92
3rd	22	63	109
4th	48	107	123
5th	56	125	128
6th	60	160	129
7th	69	163	133
8th	76	296	148
9th	76	305	171
10th	78	308	186

AUSTRALIAN XI v M.C.C.

Played at Brisbane Cricket Ground (Woolloongabba) on December 6, 7, 9 (no play), 1907. (Three-day match)
Toss : Australian XI.   Result : MATCH DRAWN.
Debuts: Nil.
12th Men: G.A.L.Brown (Aust XI) and J.B.Hobbs (MCC).
Umpires: W.H.Carvosso and T.Muir.
Attendances: 3500, 8000, 800 awaited admission.   Total: About 11,500.   Receipts: £518.
Close of Play: 1st day MCC 1/61 (Young 34, Humphries 0); 2nd day Aust XI (2) 2/110 (Hartigan 55, McAlister 51).

This match gave Queensland cricket followers their first taste of "semi-test match" (*Queensland Times*) cricket. The attendance encouraged the inclusion of such a fixture in each of the four following international tours (1910/11, 1911/12, 1920/21, 1924/25) and ultimately led to Brisbane's inaugural Test match in November 1928. Rain intervened on the second day and prevented any play on the third day when the match was abandoned, there being no provisions or an extension of time due to the visitors' travel arrangements to Sydney for the First Test. McAlister (57 in 79 minutes, 9 fours and 51 not out in 64 minutes, 5 fours), Redgrave (66 in 47 minutes, 12 fours) and Hartigan (55 not out in 78 minutes, 5 fours) hit half-centuries for the Australian XI. Hutchings (72 in 81 minutes, 12 fours) "gave a delightful display" (*Courier*) but was the only MCC batsman to impress. Sources: *Wisden, Sydney Morning Herald, Brisbane Courier, Queensland Times, The Queenslander.*

AUSTRALIAN XI

R.J.Hartigan	c & b Braund	16	not out		55
C.G.Macartney	c & b Braund	42			
F.A.Tarrant	c Humphries b Braund	2	c Humphries b Fielder		3
*P.A.McAlister	c Fielder b Braund	57	not out		51
W.W.Armstrong	st Humphries b Braund	6			
S.E.Gregory	lbw b Blythe	27	(2) c Braund b Fielder		0
J.S.Redgrave	b Fielder	66			
W.B.Hayes	run out (Young/Humphries)	32			
A.Cotter	c Crawford b Braund	35			
†W.T.Evans	not out	13			
J.V.Saunders	c Rhodes b Braund	1			
Extras	(b1, nb1)	2	(lb1)		1
Total	(67.5 overs, 203 mins)	299	(27.0 overs, 78 mins) (2 wkts)		110

M.C.C.

R.A.Young	lbw b Armstrong	34
*F.L.Fane	c Tarrant b Saunders	21
†J.Humphries	lbw b Armstrong	1
E.G.Hayes	c Hartigan b Saunders	13
K.L.Hutchings	run out (Armstrong)	72
J.Hardstaff, sr	b Macartney	9
L.C.Braund	b Macartney	17
W.Rhodes	b Macartney	8
J.N.Crawford	c Saunders b Armstrong	30
C.Blythe	c McAlister b Macartney	9
A.Fielder	not out	2
Extras	(b1, lb5, nb1)	7
Total	(74.1 overs, 216 mins)	223

M.C.C.	O	M	R	W	w,nb		O	M	R	W	w,nb
Fielder	16	4	50	1	-,1		10	1	46	2	-,-
Blythe	15	1	60	1	-,-	(3)	4	1	8	0	-,-
Braund	22.5	4	117	7	-,-	(2)	7	1	31	0	-,-
Rhodes	8	1	29	0	-,-	(5)	3	0	3	0	-,-
Crawford	6	0	41	0	-,-	(4)	3	0	21	0	-,-

AUSTRALIAN XI	O	M	R	W	w,nb
Cotter	12	0	72	0	-,1
Saunders	21	6	57	2	-,-
Armstrong	23.1	8	43	3	-,-
Macartney	16	6	36	4	-,-
Redgrave	2	0	8	0	-,-

FALL OF WICKETS

	AUST	MCC	AUST
Wkt	1st	1st	2nd
1st	33	51	7
2nd	39	61	11
3rd	72	64	-
4th	78	100	-
5th	137	129	-
6th	163	172	-
7th	235	175	-
8th	279	193	-
9th	289	205	-
10th	299	223	-

NEW SOUTH WALES v SOUTH AUSTRALIA (Shield Match 2)

Played at Sydney Cricket Ground on December 6, 7, 9, 10, 11, 12, 1907. (Timeless match)
Toss : South Australia.   Result : SOUTH AUSTRALIA WON BY 20 RUNS.
Debuts: New South Wales - C.Kelleway, H.Whiddon (both f/c).
12th Men: R.N.Hickson (NSW) and R.J.B.Townsend (SA).
Umpires: W.J.Bruton and J.Laing.
Attendances: 3205, 7871, 2339, 1860, 2820, 312.   Total: 18,407.   Receipts: £591.
Close of Play: 1st day SA 349 all out; 2nd day SA (2) 1/26 (Claxton 7, Wright 2); 3rd day SA (2) 5/351 (Dolling 63, Jennings 18);
      4th day NSW (2) 3/214 (Trumper 112, Johnson 0); 5th day NSW (2) 9/572 (Kelleway 31, Whiddon 11).

The first match in Australia to reach a sixth playing day, only three balls were required on the last day to obtain a result. The New South Wales second innings of 572, at the time the highest fourth-innings total ever recorded in the world, remains the Australian record for the fourth innings. Hill (92 in 106 minutes, 15 fours and 94 in 135 minutes, 12 fours) was twice dismissed within sight of a century for South Australia. Dolling scored 113 in 195 minutes and hit 1 six and 16 fours. Wright, batting as a night-watchman in the second innings, scored 53 in 77 minutes after surviving an early chance; his previous 20 innings in first-class cricket had yielded an aggregate of just 42 runs, the first six of which were ducks. Jennings kept wickets on the second day in place of Gehrs, who had sore hands. For New South Wales, Noble scored 93 in 137 minutes with 12 fours in the first innings. Chasing 593, Trumper (135 in 179 minutes, 20 fours) and Carter (125 in 128 minutes, 17 fours) scored centuries. Sources: *Wisden, C.B.O'Reilly, NSWCA Report, Sydney Morning Herald, Town & Country Journal.*

SOUTH AUSTRALIA

†D.R.A.Gehrs	b Kelleway	18	(11)	not out	8
R.E.Mayne	c Carter b Whiddon	91	(1)	b Whiddon	17
*C.Hill	b Kelleway	92	(4)	st Carter b Kelleway	94
C.E.Dolling	st Carter b Whiddon	2	(5)	c Duff b Whiddon	113
C.B.Jennings	lbw b Hopkins	56	(7)	c Blaxland b Hopkins	52
J.H.Pellew	b Noble	17		b Whiddon	10
N.Claxton	st Carter b Whiddon	15	(2)	lbw b Kelleway	75
L.R.Hill	not out	50		b Kelleway	28
W.L.Chamberlain	b Hopkins	0		b Johnson	36
J.D.A.O'Connor	b Whiddon	0		b Whiddon	6
A.W.Wright	run out	1	(3)	b Hopkins	53
Extras	(b3, w3, nb1)	7		(b13, lb7, w4, nb3)	27
Total	(97.0 overs, 279 mins)	349		(167.5 overs, 449 mins)	519

NEW SOUTH WALES

V.T.Trumper	b Claxton	44		c Chamberlain b Wright	135
A.Diamond	b Wright	22	(4)	c Chamberlain b O'Connor	8
*M.A.Noble	c Jennings b L.R.Hill	93		b O'Connor	51
M.H.Blaxland	b L.R.Hill	6	(6)	c Pellew b L.R.Hill	29
R.A.Duff	b L.R.Hill	7	(2)	b Claxton	37
E.L.Waddy	c L.R.Hill b O'Connor	39	(7)	b O'Connor	49
A.J.Y.Hopkins	c Jennings b L.R.Hill	5	(8)	c C.Hill b Claxton	62
†H.Carter	st Jennings b Wright	46	(9)	c Wright b O'Connor	125
C.Kelleway	b L.R.Hill	1	(10)	not out	31
H.Whiddon	b Wright	10	(11)	c Chamberlain b Wright	11
F.B.Johnson	not out	1	(5)	b O'Connor	19
Extras	(b2)	2		(b4, lb4, w3, nb4)	15
Total	(87.1 overs, 246 mins)	276		(155.3 overs, 390 mins)	572

NEW SOUTH WALES	O	M	R	W	w,nb		O	M	R	W	w,nb			FALL OF WICKETS		
Kelleway	25	8	78	2	1,1		46	9	114	3	1,2			SA	NSW	SA	NSW
Johnson	19	4	52	0	-,-	(3)	23.5	2	62	1	-,-	Wkt	1st	1st	2nd	2nd
Noble	20	2	74	1	-,-	(4)	26	4	58	0	1,-	1st	57	51	23	89
Hopkins	13	3	65	2	-,-	(5)	23	1	70	2	1,1	2nd	201	71	118	175
Whiddon	20	3	73	4	2,-	(2)	38	6	140	4	-,-	3rd	203	96	200	213
Duff							11	3	48	0	1,-	4th	208	114	267	249
												5th	241	211	296	260
SOUTH AUSTRALIA	O	M	R	W	w,nb		O	M	R	W	w,nb	6th	266	217	433	312
L.R.Hill	21	3	82	5	-,-		28	3	79	1	-,2	7th	329	231	441	356
O'Connor	30	4	80	1	-,-		57	11	172	5	2,2	8th	329	233	481	474
Wright	18.1	2	54	3	-,-		27.3	1	123	2	-,-	9th	330	269	494	554
Claxton	11	1	34	1	-,-		27	4	104	2	1,-	10th	349	276	519	572
Chamberlain	2	0	13	0	-,-											
Pellew	5	1	11	0	-,-	(5)	16	0	79	0	-,-					

AUSTRALIA v ENGLAND (1st Test)

Played at Sydney Cricket Ground on December 13, 14, 16, 17, 18 (no play), 19, 1907. (Timeless match)
Toss : England.   Result : AUSTRALIA WON BY TWO WICKETS.
Debuts: Australia - H.Carter, G.R.Hazlitt, C.G.Macartney, V.S.Ransford (all Test). England - G.Gunn, J.Hardstaff, sr, K.L.Hutchings,
    R.A.Young (all Test).
12th Men: R.A.Duff (Aust) and J.B.Hobbs (Eng).
Umpires: R.M.Crockett and W.Hannah.
Attendances: 12324, 27776, 11138, 8556, no play, 3364.   Total: 63,158.   Receipts: £3005.
Close of Play: 1st day Aust 1/50 (Trumper 31, Hill 16); 2nd day Eng (2) 0/19 (Rhodes 10, Fane 8); 3rd day Eng (2) 9/293 (Braund 31);
    4th day Aust (2) 3/63 (Noble 27, Armstrong 17); 5th day no play.

With England's captain A.O.Jones unavailable through illness, George Gunn, who was in Australia for his own health reasons and was not a member of the MCC touring party, was brought into the team. His selection ahead of E.G.Hayes and J.B.Hobbs proved to be an inspired one. In his first innings on Australian soil, which was also his first Test, he survived stumping chances at 21 and 117 to score 119 in 150 minutes with 20 fours. He moved from 78 to 102 with boundaries, spread over several overs, and added 117 with Braund in 92 minutes. Gunn's share being 91. He again topscored in the second innings (74 in 167 minutes, 11 fours) and added 113 in 98 minutes with Hardstaff (63 in 98 minutes, 10 fours) to complete a century stand for the fourth wicket in each innings. Hill (87 in 146 minutes, 8 fours) and Carter (61 in 77 minutes, 8 fours) scored half-centuries for Australia while fast bowlers, Cotter and Fielder, for once did the major wicket-taking. Rain shortened the fourth day's play and prevented any play at all on the fifth, however the wicket dried evenly on the last day, there being little sun, and few problems were encountered by batsmen. The outcome was resolved through a cavalier ninth-wicket stand of 56 between Cotter (33 not out in 66 minutes, 1 four) and Hazlitt (34 not out in 39 minutes, 6 fours). Recent publications give Aust (1) 4/171, 8/279. Sources: *Wisden, NSWCA Report, The Australasian, Sydney Morning Herald, Town & Country Journal.*

ENGLAND

Batsman	Dismissal		Runs		2nd Dismissal	Runs
†R.A.Young	c Carter b Cotter		13	(7)	b Noble	3
*F.L.Fane	c Trumper b Cotter		2		c Noble b Saunders	33
G.Gunn	c Hazlitt b Cotter		119		c Noble b Cotter	74
K.L.Hutchings	c & b Armstrong		42		c Armstrong b Saunders	17
L.C.Braund	b Cotter		30	(6)	not out	32
J.Hardstaff, sr	b Armstrong		12	(5)	b Noble	63
W.Rhodes	run out (Macartney/Carter)		1	(1)	c McAlister b Macartney	29
J.N.Crawford	b Armstrong		31		c Hazlitt b Cotter	5
S.F.Barnes	b Cotter		1		b Saunders	11
C.Blythe	b Cotter		5		c Noble b Saunders	15
A.Fielder	not out		1		lbw b Armstrong	6
Extras	(b7, lb6, w1, nb2)		16		(b2, w3, nb7)	12
Total	(76.5 overs, 250 mins)		273		(109.0 overs, 308 mins)	300

AUSTRALIA

Batsman	Dismissal		Runs		2nd Dismissal	Runs
V.T.Trumper	b Fielder		43		b Barnes	3
P.A.McAlister	c Hutchings b Barnes		3	(7)	b Crawford	41
C.Hill	c Gunn b Fielder		87		b Fielder	1
*M.A.Noble	c Braund b Fielder		37		b Barnes	27
W.W.Armstrong	c Braund b Fielder		7		b Crawford	44
V.S.Ransford	c Braund b Rhodes		24		c & b Blythe	13
C.G.Macartney	c Young b Fielder		35	(2)	c Crawford b Fielder	9
†H.Carter	b Braund		25		c Young b Fielder	61
G.R.Hazlitt	not out		18	(10)	not out	34
A.Cotter	b Braund		2	(9)	not out	33
J.V.Saunders	c Braund b Fielder		9			
Extras	(b4, lb2, w2, nb2)		10		(b6, lb3)	9
Total	(91.2 overs, 293 mins)		300		(98.3 overs, 280 mins) (8 wkts)	275

AUSTRALIA	O	M	R	W	w,nb		O	M	R	W	w,nb
Cotter	21.5	0	101	6	-,2		26	1	101	2	3,4
Hazlitt	9	2	32	0	-,-	(5)	4	2	24	0	-,-
Saunders	11	0	42	0	1,-	(2)	23	6	68	4	-,-
Armstrong	26	10	63	3	-,-	(3)	27	14	33	1	-,1
Macartney	3	0	5	0	-,-	(4)	14	2	39	1	-,-
Noble	6	1	14	0	-,-		15	5	23	2	-,2

ENGLAND	O	M	R	W	w,nb		O	M	R	W	w,nb
Fielder	30.2	4	82	6	2,2		27.3	4	88	3	-,-
Barnes	22	3	74	1	-,-		30	7	63	2	-,-
Blythe	12	1	33	0	-,-		19	5	55	1	-,-
Braund	17	2	74	2	-,-	(6)	7	2	14	0	-,-
Crawford	5	1	14	0	-,-	(4)	8	2	33	2	-,-
Rhodes	5	2	13	1	-,-	(5)	7	3	13	0	-,-

FALL OF WICKETS

Wkt	ENG 1st	AUST 1st	ENG 2nd	AUST 2nd
1st	11	4	56	7
2nd	18	72	82	12
3rd	91	164	105	27
4th	208	177	218	75
5th	221	184	223	95
6th	223	222	227	124
7th	246	253	241	185
8th	253	277	262	219
9th	271	281	293	-
10th	273	300	300	-

VICTORIAN XI v M.C.C.

Played at South Melbourne Cricket Ground on December 21, 23, 24, 1907. (Three-day match)
Toss : M.C.C.   Result : MATCH DRAWN
Debuts: Victoria - L.P.Smith (f/c).
12th Men: No 12th men or emergency fieldsmen named.
Umpires: D.A.Elder and W.A.Young.
Attendances: 12000, 4000, 2000.   Total: About 18,000.   Receipts: £210.
Close of Play: 1st day MCC 7/321 (Rhodes 12, Barnes 3); 2nd day Vic 3/156 (Tarrant 30, Armstrong 32).

The first of two first-class matches staged at the ground, this fixture was the result of a request from the South Melbourne Cricket Club to the Australian Board of Control, via the Victorian Cricket Association, for a match in MCC's tour itinerary. It was thought at the time of designation that Victoria's leading players would be unavailable for the match, hence its title. However, only G.R.Hazlitt (injured finger) and L.P.Vernon (hurt in a bicycle accident) could not play and the team was fully representative. McKenzie and Collins, originally named as 12th man, were the replacements. Scheduled to be played over four days, the first day had to be dropped due to the late finish to the First Test in Sydney. For MCC, Hobbs (77 in 145 minutes, 11 fours), Hayes (98 in 148 minutes, 2 sixes and 15 fours), Rhodes (105 not out in 146 minutes, 1 six and 10 fours) and Fielder (50 not out in 33 minutes, 2 sixes and 5 fours) succeeded with the bat, the last two adding an unbeaten 95 for the tenth wicket. Tarrant (159 in 339 minutes, 14 fours), Armstrong (117 in 136 minutes, 13 fours) and Horan (75 in 142 minutes, 7 fours) stood out for the home team. Sources: *Wisden, The Age, The Argus, The Herald, The Australasian.*

M.C.C.

J.B.Hobbs	b Armstrong	77
J.N.Crawford	c Horan b Collins	43
E.G.Hayes	c Warne b Armstrong	98
K.L.Hutchings	c McKenzie b Armstrong	4
G.Gunn	c Saunders b Tarrant	24
J.Hardstaff, sr	c Horan b Tarrant	34
*F.L.Fane	b Tarrant	17
W.Rhodes	not out	105
S.F.Barnes	lbw b Armstrong	15
†J.Humphries	c McAlister b Collins	15
A.Fielder	not out	50
Extras	(b15, lb6)	21
Total	(148.0 overs, 383 mins) (9 wkts dec)	503

VICTORIAN XI

T.S.Warne	c Gunn b Rhodes	31
C.McKenzie	b Rhodes	19
F.A.Tarrant	c Crawford b Gunn	159
V.S.Ransford	b Barnes	38
W.W.Armstrong	c Hayes b Rhodes	117
*P.A.McAlister	b Fielder	11
J.F.Horan	b Crawford	75
L.P.Smith	lbw b Hayes	6
†J.R.H.Woodford	st Humphries b Crawford	0
F.B.Collins	not out	14
J.V.Saunders	did not bat	
Extras	(b1, lb4, w4, nb9)	18
Total	(163.0 overs, 445 mins) (9 wkts)	488

VICTORIAN XI	O	M	R	W	w,nb
Saunders	27	4	100	0	-,-
Armstrong	40	9	104	4	-,-
Collins	33	8	111	2	-,-
Smith	10	2	36	0	-,-
Warne	8	0	39	0	-,-
Tarrant	30	6	92	3	-,-

M.C.C.	O	M	R	W	w,nb
Fielder	25	3	82	1	-,4
Barnes	27	9	61	1	-,5
Rhodes	40	9	90	3	-,-
Crawford	28	1	89	2	4,-
Hayes	18	0	66	1	-,-
Hobbs	5	0	22	0	-,-
Hutchings	12	4	44	0	-,-
Gunn	8	3	16	1	-,-

FALL OF WICKETS

Wkt	MCC 1st	VIC 1st
1st	63	32
2nd	181	58
3rd	199	109
4th	242	279
5th	279	317
6th	286	445
7th	318	458
8th	361	459
9th	408	488
10th	-	-

VICTORIA v NEW SOUTH WALES (Shield Match 3)

Played at Melbourne Cricket Ground on December 26, 27 (no play), 28 (no play), 30, 31, 1907. (Timeless match)
Toss : Victoria.   Result : NEW SOUTH WALES WON BY EIGHT WICKETS.
Debuts: Nil.
12th Men: T.R.Rush (Vic) and C.Kelleway (NSW).
Umpires: R.M.Crockett and W.A.Young.
Attendances: 7000, no play, no play, 4200, 4500.   Total: about 15,700.   Receipts: £461.
Close of Play: 1st day Vic 6/193 (McAlister 70, Carroll 5); 2nd day no play; 3rd day no play; 4th day Vic (2) 2/20 (McKenzie 15).

Horan and Collins replaced L.P.Vernon (injured) and W.W.Armstrong in the Victorian side. Armstrong had made himself unavailable following a dispute with the Victorian Cricket Association over expenses from a previous match. Rain and bad light prevented any play on the first day after 5.10pm and led to the cancellation of the scheduled second and third day's play. As a result, the wicket assisted bowlers initially but dried quickly and was not a factor in the Victorian collapse in the second innings. Noble (101 in 144 minutes, 9 fours) and Trumper (119 in 105 minutes, 19 fours) scored centuries for New South Wales. McAlister (72 in 152 minutes, 9 fours) recorded the only other innings over 50 in the match. Saunders bowled Hickson with the second ball of the first innings. *Wisden* gives incorrect bowling in Vic (1) for Johnson. Sources: *Wisden, NSWCA Report, VCA Report, The Age, The Argus, The Herald, The Australasian.*

VICTORIA

T.S.Warne	c Noble b Whiddon	15		b Whiddon	5
C.McKenzie	run out (Macartney)	29		c Trumper b Cotter	29
F.A.Tarrant	b Cotter	16	(4)	c Trumper b Cotter	46
V.S.Ransford	c Noble b Johnson	23	(5)	c Carter b Cotter	7
*P.A.McAlister	lbw b Macartney	72	(6)	b Whiddon	17
J.F.Horan	c Hopkins b Johnson	20	(7)	b Cotter	12
G.R.Hazlitt	c Hopkins b Macartney	4	(9)	b Whiddon	7
E.V.Carroll	b Macartney	20		c & b Whiddon	4
†W.Carkeek	c Gregory b Noble	9	(10)	not out	7
F.B.Collins	run out (Waddy)	7	(3)	b Johnson	0
J.V.Saunders	not out	5		b Cotter	1
Extras	(b2, lb3, nb7)	12		(lb2, nb4)	6
Total	(86.3 overs, 274 mins)	232		(49.2 overs, 151 mins)	141

NEW SOUTH WALES

R.N.Hickson	b Saunders	0		c McAlister b Saunders	2
V.T.Trumper	b McAlister b Saunders	29		c Collins b Tarrant	119
*M.A.Noble	c & b Collins	101		not out	41
C.G.Macartney	c Saunders b Hazlitt	13		not out	4
S.E.Gregory	c Carkeek b Saunders	3			
E.L.Waddy	c & b Collins	13			
A.J.Y.Hopkins	c Carroll b Collins	0			
†H.Carter	c Carkeek b Saunders	0			
A.Cotter	b Saunders	22			
H.Whiddon	b Collins	11			
F.B.Johnson	not out	0			
Extras	(b14, nb1)	15		(lb2)	2
Total	(60.0 overs, 174 mins)	207		(44.0 overs, 111 mins) (2 wkts)	168

NEW SOUTH WALES	O	M	R	W	w,nb		O	M	R	W	w,nb
Cotter	18	4	36	1	-,4		17.2	2	52	5	-,4
Noble	15.3	6	31	1	-,3						
Hopkins	7	1	20	0	-,-						
Whiddon	6	0	25	1	-,-		15	2	53	4	-,-
Johnson	15	3	33	2	-,-	(3)	8	1	13	1	-,-
Macartney	23	8	62	3	-,-	(2)	9	4	17	0	-,-
Hickson	2	0	13	0	-,-						

VICTORIA	O	M	R	W	w,nb		O	M	R	W	w,nb
Saunders	24	8	51	5	-,-		16	3	54	1	-,-
Tarrant	9	2	43	0	-,-	(5)	7	1	28	1	-,-
Hazlitt	13	3	39	1	-,-		6	3	32	0	-,-
Collins	14	1	59	4	-,1	(2)	7	1	23	0	-,-
Warne						(4)	8	1	29	0	-,-

FALL OF WICKETS				
Wkt	VIC 1st	NSW 1st	VIC 2nd	NSW 2nd
1st	49	0	19	2
2nd	58	41	20	150
3rd	75	72	45	-
4th	106	89	55	-
5th	166	140	102	-
6th	175	158	120	-
7th	196	163	125	-
8th	220	166	125	-
9th	220	199	140	-
10th	232	207	141	-

NEW SOUTH WALES v QUEENSLAND

Played at Sydney Cricket Ground on December 26, 27, 28, 30, 1907. (Timeless match)
Toss : New South Wales.   Result : NEW SOUTH WALES WON BY SEVEN WICKETS.
Debuts: New South Wales - J.B.Lane, P.A.Newton, W.J.Whitty (all f/c). Queensland - W.Armstrong (f/c).
12th Men: D.C.Reid (NSW) and S.C.Whittred (Qld).
Umpires: W.G.Curran and A.C.Jones.
Attendances: 3500, 1600, 1300, "small".   Total: About 6500.   Receipts: £230.
Close of Play: 1st day NSW 7/458 (Fisher 43, Bowden 72); 2nd day Qld 7/254 (Evans 6); 3rd day Qld (2) 8/305 (Thomson 56).

New South Wales won their eleventh successive match against Queensland to establish a record sequence of victories between these States which still stands. It was their 17th win from the last 18 matches in this series (the other being drawn). Waddy's century (106 in 114 minutes, 14 fours) included 88 runs before lunch on the first day. Bowden (149 in 145 minutes, 1 five and 14 fours) scored his sole first-class century with the benefit of chances at 57, 84 (twice) and 147. The Queensland fielding was "indifferent" (*SMH*). Queensland provided the second instance in Australia (also MCC v Tas at Launceston 1903-04) of all eleven men bowling in an innings. Hartigan (104 in 115 minutes, 15 fours) scored his maiden first-class century; his only other century in his 45-match first-class career came immediately afterwards, in his Test debut at Adelaide. In the Queensland follow-on Thomson (19) retired hurt at 4/167 and resumed shortly after at 5/178. Whittred, the Queensland manager, was not required to act in his emergency capacity as 12th man. *Cricket* incorrectly gives Qld (2) Redgrave 5, Hayes 34. Sources: *Cricket, NSWCA Report, Sydney Referee, Sydney Morning Herald, Town & Country Journal, Sydney Mail.*

NEW SOUTH WALES

E.F.Waddy	run out (Barstow/Redgrave)	106			
*A.Diamond	run out (Evans)	41	(4) not out		0
M.H.Blaxland	c Thomson b Hayes	78			
C.W.Gregory	b Hartigan	14			
J.C.Barnes	run out (Thomson)	27	(1) c Redgrave b McLaren		6
W.Bardsley	c Hartigan b Redgrave	23	(2) c Redgrave b McLaren		9
†J.B.Lane	c Barstow b Redgrave	27	(3) run out		4
A.D.W.Fisher	c Thomson b Hartigan	63	(5) not out		3
A.J.Bowden	c Redgrave b Armstrong	149			
P.A.Newton	not out	27			
W.J.Whitty	b Evans	1			
Extras	(b19, lb14, w2)	35	(lb3)		3
Total	(127.2 overs, 373 mins)	591	(5.4 overs, 20 mins) (3 wkts)		25

QUEENSLAND

R.J.Hartigan	c Bowden b Fisher	104	c Bardsley b Fisher		17
G.F.Martin	b Whitty	10	st Lane b Bowden		23
J.S.Redgrave	c Blaxland b Bowden	21	c Fisher b Bowden		44
W.B.Hayes	c Bardsley b Newton	46	c & b Fisher		35
E.R.Crouch	st Lane b Bowden	4	b Blaxland		53
J.Thomson	c Blaxland b Barnes	25	c Diamond b Newton		70
M.M.F.Dunn	b Bowden	19	b Barnes		0
*†W.T.Evans	c Waddy b Bowden	27	c Waddy b Bowden		37
W.Armstrong	c Diamond b Whitty	9	b Newton		1
J.W.McLaren	c Waddy b Whitty	1	b Newton		6
C.B.Barstow	not out	0	not out		0
Extras	(b11, lb1, nb7)	19	(b22, lb6, w3, nb11)		42
Total	(74.1 overs, 220 mins)	285	(90.2 overs, 271 mins)		328

QUEENSLAND	O	M	R	W	w,nb		O	M	R	W	w,nb			FALL OF WICKETS			
McLaren	27	7	114	0	-,-		3	0	6	2	-,-			NSW	QLD	QLD	NSW
Redgrave	21	2	87	2	1,-							Wkt		1st	1st	2nd	2nd
Hayes	23	2	102	1	-,-							1st		119	25	30	10
Dunn	1	0	9	0	-,-							2nd		201	105	55	21
Barstow	16	0	68	0	-,-	(3)	0.4	0	4	0	-,-	3rd		233	165	112	22
Crouch	2	0	12	0	-,-							4th		284	184	152	-
Thomson	13	0	79	0	1,-							5th		290	199	178	-
Hartigan	16	3	64	2	-,-	(2)	2	0	12	0	-,-	6th		338	243	241	-
Martin	7	0	20	0	-,-							7th		340	254	303	-
Armstrong	1	0	1	1	-,-							8th		515	275	305	-
Evans	0.2	0	0	1	-,-							9th		586	285	327	-
												10th		591	285	328	-

NEW SOUTH WALES	O	M	R	W	w,nb		O	M	R	W	w,nb
Whitty	21.1	3	86	3	-,1		21	6	59	0	-,1
Newton	18	2	58	1	-,-		15.2	3	52	3	1,-
Fisher	15	1	63	1	-,5		21	2	75	2	2,10
Bowden	18	1	53	4	-,-		20	2	51	3	-,-
Barnes	2	1	6	1	-,1		11	1	33	1	-,-
Blaxland							2	0	16	1	-,-

AUSTRALIA v ENGLAND (2nd Test)

Played at Melbourne Cricket Ground on January 1, 2, 3, 4, 6, 7, 1908. (Timeless match)
Toss : Australia.   Result : ENGLAND WON BY ONE WICKET.
Debuts: England - J.B.Hobbs, J.Humphries (both Test).
12th Men: R.J.Hartigan (Aust - see below).
Umpires: P.Argall and R.M.Crockett.
Attendances: 26789, 18227, 10208, 20073, 9089, 7000.   Total: 91,386.   Receipts: £4070.
Close of Play: 1st day Aust 7/255 (Ransford 22, Carter 10); 2nd day Eng 3/246 (Hutchings 117, Braund 15); 3rd day Aust (2) 0/96
    (Noble 50, Trumper 46); 4th day Aust (2) 7/360 (Carter 22, Cotter 27); 5th day Eng (2) 4/159 (Braund 17, Hardstaff 17).

Hartigan, nominated as 12th man for Australia, was not required to attend the match and remained at home in Brisbane. Hutchings (chanceless 126 in 163 minutes, 1 six and 21 fours) reached 50 in 85 minutes and 100 in 128 minutes, progressing from 24 at tea to 117 at stumps (including 3 fours off Cotter in the last over of the day) and sharing lengthy stands with Hobbs (83 in 192 minutes, 8 fours) and Braund (49 in 144 minutes, 5 fours) to see England ahead on the first innings with just three wickets down. Trumper (49 in 81 minutes, 5 fours and 63 in 110 minutes, 7 fours), Macartney (54 in 147 minutes, 5 fours) and Carter (53 in 83 minutes, 7 fours) all did the hard work for Australia but none went on to three figures. Fane (50 in 160 minutes, 2 fours) alone reached the half-century in England's second innings. Barnes added 34 in 45 minutes with Humphries for the ninth wicket and knocked off the winnings runs with Fielder in an unlikely tenth-wicket stand of 39. The match would have been tied had Hazlitt fielding at cover, thrown accurately to Carter while the batsmen were negotiating the winning run at 3.28pm. Sources: *Wisden, The Age, The Argus, The Herald, The Australasian, The Leader.*

AUSTRALIA

V.T.Trumper	c Humphries b Crawford	49	(2) lbw b Crawford	63
C.G.Macartney	b Crawford	37	(6) c Humphries b Barnes	54
C.Hill	b Fielder	16	b Fielder	3
*M.A.Noble	c Braund b Rhodes	61	(1) b Crawford	64
W.W.Armstrong	c Hutchings b Crawford	31	b Barnes	77
P.A.McAlister	run out (Hobbs/Humphries)	10	(4) run out (Fielder/Humphries)	15
V.S.Ransford	run out (Hobbs/Humphries)	27	c Hutchings b Barnes	18
A.Cotter	b Crawford	17	(9) lbw b Crawford	27
†H.Carter	not out	15	(8) c Fane b Barnes	53
G.R.Hazlitt	b Crawford	1	b Barnes	3
J.V.Saunders	b Fielder	0	not out	0
Extras	(lb1, w1)	2	(b12, lb8)	20
Total	(100.5 overs, 308 mins)	266	(121.4 overs, 395 mins)	397

ENGLAND

*F.L.Fane	b Armstrong	13	(2) b Armstrong	50
J.B.Hobbs	b Cotter	83	(1) b Noble	28
G.Gunn	lbw b Cotter	15	lbw b Noble	0
K.L.Hutchings	b Cotter	126	c Cotter b Macartney	39
L.C.Braund	b Cotter	49	b Armstrong	30
J.Hardstaff, sr	b Saunders	12	c Ransford b Cotter	19
W.Rhodes	b Saunders	32	run out (Armstrong/Carter)	15
J.N.Crawford	c Ransford b Saunders	16	c Armstrong b Saunders	10
S.F.Barnes	c Hill b Armstrong	14	not out	38
†J.Humphries	b Cotter	6	lbw b Armstrong	16
A.Fielder	not out	6	not out	18
Extras	(b3, lb3, w1, nb3)	10	(b9, lb7, w1, nb2)	19
Total	(135.2 overs, 422 mins)	382	(121.4 overs, 363 mins) (9 wkts)	282

ENGLAND	O	M	R	W	w,nb		O	M	R	W	w,nb
Fielder	27.5	4	77	2	1,-		27	6	74	1	-,-
Barnes	17	7	30	0	-,-	(3)	27.4	4	72	5	-,-
Rhodes	11	0	37	1	-,-	(5)	16	6	38	0	-,-
Braund	16	5	41	0	-,-		18	2	68	0	-,-
Crawford	29	1	79	5	-,-	(2)	33	6	125	3	-,-

AUSTRALIA	O	M	R	W	w,nb		O	M	R	W	w,nb
Cotter	33	4	142	5	-,3		28	3	82	1	1,1
Saunders	34	7	100	3	-,-		30	9	58	1	-,-
Noble	9	3	26	0	-,-	(4)	22	7	41	2	-,1
Armstrong	34.2	15	36	2	-,-	(3)	30.4	10	53	3	-,-
Hazlitt	13	1	34	0	1,-		2	1	8	0	-,-
Macartney	12	2	34	0	-,-		9	3	21	1	-,-

FALL OF WICKETS

Wkt	AUST 1st	ENG 1st	AUST 2nd	ENG 2nd
1st	84	27	126	54
2nd	93	61	131	54
3rd	111	160	135	121
4th	168	268	162	131
5th	197	287	268	162
6th	214	325	303	196
7th	240	353	312	198
8th	261	360	361	209
9th	265	369	392	243
10th	266	382	397	-

AUSTRALIA v ENGLAND (3rd Test)

Played at Adelaide Oval on January 10, 11, 13, 14, 15, 16, 1908. (Timeless match)
Toss : Australia.   Result : AUSTRALIA WON BY 245 RUNS.
Debuts: Australia - R.J.Hartigan, J.D.A.O'Connor (both Test).
12th Men: L.R.Hill (Aust) and R.A.Young (Eng).
Umpires: R.M.Crockett and J.Laing.
Attendances: 6251, 15000, 4800, 3200, 4000, 500.   Total: 33,751.   Receipts: £1758.
Close of Play: 1st day Aust 9/279 (O'Connor 5, Saunders 1); 2nd day Eng 5/259 (Hardstaff 51, Rhodes 34); 3rd day Aust (2) 4/133
    (Noble 63, O'Connor 4); 4th day Aust (2) 7/397 (Hartigan 105, Hill 106); 5th day Eng (2) 5/139 (Braund 41, Crawford 1).

A remarkable eighth-wicket partnership - the highest stand for any Test wicket so far - was established between Roger Hartigan (116 in 254 minutes, 12 fours) and Clem Hill (160 in 319 minutes, 18 fours) in great heat on the fourth (107°F) and fifth (111.4°F) days. They added 243 in 245 minutes and took Australia to a match-winning lead in the process. Hartigan was the fourth Australian to score a century on his Test debut. He gave three chances, when 32 to Fielder at point off Crawford, 110 to Barnes at mid-off off Crawford and 112, a stumping chance off Barnes. Hill "was sick on the field" (*Register*) two or three times on the fourth day and "was on the verge of collapse" at one stage. He did not field, his brother Roy taking his place. Macartney (75 in 153 minutes, 9 fours) and Noble (65 in 173 minutes, 5 fours) accumulated half-centuries for Australia while Gunn (65 in 130 minutes, 1 six and 3 fours), Hardstaff (61 in 127 minutes, 9 fours) and Crawford (62 in 115 minutes, 8 fours) did so in England's first innings. Hobbs, after scoring a single in the opening over of the second innings, received a painful knock from Saunders's first ball at the other end and retired "at Noble's suggestion" (*Register*). Gunn took his place after an interval of nearly 10 minutes and Hobbs resumed the following day at 6/146. Braund (47 in 160 minutes, 7 fours) and Hardstaff (72 in 90 minutes, 7 fours) added 113, 62 per cent of the eventual total, in the time for Hardstaff's innings. A.Cotter, who had suffered a leg strain during the Second Test, accompanied the Australian team to Adelaide, however his injury did not mend in time and O'Connor was brought in as a late replacement. He took eight wickets. Sources: *Wisden, The Australasian, Adelaide Advertiser, South Australian Register.*

AUSTRALIA

V.T.Trumper	b Fielder	4		b Barnes	0
*M.A.Noble	c Hutchings b Barnes	15		c Gunn b Fielder	65
C.G.Macartney	lbw b Braund	75		b Barnes	9
P.A.McAlister	c Hutchings b Crawford	28		c Hutchings b Crawford	17
W.W.Armstrong	c Humphries b Fielder	17		c Hutchings b Braund	34
V.S.Ransford	b Barnes	44	(7)	c Rhodes b Braund	25
C.Hill	c Humphries b Barnes	5	(9)	c Gunn b Crawford	160
R.J.Hartigan	b Fielder	48		c sub (R.A.Young) b Barnes	116
†H.Carter	lbw b Hutchings	24	(10)	not out	31
J.D.A.O'Connor	not out	10	(6)	b Crawford	20
J.V.Saunders	b Fielder	1		run out (Hardstaff/Humphries)	0
Extras	(b3, lb5, w3, nb3)	14		(b20, lb7, w2)	29
Total	(94.5 overs, 290 mins)	285		(167.5 overs, 560 mins)	506

ENGLAND

J.B.Hobbs	c Carter b Saunders	26		not out	23
*F.L.Fane	run out (Trumper/Carter)	48		b Saunders	0
G.Gunn	b O'Connor	65		c Trumper b O'Connor	11
K.L.Hutchings	c & b Macartney	23		b O'Connor	0
L.C.Braund	b Macartney	0		c Hartigan b O'Connor	47
J.Hardstaff, sr	b O'Connor	61		c Macartney b Saunders	72
W.Rhodes	c Carter b O'Connor	38		c Armstrong b O'Connor	9
J.N.Crawford	b Armstrong	62		c & b Saunders	7
S.F.Barnes	c & b Armstrong	12		c McAlister b Saunders	8
†J.Humphries	run out (Macartney)	7		b O'Connor	1
A.Fielder	not out	0		c Ransford b Saunders	1
Extras	(b12, lb2, w2, nb5)	21		(b3, nb1)	4
Total	(132.0 overs, 393 mins)	363		(63.4 overs, 200 mins)	183

ENGLAND	O	M	R	W	w,nb		O	M	R	W	w,nb			FALL OF WICKETS		
Fielder	27.5	5	80	4	2,1		23	3	81	1	1,-			AUST	ENG AUST	ENG
Barnes	27	8	60	3	-,2		42	9	83	3	-,-	Wkt	1st	1st 2nd	2nd
Rhodes	15	5	35	0	-,-	(5)	27	9	81	0	-,-	1st	11	58 7	8
Crawford	14	0	65	1	1,-	(3)	45.5	4	113	3	1,-	2nd	35	98 35	9
Braund	9	1	26	1	-,-	(4)	23	3	85	2	-,-	3rd	114	138 71	15
Hutchings	2	1	5	1	-,-		7	0	34	0	-,-	4th	140	138 127	128
												5th	160	194 135	138
AUSTRALIA	O	M	R	W	w,nb		O	M	R	W	w,nb	6th	191	277 179	146
O'Connor	40	8	110	3	1,4		21	6	40	5	-,1	7th	215	282 180	162
Saunders	36	6	83	1	1,-		21.4	4	65	5	-,-	8th	273	320 423	177
Noble	18	4	38	0	-,1	(5)	7	1	14	0	-,-	9th	275	363 501	182
Armstrong	18	4	55	2	-,-	(3)	10	1	43	0	-,-	10th	285	363 506	183
Macartney	18	3	49	2	-,-	(4)	4	1	17	0	-,-				
Hartigan	2	0	7	0	-,-										

TASMANIA v M.C.C.

Played at N.T.C.A. Ground, Launceston, on January 18, 20, 21, 1908. (Three-day match)
Toss : M.C.C.   Result : M.C.C. WON BY 120 RUNS.
Debuts: Tasmania - H.J.T.Henri, C.W.B.Martin, H.O.Smith, L.K.Ward (all f/c).
12th Men: A.O.Jones (MCC). No 12th named for Tasmania.
Umpires: W.Lawrence and G.E.Pennefather.
Attendances: 2500, 3000, 1500.   Total: About 7000.   Receipts: No figures published.
Close of Play: 1st day Tas 0/13 (Hawson 4, Tabart 5); 2nd day MCC (2) 1/5 (Blythe 4).

The match did not start until 2.15pm on the first day because the ship carrying the Englishmen from Adelaide was delayed by fog. Hobbs survived a chance at 40 to score his first first-class hundred in Australia. He batted 173 minutes and hit 16 fours. Hardstaff (66 in 70 minutes, 10 fours and 85 in 78 minutes, 12 fours) and Windsor for Tasmania (75 in 92 minutes, 13 fours) compiled other innings of note. Heat exhaustion prevented Gunn from batting or fielding in the second innings. Jones, substituting in his place, made his first appearance on a cricket field since becoming ill in early December. Due to illness, Dodds was replaced as wicket-keeper on the last day by Ward and Henri was unable to bat. Henri had been the nominated 12th man but was introduced in the team at the last minute to replace the N.T.C.A. coach J.P.O'Halloran (unavailable). *Wisden* incorrectly gives MCC (2) Braund c Harrison. Sources: *Wisden, Launceston Examiner, Launceston Daily Telegraph, Hobart Mercury.*

M.C.C.

*F.L.Fane	c Dodds b Richardson	14	(9) c Tabart b Martin	7
J.B.Hobbs	st Dodds b Tabart	104	(3) c Frost b Windsor	65
E.G.Hayes	lbw b Richardson	6	(8) c Martin b Windsor	4
K.L.Hutchings	c Smith b Richardson	37	b Windsor	15
J.Hardstaff, sr	b Martin	66	c Hawson b Martin	85
G.Gunn	c Harrison b Windsor	46	absent ill	-
†R.A.Young	c & b Tabart	8	(2) b Richardson	1
L.C.Braund	c Tabart b Richardson	16	(6) c Hawson b Windsor	9
J.N.Crawford	c Richardson b Tabart	11	(7) b Martin	22
W.Rhodes	not out	7	not out	8
C.Blythe	b Richardson	0	(1) b Windsor	21
Extras		6		12
Total	(60.4 overs, 185 mins)	321	(50.3 overs, 163 mins)	249

TASMANIA

R.J.Hawson	b Crawford	41	b Blythe	41
T.A.Tabart	c Hardstaff b Crawford	57	b Crawford	4
C.W.B.Martin	run out (Gunn/Young)	0	c & b Braund	10
E.W.Harrison	b Crawford	54	(10) not out	11
*E.A.C.Windsor	b Crawford	18	(6) st Young b Braund	75
†N.Dodds	b Hayes	6	(5) b Crawford	6
W.B.Richardson	c & b Braund	15	(4) b Crawford	1
L.K.Ward	run out (Hardstaff/Crawford)	8	c Rhodes b Blythe	16
H.O.Smith	not out	36	(7) b Crawford	4
H.J.T.Henri	c Young b Braund	15	absent ill	-
A.E.Frost	c & b Braund	3	(9) b Blythe	0
Extras		23		6
Total	(100.1 overs, 260 mins)	276	(48.0 overs, 138 mins)	174

TASMANIA	O	M	R	W	w,nb		O	M	R	W	w,nb	FALL OF WICKETS				
Richardson	14.4	1	87	5			12	1	60	1			MCC	TAS	MCC	TAS
Windsor	15	1	79	1			19	2	85	5		Wkt	1st	1st	2nd	2nd
Hawson	9	1	26	0		(5)	2	0	9	0		1st	33	78	5	9
Frost	5	0	36	0		(3)	4	0	23	0		2nd	45	83	39	32
Martin	6	1	41	1		(6)	8.3	0	38	3		3rd	87	124	61	47
Tabart	11	0	46	3		(4)	5	1	22	0'		4th	224	152	176	63
												5th	232	165	207	63
M.C.C.	O	M	R	W	w,nb		O	M	R	W	w,nb	6th	266	185	208	79
Blythe	20	6	46	0		(3)	14	4	35	3		7th	302	209	217	118
Crawford	34	11	75	4		(1)	18	6	50	4		8th	313	241	234	125
Braund	21.1	4	66	3		(2)	10	1	54	2		9th	321	268	249	174
Rhodes	11	2	27	0		(5)	3	1	6	0		10th	321	276	-	-
Hutchings	7	3	19	0		(4)	3	0	23	0						
Hayes	4	0	13	1												
Hardstaff	3	1	7	0												

TASMANIA v M.C.C.

Played at T.C.A. Ground, Hobart, on January 24, 25, 27, 1908. (Three-day match)
Toss : M.C.C.   Result : MATCH DRAWN.
Debuts: Tasmania - W.R.Forster (f/c).
12th Men: T.D.Carroll (Tas) and J.Humphries (MCC).
Umpires: W.M.Bradshaw and T.R.Marsden.
Attendances: 2500, 3500, 1500.   Total: About 7500.   Receipts: No figures published.
Close of Play: 1st day MCC 8/427 (Young 7); 2nd day Tas (2) 1/96 (Tabart 47, Burn 23).

E.A.C.Windsor declared at the time of selection that he would be unable to represent Tasmania because of work commitments. However, he later found that leave was possible and was included in the team at the expense of H.Hale. Burn, aged 44, scored 112 in 218 minutes in the second innings, hitting 2 sixes and 14 fours. Eady (66 in 100 minutes, 9 fours) survived three chances to partner him in a fourth-wicket stand of 122, a new Tasmanian record for that wicket. Hardstaff (106 in 130 minutes, 1 five and 16 fours) and Rhodes (119 in 125 minutes, 17 fours, 2 chances) scored centuries for MCC. Hobbs (58 in 70 minutes, 1 five and 7 fours), Fane (62 in 132 minutes, 6 fours) and Hutchings (51 in 28 minutes, 1 five and 9 fours) also batted well. Hawson was dismissed by Fielder in the first over of Tasmania's first innings. *Wisden* incorrectly gives MCC Martin 1/15. Sources: *Wisden, Launceston Examiner, Hobart Mercury.*

M.C.C.

J.B.Hobbs	c Forster b Paton	58
*F.L.Fane	c Martin b Eady	62
E.G.Hayes	lbw b Eady	1
K.L.Hutchings	c Hawson b Paton	51
L.C.Braund	c Martin b Richardson	14
J.Hardstaff, sr	c Tabart b Richardson	106
W.Rhodes	c Paton b Windsor	119
G.Gunn	c Eady b Windsor	1
†R.A.Young	lbw b Eady	20
C.Blythe	c & b Eady	10
A.Fielder	not out	5
Extras	(b6, lb2)	8
Total	(108.2 overs, 293 mins)	455

TASMANIA

R.J.Hawson	c Braund b Fielder	0	(2)	b Hutchings	25
T.A.Tabart	b Braund	11	(1)	st Young b Braund	55
W.R.Forster	b Fielder	0	(8)	not out	9
E.A.C.Windsor	c Hobbs b Braund	34		b Hardstaff	21
C.J.Eady	c Hayes b Braund	29		c Hutchings b Rhodes	66
C.W.B.Martin	c Fane b Blythe	0		b Rhodes	7
†N.Dodds	st Young b Blythe	6		c Hutchings b Braund	4
*E.J.K.Burn	b Braund	8	(3)	c & b Rhodes	112
W.B.Richardson	c Hutchings b Braund	6		b Braund	0
G.D.Paton	b Hutchings	7		not out	10
F.J.Hanson	not out	8			
Extras	(b3, lb1)	4		(b7, lb1)	8
Total	(51.5 overs, 150 mins)	113		(110.0 overs, 305 mins) (8 wkts)	317

TASMANIA	O	M	R	W	w,nb
Eady	32.2	4	127	4	-,-
Windsor	27	7	113	2	-,-
Paton	18	3	58	2	-,-
Richardson	13	1	55	2	-,-
Martin	4	1	15	0	-,-
Hanson	6	0	25	0	-,-
Hawson	4	0	18	0	-,-
Tabart	4	0	36	0	-,-

M.C.C.	O	M	R	W	w,nb		O	M	R	W	w,nb
Fielder	7	3	17	2	-,-		24	3	69	0	-,-
Blythe	24	11	34	2	-,-	(5)	21	6	48	0	-,-
Braund	19	5	55	5	-,-		31	5	103	3	-,-
Hutchings	1.5	0	3	1	-,-		8	1	48	1	-,-
Rhodes						(2)	22	10	29	3	-,-
Hardstaff							4	1	12	1	-,-

FALL OF WICKETS

	MCC	TAS	TAS
Wkt	1st	1st	2nd
1st	87	0	52
2nd	101	2	109
3rd	170	25	159
4th	180	71	281
5th	197	71	291
6th	407	75	296
7th	408	89	299
8th	427	89	302
9th	446	101	-
10th	455	113	-

NEW SOUTH WALES v VICTORIA (Shield Match 4)

Played at Sydney Cricket Ground on January 24, 25, 27, 28, 29, 30 (no play), 31, 1908. (Timeless match)
Toss : Victoria.   Result : VICTORIA WON BY 211 RUNS.
Debuts: Nil.
12th Men: W.Bardsley (NSW) and E.V.Carroll (Vic).
Umpires: W.J.Bruton and J.Laing.
Attendances: 3788, 5172, 8683, 2415, 2000, no play, 512.   Total: 22,770.   Receipts: £889.
Close of Play: 1st day Vic 4/333 (Armstrong 75, Horan 34); 2nd day NSW 3/234 (Noble 100, Gregory 70); 3rd day Vic (2) 2/64
   (Tarrant 11, Ransford 19); 4th day Vic (2) 7/363 (Tarrant 129, Warne 15); 5th day NSW (2) 3/185 (Noble 101, Gregory 40);
   6th day no play.

A wicket that "was in splendid run-getting order" (*SMH*) contributed in no small way to a high scoring match. Seven days were required to complete a first-class match for the first time. Armstrong (110 in 166 minutes, 10 fours), Tarrant (79 in 106 minutes, 10 fours and 206 in 437 minutes, 22 fours), Ransford (129 in 127 minutes, 16 fours), McKenzie (51 in 80 minutes, 5 fours) and McAlister (69 in 125 minutes, 1 six and 5 fours) led the scoring for Victoria. Noble (176 in 337 minutes, 16 fours and 123 in 222 minutes, 14 fours) and Gregory (201 in 287 minutes, 24 fours and 63 in 109 minutes, 8 fours) were the only home batsmen to offer serious resistance. Rain prevented any play on the scheduled sixth day and changed the character of the wicket which Saunders was able to exploit. V.T.Trumper (ill) had been unavailable for New South Wales. Sources: *Wisden, NSWCA Report, VCA Report, Sydney Referee, Sydney Morning Herald, Town & Country Journal.*

VICTORIA

C.McKenzie	c Carter b Noble	51	(2)	c Noble b Whiddon		21
*P.A.McAlister	c E.L.Waddy b Johnson	69	(1)	c Hopkins b Johnson		8
F.A.Tarrant	st Carter b Barnes	79		c & b Johnson		206
V.S.Ransford	b Kelleway	11		c Carter b Noble		129
W.W.Armstrong	c E.F.Waddy b Kelleway	110		b Noble		13
T.I.B.Horan	c Hopkins b Noble	35		b Hopkins		8
T.S.Warne	c E.L.Waddy b Noble	2	(9)	b Barnes		46
L.P.Vernon	b Johnson	7	(7)	b Hopkins		2
†W.Carkeek	b Johnson	3	(8)	run out (sub W.Bardsley/Carter)		26
F.B.Collins	not out	10		c Gregory b Whiddon		26
J.V.Saunders	c E.L.Waddy b Whiddon	9		not out		10
Extras	(b5, lb7, w3, nb1)	16		(b11, lb3, nb2)		16
Total	(118.0 overs, 339 mins)	402		(169.2 overs, 464 mins)		511

NEW SOUTH WALES

E.F.Waddy	b Collins	28	(7)	c Horan b Tarrant		5
A.J.Y.Hopkins	run out (Warne)	6		b Vernon		7
*M.A.Noble	b Vernon	176	(1)	c Carkeek b Saunders		123
C.G.Macartney	c Carkeek b Saunders	21	(8)	c Horan b Saunders		0
S.E.Gregory	c McAlister b Vernon	201		b Tarrant		63
E.L.Waddy	b Collins	8	(4)	c McKenzie b Saunders		3
†H.Carter	c McKenzie b Vernon	9	(3)	c Carkeek b Saunders		23
J.C.Barnes	b Collins	0	(6)	c & b Saunders		5
C.Kelleway	run out (Ransford)	1		c Vernon b Tarrant		0
H.Whiddon	c McKenzie b Vernon	0		c Horan b Saunders		1
F.B.Johnson	not out	1		not out		0
Extras	(b4, lb2, w4)	10		(b1, lb3, w7)		11
Total	(142.4 overs, 408 mins)	461		(79.2 overs, 229 mins)		241

NEW SOUTH WALES	O	M	R	W	w,nb		O	M	R	W	w,nb
Kelleway	21	4	67	2	3,-		32	10	70	0	-,1
Johnson	25	3	73	3	-,-		40	10	96	2	-,-
Whiddon	11	0	52	1	-,-	(6)	23.2	0	77	2	-,-
Hopkins	13	3	36	0	-,-	(6)	25	5	75	2	-,-
Noble	20	4	54	3	-,1		24	6	58	2	-,1'
Barnes	11	0	65	1	-,-	(4)	20	2	106	1	-,-
Macartney	12	2	15	0	-,-		5	2	13	0	-,-
Gregory	5	0	24	0	-,-						

VICTORIA	O	M	R	W	w,nb		O	M	R	W	w,nb
Vernon	21.4	2	87	4	3,-		13	2	40	1	5,-
Armstrong	40	8	86	0	-,-	(5)	12	5	18	0	-,-
Collins	27	4	90	3	1,-	(2)	15	0	40	0	2,-
Saunders	20	1	92	1	-,-	(3)	21.2	8	61	6	-,-
Tarrant	23	4	56	0	-,-	(4)	14	2	47	3	-,-
Warne	11	1	40	0	-,-	(7)	2	0	12	0	-,-
Ransford						(6)	2	0	12	0	-,-

FALL OF WICKETS

Wkt	VIC 1st	NSW 1st	VIC 2nd	NSW 2nd
1st	104	17	15	30
2nd	162	51	42	70
3rd	181	95	217	84
4th	243	410	243	220
5th	342	449	259	233
6th	344	451	261	238
7th	372	459	310	240
8th	382	460	432	240
9th	382	460	497	240
10th	402	461	511	241

VICTORIA v M.C.C.

Played at Melbourne Cricket Ground on February 1, 3, 4, 1908. (Timeless match)
Toss : M.C.C.   Result : M.C.C. WON BY 330 RUNS.
Debuts: Victoria - F.T.Delves, G.E.J.Healy, N.L.Speirs (all f/c).
12th Men: R.A.Young (MCC). J.H.Kyle and R.S.Stephens were named as Victorian emergencies.
Umpires: E.Barrass and W.Hannah (see below).
Attendances: 6633, 1500, 200.   Total: About 8333.   Receipts: £253.
Close of Play: 1st day Vic 2/28 (Vaughan 13, Healy 4); 2nd day Vic (2) 1/35 (Healy 7, Woodford 13).

The match was scheduled to start on January 31st but was put back a day in the hope that the Victorian players engaged in the Sheffield Shield match in Sydney could return in time. When that match went into an unprecedented seventh day, the Victorian selectors were forced to name what amounted to a second eleven for this match. The only player to return from Sydney in time for inclusion was the 12th man, Carroll. A further late change in the team saw Woodford replace T.J.Hastings, who was unavailable. A.O.Jones returned after his illness of two months to lead MCC. Trott, aged 41, marked his final first-class appearance with a five-wicket analysis. MCC outplayed the Victorians in all departments of the game. Hardstaff (122 in 125 minutes, 1 six and 13 fours), Crawford (69 in 50 minutes, 1 six and 12 fours), Hobbs (115 in 143 minutes, 1 six and 12 fours) and Hutchings (51 in 27 minutes, 8 fours) all scored freely while Barnes (10 for 67) and Blythe (6 for 93) accounted for the home batsmen. Only Carroll (61 in 115 minutes, 6 fours) resisted for any length of time. Umpire Barrass became ill during the match and was replaced at the commencement of MCC's second innings by R.M.Crockett, who officiated with Hannah for the remainder of the game. Sources: *Wisden, VCA Report, The Age, The Argus, The Australasian.*

M.C.C.

J.B.Hobbs	b Trott	30	c Delves b Laver		115
G.Gunn	lbw b Trott	7	c Laver b Carroll		48
E.G.Hayes	c Delves b Trott	30	b Carroll		7
K.L.Hutchings	c Carroll b Hazlitt	12	c Laver b Carroll		51
J.Hardstaff, sr	c Fry b Laver	122	not out		12
F.L.Fane	c & b Laver	36	not out		0
J.N.Crawford	c Delves b Carroll	69			
*A.O.Jones	c Vaughan b Laver	9			
S.F.Barnes	not out	7			
†J.Humphries	c Fry b Trott	7			
C.Blythe	c Delves b Trott	2			
Extras	(b5, lb2)	7	(b6, lb2)		8
Total	(81.0 overs, 218 mins)	338	(52.0 overs, 145 mins) (4 wkts dec)		241

VICTORIA

G.H.S.Trott	b Blythe	4	(5) b Blythe		30
F.Vaughan	b Barnes	16	(1) b Barnes		15
E.V.Carroll	b Blythe	6	(6) c Jones b Barnes		61
G.E.J.Healy	c Gunn b Blythe	14	(2) b Blythe		11
F.T.Delves	c Fane b Barnes	4	(4) run out (Barnes/Humphries)		4
H.J.Fry	c Crawford b Barnes	8	(7) b Crawford		1
T.R.Rush	run out (/Barnes)	0	(8) c Barnes b Crawford		9
*F.J.Laver	c Hardstaff b Barnes	2	(9) c Hobbs b Barnes		20
G.R.Hazlitt	lbw b Barnes	8	(10) c Jones b Barnes		0
N.L.Speirs	c Hobbs b Blythe	10	(11) not out		1
†J.R.H.Woodford	not out	4	(3) c Jones b Barnes		13
Extras	(lb1)	1	(lb7)		7
Total	(41.2 overs, 125 mins)	77	(64.5 overs, 184 mins)		172

VICTORIA	O	M	R	W	w,nb		O	M	R	W	w,nb					
Speirs	11	3	49	0	-,-	(4)	7	2	23	0	-,-					
Trott	25	1	116	5	-,-	(1)	8	0	39	0	-,-					
Hazlitt	20	3	84	1	-,-		10	1	49	0	-,-					
Fry	5	0	33	0	-,-	(5)	4	1	12	0	-,-					
Laver	14	3	38	3	-,-	(2)	12	4	48	1	-,-					
Carroll	6	1	11	1	-,-		11	0	62	3	-,-					

FALL OF WICKETS

Wkt	MCC 1st	VIC 1st	MCC 2nd	VIC 2nd
1st	14	5	118	21
2nd	60	13	130	35
3rd	77	31	201	43
4th	89	35	237	43
5th	197	47	-	97
6th	300	47	-	98
7th	314	55	-	122
8th	324	55	-	171
9th	336	65	-	171
10th	338	77	-	172

M.C.C.	O	M	R	W	w,nb		O	M	R	W	w,nb
Barnes	21	10	32	5	-,-		21.5	13	35	5	-,-
Blythe	19.2	5	41	4	-,-		20	6	52	2	-,-
Crawford	1	0	3	0	-,-		20	4	63	2	-,-
Hayes							3	0	15	0	-,-

AUSTRALIA v ENGLAND (4th Test)

Played at Melbourne Cricket Ground on February 7, 8, 10, 11, 1908. (Timeless match)
Toss : Australia.   Result : AUSTRALIA WON BY 308 RUNS.
Debuts: Nil.
12th Men: C.McKenzie (Aust) and C.Blythe (Eng).
Umpires: P.Argall and R.M.Crockett.
Attendances: 9928, 19797, 12088, 10948.   Total: 52,761.   Receipts: £2003.
Close of Play: 1st day Eng 0/9 (Hobbs 9, Gunn 0); 2nd day Aust (2) 3/49 (Hill 18, Gregory 13); 3rd day Aust (2) 8/358 (Armstrong 114, O'Connor 12).

R.J.Hartigan (business) and A.Cotter (injured) were unavailable for Australia. England's bowlers, led by Crawford and Fielder, began well by restricting the strong Australian line-up on the first day. Noble (48 in 111 minutes, 4 fours) and Ransford (51 in 90 minutes, 6 fours) batted well. However, heavy rain ruined the pitch for England's batsmen. Hobbs (57 in 75 minutes, 10 fours, out at 88) "went along as if the state of the wicket made no difference to him" (*Felix* in *The Australasian*) but, after his dismissal, 7 for 15 fell in 41 minutes (Saunders 5 for 10 from 8.2 overs) which included a brief stoppage when Carter, keeping wicket, was struck by a ball from Noble. England's ill-fortune continued when the wicket and outfield improved under the fine Sunday weather for Australia's second innings. Armstrong (133 not out in 289 minutes, 2 sixes and 14 fours) gave his sole chance when 44, to Crawford at slip off Braund, and put on 85 with Ransford (54 in 103 minutes, 1 five and 3 fours) and 112 with Carter (66 in 82 minutes, 11 fours) for the eighth wicket. Hobbs was out in the third over of England's second innings before a run was on the board and the Ashes were not long after relinquished to Noble's men. Some recent publications incorrectly give Aust (1) 3/84, 4/100, Eng (2) 5/85, 6/85. Sources: *Wisden, The Age, The Argus, The Herald, The Australasian, The Leader.*

AUSTRALIA

*M.A.Noble	b Crawford	48	b Crawford		10
V.T.Trumper	c Crawford b Fielder	0	b Crawford		0
C.Hill	b Barnes	7	run out (Barnes/Humphries)		25
P.A.McAlister	c Jones b Fielder	37	c Humphries b Fielder		4
S.E.Gregory	c Fielder b Crawford	10	lbw b Fielder		29
W.W.Armstrong	b Crawford	32	not out		133
V.S.Ransford	c Braund b Fielder	51	c Humphries b Rhodes		54
C.G.Macartney	c Hardstaff b Fielder	12	c Gunn b Crawford		29
†H.Carter	c & b Crawford	2	c Braund b Fielder		66
J.D.A.O'Connor	c Fielder b Crawford	2	c Humphries b Barnes		18
J.V.Saunders	not out	1	c Jones b Fielder		2
Extras	(b1, lb10, nb1)	12	(b7, lb2, nb6)		15
Total	(85.5 overs, 274 mins)	214	(124.0 overs, 375 mins)		385

ENGLAND

J.B.Hobbs	b Noble	57	c & b Saunders		0
G.Gunn	c & b Saunders	13	b Saunders		43
J.Hardstaff, sr	c Carter b O'Connor	8	c Carter b Saunders		39
K.L.Hutchings	b Saunders	8	b Noble		3
L.C.Braund	run out (Noble)	4	b Macartney		10
W.Rhodes	c McAlister b Saunders	0	c Carter b O'Connor		2
J.N.Crawford	b Saunders	1	c Carter b O'Connor		0
*A.O.Jones	b Noble	3	c Saunders b O'Connor		31
S.F.Barnes	c O'Connor b Noble	3	not out		22
†J.Humphries	not out	3	c Carter b Saunders		11
A.Fielder	st Carter b Saunders	1	b Armstrong		20
Extras	(b1, lb2, nb1)	4	(lb4, nb1)		5
Total	(34.2 overs, 126 mins)	105	(68.1 overs, 203 mins)		186

ENGLAND	O	M	R	W	w,nb		O	M	R	W	w,nb		FALL OF WICKETS			
Fielder	22	3	54	4	-,1	(3)	31	2	91	4	-,6			AUST	ENG AUST	ENG
Barnes	23	11	37	1	-,-	(1)	35	13	69	1	-,-		Wkt	1st	1st 2nd	2nd
Braund	12	3	42	0	-,-	(5)	7	0	48	0	-,-		1st	1	58 4	0
Crawford	23.5	3	48	5	-,-	(2)	25	5	72	3	-,-		2nd	14	69 21	61
Rhodes	5	0	21	0	-,-	(4)	24	5	66	1	-,-		3rd	89	88 28	64
Hutchings						(2)	2	0	24	0	-,-		4th	103	90 65	79
													5th	105	90 77	88
AUSTRALIA	O	M	R	W	w,nb		O	M	R	W	w,nb		6th	196	92 162	88
O'Connor	6	1	40	1	-,1	(2)	21	3	58	3	-,1		7th	196	96 217	128
Armstrong	1	0	4	0	-,-	(4)	3.1	0	18	1	-,-		8th	198	100 329	132
Macartney	6	1	18	0	-,-	(5)	6	1	15	1	-,-		9th	212	103 374	146
Saunders	15.2	8	28	5	-,-	(1)	26	2	76	4	-,-		10th	214	105 385	186
Noble	6	0	11	3	-,-	(3)	12	6	14	1	-,-					

NEW SOUTH WALES v M.C.C.

Played at Sydney Cricket Ground on February 14, 15, 17, 18, 19, 20 (no play), 1908. (Timeless match)
Toss : M.C.C.   Result : MATCH DRAWN.
Debuts: New South Wales - C.R.Gorry, L.A.Minnett (both f/c).
12th Men: W.J.Whitty (NSW). No 12th named for MCC.
Umpires: W.G.Curran and A.C.Jones.
Attendances: 4289, 9460, 4360, 3802, 3121, no play.   Total: 25,032.   Receipts: £886.
Close of Play: 1st day NSW 1/10 (Barnes 7); 2nd day NSW 9/355 (Waddy 101, Gorry 1); 3rd day MCC (2) 4/255 (Hardstaff 65,
    Braund 34); 4th day NSW (2) 2/78 (Bardsley 27, Trumper 21); 5th day NSW (2) 9/375 (Minnett 18, Gorry 1).

Scheduled to be played over four days, the match was extended to obtain a result but had to be abandoned following the washout of the sixth day's play, so the Fifth Test could start on time. H.Carter, business commitments, was unavailable for New South Wales. In addition, A.Cotter, S.E.Gregory and F.B.Johnson all withdrew from the selected eleven before the match for various reasons. Hopkins, Newton and Waddy were the replacements. Fane (101 in 195 minutes, 11 fours) and Braund (132 not out in 270 minutes, 13 fours) scored centuries for MCC while Macartney (96 in 156 minutes, 10 fours), Waddy (107 not out in 208 minutes, 7 fours), Bowden (87 in 100 minutes, 13 fours) and Bardsley (108 in 176 minutes, 12 fours) were the main contributors for New South Wales. Play on the fifth day - the last, as it turned out - ended when an appeal against the light by New South Wales, 12 runs short of victory, was upheld, Fielder was unable to bat or bowl in either second innings due to a strained arm. Sources: *Wisden, NSWCA Report, Sydney Referee, Sydney Morning Herald, Town & Country Journal.*

M.C.C.

J.B.Hobbs	c Gorry b Minnett	4	c Waddy b Minnett		12
F.L.Fane	st Gorry b Bowden	2	c Diamond b Hopkins		101
E.G.Hayes	c Waddy b Minnett	10	c Bardsley b Bowden		33
K.L.Hutchings	c Diamond b Minnett	73	c Macartney b Bowden		5
J.Hardstaff, sr	c Diamond b Minnett	32	b Minnett		73
L.C.Braund	c Trumper b Bowden	4	not out		132
W.Rhodes	c Waddy b Minnett	45	c Diamond b Macartney		53
†R.A.Young	c & b Minnett	59	c Macartney b Bowden		7
*A.O.Jones	not out	57	c Trumper b Barnes		17
C.Blythe	c Waddy b Minnett	1	b Bowden		15
A.Fielder	c Diamond b Hopkins	4	absent hurt		-
Extras	(b1, lb1, w1, nb4)	7	(b3, lb3, nb2)		8
Total	(83.5 overs, 250 mins)	298	(175.3 overs, 454 mins)		456

NEW SOUTH WALES

J.C.Barnes	c Rhodes b Blythe	19	(2) b Blythe		9
W.Bardsley	c Braund b Blythe	3	(3) b Blythe		108
C.G.Macartney	b Braund	96	(1) c & b Hobbs		20
*V.T.Trumper	b Blythe	14	c Jones b Hardstaff		74
A.Diamond	c Young b Blythe	7	(6) c Hayes b Rhodes		30
A.J.Y.Hopkins	c Hutchings b Fielder	13	(7) st Young b Rhodes		3
E.F.Waddy	not out	107	(5) c Young b Rhodes		57
A.J.Bowden	c Jones b Hobbs	87	c Hayes b Rhodes		22
P.A.Newton	c Hutchings b Hobbs	0	c Hardstaff b Rhodes		20
L.A.Minnett	b Fielder	3	not out		18
†C.R.Gorry	b Blythe	7	not out		1
Extras	(b7, lb2, w2, nb1)	12	(b5, lb2, w2, nb4)		13
Total	(117.3 overs, 318 mins)	368	(135.0 overs, 330 mins) (9 wkts)		375

NEW SOUTH WALES	O	M	R	W	w,nb		O	M	R	W	w,nb		FALL OF WICKETS				
Minnett	30	7	131	7	1,3		43	15	92	2	-,2			MCC	NSW	MCC	NSW
Bowden	27	7	77	2	-,-	(3)	48.3	8	119	4	-,-	Wkt	1st	1st	2nd	2nd
Newton	10	3	23	0	-,-	(5)	27	4	78	0	-,-	1st	4	10	23	29
Hopkins	8.5	1	35	1	-,1		23	3	82	1	-,-	2nd	17	44	94	30
Macartney	6	1	21	0	-,-	(2)	26	9	40	1	-,-	3rd	25	74	99	199
Barnes	2	0	4	0	-,-		8	1	37	1	-,-	4th	105	85	193	239
												5th	130	106	268	301
M.C.C.	O	M	R	W	w,nb		O	M	R	W	w,nb	6th	132	192	369	306
Blythe	37.3	7	93	5	1,-		42	10	99	2	-,-	7th	228	345	385	316
Fielder	31	7	78	2	-,1							8th	251	348	429	340
Braund	14	0	78	1	-,-		13	0	58	0	-,-	9th	269	353	456	359
Rhodes	20	3	63	0	1,-	(5)	40	11	73	5	2,-	10th	298	368	-	-
Hardstaff	4	0	16	0	-,-	(6)	18	5	51	1	-,3					
Hobbs	7	2	14	2	-,-	(2)	13	2	41	1	-,-					
Hayes	4	0	14	0	-,-											
Hutchings						(4)	9	0	40	0	-,1					

AUSTRALIA v ENGLAND (5th Test)

Played at Sydney Cricket Ground on February 21, 22, 24, 25, 26, 27, 1908. (Timeless match)
Toss : England.   Result : AUSTRALIA WON BY 49 RUNS.
Debuts: Nil.
12th Men: E.F.Waddy (Aust) and C.Blythe (Eng).
Umpires: W.Hannah and A.C.Jones.
Attendances: 7110, 12141, 2544, 8130, 8635, 2097.   Total: 40,657.   Receipts: £1605.
Close of Play: 1st day Eng 1/116 (Hobbs 65, Gunn 50); 2nd day Eng 3/187 (Gunn 77, Hardstaff 17); 3rd day Aust (2) 0/18 (Noble 11,
     O'Connor 4); 4th day Aust (2) 6/357 (Armstrong 19, Ransford 4); 5th day Eng (2) 6/117 (Rhodes 32, Young 9).

Rain was a factor throughout the match. Jones sent Australia in and the wicket was never easy at any stage, except for the fourth day after lunch. Frequent showers prevented it from drying out: there was no play on the second day after 2.35pm and none on the third day before 3.30pm. Gunn (122 not out in 287 minutes, 1 six and 7 fours) batted for all but the first three balls of the England first innings. He gave one chance, a hot one to Trumper at silly point off Saunders, and put on 134 with Hobbs (72 in 143 minutes, 7 fours) for the second wicket. Noble (35 in 62 minutes, 5 fours) and Gregory (44 in 101 minutes, 5 fours) topscored for Australia on the first day when the *Town & Country Journal* quoted Jennings, the curator as saying that the wicket was "funny". Trumper's match-winning innings of 166 (241 minutes, 18 fours) included a sole chance when the batsman was 1 (a sharp catch to Rhodes's right hand at short-leg off Barnes). When 144, Trumper reached 2000 Test runs. He shared century partnerships with Gregory for the third wicket (114 in 85 minutes) and with Hill for the fifth (108 in 72 minutes). Saunders bagged a pair off the first and second balls he faced respectively. Rhodes (69 in 160 minutes, 4 fours) was England's top scorer in the second innings, when rain again damaged the pitch. A.Fielder (injured right elbow) and J.Humphries (ill) were unavailable for England. Sources: *Wisden, NSWCA Report, The Australasian, Sydney Referee, Sydney Morning Herald, Town & Country Journal.*

AUSTRALIA

*M.A.Noble	b Barnes	35		lbw b Rhodes	34
C.G.Macartney	c Crawford b Barnes	1	(5)	c Jones b Crawford	12
J.D.A.O'Connor	c Young b Crawford	9	(2)	b Barnes	6
S.E.Gregory	c & b Barnes	44		b Crawford	56
C.Hill	c Hutchings b Barnes	12	(6)	c Young b Crawford	44
W.W.Armstrong	c & b Crawford	3	(7)	c Gunn b Crawford	32
V.T.Trumper	c Braund b Barnes	10	(3)	c Gunn b Rhodes	166
V.S.Ransford	c Gunn b Barnes	11		not out	21
R.J.Hartigan	c & b Crawford	1		b Crawford	5
†H.Carter	not out	1		c Hobbs b Rhodes	22
J.V.Saunders	c Young b Barnes	0		c Young b Rhodes	0
Extras	(b9, lb1)	10		(b21, lb3)	24
Total	(50.4 overs, 155 mins)	137		(127.4 overs, 358 mins)	422

ENGLAND

J.B.Hobbs	b Saunders	72		c Gregory b Saunders	13
F.L.Fane	b Noble	0		b Noble	46
G.Gunn	not out	122		b Macartney	0
K.L.Hutchings	run out (Trumper/Carter/Saunders)	13		b Macartney	2
J.Hardstaff, sr	c O'Connor b Saunders	17		b Saunders	8
J.N.Crawford	c Hill b Saunders	6	(10)	not out	24
L.C.Braund	st Carter b Macartney	31	(6)	c Noble b Saunders	0
W.Rhodes	c Noble b Armstrong	10	(7)	b Noble	69
†R.A.Young	st Carter b Macartney	0	(8)	c O'Connor b Saunders	11
*A.O.Jones	b Macartney	0	(9)	b Armstrong	34
S.F.Barnes	run out (Macartney)	1		b Saunders	11
Extras	(b6, lb3)	9		(b5, lb6)	11
Total	(96.1 overs, 292 mins)	281		(105.1 overs, 292 mins)	229

ENGLAND	O	M	R	W	w,nb		O	M	R	W	w,nb		FALL OF WICKETS				
Rhodes	10	5	15	0	-,-	(3)	37.4	7	102	4	-,-			AUST	ENG	AUST	ENG
Barnes	22.4	6	60	7	-,-	(1)	27	6	78	1	-,-	Wkt	1st	1st	2nd	2nd
Crawford	18	4	52	3	-,-	(2)	36	10	141	5	-,-	1st	10	1	25	21
Braund							20	3	64	0	-,-	2nd	46	135	52	26
Hobbs							7	3	13	0	-,-	3rd	46	168	166	30
												4th	64	189	192	51
AUSTRALIA	O	M	R	W	w,nb		O	M	R	W	w,nb	5th	73	197	300	57
Noble	28	9	62	1	-,-		24	6	56	2	-,-	6th	94	245	342	87
Saunders	35	5	114	3	-,-		35.1	9	82	5	-,-	7th	124	264	373	123
O'Connor	6	0	23	0	-,-	(5)	13	3	29	0	-,-	8th	129	271	387	176
Macartney	15.1	3	44	3	-,-	(3)	15	5	24	2	-,-	9th	137	271	422	198
Armstrong	12	2	29	1	-,-	(4)	18	7	27	1	-,-	10th	137	281	422	229

VICTORIA v TASMANIA

Played at Melbourne Cricket Ground on February 28, 29, March 2, 3, 1908. (Timeless match)
Toss : Victoria.   Result : VICTORIA WON BY 158 RUNS.
Debuts: Victoria - W.L.Kelly, J.H.Kyle (both f/c). Tasmania - T.D.Carroll, C.P.Payne (both f/c).
12th Men: H.H.Bowden (Vic) and G.K.B.Bailey (Tas).
Umpires: E.Barrass and C.E.Over.
Attendances: No figures published; descriptions "very small", "few".   Total: About 1500.   Receipts: £56.
Close of Play: 1st day Vic 337 all out; 2nd day Tas 6/271 (Dodds 65, Payne 7); 3rd day Vic (2) 7/327 (Kelly 22, Collins 4).

This match was given scant coverage in the Press due to the concentration of interest on the Fifth Test in Sydney; consequently some important details, including many falls of wickets, were unreported. W.W.Armstrong, V.S.Ransford and J.V.Saunders, who all played in the Test, were not considered by the Victorian selectors although Ransford returned from Sydney in time to field on the second day when Carkeek (wicket-keeping) injured a finger, McAlister and later Kyle deputising with the gloves. Horan's 165, his sole first-class century, occupied 185 minutes (1 six and 20 fours) and included 3 chances. Laver (86 in 150 minutes, 8 fours) and Carroll (81 in 70 minutes, 11 fours) were Victoria's other major run-getters. Harrison topscored in each Tasmanian innings with a career-best 97 (198 minutes, 5 fours) and 52 (95 minutes, 7 fours) while Dodds (81 in 130 minutes, 11 fours) also hit his best score at first-class level. T.S.Warne (ill) and L.P.Vernon (business) were unavailable for Victoria in addition to the Test representatives, while Kelly (originally 12th man) was a replacement for J.H.Stuckey (business) in the side selected for the match. *The Age* and *The Australasian* incorrectly give Vic (1) Horan c Harrison. Sources: *Cricket, VCA Report, The Age, The Argus, The Herald, The Australasian, The Leader.*

VICTORIA

J.F.Horan	c Hawson b Eady	165	c Hawson b Windsor		2
*P.A.McAlister	b Eady	12	b Hawson		73
C.McKenzie	c Tabart b Eady	1	lbw b Windsor		56
E.V.Carroll	c Windsor b Eady	9	c Payne b Windsor		81
F.T.Delves	st Dodds b Chancellor	26	run out		52
L.P.Smith	c & b Chancellor	5	b Windsor	(7)	2
F.J.Laver	c Burn b Windsor	86	c Paton b Hawson	(6)	27
†W.Carkeek	st Dodds b Windsor	6	not out	(11)	0
W.L.Kelly	st Dodds b Windsor	5	c Dodds b Windsor	(8)	30
F.B.Collins	c Hawson b Windsor	15	b Windsor	(9)	25
J.H.Kyle	not out	4	c Burn b Eady	(10)	1
Extras	(lb3)	3	(b1, lb7)		8
Total	(98.2 overs, 277 mins)	337	(93.3 overs, in about 270 mins)		357

TASMANIA

T.A.Tabart	c Kyle b Collins	1	b Kyle		30
R.J.Hawson	c Carkeek b Kyle	4	c Kyle b Carroll		14
E.W.Harrison	c sub (V.S.Ransford) b Collins	97	c Delves b Kelly		52
*E.J.K.Burn	c Smith b Laver	27	c & b Kyle		3
E.A.C.Windsor	c Kyle b Smith	58	c Laver b Collins		12
C.J.Eady	b Kyle	10	c McAlister b Kyle		18
†N.Dodds	b Laver	81	c Collins b Kyle		27
C.P.Payne	c & b Laver	7	not out	(11)	15
T.D.Carroll	run out (Collins/Laver)	3	b Laver		14
F.E.Chancellor	c Smith b Laver	1	c Laver b Kyle		29
G.D.Paton	not out	7	c sub (H.H.Bowden) b Kyle	(8)	4
Extras	(lb5, w1)	6	(b13, lb3)		16
Total	(108.1 overs, in about 315 mins)	302	(74.0 overs, in about 210 mins)		234

TASMANIA	O	M	R	W	w,nb		O	M	R	W	w,nb
Eady	29	4	81	4	-,-		28	12	49	1	-,-
Windsor	25.2	3	71	4	-,-		39.3	6	173	6	-,-
Paton	15	1	57	0	-,-		6	1	35	0	-,-
Hawson	11	1	41	0	-,-	(5)	11	2	42	2	-,-
Chancellor	11	1	51	2	-,-	(4)	6	1	42	0	-,-
Tabart	3	0	20	0	-,-						
Carroll	4	1	13	0	-,-	(6)	3	1	8	0	-,-

VICTORIA	O	M	R	W	w,nb		O	M	R	W	w,nb
Collins	30	7	70	2	-,-	(4)	13	2	49	1	-,-
Kyle	22	2	83	2	-,-		29	11	51	6	-,-
Laver	31.1	11	66	4	-,-	(1)	12	1	52	1	-,-
Kelly	13	5	33	0	1,-	(5)	8	1	25	1	-,-
Smith	8	0	35	1	-,-						
McAlister	4	1	9	0	-,-						
Carroll						(3)	12	1	41	1	-,-

FALL OF WICKETS				
Wkt	VIC 1st	TAS 1st	VIC 2nd	TAS 2nd
1st	44	5	4	37
2nd	52	5	107	59
3rd	64	63		75
4th	147	152		114
5th	161	165		
6th	258	254		
7th		273		
8th		280		
9th		283		193
10th	337	302	357	234

SOUTH AUSTRALIA v M.C.C.

Played at Adelaide Oval on March 2, 3, 4, 1908. (Three-day match)
Toss : M.C.C.   Result : MATCH DRAWN.
Debuts: Nil.
12th Men: A.W.Wright (SA) and E.G.Hayes (MCC).
Umpires: P.Argall and G.A.Watson.
Attendances: 1300, 1000, 1000.   Total: About 3300.   Receipts: No figures published.
Close of Play: 1st day MCC 7/261 (Rhodes 18, Crawford 0); 2nd day SA 4/244 (Dolling 48, Claxton 19).

Originally scheduled as a four-day match to start on February 29th, play began two days late because of the duration of the Fifth Test in Sydney and the prohibition on play on Sunday, March 1st. The selection of Hewer in the South Australian side at the expense of A.W.Wright was considered a surprise. Gunn changed his bat five times during the first 50 of his 102 (191 minutes, 5 fours) on a sultry opening day. Fane (59 in 124 minutes, 5 fours), Rhodes (78 not out in 130 minutes, 6 fours) and Crawford (54 in 55 minutes, 1 six and 6 fours) hit half-centuries. South Australia took a first innings lead through consistent batting, Dolling (140 in 190 minutes, 15 fours, 2 chances) and Mayne (74 in 118 minutes, 6 fours) headed the scoring. Hardstaff (63 in 103 minutes, 8 fours) enlivened the final session of a match destined to be a draw. Hot and oppressive conditions persisted on all three days. Sources: *Wisden, C.B.O'Reilly, The Australasian, Adelaide Advertiser, South Australian Register.*

M.C.C.

J.B.Hobbs	b O'Connor	7	(4) c O'Connor b C.Hill	12
F.L.Fane	c Claxton b Hewer	59		
G.Gunn	c Chamberlain b L.R.Hill	102	(5) not out	5
K.L.Hutchings	c Gehrs b Hewer	9	(1) c Dolling b O'Connor	13
J.Hardstaff, sr	b Hewer	43	(2) c Jennings b Mayne	63
L.C.Braund	c Gehrs b Hewer	8		
W.Rhodes	not out	78	(3) c C.Hill b Claxton	39
†R.A.Young	c & b Hewer	4		
J.N.Crawford	b O'Connor	54		
*A.O.Jones	c O'Connor b Chamberlain	18		
C.Blythe	b O'Connor	9		
Extras	(b6, w2, nb5)	13	(b2)	2
Total	(132.3 overs, 350 mins)	404	(44.0 overs, 115 mins) (4 wkts)	134

SOUTH AUSTRALIA

R.E.Mayne	st Young b Rhodes	74
†C.B.Jennings	c Young b Blythe	13
D.R.A.Gehrs	c Hobbs b Braund	34
J.H.Pellew	c Gunn b Hobbs	41
C.E.Dolling	c Young b Braund	140
N.Claxton	c & b Braund	45
L.R.Hill	b Braund	7
*C.Hill	st Young b Braund	33
W.L.Chamberlain	st Young b Braund	8
W.A.Hewer	b Crawford	9
J.D.A.O'Connor	not out	12
Extras	(b22, lb4, w2, nb1)	29
Total	(122.0 overs, 330 mins)	445

SOUTH AUSTRALIA	O	M	R	W	w,nb	O	M	R	W	w,nb
O'Connor	39.3	14	95	3	2,-	8	2	20	1	-,-
L.R.Hill	28	8	62	1	-,5	3	0	22	0	-,-
Hewer	34	1	149	5	-,-	7	1	18	0	-,-
Claxton	17	0	56	0	-,-	6	1	21	1	-,-
Chamberlain	7	2	15	1	-,-	6	2	14	0	-,-
Gehrs	7	4	14	0	-,-	5	2	12	0	-,-
C.Hill						2	0	10	1	-,-
Dolling						2	1	3	0	-,-
Mayne						5	3	12	1	-,-

M.C.C.	O	M	R	W	w,nb
Crawford	32	6	101	1	-,-
Blythe	32	7	81	1	-,1
Braund	37	3	149	6	-,-
Rhodes	10	2	33	1	-,-
Hobbs	5	0	36	1	2,-
Hutchings	6	1	16	0	-,-

FALL OF WICKETS

	MCC	SA	MCC
Wkt	1st	1st	2nd
1st	9	30	13
2nd	128	91	113
3rd	142	154	121
4th	217	196	134
5th	231	306	-
6th	248	338	-
7th	261	402	-
8th	356	410	-
9th	380	423	-
10th	404	445	-

WESTERN AUSTRALIA v M.C.C.

Played at W.A.C.A. Ground, Perth on March 13, 14, 16, 1908. (Three-day match)
Toss : Western Australia.   Result : MATCH DRAWN.
Debuts: Western Australia - G.B.Moysey (f/c).
12th Men: No reserves named for either team.
Umpires: J.C.Brickhill and J.F.Dwyer.
Attendances: 2000, 5000, 500.   Total: About 7500.   Receipts: £395.
Close of Play: 1st day WA 256 all out; 2nd day MCC 7/362 (Gunn 122, Braund 5).

The tour itinerary intended that the game start on March 12, but it was delayed until the following day at the request of the WA Cricket Association for financial reasons. The change required that stumps be drawn at 4pm on the last day to allow the visitors to embark for home. Injuries to Humphries and Young meant that MCC were without a regular wicket-keeper for the match: Jones, Hardstaff and Hayes took the gloves for one session each in the first innings, while Braund and Hardstaff shared the position in the second innings. Gunn gave two chances when 42 during his innings which took 150 minutes with 3 sixes and 15 fours. Barnes batted for 125 minutes, hitting 2 sixes and 8 fours in what was to be the highest score of his career. Rowe scored the first century by a WA batsman against a touring team, batting for 178 minutes with 1 five and 11 fours. Howard was run out in unusual circumstances: Rowe hit Barnes to Hutchings in the deep, whose throw passed the stumps and went to the boundary flags, and while Howard strolled down the pitch the ball was returned to Barnes, who whipped off the bails. Sources: *Wisden, Cricket, The West Australian, Daily News.*

WESTERN AUSTRALIA

*T.H.Hogue	b Crawford	33	(8)	b Hayes	10
S.H.D.Rowe	b Crawford	14	(1)	c Jones b Rhodes	105
G.B.Moysey	b Crawford	8	(6)	c Jones b Rhodes	5
H.C.Howard	c Jones b Crawford	69	(2)	run out (Hutchings/ ? /Barnes)	49
O.H.Kelly	c Hutchings b Rhodes	22	(9)	not out	13
L.Gouly	b Rhodes	2	(7)	not out	30
A.H.Christian	c Gunn b Braund	19	(3)	b Crawford	3
T.H.Coyne	c Hardstaff b Braund	4			
R.M.Evans	st Hayes b Braund	13			
W.W.Hogue	not out	24	(4)	c Jones b Barnes	4
†H.A.Evers	c Jones b Braund	19	(5)	c & b Hayes	13
Extras	(b26, lb2, w1)	29		(b31, lb2)	33
Total	(91.1 overs, 251 mins)	256		(76.0 overs, 215 mins) (7 wkts)	265

M.C.C.

J.B.Hobbs	b Christian	40
F.L.Fane	b Christian	22
J.Hardstaff, sr	lbw b Coyne	4
K.L.Hutchings	c Evans b Coyne	46
G.Gunn	not out	122
W.Rhodes	b Christian	4
S.F.Barnes	c Evans b T.H.Hogue	93
J.N.Crawford	c Christian b T.H.Hogue	9
L.C.Braund	not out	5
*A.O.Jones	) did not bat	
E.G.Hayes	)	
Extras	(b9, lb4, w4)	17
Total	(97.0 overs, 265 mins) (7 wkts dec)	362

M.C.C.	O	M	R	W	w,nb		O	M	R	W	w,nb
Braund	25.1	3	84	4	-,-	(6)	6	0	27	0	-,-
Crawford	40	14	85	4	-,-		19	5	52	1	-,-
Rhodes	23	8	56	2	1,-		15	1	39	2	-,-
Gunn	3	1	2	0	-,-	(5)	5	1	25	0	-,-
Hutchings						(4)	6	0	23	0	-,-
Barnes						(1)	18	6	31	1	-,-
Hayes							7	1	35	2	-,-

WESTERN AUSTRALIA	O	M	R	W	w,nb
Evans	12	2	35	0	4,-
Christian	32	4	130	3	-,-
Coyne	22	6	68	2	-,-
T.H.Hogue	14	1	48	2	-,-
W.W.Hogue	14	1	41	0	-,-
Howard	3	0	23	0	-,-

	FALL OF WICKETS		
	WA	MCC	WA
Wkt	1st	1st	2nd
1st	38	58	175
2nd	50	69	179
3rd	73	123	186
4th	116	123	196
5th	119	128	206
6th	156	331	226
7th	170	354	250
8th	195	-	-
9th	211	-	-
10th	256	-	-

AUSTRALIAN XI v THE REST

Played at Sydney Cricket Ground on March 20, 21, 23, 24, 1908. (Timeless match)
Toss : The Rest.   Result : AUSTRALIAN XI WON BY AN INNINGS AND 3 RUNS.
Debuts: Nil.
12th Men: F.S.Middleton (both teams).
Umpires: A.C.Jones and J.Laing.
Attendances: 1600, 7000, 2000, 1000.   Total: About 11,600.   Receipts: £529.
Close of Play: 1st day Rest 9/267 (Laver 54, Gorry 0); 2nd day Aust 8/412 (Armstrong 37, Windsor 31); 3rd day Rest (2) 4/175
    (Dolling 13, Gorry 0).

The match was arranged as a testimonial benefit for M.A.Noble and, although poorly attended, raised £2000 in his favour. Windsor replaced J.D.A.O'Connor (unavailable) in the Australian side. F.B.Johnson and P.A.McAlister (business) made themselves unavailable for The Rest and were replaced by Barnes and Laver. The Rest batted steadily on the opening day with most of the leading batsmen getting a start but only Warne (53 in 140 minutes, 6 fours) and Laver (61 not out in 100 minutes, 6 fours) reaching the half-century. Ransford (63 in 85 minutes, 9 fours) and Hill (52 in 44 minutes, 8 fours) established the momentum of the Australian innings with "some beautiful cricket" (*SMH*). Two late-order partnerships, 192 for the seventh wicket between Noble (87 in 130 minutes, 10 fours) and Gregory (106 in 106 minutes, 17 fours), and 225 for the ninth wicket between Armstrong (146 not out in 140 minutes, 1 six and 17 fours) and Windsor (78 in 135 minutes, 10 fours), put the Australians in a winning position. Half-centuries from Bardsley (67 in 110 minutes, 8 fours) and Barnes (58 not out in 66 minutes) were unable to prevent an innings defeat for The Rest. *Wisden* incorrectly gives Rest (1) McKenzie c Carter.
Sources: *Wisden, NSWCA Report, Sydney Referee, Sydney Morning Herald, Town & Country Journal, Sydney Mail.*

THE REST

C.McKenzie	st Carter b Noble	33		b Windsor		30
T.S.Warne	c Armstrong b Noble	53		b Saunders		21
W.Bardsley	c Trumper b Armstrong	34		b Saunders		67
R.E.Mayne	b Macartney	32		c Carter b Noble		36
C.E.Dolling	b Macartney	30		c Ransford b Saunders		16
A.J.Y.Hopkins	b Macartney	0	(8)	b Macartney		18
*F.J.Laver	not out	61		run out		0
J.C.Barnes	c Ransford b Saunders	18	(9)	not out		58
L.A.Minnett	b Noble	1	(10)	c Ransford b Macartney		5
F.B.Collins	c Armstrong b Saunders	6	(11)	c Gregory b Trumper		16
†C.R.Gorry	c Ransford b Saunders	15	(6)	c Trumper b Saunders		0
Extras	(b1, lb4, w1)	6		(b6, lb4)		10
Total	(109.1 overs, 315 mins)	289		(88.2 overs, 239 mins)		277

AUSTRALIAN XI

E.F.Waddy	b Warne	12
C.G.Macartney	st Gorry b Warne	5
V.S.Ransford	c & b Laver	63
†H.Carter	lbw b Warne	14
C.Hill	b Collins	52
*M.A.Noble	c Hopkins b McKenzie	87
V.T.Trumper	c Collins b Laver	0
S.E.Gregory	c & b Barnes	106
W.W.Armstrong	not out	146
E.A.C.Windsor	b Hopkins	78
J.V.Saunders	run out	0
Extras	(b3, w2, nb1)	6
Total	(121.0 overs, 362 mins)	569

AUSTRALIAN XI	O	M	R	W	w,nb		O	M	R	W	w,nb		FALL OF WICKETS			
Windsor	27	4	102	0	1,-	(2)	22	1	91	1	-,-			REST	AUST	REST
Saunders	19.1	2	45	3	-,-	(1)	22	6	58	4	-,-	Wkt	1st	1st	2nd
Macartney	24	3	65	3	-,-		13	2	33	2	-,-	1st	62	17	56
Noble	23	7	56	3	-,-		9	1	29	1	-,-	2nd	121	22	56
Armstrong	16	6	15	1	-,-		11	5	15	0	-,-	3rd	125	54	134
Hill							3	1	8	0	-,-	4th	176	130	175
Gregory							3	2	1	0	-,-	5th	176	152	178
Waddy							3	0	23	0	-,-	6th	197	152	183
Trumper							2.2	0	9	1	-,-	7th	244	344	183
												8th	250	344	224
THE REST	O	M	R	W	w,nb							9th	267	569	234
Minnett	22	5	111	0	-,-							10th	289	569	277
Warne	25	0	143	3	-,-										
Collins	17	1	82	1	-,1										
Laver	23	4	82	2	1,-										
Barnes	12	1	49	1	-,-										
Hopkins	11	0	45	1	-,-										
McKenzie	11	3	51	1	1,-										

QUEENSLAND v NEW SOUTH WALES

Played at Brisbane Cricket Ground (Woolloongabba) on April 18, 20, 21, 22, 1908. (Timeless match)
Toss : Queensland.   Result : QUEENSLAND WON BY 171 RUNS.
Debuts: New South Wales - O.H.Dean, T.J.Hartigan, D.Taylor, C.Wordsworth (all f/c).
12th Men: G.T.White (Qld) and C.Kelleway (NSW).
Umpires: A.L.Cossart and J.W.Roberts.
Attendances: 3000, other days reported as "small".   Receipts: No figures published.
Close of Play: 1st day NSW 2/65 (Carter 35, Macartney 4); 2nd day Qld (2) 4/120 (Hayes 10, Hutcheon 0); 3rd day NSW (2) 2/121
   (Waddy 70, Bardsley 7).

Queensland's first victory in any class of cricket at 'the Gabba'. T.J.Hartigan, the New South Wales manager and brother of the Queensland captain, came into the team to replace Kelleway who injured a hand at practice. Hayes survived a chance at 51 to make 98 in 122 minutes with 18 fours. In the second innings Simpson received a knock while batting late on the second day; he retired hurt at 4/120 and resumed next morning at 5/128. Evans, batting at number nine, scored 103 not out in 102 minutes with 2 sixes and 13 fours, reaching his century with a six. Waddy top scored for New South Wales with 86 in 147 minutes, including 8 fours. R.J.Hartigan and Hayes were both off the field on the last day. White and Carter, the New South Wales captain, substituted. *Cricket* gives incorrect match dates. *NSWCA Report* incorrectly gives NSW (2) extras 19 (b10, lb9), total 234. Sources: *Cricket, NSWCA Report, Sydney Referee, Brisbane Courier, Queensland Times, The Queenslander.*

QUEENSLAND

*R.J.Hartigan	c Minnett b Barnes	58		b Macartney	10
G.A.L.Brown	b Barnes	4		c Blaxland b Minnett	15
J.S.Redgrave	run out (Waddy/Macartney)	14		b Macartney	44
C.E.Simpson	c Minnett b Wordsworth	10	(6)	run out	24
J.Thomson	c Hartigan b Wordsworth	21	(4)	c Bardsley b Minnett	21
W.B.Hayes	run out (/Carter)	98	(5)	b Minnett	36
E.R.Crouch	lbw b Wordsworth	0	(8)	c Carter b Wordsworth	16
J.S.Hutcheon	c Carter b Minnett	29	(7)	c Carter b Blaxland	8
G.F.Martin	c Blaxland b Minnett	0	(10)	c Waddy b Barnes	40
†W.T.Evans	b Blaxland	4	(9)	not out	103
J.W.McLaren	not out	10		run out	6
Extras	(b6, lb4)	10		(b13, lb5)	18
Total	(61.3 overs, 191 mins)	258		(86.1 overs, 294 mins)	341

NEW SOUTH WALES

*†H.Carter	c Martin b McLaren	69		c Hartigan b McLaren	16
E.L.Waddy	b McLaren	13		b Simpson	86
M.H.Blaxland	b McLaren	8	(5)	c Brown b Redgrave	7
C.G.Macartney	c Hayes b McLaren	4	(3)	lbw b Redgrave	24
W.Bardsley	c Brown b Hayes	24	(4)	c Evans b Redgrave	30
J.C.Barnes	c Brown b Redgrave	26		lbw b Simpson	0
D.Taylor	c Hartigan b Simpson	11		b Simpson	0
O.H.Dean	run out (Hutcheon/Evans)	0		b Simpson	23
C.Wordsworth	not out	12		b Simpson	4
L.A.Minnett	c Brown b McLaren	9		c Hutcheon b Redgrave	25
T.J.Hartigan	lbw b Simpson	4		not out	0
Extras	(b9, lb6)	15		(b10, lb7, nb1)	18
Total	(41.5 overs, 144 mins)	195		(69.5 overs, 217 mins)	233

NEW SOUTH WALES	O	M	R	W	w,nb		O	M	R	W	w,nb					
Minnett	18	2	68	2	-,-	(2)	26	8	61	3	-,-					
Barnes	17.3	1	99	2	-,-	(4)	13.1	0	102	1	-,-					
Macartney	7	1	21	0	-,-	(1)	26	10	67	2	-,-					
Wordsworth	13	4	24	3	-,-	(3)	8	1	48	1	-,-					
Hartigan	1	0	4	0	-,-	(6)	2	1	11	0	-,-					
Blaxland	5	0	32	1	-,-	(5)	11	2	34	1	-,-					

												FALL OF WICKETS			
											Wkt	QLD 1st	NSW 1st	QLD 2nd	QLD 2nd
											1st	30	27	29	44
											2nd	63	41	31	91
											3rd	83	67	96	165
											4th	93	126	98	173
											5th	125	128	128	176

QUEENSLAND	O	M	R	W	w,nb		O	M	R	W	w,nb					
McLaren	18	4	83	5	-,-		17	0	70	1	-,-	6th	125	165	165	176
Redgrave	12	1	40	1	-,-		29.5	0	73	4	-,1	7th	213	166	177	177
Hayes	5	1	31	1	-,-		5	1	20	0	-,-	8th	213	175	204	188
Thomson	1	0	10	0	-,-	(5)	1	0	2	0	-,-	9th	220	186	288	229
Simpson	5.5	0	16	2	-,-	(4)	17	3	50	5	-,-	10th	258	195	341	233

1908-09 SEASON (15 MATCHES)

The return to a season of purely domestic cricket led to a sharp drop in the number of first-class matches played. But even so, 15 were staged, highlighting the gradual increase in the cricket program over the past decade with the expansion to the minor States.

New South Wales regained the Sheffield Shield from Victoria. The result of the competition again hinged on the outcome of New South Wales's last match against Victoria at Sydney, where a loss would have seen all three States tied on two wins apiece and percentages deciding the Shield winner. The match ran into a sixth day of play and a record 1911 runs were aggregated before New South Wales emerged victorious. South Australia had blown their chance to win the Shield outright a fortnight earlier in their match at Sydney, where they were defeated by nine wickets.

The strong New South Wales batting failed only once, against Victoria at Melbourne in a match which began on a rain-affected wicket. Bardsley, Noble, Hopkins, Macartney and Syd Gregory formed a formidable combination and were the chief contributors to the 2457 runs compiled at an average of 44.67 during the campaign. Wickets were spread evenly between the bowlers.

Ransford, Armstrong and McAlister batted well to lead the Victorian aggregates, Ransford becoming the first batsman to record a century in each innings for the State. Armstrong completed a fine allround season and shared the bowling honours with Hazlitt and Vernon. South Australia were best served by Mayne, Gehrs and Clem Hill (batting) and O'Connor and Whitty (bowling).

New South Wales continued to use their matches against Queensland as trials for their promising players, despite intermittent QCA appeals for New South Wales to field more representative teams. This season both States won their matches away from home.

Victoria honoured their agreement of the previous year with Tasmania by playing matches at both Launceston and Hobart during their visit. In common with New South Wales, the VCA used these encounters to try out young players. Victoria won both games comfortably.

The VCA accepted an invitation to send a team to Western Australia for two matches in early March. However, they cancelled the trip when a number of Victorian players found it impossible to arrange leave. The resulting team would have been a weak one. South Australia compensated by visiting the West a month later for three representative matches, all of which were drawn.

Clem Hill (South Australia), Frank Iredale (New South Wales) and Peter McAlister (Victoria) were appointed to select the 13th Australian team to tour England in 1909. Hill announced immediately that he would not be available as a player. The names of five certainties were announced in January - Noble, Trumper, Armstrong, Ransford and Hartigan - and they were soon followed by O'Connor, Carter, Cotter and Macartney. Two trial matches between teams styled 'Australia' and 'The Rest' were staged in February to help the selectors determine the remaining five team members. Bardsley and Whitty (a surprise to most critics) were added after these trials, while McAlister, Carkeek and Gregory formed the last batch of names announced. It was reported that Hill had wanted Dodds (or Gorry) as the reserve keeper instead of Carkeek, and preferred Gehrs to McAlister, but had been outvoted. Hopkins was added as a 15th team member after approval had been granted from the Board of Control to include another player.

Leading Aggregates

Batsmen	M	I	NO	Runs	HS	Ave.	Bowlers	Runs	Wkts	Ave.
V.S.Ransford (V)	6	10	2	825	182	103.12	J.D.A.O'Connor (SA)	920	40	23.00
W.Bardsley (NSW)	6	9	0	748	264	83.11	W.W.Armstrong (V)	451	26	17.34
D.R.A.Gehrs (SA)	9	16	0	720	113	45.00	A.H.Christian (WA)	432	25	17.28
M.A.Noble (V)	6	9	1	714	213	89.25	C.Kelleway (NSW)	599	20	29.95
S.E.Gregory (NSW)	6	9	1	547	179	68.37	A.Cotter (NSW)	651	19	34.26
R.E.Mayne (SA)	6	12	1	457	142	41.54				
A.J.Y.Hopkins (NSW)	5	9	1	410	218	51.25				

SHEFFIELD SHIELD TABLE

	P	W	L	D	Pts	Quotient	Runs Scored	Wkts Lost	Runs Conceded	Wkts Taken
NEW SOUTH WALES	4	3	1	-	2	1.538	2457	55	1974	68
SOUTH AUSTRALIA	4	2	2	-	0	0.621	1759	76	2272	61
VICTORIA	4	1	3	-	-2	1.041	2417	70	2387	72
TOTAL	6	6	6	-	0	1.000	6633	201	6633	201

SOUTH AUSTRALIA v VICTORIA (Shield Match 1)

Played at Adelaide Oval on November 7, 9, 10, 11, 12, 1908. (Timeless match)
Toss : Victoria.   Result : SOUTH AUSTRALIA WON BY TWO WICKETS.
Debuts: South Australia - W.J.Whitty, J.R.H.Woodford (both SA only).
12th Men: A.W.Jenkins (SA) and T.I.B.Horan (Vic).
Umpires: P.Argall and F.J.C.Thomas.
Attendances: 1000, 2000, 500, 200, 200.   Total: About 3900.   Receipts: No figures published.
Close of Play: 1st day SA 1/37 (Mayne 11, Claxton 23); 2nd day SA 6/394 (C.Hill 134, Chamberlain 10); 3rd day Vic (2) 4/145
    (Ransford 48, Vernon 3); 4th day SA (2) 2/34 (Mayne 15).

C.E.Dolling (university exams) was unavailable for South Australia and Hastings replaced W.Carkeek (ill) in the Victorian team. The Victorian batsmen, apart from Carroll (80 in 137 minutes, 6 fours) and Vernon (57 in 94 minutes, 7 fours), failed to take advantage of the "splendid wicket" (*Register*) after winning the toss. O'Connor "mixed his pace and length admirably" (*Register*) and was never mastered. Hewer was out in the first over of the South Australian reply but Clem Hill (141 in 225 minutes, 13 fours), Claxton (80 in 160 minutes, 4 fours), Gehrs (70 in 90 minutes, 9 fours) and Mayne (51 in 135 minutes, 5 fours) recovered the initiative and built a substantial lead. Ransford (131 in 315 minutes, 10 fours), Warne (58 in 128 minutes, 6 fours) and Vernon (67 in 123 minutes, 8 fours) led a spirited Victorian reply which set a target of 135 for the home side. Mayne (77 not out in 178 minutes, 9 fours) steered them to victory despite the regular loss of wickets on a wicket that had "stood the strain of 1,261 runs splendidly" (*Register*). Whitty and Woodford had previously represented New South Wales and Victoria respectively. Sources: *Wisden, C.B.O'Reilly, VCA Report, The Australasian, Adelaide Advertiser, South Australian Register.*

VICTORIA

T.S.Warne	c C.Hill b O'Connor	17		b O'Connor	58
C.McKenzie	b O'Connor	21		c sub (A.W.Jenkins) b Hewer	24
V.S.Ransford	c & b O'Connor	2		lbw b Hewer	131
*P.A.McAlister	b L.R.Hill	4	(7)	b O'Connor	30
W.W.Armstrong	c Woodford b O'Connor	13		c & b Hewer	1
E.V.Carroll	b O'Connor	80	(4)	c L.R.Hill b Hewer	0
F.J.Laver	b L.R.Hill	5	(8)	c Gehrs b O'Connor	47
L.P.Vernon	c Gehrs b O'Connor	57	(6)	st Woodford b O'Connor	67
†T.J.Hastings	lbw b L.R.Hill	1		b Whitty	11
F.B.Collins	c Gehrs b O'Connor	8		not out	6
J.V.Saunders	not out	3		run out	4
Extras	(b3, lb1, nb4)	8		(b28, lb3, nb1)	32
Total	(73.0 overs, 216 mins)	219		(139.4 overs, 398 mins)	411

SOUTH AUSTRALIA

R.E.Mayne	b Laver	51		not out	77
W.A.Hewer	b Vernon	0	(10)	not out	5
N.Claxton	c Armstrong b Laver	80	(2)	lbw b Saunders	7
*C.Hill	c McKenzie b Laver	141	(5)	lbw b Armstrong	13
J.H.Pellew	c Hastings b Laver	20	(3)	run out (Ransford/Hastings)	9
L.R.Hill	b McKenzie	18	(7)	c & b Armstrong	2
D.R.A.Gehrs	c Armstrong b Saunders	70	(6)	run out (Hastings/Armstrong)	15
W.L.Chamberlain	b Laver	25	(9)	b Laver	1
J.D.A.O'Connor	not out	40	(8)	b Armstrong	1
†J.R.H.Woodford	b Laver	7	(4)	lbw b Saunders	0
W.J.Whitty	lbw b Warne	23			
Extras	(b12, lb4, nb5)	21		(b4, nb1)	5
Total	(151.2 overs, 441 mins)	496		(70.0 overs, 178 mins) (8 wkts)	135

SOUTH AUSTRALIA	O	M	R	W	w,nb		O	M	R	W	w,nb		FALL OF WICKETS			
														VIC	SA	VIC	SA
O'Connor	29	6	92	7	-,2	(2)	55	12	150	4	-,-	Wkt	1st	1st	2nd	2nd
L.R.Hill	22	7	41	3	-,2	(1)	16	2	52	0	-,1	1st	25	3	46	14
Whitty	10	2	36	0	-,-	(4)	35.4	11	75	1	-,-	2nd	28	118	116	33
Claxton	5	1	19	0	-,-							3rd	40	149	127	34
Hewer	7	0	23	0	-,-	(3)	31	3	94	4	-,-	4th	59	186	133	71
Gehrs						(5)	2	0	8	0	-,-	5th	60	230	280	101
												6th	66	368	334	106
VICTORIA	O	M	R	W	w,nb		O	M	R	W	w,nb	7th	199	414	346	116
Vernon	26	4	75	1	-,1							8th	200	429	394	123
Saunders	30	7	113	1	-,2		16	2	42	2	-,1	9th	209	453	398	-
Collins	12	1	45	0	-,2							10th	219	496	411	-
Armstrong	19	7	31	0	-,-	(3)	21	10	26	3	-,-					
Laver	46	10	128	6	-,-	(1)	33	10	62	1	-,-					
McKenzie	7	0	34	1	-,-											
Warne	11.2	1	49	1	-,-											

QUEENSLAND v NEW SOUTH WALES

Played at Brisbane Cricket Ground (Woolloongabba) on December 12, 14, 15, 16, 1908. (Timeless match)
Toss : Queensland.   Result : NEW SOUTH WALES WON BY SEVEN WICKETS
Debuts: Queensland - W.I.Sewart (f/c). New South Wales - J.E.Hodgkinson, A.J.Nicholls, D.C.Reid, J.D.Scott (all f/c).
12th Men: W.H.Sullivan (Qld) and A.W.Farnsworth (NSW).
Umpires: T.Muir and J.W.Roberts.
Attendances: 3000, no other days given.   Total & Receipts: No figures published.
Close of Play: 1st day NSW 1/86 (White 20, Reid 21); 2nd day Qld (2) 1/20 (Thomson 12, Brown 1); 3rd day NSW (2) 3/15 (Bubb 10).
H.Whiddon withdrew from the New South Wales side and was replaced by Deane. A.Diamond, also named to play in the match, was withdrawn by the selectors to replace A.J.Bowden (unavailable) in the Sheffield Shield match against South Australia in Adelaide. Goddard took his place and Farnsworth was made 12th man. White (147 in 250 minutes, 15 fours), Goddard (87 not out in 111 minutes, 10 fours) and Nicholls (58 in 81 minutes, 7 fours) were chiefly responsible for New South Wales establishing a match-winning lead. A new Queensland eighth-wicket record of 101 was established in the second innings between Hutcheon (64 in 74 minutes, 2 sixes and 5 fours) and Crouch (67 in 89 minutes, 7 fours). *Cricket* and *NSWCA Report* incorrectly give Qld (2) Hutcheon b Johnson. Sources: *Cricket, NSWCA Report, Sydney Morning Herald, Brisbane Courier, Queensland Times, The Queenslander.*

QUEENSLAND

R.J.Hartigan	b Johnson	37	(4)	b Kelleway	29
W.B.Hayes	c Kelleway b Johnson	0	(6)	b Johnson	14
C.E.Simpson	run out (Goddard/Gorry)	34	(5)	b Kelleway	20
*J.S.Redgrave	b Johnson	0	(7)	b Kelleway	14
G.A.L.Brown	b Kelleway	4	(3)	c Gorry b Kelleway	40
J.Thomson	run out (Gorry)	21	(1)	c Hodgkinson b Deane	36
J.S.Hutcheon	c Gorry b Johnson	1	(8)	c & b Johnson	64
E.R.Crouch	b Kelleway	11	(9)	b Deane	67
W.I.Sewart	run out (/Gorry)	22	(10)	run out	2
†W.T.Evans	lbw b Johnson	5	(11)	not out	7
J.W.McLaren	not out	15	(2)	c Kelleway b Johnson	7
Extras	(b10, lb6)	16		(b9, lb1, nb1)	11
Total	(49.4 overs, 156 mins)	166		(69.0 overs, 247 mins)	311

NEW SOUTH WALES

E.R.Bubb	b Hayes	35		not out	25
A.B.S.White	lbw b Thomson	147	(5)	not out	16
D.C.Reid	b McLaren	23		b Simpson	0
*N.Y.Deane	lbw b Hayes	8			
J.E.Hodgkinson	c Redgrave b Hayes	18	(2)	b McLaren	2
A.J.Nicholls	c Sewart b Hayes	58	(4)	b Simpson	3
H.Goddard	not out	87			
C.Kelleway	c & b McLaren	2			
F.B.Johnson	c Brown b McLaren	6			
†C.R.Gorry	c Evans b Hayes	16			
J.D.Scott	c Sewart b Hayes	4			
Extras	(b19, lb2, nb2)	23		(b6)	6
Total	(93.0 overs, 305 mins)	427		(26.1 overs, 75 mins) (3 wkts)	52

NEW SOUTH WALES	O	M	R	W	w,nb	O	M	R	W	w,nb
Scott	8	2	29	0	-,-	10	1	42	0	-,1
Johnson	24	1	93	5	-,-	24	1	122	3	-,-
Kelleway	17	7	24	2	-,-	20	9	56	4	-,-
Deane	0.4	0	4	0	-,-	12	1	52	2	-,-
Goddard						3	0	28	0	-,-

QUEENSLAND	O	M	R	W	w,nb	O	M	R	W	w,nb
McLaren	33	8	120	3	-,2	13.1	6	16	1	-,-
Simpson	8	1	54	0	-,-	13	1	30	2	-,-
Hayes	27	0	125	6	-,-					
Redgrave	11	2	38	0	-,-					
Sewart	6	0	16	0	-,-					
Thomson	8	1	51	1	-,-					

FALL OF WICKETS

Wkt	QLD 1st	NSW 1st	QLD 2nd	NSW 2nd
1st	2	51	14	6
2nd	61	92	68	11
3rd	74	103	115	15
4th	75	147	120	-
5th	87	256	137	-
6th	94	348	158	-
7th	109	360	174	-
8th	129	368	275	-
9th	138	419	286	-
10th	166	427	311	-

SOUTH AUSTRALIA v NEW SOUTH WALES (Shield Match 2)

Played at Adelaide Oval on December 18, 19, 21, 1908. (Timeless match)
Toss : New South Wales.   Result : NEW SOUTH WALES WON BY AN INNINGS AND 527 RUNS.
Debuts: South Australia - A.H.Pretty (f/c); K.H.Quist (SA only). New South Wales - S.H.Emery (f/c).
12th Men: A.W.Wright (SA) and A.Diamond (NSW).
Umpires: P.Argall and G.A.Watson.
Attendances: 1000, 2000, 500.   Total: About 3500.   Receipts: No figures published.
Close of Play: 1st day NSW 1/410 (Hopkins 218, Noble 124); 2nd day SA 1/21 (Quist 7, Pellew 5).

V.T.Trumper (influenza) was unavailable and A.J.Bowden withdrew from the New South Wales squad of twelve to be replaced by Diamond. Due to business commitments, N.Claxton was replaced in the South Australian side by W.L.Chamberlain, who in turn was unable to obtain leave from work and gave way to Quist. In his first match for South Australia, Quist had now represented three States, playing for New South Wales and Western Australia previously. Hopkins, missed in slips by Pellew off the first ball of the match, batted through the first day's play to compile a career-best 218 in 278 minutes, hitting 1 six and 18 fours. With Noble (213 in 274 minutes, 22 fours) he shared a second-wicket partnership of 283 in 170 minutes after putting on 131 for the first wicket with Bardsley. Heavy rain fell overnight following the second day, softening the pitch and and leading to the landslide result. Woodford, who injured a foot while keeping wickets, used a runner (Dolling) in his first innings. O'Connor and Quist both suffered first ball dismissals. Gehrs, who became ill during the New South Wales innings, stayed at the ground until the end of the match but was unable to bat. Sources: *Wisden, C.B.O'Reilly, NSWCA Report, Adelaide Advertiser, South Australian Register.*

NEW SOUTH WALES

A.J.Y.Hopkins	c Woodford b O'Connor	218
W.Bardsley	c L.R.Hill b Whitty	56
*M.A.Noble	c C.Hill b O'Connor	213
E.F.Waddy	b Quist	64
S.E.Gregory	c Mayne b O'Connor	21
E.L.Waddy	b O'Connor	0
J.C.Barnes	c & b Pretty	44
C.G.Macartney	b Whitty	29
†H.Carter	b Pretty	15
A.Cotter	not out	24
S.H.Emery	b Pretty	5
Extras	(b6, lb11, w1, nb6)	24
Total	(171.3 overs, 510 mins)	713

SOUTH AUSTRALIA

R.E.Mayne	c Cotter b Emery	8	(5)	c Barnes b Macartney	0
K.H.Quist	st Carter b Macartney	8	(7)	b Noble	0
J.H.Pellew	c Gregory b Hopkins	11		c Cotter b Noble	37
*C.Hill	c E.L.Waddy b Hopkins	28	(6)	c Macartney b Noble	1
C.E.Dolling	lbw b Noble	0	(1)	c Bardsley b Macartney	11
L.R.Hill	run out (E.L.Waddy/Noble)	11	(4)	st Carter b Macartney	6
J.D.A.O'Connor	c Emery b Hopkins	0	(2)	c Barnes b Emery	16
†J.R.H.Woodford	not out	18		b Noble	4
A.H.Pretty	c Barnes b Macartney	1	(10)	run out	0
W.J.Whitty	b Macartney	4	(9)	not out	3
D.R.A.Gehrs	absent ill	-		absent ill	-
Extras	(b5, lb2, nb1)	8		(b9, nb2)	11
Total	(40.1 overs, 135 mins)	97		(34.4 overs, 105 mins)	89

SOUTH AUSTRALIA	O	M	R	W	w,nb
O'Connor	54	11	173	4	-,-
L.R.Hill	27	3	90	0	-,6
Whitty	29	3	142	2	-,-
Pretty	23.3	0	113	3	-,-
Gehrs	7	2	18	0	1,-
Pellew	11	0	74	0	-,-
Quist	16	1	56	1	-,-
C.Hill	2	0	11	0	-,-
Dolling	2	0	12	0	-,-

NEW SOUTH WALES	O	M	R	W	w,nb		O	M	R	W	w,nb
Cotter	5	1	7	0	-,-	(3)	6	1	15	0	-,1
Emery	5	2	12	1	-,-	(4)	2	0	6	1	-,-
Macartney	11.1	2	32	3	-,1	(2)	15	4	28	3	-,1
Hopkins	14	3	31	3	-,-	(1)	2	0	8	0	-,-
Noble	5	2	7	1	-,-		9.4	1	21	4	-,-

FALL OF WICKETS

Wkt	NSW 1st	SA 1st	SA 2nd
1st	131	11	16
2nd	414	25	47
3rd	563	44	71
4th	576	45	79
5th	581	67	80
6th	592	71	80
7th	668	71	86
8th	670	76	87
9th	703	97	89
10th	713	-	-

VICTORIA v NEW SOUTH WALES (Shield Match 3)

Played at Melbourne Cricket Ground on December 26, 28, 29, 1908. (Timeless match)
Toss : New South Wales.   Result : VICTORIA WON BY AN INNINGS AND 47 RUNS.
Debuts: Nil.
12th Men: E.L.Waddy (NSW). T.I.B.Horan and J.H.Kyle were named as Victorian emergencies.
Umpires: R.M.Crockett and W.Hannah.
Attendances: 9148, 10640, 4879.   Total: 24,667.   Receipts: £731.
Close of Play: 1st day Vic 0/29 (Warne 8, Hastings 10); 2nd day Vic 8/326 (Laver 19).

Rain delayed the start of the match until after the luncheon adjournment and the soft wicket contributed to the failure of the New South Wales batting. Ransford (94 in 147 minutes, 7 fours), McAlister (79 in 133 minutes, 6 fours) and Carroll (60 in 121 minutes, 5 fours) took advantage of the improved conditions on the second day when the "wicket and weather were all that could be desired" (*Australasian*). New South Wales collapsed unaccountably on the third day, with the wicket again playing truly, to be defeated in a single innings. *Wisden* incorrectly gives Vernon c Noble in the Victorian innings. Sources: *Wisden, VCA Report, The Age, The Argus, The Herald, The Australasian, The Leader.*

NEW SOUTH WALES

A.J.Y.Hopkins	c Warne b Vernon	5		b Laver	7
S.E.Gregory	c Laver b Saunders	44	(5)	lbw b Laver	11
*M.A.Noble	b Hazlitt	16		b Vernon	4
†H.Carter	c Ransford b Laver	7	(10)	b Vernon	1
A.Cotter	run out (McAlister/Hastings)	0	(9)	c Carroll b Saunders	8
E.F.Waddy	c McKenzie b Saunders	47	(4)	c Laver b Hazlitt	12
W.Bardsley	c Vernon b Armstrong	8	(2)	c McAlister b Hazlitt	31
C.G.Macartney	c Warne b Armstrong	22	(6)	not out	39
A.Diamond	st Hastings b Armstrong	15	(8)	lbw b Vernon	3
J.C.Barnes	not out	0	(7)	run out (Hastings)	9
S.H.Emery	c McAlister b Armstrong	4		c McAlister b Saunders	13
Extras	(b4, lb3, w1)	8		(b7, w1)	8
Total	(50.3 overs, 152 mins)	176		(47.2 overs, 141 mins)	146

VICTORIA

T.S.Warne	c Carter b Emery	27
†T.J.Hastings	lbw b Emery	13
C.McKenzie	c & b Emery	0
V.S.Ransford	c Waddy b Hopkins	94
W.W.Armstrong	b Cotter	4
*P.A.McAlister	c & b Macartney	79
E.V.Carroll	c Noble b Hopkins	60
L.P.Vernon	c Waddy b Hopkins	0
F.J.Laver	b Cotter	35
G.R.Hazlitt	not out	27
J.V.Saunders	c Carter b Hopkins	0
Extras	(b20, lb10)	30
Total	(118.4 overs, 329 mins)	369

VICTORIA	O	M	R	W	w,nb	O	M	R	W	w,nb
Vernon	6	0	17	1	1,-	14	2	50	3	-,-
Laver	11	3	31	1	-,-	15	2	35	2	-,-
Hazlitt	8	0	29	1	-,-	10	2	26	2	1,-
Saunders	14	1	50	2	-,-	8.2	2	27	2	-,-
Armstrong	11.3	1	41	4	-,-					

NEW SOUTH WALES	O	M	R	W	w,nb
Noble	18	5	45	0	-,-
Macartney	23	8	41	1	-,-
Emery	31	3	115	3	-,-
Cotter	22	1	82	2	-,-
Hopkins	24.4	8	56	4	-,-

FALL OF WICKETS

Wkt	NSW 1st	VIC 1st	NSW 2nd
1st	16	36	9
2nd	41	36	16
3rd	54	119	48
4th	54	126	67
5th	118	206	69
6th	131	268	104
7th	138	269	108
8th	165	326	123
9th	172	368	125
10th	176	369	146

VICTORIA v SOUTH AUSTRALIA (Shield Match 4)

Played at Melbourne Cricket Ground on January 1, 2, 4 (no play), 5 (no play), 6, 7, 1909. (Timeless match)
Toss : South Australia.   Result : SOUTH AUSTRALIA WON BY 15 RUNS.
Debuts: Nil.
12th Men: A.W.Jenkins (SA). T.I.B.Horan and J.H.Kyle were named as Victorian emergencies.
Umpires: R.M.Crockett and W.A.Young.
Attendances: 10000, 8000, no play, no play, 2000, 800.   Total: About 20,800.   Receipts: £562.
Close of Play: 1st day Vic 3/113 (Ransford 42, McAlister 42); 2nd day SA (2) 0/34 (Mayne 9, L.R.Hill 25); 3rd day no play; 4th day no
     play; 5th day SA (2) 9/351 (Mayne 142, Wright 4).

South Australia squandered the advantage of batting first in ideal conditions on the first day, Woodford (32 in 61 minutes, 2 fours) alone resisting for any time. Ransford (unbeaten 171 in 342 minutes, 17 fours, chance at 88) and McAlister (50 in 78 minutes, 6 fours) took Victoria into the lead while Vernon and Laver played supporting roles late in the order to build a substantial first innings advantage. Rain washed out the third and fourth days' play but when play resumed on the fifth day in fine weather there was no indication of any malice in the wicket. Mayne (142 in 326 minutes, 5 fours) held the South Australian innings together while Gehrs (75 in 77 minutes, 8 fours) played a "masterly and attractive innings" (*Australasian*). Requiring only 133 for victory, the home batsmen were unable to withstand the sustained accuracy and variations of the medium-paced O'Connor. Hazlitt had performed a similar role for the home team. Sources: *Wisden, C.B.O'Reilly, VCA Report, The Age, The Argus, The Herald, The Australasian.*

SOUTH AUSTRALIA

R.E.Mayne	b Laver	8		b Armstrong	142
C.E.Dolling	b Vernon	5	(4)	c Laver b Saunders	0
*C.Hill	b Vernon	1		b Hazlitt	12
N.Claxton	b Vernon	4	(5)	c Laver b Hazlitt	35
J.H.Pellew	b Saunders	21	(6)	b Hazlitt	0
D.R.A.Gehrs	b Hazlitt	18	(7)	b McKenzie	75
L.R.Hill	st Hastings b Hazlitt	5	(2)	c Vernon b Hazlitt	26
J.D.A.O'Connor	b Vernon	16		c & b Hazlitt	5
W.J.Whitty	c Saunders b Hazlitt	0	(10)	b Vernon	2
†J.R.H.Woodford	b Vernon	32	(9)	lbw b Armstrong	21
A.W.Wright	not out	1		not out	4
Extras	(b13, lb3)	16		(b23, lb4, nb2)	29
Total	(48.4 overs, 159 mins)	127		(121.4 overs, 326 mins)	351

VICTORIA

T.S.Warne	b O'Connor	14	b O'Connor	3
C.McKenzie	c Woodford b O'Connor	4	run out (Gehrs/Woodford)	9
V.S.Ransford	not out	171	c Gehrs b O'Connor	30
W.W.Armstrong	run out (Gehrs)	7	b O'Connor	19
*P.A.McAlister	c & b L.R.Hill	50	c Woodford b O'Connor	5
E.V.Carroll	c Woodford b Claxton	7	b O'Connor	0
G.R.Hazlitt	c Mayne b Claxton	10	c Gehrs b Whitty	14
L.P.Vernon	b Whitty	25	st Woodford b O'Connor	8
F.J.Laver	b Whitty	23	not out	10
†T.J.Hastings	b Whitty	9	c Gehrs b O'Connor	0
J.V.Saunders	c C.Hill b Wright	17	run out (/Woodford)	0
Extras	(b7, lb2)	9	(b14, lb2, nb3)	19
Total	(123.0 overs, 360 mins)	346	(57.0 overs, 160 mins)	117

VICTORIA	O	M	R	W	w,nb		O	M	R	W	w,nb		FALL OF WICKETS			
Vernon	12.4	4	24	5	-,-		22	2	67	1	-,-			SA	VIC	SA	VIC
Laver	8	2	26	1	-,-		18	6	36	0	-,-	Wkt	1st	1st	2nd	2nd
Hazlitt	12	3	19	3	-,-		28	5	80	5	-,-	1st	11	10	41	20
Saunders	10	4	21	1	-,-	(5)	24	7	48	1	-,1	2nd	19	35	60	22
Armstrong	6	0	21	0	-,-	(6)	19.4	7	36	2	-,1	3rd	23	55	63	50
Warne						(4)	3	0	20	0	-,-	4th	23	134	135	56
McKenzie						(7)	7	0	35	1	-,-	5th	58	155	135	56
												6th	67	183	265	80
SOUTH AUSTRALIA	O	M	R	W	w,nb		O	M	R	W	w,nb	7th	74	253	289	101
L.R.Hill	19	5	52	1	-,-		13	4	27	0	-,3	8th	80	311	340	106
O'Connor	38	8	121	2	-,-	(3)	24	14	36	7	-,-	9th	124	321	343	108
Whitty	33	10	71	3	-,-	(2)	20	6	35	1	-,-	10th	127	346	351	117
Wright	15	2	32	1	-,-											
Claxton	13	3	46	2	-,-											
Pellew	1	0	8	0	-,-											
Gehrs	4	0	7	0	-,-											

NEW SOUTH WALES v QUEENSLAND

Played at Sydney Cricket Ground on January 1, 2, 4, 5, 6, 1909. (Timeless match)
Toss : New South Wales.   Result : QUEENSLAND WON BY TWO WICKETS.
Debuts: New South Wales - E.P.Barbour, A.W.Farnsworth (both f/c). Queensland - W.H.Sullivan (f/c).
12th Men: J.E.Hodgkinson (NSW). No 12th named for Queensland.
Umpires: W.G.Curran and R.M.Wallace.
Attendances: 2500, 2500, 500, 50, 20.   Total: About 5570.   Receipts: £186.
Close of Play: 1st day Qld 2/24 (Hartigan 11, Thomson 1); 2nd day NSW (2) 3/92 (Bubb 50, Goddard 0); 3rd day Qld (2) 4/141 (Evans 9, Hayes 3); 4th day Qld (2) 6/234 (Hayes 25, Hutcheon 10).

A.J.Bowden, who again became unavailable for New South Wales after the naming of the side, was replaced by Nicholls. Rain washed out play on the fourth day at 1.00pm. Farnsworth, making his only appearance for New South Wales, scored 69 in 99 minutes and hit 9 fours. Bubb (48 in 105 minutes, 3 fours and 77 in 159 minutes, 10 fours) batted soundly in both innings. Sullivan, also on debut, was out to the first ball he received in the first innings. Queensland's notable batting performances came from Thomson (68 in 138 minutes, 9 fours), Hayes (52 in 81 minutes, 9 fours) and Simpson (68 not out in 49 minutes, 13 fours and 43 in 46 minutes, 7 fours). Poor fielding by New South Wales on the last day did not help their cause; Hutcheon survived three chances. *SMH* gives NSW (2) Bubb c Sullivan, all other sources as shown here. Sources: *Cricket, NSWCA Report, Sydney Referee, Sydney Morning Herald, Town & Country Journal, Sydney Daily Telegraph, Newcastle Herald.*

NEW SOUTH WALES

D.C.Reid	c McLaren b Simpson	38	(3) run out (Simpson/Evans)		23
E.R.Bubb	c Hutcheon b Redgrave	48	c McLaren b Hayes		77
*A.B.S.White	c McLaren b Redgrave	21	(1) b McLaren		8
A.J.Nicholls	b Hayes	16	b Hayes		7
H.Goddard	b Simpson	30	c & b Hayes		33
A.W.Farnsworth	c & b Hayes	6	st Evans b Hayes		69
E.P.Barbour	c Evans b Simpson	40	c & b Hayes		0
C.Kelleway	c Thomson b Simpson	3	lbw b McLaren		28
L.A.Minnett	c Simpson b Redgrave	24	b McLaren		5
F.B.Johnson	b Hayes	13	not out		6
†C.R.Gorry	not out	2	run out		2
Extras	(b10, lb5)	15	(b12, lb5, w1, nb4)		22
Total	(81.0 overs, 235 mins)	256	(85.1 overs, 242 mins)		280

QUEENSLAND

*R.J.Hartigan	c White b Kelleway	26	run out (Goddard)		43
W.I.Sewart	c Johnson b Kelleway	11	c Nicholls b Barbour		19
J.W.McLaren	b Kelleway	0			
J.Thomson	b Barbour	68	b Goddard		14
W.B.Hayes	c Kelleway b Johnson	52	(6) c Nicholls b Kelleway		31
J.S.Redgrave	c White b Minnett	11	(7) b Kelleway		5
C.E.Simpson	not out	68	(3) st Gorry b Goddard		43
J.S.Hutcheon	st Gorry b Barbour	1	b Kelleway		36
E.R.Crouch	c Gorry b Minnett	8	not out		4
W.H.Sullivan	b Minnett	0	not out		2
†W.T.Evans	c Nicholls b Johnson	7	(5) b Johnson		55
Extras	(b5, lb3, nb5)	13	(b14, lb2, w1, nb3)		20
Total	(70.5 overs, 216 mins)	265	(73.4 overs, 225 mins) (8 wkts)		272

QUEENSLAND	O	M	R	W	w,nb		O	M	R	W	w,nb			FALL OF WICKETS		
McLaren	16	0	48	0	-,-		23	8	44	3	-,2			NSW	QLD	NSW	QLD
Redgrave	19	3	79	3	-,-		21	0	71	0	1,-	Wkt	1st	1st	2nd	2nd
Simpson	21	5	54	4	-,-		9	0	35	0	-,-	1st	64	23	16	66
Hayes	22	5	48	3	-,-		21.1	4	76	5	-,2	2nd	110	23	48	68
Sewart	3	0	12	0	-,-		11	3	32	0	-,-	3rd	111	50	81	110
												4th	139	157	144	133
NEW SOUTH WALES	O	M	R	W	w,nb		O	M	R	W	w,nb	5th	153	179	163	207
Minnett	21	5	57	3	-,3	(3)	16	3	36	0	1,-	6th	169	189	168	214
Kelleway	20	4	70	3	-,1		18.4	1	72	3	-,3	7th	173	196	261	244
Johnson	19.5	3	67	2	-,-	(1)	24	3	86	1	-,-	8th	223	214	268	269
Barbour	10	0	58	2	-,1		5	0	22	1	-,-	9th	254	214	272	-
Goddard							10	2	36	2	-,-	10th	256	265	280	-

NEW SOUTH WALES v SOUTH AUSTRALIA (Shield Match 5)

Played at Sydney Cricket Ground on January 9, 11, 12, 1909. (Timeless match)
Toss : South Australia.　　　　　Result : NEW SOUTH WALES WON BY NINE WICKETS.
Debuts: Nil.
12th Men: A.Diamond (NSW) and A.W.Jenkins (SA).
Umpires: W.G.Curran and A.C.Jones.
Attendances: 6809, 4128, 2246.　　　Total: 13,183.　　　Receipts: £506.
Close of Play: 1st day NSW 0/88 (Bardsley 44, Macartney 36); 2nd day NSW 9/445 (Kelleway 22, Gorry 7).

It was reported that H.Carter stood down for this match "to enable the selectors of the Australian XI to see Gorry behind the wickets" (*SMH*) and assist them in chosing the second wicket-keeper for the England tour. V.T.Trumper was unavailable. Gehrs, who gave a chance at 23, scored 102 in 133 minutes and hit 17 fours. Claxton was bowled first ball by Kelleway. Dolling batted for 120 minutes in the second innings and hit 10 fours. Bardsley (119 in 200 minutes, 10 fours) and Macartney (100 in 150 minutes, 12 fours) put on 203 for the New South Wales first wicket. Gregory, who made 94 in 142 minutes with 10 fours, compiled the only other innings of note for New South Wales. A.J.Y.Hopkins was unavailable for New South Wales due to injury. *SMH* gives NSW (1) Gregory 93 extras 17, Claxton 0/44. Sources: *Wisden, C.B.O'Reilly, Sydney Referee, Sydney Morning Herald, Town & Country Journal, Newcastle Herald.*

SOUTH AUSTRALIA

R.E.Mayne	c Gorry b Cotter	12	c Gorry b Kelleway		0
L.R.Hill	run out (Barnes/Emery)	21	b Cotter		16
*C.Hill	b Kelleway	22	c E.L.Waddy b Cotter		2
D.R.A.Gehrs	b Cotter	102	c E.F.Waddy b Emery		46
C.E.Dolling	lbw b Emery	27	b Cotter		78
J.H.Pellew	c Gorry b Kelleway	3	b Emery		2
N.Claxton	b Kelleway	0	c Emery b Noble		5
J.D.A.O'Connor	b Noble	7	b Noble		0
†J.R.H.Woodford	run out (Bardsley/Emery)	35	b Cotter		25
W.J.Whitty	not out	10	not out		4
A.W.Wright	b Kelleway	0	c Gorry b Cotter		0
Extras	(b15, lb11, w3, nb4)	33	(b7, lb3, w1, nb3)		14
Total	(64.2 overs, 203 mins)	272	(46.5 overs, 140 mins)		192

NEW SOUTH WALES

W.Bardsley	c Mayne b O'Connor	119			
C.G.Macartney	lbw b L.R.Hill	100			
*M.A.Noble	lbw b L.R.Hill	3			
E.F.Waddy	c Woodford b O'Connor	20			
S.E.Gregory	b Whitty	94			
E.L.Waddy	b Gehrs	33			
J.C.Barnes	c Woodford b Gehrs	2			
A.Cotter	c Dolling b Wright	11			
S.H.Emery	st Woodford b Wright	18	(1) b C.Hill		4
C.Kelleway	not out	22	(3) not out		2
†C.R.Gorry	c Claxton b Wright	9	(2) not out		9
Extras	(b12, w2, nb2)	16	(b4)		4
Total	(119.4 overs, 305 mins)	447	(4.0 overs, 10 mins) (1 wkt)		19

NEW SOUTH WALES	O	M	R	W	w,nb		O	M	R	W	w,nb						
Cotter	20	2	78	2	2,4		14.5	1	65	5	-,3				FALL OF WICKETS		
Emery	19	2	80	1	-,-	(3)	9	1	38	2	-,-	Wkt	SA 1st	NSW 1st	SA 2nd	NSW 2nd	
Noble	13	3	35	1	1,-	(4)	10	2	28	2	-,-	1st	34	203	1	12	
Kelleway	10.2	5	33	4	-,-	(2)	13	1	47	1	1,-	2nd	55	207	5	-	
Macartney	2	0	13	0	-,-							3rd	81	251	35	-	
												4th	132	260	117	-	
SOUTH AUSTRALIA	O	M	R	W	w,nb		O	M	R	W	w,nb	5th	142	323	121	-	
L.R.Hill	24	2	83	2	1,2							6th	142	335	130	-	
O'Connor	25	0	113	2	-,-							7th	189	352	130	-	
Whitty	15	1	57	1	-,-							8th	234	392	177	-	
Claxton	11	0	45	0	1,-							9th	272	430	192	-	
Wright	39.4	7	124	3	-,-							10th	272	447	192	-	
Gehrs	5	2	9	2	-,-												
C.Hill						(1)	2	0	7	1	-,-						
Mayne						(2)	2	0	8	0	-,-						

NEW SOUTH WALES v VICTORIA (Shield Match 6)

Played at Sydney Cricket Ground on January 23, 25, 26, 27, 28, 29, 1909. (Timeless match)
Toss : New South Wales.   Result : NEW SOUTH WALES WON BY SIX WICKETS.
Debuts: Victoria - D.B.M.Smith (f/c).
12th Men: E.L.Waddy (NSW) and J.H.Kyle (Vic).
Umpires: W.J.Bruton and A.C.Jones.
Attendances: 8620, 5301, 10738, 2663, 1552, 1355.   Total: 30,229.   Receipts: £1233.
Close of Play: 1st day NSW 3/365 (Noble 127); 2nd day NSW 9/811 (Emery 55, Kelleway 41); 3rd day Vic 3/265 (Ransford 136, McAlister 24); 4th day Vic (2) 2/120 (Armstrong 66, Smith 20); 5th day Vic (2) 7/446 (Vernon 26, Hazlitt 39).

A run feast which saw seven centuries and a new first-class record aggregate of 1911 runs scored over six days. The New South Wales total remains their highest against Victoria. Centuries were made by Bardsley (192 in 266 minutes, 1 six and 29 fours), Noble (213 in 356 minutes, 24 fours) and Gregory (179 in 202 minutes, 26 fours). The second-wicket partnership of 304 between Bardsley and Noble was the highest for that wicket yet recorded in Australia. Carroll was out to the third ball of Victoria's first innings and it was reported that Horan's 55, made in 184 minutes with 4 fours, was composed entirely of scoring shots on the leg side. Ransford became the first Victorian to score a century in each innings (182 in 360 minutes, 24 fours and 110 in 193 minutes, 9 fours). McAlister scored 108 in 200 minutes and hit 14 fours, while Armstrong made 171 in 243 minutes with 1 six and 24 fours. Noble bowled 10 successive maidens, 64 balls in a row without conceding a run, on the third day. Sources: *Wisden, NSWCA Report, Sydney Referee, Sydney Morning Herald, Town & Country Journal, Newcastle Herald.*

NEW SOUTH WALES

Batsman	1st innings	Runs	2nd innings	Runs
W.Bardsley	c & b Ransford	192	c Hazlitt b Saunders	24
A.J.Y.Hopkins	c Horan b Hazlitt	21	b Vernon	10
*M.A.Noble	b Saunders	213	not out	69
A.Cotter	c Smith b Armstrong	13		
E.F.Waddy	c Vernon b Laver	14	(4) c & b Armstrong	14
S.E.Gregory	b Ransford	179	(5) b Hazlitt	14
C.G.Macartney	c Hazlitt b Vernon	28	(6) not out	1
J.C.Barnes	run out (Carroll/Carkeek)	15		
†H.Carter	b Armstrong	11		
S.H.Emery	not out	58		
C.Kelleway	run out (Hazlitt/Carkeek)	42		
Extras	(b11, lb13, w3, nb2)	29	(b8, lb1)	9
Total	(193.3 overs, 570 mins)	815	(50.0 overs, 136 mins) (4 wkts)	141

VICTORIA

Batsman	1st innings	Runs	2nd innings	Runs
E.V.Carroll	c Carter b Cotter	0	b Barnes	7
T.I.B.Horan	b Cotter	55	b Barnes	19
V.S.Ransford	b Barnes	182	(5) c Carter b Noble	110
W.W.Armstrong	c Kelleway b Noble	20	(3) lbw b Noble	171
*P.A.McAlister	st Carter b Barnes	108	(6) b Emery	4
D.B.M.Smith	b Barnes	11	(4) b Barnes	22
G.R.Hazlitt	b Barnes	4	(9) c Noble b Cotter	56
L.P.Vernon	c Bardsley b Barnes	2	b Cotter	26
F.J.Laver	c Hopkins b Emery	22	(7) b Barnes	21
†W.Carkeek	c Kelleway b Barnes	15	not out	13
J.V.Saunders	not out	4	c Cotter b Barnes	7
Extras	(b22, lb12, w5, nb6)	45	(b12, lb15, w2, nb2)	31
Total	(149.2 overs, 447 mins)	468	(141.5 overs, 427 mins)	487

VICTORIA	O	M	R	W	w,nb		O	M	R	W	w,nb
Vernon	34	3	154	1	3,2	(2)	4	0	28	1	-,-
Laver	31	5	113	1	-,-						
Hazlitt	29	6	129	1	-,-		12	5	23	1	-,-
Saunders	42.3	6	178	1	-,-	(1)	22	5	57	1	-,-
Armstrong	38	5	104	2	-,-	(4)	12	3	24	1	-,-
Ransford	13	1	61	2	-,-						
Carroll	3	0	26	0	-,-						
McAlister	3	0	21	0	-,-						

NEW SOUTH WALES	O	M	R	W	w,nb		O	M	R	W	w,nb
Cotter	38	8	123	2	1,6		20	3	52	2	1,1
Emery	24	3	79	1	-,-	(6)	24	8	61	1	-,-
Hopkins	24	7	63	0	-,-	(5)	18	2	55	0	-,-
Kelleway	20	4	53	0	4,-	(3)	16	3	53	0	-,-
Noble	22	14	28	1	-,-	(7)	18	5	41	2	-,1
Macartney	7	2	18	0	-,-	(4)	12	1	47	0	-,-
Barnes	14.2	0	59	6	-,-	(2)	33.5	2	147	5	1,-

FALL OF WICKETS

Wkt	NSW 1st	VIC 1st	VIC 2nd	NSW 2nd
1st	42	0	14	25
2nd	346	178	55	49
3rd	365	225	123	98
4th	401	356	330	127
5th	526	370	343	-
6th	600	384	355	-
7th	644	394	380	-
8th	677	428	447	-
9th	729	463	472	-
10th	815	468	487	-

AUSTRALIAN XI v THE REST

Played at Sydney Cricket Ground on February 5, 6, 8, 9, 1909. (Timeless match)
Toss : The Rest.   Result : AUSTRALIAN XI WON BY EIGHT WICKETS.
Debuts: Nil.
12th Men: F.J.Laver (both teams).
Umpires: W.G.Curran and R.M.Wallace.
Attendances: 3000, 8000, 5500, 1300.   Total: About 17,800.   Receipts: £700.
Close of Play: 1st day Rest 5/174 (Hazlitt 17); 2nd day Aust 8/177 (Cotter 4, O'Connor 2); 3rd day Aust (2) 1/95 (Gregory 38, Noble 56).
This and the following match in Melbourne were staged as 'Test trials' for the forthcoming tour of England. The Australian XI comprised eight players already named to tour plus Carkeek, Gregory and McAlister, who were vying for the remaining positions along with those representing The Rest. C.Hill and R.J.Hartigan both announced their unavailability for these two matches. Rain delayed the start until 2.40pm on the first day. Hopkins scored 91 not out in 137 minutes and hit 1 six and 9 fours. Parker, who had travelled from Western Australia for the trials, was dismissed first ball in the second innings. Gregory (126 not out in 190 minutes, with 13 fours) and Noble (125 in 166 minutes, 15 fours) shared a second-wicket stand of 246 for the Australian XI to secure victory. Saunders was unable to take the field on the last day due to illness. Sources: *Wisden, NSWCA Report, Sydney Morning Herald, Town & Country Journal.*

THE REST

*A.J.Y.Hopkins	b O'Connor	55	(4) not out		91
W.Bardsley	c Carkeek b O'Connor	48	b Cotter		6
D.R.A.Gehrs	c Ransford b O'Connor	37	c Carkeek b O'Connor		13
R.E.Mayne	b Macartney	3	(1) b Armstrong		12
E.F.Parker	b Macartney	6	c Carkeek b O'Connor		0
G.R.Hazlitt	c Cotter b O'Connor	62	b Armstrong		10
C.E.Simpson	c Ransford b O'Connor	13	b Armstrong		0
J.C.Barnes	b Cotter	34	b Cotter		12
C.Kelleway	not out	12	lbw b Armstrong		7
†C.R.Gorry	b Cotter	15	b O'Connor		4
J.V.Saunders	b O'Connor	8	b Armstrong		0
Extras	(b6, lb8, nb4)	18	(b1, lb1, nb2)		4
Total	(99.2 overs, 280 mins)	311	(62.4 overs, 173 mins)		159

AUSTRALIAN XI

*M.A.Noble	run out (Simpson/Gorry)	9	(3) b Barnes		125
V.T.Trumper	c Gorry b Saunders	0			
V.S.Ransford	b Saunders	21	(4) not out		9
W.W.Armstrong	b Saunders	19			
S.E.Gregory	c Gehrs b Kelleway	41	(2) not out		126
P.A.McAlister	st Gorry b Barnes	30	(1) run out (Barnes/Gorry)		0
C.G.Macartney	lbw b Kelleway	28			
H.Carter	c Mayne b Simpson	10			
A.Cotter	st Gorry b Barnes	22			
J.D.A.O'Connor	c Parker b Barnes	5			
†W.Carkeek	not out	3			
Extras	(b8, lb3, w2, nb1)	14	(b4, lb2, w3)		9
Total	(53.5 overs, 173 mins)	202	(70.2 overs, 190 mins) (2 wkts)		269

AUSTRALIAN XI	O	M	R	W	w,nb		O	M	R	W	w,nb
Macartney	20	7	54	2	-,-	(4)	7	2	17	0	-,-
Noble	7	0	29	0	-,-						
O'Connor	34.2	8	106	6	-,-		17	4	49	3	-,-
Cotter	19	1	58	2	-,4	(1)	15	1	52	2	-,2
Armstrong	15	2	34	0	-,-	(2)	23.4	10	37	5	-,-
Ransford	4	0	12	0	-,-						

THE REST	O	M	R	W	w,nb		O	M	R	W	w,nb
Saunders	17	2	54	3	1,1		6	0	30	0	-,-
Kelleway	15	2	49	2	1,-	(4)	10	1	45	0	1,-
Hazlitt	5	0	26	0	-,-		10	0	45	0	1,-
Hopkins	4	0	10	0	-,-	(6)	12	3	34	0	-,-
Barnes	6.5	0	35	3	-,-	(2)	17	0	68	1	1,-
Simpson	6	1	14	1	-,-	(5)	15.2	2	38	0	-,-

	FALL OF WICKETS			
	REST	AUST	REST	AUST
Wkt	1st	1st	2nd	2nd
1st	104	3	16	0
2nd	111	31	25	246
3rd	130	55	50	-
4th	138	55	50	-
5th	174	123	89	-
6th	203	150	89	-
7th	268	167	109	-
8th	271	173	127	-
9th	295	199	158	-
10th	311	202	159	-

AUSTRALIAN XI v THE REST

Played at Melbourne Cricket Ground on February 12, 13, 15, 1909. (Timeless match)
Toss : Australian XI.   Result : AUSTRALIAN XI WON BY AN INNINGS AND 158 RUNS.
Debuts: Nil.
12th Men: F.J.Laver (both teams).
Umpires: W.Hannah and W.A.Young.
Attendances: 4000, 7200, 2000.   Total: About 13,200.   Receipts: £349.
Close of Play: 1st day Aust 5/417 (Bardsley 180, Macartney 65); 2nd day Rest 3/178 (Mayne 68, Carroll 17).

W.Carkeek, H.Carter, V.T.Trumper and L.P.Vernon were unavailable to represent the Australian XI. C.E.Dolling and L.R.Hill withdrew from The Rest and were replaced by Carroll and Kelleway. Bardsley, who batted throughout the first day, compiled a career-best 264 in 373 minutes and hit 29 fours. Dodds scored 80 not out in 66 minutes with 15 fours, while Ransford made 75 in 90 minutes with 8 fours. Mayne (101 in 199 minutes, 9 fours) and Parker (65 in 88 minutes, 6 fours) shared an opening stand of 119 for The Rest. Following on, Gehrs (62 in 46 minutes, 11 fours) and Mayne again (43 in 73 minutes, 3 fours) made the highest scores after Hopkins was out to the first ball of the innings. Laver substituted for Kelleway (injured knee) on the second day. Sources: *Wisden, NSWCA Report, The Age, The Argus, The Herald, The Australasian*.

AUSTRALIAN XI

P.A.McAlister	c Whitty b Saunders	2
W.Bardsley	c Gorry b Hopkins	264
*M.A.Noble	c & b Kelleway	62
V.S.Ransford	c Hopkins b Gehrs	75
S.E.Gregory	lbw b Whitty	17
W.W.Armstrong	c Parker b Whitty	3
C.G.Macartney	b Simpson	72
G.R.Hazlitt	c Simpson b Saunders	0
A.Cotter	c Barnes b Whitty	43
†N.Dodds	not out	80
J.D.A.O'Connor	b Saunders	12
Extras	(b18)	18
Total	(127.0 overs, 419 mins)	648

THE REST

R.E.Mayne	b Hazlitt	101	(4)	c Noble b Armstrong	43
E.F.Parker	b Hazlitt	65	(3)	c Hazlitt b Armstrong	8
D.R.A.Gehrs	b Armstrong	7	(2)	st Dodds b O'Connor	62
*A.J.Y.Hopkins	b Armstrong	3	(1)	b Cotter	0
E.V.Carroll	c Noble b Armstrong	69		c Macartney b O'Connor	9
J.C.Barnes	c Dodds b Hazlitt	11		b Hazlitt	28
C.E.Simpson	b Armstrong	0		b O'Connor	19
C.Kelleway	c Dodds b Armstrong	14		c McAlister b O'Connor	1
W.J.Whitty	b Cotter	8		b Armstrong	12
†C.R.Gorry	not out	0		c Dodds b O'Connor	0
J.V.Saunders	c Cotter b Armstrong	2		not out	0
Extras	(b18, lb5, nb2)	25		(lb1, w2)	3
Total	(99.5 overs, 269 mins)	305		(50.2 overs, 150 mins)	185

THE REST	O	M	R	W	w,nb
Saunders	25	1	131	3	-,-
Kelleway	19	3	97	1	-,-
Hopkins	20	2	79	1	-,-
Whitty	34	10	123	3	-,-
Barnes	16	0	106	0	-,-
Simpson	16	1	64	1	-,-
Gehrs	7	0	30	1	-,-

AUSTRALIAN XI	O	M	R	W	w,nb		O	M	R	W	w,nb
Cotter	21	2	66	1	-,1		8	0	53	1	2,-
Armstrong	30.5	6	59	6	-,-		11.2	1	38	3	-,-
O'Connor	10	1	39	0	-,-	(4)	15	3	41	5	-,-
Hazlitt	29	5	80	3	-,1	(3)	11	0	37	1	-,-
Noble	7	2	30	0	-,-						
Macartney	2	0	6	0	-,-	(5)	5	1	13	0	-,-

FALL OF WICKETS

Wkt	AUST 1st	REST 1st	REST 2nd
1st	4	119	0
2nd	123	132	20
3rd	271	143	85
4th	294	249	97
5th	310	261	134
6th	431	262	167
7th	434	286	168
8th	510	303	183
9th	595	303	183
10th	648	305	185

TASMANIA v VICTORIA

Played at T.C.A. Ground, Hobart, on February 12, 13, 15, 16, 1909. (Timeless match)
Toss : Tasmania,   Result : VICTORIA WON BY FOUR WICKETS.
Debuts: Tasmania - A.Braithwaite, A.C.Facy, H.Parkinson (all f/c). Victoria - H.F.Parsons (f/c).
12th Men: T.J.Matthews (Vic). No 12th man or emergency fieldsmen named for Tasmania.
Umpires: W.M.Bradshaw and E.J.K.Burn.
Attendances: No figures published, comments included "meagre" and "poor".   Receipts: £39.
Close of Play: 1st day Tas 7/349 (Carroll 13, Martin 25); 2nd day Vic 340 all out; 3rd day Vic (2) 0/16 (Horan 6, Ainslie 10).

N.Dodds, in Melbourne playing for the Australian XI v The Rest, N.R.Westbrook and E.A.C.Windsor were unavailable for Tasmania. Stuckey replaced E.V.Carroll (unavailable) in the Victorian side. Hawson, 139 in 210 minutes with 18 fours, gave his only chance at 137 and shared a new Tasmanian third-wicket record partnership of 183 with Paton (81 in 130 minutes, 7 fours). Hudson (82 not out in 200 minutes, 6 fours) and Chancellor (99 in 155 minutes, 13 fours) also established a new seventh-wicket record of 183 in 155 minutes in the second innings. Ainslie, 107 not out in 180 minutes with 16 fours, narrowly missed a second century (92 in about 165 minutes, 8 fours) in the match when he was run out after surviving two chances in the field. Smith hit 77 in 60 minutes with 1 six and 12 fours and 94 in 125 minutes with 16 fours and three chanecs. Facy and Parsons were both out first ball in the second innings; Parsons staying at the crease to act as runner for Delves, who batted down the order after sustaining an injury while fielding. *ACS* incorrectly gives Vic (1) fall of 5th, 7th and 9th wkts; Vic (1) Facy 4/136. *VCA Report* incorrectly gives Tas (1) Harrison c Ainslie. Sources: *A.C.S., VCA Report, The Age, The Argus, Hobart Mercury, Launceston Examiner.*

TASMANIA

R.J.Hawson	run out (Parsons/Reeves)	139	(2)	b Kyle	1
E.W.Harrison	c Collins b McKenzie	19	(3)	b Kyle	1
J.L.Hudson	c Ainslie b Collins	2	(7)	not out	82
G.D.Paton	c Ainslie b Collins	81		b McKenzie	28
*T.A.Tabart	b McKenzie	22	(1)	b Collins	38
A.Braithwaite	lbw b McKenzie	10	(10)	c Kyle b Stuckey	0
A.C.Facy	c McKenzie b Parsons	8	(6)	b McKenzie	0
T.D.Carroll	c McKenzie b Collins	16	(9)	b Collins	0
C.W.B.Martin	b Collins	26	(5)	c Ainslie b McKenzie	9
F.E.Chancellor	not out	8	(8)	b Stuckey	99
†H.Parkinson	b Collins	0		c & b Collins	0
Extras	(b26, lb4)	30		(b17, lb7, w1)	25
Total	(114.0 overs, 310 mins)	361		(108.1 overs, 290 mins)	283

VICTORIA

C.McKenzie	c Paton b Braithwaite	32	(5)	b Carroll	23
F.T.Delves	c Hawson b Facy	48	(8)	not out	2
J.F.Horan	b Facy	0	(1)	c Tabart b Facy	10
*F.Vaughan	c Parkinson b Facy	14	(3)	c Parkinson b Facy	51
D.B.M.Smith	c Braithwaite b Chancellor	77	(4)	b Facy	94
J.Ainslie	not out	107	(2)	run out	92
J.H.Stuckey	c Hawson b Facy	19	(6)	not out	17
H.F.Parsons	c Tabart b Chancellor	11	(7)	b Facy	0
J.H.Kyle	c Carroll b Braithwaite	3			
F.B.Collins	c Braithwaite b Facy	14			
†W.H.Reeves	b Facy	11			
Extras	(b2, lb2)	4		(b12, lb3, nb1)	16
Total	(88.1 overs, 260 mins)	340		(92.5 overs, 270 mins) (6 wkts)	305

VICTORIA	O	M	R	W	w,nb		O	M	R	W	w,nb
Kyle	28	9	55	0	-,-		33	12	61	2	-,-
Parsons	23	2	96	1	-,-		19	7	59	0	-,-
McKenzie	25	4	67	3	-,-	(4)	20	6	30	3	-,-
Collins	29	6	91	5	-,-	(3)	25.1	4	87	3	-,-
Ainslie	5	1	6	0	-,-		3	0	7	0	1,-
Delves	4	0	16	0	-,-						
Horan						(6)	3	0	7	0	-,-
Stuckey						(7)	5	2	7	2	-,-

TASMANIA	O	M	R	W	w,nb		O	M	R	W	w,nb
Facy	34.1	4	134	6	-,-		33	8	92	4	-,-
Paton	15	1	41	0	-,-		16	4	39	0	-,-
Braithwaite	16	2	69	2	-,-		16	1	59	0	-,-
Chancellor	12	1	54	2	-,-		11	1	40	0	-,1
Carroll	11	2	38	0	-,-	(6)	12.5	1	49	1	-,-
Martin						(5)	4	0	10	0	-,-

FALL OF WICKETS

Wkt	TAS 1st	VIC 1st	TAS 2nd	VIC 2nd
1st	58	63	7	26
2nd	61	63	13	132
3rd	244	95	71	190
4th	276	95	73	231
5th	299	207	73	297
6th	300	233	88	297
7th	312	259	271	-
8th	352	272	275	-
9th	361	320	282	-
10th	361	340	283	-

TASMANIA v VICTORIA

Played at N.T.C.A. Ground, Launceston, on February 19, 20, 22, 1909. (Timeless match)
Toss : Tasmania.   Result : VICTORIA WON BY AN INNINGS AND 287 RUNS.
Debuts: Tasmania - T.H.Elliott, W.Reid, H.Woolley (all f/c). Victoria - A.W.Lampard (f/c).
12th Men: F.Vaughan (Vic). No 12th named for Tasmania.
Umpires: See below.
Attendances & Receipts: No figures published.
Close of Play: 1st day Vic 0/78 (Ainslie 33, Delves 44); 2nd day Vic 7/581 (Stuckey 118).

F.E.Chancellor (business), N.Dodds and J.L.Hudson were all unavailable for Tasmania. Reid, who had had no wicket-keeping experience whatsoever prior to this season, was called up on the day of the match to replace A.J.Badcock (unavailable); *Launceston Weekly Courier* reported that two Launceston keepers (L.Thomas and H.C.Pilbeam) refused to play because Dodds had been the first asked to do the job. Matthews did the hat-trick in the first innings, dismissing Harrison, Martin and Elliott, and achieved his only ten-wicket-match (12 for 91) in first-class cricket. Westbrook (67 in 125 minutes, 8 fours) topscored for Tasmania, who lost 8 for 13 (6 for 2) in their dramatic first-innings collapse. Ainslie (67 in 130 minutes, 8 fours) and Delves (162 in 185 minutes, 32 fours, 4 chances - his sole first-class century) established a new first-wicket record for Victoria, the visitors mounting their highest total against Tasmania yet. The 39-year-old Stuckey scored the last of his four first-class hundreds (129 in 155 minutes, 21 fours). The umpires for this match remain something of an enigma: *Launceston Telegraph* names W.Reeves, H.G.Tevelein and H.Wilson (first day), none on the second day, and F.Vaughan and "Jordan" (third day); *Cricket* reports that eight different umpires officiated but gives no details, and no other source gives any names or reasons for the changes. Sources: *Cricket, The Age, The Argus, Hobart Mercury, Launceston Examiner, Launceston Daily Telegraph, Launceston Weekly Courier.*

TASMANIA

R.J.Hawson	st Lampard b Parsons	39	(8)	not out	26
N.R.Westbrook	c Lampard b Kyle	67	(7)	c Collins b Ainslie	23
G.D.Paton	hit wkt b Matthews	10	(1)	c & b Collins	25
E.A.C.Windsor	c & b Matthews	1	(9)	b Ainslie	0
*E.W.Harrison	b Matthews	1	(11)	c & b Matthews	4
C.W.B.Martin	c & b Matthews	0		c Kyle b McKenzie	28
T.H.Elliott	lbw b Matthews	0	(4)	c Horan b Matthews	15
A.Braithwaite	b Matthews	0	(5)	b Matthews	6
A.C.Facy	not out	26	(10)	c Collins b Kyle	15
H.Woolley	b Matthews	4	(3)	c Smith b Matthews	4
†W.Reid	b Kyle	4	(2)	c Parsons b Matthews	11
Extras	(b11)	11		(b15, lb3, w1)	19
Total	(68.4 overs, 185 mins)	163		(57.2 overs, 165 mins)	176

VICTORIA

J.Ainslie	c Reid b Facy	67
F.T.Delves	b Paton	162
D.B.M.Smith	c Reid b Facy	47
C.McKenzie	c Hawson b Facy	59
*J.F.Horan	b Windsor	12
J.H.Stuckey	c Braithwaite b Windsor	129
T.J.Matthews	c Harrison b Windsor	18
H.F.Parsons	b Martin	64
†A.W.Lampard	b Windsor	4
J.H.Kyle	c Facy b Windsor	20
F.B.Collins	not out	10
Extras	(b24, lb10)	34
Total	(139.0 overs, 405 mins)	626

VICTORIA	O	M	R	W	w,nb		O	M	R	W	w,nb			FALL OF WICKETS		
														TAS	VIC	TAS
Kyle	22.4	9	40	2	-,-		6	1	15	1	-,-	Wkt	1st	1st	2nd
Matthews	20	4	49	7	-,-	(3)	19.2	7	42	5	-,-	1st	81	186	29
Parsons	10	4	15	1	-,-							2nd	123	273	34
Collins	4	1	11	0	-,-		6	1	30	1	-,-	3rd	123	305	49
McKenzie	8	2	18	0	-,-	(2)	17	5	47	1	-,-	4th	125	340	69
Ainslie	4	0	19	0	-,-	(5)	9	3	23	2	1,-	5th	125	389	78
												6th	125	432	108
TASMANIA	O	M	R	W	w,nb							7th	125	581	132
Facy	31	5	127	3	-,-							8th	132	594	132
Windsor	37	6	142	5	-,-							9th	136	599	157
Paton	22	4	80	1	-,-							10th	163	626	176
Braithwaite	14	2	70	0	-,-										
Elliott	10	1	56	0	-,-										
Woolley	6	0	34	0	-,-										
Martin	11	0	50	1	-,-										
Hawson	7	1	25	0	-,-										
Harrison	1	0	8	0	-,-										

WESTERN AUSTRALIA v SOUTH AUSTRALIA

Played at Fremantle Oval on April 3 (no play), 5, 6, 7, 1909. (Three-day match)
Toss : Western Australia.   Result : MATCH DRAWN.
Debuts: Western Australia - A.J.Banks, C.W.Harper, A.S.Patfield (all f/c). South Australia - G.T.Bloomfield. L.E.Howard (both f/c).
12th Men: W.S.Stirling (SA). No 12th named for Western Australia.
Umpires: J.C.Brickhill and J.W.Drew.
Attendances: Several, 1500, 500, 200.   Total: About 2200.   Receipts: £103.
Close of Play: 1st day no play; 2nd day SA 4/25 (Chamberlain 8); 3rd day WA (2) 4/21 (Rowe 1, Hogue 0).

Patfield replaced Evers (injured) in the Western Australian team. Rain prevented play on the first day: the few spectators present were given passes for the second day and officials decreed that the day's play be made up. Hogue (70 in 143 minutes, 8 fours) and Coyne (62 in 140 minutes, 4 fours) were engaged in a fourth wicket partnership of 125. Gehrs's century was his third in successive innings in Western Australia, his innings lasting 181 minutes with 12 fours. High winds on the last day dislodged the bails several times. Play was called off at 5.45pm when the pavilion shadow was on the pitch. Sources: *C.B.O'Reilly, The West Australian, Daily News, Western Mail.*

WESTERN AUSTRALIA

Batsman	Dismissal	R		Dismissal	R
H.C.Howard	c & b Claxton	3	(8)	c Woodford b Quist	10
E.F.Parker	lbw b Reedman	14	(7)	c Hack b Quist	35
S.H.D.Rowe	run out (Hack/Reedman)	17	(5)	st Woodford b Quist	20
T.H.Hogue	c Howard b Quist	70	(6)	b Howard	22
T.H.Coyne	st Woodford b Quist	62	(9)	run out (Wright/Woodford)	13
R.M.Evans	lbw b Quist	5	(3)	b Claxton	10
*A.H.Christian	b Quist	9	(1)	c Quist b Claxton	2
A.J.Banks	c Chamberlain b Claxton	19	(4)	c Stuart b Claxton	0
†A.S.Patfield	not out	21	(2)	c Reedman b Howard	8
C.W.Harper	c Woodford b Claxton	0	(11)	not out	11
R.A.Selk	b Howard	28	(10)	b Quist	13
Extras	(b4, lb3)	7		(b6, lb4)	10
Total	(79.2 overs, 248 mins)	255		(77.1 overs, 225 mins)	154

SOUTH AUSTRALIA

Batsman	Dismissal	R		Dismissal	R
F.T.Hack	st Patfield b Selk	7	(3)	not out	10
K.H.Quist	lbw b Christian	3			
W.L.Chamberlain	b Christian	59	(2)	c Banks b Hogue	40
W.P.Stuart	b Christian	3		not out	0
J.C.Reedman	b Selk	4			
D.R.A.Gehrs	c Banks b Hogue	106	(1)	c Rowe b Selk	7
G.T.Bloomfield	b Coyne	38			
*N.Claxton	b Hogue	38			
†J.R.H.Woodford	b Hogue	2			
A.W.Wright	b Hogue	2			
L.E.Howard	not out	0			
Extras	(b12, lb6)	18		(b2)	2
Total	(82.0 overs, 230 mins)	280		(26.0 overs, 75 mins) (2 wkts)	59

SOUTH AUSTRALIA	O	M	R	W	w,nb		O	M	R	W	w,nb
Howard	19.2	4	55	1	-,-	(2)	22	5	57	2	-,-
Claxton	16	4	47	3	-,-	(1)	14	3	23	3	-,-
Reedman	21	7	58	1	-,-		13	4	16	0	-,-
Wright	8	0	26	0	-,-	(6)	8	2	12	0	-,-
Gehrs	3	1	3	0	-,-						
Chamberlain	2	0	17	0	-,-						
Hack	3	1	7	0	-,-	(5)	4	1	3	0	-,-
Quist	7	0	35	4	-,-	(4)	16.1	3	33	4	-,-

WESTERN AUSTRALIA	O	M	R	W	w,nb		O	M	R	W	w,nb
Selk	19	5	53	2	-,-	(2)	11	2	16	1	-,-
Christian	27	5	79	3	-,-	(1)	10	2	30	0	-,-
Coyne	10	1	24	1	-,-						
Harper	9	0	37	0	-,-						
Hogue	10	2	26	4	-,-	(3)	3	0	6	1	-,-
Evans	4	1	22	0	-,-	(4)	2	1	5	0	-,-
Banks	3	0	21	0	-,-						

FALL OF WICKETS

Wkt	WA 1st	SA 1st	WA 2nd	SA 2nd
1st	17	8	10	17
2nd	26	10	11	57
3rd	45	17	12	-
4th	170	25	21	-
5th	178	118	62	-
6th	179	195	74	-
7th	188	273	104	-
8th	217	277	126	-
9th	220	279	139	-
10th	255	280	154	-

WESTERN AUSTRALIA v SOUTH AUSTRALIA

Played at W.A.C.A. Ground, Perth, on April 10, 12, 13, 1909. (Three-day match)
Toss : Western Australia   Result : MATCH DRAWN.
Debuts: Western Australia - J.T.Anderson (WA only). South Australia - W.S.Stirling (f/c).
12th Men: A.W.Wright (SA). No 12th named for Western Australia.
Umpires: T.Coombe and T.Shiells.
Attendances: 800, 2000, 800.   Total: About 3600.   Receipts: £195.
Close of Play: 1st day SA 4/118 (Claxton 40, Quist 16); 2nd day SA (2) 3/63 (Stuart 32, Stirling 2).

Anderson had previously represented Scotland in first-class cricket. Rain restricted play on the first day to 150 minutes. "On Monday, runs were difficult to make, but on Tuesday the wicket had quite recovered and played fast and true" (*West Australian*). Stirling dismissed Parker with his second ball in first-class cricket. Bloomfield's catch to dismiss Rowe was controversial - fielding at point, he let go of the ball as he fell, but umpire Shiells ruled that the ball had been held long enough to justify a catch, a decision which was greeted with disapproval by the spectators. In the concluding stages of the match Hack bowled deliveries "timed to fall right on the wicket". Sources: *C.B.O'Reilly, The West Australian, Daily News, Western Mail.*

SOUTH AUSTRALIA

F.T.Hack	b Christian	16		b Christian	5
D.R.A.Gehrs	c Anderson b Christian	27	(6)	b Christian	0
W.L.Chamberlain	run out	12		b Christian	20
W.P.Stuart	c Anderson b Coyne	6		st Evers b Christian	38
*N.Claxton	c Parker b Christian	40	(8)	c Evans b Harper	56
K.H.Quist	c Rowe b Hogue	17	(2)	c Howard b Christian	0
G.T.Bloomfield	c Rowe b Hogue	19		c Anderson b Christian	4
J.C.Reedman	st Evers b Christian	15	(9)	c & b Selk	19
W.S.Stirling	not out	5	(5)	c Christian b Coyne	2
†J.R.H.Woodford	c Howard b Christian	2		c Rowe b Harper	3
L.E.Howard	c & b Hogue	5		not out	2
Extras	(b5, lb1, w2)	8		(b4, lb4)	8
Total	(74.0 overs, 230 mins)	172		(48.0 overs, 150 mins)	157

WESTERN AUSTRALIA

E.F.Parker	c Chamberlain b Stirling	17		c Hack b Reedman	11
H.C.Howard	st Woodford b Reedman	1	(7)	not out	14
S.H.D.Rowe	c Reedman b Howard	9		c Bloomfield b Howard	5
*T.H.Hogue	c Reedman b Howard	19	(2)	b Howard	46
T.H.Coyne	run out (Bloomfield)	14	(4)	b Reedman	25
R.M.Evans	b Reedman	12		not out·	34
A.H.Christian	c Howard b Reedman	0	(5)	b Reedman	28
†H.A.Evers	c Bloomfield b Reedman	6			
J.T.Anderson	c Howard b Reedman	0			
R.A.Selk	c Chamberlain b Reedman	2			
C.W.Harper	not out	1			
Extras	(lb4, w1)	5		(b7)	7
Total	(40.5 overs, 110 mins)	86		(66.0 overs, 210 mins) (5 wkts)	170

WESTERN AUSTRALIA	O	M	R	W	w,nb		O	M	R	W	w,nb
Selk	13	3	28	0	-,-	(3)	14	2	40	1	-,-
Christian	31	11	67	5	2,-		18	3	56	6	-,-
Coyne	11	2	26	1	-,-	(5)	4	0	19	1	-,-
Hogue	15	1	40	3	-,-		3	1	10	0	-,-
Anderson	3	2	1	0	-,-	(1)	3	0	8	0	-,-
Harper	1	0	2	0	-,-		6	0	16	2	-,-

SOUTH AUSTRALIA	O	M	R	W	w,nb		O	M	R	W	w,nb
Claxton	3	0	17	0	-,-						
Reedman	12.5	5	26	6	-,-		26	5	62	3	-,-
Stirling	8	2	16	1	1,-		6	2	14	0	-,-
Howard	12	6	17	2	-,-	(1)	17	2	47	2	-,-
Hack	5	4	5	0	-,-		7	3	7	0	-,-
Quist						(4)	7	2	25	0	-,-
Chamberlain						(6)	3	1	8	0	-,-

FALL OF WICKETS				
	SA	WA	SA	WA
Wkt	1st	1st	2nd	2nd
1st	39	13	2	14
2nd	47	21	17	25
3rd	60	46	42	84
4th	73	61	69	106
5th	120	71	69	128
6th	128	72	69	-
7th	150	80	91	-
8th	163	80	130	-
9th	165	85	154	-
10th	172	86	157	-

WESTERN AUSTRALIA v SOUTH AUSTRALIA

Played at Fremantle Oval on April 16, 17, 19, 1909. (Three-day match)
Toss : South Australia. Result : MATCH DRAWN.
Debuts: Western Australia - T.C.M.Hantke (f/c).
12th Men: N.Claxton (SA). No 12th named for Western Australia.
Umpires: J.C.Brickhill and T.Shiells.
Attendances: 300, 1200, 300. Total: About 1800. Receipts: £97.
Close of Play: 1st day SA 5/324 (Stuart 9); 2nd day WA 7/243 (Christian 61, Anderson 4).

Hantke replaced Coyne (unavailable) in the Western Australian team, while Claxton, the South Australian captain, stood down due to a leg injury. Gehrs batted for 156 minutes and hit 12 fours in making 113; he gave a chance when 7. Play started half an hour late on the second day when some WA players missed their train to the ground. Parker survived three chances during his innings of 86 in 122 minutes. Harper sustained a hand injury during the South Australian first innings which prevented him bowling again in the match. Quist was dismissed from the first ball of the South Australian second innings. Last first-class appearance by J.C.Reedman. Sources: *C.B.O'Reilly, The West Australian, Daily News, Western Mail.*

SOUTH AUSTRALIA

K.H.Quist	c Parker b Christian	41	c Hogue b Selk		0
W.L.Chamberlain	b Christian	41	st Evers b Christian		61
F.T.Hack	b Christian	52	c & b Christian		23
*D.R.A.Gehrs	c Rowe b Anderson	113	c Rowe b Christian		22
G.T.Bloomfield	b Anderson	65	c Rowe b Christian		6
W.P.Stuart	c Rowe b Christian	25	not out		2
J.C.Reedman	b Selk	20			
W.S.Stirling	b Christian	0			
†J.R.H.Woodford	lbw b Christian	10			
A.W.Wright	c Hogue b Christian	10			
L.E.Howard	not out	5			
Extras	(b4, lb1, nb1)	6	(lb2)		2
Total	(108.0 overs, 311 mins)	388	(43.2 overs, 110 mins) (5 wkts dec)		116

WESTERN AUSTRALIA

T.H.Hogue	c Hack b Reedman	21	lbw b Reedman		33
E.F.Parker	c Woodford b Reedman	86	b Howard		16
S.H.D.Rowe	c & b Howard	4	(5) c Quist b Wright		21
H.C.Howard	b Reedman	30	(6) not out		5
R.M.Evans	st Woodford b Quist	28	(3) run out (/Woodford)		16
A.H.Christian	lbw b Reedman	73	(4) c Gehrs b Howard		57
*†H.A.Evers	c & b Stirling	1			
T.C.M.Hantke	b Reedman	2	(7) b Wright		0
J.T.Anderson	b Howard	8	(8) not out		3
R.A.Selk	b Howard	5			
C.W.Harper	not out	4			
Extras	(b3, lb3, w1)	7			-
Total	(77.5 overs, 227 mins)	269	(49.0 overs, 135 mins) (6 wkts)		151

WESTERN AUSTRALIA	O	M	R	W	w,nb		O	M	R	W	w,nb
Christian	37	7	144	7	-,-	(2)	18.2	2	56	4	-,-
Selk	32	7	95	1	-,1	(1)	21	5	41	1	-,-
Anderson	9	1	42	2	-,-	(4)	1	0	5	0	-,-
Harper	13	4	34	0	-,-						
Hantke	4	0	16	0	-,-		1	0	4	0	-,-
Hogue	7	1	24	0	-,-	(3)	2	0	8	0	-,-
Evans	4	0	19	0	-,-						
Parker	2	0	8	0	-,-						

SOUTH AUSTRALIA	O	M	R	W	w,nb		O	M	R	W	w,nb
Howard	22	6	78	3	1,-		9	3	32	2	-,-
Reedman	21.5	1	76	5	-,-		17	2	56	1	-,-
Wright	11	3	30	0	-,-		11	3	29	2	-,-
Stirling	8	1	34	1	-,-	(5)	4	0	19	0	-,-
Hack	3	0	14	0	-,-	(4)	3	1	5	0	-,-
Quist	12	4	30	1	-,-		5	2	10	0	-,-

FALL OF WICKETS

Wkt	SA 1st	WA 1st	SA 2nd	WA 2nd
1st	80	25	0	27
2nd	89	34	61	58
3rd	177	131	87	71
4th	299	152	110	131
5th	324	191	116	145
6th	360	196	-	145
7th	360	221	-	-
8th	360	250	-	-
9th	379	257	-	-
10th	388	269	-	-

South Australia ended a 15-year hiatus to win the Sheffield Shield for only the second time. The signing of J.N.Crawford, the Surrey and England allrounder, played a major part in events. Crawford's allround form, aligned to the bowling of O'Connor and Whitty and the batting of Clem Hill - who had a vintage season - gave the South Australians a significant edge over the other States. Innings victories were recorded in both their home matches at the outset of the season, and a defeat at the hands of Victoria at Melbourne proved to be the only setback for the eventual Shield-winners. They comprehensively defeated New South Wales at Sydney one week after their loss at Melbourne.

Victoria's win at home against South Australia was their only success in the Shield season. Armstrong and Smith were the best of a brittle batting lineup. Ransford, who appeared only twice, was unable to find form, and the experienced McAlister played just once. Saunders and Armstrong came to the fore in the bowling.

New South Wales's prospects of retaining the Shield were dealt a blow prior to the season, with the retirement of Noble on returning from the Australian tour of England. The NSWCA departed from tradition by appointing Austin Diamond as the new captain, and this brought the association into dispute with Victor Trumper which led to Trumper making himself unavailable for the season. It had previously been accepted that a senior player acceded to the leadership, and Trumper was in that category. It had also been the prerogative of the players in the past to elect their captain. Syd Gregory and Bert Hopkins played only one match each for New South Wales, Charlie Macartney was coaching in New Zealand and their experience was also missed. Young players vied for places and of these, Emery, Scott, Kelleway, Stack and the Minnett brothers impressed the most. Under the circumstances, New South Wales's two wins (both achieved against Victoria) were considered a reasonable return.

New South Wales and Queensland each won a match against the other. Roy Minnett and E.P.Barbour hit centuries and shared a double-century stand for the fourth wicket at Sydney, but New South Wales, having conceded a first-innings deficit, were unable to save the match. Queensland played their third match when the Victorian Shield side travelled to Brisbane after their engagement at Sydney. Arthur Kenny, in only his third first-class match, hit a century in each innings for Victoria. Bert Kortlang also impressed with a century in the first innings and shared a record sixth-wicket stand of 262 with Kenny. Victoria won easily.

The NSWCA staged a match at Sydney between New South Wales and The Rest as a benefit for C.T.B.Turner. Noble and Trumper made their only appearances for the season with contrasting results: Noble registered a pair but Trumper scored a century.

Tasmania were heavily defeated by both Victoria and New South Wales in their only two matches this year. Healy (218) and Vaughan (150) saw Victoria well on their way to their innings victory while Barbour (160) scored freely for New South Wales in their match at Hobart.

Victoria concluded the season by making their first visit to Western Australia, 12 months after originally planned. Three representative matches were played, with the results 2-1 in favour of Victoria. Kortlang compiled 474 runs in his five innings, three of which were unfinished. Selk captured 19 wickets for Western Australia.

An Australian team was selected to tour New Zealand at the end of January under the auspices of the Board of Control. The named team comprised W.W.Armstrong (captain), W.Bardsley, N.Dodds, S.H.Emery, A.C.Facy, C.R.Gorry, S.Hill, A.J.Y.Hopkins, C.Kelleway, R.E.Mayne, D.B.M.Smith, E.L.Waddy and W.J.Whitty. Hill and Waddy were subsequently unable to arrange leave and were replaced by C.E.Simpson and T.S.Warne. Earlier, E.A.C.Windsor had been invited but declined, and Facy accepted an invitation to take his place.

Leading Aggregates

Batsmen	M	I	NO	Runs	HS	Ave.	Bowlers	Runs	Wkts	Ave.
H.H.L.Kortlang (V)	5	9	4	656	197	131.20	J.V.Saunders (V)	849	49	17.32
C.Hill (SA)	3	4	0	609	205	152.25	J.D.Scott (NSW)	314	25	12.56
E.L.Waddy (NSW)	6	12	1	473	133	43.00	S.H.Emery (NSW)	430	25	17.20
W.Bardsley (NSW)	5	10	0	460	149	46.00	W.W.Armstrong (V)	457	22	20.77
A.Kenny (V)	6	11	1	413	164	41.30	A.Kenny (V)	405	21	19.28
C.McKenzie (V)	5	8	0	377	211	47.12	J.N.Crawford (SA)	378	20	18.90
W.W.Armstrong (V)	4	8	0	339	124	42.37	W.J.Stack (NSW)	571	20	28.55
E.P.Barbour (NSW)	2	4	1	329	160	109.66				

SHEFFIELD SHIELD TABLE

	P	W	L	D	Pts	Quotient	Runs Scored	Wkts Lost	Runs Conceded	Wkts Taken
SOUTH AUSTRALIA	4	3	1	-	2	1.602	1955	53	1819	79
NEW SOUTH WALES	4	2	2	-	0	0.999	1784	74	1519	63
VICTORIA	4	1	3	-	-2	0.661	1782	79	2183	64
TOTAL	6	6	6	-	0	1.000	5521	206	5521	206

SOUTH AUSTRALIA v VICTORIA (Shield Match 1)

Played at Adelaide Oval on November 13 (no play), 15, 16, 17, 18, 1909. (Timeless match)
Toss : South Australia.　　　　　Result : SOUTH AUSTRALIA WON BY AN INNINGS AND 209 RUNS.
Debuts: South Australia - G.C.Campbell, S.Hill, A.H.Woolcock (all f/c).
12th Men: P.H.Coombe (SA) and W.H.Cannon (Vic).
Umpires: P.Argall and T.G.Ward.
Attendances: no play, 2000, 800, 400, 100.　　　　Total: About 3300.　　　Receipts: No figures published.
Close of Play: 1st day no play; 2nd day SA 3/356 (C.Hill 171, Claxton 10); 3rd day Vic 5/75 (Warne 24); 4th day Vic (2) 0/5 (Speirs 2, Hazlitt 1).

Woolcock replaced W.L.Chamberlain (unavailable) in the South Australian side. Solly Hill became the sixth, and last, of the Hill brotherhood to appear for South Australia. Rain washed out play on the opening day. South Australia reached 590 due to the efforts of C.Hill (176 in 280 minutes, 14 fours), Gehrs (118 in 185 minutes, 17 fours, 2 chances), Claxton (88 in 135 minutes, 9 fours) and Hewer (83 not out in 125 minutes, 11 fours). The partnership of 253 between Hill and Gehrs was a new South Australian third-wicket record. Warne kept wickets for a time on the second day in the absence of Reeves through illness. McKenzie and Reeves were each out to the first ball they faced in the second innings. Rain delayed the start on the last day until 3.00pm and the Victorians collapsed on the "sloppy, sticky and treacherous wicket" (*Register*). Sources: *Wisden, C.B.O'Reilly, The Australasian, Adelaide Advertiser, South Australian Register*.

SOUTH AUSTRALIA

R.E.Mayne	b Saunders	32
L.R.Hill	b Saunders	5
*C.Hill	run out (Delves/Reeves)	176
D.R.A.Gehrs	b Scott	118
N.Claxton	c Ainslie b Saunders	88
S.Hill	b Scott	18
A.H.Woolcock	lbw b Scott	7
W.A.Hewer	not out	83
R.B.C.Rees	c Delves b Saunders	26
†G.C.Campbell	c & b Scott	5
L.E.Howard	b Scott	0
Extras	(b16, lb10, w3, nb3)	32
Total	(158.2 overs, 427 mins)	590

VICTORIA

J.Ainslie	b Rees	19	(8)	c Campbell b L.R.Hill	4
F.T.Delves	c Hewer b Rees	8	(3)	c Claxton b Rees	16
*T.S.Warne	st Campbell b Hewer	57	(7)	not out	24
C.McKenzie	b L.R.Hill	7	(5)	st Campbell b Rees	0
D.B.M.Smith	c Gehrs b Rees	2	(4)	c Gehrs b Claxton	3
J.F.Horan	lbw b Rees	11		c & b L.R.Hill	15
W.J.Scott	c Claxton b Howard	19	(9)	c S.Hill b L.R.Hill	0
G.R.Hazlitt	not out	82	(2)	c Howard b Claxton	8
N.L.Speirs	c Gehrs b Woolcock	49	(1)	c Gehrs b Rees	19
J.V.Saunders	b Rees	5		b Rees	1
†W.H.Reeves	absent ill	-		c Mayne b Rees	0
Extras	(b3, lb16, w3, nb3)	25		(b3, lb3, nb1)	7
Total	(89.1 overs, 262 mins)	284		(34.0 overs, 120 mins)	97

VICTORIA	O	M	R	W	w,nb		O	M	R	W	w,nb
Saunders	56	15	173	4	-,1						
Hazlitt	39	8	132	0	1,2						
Speirs	18	3	53	0	-,-						
Scott	24.2	1	91	5	-,-						
McKenzie	9	0	53	0	-,-						
Warne	11	0	46	0	-,-						
Ainslie	1	0	10	0	2,-						

SOUTH AUSTRALIA	O	M	R	W	w,nb		O	M	R	W	w,nb
Howard	20	6	64	1	2,2	(4)	1	0	6	0	-,-
Rees	31.1	6	88	5	-,-	(3)	13	0	41	5	-,-
L.R.Hill	19	6	36	1	1,1	(1)	7	1	14	3	-,1
Hewer	10	0	39	1	-,-	(5)	3	1	5	0	-,-
Claxton	6	0	12	0	-,-	(2)	10	3	24	2	-,-
Woolcock	3	0	20	1	-,-						

FALL OF WICKETS			
	SA	VIC	VIC
Wkt	1st	1st	2nd
1st	11	12	25
2nd	74	39	32
3rd	327	54	45
4th	371	57	45
5th	410	75	55
6th	426	121	78
7th	484	140	94
8th	519	266	94
9th	586	284	97
10th	590	-	97

QUEENSLAND v NEW SOUTH WALES

Played at Brisbane Cricket Ground (Woolloongabba) on December 11, 13, 14, 1909. (Timeless match)
Toss : Queensland.   Result : NEW SOUTH WALES WON BY SEVEN WICKETS.
Debuts: Queensland - B.W.Cook, S.J.Fennelly, F.Fett, J.W.Fletcher (all f/c). New South Wales - H.Cranney, C.T.Docker, G.G.Harvey,
    R.V.Minnett, J.A.Randell, J.Smith, G.A.Thomas (all f/c).
12th Men: J.S.Hutcheon (Qld) and A.W.Farnsworth (NSW).
Umpires: A.H.Benjamin and E.W.Jones.
Attendances: & Receipts: No figures published.
Close of Play: 1st day NSW 5/219 (Hodgkinson 18, Goddard 17,); 2nd day Qld (2) 7/153 (Fennelly 60).

Business responsibilities forced R.J.Hartigan, the nominated captain, to withdraw from the Queensland squad of thirteen. New South Wales
brought Farnsworth, Harvey and Smith into their twelve as replacements for C.R.Gorry, F.K.Gow and R.B.Minnett who were required to
reinforce their Sheffield Shield squad in Adelaide. E.P.Barbour had previously notified his unavailability. Docker, on debut, captured
wickets in his opening over in each innings, the fifth ball in the first (Crouch) and the sixth ball of the second (Fletcher). Thomas (96 in
96 minutes, 2 sixes and 9 fours) and Fennelly (97 in 147 minutes, 13 fours) each narrowly missed a century on debut. Hodgkinson (62 in
97 minutes, 6 fours) and Goddard (108 in 169 minutes, 12 fours, chance at 84) contributed to the substantial New South Wales first
innings lead. Sources: *Cricket, NSWCA Report, Sydney Morning Herald, Queensland Times, Brisbane Courier, The Queenslander.*

QUEENSLAND

J.W.Fletcher	b Randell	35		b Docker	1
*E.R.Crouch	b Docker	4	(7)	b Docker	0
W.B.Hayes	st Harvey b Randell	0		b Docker	21
J.S.Redgrave	lbw b Randell	15	(6)	b Docker	0
J.Thomson	c Randell b Smith	47	(2)	b Docker	27
S.J.Fennelly	c & b Middleton	41	(4)	c Cranney b Goddard	97
W.Armstrong	b Docker	19	(5)	run out (/Harvey)	0
†W.T.Evans	c Goddard b Smith	12		c Reid b Randell	33
J.W.McLaren	not out	1		not out	40
B.W.Cook	c Thomas b Docker	1		b Goddard	23
F.Fett	b Docker	0		c Minnett b Goddard	2
Extras	(b1, lb3, nb1)	5		(b10, lb3, w3)	16
Total	(32.2 overs, 127 mins)	180		(63.4 overs, 222 mins)	260

NEW SOUTH WALES

H.Cranney	b McLaren	30	(4)	not out	17
G.A.Thomas	b McLaren	96	(5)	not out	11
D.C.Reid	b McLaren	3	(1)	c & b Hayes	23
R.V.Minnett	c & b Hayes	42			
F.S.Middleton	b McLaren	2	(2)	b Hayes	5
*J.E.Hodgkinson	run out (Hayes/Evans)	62			
H.Goddard	not out	108			
C.T.Docker	c & b Hayes	15			
†G.G.Harvey	b Fett	3	(3)	b McLaren	5
J.A.Randell	c Cook b Redgrave	6			
J.Smith	c & b Redgrave	1			
Extras	(b2, lb6, nb4)	12		(lb2)	2
Total	(94.0 overs, 286 mins)	380		(12.0 overs, 35 mins) (3 wkts)	63

NEW SOUTH WALES	O	M	R	W	w,nb		O	M	R	W	w,nb			FALL OF WICKETS			
Docker	11.2	1	65	4	-,1		21	3	67	5	3,-			QLD	NSW	QLD	NSW
Randell	8	0	55	3	-,-		9	1	52	1	-,-		Wkt	1st	1st	2nd	2nd
Smith	8	0	36	2	-,-		16	1	54	0	-,-		1st	5	71	4	26
Middleton	5	0	19	1	-,-		7	2	20	0	-,-		2nd	8	81	40	31
Goddard							10.4	0	51	3	-,-		3rd	38	165	55	36
													4th	72	176	56	-
QUEENSLAND	O	M	R	W	w,nb		O	M	R	W	w,nb		5th	131	188	57	-
McLaren	27	3	107	4	-,4	(3)	3	1	10	1	-,-		6th	146	308	67	-
Hayes	24	2	101	2	-,-		6	0	35	2	-,-		7th	175	338	152	-
Redgrave	14	2	54	2	-,-								8th	179	349	199	-
Fett	14	1	58	1	-,-	(1)	3	0	16	0	-,-		9th	180	364	256	-
Cook	4	1	19	0	-,-								10th	180	380	260	-
Thomson	8	2	23	0	-,-												
Fletcher	3	0	6	0	-,-												

SOUTH AUSTRALIA v NEW SOUTH WALES (Shield Match 2)

Played at Adelaide Oval on December 18, 20, 21, 1909. (Timeless match)
Toss : New South Wales.   Result : SOUTH AUSTRALIA WON BY AN INNINGS AND 4 RUNS.
Debuts: South Australia - J.N.Crawford (SA only). New South Wales - H.L.Collins, F.K.Gow, W.J.Stack (all f/c).
12th Men: A.H.Woolcock (SA) and S.H.Emery (NSW).
Umpires: F.J.C.Thomas and G.A.Watson.
Attendances: 5000, 2000, 1000.   Total: About 8000.   Receipts: No figures published.
Close of Play: 1st day SA 4/184 (C.Hill 94); 2nd day NSW (2) 4/145 (Diamond 35, Barnes 25).

John Neville Crawford, the brilliant Surrey and England all-rounder, made his debut for South Australia in this match. Following a dispute with the Surrey C.C.C. during the previous winter, he had emigrated to Adelaide, and was to represent South Australia with much success until 1913-14. Thomas was appointed to replace P.Argall (ill) as umpire on the day prior to the game. W.A.Hewer announced himself unavailable after the naming of the South Australian side and was replaced in the team by Wright. C.Kelleway (injured), H.Carter and V.T.Trumper were all unavailable for New South Wales. Three sets of brothers took part, the Minnetts and Waddys for New South Wales and three Hills for South Australia. Bardsley was out to the third ball of the match. E.L.Waddy scored 118 in 135 minutes and hit 1 six and 18 fours, contributing 64 per cent of his side's first-innings total. C.Hill (205 in about 250 minutes, 2 fives and 20 fours) made a similar contribution for South Australia and was supported by Gehrs (72 in 105 minutes, 10 fours). Campbell, sent in as night-watchman on the first day, was out first ball. Sources: *Wisden, C.B.O'Reilly, NSWCA Report, Adelaide Advertiser, South Australian Register.*

NEW SOUTH WALES

W.Bardsley	lbw b L.R.Hill	2	(2)	c O'Connor b Wright	31
E.L.Waddy	c O'Connor b Whitty	118	(1)	b Crawford	31
F.K.Gow	b O'Connor	11		b Crawford	8
E.F.Waddy	c & b Wright	10		b Crawford	0
*A.Diamond	st Campbell b Wright	0		c O'Connor b Whitty	47
J.C.Barnes	b Crawford	5		c Whitty b Crawford	46
H.L.Collins	b Crawford	3		c Crawford b Whitty	1
R.B.Minnett	c Crawford b Whitty	11		c Campbell b Crawford	15
W.J.Stack	run out (L.R.Hill/Campbell)	4		c Mayne b Whitty	0
L.A.Minnett	c Mayne b O'Connor	2		b Crawford	12
†C.R.Gorry	not out	10		not out	3
Extras	(b4, lb2, nb2)	8		(b4, lb7, nb4)	15
Total	(45.2 overs, 150 mins)	184		(67.1 overs, 210 mins)	209

SOUTH AUSTRALIA

R.E.Mayne	b L.A.Minnett	4
L.R.Hill	c E.F.Waddy b L.A.Minnett	3
*C.Hill	b R.B.Minnett	205
D.R.A.Gehrs	c E.L.Waddy b R.B.Minnett	72
†G.C.Campbell	b R.B.Minnett	0
N.Claxton	b Stack	0
J.N.Crawford	c Barnes b L.A.Minnett	14
S.Hill	b L.A.Minnett	29
J.D.A.O'Connor	c Diamond b Collins	24
W.J.Whitty	c E.F.Waddy b L.A.Minnett	23
A.W.Wright	not out	2
Extras	(b16, lb1, nb4)	21
Total	(90.2 overs, 300 mins)	397

SOUTH AUSTRALIA	O	M	R	W	w,nb		O	M	R	W	w,nb
L.R.Hill	4	0	22	1	-,2		8	1	24	0	-,3
O'Connor	11.2	2	34	2	-,-		7	1	31	0	-,-
Whitty	10	2	38	2	-,-	(4)	14	3	42	3	-,1
Crawford	11	2	31	2	-,-	(3)	24.1	5	59	6	-,-
Wright	9	2	51	2	-,-		11	1	31	1	-,-
Claxton							3	1	7	0	-,-

NEW SOUTH WALES	O	M	R	W	w,nb
L.A.Minnett	23.2	3	90	5	-,3
Stack	25	1	122	1	-,-
R.B.Minnett	21	5	69	3	-,1
Collins	12	3	35	1	-,-
Barnes	9	0	60	0	-,-

FALL OF WICKETS

	NSW	SA	NSW
	1st	1st	2nd
Wkt			
1st	2	4	58
2nd	33	13	70
3rd	69	184	72
4th	69	184	80
5th	80	191	169
6th	90	216	176
7th	145	323	187
8th	157	361	187
9th	170	391	197
10th	184	397	209

VICTORIA v NEW SOUTH WALES (Shield Match 3)

Played at Melbourne Cricket Ground on December 27, 28, 29, 1909. (Timeless match)
Toss : New South Wales.   Result : NEW SOUTH WALES WON BY 272 RUNS.
Debuts: Victoria - W.I.Sewart (Vic only).
12th Men: T.J.Matthews (Vic) and F.K.Gow (NSW).
Umpires: R.M.Crockett and W.Hannah.
Attendances: 8031, 4600, 3395.   Total: 16,026.   Receipts: £452.
Close of Play: 1st day Vic 0/8 (Sewart 0, Carkeek 7); 2nd day NSW (2) 3/111 (Bardsley 59, Emery 11).

T.S.Warne (leg injury) and T.J.Matthews were omitted from the thirteen players nominated by the Victorian selector and captain, P.A.McAlister. Bardsley dominated the batting in the match with innings of 78 (139 minutes, 1 five and 5 fours) and 149 (260 minutes, 16 fours). Laver dismissed E.L.Waddy with the third ball of the New South Wales second innings. McAlister was dismissed in the first over of Victoria's second innings, in which Armstrong (67 in 94 minutes, 7 fours) similarly compiled the highest score. The wicket was "in excellent order" (*Age*) throughout and could not be blamed for the low-scoring. Emery's first innings bowling figures of 7 for 28 remained the best of his career. Sewart had previously played for Queensland. *NSWCA Report* incorrectly gives NSW (2) Laver 1/60, Saunders 4/65. Sources: *Wisden, NSWCA Report, The Age, The Argus, The Herald, The Australasian.*

NEW SOUTH WALES

E.L.Waddy	c & b Laver	26		c Carkeek b Laver	0
W.Bardsley	b Laver	78		lbw b Armstrong	149
E.F.Waddy	c Armstrong b Hazlitt	27		b Armstrong	7
*A.Diamond	c & b Armstrong	22		b Saunders	31
J.C.Barnes	c Carkeek b Kyle	33	(6)	lbw b Armstrong	24
H.L.Collins	b Kyle	17	(7)	b Saunders	11
R.B.Minnett	not out	41	(8)	c Carroll b Saunders	7
S.H.Emery	run out (Sewart/Carkeek)	5	(5)	c Sewart b Kyle	11
W.J.Stack	c Armstrong b Laver	22		c Armstrong b Saunders	8
L.A.Minnett	c Ransford b Laver	11		not out	6
†C.R.Gorry	hit wkt b Armstrong	0		c Carkeek b Armstrong	6
Extras	(lb2, w1, nb2)	5		(b1, lb2)	3
Total	(83.2 overs, 249 mins)	287		(92.5 overs, 262 mins)	263

VICTORIA

W.I.Sewart	b Emery	26	(6)	b Emery	7
†W.Carkeek	st Gorry b Stack	7	(9)	c Emery b Stack	26
E.V.Carroll	run out (Collins/Gorry)	2		b Emery	7
V.S.Ransford	lbw b Emery	20		c Gorry b Emery	2
W.W.Armstrong	b Emery	2		lbw b Stack	67
D.B.M.Smith	b Emery	9	(2)	c Diamond b L.A.Minnett	36
*P.A.McAlister	c R.B.Minnett b Emery	7	(1)	b L.A.Minnett	0
G.R.Hazlitt	c & b Emery	6	(7)	c Barnes b Emery	0
F.J.Laver	b R.B.Minnett	1	(8)	b L.A.Minnett	10
J.H.Kyle	c Bardsley b Emery	8		not out	18
J.V.Saunders	not out	1		b Emery	4
Extras	(b2, lb2)	4		(b4, w3, nb1)	8
Total	(37.0 overs, 127 mins)	93		(42.1 overs, 138 mins)	185

VICTORIA	O	M	R	W	w,nb		O	M	R	W	w,nb
Laver	26	6	90	4	-,-		26	5	62	1	-,-
Armstrong	27.2	7	68	2	-,-		21.5	8	44	4	-,-
Saunders	3	0	17	0	-,-		22	5	63	4	-,-
Hazlitt	15	4	57	1	1,2		13	2	50	0	-,-
Kyle	11	1	46	2	-,-		10	1	41	1	-,-
Ransford	1	0	4	0	-,-						

NEW SOUTH WALES	O	M	R	W	w,nb		O	M	R	W	w,nb
L.A.Minnett	8	4	10	0	-,-		13	3	41	3	-,-
Emery	12	1	28	7	-,-		19.1	3	85	5	1,-
Stack	7	0	27	1	-,-	(4)	6	1	28	2	-,-
R.B.Minnett	10	3	24	1	-,-	(3)	4	0	23	0	-,1

FALL OF WICKETS

Wkt	NSW 1st	VIC 1st	NSW 2nd	VIC 2nd
1st	46	9	0	0
2nd	97	13	23	38
3rd	151	48	92	47
4th	175	60	111	51
5th	206	63	160	64
6th	207	74	182	64
7th	225	83	196	83
8th	265	84	218	159
9th	287	92	257	180
10th	287	93	263	185

NEW SOUTH WALES v QUEENSLAND

Played at Sydney Cricket Ground on December 31, 1909, January 1, 3, 4, 1910. (Timeless match)
Toss : New South Wales.   Result : QUEENSLAND WON BY THREE WICKETS.
Debuts: Queensland - E.A.Benbow (f/c).
12th Men: W.C.Whitting (NSW) and G.G.Armstrong (Qld).
Umpires: R.Callaway and A.C.Jones.
Attendances: 1300, 2000, 1200, 100.   Total: About 4600.   Receipts: £172.
Close of Play: 1st day Qld 2/154 (Redgrave 70, Crouch 10); 2nd day NSW (2) 2/145 (Minnett 69, Hodgkinson 7); 3rd day Qld (2) 1/56
    (Thomson 41, Crouch 14).

Armstrong replaced S.J.Fennelly (unavailable) in the Queensland twelve and Scott was brought into the New South Wales team when C.T.Docker (work) withdrew. Cranney was missed by Fletcher at slip off McLaren from the first ball of the match. Minnett (36) was struck in the mouth during Thomson's first over of the first innings and retired at 2/65, returning at 5/143. Thomson (6) was hit on the body during a fiery spell from Scott later in the day and was forced to retire at about 1/20, resuming on the following day at 3/185. Scott also scored hits on Hartigan, Redgrave (twice), Fletcher (twice) and Crouch, as well as dislocating his wicket-keeper Harvey's finger, causing him to give the gloves to, first Goddard and later Cranney. Harvey did not return until the second day. Redgrave (92 in 105 minutes, 16 fours), Crouch (67 in 195 minutes), Evans (52 in 46 minutes, 8 fours) and Hutcheon (63 in 59 minutes, 1 five and 7 fours) hit half-centuries for Queensland. Minnett (169 in 261 minutes, 15 fours, chance at 128) shared century stands with Thomas (65 in 90 minutes, 9 fours) for the second wicket, and Barbour (124 not out in 208 minutes, 13 fours, 3 chances) for the fourth wicket. Hartigan returned to Brisbane on business late on the third day before the Queensland second innings began. *Cricket* incorrectly gives NSW (2) Minnett c Evans b Hayes. Sources: *Cricket, NSWCA Report, Sydney Referee, Sydney Morning Herald, Town & Country Journal, Sydney Mail, Sydney Daily Telegraph.*

NEW SOUTH WALES

H.Cranney	c Hartigan b Redgrave	19		run out (Thomson/Evans)	2
G.A.Thomas	st Evans b Hayes	4		st Evans b Hayes	65
R.V.Minnett	c Hayes b Redgrave	39		c Evans b Lewis	169
E.P.Barbour	b Thomson	13	(5)	not out	124
F.S.Middleton	run out (Benbow/Evans)	1	(6)	b Lewis	5
H.Goddard	c Hutcheon b Redgrave	52	(7)	b Redgrave	0
*J.E.Hodgkinson	c Thomson b Lewis	27	(4)	run out (Crouch/Evans)	12
J.D.Scott	c Hutcheon b Redgrave	3	(10)	b McLaren	0
†G.G.Harvey	b Lewis	2	(8)	run out (/Evans)	12
J.A.Randell	c Hutcheon b McLaren	10	(9)	c Redgrave b McLaren	7
J.Smith	not out	7		lbw b Hayes	2
Extras	(b5, lb3)	8		(b17, lb1, w1)	19
Total	(56.4 overs, 169 mins)	185		(114.0 overs, 328 mins)	417

QUEENSLAND

*R.J.Hartigan	b Scott	5			
J.Thomson	b Goddard	18		b Scott	44
J.W.Fletcher	c sub (W.C.Whitting) b Middleton	47	(1)	run out (Thomas/Smith)	1
J.S.Redgrave	c Harvey b Scott	92		c Barbour b Smith	30
E.R.Crouch	b Goddard	67	(3)	c Barbour b Scott	35
W.B.Hayes	c Cranney b Smith	3	(5)	c Harvey b Scott	1
E.A.Benbow	c Smith b Goddard	0	(8)	b Goddard	0
J.W.Lewis	c Barbour b Smith	3			
J.S.Hutcheon	c & b Scott	27	(7)	c Barbour b Smith	63
†W.T.Evans	c Minnett b Goddard	52	(9)	not out	3
J.W.McLaren	not out	43	(6)	not out	40
Extras	(b19, lb1, w1, nb1)	22		(b4, lb1, w5)	10
Total	(89.5 overs, 286 mins)	379		(53.3 overs, 170 mins) (7 wkts)	227

QUEENSLAND	O	M	R	W	w,nb		O	M	R	W	w,nb
McLaren	13.4	1	51	1	-,-		26	3	90	2	1,-
Hayes	15	1	49	1	-,-		25	2	91	2	-,-
Redgrave	15	3	30	4	-,-		29	6	78	1	-,-
Thomson	3	0	13	1	-,-		14	0	67	0	-,-
Lewis	10	3	34	2	-,-		12	1	50	2	-,-
Fletcher							8	0	22	0	-,-

NEW SOUTH WALES	O	M	R	W	w,nb		O	M	R	W	w,nb
Scott	27	4	81	3	-,-		22	3	75	3	5,-
Randell	11	1	46	0	-,-	(3)	7	0	37	0	-,-
Smith	19	1	113	2	-,-	(2)	12.3	2	53	2	-,-
Barbour	8	1	36	0	-,-		3	0	11	0	-,-
Middleton	10	3	32	1	-,1		3	1	17	0	-,-
Goddard	14.5	0	49	4	1,-		6	0	24	1	-,-

FALL OF WICKETS

Wkt	NSW 1st	QLD 1st	NSW 2nd	QLD 2nd
1st	12	6	2	14
2nd	48	141	133	69
3rd	74	185	154	108
4th	82	204	364	114
5th	143	207	365	119
6th	158	209	370	215
7th	163	212	393	219
8th	168	243	414	-
9th	173	298	414	-
10th	185	379	417	-

VICTORIA v SOUTH AUSTRALIA (Shield Match 4)

Played at Melbourne Cricket Ground on January 1, 3, 4, 5, 6, 1910. (Timeless match)
Toss : Victoria.   Result : VICTORIA WON BY 81 RUNS,
Debuts: Victoria - A.Kenny (f/c).
12th Men: G.R.Hazlitt (Vic) and P.C.Desmazeures (SA).
Umpires: E.Barrass and R.M.Crockett.
Attendances: 8247, 7197, 4691, 4015, 850.   Total: About 25,000.   Receipts: £647.
Close of Play: 1st day SA 2/143 (C.Hill 92, Crawford 23); 2nd day Vic (2) 0/25 (Sewart 3, Delves 18); 3rd day Vic (2) 7/429
   (Armstrong 119, Laver 6); 4th day SA (2) 7/201 (Quist 18).

T.S.Warne (ill), N.Claxton, D.R.A.Gehrs, W.A.Hewer and L.R.Hill were unavailable for their respective States. P.A.McAlister, Victoria's sole selector, omitted himself from the thirteen named for the match. Sewart, batting without gloves, was hit on the hand from the fifth ball of the match and forced to retire hurt at 0/0. He resumed at 7/155 but did not field at all during the match; Hazlitt acted as substitute throughout. Clem Hill (185 in 240 minutes, 1 six and 19 fours, chance at 150) dominated South Australia's first innings. Smith (146 in 160 minutes, 1 six and 19 fours) and Armstrong (124 in 200 minutes, 13 fours) added 170 for the fourth wicket to turn the match in Victoria's favour. Clem Hill again (43 in 35 minutes, 5 fours) and brother Solly (58 in 140 minutes, 5 fours) batted in contrasting roles in the second innings. Sources: *Wisden, C.B.O'Reilly, VCA Report, The Age, The Argus, The Herald, The Australasian.*

VICTORIA

W.I.Sewart	c Crawford b O'Connor	9	b Whitty	6
F.T.Delves	c Leak b Whitty	36	c C.Hill b Crawford	28
V.S.Ransford	b Wright	37	st Campbell b Wright	45
D.B.M.Smith	c Mayne b O'Connor	2	b Crawford	146
W.W.Armstrong	b Whitty	1	b Whitty	124
W.J.Scott	c Mayne b Crawford	27	st Campbell b Wright	24
A.Kenny	b Crawford	7	c Quist b O'Connor	27
T.J.Matthews	c Whitty b O'Connor	31	lbw b O'Connor	5
*F.J.Laver	st Campbell b Whitty	0	not out	23
†W.Carkeek	c Crawford b Wright	11	b O'Connor	3
J.V.Saunders	not out	23	b O'Connor	2
Extras	(b16, lb6)	22	(b16, lb7, w1, nb1)	25
Total	(50.5 overs, 160 mins)	206	(111.2 overs, 345 mins)	458

SOUTH AUSTRALIA

R.E.Mayne	st Carkeek b Armstrong	6	st Carkeek b Saunders	14
E.H.Leak	b Laver	18	c Kenny b Armstrong	11
*C.Hill	c Scott b Armstrong	185	c Delves b Matthews	43
J.N.Crawford	c Laver b Kenny	75	c Delves b Laver	4
S.Hill	run out (/Kenny)	19	st Carkeek b Saunders	58
A.H.Woolcock	c sub (G.R.Hazlitt) b Kenny	8	c Smith b Armstrong	37
K.H.Quist	b Kenny	16	c Scott b Armstrong	24
J.D.A.O'Connor	not out	15	lbw b Saunders	5
†G.C.Campbell	lbw b Saunders	7	c Carkeek b Saunders	7
W.J.Whitty	b Saunders	0	b Saunders	9
A.W.Wright	b Saunders	0	not out	0
Extras	(b6, lb4, nb1)	11	(b6, lb3, nb2)	11
Total	(132.4 overs, 370 mins)	360	(97.2 overs, 266 mins)	223

SOUTH AUSTRALIA	O	M	R	W	w,nb		O	M	R	W	w,nb					
Crawford	13	1	63	2	-,-		27	3	120	2	-,1					
Whitty	21	2	77	3	-,-		34	5	109	2	-,-					
O'Connor	13	5	31	3	-,-	(4)	28.2	5	95	4	-,-					
Wright	3.5	2	13	2	-,-	(3)	18	1	81	2	-,-					
Woolcock							3	1	17	0	1,-					
Quist							1	0	11	0	-,-					

VICTORIA	O	M	R	W	w,nb		O	M	R	W	w,nb	
Saunders	28.4	10	70	3	-,-		27.2	6	69	5	-,-	
Armstrong	34	8	72	2	-,1		28	9	59	3	-,2	
Matthews	15	1	58	0	-,-	(4)	15	4	36	1	-,-	
Laver	27	6	64	1	-,-	(3)	17	6	25	1	-,-	
Ransford	3	0	8	0	-,-							
Kenny	19	3	58	3	-,-	(5)	3	0	11	0	-,-	
Scott	6	1	19	0	-,-	(6)	7	4	12	0	-,-	

FALL OF WICKETS

Wkt	VIC 1st	SA 1st	VIC 2nd	SA 2nd
1st	52	9	33	23
2nd	72	88	51	39
3rd	73	277	135	70
4th	92	296	305	75
5th	105	319	362	153
6th	138	319	411	195
7th	155	341	421	201
8th	163	360	435	211
9th	166	360	448	218
10th	206	360	458	223

NEW SOUTH WALES v SOUTH AUSTRALIA (Shield Match 5)

Played at Sydney Cricket Ground on January 8, 10, 11, 1910. (Timeless match)
Toss : New South Wales.   Result : SOUTH AUSTRALIA WON BY SEVEN WICKETS.
Debuts: South Australia - P.C.Desmazeures (SA only).
12th Men: F.K.Gow (NSW). No 12th named for SA, only 11 in party.
Umpires: W.J.Bruton and W.G.Curran.
Attendances: 5625, 3162, 784.   Total: 9571.   Receipts: £373.
Close of Play: 1st day SA 9/184 (Whitty 28, Wright 18); 2nd day NSW (2) 289 all out.

V.T.Trumper withdrew from the selected New South Wales side and was replaced by R.V.Minnett, the nominated 12th man. Clem Hill had returned to Adelaide after the match with Victoria (a previously agreed condition of his availability for that match) leaving the South Australians without a reserve. The West Adelaide player A.D.G.Sands, who was in Sydney at the time, substituted when Wright was forced from the field after injuring a foot while attempting to field a hard drive by Waddy from his own bowling. Whitty bowled throughout the New South Wales first innings, bowling Diamond and R.V.Minnett with consecutive deliveries. He later combined with Wright to add a vital 68 for the last wicket and extend South Australia's first-innings advantage. Admirable pace bowling by Crawford removed New South Wales a second time despite the efforts of Kelleway (108 in 163 minutes, 13 fours). He followed up with a match-winning innings (73 not out in 135 minutes, 4 fours) on a wicket drenched by frequent showers of rain. "Solly" Hill (62 in 70 minutes, 5 fours) gave great support and the win secured the Sheffield Shield. Desmazeures, whose previous first-class appearance was for Victoria in 1906-07, played his sole match for South Australia. Sources: *Wisden, C.B.O'Reilly, NSWCA Report, Sydney Referee, Sydney Morning Herald, Town & Country Journal, Sydney Mail.*

NEW SOUTH WALES

E.L.Waddy	c Desmazeures b Whitty	30	(4)	c Quist b Crawford	9
W.Bardsley	lbw b O'Connor	8		c Leak b Crawford	11
J.C.Barnes	b O'Connor	0		c Campbell b Crawford	10
*A.Diamond	b Whitty	12	(1)	c Campbell b O'Connor	30
R.V.Minnett	b Whitty	0		b Crawford	6
C.Kelleway	b O'Connor	0		c Woolcock b Crawford	108
A.J.Y.Hopkins	b Whitty	13		lbw b O'Connor	8
S.H.Emery	run out (Crawford/Campbell)	7		c Leak b Quist	30
W.J.Stack	c O'Connor b Whitty	6		b Crawford	8
†C.R.Gorry	b Crawford	10	(11)	not out	1
L.A.Minnett	not out	0	(10)	b Crawford	37
Extras	(b1, lb4, nb1)	6		(b23, lb4, nb4)	31
Total	(32.0 overs, 99 mins)	92		(85.0 overs, 244 mins)	289

SOUTH AUSTRALIA

*R.E.Mayne	c Waddy b L.A.Minnett	61		c L.A.Minnett b Hopkins	35
E.H.Leak	c Gorry b Kelleway	10		b Emery	0
J.N.Crawford	b Stack	12		not out	73
S.Hill	b Emery	15		st Gorry b Waddy	62
A.H.Woolcock	b Emery	18		not out	4
K.H.Quist	c Gorry b Hopkins	3			
P.C.Desmazeures	b Emery	0			
J.D.A.O'Connor	c Bardsley b Hopkins	2			
†G.C.Campbell	b Emery	4			
W.J.Whitty	b Emery	34			
A.W.Wright	not out	28			
Extras	(b10, lb8, w1, nb1)	20		(b3, lb1)	4
Total	(61.1 overs, 179 mins)	207		(52.3 overs, 140 mins) (3 wkts)	178

SOUTH AUSTRALIA	O	M	R	W	w,nb		O	M	R	W	w,nb
Whitty	16	4	43	5	-,-		25	7	54	0	-,1
O'Connor	11	4	30	3	-,-		22	2	76	2	-,-
Crawford	5	0	13	1	-,1		27	2	92	7	-,3
Wright							3	1	8	0	-,-
Quist							7	1	24	1	-,-
Desmazeures							1	0	4	0	-,-

NEW SOUTH WALES	O	M	R	W	w,nb		O	M	R	W	w,nb
L.A.Minnett	8	0	47	1	-,1		16	1	58	0	-,-
Emery	17.1	3	55	5	-,-		14	0	39	1	-,-
Kelleway	13	3	31	1	-,-	(4)	10	0	27	0	-,-
Stack	17	3	39	1	1,-	(5)	3	0	14	0	-,-
Hopkins	6	1	15	2	-,-	(3)	9	0	32	1	-,-
Waddy							0.3	0	4	1	-,-

	FALL OF WICKETS			
	NSW	SA	NSW	SA
Wkt	1st	1st	2nd	2nd
1st	23	55	22	10
2nd	23	78	45	65
3rd	44	101	60	174
4th	44	128	68	-
5th	53	131	84	-
6th	53	131	116	-
7th	73	133	161	-
8th	74	138	188	-
9th	80	139	288	-
10th	92	207	289	-

NEW SOUTH WALES v THE REST

Played at Sydney Cricket Ground on January 21, 22, 24, 25, 1910. (Timeless match)
Toss : New South Wales.   Result : NEW SOUTH WALES WON BY 35 RUNS.
Debuts: Nil.
12th Men: E.F.Waddy (NSW) and R.V.Minnett (Rest).
Umpires: A.Lucas and R.M.Wallace.
Attendances: 3000, 5700, 2300, 1000.   Total: About 12,000.   Receipts: £479 (plus £55 in "collections").
Close of Play: 1st day NSW 7/258 (Trumper 87, Cotter 7); 2nd day Rest 6/99 (Laver 8, Facy 4); 3rd day NSW (2) 275 all out.

The match was staged as a benefit for C.T.B.Turner, aged 47, who was actively involved in coaching for many years following his retirement from first-class cricket in 1897. It raised £331 in his favour and was his only first-class match in the 20th century. Gow, Hutcheon and Simpson replaced C.Hill, V.S.Ransford and J.S.Redgrave (all unavailable) for The Rest. Trumper, who scored 105 in 127 minutes with 12 fours and offered a chance at 92, was unable to bat in the second innings because of a heavy cold. Noble, who came out of retirement to captain New South Wales in this match, suffered the ignominy of a pair, being bowled first ball and third ball respectively in each innings. Waddy (133 in 156 minutes, 13 fours) and Bardsley (55 in 81 minutes, 8 fours) added 124 for the first wicket in the second innings. The Rest began badly - Turner opened with a maiden to Mayne, Simpson fell in the next over bowled by Kelleway, followed by Mayne in Turner's second over and Smith to the first ball of Kelleway's second over. Batting again, Mayne (63 in 99 minutes, 4 fours), Simpson (102 in 102 minutes, 13 fours) and Armstrong (85 in 105 minutes, 10 fours) atoned for their first innings failures. Sources: *Wisden, NSWCA Report, Sydney Referee, Sydney Morning Herald, Town & Country Journal, Sydney Mail.*

NEW SOUTH WALES

E.L.Waddy	c & b Laver	43		c Smith b Armstrong	133
W.Bardsley	c Mayne b Laver	28		c Armstrong b O'Connor	55
*M.A.Noble	b Facy	0		b Whitty	0
C.Kelleway	b Armstrong	65		c O'Connor b Whitty	11
S.E.Gregory	c O'Connor b Laver	14		b Whitty	0
V.T.Trumper	c O'Connor b Armstrong	105		absent ill	-
C.T.B.Turner	b Laver	8	(6)	b Facy	19
S.H.Emery	c Laver b Armstrong	2		c Carkeek b Facy	2
A.Cotter	st Carkeek b Armstrong	23	(7)	c Hutcheon b Armstrong	27
W.J.Stack	c Simpson b Armstrong	8	(9)	not out	16
†C.R.Gorry	not out	0	(10)	c Carkeek b Armstrong	0
Extras	(b2, lb4)	6		(b3, lb9)	12
Total	(86.2 overs, 237 mins)	302		(68.1 overs, 207 mins)	275

THE REST

R.E.Mayne	b Turner	0		run out (Gregory)	63
C.E.Simpson	c E.L.Waddy b Kelleway	0		run out (Gregory)	102
D.B.M.Smith	c Gorry b Kelleway	0		b Kelleway	24
F.K.Gow	c Noble b Stack	34	(6)	lbw b Emery	13
W.W.Armstrong	c Emery b Kelleway	7		c Gorry b Noble	85
J.S.Hutcheon	c Trumper b Stack	36	(4)	st Gorry b Stack	17
*F.J.Laver	b Cotter	33	(11)	not out	0
A.C.Facy	not out	21	(7)	b Kelleway	44
†W.Carkeek	c Gregory b Emery	17		b Kelleway	0
J.D.A.O'Connor	st Gorry b Stack	0	(8)	c sub (E.F.Waddy) b Kelleway	13
W.J.Whitty	run out (/Emery)	0	(10)	c Cotter b Stack	2
Extras	(b7, lb2, w2, nb1)	12		(b16, lb1, w1, nb1)	19
Total	(43.2 overs, 135 mins)	160		(84.3 overs, 256 mins)	382

THE REST	O	M	R	W	w,nb		O	M	R	W	w,nb
Whitty	14	2	43	0	-,-		16	1	78	3	-,-
O'Connor	11	1	60	0	-,-	(3)	16	5	51	1	-,-
Laver	27	4	75	4	-,-	(4)	7	1	24	0	-,-
Facy	11	1	24	1	-,-	(2)	18	0	49	2	-,-
Armstrong	18.2	3	67	5	-,-		11.1	0	61	3	-,-
Simpson	5	0	27	0	-,-						

NEW SOUTH WALES	O	M	R	W	w,nb		O	M	R	W	w,nb
Turner	8	2	21	1	-,-						
Kelleway	9	1	34	3	-,-	(3)	22	3	88	4	-,-
Noble	3	0	7	0	-,-	(4)	20	3	67	1	-,-
Stack	12	1	57	3	-,-	(5)	10.3	0	56	2	-,-
Emery	4.2	0	16	1	2,-	(2)	16	1	74	1	-,-
Cotter	7	1	13	1	-,1	(1)	16	1	78	0	1,1

FALL OF WICKETS

Wkt	NSW 1st	REST 1st	NSW 2nd	REST 2nd
1st	70	0	124	167
2nd	71	0	125	170
3rd	77	0	149	205
4th	105	8	149	217
5th	225	79	213	258
6th	238	81	249	359
7th	249	132	253	371
8th	275	133	264	371
9th	299	160	275	382
10th	302	160	-	382

NEW SOUTH WALES v VICTORIA (Shield Match 6)

Played at Sydney Cricket Ground on January 26, 27, 28 (no play), 29, 1910. (Timeless match)
Toss : Victoria.   Result : NEW SOUTH WALES WON BY SIX WICKETS.
Debuts: New South Wales - C.E.Simpson (NSW only). Victoria - H.H.L.Kortlang (f/c).
12th Men: J.C.Barnes (NSW) and F.J.Laver (Vic).
Umpires: W.J.Bruton and W.G.Curran.
Attendances: 5371, 1583, no play, 1934.   Total: 8888.   Receipts: £341.
Close of Play: 1st day NSW 161 all out; 2nd day NSW (2) 0/34 (Bardsley 10, Gregory 24); 3rd day no play.

A.J.Y.Hopkins (unavailable) and V.T.Trumper (ill) were replaced in the New South Wales side by Minnett and Simpson. Victorian player V.S.Ransford remained in Melbourne for business reasons and appeared for his State against Tasmania. Chief batting contributions for Victoria in this match came from Delves (57 in 95 minutes, 6 fours), Ainslie (50 in 95 minutes, 7 fours) and Scott (81 in 122 minutes, 8 fours). Barnes and R.E.Mayne, who had remained in Sydney after the NSW v The Rest match in order to leave with the touring team to New Zealand, acted alternately as substitute for D.B.M.Smith (foot injury while batting) on the first day. Laver had been left out of the Victorian team because of a leg injury. Rain prevented any play on the third day. Gregory led New South Wales to victory by scoring 169 not out in 255 minutes, hitting 15 fours. Simpson, playing his first match for New South Wales, had previously represented Queensland. *Wisden* incorrectly gives Vic (1) Stack 0/44; Vic (2) Armstrong st Gorry b Scott, Scott 7/48, Stack 1/68. Sources: *Wisden, NSWCA Report, VCA Report, Sydney Referee, Sydney Morning Herald, Town & Country Journal, Sydney Mail, Newcastle Herald.*

VICTORIA

T.S.Warne	c Waddy b Scott	0	b Simpson		37
F.T.Delves	c Gorry b Scott	57	c Gregory b Scott		10
D.B.M.Smith	b Kelleway	32	b Emery		0
J.Ainslie	run out (Bardsley)	5	c Gow b Stack		50
*W.W.Armstrong	c Emery b Scott	6	st Gorry b Stack		47
W.J.Scott	b Stack	3	c Gorry b Scott		81
H.H.L.Kortlang	not out	34	c Simpson b Scott		15
A.Kenny	b Emery	10	b Scott		7
T.J.Matthews	b Emery	13	c Gorry b Scott		0
†W.Carkeek	b Emery	11	c Simpson b Scott		0
J.V.Saunders	c Gorry b Emery	0	not out		18
Extras	(b7, lb2)	9	(b8, lb5, w1)		14
Total	(60.1 overs, 168 mins)	180	(78.3 overs, 242 mins)		279

NEW SOUTH WALES

W.Bardsley	c Armstrong b Saunders	51	b Kenny		47
E.L.Waddy	b Saunders	3	(6) not out		2
C.E.Simpson	b Armstrong	6	b Armstrong		13
C.Kelleway	c sub (J.C.Barnes) b Saunders	3	st Carkeek b Warne		50
*S.E.Gregory	run out(/Matthews)	22	(2) not out		169
F.K.Gow	c Ainslie b Saunders	38	(5) c Warne b Kortlang		4
R.V.Minnett	b Armstrong	6			
S.H.Emery	c Kenny b Saunders	4			
W.J.Stack	c sub (R.E.Mayne) b Saunders	7			
J.D.Scott	not out	9			
†C.R.Gorry	run out	8			
Extras	(b4)	4	(b6, lb4, w1, nb3)		14
Total	(34.2 overs, 115 mins)	161	(88.2 overs, 255 mins) (4 wkts)		299

NEW SOUTH WALES	O	M	R	W	w,nb		O	M	R	W	w,nb			FALL OF WICKETS			
														VIC	NSW	VIC	NSW
Scott	14	3	41	3	-,-		16.3	3	48	6	1,-		Wkt	1st	1st	2nd	2nd
Stack	13	1	44	1	-,-	(5)	17	3	68	2	-,-		1st	2	13	22	118
Kelleway	15	1	41	1	-,-		14	3	44	0	-,-		2nd	63	20	23	143
Emery	18.1	1	45	4	-,-	(2)	25	3	88	1	-,-		3rd	80	31	79	280
Simpson						(4)	6	3	17	1	-,-		4th	97	65	138	293
													5th	104	110	170	-
VICTORIA	O	M	R	W	w,nb		O	M	R	W	w,nb		6th	106	131	202	-
Saunders	13.2	0	76	6	-,-		24	1	86	0	-,-		7th	132	131	218	-
Armstrong	14	4	34	2	-,-		30	11	52	1	-,3		8th	156	140	218	-
Scott	4	1	20	0	-,-	(4)	12	1	45	0	1,-		9th	180	144	218	-
Matthews	3	0	27	0	-,-	(5)	3	0	27	0	-,-		10th	180	161	279	-
Kenny						(3)	10	1	31	1	-,-						
Kortlang							7	1	32	1	-,-						
Warne							2.2	0	12	1	-,-						

VICTORIA v TASMANIA

Played at Melbourne Cricket Ground on January 29, 31, February 1, 2, 1910. (Timeless match)

Toss : Victoria.   Result : VICTORIA WON BY AN INNINGS AND 126 RUNS.

Debuts: Victoria - E.J.Binney, H.W.Hart, C.Kiernan (all f/c). Tasmania - W.K.Eltham, E.A.McDonald, M.S.McKenzie, K.R.Westbrook (all f/c).

12th Men: N.L.Speirs (Vic) and S.R.Frost (Tas).

Umpires: E.Barrass and D.A.Elder.

Attendances: 1955, 2082, 400, "handful".   Total: About 4500.   Receipts: £85.

Close of Play: 1st day Vic 4/400 (Healy 167, Vaughan 46); 2nd day Tas 3/63 (Burn 31, Eltham 4); 3rd day Tas (2) 0/41 (Hawson 15, McKenzie 21).

Healy (218 in 377 minutes, 14 fours, chance at 36) and Vaughan (150 in 182 minutes, 1 five and 19 fours) established a new Victorian fifth-wicket record partnership of 255. Vaughan did not field at all during the match as he was sent to Brisbane on the second day to reinforce the Victorian team to play Queensland commencing on February 4. Speirs acted as substitute in his place and C.R.Sheldon was called on to field for Kiernan (ill) in the pre-lunch session on the third day. McKenzie (96 in 97 minutes, 13 fours) and Ransford (74 in 87 minutes, 7 fours) scored at will. Facy (3), the non-striker, was struck on the arm by a straight drive from Hale and retired hurt at 5/122 in the first innings. He returned at 6/180 and batted in all for 97 minutes, hitting 7 fours. Burn (53 in 113 minutes, 5 fours) and Hale (53 in 70 minutes, 7 fours) also scored fifties for Tasmania. Westbrook's debut innings lasted 123 minutes. Sources: *Cricket, VCA Report, The Age, The Argus, The Herald, The Australasian, Sydney Referee.*

VICTORIA

E.V.Carroll	c & b Facy	9
G.E.J.Healy	lbw b Chancellor	218
V.S.Ransford	c McDonald b Facy	74
*J.H.Stuckey	c Parkinson b Chancellor	5
C.McKenzie	c Parkinson b Chancellor	96
F.Vaughan	c Hawson b Chancellor	150
C.Kiernan	c Martin b Chancellor	2
H.F.Parsons	c Burn b Facy	1
†A.W.Lampard	not out	55
H.W.Hart	b Facy	6
E.J.Binney	b McDonald	29
Extras	(b13, lb2)	15
Total	(160.1 overs, 468 mins)	660

TASMANIA

R.J.Hawson	b Hart	0		c Lampard b Parsons	36
*E.J.K.Burn	b Parsons	53	(10)	not out	12
C.W.B.Martin	b Hart	21	(4)	lbw b Parsons	11
F.E.Chancellor	b Hart	3	(3)	b Hart	28
W.K.Eltham	b Ransford	20	(7)	st Lampard b Parsons	21
H.Hale	c Kiernan b Ransford	53	(5)	st Lampard b Ransford	18
A.C.Facy	c & b Kiernan	67	(6)	c McKenzie b Parsons	8
K.R.Westbrook	c & b Kiernan	35	(9)	lbw b McKenzie	25
M.S.McKenzie	not out	14	(2)	st Lampard b Parsons	40
E.A.McDonald	b Hart	9	(8)	b Parsons	2
†H.Parkinson	b Parsons	19		c Binney b McKenzie	4
Extras	(b15, lb6, w3)	24		(b8, lb3)	11
Total	(114.2 overs, 317 mins)	318		(85.2 overs, 220 mins)	216

TASMANIA	O	M	R	W	w,nb
Facy	54	13	181	4	-,-
Chancellor	41	6	167	5	-,-
Martin	15	0	79	0	-,-
McDonald	22.1	0	107	1	-,-
McKenzie	6	1	28	0	-,-
Westbrook	16	1	51	0	-,-
Eltham	3	0	10	0	-,-
Hawson	3	0	22	0	-,-

VICTORIA	O	M	R	W	w,nb		O	M	R	W	w,nb
Binney	19	6	49	0	2,-	(2)	11	2	23	0	-,-
Hart	35	8	88	4	-,-	(6)	16	2	50	1	-,-
McKenzie	4	0	19	0	-,-		9.2	2	17	2	-,-
Kiernan	17	4	46	2	1,-	(1)	12	2	32	0	-,-
Parsons	11.2	1	35	2	-,-	(4)	31	5	63	6	-,-
Ransford	21	9	41	2	-,-	(5)	6	2	20	1	-,-
Carroll	5	2	12	0	-,-						
Stuckey	2	1	4	0	-,-						

FALL OF WICKETS

Wkt	VIC 1st	TAS 1st	TAS 2nd
1st	13	1	76
2nd	115	41	95
3rd	128	57	125
4th	298	106	125
5th	553	110	139
6th	561	180	153
7th	564	273	156
8th	564	273	194
9th	588	288	206
10th	660	318	216

QUEENSLAND v VICTORIA

Played at Brisbane Cricket Ground (Woolloongabba) on February 4, 5, 7, 1910. (Timeless match)
Toss : Victoria.   Result : VICTORIA WON BY 352 RUNS.
Debuts: Queensland - G.G.Armstrong, H.Ironmonger (both f/c).
12th Men: J.J.Fitzgerald (Qld). No 12th named for Victoria; only 11 men in party.
Umpires: G.A.Carter and T.Muir.
Attendances & Receipts: No figures published.
Close of Play: 1st day Vic 9/370 (Kyle 2); 2nd day Vic (2) 3/94 (Vaughan 30, Kortlang 1).

W.W.Armstrong, D.B.M.Smith and T.S.Warne, all touring New Zealand with an Australian side, were unavailable for Victoria and were replaced by Kyle, Sewart and Vaughan. Kenny became the second Victorian after V.S.Ransford to register a century in each innings of a first-class match, making 164 in 164 minutes with 25 fours and 100 not out in 142 minutes with 12 fours, giving a chance at 46 in the second innings. With Kortlang (116 in 210 minutes, 10 fours) he established a new Victorian sixth-wicket record partnership of 262 runs in the first innings. Hartigan, Queensland's only batsman to register a half-century in the match (58 in 81 minutes, 8 fours), was out to the first ball of the second innings, through which Saunders bowled unchanged. *Cricket* incorrectly gives Qld (2) Hartigan c & b Saunders.
Sources: *Cricket, VCA Report, Brisbane Courier, The Queenslander, Queensland Times.*

VICTORIA

F.Vaughan	run out (McLaren/Pyke)	3	run out (McLaren)		32
F.T.Delves	b McLaren	26	b Ironmonger		19
J.Ainslie	run out (Thomson/Pyke)	0	b McLaren		1
W.I.Sewart	c Fletcher b McLaren	13	(8) c Pyke b Hartigan		11
W.J.Scott	b Thomson	12	(4) run out (Hutcheon)		35
H.H.L.Kortlang	c & b Ironmonger	116	(5) lbw b Lewis		17
A.Kenny	run out (Hutcheon/Pyke)	164	(6) not out		100
T.J.Matthews	c Hutcheon b Ironmonger	9	(7) b Lewis		0
*†W.Carkeek	c Hutcheon b Hartigan	9	c Fennelly b Hartigan		0
J.H.Kyle	not out	7	b McLaren		44
J.V.Saunders	c Hutcheon b Hartigan	0	c Fletcher b Hartigan		0
Extras	(b10, lb2, w4)	16	(b14, lb3)		17
Total	(97.5 overs, 279 mins)	375	(79.5 overs, 248 mins)		276

QUEENSLAND

*R.J.Hartigan	c Ainslie b Kyle	58	c Scott b Saunders		0
J.Thomson	b Kyle	31	c & b Matthews		11
J.W.Fletcher	b Kenny	3	c Kyle b Saunders		10
S.J.Fennelly	b Kenny	15	lbw b Saunders		15
J.S.Hutcheon	c Carkeek b Saunders	7	c Kortlang b Saunders		18
J.W.McLaren	run out (/Carkeek)	8	c Ainslie b Saunders		1
G.G.Armstrong	c Kyle b Matthews	16	(8) c Kortlang b Saunders		0
E.A.Benbow	b Kyle	33	(7) b Kyle		20
J.W.Lewis	c & b Matthews	5	b Kyle		8
†R.D.Pyke	not out	10	not out		2
H.Ironmonger	c & b Kenny	9	b Kyle		2
Extras	(b5, lb5)	10	(b6, lb1)		7
Total	(52.0 overs, 166 mins)	205	(26.0 overs, 87 mins)		94

QUEENSLAND	O	M	R	W	w,nb		O	M	R	W	w,nb			
McLaren	25	1	83	2	4,-		22	2	70	2	-,-			
Ironmonger	20	3	72	2	-,-		22	5	52	1	-,-			
Thomson	12	1	49	1	-,-	(4)	7	0	39	0	-,-			
Lewis	15	3	48	0	-,-	(5)	15	2	65	2	-,-			
Hartigan	12.5	4	36	2	-,-	(3)	11.5	4	27	3	-,-			
Fennelly	8	1	50	0	-,-		2	0	6	0	-,-			
Fletcher	5	0	21	0	-,-									

												FALL OF WICKETS			
											Wkt	VIC 1st	QLD 1st	VIC 2nd	QLD 2nd
											1st	4	60	28	0
											2nd	4	71	35	16
											3rd	36	91	93	26
											4th	45	115	103	57
											5th	66	127	123	59
											6th	328	128	123	68
VICTORIA	O	M	R	W	w,nb		O	M	R	W	w,nb	7th	353	150	162	72
Saunders	11	2	38	1	-,-		13	3	35	6	-,-	8th	364	167	162	85
Matthews	15	1	50	2	-,-		9	2	32	1	-,-	9th	370	192	274	92
Kenny	11	1	37	3	-,-							10th	375	205	276	94
Kyle	15	1	70	3	-,-	(3)	4	0	20	3	-,-					

TASMANIA v NEW SOUTH WALES

Played at T.C.A. Ground, Hobart, on February 25, 26, 1910. (Timeless match)
Toss : New South Wales.   Result : NEW SOUTH WALES WON BY 333 RUNS.
Debuts: Tasmania - E.P.Free, T.F.E.Rockliffe (both f/c).
12th Men: A.G.McLean (NSW). No 12th man or emergency fieldsman named for Tasmania.
Umpires: T.Marshall and F.Price.
Attendances: No figures published, but considered poor on both days.   Receipts: £31.
Close of Play: 1st day NSW (2) 1/44 (Barbour 27, Cranney 10).

The Tasmanian side was drawn solely from players in the south of the island due to the continuing refusal of the NTCA to co-operate with and recognise the TCA as the ruling body of Tasmanian cricket. Consequently without players from the north such as J.H.Savigny and E.A.C.Windsor and the absence of N.Dodds and A.C.Facy (in New Zealand with an Australian team), the side which appeared here was not a truly representative one. New South Wales were also below full strength, with Barbour and R.B.Minnett replacing Trumper and E.F.Waddy, who withdrew soon after selection in in the team. Barbour (160 in 162 minutes, 20 fours, 3 chances) and Waddy (65 in 32 minutes, 1 six and 12 fours) added 97 for the third wicket in 32 minutes, contributing towards a total of 536 runs on the second day. Jack Scott, a right-arm fast bowler who later umpired in 10 Tests, bowled Hale first ball in the second innings and collected the only 10-wicket-match haul of his career. The match marked the last first-class appearance by E.J.K.Burn, who had debuted in 1883-84, Tasmania in New Zealand. Sources: *Cricket, NSWCA Report, TCA Report, Hobart Mercury.*

NEW SOUTH WALES

E.L.Waddy	c Paton b Rockliffe	13	(4)	c Hawson b Chancellor	65
*A.Diamond	b Paton	0	(7)	lbw b Rockliffe	17
H.Cranney	st Free b Meech	18		b Meech	37
J.C.Barnes	b Meech	39	(5)	lbw b Carroll	31
E.P.Barbour	c Free b Paton	32	(1)	c Hale b Rockliffe	160
F.K.Gow	c Free b Paton	10		c Hudson b Meech	9
R.B.Minnett	c Meech b Chancellor	30	(8)	c Free b Chancellor	29
W.J.Stack	c Rockliffe b Chancellor	4	(9)	not out	58
†G.G.Harvey	not out	6	(10)	c Free b Chancellor	7
L.A.Minnett	run out (Chancellor)	0	(2)	b Rockliffe	7
J.D.Scott	c Hale b Chancellor	2		b Chancellor	13
Extras	(b2)	2		(b12, lb3)	15
Total	(34.2 overs, 125 mins)	156		(67.3 overs, 209 mins)	448

TASMANIA

F.E.Chancellor	b Scott	14		b Stack	3
*E.J.K.Burn	lbw b Stack	22		b L.A.Minnett	30
W.K.Eltham	b Stack	20		c Waddy b Scott	13
J.L.Hudson	c Harvey b Scott	6	(6)	b Stack	28
R.J.Hawson	b Scott	5		b Scott	9
H.Hale	c Harvey b Stack	3	(4)	b Scott	0
G.D.Paton	b Scott	9		st Harvey b Stack	3
T.D.Carroll	b L.A.Minnett	8		b Scott	8
†E.P.Free	b L.A.Minnett	12		c Barbour b Scott	11
T.F.E.Rockliffe	not out	3		not out	12
J.R.Meech	b Scott	11		c Cranney b Stack	5
Extras	(b17, nb4)	21		(b4, lb2, nb4)	10
Total	(36.3 overs, 123 mins)	139		(31.4 overs, 105 mins)	132

TASMANIA	O	M	R	W	w,nb		O	M	R	W	w,nb
Rockliffe	10	1	42	1	-,-		19	0	108	3	-,-
Paton	10	1	42	3	-,-		16	0	87	0	-,-
Meech	7	0	38	2	-,-		13	0	90	2	-,-
Carroll	2	0	10	0	-,-	(5)	5	0	46	1	-,-
Chancellor	5.2	0	22	3	-,-	(4)	14.3	1	102	4	-,-

NEW SOUTH WALES	O	M	R	W	w,nb		O	M	R	W	w,nb
Scott	11.3	1	35	5	-,2		11	2	34	5	-,2
Stack	17	3	63	3	-,-		11.4	1	53	4	-,-
L.A.Minnett	7	2	16	2	-,2	(4)	5	0	11	1	-,1
Barbour	1	0	4	0	-,-	(3)	4	0	24	0	-,1

FALL OF WICKETS

Wkt	NSW 1st	TAS 1st	NSW 2nd	TAS 2nd
1st	6	32	15	14
2nd	20	53	82	29
3rd	44	69	179	29
4th	97	77	247	44
5th	113	79	266	82
6th	128	92	310	93
7th	139	98	345	94
8th	152	111	401	109
9th	153	121	425	127
10th	156	139	448	132

WESTERN AUSTRALIA v VICTORIA

Played at W.A.C.A. Ground, Perth on February 26, 28, March 1, 2, 1910. (Timeless match)
Toss : Western Australia.   Result : VICTORIA WON BY AN INNINGS AND 5 RUNS.
Debuts: Western Australia - R.C.Carter, J.S.Everett, W.H.Hennah, H.E.Walkerden (all f/c). Victoria - T.F.Scannell (f/c).
12th Men: R.G.Johnstone (Vic). W.Brine and R.N.S.Good were named as WA emergencies.
Umpires: J.F.Dwyer and T.Shiells.
Attendances: 2000, 400, 400, 200.   Total: About 3000.   Receipts: £115.
Close of Play: 1st day Vic 1/144 (Kortlang 61, McKenzie 32); 2nd day Vic 6/524 (Scannell 1, Kyle 0); 3rd day WA (2) 4/276 (Rowe 10, Christian 25).

Hart, Johnstone, Lampard and Scannell were last minute replacements for F.T.Delves, T.J.Matthews, W.I.Sewart and T.S.Warne in the first Victorian team to tour Western Australia. The second-wicket partnership of 358 in 227 minutes by Kortlang and McKenzie was at the time the highest partnership for any wicket outside England and the fourth-highest partnership for the second wicket in the world. Kortlang batted for 328 minutes, hitting 3 sixes and 21 fours, while McKenzie's innings lasted 227 minutes, with 5 sixes and 20 fours. In the Western Australian second innings Ernie Parker gave a brilliant exhibition of batting racing to 117 in 82 minutes with 22 fours. When he brought up his century, in 61 minutes with 20 fours, Parker had scored 101 out of the team's 110; he was out with the score at 133. The match provided only the second instance of 20 bowlers being used in a match, the first being at Southampton in 1897. A severe cold prevented Saunders from participating after the first day. Hennah is shown in some newspapers as having conceded two no-balls. Sources: *Cricket, VCA Report, The West Australian, Western Mail.*

WESTERN AUSTRALIA

H.C.Howard	c Carkeek b Hart	7	(2)	lbw b Kenny	5
E.F.Parker	c Horan b Saunders	1	(1)	c Carkeek b Kortlang	117
T.H.Hogue	c Kyle b Saunders	0		b Horan	76
W.H.Hennah	b Saunders	0	(7)	b Kenny	0
S.H.D.Rowe	c Saunders b McKenzie	34		b Kenny	31
*A.H.Christian	c McKenzie b Hart	31		b Kyle	97
R.C.Carter	not out	28	(4)	run out (McKenzie)	32
J.S.Everett	c Horan b Kenny	13		b Kenny	0
W.W.Hogue	c & b Saunders	12		b Kenny	15
C.Munro	b Saunders	5		not out	26
†H.E.Walkerden	b Saunders	0		b Kenny	6
Extras	(b1, lb2)	3		(b12, lb6, nb1)	19
Total	(51.0 overs, 156 mins)	134		(105.3 overs, 320 mins)	424

VICTORIA

J.H.Stuckey	b Christian	46
H.H.L.Kortlang	b Howard	197
C.McKenzie	c W.W.Hogue b Christian	211
J.F.Horan	c Everett b T.H.Hogue	19
A.W.Lampard	c T.H.Hogue b Howard	2
A.Kenny	lbw b Howard	22
T.F.Scannell	b T.H.Hogue	16
J.H.Kyle	b Christian	10
*†W.Carkeek	c Hennah b Christian	0
H.W.Hart	not out	10
J.V.Saunders	absent ill	-
Extras	(b17, lb10, w2, nb1)	30
Total	(159.5 overs, 390 mins)	563

VICTORIA	O	M	R	W	w,nb		O	M	R	W	w,nb	
Saunders	14	3	37	6	-,-							
Kyle	9	3	20	0	-,-		24	7	74	1	-,-	
Hart	12	4	31	2	-,-	(1)	24	5	90	0	-,1	
Kenny	9	3	21	1	-,-	(3)	20.3	6	59	6	-,-	
McKenzie	6	1	22	1	-,-	(4)	6	0	63	0	-,-	
Scannell	1	1	0	0	-,-		3	0	24	0	-,-	
Kortlang						(5)	9	3	32	1	-,-	
Lampard						(7)	12	3	35	0	-,-	
Horan						(8)	4	1	24	1	-,-	
Stuckey						(9)	3	2	4	0	-,-	

WESTERN AUSTRALIA	O	M	R	W	w,nb
W.W.Hogue	17	2	63	0	-,-
Christian	44	6	149	4	-,-
Hennah	14	0	52	0	-,-
Everett	13	0	48	0	-,-
Munro	14	2	48	0	-,-
T.H.Hogue	29.5	5	76	2	-,-
Carter	4	2	14	0	-,-
Howard	16	3	52	3	2,1
Parker	4	1	11	0	-,-
Rowe	4	0	20	0	-,-

FALL OF WICKETS

	WA	VIC	WA
Wkt	1st	1st	2nd
1st	1	81	82
2nd	1	439	133
3rd	1	490	225
4th	8	496	244
5th	62	508	317
6th	74	522	327
7th	94	549	327
8th	122	549	343
9th	134	563	401
10th	134	-	424

WESTERN AUSTRALIA v VICTORIA

Played at Fremantle Oval on March 5, 7, 8, 1910. (Timeless match)
Toss : Western Australia.   Result : WESTERN AUSTRALIA WON BY 79 RUNS.
Debuts: Western Australia - R.N.S.Good (f/c). Victoria - R.G.Johnstone (f/c).
12th Men: T.F.Scannell (Vic). No 12th named for WA.
Umpires: J.F.Dwyer and T.Shiells.
Attendances: 1500, 800, 200.   Total: About 2500.   Receipts: £117.
Close of Play: 1st day WA (2) 0/7 (Hogue 4, Howard 3); 2nd day Vic (2) 3/30 (Kenny 11, Hart 2).

The match was played on a very dry wicket that was sympathetic to spin from the beginning, 20 wickets falling on the opening day. Bowling on his "home" wicket, "Bobby" Selk utilised the conditions to the full with his varied spin. His match analysis of 13 for 77 was not bettered for Western Australia until Alderman's 14 for 87 against New South Wales in 1981-82 and was the key factor in the defeat of the Victorians. Hogue (64 in 138 minutes, 4 fours) batted soundly in the second innings while Parker (40 in 37 minutes, 5 fours) "displayed much of his usual brilliancy" (*West Australian*). Kortlang (72 not out in 85 minutes, 8 fours) alone showed any capacity to survive on the final day. Lampard was run out in most unusual circumstances in the second innings. Patfield attempted to stump him from the bowling of Christian and Lampard started for the pavilion, thinking that he was out. The umpire, however, had negatived the appeal and Patfield pulled out a stump to effect a run out. Sources: *Cricket, VCA Report, The West Australian, Western Mail, Daily News*.

WESTERN AUSTRALIA

H.C.Howard	run out (McKenzie/Carkeek)	9	(2) b Kenny	14
E.F.Parker	b Kyle	9	(4) b McKenzie	40
T.H.Hogue	b Kyle	23	(1) c Horan b Johnstone	64
R.C.Carter	b Saunders	6	(5) run out (Kenny/Carkeek)	4
S.H.D.Rowe	c Johnstone b Saunders	8	(3) b Kenny	2
*A.H.Christian	c & b Saunders	9	c Kortlang b McKenzie	9
R.N.S.Good	b Saunders	0	b Johnstone	4
R.M.Evans	c Carkeek b Saunders	0	c Carkeek b Hart	29
†A.S.Patfield	b Kyle	10	b Johnstone	5
J.T.Anderson	c Carkeek b Kyle	2	b Saunders	11
R.A.Selk	not out	7	not out	23
Extras	(b3, lb3)	6	(b6, lb6)	12
Total	(37.2 overs, 116 mins)	89	(73.1 overs, 208 mins)	217

VICTORIA

J.H.Stuckey	b Selk	16	(7) b Christian	7
H.H.L.Kortlang	st Patfield b Selk	25	(6) not out	72
C.McKenzie	st Patfield b Selk	9	(2) st Patfield b Selk	5
J.F.Horan	lbw b Hogue	11	(1) b Selk	5
A.Kenny	c & b Selk	8	(4) c Carter b Selk	12
A.W.Lampard	not out	11	(3) run out (Patfield)	2
R.G.Johnstone	b Selk	0	(8) b Howard	8
J.H.Kyle	b Selk	0	(9) b Selk	5
*†W.Carkeek	b Christian	3	(10) b Hogue	3
H.W.Hart	b Selk	1	(5) b Selk	10
J.V.Saunders	b Selk	0	run out (/Hogue)	1
Extras	(b3)	3	(b10)	10
Total	(38.5 overs, 112 mins)	87	(52.5 overs, 140 mins)	140

VICTORIA	O	M	R	W	w,nb		O	M	R	W	w,nb			FALL OF WICKETS		
														WA	VIC	WA	VIC
Saunders	19	5	45	5	-,-		17	4	44	1	-,-		Wkt	1st	1st	2nd	2nd
Kyle	13.2	2	29	4	-,-		8	3	19	0	-,-		1st	11	33	52	5
Kenny	5	2	9	0	-,-	(4)	17	2	70	2	-,-		2nd	27	49	54	12
Hart						(3)	12.1	2	20	1	-,-		3rd	38	64	117	14
Stuckey							1	0	2	0	-,-		4th	60	64	129	34
McKenzie							10	3	19	2	-,-		5th	70	77	136	53
Johnstone							8	0	31	3	-,-		6th	70	77	141	62
													7th	70	81	145	104
WESTERN AUSTRALIA	O	M	R	W	w,nb		O	M	R	W	w,nb		8th	80	84	150	123
Anderson	3	0	8	0	-,-								9th	80	87	182	126
Christian	9	0	20	1	-,-	(3)	14	3	37	1	-,-		10th	89	87	217	140
Selk	16.5	5	28	8	-,-	(2)	23	10	49	5	-,-						
Howard	5	0	21	0	-,-		5	1	17	1	-,-						
Hogue	5	2	7	1	-,-		2.5	0	11	1	-,-						
Evans						(1)	8	3	16	0	-,-						

WESTERN AUSTRALIA v VICTORIA

Played at W.A.C.A. Ground, Perth on March 12, 14, 15, 16, 1910. (Timeless match)
Toss : Western Australia.   Result : VICTORIA WON BY TWO WICKETS.
Debuts: Nil.
12th Men: H.W.Hart (Vic). No 12th named for WA.
Umpires: J.F.Dwyer and T.Shiells.
Attendances: 1800, 1000, 500, 500.   Total: About 3800.   Receipts: £178.
Close of Play: 1st day WA 8/321 (Anderson 14); 2nd day WA (2) 2/25 (Hogue 1); 3rd day Vic (2) 4/143 (Kyle 3).

Howard (54 in 144 minutes, 6 fours), Hogue (119 in 139 minutes, 19 fours) and Good (48 in 78 minutes, 7 fours) put their team in a sound position on the opening day. Kortlang (82 in 171 minutes, 11 fours) batted throughout the Victorian first innings in the face of fine bowling from Selk. Saunders and Kenny put Victoria back in the match when they accounted for the Western Australians second innings in just under two hours. Kortlang (36) was struck in the face by a short-pitched ball from Anderson and retired hurt at 2/75 in the second innings. He resumed at the start of play on the following day to bat in all for 180 minutes (17 fours) and steer his team to victory. Last first-class appearance by J.H.Stuckey. Sources: *Cricket, VCA Report, The West Australian, Western Mail, Daily News.*

WESTERN AUSTRALIA

S.H.D.Rowe	c & b Saunders	11	(4) c Kortlang b Kenny		0
H.C.Howard	lbw b Kyle	54	(1) lbw b Kenny		6
R.C.Carter	b Saunders	27	(5) c McKenzie b Kenny		0
E.F.Parker	c Kenny b Lampard	14	(2) c Kortlang b Kenny		18
T.H.Hogue	run out (Kyle/Carkeek)	119	(3) c Kenny b Saunders		1
*A.H.Christian	b Kyle	15	(7) c Kenny b Kyle		46
R.M.Evans	c Scannell b Saunders	7	(6) c Scannell b Saunders		11
R.N.S.Good	b Kyle	48	b Kenny		0
J.T.Anderson	c Kenny b Kyle	14	c Horan b Saunders		2
R.A.Selk	c Horan b Saunders	5	(11) not out		0
†A.S.Patfield	not out	4	(10) b Saunders		13
Extras	(b8, lb6)	14	(b5, lb3)		8
Total	(89.3 overs, 276 mins)	332	(38.4 overs, 115 mins)		105

VICTORIA

H.H.L.Kortlang	not out	82	not out		98
J.H.Stuckey	b Selk	5	(3) run out (Rowe/Patfield)		8
A.W.Lampard	c Patfield b Selk	2	(2) c Patfield b Hogue		4
C.McKenzie	st Patfield b Christian	1	(5) b Christian		48
J.F.Horan	c Rowe b Hogue	28	(4) b Christian		29
A.Kenny	b Selk	40	(7) b Hogue		16
R.G.Johnstone	b Selk	0	(8) b Selk		4
T.F.Scannell	b Selk	0	(9) b Christian		4
J.H.Kyle	b Howard	10	(6) b Christian		8
*†W.Carkeek	b Hogue	14	not out		0
J.V.Saunders	b Hogue	2			
Extras	(b5, lb4, w2, nb1)	12	(b22, lb3)		25
Total	(62.3 overs, 171 mins)	196	(100.4 overs, 250 mins) (8 wkts)		244

VICTORIA	O	M	R	W	w,nb		O	M	R	W	w,nb		FALL OF WICKETS			
													WA	VIC	WA	VIC
Kyle	16	8	48	4	-,-	(2)	5	1	13	1	-,-	Wkt	1st	1st	2nd	2nd
Saunders	26.3	12	59	4	-,-	(1)	19.4	8	37	4	-,-	1st	21	5	18	8
Kenny	13	2	62	0	-,-		14	3	47	5	-,-	2nd	75	11	25	23
Lampard	11	1	42	1	-,-							3rd	90	16	25	122
McKenzie	3	0	21	0	-,-							4th	156	58	29	143
Johnstone	11	2	41	0	-,-							5th	182	108	33	148
Scannell	4	0	25	0	-,-							6th	202	108	48	185
Kortlang	5	0	20	0	-,-							7th	281	108	48	213
												8th	321	157	67	235
WESTERN AUSTRALIA	O	M	R	W	w,nb		O	M	R	W	w,nb	9th	322	194	105	-
Selk	24	9	73	5	-,1		30	9	84	1	-,-	10th	332	196	105	-
Christian	18	1	52	1	-,-	(3)	25.4	7	49	4	-,-					
Evans	5	2	11	0	-,-											
Hogue	8.3	2	22	3	-,-	(2)	29	11	53	2	-,-					
Howard	7	2	26	1	2,-		5	1	15	0	-,-					
Anderson						(4)	11	6	18	0	-,-					

1910-11 SEASON (25 MATCHES)

The first tour by a South African team to Australia created widespread interest. They played 22 matches, including five Tests and 10 other matches of first-class status. Many of the tourists, who had been raised on matting wickets, had problems in adjusting to Australian pitches - this was particularly evident in their bowling. The strong Australian team completely outplayed the visitors in the Tests to take the series 4-1. Trumper, Hill, Bardsley and Armstrong led the prolific Australian batting card and the bowling of Whitty and Cotter - and later in the series Hordern - made life unpleasant for the South African batsmen. Whitty captured 37 wickets in the five Tests, an Australian record which remained until 1935-36 (broken by Grimmett in South Africa). Similarly, Trumper's aggregate of 661 runs established a batting record which remained until 1930 (broken by Bradman in England).

Of the other 10 first-class tour matches, the South Africans won five, lost three and drew two. Faulkner, Nourse and Zulch headed the batting in both the Tests and all first-class games. Faulkner also performed outstandingly with the ball and was the pick of the bowlers, along with Schwarz. Illness limited Hathorn's appearances.

Percentages, or quotients, decided the Sheffield Shield winners for the first time, New South Wales and South Australia being tied on two wins apiece. Superior averages in both batting and bowling enabled New South Wales to regain the crown which they had surrendered to South Australia the previous season. The situation would not have arisen had South Australia and New South Wales not agreed pre-season to forgo their fixture in Adelaide because of the South African tour.

Queensland's opportunities in first-class cricket increased. In addition to their annual home and away encounters with New South Wales, they met the South Africans and travelled to Melbourne for a match against Victoria. The results were more than encouraging, as all three interstate fixtures were won. Marshal, Fennelly, Hutcheon, McLaren and Barstow took advantage of the extra chances to demonstrate their ability. Brisbane also hosted an 'Australian XI' match against the South Africans in which six places were allocated to Queensland players in the Australian side.

Tasmania also anticipated an increased program. They travelled to Sydney to meet New South Wales over the New Year, only to be heavily defeated. A fortnight later, the South Africans arrived on the island for matches at Launceston and Hobart. The Tasmanians again suffered a comprehensive defeat in the first match, but made a much better showing in the second to hold out for a draw. Arrangements for a visit by a Victorian team, incorporating matches at Hobart and Launceston, had not been finalised when the season commenced, and the games were eventually abandoned due to the increase in fixtures with the South African tour.

The first-class season came to an end with a match between an Australian XI and The Rest at Melbourne, staged as a benefit for T.S.Warne, the long-serving Victorian player. Western Australia had hoped to arrange a fixture against the South Africans but were unable to do so.

Leading Aggregates

Batsmen	M	I	NO	Runs	HS	Ave.	Bowlers	Runs	Wkts	Ave.
G.A.Faulkner (SAf)	14	27	1	1534	204	59.00	W.J.Whitty (SA)	1419	70	20.27
A.W.Nourse (SAf)	15	29	5	1454	201*	60.58	R.O.Schwarz (SAf)	1475	59	25.00
V.T.Trumper (NSW)	11	20	2	1246	214*	69.22	H.V.Hordern (NSW)	860	58	14.82
W.Bardsley (NSW)	10	19	1	1233	191*	68.50	G.A.Faulkner (SAf)	1254	49	25.59
C.Hill (SA)	11	19	1	903	191	50.16	W.W.Armstrong (V)	1189	41	29.00
J.W.Zulch (SAf)	13	25	1	724	150	30.16	A.Cotter (NSW)	1120	35	32.00
W.W.Armstrong (V)	12	18	1	710	132	41.76	C.Kelleway (NSW)	1032	34	30.35
C.Kelleway (NSW)	12	22	3	678	65	35.68	A.E.E.Vogler (SAf)	1197	31	38.61
L.A.Stricker (SAf)	14	28	2	667	146	25.65	C.B.Llewellyn (SAf)	854	30	28.46
D.R.A.Gehrs (SA)	10	18	1	621	120	36.52				

SHEFFIELD SHIELD TABLE

	P	W	L	D	Pts	Quotient	Runs Scored	Wkts Lost	Runs Conceded	Wkts Taken
NEW SOUTH WALES	3	2	1	-	1	1.180	2007	60	1643	58
SOUTH AUSTRALIA	3	2	1	-	1	1.045	1790	54	1586	50
VICTORIA	4	1	3	-	-2	0.830	1832	68	2400	74
TOTAL	5	5	5	-	0	1.000	5629	182	5629	182

SOUTH AUSTRALIA v VICTORIA (Shield Match 1)

Played at Adelaide Oval on October 28 (no play), 29, 31, November 1, 1910. (Timeless match)
Toss : South Australia.   Result : SOUTH AUSTRALIA WON BY SIX WICKETS.
Debuts: South Australia - P.W.Zschorn (f/c).
12th Men: G.S.Down (SA) and T.J.Matthews (Vic).
Umpires: A.McIntyre and G.A.Watson.
Attendances: no play, 3000, 1000, 300.   Total: About 4300.   Receipts: No figures published.
Close of Play: 1st day no play; 2nd day SA 8/135 (Crawford 31); 3rd day Vic (2) 4/250 (Kortlang 30).

N.Claxton, C.E.Dolling, L.R.Hill and R.E.Mayne were all unavailable for South Australia. After the first day's play was lost to the elements, Victoria was sent in to bat on a rain-affected pitch and lost Warne (second ball) and Ransford in the first over of the match. In the second innings, Smith (96 in 105 minutes, 11 fours), Ransford (71 in 180 minutes) and Kortlang (69 not out in 150 minutes) registered fifties. Kenny suffered a first ball dismissal. South Australia's first innings was dominated by Crawford's unbeaten 79 in 120 minutes with 8 fours. Gehrs, who was held back until the second day due to a heavy cold, recovered to score a brilliant second-innings century in 93 minutes with 2 sixes and 9 fours. On 90 not out, he hit a four to level the scores and then lifted the ball over square leg to win the match with a six, thereby bringing up his hundred. P.A.McAlister's last first-class appearance. Sources: *Wisden, C.B.O'Reilly, SACA Report, Adelaide Advertiser, South Australian Register.*

VICTORIA

T.S.Warne	c Crawford b Whitty	0	c Gehrs b Rees		18
D.B.M.Smith	c S.Hill b Crawford	2	c Campbell b Hewer		96
V.S.Ransford	run out (Chamberlain)	3	b Crawford		71
W.W.Armstrong	b Crawford	35	c Rees b Whitty		27
H.H.L.Kortlang	c C.Hill b Whitty	0	not out		69
*P.A.McAlister	lbw b Crawford	1	b Wright		4
F.T.Delves	c Zschorn b Crawford	4	c Crawford b Rees		6
A.Kenny	c Campbell b Whitty	2	b Crawford		0
G.R.Hazlitt	c Chamberlain b Crawford	30	st Campbell b Rees		6
F.J.Laver	b Whitty	19	b Whitty		0
†W.Carkeek	not out	2	c Crawford b Rees		0
Extras	(b11, lb1, nb1)	13	(b8)		8
Total	(34.1 overs, 115 mins)	111	(99.3 overs, 290 mins)		305

SOUTH AUSTRALIA

W.A.Hewer	c Laver b Hazlitt	14	(2) b Armstrong		5
†G.C.Campbell	c Kortlang b Laver	2			
W.J.Whitty	c Ransford b Laver	4			
R.B.C.Rees	c Delves b Laver	16			
S.Hill	b Hazlitt	9	(1) b Armstrong		1
*C.Hill	b Armstrong	26	(3) b Kenny		68
J.N.Crawford	not out	79	(4) b Armstrong		23
W.L.Chamberlain	st Carkeek b Kenny	24	(6) not out		3
A.W.Wright	c Warne b Kenny	2			
D.R.A.Gehrs	b Armstrong	36	(5) not out		100
P.W.Zschorn	c Warne b Hazlitt	1			
Extras	(b2, lb4, nb1)	7	(b1, lb1)		2
Total	(69.0 overs, 205 mins)	220	(49.2 overs, 150 mins) (4 wkts)		202

SOUTH AUSTRALIA	O	M	R	W	w,nb		O	M	R	W	w,nb
Whitty	17.1	4	41	4	-,1		25	6	68	2	-,-
Crawford	15	5	42	5	-,-	(3)	29	5	87	2	-,-
Rees	2	0	15	0	-,-	(4)	16.3	3	66	4	-,-
Wright						(2)	22	3	52	1	-,-
Chamberlain							2	0	6	0	-,-
Hewer							5	0	18	1	-,-

VICTORIA	O	M	R	W	w,nb		O	M	R	W	w,nb
Laver	17	5	69	3	-,-	(3)	13	3	52	0	-,-
Hazlitt	30	8	74	3	-,-	(1)	12	0	45	0	-,-
Armstrong	13	2	31	2	-,1	(2)	20	2	68	3	-,-
Kenny	9	0	39	2	-,-		2.2	0	25	1	-,-
Warne							2	0	10	0	-,-

FALL OF WICKETS				
	VIC	SA	VIC	SA
Wkt	1st	1st	2nd	2nd
1st	0	13	54	5
2nd	4	21	141	8
3rd	6	24	190	50
4th	6	38	250	177
5th	13	75	263	-
6th	21	75	281	-
7th	27	131	282	-
8th	78	135	297	-
9th	105	193	304	-
10th	111	220	305	-

QUEENSLAND v NEW SOUTH WALES

Played at Brisbane Cricket Ground (Woolloongabba) on November 4, 5, 7, 1910. (Timeless match)
Toss : Queensland.   Result : QUEENSLAND WON BY 19 RUNS.
Debuts: Queensland - W.S.S.McCloy (f/c); C.B.Jennings (Qld only).
12th Men: No 12th men or emergency fieldsmen named.
Umpires: W.H.Carvosso and A.T.Horrigan.
Attendances & Receipts: No figures published..
Close of Play: 1st day NSW 6/179 (Collins 43, Hopkins 1); 2nd day NSW (2) 1/18 (Diamond 12, Gorry 0).

Hutcheon assumed the Queensland captaincy when R.J.Hartigan withdrew for business reasons, along with W.B.Hayes, J.W.McLaren, J.S.Redgrave and J.Thomson. Strong hitting by Evans (82 in 92 minutes, 1 six and 11 fours) for Queensland and Gow (67 in 76 minutes, 10 fours) for New South Wales highlighted a first day on which the bowlers were mostly in control. Hutcheon's second-innings 64 included 18 runs from one over by Scott. New South Wales had the misfortune to be caught on a wicket "resembling a soft pudding" (*Courier*) on the last day after heavy overnight rain. Barstow, right-arm medium-pace, became the first Queensland bowler to take 12 wickets in a first-class match; bowling unchanged throughout the second innings, his 8 for 51 was bettered only by R.Wilson's 8 for 35 v Auckland in New Zealand in 1896-97 among Queenslanders at the time. Jennings made his first appearance for Queensland, having previously played for South Australia. *Cricket* incorrectly gives Qld (1) G.G.Armstrong c Hordern b Scott. Sources: *Cricket, NSWCA Report, Sydney Morning Herald, Brisbane Courier, Queensland Times, The Queenslander.*

QUEENSLAND

J.W.Lewis	b Scott	8		c Hordern b Scott	14
S.J.Fennelly	st Gorry b Hordern	22		c Gorry b Scott	14
C.B.Jennings	b Scott	6		st Gorry b Hordern	37
A.Marshal	b Hordern	2		b Kelleway	27
*J.S.Hutcheon	c Hordern b Kelleway	8		b Hordern	64
†W.T.Evans	b Collins	82		b Hordern	0
W.Armstrong	c & b Scott	2		c Kelleway b Minnett	27
W.S.S.McCloy	c Gow b Hordern	0	(9)	c Gorry b Minnett	8
G.G.Armstrong	c Scott b Hordern	13	(8)	c Diamond b Hordern	7
C.B.Barstow	not out	13		c Simpson b Hordern	1
H.Ironmonger	c Gorry b Scott	1		not out	1
Extras	(b4, lb1, nb1)	6		(lb2, w1)	3
Total	(47.0 overs, 140 mins)	163		(58.4 overs, 175 mins)	203

NEW SOUTH WALES

E.L.Waddy	c Jennings b Barstow	29	(4)	c & b Barstow	12
F.K.Gow	st Evans b Barstow	67	(5)	b Barstow	0
C.Kelleway	c McCloy b Ironmonger	0	(6)	c Marshal b Barstow	22
C.E.Simpson	run out (McCloy/Evans)	5	(8)	c Lewis b Barstow	55
H.L.Collins	c & b Lewis	59	(2)	lbw b Ironmonger	5
R.B.Minnett	b Barstow	0	(9)	c Hutcheon b Barstow	8
*A.Diamond	b Lewis	25	(1)	c McCloy b Barstow	18
A.J.Y.Hopkins	c McCloy b Barstow	1	(10)	c Lewis b Barstow	10
H.V.Hordern	c Evans b Marshal	10	(7)	b Barstow	0
J.D.Scott	c Jennings b Marshal	7	(11)	not out	0
†C.R.Gorry	not out	0	(3)	b Ironmonger	0
Extras	(b6, lb2, w1)	9		(b5)	5
Total	(51.1 overs, 151 mins)	212		(40.4 overs, 125 mins)	135

NEW SOUTH WALES	O	M	R	W	w,nb		O	M	R	W	w,nb
Scott	15	1	47	4	-,-		14	4	63	2	1,-
Hordern	16	1	60	4	-,-		21	4	70	5	-,-
Collins	5	0	24	1	-,-		4	1	10	0	-,-
Kelleway	7	4	12	1	-,1		4	0	15	1	-,-
Simpson	4	1	14	0	-,-						
Minnett						(5)	11.4	4	30	2	-,-
Hopkins						(6)	4	0	12	0	-,-

QUEENSLAND	O	M	R	W	w,nb		O	M	R	W	w,nb
Barstow	17	2	63	4	-,-		20.4	5	51	8	-,-
McCloy	4	0	34	0	-,-						
Ironmonger	15	4	55	1	1,-	(2)	11	2	44	2	-,-
Marshal	10.1	3	24	2	-,-	(3)	7	2	21	0	-,-
W.Armstrong	2	0	17	0	-,-						
Lewis	3	1	10	2	-,-	(4)	2	0	14	0	-,-

FALL OF WICKETS

Wkt	QLD 1st	NSW 1st	QLD 2nd	NSW 2nd
1st	10	70	16	12
2nd	34	76	41	18
3rd	43	92	90	28
4th	44	125	109	28
5th	65	125	109	41
6th	101	178	177	48
7th	102	179	189	105
8th	148	202	197	115
9th	156	212	200	133
10th	163	212	203	135

SOUTH AUSTRALIA v SOUTH AFRICAN XI

Played at Adelaide Oval on November 4 (no play), 5, 7, 8, 1910. (Timeless match)
Toss : South Australia.　　　　Result : SOUTH AFRICAN XI WON BY 281 RUNS.
Debuts: Nil.
12th Men: G.S.Down (SA) and J.M.M.Commaille (SAF).
Umpires: F.J.C.Thomas and G.A.Watson.
Attendances: no play, 4000, 1500, 1500.　　　Total: About 7000.　　　Receipts: No figures published.
Close of Play: 1st day no play; 2nd day SA 9/169 (Whitty 31, Wright 6); 3rd day SAF (2) 6/371 (Nourse 136, Schwarz 9).

Rain prevented any play on the first day of South Africa's inaugural first-class match in Australia. Stricker (146 in 209 minutes, 21 fours) and Nourse (201 not out in 302 minutes, 1 five and 22 fours, chances at 17 and 126) recorded a stand of 242 for the third wicket. Faulkner (54 in 90 minutes, 1 six and 8 fours) and Schwarz (64 in 56 minutes, 1 six and 6 fours) also scored fifties for the visitors, Schwarz in addition capturing 11 wickets. Vogler (right-arm leg-breaks and googlies) dismissed Zschorn with the first ball he sent down in Australia. Crawford (66 in 63 minutes, 9 fours) and Gehrs (60 in 65 minutes, 5 fours) made quick fifties for South Australia. W.L.Chamberlain, C.E.Dolling and W.A.Hewer all had work commitments and were unavailable for South Australia. Sources: *Wisden, Luckin, C.B.O'Reilly, SACA Report, The Age, Adelaide Advertiser, South Australian Register.*

SOUTH AFRICAN XI

L.A.Stricker	c Zschorn b Whitty	3	(2) c C.Hill b Chamberlain	146
J.W.Zulch	c Mayne b Whitty	0	(1) b Whitty	13
*†P.W.Sherwell	b Whitty	8	lbw b Crawford	14
A.W.Nourse	run out (Campbell/Crawford)	4	not out	201
G.A.Faulkner	c S.Hill b Rees	54	c Crawford b Wright	4
S.J.Snooke	c C.Hill b Crawford	4	b Crawford	7
C.B.Llewellyn	c Campbell b Crawford	3	c Campbell b Gehrs	17
R.O.Schwarz	b Whitty	22	b Rees	64
C.O.C.Pearse	b Wright	21	c sub (G.S.Down) b Wright	8
A.E.E.Vogler	not out	5	b Wright	0
S.J.Pegler	c Zschorn b Wright	0	b Crawford	4
Extras	(b8, lb1)	9	(b18, lb10, nb1)	29
Total	(46.0 overs, 115 mins)	133	(114.5 overs, 345 mins)	507

SOUTH AUSTRALIA

R.E.Mayne	b Schwarz	9	run out (Pearse)	24
P.W.Zschorn	c Sherwell b Vogler	0	c Snooke b Vogler	12
*C.Hill	c Schwarz b Vogler	15	st Sherwell b Schwarz	12
D.R.A.Gehrs	st Sherwell b Schwarz	1	b Schwarz	60
J.N.Crawford	c Snooke b Schwarz	66	c & b Vogler	9
S.Hill	c Vogler b Schwarz	11	c & b Schwarz	4
C.T.Chamberlain	lbw b Schwarz	6	b Pegler	18
†G.C.Campbell	c Sherwell b Vogler	8	lbw b Pegler	14
R.B.C.Rees	st Sherwell b Schwarz	7	b Schwarz	2
W.J.Whitty	b Pegler	38	c Nourse b Schwarz	2
A.W.Wright	not out	13	not out	0
Extras	(b6, lb3)	9	(b15, lb2, nb2)	19
Total	(51.0 overs, 147 mins)	183	(41.5 overs, 131 mins)	176

SOUTH AUSTRALIA	O	M	R	W	w,nb		O	M	R	W	w,nb		FALL OF WICKETS			
Whitty	21	5	57	4	-,-		30	4	121	1	-,-			SAF	SA	SAF	SA
Crawford	14	7	31	2	-,-	(4)	28.5	4	135	3	-,-	Wkt	1st	1st	2nd	2nd
Rees	9	1	30	1	-,-		14	1	81	1	-,-	1st	5	0	22	34
Wright	2	1	6	2	-,-	(2)	22	4	66	3	-,-	2nd	8	28	52	44
Chamberlain							14	3	59	1	-,1	3rd	19	30	294	52
Mayne							2	1	2	0	-,-	4th	20	31	299	65
Gehrs							4	0	14	1	-,-	5th	25	63	316	70
												6th	40	89	357	122
SOUTH AFRICAN XI	O	M	R	W	w,nb		O	M	R	W	w,nb	7th	101	118	466	156
Nourse	3	1	9	0	-,-							8th	109	127	478	164
Vogler	14	3	43	3	-,-		15	1	58	2	-,-	9th	133	147	478	174
Schwarz	20	4	66	6	-,-		16	1	64	5	-,1	10th	133	183	507	176
Faulkner	10	1	39	0	-,-		4	0	18	0	-,1					
Pegler	4	0	17	1	-,-		3.5	0	12	2	-,-					
Snooke						(1)	3	0	5	0	-,-					

VICTORIA v SOUTH AFRICAN XI

Played at Melbourne Cricket Ground on November 11, 12, 14, 15, 16, 1910. (Timeless match)
Toss : South African XI.   Result : VICTORIA WON BY FIVE WICKETS.
Debuts: Victoria - A.C.Facy, J.A.Seitz (both Vic only).
12th Men: A.Kenny (Vic) and C.O.C.Pearse (SAF).
Umpires: R.M.Crockett and W.Hannah.
Attendances: 1575, 12795, 6490, 4602, 200.   Total: 25,662.   Receipts: £673.
Close of Play: 1st day SAF 0/1 (Zulch 1, Stricker 0); 2nd day Vic 3/75 (Warne 49); 3rd day SAF (2) 3/56 (Nourse 15, Faulkner 13);
     4th day Vic (2) 4/58 (Kortlang 4, Carkeek 2).

V.S.Ransford (ill) was replaced in the Victorian side by Scott, the nominated 12th man. Stricker (0) was hit on the hand by a ball from
Facy on the severely rain-affected first day and was unable to resume his innings next morning. He returned at 9/170 but did not field in
Victoria's first innings, Pearse substituting in his place. Nourse (51 in 103 minutes, 5 fours) and Faulkner (50 in 101 minutes, 6 fours)
combined to add 106 runs out of 189. Faulkner also hit 69 in 115 minutes with 6 fours in the second innings. Pegler completed the first
pair by a South African in Australia when he was dismissed first ball in the second innings. Warne (84 in 138 minutes, 6 fours), Kortlang
(60 in 106 minutes, 2 fours) and Matthews (51 in 56 minutes, 3 fours) scored fifties for Victoria. Facy and Seitz made their debuts for
Victoria after previous first-class appearances for Tasmania and Oxford University respectively. *Luckin* incorrectly gives Vic (2) Facy
batting instead of Laver. Sources: *Wisden, Luckin, VCA Report, The Age, The Argus, The Herald, The Australasian, Sydney Referee.*

SOUTH AFRICAN XI

J.W.Zulch	c Hazlitt b Armstrong	1		b Armstrong	13
L.A.Stricker	not out	1	(8)	run out (Smith/Carkeek)	41
*†P.W.Sherwell	c Scott b Hazlitt	5		b Facy	1
A.W.Nourse	c Armstrong b Hazlitt	51		lbw b Laver	40
G.A.Faulkner	c Armstrong b Laver	50		c & b Matthews	69
S.J.Snooke	lbw b Armstrong	4	(2)	c Carkeek b Hazlitt	6
C.B.Llewellyn	c Armstrong b Laver	13		c Scott b Matthews	16
R.O.Schwarz	c Seitz b Matthews	26	(6)	c Matthews b Laver	0
J.M.M.Commaille	lbw b Laver	0	(10)	not out	23
A.E.E.Vogler	b Matthews	29	(9)	c & b Matthews	12
S.J.Pegler	b Matthews	0		b Armstrong	0
Extras	(b6, lb3)	9		(b5, lb9, w1)	15
Total	(72.3 overs, 228 mins)	189		(102.5 overs, 277 mins)	236

VICTORIA

T.S.Warne	st Sherwell b Llewellyn	84	(2)	b Vogler	16
D.B.M.Smith	run out (Zulch/Vogler)	5	(1)	b Schwarz	21
J.A.Seitz	c Faulkner b Vogler	18		run out (Faulkner/Sherwell)	14
†W.Carkeek	c & b Vogler	3	(6)	not out	38
H.H.L.Kortlang	c Sherwell b Vogler	60	(4)	lbw b Schwarz	10
*W.W.Armstrong	c Nourse b Schwarz	30	(7)	not out	20
G.R.Hazlitt	run out (Commaille/Sherwell)	21			
W.J.Scott	st Sherwell b Schwarz	5			
T.J.Matthews	c Sherwell b Vogler	51			
F.J.Laver	not out	12	(5)	lbw b Pegler	0
A.C.Facy	c Faulkner b Vogler	6			
Extras	(b4, lb2)	6		(b5, lb2)	7
Total	(108.4 overs, 265 mins)	301		(31.0 overs, 96 mins) (5 wkts)	126

VICTORIA	O	M	R	W	w,nb		O	M	R	W	w,nb
Facy	6	3	13	0	-,-		16	4	46	1	1,-
Hazlitt	21	9	45	2	-,-		19	10	29	1	-,-
Armstrong	20	5	44	2	-,-		14.5	3	42	2	-,-
Laver	17	5	56	3	-,-		32	12	65	2	-,-
Scott	1	0	9	0	-,-						
Matthews	7.3	2	13	3	-,-	(5)	18	3	33	3	-,-
Warne						(6)	3	1	6	0	-,-

SOUTH AFRICAN XI	O	M	R	W	w,nb		O	M	R	W	w,nb
Schwarz	34	6	85	2	-,-		12	2	54	2	-,-
Vogler	35.4	6	104	5	-,-		11	1	42	1	-,-
Faulkner	18	0	64	0	-,-						
Nourse	4	1	7	0	-,-						
Pegler	11	3	18	0	-,-	(3)	8	2	23	1	-,-
Llewellyn	6	0	17	1	-,-						

FALL OF WICKETS

Wkt	SAF 1st	VIC 1st	SAF 2nd	VIC 2nd
1st	6	17	13	28
2nd	7	65	14	47
3rd	113	75	39	56
4th	118	143	123	56
5th	118	197	123	84
6th	139	202	152	-
7th	139	209	157	-
8th	169	263	175	-
9th	170	291	236	-
10th	189	301	236	-

NEW SOUTH WALES v SOUTH AFRICAN XI

Played at Sydney Cricket Ground on November 18, 19, 21, 1910. (Timeless match)
Toss : South African XI.   Result : NEW SOUTH WALES WON BY THREE WICKETS.
Debuts: New South Wales - B.J.Folkard (f/c).
12th Men: F.K.Gow (NSW) and S.J.Pegler (SAF).
Umpires: W.J.Bruton and W.G.Curran.
Attendances: 7795, 20523, 6815.   Total: 35,133.   Receipts: £1738.
Close of Play: 1st day NSW 0/76 (Trumper 41, Bardsley 35); 2nd day SAF (2) 6/139 (Pearse 19, Commaille 3).

Folkard, brought in as a late replacement for J.D.Scott (leg injury), captured 8 wickets on debut including those of Llewellyn and Schwarz with successive deliveries in the first innings. Trumper (70 in 94 minutes, 7 fours and 78 in 62 minutes, 11 fours) and Bardsley (70 in 69 minutes, 1 five and 6 fours and 45 in 97 minutes) began each New South Wales innings with a century partnership but the rest of the batting disappointed. South Africa's leading scorers were Stricker (73 in 140 minutes, 10 fours), Faulkner (74 in 98 minutes, 12 fours) and Pearse (45 in 46 minutes, 1 six, 5 fours and 52 in 100 minutes, 6 fours). The overall failure of the batting of both sides surprised those present, as the "weather was ideal, and the wicket was of the very best" (*Town & Country Journal*). *Wisden* incorrectly gives SAF (2) Commaille b Folkard; NSW (2) E.L.Waddy c Sherwell. *Luckin* incorrectly gives SAF (2) Zulch c Bardsley b Folkard, Stricker c & b Kelleway; NSW (1) Emery not out 4, Hordern run out 6; NSW (2) E.F.Waddy 13, Folkard 8. Sources: *Wisden, Luckin, NSWCA Report, Sydney Referee, Sydney Morning Herald, Town & Country Journal, Sydney Daily Telegraph.*

SOUTH AFRICAN XI

J.W.Zulch	c Folkard b Kelleway	14	c Bardsley b Kelleway	29
L.A.Stricker	b Kelleway	73	c Kelleway b Folkard	38
S.J.Snooke	c Emery b Kelleway	6	b Folkard	19
A.W.Nourse	c Kelleway b Emery	40	b Folkard	6
G.A.Faulkner	b Emery	74	c E.F.Waddy b Emery	1
C.B.Llewellyn	b Folkard	13	b Folkard	8
R.O.Schwarz	b Folkard	0	(9) st Carter b Folkard	3
A.E.E.Vogler	b Cotter	12	(10) c Carter b Folkard	11
C.O.C.Pearse	c & b Kelleway	45	(7) not out	52
J.M.M.Commaille	lbw b Kelleway	0	(8) b Kelleway	3
*†P.W.Sherwell	not out	5	st Carter b Hordern	10
Extras	(b3, lb7, nb8)	18	(b5, lb8, w4, nb1)	18
Total	(75.5 overs, 231 mins)	300	(78.0 overs, 208 mins)	198

NEW SOUTH WALES

*V.T.Trumper	c Vogler b Faulkner	70	st Sherwell b Faulkner	78
W.Bardsley	c Faulkner b Vogler	70	lbw b Faulkner	45
C.G.Macartney	run out (Commaille/Sherwell)	23	b Vogler	4
E.L.Waddy	c & b Faulkner	15	st Sherwell b Schwarz	32
E.F.Waddy	b Faulkner	3	lbw b Schwarz	8
B.J.Folkard	b Schwarz	28	st Sherwell b Vogler	13
C.Kelleway	c Llewellyn b Faulkner	37	not out	19
†H.Carter	b Nourse	19	b Snooke	9
A.Cotter	c Llewellyn b Faulkner	1	not out	1
S.H.Emery	run out (Llewellyn/Sherwell)	4		
H.V.Hordern	not out	6		
Extras	(b4, lb4, w3)	11	(lb2, nb1)	3
Total	(65.1 overs, 197 mins)	287	(45.3 overs, 135 mins) (7 wkts)	212

NEW SOUTH WALES	O	M	R	W	w,nb		O	M	R	W	w,nb			FALL OF WICKETS			
Cotter	17	1	66	1	-,3		17	5	50	0	1,1			SAF	NSW	SAF	NSW
Kelleway	24.5	9	60	5	-,5		19	6	42	2	2,-	Wkt	1st	1st	2nd	2nd
Hordern	4	0	31	0	-,-	(5)	3	0	10	1	-,-	1st	29	122	53	121
Macartney	3	2	1	0	-,-							2nd	40	164	90	126
Folkard	13	1	53	2	-,-	(4)	26	15	37	6	1,-	3rd	122	176	104	128
Emery	14	2	71	2	-,-	(3)	9	0	41	1	-,-	4th	166	181	107	154
												5th	192	191	115	175
SOUTH AFRICAN XI	O	M	R	W	w,nb		O	M	R	W	w,nb	6th	192	227	117	198
Nourse	14.1	1	45	1	3,-	(5)	5	1	23	0	-,-	7th	221	260	139	211
Vogler	18	2	105	1	-,-	(1)	11	0	58	2	-,-	8th	292	265	150	-
Schwarz	17	0	69	1	,		9	0	42	2	-,1	9th	295	276	173	-
Llewellyn	2	0	13	0	-,-							10th	300	287	198	-
Snooke	1	0	4	0	-,-	(6)	1.3	0	2	1	-,-					
Faulkner	13	1	40	5	-,-	(2)	18	0	74	2	-,-					
Stricker						(4)	1	0	10	0	-,-					

QUEENSLAND v SOUTH AFRICAN XI

Played at Brisbane Cricket Ground (Woolloongabba) on November 25, 26, 28, 1910. (Three-day match)
Toss : South African XI.   Result : SOUTH AFRICAN XI WON BY 122 RUNS.
Debuts: Queensland - A.E.Sims (f/c).
12th Men: E.R.Crouch (Qld) and J.M.M.Commaille (SAF).
Umpires: G.A.Carter and W.H.Carvosso.
Attendances: 2000, 5000, 1500.   Total: About 8500.   Receipts: £342.
Close of Play: 1st day Qld 5/114 (Marshal 49, McCloy 12); 2nd day SAF (2) 8/339 (Llewellyn 59, Schwarz 38).

A heavy thunderstorm caused a 40-minute delay between the end of the South African innings and the start of the Queensland innings. It was preceded by a dust storm and light rain during the closing stages of the South African innings. Zulch (99 in 115 minutes, 16 fours) and Llewellyn (88 not out in 67 minutes, 11 fours) were responsible for the fast rate of scoring in the second innings. Zulch, looking for his century, played a ball to cover and set off for a single but the field had been brought in, Faulkner did not respond, and Zulch slipped in attempting to regain his crease. Faulkner became the first touring cricketer to do the match double in Australia, scoring 54 in 60 minutes (7 fours) and 73 in 100 minutes (6 fours) and taking 10 wickets. Schwarz hit 51 in 63 minutes (8 fours). Hartigan (65 in 80 minutes, 9 fours) and Jennings (67 in 98 minutes, 6 fours) established a new Queensland first-wicket record. Armstrong replaced W.T.Evans (leg injury) in the Queensland side prior to the start. *Luckin gives incorrect match dates.* Sources: *Wisden, Luckin, Brisbane Courier, The Queenslander, Queensland Times.*

SOUTH AFRICAN XI

L.A.Stricker	c Redgrave b McLaren	5	(2)	c & b Barstow	0
J.W.Zulch	c Jennings b McLaren	7	(1)	run out (Hutcheon/Sims)	99
C.M.H.Hathorn	c Jennings b Barstow	15		b McCloy	3
A.W.Nourse	b Barstow	38	(5)	c Hartigan b McLaren	1
G.A.Faulkner	c Marshal b Redgrave	54	(6)	c Jennings b McLaren	73
C.O.C.Pearse	c Fennelly b McCloy	1	(7)	c Hutcheon b McCloy	33
S.J.Snooke	c Fennelly b McLaren	13	(8)	b McLaren	14
C.B.Llewellyn	c Marshal b Redgrave	31	(9)	not out	88
*R.O.Schwarz	b McLaren	4	(10)	b Barstow	51
A.E.E.Vogler	c Sims b McLaren	3	(11)	c Jennings b Barstow	1
†T.Campbell	not out	9	(4)	c Fennelly b Redgrave	6
Extras	(b18, lb4)	22		(b8, lb3, w2)	13
Total	(47.2 overs, 160 mins)	202		(83.0 overs, 254 mins)	382

QUEENSLAND

R.J.Hartigan	c Faulkner b Vogler	2		b Faulkner	65
C.B.Jennings	lbw b Schwarz	24		b Nourse	67
S.J.Fennelly	c Vogler b Llewellyn	15	(4)	b Faulkner	37
A.Marshal	c Vogler b Faulkner	50	(3)	c Campbell b Vogler	34
J.S.Redgrave	b Schwarz	1		b Schwarz	4
*J.S.Hutcheon	st Campbell b Faulkner	9		c Hathorn b Faulkner	39
W.S.S.McCloy	c Vogler b Faulkner	15		b Faulkner	7
J.W.McLaren	st Campbell b Vogler	0	(10)	not out	17
W.Armstrong	not out	14	(8)	c Campbell b Vogler	19
C.B.Barstow	b Faulkner	4	(9)	c & b Faulkner	1
†A.E.Sims	b Faulkner	5		b Vogler	3
Extras	(b4, nb2)	6		(b16, lb7, w1)	24
Total	(44.1 overs, 128 mins)	145		(77.4 overs, 200 mins)	317

QUEENSLAND	O	M	R	W	w,nb		O	M	R	W	w,nb		FALL OF WICKETS			
McLaren	18	2	55	5	-,-	(2)	25	4	75	3	1,-			SAF	QLD	SAF	QLD
McCloy	7	0	27	1	-,-	(3)	14	0	92	2	-,-	Wkt	1st	1st	2nd	2nd
Barstow	11	0	50	2	-,-	(1)	17	1	68	3	-,-	1st	6	2	1	137
Marshal	3	0	10	0	-,-	(5)	3	0	25	0	-,-	2nd	13	40	14	151
Redgrave	8.2	1	38	2	-,-	(4)	18	3	75	1	1,-	3rd	51	56	25	217
Armstrong							4	0	25	0	-,-	4th	78	64	43	222
Hartigan							2	0	9	0	-,-	5th	94	82	149	232
												6th	146	116	207	266
SOUTH AFRICAN XI	O	M	R	W	w,nb		O	M	R	W	w,nb	7th	146	117	240	289
Vogler	16	4	60	2	-,-	(5)	16.4	2	66	3	1,-	8th	152	125	240	290
Faulkner	16.1	2	32	5	-,-	(3)	28	2	106	5	-,-	9th	162	129	378	311
Schwarz	8	0	29	2	-,2	(4)	13	2	47	1	-,-	10th	202	145	382	317
Llewellyn	4	0	18	1	-,-	(6)	1	0	2	0	-,-					
Nourse						(1)	15	2	60	1	-,-					
Snooke						(2)	4	1	12	0	-,-					

VICTORIA v SOUTH AUSTRALIA (Shield Match 2)

Played at Melbourne Cricket Ground on November 25, 26, 28, 29, 1910. (Timeless match)
Toss : South Australia.   Result : VICTORIA WON BY AN INNINGS AND 87 RUNS.
Debuts: South Australia - C.R.Moyle (f/c).
12th Men: F.T.Delves (Vic) and W.A.Hewer (SA).
Umpires: R.M.Crockett and W.A.Young.
Attendances: 2337, 7812, 2493, 439.   Total: 13,081.   Receipts: £303.
Close of Play: 1st day Vic 1/90 (Scott 40, Carkeek 0); 2nd day Vic 6/423 (Armstrong 73, Matthews 33); 3rd day SA (2); 4/138
    (Crawford 13, S.Hill 4).

Kenny and Scott (originally 12th) replaced A.C.Facy (unavailable) and V.S.Ransford (ill) in the selected Victorian team. The South Australian batsmen failed to take advantage of ideal conditions on the first day and their team was never in the match thereafter. Scott (117 in 261 minutes, 12 fours), Kortlang (94 in 149 minutes, 7 fours) and Armstrong (76 in 110 minutes, 1 five and 5 fours) assisted Victoria beyond 400 but it was a record ninth-wicket partnership of 143 by Hazlitt (77 in 96 minutes, 10 fours) and Kenny (73 in 132 minutes, 6 fours) that put the game beyond doubt. Victoria's leg-spinning allrounders, Armstrong and Kenny, both put in match-winning performances. Sources: *Wisden, C.B.O'Reilly, SACA Report, The Age, The Argus, The Australasian.*

SOUTH AUSTRALIA

R.E.Mayne	b Laver	45	c Armstrong b Laver	17
C.E.Dolling	c Seitz b Hazlitt	38	c Carkeek b Armstrong	11
*C.Hill	b Hazlitt	4	c Hazlitt b Kenny	35
D.R.A.Gehrs	st Carkeek b Armstrong	27	b Laver	52
J.N.Crawford	c Hazlitt b Armstrong	69	c Armstrong b Laver	25
S.Hill	c Carkeek b Armstrong	7	c Smith b Kenny	42
L.R.Hill	b Armstrong	5	c Laver b Kenny	51
R.B.C.Rees	c Hazlitt b Armstrong	11	b Kenny	15
†C.R.Moyle	c Warne b Hazlitt	24	run out (Hazlitt/Carkeek)	2
W.J.Whitty	b Hazlitt	3	not out	19
A.W.Wright	not out	5	c Matthews b Kenny	6
Extras	(b3, lb1, w1)	5	(b5, lb4)	9
Total	(72.2 overs, 201 mins)	243	(89.3 overs, 236 mins)	284

VICTORIA

W.J.Scott	c Crawford b Mayne	117
D.B.M.Smith	c Mayne b Gehrs	49
†W.Carkeek	c Moyle b Crawford	29
J.A.Seitz	c Moyle b Whitty	1
H.H.L.Kortlang	b Whitty	94
*W.W.Armstrong	b Whitty	76
T.S.Warne	b Crawford	8
T.J.Matthews	b Rees	42
G.R.Hazlitt	c & b Rees	77
A.Kenny	st Moyle b Whitty	73
F.J.Laver	not out	17
Extras	(b17, lb13, w1)	31
Total	(185.5 overs, 513 mins)	614

VICTORIA	O	M	R	W	w,nb		O	M	R	W	w,nb	
Hazlitt	21.2	4	73	4	1,-	(5)	9	0	30	0	-,-	
Armstrong	22	6	59	5	-,-		22	5	62	1	-,-	
Matthews	10	0	44	0	-,-	(4)	6	0	22	0	-,-	
Laver	18	2	60	1	-,-	(1)	36	2	112	3	-,-	
Warne	1	0	2	0	-,-							
Kenny						(3)	16.3	3	49	5	-,-	

SOUTH AUSTRALIA	O	M	R	W	w,nb
L.R.Hill	16	2	73	0	-,-
Whitty	53.5	15	142	4	1,-
Crawford	33	7	90	2	-,-
Wright	27	2	84	0	-,-
Rees	39	4	128	2	-,-
Gehrs	9	1	39	1	-,-
Mayne	7	1	23	1	-,-
C.Hill	1	0	4	0	-,-

FALL OF WICKETS

Wkt	SA 1st	VIC 1st	SA 2nd
1st	71	86	24
2nd	82	140	34
3rd	93	144	92
4th	120	278	134
5th	142	334	161
6th	148	354	241
7th	170	435	244
8th	233	437	250
9th	237	580	266
10th	243	614	284

AUSTRALIAN XI v SOUTH AFRICAN XI

Played at Brisbane Cricket Ground (Woolloongabba) on December 2, 3, 5, 1910. (Three-day match)
Toss : Australian XI.   Result : MATCH DRAWN.
Debuts: Nil.
12th Men: J.S.Hutcheon (Aust XI). No 12th named for South Africa.
Umpires: G.A.Carter and T.Muir.
Attendances: 2000, 7000, 2000.   Total: About 11,000.   Receipts: No figures published.
Close of Play: 1st day Aust XI 0/7 (Matthews 6, Hordern 1); 2nd day SAF (2) 3/57 (Zulch 20, Faulkner 13).

The South Africans were sent in on a wicket softened by heavy overnight rain and lost four wicket before lunch. Faulkner (70 in 89 minutes, 8 fours), Llewellyn (50 in 84 minutes, 7 fours) and Sherwell (76 in 90 minutes, 12 fours) led the recovery. Hordern, sent in with Matthews late on the first day, hit a half-century (54 in 82 minutes, 7 fours) but thereafter only Jennings (95 in 123 minutes, 7 fours) made any impression. Further rain during the night preceding the final day caused the wicket to play slowly. Batsmen of both sides hit out in an attempt to achieve a result but there was insufficient time for either team to do so. Marshal (106 in 130 minutes, 13 fours) took 80 minutes to reach 50 but went to his century in only a further 31 minutes, "his driving in particular being brilliant" (*Courier*). Sources: *Wisden, Luckin, Sydney Referee, Sydney Morning Herald, Brisbane Courier, Queensland Times, The Queenslander.*

SOUTH AFRICAN XI

J.W.Zulch	b Macartney	2	run out (Macartney)		58
L.A.Stricker	b McLaren	1	b Hordern		3
S.J.Snooke	c Jennings b McLaren	0	c Marshal b McLaren		5
A.W.Nourse	c Marshal b McLaren	26	b Hordern		2
G.A.Faulkner	c Jennings b Matthews	70	run out (McLaren/Matthews)		21
C.B.Llewellyn	b Matthews	50	c Matthews b Hordern		42
C.O.C.Pearse	b Macartney	5	c Jennings b Matthews		4
J.H.Sinclair	b McLaren	47	c Kortlang b Matthews		11
*†P.W.Sherwell	not out	76	not out		13
A.E.E.Vogler	c Kortlang b Hordern	41	not out		18
S.J.Pegler	b Hordern	8			
Extras	(b10, lb2, w2, nb3)	17	(b16, lb4)		20
Total	(74.4 overs, 248 mins)	343	(68.0 overs, 210 mins) (8 wkts dec)		197

AUSTRALIAN XI

T.J.Matthews	lbw b Sinclair	13			
H.V.Hordern	st Sherwell b Vogler	54			
R.J.Hartigan	b Pegler	11			
A.Marshal	b Vogler	0	(1) st Sherwell b Vogler		106
H.H.L.Kortlang	lbw b Faulkner	39	(6) not out		33
C.B.Jennings	c Llewellyn b Sinclair	95	(4) c Sherwell b Faulkner		9
D.B.M.Smith	b Llewellyn	17	(2) c Nourse b Faulkner		15
C.G.Macartney	c Zulch b Sinclair	22	(3) st Sherwell b Faulkner		2
S.J.Fennelly	lbw b Sinclair	0	(5) c & b Pegler		25
J.W.McLaren	run out	6			
*†W.T.Evans	not out	0			
Extras	(b3, lb3, w1, nb1)	8	(b4, lb7, w1, nb1)		13
Total	(82.0 overs, 224 mins)	265	(45.1 overs, 130 mins) (5 wkts)		203

AUSTRALIAN XI	O	M	R	W	w,nb		O	M	R	W	w,nb
McLaren	24	4	85	4	2,3		14	5	35	1	-,-
Macartney	21	4	74	2	-,-	(3)	19	8	25	0	-,-
Hordern	9.4	0	54	2	-,-	(2)	18	3	71	3	-,-
Hartigan	2	0	12	0	-,-						
Matthews	16	2	83	2	-,-	(4)	13	3	34	2	-,-
Marshal	2	0	18	0	-,-	(5)	3	0	10	0	-,-
Fennelly						(6)	1	0	2	0	-,-

SOUTH AFRICAN XI	O	M	R	W	w,nb		O	M	R	W	w,nb
Snooke	8	0	16	0	-,-	(2)	3	0	10	0	-,-
Pegler	11	1	53	1	-,-	(4)	4	0	22	1	-,-
Sinclair	24	2	67	4	-,-	(5)	9	0	31	0	1,-
Vogler	17	2	46	2	-,-	(3)	11.1	1	54	1	-,1
Faulkner	14	2	44	1	-,1	(1)	14	3	52	3	-,-
Nourse	3	0	12	0	1,-	(7)	2	0	11	0	-,-
Llewellyn	5	1	19	1	-,-	(6)	2	1	10	0	-,-

FALL OF WICKETS

	SAF	AUST	SAF	AUST
Wkt	1st	1st	2nd	2nd
1st	2	23	14	30
2nd	3	62	25	36
3rd	10	80	32	64
4th	75	83	66	124
5th	126	158	143	203
6th	145	196	153	-
7th	178	254	159	
8th	246	254	164	
9th	330	265	-	
10th	343	265	-	

NEW SOUTH WALES v SOUTH AUSTRALIA (Shield Match 3)

Played at Sydney Cricket Ground on December 2, 3, 5, 6, 1910. (Timeless match)
Toss : New South Wales.   Result : SOUTH AUSTRALIA WON BY 285 RUNS.
Debuts: Nil.
12th Men: E.L.Waddy (NSW). No 12th named for SA - see below.
Umpires: W.J.Bruton and A.C.Jones.
Attendances: 2850, 6850, 2700, 800.   Total: About 13,200.   Receipts: £495.
Close of Play: 1st day NSW 0/44 (Trumper 29, Bardsley 13); 2nd day SA (2) 4/209 (C.Hill 90); 3rd day NSW (2) 2/62 (Bardsley 31, Collins 23).

Chamberlain was brought from Adelaide to replace J.N.Crawford and R.B.C.Rees, who announced their unavailability after the match in Melbourne. South Australia were consequently left without a 12th man for this match; V.S.Ransford, the Victorian player who had arrived in Sydney for the First Test against South Africa, was called upon to substitute on the last day. C.Hill (87 in 135 minutes, 12 fours) and Gehrs (120 in 146 minutes, 18 fours) added 168 for South Australia's third wicket. Trumper (75 in 88 minutes, 9 fours) shone in the New South Wales first innings but was out second ball in the second innings. Whitty followed up by then bowling Gow next ball. Clem Hill (156 in 186 minutes, 21 fours) survived three early chances to complete a fine match double. Leslie Hill, a brother, also registered a century, making 123 in 118 minutes with 21 fours and three chances. Bardsley (191 not out in 351 minutes, 1 five and 21 fours) carried his bat. *Wisden* incorrectly gives NSW (2) Wright 6/103. Sources: *Wisden, C.B.O'Reilly, NSWCA Report, Sydney Referee, Sydney Morning Herald, Town & Country Journal, Sydney Telegraph, Newcastle Herald.*

SOUTH AUSTRALIA

Batsman	Dismissal	R		Dismissal	R
R.E.Mayne	c Trumper b Collins	2		b Kelleway	28
C.E.Dolling	c Folkard b Emery	24		b Emery	67
*C.Hill	c Folkard b Scott	87		b Kelleway	156
D.R.A.Gehrs	c Collins b Emery	120		b Cotter	11
S.Hill	b Scott	0	(6)	b Emery	25
W.A.Hewer	b Kelleway	7	(9)	b Kelleway	30
W.L.Chamberlain	b Scott	35		b Kelleway	23
L.R.Hill	b Emery	0		c Collins b Kelleway	123
†C.R.Moyle	run out (Kelleway/Gorry)	22	(5)	b Kelleway	1
W.J.Whitty	b Scott	5		c Emery b Cotter	0
A.W.Wright	not out	5		not out	1
Extras	(b25, lb7, w2, nb1)	35		(b19, lb4, w6, nb5)	34
Total	(83.0 overs, 246 mins)	342		(104.2 overs, 330 mins)	499

NEW SOUTH WALES

Batsman	Dismissal	R	Dismissal	R
*V.T.Trumper	c Moyle b Whitty	75	b Whitty	0
W.Bardsley	c Mayne b L.R.Hill	26	not out	191
F.K.Gow	b Wright	23	b Whitty	0
H.L.Collins	c Chamberlain b Wright	0	b Whitty	26
H.Cranney	c Chamberlain b Whitty	1	c Moyle b Wright	26
C.Kelleway	c Mayne b Chamberlain	26	c C.Hill b Wright	65
B.J.Folkard	c L.R.Hill b Wright	15	c Moyle b Wright	1
A.Cotter	c Mayne b Chamberlain	12	c sub (V.S.Ransford) b Wright	8
S.H.Emery	c Gehrs b Wright	11	c Moyle b Whitty	21
J.D.Scott	c Moyle b Wright	0	hit wkt b Wright	0
†C.R.Gorry	not out	0	c sub (V.S.Ransford) b Wright	0
Extras	(b2, lb1, w1, nb2)	6	(b16, lb5, w2)	23
Total	(61.1 overs, 172 mins)	195	(100.0 overs, 351 mins)	361

NEW SOUTH WALES	O	M	R	W	w,nb		O	M	R	W	w,nb
Folkard	23	3	85	0	-,-	(5)	14	0	57	0	-,-
Collins	3	0	11	1	,	(6)	5	1	17	0	-,-
Kelleway	18	4	45	1	2,-		29.2	6	72	6	4,-
Emery	19	0	100	3	-,-	(2)	14	1	95	2	-,-
Scott	16	3	48	4	-,-	(1)	15	1	108	0	1,1
Cotter	4	0	18	0	-,1	(4)	25	2	104	2	1,4
Cranney							2	0	12	0	-,-

SOUTH AUSTRALIA	O	M	R	W	w,nb		O	M	R	W	w,nb
Whitty	21	6	63	2	-,-		37	6	123	4	1,-
Wright	22.1	3	75	5	-,-		37	8	101	6	-,-
L.R.Hill	9	1	33	1	-,2		10	2	39	0	-,-
Chamberlain	9	3	18	2	1,-		10	2	31	0	1,-
Gehrs							4	0	27	0	-,-
Hewer							2	0	17	0	-,-

FALL OF WICKETS

Wkt	SA 1st	NSW 1st	SA 2nd	NSW 2nd
1st	11	62	68	0
2nd	57	126	167	0
3rd	225	126	208	76
4th	225	126	209	126
5th	237	132	289	267
6th	293	164	327	279
7th	300	179	352	295
8th	316	187	476	346
9th	326	195	481	361
10th	342	195	499	361

AUSTRALIA v SOUTH AFRICA (1st Test)

Played at Sydney Cricket Ground on December 9, 10, 12 (no play), 13, 14, 1910. (Timeless match)
Toss : Australia.   Result : AUSTRALIA WON BY AN INNINGS AND 114 RUNS.
Debuts: Australia - C.Kelleway (Test). South Africa - C.O.C.Pearse (Test).
12th Men: S.H.Emery (Aust) and S.J.Pegler (SAF).
Umpires: R.M.Crockett and W.G.Curran.
Attendances: 9617, 20579, no play, 280, 4549.   Total: 35,025.   Receipts: £1757.
Close of Play: 1st day Aust 6/494 (Armstrong 43, Kelleway 0); 2nd day SAF 7/140 (Faulkner 45, Schwarz 52); 3rd day no play; 4th day
    SAF 7/146 (Faulkner 45, Schwarz 58).

Australia's 494 runs in 5 hours is unlikely to be exceeded as the record for most runs on the opening day of a Test match. The score raced
from 1/147 at lunch (Bardsley 61, Hill 55) to 2/355 at tea (Hill 150, Gehrs 38) while Bardsley (chanceless 132 in 135 minutes, 16 fours)
and Hill (191 in 202 minutes, 18 fours, chance when 113) took 224 runs off the South African attack in just 105 minutes to create a new
second-wicket record for Australia. Hill and Gehrs (67 in 64 minutes, 9 fours) put on a further 144 in 64 minutes for the next wicket.
Faulkner (62 in 146 minutes, 10 fours) and Schwarz (61 in 87 minutes, 6 fours) replied by adding 100 in 87 minutes for the visitor's
eighth wicket while the pitch was still largely intact, Cotter capturing six of the first seven Springbok wickets to fall. Rain set in after the
second day - no play was possible on the third and only 13 minutes of action took place on the fourth. The wicket never recovered "and
was inclined to do a bit" (*SMH*) on the last day. Sherwell (60 in 78 minutes, 1 six and 7 fours), Faulkner (43 in 67 minutes, 8 fours) and
Nourse (64 not out in 119 minutes, 5 fours) batted well, while Vogler completed a king pair. *NSWCA Report* incorrectly gives SAF (1)
Whitty 4/38, Macartney 0/16. Some recent publications incorrectly give SAF (2) 2/28, 8/185. Sources: *Wisden, Luckin, NSWCA
Report, Sydney Referee, Sydney Morning Herald, Town & Country Journal.*

AUSTRALIA

V.T.Trumper	run out (Llewellyn)	27
W.Bardsley	b Pearse	132
*C.Hill	b Pearse	191
D.R.A.Gehrs	b Pearse	67
W.W.Armstrong	b Schwarz	48
V.S.Ransford	b Schwarz	11
C.G.Macartney	b Schwarz	1
C.Kelleway	not out	14
†H.Carter	st Sherwell b Schwarz	5
A.Cotter	st Sherwell b Schwarz	0
W.J.Whitty	c Snooke b Sinclair	15
Extras	(b12, lb4, nb1)	17
Total	(109.4 overs, 322 mins)	528

SOUTH AFRICA

L.A.Stricker	b Cotter	2	(7)	lbw b Whitty	4
J.W.Zulch	b Cotter	4	(4)	run out (Cotter/Armstrong)	1
C.O.C.Pearse	c Trumper b Cotter	16	(10)	run out (Gehrs/Kelleway)	31
A.W.Nourse	c Kelleway b Cotter	5	(6)	not out	64
G.A.Faulkner	c Kelleway b Whitty	62		c Bardsley b Whitty	43
C.B.Llewellyn	b Cotter	0	(8)	c Macartney b Whitty	19
S.J.Snooke	b Whitty	3	(3)	b Cotter	4
J.H.Sinclair	b Cotter	1	(2)	b Cotter	6
R.O.Schwarz	c Trumper b Whitty	61		c Carter b Whitty	0
*†P.W.Sherwell	not out	8	(1)	c Whitty b Kelleway	60
A.E.E.Vogler	b Whitty	0		b Kelleway	0
Extras	(lb6, nb6)	12		(lb1, nb7)	8
Total	(68.0 overs, 193 mins)	174		(67.1 overs, 199 mins)	240

SOUTH AFRICA	O	M	R	W	w,nb
Llewellyn	14	0	54	0	-,-
Sinclair	19.4	0	80	1	-,-
Schwarz	25	6	102	5	-,1
Vogler	15	0	87	0	-,-
Faulkner	12	0	71	0	-,-
Nourse	12	0	61	0	-,-
Pearse	12	0	56	3	-,-

AUSTRALIA	O	M	R	W	w,nb		O	M	R	W	w,nb
Cotter	20	2	69	6	-,4	(3)	17	2	73	2	-,4
Whitty	24	11	33	4	-,-	(1)	21	4	75	4	-,-
Armstrong	8	3	16	0	-,1	(4)	9	1	35	0	-,1
Kelleway	9	1	33	0	-,1	(5)	15.1	4	37	2	-,2
Macartney	7	4	11	0	-,-	(2)	5	1	12	0	-,-

FALL OF WICKETS

	AUST	SAF	SAF
Wkt	1st	1st	2nd
1st	52	5	24
2nd	276	10	38
3rd	420	29	44
4th	427	38	98
5th	445	38	124
6th	453	44	144
7th	499	49	183
8th	511	149	183
9th	511	174	237
10th	528	174	240

VICTORIA v QUEENSLAND

Played at Melbourne Cricket Ground on December 16, 17, 19, 1910. (Timeless match)
Toss : Queensland.   Result : QUEENSLAND WON BY 66 RUNS.
Debuts: L.P.R.Miller - (f/c). Note: not L.F.Miller (see below).
12th Men: N.L.Speirs (Vic) and J.T.Bolton (Qld).
Umpires: E.Barrass and W.A.Young.
Attendances: 1500, 3450, 500.   Total: About 5450.   Receipts: £114.
Close of Play: 1st day Vic 3/103 (Seitz 45, Kenny 45); 2nd day Qld (2) 9/194 (Barstow 0).

R.J.Hartigan and C.B.Jennings were unavailable for Queensland. F.J.Laver (also unavailable), D.B.M.Smith (just married) and T.S.Warne (hand injury) all withdrew from the Victorian side named for the match and were replaced by Delves, Parsons and Seitz, who was originally nominated to be 12th man. Kenny survived six chances, four of them before 45, in making 121 not out in 180 minutes with 15 fours. Vaughan, bowled first ball in the first innings, topscored in the second innings with 66 in 155 minutes, 2 fours. Hutcheon scored 73 in 75 minutes and hit 5 fours. Carkeek captained Victoria on the last day in the absence of Armstrong, who had contracted mumps. L.P.R.Miller, a Richmond player making his debut, was erroneously listed in the ACS "Victorian Cricketers" booklet as L.F.Miller, an entirely different player who had represented the University club. *Cricket* incorrectly give Vic (2) Cook 1/23. Sources: *Cricket, VCA Report, The Age, The Argus, The Herald, The Australasian.*

QUEENSLAND

S.J.Fennelly	c Kenny b Scott	35	c Seitz b Parsons	14
A.Marshal	b Parsons	51	c Matthews b Parsons	66
J.S.Redgrave	c Armstrong b Parsons	37	lbw b Parsons	2
*J.S.Hutcheon	b Parsons	20	c Kortlang b Scott	73
†W.T.Evans	c Kortlang b Parsons	6	lbw b Parsons	6
A.H.Jones	c sub (N.L.Speirs) b Armstrong	67	c Vaughan b Matthews	6
J.W.McLaren	lbw b Scott	6	b Armstrong	25
W.S.S.McCloy	c Carkeek b Matthews	17	(10) c Seitz b Armstrong	1
J.W.Lewis	lbw b Seitz	9	(11) not out	29
B.W.Cook	run out (Matthews)	4	(9) c Kortlang b Scott	0
C.B.Barstow	not out	5	(8) c Miller b Scott	29
Extras	(b3, lb1, w1)	5	(lb1)	1
Total	(78.0 overs, 205 mins)	262	(65.2 overs, 182 mins)	252

VICTORIA

W.J.Scott	c Evans b McLaren	0	lbw b Cook	12
F.Vaughan	b McLaren	0	c McCloy b Redgrave	66
J.A.Seitz	run out (Hutcheon/Evans)	59	c Fennelly b Barstow	27
H.H.L.Kortlang	b McCloy	6	b Redgrave	9
A.Kenny	not out	121	c Hutcheon b Redgrave	4
*W.W.Armstrong	c Redgrave b Barstow	18	absent ill	-
T.J.Matthews	c Lewis b Cook	18	not out	35
F.T.Delves	b Cook	21	(11) c Evans b Redgrave	1
†W.Carkeek	c & b Cook	3	(8) b McLaren	10
H.F.Parsons	c McCloy b Barstow	3	(9) b McLaren	0
L.P.R.Miller	b Barstow	10	(10) b McLaren	2
Extras	(b3, lb8, nb3)	14	(b5, lb1, w1, nb2)	9
Total	(73.0 overs, 216 mins)	273	(68.5 overs, 185 mins)	175

VICTORIA	O	M	R	W	w,nb		O	M	R	W	w,nb		FALL OF WICKETS			
Miller	12	1	43	0	-,-	(5)	7	0	41	0	-,-			QLD	VIC	QLD	VIC
Kenny	9	0	43	0	-,-	(6)	3	0	13	0	-,-	Wkt	1st	1st	2nd	2nd
Matthews	10	0	31	1	-,-	(4)	9	3	21	1	-,-	1st	69	1	51	19
Scott	22	4	69	2	1,-	(1)	10.2	1	50	3	-,-	2nd	96	10	57	77
Parsons	21	5	54	4	-,-	(3)	19	2	79	4	-,-	3rd	128	23	94	113
Seitz	2	0	7	1	-,-							4th	138	126	104	119
Armstrong	2	0	10	1	-,-	(2)	17	3	47	2	-,-	5th	166	163	119	123
												6th	183	195	193	136
QUEENSLAND	O	M	R	W	w,nb		O	M	R	W	w,nb	7th	216	246	193	171
McLaren	24	1	112	2	-,2		11.5	1	30	3	-,2	8th	244	254	193	171
McCloy	8	0	32	1	-,1	(4)	1	0	3	0	-,-	9th	249	257	194	175
Barstow	12	0	47	3	-,-		9	0	36	1	-,-	10th	262	273	252	-
Redgrave	11	0	28	0	-,-	(5)	14	2	33	4	1,-					
Lewis	7	2	16	0	-,-											
Cook	11	1	24	3	-,-	(2)	23	8	34	1	-,-					
Marshal						(6)	10	0	30	0	-,-					

AFCM No. 415/85
SSM No. 108/37

VICTORIA v NEW SOUTH WALES (Shield Match 4)

Played at Melbourne Cricket Ground on December 24, 26, 27, 28, 1910. (Timeless match)
Toss : Victoria.   Result : NEW SOUTH WALES WON BY 193 RUNS.
Debuts: New South Wales - F.E.McElhone (f/c).
12th Men: H.Goddard (NSW). No 12th man or emergency fieldsman named for Victoria.
Umpires: R.M.Crockett and D.A.Elder.
Attendances: 6802, 8880, 7885, 3965.   Total: 27,532.   Receipts: £827.
Close of Play: 1st day Vic 0/1 (Laver 1, Kyle 0); 2nd day NSW (2) 3/70 (Barbour 13, Emery 0); 3rd day Vic (2) 1/54 (Seitz 23, Kyle 20).

W.W.Armstrong (mumps) and H.F.Parsons (mistakenly thought to have retired) were not considered for Victorian selection. Hart and Seitz (originally 12th man) were late replacements for L.P.Vernon and T.S.Warne (unavailable). Heavy overnight rain prompted Laver to put New South Wales in on winning the toss, but Trumper (52 in 95 minutes, 4 fours) and Bardsley (124 in 143 minutes, 14 fours) "showed exceptional skill in mastering the difficulty of the wicket" (*Age*) to negate any advantage gained. Victoria batted on an improved wicket but only Kortlang (58 in 102 minutes, 4 fours), Kyle (50 in 65 minutes, 4 fours) and Matthews (50 in 64 minutes, 5 fours) reached 50 in either innings against a well-balanced New South Wales attack. Trumper (142 in 200 minutes, 16 fours) and Barbour (82 in 138 minutes, 7 fours) led the scoring in the New South Wales second innings. Macartney's 36 included a seven (three plus four overthrows). Sources: *Wisden, NSWCA Report, The Age, The Argus, The Herald.*

NEW SOUTH WALES

*V.T.Trumper	b Kyle	52	(6)	c Matthews b Ransford	142
W.Bardsley	c & b Laver	124		c Kenny b Laver	1
C.G.Macartney	c Matthews b Kyle	43		c Carkeek b Matthews	36
E.L.Waddy	c & b Laver	9	(1)	lbw b Kenny	20
C.Kelleway	lbw b Laver	15	(7)	c Scott b Matthews	38
F.E.McElhone	c Smith b Kyle	26	(9)	c Scott b Kenny	23
E.P.Barbour	c Scott b Hart	8	(4)	c Ransford b Laver	82
H.L.Collins	not out	32		c & b Matthews	0
†H.Carter	c Seitz b Laver	11	(10)	not out	6
A.Cotter	run out (Ransford/Carkeek)	0	(11)	b Laver	17
S.H.Emery	c Hart b Kyle	5	(5)	c Seitz b Laver	7
Extras	(b3, lb3)	6		(b8, lb2)	10
Total	(101.3 overs, 280 mins)	331		(141.1 overs, 305 mins)	382

VICTORIA

*F.J.Laver	b Barbour	42	(9)	b Cotter	16
J.H.Kyle	b Kelleway	10	(3)	b Cotter	50
V.S.Ransford	c Kelleway b Cotter	33	(4)	c Carter b Cotter	15
D.B.M.Smith	c McElhone b Cotter	33	(5)	b Macartney	33
H.H.L.Kortlang	b Kelleway	58	(6)	c Waddy b Kelleway	34
J.A.Seitz	lbw b Barbour	2	(2)	c Carter b Cotter	32
A.Kenny	c Kelleway b Emery	20		b Macartney	4
W.J.Scott	b Emery	0	(1)	b Kelleway	10
T.J.Matthews	b Cotter	39	(8)	not out	50
†W.Carkeek	b Cotter	4		b Emery	6
H.W.Hart	not out	4		c Kelleway b Emery	2
Extras	(b5, nb2)	7		(b5, lb6, nb5)	16
Total	(71.1 overs, 215 mins)	252		(70.3 overs, 202 mins)	268

VICTORIA	O	M	R	W	w,nb		O	M	R	W	w,nb					
Hart	18	3	52	1	-,-	(5)	25	2	42	0	-,-					
Laver	36	10	86	4	-,-		35.1	8	83	4	-,-					
Kyle	26.3	6	70	4	-,-	(1)	30	12	52	0	-,-					
Matthews	6	0	41	0	-,-		25	3	89	3	-,-					
Kenny	9	1	39	0	-,-	(3)	15	1	63	2	-,-					
Ransford	3	0	19	0	-,-		5	2	15	1	-,-					
Scott	3	0	18	0	-,-		6	1	28	0	-,-					

FALL OF WICKETS

Wkt	NSW 1st	VIC 1st	NSW 2nd	VIC 2nd
1st	120	17	6	23
2nd	214	84	36	70
3rd	232	97	65	106
4th	232	148	90	113
5th	261	154	206	171
6th	276	184	302	185
7th	300	184	306	187
8th	320	235	354	231
9th	321	247	358	262
10th	331	252	382	268

NEW SOUTH WALES	O	M	R	W	w,nb		O	M	R	W	w,nb
Cotter	21.1	3	60	4	-,1		24	1	85	4	-,2
Macartney	8	2	26	0	-,-	(5)	12	1	26	2	-,-
Kelleway	23	6	58	2	-,1	(2)	17	3	53	2	-,3
Emery	8	0	40	2	-,-		11.3	0	45	2	-,-
Barbour	11	1	61	2	-,-	(3)	6	0	43	0	-,-

448

NEW SOUTH WALES v QUEENSLAND

Played at Sydney Cricket Ground on December 24, 26, 27, 1910. (Timeless match)
Toss : New South Wales.　　　　　Result : QUEENSLAND WON BY FOUR WICKETS.
Debuts: New South Wales - P.W.Docker, W.S.Makin, W.Watson (all f/c).
12th Men: J.T.Bolton (Qld). No 12th man or emergency fieldsman named for NSW.
Umpires: W.G.Curran and W.G.French.
Attendances: 2000, 2400, 200 .　　　Total: About 4600.　　　Receipts: £171.
Close of Play: 1st day Qld 7/122 (McLaren 2); 2nd day Qld (2) 3/98 (Fennelly 53, Jones 2).

Although the match was played on a firm pitch under ideal conditions batsmen from both sides struggled throughout. Barnes (62 in 67 minutes, 10 fours), Makin (71 in 82 minutes, 11 fours) and the New South Wales-born Fennelly (61 in 102 minutes, 7 fours) registered the only fifties. Makin was nominated 12th man before the start but came into the New South Wales team when C.E.Simpson declared himself unavailable. Barney Cook (right-arm off-cutters) was forced from the field with a leg strain in the first innings after taking four early wickets. He returned to complete his only five-wicket analysis and played the rest of the match without discomfort. Jones began the New South Wales second innings in the role of wicket-keeper but soon gave way to Evans who remained there until the end of the innings. Queensland's victory was their third in successive matches in Sydney. Sources: *Cricket, NSWCA Report, Sydney Referee, Sydney Morning Herald, Town & Country Journal, Sydney Daily Telegraph, Newcastle Herald.*

NEW SOUTH WALES

F.K.Gow	b Cook	0	(7)	c Lewis b Cook		16
H.Cranney	b Cook	4		c & b Barstow		15
*E.F.Waddy	b Cook	8	(6)	b Cook		0
J.C.Barnes	c McCloy b Barstow	62	(3)	b Barstow		3
R.B.Minnett	lbw b Cook	5	(4)	c Marshal b Redgrave		15
W.Watson	c Marshal b McCloy	38	(1)	c Evans b Redgrave		28
W.S.Makin	b McLaren	71	(5)	b Cook		1
P.W.Docker	lbw b Cook	0	(9)	run out (Evans)		1
H.V.Hordern	not out	13	(8)	c Evans b Redgrave		18
†G.G.Harvey	b McLaren	1		c McCloy b Redgrave		4
J.D.Scott	c McCloy b McLaren	0		not out		0
Extras	(b1, lb1, w1, nb2)	5		(lb2, w1, nb3)		6
Total	(51.4 overs, 167 mins)	207		(40.1 overs, 120 mins)		107

QUEENSLAND

S.J.Fennelly	lbw b Hordern	27		b Scott		61
A.Marshal	c Harvey b Docker	34		c Cranney b Minnett		1
J.S.Redgrave	run out (Barnes/Hordern)	5		c Harvey b Minnett		14
*J.S.Hutcheon	c Waddy b Scott	13		c Hordern b Minnett		19
†W.T.Evans	b Hordern	10	(8)	not out		12
A.H.Jones	c Hordern b Minnett	10	(5)	st Harvey b Hordern		2
W.S.S.McCloy	b Hordern	15	(7)	c Waddy b Scott		4
J.W.McLaren	c Makin b Scott	17	(6)	not out		9
J.W.Lewis	c Scott b Docker	22				
B.W.Cook	not out	9				
C.B.Barstow	b Docker	11				
Extras	(lb4, w1, nb4)	9		(b3, lb4, w1, nb3)		11
Total	(48.2 overs, 162 mins)	182		(41.3 overs, 126 mins) (6 wkts)		133

QUEENSLAND	O	M	R	W	w,nb		O	M	R	W	w,nb
Cook	12	1	34	5	-,-		13.1	3	26	3	-,-
McLaren	16.4	3	61	3	-,2		5	0	21	0	-,2
Redgrave	11	0	47	0	-,-	(4)	11	3	19	4	1,-
Marshal	3	0	10	0	1,-						
Barstow	6	0	34	1	-,-	(3)	7	0	23	2	-,-
McCloy	3	0	16	1	-,-	(5)	4	0	12	0	-,1

NEW SOUTH WALES	O	M	R	W	w,nb		O	M	R	W	w,nb
Scott	18	2	59	2	1,2	(2)	16	3	38	2	-,3
Hordern	14	0	59	3	-,-	(5)	7.3	0	25	1	-,-
Docker	12.2	0	47	3	-,-		5	1	19	0	-,-
Minnett	4	1	8	1	-,2	(1)	12	3	27	3	1,-
Watson						(4)	1	0	13	0	-,-

FALL OF WICKETS

Wkt	NSW 1st	QLD 1st	NSW 2nd	QLD 2nd
1st	4	50	27	3
2nd	15	66	32	45
3rd	25	67	63	92
4th	37	82	66	106
5th	93	93	66	106
6th	152	111	69	117
7th	159	122	98	-
8th	202	162	101	-
9th	207	162	107	-
10th	207	182	107	-

AUSTRALIA v SOUTH AFRICA (2nd Test)

Played at Melbourne Cricket Ground on December 31, 1910, January 2, 3, 4, 1911. (Timeless match)
Toss : Australia.   Result : AUSTRALIA WON BY 89 RUNS.
Debuts: Nil.
12th Men: T.J.Matthews (Aust) and J.M.M.Commaille (SAF).
Umpires: R.M.Crockett and W.Hannah.
Attendances: 15974, 18850, 13627, 9095.   Total: 57,546.   Receipts: £2256.
Close of Play: 1st day SAF 0/17 (Zulch 5, Sherwell 10); 2nd day SAF 5/352 (Faulkner 188, Snooke 18); 3rd day Aust (2) 5/208
    (Trumper 133, Kelleway 6).

Faulkner (204 in 315 minutes, 26 fours) survived chances at 64 and 126 but gave an otherwise masterly display in scoring South Africa's first Test double century. Zulch (42 in 124 minutes, 5 fours), Snooke (77 in 150 minutes, 10 fours) and Sinclair (58 not out in 90 minutes, 2 sixes and 6 fours) also batted well. South Africa;s second-innings collapse occurred when the wicket was still in good condition, "all credit to the fine bowling of Whitty and Cotter" (*Age*). Bardsley (85 in 115 minutes, 8 fours) gave a polished display in Australia's first innings, sharing a century second-wicket stand with Hill (39 in 49 minutes, 2 fours), who was out to the first ball he received in the second innings. Ransford (58 in 77 minutes, 1 five and 6 fours) and Armstrong (75 in 120 minutes, 5 fours) made other important contributions. However, the innings of the match was considered to be Trumper's chanceless 159 in 171 minutes, with 1 six and 15 fours. He reached 50 in 63 minutes and 100 in 117 minutes and it was plainly stated: "During his stay at the wicket he never made a false stroke" (*Age*). As Australia's second innings began at 3.30pm after an early tea break, Trumper's 133* in 154 minutes can be considered to have occupied one session. *Luckin* incorrectly records the order of some dismissals in Aust (2). More recent publications incorrectly give Aust (1) 5/183. Sources: *Wisden, Luckin, NSWCA Report, The Age, The Argus, The Herald, The Australasian, The Leader.*

AUSTRALIA

V.T.Trumper	b Pegler	34	b Faulkner		159
W.Bardsley	c Snooke b Sinclair	85	st Sherwell b Schwarz		14
*C.Hill	b Llewellyn	39	b Schwarz		0
D.R.A.Gehrs	b Llewellyn	4	st Sherwell b Schwarz		22
C.G.Macartney	run out (Zulch/Sherwell)	7	c Snooke b Llewellyn		5
V.S.Ransford	run out (Sinclair/Sherwell)	58	c Sinclair b Schwarz		23
W.W.Armstrong	c Sherwell b Faulkner	75	(8) b Llewellyn		29
C.Kelleway	c Faulkner b Stricker	18	(7) b Pegler		48
†H.Carter	not out	15	c Sherwell b Llewellyn		0
A.Cotter	c Stricker b Schwarz	3	c sub (J.M.M.Commaille) b Llewellyn		15
W.J.Whitty	c Nourse b Faulkner	6	not out		5
Extras	(lb3, nb1)	4	(lb6, nb1)		7
Total	(79.4 overs, 246 mins)	348	(79.3 overs, 248 mins)		327

SOUTH AFRICA

J.W.Zulch	b Cotter	42	(8) not out		6
*†P.W.Sherwell	c Carter b Cotter	24	(1) b Whitty		16
G.A.Faulkner	c Armstrong b Whitty	204	c Kelleway b Whitty		8
A.W.Nourse	b Kelleway	33	lbw b Cotter		2
L.A.Stricker	b Armstrong	26	(2) lbw b Cotter		0
C.B.Llewellyn	b Armstrong	5	b Cotter		17
S.J.Snooke	b Whitty	77	c Armstrong b Whitty		9
J.H.Sinclair	not out	58	(5) lbw b Whitty		3
R.O.Schwarz	b Whitty	0	c Kelleway b Cotter		7
C.O.C.Pearse	b Armstrong	6	c Kelleway b Whitty		0
S.J.Pegler	lbw b Armstrong	8	lbw b Whitty		0
Extras	(b2, lb10, w2, nb9)	23	(b6, lb3, nb3)		12
Total	(153.0 overs, 442 mins)	506	(32.0 overs, 100 mins)		80

SOUTH AFRICA	O	M	R	W	w,nb		O	M	R	W	w,nb		FALL OF WICKETS			
Nourse	8	3	24	0	-,-		5	1	18	0	-,-			AUST	SAF	AUST	SAF
Snooke	5	1	19	0	-,-		8	1	24	0	-,-	Wkt	1st	1st	2nd	2nd
Pegler	10	0	43	1	-,-	(5)	6.3	1	24	1	-,-	1st	59	34	35	1
Schwarz	13	0	66	1	-,-	(3)	22	2	76	4	-,-	2nd	160	141	35	28
Llewellyn	10	0	69	2	-,-	(4)	16	0	81	4	-,-	3rd	164	251	89	31
Sinclair	13	1	53	1	-,-		8	0	32	0	-,-	4th	164	298	94	34
Stricker	10	0	36	1	-,-	(8)	2	1	10	0	-,-	5th	188	312	176	46
Faulkner	10.4	0	34	2	-,1	(7)	12	1	55	1	-,1	6th	262	402	237	66
												7th	309	469	279	69
AUSTRALIA	O	M	R	W	w,nb		O	M	R	W	w,nb	8th	337	469	279	77
Cotter	43	5	158	2	1,6		15	3	47	4	-,3	9th	340	482	305	80
Whitty	29	6	81	3	-,-		16	7	17	6	-,-	10th	348	506	327	80
Kelleway	17	3	67	1	1,2											
Armstrong	48	9	134	4	-,1	(3)	1	0	4	0	-,-					
Macartney	16	5	43	0	-,-											

NEW SOUTH WALES v TASMANIA

Played at Sydney Cricket Ground on December 31, 1910, January 2, 1911. (Three-day match)
Toss : Tasmania.   Result : NEW SOUTH WALES WON BY AN INNINGS AND 113 RUNS.
Debuts: Tasmania - S.R.Frost (f/c).
12th Men: E.F.Waddy (NSW). No 12th named for Tasmania (only 11 men in party).
Umpires: R.Callaway and A.Lucas.
Attendances: 1600, 1500.   Total: About 3100.   Receipts: £121.
Close of Play: 1st day NSW 406 all out.

Drizzle fell at regular intervals on both days of the match but did not force the players from the field at any stage. It did however make conditions difficult for batting on the second day, in which Tasmania were dismissed for their lowest total against New South Wales. Dr 'Ranji' Hordern's leg-breaks and googlies accounted for 12 of the 20 wickets which fell on the day. Tasmania's captain Hawson, accused of an error in judgement in not batting first, justified his decision on the fact that his team had just disembarked from their ship. Barnes took over as wicket-keeper for the rest of the game when Harvey injured a hand while catching Hawson in the second innings. Eltham (78 in 100 minutes, 7 fours, chance at 0) and Hudson (94 in 103 minutes, 10 fours, 2 chances at 14) established a new Tasmanian fourth-wicket record. All three chances came in one over by Minnett, who had earlier batted 151 minutes and hit 1 six and 24 fours. Docker and Scott shared a tenth-wicket partnership of 78 in 28 minutes. Sources: *Cricket, NSWCA Report, Sydney Morning Herald, Town & Country Journal, Sydney Mail, Sydney Daily Telegraph, Hobart Mercury.*

NEW SOUTH WALES

E.P.Barbour	c Harrison b Frost	34
F.E.McElhone	c Hudson b Frost	51
J.C.Barnes	c Harrison b Carroll	13
W.S.Makin	c Payne b Paton	30
R.B.Minnett	b Paton	151
*H.Goddard	c Parkinson b Martin	2
W.Watson	b Carroll	18
H.V.Hordern	c & b Carroll	1
P.W.Docker	not out	41
†G.G.Harvey	c Harrison b Paton	6
J.D.Scott	c Carroll b Eltham	50
Extras	(b6, lb2, nb1)	9
Total	(92.2 overs, 290 mins)	406

TASMANIA

*R.J.Hawson	b Hordern	9	(3) c Harvey b Minnett	0
J.L.Hudson	b Hordern	16	(5) b Hordern	94
W.K.Eltham	b Scott	3	(4) c Hordern b Docker	78
H.Hale	b Hordern	0	(6) run out (McElhone)	4
G.D.Paton	b Scott	0	(7) st Barnes b Hordern	2
E.W.Harrison	b Scott	0	(9) c Scott b Docker	1
T.D.Carroll	b Hordern	5	(8) c Scott b Hordern	22
C.W.B.Martin	st Harvey b Hordern	9	(2) b Scott	11
S.R.Frost	not out	5	(1) b Hordern	11
C.P.Payne	b Hordern	2	not out	5
†H.Parkinson	c Scott b Hordern	0	c McElhone b Hordern	6
Extras		-	(b9, lb1)	10
Total	(19.2 overs, 70 mins)	49	(63.2 overs, 191 mins)	244

TASMANIA	O	M	R	W	w,nb
Paton	26	5	98	3	-,-
Carroll	30	5	126	3	-,1
Frost	24	3	111	2	-,-
Martin	10	1	45	1	,
Eltham	2.2	0	17	1	-,-

NEW SOUTH WALES	O	M	R	W	w,nb	O	M	R	W	w,nb
Scott	10	1	18	3	-,-	11	2	31	1	-,-
Hordern	9.2	1	31	7	-,-	15.2	0	67	5	-,-
Minnett						10	0	44	1	-,-
Watson						6	1	28	0	-,-
Barbour						3	0	18	0	-,-
Makin						3	0	6	0	-,-
Goddard						7	1	27	0	-,-
Docker						8	3	13	2	-,-

FALL OF WICKETS

Wkt	NSW 1st	TAS 1st	TAS 2nd
1st	78	15	21
2nd	99	18	23
3rd	105	27	24
4th	173	28	187
5th	197	28	192
6th	260	28	202
7th	266	44	209
8th	318	45	214
9th	328	47	234
10th	406	49	244

AUSTRALIA v SOUTH AFRICA (3rd Test)

Played at Adelaide Oval on January 7, 9, 10, 11, 12, 13, 1911. (Timeless match)
Toss : South Africa.   Result : SOUTH AFRICA WON BY 38 RUNS.
Debuts: Nil.
12th Men: T.J.Matthews (Aust) and C.O.C.Pearse (SAF).
Umpires: R.M.Crockett and G.A.Watson.
Attendances: 10000, 7000, 6000, 3500, 3000, 1500.   Total: 31,336.   Receipts: £1194.
Close of Play: 1st day SAF 5/279 (Llewellyn 36, Snooke 36); 2nd day Aust 1/72 (Kelleway 39, Ransford 31); 3rd day Aust 8/458
    (Trumper 208, Cotter 8); 4th day SAF (2) 5/232 (Llewellyn 44, Pegler 2); 5th day Aust (2) 4/187 (Kelleway 33, Carter 11).

South Africa achieved their first Test win against Australia, a feat they did not repeat until 1952-53, 25 matches later. Poor fielding by
Australia let the tourists off early. Zulch (105 in 185 minutes, 1 five and 9 fours) survived chances at 12, 18, 68 and 84 and Snooke (103
in 215 minutes, 12 fours) was given a life at 13. Trumper (214 not out in 242 minutes, 26 fours) was at his brilliant best. His innings,
which established a new record for an Australian batsman in Test matches, was acclaimed by "old cricketers" as "the most perfect innings
they had seen on the Adelaide Oval"; he "never gave the semblance of a chance" (*Register*) as he progressed from 11* at lunch to 109* at tea
to 208* at stumps on the third day, bringing up his milestones of 50 in 61 minutes, 100 in 126 minutes, 150 in 176 minutes and 200 in
226 minutes. During the second innings Hill became the first batsman to score 3000 Test runs. Faulkner scored a fine double for South
Africa with 56 (105 minutes, 7 fours) and a chanceless 115 (236 minutes, 10 fours). Llewellyn also making 80 (218 minutes, 4 fours).
Luckin incorrectly gives SAF (2) Zulch c Cotter. Some recent publications give SAF (1) 6/303; Aust (1) 4/229. Sources: *Wisden,*
Luckin, SACA Report, The Age, The Australasian, Adelaide Advertiser, South Australian Register.

SOUTH AFRICA

*†P.W.Sherwell	lbw b Armstrong	11		lbw b Whitty	1
J.W.Zulch	c Macartney b Whitty	105		c Carter b Whitty	14
G.A.Faulkner	c Hill b Armstrong	56		c Armstrong b Whitty	115
A.W.Nourse	b Cotter	10		c Armstrong b Kelleway	39
C.M.H.Hathorn	b Whitty	9	(10)	b Whitty	2
C.B.Llewellyn	run out (Carter/Armstrong)	43		b Whitty	80
S.J.Snooke	c Kelleway b Cotter	103	(8)	run out (Whitty/Carter)	25
J.H.Sinclair	c Armstrong b Kelleway	20	(9)	c Hill b Whitty	29
L.A.Stricker	c Kelleway b Armstrong	48	(5)	b Macartney	6
R.O.Schwarz	b Armstrong	15	(11)	not out	11
S.J.Pegler	not out	24	(7)	c Cotter b Kelleway	26
Extras	(b6, lb10, w4, nb18)	38		(b4, lb2, w1, nb5)	12
Total	(166.4 overs, 493 mins)	482		(130.2 overs, 392 mins)	360

AUSTRALIA

C.G.Macartney	b Llewellyn	2	(9)	lbw b Schwarz	0
C.Kelleway	c Sherwell b Llewellyn	47	(4)	c Sherwell b Sinclair	65
V.S.Ransford	b Llewellyn	50	(5)	c Llewellyn b Schwarz	0
W.Bardsley	lbw b Nourse	54	(2)	c & b Faulkner	58
V.T.Trumper	not out	214	(1)	b Llewellyn	28
D.R.A.Gehrs	c Schwarz b Faulkner	20	(8)	c Sherwell b Schwarz	22
*C.Hill	c Snooke b Schwarz	16	(3)	c Schwarz b Sinclair	55
W.W.Armstrong	b Sinclair	30	(7)	b Schwarz	48
†H.Carter	lbw b Schwarz	17	(6)	c Llewellyn b Faulkner	11
A.Cotter	c Snooke b Llewellyn	8		not out	36
W.J.Whitty	c Sherwell b Sinclair	1		c Schwarz b Pegler	11
Extras	(b4, lb2)	6		(lb5)	5
Total	(119.5 overs, 350 mins)	465		(83.4 overs, 267 mins)	339

AUSTRALIA	O	M	R	W	w,nb		O	M	R	W	w,nb			FALL OF WICKETS		
Cotter	38	4	100	2	1,9	(2)	23	3	64	0	1,-		SAF	AUST	SAF	AUST
Whitty	34	7	114	2	-,-	(1)	39.2	5	104	6	-,-	Wkt	1st	1st	2nd	2nd
Armstrong	42.4	9	103	4	-,-		33	9	90	0	-,-	1st	31	7	10	63
Kelleway	24	6	72	1	3,8		23	4	64	2	-,5	2nd	166	94	29	122
Macartney	27	9	51	0	-,1		12	3	26	1	-,-	3rd	189	111	106	170
Gehrs	1	0	4	0	-,-							4th	191	227	119	171
												5th	205	276	228	187
SOUTH AFRICA	O	M	R	W	w,nb		O	M	R	W	w,nb	6th	302	319	273	263
Llewellyn	31	4	107	4	-,-	(3)	12	0	48	1	-,-	7th	338	384	317	285
Pegler	20	2	92	0	-,-	(4)	10.4	0	58	1	-,-	8th	400	430	319	285
Schwarz	19	2	68	2	-,-	(5)	15	3	48	4	-,-	9th	429	458	327	292
Faulkner	11	0	59	1	-,-	(6)	15	3	56	2	-,-	10th	482	465	360	339
Stricker	1	0	4	0	-,-											
Sinclair	25.5	3	86	2	-,-	(7)	21	2	72	2	-,-					
Nourse	12	2	43	1	-,-	(2)	5	0	31	0	-,-					
Snooke						(1)	5	0	21	0	-,-					

TASMANIA v SOUTH AFRICAN XI

Played at N.T.C.A. Ground, Launceston, on January 17, 18, 19, 1911. (Three-day match)
Toss : Tasmania.   Result : SOUTH AFRICAN XI WON BY 209 RUNS.
Debuts: Tasmania - C.G.Russen, L.Thomas, R.A.Westbrook (all f/c).
12th Men: No 12th men or emergency fieldsmen named (see below).
Umpires: H.Barnes and H.James.
Attendances & Receipts: No figures published.
Close of Play: 1st day SAF 8/364 (Commaille 11, Vogler 1); 2nd day SAF (2) 4/14 (Commaille 5, Sherwell 6).

Scheduled to commence on the 14th, the match was delayed due to the protracted Third Test and was poorly attended because of the Tuesday start. R.J.Hawson and J.L.Hudson were unavailable for Tasmania and E.T.Boddam, who withdrew, was replaced by Westbrook. J.H.Savigny was expected to play but did not front on the first day so Russen, a local, substituted in the field. When Savigny failed to arrive on the second day Russen was brought into the team with the consent of the South Africans, Zulch (0) retired at 0/3 after suffering a blow to the head and resumed at 4/127. Nourse (141 in 147 minutes, 22 fours, chance at 30) and Sherwell (144 in 94 minutes, 1 six and 25 fours, chance at 32) compiled quick centuries for the visitors, Sherwell scoring his last 138 runs before lunch on the third day. Pegler (14 minutes, 2 sixes and 7 fours) raced to the fastest fifty in Australian first-class cricket; it was also at the time a record for all first-class matches. Sinclair (66 in 22 minutes, 1 six and 12 fours) was not far behind Pegler's rate, hitting 20 runs (5 fours) off one over from McDonald. Chancellor was out to the fifth ball of the first over while Smith (62 in 150 minutes, 6 fours and 124 not out in 172 minutes, 17 fours) and Martin (103 in 118 minutes, 1 six and 14 fours) did the bulk of the scoring for Tasmania, Smith being the first to carry his bat for the island. Sources: *Wisden, Luckin, Launceston Examiner, Launceston Daily Telegraph, Hobart Mercury.*

SOUTH AFRICAN XI

J.H.Sinclair	st Thomas b Windsor		24	(8) not out		66
J.W.Zulch	st Thomas b Chancellor		76			
R.O.Schwarz	lbw b McDonald		8			
A.W.Nourse	c Westbrook b Chancellor		141	(7) not out		61
S.J.Snooke	c sub (C.G.Russen) b Windsor		2			
C.O.C.Pearse	c Carroll b Chancellor		41	(5) b Windsor		3
*P.W.Sherwell	run out (Westbrook/Thomas)		9	(6) b McDonald		144
J.M.M.Commaille	lbw b McDonald		11	(2) c Harrison b Windsor		10
S.J.Pegler	b McDonald		50	(4) c McDonald b Windsor		0
A.E.E.Vogler	run out (/McDonald)		1	(3) b McDonald		0
†T.Campbell	not out		0	(1) c Martin b Windsor		0
Extras	(nb1)		1	(b3, lb1)		4
Total	(64.5 overs, 193 mins)		364	(47.0 overs, 157 mins) (6 wkts dec)		288

TASMANIA

F.E.Chancellor	b Vogler		0	(9) b Pegler		2
H.O.Smith	c & b Schwarz		62	(1) not out		124
C.W.B.Martin	b Pearse		103	b Nourse		22
W.K.Eltham	st Campbell b Schwarz		8	(2) b Nourse		1
E.A.C.Windsor	st Campbell b Schwarz		0	(4) lbw b Schwarz		1
*E.W.Harrison	b Sinclair		22	(7) b Nourse		13
R.A.Westbrook	c Vogler b Sinclair		16	(6) c Sherwell b Schwarz		14
T.D.Carroll	b Sinclair		2	b Nourse		7
E.A.McDonald	c Zulch b Schwarz		11	(10) b Nourse		1
†L.Thomas	not out		7	(5) lbw b Sinclair		9
C.G.Russen	b Sinclair		0	lbw b Schwarz		0
J.H.Savigny	absent		-	absent		-
Extras	(b7, lb1)		8	(b6, lb4)		10
Total	(85.5 overs, 226 mins)		239	(69.5 overs, 173 mins)		204

TASMANIA	O	M	R	W	w,nb		O	M	R	W	w,nb
McDonald	13.5	0	64	3	-,-		17	3	97	2	-,-
Windsor	16	0	96	2	-,-		16	1	71	4	-,-
Carroll	7	0	46	0	-,-	(4)	8	0	49	0	-,-
Chancellor	14	1	73	3	-,1	(3)	4	0	46	0	-,-
Martin	11	1	72	0	-,-		2	0	21	0	-,-
Eltham	3	0	12	0	-,-						

SOUTH AFRICAN XI	O	M	R	W	w,nb		O	M	R	W	w,nb
Vogler	17	1	53	1	-,-	(5)	8	1	25	0	-,-
Nourse	4	2	10	0	-,-		27	10	47	5	-,-
Schwarz	27	7	72	4	-,-		16.5	2	56	3	-,-
Sinclair	20.5	3	53	4	-,-		7	1	16	1	-,-
Pegler	10	2	29	0	-,-	(6)	7	0	28	1	-,-
Pearse	7	2	14	1	-,-						
Snooke						(1)	4	0	22	0	-,-

FALL OF WICKETS

Wkt	SAF 1st	TAS 1st	SAF 2nd	TAS 2nd
1st	29	0	1	3
2nd	33	154	1	47
3rd	37	165	2	60
4th	127	165	5	81
5th	293	182	45	110
6th	302	215	204	147
7th	302	220	-	167
8th	355	223	-	192
9th	364	235	-	196
10th	364	239	-	204

453

TASMANIA v SOUTH AFRICAN XI

Played at T.C.A. Ground, Hobart, on January 20, 21, 23, 1911. (Three-day match)
Toss : South African XI.　　　　　　Result : MATCH DRAWN.
Debuts: Tasmania - E.T.Boddam (f/c).
12th Men: No 12th men or emergency fieldsmen named.
Umpires: F.Price and H.Malvino.
Attendances: "very small", 1200, ?　.　　　Total: About 2500.　　Receipts: £125.
Close of Play: 1st day Tas 1/28 (Smith 9, Martin 5); 2nd day SAF (2) 2/184 (Stricker 84, Nourse 4).

Frost, the nominated 12th man, replaced F.E.Chancellor, a late withdrawal from the Tasmanian side. Snooke scored 71 in 65 minutes and hit 1 six and 11 fours on the first day, which was shortened by three hours because of rain. The third day saw 462 runs scored for the loss of 10 wickets. South Africa's second innings included notable performances from Stricker (88 in 95 minutes, 13 fours), Faulkner (87 in 60 minutes, 14 fours), Nourse (112 not out in 116 minutes, 19 fours) and Snooke again (88 in 55 minutes, 18 fours). Best for Tasmania were Hawson (82 in 144 minutes, 9 fours), Eltham (51 in 104 minutes, 7 fours) and Windsor (83 in 93 minutes, 7 fours). Windsor also bowled unchanged through the first innings and captured career-best figures of 7 for 95. Sources: *Wisden, Luckin, Launceston Examiner, Launceston Daily Telegraph, Hobart Mercury.*

SOUTH AFRICAN XI

J.M.M.Commaille	c Boddam b Windsor	2	lbw b Boddam		9
L.A.Stricker	c Frost b Boddam	11	b Windsor		88
G.A.Faulkner	lbw b Windsor	6	c Martin b Windsor		87
A.W.Nourse	c Hudson b Windsor	18	not out		112
S.J.Snooke	c Boddam b Windsor	71	c Hawson b Windsor		88
C.B.Llewellyn	c Boddam b Windsor	15	c Eltham b Frost		11
J.H.Sinclair	c Hudson b Windsor	23	b Frost		4
C.O.C.Pearse	c Frost b Carroll	16	not out		25
*P.W.Sherwell	c Parkinson b Carroll	8			
A.E.E.Vogler	b Windsor	3			
†T.Campbell	not out	1			
Extras	(b3, lb1)	4	(b5, w1)		6
Total	(31.1 overs, 105 mins)	178	(69.0 overs, 207 mins) (6 wkts dec)		430

TASMANIA

W.K.Eltham	b Nourse	13	(3) c Campbell b Pearse		51
H.O.Smith	b Llewellyn	29	(1) c Campbell b Llewellyn		11
C.W.B.Martin	c Campbell b Faulkner	19	(2) c Pearse b Vogler		29
J.L.Hudson	b Llewellyn	12	(5) b Llewellyn		5
*R.J.Hawson	b Llewellyn	82	(4) c Sherwell b Vogler		8
E.A.C.Windsor	c Campbell b Llewellyn	2	c Sherwell b Llewellyn		83
E.T.Boddam	b Vogler	2			
T.D.Carroll	c Vogler b Llewellyn	1	not out		9
G.D.Paton	b Llewellyn	25	(7) not out		15
S.R.Frost	c Sinclair b Llewellyn	3			
†H.Parkinson	not out	1			
Extras	(b1, lb5)	6	(b2, lb2, nb1)		5
Total	(76.5 overs, 203 mins)	195	(59.0 overs, 157 mins) (6 wkts)		216

TASMANIA	O	M	R	W	w,nb		O	M	R	W	w,nb					
Boddam	7	1	26	1	-,-	(4)	14	2	93	1	-,-					
Windsor	15.1	1	95	7	-,-		23	1	117	3	1,-					
Paton	5	0	37	0	-,-		7	0	48	0	-,-					
Carroll	4	0	16	2	-,-		8	1	60	0	-,-					
Frost							14	1	77	2	-,-					
Martin							3	0	29	0	-,-					

FALL OF WICKETS

Wkt	SAF 1st	TAS 1st	SAF 2nd	TAS 2nd
1st	4	17	16	28
2nd	10	62	158	44
3rd	26	68	193	58
4th	50	81	343	65
5th	72	95	355	174
6th	132	106	359	198
7th	154	107	-	-
8th	169	190	-	-
9th	176	194	-	-
10th	178	195	-	-

SOUTH AFRICAN XI	O	M	R	W	w,nb		O	M	R	W	w,nb
Nourse	11	2	32	1	-,-	(4)	6	2	18	0	-,-
Vogler	16	2	38	1	-,-		19	2	82	2	-,-
Pearse	2	1	1	0	-,-	(6)	3	0	18	1	-,-
Faulkner	10	1	42	1	-,-	(5)	6	1	16	0	-,-
Llewellyn	24.5	6	50	7	-,-	(1)	22	4	66	3	-,-
Snooke	6	3	7	0	-,-	(3)	3	1	11	0	-,1
Sinclair	7	3	19	0	-,-						

NEW SOUTH WALES v VICTORIA (Shield Match 5)

Played at Sydney Cricket Ground on January 26 (no play), 27, 28, 30, 31, 1911. (Timeless match)
Toss : New South Wales.   Result : NEW SOUTH WALES WON BY 456 RUNS.
Debuts: Nil.
12th Men: E.F.Waddy (NSW) and W.J.Scott (Vic).
Umpires: W.G.Curran and A.C.Jones.
Attendances: no play, 1988, 5758, 1773, 340.   Total: 9859   Receipts: £383.
Close of Play: 1st day no play; 2nd day Vic 0/7 (Kyle 5, Carkeek 0); 3rd day NSW (2) 2/131 (Bardsley 43, Emery 0); 4th day Vic (2) 4/59 (Carkeek 1).

New South Wales omitted W.S.Makin, R.J.A.Massie, C.J.Tozer and E.F.Waddy from a squad of fifteen named for the match. H.F.Parsons declared himself unavailable for Victoria and T.S.Warne (injured) was replaced by McKenzie. Rain washed out play on the opening day. Laver became ill with appendicitis and took no further part after the conclusion of the New South Wales first innings. Bardsley (78 in 121 minutes, 11 fours) held the first innings together early on. McElhone (101 in 118 minutes, 14 fours) and Barbour (113 not out in 172 minutes, 17 fours) scored centuries for New South Wales, the latter sharing a ninth-wicket partnership of 123 with Hordern (64 in 78 minutes, 1 six and 7 fours). Hordern also took 13 wickets and bowled unchanged through the second innings. Trumper scored 82 in 78 minutes and hit 12 fours. Sources: *Wisden, NSWCA Report, Sydney Morning Herald, Town & Country Journal, Newcastle Herald.*

NEW SOUTH WALES

Batsman	1st innings	R		2nd innings	R
*V.T.Trumper	b Laver	4		c Healy b Kyle	82
W.Bardsley	c Healy b Matthews	78		c & b Armstrong	43
C.Kelleway	c & b Kyle	24	(5)	b Armstrong	4
C.G.Macartney	c Kenny b Kyle	0	(6)	b Kyle	8
E.P.Barbour	c Kyle b Matthews	26	(7)	not out	113
E.L.Waddy	c Carkeek b Matthews	36	(8)	run out (Kyle/Matthews)	30
F.E.McElhone	c Ransford b Laver	101	(9)	b Kyle	34
H.V.Hordern	lbw b Armstrong	27	(10)	c Healy b Kyle	64
†H.Carter	c Carkeek b Armstrong	10	(3)	b Kyle	0
A.Cotter	lbw b Armstrong	22	(11)	c McKenzie b Armstrong	0
S.H.Emery	not out	1	(4)	b Kyle	10
Extras	(b1, w4, nb3)	8		(b9, lb4)	13
Total	(99.0 overs, 264 mins)	337		(102.4 overs, 278 mins)	401

VICTORIA

Batsman	1st innings	R		2nd innings	R
J.H.Kyle	c McElhone b Hordern	17	(4)	b Macartney	1
†W.Carkeek	c Kelleway b Hordern	3	(5)	c Cotter b Hordern	9
V.S.Ransford	c & b Cotter	33	(8)	not out	5
H.H.L.Kortlang	st Carter b Hordern	41	(1)	c Kelleway b Hordern	30
*W.W.Armstrong	b Hordern	41	(7)	b Hordern	6
T.J.Matthews	not out	32		lbw b Hordern	2
D.B.M.Smith	b Hordern	8	(9)	c McElhone b Hordern	1
G.E.J.Healy	c Carter b Cotter	4	(3)	b Hordern	0
A.Kenny	c Trumper b Hordern	1	(10)	run out (Barbour)	1
C.McKenzie	b Hordern	0	(2)	b Macartney	22
F.J.Laver	absent ill	-		absent ill	-
Extras	(b10, lb1, nb3)	14		(b6, lb5)	11
Total	(66.0 overs, 191 mins)	194		(36.3 overs, 111 mins)	88

VICTORIA	O	M	R	W	w,nb		O	M	R	W	w,nb
Laver	21	3	70	2	-,-						
Armstrong	22	2	55	3	-,3	(3)	31.4	8	94	3	-,-
Matthews	23	5	85	3	-,-	(2)	18	1	67	0	-,-
Kyle	27	6	90	2	-,-	(1)	33	4	129	6	-,-
Kenny	4	0	10	0	-,-	(4)	14	1	75	0	-,-
McKenzie	2	0	19	0	-,-						
Ransford						(5)	6	0	23	0	-,-

FALL OF WICKETS	NSW 1st	VIC 1st	NSW 2nd	VIC 2nd
1st	4	13	131	51
2nd	64	39	131	51
3rd	75	88	131	58
4th	126	141	135	59
5th	153	154	146	66
6th	192	172	155	76
7th	257	191	214	81
8th	293	194	278	87
9th	329	194	401	88
10th	337	-	401	-

NEW SOUTH WALES	O	M	R	W	w,nb		O	M	R	W	w,nb
Cotter	18	3	42	2	-,3		6	0	27	0	-,-
Hordern	25	8	55	7	-,-		18	5	32	6	-,-
Kelleway	12	1	41	0	-,-						
Emery	8	1	33	0	-,-						
Macartney	3	0	9	0	-,-	(3)	12.3	5	18	2	-,-

VICTORIA v SOUTH AFRICAN XI

Played at Melbourne Cricket Ground on February 3, 4, 6 (no play), 7, 1911. (Four-day match)
Toss : Victoria.   Result : SOUTH AFRICAN XI WON BY EIGHT WICKETS.
Debuts: Victoria - F.J.Pitcher (f/c).
12th Men: G.E.J.Healy (Vic) and R.O.Schwarz (SAF).
Umpires: R.M.Crockett and W.A.Young.
Attendances: 2995, 5741, no play, 1210.   Total: 9946.   Receipts: £238.
Close of Play: 1st day SAF 1/67 (Zulch 30, Faulkner 30); 2nd day SAF 324 all out; 3rd day no play.

The aptly-named Pitcher, in his sole first-class appearance, was no-balled by Crockett for throwing his first three balls of the match. A fourth no-ball was called later in the over and Young called him for a fifth time during his second over, which was delivered the following day. Two of Pitcher's five no-balls were scored from. Nourse scored 128 in 212 minutes and hit 13 fours. Sinclair was out first ball. Rain washed out play on the third day. Kortlang (2) received a blow on the knee from Faulkner and retired at 3/42 in the second innings, resuming at 5/67. Faulkner, South Africa's premier all-rounder, returned career-best figures of 7 for 26, bowling unchanged through the second innings. Sources: *Wisden, Luckin, The Age, The Argus, The Herald, The Australasian, The Leader.*

VICTORIA

T.S.Warne	run out (Zulch/Vogler)	55	(6) c Pegler b Sinclair		16
A.Kenny	b Faulkner	43	(7) st Campbell b Faulkner		11
V.S.Ransford	b Faulkner	8	c Pegler b Faulkner		3
T.J.Matthews	c Pegler b Faulkner	35	run out		4
H.H.L.Kortlang	lbw b Vogler	0	c Snooke b Faulkner		10
*W.W.Armstrong	c Nourse b Stricker	17	(1) b Faulkner		30
D.B.M.Smith	c Zulch b Pegler	30	(2) c Vogler b Faulkner		5
H.F.Parsons	st Campbell b Faulkner	2	c Snooke b Sinclair		0
F.J.Pitcher	b Pearse	18	b Faulkner		0
J.H.Kyle	not out	18	b Faulkner		0
†W.Carkeek	b Sinclair	13	not out		4
Extras	(lb2, w1)	3	(b5, lb1, nb1)		7
Total	(69.2 overs, 192 mins)	242	(33.2 overs, 106 mins)		90

SOUTH AFRICAN XI

J.W.Zulch	b Kyle	31	lbw b Ransford		3
L.A.Stricker	c & b Kyle	4	st Carkeek b Armstrong		2
G.A.Faulkner	c & b Kyle	32			
A.W.Nourse	c Kyle b Parsons	128			
S.J.Snooke	c Kortlang b Armstrong	39			
J.H.Sinclair	c Kenny b Armstrong	0			
*P.W.Sherwell	c Ransford b Armstrong	17	(3) not out		4
C.O.C.Pearse	c Armstrong b Kyle	31			
S.J.Pegler	c Ransford b Kyle	23	•		
†T.Campbell	c & b Armstrong	6	(4) not out		0
A.E.E.Vogler	not out	5			
Extras	(b2, lb2, w1, nb3)	8			-
Total	(108.3 overs, 297 mins)	324	(2.4 overs, 7 mins) (2 wkts)		9

SOUTH AFRICAN XI	O	M	R	W	w,nb		O	M	R	W	w,nb
Nourse	6	1	14	0	-,-	(5)	2	1	1	0	-,-
Snooke	1	0	3	0	-,-						
Vogler	14	0	72	1	1,-		4	1	18	0	-,-
Sinclair	5.2	0	27	1	-,-		4	1	13	2	-,-
Faulkner	21	1	55	4	-,-	(2)	16.2	4	26	7	-,1
Pegler	11	4	23	1	-,-	(1)	7	2	25	0	-,-
Stricker	8	1	30	1	-,-						
Pearse	3	0	15	1	-,-						

VICTORIA	O	M	R	W	w,nb		O	M	R	W	w,nb
Pitcher	2	0	11	0	1,3						
Kyle	41	9	111	5	-,-						
Armstrong	39	8	110	4	-,-	(1)	1.4	0	9	1	-,-
Parsons	7.3	0	31	1	-,-						
Warne	4	2	10	0	-,-						
Matthews	13	1	36	0	-,-						
Kenny	2	1	7	0	-,-						
Ransford						(2)	1	1	0	1	-,-

FALL OF WICKETS

Wkt	VIC 1st	SAF 1st	VIC 2nd	SAF 2nd
1st	86	9	14	5
2nd	96	69	18	5
3rd	120	74	25	-
4th	121	148	51	-
5th	155	148	67	-
6th	159	168	75	-
7th	172	246	75	-
8th	209	278	78	-
9th	218	291	84	-
10th	242	324	90	-

AUSTRALIA v SOUTH AFRICA (4th Test)

Played at Melbourne Cricket Ground on February 17, 18, 20, 21, 1911. (Timeless match)
Toss : South Africa.   Result : AUSTRALIA WON BY 530 RUNS.
Debuts: Australia - H.V.Hordern (Test).
12th Men: T.J.Matthews (Aust) and J.M.M.Commaille (SAF).
Umpires: R.M.Crockett and W.Hannah.
Attendances: 8433, 21897, 12477, 6620.   Total: 49,427.   Receipts: £1677.
Close of Play: 1st day Aust 8/317 (Hordern 1); 2nd day Aust (2) 1/48 (Gehrs 30); 3rd day Aust (2) 7/476 (Ransford 38, Hordern 23).

Rain during the week which led up to the match influenced Sherwell to send Australia in, but the wicket "was a much better one than might have been expected" (*Age*) and the weather throughout the match was perfect. Bardsley (82 in 154 minutes, 5 fours), Armstrong (48 in 76 minutes, 2 fours), Kelleway (59 in 142 minutes, 1 four) and Ransford (75 in 126 minutes, 3 fours) topscored in Australia's first innings. Llewellyn damaged a finger when he attempted to stop a hard drive by Armstrong off his own bowling before lunch on the first day. He returned after the adjournment with his left hand bandaged, but took no further part in the match after batting in South Africa's first innings. Hordern, who took the wicket of Stricker with the first ball of his second over in Tests, dislocated the middle finger of his right hand in the lunch-tea session on the second day and retired from the field. However, he suffered no ill-effects and was again fit from the following day. He finished with eight wickets on debut. South Africa's only major batting came from Nourse (92 not out in 176 minutes, 6 fours) in the first innings and Faulkner (80 in 131 minutes, 1 six and 9 fours) in the second. Armstrong (132 in 208 minutes, 13 fours, sharp return catch to Sinclair when 84) and Hill (chanceless 100 in 101 minutes, 13 fours) shared a fourth-wicket partnership of 154 in 101 minutes. Gehrs (58 in 75 minutes, 6 fours), Trumper (87 in 79 minutes, 11 fours) and Ransford (95 in 123 minutes, 9 fours) also batted brightly. W.L.Murdoch, the former New South Wales and Australian captain, collapsed and died while attending the match on the second day. Recent publications incorrectly give umpires as Crockett and D.A.Elder. Sources: *Wisden, Luckin, NSWCA Report, The Age, The Argus, The Herald, The Australasian, Sydney Referee, Sydney Morning Herald.*

AUSTRALIA

V.T.Trumper	b Faulkner	7	(6) c Sherwell b Vogler		87
W.Bardsley	c Schwarz b Pegler	82	(3) run out (Vogler)		15
*C.Hill	b Llewellyn	11	(5) st Sherwell b Pegler		100
W.W.Armstrong	run out (Snooke/Sherwell)	48	c Sherwell b Vogler		132
D.R.A.Gehrs	st Sherwell b Vogler	9	(2) c Snooke b Faulkner		58
C.Kelleway	run out	59	(1) run out (Faulkner/Sherwell)		18
V.S.Ransford	lbw b Schwarz	75	b Faulkner		95
A.Cotter	b Pegler	10	c sub (C.O.C.Pearse) b Vogler		0
H.V.Hordern	c Vogler b Pegler	7	c sub (C.O.C.Pearse) b Schwarz		24
†H.Carter	run out (Stricker/Sherwell)	5	c Snooke b Faulkner		2
W.J.Whitty	not out	0	not out		39
Extras	(b7, lb7, w1)	15	(b4, lb3, nb1)		8
Total	(94.4 overs, 296 mins)	328	(126.2 overs, 389 mins)		578

SOUTH AFRICA

J.W.Zulch	run out (Gehrs/Carter)	2	c Trumper b Cotter		15
L.A.Stricker	b Hordern	4	c Carter b Cotter		0
G.A.Faulkner	c Gehrs b Hordern	20	b Whitty		80
A.W.Nourse	not out	92	c & b Hordern		28
S.J.Snooke	b Whitty	1	b Hordern		7
J.H.Sinclair	b Hordern	0	lbw b Hordern		19
R.O.Schwarz	b Whitty	18	c Carter b Whitty		1
*†P.W.Sherwell	c sub (T.J.Matthews) b Whitty	41	c Kelleway b Hordern		0
C.B.Llewellyn	b Whitty	7	absent hurt		-
S.J.Pegler	c Hill b Cotter	15	(9) c Gehrs b Hordern		8
A.E.E.Vogler	b Cotter	0	(10) not out		2
Extras	(b4, lb1)	5	(b7, lb1, w2, nb1)		11
Total	(62.5 overs, 204 mins)	205	(40.2 overs, 135 mins)		171

SOUTH AFRICA	O	M	R	W	w,nb		O	M	R	W	w,nb		FALL OF WICKETS			
														AUST	SAF	AUST	SAF
Llewellyn	15	1	65	1	-,-								Wkt	1st	1st	2nd	2nd
Faulkner	18	2	82	1	-,-	(4)	28.2	5	101	3	-,-		1st	9	7	48	2
Schwarz	15	2	34	1	-,-	(2)	38	4	168	1	-,1		2nd	24	23	88	25
Vogler	8	2	30	1	-,-	(9)	15	3	59	3	-,-		3rd	126	36	106	88
Sinclair	14	2	40	0	1,-	(1)	13	1	71	0	-,-		4th	146	37	260	108
Pegler	17.4	3	40	3	-,-	(3)	17	1	88	1	-,-		5th	182	38	403	151
Stricker	5	1	18	0	-,-	(8)	3	0	14	0	-,-		6th	289	65	418	158
Nourse	2	0	4	0	-,-	(6)	7	0	31	0	-,-		7th	310	156	420	161
Zulch						(5)	3	0	26	0	-,-		8th	317	171	491	165
Snooke						(7)	2	0	12	0	-,-		9th	328	205	496	171
													10th	328	205	578	-

AUSTRALIA	O	M	R	W	w,nb		O	M	R	W	w,nb
Cotter	6.5	0	16	2	-,-		6	1	22	2	1,-
Whitty	22	5	78	4	-,-		9	2	32	2	-,-
Hordern	15	1	39	3	-,-	(4)	14.2	2	66	5	-,-
Armstrong	8	2	25	0	-,-	(5)	3	0	15	0	-,1
Kelleway	11	1	42	0	-,-	(3)	8	0	25	0	1,-

NEW SOUTH WALES v SOUTH AFRICAN XI

Played at Sydney Cricket Ground on February 24, 25, 27, 28, March 1, 1911. (Timeless match)
Toss : New South Wales.   Result : NEW SOUTH WALES WON BY 44 RUNS.
Debuts: New South Wales - R.J.A.Massie, C.J.Tozer (both f/c).
12th Men: E.L.Waddy (NSW). No 12th named for SAF.
Umpires: R.Callaway and A.C.Jones.
Attendances: 4356, 10198, 2975, 2344, 1083.   Total: 20,956.   Receipts: £976.
Close of Play: 1st day NSW 9/415 (Emery 52); 2nd day SAF 8/315 (Stricker 32, Pegler 8); 3rd day NSW (2) 5/255 (Macartney 67,
   Tozer 25); 4th day SAF (2) 2/232 (Faulkner 102, Nourse 112).

The match aggregate of 1744 runs, which included 14 individual fifties, had been bettered only once in all first-class cricket to this time.
Macartney, who survived a confident appeal for leg before wicket when 1 in the first innings, went on to become the first player to register
a century in each innings against a team touring Australia. He hit 119 in 135 minutes with 16 fours and 126 in 128 minutes, 9 fours.
McElhone scored 94 in 121 minutes, hitting 12 fours. Emery (58 in 61 minutes, 1 six and 8 fours; 80 in 46 minutes, 1 six and 7 fours)
hit hard in both innings. Faulkner (144 in 234 minutes, 22 fours) and Nourse (160 in 224 minutes, 16 fours) shared a partnership of 318
in the second innings, a new record for the third wicket in Australia. Sources: *Wisden, Luckin, NSWCA Report, Sydney Referee, Sydney
Morning Herald, Town & Country Journal.*

NEW SOUTH WALES

W.Bardsley	c Snooke b Pearse	9	b Sinclair	73
*V.T.Trumper	b Pearse	5	b Sinclair	15
C.Kelleway	lbw b Pegler	33	b Faulkner	65
F.E.McElhone	hit wkt b Sinclair	94	c Schwarz b Faulkner	2
C.G.Macartney	c Pegler b Faulkner	119	b Schwarz	126
H.L.Collins	c Stricker b Nourse	83	c Snooke b Faulkner	2
C.J.Tozer	c Stricker b Sinclair	2	b Stricker	37
L.A.Minnett	b Faulkner	2	c & b Schwarz	23
S.H.Emery	not out	58	not out	80
R.J.A.Massie	b Nourse	0	b Faulkner	19
†G.G.Harvey	b Pegler	11	c Vogler b Pegler	7
Extras	(b13, lb7)	20	(b2, lb6, w1)	9
Total	(113.0 overs, 298 mins)	436	(112.0 overs, 297 mins)	458

SOUTH AFRICAN XI

C.O.C.Pearse	c Macartney b Emery	54		b Macartney	9
J.M.M.Commaille	c Bardsley b Minnett	29		b Macartney	1
G.A.Faulkner	b Minnett	2		c Kelleway b Macartney	144
A.W.Nourse	b Emery	81		c Collins b Kelleway	160
S.J.Snooke	c Minnett b Kelleway	13	(7)	b Kelleway	4
J.H.Sinclair	b Massie	65	(5)	b Kelleway	4
L.A.Stricker	not out	82	(6)	b Massie	18
A.E.E.Vogler	c Macartney b Emery	0	(11)	run out (McElhone/Harvey)	2
*R.O.Schwarz	b Macartney	13		not out	45
S.J.Pegler	c Kelleway b Minnett	16	(8)	b Kelleway	16
†T.Campbell	c McElhone b Kelleway	32	(10)	c Minnett b Massie	3
Extras	(b12, lb4, w1, nb4)	21		(b24, lb4, w2, nb6)	36
Total	(123.5 overs, 347 mins)	408		(114.0 overs, 330 mins)	442

SOUTH AFRICAN XI	O	M	R	W	w,nb		O	M	R	W	w,nb		FALL OF WICKETS				
														NSW	SAF	NSW	SAF
Vogler	21	6	53	0	-,-		7	0	44	0	1,-	Wkt	1st	1st	1st	2nd	2nd
Pearse	11	0	54	2	-,-		9	1	36	0	-,-	1st	10	76	40	6
Sinclair	19	0	72	2	-,-		29	4	92	2	-,-	2nd	23	84	159	19
Pegler	15	1	71	2	-,-		16	1	61	1	-,-	3rd	79	91	159	337
Schwarz	14	2	68	0	-,-	(6)	12	0	77	2	-,-	4th	215	119	174	337
Faulkner	19	2	61	2	-,-	(7)	22	3	71	4	-,-	5th	320	239	189	344
Nourse	10	3	24	2	-,-	(5)	8	2	23	0	-,-	6th	320	281	293	348
Stricker	4	0	13	0	-,-	(9)	8	1	43	1	-,-	7th	333	281	340	371
Snooke						(8)	1	0	2	0	-,-	8th	407	301	357	412
												9th	415	331	423	420
NEW SOUTH WALES	O	M	R	W	w,nb		O	M	R	W	w,nb	10th	436	408	458	442
Minnett	36	6	140	3	1,1		11	0	56	0	1,1					
Kelleway	23.5	6	49	2	-,1	(5)	33	6	120	4	-,-					
Emery	30	2	101	3	-,1		14	2	53	0	-,-					
Massie	19	3	55	1	-,1		20	4	64	2	1,2					
Macartney	16	2	42	1	-,-	(2)	35	5	113	3	-,3					
Collins							1	1	0	0	-,-					

AUSTRALIA v SOUTH AFRICA (5th Test)

Played at Sydney Cricket Ground on March 3, 4, 6, 7, 1911. (Timeless match)
Toss : South Africa. Result : AUSTRALIA WON BY SEVEN WICKETS.
Debuts: Nil.
12th Men: D.R.A.Gehrs (Aust). No 12th named for SAF.
Umpires: R.M.Crockett and A.C.Jones.
Attendances: 6900, 24221, 5330, 3808.   Total: 40,259.   Receipts: £1994.
Close of Play: 1st day Aust 3/281 (Bardsley 83, Whitty 2); 2nd day SA (2) 1/33 (Zulch 7, Pegler 10); 3rd day SA (2) 6/368 (Snooke 2).

Heavy overnight rain delayed the start until after lunch, however "the wicket rolled out fairly easy" (*SMH*), again upsetting the calculations of Sherwell. Macartney (chanceless 137 in 193 minutes, 16 fours) recorded his third century in successive first-class innings, all against the South Africans at Sydney. He reached 50 in 72 minutes and 100 in 152 minutes. With Hordern (50 in 87 minutes, 4 fours), who had been sent in while the pitch dried after the loss of Kelleway to the second ball of the match, he added 124 and with Bardsley (94 in 137 minutes, 9 fours) he added 145 in 105 minutes. Zulch (150 in 298 minutes, 15 fours) benefited from chances at 22, 39 and 69. Faulkner's pair of half-centuries 52 (81 minutes) and 92 (107 minutes, 10 fours), brought his aggregate of runs in the Test series to 732, average 73.20, a new record for any country, while Trumper (74 not out in 84 minutes) finished with 661 runs, average 94.43, a new record for an Australian batsman. In the second innings Macartney took just 35 minutes to reach his fifty. Whitty's 37 wickets, at 17.08 apiece, was until 1924-25 a record for a Test series in Australia. Recent publications incorrectly give umpires as Crockett and D.A.Elder. Sources: *Wisden, Luckin, NSWCA Report, Sydney Referee, Sydney Morning Herald, Town & Country Journal, Newcastle Herald.*

AUSTRALIA

C.Kelleway	c Snooke b Llewellyn	2	(5) not out	24
C.G.Macartney	lbw b Schwarz	137	c Nourse b Schwarz	56
H.V.Hordern	lbw b Sinclair	50		
W.Bardsley	c & b Sinclair	94	(1) b Nourse	39
W.J.Whitty	c Nourse b Llewellyn	13		
V.T.Trumper	b Schwarz	31	(3) not out	74
*C.Hill	st Sherwell b Schwarz	13		
W.W.Armstrong	c Pearse b Schwarz	0		
V.S.Ransford	st Sherwell b Schwarz	6	(4) b Nourse	0
A.Cotter	st Sherwell b Schwarz	8		
†H.Carter	not out	1		
Extras	(b7, lb2)	9	(b1, lb3, w1)	5
Total	(96.4 overs, 278 mins)	364	(43.1 overs, 126 mins) (3 wkts)	198

SOUTH AFRICA

J.W.Zulch	st Carter b Hordern	15	(2) b Ransford	150
C.O.C.Pearse	b Whitty	0	(11) lbw b Hordern	2
G.A.Faulkner	b Armstrong	52	(4) b Cotter	92
A.W.Nourse	b Armstrong	3	(5) c Cotter b Whitty	28
L.A.Stricker	c Macartney b Hordern	19	(6) b Cotter	42
J.H.Sinclair	c Ransford b Hordern	1	(8) c & b Whitty	12
S.J.Snooke	b Hordern	18	c Carter b Whitty	12
C.B.Llewellyn	c Carter b Kelleway	24	(9) b Whitty	3
R.O.Schwarz	run out (Cotter)	13	(10) not out	6
*†P.W.Sherwell	c Bardsley b Whitty	5	(1) b Armstrong	14
S.J.Pegler	not out	0	(3) c Cotter b Hordern	26
Extras	(b1, lb8, nb1)	10	(b3, lb4, w2, nb5)	14
Total	(50.1 overs, 165 mins)	160	(122.1 overs, 369 mins)	401

SOUTH AFRICA	O	M	R	W	w,nb		O	M	R	W	w,nb
Llewellyn	25	0	92	2	-,-	(2)	8	1	43	0	-,-
Faulkner	12	2	38	0	-,-	(6)	5	0	18	0	-,-
Sinclair	27	6	83	2	-,-	(4)	6	1	22	0	-,-
Pegler	6	1	31	0	-,-	(5)	4	0	22	0	1,-
Schwarz	11.4	0	47	6	-,-	(3)	9	0	42	1	-,-
Nourse	5	1	26	0	-,-	(7)	8.1	0	32	2	-,-
Pearse	9	0	36	0	-,-	(1)	3	0	14	0	-,-
Zulch	1	0	2	0	-,-						

AUSTRALIA	O	M	R	W	w,nb		O	M	R	W	w,nb
Cotter	8	2	24	0	-,-		18	1	60	2	2,5
Whitty	11.1	3	32	2	-,-	(4)	27	5	66	4	-,-
Hordern	21	3	73	4	-,-		30.1	1	117	2	-,-
Kelleway	4	1	4	1	-,-	(5)	7	1	46	0	-,-
Armstrong	6	1	17	2	-,1	(2)	26	4	68	1	-,-
Macartney							10	0	21	0	-,-
Ransford							4	2	9	1	-,-

FALL OF WICKETS

	AUST	SAF	SAF	AUST
Wkt	1st	1st	2nd	2nd
1st	2	4	19	74
2nd	126	47	64	134
3rd	271	70	207	134
4th	296	81	278	-
5th	317	87	357	-
6th	346	115	368	-
7th	346	128	385	-
8th	351	144	392	-
9th	361	160	398	-
10th	364	160	401	-

SOUTH AUSTRALIA v SOUTH AFRICAN XI

Played at Adelaide Oval on March 10, 11, 13, 1911. (Three-day match)
Toss : South Australia.   Result : SOUTH AFRICAN XI WON BY SIX WICKETS.
Debuts: South Australia - H.W.Webster (f/c).
12th Men: W.L.Chamberlain (SA). No 12th named for SAF.
Umpires: F.Adams and A.T.Haddrick.
Attendances: 2800, 5900, 300.   Total: About 9000.   Receipts: No figures published.
Close of Play: 1st day SAF 3/29 (Zulch 20); 2nd day SAF (2) 1/8 (Commaille 5).

A tenth-wicket partnership of 93 between Llewellyn (48 in 54 minutes, 7 fours) and Sherwell (46 not out in 41 minutes, 7 fours) gave the South Africans a first-innings lead in their last first-class match on tour. Only half an hour was needed on the final day for the visitors to wrap the match up. Whitty's seven-wicket haul - all of them bowled - took his season's tally against the South Africans to 49, 37 in the Tests and 12 in the two South Australian fixtures. Sources: *Wisden, Luckin, C.B.O'Reilly, SACA Report, The Age, Adelaide Advertiser, South Australian Register.*

SOUTH AUSTRALIA

R.E.Mayne	lbw b Schwarz	15	c Faulkner b Schwarz		7
C.E.Dolling	st Sherwell b Llewellyn	45	run out (Snooke/Schwarz)		8
*C.Hill	b Nourse	54	c Llewellyn b Nourse		8
D.R.A.Gehrs	b Schwarz	2	c Llewellyn b Schwarz		3
J.N.Crawford	c Snooke b Pegler	57	not out		40
L.R.Hill	b Nourse	3	c Sherwell b Llewellyn		9
R.B.C.Rees	b Pegler	29	c Nourse b Llewellyn		5
W.J.Whitty	b Pegler	1	b Pegler		3
†H.W.Webster	b Pegler	23	c Llewellyn b Pegler		0
W.S.Stirling	b Pegler	5	b Pegler		3
A.W.Wright	not out	1	b Pegler		6
Extras	(b3, lb2)	5	(b8)		8
Total	(59.1 overs, 171 mins)	240	(25.5 overs, 85 mins)		100

SOUTH AFRICAN XI

J.W.Zulch	b Whitty	21	b Whitty		3
J.M.M.Commaille	b Whitty	4	b Whitty		7
L.A.Stricker	b Whitty	0	(5) b Rees		0
S.J.Pegler	b Whitty	5			
G.A.Faulkner	c Gehrs b Rees	33	(3) not out		28
A.W.Nourse	b Whitty	40	(4) b Rees		0
S.J.Snooke	c Whitty b Rees	55			
R.O.Schwarz	c Dolling b Rees	12			
J.H.Sinclair	c Dolling b Rees	14	(6) not out		12
C.B.Llewellyn	b Mayne	48			
*†P.W.Sherwell	not out	46			
Extras	(b11, lb3)	14	(lb1)		1
Total	(60.5 overs, 190 mins)	292	(15.2 overs, 45 mins) (4 wkts)		51

SOUTH AFRICAN XI	O	M	R	W	w,nb		O	M	R	W	w,nb		FALL OF WICKETS			
Llewellyn	16	0	73	1	-,-	(3)	6	0	27	2	-,-			SA	SAF	SA	SAF
Sinclair	8	3	19	0	-,-							Wkt	1st	1st	2nd	2nd
Schwarz	16	0	67	2	-,-	(1)	7	0	28	2	-,-	1st	42	9	10	8
Nourse	8	2	22	2	-,-	(2)	7	0	23	1	-,-	2nd	70	9	16	19
Pegler	11.1	1	54	5	-,-	(4)	5.5	2	14	4	-,-	3rd	73	29	20	20
												4th	145	38	36	20
SOUTH AUSTRALIA	O	M	R	W	w,nb		O	M	R	W	w,nb	5th	157	70	55	-
Whitty	22	3	79	5	-,-		8	1	14	2	-,-	6th	192	164	65	-
Crawford	6	0	33	0	-,-							7th	206	166	68	-
Wright	8	0	42	0	-,-							8th	207	185	76	-
Rees	17	1	84	4	-,-	(2)	7	0	28	2	-,-	9th	227	199	82	-
Stirling	5	0	33	0	-,-							10th	240	292	100	-
L.R.Hill	2	0	5	0	-,-											
Mayne	0.5	0	2	1	-,-											
C.Hill						(3)	0.2	0	8	0	-,-					

AUSTRALIAN XI v THE REST

Played at Melbourne Cricket Ground on March 17, 18, 20 (no play), 1911. (Three-day match)
Toss : The Rest.   Result : MATCH DRAWN.
Debuts: The Rest - W.C.Ivory (f/c).
12th Men: no 12th men or emergency fieldsmen named.
Umpires: R.M.Crockett and W.Hannah.
Attendances: No figures published, but considered small.   Receipts: £162.
Close of Play: 1st day Rest 364 all out; 2nd day Aust 6/267 (Matthews 92, Hill 13).

Staged as a benefit for T.S.Warne, the contest raised £234 in his favour but was marred by inclement weather. Rain halted play at 3.40pm on the second day and made play impossible on the last day. H.Carter and H.V.Hordern withdrew from the Australian XI before the start and were replaced by Gehrs and Carkeek, who transferred from The Rest to fill the position of wicket-keeper, left vacant by Carter. Ivory, in turn chosen to replace Carkeek, kept wickets in his only first-class match. Mayne (105 in 191 minutes, 7 fours), Smith (75 in 94 minutes, 11 fours) and Minnett (59 in 60 minutes, 6 fours) led the scoring for The Rest. McElhone's innings included an eight - an all-run four plus four overthrows. Matthews (92 not out in 110 minutes, 9 fours) and Trumper (5 fours) added 125 for the sixth wicket in only 59 minutes on the second day. Sources: *Wisden, The Age, The Argus, The Herald, The Australasian, The Leader, Sydney Referee.*

THE REST

R.E.Mayne	run out (Gehrs/Whitty)	105
C.E.Dolling	c Cotter b Whitty	1
F.E.McElhone	b Whitty	16
H.H.L.Kortlang	c Kelleway b Armstrong	8
*M.A.Noble	c Armstrong b Matthews	23
T.S.Warne	c Carkeek b Kelleway	29
D.B.M.Smith	c Kelleway b Whitty	75
R.B.Minnett	b Whitty	59
S.H.Emery	c Kelleway b Matthews	15
J.H.Kyle	not out	17
†W.C.Ivory	b Whitty	0
Extras	(b8, lb3, w1, nb4)	16
Total	(98.3 overs, 290 mins)	364

AUSTRALIAN XI

C.G.Macartney	c & b Emery	18
C.Kelleway	st Ivory b Warne	35
V.S.Ransford	b Emery	16
D.R.A.Gehrs	run out (Emery/Ivory)	7
†W.Carkeek	st Ivory b Warne	16
T.J.Matthews	not out	92
V.T.Trumper	b Noble	62
*C.Hill	not out	13
W.W.Armstrong	)	
A.Cotter	) did not bat	
W.J.Whitty	)	
Extras	(b5, lb3)	8
Total	(54.0 overs, 166 mins) (6 wkts)	267

AUSTRALIAN XI	O	M	R	W	w,nb
Cotter	12	1	35	0	1,1
Whitty	25.3	4	79	5	-,-
Armstrong	17	4	51	1	-,-
Kelleway	20	1	75	1	-,3
Macartney	11	0	51	0	-,-
Matthews	11	1	49	2	-,-
Ransford	2	0	8	0	-,-

THE REST	O	M	R	W	w,nb
Emery	15	0	95	2	-,-
Minnett	8	0	49	0	-,-
Kyle	15	0	41	0	-,-
Warne	9	0	46	2	-,-
Noble	7	3	28	1	-,-

FALL OF WICKETS

Wkt	REST 1st	AUST 1st
1st	4	34
2nd	30	62
3rd	48	75
4th	112	79
5th	163	115
6th	218	240
7th	316	-
8th	332	-
9th	360	-
10th	364	-

1911-12 SEASON (24 MATCHES)

The 18th English team to tour Australia swept all before them, taking the Test series 4-1 and winning seven of the remaining nine first-class matches, the other two being drawn. Comprehensive victories were achieved by MCC at every turn despite the loss of their captain, P.F.Warner, through illness after the opening match at Adelaide. J.W.H.T.Douglas assumed the captaincy for the remainder of the tour. The itinerary initially released in November featured 20 matches, but the program was pruned to 18 with the cancellation of first-class games against South Australia (starting March 1) and Western Australia (March 12), owing to the later-than-expected finish to the Fifth Test and travel arrangements for home.

Australia's victory in the First Test proved to be a misleading pointer to the outcome of the series and the form of the home players. The local batsmen were unable to find an answer to the England attack of Barnes, Foster and Douglas, and England's batting lineup of Hobbs, Rhodes, Hearne, Gunn and Woolley had strength and depth.

The Australians morale was also being eroded by off-field clashes with officials. The conflict continued throughout the season and culminated in a 20-minutes fight in the NSWCA offices between Clem Hill and Peter McAlister during selection of the team for the Fourth Test. At the root of the conflict was the ongoing struggle between players and administrators for control of the organisation and financial management of tours to and from Australia. This latest episode had been smouldering since the 1909 tour of England, and it went on for some time yet. As a result, six leading Australian players - Clem Hill, Trumper, Armstrong, Ransford, Carter and Cotter - declined invitations to tour England for the 1912 triangular tournament. The final team selected for the tour was: S.E.Gregory (captain), W.Bardsley, W.Carkeek, S.H.Emery, G.R.Hazlitt, C.B.Jennings, C.Kelleway, J.W.McLaren, C.G.Macartney, T.J.Matthews, R.E.Mayne, R.B.Minnett, D.B.M.Smith, H.W.Webster and W.J.Whitty. The team is acknowledged as one of the weakest to ever leave Australia.

The Sheffield Shield program was forced into the background by the English visit and the off-field turmoil. New South Wales retained the title, winning all their four matches by comfortable margins. The other two placings were equally clear-cut, Victoria winning two matches and South Australia none.

Queensland were unable to repeat their successes of the previous season and lost all their matches - once to MCC and twice to New South Wales. Tasmania were no match for the visiting Englishmen either, Woolley hitting an unbeaten 305 at Hobart, though the islanders finished the season on a high note by winning both their games against Victoria.

One of the most acrimonious and controversial seasons in the history of Australian first-class cricket had come to an end. Western Australia were the only State not to take any part.

Leading Aggregates

Batsmen	M	I	NO	Runs	HS	Ave.	Bowlers	Runs	Wkts	Ave.
W.Rhodes (MCC)	14	24	4	1098	179	54.90	F.R.Foster (MCC)	1252	62	20.19
W.W.Armstrong (V)	12	22	3	954	250	50.21	S.F.Barnes (MCC)	1231	59	20.86
J.B.Hobbs (MCC)	11	18	1	943	187	55.47	A.Cotter (NSW)	1166	50	23.32
R.B.Minnett (NSW)	11	17	3	882	216*	63.00	J.W.H.T.Douglas (MCC)	803	37	21.70
J.W.Hearne (MCC)	13	22	4	808	143	44.88	H.V.Hordern (NSW)	842	35	24.05
F.E.Woolley (MCC)	14	18	4	781	305*	55.78	G.R.Hazlitt (NSW)	623	29	21.48
G.Gunn (MCC)	9	15	2	665	106	51.15	J.W.Hitch (MCC)	548	27	20.29
F.R.Foster (MCC)	13	19	1	641	158	35.61	W.W.Armstrong (V)	764	26	29.38
V.T.Trumper (NSW)	12	20	3	583	113	34.29	C.Kelleway (NSW)	635	23	27.60
S.E.Gregory (NSW)	8	13	2	563	186*	51.18				
W.Bardsley (NSW)	11	18	2	558	177	34.87				

SHEFFIELD SHIELD TABLE

	P	W	L	D	Pts	Quotient	Runs Scored	Wkts Lost	Runs Conceded	Wkts Taken
NEW SOUTH WALES	4	4	-	-	4	1.794	2098	54	1732	80
VICTORIA	4	2	2	-	0	1.005	2034	66	1901	62
SOUTH AUSTRALIA	4	-	4	-	-4	0.572	1873	80	2372	58
TOTAL	6	6	6	-	0	1.000	6005	200	6005	200

NEW SOUTH WALES v QUEENSLAND

Played at Sydney Cricket Ground on November 3, 4, 6, 1911. (Timeless match)
Toss : New South Wales.   Result : NEW SOUTH WALES WON BY AN INNINGS AND 56 RUNS.
Debuts: Queensland - R.K.Oxenham (f/c).
12th Men: J.C.Barnes (NSW) and A.E.Oxenham (Qld - team manager)
Umpires: A.C.Jones and R.Thornthwaite.
Attendances: 1500, 4500, 300.   Total: About 6300.   Receipts: £219.
Close of Play: 1st day NSW 7/439 (Minnett 37, Emery 16); 2nd day Qld (2) 0/86 (Jennings 36, Fennelly 42).

A.Marshal was omitted from the Queensland side over an incident in a recent trial match when, after disputing his lbw dismissal, he refused to apologise to the umpires. W.T.Evans and R.J.Hartigan were both unavailable for Queensland for business reasons and H.Carter, G.R.Hazlitt, H.V.Hordern, C.Kelleway and R.V.Minnett were all unavailable for New South Wales. Macartney, who scored 122 in 93 minutes and hit 1 six and 22 fours, was one of five players to reach 50 for New South Wales. Fennelly (71 in 126 minutes, 10 fours and 78 in 107 minutes, 14 fours) made a big contribution for the visitors, establishing a new Queensland first-wicket record of 184 with Jennings (123 in 146 minutes, 19 fours). McElhone deputised as wicket-keeper on the last day when Harvey sustained a hand injury.
Sources: *Cricket, NSWCA Report, Sydney Referee, Sydney Morning Herald, Town & Country Journal.*

NEW SOUTH WALES

*V.T.Trumper	c Cook b Redgrave	59
W.Bardsley	c Sims b Lewis	59
C.G.Macartney	c Lewis b Oxenham	122
S.E.Gregory	c Cook b McLaren	32
E.P.Barbour	c Sims b Oxenham	57
F.E.McElhone	run out (/Sims)	38
B.J.Folkard	st Sims b Cook	5
R.B.Minnett	b Cook	57
S.H.Emery	c Oxenham b Barstow	39
A.Cotter	not out	5
†G.G.Harvey	b Barstow	4
Extras	(b14, lb7)	21
Total	(115.3 overs, 324 mins)	498

QUEENSLAND

*C.B.Jennings	run out (Emery/Harvey)	1		c Macartney b Cotter	123
S.J.Fennelly	st Harvey b Macartney	71		b Macartney	78
J.W.Lewis	c Harvey b Emery	9		c Trumper b Cotter	11
J.S.Redgrave	b Emery	6		b Cotter	4
E.K.Armstrong	b Folkard	7	(6)	b Cotter	0
J.W.McLaren	c Harvey b Minnett	6	(7)	c McElhone b Cotter	13
R.K.Oxenham	not out	26	(5)	b Macartney	0
C.B.Barstow	c Folkard b Emery	7	(9)	b Macartney	0
B.W.Cook	c Trumper b Folkard	4	(8)	c Bardsley b Cotter	4
M.F.McCaffrey	b Folkard	1		b Macartney	8
‖A.E.Sims	run out (McElhone/Harvey)	4		not out	11
Extras	(b9, lb10, nb1)	20		(b20, lb3, nb5)	28
Total	(60.2 overs, 192 mins)	162		(69.2 overs, 205 mins)	280

QUEENSLAND	O	M	R	W	w,nb
McLaren	25	0	115	1	-,-
Barstow	31.3	3	112	2	-,-
Redgrave	17	1	93	1	-,-
Cook	14	3	62	2	-,-
McCaffrey	9	4	29	0	-,-
Lewis	10	2	31	1	-,-
Oxenham	9	1	35	2	-,-

NEW SOUTH WALES	O	M	R	W	w,nb		O	M	R	W	w,nb
Cotter	12	3	18	0	-,-		19	2	76	6	-,5
Macartney	9	3	21	1	-,-	(3)	23.2	5	60	4	-,-
Folkard	12.2	5	28	3	-,-	(2)	15	3	50	0	-,-
Emery	18	3	48	3	-,1		7	0	48	0	-,-
Minnett	9	1	27	1	-,-	(6)	4	0	18	0	-,-
Barbour						(5)	1	1	0	0	-,-

FALL OF WICKETS

Wkt	NSW 1st	QLD 1st	QLD 2nd
1st	100	8	184
2nd	192	30	225
3rd	270	42	233
4th	305	87	236
5th	364	108	237
6th	382	135	246
7th	395	142	252
8th	481	155	253
9th	485	157	265
10th	498	162	280

AFCM No. 430/49
SSM No. 110/36

SOUTH AUSTRALIA v VICTORIA (Shield Match 1)

Played at Adelaide Oval on November 3, 4, 6, 7, 1911. (Timeless match)
Toss : South Australia.　　　　　　　Result : VICTORIA WON BY FOUR WICKETS.
Debuts: South Australia - G.S.Down (f/c). Victoria - N.E.Brown, W.R.F.Macrow (both f/c).
12th Men: P.W.Zschorn (SA) and T.S.Warne (Vic).
Umpires: A.T.Haddrick and G.A.Watson.
Attendances: 600, 4000, 1000, 400.　　　Total: About 6000.　　　Receipts: No figures published.
Close of Play: 1st day SA 305 all out; 2nd day SA (2) 2/29 (Stirling 10, Webster 9); 3rd day Vic (2) 0/37 (Seitz 23, Kortlang 14).

Macrow replaced H.F.Parsons (influenza) in the Victorian side and Warne was made 12th man due to injury. C.E.Dolling, C.F.Drew, D.R.A.Gehrs and R.B.C.Rees were all unavailable for South Australia and Down was a late replacement for W.A.Hewer. Mayne (95 in 182 minutes, 1 six and 4 fours), Stirling (52 in 101 minutes, 4 fours) and Crawford (126 in 160 minutes, 1 six and 18 fours) achieved best results with the bat for South Australia, Stirling hitting 16 runs (4 fours) in one over from Macrow. Mayne, after cutting a ball from Kyle and moving off for a run, was sent back by Crawford and stood petrified three steps out of the crease while Carkeek removed the bails. He immediately walked but umpire Watson, noticing Carkeek had prematurely broken the wicket, ruled 'not out'. Carkeek then pulled out a stump but still did not have the ball. Laver finally settled the issue by uprooting another stump with the ball in his hand, and all the while Mayne had not stopped his walk towards the pavilion. Seitz (75 in 173 minutes, 8 fours and 107 in 240 minutes, 10 fours) and Ransford (55 in 74 minutes, 6 fours and 72 in 70 minutes, 8 fours) dominated the scoring for Victoria. Webster, keeping wickets on the last day, was struck in the chest by a rising ball during the lunch-tea session and then hit on the thumb, causing him (although standing back) to concede 12 byes in rapid succession. Sources: *Wisden, C.B.O'Reilly, VCA Report, SACA Report, The Age, Adelaide Advertiser, South Australian Register.*

SOUTH AUSTRALIA

S.Hill	b Matthews	19		b Armstrong	8
H.P.Kirkwood	run out (　　/Carkeek)	27		lbw b Armstrong	0
*C.Hill	st Carkeek b Matthews	16	(7)	c & b Kyle	33
J.N.Crawford	b Macrow	35	(6)	c Ransford b Laver	126
W.L.Chamberlain	lbw b Kyle	32	(8)	run out (Matthews/Carkeek)	21
R.E.Mayne	c & b Matthews	95	(5)	run out (Kortlang/Carkeek/Laver)	12
G.S.Down	b Brown	10	(9)	not out	12
W.S.Stirling	b Kyle	52	(3)	b Macrow	13
W.J.Whitty	b Kyle	0	(10)	c Ransford b Armstrong	12
†H.W.Webster	c & b Kyle	6	(4)	c & b Laver	21
A.W.Wright	not out	1		c & b Armstrong	31
Extras	(b2, lb7, nb3)	_12_		(lb7)	_7_
Total	(99.4 overs, 285 mins)	305		(94.3 overs, 281 mins)	296

VICTORIA

J.A.Seitz	c Stirling b Whitty	75		b Crawford	107
H.H.L.Kortlang	lbw b Wright	6		b Whitty	24
T.J.Matthews	c Stirling b Wright	20	(6)	b Crawford	44
D.B.M.Smith	c Kirkwood b Wright	48		b Crawford	9
*W.W.Armstrong	lbw b Crawford	9		lbw b Whitty	13
V.S.Ransford	c Webster b Crawford	55	(3)	c Kirkwood b Whitty	72
N.E.Brown	run out (Stirling/Webster)	18		not out	20
F.J.Laver	b Crawford	2		not out	23
J.H.Kyle	b Whitty	6			
†W.Carkeek	not out	11			
W.R.F.Macrow	b Crawford	5			
Extras	(b5, lb3, w1, nb1)	_10_		(b24, lb2)	_26_
Total	(84.0 overs, 256 mins)	265		(91.4 overs, 270 mins) (6 wkts)	338

VICTORIA	O	M	R	W	w,nb		O	M	R	W	w,nb
Macrow	18	3	67	1	-,3		7	1	25	1	-,-
Laver	23	3	69	0	-,-	(5)	30	7	78	2	-,-
Matthews	16	0	41	3	-,-	(4)	9	0	38	0	-,-
Kyle	30.4	11	64	4	-,-	(3)	21	5	50	1	-,-
Brown	5	0	23	1	-,-	(6)	5	0	22	0	-,-
Armstrong	7	0	29	0	-,-	(2)	22.3	7	76	4	-,-

SOUTH AUSTRALIA	O	M	R	W	w,nb		O	M	R	W	w,nb
Whitty	25	9	52	2	-,-		32.4	7	94	3	-,-
Wright	21	4	62	3	-,-		14	1	58	0	-,-
Crawford	21	3	76	4	-,-		32	12	81	3	-,-
Stirling	10	3	37	0	1,-		6	2	33	0	-,-
Down	1	0	6	0	-,1						
Chamberlain	5	1	11	0	-,-	(5)	5	0	27	0	-,-
Kirkwood	1	0	11	0	-,-						
Mayne						(6)	2	0	19	0	-,-

FALL OF WICKETS

Wkt	SA 1st	VIC 1st	SA 2nd	VIC 2nd
1st	34	12	8	53
2nd	55	44	11	160
3rd	69	112	34	172
4th	113	135	50	197
5th	155	193	89	276
6th	172	240	162	293
7th	287	242	240	-
8th	289	242	240	-
9th	303	254	256	-
10th	305	265	296	-

SOUTH AUSTRALIA v M.C.C.

Played at Adelaide Oval on November 10, 11, 13, 14, 1911. (Four-day match)
Toss : MCC   Result : MCC WON BY AN INNINGS AND 194 RUNS.
Debuts: South Australia - C.J.Backman (f/c).
12th Men: P.W.Zschorn (SA). No 12th named for MCC.
Umpires: F.J.C.Thomas and G.A.Watson.
Attendances: 3000, 6000, 1750, 500.   Total: About 11,250.   Receipts: £419.
Close of Play: 1st day MCC 4/331 (Warner 112, Foster 34); 2nd day SA 4/85 (C.Hill 49, Down 4); 3rd day SA (2) 5/204 (Mayne 82).

Four players, C.E.Dolling, C.F.Drew, D.R.A.Gehrs and L.R.Hill were unavailable for South Australia. In addition, W.L.Chamberlain and A.W.Wright withdrew after being named in the side and were replaced by Kirkwood and Backman respectively. Centuries were scored by Gunn (106 in 180 minutes, 10 fours) Warner (112 in 295 minutes, 12 fours, chance at 73) and Foster (158 in 162 minutes, 18 fours). Nine South Australians registered ducks in the match. Mayne (84 in 215 minutes, 8 fours) and Crawford (63 in 83 minutes, 12 fours) topscored in the second innings. Due to a blistered hand, J.W.Hearne was unavailable for MCC. After this match, P.F.Warner, the MCC captain, became seriously ill. He did not play again on the tour, J.W.H.T.Douglas taking over the captaincy. *The Age* incorrectly lists umpire A.McIntyre instead of F.J.C.Thomas. Sources: *Wisden, C.B.O'Reilly, SACA Report, The Age, Adelaide Advertiser, South Australian Register.*

M.C.C.

J.B.Hobbs	c Kirkwood b Rees	36
W.Rhodes	b Whitty	7
G.Gunn	c Backman b Whitty	106
*P.F.Warner	b Backman	151
C.P.Mead	st Webster b Rees	20
F.R.Foster	b Crawford	158
J.W.H.T.Douglas	c & b Crawford	10
F.E.Woolley	c Stirling b Backman	15
J.Vine	c Mayne b Backman	5
S.F.Barnes	not out	16
†H.Strudwick	c Whitty b Stirling	20
Extras	(b13, lb5, w1)	19
Total	(169.0 overs, 465 mins)	563

SOUTH AUSTRALIA

R.E.Mayne	b Foster	0		c Douglas b Woolley	84
W.S.Stirling	run out (Hobbs/Strudwick)	1	(5)	lbw b Barnes	0
*C.Hill	c Rhodes b Foster	51		b Douglas	0
S.Hill	b Barnes	9	(6)	b Douglas	0
J.N.Crawford	run out (Hobbs/Strudwick)	14	(4)	c Vine b Barnes	63
G.S.Down	b Vine	22	(2)	b Foster	0
H.P.Kirkwood	b Foster	0	(11)	not out	13
C.J.Backman	c Rhodes b Foster	16	(7)	st Strudwick b Douglas	0
R.B.C.Rees	b Barnes	0		c Strudwick b Woolley	44
†H.W.Webster	c Hobbs b Barnes	1		b Douglas	8
W.J.Whitty	not out	8	(8)	b Douglas	0
Extras	(b11, lb3, nb5)	19		(b10, lb4, nb2)	16
Total	(56.1 overs, 175 mins)	141		(69.1 overs, 230 mins)	228

SOUTH AUSTRALIA	O	M	R	W	w,nb
Whitty	41	11	116	2	-,-
Crawford	47	9	132	2	-,-
Rees	38	2	154	2	-,-
Stirling	22	4	66	1	1,-
Backman	16	2	53	3	-,-
Kirkwood	3	0	15	0	-,-
Down	1	0	5	0	-,-
Mayne	1	0	3	0	-,-

MCC	O	M	R	W	w,nb		O	M	R	W	w,nb
Foster	20	3	58	4	-,2		6	1	24	1	-,2
Barnes	24	11	38	3	-,-	(5)	12	5	26	2	-,-
Douglas	8	4	17	0	-,3	(2)	26.1	5	65	5	-,-
Woolley	1	1	0	0	-,-		12	3	37	2	-,-
Vine	3.1	1	9	1	-,-	(3)	7	0	40	0	-,-
Rhodes							5	1	16	0	-,-
Hobbs							1	0	4	0	-,-

FALL OF WICKETS

Wkt	MCC 1st	SA 1st	SA 2nd
1st	13	2	4
2nd	68	3	7
3rd	235	21	104
4th	278	75	108
5th	435	89	111
6th	495	91	115
7th	508	119	115
8th	525	124	204
9th	532	126	212
10th	563	141	228

VICTORIA v M.C.C.

Played at Melbourne Cricket Ground on November 17, 18, 20, 21, 22, 1911. (Timeless match)
Toss : MCC   Result : MCC WON BY 49 RUNS.
Debuts: Nil.
12th Men: E.L.Spencer (Vic) and J.Vine (MCC).
Umpires: R.M.Crockett and W.A.Young.
Attendances: 6160, 17362, 6148, 4565, 200.   Total: 34,435.   Receipts: £1178.
Close of Play: 1st day MCC 6/247 (Douglas 18, Smith 1); 2nd day Vic 3/219 (Kortlang 67, Laver 2); 3rd day MCC (2) 3/173
    (Rhodes 58, Hitch 4); 4th day Vic (2) 8/210 (Laver 11, Carkeek 0).

Foster scored 101 in 134 minutes and hit 13 fours, surviving chances at 1 and 50. An unbeaten innings of 33 in 189 minutes with 1 four by Douglas, in his new role as captain following Warner's illness, gave first rise to the quip "Johnny Won't Hit Today" in the press, and the nickname stuck. Kyle (7) received a heavy blow on the arm from Foster in the first innings and retired at 3/208; he resumed at 9/264. Kortlang (74 in 205 minutes, 3 fours) and Smith (68 in 85 minutes, 10 fours and 84 in 95 minutes, 10 fours) compiled notable innings for Victoria. Hobbs (88 in 181 minutes, 6 fours) and Rhodes (66 in 178 minutes, 2 fours) shared a partnership of 123 in MCC's second innings. T.S.Warne (back injury) was unavailable for Victoria. Sources: *Wisden, VCA Report, The Age, The Argus, The Herald, The Australasian.*

M.C.C.

J.B.Hobbs	c Laver b Matthews	21	c Matthews b Armstrong		88
S.Kinneir	c Kyle b Macrow	32	lbw b Laver		12
W.Rhodes	lbw b Laver	28	lbw b Armstrong		66
C.P.Mead	c Carkeek b Kyle	34	(6) b Laver		22
J.W.Hearne	b Matthews	6	(7) c & b Laver		0
F.R.Foster	c Armstrong b Laver	101	(8) b Armstrong		0
*J.W.H.T.Douglas	not out	33	(9) not out		5
†E.J.Smith	c Smith b Laver	22	(4) b Kyle		1
F.E.Woolley	c & b Matthews	5	(10) b Macrow		15
J.Iremonger	run out (Carkeek)	14	(11) b Macrow		0
J.W.Hitch	run out (Seitz/Carkeek)	15	(5) b Armstrong		13
Extras	(b5, lb2)	7	(b7, lb4, nb1)		12
Total	(138.4 overs, 368 mins)	318	(101.4 overs, 277 mins)		234

VICTORIA

J.A.Seitz	b Foster	14	b Douglas		3
H.H.L.Kortlang	b Hitch	74	run out (Hobbs)		7
V.S.Ransford	b Hearne	34	c Foster b Iremonger		34
D.B.M.Smith	b Douglas	68	run out (Rhodes/Smith)		84
J.H.Kyle	not out	7	(9) run out (/Smith)		6
F.J.Laver	c Hitch b Douglas	14	(8) b Douglas		11
*W.W.Armstrong	c Smith b Douglas	0	(5) b Iremonger		9
T.J.Matthews	b Hitch	9	(6) b Douglas		24
N.E.Brown	c Smith b Douglas	21	(7) b Foster		26
†W.Carkeek	b Hitch	0	lbw b Douglas		10
W.R.F.Macrow	c Rhodes b Hitch	2	not out		4
Extras	(b24, lb4, w1, nb2)	31	(b3, lb8)		11
Total	(75.2 overs, 253 mins)	274	(69.3 overs, 237 mins)		229

VICTORIA	O	M	R	W	w,nb		O	M	R	W	w,nb				FALL OF WICKETS		
Macrow	23	4	51	1	-,-	(2)	10.4	1	30	2	-,1			MCC	VIC	MCC	VIC
Laver	44	17	88	3	-,-	(1)	19	12	23	3	-,-	Wkt	1st	1st	2nd	2nd
Matthews	26	6	65	3	-,-		9	1	25	0	-,-	1st	32	27	41	3
Kyle	25	13	59	1	-,-		32	9	69	1	-,-	2nd	81	76	164	15
Brown	6	1	17	0	-,-		4	0	19	0	-,-	3rd	83	189	169	75
Armstrong	14.4	2	31	0	-,-		27	9	56	4	-,-	4th	113	240	184	103
												5th	139	240	199	156
MCC	O	M	R	W	w,nb		O	M	R	W	w,nb	6th	246	240	204	179
Foster	20	4	65	1	-,-		20	7	55	1	-,-	7th	274	251	213	189
Douglas	18.2	5	41	4	1,-		19.3	9	37	4	-,-	8th	280	251	213	209
Hitch	15	4	54	4	-,1		7	1	33	0	-,-	9th	302	264	234	218
Hearne	7	0	39	1	-,-	(5)	8	0	51	0	-,-	10th	318	274	234	229
Woolley	5	0	15	0	-,1											
Iremonger	10	1	29	0	-,-	(4)	15	1	42	2	-,-					

NEW SOUTH WALES v M.C.C.

Played at Sydney Cricket Ground on November 24, 25 (no play), 27, 28 (no play), 1911. (Four-day match)
Toss : New South Wales.   Result : MATCH DRAWN.
Debuts: Nil.
12th Men: E.L.Waddy (NSW) and J.Vine (MCC).
Umpires: W.G.Curran and A.C.Jones.
Attendances: 10091, 8000 awaited admission, 11495, no play.   Total: 21,586.   Receipts: £986.
Close of Play: 1st day MCC 4/151 (Mead 41, Foster 15); 2nd day no play; 3rd day NSW 8/198 (Minnett 52, Carter 1).

Over half the possible playing time, including all of the second and fourth days was lost to rain. Gunn was struck a painful blow on his gloveless left hand by a ball from Minnett shortly before the tea break on the first day. He continued batting but an examination of his hand later revealed a broken bone; he was unable to field during the New South Wales innings - Vine substituted. Gregory (66 in 82 minutes, 8 fours) and Minnett (52 not out in 76 minutes), topscored in the unfinished New South Wales innings after Trumper was dismissed in the first over. Gregory also substituted for a short time against his own team late on the third day when Douglas was off the field, there being no other MCC player in attendance. S.H.Emery (hand injury), C.Kelleway (ill) and R.V.Minnett were all unavailable for New South Wales. Sources: *Wisden, NSWCA Report, The Age, Sydney Morning Herald, Town & Country Journal.*

M.C.C.

J.B.Hobbs	c Bardsley b Folkard	15
W.Rhodes	c Cotter b Hordern	15
G.Gunn	run out (Gregory/Carter)	50
C.P.Mead	c Carter b Cotter	46
J.W.Hearne	c Carter b Cotter	2
F.R.Foster	c Gregory b Cotter	22
*J.W.H.T.Douglas	lbw b Hordern	0
F.E.Woolley	not out	43
S.F.Barnes	b Folkard	12
†H.Strudwick	b Cotter	5
J.W.Hitch	b Hordern	9
Extras	(b9, lb4, nb6)	19
Total	(104.1 overs, 298 mins)	238

NEW SOUTH WALES

*V.T.Trumper	c Strudwick b Foster	1
W.Bardsley	c Strudwick b Foster	24
C.G.Macartney	lbw b Douglas	1
S.E.Gregory	c Foster b Douglas	66
E.P.Barbour	b Hitch	37
F.E.McElhone	lbw b Douglas	0
R.B.Minnett	not out	52
H.V.Hordern	c sub (S.E.Gregory) b Hitch	3
B.J.Folkard	b Foster	6
†H.Carter	not out	1
A.Cotter	did not bat	
Extras	(b2, lb2, nb3)	7
Total	(57.0 overs, 170 mins) (8 wkts)	198

NEW SOUTH WALES	O	M	R	W	w,nb
Macartney	15	9	9	0	-,1
Folkard	16	6	45	2	-,-
Hordern	36.1	13	62	3	-,-
Cotter	17	5	45	4	-,4
Minnett	20	8	58	0	-,1

MCC	O	M	R	W	w,nb
Foster	13	2	35	3	-,2
Douglas	18	5	35	3	-,-
Woolley	3	1	14	0	-,-
Barnes	13	3	43	0	-,-
Hearne	4	0	34	0	-,-
Hitch	6	0	30	2	-,1

FALL OF WICKETS

	MCC	NSW
Wkt	1st	1st
1st	25	2
2nd	43	15
3rd	116	38
4th	124	119
5th	160	119
6th	166	145
7th	168	164
8th	213	190
9th	221	-
10th	238	-

VICTORIA v SOUTH AUSTRALIA (Shield Match 2)

Played at Melbourne Cricket Ground on November 24, 25, 27, 28, 1911. (Timeless match)
Toss : Victoria.   Result : VICTORIA WON BY AN INNINGS AND 135 RUNS.
Debuts: Nil.
12th Men: E.L.Spencer (Vic) and A.W.Wright (SA).
Umpires: R.M.Crockett and W.Hannah.
Attendances: 1881, 8239, 1117, 100.   Total: 11,337.   Receipts: £349.
Close of Play: 1st day Vic 6/393 (Armstrong 173, Kyle 4); 2nd day SA 7/131 (Dolling 66, Rees 1); 3rd day SA (2) 8/171 (Stirling 2).

The batting of Armstrong overshadowed all else in the match. He began his innings with Victoria precariously placed at 3/59 and batted for 355 minutes (1 six and 29 fours) to score 250 out of 494 added during his presence. He had partnerships of 145 for the fourth wicket with Seitz (101 in 145 minutes, 14 fours), 127 for the sixth wicket with Brown (48 in 90 minutes, 6 fours) and 141 for the ninth wicket with Carkeek (68 in 100 minutes, 7 fours). The sustained accuracy of Macrow, Matthews and Kyle proved too much for the South Australian batsmen, who were unable to avoid the follow-on despite the stubborn efforts of Dolling (94 in 205 minutes, 10 fours). Only Clem Hill (55 in 110 minutes, 3 fours) offered other than token resistance in the second innings, leaving the home team emphatic victors. 'Felix', writing in *The Australasian*, was loud in his praise of Kyle's bowling and suggested his 'consideration in connection with the selection of the Australian representative team'. Sources: *Wisden, C.B.O'Reilly, VCA Report, SACA Report, The Age, The Argus, The Herald, The Australasian.*

VICTORIA

J.A.Seitz	b Whitty	101
H.H.L.Kortlang	c Webster b Rees	17
V.S.Ransford	c Mayne b Rees	8
D.B.M.Smith	c Rees b Whitty	13
*W.W.Armstrong	c Mayne b Chamberlain	250
T.J.Matthews	c & b Rees	17
N.E.Brown	b Whitty	48
J.H.Kyle	lbw b Rees	4
H.W.Hart	c C.Hill b Rees	2
†W.Carkeek	b Chamberlain	68
W.R.F.Macrow	not out	5
Extras	(b19, lb1)	20
Total	(144.1 overs, 423 mins)	553

SOUTH AUSTRALIA

R.E.Mayne	c Hart b Matthews	3	(3)	b Macrow	22
C.E.Dolling	lbw b Matthews	94		c & b Macrow	20
*C.Hill	c Armstrong b Kyle	17	(4)	c Armstrong b Matthews	55
J.N.Crawford	b Kyle	9	(5)	c Seitz b Kyle	13
W.L.Chamberlain	b Kyle	4	(6)	c Macrow b Matthews	16
G.S.Down	b Macrow	23	(7)	run out (Matthews)	6
S.Hill	b Macrow	0	(9)	b Macrow	7
W.S.Stirling	b Matthews	1		not out	3
R.B.C.Rees	not out	42	(1)	b Armstrong	8
†H.W.Webster	b Ransford	25		b Kyle	5
W.J.Whitty	c Hart b Ransford	3		b Kyle	1
Extras	(b5, lb3, w1, nb2)	11		(b21, lb4, w2, nb3)	30
Total	(80.5 overs, 235 mins)	232		(65.6 overs, 220 mins)	186

SOUTH AUSTRALIA	O	M	R	W	w,nb
Whitty	38	11	116	3	-,-
Crawford	38	7	128	0	-,-
Rees	38	4	166	5	-,-
Chamberlain	10.1	1	51	2	-,-
Stirling	19	4	65	0	-,-
Mayne	1	0	7	0	-,-

VICTORIA	O	M	R	W	w,nb		O	M	R	W	w,nb
Macrow	15	3	27	2	-,2	(3)	13	3	40	3	2,3
Matthews	24	5	68	3	-,-	(5)	12	2	37	2	-,-
Kyle	27	12	47	3	-,-	(2)	26.5	5	54	3	-,-
Hart	6	0	29	0	1,-		5	0	19	0	-,-
Brown	4	0	22	0	-,-						
Ransford	2.5	0	22	2	-,-						
Armstrong	2	1	6	0	-,-	(1)	9	6	6	1	-,-

FALL OF WICKETS

Wkt	VIC 1st	SA 1st	SA 2nd
1st	34	7	12
2nd	44	31	54
3rd	59	49	58
4th	204	61	92
5th	249	113	138
6th	376	115	161
7th	395	124	161
8th	397	183	171
9th	538	228	179
10th	553	232	186

QUEENSLAND v M.C.C.

Played at Brisbane Cricket Ground (Woolloongabba) on December 1, 2, 4, 1911. (Three-day match)
Toss : Queensland.   Result : MCC WON BY SEVEN WICKETS.
Debuts: Queensland - J.T.Bolton (f/c).
12th Men: R.K.Oxenham (Qld) and S.Kinneir (MCC).
Umpires: G.A.Carter and W.R.Shillington.
Attendances: 3000, 8000, 2000.   Total: About 13,000.   Receipts: £529.
Close of Play: 1st day MCC 2/62 (Hearne 15, Mead 13); 2nd day Qld (2) 2/65 (Jennings 43, Bolton 4).

G.Gunn (hand injury) preferred to remain in Sydney after the match against New South Wales and J.W.Hitch (strained groin) was also unavailable for the tourists. Jennings (91 in 132 minutes, 14 fours) and Hartigan (59 in 54 minutes, 2 sixes and 7 fours) shared a third-wicket partnership of 102 in 60 minutes on the first day. Mead topscored in each innings for MCC with 79 in 119 minutes (5 fours) and 54 not out in 77 minutes (7 fours). The original tour itinerary provided four days for the match, starting November 30th, but it was later amended to a three-day contest because of travel arrangements. Following their victory the Englishmen embarked on a five-hour train journey to Toowoomba for a two-day match against a local team. Sources: *Wisden, Brisbane Courier, Queensland Times, The Queenslander.*

QUEENSLAND

*C.B.Jennings	b Foster	91	(2) b Foster		44
S.J.Fennelly	c Rhodes b Hearne	29	(5) c Iremonger b Barnes		38
A.Marshal	c Woolley b Barnes	11	(1) b Foster		8
R.J.Hartigan	run out (Douglas/)	59	(3) c Douglas b Foster		8
W.T.Evans	run out (Hobbs/Smith)	4	(8) c Barnes b Foster		6
W.B.Hayes	c Smith b Douglas	5	c Iremonger b Barnes		1
J.W.McLaren	b Foster	29	c Iremonger b Barnes		0
†J.T.Bolton	b Douglas	0	(4) b Foster		5
C.B.Barstow	not out	43	c Smith b Foster		0
B.W.Cook	b Barnes	7	not out		0
F.Fett	b Barnes	0	st Smith b Barnes		1
Extras	(b1, lb10, nb1)	12	(b6, lb5, nb2)		13
Total	(62.5 overs, 236 mins)	290	(45.1 overs, 139 mins)		124

M.C.C.

J.B.Hobbs	c Marshal b McLaren	26	b McLaren		14
J.Vine	b McLaren	3			
J.W.Hearne	c McLaren b Hayes	53	c Jennings b McLaren		9
C.P.Mead	b Cook	79	not out		54
W.Rhodes	not out	64	(2) b McLaren		26
F.R.Foster	lbw b Cook	4	(5) not out		33
F.E.Woolley	c Jennings b Hartigan	1			
*J.W.H.T.Douglas	c & b Hayes	20			
J.Iremonger	c & b Hayes	0			
S.F.Barnes	b McLaren	0			
‡E.J.Smith	st Bolton b Hayes	7			
Extras	(b7, lb5, w6)	18	(b4)		4
Total	(77.2 overs, 255 mins)	275	(30.3 overs, 106 mins) (3 wkts)		140

MCC	O	M	R	W	w,nb		O	M	R	W	w,nb
Foster	17	3	67	2	-,-		19	9	31	6	-,-
Douglas	12	2	53	2	-,1		6	2	20	0	-,1
Barnes	14.5	2	52	3	-,-		13.1	4	49	4	-,1
Hearne	7	0	39	1	-,-	(5)	3	0	9	0	-,-
Iremonger	8	1	36	0	-,-						
Vine	4	0	31	0	-,-						
Woolley						(4)	4	2	2	0	-,-

QUEENSLAND	O	M	R	W	w,nb		O	M	R	W	w,nb
McLaren	17	2	55	3	1,-	(2)	9	0	46	3	-,-
Barstow	16	4	51	0	5,-	(1)	9.3	1	43	0	-,-
Hayes	15.2	2	69	4	-,-	(5)	3	0	21	0	-,-
Fett	6	1	18	0	-,-						
Cook	14	1	41	2	-,-	(3)	6	1	18	0	-,-
Marshal	3	0	7	0	-,-						
Hartigan	5	1	15	1	-,-	(4)	3	0	8	0	-,-
Evans	1	0	1	0	-,-						

FALL OF WICKETS

Wkt	QLD 1st	MCC 1st	QLD 2nd	MCC 2nd
1st	61	32	23	20
2nd	86	35	31	34
3rd	188	140	67	87
4th	197	180	90	-
5th	202	186	91	-
6th	214	189	91	-
7th	214	255	116	-
8th	271	261	123	-
9th	290	268	123	-
10th	290	275	124	-

NEW SOUTH WALES v SOUTH AUSTRALIA (Shield Match 3)

Played at Sydney Cricket Ground on December 1, 2 (no play), 4, 5, 6, 1911. (Timeless match)
Toss : South Australia.   Result : NEW SOUTH WALES WON BY 361 RUNS.
Debuts: New South Wales - E.J.Long (f/c); G.R.Hazlitt (NSW only).
12th Men: S.Hill (SA). No 12th man or emergency fieldsman named for NSW.
Umpires: W.G.French and A.C.Jones.
Attendances: 1138, no play, 4179, 2239, 799.   Total: 8355.   Receipts: £295.
Close of Play: 1st day NSW 0/79 (Trumper 45, Bardsley 31); 2nd day no play; 3rd day SA 5/164 (Chamberlain 26, Rees 13); 4th day
  NSW (2) 8/323 (Minnett 67, Long 15).

Rain prevented any play after lunch on the first day and saturated the wicket area to such an extent that a resumption was not possible until
the third day. That afternoon Cotter hit 82 in 50 minutes with 4 sixes and 6 fours; he arrived at the crease 9 minutes before lunch and was
2 at the adjournment, then scored 80 in 41 minutes, including 50 in four overs by Rees. Gregory (76 in 135 minutes, 6 fours) and Minnett
(87 not out in 96 minutes, 15 fours) topscored in the second innings. R.J.A.Massie (exams), H.Carter, B.J.Folkard and H.V.Hordern were
unavailable for New South Wales and Waddy, the nominated 12th man, was included at the last minute to replace S.H.Emery, who had not
fully recovered from a hand injury. Hazlitt's previous matches were for Victoria. *Wisden* and *O'Reilly* incorrectly give SA (1) Stirling c
Randell. Sources: *Wisden, C.B.O'Reilly, NSWCA Report, SACA Report, Sydney Referee, Sydney Morning Herald.*

NEW SOUTH WALES

*V.T.Trumper	b Whitty	47	c Stirling b Whitty	37
W.Bardsley	b Rees	58	c Dolling b Whitty	38
C.G.Macartney	st Webster b Rees	2	b Rees	3
S.E.Gregory	b Rees	6	lbw b Crawford	76
E.P.Barbour	c Crawford b Whitty	5	c Chamberlain b Crawford	18
E.L.Waddy	not out	78	b Chamberlain	40
R.B.Minnett	lbw b Rees	9	not out	87
G.R.Hazlitt	c Mayne b Wright	6	b Crawford	3
A.Cotter	b Wright	82	c Stirling b Chamberlain	21
†E.J.Long	c Wright b Crawford	0	b Rees	24
J.A.Randell	lbw b Wright	16	c Webster b Whitty	0
Extras	(b4, lb2, w1)	7	(b2, lb2, w1)	5
Total	(77.4 overs, 231 mins)	316	(90.4 overs, 271 mins)	352

SOUTH AUSTRALIA

R.E.Mayne	c Hazlitt b Minnett	21	b Cotter	18
C.E.Dolling	b Minnett	28	b Hazlitt	10
*C.Hill	b Hazlitt	59	(4) not out	32
J.N.Crawford	c Trumper b Randell	11	(3) c Long b Cotter	0
W.L.Chamberlain	c Cotter b Hazlitt	36	b Cotter	0
G.S.Down	b Randell	2	b Cotter	4
R.B.C.Rees	b Hazlitt	31	b Hazlitt	11
W.S.Stirling	c Hazlitt b Minnett	5	b Cotter	0
†H.W.Webster	b Hazlitt	5	b Hazlitt	1
W.J.Whitty	c Bardsley b Hazlitt	2	b Hazlitt	0
A.W.Wright	not out	1	run out (Macartney/Long)	5
Extras	(b3, lb1, w1, nb3)	8	(b10, lb5, w1, nb1)	17
Total	(59.4 overs, 177 mins)	209	(27.5 overs, 96 mins)	98

SOUTH AUSTRALIA	O	M	R	W	w,nb		O	M	R	W	w,nb
Whitty	29	6	94	2	-,-		23.4	3	76	3	-,-
Crawford	19	5	69	1	1,-		23	4	82	3	-,-
Rees	17	1	94	4	-,-	(4)	18	1	76	2	-,-
Wright	10.4	2	40	3	-,-	(3)	12	1	50	0	-,-
Stirling	2	0	12	0	-,-	(6)	7	2	28	0	1,-
Chamberlain						(5)	7	0	35	2	-,-

NEW SOUTH WALES	O	M	R	W	w,nb		O	M	R	W	w,nb
Cotter	10	1	37	0	-,2		14	3	34	5	1,1
Hazlitt	20.4	3	57	5	-,-		13.5	2	47	4	-,-
Minnett	13	2	48	3	1,1						
Macartney	8	2	20	0	-,-						
Randell	8	1	39	2	-,-						

FALL OF WICKETS

Wkt	NSW 1st	SA 1st	NSW 2nd	SA 2nd
1st	81	44	78	16
2nd	96	79	78	31
3rd	119	101	82	32
4th	124	139	120	36
5th	124	142	206	40
6th	148	192	236	66
7th	159	197	240	67
8th	283	206	267	86
9th	284	206	345	88
10th	316	209	352	98

AUSTRALIAN XI v M.C.C.

Played at Brisbane Cricket Ground (Woolloongabba) on December 8, 9, 11, 1911. (Three-day match)
Toss : MCC   Result : MATCH DRAWN.
Debuts: Nil.
12th Men: A.Marshal (Aust) and E.J.Smith (MCC).
Umpires: G.A.Carter and W.H.Carvosso.
Attendances: 5000, 10000, 1500.   Total: About 16,500.   Receipts: £767.
Close of Play: 1st day MCC 8/236 (Douglas 89, Barnes 4); 2nd day Aust 8/277 (Crawford 56, McLaren 10).

McLaren, right-arm fast, dismissed Rhodes and Vine in the first over of the match, Mead in the third over and Foster soon afterwards. The Englishmen recovered due to cautious innings from Kinneir (63 in 140 minutes, 10 fours) and Douglas (101 not out in 293 minutes, 10 fours). Barnes dismissed Jennings and Armstrong with successive balls in the Australian innings. Crawford reached 50 in 43 minutes, 100 in 106 minutes and batted for 109 minutes in all, hitting 2 sixes and 15 fours. Prior to reaching fifty he had lofted a ball from Barnes to Mead on the boundary who took the catch. However, umpire Carter ran to the spot and disallowed the catch, ruling that Mead's foot infringed on the asphalt bicycle track surrounding the playing arena, Carter then signalled a four. Kelleway (66 in 162 minutes, 4 fours) and Minnett (69 in 78 minutes, 1 six and 5 fours), who were brought into the team when W.Bardsley and C.Hill declined invitations to play, also contributed to the Australian first-innings lead. Hearne scored 89 not out in 159 minutes with 11 fours in the second innings. Jennings kept wickets after tea in the unexplained absence of Evans. Sources: *Wisden, Sydney Morning Herald, Brisbane Courier, Queensland Times, The Queenslander.*

M.C.C.

Batsman	Dismissal	Runs		2nd innings	Runs
S.Kinneir	c Barstow b Armstrong	63	(2)	b Kelleway	18
W.Rhodes	c Crawford b McLaren	0	(1)	b Armstrong	34
J.Vine	b McLaren	0			
C.P.Mead	b McLaren	0		b Kelleway	50
F.R.Foster	b McLaren	9		c Crawford b Fennelly	37
*J.W.H.T.Douglas	not out	101			
F.E.Woolley	c Evans b Barstow	9	(6)	not out	30
J.W.Hearne	lbw b Crawford	43	(3)	not out	89
J.Iremonger	b Minnett	0			
S.F.Barnes	run out (Jennings/Evans)	14			
†H.Strudwick	b Minnett	3			
Extras	(b8, lb7, w4, nb6)	25		(b11, lb2, w1, nb7)	21
Total	(107.1 overs, 322 mins)	267		(71.0 overs, 225 mins) (4 wkts)	279

AUSTRALIAN XI

Batsman	Dismissal	Runs
S.J.Fennelly	c Strudwick b Iremonger	22
C.B.Jennings	b Barnes	5
R.J.Hartigan	c Vine b Iremonger	0
C.Kelleway	c Strudwick b Barnes	66
W.W.Armstrong	b Barnes	0
*V.T.Trumper	c Hearne b Iremonger	30
R.B.Minnett	c Woolley b Hearne	69
J.N.Crawford	c Strudwick b Barnes	110
†W.T.Evans	b Barnes	10
J.W.McLaren	c Strudwick b Woolley	17
C.B.Barstow	not out	7
Extras	(b4, lb5, nb2)	11
Total	(92.2 overs, 280 mins)	347

AUSTRALIAN XI	O	M	R	W	w,nb		O	M	R	W	w,nb
McLaren	21	5	59	4	3,1		8	1	29	0	-,2
Barstow	20	5	53	1	-,-	(6)	5	1	17	0	-,-
Crawford	26	9	44	1	1,-		15	2	40	0	-,-
Minnett	17.1	7	41	2	-,2	(7)	9	2	28	0	-,-
Kelleway	7	4	6	0	-,-	(2)	13	0	52	2	1,4
Armstrong	16	2	39	1	-,3	(4)	13	5	31	1	-,-
Fennelly						(5)	5	0	52	1	-,1
Hartigan							3	0	9	0	-,-

MCC	O	M	R	W	w,nb
Barnes	28.2	8	89	5	-,-
Iremonger	28	6	79	3	-,-
Hearne	12	0	51	1	-,-
Rhodes	10	2	45	0	-,-
Foster	10	1	50	0	-,1
Woolley	4	0	22	1	-,1

FALL OF WICKETS

Wkt	MCC 1st	AUST 1st	MCC 2nd
1st	1	29	47
2nd	1	31	63
3rd	9	32	168
4th	21	32	231
5th	115	73	-
6th	131	182	-
7th	219	237	-
8th	220	257	-
9th	264	315	-
10th	267	347	-

AUSTRALIA v ENGLAND (1st Test)

Played at Sydney Cricket Ground on December 15, 16, 18, 19, 20, 21, 1911. (Timeless match)
Toss : Australia.   Result : AUSTRALIA WON BY 146 RUNS.
Debuts: Australia - R.B.Minnett (Test). England - J.W.H.T.Douglas, F.R.Foster, J.W.Hearne, S.Kinneir, C.P.Mead (all Test).
12th Men: C.G.Macartney (Aust) and J.Vine (Eng).
Umpires: R.M.Crockett and W.G.Curran.
Attendances: 17171, 35526, 13151, 8445, 5690, 486.   Total: 80,469.   Receipts: £4253.
Close of Play: 1st day Aust 5/317 (Trumper 95, Minnett 22); 2nd day Eng 4/142 (Hobbs 63, Hearne 9); 3rd day Aust (2) 1/119
       (Kelleway 47, Hill 49); 4th day Eng (2) 1/65 (Kinneir 27, Gunn 16); 5th day Eng (2) 8/263 (Douglas 32).

Trumper (chanceless 113 in 226 minutes, 12 fours) and Minnett on debut (90 in 111 minutes, 14 fours, chance at 51) consolidated Australia's position in the first innings, adding 109 in 79 minutes. In the process Trumper became the second batsman - after his current captain - to reach 3000 runs in Test matches. Armstrong (60 in 103 minutes, 7 fours) also batted well. Kelleway (70 in 183 minutes, 9 fours) and Hill (65 in 119 minutes, 7 fours) shared a stand of 121 in the second innings. On the third day Hill, with his 45th run, became the first batsman to aggregate 10,000 runs in first-class cricket in Australia, a feat not equalled until 1935-36 (by Bradman). Hearne batted coolly in both innings of his Test debut. He made 76 (165 minutes, 8 fours) in the first, while in the second he was out to the final ball of the fifth day's play after 143 minutes' resistance. He alone played the deliveries of Hordern with confidence; the googly bowler captured 12 for 175 in his first Test against England. Hobbs (63 in 167 minutes, 1 five and 5 fours), Foster (56 in 62 minutes, 9 fours) and Gunn (62 in 171 minutes) scored half-centuries for England, who were unable to consider their captain P.F.Warner (ill) and J.W.Hitch (groin strain) for selection. *NSWCA Report* incorrectly gives umpires as Crockett and A.C.Jones. Sources: *Wisden, NSWCA Report, The Age, Sydney Morning Herald.*

AUSTRALIA

W.Bardsley	c Strudwick b Douglas	30		b Foster	12
C.Kelleway	c & b Woolley	20		b Douglas	70
*C.Hill	run out (Rhodes/Strudwick)	46		b Foster	65
W.W.Armstrong	st Strudwick b Hearne	60		b Foster	28
V.T.Trumper	c Hobbs b Woolley	113		c & b Douglas	14
V.S.Ransford	c Hearne b Barnes	26		c Rhodes b Barnes	34
R.B.Minnett	c Foster b Barnes	90	(8)	b Douglas	17
H.V.Hordern	not out	17	(7)	b Foster	18
A.Cotter	c & b Barnes	6		lbw b Douglas	2
†H.Carter	b Foster	13		c Gunn b Foster	15
W.J.Whitty	b Foster	0		not out	9
Extras	(b9, lb15, nb2)	26		(b16, lb7, nb1)	24
Total	(127.0 overs, 394 mins)	447		(104.3 overs, 350 mins)	308

ENGLAND

J.B.Hobbs	c Hill b Whitty	63		c Carter b Cotter	22
S.Kinneir	b Kelleway	22		c Trumper b Hordern	30
G.Gunn	b Cotter	4		c Whitty b Hordern	62
W.Rhodes	c Hill b Hordern	41	(5)	c Trumper b Hordern	0
C.P.Mead	c & b Hordern	0	(4)	run out (Hill/Whitty)	25
J.W.Hearne	c Trumper b Kelleway	76	(7)	b Hordern	43
F.R.Foster	b Hordern	56	(6)	c Ransford b Hordern	21
F.E.Woolley	b Hordern	39		c Armstrong b Cotter	7
*J.W.H.T.Douglas	c Trumper b Hordern	0		b Hordern	32
S.F.Barnes	b Kelleway	9		b Hordern	14
†H.Strudwick	not out	0		not out	12
Extras	(b3, lb3, w1, nb1)	8		(b14, lb8, nb1)	23
Total	(101.5 overs, 317 mins)	318		(123.2 overs, 375 mins)	291

ENGLAND	O	M	R	W	w,nb		O	M	R	W	w,nb
Foster	29	6	105	2	-,1		31.3	5	92	5	-,1
Douglas	24	5	62	1	-,-		21	3	50	4	-,-
Barnes	35	5	107	3	-,-		30	8	72	1	-,-
Hearne	10	0	44	1	-,-	(5)	13	2	51	0	-,-
Woolley	21	2	77	2	-,1	(4)	6	1	15	0	-,-
Rhodes	8	0	26	0	-,-		3	1	4	0	-,-

AUSTRALIA	O	M	R	W	w,nb		O	M	R	W	w,nb
Cotter	19	0	88	1	-,1	(2)	27	3	71	2	-,1
Whitty	28	13	60	1	-,-	(1)	20	8	41	0	-,-
Kelleway	16.5	3	46	3	1,-	(4)	19	6	27	0	-,-
Hordern	27	5	85	5	-,-	(3)	42.2	11	90	7	-,-
Armstrong	9	3	28	0	-,-		15	3	39	0	-,-
Minnett	2	1	3	0	-,-						

FALL OF WICKETS

	AUST	ENG	AUST	ENG
Wkt	1st	1st	2nd	2nd
1st	44	45	29	29
2nd	77	53	150	69
3rd	121	115	169	141
4th	198	129	191	141
5th	278	142	218	148
6th	387	231	246	167
7th	420	293	268	177
8th	426	293	274	263
9th	447	310	283	276
10th	447	318	308	291

VICTORIA v NEW SOUTH WALES (Shield Match 4)

Played at Melbourne Cricket Ground on December 23, 26, 27, 1911. (Timeless match)
Toss : Victoria.   Result : NEW SOUTH WALES WON BY TEN WICKETS.
Debuts: Victoria - A.E.V.Hartkopf (f/c).
12th Men: E.L.Spencer (Vic) and R.B.Minnett (Aust).
Umpires: W.J.Bruton and D.A.Elder.
Attendances: 9527, 12844, 8658.   Total: 31,029.   Receipts: £911.
Close of Play: 1st day NSW 1/11 (Emery 2); 2nd day NSW 341 all out.

Victoria began the match disastrously with Seitz caught at the wicket off the first ball of the match. Ransford and Smith fell to Macartney's first and third balls at the other end and Kortlang, who was dismissed in Cotter's second over, had to be assisted from the field after being struck just above the knee. Armstrong (51 in 90 minutes, 8 fours) and Hartkopf (42 not out in 122 minutes, 3 fours, chance at 0) led a partial recovery. Bardsley received a severe blow in the rib cage at 1/81 from Macrow's first ball of the match and retired at 2/103. Kelleway was run out in 16 minutes and hit 6 fours. Waddy was run out without facing a ball. Kortlang (67 in 107 minutes, 6 fours) and Matthews (65 in 49 minutes, 8 fours) bolstered the second innings. H.V.Hordern was unavailable for New South Wales and R.B.Minnett was made 12th man because of a foot injury sustained at practice before the match. Sources: *Wisden, NSWCA Report, VCA Report, The Age, The Argus, The Herald, The Australasian.*

VICTORIA

J.A.Seitz	c Carter b Cotter	0	c Carter b Cotter		10
H.H.L.Kortlang	lbw b Cotter	0	c Carter b Emery		67
V.S.Ransford	c & b Macartney	1	c Trumper b Cotter		2
D.B.M.Smith	b Macartney	0	b Emery		22
*W.W.Armstrong	c Bardsley b Kelleway	51	c Carter b Cotter		16
T.J.Matthews	c Carter b Cotter	16	b Kelleway		65
N.E.Brown	b Cotter	6	not out		26
A.E.V.Hartkopf	not out	42	b Kelleway		0
J.H.Kyle	c Trumper b Kelleway	17	c Carter b Cotter		0
†W.Carkeek	st Carter b Macartney	21	b Cotter		0
W.R.F.Macrow	b Kelleway	2	b Cotter		0
Extras	(b5, lb1, nb4)	10	(b1, lb3, w1, nb4)		9
Total	(62.2 overs, 197 mins)	166	(46.2 overs, 152 mins)		217

NEW SOUTH WALES

†H.Carter	lbw b Armstrong	9			
S.H.Emery	c Kyle b Macrow	43			
W.Bardsley	retired hurt	34			
C.Kelleway	st Carkeek b Hartkopf	101			
*V.T.Trumper	c Hartkopf b Matthews	58			
S.E.Gregory	c sub (E.L.Spencer) b Matthews	39			
C.G.Macartney	st Carkeek b Matthews	6	(1) not out		28
E.P.Barbour	lbw b Hartkopf	27			
A.Cotter	c Brown b Kyle	10			
E.L.Waddy	run out (Macrow/Carkeek)	0	(2) not out		15
G.R.Hazlitt	not out	0			
Extras	(b1, lb6, w2, nb5)	14			-
Total	(98.0 overs, 290 mins)	341	(6.0 overs, 17 mins) (0 wkts)		43

NEW SOUTH WALES	O	M	R	W	w,nb		O	M	R	W	w,nb
Cotter	17	6	38	4	-,3		17.2	2	86	6	1,2
Macartney	29	11	68	3	-,1		7	2	17	0	-,1
Kelleway	14.2	5	42	3	-,-	(5)	7	1	32	2	-,1
Emery	2	0	8	0	-,-		9	0	50	2	-,-
Hazlitt						(3)	6	2	23	0	-,-

VICTORIA	O	M	R	W	w,nb		O	M	R	W	w,nb
Kyle	33	6	109	1	-,-						
Armstrong	11	4	24	1	-,-	(1)	3	0	28	0	-,-
Matthews	22	6	63	3	-,-						
Macrow	19	3	87	1	2,5	(2)	3	0	15	0	-,-
Brown	5	1	24	0	-,-						
Hartkopf	8	1	20	2	-,-						

FALL OF WICKETS

Wkt	VIC 1st	NSW 1st	VIC 2nd	NSW 2nd
1st	0	11	16	-
2nd	1	85	21	-
3rd	1	180	73	-
4th	1	253	114	-
5th	36	265	135	-
6th	50	322	206	-
7th	86	335	211	-
8th	116	339	213	-
9th	161	341	213	-
10th	166	-	217	-

AUSTRALIA v ENGLAND (2nd Test)

Played at Melbourne Cricket Ground on December 30, 1911, January 1, 2, 3, 1912. (Timeless match)
Toss : Australia,   Result : ENGLAND WON BY EIGHT WICKETS.
Debuts: England - J.W.Hitch, E.J.Smith (both Test).
12th Men: C.G.Macartney (Aust) and S.Kinneir (Eng).
Umpires: R.M.Crockett and D.A.Elder.
Attendances: 26391, 31453, 20093, 18518.   Total: 96,455.   Receipts: £4353.
Close of Play: 1st day Eng 1/38 (Rhodes 16, Hearne 12); 2nd day Eng 265 all out; 3rd day Aust (2) 8/269 (Cotter 18, Carter 12).

The 38-year-old Barnes bowled Bardsley with his first delivery of the match and returned 4 for 1 from 7 overs in his opening spell. Resuming after lunch - the first session was briefly shortened by rain - he took the wicket of Minnett to have 5 for 6 from 11 overs (7 maidens). He was advised by the crowd to "bowl up" when adjusting his field during the lunch-tea session and in response he threw the ball on the ground in protest, but was persuaded by his team-mates to continue; only a minute or two was lost. Barnes's bowling was outstanding throughout the match. "at no stage was it anything like loose (*Age*). Ransford (43 in 90 minutes, 2 fours) and Hordern (49 not out in 141 minutes, 6 fours) were the top scorers on the first day. Hearne, at 20 years and 324 minutes of age, was the youngest batsman to score a Test hundred for England in Australia (a chanceless 114 in 225 minutes with 11 fours). He put on 127 with Rhodes (61 in 130 minutes, 4 fours) for the second wicket. Armstrong (90 in 148 minutes, 14 fours) batted determinedly in Australia's second innings. Hobbs (chanceless 126 not out in 207 minutes, 8 fours) steered England to victory with the first of his 12 Test centuries against Australia. He "never looked like getting out" (*Age*). Sources: *Wisden, VCA Report, The Age, The Argus, The Herald, The Australasian.*

AUSTRALIA

C.Kelleway	lbw b Barnes	2		c Gunn b Foster	13
W.Bardsley	b Barnes	0		run out (Hobbs)	16
*C.Hill	b Barnes	4		c Gunn b Barnes	0
W.W.Armstrong	c Smith b Barnes	4		b Foster	90
V.T.Trumper	b Foster	13		b Barnes	2
V.S.Ransford	c Smith b Hitch	43		c Smith b Foster	32
R.B.Minnett	c Hobbs b Barnes	2	(8)	b Foster	34
H.V.Hordern	not out	49	(7)	c Mead b Foster	31
A.Cotter	run out (Hearne/Woolley)	14		c Hobbs b Foster	41
†H.Carter	c Smith b Douglas	29		b Barnes	16
W.J.Whitty	b Woolley	14		not out	0
Extras	(b5, lb4, nb1)	10		(b14, lb7, w1, nb2)	24
Total	(62.1 overs, 222 mins)	184		(91.1 overs, 296 mins)	299

ENGLAND

W.Rhodes	c Trumper b Cotter	61		c Carter b Cotter	28
J.B.Hobbs	c Carter b Cotter	6		not out	126
J.W.Hearne	c Carter b Cotter	114	(4)	not out	12
G.Gunn	lbw b Armstrong	10	(3)	c Carter b Whitty	43
C.P.Mead	c Armstrong b Whitty	11			
F.R.Foster	c Hill b Cotter	9			
*J.W.H.T.Douglas	b Hordern	9			
F.E.Woolley	c Ransford b Hordern	23			
†E.J.Smith	b Hordern	5			
S.F.Barnes	lbw b Hordern	1			
J.W.Hitch	not out	0			
Extras	(b2, lb10, nb4)	16		(b5, lb5)	10
Total	(98.1 overs, 305 mins)	265		(67.1 overs, 207 mins) (2 wkts)	219

ENGLAND	O	M	R	W	w,nb		O	M	R	W	w,nb		FALL OF WICKETS			
Foster	16	2	52	1	-,-		38	9	91	6	1,-			AUST	ENG	AUST	ENG
Barnes	23	9	44	5	-,-		32.1	7	96	3	-,1		Wkt	1st	1st	2nd	2nd
Hitch	7	0	37	1	-,1	(6)	5	0	21	0	-,1		1st	0	10	28	57
Douglas	15	4	33	1	-,-	(3)	10	0	38	0	-,-		2nd	5	137	34	169
Hearne	1	0	8	0	-,-	(4)	1	0	5	0	-,-		3rd	8	174	34	-
Woolley	0.1	0	0	1	-,-	(5)	3	0	21	0	-,-		4th	11	213	38	-
Rhodes							2	1	3	0	-,-		5th	33	224	135	-
													6th	38	227	168	-
AUSTRALIA	O	M	R	W	w,nb		O	M	R	W	w,nb		7th	80	258	232	-
Cotter	21	2	73	4	-,3		14	5	45	1	-,-		8th	97	260	235	-
Whitty	19	2	47	1	-,-		18	3	37	0	-,-		9th	140	262	298	-
Hordern	23.1	1	66	4	-,-		17	0	66	0	-,-		10th	184	265	299	-
Kelleway	15	7	27	0	-,-	(5)	7	0	15	0	-,-						
Armstrong	15	4	20	1	-,-	(4)	8	1	22	0	-,-						
Minnett	5	0	16	0	-,1		2	0	13	0	-,-						
Ransford							1.1	0	11	0	-,-						

SOUTH AUSTRALIA v NEW SOUTH WALES (Shield Match 5)

Played at Adelaide Oval on January 6, 8, 9, 10, 1912. (Timeless match)
Toss : South Australia.   Result : NEW SOUTH WALES WON BY EIGHT WICKETS.
Debuts: South Australia - C.F.Drew, J.T.Murray, D.M.Steele (all f/c).
12th Men: E.J.Long (NSW). No 12th named for SA.
Umpires: F.J.C.Thomas and G.A.Watson.
Attendances: 4000, 2500, 1500, 500.   Total: About 8500.   Receipts: £280.
Close of Play: 1st day NSW 1/19 (Barbour 7, Emery 5); 2nd day NSW 4/312 (Bardsley 104, Minnett 39); 3rd day SA (2) 5/152
          (Murray 25).

New South Wales rested their regular wicket-keeper, H.Carter, for the Test match which immediately followed and, somewhat surprisingly, also left out their No. 2 keeper, Long, for part-timer Waddy. Dolling topscored in both South Australian innings, making 105 (196 minutes, 12 fours) and 66 (105 minutes, 6 fours). Barbour (122 in 244 minutes, 14 fours), missed at 2, put on 140 for the fourth wicket with Bardsley (177 in 235 minutes, 19 fours, chance at 116), who in turn added 190 with Minnett (87 in 117 minutes, 14 fours) for the fifth wicket. Emery caught a team-mate, Hazlitt, while fielding for Mayne on the third day. Stirling's pair included a second-ball dismissal in the second innings. Sources: *Wisden, C.B.O'Reilly, NSWCA Report, SACA Report, Adelaide Advertiser, South Australian Register.*

SOUTH AUSTRALIA

R.E.Mayne	c Bardsley b Kelleway	22	b Hazlitt		29
C.E.Dolling	b Cotter	105	lbw b Emery		66
*C.Hill	b Emery	10	c Bardsley b Emery		1
J.N.Crawford	b Emery	9	c Kelleway b Hazlitt		0
D.M.Steele	b Emery	16	b Cotter		6
J.T.Murray	b Cotter	48	b Emery		36
C.F.Drew	b Cotter	18	b Hazlitt		9
K.H.Quist	c Hazlitt b Kelleway	1	not out		44
W.S.Stirling	b Kelleway	0	b Emery		0
†H.W.Webster	b Cotter	2	b Cotter		39
W.J.Whitty	not out	3	b Kelleway		14
Extras	(b9, lb9, nb9)	27	(b31, lb7, w1, nb3)		42
Total	(72.4 overs, 236 mins)	261	(72.2 overs, 228 mins)		286

NEW SOUTH WALES

E.P.Barbour	c Murray b Stirling	122			
†E.L.Waddy	b Crawford	5			
S.H.Emery	c Webster b Whitty	23	(1) b Whitty		5
C.Kelleway	c & b Crawford	11			
W.Bardsley	c Webster b Hill	177			
R.B.Minnett	b Quist	87			
G.R.Hazlitt	c sub (S.H.Emery) b Crawford	9			
S.E.Gregory	b Crawford	2	(3) not out		13
*V.T.Trumper	not out	21	(4) not out		1
C.G.Macartney	c Drew b Crawford	18			
A.Cotter	c Dolling b Crawford	37	(2) c Quist b Crawford		9
Extras	(b4, lb4)	8			---
Total	(144.0 overs, 441 mins)	520	(6.0 overs, 20 mins) (2 wkts)		28

NEW SOUTH WALES	O	M	R	W	w,nb		O	M	R	W	w,nb
Cotter	15.4	0	67	4	-,6		18	1	90	2	-,3
Kelleway	24	10	44	3	-,3		10.2	1	34	1	-,-
Hazlitt	14	3	35	0	-,-	(4)	25	5	66	3	-,-
Emery	12	0	63	3	-,-	(5)	18	3	47	4	1,-
Minnett	7	1	25	0	-,-	(3)	1	0	7	0	-,-

SOUTH AUSTRALIA	O	M	R	W	w,nb		O	M	R	W	w,nb
Whitty	49	17	147	1	-,-		3	0	10	1	-,-
Crawford	52	11	141	6	-,-		3	1	18	1	-,-
Stirling	18	3	80	1	-,-						
Murray	8	0	51	0	-,-						
Quist	7	0	36	1	-,-						
Mayne	3	0	18	0	-,-						
Dolling	2	0	23	0	-,-						
Hill	5	1	16	1	-,-						

FALL OF WICKETS

Wkt	SA 1st	NSW 1st	SA 2nd	NSW 2nd
1st	49	8	69	11
2nd	63	40	74	21
3rd	79	91	86	-
4th	105	231	113	-
5th	213	421	152	-
6th	218	441	171	-
7th	239	442	177	-
8th	245	445	177	-
9th	254	475	263	-
10th	261	520	286	-

AUSTRALIA v ENGLAND (3rd Test)

Played at Adelaide Oval on January 12, 13, 15, 16, 17, 1912. (Timeless match)
Toss : Australia.   Result : ENGLAND WON BY SEVEN WICKETS.
Debuts: Australia - T.J.Matthews (Test).
12th Men: C.G.Macartney (Aust) and J.Vine (Eng).
Umpires: R.M.Crockett and G.A.Watson.
Attendances: 7000, 12000, 6000, 6500, 4500.   Total: 36,350.   Receipts: £1797.
Close of Play: 1st day Eng 0/49 (Hobbs 29, Rhodes 20); 2nd day Eng 4/327 (Mead 31, Foster 0); 3rd day Aust (2) 1/96 (Bardsley 46, Carter 4); 4th day Aust (2) 5/360 (Minnett 38, Hordern 3).

Australia were bowled out on a perfect first-day wicket for 133 in 197 minutes. Ransford (6) retired at 2/17 after being struck on the thumb by Foster; he resumed at 8/113. Hobbs (187 in 334 minutes, 16 fours) and Rhodes (59 in 159 minutes, 5 fours) saw England to a lead with their first-wicket stand. Hobb's dismissal - he was caught at point after giving chances at 116, 118, 158, 170 and 173 - ended the first unbroken sequence of 300 runs or more in Test cricket by a batsman. Mead, Vine and Macartney all fielded as substitutes at various times in the England first innings in the absence of Trumper, who injured a leg while fielding, and Ransford. Carter (72 in 176 minutes, 8 fours) and Hill (98 in 155 minutes, 11 fours) shared a third-wicket stand of 157 in 126 minutes in the second innings. Matthews (53 in 114 minutes, 5 fours) batted well on debut. Other half-centuries were scored by Bardsley (63 in 128 minutes, 5 fours) and, for England, Foster (71 in 134 minutes, 6 fours) and Rhodes (57 not out in 120 minutes, 6 fours). Sources: *Wisden, SACA Report, The Age, Sydney Morning Herald, Adelaide Advertiser, South Australian Register.*

AUSTRALIA

W.Bardsley	c Smith b Barnes	5		b Foster	63
C.Kelleway	b Foster	1		b Douglas	37
H.V.Hordern	c Rhodes b Foster	25	(7)	c & b Barnes	5
V.S.Ransford	not out	8	(8)	b Hitch	38
W.W.Armstrong	b Foster	33		b Douglas	25
V.T.Trumper	b Hitch	26	(11)	not out	1
*C.Hill	st Smith b Foster	0	(4)	c Hitch b Barnes	98
R.B.Minnett	b Foster	0	(6)	c Hobbs b Barnes	38
T.J.Matthews	c Mead b Barnes	5		b Barnes	53
A.Cotter	b Barnes	11		b Barnes	15
†H.Carter	c Gunn b Douglas	8	(3)	c Smith b Woolley	72
Extras	(b3, lb6, nb2)	11		(b26, lb3, nb2)	31
Total	(60.0 overs, 197 mins)	133		(153.4 overs, 497 mins)	476

ENGLAND

J.B.Hobbs	c Hordern b Minnett	187	lbw b Hordern	3
W.Rhodes	lbw b Cotter	59	not out	57
G.Gunn	c Hill b Cotter	29	c Cotter b Kelleway	45
J.W.Hearne	c Hill b Kelleway	12	c Kelleway b Matthews	2
C.P.Mead	c & b Hordern	46	not out	2
F.R.Foster	b Armstrong	71		
*J.W.H.T.Douglas	b Minnett	35		
F.E.Woolley	b Cotter	20		
†E.J.Smith	c sub (J.Vine) b Cotter	22		
S.F.Barnes	not out	2		
J.W.Hitch	c sub (C.G.Macartney) b Hordern	0		
Extras	(b7, lb8, nb3)	18	(b1, lb1, nb1)	3
Total	(177.1 overs, 514 mins)	501	(42.2 overs, 120 mins) (3 wkts)	112

ENGLAND	O	M	R	W	w,nb		O	M	R	W	w,nb
Foster	26	9	36	5	-,2		49	15	103	1	-,1
Barnes	23	4	71	3	-,-		46.4	7	105	5	-,-
Douglas	7	2	7	1	-,-		29	10	71	2	-,-
Hearne	2	0	6	0	-,-		10	0	61	0	-,-
Hitch	2	1	2	1	-,-		11	0	69	1	-,-
Woolley							7	1	30	1	-,1
Rhodes							1	0	6	0	-,-

AUSTRALIA	O	M	R	W	w,nb		O	M	R	W	w,nb
Cotter	43	11	125	4	-,3		5	0	21	0	-,-
Hordern	47.1	4	143	2	-,-		11	3	32	1	-,-
Kelleway	23	3	46	1	-,-	(6)	7	3	8	1	-,-
Matthews	33	8	72	0	-,-	(5)	9.2	3	24	1	-,-
Minnett	17	3	54	2	-,-	(4)	4	1	12	0	-,1
Armstrong	14	0	43	1	-,-	(3)	6	1	12	0	-,-

FALL OF WICKETS

Wkt	AUST 1st	ENG 1st	AUST 2nd	ENG 2nd
1st	6	147	86	5
2nd	6	206	122	102
3rd	65	260	279	105
4th	84	323	303	-
5th	88	350	342	-
6th	88	435	360	-
7th	97	455	363	-
8th	113	492	447	-
9th	123	501	475	-
10th	133	501	476	-

TASMANIA v M.C.C.

Played at N.T.C.A. Ground, Launceston, on January 23, 24, 25, 1912. (Three-day match)
Toss : Tasmania.   Result : MCC WON BY EIGHT WICKETS.
Debuts: Tasmania - L.L.Gill, L.R.Tumilty, N.H.Vincent (all f/c).
12th Men: E.W.Harrison (Tas). No 12th named for MCC.
Umpires: H.James and T.Neuman.
Attendances & Receipts: No figures published.
Close of Play: 1st day Tas 217 all out; 2nd day Tas (2) 1/37 (Gill 18, Vincent 5).

Play did not start on the first day until 2.10pm because the ship carrying the Englishmen had arrived only that morning. Notable innings for Tasmania were made by Martin (48 in 83 minutes, 9 fours), McKenzie (59 in 129 minutes) and Tumilty (56 in 72 minutes, 6 fours). Mead batted about 150 minutes and hit 1 six and 10 fours. Gill was denied the wicket of Woolley with his second ball in first-class cricket when Thomas missed a chance behind the wicket. Hawson topscored in the second innings for Tasmania with 36 not out in 156 minutes (4 fours). *Wisden* incorrectly gives Tas (1) Hearne 2/66. Sources: *Wisden, Launceston Examiner, Launceston Daily Telegraph, Hobart Mercury*.

TASMANIA

R.J.Hawson	c Strudwick b Iremonger	13	(4)	not out	36
C.W.B.Martin	b Hitch	48	(5)	run out (Hitch/Strudwick)	0
M.S.McKenzie	c Strudwick b Hearne	59	(6)	c Kinneir b Barnes	26
G.D.Paton	b Hitch	0	(9)	b Hearne	7
L.R.Tumilty	run out (Hitch/Strudwick)	56	(7)	b Hitch	16
*E.A.C.Windsor	b Hearne	7	(8)	c Woolley b Hitch	4
W.K.Eltham	c Strudwick b Iremonger	13	(1)	c Mead b Hearne	11
N.H.Vincent	c Woolley b Iremonger	7	(3)	c Strudwick b Hearne	29
†L.Thomas	lbw b Iremonger	0	(10)	c Barnes b Woolley	2
T.H.Elliott	c & b Iremonger	0	(11)	b Woolley	0
L.L.Gill	not out	2	(2)	b Hearne	28
Extras	(b9, lb2, nb1)	12		(lb3, w1, nb2)	6
Total	(65.2 overs, 199 mins)	217		(81.5 overs, 212 mins)	165

M.C.C.

S.F.Barnes	c Thomas b Windsor	35			
S.Kinneir	lbw b Windsor	16			
C.P.Mead	b McKenzie	98			
F.E.Woolley	c McKenzie b Windsor	45			
J.Iremonger	b Martin	31			
W.Rhodes	c Elliott b McKenzie	14	(4)	not out	13
J.Vine	b Martin	1	(2)	c Gill b Windsor	1
J.W.Hearne	c Paton b Martin	13	(3)	not out	34
*F.R.Foster	c Gill b Martin	12	(1)	b Paton	8
J.W.Hitch	not out	33			
†H.Strudwick	run out (Vincent/Thomas)	28			
Extras	(b4, lb2)	6			-
Total	(69.0 overs, 239 mins)	332		(13.2 overs, 37 mins) (2 wkts)	56

MCC	O	M	R	W	w,nb		O	M	R	W	w,nb		FALL OF WICKETS			
														TAS	MCC	TAS	MCC
Iremonger	20.2	5	52	5	-,-	(2)	27	15	32	0	-,-	Wkt	1st	1st	2nd	2nd
Hitch	20	4	43	2	-,-	(5)	12	1	26	2	1,1	1st	38	49	16	4
Woolley	3	0	22	0	-,1	(6)	1.5	0	3	2	-,1	2nd	83	58	67	14
Vine	2	0	15	0	-,-							3rd	83	127	74	-
Rhodes	11	2	40	0	-,-							4th	186	212	74	-
Hearne	9	2	33	2	-,-	(3)	26	4	66	4	-,-	5th	192	240	119	-
Foster						(1)	4	1	12	0	-,-	6th	199	241	140	-
Barnes						(4)	11	5	20	1	-,-	7th	206	245	148	-
												8th	206	269	162	-
TASMANIA	O	M	R	W	w,nb		O	M	R	W	w,nb	9th	206	272	165	-
Paton	12	2	46	0	-,-		7	0	16	1	-,-	10th	217	332	165	-
McKenzie	17	1	65	2	-,-											
Windsor	12	0	40	3	-,-	(2)	5	0	23	1	-,-					
Martin	19	1	127	4	-,-	(3)	1.2	0	17	0	-,-					
Elliott	3	0	15	0	-,-											
Gill	6	0	33	0	-,-											

TASMANIA v M.C.C.

Played at T.C.A. Ground, Hobart, on January 26, 27, 29, 1912. (Three-day match)
Toss : Tasmania.　　　　　　Result : MCC WON BY AN INNINGS AND 95 RUNS.
Debuts: Nil.
12th Men: A.C.Newton (Tas). No 12th named for MCC.
Umpires: T.Harper and A.Williams.
Attendances: No figures published.　　　Receipts: £146.
Close of Play: 1st day MCC 1/191 (Rhodes 71, Woolley 79); 2nd day Tas (2) 3/113 (Hudson 35).

Woolley's 305 not out in 229 minutes included 2 sixes and 43 fours and a chance at 72. It remains the highest first-class innings scored in Tasmania and has been surpassed only by M.C.Cowdrey's 307 v South Australia in 1962-63 among Englishmen touring Australia. Listed to bat at no. 9, Woolley disobeyed his captain by going out to bat when the first wicket fell. He reached 50 in 24 minutes, 100 in 84 minutes, 200 in 154 minutes and 300 in 219 minutes and along the way shared partnerships of 206 in 100 minutes with Rhodes (102 in 148 minutes, 11 fours) and a whirlwind 264 in 100 minutes with Hearne (97 in 100 minutes, 1 six and 12 fours). Woolley's innings included 117 out of 202 before lunch on the second day, and not one of the 88 completed overs bowled by the Tasmanians was a maiden. Eltham, who was out to the first ball of the match, retired at 6/346 in the second innings when he was struck on the hand by a ball from Hitch; a subsequent examination revealed several broken bones. Martin (54 in 107 minutes, 8 fours), Hudson (51 in 140 minutes, 8 fours), Paton (112 in 215 minutes, 16 fours) and Boddam (52 in 43 minutes, 9 fours) were responsible for Tasmania achieving a credible second-innings total. *Wisden* incorrectly gives MCC McKenzie 1/65 Tas (2) Carroll 4, extras 35. Sources: *Wisden, Launceston Examiner, Launceston Daily Telegraph, Hobart Mercury.*

TASMANIA

W.K.Eltham	c Foster b Barnes	0	(8) retired hurt	0
M.S.McKenzie	c Barnes b Hitch	0	(6) lbw b Vine	29
C.W.B.Martin	b Hitch	12	(2) c Rhodes b Foster	54
*R.J.Hawson	c Barnes b Foster	13	(1) b Barnes	9
J.L.Hudson	b Hitch	14	(4) b Vine	51
E.A.C.Windsor	b Hitch	24	(3) b Foster	4
G.D.Paton	c Vine b Hearne	22	(5) c Rhodes b Hitch	112
F.E.Chancellor	c Strudwick b Iremonger	9	(9) b Hitch	0
T.D.Carroll	b Hearne	5	(10) not out	3
E.T.Boddam	not out	8	(7) b Hitch	52
†H.Parkinson	b Hearne	2	c Foster b Hitch	5
Extras	(b11, lb2, nb2)	15	(b19, lb14, nb3)	36
Total	(49.3 overs, 165 mins)	124	(113.1 overs, 355 mins)	355

M.C.C.

S.Kinneir	lbw b Paton	26
W.Rhodes	b Martin	102
F.E.Woolley	not out	305
J.W.Hearne	c Boddam b Eltham	97
*F.R.Foster	c Hudson b Carroll	21
C.P.Mead	)	
J.Iremonger	)	
J.Vine	) did not bat	
†H.Strudwick	)	
S.F.Barnes	)	
J.W.Hitch	)	
Extras	(b14, lb5, w4)	23
Total	(88.2 overs, 270 mins) (4 wkts dec)	574

MCC	O	M	R	W	w,nb		O	M	R	W	w,nb
Barnes	8	2	16	1	-,-		15	3	36	1	-,-
Hitch	18	3	41	4	-,2	(4)	15.1	5	42	4	-,1
Hearne	8.3	3	12	3	-,-		22	1	88	0	-,-
Foster	4	1	14	1	-,-	(2)	27	6	60	2	-,-
Iremonger	11	3	26	1	-,-		14	8	23	0	-,-
Vine							11	3	36	2	-,-
Woolley							9	4	34	0	-,2

TASMANIA	O	M	R	W	w,nb
Carroll	19.2	0	83	1	-,-
Windsor	18	0	112	0	4,-
Paton	11	0	86	1	-,-
Boddam	11	0	66	0	-,-
McKenzie	11	0	65	0	-,-
Martin	11	0	76	1	-,-
Chancellor	4	0	39	0	-,-
Eltham	3	0	24	1	-,-

FALL OF WICKETS

Wkt	TAS 1st	MCC 1st	TAS 2nd
1st	0	62	18
2nd	2	268	25
3rd	19	532	113
4th	36	574	180
5th	61	-	260
6th	72	-	346
7th	87	-	346
8th	110	-	347
9th	119	-	355
10th	124	-	-

NEW SOUTH WALES v VICTORIA (Shield Match 6)

Played at Sydney Cricket Ground on January 26, 27, 29, 1912. (Timeless match)
Toss : Victoria.   Result : NEW SOUTH WALES WON BY SEVEN WICKETS.
Debuts: New South Wales - C.G.McKew (f/c). Victoria - E.A.McDonald (Vic only).
12th Men: B.J.Folkard (NSW) and E.L.Spencer (Vic).
Umpires: R.Callaway and A.C.Jones.
Attendances: 7150, 5732, 219.   Total: 13,101.   Receipts: £561.
Close of Play: 1st day NSW 7/240 (Minnett 65, Cotter 58); 2nd day Vic (2) 6/176 (McKenzie 51, McDonald 3).

H.Carter, H.V.Hordern and V.T.Trumper (injured) were unavailable for New South Wales and V.S.Ransford for Victoria. Minnett scored a career-best 216 not out in 197 minutes, hitting 3 sixes and 27 fours. He survived chances at 148 and 170 and shared in two quick partnerships in the late order for New South Wales - 108 in 39 minutes for the eighth wicket with Cotter (79 including 6 sixes and 5 fours) and 169 in 83 minutes for the tenth wicket (a new State record) with McKew. McKenzie (121 in 164 minutes, 21 fours) and Armstrong (60 not out in 81 minutes, 12 fours) topscored for Victoria. Matthews (muscle strain) and Armstrong (ill) batted late in the order due to their indispositions. McDonald, a native-born Tasmanian, had played two matches for the State before moving to Victoria in 1911. *Wisden* incorrectly gives NSW (2) McDonald 1/42. Sources: *Wisden, NSWCA Report, VCA Report, Sydney Referee, Sydney Morning Herald.*

VICTORIA

J.A.Seitz	c McKew b Cotter	4		b Hazlitt	19
H.H.L.Kortlang	c Barbour b Cotter	14		c Gregory b Emery	29
T.J.Matthews	c Waddy b Hazlitt	7	(9)	b Emery	24
D.B.M.Smith	b Emery	20		c McKew b Hazlitt	15
*W.W.Armstrong	b Kelleway	51	(10)	not out	60
N.E.Brown	c McKew b Kelleway	6	(5)	b Cotter	31
C.McKenzie	b Emery	4	(6)	c Minnett b Hazlitt	121
A.E.V.Hartkopf	b Kelleway	17	(3)	b Cotter	5
J.H.Kyle	c Bardsley b Hazlitt	0	(7)	lbw b Cotter	0
E.A.McDonald	c & b Hazlitt	1	(8)	b Cotter	7
†W.Carkeek	not out	3		b Cotter	28
Extras	(lb2)	2		(b9, lb13, w1, nb4)	27
Total	(40.5 overs, 131 mins)	129		(96.0 overs, 282 mins)	366

NEW SOUTH WALES

*S.E.Gregory	lbw b Armstrong	48	(3)	lbw b Brown	18
W.Bardsley	c Armstrong b McDonald	23	(5)	not out	6
C.G.Macartney	c Carkeek b Brown	15	(4)	not out	10
E.P.Barbour	c Carkeek b Kyle	6			
R.B.Minnett	not out	216			
C.Kelleway	b Armstrong	0			
E.L.Waddy	b Armstrong	0	(1)	b Brown	3
S.H.Emery	b Armstrong	22	(2)	b McDonald	11
A.Cotter	b Armstrong	79			
G.R.Hazlitt	c & b Kyle	0			
†C.G.McKew	run out (Smith/McDonald)	29			
Extras	(b7, lb3)	10		(lb1, w1)	2
Total	(85.4 overs, 269 mins)	448		(9.0 overs, 30 mins) (3 wkts)	50

NEW SOUTH WALES	O	M	R	W	w,nb		O	M	R	W	w,nb		FALL OF WICKETS			
Cotter	9	3	17	2	-,-		27	4	110	5	-,4			VIC	NSW	VIC	NSW
Hazlitt	13.5	2	50	3	-,-		29	5	90	3	-,-		Wkt	1st	1st	2nd	2nd
Emery	9	1	42	2	-,-		16	2	62	2	-,-		1st	14	35	25	3
Kelleway	9	3	18	3	-,-		20	4	65	0	-,-		2nd	25	56	38	25
Macartney							2	0	6	0	-,-		3rd	27	93	78	34
Minnett							2	0	6	0	1,-		4th	58	93	78	-
													5th	77	100	160	-
VICTORIA	O	M	R	W	w,nb		O	M	R	W	w,nb		6th	96	100	160	-
McDonald	19.4	3	74	1	-,-		5	0	24	1	1,-		7th	122	170	180	-
Matthews	4	0	17	0	-,-								8th	125	278	232	-
Brown	13	1	66	1	-,-	(2)	4	0	24	2	-,-		9th	126	279	283	-
Kyle	18	3	109	2	-,-								10th	129	448	366	-
Armstrong	20	1	104	5	-,-												
Hartkopf	8	1	48	0	-,-												
McKenzie	3	1	20	0	-,-												

VICTORIA v M.C.C.

Played at Melbourne Cricket Ground on February 2, 3, 5, 6, 1912. (Four-day match)
Toss : MCC   Result : MCC WON BY EIGHT WICKETS.
Debuts: Victoria - F.A.Baring, E.L.Spencer (both f/c).
12th Men: J.H.Kyle (Vic) and J.Vine (MCC).
Umpires: R.M.Crockett and W.Hannah.
Attendances: 1906, 4537, 2159, 599.   Total: 9201.   Receipts: £290.
Close of Play: 1st day MCC 5/293 (Hearne 125, Douglas 58); 2nd day Vic 6/84 (McDonald 4); 3rd day Vic (2) 5/132 (McKenzie 51, Armstrong 14).

The match was staged as a benefit for J.M.Blackham, then aged 57, and raised £1359. Due to a thumb injury, V.S.Ransford was replaced in the Victorian side by Seitz. Matthews was absent after MCC's first innings because of the death of his young son. Centuries were scored by Hearne (143 in 228 minutes, 20 fours) and Douglas (140 in 327 minutes, 1 five and 14 fours) for the tourists, while McKenzie (78 in 165 minutes, 7 fours) and Armstrong (120 not out in 135 minutes, 17 fours) made the highest scores for Victoria after Baring was given out to the first ball of the second innings. *VCA Report* incorrectly gives MCC (1) Mead 3, Hitch 0; Vic (1) Barnes 4/28, Hitch 3/56. Sources: *Wisden, VCA Report, The Age, The Argus, The Herald, The Australasian*.

M.C.C.

J.B.Hobbs	b Brown	29			
W.Rhodes	c Armstrong b Scott	16		not out	22
G.Gunn	b McDonald	29	(4)	not out	16
J.W.Hearne	b Matthews	143			
C.P.Mead	lbw b Brown	2	(1)	b McDonald	0
F.E.Woolley	b Matthews	21			
*J.W.H.T.Douglas	c Seitz b Scott	140			
†E.J.Smith	lbw b Brown	47			
J.Iremonger	c Armstrong b Scott	9	(3)	c Smith b Scott	3
S.F.Barnes	not out	4			
J.W.Hitch	c Brown b Matthews	1			
Extras	(b6, lb8, w12)	26		(lb1, w1)	2
Total	(154.3 overs, 449 mins)	467		(11.2 overs, 30 mins) (2 wkts)	43

VICTORIA

F.A.Baring	c Gunn b Hitch	11		lbw b Douglas	0
J.A.Seitz	lbw b Barnes	0		c sub (J.Vine) b Woolley	40
D.B.M.Smith	c & b Barnes	20		b Douglas	12
E.L.Spencer	b Barnes	18	(8)	c Smith b Hobbs	0
C.McKenzie	b Barnes	5		c Smith b Woolley	78
W.J.Scott	run out (Hobbs/Smith)	15	(4)	run out (Rhodes/Douglas)	0
E.A.McDonald	b Hitch	6	(10)	c Hobbs b Iremonger	38
*W.W.Armstrong	not out	51	(7)	not out	120
N.E.Brown	b Hearne	35	(6)	b Hitch	14
†W.Carkeek	c Smith b Hitch	19	(9)	b Woolley	0
T.J.Matthews	absent	-		absent	-
Extras	(b9, lb5, nb1)	15		(b10, lb2)	12
Total	(61.3 overs, 204 mins)	195		(79.3 overs, 253 mins)	314

VICTORIA	O	M	R	W	w,nb		O	M	R	W	w,nb
McDonald	32	4	106	1	2,-		5	0	19	1	-,-
Scott	37	8	100	3	8,-		5	1	11	1	1,-
Matthews	35.3	9	99	3	1,-						
Brown	31	3	100	3	1,-	(3)	1	0	8	0	-,-
McKenzie	3	0	10	0	-,-						
Spencer	14	6	24	0	-,-						
Seitz	1	0	2	0	-,-	(4)	0.2	0	3	0	-,-
Smith	1	1	0	0	-,-						

MCC	O	M	R	W	w,nb		O	M	R	W	w,nb
Barnes	14	5	26	4	-,-						
Hitch	16.3	2	58	3	-,1	(3)	10	1	38	1	-,-
Woolley	4	0	10	0	-,-	(4)	14	3	71	3	-,-
Iremonger	10	0	32	0	-,-	(2)	16.3	5	46	1	-,-
Hearne	8	0	36	1	-,-		4	0	31	0	-,-
Douglas	9	1	18	0	-,-	(1)	20	4	52	2	-,-
Hobbs						(6)	8	0	33	1	-,-
Rhodes						(7)	7	0	31	0	-,-

FALL OF WICKETS

	MCC	VIC	VIC	MCC
Wkt	1st	1st	2nd	2nd
1st	22	3	0	7
2nd	75	23	28	10
3rd	79	37	28	-
4th	90	49	71	-
5th	125	80	98	-
6th	239	84	236	-
7th	427	90	237	-
8th	456	156	246	-
9th	465	195	314	-
10th	467	-	-	-

AUSTRALIA v ENGLAND (4th Test)

Played at Melbourne Cricket Ground on February 9, 10, 12, 13, 1912. (Timeless match)
Toss : England.   Result : ENGLAND WON BY AN INNINGS AND 225 RUNS.
Debuts: England - J.Vine (Test).
12th Men: J.W.McLaren (Aust) and S.Kinneir (Eng).
Umpires: R.M.Crockett and W.A.Young.
Attendances: 16443, 31795, 13424, 12217.   Total: 73,879.   Receipts: £3021.
Close of Play: 1st day Eng 0/54 (Hobbs 30, Rhodes 23); 2nd day Eng 1/370 (Rhodes 157, Gunn 22); 3rd day Aust (2) 0/8 (Kelleway 2, Carter 5).

Rain during the two preceding days left a green-looking wicket and Douglas elected to field upon winning the toss. Although conditions on the first day were found to be never really difficult, England's advantage was strengthened by overnight rain after the third day which slowed the pace of the wicket and made batting arduous for the Australians in their second innings. The stand of 323 between Hobbs (178 in 268 minutes, 22 fours) and Rhodes (179 in 417 minutes, 14 fours) remained the first-wicket record in England-Australia tests until 1989. Both gave chances, Hobbs at 101, 126 and 178 (the ball prior to his dismissal) and Rhodes at 27, when Trumper at square-leg moved in quickly in anticipation of a stroke off Hordern's bowling, only for the ball to lob just over his head. Rhodes shared a further century partnership with Gunn (75 in 174 minutes, 6 fours) while Foster (50 in 82 minutes) and Woolley (56 in 76 minutes, 1 six and 4 fours) scored fifties. Douglas fell second ball. Minnett (56 in 80 minutes, 6 fours) topscored for Australia. Controversy surrounded McLaren's selection in the twelve. The Trades Hall Council called for a boycott of the Test in protest over McLaren's appointment as a special constable during a bitter strike by Brisbane wharf labourers. McLaren claimed he had not participated, and it is doubtful that the boycott would have been taken seriously by Melbourne patrons had he been included in the final side. England did not consider J.W.Hitch (slight strain) for selection. Sources: *Wisden, VCA Report, The Age, The Argus, The Herald, The Australasian.*

AUSTRALIA

H.V.Hordern	b Barnes	19	(11)	c Foster b Douglas	5
C.Kelleway	c Hearne b Woolley	29	(1)	c Smith b Barnes	5
W.Bardsley	b Foster	0		b Foster	3
V.T.Trumper	b Foster	17		b Barnes	28
*C.Hill	c Hearne b Barnes	22		b Douglas	11
W.W.Armstrong	b Barnes	7		b Douglas	11
R.B.Minnett	c Rhodes b Foster	56		b Douglas	7
V.S.Ransford	c Rhodes b Foster	4		not out	29
T.J.Matthews	c Gunn b Barnes	3	(10)	b Foster	10
A.Cotter	b Barnes	15	(9)	c Mead b Foster	8
†H.Carter	not out	6	(2)	c Hearne b Douglas	38
Extras	(b1, lb5, nb7)	13		(b9, lb2, nb7)	18
Total	(65.1 overs, 224 mins)	191		(61.5 overs, 210 mins)	173

ENGLAND

J.B.Hobbs	c Carter b Hordern	178
W.Rhodes	c Carter b Minnett	179
G.Gunn	c Hill b Armstrong	75
J.W.Hearne	c Armstrong b Minnett	0
F.R.Foster	c Hordern b Armstrong	50
*J.W.H.T.Douglas	c Bardsley b Armstrong	0
F.E.Woolley	c Kelleway b Minnett	56
C.P.Mead	b Hordern	21
J.Vine	not out	4
†E.J.Smith	c Matthews b Kelleway	7
S.F.Barnes	c Hill b Hordern	0
Extras	(b2, lb4, w4, nb9)	19
Total	(190.5 overs, 570 mins)	589

ENGLAND	O	M	R	W	w,nb		O	M	R	W	w,nb		FALL OF WICKETS			
Foster	22	2	77	4	-,5		19	3	38	3	-,7			AUST	ENG	AUST
Barnes	29.1	4	74	5	-,1		20	6	47	2	-,-	Wkt	1st	1st	2nd
Woolley	11	3	22	1	-,1	(5)	2	0	7	0	-,-	1st	53	323	12
Rhodes	2	1	1	0	-,-							2nd	53	425	20
Hearne	1	0	4	0	-,-	(4)	3	0	17	0	-,-	3rd	69	425	76
Douglas						(3)	17.5	6	46	5	-,-	4th	74	486	86
												5th	83	486	101
AUSTRALIA	O	M	R	W	w,nb							6th	124	513	112
Cotter	37	5	125	0	1,7							7th	152	565	117
Kelleway	26	2	80	1	-,2							8th	165	579	127
Armstrong	36	12	93	3	-,-							9th	170	589	156
Matthews	22	1	68	0	-,-							10th	191	589	173
Hordern	47.5	5	137	3	-,-										
Minnett	20	5	59	3	3,-										
Ransford	2	1	8	0	-,-										

NEW SOUTH WALES v M.C.C.

Played at Sydney Cricket Ground on February 16, 17, 19, 20, 1912. (Four-day match)
Toss : New South Wales.   Result : MCC WON BY EIGHT WICKETS.
Debuts: Nil.
12th Men: E.L.Waddy (NSW) and E.J.Smith (MCC).
Umpires: W.G.French and A.C.Jones.
Attendances: 6464, 11554, 4224, 2256.   Total: 24,498.   Receipts: £1121.
Close of Play: 1st day MCC 2/183 (Rhodes 88, Hearne 16); 2nd day NSW (2) 1/93 (Gregory 36, Bardsley 5); 3rd day NSW (2) 403 all out.

Rhodes became the second Englishman after A.C.MacLaren (1897-98) to register three centuries in consecutive innings in Australia. He scored 119 (208 minutes, 12 fours) and 109 (140 minutes, 15 fours) to follow his hundred in the Fourth Test at Melbourne. He was also the second touring batsman after MacLaren to make a hundred in each innings in this country. Gregory (186 not out in 346 minutes, 18 fours) carried his bat through the second innings, sharing an eighth-wicket stand of 144 with Emery (65 in 98 minutes, 11 fours) along the way. McKew was absent on the third day due to the death of his sister. In the absence of Waddy, T.J.E.Andrews substituted for Trumper on the last day. H.Carter, A.Cotter, H.V.Hordern and R.B.Minnett were all unavailable for New South Wales. *Wisden* incorrectly gives MCC (2) Scott 0/33, Barbour 0/6. Sources: *Wisden, NSWCA Report, Sydney Referee, Sydney Morning Herald.*

NEW SOUTH WALES

W.Bardsley	c Gunn b Foster	2	(3)	b Foster	8
H.L.Collins	b Foster	0	(7)	c Strudwick b Hobbs	3
S.E.Gregory	c Foster b Barnes	5	(2)	not out	186
C.G.Macartney	st Strudwick b Douglas	18		b Douglas	24
*V.T.Trumper	b Woolley	7	(1)	run out (Hobbs/Strudwick)	53
C.Kelleway	c Hobbs b Foster	9		b Hobbs	2
E.P.Barbour	b Foster	29	(5)	c Woolley b Hobbs	10
G.R.Hazlitt	c Douglas b Foster	7		c Woolley b Vine	12
S.H.Emery	c Woolley b Foster	4		b Foster	65
J.D.Scott	not out	13		c & b Hobbs	1
†C.G.McKew	b Foster	0		absent	-
Extras	(b6, lb1, nb5)	12		(b17, lb13, nb9)	39
Total	(44.3 overs, 145 mins)	106		(120.1 overs, 346 mins)	403

M.C.C.

J.B.Hobbs	c Hazlitt b Kelleway	38		c sub (T.J.E.Andrews) b Kelleway	14
W.Rhodes	c Kelleway b Hazlitt	119		c Collins b Kelleway	109
G.Gunn	c Kelleway b Hazlitt	27		not out	56
J.W.Hearne	c Emery b Hazlitt	32		not out	6
F.R.Foster	c & b Hazlitt	10			
*J.W.H.T.Douglas	run out (Bardsley)	5			
F.E.Woolley	b Hazlitt	3			
C.P.Mead	c Bardsley b Hazlitt	21			
J.Vine	c Kelleway b Hazlitt	22			
S.F.Barnes	c Kelleway b Hazlitt	10			
†H.Strudwick	not out	0			
Extras	(b18, lb7, w2, nb1)	28		(b9, w1)	10
Total	(96.3 overs, 290 mins)	315		(49.3 overs, 150 mins) (2 wkts)	195

MCC	O	M	R	W	w,nb		O	M	R	W	w,nb
Foster	19.3	6	36	7	-,5		30	8	53	2	-,8
Barnes	10	3	20	1	-,-		12	3	38	0	-,-
Douglas	12	2	34	1	-,-	(4)	28	5	76	1	-,-
Woolley	3	0	4	1	-,-	(3)	15	1	60	0	-,1
Vine							11	1	51	1	-,-
Hearne							4	0	16	0	-,-
Hobbs							9.1	3	25	4	-,-
Rhodes							11	1	45	0	-,-

NEW SOUTH WALES	O	M	R	W	w,nb		O	M	R	W	w,nb
Scott	19	1	66	0	1,-		7	2	32	0	-,-
Hazlitt	39	13	95	7	1,-		8	0	33	0	1,-
Macartney	6	0	26	0	-,-	(5)	5	1	14	0	-,-
Emery	15.3	1	49	1	-,-	(3)	9	1	35	0	-,-
Kelleway	17	5	51	1	-,1	(4)	14	4	42	2	-,-
Collins							5	0	22	0	-,-
Barbour							1.1	0	7	0	-,-

FALL OF WICKETS

Wkt	NSW 1st	MCC 1st	NSW 2nd	MCC 2nd
1st	2	94	81	47
2nd	7	157	100	184
3rd	16	213	182	-
4th	39	231	201	-
5th	41	251	217	-
6th	74	254	229	-
7th	83	269	257	-
8th	89	296	401	-
9th	106	315	403	-
10th	106	315	-	-

TASMANIA v VICTORIA

Played at N.T.C.A. Ground, Launceston, on February 16, 17, 19, 20, 1912. (Timeless match)
Toss : Tasmania.   Result : TASMANIA WON BY 2 RUNS.
Debuts: Tasmania - A.C.Newton, A.Thomlinson (both f/c). Victoria - R.L.Braid, J.C.Dwyer, A.E.Liddicut (all f/c).
12th Men: No 12th men or emergency fieldsmen named; only 11 men in Victorian party.
Umpires: H.C.George and H.R.Purse.
Attendances & Receipts: No figures published.
Close of Play: 1st day Tas 208 all out; 2nd day Tas (2) 1/100 (Thomlinson 38, Thomas 17); 3rd day Vic (2) 3/81 (Lampard 35).

Seven players - F.A.Baring, N.E.Brown, J.H.Kyle, H.C.A.Sandford, W.J.Scott, J.A.Seitz and D.B.M.Smith - withdrew from the selected Victorian team for various reasons. The replacements were Dwyer, Hartkopf, Healy, Lampard, McDonald and Warne, reducing the team to eleven. J.L.Hudson and G.D.Paton declined selection for Tasmania and Thomlinson replaced E.T.Boddam (unavailable). The match was scheduled to start on the 17th but as the Victorians travelled on the 14th the N.T.C.A. requested that it commence a day early, and the Victorians agreed. Fifties were scored by Windsor (52 in 80 minutes, 7 fours) for Tasmania and Warne (76 in 153 minutes, 8 fours), Facy (74 in 115 minutes, 1 six and 9 fours), Lampard (80 in 140 minutes, 11 fours) and Hartkopf (77 in 160 minutes) for Victoria. Purse was unable to officiate on the last day due to other commitments; L.Gatenby, the official scorer on the first three days, stood in his place. M.S.McKenzie and Westbrook were absent on the final day, local club players, Byfield and Dyer substituting. J.R.Byfield took a magnificent catch running in from third man to give Tasmania victory by a narrow margin. Last first-class appearance by E.A.C.Windsor. *Cricket* and *Mercury* give Vic (1) McDonald 3, total 218, Thomlinson 0/18; Tas (1) Tumilty 35, extras 15, Dwyer 0/31; but the scores here are believed correct. Sources: *Cricket, VCA Report, Launceston Examiner, Launceston Daily Telegraph, Hobart Mercury*.

TASMANIA

M.S.McKenzie	c Braid b McDonald	11	(9)	b Hartkopf	7
N.H.Vincent	b McDonald	9	(10)	c Woodford b Liddicut	0
C.W.B.Martin	c Liddicut b Hartkopf	43	(1)	st Woodford b Braid	42
*R.J.Hawson	c McDonald b McKenzie	8		b McKenzie	28
R.A.Westbrook	b Facy	29	(8)	lbw b Liddicut	41
L.R.Tumilty	b Facy	36	(5)	c Dwyer b Braid	12
E.A.C.Windsor	b Facy	16	(6)	lbw b Liddicut	52
L.L.Gill	c Lampard b Braid	11	(11)	not out	6
†L.Thomas	c Liddicut b Braid	24	(3)	b McDonald	42
A.Thomlinson	not out	7	(2)	c & b Braid	45
A.C.Newton	c & b Braid	0	(7)	st Woodford b Warne	16
Extras	(b9, lb2, w2, nb1)	14		(b11, lb12, w3, nb1)	27
Total	(57.5 overs, 188 mins)	208		(110.3 overs, 303 mins)	318

VICTORIA

C.McKenzie	b Martin	8		c & b Windsor	12
G.E.J.Healy	run out (Hawson/Thomas)	0	(6)	c Martin b Windsor	9
A.E.V.Hartkopf	c Martin b Windsor	6	(5)	run out (Vincent/Windsor)	77
A.W.Lampard	c Thomas b Martin	10	(3)	c Martin b Windsor	80
*T.S.Warne	c Vincent b Martin	76	(2)	run out (Vincent/Thomas)	17
A.E.Liddicut	lbw b Windsor	4	(7)	lbw b Newton	44
J.C.Dwyer	lbw b Windsor	0	(9)	c McKenzie b Windsor	0
R.L.Braid	b Martin	17	(10)	not out	31
E.A.McDonald	c McKenzie b Windsor	2	(4)	c Windsor b Martin	13
A.C.Facy	c Hawson b Martin	74	(8)	c Thomas b Windsor	0
†J.R.H.Woodford	not out	8		c sub (J.R.Byfield) b Windsor	9
Extras	(b5, lb6, w1)	12		(b15)	15
Total	(74.2 overs, 200 mins)	217		(103.3 overs, 266 mins)	307

VICTORIA	O	M	R	W	w,nb		O	M	R	W	w,nb
McDonald	9	0	45	2	-,-		19	7	40	1	-,-
Braid	15.5	5	48	3	-,-		30	10	68	3	2,1
McKenzie	7	2	11	1	-,-	(4)	13	4	32	1	-,-
Hartkopf	7	3	12	1	-,-	(3)	11.3	4	24	1	-,-
Dwyer	6	0	32	0	-,-	(6)	5	0	11	0	1,-
Facy	10	2	35	3	2,1	(7)	11	7	36	0	-,-
Warne	3	0	11	0	-,-	(8)	11	1	36	1	-,-
Lampard						(5)	3	0	15	0	-,-
Liddicut							7	1	29	3	-,-

TASMANIA	O	M	R	W	w,nb		O	M	R	W	w,nb
Windsor	22	5	64	4	-,-		43.3	15	132	6	-,-
Martin	26.2	4	69	5	-,-		29	6	88	1	-,-
McKenzie	7	0	27	0	-,-	(5)	8	1	33	0	-,-
Newton	10	2	22	0	-,-	(3)	18	6	30	1	-,-
Thomlinson	5	1	17	0	1,-						
Gill	4	3	6	0	-,-	(4)	5	2	9	0	-,-

FALL OF WICKETS

Wkt	TAS 1st	VIC 1st	TAS 2nd	VIC 2nd
1st	15	1	48	19
2nd	32	11	107	66
3rd	69	26	152	81
4th	75	26	180	152
5th	137	33	184	186
6th	146	35	221	245
7th	167	56	302	245
8th	191	61	311	245
9th	208	207	311	291
10th	208	217	318	307

AUSTRALIA v ENGLAND (5th Test)

Played at Sydney Cricket Ground on February 23, 24, 26 (no play), 27, 28, 29 (no play), March 1, 1912. (Timeless match)
Toss : England.   Result : ENGLAND WON BY 70 RUNS.
Debuts: Australia - J.W.McLaren (Test).
12th Men: T.J.Matthews (Aust) and C.P.Mead (Eng).
Umpires: R.M.Crockett and A.C.Jones.
Attendances: 11806, 28485, no play, 5883, 6344, no play, 2499.   Total: 55,017.   Receipts: £2854.
Close of Play: 1st day Eng 6/204 (Woolley 62, Vine 8); 2nd day Aust 5/133 (Ransford 28, Carter 0); 3rd day no play; 4th day Eng (2)
    9/209 (Vine 5); 5th day Aust (2) 3/193 (Armstrong 23, Minnett 49); 6th day no play.

Woolley's undefeated 133 - the first century by an English left-hander against Australia - occupied 215 minutes (12 fours) and included chances at 63 and 128. With Vine he established a new England seventh-wicket record of 143 in 147 minutes. Woolley also held two memorable catches in the second innings, dismissing Trumper by diving forward from short-leg and Minnett at slip from a late cut: "doubling up like an acrobat, he shot out his left hand and effected another magnificent catch" (*SMH*). Minnett (61 in 132 minutes, 9 fours) was Australia's highest scorer. McLaren had the distinction of becoming the first native-born Queenslander to represent Australia in Test cricket. Trumper and Hill, Australia's premier run-scorers, were both playing what conspired to be their final Tests. Heavy overnight rain drenched the wicket but, in the absence of sun, it played fairly easily on the second day. Another storm on Sunday prevented play on Monday and sun on Tuesday produced a 'sticky'. It had improved by the Wednesday but further storms again made it difficult and Australia did well to score 292 in the fourth innings. The late finish resulted in the cancellation of the final tour match, against South Australia, prior to the MCC's departure for home. Sources: *Wisden, NSWCA Report, The Australasian, Sydney Morning Herald.*

ENGLAND

J.B.Hobbs	c Ransford b Hordern	32	c Hazlitt b Hordern		45
W.Rhodes	b Macartney	8	lbw b Armstrong		30
G.Gunn	st Carter b Hordern	52	b Hordern		61
J.W.Hearne	c Macartney b Armstrong	4	b Hordern		18
F.R.Foster	st Carter b Hazlitt	15	b McLaren		4
*J.W.H.T.Douglas	c Ransford b Hordern	18	b Armstrong		8
F.E.Woolley	not out	133	c Armstrong b Hazlitt		11
J.Vine	b Hordern	36	not out		6
†E.J.Smith	b Hordern	0	b Hordern		13
S.F.Barnes	c Hordern b Hazlitt	5	b Hordern		4
J.W.Hitch	c Hill b Hazlitt	4	c Ransford b Armstrong		4
Extras	(b10, lb4, w1,nb2)	17	(b8, nb2)		10
Total	(129.0 overs, 389 mins)	324	(70.3 overs, 218 mins)		214

AUSTRALIA

V.T.Trumper	c Woolley b Barnes	5		c Woolley b Barnes	50
S.E.Gregory	c Gunn b Douglas	32		c Smith b Barnes	40
*C.Hill	c Smith b Hitch	20		b Foster	8
W.W.Armstrong	lbw b Barnes	33		b Barnes	33
R.B.Minnett	c Douglas b Hitch	0		c Woolley b Barnes	61
V.S.Ransford	c Hitch b Foster	29		b Woolley	9
†H.Carter	c sub (C.P.Mead) b Barnes	11	(8) c Woolley b Foster		23
C.G.Macartney	c & b Woolley	26	(7) c Woolley b Foster		27
H.V.Hordern	b Woolley	0		run out (Hobbs)	4
G.R.Hazlitt	run out (Hobbs/Smith)	1		c Rhodes b Foster	4
J.W.McLaren	not out	0		not out	0
Extras	(b14, lb2, w2, nb1)	19	(b22, lb8, w1, nb2)		33
Total	(53.0 overs, 180 mins)	176	(102.1 overs, 270 mins)		292

AUSTRALIA	O	M	R	W	w,nb		O	M	R	W	w,nb		FALL OF WICKETS			
														ENG	AUST	ENG	AUST
McLaren	16	2	47	0	1,-	(5)	8	1	23	1	-,1	Wkt	1st	1st	2nd	2nd
Macartney	12	3	26	1	-,2	(1)	7	0	28	0	-,1	1st	15	17	76	88
Hordern	37	8	95	5	-,-	(4)	25	5	66	5	-,-	2nd	69	59	76	101
Hazlitt	31	6	75	3	-,-	(2)	12	2	52	1	-,-	3rd	83	81	105	117
Armstrong	25	8	42	1	-,-	(3)	17.3	7	35	3	-,-	4th	114	82	110	209
Minnett	8	1	22	0	-,-		1	1	0	0	-,-	5th	125	133	146	220
												6th	162	133	178	231
ENGLAND	O	M	R	W	w,nb		O	M	R	W	w,nb	7th	305	171	185	278
Foster	16	0	55	1	-,1		30.1	7	43	4	-,1	8th	305	175	201	287
Barnes	19	2	56	3	1,-		39	12	106	4	1,-	9th	312	176	209	287
Hitch	9	0	31	2	-,-	(4)	6	1	23	0	-,-	10th	324	176	214	292
Douglas	7	0	14	1	-,-	(3)	9	0	34	0	-,-					
Woolley	2	1	1	2	1,-		16	5	36	1	-,1					
Rhodes							2	0	17	0	-,-.					

TASMANIA v VICTORIA

Played at T.C.A. Ground, Hobart, on February 23, 24, 26, 27, 1912. (Timeless match)
Toss : Tasmania.   Result : TASMANIA WON BY 72 RUNS.
Debuts: Tasmania - A.B.Crowder, E.S.Headlam, R.J.Pennycuick (all f/c).
12th Men: No 12th men or emergency fieldsmen named; only 11 men in Victorian party.
Umpires: F.Price and A.Williams.
Attendances: No figures published.   Receipts: £26.
Close of Play: 1st day Tas 7/285 (Watt 12, Crowder 0); 2nd day Vic 162 all out 3rd day Vic (2) 3/141 (Warne 61, Liddicut 35).

E.A.C.Windsor was unavailable for Tasmania and H.Hale, J.L.Hudson, H.Parkinson, C.H.Robinson and L.R.Tumilty all withdrew from the named side. The replacements were Crowder, Headlam, Martin (originally unavailable), Pennycuick (the nominated 12th man) and Richardson. After Martin was out to the third ball of the match Hawson (96 in 220 minutes, 15 fours) and Paton (109 in 205 minutes, 13 fours) established a new second-wicket record for Tasmania. Watt scored 79 in 108 minutes and hit 11 fours. Martin, who completed his pair when dismissed second ball in the second innings, substituted for Victoria on the first day when Liddicut twisted his leg after one over and was forced from the field. Warne, making his last first-class appearance, opened the second innings and was last out for a career-best 153 (325 minutes, 22 fours, chance at 75) . *Cricket* incorrectly gives Tas (1) extras 17, total 435; Vic (2) Headlam 0/13. Sources: *Cricket, VCA Report, TCA Report, Launceston Examiner, Launceston Daily Telegraph, Hobart Mercury.*

TASMANIA

*R.J.Hawson	c & b Hartkopf	96	b McDonald	15
C.W.B.Martin	b Facy	0	(4) b McDonald	0
G.D.Paton	b Braid	109	(2) c Hartkopf b McDonald	17
E.T.Boddam	c & b Braid	19	(9) b Hartkopf	27
A.C.Newton	b Hartkopf	4	(11) b Facy	0
E.S.Headlam	c Braid b Facy	15	(8) not out	32
W.B.Richardson	c & b Braid	13	(10) b Facy	0
A.K.E.Watt	b Warne	79	(3) run out (/Woodford)	11
†A.B.Crowder	b Braid	18	(6) b McDonald	11
T.D.Carroll	c Hartkopf b Braid	41	(7) b Lampard	7
R.J.Pennycuick	not out	24	(5) st Woodford b Braid	24
Extras	(b15, lb3)	18	(b5, lb3, nb2)	10
Total	(126.5 overs, 400 mins)	436	(32.3 overs, 170 mins)	154

VICTORIA

C.McKenzie	c Watt b Carroll	12	(2) c & b Martin	5
A.W.Lampard	b Martin	10	(3) c Crowder b Boddam	38
A.E.V.Hartkopf	b Martin	7	(4) b Boddam	1
A.E.Liddicut	b Martin	11	(5) run out (/Crowder/Watt)	53
*T.S.Warne	c Newton b Martin	31	(1) c Carroll b Martin	153
G.E.J.Healy	b Martin	12	(7) b Hawson	17
R.L.Braid	c Hawson b Martin	19	(8) b Paton	13
J.C.Dwyer	not out	41	(6) c Richardson b Pennycuick	62
A.C.Facy	b Watt	0	lbw b Paton	0
E.A.McDonald	c Boddam b Watt	13	b Martin	1
†J.R.H.Woodford	lbw b Paton	4	not out	1
Extras	(nb2)	2	(b12)	12
Total	(49.3 overs, 150 mins)	162	(143.0 overs, 325 mins)	356

VICTORIA	O	M	R	W	w,nb		O	M	R	W	w,nb
Facy	20	2	66	2	-,-	(4)	4.3	0	17	2	-,1
Braid	27.5	5	82	5	-,-		11	1	35	1	-,-
Hartkopf	24	5	82	2	-,-	(5)	2	0	10	1	-,-
McKenzie	8	5	7	0	-,-						
Lampard	11	1	41	0	-,-	(3)	3	1	30	1	-,-
Warne	4	0	25	1	-,-						
McDonald	17	5	41	0	-,-	(1)	12	4	52	4	-,1
Liddicut	1	1	0	0	-,-						
Dwyer	14	1	74	0	-,-						

TASMANIA	O	M	R	W	w,nb		O	M	R	W	w,nb
Carroll	19	4	51	1	-,2		26	6	52	0	-,-
Martin	23	4	78	6	-,-		36	9	89	3	-,-
Boddam	1	0	3	0	-,-	(5)	18	4	53	2	-,-
Watt	5	2	21	2	-,-	(3)	21	1	51	0	-,-
Paton	1.3	0	7	1	-,-	(4)	21	8	42	2	-,-
Newton							6	0	10	0	-,-
Pennycuick							4	1	15	1	-,-
Richardson							4	1	5	0	-,-
Hawson							3	0	13	1	-,-
Headlam							4	0	14	0	-,-

FALL OF WICKETS

Wkt	TAS 1st	VIC 1st	TAS 2nd	VIC 2nd
1st	1	18	22	10
2nd	204	29	40	76
3rd	232	34	40	78
4th	236	43	59	174
5th	242	63	78	258
6th	257	85	84	323
7th	274	116	92	343
8th	319	120	150	343
9th	394	150	153	348
10th	436	162	154	356

QUEENSLAND v NEW SOUTH WALES

Played at Brisbane Cricket Ground (Woolloongabba) on March 8, 9, 1912. (Timeless match)
Toss : Queensland.   Result : NEW SOUTH WALES WON BY TEN WICKETS.
Debuts: Queensland - H.G.S.Smith (f/c). New South Wales - P.S.Arnott, H.H.Davis, H.Shortland, J.S.Taylor (all f/c).
12th Men: A.N.Bolton (Qld) and F.Buckle (NSW).
Umpires: G.A.Carter and A.T.Horrigan.
Attendances: 500, 3000.   Total: About 3500.   Receipts: £160.
Close of Play: 1st day NSW 6/91 (Diamond 32).

Originally scheduled to start on February 9th, the match was postponed due to a prolonged industrial strike by wharf labourers in Brisbane. The New South Wales team was consequently reselected with Arnott, Buckle and Davis being included in the twelve at the expense of H.L.Collins, H.Cranney and A.J.Y.Hopkins. W.T.Evans and R.J.Hartigan were unavailable for Queensland selection. Redgrave (107 in 151 minutes, 11 fours) and Diamond (105 not out in 140 minutes, 1 five and 14 fours) scored hundreds for their respective sides. Waddy was dropped at slip by Armstrong off the third ball of the New South Wales first innings. Smith dismissed Shortland and McKew with successive balls. Despite heavy rain in the week leading up to the match, the pitch was reported to be in perfect condition. There were no interruptions in play and the game ended at 5.12pm on the second day, having lasted a mere seven and a half hours. Carter replaced T.Muir after the original umpire appointments. *Cricket* gives incorrect details for NSW (1) McKew, Randell; Qld (2) Bolton, Smith. Sources: *Cricket, NSWCA Report, Sydney Referee, Sydney Morning Herald, Queensland Times, Brisbane Courier.*

QUEENSLAND

Batsman	Dismissal	Runs	2nd Dismissal	Runs
*C.B.Jennings	c Barbour b Arnott	14	b Scott	4
S.J.Fennelly	c Folkard b Scott	2	b Randell	24
A.Marshal	b Folkard	4	b Scott	8
J.S.Redgrave	b Scott	107	c McKew b Folkard	1
W.B.Hayes	c Arnott b Folkard	23	st McKew b Randell	14
W.Armstrong	b Arnott	4	(7) c Barbour b Scott	2
R.K.Oxenham	run out	13	(8) b Randell	2
†J.T.Bolton	not out	5	(6) c McKew b Scott	1
B.W.Cook	b Scott	0	(10) not out	2
C.B.Barstow	st McKew b Randell	0	(9) b Scott	11
H.G.S.Smith	b Scott	0	st McKew b Randell	0
Extras	(b2, lb3, nb4)	9	(b3, lb2, w1, nb4)	10
Total	(58.5 overs, 166 mins)	181	(29.2 overs, 85 mins)	79

NEW SOUTH WALES

Batsman	Dismissal	Runs	2nd Dismissal	Runs
E.L.Waddy	b Smith	21		
E.P.Barbour	b Barstow	7		
B.J.Folkard	c sub (A.N.Bolton) b Barstow	8		
J.S.Taylor	b Cook	13	(1) not out	14
*A.Diamond	not out	105		
P.S.Arnott	lbw b Cook	0	(2) not out	18
H.H.Davis	lbw b Hayes	10		
J.D.Scott	c J.T.Bolton b Marshal	44		
H.Shortland	b Smith	14		
†C.G.McKew	b Smith	0		
J.A.Randell	b Barstow	2		
Extras	(b2, lb1, w1)	4	(lb1)	1
Total	(61.3 overs, 178 mins)	228	(4.1 overs, 12 mins) (0 wkts)	33

NEW SOUTH WALES	O	M	R	W	w,nb		O	M	R	W	w,nb
Scott	13.5	4	28	4	-,2		11	2	28	5	1,4
Folkard	13	4	28	2	-,-	(3)	6	2	7	1	-,-
Shortland	10	0	36	0	-,2	(4)	4	1	8	0	-,-
Arnott	7	0	27	2	-,-	(2)	3	0	15	0	-,-
Randell	12	0	49	1	-,-		5.2	0	11	4	-,-
Davis	3	0	4	0	-,-						

QUEENSLAND	O	M	R	W	w,nb		O	M	R	W	w,nb
Smith	19	1	50	3	1,-		2	0	12	0	-,-
Barstow	16.3	1	68	3	-,-						
Cook	8	1	20	2	-,-	(2)	2	0	16	0	-,-
Oxenham	5	0	22	0	-,-						
Hayes	6	1	30	1	-,-						
Armstrong	3	0	16	0	-,-						
Marshal	4	1	18	1	-,-						
Fennelly						(3)	0.1	0	4	0	-,-

FALL OF WICKETS

Wkt	QLD 1st	NSW 1st	QLD 2nd	QLD 2nd
1st	4	28	8	-
2nd	9	28	32	-
3rd	46	49	33	-
4th	110	49	51	-
5th	117	49	60	-
6th	156	91	60	-
7th	179	183	64	-
8th	179	225	64	-
9th	180	225	78	-
10th	181	228	79	-

Domestic cricket returned to the fore in the absence of a visiting team from overseas, and all six State associations took the opportunity to arrange fixtures outside the Sheffield Shield program. The chief innovation was Western Australia's extensive tour of the Eastern States which included their maiden visit to New South Wales. The trip incorporated five first-class matches against South Australia, Victoria and New South Wales. It was very much a learning process for the westerners, who failed to win a match. It provided them with an opportunity to develop closer links with the major States, with a view to playing interstate fixtures on a regular basis and being admitted to the Board of Control.

South Australia emerged to win the Sheffield Shield for the third time. They began by defeating New South Wales by an innings at Adelaide and then accounted for Victoria at Melbourne, before losing to New South Wales in their return match at Sydney. A fortnight later, New South Wales overcame Victoria at Sydney to draw level with South Australia at the head of the table. South Australia grabbed the chance to win the Shield outright when Victoria arrived in Adelaide for the final match in late February. Jack Crawford scored an inspired 163 and then captured 8 for 66, establishing a first-innings advantage which eventually proved decisive. Crawford's allround talents played a major part in South Australia's success during the course of the season, but he also received strong support from Clem Hill, Mayne, Gehrs and Moyes in the batting lineup which rarely failed. The bowling relied almost solely on the ability of Crawford and Whitty to perform.

New South Wales undertook their away matches in the Shield with a significantly depleted side, and it proved costly. Their performances were marked by the outstanding bowling of Massie, a left-arm paceman who seemed destined for greatness. Trumper, Macartney, Barbour and Bardsley played some fine innings at home in the second half of the Shield season.

Victoria caught New South Wales on a rain-affected wicket at Melbourne to bring off their only win this year. Ryder and Armstrong were their finest players.

New South Wales and Queensland played their annual home and away fixtures and New South Wales proved far too strong on both occasions. Massie captured 18 wickets in these games. Queensland lost again in their home match against Victoria.

Tasmania journeyed to Melbourne for their annual clash with Victoria and were led to an outstanding victory by an unbeaten 199 from Reg Hawson in the second innings. New South Wales sent a strong team to Tasmania in March and duly thrashed the islanders inside two days. Collins hit 282 and Trumper scored 87 not out in less than an hour to delight the crowd.

The NSWCA accorded Trumper a benefit in the form of a match between New South Wales and The Rest. It was a huge success, and Trumper marked the occasion by scoring a century in the first innings and 61 in an hour in the second.

R.E.Mayne organised an Australian team to tour the United States and Canada at the close of the 1912-13 season. It was a private venture, as Mayne was unable to obtain Board of Control approval. The team was: A.Diamond (captain), P.S.Arnott, W.Bardsley, G.C.Campbell, L.A.Cody, H.L.Collins, J.N.Crawford, G.S.Down, S.H.Emery, C.G.Macartney, A.A.Mailey and R.E.Mayne.

Leading Aggregates

Batsmen	M	I	NO	Runs	HS	Ave.	Bowlers	Runs	Wkts	Ave.
V.T.Trumper (NSW)	7	13	3	843	201*	84.30	R.J.A.Massie (NSW)	1101	59	18.66
C.G.Macartney (NSW)	4	7	1	646	154	107.66	J.Ryder (V)	579	35	16.54
H.L.Collins (NSW)	10	17	3	598	282	42.71	J.N.Crawford (SA)	772	33	23.39
R.E.Mayne (SA)	5	9	0	542	124	60.22	W.J.Whitty (SA)	658	29	22.68
J.Ryder (V)	7	13	1	521	110	43.41	W.W.Armstrong (V)	510	24	21.25
C.Hill (SA)	6	11	0	476	138	43.27	A.A.Mailey (NSW)	337	21	16.04
A.G.Moyes (SA)	6	11	0	452	104	41.09	A.H.Christian (WA)	605	20	30.25
E.P.Barbour (NSW)	4	8	1	450	146	64.28				
W.W.Armstrong (V)	7	12	2	402	118*	40.20				

SHEFFIELD SHIELD TABLE

	P	W	L	D	Pts	Quotient	Runs Scored	Wkts Lost	Runs Conceded	Wkts Taken
SOUTH AUSTRALIA	4	3	1	-	2	1.220	2339	70	2136	78
NEW SOUTH WALES	4	2	2	-	0	0.900	2299	72	2269	64
VICTORIA	4	1	3	-	-2	0.882	1750	72	1983	72
TOTAL	6	6	6	-	0	1.000	6388	214	6388	214

SOUTH AUSTRALIA v WESTERN AUSTRALIA

Played at Adelaide Oval on October 25, 26, 28, 1912. (Three-day match)
Toss : South Australia   Result : SOUTH AUSTRALIA WON BY 365 RUNS.
Debuts: South Australia - N.L.Gooden, E.H.Kitson, S.G.Leak, A.G.Moyes (all f/c). Western Australia - L.C.Bott, W.C.Hughes,
    C.A.Lehmann (all f/c).
12th Men: G.S.Down (SA) and A.C.Randell (WA).
Umpires: A.T.Haddrick and F.J.C.Thomas.
Attendances: "poor", 1000, "little public interest".   Total: 1442.   Receipts: No figures published.
Close of Play: 1st day SA (2) 0/11 (Leak 2, Kitson 7); 2nd day WA (2) 3/69 (Edmondson 12, Bott 9).

Crawford's 7 for 31 included the hat-trick, Christian to the last ball of an over followed by Hogue and Bott to the first two balls of a new
over. Bott was bowled by the first ball he received in first-class cricket. Moyes (104 in 103 minutes, 1 six and 17 fours) and Gooden (102
in 146 minutes, 10 fours, chance at 34) each recorded a century on debut. Gehrs (119 in 60 minutes, 21 fours, chance at 64) reached 50 in
25 minutes and 100 in only 50 minutes. Leak (8) was hit in the face by a ball from Hughes in the second innings and retired at 0/21,
resuming at 4/293. Edmondson, WA's player-manager, scored 57 in 100 minutes and hit 5 fours. He replaced Evers (sore hands) as
wicket-keeper after lunch on the second day. Sources: *Cricket, C.B.O'Reilly, SACA Report, The Age, Adelaide Advertiser, South
Australian Register.*

SOUTH AUSTRALIA

S.G.Leak	lbw b Selk	7	st Edmondson b Lehmann	23
E.H.Kitson	lbw b T.H.Hogue	34	b Christian	22
N.L.Gooden	c Edmondson b Christian	49	c Rowe b Lehmann	102
A.G.Moyes	b Hughes	104	b Selk	38
D.R.A.Gehrs	b Christian	0	b Lehmann	119
J.N.Crawford	b Christian	28	c Evers b Lehmann	7
*C.Hill	b Hughes	28	c sub (A.C.Randell) b T.H.Hogue	28
†G.C.Campbell	b Hughes	0	c Lehmann b Selk	24
R.B.C.Rees	b Edmondson	3	run out (Rowe)	21
W.S.Stirling	c Lehmann b Edmondson	3	b Hughes	16
L.E.Howard	not out	4	not out	0
Extras	(b2, lb7, nb1)	10	(b4, lb2, nb4)	10
Total	(55.5 overs, 170 mins)	270	(80.4 overs, 225 mins)	410

WESTERN AUSTRALIA

H.C.Howard	c Gehrs b Crawford	3	c Gooden b Rees	6
S.H.D.Rowe	c Hill b Crawford	1	(6) c Moyes b Rees	31
T.H.Hogue	c Leak b Crawford	4	c Howard b Rees	0
A.H.Christian	c Stirling b Crawford	2	(2) c Crawford b Rees	37
H.P.D.Edmondson	c Moyes not out	1	(4) c & b Rees	57
L.C.Bott	b Crawford	0	(5) b Crawford	21
*†H.A.Evers	b Crawford	4	c & b Crawford	43
W.W.Hogue	b Howard	33	b Crawford	4
W.C.Hughes	c Campbell b Howard	2	not out	13
R.A.Selk	b Crawford	11	c Leak b Crawford	0
C.A.Lehmann	not out	6	c Leak b Rees	10
Extras	(lb1, nb1)	2	(b7, lb15, w2)	24
Total	(19.0 overs, 75 mins)	69	(66.0 overs, 185 mins)	246

WESTERN AUSTRALIA	O	M	R	W	w,nb		O	M	R	W	w,nb
Selk	14	3	58	1	-,-	(4)	12	1	77	2	-,-
Christian	19	3	87	3	-,-		21	2	83	1	-,-
Hughes	11	2	38	3	-,-	(1)	12.4	1	73	1	-,-
T.H.Hogue	4	0	35	1	-,-	(3)	15	1	59	1	-,-
Lehmann	3	0	21	0	-,1	(6)	15	2	64	4	-,4
Edmondson	4.5	0	21	2	-,-	(7)	3	0	18	0	-,-
W.W.Hogue						(5)	2	0	26	0	-,-

SOUTH AUSTRALIA	O	M	R	W	w,nb		O	M	R	W	w,nb
Howard	10	2	36	3	-,1	(5)	9	0	49	0	2,-
Crawford	9	1	31	7	-,-	(4)	17	5	40	4	-,-
Rees						(1)	26	5	91	6	-,-
Stirling						(2)	10	2	32	0	-,-
Moyes						(3)	4	1	10	0	-,-

FALL OF WICKETS

Wkt	SA 1st	WA 1st	SA 2nd	WA 2nd
1st	23	2	44	22
2nd	64	8	95	26
3rd	148	10	269	55
4th	149	12	293	88
5th	189	12	312	164
6th	246	16	328	181
7th	246	16	357	190
8th	264	39	380	227
9th	264	53	403	227
10th	270	69	410	246

VICTORIA v WESTERN AUSTRALIA

Played at Melbourne Cricket Ground on November 1, 2 (no play), 4, 1912. (Three-day match)
Toss : Western Australia.   Result : MATCH DRAWN.
Debuts: Victoria - J.Ryder (f/c). Western Australia - A.C.Randell (f/c).
12th Men: L.C.Bott (WA). H.W.Hart, W.R.F.Macrow and W.J.Scott were named as Victorian emergencies.
Umpires: W.J.Bruton and W.A.Young.
Attendances: 500, no play, 500.   Total: About 1000.   Receipts: £30.
Close of Play: 1st day Vic 4/187 (Ryder 56, Facy 0); 2nd day no play.

Western Australia's second first-class match in Victoria was ruined by rain which prevented any play on the second day and interrupted the third with WA 1/61 in their second innings. Further rain caused the match to be abandoned at 5.00pm after a token resumption. Victoria were without W.Carkeek, T.J.Matthews and D.B.M.Smith who all had not yet returned from England. D.A.Elder (unavailable) was replaced as umpire by Bruton after the original appointments. Facy dismissed Howard and Hogue with successive deliveries. Randell, who later became a prominent administrator, scored 61 in 58 minutes and hit 10 fours on debut. Woodford, standing well back to Ryder, stumped Selk with a shy at the wicket. Seitz, who batted about 80 minutes, scored an all-run five with a leg-hit off Christian and hit 3 fours. Carroll (54 in 50 minutes, 6 fours), Ryder (74 in about 90 minutes, 11 fours) and Facy (77 in about 100 minutes, 11 fours) also scored fifties. No details for Hartkopf's innings survive. *West Australian* incorrectly gives WA (1) T.H.Hogue c Armstrong. Sources: *Cricket, VCA Report, The Age, The Argus, The Herald, The Australasian, The Leader, The West Australian.*

WESTERN AUSTRALIA

S.H.D.Rowe	b Facy	14	(2) not out		26
H.C.Howard	c Armstrong b Facy	8	(4) not out		1
T.H.Hogue	c Hartkopf b Facy	0			
A.H.Christian	b Brown	5	(1) c Seitz b Facy		31
H.P.D.Edmondson	c Hartkopf b Facy	23	(3) b Braid		14
A.C.Randell	c Woodford b Facy	61			
*†H.A.Evers	b Ransford	19			
W.W.Hogue	b Ransford	9			
W.C.Hughes	not out	3			
R.A.Selk	st Woodford b Ryder	3			
C.A.Lehmann	c Braid b Ryder	1			
Extras	(b7, lb1)	8			-
Total	(53.0 overs, 170 mins)	154	(31.0 overs, 90 mins) (2 wkts)		72

VICTORIA

E.V.Carroll	b Selk	54
J.A.Seitz	c Selk b Hughes	63
F.A.Baring	b Selk	2
N.E.Brown	b Selk	7
J.Ryder	lbw b Christian	74
A.C.Facy	b Selk	77
A.E.V.Hartkopf	not out	74
*W.W.Armstrong	)	
V.S.Ransford	)	
R.L.Braid	) did not bat	
†J.R.H.Woodford	)	
Extras	(b2, lb6)	8
Total	(89.5 overs, 245 mins) (6 wkts dec)	359

VICTORIA	O	M	R	W	w,nb		O	M	R	W	w,nb
Facy	20	4	40	5	-,-	(3)	7	2	11	1	-,-
Braid	14	4	41	0	-,-	(4)	8	2	21	1	-,-
Ryder	7	3	14	2	-,-	(2)	8	2	19	0	-,-
Brown	8	1	35	1	-,-						
Ransford	3	0	13	2	-,-						
Carroll	1	0	3	0	-,-						
Armstrong						(1)	8	3	21	0	-,-

WESTERN AUSTRALIA	O	M	R	W	w,nb		O	M	R	W	w,nb
Selk	22.5	4	77	4	-,-						
Hughes	15	0	77	1	-,-						
Lehmann	9	1	68	0	-,-						
Christian	20	1	68	1	-,-						
Edmondson	4	0	20	0	-,-						
T.H.Hogue	19	5	41	0	-,-						

FALL OF WICKETS

Wkt	WA 1st	VIC 1st	WA 2nd
1st	21	77	51
2nd	21	85	70
3rd	24	97	-
4th	32	186	-
5th	118	215	-
6th	119	359	-
7th	140	-	-
8th	147	-	-
9th	150	-	-
10th	154	-	-

NEW SOUTH WALES v WESTERN AUSTRALIA

Played at Sydney Cricket Ground on November 8 (no play), 9, 11, 1912. (Three-day match)
Toss : Western Australia.   Result : MATCH DRAWN.
Debuts: New South Wales - L.A.Cody, A.A.Mailey, C.V.Single (all f/c); S.Hill (NSW only).
12th Men: J.C.Barnes (NSW) and C.A.Lehmann (WA).
Umpires: R.Thornthwaite and J.A.Turnbull.
Attendances: no play, 1500, 500.   Total: About 2000.   Receipts: £72.
Close of Play: 1st day no play; 2nd day NSW (2) 1/9 (McKew 2).

New South Wales were forced to field an understrength side for their first match at home against Western Australia. W.Bardsley, S.H.Emery, S.E.Gregory, G.R.Hazlitt, C.Kelleway, C.G.Macartney and R.B.Minnett had not yet returned from the tour of England, and in addition E.P.Barbour, H.Carter, A.Cotter and J.D.Scott all announced their unavailability after being selected in the team. Sent in on a rain-affected wicket (there being no play on the first day), New South Wales were dismissed for what was their lowest total against Western Australia until 1985-86. Trumper (51 in 55 minutes, 4 fours) got more than half the runs. However, the visitors also struggled in the conditions, Christian (30 in 33 minutes, 4 fours) topscoring; 21 wickets fell in the day's play. In the second innings Arnott (80 not out in 64 minutes, 14 fours, chance at 73) and Single (72 in 54 minutes, 9 fours) both hit their highest first-class scores, adding 160 in just 54 minutes for the ninth wicket, a record stand in matches between these teams. Trumper (55in 73 minutes, 6 fours), Waddy (52 in 37 minutes, 8 fours) and Christian (55 not out in 55 minutes) also scored second-innings fifties. Hill, one of six South Australian-born brothers to play first-class cricket, played his only match for New South Wales. *Cricket* incorrectly gives NSW (2) Selk 2/89. Sources: *Cricket, NSWCA Report, Sydney Referee, Sydney Morning Herald, Town & Country Journal, Sydney Daily Telegraph.*

NEW SOUTH WALES

*V.T.Trumper	c Rowe b T.H.Hogue	51	(3) c Rowe b Edmondson	55
E.L.Waddy	c Rowe b Christian	1	(4) lbw b Selk	52
S.Hill	c T.H.Hogue b Selk	12	(5) c Evers b Christian	17
H.L.Collins	c Hughes b Christian	7	(7) c Evers b Hughes	21
H.Cranney	st Evers b Christian	5	(8) b Christian	8
L.A.Cody	c Hughes b Christian	2	b Selk	13
P.S.Arnott	c Randell b T.H.Hogue	4	(9) not out	80
C.V.Single	c Selk b Christian	0	(10) b T.H.Hogue	72
R.J.A.Massie	c Evers b T.H.Hogue	11	(11) b T.H.Hogue	5
†C.G.McKew	c Hughes b Christian	0	(1) c Bott b Hughes	5
A.A.Mailey	not out	0	(2) st Evers b Hughes	7
Extras	(b1, lb1)	2	(b9, lb4)	13
Total	(27.1 overs, 84 mins)	95	(72.5 overs, 204 mins)	348

WESTERN AUSTRALIA

H.C.Howard	b Massie	9	(2) not out	21
S.H.D.Rowe	b Massie	1	(1) c Trumper b Collins	0
H.P.D.Edmondson	b Massie	0	c McKew b Collins	0
A.H.Christian	b Massie	30	not out	55
A.C.Randell	st McKew b Mailey	16		
T.H.Hogue	st McKew b Mailey	4		
*†H.A.Evers	b Mailey	0		
L.C.Bott	b Mailey	23		
W.W.Hogue	st McKew b Mailey	0		
W.C.Hughes	c McKew b Massie	7		
R.A.Selk	not out	0		
Extras	(b13, lb2)	15	(b5, lb1, nb1)	7
Total	(30.5 overs, 102 mins)	105	(23.0 overs, 60 mins) (2 wkts)	83

WESTERN AUSTRALIA	O	M	R	W	w,nb		O	M	R	W	w,nb
Selk	7	0	35	1	-,-	(3)	9	0	45	2	-,-
Christian	13.1	2	40	6	-,-	(1)	25	7	52	2	-,-
T.H.Hogue	7	2	18	3	-,-	(4)	8.5	0	61	2	-,-
Hughes						(2)	13	0	89	3	-,-
Edmondson							12	1	49	1	-,-
W.W.Hogue							3	0	24	0	-,-
Howard							2	0	15	0	-,-

NEW SOUTH WALES	O	M	R	W	w,nb		O	M	R	W	w,nb
Single	6	2	20	0	-,-	(5)	1	0	9	0	-,-
Massie	15	8	24	5	-,-		6	1	30	0	-,-
Mailey	9.5	0	46	5	-,-		5	1	12	0	-,-
Collins						(1)	9	3	21	2	-,1
Arnott						(4)	2	0	4	0	-,-

FALL OF WICKETS

	NSW	WA	NSW	WA
Wkt	1st	1st	2nd	2nd
1st	3	2	9	0
2nd	26	4	16	6
3rd	58	50	104	-
4th	76	55	139	-
5th	78	69	145	-
6th	79	69	166	-
7th	83	78	182	-
8th	83	78	182	-
9th	95	97	342	-
10th	95	105	348	-

NEW SOUTH WALES v WESTERN AUSTRALIA

Played at Sydney Cricket Ground on November 15, 16, 18, 1912. (Three-day match)
Toss : New South Wales.   Result : NEW SOUTH WALES WON BY 155 RUNS.
Debuts: New South Wales - T.J.E.Andrews, R.A.Munn (both f/c).
12th Men: O.S.Smith (NSW) and C.A.Lehmann (WA).
Umpires: W.G.French and A.Seymour.
Attendances: 500, 1200, 300.   Total: About 2000.   Receipts: £55.
Close of Play: 1st day WA 4/122 (Randell 15, Bott 1); 2nd day NSW (2) 6/264 (Single 45, Munn 14).

New South Wales batted with remarkable consistency in this match, 20 out of 21 individual innings exceeding double figures. Cody (42) severely strained a leg while running between wickets on the first day and retired at 1/72; he resumed at 6/190 with Andrews as his runner, his eventual 84 in 83 minutes included 13 fours. He was unable to field, Smith substituting for him on the first and third days, W.S.S.McCloy on the second. He again required a runner (E.L.Waddy) in the second innings. The hard hitting Arnott (70 in 56 minutes, 1 six and 11 fours) took over from where he had left off earlier in the week. The second day saw 460 runs scored in five hours, Christian (58 in 82 minutes, 9 fours) and Edmondson (68 in 78 minutes, 12 fours) establishing a new Western Australian seventh-wicket record (118). Andrews (62 in 80 minutes, 6 fours), Tozer (54 in 80 minutes), Single (54 in 58 minutes, 7 fours) and Massie (50 not out in 48 minutes, 1 six and 7 fours) registered half-centuries in the second innings. In his second first-class match Mailey (13 for 152) captured the best match figures by a bowler on either side in this series until 1981-82. Howard (71 in 178 minutes, 5 fours) was first in and last out in Western Australia's second innings. *NSWCA Report* gives NSW (1) Barnes 14, Mailey 14. Sources: *Cricket, NSWCA Report, Sydney Referee, Sydney Morning Herald, Town & Country Journal, Sydney Daily Telegraph.*

NEW SOUTH WALES

H.L.Collins	c Selk b Christian	19	(2) c Bott b Hughes		27
L.A.Cody	c Howard b Selk	84	(9) not out		37
*E.L.Waddy	b T.H.Hogue	11	(1) c Howard b Selk		20
J.C.Barnes	b Christian	13	(3) c Howard b T.H.Hogue		14
T.J.E.Andrews	c Evers b Christian	16	(4) c Randell b Christian		62
P.S.Arnott	b Hughes	70	(5) c & b Hughes		17
C.J.Tozer	b Hughes	19	(6) c Evers b Hughes		54
C.V.Single	c Randell b Edmondson	12	(7) b T.H.Hogue		54
†R.A.Munn	not out	32	(8) c T.H.Hogue b Christian		23
R.J.A.Massie	b T.H.Hogue	6	not out		50
A.A.Mailey	b T.H.Hogue	15			
Extras	(b7, lb1)	8	(b12, lb5)		17
Total	(65.0 overs, 185 mins)	305	(85.0 overs, 266 mins) (8 wkts dec)		375

WESTERN AUSTRALIA

S.H.D.Rowe	b Collins	6	c Mailey b Massie		10
H.C.Howard	c Andrews b Mailey	26	b Mailey		71
T.H.Hogue	st Munn b Mailey	48	st Munn b Collins		14
A.C.Randell	b Massie	43	(6) c sub (O.S.Smith) b Massie		10
W.C.Hughes	c Waddy b Mailey	6	(9) b Mailey		0
L.C.Bott	b Massie	4	(7) b Mailey		27
A.H.Christian	c Tozer b Mailey	58	(5) c Barnes b Mailey		20
H.P.D.Edmondson	b Mailey	68	(4) c sub (O.S.Smith) b Mailey		26
*†H.A.Evers	b Mailey	28	(8) c Barnes b Mailey		0
W.W.Hogue	c Tozer b Mailey	1	run out (Tozer)		7
R.A.Selk	not out	1	not out		2
Extras	(b21, lb7, nb1)	29	(b14, lb4, nb2)		20
Total	(70.1 overs, 223 mins)	318	(55.1 overs, 178 mins)		207

WESTERN AUSTRALIA	O	M	R	W	w,nb		O	M	R	W	w,nb
Christian	22	5	80	3	-,-	(2)	23	2	99	2	-,-
Selk	15	1	72	1	-,-	(1)	16	2	68	1	-,-
Hughes	7	0	54	2	-,-	(4)	18	1	98	3	-,-
T.H.Hogue	13	3	59	3	-,-	(3)	22	5	50	2	-,-
Edmondson	8	2	32	1	-,-		3	0	16	0	-,-
Howard							3	0	27	0	-,-

NEW SOUTH WALES	O	M	R	W	w,nb		O	M	R	W	w,nb
Massie	29	10	95	2	-,1		17	0	58	2	-,-
Collins	8	1	27	1	-,-		8	2	21	1	-,2
Single	5	0	25	0	-,-		12	3	42	0	-,-
Mailey	22.1	4	105	7	-,-		14.1	2	47	6	-,-
Andrews	4	1	17	0	-,-						
Arnott	2	0	20	0	-,-	(5)	4	0	19	0	-,-

FALL OF WICKETS

Wkt	NSW 1st	WA 1st	NSW 2nd	WA 2nd
1st	52	6	28	21
2nd	79	90	59	40
3rd	99	93	69	92
4th	106	110	99	118
5th	153	140	178	133
6th	190	159	234	189
7th	211	277	277	191
8th	260	303	287	191
9th	283	307	-	205
10th	305	318	-	207

VICTORIA v WESTERN AUSTRALIA

Played at Melbourne Cricket Ground on November 20, 21, 22, 1912. (Three-day match)
Toss : Western Australia.   Result : MATCH DRAWN.
Debuts: Victoria - E.S.Boulter, E.L.Carroll, W.F.Delves, C.R.Hendrie, M.D.Hotchin, R.L.Park, H.C.A.Sandford (all f/c).
12th Men: C.B.Willis (Vic emergency). No 12th for WA.
Umpires: E.Barrass and J.O'Connor.
Attendances: No daily figures published.   Total: About 500.   Receipts: £13.
Close of Play: 1st day WA 1/57 (Rowe 26); 2nd day Vic (2) 2/232 (Ryder 86).

F.A.Baring (business) was replaced by Sandford in the Victorian team selected for the match. C.A.Lehmann, the 12th member of the Western Australian touring party, had returned home (presumably to attend to his business); a Perth merchant, he had contributed £200 towards the team's travelling costs for their second, and more extensive, tour of the Eastern States. Ryder scored 57 (80 minutes, 7 fours) and 110 (185 minutes, 8 fours) for the home team, offering his only chance in the second innings at 36, when Evers failed to take a skied edge, catching the sun instead. One of Ryder's powerful drives broke a stump at the non-striker's end. With Hotchin (86 in 105 minutes, 3 fours) he added 147 for the first wicket. Rowe (50 in 140 minutes, 3 fours) alone offered serious resistance for the visitors, whose first three wickets fell to a team "hat-trick", Howard being run out off the last ball of the first day, followed by Edmondson and T.H.Hogue with Macrow's opening deliveries on the second day. Randell, fielding at second slip on the last day, was struck a nasty blow on the forehead and had to retire. Rain caused the abandonment of the match at 2.15pm. The combined attendance, a mere 500 people, is one of the smallest on record in Australian first-class cricket. Sources: *Cricket, VCA Report, The Age, The Argus, The Herald, The Australasian, The Leader, The West Australian.*

VICTORIA

J.Ryder	c Evers b Hughes	57	b T.H.Hogue	110
M.D.Hotchin	b Selk	21	st Evers b Christian	86
A.E.Liddicut	c Hughes b Christian	25	(5) not out	29
*R.L.Park	c Evers b Hughes	2	c Howard b Hughes	18
E.L.Carroll	c Bott b Selk	40	(6) c Evers b Hughes	1
†W.F.Delves	not out	28	(7) not out	16
H.C.A.Sandford	b T.H.Hogue	9	(3) st Evers b W.W.Hogue	47
H.W.Hart	c Hughes b T.H.Hogue	0		
E.S.Boulter	c Evers b Hughes	0		
C.R.Hendrie	b Hughes	0		
W.R.F.Macrow.	b T.H.Hogue	1		
Extras	(b5, lb3)	8	(b13, lb3)	16
Total	(80.3 overs, 205 mins)	191	(80.0 overs, 210 mins) (5 wkts)	323

WESTERN AUSTRALIA

H.C.Howard	run out (/Carroll)	18
S.H.D.Rowe	run out (Boulter/Delves)	50
H.P.D.Edmondson	c Carroll b Macrow	0
T.H.Hogue	c Delves b Macrow	0
L.C.Bott	c Delves b Macrow	5
A.H.Christian	c Carroll b Ryder	29
A.C.Randell	b Carroll	9
*†H.A.Evers	c Ryder b Hart	15
W.W.Hogue	not out	27
W.C.Hughes	b Hart	7
R.A.Selk	c Hart b Boulter	1
Extras	(b13, lb3, w2, nb4)	22
Total	(62.2 overs, 173 mins)	183

WESTERN AUSTRALIA	O	M	R	W	w,nb		O	M	R	W	w,nb
T.H.Hogue	15.3	5	31	3	-,-	(4)	14	2	49	1	-,-
Christian	28	13	40	1	-,-		21	7	56	1	-,-
Selk	17	3	48	2	-,-		7	2	38	0	-,-
Edmondson	3	0	23	0	-,-	(6)	10	0	31	0	-,-
Hughes	17	3	41	4	-,-	(1)	20	0	85	2	-,-
Howard						(5)	2	0	17	0	-,-
Bott							3	0	16	0	-,-
W.W.Hogue							3	0	15	1	-,-

VICTORIA	O	M	R	W	w,nb		O	M	R	W	w,nb
Macrow	17	4	44	3	2,4						
Hendrie	8	0	23	0	-,-						
Ryder	9	3	18	1	-,-						
Hart	13	4	19	2	-,-						
Boulter	9.2	2	40	1	-,-						
Carroll	6	2	17	1	-,-						

FALL OF WICKETS

Wkt	VIC 1st	WA 1st	VIC 2nd
1st	56	57	147
2nd	95	57	232
3rd	97	57	275
4th	129	67	281
5th	168	108	286
6th	186	117	-
7th	186	142	-
8th	186	150	-
9th	186	180	-
10th	191	183	-

QUEENSLAND v NEW SOUTH WALES

Played at Brisbane Cricket Ground (Woolloongabba) on November 22 (no play), 23, 25, 26, 1912. (Timeless match)
Toss : New South Wales.   Result : NEW SOUTH WALES WON BY EIGHT WICKETS.
Debuts: Queensland - J.A.Downey, W.Rowe, J.F.Sheppard, F.C.Thompson (all f/c). New South Wales - G.S.Moore (f/c).
12th Men: L.A.Cody (NSW). No Qld reserve named after withdrawal of R.W.Law, the nominated 12th man.
Umpires: W.H.Carvosso and R.Haigh.
Attendances: no play, 2000, 600, 50.   Total: About 2650.   Receipts: £160.
Close of Play: 1st day no play; 2nd day Qld (2) 0/21 (Bolton 9, Smith 5); 3rd day NSW (2) 2/81 (Barbour 40).

B.W.Cook and W.T.Evans were unavailable for Queensland. Rowe and Sheppard, selected when W.B.Hayes and R.K.Oxenham (ill) withdrew, performed notably on debut. Sheppard (63 in about 65 minutes, 3 sixes and 4 fours) compiled Queensland's only fifty on a rain-affected wicket, the first day and part of the third being lost to the elements. Rowe introduced at 3/76, bowled Folkard with his fourth ball and then removed Arnott and Scott with consecutive balls in his next over. It remained his career-best analysis. Barbour (68 not out in 180 minutes) guided New South Wales to victory. *Cricket* incorrectly gives Qld (1) Massie 2/24; NSW (2) Downey 0/24. Some sources incorrectly give Qld (2) Bolton lbw b Scott. Sources: *Cricket, NSWCA Report, Sydney Morning Herald, Brisbane Courier, Queensland Times.*

QUEENSLAND

*R.J.Hartigan	c Mailey b Folkard	14	(5) b Massie	4
A.Marshal	c Barnes b Massie	4	(3) lbw b Scott	1
J.S.Redgrave	c Collins b Massie	5	(6) b Scott	0
S.J.Fennelly	b Folkard	0	b Massie	0
F.C.Thompson	b Scott	21	(7) c Collins b Scott	0
J.Thomson	b Folkard	4	(10) not out	29
W.Rowe	st McKew b Mailey	21	(9) b Massie	13
J.F.Sheppard	not out	63	b Scott	5
†J.T.Bolton	c Massie b Scott	8	(1) c McKew b Scott	19
J.A.Downey	b Massie	3	(11) c Barbour b Massie	10
H.G.S.Smith	b Folkard	2	(2) c Scott b Massie	7
Extras	(b13, lb1)	14	(b9, lb2, nb1)	12
Total	(46.2 overs, 140 mins)	159	(46.1 overs, 132 mins)	100

NEW SOUTH WALES

G.S.Moore	b Smith	22	(2) c Rowe b Marshal	9
E.P.Barbour	c Redgrave b Smith	0	(1) not out	68
*E.L.Waddy	c Hartigan b Downey	32	c Sheppard b Hartigan	28
H.L.Collins	c Thompson b Downey	25	not out	25
B.J.Folkard	b Rowe	1		
P.S.Arnott	c Marshal b Rowe	2		
J.C.Barnes	not out	31		
J.D.Scott	b Rowe	0		
R.J.A.Massie	b Rowe	8		
A.A.Mailey	b Rowe	0		
†C.G.McKew	b Rowe	1		
Extras	(lb1)	1	(b5, lb1, w1)	7
Total	(31.2 overs, 103 mins)	123	(49.1 overs, 180 mins) (2 wkts)	137

NEW SOUTH WALES	O	M	R	W	w,nb		O	M	R	W	w,nb
Massie	13	4	24	3	-,-	(2)	20.1	7	36	5	-,-
Folkard	14.2	3	51	4	-,-	(3)	4	2	8	0	-,-
Collins	2	1	11	0	-,-						
Scott	7	1	18	2	-,-	(1)	18	7	34	5	-,1
Mailey	10	0	41	1	-,-	(4)	4	1	10	0	-,-

QUEENSLAND	O	M	R	W	w,nb		O	M	R	W	w,nb
Redgrave	6	1	28	0	-,-	(3)	6	1	16	0	-,-
Smith	8	1	25	2	-,-		9	1	27	0	-,-
Downey	10	0	54	2	-,-	(6)	8.1	0	26	0	-,-
Rowe	7.2	3	15	6	-,-	(1)	15	2	30	0	-,-
Marshal						(4)	7	1	19	1	1,-
Hartigan						(5)	4	1	12	1	-,-

FALL OF WICKETS

Wkt	QLD 1st	NSW 1st	QLD 2nd	NSW 2nd
1st	9	2	32	31
2nd	21	37	34	81
3rd	21	67	35	-
4th	26	80	37	-
5th	30	80	37	-
6th	65	83	39	-
7th	95	83	39	-
8th	113	109	46	-
9th	152	109	66	-
10th	159	123	100	-

SOUTH AUSTRALIA v NEW SOUTH WALES (Shield Match 1)

Played at Adelaide Oval on December 20, 21, 23, 1912. (Timeless match)
Toss : South Australia.   Result : SOUTH AUSTRALIA WON BY BY AN INNINGS AND 53 RUNS.
Debuts: South Australia - H.H.M.Bridgman, H.J.McKay, P.D.Rundell (all f/c).
12th Men: L.S.Waye (SA) and L.A.Cody (NSW).
Umpires: A.T.Haddrick and F.J.C.Thomas.
Attendances: No individual figures published.   Total: 4314.   Receipts: No figures published.
Close of Play: 1st day SA 6/420 (Steele 35); 2nd day NSW 4/177 (Barnes 17, McKew 1).

Eight established players - E.P.Barbour, W.Bardsley, H.Carter, A.Cotter, G.R.Hazlitt, H.V.Hordern, C.Kelleway and C.G.Macartney - were unavailable for New South Wales, significantly depleting the strength of the side. Bridgman, McKay and Rundell were late replacements in the home team for D.R.A.Gehrs, N.L.Gooden and R.B.C.Rees (all unavailable). Mayne (124 in 245 minutes, 11 fours), Chamberlain (103 in 130 minutes, 11 fours) and Steele (113 not out in 175 minutes, 15 fours, 1 chance) scored centuries for South Australia, Chamberlain and Steele both achieving their career-best scores. Collins (79 in 140 minutes, 11 fours) topscored in the first innings for New South Wales, Following on, Whitty dismissed Collins and Minnett with consecutive balls before Arnott (60 in 135 minutes, 3 fours) and Folkard (61 in 60 minutes, 1 six and 6 fours) made notable scores in the late order. *Wisden* incorrectly lists K.N.Steele instead of D.M.Steele in SA team. *Wisden* and *C.B.O'Reilly* incorrectly give NSW (1) Barnes 38, Arnott 21. Sources: *Wisden, C.B.O'Reilly, NSWCA Report, SACA Report, Adelaide Advertiser, South Australian Register.*

SOUTH AUSTRALIA

R.E.Mayne	c Waddy b Moore	124
J.N.Crawford	b Folkard	47
*C.Hill	c McKew b Folkard	8
A.G.Moyes	run out (Waddy/McKew)	64
W.L.Chamberlain	c Arnott b Barnes	103
D.M.Steele	not out	113
†G.C.Campbell	lbw b Emery	19
P.D.Rundell	b Minnett	36
H.H.M.Bridgman	b Minnett	11
W.J.Whitty	c Moore b Arnott	4
H.J.McKay	c Minnett b Massie	17
Extras	(b10, lb9, nb4)	23
Total	(141.3 overs, 420 mins)	569

NEW SOUTH WALES

*V.T.Trumper	b Whitty	0		b Whitty	11
E.L.Waddy	b Chamberlain	35		b Crawford	6
H.L.Collins	c Chamberlain b Bridgman	79		b Whitty	1
R.B.Minnett	c Bridgman b Rundell	39		c Crawford b Whitty	0
J.C.Barnes	c Campbell b Rundell	42		b Crawford	5
†C.G.McKew	b Crawford	1	(11)	not out	3
G.S.Moore	b Whitty	19	(6)	c & b McKay	48
P.S.Arnott	b Chamberlain	17	(7)	c Mayne b Whitty	60
S.H.Emery	not out	25		c Rundell b Crawford	23
B.J.Folkard	c Moyes b Rundell	5	(8)	c & b Crawford	61
R.J.A.Massie	b Chamberlain	5	(10)	run out (Steele/Whitty)	2
Extras	(b3, lb5, nb1)	9		(b8, lb6, w2, nb4)	20
Total	(89.0 overs, 250 mins)	276		(64.0 overs, 185 mins)	240

NEW SOUTH WALES	O	M	R	W	w,nb		O	M	R	W	w,nb
Massie	36.3	7	120	1	-,4						
Minnett	24	5	77	2	-,-						
Folkard	35	6	121	2	-,-						
Emery	21	3	96	1	-,-						
Arnott	9	0	68	1	-,-						
Moore	10	2	41	1	-,-						
Barnes	4	0	21	1	-,-						
Collins	2	0	2	0	-,-						

SOUTH AUSTRALIA	O	M	R	W	w,nb		O	M	R	W	w,nb
Whitty	22	7	62	2	-,-		15	4	37	4	-,3
Crawford	22	4	55	1	-,-		22	5	78	4	2,-
McKay	12	3	33	0	-,-		9	1	21	1	-,-
Chamberlain	21	5	76	3	-,1	(5)	3	0	16	0	-,1
Rundell	10	0	34	3	-,-	(6)	8	0	42	0	-,-
Bridgman	2	0	7	1	-,-	(4)	7	0	26	0	-,-

FALL OF WICKETS

Wkt	SA 1st	NSW 1st	NSW 2nd
1st	69	0	10
2nd	77	68	13
3rd	173	140	13
4th	343	170	20
5th	382	177	34
6th	420	201	95
7th	493	240	188
8th	525	240	222
9th	530	270	228
10th	569	276	240

VICTORIA v NEW SOUTH WALES (Shield Match 2)

Played at Melbourne Cricket Ground on December 26, 27, 28, 1912. (Timeless match)
Toss : Victoria.   Result : VICTORIA WON BY SIX WICKETS.
Debuts: Victoria - W.H.Cannon, J.L.McNaughton (both f/c).
12th Men: A.E.V.Hartkopf (Vic) and L.A.Cody (NSW).
Umpires: R.M.Crockett and D.A.Elder.
Attendances: 9651, 3722, 1516.   Total: 14,889.   Receipts: £446.
Close of Play: 1st day Vic 9/181 (Baring 36); 2nd day Vic (2) 3/75 (Seitz 15, Baring 29).

New South Wales, put in to bat on a damp wicket, were dismissed for a decisively low total. Minnett captured a wicket in the first over of each Victorian innings, Seitz with his fifth ball in the first and Carroll with his fourth ball in the second. Carroll topscored in the match, making 73 in 90 minutes with 5 fours. Cannon fell to the second ball of the second day. Barnes (53 in 79 minutes, 5 fours) and Moore (42 not out in 68 minutes, 5 fours) batted well in the New South Wales second innings while Ryder, right-arm fast-medium in his first season, took 6 for 44. Ransford received a heavy blow over the heart by a ball from Massie and retired at 1/3; he recovered the following day and was ready to bat if needed. McKew, who sustained a hand injury when he took a delivery from Massie early in the second innings, left the field and was replaced behind the stumps by Waddy with Cody fielding as substitute. *NSWCA Report* incorrectly gives NSW (1) Moore b Matthews. Sources: *Wisden, NSWCA Report, VCA Report, The Age, The Argus, The Herald, The Australasian.*

NEW SOUTH WALES

*V.T.Trumper	c & b Matthews	25	c Carkeek b McNaughton	10
E.L.Waddy	c Matthews b Ryder	6	b Ryder	10
H.L.Collins	c Armstrong b McNaughton	15	c Seitz b Ryder	44
R.B.Minnett	lbw b Armstrong	4	c Carkeek b Matthews	26
J.C.Barnes	b McNaughton	10	b Armstrong	53
G.S.Moore	c Brown b Matthews	16	not out	42
P.S.Arnott	c Armstrong b McNaughton	0	c Baring b Ryder	12
B.J.Folkard	c Baring b Matthews	1	c Ryder b McNaughton	19
S.H.Emery	st Carkeek b Matthews	0	c Carkeek b Ryder	5
R.J.A.Massie	c Carkeek b Matthews	0	c Carkeek b Ryder	7
†C.G.McKew	not out	5	c Carkeek b Ryder	0
Extras	(b1, lb1)	2	(b4)	4
Total	(47.1 overs, 125 mins)	84	(65.4 overs, 178 mins)	232

VICTORIA

E.V.Carroll	c Arnott b Moore	73	c Moore b Minnett	0
*J.A.Seitz	c Massie b Minnett	0	not out	35
V.S.Ransford	c Massie b Emery	37	retired hurt	1
J.Ryder	c Barnes b Emery	0	c sub (L.A.Cody) b Minnett	14
W.W.Armstrong	c Folkard b Moore	15	b Minnett	7
F.A.Baring	not out	36	c & b Massie	42
N.E.Brown	b Massie	0	not out	21
T.J.Matthews	c Moore b Massie	14		
J.L.McNaughton	b Massie	0		
†W.Carkeek	c Minnett b Emery	4		
W.H.Cannon	b Emery	0		
Extras	(b1, lb1)	2	(b13, lb4)	17
Total	(46.3 overs, 138 mins)	181	(43.4 overs, 116 mins) (4 wkts)	137

VICTORIA	O	M	R	W	w,nb		O	M	R	W	w,nb
McNaughton	16	6	29	3	-,-		15	3	72	2	-,-
Ryder	7	3	17	1	-,-		19.4	4	44	6	-,-
Matthews	16.1	6	25	5	-,-	(4)	8	1	32	1	-,-
Armstrong	8	4	11	1	-,-	(3)	17	3	48	1	-,-
Cannon							6	1	32	0	-,-

NEW SOUTH WALES	O	M	R	W	w,nb		O	M	R	W	w,nb
Minnett	5	0	27	1	-,-		15	3	40	3	-,-
Massie	14	1	46	3	-,-		19.4	5	45	1	-,-
Folkard	9	0	31	0	-,-		4	0	16	0	-,-
Emery	12.3	1	48	4	-,-		5	0	19	0	-,-
Moore	6	0	27	2	-,-						

FALL OF WICKETS

	NSW	VIC	NSW	VIC
Wkt	1st	1st	2nd	2nd
1st	21	1	21	0
2nd	36	84	21	32
3rd	43	86	60	40
4th	57	119	147	95
5th	66	128	147	-
6th	66	140	147	-
7th	73	166	219	-
8th	79	166	224	-
9th	79	181	232	-
10th	84	181	232	-

VICTORIA v SOUTH AUSTRALIA (Shield Match 3)

Played at Melbourne Cricket Ground on January 1, 2, 3, 1913. (Timeless match)
Toss : South Australia.   Result : SOUTH AUSTRALIA WON BY 68 RUNS.
Debuts: South Australia - L.S.Waye (f/c).
12th Men: R.L.Braid (Vic) and H.J.McKay (SA).
Umpires: R.M.Crockett and W.A.Young.
Attendances: 10419, 7934, 6342.   Total: 24,695.   Receipts: £722.
Close of Play: 1st day Vic 0/5 (Matthews 2, Carkeek 0); 2nd day SA (2) 5/39 (Mayne 30, Whitty 0).

Mayne (77 in 93 minutes, 11 fours and 52 in 80 minutes, 4 fours) and Crawford (83 in 113 minutes, 12 fours) shared the honours for South Australia with the bat. Matthews was struck a painful blow on the left wrist by a ball from Crawford late on the first day and stumps were drawn when he was forced to retire hurt. He was unable to take any further part in the match. Overnight rain made batting difficult on the last day; Baring did exceptionally well to make 76 in 108 minutes with 10 fours. Ryder, in outstanding form with the ball in his first season, took 13 wickets including a career-best 7 for 53 in the second innings. It was his only 10-wicket match haul in a first-class career which was to last a further 23 years. *VCA Report* incorrectly lists K.N.Steele instead of D.M.Steele in SA team. *SACA Report* incorrectly gives Vic (1) Ryder 44, extras 18. Sources: *Wisden, C.B.O'Reilly, VCA Report, SACA Report, The Age, The Argus, The Herald, The Australasian, The Leader.*

SOUTH AUSTRALIA

R.E.Mayne	lbw b Ryder	77		c Carkeek b Ryder	52
†G.C.Campbell	c Hartkopf b Ryder	37		b Seitz b Ryder	1
*C.Hill	c Matthews b Ransford	53	(10)	c Brown b Armstrong	17
J.N.Crawford	c Matthews b Armstrong	83	(8)	c Carkeek b Ryder	0
D.M.Steele	lbw b Ryder	7	(6)	c Carkeek b Ryder	4
D.R.A.Gehrs	c & b Ryder	11	(9)	not out	31
A.G.Moyes	b Armstrong	11	(3)	c Carroll b Ryder	3
W.L.Chamberlain	b Armstrong	14	(11)	c Brown b Armstrong	1
H.H.M.Bridgman	not out	8	(4)	b Ryder	0
L.C.Waye	c Hartkopf b Ryder	2	(5)	c Carkeek b Ryder	0
W.J.Whitty	c Matthews b Ryder	0	(7)	c Ryder b Armstrong	14
Extras	(b5, lb1)	6		(b2, lb2, nb1)	5
Total	(90.0 overs, 256 mins)	309		(38.1 overs, 145 mins)	128

VICTORIA

T.J.Matthews	retired hurt	2		absent hurt	-
†W.Carkeek	c Crawford b Chamberlain	46	(1)	c Mayne b Whitty	0
E.V.Carroll	c Waye b Whitty	55	(8)	b Whitty	8
V.S.Ransford	b Chamberlain	11	(7)	c Mayne b Chamberlain	21
W.W.Armstrong	c Crawford b Moyes	24	(6)	c Moyes b Whitty	1
F.A.Baring	run out (Crawford/Campbell)	15	(5)	b Crawford	76
A.E.V.Hartkopf	b Whitty	18	(9)	lbw b Whitty	7
*J.A.Seitz	b Moyes	0	(2)	run out (Waye/Campbell)	2
J.Ryder	not out	40	(4)	b Crawford	16
N.E.Brown	c Campbell b Crawford	6		not out	1
J.L.McNaughton	b Chamberlain	0	(3)	c Gehrs b Whitty	0
Extras	(b12)	12		(b5, lb3)	8
Total	(78.0 overs, 223 mins)	229		(36.4 overs, 120 mins)	140

VICTORIA	O	M	R	W	w,nb		O	M	R	W	w,nb		SA	VIC	SA	VIC
												FALL OF WICKETS				
McNaughton	14	4	54	0	-,-		9	2	36	0	-,-	Wkt	1st	1st	2nd	2nd
Ryder	28	7	102	6	-,-		19	6	53	7	-,-	1st	96	68	10	0
Armstrong	27	6	55	3	-,-		10.1	2	34	3	-,1	2nd	129	98	18	0
Matthews	12	2	54	0	-,-							3rd	200	136	18	9
Brown	4	0	25	0	-,-							4th	230	159	22	36
Ransford	5	1	13	1	-,-							5th	274	165	32	37
												6th	274	165	69	99
SOUTH AUSTRALIA	O	M	R	W	w,nb		O	M	R	W	w,nb	7th	299	206	74	110
Whitty	23	6	60	2	-,-		16	4	65	5	-,-	8th	300	219	105	138
Crawford	20	2	73	1	-,-		16.4	1	49	2	-,-	9th	307	229	126	140
Moyes	12	2	22	2	-,-							10th	309	-	128	-
Chamberlain	16	6	36	3	-,-	(3)	4	1	18	1	-,-					
Bridgman	4	0	15	0	-,-											
Gehrs	2	0	5	0	-,-											
Waye	1	0	6	0	-,-											

NEW SOUTH WALES v SOUTH AUSTRALIA (Shield Match 4)

Played at Sydney Cricket Ground on January 10, 11, 13, 14, 1913. (Timeless match)
Toss : New South Wales.   Result : NEW SOUTH WALES WON BY BY 84 RUNS.
Debuts: New South Wales - D.R.Cullen (f/c).
12th Men: G.S.Moore (NSW) and L.S.Waye (SA).
Umpires: W.G.Curran and A.C.Jones.
Attendances: 4052, 8345, 3205, 1861.   Total: 17,463.   Receipts: £767.
Close of Play: 1st day NSW 6/428 (Trumper 139, Lane 20); 2nd day SA 9/295 (Bridgman 42, McKay 1); 3rd day NSW (2) 314 all out.
New South Wales scored 428 runs in 288 minutes from 110.0 overs on the first day. Trumper's 201 not out occupied 209 minutes and included 21 fours and a chance at 103. Macartney (125 in 127 minutes and 136 balls, 18 fours and 96 in 144 minutes, 11 fours) dominated in each innings with support from Barbour (56 in 81 minutes, 8 fours and 60 in 75 minutes) and Bardsley (90 in 150 minutes, 9 fours). Hill replied for South Australia with 138 (168 minutes, 19 fours) and 77 (108 minutes, 9 fours). Mayne (67 in 103 minutes, 10 fours) and Moyes (95 in 101 minutes, 12 fours) also batted well. A.Cotter (knee injury), H.Carter, S.E.Gregory and H.V.Hordern were all unavailable for New South Wales. Cullen was a late replacement for J.D.Scott (work). *Wisden* and *O'Reilly* incorrectly give NSW (2) Whitty 5/90, Bridgman 0/14; SA (2) Steele c Kelleway. Sources: *Wisden, C.B.O'Reilly, NSWCA Report, SACA Report, Sydney Referee, Sydney Morning Herald, Town & Country Journal.*

NEW SOUTH WALES

Batsman	Dismissal (1st)	Runs	Dismissal (2nd)	Runs
C.Kelleway	run out (Whitty)	38	b Whitty	7
E.P.Barbour	b Crawford	56	c Mayne b McKay	60
C.G.Macartney	c Bridgman b Crawford	125	lbw b Crawford	96
W.Bardsley	c Bridgman b McKay	8	c Campbell b McKay	90
*V.T.Trumper	not out	201	b Whitty	25
H.L.Collins	c Steele b McKay	5	lbw b Whitty	13
R.B.Minnett	c Campbell b Bridgman	28	c Moyes b McKay	0
†J.B.Lane	b Whitty	20	c Campbell b Whitty	0
W.J.Stack	b Whitty	0	b McKay	1
D.R.Cullen	st Campbell b Crawford	8	c Crawford b Whitty	8
R.J.A.Massie	c Gehrs b Chamberlain	14	not out	4
Extras	(b1, lb9)	10	(b6, lb2, nb2)	10
Total	(129.2 overs, 347 mins)	513	(83.2 overs, 240 mins)	314

SOUTH AUSTRALIA

Batsman	Dismissal (1st)	Runs	Dismissal (2nd)	Runs
R.E.Mayne	c Stack b Massie	7	c Macartney b Massie	67
D.R.A.Gehrs	b Macartney	39	b Stack	25
*C.Hill	c Bardsley b Stack	138	b Massie	77
J.N.Crawford	c Bardsley b Cullen	19	b Massie	8
D.M.Steele	b Massie	0	(6) c Stack b Barbour	15
A.G.Moyes	b Cullen	0	(7) c Cullen b Stack	95
W.L.Chamberlain	c Massie b Cullen	9	(5) b Barbour	39
†G.C.Campbell	b Stack	14	c Minnett b Kelleway	43
H.H.M.Bridgman	c Trumper b Massie	59	b Macartney	0
W.J.Whitty	b Collins	10	not out	10
H.J.McKay	not out	13	b Kelleway	4
Extras	(b8, lb1, w8, nb6)	23	(b16, lb9, w1, nb3)	29
Total	(79.5 overs, 240 mins)	331	(102.3 overs, 300 mins)	412

SOUTH AUSTRALIA	O	M	R	W	w,nb		O	M	R	W	w,nb
Whitty	33	6	115	2	-,-		28.2	1	92	5	-,-
Moyes	5	1	31	0	-,-	(5)	2	1	12	0	-,-
Chamberlain	28.2	7	101	1	-,-	(2)	13	3	44	0	-,-
Crawford	30	0	124	3	-,-	(3)	16	1	68	1	-,-
McKay	22	3	70	2	-,-	(4)	21	1	76	4	-,2
Gehrs	5	0	31	0	-,-						
Bridgman	6	0	31	1	-,-	(6)	3	0	12	0	-,-

NEW SOUTH WALES	O	M	R	W	w,nb		O	M	R	W	w,nb
Cullen	18	2	79	3	6,-		18	0	79	0	1,-
Massie	21.5	3	74	3	2,2	(4)	27	5	62	3	-,2
Macartney	6	1	14	1	-,-	(7)	6	1	18	1	-,-
Stack	14	0	67	2	-,-	(3)	21	1	108	2	-,-
Kelleway	12	1	56	0	-,2		14.3	1	57	2	-,1
Collins	2	0	9	1	-,-	(2)	9	3	23	0	-,-
Minnett	6	3	9	0	-,2						
Barbour						(6)	7	0	36	2	-,-

FALL OF WICKETS

Wkt	NSW 1st	SA 1st	NSW 2nd	SA 2nd
1st	88	26	18	45
2nd	119	117	100	149
3rd	154	171	219	171
4th	296	173	262	186
5th	310	174	300	240
6th	365	202	300	259
7th	428	237	300	384
8th	436	258	302	389
9th	457	287	310	396
10th	513	331	314	412

NEW SOUTH WALES v VICTORIA (Shield Match 5)

Played at Sydney Cricket Ground on January 24, 25, 27, 28, 1913. (Timeless match)
Toss : Victoria.   Result : NEW SOUTH WALES WON BY EIGHT WICKETS.
Debuts: Victoria - H.H.G.Bracher (f/c).
12th Men: E.L.Waddy (NSW) and N.E.Brown (Vic).
Umpires: W.G.Curran and A.C.Jones.
Attendances: 4267, 8230, 8067, 702.   Total: 21,266.   Receipts: £994.
Close of Play: 1st day NSW 2/41 (Hordern 23, Cody 9); 2nd day NSW 8/473 (Barbour 144, Collins 12); 3rd day Vic (2) 9/335 (Matthews 68).

Victor Trumper (a chanceless 138 in 163 minutes, 23 fours) and Eric Barbour (146 in 174 minutes, 20 fours, 4 chances) established the all-time eighth-wicket record partnership in Australian first-class cricket by adding 270 in 147 minutes. Trumper had adopted the tactic of sending most of his bowlers in first, for no apparent reason other than experimentation. *The Referee* questioned 'why they were sent in puzzled every one'. Macartney continued his excellent form with 94 in 106 minutes (13 fours) and 76 in 76 minutes (10 fours). Armstrong (118 in 191 minutes, 11 fours) and Matthews (74 in 115 minutes, 11 fours and 81 in 90 minutes, 9 fours) dominated the batting for Victoria. Massie took a career-best 7 for 110 in the second innings. A.C.Facy and V.S.Ransford both withdrew after being selected to play for Victoria. Sources: *Wisden, NSWCA Report, The Age, The Australasian, Sydney Referee, Sydney Morning Herald*.

VICTORIA

Batsman	Dismissal	Runs	Dismissal	Runs
E.V.Carroll	c Kelleway b Massie	12	c Macartney b Massie	22
H.H.G.Bracher	b Massie	7	c Cotter b Massie	16
F.A.Baring	b Kelleway	19	c Hordern b Massie	36
*J.A.Seitz	st Lane b Hordern	13	c Hordern b Kelleway	44
W.W.Armstrong	not out	118	c Macartney b Massie	12
J.Ryder	st Lane b Hordern	2	c Kelleway b Massie	53
E.L.Carroll	b Massie	5	b Collins	43
T.J.Matthews	c Lane b Cotter	74	c Collins b Hordern	81
†W.Carkeek	c & b Massie	0	b Massie	2
H.W.Hart	b Hordern	3	b Massie	1
W.H.Cannon	c Kelleway b Hordern	9	not out	13
Extras	(b1, lb8, nb3)	12	(b27, lb13, w1, nb1)	42
Total	(80.0 overs, 232 mins)	274	(104.5 overs, 285 mins)	365

NEW SOUTH WALES

Batsman	Dismissal	Runs	Dismissal	Runs
H.V.Hordern	st Carkeek b Cannon	25		
†J.B.Lane	c Armstrong b Cannon	0		
R.J.A.Massie	c Seitz b Cannon	9		
L.A.Cody	c Carkeek b Matthews	39		
C.G.Macartney	c Seitz b Ryder	94	(3) not out	76
W.Bardsley	b Matthews	0	(4) not out	46
C.Kelleway	c & b Cannon	8	(1) b Cannon	7
*V.T.Trumper	b Matthews	138		
E.P.Barbour	b Cannon	146	(2) b Ryder	30
H.L.Collins	not out	12		
A.Cotter	b Cannon	2		
Extras	(b1, lb2, nb1)	4	(lb4)	4
Total	(117.0 overs, 326 mins)	477	(36.0 overs, 101 mins) (2 wkts)	163

NEW SOUTH WALES	O	M	R	W	w,nb		O	M	R	W	w,nb
Cotter	16	3	49	1	-,1		14	4	47	0	-,1
Massie	25	3	85	4	-,2		31	7	110	7	-,-
Kelleway	14	2	52	1	-,-	(4)	19	8	31	1	1,-
Hordern	22	4	69	4	-,-	(3)	26.5	2	87	1	-,-
Macartney	2	1	4	0	-,-		9	0	31	0	-,-
Barbour	1	0	3	0	-,-						
Collins						(6)	5	0	17	1	-,-

VICTORIA	O	M	R	W	w,nb		O	M	R	W	w,nb
Ryder	35	6	109	1	-,1		14	3	47	1	-,-
Cannon	23	4	107	6	-,-		11	2	57	1	-,-
Matthews	28	4	111	3	-,-		7	3	19	0	-,-
Armstrong	13	3	46	0	-,-		1	0	8	0	-,-
Hart	9	0	55	0	-,-		3	0	28	0	-,-
E.L.Carroll	6	0	25	0	-,-						
E.V.Carroll	3	0	20	0	-,-						

FALL OF WICKETS

Wkt	VIC 1st	NSW 1st	VIC 2nd	NSW 2nd
1st	10	0	40	37
2nd	27	22	61	45
3rd	39	44	98	-
4th	61	129	118	-
5th	73	129	162	-
6th	78	163	219	-
7th	234	181	322	-
8th	246	451	327	-
9th	263	475	335	-
10th	274	477	365	-

VICTORIA v TASMANIA

Played at Melbourne Cricket Ground on January 24, 25, 27, 28, 29, 1913. (Timeless match)
Toss : Tasmania.   Result : TASMANIA WON BY 54 RUNS.
Debuts: Victoria - R.H.Bailey, P.A.Shea (both f/c); H.O.Smith (Vic only). Tasmania - R.A.Davis, C.H.Robinson (both f/c).
12th Men: No 12th men or emergency fieldsmen; only 11 men in Tasmanian party.
Umpires: E.Barrass and D.A.Elder.
Attendances: Match total approximately 1500. No breakdowns published.   Receipts: £67.
Close of Play: 1st day Tas 331 all out ; 2nd day Vic 5/374 (Sewart 101, Spencer 43); 3rd day Tas (2) 5/170 (Hawson 74, Eltham 6);
    4th day Vic (2) 4/102 (Spencer 14).

Victorian teams were engaged in three simultaneous matches; this one, a Shield match in Sydney and a Colts match at the East Melbourne Ground against NSW. The Colts match, though not rated first-class, included five players who represented Victoria this season and a further four who went on to First-Class representation in the following season. Selection problems were compounded by several players' work commitments. Johnstone, expecting the match to finish inside three days, was forced to leave for Sydney on business on the last day, leaving his team to bat a man short. McKenzie fell to the fourth ball of the match, but thereafter consistent scoring saw substantial totals from both teams. Hawson (chanceless 199 in 270 minutes, 18 fours) compiled the highest innings by a Tasmanian to date and, with support from the late order, put his team in a winning position. Sewart (143 in 182 minutes, 14 fours and 69 not out in 70 minutes, 5 fours) enjoyed his most successful game of a 13 match career at this level but his efforts were to no avail. Shea kept wickets while Woodford bowled. Smith had previously represented Tasmania. *VCA Report* incorrectly gives Tas (1) Thomas c Sewart. Sources: *VCA Report, The Age, The Argus, The Herald, The Australasian, The Leader, Sydney Referee, Weekly Times.*

TASMANIA

M.S.McKenzie	b McNaughton	0	(6)	b McNaughton	25
G.D.Paton	b McNaughton	40	(3)	c Smith b McNaughton	1
*R.J.Hawson	b McNaughton	41	(4)	not out	199
C.H.Robinson	c McNaughton b Johnstone	12	(1)	b McNaughton	3
W.K.Eltham	c Shea b Spencer	58	(7)	b McNaughton	21
†L.Thomas	c Smith b McNaughton	59	(5)	c McNaughton b Johnstone	8
R.J.Pennycuick	c Dwyer b McNaughton	6	(9)	c Woodford b Kiernan	2
A.K.E.Watt	lbw b Shea	23	(10)	c Braid b Woodford	53
R.A.Davis	b Dwyer	18	(11)	b Bailey	22
C.P.Payne	b Kiernan	43	(8)	c Sewart b Kiernan	35
L.L.Gill	not out	21	(2)	b Johnstone	42
Extras	(lb6, w4)	10		(b26, lb10, nb1)	37
Total	(104.5 overs, 290 mins)	331		(146.4 overs, 330 mins)	448

VICTORIA

H.O.Smith	c Hawson b Robinson	37	(4)	b Eltham	20
R.G.Johnstone	c & b Watt	45		absent	-
J.C.Dwyer	c & b Pennycuick	67		c Thomas b Watt	52
C.Kiernan	st Thomas b Watt	58	(6)	b Watt	7
W.I.Sewart	b Eltham	143	(7)	not out	69
P.A.Shea	c Hawson b Watt	14	(1)	c McKenzie b Watt	7
E.L.Spencer	c & b Watt	52	(5)	b Eltham	14
R.I.Braid	lbw b Watt	10		lbw b Watt	29
R.H.Bailey	c McKenzie b Paton	9	(2)	c Watt b Robinson	4
J.L.McNaughton	not out	5	(9)	b Robinson	26
*†J.R.H.Woodford	c Hawson b Robinson	20	(10)	b Robinson	10
Extras	(b10, lb4, w1)	15		(b5, lb5, w1, nb1)	12
Total	(143.3 overs, 330 mins)	475		(59.2 overs, 170 mins)	250

VICTORIA	O	M	R	W	w,nb		O	M	R	W	w,nb		FALL OF WICKETS			
														TAS	VIC	TAS	VIC
McNaughton	32	7	82	5	4,-		44	16	94	4	-,-		Wkt	1st	1st	2nd	2nd
Bailey	11	2	33	0	-,-		15.4	4	39	1	-,-		1st	0	69	16	11
Dwyer	14	2	53	1	-,-		15	3	54	0	-,-		2nd	74	111	22	11
Braid	10	0	37	0	-,-		19	3	54	0	-,-		3rd	98	203	79	78
Johnstone	20	5	46	1	-,-		17	6	34	2	-,-		4th	100	227	95	102
Shea	8	0	34	1	-,-		4	0	22	0	-,-		5th	217	250	161	102
Spencer	7	1	30	1	-,-		7	1	18	0	-,1		6th	219	403	189	124
Kiernan	2.5	1	6	1	-,-		10	0	45	2	-,-		7th	224	425	264	192
Woodford							15	0	51	1	-,-		8th	261	446	269	227
TASMANIA	O	M	R	W	w,nb		O	M	R	W	w,nb		9th	284	446	385	250
Paton	29	7	57	1	-,-	(5)	7	2	20	0	-,-		10th	331	475	448	-
McKenzie	9	0	37	0	-,-												
Robinson	33.3	9	86	2	1,-	(1)	21.2	2	80	3	1,1						
Davis	15	0	64	0	-,-												
Watt	32	3	102	5	-,-	(2)	20	1	85	4	-,-						
Gill	6	1	34	0	-,-												
Pennycuick	8	1	30	1	-,-	(3)	2	0	14	0	-,-						
Hawson	5	1	21	0	-,-												
Eltham	6	1	29	1	-,-	(4)	9	0	39	2	-,-						

QUEENSLAND v VICTORIA

Played at Brisbane Cricket Ground (Woolloongabba) on January 31, February 1, 3, 1913. (Timeless match)
Toss : Queensland.   Result : VICTORIA WON BY SIX WICKETS.
Debuts: Queensland - R.W.Law, L.P.D.O'Connor (both f/c).
12th Men: H.W.Hart (Vic). No 12th for Qld.
Umpires: W.H.Carvosso and W.R.Shillington.
Attendances & Receipts: No figures published.
Close of Play: 1st day Vic 1/10 (Carkeek 4); 2nd day Qld (2) 2/40 (Sheppard 20, Smith 3).

Thomson's sole first-class century occupied 148 minutes (16 fours) and was responsible for Queensland's highest total against Victoria so far. The catalyst for a spectacular innings by Evans (75 in 39 minutes, 5 sixes and 7 fours) occurred before the batsman had scored, when umpire Carvosso adjudged him to be lbw, only for Seitz to recall him because the ball had hit bat before pad. Evans scored his runs out of 85 made while he was at the crease and took 8, 17 and 18 runs off successive overs from Cannon and 16 off an over from Matthews (4 successive fours). Other half-centuries in the match were scored by Law (50 not out in 60 minutes, 5 fours), Armstrong (60 in 85 minutes, 5 fours), Brown (63 in 90 minutes, 6 fours) and Carroll (90 not out in 107 minutes, 1 six and 9 fours). R.J.Hartigan and A.H.Jones were unavailable for Queensland and F.C.Thompson and J.W.McLaren withdrew after being named in the side. They were replaced by O'Connor (originally 12th man) and Smith. O'Connor, who served Queensland with distinction over the next 17 years as a batsman, wicket-keeper and captain, replaced Evans with the gloves from lunch on the second day onwards in his debut match. *Cricket* incorrectly gives Qld (1) Oxenham 9, extras 13, Ryder 1/65; Qld (2) Law 54*, Oxenham 7, Evans 0; Vic (1) Carkeek 8, Cannon 4. Sources: *Cricket, VCA Report, Brisbane Courier, Queensland Times.*

QUEENSLAND

S.J.Fennelly	c Seitz b Matthews	15		lbw b Matthews	16
J.F.Sheppard	c Bracher b Armstrong	42		c Seitz b Brown	45
J.Thomson	b Cannon	116		b Armstrong	0
R.W.Law	c E.L.Carroll b Ryder	3	(5)	not out	50
L.P.D.O'Connor	lbw b Armstrong	14	(6)	c Baring b Brown	0
W.Rowe	b Bracher	12	(7)	b Brown	6
R.K.Oxenham	c Carkeek b Matthews	8	(8)	b Armstrong	4
*†W.T.Evans	lbw b Matthews	75	(9)	b Armstrong	7
B.W.Cook	b Armstrong	7	(10)	b Armstrong	0
J.A.Downey	not out	9	(11)	lbw b Armstrong	0
H.G.S.Smith	c Matthews b Armstrong	15	(4)	b Ryder	5
Extras	(b4, lb10)	13		(b7, lb1, nb3)	11
Total	(100.5 overs, 275 mins)	330		(56.3 overs, 150 mins)	144

VICTORIA

†W.Carkeek	c Sheppard b Downey	6			
W.H.Cannon	b Downey	6			
E.V.Carroll	c Downey b Rowe	31	(4)	not out	90
F.A.Baring	c Fennelly b Smith	5	(3)	b Cook	34
W.W.Armstrong	b Downey	60	(1)	b Cook	33
J.Ryder	lbw b Downey	21	(2)	b Law	25
H.H.G.Bracher	st Evans b Downey	0			
*J.A.Seitz	b Downey	3	(5)	lbw b Oxenham	37
E.L.Carroll	st O'Connor b Downey	29	(6)	not out	0
N.E.Brown	c O'Connor b Smith	63			
T.J.Matthews	not out	19			
Extras	(b4, lb8, nb1)	13		(b2, lb2)	4
Total	(72.1 overs, 210 mins)	256		(51.1 overs, 147 mins) (4 wkts)	223

VICTORIA	O	M	R	W	w,nb		O	M	R	W	w,nb
Ryder	24	9	64	1	-,-	(3)	4	1	4	1	-,-
Matthews	35	6	107	3	-,-		17	6	46	1	-,-
Armstrong	26.5	8	73	4	-,-	(1)	27.3	6	48	5	-,3
Cannon	10	2	61	1	-,-						
Brown	4	2	6	0	-,-	(4)	8	0	35	3	-,-
Bracher	1	0	5	1	-,-						

QUEENSLAND	O	M	R	W	w,nb		O	M	R	W	w,nb
Smith	7.1	1	22	2	-,-		10	1	50	0	-,-
Downey	29	1	98	7	-,-		8.1	0	65	0	-,-
Rowe	18	0	66	1	-,-	(5)	1	0	2	0	-,-
Cook	8	0	31	0	-,-		11	1	35	2	-,-
Oxenham	3	0	12	0	-,-	(6)	4	1	16	1	-,-
Law	7	1	14	0	-,1	(3)	15	4	39	1	-,-
Thomson							2	0	12	0	-,-

FALL OF WICKETS

Wkt	QLD 1st	VIC 1st	QLD 2nd	VIC 2nd
1st	47	10	30	52
2nd	67	14	31	60
3rd	84	29	52	123
4th	140	67	98	217
5th	196	116	98	-
6th	211	120	108	-
7th	296	132	126	-
8th	305	145	140	-
9th	307	202	144	-
10th	330	256	144	-

NEW SOUTH WALES v THE REST

Played at Sydney Cricket Ground on February 7, 8, 10, 11 (no play), 12, 1913. (Four-day match)
Toss : The Rest.   Result : MATCH DRAWN.
Debuts: Nil.
12th Men: No 12th men or emergency fieldsmen named.
Umpires: J.Laing and C.W.Waugh.
Attendances: 8035, 12890, 7361, no play, 1965.   Total: 30,251.   Receipts: £1552.
Close of Play: 1st day Rest 9/356 (Matthews 17, Whitty 9); 2nd day NSW 3/214 (Trumper 27, Bardsley 4); 3rd day Rest (2) 6/165
    (Armstrong 33, Ryder 23); 4th day no play.

Arranged as a benefit for V.T.Trumper the match raised £2950, easily a record in Australia to that time. The great batsman marked the occasion by scoring an unbeaten 126 in 166 minutes with 16 fours after surviving two difficult caught-and-bowled chances, the first to Armstrong when about 30 and the second to Crawford when 50. Trumper was also bowled by a Whitty no-ball before he had scored; in the second innings he batted 61 minutes and hit 10 fours. Kelleway was out to the fourth ball of the first innings. Barbour (86 in 143 minutes, 10 fours) and Macartney (91 in 100 minutes, 13 fours) made good contributions while Noble came out of brief retirement to score 46 in 57 minutes and share a partnership of 108 with Trumper for the fifth wicket. Hill (66 in 103 minutes, 6 fours), Moyes (76 in 109 minutes, 1 six and 10 fours) and Ryder (71 in 109 minutes, 9 fours) scored fifties for the Rest. Ryder captured his wickets in the first innings in 4 overs for 4 runs. Rain disrupted the second day and washed out the fourth, resulting in a one-day extension which was also reduced by rain. G.R.Hazlitt (teaching duties) was absent on the final day and the Gloucestershire player F.H.Bateman-Champain, who was in Sydney on holiday, took the field in his stead. F.A.Baring (unavailable) withdrew from the Rest. His replacements, first E.V.Carroll and then J.A.Seitz announced their unavailability and Cody was brought in instead. *NSWCA Report* incorrectly gives NSW (2) Noble c Crawford. Sources: *Wisden, NSWCA Report, Sydney Referee, Sydney Morning Herald, Town & Country Journal.*

THE REST

R.E.Mayne	c & b Hazlitt	40		c Barbour b Kelleway	26
†G.C.Campbell	b Hordern	14	(10)	lbw b Massie	9
*C.Hill	b Massie	66		st Carter b Noble	34
W.W.Armstrong	b Kelleway	1	(6)	b Macartney	42
V.S.Ransford	c Carter b Massie	38		b Hordern	0
A.G.Moyes	b Macartney	76	(4)	st Carter b Hordern	25
J.N.Crawford	c Bardsley b Noble	0	(9)	c Noble b Massie	20
L.A.Cody	lbw b Hordern	42	(2)	b Kelleway	18
J.Ryder	c Collins b Hordern	38	(8)	c Carter b Collins	71
T.J.Matthews	not out	18	(7)	c Noble b Hordern	0
W.J.Whitty	b Collins	10		not out	8
Extras	(b5, lb8, w1, nb1)	15		(b7, lb5)	12
Total	(97.3 overs, 283 mins)	358		(80.0 overs, 231 mins)	265

NEW SOUTH WALES

C.Kelleway	c Campbell b Whitty	0	(7)	c Armstrong b Ryder	1
E.P.Barbour	c Matthews b Armstrong	86	(1)	c Hill b Whitty	4
C.G.Macartney	c Moyes b Whitty	91		c Matthews b Whitty	10
*V.T.Trumper	not out	126		c Crawford b Matthews	61
W.Bardsley	c Crawford b Armstrong	24	(2)	c Crawford b Armstrong	45
M.A.Noble	c Armstrong b Ryder	46	(5)	c Campbell b Ryder	8
H.L.Collins	c Crawford b Ryder	0	(6)	not out	9
†H.Carter	c Hill b Ryder	5	(9)	not out	0
H.V.Hordern	c Mayne b Ryder	0	(8)	c Campbell b Ryder	1
G.R.Hazlitt	c Campbell b Ryder	2			
R.J.A.Massie	lbw b Crawford	3			
Extras	(b5, lb1)	6		(b4, lb2, nb1)	7
Total	(97.0 overs, 278 mins)	389		(44.0 overs, 135 mins) (7 wkts)	146

NEW SOUTH WALES	O	M	R	W	w,nb		O	M	R	W	w,nb
Massie	27	3	83	2	1,-		17	9	23	2	-,-
Hordern	21	3	67	3	-,-	(4)	18	1	72	3	-,-
Hazlitt	15	3	54	1	-,-	(2)	7	1	24	0	-,-
Kelleway	17	4	67	1	-,1	(3)	11	2	35	2	-,-
Noble	10	0	51	1	-,-		7	1	24	1	-,-
Macartney	6	0	21	1	-,-	(7)	10	3	34	1	-,-
Collins	1.3	1	0	1	-,-	(6)	10	0	41	1	-,-

THE REST	O	M	R	W	w,nb		O	M	R	W	w,nb
Whitty	29	5	113	2	-,-		15	3	38	2	-,-
Armstrong	22	2	72	2	-,-	(3)	8	3	24	1	-,-
Crawford	17	1	73	1	-,-	(4)	7	0	45	0	-,1
Matthews	10	2	59	0	-,-	(5)	2	0	10	1	-,-
Ryder	19	3	66	5	-,-	(2)	12	2	22	3	-,-

FALL OF WICKETS

Wkt	REST 1st	NSW 1st	REST 2nd	NSW 2nd
1st	31	0	39	11
2nd	89	138	60	35
3rd	90	198	95	100
4th	152	242	103	135
5th	179	350	125	140
6th	184	350	126	142
7th	281	358	178	146
8th	308	358	231	-
9th	335	366	245	-
10th	358	389	265	-

NEW SOUTH WALES v QUEENSLAND

Played at Sydney Cricket Ground on February 14, 15, 17, 1913. (Timeless match)
Toss : Queensland,   Result : NEW SOUTH WALES WON BY AN INNINGS AND 92 RUNS.
Debuts: New South Wales - N.M.Gregg, W.S.Prentice (both f/c). Queensland - C.Hanify (f/c).
12th Men: P.S.Arnott (NSW) and S.W.Ayres (Qld).
Umpires: W.G.Curran and W.G.French.
Attendances: 1147, 3355, 200.   Total: About 4700.   Receipts: £178.
Close of Play: 1st day NSW 1/73 (Cody 34, Moore 22); 2nd day Qld (2) 0/5 (Law 2, Bolton 1).

Thomson (62 in 83 minutes, 10 fours) and Thompson (100 in 118 minutes, 13 fours) stood out for Queensland on the first day, Thompson's maiden first-class century came in his first innings in Sydney. Ayres substituted in the field for Thomson (ill) on the second day. Massie, a left-arm fast-medium giant, bowled eight batsmen in the match and finished with the figures of 10 for 106. Macartney (154 in 164 minutes, 20 fours) shared century partnerships with Trumper for the fifth wicket and Tozer (78 not out in 97 minutes, 8 fours) for the sixth wicket. *Cricket* gives incorrect match dates and Qld (1) Mailey 0/50. *NSWCA Report* incorrectly gives Qld (1) Barstow b Massie. Sources: *Cricket, NSWCA Report, Sydney Referee, Sydney Morning Herald, Town & Country Journal.*

QUEENSLAND

Batsman	Dismissal	Runs		Dismissal	Runs
S.J.Fennelly	c Moore b Scott	3	(3)	b Massie	0
J.Thomson	b Massie	62	(6)	b Massie	39
J.F.Sheppard	b Massie	2	(5)	b Scott	0
F.C.Thompson	b Collins	100		b Mailey	16
R.W.Law	b Scott	10	(2)	c Prentice b Scott	2
*J.S.Redgrave	b Scott	1	(9)	lbw b Mailey	4
W.Rowe	b Massie	30		b Massie	1
C.Hanify	b Massie	9		run out (Collins)	18
†J.T.Bolton	b Massie	26	(1)	c Prentice b Massie	15
C.B.Barstow	c Tozer b Massie	3		b Scott	10
J.A.Downey	not out	3		not out	2
Extras	(b14, lb7, w2, nb4)	27		(b1, lb3, w1, nb3)	8
Total	(68.0 overs, 209 mins)	276		(29.5 overs, 101 mins)	115

NEW SOUTH WALES

Batsman	Dismissal	Runs
H.L.Collins	run out (Fennelly)	14
L.A.Cody	c Law b Barstow	39
G.S.Moore	b Rowe	52
N.M.Gregg	b Hanify	33
C.G.Macartney	st Bolton b Rowe	154
*V.T.Trumper	b Rowe	53
C.J.Tozer	not out	78
†W.S.Prentice	b Downey	0
J.D.Scott	c Redgrave b Hanify	20
A.A.Mailey	c sub (S.W.Ayres) b Barstow	0
R.J.A.Massie	c Redgrave b Downey	24
Extras	(b7, lb7, w2)	16
Total	(104.4 overs, 293 mins)	483

NEW SOUTH WALES	O	M	R	W	w,nb		O	M	R	W	w,nb
Scott	21	5	81	3	-,3		12.5	3	47	3	1,1
Massie	26	6	73	6	1,1		11	1	33	4	-,2
Mailey	10	0	56	0	-,-	(4)	3	0	20	2	-,-
Moore	4	1	13	0	-,-						
Collins	7	1	26	1	1,-	(3)	3	0	7	0	-,-

QUEENSLAND	O	M	R	W	w,nb
Barstow	24	1	110	2	-,-
Downey	27.4	3	114	2	-,-
Hanify	15	2	52	2	2,-
Redgrave	13	1	51	0	-,-
Rowe	22	2	117	3	-,-
Law	3	0	23	0	-,-

FALL OF WICKETS

Wkt	QLD 1st	NSW 1st	QLD 2nd
1st	24	35	10
2nd	31	98	11
3rd	116	123	35
4th	149	166	38
5th	153	280	38
6th	213	385	44
7th	232	388	98
8th	249	429	99
9th	260	430	107
10th	276	483	115

SOUTH AUSTRALIA v VICTORIA (Shield Match 6)

Played at Adelaide Oval on February 28, March 1, 3, 4, 1913. (Timeless match)
Toss : South Australia.　　　　　Result : SOUTH AUSTRALIA WON BY 166 RUNS.
Debuts: South Australia - R.F.Middleton (f/c).
12th Men: N.L.Gooden (SA) and N.E.Brown (Vic).
Umpires: A.McIntyre and F.J.C.Thomas.
Attendances: 2500, 5000, 500,　? .　　　　Total: About 8000.　　　Receipts: £233.
Close of Play: 1st day SA 368 all out; 2nd day SA (2) 1/70 (Mayne 51, Hill 10); 3rd day Vic (2) 4/139 (Matthews 56, McKenzie 29).

Jack Crawford, South Australia's prized all-rounder from Surrey, registered his Australian best with both bat and ball, leading South Australia to their third Sheffield Shield in the process. Offering a chance at 11, Crawford scored 163 in 171 minutes including 1 six and 18 fours. His right-arm fast-medium deliveries then accounted for eight Victorian batsmen, seven bowled, to give his team a decisive first-innings lead. Ransford (65 in 88 minutes, 7 fours) and Armstrong (72 in 134 minutes, 6 fours) made Victoria's highest scores. Mayne (106 in 165 minutes, 1 six and 9 fours) dominated a second innings in which Armstrong dismissed Hill and Gehrs with successive balls. Overnight rain precipitated Victoria's demise on a wet wicket on the last day. H.H.M.Bridgman (unavailable) was replaced in the home side by Middleton, originally nominated for 12th man duties. J.Ryder and J.A.Seitz withdrew after being selected for Victoria and were replaced by McKenzie and McNaughton.　Sources: *Wisden, C.B.O'Reilly, VCA Report, SACA Report, Sydney Morning Herald, Adelaide Advertiser, South Australian Register.*

SOUTH AUSTRALIA

R.E.Mayne	st Carkeek b Matthews	43	lbw b McKenzie		106
†G.C.Campbell	st Carkeek b Matthews	27	b McNaughton		9
*C.Hill	lbw b McNaughton	16	c Matthews b Armstrong		11
D.R.A.Gehrs	b McNaughton	13	b Armstrong		0
A.G.Moyes	b Matthews	19	b Armstrong		17
J.N.Crawford	c Baring b Cannon	163	b McKenzie		18
R.F.Middleton	b Matthews	20	b Cannon		14
P.D.Rundell	c Cannon b McNaughton	31	c Carkeek b Cannon		13
R.B.C.Rees	b McNaughton	8	not out		20
W.J.Whitty	c Matthews b Cannon	14	b Armstrong		1
H.J.McKay	not out	0	c & b Cannon		10
Extras	(b10, lb4)	14	(lb3)		3
Total	(111.2 overs, 290 mins)	368	(73.2 overs, 205 mins)		222

VICTORIA

E.V.Carroll	b Crawford	6		b Rundell	21
E.L.Carroll	b Crawford	0	(8)	c McKay b Rees	17
F.A.Baring	b Crawford	22		b Rundell	19
*V.S.Ransford	b Whitty	65	(5)	c Hill b Rundell	6
W.W.Armstrong	b Crawford	72	(7)	not out	17
T.J.Matthews	run out (Gehrs)	8	(4)	b Crawford	56
M.D.Hotchin	b Crawford	3	(2)	b Whitty	1
C.McKenzie	not out	17	(6)	b Whitty	34
†W.Carkeek	c Gehrs b Crawford	0		run out (Rundell/Campbell)	11
J.L.McNaughton	b Crawford	1		b Whitty	1
W.H.Cannon	b Crawford	0		c Gehrs b Whitty	1
Extras	(b14, nb1)	15		(b19, lb7, nb5)	31
Total	(68.5 overs, 211 mins)	209		(73.4 overs, 215 mins)	215

VICTORIA	O	M	R	W	w,nb		O	M	R	W	w,nb					
McNaughton	32	6	101	4	-,-		21	2	72	1	-,-			SA	VIC	SA	VIC
Cannon	16.2	2	67	2	-,-	(3)	13.2	0	47	3	-,-	Wkt	1st	1st	2nd	2nd
Matthews	40	7	111	4	-,-	(5)	2	1	8	0	-,-	1st	69	4	31	1
McKenzie	20	3	66	0	-,-		8	2	22	2	-,-	2nd	80	21	71	38
Baring	3	0	9	0	-,-							3rd	100	60	71	45
Armstrong						(2)	29	5	70	4	-,-	4th	123	124	93	51
												5th	123	140	124	141
SOUTH AUSTRALIA	O	M	R	W	w,nb		O	M	R	W	w,nb	6th	155	160	153	145
Whitty	21	1	46	1	-,1		23.4	10	30	4	-,5	7th	250	205	191	180
Crawford	22.5	7	66	8	-,-		23	5	60	1	-,-	8th	276	205	194	204
McKay	7	1	18	0	-,-	(5)	8	0	25	0	-,-	9th	368	209	199	205
Rees	10	0	30	0	-,-		7	0	25	1	-,-	10th	368	209	222	215
Rundell	7	0	27	0	-,-	(3)	12	3	44	3	-,-					
Gehrs	1	0	7	0	-,-											

TASMANIA v NEW SOUTH WALES

Played at T.C.A. Ground, Hobart, on March 1, 3, 1913. (Timeless match)
Toss : Tasmania.   Result : NEW SOUTH WALES WON BY AN INNINGS AND 289 RUNS.
Debuts: Tasmania - H.E.Allen, G.F.Linney (both f/c).
12th Men: R.Wilkins (Tas) and T.J.E.Andrews (NSW).
Umpires: T.Harper and A.J.Williams.
Attendances: 1500, 500.   Total: About 2000.   Receipts: £106.
Close of Play: 1st day NSW 3/293 (Collins 141, Davis 4).

Tasmania fielded a team drawn solely from the south of the island due to the non-participation of players from the Northern Tasmanian Cricket Association. L.Thomas, considered Tasmania's leading wicket-keeper, announced his unavailability while other Launceston players, M.S.McKenzie and L.R.Tumilty, withdrew after being selected in the team. *The Hobart Mercury* was 'heartily sick and tired of the apathy shown by Northern players' towards the match. F.Price, appointed to umpire with Williams, had a disagreement over match fees and was replaced by Harper before the game got underway. C.Kelleway and E.L.Waddy withdrew from the selected New South Wales team and were replaced by Andrews and Davis when J.C.Barnes and E.A.Bull declined invitations to take part. Robinson, who sustained a heavy knock on the knee from Massie on the first day, took no further part in the match after being dismissed and was replaced in the field by Wilkins. Collins scored the highest of his 32 first-class hundreds. He batted 290 minutes and survived four chances, mid-50s, 111 (twice) and 207, hitting 1 five and 31 fours, sharing century partnerships with Gregg (79 in 54 minutes, 10 fours), Cody (42 in 55 minutes, 7 fours), Davis (77 in 100 minutes, 8 fours) and Trumper (87 not out in 55 minutes, 9 fours). It was reported that Trumper should not have batted because of a split finger while fielding but he felt he 'could not disappoint the crowd'. He was unable to field in the second innings, Andrews acting as substitute. Eltham and Pennycuick put on 85 for the first wicket in 60 minutes and Hawson made 42 in 30 minutes with 9 fours. Altogether 507 runs were scored on the second day to conclude the match, somewhat surprising haste for a "timeless" match. *Cricket* and *SMH* give Tas (2) Massie 6/59, Hordern 1/57. Sources: *Cricket, NSWCA Report, Sydney Morning Herald, Hobart Mercury.*

TASMANIA

*R.J.Hawson	b Hordern	11	(5) c Cody b Scott		42
G.D.Paton	b Scott	17	(4) b Scott		12
W.K.Eltham	b Hordern	0	(1) c Carter b Hordern		30
C.H.Robinson	st Carter b Hordern	11	absent hurt		-
A.K.E.Watt	b Scott	0	(8) c Hordern b Massie		4
R.J.Pennycuick	c Davis b Hordern	27	(2) c Gregg b Massie		49
A.C.Newton	c Carter b Scott	32	(3) b Massie		1
E.T.Boddam	c Minnett b Hordern	10	(7) c Collins b Massie		0
C.P.Payne	c Carter b Hordern	4	(10) c Gregg b Massie		10
H.E.Allen	b Scott	8	(9) not out		21
†G.F.Linney	not out	1	(6) b Massie		4
Extras	(b11, lb6, nb1)	18	(b4, lb4, nb5)		13
Total	(41.0 overs, 135 mins)	139	(35.4 overs, 125 mins)		186

NEW SOUTH WALES

C.J.Tozer	lbw b Allen	15
H.L.Collins	b Eltham	282
N.M.Gregg	c Allen b Pennycuick	79
L.A.Cody	c & b Boddam	42
H.H.Davis	b Boddam	77
*V.T.Trumper	not out	87
R.B.Minnett	)	
†H.Carter	)	
H.V.Hordern	) did not bat	
J.D.Scott	)	
R.J.A.Massie	)	
Extras	(b23, lb8, nb1)	32
Total	(107.3 overs, 290 mins) (5 wkts dec)	614

NEW SOUTH WALES	O	M	R	W	w,nb		O	M	R	W	w,nb
Massie	7	2	17	0	-,-	(3)	13.4	2	63	6	-,2
Hordern	20	4	67	6	-,-		12	2	53	1	-,-
Scott	14	2	37	4	-,1	(1)	10	0	57	2	-,3

TASMANIA	O	M	R	W	w,nb
Boddam	29	1	125	2	-,1
Allen	24	0	133	1	-,-
Paton	15	0	82	0	-,-
Watt	16	0	86	0	-,-
Newton	5	0	52	0	-,-
Pennycuick	15	1	67	1	-,-
Eltham	3.3	0	37	1	-,-

FALL OF WICKETS

Wkt	TAS 1st	NSW 1st	TAS 2nd
1st	21	39	85
2nd	27	153	85
3rd	35	258	96
4th	35	446	144
5th	63	614	149
6th	86	-	150
7th	103	-	150
8th	110	-	161
9th	138	-	186
10th	139	-	-

1913-14 SEASON (16 MATCHES)

New Zealand's second tour of Australia's Eastern States comprised nine matches, four of which were first-class. The team arrived in December and began brightly by recording a narrow win over Queensland, but then lost successive matches against New South Wales and Victoria - each by an innings - before drawing the final match against South Australia. Dan Reese, the New Zealand captain, was by far their most accomplished performer.

New South Wales regained the Sheffield Shield from South Australia, Victoria finishing in last place for the fifth time in six seasons. The champions overcame the initial setback of losing their opening match at Adelaide to win their last three and take the Shield outright. Their strongest players were Macartney, Bardsley and Collins (batting), Kelleway (allround) and Massie (bowling). Macartney had a phenomenal run of success at the Sydney Cricket Ground. In the five matches there he hit 195, 117, 54, 142, 201 and 110. He scored at least 100 runs in a session in four of his five centuries.

Crawford again experienced a fine year for South Australia with bat and ball. Clem Hill gave glimpses of his ability but the other batsmen were not as prolific as before. In addition, Whitty was available for only one match and his bowling was sorely missed. Victoria relied heavily on the allround efforts of Armstrong and Ryder, although the batting of Baring and Park fostered hope for the future.

Queensland were comprehensively beaten in their three interstate fixtures after their narrow defeat by New Zealand. Fennelly was their best batsman, while Ironmonger's bowling resulted in an invitation to play for Victoria. As a consequence he played for two States this season.

Tasmania were completely outclassed by New south Wales when they travelled to Sydney in February. Later that month they hosted two matches against Victoria, only to suffer a similar fate in both encounters. Stan Stephens, in the second of his three first-class matches, hit a century in each innings for Victoria at Launceston.

Western Australia invited teams from both New South Wales and South Australia to visit Perth this year. Neither came, although South Australia withdrew only after failing to assemble a reasonably representative team. A number of their players were unable to obtain leave. Western Australia had some satisfaction later in the year when, on October 15, they were admitted to the Board of Control.

New Zealand cricketer-businessman Arthur Sims offered to cover expenses for a visit by an Australian XI to New Zealand in February 1914. Monty Noble and Frank Laver acted as his agents and the Board of Control sanctioned the tour after some initial reluctance. The full team comprised A.Sims (captain), W.W.Armstrong, L.A.Cody, H.L.Collins, J.N.Crawford, C.E.Dolling, F.J.Laver, W.MacGregor, C.McKenzie, A.A.Mailey, M.A.Noble, V.S.Ransford, V.T.Trumper and E.L.Waddy.

An Australian team was also named to tour South Africa the following season. Clem Hill, H.V.Hordern, R.J.A.Massie, V.S.Ransford and V.T.Trumper all announced their inability to tour. The team was selected by E.E.Bean, Hill and L.O.S.Poidevin and comprised W.W.Armstrong (captain), T.J.E.Andrews, E.P.Barbour, W.Bardsley, F.A.Baring, W.Carkeek, G.R.Hazlitt, C.Kelleway, C.G.Macartney, R.E.Mayne, A.G.Moyes, J.Ryder, W.J.Whitty and G.C.Campbell (player-manager). Barbour and Hazlitt subsequently withdrew and were replaced by B.J.Folkard and R.L.Park. The outbreak of war in Europe caused the Board of Control to cancel the tour on August 17. This was particularly unfortunate for Baring, Folkard, Campbell, Barbour and Moyes - all destined never to represent Australia.

Leading Aggregates

Batsmen	M	I	NO	Runs	HS	Ave.	Bowlers	Runs	Wkts	Ave.
C.G.Macartney (NSW)	7	9	1	892	201	111.50	C.Kelleway (NSW)	571	45	12.68
W.W.Armstrong (V)	5	8	2	555	202*	92.50	R.J.A.Massie (NSW)	604	37	16.32
H.L.Collins (NSW)	6	8	1	482	111	68.85	J.N.Crawford (SA)	697	34	20.50
R.L.Park (V)	6	12	0	417	104	34.75	H.Ironmonger (Q & V)	566	30	18.86
R.S.Stephens (V)	2	4	1	358	181	119.33	J.Ryder (V)	714	28	25.50
T.J.E.Andrews (NSW)	7	8	0	315	96	39.37	B.J.Folkard (NSW)	406	20	20.30
J.N.Crawford (SA)	5	9	1	313	91	39.12				
F.A.Baring (V)	4	8	0	310	122	38.75				
D.Reese (NZ)	4	8	1	307	130*	43.85				
S.J.Fennelly (Q)	4	8	0	303	131	37.87				

SHEFFIELD SHIELD TABLE

	P	W	L	D	Pts	Quotient	Runs Scored	Wkts Lost	Runs Conceded	Wkts Taken
NEW SOUTH WALES	4	3	1	-	2	1.610	1945	51	1871	79
SOUTH AUSTRALIA	4	2	2	-	0	0.868	1992	80	1892	66
VICTORIA	4	1	3	-	-2	0.746	2024	74	2198	60
TOTAL	6	6	6	-	0	1.000	5961	205	5961	205

QUEENSLAND v NEW SOUTH WALES

Played at Brisbane Cricket Ground (Woolloongabba) on November 21, 22, 24, 1913. (Timeless match)
Toss : Queensland.   Result : NEW SOUTH WALES WON BY EIGHT WICKETS.
Debuts: Queensland - S.W.Ayres, R.J.Willcocks (both f/c). New South Wales - H.G.Pratten (f/c).
12th Men: J.K.Farquhar (Qld) and A.T.Ratcliffe (NSW).
Umpires: G.A.Carter and W.H.Carvosso (R.Haigh deputised).
Attendances: "not large", 3000, 250.   Total: About 4000.   Receipts: No figures published.
Close of Play: 1st day NSW 5/182 (Pratten 38); 2nd day Qld (2) 8/208 (Oxenham 0).

C.Kelleway captured the earliest detected split hat-trick in Australian first-class cricket when he dismissed Ayres (first innings) and Sheppard and Thomson (second innings). The feat went unnoticed by all at the ground, including the Press, and it has never before been listed as a hat-trick in any record book. Probably such hat-tricks were not recognised in Australia until after the First World War. Kelleway almost made it "four in four" by inducing a caught-and-bowled chance from Thompson next ball. He took two wickets in two balls on two other separate occasions in the match, dismissing Oxenham and Barstow (first innings) and Ayres and Barstow (second innings) in succession, Barstow bagging a king pair in the process. Kelleway finished with his only ten-wicket-match at first-class level. Cranney (56 in 46 minutes, 10 fours), Collins (54 in 110 minutes) and Pratten (50 in 100 minutes, 4 fours) scored half-centuries in New South Wales's first innings while Collins (64 not out in 94 minutes) and Waddy (63 not out in 70 minutes) in the second gave the visitors their fifth win in a row over Queensland with an unfinished stand of 119. Fennelly's sole first-class century (131 in 203 minutes, 11 fours) included a stumping chance off Mailey when he was 73. He was seventh out at 208. Haigh stood for umpire Carvosso (ill) on the last day. W.T.Evans, J.W.McLaren and J.S.Redgrave were all unavailable for Queensland. E.P.Barbour, R.J.A.Massie and C.J.Tozer, who all had university exams, were unavailable for New South Wales while Ratcliffe, selected to keep wicket, was left out of the eleven because of a hand injury he sustained at practice. It was reported in the *Sydney Morning Herald* that other leading New South Wales players (no names given) had made themselves unavailable for the trip because compulsory inoculations were required before the team departed. *NSWCA Report* gives Qld (2) some incorrect falls of wickets. Sources: *NSWCA Report, Sydney Morning Herald, Brisbane Courier, Queensland Times.*

QUEENSLAND

S.J.Fennelly	c Cody b Mailey	26	c Cranney b Kelleway		131
J.F.Sheppard	b Mailey	36	b Kelleway		1
*J.Thomson	c Taylor b Cullen	38	b Kelleway		0
F.C.Thompson	b Mailey	0	c Cody b Mailey		7
†L.P.D.O'Connor	c & b Cullen	18	lbw b Gee		26
W.Rowe	st Waddy b Mailey	16	c Cody b Collins		24
S.W.Ayres	b Kelleway	14	c Waddy b Kelleway		0
R.K.Oxenham	b Kelleway	1	b Kelleway		1
C.B.Barstow	b Kelleway	0	c Cody b Kelleway		0
R.J.Willcocks	c Collins b Kelleway	0	c Mailey b Kelleway		0
J.A.Downey	not out	1	not out		9
Extras	(b19, lb5, nb2)	26	(b10, lb3, w2, nb5)		20
Total	(46.4 overs, 165 mins)	176	(81.5 overs, 220 mins)		219

NEW SOUTH WALES

C.Kelleway	lbw b Barstow	2			
H.Cranney	c & b Downey	56	(1) st O'Connor b Downey		20
H.L.Collins	c Ayres b Willcocks	54	not out		64
*†E.L.Waddy	c & b Rowe	5	not out		63
H.G.Pratten	c Sheppard b Oxenham	50			
J.S.Taylor	c O'Connor b Oxenham	19			
L.A.Cody	b Barstow	0	(2) b Barstow		0
H.H.Davis	b Barstow	20			
D.A.Gee	c Sheppard b Barstow	24			
A.A.Mailey	b Barstow	0			
D.R.Cullen	not out	4			
Extras	(b9, lb4)	13	(lb3)		3
Total	(71.2 overs, 192 mins)	247	(36.0 overs, 96 mins) (2 wkts)		150

NEW SOUTH WALES	O	M	R	W	w,nb		O	M	R	W	w,nb
Kelleway	12.4	3	34	4	-,2	(2)	23.5	7	48	7	-,4
Cullen	12	1	54	2	-,-	(1)	12	2	42	0	2,1
Mailey	18	3	51	4	-,-		23	2	66	1	-,-
Collins	4	1	11	0	-,-		15	7	22	1	-,-
Gee							7	2	17	1	-,-
Cranney							1	0	4	0	-,-

QUEENSLAND	O	M	R	W	w,nb		O	M	R	W	w,nb
Willcocks	16	4	58	1	-,-	(4)	3	0	18	0	-,-
Barstow	23.2	0	91	5	-,-	(1)	14	2	42	1	-,-
Rowe	12	3	37	1	-,-		3	0	18	0	-,-
Downey	10	2	25	1	-,-	(2)	11	0	38	1	-,-
Ayres	2	0	3	0	-,-		4	0	26	0	-,-
Oxenham	8	2	20	2	-,-		1	0	5	0	-,-

FALL OF WICKETS

Wkt	QLD 1st	NSW 1st	QLD 2nd	NSW 2nd
1st	73	21	2	1
2nd	82	72	2	31
3rd	82	83	40	-
4th	135	152	124	-
5th	144	182	200	-
6th	160	191	205	-
7th	168	205	208	-
8th	168	234	208	-
9th	169	238	210	-
10th	176	247	219	-

VICTORIA v QUEENSLAND

Played at Melbourne Cricket Ground on December 5, 6, 8, 1913. (Timeless match)
Toss : Queensland.   Result : VICTORIA WON BY AN INNINGS AND 209 RUNS.
Debuts: Nil.
12th Men: R.L.Park (Vic) and S.W.Ayres (Qld).
Umpires: R.M.Crockett and J.O'Connor.
Attendances: 900, 3500, 300.   Total: About 4700.   Receipts: £118.
Close of Play: 1st day Vic 4/221 (Armstrong 83, Ransford 78); 2nd day Qld (2) 5/95 (Rowe 32, Redgrave 11).

F.A.Baring (unavailable) was replaced in the Victorian side by Kiernan. C.B.Barstow and W.T.Evans, the nominated captain, withdrew from the Queensland side for the southern tour of Victoria and New South Wales and were replaced by Ironmonger and O'Connor. The match began with several maidens from McNaughton and Ryder, Fennelly being dismissed by the second ball of McNaughton's second over and Thomson falling to the second ball of his third over. Armstrong's unbeaten 202 occupied 315 minutes and included 17 fours. He shared big partnerships with Ransford (82 in 112 minutes, 9 fours, chances at 4 and 7) and Matthews (62 in 88 minutes, 4 fours) for the fifth and seventh wickets A foot injury prevented Matthews taking the field on the last day; Park substituted. Sources: *VCA Report, The Age, The Argus, The Herald, The Australasian, The Leader.*

QUEENSLAND

S.J.Fennelly	b McNaughton	0	b Ryder	9
J.F.Sheppard	c Ryder b Cannon	13	c Carroll b McNaughton	13
J.Thomson	b McNaughton	0	c Matthews b Ryder	21
F.C.Thompson	c Armstrong b McNaughton	4	lbw b McNaughton	1
W.Rowe	run out (Kiernan)	25	c Kiernan b Cannon	54
†L.P.D.O'Connor	c Armstrong b Cannon	3	lbw b Cannon	4
*J.S.Redgrave	c Carkeek b McNaughton	20	b Ryder	15
R.K.Oxenham	b Ryder	8	not out	17
J.W.McLaren	b Cannon	15	c Kiernan b Cannon	4
J.A.Downey	c Matthews b Ryder	13	b Armstrong	1
H.Ironmonger	not out	1	st Carkeek b Cannon	11
Extras	(b5, lb2, w1)	8	(b5, lb1)	6
Total	(47.1 overs, 147 mins)	110	(52.3 overs, 150 mins)	156

VICTORIA

W.I.Sewart	c O'Connor b McLaren	0
E.V.Carroll	c O'Connor b McLaren	33
A.E.V.Hartkopf	c O'Connor Ironmonger	2
C.Kiernan	b Downey	22
W.W.Armstrong	not out	202
*V.S.Ransford	b McLaren	82
J.Ryder	c & b Redgrave	36
T.J.Matthews	b McLaren	62
†W.Carkeek	c Redgrave b Downey	17
J.L.McNaughton	b Rowe	1
W.H.Cannon	run out (/O'Connor)	0
Extras	(b11, lb5, w2)	18
Total	(107.2 overs, 360 mins)	475

VICTORIA	O	M	R	W	w,nb		O	M	R	W	w,nb
McNaughton	15	8	23	4	1,-		15	3	52	2	-,-
Ryder	17.1	4	36	2	-,-		18	3	49	3	-,-
Cannon	9	2	25	3	-,-		11.3	1	39	4	-,-
Matthews	6	0	18	0	-,-						
Hartkopf						(4)	4	1	3	0	-,-
Armstrong						(5)	4	1	7	1	-,-

QUEENSLAND	O	M	R	W	w,nb
McLaren	26	1	116	4	2,-
Ironmonger	25	1	99	1	-,-
Downey	28	0	119	2	-,-
Rowe	8.2	1	44	1	-,-
Oxenham	11	0	50	0	-,-
Redgrave	9	1	29	1	-,-

FALL OF WICKETS

	QLD	VIC	QLD
Wkt	1st	1st	2nd
1st	0	2	17
2nd	0	11	25
3rd	10	50	46
4th	38	70	49
5th	43	232	61
6th	68	312	100
7th	78	426	136
8th	88	460	140
9th	106	475	143
10th	110	475	156

NEW SOUTH WALES v QUEENSLAND

Played at Sydney Cricket Ground on December 12, 13, 15, 1913. (Timeless match)
Toss : Queensland.   Result : NEW SOUTH WALES WON BY AN INNINGS AND 28 RUNS.
Debuts: Nil.
12th Men: E.L.Waddy (NSW) and J.W.McLaren (Qld).
Umpires: W.G.Curran and R.M.Wallace.
Attendances: 979, 3533, 250.   Total: About 4800.   Receipts: £179.
Close of Play: 1st day NSW 2/71 (Davis 28, Andrews 18); 2nd day 571 all out.

New South Wales scored precisely 500 runs on the second day including 202 in the last session. Macartney (195 in 150 minutes, 26 fours) and Scott (100 in 130 minutes, 10 fours) added 218 runs for the eighth wicket in 97 minutes. Macartney commenced his innings immediately after lunch and was 104 not out in 105 minutes at tea. Davis (71 in 100 minutes, 8 fours) and Andrews (96 in 113 minutes, 11 fours) had earlier stabilised the innings. Fennelly (78 in 120 minutes, 10 fours) and Rowe (53 in 78 minutes, 7 fours) topscored for Queensland after Folkard dismissed Sheppard and Thomson with successive deliveries. Fennelly also led the second innings, batting 90 minutes. E.P.Barbour, F.E.McElhone and C.J.Tozer were all unavailable for New South Wales and W.Bardsley, H.V.Hordern (ill) and R.J.A.Massie withdrew after being selected. Mailey, Scott and G.S.Moore were the nominated replacements but Moore also announced his unavailability and Davis, the named 12th man, came in. H.W.Webster (unavailable) was replaced as wicket-keeper by Munn. Sources: *NSWCA Report, Sydney Referee, Sydney Morning Herald, Sydney Daily Telegraph, Brisbane Courier, Town & Country Journal.*

QUEENSLAND

J.F.Sheppard	c Davis b Folkard	40		b Kelleway	20
S.J.Fennelly	b Kelleway	78		c Mailey b Scott	57
J.Thomson	b Folkard	0	(4)	b Kelleway	12
W.Rowe	c Scott b Folkard	53	(3)	b Kelleway	19
F.C.Thompson	c Scott b Mailey	38		b Folkard	6
*J.S.Redgrave	b Folkard	48		c Munn b Kelleway	6
R.K.Oxenham	b Mailey	0		b Davis	18
S.W.Ayres	c Macartney b Folkard	30		b Kelleway	30
†L.P.D.O'Connor	b Folkard	4	(10)	b Kelleway	13
J.A.Downey	not out	2	(9)	b Kelleway	1
H.Ironmonger	b Folkard	0		not out	0
Extras	(b14, lb3, w1)	18		(b41, lb7, nb2)	50
Total	(73.3 overs, 216 mins)	311		(71.1 overs, 206 mins)	232

NEW SOUTH WALES

L.A.Cody	b Downey	9
H.L.Collins	c Thompson b Ironmonger	8
H.H.Davis	c Fennelly b Rowe	71
T.J.E.Andrews	b Ironmonger	96
C.Kelleway	lbw b Ironmonger	34
C.G.Macartney	c Ayres b Redgrave	195
*V.T.Trumper	c O'Connor b Ironmonger	13
B.J.Folkard	b Ironmonger	0
J.D.Scott	c Oxenham b Downey	100
†R.A.Munn	b Redgrave	7
A.A.Mailey	not out	19
Extras	(b16, lb3)	19
Total	(117.2 overs, 326 mins)	571

NEW SOUTH WALES	O	M	R	W	w,nb		O	M	R	W	w,nb		FALL OF WICKETS		
Scott	17	0	75	0	1,-		16	4	50	1	-,2		QLD	NSW	QLD
Kelleway	16	3	68	1	-,-	(3)	23.1	10	35	7	-,-	Wkt	1st	1st	2nd
Mailey	18	1	79	2	-,-	(5)	8	2	23	0	-,-	1st	81	13	71
Folkard	21.3	2	65	7	-,-		16	5	50	1	-,-	2nd	81	25	108
Davis	1	0	6	0	-,-	(6)	1	0	6	1	-,-	3rd	166	168	133
Collins						(2)	7	2	18	0	-,-	4th	200	212	146
												5th	261	261	156
QUEENSLAND	O	M	R	W	w,nb							6th	261	287	164
Ironmonger	38	3	158	5	-,-							7th	301	291	213
Downey	24.2	0	112	2	-,-							8th	306	509	219
Redgrave	21	3	85	2	-,-							9th	311	522	219
Rowe	17	0	90	1	-,-							10th	311	572	232
Ayres	7	0	44	0	-,-										
Oxenham	7	0	47	0	-,-										
Thomson	3	0	16	0	-,-										

QUEENSLAND v NEW ZEALAND XI

Played at Brisbane Cricket Ground (Woolloongabba) on December 19 (no play), 20, 22, 1913. (Three-day match)
Toss : Queensland.   Result : NEW ZEALAND XI WON BY 12 RUNS.
Debuts: Queensland - C.E.Cossart, J.K.Farquhar, C.Griffiths, J.A.Prout (all f/c).
12th Men: J.T.Bolton (Qld). No 12th named for New Zealand XI.
Umpires: W.H.Carvosso and A.T.Horrigan.
Attendances: no play, 1500, 500.   Total: About 2000.   Receipts: No figures published.
Close of Play: 1st day no play; 2nd day NZ(2) 4/64 (Taylor 8, Patrick 4).

Heavy rain caused the abandonment of play on the opening day and damaged the pitch to such an extent that batting was difficult throughout. Barstow and Ironmonger took advantage of the softened wicket when the match began in sunny conditions, making the ball bump awkwardly. Marshal's 42 (70 minutes, 2 sixes and 1 four) and unbeaten 66 (117 minutes, 6 fours) were masterly under the circumstances. Patrick, not out at the close of play, was delayed by his transport to the ground on the last day and had not arrived when play began. Reese joined Taylor at the crease and Patrick was permitted to resume his innings at 6/111. Fennelly was out to the first ball of the second innings which saw no catches taken. Sandman bowled Evans and Cossart with successive balls and Downey three balls later. R.J.Hartigan had been invited to captain the home team but was unavailable and was replaced by Prout, the nominated 12th man. *Reese incorrectly gives NZ (2) Ironmonger 0/45; Qld (2) Reese 2/15. Sources: T.W.Reese, Sydney Referee, Brisbane Courier, Queensland Times.*

NEW ZEALAND XI

L.G.Hemus	lbw b Barstow	14		b Griffiths	25
A.N.C.Snedden	c Marshal b Ironmonger	2		st Evans b Barstow	0
B.J.Tuckwell	c Cossart b Barstow	9		b Barstow	18
R.G.Hickmott	c Downey b Ironmonger	19		c Farquhar b Griffiths	1
*D.Reese	c Fennelly b Ironmonger	7	(7)	b Barstow	4
W.R.Patrick	run out (Downey)	10		c Rowe b Barstow	27
D.M.Sandman	c Rowe b Barstow	9	(9)	st Evans b Downey	4
L.G.Taylor	st Evans b Ironmonger	5	(5)	c & b Downey	22
C.W.Robinson	c & b Barstow	2	(8)	st Evans b Downey	27
J.H.Bennett	st Evans b Barstow	1		lbw b Barstow	16
†C.Boxshall	not out	7		not out	3
Extras	(b2, lb2)	4		(b11, lb3)	14
Total	(31.0 overs, 95 mins)	89		(45.3 overs, 140 mins)	161

QUEENSLAND

S.J.Fennelly	c Robinson b Reese	2		b Robinson	0
A.Marshal	b Reese	42		not out	66
W.Rowe	b Reese	3	(4)	b Reese	0
J.K.Farquhar	c Tuckwell b Bennett	3	(3)	b Reese	3
J.A.Prout	c Tuckwell b Bennett	14		b Sandman	18
*†W.T.Evans	c Hickmott b Reese	30		b Sandman	8
C.E.Cossart	c Bennett b Reese	0		b Sandman	0
J.A.Downey	st Boxshall b Reese	3		b Sandman	0
C.B.Barstow	c Hickmott b Bennett	0		run out	5
C.Griffiths	b Reese	0		b Robinson	3
H.Ironmonger	not out	3		b Sandman	1
Extras	(b24)	24		(b5, lb4, nb1)	10
Total	(35.2 overs, 98 mins)	124		(44.2 overs, 117 mins)	114

QUEENSLAND	O	M	R	W	w,nb		O	M	R	W	w,nb				
Barstow	16	4	47	5	-,-	(2)	11.3	1	45	5	-,-				
Ironmonger	15	4	38	4	-,-	(1)	6	1	14	0	-,-				
Downey							9	1	50	3	-,-				
Griffiths							15	4	26	2	-,-				
Marshal							2	0	4	0	-,-				
Rowe							2	0	8	0	-,-				

NEW ZEALAND XI	O	M	R	W	w,nb		O	M	R	W	w,nb
Reese	17.2	3	53	7	-,-	(2)	6	1	17	2	-,-
Bennett	17	6	40	3	-,-	(3)	4	1	9	0	-,-
Snedden	1	0	7	0	-,-						
Robinson						(1)	17	1	37	2	-,1
Sandman						(4)	17.2	1	41	5	-,-

FALL OF WICKETS

Wkt	NZ 1st	QLD 1st	NZ 2nd	QLD 2nd
1st	9	7	5	0
2nd	26	19	29	7
3rd	29	22	48	7
4th	42	73	51	57
5th	54	83	69	71
6th	65	90	111	71
7th	77	110	120	71
8th	80	111	126	95
9th	80	115	152	105
10th	89	124	161	114

NEW SOUTH WALES v SOUTH AUSTRALIA (Shield Match 1)

Played at Sydney Cricket Ground on December 19, 20, 22, 23, 1913. (Timeless match)
Toss : South Australia.   Result : SOUTH AUSTRALIA WON BY 19 RUNS.
Debuts: South Australia - C.E.Pellew, K.N.Steele, C.L.Winser (all f/c).
12th Men: H.L.Collins (NSW) and H.H.M.Bridgman (SA).
Umpires: W.G.Curran and C.W.Waugh.
Attendances: 2477, 5997, 1325, "very small".   Total: 9799 (excluding final day).   Receipts: £388.
Close of Play: 1st day NSW 2/149 (Macartney 104, Trumper 19); 2nd day SA (2) 7/183 (Rundell 6); 3rd day NSW (2) 7/197 (Folkard 17).

Crawford (91 in 89 minutes, 17 fours) and Pellew (57 in 61 minutes, 10 fours) held the South Australian first innings together. Middleton (2) was hit in the groin by a ball from Massie and retired between 185 and 190, resuming at 9/247. New South Wales began their reply immediately after the tea adjournment. Bardsley was out first ball in the second over which brought Macartney to the crease. He proceeded to 50 in 35 minutes, and his century in 75 minutes just before stumps. He was out early next day after 107 minutes, hitting 20 fours. Mayne (68 in 133 minutes) batted defensively. Macartney in the second innings hit 54 in 63 minutes with 7 fours. No charge was made for admission on the final day. McKew was included for New South Wales as a replacement for H.W.Webster, who was again unavailable. Webster was never again asked to play and therefore did not represent the State of his birth, all his first-class cricket being restricted to his appearances with South Australia and the 1912 Australians in England. Pre-match reports in *SMH* mention A.C.Jones instead of Waugh who is given in the annual *NSWCA Report*. Sources: *Wisden, C.B.O'Reilly, NSWCA Report, SACA Report, Sydney Referee, Sydney Morning Herald, Sydney Daily Telegraph, Town & Country Journal, Newcastle Herald*.

SOUTH AUSTRALIA

*R.E.Mayne	b Folkard	28		st McKew b Mailey	68
W.L.Chamberlain	b Massie	5		b Massie	0
J.N.Crawford	c McKew b Massie	91	(5)	b Andrews	40
D.M.Steele	b Kelleway	28	(3)	b Kelleway	1
A.G.Moyes	b Kelleway	9	(4)	c Mailey b Folkard	41
R.F.Middleton	not out	16	(9)	c Massie b Folkard	14
P.D.Rundell	b Kelleway	0		not out	47
H.P.Kirkwood	st McKew b Mailey	14	(10)	b Folkard	36
C.E.Pellew	b Massie	57	(6)	b Mailey	23
K.N.Steele	b Folkard	6	(11)	c Trumper b Massie	11
†C.L.Winser	b Folkard	0	(8)	b Folkard	1
Extras	(b18, lb5, w4)	27		(b4, lb2, nb2)	8
Total	(70.1 overs, 196 mins)	281		(97.1 overs, 251 mins)	290

NEW SOUTH WALES

C.Kelleway	b Crawford	21	b Chamberlain	12
W.Bardsley	c Mayne b Crawford	0	c Winser b Kirkwood	41
C.G.Macartney	c Chamberlain b Crawford	117	b Crawford	54
*V.T.Trumper	c D.M.Steele b Kirkwood	20	b Crawford	18
H.H.Davis	c Winser b Kirkwood	11	c Chamberlain b Crawford	22
T.J.E.Andrews	c Pellew b Rundell	43	c Pellew b Crawford	21
E.P.Barbour	c Mayne b Kirkwood	52	st Winser b Moyes	5
B.J.Folkard	not out	25	b Kirkwood	42
R.J.A.Massie	b Crawford	7	c Kirkwood b Crawford	5
A.A.Mailey	b Crawford	0	c Chamberlain b Kirkwood	11
†C.G.McKew	run out (Rundell/Kirkwood)	2	not out	0
Extras	(b2, lb3, nb4)	9	(b12, lb1, nb1)	14
Total	(84.3 overs, 221 mins)	307	(80.3 overs, 210 mins)	245

NEW SOUTH WALES	O	M	R	W	w,nb		O	M	R	W	w,nb					
Massie	23.1	4	80	3	4,-		27.1	4	85	2	-,-					
Kelleway	17	3	51	3	-,-		20	8	34	1	-,2					
Folkard	18	3	63	3	-,-		24	10	61	4	-,-					
Mailey	12	1	60	1	-,-	(5)	16	1	65	2	-,-					
Andrews						(4)	9	0	36	1	-,-					
Davis							1	0	1	0	-,-					

													FALL OF WICKETS			
													SA	NSW	SA	NSW
												Wkt	1st	1st	2nd	2nd
												1st	11	4	1	29
												2nd	95	77	2	83
												3rd	169	150	75	125
												4th	170	174	133	126
												5th	179	175	171	167
SOUTH AUSTRALIA	O	M	R	W	w,nb		O	M	R	W	w,nb	6th	179	245	176	174
K.N.Steele	11	1	48	0	-,4	(4)	4	0	22	0	-,-	7th	222	283	183	197
Crawford	36	7	89	5	-,-	(1)	35	8	71	5	-,1	8th	247	300	207	205
Rundell	11	0	61	1	-,-							9th	247	300	275	244
Chamberlain	5	0	24	0	-,-	(2)	21	1	72	1	-,-	10th	281	307	290	245
Kirkwood	21.3	3	76	3	-,-	(3)	6.3	0	38	3	-,-					
Moyes						(5)	14	2	28	1	-,-					

NEW SOUTH WALES v NEW ZEALAND XI

Played at Sydney Cricket Ground on December 26, 27, 1913. (Three-day match)
Toss : New South Wales.   Result : NEW SOUTH WALES WON BY AN INNINGS AND 247 RUNS.
Debuts: Nil.
12th Men: No 12th men or emergencies named.
Umpires: W.G.French and J.C.Gairns.
Attendances: 3299, 3220.   Total: 6519.   Receipts: £272.
Close of Play: 1st day NSW 5/234 (Scott 25).

Trumper was "temporarily detained" on the first morning, Bardsley tossing with Reese in his absence. Kelleway took the wickets of Hemus (third ball) and Tuckwell (fifth ball) in his opening over, following a maiden from Scott, and bowled unchanged throughout the innings. Collins (104 in 125 minutes, 1 five and 9 four), Scott (84 in 86 minutes, 10 fours) and Macartney (142 in 103 minutes, 20 fours) made quick runs for New South Wales. Macartney began his innings at the start of the second day, a minute or two after midday, and added 171 for the sixth wicket in 73 minutes with Scott. He brought up his 50 in 38 minutes, 100 in 68 minutes, and was not out at lunch (1.30) when the total was 439; his score at that stage, though not given, was well over the century. Snedden (44 in 82 minutes, 6 fours) and Sandman (53 not out in 74 minutes, 8 fours) made the highest score for New Zealand who had not yet become accustomed to the faster pace of Australian pitches. Sources: *T.W.Reese, NSWCA Report, Sydney Referee, Sydney Morning Herald, Sydney Daily Telegraph, Town & Country Journal, Newcastle Herald.*

NEW ZEALAND XI

A.N.C.Snedden	b Kelleway	44	c Trumper b Kelleway	7
L.G.Hemus	c McKew b Kelleway	0	c Scott b Mailey	7
B.J.Tuckwell	b Kelleway	0	b Mailey	7
R.G.Hickmott	b Scott	0	c Trumper b Mailey	7
*D.Reese	b Kelleway	6	st McKew b Mailey	5
W.R.Patrick	b Kelleway	6	run out (Andrews/McKew)	2
D.M.Sandman	not out	53	run out (Bardsley/Andrews/McKew)	33
T.A.Carlton	lbw b Kelleway	3	not out	22
C.W.Robinson	b Kelleway	31	c & b Andrews	0
J.H.Bennett	c Bardsley b Andrews	7	b Andrews	5
†C.Boxshall	c Mailey b Andrews	1	b Andrews	0
Extras	(b4, lb5, nb1)	10	(b6, lb3, nb1)	10
Total	(42.2 overs, 134 mins)	161	(34.5 overs, 106 mins)	105

NEW SOUTH WALES

W.Bardsley	b Robinson	7
T.J.E.Andrews	c Tuckwell b Bennett	48
H.L.Collins	b Robinson	104
L.A.Cody	lbw b Sandman	41
H.H.Davis	c Carlton b Reese	5
J.D.Scott	run out (Hickmott)	84
C.G.Macartney	c Reese b Robinson	142
*V.T.Trumper	b Sandman	32
C.Kelleway	not out	31
A.A.Mailey	run out (Hemus/Boxshall)	1
†C.G.McKew	b Robinson	2
Extras	(b15, lb1)	16
Total	(96.5 overs, 255 mins)	513

NEW SOUTH WALES	O	M	R	W	w,nb	O	M	R	W	w,nb
Scott	10	3	37	1	-,1	1	0	3	0	-,-
Kelleway	21	6	53	7	-,-	11	4	15	1	-,-
Mailey	10	0	55	0	-,-	15	1	41	4	-,-
Andrews	1.2	0	6	2	-,-	5.5	0	24	3	-,-
Davis						2	0	12	0	-,1

NEW ZEALAND XI	O	M	R	W	w,nb
Robinson	21.5	1	129	4	-,-
Reese	12	0	82	1	-,-
Carlton	14	0	64	0	-,-
Sandman	28	3	131	2	-,-
Bennett	17	0	70	1	-,-
Hickmott	3	0	18	0	-,-
Hemus	1	0	3	0	-,-

FALL OF WICKETS

Wkt	NZ 1st	NSW 1st	NZ 2nd
1st	0	10	20
2nd	0	98	20
3rd	10	175	32
4th	27	192	35
5th	35	234	37
6th	70	405	50
7th	84	457	98
8th	142	487	98
9th	159	492	105
10th	161	513	105

VICTORIA v SOUTH AUSTRALIA (Shield Match 2)

Played at Melbourne Cricket Ground on December 26, 27, 29, 30, 1913. (Timeless match)
Toss : South Australia.　　　　Result : VICTORIA WON BY FIVE WICKETS.
Debuts: Nil.
12th Men: W.I.Sewart (Vic) and R.F.Middleton (SA).
Umpires: W.J.Bruton and R.M.Crockett.
Attendances: 10612, 11773, 5853, 3904.　　Total: 32,142.　　Receipts: £1053.
Close of Play: 1st day SA 245 all out; 2nd day SA (2) 5/128 (D.M.Steele 39, Chamberlain 6); 3rd day Vic (2) 3/145 (Park 65, Armstrong 30).

Armstrong left his stamp on the match with a fine all-round performance. Although weakened by a malarial attack, he teamed with Ryder to hold the South Australian batting in check on the opening day. Mayne (58 in 108 minutes, 4 fours), Moyes (53 in 60 minutes, 6 fours) and Chamberlain (43 in 94 minutes, 6 fours) alone offered any serious resistance. The Victorian batting collapsed despite ideal conditions on the second day, Armstrong (51 in 82 minutes, 3 fours) remaining undefeated. Steele (84 in 245 minutes, 5 fours) and Kirkwood (58 in 99 minutes, 7 fours) arrested a collapse of the South Australian second innings with an eighth wicket stand of 108. Set 352 to win, the Victorians entered the final day requiring a further 207 with 7 wickets in hand. Park (104 in 248 minutes, 10 fours) and Armstrong (132 in 250 minutes, 6 fours) added 153 in a crucial fourth wicket stand that set up the final victory. Sources: *Wisden, C.B.O'Reilly, VCA Report, SACA Report, The Age, The Argus, The Herald, The Australasian, The Leader.*

SOUTH AUSTRALIA

*R.E.Mayne	lbw b Armstrong	58	c Carkeek b Matthews		28
D.M.Steele	b Armstrong	8	(3) c sub (R.L.Braid) b Matthews		84
A.G.Moyes	c Ransford b Ryder	53	(6) c Park b Cannon		7
J.N.Crawford	c Matthews b Ryder	24	(5) c & b Cannon		20
W.L.Chamberlain	b Armstrong	43	(7) b Ryder		8
C.E.Pellew	c Ryder b McNaughton	17	(8) b Armstrong		1
P.D.Rundell	run out (Matthews/Carkeek)	8	(2) b Ryder		8
H.P.Kirkwood	b Armstrong	7	(9) c Armstrong b Ryder		58
H.H.M.Bridgman	not out	25	(4) lbw b Cannon		11
K.N.Steele	b Ryder	1	c Bracher b Matthews		0
†C.L.Winser	b Ryder	0	not out		6
Extras	(lb1)	1	(b6, lb9)		15
Total	(105.2 overs, 285 mins)	245	(105.5 overs, 275 mins)		246

VICTORIA

R.L.Park	c Winser b Crawford	3	b Crawford		104
H.H.G.Bracher	c & b Kirkwood	15	(6) not out		42
F.A.Baring	c Winser b Crawford	7	st Winser b Kirkwood		17
*V.S.Ransford	c D.M.Steele b Crawford	25	b Chamberlain		11
T.J.Matthews	lbw b Kirkwood	0			
J.Ryder	c Crawford b Kirkwood	0	(7) not out		9
W.W.Armstrong	not out	51	(5) c Pellew b Moyes		132
E.V.Carroll	c Bridgman b Kirkwood	24	(2) b Kirkwood		15
†W.Carkeek	b Kirkwood	6			
J.L.McNaughton	b Crawford	3			
W.H.Cannon	st Winser b Kirkwood	5			
Extras	(lb1)	1	(b16, lb7, nb1)		24
Total	(45.1 overs, 135 mins)	140	(119.1 overs, 360 mins) (5 wkts)		354

VICTORIA	O	M	R	W	w,nb		O	M	R	W	w,nb		FALL OF WICKETS			
													SA	VIC	SA	VIC
McNaughton	22	3	76	1	-,-		21	12	40	0	-,-	Wkt	1st	1st	2nd	2nd
Ryder	35.2	6	93	4	-,-		29	9	64	3	-,-	1st	39	16	18	23
Armstrong	41	19	51	4	-,-	(5)	11	5	23	1	-,-	2nd	120	26	49	61
Cannon	6	0	11	0	-,-		22	3	58	3	-,-	3rd	120	26	68	91
Baring	1	0	13	0	-,-							4th	186	27	96	244
Matthews						(3)	22.5	7	46	3	-,-	5th	194	29	114	326
												6th	212	69	131	-
SOUTH AUSTRALIA	O	M	R	W	w,nb		O	M	R	W	w,nb	7th	212	108	132	-
Crawford	23	5	63	4	-,-		36	6	111	1	-,-	8th	236	122	240	-
Kirkwood	22.1	4	76	6	-,-		27	4	76	2	-,-	9th	245	129	240	-
K.N.Steele							8	0	29	0	-,-	10th	245	140	246	-
Rundell							8	1	29	0	-,-					
Chamberlain							25	5	50	1	-,-					
Pellew							6	2	8	0	-,1					
Moyes							9.1	5	27	1	-,-					

VICTORIA v NEW SOUTH WALES (Shield Match 3)

Played at Melbourne Cricket Ground on January 1, 2, 3, 1914. (Timeless match)
Toss : New South Wales.　　　　　Result : NEW SOUTH WALES WON BY AN INNINGS AND 59 RUNS.
Debuts: Nil.
12th Men: C.Kiernan (Vic) and H.H.Davis (NSW).
Umpires: H.J.Alessio and R.M.Crockett.
Attendances: 13717, 10907, 8112.　　　　Total: 32,736.　　　Receipts: £1044.
Close of Play: 1st day NSW 6/285 (Bardsley 81, Massie 0); 2nd day Vic (2) 2/3 (Carkeek 1).

Armstrong, who assumed the home captaincy when V.S.Ransford was unable to play due to illness, led Victoria only until lunch on the first day; an argument with the selectors E.E.Bean, M.Ellis and P.A.McAlister, who refused to promise him the captaincy for the remainder of the season, resulted in Armstrong refusing to continue in the position and Carroll deputised - reluctantly - for the rest of the match. Further talks after the game brought about a compromise, and Armstrong captained Victoria in their next match. Collins (73 in 115 minutes, 7 fours) and Bardsley (124 not out in 277 minutes, 9 fours) topscored for New South Wales. Bracher (knee) and Sewart (hand) sustained fielding injuries on the first day, Kiernan and G.E.J.Healy substituting for the remainder of the innings. Sewart, who had been included in the side for Ransford, was unable to bat in the first innings and Bracher required a runner in both. Baring's maiden first-class hundred (122 in 160 minutes, 13 fours) accounted for 61.3 per cent of Victoria's second-innings total . Sources: *Wisden, NSWCA Report, VCA Report, The Age, The Argus, The Herald, The Australasian.*

NEW SOUTH WALES

H.L.Collins	c Baring b Ryder	73
L.A.Cody	lbw b Ryder	68
*W.Bardsley	not out	124
C.Kelleway	c Matthews b Ryder	47
T.J.E.Andrews	lbw b Armstrong	0
B.J.Folkard	c Ryder b Armstrong	10
A.Cotter	c Ryder b Armstrong	3
R.J.A.Massie	run out (Carroll/Ryder)	9
C.G.Macartney	b Matthews	53
A.A.Mailey	c Armstrong b Ryder	18
†C.G.McKew	c Park b Ryder	0
Extras	(w2, nb2)	4
Total	(137.5 overs, 402 mins)	409

VICTORIA

E.V.Carroll	c Macartney b Massie	26	(7)	b Cotter	25
R.L.Park	c McKew b Massie	25	(4)	c Bardsley b Massie	3
F.A.Baring	c & b Massie	14	(5)	c Mailey b Kelleway	122
T.J.Matthews	run out (Andrews/Massie)	27	(8)	st McKew b Mailey	27
*W.W.Armstrong	c Massie b Folkard	34	(6)	b Cotter	0
J.Ryder	b Kelleway	0	(9)	b Kelleway	1
H.H.G.Bracher	c Massie b Folkard	7	(10)	b Kelleway	0
†W.Carkeek	b Kelleway	1	(1)	b Cotter	8
J.L.McNaughton	not out	0	(2)	b Massie	1
W.H.Cannon	b Kelleway	0	(3)	c McKew b Massie	0
W.I.Sewart	absent hurt	-		not out	2
Extras	(b11, lb5, nb1)	17		(b5, lb4, nb1)	10
Total	(46.6 overs, 147 mins)	151		(64.2 overs, 184 mins)	199

VICTORIA	O	M	R	W	w,nb
McNaughton	20	1	73	0	2,-
Cannon	19	0	76	0	-,-
Armstrong	39	8	62	3	-,1
Ryder	38.5	4	138	5	-,1
Matthews	19	1	49	1	-,-
Sewart	2	0	7	0	-,-

NEW SOUTH WALES	O	M	R	W	w,nb		O	M	R	W	w,nb
Cotter	10	1	43	0	-,1		13	3	51	3	-,1
Massie	18	2	59	3	-,-		17	4	49	3	-,-
Kelleway	12.4	4	15	3	-,-	(4)	8.2	2	16	3	-,-
Folkard	5	0	13	2	-,-	(5)	9	1	30	0	-,-
Mailey	1	0	4	0	-,-	(3)	17	4	43	1	-,-

FALL OF WICKETS

Wkt	NSW 1st	VIC 1st	VIC 2nd
1st	140	55	3
2nd	144	62	3
3rd	262	89	14
4th	263	124	20
5th	275	124	24
6th	281	150	108
7th	299	151	175
8th	378	151	180
9th	409	151	184
10th	409	-	199

VICTORIA v NEW ZEALAND XI

Played at Melbourne Cricket Ground on January 9, 10, 1914. (Timeless match)
Toss : New Zealand XI.   Result : VICTORIA WON BY AN INNINGS AND 110 RUNS.
Debuts: Victoria - F.L.Lugton, C.B.Willis (both f/c); P.J.Heather (Vic only).
12th Men: W.Carlton (Vic). No 12th named for NZ.
Umpires: E.Barrass and R.M.Crockett.
Attendances: 2575, 4726.   Total: 7301.   Receipts: £156.
Close of Play: 1st day Vic 5/235 (Lugton 32).

The New Zealanders struggled from the outset on a pacy wicket. Patrick was missed by Armstrong and Heather off the first two balls he faced, only to be bowled next ball without scoring. Snedden (51 in 88 minutes, 4 fours) left a good impression in the second innings. The Victorians scored their runs rapidly, Kiernan (61 in 80 minutes, 6 fours), Heather (65 in 40 minutes, 9 fours, 2 chances), McDonald (64 in 50 minutes, 9 fours) and Matthews (63 not out in 50 minutes) being the leading contributors in an even performance. Heather had played 12 first-class matches in South Africa (Natal 1904-05 and Transvaal 1910-11 to 1912-13) prior to this appearance, his sole first-class match in Australia. H.H.G.Bracher (injured knee), F.A.Baring, N.E.Brown (the nominated 12th man), R.L.Park, V.S.Ransford (ill) and J.Ryder were all unavailable for Victorian selection while J.H.Bennett (injured) could not be considered for the visitors. Sources: *T.W.Reese, VCA Report, The Age, The Argus, The Herald, The Australasian, The Leader, Sydney Referee.*

NEW ZEALAND XI

L.G.Hemus	c Armstrong b Lampard	7	(5)	b Armstrong	19
W.R.Patrick	b McDonald	0	(8)	run out (sub W.Carlton/Matthews)	8
A.N.C.Snedden	b McDonald	0		c Kiernan b Lampard	51
B.J.Tuckwell	b Lampard	3	(6)	c Carkeek b Armstrong	33
R.G.Hickmott	c Armstrong b McDonald	46	(2)	st Carkeek b Lampard	9
*D.Reese	b Lampard	47	(1)	b McDonald	12
D.M.Sandman	c Carkeek b Lampard	9		c Kiernan b Matthews	6
L.G.Taylor	run out	6	(4)	c Armstrong b Lugton	14
T.A.Carlton	c Carkeek b Lampard	9		c Armstrong b Willis	21
C.W.Robinson	not out	7		st Carkeek b Willis	4
†C.Boxshall	b Lugton	4		not out	2
Extras	(lb3)	3		(b2, lb7)	9
Total	(50.1 overs, 175 mins)	141		(56.3 overs, 172 mins)	188

VICTORIA

E.V.Carroll	c Hickmott b Robinson	2
W.I.Sewart	c & b Sandman	25
C.Kiernan	c Tuckwell b Carlton	61
C.B.Willis	c Taylor b Robinson	40
P.J.Heather	b Sandman	65
F.J.Lugton	b Sandman	36
A.W.Lampard	b Snedden	36
E.A.McDonald	c Taylor b Snedden	64
T.J.Matthews	not out	63
*W.W.Armstrong	c & b Sandman	18
†W.Carkeek	b Robinson	6
Extras	(b22, lb1,)	23
Total	(84.4 overs, 260 mins)	439

VICTORIA	O	M	R	W	w,nb		O	M	R	W	w,nb
McDonald	20	6	50	3	-,-		9	3	32	1	-,-
Lampard	20	5	41	5	-,-		13	4	50	2	-,-
Lugton	5.1	1	21	1	-,-		8	2	21	1	-,-
Matthews	5	1	26	0	-,-	(5)	8	1	33	1	-,-
Armstrong						(4)	17	5	33	2	-,-
Willis							1.3	0	10	2	-,-

NEW ZEALAND XI	O	M	R	W	w,nb		O	M	R	W	w,nb
Robinson	24.4	4	113	3	-,-						
Carlton	19	3	79	1	-,-						
Sandman	21	2	103	4	-,-						
Reese	5	0	29	0	-,-						
Hickmott	3	0	26	0	-,-						
Snedden	10	0	51	2	-,-						
Tuckwell	2	0	15	0	-,-						

FALL OF WICKETS

Wkt	NZ 1st	VIC 1st	NZ 2nd
1st	5	4	22
2nd	5	52	22
3rd	7	124	63
4th	24	150	107
5th	96	235	114
6th	114	244	123
7th	115	334	147
8th	122	362	182
9th	132	422	182
10th	141	439	188

SOUTH AUSTRALIA v NEW SOUTH WALES (Shield Match 4)

Played at Adelaide Oval on January 9, 10, 12, 1914. (Timeless match)
Toss : South Australia.   Result : NEW SOUTH WALES WON BY NINE WICKETS.
Debuts: South Australia - A.Smith (f/c).
12th Men: N.L.Gooden (SA) and H.H.Davis (NSW).
Umpires: A.McIntyre and J.G.Wagstaff.
Attendances: 1500, 6000, 500.   Total: About 8000.   Receipts: £334.
Close of Play: 1st day NSW 3/95 (Collins 51, McKew 2); 2nd day SA (2) 7/66 (Crawford 11).

South Australia failed in both innings to combat the pace of Massie (10 for 125), Kelleway (5 for 97) and Cotter (3 for 41). After scoring 111 in 180 minutes and hitting 8 fours, Collins was run out in the first over of the second innings without facing a ball. He failed to make his ground when Macartney forced a ball back past the bowler and called for two, the umpires also signalled the first run short. Bardsley scored 79 in 170 minutes and hit 4 fours. Massie bowled unchanged through the second South Australian innings. Smith was a last-minute replacement for P.D.Rundell (unavailable). *Wisden* and *O'Reilly* incorrectly give Chamberlain (1) c Collins. Sources: *Wisden, C.B.O'Reilly, NSWCA Report, SACA Report, Sydney Referee, Adelaide Advertiser, South Australian Register.*

SOUTH AUSTRALIA

R.E.Mayne	c McKew b Kelleway	10		c McKew b Massie	28
D.M.Steele	c Cotter b Massie	42		b Cotter	6
J.N.Crawford	c Collins b Massie	11	(6)	c Cody b Massie	34
A.G.Moyes	b Kelleway	21	(3)	c & b Massie	11
W.L.Chamberlain	c & b Massie	11	(4)	c Collins b Massie	1
*C.Hill	c McKew b Kelleway	12	(5)	b Kelleway	7
C.E.Pellew	c & b Massie	9		b Kelleway	1
H.P.Kirkwood	not out	36		run out (Andrews/McKew)	0
A.Smith	b Massie	11		run out (Andrews/McKew)	8
W.J.Whitty	b Massie	0		not out	15
†C.L.Winser	b Cotter	23		b Cotter	2
Extras	(w1, nb2)	3		(b2, lb1, w1, nb1)	5
Total	(65.0 overs, 195 mins)	189		(44.2 overs, 145 mins)	118

NEW SOUTH WALES

L.A.Cody	b Crawford	0			
H.L.Collins	run out (Kirkwood/Winser)	111		run out (Pellew/Moyes)	0
C.G.Macartney	c Smith b Crawford	15	(1)	not out	5
T.J.E.Andrews	c Winser b Whitty	20			
†C.G.McKew	c & b Whitty	2			
*W.Bardsley	c Kirkwood b Crawford	79	(3)	not out	3
C.Kelleway	c Chamberlain b Crawford	14			
B.J.Folkard	c & b Crawford	0			
A.Cotter	b Crawford	29			
R.J.A.Massie	c & b Crawford	3			
A.A.Mailey	not out	3			
Extras	(h17, lh2, w2)	21		(b4)	4
Total	(96.2 overs, 280 mins)	297		(4.0 overs, 11 mins) (1 wkt)	12

NEW SOUTH WALES	O	M	R	W	w,nb	O	M	R	W	w,nb
Cotter	5	0	17	1	-,1	5.2	0	24	2	1,-
Massie	26	2	68	6	1,-	22	4	57	4	-,-
Kelleway	22	6	65	3	-,1	17	6	32	2	-,1
Mailey	6	2	19	0	-,-					
Folkard	6	1	17	0	-,-					

SOUTH AUSTRALIA	O	M	R	W	w,nb	O	M	R	W	w,nb
Whitty	30	4	68	2	1,-	2	0	3	0	-,-
Crawford	32.2	8	78	7	-,-	2	0	5	0	-,-
Kirkwood	15	0	71	0	-,-					
Chamberlain	11	1	35	0	1,-					
Moyes	7	3	14	0	-,-					
Smith	1	0	10	0	-,-					

FALL OF WICKETS

Wkt	SA 1st	NSW 1st	SA 2nd	NSW 2nd
1st	22	1	12	0
2nd	60	37	37	-
3rd	79	72	47	-
4th	87	101	48	-
5th	109	180	54	-
6th	119	206	56	-
7th	119	216	66	-
8th	130	280	97	-
9th	130	286	102	-
10th	189	297	118	-

SOUTH AUSTRALIA v NEW ZEALAND XI

Played at Adelaide Oval on January 16, 17, 19, 1914. (Three-day match)
Toss : New Zealand XI.   Result : MATCH DRAWN.
Debuts: South Australia - H.B.Willsmore (f/c).
12th Men: H.M.Beresford (SA). No 12th named for NZ.
Umpires: F.J.C.Thomas and J.G.Wagstaff.
Attendances: "fair", 3000, "fair".   Total: 5144.   Receipts: No figures published.
Close of Play: 1st day SA 1/54 (Steele 38, Smith 4); 2nd day NZ (2) 2/28 (Sandman 19, Tuckwell 2).

D.Reese, New Zealand's left-handed captain, registered the first first-class century by a New Zealander in Australia, compiling an unbeaten 130 in 140 minutes with 12 fours and a six. His first innings occupied 145 minutes, included 11 fours, and was supported by Snedden (88 in 125 minutes, 6 fours) and Sandman (56 in 80 minutes, 8 fours). South Australia's best innings came from Steele (90 minutes, 1 six and 7 fours), Pellew (95 minutes, 1 six and 9 fours), Hill (100 minutes, 9 fours) and in the second innings Smith (74 in 95 minutes, 7 fours). Somervell was caught from the third ball of the New Zealand second innings. Sources: *T.W.Reese, C.B.O'Reilly, SACA Report, Adelaide Advertiser, South Australian Register.*

NEW ZEALAND XI

L.G.Hemus	st Campbell b Smith	46		c Crawford b Willsmore	6
R.G.Hickmott	c Hill b Rundell	7	(5)	b Howard	5
A.N.C.Snedden	c Campbell b Mayne	88		lbw b Mayne	52
B.J.Tuckwell	run out (Steele)	6		c Campbell b Howard	21
*D.Reese	b Howard	96	(6)	not out	130
L.G.Taylor	b Pellew	16	(7)	c Crawford b Howard	43
D.M.Sandman	b Willsmore	56	(8)	not out	12
R.C.Somervell	run out	0	(2)	c Smith b Crawford	0
C.W.Robinson	b Howard	13			
J.H.Bennett	c Rundell b Howard	4			
†C.Boxshall	not out	5			
Extras	(b4, lb8, w4, nb9)	25		(b8, lb7, nb3)	18
Total	(78.0 overs, 240 mins)	362		(78.0 overs, 220 mins) (6 wkts dec)	287

SOUTH AUSTRALIA

P.D.Rundell	lbw b Bennett	12	(3)	c & b Robinson	19
D.M.Steele	c Taylor b Reese	73			
A.Smith	c Sandman b Bennett	37	(2)	not out	74
R.E.Mayne	b Sandman	3	(1)	b Bennett	19
C.E.Pellew	c Sandman b Bennett	94			
N.L.Gooden	lbw b Sandman	9	(5)	not out	36
H.B.Willsmore	c Reese b Sandman	57	(4)	b Robinson	8
*C.Hill	c Reese b Robinson	92			
J.N.Crawford	not out	48			
†G.C.Campbell	c Snedden b Robinson	0			
L.E.Howard	b Robinson	0			
Extras	(b6, lb2)	8		(b5)	5
Total	(99.1 overs, 265 mins)	433		(37.0 overs, 95 mins) (3 wkts)	161

SOUTH AUSTRALIA	O	M	R	W	w,nb		O	M	R	W	w,nb		FALL OF WICKETS			
Howard	19	2	82	3	4,8	(2)	17	1	66	3	-,3		SA	NZ	SA	NZ
Rundell	8	1	36	1	-,-	(5)	10	2	43	0	-,-	Wkt	1st	1st	2nd	2nd
Crawford	22	3	80	0	-,1	(1)	23	5	55	1	-,-	1st	15	40	1	31
Smith	9	0	53	1	-,-	(6)	3	0	18	0	-,-	2nd	78	113	23	68
Willsmore	11	1	38	1	-,-	(3)	12	0	46	1	-,-	3rd	101	130	69	80
Mayne	4	0	20	1	-,-	(4)	10	2	19	1	-,-	4th	213	132	79	-
Pellew	4	0	23	1	-,-		2	0	13	0	-,-	5th	246	158	104	-
Hill	1	0	5	0	-,-		1	0	9	0	-,-	6th	321	276	253	-
												7th	325	312	-	-
NEW ZEALAND XI	O	M	R	W	w,nb		O	M	R	W	w,nb	8th	338	429	-	-
Robinson	15.1	2	72	3	-,-	(3)	7	1	45	2	-,-	9th	346	429	-	-
Bennett	31	7	101	3	-,-		17	3	48	1	-,-	10th	362	433	-	-
Sandman	28	0	135	3	-,-	(1)	10	0	47	0	-,-					
Reese	15	0	57	1	-,-		1	0	8	0	-,-					
Hemus	1	0	3	0	-,-	(6)	1	0	2	0	-,-					
Snedden	5	0	35	0	-,-											
Hickmott	2	0	14	0	-,-											
Somervell	2	1	8	0	-,-	(5)	1	0	6	0	-,-					

NEW SOUTH WALES v VICTORIA (Shield Match 5)

Played at Sydney Cricket Ground on January 23, 24, 26, 27, 28, 1914. (Timeless match)
Toss : New South Wales.   Result : NEW SOUTH WALES WON BY AN INNINGS AND 32 RUNS.
Debuts: Nil.
12th Men: L.A.Cody (NSW) and H.H.G.Bracher (Vic).
Umpires: A.C.Jones and C.W.Waugh.
Attendances: 3298, 7270, 4881, 600, ?   Total: 16,049 (excluding final day).   Receipts: £655.
Close of Play: 1st day NSW 3/430 (Macartney 184, Mailey 0); 2nd day Vic 3/49 (Park 19, Matthews 14); 3rd day Vic (2) 0/2 (Ryder 2, Carkeek 0); 4th day Vic (2) 8/269 (Matthews 22).

Kelleway (138 in 247 minutes, 16 fours) shared partnerships of 136 in 118 minutes for the first wicket with Collins (9 fours) and 221 in 129 minutes for the second wicket with Macartney (201 in 186 minutes, 29 fours). Macartney brought up 50 in 50 minutes, 100 in 103 minutes, 150 in 138 minutes and 200 in 185 minutes, moving from 63 to 184 between tea and stumps on the first day. Matthews (62 in 190 minutes, 6 fours) and Armstrong (87 in 84 minutes, 7 fours) in the first innings and Baring (71 in 131 minutes, 9 fours) in the second were the only Victorians to exceed fifty. Massie claimed 10 wickets in his last Sheffield Shield match including that of Lampard with his fourth ball. There was no admittance fee on the last day. Destiny decreed that it was to be V.T.Trumper's last first-class match in Australia. V.S.Ransford (ill) was unavailable for Victoria and E.A.McDonald (injured knee) was replaced by Lugton. Sources: *Wisden, NSWCA Report, VCA Report, Sydney Referee, Sydney Morning Herald, Town & Country Journal*.

NEW SOUTH WALES

H.L.Collins	c Carroll b Armstrong	68
C.Kelleway	b Lugton	138
C.G.Macartney	c Lampard b Ryder	201
W.Bardsley	c & b Matthews	28
A.A.Mailey	b Ryder	66
*V.T.Trumper	c Armstrong b Lugton	24
T.J.E.Andrews	lbw b Matthews	20
E.P.Barbour	not out	65
B.J.Folkard	c Carkeek b Armstrong	15
R.J.A.Massie	lbw b Armstrong	8
†C.G.McKew	c & b Armstrong	22
Extras	(b6, lb13, nb1)	20
Total	(173.2 overs, 490 mins)	675

VICTORIA

R.L.Park	c Folkard b Kelleway	25	(4) c Mailey b Massie		47
A.W.Lampard	b Massie	0	(11) b Folkard		10
W.I.Sewart	b Massie	0	(5) b Macartney		1
E.V.Carroll	lbw b Kelleway	12	(7) c Kelleway b Massie		35
T.J.Matthews	c McKew b Massie	62	(8) not out		43
*W.W.Armstrong	b Massie	87	c Folkard b Mailey		31
F.A.Baring	b Massie	1	(3) c Andrews b Massie		71
C.Kiernan	b Macartney	44	(9) b Mailey		5
F.J.Lugton	b Massie	35	(10) b Massie		7
J.Ryder	b Folkard	15	(1) c & b Kelleway		30
†W.Carkeek	not out	22	(2) c Mailey b Folkard		8
Extras	(b17, lb11, nb1)	29	(b10, lb8, w1, nb4)		23
Total	(136.1 overs, 342 mins)	332	(107.2 overs, 285 mins)		311

VICTORIA	O	M	R	W	w,nb
Ryder	52	14	163	2	-,-
Armstrong	46.2	9	127	4	-,1
Lampard	20	1	128	0	-,-
Lugton	20	2	96	2	-,-
Matthews	27	7	102	2	-,-
Kiernan	3	0	14	0	-,-
Baring	2	0	7	0	-,-
Park	3	0	18	0	-,-

NEW SOUTH WALES	O	M	R	W	w,nb		O	M	R	W	w,nb
Kelleway	24	10	51	2	-,1	(3)	21	4	54	1	-,4
Massie	41	13	93	6	-,-		31	9	75	4	1,-
Mailey	33	10	67	0	-,-	(5)	15	4	41	2	-,-
Folkard	23.1	9	46	1	-,-		20.2	7	61	2	-,-
Andrews	5	1	21	0	-,-	(6)	2	0	11	0	-,-
Barbour	2	1	6	0	-,-						
Macartney	8	2	19	1	-,-	(1)	18	7	46	1	-,-

FALL OF WICKETS

Wkt	NSW 1st	VIC 1st	VIC 2nd
1st	136	0	32
2nd	357	2	66
3rd	416	23	169
4th	451	66	170
5th	495	172	171
6th	535	174	235
7th	569	220	260
8th	605	288	269
9th	629	288	285
10th	675	332	311

NEW SOUTH WALES v TASMANIA

Played at Sydney Cricket Ground on February 6, 7, 9, 1914. (Timeless match)
Toss : Tasmania.   Result : NEW SOUTH WALES WON BY AN INNINGS AND 180 RUNS.
Debuts: New South Wales - E.B.Berrie, F.Buckle, E.A.Bull, A.T.Ratcliffe, J.M.Taylor (all f/c). Tasmania - E.L.A.Butler, T.D.Freeman,
    H.C.Smith, J.A.Woods (all f/c).
12th Men: H.G.Pratten (NSW). No 12th for Tas; only 11 men in party.
Umpires: R.Callaway and R.Thornwaite.
Attendances: No figures published.   Total: About 2500.   Receipts: £63.
Close of Play: 1st day NSW 1/37 (Cranney 16, Ratcliffe 15); 2nd day NSW 5/403 (Macartney 101, Andrews 43).

A thunderstorm reduced the second day's play by 75 minutes but did nothing to halt New South Wales rate of scoring. Davis was out in the second over but Cranney (75 in 107 minutes, 8 fours) and Ratcliffe (51 in 94 minutes) retrieved the position and paved the way for Taylor (83 in 95 minutes, 8 fours), Bull (42 in 68 minutes) and Macartney (110 in 95 minutes, 4 chances) and Andrews (67 in 73 minutes) to up the run-rate. Macartney began his innings an hour after lunch and brought up his fifty in 43 minutes, just prior to a stoppage for rain at 3.50pm. When play resumed at 5.15pm he went to his century in 83 minutes and added 97 in the last 45 minutes with Andrews. Scott took a spell of 3 for 4 late in the match, dismissing Thomas, Butler and Smith all in the same over (1st, 4th and 6th balls). H.Cranney had replaced G.S.Moore (unavailable) in the New South Wales team. Sources: *Cricket, NSWCA Report, Sydney Referee, Sydney Morning Herald, Sydney Daily Telegraph, Town & Country Journal, Hobart Mercury.*

TASMANIA

H.Myers	b Massie	31		c Ratcliffe b Scott	0
C.H.Robinson	lbw b Andrews	33	(3)	b Massie	21
R.A.Westbrook	b Scott	1	(5)	b Massie	1
*R.J.Hawson	b Massie	4		c Andrews b Cranney	32
G.D.Paton	c Buckle b Andrews	19	(6)	c Davis b Massie	19
W.K.Eltham	b Andrews	46	(2)	c Massie b Berrie	7
E.L.A.Butler	c Massie b Berrie	13	(9)	b Scott	4
J.A.Woods	b Berrie	0	(7)	b Massie	6
H.C.Smith	c Ratcliffe b Scott	0	(10)	b Scott	0
†L.Thomas	not out	3	(8)	b Scott	4
T.D.Freeman	c Andrews b Berrie	4		not out	0
Extras	(b2, lb4, w1, nb2)	9		(b6, lb4, nb4)	14
Total	(81.4 overs, 224 mins)	163		(43.5 overs, 127 mins)	108

NEW SOUTH WALES

H.Cranney	c Hawson b Paton	75
H.H.Davis	c Thomas b Myers	1
†A.T.Ratcliffe	c Freeman b Paton	51
J.M.Taylor	b Paton	83
E.A.Bull	b Paton	42
*C.G.Macartney	c Hawson b Robinson	110
T.J.E.Andrews	c Thomas b Robinson	67
F.Buckle	c Westbrook b Myers	10
J.D.Scott	c Freeman b Myers	5
R.J.A.Massie	not out	0
E.B.Berrie	c Thomas b Myers	0
Extras	(b4, lb3)	7
Total	(105.3 overs, 294 mins)	451

NEW SOUTH WALES	O	M	R	W	w,nb		O	M	R	W	w,nb
Scott	18	3	35	2	-,2		11	3	20	4	-,4
Berrie	23.4	7	45	3	-,-		11	4	21	1	-,-
Bull	11	6	14	0	-,-						
Massie	16	6	23	2	1,-		10.5	6	15	4	-,-
Andrews	10	3	27	3	-,-	(3)	7	1	19	0	-,-
Davis	3	1	10	0	-,-						
Cranney						(5)	4	0	19	1	-,-

TASMANIA	O	M	R	W	w,nb
Robinson	25	4	84	2	-,-
Myers	35.3	6	132	4	-,-
Paton	28	2	129	4	-,-
Freeman	6	0	42	0	-,-
Eltham	9	1	43	0	-,-
Westbrook	2	0	14	0	-,-

FALL OF WICKETS

Wkt	TAS 1st	NSW 1st	TAS 2nd
1st	48	2	1
2nd	55	131	10
3rd	70	136	73
4th	84	232	74
5th	103	285	75
6th	127	423	89
7th	127	442	102
8th	134	447	106
9th	156	451	106
10th	163	451	108

SOUTH AUSTRALIA v VICTORIA (Shield Match 6)

Played at Adelaide Oval on February 13, 14, 16, 17, 1914. (Timeless match)
Toss : South Australia.   Result : SOUTH AUSTRALIA WON BY 86 RUNS.
Debuts: South Australia - S.H.Clutterbuck, W.D.Price (both f/c). Victoria - J.M.Fitzpatrick, V.J.Souter (both f/c).
12th Men: H.H.M.Bridgman (SA) and P.J.Heather (Vic).
Umpires: A.W.Hele and A.McIntyre.
Attendances: No individual figures published.   Total: 4316.   Receipts: £74.
Close of Play: 1st day Vic 2/28 (Carroll 10); 2nd day SA (2) 2/112 (Smith 18, Willsmore 20); 3rd day Vic (2) 2/96 (Park 39, Kiernan 26).

Victoria were without W.W.Armstrong and V.S.Ransford, both in New Zealand with an Australian side, and H.H.G.Bracher (unavailable) who was replaced by Heather. D.M.Steele was unavailable for South Australia and Clutterbuck was a late replacement for W.J.Whitty (business). Hill (105 in 163 minutes, 15 fours) and Baring (71 in 120 minutes, 7 fours) were the leading batsmen for their respective teams in the first innings. Hill also scored 60 in 95 minutes in the second innings with 7 fours. T.J.Keppell of the Adelaide club substituted in the first innings for Pellew who had injured a finger attempting to field a ball. Ryder followed his nine wickets by scoring 105 in 155 minutes (1 six and 11 fours), adding 113 for the ninth wicket with Souter. *Wisden* and *O'Reilly* incorrectly give Vic (1) Park c Pellew. Sources: *Wisden, C.B.O'Reilly, VCA Report, SACA Report, Adelaide Advertiser, South Australian Register.*

SOUTH AUSTRALIA

R.E.Mayne	b Ryder	8		lbw b Fitzpatrick	44
R.F.Middleton	c Willis b Ryder	34		b Lugton	27
*C.Hill	c & b Ryder	105	(5)	c Kiernan b Ryder	60
J.N.Crawford	c Lugton b Souter	27	(6)	c Ryder b Fitzpatrick	18
A.G.Moyes	c Matthews b Ryder	41	(7)	st Carkeek b Kiernan	32
C.E.Pellew	b Lugton	1	(9)	c Park b Souter	47
A.Smith	c Souter b Matthews	9	(3)	b Matthews	34
H.B.Willsmore	c Souter b Ryder	14	(4)	c Fitzpatrick b Ryder	39
W.D.Price	b Ryder	7	(10)	not out	5
†G.C.Campbell	not out	17	(8)	b Fitzpatrick	28
S.H.Clutterbuck	c Baring b Ryder	2	(11)	b Fitzpatrick	0
Extras	(lb8, nb1)	9		(b9, lb2, w1, nb3)	15
Total	(74.3 overs, 260 mins)	274		(83.3 overs, 270 mins)	349

VICTORIA

*E.V.Carroll	c Pellew b Price	35		b Crawford	19
R.L.Park	c Price b Crawford	10		c Campbell b Willsmore	59
T.J.Matthews	b Crawford	4	(5)	lbw b Crawford	10
C.Kiernan	b Crawford	0		c & b Crawford	27
F.A.Baring	b Crawford	71	(3)	b Crawford	7
C.B.Willis	b Price	0	(7)	b Crawford	0
J.M.Fitzpatrick	st Campbell b Mayne	40	(8)	c Moyes b Willsmore	24
J.Ryder	not out	36	(6)	c & b Willsmore	105
F.J.Lugton	c Moyes b Mayne	0		c & b Crawford	1
V.J.Souter	c sub (T.J.Keppell) b Mayne	4		not out	48
†W.Carkeek	c Willsmore b Crawford	4		c Moyes b Willsmore	9
Extras	(lb8, w1)	9		(b11, lb1, nb3)	15
Total	(71.3 overs, 210 mins)	213		(98.3 overs, 288 mins)	324

VICTORIA	O	M	R	W	w,nb		O	M	R	W	w,nb			FALL OF WICKETS		
														SA	VIC	SA	VIC
Ryder	23.3	2	88	7	-,1		20	1	83	2	-,2		Wkt	1st	1st	2nd	2nd
Matthews	20	3	83	1	-,-	(4)	19	4	74	1	-,-		1st	8	17	68	24
Souter	16	3	47	1	-,-	(2)	15	3	58	1	-,-		2nd	82	28	88	36
Lugton	13	4	38	1	-,-	(3)	17	0	50	1	-,-		3rd	133	28	147	99
Kiernan	2	0	9	0	-,-	(6)	5	0	26	1	1,-		4th	214	85	172	117
Fitzpatrick						(5)	7.3	0	43	4	-,1		5th	221	85	213	132
													6th	223	144	258	133
SOUTH AUSTRALIA	O	M	R	W	w,nb		O	M	R	W	w,nb		7th	241	200	264	187
Crawford	23.3	5	48	5	-,-		33	4	97	6	-,3		8th	250	200	336	189
Clutterbuck	13	0	44	0	1,-		8	1	34	0	-,-		9th	256	208	349	302
Price	13	4	36	2	-,-	(4)	17	3	36	0	-,-		10th	274	213	349	324
Willsmore	9	0	30	0	-,-	(5)	20.3	3	65	4	-,-						
Moyes	7	1	20	0	-,-	(6)	6	1	24	0	-,-						
Smith	3	0	20	0	-,-	(7)	2	0	14	0	-,-						
Mayne	3	1	6	3	-,-	(3)	12	0	39	0	-,-						

TASMANIA v VICTORIA

Played at T.C.A. Ground, Hobart, on February 27, 28, March 2, 1914. (Timeless match)
Toss : Tasmania.   Result : VICTORIA WON BY EIGHT WICKETS.
Debuts: Tasmania - L.F.Gatenby (f/c). Victoria - A.E.Brown, B.J.Sheppard, R.S.Stephens (all f/c); H.Ironmonger (Vic Only).
12th Men: B.L.Cohen (Vic). No 12th man or emergency fieldsman named for Tasmania.
Umpires: W.M.McHugo and A.Williams.
Attendances: No figures published.   Receipts: £16.
Close of Play: 1st day Vic 3/186 (Willis 79, Brown 1); 2nd day Tas (2) 4/191 (Myers 13, Boddam 4).

In the Victorian first innings Park (96 in 95 minutes, 13 fours), Willis (93 in 143 minutes, 9 fours) and Souter (55 in 54 minutes, 10 fours) were the main contributors. Robinson (57 in 105 minutes, 8 fours) and Hawson (90 in 155 minutes, 11 fours) raised an opening partnership of 140 for Tasmania. H.Ironmonger, who had moved to Victoria from Queensland earlier in the season to improve his prospects of playing international cricket at the age of 32, took 10 for 162 in the match with his left-arm orthodox deliveries. He had represented Queensland against New South Wales, Victoria and New Zealand in December and his eligibility for Victoria was questioned by "Not Out" in the *Sydney Referee*. However, there was no official complaint. Carlton gave chances to the wicket-keeper at 7 and again at 13 in the second innings and added an unbroken 132 for the third wicket with Stephens to finish the match. Sources: *VCA Report, TCA Report, Hobart Mercury, Launceston Examiner, Sydney Referee*.

TASMANIA

C.H.Robinson	b Souter	6		c & b Ironmonger	57
H.Myers	c Stephens b Ironmonger	11	(5)	run out (Willis/Sheppard)	38
W.K.Eltham	run out (/Sheppard)	10		c Willis b Lugton	5
L.F.Gatenby	c Sheppard b Ironmonger	1	(8)	b Stephens	13
*R.J.Hawson	b Ironmonger	25	(2)	b Hart	90
A.C.Newton	b Ironmonger	13	(7)	b Ironmonger	44
E.T.Boddam	b Ironmonger	27	(6)	c & b Hart	30
R.A.Davis	b Ironmonger	0	(10)	b Lugton	17
T.D.Carroll	b Ironmonger	9		b Ironmonger	10
H.E.Allen	not out	31	(4)	b Lugton	6
†H.Parkinson	st Sheppard b Willis	24		not out	6
Extras	(b4, lb10)	14		(b21, lb13, nb2)	36
Total	(54.3 overs, 165 mins)	171		(99.1 overs, 280 mins)	352

VICTORIA

R.L.Park	c Robinson b Davis	96		lbw b Boddam	9
*E.V.Carroll	c & b Myers	1		c Parkinson b Boddam	30
C.B.Willis	c Davis b Boddam	93			
W.Carlton	b Myers	4	(3)	not out	66
A.E.Brown	lbw b Myers	21			
R.S.Stephens	b Myers	7	(4)	not out	62
V.J.Souter	b Myers	55			
F.J.Lugton	b Newton	25			
†B.J.Sheppard	c Allen b Newton	17			
H.W.Hart	c Allen b Myers	0			
H.Ironmonger	not out	13			
Extras	(b13, lb5, w1)	19		(b4, lb1, w1)	6
Total	(81.2 overs, 238 mins)	351		(47.4 overs, 130 mins) (2 wkts)	173

VICTORIA	O	M	R	W	w,nb		O	M	R	W	w,nb		FALL OF WICKETS			
Ironmonger	22	7	53	7	-,-		37	7	109	3	-,1			TAS	VIC	TAS	VIC
Souter	11	5	26	1	-,-		19	1	71	0	-,-		Wkt	1st	1st	2nd	2nd
Lugton	13	2	34	0	-,-		21.1	5	45	3	-,1		1st	13	7	140	38
Hart	5	0	26	0	-,-		16	4	59	2	-,-		2nd	23	158	158	41
Carlton	2	0	12	0	-,-								3rd	28	184	168	-
Willis	1.3	0	6	1	-,-	(5)	3	0	8	0	-,-		4th	30	210	183	-
Stephens						(6)	3	0	24	1	-,-		5th	44	221	239	-
													6th	90	236	249	-
TASMANIA	O	M	R	W	w,nb		O	M	R	W	w,nb		7th	90	299	266	-
Robinson	9	0	50	0	-,-		4	0	23	0	-,-		8th	109	319	317	-
Myers	24	1	101	6	-,-		10	0	40	0	-,-		9th	120	321	340	-
Allen	11	3	28	0	1,-	(5)	4	1	7	0	-,-		10th	171	351	352	-
Newton	11.2	1	52	2	-,-		3	0	11	0	-,-						
Boddam	10	2	38	1	-,-	(3)	10.4	0	29	2	-,-						
Carroll	8	0	36	0	-,-	(7)	7	1	14	0	1,-						
Davis	8	1	27	1	-,-	(6)	3	0	26	0	-,-						
Hawson							2	0	7	0	-,-						
Eltham							4	1	10	0	-,-						

TASMANIA v VICTORIA

Played at N.T.C.A. Ground, Launceston, on March 6, 7, 9, 10, 1914. (Timeless match)
Toss : Victoria.   Result : VICTORIA WON BY 550 RUNS.
Debuts: Tasmania - R.C.A.V.Bayles, W.H.Bayles, A.P.Findlay, F.E.Headlam, J.A.Jakins, P.Shawe (all f/c). Victoria - B.L.Cohen (f/c).
12th Men: A.E.Brown (Vic). No 12th man or emergency fieldsman named for Tasmania.
Umpires: E.Armitage and C.McAllen.
Attendances & Receipts: No figures published.
Close of Play: 1st day Tas 0/10 (Martin 5, Gatenby 2); 2nd day Vic (2) 1/180 (Stephens 90, Willis 58); 3rd day Tas (2) 0/13 (Shawe 9, Elliott 0).

The T.C.A. nominated A.C.Facy, W.K.Eltham and A.C.Newton for inclusion in the Tasmanian team but all announced their unavailability. Jakins (North Coast) was consequently the sole member selected from outside the N.T.C.A. by the N.T.C.A. match selectors and only Gatenby and Davis remained of the team which played earlier in the week. The brothers Bayles and their cousin F.E.Headlam were among the debutants, Headlam capturing wickets with his second and fourth deliveries in first-class cricket. Stephens compiled a century in each innings in only his second first-class match. His 108 (150 minutes, 12 fours) included a chance at 13 but his second-innings 181 (255 minutes, 16 fours) was chanceless. Lugton's unbeaten 94 took about 100 minutes and included 11 fours. Martin (84 in 116 minutes, 1 six and 14 fours) was the only local batsman to surpass 20. His runs came from 126 scored whilst he was at the crease. Sources: *VCA Report, Launceston Daily Telegraph, Launceston Examiner, Hobart Mercury.*

VICTORIA

R.S.Stephens	st Thomas b Davis	108	b Headlam	181
R.L.Park	b Elliott	10	c Thomas b Jakins	26
C.B.Willis	c Findlay b Shawe	6	b Jakins	61
*E.V.Carroll	b Shawe	4	c Thomas b Jakins	4
W.Carlton	c Martin b Shawe	2	b Shawe	52
B.L.Cohen	c R.C.A.V.Bayles b Davis	20	c R.C.A.V.Bayles b Elliott	69
V.J.Souter	c W.H.Bayles b Davis	10	c R.C.A.V.Bayles b Elliott	57
F.J.Lugton	not out	94	c Findlay b Elliott	20
†B.J.Sheppard	b Headlam	30	c Gatenby b Elliott	13
H.W.Hart	c Davis b Headlam	0	c Headlam b Gatenby	11
H.Ironmonger	lbw b Findlay	1	not out	6
Extras	(b7, lb3)	10	(b10, lb7, w4)	21
Total	(75.0 overs, 210 mins)	295	(128.3 overs, 400 mins)	521

TASMANIA

C.W.B.Martin	b Ironmonger	84	(3) b Ironmonger	6
L.F.Gatenby	c Carlton b Souter	11	(5) c sub (A.E.Brown) b Carlton	10
A.P.Findlay	b Souter	0	(4) c Ironmonger b Souter	4
R.A.Davis	c Sheppard b Souter	17	(6) c Souter b Carlton	5
F.E.Headlam	b Souter	1	(8) b Ironmonger	20
*†L.Thomas	c Willis b Ironmonger	18	(7) c Park b Carlton	14
W.H.Bayles	b Souter	0	(10) not out	11
T.H.Elliott	b Ironmonger	10	(2) c & b Souter	10
R.C.A.V.Bayles	c Souter b Ironmonger	3	c Willis b Ironmonger	2
J.A.Jakins	not out	0	(11) c Souter b Ironmonger	0
P.Shawe	c Cohen b Ironmonger	2	(1) b Ironmonger	12
Extras	(b11, lb4)	15	(b10, lb1)	11
Total	(48.5 overs, 161 mins)	161	(38.0 overs, 115 mins)	105

TASMANIA	O	M	R	W	w,nb		O	M	R	W	w,nb
Elliott	13	1	45	1	-,-	(8)	13	1	58	4	2,-
Shawe	15	2	63	3	-,-	(1)	14	5	57	1	1,-
Findlay	8	0	38	1	-,-		9	1	40	0	-,-
Davis	17	2	58	3	-,-	(2)	20	3	66	0	-,-
Martin	11	1	49	0	-,-	(7)	4	0	23	0	-,-
W.H.Bayles	6	3	6	0	-,-	(5)	11	1	53	0	-,-
Jakins	3	0	18	0	-,-	(4)	26	2	85	3	-,-
Headlam	2	0	8	2	-,-	(6)	12	2	31	1	1,-
Gatenby							13.3	0	58	1	-,-
R.C.A.V.Bayles							6	1	29	0	-,-

VICTORIA	O	M	R	W	w,nb		O	M	R	W	w,nb
Ironmonger	19.5	7	53	5	-,-		19	7	42	5	-,-
Souter	18	2	54	5	-,-		6	1	20	2	-,-
Hart	5	1	16	0	-,-		3	3	0	0	-,-
Stephens	5	0	22	0	-,-						
Lugton	1	0	1	0	-,-						
Carlton						(4)	10	0	32	3	-,-

FALL OF WICKETS

Wkt	VIC 1st	TAS 1st	VIC 2nd	TAS 2nd
1st	22	26	39	26
2nd	33	26	192	32
3rd	39	96	208	32
4th	47	122	313	36
5th	83	126	343	51
6th	107	127	469	59
7th	198	154	476	73
8th	284	157	504	101
9th	284	158	509	105
10th	295	161	521	105

1914-15 SEASON (10 MATCHES)

The declaration of war in Europe in August cast a shadow over the commencement of the season. The Board of Control allowed the program of matches to continue as normal despite the worsening situation overseas. Ten matches of first-class ranking were played.

After six lean years, Victoria bounced back to win the Sheffield Shield on batting and bowling averages from New South Wales. The title-holders, New South Wales, began well by winning both their away matches, and kept their unblemished record intact with a 16-run victory over South Australia at Sydney. Victoria in the meantime achieved a win over South Australia at Melbourne and, having already lost to New South Wales at home, journeyed to Sydney needing to defeat New South Wales to keep the Shield race alive. The teams engaged in a hard-fought, low-scoring contest, in which Victoria emerged winners by 16 runs - coincidentally the same margin achieved by New South Wales in the previous match at the ground. Victoria then needed to defeat South Australia at Adelaide in order to equal New South Wales's record of three wins. They achieved this by the comfortable margin of 10 wickets, and in the process took a percentage advantage to overtake New South Wales at the death.

Armstrong, Ryder, Park and Baring were again at the forefront for Victoria, but the crucial factor this year was the bowling of Ironmonger and McDonald. Both went on to achieve Test recognition and fame in the 1920s and '30s.

New South Wales performed well despite the absence of Trumper (illness), Massie, Collins and Cotter (all in military service). Bardsley, Kelleway, Macartney, Andrews, Mailey and Roy Minnett all recorded notable achievements, but they were not always available.

South Australia failed to win a match. The retirement of Clem Hill and the departure of Jack Crawford to take up an overseas coaching appointment were severe losses. Whitty and Wright virtually carried the bowling on their own and the batting, apart from Pellew and Steele, was generally disappointing. It marked the start of South Australia's darkest years in Sheffield Shield cricket.

Queensland met New South Wales (twice) and Victoria, but put up little resistance. The first of the matches against New South Wales at Brisbane went into a third day, but the remaining two were over inside two days. McAndrew's left-arm pace bowling was the only encouraging sign for the future.

Tasmania met Victoria in Melbourne in their sole first-class fixture this season. They also offered little resistance to a Victorian team which was barely Second-XI strength. Tasmania's first innings lasted just on an hour and their bowling struggled to dismiss the home side. Arrangements had been made for New South Wales to visit Tasmania but, as the season developed, the NSWCA reported that 'it was found impractical to send a team'.

The Western Australian Cricket Association also invited New South Wales to send a team west this season. However, the associations were unable to agree on financial terms for the visit. A further approach to the NSWCA was made by the Early Worker Newspaper Company in Perth, but they were advised that negotiations would only be conducted between the associations. Nothing came of the move.

The war situation and the need to concentrate on the general war effort led to the indefinite suspension of all interstate cricket until peace returned.

Leading Aggregates

Batsmen	M	I	NO	Runs	HS	Ave.	Bowlers	Runs	Wkts	Ave.
J.Ryder (V)	5	10	4	445	151	74.16	H.Ironmonger (V)	631	36	17.52
W.Bardsley (NSW)	4	8	1	334	103	47.71	E.A.McDonald (V)	252	19	13.26
R.L.Park (V)	4	8	2	311	134	51.83	W.J.Whitty (SA)	514	18	28.55
C.E.Pellew (SA)	4	8	0	287	97	35.87	J.W.McAndrew (Q)	251	17	14.76
D.M.Steele (SA)	4	8	0	268	100	33.50	T.J.E.Andrews (NSW)	312	16	19.50
W.W.Armstrong (V)	5	8	0	272	71	34.00				

SHEFFIELD SHIELD TABLE

	P	W	L	D	Pts	Quotient	Runs Scored	Wkts Lost	Runs Conceded	Wkts Taken
VICTORIA	4	3	1	-	2	1.234	1810	70	1550	74
NEW SOUTH WALES	4	3	1	-	2	1.196	1851	74	1673	80
SOUTH AUSTRALIA	4	-	4	-	4	0.707	1847	80	2285	70
TOTAL	6	6	6	-	0	1.000	5508	224	5508	224

QUEENSLAND v NEW SOUTH WALES

Played at Brisbane Cricket Ground (Woolloongabba) on November 6, 7, 9, 1914. (Timeless match)
Toss : New South Wales.   Result : NEW SOUTH WALES WON BY 86 RUNS.
Debuts: Queensland - J.W.McAndrew (f/c). New South Wales - J.P.Flynn (f/c).
12th Men: J.K.Farquhar (Qld). Only 11 players in NSW party.
Umpires: G.A.Carter and W.R.Shillington.
Attendances: "small", 1000,   ?   Total: About 2000.   Receipts: £113.
Close of Play: 1st day Qld 6/75 (Ayres 0); 2nd day Qld (2) 1/34 (Ayres 20, Prout 7).

Sheppard, fielding at slip, held an Australian record six catches in the first innings including a running catch towards fine leg to dismiss Minnett from a skier. Davis (60 in 93 minutes, 3 fours) and Cranney (75 in 80 minutes, 7 fours) topscored for New South Wales. Hopkins, playing in his last first-class match, captured three wickets in four balls late on the first day, bowling Prout, Downes and McAndrew with his first, third and fourth balls. Stumps were drawn upon McAndrew's dismissal and when play resumed the next morning Ayres was run out off the sixth ball, thus four wickets were lost in one over. In the following over, Andrews' fourth ball was no-balled "evidently because it appeared to the umpire to be a throw" (*Courier*), Bolton hit two runs from it. McAndrew's first-innings analysis remains the record for a Queensland bowler on debut in Australia. Ayres (74 in 76 minutes, 11 fours) and Hartigan (88 in 110 minutes, 1 six and 12 fours) led a fightback in the fourth innings but to no avail. C.McMillan, New South Wales manager, fielded for Davis on the last day. W.Bardsley (nominated captain), C.Kelleway and R.B.Minnett had announced their unavailability for New South Wales and J.D.Scott withdrew before the team departed. Farquhar replaced J.S.Redgrave (business) in the Queensland twelve. *QCA Report* gives umpire W.H.Carvosso instead of Shillington but the latter is believed correct. *NSWCA Report* incorrectly gives NSW (2) Davis 22, Flynn 16. Sources: *NSWCA Report, QCA Report, Sydney Morning Herald, Brisbane Courier.*

NEW SOUTH WALES

H.H.Davis	c Downey b Barstow	60	hit wkt b Downey	32
E.P.Barbour	c Thomson b McAndrew	7	c Ayres b McAndrew	11
T.J.E.Andrews	b Downey	36	b Barstow	45
H.Cranney	c Sheppard b Barstow	28	c sub (J.K.Farquhar) b Downey	75
H.G.Pratten	c Sheppard b McAndrew	21	c Bolton b McAndrew	36
N.M.Gregg	c Sheppard b McAndrew	0	b Downey	4
B.J.Folkard	c Sheppard b McAndrew	0	c & b Barstow	16
R.V.Minnett	c Sheppard b McAndrew	51	lbw b Barstow	10
*A.J.Y.Hopkins	not out	33	(11) st Bolton b Ayres	4
†A.T.Ratcliffe	c Downey b McAndrew	3	(9) b Ayres	16
J.P.Flynn	c Sheppard b McAndrew	5	(10) not out	6
Extras	(b4, lb7)	11	(b6)	6
Total	(68.4 overs, 200 mins)	255	(67.0 overs, 180 mins)	261

QUEENSLAND

*R.J.Hartigan	st Ratcliffe b Andrews	33	(5) c Gregg b Barbour	88
J.F.Sheppard	st Ratcliffe b Andrews	32	(6) c Ratcliffe b Cranney	41
J.Thomson	lbw b Folkard	0	(7) c Minnett b Barbour	45
J.A.Prout	b Hopkins	10	(3) c Cranney b Davis	43
S.W.Ayres	run out (/Ratcliffe)	0	(1) c sub (C.McMillan) b Folkard	74
J.A.Downey	b Hopkins	0	(11) not out	0
J.W.McAndrew	b Hopkins	0	(10) b Flynn	0
†J.T.Bolton	c Flynn b Hopkins	9	(2) b Andrews	2
W.Rowe	not out	18	(4) b Folkard	0
C.B.Barstow	b Hopkins	0	(8) run out	2
J.W.McLaren	run out (Andrews)	4	(9) run out	0
Extras	(b1, lb1, nb2)	4	(b17, lb1, nb7)	25
Total	(33.2 overs, 100 mins)	110	(71.1 overs, 207 mins)	320

QUEENSLAND	O	M	R	W	w,nb		O	M	R	W	w,nb
McLaren	9	1	36	0	-,-						
McAndrew	21.4	4	51	7	-,-	(1)	24	4	69	2	-,-
Ayres	5	0	21	0	-,-	(4)	10	0	43	2	-,-
Barstow	18	2	63	2	-,-	(2)	20	3	74	3	-,-
Downey	11	0	55	1	-,-	(3)	13	0	69	3	-,-
Rowe	4	0	18	0	-,-						

NEW SOUTH WALES	O	M	R	W	w,nb		O	M	R	W	w,nb
Flynn	6	2	26	0	-,-		12	2	33	1	-,3
Folkard	12	2	46	1	-,-		23	5	63	2	-,2
Andrews	7	1	17	2	-,1		10	1	44	1	-,-
Hopkins	8.2	3	17	5	-,1	(5)	6	0	32	0	-,-
Barbour						(4)	6.1	1	32	2	-,2
Gregg							2	0	16	0	-,-
Davis							6	0	44	1	-,-
Cranney							6	0	31	1	-,-

FALL OF WICKETS

Wkt	NSW 1st	QLD 1st	NSW 2nd	QLD 2nd
1st	14	44	43	15
2nd	82	45	47	119
3rd	134	75	142	125
4th	134	75	182	129
5th	136	75	193	256
6th	136	75	213	299
7th	201	76	228	303
8th	226	103	243	312
9th	231	103	257	319
10th	255	110	261	320

SOUTH AUSTRALIA v NEW SOUTH WALES (Shield Match 1)

Played at Adelaide Oval on December 18, 19, 21, 22, 1914. (Timeless match)
Toss : New South Wales.   Result : NEW SOUTH WALES WON BY 174 RUNS.
Debuts: South Australia - W.O.Cooper, A.P.James (both f/c).
12th Men: W.D.Price (SA) and C.Sheppard (NSW).
Umpires: A.T.Haddrick and F.J.C.Thomas.
Attendances: 1000, 2000, 800, 200.   Total: About 4000.   Receipts: No figure published.
Close of Play: 1st day SA 4/40 (Pellew 0); 2nd day NSW (2) 5/211 (Andrews 17, Kelleway 3); 3rd day SA (2) 6/168 (Steele 70, Stirling 3).

Taylor (69 in 118 minutes, 8 fours) and Pratten (53 in 100 minutes, 6 fours) were the only New South Welshmen to score half-centuries, despite the top nine in the second innings all reaching well into double figures, catches accounting for the entire ten wickets to fall. Steele (100 in 135 minutes) benefitted from chances at 9 and 18 to easily topscore for South Australia. Stirling (54 in 85 minutes, 8 fours) also batted well. J.P.Flynn, A.J.Y.Hopkins and C.G.Macartney had all announced their unavailability for New South Wales after being selected to play. Cranney, Randell and Sheppard were the replacements. Sources: *Wisden, C.B.O'Reilly, NSWCA Report, SACA Report, Adelaide Advertiser, South Australian Register.*

NEW SOUTH WALES

C.Kelleway	run out (Steele/Campbell)	22	(7)	c Pellew b Mayne	32
H.H.Davis	lbw b Wright	7		c Pellew b Willsmore	32
J.M.Taylor	c & b Stirling	69		c Moyes b Wright	35
R.B.Minnett	lbw b James	21		c Willsmore b Moyes	27
*W.Bardsley	c Mayne b Cooper	27		c Middleton b Mayne	42
T.J.E.Andrews	c Pellew b Stirling	0		c & b Stirling	33
H.Cranney	c Pellew b James	31	(1)	c Mayne b James	45
H.G.Pratten	b Stirling	11		c Campbell b Cooper	53
J.D.Scott	c Pellew b Wright	0		not out	45
†A.T.Ratcliffe	not out	31		c James b Stirling	5
J.A.Randell	c Willsmore b Cooper	9		c James b Cooper	0
Extras	(b3, lb9, nb1)	13		(b9, lb2, w1, nb5)	17
Total	(76.1 overs, 220 mins)	241		(108.3 overs, 305 mins)	366

SOUTH AUSTRALIA

*R.E.Mayne	b Randell	21		c & b Minnett	6
R.F.Middleton	run out (Minnett/Ratcliffe)	8	(6)	c Cranney b Scott	9
A.G.Moyes	c Minnett b Kelleway	3		c Bardsley b Minnett	14
D.M.Steele	c & b Randell	4	(5)	c Bardsley b Minnett	100
C.E.Pellew	b Scott	30	(2)	lbw b Kelleway	7
†G.C.Campbell	lbw b Scott	19	(4)	c Ratcliffe b Scott	25
H.B.Willsmore	b Scott	5		c Randell b Kelleway	19
W.S.Stirling	b Scott	3		b Kelleway	54
W.O.Cooper	c Andrews b Randell	25	(10)	not out	16
A.P.James	not out	19	(9)	c Kelleway b Randell	6
A.W.Wright	b Randell	4		c Ratcliffe b Andrews	6
Extras	(b2, lb5, nb3)	10		(b3, lb3, nb14)	20
Total	(51.4 overs, 147 mins)	151		(73.3 overs, 230 mins)	282

SOUTH AUSTRALIA	O	M	R	W	w,nb		O	M	R	W	w,nb
James	20	8	49	2	-,1	(3)	24	5	77	1	-,4
Wright	24	4	75	2	-,-		16	1	60	1	-,-
Stirling	16	4	52	3	-,-	(4)	22	2	70	2	-,-
Cooper	9.1	0	33	2	-,-	(1)	17.3	3	60	2	-,-
Willsmore	4	0	9	0	-,-		7	0	28	1	-,1
Moyes	3	1	10	0	-,-		10	3	20	1	1,-
Mayne							12	2	34	2	-,-

NEW SOUTH WALES	O	M	R	W	w,nb		O	M	R	W	w,nb
Kelleway	13	3	32	1	-,3		14	3	47	3	-,5
Minnett	6	2	14	0	-,-		17	6	59	3	-,3
Randell	20.4	3	73	4	-,-		14	2	62	1	-,-
Scott	11	3	20	4	-,-		17	3	44	2	-,6
Andrews	1	0	2	0	-,-		7.3	1	31	1	-,-
Davis							4	0	19	0	-,-

FALL OF WICKETS

Wkt	NSW 1st	SA 1st	NSW 2nd	SA 2nd
1st	11	23	76	17
2nd	62	30	79	19
3rd	110	37	134	47
4th	153	40	176	72
5th	157	87	205	108
6th	158	90	235	157
7th	185	96	284	225
8th	186	103	340	247
9th	215	132	365	266
10th	241	151	366	282

VICTORIA v NEW SOUTH WALES (Shield Match 2)

Played at Melbourne Cricket Ground on 26, 28, December 1914. (Timeless match)
Toss : New South Wales.   Result : NEW SOUTH WALES WON BY SIX WICKETS.
Debuts: Nil.
12th Men: W.M.Allen (Vic) and C.Sheppard (NSW).
Umpires: R.M.Crockett and E.J.Martin.
Attendances: 10995, 9881.   Total: 20,876.   Receipts: £644.
Close of Play: 1st day NSW 4/125 (Pratten 22).

R.L.Park withdrew from the Victorian side due to the death of his father and was replaced by Hotchin. Ryder strained neck muscles while bowling on the first day and did not field at all on the second. Armstrong (152 minutes, 3 fours) compiled the only fifty of the match, batting for all but 8 minutes of the first innings; heavy rain on Christmas Day spoiled the wicket and was responsible for the low scoring throughout. Failing light and smoke from passing steam engines further handicapped New South Wales batsmen late on the first day. Minnett (right-arm fast-medium) captured career-best figures in the first innings and dismissed Hotchin with the first ball of the second innings. Kelleway also claimed a wicket (Bracher) with his first ball in the second innings. Sources: *Wisden, NSWCA Report, VCA Report, The Age, The Argus, The Australasian, The Leader.*

VICTORIA

*W.W.Armstrong	b Andrews	62	(7)	b Minnett	1
F.A.Baring	c Randell b Minnett	10	(5)	b Kelleway	0
V.S.Ransford	b Minnett	11		c Ratcliffe b Kelleway	10
J.Ryder	c Randell b Minnett	10	(10)	not out	11
T.J.Matthews	c Randell b Minnett	2	(6)	c Ratcliffe b Kelleway	23
V.J.Souter	c Pratten b Minnett	0	(8)	c Minnett b Randell	20
A.E.Brown	b Minnett	0	(4)	run out (Minnett)	6
H.H.G.Bracher	c Taylor b Kelleway	11	(2)	lbw b Kelleway	16
M.D.Hotchin	c Ratcliffe b Minnett	13	(1)	b Minnett	0
†W.Carkeek	b Minnett	1	(9)	b Kelleway	17
H.Ironmonger	not out	2		b Randell	13
Extras	(b17, lb1, w1, nb1)	20		(b1, lb4, nb2)	7
Total	(48.2 overs, 160 mins)	142		(40.2 overs, 145 mins)	124

NEW SOUTH WALES

*W.Bardsley	c Carkeek b Armstrong	34		b Ironmonger	16
H.Cranney	c Ransford b Ironmonger	19	(6)	not out	4
C.Kelleway	c Carkeek b Ironmonger	21			
H.G.Pratten	c Baring b Armstrong	22	(5)	c Carkeek b Ironmonger	0
†A.T.Ratcliffe	c Armstrong b Baring	20	(4)	not out	2
T.J.E.Andrews	c Carkeek b Baring	30	(3)	run out (sub W.M.Allen)	24
J.M.Taylor	st Carkeek b Ironmonger	1	(2)	c & b Souter	5
R.B.Minnett	c sub (W.M.Allen) b Armstrong	3			
H.H.Davis	lbw b Armstrong	12			
J.D.Scott	b Armstrong	28			
J.A.Randell	not out	5			
Extras	(b8, lb8, nb1)	17		(b6, lb1,)	7
Total	(74.4 overs, 220 mins)	212		(21.5 overs, 60 mins) (4 wkts)	58

NEW SOUTH WALES	O	M	R	W	w,nb		O	M	R	W	w,nb
Minnett	24.2	9	50	8	1,1		12	4	34	2	-,2
Kelleway	15	2	52	1	-,-	(3)	16	4	35	5	-,-
Scott	7	2	16	0	-,-	(2)	4	0	19	0	-,-
Andrews	2	0	4	1	-,-						
Randell						(4)	8.2	1	29	2	-,-

VICTORIA	O	M	R	W	w,nb		O	M	R	W	w,nb
Souter	11	1	42	0	-,-		11	2	30	1	-,-
Ironmonger	30	7	70	3	-,-		10.5	3	21	2	-,-
Ryder	7	1	18	0	-,-						
Armstrong	19.4	10	34	5	-,1						
Matthews	2	1	8	0	-,-						
Baring	5	0	23	2	-,-						

FALL OF WICKETS

Wkt	VIC 1st	NSW 1st	VIC 2nd	NSW 2nd
1st	22	40	0	11
2nd	38	78	29	49
3rd	59	82	30	53
4th	61	125	30	54
5th	65	130	45	-
6th	66	136	46	-
7th	103	139	72	-
8th	136	164	96	-
9th	137	200	104	-
10th	142	212	124	-

AFCM No. 489/55
SSM No. 130/42

VICTORIA v SOUTH AUSTRALIA (Shield Match 3)

Played at Melbourne Cricket Ground on January 1, 2, 4, 5, 1915. (Timeless match)
Toss : Victoria.   Result : VICTORIA WON BY 247 RUNS.
Debuts: Victoria - W.M.Allen (f/c).
12th Men: R.F.Middleton (SA). A.E.Brown and E.A.McDonald were named as Victorian emergencies.
Umpires: H.J.Alessio and R.M.Crockett.
Attendances: 10584, 11909, 5428, 3967.   Total: 31,888.   Receipts: £881.
Close of Play: 1st day Vic 7/366 (Matthews 44, Carkeek 8); 2nd day SA 5/265 (Pellew 72, Willsmore 30); 3rd day Vic (2) 4/254
(Park 130, Allen 0).

Baring (80 in 120 minutes, 10 fours), Armstrong (71 in 95 minutes, 5 fours) and Matthews (65 in 125 minutes, 5 fours) were the leading scorers in an even Victorian first innings. Park (134 in 240 minutes, 13 fours) topscored in the second innings, during which Allen (run out), Bracher and Matthews were dismissed in one over by Wright. Fifties were scored for South Australia by Steele (85 in 145 minutes, 6 fours), Pellew (72 in 130 minutes, 9 fours) and Mayne (68 in 190 minutes, 9 fours). *O'Reilly* incorrectly gives Vic (1) Wright 5-0-39-1.
SACA Report incorrectly gives SA (2) Willsmore c Matthews b Allen. Sources: *Wisden, C.B.O'Reilly, VCA Report, SACA Report, The Age, The Argus, The Herald, The Australasian.*

VICTORIA

R.L.Park	c Moyes b Whitty	20	b Whitty		134
J.Ryder	c Wright b Stirling	58	st Campbell b Stirling		40
F.A.Baring	c Moyes b Mayne	80	b Whitty		49
V.S.Ransford	c Whitty b Mayne	33	lbw b Whitty		4
*W.W.Armstrong	b Rundell	71	(9) c Rundell b Wright		12
H.H.G.Bracher	lbw b Wright	13	(7) lbw b Wright		0
T.J.Matthews	c Campbell b Whitty	65	(8) b Wright		0
V.J.Souter	c & b Rundell	25	(5) lbw b Wright		24
†W.Carkeek	c Campbell b James	14	(10) not out		25
W.M.Allen	b James	6	(6) run out (Steele/Campbell)		5
H.Ironmonger	not out	0	b James		13
Extras	(b4, lb7, w3, nb1)	15	(b2, lb2, w3, nb1)		8
Total	(115.2 overs, 325 mins)	400	(97.5 overs, 290 mins)		314

SOUTH AUSTRALIA

*R.E.Mayne	c Baring b Ryder	30	c Carkeek b Ironmonger		68
†G.C.Campbell	c Baring b Ryder	11	(6) c Armstrong b Ironmonger		8
D.M.Steele	c Souter b Ironmonger	85	c Souter b Armstrong		3
A.G.Moyes	c Souter b Ironmonger	13	(8) c Armstrong b Ironmonger		2
P.D.Rundell	run out (Matthews)	9	(4) c Carkeek b Ironmonger		6
C.E.Pellew	c Ryder b Ironmonger	72	(5) lbw b Ironmonger		19
H.B.Willsmore	c Allen b Ironmonger	39	c Matthews b Ryder		1
W.S.Stirling	b Ryder	5	(9) b Ryder		5
A.P.James	b Ironmonger	17	(2) b Ironmonger		15
W.J.Whitty	b Ironmonger	23	not out		6
A.W.Wright	not out	1	b Ironmonger		4
Extras	(b3, lb7, w6, nb3)	19	(b4, w2)		6
Total	(113.4 overs, 330 mins)	324	(68.0 overs, 200 mins)		143

SOUTH AUSTRALIA	O	M	R	W	w,nb		O	M	R	W	w,nb					
Whitty	31.2	4	112	2	1,-		39	12	101	3	2,-			VIC	SA	VIC	SA
James	20	3	72	2	-,1	(3)	12.5	2	46	1	1,1	Wkt	1st	1st	2nd	2nd
Rundell	13	1	54	2	-,-	(5)	7	1	34	0	-,-	1st	47	34	91	37
Wright	25	7	49	1	-,-		20	5	53	4	-,-	2nd	112	57	182	40
Stirling	12	2	38	1	1,-	(6)	5	0	27	1	-,-	3rd	185	80	198	58
Mayne	14	3	60	2	1,-	(2)	4	1	19	0	-,-	4th	216	120	253	90
Willsmore							6	0	24	0	-,-	5th	270	184	259	102
Moyes							4	3	2	0	-,-	6th	293	269	259	103
												7th	339	274	259	116

VICTORIA	O	M	R	W	w,nb		O	M	R	W	w,nb					
Allen	11	1	28	0	4,-	(4)	10	4	17	0	-,-	8th	380	282	273	125
Ironmonger	46.4	15	112	6	1,-		29	10	69	7	2,-	9th	398	323	275	139
Ryder	30	4	88	3	1,-	(1)	16	4	40	2	-,-	10th	400	324	314	143
Armstrong	9	1	29	0	-,3	(3)	13	8	11	1	-,-					
Souter	9	3	24	0	-,-											
Matthews	8	2	24	0	-,-											

NEW SOUTH WALES v SOUTH AUSTRALIA (Shield Match 4)

Played at Sydney Cricket Ground on January 8, 9 (no play), 11, 12, 13, 14, 1915. (Timeless match)
Toss : New South Wales.   Result : NEW SOUTH WALES WON BY 16 RUNS.
Debuts: New South Wales - L.Best (f/c).
12th Men: H.Cranney (NSW) and R.F.Middleton (SA).
Umpires: W.G.Curran and A.C.Jones (see below).
Attendances: 1816, no play, 2231, 301, 793, 565.   Total: 5706.   Receipts: £198.
Close of Play: 1st day NSW 2/166 (Bardsley 80, Andrews 51); 2nd day no play; 3rd day SA 5/109 (Rundell 12, Stirling 12); 4th day
    NSW (2) 2/74 (Bardsley 38, Randell 3); 5th day SA (2) 1/69 (Mayne 31, Willsmore 16).

E.P.Barbour, H.Carter and R.B.Minnett withdrew from the selected New South Wales side and were replaced by Best (originally 12th man),
L.A.Minnett and Ratcliffe. Rain caused several interruptions on the first day and prevented any play on the second. Bardsley (103 in 202
minutes, 3 fours) for New South Wales and Pellew (97 in 180 minutes, 7 fours) for South Australia compiled the top scores. Ratcliffe and
Best, in his sole match, shared a tenth-wicket stand of 87 in New South Wales's second innings. Due to injury, Best was later unable to
complete his fourth over. Whitty (left-arm fast-medium) took his only 10-wicket-match for South Australia. W.G.French deputized for
umpire Curran on the last day. *O'Reilly* and *NSWCA Report* give NSW (1) Ratcliffe 30, Randell 12. Sources: *Wisden, C.B.O'Reilly,
NSWCA Report, SACA Report, Sydney Referee, Sydney Morning Herald, Sydney Daily Telegraph, Town & Country Journal.*

NEW SOUTH WALES

*W.Bardsley	run out (Pellew/Whitty)	103		c Whitty b James	45
C.Kelleway	b Whitty	2	(7)	b Wright	29
C.G.Macartney	c Moyes b Wright	24	(2)	b Mayne	15
T.J.E.Andrews	b James	52	(5)	b Whitty	5
J.M.Taylor	c James b Whitty	22	(8)	b Whitty	27
H.G.Pratten	b Whitty	22	(3)	c Moyes b Whitty	6
J.D.Scott	c James b Wright	4	(9)	b Whitty	2
†A.T.Ratcliffe	b James	29	(10)	st Campbell b Willsmore	59
L.Best	c Whitty b James	7	(11)	not out	24
L.A.Minnett	not out	11	(6)	b Whitty	1
J.A.Randell	c Campbell b Whitty	13	(4)	c Willsmore b Whitty	17
Extras	(b9, lb3, w2, nb4)	18		(b22, lb2, w1)	25
Total	(104.1 overs, 300 mins)	307		(95.3 overs, 271 mins)	255

SOUTH AUSTRALIA

*R.E.Mayne	c Bardsley b Kelleway	5		c Kelleway b Randell	39
A.G.Moyes	run out (Kelleway/Ratcliffe)	27		c Macartney b Randell	17
D.M.Steele	c Kelleway b Minnett	13	(4)	b Minnett	18
P.D.Rundell	c Minnett b Scott	12	(6)	b Best	36
H.B.Willsmore	c & b Minnett	0	(3)	b Randell	16
C.E.Pellew	st Ratcliffe b Andrews	24	(5)	c Taylor b Andrews	97
W.S.Stirling	b Minnett	43	(8)	c & b Andrews	44
†G.C.Campbell	b Scott	7	(9)	st Ratcliffe b Andrews	16
A.P.James	c Andrews b Minnett	12	(10)	b Scott	1
W.J.Whitty	not out	39	(7)	b Kelleway	28
A.W.Wright	c Ratcliffe b Kelleway	7		not out	0
Extras	(b7, lb8, w6, nb5)	26		(b7, lb8, nb4)	19
Total	(88.1 overs, 259 mins)	215		(128.4 overs, 360 mins)	331

SOUTH AUSTRALIA	O	M	R	W	w,nb		O	M	R	W	w,nb		FALL OF WICKETS			
													NSW	SA	NSW	SA
Whitty	37.1	3	113	4	-,-		40	7	103	6	1,-	Wkt	1st	1st	2nd	2nd
James	42	12	105	3	-,4		22	4	48	1	-,-	1st	16	9	45	33
Wright	11	2	33	2	-,-	(5)	10	4	25	1	-,-	2nd	64	41	60	71
Stirling	3	1	5	0	,	(3)	4	0	11	0	-,-	3rd	173	55	96	82
Moyes	4	0	19	0	2,-							4th	218	55	98	136
Mayne	7	1	14	0	-,-	(4)	15	2	27	1	-,-	5th	219	88	105	232
Rundell						(6)	4	0	16	0	-,-	6th	228	109	107	256
Willsmore						(7)	0.3	0	0	1	-,-	7th	269	135	146	273
												8th	281	155	154	330
NEW SOUTH WALES	O	M	R	W	w,nb		O	M	R	W	w,nb	9th	284	171	168	331
Scott	23	4	46	2	4,3		26.3	6	58	1	-,-	10th	307	215	255	331
Kelleway	27.1	7	52	2	-,2		27	9	64	1	-,1					
Minnett	18	9	23	4	2,-	(4)	23	5	59	1	-,3					
Randell	9	2	30	0	-,-	(3)	24	2	74	3	-,-					
Andrews	9	0	36	1	-,-	(6)	16	4	33	3	-,-					
Best	1	0	2	0	-,-	(7)	3.1	0	12	1	-,-					
Macartney	1	1	0	0	-,-	(5)	9	3	12	0	-,-					

NEW SOUTH WALES v VICTORIA (Shield Match 5)

Played at Sydney Cricket Ground on January 23, 25, 26, 27, 1915. (Timeless match)
Toss : Victoria.   Result : VICTORIA WON BY 16 RUNS.
Debuts: New South Wales - F.M.Farrar (f/c). Victoria - L.A.Cody (Vic only).
12th Men: C.C.O'Connor (NSW) and R.S.Stephens (Vic).
Umpires: W.G.French and R.M.Wallace.
Attendances: 3938, 2128, 3164, 623.   Total: 9853.   Receipts: £399.
Close of Play: 1st day NSW 0/10 (Bardsley 4, Mailey 2); 2nd day Vic (2) 0/25 (Cody 11, Park 14); 3rd day NSW (2) 3/78 (Macartney 37, Kelleway 3).

V.S.Ransford (ill) was unavailable for Victoria and Stephens was a late replacement for M.D.Hotchin (work) just before the team left for Sydney. New South Wales brought Flynn into their side when J.D.Scott was unable to obtain leave from his employer. On a true pitch batsmen of both sides were held in check by accurate bowling and excellent fielding. Ryder forsook his normally attacking game for a defensive role and topscored in both innings with 55 in 135 minutes and an unbeaten 93 in 170 minutes with 4 fours. Cody had previously played for New South Wales. *NSWCA Report & VCA Report* incorrectly give Vic (1) Kelleway 0/29, Mailey 6/64. Sources: *Wisden, NSWCA Report, VCA Report, Sydney Referee, Sydney Morning Herald, Sydney Daily Telegraph, Town & Country Journal.*

VICTORIA

R.L.Park	b Andrews	35	(2) c Collins b Andrews	17
J.Ryder	c Ratcliffe b Mailey	55	(3) not out	93
F.A.Baring	c Bardsley b Mailey	27	(4) b Flynn	38
L.A.Cody	c & b Farrar	48	(1) b Flynn	16
*W.W.Armstrong	c Ratcliffe b Flynn	27	c Ratcliffe b Andrews	8
T.J.Matthews	c Mailey b Farrar	9	c Kelleway b Andrews	1
V.J.Souter	b Mailey	15	b Mailey	0
A.E.Brown	c Bardsley b Mailey	0	b Mailey	0
E.A.McDonald	c Farrar b Mailey	0	b Bull	13
†W.Carkeek	c Flynn b Mailey	7	c Farrar b Bull	0
H.Ironmonger	not out	0	c Farrar b Andrews	0
Extras	(b10, lb5, w1, nb1)	17	(b1, lb1)	3
Total	(107.0 overs, 276 mins)	240	(88.5 overs, 221 mins)	188

NEW SOUTH WALES

*W.Bardsley	c Carkeek b McDonald	8	(6) not out	59
A.A.Mailey	b McDonald	3	(10) c Ryder b Ironmonger	18
C.G.Macartney	run out (Park)	9	c Carkeek b McDonald	40
F.M.Farrar	c Carkeek b Ironmonger	10	(2) b Souter	25
T.J.E.Andrews	c Ryder b Ironmonger	0	(7) c Armstrong b Ironmonger	10
J.M.Taylor	b Ryder	32	(4) b Ironmonger	5
H.L.Collins	b Ryder	36	(1) c Park b Armstrong	1
†A.T.Ratcliffe	c Baring b McDonald	16	b Ironmonger	0
C.Kelleway	not out	43	(5) b Ironmonger	7
E.A.Bull	run out (Matthews/Carkeek)	26	(9) c Park b Ironmonger	21
J.P.Flynn	c Ironmonger b Armstrong	2	b Armstrong	4
Extras	(b5, lb7, w2)	14	(b14, lb4, w4, nb1)	23
Total	(83.0 overs, 252 mins)	199	(114.5 overs, 344 mins)	213

NEW SOUTH WALES	O	M	R	W	w,nb		O	M	R	W	w,nb
Flynn	25	14	38	1	-,-		23	7	43	2	-,-
Kelleway	23	10	31	0	1,1	(4)	8	5	5	0	-,-
Mailey	20	0	62	6	-,-		23	2	72	2	-,-
Macartney	6	1	9	0	-,-						
Bull	9	1	26	0	-,-	(7)	6	1	8	2	-,-
Andrews	17	2	41	1	-,-	(5)	21.5	7	45	4	-,-
Farrar	7	2	16	2	-,-	(2)	4	1	6	0	-,-
Collins						(6)	3	0	7	0	-,-

VICTORIA	O	M	R	W	w,nb		O	M	R	W	w,nb
McDonald	22	4	59	3	1,-	(5)	18	3	31	1	1,1
Ironmonger	30	7	64	2	-,-		48	21	73	6	-,-
Armstrong	17	4	36	1	1,-	(1)	27.5	10	46	2	-,-
Souter	4	3	3	0	-,-	(3)	16	5	20	1	2,-
Matthews	1	0	4	0	-,-						
Ryder	9	0	19	2	-,-		3	0	15	0	-,-
Cody						(4)	2	0	5	0	1,-

FALL OF WICKETS

Wkt	VIC 1st	NSW 1st	VIC 2nd	NSW 2nd
1st	80	11	31	2
2nd	118	26	39	52
3rd	143	27	122	59
4th	190	27	140	85
5th	208	44	142	87
6th	229	102	142	106
7th	230	111	144	106
8th	231	142	182	165
9th	240	186	188	204
10th	240	199	188	213

VICTORIA v TASMANIA

Played at Melbourne Cricket Ground on January 29, 30, February 1, 1915. (Timeless match)
Toss : Tasmania.   Result : VICTORIA WON BY AN INNINGS AND 130 RUNS.
Debuts: Victoria - F.W.Hyett, R.J.Junor, W.J.G.Woodbury, F.C.Yeomans (all f/c). Tasmania - W.Arnold, S.Lord, R.H.Powell (all f/c).
12th Men: F.W.Flewellen (Vic) and R.McKenzie (Tas).
Umpires: E.Barrass and R.M.Crockett.
Attendances: 837, 600, 200.   Total: 1637.   Receipts: £26.
Close of Play: 1st day Vic 8/300 (Yeomans 24, Hyett 33); 2nd day Tas (2) 4/172 (Lord 26, Carroll 8).

Opting to bat on a good wicket in fine weather, Tasmania lost Myers to the third ball of the match and collapsed to be all out on the hour. Victoria then set about scoring rapidly with Willis (82 in 90 minutes, 12 fours), Kiernan (59 in 75 minutes, 7 fours), Brown (45 in 40 minutes, 2 sixes and 3 fours) and Yeomans (48, 3 fours) setting up a century on debut for No. 10 batsman Hyett (108 not out in 125 minutes, 1 all-run five and 9 fours). Hyett shared partnerships of 117 for the ninth wicket with Yeomans in 110 minutes and 81 for the tenth wicket with Allen in 40 minutes. Hyett used a VCA bat which was later presented to him in recognition of his feat. Smith (64 in 109 minutes, 6 fours) and Lord (78 in 138 minutes, 9 fours) scored second-innings fifties for Tasmania. Many players were unavailable for the match: R.J.Hawson, A.C.Newton, R.J.Pennycuick and R.Wilkins were absent from Tasmania, while Brown, Cohen (originally 12th man) and Yeomans replaced H.H.G.Bracher, G.E.J.Healy and W.J.Scott in the Victorian side. *The Australasian* names Watt as Tasmanian captain but *TCA Report* records Lord and as there is no mention in other sources, this has been accepted. Sources: *VCA Report, TCA Report, The Age, The Argus, The Herald, The Australasian, The Leader, The Mercury.*

TASMANIA

H.Myers	b Allen	0	c Woodbury b Junor		19
A.K.E.Watt	b Hart	0	b Hart		12
W.Arnold	c Hyett b Allen	5	c & b Junor		30
H.O.Smith	c Hart b Allen	0	b Woodbury		64
*†S.Lord	b Hart	25	b Woodbury		78
T.D.Carroll	b Hart	0	c Hyett b Allen		8
E.L.A.Butler	c Hyett b Allen	7	lbw b Allen		0
R.A.Davis	c Willis b Hart	0	b Junor		10
F.E.Headlam	b Hart	7	c Woodbury b Allen		19
P.Shawe	b Hart	1	(11) not out		3
R.H.Powell	not out	1	(10) c & b b Woodbury		6
Extras	(lb2)	2	(b9, lb6, w2)		17
Total	(15.2 overs, 59 mins)	48	(104.5 overs, 310 mins)		266

VICTORIA

B.L.Cohen	c Davis b Shawe	29
M.D.Hotchin	c Watt b Carroll	7
C.B.Willis	lbw b Myers	82
*C.Kiernan	b Myers	59
W.J.G.Woodbury	b Shawe	5
N.E.Brown	c Davis b Myers	45
F.C.Yeomans	c Lord b Myers	48
H.W.Hart	c Smith b Carroll	2
R.J.Junor	b Myers	1
†F.W.Hyett	not out	108
W.M.Allen	b Shawe	41
Extras	(b6, lb5, w3, nb3)	17
Total	(105.3 overs, 305 mins)	444

VICTORIA	O	M	R	W	w,nb	O	M	R	W	w,nb		FALL OF WICKETS		
Allen	8	3	23	4	-,-	33	10	67	3	1,-		TAS	VIC	TAS
Hart	7.2	2	23	6	-,-	35	13	72	1	-,-	Wkt	1st	1st	2nd
Junor						19	4	64	3	1,-	1st	0	19	24
Brown						3	0	11	0	-,-	2nd	6	93	43
Woodbury						11.5	1	33	3	-,-	3rd	6	139	121
Kiernan						3	2	2	0	-,-	4th	6	158	164
											5th	12	210	172
TASMANIA	O	M	R	W	w,nb						6th	37	237	172
Carroll	19	1	79	2	2,3						7th	37	245	189
Powell	6	0	24	0	-,-						8th	40	246	232
Watt	20	0	100	0	-,-						9th	41	363	263
Shawe	26.3	4	95	3	-,-						10th	48	444	266
Davis	17	2	65	0	1,-									
Myers	17	3	64	5	-,-									

QUEENSLAND v VICTORIA

Played at Brisbane Cricket Ground (Woolloongabba) on January 29, 30, 1915. (Timeless match)
Toss : Victoria.   Result : VICTORIA WON BY TEN WICKETS.
Debuts: Nil.
12th Men: W.J.Thompson (Qld). Only 11 players in Victorian party.
Umpires: R.Haigh and A.T.Horrigan.
Attendances: 300, 1000.   Total: About 1300.   Receipts: £142.
Close of Play: 1st day Vic 179 all out.

Queensland omitted J.T.Bolton, R.K.Oxenham, G.A.Poeppel and W.J.Thompson from an original squad of 15. The Victorians requested that the start of the match be postponed until the 30th so that the players could rest after a hot and tiring train journey from Sydney, but the Queensland Cricket Association was unable to alter arrangements at such short notice. Farquhar replaced W.T.Evans (knee injury) in the home side. The Queensland lineup failed in either innings to cope with the pace of McDonald, who bowled nine of his ten wickets in the match. Thomson completed a pair by being dismissed first ball and fifth ball respectively and Hartigan was out in the first over of the second innings. Armstrong scored the only fifty of the match, batting 68 minutes with 3 fours. Stephens was dismissed first ball in what was to be his final first-class appearance. His three-match career included a century in each innings against Tasmania the previous season. *VCA Report* incorrectly gives Qld (1) Downey b Ironmonger. Due to the early finish midway through the second day, a non-first-class exhibition match was played on January 30th and February 1st. Scores: Victoria 9/260 decl. (Cody 148, Souter 57, McLaren 6/54) and 6/110 (Park 39*, Souter 26*, Rowe 3/22); Queensland 165 (Prout 49, Armstrong 7/76). Sources: *VCA Report, QCA Report, The Age, The Argus, Brisbane Courier, Queensland Times.*

QUEENSLAND

†J.K.Farquhar	b McDonald	2	(6) c Carkeek b Ironmonger		17
J.F.Sheppard	c Stephens b Matthews	33	c Carkeek b McDonald		2
J.Thomson	b McDonald	0	(5) b McDonald		0
S.W.Ayres	b McDonald	14	run out (/Carkeek)		35
*R.J.Hartigan	b Ironmonger	7	(1) b McDonald		1
W.Rowe	b Souter	6	(7) b McDonald		19
J.A.Prout	not out	20	(3) b Ironmonger		0
J.W.McLaren	b McDonald	0	b McDonald		26
J.A.Downey	c Ryder b Ironmonger	0	c Matthews b Stephens		9
C.B.Barstow	run out (Cody/Carkeek)	1	b Stephens		0
J.W.McAndrew	b McDonald	0	not out		25
Extras	(b4, lb1, nb1)	6	(b1, lb2, nb1)		4
Total	(28.3 overs, 97 mins)	89	(32.5 overs, 125 mins)		138

VICTORIA

R.L.Park	st Farquhar b McAndrew	2	not out		29
J.Ryder	c Farquhar b McAndrew	1	not out		19
L.A.Cody	b McLaren	35			
R.S.Stephens	b McAndrew	0			
A.E.Brown	c Ayres b Downey	19			
V.J.Souter	c Rowe b Downey	3			
T.J.Matthews	c McAndrew b Barstow	32			
*W.W.Armstrong	b Barstow	56			
E.A.McDonald	c Ayres b Barstow	9			
†W.Carkeek	not out	7			
H.Ironmonger	st Farquhar b Barstow	4			
Extras	(b7, lb3, nb1)	11	(lb1)		1
Total	(53.4 overs, 158 mins)	179	(15.3 overs, 48 mins) (0 wkts)		49

VICTORIA	O	M	R	W	w,nb		O	M	R	W	w,nb			FALL OF WICKETS		
McDonald	10.3	3	33	5	-,1		7.5	2	22	5	-,1			QLD	VIC	QLD	VIC
Ironmonger	10	2	26	2	-,-		14	1	57	2	-,-	Wkt	1st	1st	2nd	2nd
Stephens	1	0	8	0	-,-	(6)	4	0	17	2	-,-	1st	8	2	2	-
Ryder	3	0	8	0	-,-	(3)	2	0	18	0	-,-	2nd	8	17	3	-
Souter	3	0	8	1	-,-	(4)	3	0	18	0	-,-	3rd	34	17	3	-
Matthews	1	1	0	1	-,-	(5)	2	0	2	0	-,-	4th	43	58	3	-
												5th	61	66	44	-
QUEENSLAND	O	M	R	W	w,nb		O	M	R	W	w,nb	6th	67	68	70	-
McAndrew	18	3	39	3	-,-		4	1	9	0	-,-	7th	70	157	78	-
Barstow	13.4	1	42	4	-,-	(3)	4.3	1	12	0	-,-	8th	71	167	96	-
Downey	13	0	56	2	-,-	(2)	3	0	13	0	-,-	9th	82	170	99	-
McLaren	5	1	15	1	-,1							10th	89	179	138	-
Ayres	4	1	16	0	-,-	(4)	4	0	14	0	-,-					

NEW SOUTH WALES v QUEENSLAND

Played at Sydney Cricket Ground on February 19, 20, 1915. (Timeless match)
Toss : Queensland.   Result : NEW SOUTH WALES WON BY AN INNINGS AND 231 RUNS.
Debuts: New South Wales - N.F.Callaway, W.Cullen, J.L.Wall (all f/c). Queensland - G.A.Poeppel, W.J.Thompson (both f/c).
12th Men: None named. Only 11 players in Queensland party.
Umpires: A.C.Jones and J.A.Turnbull.
Attendances: "very small", 1000.   Total: About 1500.   Receipts: No figures published.
Close of Play: 1st day NSW 4/228 (Callaway 125, Macartney 57).

Cullen, Pite and Waddy replaced C.Kelleway, J.D.Scott and J.M.Taylor (all unavailable) in the selected New South Wales team. Callaway (207 in 214 minutes, 26 fours) batted brilliantly in his sole first-class match: he was killed in France in 1917 before his next chance in big cricket would have arrived. His attacking innings - the highest on debut in Australia so far - included chances at 41, 149, 163, 175 and 180 and featured strong driving and deft cutting. He reached 50 in 67 minutes and 100 in 94 minutes and shared a fifth-wicket stand of 256 with Macartney (103 in 155 minutes, 5 fours) after Macartney had been missed from his first ball, by Sheppard of McLaren. The Queenslanders fielded very poorly, for in addition to the chances given by Callaway and Macartney, Pite (who was making his second and last first-class appearance 13 years after his debut) was allowed two lives in his 56. Farquhar was struck on the brow while keeping wicket and retired from the game, Sheppard deputising for the remainder of the New South Wales innings and Andrews, Farrar and Mailey taking turns to field in the absence of a Queensland reserve. Redgrave replaced J.A.Downey (unavailable) in the Queensland side selected for the match.
Sources: *NSWCA Report, Sydney Referee, Sydney Morning Herald, Sydney Daily Telegraph.*

QUEENSLAND

J.F.Sheppard	c Farrar b Cullen	40		c Macartney b Mailey	28
S.W.Ayres	c Callaway b Cullen	7		b Wall	6
F.C.Thompson	c & b Wall	18		b Andrews	2
†J.K.Farquhar	c Wall b Cullen	15		absent hurt	-
W.Rowe	c Pite b Wall	2	(4)	b Mailey	7
W.J.Thompson	c Callaway b Cullen	1	(7)	b Mailey	0
J.S.Redgrave	b Wall	11	(6)	b Mailey	3
G.A.Poeppel	c & b Bull	3		st Ratcliffe b Mailey	13
J.W.McAndrew	not out	16	(5)	c Andrews b Cullen	19
C.B.Barstow	lbw b Bull	9		not out	3
*J.W.McLaren	b Wall	11	(9)	st Ratcliffe b Andrews	18
Extras	(lb2, w2)	4		(lb1)	1
Total	(50.0 overs, 143 mins)	137		(52.0 overs, 131 mins)	100

NEW SOUTH WALES

F.M.Farrar	c Farquhar b McLaren	27
E.L.Waddy	b McAndrew	0
T.J.E.Andrews	b McAndrew	8
†A.T.Ratcliffe	b McAndrew	0
N.F.Callaway	c Ayres b McLaren	207
*C.G.Macartney	c Barstow b Redgrave	103
W.E.Pite	c Ayres b Barstow	56
E.A.Bull	b McAndrew	22
A.A.Mailey	not out	9
J.L.Wall	c Sheppard b McAndrew	0
W.Cullen	b Barstow	11
Extras	(b11, lb11, w2, nb1)	25
Total	(103.5 overs, 294 mins)	468

NEW SOUTH WALES	O	M	R	W	w,nb		O	M	R	W	w,nb
Cullen	15	8	20	4	2,-		10	4	19	1	-,-
Farrar	3	1	3	0	-,-	(5)	5	1	14	0	-,-
Wall	19	5	44	4	-,-	(2)	10	5	13	1	-,-
Andrews	6	0	37	0	-,-	(3)	9	1	22	2	-,-
Mailey	3	1	4	0	-,-	(4)	18	2	31	5	-,-
Bull	4	0	25	2	-,-						

QUEENSLAND	O	M	R	W	w,nb
McAndrew	24	0	83	5	-,1
Barstow	24.5	1	132	2	-,-
McLaren	19	0	66	2	1,-
Redgrave	21	0	90	1	1,-
Rowe	4	0	26	0	-,-
Ayres	11	0	46	0	-,-

FALL OF WICKETS

Wkt	QLD 1st	NSW 1st	QLD 2nd
1st	10	1	12
2nd	50	17	15
3rd	74	17	34
4th	83	58	47
5th	84	314	55
6th	92	387	55
7th	100	437	67
8th	104	445	96
9th	115	449	100
10th	137	468	-

AFCM No. 495/56
SSM No. 133/43

SOUTH AUSTRALIA v VICTORIA (Shield Match 6)

Played at Adelaide Oval on February 19, 20, 22, 1915. (Timeless match)
Toss : South Australia.   Result : VICTORIA WON BY TEN WICKETS.
Debuts: Nil.
12th Men: W.D.Price (SA) and C.B.Willis (Vic).
Umpires: A.W.Hele and A.McIntyre.
Attendances: No daily figures published.   Total: 4513   Receipts: No figures published.
Close of Play: 1st day Vic 0/114 (Park 51, Ryder 59); 2nd day SA (2) 0/33 (Mayne 9, Pellew 21).

Mayne was out to the fifth ball of the match. Moyes (61 in 77 minutes, 11 fours) alone exceeded fifty for South Australia. Park (62 with 6 fours) and Ryder (151 in 277 minutes, 17 fours) surpassed the first innings target with all wickets intact, sharing an opening stand of 149 in 160 minutes. Park kept wickets after lunch on the last day when Hyett aggravated a hand injury sustained in the match against Tasmania earlier in the month. R.L.Braid, unavailable, was replaced by Willis after the sides were selected. *Wisden* incorrectly gives SA (2) Steele 49, Campbell 31. Sources: *Wisden, C.B.O'Reilly, The Age, Adelaide Advertiser, South Australian Register.*

SOUTH AUSTRALIA

R.E.Mayne	c Souter b McDonald	0		b McDonald	16
A.G.Moyes	c- Baring b Ironmonger	5	(4)	b Ironmonger	61
D.M.Steele	c Armstrong b Ironmonger	2		b Souter	43
C.E.Pellew	c Baring b Ryder	12	(2)	c Souter b McDonald	26
R.F.Middleton	b Ironmonger	2	(8)	c Armstrong b McDonald	7
H.B.Willsmore	c Hyett b Ironmonger	23	(5)	c Baring b Ironmonger	20
*†G.C.Campbell	c Cody b Armstrong	32		not out	37
W.S.Stirling	c Ironmonger b Souter	42	(6)	lbw b Armstrong	2
W.J.Whitty	c Souter b Armstrong	7		c Ryder b Armstrong	14
A.P.James	c Armstrong b Souter	0		c Souter b Armstrong	23
P.H.Coombe	not out	0		b McDonald	0
Extras	(b16, lb1, nb1)	18		(b6, lb2, w1)	9
Total	(52.1 overs, 167 mins)	143		(93.4 overs, 290 mins)	258

VICTORIA

R.L.Park	c & b Willsmore	62	not out	12
J.Ryder	c Moyes b James	151	not out	7
F.A.Baring	c & b James	7		
L.A.Cody	c James b Willsmore	4		
G.E.J.Healy	b Whitty	16		
C.Kiernan	st Campbell b Coombe	22		
*W.W.Armstrong	st Campbell b Whitty	35		
V.J.Souter	lbw b Willsmore	30		
†F.W.Hyett	b Whitty	2		
E.A.McDonald	not out	15		
H.Ironmonger	b James	20		
Extras	(b13, lb1, w1)	15	(b4)	4
Total	(132.0 overs, 360 mins)	379	(5.3 overs, 15 mins) (0 wkts)	23

VICTORIA	O	M	R	W	w,nb		O	M	R	W	w,nb
McDonald	14	2	39	1	-,-		23.4	4	68	4	-,-
Ironmonger	20	6	41	4	-,1		35	9	98	2	-,-
Ryder	9	1	26	1	-,-	(4)	10	2	23	0	-,-
Armstrong	6	3	11	2	-,-	(3)	23	9	50	3	1,-
Souter	3.1	1	8	2	-,-		2	0	10	1	-,-

SOUTH AUSTRALIA	O	M	R	W	w,nb	O	M	R	W	w,nb
Whitty	40	12	80	3	-,-	3	2	5	0	-,-
James	21	6	56	3	1,-	2.3	0	14	0	-,-
Stirling	12	0	47	0	-,-					
Coombe	25	3	79	1	-,-					
Moyes	4	0	8	0	-,-					
Willsmore	25	3	75	3	-,-					
Mayne	5	1	19	0	-,-					

FALL OF WICKETS

Wkt	SA 1st	VIC 1st	SA 2nd	VIC 2nd
1st	0	149	45	-
2nd	3	158	48	-
3rd	10	167	125	-
4th	14	204	166	-
5th	42	251	169	-
6th	52	271	180	-
7th	135	338	203	-
8th	143	340	224	-
9th	143	342	258	-
10th	143	379	258	-

1918-19 SEASON (3 MATCHES)

The New South Wales and Victorian Cricket Associations met within a week of the signing of the Armistice that brought hostilities in the First World War to an end. They decided that a program of return matches between the Sheffield Shield States should be played this season, but that competition for the Shield itself should not recommence until the following year. The South Australian Cricket Association agreed to the proposals.

The first meeting of the Board of Control was held in Sydney on December 6 to ratify the proposals and discuss other matters concerning the resumption of first-class cricket. A suggestion by New South Wales that interstate matches be restricted to three days was rejected, and it was determined that all games should be played out - as had been the case before the War. It was further agreed that eight-ball overs should be introduced. Victoria caused a surprise with a recommendation to discontinue the Sheffield Shield competition, contending that 'other States were tired of it'. South Australia opposed the move and the proposal was deferred. It was given further consideration at Board meetings in October and November 1919 before final agreement was reached to continue the competition.

M.A.Noble, who turned 46 in January 1919, returned to the first-class scene to lead New South Wales against Victoria at Melbourne. His team was outplayed by the Victorians but Noble's five wickets in the first innings and a fighting half-century on the final day indicated little diminution of his skill with the passing years. Mayne (on debut for Victoria) and Baring hit centuries for the home team while McDonald, Ironmonger, Ryder and Armstrong shared the majority of the wickets.

The South Australians arrived in Melbourne a day or two later. Clem Hill had also emerged from retirement in order to help re-establish first-class cricket after the enforced layoff. He led the visitors. Only 15 runs separated the teams after the first innings, but the Victorians finished stronger to record a convincing win. The fast bowling of McDonald (6 for 111 and 6 for 69) proved the decisive factor.

The return New South Wales-Victoria match at Sydney began in sensational fashion, both teams completing their first innings before the first day was through. McDonald continued his destructive form, capturing 8 for 42 in the New South Wales innings. That Victoria were able to set the home team a target of 386 was chiefly due to Les Keating's innings of 154. Centuries from Bogle (on debut) and Andrews saw New South Wales home with surprising ease.

An epidemic of Spanish pneumonic influenza broke out in Europe in November and troops returning from the war quickly spread the disease throughout the Australian community. Travel restrictions were imposed in January to help quarantine, but thousands of deaths were still recorded throughout the country. The Victorian wicket-keeper, Frank Hyett, was among them. As a direct result of the epidemic, all further interstate matches this season were at first postponed and then later abandoned. The South Australian and Western Australian associations had commenced negotiations for a match at Perth, and New South Wales and Queensland had a similar arrangement. The QCA had proposed Brisbane as the venue, the match was scheduled to follow the New South Wales-Victoria clash at Sydney. New South Wales had agreed to send the same full-strength XI that met Victoria under Noble's leadership. The game was put off until Easter before being finally scratched.

The Tasmanian and Victorian associations came the closest to staging a fixture amidst the epidemic - they scheduled a match for Hobart on February 7, 8, and 10. The Victorian selectors followed a VCA suggestion to 'give preference to the younger players' and subsequently announced the following team: J.L.McNaughton (captain), E.L.Carroll, J.L.Ellis, L.F.Freemantle, H.Joyce, A.E.Liddicut, W.H.Ponsford, W.L.Rush, W.D.Saltau, F.G.Truman, W.J.G.Woodbury and F.C.Yeomans. The TCA named a practice squad of 16 comprising C.Cameron, V.R.Driscoll, W.Ellis, H.P.Facy, A.P.Findlay, H.Forster, J.Gardiner, A.C.Newton, R.J.Pennycuick, R.H.Powell, H.C.Smith, J.Trebilcock, D.M.Vautin, A.K.E.Watt, S.L.Wellington and R.Wilkins. A final selection was never made due to the postponement and later abandonment of the fixture.

Leading Aggregates

Batsmen	M	I	NO	Runs	HS	Ave.	Bowlers	Runs	Wkts	Ave.
W.W.Armstrong (V)	2	4	1	249	162*	83.00	E.A.McDonald (V)	393	25	15.72
J.L.Keating (V)	2	4	0	231	154	57.75	M.A.Noble (NSW)	133	9	14.77
J.Ryder (V)	3	6	0	217	78	36.16	T.J.E.Andrews (NSW)	147	8	18.37
F.A.Baring (V)	2	4	0	199	131	49.75	H.Ironmonger (V)	231	8	28.87
V.S.Ransford (V)	3	6	0	162	62	27.00	W.W.Armstrong (V)	119	7	17.00
J.Bogle (NSW)	1	2	0	161	145	80.50	R.Norman (NSW)	211	7	30.14
R.E.Mayne (V)	2	4	0	160	105	40.00	W.J.Whitty (SA)	149	6	24.83

VICTORIA v NEW SOUTH WALES

Played at Melbourne Cricket Ground on December 26, 27, 28, 30, 1918. (Timeless match)
Toss : New South Wales.   Result : VICTORIA WON BY 216 RUNS.
Debuts: Victoria - J.L.Ellis (f/c); P.R.Le Couteur, R.E.Mayne (both Vic only). New South Wales - W.L.Berry, E.A.Dwyer,
   H.S.T.L.Hendry, A.F.Kippax, R.Norman (all f/c).
12th Men: J.L.Keating (Vic) and E.W.Adams (NSW).
Umpires: W.J.R.Bowes and R.M.Crockett.
Attendances: 6200, 7738, 7631, 4000.   Total: About 25,500.   Receipts: £1277.
Close of Play: 1st day Vic 7/250 (Sewart 3, Ellis 0); 2nd day NSW 123 all out; 3rd day NSW (2) 0/31 (Bardsley 14, Dwyer 9).

The first match after the War saw the introduction of eight-ball overs to Australian first-class cricket. Rain prior to the start of the match provided conditions favourable to the bowlers for the first two days. Ironmonger bowled unchanged through the first innings and dismissed Ratcliffe and Norman first ball, though not with successive deliveries. Baring scored 131 (his highest first-class score) in 206 minutes and hit 11 fours. Mayne, on debut for Victoria after 37 matches for South Australia, scored 105 in 208 minutes, and hit 4 fours. At 36 he played a ball into his stumps without dislodging the bails. He used Keating as a runner for the last 30 runs of his innings after suffering a leg strain at the crease. Le Couteur had previously represented Oxford University. Ellis replaced F.W.Hyett (sprained ankle) in the Victorian side. *Age* and *Argus* give umpires as Crockett and D.A.Elder in their pre-match coverage but the above, from later reports, is believed correct. *Wisden* incorrectly gives Vic (1) McDonald 0*, Ironmonger 4; Vic (2) Sewart 4, McDonald 0. Sources: *Wisden, VCA Report, The Age, The Argus, The Herald, The Australasian, Sydney Morning Herald.*

VICTORIA

F.A.Baring	b Noble	131		c Kippax b Hendry	11
C.Kiernan	c Diamond 'b Norman	4	(6)	b Andrews	44
J.Ryder	c Mailey b Norman	3	(4)	c Ratcliffe b Norman	74
R.E.Mayne	c Kippax b Noble	15	(2)	c Andrews b Noble	105
V.S.Ransford	b Noble	4	(3)	b Norman	10
*W.W.Armstrong	run out (Kippax)	68	(8)	c Mailey b Norman	17
W.I.Sewart	run out (Kippax/Ratcliffe)	12	(5)	b Noble	2
P.R.Le Couteur	c & b Norman	1	(7)	run out (Norman/Noble/Ratcliffe)	4
†J.L.Ellis	lbw b Noble	0		not out	10
E.A.McDonald	not out	4		c Diamond b Andrews	2
H.Ironmonger	c Diamond b Noble	0		b Andrews	8
Extras	(b12, lb8, nb4)	24		(b5, lb5, nb2)	12
Total	(61.6 overs, 246 mins)	266		(76.0 overs, 281 mins)	299

NEW SOUTH WALES

W.Bardsley	lbw b Baring	18		st Ellis b Ironmonger	23
E.A.Dwycr	c Ellis b McDonald	11		b McDonald	9
T.J.E.Andrews	c Ellis b Ironmonger	3	(6)	c Baring b Armstrong	20
†A.T.Ratcliffe	b Ironmonger	0		c Ellis b McDonald	1
*M.A.Noble	c & b Ryder	16		c & b Le Couteur	52
R.Norman	lbw b Ironmonger	0	(10)	c Ransford b Armstrong	13
A.Diamond	c Le Couteur b Ironmonger	0	(3)	b McDonald	11
A.F.Kippax	c Ellis b Ryder	20	(7)	b McDonald	14
W.L.Berry	c Ironmonger b Ryder	26	(8)	c Sewart b Le Couteur	17
H.S.T.L.Hendry	run out (Kiernan)	15	(9)	lbw b Armstrong	40
A.A.Mailey	not out	5		not out	9
Extras	(b7, lb1, nb1)	9		(b14, lb2, w1)	17
Total	(35.4 overs, 148 mins)	123		(66.1 overs, 251 mins)	226

NEW SOUTH WALES	O	M	R	W	w,nb		O	M	R	W	w,nb
Norman	18	4	53	3	-,4	(3)	18	1	84	3	-,2
Hendry	12	1	57	0	-,-	(1)	16	0	54	1	-,-
Noble	17.6	3	58	5	-,-	(5)	16	3	23	2	-,-
Mailey	8	0	42	0	-,-	(2)	20	1	91	0	-,-
Kippax	5	0	30	0	-,-						
Andrews	1	0	2	0	-,-	(4)	6	0	35	3	-,-

VICTORIA	O	M	R	W	w,nb		O	M	R	W	w,nb
McDonald	8	0	22	1	-,1		21	5	47	4	-,-
Ironmonger	17.4	3	52	4	-,-		11	0	43	1	-,-
Baring	2	0	8	1	-,-						
Ryder	8	2	32	3	-,-	(3)	8	0	31	0	1,-
Le Couteur						(4)	15	2	59	2	-,-
Armstrong						(5)	11.1	1	29	3	-,-

FALL OF WICKETS

Wkt	VIC 1st	NSW 1st	VIC 2nd	NSW 2nd
1st	25	26	16	37
2nd	34	33	36	50
3rd	65	33	182	53
4th	77	41	189	56
5th	243	41	229	105
6th	245	41	237	140
7th	250	70	263	146
8th	262	75	289	167
9th	266	113	291	199
10th	266	123	299	226

VICTORIA v SOUTH AUSTRALIA

Played at Melbourne Cricket Ground on January 1, 2, 3, 4, 1919. (Timeless match)
Toss : Victoria.   Result : VICTORIA WON BY 108 RUNS.
Debuts: Victoria - J.L.Keating, F.G.Truman (both f/c). South Australia - G.E.Jose, D.E.Pritchard, A.J.Richardson, V.Y.Richardson,
 V.P.Selth (all f/c).
12th Men: C.V.Grimmett (Vic) and D.E.Pritchard (SA - see below).
Umpires: H.J.Alessio and R.M.Crockett.
Attendances: 12000, 6510, 7500, 3000.   Total: About 29,000.   Receipts: £919.
Close of Play: 1st day SA 2/19 (Gehrs 8, Selth 0); 2nd day Vic (2) 2/15 (Truman 0, Keating 1); 3rd day SA (2) 1/104 (V.Y.Richardson 49,
 Rundell 16).

F.W.Hyett, H.Ironmonger and R.E.Mayne all had leg injuries which prevented their selection for Victoria. Willsmore badly twisted a knee while attempting to field a ball only half an hour into the match; permission was granted by the Victorians for Pritchard to take his place as a full member of the side for the remainder. Following one bye and a single to Sewart, Kiernan was out to the last ball of the opening over. Ryder (78 in 132 minutes, 9 fours) played a lone hand in the early part but it was left to Armstrong (162 not out in 183 minutes, 18 fours) to rescue the Victorian first innings. He added 72 with McDonald for the ninth wicket and 101 in 65 minutes with Truman for the tenth wicket. In the second innings Truman scored 46 in 115 minutes and hit 2 fours in the role of night-watchman. Gehrs (96 in 149 minutes, 9 fours), Rundell (100 in 167 minutes, 7 fours) and V.Y.Richardson on debut (72 in 123 minutes, 8 fours) led a recovery for South Australian after Townsend was run out to the fourth ball of the innings. Jose, another debutant, was thrown out attempting a run from his first ball in the first innings and was bowled second ball in the second innings. *Wisden* and *O'Reilly* incorrectly give Vic (2) Ransford c Rundell. Sources: *Wisden, C.B.O'Reilly, VCA Report, The Age, The Argus, The Herald, The Australasian.*

VICTORIA

C.Kiernan	lbw b Whitty	0		b Whitty	11
W.I.Sewart	c Hill b Rundell	18	(9)	c Rundell b Townsend	7
P.R.Le Couteur	b Rundell	12	(10)	b Townsend	8
J.Ryder	lbw b Whitty	78	(6)	c V.Y.Richardson b Townsend	40
J.L.Keating	c V.Y.Richardson b Bridgman	12	(4)	b Bridgman	54
V.S.Ransford	c V.Y.Richardson b Bridgman	16	(7)	b Townsend	17
F.A.Baring	c Townsend b A.J.Richardson	8	(5)	b Townsend	49
*W.W.Armstrong	not out	162		c Selth b Whitty	2
†J.L.Ellis	b Whitty	0	(2)	lbw b Whitty	3
E.A.McDonald	b A.J.Richardson	38	(11)	not out	8
F.G.Truman	b Hill	24	(3)	c Townsend b Bridgman	46
Extras	(b4, lb1, w1)	6		(b3, lb4)	7
Total	(76.0 overs, 290 mins)	374		(69.4 overs, 249 mins)	252

SOUTH AUSTRALIA

R.J.B.Townsend	b McDonald	0	(9)	b Armstrong	15
A.J.Richardson	b McDonald	4	(4)	st Ellis b Armstrong	1
D.R.A.Gehrs	b Ryder	96	(1)	lbw b Le Couteur	37
†V.P.Selth	c Ryder b McDonald	4	(11)	not out	1
P.D.Rundell	b Armstrong	100	(3)	b McDonald	16
V.Y.Richardson	c & b McDonald	72	(2)	b McDonald	48
H.H.M Bridgman	run out (Truman)	1	(5)	c Ellis b McDonald	26
*C.Hill	b McDonald	42	(7)	lbw b McDonald	4
G.E.Jose	run out (Truman)	0	(8)	b McDonald	0
D.E.Pritchard	c Ellis b McDonald	3	(6)	b McDonald	3
W.J.Whitty	not out	19	(10)	c McDonald b Armstrong	5
H.B.Willsmore	absent hurt	-		absent hurt	-
Extras	(b12, lb6)	18		(b1, lb1, w1)	3
Total	(76.6 overs, 310 mins)	359		(35.6 overs, 153 mins)	159

SOUTH AUSTRALIA	O	M	R	W	w,nb		O	M	R	W	w,nb
Whitty	23	3	77	3	-,-		23	1	72	3	-,-
A.J.Richardson	12	0	52	2	-,-		13	1	48	0	-,-
Rundell	18	0	117	2	-,-		9	0	47	0	-,-
Bridgman	16	1	87	2	1,-		12	1	51	2	-,-
Townsend	4	2	14	0	-,-		12.4	2	27	5	-,-
V.Y.Richardson	2	0	14	0	-,-						
Hill	1	0	7	1	-,-						

VICTORIA	O	M	R	W	w,nb			O	M	R	W	w,nb
McDonald	20.6	2	111	6	-,-			12	0	69	6	1,-
Truman	15	0	70	0	-,-							
Le Couteur	4	0	21	0	-,-	(4)		5	0	20	1	-,-
Ryder	13	1	59	1	-,-	(3)		6	1	22	0	-,-
Armstrong	14	2	45	1	-,-	(2)		12.6	1	45	3	-,-
Keating	4	0	12	0	-,-							
Baring	6	0	23	0	-,-							

FALL OF WICKETS

Wkt	VIC 1st	SA 1st	VIC 2nd	SA 2nd
1st	2	0	13	76
2nd	31		14	104
3rd	32	24	111	105
4th	51	194	122	107
5th	87	234	204	110
6th	100	240	209	118
7th	199	325	213	118
8th	201	325	222	147
9th	273	330	241	157
10th	374	359	252	159

NEW SOUTH WALES v VICTORIA

Played at Sydney Cricket Ground on January 25, 27, 28, 1919. (Timeless match)
Toss : Victoria.   Result : NEW SOUTH WALES WON BY SIX WICKETS.
Debuts: New South Wales - J.Bogle (f/c); W.S.S.McCloy (NSW only). Victoria - B.A.Onyons (f/c); C.V.Grimmett (Vic only).
12th Men: W.S.Prentice (NSW) and G.Spicer (Vic).
Umpires: A.C.Jones and A.P.Williams.
Attendances: 9839, 12212, 3108.   Total: 25,159.   Receipts: £1404.
Close of Play: 1st day Vic (2) 2/138 (Ransford 52, Keating 54); 2nd day NSW (2) 2/156 (Kippax 26, Bogle 74).

A vacancy in the Victorian side brought about by W.W.Armstrong's unavailability gave Grimmett his introduction to Australian first-class cricket. F.A.Baring became captain but then withdrew for business reasons and Spicer came into the twelve in his place. Mayne assumed the captaincy in only his second match for the State. Keating gave no chances in compiling 154 in 250 minutes with 12 fours, his only first-class century. Onyons registered a pair on debut. McDonald's first innings figures were his best for Victoria. Bogle scored a century on debut, batting 326 minutes with 1 five and 8 fours. With Andrews (112 not out in 180 minutes, 1 five and 11 fours) he shared a fourth-wicket partnership of 157 to ensure victory for New South Wales. McCloy (ex-Queensland) was bowled second ball in his only match for New South Wales. Grimmett, who had played nine first-class matches for Wellington in New Zealand before the War, went on to better things. *VCA Report* and *Age* incorrectly give Vic (1) Hyett c Ratcliffe. Sources: *Wisden, VCA Report, The Age, The Argus, Sydney Referee, Sydney Morning Herald.*

VICTORIA

*R.E.Mayne	b Norman	32		b Scott	8
B.A.Onyons	c Ratcliffe b Scott	0	(7)	c & b Andrews	0
J.Ryder	c sub (W.S.Prentice) b Scott	0	(2)	b Hendry	22
J.L.Keating	b Mailey	11		c McCloy b Mailey	154
V.S.Ransford	b Scott	53	(3)	c Andrews b Noble	62
P.R.Le Couteur	st Ratcliffe b Andrews	3		b Hendry	17
W.I.Sewart	c McCloy b Andrews	0	(5)	lbw b Noble	30
E.A.McDonald	c Ratcliffe b Andrews	4	(10)	st Ratcliffe b Mailey	13
†F.W.Hyett	st Ratcliffe b Andrews	5	(8)	b Mailey	14
C.V.Grimmett	b Scott	7	(9)	b Mailey	0
H.Ironmonger	not out	0		not out	1
Extras	(b3, lb6, nb1)	10		(b17, lb5, nb3)	25
Total	(27.0 overs, 112 mins)	125		(76.4 overs, 293 mins)	346

NEW SOUTH WALES

W.Bardsley	b McDonald	3	(2)	c Hyett b Ryder	49
H.S.T.L.Hendry	c Le Couteur b Ironmonger	13	(6)	not out	19
J.Bogle	b McDonald	16		b Keating	145
T.J.E.Andrews	b McDonald	3	(5)	not out	112
A.F.Kippax	c Onyons b McDonald	18	(4)	b Ironmonger	45
*M.A.Noble	c Grimmett b McDonald	5	(1)	b Ironmonger	7
W.S.S.McCloy	b McDonald	0			
†A.T.Ratcliffe	not out	14			
J.D.Scott	b McDonald	0			
R.Norman	b McDonald	0			
A.A.Mailey	b Le Couteur	9			
Extras	(b3, lb2)	5		(b7, lb3)	10
Total	(21.1 overs, 99 mins)	86		(91.2 overs, 355 mins) (4 wkts)	387

NEW SOUTH WALES	O	M	R	W	w,nb		O	M	R	W	w,nb
Scott	6	0	19	4	-,-		4	0	35	1	-,-
Mailey	5	0	26	1	-,-		13.4	0	59	4	-,-
Andrews	8	0	45	4	-,-		14	1	65	1	-,-
Norman	8	2	25	1	-,1		11	0	49	0	-,3
Hendry							20	1	61	2	-,-
Noble							14	3	52	2	-,-

VICTORIA	O	M	R	W	w,nb		O	M	R	W	w,nb
McDonald	11	1	42	8	-,-		22	0	102	0	-,-
Ironmonger	10	0	39	1	-,-		32	1	97	2	-,-
Le Couteur	0.1	0	0	1	-,-	(4)	6	0	48	0	-,-
Ryder						(3)	22	2	83	1	-,-
Grimmett							5	0	34	0	-,-
Keating							4.2	1	13	1	-,-

FALL OF WICKETS

Wkt	VIC 1st	NSW 1st	VIC 2nd	NSW 2nd
1st	9	6	8	11
2nd	9	34	49	109
3rd	22	34	178	191
4th	55	44	249	348
5th	75	58	279	-
6th	75	58	282	-
7th	85	65	330	-
8th	99	65	330	-
9th	124	65	333	-
10th	125	86	346	-

1919-20 SEASON (12 MATCHES)

Competition for the Sheffield Shield resumed, five years after the wartime suspension. New South Wales headed Victoria on averages - an exact reversal of the previous result in 1914-15. Heavy scoring was a feature of the season. More than 7000 Shield runs were tallied - the first such instance - and double-centuries came from the bats of Bogle and Andrews (New South Wales), Park (Victoria) and Pellew (South Australia).

Victoria began their campaign by recording emphatic victories in both home games. New South Wales drew level with equally emphatic victories in both their matches against South Australia, and then went ahead with an innings victory over Victoria at Sydney. Victoria defeated South Australia at Adelaide in the final game to draw level on points, but their averages were vastly inferior to those of New South Wales and this proved decisive.

The Australian Imperial Forces team returned home on January 2 from their successful tour of England and South Africa. They were scheduled to play a match against the three major States, however their arrival in Adelaide coincided with South Australia's absence in Melbourne for the Sheffield Shield clash against Victoria. The AIF, unable to alter their itinerary, cancelled the match against South Australia and juggled the dates of the remaining matches against Victoria and New South Wales in order to fit in a new match against Queensland. The team played attractive, attacking cricket, and became instantly popular with spectators, the chief drawcard being Jack Gregory. His fame from his overseas exploits had preceded him, and Australian crowds were not disappointed. Fiery fast bowling at Melbourne, a century in each innings at Sydney, and brilliant athletic slip fielding confirmed the dawning of an outstanding allround career.

There were suggestions that a 'Test' be played between the AIF team and the Rest of Australia, and that players such as Kelleway, Macartney and Tozer be added to strengthen the AIF. However, the tight schedule of the AIF team could not be changed and no firm arrangements were initiated.

Queensland returned to the first-class scene after the war by resuming their regular home and away matches with New South Wales, as well as games against Victoria and the AIF. Rain helped them draw home matches against the AIF and New South Wales, but they were heavily defeated by Victoria at Brisbane and then by New South Wales at Sydney. McAndrew confirmed pre-war impressions of his left-arm pace bowling and Cecil Thompson's consistency hinted at a promising batting career.

An attempt was made to resume matches between Victoria and Tasmania. Arrangements were completed for a fixture at Launceston on January 24, 26 and 27, but a prolonged shipping strike isolated Tasmania, resulting in the match being at first postponed and then abandoned. The Tasmanian team comprised R.C.A.V.Bayles, F.L.Butler, B.J.J.Davie, A.H.Davis, T.H.Elliott, A.P.Findlay, G.W.Martin, A.C.Newton, R.J.Pennycuick, L.Thomas, A.K.E.Watt and E.S.Headlam (12th man). No captain was nominated in the Press. The Victorian team originally comprised B.J.Sheppard (captain), A.H.Dean, L.Downs, L.D.Ferguson, L.F.Freemantle, C.V.Grimmett, W.J.Johnson, A.E.Liddicut, A.G.Moyes, B.A.Onyons, W.J.Rayson and H.C.A.Sandford. Shortly after the team was named, Dean and Freemantle were transferred to the Victorian Shield team to play New South Wales at Sydney, as replacements, and Grimmett also announced he was unavailable. S.Anderson, R.Love and W.H.Ponsford were named to fill their spots in the twelve.

Leading Aggregates

Batsmen	M	I	NO	Runs	HS	Ave.	Bowlers	Runs	Wkts	Ave.
R.L.Park (V)	5	9	0	648	228	72.00	H.S.T.L.Hendry (NSW)	526	29	18.13
T.J.E.Andrews (NSW)	6	9	2	609	247*	87.00	W.W.Armstrong (V)	615	25	24.60
R.E.Mayne (V)	6	12	1	591	131	53.72	R.Norman (NSW)	621	24	25.87
W.Bardsley (NSW)	5	7	0	412	106	58.85	A.A.Mailey (NSW)	704	24	29.33
H.L.Collins (AIF/NSW)	4	7	0	408	135	58.28	J.M.Gregory (AIF)	283	19	14.89
C.E.Pellew (AIF/SA)	4	8	0	400	271	50.00				
W.W.Armstrong (V)	6	9	1	388	143	48.50				
J.M.Gregory (AIF)	3	6	1	375	122	75.00				

SHEFFIELD SHIELD TABLE

	P	W	L	D	Pts	Quotient	Runs Scored	Wkts Lost	Runs Conceded	Wkts Taken
NEW SOUTH WALES	4	3	1	-	2	1.650	2432	54	2129	78
VICTORIA	4	3	1	-	2	1.143	2583	62	2551	70
SOUTH AUSTRALIA	4	-	4	-	-4	0.522	2242	80	2577	48
TOTAL	6	6	6	-	0	1.000	7257	196	7257	196

QUEENSLAND v NEW SOUTH WALES

Played at Brisbane Cricket Ground (Woolloongabba) on November 29, December 1, 2, 1919. (Three-day match)
Toss : New South Wales.   Result : MATCH DRAWN.
Debuts: Queensland - R.R.Barbour, C.E.R.Maddock, L.E.Oxenham (all f/c). New South Wales - O.P.Asher, K.B.Docker, W.F.Ives, A.T.E.Punch (all f/c).
12th Men: J.W.Anderson (Qld) and E.W.Adams (NSW).
Umpires: W.H.Carvosso and R.Haigh.
Attendances: 3500, 5000, 500.   Total: About 9000.   Receipts: £506.
Close of Play: 1st day Qld 2/90 (Thomson 22, Barbour 1); 2nd day NSW (2) 3/230 (Kippax 7, Berry 2).

Rain interrupted play on the last day and led to an abandonment at 5.30pm. Noble, in his last first-class match, injured a leg after scoring 2 in the second innings and called for a runner who, though not identified in press reports brought about Noble's dismissal when a sharp return from Sheppard at cover to the non-striker's end found the runner well out of his ground. The injury also prevented Noble taking the field in the second Queensland innings, Berry leading the side in his absence. Kippax scored 93 in 102 minutes with 9 fours and was out to the first ball after the tea adjournment. Centuries were scored by Tozer (103 in 146 minutes, 3 fours - his only first-class hundred) and Ratcliffe (107 in 110 minutes, 11 fours). *NSWCA Report* incorrectly gives NSW (2) Docker 11, Barstow 2/92. Sources: *A.C.S., NSWCA Report, Sydney Morning Herald, Brisbane Courier.*

NEW SOUTH WALES

C.J.Tozer	c Farquhar b Ayres	51	(2) c sub (J.W.Anderson) b Thompson	103
H.S.T.L.Hendry	c Ayres b McAndrew	8	(8) not out	32
A.T.E.Punch	b Barstow	38	(7) b McAndrew	4
†A.T.Ratcliffe	b Ayres	21	(3) c sub (J.W.Anderson) b Thompson	107
A.F.Kippax	c & b Ayres	93	(4) b McAndrew	13
K.B.Docker	st Farquhar b Ayres	15	c Farquhar b Barstow	1
*M.A.Noble	st Farquhar b Ayres	3	(1) run out (Sheppard/Barstow)	10
W.L.Berry	c Rowe b Maddock	37	(5) c & b Barstow	11
O.P.Asher	not out	15		
W.F.Ives	c Maddock b Ayres	13	(9) not out	41
R.Norman	lbw b Ayres	4		
Extras	(b1, nb1)	2	(b2, lb1)	3
Total	(59.0 overs, 222 mins)	300	(94.2 overs, 270 mins) (7 wkts dec)	325

QUEENSLAND

*J.F.Sheppard	c Asher b Noble	54	c Kippax b Norman	8
L.E.Oxenham	run out (Norman)	13	c Asher b Norman	9
J.Thomson	c Norman b Hendry	54	b Hendry	25
R.R.Barbour	c Ratcliffe b Norman	41	b Asher	25
F.C.Thompson	c & b Norman	11	not out	44
†J.K.Farquhar	c Tozer b Norman	8	c Ives b Asher	3
W.Rowe	c Hendry b Norman	6	c Asher b Norman	0
S.W.Ayres	lbw b Asher	15	not out	0
J.W.McAndrew	b Norman	9		
C.E.R.Maddock	c Kippax b Asher	13		
C.B.Barstow	not out	0		
Extras	(b3, nb9)	12	(b10, nb5)	15
Total	(57.2 overs, 210 mins)	236	(38.0 overs, 150 mins) (6 wkts)	129

QUEENSLAND	O	M	R	W	w,nb		O	M	R	W	w,nb
McAndrew	22	2	97	1	-,1		44	5	106	2	-,-
Ayres	16	0	83	7	-,-	(3)	6	0	46	0	-,-
Barstow	10	0	53	1	-,-	(2)	27.2	0	91	2	-,-
Rowe	4	0	12	0	-,-	(6)	4	0	26	0	-,-
Maddock	4	0	41	1	-,-		3	0	25	0	-,-
Thompson	3	0	12	0	-,-	(4)	10	1	28	2	-,-

NEW SOUTH WALES	O	M	R	W	w,nb		O	M	R	W	w,nb
Norman	17.2	1	61	5	-,9		11	0	43	3	-,5
Asher	6	0	40	2	-,-	(5)	6	2	5	2	-,-
Hendry	12	0	51	1	-,-		9	1	33	1	-,-
Noble	15	1	50	1	-,-						
Ives	7	0	22	0	-,-	(2)	9	3	27	0	-,-
Kippax						(4)	3	0	6	0	-,-

FALL OF WICKETS

Wkt	NSW 1st	QLD 1st	NSW 2nd	QLD 2nd
1st	13	45	18	13
2nd	70	86	209	49
3rd	112	139	226	49
4th	123	171	244	119
5th	153	189	249	127
6th	165	193	251	127
7th	238	209	254	-
8th	279	222	-	-
9th	293	236	-	-
10th	300	236	-	-

SOUTH AUSTRALIA v NEW SOUTH WALES (Shield Match 1)

Played at Adelaide Oval on December 19, 20, 22, 1919. (Timeless match)
Toss : New South Wales.   Result : NEW SOUTH WALES WON BY AN INNINGS AND 330 RUNS.
Debuts: South Australia - F.R.Lucas, N.L.Williams (both f/c).
12th Men: H.H.M.Bridgman (SA) and E.A.Dwyer (NSW).
Umpires: A.McIntyre and F.J.C.Thomas.
Attendances: No daily figures published.   Total: 8376.   Receipts: £394.
Close of Play: 1st day NSW 4/414 (Andrews 73); 2nd day SA 6/126 (Rundell 58, Williams 1).

G.C.Campbell (South Australia), K.B.Docker, C.G.Macartney and C.J.Tozer (New South Wales) all announced their unavailability prior to the match. Bridgman replaced H.B.Willsmore (hand injury) in the South Australian twelve. Bardsley, dropped first ball by Selth went on to score 106 in 174 minutes with 1 five and 10 fours. Selth was hit in the eye soon afterwards and taken to hospital; Gehrs replaced him as wicket-keeper for the rest of the innings and caught Kippax in the role. Bogle, who had scored a hundred on debut the previous season, improved by compiling a double century in only his second first-class match. He batted 240 minutes and hit 29 fours, giving a chance at 126. Other centuries were scored by Andrews (103 in 161 minutes, 14 fours) and Kelleway (121 not out in 125 minutes, 19 fours, stumping chance at 46). Norman claimed a wicket in the first over of each South Australian innings, dismissing V.Y.Richardson second ball and Gehrs eighth ball respectively. *Wisden* and *O'Reilly* incorrectly give NSW Kippax b Whitty. *NSWCA Report* and *Daily Herald* incorrectly give SA (1) Townsend c Kippax b Mailey. Sources: *Wisden, C.B.O'Reilly, NSWCA Report, Adelaide Advertiser, South Australian Register, Adelaide Daily Herald.*

NEW SOUTH WALES

*†H.Carter	b Lucas	21
W.Bardsley	b Lucas	106
J.Bogle	c & b Williams	200
A.F.Kippax	c Gehrs b Whitty	0
T.J.E.Andrews	b Lucas	103
A.T.Ratcliffe	c & b Williams	23
H.S.T.L.Hendry	b Lucas	22
C.Kelleway	not out	121
W.F.Ives	b Lucas	1
A.A.Mailey	c Pritchard b V.Y.Richardson	40
R.Norman	c Rundell b Williams	20
Extras	(b25, lb5, w2, nb1)	33
Total	(114.0 overs, 460 mins)	690

SOUTH AUSTRALIA

V.Y.Richardson	b Norman	0	(8)	not out	51
D.E.Pritchard	st Carter b Mailey	13		b Hendry	17
P.D.Rundell	c Hendry b Mailey	58	(4)	b Mailey	6
D.M.Steele	c Carter b Mailey	3	(5)	b Mailey	15
A.J.Richardson	b Mailey	28	(6)	c Mailey b Kelleway	13
R.J.B.Townsend	c Ratcliffe b Mailey	8	(7)	c Kippax b Mailey	0
*D.R.A.Gehrs	c Carter b Norman	0	(1)	c Kelleway b Norman	4
N.L.Williams	run out (Andrews/Carter)	50	(9)	b Kelleway	0
†V.P.Selth	b Ives	25	(3)	c Mailey b Hendry	18
W.J.Whitty	not out	0		c Kippax b Mailey	5
F.R.Lucas	c Kelleway b Ives	0		c Ratcliffe b Kelleway	1
Extras	(b14, lb2, nb6)	22		(b17, lb4, nb2)	23
Total	(44.6 overs, 175 mins)	207		(40.4 overs, 165 mins)	153

SOUTH AUSTRALIA	O	M	R	W	w,nb
Whitty	26	3	95	1	2,-
Lucas	25	3	152	5	-,-
Townsend	12	1	82	0	-,-
Rundell	10	0	83	0	-,-
A.J.Richardson	20	1	102	0	-,-
Williams	19	0	138	3	-,1
V.Y.Richardson	2	1	5	1	-,-

NEW SOUTH WALES	O	M	R	W	w,nb		O	M	R	W	w,nb
Norman	11	4	35	2	-,5		8	0	24	1	-,2
Kelleway	8	3	25	0	-,-	(5)	8.4	0	18	3	-,-
Mailey	18	0	87	5	-,-		13	2	46	4	-,-
Ives	4.6	0	21	2	-,-	(2)	4	1	17	0	-,-
Andrews	3	0	17	0	-,1						
Hendry						(4)	7	1	25	2	-,-

	FALL OF WICKETS			
		NSW	SA	SA
Wkt		1st	1st	2nd
1st		44	0	5
2nd		247	27	36
3rd		248	37	53
4th		414	86	57
5th		454	107	74
6th		493	112	74
7th		494	131	132
8th		518	207	142
9th		637	207	151
10th		690	207	153

VICTORIA v NEW SOUTH WALES (Shield Match 2)

Played at Melbourne Cricket Ground on December 26, 27, 29, 30, 31, 1919, January 1, 1920. (Timeless match)
Toss : Victoria.   Result : VICTORIA WON BY 116 RUNS.
Debuts: Nil.
12th Men: L.A.Cody (Vic) and E.A.Dwyer (NSW).
Umpires: R.M.Crockett and D.A.Elder.
Attendances: 14006, 4304, 12294, 7706, 7653, 11868.   Total: 57,831.   Receipts: £2574.
Close of Play: 1st day Vic 6/360 (Hartkopf 13, Ellis 11); 2nd day Vic 6/376 (Hartkopf 24, Ellis 16); 3rd day NSW 6/233 (Ratcliffe 44,
    Kelleway 32); 4th day Vic (2) 6/252 (McDonald 8); 5th day NSW (2) 3/221 (Bogle 3).

A second-wicket stand of 215 between Mayne (131 in 177 minutes, 16 fours) and Park (92 in 147 minutes, 9 fours) for Victoria highlighted the first day's play. Ransford, in attempting to hit a Kelleway full toss, edged the ball into his face and suffered a broken nose. He retired at 4/252 (Baring was just out) and took no further part in the match. Park's second innings of 77 occupied 132 minutes and included 9 fours. Rain severely curtailed proceedings on the second day. Century opening stands were raised in each New South Wales innings, first between Carter (61 in 75 minutes, 3 fours) and Bardsley (53 in 93 minutes, 4 fours) and then between Kelleway (104 in 208 minutes, 8 fours, chance at 87) and Bardsley (106 in 218 minutes, 1 five and 3 fours, 2 chances) in the second innings. *NSWCA Report* incorrectly gives Vic (1) Ryder 9. Sources: *Wisden, NSWCA Report, VCA Report, The Age, The Argus, The Herald, The Australasian, The Leader.*

VICTORIA

Batsman	Dismissal	Score		2nd Innings	Score
R.E.Mayne	c sub (E.A.Dwyer) b Kelleway	131		c Mailey b Norman	22
J.Ryder	c Bogle b Hendry	0	(5)	run out (/Carter)	11
R.L.Park	c Carter b Hendry	92		c Bogle b Norman	77
F.A.Baring	c Carter b Mailey	20		c & b Norman	67
V.S.Ransford	retired hurt	6		absent hurt	-
*W.W.Armstrong	c Kelleway b Mailey	46	(8)	c Mailey b Hendry	33
J.L.Keating	c & b Mailey	36	(9)	b Hendry	51
A.E.V.Hartkopf	c Kelleway b Ives	53	(2)	c Bardsley b Hendry	49
†J.L.Ellis	c Norman b Ives	33	(6)	lbw b Norman	0
E.A.McDonald	not out	25	(7)	run out (Bardsley/Carter)	8
H.Ironmonger	b Mailey	13	(10)	not out	0
Extras	(b5, lb2, nb2)	9		(b10, lb5, nb3)	18
Total	(107.2 overs, 392 mins)	464		(73.1 overs, 272 mins)	336

NEW SOUTH WALES

Batsman	Dismissal	Score		2nd Innings	Score
*†H.Carter	c Keating b Ryder	61	(5)	lbw b Armstrong	13
W.Bardsley	c Ellis b Ryder	53		run out (Ironmonger/Ellis)	106
J.Bogle	c Ellis b Ryder	1		c Ellis b McDonald	20
T.J.E.Andrews	c Ellis b Ryder	5	(6)	b Armstrong	1
A.F.Kippax	lbw b Ryder	23	(7)	c Ellis b McDonald	16
A.T.Ratcliffe	b McDonald	62	(8)	lbw b Ryder	34
H.S.T.L.Hendry	run out (Hartkopf/Armstrong)	5	(9)	not out	55
C.Kelleway	c Ellis b McDonald	37	(1)	c Armstrong b Hartkopf	104
W.F.Ives	not out	13	(4)	lbw b Armstrong	1
A.A.Mailey	c Armstrong b Ironmonger	5		b Ryder	0
R.Norman	b McDonald	18		c sub (L.A.Cody) b McDonald	28
Extras	(b8, lb3, nb1)	12		(b5, lb2, w4)	11
Total	(72.1 overs, 295 mins)	295		(102.4 overs, 420 mins)	389

NEW SOUTH WALES	O	M	R	W	w,nb		O	M	R	W	w,nb
Norman	18	2	96	0	-,2		21	2	123	4	-,3
Hendry	17	0	56	2	-,-		16.1	5	42	3	-,-
Kelleway	22	2	84	1	-,-	(5)	5	2	10	0	-,-
Mailey	29.2	2	99	4	-,-	(3)	17	2	82	0	-,-
Ives	10	0	68	2	-,-	(6)	5	0	15	0	-,-
Andrews	11	0	52	0	-,-	(4)	9	0	46	0	-,-

VICTORIA	O	M	R	W	w,nb		O	M	R	W	w,nb
McDonald	17.1	0	93	3	-,1		17.4	1	69	3	-,-
Ironmonger	23	3	77	1	-,-		21	3	87	0	2,-
Armstrong	13	1	44	0	-,-	(7)	26	8	47	3	2,-
Ryder	16	3	56	5	-,-	(3)	12	0	65	2	-,-
Keating	2	0	4	0	-,-						
Hartkopf	1	0	9	0	-,-	(4)	23	1	96	1	-,-
Baring						(5)	2	0	9	0	-,-
Park						(6)	1	0	5	0	-,-

FALL OF WICKETS

Wkt	1st VIC	1st NSW	2nd VIC	2nd NSW
1st	2	110	68	216
2nd	217	111	89	220
3rd	231	118	232	221
4th	252	123	237	237
5th	331	161	237	247
6th	336	181	251	268
7th	425	245	252	269
8th	436	261	333	316
9th	464	266	336	316
10th	-	295	-	389

VICTORIA v SOUTH AUSTRALIA (Shield Match 3)

Played at Melbourne Cricket Ground on January 2, 3, 5, 6, 1920. (Timeless match)
Toss : South Australia.   Result : VICTORIA WON BY TEN WICKETS.
Debuts: Victoria - L.D.Ferguson (f/c). South Australia - J.W.E.Schultz (f/c).
12th Men: H.H.M.Bridgman (SA). No 12th man or emergency fieldsman named for Victoria.
Umpires: W.J.R.Bowes and R.M.Crockett.
Attendances: 7224, 13698, 6080, 1668.   Total: 28,670.   Receipts: £1238.
Close of Play: 1st day Vic 1/50 (Mayne 31, McNaughton 3); 2nd day Vic 7/414 (Park 171, Armstrong 45); 3rd day SA (2) 2/167
      (V.Y.Richardson 84, Pritchard 67).

Cody, Ferguson and McNaughton replaced F.A.Baring (business), H.Ironmonger and V.S.Ransford (both injured) in the Victorian side. Rundell (122 not out in 228 minutes, 10 fours) and V.Y.Richardson (134 in 225 minutes, 18 fours) compiled centuries for South Australia while Pritchard scored 91 in 156 minutes with 12 fours. A.J.Richardson was hit by a McDonald delivery and forced to retire at 4/103. He resumed at 6/185 but was bowled first ball, McDonald taking three wickets (Williams, A.J.Richardson, ball, Schultz) in four balls. Park (a career-highest 228 in 405 minutes, 21 fours) and Armstrong (143 in 256 minutes, 9 fours) shared an eighth-wicket partnership of 215 for Victoria, a State record which still stands. Schultz registered a pair on debut - out second ball in the first innings and first ball in the second. Sources: *Wisden, C.B.O'Reilly, VCA Report, The Age, The Argus, The Herald, The Australasian, Bendigo Advertiser, The Leader.*

SOUTH AUSTRALIA

*D.R.A.Gehrs	b McDonald	13		b McDonald	5
D.E.Pritchard	b McNaughton	4	(4)	lbw b Ryder	91
P.D.Rundell	not out	122		b McDonald	0
V.Y.Richardson	b Park	20	(2)	b Park	134
D.M.Steele	c Armstrong b McNaughton	17		c Hartkopf b Ryder	73
A.J.Richardson	b McDonald	0		c Park b Armstrong	29
R.J.B.Townsend	b Armstrong	46		c Park b Armstrong	4
N.L.Williams	b McDonald	4		not out	20
†J.W.E.Schultz	c Armstrong b McDonald	0		b Ryder	0
W.J.Whitty	c Armstrong b McNaughton	3		c Ellis b Armstrong	5
F.R.Lucas	b Armstrong	10		run out (Ferguson)	0
Extras	(b6, lb2)	8		(b4, lb13)	17
Total	(60.2 overs, 239 mins)	247		(82.1 overs, 323 mins)	378

VICTORIA

R.E.Mayne	c Schultz b A.J.Richardson	70	not out	13
L.A.Cody	b Whitty	15	not out	8
J.L.McNaughton	c Whitty b Lucas	5		
J.L.Keating	c Steele b Rundell	3		
R.L.Park	c Pritchard b Lucas	228		
J.Ryder	c Townsend b Rundell	18		
L.D.Ferguson	b Whitty	29		
A.E.V.Hartkopf	b Rundell	49		
*W.W.Armstrong	b Williams	143		
†J.L.Ellis	b Williams	17		
E.A.McDonald	not out	11		
Extras	(b8, lb8, w1)	17		—
Total	(140.5 overs, 530 mins)	605	(2.0 overs, 6 mins) (0 wkts)	21

VICTORIA	O	M	R	W	w,nb		O	M	R	W	w,nb					
McNaughton	23	6	88	3	-,-		16	4	58	0	-,-					
McDonald	18	1	71	4	-,-		20	2	84	2	-,-	Wkt	1st	1st	2nd	2nd
Ryder	9	1	39	0	-,-		11.1	0	54	3	-,-	1st	9	43	5	-
Park	3	0	15	1	-,-	(8)	5	0	17	1	-,-	2nd	21	62	9	-
Hartkopf	3	0	20	0	-,-	(4)	10	1	57	0	-,-	3rd	58	78	209	-
Armstrong	4.2	0	6	2	-,-	(7)	17	1	69	3	-,-	4th	102	101	260	-
Keating						(5)	2	0	16	0	-,-	5th	180	126	330	-
Mayne						(6)	1	0	6	0	-,-	6th	185	186	340	-
												7th	185	319	364	-
SOUTH AUSTRALIA	O	M	R	W	w,nb		O	M	R	W	w,nb	8th	185	534	364	-
Whitty	36	4	104	2	-,-							9th	220	590	377	-
Lucas	18	1	88	2	-,-							10th	247	605	378	-
Townsend	14	0	50	0	-,-											
Rundell	27	1	147	3	-,-											
A.J.Richardson	26	3	92	1	-,-											
Williams	15.5	0	87	2	1,-											
V.Y.Richardson	3	0	15	0	-,-	(2)	1	0	13	0	-,-					
Pritchard	1	0	5	0	-,-											
Gehrs						(1)	1	0	8	0	-,-					

FALL OF WICKETS
| | | SA | VIC | SA | VIC |

NEW SOUTH WALES v SOUTH AUSTRALIA (Shield Match 4)

Played at Sydney Cricket Ground on January 9, 10, 12, 1920. (Timeless match)
Toss : South Australia.   Result : NEW SOUTH WALES WON BY SIX WICKETS.
Debuts: New South Wales - F.A.O'Keeffe (f/c).
12th Men: A.T.E.Punch (NSW) and R.J.B.Townsend (SA).
Umpires: A.C.Jones and A.P.Williams.
Attendances: 3884, 8307, 1439.   Total: 13,630.   Receipts: £696.
Close of Play: 1st day NSW 3/75 (Tozer 27, Andrews 10); 2nd day SA (2) 5/122 (Steele 56, A.J.Richardson 32).

South Australia suffered early setbacks in both innings, Pritchard faring the worst with a pair of ducks. Vic Richardson (45 in 126 minutes, 5 fours), Bridgman (65 in 96 minutes, 10 fours) and Williams (54 in 54 minutes, 7 fours) held the first innings together. Steele (76 in 131 minutes, 9 fours) and Arthur Richardson (95 in 154 minutes, 10 fours) played major roles in the second innings. New South Wales also began shakily, but half-centuries on the second day from Andrews (69 in 92 minutes), Kippax (68 in 95 minutes, 5 fours) and Hendry (81 in 113 minutes, 12 fours) provided a healthy lead on the first innings. Bardsley was unable to bat on the third day due to injury, Bogle (55 in 88 minutes, 7 fours) and Andrews (69 not out) putting on 100 for the third wicket to effectively seal the result. H.Carter (injured) was unavailable for New South Wales. *Wisden* and *O'Reilly* incorrectly gives SA (2) extras 7, total 282; NSW (1) A.J.Richardson 1/68, Williams 1/37. *NSWCA Report* incorrectly gives SA (2) Schultz 10*. Sources: *Wisden, C.B.O'Reilly, NSWCA Report, Sydney Referee, Sydney Morning Herald, Sydney Daily Telegraph.*

SOUTH AUSTRALIA

V.Y.Richardson	b Hendry	45		b Hendry	4
D.E.Pritchard	c Hendry b Kelleway	0		b Hendry	0
P.D.Rundell	b Kelleway	7	(4)	c Ratcliffe b Hendry	1
D.M.Steele	b Ives	7	(3)	c Kelleway b Ives	76
A.J.Richardson	c Hendry b Kelleway	18	(7)	c Mailey b O'Keeffe	95
*D.R.A.Gehrs	c Bogle b Andrews	30		c O'Keeffe b Ives	17
H.H.M.Bridgman	b Hendry	65	(5)	c Hendry b Ives	11
N.L.Williams	c Ratcliffe b Hendry	54		run out (sub A.T.E.Punch)	28
W.J.Whitty	c Ratcliffe b Hendry	9		b Ives	19
†J.W.E.Schultz	not out	7		not out	19
F.R.Lucas	run out (Andrews/Ratcliffe)	0		c sub (A.T.E.Punch) b O'Keeffe	5
Extras	(b5, lb1, nb1)	7		(b4, lb8)	12
Total	(66.1 overs, 244 mins)	249		(66.2 overs, 235 mins)	287

NEW SOUTH WALES

*C.Kelleway	c Schultz b Whitty	7		c Schultz b Lucas	1
W.Bardsley	b Whitty	14			
C.J.Tozer	run out (A.J.Richardson/Schultz)	37	(2)	b Whitty	14
J.Bogle	b A.J.Richardson	8	(3)	c Schultz b Bridgman	55
T.J.E.Andrews	b Lucas	69	(4)	not out	69
†A.T.Ratcliffe	b Bridgman	17	(5)	c Steele b Bridgman	2
A.F.Kippax	st Schultz b Williams	68	(6)	not out	18
H.S.T.L.Hendry	c & b Lucas	81			
F.A.O'Keeffe	lbw b Rundell	28			
W.F.Ives	not out	7			
A.A.Mailey	b Rundell	1			
Extras	(b31, lb7)	38		(lb2, w1)	3
Total	(77.7 overs, 296 mins)	375		(30.6 overs, 120 mins) (4 wkts)	162

NEW SOUTH WALES	O	M	R	W	w,nb		O	M	R	W	w,nb			FALL OF WICKETS		
														SA	NSW	SA	NSW
Hendry	19.1	6	30	4	-,-	(2)	13	0	40	3	-,-	Wkt	1st	1st	2nd	2nd
Kelleway	16	3	71	3	-,-	(1)	14	3	49	0	-,-	1st	6	18	2	1
Mailey	14	1	61	0	-,-	(4)	17	1	69	0	-,-	2nd	14	31	5	17
Ives	9	3	21	1	-,-	(3)	15	1	69	4	-,-	3rd	35	42	7	117
Andrews	6	0	43	1	-,1		4	0	31	0	-,-	4th	76	95	33	129
O'Keeffe	2	0	16	0	-,-		3.2	0	17	2	-,-	5th	95	152	63	-
												6th	141	206	148	-
SOUTH AUSTRALIA	O	M	R	W	w,nb		O	M	R	W	w,nb	7th	227	303	187	-
Whitty	26	3	105	2	-,-		13	1	52	1	-,-	8th	236	362	241	-
Lucas	10	0	51	2	-,-		6.6	0	29	1	-,-	9th	247	370	281	-
Rundell	7.7	1	40	2	-,-	(4)	2	0	20	0	-,-	10th	249	375	287	-
A.J.Richardson	18	4	58	1	-,-	(3)	3	0	22	0	1,-					
Williams	8	0	47	1	-,-		2	0	11	0	-,-					
Bridgman	8	0	36	1	-,-		4	0	25	2	-,-					

VICTORIA v A.I.F.

Played at Melbourne Cricket Ground on January 16, 17, 19, 1920. (Three-day match)
Toss : A.I.F.   Result : A.I.F. WON BY SIX WICKETS.
Debuts: Victoria - T.A.Carlton (Vic only).
12th Men: L.F.Freemantle (Vic) and J.T.Murray (AIF).
Umpires: H.J.Alessio and R.M.Crockett.
Attendances: 7000, 18000, 4000.   Total: About 29,000.   Receipts: £1200.
Close of Play: 1st day AIF 1/27 (Trenerry 13, Winning 4); 2nd day Vic (2) 1/31 (Mayne 20, Keating 9).

After 28 first-class matches in England and 8 in South Africa, representatives of the Australian Imperial Forces played their first match on home soil. On a rain-affected pitch, J.M.Gregory (right-arm fast) proved virtually unplayable on the first day. Gregory, Oldfield, Trenerry and Winning were all playing their first first-class matches in Australia. Willis scored 111 in 162 minutes and hit 11 fours, giving a chance at 51. Mayne (54 in 117 minutes, 3 fours) topscored for Victoria. A tenth-wicket partnership of 88 between Ellis and Carlton, who had played for Canterbury and for New Zealand in Australia before the War, took the match to a fourth innings, in which Collins was dismissed first ball. Freemantle and Liddicut replaced A.E.V.Hartkopf and R.L.Park (both unavailable) in the Victorian twelve. *Wisden incorrectly gives AIF (1) Trenerry b McDonald.* Sources: *Wisden, VCA Report, The Age, The Argus, The Herald, The Australasian, The Leader.*

VICTORIA

R.E.Mayne	c Gregory b Winning	24		c Gregory b Lampard	54
*W.W.Armstrong	c Docker b Gregory	23	(6)	c Oldfield b Lampard	0
F.A.Baring	c Stirling b Gregory	6	(5)	b Lampard	9
J.Ryder	b Gregory	19		b Lampard	0
L.A.Cody	c Oldfield b Winning	3	(2)	lbw b Docker	2
J.L.Keating	c Collins b Gregory	8	(3)	c Oldfield b Gregory	17
A.E.Liddicut	c Pellew b Gregory	2		c Oldfield b Lampard	47
L.D.Ferguson	c Collins b Gregory	3		b Collins	35
†J.L.Ellis	b Gregory	1	(10)	not out	52
E.A.McDonald	c Stirling b Winning	24	(9)	c Pellew b Lampard	14
T.A.Carlton	not out	0		c Gregory b Lampard	36
Extras	(b2, w1)	3		(b2, lb1, w1)	4
Total	(36.0 overs, 137 mins)	116		(76.7 overs, 288 mins)	270

A.I.F.

*H.L.Collins	c Carlton b McDonald	9		c Armstrong b McDonald	0
W.L.Trenerry	c Ellis b McDonald	16	(4)	c Ellis b Armstrong	3
C.S.Winning	c Baring b McDonald	7			
C.B.Willis	c Mayne b Carlton	111			
C.E.Pellew	b Carlton	46	(2)	c Carlton b McDonald	19
J.M.Taylor	lbw b Liddicut	8	(3)	c Ryder b Armstrong	24
A.W.Lampard	c Ryder b Liddicut	45			
J.M.Gregory	c Carlton b Liddicut	44	(5)	not out	23
C.T.Docker	c Baring b Armstrong	8	(6)	not out	2
W.S.Stirling	lbw b Liddicut	2			
†W.A.S.Oldfield	not out	1			
Extras	(b4, lb6, w1, nb3)	14		(b4, lb1, w1)	6
Total	(70.6 overs, 274 mins)	311		(16.5 overs, 59 mins) (4 wkts)	77

A.I.F.	O	M	R	W	w,nb		O	M	R	W	w,nb		FALL OF WICKETS			
Collins	6	0	16	0	-,-	(5)	9	2	29	1	-,-		VIC	AIF	VIC	AIF
Stirling	3	0	12	0	1,-							Wkt	1st	1st	2nd	2nd
Winning	15	2	63	3	-,-	(6)	2	0	16	0	1,-	1st	49	9	8	0
Gregory	12	3	22	7	-,-	(1)	21	4	79	1	-,-	2nd	55	31	53	37
Docker						(2)	17	4	30	1	-,-	3rd	57	40	54	47
Lampard						(3)	24.7	3	99	7	-,-	4th	75	140	72	59
Trenerry						(4)	3	0	13	0	-,-	5th	85	173	72	-
												6th	87	223	97	-
VICTORIA	O	M	R	W	w,nb		O	M	R	W	w,nb	7th	88	265	150	-
Carlton	13	1	42	2	-,-							8th	91	284	176	-
McDonald	16	1	76	3	-,2	(1)	5	0	28	2	-,-	9th	104	300	182	-
Armstrong	17	1	68	1	-,1	(2)	8	2	20	2	-,-	10th	116	311	270	-
Ryder	8	0	56	0	-,-											
Liddicut	16.6	2	55	4	1,-	(3)	3.5	0	23	0	1,-					

NEW SOUTH WALES v VICTORIA (Shield Match 5)

Played at Sydney Cricket Ground on January 24, 26, 27, 28, 1920. (Timeless match)
Toss : New South Wales.   Result : NEW SOUTH WALES WON BY AN INNINGS AND 88 RUNS.
Debuts: Victoria - L.F.Freemantle (f/c).
12th Men: E.Trenerry (NSW) and A.H.Dean (Vic).
Umpires: W.G.Curran and J.G.Gairns.
Attendances: 9849, 10283, 1391, 1429.   Total: 22,952.   Receipts: £1180.
Close of Play: 1st day NSW 8/468 (Andrews 207, Norman 18); 2nd day Vic 1/62 (Mayne 40, Ransford 22); 3rd day Vic 4/125 (Mayne 70, Carlton 2).

J.Bogle and C.J.Tozer were unavailable for New South Wales and F.A.Baring and A.E.V.Hartkopf could not play for Victoria owing to work commitments. Shea was a late replacement for E.A.McDonald, also unavailable, before the team left for Sydney. Andrews' career-best score of 247 not out occupied 299 minutes and included 33 fours; his score progressed from 16 at lunch to 121 at tea and 207 at stumps as New South Wales tallied 468 runs on the first day. Bardsley (71 in 122 minutes, 6 fours) and Kippax (47 in 57 minutes, 8 fours) supported Andrews during his brilliant innings. Heavy rain severely restricted playing time on the second and third days, giving the Victorians the worst of the wicket for their batting. Mayne (82 in 180 minutes, 12 fours), Carlton (39 in 96 minutes, 3 fours) and Armstrong (48 in 80 minutes, 6 fours) made the highest scores in the first innings. Park (65 in 142 minutes, 8 fours) topscored after the follow-on was enforced. *Wisden* incorrectly gives NSW Macartney c Ellis b Carlton, Carlton 4/140, Shea 1/105. Sources: *Wisden, NSWCA Report, VCA Report, Sydney Referee, Sydney Morning Herald, Sydney Daily Telegraph.*

NEW SOUTH WALES

*†H.Carter	c Mayne b Carlton	3
W.Bardsley	c Ellis b Carlton	71
C.G.Macartney	c Ellis b Shea	37
T.J.E.Andrews	not out	247
C.Kelleway	c Armstrong b Ryder	8
A.F.Kippax	c Mayne b Park	47
H.S.T.L.Hendry	b Ryder	0
A.T.Ratcliffe	c Ryder b Carlton	21
A.T.E.Punch	c & b Armstrong	47
R.Norman	run out (/Shea/Ellis)	18
A.A.Mailey	b Shea	13
Extras	(b3, lb4, nb2)	9
Total	(97.2 overs, 420 mins)	521

VICTORIA

R.E.Mayne	c & b Kelleway	82	c & b Hendry	4
L.A.Cody	lbw b Hendry	0	c Carter b Hendry	9
V.S.Ransford	c Hendry b Kelleway	22	c Mailey b Hendry	13
R.L.Park	b Macartney	11	c Andrews b Hendry	65
J.Ryder	c Punch b Kelleway	15	c Mailey b Hendry	4
T.A.Carlton	c Macartney b Mailey	39	(11) not out	6
*W.W.Armstrong	c Hendry b Norman	48	(6) b Hendry	5
J.L.Keating	c Andrews b Norman	4	(7) b Norman	23
L.F.Freemantle	not out	0	(8) b Norman	4
P.A.Shea	c Ratcliffe b Norman	13	(9) c Kippax b Hendry	22
†J.L.Ellis	b Norman	0	(10) run out	14
Extras	(b4, lb5, nb2)	11	(b9, lb5, nb5)	19
Total	(79.0 overs, 295 mins)	245	(41.5 overs, 159 mins)	188

VICTORIA	O	M	R	W	w,nb
Carlton	27	1	140	3	-,1
Armstrong	17	1	83	1	-,-
Ryder	26	2	92	2	-,1
Shea	14.2	0	105	2	-,-
Park	3	0	17	1	-,-
Freemantle	5	0	37	0	-,-
Ransford	5	0	38	0	-,-

NEW SOUTH WALES	O	M	R	W	w,nb		O	M	R	W	w,nb
Norman	10	1	36	4	-,-		12	2	56	2	-,3
Hendry	16	6	43	1	-,-		12.5	3	34	7	-,-
Macartney	20	1	62	1	-,-						
Kelleway	20	6	43	3	-,-	(3)	4	2	7	0	-,1
Mailey	12	2	46	1	-,-	(4)	10	1	47	0	-,-
Andrews	1	0	4	0	-,2	(5)	3	0	25	0	-,1

FALL OF WICKETS

Wkt	NSW 1st	VIC 1st	VIC 2nd
1st	4	14	10
2nd	86	62	20
3rd	149	79	32
4th	178	113	38
5th	277	167	48
6th	294	218	89
7th	336	230	95
8th	439	231	157
9th	473	245	176
10th	521	245	188

QUEENSLAND v A.I.F.

Played at Brisbane Cricket Ground (Woolloongabba) on January 24, 26, 27, 1920. (Three-day match)
Toss : A.I.F.   Result : MATCH DRAWN.
Debuts: Queensland - W.M.Kay (f/c).
12th Men: J.A.Prout (Qld) and W.S.Stirling (AIF).
Umpires: W.H.Carvosso and G.Casperson.
Attendances: 4000, 5000, "small".   Total: About 9500.   Receipts: No figures published.
Close of Play: 1st day Qld 3/96 (Oxenham 34, Farquhar 11); 2nd day AIF (2) 5/273 (Lampard 11, Murray 1).

Kay replaced J.S.Redgrave (unavailable) in the Queensland side. Heavy rain on the preceding days cast doubts on the quality of the wicket which did not eventuate as it "rolled out firm and fairly fast" (*Courier*). Few details of individual innings were reported. Collins (135 in 171 minutes, 5 fours) led the scoring "by very sound and well-judged batting" (*Courier*) while Taylor hit a stylish half-century in each innings. McAndrew captured the wickets of Lampard and Murray in the first innings with consecutive deliveries. Oxenham (50 in 175 minutes) and Thompson (55 in 64 minutes, 8 fours) registered half-centuries for the home team. A severe thunderstorm on the final afternoon denied the A.I.F. possible victory when the match was abandoned just after tea. Maddock was absent on the final day due to a court appearance on a charge of stealing twelve shillings and ninepence-ha'penny and other minor items from the players' change rooms at the Brisbane Cricket Ground. *VCA Report, Courier* and *Daily Mail* scoresheets give Qld (2) Rowe c Murray b Gregory, Gregory 3/33, Lampard 1/34. Sources: *Wisden, VCA Report, Brisbane Courier, Brisbane Daily Mail.*

A.I.F.

*H.L.Collins	c McAndrew b Kay	18		c & b Ayres	135
J.M.Gregory	b Rowe	45		c Oxenham b McAndrew	39
W.L.Trenerry	c Barbour b Kay	13		b McAndrew	4
J.M.Taylor	c & b Rowe	60	(5)	c Maddock b McAndrew	67
C.E.Pellew	b Kay	26	(4)	b McAndrew	4
A.W.Lampard	c Farquhar b McAndrew	26		not out	26
J.T.Murray	b McAndrew	0		not out	28
E.A.Bull	b Rowe	2			
†W.A.S.Oldfield	b Rowe	0			
C.T.Docker	b McAndrew	11			
C.S.Winning	not out	3			
Extras	(b2, lb9)	11		(b13, lb3)	16
Total	(40.6 overs, 160 mins)	215		(68.0 overs, 246 mins) (5 wkts dec)	319

QUEENSLAND

*J.F.Sheppard	b Gregory	2		c Oldfield b Gregory	7
L.E.Oxenham	st Oldfield b Winning	50		c Oldfield b Gregory	8
J.Thomson	c Winning b Collins	0		c Docker b Winning	20
F.C.Thompson	lbw b Docker	44		c Murray b Collins	55
†J.K.Farquhar	c Gregory b Lampard	30		not out	28
R.R.Barbour	c Oldfield b Winning	6		c Oldfield b Lampard	2
W.Rowe	c Oldfield b Winning	2		c Murray b Lampard	21
S.W.Ayres	lbw b Lampard	1		not out	0
C.E.R.Maddock	c Taylor b Lampard	4			
J.W.McAndrew	c Murray b Winning	0			
W.M.Kay	not out	0			
Extras	(b4, lb2, nb1)	7		(lb3)	3
Total	(59.1 overs, 210 mins)	146		(44.0 overs, 165 mins) (6 wkts)	144

QUEENSLAND	O	M	R	W	w,nb		O	M	R	W	w,nb
McAndrew	12.6	2	44	3	-,-		23	2	74	4	-,-
Ayres	8	0	55	0	-,-		5	0	26	1	-,-
Kay	10	0	75	3	-,-	(4)	16	0	91	0	-,-
Rowe	10	1	30	4	-,-	(3)	8	0	33	0	-,-
Maddock							16	0	79	0	-,-

A.I.F	O	M	R	W	w,nb		O	M	R	W	w,nb
Gregory	8	2	19	1	-,1		13	4	33	2	-,-
Collins	16	3	40	1	-,-		8	2	29	1	-,-
Lampard	15.1	4	43	3	-,-		8	0	34	2	-,-
Winning	13	2	24	4	-,-		10	0	34	1	-,-
Docker	7	1	13	1	-,-		4	1	9	0	-,-
Trenerry							1	0	2	0	-,-

FALL OF WICKETS

Wkt	AIF 1st	QLD 1st	AIF 2nd	QLD 2nd
1st	55	2	103	15
2nd	79	3	114	25
3rd	85	78	132	39
4th	123	129	227	108
5th	185	135	270	112
6th	185	141	-	142
7th	200	142	-	-
8th	200	146	-	-
9th	201	146	-	-
10th	215	146	-	-

NEW SOUTH WALES v A.I.F.

Played at Sydney Cricket Ground on January 31, February 2, 3, 1920. (Three-day match)
Toss : A.I.F.   Result : A.I.F. WON BY 203 RUNS.
Debuts: New South Wales - E.Trenerry (f/c).
12th Men: F.A.O'Keeffe (NSW) and E.A.Bull (AIF).
Umpires: W.H.C.Davis and A.C.Jones.
Attendances: 13179, 6000, 5000.   Total: About 24,179.   Receipts: £1086.
Close of Play: 1st day NSW 3/185 (Andrews 19); 2nd day AIF (2) 6/340 (Murray 5).

Norman bowled Collins with the first ball of the match, Gregory gave a superb all-round performance, scoring 122 (170 minutes, 19 fours) and 102 (101 minutes, 16 fours), capturing eight wickets and taking three fine catches. Collins atoned for his first-ball failure by scoring 129 in the second innings in 176 minutes with 15 fours. New South Wales were unable to field their best side due to the unavailability of C.Kelleway, J.Bogle and C.G.Macartney. Two sets of brothers, Dockers and Trenerrys, took part with one from each family on each side, an occasion unique in Australian first-class cricket. *Wisden* incorrectly gives AIF (1) Murray lbw b Mailey; AIF (2) Pellew c Carter b Mailey. *NSWCA Report* incorrectly gives AIF (2) Hendry 0/63, Mailey 4/92. Sources: *Wisden, NSWCA Report, Sydney Referee, Sydney Morning Herald, Sydney Daily Telegraph.*

A.I.F.

*H.L.Collins	b Norman	0		c & b Mailey	129
J.M.Gregory	c Carter b Norman	122	(4)	st Carter b Mailey	102
C.E.Pellew	c Trenerry b Hendry	1	(5)	c Carter b Norman	10
A.W.Lampard	c Mailey b Trenerry	45	(3)	c Trenerry b Mailey	18
J.M.Taylor	c Mailey b Trenerry	7	(6)	b Mailey	32
W.L.Trenerry	st Carter b Mailey	31	(2)	b Trenerry	26
J.T.Murray	hit wkt b Mailey	0		c Trenerry b Mailey	29
†W.A.S.Oldfield	c Mailey b Hendry	12		b Hendry	2
W.S.Stirling	lbw b Hendry	0	(10)	c Carter b Mailey	12
C.T.Docker	c Carter b Mailey	38	(9)	lbw b Mailey	1
C.S.Winning	not out	2		not out	13
Extras	(b1, lb4, nb2)	7		(b9, lb10, nb2)	21
Total	(50.5 overs, 195 mins)	265		(72.7 overs, 269 mins)	395

NEW SOUTH WALES

*†H.Carter	b Gregory	17		c Oldfield b Gregory	15
W.Bardsley	c Oldfield b Collins	60		b Gregory	2
H.S.T.L.Hendry	b Gregory	85	(4)	c Gregory b Collins	3
T.J.E.Andrews	c Docker b Gregory	39	(3)	b Winning	65
A.F.Kippax	c Winning b Gregory	17	(8)	run out (Winning/Oldfield)	2
K.B.Docker	lbw b Lampard	0	(5)	c Lampard b Docker	27
A.T.E.Punch	b Docker	30	(6)	c Oldfield b Docker	6
A.T.Ratcliffe	c Oldfield b Gregory	22	(7)	c Winning b Gregory	12
R.Norman	c Gregory b Winning	3		c Gregory b Lampard	24
E.Trenerry	run out (Winning)	0		not out	15
A.A.Mailey	not out	0		c Taylor b Winning	1
Extras	(b4, lb1, w1)	6		(b5, lb1)	6
Total	(57.3 overs, 238 mins)	279		(49.7 overs, 200 mins)	178

NEW SOUTH WALES	O	M	R	W	w,nb		O	M	R	W	w,nb					
Norman	16	3	66	2	-,-		15	0	81	1	-,2					
Hendry	10	2	62	3	-,2		20	3	85	1	-,-					
Trenerry	14	1	85	2	-,-	(4)	9	0	69	1	-,-					
Mailey	10.5	1	45	3	-,-	(3)	26.7	0	122	7	-,-					
Andrews							2	0	17	0	-,-					

A.I.F.	O	M	R	W	w,nb		O	M	R	W	w,nb
Gregory	15.3	1	65	5	-,-		15	3	65	3	-,-
Collins	11	0	59	1	-,-		20	1	52	1	-,-
Docker	9	0	34	1	-,-		8	1	28	2	-,-
Winning	10	0	45	1	-,-		4.7	1	19	2	-,-
Lampard	12	0	70	1	1,-		2	0	8	1	-,-

FALL OF WICKETS

Wkt	AIF 1st	NSW 1st	AIF 2nd	NSW 2nd
1st	0	30	54	5
2nd	3	151	101	28
3rd	110	185	289	37
4th	118	218	296	100
5th	175	219	328	122
6th	175	227	340	122
7th	218	276	343	125
8th	218	279	344	154
9th	236	279	366	173
10th	265	279	395	178

QUEENSLAND v VICTORIA

Played at Exhibition Ground, Brisbane, on January 31, February 2, 3, 1920. (Timeless match)
Toss : Victoria.   Result : VICTORIA WON BY 153 RUNS.
Debuts: Queensland - J.W.Anderson, J.H.Fletcher, P.M.Hornibrook, A.J.Marsden (all f/c). Victoria - A.H.Dean (f/c).
12th Men: W.Rowe (Qld) and L.A.Cody (Vic).
Umpires: W.H.Carvosso and A.E.Wyeth (see below).
Attendances: 5000, 1600, 1200.   Total: About 7800.   Receipts: £310.
Close of Play: 1st day Qld 4/54 (Thompson 8, Anderson 4); 2nd day Vic (2) 5/230 (Keating 20, Ellis 3).

First-class cricket returned to the Exhibition ground after a hiatus of nearly 23 years. McAndrew bowled Mayne with the second ball of the match. Ransford (115 in 127 minutes, 1 six and 12 fours) and Armstrong (86 not out in 85 minutes, 10 fours) topscored in the Victorian first innings. Mayne atoned for his duck by scoring 129 in 137 minutes in the second innings, hitting 1 six and 13 fours and sharing a first-wicket stand of 170 in 120 minutes with Parks (3 fours). Thompson (47 in 83 minutes, 6 fours) and Hartigan (63 in 51 minutes, 1 six and 7 fours) topscored in Queensland's first innings while Oxenham (50 in 120 minutes, 5 fours) and Thompson (57 in 85 minutes, 6 fours) scored fifties in the second innings. R.Haigh umpired in place of Wyeth on the second and third days though no explanation was offered in the press. *ACS* incorrectly gives some falls of wickets and Qld (1) breakdown of extras. Sources: *A.C.S., VCA Report, The Australasian, Brisbane Courier, Brisbane Daily Mail, Darling Downs Gazette.*

VICTORIA

R.E.Mayne	b McAndrew	0	c Thompson b Fletcher		129
†J.L.Ellis	c Hartigan b Marsden	5	(7) not out		15
V.S.Ransford	c McAndrew b Marsden	115	(10) not out		2
A.H.Dean	c Oxenham b Anderson	13	(3) b Hornibrook		5
J.L.Keating	c Sheppard b McAndrew	35	(6) c Prout b Hornibrook		25
R.L.Park	c Anderson b McAndrew	0	(2) st Farquhar b Fletcher		62
J.Ryder	c Anderson b Fletcher	20	(5) c Oxenham b Fletcher		5
*W.W.Armstrong	not out	86			
P.A.Shea	c Thompson b McAndrew	28	(4) b Hornibrook		0
L.F.Freemantle	st Farquhar b Marsden	0	(8) b McAndrew		3
T.A.Carlton	b Hornibrook	6	(9) c Sheppard b McAndrew		2
Extras	(b8, lb5)	13	(b4, lb2)		6
Total	(54.6 overs, 216 mins)	321	(58.0 overs, 215 mins) (8 wkts dec)		254

QUEENSLAND

J.F.Sheppard	c Keating b Freemantle	13	lbw b Armstrong		6
L.E.Oxenham	run out	13	c Ransford b Freemantle		50
J.A.Prout	run out	10	c Freemantle b Shea		3
F.C.Thompson	c Shea b Armstrong	47	c Armstrong b Freemantle		57
†J.K.Farquhar	lbw b Shea	5	b Armstrong		8
J.W.Anderson	c Carlton b Freemantle	6	(8) c Armstrong b Freemantle		16
*R.J.Hartigan	c Mayne b Ryder	63	(6) b Armstrong		27
J.H.Fletcher	lbw b Armstrong	29	(7) b Armstrong		0
J.W.McAndrew	c Keating b Armstrong	23	run out		22
A.J.Marsden	c Ellis b Armstrong	8	c Ransford b Armstrong		0
P.M.Hornibrook	not out	0	not out		2
Extras	(lb1, nb4)	5	(b6, lb2, w1)		9
Total	(42.5 overs, 157 mins)	222	(46.4 overs, 165 mins)		200

QUEENSLAND	O	M	R	W	w,nb		O	M	R	W	w,nb
McAndrew	18	2	60	4	-,-		15	1	41	2	-,-
Marsden	15	0	86	3	-,-		9	0	37	0	-,-
Anderson	9	2	67	1	-,-	(4)	7	0	40	0	-,-
Fletcher	6	0	55	1	-,-	(5)	8	0	65	3	-,-
Hornibrook	6.6	0	40	1	-,-	(3)	19	1	65	3	-,-

VICTORIA	O	M	R	W	w,nb		O	M	R	W	w,nb
Carlton	4	2	8	0	-,1		6	1	15	0	-,-
Freemantle	10	0	67	2	-,-	(5)	10.4	0	73	3	-,-
Shea	8	2	23	1	-,-	(4)	7	1	35	1	1,-
Dean	3	0	32	0	-,-						
Keating	3	2	12	0	-,3						
Ryder	8	2	40	1	-,-	(2)	6	4	10	0	-,-
Armstrong	6.5	0	35	4	-,-	(3)	17	2	58	5	-,-

FALL OF WICKETS

Wkt	VIC 1st	QLD 1st	VIC 2nd	QLD 2nd
1st	0	17	170	19
2nd	8	35	195	31
3rd	46	40	201	123
4th	161	48	203	126
5th	161	63	221	135
6th	185	160	242	145
7th	204	162	245	164
8th	279	201	249	194
9th	279	220	-	194
10th	321	222	-	200

SOUTH AUSTRALIA v VICTORIA (Shield Match 6)

Played at Adelaide Oval on February 27, 28, March 1, 2, 3, 1920. (Timeless match)
Toss : Victoria.   Result : VICTORIA WON BY SIX WICKETS.
Debuts: South Australia - G.M.Hone, L.V.Pellew, E.L.Phillips (all f/c). Victoria - L.T.Mullett (f/c); A.G.Moyes (Vic only).
12th Men: D.E.Pritchard (SA) and J.L.Keating (Vic).
Umpires: G.I.Colyer and A.McIntyre.
Attendances: 3500, 7000, 3000, 3000, 500.   Total: About 17,000.   Receipts: £734.
Close of Play: 1st day Vic 6/365 (Moyes 50, Liddicut 32); 2nd day SA (2) 0/45 (Smith 15, C.E.Pellew 26); 3rd day SA (2) 5/479
    (L.V.Pellew 43, A.J.Richardson 23); 4th day Vic (2) 3/254 (Park 88, Ellis 7).

W.J.Whitty (unavailable) withdrew from the South Australian team. His replacement, W.S.Stirling, also announced his unavailability and the spot went to Phillips. Ransford (70 in 126 minutes, 7 fours) and Ryder (87 in 120 minutes, 1 six and 9 fours) did well on the first day. Lampard (46) retired at 6/284 due to a recurring back injury and resumed next day at 8/374. He batted in all for 100 minutes and hit 10 fours. Pellew (a chanceless 271 in 286 minutes, 37 fours) played the innings of his life for South Australia after the team followed on. Resuming the third day on 26 he reached his 50 in 51 minutes, 100 in 96 minutes, was 119 at lunch after an hour's play, brought up his 100 in the day in 66 minutes, reached 200 in 200 minutes, was 219 at tea and reached 250 in 265 minutes. He went through four bats in what was his only century in 23 games for the State. Victoria won the match with innings from Ransford (99 in 174 minutes, 12 fours) and Park (104 in 205 minutes, 12 fours). Sources: *Wisden, C.B.O'Reilly, VCA Report, Adelaide Advertiser, South Australian Register.*

VICTORIA

R.E.Mayne	b A.J.Richardson	23		lbw b A.J.Richardson	39
R.L.Park	c Phillips b A.J.Richardson	9	(4)	b V.Y.Richardson	104
V.S.Ransford	run out (V.Y.Richardson/Schultz)	70		lbw b Phillips	99
C.B.Willis	c Schultz b Phillips	36	(6)	not out	12
*W.W.Armstrong	b Rundell	4			
J.Ryder	run out (Rundell/Schultz)	87			
A.W.Lampard	not out	66	(2)	c & b A.J.Richardson	6
A.G.Moyes	b Phillips	55			
A.E.Liddicut	b Phillips	34			
†J.L.Ellis	b Phillips	3	(5)	not out	33
L.T.Mullett	b Rundell	7			
Extras	(b8, lb2, w2)	12		(b20, lb4, w1)	25
Total	(88.7 overs, 330 mins)	406		(69.3 overs, 270 mins) (4 wkts)	318

SOUTH AUSTRALIA

A.Smith	c Armstrong b Mullett	11	c Lampard b Mullett	50
C.E.Pellew	b Ryder	23	c Lampard b Ransford	271
G.M.Hone	b Mullett	2	lbw b Armstrong	18
P.D.Rundell	c Armstrong b Ryder	13	b Mullett	53
V.Y.Richardson	lbw b Liddicut	30	run out (Liddicut)	0
L.V.Pellew	b Armstrong	25	run out (/Ellis)	57
A.J.Richardson	b Ryder	26	lbw b Mullett	40
*H.H.M.Bridgman	c & b Mullett	2	c Liddicut b Mullett	6
N.L.Williams	c Ellis b Ryder	32	c Ryder b Armstrong	7
E.L.Phillips	c Ellis b Mullett	6	not out	11
†J.W.E.Schultz	not out	1	st Ellis b Armstrong	7
Extras	(b4, lb2, w1)	7	(b15, lb6, w2)	23
Total	(41.6 overs, 172 mins)	178	(93.4 overs, 382 mins)	543

SOUTH AUSTRALIA	O	M	R	W	w,nb		O	M	R	W	w,nb		FALL OF WICKETS			
														VIC	SA	SA	VIC
A.J.Richardson	24	2	89	2	-,-	(2)	23	2	65	2	-,-	Wkt	1st	1st	2nd	2nd
Phillips	21	2	87	4	1,-	(1)	15	2	73	1	1,-	1st	25	29	174	32
Hone	2	0	21	0	-,-							2nd	40	35	219	73
Williams	10	0	58	0	-,-	(3)	11	0	48	0	-,-	3rd	120	45	368	236
Rundell	16.7	1	69	2	-,-		10	0	43	0	-,-	4th	125	52	369	300
Bridgman	7	1	25	0	-,-	(4)	4	0	27	0	-,-	5th	185	103	434	-
C.E.Pellew	6	0	22	0	1,-	(6)	2	0	16	0	-,-	6th	283	111	502	-
Smith	2	0	23	0	-,-							7th	371	127	513	-
L.V.Pellew						(7)	2	0	8	0	-,-	8th	374	147	524	-
V.Y.Richardson						(8)	2.3	0	13	1	-,-	9th	379	172	528	-
												10th	406	178	543	-

VICTORIA	O	M	R	W	w,nb		O	M	R	W	w,nb
Mullett	15.6	2	45	4	1,-		26	0	128	4	2,-
Ryder	15	2	82	4	-,-	(4)	13	1	81	0	-,-
Armstrong	6	0	27	1	-,-	(2)	33.4	4	158	3	-,-
Liddicut	5	0	17	1	-,-	(3)	13	0	61	0	-,-
Lampard							7	0	79	0	-,-
Ransford							1	0	13	1	-,-

NEW SOUTH WALES v QUEENSLAND

Played at Sydney Cricket Ground on April 3, 5, 1920. (Three-day match)
Toss : New South Wales.　　　　Result : NEW SOUTH WALES WON BY AN INNINGS AND 157 RUNS.
Debuts: New South Wales - E.W.Adams, W.G.F.Brown, P.M.King (all f/c); W.A.S.Oldfield (NSW only). Queensland - E.H.Hutcheon
　　(f/c).
12th Men: J.W.McLaren (Qld - manager). No 12th named for NSW.
Umpires: M.Carney and A.C.Jones.
Attendances: 4000, 2000.　　　　Total: About 6000.　　　Receipts: £242.
Close of Play: 1st day Qld 3/40 (Thompson 9, Sheppard 0).

Collins (117 in 124 minutes, 19 fours) was missed at the wicket off Ayres when only 8 and went on to score 109 before lunch on the first day. King who was playing in his sole first-class match, (72 in 106 minutes, 8 fours) and Punch (55 in 65 minutes, 7 fours) added 107 for the fifth wicket. Adams and Oldfield replaced C.Kelleway and A.T.Ratcliffe when they withdrew from the named New South Wales side. King, the nominated 12th man, was a late replacement for A.F.Kippax. Ted Trenerry (right-arm fast-medium) achieved his only ten-wicket match analysis. Oldfield had previously played for the AIF Services team. The match was a financial failure and dissuaded the NSW Cricket Association from organizing further matches in April. *NSWCA Report* incorrectly gives NSW Trenerry 11, fall 1/71; Qld (2) Hutcheon c Berry. Sources: *NSWCA Report, Sydney Referee, Sydney Morning Herald, Sydney Daily Telegraph.*

NEW SOUTH WALES

*H.L.Collins	c Farquhar b Anderson	117	
O.P.Asher	c Hornibrook b Rowe	29	
T.J.E.Andrews	c Hutcheon b Anderson	11	
H.S.T.L.Hendry	b Marsden	5	
P.M.King	b Rowe	72	
A.T.E.Punch	b Marsden	55	
W.G.F.Brown	run out (Hartigan/Rowe)	41	
W.L.Berry	c & b Ayres	7	
†W.A.S.Oldfield	b Anderson	14	
E.W.Adams	not out	18	
E.Trenerry	b Anderson	1	
Extras	(b4, lb7)	11	
Total	(70.2 overs, 255 mins)	381	

QUEENSLAND

*R.J.Hartigan	run out (Andrews/Trenerry)	11	(5)	b Asher	2
L.E.Oxenham	c Hendry b Trenerry	15		st Oldfield b Trenerry	38
W.Rowe	b Asher	5		c Hendry b Asher	1
F.C.Thompson	b Trenerry	15		c Punch b Trenerry	8
J.F.Sheppard	c Hendry b Trenerry	0	(1)	b Asher	14
A.J.Marsden	b Hendry	37	(10)	c Hendry b Trenerry	2
†J.K.Farquhar	c Asher b Trenerry	5	(8)	not out	14
E.H.Hutcheon	c Berry b Trenerry	2	(6)	c Oldfield b Trenerry	8
S.W.Ayres	st Oldfield b Asher	6		b Asher	1
J.W.Anderson	c Andrews b Trenerry	13	(7)	b Trenerry	1
P.M.Hornibrook	not out	19		c Oldfield b Trenerry	0
Extras	(b1)	1		(lb4, w2)	6
Total	(47.2 overs, 160 mins)	129		(34.6 overs, 120 mins)	95

QUEENSLAND	O	M	R	W	w,nb
Hornibrook	16	1	83	0	-,-
Ayres	14	0	106	1	-,-
Anderson	18.2	1	88	4	-,-
Rowe	10	0	36	2	-,-
Marsden	12	0	57	2	-,-

NEW SOUTH WALES	O	M	R	W	w,nb		O	M	R	W	w,nb
Adams	9	1	36	0	-,-	(2)	5	0	17	0	-,-
Trenerry	23	2	64	6	-,-	(4)	7.6	1	19	6	1,-
Asher	15	4	28	2	-,-		12	2	28	4	-,-
Hendry	0.2	0	0	1	-,-	(1)	10	3	25	0	1,-

FALL OF WICKETS

Wkt	NSW 1st	QLD 1st	QLD 2nd
1st	77	18	38
2nd	126	28	46
3rd	133	40	64
4th	181	55	67
5th	288	55	67
6th	308	61	76
7th	317	65	77
8th	342	74	84
9th	370	97	95
10th	381	129	95

1920-21 SEASON (22 MATCHES)

The presence of a full-strength English team brought about the busiest first-class season in Australia in 10 years. The Board of Control had invited MCC to send a team in 1919-20 but this proved impracticable so soon after the war. English cricket had still not completely recovered but MCC felt bound not to refuse a second time.

R.H.Spooner was unable to accept an invitation to lead the MCC team and Douglas assumed the captaincy. The original tour itinerary had to be modified when the team was quarantined upon arrival in Western Australia because of a reported case of typhoid on their ship. The proposed four-day fixture against Western Australia was shortened to a one-day affair. A further change was required in January when a shipping strike prevented their travel to Tasmania for first-class matches at Launceston and Hobart against the island State. In all, 22 matches were played of which 13, including five Tests, ranked as first-class. England had no answer to the batting of Armstrong, Collins, Macartney and Pellew, the bowling of Mailey or the allround skills of Gregory and Kelleway in the Test matches, and lost all five by substantial margins. They were more successful against the States, winning five matches and drawing two, losing only once to New South Wales. Hendren hit over 1000 runs in the first-class matches and Hobbs, Russell, Douglas, Rhodes and Woolley also scored well. The bowling relied too heavily on the abilities of Parkin.

New South Wales retained the Sheffield Shield, achieving three wins and a draw from their four matches. The drawn game between New South Wales and South Australia at Sydney was the first in the Sheffield Shield not to be truly played to a finish. Victoria, though defeating South Australia twice, were no match for the powerful New South Wales combination. The scoring was thick in most matches and the hapless South Australians fielded out to totals of 639, 724, 802 and 770 in their four losing encounters.

Queensland made little impression in their three first-class matches. They conceded a big total to New South Wales at Sydney before the match was abandoned early because of rain, and were well beaten in the return game at Brisbane. They failed to extend the Englishmen in their clash at the Exhibition Ground in November.

The Western Australian Cricket Association invited New South Wales to send a team to Perth but the NSWCA declined due to the heavy program with the Englishmen in Australia. Western Australia finally got their long-sought first-class match when the Australian team stopped en route to England, but the game was completely ruined by rain.

The maritime strike that prevented MCC playing in Tasmania also prevented a Victorian team accepting a TCA invitation. No teams were named.

Selection of the 15th Australian team to tour England brought no surprises in view of the success in the Test series just concluded. The team was: W.W.Armstrong (captain), T.J.E.Andrews, W.Bardsley, H.Carter, H.L.Collins, J.M.Gregory, H.S.T.L.Hendry, C.G.Macartney, E.A.McDonald, A.A.Mailey, R.E.Mayne, W.A.S.Oldfield, C.E.Pellew, J.Ryder and J.M.Taylor. Hendry had replaced C.Kelleway (unavailable).

The Board of Control earlier accepted an invitation to send another Australian team to New Zealand in February-March. The selected team comprised D.M.Steele (captain), O.P.Asher, J.L.Ellis, H.S.T.L.Hendry, H.Ironmonger, A.W.Lampard, A.E.Liddicut, L.V.Pellew, V.S.Ransford, A.T.Ratcliffe, A.J.Richardson, V.Y.Richardson and C.B.Willis. A.E.V.Hartkopf and A.G.Moyes both declined invitations. J.Bogle, E.E.B.Forssberg, P.M.Hornibrook, A.F.Kippax and E.L.Waddy were later added when Ellis, Hendry, A.J.Richardson, Steele and Willis withdrew for various reasons. Ransford assumed the captaincy.

Leading Aggregates

Batsmen	M	I	NO	Runs	HS	Ave.	Bowlers	Runs	Wkts	Ave.
E.H.Hendren (MCC)	12	20	1	1178	271	62.00	A.A.Mailey (NSW)	1825	81	22.53
W.W.Armstrong (V)	10	15	3	1069	245	89.08	J.M.Gregory (NSW)	962	43	22.37
W.Bardsley (NSW)	12	19	2	979	235	57.58	C.H.Parkin (MCC)	1344	43	31.25
H.L.Collins (NSW)	12	20	0	939	162	46.95	E.A.McDonald (V)	1158	42	27.57
J.B.Hobbs (MCC)	12	19	1	924	131	51.33	P.G.H.Fender (MCC)	983	32	30.71
J.M.Taylor (NSW)	12	17	2	906	180	60.40	F.E.Woolley (MCC)	1051	31	33.90
J.Ryder (V)	12	20	2	869	135*	48.27	J.W.H.T.Douglas (MCC)	918	27	34.00
J.M.Gregory (NSW)	12	18	4	844	130	60.28	C.Kelleway (NSW)	620	23	26.95
C.A.G.Russell (MCC)	10	15	1	818	201	58.42				
J.W.H.T.Douglas (MCC)	13	18	4	816	133*	58.28				

SHEFFIELD SHIELD TABLE

	P	W	L	D	Pts	Quotient	Runs Scored	Wkts Lost	Runs Conceded	Wkts Taken
NEW SOUTH WALES	4	3	-	1	3	1.964	2985	63	1640	68
VICTORIA	4	2	2	-	0	1.205	2680	70	2318	73
SOUTH AUSTRALIA	4	-	3	1	-3	0.457	1842	68	3549	60
TOTAL	6	5	5	1	0	1.000	7507	201	7507	201

SOUTH AUSTRALIA v VICTORIA (Shield Match 1)

Played at Adelaide Oval on October 29, 30, November 1, 2, 1920. (Timeless match)
Toss : South Australia.   Result : VICTORIA WON BY AN INNINGS AND 79 RUNS.
Debuts: South Australia - A.M.Ambler (f/c).
12th Men: D.M.Henry (SA) and A.G.Moyes (Vic).
Umpires: G.I.Colyer and F.J.C.Thomas.
Attendances: 2990, 6411, 2505, 223.   Total: 12,129.   Receipts: £570.
Close of Play: 1st day Vic 0/14 (Mayne 8, Park 2); 2nd day Vic 4/363 (Ransford 54, Armstrong 45); 3rd day SA (2) 4/82 (Gehrs 12, Phillips 6).

Whitty (81 in 76 minutes, 1 six and 9 fours) dominated a ninth-wicket partnership of 122 with Steele; it remains South Australia's record for that wicket against Victoria. Park (152 in 222 minutes, 18 fours and 0 chances) and Ryder (127 in 158 minutes, 2 sixes and 10 fours) registered centuries for Victoria and were supported by Ransford (93 in 154 minutes, 8 fours) and Lampard (65 in 87 minutes, 5 fours). Ransford assumed the captaincy in the second innings when Armstrong was absent due to fibrositis. J.T.Murray and L.V.Pellew were unavailable for South Australia and Henry replaced V.Y.Richardson (ill) in the twelve. The withdrawal of E.A.McDonald (unavailable) left a vacancy for Liddicut in the Victorian side. *Wisden* and *VCA Report* incorrectly give Vic (1) Lampard c & b Pritchard; SA (1) Pellew c Ellis b Armstrong, Rundell c Park b Ironmonger, Ironmonger 4/84. Sources: *Wisden, C.B.O'Reilly, VCA Report, SACA Report, Adelaide Advertiser, South Australian Register.*

SOUTH AUSTRALIA

C.E.Pellew	b Ryder	68		c Ellis b Ironmonger	43
A.Smith	b Ryder	29		c Mayne b Liddicut	18
D.M.Steele	not out	63	(7)	b Lampard	50
D.E.Pritchard	c Ransford b Ryder	18		b Ironmonger	0
P.D.Rundell	b Ryder	0	(8)	c Park b Lampard	14
A.J.Richardson	lbw b Armstrong	8	(9)	not out	53
*D.R.A.Gehrs	b Ironmonger	0	(3)	b Liddicut	43
H.B.Willsmore	c Ellis b Armstrong	7	(10)	c Lampard b Ryder	9
E.L.Phillips	b Armstrong	1	(6)	lbw b Ironmonger	19
W.J.Whitty	b Liddicut	81	(11)	run out	17
†A.M.Ambler	lbw b Armstrong	1	(5)	b Ironmonger	0
Extras	(b9, lb5)	14		(b2, nb2)	4
Total	(63.0 overs, 250 mins)	290		(65.4 overs, 246 mins)	270

VICTORIA

R.E.Mayne	c Pritchard b Richardson	42
R.L.Park	c & b Smith	152
C.B.Willis	b Willsmore	20
F.A.Baring	c Steele b Smith	39
V.S.Ransford	b Willsmore	93
*W.W.Armstrong	lbw b Whitty	53
J.Ryder	c Willsmore b Richardson	127
A.W.Lampard	b Pritchard	65
A.E.Liddicut	st Ambler b Smith	16
†J.L.Ellis	c & b Smith	3
H.Ironmonger	not out	12
Extras	(b6, lb10, nb1)	17
Total	(129.3 overs, 497 mins)	639

VICTORIA	O	M	R	W	w,nb		O	M	R	W	w,nb		FALL OF WICKETS		
Ryder	16	0	68	4	-,-		15	0	81	1	-,-		SA	VIC	SA
Ironmonger	18	1	86	1	-,-		22	1	82	4	-,2	Wkt	1st	1st	2nd
Armstrong	18	2	60	4	-,-							1st	103	83	55
Lampard	10	0	61	0	-,-		17	1	70	2	-,-	2nd	110	127	75
Liddicut	1	0	1	1	-,-	(3)	11	2	29	2	-,-	3rd	134	240	75
Willis						(5)	0.4	0	4	0	-,-	4th	134	279	75
												5th	147	380	106
SOUTH AUSTRALIA	O	M	R	W	w,nb							6th	148	430	159
Whitty	26	0	103	1	-,-							7th	159	574	180
Phillips	18	2	64	0	-,-							8th	161	615	203
Richardson	25	0	118	2	-,-							9th	283	622	228
Rundell	13	0	93	0	-,-							10th	290	639	270
Willsmore	15	0	82	2	-,1										
Pellew	13	0	42	0	-,-										
Smith	14.3	0	103	4	-,-										
Pritchard	5	1	17	1	-,-										

SOUTH AUSTRALIA v M.C.C.

Played at Adelaide Oval on November 5, 6, 8, 9, 1920. (Timeless match)
Toss : M.C.C.   Result : M.C.C. WON BY AN INNINGS AND 55 RUNS.
Debuts: South Australia - D.M.Henry, W.J.Thurgarland (both f/c).
12th Men: D.E.Pritchard (SA) and P.G.H.Fender (MCC).
Umpires: G.I.Colyer and F.K.Lindow.
Attendances: 4186, 10297, 2315, 265.   Total: 17,063.   Receipts: £997.
Close of Play: 1st day MCC 1/201 (Russell 101, Hearne 46); 2nd day SA (2) 0/50 (Pellew 33, Smith 15); 3rd day SA (2) 7/315
    (A.J.Richardson 109).

Sent in on a soft wicket, South Australia lost Pellew to the second ball of the match. Parkin (right-arm off-breaks) played a part in nine of the dismissals in the first innings. The visiting batsmen were given many chances: Russell (156 in 237 minutes, 1 six and 17 fours) gave chances at 24, 64 and 145, Hearne (182 in 232 minutes, 22 fours) was let off at 70 and Hendren (79 in 130 minutes, 1 six and 7 fours) was also given an early reprieve. In the second innings Pellew (64 in 140 minutes, 7 fours), A.J.Richardson (111 in 189 minutes, 12 fours, chance at 36) and Rundell (75 in 129 minutes, 8 fours) stood out. D.M.Steele (work), W.J.Whitty and H.B.Willsmore were all unavailable for South Australia. Last first-class appearance by D.R.A.Gehrs. *Wisden* and *O'Reilly* incorrectly give SA (2) Pellew b Douglas. *O'Reilly* incorrectly gives MCC Russell b Smith. Sources: *Wisden, C.B.O'Reilly, SACA Report, The Age, Adelaide Advertiser, South Australian Register.*

SOUTH AUSTRALIA

C.E.Pellew	c Parkin b Woolley	0		c & b Douglas	64
A.Smith	b Parkin	1		b Howell	15
W.S.Stirling	c Russell b Parkin	0	(7)	b Howell	0
V.Y.Richardson	b Woolley	38		c Hobbs b Douglas	11
*D.R.A.Gehrs	b Parkin	0	(6)	b Howell	14
D.M.Henry	b Parkin	24	(3)	b Wilson	17
A.J.Richardson	c Hobbs b Parkin	7	(5)	b Hearne	111
P.D.Rundell	b Parkin	1		b Hearne	75
E.L.Phillips	b Parkin	6	(10)	b Howell	0
W.J.Thurgarland	b Parkin	26	(9)	b Hearne	11
†A.M.Ambler	not out	8		not out	10
Extras	(b3, lb1, nb3)	7		(b1, lb3, w1, nb6)	11
Total	(37.4 overs, 121 mins)	118		(117.5 overs, 350 mins)	339

M.C.C.

J.B.Hobbs	c Pellew b Smith	48
C.A.G.Russell	c & b Smith	156
J.W.Hearne	c Phillips b Smith	182
E.H.Hendren	st Ambler b Smith	79
J.W.H.Makepeace	not out	38
C.H.Parkin	st Ambler b Smith	0
*J.W.H.T.Douglas	)	
F.E.Woolley	)	
E.R.Wilson	) did not bat	
†H.Strudwick	)	
H.Howell	)	
Extras	(b6, lb3)	9
Total	(141.0 overs, 372 mins) (5 wkts dec)	512

M.C.C.	O	M	R	W	w,nb		O	M	R	W	w,nb
Woolley	19	4	56	2	-,-	(6)	7	1	22	0	-,1
Parkin	18.4	6	55	8	-,3	(4)	14	3	41	0	1,1
Howell						(1)	32	7	81	4	-,2
Douglas						(2)	20	3	67	2	-,2
Hearne						(3)	20.5	5	63	3	-,-
Wilson						(5)	24	8	54	1	-,-

SOUTH AUSTRALIA	O	M	R	W	w,nb
Phillips	20	3	51	0	-,-
Thurgarland	15	3	43	0	-,-
A.J.Richardson	28	5	88	0	-,-
Stirling	18	0	57	0	-,-
Smith	19	0	120	5	-,-
Pellew	17	1	57	0	-,-
Rundell	17	1	61	0	-,-
V.Y.Richardson	7	1	26	0	-,-

FALL OF WICKETS

Wkt	SA	MCC	SA 2nd
1st	0	116	51
2nd	3	325	94
3rd	4	432	107
4th	4	512	125
5th	55	512	149
6th	63	-	149
7th	68	-	315
8th	78	-	318
9th	99	-	319
10th	118	-	339

VICTORIA v M.C.C.

Played at Melbourne Cricket Ground on November 12, 13, 15 (no play), 16, 1920. (Timeless match)
Toss : Victoria.   Result : M.C.C. WON BY AN INNINGS AND 59 RUNS.
Debuts: Nil.
12th Men: F.C.Yeomans (Vic). No 12th named for MCC.
Umpires: F.Benson and R.M.Crockett.
Attendances: 9925, 20839, no play, 4261.   Total: 35,025.   Receipts: £2927.
Close of Play: 1st day MCC 0/24 (Hobbs 11, Russell 13); 2nd day MCC 2/343 (Hearne 82, Hendren 77); 3rd day no play.

W.W.Armstrong (ill) and F.A.Baring (business) were replaced in the Victorian side by Moyes, the nominated 12th man, and Mullett. Howell dismissed Park in his first over while Parkin took the wickets of Willis and Ransford with successive balls. Lampard (111 in 174 minutes, 12 fours, chance at 63) and Liddicut (56 in 144 minutes, 4 fours) shared a seventh-wicket partnership of 142. For the second successive match the Englishmen registered century partnerships for the first three wickets, Hobbs (131 in 213 minutes, 8 fours), Hearne (87 in 210 minutes, 3 fours) and Hendren (106 not out in 155 minutes, 8 fours) leading the way. Rain washed out the scheduled third day and severely affected the condition of the pitch for play the next day. Moyes and Mullett both sustained first-ball dismissals. Sources: *Wisden, VCA Report, The Age, The Argus, The Herald, The Australasian.*

VICTORIA

Batsman	Dismissal	R		Dismissal	R
*R.E.Mayne	b Parkin	43		c Hendren b Rhodes	11
R.L.Park	c Dolphin b Howell	0		lbw b Rhodes	12
C.B.Willis	lbw b Parkin	20		c Fender b Woolley	9
V.S.Ransford	c Woolley b Parkin	0	(6)	c Fender b Rhodes	21
J.Ryder	c Dolphin b Fender	8		b Rhodes	0
A.W.Lampard	c Parkin b Woolley	111	(4)	c Hendren b Woolley	2
A.G.Moyes	c Hendren b Parkin	19		st Dolphin b Rhodes	0
A.E.Liddicut	hit wkt b Woolley	56		not out	23
E.A.McDonald	c Dolphin b Woolley	8		c Douglas b Rhodes	3
†J.L.Ellis	c Rhodes b Howell	2		st Dolphin b Woolley	1
L.T.Mullett	not out	1		b Woolley	0
Extras	(b3, lb2, w1)	6		(b3)	3
Total	(71.1 overs, 228 mins)	274		(38.3 overs, 115 mins)	85

M.C.C.

Batsman	Dismissal	R
J.B.Hobbs	c Moyes b Ryder	131
C.A.G.Russell	c Mullett b McDonald	49
J.W.Hearne	c Ryder b McDonald	87
E.H.Hendren	not out	106
F.E.Woolley	not out	36
*J.W.H.T.Douglas	)	
W.Rhodes	)	
P.G.H.Fender	)	
C.H.Parkin	) did not bat	
†A.Dolphin	)	
H.Howell	)	
Extras	(b1, lb5, w2, nb1)	9
Total	(120.0 overs, 365 mins) (3 wkts dec)	418

M.C.C.	O	M	R	W	w,nb		O	M	R	W	w,nb
Douglas	18	0	62	0	1,-						
Howell	19.1	2	70	2	-,-						
Parkin	13	1	58	4	-,-		4	0	16	0	-,-
Fender	9	0	49	1	-,-						
Woolley	12	4	29	3	-,-	(1)	15.3	6	27	4	-,-
Rhodes						(2)	19	4	39	6	-,-

VICTORIA	O	M	R	W	w,nb
McDonald	29	3	85	2	-,1
Mullett	20	0	73	0	-,-
Lampard	17	1	59	0	1,-
Ryder	23	0	76	1	-,-
Liddicut	14	1	43	0	1,-
Park	4	1	18	0	-,-
Moyes	6	0	21	0	-,-
Willis	4	0	22	0	-,-
Ransford	3	0	12	0	-,-

	FALL OF WICKETS		
	VIC	MCC	VIC
Wkt	1st	1st	2nd
1st	5	114	23
2nd	68	232	23
3rd	68	355	33
4th	77	-	34
5th	77	-	34
6th	105	-	34
7th	247	-	69
8th	263	-	84
9th	270	-	85
10th	274	-	85

NEW SOUTH WALES v M.C.C.

Played at Sydney Cricket Ground on November 19, 20, 22, 1920. (Timeless match)
Toss : M.C.C.   Result : NEW SOUTH WALES WON BY SIX WICKETS.
Debuts: New South Wales - J.M.Gregory (NSW only).
12th Men: A.T.E.Punch (NSW) and A.Waddington (MCC).
Umpires: A.C.Jones and A.P.Williams.
Attendances: 15709, 33283, 18264.   Total: 67,256.   Receipts: £5123.
Close of Play: 1st day NSW 3/50 (Kelleway 19, Bardsley 6); 2nd day MCC (2) 7/220 (Rhodes 22, Fender 35).

Hobbs (112 in 168 minutes, 12 fours) and Hendren (67 in 77 minutes, 6 fours) added 134 out of 236 in the first innings. Howell claimed the wickets of Macartney and Andrews with consecutive balls. Hearne scored 81 in 124 minutes and hit 9 fours. Gregory, whose bowling for the AIF had created a sensation the previous year, earned himself a spot in the First Test team with a nine-wicket haul in his first match for New South Wales. Against all expectations Collins (106 in 186 minutes, 12 fours, chance at 103) and Macartney (161 in 212 minutes, 18 fours) paved the way for an upset with an opening stand of 244 in the second innings. Kelleway's score at stumps on the first day was reduced from 21 at the direction of the umpires due to two leg byes having been incorrectly credited to him earlier. Punch replaced C.J.Tozer (ill) as New South Wales 12th man. *Wisden* incorrectly gives W.L.Trenerry instead of E.Trenerry in NSW side. Sources: *Wisden, NSWCA Report, VCA Report, The Age, Sydney Referee, Sydney Morning Herald.*

M.C.C.

J.B.Hobbs	c & b Mailey	112	c Hendry b Gregory	5
C.A.G.Russell	b Gregory	8	b Gregory	1
J.W.Hearne	lbw b Kelleway	2	c Gregory b Mailey	81
E.H.Hendren	run out (Oldfield/Gregory)	67	b Mailey	27
J.W.H.Makepeace	st Oldfield b Mailey	20	c Hendry b Gregory	3
F.E.Woolley	b Mailey	11	b Gregory	26
*J.W.H.T.Douglas	b Mailey	0	c Taylor b Mailey	11
W.Rhodes	b Gregory	4	lbw b Kelleway	26
P.G.H.Fender	not out	1	c Collins b Kelleway	54
†H.Strudwick	b Gregory	0	c Collins b Gregory	3
H.Howell	b Gregory	5	not out	0
Extras	(b2, lb4)	6	(b12, lb1)	13
Total	(68.1 overs, 197 mins)	236	(69.2 overs, 206 mins)	250

NEW SOUTH WALES

*H.L.Collins	b Hearne	18	c Russell b Fender	106
C.G.Macartney	b Howell	3	lbw b Hearne	161
T.J.E.Andrews	b Howell	0	c Hearne b Woolley	34
C.Kelleway	c Woolley b Douglas	21	lbw b Hearne	9
W.Bardsley	c Woolley b Fender	6	not out	3
J.M.Gregory	b Fender	46	not out	11
J.M.Taylor	c & b Douglas	11		
H.S.T.L.Hendry	b Douglas	4		
†W.A.S.Oldfield	not out	19		
E.Trenerry	c Russell b Fender	0		
A.A.Mailey	b Fender	12		
Extras	(b4, lb6, w1, nb2)	13	(b1, lb7, w2, nb1)	11
Total	(48.0 overs, 163 mins)	153	(84.5 overs, 259 mins) (4 wkts)	335

NEW SOUTH WALES	O	M	R	W	w,nb		O	M	R	W	w,nb
Gregory	18.1	1	52	4	-,-		23	4	67	5	-,-
Kelleway	17	2	45	1	-,-		11.2	3	33	2	-,-
Trenerry	10	0	34	0	-,-	(4)	3	0	9	0	-,-
Mailey	17	5	69	4	-,-	(3)	21	1	100	3	-,-
Hendry	6	1	30	0	-,-		11	2	28	0	-,-

M.C.C.	O	M	R	W	w,nb		O	M	R	W	w,nb
Douglas	14	3	41	3	-,-		12	0	68	0	-,-
Howell	13	2	38	2	1,1		18	1	58	0	-,-
Hearne	12	2	35	1	-,-		14	3	44	2	-,1
Fender	9	1	26	4	-,1		11	1	74	1	-,-
Woolley							22.5	4	66	1	2,-
Rhodes							3	1	6	0	-,-
Hobbs							4	0	8	0	-,-

FALL OF WICKETS

Wkt	MCC 1st	NSW 1st	MCC 2nd	NSW 2nd
1st	27	5	7	244
2nd	36	5	14	292
3rd	170	27	89	312
4th	202	50	92	319
5th	215	58	126	-
6th	223	84	152	-
7th	228	88	161	-
8th	230	132	243	-
9th	230	132	250	-
10th	236	153	250	-

VICTORIA v SOUTH AUSTRALIA (Shield Match 2)

Played at Melbourne Cricket Ground on November 26, 27, 29, 30, December 1, 1920. (Timeless match)
Toss : Victoria.   Result : VICTORIA WON BY 385 RUNS.
Debuts: South Australia - H.M.Fisher (f/c).
12th Men: F.C.Yeomans (Vic) and D.M.Henry (SA).
Umpires: H.J.Alessio and R.M.Crockett.
Attendances: 4493, 9797, 4842, 3125, 1367.   Total: 23,624.   Receipts: £892.
Close of Play: 1st day SA 0/18 (C.E.Pellew 13, V.Y.Richardson 5); 2nd day Vic (2) 0/49 (Mayne 23, Baring 25); 3rd day Vic (2) 7/375
     (Armstrong 127); 4th day SA (2) 1/54 (C.E.Pellew 29, L.V.Pellew 12).

Warwick Windridge Armstrong, aged 41, became the first Australian to score 400 runs in one match and only the second to have done so in all first-class cricket. He scored 157 not out in 165 minutes (17 fours) and 245 in 320 minutes (13 fours). Mayne (82 in 149 minutes, 9 fours) and Liddicut (152 in 255 minutes, 12 fours) also made contributions to the then highest second-innings total in all first-class cricket. A fifth-wicket partnership of 190 for South Australia between Rundell (116 in 156 minutes, 6 fours, chance at 12) and Steele (107 not out in 193 minutes, 6 fours) set a new State record for that wicket against Victoria. J.T.Murray, A.Smith, W.J.Whitty and H.B.Willsmore were all unavailable for South Australia and Bridgman replaced N.L.Williams, also unavailable, in the selected side. *Wisden* and *VCA Report* incorrectly give SA (1) McDonald 3/47; SA (2) McDonald 6/128; Vic (2) Fisher 1/104. Sources: *Wisden, C.B.O'Reilly, VCA Report, SACA Report, The Age, The Argus, The Herald, Geelong Advertiser.*

VICTORIA

Batsman	Dismissal	Runs		Dismissal	Runs
R.E.Mayne	st Winser b A.J.Richardson	16		st Winser b Wright	82
R.L.Park	lbw b A.J.Richardson	18	(4)	c Winser b Rundell	48
A.W.Lampard	run out (C.E.Pellew/Winser)	47		c Steele b Fisher	20
J.Ryder	c & b C.E.Pellew	36	(7)	c Bridgman b A.J.Richardson	31
*W.W.Armstrong	not out	157	(6)	b A.J.Richardson	245
V.S.Ransford	b Wright	1	(5)	c & b Wright	8
F.A.Baring	b A.J.Richardson	3	(2)	lbw b A.J.Richardson	29
C.B.Willis	c Winser b Fisher	14		c Pritchard b A.J.Richardson	25
A.E.Liddicut	st Winser b Wright	13		c & b Rundell	152
†J.L.Ellis	b A.J.Richardson	2		b Wright	38
E.A.McDonald	c Winser b Wright	0		not out	24
Extras	(lb2, w1)	3		(b16, lb5, w1)	22
Total	(73.0 overs, 277 mins)	310		(168.7 overs, 608 mins)	724

SOUTH AUSTRALIA

Batsman	Dismissal	Runs		Dismissal	Runs
C.E.Pellew	c & b Ryder	26		c Mayne b Liddicut	52
V.Y.Richardson	st Ellis b Willis	66		b McDonald	9
P.D.Rundell	c Ellis b Ryder	7	(5)	b McDonald	116
A.J.Richardson	c Ryder b Armstrong	14	(7)	b McDonald	17
*D.M.Steele	c Ellis b McDonald	20	(6)	not out	107
D.E.Pritchard	c Armstrong b McDonald	4	(4)	b Baring	22
L.V.Pellew	c Ellis b McDonald	69	(3)	b McDonald	53
H.H.M.Bridgman	c Ellis b Ryder	11		c Ellis b McDonald	0
†C.L.Winser	c Ryder b Armstrong	12		b McDonald	5
H.M.Fisher	lbw b Armstrong	8		b Liddicut	4
A.W.Wright	not out	1		b Liddicut	0
Extras	(b5, lb2, nb1)	8		(b11, lb6, nb1)	18
Total	(66.1 overs, 252 mins)	246		(81.6 overs, 330 mins)	403

SOUTH AUSTRALIA	O	M	R	W	w,nb		O	M	R	W	w,nb
Fisher	15	1	69	1	1,-		27	2	103	1	1,-
A.J.Richardson	21	3	66	4	-,-		43	6	153	4	-,-
Wright	18	0	89	3	-,-		39	1	184	3	-,-
C.E.Pellew	6	0	30	1	-,-	(5)	20	3	67	0	-,-
Bridgman	7	1	20	0	-,-	(6)	14	0	72	0	-,-
Rundell	6	0	33	0	-,-	(4)	21.7	1	92	2	-,-
L.V.Pellew							2	0	11	0	-,-
V.Y.Richardson							2	0	20	0	-,-

VICTORIA	O	M	R	W	w,nb		O	M	R	W	w,nb
McDonald	18.1	3	46	3	-,1		27	2	127	6	-,1
Lampard	9	0	51	0	-,-		9	0	58	0	-,-
Ryder	14	0	62	3	-,-		14	0	56	0	-,-
Armstrong	20	2	58	3	-,-						
Liddicut	1	0	1	0	-,-	(4)	12.6	2	42	3	-,-
Willis	4	0	20	1	-,-		3	0	23	0	-,-
Baring						(5)	11	1	52	1	-,-
Ransford						(7)	5	0	27	0	-,-

FALL OF WICKETS

Wkt	VIC 1st	SA 1st	VIC 2nd	SA 2nd
1st	34	48	64	15
2nd	37	60	118	120
3rd	106	95	153	138
4th	127	126	167	168
5th	137	139	210	358
6th	144	170	281	362
7th	202	186	375	386
8th	266	209	568	396
9th	280	230	677	403
10th	310	246	724	403

QUEENSLAND v M.C.C.

Played at Exhibition Ground, Brisbane, on November 27, 29, 30, 1920. (Three-day match)
Toss : Queensland.   Result : M.C.C. WON BY AN INNINGS AND 41 RUNS.
Debuts: Queensland - G.S.Moore (Qld only).
12th Men: E.H.Hutcheon (Qld) and A.Waddington (MCC).
Umpires: G.A.Carter and W.H.Carvosso.
Attendances: 7000, 2500, 3500.   Total: About 13,000.   Receipts: £903.
Close of Play: 1st day MCC 1/71 (Russell 35, Rhodes 10); 2nd day MCC 419 all out.

J.K.Farquhar and J.F.Sheppard were omitted from the Queensland thirteen selected for the match, with Hutcheon later added as 12th man. Hartigan led the home side in his final first-class appearance but was out to the third ball of the match. The ex-New South Welshman, Moore (85 in 103 minutes, 1 six and 6 fours) and Oxenham added 116 for the second wicket but there was little resistance to the varied English attack thereafter. Russell (73 in 125 minutes, 9 fours), Rhodes (162 in 306 minutes, 4 fours) and Douglas (84 in 143 minutes, 7 fours) then batted their team into an impregnable position, Rhodes having survived a chance to slip before reaching double figures. The Queensland batting capitulated for a second time, O'Connor (66 not out in 105 minutes, 6 fours) and Ayres (41, 5 fours) alone providing any worthwhile resistance, and the match was over at 3.45pm on the third day. A "scratch match" was then played "in order to give the spectators an opportunity of seeing some of the Englishmen at the wickets". Hendren, Waddington, Hitch and Parkin batted, in turn, to the bowling of Ayres, Moore, Rowe, Fennelly and C.B.Barstow in what turned out to be little more than "an exhibition of slogging". No scores were kept. *Wisden* incorrectly gives Hendren lbw b Ayres in the MCC innings. Sources: *Wisden, VCA Report, The Age, Sydney Morning Herald, Brisbane Courier.*

QUEENSLAND

*R.J.Hartigan	c Russell b Howell	0	(5)	b Parkin	16
L.E.Oxenham	run out	29	(1)	st Dolphin b Woolley	1
G.S.Moore	c Hendren b Rhodes	85		b Parkin	20
F.C.Thompson	c Wilson b Rhodes	11		run out	3
S.J.Fennelly	c Woolley b Parkin	3	(2)	st Dolphin b Woolley	17
W.Rowe	not out	23		c Wilson b Parkin	2
†L.P.D.O'Connor	lbw b Hearne	10		not out	66
S.W.Ayres	lbw b Wilson	7		c Hearne b Woolley	41
J.W.McAndrew	b Wilson	2		run out (/Dolphin)	4
A.J.Marsden	b Parkin	0	(11)	b Parkin	0
P.M.Hornibrook	b Parkin	5	(10)	c Hendren b Woolley	6
Extras	(b6, lb2, w1, nb2)	11		(b4, lb8, w3, nb1)	16
Total	(74.2 overs, 201 mins)	186		(58.2 overs, 171 mins)	192

M.C.C.

J.W.H.Makepeace	c O'Connor b Marsden	22
C.A.G.Russell	b Hornibrook	73
W.Rhodes	c & b Ayres	162
F.E.Woolley	c Fennelly b Marsden	12
*J.W.H.T.Douglas	c & b Hornibrook	84
E.R.Wilson	c Thompson b Hornibrook	8
J.W.Hearne	c O'Connor b Ayres	11
E.H.Hendren	c Fennelly b Ayres	21
C.H.Parkin	c Hartigan b Ayres	2
†A.Dolphin	not out	6
H.Howell	c Rowe b Ayres	0
Extras	(b10, lb6, nb2)	18
Total	(136.4 overs, 375 mins)	419

M.C.C.	O	M	R	W	w,nb		O	M	R	W	w,nb
Howell	11	1	34	1	-,-		10	0	41	0	-,1
Douglas	4	1	10	0	-,2						
Parkin	16.2	5	40	3	1,-		16.2	4	54	4	-,-
Wilson	9	4	18	2	-,-		11	4	23	0	-,-
Woolley	6	0	17	0	-,-	(2)	18	6	43	4	-,-
Hearne	11	4	26	1	-,-						
Rhodes	17	7	30	2	-,-						
Hendren						(5)	3	1	15	0	3,-

QUEENSLAND	O	M	R	W	w,nb
McAndrew	27	2	73	0	-,1
Ayres	20.4	6	112	5	-,1
Marsden	25	2	75	2	-,-
Rowe	22	5	47	0	-,-
Hornibrook	39	4	89	3	-,-
Thompson	3	0	5	0	-,-

FALL OF WICKETS

	QLD	MCC	QLD
Wkt	1st	1st	2nd
1st	0	48	1
2nd	116	147	33
3rd	123	170	41
4th	126	344	58
5th	136	364	59
6th	149	386	66
7th	169	395	161
8th	175	397	170
9th	180	419	183
10th	186	419	192

AUSTRALIAN XI v M.C.C.

Played at Brisbane Cricket Ground (Woolloongabba) on December 3, 4, 6, 1920. (3-day match)
Toss : Australian XI.   Result : MATCH DRAWN.
Debuts: Nil.
12th Men: L.E.Oxenham (Aust) and A.Dolphin (MCC).
Umpires: G.A.Carter and W.H.Carvosso.
Attendances: 4000, 12000, 4000.   Total: About 20,000.   Receipts: £1705.
Close of Play: 1st day MCC 0/24 (Hobbs 14, Russell 10); 2nd day MCC 9/285 (Wilson 22, Waddington 15).

Kippax and Trenerry were called up to replace A.W.Lampard and J.Ryder (both unavailable) in the Australian XI. Tozer (51 in 115 minutes, 4 fours), Macartney (96 in 137 minutes, 11 fours) and Armstrong (53 in 120 minutes, 5 fours) hit half-centuries on the opening day. Collins had an early escape when caught from a no-ball, only to be bowled by the next ball. Russell (72 in 153 minutes, 4 fours) and Hendren (96 in 182 minutes, 10 fours) batted well for M.C.C. but the first innings advantage was entirely due to a last wicket stand of 97 from Wilson and Waddington. Carter (50 in 89 minutes, 6 fours) and Tozer (53 in 145 minutes, 3 fours) recorded half-centuries on the last day but there was no time for a result and bad light caused the abandonment of the game at 5.20pm. Moore was out first ball in each innings. *Wisden* incorrectly names W.L.Trenerry instead of E.Trenerry in the Australian XI and also has Trenerry lbw b Douglas in Aust (1). Sources: *Wisden, VCA Report, Sydney Morning Herald, Brisbane Courier.*

AUSTRALIAN XI

H.L.Collins	b Waddington	3			
C.J.Tozer	c Hendren b Waddington	51		b Rhodes	53
G.S.Moore	b Waddington	0		c & b Rhodes	0
A.F.Kippax	b Woolley	18		b Hitch	17
C.G.Macartney	lbw b Douglas	96		b Woolley	30
*W.W.Armstrong	c Strudwick b Douglas	53		not out	16
†H.Carter	c Hitch b Douglas	8	(1)	c Woolley b Rhodes	50
E.Trenerry	c Strudwick b Douglas	2	(7)	not out	6
A.J.Marsden	lbw b Woolley	0			
J.W.McAndrew	not out	1			
P.M.Hornibrook	c Strudwick b Douglas	0			
Extras	(b7, lb11, nb5)	23		(b3, lb1, nb6)	10
Total	(80.0 overs, 240 mins)	255		(60.0 overs, 175 mins) (5 wkts)	182

M.C.C.

J.B.Hobbs	c McAndrew b Trenerry	26
C.A.G.Russell	c Macartney b Hornibrook	72
W.Rhodes	lbw b Trenerry	3
E.H.Hendren	b Hornibrook	96
F.E.Woolley	run out (Armstrong)	26
*J.W.H.T.Douglas	lbw b Marsden	0
P.G.H.Fender	c Trenerry b McAndrew	8
E.R.Wilson	c sub (L.E.Oxenham) b McAndrew	56
J.W.Hitch	c Moore b Hornibrook	2
†H.Strudwick	c & b Hornibrook	4
A.Waddington	not out	51
Extras	(b11, lb2)	13
Total	(140.2 overs, 380 mins)	357

M.C.C.	O	M	R	W	w,nb		O	M	R	W	w,nb
Waddington	25	7	63	3	-,5	(3)	8	3	26	0	-,6
Hitch	9	0	31	0	-,-	(1)	13	2	40	1	-,-
Douglas	18	6	45	5	-,-	(2)	1	1	0	0	-,-
Woolley	15	2	37	2	-,-	(6)	5	0	17	1	-,-
Fender	6	0	29	0	-,-		7	0	37	0	-,-
Wilson	7	1	27	0	-,-						
Rhodes						(4)	26	6	52	3	-,-

AUSTRALIAN XI	O	M	R	W	w,nb
McAndrew	42.2	10	98	2	-,-
Trenerry	28	4	78	2	-,-
Marsden	17	4	45	1	-,-
Hornibrook	32	8	80	4	-,-
Macartney	11	2	23	0	-,-
Armstrong	10	3	20	0	-,-

FALL OF WICKETS

	AUST	MCC	AUST
Wkt	1st	1st	2nd
1st	17	61	93
2nd	17	67	93
3rd	59	154	118
4th	112	199	154
5th	224	199	172
6th	234	219	-
7th	244	249	-
8th	251	253	-
9th	255	260	-
10th	255	357	-

NEW SOUTH WALES v SOUTH AUSTRALIA (Shield Match 3)

Played at Sydney Cricket Ground on December 3, 4, 6 (no play), 7, 8 & 9 (no play), 1920. (Timeless match)
Toss : New South Wales.   Result : MATCH DRAWN.
Debuts: Nil.
12th Men: W.G.F.Brown (NSW) and D.E.Pritchard (SA).
Umpires: W.G.Curran and A.C.Jones.
Attendances: 2752, 8159, no play, 2798, no play, no play.   Total: 13,709.   Receipts: £767.
Close of Play: 1st day NSW 3/224 (Bogle 94, Bardsley 20); 2nd day NSW 7/675 (Gregory 20, Hendry 14); 3rd day no play; 4th day SA (2) 0/6 (C.E.Pellew 3, V.Y.Richardson 2); 5th day no play.

H.Carter, H.L.Collins, C.G.Macartney, C.J.Tozer and E.Trenerry were all unavailable for New South Wales due to their selection in the Australian XI v MCC match in Brisbane. Brown was brought into the twelve when A.F.Kippax was a late inclusion in that match. The South Australians were unable to reach Sydney until the scheduled starting date of December 3rd because their previous match, against Victoria, had stretched into a fifth day. They requested that the match be delayed until the following day but N.S.W.C.A. officials set the start at 2.00pm on the 3rd. A further delay was caused by the non-arrival of some of the South Australian's baggage and the game did not finally get underway until 3.15pm. Bogle (103 in 200 minutes, 9 fours), Taylor (95 in 128 minutes, 10 fours), Bardsley (235 in 319 minutes, 28 fours), Kelleway (168 in 290 minutes, 15 fours) and Hendry (82 in 102 minutes, 8 fours) all made contributions to the massive New South Wales total, 451 runs being scored on the second day. Bardsley and Kelleway added 397 for the fifth wicket, the highest partnership for any wicket recorded in Australia up to this time. It remained the fifth wicket record until 1946-47. Heavy rain prevented any play on the third day and returned to cause the cancellation of the fifth and sixth days. Many of the visiting players had work commitments and, at the request of the S.A.C.A., it was agreed to abandon the match. It was the first game since the inception of the Sheffield Shield not to be played to a finish. Some records incorrectly state a NSW victory. *Wisden* incorrectly gives NSW Kelleway c & b C.E.Pellew; SA (1) L.V.Pellew 8, Henry 12, Winser 14; and omits extras 7. Sources: *Wisden, C.B.O'Reilly, NSWCA Report, SACA Report, Sydney Referee, Sydney Morning Herald.*

NEW SOUTH WALES

A.T.E.Punch	b Fisher	4
J.Bogle	c Bridgman b Fisher	103
T.J.E.Andrews	c & b A.J.Richardson	10
J.M.Taylor	c Steele b C.E.Pellew	95
W.Bardsley	c A.J.Richardson b C.E.Pellew	235
*C.Kelleway	b C.E.Pellew	168
J.M.Gregory	b Wright	43
F.A.O'Keeffe	lbw b Wright	3
H.S.T.L.Hendry	c C.E.Pellew b Rundell	82
†W.A.S.Oldfield	b Wright	8
A.A.Mailey	not out	26
Extras	(b19, lb5, nb1)	25
Total	(156.3 overs, 612 mins)	802

SOUTH AUSTRALIA

C.E.Pellew	st Oldfield b Mailey	73	not out	3
V.Y.Richardson	b Hendry	22	not out	2
L.V.Pellew	run out (Punch/Oldfield)	2		
P.D.Rundell	c Gregory b Mailey	7		
*D.M.Steele	st Oldfield b Mailey	17		
A.J.Richardson	c O'Keeffe b Mailey	34		
D.M.Henry	b Mailey	10		
H.H.M.Bridgman	st Oldfield b Mailey	1		
†C.L.Winser	c Oldfield b Mailey	15		
H.M.Fisher	not out	3		
A.W.Wright	b Mailey	0		
Extras	(b5, lb2)	7	(lb1)	1
Total	(53.7 overs, 196 mins)	191	(4.0 overs, 10 mins) (0 wkts)	6

SOUTH AUSTRALIA	O	M	R	W	w,nb
Fisher	25	0	137	2	-,-
A.J.Richardson	39	4	175	1	-,-
Wright	36	4	164	3	-,-
C.E.Pellew	29	3	119	3	-,1
Rundell	13.3	0	82	1	-,-
Bridgman	9	0	65	0	-,-
V.Y.Richardson	2	0	16	0	-,-
L.V.Pellew	3	0	19	0	-,-

NEW SOUTH WALES	O	M	R	W	w,nb		O	M	R	W	w,nb
Gregory	7	0	29	0	-,-						
Kelleway	14	3	32	0	-,-						
Mailey	19.7	3	81	8	-,-	(2)	2	0	4	0	-,-
Hendry	9	2	27	1	-,-	(1)	2	1	1	0	-,-
O'Keeffe	4	1	15	0	-,-						

FALL OF WICKETS

		NSW	SA	SA
Wkt		1st	1st	2nd
1st		10	55	-
2nd		25	67	-
3rd		186	85	-
4th		239	123	-
5th		636	132	-
6th		647	160	-
7th		658	168	-
8th		705	175	-
9th		725	191	-
10th		802	191	-

AUSTRALIA v ENGLAND (1st Test)

Played at Sydney Cricket Ground on December 17, 18, 20, 21, 22, 1920. (Timeless match)
Toss : Australia.　　　　　　　Result : AUSTRALIA WON BY 377 RUNS.
Debuts: Australia - H.L.Collins, J.M.Gregory, A.A.Mailey, W.A.S.Oldfield, C.E.Pellew, J.Ryder, J.M.Taylor (all Test). England -
　　E.H.Hendren, C.H.Parkin, C.A.G.Russell, A.Waddington (all Test).
12th Men: R.E.Mayne (Aust) and P.G.H.Fender (Eng).
Umpires: R.M.Crockett and A.C.Jones.
Attendances: 22316, 40005, 25807, 15257, 7817.　　　Total: 111,202.　　　Receipts: £10,386.
Close of Play: 1st day Aust 8/250 (Ryder 5, Oldfield 0); 2nd day Aust (2) 0/46 (Collins 17, Bardsley 23); 3rd day Aust (2) 5/332
　　(Kelleway 23); 4th day Eng (2) 1/47 (Hobbs 18, Hearne 23).

Armstrong began his highly-successful tenure as Australian captain with a chanceless hundred (158 in 205 minutes, 1 five and 17 fours).
He shared a sixth-wicket partnership of 187 with Kelleway (78 in 207 minutes, 2 fours) in 155 minutes. Collins, making his international
debut at the age of 31 years 11 months, scored 70 (150 minutes, 8 fours, chances at 16 and 42) and 104 (219 minutes, 11 fours, chances at
48 and 69). He was the fifth Australian to score a century in his first Test. Bardsley (57 in 122 minutes, 4 fours), Macartney (69 in 104
minutes, 9 fours) and Taylor (51 in 102 minutes, 6 fours) scored half-centuries in Australia's match-winning second-innings total. Russell,
on debut for England, played on to his first ball in Tests and was out to the second ball of the second over in the second innings. Hobbs
(59 in 105 minutes, 1 six and 2 fours), Hearne (57 in 160 minutes, 4 fours) and Hendren (56 in 125 minutes, 7 fours) topscored for
England. *Wisden* incorrectly gives Eng (2) Rhodes b Mailey. *VCA Report* gives Aust (2) Woolley 10 maidens. Sources: *Wisden, VCA
Report, The Age, The Argus, Sydney Referee, Sydney Morning Herald.*

AUSTRALIA

C.G.Macartney	b Waddington	19	(3) b Douglas		69
H.L.Collins	run out (Hitch)	70	(1) c Waddington b Douglas		104
W.Bardsley	c Strudwick b Hearne	22	(2) b Hearne		57
C.Kelleway	run out (Hendren/Strudwick)	33	(6) c Russell b Woolley		78
*W.W.Armstrong	st Strudwick b Woolley	12	(7) b Parkin		158
J.M.Gregory	c Strudwick b Woolley	8	(9) run out (Hendren/Strudwick)		0
J.M.Taylor	lbw b Hearne	34	(4) c Woolley b Parkin		51
C.E.Pellew	c Hendren b Hearne	36	(5) lbw b Woolley		16
J.Ryder	run out (Hobbs/Hearne)	5	(8) run out (Parkin/Strudwick)		6
†W.A.S.Oldfield	c Hobbs b Parkin	7	c Strudwick b Parkin		16
A.A.Mailey	not out	10	not out		0
Extras	(b4, lb6, nb1)	11	(b17, lb7, nb2)		26
Total	(114.5 overs, 317 mins)	267	(192.3 overs, 538 mins)		581

ENGLAND

C.A.G.Russell	b Kelleway	0	c Oldfield b Gregory		5
J.B.Hobbs	b Gregory	49	lbw b Armstrong		59
J.W.Hearne	c Gregory b Mailey	14	b Gregory		57
E.H.Hendren	c Gregory b Ryder	28	b Kelleway		56
F.E.Woolley	c Mailey b Ryder	52	st Oldfield b Mailey		16
*J.W.H.T.Douglas	st Oldfield b Mailey	21	c Armstrong b Mailey		7
W.Rhodes	c Gregory b Mailey	3	c Ryder b Mailey		45
J.W.Hitch	c Kelleway b Gregory	3	c Taylor b Gregory		19
A.Waddington	run out (Pellew/Mailey)	7	b Kelleway		3
C.H.Parkin	not out	4	b Kelleway		4
†H.Strudwick	lbw b Gregory	2	not out		1
Extras	(b3, lb4)	7	(b6, lb3)		9
Total	(59.1 overs, 189 mins)	190	(102.5 overs, 301 mins)		281

ENGLAND	O	M	R	W	w,nb		O	M	R	W	w,nb		FALL OF WICKETS			
Hitch	10	0	37	0	-,-		8	0	40	0	-,-			AUST	ENG	AUST	ENG
Waddington	18	3	35	1	-,1		23	4	53	0	-,1		Wkt	1st	1st	2nd	2nd
Parkin	26.5	5	58	1	-,-		35.3	5	102	3	-,-		1st	40	0	123	5
Hearne	34	8	77	3	-,-		42	7	124	1	-,1		2nd	80	50	234	105
Woolley	23	7	35	2	-,-	(6)	36	11	90	2	-,-		3rd	140	70	241	149
Douglas	3	0	14	0	-,-	(5)	26	3	79	2	-,-		4th	162	143	282	170
Rhodes							22	2	67	0	-,-		5th	173	145	332	178
													6th	176	158	519	231
AUSTRALIA	O	M	R	W	w,nb		O	M	R	W	w,nb		7th	244	165	536	264
Kelleway	6	2	10	1	-,-		15.5	3	45	3	-,-		8th	249	180	540	271
Gregory	23.1	3	56	3	-,-		33	6	70	3	-,-		9th	250	188	578	279
Mailey	23	4	95	3	-,-	(4)	24	2	105	3	-,-		10th	267	190	581	281
Ryder	6	1	20	2	-,-	(5)	17	6	24	0	-,-						
Armstrong	1	0	2	0	-,-	(6)	10	0	21	1	-,-						
Macartney						(3)	3	0	7	0	-,-						

VICTORIA v NEW SOUTH WALES (Shield Match 4)

Played at Melbourne Cricket Ground on December 24, 27, 28, 29, 1920. (Timeless match)
Toss : New South Wales.   Result : NEW SOUTH WALES WON BY 101 RUNS.
Debuts: Nil.
12th Men: F.C.Yeomans (Vic) and A.F.Kippax (NSW).
Umpires: R.M.Crockett and A.D.Reaburn.
Attendances: 4766, 19068, 17630, 13677.   Total: 55,141.   Receipts: £2692.
Close of Play: 1st day NSW 7/314 (Hendry 26, Gregory 25); 2nd day Vic 5/228 (Ryder 39); 3rd day NSW (2) 7/209 (Taylor 102).

New South Wales omitted H.Carter and A.F.Kippax from their thirteen but both were required as substitutes in Victoria's second innings in the absence of Gregory (bruised heel) and Macartney (gastritis). Ironmonger was a late inclusion for V.S.Ransford (injured hand). Mayne tossed for Victoria and led the home side on the first day in the absence of Armstrong (family bereavement). Bardsley (125 in 262 minutes, 9 fours), Park (111 in 213 minutes, 7 fours) and Taylor (118 in 178 minutes, 11 fours) compiled centuries. Macartney was also impressive in his 94-minutes stay in the first innings, hitting 8 fours. *Wisden* and *VCA Report* incorrectly give NSW (1) McDonald 3/92; Vic (1) Collins 0/17. *VCA Report* also incorrectly gives NSW (2) McDonald 5/83, Ironmonger 2/66. Sources: *Wisden, NSWCA Report, VCA Report, The Age, The Argus, The Herald, The Australasian.*

NEW SOUTH WALES

*H.L.Collins	c Baring b Ryder	26		b Ironmonger	8
W.Bardsley	c McDonald b Ryder	125		lbw b Ryder	41
C.G.Macartney	b Liddicut	68		absent ill	-
C.Kelleway	c Ellis b Ironmonger	10		b McDonald	2
T.J.E.Andrews	c Ellis b McDonald	15	(3)	b McDonald	2
J.M.Taylor	b Ironmonger	9	(5)	st Ellis b Ironmonger	118
J.Bogle	b Ironmonger	8	(6)	b Liddicut	28
H.S.T.L.Hendry	b McDonald	37	(7)	b McDonald	7
J.M.Gregory	not out	46	(8)	b McDonald	5
†W.A.S.Oldfield	b McDonald	0	(9)	c Ellis b McDonald	2
A.A.Mailey	b Ironmonger	13	(10)	not out	7
Extras	(b6, lb1, nb2)	9		(b5, lb7, w1, nb2)	15
Total	(82.5 overs, 367 mins)	366		(55.0 overs, 233 mins)	235

VICTORIA

R.E.Mayne	b Gregory	10		lbw b Mailey	40
A.W.Lampard	c Collins b Gregory	1	(7)	c Oldfield b Kelleway	12
F.A.Baring	b Gregory	8	(6)	c Taylor b Mailey	12
R.L.Park	c Taylor b Mailey	111	(2)	c Hendry b Mailey	22
*W.W.Armstrong	b Hendry	51		c Collins b Mailey	12
J.Ryder	c Collins b Mailey	59	(4)	c Taylor b Mailey	13
A.E.Liddicut	st Oldfield b Mailey	4	(8)	c Oldfield b Hendry	18
C.B.Willis	not out	33	(3)	st Oldfield b Mailey	43
†J.L.Ellis	st Oldfield b Mailey	2		run out (Bogle)	14
E.A.McDonald	b Mailey	0		run out (sub A.F.Kippax)	1
H.Ironmonger	st Oldfield b Mailey	10		not out	4
Extras	(b5, lb3, nb5)	13		(b4, lb3)	7
Total	(93.1 overs, 335 mins)	302		(61.3 overs, 230 mins)	198

VICTORIA	O	M	R	W	w,nb		O	M	R	W	w,nb
McDonald	20	0	90	3	-,2		19	0	81	5	-,2
Ironmonger	33.5	1	127	4	-,-		20	3	62	2	-,-
Ryder	14	0	57	2	-,-		4	0	21	1	1,-
Liddicut	10	0	46	1	-,-	(5)	6	0	21	1	-,-
Baring	2	0	10	0	-,-	(6)	4	0	20	0	-,-
Willis	1	0	9	0	-,-						
Lampard	2	0	18	0	-,-	(4)	2	0	15	0	-,-

NEW SOUTH WALES	O	M	R	W	w,nb		O	M	R	W	w,nb
Gregory	13	0	49	3	-,-						
Kelleway	28	8	61	0	-,1		20.3	4	44	1	-,-
Mailey	26.1	2	97	6	-,-		23	0	99	6	-,-
Hendry	20	3	52	1	-,-	(1)	18	3	48	1	-,-
Andrews	2	0	16	0	-,1						
Collins	4	1	14	0	-,3						

FALL OF WICKETS				
Wkt	NSW 1st	VIC 1st	NSW 2nd	VIC 2nd
1st	50	5	34	47
2nd	169	14	39	84
3rd	199	22	41	108
4th	228	142	74	122
5th	247	228	162	133
6th	263	234	201	148
7th	263	275	209	167
8th	347	282	211	181
9th	347	282	235	188
10th	366	302	-	198

AUSTRALIA v ENGLAND (2nd Test)

Played at Melbourne Cricket Ground on December 31, 1920, January 1, 3, 4, 1921. (Timeless match)
Toss : Australia.   Result : AUSTRALIA WON BY AN INNINGS AND 91 RUNS.
Debuts: Australia - R.L.Park (Test). England - H.Howell, J.W.H.Makepeace (both Test).
12th Men: R.E.Mayne (Aust) and J.W.Hitch (Eng).
Umpires: R.M.Crockett and D.A.Elder.
Attendances: 32499, 32444, 34963, 5619.   Total: 105,525.   Receipts: £10,201.
Close of Play: 1st day Aust 6/282 (Pellew 33, Ryder 13); 2nd day Eng 2/93 (Hobbs 53, Hendren 29); 3rd day Eng (2) 5/76 (Woolley 15, Douglas 0).

C.G.Macartney (ill with gastritis) was replaced at the last moment by Park (originally 12th man). Mailey was selected despite reporting some soreness in his arm but was not required to bowl at all during the match. Hearne became ill with lumbago on the first day and took no further part in the match or tour. Collins (64 in 100 minutes, 6 fours) was missed by Rhodes at third slip from the fourth ball of the match and went on to add 116 with Bardsley (51 in 111 minutes, 5 fours) for the opening wicket. Park was out first ball in his only Test. Pellew (116 in 203 minutes, 1 five and 8 fours, missed at 3 off Douglas) and Gregory (chanceless 100 in 137 minutes, 12 fours) added 173 for the eighth wicket in 124 minutes to boost Australia's score from 7/282 to 8/455. Taylor (68 in 130 minutes, 5 fours) earlier scored a studious half-century. An overnight storm after the second day flooded the ground and the following sunshine produced a wicket that was at its most difficult when Hobbs and Hendren resumed their stand on Monday. Hobbs's innings (122 in 210 minutes, 10 fours) was considered a masterly affair in which he did not give a chance until after reaching the century (when 110); in all he put on 142 in 132 minutes with Hendren (67 in 132 minutes, 3 fours). Thereafter the pitch caught up with the batsmen and only Woolley in the second innings (50 in 109 minutes, 3 fours) batted with any distinction. Gregory was the first all-rounder to score a century and take seven wickets in an innings in a Test match. Sources: *Wisden, VCA Report, The Age, The Argus, The Australasian, Sydney Morning Herald.*

AUSTRALIA

H.L.Collins	c Hearne b Howell	64
W.Bardsley	c Strudwick b Woolley	51
R.L.Park	b Howell	0
J.M.Taylor	c Woolley b Parkin	68
*W.W.Armstrong	lbw b Douglas	39
C.Kelleway	c Strudwick b Howell	9
C.E.Pellew	b Parkin	116
J.Ryder	c Woolley b Douglas	13
J.M.Gregory	c Russell b Woolley	100
†W.A.S.Oldfield	c & b Rhodes	24
A.A.Mailey	not out	8
Extras	(b1, lb3, w1, nb2)	7
Total	(137.3 overs, 452 mins)	499

ENGLAND

J.B.Hobbs	c Ryder b Gregory	122	b Kelleway	20
W.Rhodes	b Gregory	7	c Collins b Armstrong	28
J.W.H.Makepeace	lbw b Armstrong	4	c Gregory b Armstrong	4
E.H.Hendren	c Taylor b Gregory	67	c & b Collins	1
C.A.G.Russell	c Collins b Gregory	0	c Armstrong b Collins	5
F.E.Woolley	b Gregory	5	b Ryder	50
*J.W.H.T.Douglas	lbw b Gregory	15	b Gregory	9
C.H.Parkin	c Mailey b Gregory	4	c Taylor b Armstrong	9
†H.Strudwick	not out	21	c Oldfield b Armstrong	24
H.Howell	st Oldfield b Armstrong	5	not out	0
J.W.Hearne	absent ill	-	absent ill	-
Extras	(nb1)	1	(b3, lb3, nb1)	7
Total	(87.3 overs, 265 mins)	251	(67.2 overs, 204 mins)	157

ENGLAND	O	M	R	W	w,nb
Howell	37	5	142	3	-,-
Douglas	24	1	83	2	-,-
Parkin	27	0	116	2	1,-
Hearne	14	0	38	0	-,-
Woolley	27	8	87	2	-,2
Rhodes	8.3	1	26	1	-,-

AUSTRALIA	O	M	R	W	w,nb		O	M	R	W	w,nb
Kelleway	19	1	54	0	-,-		12	1	25	1	-,-
Gregory	20	1	69	7	-,-		12	0	32	1	-,-
Armstrong	24.3	8	50	2	-,-		15.2	5	26	4	-,-
Ryder	14	2	31	0	-,-	(5)	10	2	17	1	-,-
Park	1	0	9	0	-,-						
Collins	9	0	37	0	-,1	(4)	17	5	47	2	-,1
Pellew						(6)	1	0	3	0	-,-

	FALL OF WICKETS		
	AUST	ENG	ENG
Wkt	1st	1st	2nd
1st	116	20	36
2nd	116	32	53
3rd	118	174	54
4th	194	185	58
5th	220	201	70
6th	251	208	104
7th	282	213	141
8th	455	232	151
9th	469	251	157
10th	499	-	-

NEW SOUTH WALES v QUEENSLAND

Played at Sydney Cricket Ground on January 1, 3, 4 (no play), 1921. (Three-day match)
Toss : New South Wales.   Result : MATCH DRAWN.
Debuts: South Wales - E.E.B.Forssberg, H.S.B.Love, A.P.Wells (all f/c).
12th Men: A.E.Scanes (NSW) and G.S.L.Burns (Qld).
Umpires: R.Callaway and C.W.Waugh.
Attendances: 3500, 300, no play.   Total: About 3800.   Receipts: About £200.
Close of Play: 1st day NSW 506 all out; 2nd day Qld 3/156 (Thompson 21, Thomson 1).

New South Wales were forced to pick a new captain for this match following the murder of C.J.Tozer, who had been nominated for the job, on December 21st by a Mrs. Dorothy Mort (wife of H.S.Mort, a member of the family that founded Goldsborough-Mort - later Elders), Tozer had wanted to end their affair. At her trial Mrs. Mort, who had lain in Tozer's arms for several hours after shooting him in the head and chest, was found not guilty due to insanity. Prentice, brought into the team in Tozer's place and made captain, was dismissed first ball. New South Wales flayed 506 runs on the first day, including 189 after tea; the score raced from 400 to 500 in 35 minutes. Debutants Forssberg (143 in 147 minutes) and Love (91 in 123 minutes, 5 fours) added 201 in 123 minutes, a record ninth-wicket partnership in matches between these teams. Forssberg reached his hundred (his sole first-class hundred) in 116 minutes and gave two chances, the first at 55. O'Keeffe (83 in 116 minutes, 8 fours) and Trenerry (70 in 84 minutes, 6 fours) had earlier put on 115 for the sixth wicket, both making their highest scores for New South Wales in the process. Kay (fast-medium swingers) made early inroads and finished with 7 for 194, his best return in a three-match career and the best analysis by a Queenslander at Sydney until 1968-69. Rain restricted play on the second day to the pre-lunch session (two hours), Sheppard (80 in 102 minutes, 10 fours) batted fluently for the visitors. Further overnight rain prevented any further play, the match being called off at 1.45pm on the third day. Queensland then travelled to Bathurst to play a previously-arranged two-day match. Sources: *The Cricketer, NSWCA Report, Sydney Referee, Sydney Morning Herald, Sydney Daily Telegraph.*

NEW SOUTH WALES

†A.T.Ratcliffe	c Fennelly b Kay	27
O.P.Asher	b Kay	19
A.T.E.Punch	st Farquhar b Rowe	1
*W.S.Prentice	b Kay	0
F.A.O'Keeffe	c & b Kay	83
W.G.F.Brown	b Kay	17
W.L.Trenerry	st Farquhar b Rowe	70
A.P.Wells	b Kay	4
E.E.B.Forssberg	run out (Kay)	143
H.S.B.Love	c Rowe b Kay	91
W.F.Ives	not out	33
Extras	(b10, lb8)	18
Total	(96.0 overs, 320 mins)	506

QUEENSLAND

J.F.Sheppard	c & b Ives	80
*L.E.Oxenham	c Ives b Asher	20
G.S.Moore	c Ives b Forssberg	26
F.C.Thompson	not out	21
J.Thomson	not out	1
S.J.Fennelly	)	
W.Rowe	)	
P.M.Hornibrook	)	
†J.K.Farquhar	) did not bat	
J.W.McAndrew	)	
W.M.Kay	)	
Extras	(b5, lb2, nb1)	8
Total	(29.0 overs, 120 mins) (3 wkts)	156

QUEENSLAND	O	M	R	W	w,nb
McAndrew	21	1	84	0	-,-
Kay	33	1	194	7	-,-
Rowe	18	1	61	2	-,-
Hornibrook	17	0	92	0	-,-
Thompson	3	0	29	0	-,-
Oxenham	4	0	28	0	-,-

NEW SOUTH WALES	O	M	R	W	w,nb
Ives	10	1	40	1	-,1
Asher	9	0	60	1	-,-
Forssberg	7	0	33	1	-,-
Brown	3	0	15	0	-,-

FALL OF WICKETS

Wkt	NSW 1st	QLD 1st
1st	48	50
2nd	49	120
3rd	49	152
4th	49	-
5th	101	-
6th	216	-
7th	229	-
8th	232	-
9th	433	-
10th	506	-

SOUTH AUSTRALIA v NEW SOUTH WALES (Shield Match 5)

Played at Adelaide Oval on January 7, 8, 10, 11, 12, 1921. (Timeless match)
Toss : New South Wales.   Result : NEW SOUTH WALES WON BY 638 RUNS.
Debuts: Nil.
12th Men: G.W.Harris (SA) and W.A.S.Oldfield (NSW).
Umpires: A.H.Kruss and F.K.Lindow.
Attendances: 4713, 10064, 3155, 3417, 1406.   Total: 22,755.   Receipts: £1078.
Close of Play: 1st day SA 0/34 (C.E.Pellew 19, Smith 12); 2nd day NSW (2) 1/20 (Bardsley 12, Bogle 3); 3rd day NSW (2) 3/400
    (Bardsley 185, Andrews 17); 4th day SA (2) 0/13 (C.E.Pellew 3, Smith 7).

P.D.Rundell, C.L.Winser and A.W.Wright were all unavailable for South Australia. New South Wales rested A.A.Mailey and Oldfield because of the ensuing Test. Whitty injured his bowling hand on the first day and was restricted for the rest of the match; he did not attempt to bat. Taylor (61 in 93 minutes, 9 fours) and Gregory (130 in 152 minutes, 20 fours) for New South Wales and C.E.Pellew (91 in 162 minutes, 5 fours) for South Australia were the leading scorers in the first innings. The third-wicket stand of 345 in 252 minutes between Bardsley (235 in 383 minutes, 23 fours) and Taylor (180 in 252 minutes, 20 fours) on the third day was a new Australian record for that wicket. Hendry (65 in 91 minutes, 6 fours), Kelleway (103 not out in 143 minutes, 10 fours) and Carter (53 in 60 minutes, 8 fours) also contributed towards the highest second-innings total in all first-class cricket. Kelleway and Carter added 112 for the tenth wicket. *Wisden* incorrectly gives NSW (2) A.J.Richardson 1/168. *O'Reilly* incorrectly gives NSW (1) Waddy c Henry b Smith. Sources: *Wisden, C.B.O'Reilly, NSWCA Report, SACA Report, The Age, Adelaide Advertiser, South Australian Register.*

NEW SOUTH WALES

*H.L.Collins	c Ambler b Whitty	1		c Henry b A.J.Richardson	5
W.Bardsley	run out (Fisher)	12		c Steele b Smith	235
C.Kelleway	c Ambler b A.J.Richardson	16	(9)	not out	103
J.M.Taylor	st Ambler b Smith	61		c Fisher b C.E.Pellew	180
T.J.E.Andrews	c Fisher b Smith	9		c Steele b C.E.Pellew	44
J.M.Gregory	lbw b A.J.Richardson	130	(8)	c Steele b Willsmore	15
H.S.T.L.Hendry	lbw b Whitty	32	(6)	lbw b A.J.Richardson	65
J.Bogle	run out (C.E.Pellew/Whitty)	8	(3)	lbw b A.J.Richardson	8
A.F.Kippax	c Fisher b Smith	9	(7)	b Whitty	11
E.L.Waddy	c sub (G.W.Harris) b Smith	14		c Henry b Willsmore	44
†H.Carter	not out	0		c V.Y.Richardson b Willsmore	53
Extras	(b10, lb2)	12		(b5, lb2)	7
Total	(51.2 overs, 222 mins)	304		(137.0 overs, 560 mins)	770

SOUTH AUSTRALIA

C.E.Pellew	b Kelleway	91		b Collins	3
A.Smith	c & b Andrews	34		c Hendry b Kelleway	11
V.Y.Richardson	b Andrews	9		c Bogle b Collins	52
L.V.Pellew	c & b Andrews	33		c Gregory b Hendry	46
A.J.Richardson	c Taylor b Kelleway	42	(6)	c Kippax b Andrews	35
H.B.Willsmore	c Gregory b Collins	14	(7)	st Carter b Andrews	0
*D.M.Steele	b Hendry	20	(5)	b Kelleway	3
D.M.Henry	not out	7		c Collins b Andrews	5
†A.M.Ambler	b Andrews	1		st Carter b Andrews	7
H.M.Fisher	b Andrews	1		not out	5
W.J.Whitty	absent hurt	-		absent hurt	-
Extras	(b1, lb8, nb4)	13		(lb4)	4
Total	(66.0 overs, 260 mins)	265		(51.3 overs, 190 mins)	171

SOUTH AUSTRALIA	O	M	R	W	w,nb		O	M	R	W	w,nb			NSW	SA	NSW	SA
Fisher	7	0	57	0	-,-		11	0	75	0	-,-		Wkt	1st	1st	2nd	2nd
Whitty	12	2	47	2	-,-	(6)	24	2	146	1	-,-		1st	7	71	7	14
A.J.Richardson	17	2	88	2	-,-	(2)	35	4	168	3	-,-		2nd	13	83	25	21
Smith	10.2	0	71	4	-,-	(3)	23	0	167	1	-,-		3rd	39	172	370	115
C.E.Pellew	2	1	5	0	-,-		21	2	91	2	-,-		4th	56	176	458	115
Willsmore	3	0	24	0	-,-	(4)	20	0	105	3	-,-		5th	127	211	497	141
L.V.Pellew							3	0	11	0	-,-		6th	211	240	522	148
													7th	236	260	547	154
NEW SOUTH WALES	O	M	R	W	w,nb		O	M	R	W	w,nb		8th	271	263	584	159
Hendry	17	2	55	1	-,-		16	4	41	1	-,-		9th	300	265	658	171
Kelleway	17	2	67	2	-,-		11	3	23	2	-,-		10th	304	-	770	-
Andrews	20	0	89	5	-,2	(4)	12.3	0	67	4	-,-						
Collins	8	1	26	1	-,-	(3)	12	2	36	2	-,-						
Gregory	4	0	15	0	-,-												

FALL OF WICKETS

AUSTRALIA v ENGLAND (3rd Test)

Played at Adelaide Oval on January 14, 15, 17, 18, 19, 20, 1921. (Timeless match)
Toss : Australia.   Result : AUSTRALIA WON BY 119 RUNS.
Debuts: Australia - E.A.McDonald (Test). England - P.G.H.Fender (Test).
12th Men: R.L.Park (Aust) and J.W.Hitch (Eng).
Umpires: R.M.Crockett and D.A.Elder.
Attendances: 19170, 34487, 17649, 14607, 14232, 9559.   Total: 109,704.   Receipts: £6948.
Close of Play: 1st day Aust 7/313 (Ryder 36, Oldfield 22); 2nd day Eng 4/233 (Woolley 73, Russell 21); 3rd day Aust (2) 3/71
   (Kelleway 19); 4th day Aust (2) 5/364 (Kelleway 115, Pellew 26); 5th day Eng (2) 1/66 (Hobbs 50, Makepeace 11).

More runs (1753) were scored in this Test than any other in Australia until 1968-69. Collins (162 in 258 minutes, 20 fours, chances at 53 and 61) scored his second century in his third match for Australia. Kelleway's highest innings in Tests (147 in 417 minutes, 13 fours) included a sole chance, before he had scored, to Fender at third slip off Howell. With Armstrong (chanceless 121 in 206 minutes, 11 fours), Kelleway added 194 for the fourth wicket, and with Pellew (104 in 128 minutes, 13 fours, chance at 42) he put on 126 for the sixth wicket. Oldfield (50 in 76 minutes, 7 fours) and Gregory (78 not out in 112 minutes, 8 fours) scored half-centuries for Australia. Mailey was the first bowler to concede 300 runs in a Test match. England's scoring was led by Makepeace (60 in 108 minutes, 6 fours), Woolley (79 in 124 minutes, 1 six and 10 fours), Russell (135 not out in 250 minutes, 1 six and 10 fours, chances at 32 and 52) and Douglas (60 in 113 minutes, 7 fours) in the first innings and Hobbs (a chanceless 123 in 151 minutes, 13 fours), Hendren (51 in 106 minutes, 1 six and 2 fours) and Russell (59 in 107 minutes, 4 fours) in the second. This was the first time in an Australian-England series of five Tests that the fate of the Ashes had been decided as early as the Third Test. Sources: *Wisden, VCA Report, SACA Report, Adelaide Advertiser, South Australian Register.*

AUSTRALIA

H.L.Collins	c Rhodes b Parkin	162		c Hendren b Parkin	24
W.Bardsley	st Strudwick b Douglas	14		b Howell	16
C.Kelleway	c Fender b Parkin	4		b Howell	147
J.M.Taylor	run out (Hendren/Strudwick)	5	(6)	c Strudwick b Fender	38
*W.W.Armstrong	c Strudwick b Douglas	11		b Howell	121
C.E.Pellew	run out (Hobbs/Fender)	35	(7)	c Strudwick b Parkin	104
J.M.Gregory	c Strudwick b Fender	10	(8)	not out	78
J.Ryder	c Douglas b Parkin	44	(4)	c Woolley b Howell	3
†W.A.S.Oldfield	lbw b Parkin	50		b Rhodes	10
E.A.McDonald	b Parkin	2		b Rhodes	4
A.A.Mailey	not out	3		b Rhodes	13
Extras	(b6, lb8)	14		(b5, lb10, w4, nb5)	24
Total	(108.0 overs, 336 mins)	354		(185.5 overs, 560 mins)	582

ENGLAND

J.B.Hobbs	c & b Mailey	18		b Gregory	123
W.Rhodes	run out (McDonald)	16		lbw b McDonald	4
J.W.H.Makepeace	c Gregory b Armstrong	60		c & b McDonald	30
E.H.Hendren	b Gregory	36		b Mailey	51
F.E.Woolley	c Kelleway b Gregory	79		b Gregory	0
C.A.G.Russell	not out	135		b Mailey	59
*J.W.H.T.Douglas	lbw b Mailey	60		c Armstrong b Gregory	32
P.G.H.Fender	b McDonald	2		c Ryder b Mailey	42
C.H.Parkin	st Oldfield b Mailey	12		st Oldfield b Mailey	17
†H.Strudwick	c Pellew b Mailey	9		c Armstrong b Mailey	1
H.Howell	c Gregory b Mailey	2		not out	4
Extras	(b8, lb5, nb5)	18		(lb3, nb4)	7
Total	(132.1 overs, 398 mins)	447		(106.2 overs, 326 mins)	370

ENGLAND	O	M	R	W	w,nb		O	M	R	W	w,nb		FALL OF WICKETS			
Howell	26	1	89	0	-,-		34	6	115	4	4,4			AUST	ENG AUST	ENG
Douglas	24	6	69	2	-,-		19	2	61	0	-,1	Wkt	1st	1st 2nd	2nd
Parkin	20	2	60	5	-,-	(4)	40	8	109	2	-,-	1st	32	25 34	20
Woolley	21	6	47	0	-,-	(3)	38	4	91	0	-,-	2nd	45	49 63	125
Fender	12	0	52	1	-,-		22	0	105	1	-,-	3rd	55	111 71	183
Rhodes	5	1	23	0	-,-		25.5	8	61	3	-,-	4th	96	161 265	185
Hobbs							7	2	16	0	-,-	5th	176	250 328	243
												6th	209	374 454	292
AUSTRALIA	O	M	R	W	w,nb		O	M	R	W	w,nb	7th	285	391 477	308
McDonald	24	1	78	1	-,2		24	0	95	2	-,3	8th	347	416 511	321
Gregory	36	5	108	2	-,1	(6)	20	2	50	3	-,-	9th	349	437 570	341
Kelleway	11	4	25	0	-,2	(2)	8	2	16	0	-,1	10th	354	447 582	370
Mailey	32.1	3	160	5	-,-	(3)	29.2	3	142	5	-,-				
Armstrong	23	10	29	1	-,-	(4)	16	1	41	0	-,-				
Ryder	6	0	29	0	-,-	(5)	9	2	19	0	-,-				

NEW SOUTH WALES v VICTORIA (Shield Match 6)

Played at Sydney Cricket Ground on January 25, 26, 27, 28, 1921. (Timeless match)
Toss : Victoria.   Result : NEW SOUTH WALES WON BY SIX WICKETS.
Debuts: Nil.
12th Men: A.F.Kippax (NSW) and A.G.Moyes (Vic).
Umpires: W.G.Curran and A.C.Jones.
Attendances: 4339, 8282, 1063, 660.   Total: 14,344.   Receipts: £815.
Close of Play: 1st day NSW 3/170 (Collins 100, Andrews 40); 2nd day Vic (2) 2/56 (Sandford 31, Park 6); 3rd day Vic (2) 6/294
      (Ryder 117, Liddicut 9).

C.G.Macartney (ill), C.Kelleway and W.A.S.Oldfield (both unavailable) were replaced in the New south Wales side by O'Keeffe (originally 12th man), Ratcliffe and Trenerry. W.W.Armstrong withdrew from the Victorian eleven on the morning of the match because of bruising from the Third Test. Ryder led the Victorian batting with innings of 64 (134 minutes, 5 fours) and 135 (227 minutes, 1 six and 11 fours). Park recovered from his first-innings duck to score an even hundred in 185 minutes with 9 fours. Collins (146 in 206 minutes, 21 fours) and Andrews (90 in 183 minutes, 10 fours) swung the match with a fourth-wicket partnership of 172 for New South Wales. W.G.F.Brown substituted for Bardsley on the last day in the absence of Kippax. Sources: *Wisden, NSWCA Report, VCA Report, The Age, The Argus, Sydney Referee, Sydney Morning Herald.*

VICTORIA

*R.E.Mayne	b Gregory	19		b Gregory	8
R.L.Park	c Gregory b Trenerry	0	(4)	b Hendry	100
C.B.Willis	c Bardsley b Gregory	8	(5)	b Gregory	7
A.W.Lampard	b Gregory	4	(7)	c Gregory b Hendry	3
J.Ryder	b Forssberg	64	(6)	not out	135
A.E.Liddicut	b Gregory	12	(8)	c sub (W.G.F.Brown) b Hendry	26
J.L.Keating	st Ratcliffe b Mailey	20	(3)	b Mailey	11
H.C.A.Sandford	st Ratcliffe b Mailey	5	(2)	b Mailey	31
†J.L.Ellis	b Andrews	40		run out (Taylor/Ratcliffe)	1
E.A.McDonald	st Ratcliffe b Andrews	0		c Gregory b Mailey	0
H.Ironmonger	not out	0		c O'Keeffe b Mailey	0
Extras	(b2, lb2)	4		(b5, lb1, w1, nb2)	9
Total	(42.1 overs, 167 mins)	176		(73.6 overs, 280 mins)	331

NEW SOUTH WALES

*H.L.Collins	lbw b Liddicut	146	(4)	c Ellis b Ironmonger	0
J.M.Taylor	c Mayne b McDonald	21	(5)	not out	22
J.M.Gregory	b Liddicut	4			
W.Bardsley	c Ryder b Liddicut	0			
T.J.E.Andrews	lbw b Sandford	90			
H.S.T.L.Hendry	b Ironmonger	63		not out	3
F.A.O'Keeffe	b Ironmonger	2	(1)	b McDonald	26
E.E.B.Forssberg	c Liddicut b Ironmonger	21	(3)	c Ellis b McDonald	4
†A.T.Ratcliffe	not out	54	(2)	c sub (A.G.Moyes) b McDonald	19
A.A.Mailey	c Liddicut b McDonald	4			
E.Trenerry	b Liddicut	13			
Extras	(b9, lb2, w4)	15		(b1)	1
Total	(86.4 overs, 355 mins)	433		(21.3 overs, 85 mins) (4 wkts)	75

NEW SOUTH WALES	O	M	R	W	w,nb		O	M	R	W	w,nb
Gregory	13	0	61	4	-,-		11	0	56	2	-,-
Trennery	7	0	27	1	-,-		15	1	66	0	-,1
Mailey	11	1	37	2	-,-		17.6	0	86	4	-,1
Hendry	8	0	32	0	-,-		15	0	59	3	-,-
Andrews	3	0	15	2	-,-	(6)	1	0	13	0	-,-
Forssberg	0.1	0	0	1	-,-	(5)	6	0	20	0	-,-
Collins							5	2	18	0	1,-
O'Keeffe							3	1	4	0	-,-

VICTORIA	O	M	R	W	w,nb		O	M	R	W	w,nb
McDonald	22	1	95	2	-,-		11	1	49	3	-,-
Ironmonger	25	3	109	3	4,-		10.3	3	25	1	-,-
Liddicut	12.4	0	50	4	-,-						
Ryder	16	1	78	0	-,-						
Keating	5	0	44	0	-,-						
Sandford	6	0	42	1	-,-						

FALL OF WICKETS

Wkt	VIC 1st	NSW 1st	VIC 2nd	NSW 2nd
1st	4	63	8	33
2nd	23	68	43	37
3rd	30	74	56	38
4th	37	246	78	66
5th	53	318	265	-
6th	92	321	277	-
7th	98	354	325	-
8th	176	367	326	-
9th	176	376	331	-
10th	176	433	331	-

VICTORIA v M.C.C.

Played at Melbourne Cricket Ground on February 4, 5, 7, 8, 1921. (Timeless match)
Toss : Victoria.　　　　　　　Result : M.C.C. WON BY SEVEN WICKETS.
Debuts: Victoria - G.A.Davies, W.H.Ponsford (both f/c).
12th Men: W.J.G.Woodbury (Vic) and A.Waddington (MCC).
Umpires: R.M.Crockett and A.D.Reaburn.
Attendances: 7354, 15775, 5745, 2006.　　　Total: 30,880.　　　Receipts: £1687.
Close of Play: 1st day MCC 1/17 (Rhodes 5); 2nd day MCC 5/445 (Hendren 262, Douglas 112); 3rd day Vic (2) 5/217 (Ryder 69, Keating 1).

W.W.Armstrong was omitted by the Victorian selectors as a disciplinary measure for standing down from the interstate match in Sydney. The V.C.A. later vindicated Armstrong after hearing evidence from R.E.Mayne and Dr. R.L.Park on the bruising he suffered while batting in the Third Test. A mid-afternoon protest outside the ground by Armstrong's supporters attracted about 8000 spectators of the second-day crowd. Due to medical duties A.E.V.Hartkopf was replaced by Davies, originally named as 12th man. Hitch strained his back while bowling in the first innings and took no further part in the match. Hendren (271 in 271 minutes, 3 sixes and 31 fours) and Douglas (133 not out in 225 minutes, 14 fours) added 323 in 210 minutes for M.C.C., their sixth-wicket partnership accounting for 66.5 per cent of the total. Hendren went from 63 at lunch to 144 at tea and 262 at stumps on the second day. Ryder (54 in 104 minutes, 1 five and 6 fours) and Davies (61 in 87 minutes, 8 fours) scored first-innings fifties for Victoria, Sandford (72 in 67 minutes, 1 six and 9 fours) and Ryder (108 in 223 minutes, 6 fours) topscoring in the second. Sources: *Wisden, VCA Report, The Age, The Argus, The Herald, The Australasian.*

VICTORIA

*R.E.Mayne	b Hitch	27	(2)	b Parkin	33
H.C.A.Sandford	b Hitch	3	(1)	b Parkin	72
R.L.Park	c Hendren b Douglas	2	(4)	c Fender b Woolley	1
J.Ryder	c & b Woolley	54	(3)	c Hobbs b Parkin	108
W.H.Ponsford	c Parkin b Woolley	6	(6)	st Dolphin b Fender	19
J.L.Keating	c Douglas b Hitch	15	(7)	lbw b Rhodes	28
L.D.Ferguson	c Dolphin b Hitch	6	(8)	run out (Hobbs/Dolphin)	2
G.A.Davies	c Dolphin b Douglas	61	(5)	c Hobbs b Wilson	20
†J.L.Ellis	st Dolphin b Parkin	8		b Rhodes	0
C.V.Grimmett	not out	31		not out	3
E.A.McDonald	b Rhodes	42		c sub (A.Waddington) b Parkin	6
Extras	(b4, lb8, nb1)	13		(nb3)	3
Total	(76.4 overs, 243 mins)	268		(113.2 overs, 308 mins)	295

M.C.C.

J.B.Hobbs	c Ellis b Ryder	12		not out	26
W.Rhodes	lbw b McDonald	15		c Ellis b McDonald	5
J.W.H.Makepeace	c Ryder b McDonald	3		c Ellis b McDonald	11
E.H.Hendren	c Park b McDonald	271		b McDonald	24
F.E.Woolley	b Ryder	20		not out	9
P.G.H.Fender	c Ryder b McDonald	10			
*J.W.H.T.Douglas	not out	133			
E.R.Wilson	c Ellis b McDonald	0			
†A.Dolphin	b McDonald	2			
C.H.Parkin	lbw b Grimmett	8			
J.W.Hitch	absent hurt	-			
Extras	(b5, lb5, nb2)	12		(b2, nb1)	3
Total	(115.3 overs, 355 mins)	486		(17.0 overs, 62 mins) (3 wkts)	78

M.C.C.	O	M	R	W	w,nb		O	M	R	W	w,nb
Hitch	15	3	28	4	-,-						
Douglas	19	2	58	2	-,-		12	1	38	0	-,-
Parkin	13	0	59	1	-,-	(6)	26.2	4	76	4	-,-
Woolley	17	2	57	2	-,1	(3)	26	8	63	1	-,2
Rhodes	3.4	0	19	1	-,-	(7)	12	4	20	2	-,-
Wilson	9	0	34	0	-,-	(5)	23	8	33	1	-,-
Hobbs						(1)	3	1	11	0	-,-
Fender						(4)	11	0	51	1	-,1

VICTORIA	O	M	R	W	w,nb		O	M	R	W	w,nb
McDonald	41	4	145	6	-,2		9	0	32	3	-,1
Ryder	29	6	94	2	-,-		5	0	30	0	-,-
Grimmett	19.3	0	104	1	-,-		1	0	6	0	-,-
Keating	12	0	38	0	-,-		2	0	7	0	-,-
Park	3	0	19	0	-,-						
Sandford	4	1	31	0	-,-						
Davies	3	0	17	0	-,-						
Mayne	4	0	26	0	-,-						

FALL OF WICKETS

Wkt	VIC 1st	MCC 1st	VIC 2nd	MCC 2nd
1st	13	17	101	13
2nd	26	28	108	25
3rd	38	69	111	66
4th	59	114	171	-
5th	92	132	216	-
6th	106	455	282	-
7th	136	455	286	-
8th	150	457	286	-
9th	213	486	286	-
10th	268	-	295	-

AUSTRALIA v ENGLAND (4th Test)

Played at Melbourne Cricket Ground on February 11, 12, 14, 15, 16, 1921. (Timeless match)
Toss : England.   Result : AUSTRALIA WON BY EIGHT WICKETS.
Debuts: England - A.Dolphin (Test).
12th Men: T.J.E.Andrews (Aust) and H.Strudwick (Eng).
Umpires: R.M.Crockett and D.A.Elder.
Attendances: 18138, 31979, 20384, 12785, 4882.   Total: 88,168.   Receipts: £7583.
Close of Play: 1st day Eng 6/270 (Douglas 50); 2nd day Aust 5/267 (Gregory 67, Armstrong 54); 3rd day Eng (2) 1/123 (Rhodes 66,
    Makepeace 40); 4th day Aust (2) 2/92 (Ryder 12, Gregory 6).

England were unable to consider J.W.Hearne (ill), J.W.Hitch (strained side) and C.A.G.Russell (badly bruised thumb), while Australia were still without C.G.Macartney (ill). Makepeace (a chanceless 117 in 260 minutes, 4 fours) and Douglas (50 in 140 minutes, 4 fours) added 106 for England's fifth wicket late on the first day. Australia's first-innings lead was solely due to two partnerships, Collins (59 in 105 minutes, 5 fours) and Bardsley (56 in 87 minutes, 1 four) putting on 117 at the start, and Gregory (77 in 162 minutes, 8 fours) and Armstrong (chanceless 123 not out in 214 minutes, 9 fours) adding 145 for the sixth wicket. Armstrong scored his third century of the series despite an attack of malaria, which rendered him incapable of taking any further part, Collins deputising as captain for the rest of the game. Half-centuries in England's second innings by Rhodes (73 in 185 minutes, 4 fours), Makepeace (54 in 149 minutes, 2 fours), Douglas (60 in 134 minutes, 3 fours) and Fender (59 in 88 minutes, 1 six and 2 fours) produced a target which was easily overcome by Ryder (52 not out in 114 minutes, 5 fours) and Gregory (76 not out in 103 minutes, 10 fours), who added an unfinished 130 to win the match. Mailey was the first Australian to take nine wickets in a Test innings. Sources: *Wisden, VCA Report, The Age, The Argus, The Herald, The Australasian, Sydney Morning Herald.*

ENGLAND

J.B.Hobbs	c Carter b McDonald	27		lbw b Mailey	13
W.Rhodes	c Carter b Gregory	11		c Gregory b Mailey	73
J.W.H.Makepeace	c Collins b Mailey	117		lbw b Mailey	54
E.H.Hendren	c Carter b Mailey	30		b Kelleway	32
F.E.Woolley	lbw b Kelleway	29		st Carter b Mailey	0
*J.W.H.T.Douglas	c & b Mailey	50		st Carter b Mailey	60
A.Waddington	b Mailey	0	(8)	st Carter b Mailey	6
P.G.H.Fender	c Gregory b Kelleway	3	(7)	c Collins b Mailey	59
†A.Dolphin	b Kelleway	1		c Gregory b Mailey	0
C.H.Parkin	run out (Pellew)	10		c Bardsley b Mailey	4
H.Howell	not out	0		not out	0
Extras	(b1, lb5)	6		(b5, lb5, w1, nb3)	14
Total	(99.2 overs, 308 mins)	284		(117.0 overs, 341 mins)	315

AUSTRALIA

H.L.Collins	c Rhodes b Woolley	59		c Rhodes b Parkin	32
W.Bardsley	b Fender	56		run out (Hendren/Dolphin)	38
J.Ryder	lbw b Woolley	7		not out	52
J.M.Taylor	hit wkt b Fender	2			
J.M.Gregory	c Dolphin b Parkin	77	(4)	not out	76
C.E.Pellew	b Fender	12			
*W.W.Armstrong	not out	123			
C.Kelleway	b Fender	27			
†H.Carter	b Fender	0			
A.A.Mailey	run out (Fender/Woolley)	13			
E.A.McDonald	b Woolley	0			
Extras	(b1, lb6, w1, nb5)	13		(b5, lb5, w2, nb1)	13
Total	(112.1 overs, 348 mins)	389		(64.2 overs, 175 mins) (2 wkts)	211

AUSTRALIA	O	M	R	W	w,nb		O	M	R	W	w,nb
McDonald	19	2	46	1	-,-	(2)	23	2	77	0	-,1
Gregory	18	1	61	1	-,-	(1)	14	4	31	0	1,-
Mailey	29.2	1	115	4	-,-		47	8	121	9	-,-
Ryder	10	5	10	0	-,-	(5)	10	3	25	0	-,-
Armstrong	5	1	9	0	-,-						
Kelleway	18	2	37	3	-,-	(4)	23	8	47	1	-,2

ENGLAND	O	M	R	W	w,nb		O	M	R	W	w,nb
Howell	17	2	86	0	1,1		10	1	36	0	2,-
Douglas	4	0	17	0	-,-		5	1	13	0	-,-
Waddington	5	0	31	0	-,-						
Parkin	22	5	64	1	-,-		12	2	46	1	-,-
Fender	32	3	122	5	-,3		13.2	2	39	0	-,1
Woolley	32.1	14	56	3	-,1	(3)	14	4	39	0	-,-
Rhodes						(6)	10	2	25	0	-,-

FALL OF WICKETS				
	ENG	AUST	ENG	AUST
Wkt	1st	1st	2nd	2nd
1st	18	117	32	71
2nd	61	123	145	81
3rd	104	128	152	-
4th	164	133	152	-
5th	270	153	201	-
6th	270	298	305	-
7th	273	335	307	-
8th	274	335	307	-
9th	275	376	315	-
10th	284	389	315	-

NEW SOUTH WALES v M.C.C.

Played at Sydney Cricket Ground on February 18, 19, 21, 22, 1921. (Four-day match)
Toss : M.C.C.   Result : MATCH DRAWN.
Debuts: Nil.
12th Men: W.G.F.Brown (NSW) and A.Dolphin (MCC).
Umpires: W.G.Curran and A.C.Jones.
Attendances: 8933, 17370, 8815, 6180.   Total: 41,298.   Receipts: £2730.
Close of Play: 1st day MCC 6/402 (Fender 58, Wilson 4); 2nd day NSW 5/268 (Taylor 10); 3rd day MCC (2) 3/220 (Woolley 130, Douglas 4).

Quickfire centuries by Hendren (102 in 101 minutes, 1 six and 9 fours) and Woolley (138 in 138 minutes, 1 six and 13 fours, chances at 0 and 64) were not enough for the Englishmen to beat the star-studded New South Wales side in the time given. The home team would have been even stronger had not C.Kelleway withdrawn, his place going to Folkard at the last moment. Douglas complemented his 128 runs (once out) with a hat-trick: he dismissed Hendry (26th over) and Oldfield and Mailey (27th over) to finish the New South Wales first innings. Macartney (130 in 225 minutes, 7 fours) and Taylor (107 not out in 171 minutes, 7 fours) scored hundreds for New South Wales. Hobbs took no further part after tearing a leg muscle while fielding on the second day. Waddington bowled Folkard in the opening over of the second innings and Macartney soon afterwards to give the tourists a glimmer of hope, but an unbroken stand of 140 in 83 minutes between Hendry and Punch left honours even. *SMH* incorrectly gives MCC (2) Waddington c Hendry. Sources: *Wisden, NSWCA Report, VCA Report, The Age, Sydney Referee, Sydney Morning Herald.*

M.C.C.

J.B.Hobbs	c Collins b Mailey	41		absent hurt	-
W.Rhodes	c Oldfield b Mailey	50		c Mailey b Hendry	17
J.W.H.Makepeace	c Oldfield b Mailey	73		c Punch b Gregory	0
E.H.Hendren	b Mailey	102		c Oldfield b Gregory	66
F.E.Woolley	c Gregory b Punch	20	(1)	b Hendry	138
P.G.H.Fender	lbw b Mailey	60		c Hendry b Mailey	27
*J.W.H.T.Douglas	c Folkard b Andrews	46	(5)	not out	82
E.R.Wilson	b Hendry	9		c Bardsley b Andrews	30
A.Waddington	not out	12	(7)	c Andrews b Mailey	3
†H.Strudwick	c Gregory b Mailey	4	(9)	c Taylor b Andrews	4
C.H.Parkin	c Hendry b Mailey	1	(10)	st Oldfield b Andrews	2
Extras	(b7, lb1, nb1)	9		(b4, lb8)	12
Total	(126.0 overs, 334 mins)	427		(113.1 overs, 320 mins)	381

NEW SOUTH WALES

*H.L.Collins	b Douglas	2			
W.Bardsley	c Woolley b Douglas	4			
C.G.Macartney	b Douglas	130	(2)	b Waddington	6
J.M.Gregory	c Strudwick b Wilson	52			
T.J.E.Andrews	c Strudwick b Douglas	54			
J.M.Taylor	not out	107			
A.T.E.Punch	c sub (A.Dolphin) b Fender	59	(4)	not out	63
B.J.Folkard	c Strudwick b Parkin	9	(1)	b Waddington	0
H.S.T.L.Hendry	c Strudwick b Douglas	5	(3)	not out	66
†W.A.S.Oldfield	b Douglas	0			
A.A.Mailey	b Douglas	0			
Extras	(b13, lb11, w1)	25		(b10, lb4, nb2)	16
Total	(129.2 overs, 369 mins)	447		(34.0 overs, 90 mins) (2 wkts)	151

NEW SOUTH WALES	O	M	R	W	w,nb		O	M	R	W	w,nb
Hendry	27	5	63	1	-,-	(2)	15	3	50	2	-,-
Folkard	12	0	53	0	-,-	(4)	12	3	29	0	-,-
Mailey	45	3	172	7	-,-		32	2	122	2	-,-
Macartney	17	3	43	0	-,1	(5)	9	1	25	0	-,-
Andrews	11	0	50	1	-,-	(6)	9.1	0	44	3	-,-
Collins	5	1	9	0	-,-	(7)	6	1	12	0	-,-
Punch	9	2	28	1	-,-	(8)	8	2	18	0	-,-
Gregory						(1)	22	4	69	2	-,-

SOUTH AUSTRALIA	O	M	R	W	w,nb		O	M	R	W	w,nb
Douglas	26.2	3	98	7	1,-						
Waddington	8	1	31	0	-,-	(1)	10	1	30	2	-,1
Woolley	21	4	47	0	-,-						
Parkin	32	5	105	1	-,-	(2)	6	1	31	0	-,-
Wilson	24	8	47	1	-,-		1	0	1	0	-,-
Fender	15	1	73	1	-,-	(3)	10	0	50	0	-,1
Rhodes	3	0	21	0	-,-	(4)	7	1	23	0	-,-

FALL OF WICKETS

Wkt	MCC 1st	NSW 1st	MCC 2nd	NSW 2nd
1st	89	6	28	2
2nd	104	11	29	11
3rd	253	105	211	-
4th	292	243	238	-
5th	298	268	272	-
6th	382	381	296	-
7th	404	420	365	-
8th	410	445	369	-
9th	423	447	381	-
10th	427	447	-	-

QUEENSLAND v NEW SOUTH WALES

Played at Brisbane Cricket Ground (Woolloongabba) on February 19, 21, 22, 1921. (Three-day match)
Toss : New South Wales.   Result : NEW SOUTH WALES WON BY 102 RUNS.
Debuts: New South Wales - R.Bardsley, E.K.Brown, R.E.Gostelow, B.L.McCoy, B.L.Russell, A.N.Thatcher (all f/c).
12th Men: C.R.H.MacDonnell (Qld) and A.R.Rowe (NSW).
Umpires: W.H.Carvosso and G.Casperson.
Attendances & Receipts: No figures published.
Close of Play: 1st day Qld 5/57 (Rowe 4); 2nd day NSW (2) 268 all out.

O'Connor (originally 12th man) replaced J.Thomson (unavailable) in the Queensland side named for this match. Bardsley on debut (70 in 119 minutes, 5 fours) and O'Keeffe (72 in 92 minutes, 6 fours) registered half-centuries for New South Wales. Wells (6) retired hurt at 3/31 in the first innings and resumed at 5/137. Oxenham (66 in 120 minutes, 4 fours) was the only Queenslander to exceed 50. Ayres became the first bowler to twice take seven wickets in an innings for Queensland (also 7 for 83 v NSW 1919-20), a feat not repeated for the State until 1945-46 by C.L.McCool. *The Courier* reported that the wicket-keeping of Gostelow compared unfavourably with the sharp, sure work of his counterpart, Farquhar. Gostelow twice failed to stump Sheppard early in the second innings and was replaced by Love for the remainder of the match. *Cricketer, NSWCA Report, VCA Report* and *SMH* all incorrectly give NSW (2) Ives b Ayres, Randell c & b Ayres. In addition, *NSWCA Report* incorrectly gives Qld (1) Kay c & b Ives, *VCA Report* Kay b Ives. *Cricketer* and *VCA Report* both incorrectly give NSW (2) Brown (instead of O'Keeffe) 1 maiden. Sources: *The Cricketer, NSWCA Report, VCA Report, Sydney Morning Herald, Brisbane Courier, Brisbane Daily Mail.*

NEW SOUTH WALES

B.L.McCoy	b Kay	4		c Oxenham b Ayres	16
H.S.B.Love	run out (Marsden/Kay)	17		lbw b Marsden	34
F.A.O'Keeffe	c Farquhar b McAndrew	4		lbw b Kay	72
A.P.Wells	b Kay	6	(10)	c Sheppard b Ayres	3
E.K.Brown	st Farquhar b Marsden	15		b Ayres	25
R.Bardsley	c Marsden b Rowe	70	(4)	b Kay	27
W.F.Ives	b Kay	20	(6)	st Farquhar b Ayres	38
†R.E.Gostelow	c Farquhar b Marsden	28	(7)	st Farquhar b Ayres	9
A.N.Thatcher	c Farquhar b Kay	2	(8)	not out	31
B.L.Russell	b Kay	25	(9)	b Ayres	0
*J.A.Randell	not out	1		st Farquhar b Ayres	3
Extras	(b9, lb1)	10		(b3, lb7)	10
Total	(62.0 overs, 208 mins)	202		(56.4 overs, 193 mins)	268

QUEENSLAND

J.F.Sheppard	b Russell	8		lbw b Ives	40
*L.E.Oxenham	b Russell	13		lbw b Randell	66
S.J.Fennelly	c Ives b Randell	15		b Russell	22
G.S.Moore	b Russell	4		c Love b Randell	0
†J.K.Farquhar	b Russell	10	(6)	b Ives	3
W.Rowe	b Randell	14	(7)	lbw b Ives	6
L.P.D.O'Connor	c Gostelow b Ives	39	(5)	c Bardsley b Randell	19
S.W.Ayres	c Brown b Ives	19		lbw b Ives	0
J.W.McAndrew	not out	36		b Randell	13
A.J.Marsden	b Thatcher	2		not out	8
W.M.Kay	c O'Keeffe b Ives	7		st Love b Randell	3
Extras	(b7, lb3, nb2)	12		(b2, lb5, nb2)	9
Total	(39.0 overs, 143 mins)	179		(51.0 overs, 185 mins)	189

QUEENSLAND	O	M	R	W	w,nb		O	M	R	W	w,nb		FALL OF WICKETS			
														NSW	QLD	NSW	QLD
McAndrew	19	2	51	1	-,-	(3)	8	0	46	0	-,-	Wkt	1st	1st	2nd	2nd
Kay	23	2	79	5	-,-	(1)	19	0	77	2	-,-	1st	7	10	25	68
Marsden	12	1	42	2	-,-	(4)	6	1	30	1	-,-	2nd	12	31	86	116
Rowe	8	1	20	1	-,-	(5)	4	1	17	0	-,-	3rd	31	41	152	119
Ayres						(2)	19.4	1	88	7	-,-	4th	89	46	155	143
												5th	137	57	205	146
NEW SOUTH WALES	O	M	R	W	w,nb		O	M	R	W	w,nb	6th	139	77	219	156
Russell	13	2	59	4	-,2		12	1	28	1	-,1	7th	143	112	232	156
Randell	13	1	45	2	-,-		23	1	97	5	-,-	8th	146	153	234	174
Ives	9	0	41	3	-,-		13	2	43	4	-,1	9th	190	156	246	184
Thatcher	4	1	22	1	-,-		2	0	12	0	-,-	10th	202	179	268	189
O'Keeffe							1	1	0	0	-,-					

AUSTRALIA v ENGLAND (5th Test)

Played at Sydney Cricket Ground on February 25, 26, 28, March 1, 1921. (Timeless match)
Toss : England.   Result : AUSTRALIA WON BY NINE WICKETS.
Debuts: England - E.R.Wilson (Test).
12th Men: T.J.E.Andrews (Aust) and A.Waddington (Eng).
Umpires: R.M.Crockett and D.A.Elder.
Attendances: 16586, 32820, 12654, 1361.   Total: 63,421.   Receipts: £5610.
Close of Play: 1st day Aust 2/70 (Macartney 31, Taylor 22); 2nd day Eng (2) 2/24 (Rhodes 10, Wilson 4); 3rd day Aust (2) 0/25
    (Collins 7, Bardsley 17).

Macartney returned to the Australian side after a break through illness to compile his highest Test score, a chanceless 170 in 244 minutes with 20 fours. He added 198 for the fourth wicket with Gregory (93 in 133 minutes, 8 fours) to put Australia ahead with seven wickets in hand. Among those who saw this partnership on the second day were Bowral residents George Bradman and his 12-year-old son Donald, who was inspired by his first glimpse of first-class cricket. England had again been unable to consider J.W.Hearne and J.W.Hitch due to illness and injury, Howell (muscle strain) also being unavailable. Hobbs (thigh) and Russell (thumb) carried injuries into the match. Woolley (53 in 60 minutes, 7 fours) and Douglas (68 in 167 minutes, 1 five and 6 fours) scored half-centuries for the tourists. Bardsley (50 not out in 101 minutes, 4 fours) knocked off most of the required runs for Australia, who gained the first 5-0 result in a Test series. Gregory was the first fielder to take 15 catches in a Test series while Mailey's 36 wickets fell just one short of the record in a series in Australia to this time. Sources: *Wisden, VCA Report, The Herald, The Australasian, Sydney Referee, Sydney Morning Herald.*

ENGLAND

J.B.Hobbs	lbw b Gregory	40	(5) c Taylor b Mailey	34
W.Rhodes	c Carter b Kelleway	26	run out (Mailey)	25
J.W.H.Makepeace	c Gregory b Mailey	3	c Gregory b Kelleway	7
E.H.Hendren	c Carter b Gregory	5	(6) st Carter b Mailey	13
F.E.Woolley	b McDonald	53	(1) c & b Kelleway	1
C.A.G.Russell	c Gregory b Mailey	19	(8) c Gregory b Armstrong	35
*J.W.H.T.Douglas	not out	32	c & b Mailey	68
P.G.H.Fender	c Gregory b Kelleway	2	(9) c Kelleway b McDonald	40
E.R.Wilson	c Carter b Kelleway	5	(4) st Carter b Mailey	5
C.H.Parkin	c Taylor b Kelleway	9	c Gregory b Mailey	36
†H.Strudwick	b Gregory	2	not out	5
Extras	(b3, lb2, w1, nb2)	8	(b3, lb5, nb3)	11
Total	(70.1 overs, 206 mins)	204	(101.2 overs, 287 mins)	280

AUSTRALIA

H.L.Collins	c Fender b Parkin	5	c Strudwick b Wilson	37
W.Bardsley	c Fender b Douglas	7	not out	50
C.G.Macartney	c Hobbs b Fender	170	not out	2
J.M.Taylor	c Hendren b Douglas	32		
J.M.Gregory	c Strudwick b Fender	93		
*W.W.Armstrong	c Woolley b Fender	0		
J.Ryder	b Fender	2		
C.Kelleway	c Strudwick b Wilson	32		
†H.Carter	c Woolley b Fender	17		
A.A.Mailey	b Wilson	5		
E.A.McDonald	not out	3		
Extras	(b18, lb6, nb2)	26	(b3, nb1)	4
Total	(91.3 overs, 289 mins)	392	(34.2 overs, 101 mins) (1 wkt)	93

AUSTRALIA	O	M	R	W	w,nb		O	M	R	W	w,nb
Gregory	16.1	4	42	3	-,-	(4)	16	3	37	0	-,-
McDonald	11	2	38	1	1,1	(1)	25	3	58	1	-,-
Kelleway	20	6	27	4	-,1	(2)	14	3	29	2	-,3
Mailey	23	1	89	2	-,-	(3)	36.2	5	119	5	-,-
Ryder							2	2	0	0	-,-
Armstrong							8	1	26	1	-,-

ENGLAND	O	M	R	W	w,nb		O	M	R	W	w,nb
Douglas	16	0	84	2	-,-						
Parkin	19	1	83	1	-,-	(1)	9	1	32	0	-,-
Woolley	15	1	58	0	-,1	(2)	11	3	27	0	-,-
Wilson	14.3	4	28	2	-,-	(5)	6	1	8	1	-,-
Fender	20	1	90	5	-,1	(3)	1	0	2	0	-,1
Rhodes	7	0	23	0	-,-	(4)	7.2	1	20	0	-,-

FALL OF WICKETS				
	ENG	AUST	ENG	AUST
Wkt	1st	1st	2nd	2nd
1st	54	16	1	91
2nd	70	22	14	-
3rd	74	89	29	-
4th	76	287	75	-
5th	125	287	82	-
6th	161	313	91	-
7th	164	356	160	-
8th	172	384	224	-
9th	201	384	251	-
10th	204	392	280	-

SOUTH AUSTRALIA v M.C.C.

Played at Adelaide Oval on March 11, 12, 14, 15, 1921. (Four-day match)
Toss : South Australia.   Result : M.C.C. WON BY AN INNINGS AND 63 RUNS.
Debuts: South Australia - G.W.Harris, E.A.Loveridge, R.Moroney, L.J.Power (all f/c).
12th Men: D.G.McKenzie (SA) and J.W.Hitch (MCC).
Umpires: G.A.Hele and S.W.Smith.
Attendances: 4499, 5540, 1974, 915.   Total: 12,928.   Receipts: £514.
Close of Play: 1st day MCC 1/128 (Rhodes 70, Russell 35); 2nd day MCC 5/540 (Douglas 58, Woolley 27); 3rd day SA (2) 4/253
     (Rundell 119, Murray 11).

South Australia were well below full strength due to the absence of L.V.Pellew and V.Y.Richardson (both in New Zealand), C.E.Pellew (personal affairs), D.M.Steele (medical duties) and H.B.Willsmore and A.W.Wright (both unavailable). Rhodes (210 in 315 minutes, 17 fours) and Russell (201 in 260 minutes, 23 fours) shared a second-wicket stand of 368 in 260 minutes for M.C.C., still the highest partnership for that wicket by an English team in Australia. An unbeaten 106 by Douglas occupied 185 minutes and included 11 fours. McKenzie, son of former South Australia player J.McKenzie, caught Hobbs while substituting for Richardson (ricked back) late on the first day. Harris on debut made 40 (82 minutes, 3 fours) and 84 (152 minutes, 7 fours). Aided by a dashing innings from Rundell (121 in 97 minutes, 15 fours) he added 143 for the third wicket. Fender captured 12 for 184 with his leg breaks. Sources: *Wisden, C.B.O'Reilly, VCA Report, SACA Report, Adelaide Advertiser, South Australian Register.*

SOUTH AUSTRALIA

*A.Smith	c Howell b Parkin	45		b Howell	8
G.W.Harris	b Fender	40		b Fender	84
L.J.Power	c Dolphin b Fender	7	(7)	lbw b Woolley	44
P.D.Rundell	b Parkin	20		lbw b Waddington	121
A.J.Richardson	run out (Rhodes/Fender)	46	(3)	st Dolphin b Fender	19
G.E.Jose	c Russell b Fender	16	(5)	lbw b Woolley	2
J.T.Murray	c & b Fender	4	(6)	b Fender	20
E.A.Loveridge	c Douglas b Fender	3		st Dolphin b Fender	38
R.Moroney	b Fender	1		c Dolphin b Fender	9
N.L.Williams	b Fender	8		run out	1
†A.M.Ambler	not out	3		not out	0
Extras	(b1, nb1)	2		(b18, lb2, w1, nb2)	23
Total	(62.3 overs, 192 mins)	195		(114.1 overs, 313 mins)	369

M.C.C.

J.B.Hobbs	c sub (D.G.McKenzie) b Williams	18
W.Rhodes	st Ambler b Smith	210
C.A.G.Russell	b Murray	201
A.Waddington	c Ambler b Loveridge	0
*J.W.H.T.Douglas	not out	106
P.G.H.Fender	c Murray b Smith	17
F.E.Woolley	c & b Richardson	36
E.R.Wilson	run out (Ambler)	11
C.H.Parkin	c & b Loveridge	12
†A.Dolphin	c & b Loveridge	0
H.Howell	b Loveridge	6
Extras	(b5, lb4, w1)	10
Total	(169.2 overs, 391 mins)	627

M.C.C.	O	M	R	W	w,nb		O	M	R	W	w,nb
Howell	5	2	10	0	-,-		16	2	56	1	-,-
Waddington	8	2	17	0	-,-		17	4	41	1	-,2
Douglas	4	0	11	0	,-						
Fender	24.3	4	75	7	-,-		30.1	3	109	5	-,-
Parkin	15	3	63	2	-,1	(3)	19	2	76	0	-,-
Wilson	6	1	17	0	-,-						
Rhodes						(5)	9	3	24	0	-,-
Woolley						(6)	23	6	40	2	1,-

SOUTH AUSTRALIA	O	M	R	W	w,nb
Moroney	28	4	68	0	1,-
Murray	15	0	51	1	-,-
Williams	26	1	108	1	-,-
Loveridge	26.2	4	102	4	-,-
Smith	31	0	119	2	-,-
Rundell	7	0	44	0	-,-
Richardson	33	2	110	1	-,-
Jose	3	0	15	0	-,-

FALL OF WICKETS

Wkt	SA 1st	MCC 1st	SA 2nd
1st	73	29	19
2nd	94	397	57
3rd	100	398	200
4th	116	456	217
5th	137	482	264
6th	165	565	264
7th	169	588	354
8th	171	615	368
9th	191	615	369
10th	195	627	369

WESTERN AUSTRALIA v AUSTRALIAN XI

Played at W.A.C.A. Ground, Perth, on March 19, 21, 22 (no play), 1921. (Three-day match)
Toss : Australian XI.   Result : MATCH DRAWN.
Debuts: Western Australian - F.R.Buttsworth, E.N.Healy, A.B.Meek (all f/c); C.H.Robinson (WA only).
12th Men: V.C.Carlson (WA). H.S.T.L.Hendry and R.E.Mayne were reserves for Australian XI.
Umpires: A.P.Collis and A.E.Lawrence.
Attendances: 10000, 2000, 100.   Total: About 12,100.   Receipts: £1023.
Close of Play: 1st day WA 2/16 (Howard 7); 2nd day WA 9/88 (Meek 12, Buttsworth 5).

The Australians, fresh from a 5-0 win over England, were the first team to visit Western Australia by train, the trans-continental railway having been completed in 1917. Evans, originally named 12th man for Western Australia, replaced L.Packham who took ill before the match. Robinson had previously represented Tasmania in first-class cricket. Ryder's chanceless century in 135 minutes included 11 fours, while Taylor and Gregory each hit 2 sixes and 5 fours to compile their half-centuries in even time. Rain early on the second day made batting difficult and a severe storm soon after the luncheon adjournment washed out play for the day and prevented any play at all on the third day. The attendance and takings of £800 on the first day were easily a record for the ground. At 4.00pm on the third day the Australians joined the M.C.C. tourists on board the *R.M.S.Osterley* for the journey to England. Contrary to the statement in *Wisden 1922*, p 639, this match is first-class. Sources: *Wisden, Adelaide Advertiser, The West Australian, Daily News.*

AUSTRALIAN XI

H.L.Collins	b Robinson	67
W.Bardsley	b Buttsworth	7
T.J.E.Andrews	c Evers b Bank	54
J.Ryder	st Evers b Robinson	102
C.G.Macartney	c & b Buttsworth	30
*W.W.Armstrong	c Rowe b Buttsworth	18
J.M.Taylor	b Banks	52
J.M.Gregory	b Christian	50
†W.A.S.Oldfield	not out	9
A.A.Mailey	b Christian	1
E.A.McDonald	b Banks	0
Extras	(b2, lb4)	6
Total	(66.4 overs, 270 mins)	396

WESTERN AUSTRALIA

H.C.Howard	c Collins b McDonald	8
L.C.Bott	st Oldfield b Mailey	1
S.H.D.Rowe	b Mailey	8
A.H.Christian	b McDonald	4
E.N.Healy	c Ryder b Mailey	1
A.J.Banks	c Bardsley b McDonald	4
*†H.A.Evers	c Collins b Armstrong	8
C.H.Robinson	b Macartney	16
R.M.Evans	c Collins b Macartney	7
A.B.Meek	not out	12
F.R.Buttsworth	not out	5
Extras	(b14)	14
Total	(30.0 overs, 115 mins) (9 wkts)	88

WESTERN AUSTRALIA	O	M	R	W	w,nb
Buttsworth	15	1	89	3	-,-
Christian	11	0	49	2	-,-
Meek	7	1	28	0	-,-
Robinson	19	0	125	2	-,-
Banks	11.4	0	84	3	-,-
Bott	3	0	15	0	-,-

AUSTRALIAN XI	O	M	R	W	w,nb
McDonald	6	0	16	3	-,-
Mailey	5	1	12	3	-,-
Gregory	4	0	8	0	-,-
Andrews	3	2	5	0	-,-
Macartney	7	1	9	2	-,-
Armstrong	5	0	24	1	-,-

FALL OF WICKETS

	AUST	WA
Wkt	1st	1st
1st	9	8
2nd	115	16
3rd	137	18
4th	216	19
5th	256	26
6th	310	31
7th	365	52
8th	389	67
9th	391	76
10th	396	-

1921-22 SEASON (10 MATCHES)

Victoria won the Sheffield Shield decisively and were rarely troubled at any stage of their campaign. An insignificant first-innings deficit in their match against New South Wales at Sydney raised the only doubt about the final result of a match involving Victoria. They fielded batsmen of the calibre of Ryder, Ransford, Park, Willis, Mayne and Armstrong, but the form of Frank O'Keeffe was a revelation. He forced his way into the Shield side for the final two matches by weight of his run-scoring for Carlton in club cricket, having moved from New South Wales to Victoria at the start of the season. His three innings for Victoria produced scores of 87, 79 and 180, and he further bolstered a strong bowling attack - which included Ted McDonald - by taking 5 for 45 against South Australia in addition to his fine century.

O'Keeffe reserved his greatest triumph for the Frank Iredale testimonial match at Sydney in February, which the NSWCA arranged between the 1921 Australians and The Rest. O'Keeffe was included for The Rest on the basis of his 87 and 79 against New South Wales a few days beforehand. He hit 177 and 144 in the drawn match and appeared to be on the verge of a distinguished career. But peritonitis tragically cut short his life two tears later in England.

New South Wales, who contributed 10 players to the 1921 Australian team that toured England, appeared on paper to be the strongest team in the Shield competition. Collins, Andrews, Cranney, Love, Gregory, Wall, Oldfield, Kelleway and Scott all had their moments but were unable to edge out the consistent Victorians. South Australia failed to win a match for the fourth successive season despite some fine individual performances from Smith, Townsend, Pritchard and Whitty.

Tasmania returned to the first-class arena for their first match since 1914-15. Victoria sent a team, comprised mainly of promising colts, to Launceston where they had the better of a drawn game. Bill Ponsford appeared on the list of century-makers for Victoria for the first time.

Western Australia hosted the Victorian Shield team, who followed on from their match at Adelaide, but were no match for the visitors, losing by an innings. Young Victorians Woodfull (153) and Wallace (8 for 67) recorded notable returns but the highlight from a statistical and Western Australian viewpoint was a last-wicket stand of 154 in the first innings between Buttsworth (100) and Lanigan (64*).

Queensland defeated New South Wales for the first time since December 1910 when they met at Brisbane. Although Sheppard hit a century, the bowling of Hornibrook (3 for 37 and 8 for 60) proved to be the chief contributing factor to the outcome.

New South Wales were scheduled to play Queensland at the Sydney Cricket Ground on December 31, January 2 and 3 but heavy rain before the game prevented a start and the match had to be abandoned when, after the third scheduled day, the rain had not abated. New South Wales named R.Bardsley (captain), J.Bogle, R.A.Bubb, E.E.B.Forssberg, A.T.Gray, W.F.Ives, A.F.Kippax, G.Parnell, A.T.Ratcliffe, A.E.Scanes and A.C.Yates. Forssberg withdrew prior to the scheduled start and was replaced by G.A.N.Chapman. Queensland named J.K.Farquhar (captain), S.W.Ayres, S.J.Fennelly, W.M.Forbes, P.M.Hornibrook, E.H.Hutcheon, L.P.D.O'Connor, C.B.Page, J.S.Redgrave, W.Rowe, T.H.Smith and L.E.Oxenham (12th man). No toss took place.

Leading Aggregates

Batsmen	M	I	NO	Runs	HS	Ave.	Bowlers	Runs	Wkts	Ave.
F.A.O'Keeffe (V)	4	6	0	708	180	118.00	E.A.McDonald (V)	602	28	21.50
J.Ryder (V)	4	8	2	611	242	101.83	J.L.Wall (NSW)	603	22	27.40
H.S.B.Love (NSW)	4	8	0	424	102	53.00	P.H.Wallace (V)	357	20	17.85
T.J.E.Andrews (NSW)	4	8	0	402	129	50.25	P.M.Hornibrook (Q)	310	18	17.22
A.Smith (SA)	4	8	0	379	122	47.37				
H.L.Collins (NSW)	3	6	0	374	117	62.33				

SHEFFIELD SHIELD TABLE

	P	W	L	D	Pts	Quotient	Runs Scored	Wkts Lost	Runs Conceded	Wkts Taken
VICTORIA	4	4	-	-	4	1.652	2344	58	1956	80
NEW SOUTH WALES	4	2	2	-	0	0.956	2286	73	2423	74
SOUTH AUSTRALIA	4	-	4	-	-4	0.640	2238	80	2489	57
TOTAL	6	6	6	-	0	1.000	6868	211	6868	211

QUEENSLAND v NEW SOUTH WALES

Played at Brisbane Cricket Ground (Woolloongabba) on December 3, 5, 6, 1921. (Three-day match)
Toss : New South Wales.   Result : QUEENSLAND WON BY 165 RUNS.
Debuts: Queensland - W.C.Browne, C.B.Page, T.H.Smith (all f/c). New South Wales - C.S.Achurch, R.C.M.Boyce, S.C.Everett, A.E.Scanes (all f/c).
12th Men: E.Francis (Qld) and J.Bogle (NSW).
Umpires: J.P.Orr and A.E.Wyeth.
Attendances & Receipts: No figures published..
Close of Play: 1st day NSW 3/36 (Achurch 4); 2nd day Qld (2) 4/150 (Sheppard 54, Page 17).

O'Connor, originally named as 12th man, replaced the nominated captain G.S.Moore (work) in the Queensland side. New South Wales were forced to leave out Bogle on account of an injured finger not healing as expected. Rain in the week leading up to the match severely handicapped pitch preparation, resulting in a fiery wicket on the first day and a slow outfield throughout. Redgrave was out in the first over of the match and Smith (10) was struck on the hand by a lifter from Everett and retired at 1/13; he resumed at 3/43. O'Connor (52 in 103 minutes, 5 fours) batted courageously. Hornibrook, bowling left-arm fast, also gained steep bounce early in the New South Wales innings, Farquhar (wicket-keeping) being struck over the right eye and leaving the field for stitches. O'Connor took his position for the remainder of the match and Ayres became captain, Francis fielding as substitute. Farquhar's only further participation in the match was to bat at number 11 in the 2nd innings so that Sheppard (101 in 235 minutes, 3 fours) could reach his first and only century. Soon after Farquhar's mishap, Scanes (4) was hit on the body by another vicious ball from Hornibrook and retired about 1/15. He resumed next day at 3/36. Though the wicket eased slightly, there was enough left in it for Hornibrook to take career-best figures on the last day. Flags were set at half-mast at the start of the match to respect J.W.McLaren, 33, who had succumbed to diabetes two weeks previously. *NSWCA Report* incorrectly gives Qld (1) Redgrave c Wall. Sources: *The Cricketer, NSWCA Report, Sydney Referee, Brisbane Courier, Brisbane Daily Mail.*

QUEENSLAND

J.S.Redgrave	c Russell b Everett	0	(2) b Asher		2
T.H.Smith	lbw b Wall	17	(1) run out		21
J.F.Sheppard	b Forssberg	6	not out		101
E.H.Hutcheon	c Wall b Forssberg	6	(7) b Forssberg		19
C.B.Page	c Trenerry b Wall	30	(6) c Russell b Asher		35
L.P.D.O'Connor	b Everett	52	(5) c Russell b Asher		28
*†J.K.Farquhar	run out (Scanes)	5	(11) not out		4
W.Rowe	b Russell	25	(4) c Gostelow b Wall		13
W.C.Browne	st Gostelow b Asher	6	c Scanes b Forssberg		1
S.W.Ayres	not out	3	(8) lbw b Wall		2
P.M.Hornibrook	c Trenerry b Asher	1	(10) b Wall		4
Extras	(b11, lb5, nb4)	20	(b7, lb14, nb1)		22
Total	(46.0 overs, 187 mins)	171	(78.0 overs, 245 mins) (9 wkts dec)		252

NEW SOUTH WALES

H.Cranney	c Hutcheon b Redgrave	5	st O'Connor b Ayres		40
W.L.Trenerry	c Sheppard b Redgrave	8	(5) b Hornibrook		9
A.E.Scanes	c O'Connor b Ayres	8	(4) b Hornibrook		4
E.E.B.Forssberg	lbw b Redgrave	9	(3) b Hornibrook		46
C.S.Achurch	c Redgrave b Hornibrook	37	(6) b Hornibrook		1
*R.C.M.Boyce	c Sheppard b Ayres	50	(7) c Page b Hornibrook		8
O.P.Asher	lbw b Hornibrook	2	(2) c Rowe b Hornibrook		7
S.C.Everett	c O'Connor b Ayres	0	(9) b Ayres		5
†R.E.Gostelow	c sub (E.Francis) b Ayres	3	(11) not out		0
B.L.Russell	b Hornibrook	4	c & b Hornibrook		0
J.L.Wall	not out	0	(8) st O'Connor b Hornibrook		1
Extras	(b3, lb4, nb1)	8	(b2, lb1)		3
Total	(49.4 overs, 190 mins)	134	(39.1 overs, 150 mins)		124

NEW SOUTH WALES	O	M	R	W	w,nb		O	M	R	W	w,nb
Everett	10	2	27	2	-,4		10	0	23	0	-,1
Russell	13	2	41	1	-,-		14	3	38	0	-,-
Forssberg	10	1	41	2	-,-	(5)	10	0	48	2	-,-
Wall	7	0	25	2	-,-	(3)	17	6	21	3	-,-
Asher	6	0	17	2	-,-	(4)	23	1	81	3	-,-
Trenerry							4	0	19	0	-,-

QUEENSLAND	O	M	R	W	w,nb		O	M	R	W	w,nb
Hornibrook	22	6	37	3	-,1		20	1	60	8	-,-
Redgrave	11	4	28	3	-,-		6	0	18	0	-,-
Ayres	12.4	1	50	4	-,-		11.1	3	43	2	-,-
Rowe	4	1	11	0	-,-		2	2	0	0	-,-

FALL OF WICKETS				
	QLD	NSW	QLD	NSW
Wkt	1st	1st	2nd	2nd
1st	0	12	7	18
2nd	22	23	34	56
3rd	43	36	61	70
4th	61	45	125	84
5th	76	117	185	86
6th	88	127	218	115
7th	148	127	225	119
8th	167	127	228	124
9th	169	134	233	124
10th	171	134	-	124

SOUTH AUSTRALIA v NEW SOUTH WALES (Shield Match 1)

Played at Adelaide Oval on December 16, 17, 19, 20, 21, 1921. (Timeless match)
Toss : New South Wales.   Result : NEW SOUTH WALES WON BY 17 RUNS.
Debuts: South Australia - C.Braybrook, C.D.Gray (both f/c). New South Wales - J.G.Morgan (f/c).
12th Men: G.W.Harris (SA) and H.O.Rock (NSW).
Umpires: G.A.Hele and S.W.Smith.
Attendances: 3226, 5357, 2314, 1716, 1346.   Total: 13,959.   Receipts: £484.
Close of Play: 1st day SA 1/14 (V.Y.Richardson 11, Williams 1); 2nd day NSW (2) 0/18 (Achurch 11, Asher 7); 3rd day NSW (2) 5/375
   (Love 71, Boyce 4); 4th day SA (2) 4/304 (Smith 102, Townsend 102).

Pellew was a late replacement for J.T.Murray (unavailable) in the South Australian side. Boyce captained New South Wales in his only Shield match. Cranney topscored in each innings for New South Wales with 70 (103 minutes, 8 fours) and 144 (161 minutes, 1 six and 17 fours, stumping chance at 26) his only first-class century. Morgan, on debut, (75 in 114 minutes, 9 fours) and Love (95 in 189 minutes, 3 fours) provided support. A muscle strain prevented Russell from completing his 12th over; he took no further part in the match. H.O.Rock substituted in his place but was himself absent on the last day, S.E.Hall (North Adelaide) taking over as substitute fieldsman. South Australia's chief scorers were Pellew (77 in 97 minutes, 12 fours) and Pritchard (100 in 132 minutes, 14 fours) in the first innings and Smith (104 in 154 minutes, 13 fours) and Townsend (a career-best 117 in 125 minutes, 18 fours) in the second. *O'Reilly* incorrectly gives NSW (2) Cranney c V.Y.Richardson. Sources: *Wisden, C.B.O'Reilly, NSWCA Report, SACA Report, Sydney Morning Herald, Adelaide Advertiser, South Australian Register.*

NEW SOUTH WALES

H.Cranney	b Townsend	70	(5) c A.J.Richardson b Braybrook	144
O.P.Asher	c & b Townsend	6	c Ambler b A.J.Richardson	18
†H.S.B.Love	lbw b Townsend	43	(6) b Williams	95
A.T.E.Punch	b Williams	34	b Townsend	33
J.G.Morgan	st Ambler b Williams	11	(3) b Townsend	75
C.S.Achurch	b Rundell	2	(1) c Rundell b A.J.Richardson	24
A.P.Wells	c Gray b Townsend	55	(8) b Williams	11
*R.C.M.Boyce	b Townsend	39	(7) c Pritchard b Braybrook	29
J.L.Wall	c V.Y.Richardson b A.J.Richardson	61	c V.Y.Richardson b Braybrook	2
B.L.Russell	c Ambler b A.J.Richardson	34	absent hurt	-
S.C.Everett	not out	0	(10) not out	0
Extras	(b2, lb3)	5	(b5, lb3)	8
Total	(74.0 overs, 270 mins)	360	(103.5 overs, 368 mins)	439

SOUTH AUSTRALIA

V.Y.Richardson	b Wall	26	b Wall	27
*A.Smith	b Wall	1	(5) c Love b Wall	104
N.L.Williams	c Asher b Wall	43	(8) b Everett	1
P.D.Rundell	b Wall	5	(3) st Love b Asher	14
A.J.Richardson	b Wall	5	(4) run out (Cranney)	31
R.J.B.Townsend	b Russell	46	c Achurch b Everett	117
L.V.Pellew	c sub (H.O.Rock) b Asher	77	(2) b Everett	12
D.E.Pritchard	c & b Wall	100	(7) st Love b Asher	22
C.D.Gray	lbw b Morgan	21	not out	30
†A.M.Ambler	c Everett b Wall	41	c Boyce b Wall	1
C.Braybrook	not out	1	b Wall	26
Extras	(b1, lb6, w2, nb1)	10	(b10, lb9, w2)	21
Total	(65.3 overs, 255 mins)	376	(86.6 overs, 320 mins)	406

SOUTH AUSTRALIA	O	M	R	W	w,nb		O	M	R	W	w,nb
Townsend	18	1	60	5	-,-		29	3	94	2	-,-
Gray	5	0	34	0	-,-	(4)	4	0	30	0	-,-
A.J.Richardson	22	4	79	2	-,-	(2)	28	5	91	2	-,-
Braybrook	5	0	51	0	-,-	(6)	11.5	1	52	3	-,-
Smith	5	0	34	0	-,-	(8)	3	0	18	0	-,-
Williams	13	2	67	2	-,-	(3)	16	1	76	2	-,-
Rundell	6	1	30	1	-,-	(5)	6	0	38	0	-,-
V.Y.Richardson						(7)	4	1	18	0	-,-
Pellew							2	0	14	0	-,-

NEW SOUTH WALES	O	M	R	W	w,nb		O	M	R	W	w,nb
Everett	9	0	52	0	1,1		17	1	71	3	-,-
Wall	25.6	4	133	7	-,-		34.6	4	123	4	-,-
Russell	11.5	1	70	1	1,-						
Asher	11	0	67	1	-,-	(3)	22	3	95	2	-,-
Punch	2	0	7	0	-,-		3	0	13	0	-,-
Morgan	6	0	37	1	-,-	(4)	4	0	31	0	-,-
Cranney						(6)	6	0	52	0	2,-

		FALL OF WICKETS			
		NSW	SA	NSW	SA
Wkt	1st	1st	2nd	2nd	
1st	8	5	42	31	
2nd	114	62	43	57	
3rd	125	74	137	67	
4th	150	80	180	129	
5th	159	81	368	308	
6th	183	166	420	334	
7th	246	253	432	338	
8th	267	318	439	355	
9th	360	358	439	360	
10th	360	376	-	406	

VICTORIA v NEW SOUTH WALES (Shield Match 2)

Played at Melbourne Cricket Ground on December 24, 26, 27, 28, 1921. (Timeless match)
Toss : New South Wales.   Result : VICTORIA WON BY SIX WICKETS.
Debuts: Nil.
12th Men: J.G.Morgan (NSW). No 12th or emergency fieldsman named for Victoria.
Umpires: R.M.Crockett and C.Garing.
Attendances: 13832, 17736, 17713, 14179.   Total: 63,460.   Receipts: £2859.
Close of Play: 1st day NSW 6/191 (Andrews 87, Hendry 36); 2nd day Vic 9/292 (Ellis 8, McDonald 5); 3rd day Vic (2) 0/4 (Ryder 1, Lampard 3).

W.Bardsley, C.G.Macartney and W.A.S.Oldfield were unavailable for New South Wales and Victoria were without W.W.Armstrong (leg injury). Andrews (115 in 202 minutes, 8 fours), Love (102 in 195 minutes, 4 fours) and Collins (111 in 150 minutes, 8 fours) scored centuries for the visitors. Punch (8) was struck on the head by a ball from McDonald and forced to retire at 1/17. He resumed later at 4/73. Park with 122 (162 minutes, 13 fours, no chances) and Ryder with 85 (157 minutes, 6 fours) led the way for Victoria. Morgan substituted for Cranney (leg injury) in the second innings. *Wisden* incorrectly gives NSW (2) Punch 14, Gregory 17. Sources: *Wisden, NSWCA Report, VCA Report, The Age, The Argus, Sydney Morning Herald, The Australasian.*

NEW SOUTH WALES

H.Cranney	b McDonald	1	c Ellis b McDonald		6
A.T.E.Punch	b McDonald	23	c Mayne b Liddicut		17
H.S.B.Love	c Ellis b Hartkopf	5	c Liddicut b Hartkopf		102
*H.L.Collins	c Ryder b Liddicut	29	c Lampard b McDonald		111
T.J.E.Andrews	b Lampard	115	run out (Liddicut)		7
J.M.Taylor	c & b Hartkopf	1	c & b Hartkopf		7
J.M.Gregory	b McDonald	0	c Hartkopf b McDonald		4
H.S.T.L.Hendry	c Ellis b McDonald	38	not out		9
†H.Carter	c Ellis b McDonald	4	c McDonald b Hartkopf		4
J.L.Wall	not out	19	st Ellis b Hartkopf		0
A.A.Mailey	b Lampard	10	st Ellis b Hartkopf		5
Extras	(b5, lb3, nb1)	9	(b2, lb5, nb1)		8
Total	(63.6 overs, 239 mins)	254	(60.6 overs, 237 mins)		280

VICTORIA

R.L.Park	c Mailey b Punch	122	(3) c Carter b Hendry		53
H.C.A.Sandford	b Gregory	0	(4) run out (Andrews/Carter)		1
C.B.Willis	b Gregory	4	(5) not out		35
A.E.Liddicut	b Gregory	22	(6) not out		8
J.Ryder	c & b Hendry	38	(1) c Collins b Mailey		85
V.S.Ransford	c Gregory b Punch	53			
*R.E.Mayne	lbw b Punch	1			
A.E.V.Hartkopf	c Gregory b Mailey	18			
A.W.Lampard	c Wall b Mailey	16	(2) c sub (J.G.Morgan) b Mailey		44
†J.L.Ellis	not out	17			
E.A.McDonald	c Wall b Gregory	6			
Extras	(b3, lb2)	5	(b5, lb2)		7
Total	(60.5 overs, 228 mins)	302	(58.4 overs, 201 mins) (4 wkts)		233

VICTORIA	O	M	R	W	w,nb		O	M	R	W	w,nb		FALL OF WICKETS			
McDonald	17	0	65	5	-,1		21	0	76	3	-,1		NSW	VIC	NSW	VIC
Liddicut	13	4	32	1	-,-		14	0	47	1	-,-	Wkt	1st	1st	2nd	2nd
Hartkopf	17	0	80	2	-,-		14.6	0	86	5	-,-	1st	8	7	12	89
Ryder	8	0	20	0	-,-		7	0	36	0	-,-	2nd	22	25	24	176
Sandford	2	0	12	0	-,-							3rd	70	69	229	202
Lampard	6.6	0	36	2	-,-	(5)	4	0	27	0	-,-	4th	73	145	240	203
												5th	96	235	254	-
NEW SOUTH WALES	O	M	R	W	w,nb		O	M	R	W	w,nb	6th	96	237	259	-
Gregory	12.5	0	71	4	-,-		9	1	35	0	-,-	7th	200	250	259	-
Wall	12	0	69	0	-,-	(4)	14.4	2	50	0	-,-	8th	204	275	264	-
Hendry	8	2	38	1	-,-	(2)	10	0	34	1	-,-	9th	232	280	268	-
Mailey	20	2	82	2	-,-	(3)	15	1	75	2	-,-	10th	254	302	280	-
Punch	8	1	37	3	-,-		10	2	32	0	-,-					

VICTORIA v SOUTH AUSTRALIA (Shield Match 3)

Played at Melbourne Cricket Ground on December 31, 1921, January 2, 3, 4, 1922. (Timeless match)
Toss : Victoria.   Result : VICTORIA WON BY SIX WICKETS.
Debuts: Nil.
12th Men: J.L.Keating (Vic) and W.S.Stirling (SA).
Umpires: H.J.Alessio and D.A.Elder.
Attendances: 18897, 20411, 8901, 1000.   Total: About 49,209.   Receipts: £2345.
Close of Play: 1st day Vic 3/388 (Ryder 232, Ransford 68); 2nd day SA 5/207 (Pellew 40, Pritchard 24); 3rd day SA (2) 6/250 (Smith 85, Loveridge 83).

Sandford, originally named 12th man for Victoria, was a late replacement for R.E.Mayne (injured hand). G.W.Harris was unavailable for South Australia and Stirling came into the side to replace C.E.Pellew, who withdrew despite being named captain. Ryder (242 in 304 minutes, 1 six and 24 fours) survived an appeal for caught behind when 76 and a stumping chance off Loveridge when 116; he took his score from 136 at tea to 232 at stumps on the first day. With Ransford (87 in 177 minutes, 7 fours) he shared a fourth-wicket stand of 187. Smith (122 in 318 minutes, 9 fours) and Loveridge (94 in 162 minutes, 9 fours) made career-best scores for South Australia. Batting out of his crease in the first innings, Loveridge survived a confident appeal for lbw off Liddicut only to see his stumps thrown down by the wicket-keeper while awaiting the umpire's decision. The match was Warwick Armstrong's last for Victoria. Sources: *Wisden, C.B.O'Reilly, VCA Report, SACA Report, The Age, The Argus, The Herald, The Australasian.*

VICTORIA

R.L.Park	c Pritchard b Townsend	39		b A.J.Richardson	33
J.Ryder	c V.Y.Richardson b Whitty	242	(4)	not out	18
C.B.Willis	c Loveridge b A.J.Richardson	44		lbw b Loveridge	1
A.W.Lampard	c Ambler b A.J.Richardson	1	(5)	c Ambler b A.J.Richardson	1
V.S.Ransford	b Williams	87	(6)	not out	4
H.C.A.Sandford	st Ambler b Williams	10	(2)	c Pritchard b Loveridge	39
A.E.Liddicut	c V.Y.Richardson b A.J.Richardson	19			
*W.W.Armstrong	b A.J.Richardson	1			
A.E.V.Hartkopf	c V.Y.Richardson b Williams	22			
†J.L.Ellis	b A.J.Richardson	1			
E.A.McDonald	not out	0			
Extras	(b5, lb3)	8		(lb1)	1
Total	(97.1 overs, 375 mins)	474		(26.1 overs, 96 mins) (4 wkts)	97

SOUTH AUSTRALIA

*V.Y.Richardson	run out (Liddicut/McDonald)	13	(2)	c Ellis b McDonald	0
A.Smith	c Ryder b Hartkopf	49	(1)	b Liddicut	122
P.D.Rundell	c Ellis b Hartkopf	6		b McDonald	7
R.J.B.Townsend	c Hartkopf b McDonald	41	(5)	b Hartkopf	24
A.J.Richardson	c Ellis b Armstrong	22	(4)	c Ryder b Liddicut	16
L.V.Pellew	b McDonald	41		b Hartkopf	9
D.E.Pritchard	b Liddicut	29		b Hartkopf	6
E.A.Loveridge	run out (Ellis)	0		b McDonald	94
N.L.Williams	b Liddicut	10		c Willis b Liddicut	33
W.J.Whitty	b McDonald	0		not out	12
†A.M.Ambler	not out	0		run out (Ransford/Ellis)	4
Extras	(lb6, nb2)	8		(b12, lb10, nb2)	24
Total	(57.4 overs, 230 mins)	219		(88.3 overs, 327 mins)	351

SOUTH AUSTRALIA	O	M	R	W	w,nb		O	M	R	W	w,nb
Whitty	20	1	64	1	-,-		5	1	19	0	-,-
Townsend	16	1	104	1	-,-		3	0	20	0	-,-
A.J.Richardson	24	2	112	5	-,-	(4)	8.1	2	11	2	-,-
Williams	20.1	3	102	3	-,-	(3)	3	0	29	0	-,-
Smith	4	0	26	0	-,-						
Loveridge	10	1	41	0	-,-	(5)	7	1	17	2	-,-
Rundell	3	0	17	0	-,-						

VICTORIA	O	M	R	W	w,nb		O	M	R	W	w,nb
McDonald	15	2	52	3	-,2		21	0	78	3	-,2
Liddicut	12.4	2	45	2	-,-		20.3	1	79	3	-,-
Armstrong	10	3	29	1	-,-	(6)	12	2	42	0	-,-
Hartkopf	13	0	64	2	-,-	(3)	16	2	45	3	-,-
Ryder	5	0	16	0	-,-	(4)	7	0	28	0	-,-
Lampard	2	0	5	0	-,-	(5)	3	0	13	0	-,-
Sandford							3	0	18	0	-,-
Ransford							3	0	7	0	-,-
Willis							3	0	17	0	-,-

FALL OF WICKETS

	VIC	SA	SA	VIC
Wkt	1st	1st	2nd	2nd
1st	100	33	5	71
2nd	217	61	17	72
3rd	220	86	38	78
4th	407	119	71	82
5th	420	163	93	-
6th	443	209	109	-
7th	446	209	271	-
8th	465	212	328	-
9th	474	213	335	-
10th	474	219	351	-

NEW SOUTH WALES v SOUTH AUSTRALIA (Shield Match 4)

Played at Sydney Cricket Ground on January 6, 7, 9, 10, 11, 1922. (Timeless match)
Toss : South Australia.   Result : NEW SOUTH WALES WON BY SIX WICKETS.
Debuts: New South Wales - H.Savage (f/c).
12th Men: S.M.Smith (NSW) and W.S.Stirling (SA).
Umpires: W.G.French and A.C.Jones.
Attendances: 3186, 1894, 4293, 2867, "considerable interest".   Total: 12,240 (excluding last day).   Receipts: £595.
Close of Play: 1st day SA 6/208 (Rundell 72, Pritchard 34); 2nd day SA 9/256 (Whitty 5, Ambler 3); 3rd day SA (2) 6/116 (A.J.Richardson 13); 4th day NSW (2) 3/256 (Andrews 123, Morgan 1).

V.Y.Richardson was caught at the wicket from the sixth ball of the match. Delays caused by inclement weather took the first innings into the third day. Pellew (81 in 176 minutes, 8 fours, chance at 0) and Rundell (78 in 124 minutes, 9 fours) topscoring for South Australia. Hendry dismissed Rundell and Whitty with successive balls in the second innings and was denied the hat-trick when Ives missed Smith next ball. Whitty (left-arm fast-medium) captured 7 for 66, his best analysis in 43 matches for South Australia, including the wicket of Morgan (52 in 88 minutes, 5 fours). The New South Wales victory was set up by Andrews (129 in 200 minutes, 14 fours) with support from Punch (65 in 88 minutes, 8 fours). The gates were thrown open for the final day, only 64 minutes being required to finish the match. Savage was a late inclusion for New South Wales due to the unavailability of H.Carter, H.S.B.Love, W.A.S.Oldfield and A.T.Ratcliffe. He came from a mainly Second Eleven career for Waverley, Carter's club, and returned there after an undistinguished effort behind the stumps. W.Bardsley, H.L.Collins, E.E.B.Forssberg, J.M.Gregory, C.G.Macartney and J.M.Taylor were also unavailable for New South Wales. *Wisden* and *O'Reilly* give incorrect match dates. *VCA Report* incorrectly gives NSW (1) 7/117, 8/118. Sources: *Wisden, C.B.O'Reilly, NSWCA Report, VCA Report, SACA Report, The Age, Sydney Referee, Sydney Morning Herald.*

SOUTH AUSTRALIA

Batsman	1st innings		2nd innings	
*V.Y.Richardson	c Savage b Scott	0	(4) b Ives	20
A.Smith	c Hendry b Scott	3	(11) b Scott	2
L.V.Pellew	lbw b Punch	81	c Morgan b Ives	40
A.J.Richardson	c Punch b Hendry	34	(5) c Mailey b Ives	28
R.J.B.Townsend	b Wall	1	(1) c Savage b Wall	7
P.D.Rundell	b Hendry	78	(8) c Scott b Hendry	55
E.A.Loveridge	b Scott	3	(2) st Savage b Mailey	28
D.E.Pritchard	b Hendry	34	(9) not out	35
N.L.Williams	c Punch b Hendry	0	(6) b Ives	0
W.J.Whitty	not out	11	c Punch b Hendry	0
†A.M.Ambler	c Savage b Scott	4	(7) b Wall	6
Extras	(b13, lb2)	15	(b6, lb2)	8
Total	(78.5 overs, 278 mins)	264	(70.2 overs, 248 mins)	229

NEW SOUTH WALES

Batsman	1st innings		2nd innings	
H.Cranney	b Whitty	6	(3) run out	49
A.T.E.Punch	b Whitty	1	(4) lbw b Townsend	65
T.J.E.Andrews	c V.Y.Richardson b Whitty	24	(1) b Whitty	129
H.S.T.L.Hendry	b Whitty	2	(2) c Ambler b Whitty	13
J.G.Morgan	c Ambler b Whitty	52	not out	39
A.P.Wells	b Whitty	5	not out	33
J.D.Scott	c A.J.Richardson b Whitty	25		
J.L.Wall	c Williams b A.J.Richardson	22		
W.F.Ives	c Ambler b Loveridge	9		
†H.Savage	lbw b A.J.Richardson	2		
*A.A.Mailey	not out	12		
Extras		-	(lb5, nb1)	6
Total	(40.7 overs, 163 mins)	160	(66.6 overs, 256 mins) (4 wkts)	334

NEW SOUTH WALES	O	M	R	W	w,nb		O	M	R	W	w,nb
Scott	17.5	5	35	4	-,-		14.2	1	44	1	-,-
Wall	23	3	77	1	-,-		13	3	38	2	-,-
Hendry	20	3	58	4	-,-		13	1	38	2	-,-
Mailey	12	0	49	0	-,-		17	2	63	1	-,-
Ives	3	0	18	0	-,-		12	1	31	4	-,-
Punch	3	1	12	1	-,-		1	0	7	0	-,-

SOUTH AUSTRALIA	O	M	R	W	w,nb		O	M	R	W	w,nb
Whitty	18	2	66	7	-,-		22	3	82	2	-,1
A.J.Richardson	8.7	0	38	2	-,-		17	0	95	0	-,-
Townsend	1	0	6	0	-,-		13.6	1	62	1	-,-
Loveridge	13	1	50	1	-,-	(5)	10	0	53	0	-,-
Williams						(4)	4	0	36	0	-,-

FALL OF WICKETS

Wkt	SA 1st	NSW 1st	SA 2nd	NSW 2nd
1st	0	3	13	33
2nd	7	8	62	125
3rd	89	10	82	252
4th	90	43	99	265
5th	191	53	99	-
6th	200	111	116	-
7th	225	118	140	-
8th	231	141	222	-
9th	248	151	222	-
10th	264	160	229	-

NEW SOUTH WALES v VICTORIA (Shield Match 5)

Played at Sydney Cricket Ground on January 26, 27, 28, 30, 1922. (Timeless match)
Toss : Victoria.   Result : VICTORIA WON BY 154 RUNS.
Debuts: Victoria - F.A.O'Keeffe (Vic only).
12th Men: C.S.Achurch (NSW) and J.L.Keating (Vic).
Umpires: C.W.Waugh and A.P.Williams.
Attendances: 15888, 6742, 9491, 4337.   Total: 36,458.   Receipts: £2256.
Close of Play: 1st day NSW 1/46 (Collins 32, Andrews 0); 2nd day Vic (2) 0/42 (Mayne 23, O'Keeffe 15); 3rd day Vic (2) 9/344
   (Ellis 10, McDonald 0).

J.M.Gregory (back injury), C.G.Macartney and J.M.Taylor were all unavailable for New South Wales. Keating was a late replacement in the Victorian twelve for R.L.Park. O'Keeffe made a fine debut for his adopted State having recently moved from Sydney, scoring 87 (204 minutes, 6 fours) and 79 (172 minutes, 9 fours). He shared a valuable 120-run partnership with Ryder (95 in 206 minutes, 5 fours). Sandford (48 in 49 minutes, 5 fours) was dismissed second ball in the second innings. Love (69 in 182 minutes, 5 fours) was the topscorer for New South Wales. McDonald returned his best innings and match analyses in the Sheffield Shield. *Wisden* incorrectly gives Vic (1) O'Keeffe st Oldfield b Mailey. *VCA Report* incorrectly gives NSW (1) 1/40, 8/254, 9/254. Sources: *Wisden, NSWCA Report, VCA Report, The Age, The Argus, Sydney Referee, Sydney Morning Herald.*

VICTORIA

J.Ryder	c Mailey b Scott	6	(3) lbw b Wall	95
*R.E.Mayne	b Scott	2	(1) b Scott	27
C.B.Willis	c Mailey b Kelleway	4	(7) lbw b Mailey	22
F.A.O'Keeffe	b Scott	87	(2) run out (Kelleway/Oldfield)	79
H.C.A.Sandford	st Oldfield b Mailey	48	(4) b Mailey	0
V.S.Ransford	b Scott	18	st Oldfield b Mailey	34
A.E.Liddicut	b Scott	13	(9) c Mailey b Kelleway	21
A.W.Lampard	c & b Punch	29	b Wall	7
A.E.V.Hartkopf	c Oldfield b Kelleway	34	(5) b Wall	30
†J.L.Ellis	not out	11	not out	10
E.A.McDonald	b Kelleway	2	b Kelleway	0
Extras	(b2, lb9)	11	(b13, lb5, w1, nb4)	23
Total	(68.0 overs, 249 mins)	265	(97.0 overs, 330 mins)	348

NEW SOUTH WALES

*H.L.Collins	c & b Ryder	42	c Ellis b McDonald	34
W.Bardsley	c Ellis b Ryder	9	c Ryder b McDonald	0
T.J.E.Andrews	c Ellis b McDonald	19	b Hartkopf	33
H.S.B.Love	c Ellis b Ryder	69	b McDonald	19
A.T.E.Punch	c Ellis b Ryder	3	b McDonald	3
C.Kelleway	run out (O'Keeffe)	54	b McDonald	45
H.S.T.L.Hendry	b Ryder	36	b McDonald	8
J.D.Scott	b Ryder	4	b McDonald	4
†W.A.S.Oldfield	b McDonald	3	c Ellis b Ryder	11
A.A.Mailey	b McDonald	0	b McDonald	4
J.L.Wall	not out	0	not out	8
Extras	(b15, lb9, w1, nb3)	28	(b12, lb7, w1, nb3)	23
Total	(82.5 overs, 328 mins)	267	(52.2 overs, 230 mins)	192

NEW SOUTH WALES	O	M	R	W	w,nb		O	M	R	W	w,nb
Scott	17	1	74	5	-,-		18	1	73	1	1,3
Kelleway	15	1	42	3	-,-		21	2	65	2	-,1
Mailey	14	1	66	1	-,-		31	3	97	3	-,-
Wall	11	2	30	0	-,-	(5)	17	5	37	3	-,-
Hendry	6	1	14	0	-,-	(4)	9	0	48	0	-,-
Punch	5	0	28	1	-,-		1	0	5	0	-,-

VICTORIA	O	M	R	W	w,nb		O	M	R	W	w,nb
McDonald	27	6	100	3	-,2		21.2	0	84	8	-,3
Liddicut	11	4	19	0	-,-	(4)	3	1	9	0	-,-
Ryder	22.5	3	60	6	1,1	(2)	21	4	49	1	1,-
Hartkopf	11	3	29	0	-,-	(3)	7	0	27	1	-,-
Lampard	6	0	19	0	-,-						
Ransford	5	1	12	0	-,-						

FALL OF WICKETS

Wkt	VIC 1st	NSW 1st	VIC 2nd	NSW 2nd
1st	7	42	51	1
2nd	12	83	171	60
3rd	14	83	171	87
4th	81	89	242	98
5th	114	207	255	105
6th	134	227	287	125
7th	196	231	310	135
8th	235	250	312	165
9th	263	250	344	177
10th	265	267	348	192

AUSTRALIAN XI v THE REST

Played at Sydney Cricket Ground on February 3, 4, 6, 7, 1922. (Four-day match)
Toss : The Rest.   Result : MATCH DRAWN.
Debuts: Nil.
12th Men: H.S.T.L.Hendry (Aust) and C.S.Achurch (Rest).
Umpires: A.C.Jones and A.P.Williams.
Attendances: 5776, 8981, 6876, 4787.   Total: 26,420.   Receipts: £1741 (including "collections").
Close of Play: 1st day Rest 393 all out; 2nd day Aust 6/227 (Ryder 44, Oldfield 9); 3rd day Rest (2) 2/179 (O'Keeffe 87, Love 48).

Arranged by the N.C.W.C.A. Executive as a benefit for F.A.Iredale, the Association secretary. Kelleway, dismissed by the fourth ball of the match, suffered a strain while bowling on the second day and took no further part in the match. O'Keeffe scored his first and second centuries at this level, 177 (261 minutes, 19 fours) and 144 (272 minutes, 6 fours). Willis (133 in 156 minutes, 17 fours) and Love (63 in 105 minutes, 4 fours) also made runs for the Rest. Armstrong (unbeaten 77 in 139 minutes, 6 fours) and Collins (117 in 162 minutes, 8 fours) topscored for the Australian side, Armstrong playing his last first-class match at the age of 42. Achurch and Punch were late replacements for A.E.V.Hartkopf and A.E.Liddicut in the selected twelve for the Rest. *Wisden* incorrectly gives Rest (2) O'Keeffe 141, Willis 34*; Aust (2) Gregory 6, Ryder 63*. Sources: *Wisden, NSWCA Report, VCA Report, The Age, The Argus, Sydney Referee, Sydney Morning Herald.*

THE REST

Batsman	Dismissal	Runs	Dismissal (2)	Runs (2)
C.Kelleway	c Oldfield b Gregory	0		
F.A.O'Keeffe	b McDonald	177	b Macartney	144
V.Y.Richardson	c Oldfield b Gregory	8	b Ryder	5
†H.S.B.Love	b Gregory	28	c Mailey b McDonald	63
E.P.Barbour	c Oldfield b Gregory	20	c Andrews b Mailey	16
C.B.Willis	c & b Gregory	133	not out	31
A.T.E.Punch	c Ryder b McDonald	4		
*V.S.Ransford	c Oldfield b Macartney	0		
A.W.Lampard	not out	21	(1) lbw b Ryder	32
J.D.Scott	c Mailey b Gregory	0		
P.M.Hornibrook	c Oldfield b Gregory	0		
Extras	(lb1, nb1)	2	(b7, lb2, w1, nb1)	11
Total	(83.0 overs, 330 mins)	393	(75.0 overs, 272 mins) (5 wkts dec)	302

AUSTRALIAN XI

Batsman	Dismissal	Runs	Dismissal (2)	Runs (2)
H.L.Collins	lbw b Kelleway	41	(2) b Hornibrook	117
W.Bardsley	c Love b Scott	25		
C.G.Macartney	c Kelleway b O'Keeffe	47	(1) b Hornibrook	9
T.J.E.Andrews	run out (Hornibrook/Love)	30	(3) c Love b Scott	45
J.M.Gregory	c Love b Kelleway	1	c Ransford b Hornibrook	4
J.M.Taylor	c Love b Hornibrook	19		
J.Ryder	c sub (C.S.Achurch) b Scott	62	(4) not out	65
†W.A.S.Oldfield	c & b Hornibrook	63		
*W.W.Armstrong	not out	77		
A.A.Mailey	c Barbour b Hornibrook	6		
E.A.McDonald	b Hornibrook	14		
Extras	(b12, lb4, w1, nb1)	18	(b9, lb4, w5, nb2)	20
Total	(88.3 overs, 375 mins)	403	(45.2 overs, 173 mins) (4 wkts)	260

AUSTRALIAN XI	O	M	R	W	w,nb		O	M	R	W	w,nb
Gregory	19	3	95	7	-,-		9	0	51	0	-,-
McDonald	19	1	95	2	-,1		14	1	52	1	-,1
Mailey	12	1	66	0	-,-	(6)	18	1	81	1	-,-
Armstrong	9	3	29	0	-,-						
Ryder	7	2	27	0	-,-		11	1	42	2	1,-
Andrews	5	0	35	0	-,-	(3)	4	0	25	0	-,-
Collins	3	0	6	0	-,-	(4)	8	1	14	0	-,-
Macartney	9	2	38	1	-,-	(7)	11	0	26	1	-,-

THE REST	O	M	R	W	w,nb		O	M	R	W	w,nb
Scott	24	4	109	2	1,1		13	1	71	1	5,2
Kelleway	17	1	68	2	-,-						
Hornibrook	30.3	5	107	4	-,-	(2)	21.2	1	106	3	-,-
Richardson	1	0	13	0	-,-						
O'Keeffe	7	0	41	1	-,-						
Barbour	9	0	47	0	-,-						
Lampard						(3)	5	0	29	0	-,-
Punch						(4)	6	0	34	0	-,-

FALL OF WICKETS

Wkt	REST 1st	AUST 1st	REST 2nd	AUST 2nd
1st	0	55	70	26
2nd	32	87	78	126
3rd	121	145	208	250
4th	167	149	237	260
5th	332	153	302	-
6th	336	212	-	-
7th	339	250	-	-
8th	393	346	-	-
9th	393	373	-	-
10th	393	403	-	-

TASMANIA v VICTORIA

Played at N.T.C.A.Ground, Launceston, on February 14, 15, 16, 1922. (Three-day match)
Toss : Victoria.   Result : MATCH DRAWN.
Debuts: Tasmania - B.J.J.Davie, G.W.Martin, L.L.Richardson, F.J.Toby (all f/c); F.L.Butler (Tas only). Victoria - J.A.Atkinson,
    A.W.Dummett, V.C.Monohan, S.G.Rimington, E.K.Tolhurst, P.H.Wallace (all f/c).
12th Men: G.H.Allan (Tas) and W.H.Bailey (Vic).
Umpires: E.Armitage and F.C.Tabart.
Attendances: No figures published, described as "fair" throughout.   Receipts: No figures published.
Close of Play: 1st day Vic 7/323 (Ponsford 15, Monohan 3); 2nd day Tas 8/172 (Smith 11).

Arranged at short notice, the match was limited to three days to avoid clashing with upcoming Victorian matches against South Australia and Western Australia. Although Tasmania narrowly avoided the follow-on under the laws of the day, they batted again "through some misunderstanding of the rules" according to the *VCA Report*. Toby, who twisted an ankle at practice prior to the game, aggravated the injury on the first day and was unable to continue in the field on the second day. As C.W.B.Martin was also absent with a damaged ankle (sustained while attempting to stop the ball with his foot), Allan and N.W.Davis were required as substitute fieldsmen. Both century-makers, Ponsford (162 in 175 minutes, 17 fours) for Victoria and Newton (117 in 95 minutes, 2 sixes and 19 fours) for Tasmania, scored a pre-lunch hundred. Ponsford scored 147 out of his side's 227 on the second day and although no figures were published, 100-110 of these must have been compiled before lunch. Newton's first 110 runs were scored in the third day's pre-lunch session, in which he and Smith added Tasmania's all-time ninth-wicket record partnership of 148. Altogether 461 runs were totted up on the last day. No details survive of Rimington's 91, his only first-class innings. Butler represented Canterbury in 1914-15. Sources: *A.C.S., VCA Report, Launceston Examiner, Launceston Daily Telegraph, Hobart Mercury.*

VICTORIA

E.K.Tolhurst	b Toby	61	
†J.A.Atkinson	b Newton	28	
A.E.Brown	c Newton b Smith	33	
*E.V.Carroll	c Thomas b Newton	38	
R.L.Braid	st Thomas b Toby	3	
S.G.Rimington	c Thomas b Toby	91	
A.W.Dummett	b Carroll	43	
W.H.Ponsford	b Newton	162	
V.C.Monohan	c Davie b Findlay	36	
C.V.Grimmett	c Richardson b Davie	23	
P.H.Wallace	not out	19	
Extras	(b11, nb2)	13	
Total	(94.4 overs, 350 mins)	550	

TASMANIA

C.W.B.Martin	c Atkinson b Grimmett	12	(2)	b Braid	4
B.J.J.Davie	c Atkinson b Dummett	56	(1)	c & b Grimmett	56
F.L.Butler	b Wallace	54		c Carroll b Monohan	48
L.L.Richardson	st Atkinson b Grimmett	13	(6)	b Braid	37
†L.Thomas	c & b Grimmett	7	(4)	c & b Wallace	11
G.W.Martin	b Dummett	1	(7)	not out	82
*T.D.Carroll	b Wallace	8	(5)	b Grimmett	8
H.C.Smith	c & b Dummett	59		not out	12
A.P.Findlay	c Atkinson b Wallace	1			
A.C.Newton	c Brown b Grimmett	117			
F.J.Toby	not out	9			
Extras	(b13, lb5, w1, nb2)	21		(b16, lb1)	17
Total	(80.0 overs, 305 mins)	358		(47.0 overs, 200 mins) (6 wkts)	275

TASMANIA	O	M	R	W	w,nb
Newton	26.4	1	142	3	-,-
Carroll	14	0	85	1	-,2
C.W.B.Martin	7	1	37	0	-,-
Smith	11	0	95	1	-,-
Findlay	16	1	83	1	-,-
Toby	11	0	48	3	-,-
Davie	9	1	47	1	-,-

VICTORIA	O	M	R	W	w,nb		O	M	R	W	w,nb
Wallace	23	3	106	3	-,-		12	0	61	1	-,-
Grimmett	25	2	89	4	1,-	(4)	15	0	72	2	-,-
Dummett	17	1	68	3	-,2	(5)	3	0	24	0	-,-
Monohan	1	0	5	0	-,-	(3)	6	0	33	1	-,-
Rimington	5	0	35	0	-,-	(6)	3	0	22	0	-,-
Braid	9	1	34	0	-,-	(2)	8	1	46	2	-,-

FALL OF WICKETS

Wkt	VIC 1st	TAS 1st	TAS 2nd
1st	47	18	8
2nd	95	85	91
3rd	149	140	125
4th	163	140	129
5th	177	145	160
6th	256	150	221
7th	320	168	-
8th	399	172	-
9th	479	320	-
10th	550	358	-

SOUTH AUSTRALIA v VICTORIA (Shield Match 6)

Played at Adelaide Oval on February 24, 25, 27, 28, 1922. (Timeless match)
Toss : South Australia.   Result : VICTORIA WON BY AN INNINGS AND 232 RUNS.
Debuts: South Australia - F.L.Morton, J.W.Rymill (both f/c). Victoria - M.A.Schade, W.M.Woodfull (both f/c).
12th Men: F.K.Gould (SA) and G.A.Davies (Vic).
Umpires: T.W.Cook and S.W.Smith.
Attendances: 4015, 5895, 2294, 136.   Total: 12,340.   Receipts: £496.
Close of Play: 1st day Vic 0/141 (Mayne 82, O'Keeffe 51); 2nd day Vic 4/523 (Ransford 117, Cody 78); 3rd day SA (2) 6/194
    (Townsend 27, Rymill 22).

A.M.Ambler (ill) and C.E.Pellew for South Australia and M.D.Hotchin, R.L.Park, E.A.McDonald and J.Ryder for Victoria were all unavailable. Mayne (85 in 114 minutes, 7 fours), O'Keeffe (career-best 180 in 273 minutes, 20 fours, two chances after 100) and Ransford (129 in 217 minutes, 1 six and 17 fours, three chances after 120) played major innings for Victoria. Cody (107 in 183 minutes, 13 fours) scored his only century in 30 matches as a specialist batsman. Woodfull, on debut, injured a hand while fielding on the first day and consequently batted at number 8. The only South Australian to exceed fifty was Smith (72 in 123 minutes, 8 fours). O'Keeffe captured three wickets in four balls (Murray, ball, Smith, Loveridge) in his 5 for 45, the only five-wicket haul of his short career. Loveridge was dismissed first ball in each innings. *Wisden* and *O'Reilly* incorrectly give Vic (1) Woodfull 17*, Morton 29.6 overs, Loveridge 0/103, total 620; SA (2) Richardson 22, Pritchard 5. Sources: *Wisden, C.B.O'Reilly, VCA Report, SACA Report, Adelaide Advertiser, South Australian Register.*

SOUTH AUSTRALIA

*A.Smith	b Hartkopf	26		c Woodfull b O'Keeffe	72
A.J.Richardson	c Ellis b Wallace	3		c Ellis b Wallace	21
E.A.Loveridge	b Wallace	0	(7)	c & b O'Keeffe	0
P.D.Rundell	b Wallace	45	(3)	b O'Keeffe	30
J.T.Murray	c Ellis b Wallace	17		lbw b O'Keeffe	13
R.J.B.Townsend	b Keating	29		c Ellis b Wallace	31
D.E.Pritchard	b Keating	13	(4)	c Woodfull b O'Keeffe	6
J.W.Rymill	b Schade	4		c Cody b Keating	28
†J.W.E.Schultz	c Hartkopf b Keating	5	(10)	c & b Keating	5
W.J.Whitty	not out	10	(9)	b Wallace	20
F.L.Morton	c Schade b Keating	0		not out	1
Extras	(b5, lb2, w1)	8		(b2, lb4)	6
Total	(42.0 overs, 176 mins)	160		(46.4 overs, 186 mins)	233

VICTORIA

*R.E.Mayne	c Townsend b Whitty	85
F.A.O'Keeffe	c Schultz b Richardson	180
C.B.Willis	b Townsend	15
A.E.V.Hartkopf	b Morton	32
V.S.Ransford	c Murray b Morton	129
L.A.Cody	b Townsend	107
J.L.Keating	lbw b Townsend	17
W.M.Woodfull	not out	22
†J.L.Ellis	run out (Rundell)	11
P.H.Wallace	c Morton b Whitty	5
M.A.Schade	c Pritchard b Morton	4
Extras	(b14, lb4)	18
Total	(124.6 overs, 503 mins)	625

VICTORIA	O	M	R	W	w,nb		O	M	R	W	w,nb
Wallace	12	4	24	4	-,-		17.4	2	62	3	-,-
Schade	8	0	35	1	-,-		9	1	47	0	-,-
Hartkopf	11	1	52	1	1,-						
Keating	9	3	28	4	-,-	(3)	14	0	73	2	-,-
O'Keeffe	2	0	13	0	-,-	(4)	6	0	45	5	-,-

SOUTH AUSTRALIA	O	M	R	W	w,nb
Morton	24.6	2	132	3	-,-
Whitty	36	4	135	2	-,-
Townsend	20	0	102	3	-,-
Richardson	15	2	61	1	-,-
Loveridge	19	0	108	0	-,-
Smith	4	0	33	0	-,-
Murray	3	0	13	0	-,-
Rundell	3	0	23	0	-,-

FALL OF WICKETS

Wkt	SA 1st	VIC 1st	SA 2nd
1st	5	144	35
2nd	5	182	109
3rd	71	270	125
4th	94	378	143
5th	102	557	144
6th	139	578	144
7th	144	587	201
8th	144	609	224
9th	160	618	231
10th	160	625	233

WESTERN AUSTRALIA v VICTORIA

Played at W.A.C.A. Ground, Perth, on March 10, 11, 13, 1922. (Three-day match)
Toss : Victoria.   Result : VICTORIA WON BY AN INNINGS AND 72 RUNS.
Debuts: Western Australia - G.R.Blundell, W.J.Butler, W.A.Evans, J.P.Lanigan, L.Packham, W.Stokes (all f/c). Victoria -
 W.H.McDonald (f/c).
12th Men: S.H.D.Rowe (WA) and M.A.Schade (Vic).
Umpires: C.Sinclair and E.A.Walker.
Attendances: 3000, 5000, 1000.   Total: About 9000.   Receipts: £554.
Close of Play: 1st day Vic 5/335 (Woodfull 122, Davies 6); 2nd day WA 9/146 (Buttsworth 54, Lanigan 10).

Woodfull, in his second first-class match, batted 246 minutes and hit 18 fours in compiling 153, an innings made with the benefit of two chances. A remarkable 10th-wicket partnership of 154 in 105 minutes between Buttsworth (119 minutes, 1 six and 15 fours) and Lanigan (7 fours) still stands as the Western Australian record for the last wicket. Howard carried his bat in the second innings for 77, with 8 fours; he "ricked his loin" shortly before tea on the last day and resumed after the interval with a runner (Blundell) with his score at 32. Howard's partnership with Packham, who had twisted an ankle while fielding on the first day, was most unusual, requiring the assistance of runners at each end (Evans ran for Packham). The ninth wicket in the innings fell at 5.59pm, but the umpires permitted another over to be bowled to give the Victorians a chance of winning the match before they caught their train to Kalgoorlie that night. Perth's official temperature on the third day reached 105.9°(41.0°C). Sources: *The Cricketer, VCA Report, The West Australian, Daily News*.

VICTORIA

*R.E.Mayne	c Stokes b Buttsworth	73		
F.A.O'Keeffe	lbw b Lanigan	41		
L.A.Cody	b Bott	34		
W.M.Woodfull	run out (Blundell/Stokes)	153		
E.K.Tolhurst	b Bott	5		
J.L.Keating	b Lanigan	52		
G.A.Davies	run out (Evans)	11		
H.H.G.Bracher	b Howard	75		
†J.L.Ellis	lbw b Lanigan	10		
W.H.McDonald	run out (Blundell/Stokes)	5		
P.H.Wallace	not out	10		
Extras	(b8, lb6, w1, nb1)	16		
Total	(131.2 overs, 436 mins)	485		

WESTERN AUSTRALIA

H.C.Howard	c Keating b Wallace	12	(2) not out	77
W.J.Butler	c McDonald b Wallace	4	(10) b McDonald	6
A.C.Randell	lbw b McDonald	9	c Wallace b O'Keeffe	8
L.C.Bott	lbw b McDonald	3	(6) run out	16
G.R.Blundell	c Woodfull b Wallace	4	(1) run out (Woodfull/Ellis)	31
*A.H.Christian	c Keating b Wallace	15	(7) c Ellis b Keating	2
†W.Stokes	c Cody b Wallace	7	(11) b Wallace	1
W.A.Evans	b Wallace	0	c Bracher b O'Keeffe	14
L.Packham	c Keating b Wallace	19	b O'Keeffe	8
F.R.Buttsworth	c Ellis b Wallace	100	(5) c & b O'Keeffe	2
J.P.Lanigan	not out	64	(4) b McDonald	1
Extras	(b6, lb2)	8	(b1, nb1)	2
Total	(49.5 overs, 191 mins)	245	(51.3 overs, 220 mins)	168

WESTERN AUSTRALIA	O	M	R	W	w,nb
Buttsworth	29	6	85	1	-,-
Lanigan	38	7	124	3	1,-
Packham	11	1	54	0	-,-
Christian	27	4	71	0	-,1
Blundell	9	1	58	0	-,-
Evans	8	1	28	0	-,-
Bott	8	0	43	2	-,-
Howard	1.2	0	6	1	-,-

VICTORIA	O	M	R	W	w,nb		O	M	R	W	w,nb
Wallace	20.5	1	67	8	-,-		12.3	3	37	1	-,-
McDonald	19	2	117	2	-,-	(3)	14	2	42	2	-,-
Keating	4	0	19	0	-,-	(5)	7	5	8	1	-,1
O'Keeffe	4	0	21	0	-,-		12	1	58	4	-,-
Cody	2	0	13	0	-,-	(2)	4	1	8	0	-,-
Mayne							2	0	13	0	-,-

FALL OF WICKETS

	VIC	WA	WA
Wkt	1st	1st	2nd
1st	96	11	46
2nd	134	22	59
3rd	211	30	66
4th	229	34	69
5th	317	34	93
6th	354	53	100
7th	398	53	121
8th	442	68	131
9th	463	91	167
10th	485	245	168

A.C.MacLaren led an MCC team to New Zealand this season which stopped off twice in Australia - on the way there and on the way back. They played eight matches in this country, seven of which are considered first-class. The leading English players had been selected for a concurrent tour of South Africa and MacLaren's team was considered well below true representative strength. They failed to win a game in Australia and rarely worried the opposition. The brilliant hitting of Percy Chapman and the legspin bowling of 'Tich' Freeman stood out.

Batting and bowling averages, or percentages, were required to determine the winner of the Sheffield Shield for the fourth time. New South Wales and Victoria remained deadlocked throughout the season and finished on three wins each. The bowling averages were much the same for both teams, but the powerful New South Wales batting (2233 runs at 43.78) conclusively outperformed that of Victoria (2029 runs at 30.74) to decide who should take the title. Collins, Bardsley, Macartney, Andrews, Kippax, Hendry, Taylor and Oldfield all scored heavily for the champions, whose depth in batting was worthy of comparison with the New South Wales XIs at the turn of the century. Woodfull, in his first big year, led the Victorian batting but lacked support. South Australia finished a distant third in the competition again.

Tall scoring had become a feature of Australian cricket by now, but all previous efforts paled into insignificance during the Victoria-Tasmania match at Melbourne in February. Victoria became the first team to exceed 1000 runs in a first-class innings and Bill Ponsford's 429 displaced A.C.MacLaren's 424 in England in 1895 as the highest individual score. Both Victoria and Ponsford were to improve their records before the decade was over. Victoria's winning margin, an innings and 666 runs, established a new record in Australian first-class cricket.

Rain prevented a result from being obtained in the Queensland-New South Wales encounter at Brisbane. It was Queensland's sole match for the season. Barstow, Hornibrook and Mailey all had impressive returns in a match where batsmen of both sides struggled to come to terms with difficult conditions. Hornibrook, in particular, impressed the visitors.

Western Australia continued their attempts to increase participation in interstate cricket. Persistent invitations from the WACA to the New South Wales Cricket Association, which had stretched back 10 years without success, finally resulted in a visit in March 1923. It was New South Wales's second trip to Western Australia following their previous tour in 1906-07. The results were sadly one-sided, New South Wales winning both matches by an innings. Hendry, Bardsley, Andrews, Macartney and Mailey all demonstrated their class above the local players.

The Queensland Cricket Association sought the support of the New South Wales Cricket Association in their endeavours to gain admittance to the Sheffield Shield. The NSWCA, although sympathetic to Queensland's cause, failed to influence the majority of delegates to the Board of Control. A further three seasons passed before a successful application was made.

Leading Aggregates

Batsmen	M	I	NO	Runs	HS	Ave.	Bowlers	Runs	Wkts	Ave.
A.P.F.Chapman (MCC)	7	13	1	782	134*	65.16	A.A.Mailey (NSW)	1187	55	21.58
A.J.Richardson (SA)	6	11	1	758	280	75.80	A.P.Freeman (MCC)	989	30	32.96
A.F.Kippax (NSW)	6	9	2	631	197	90.14	A.E.V.Hartkopf (V)	647	28	23.10
W.H.Ponsford (V)	3	4	0	616	429	154.00	P.H.Wallace (V)	630	25	25.20
W.M.Woodfull (V)	6	11	3	598	123	74.75	H.S.T.L.Hendry (NSW)	504	23	21.91
H.S.T.L.Hendry (NSW)	9	11	0	591	146	53.72	J.D.Scott (NSW)	450	21	21.42
T.J.E.Andrews (NSW)	8	12	1	535	179	48.63	C.H.Gibson (MCC)	913	21	43.47
H.L.Collins (NSW)	7	12	0	475	133	39.58	A.E.Liddicut (V)	421	20	21.05
H.S.B.Love (V)	3	4	0	418	192	104.50				
G.Wilson (MCC)	6	12	2	417	142*	41.70				

SHEFFIELD SHIELD TABLE

	P	W	L	D	Pts	Quotient	Runs Scored	Wkts Lost	Runs Conceded	Wkts Taken
NEW SOUTH WALES	4	3	1	-	2	1.686	2233	51	1895	73
VICTORIA	4	3	1	-	2	1.204	2029	66	1787	70
SOUTH AUSTRALIA	4	-	4	-	-4	0.522	1985	80	2565	54
TOTAL	6	6	6	-	0	1.000	6247	197	6247	197

WESTERN AUSTRALIA v M.C.C.

Played at W.A.C.A. Ground, Perth, on November 3, 4, 1922. (Two-day match)
Toss : M.C.C.   Result : MATCH DRAWN.
Debuts: Western Australia - V.C.Carlson, C.W.E.J.Fleay, A.H.J.C.Heindricks (all f/c). MCC - H.D.Swan (f/c).
12th Men: A.C.Randell (WA). No 12th named for MCC.
Umpires: A.E.Lawrence and E.A.Walker.
Attendances & Receipts: No figures published.
Close of Play: 1st day WA 2/54 (Howard 23, Heindricks 14).

The match was restricted to two days because of the tight travelling schedule of the England team. A.C.MacLaren, F.S.G.Calthorpe, J.F.Maclean and G.Wilson continued on to Adelaide by ship during the game. H.D.Swan the MCC's honorary manager made his sole first-class appearance; in the words of E.W.Swanton he was "comfortably the worst cricketer I ever saw". Chapman gave a fine exhibition in the match, hitting 75 in 77 minutes with 9 fours in the first innings and 58 in 39 minutes with 11 fours in the second. Dolph Heindricks, aged 39, was unlucky not to reach a century on debut, his 91 not out taking 220 minutes and including 9 fours. He played only one further first-class match. Hill-Wood was out in identical fashion in each innings to outstanding catches by Fleay at slip.
Sources: *Wisden, VCA Report, The Age, Sydney Morning Herald, The West Australian, Daily News, Western Mail, Sunday Times.*

M.C.C.

C.H.Titchmarsh	lbw b Lanigan	4	not out		50
W.W.Hill-Wood	c Fleay b Buttsworth	13	c Fleay b Buttsworth		6
W.A.C.Wilkinson	c Blundell b Buttsworth	40	c Howard b Buttsworth		0
A.P.F.Chapman	run out (Meek/Buttsworth)	75	c Blundell b Evans		58
D.F.Brand	c Evans b Fleay	21	not out		13
†T.C.Lowry	c Carlson b Buttsworth	20			
H.Tyldesley	c Buttsworth b Evans	0			
*J.C.Hartley	b Fleay	3			
C.H.Gibson	not out	4			
A.P.Freeman	b Bott	6			
H.D.Swan	b Bott	0			
Extras	(b2, lb2)	4	(b2, lb3)		5
Total	(67.4 overs, 190 mins)	190	(41.0 overs, 95 mins) (3 wkts)		132

WESTERN AUSTRALIA

H.C.Howard	b Freeman	24
G.R.Blundell	c Wilkinson b Gibson	10
V.C.Carlson	b Freeman	4
A.H.J.C.Heindricks	not out	91
*L.C.Bott	b Freeman	8
W.A.Evans	b Gibson	53
A.B.Meek	run out	3
C.W.E.J.Fleay	c Chapman b Gibson	4
F.R.Buttsworth	c Titchmarsh b Gibson	12
†W.Stokes	c Gibson b Freeman	5
J.P.Lanigan	st Lowry b Brand	11
Extras	(b5, lb4)	9
Total	(96.3 overs, 271 mins)	234

WESTERN AUSTRALIA	O	M	R	W	w,nb	O	M	R	W	w,nb
Buttsworth	17	3	45	3	-,-	10	0	29	2	-,-
Lanigan	15	1	60	1	-,-	8	3	20	0	-,-
Meek	11	1	29	0	-,-	5	1	14	0	-,-
Evans	15	3	39	1	-,-	9	1	31	1	-,-
Fleay	6	2	10	2	-,-	3	0	26	0	-,-
Bott	3.4	1	3	2	-,-	3	2	2	0	-,-
Carlson						3	0	5	0	-,-

M.C.C	O	M	R	W	w,nb
Gibson	38	11	68	4	-,-
Freeman	38	13	101	4	-,-
Brand	9.3	2	22	1	-,-
Hill-Wood	2	0	6	0	-,-
Tyldesley	9	0	28	0	-,-

FALL OF WICKETS

	MCC	WA	MCC
Wkt	1st	1st	2nd
1st	19	19	21
2nd	19	24	21
3rd	129	55	116
4th	137	63	-
5th	160	154	-
6th	164	164	-
7th	174	172	-
8th	180	188	-
9th	190	199	-
10th	190	234	-

SOUTH AUSTRALIA v M.C.C.

Played at Adelaide Oval on November 10, 11, 13, 1922. (Three-day match)
Toss : South Australia.　　　　Result : SOUTH AUSTRALIA WON BY SIX WICKETS.
Debuts: South Australia - R.L.Bennett (f/c).
12th Men: D.E.Pritchard (SA). No 12th named for MCC.
Umpires: T.W.Cook and G.A.Hele.
Attendances: 5317, 7563, 1702.　　　Total: 14,582.　　　Receipts: £503.
Close of Play: 1st day MCC 0/7 (Hill-Wood 6, Wilkinson 1); 2nd day MCC (2) 1/38 (Wilson 18, Titchmarsh 9).

An opening stand of 256 in 125 minutes for South Australia between A.J.Richardson (150 in 144 minutes, 25 fours, chance at 106) and V.Y.Richardson (118 with 19 fours) included 24 runs off an over from Hill-Wood, 19 of which were scored by the former. Titchmarsh replaced Lowry as M.C.C.'s wicket-keeper from 0/192 through to the end of the match. Wilkinson (64 in 140 minutes, 5 fours), Wilson (61 in 150 minutes, 3 fours) and Chapman (53 in 102 minutes, 5 fours) each surpassed fifty for the tourists. South Australia won the game with just two minutes to spare thanks to some hard hitting and despite Freeman recording a hat-trick (Murray, V.Y.Richardson, Dolling) along the way. C.E.Pellew, L.V.Pellew, P.D.Rundell, A.E.Smith and W.J.Whitty had all announced their unavailability for South Australia. Sources: *Wisden, C.B.O'Reilly, SACA Report, Adelaide Advertiser, South Australian Register.*

SOUTH AUSTRALIA

A.J.Richardson	c Wilkinson b Tyldesley	150		b Freeman	15
V.Y.Richardson	c Tyldesley b Calthorpe	118	(3)	lbw b Freeman	0
J.T.Murray	c Chapman b Freeman	48	(2)	c Chapman b Freeman	28
*C.E.Dolling	c Lowry b Tyldesley	24		c Tyldesley b Freeman	0
E.A.Loveridge	run out (Hill-Wood)	29			
R.J.B.Townsend	c Calthorpe b Freeman	18	(5)	not out	10
J.W.Rymill	c Freeman b Tyldesley	23	(6)	not out	1
C.D.Gray	lbw b Tyldesley	16			
N.L.Williams	c Calthorpe b Tyldesley	5			
†R.L.Bennett	b Freeman	5			
F.L.Morton	not out	0			
Extras	(b2, lb4)	6		(b3, lb3)	6
Total	(77.0 overs, 258 mins)	442		(4.5 overs, 19 mins) (4 wkts)	60

M.C.C.

W.W.Hill-Wood	c Bennett b A.J.Richardson	15	(4)	lbw b Townsend	30
W.A.C.Wilkinson	c Bennett b Williams	64		b Gray	6
C.H.Titchmarsh	run out (V.Y.Richardson)	9		b A.J.Richardson	41
F.S.G.Calthorpe	c & b Loveridge	0	(5)	c & b A.J.Richardson	17
A.P.F.Chapman	c Bennett b Townsend	32	(6)	c Bennett b Townsend	53
G.Wilson	b A.J.Richardson	38	(1)	b Townsend	61
*A.C.MacLaren	c & b Townsend	12		st Bennett b Williams	41
†T.C.Lowry	st Bennett b Williams	1		b A.J.Richardson	20
C.H.Gibson	lbw b A.J.Richardson	17		lbw b Williams	3
H.Tyldesley	c Dolling b Gray	6		lbw b Williams	7
A.P.Freeman	not out	0		not out	3
Extras	(b6, lb4, w1)	11		(b7, lb4, w1)	12
Total	(58.4 overs, 225 mins)	205		(76.5 overs, 290 mins)	294

M.C.C.	O	M	R	W	w,nb		O	M	R	W	w,nb
Gibson	10	0	53	0	-,-						
Calthorpe	11	1	75	1	-,-						
Freeman	29	0	169	3	-,-	(2)	2	0	23	4	-,-
Tyldesley	24	3	100	5	-,-	(1)	2.5	0	31	0	-,-
Chapman	2	0	15	0	-,-						
Hill-Wood	1	0	24	0	-,-						

SOUTH AUSTRALIA	O	M	R	W	w,nb		O	M	R	W	w,nb
Morton	13	0	51	0	1,-		8	2	27	0	1,-
Townsend	13	2	35	2	-,-	(6)	15	0	75	3	-,-
A.J.Richardson	16.4	4	40	3	-,-	(5)	16	4	37	3	-,-
Murray	2	1	1	0	-,-	(7)	5	0	14	0	-,-
Williams	11	1	44	2	-,-	(4)	9.5	0	62	3	-,-
Loveridge	2	0	20	1	-,-	(3)	10	1	37	0	-,-
Gray	1	0	3	1	-,-	(2)	13	2	30	1	-,-

FALL OF WICKETS

	SA	MCC	SA	MCC
Wkt	1st	1st	2nd	2nd
1st	256	33	7	42
2nd	276	76	82	42
3rd	333	79	137	42
4th	351	124	152	45
5th	373	128	174	-
6th	414	143	254	-
7th	414	143	270	-
8th	433	198	284	-
9th	440	205	284	-
10th	442	205	294	-

VICTORIA v M.C.C.

Played at Melbourne Cricket Ground on November 17, 18, 20, 1922. (Three-day match)
Toss : M.C.C.   Result : VICTORIA WON BY TWO WICKETS.
Debuts: Nil.
12th Men: W.H.Ponsford (Vic) and T.C.Lowry (MCC).
Umpires: R.M.Crockett and C.Garing.
Attendances: 3948, 14054, 3372.   Total: 21,374.   Receipts: No figures published.
Close of Play: 1st day Vic 5/44 (Woodfull 11); 2nd day MCC (2) 2/100 (Titchmarsh 57, Tyldesley 0).

J.Ryder (leg injury) and Ponsford were omitted from the Victorian 13. Chapman scored 73 (112 minutes, 4 fours) and 69 (95 minutes, 1 six and 4 fours) to complete a fine double. Titchmarsh made 82 in 135 minutes and hit 6 fours. Liddicut was unluckily run out at the non-striker's end late on the first day when a hard drive from Woodfull was deflected by the bowler Freeman's hand into the stumps. Woodfull (74 in 165 minutes, 3 fours) and Hartkopf (86 in 112 minutes, 9 fours) shared a sixth-wicket partnership of 144 out of 278. Hartkopf also had an outstanding match in the field, holding three catches and taking 13 wickets with his leg-breaks including a career-best 8/105 in the second innings Willis (60 in 75 minutes, 7 fours) helped Victoria to a narrow win. Sources: *Wisden, VCA Report, The Age, The Argus, The Herald, The Sporting Globe.*

M.C.C.

G.Wilson	b Wallace	9	(6)	c Mayne b Hartkopf	3
C.H.Titchmarsh	c Willis b Wallace	11	(1)	c & b Hartkopf	82
F.S.G.Calthorpe	c Mayne b Wallace	10		b Grimmett	19
W.A.C.Wilkinson	c Hartkopf b Keating	62	(2)	c Willis b Hartkopf	20
A.P.F.Chapman	st Ellis b Hartkopf	73		c Willis b Hartkopf	69
D.F.Brand	c Mayne b Hartkopf	17	(7)	b Liddicut	1
*A.C.MacLaren	c Ellis b Grimmett	5	(8)	c Mayne b Hartkopf	0
C.H.Gibson	b Hartkopf	2	(10)	c & b Hartkopf	11
†J.F.Maclean	not out	11		c Wallace b Hartkopf	8
H.Tyldesley	st Ellis b Hartkopf	4	(4)	b Hartkopf	3
A.P.Freeman	c Ransford b Hartkopf	0		not out	6
Extras	(b3, w3)	6		(b4, lb4, w1)	9
Total	(54.5 overs, 202 mins)	210		(50.6 overs, 200 mins)	231

VICTORIA

*R.E.Mayne	lbw b Gibson	17		c Maclean b Gibson	15
R.L.Park	b Freeman	11		b Tyldesley	11
C.B.Willis	c MacLaren b Gibson	5		b Calthorpe	60
W.M.Woodfull	run out (Chapman/Maclean)	74	(10)	not out	4
†J.L.Ellis	c Calthorpe b Gibson	0	(8)	b Tyldesley	16
A.E.Liddicut	run out (Freeman)	0	(7)	c Chapman b Calthorpe	1
A.E.V.Hartkopf	c & b Freeman	86	(9)	not out	14
V.S.Ransford	c MacLaren b Brand	26	(5)	b Calthorpe	15
J.L.Keating	c Chapman b Brand	25	(4)	st Maclean b Calthorpe	22
C.V.Grimmett	not out	18	(6)	c & b Brand	5
P.H.Wallace	b Tyldesley	0			
Extras	(b14, lb2)	16		(lb1)	1
Total	(83.3 overs, 256 mins)	278		(43.4 overs, 150 mins) (8 wkts)	164

VICTORIA	O	M	R	W	w,nb		O	M	R	W	w,nb
Wallace	13	1	64	3	-,-		14	0	50	0	1,-
Keating	12	2	33	1	3,-	(4)	4	1	19	0	-,-
Liddicut	12	2	41	0	-,-	(2)	11	0	41	1	-,-
Grimmett	11	0	43	1	-,-	(5)	1	0	7	1	-,-
Hartkopf	6.5	0	23	5	-,-	(3)	20.6	2	105	8	-,-

M.C.C.	O	M	R	W	w,nb		O	M	R	W	w,nb
Gibson	23	4	58	3	-,-		14.4	0	61	1	-,-
Freeman	23	4	81	2	-,-		4	0	16	0	-,-
Tyldesley	13.3	3	25	1	-,-		5	0	21	2	-,-
Calthorpe	14	1	60	0	-,-		12	2	41	4	-,-
Brand	9	2	33	2	-,-		8	3	24	1	-,-
Chapman	1	0	5	0	-,-						

FALL OF WICKETS

Wkt	MCC 1st	VIC 1st	MCC 2nd	VIC 2nd
1st	15	24	61	20
2nd	23	28	99	36
3rd	37	44	122	90
4th	143	44	145	124
5th	184	44	149	125
6th	191	188	156	127
7th	195	220	157	132
8th	199	248	165	159
9th	210	278	206	-
10th	210	278	231	-

NEW SOUTH WALES v M.C.C.

Played at Sydney Cricket Ground on November 24, 25, 27, 1922. (Three-day match)
Toss : M.C.C.   Result : NEW SOUTH WALES WON BY FIVE WICKETS.
Debuts: Nil.
12th Men:
Umpires: W.G.French and A.C.Jones.
Attendances: 6315, 17787, 6806.   Total: 30,908.   Receipts: £2150.
Close of Play: 1st day NSW 0/10 (Bardsley 3, Collins 7); 2nd day MCC (2) 9/117 (MacLaren 26, Tyldesley 3).

Oldfield and Scanes replaced H.Carter (ill) and J.M.Taylor (dentistry exams) in the New South Wales side. A quickfire hundred by Chapman (77 minutes, 15 fours) highlighted the M.C.C. batting on the first day while Titchmarsh (79 in 131 minutes, 7 fours) and MacLaren (54 in 60 minutes, 6 fours) chipped in with fifties. Macartney (63 in 54 minutes, 10 fours and 84 in 115 minutes, 8 fours) topscored for New South Wales, adding 135 in 79 minutes, with Andrews (74 in 79 minutes, 12 fours) in the second innings to set up a win. Sources: *Wisden, NSWCA Report, VCA Report, The Argus, Sydney Morning Herald, Sydney Referee.*

M.C.C.

W.A.C.Wilkinson	b Hendry	10	b Kelleway		8
C.H.Titchmarsh	b Kelleway	79	b Hendry		17
F.S.G.Calthorpe	c Asher b Hendry	11	b Macartney		21
A.P.F.Chapman	c Bardsley b Asher	100	c Oldfield b Kelleway		24
G.Wilson	c Oldfield b Hendry	29	c Macartney b Kelleway		2
D.F.Brand	b Kelleway	6	c Asher b Hendry		4
*A.C.MacLaren	b Hendry	54	not out		28
†J.F.Maclean	c Oldfield b Kelleway	33	b Macartney		1
C.H.Gibson	c Collins b Kelleway	5	c Andrews b Mailey		3
H.Tyldesley	run out (Andrews)	0	(11) b Kelleway		4
A.P.Freeman	not out	26	(10) c Hendry b Mailey		0
Extras	(lb5, nb2)	7	(b3, lb1, w2, nb3)		9
Total	(76.1 overs, 270 mins)	360	(39.3 overs, 148 mins)		121

NEW SOUTH WALES

W.Bardsley	c Wilson b Freeman	6	b Gibson		7
*H.L.Collins	b Freeman	24	lbw b Tyldesley		22
C.G.Macartney	c & b Tyldesley	63	b Gibson		84
A.F.Kippax	c Maclean b Brand	34	(5) b Gibson		41
T.J.E.Andrews	b Brand	36	(4) lbw b Calthorpe		74
C.Kelleway	c Maclean b Tyldesley	15	not out		32
A.E.Scanes	b Tyldesley	3	not out		13
H.S.T.L.Hendry	run out (Freeman/Tyldesley)	9			
O.P.Asher	not out	6			
†W.A.S.Oldfield	c MacLaren b Brand	0			
A.A.Mailey	b Brand	0			
Extras	(b1, lb4)	5	(b7, lb3)		10
Total	(50.5 overs, 161 mins)	201	(58.6 overs, 195 mins) (5 wkts)		283

NEW SOUTH WALES	O	M	R	W	w,nb		O	M	R	W	w,nb
Kelleway	24.1	6	81	4	-,1		13.3	2	39	4	1,3
Hendry	20	5	64	4	-,1		11	1	48	2	-,-
Mailey	13	0	106	0	-,-		9	2	17	2	1,-
Asher	16	0	70	1	-,-						
Andrews	3	0	32	0	-,-						
Macartney						(4)	6	2	8	2	-,-

M.C.C.	O	M	R	W	w,nb		O	M	R	W	w,nb
Gibson	11	1	46	0	-,-		20.6	2	80	3	-,-
Freeman	9	1	41	2	-,-		6	1	36	0	-,-
Calthorpe	6	0	19	0	-,-		13	0	66	1	-,-
Tyldesley	15	2	47	3	-,-		13	1	67	1	-,-
Brand	9.5	0	43	4	-,-		6	1	24	0	-,-

FALL OF WICKETS

Wkt	MCC 1st	NSW 1st	MCC 2nd	NSW 2nd
1st	13	17	27	20
2nd	33	58	29	56
3rd	181	113	60	191
4th	212	150	67	197
5th	222	169	77	265
6th	278	172	93	-
7th	299	191	99	-
8th	318	197	108	-
9th	318	201	108	-
10th	360	201	121	-

QUEENSLAND v NEW SOUTH WALES

Played at Brisbane Cricket Ground (Woolloongabba) on December 2, 4, 5 (no play), 1922. (Three-day match)
Toss : New South Wales.   Result : MATCH DRAWN.
Debuts: New South Wales - C.R.Campling, O.E.Nothling (both f/c).
12th Men: W.Cain (Qld) and J.G.Morgan (NSW).
Umpires: J.P.Orr and J.W.Ward.
Attendances: 5000, 5000, no play.   Total: About 10,000.   Receipts: £661.
Close of Play: 1st day Qld 6/126 (R.K.Oxenham 22, Farquhar 6); 2nd day Qld (2) 1/23 (R.K.Oxenham 7, O'Connor 10).

Campling replaced A.T.E.Punch and Barstow was brought in for J.S.Redgrave (unavailable) prior to the start. Nothling, on debut, was dismissed second ball in the first innings. Rowe (77 minutes, 5 fours) registered the only fifty of the match. An Overnight storm after the second day flooded the ground and made play on the last day impossible. *Cricketer* incorrectly gives NSW (2) Campling 18; Qld (2) L.E.Oxenham 8*. *NSWCA Report* incorrectly gives NSW (2) Wells 1, Nothling 2, extras 12, Rowe 0/14; Qld (2) L.E.Oxenham 8*, O'Connor 9*. Sources: *The Cricketer, NSWCA Report, QCA Report, Sydney Morning Herald, Brisbane Courier, Brisbane Mail.*

NEW SOUTH WALES

*H.L.Collins	c & b Ayres	7		lbw b Barstow	30
A.E.Scanes	c Ayres b Barstow	5	(6)	c Hutcheon b R.K.Oxenham	20
C.G.Macartney	b Hornibrook	46		b Hornibrook	1
A.P.Wells	b Barstow	15		c Rowe b Hornibrook	8
H.S.T.L.Hendry	c Hutcheon b Barstow	30		b Hornibrook	45
O.P.Asher	not out	18	(2)	run out (Farquhar/Hornibrook)	41
O.E.Nothling	b Barstow	0		b R.K.Oxenham	3
†W.A.S.Oldfield	c Ayres b Hornibrook	7		lbw b Barstow	3
A.A.Mailey	b Barstow	0		c Barstow b R.K.Oxenham	17
C.R.Campling	st Farquhar b Hornibrook	1		c R.K.Oxenham b Hornibrook	19
S.C.Everett	c Ayres b Barstow	1		not out	2
Extras	(b5, lb4, nb1)	10		(b5, lb6)	11
Total	(35.4 overs, 129 mins)	140		(52.4 overs, 194 mins)	200

QUEENSLAND

L.P.D.O'Connor	st Oldfield b Mailey	4	(3)	not out	10
L.E.Oxenham	b Everett	4			
E.H.Hutcheon	c Hendry b Everett	6			
F.C.Thompson	c & b Mailey	28			
T.H.Smith	c Scanes b Mailey	1	(1)	b Hendry	4
W.Rowe	run out (Wells)	52			
R.K.Oxenham	st Oldfield b Mailey	23	(2)	not out	7
*†J.K.Farquhar	c Hendry b Mailey	8			
P.M.Hornibrook	c Oldfield b Everett	0			
S.W.Ayres	not out	2			
C.B.Barstow	c Scanes b Mailey	3			
Extras	(lb1, nb2)	3		(b1, nb1)	2
Total	(42.0 overs, 157 mins)	134		(5.0 overs, 20 mins) (1 wkt)	23

QUEENSLAND	O	M	R	W	w,nb		O	M	R	W	w,nb
Hornibrook	16	5	40	3	-,-		21.4	2	50	4	-,-
Barstow	12.4	0	45	6	-,-		18	1	86	2	-,-
Ayres	5	0	41	1	-,1		3	0	24	0	-,-
Rowe	2	0	4	0	-,-		5	1	15	0	-,-
R.K.Oxenham							5	1	14	3	-,-

NEW SOUTH WALES	O	M	R	W	w,nb		O	M	R	W	w,nb
Everett	13	0	34	3	-,2	(2)	2	0	12	0	-,-
Campling	7	2	13	0	-,-						
Mailey	13	1	45	6	-,-						
Nothling	4	0	23	0	-,-						
Asher	5	0	16	0	-,-						
Hendry						(1)	3	0	9	1	-,1

FALL OF WICKETS				
	NSW	QLD	NSW	QLD
Wkt	1st	1st	2nd	2nd
1st	11	9	65	7
2nd	44	13	68	-
3rd	65	23	82	-
4th	101	24	92	-
5th	118	58	138	-
6th	118	113	144	-
7th	133	128	152	-
8th	134	129	166	-
9th	139	131	196	-
10th	140	134	200	-

SOUTH AUSTRALIA v NEW SOUTH WALES (Shield Match 1)

Played at Adelaide Oval on December 15, 16, 18 (no play), 19, 20, 1922. (Timeless match)
Toss : New South Wales.　　　　Result : NEW SOUTH WALES WON BY AN INNINGS AND 310 RUNS.
Debuts: South Australia - F.K.Gould (f/c).
12th Men: J.W.Rymill (SA) and A.T.Gray (NSW).
Umpires: T.W.Cook and C.R.O'Connor.
Attendances: 3900, 6674, 275, 2115, 132.　　　Total: 13,096.　　　Receipts: £611.
Close of Play: 1st day NSW 5/450 (Kippax 132, Hendry 26); 2nd day SA 1/86 (V.Y.Richardson 32, Dolling 20); 3rd day no play; 4th day
　SA (2) 4/54 (Pellew 16).

For the third time, four New South Wales batsmen scored hundreds in a single innings against South Australia: Taylor (159 in 149
minutes, 2 sixes, 3 fives and 16 fours), Kippax (170 in 207 minutes, 1 five and 19 fours, stumping chance at 16), Hendry (146 in 168
minutes, 15 fours) and Oldfield (118 in 152 minutes, 14 fours). Collins had earlier scored 64 in 129 minutes with 6 fours. Dolling (54 in
73 minutes, 8 fours), A.J.Richardson (60 not out in 140 minutes, 5 fours) and Williams (51 not out in 55 minutes) scored fifties for South
Australia. Gould on debut was out to the fourth ball of the second innings, after rain had prevented any play on the third day. Gray and
Campling replaced O.P.Asher and C.Kelleway (both unavailable) for New South Wales, while J.T.Murray, C.E.Pellew, P.D.Rundell,
A.Smith and W.J.Whitty all announced their unavailability for South Australia. *Wisden* and *O'Reilly* incorrectly give SA (1) Townsend b
Everett. Sources: *Wisden, C.B.O'Reilly, NSWCA Report, SACA Report, Sydney Morning Herald, Adelaide Advertiser, South Australian
Register.*

NEW SOUTH WALES

*H.L.Collins	b Bennett b A.J.Richardson	64
W.Bardsley	run out (V.Y.Richardson)	40
C.G.Macartney	c Williams b Morton	6
T.J.E.Andrews	lbw b A.J.Richardson	14
J.M.Taylor	c Townsend b Morton	159
A.F.Kippax	b Williams	170
H.S.T.L.Hendry	st Bennett b A.J.Richardson	146
†W.A.S.Oldfield	st Bennett b Williams	118
C.R.Campling	c A.J.Richardson b Williams	10
A.A.Mailey	not out	38
S.C.Everett	hit wkt b Williams	4
Extras	(b12, lb4, w1)	17
Total	(128.4 overs, 480 mins)	786

SOUTH AUSTRALIA

V.Y.Richardson	c Collins b Mailey	47	(2)	c Bardsley b Hendry	6
F.K.Gould	run out (Andrews/Bardsley/Campling)	24	(1)	c Oldfield b Hendry	0
*C.E.Dolling	c Oldfield b Everett	54	(4)	c Collins b Mailey	17
L.V.Pellew	st Oldfield b Mailey	14	(5)	b Mailey	31
R.J.B.Townsend	c Mailey b Everett	4	(7)	c Andrews b Mailey	24
D.E.Pritchard	c Collins b Everett	2	(3)	st Oldfield b Mailey	14
A.J.Richardson	not out	60	(6)	lbw b Mailey	29
C.D.Gray	c Campling b Everett	18	(9)	c Oldfield b Hendry	0
N.L.Williams	c Macartney b Mailey	37	(8)	not out	51
†R.L.Bennett	lbw b Everett	6		b Mailey	5
F.L.Morton	b Everett	3		b Campling	19
Extras	(b5)	5		(b2, lb4)	6
Total	(77.6 overs, 292 mins)	274		(51.4 overs, 195 mins)	202

SOUTH AUSTRALIA	O	M	R	W	w,nb
Morton	23	0	134	2	1,-
A.J.Richardson	33	2	135	3	-,-
Townsend	29	1	176	0	-,-
Williams	25.4	0	206	4	-,-
V.Y.Richardson	3	0	13	0	-,-
Gray	11	0	78	0	-,-
Pellew	4	0	27	0	-,-

NEW SOUTH WALES	O	M	R	W	w,nb		O	M	R	W	w,nb
Everett	20.6	2	59	6	-,-	(2)	2	1	5	0	-,-
Campling	9	1	41	0	-,-	(3)	16.4	1	62	1	-,-
Mailey	29	1	106	3	-,-	(4)	20	1	77	6	-,-
Hendry	9	2	27	0	-,-	(1)	13	4	52	3	-,-
Macartney	9	3	28	0	-,-						
Andrews	1	0	8	0	-,-						

FALL OF WICKETS

Wkt	NSW 1st	SA 1st	SA 2nd
1st	88	39	0
2nd	104	117	11
3rd	122	137	35
4th	141	142	54
5th	404	146	85
6th	518	149	126
7th	698	182	127
8th	711	245	131
9th	776	264	138
10th	786	274	202

VICTORIA v NEW SOUTH WALES (Shield Match 2)

Played at Melbourne Cricket Ground on December 23, 26, 27, 1922. (Timeless match)
Toss : Victoria.   Result : VICTORIA WON BY SEVEN WICKETS.
Debuts: New South Wales - A.T.Gray (f/c).
12th Men: J.L.Keating (Vic) and S.C.Everett (NSW).
Umpires: R.M.Crockett and C.Garing
Attendances: 12824, 13108, 11345.   Total: 37,277.   Receipts: £1618.
Close of Play: 1st day Vic 4/94 (Freemantle 6, Ellis 3); 2nd day Vic (2) 0/4 (Mayne 4, Woodfull 0).

Everett had not recovered from a leg strain sustained while bowling in the previous match in Adelaide and was made 12th man. A rain-affected pitch was responsible for only two batsmen reaching fifty, Kippax (68 in 102 minutes, 6 fours) for New South Wales and Woodfull (84 not out in 222 minutes, 2 fours) for Victoria. Macartney cleaned up the Victorian tail with remarkable efficiency. Liddicut was twice on a hat-trick; he dismissed Bardsley and Macartney in succession in the first innings and Macartney and Taylor in the second. *Wisden* incorrectly gives NSW (2) extras 14, total 141. Sources: *Wisden, NSWCA Report, VCA Report, The Age, The Argus, The Herald, Sydney Morning Herald.*

NEW SOUTH WALES

*H.L.Collins	c Ryder b Wallace	7		b Wallace	29
W.Bardsley	c & b Liddicut	10	(4)	c & b Liddicut	10
C.G.Macartney	c Hartkopf b Liddicut	0	(2)	lbw b Liddicut	15
T.J.E.Andrews	c Ellis b Wallace	7	(5)	lbw b Liddicut	0
J.M.Taylor	c Ellis b Wallace	34	(3)	c Freemantle b Liddicut	0
A.F.Kippax	b Hartkopf	68		c & b Ryder	5
H.S.T.L.Hendry	st Ellis b Liddicut	1		c & b Wallace	22
A.T.Gray	st Ellis b Liddicut	1		c Hartkopf b Wallace	28
†W.A.S.Oldfield	c Freemantle b Ryder	12		c Ellis b Freemantle	11
C.R.Campling	c Hartkopf b Ryder	12		c Wallace b Freemantle	7
A.A.Mailey	not out	0		not out	0
Extras	(b7, lb1)	8		(b10, lb4, nb1)	15
Total	(35.6 overs, 150 mins)	160		(47.2 overs, 185 mins)	142

VICTORIA

*R.E.Mayne	c Campling b Gray	24		st Oldfield b Mailey	8
W.M.Woodfull	c Hendry b Mailey	47		not out	84
C.B.Willis	c Mailey b Gray	8			
L.F.Freemantle	c Hendry b Mailey	13			
J.Ryder	c Oldfield b Gray	5	(3)	b Gray	36
†J.L.Ellis	c Hendry b Macartney	9			
A.E.V.Hartkopf	c Oldfield b Macartney	6	(4)	c Macartney b Gray	17
R.L.Park	b Macartney	7	(5)	not out	30
V.S.Ransford	st Oldfield b Macartney	0			
A.E.Liddicut	b Macartney	3			
P.H.Wallace	not out	1			
Extras	(lb1, w1)	2		(lb2, w1)	3
Total	(49.6 overs, 161 mins)	125		(74.2 overs, 222 mins) (3 wkts)	178

VICTORIA	O	M	R	W	w,nb		O	M	R	W	w,nb
Wallace	10	0	32	3	-,-		18	1	54	3	-,-
Liddicut	13	0	56	4	-,-		17	3	39	4	-,-
Hartkopf	4.6	0	34	1	-,-						
Ryder	7	0	26	2	-,-	(3)	6	0	18	1	-,1
Freemantle	1	0	4	0	-,-		3.2	1	8	2	-,-
Ransford						(4)	3	0	8	0	-,-

NEW SOUTH WALES	O	M	R	W	w,nb		O	M	R	W	w,nb
Hendry	6	0	17	0	-,-	(2)	5	0	19	0	-,-
Campling	8	4	12	0	-,-	(5)	6.2	0	18	0	-,-
Mailey	19	1	53	2	-,-		28	3	57	1	1,-
Gray	11	0	33	3	-,-		19	2	58	2	-,-
Macartney	5.6	1	8	5	-,-	(1)	16	5	23	0	-,-

FALL OF WICKETS

Wkt	NSW 1st	VIC 1st	NSW 2nd	VIC 2nd
1st	11	58	28	15
2nd	11	70	28	92
3rd	26	86	42	118
4th	33	91	42	-
5th	96	107	62	-
6th	99	107	77	-
7th	107	118	102	-
8th	120	118	133	-
9th	142	124	135	-
10th	160	125	142	-

VICTORIA v SOUTH AUSTRALIA (Shield Match 3)

Played at Melbourne Cricket Ground on December 30 (no play), 1922, January 1, 2, 3, 4, 1923. (Timeless match)
Toss : Victoria.   Result : VICTORIA WON BY 268 RUNS.
Debuts: Nil.
12th Men: J.L.Keating (Vic) and H.H.M.Bridgman (SA).
Umpires: R.M.Crockett and D.A.Elder.
Attendances: no play, 16598, 13483, 7421, 2532.   Total: 40,034.   Receipts: £1800.
Close of Play: 1st day no play; 2nd day Vic 7/289 (Freemantle 11, Liddicut 6); 3rd day SA 8/232 (Gould 39, Bennett 20); 4th day Vic (2)
  287 all out.

C.E.Dolling, J.T.Murray, C.E.Pellew and D.E.Pritchard were all unavailable for South Australia. Fifties were registered for Victoria by
Ryder (64 in 123 minutes, 4 fours), Hartkopf (98 in 158 minutes, 12 fours) and Ransford (73 in 128 minutes, 5 fours) in the first innings
and Liddicut (71 in 111 minutes, 7 fours) in the second innings. Liddicut shared a decisive seventh-wicket partnership of 155 with the
promising Woodfull (115 in 249 minutes, 4 fours, chances at 79 and 97). Gould sustained a leg injury on the second day and used Rymill
for a runner in the first innings; he did not field again in the match. V.Y.Richardson apart, the visitors' batting was disappointing.
A.J.Richardson was out to the fourth ball of the second innings. *Wisden* and *O'Reilly* give incorrect match dates, also Vic (2) Ellis st
Bennett b Williams. Sources: *Wisden, C.B.O'Reilly, VCA Report, SACA Report, The Age, The Argus, The Herald, The Australasian,*
The Sporting Globe.

VICTORIA

*R.E.Mayne	b Whitty	18	c Bennett b Morton		0
W.M.Woodfull	c Townsend b Morton	0	c V.Y.Richardson b Williams		115
J.Ryder	run out (Rymill/Bennett)	64	lbw b Whitty		3
A.E.V.Hartkopf	c sub (H.H.M.Bridgman) b Whitty	98	b Morton		1
R.L.Park	run out (Whitty/Bennett)	0	b Williams		12
V.S.Ransford	c Rundell b Whitty	73	run out (Williams/Bennett)		14
C.B.Willis	b Morton	10	st Bennett b Williams		19
L.F.Freemantle	b Whitty	11	(9) lbw b Whitty		23
A.E.Liddicut	not out	37	(8) c sub (H.H.M.Bridgman) b Morton		71
†J.L.Ellis	b Whitty	0	b Williams		18
P.H.Wallace	st Bennett b Williams	6	not out		0
Extras	(b4, lb6, w1)	11	(b6, lb2, nb3)		11
Total	(78.1 overs, 329 mins)	328	(71.3 overs, 255 mins)		287

SOUTH AUSTRALIA

A.J.Richardson	b Ryder	30	b Wallace		0
*V.Y.Richardson	c Woodfull b Hartkopf	50	st Ellis b Hartkopf		34
L.V.Pellew	lbw b Hartkopf	8	b Wallace		1
P.D.Rundell	c Freemantle b Liddicut	44	b Liddicut		15
J.W.Rymill	st Ellis b Hartkopf	12	(7) st Ellis b Hartkopf		1
R.J.B.Townsend	c Liddicut b Freemantle	10	b Hartkopf		16
N.L.Williams	lbw b Freemantle	11	(8) c Ryder b Hartkopf		3
F.K.Gould	c Ellis b Liddicut	44	(5) c Mayne b Ryder		6
W.J.Whitty	c Hartkopf b Freemantle	2	(10) b Liddicut		2
†R.L.Bennett	not out	28	(9) not out		2
F.L.Morton	lbw b Liddicut	6	hit wkt b Hartkopf		0
Extras	(b6, lb6)	12	(b2, lb7, w1)		10
Total	(69.0 overs, 267 mins)	257	(25.3 overs, 114 mins)		90

SOUTH AUSTRALIA	O	M	R	W	w,nb		O	M	R	W	w,nb		FALL OF WICKETS			
														VIC	SA	VIC	SA
Whitty	28	7	82	5	-,-		19	6	41	2	-,-		Wkt	1st	1st	2nd	2nd
Morton	16	2	69	2	-,-		11	2	52	3	-,-		1st	2	70	3	0
A.J.Richardson	15	3	63	0	-,-	(4)	13	3	36	0	-,-		2nd	62	91	6	8
Townsend	10	0	40	0	-,-	(5)	4	0	17	0	-,-		3rd	98	94	9	47
Williams	8.1	0	58	1	1,-	(3)	20.3	1	111	4	-,3		4th	101	118	35	54
Rundell	1	0	5	0	-,-		4	0	19	0	-,-		5th	247	137	59	75
													6th	270	158	84	77
VICTORIA	O	M	R	W	w,nb		O	M	R	W	w,nb		7th	270	180	239	83
Wallace	16	2	72	0	-,-		5	0	24	2	1,-		8th	289	189	250	83
Liddicut	11	2	31	3	-,-		8	3	9	2	-,-		9th	289	242	285	89
Ryder	7	0	25	1	-,-	(4)	4	0	23	1	-,-		10th	328	257	287	90
Freemantle	15	3	51	3	-,-												
Hartkopf	20	3	66	3	-,-	(3)	8.3	1	24	5	-,-						

NEW SOUTH WALES v SOUTH AUSTRALIA (Shield Match 4)

Played at Sydney Cricket Ground on January 6, 8, 9, 10, 1923. (Timeless match)
Toss : New South Wales.　　　　　Result : NEW SOUTH WALES WON BY NINE WICKETS.
Debuts: Nil.
12th Men: E.E.B.Forssberg (NSW) and F.K.Gould (SA).
Umpires: A.H.Farrow and A.P.Williams.
Attendances: 6933, 3572, 932, 20.　　　Total: 11,457.　　　Receipts: £725.
Close of Play: 1st day NSW 6/455 (Hendry 40, Gray 5); 2nd day SA (2) 2/87 (A.J.Richardson 43, Williams 6); 3rd day NSW (2) 0/64
　　(Collins 22, Bardsley 35).

Gould, who had not recovered from his recent leg injury was named 12th man for South Australia but was unable to field; Forssberg instead substituted when Pellew (minor leg strain) left the field on the first day. Collins (133 in 163 minutes, 14 fours) and Andrews (179 in 223 minutes, 18 fours) added 165 for New South Wales second wicket. Rundell (56 in 139 minutes, 3 fours) and A.J.Richardson (155 in 237 minutes, 1 six and 18 fours) dominated the batting for South Australia. V.Y.Richardson kept wickets instead of Bennett for the 39 minutes of play on the last day. Sources: *Wisden, C.B.O'Reilly, NSWCA Report, SACA Report, Sydney Morning Herald, Sydney Referee.*

NEW SOUTH WALES

*H.L.Collins	c V.Y.Richardson b A.J.Richardson	133	b Whitty	37
W.Bardsley	b Williams	26	not out	55
T.J.E.Andrews	c V.Y.Richardson b A.J.Richardson	179	not out	0
J.M.Taylor	b Whitty	3		
A.F.Kippax	c sub (E.E.B.Forssberg) b Townsend	51		
A.T.E.Punch	b Rundell	0		
H.S.T.L.Hendry	lbw b Morton	47		
A.T.Gray	b Whitty	7		
†W.A.S.Oldfield	c V.Y.Richardson b Whitty	4		
J.D.Scott	c & b Morton	9		
A.A.Mailey	not out	4		
Extras	(b15, lb3, nb5)	23	(b5, lb1, nb1)	7
Total	(85.4 overs, 335 mins)	486	(25.3 overs, 104 mins) (1 wkt)	99

SOUTH AUSTRALIA

A.J.Richardson	c & b Scott	2	st Oldfield b Mailey	155
*V.Y.Richardson	b Mailey	21	c Oldfield b Hendry	32
H.H.M.Bridgman	b Scott	2	(9) b Mailey	13
P.D.Rundell	c Hendry b Mailey	56	(5) c Oldfield b Andrews	15
L.V.Pellew	b Scott	2	(7) c & b Mailey	3
J.W.Rymill	c Oldfield b Gray	8	(8) not out	50
R.J.B.Townsend	c Punch b Gray	15	(6) c Taylor b Mailey	25
N.L.Williams	b Scott	5	(4) lbw b Punch	53
†R.L.Bennett	b Mailey	17	(3) b Mailey	1
W.J.Whitty	b Mailey	40	b Mailey	1
F.L.Morton	not out	23	c Bardsley b Andrews	22
Extras	(b2, lb5)	7	(b4, lb9, w2, nb1)	16
Total	(52.5 overs, 219 mins)	198	(83.6 overs, 306 mins)	386

SOUTH AUSTRALIA	O	M	R	W	w,nb		O	M	R	W	w,nb
Whitty	24.4	1	97	3	-,1		13	0	46	1	-,-
Morton	7	0	42	2	-,3		7	1	29	0	-,-
A.J.Richardson	15	0	56	2	-,-		3	0	7	0	-,1
Williams	11	0	109	1	-,1						
Rundell	11	0	54	1	-,-						
Townsend	12	0	73	1	-,-	(4)	2.3	0	10	0	-,-
Bridgman	5	0	32	0	-,-						

NEW SOUTH WALES	O	M	R	W	w,nb		O	M	R	W	w,nb
Scott	13	0	46	4	-,-		3	0	22	0	1,-
Hendry	8	0	36	0	-,-		15	1	57	1	-,-
Mailey	17.5	1	67	4	-,-	(4)	30	2	128	6	1,-
Gray	14	4	42	2	-,-	(3)	19	1	82	0	-,-
Punch							5	0	22	1	-,1
Andrews							4.6	0	41	2	-,-
Collins							7	0	18	0	-,-

FALL OF WICKETS

Wkt	NSW 1st	SA 1st	SA 2nd	NSW 2nd
1st	76	8	68	93
2nd	241	25	69	-
3rd	260	29	173	-
4th	386	32	205	-
5th	387	46	256	-
6th	436	66	272	-
7th	468	83	301	-
8th	468	117	321	-
9th	481	146	325	-
10th	486	198	386	-

NEW SOUTH WALES v VICTORIA (Shield Match 5)

Played at Sydney Cricket Ground on January 26, 27, 29, 30, 1923. (Timeless match)
Toss : Victoria.   Result : NEW SOUTH WALES WON BY AN INNINGS AND 28 RUNS.
Debuts: Nil.
12th Men: A.T.Gray (NSW) and T.A.Carlton (Vic).
Umpires: W.G.French and A.C.Jones.
Attendances: 13181, 18338, 7592, 1561.   Total: 40,672.   Receipts: £2985.
Close of Play: 1st day Vic 5/320 (Park 65, Willis 24); 2nd day NSW 6/291 (Kippax 60, Hendry 25); 3rd day Vic (2) 4/88 (Liddicut 7, Keating 3).

The Victorian middle order batting, led by Ryder (71 in 112 minutes, 2 sixes and 3 fours), Hartkopf (63 in 80 minutes, 7 fours) and Park (66 in 120 minutes, 6 fours) put their team in a strong position on the first day. Thereafter, the game slipped away from them and New South Wales won with ease. Collins (106 in 228 minutes, 8 fours) and Macartney (65 in 84 minutes, 9 fours) added 111 for the second wicket but it was the 168 added for the seventh wicket by Kippax (197 in 319 minutes, 21 fours) and Hendry (93 in 132 minutes, 9 fours) that turned the game in favour of the home team. The unexpected collapse of the Victorian second innings in the face of some fine bowling from Mailey saw completion of the match before lunch on the fourth day. Sources: *Wisden, NSWCA Report, VCA Report, Sydney Morning Herald, Sydney Referee, Sydney Daily Telegraph.*

VICTORIA

*R.E.Mayne	b Kelleway	17		lbw b Scott	2
W.M.Woodfull	c Oldfield b Scott	27		c & b Mailey	24
J.Ryder	b Mailey	71	(7)	c Andrews b Mailey	3
A.E.V.Hartkopf	c & b Macartney	63	(8)	b Kelleway	18
R.L.Park	c Hendry b Mailey	66	(3)	b Scott	5
V.S.Ransford	c & b Andrews	40	(4)	c Collins b Scott	36
C.B.Willis	c Mailey b Scott	42	(9)	run out (Kelleway)	23
A.E.Liddicut	b Mailey	6	(5)	c Hendry b Mailey	12
J.L.Keating	c Oldfield b Scott	7	(6)	st Oldfield b Mailey	34
†J.L.Ellis	not out	1		st Oldfield b Mailey	3
P.H.Wallace	run out (Andrews/Oldfield)	0		not out	2
Extras	(b5, lb5, w1, nb2)	13		(b6, lb3, w1, nb7)	17
Total	(81.2 overs, 333 mins)	353		(51.4 overs, 202 mins)	179

NEW SOUTH WALES

*H.L.Collins	c Ellis b Wallace	106
W.Bardsley	c Ellis b Wallace	7
C.G.Macartney	c & b Hartkopf	65
T.J.E.Andrews	lbw b Ryder	4
C.Kelleway	c Hartkopf b Ryder	7
J.M.Taylor	b Wallace	9
A.F.Kippax	c Mayne b Liddicut	197
H.S.T.L.Hendry	b Ransford	93
J.D.Scott	c Keating b Ryder	19
†W.A.S.Oldfield	b Keating	15
A.A.Mailey	not out	20
Extras	(b4, lb9, w2, nb3)	18
Total	(119.2 overs, 473 mins)	560

NEW SOUTH WALES	O	M	R	W	w,nb		O	M	R	W	w,nb
Scott	22	3	83	3	-,1		17	3	56	3	1,7
Kelleway	17	2	64	1	-,1		12	3	21	1	-,-
Mailey	20.2	0	95	3	-,-	(4)	18.4	2	73	5	-,-
Hendry	6	1	25	0	1,-	(3)	4	0	12	0	-,-
Andrews	9	0	47	1	-,-						
Macartney	7	1	26	1	-,-						

VICTORIA	O	M	R	W	w,nb
Wallace	24	1	104	3	-,-
Liddicut	19.2	2	86	1	-,-
Hartkopf	29	0	158	1	-,-
Ryder	28	3	103	3	-,2
Keating	14	0	66	1	1,1
Ransford	5	0	25	1	-,-

FALL OF WICKETS

Wkt	VIC 1st	NSW 1st	VIC 2nd
1st	32	10	10
2nd	64	121	18
3rd	182	132	65
4th	188	146	81
5th	267	164	106
6th	326	250	110
7th	332	418	135
8th	352	449	169
9th	353	499	174
10th	353	560	174

VICTORIA v TASMANIA

Played at Melbourne Cricket Ground on February 2, 3, 5, 6, 1923. (Timeless match)

Toss : Tasmania. Result : VICTORIA WON BY AN INNINGS AND 666 RUNS.

Debuts: Victoria - W.H.Bailey, H.S.Gamble, R.W.Herring, A.J.W.Lansdown, J.Mathers, K.J.Schneider (all f/c); H.S.B.Love (Vic only).
    Tasmania - G.H.Allan, G.G.Goodrick, P.G.Henty, G.S.Loney, A.W.Rushforth (all f/c).

12th Men: W.M.Irvine (Vic) and N.W.Davis (Tas).

Umpires: C.Garing and A.D.Reaburn.

Attendances: 2135, 5000, 2200, 100. Total: About 9435. Receipts: £371.

Close of Play: 1st day Vic 1/166 (Herring 65, Brown 70); 2nd day Vic 5/672 (Ponsford 234, Bailey 33); 3rd day Tas (2) 5/61 (Butler 20).

Ponsford, who assumed the captaincy in only his third first-class match, compiled the highest individual innings to that time as Victoria became the first team to exceed 1000 in first-class cricket. All batsmen reached double figures and a rapid scoring rate was maintained throughout, with 506 runs made on the second day. Chief contributors were Ponsford (429 in 477 minutes, 42 fours), Love (156 in 184 minutes, 9 fours), Brown (87 in 93 minutes, 1 six and 9 fours), Bailey (82 in 96 minutes, 11 fours), Herring (66 in 93 minutes, 5 fours) and Schneider (55 in 109 minutes, 4 fours). Ponsford went from 25 at lunch on day two to 121 at tea, 234 at stumps, to 375 at lunch on day three, and finally out at 8/1001 before tea. Shortly before, Mullett denied himself a single to allow Ponsford the distinction of scoring the 1000th run of the innings. Two hard chances, to Facy off Davis at 60 and Martin off Allan at 115, were the only blemishes. Bailey (43) was struck a severe blow on the body by a ball from Facy. He was able to continue after four minutes but sought further treatment in the pavilion by a doctor after being dismissed, "leeches having to be applied" according to the *Australasian* correspondent. He was unable to field in the second innings, Irvine substituting. Newton scored unbeaten innings of 49 (75 minutes, 3 fours) and 63 (103 minutes, 7 fours) for Tasmania. T.A.Carlton and C.V.Grimmett were omitted from the Victorian 13. L.F.Freemantle, the nominated captain, withdrew at the last moment and Lansdown replaced him. Starting times were brought forward an hour to 11.00am on the last two days. Love had previously played for New South Wales. Sources: *The Cricketer, VCA Report, The Age, The Argus, The Herald, Melbourne Sun, The Australasian*.

TASMANIA

A.W.Rushforth	b Lansdown	22	c & b Gamble		0
B.J.J.Davie	c & b Lansdown	36	b Lansdown		6
C.W.B.Martin	c Mullett b Bailey	24	run out (sub W.M.Irvine/		0
G.H.Allan	c Mathers b Gamble	5	run out		15
G.G.Goodrick	c Mathers b Bailey	1	st Love b Schneider		20
F.L.Butler	b Lansdown	7	b Gamble		24
*H.C.Smith	c Love b Bailey	29	(8) b Mullett		11
A.C.Newton	not out	49	(7) not out		63
G.S.Loney	c Mathers b Schneider	12	c Love b Gamble		18
†P.G.Henty	c Love b Lansdown	25	c Mathers b Martin		14
A.C.Facy	c Love b Gamble	1	b Sandford		0
Extras	(b2, lb4)	6	(b5)		5
Total	(52.3 overs, 191 mins)	217	(44.5 overs, 170 mins)		176

VICTORIA

H.C.A.Sandford	st Henty b Newton	23
R.W.Herring	c Martin b Newton	66
A.E.Brown	c Henty b Facy	87
J.Mathers	c Henty b Facy	46
*W.H.Ponsford	c Davie b Allan	429
†H.S.B.Love	c Rushforth b Loney	156
W.H.Bailey	b Martin	82
K.J.Schneider	run out	55
L.T.Mullett	b Allan	16
A.J.W.Lansdown	not out	25
H.S.Gamble	c Rushforth b Martin	32
Extras	(b32, lb9, nb1)	42
Total	(186.0 overs, 641 mins)	1059

VICTORIA	O	M	R	W	w,nb		O	M	R	W	w,nb		FALL OF WICKETS			
Gamble	13.3	1	41	2	-,-		14	2	55	3	-,-			TAS	VIC	TAS
Mullett	12	1	48	0	-,-	(4)	12	3	25	2	-,-	Wkt	1st	1st	2nd
Lansdown	14	0	53	4	-,-	(2)	10	1	49	1	-,-	1st	51	43	6
Bailey	10	0	47	3	-,-							2nd	84	168	6
Schneider	3	0	22	1	-,-	(3)	6	0	39	1	-,-	3rd	84	200	6
Sandford						(5)	2.5	0	3	1	-,-	4th	85	259	36
												5th	94	595	61
TASMANIA	O	M	R	W	w,nb							6th	102	792	74
Facy	38	1	228	2	-,-							7th	145	956	103
Newton	40	1	182	2	-,-							8th	177	1001	146
Davie	11	0	97	0	-,-							9th	210	1002	175
Goodrick	22	1	114	0	-,-							10th	217	1059	176
Allan	29	0	154	2	-,-										
Martin	32	1	161	2	-,1										
Loney	13	0	70	1	-,-										
Smith	1	0	11	0	-,-										

SOUTH AUSTRALIA v VICTORIA (Shield Match 6)

Played at Adelaide Oval on February 16, 17, 19, 20, 1923. (Timeless match)
Toss : South Australia.　　　　　　Result : VICTORIA WON BY SEVEN WICKETS.
Debuts: South Australia - E.J.Carragher (f/c).
12th Men: J.W.Rymill (SA) and J.L.Keating (Vic).
Umpires: T.W.Cook and G.A.Hele.
Attendances: 5582, 11851, 5643, 3085.　　　Total: 26,161.　　　Receipts: £1310.
Close of Play: 1st day Vic 1/10 (Woodfull 9, Ellis 1); 2nd day Vic 7/308 (Mayne 10, Liddicut 8); 3rd day SA (2) 5/209 (Murray 110).

In their first match together at first-class level, Woodfull (123 in 188 minutes, 9 fours, chance at 22) and Ponsford (108 in 162 minutes, 10 fours) shared a partnership of 133 for the Victorian fourth wicket, the first 100 runs arriving in 72 minutes. The second innings saw Woodfull (chanceless 94 not out in 149 minutes, 11 fours) and Love (70 in 80 minutes, 6 fours) add 132 for the third wicket. V.Y.Richardson (95 in 163 minutes, 10 fours), Hill (66 in 163 minutes, 2 fours in his last match for the State) and Whitty (43 in 45 minutes, 2 sixes and 4 fours) topscored for South Australia in the first innings. Murray (career-best 152 in 234 minutes, 17 fours) dominated the second innings, a chance at 120 being his only blemish. R.L.Park and J.Ryder were both unavailable for Victoria. Rymill and R.J.B.Townsend were omitted from South Australia's 13. Proceeds of the match £2020 including donations, were directed to the benefit of George Giffen. *Wisden* gives incorrect match dates and dismissal of Gould in SA (2). *Wisden* and *O'Reilly* incorrectly give Vic (1) Ponsford dismissal; SA (2) Gould 5, V.Y.Richardson 9, Pellew 7. Sources: *Wisden, C.B.O'Reilly, VCA Report, SACA Report, The Age, Adelaide Advertiser, South Australian Register.*

SOUTH AUSTRALIA

A.J.Richardson	c Liddicut b Carlton	5		c Ellis b Liddicut	32
F.K.Gould	c Ellis b Wallace	21		c Mayne b Wallace	4
V.Y.Richardson	st Ellis b Hartkopf	95		b Carlton	5
C.E.Pellew	lbw b Wallace	0	(6)	c Liddicut b Carlton	12
J.T.Murray	run out (Willis)	6	(4)	b Carlton	152
*C.Hill	c Love b Hartkopf	66	(5)	b Ransford	39
N.L.Williams	c Willis b Hartkopf	19		c Ellis b Wallace	7
†R.L.Bennett	b Wallace	0	(9)	b Carlton	14
W.J.Whitty	run out (Ponsford)	43	(8)	b Carlton	11
H.M.Fisher	st Ellis b Hartkopf	0		c Ellis b Hartkopf	12
A.J.Carragher	not out	17		not out	4
Extras	(b1, lb2)	3		(b4, lb6, w1)	11
Total	(58.3 overs, 250 mins)	275		(63.2 overs, 272 mins)	303

VICTORIA

W.M.Woodfull	c V.Y.Richardson b Whitty	123	(2)	not out	94
H.S.B.Love	b Fisher	0	(4)	lbw b Fisher	70
†J.L.Ellis	c Gould b Carragher	17			
A.E.V.Hartkopf	run out (V.Y.Richardson/Bennett)	14			
W.H.Ponsford	b A.J.Richardson	108	(3)	c V.Y.Richardson b A.J.Richardson	17
V.S.Ransford	b Whitty	6	(5)	not out	5
C.B.Willis	b Carragher	18			
*R.E.Mayne	run out (/Bennett)	40	(1)	lbw b Fisher	1
A.E.Liddicut	c A.J.Richardson b Whitty	28			
T.A.Carlton	c V.Y.Richardson b A.J.Richardson	20			
P.H.Wallace	not out	1			
Extras	(b9, lb2)	11		(b4, nb2)	6
Total	(95.5 overs, 351 mins)	386		(37.5 overs, 149 mins) (3 wkts)	193

VICTORIA	O	M	R	W	w,nb		O	M	R	W	w,nb			FALL OF WICKETS		
														SA	VIC	SA	VIC
Wallace	14	0	77	3	-,-		11	1	49	2	-,-		Wkt	1st	1st	2nd	2nd
Carlton	12	1	49	1	-,-		17	2	67	5	-,-	Wkt	1st	15	4	5	3
Liddicut	12	2	33	0	-,-		8	3	25	1	1,-	1st	1st	15	4	5	3
Hartkopf	17	0	105	4	-,-		22.2	0	132	1	-,-	2nd	2nd	33	48	18	44
Ransford	3.3	0	8	0	-,-		5	0	19	1	-,-	3rd	3rd	33	84	86	176
													4th	41	217	167	-
SOUTH AUSTRALIA	O	M	R	W	w,nb		O	M	R	W	w,nb		5th	190	241	209	-
Whitty	25	5	72	3	-,-		10	0	46	0	-,-	6th	6th	212	273	226	-
Fisher	15	3	61	1	-,-		8	0	31	2	-,-	7th	7th	213	293	257	-
Carragher	22	1	102	2	-,-	(4)	3	0	22	0	-,-	8th	8th	213	341	278	-
A.J.Richardson	23.5	4	83	2	-,-	(3)	11	1	51	1	-,-	9th	9th	214	383	293	-
Williams	7	0	43	0	-,-		5.5	0	37	0	-,2	10th	10th	275	386	303	-
Pellew	3	0	14	0	-,-												

NEW SOUTH WALES v M.C.C.

Played at Sydney Cricket Ground on March 2, 3, 5, 1923. (Three-day match)
Toss : M.C.C.   Result : MATCH DRAWN.
Debuts: Nil.
12th Men: A.T.Gray (NSW) and H.Tyldesley (MCC).
Umpires: W.J.R.Bowes and E.Whalley.
Attendances: 4432, 13452, 3928.   Total: 21,812.   Receipts: £1426.
Close of Play: 1st day NSW 0/18 (Collins 4, Bardsley 13); 2nd day MCC (2) 1/62 (Hill-Wood 37, Calthorpe 25).

Titchmarsh was struck in the face by a short-pitched ball from Scott in the third over of the match and retired at 0/2. He was unable to field in the New South Wales first innings; Tyldesley substituted in his place. Chapman (91 in 119 minutes, 7 fours), Hartley (48 in 95 minutes, 4 fours) and Brand (60 in 112 minutes, 8 fours) batted well on the first day. The topscorers for New South Wales were Bardsley (90 in 155 minutes, 4 fours), Taylor (73 in 74 minutes, 9 fours) and Kippax (59 not out in 72 minutes, 8 fours). Taylor continued his form in the second innings with 52 in 45 minutes, the match being abandoned upon his dismissal. Wilson fell victim to the eighth and last ball of Scott's first over in the MCC second innings. Calthorpe gave chances at 39 and 62 in scoring 110 in 218 minutes with 8 fours. Sources: *Wisden, NSWCA Report, The Age, The Argus, Sydney Morning Herald, Sydney Referee.*

M.C.C.

C.H.Titchmarsh	retired hurt	2	(6) lbw b Mailey	36
W.W.Hill-Wood	c Oldfield b Scott	18	(1) c Oldfield b Scott	46
F.S.G.Calthorpe	c Mailey b Scott	0	b Hendry	110
A.P.F.Chapman	b Andrews	91	(5) c Hendry b Mailey	18
T.C.Lowry	c Kippax b Mailey	10	(4) c Oldfield b Mailey	0
G.Wilson	c Oldfield b Scott	33	(2) b Scott	0
†J.F.Maclean	b Scott	6	c Kelleway b Mailey	0
*J.C.Hartley	lbw b Kelleway	48	c Hendry b Mailey	4
D.F.Brand	c Andrews b Mailey	60	lbw b Andrews	22
C.H.Gibson	not out	4	not out	30
A.P.Freeman	c Taylor b Mailey	1	lbw b Andrews	22
Extras	(lb1, w1)	2	(b1, w3, nb4)	8
Total	(68.1 overs, 251 mins)	275	(73.7 overs, 258 mins)	296

NEW SOUTH WALES

*H.L.Collins	c Calthorpe b Gibson	10	b Freeman	6
W.Bardsley	lbw b Freeman	90	c Maclean b Gibson	26
C.G.Macartney	c Chapman b Gibson	18	b Freeman	0
T.J.E.Andrews	c Chapman b Gibson	37	st Maclean b Freeman	8
J.M.Taylor	c Hill-Wood b Gibson	73	c Gibson b Chapman	52
A.F.Kippax	not out	59	not out	6
C.Kelleway	lbw b Gibson	0		
H.S.T.L.Hendry	c Gibson b Freeman	13		
†W.A.S.Oldfield	st Maclean b Freeman	0		
J.D.Scott	c Chapman b Gibson	4		
A.A.Mailey	b Freeman	0		
Extras	(b6, lb3, w1)	10	(b3, lb1)	4
Total	(68.0 overs, 248 mins)	314	(25.7 overs, 83 mins) (5 wkts)	102

NEW SOUTH WALES	O	M	R	W	w,nb		O	M	R	W	w,nb					
Scott	19	1	68	4	1,-		21	1	76	2	-,4			FALL OF WICKETS		
Kelleway	21	5	53	1	-,-		14	1	42	0	1,-			MCC	NSW	MCC	NSW
Mailey	16.1	0	91	3	-,-		29	1	118	5	2,-		Wkt	1st	1st	2nd	2nd
Hendry	3	0	21	0	-,-		6	1	34	1	-,-		1st	2	34	1	20
Andrews	7	0	40	1	-,-		3.7	0	18	2	-,-		2nd	55	56	80	30
Macartney	2	2	0	0	-,-								3rd	74	120	85	40
													4th	135	216	122	52
													5th	145	249	182	102
M.C.C.	O	M	R	W	w,nb		O	M	R	W	w,nb		6th	170	250	182	-
Gibson	32	1	140	6	1,-		12	1	42	1	-,-		7th	245	295	192	-
Freeman	23	2	99	4	-,-		10	1	34	3	-,-		8th	273	300	235	-
Brand	5	0	28	0	-,-								9th	275	307	250	-
Calthorpe	8	0	37	0	-,-								10th	-	314	296	-
Chapman						(3)	2.7	0	10	1	-,-					
Hill-Wood						(4)	1	0	12	0	-,-					

VICTORIA v M.C.C.

Played at Melbourne Cricket Ground on March 9, 10, 12, 1923. (Three-day match)
Toss : M.C.C.   Result : MATCH DRAWN.
Debuts: Nil.
12th Men: None named.
Umpires: R.M.Crockett and (probably) C.Garing.
Attendances: 2792, 7810, 1448.   Total: 12,050.   Receipts: No figures published.
Close of Play: 1st day Vic 3/189 (Love 105, Park 4); 2nd day Vic 6/617 (Ransford 118, Bailey 11).

C.V.Grimmett, A.E.V.Hartkopf, G.E.J.Healy, R.E.Mayne and K.J.Schneider were all unavailable for Victoria. According to the *Argus*, the visitors "practically committed suicide in feeling for deliveries pitched wide outside the off stump," the pitch being in excellent condition. Love (career-best 192 in 285 minutes, 13 fours). Ponsford (62 in 97 minutes, 6 fours), Park (101 in 155 minutes, 8 fours), Ransford (118 not out in 145 minutes, 11 fours) and Liddicut (102 in 138 minutes, 8 fours, chance at 11) gave Victoria an unassailable first-innings lead. Hill-Wood (16 fours) and Wilson (14 fours) saved the match by batting through the last day, Wilson's 100 his only first-class century in 115 matches. Both were barracked for slow play early in their stand (Hill-Wood reached 50 in 173 minutes and 100 in 245 minutes, Wilson 50 in 121 minutes and 100 in 197 minutes) and Liddicut bowled an underarm grubber "in frustration at the stonewalling" shortly after tea. Though no mention is made of umpire Garing in the match, a Melbourne newspaper report in early March specified the following appointments for forthcoming M.C.C. matches: Combined Universities, Crockett and Garing; Victoria D.A.Elder and A.D.Reaburn. Reports here mention Crockett in commentary and it is assumed, also considering the status of the umpires at the time, that the appointments were printed in reverse. The V.C.A. directed that its share of the gate be divided between W.Carkeek and T.J.Matthews who were both in ill-health at the time; each received about £300. Sources: *Wisden, VCA Report, The Age, The Argus, The Herald, Melbourne Sun, The Sporting Globe, The Leader, The Australasian.*

M.C.C.

W.W.Hill-Wood	c Ryder b Wallace	10	not out		122
C.H.Titchmarsh	c Ryder b Liddicut	1			
F.S.G.Calthorpe	b Wallace	20			
A.P.F.Chapman	c Ryder b Liddicut	6			
T.C.Lowry	c Woodfull b Liddicut	5			
G.Wilson	c Ellis b Wallace	16	(2) not out		142
†J.F.Maclean	c Woodfull b Liddicut	0			
*J.C.Hartley	lbw b Wallace	3			
D.F.Brand	c Ryder b Wallace	2			
C.H.Gibson	not out	3			
A.P.Freeman	c Ryder b Wallace	0			
Extras	(lb3, w2)	5	(b11, lb1, w2, nb4)		18
Total	(30.5 overs, 127 mins)	71	(85.0 overs, 282 mins) (0 wkts)		282

VICTORIA

W.M.Woodfull	c Chapman b Gibson	6
H.S.B.Love	b Chapman	192
W.H.Ponsford	st Maclean b Brand	62
*J.Ryder	run out (Chapman/Maclean)	11
R.L.Park	c Wilson b Calthorpe	101
V.S.Ransford	not out	118
A.E.Liddicut	c Hill-Wood b Wilson	102
W.H.Bailey	not out	11
†J.L.Ellis	)	
T.A.Carlton	) did not bat	
P.H.Wallace	)	
Extras	(b7, lb7)	14
Total	(138.0 overs, 445 mins) (6 wkts dec)	617

VICTORIA	O	M	R	W	w,nb	O	M	R	W	w,nb
Wallace	15.5	1	50	6	2,-	18	4	54	0	-,-
Liddicut	15	5	16	4	-,-	19	9	44	0	1,-
Ryder						11	2	36	0	-,-
Carlton						16	2	51	0	-,3
Bailey						6	0	25	0	1,-
Ransford						9	2	34	0	-,-
Love						2	0	19	0	-,1
Park						4	3	1	0	-,-

M.C.C.	O	M	R	W	w,nb
Gibson	42	4	151	1	-,-
Calthorpe	18	0	90	1	-,-
Freeman	33	4	121	0	-,-
Brand	20	0	108	1	-,-
Chapman	9	0	36	1	-,-
Wilson	7	0	44	1	-,-
Hill-Wood	9	1	53	0	-,-

FALL OF WICKETS

	MCC	VIC	MCC
Wkt	1st	1st	2nd
1st	6	18	-
2nd	18	143	-
3rd	25	177	-
4th	45	375	-
5th	45	385	-
6th	45	601	-
7th	56	-	-
8th	62	-	-
9th	71	-	-
10th	71	-	-

SOUTH AUSTRALIA v M.C.C.

Played at Adelaide Oval on March 15, 16, 17, 1923. (Three-day match)
Toss : South Australia. Result : MATCH DRAWN.
Debuts: South Australia - E.L.Bowley (f/c).
12th Men: C.Seager (SA) and H.Tyldesley (MCC).
Umpires: G.A.Hele and S.W.Smith.
Attendances: 3700, 4200, 6192. Total: 14,092. Receipts: £277 (excluding 3rd day unpublished).
Close of Play: 1st day SA 495 all out; 2nd day MCC 9/360 (Hartley 22, Freeman 51).

A.J.Richardson's career-best 280 took just 242 minutes and included 2 sixes, a five and 36 fours. He reached his century before lunch on the first day (104 out of 3/133) and he had 224 by tea-time out of 4/328. His innings included chances at 1, 140 and 153. Bowley on debut scored 76 in 91 minutes, with 12 fours and Rymill scored 50 in 47 minutes with 8 fours. Wilson (78 in 150 minutes, 7 fours), Calthorpe (96 in 144 minutes, 11 fours), Chapman (49 in 71 minutes, 6 fours) and Freeman (57 in 63 minutes, 1 six and 9 fours) contributed scores for M.C.C.. Freeman and Hartley adding 85 for the last wicket after Fisher had dismissed Maclean, Brand and Gibson in the space of four balls. Pellew (69 in 65 minutes, 1 six and 9 fours) and Chapman (134 not out in 142 minutes, 3 sixes and 12 fours) hit hard in the second innings. In all, 1319 runs were scored over three days at a rate of 78 per 100 balls. Five players - F.K.Gould, L.V.Pellew, P.D.Rundell, W.J.Whitty and N.L.Williams - announced their unavailability for South Australia. *O'Reilly* incorrectly gives MCC (2) Pellew 0/19 instead of Harris. Sources: *Wisden, C.B.O'Reilly, SACA Report, Adelaide Advertiser, South Australian Register.*

SOUTH AUSTRALIA

A.J.Richardson	c Lowry b Chapman	280			
V.Y.Richardson	run out (Wilson/Maclean)	1			
*C.E.Dolling	b Calthorpe	10	(5)	lbw b Gibson	33
J.T.Murray	c & b Freeman	8		not out	36
C.E.Pellew	c Maclean b Freeman	26	(1)	c Chapman b Freeman	69
E.L.Bowley	run out (Wilson/Maclean)	76	(3)	c Lowry b Freeman	35
G.W.Harris	c Hill-Wood b Freeman	4	(2)	c Hill-Wood b Gibson	27
J.W.Rymill	st Maclean b Freeman	50			
H.M.Fisher	c & b Freeman	22			
A.J.Carragher	st Maclean b Freeman	11			
†A.M.Ambler	not out	0			
Extras	(b2, lb5)	7		(b4)	4
Total	(74.7 overs, 272 mins)	495		(30.2 overs, 103 mins) (4 wkts dec)	204

M.C.C.

W.W.Hill-Wood	c Ambler b A.J.Richardson	3		b Murray	41
G.Wilson	st Ambler b Murray	78	(6)	not out	6
F.S.G.Calthorpe	c A.J.Richardson b Carragher	96	(4)	b Murray	12
A.P.F.Chapman	b Fisher	49	(2)	not out	134
T.C.Lowry	b Bowley	17		b Carragher	45
C.H.Titchmarsh	b Fisher	0	(3)	lbw b Fisher	5
†J.F.Maclean	c & b Fisher	37			
*J.C.Hartley	not out	28			
D.F.Brand	b Fisher	0			
C.H.Gibson	b Fisher	0			
A.P.Freeman	c Fisher b Carragher	57			
Extras	(b1, lb6)	7		(b3, lb2)	5
Total	(73.7 overs, 320 mins)	372		(32.0 overs, 142 mins) (4 wkts)	248

M.C.C.	O	M	R	W	w,nb		O	M	R	W	w,nb
Gibson	27	3	127	0	-,-		15.2	1	87	2	-,-
Freeman	27.7	0	176	6	-,-		12	0	92	2	-,-
Calthorpe	11	0	101	1	-,-		3	0	21	0	-,-
Brand	3	0	51	0	-,-						
Chapman	6	0	33	1	-,-						

SOUTH AUSTRALIA	O	M	R	W	w,nb		O	M	R	W	w,nb
Fisher	20	1	96	5	-,-		8	0	59	1	-,-
A.J.Richardson	21	4	60	1	-,-						
Carragher	18.7	1	123	2	-,-	(4)	7	0	69	1	-,-
Bowley	7	1	52	1	-,-	(2)	4	0	33	0	-,-
Murray	5	0	27	1	-,-	(3)	10	0	63	2	-,-
Pellew	2	0	7	0	-,-						
Harris						(5)	3	0	19	0	-,-

FALL OF WICKETS

	SA	MCC	SA	MCC
Wkt	1st	1st	2nd	2nd
1st	15	17	89	87
2nd	51	182	126	98
3rd	65	200	153	131
4th	169	235	204	238
5th	366	237	-	-
6th	371	282	-	-
7th	446	287	-	-
8th	484	287	-	-
9th	484	287	-	-
10th	495	372	-	-

WESTERN AUSTRALIA v NEW SOUTH WALES

Played at W.A.C.A. Ground, Perth, on March 17, 19, 20, 1923. (Three-day match)

Toss : New South Wales. Result : NEW SOUTH WALES WON BY AN INNINGS AND 11 RUNS.

Debuts: Western Australia - H.J.Clark, A.E.Hardie, H.J.Herbert, F.H.Taaffe (all f/c). New South Wales - N.E.Phillips (f/c).

12th Men: L.C.Renfrey (WA) and S.C.Everett (NSW).

Umpires: A.E.Lawrence and C.Sinclair.

Attendances: 4000, 1500, "a few enthusiasts". Total: About 6000. Receipts: £420.

Close of Play: 1st day WA 3/55 (Taaffe 30, Hardie 1); 2nd day WA (2) 8/159 (Herbert 4, Buttsworth 6).

Phillips replaced E.E.B.Forssberg (unavailable) in the New South Wales twelve selected to tour Western Australia, while Renfrey replaced A.B.Meek (also unavailable) in the WA line-up. New South Wales scored at a fast rate on the first day with Macartney (60 minutes, 5 fours), Andrews (70 minutes, 1 six and 14 fours) and Hendry (115 minutes, 1 six and 16 fours) the main contributors. Western Australia collapsed in the face of Mailey's leg-spin in both innings. Taaffe (101 minutes, 5 fours) fought hard in the first innings but was unable to avoid the follow-on being enforced. Blundell (100 minutes, 4 fours) and Bott (72 minutes, 1 six and 2 fours) hit half-centuries but the last eight wickets fell with the addition of only 61 runs. There was no admission for the third day, 15 minutes being sufficient to decide the match. *Cricketer* gives incorrect match dates. Sources: *The Cricketer, NSWCA Report, The West Australian, Daily News.*

NEW SOUTH WALES

W.Bardsley	run out (Rowe/Hardie)	11
J.G.Morgan	lbw b Hardie	16
*C.G.Macartney	run out (Taaffe)	44
T.J.E.Andrews	hit wkt b Hardie	89
N.E.Phillips	run out (Evans/Taaffe)	0
H.S.T.L.Hendry	c Evans b Herbert	123
A.T.Gray	run out (Herbert)	0
J.D.Scott	c Stokes b Hardie	6
†W.A.S.Oldfield	lbw b Hardie	24
J.L.Wall	b Herbert	5
A.A.Mailey	not out	16
Extras	(b7, lb2)	9
Total	(55.0 overs, 207 mins)	343

WESTERN AUSTRALIA

A.H.J.C.Heindricks	c Morgan b Wall	12		b Scott	24
F.H.Taaffe	c Oldfield b Macartney	44		c Oldfield b Scott	3
G.R.Blundell	b Macartney	11		st Oldfield b Mailey	52
L.C.Bott	c Macartney b Mailey	0		c Scott b Macartney	54
A.E.Hardie	b Mailey	17		run out	6
*S.H.D.Rowe	b Scott	30	(7)	b Macartney	0
W.A.Evans	b Mailey	6	(9)	st Oldfield b Mailey	0
H.J.Herbert	not out	19		b Scott	4
F.R.Buttsworth	b Scott	7	(10)	not out	17
H.J.Clark	st Oldfield b Mailey	1	(6)	b Mailey	0
†W.Stokes	st Oldfield b Mailey	12		c Bardsley b Mailey	2
Extras	(nb1)	1		(b5, lb3, w1, nb1)	10
Total	(54.5 overs, 185 mins)	160		(44.3 overs, 167 mins)	172

WESTERN AUSTRALIA	O	M	R	W	w,nb
Buttsworth	15	1	68	0	-,-
Hardie	17	0	112	4	-,-
Taaffe	12	1	74	0	-,-
Evans	3	0	24	0	-,-
Clark	3	0	18	0	-,-
Herbert	5	0	38	2	-,-

NEW SOUTH WALES	O	M	R	W	w,nb		O	M	R	W	w,nb
Scott	12	2	42	2	-,1		10	2	21	3	1,1
Wall	6	1	19	1	-,-	(3)	3	1	6	0	-,-
Macartney	15	5	28	2	-,-	(2)	7	2	25	2	-,-
Mailey	20.5	4	66	5	-,-	(6)	14.3	1	53	4	-,-
Gray	1	0	4	0	-,-	(7)	3	0	19	0	-,-
Andrews						(5)	3	0	24	0	-,-
Phillips						(4)	4	1	14	0	-,-

FALL OF WICKETS

	NSW	WA	WA
Wkt	1st	1st	2nd
1st	30	14	4
2nd	37	53	64
3rd	148	54	111
4th	152	77	135
5th	179	101	142
6th	179	121	149
7th	188	121	152
8th	259	128	153
9th	290	133	159
10th	343	160	172

WESTERN AUSTRALIA v NEW SOUTH WALES

Played at W.A.C.A. Ground, Perth, on March 23, 24, 26, 1923. (Three-day match)
Toss : Western Australia.   Result : NEW SOUTH WALES WON BY AN INNINGS AND 129 RUNS.
Debuts: Western Australia - L.C.Renfrey (f/c).
12th Men: V.C.Carlson (WA) and N.E.Phillips (NSW).
Umpires: C.Sinclair and E.A.Walker.
Attendances: 1500, 3000, "a handful".   Total:About 5000.   Receipts: £260.
Close of Play: 1st day NSW 1/42 (Gray 25, Hendry 8); 2nd day WA (2) 1/9 (Hardie 6, Stokes 3).

Howard replaced A.H.J.C.Heindricks (injured in the team for Western Australia and topscored for his side, batting 180 minutes and striking 11 fours. As in the previous match the New South Wales batsmen scored at a rapid rate. Hendry (75 minutes, 3 fours), Bardsley (153 minutes, 12 fours, chance at 15) and Andrews (85 minutes, 1 six and 8 fours) were the main contributors Western Australia capitulated on a wet wicket on the last day. Howard was bowled by the first ball of the innings; Taaffe and Buttsworth suffered first-ball dismissals. Rowe batted down the order because of an ankle injury. *Cricketer* gives incorrect NSW bowling (1) Mailey 0/38. Sources: *The Cricketer, NSWCA Report, The West Australian, Daily News.*

WESTERN AUSTRALIA

H.C.Howard	c Oldfield b Hendry	74		b Everett	0
F.H.Taaffe	b Everett	8	(4)	c Wall b Hendry	0
G.R.Blundell	c Scott b Hendry	31	(5)	c Hendry b Wall	14
L.C.Bott	run out	47	(6)	c & b Hendry	2
A.E.Hardie	b Hendry	13	(2)	c Morgan b Wall	13
*S.H.D.Rowe	c & b Wall	14	(10)	st Oldfield b Wall	0
A.B.Meek	c Mailey b Hendry	5		c Wall b Hendry	10
H.J.Herbert	c Oldfield b Hendry	0		b Hendry	1
F.R.Buttsworth	c Hendry b Everett	2		c Mailey b Hendry	0
L.C.Renfrey	st Oldfield b Wall	20	(11)	not out	0
†W.Stokes	not out	10	(3)	c Andrews b Hendry	3
Extras	(b3, lb3, w1, nb2)	9		(b5, lb1)	6
Total	(67.3 overs, 240 mins)	233		(20.1 overs, 70 mins)	49

NEW SOUTH WALES

J.G.Morgan	b Hardie	8
A.T.Gray	c Renfrey b Hardie	45
H.S.T.L.Hendry	lbw b Taaffe	62
†W.A.S.Oldfield	b Renfrey	40
*C.G.Macartney	lbw b Taaffe	8
W.Bardsley	c Rowe b Taaffe	112
T.J.E.Andrews	lbw b Taaffe	87
J.D.Scott	b Renfrey	14
J.L.Wall	run out (Buttsworth)	9
A.A.Mailey	c Rowe b Taaffe	4
S.C.Everett	not out	0
Extras	(b17, lb5)	22
Total	(66.3 overs, 263 mins)	411

NEW SOUTH WALES	O	M	R	W	w,nb		O	M	R	W	w,nb
Scott	7	1	36	0	1,2						
Everett	12	1	47	2	-,-	(1)	1	0	7	1	-,-
Hendry	26	5	68	5	-,-		9.1	4	15	6	-,-
Wall	16.3	4	38	2	-,-	(2)	10	2	21	3	-,-
Mailey	6	1	35	0	-,-						

WESTERN AUSTRALIA	O	M	R	W	w,nb
Buttsworth	9	1	61	0	-,-
Hardie	11	0	89	2	-,-
Renfrey	23	0	119	2	-,-
Taaffe	17.3	1	89	5	-,-
Herbert	3	0	14	0	-,-
Bott	3	0	17	0	-,-

FALL OF WICKETS			
	WA	NSW	WA
Wkt	1st	1st	2nd
1st	11	13	0
2nd	72	97	16
3rd	153	133	16
4th	181	161	20
5th	190	181	28
6th	198	349	48
7th	198	375	49
8th	203	395	49
9th	203	411	49
10th	233	411	49

This purely domestic season comprised 11 first-class matches, all of them interstate based. Five States shared in the matches, only Western Australia neither hosting nor appearing in a fixture. The games between Victoria and New South Wales continued to generate huge public interest. Nearly 90,000 people attended their Sheffield Shield clash at Melbourne over the New Year, while 25,000 turned out for the opening day of their return match at Sydney commencing on Australia Day.

Victoria won all four of their engagements to regain the Shield which they had surrendered to New South Wales the previous year. Their strong batting, led by Mayne, Ponsford, Woodfull and Love, ensured they were never in danger of being defeated. Hartkopf, Wallace and Liddicut spearheaded a varied attack which had the measure of opposition batting throughout the campaign.

New South Wales twice accounted for South Australia - in the second instance by an innings - and came close to winning their momentous match against Victoria at Melbourne. Their formidable-looking batting lineup was not quite as prolific as in recent seasons. Kippax, Collins, Bardsley and Andrews all showed form but the consistency was not there. The bowling returns were also down on previous years. Gregory was again absent through injury and Mailey's reduced wicket tally was obtained at greater cost. Hendry proved to be the most effective member of the attack.

The South Australians continued to be outclassed by the two senior States and again failed to win a match. Their last win in a Sheffield Shield match had occurred some 10 years previously, in February 1914. The two Richardsons were the most consistent of the batsmen but the bowling, as had often been the case in past years, lacked the penetration to trouble the best opposition.

Queensland continued their efforts to gain admission to the Shield competition by playing as much first-class cricket as possible. They visited Adelaide for the first time to play South Australia, and also met Victoria at Melbourne and New South Wales at Sydney on an extensive tour south. However, they were unable to extend the three Shield teams and demonstrated that they did not yet possess the depth of ability to be competitive at the highest level. O'Connor, Thompson and Hornibrook stood head-and-shoulders above the rest. Griffiths, who took 10 wickets in the match against New South Wales at Brisbane, failed to take a wicket on the southern tour. Mayne and Ponsford, the Victorian openers, punished the Queensland attack to devastating effect in Melbourne to establish a new all-wicket record partnership for Australian first-class cricket.

Victoria journeyed to Hobart for their annual fixture against Tasmania and emerged victorious by five wickets. The match was chiefly notable for a century by Wootton in what proved to be his sole innings in first-class cricket. Hans Ebeling, later to play a sole Test for Australia, also secured seven wickets on debut.

The New Zealand Cricket Council invited the Board of Control to select an Australian XI for a six-week tour in February/March, but negotiations broke down over terms. The New South Wales Cricket Association then agreed to send their State team, with Board approval, as a substitute. Although H.L.Collins, State captain, C.Kelleway, J.D.Scott and J.M.Taylor were unavailable, a strong side was still able to be assembled. It was: C.G.Macartney (captain), T.J.E.Andrews, R.Bardsley, W.Bardsley, S.C.Everett, H.S.T.L.Hendry, A.F.Kippax, A.A.Mailey, D.A.Mullarkey, W.A.S.Oldfield, A.T.E.Punch and A.T.Ratcliffe.

Leading Aggregates

Batsmen	M	I	NO	Runs	HS	Ave.	Bowlers	Runs	Wkts	Ave.
W.H.Ponsford (V)	5	8	1	777	248	111.00	A.E.V.Hartkopf (V)	639	26	24.57
R.E.Mayne (V)	5	8	1	576	209	82.28	N.L.Williams (SA)	699	26	26.88
A.F.Kippax (NSW)	4	7	0	452	248	64.57	P.H.Wallace (V)	496	19	26.10
F.C.Thompson (Q)	4	8	0	397	134	49.62	H.S.T.L.Hendry (NSW)	406	18	22.55
A.J.Richardson (SA)	5	10	1	371	144	41.22	A.A.Mailey (NSW)	682	18	37.88
L.P.D.O'Connor (Q)	4	8	0	360	184	45.00				

SHEFFIELD SHIELD TABLE

	P	W	L	D	Pts	Quotient	Runs Scored	Wkts Lost	Runs Conceded	Wkts Taken
VICTORIA	4	4	-	-	4	1.381	2269	62	2119	80
NEW SOUTH WALES	4	2	2	-	0	1.141	2307	70	2078	72
SOUTH AUSTRALIA	4	-	4	-	-4	0.617	1768	80	2147	60
TOTAL	6	6	6	-	0	1.000	6344	212	6344	212

QUEENSLAND v NEW SOUTH WALES

Played at Exhibition Ground, Brisbane, on November 30, December 1, 3, 1923. (Three-day match)
Toss : New South Wales.   Result : MATCH DRAWN.
Debuts: Queensland - M.H.Blaxland (Qld only). New South Wales - D.A.Mullarkey (f/c).
12th Men: H.R.G.Poon (Qld) and H.Cranney (NSW).
Umpires: W.H.Carvosso and A.E.Wyeth.
Attendances: 3000, 10000, 3000.   Total: About 16,000.   Receipts: £950.
Close of Play: 1st day Qld 3/158 (O'Connor 58, Rowe 5); 2nd day NSW (2) 3/194 (Mullarkey 115, Bardsley 43).

Mullarkey, a late inclusion in the New South Wales side for W.L.Berry who was unavailable, scored a century on debut (130 in 225 minutes, 14 fours) after surviving a chance to the keeper off Ron Oxenham when 55. Macartney (60 in 72 minutes, 8 fours) and Wells (40 not out in 73 minutes, 3 fours) were chief contributors to the meagre New South Wales first innings while Bardsley (46 in 103 minutes, 3 fours) and Wells (45 in 67 minutes, 4 fours) provided the most support to Mullarkey in the second. Queensland, who omitted Poon and S.J.Fennelly from their thirteen, gave the 39-year-old Blaxland - who last played first-class cricket for New South Wales in 1907-08 - his sole match for the State. Lionel Oxenham was run out without facing a ball while attempting a third run for Farquhar in the first over. Farquhar (40 in 43 minutes, 5 fours), O'Connor (61 in 132 minutes, 1 fours) and Thompson (46 in 60 minutes, 6 fours) saw Queensland to a lead. O'Connor (69 in 104 minutes, 1 six and 4 fours) and Thompson (61 in 88 minutes, 8 fours) held the second innings together with a century partnership. Worsening light caused the abandonment of the game at 5.30pm. *Cricketer, NSWCA Report* and *SMH* all incorrectly give NSW (1) Mullarkey st Farquhar, Mailey st Farquhar. Sources: *The Cricketer, NSWCA Report, Sydney Morning Herald, Brisbane Courier, Brisbane Daily Mail.*

NEW SOUTH WALES

D.A.Mullarkey	c Farquhar b Hornibrook	6	b Hornibrook	130
W.G.F.Brown	c Blaxland b Ayres	17	c O'Connor b Hornibrook	1
*C.G.Macartney	c Sheppard b Griffiths	60	b Hornibrook	5
H.S.T.L.Hendry	st Farquhar b Griffiths	24	c Thompson b Griffiths	25
R.Bardsley	lbw b R.K.Oxenham	1	b Griffiths	46
A.P.Wells	not out	40	b Griffiths	45
†W.A.S.Oldfield	lbw b Hornibrook	15	c O'Connor b R.K.Oxenham	21
A.N.Thatcher	b Hornibrook	0	b Griffiths	19
A.T.Gray	c L.E.Oxenham b Griffiths	1	b Griffiths	5
J.D.Scott	b Griffiths	8	b Griffiths	10
A.A.Mailey	c Farquhar b R.K.Oxenham	1	not out	11
Extras	(b3)	3	(b2, lb7)	9
Total	(35.6 overs, 141 mins)	176	(74.0 overs, 289 mins)	327

QUEENSLAND

*†J.K.Farquhar	c Oldfield b Thatcher	40		st Oldfield b Gray	14
L.E.Oxenham	run out (Gray/Oldfield)	0	(5)	not out	11
L.P.D.O'Connor	run out (Mullarkey)	61		b Gray	69
F.C.Thompson	b Thatcher	46		lbw b Gray	61
W.Rowe	b Hendry	37	(6)	not out	8
J.F.Sheppard	b Hendry	18	(2)	c Oldfield b Hendry	1
R.K.Oxenham	c Oldfield b Scott	12			
M.H.Blaxland	b Hendry	1			
P.M.Hornibrook	c Oldfield b Gray	1			
S.W.Ayres	c & b Hendry	5			
C.Griffiths	not out	0			
Extras	(b6, lb6, nb6)	18		(b4, lb3, w1, nb1)	9
Total	(64.4 overs, 224 mins)	239		(43.0 overs, 129 mins) (4 wkts)	173

QUEENSLAND	O	M	R	W	w,nb		O	M	R	W	w,nb
Hornibrook	11	1	49	3	-,-		27	2	114	3	-,-
Griffiths	15	1	67	4	-,-		21	1	71	6	-,-
Ayres	3	0	29	1	-,-	(5)	5	0	57	0	-,-
R.K.Oxenham	6.6	0	28	2	-,-	(3)	15	4	37	1	-,-
Rowe						(4)	6	0	39	0	-,-

NEW SOUTH WALES	O	M	R	W	w,nb		O	M	R	W	w,nb
Scott	18	2	55	1	-,6		5	0	19	0	1,-
Hendry	12.4	1	28	4	-,-		12	3	29	1	-,1
Thatcher	20	0	91	2	-,-	(5)	7	0	37	0	-,-
Mailey	5	1	18	0	-,-		9	0	45	0	-,-
Gray	9	1	29	1	-,-	(3)	10	2	34	3	-,-

FALL OF WICKETS

Wkt	NSW 1st	QLD 1st	NSW 2nd	QLD 2nd
1st	12	6	3	5
2nd	45	57	15	31
3rd	97	135	74	143
4th	100	172	203	158
5th	118	215	231	-
6th	153	218	256	-
7th	153	220	297	-
8th	154	230	304	-
9th	169	239	311	-
10th	176	239	327	-

SOUTH AUSTRALIA v NEW SOUTH WALES (Shield Match 1)

Played at Adelaide Oval on December 14, 15, 17, 18, 1923. (Timeless match)
Toss : South Australia.   Result : NEW SOUTH WALES WON BY 170 RUNS.
Debuts: South Australia - P.A.P.Ohlstrom, N.A.Walsh (both f/c); H.F.T.Heath (SA only).
12th Men: D.E.Pritchard (SA) and A.T.Gray (NSW).
Umpires: T.W.Cook and S.W.Smith.
Attendances: 3989, 10288, 3313, 3751.   Total: 21,341.   Receipts: £1019.
Close of Play: 1st day SA 6/79 (Heath 2); 2nd day NSW (2) 9/198 (Oldfield 4); 3rd day NSW (2) 9/332 (Oldfield 83, Mailey 53).

On a rain-affected pitch Oldfield (84 in 122 minutes, 8 fours) and Mailey (53 in 110 minutes, 5 fours) scored the only fifties and added a record 135 for the tenth wicket. Mailey (24) was missed by Murray off the bowling of Townsend at 238. Heath, brought in to replace the nominated South Australian captain V.Y.Richardson (business commitments), made his Sheffield Shield debut aged 37 years 361 days. His only previous first-class experience was for A.I.F. v Oxford University in 1919 and he was destined to play just one more match for South Australia. Rain ended play on the third day 20 minutes into the lunch-tea session. *Wisden* and *O'Reilly* incorrectly give SA (1) Bowley c Mailey. Sources: *Wisden, C.B.O'Reilly, NSWCA Report, Adelaide Advertiser, South Australian Register.*

NEW SOUTH WALES

*H.L.Collins	c Murray b Heath	7		c Heath b Townsend	1
W.Bardsley	c Fisher b Townsend	14	(4)	c Ambler b Fisher	2
C.G.Macartney	c Bowley b Heath	4	(2)	c Heath Richardson	34
T.J.E.Andrews	c Ambler b Heath	13	(3)	c Bowley b Fisher	47
J.M.Taylor	run out (Walsh)	12		c Richardson b Townsend	33
A.F.Kippax	c Richardson b Heath	11		hit wkt b Ohlstrom	20
C.Kelleway	c Fisher b Heath	13		st Ambler b Williams	26
H.S.T.L.Hendry	b Townsend	0		c Townsend b Williams	26
†W.A.S.Oldfield	c Bowley b Townsend	9		c & b Townsend	84
J.D.Scott	not out	15		c Heath b Williams	1
A.A.Mailey	lbw b Townsend	0		not out	53
Extras		-		(b3, lb2, nb1)	6
Total	(24.4 overs, 115 mins)	98		(70.4 overs, 278 mins)	333

SOUTH AUSTRALIA

E.L.Bowley	c Bardsley b Hendry	33	c Mailey b Scott	18
A.J.Richardson	c Andrews b Kelleway	16	b Scott	0
*J.T.Murray	c Oldfield b Kelleway	8	c Oldfield b Kelleway	4
R.J.B.Townsend	c Oldfield b Kelleway	12	run out (Kelleway/Oldfield)	2
J.W.Rymill	st Oldfield b Kelleway	5	c Taylor b Scott	44
N.A.Walsh	b Hendry	2	c & b Mailey	3
H.F.T.Heath	c Taylor b Macartney	11	b Mailey	21
N.L.Williams	hit wkt b Kelleway	7	b Mailey	23
H.M.Fisher	c Collins b Hendry	4	not out	3
†A.M.Ambler	c & b Macartney	16	c Bardsley b Kelleway	7
P.A.P.Ohlstrom	not out	1	hit wkt b Mailey	3
Extras	(b1)	1	(b10, lb5, nb2)	17
Total	(31.4 overs, 134 mins)	116	(35.2 overs, 143 mins)	145

SOUTH AUSTRALIA	O	M	R	W	w,nb		O	M	R	W	w,nb					
Fisher	5	0	21	0	-,-	(4)	10	0	67	2	-,-					
Heath	12	3	43	5	-,-	(1)	14	0	78	0	-,-					
Townsend	6.4	0	33	4	-,-	(2)	20.4	4	63	3	-,-					
Richardson	1	0	1	0	-,-	(3)	10	0	50	1	-,-					
Ohlstrom							7	0	25	1	-,-					
Williams							9	0	44	3	-,1					

FALL OF WICKETS

	NSW	SA	NSW	SA
Wkt	1st	1st	2nd	2nd
1st	12	42	5	1
2nd	20	56	65	8
3rd	38	58	73	11
4th	39	74	86	71
5th	56	77	134	81
6th	66	79	146	83
7th	66	88	187	112
8th	74	95	196	131
9th	98	113	198	133
10th	98	116	333	145

NEW SOUTH WALES	O	M	R	W	w,nb		O	M	R	W	w,nb
Kelleway	16	3	40	5	-,-	(2)	10	0	22	2	-,1
Macartney	5.4	0	31	2	-,-	(3)	4	0	16	0	-,-
Hendry	10	0	44	3	-,-						
Scott						(1)	12	0	48	3	-,1
Mailey						(4)	9.2	0	42	4	-,-

VICTORIA v QUEENSLAND

Played at Melbourne Cricket Ground on December 21, 22, 24, 1923. (Three-day match)
Toss : Queensland.   Result : VICTORIA WON BY AN INNINGS AND 241 RUNS.
Debuts: Queensland - H.R.G.Poon (f/c).
12th Men: J.Mathers (Vic) and E.C.Bensted (Qld).
Umpires: H.J.Alessio and J.Richards.
Attendances: 5000, 10000, 2000.   Total: About 17,000.   Receipts: £611.
Close of Play: 1st day Vic 0/108 (Mayne 47, Ponsford 59); 2nd day Vic 2/538 (Woodfull 46, Love 17).

Edgar Mayne (209 in 378 minutes, 12 fours) and Bill Ponsford (248 in 359 minutes, 22 fours) established a new record partnership for any wicket in Australian first-class cricket which was to stand until the 1986-87 season. Ponsford offered two chances during his innings, a return catch to Hornibrook when 132 and a chance to Griffiths off R.K.Oxenham when 170. Woodfull, called up to replace E.V.Carroll (eye injury) at the last moment, arrived at the ground half an hour after the match began. Freemantle also arrived late for the start and as no 12th man was present (Mathers being present only late in the match) two Queenslanders were forced to act as substitutes against their side early on. Rowe contributed to each Queensland innings with scores of 42 (86 minutes, 1 four) and 55 not out (107 minutes, 3 fours). L.E.Oxenham's 43 occupied 86 minutes and included 3 fours. Gamble took the wickets of L.E.Oxenham and Sheppard with successive balls in the second innings, Mathers substituting for Willis at the time. Sources: *The Cricketer, VCA Report, The Age, The Argus, The Herald, Melbourne Sun, The Australasian, Brisbane Courier.*

QUEENSLAND

†J.K.Farquhar	b Gamble	1	(2)	c Carlton b Gamble	7
L.E.Oxenham	c Love b Hartkopf	43	(1)	b Gamble	2
J.F.Sheppard	c Liddicut b Gamble	8		c sub (J.Mathers) b Gamble	0
F.C.Thompson	c & b Liddicut	14		b Gamble	23
*L.P.D.O'Connor	c & b Hartkopf	16		b Liddicut	11
W.Rowe	st Love b Ransford	42		not out	55
R.K.Oxenham	c Love b Liddicut	24		c Love b Gamble	8
H.R.G.Poon	b Ransford	2		b Carlton	10
P.M.Hornibrook	b Gamble	10		b Hartkopf	8
C.B.Barstow	b Gamble	0		b Carlton	0
C.Griffiths	not out	1		st Love b Hartkopf	3
Extras	(lb1)	1		(b6, lb1, nb1)	8
Total	(55.6 overs, 195 mins)	162		(42.1 overs, 160 mins)	135

VICTORIA

*R.E.Mayne	b Barstow	209
W.H.Ponsford	lbw b R.K.Oxenham	248
W.M.Woodfull	not out	46
†H.S.B.Love	not out	17
C.B.Willis	)	
V.S.Ransford	)	
A.E.V.Hartkopf	)	
L.F.Freemantle	) did not bat	
T.A.Carlton	)	
A.E.Liddicut	)	
H.S.Gamble	)	
Extras	(b14, lb4)	18
Total	(124.0 overs, 422 mins) (2 wkts dec)	538

VICTORIA	O	M	R	W	w,nb		O	M	R	W	w,nb
Gamble	12.6	1	27	4	-,-		12	2	38	5	-,1
Carlton	12	5	16	0	-,-		8	4	25	2	-,-
Liddicut	10	2	27	2	-,-	(4)	4	1	10	1	-,-
Freemantle	10	1	40	0	-,-	(3)	4	0	22	0	-,-
Hartkopf	8	0	39	2	-,-		11.1	2	22	2	-,-
Ransford	3	0	12	2	-,-		3	0	10	0	-,-

QUEENSLAND	O	M	R	W	w,nb
Hornibrook	39	2	144	0	-,-
Barstow	24	1	110	1	-,-
Griffiths	29	4	115	0	-,-
R.K.Oxenham	17	0	87	1	-,-
Poon	8	0	29	0	-,-
L.E.Oxenham	6	1	27	0	-,-
Thompson	1	0	8	0	-,-

FALL OF WICKETS

Wkt	QLD 1st	VIC 1st	QLD 2nd
1st	2	456	5
2nd	19	480	5
3rd	49	-	14
4th	77	-	33
5th	96	-	86
6th	149	-	106
7th	149	-	120
8th	155	-	131
9th	161	-	132
10th	162	-	135

VICTORIA v NEW SOUTH WALES (Shield Match 2)

Played at Melbourne Cricket Ground on December 26, 27, 28, 29, 31, 1923, January 1, 1924. (Timeless match)
Toss : Victoria.   Result : VICTORIA WON BY 43 RUNS.
Debuts: Nil.
12th Men: H.S.B.Love (Vic) and A.T.Gray (NSW).
Umpires: R.M.Crockett and C.Garing.
Attendances: 14214, 16871, 14298, 19574, 15027, 9402.   Total: 89,386.   Receipts: £4365.
Close of Play: 1st day Vic 8/268 (Liddicut 12); 2nd day NSW 7/185 (Collins 94, Oldfield 13); 3rd day Vic (2) 2/136 (Woodfull 37,
    Ryder 54); 4th day Vic (2) 8/371 (Park 46, Ellis 11); 5th day NSW (2) 5/223 (Kippax 49, Kelleway 32).

Mayne (106 in 217 minutes, 5 fours) held the Victorian batting together on the first day, a performance emulated by Collins (108 in 298 minutes, 4 fours) for New South Wales. Andrews, yet to get off the mark, skied a ball behind the wicket and was dropped by Ellis; Ryder then seized the ball and threw the wicket down. A cautious innings by Woodfull (117 in 281 minutes, 3 fours) with assistance from Ryder (54 in 82 minutes, 1 four), Willis (59 in 110 minutes, 4 fours) and Park (50 in 172 minutes, 4 fours) put Victoria in a winning position on the fifth day. Bardsley (74 in 165 minutes, 4 fours) batted well in reply but the match appeared lost at 5/153, only to be revived with a sixth-wicket stand of 127 between Kippax (72 in 159 minutes, 6 fours) and Kelleway (98 in 223 minutes, 6 fours). Nearly 90,000 people watched the match unfold over six days. *Wisden* incorrectly gives NSW (2) Hendry b Ransford. Sources: *Wisden, NSWCA Report, VCA Report, The Age, The Argus, The Herald, The Australasian.*

VICTORIA

*R.E.Mayne	c Collins b Scott	106	st Oldfield b Mailey	20
W.H.Ponsford	lbw b Scott	45	b Kelleway	24
W.M.Woodfull	c Mailey b Kelleway	23	b Macartney	117
J.Ryder	c Scott b Hendry	42	st Oldfield b Mailey	54
C.B.Willis	c Hendry b Scott	3	c Oldfield b Hendry	59
R.L.Park	c Hendry b Scott	7	b Kelleway	50
A.E.V.Hartkopf	b Scott	2	c Hendry b Macartney	0
V.S.Ransford	b Hendry	20	b Kelleway	17
A.E.Liddicut	c Hendry b Kelleway	12	c Hendry b Mailey	15
†J.L.Ellis	not out	4	not out	27
P.H.Wallace	c Collins b Kelleway	13	c Oldfield b Mailey	14
Extras	(b5, lb1, w2)	8	(b4, lb9, w1, nb1)	15
Total	(88.0 overs, 313 mins)	285	(145.2 overs, 498 mins)	412

NEW SOUTH WALES

*H.L.Collins	c Hartkopf b Liddicut	108	b Wallace	24
W.Bardsley	c Ellis b Wallace	3	b Wallace	74
C.G.Macartney	c Ellis b Liddicut	0	c & b Ryder	6
T.J.E.Andrews	run out (Ryder)	0	b Ryder	2
J.M.Taylor	c Willis b Liddicut	3	b Ryder	22
A.F.Kippax	c Ellis b Liddicut	35	lbw b Hartkopf	72
C.Kelleway	c Park b Hartkopf	19	lbw b Hartkopf	98
H.S.T.L.Hendry	c Park b Ryder	17	lbw b Ransford	31
†W.A.S.Oldfield	b Wallace	49	b Ryder	13
J.D.Scott	c Liddicut b Hartkopf	11	st Ellis b Hartkopf	11
A.A.Mailey	not out	15	not out	4
Extras	(b5, lb3)	8	(b19, lb6, w1, nb3)	29
Total	(98.5 overs, 341 mins)	268	(105.3 overs, 400 mins)	386

NEW SOUTH WALES	O	M	R	W	w,nb		O	M	R	W	w,nb			FALL OF WICKETS		
Scott	29	3	107	5	2,-		25	3	100	0	-,1			VIC	NSW	VIC	NSW
Kelleway	21	6	38	3	-,-		39	7	90	3	-,-	Wkt	1st	1st	2nd	2nd
Macartney	1	0	2	0	-,-	(6)	11	3	28	2	-,-	1st	99	12	44	64
Mailey	23	0	89	0	-,-	(3)	45.2	8	123	4	1,-	2nd	155	13	44	78
Hendry	14	2	41	2	-,-	(4)	21	2	45	1	-,-	3rd	211	15	137	80
Kippax						(5)	4	0	11	0	-,-	4th	227	23	253	116
												5th	229	72	294	153
VICTORIA	O	M	R	W	w,nb		O	M	R	W	w,nb	6th	233	107	294	280
Wallace	20.5	0	66	2	-,-		27	6	80	2	1,2	7th	242	163	320	334
Liddicut	31	10	50	4	-,-		26	3	59	0	-,1	8th	264	218	343	363
Ryder	18	5	44	1	-,-	(4)	21	2	81	4	-,-	9th	269	242	378	377
Hartkopf	26	2	87	2	-,-	(3)	20.3	1	101	3	-,-	10th	285	268	412	386
Ransford	3	0	13	0	-,-		11	2	36	1	-,-					

SOUTH AUSTRALIA v QUEENSLAND

Played at Adelaide Oval on December 26, 27, 28, 1923. (Three-day match)
Toss : Queensland.   Result : SOUTH AUSTRALIA WON BY TEN WICKETS.
Debuts: South Australia - E.G.C.Wainwright (f/c). Queensland - E.C.Bensted (f/c).
12th Men: F.K.Gould (SA) and T.H.Smith (Qld).
Umpires: C.L.Cornish and S.W.Smith.
Attendances: 4906, 7630, 4300.   Total: 16,836.   Receipts: £792.
Close of Play: 1st day Qld 7/357 (O'Connor 173, Hornibrook 7); 2nd day SA 3/341 (Bowley 152, Pritchard 35).

Queensland's first match on South Australian soil and the first meeting between the teams in 25 years was restricted to three days because of upcoming Shield fixtures. H.M.Fisher and H.F.T.Heath announced their unavailability for South Australia and Wainwright was a late replacement for W.J.Whitty (ill). O'Connor (184 in 305 minutes, 20 fours) and Thompson (54 in 78 minutes, 6 fours) for Queensland and Bowley (192 in 305 minutes, 19 fours), Murray (113 in 160 minutes, 13 fours) and Pritchard (65 in 69 minutes, 1 six and 8 fours) for South Australia compiled the most noteworthy innings. Smith substituted in the field for Griffiths early on the last day when Griffiths injured a finger attempting to catch Pritchard. Williams wrapped up the second innings by twice taking two wickets with consecutive balls. A.J.Richardson finished the match with a six. Sources: *The Cricketer, C.B.O'Reilly, SACA Report, Adelaide Advertiser, South Australian Register, Adelaide Daily Herald, The News.*

QUEENSLAND

†J.K.Farquhar	c Ambler b A.J.Richardson	0	run out (V.Y.Richardson/Ambler)		10
L.E.Oxenham	st Ambler b Williams	7	b Townsend		7
*L.P.D.O'Connor	b Williams	184	c Walsh b A.J.Richardson		3
F.C.Thompson	st Ambler b Williams	54	b Williams		32
W.Rowe	b Williams	12	not out		41
J.F.Sheppard	c Ambler b Townsend	37	c Wainwright b Williams		1
R.K.Oxenham	b A.J.Richardson	24	b Townsend		0
E.C.Bensted	st Ambler b Williams	31	c Ambler b Williams		11
P.M.Hornibrook	b Williams	18	b Williams		0
C.B.Barstow	b Townsend	10	c Townsend b Williams		1
C.Griffiths	not out	13	c & b Williams		0
Extras	(b2, lb9, nb3)	14	(b3, lb5, nb1)		9
Total	(91.0 overs, 327 mins)	404	(35.2 overs, 138 mins)		115

SOUTH AUSTRALIA

E.L.Bowley	st Farquhar b Hornibrook	192		
*V.Y.Richardson	b Barstow	13		
J.T.Murray	c Thompson b Hornibrook	113		
A.J.Richardson	b Hornibrook	18	(1) not out	26
D.E.Pritchard	c L.E.Oxenham b Hornibrook	65		
R.J.B.Townsend	run out (sub T.H.Smith)	15	(2) not out	25
N.A.Walsh	c Bensted b Barstow	4		
J.W.Rymill	run out (/Barstow)	11		
E.G.C.Wainwright	lbw b Hornibrook	2		
N.L.Williams	b Hornibrook	17		
†A.M.Ambler	not out	0		
Extras	(b2, lb11, nb1)	14	(b2, lb3, w1)	6
Total	(80.3 overs, 327 mins)	464	(5.7 overs, 29 mins) (0 wkts)	57

SOUTH AUSTRALIA	O	M	R	W	w,nb	O	M	R	W	w,nb
Townsend	25	10	74	2	-,-	12	4	24	2	-,-
A.J.Richardson	19	3	69	2	-,-	7	0	17	1	-,-
Williams	29	3	155	6	-,3	12.2	1	40	6	-,1
Wainwright	11	1	41	0	-,-	4	0	25	0	-,-
Bowley	3	0	19	0	-,-					
Murray	2	0	15	0	-,-					
Pritchard	2	0	17	0	-,-					

QUEENSLAND	O	M	R	W	w,nb		O	M	R	W	w,nb
Hornibrook	29.3	1	160	6	-,-		2	0	19	0	-,-
Barstow	19	0	109	2	-,1						
R.K.Oxenham	10	1	57	0	-,-	(2)	2.7	0	22	0	-,-
Griffiths	11	0	57	0	-,-						
Rowe	9	1	52	0	-,-						
Bensted	2	0	15	0	-,-						
L.E.Oxenham						(3)	1	0	10	0	1,-

FALL OF WICKETS

Wkt	QLD 1st	SA 1st	QLD 2nd	SA 2nd
1st	3	34	15	-
2nd	19	263	20	-
3rd	114	298	31	-
4th	152	397	90	-
5th	221	427	96	-
6th	287	432	97	-
7th	338	444	111	-
8th	375	444	111	-
9th	386	455	115	-
10th	404	464	115	-

NEW SOUTH WALES v QUEENSLAND

Played at Sydney Cricket Ground on December 31, 1923, January 1, 2, 1924. (Three-day match)
Toss : Queensland.   Result : MATCH DRAWN.
Debuts: Nil.
12th Men: C.C.O'Connor (NSW) and H.R.G.Poon (Qld).
Umpires: E.R.Kent and E.Whalley.
Attendances: 6000, 4700, 1000.   Total: About 11,700.   Receipts: £591.
Close of Play: 1st day NSW 1/59 (Mullarkey 35, Thatcher 0); 2nd day NSW 442 all out.

Ratcliffe, chosen to replace H.Carter (unavailable) as New South Wales captain and wicket-keeper, pulled off a remarkable dismissal on the first day when he chased a ball to the boundary edge, removed his glove and threw in a powerful return to run out O'Connor, attempting a fourth run. Sheppard (56 in 66 minutes, 6 fours), Thompson (134 in 224 minutes, 1 five and 13 fours) and Bensted (54 in 85 minutes, 7 fours) topscored for Queensland. Five fifties were registered for New South Wales, Mullarkey (64 in 147 minutes, 4 fours), Punch (74 in 86 minutes, 9 fours), Ratcliffe (74 in 162 minutes, 8 fours), Wells (70 in 114 minutes, 5 fours) and Brown (60 not out in 50 minutes, 7 fours). Wall captured the wickets of Thompson and Hornibrook with successive balls. Sources: *NSWCA Report, Sydney Morning Herald, Sydney Referee*.

QUEENSLAND

†J.K.Farquhar	c Wall b Punch	46	b McCoy	12
L.E.Oxenham	run out (Mullarkey/Ratcliffe)	38	b Everett	6
*L.P.D.O'Connor	run out (Ratcliffe/McCoy)	12	c Ratcliffe b Wall	4
F.C.Thompson	st Ratcliffe b Thatcher	33	lbw b Wall	134
W.Rowe	b Everett	44	b Wall	3
J.F.Sheppard	b Punch	56	c Bardsley b Punch	18
T.H.Smith	b McCoy	17	(8) b Thatcher	1
R.K.Oxenham	hit wkt b Punch	11	(9) not out	38
E.C.Bensted	not out	27	(7) c Wall b Thatcher	54
P.M.Hornibrook	b Punch	9	c & b Wall	0
C.B.Barstow	c Wall b Punch	7	c Wall b Thatcher	1
Extras	(lb4, w1, nb4)	9	(b4, lb4, w3, nb3)	14
Total	(62.7 overs, 252 mins)	309	(73.0 overs, 270 mins)	285

NEW SOUTH WALES

B.L.McCoy	c O'Connor b Hornibrook	21	c Hornibrook Barstow	5
D.A.Mullarkey	c Farquhar b R.K.Oxenham	64		
A.N.Thatcher	b Rowe	26	(2) not out	15
R.Bardsley	lbw b Rowe	0		
H.H.Davis	c Farquhar b Hornibrook	15		
A.T.E.Punch	c Bensted b R.K.Oxenham	74		
*†A.T.Ratcliffe	c & b L.E.Oxenham	74		
A.P.Wells	c Bensted b Rowe	70		
W.G.F.Brown	not out	60		
J.L.Wall	c Rowe b Hornibrook	5	(3) not out	3
S.C.Everett	b R.K.Oxenham	23		
Extras	(b1, lb7, w1, nb1)	10	(b2)	2
Total	(99.5 overs, 400 mins)	442	(10.0 overs, 50 mins) (1 wkt)	25

NEW SOUTH WALES	O	M	R	W	w,nb		O	M	R	W	w,nb
Everett	19	2	91	1	1,1		20	3	48	1	2,2
Wall	14	0	60	0	-,-		22	6	67	4	-,-
Thatcher	17	0	80	1	-,-	(4)	14	0	76	3	-,-
McCoy	7	0	34	1	-,-	(3)	8	1	23	1	1,-
Punch	5.7	0	33	5	-,3		9	0	57	1	-,1

QUEENSLAND	O	M	R	W	w,nb		O	M	R	W	w,nb
Hornibrook	34	3	158	3	-,-		4	1	4	0	-,-
Barstow	20	1	88	0	-,1		5	0	11	1	-,-
Rowe	18	4	59	3	-,-						
R.K.Oxenham	17.5	2	70	3	-,-	(3)	1	0	8	0	-,-
L.E.Oxenham	4	0	19	1	1,-						
Bensted	4	0	28	0	-,-						
Thompson	2	0	10	0	-,-						

	FALL OF WICKETS			
	QLD	NSW	QLD	NSW
Wkt	1st	1st	2nd	2nd
1st	71	58	13	10
2nd	99	112	23	-
3rd	115	112	23	-
4th	157	128	41	-
5th	201	141	66	-
6th	228	242	191	-
7th	264	322	197	-
8th	270	385	280	-
9th	284	394	280	-
10th	309	442	285	-

VICTORIA v SOUTH AUSTRALIA (Shield Match 3)

Played at Melbourne Cricket Ground on January 2, 3, 4, 5, 1924. (Timeless match)
Toss : Victoria.   Result : VICTORIA WON BY 98 RUNS.
Debuts: Nil.
12th Men: T.A.Carlton (Vic) and N.A.Walsh (SA).
Umpires: D.A.Elder and A.D.Reaburn.
Attendances: 7325, 6469, 5958, 16910.   Total: 36,662.   Receipts: £1567.
Close of Play: 1st day Vic 6/182 (Park 2, Hartkopf 6); 2nd day SA 3/214 (A.J.Richardson 84, Gould 10); 3rd day Vic (2) 2/216
    (Ponsford 144, Love 40).

Ponsford, the mainstay of both Victorian innings, scored 81 (124 minutes, 3 fours) and 159 (213 minutes, 8 fours) and shared a third-wicket partnership of 149 with Love (105 in 183 minutes, 4 fours) to establish a match-winning lead. A.J.Richardson (144 in 295 minutes, 1 six and 6 fours, chance at 120) and V.Y.Richardson (100 in 140 minutes, 8 fours, two chances) added 152 out of 309 and scored 79 per cent of South Australia's first innings between them. Sources: *Wisden, C.B.O'Reilly, VCA Report, The Age, The Argus, The Herald, The Australasian.*

VICTORIA

*R.E.Mayne	st Ambler b Williams	32	c Williams b A.J.Richardson		20
W.H.Ponsford	b Whitty	81	c Ambler b Whitty		159
W.M.Woodfull	run out (V.Y.Richardson)	14	b A.J.Richardson		8
H.S.B.Love	b Fisher	31	c Ambler b Williams		105
C.B.Willis	c Townsend b Whitty	0	lbw b Whitty		3
J.Ryder	b A.J.Richardson	14	st Ambler b Williams		10
R.L.Park	c Townsend b Fisher	6	b Townsend		7
A.E.V.Hartkopf	lbw b Whitty	23	b Williams		4
A.E.Liddicut	b Whitty	11	not out		27
†J.L.Ellis	c Townsend b Whitty	5	st Ambler b Williams		4
P.H.Wallace	not out	0	st Ambler b Williams		1
Extras	(b1, lb2, nb1)	4	(b3, lb5, nb1)		9
Total	(61.0 overs, 240 mins)	221	(82.3 overs, 315 mins)		357

SOUTH AUSTRALIA

E.L.Bowley	b Liddicut	5	c Ryder b Hartkopf		30
A.J.Richardson	c Ellis b Liddicut	144	(5) b Ryder		3
*V.Y.Richardson	b Liddicut	100	b Ryder		15
D.E.Pritchard	c Willis b Liddicut	14	lbw b Wallace		33
F.K.Gould	st Ellis b Hartkopf	23	(2) b Hartkopf		27
R.J.B.Townsend	c Woodfull b Hartkopf	2	run out (Hartkopf)		20
J.W.Rymill	b Wallace	6	b Wallace		5
N.L.Williams	c Ryder b Liddicut	5	c Ponsford b Hartkopf		14
W.J.Whitty	c Ellis b Liddicut	2	st Ellis b Hartkopf		10
H.M.Fisher	not out	6	c Woodfull b Hartkopf		2
†A.M.Ambler	b Hartkopf	0	not out		2
Extras	(lb1, w1)	2	(b5, lb5)		10
Total	(75.5 overs, 298 mins)	309	(39.7 overs, 169 mins)		171

SOUTH AUSTRALIA	O	M	R	W	w,nb		O	M	R	W	w,nb
Whitty	20	4	49	5	-,-		19	1	69	2	-,-
Fisher	15	1	60	2	-,-		10	0	61	0	-,-
Townsend	4	0	14	0	-,-	(5)	13	1	44	1	-,-
Williams	11	0	78	1	-,1	(3)	18.3	0	117	5	-,1
A.J.Richardson	11	4	16	1	-,-	(4)	22	1	57	2	-,-

VICTORIA	O	M	R	W	w,nb		O	M	R	W	w,nb
Wallace	20	0	67	1	-,-		9	0	47	2	-,-
Liddicut	26	4	65	6	1,-		12	3	34	0	-,-
Ryder	8	0	40	0	-,-	(4)	6	0	24	2	-,-
Hartkopf	20.5	0	128	3	-,-	(3)	12.7	1	56	5	-,-
Willis	1	0	7	0	-,-						

FALL OF WICKETS

Wkt	VIC 1st	SA 1st	VIC 2nd	SA 2nd
1st	79	7	78	53
2nd	106	159	111	72
3rd	142	197	260	78
4th	142	238	264	85
5th	167	242	280	137
6th	175	253	316	138
7th	186	276	320	157
8th	213	290	325	157
9th	220	308	331	168
10th	221	309	357	171

NEW SOUTH WALES v SOUTH AUSTRALIA (Shield Match 4)

Played at Sydney Cricket Ground on January 11, 12, 14, 1924. (Timeless match)
Toss : South Australia.   Result : NEW SOUTH WALES WON BY AN INNINGS AND 104 RUNS.
Debuts: Nil.
12th Men: D.A.Mullarkey (NSW) and N.A.Walsh (SA).
Umpires: A.H.Farrow and A.C.Jones.
Attendances: 4829, 15753, 6164.   Total: 26,746.   Receipts: £2001.
Close of Play: 1st day NSW 0/25 (Collins 13, Bardsley 11); 2nd day NSW 5/500 (Kippax 140, Hendry 24).

South Australia started brightly through A.J.Richardson (90 in 122 minutes, 1 six and 6 fours), V.Y.Richardson (135 in 193 minutes, 19 fours) and Pritchard (62 in 77 minutes, 6 fours) but collapsed to lose their last seven wickets for 23, including Rymill and Fisher first ball. Bardsley (144 in 234 minutes, 11 fours), Kippax (248 in 316 minutes, 32 fours) and Punch (84 in 84 minutes, 12 fours) contributed towards New South Wales' 475 runs on the second day. Kippax's solitary chance, a stumping off Williams, came with his score at 226 in an otherwise faultless display. Everett bowled Bowley with the second ball of the second innings. C.Kelleway, C.G.Macartney and J.D.Scott were all unavailable for New South Wales. *Wisden* incorrectly gives reversed dismissals for Gould and Rymill in SA (1).
Sources: *Wisden, C.B.O'Reilly, NSWCA Report, Sydney Morning Herald, Sydney Referee.*

SOUTH AUSTRALIA

E.L.Bowley	c Oldfield b Mailey	33		b Everett	0
A.J.Richardson	st Oldfield b Mailey	90		b Everett	41
*V.Y.Richardson	b Mailey	135		c Hendry b Punch	67
D.E.Pritchard	st Oldfield b Punch	62		b Hendry	20
F.K.Gould	b Mailey	24	(6)	b Everett	23
R.J.B.Townsend	c Mailey b Hendry	0	(5)	b Punch	1
J.W.Rymill	st Oldfield b Mailey	0		st Oldfield b Mailey	13
N.L.Williams	not out	9		b Everett	2
W.J.Whitty	c Collins b Mailey	3		not out	9
H.M.Fisher	c Everett b Hendry	0		b Everett	1
†A.M.Ambler	c Hendry b Mailey	8		lbw b Everett	4
Extras	(b3, lb13, nb3)	19		(b7, lb7, w1, nb1)	16
Total	(74.4 overs, 273 mins)	383		(49.0 overs, 185 mins)	197

NEW SOUTH WALES

*H.L.Collins	c Ambler b Whitty	19
W.Bardsley	c Ambler b Williams	144
T.J.E.Andrews	b A.J.Richardson	47
J.M.Taylor	st Ambler b Williams	29
A.F.Kippax	c Whitty b Williams	248
A.T.E.Punch	b A.J.Richardson	84
H.S.T.L.Hendry	c Bowley b Whitty	47
A.T.Gray	b Townsend	8
†W.A.S.Oldfield	b Whitty	36
A.A.Mailey	c Ambler b Williams	0
S.C.Everett	not out	2
Extras	(b12, lb5, nb3)	20
Total	(121.4 overs, 482 mins)	684

NEW SOUTH WALES	O	M	R	W	w,nb	O	M	R	W	w,nb
Everett	11	0	64	0	-,-	14	1	54	6	1,1
Hendry	22	2	68	2	-,-	12	1	35	1	-,-
Gray	7	0	45	0	-,-	1	0	3	0	-,-
Mailey	25.4	1	133	7	-,1	15	0	60	1	-,-
Punch	7	0	42	1	-,2	7	0	29	2	-,-
Kippax	2	0	12	0	-,-					

SOUTH AUSTRALIA	O	M	R	W	w,nb
Whitty	37	2	153	3	-,-
Fisher	15	1	113	0	-,3
Williams	24.4	0	196	4	-,-
Townsend	25	2	97	1	-,-
A.J.Richardson	20	0	105	2	-,-

FALL OF WICKETS

Wkt	SA 1st	NSW 1st	SA 2nd
1st	64	45	0
2nd	199	142	79
3rd	314	187	130
4th	360	300	146
5th	363	441	149
6th	363	564	173
7th	363	577	181
8th	374	668	181
9th	374	669	184
10th	383	684	197

NEW SOUTH WALES v VICTORIA (Shield Match 5)

Played at Sydney Cricket Ground on January 26, 28, 29, 30, 1924. (Timeless match)
Toss : Victoria.   Result : VICTORIA WON BY EIGHT WICKETS.
Debuts: Nil.
12th Men: D.A.Mullarkey (NSW) and C.B.Willis (Vic).
Umpires: A.C.Jones and A.P.Williams.
Attendances: 25408, 10367, 11373, 6463.   Total: 53,611.   Receipts: £4081.
Close of Play: 1st day Vic 1/41 (Mayne 18, Love 23); 2nd day Vic 9/323 (Mayne 135, Wallace 2); 3rd day NSW (2) 5/254 (Kippax 55, Hendry 28).

The match was scheduled to start on January 25th but rain prevented an adequate preparation of the pitch in time and it was postponed one day. Victoria omitted Willis and C.V.Grimmett from their squad of thirteen on the first morning; both were required as substitutes when mishaps befell two of the team members. Ryder sustained a back injury while bowling midway through the first day and did not field again in the match and Ellis was absent in the second innings due to gastritis. Scott strained a leg late on the first day and did not field again in the match; Mullarkey substituted throughout. Andrews (96 in 167 minutes, 11 fours) and Collins (81 in 194 minutes, 5 fours) topscored for New South Wales while Bardsley was out to the first ball of the second innings. Mayne survived four chances to carry his bat, hitting 10 fours. Ponsford (110 in 167 minutes, 11 fours and 110 not out in 183 minutes, 10 fours) achieved three centuries in successive first-class innings, following his 159 v South Australia in the previous match. Love kept wicket throughout the New South Wales second innings. *Wisden* incorrectly gives NSW (1) Wallace 3/47, Carlton 1/37, Liddicut 2/49. Sources: *Wisden, NSWCA Report, VCA Report, The Argus, Sydney Morning Herald, Sydney Referee.*

NEW SOUTH WALES

*H.L.Collins	c Ryder b Liddicut	16	(2) c Woodfull b Liddicut		81
W.Bardsley	c Ellis b Wallace	4	(1) b Wallace		0
C.G.Macartney	b Wallace	30	c Love b Wallace		35
T.J.E.Andrews	c Woodfull b Hartkopf	96	c Wallace b Hartkopf		44
A.F.Kippax	c Ellis b Wallace	1	c Ponsford b Wallace		65
A.T.E.Punch	c Ellis b Liddicut	10	b Hartkopf		6
H.S.T.L.Hendry	b Carlton	6	b Hartkopf		73
†W.A.S.Oldfield	c & b Hartkopf	4	c Love b Wallace		0
J.D.Scott	c sub (C.B.Willis) b Hartkopf	6	(11) not out		2
A.A.Mailey	not out	22	(9) b Wallace		0
J.L.Wall	c Ransford b Hartkopf	9	(10) b Hartkopf		9
Extras	(b1, lb11, w1)	13	(b4, lb1, nb1)		6
Total	(62.2 overs, 221 mins)	217	(87.4 overs, 330 mins)		321

VICTORIA

*R.E.Mayne	not out	154	c Mailey b Hendry		10
W.M.Woodfull	c Mailey b Hendry	0	(3) c Hendry b Wall		30
H.S.B.Love	lbw b Mailey	31	(4) not out		43
W.H.Ponsford	b Macartney	110	(2) not out		110
J.Ryder	b Hendry	3			
A.E.V.Hartkopf	c Kippax b Macartney	2			
V.S.Ransford	b Hendry	10			
A.E.Liddicut	c Mailey b Wall	14			
T.A.Carlton	st Oldfield b Mailey	1			
†J.L.Ellis	b Punch	2			
P.H.Wallace	b Macartney	4			
Extras	(b9, lb2, w1, nb2)	14	(lb1, w1)		2
Total	(129.7 overs, 419 mins)	345	(59.2 overs, 183 mins) (2 wkts)		195

VICTORIA	O	M	R	W	w,nb		O	M	R	W	w,nb
Wallace	16	3	48	3	1,-		27	4	99	5	-,-
Carlton	9	2	38	1	-,-		12	2	37	0	-,1
Liddicut	17	1	47	2	-,-		20	5	50	1	-,-
Ryder	6	0	22	0	-,-						
Hartkopf	14.2	1	49	4	-,-	(4)	28.4	0	129	4	-,-

NEW SOUTH WALES	O	M	R	W	w,nb		O	M	R	W	w,nb
Scott	4	0	11	0	-,-						
Hendry	35	4	81	3	-,1	(1)	13	3	35	1	-,-
Wall	14	4	35	1	-,-	(4)	17.2	1	55	1	1,-
Mailey	37	6	125	2	1,-	(3)	10	0	47	0	-,-
Punch	7	1	26	1	-,1		7	0	21	0	-,-
Andrews	3	0	17	0	-,-						
Macartney	29.7	12	36	3	-,-	(2)	12	3	35	0	-,-

FALL OF WICKETS

Wkt	NSW 1st	VIC 1st	NSW 2nd	VIC 2nd
1st	11	2	0	16
2nd	30	49	53	105
3rd	68	225	129	-
4th	72	234	192	-
5th	89	237	199	-
6th	114	265	279	-
7th	131	295	279	-
8th	145	300	279	-
9th	205	308	300	-
10th	217	345	321	-

SOUTH AUSTRALIA v VICTORIA (Shield Match 6)

Played at Adelaide Oval on February 15, 16, 18, 19 (no play), 20, 1924. (Timeless match)
Toss : South Australia.   Result : VICTORIA WON BY AN INNINGS AND 7 RUNS.
Debuts: Nil.
12th Men: P.K.Lee (SA) and A.E.Brown (Vic).
Umpires: F.K.Lindow and S.W.Smith.
Attendances: 3572, 8294, 2810, no play, 1736.   Total: 16,412.   Receipts: £775.
Close of Play: 1st day Vic 7/354 (Liddicut 42, Ellis 35); 2nd day Vic 9/444 (Ellis 88, Wallace 0); 3rd day SA 8/145 (Pritchard 43, Williams 1); 4th day no play.

South Australia concluded their sixth consecutive season of losing every Sheffield Shield match: a run of failure without equal in the history of the competition. V.Y.Richardson was unavailable for the home side and Heath replaced W.J.Whitty (also unavailable) after the team was selected. The Victorian selectors had to withdraw Brown and Keating from the side to play Tasmania to replace H.S.B.Love (unavailable) and J.Ryder (not recovered from back injury). Heath dismissed Ponsford (out to his second ball) with the third delivery of the match. Half-centuries in the lower order by Hartkopf (99 with 1 six and 14 fours), Liddicut (73 in 127 minutes, 7 fours) and Ellis (94 in 148 minutes, 8 fours) restored the batting from 5/144, the Liddicut/Ellis stand realised 134 for the eighth wicket. Pritchard (73 not out) and Murray (91 in 155 minutes, 10 fours) scored half-centuries for South Australia. Grimmett - playing the last of five matches for Victoria before he transferred to South Australia - began his record-breaking career in the Sheffield Shield by capturing the best innings figures by a bowler on debut in the competition. The previous best had been established by G.M.Pierce (8 for 111, NSW v SA at Adelaide 1892-93) in the first Shield match of all. Rain restricted play on the second day and washed out the fourth. *Wisden* and *VCA Report* incorrectly give SA (1) Wainwright lbw. Sources: *Wisden, C.B.O'Reilly, VCA Report, The Age, The Argus, Adelaide Advertiser, South Australian Register.*

VICTORIA

*R.E.Mayne	b Richardson	25
W.H.Ponsford	c Wainwright b Heath	0
W.M.Woodfull	c & b Wainwright	62
R.L.Park	b Williams	22
J.L.Keating	c Wainwright b Heath	1
C.B.Willis	c Bowley b Townsend	61
A.E.V.Hartkopf	lbw b Wainwright	99
A.E.Liddicut	run out (Walsh/Ambler)	73
†J.L.Ellis	c Murray b Pritchard	94
C.V.Grimmett	b Wainwright	3
P.H.Wallace	not out	3
Extras	(b6, lb3, w2)	11
Total	(96.1 overs, 361 mins)	454

SOUTH AUSTRALIA

E.L.Bowley	c Woodfull b Wallace	4	(4)	st Ellis b Grimmett	23
A.J.Richardson	lbw b Wallace	32		c Grimmett b Wallace	1
J.T.Murray	c Wallace b Keating	23	(5)	c Willis b Grimmett	91
D.E.Pritchard	not out	73	(1)	c Hartkopf b Grimmett	47
*P.D.Rundell	c Hartkopf b Keating	0	(3)	st Ellis b Grimmett	34
N.A.Walsh	b Grimmett	17		c Woodfull b Hartkopf	33
E.G.C.Wainwright	b Keating	1		c Ellis b Grimmett	4
R.J.B.Townsend	b Keating	11		st Ellis b Grimmett	4
H.F.T.Heath	b Keating	0	(10)	not out	3
N.L.Williams	c Liddicut b Wallace	13	(9)	c Ponsford b Grimmett	0
†A.M.Ambler	c Hartkopf b Keating	2		c & b Grimmett	5
Extras	(b8, lb2, w3, nb2)	15		(b2, lb2, w1, nb6)	11
Total	(53.0 overs, 210 mins)	191		(63.1 overs, 236 mins)	256

SOUTH AUSTRALIA	O	M	R	W	w,nb		O	M	R	W	w,nb
Heath	19	2	93	2	-,-						
Townsend	20	0	103	1	-,-						
Richardson	15	2	61	1	-,-						
Williams	14	0	69	1	2,-						
Murray	5	0	24	0	-,-						
Wainwright	16	1	52	3	-,-						
Rundell	4	0	37	0	-,-						
Pritchard	3.1	1	4	1	-,-						

VICTORIA	O	M	R	W	w,nb		O	M	R	W	w,nb
Wallace	17	4	36	3	2,-	(2)	13	0	53	1	1,5
Liddicut	17	4	56	0	1,1	(3)	15	2	41	0	-,1
Keating	16	2	72	6	-,1	(1)	9	0	37	0	-,-
Grimmett	3	0	12	1	-,-		19.1	1	86	8	-,-
Hartkopf							7	1	28	1	-,-

FALL OF WICKETS

Wkt	VIC 1st	SA 1st	SA 2nd
1st	1	4	9
2nd	40	50	82
3rd	87	68	85
4th	90	70	116
5th	144	104	198
6th	245	117	218
7th	287	139	222
8th	421	139	222
9th	442	185	250
10th	454	191	256

TASMANIA v VICTORIA

Played at T.C.A. Ground, Hobart, on February 21, 22, 23, 1924. (Timeless match)
Toss : Victoria.   Result : VICTORIA WON BY FIVE WICKETS.
Debuts: Tasmania - A.O.Burrows, N.W.Davis, A.Limb, C.E.Lucas (all f/c). Victoria - H.W.de Gruchy, H.I.Ebeling, W.J.Johnson,
    H.C.Lansdown, H.J.Richardson, C.A.H.Sindrey, W.A.Wilkinson, S.E.Wootton (all f/c).
12th Men: G.S.Loney (Tas) and K.J.Millar (Vic).
Umpires: W.M.McHugo and A.O'Leary.
Attendances: No figures were published; 150, 175 and 250 were estimated by a journalist.   Receipts: No figures published.
Close of Play: 1st day Vic 1/10 (Johnson 3, Ebeling 2); 2nd day Tas (2) 0/65 (Rushforth 28, Allan 28).

Limb was Tasmania's first choice as wicket-keeper but the late addition of Henty to the team saw him played as a batsman only, with Loney relegated to 12th man. Victoria had great difficulty in selecting a team to travel to Tasmania. T.A.Carlton, B.L.Cohen, L.F.Freemantle and H.S.Gamble all withdrew after being named for the trip and A.E.Brown and J.L.Keating were needed in Adelaide for the Shield side. De Gruchy, Ebeling, Ferguson, W.J.Rayson, K.J.Schneider, H.C.Schrader and Sindrey were nominated but Rayson, Schneider and Schrader declared their unavailability and were in turn replaced by Johnson, Lansdown and Richardson. Limb was dismissed second ball on debut. Burrows claimed the wickets of Ebeling and Herring with successive balls. Wootton's chanceless century on debut (destined to be his only innings in first-class cricket) took only 90 minutes in all and included 16 fours. He was struck a severe blow on the body by a ball from Newton when 97, was dismissed soon after, and took no further part in the match; Herring deputising as wicket-keeper in the second innings. Wootton remained unwell for some time after returning to Melbourne. Carroll (53 in 75 minutes, 5 fours) and Lansdown (47 in 65 minutes, 4 fours) also did well for Victoria. *Cricketer* incorrectly gives Tas (1) Ebeling 2/55. Sources: *The Cricketer, VCA Report, The Sporting Globe, Hobart Mercury, Launceston Examiner*.

TASMANIA

*A.W.Rushforth	st Wootton b Johnson	14		b Ebeling	31
G.H.Allan	c Richardson b Ebeling	24		b Ebeling	31
F.L.Butler	b Wilkinson	43		c Carroll b de Gruchy	3
A.C.Newton	b Richardson	9	(5)	b de Gruchy	0
A.K.E.Watt	st Wootton b Wilkinson	13	(6)	c Richardson b de Gruchy	7
N.W.Davis	c de Gruchy b Richardson	0	(7)	b Ebeling	39
A.Limb	b Richardson	0	(8)	c Herring b Richardson	10
G.W.Martin	c Ebeling b Wilkinson	40	(4)	c Herring b Ebeling	42
†P.G.Henty	b Richardson	9		b Ebeling	6
A.O.Burrows	c Wootton b Ebeling	8		run out (/Herring)	3
C.E.Lucas	not out	14		not out	0
Extras	(b3, lb3, nb1)	7		(b15, lb4, w1, nb7)	27
Total	(58.2 overs, 288 mins)	181		(55.6 overs, 202 mins)	199

VICTORIA

W.J.Johnson	b Newton	24		c Rushforth b Lucas	43
C.A.H.Sindrey	c Rushforth b Newton	4		c Rushforth b Burrows	13
H.I.Ebeling	b Burrows	5			
R.W.Herring	c Rushforth b Burrows	0	(3)	c Henty b Newton	1
*E.V.Carroll	c Henty b Lucas	53	(4)	c Lucas b Burrows	2
L.D.Ferguson	st Henty b Watt	10	(5)	b Newton	15
†S.E.Wootton	c Rushforth b Watt	105			
H.J.Richardson	c & b Lucas	2	(6)	not out	29
H.C.Lansdown	b Watt	47	(7)	not out	18
H.W.de Gruchy	st Henty b Watt	1			
W.A.Wilkinson	not out	1			
Extras	(b2, lb1, w1)	4		(b3, w1)	4
Total	(51.5 overs, 206 mins)	256		(35.5 overs, 135 mins) (5 wkts)	125

VICTORIA	O	M	R	W	w,nb		O	M	R	W	w,nb			FALL OF WICKETS		
Ebeling	17.2	1	57	2	-,-		20	3	59	5	1,1			TAS	VIC	TAS	VIC
Wilkinson	16	2	52	3	-,-		5	0	17	0	-,-	Wkt	1st	1st	2nd	2nd
Johnson	9	3	27	1	-,-		3	0	8	0	-,-	1st	37	8	74	21
de Gruchy	3	1	4	0	-,1	(5)	14	1	52	3	-,6	2nd	51	17	75	22
Richardson	13	2	34	4	-,-	(4)	13.6	5	36	1	-,-	3rd	78	17	77	25
												4th	106	61	77	52
TASMANIA	O	M	R	W	w,nb		O	M	R	W	w,nb	5th	107	96	87	104
Newton	18	0	67	2	-,-		14	0	36	2	-,-	6th	107	106	171	-
Burrows	11	0	57	2	1,-		8	0	28	2	1,-	7th	111	121	189	-
Lucas	8	0	38	2	-,-	(4)	4.5	1	17	1	-,-	8th	130	254	189	-
Watt	8.5	0	45	4	-,-	(3)	5	0	18	0	-,-	9th	159	255	198	-
Allan	6	0	45	0	-,-		0		22	0	-,-	10th	181	256	199	-

A.E.R.Gilligan led a full-strength MCC team which held high hopes of defeating the Australians in the five-Test series, only to lose 4-1. However, the contest was not as one-sided as might appear at first glance. Australia won the first two Tests, both high-scoring affairs, by reasonably comfortable margins. They also won the third, but only by 11 runs, after England had appeared better placed late on the sixth day. An England victory by an innings in the Fourth Test confirmed that, with luck, the series could have been 2-2 at that point. Australia, through the bowling of Grimmett (11 for 82 on debut), won the final Test convincingly.

The batting of both sides bore a formidable look throughout the series, with Ryder, Ponsford and Taylor (Australia) and Hobbs, Sutcliffe, Hendren and Woolley (England) all performing prominently. It followed that the bowlers paid a higher price than normal for their wickets - this was true with the notable exception of Maurice Tate. He virtually carried the English bowling on his own and his 38 wickets established a record for England in Australia.

The MCC team played 23 matches in all on their tour of Australia, 17 of which were first-class (eight won, six lost, three drawn). Losses to South Australia and Victoria complemented their four Test defeats. Sutcliffe, Hendren, Hobbs and Sandham all exceeded 1000 runs (Sutcliffe and Hendren did it in first-class games alone), while Tate secured almost twice as many wickets as the next bowler (85 including 77 first-class).

The presence of an English team in the country decreased interest in the Sheffield Shield to some extent. Victoria retained the title by winning three of their four encounters, their sole loss being at the hands of New South Wales in the final match. South Australia recorded their first win in a Shield match since February 1914 when they accounted for New South Wales at Adelaide. New South Wales won a match each against South Australia and Victoria.

Batting generally predominated over bowling in the Shield season, as it had in the Test matches. Victoria's more consistent performances allround carried the day, despite some fine individual performances from Kippax, Rock, Mailey and Gregory (New South Wales) and Grimmett and the two Richardsons (South Australia). Rock was selected for only two matches due to the depth of the New South Wales lineup, but in these he returned innings of 127, 27 not out, 235 and 51 - a brilliant start to his first-class career. His medical career severely limited further opportunities. New South Wales (and Australia) missed the services of C.G.Macartney, who was unable to play at all after November due to a nervous breakdown, despite later claims to the contrary in his autobiography.

Return matches between New South Wales and Queensland were played, Queensland winning at Brisbane but a draw resulting in Sydney. There was no meeting of Tasmania and Victoria due to the presence of the MCC team. A match between New South Wales and an Australian XI was staged in October as a benefit for W.P.Howell. In all, 26 matches of first-class status were played - equalling the record for an Australian season set in 1907-08.

A Victorian team undertook a six-week tour of New Zealand from the end of February at the invitation of the New Zealand Cricket Council. Leading players, H.S.T.L.Hendry, W.H.Ponsford, J.Ryder and F.A.Tarrant were unavailable and the final selection blended youth with experience. The team was: R.E.Mayne [captain], E.T.Austen, H.M.Austin, H.I.Ebeling, J.L.Ellis, A.E.V.Hartkopf, A.E.Liddicut, K.J.Millar, V.S.Ransford, P.H.Wallace, C.B.Willis and W.M.Woodfull. Both E.T.Austen and H.M.Austin made their initial Victorian appearances on the tour but E.T.Austen was the only one of the pair to do so again in the future. H.M.Austin had previous first-class experience with Cambridge University in 1924.

Leading Aggregates

Batsmen	M	I	NO	Runs	HS	Ave.	Bowlers	Runs	Wkts	Ave.
H.Sutcliffe (MCC)	12	18	0	1250	188	69.44	M.W.Tate (MCC)	1464	77	19.01
E.H.Hendren (MCC)	14	22	3	1233	168	64.89	C.V.Grimmett (SA)	1300	59	22.03
W.H.Ponsford (V)	10	18	0	926	166	51.44	A.A.Mailey (NSW)	1797	59	30.45
A.Sandham (MCC)	12	19	0	866	137	45.57	R.Kilner (MCC)	1007	40	25.17
J.B.Hobbs (MCC)	10	17	1	865	154	54.06	A.P.Freeman (MCC)	1209	40	30.22
A.F.Kippax (NSW)	8	13	2	853	212*	77.54	J.M.Gregory (NSW)	1132	33	34.30
V.Y.Richardson (SA)	10	19	0	827	138	43.52	J.W.Hearne (MCC)	979	30	32.63
A.J.Richardson (SA)	11	21	1	785	200*	39.25	A.E.R.Gilligan (MCC)	1075	28	38.39
T.J.E.Andrews (NSW)	9	15	1	776	224	55.42				

SHEFFIELD SHIELD TABLE

	P	W	L	D	Pts	Quotient	Runs Scored	Wkts Lost	Runs Conceded	Wkts Taken
VICTORIA	4	3	1	-	2	1.242	2460	62	2458	77
NEW SOUTH WALES	4	2	2	-	0	1.007	2415	68	2574	73
SOUTH AUSTRALIA	4	1	3	-	-2	0.798	2598	80	2441	60
TOTAL	6	6	6	-	0	1.000	7473	210	7473	210

NEW SOUTH WALES v AUSTRALIAN XI

Played at Sydney Cricket Ground on October 17, 18, 20, 1924. (Three-day match)
Toss : New South Wales.   Result : MATCH DRAWN.
Debuts: Australian XI - L.W.Gwynne (f/c).
12th Men: No 12th men or emergency fieldsmen named.
Umpires: A.C.Jones and G.P.Worth.
Attendances: 5300, 11300, 2800.   Total: About 19,400.   Receipts: About £1150.
Close of Play: 1st day NSW 7/476 (Kelleway 18, Nothling 3); 2nd day Aust 7/240 (Ratcliffe 132, Hornibrook 4).

The match raised £950 for the benefit of W.P.Howell, aged 54, who sent down the first ball (unrecorded in the score) before retiring to the pavilion. W.W.Armstrong was invited to captain the Australian side but the V.C.A. refused to take any part in the match and barred Victorian players from participating. Hill and Carter came out of retirement, Hill leading the Australian XI in Armstrong's absence. Collins (106 in 120 minutes, 12 fours), Bardsley (90 in 161 minutes, 9 fours), Taylor (111 in 120 minutes, 12 fours), Kippax (115 in 130 minutes, 2 sixes and 10 fours) and Kelleway (101 in 125 minutes, 7 fours) scored rapid innings for New South Wales. Barbour was run out off the fourth ball of the Australian first innings after being missed by the same fielder from the second ball. Ratcliffe's 161 occupied 252 minutes and included 17 fours and 2 chances. With the Australian side facing imminent defeat in mid-afternoon on the last day, the match was abandoned in favour of a second, unofficial, New South Wales innings. Score: NSW 1/118 (Macartney lbw b Hornibrook 8, Andrews 50*, Gregory 56*, extras 4); fall 1/8; bowling : Everett 3-0-25-0, Hornibrook 6-0-41-1, Grimmett 6-0-36-0, A.J.Richardson 2-0-10-0. (Bowling figures do not tally). Despite its unusual features the match was played seriously and was regarded as a trial for the forthcoming Test series. Sources: *The Cricketer, NSWCA Report, The Age, Sydney Morning Herald, Sydney Referee, Sydney Daily Telegraph.*

NEW SOUTH WALES

*H.L.Collins	c V.Y.Richardson b Hornibrook	106
W.Bardsley	c Hornibrook b Grimmett	90
C.G.Macartney	b Hornibrook	7
T.J.E.Andrews	b Grimmett	8
J.M.Taylor	st Ratcliffe b A.J.Richardson	111
A.F.Kippax	c V.Y.Richardson b Barbour	115
C.Kelleway	b Everett	101
J.M.Gregory	c V.Y.Richardson b A.J.Richardson	9
O.E.Nothling	b Grimmett	5
†H.Carter	c Gwynne b Murray	58
A.A.Mailey	not out	25
Extras	(b3, lb7)	10
Total	(102.4 overs, 420 mins)	645

AUSTRALIAN XI

E.P.Barbour	run out (Carter)	0		c Kelleway b Nothling	1
†A.T.Ratcliffe	lbw b Kelleway	161			
A.J.Richardson	b Kelleway	3	(4)	st Carter b Macartney	31
J.T.Murray	c & b Mailey	14	(3)	c Gregory b Mailey	24
V.Y.Richardson	b Mailey	22		c Andrews b Mailey	25
*C.Hill	b Mailey	40			
F.C.Thompson	c Gregory b Mailey	2	(6)	st Carter b Mailey	1
S.C.Everett	c Gregory b Mailey	9		c Gregory b Mailey	11
P.M.Hornibrook	b Kelleway	25		not out	4
L.W.Gwynne	not out	10	(2)	b Mailey	33
C.V.Grimmett	b Macartney	9	(7)	c Collins b Macartney	7
Extras	(b8, lb4, nb3)	15		(b1, lb3, nb1)	5
Total	(78.4 overs, 278 mins)	310		(34.0 overs, 120 mins) (8 wkts)	142

AUSTRALIAN XI	O	M	R	W	w,nb
Everett	19.4	1	125	1	-,-
Hornibrook	22	1	141	2	-,-
Grimmett	25	1	138	3	-,-
A.J.Richardson	21	0	113	2	-,-
Murray	8	0	51	1	-,-
Barbour	7	0	67	1	-,-

NEW SOUTH WALES	O	M	R	W	w,nb		O	M	R	W	w,nb
Gregory	9	1	41	0	-,-						
Kelleway	17	1	52	3	-,1	(1)	4	0	11	0	-,-
Mailey	23	1	97	5	-,-		13	0	72	5	-,-
Nothling	11	0	42	0	-,2	(2)	11	1	35	1	-,1
Macartney	13.4	4	34	1	-,-	(4)	6	2	19	2	-,-
Andrews	5	0	29	0	-,-						

FALL OF WICKETS

	NSW	AUST	AUST
Wkt	1st	1st	2nd
1st	181	0	1
2nd	204	11	58
3rd	215	44	67
4th	216	119	111
5th	435	217	120
6th	447	219	122
7th	466	229	138
8th	487	285	142
9th	586	292	-
10th	645	310	-

WESTERN AUSTRALIA v M.C.C.

Played at W.A.C.A. Ground, Perth, on October 17 (no play), 18, 20, 1924. (Three-day match)
Toss : Western Australia.　　　　　Result : MATCH DRAWN.
Debuts: Western Australia - R.J.Bryant, H.E.Fidock, R.H.Hewson, W.E.Miller (all f/c); L.F.Freemantle (WA only).
12th Men: J.Hanley (WA). No 12th named for M.C.C.
Umpires: A.D.McIntyre and E.Walker.
Attendances: No play, 6000, 2000.　　　　Total: About 8000.　　　Receipts: £680.
Close of Play: 1st day no play; 2nd day MCC 7/330 (Gilligan 20, Tate 18).

Rain washed out all of the first day's play. Kilner offered no chances in batting 93 minutes; his innings included 10 fours and 4 sixes and he reached his century with 18 runs in one over from Freemantle (who had previously represented Victoria at first-class level). Douglas took 145 minutes over his 62 which included 3 fours. Howard was caught off a no-ball from Gilligan's second delivery in the Western Australian first innings. Taaffe's 71 came in 179 minutes, with 5 fours. Together with Bryant, he was nominated by the WA Cricket Association for selection in the Australian XI to play M.C.C. in Brisbane in December. Sources: *Wisden, WACA Report, The Age, Sydney Morning Herald, The West Australian, Daily News.*

M.C.C.

A.Sandham	c Bott b Taaffe	28
H.Sutcliffe	c & b Freemantle	36
J.W.Hearne	c Hewson b Freemantle	15
F.E.Woolley	run out (Bryant)	7
A.P.F.Chapman	c Fidock b Miller	34
J.W.H.T.Douglas	b Freemantle	62
R.Kilner	c Fidock b Freemantle	103
*A.E.R.Gilligan	not out	20
M.W.Tate	not out	18
†H.Strudwick	)	
R.K.Tyldesley	) did not bat	
Extras	(b3, lb4)	7
Total	(74.0 overs, 285 mins) (7 wkts dec)	330

WESTERN AUSTRALIA

H.C.Howard	run out (Sutcliffe/Sandham)	4	lbw b Hearne	15
F.H.Taaffe	b Gilligan	4	c Gilligan b Woolley	71
H.J.Herbert	b Gilligan	0	b Tyldesley	3
L.F.Freemantle	b Tate	0	b Tate	14
W.A.Evans	b Gilligan	2	st Strudwick b Tyldesley	11
*L.C.Bott	c Hearne b Gilligan	5	st Strudwick b Hearne	16
R.J.Bryant	b Tate	0	c Strudwick b Chapman	24
†R.H.Hewson	b Tyldesley	8	not out	0
L.C.Renfrey	lbw b Tyldesley	11		
W.E.Miller	c Tyldesley b Woolley	14		
H.E.Fidock	not out	4		
Extras	(b2, lb1, nb2)	5	(b2, lb1)	3
Total	(22.0 overs, 93 mins)	57	(55.2 overs, 179 mins) (7 wkts)	157

WESTERN AUSTRALIA	O	M	R	W	w,nb
Fidock	9	1	25	0	-,-
Renfrey	10	1	31	0	-,-
Taaffe	17	3	76	1	-,-
Freemantle	22	1	118	4	-,-
Evans	8	0	34	0	-,-
Miller	7	1	23	1	-,-
Bott	1	0	16	0	-,-

M.C.C.	O	M	R	W	w,nb		O	M	R	W	w,nb
Gilligan	6	1	12	4	-,1	(6)	3	0	13	0	-,-
Tate	5	1	9	2	-,-	(5)	9	2	22	1	-,-
Douglas	4	1	10	0	-,-	(1)	5	3	5	0	-,-
Tyldesley	5	1	13	2	-,-		11	1	25	2	-,-
Woolley	2	0	8	1	-,1	(7)	1	1	0	1	-,-
Kilner						(2)	11	1	30	0	-,-
Hearne						(3)	15	2	59	2	-,-
Chapman							0.2	0	0	1	-,-

FALL OF WICKETS

	MCC	WA	WA
Wkt	1st	1st	2nd
1st	61	6	30
2nd	65	8	47
3rd	81	9	63
4th	99	12	86
5th	147	16	109
6th	266	18	157
7th	295	18	157
8th	-	33	-
9th	-	44	-
10th	-	57	-

WESTERN AUSTRALIA v M.C.C.

Played at W.A.C.A. Ground, Perth, on October 25, 27, 28, 1924. (Three-day match)
Toss : M.C.C.   Result : M.C.C. WON BY AN INNINGS AND 190 RUNS.
Debuts: Western Australia - H.R.Cantwell, A.D.Drew, M.W.Loton (all f/c).
12th Men: J.Hanley (WA) and E.H.Hendren (MCC).
Umpires: A.E.Lawrence and E.Walker.
Attendances: 6000, 2000, 200.   Total: About 8200.   Receipts: £654.
Close of Play: 1st day MCC 397 all out; 2nd day WA (2) 3/34 (Blundell 14, Evans 2).

Western Australia fielded atrociously on the opening day. Freemantle, at first slip, dropped Whysall from the third ball of the match. Gilligan (130 minutes, 5 sixes and 10 fours) survived six chances to make 138, while Hearne (88 minutes, 6 fours), Chapman (61 minutes, 1 six and 4 fours) and Tate (74 minutes, 4 fours) were also let off in the field. Loton batted 105 minutes and hit 3 fours to reach 38, but Western Australia were forced to follow on and overnight rain caught them on a soft pitch on the last day. Bryant (0) was struck on the hand by a ball from Tate and retired hurt at 6/55; he resumed at 9/67. *Wisden* gives incorrect match dates. Sources: *Wisden, WACA Report, The Age, Sydney Morning Herald, The West Australian, Daily News.*

M.C.C.

J.B.Hobbs	c Evans b Fidock	17
W.W.Whysall	c Cantwell b Taaffe	32
J.W.Hearne	lbw b Blundell	54
A.P.F.Chapman	c Bryant b Blundell	44
J.W.H.T.Douglas	run out (Blundell/Hewson)	9
J.L.Bryan	c Hewson b Blundell	20
*A.E.R.Gilligan	c Freemantle b Blundell	138
M.W.Tate	c Freemantle b Drew	44
A.P.Freeman	c Loton b Renfrey	8
†H.Strudwick	not out	16
H.Howell	c Taaffe b Blundell	4
Extras	(b6, lb4 w1)	11
Total	(78.5 overs, 285 mins)	397

WESTERN AUSTRALIA

F.H.Taaffe	b Freeman	11		b Tate	1
M.W.Loton	b Freeman	38		b Tate	2
G.R.Blundell	b Freeman	2		c Chapman b Tate	23
R.J.Bryant	c Chapman b Gilligan	5	(7)	c Gilligan b Freeman	1
A.D.Drew	lbw b Freeman	18	(6)	c sub (Hendren) b Freeman	0
H.R.Cantwell	c Douglas b Freeman	0	(8)	c & b Freeman	0
L.F.Freemantle	b Howell	11	(4)	run out	10
*R.M.Evans	b Freeman	21	(5)	run out (Hearne/Strudwick)	14
L.C.Renfrey	c Strudwick b Gilligan	11	(10)	not out	6
†R.H.Hewson	not out	3	(9)	c Chapman b Douglas	0
H.E.Fidock	b Gilligan	4		run out (Hobbs)	7
Extras	(b10, lb4)	14		(b3, lb2)	5
Total	(55.4 overs, 202 mins)	138		(34.5 overs, 134 mins)	69

WESTERN AUSTRALIA	O	M	R	W	w,nb
Fidock	15	0	73	1	-,-
Freemantle	15	1	88	0	-,-
Renfrey	11	1	46	1	1,-
Evans	8	2	24	0	-,-
Taaffe	13	1	72	1	-,-
Blundell	12.5	0	59	5	-,-
Drew	4	0	24	1	-,-

M.C.C.	O	M	R	W	w,nb		O	M	R	W	w,nb
Gilligan	9.4	2	20	3	-,-	(6)	4	0	8	0	-,-
Tate	3	1	7	0	-,-		8	2	10	3	-,-
Howell	7	0	15	1	-,-						
Douglas	9	2	26	0	-,-	(1)	10	2	13	1	-,-
Freeman	21	5	47	6	-,-		9.5	2	23	3	-,-
Hearne	6	1	9	0	-,-	(3)	2	0	4	0	-,-
Chapman						(4)	1	0	6	0	-,-

FALL OF WICKETS			
	MCC	WA	WA
Wkt	1st	1st	2nd
1st	24	40	7
2nd	66	44	10
3rd	147	55	27
4th	152	65	52
5th	172	65	55
6th	190	79	55
7th	317	110	55
8th	340	129	55
9th	393	129	67
10th	397	138	69

SOUTH AUSTRALIA v VICTORIA (Shield Match 1)

Played at Adelaide Oval on October 31, November 1, 3, 4, 5, 6, 1924. (Timeless match)
Toss : South Australia.　　　Result : VICTORIA WON BY THREE WICKETS.
Debuts: South Australia - T.W.Wall (f/c); C.V.Grimmett (SA only). Victoria - H.S.T.L.Hendry (Vic only).
12th Men: L.T.Gun (SA) and J.L.Keating (Vic).
Umpires: C.L.Cornish and S.W.Smith.
Attendances: 3808, 9272, 3813, 4509, 4076, 3277.　　　Total: 28,755.　　　Receipts: £1257.
Close of Play: 1st day SA 3/263 (V.Y.Richardson 29, Grimmett 3); 2nd day Vic 2/32 (Tarrant 5, Ellis 6); 3rd day Vic 6/210 (Ryder 5, Love 1); 4th day SA (2) 4/130 (Walsh 14, Grimmett 9); 5th day Vic (2) 1/118 (Ponsford 58, Woodfull 34).

After Wainwright fell to the third ball of the match, Harris (98 in 191 minutes, 8 fours, 2 chances), Murray (chanceless 126 in 232 minutes, 16 fours) and V.Y.Richardson (123 in 145 minutes, 19 fours) consolidated to set up a big total for South Australia. In the second innings Wainwright (45 in 69 minutes, 1 six and 3 fours) and A.J.Richardson (46 in 90 minutes, 2 fours) topscored for the side. Murray was unluckily run out when, in stretching for his crease, he deflected a wayward throw from Liddicut into the stumps with his bat. Tarrant (86 in 205 minutes, 1 six and 11 fours) and Ellis (69 in 200 minutes, 7 fours) scored first-innings fifties for Victoria who, despite a 175-run deficit, won the match at 5.30pm on the last day through contributions from Ponsford (77 in 189 minutes, 4 fours), Woodfull (67 in 173 minutes, 4 fours), Hendry (109 not out in 166 minutes, 11 fours) and Liddicut (45 not out in 72 minutes, 3 fours). Grimmett captured nine wickets in his first match against his old State while Hendry, in his debut for Victoria after five seasons with New South Wales, took seven. Though scheduled to be played to a finish, both teams agreed after the fifth day that only one further day would be played so that the match against M.C.C. at the ground would not be delayed. A.E.V.Hartkopf was unavailable for Victoria and Gun replaced J.W.Rymill in the local twelve. *Wisden* incorrectly gives SA (1) Tarrant 0/54, Liddicut 0/93. Sources: *Wisden, C.B.O'Reilly, VCA Report, SACA Report, South Australian Register, Adelaide Advertiser.*

SOUTH AUSTRALIA

Batsman	Dismissal (1st)	Runs	Dismissal (2nd)	Runs
G.W.Harris	run out (Park/Ellis)	98	(2) b Hendry	15
E.G.C.Wainwright	b Wallace	0	(8) c Ellis b Hendry	45
J.T.Murray	c Ryder b Hendry	126	run out (Liddicut)	24
*V.Y.Richardson	c Ellis b Hendry	123	c Mayne b Wallace	17
C.V.Grimmett	c Woodfull b Hendry	49	(6) c Love b Tarrant	22
A.J.Richardson	b Ryder	24	(1) b Ryder	46
N.A.Walsh	c Mayne b Hendry	27	(5) c & b Tarrant	33
E.L.Bowley	run out (Woodfull/Ellis)	1	(7) c Park b Hendry	0
N.L.Williams	not out	30	b Tarrant	2
T.W.Wall	run out (Woodfull/Ellis)	13	not out	2
†A.M.Ambler	lbw b Wallace	15	c Mayne b Wallace	16
Extras	(b2, lb3, w1, nb6)	12	(b2, lb1, nb8)	11
Total	(118.3 overs, 458 mins)	518	(77.0 overs, 289 mins)	233

VICTORIA

Batsman	Dismissal (1st)	Runs	Dismissal (2nd)	Runs
*R.E.Mayne	c & b Grimmett	12	st Ambler b Grimmett	22
R.L.Park	c Bowley b Wall	7	(8) st Ambler b Grimmett	38
F.A.Tarrant	st Ambler b Grimmett	86	(5) c Harris b A.J.Richardson	19
†J.L.Ellis	c Ambler b Grimmett	69		
W.M.Woodfull	c V.Y.Richardson b Murray	6	(3) c V.Y.Richardson b Grimmett	67
W.H.Ponsford	b Grimmett	10	(2) b Grimmett	77
J.Ryder	run out (A.J.Richardson/Ambler)	42	(4) c V.Y.Richardson b A.J.Richardson	11
H.S.B.Love	b Wainwright	22	(6) lbw b Wall	10
H.S.T.L.Hendry	c Murray b Grimmett	18	(7) not out	109
A.E.Liddicut	c V.Y.Richardson b A.J.Richardson	43	(9) not out	45
P.H.Wallace	not out	10		
Extras	(b6, lb6, w4, nb2)	18	(b8, lb3)	11
Total	(112.2 overs, 404 mins)	343	(120.3 overs, 415 mins) (7 wkts)	409

VICTORIA bowling

Bowler	O	M	R	W	w,nb		O	M	R	W	w,nb
Wallace	24.3	2	123	2	-,2		19	3	70	2	-,5
Tarrant	15	1	64	0	-,-	(4)	20	5	50	3	-,-
Liddicut	25	4	82	0	-,1		4	1	6	0	-,-
Ryder	18	1	83	1	-,-	(5)	7	2	13	1	-,-
Hendry	32	5	134	4	-,3	(2)	27	5	83	3	-,3
Park	4	0	20	0	1,-						

SOUTH AUSTRALIA bowling

Bowler	O	M	R	W	w,nb		O	M	R	W	w,nb
Wall	22	5	83	1	1,1		11.3	0	44	1	-,-
A.J.Richardson	27.2	9	61	1	-,-		37	10	81	2	-,-
Grimmett	42	10	97	5	-,-		50	6	170	4	-,-
Wainwright	12	1	35	1	2,-	(5)	7	0	25	0	-,-
Williams	4	0	29	0	-,1	(4)	14	1	68	0	-,-
Murray	5	1	20	1	1,-		1	0	10	0	-,-

FALL OF WICKETS

Wkt	SA 1st	VIC 1st	SA 2nd	VIC 2nd
1st	1	20	27	47
2nd	206	26	82	156
3rd	252	183	89	175
4th	392	186	119	199
5th	410	202	155	205
6th	452	208	155	236
7th	458	268	179	313
8th	460	272	187	-
9th	488	307	215	-
10th	518	343	233	-

SOUTH AUSTRALIA v M.C.C.

Played at Adelaide Oval on November 7, 8, 10, 11, 1924. (Four-day match)
Toss : South Australia.   Result : M.C.C. WON BY NINE WICKET.
Debuts: Nil.
12th Men: L.T.Gun (SA) and A.P.Freeman (MCC).
Umpires: G.I.Colyer and S.W.Smith.
Attendances: 6486, 16170, 3454, 1659.   Total: 27,769.   Receipts: £1584.
Close of Play: 1st day SA 4/334 (A.J.Richardson 192, Walsh 31); 2nd day MCC 2/230 (Hearne 58, Woolley 25); 3rd day SA (2) 103 all out.

Vic Richardson became the first captain to lose a first-class match in Australia after declaring an innings closed. Tate had dismissed both Harris and Murray in his third over on the first morning before Arthur Richardson (chanceless 200 not out in 298 minutes, 3 sixes and 18 fours) and Vic, his unrelated captain (87 in 160 minutes, 8 fours), came together to add 214 runs, South Australia's highest partnership for the third-wicket against any touring team and the second double-century stand to be shared by the Richardsons in three matches against the Englishmen. Arthur had scored 280 in his previous innings for South Australia against M.C.C. Hobbs (50 in 84 minutes, 7 fours), Sutcliffe (75 in 195 minutes, 7 fours), Hearne (78 in 212 minutes, 2 fours) and Woolley (90 in 133 minutes, 8 fours) scored half-centuries for the tourists. Ambler was struck in the eye by a ball from Whitty after lunch on the second day and Harris deputised as wicket-keeper until he recovered. South Australia's second innings collapse on the third afternoon contained five ducks (including Arthur Richardson to his first ball) and a spell of 5 for 17 by Hearne. Gun replaced N.L.Williams (exams) in the local twelve selected for the game. *Wisden* and *O'Reilly* incorrectly give SA (2) V.Y.Richardson b Hearne. Sources: *Wisden, C.B.O'Reilly, VCA Report, Adelaide Advertiser, South Australian Register.*

SOUTH AUSTRALIA

A.J.Richardson	not out	200	(6)	lbw b Hearne	0
G.W.Harris	b Tate	5	(1)	c Hearne b Gilligan	0
J.T.Murray	lbw b Tate	0		b Gilligan	8
*V.Y.Richardson	hit wkt b Gilligan	87		lbw b Hearne	28
D.E.Pritchard	b Gilligan	4		c Sutcliffe b Hearne	31
N.A.Walsh	not out	34	(2)	b Tate	2
E.G.C.Wainwright	)			c Douglas b Hearne	6
C.V.Grimmett	)			c Hearne b Douglas	0
W.J.Whitty	) did not bat			lbw b Hearne	0
T.W.Wall	)			lbw b Douglas	0
†A.M.Ambler	)			not out	19
Extras	(b4, lb11, nb1)	16		(b6, lb3)	9
Total	(81.0 overs, 298 mins) (4 wkts dec)	346		(27.6 overs, 121 mins)	103

M.C.C.

J.B.Hobbs	b Wall	50	not out	18
H.Sutcliffe	b Grimmett	75	st Ambler b Grimmett	24
J.W.Hearne	lbw b Grimmett	78	not out	2
F.E.Woolley	b Grimmett	90		
E.H.Hendren	run out (V.Y.Richardson)	42		
A.P.F.Chapman	b Grimmett	10		
*A.E.R.Gilligan	b Whitty	3		
J.W.H.T.Douglas	not out	19		
M.W.Tate	c A.J.Richardson b Whitty	13		
R.K.Tyldesley	c Pritchard b Whitty	1		
†H.Strudwick	c Pritchard b Whitty	0		
Extras	(b20, lb4, nb1)	25		–
Total	(99.7 overs, 392 mins)	406	(10.1 overs, 40 mins) (1 wkt)	44

M.C.C.	O	M	R	W	w,nb		O	M	R	W	w,nb
Gilligan	13	1	51	2	-,-		5	0	15	2	-,-
Tate	21	5	56	2	-,-		4	0	7	1	-,-
Tyldesley	13	2	60	0	-,1		4	0	14	0	-,-
Douglas	11	1	56	0	-,-		5	1	29	2	-,-
Hearne	12	2	62	0	-,-		5.6	2	17	5	-,-
Woolley	10	0	43	0	-,-		4	0	12	0	-,-
Chapman	1	0	2	0	-,-						

SOUTH AUSTRALIA	O	M	R	W	w,nb		O	M	R	W	w,nb
Whitty	27.7	1	113	4	-,-		4	0	19	0	-,-
A.J.Richardson	19	4	71	0	-,-	(4)	1	0	2	0	-,-
Murray	2	0	11	0	-,-						
Wall	22	0	85	1	-,1	(2)	4	0	21	0	-,-
Grimmett	26	4	87	4	-,-	(3)	1.1	0	2	1	-,-
Wainwright	3	0	14	0	-,-						

FALL OF WICKETS

Wkt	SA 1st	MCC 1st	SA 2nd	MCC 2nd
1st	8	89	0	41
2nd	8	189	14	-
3rd	222	299	16	-
4th	248	344	54	-
5th	-	368	54	-
6th	-	369	70	-
7th	-	373	73	-
8th	-	397	74	-
9th	-	406	81	-
10th	-	406	103	-

VICTORIA v M.C.C.

Played at Melbourne Cricket Ground on November 14, 15, 17, 18, 19, 1924. (Timeless match)
Toss : M.C.C.   Result : VICTORIA WON BY SIX WICKETS.
Debuts: Nil.
12th Men: H.S.B.Love (Vic) and M.W.Tate (MCC).
Umpires: R.M.Crockett and C.Garing.
Attendances: 11991, 33567, 13346, 9991, 8094.   Total: 76,989.   Receipts: £6416.
Close of Play: 1st day MCC 3/113 (Woolley 40, Hendren 16); 2nd day Vic 2/44 (Hendry 24, Ellis 0); 3rd day MCC (2) 2/83
    (Sandham 30, Woolley 11); 4th day Vic (2) 1/111 (Mayne 55, Woodfull 54).

Several rain interruptions restricted play on the first day to 155 minutes, and led to the low-scoring match. Fifties were registered for M.C.C. by Douglas (59 not out in 89 minutes, 6 fours) in the first innings and Sandham (66 in 179 minutes, 4 fours) and Hendren (54 in 138 minutes, 4 fours) in the second innings. Eight different fielders held catches in the first innings. Hearne strained a leg muscle while fielding on the third day and took no further part in the match. Ryder tore a ligament in his side while bowling his fourth over and also took no further part. Hendry's 63 in 182 minutes with 3 fours included four chances, three of them before reaching 20. Mayne (87 in 160 minutes, 7 fours), Woodfull (61 in 106 minutes, 1 four) and Hartkopf (56 not out in 85 minutes, 5 fours) led Victoria to victory. The match was originally scheduled for four days but the teams agreed to extend play for up to two hours on a fifth day which enabled Victoria to win from the third ball of the final over and the Englishmen to still catch their train to Sydney. Sources: *Wisden, VCA Report, The Age, The Argus, The Herald, Melbourne Sun, The Australasian.*

M.C.C.

J.B.Hobbs	c Ellis b Ryder	30	lbw b Tarrant		37
A.Sandham	c Ryder b Wallace	4	b Hendry		66
J.W.Hearne	c Mayne b Liddicut	18	absent hurt		-
F.E.Woolley	c Wallace b Tarrant	45	c Woodfull b Tarrant		24
E.H.Hendren	c Woodfull b Hendry	20	b Hendry		54
†W.W.Whysall	c Ryder b Liddicut	7	(3) b Tarrant		1
R.Kilner	c Ponsford b Tarrant	20	(6) lbw b Wallace		9
J.W.H.T.Douglas	not out	59	(7) b Tarrant		5
J.L.Bryan	c Liddicut b Ryder	15	(8) not out		18
*A.E.R.Gilligan	b Ryder	11	(9) b Hendry		8
A.P.Freeman	c Tarrant b Ryder	1	(10) run out (	/Ellis)	1
Extras	(b4, lb5, nb1)	10	(b10, w1, nb7)		18
Total	(75.0 overs, 296 mins)	240	(73.6 overs, 286 mins)		241

VICTORIA

*R.E.Mayne	b Kilner	1	c Freeman b Gilligan		87
R.L.Park	b Woolley	17	b Gilligan		1
H.S.T.L.Hendry	lbw b Freeman	63	(6) not out		36
†J.L.Ellis	c Freeman b Hearne	36			
W.M.Woodfull	c Kilner b Woolley	14	(3) c Whysall b Gilligan		61
W.H.Ponsford	st Whysall b Freeman	6			
J.Ryder	c & b Woolley	11			
F.A.Tarrant	lbw b Douglas	35			
A.E.V.Hartkopf	c Douglas b Freeman	2	(5) not out		56
A.E.Liddicut	not out	31	(4) b Gilligan		7
P.H.Wallace	lbw b Douglas	4			
Extras	(b1, lb6, nb2)	9	(b4, nb1)		5
Total	(83.4 overs, 296 mins)	229	(58.3 overs, 218 mins) (4 wkts)		253

VICTORIA	O	M	R	W	w,nb		O	M	R	W	w,nb		FALL OF WICKETS			
													MCC	VIC	MCC	VIC
Wallace	11	2	40	1	-,1		19	3	40	1	-,6	Wkt	1st	1st	2nd	2nd
Liddicut	27	8	63	2	-,-	(4)	6	1	22	0	-,-	1st	7	1	65	4
Ryder	10	2	33	4	-,-	(2)	3.4	0	12	0	-,-	2nd	48	39	67	124
Hendry	13	1	50	1	-,-	(6)	9	1	23	3	-,1	3rd	58	98	109	136
Tarrant	14	1	44	2	-,-		15.2	6	33	4	-,-	4th	118	133	163	171
Hartkopf						(3)	21	1	93	0	1,-	5th	125	135	175	-
M.C.C.	O	M	R	W	w,nb		O	M	R	W	w,nb	6th	143	153	191	
Gilligan	15	2	36	0	-,-	(2)	17.3	0	89	4	-,-	7th	155	159	222	
Kilner	6	3	10	1	-,-	(5)	21	0	79	0	-,-	8th	209	161	240	
Freeman	15	3	37	3	-,-	(4)	9	0	34	0	-,-	9th	234	223	241	
Woolley	30	12	62	3	-,2	(3)	5	0	21	0	-,1	10th	240	229	-	-
Hearne	12	2	50	1	-,-											
Douglas	5.4	0	25	2	-,-	(1)	6	0	25	0	-,-					

NEW SOUTH WALES v M.C.C.

Played at Sydney Cricket Ground on November 21, 22, 24, 25, 1924. (Four-day match)
Toss : New South Wales.   Result : M.C.C. WON BY THREE WICKETS.
Debuts: Nil.
12th Men: J.G.Morgan (NSW) and H.Howell (MCC).
Umpires: A.C.Jones and A.P.Williams.
Attendances: 16424, 34094, 16899, 17702.   Total: 85,119.   Receipts: £7947.
Close of Play: 1st day NSW 7/242 (Bardsley 142, Nothling 4); 2nd day NSW (2) 0/0 (Mailey 0, Nothling 0) 3rd day NSW (2) 8/179
    (Andrews 63, Oldfield 6).

C.Kelleway declared unavailable for New South Wales because of a dispute with the N.S.W.C.A. over match payments and was replaced by
Scott. Bardsley's chanceless 160 (258 minutes, 10 fours) dominated the first innings. Hendren (75 not out in 162 minutes, 4 fours),
Hobbs (81 in 114 minutes, 4 fours) and Chapman (72 in 71 minutes, 10 fours) scored fifties for the tourists. A light appeal by the
batsmen ended the second day before a ball had been bowled in the New South Wales second innings. Andrews atoned for his first-ball
dismissal in the first innings with an unbeaten 86 (149 minutes, 8 fours). J.W.Hearne and F.E.Woolley were unavailable for M.C.C. due
to injury. Rain interrupted play several times on the third day. Sources: *Wisden, NSWCA Report, VCA Report, Sydney Referee, Sydney
Morning Herald.*

NEW SOUTH WALES

*H.L.Collins	lbw b Tyldesley	32	(4) c Strudwick b Gilligan	32
W.Bardsley	c & b Tyldesley	160	(3) c Strudwick b Tyldesley	14
C.G.Macartney	c Hendren b Tate	0	(5) b Tyldesley	4
T.J.E.Andrews	lbw b Tate	0	(7) not out	86
J.M.Taylor	c Kilner b Tate	51	(6) c Strudwick b Tyldesley	19
A.F.Kippax	c Kilner b Tate	0	(8) b Tate	14
J.M.Gregory	c Hendren b Tate	6	(9) c Gilligan b Tyldesley	6
†W.A.S.Oldfield	c Hendren b Tate	1	(10) b Tyldesley	19
O.E.Nothling	c Chapman b Tate	12	(2) b Tate	4
J.D.Scott	c Douglas b Tyldesley	0	(11) b Tyldesley	2
A.A.Mailey	not out	2	(1) st Strudwick b Tate	13
Extras	(b6, lb1)	7	(b5, lb3)	8
Total	(65.5 overs, 266 mins)	271	(77.3 overs, 279 mins)	221

M.C.C.

J.B.Hobbs	c Gregory b Scott	8	c Nothling b Scott	81
H.Sutcliffe	c Kippax b Gregory	17	b Gregory	45
A.Sandham	c Nothling b Mailey	21	c Oldfield b Macartney	1
R.Kilner	c Gregory b Scott	2	c & b Nothling	19
E.H.Hendren	not out	75	b Mailey	46
J.W.H.T.Douglas	c Gregory b Mailey	1	c Collins b Mailey	8
A.P.F.Chapman	c Collins b Mailey	4	c Taylor b Mailey	72
M.W.Tate	c Scott b Mailey	13	not out	15
*A.E.R.Gilligan	c Gregory b Macartney	5	not out	7
R.K.Tyldesley	b Gregory	36		
†H.Strudwick	run out (Andrews)	3		
Extras	(lb2, w1, nb5)	8	(b1, lb4, nb2)	7
Total	(52.5 overs, 206 mins)	193	(66.3 overs, 255 mins) (7 wkts)	301

M.C.C.	O	M	R	W	w,nb		O	M	R	W	w,nb						
Douglas	4	0	18	0	-,-												
Tate	19.5	0	74	7	-,-		26	6	59	3	-,-						
Gilligan	13	1	46	0	-,-		18	4	60	1	-,-						
Tyldesley	16	2	74	3	-,-		26.3	2	83	6	-,-						
Kilner	13	1	52	0	-,-	(1)	7	2	11	0	-,-						

FALL OF WICKETS

Wkt	NSW 1st	MCC 1st	NSW 2nd	MCC 2nd
1st	81	17	19	91
2nd	84	34	22	114
3rd	84	37	36	132
4th	206	84	42	166
5th	206	88	74	183
6th	218	94	106	245
7th	224	114	151	294
8th	269	121	158	-
9th	269	180	219	-
10th	271	193	221	-

NEW SOUTH WALES	O	M	R	W	w,nb		O	M	R	W	w,nb
Gregory	12.5	0	46	2	-,-		14.3	0	74	1	-,-
Scott	9	2	37	2	1,5		12	1	66	1	-,2
Macartney	15	4	33	1	-,-	(5)	17	3	31	1	-,-
Mailey	12	1	55	4	-,-		11	0	94	3	-,-
Nothling	4	0	14	0	-,-	(3)	12	1	29	1	-,-

VICTORIA v SOUTH AUSTRALIA (Shield Match 2)

Played at Melbourne Cricket Ground on November 21, 22, 24, 25, 26, 27, 1924. (Timeless match)
Toss : Victoria.   Result : VICTORIA WON BY EIGHT WICKETS.
Debuts: South Australia - G.H.Palmer (f/c).
12th Men: K.J.Millar (Vic) and J.W.Rymill (SA).
Umpires: D.A.Elder and A.D.Reaburn (see below).
Attendances: 2098, 19615, 4780, 3911, 1428, ?   Total: 31,832.   Receipts: £1247.
Close of Play: 1st day SA 4/163 (Pritchard 61, Grimmett 1); 2nd day Vic 2/156 (Ponsford 63, Love 32); 3rd day Vic 4/280 (Ponsford 120, Hendry 6); 4th day SA (2) 6/156 (Gould 18, Grimmett 6); 5th day Vic (2) 1/68 (Mayne 48, Woodfull 19).

A.J.Richardson (81 in 125 minutes, 11 fours) and Pritchard (115 in 175 minutes, 14 fours) made major contributions to the first South Australian innings. Ponsford, last out in the Victorian first innings, scored 166 in 338 minutes and hit 12 fours but was dismissed by the last ball of the first over in the second innings. Rain caused delays on the first, third and fifth days. C.Garing replaced umpire Elder (ill) from the start of play on the third day to the end of the match. After suffering a first-ball dismissal in the first innings, Gould scored 55 not out in 72 minutes and hit 3 fours in the second. Ground admission was free on the last day. *Wisden* and *O'Reilly* incorrectly give Vic (1) Ellis st Ambler; SA (2) Harris 4, Pritchard 51; incorrect match dates. Sources: *Wisden, C.B.O'Reilly, VCA Report, The Age, The Argus, The Australasian.*

SOUTH AUSTRALIA

A.J.Richardson	c Woodfull b Tarrant	81		c Tarrant b Hendry	25
G.W.Harris	b Liddicut	0		c & b Liddicut	0
N.A.Walsh	c Ellis b Liddicut	2	(5)	lbw b Hartkopf	14
*V.Y.Richardson	c Ellis b Keating	14		c Ellis b Tarrant	28
D.E.Pritchard	b Wallace	115	(3)	c & b Wallace	55
C.V.Grimmett	c Mayne b Wallace	9	(8)	c Ellis b Wallace	6
F.K.Gould	c Hartkopf b Wallace	0		not out	55
E.G.C.Wainwright	b Tarrant	19	(6)	lbw b Hartkopf	4
T.W.Wall	st Ellis b Hartkopf	8		c Liddicut b Tarrant	3
†A.M.Ambler	not out	21		lbw b Tarrant	2
G.H.Palmer	b Hartkopf	4		c Hendry b Liddicut	3
Extras	(b5, lb4, nb6)	15		(b3, lb2, w1, nb1)	7
Total	(62.0 overs, 263 mins)	288		(52.3 overs, 215 mins)	202

VICTORIA

*R.E.Mayne	run out (Wall)	22	b Palmer	68
W.H.Ponsford	b Grimmett	166	c V.Y.Richardson b Wall	0
W.M.Woodfull	run out (Wall/Ambler)	28	not out	55
H.S.B.Love	b Grimmett	54	not out	5
F.A.Tarrant	c Palmer b A.J.Richardson	36		
H.S.T.L.Hendry	lbw b Wall	6		
A.E.V.Hartkopf	c Walsh b Wall	11		
A.E.Liddicut	c Harris b Grimmett	15		
J.L.Keating	c Palmer b Grimmett	3		
†J.L.Ellis	c Ambler b Grimmett	0		
P.H.Wallace	not out	1		
Extras	(b9, lb8)	17	(b5, lb1)	6
Total	(92.6 overs, 338 mins)	357	(40.2 overs, 145 mins) (2 wkts)	134

VICTORIA	O	M	R	W	w,nb		O	M	R	W	w,nb		FALL OF WICKETS			
Wallace	21	0	105	3	-,5		13	0	58	2	1,1		SA	VIC	SA	VIC
Liddicut	12	3	30	2	-,-		6.3	2	18	2	-,-	Wkt	1st	1st	2nd	2nd
Tarrant	7	0	25	2	-,-	(6)	16	1	49	3	-,-	1st	2	46	4	1
Hartkopf	10	1	49	2	-,-		10	2	37	2	-,-	2nd	8	94	61	117
Keating	5	1	22	1	-,-		2	0	8	0	-,-	3rd	47	192	106	-
Hendry	7	1	42	0	-,1	(3)	5	0	25	1	-,-	4th	162	249	128	-
												5th	188	280	132	-
SOUTH AUSTRALIA	O	M	R	W	w,nb		O	M	R	W	w,nb	6th	188	304	132	-
Wall	19	4	96	2	-,-		6	0	20	1	-,-	7th	229	336	159	-
Palmer	14	1	50	0	-,-		10	0	35	1	-,-	8th	259	342	172	-
A.J.Richardson	23	1	80	1	-,-	(4)	9	3	30	0	-,-	9th	263	348	183	-
Grimmett	33.6	4	97	5	-,-	(3)	15.2	0	43	0	-,-	10th	288	357	202	-
Wainwright	3	0	17	0	-,-											

QUEENSLAND v NEW SOUTH WALES

Played at Brisbane Cricket Ground (Woolloongabba) on November 22, 24, 25, 1924. (Three-day match)
Toss : Queensland.   Result : QUEENSLAND WON BY 152 RUNS.
Debuts: Queensland - W.Cain, F.U.Hefferan, C.B.P.McFarlane (all f/c); W.H.McDonald (Qld only). New South Wales - A.D.A.Mayes,
    C.V.Morrissey, R.H.Osborne, B.M.Salmon (all f/c); L.W.Gwynne (NSW only).
12th Men: N.C.Beeston (Qld) and L.W.Sieler (NSW).
Umpires: C.G.Mannion and J.W.Ward.
Attendances: 5000, ? , ? .   Total: About 7000.   Receipts: £346.
Close of Play: 1st day Qld (2) 0/0 (Bensted 0, McAndrew 0); 2nd day Qld (2) 9/295 (McDonald 17).

O.P.Asher, J.V.Foskett, J.G.Morgan, A.T.Ratcliffe and A.P.Wells all withdrew from the New South Wales side. J.D.Scott, in addition,
was withdrawn by the selectors to act as a replacement for C.Kelleway in the match against M.C.C. Oxenham, whose second-innings
analysis remained his best in 70 matches for Queensland, took the wickets of Salmon, Mayes and Gray with the first, third and fifth balls
of one over in the first innings. Rowe (94 in 134 minutes, 5 fours, chance at 53) and Bensted (76 in 130 minutes, 6 fours) topscored for
Queensland while Punch (52 in 76 minutes, 2 fours) and Gray (51 in 102 minutes, 2 sixes and 3 fours) did so for the visitors. Hefferan
suffered a first-ball dismissal. Sieler, the New South Wales reserve, was destined never to appear in first-class cricket but his grandson,
A.J.Sieler, played for Victoria in the early 1970s. McDonald (Victoria 1921-22) and Gwynne (Howell testimonial in October 1924) had
each played one first-class match prior to their State debuts in this match. *Cricketer* gives incorrect dismissal for Qld (1) Hornibrook.
Sources: *The Cricketer, NSWCA Report, QCA Report, Sydney Morning Herald, Brisbane Courier, Brisbane Daily Mail.*

QUEENSLAND

R.K.Oxenham	b Bubb	1	(6)	run out (Gray)	34
W.H.McDonald	c Bubb b Morrissey	0	(8)	b Morrissey	18
*†L.P.D.O'Connor	run out (Trenerry/Morrissey)	32		b Bubb	2
F.C.Thompson	c Trenerry b Mayes	37		b Morrissey	43
F.U.Hefferan	c Morrissey b Bubb	20		b Gray	0
W.Rowe	c Trenerry b Morrissey	9	(7)	b Mayes	94
C.B.P.McFarlane	c Mayes b Morrissey	3	(9)	b Mayes	0
W.Cain	c Osborne b Morrissey	3	(10)	run out (/Osborne)	14
E.C.Bensted	not out	8	(1)	c Osborne b Gray	76
J.W.McAndrew	b Morrissey	3	(2)	b Morrissey	0
P.M.Hornibrook	b Morrissey	2		not out	0
Extras	(b2, lb4, w1)	7		(b10, lb3, nb2)	15
Total	(35.2 overs, 132 mins)	125		(76.5 overs, 291 mins)	296

NEW SOUTH WALES

H.H.Davis	c O'Connor b Oxenham	22		c O'Connor b Oxenham	6
L.W.Gwynne	st O'Connor b Hornibrook	16		b Hornibrook	3
B.M.Salmon	b Oxenham	13	(9)	not out	27
A.T.E.Punch	c Rowe b Oxenham	8		lbw b Oxenham	52
*W.L.Trenerry	b Hornibrook	2	(3)	c Hornibrook b Oxenham	1
A.D.A.Mayes	lbw b Oxenham	0		b Oxenham	3
A.T.Gray	lbw b Oxenham	0	(5)	c sub (N.C.Beeston) b Oxenham	51
C.V.Morrissey	b McAndrew	14	(7)	b Oxenham	1
R.A.Bubb	lbw b Hornibrook	22	(8)	c Oxenham b McAndrew	1
T.C.W.Egan	not out	0		lbw b McDonald	7
†R.H.Osborne	b Hornibrook	1		b McDonald	0
Extras	(b9, lb4)	13		(b1, lb5)	6
Total	(33.7 overs, 133 mins)	111		(47.2 overs, 167 mins)	158

NEW SOUTH WALES	O	M	R	W	w,nb		O	M	R	W	w,nb
Bubb	11	2	36	2	-,-	(3)	16	4	52	1	-,-
Morrissey	13.2	2	30	6	-,-		16.5	2	63	3	-,-
Egan	4	0	37	0	1,-	(5)	2	0	17	0	-,-
Mayes	7	1	15	1	-,-	(1)	16	5	34	2	-,2
Punch						(4)	4	0	28	0	-,-
Gray							15	4	54	2	-,-
Trenerry							7	0	33	0	-,-

QUEENSLAND	O	M	R	W	w,nb		O	M	R	W	w,nb
Hornibrook	13.7	0	38	4	-,-		12	1	59	1	-,-
McDonald	6	0	18	0	-,-	(4)	3.2	0	7	2	-,-
McAndrew	7	1	15	1	-,-		10	0	23	1	-,-
Oxenham	7	1	27	5	-,-	(2)	17	4	45	6	-,-
Rowe							5	0	18	0	-,-

FALL OF WICKETS

	QLD	NSW	QLD	NSW
Wkt	1st	1st	2nd	2nd
1st	2	31	0	9
2nd	2	53	9	9
3rd	59	69	116	20
4th	90	72	130	111
5th	104	72	130	124
6th	109	72	223	140
7th	112	106	273	142
8th	113	110	273	145
9th	123	110	295	158
10th	125	111	296	158

NEW SOUTH WALES v SOUTH AUSTRALIA (Shield Match 3)

Played at Sydney Cricket Ground on November 28, 29, December 1, 2, 1924. (Timeless match)
Toss : New South Wales.　　　Result : NEW SOUTH WALES WON BY NINE WICKETS.
Debuts: New South Wales - H.O.Rock (f/c).
12th Men: D.A.Mullarkey (NSW) and G.W.Harris (SA).
Umpires: W.J.R.Bowes and W.G.French.
Attendances: 3169, 11432, 1478, 549.　　　Total: 16,628.　　　Receipts: £1020.
Close of Play: 1st day NSW 4/312 (Kippax 21, Morgan 15); 2nd day SA 5/194 (Rymill 9, Wainwright 3); 3rd day SA (2) 5/222 (Wall 0, Wainwright 0).

Rock, brought into the New South Wales team along with Morgan, Morrissey and Ratcliffe as replacements for H.L.Collins, C.G.Macartney, J.D.Scott and J.M.Taylor (all unavailable), scored 127 on debut in 140 minutes with 14 fours. His innings included a chance at 73. W.Bardsley, the nominated captain, withdrew through injury on the morning of the match and was replaced by Brown, Andrews (99 in 104 minutes, 12 fours) assuming the captaincy. Kippax (127 in 170 minutes, 13 fours) and Morgan (74 in 95 minutes, 7 fours) helped put New South Wales in a winning position with a fifth-wicket partnership of 140 runs. Richardson, who became the second South Australian to register a hundred in each innings, (100 in 136 minutes, 15 fours and 125 in 184 minutes, 11 fours), shared third-wicket stands with Pritchard (71 in 133 minutes, 5 fours and 85 in 147 minutes, 8 fours) in each innings. Rymill's 62 occupied 60 minutes and included 1 six and 6 fours. Gregory (7 for 88) forced South Australia to follow on shortly before lunch on the third day. Wall did not bowl after pulling a leg muscle in his first over. Sources: *Wisden, C.B.O'Reilly, NSWCA Report, Sydney Referee, Sydney Morning Herald, Sydney Daily Telegraph.*

NEW SOUTH WALES

H.O.Rock	c Walsh b Palmer	127	not out		27
A.T.Ratcliffe	c V.Y.Richardson b A.J.Richardson	29	b Palmer b Wainwright		3
*T.J.E.Andrews	c V.Y.Richardson b Palmer	99			
A.F.Kippax	c & b Grimmett	127			
J.M.Gregory	c Wainwright b Grimmett	16			
J.G.Morgan	b Walsh	74			
O.E.Nothling	c sub (G.W.Harris) b Grimmett	12			
†W.A.S.Oldfield	b Grimmett	13			
C.V.Morrissey	b Grimmett	2			
W.G.F.Brown	run out (Wainwright)	1	(3) not out		21
A.A.Mailey	not out	0			
Extras	(b3, lb5, w2)	10	(b1, lb1, w1,)		3
Total	(82.7 overs, 326 mins)	510	(16.0 overs, 56 mins) (1 wkt)		54

SOUTH AUSTRALIA

A.J.Richardson	b Gregory	4	(8) b Mailey		5
F.K.Gould	b Gregory	3	(1) c Mailey b Nothling		1
D.E.Pritchard	c & b Gregory	71	b Morrissey		83
*V.Y.Richardson	c Gregory b Mailey	100	b Mailey		125
N.A.Walsh	lbw b Gregory	0	(10) c Mailey b Kippax		11
J.W.Rymill	b Gregory	24	(9) c Andrews b Mailey		62
E.G.C.Wainwright	c Oldfield b Mailey	26	b Mailey		7
C.V.Grimmett	b Gregory	12	(2) b Gregory		0
†A.M.Ambler	run out (Morgan/Mailey/Oldfield)	1	(5) st Oldfield b Mailey		3
T.W.Wall	b Gregory	0	(6) b Mailey		0
G.H.Palmer	not out	1	not out		4
Extras	(b1, lb4, nb1)	6	(b1, lb5, w3, nb2)		11
Total	(57.0 overs, 215 mins)	248	(68.5 overs, 282 mins)		314

SOUTH AUSTRALIA	O	M	R	W	w,nb		O	M	R	W	w,nb
Wall	1	0	6	0	1,-						
A.J.Richardson	30	1	161	1	1,-						
Palmer	15	1	103	2	-,-	(2)	6	1	8	0	-,-
Grimmett	26.7	1	137	5	-,-						
Wainwright	7	0	68	0	-,-	(1)	6	1	22	1	1,-
Walsh	3	0	25	1	-,-	(4)	2	0	14	0	-,-
Pritchard						(3)	2	1	7	0	-,-

NEW SOUTH WALES	O	M	R	W	w,nb		O	M	R	W	w,nb
Gregory	19	0	88	7	-,-		16	2	67	1	2,-
Morrissey	12	0	44	0	-,-	(3)	17	6	42	1	1,-
Mailey	18	0	69	2	-,-	(4)	19.5	0	99	6	-,-
Nothling	7	0	31	0	-,-	(2)	12	1	59	1	-,1
Andrews	1	0	10	0	-,1		2	0	28	0	-,1
Kippax							2	0	8	1	-,-

FALL OF WICKETS

	NSW	SA	NSW	SA
Wkt	1st	1st	2nd	2nd
1st	61	7	1	7
2nd	245	10	2	-
3rd	262	180	204	-
4th	294	180	221	-
5th	434	190	222	-
6th	467	220	225	-
7th	499	246	234	-
8th	501	247	255	-
9th	510	247	304	-
10th	510	248	314	-

QUEENSLAND v M.C.C.

Played at Exhibition Ground, Brisbane on November 29, December 1, 2, 1924. (Three-day match)
Toss : M.C.C.   Result : MATCH DRAWN.
Debuts: Queensland - L.J.Shewan (f/c).
12th Men: N.C.Beeston (Qld). No 12th named for MCC.
Umpires: J.P.Orr and A.E.Wyeth.
Attendances: 12000, 6000, 1000.   Total: About 19,000.   Receipts: £1113.
Close of Play: 1st day MCC 5/391 (Hendren 153, Whysall 13); 2nd day Qld 8/218 (Cain 18, Hornibrook 5).

S.W.Ayres and J.W.McAndrew were unavailable for Queensland. Hobbs (51 in 90 minutes, 1 six and 3 fours), Sandham (64 in 110 minutes, 7 fours), Hendren (168 in 192 minutes, 1 six and 20 fours) and Chapman (80 in 70 minutes, 1 six and 10 fours) all surpassed 50 for M.C.C. Bensted topscored in Queensland's first innings (40 in 82 minutes, 3 fours) while Cain (39 in 50 minutes, 1 six and 4 fours) and Hornibrook (36 in 45 minutes, 4 fours) added 59 for the ninth wicket. Tate dismissed Thompson and Hefferan with successive balls. The match was abandoned at 5.00pm on the last day following a storm and associated bad light. Sources: *Wisden, QCA Report, Brisbane Courier, Brisbane Daily Mail.*

M.C.C.

J.B.Hobbs	c O'Connor b Hornibrook	51
H.Sutcliffe	c Bensted b McDonald	24
A.Sandham	c & b Oxenham	64
J.L.Bryan	c & b Hornibrook	4
E.H.Hendren	c Oxenham b Hornibrook	168
A.P.F.Chapman	c Rowe b Bensted	80
†W.W.Whysall	b Hornibrook	46
M.W.Tate	c Shewan b Hornibrook	20
*A.E.R.Gilligan	b Oxenham	3
R.K.Tyldesley	c Oxenham b Brew	39
A.P.Freeman	not out	21
Extras	(b2)	2
Total	(98.3 overs, 385 mins)	522

QUEENSLAND

*†L.P.D.O'Connor	b Tyldesley	29	not out		66
E.C.Bensted	lbw b Freeman	40	lbw b Freeman		12
W.Rowe	run out (Tate)	32	b Tate		3
F.C.Thompson	b Tate	39	c & b Freeman		2
R.K.Oxenham	b Tyldesley	26	not out		45
F.U.Hefferan	b Tate	0			
W.H.McDonald	b Tate	8			
C.B.P.McFarlane	c Gilligan b Tate	7			
W.Cain	b Freeman	39			
P.M.Hornibrook	b Freeman	36			
L.J.Shewan	not out	3			
Extras	(b7, lb8, nb1)	16	(b1, lb1, w1)		3
Total	(68.0 overs, 249 mins)	275	(43.0 overs, 135 mins) (3 wkts)		131

QUEENSLAND	O	M	R	W	w,nb
Hornibrook	34	3	210	5	-,-
Shewan	13	0	71	0	-,-
Oxenham	29	3	114	2	-,-
McDonald	12	0	63	1	-,-
Rowe	7.3	0	41	1	-,-
Bensted	3	0	21	1	-,-

M.C.C.	O	M	R	W	w,nb		O	M	R	W	w,nb
Gilligan	16	4	44	0	-,1	(5)	4	0	13	0	-,-
Tate	15	2	64	4	-,-		9	2	23	1	-,-
Tyldesley	17	3	67	2	-,-	(4)	9	3	18	0	1,-
Freeman	19	1	79	3	-,-	(3)	15	0	49	2	-,-
Bryan	1	0	5	0	-,-						
Hobbs						(1)	3	0	13	0	-,-
Sutcliffe						(6)	3	0	12	0	-,-

FALL OF WICKETS

	MCC	QLD	QLD
Wkt	1st	1st	2nd
1st	64	58	37
2nd	83	86	40
3rd	99	124	43
4th	197	161	-
5th	331	161	-
6th	418	185	-
7th	425	185	-
8th	460	211	-
9th	468	270	-
10th	522	275	-

AUSTRALIAN XI v M.C.C.

Played at Exhibition Ground, Brisbane on December 4, 5, 6, 8, 1924. (Four-day match)
Toss : Australian XI.   Result : MATCH DRAWN.
Debuts: Nil.
12th Men: W.Rowe (Aust) and W.W.Whysall (MCC).
Umpires: J.P.Orr and A.E.Wyeth.
Attendances: 6000, 8000, 15,000, ? .   Total & Receipts: No figures published.
Close of Play: 1st day Aust XI 5/299 (Oxenham 47); 2nd day MCC 0/4 (Douglas 1, Strudwick 1); 3rd day MCC 6/292 (Hendren 71).

O'Connor and Ponsford (81 in 152 minutes, 5 fours) shared an opening stand of 121 in 120 minutes on the first day. Hendry and Oxenham added 111 for the fifth wicket in 75 minutes and Thompson (114 in 209 minutes, 7 fours) and Taaffe (86 not out in 232 minutes, 4 fours) continued on by adding 170 in 172 minutes for the seventh wicket next morning. Hendren (100 in 209 minutes, 1 six and 10 fours) and Chapman (92 in 104 minutes, 1 six and 10 fours) topscored for M.C.C. Tyldesley's 29 included 20 (6464) off four consecutive balls from Grimmett. Taaffe, attempting to catch Kilner in the deep on the last day, overbalanced and struck his head on the fence, momentarily losing consciousness; he was assisted from the field but quickly recovered. All eleven Englishmen bowled in the second innings, Strudwick taking his sole first-class wicket and combining with Freeman to dismiss Oxenham in a reversal of the first innings unique in Australian matches. Richardson (83 in 74 minutes, 10 fours) and Kippax (82 not out) added 113 for the third wicket. Sources: *Wisden, QCA Report, Brisbane Courier, Brisbane Daily Mail.*

AUSTRALIAN XI

†L.P.D.O'Connor	lbw b Freeman	50	(2)	b Howell	40
W.H.Ponsford	c Sandham b Howell	81			
A.J.Richardson	lbw b Tyldesley	35		st Strudwick b Chapman	83
A.F.Kippax	st Strudwick b Tyldesley	14		not out	82
*H.S.T.L.Hendry	c Strudwick b Freeman	68	(1)	lbw b Tyldesley	26
R.K.Oxenham	st Strudwick b Freeman	54		st Freeman b Strudwick	0
F.C.Thompson	c Sutcliffe b Freeman	114	(5)	c Bryan b Chapman	12
F.H.Taaffe	not out	86	(7)	not out	10
P.M.Hornibrook	b Freeman	16			
C.V.Grimmett	b Freeman	0			
P.H.Wallace	b Howell	1			
Extras	(b1, lb4, nb2)	7		(b1, lb2, w1)	4
Total	(157.0 overs, 565 mins)	526		(50.0 overs, 175 mins) (5 wkts)	257

M.C.C.

*J.W.H.T.Douglas	b Grimmett	54
†H.Strudwick	b Wallace	6
H.Sutcliffe	lbw b Richardson	19
J.L.Bryan	c & b Grimmett	29
E.H.Hendren	lbw b Oxenham	100
A.Sandham	lbw b Oxenham	10
A.P.F.Chapman	st O'Connor b Grimmett	92
R.Kilner	c O'Connor b Oxenham	52
R.K.Tyldesley	c Hendry b Grimmett	29
A.P.Freeman	not out	12
H.Howell	b Oxenham	1
Extras	(b10, lb3, nb4)	17
Total	(102.1 overs, 400 mins)	421

M.C.C.	O	M	R	W	w,nb		O	M	R	W	w,nb
Howell	35	2	123	2	-,2	(5)	5	0	21	1	-,-
Douglas	12	0	53	0	-,-	(1)	5	0	29	0	-,-
Kilner	18	2	69	0	-,-	(2)	5	0	17	0	-,-
Tyldesley	37	5	105	2	-,-	(3)	5	0	19	1	-,-
Freeman	53	6	160	6	-,-	(4)	7	0	29	0	-,-
Bryan	2	0	9	0	-,-		3	0	25	0	-,-
Sutcliffe							3	0	13	0	-,-
Hendren							4	0	34	0	1,-
Sandham							4	0	24	0	-,-
Chapman							6	0	33	2	-,-
Strudwick							3	0	9	1	-,-

AUSTRALIAN XI	O	M	R	W	w,nb
Wallace	14	1	54	1	-,4
Hornibrook	25	5	87	0	-,-
Grimmett	36	3	176	4	-,-
Richardson	11	2	40	1	-,-
Oxenham	12.1	3	25	4	-,-
Hendry	4	0	22	0	-,-

FALL OF WICKETS

Wkt	AUST 1st	MCC 1st	AUST 2nd
1st	121	15	48
2nd	145	52	89
3rd	175	105	202
4th	188	116	234
5th	299	146	239
6th	312	292	-
7th	482	357	-
8th	513	386	-
9th	523	420	-
10th	526	421	-

AUSTRALIA v ENGLAND (1st Test)

Played at Sydney Cricket Ground on December 19, 20, 22, 23, 24, 26, 27, 1924. (Timeless match)
Toss : Australia.   Result : AUSTRALIA WON BY 193 RUNS.
Debuts: Australia - W.H.Ponsford, A.J.Richardson, V.Y.Richardson (all Test). England - A.P.Freeman (Test).
12th Men: T.J.E.Andrews (Aust) and R.Kilner (Eng).
Umpires: A.C.Jones and A.P.Williams.
Attendances: 33911, 47152, 16368, 7717, 29094, 2760.   Total: 166,215.   Receipts: £16,302.
Close of Play: 1st day Aust 3/282 (A.J.Richardson 21, Taylor 1); 2nd day Eng 0/72 (Hobbs 42, Sutcliffe 28); 3rd day Aust (2) 1/61
    (A.J.Richardson 30, Kelleway 9); 4th day Aust (2) 5/258 (Collins 58, Hendry 6); 5th day Eng (2) 0/42 (Hobbs 13, Sutcliffe 27)
    6th day Eng (2) 8/362 (Woolley 94, Freeman 33).

Ponsford (110 in 230 minutes, 8 fours) was the sixth Australian to score a century on his Test debut and the third to do so in his first innings. Although he gave no actual chance he was considered fortunate to survive the early part of his innings. Arthur Richardson (98 in 169 minutes, 9 fours) missed by a whisker emulating his feat in the second innings. A record tenth-wicket stand for Australia in all Tests - 127 in 79 minutes - was established between Taylor (chanceless 108 in 166 minutes, 8 fours) and Mailey (46 not out with 4 fours) on the fifth day. Taylor scored his runs - his second 50 took just 32 minutes - under the hindrance of a boil on his leg, which prevented him fielding from the third day on. Andrews took his place. Collins (114 in 235 minutes, 9 fours, chance at 42) was absent on the third day due to the death of his sister. Bardsley stood as acting captain while J.Ryder fielded as substitute. Hobbs and Sutcliffe became only the third pair of openers (the first in Tests) to put up century partnerships for the first wicket in both innings of a first-class match in Australia. Hobbs scored a chanceless 115 (219 minutes, 7 fours) and 57 (111 minutes, 1 five and 1 four); Sutcliffe 59 (160 minutes, 5 fours) and a chanceless 115 (247 minutes, 9 fours). Woolley (123 in 146 minutes, 1 six and 15 fours, chance at 93) and Freeman (50 not out in 87 minutes, 9 fours) shared a ninth-wicket stand of 128 in 82 minutes. Hendren (74 not out in 113 minutes, 1 six and 6 fours) and Collins (60 in 154 minutes, 3 fours) scored other half-centuries. Hearne injured his hand in the pre-lunch session on the second day while attempting to stop a hard drive by Taylor off the first ball of his 13th over. C.G.Macartney (ill) was unavailable for Australia. Sources: *Wisden, NSWCA Report, Sydney Morning Herald, Sydney Referee, The Australasian.*

AUSTRALIA

*H.L.Collins	c Hendren b Tate	114	(4) c Chapman b Tate	60
W.Bardsley	c Woolley b Freeman	21	(1) b Tate	22
W.H.Ponsford	b Gilligan	110	(5) c Woolley b Freeman	27
A.J.Richardson	b Hearne	22	(2) c & b Freeman	98
J.M.Taylor	c Strudwick b Tate	43	(8) b Tate	108
V.Y.Richardson	b Freeman	42	c Hendren b Tate	18
C.Kelleway	c Woolley b Tate	17	(3) b Gilligan	23
H.S.T.L.Hendry	c Strudwick b Tate	3	(7) c Strudwick b Tate	22
J.M.Gregory	c Strudwick b Tate	0	c Woolley b Freeman	2
†W.A.S.Oldfield	not out	39	c Strudwick b Gilligan	18
A.A.Mailey	b Tate	21	not out	46
Extras	(b10, lb8)	18	(b2, lb5, w1)	8
Total	(152.2 overs, 500 mins)	450	(125.7 overs, 425 mins)	452

ENGLAND

J.B.Hobbs	c Kelleway b Gregory	115	c Hendry b Mailey	57
H.Sutcliffe	c V.Y.Richardson b Mailey	59	c Gregory b Mailey	115
J.W.Hearne	c sub (T.J.E.Andrews) b Mailey	7	b Gregory	0
F.E.Woolley	b Gregory	0	(6) c Mailey b Gregory	123
E.H.Hendren	not out	74	c Gregory b Hendry	9
A.Sandham	b Mailey	7	(7) c Oldfield b Mailey	2
A.P.F.Chapman	run out (sub T.J.E.Andrews)	13	(4) c Oldfield b Hendry	44
M.W.Tate	c sub (T.J.E.Andrews) b Mailey	7	c Ponsford b Kelleway	0
*A.E.R.Gilligan	b Gregory	1	b Kelleway	1
A.P.Freeman	b Gregory	0	not out	50
†H.Strudwick	lbw b Gregory	6	c Oldfield b Hendry	2
Extras	(b1, lb5, nb3)	9	(b4, lb3, nb1)	8
Total	(79.7 overs, 302 mins)	298	(96.7 overs, 374 mins)	411

ENGLAND	O	M	R	W	w,nb		O	M	R	W	w,nb
Tate	55.1	11	130	6	-,-	(2)	33.7	8	98	5	-,-
Gilligan	23	0	92	1	-,-	(1)	27	6	114	2	-,-
Freeman	49	11	124	2	-,-		37	4	134	3	-,-
Hearne	12.1	3	28	1	-,-		25	2	88	0	1,-
Woolley	9	0	35	0	-,-						
Hobbs	2	0	13	0	-,-						
Chapman	2	0	10	0	-,-	(5)	3	1	10	0	-,-

AUSTRALIA	O	M	R	W	w,nb		O	M	R	W	w,nb
Gregory	28.7	2	111	5	-,-		28	2	115	2	-,-
Kelleway	14	3	44	0	-,3		21	5	60	2	-,1
Mailey	31	3	129	4	-,-		32	0	179	3	-,-
Hendry	5	1	5	0	-,-	(5)	10.7	2	36	3	-,-
A.J.Richardson	1	1	0	0	-,-	(4)	5	0	13	0	-,-

FALL OF WICKETS

	AUST	ENG	AUST	ENG
Wkt	1st	1st	2nd	2nd
1st	46	157	40	110
2nd	236	171	115	127
3rd	275	172	168	195
4th	286	202	210	212
5th	364	235	241	263
6th	374	254	260	269
7th	387	272	281	270
8th	387	274	286	276
9th	388	274	325	404
10th	450	298	452	411

NEW SOUTH WALES v QUEENSLAND

Played at Sydney Cricket Ground on December 31, 1924, January 1, 2, 1925. (Three-day match)
Toss : Queensland.   Result : MATCH DRAWN.
Debuts: New South Wales - G.A.N.Chapman, P.W.Dive, J.E.H.Hooker, F.W.Rowland (all f/c). Queensland - N.C.Beeston, F.M.Brew,
    F.J.Gough, H.D.Noyes, H.W.Rahmann (all f/c).
12th Men: R.G.L.Harris (NSW) and F.U.Hefferan (Qld).
Umpires: Not known.
Attendances & Receipts: No figures published.
Close of Play: 1st day Qld 406 all out; 2nd day Qld (2) 4/74 (O'Connor 17).

Rowland, a last-minute inclusion in the New South Wales team to replace B.L.McCoy (injured knee), was unable to get to the ground
before lunch on the first day and Harris substituted until he arrived. A new Queensland third-wicket record of 160 was established by
O'Connor (chanceless 141 in 200 minutes, 9 fours) and Thompson (57 in 107 minutes, 3 fours) who guided the team towards their highest
total against New South Wales so far. Brew was out to his first ball on debut. Punch and Salmon shared a century partnership in each
innings for New South Wales 117 (fourth wicket) and 160 (third wicket) respectively. Punch scoring 87 (92 minutes, 9 fours) and 94 (135
minutes, 9 fours) and Salmon 68 (142 minutes, 6 fours) and a career-best 94 (135 minutes, 11 fours). Wall was out to the only ball he
faced. O'Connor (47 in 140 minutes, 2 fours) and Oxenham (41 in 90 minutes, 2 fours) topscored in Queensland's second innings. This is
the only Australian match in the 20th Century for which the names of the umpires have not been found. Sources: *The Cricketer, NSWCA
Report, Sydney Sun, Sydney Morning Herald, NSWCA Scorebook, Sydney Referee, Sydney Daily Telegraph.*

QUEENSLAND

*†L.P.D.O'Connor	c Rowland b Wall	141		b Bubb	47
R.K.Oxenham	c & b Dive	17	(6)	lbw b Punch	41
W.Rowe	c Gostelow b Bubb	14		b Morrissey	0
F.C.Thompson	lbw b Hooker	57		b Hooker	10
F.M.Brew	b Hooker	0	(7)	b Bubb	2
F.J.Gough	run out	31	(2)	c Gostelow b Morrissey	0
S.W.Ayres	c Gostelow b Hooker	17	(8)	not out	25
W.Cain	c Gostelow b Hooker	12	(10)	not out	4
N.C.Beeston	c Dive b Hooker	37		b Hooker	28
H.D.Noyes	c Brown b Punch	35	(5)	c Punch b Wall	27
H.W.Rahmann	not out	19			
Extras	(b9, lb11, w1, nb5)	26		(b19, lb8)	27
Total	(79.4 overs, 310 mins)	406		(60.0 overs, 225 mins) (8 wkts dec)	211

NEW SOUTH WALES

W.G.F.Brown	c O'Connor b Ayres	2	(6)	not out	1
†R.E.Gostelow	c O'Connor b Noyes	8	(1)	lbw b Oxenham	1
G.A.N.Chapman	c Noyes b Ayres	6		c sub (F.U.Hefferan) b Thompson	28
*A.T.E.Punch	b Oxenham	87		c O'Connor b Brew	94
B.M.Salmon	c & b Ayres	68	(2)	b Noyes	94
F.W.Rowland	c Oxenham b Ayres	22	(5)	not out	20
J.E.H.Hooker	c Gough b Oxenham	28			
C.V.Morrissey	b Oxenham	32			
J.L.Wall	b Oxenham	0			
R.A.Bubb	not out	24			
P.W.Dive	run out	2			
Extras	(b2, lb8, nb1)	11		(b12, lb3, w1, nb1)	17
Total	(63.7 overs, 255 mins)	290		(42.0 overs, 180 mins) (4 wkts)	255

NEW SOUTH WALES	O	M	R	W	w,nb		O	M	R	W	w,nb
Morrissey	16	0	53	0	-,1		16	2	48	2	-,-
Hooker	19.4	1	81	5	1,-		12	1	31	2	-,-
Dive	13	0	90	1	-,3						
Bubb	8	0	47	1	-,1	(5)	12	1	44	2	-,-
Wall	17	1	68	1	-,-	(3)	7	1	30	1	-,-
Punch	6	0	41	1	-,-	(4)	13	2	31	1	-,-

QUEENSLAND	O	M	R	W	w,nb		O	M	R	W	w,nb
Noyes	16	2	62	1	-,-		13	1	67	1	-,-
Ayres	17.7	2	95	4	-,1	(6)	3	0	24	0	-,-
Oxenham	15	1	68	4	-,-	(2)	10	0	40	1	-,-
Rahmann	5	0	16	0	-,-	(5)	6	0	41	0	-,1
Rowe	6	0	25	0	-,-	(4)	4	0	23	0	-,-
Thompson	4	0	13	0	-,-	(3)	4	1	23	1	1,-
Brew							1	0	8	1	-,-
Gough							1	0	12	0	-,-

FALL OF WICKETS

	QLD	NSW	QLD	NSW
Wkt	1st	1st	2nd	2nd
1st	49	5	5	9
2nd	77	15	7	54
3rd	237	25	22	214
4th	237	142	74	243
5th	247	200	138	-
6th	270	201	152	-
7th	288	248	154	-
8th	311	248	203	-
9th	354	285	-	-
10th	406	290	-	-

AUSTRALIA v ENGLAND (2nd Test)

Played at Melbourne Cricket Ground on January 1, 2, 3, 5, 6, 7, 8, 1925. (Timeless match)
Toss : Australia.   Result : AUSTRALIA WON BY 81 RUNS.
Debuts: Australia - A.E.V.Hartkopf (Test).
12th Men: T.J.E.Andrews (Aust) and A.Sandham (Eng).
Umpires: R.M.Crockett and C.Garing.
Attendances: 48321, 45015, 47875, 33524, 23335, 22151, 16037.   Total: 236,258.   Receipts: £22,599.
Close of Play: 1st day Aust 4/300 (Ponsford 128, V.Y.Richardson 39); 2nd day Aust 600 all out; 3rd day Eng 0/283 (Hobbs 154,
    Sutcliffe 123); 4th day Aust (2) 3/63 (Collins 17, Taylor 25); 5th day Eng (2) 1/54 (Sutcliffe 12, Strudwick 15); 6th day Eng (2)
    6/259 (Sutcliffe 114, Douglas 0).

Australia became the first team to score 600 runs in a Test innings. Ponsford (128 in 222 minutes, 6 fours) was the first batsman to score centuries in each of his first two Tests. He gave a chance on 63, to Tyldesley at forward square-leg off Hearne, before playing on to his first ball of the second day. Vic Richardson (138 in 198 minutes, 13 fours) was missed on 67, by Douglas at wide mid-off off Tyldesley. Taylor (72 in 130 minutes, 3 fours) and Hartkopf on debut (80 in 162 minutes, 8 fours) scored solid half-centuries. Hobbs (chanceless 154 in 289 minutes, 11 fours) and Sutcliffe (chanceless 176 in 431 minutes, 18 fours) became the first pair to bat undefeated through an uninterrupted day's play in a first-class match in Australia, adding 283 in 288 minutes. When play resumed on the fourth day, after rest on Sunday, Hobbs was bowled second ball by a Mailey full-toss. Sutcliffe repeated his feat in the second innings to become the first to score a century in each innings of a Test in Australia (127 in 379 minutes, 12 fours) and bat through another full day (the sixth). He gave two chances, when 12 to Gregory (a difficult one) off Mailey, and 94 to Kelleway at first slip off Gregory. Woolley (50 in 165 minutes, 6 fours) was the only other batsman to reach a half-century for England. Taylor (90 in 149 minutes, 1 five and 7 fours) earlier held Australia's second innings together. This was the first cricket match in the world to attract in excess of 200,000 spectators. Sources: *Wisden, VCA Report, The Age, The Argus, The Herald, Melbourne Sun, The Australasian.*

AUSTRALIA

*H.L.Collins	c Strudwick b Tate	9	b Hearne		30
W.Bardsley	c Strudwick b Gilligan	19	lbw b Tate		2
A.J.Richardson	run out (Hobbs/Gilligan)	14	b Tate		9
W.H.Ponsford	b Tate	128	b Tate		4
J.M.Taylor	run out (Hobbs)	72	b Tate		90
V.Y.Richardson	run out (Chapman)	138	c Strudwick b Hearne		8
C.Kelleway	c Strudwick b Gilligan	32	c & b Hearne		17
A.E.V.Hartkopf	c Chapman b Gilligan	80	lbw b Tate		0
J.M.Gregory	c Gilligan b Tate	44	not out		36
†W.A.S.Oldfield	not out	39	lbw b Tate		39
A.A.Mailey	lbw b Douglas	1	b Tate		3
Extras	(b18, lb5, nb1)	24	(b11, lb1)		12
Total	(149.5 overs, 578 mins)	600	(79.3 overs, 284 mins)		250

ENGLAND

J.B.Hobbs	b Mailey	154	lbw b Mailey		22
H.Sutcliffe	b Kelleway	176	c Gregory b Mailey		127
F.E.Woolley	b Gregory	0	(5) lbw b A.J.Richardson		50
J.W.Hearne	b Mailey	9	lbw b Gregory		23
E.H.Hendren	c Oldfield b Kelleway	32	(6) b Gregory		18
A.P.F.Chapman	c Oldfield b Gregory	28	(9) not out		4
J.W.H.T.Douglas	c Collins b A.J.Richardson	8	(8) b Mailey		14
R.K.Tyldesley	c Collins b Gregory	5	(7) c Ponsford b Mailey		0
M.W.Tate	b A.J.Richardson	34	(11) b Gregory		0
*A.E.R.Gilligan	not out	17	c & b Mailey		0
†H.Strudwick	b Hartkopf	4	(3) lbw b Gregory		22
Extras	(b4, lb4, nb4)	12	(b6, lb2, nb2)		10
Total	(138.0 overs, 499 mins)	479	(106.3 overs, 397 mins)		290

ENGLAND	O	M	R	W	w,nb		O	M	R	W	w,nb			FALL OF WICKETS		
Tate	45	10	142	3	-,-		33.3	8	99	6	-,-			AUST	ENG	AUST	ENG
Douglas	19.5	0	95	1	-,-	(5)	4	0	9	0	-,-	Wkt	1st	1st	2nd	2nd
Tyldesley	35	3	130	0	-,-		2	0	6	0	-,-	1st	22	283	3	36
Gilligan	26	1	114	3	-,-	(2)	11	2	40	0	-,-	2nd	47	284	13	75
Hearne	13	1	69	0	-,-	(4)	29	5	84	4	-,-	3rd	47	305	27	121
Woolley	11	3	26	0	-,1							4th	208	373	106	211
												5th	301	404	126	254
AUSTRALIA	O	M	R	W	w,nb		O	M	R	W	w,nb	6th	424	412	166	255
Gregory	34	4	124	3	-,-		27.3	6	87	4	-,-	7th	439	418	168	280
Kelleway	30	10	62	2	-,4		18	4	42	0	-,2	8th	499	453	168	289
Mailey	34	5	141	2	-,-	(4)	24	2	92	5	-,-	9th	599	458	239	289
Hartkopf	26	1	120	1	-,-	(5)	4	1	14	0	-,-	10th	600	479	250	290
A.J.Richardson	14	6	20	2	-,-	(3)	22	7	35	1	-,-					
Collins							11	3	10	0	-,-					

SOUTH AUSTRALIA v NEW SOUTH WALES (Shield Match 4)

Played at Adelaide Oval on January 9, 10, 12, 13, 14, 1925. (Timeless match)
Toss : South Australia.   Result : SOUTH AUSTRALIA WON BY 161 RUNS.
Debuts: South Australia - L.T.Gun (f/c).
12th Men: L.S.Walsh (SA) and B.M.Salmon (NSW).
Umpires: G.I.Colyer and C.L.Cornish.
Attendances: 4009, 6239, 2716, 2880, 666.   Total: 16,510.   Receipts: £791.
Close of Play: 1st day SA 9/376 (Gun 127); 2nd day NSW 5/328 (Kippax 81, Nothling 0); 3rd day SA (2) 4/137 (Pritchard 27, Rundell 15); 4th day NSW (2) 5/111 (Punch 4, Nothling 3).

Despite the unavailability of A.J.Richardson, South Australia recorded their first victory in the Shield competition since the 1913-14 season. Murray tossed for the home side in the absence of V.Y.Richardson who arrived at the ground late upon returning from the Second Test in Melbourne. Gun, included at the last minute when N.A.Walsh, the original 12th man, was unable to obtain leave, scored an unbeaten 136 on debut in 199 minutes with 16 fours. Pritchard (101 in 141 minutes, 8 fours) and Rymill (110 in 139 minutes, 13 fours) also scored centuries for South Australia while Rundell was out first ball. Grimmett, struck on the knee attempting to field the third ball of the New South Wales innings, was off the field for the rest of the second day. Gwynne (chanceless 138 in 223 minutes, 1 five and 16 fours) and Kippax (122 in 198 minutes, 9 fours) scored centuries for New South Wales. *Wisden* and *O'Reilly* incorrectly give SA (1) Nothling 1/36, Morgan 0/25, omit Punch; NSW (2) Scott c & b Palmer 16, Morrissey c Palmer, extras 6, Murray 0/17. Sources: *Wisden, C.B.O'Reilly, NSWCA Report, South Australian Register, Adelaide Advertiser.*

SOUTH AUSTRALIA

J.W.Rymill	b Scott	9	(7) st Ratcliffe b Randell	110
E.G.C.Wainwright	c Ratcliffe b Scott	15	(1) c Scott b Morrissey	31
J.T.Murray	c Punch b Randell	46	c Scott b Andrews	17
D.E.Pritchard	c Ratcliffe b Andrews	101	lbw b Morrissey	61
P.D.Rundell	b Scott	0	(6) b Morrissey	69
*V.Y.Richardson	c Morrissey b Scott	4	(5) st Ratcliffe b Andrews	1
L.T.Gun	not out	136	(2) c Ratcliffe b Morrissey	36
C.V.Grimmett	b Andrews	38	(9) lbw b Randell	29
T.W.Wall	b Nothling	2	(8) c Randell b Andrews	23
†A.M.Ambler	run out (Morgan)	19	c Punch b Mayes	5
G.H.Palmer	b Scott	3	not out	0
Extras	(b9, lb3, nb4)	16	(b10, lb9, nb5)	24
Total	(74.2 overs, 303 mins)	389	(85.7 overs, 340 mins)	406

NEW SOUTH WALES

†A.T.Ratcliffe	b Wall	37	(5) c Gun b Grimmett	12
L.W.Gwynne	c Wainwright b Gun	138	(1) st Ambler b Grimmett	41
J.G.Morgan	b Wall	1	(2) c Rundell b Wall	4
*T.J.E.Andrews	b Gun	38	(3) c Pritchard b Palmer	13
A.F.Kippax	st Ambler b Grimmett	122	(4) st Ambler b Grimmett	31
A.T.E.Punch	c Murray b Rundell	18	lbw b Grimmett	32
O.E.Nothling	b Wall	9	b Palmer	25
A.D.A.Mayes	b Grimmett	6	(9) not out	29
J.D.Scott	b Grimmett	3	(10) c Pritchard b Palmer	15
C.V.Morrissey	not out	14	(8) c Pritchard b Grimmett	16
J.A.Randell	c Grimmett b Murray	2	c Richardson b Grimmett	1
Extras	(b9, lb6, w4, nb1)	20	(b4, lb2, w1)	7
Total	(87.1 overs, 350 mins)	408	(54.0 overs, 220 mins)	226

NEW SOUTH WALES	O	M	R	W	w,nb		O	M	R	W	w,nb
Scott	17.2	0	92	5	-,2		19	1	70	0	-,4
Mayes	11	2	38	0	-,1		12	1	43	1	-,1
Randell	14	0	75	1	-,-	(6)	9.7	0	53	2	-,-
Morrissey	7	0	38	0	-,-	(5)	21	1	87	4	-,-
Kippax	3	0	13	0	-,-	(7)	5	0	34	0	-,-
Nothling	7	1	26	1	-,-						
Andrews	9	0	56	2	-,1	(4)	18	1	92	3	-,-
Morgan	4	0	26	0	-,-						
Punch	2	0	9	0	-,-	(3)	1	0	3	0	-,-

SOUTH AUSTRALIA	O	M	R	W	w,nb		O	M	R	W	w,nb
Wall	24	2	100	3	-,1		8	0	39	1	-,-
Palmer	10	0	72	0	-,-		17	3	61	3	1,-
Murray	13.1	0	46	1	2,-	(4)	6	1	16	0	-,-
Wainwright	6	0	48	0	-,-						
Gun	11	1	38	2	1,-						
Rundell	8	0	28	1	1,-						
Richardson	2	0	13	0	-,-						
Grimmett	13	1	43	3	-,-	(3)	23	3	103	6	-,-

FALL OF WICKETS

Wkt	SA 1st	NSW 1st	SA 2nd	NSW 2nd
1st	10	71	68	5
2nd	33	73	81	40
3rd	122	162	97	83
4th	122	277	99	99
5th	126	324	214	107
6th	227	350	237	165
7th	296	361	298	165
8th	309	373	392	195
9th	376	402	403	221
10th	389	408	406	226

AUSTRALIA v ENGLAND (3rd Test)

Played at Adelaide Oval on January 16, 17, 19, 20, 21, 22, 23, 1925. (Timeless match)
Toss : Australia.   Result : AUSTRALIA WON BY 11 RUNS.
Debuts: England - W.W.Whysall (Test).
12th Men: W.Bardsley (Aust) and A.Sandham (Eng).
Umpires: R.M.Crockett and D.A.Elder.
Attendances: 18755, 34851, 21000, 11916, 12116, 8341, 12000.   Total: 118,979.   Receipts: £10,821.
Close of Play: 1st day Aust 7/275 (Ryder 72, Kelleway 8); 2nd day Eng 2/36 (Tate 14, Chapman 7); 3rd day Eng 6/270 (Hobbs 99,
    Hendren 47); 4th day Aust (2) 3/211 (Ryder 86, Ponsford 40); 5th day Eng (2) 3/133 (Sutcliffe 56, Whysall 22); 6th day Eng (2) 8/348
    (Gilligan 29, Freeman 17).

A splendid double by Ryder - 201 not out (395 minutes, 1 six, 1 five and 12 fours) and 88 (125 minutes, 7 fours) - enabled Australia to
clinch their third successive Test and retain the Ashes. Fully 12,000 people turned up to see the tense finish on the seventh day: admittance
was free and 20 minutes sufficed to decide events. Ryder's sole chance in his double-century occurred on 145, when he drove a ball fiercely
to Freeman at mid-on from the bowling of Kilner. The fielder sustained a badly-bruised wrist in attempting to take the catch and was forced
from the field. "So great was the pain that Freeman fainted on reaching the dressing room" (*Register*). Ryder carried the Australian total
from 6/119 to 489 through associations of 134 in 112 minutes with Andrews (9 fours) for the seventh wicket, 108 in 118 minutes with
Oldfield (3 fours) for the ninth and 73 in 77 minutes with Mailey for the tenth. Arthur Richardson (69 in 176 minutes, 7 fours) had earlier
batted well. England's bowling was greatly depleted by the absence of Gilligan, who strained a groin muscle while bowling his eighth
over, in addition to Tate (injured toe) and Freeman. Hobbs (chanceless 119 in 294 minutes, 7 fours) and Hendren (92 in 193 minutes, 8
fours) were the mainstay of the English batting while Sutcliffe (59 in 184 minutes, 8 fours), Whysall on debut (75 in 159 minutes, 4
fours) and Chapman (58 in 88 minutes, 2 sixes and 7 fours) scored half-centuries in the second innings. Early morning rain on the fifth day
gave temporary help to Woolley and Kilner's left-arm deliveries as Australia lost their last 7 for 35. Sources: *Wisden, VCA Report,
Sydney Referee, Adelaide Advertiser, South Australian Register*.

AUSTRALIA

*H.L.Collins	b Tate	3		b Freeman	26
A.J.Richardson	b Kilner	69		c Kilner Woolley	14
J.M.Gregory	b Freeman	6	(9)	c Hendren b Woolley	2
J.M.Taylor	lbw b Tate	0		b Freeman	34
W.H.Ponsford	c Strudwick b Gilligan	31		c Hendren b Kilner	43
V.Y.Richardson	c Whysall b Kilner	4	(7)	c Tate b Woolley	0
J.Ryder	not out	201	(3)	c & b Woolley	88
T.J.E.Andrews	b Kilner	72	(6)	c Whysall b Kilner	1
C.Kelleway	c Strudwick b Woolley	16	(8)	not out	22
†W.A.S.Oldfield	lbw b Kilner	47		b Kilner	4
A.A.Mailey	st Strudwick b Hendren	27		c Sutcliffe b Kilner	5
Extras	(lb9, nb4)	13		(b4, lb4, nb3)	11
Total	(153.0 overs, 523 mins)	489		(68.1 overs, 244 mins)	250

ENGLAND

W.W.Whysall	b Gregory	9	(5)	c & b Gregory	75
M.W.Tate	c Andrews b Mailey	27	(8)	b Mailey	21
†H.Strudwick	c Gregory b Kelleway	1	(11)	not out	2
A.P.F.Chapman	b Gregory	26	(6)	c Ryder b Kelleway	58
J.B.Hobbs	c Gregory b Mailey	119	(1)	c Collins b A.J.Richardson	27
H.Sutcliffe	c Oldfield b Ryder	33	(2)	c Ponsford b Mailey	59
F.E.Woolley	c Andrews b Mailey	16	(3)	b Kelleway	21
E.H.Hendren	c Taylor b Gregory	92	(4)	lbw b Kelleway	4
R.Kilner	lbw b A.J.Richardson	6	(7)	c V.Y.Richardson b A.J.Richardson	24
*A.E.R.Gilligan	c Collins b A.J.Richardson	9	(9)	c V.Y.Richardson b Gregory	31
A.P.Freeman	not out	6	(10)	c Oldfield b Mailey	24
Extras	(b8, lb10, nb3)	21		(b5, lb5, w1, nb6)	17
Total	(117.2 overs, 427 mins)	365		(111.2 overs, 405 mins)	363

ENGLAND	O	M	R	W	w,nb		O	M	R	W	w,nb		FALL OF WICKETS			
Tate	18	1	43	2	-,-		10	4	17	0	-,-			AUST	ENG	AUST	ENG
Gilligan	7.7	1	17	1	-,-								Wkt	1st	1st	2nd	2nd
Freeman	18	0	107	1	-,-		17	1	94	2	-,-		1st	10	15	36	63
Woolley	43	5	135	1	-,4		19	1	77	4	-,3		2nd	19	18	63	92
Kilner	56	7	127	4	-,-	(2)	22.1	7	51	4	-,-		3rd	22	67	126	96
Hobbs	3	0	11	0	-,-								4th	114	69	215	155
Hendren	5.1	0	27	1	-,-								5th	118	159	216	244
Whysall	2	0	9	0	-,-								6th	119	180	217	254
													7th	253	297	217	279
AUSTRALIA	O	M	R	W	w,nb		O	M	R	W	w,nb		8th	308	316	220	312
Gregory	26.2	0	111	3	-,-		23	6	71	2	-,-		9th	416	326	242	357
Kelleway	15	6	24	1	-,3	(3)	22	4	57	3	-,6		10th	489	365	250	363
Mailey	44	5	133	3	-,-	(6)	30.2	4	126	3	1,-						
A.J.Richardson	21	7	42	2	-,-	(5)	25	5	62	2	-,-						
Ryder	6	2	15	1	-,-	(4)	2	0	11	0	-,-						
Collins	5	1	19	0	-,-	(2)	9	4	19	0	-,-						

NEW SOUTH WALES v VICTORIA (Shield Match 5)

Played at Sydney Cricket Ground on January 24, 26, 27, 28, 29, 1925. (Timeless match)
Toss : New South Wales.   Result : VICTORIA WON BY SEVEN WICKETS.
Debuts: New South Wales - M.W.Bosley, C.H.W.Lawes (both f/c). Victoria - D.D.Blackie (f/c).
12th Men: J.E.H.Hooker (NSW) and K.J.Millar (Vic).
Umpires: W.J.R.Bowes and W.G.French.
Attendances: 6271, 10876, 2270, 1071, 630.   Total: 21,118.   Receipts: £1301.
Close of Play: 1st day NSW 2/393 (Rock 187, Kippax 93); 2nd day Vic 2/69 (Woodfull 23); 3rd day Vic 7/376 (Willis 17, Ellis 10);
  4th day NSW (2) 152 all out.

A total of 14 catches were dropped by the Victorian fieldsmen in the first innings. Rock (235 in 387 minutes, 15 fours, chances at 9, 100, 201) benefited most to compile the highest score of his career, cut short when he qualified as a doctor the following year. He shared partnerships of 202 for the first wicket with Morgan (87 in 152 minutes, 5 fours, 2 chances) and 268 for the third wicket with Kippax (212 not out in 371 minutes, 15 fours, chances at 48, 113, 139 and 212). .The Victorians were led by Woodfull (81 in 229 minutes, 5 fours), Liddicut (132 in 293 minutes, 11 fours, 2 chances at 114), Hartkopf (56 in 99 minutes, 9 fours) and Willis (100 in 149 minutes, 11 fours) in the first innings. Batting again New South Wales collapsed, losing seven wickets for 28 runs, and Victoria achieved victory through Woodfull (120 not out in 272 minutes, 6 fours) and Hendry (85 in 157 minutes, 2 fours). Rock kept wickets after tea on the last day; Ratcliffe was rested in the field after taking several knocks earlier in the day and caught Liddicut at mid-on. Blackie made his first-class debut at the remarkable age of 42 years 294 days. New South Wales were severely depleted by the absence of eight players due to the length of the Adelaide Test. Sources: *Wisden, NSWCA Report, VCA Report, The Argus, Sydney Morning Herald, Sydney Referee.*

NEW SOUTH WALES

H.O.Rock	c Tarrant b Hartkopf	235		c Hartkopf b Blackie	51
J.G.Morgan	b Hendry	87		c Hartkopf b Wallace	3
*†A.T.Ratcliffe	lbw b Blackie	1	(6)	c Hartkopf b Blackie	8
A.F.Kippax	not out	212		st Ellis b Hartkopf	40
B.M.Salmon	run out (Tarrant/Hartkopf)	31	(3)	c Liddicut b Blackie	9
A.P.Wells	st Ellis b Hartkopf	9	(5)	run out (Wallace/Ellis)	14
C.V.Morrissey	c Ellis b Hartkopf	4		b Hendry	0
C.H.W.Lawes	b Hartkopf	0		st Ellis b Hartkopf	1
A.D.A.Mayes	run out (Willis/Hartkopf)	6		not out	5
J.D.Scott	b Wallace	1		c Schneider b Hartkopf	4
M.W.Bosley	st Ellis b Hartkopf	1		c Mayne b Hendry	9
Extras	(b13, lb6, w4, nb4)	27		(b6, nb2)	8
Total	(148.1 overs, 532 mins)	614		(44.6 overs, 186 mins)	152

VICTORIA

*R.E.Mayne	b Scott	12		lbw b Scott	1
W.M.Woodfull	run out (Wells/Ratcliffe)	81		not out	120
H.S.T.L.Hendry	c Mayes b Lawes	19		c Scott b Morrissey	85
A.E.Liddicut	b Scott	132		c Ratcliffe b Morgan	28
F.A.Tarrant	c Ratcliffe b Scott	23		not out	18
A.E.V.Hartkopf	c Walls b Morrissey	56			
K.J.Schneider	b Scott	1			
C.B.Willis	c Rock b Scott	100			
†J.L.Ellis	run out (Wells)	20			
D.D.Blackie	c Kippax b Lawes	23			
P.H.Wallace	not out	0			
Extras	(b9, lb10, w1, nb15)	35		(b8, lb4, nb1)	13
Total	(134.1 overs, 525 mins)	502		(78.4 overs, 272 mins) (3 wkts)	265

VICTORIA	O	M	R	W	w,nb		O	M	R	W	w,nb
Wallace	24	0	103	1	3,3		5	0	16	1	-,2
Blackie	31	1	108	1	-,-		12	2	29	2	-,-
Hendry	33	2	129	1	-,1		9.6	0	23	3	-,-
Hartkopf	23.1	0	121	5	1,-		8	0	45	3	-,-
Tarrant	20	1	69	0	-,-	(7)	6	1	13	0	-,-
Liddicut	14	1	42	0	-,-	(5)	2	0	9	0	-,-
Schneider	3	0	15	0	-,-	(6)	2	0	9	0	-,-

NEW SOUTH WALES	O	M	R	W	w,nb		O	M	R	W	w,nb
Scott	33.1	3	149	5	-,13		11	0	44	1	-,-
Lawes	33	9	82	2	-,-		16	1	47	0	-,-
Morrissey	26	4	91	1	1,2		11	0	36	1	-,1
Bosley	12	2	36	0	-,-		15.4	1	46	0	-,-
Mayes	16	3	51	0	-,-	(6)	10	3	15	0	-,-
Kippax	14	3	58	0	-,-	(5)	9	0	47	0	-,-
Morgan							6	0	17	1	-,-

FALL OF WICKETS

Wkt	NSW 1st	VIC 1st	NSW 2nd	VIC 2nd
1st	202	34	8	4
2nd	205	69	45	169
3rd	473	199	95	216
4th	550	246	124	-
5th	567	341	133	-
6th	583	345	133	-
7th	583	346	134	-
8th	609	402	134	-
9th	613	494	138	-
10th	614	502	152	-

TASMANIA v M.C.C.

Played at N.T.C.A. Ground, Launceston, on January 27, 28, 29, 1925. (Three-day match)
Toss : M.C.C.   Result : M.C.C. WON BY 119 RUNS.
Debuts: Tasmania - A.H.Davis, D.C.Green, A.W.Shugg (all f/c); R.L.Bennett (Tas only).
12th Men: A.B.Crowder (Tas) and H.Sutcliffe (MCC).
Umpires: H.C.L.Barber and F.C.Tabart.
Attendances: 2000, 5000, 700.   Total: About 7700.   Receipts: About £600.
Close of Play: 1st day Tas 3/71 (Green 30); 2nd day Tas (2) 2/30 (Green 4).

The M.C.C. party arrived by ship on the morning of the match. Sandham (116 in 155 minutes, 14 fours) was dropped off consecutive balls when 58 by Henty and Allan from the bowling of Shugg. After losing Bennett to the fourth ball of the innings, Tasmania encountered a rain-affected wicket on the second day and Kilner ran through the middle order. A.H.Davis (25) was adjudged lbw but recalled after Gilligan conferred with the umpires. However the pitch provided little trouble for the visitors batting in their second innings, Sandham (51 in 46 minutes, 5 fours), Hendren (101 not out in 94 minutes, 15 fours) and Gilligan (60 in 36 minutes, 1 six and 7 fours) all scored rapidly in contributing to the 456 runs scored in the day. A new Tasmanian record for the sixth-wicket was established by Martin (chanceless 121 in 126 minutes, 15 fours) and Findlay. Howell finished the match by dismissing Newton and Shugg with successive balls. Bennett had previously played five matches for South Australia. *Hobart Mercury* gives Tas (1) 2/47, 6/89. Sources: *Wisden, VCA Report, The Age, Launceston Examiner, Hobart Mercury.*

M.C.C.

J.L.Bryan	c Green b A.H.Davis	8		lbw b Findlay	46
A.Sandham	c Allan b A.H.Davis	116		c Henty b Findlay	51
J.W.Hearne	run out (N.W.Davis)	6		c Findlay b Shugg	7
A.P.F.Chapman	c A.H.Davis b Newton	15	(6)	c Findlay b Newton	13
E.H.Hendren	c Henty b Newton	1	(4)	not out	101
R.Kilner	c C.W.B.Martin b Shugg	21	(8)	c Newton b Findlay	39
†W.W.Whysall	c Henty b A.H.Davis	26	(5)	c N.W.Davis b A.H.Davis	9
*A.E.R.Gilligan	c G.W.Martin b Newton	1	(7)	b Findlay	60
R.K.Tyldesley	not out	13			
M.W.Tate	c Henty b A.H.Davis	0			
H.Howell	run out (G.W.Martin/Newton)	4			
Extras	(b6, nb1)	7		(b4, lb1)	5
Total	(40.4 overs, 157 mins)	218		(41.0 overs, 156 mins) (7 wkts dec)	331

TASMANIA

R.L.Bennett	c Whysall b Tate	0		c Bryan b Hearne	20
*G.H.Allan	c Whysall b Howell	23		c Tyldesley b Tate	2
D.C.Green	c Hendren b Kilner	31		c Whysall b Tyldesley	4
C.W.B.Martin	c Gilligan b Hearne	17		lbw b Tyldesley	5
N.W.Davis	c Hearne b Kilner	15		b Tyldesley	10
G.W.Martin	c Chapman b Kilner	0		c Chapman b Tate	121
A.C.Newton	c Tate b Kilner	5	(8)	c Hearne b Howell	41
A.P.Findlay	b Hearne	12	(7)	run out (Sandham/Tyldesley)	39
A.H.Davis	c Chapman b Kilner	28		b Howell	1
†P.G.Henty	c Gilligan b Tate	32		not out	7
A.W.Shugg	not out	1		c Whysall b Howell	0
Extras	(lb2)	2		(b12, lb1, nb1)	14
Total	(41.2 overs, 152 mins)	166		(53.4 overs, 204 mins)	264

TASMANIA	O	M	R	W	w,nb		O	M	R	W	w,nb		FALL OF WICKETS			
														MCC	TAS	MCC	TAS
Newton	13.4	1	60	3	-,-		9	0	52	1	-,-	Wkt	1st	1st	2nd	2nd
A.H.Davis	14	0	85	4	-,-		9	0	90	1	-,-	1st	19	0	85	5
Findlay	6	1	26	0	-,-	(4)	11	0	91	4	-,-	2nd	44	48	102	30
Shugg	4	0	28	1	-,1	(3)	7	0	48	1	-,-	3rd	69	71	106	34
C.W.B.Martin	3	0	12	0	-,-		5	0	45	0	-,-	4th	71	79	147	39
												5th	116	79	162	62
M.C.C.	O	M	R	W	w,nb		O	M	R	W	w,nb	6th	191	88	271	162
Tate	9.2	1	39	2	-,-		11	1	47	2	-,-	7th	192	93	331	240
Howell	5	0	14	1	-,-		11.4	1	43	3	-,1	8th	206	123	-	248
Tyldesley	8	0	33	0	-,-	(5)	13	2	63	3	-,-	9th	206	164	-	264
Hearne	10	1	43	2	-,-		8	1	42	1	-,-	10th	218	166	-	264
Kilner	9	2	35	5	-,-	(3)	8	0	37	0	-,-					
Bryan							2	0	18	0	-,-					

TASMANIA v M.C.C.

Played at T.C.A. Ground, Hobart, on January 30, 31, February 2, 1925. (Three-day match)
Toss : M.C.C.   Result : M.C.C. WON BY AN INNINGS AND 136 RUNS.
Debuts: Tasmania - S.V.A.James (f/c).
12th Men: A.B.Crowder (Tas). No 12th named for MCC.
Umpires: M.Leonard and A.O'Leary.
Attendances: 4000, 3500, 700.   Total: About 8200.   Receipts: £698.
Close of Play: 1st day MCC 2/217 (Sutcliffe 89, Hendren 2); 2nd day Tas (2) 2/101 (Myers 35, C.W.B.Martin 15).

A fine spell by Tate on the first morning vindicated Gilligan's decision to field on winning the toss. For the second consecutive innings, Shugg was out to the first ball he faced. Sutcliffe (188 in 230 minutes, 23 fours, chance at 13) added 161 for the first wicket with Sandham (92 in 113 minutes, 10 fours) and 129 for the third wicket with Hendren (50 in 52 minutes, 7 fours). Myers, a former Yorkshire professional from 1901-10 (201 matches), topped the batting for Tasmania (40 in 169 minutes, 2 fours) in his last first-class appearance. He was aged 50 years 31 days on the final day of the match, and the ball that ended his career sent one bail 37 yards. C.W.B.Martin (35 in 74 minutes, 5 fours) and Bennett (38 in 92 minutes, 4 fours) made other scores. Sources: *Wisden, TCA Report, The Age, Hobart Mercury, Launceston Examiner*.

TASMANIA

*H.Myers	c Sutcliffe b Tate	0	b Howell		40
G.H.Allan	b Tate	8	c Tate b Howell		22
D.C.Green	run out (Chapman/Whysall)	1	c Bryan b Chapman		16
C.W.B.Martin	c Sandham b Freeman	16	c Gilligan b Howell		35
G.W.Martin	c Freeman b Kilner	13	c Hendren b Freeman		20
†R.L.Bennett	c Tate b Freeman	0	lbw b Freeman		38
A.C.Newton	b Tate	23	b Howell		5
N.W.Davis	b Tate	12	b Howell		1
A.K.E.Watt	not out	3	(11) not out		6
A.W.Shugg	b Tate	0	(9) c Hendren b Freeman		5
S.V.A.James	b Tate	6	(10) b Howell		0
Extras	(b3, lb3, nb1)	7	(b20, lb12, w1, nb3)		36
Total	(25.2 overs, 99 mins)	89	(71.3 overs, 267 mins)		224

M.C.C.

H.Sutcliffe	st Bennett b Watt	188
A.Sandham	c Davis b Shugg	92
J.L.Bryan	lbw b Shugg	29
E.H.Hendren	c Watt b Allan	50
†W.W.Whysall	c Shugg b Allan	11
*A.E.R.Gilligan	c Myers b Allan	5
A.P.F.Chapman	b Watt	1
R.Kilner	not out	24
M.W.Tate	c James b Watt	4
A.P.Freeman	b Newton	26
H.Howell	b Newton	9
Extras	(b3, lb6, w1)	10
Total	(74.2 overs, 288 mins)	449

M.C.C.	O	M	R	W	w,nb		O	M	R	W	w,nb
Tate	8.2	2	26	6	-,-	(5)	8	2	16	0	-,-
Howell	2	1	3	0	-,-	(1)	26	1	96	6	-,1
Kilner	8	2	22	1	-,1	(2)	6	1	11	0	-,-
Freeman	7	0	31	2	-,-	(3)	26.3	10	53	3	1,-
Chapman						(4)	5	2	12	1	-,2

TASMANIA	O	M	R	W	w,nb
Newton	17.2	1	102	2	-,-
James	16	0	98	0	1,-
Watt	11	1	57	3	-,-
Shugg	13	1	61	2	-,-
C.W.B.Martin	5	1	44	0	-,-
Myers	3	0	24	0	-,-
Allan	9	0	53	3	-,-

FALL OF WICKETS			
	TAS	MCC	TAS
Wkt	1st	1st	2nd
1st	0	161	47
2nd	7	207	74
3rd	13	336	128
4th	34	378	135
5th	35	383	174
6th	40	383	183
7th	76	385	187
8th	79	401	202
9th	79	439	203
10th	89	449	224

VICTORIA v NEW SOUTH WALES (Shield Match 6)

Played at Melbourne Cricket Ground on January 30, 31, February 2, 3, 1925. (Timeless match)
Toss : Victoria.   Result : NEW SOUTH WALES WON BY THREE WICKETS.
Debuts: Victoria - K.J.Millar, W.J.Rayson (both f/c).
12th Men: A.O.Thomson (Vic) and G.A.N.Chapman (NSW).
Umpires: H.J.Alessio and A.D.Reaburn.
Attendances: 4600, 13684, 4690, 300.   Total: 23,274.   Receipts: £974.
Close of Play: 1st day Vic 6/270 (Ransford 37, Atkinson 53); 2nd day NSW 8/244 (Oldfield 10, Mailey 5); 3rd day NSW (2) 2/70
     (Bardsley 31, Andrews 32).

It was reported that the Victorian selectors wanted Warwick Armstrong to lead their team but he was "not within reach". Both States fielded entirely new elevens compared to those that appeared in the Sydney match which finished on January 29th. However, the 12th men in that match, Hooker and Millar, were included and both teams were able to include participants of the Adelaide Test - Ryder and Ponsford (Victoria) and Collins, Taylor, Andrews, Kelleway, Oldfield and Mailey (New South Wales). Ponsford (80 in 128 minutes, 4 fours) and Atkinson (53 in 55 minutes, 7 fours) were the only Victorians to exceed fifty in the match. Collins (70 in 160 minutes, 4 fours) and Bardsley (65 in 116 minutes, 3 fours) launched the New South Wales batting with a century opening stand but only Andrews (54 in 78 minutes, 7 fours) followed up. In the second innings Bardsley (59 in 120 minutes, 1 four) and Gwynne (46 not out in 122 minutes, 2 fours) led the team to victory. Gamble dismissed Bardsley and Kelleway with successive balls. No admission fee was charged on the last day despite 103 runs being required. Last first-class appearance by R.L.Park. *Wisden* gives incorrect match dates. Sources: *Wisden, NSWCA Report, VCA Report, The Age, The Argus, The Herald, Melbourne Sun, The Australasian.*

VICTORIA

*J.Ryder	c & b Mailey		42	st Oldfield b Mailey	31
W.H.Ponsford	b Everett		80	b Kelleway	38
†H.S.B.Love	run out (/Mailey)		40	b Mailey	9
K.J.Millar	c & b Mailey		8	(8) b Kelleway	3
R.L.Park	c Oldfield b Mailey		1	(4) lbw b Hooker	6
J.L.Keating	c Mailey b Hooker		3	(7) st Oldfield b Kelleway	26
V.S.Ransford	not out		44	(5) b Kelleway	21
J.A.Atkinson	b Kelleway		53	(6) b Hooker	7
H.S.Gamble	c Punch b Mailey		9	c Hooker b Mailey	2
W.J.Rayson	b Kelleway		2	not out	2
H.Ironmonger	b Mailey		0	run out	3
Extras	(b6, lb4, nb3)		13	(b4, w1, nb2)	7
Total	(66.4 overs, 244 mins)		295	(46.3 overs, 158 mins)	155

NEW SOUTH WALES

*H.L.Collins	b Ironmonger		70	b Ryder	3
W.Bardsley	lbw b Rayson		65	lbw b Gamble	59
J.M.Taylor	c Ryder b Rayson		9	b Ryder	0
T.J.E.Andrews	c Love b Ryder		54	c Ryder b Ironmonger	37
L.W.Gwynne	c & b Rayson		3	not out	46
C.Kelleway	b Keating		11	b Gamble	0
A.T.E.Punch	c & b Ryder		5	b Gamble	16
†W.A.S.Oldfield	run out (Park/Love)		25	b Gamble	1
J.E.H.Hooker	st Love b Keating		4	not out	7
A.A.Mailey	b Keating		16		
S.C.Everett	not out		8		
Extras	(b2, lb3, nb3)		8	(b1, lb3)	4
Total	(75.0 overs, 282 mins)		278	(44.5 overs, 180 mins) (7 wkts)	173

NEW SOUTH WALES	O	M	R	W	w,nb		O	M	R	W	w,nb
Everett	11	0	66	1	-,1		4	0	30	0	-,-
Kelleway	12	1	46	2	-,2		15.3	1	35	4	-,2
Mailey	22.4	3	103	5	-,-	(4)	17	1	56	3	1,-
Hooker	15	2	42	1	-,-	(3)	9	1	26	2	-,-
Punch	4	0	16	0	-,-						
Collins	2	0	9	0	-,-	(5)	1	0	1	0	-,-

VICTORIA	O	M	R	W	w,nb		O	M	R	W	w,nb
Gamble	7	0	41	0	-,1	(5)	10.5	0	38	4	-,-
Ironmonger	27	3	74	1	-,1		17	3	59	1	-,-
Ryder	11	1	35	2	-,-	(1)	11	1	35	2	-,-
Rayson	14	1	67	3	-,-	(3)	5	0	31	0	-,-
Millar	5	0	22	0	-,-						
Keating	11	3	31	3	-,1	(4)	1	0	5	0	-,-

FALL OF WICKETS

Wkt	VIC 1st	NSW 1st	VIC 2nd	NSW 2nd
1st	74	108	68	8
2nd	160	140	82	8
3rd	171	168	89	77
4th	175	173	89	116
5th	175	218	104	116
6th	182	225	135	148
7th	273	226	143	150
8th	285	235	150	-
9th	293	265	150	-
10th	295	278	155	-

VICTORIA v M.C.C.

Played at Melbourne Cricket Ground on February 6, 7, 9, 10, 1925. (Four-day match)
Toss : M.C.C.   Result : M.C.C. WON BY AN INNINGS AND 271 RUNS.
Debuts: Nil.
12th Men: K.J.Schneider (Vic) and A.P.Freeman (MCC).
Umpires: R.M.Crockett and J.Richards.
Attendances: 4876, 9186, 2408, 50.   Total: 16,520.   Receipts: £1191.
Close of Play: 1st day MCC 2/295 (Hearne 121, Whysall 57); 2nd day Vic 1/35 (Woodfull 14, Ryder 5); 3rd day Vic (2) 6/14 (Hendry 6).

H.S.Gamble and H.S.B.Love were unavailable for Victoria and Atkinson and Rayson replaced A.E.V.Hartkopf (work) and F.A.Tarrant (unavailable) after the side was selected. Sutcliffe (88 in 133 minutes, 11 fours), Hearne (193 in 356 minutes, 15 fours, chance at 23), Whysall (89 in 217 minutes, 5 fours) and Bryan (59 in 92 minutes, 6 fours) all scored prominently for M.C.C. Ironmonger did the hat-trick (Tate, Strudwick, Howell) to finish off the innings. Rayson had earlier captured three wickets in five balls, dismissing Whysall and Kilner in succession and Douglas three balls later, all in the same over. Douglas was involved in a car crash in the early hours of Sunday (the driver was killed) but escaped with severe bruising; however he did not play again on the tour. Bryan, the only other amateur in the team, assumed the captaincy for the remainder of this match. Rain on the rest day turned the wicket heavily in favour of the bowlers and apart from Woodfull (60 in 194 minutes, 2 fours) and Ransford (62 in 140 minutes, 4 fours) in the first innings the Victorians succumbed to the sticky conditions in quick succession. Hendry suffered a first-ball dismissal. Sources: *Wisden, VCA Report, The Age, The Argus, The Herald, The Australasian.*

M.C.C.

H.Sutcliffe	c Hendry b Ironmonger	88
A.Sandham	b Hendry	21
J.W.Hearne	c Ryder b Wallace	193
W.W.Whysall	c Hendry b Rayson	89
R.Kilner	c Atkinson b Rayson	0
*J.W.H.T.Douglas	c Atkinson b Rayson	0
J.L.Bryan	b Ironmonger	59
M.W.Tate	c Atkinson b Ironmonger	25
R.K.Tyldesley	not out	6
†H.Strudwick	lbw b Ironmonger	0
H.Howell	b Ironmonger	0
Extras	(b9, lb2, w4, nb4)	19
Total	(126.5 overs, 463 mins)	500

VICTORIA

*R.E.Mayne	c Tyldesley b Tate	9	(9)	b Hearne	0
W.M.Woodfull	b Hearne	60	(1)	c Hearne b Kilner	2
J.Ryder	c Sandham b Kilner	13	(8)	lbw b Hearne	15
H.S.T.L.Hendry	c Hearne b Tyldesley	0	(7)	c sub (A.P.Freeman) b Hearne	12
V.S.Ransford	c sub (A.P.Freeman) b Hearne	62	(3)	c Tate b Kilner	1
C.B.Willis	c Bryan b Hearne	3	(11)	not out	0
J.A.Atkinson	c Whysall b Kilner	13	(10)	c Tate b Hearne	15
†J.L.Ellis	c Tyldesley b Kilner	2	(2)	b Tyldesley b Kilner	1
P.H.Wallace	c Sutcliffe b Kilner	5	(4)	b Kilner	2
W.J.Rayson	b Kilner	0	(5)	c sub (A.P.Freeman) b Kilner	0
H.Ironmonger	not out	0	(6)	st Strudwick b Hearne	0
Extras	(b8, lb3, w1)	12		(b1, lb1)	2
Total	(68.2 overs, 230 mins)	179		(25.6 overs, 87 mins)	50

VICTORIA	O	M	R	W	w,nb
Wallace	21	0	114	1	4,2
Ironmonger	39.5	6	93	5	-,1
Hendry	25	6	82	1	-,-
Rayson	32	0	161	3	-,-
Ryder	7	1	25	0	-,1
Ransford	2	0	6	0	-,-

M.C.C.	O	M	R	W	w,nb		O	M	R	W	w,nb
Howell	4	0	17	0	1,-						
Tate	8	2	19	1	-,-						
Tyldesley	17	4	44	1	-,-						
Kilner	24.2	4	48	5	-,-	(1)	13	6	18	5	-,-
Hearne	15	4	39	3	-,-	(2)	12.6	3	30	5	-,-

FALL OF WICKETS

		MCC	VIC	VIC
Wkt		1st	1st	2nd
1st		58	20	2
2nd		150	48	4
3rd		366	48	5
4th		366	154	5
5th		367	158	6
6th		436	158	14
7th		488	163	34
8th		500	174	34
9th		500	179	50
10th		500	179	50

AUSTRALIA v ENGLAND (4th Test)

Played at Melbourne Cricket Ground on February 13, 14, 16, 17, 18, 1925. (Timeless match)
Toss : England.   Result : ENGLAND WON BY AN INNINGS AND 29 RUNS.
Debuts: Nil.
12th Men: V.Y.Richardson (Aust) and A.Sandham (Eng).
Umpires: R.M.Crockett and D.A.Elder.
Attendances: 15,176, 29,358, 15,563, 12,786, 7203.   Total: 80,086.   Receipts: £6640.
Close of Play: 1st day Eng 282 (Sutcliffe 141, Woolley 26); 2nd day Eng 548 all out; 3rd day Aust 5/168 (Taylor 42, Andrews 33);
    4th day Aust (2) 4/175 (Taylor 59, Kelleway 23).

Sutcliffe (143 in 293 minutes, 14 fours, chances at 9 and 83) continued his outstanding run of scoring in the Test series and became the first batsman to score four centuries in one rubber. For the third time this series he batted throughout a day's play. He shared yet another century opening stand with Hobbs (66 in 128 minutes, 5 fours), also adding 106 for the second wicket with Hearne. Later in the innings Whysall (76 in 203 minutes, 6 fours, chance at 26) and Kilner (74 in 149 minutes, 11 fours) added 133 for the seventh wicket. Hendren (65 in 114 minutes, 4 fours) also batted well. Gilligan was out first ball. Oldfield became the first wicket-keeper to complete five dismissals in a Test innings. Taylor played the leading role in each innings for Australia after several showers on the third day altered the character of the wicket to favour the bowlers. His first innings of 86 occupied 138 minutes (9 fours) and his second of 68 took 184 minutes (3 fours). This was England's first Test victory over Australia since 1912, ending a sequence of 13 unsuccessful matches against their oldest opponent. Australia had not lost against either England or South Africa in their last 16 international matches. Sources: *Wisden, VCA Report, The Age, The Argus, The Herald, Melbourne Sun, The Australasian.*

ENGLAND

J.B.Hobbs	st Oldfield b Ryder	66
H.Sutcliffe	lbw b Mailey	143
J.W.Hearne	c Bardsley b Richardson	44
F.E.Woolley	st Oldfield b Mailey	40
E.H.Hendren	b Ryder	65
A.P.F.Chapman	st Oldfield b Mailey	12
W.W.Whysall	st Oldfield b Kelleway	76
R.Kilner	lbw b Kelleway	74
*A.E.R.Gilligan	c Oldfield b Kelleway	0
M.W.Tate	c Taylor b Mailey	8
†H.Strudwick	not out	7
Extras	(b6, lb2, w3, nb2)	13
Total	(151.6 overs, 575 mins)	548

AUSTRALIA

*H.L.Collins	c Kilner b Tate	22	c Whysall b Kilner	1
A.J.Richardson	b Hearne	19	(9) lbw b Hearne	3
J.Ryder	b Tate	0	(5) lbw b Woolley	38
W.Bardsley	run out (Hobbs)	24	(2) b Tate	0
W.H.Ponsford	c Strudwick b Hearne	21	(8) b Tate	19
J.M.Taylor	c Hendren b Woolley	86	(4) c Woolley b Gilligan	68
T.J.E.Andrews	c Hearne b Kilner	35	(6) c Strudwick b Tate	3
C.Kelleway	lbw b Kilner	1	(7) c Strudwick b Tate	42
J.M.Gregory	c Woolley b Hearne	38	(3) c Sutcliffe b Kilner	45
†W.A.S.Oldfield	c Chapman b Kilner	3	b Tate	8
A.A.Mailey	not out	4	not out	8
Extras	(b13, lb2, nb1)	16	(b15)	15
Total	(63.3 overs, 238 mins)	269	(74.5 overs, 267 mins)	250

AUSTRALIA	O	M	R	W	w,nb
Gregory	22	1	102	0	1,1
Kelleway	29	5	70	3	-,-
Mailey	43.6	2	186	4	1,-
Ryder	25	3	83	2	-,1
Richardson	26	8	76	1	-,-
Collins	6	1	18	0	1,-

ENGLAND	O	M	R	W	w,nb		O	M	R	W	w,nb
Tate	16	2	70	2	-,-		25.5	6	75	5	-,-
Gilligan	6	1	24	0	-,1	(5)	7	0	26	1	-,-
Hearne	19.3	1	77	3	-,-		20	0	76	1	-,-
Kilner	13	1	29	3	-,-	(2)	16	3	41	2	-,-
Woolley	9	1	53	1	-,-	(4)	6	0	17	1	-,-

FALL OF WICKETS

Wkt	ENG 1st	AUST 1st	AUST 2nd
1st	126	38	5
2nd	232	38	5
3rd	284	64	64
4th	307	74	133
5th	346	109	190
6th	394	170	195
7th	527	172	225
8th	527	244	234
9th	529	257	238
10th	548	269	250

NEW SOUTH WALES v M.C.C.

Played at Sydney Cricket Ground on February 21, 23, 24, 25, 1925. (Four-day match)
Toss : M.C.C.   Result : MATCH DRAWN.
Debuts: Nil.
12th Men: M.W.Tate (MCC). No 12th named for NSW.
Umpires: W.G.French and A.C.Jones.
Attendances: 15775, 6632, 5762, 2521.   Total: 30,690.   Receipts: £2455.
Close of Play: 1st day MCC 3/397 (Hendren 22, Gilligan 11); 2nd day NSW 1/164 (Collins 101, Andrews 29); 3rd day NSW 5/546
(Kelleway 22, Ratcliffe 35).

This was the first instance in Australian first-class cricket of both sides scoring over 600 runs in one innings. Sandham (137 in 253 minutes, 12 fours) put on 136 with Bryan (72 in 121 minutes, 7 fours) and 202 with Woolley (149 in 154 minutes, 1 six and 17 fours) for the first two wickets. Hendren (165 in 192 minutes, 14 fours) dominated the scoring in the lower order and was last man out. Kippax (leg-breaks) returned his best first-class figures. Collins (chanceless 173 in 257 minutes, 1 five and 13 fours) and Andrews (224 in 296 minutes, 13 fours, chance at 19) established a second-wicket stand of 270 in only 178 minutes for New South Wales. In the second innings Sandham (104 in 183 minutes, 6 fours) and Woolley (80 in 102 minutes, 8 fours) again achieved a century partnership. Punch conceded 67 runs in his 6.4 overs. W.A.S.Oldfield and W.Bardsley (both rested) and J.M.Gregory (injured foot) and H.O.Rock (university exams) were missing from the New South Wales line-up and in addition J.M.Taylor (gastritis) had to be replaced by Wells after the team was selected. Sources: *Wisden, NSWCA Report, VCA Report, Sydney Morning Herald, Sydney Referee, Sydney Daily Telegraph.*

M.C.C.

A.Sandham	st Ratcliffe b Mailey	137		c Morgan b Hooker	104
J.L.Bryan	b Kelleway	72			
F.E.Woolley	st Ratcliffe b Mailey	149		c Collins b Hooker	80
E.H.Hendren	c & b Kippax	165			
*A.E.R.Gilligan	b Scott	18	(4)	c Kippax b Punch	14
A.P.F.Chapman	b Hooker	28		c Morgan b Punch	47
†W.W.Whysall	c & b Kippax	29	(2)	b Scott	28
R.Kilner	c Morgan b Kippax	9	(5)	b Hooker	1
A.P.Freeman	c Morgan b Kippax	0		c & b Punch	4
R.K.Tyldesley	b Morgan	1	(7)	b Hooker	6
H.Howell	not out	1	(8)	not out	1
Extras	(b14, lb1, w2)	17		(b4, lb1, w4, nb2)	11
Total	(118.4 overs, 441 mins)	626		(52.4 overs, 210 mins) (8 wkts)	296

NEW SOUTH WALES

*H.L.Collins	c & b Freeman	173
J.G.Morgan	c Freeman b Kilner	29
T.J.E.Andrews	b Kilner	224
A.F.Kippax	run out (Sandham/Gilligan)	46
C.Kelleway	c Hendren b Freeman	38
A.T.E.Punch	b Kilner	2
†A.T.Ratcliffe	c Gilligan b Freeman	49
A.P.Wells	c Whysall b Kilner	2
J.E.H.Hooker	c Freeman b Kilner	3
J.D.Scott	b Kilner	26
A.A.Mailey	not out	10
Extras	(b11, lb6)	17
Total	(137.6 overs, 481 mins)	619

NEW SOUTH WALES	O	M	R	W	w,nb		O	M	R	W	w,nb			FALL OF WICKETS		
Scott	23	2	120	1	2,-		10	0	68	1	2,1			MCC	NSW	NSW
Kelleway	26	5	80	1	-,-							Wkt	1st	1st	2nd
Mailey	26	0	153	2	-,-							1st	136	84	57
Hooker	17	1	92	1	-,-	(2)	12	0	47	4	1,1	2nd	338	354	206
Punch	7	0	47	0	-,-		6.4	0	67	3	-,-	3rd	375	462	232
Andrews	2	0	19	0	-,-		3	0	11	0	1,-	4th	415	493	233
Collins	3	0	15	0	-,-							5th	482	495	266
Morgan	4	0	17	1	-,-	(4)	9	2	31	0	-,-	6th	566	564	291
Kippax	10.4	0	66	4	-,-	(3)	12	1	61	0	-,-	7th	592	567	291
												8th	594	581	296
M.C.C	O	M	R	W	w,nb		O	M	R	W	w,nb	9th	599	585	-
Gilligan	17	1	81	0	-,-							10th	626	619	-
Howell	17	1	70	0	-,-										
Freeman	31	2	157	3	-,-										
Tyldesley	21	2	112	0	-,-										
Kilner	41.6	2	145	6	-,-										
Woolley	7	0	28	0	-,-										
Chapman	3	0	9	0	-,-										

AUSTRALIA v ENGLAND (5th Test)

Played at Sydney Cricket Ground on February 27, 28, March 2, 3, 4, 1925. (Timeless match)
Toss : Australia.   Result : AUSTRALIA WON BY 307 RUNS.
Debuts: Australia - C.V.Grimmett, A.F.Kippax (both Test).
12th Men: V.Y.Richardson (Aust) and A.P.F.Chapman (Eng).
Umpires: R.M.Crockett and D.A.Elder.
Attendances: 19402, 40830, 23160, 17406, 2415.   Total: 103,213.   Receipts: £9520.
Close of Play: 1st day Aust 7/239 (Kelleway 9, Oldfield 0); 2nd day Eng 167 all out; 3rd day Aust (2) 6/203 (Collins 27, Kelleway 22)
    4th day Eng (2) 5/88 (Hearne 18, Whysall 1).

England lost Hobbs (caught down the leg-side) to the fifth ball of their first innings and never recovered. They recorded the only two innings under 200 in what had been a high-scoring series by both sides. Woolley (47 in 93 minutes, 5 fours), their topscorer, provided Grimmett (who became the first bowler to take ten or more wickets on Test Debut for Australia) with his first victim. Grimmett's selection had been seen as a surprise in some circles. Ponsford (80 in 140 minutes, 6 fours) survived two chances on the first day. His century partnership for the sixth wicket with Kippax enabled Australia to recover from 5/103. Steady batting in the second innings by Andrews (80 in 170 minutes, 1 five and 5 fours), Kelleway (73 in 202 minutes, 5 fours) and Oldfield (65 not out in 117 minutes, 3 fours) put Australia in an impregnable position, the last two named adding 116 for the eighth wicket. Collins held himself back in the order after injuring a finger at practice prior to the start of the third day. New record aggregates for a Test series in Australia were established by Sutcliffe (most runs - 734) and Tate (most wickets -38). They were not broken until 1928-29 and 1978-79 respectively. *Wisden* incorrectly gives Aust (2) Kilner 10 maidens . Sources: *Wisden, NSWCA Report, Sydney Morning Herald, Sydney Referee, The Australasian.*

AUSTRALIA

*H.L.Collins	c Strudwick b Gilligan	1	(7)	lbw b Tate	28
J.Ryder	b Kilner	29		b Gilligan	7
J.M.Gregory	run out (Tate/Strudwick)	29	(1)	lbw b Hearne	22
T.J.E.Andrews	c Whysall b Kilner	26	(3)	c Woolley b Hearne	80
J.M.Taylor	c Whysall b Tate	15	(4)	st Strudwick b Tate	25
W.H.Ponsford	c Woolley b Kilner	80	(5)	run out (Gilligan/Strudwick)	5
A.F.Kippax	b Kilner	42	(6)	c Whysall b Woolley	8
C.Kelleway	lbw b Tate	9		c Whysall b Tate	73
†W.A.S.Oldfield	c Strudwick b Tate	29		not out	65
A.A.Mailey	b Tate	14		b Tate	0
C.V.Grimmett	not out	12		b Tate	0
Extras	(b2, lb5, nb2)	9		(b6, lb4, w1, nb1)	12
Total	(102.5 overs, 345 mins)	295		(118.3 overs, 394 mins)	325

ENGLAND

J.B.Hobbs	c Oldfield b Gregory	0	st Oldfield b Grimmett	13
H.Sutcliffe	c Mailey b Kelleway	22	b Gregory	0
A.Sandham	run out (Grimmett/Gregory)	4	lbw b Grimmett	15
F.E.Woolley	b Grimmett	47	c Andrews b Kelleway	28
E.H.Hendren	c Ponsford b Gregory	10	c Oldfield b Grimmett	10
J.W.Hearne	lbw b Grimmett	16	lbw b Grimmett	24
W.W.Whysall	lbw b Grimmett	8	st Oldfield b Grimmett	18
R.Kilner	st Oldfield b Grimmett	24	c Ponsford b Collins	1
M.W.Tate	b Ryder	25	c Mailey b Kelleway	33
*A.E.R.Gilligan	st Oldfield b Grimmett	5	not out	0
†H.Strudwick	not out	1	c Mailey b Grimmett	0
Extras	(lb4, nb1)	5	(b1, lb3)	4
Total	(47.7 overs, 194 mins)	167	(44.4 overs, 170 mins)	146

ENGLAND	O	M	R	W	w,nb	O	M	R	W	w,nb
Tate	39.5	6	92	4	-,-	39.3	6	115	5	-,-
Gilligan	13	1	46	1	-,1	15	2	46	1	-,-
Kilner	38	4	97	4	-,-	34	13	54	0	-,1
Hearne	7	0	33	0	-,-	22	0	84	2	-,-
Woolley	5	0	18	0	-,1	8	1	14	1	1,-

AUSTRALIA	O	M	R	W	w,nb		O	M	R	W	w,nb
Gregory	9	1	42	2	-,-		10	0	53	1	-,-
Kelleway	15	1	38	1	-,1		7	1	16	2	-,-
Mailey	5	0	13	0	-,-						
Ryder	7	0	24	1	-,-						
Grimmett	11.7	2	45	5	-,-	(3)	19.4	3	37	6	-,-
Collins						(4)	8	2	36	1	-,-

FALL OF WICKETS

Wkt	AUST 1st	ENG 1st	AUST 2nd	ENG 2nd
1st	3	0	7	3
2nd	55	15	43	31
3rd	64	28	110	32
4th	99	58	130	60
5th	103	96	152	84
6th	208	109	156	99
7th	239	122	209	100
8th	239	157	325	146
9th	264	163	325	146
10th	295	167	325	146

SOUTH AUSTRALIA v M.C.C.

Played at Adelaide Oval on March 13, 14, 16, 1925. (Four-day match)
Toss : M.C.C.   Result : SOUTH AUSTRALIA WON BY TEN WICKETS.
Debuts: Nil.
12th Men: E.G.C.Wainwright (SA) and H.Sutcliffe (MCC).
Umpires: G.I.Colyer and S.W.Smith.
Attendances: 6068, 10301, 4763.   Total: 21,132.   Receipts: £1228.
Close of Play: 1st day SA 2/76 (Pritchard 45, V.Y.Richardson 27); 2nd day MCC (2) 0/15 (Sandham 6, Whysall 9).

M.C.C. were without J.L.Bryan and A.P.F.Chapman who had both left for home via Sydney on March 12th plus H.Strudwick who was holidaying at Murtoa in Victoria and J.B.Hobbs who was resting. Palmer dismissed Whysall with his second ball and with the exception of Sandham, who was the last man dismissed (59 in 208 minutes, 3 fours), the Englishmen were quickly bundled out for 179. South Australia based their 264-run lead on big innings from Pritchard (87 in 119 minutes, 1 six and 10 fours), Rundell (90 in 156 minutes, 9 fours) and Rymill (a career-highest 146 in 173 minutes, 14 fours). A first-wicket stand of 166 between Sandham (64 in 141 minutes, 1 six and 6 fours) and Whysall (101 in 146 minutes, 9 fours) gave M.C.C. a great start in the second innings but only 98 runs were made after the first wicket fell. *Wisden* gives incorrect match dates. Sources: *Wisden, C.B.O'Reilly, SACA Report, Adelaide Advertiser, The News, South Australian Register.*

M.C.C.

†W.W.Whysall	lbw b Palmer	1	(2) c V.Y.Richardson b A.J.Richardson	101
A.Sandham	c Ambler b A.J.Richardson	59	(1) b Grimmett	64
J.W.Hearne	c Murray b Grimmett	10	c & b Grimmett	7
F.E.Woolley	c Murray b A.J.Richardson	14	c V.Y.Richardson b Grimmett	3
E.H.Hendren	c V.Y.Richardson b Palmer	38	c Grimmett b A.J.Richardson	59
R.Kilner	b Palmer	11	c Palmer b Grimmett	9
M.W.Tate	c & b A.J.Richardson	30	c Gun b Grimmett	2
A.P.Freeman	c Ambler b Palmer	3	c Murray b Grimmett	1
*A.E.R.Gilligan	c Palmer b A.J.Richardson	0	b Grimmett	0
R.K.Tyldesley	lbw b A.J.Richardson	0	c V.Y.Richardson b A.J.Richardson	14
H.Howell	not out	7	not out	1
Extras	(b5, lb1)	6	(b2, lb1)	3
Total	(54.0 overs, 208 mins)	179	(55.5 overs, 220 mins)	264

SOUTH AUSTRALIA

A.J.Richardson	b Gilligan	0		
L.T.Gun	c Tyldesley b Tate	3	(1) not out	1
D.E.Pritchard	st Whysall b Freeman	87		
*V.Y.Richardson	c Whysall b Gilligan	43		
P.D.Rundell	c Tyldesley b Tate	90		
J.W.Rymill	run out (Hendren/Whysall)	146		
J.T.Murray	lbw b Tate	2		
C.V.Grimmett	c Whysall b Tate	39		
T.W.Wall	run out (Hendren)	9		
†A.M.Ambler	c Tate b Howell	6	(2) not out	0
G.H.Palmer	not out	1		
Extras	(b7, lb10)	17		–
Total	(78.1 overs, 321 mins)	443	(0.1 overs, 1 min) (0 wkts)	1

SOUTH AUSTRALIA	O	M	R	W	w,nb		O	M	R	W	w,nb
Wall	7	0	30	0	-,-		8	1	40	0	-,-
Palmer	17	5	50	4	-,-		8	0	47	0	-,-
A.J.Richardson	13	1	52	5	-,-	(4)	15.5	1	86	3	-,-
Grimmett	17	2	40	1	-,-	(3)	23	0	85	7	-,-
Murray							1	0	3	0	-,-

M.C.C.	O	M	R	W	w,nb		O	M	R	W	w,nb
Tate	22.1	2	105	4	-,-						
Gilligan	13	1	68	2	-,-						
Hearne	13	0	85	0	-,-						
Howell	9	0	51	1	-,-						
Tyldesley	7	1	42	0	-,-						
Freeman	9	0	51	1	-,-						
Kilner	5	0	24	0	-,-						
Sandham						(1)	0.1	0	1	0	-,-

FALL OF WICKETS

	MCC	SA	MCC	SA
Wkt	1st	1st	2nd	2nd
1st	1	1	166	-
2nd	27	13	166	-
3rd	46	95	175	-
4th	97	164	186	-
5th	111	315	218	-
6th	150	321	226	-
7th	157	413	242	-
8th	158	434	243	-
9th	158	441	249	-
10th	179	443	264	-

A New Zealand team toured Australia for the first time since 1913-14, again playing nine matches, four of which were first-class. Several of their leading players were unavailable for the tour and the final party was very much below strength. A loss to Queensland by an innings early on did not augur well for the visitors, but creditable draws were then recorded against each of the three major States. Neither New South Wales nor Victoria fielded full-strength XIs, and the New Zealanders batted well enough to avoid any serious danger of defeat. Allcott hit two centuries in the first-class games and Lowry and Patrick one each.

New South Wales devastated Victoria and South Australia to regain the Sheffield Shield in the most comprehensive fashion imaginable. They won three matches by an innings and the other by over 500 runs. They had the capacity to field a virtual Test XI: Rock (two matches) and Punch (one) were the only non-representative players to play for the State during their campaign. Everett, though never a Test player, achieved national representation when he was selected in the Australian team to tour England in 1926. The return of Macartney, who had missed the previous season through illness, further strengthened an outstanding team, and in their five innings New South Wales piled up 554, 705, 642, 593 and 708. Six men hit centuries - Macartney, Collins and Kelleway (two apiece) and Oldfield, Bardsley and Kippax - and Taylor, Andrews, Gregory and Rock further added to the batting depth. Gregory, Kelleway, Macartney, Mailey and Everett formed a varied and penetrative attack.

South Australia and Victoria each took a game off the other. Victoria opted for experience by fielding virtually the same XI that won the Shield the two preceding seasons. Woodfull and Ponsford continued to score heavily and Blackie was a consistent wicket-taker. South Australia, though quite sound in batting, relied strongly on Grimmett (spin) and Scott (pace) to dismiss the opposition.

Western Australia sent a team east for the first time since 1912-13 and played a total of eight matches, those against South Australia (two), Victoria and New South Wales being accorded first-class status. Three were lost by an innings and the other by nine wickets, but the trip benefitted both as a learning exercise for several young players, and as a means to strengthen contacts in the Eastern States to assist the WACA in its quest for a more regular first-class program. Some immediate success came with the arrangement of a match in Perth against the departing Australian team to England - a fixture initiated in 1921, which continued with all subsequent Australian teams to England up until 1964.

Queensland drew both their matches against New South Wales and also met the South Australian team, who travelled on to Brisbane after their away Shield matches at Melbourne and Sydney. The visitors won a low-scoring game by 44 runs.

An Australian XI versus The Rest match was staged at Sydney to further help the selectors finalise the team to tour England. All the established players came up to scratch and little was learned from the exercise. The 16th Australian team to tour England comprised H.L.Collins (captain), W.Bardsley (vice-captain), T.J.E.Andrews, J.L.Ellis, S.C.Everett, J.M.Gregory, C.V.Grimmett, H.S.T.L.Hendry, C.G.Macartney, A.A.Mailey, W.A.S.Oldfield, A.J.Richardson, J.Ryder, W.H.Ponsford, J.M.Taylor and W.M.Woodfull. It was difficult to understand the omission of A.F.Kippax and, to a lesser extent, V.Y.Richardson.

Leading Aggregates

Batsmen	M	I	NO	Runs	HS	Ave.	Bowlers	Runs	Wkts	Ave.
A.J.Richardson (SA)	11	18	0	904	227	50.22	C.V.Grimmett (SA)	1794	59	30.40
W.M.Woodfull (V)	9	14	0	890	236	63.57	A.A.Mailey (NSW)	1232	42	29.33
C.G.Macartney (NSW)	8	10	1	795	163*	88.33	A.J.Richardson (SA)	817	41	19.92
W.H.Ponsford (V)	8	12	1	701	158	63.72	J.D.Scott (SA)	1085	34	31.91
H.L.Collins (NSW)	9	11	0	698	143	63.45	S.C.Everett (NSW)	745	33	22.57
V.Y.Richardson (SA)	8	15	0	589	107	39.26	D.D.Blackie (V)	838	29	28.89
A.F.Kippax (NSW)	6	8	1	585	271*	83.57	H.S.T.L.Hendry (V)	708	28	25.28
C.Kelleway (NSW)	5	7	1	582	145	97.00	C.G.Macartney (NSW)	453	24	18.87
H.S.T.L.Hendry (V)	8	13	2	577	325*	52.45				

SHEFFIELD SHIELD TABLE

	P	W	L	D	Pts	Quotient	Runs Scored	Wkts Lost	Runs Conceded	Wkts Taken
NEW SOUTH WALES	4	4	-	-	4	2.195	3202	50	2304	79
VICTORIA	4	1	3	-	-2	0.740	2448	78	2542	60
SOUTH AUSTRALIA	4	1	3	-	-2	0.636	2278	79	3082	68
TOTAL	6	6	6	-	0	1.000	7928	207	7928	207

SOUTH AUSTRALIA v WESTERN AUSTRALIA

Played at Adelaide Oval on October 30, 31, November 2, 1925. (Three-day match)
Toss : Western Australia.   Result : SOUTH AUSTRALIA WON BY AN INNINGS AND 281 RUNS.
Debuts: South Australia - W.C.Alexander (f/c); J.D.Scott (SA only). Western Australia - H.T.Grigg, M.Inverarity, C.V.Loton (all f/c).
    P.F.Quinlan (WA only).
12th Men: A.T.Hack (SA) and V.C.Carlson (WA).
Umpires: G.A.Hele and S.W.Smith.
Attendances: No daily figures published.   Total: 8541.   Receipts: £259.
Close of Play: 1st day SA 0/172 (A.J.Richardson 89, Gun 68); 2nd day WA (2) 0/10 (Quinlan 6, Meek 4).

L.F.Freemantle, A.E.Hardie and H.J.Herbert all withdrew from the Western Australian side selected to tour the Eastern States and F.H.Taaffe was unavailable. W.C.Alexander and A.T.Hack replaced J.T.Murray (unavailable) and C.E.Pellew (business) in the South Australian twelve. Meek was out to the fifth ball of the match and Drew to the last ball of the second over. South Australia recorded their highest total in first-class matches to date. The opening stand of 313 between A.J.Richardson (227 in 286 minutes, 1 six and 23 fours) and Gun (129 in 218 minutes, 10 fours) remains the State record for the first wicket. Scott (78 in 67 minutes, 1 six and 8 fours) and Grimmett (57 in 62 minutes) added 113 for the eighth wicket. Bryant, who hit 18 runs off an over from Wall in the first innings (4 fours and a two), scored Western Australia's only fifty (65 in 93 minutes, 1 six and 7 fours). Grimmett's 10-wicket haul included those of Inverarity and Grigg with successive balls in the second innings. Scott (ex-NSW) and Quinlan (Ireland 1912-14) had prior experience at first-class level. *Cricketer* incorrectly gives SA V.Y.Richardson 19, Scott 77. Sources: *The Cricketer, C.B.O'Reilly, SACA Report, WACA Report, South Australia Register, Adelaide Advertiser, The News.*

WESTERN AUSTRALIA

P.F.Quinlan	b Grimmett	21	st Ambler b Grimmett		28
A.B.Meek	c Grimmett b Scott	2	c Scott b Wall		4
A.D.Drew	b Wall	5	b Scott		5
L.C.Bott	st Ambler b Grimmett	41	lbw b Grimmett		27
R.J.Bryant	st Ambler b Grimmett	25	c V.Y.Richardson b A.J.Richardson		65
*S.H.D.Rowe	c A.J.Richardson b Grimmett	38	lbw b Grimmett		6
M.Inverarity	b Scott	5	b Grimmett		12
H.T.Grigg	c Scott b Grimmett	13	c Pritchard b Grimmett		0
W.A.Evans	b Wall	3	b Scott		1
L.C.Renfrey	c Ambler b Wall	11	not out		4
†C.V.Loton	not out	0	c Scott b A.J.Richardson		0
Extras	(b1, lb5)	6	(b9)		9
Total	(38.1 overs, 151 mins)	170	(37.4 overs, 134 mins)		161

SOUTH AUSTRALIA

A.J.Richardson	st Loton b Inverarity	227
L.T.Gun	c Drew b Quinlan	129
D.E.Pritchard	c Rowe b Inverarity	15
*V.Y.Richardson	b Inverarity	18
J.W.Rymill	c Drew b Inverarity	13
E.G.C.Wainwright	b Inverarity	17
W.C.Alexander	c Meek b Renfrey	17
J.D.Scott	c Bott b Meek	78
C.V.Grimmett	c Grigg b Inverarity	57
T.W.Wall	not out	4
†A.M.Ambler	b Meek	1
Extras	(b23, lb8, w4, nb1)	36
Total	(100.1 overs, 373 mins)	612

SOUTH AUSTRALIA	O	M	R	W	w,nb	O	M	R	W	w,nb
Scott	12	2	52	2	-,-	13	1	52	2	-,-
Wall	8.1	0	48	3	-,-	8	1	32	1	-,-
Grimmett	15	3	60	5	-,-	12	0	62	5	-,-
A.J.Richardson	3	2	4	0	-,-	4.4	1	6	2	-,-

WESTERN AUSTRALIA	O	M	R	W	w,nb
Quinlan	20	0	107	1	4,-
Renfrey	24	1	110	1	-,-
Meek	13.1	0	97	2	-,-
Inverarity	29	0	179	6	-,1
Evans	12	0	61	0	-,-
Bryant	1	0	4	0	-,-
Drew	1	0	18	0	-,-

FALL OF WICKETS

Wkt	WA 1st	SA 1st	WA 2nd
1st	2	313	18
2nd	11	362	35
3rd	60	418	41
4th	88	434	100
5th	112	445	110
6th	133	466	126
7th	155	483	126
8th	155	596	131
9th	169	611	161
10th	170	612	161

642

VICTORIA v WESTERN AUSTRALIA

Played at Fitzroy Cricket Ground, Melbourne, on November 6, 7, 9, 1925. (Three-day match)
Toss : Victoria. Result : VICTORIA WON BY AN INNINGS AND 282 RUNS.
Debuts: Nil.
12th Men: No 12th men or emergency fielders named.
Umpires: C.Garing and J.Stafford.
Attendances: 600, 1264, 100. Total: 1964. Receipts: £117.
Close of Play: 1st day Vic 1/167 (Ponsford 103, Love 11); 2nd day WA (2) 2/12 (Quinlan 6, Bott 2).

The Melbourne Cricket Ground was unavailable for Western Australia's first match in Victoria for nearly 13 years because heavy wear from the football season had delayed the preparation of the wickets. The Fitzroy Cricket Ground was chosen to stage its sole first-class match due to the Fitzroy Club having a bye in the Melbourne District competition. J.Ryder and F.A.Tarrant were unavailable for the home State. Western Australia were completely outclassed with bat and ball throughout the match, the highest scores coming from Quinlan (37 in 130 minutes, one four), Drew (42 in 119 minutes, 2 fours) and Rowe (55 in 91 minutes, 6 fours). Carlson was bowled by the fourth ball of the match after four byes had been conceded from the first and completed a pair when bowled by the third ball of the second innings. Ponsford, who scored his first 103 runs after tea on the first day, batted 170 minutes and hit 12 fours. He shared partnerships of 140 for the first wicket with Mayne (48 in 81 minutes, 3 fours) and 126 for the second wicket with Love (103 in 178 minutes, 3 fours and 59 singles). Willis scored 79 in 102 minutes with 4 fours. Inverarity, aged 18, took career-best figures of 6 for 162 in his second first-class match to better his 6 for 179 on debut seven days previously. Sources: *VCA Report, WACA Report, The Age, The Argus, The Australasian, The Herald, Melbourne Sun.*

WESTERN AUSTRALIA

V.C.Carlson	b Ironmonger	0		b Ironmonger	0
P.F.Quinlan	c Ironmonger b Blackie	37		c Hendry b Rayson	9
A.D.Drew	lbw b Ironmonger	42		b Blackie	3
L.C.Bott	c Love b Ironmonger	0		c Hendry b Liddicut	2
R.J.Bryant	c Love b Blackie	7		b Liddicut	2
*S.H.D.Rowe	b Ironmonger	1		c Blackie b Ironmonger	55
M.Inverarity	b Ironmonger	16		hit wkt b Rayson	11
W.A.Evans	b Blackie	1	(9)	c Ellis b Hendry	5
L.C.Renfrey	not out	29	(8)	b Hendry	3
F.R.Buttsworth	lbw b Ironmonger	0		c Love b Rayson	5
†R.H.Hewson	b Ironmonger	6		not out	2
Extras	(b5, lb4, nb3)	12		(b5, lb1)	6
Total	(54.3 overs, 194 mins)	151		(36.3 overs, 132 mins)	103

VICTORIA

*R.E.Mayne	c Hewson b Bryant	48
W.H.Ponsford	c Quinlan b Drew	158
H.S.B.Love	c Hewson b Buttsworth	103
H.S.T.L.Hendry	b Inverarity	30
C.B.Willis	c Bott b Quinlan	79
A.E.Liddicut	lbw b Inverarity	12
W.M.Woodfull	c & b Inverarity	28
†J.L.Ellis	not out	36
D.D.Blackie	c Evans b Inverarity	11
W.J.Rayson	c & b Inverarity	0
H.Ironmonger	st Hewson b Inverarity	13
Extras	(b7, lb11)	18
Total	(104.6 overs, 370 mins)	536

VICTORIA	O	M	R	W	w,nb		O	M	R	W	w,nb			FALL OF WICKETS		
Ironmonger	16.3	8	30	7	-,-		11	2	24	2	-,-			WA	VIC	WA
Blackie	18	1	57	3	-,3		3	0	7	1	-,-	Wkt	1st	1st	2nd
Rayson	5	1	13	0	-,-	(4)	11.3	1	46	3	-,-	1st	4	140	0
Hendry	4	0	9	0	-,-	(5)	7	3	12	2	-,-	2nd	88	266	7
Liddicut	8	2	17	0	-,-	(3)	4	0	8	2	-,-	3rd	88	315	12
Willis	3	1	13	0	-,-							4th	88	395	14
												5th	93	436	27
WESTERN AUSTRALIA	O	M	R	W	w,nb							6th	97	461	63
Quinlan	10	0	68	1	-,-							7th	98	491	72
Evans	6	0	23	0	-,-							8th	120	513	78
Renfrey	13	0	62	0	-,-							9th	127	513	99
Inverarity	32.6	0	162	6	-,-							10th	151	536	103
Buttsworth	15	0	81	1	-,-										
Bryant	20	1	79	1	-,-										
Drew	5	0	28	1	-,-										
Bott	3	0	15	0	-,-										

NEW SOUTH WALES v WESTERN AUSTRALIA

Played at Sydney Cricket Ground on November 13, 14, 16, 1925. (Three-day match)
Toss : Western Australia.　　　　Result : NEW SOUTH WALES WON BY AN INNINGS AND 234 RUNS.
Debuts: New South Wales - E.R.Tweeddale, L.J.Vaughan (both f/c).
12th Men: B.M.Salmon (NSW) and C.V.Loton (WA).
Umpires: M.Carney and P.M.Solomon.
Attendances: 1000, 3929, 300.　　　　Total: About 5229.　　　　Receipts: No figures published.
Close of Play: 1st day NSW 1/256 (Rock 151, Macartney 17); 2nd day WA (2) 4/71 (Hewson 13, Bott 12).

For the third successive match Western Australia were defeated by a margin exceeding an innings and 200 runs. Rock compiled his third first-class century in only his fourth match, 151 in 125 minutes with 19 fours and three chances. All his runs were scored in the tea to stumps session of the first day; he was out to the second ball of the next day. Collins (86 in 101 minutes, 9 fours), Macartney (114 in 129 minutes, 10 fours), Kippax (118 in 146 minutes, 7 fours) and Scanes (94 in 86 minutes, 15 fours) also took advantage of the weak Western Australian bowling to help New South Wales register their highest total against that State. Meek was out to the second ball of WA's second innings. Rowe was unable to bat due to a torn leg muscle sustained while fielding and Bryant was forced to use a runner (Evans) in the second innings because of a similar injury. *WACA Report* incorrectly gives WA (1) Quinlan c Scanes. Sources: *The Cricketer, NSWCA Report, WACA Report, Sydney Morning Herald, Sydney Referee, Sydney Mail, Sydney Daily Telegraph.*

WESTERN AUSTRALIA

P.F.Quinlan	c Everett b Mailey	11	(2)	run out (Vaughan/　　　)	12
A.D.Drew	c Mailey b Everett	9	(3)	b Everett	7
L.C.Bott	st Ratcliffe b Mailey	9	(6)	b Everett	21
R.J.Bryant	b Tweeddale	7	(9)	b Macartney	32
*S.H.D.Rowe	b Tweeddale	18		absent hurt	-
A.B.Meek	c Mailey b Tweeddale	4	(1)	c Mailey b Everett	0
M.Inverarity	b Tweeddale	21		c Ratcliffe b Macartney	26
H.T.Grigg	b Macartney	30	(5)	b Everett	20
L.C.Renfrey	b Macartney	10	(10)	not out	30
W.A.Evans	run out	38	(8)	b Everett	25
†R.H.Hewson	not out	20	(4)	c Ratcliffe b Mailey	16
Extras	(b5, lb3, nb9)	17		(b7, lb11, nb4)	22
Total	(50.2 overs, 196 mins)	194		(41.1 overs, 160 mins)	211

NEW SOUTH WALES

*H.L.Collins	lbw b Quinlan	86
H.O.Rock	c Renfrey b Quinlan	151
C.G.Macartney	c Rowe b Inverarity	114
A.F.Kippax	c Bott b Bryant	118
A.E.Scanes	st Hewson b Inverarity	94
J.G.Morgan	c & b Bryant	11
L.J.Vaughan	c Hewson b Evans	3
†A.T.Ratcliffe	b Renfrey	39
A.A.Mailey	c & b Evans	1
S.C.Everett	c Evans b Inverarity	10
E.R.Tweeddale	not out	0
Extras	(b7, lb2, nb3)	12
Total	(100.4 overs, 352 mins)	639

NEW SOUTH WALES	O	M	R	W	w,nb	O	M	R	W	w,nb
Everett	12	1	48	1	-,4	16	1	84	5˙	-,2
Tweeddale	17.2	6	36	4	-,5	7	0	27	0	-,-
Mailey	14	1	64	2	-,-	12	1	48	1	-,-
Macartney	7	0	29	2	-,-	5.1	2	20	2	-,2
Collins						1	0	10	0	-,-

WESTERN AUSTRALIA	O	M	R	W	w,nb
Quinlan	13	0	90	2	-,-
Inverarity	27	0	203	3	-,-
Evans	16	2	84	2	-,-
Renfrey	20.4	0	100	1	-,3
Meek	9	0	69	0	-,-
Bryant	12	1	69	2	-,-
Drew	3	0	12	0	-,-

FALL OF WICKETS

	WA	NSW	WA
Wkt	1st	1st	2nd
1st	23	210	0
2nd	27	256	13
3rd	38	430	21
4th	52	510	49
5th	61	539	82
6th	64	582	84
7th	111	590	114
8th	124	595	162
9th	146	616	211
10th	194	639	-

SOUTH AUSTRALIA v VICTORIA (Shield Match 1)

Played at Adelaide Oval on November 13, 14, 16, 17, 18, 1925. (Timeless match)
Toss : South Australia.   Result : SOUTH AUSTRALIA WON BY 123 RUNS.
Debuts: Nil.
12th Men: G.W.Harris (SA) and W.J.Rayson (Vic).
Umpires: T.W.Cook and R.B.Pounsett.
Attendances: No daily figures published.   Total: 15,670.   Receipts: £848.
Close of Play: 1st day Vic 3/138 (Ryder 52, Love 43); 2nd day SA (2) 2/114 (Pritchard 17, V.Y.Richardson 4); 3rd day SA (2) 9/371
    (Grimmett 26, Ambler 0); 4th day Vic (2) 5/100 (Ellis 1, Blackie 0).

J.T.Murray (injured knee) and C.E.Pellew (farm duties) were replaced in the South Australian twelve by Harris and Walsh. Blackie (right-arm off-breaks) bowled unchanged in the first innings for a Shield-best analysis. Victoria gained a first-innings lead due to Ryder (53 in 79 minutes, 5 fours), Love (63 in 156 minutes, 1 five and 3 fours) and Liddicut (62 not out in 68 minutes, 1 seven and 9 fours). Liddicut's seven consisted of a three plus four overthrows; he also hit 19 runs off the last, incomplete, over of the innings from Scott which included two no-balls and the wicket of Ironmonger. South Australia rallied with fifties from Gun (67 in 125 minutes, 3 fours), Pritchard (69 in 133 minutes, 6 fours), A.J.Richardson (52 in 86 minutes, 3 sixes and 2 fours) and Wainwright (56 in 137 minutes, 6 fours) and Scott followed up by dismissing Mayne with the first ball of Victoria's second innings. Scott's fast deliveries accounted for five further wickets and forced Willis to retire at 6/118 with a broken nose. Ellis, not out at the close of the fourth day, broke a thumb while leaning out of a tram on the way back to the team hotel and was unable to resume his innings on the last day. Contrasting innings from Woodfull (44 in 144 minutes, 1 four) and Hendry (65 not out in 56 minutes, 1 six and 9 fours) could not save Victoria. *Wisden* and *O'Reilly* incorrectly give Vic (1) Ponsford b Scott. Sources: *Wisden, C.B.O'Reilly, VCA Report, SACA Report, Adelaide Advertiser, South Australian Register, The News.*

SOUTH AUSTRALIA

A.J.Richardson	c Ellis b Ironmonger	23	(5) c Ellis b Hendry	52
L.T.Gun	st Ellis b Blackie	13	(1) c Willis b Blackie	67
D.E.Pritchard	c Ellis b Blackie	5	c Ryder b Hendry	69
*V.Y.Richardson	c Woodfull b Blackie	28	c & b Hendry	36
N.A.Walsh	b Ironmonger	0	(2) c Ponsford b Blackie	24
J.W.Rymill	c Liddicut b Blackie	39	run out (Willis/Ellis)	5
E.G.C.Wainwright	c Love b Blackie	4	b Ironmonger	56
J.D.Scott	b Blackie	7	b Hendry	20
C.V.Grimmett	not out	19	c Ryder b Hendry	40
G.H.Palmer	st Ellis b Blackie	17	c Love b Ironmonger	5
†A.M.Ambler	c Ironmonger b Hendry	9	not out	23
Extras	(b5, lb1)	6	(b4, lb7, nb2)	13
Total	(44.5 overs, 172 mins)	170	(114.3 overs, 463 mins)	410

VICTORIA

*R.E.Mayne	run out (V.Y.Richardson/Ambler)	23	c Palmer b Scott	0
W.H.Ponsford	c V.Y.Richardson b Scott	6	c Walsh b A.J.Richardson	19
W.M.Woodfull	c & b Grimmett	13	b Scott	44
J.Ryder	run out (A.J.Richardson/Ambler)	53	b Scott	27
H.S.B.Love	b Scott	63	c Ambler b Scott	4
H.S.T.L.Hendry	c V.Y.Richardson b Grimmett	34	(8) not out	65
C.B.Willis	c Pritchard b Grimmett	0	(9) retired hurt	2
A.E.Liddicut	not out	62	(10) b Grimmett	1
†J.L.Ellis	b Grimmett	6	(6) retired hurt	1
D.D.Blackie	c Rymill b Grimmett	2	(7) b Scott	0
H.Ironmonger	b Scott	8	c Ambler b Scott	5
Extras	(lb4, nb1)	5	(b4, lb9, nb1)	14
Total	(64.7 overs, 246 mins)	275	(51.6 overs, 205 mins)	182

VICTORIA	O	M	R	W	w,nb		O	M	R	W	w,nb
Ironmonger	17	0	66	2	-,-		23	2	76	2	-,-
Blackie	22	5	71	7	-,-		38	4	138	2	-,-
Hendry	5.5	0	27	1	-,-	(4)	27.3	4	99	5	-,2
Ryder						(3)	13	1	52	0	-,-
Liddicut							13	0	32	0	-,-

SOUTH AUSTRALIA	O	M	R	W	w,nb		O	M	R	W	w,nb
Scott	18.7	0	105	3	-,1		14.6	3	58	6	-,1
Palmer	10	1	41	0	-,-		7	0	23	0	-,-
Grimmett	26	2	95	5	-,-	(4)	15	1	60	1	-,-
A.J.Richardson	10	2	29	0	-,-	(3)	15	2	27	1	-,-

FALL OF WICKETS

Wkt	SA	VIC	SA	VIC
	1st	1st	2nd	2nd
1st	30	15	88	0
2nd	36	36	95	41
3rd	46	51	198	91
4th	46	139	205	99
5th	103	188	220	100
6th	117	192	280	110
7th	118	218	312	123
8th	127	233	364	182
9th	157	235	370	-
10th	170	275	410	-

SOUTH AUSTRALIA v WESTERN AUSTRALIA

Played at Adelaide Oval on November 21, 23, 1925. (Three-day match)
Toss : Western Australia.   Result : SOUTH AUSTRALIA WON BY NINE WICKETS.
Debuts: South Australia - A.J.Bartlett, D.R.Downey, W.N.Riley, H.N.Shepley, A.J.Ryan (all f/c).
12th Men: A.B.Meek (WA). No 12th man or emergency fieldsman named for SA.
Umpires: R.B.Pounsett and S.W.Smith.
Attendances: No daily figures published.   Total: 3032.   Receipts: No figure published.
Close of Play: 1st day SA 5/178 (Pritchard 111, Riley 26).

Selectors rested all but three of the South Australians involved in the previous match against Victoria. A.J.Richardson was a late withdrawal, leaving the team without a 12th man. Western Australia were unable to select their captain, S.H.D.Rowe, who had not recovered from the leg injury sustained in the match against New South Wales. Pritchard (167 in 192 minutes, 1 six and 17 fours) scored 111 in 125 minutes after tea on the first day and shared a sixth-wicket stand of 147 in 90 minutes with Riley. Best with the bat for the visitors were Bryant (37 in 65 minutes), Bott (41 in 26 minutes, 5 fours) and Evans (37 in 42 minutes, 4 fours) in the first innings and Bott (27 in 23 minutes, 4 fours), Renfrey (28 in 55 minutes, 3 fours) and Hewson (38 in 59 minutes, 2 fours) in the second. Carlson registered his third duck in four innings when Wall claimed his wicket with the seventh ball of the second innings. Inverarity had conceded over 100 runs in each of the four first-class innings he had bowled in to date. *Cricketer* incorrectly gives WA (1) Shepley 3/43. Sources: *The Cricketer, C.B.O'Reilly, SACA Report, WACA Report, Adelaide Advertiser, South Australian Register, The News, The West Australian.*

WESTERN AUSTRALIA

A.D.Drew	b Wall	10	(7)	c Harris b Grimmett	3
R.J.Bryant	st Downey b Grimmett	37		b Wall	8
V.C.Carlson	c Ryan b Shepley	10	(1)	lbw b Wall	0
L.C.Bott	b Wall	41	(3)	b Wall	27
M.Inverarity	b Grimmett	6	(4)	c Riley b Wall	9
H.T.Grigg	b Grimmett	6	(8)	b Grimmett	12
W.A.Evans	c Downey b Shepley	37	(5)	b Wall	0
L.C.Renfrey	c Walsh b Grimmett	14	(6)	b Grimmett	28
*†R.H.Hewson	b Grimmett	6		b Grimmett	38
F.R.Buttsworth	c Pritchard b Grimmett	3	(11)	not out	0
C.V.Loton	not out	4	(10)	lbw b Grimmett	21
Extras	(b2, lb1)	3		(b9)	9
Total	(39.3 overs, 144 mins)	177		(30.6 overs, 119 mins)	155

SOUTH AUSTRALIA

G.W.Harris	c Renfrey b Buttsworth	5			
N.A.Walsh	c Hewson b Inverarity	21	(1)	lbw b Renfrey	15
D.E.Pritchard	c Bryant b Renfrey	167			
A.J.Ryan	run out (/Hewson)	4	(2)	not out	7
A.J.Bartlett	c Drew b Renfrey	7	(3)	not out	4
*C.E.Pellew	lbw b Inverarity	1			
W.N.Riley	b Buttsworth	45			
C.V.Grimmett	b Buttsworth	9			
†D.R.Downey	lbw b Renfrey	12			
T.W.Wall	not out	11			
H.N.Shepley	not out	6			
Extras	(b1, lb11, w1)	13		(b4, lb1, w1)	6
Total	(59.0 overs, 221 mins) (9 wkts dec)	301		(12.6 overs, 40 mins) (1 wkt)	32

SOUTH AUSTRALIA	O	M	R	W	w,nb		O	M	R	W	w,nb		FALL OF WICKETS			
														WA	SA	WA	SA
Wall	10	0	42	2	-,-		9.6	0	40	6	-,-	Wkt	1st	1st	2nd	2nd
Riley	5	1	13	0	-,-		3	0	22	0	-,-	1st	26	8	0	28
Grimmett	14.3	0	76	6	-,-		12	0	57	4	-,-	2nd	52	40	25	-
Shepley	10	0	43	2	-,-		6	0	27	0	-,-	3rd	70	52	44	-
												4th	104	71	44	-
WESTERN AUSTRALIA	O	M	R	W	w,nb		O	M	R	W	w,nb	5th	108	80	51	-
Buttsworth	22	1	86	3	-,-							6th	114	227	56	-
Evans	7	1	29	0	-,-	(1)	6.6	2	12	0	-,-	7th	152	251	75	-
Inverarity	13	0	101	2	1,-							8th	167	281	115	-
Renfrey	14	3	47	3	-,-	(2)	6	2	14	1	1,-	9th	173	285	153	-
Drew	1	0	6	0	-,-							10th	177	-	155	-
Bryant	2	0	19	0	-,-											

QUEENSLAND v NEW SOUTH WALES

Played at Exhibition Ground, Brisbane, on November 28, 30, December 1, 1925. (Three-day match)
Toss : New South Wales.   Result : MATCH DRAWN.
Debuts: Queensland - H.J.R.Higgins, C.V.Sim (both f/c). New South Wales - L.P.Campbell (f/c); A.H.E.White (NSW Only).
12th Men: E.C.Knowles (Qld). No 12th named for NSW; only 11 men in party.
Umpires: W.H.Carvosso and J.P.Orr.
Attendances: 5000, 3000, 1000.   Total: 9000.   Receipts: £419.
Close of Play: 1st day NSW 287 all out; 2nd day Qld 5/322 (Thompson 72, Brew 0).

Campbell, Dwyer, White and F.S.Cummins replaced O.P.Asher, A.T.Ratcliffe, E.R.Tweeddale and L.J.Vaughan (all unavailable) in the New South Wales side. Cummins withdrew due to an injured knee before the team left, leaving only 11 players in the party. New South Wales based their first innings around Phillips (78 in 142 minutes, 8 fours), Punch (49 in 104 minutes, 2 fours) and Oldfield (52 in 102 minutes, 5 fours). Queensland's total of 9/506 was a new State record; chief contributions came from Oxenham (96 in 183 minutes, 5 fours), Higgins (54 in 75 minutes, 5 fours), O'Connor (44 in 90 minutes, 5 fours), Thompson (132 in 222 minutes, 11 fours) and Beeston (52 not out in 102 minutes, 4 fours). Rowe (8) was struck by a ball from Everett and retired at 3/223, resuming next morning at 6/322. White played his sole match for New South Wales after 19 matches for Cambridge University in 1922-24. Sources: *The Cricketer, NSWCA Report, Sydney Morning Herald, Brisbane Courier, Brisbane Daily Mail, Maryborough Chronicle*.

NEW SOUTH WALES

W.G.F.Brown	b Noyes	19	c Sim b Noyes		8
N.E.Phillips	b Rowe	78	b Noyes		9
A.E.Scanes	run out (Brew/O'Connor)	10	b Sim		0
A.T.E.Punch	run out (Noyes/O'Connor)	49	b Oxenham		11
*†W.A.S.Oldfield	c Hornibrook b Oxenham	52	not out		22
E.A.Dwyer	c O'Connor b Oxenham	20	not out		23
R.Bardsley	c O'Connor b Noyes	19			
A.H.E.White	c Brew b Oxenham	11			
C.V.Morrissey	b Oxenham	2			
L.P.Campbell	c Hutcheon b Oxenham	12			
S.C.Everett	not out	9			
Extras	(b3, lb2, nb1)	6	(b4)		4
Total	(78.3 overs, 278 mins)	287	(38.0 overs, 115 mins) (4 wkts)		77

QUEENSLAND

R.K.Oxenham	b Everett	96
H.J.R.Higgins	c Punch b Campbell	54
*†L.P.D.O'Connor	c Punch b Morrissey	44
F.C.Thompson	lbw b White	132
W.Rowe	c Oldfield b Punch	32
E.H.Hutcheon	c Scanes b Everett	30
P.M.Hornibrook	b Everett	9
F.M.Brew	b Everett	0
N.C.Beeston	not out	52
H.D.Noyes	c Scanes b Phillips	28
C.V.Sim	not out	10
Extras	(b4, lb9, nb6)	19
Total	(123.0 overs, 444 mins) (9 wkts dec)	506

QUEENSLAND	O	M	R	W	w,nb		O	M	R	W	w,nb
Hornibrook	21	2	82	0	-,1						
Noyes	19	1	86	2	-,-	(1)	14	4	37	2	-,-
Sim	16	1	65	0	-,-	(2)	10	4	8	1	-,-
Oxenham	16.3	5	37	5	-,-	(3)	6	3	5	1	-,-
Rowe	6	2	11	1	-,-		3	2	1	0	-,-
Brew						(4)	5	0	22	0	-,-

NEW SOUTH WALES	O	M	R	W	w,nb
Everett	32	1	142	4	-,5
Morrissey	31	4	94	1	-,-
White	19	3	72	1	-,1
Campbell	27	0	123	1	-,-
Punch	10	1	43	1	-,-
Phillips	4	2	13	1	-,-

FALL OF WICKETS

Wkt	NSW 1st	QLD 1st	NSW 2nd
1st	23	85	16
2nd	46	194	17
3rd	155	211	17
4th	162	300	35
5th	199	322	-
6th	248	322	-
7th	256	370	-
8th	258	437	-
9th	272	487	-
10th	287	-	-

QUEENSLAND v NEW ZEALAND XI

Played at Brisbane Cricket Ground (Woolloongabba) on December 4, 5, 7, 1925. (Three-day match)
Toss : New Zealand XI.   Result : QUEENSLAND WON BY AN INNINGS AND 92 RUNS.
Debuts: Nil.
12th Men: L.E.Oxenham (Qld). No 12th named for NZ.
Umpires: J.P.Orr and J.A.Scott.
Attendances: No daily figures published.   Total: About 6000.   Receipts: £271.
Close of Play: 1st day Qld 0/63 (O'Connor 21, Higgins 32); 2nd day Qld 7/413 (Rowe 65, Noyes 53).

New Zealand began the first match of their third Australian tour in intense heat on a hard and fast wicket. L.E.Oxenham replaced E.C.Knowles (business) as 12th man for the local side. Dacre (80 in 102 minutes, 12 fours) registered New Zealand's only fifty. Allcott retired hurt soon after commencing his innings but his score and that at which he left the field was not recorded. He resumed at 9/200. O'Connor (103 in 200 minutes, 8 fours) and Higgins (80 in 153 minutes, 7 fours, early chance) established a first-wicket stand of 167 for Queensland. An unbroken eighth-wicket partnership of 77 in 37 minutes by Rowe and Noyes included 24 by Noyes off an over from Blunt with 2 sixes and 2 fours. In their second innings New Zealand had no answer to Noyes, who brought the ball back sharply from the off and claimed his only five-wicket analysis for the State. *Reese incorrectly gives NZ (1) Blunt b R.K.Oxenham. Sources: T.W.Reese, Brisbane Courier, Brisbane Daily Mail.*

NEW ZEALAND XI

R.V.deR.Worker	b Noyes	5	(2)	b Noyes	4
R.C.Blunt	lbw b R.K.Oxenham	19	(1)	c sub (L.E.Oxenham) b Rowe	22
A.W.Alloo	lbw b Barstow	11	(10)	lbw b Sim	6
C.J.Oliver	c Higgins b Barstow	2	(8)	st O'Connor b Sim	9
C.C.R.Dacre	c O'Connor b Rowe	80	(4)	b Noyes	9
*W.R.Patrick	lbw b R.K.Oxenham	20		b Noyes	5
†T.C.Lowry	c Beeston b Noyes	42	(5)	c Brew b Noyes	16
H.D.Gillespie	b Rowe	0	(3)	b Noyes	2
C.F.W.Allcott	not out	20	(7)	b Noyes	15
D.J.McBeath	b R.K.Oxenham	5	(11)	not out	0
W.H.R.Cunningham	lbw b R.K.Oxenham	16	(9)	st O'Connor b Sim	1
Extras	(b2, lb5)	7		(b2, lb3)	5
Total	(60.7 overs, 219 mins)	227		(35.1 overs, 123 mins)	94

QUEENSLAND

*†L.P.D.O'Connor	c Lowry b Patrick	103
H.J.R.Higgins	c Allcott b Cunningham	80
F.M.Brew	b Blunt	22
F.C.Thompson	lbw b Blunt	17
R.K.Oxenham	st Lowry b McBeath	17
W.Rowe	not out	65
N.C.Beeston	b Cunningham	1
E.H.Hutcheon	lbw b Allcott	26
H.D.Noyes	not out	53
C.B.Barstow	)	
C.V.Sim	) did not bat	
Extras	(b11, lb12, w1, nb5)	29
Total	(95.0 overs, 364 mins) (7 wkts dec)	413

QUEENSLAND	O	M	R	W	w,nb		O	M	R	W	w,nb
Noyes	15	0	60	2	-,-		14	1	48	6	-,-
Barstow	15	3	33	2	-,-	(4)	4	1	4	0	-,-
R.K.Oxenham	18.7	4	64	4	-,-	(2)	6	1	17	0	-,-
Sim	7	1	44	0	-,-	(5)	5.1	1	12	3	-,-
Rowe	5	1	19	2	-,-	(3)	6	3	8	1	-,-

NEW ZEALAND XI	O	M	R	W	w,nb
McBeath	21	2	74	1	1,-
Cunningham	26	0	119	2	-,5
Blunt	18	0	104	2	-,-
Allcott	20	3	42	1	-,-
Alloo	5	0	19	0	-,-
Oliver	2	0	8	0	-,-
Patrick	3	0	18	1	-,-

FALL OF WICKETS

Wkt	NZ 1st	QLD 1st	NZ 2nd
1st	16	167	5
2nd	35	214	9
3rd	39	242	27
4th	44	243	57
5th	116	276	57
6th	155	283	70
7th	169	336	79
8th	197	-	80
9th	200	-	93
10th	227	-	94

AUSTRALIAN XI v THE REST

Played at Sydney Cricket Ground on December 4, 5, 7, 8, 1925. (Four-day match)
Toss : The Rest.   Result : THE REST WON BY 156 RUNS.
Debuts: Nil.
12th Men: D.E.Pritchard (both sides).
Umpires: W.G.French and A.C.Jones.
Attendances: 9388, 20339, 8094, not published.   Total: 37821.   Receipts: £2619.
Close of Play: 1st day Aust 0/26 (Collins 17, Ponsford 7); 2nd day Rest (2) 1/109 (Bardsley 54, Macartney 18); 3rd day Aust (2) 0/25 (Woodfull 16, Ponsford 8).

The match was arranged as a trial to aid selection for the 1926 tour to England. J.M.Taylor (university exams) was unable to take his place in the Australian side and J.L.Ellis (injured thumb) was unavailable for the Rest. Macartney (84 in 91 minutes, 10 fours), V.Y.Richardson (56 in 60 minutes, 10 fours), Kelleway (99 not out in 165 minutes, 10 fours) and Grimmett (44 in 55 minutes, 4 fours) gave the Rest a fine start. Bardsley (54 in 112 minutes, 5 fours) and Love (54 in 147 minutes, 1 four) scored fifties in the second innings. Collins, although affected by illness late in the game, completed a double success for the Australian side scoring 102 (208 minutes, 6 fours) and 81 (135 minutes, 10 fours). He shared a seventh-wicket partnership of 138 with Gregory (100 in 144 minutes, 1 six and 10 fours) in the second innings. Sources: *Wisden, NSWCA Report, VCA Report, The Age, The Argus, Sydney Morning Herald, Sydney Referee.*

THE REST

*W.Bardsley	c Mailey b Gregory	7	c Collins b Gregory	54
H.O.Rock	b Gregory	12	st Oldfield b Mailey	35
C.G.Macartney	run out (Kippax/Oldfield)	84	c Gregory b Hornibrook	28
A.J.Richardson	c Gregory b Mailey	39	c Mailey b Hendry	19
V.Y.Richardson	b Hendry	56	c Oldfield b Hendry	19
C.Kelleway	not out	99	c Kippax b Ryder	34
J.W.Rymill	b Ryder	13	c Mailey b Hendry	5
†H.S.B.Love	run out (Woodfull/Oldfield/Ryder)	3	b Hornibrook	54
C.V.Grimmett	st Oldfield b Mailey	44	run out (Andrews/Gregory)	39
J.D.Scott	c Woodfull b Mailey	4	not out	8
D.D.Blackie	run out (Hornibrook/Mailey)	12		
Extras	(lb6, w1)	7	(b2, lb1)	3
Total	(73.2 overs, 279 mins)	380	(95.0 overs, 346 mins) (9 wkts dec)	298

AUSTRALIAN XI

*H.L.Collins	c Bardsley b A.J.Richardson	102	(8) c & b Blackie	81
W.H.Ponsford	b Kelleway	17	c V.Y.Richardson b Blackie	10
W.M.Woodfull	run out (Rymill/A.J.Richardson)	11	(1) st Love b Grimmett	42
T.J.E.Andrews	b Blackie	14	b Grimmett	2
A.F.Kippax	run out (Grimmett/Love)	19	b Grimmett	0
J.Ryder	lbw b A.J.Richardson	5	(3) b Macartney	43
H.S.T.L.Hendry	st Love b Grimmett	11	c Scott b Grimmett	2
J.M.Gregory	c Love b A.J.Richardson	25	(6) c Grimmett b Blackie	100
†W.A.S.Oldfield	b A.J.Richardson	6	not out	9
A.A.Mailey	b Grimmett	3	(11) b Blackie	0
P.M.Hornibrook	not out	0	(10) hit wkt b Grimmett	1
Extras	(b3, lb3, w3, nb4)	13	(b1, lb3, w1, nb1)	6
Total	(81.2 overs, 236 mins)	226	(73.7 overs, 270 mins)	296

AUSTRALIAN XI	O	M	R	W	w,nb		O	M	R	W	w,nb
Gregory	17	3	85	2	-,-		15	1	69	1	-,-
Hornibrook	11	0	80	0	-,-	(3)	25	5	93	2	-,-
Mailey	23.2	1	127	3	-,-	(4)	24	1	60	1	-,-
Hendry	13	3	33	1	-,-	(2)	21	8	56	3	-,-
Ryder	8	0	42	1	1,-		10	3	17	1	-,-
Andrews	1	0	6	0	-,-						

THE REST	O	M	R	W	w,nb		O	M	R	W	w,nb
Scott	12	1	49	0	3,-		2	0	6	0	-,-
Grimmett	17	2	65	2	-,-	(5)	28	3	91	5	-,-
Blackie	11	3	33	1	-,1	(4)	22.7	1	71	4	-,-
Kelleway	6	0	17	1	-,3	(2)	13	3	41	0	1,1
A.J.Richardson	18.2	3	49	4	-,-	(3)	8	0	41	0	-,-
Macartney							17	7	40	1	-,-

FALL OF WICKETS

Wkt	REST 1st	AUST 1st	REST 2nd	AUST 2nd
1st	10	55	78	27
2nd	35	82	111	95
3rd	118	100	119	100
4th	176	153	148	100
5th	221	172	165	105
6th	242	185	171	129
7th	247	195	242	267
8th	330	219	278	290
9th	334	222	298	293
10th	380	226	-	296

VICTORIA v NEW ZEALAND XI

Played at Melbourne Cricket Ground on December 18, 19, 21, 1925. (Three-day match)
Toss : Victoria.   Result : MATCH DRAWN.
Debuts: Victoria - B.Cosgrave, N.F.Mitchell (both f/c). NZ - R.W.Hope (f/c).
12th Men: E.T.Austen (Vic) and H.D.Gillespie (NZ).
Umpires: H.E.Nichols and J.Richards.
Attendances: 1357, 4570, 1155.   Total: 7082.   Receipts: £276.
Close of Play: 1st day NZ 314 all out; 2nd day Vic 5/406 (Hendry 213, Lansdown 35).

F.A.Baring, F.A.Tarrant and S.E.Wootton all became unavailable after the Victorian side was chosen and were replaced by Atkinson, Lansdown and Wilkinson. Hendry's career-best unbeaten 325 in 323 minutes with 26 fours dominated the match. He went from 5 at lunch on the second day to 87 at tea, 213 at stumps and was 325 at lunch on the third day when Mayne declared the Victorian innings closed. Hendry shared partnerships of 204 for the sixth wicket with Lansdown (51 in 118 minutes, no fours) and 110 for the seventh wicket with Liddicut (47 in 63 minutes, 6 fours) and kept pace with the clock throughout his innings. Mayne scored 57 in 110 minutes with 2 fours, surviving a chance when 3. Worker (89 in 199 minutes, 5 fours) and Allcott (107 in 157 minutes, 7 fours) added 193 for New Zealand's third wicket on the first day while Worker (42 in 97 minutes, 2 fours), Blunt (57 in 47 minutes, 6 fours) and Oliver (58 in 65 minutes, 8 fours) saved New Zealand from defeat on the last day. Sources: *T.W.Reese, VCA Report, The Age, The Argus, The Australasian, The Herald.*

NEW ZEALAND XI

R.V.deR.Worker	b Wilkinson	89		c Mitchell b Lansdown	42
R.C.Blunt	c Hendry b Wilkinson	5		b Ebeling	57
†T.C.Lowry	b Ebeling	9	(6)	st Atkinson b Lansdown	1
C.F.W.Allcott	c Liddicut b Wilkinson	107	(3)	c Wilkinson b Lansdown	31
C.C.R.Dacre	lbw b Ebeling	19		c Mitchell b Lansdown	12
C.J.Oliver	run out (Gamble/Atkinson)	36	(7)	lbw b Mitchell	58
*W.R.Patrick	c Ransford b Lansdown	22			
C.G.Crawford	hit wkt b Hendry	0		not out	5
A.W.Alloo	b Hendry	3	(4)	not out	18
W.H.R.Cunningham	not out	5			
R.W.Hope	run out (Lansdown)	5			
Extras	(b8, lb4, w2)	14		(b7)	7
Total	(77.2 overs, 297 mins)	314		(53.0 overs, 195 mins) (6 wkts)	231

VICTORIA

*R.E.Mayne	c Lowry b Blunt	57
B.Cosgrave	c Crawford b Hope	33
H.S.T.L.Hendry	not out	325
†J.A.Atkinson	b Blunt	19
N.F.Mitchell	b Cunningham	21
V.S.Ransford	c Allcott b Cunningham	19
A.J.W.Lansdown	c Lowry b Cunningham	51
A.E.Liddicut	c Dacre b Allcott	47
W.A.Wilkinson	not out	8
H.S.Gamble	)	
H.I.Ebeling	) did not bat	
Extras	(b8, lb3, nb1)	12
Total	(118.0 overs, 423 mins) (7 wkts dec)	592

VICTORIA	O	M	R	W	w,nb		O	M	R	W	w,nb
Ebeling	19	2	58	2	-,-	(3)	8	0	33	1	-,-
Wilkinson	12	1	40	3	-,-		8	0	42	0	-,-
Lansdown	10.2	1	60	1	2,-	(4)	16	0	76	4	-,-
Gamble	13	1	65	0	-,-	(1)	5	0	42	0	-,-
Liddicut	7	0	28	0	-,-		11	2	21	0	-,-
Hendry	16	2	49	2	-,-						
Ransford						(6)	3	2	1	0	-,-
Mitchell						(7)	2	0	9	1	-,-

NEW ZEALAND XI	O	M	R	W	w,nb
Hope	18	0	90	1	-,1
Cunningham	33	1	173	3	-,-
Allcott	37	3	128	1	-,-
Blunt	24	0	152	2	-,-
Patrick	1	0	10	0	-,-
Alloo	5	0	27	0	-,-

FALL OF WICKETS

Wkt	NZ 1st	VIC 1st	NZ 2nd
1st	8	91	86
2nd	23	99	133
3rd	216	149	134
4th	227	205	148
5th	246	244	150
6th	281	448	226
7th	282	558	-
8th	290	-	-
9th	300	-	-
10th	314	-	-

SOUTH AUSTRALIA v NEW SOUTH WALES (Shield Match 2)

Played at Adelaide Oval on December 18, 19, 21, 22, 1925. (Timeless match)
Toss : South Australia.   Result : NEW SOUTH WALES WON BY AN INNINGS AND 99 RUNS.
Debuts: Nil.
12th Men: G.H.Palmer (SA) and H.O.Rock (NSW).
Umpires: R.B.Pounsett and S.W.Smith.
Attendances: 5000, 15000, other days not published.   Total: 25,449   Receipts: £1378.
Close of Play: 1st day NSW 1/38 (Bardsley 14, Macartney 19); 2nd day NSW 6/436 (Kippax 50, Gregory 1); 3rd day SA (2) 2/114
    (Gun 50, V.Y.Richardson 20).

Gregory dismissed Arthur Richardson with the second ball of the match and Vic Richardson (59 in 108 minutes, 5 fours) scored the sole half-century on the opening day. Contributions by Bardsley (47 in 138 minutes, 1 four), Macartney (112 in 155 minutes, 1 six and 10 fours, chance at 87), Taylor (95 in 118 minutes, 9 fours, chance at 20), Andrews (63 in 82 minutes, 5 fours), Kippax (56 in 92 minutes, 7 fours), Kelleway (50 in 68 minutes, 8 fours) and Gregory (68 in 79 minutes, 9 fours) - all good Test men at one time or another - put New South Wales in an impregnable position. Gun (59 with 5 fours) and again Vic Richardson (61 with 5 fours) scored half-centuries in the second innings. Everett had replaced O.P.Asher in the New South Wales twelve. Sources: *Wisden, C.B.O'Reilly, VCA Report, SACA Report, Adelaide Advertiser, South Australian Register.*

SOUTH AUSTRALIA

A.J.Richardson	c Everett b Gregory	0	(7)	run out (Kippax)	24
L.T.Gun	c Mailey b Everett	11		b Gregory	59
D.E.Pritchard	c Gregory b Mailey	9		b Mailey	26
*V.Y.Richardson	c Andrews b Mailey	59		st Oldfield b Mailey	61
J.W.Rymill	c Oldfield b Everett	26	(1)	b Kelleway	8
J.T.Murray	b Mailey	4		c Oldfield b Gregory	9
P.D.Rundell	not out	37	(5)	b Kelleway	34
C.V.Grimmett	c Taylor b Mailey	5		c Oldfield b Gregory	14
J.D.Scott	c Oldfield b Macartney	20		b Gregory	5
W.J.Whitty	c Gregory b Mailey	5		c Everett b Kelleway	2
†A.M.Ambler	b Mailey	0		not out	13
Extras	(b4, lb4, nb1)	9		(b7, lb8)	15
Total	(63.3 overs, 234 mins)	185		(75.1 overs, 285 mins)	170

NEW SOUTH WALES

*H.L.Collins	c Grimmett b Whitty	5
W.Bardsley	b Scott	47
C.G.Macartney	c Grimmett b A.J.Richardson	112
J.M.Taylor	c Murray b Scott	95
T.J.E.Andrews	b Scott	63
A.F.Kippax	b Whitty	56
C.Kelleway	b Murray	50
J.M.Gregory	c Pritchard b Whitty	68
†W.A.S.Oldfield	c Ambler b Scott	36
A.A.Mailey	b Scott	4
S.C.Everett	not out	4
Extras	(b6, lb5, nb3)	14
Total	(111.7 overs, 428 mins)	554

NEW SOUTH WALES	O	M	R	W	w,nb		O	M	R	W	w,nb			FALL OF WICKETS	
													SA	NSW	SA
Gregory	11	1	25	1	-,-		22	6	75	4	-,-	Wkt	1st	1st	2nd
Kelleway	8	1	16	0	-,-		17	0	57	3	-,-	1st	0	7	13
Mailey	24.3	5	79	6	-,-	(4)	20.1	3	64	2	-,-	2nd	17	145	77
Everett	10	2	35	2	-,1	(3)	11	0	52	0	-,-	3rd	31	195	131
Macartney	10	2	21	1	-,-		5	3	7	0	-,-	4th	100	333	187
												5th	105	338	202
SOUTH AUSTRALIA	O	M	R	W	w,nb							6th	122	429	212
Scott	19.7	1	117	5	-,3							7th	134	446	231
Whitty	29	4	116	3	-,-							8th	168	530	241
Grimmett	39	5	174	0	-,-							9th	185	535	244
A.J.Richardson	18	1	103	1	-,-							10th	185	554	270
Murray	5	0	24	1	-,-										
Rundell	1	0	6	0	-,-										

VICTORIA v NEW SOUTH WALES (Shield Match 3)

Played at Melbourne Cricket Ground on December 26, 28, 29, 30, 31, 1925. (Timeless match)
Toss : Victoria.   Result : NEW SOUTH WALES WON BY AN INNINGS AND 162 RUNS.
Debuts: Nil.
12th Men: A.J.W.Lansdown (Vic) and E.L.Waddy (NSW - manager).
Umpires: D.A.Elder and C.Garing.
Attendances: 23816, 26200, 17553, 11919, 3148.   Total: 82,636.   Receipts: £4085.
Close of Play: 1st day Vic 6/251 (Love 56, Baring 28); 2nd day NSW 2/140 (Andrews 40, Taylor 9); 3rd day NSW 7/466 (Kelleway 46,
    Gregory 25); 4th day Vic (2) 4/63 (Baring 22, Hendry 3).

S.C.Everett, who strained his side in the previous match against South Australia, was unable to take his place in the New South Wales twelve. Lansdown replaced J.L.Ellis, who had not recovered from a hand injury, in the Victorian twelve. A century by Love (115 in 263 minutes, 5 fours) and half-centuries by Woodfull (53 in 119 minutes, 2 fours), Ponsford (68 in 128 minutes, 1 four) and Hartkopf (54 not out in 88 minutes, 1 six and 4 fours) put Victoria in a sound position. Macartney (slow left-arm) took his best State bowling figures. A New South Wales record ninth-wicket stand of 226 between Kelleway (145 in 327 minutes, 10 fours, chances at 9 and 30) and Oldfield (129 in 194 minutes, 9 fours, chance at 101) highlighted an innings in which the lowest completed score was 29. Andrews (61 in 107 minutes, 3 fours), Taylor (66 in 117 minutes, 5 fours), Macartney (59 in 87 minutes, 4 fours) and Rock (81 in 130 minutes, 7 fours) all scored fifties. Baring strained a side muscle while bowling in the nets prior to the second day's play and batted with discomfort. He did not field at all, Lansdown substituting in his place. Last first-class appearance by R.E.Mayne. *Wisden* gives incorrect match dates. Sources: *Wisden, NSWCA Report, VCA Report, The Age, The Argus, The Herald, Melbourne Sun.*

VICTORIA

*R.E.Mayne	c Gregory b Kelleway	25		b Gregory	7
W.M.Woodfull	c Gregory b Macartney	53		lbw b Macartney	13
J.Ryder	b Macartney	5	(7)	c & b Mailey	18
H.S.T.L.Hendry	b Macartney	5	(6)	b Kelleway	5
W.H.Ponsford	c & b Macartney	68	(8)	not out	25
F.A.Tarrant	b Macartney	9	(4)	b Macartney	2
†H.S.B.Love	lbw b Macartney	115	(5)	lbw b Mailey	11
F.A.Baring	lbw b Macartney	57	(3)	b Gregory	30
A.E.V.Hartkopf	not out	54		c Oldfield b Kelleway	1
A.E.Liddicut	b Gregory	18		lbw b Mailey	4
D.D.Blackie	b Gregory	0		b Kelleway	3
Extras	(lb4)	4		(b3, lb4, nb4)	11
Total	(128.5 overs, 435 mins)	413		(33.0 overs, 131 mins)	130

NEW SOUTH WALES

*H.L.Collins	run out (Liddicut/Love)	45
W.Bardsley	b Hartkopf	45
T.J.E.Andrews	b Blackie	61
J.M.Taylor	c Tarrant b Hendry	66
C.G.Macartney	lbw b Hartkopf	59
A.F.Kippax	c Love b Ryder	29
H.O.Rock	lbw b Blackie	81
C.Kelleway	lbw b Ryder	145
J.M.Gregory	c Love b Blackie	32
†W.A.S.Oldfield	c sub (A.J.W.Lansdown) b Blackie	129
A.A.Mailey	not out	1
Extras	(b9, lb1, w2)	12
Total	(177.6 overs, 631 mins)	705

NEW SOUTH WALES	O	M	R	W	w,nb		O	M	R	W	w,nb
Gregory	31.5	3	102	2	-,-		11	1	57	2	-,-
Kelleway	27	4	74	1	-,-	(4)	6	0	12	3	-,1
Mailey	33	0	148	0	-,-		8	1	34	3	-,-
Macartney	37	6	85	7	-,-	(2)	8	3	16	2	-,3

VICTORIA	O	M	R	W	w,nb
Hendry	39	4	159	1	-,-
Blackie	38.6	0	153	4	-,-
Ryder	35	5	121	2	-,-
Tarrant	27	6	76	0	-,-
Liddicut	16	2	62	0	-,-
Hartkopf	22	0	122	2	2,-

FALL OF WICKETS

Wkt	VIC 1st	NSW 1st	VIC 2nd
1st	50	69	20
2nd	67	122	22
3rd	75	177	27
4th	102	267	52
5th	124	291	71
6th	203	323	73
7th	313	425	111
8th	367	475	116
9th	413	701	125
10th	413	705	130

NEW SOUTH WALES v QUEENSLAND

Played at Sydney Cricket Ground on December 26, 28, 29, 1925. (Three-day match)
Toss : New South Wales.　　　　Result : MATCH DRAWN.
Debuts: New South Wales - F.S.Cummins, C.O.Nicholls (both f/c). Queensland - A.Hurwood (f/c).
12th Men: L.J.Vaughan (NSW) and M.Biggs (Qld).
Umpires: W.J.R.Bowes and A.Pike.
Attendances: 4600, 3323, 654.　　　Total: 8577.　　　Receipts: £340.
Close of Play: 1st day Qld 1/0 (Higgins 0); 2nd day Qld (2) 3/102 (Thompson 25, L.E.Oxenham 29).

The last non-Sheffield Shield match between these teams prior to Queensland's admission to the national competition the following year was therefore also the last time New South Wales fielded a Second Eleven against the northerners. Scanes (67 in 71 minutes, 11 fours) and Ratcliffe (chanceless 106 in 172 minutes, 11 fours) compiled the highest scores for New South Wales. Nicholls dismissed Sim (sent in as night-watchman) in his first over in first-class cricket and Higgins fell to the first ball he received on the second day (Tweeddale's first). O'Connor, aided by a chance at 9, held out for 160 minutes (4 fours) to score 74. Queensland were saved from defeat largely by a fourth-wicket stand of 223 between Thompson (150 not out in 360 minutes, 1 five and 10 fours) and Lionel Oxenham (119 in 251 minutes, chances at 14 and 40 - his sole first-class century), who recorded the State's first partnership of 200 or more for any wicket in Australia. (A sixth-wicket stand of 238 between R.Macdonald and O.W.Cowley, Qld v Hawke's Bay at Napier, New Zealand 1896-97 was the only precedent). Thompson added a further 120 for the fifth wicket with Hutcheon (career-best 71 in 93 minutes, 7 fours). P.M.Hornibrook was unavailable for Queensland and Sim and Biggs had replaced W.Rowe and E.C.Knowles (both unavailable) after the team was announced.
Sources: *The Cricketer, NSWCA Report, Sydney Morning Herald, Sydney Referee, Sydney Daily Telegraph, Brisbane Courier.*

NEW SOUTH WALES

W.G.F.Brown	c Sim b Hurwood	34
N.E.Phillips	lbw b Sim	57
A.E.Scanes	c Hurwood b Sim	67
J.G.Morgan	c O'Connor b Sim	4
*†A.T.Ratcliffe	b Hurwood	106
R.Bardsley	c Hutcheon b Sim	35
A.T.E.Punch	c O'Connor b Thompson	58
F.S.Cummins	c Sim b Thompson	2
O.P.Asher	c L.E.Oxenham b Thompson	20
C.O.Nicholls	c sub (M.Biggs) b Thompson	12
E.R.Tweeddale	not out	1
Extras	(b5, lb6 w1)	12
Total	(85.3 overs, 275 mins)	408

QUEENSLAND

C.V.Sim	c Bardsley b Nicholls	0			
H.J.R.Higgins	c Nicholls b Tweeddale	0	(1)	b Tweeddale	5
R.K.Oxenham	run out (Asher/Ratcliffe)	6	(2)	run out	19
*†L.P.D.O'Connor	b Phillips	74	(3)	lbw b Morgan	12
F.C.Thompson	c Punch b Asher	17	(4)	not out	150
L.E.Oxenham	lbw b Asher	20	(5)	b Asher	119
E.H.Hutcheon	b Punch	10	(6)	c Tweeddale b Nicholls	71
N.C.Beeston	run out (Morgan/Ratcliffe/Punch)	16	(7)	not out	0
F.M.Brew	run out (Morgan)	8			
H.D.Noyes	c & b Morgan	8			
A.Hurwood	not out	4			
Extras	(b2, lb4, nb1)	7		(b13, w1, nb4)	18
Total	(58.6 overs, 175 mins)	170		(119.0 overs, 375 mins) (5 wkts)	394

QUEENSLAND	O	M	R	W	w,nb		O	M	R	W	w,nb
Noyes	14	1	70	0	1,-						
Hurwood	19	1	97	2	-,-						
Sim	16	0	92	4	-,-						
R.K.Oxenham	23	3	106	0	-,-						
Brew	5	0	10	0	-,-						
Thompson	8.3	0	21	4	-,-						

NEW SOUTH WALES	O	M	R	W	w,nb		O	M	R	W	w,nb
Nicholls	11	3	29	1	-,-		18	2	68	1	1,-
Tweeddale	12	0	45	1	-,1		23	3	79	1	-,3
Asher	17	3	33	2	-,-	(4)	34	6	69	1	-,-
Phillips	10	3	34	1	-,-	(6)	13	3	35	0	-,1
Punch	7	1	22	1	-,-		15	2	61	0	-,-
Morgan	1.6	1	0	1	-,-	(3)	16	2	64	1	-,-

FALL OF WICKETS

Wkt	NSW 1st	QLD 1st	QLD 2nd
1st	56	0	10
2nd	146	0	43
3rd	162	17	51
4th	173	52	274
5th	239	94	392
6th	337	130	-
7th	349	134	-
8th	389	155	-
9th	397	165	-
10th	408	170	-

SOUTH AUSTRALIA v NEW ZEALAND XI

Played at Adelaide Oval on December 26, 28, 29, 1925. (Three-day match)
Toss : South Australia.   Result : MATCH DRAWN.
Debuts: South Australia - P.K.Lee, D.G.McKay, C.N.Parry (all f/c).
12th Men: A.J.Bartlett (SA) and H.D.Gillespie (NZ).
Umpires: C.L.Cornish and G.A.Hele.
Attendances: No daily figures published.   Total: 12,849.   Receipts: No figures published.
Close of Play: 1st day NZ 0/20 (Blunt 11, Worker 9); 2nd day SA (2) 0/109 (Parry 64, A.J.Richardson 43).

Bartlett replaced G.W.Harris (unavailable) as 12th man for South Australia. V.Y.Richardson, dismissed first ball in each innings, fell to the third ball of the match. A.J.Richardson (77 in 100 minutes, 7 fours) and Alexander (130 in 176 minutes, 5 fours) topscored in the first innings. Parry (69 in 70 minutes, 1 six and 7 fours) and A.J.Richardson (104 in 150 minutes, 13 fours) shared a quick opening partnership of 118 in the second innings. Dacre (70 in 69 minutes, 2 sixes and 10 fours) and Lowry (123 in 95 minutes, 22 fours) in the first innings and Oliver (68 in 67 minutes, 1 six and 10 fours) in the second batted in brilliant style for New Zealand. *Reese* and *Age* incorrectly give NZ (1) Dacre 77, Crawford 23*; NZ (2) McKay 0/29, Murray 0/25. Sources: *T.W.Reese, C.B.O'Reilly, SACA Report, The Age, Adelaide Advertiser, South Australian Register.*

SOUTH AUSTRALIA

Batsman	Dismissal	Runs	2nd Innings	Runs
A.J.Richardson	b Hope	77	(2) b Blunt	104
*V.Y.Richardson	c Allcott b Hope	0	(4) st Lowry b Blunt	0
D.E.Pritchard	b Cunningham	2	b Blunt	13
P.K.Lee	b Cunningham	0		
J.W.Rymill	b Allcott	50	b Allcott	15
W.C.Alexander	run out (Dacre/Lowry)	130	(7) not out	34
J.T.Murray	c Lowry b Allcott	4	(6) not out	40
D.G.McKay	c Dacre b Alloo	36		
C.V.Grimmett	c Allcott b Alloo	45		
†C.N.Parry	hit wkt b Alloo	1	(1) st Lowry b Blunt	69
G.H.Palmer	not out	4		
Extras	(lb1, nb1)	2	(b13, lb5)	18
Total	(67.7 overs, 250 mins)	351	(53.0 overs, 199 mins) (5 wkts dec)	293

NEW ZEALAND XI

Batsman	Dismissal	Runs	2nd Innings	Runs
R.V.deR.Worker	c & b Grimmett	14	(6) run out (V.Y.Richardson/Grimmett)	11
R.C.Blunt	st Parry b Grimmett	65	(1) lbw b Grimmett	34
C.F.W.Allcott	c & b McKay	7	(8) not out	2
C.J.Oliver	c & b Grimmett	22	(3) st Parry b A.J.Richardson	68
C.C.R.Dacre	c V.Y.Richardson b Murray	70	(4) b A.J.Richardson	40
†T.C.Lowry	c Lee b A.J.Richardson	123	(5) b Alexander	16
*W.R.Patrick	b Palmer	4	(9) not out	2
C.G.Crawford	not out	30	(2) lbw b A.J.Richardson	3
A.W.Alloo	b A.J.Richardson	0	(7) run out (Bartlett/Parry/Pritchard)	14
W.H.R.Cunningham	b A.J.Richardson	1		
R.W.Hope	lbw b A.J.Richardson	0		
Extras	(b2, lb1)	2	(b2)	2
Total	(70.0 overs, 243 mins)	339	(42.0 overs, 150 mins) (7 wkts)	192

NEW ZEALAND XI	O	M	R	W	w,nb		O	M	R	W	w,nb
Hope	17	0	119	2	-,1		7	0	43	0	-,-
Cunningham	19	0	91	2	-,-		12	0	75	0	-,-
Allcott	12	0	40	2	-,-		12	1	43	1	-,-
Blunt	8	0	51	0	-,-	(5)	15	1	72	4	-,-
Alloo	10.7	0	41	3	-,-	(4)	5	0	33	0	-,-
Patrick	1	0	7	0	-,-		2	0	9	0	-,-

SOUTH AUSTRALIA	O	M	R	W	w,nb		O	M	R	W	w,nb
McKay	12	1	62	1	-,-		5	0	28	0	-,-
Palmer	12	1	71	1	-,-		5	0	23	0	-,-
Grimmett	31	3	130	3	-,-	(4)	11	1	35	1	-,-
A.J.Richardson	11	0	41	4	-,-	(3)	11	2	46	3	-,-
Murray	2	0	18	1	-,-		3	0	26	0	-,-
Lee	2	0	14	0	-,-		4	0	16	0	-,-
Alexander							2	0	15	1	-,-
Pritchard							1	0	1	0	-,-

FALL OF WICKETS

Wkt	SA 1st	NZ 1st	SA 2nd	NZ 2nd
1st	1	33	118	36
2nd	4	50	152	38
3rd	8	85	152	138
4th	92	152	194	149
5th	162	216	221	168
6th	178	245	-	187
7th	248	333	-	189
8th	346	334	-	-
9th	346	339	-	-
10th	351	339	-	-

NEW SOUTH WALES v NEW ZEALAND XI

Played at Sydney Cricket Ground on January 1, 2, 4, 1926. (Three-day match)
Toss : New South Wales.   Result : MATCH DRAWN.
Debuts: Nil.
12th Men: C.D.Seddon (NSW) and H.D.Gillespie (NZ).
Umpires: A.C.Jones and A.P.Williams
Attendances: 3834, 3939, 1040.   Total: 8813.   Receipts: £344.
Close of Play: 1st day NSW 7/441 (Bardsley 54, Nicholls 10); 2nd day NZ 6/282 (Patrick 71, Allcott 51).

This was the third drawn match in succession on New Zealand's tour and led the authorities to extend the duration of future tour matches in Australia to four days. Brown (168 in 232 minutes, 21 fours) hit his sole century in his ninth and last first-class match and added 229 in 159 minutes for the fourth wicket with Ratcliffe (128 in 191 minutes, 13 fours), who also compiled his highest score for New South Wales. Bardsley (career-best 87 in 126 minutes, 9 fours) also batted well. Patrick (143 in 294 minutes, 24 fours) and Allcott (116 in 229 minutes, 15 fours) shared a seventh-wicket stand of 244 for the New Zealanders, the highest partnership for that wicket yet in Australia. It remained the record until 1934-35. Blunt's 73 took only 75 minutes and included 10 fours. Phillips (102 not out in 125 minutes) reached his century with a six in the last over of the match. Seddon had replaced F.S.Cummins (unavailable) as the home side's 12th man. *Reese* incorrectly gives NSW (1) Brown b Patrick, Nicholls c Allcott b Cunningham. Sources: *T.W.Reese, NSWCA Report, Sydney Morning Herald, Sydney Referee.*

NEW SOUTH WALES

W.G.F.Brown	c Dacre b Patrick	168			
N.E.Phillips	b Cunningham	1	(1) not out		102
A.E.Scanes	b Allcott	17	(2) c Allcott b McBeath		34
J.G.Morgan	c Oliver b Cunningham	29			
*†A.T.Ratcliffe	b Allcott	128			
R.Bardsley	c Blunt b Cunningham	87			
A.T.E.Punch	c Allcott b McBeath	13	(4) b Cunningham		44
L.J.Vaughan	b Cunningham	11	(3) b Alloo		15
C.O.Nicholls	c McBeath b Cunningham	47	(5) not out		6
L.P.Campbell	not out	16			
E.R.Tweeddale	run out (McBeath/James)	2			
Extras	(b4, lb6, w2)	12	(lb3, w1)		4
Total	(108.5 overs, 390 mins)	531	(40.0 overs, 125 mins) (3 wkts)		205

NEW ZEALAND XI

R.V.deR.Worker	c & b Campbell	30
A.W.Alloo	b Nicholls	13
R.C.Blunt	c Campbell b Morgan	73
C.J.Oliver	c Vaughan b Campbell	23
T.C.Lowry	c Ratcliffe b Morgan	6
C.C.R.Dacre	b Campbell	6
*W.R.Patrick	b Campbell	143
C.F.W.Allcott	b Morgan	116
†K.C.James	lbw b Morgan	10
D.J.McBeath	c Vaughan b Campbell	16
W.H.R.Cunningham	not out	5
Extras	(b7, lb4, nb3)	14
Total	(109.4 overs, 450 mins)	455

NEW ZEALAND XI	O	M	R	W	w,nb	O	M	R	W	w,nb
Oliver	6	0	31	0	-,-	2	0	9	0	-,-
Cunningham	27.5	3	125	5	-,-	10	0	52	1	-,-
Allcott	32	4	112	2	-,-	4	0	31	0	-,-
Blunt	13	0	96	0	-,-	4	0	31	0	-,-
McBeath	15	3	76	1	1,-	7	0	28	1	-,-
Alloo	4	0	27	0	-,-	11	0	38	1	-,-
Patrick	11	0	52	1	1,-	1	0	8	0	1,-
Dacre						1	0	4	0	-,-

NEW SOUTH WALES	O	M	R	W	w,nb
Nicholls	18	0	80	1	-,-
Tweeddale	22	2	98	0	-,3
Phillips	7	0	46	0	-,-
Morgan	21	3	60	4	-,-
Campbell	31.4	4	132	5	-,-
Punch	10	2	25	0	-,-

FALL OF WICKETS

Wkt	NSW 1st	NZ 1st	NSW 2nd
1st	2	19	46
2nd	37	117	81
3rd	83	131	176
4th	312	149	-
5th	381	152	-
6th	402	162	-
7th	428	406	-
8th	494	421	-
9th	529	444	-
10th	531	455	-

VICTORIA v SOUTH AUSTRALIA (Shield Match 4)

Played at Melbourne Cricket Ground on January 1, 2, 4, 5, 6, 7 - 8 (no play), 9, 1926. (Timeless match)
Toss : Victoria.   Result : VICTORIA WON BY 287 RUNS.
Debuts: Victoria - A.O.Thomson (f/c).
12th Men: K.J.Schneider (Vic) and G.H.Palmer (SA).
Umpires: F.W.Dixon and P.E.Smith.
Attendances: 12150, 11939, 2919, 6356, 7862, no play, no play, 1436.   Total: 42,662.   Receipts: £1804.
Close of Play: 1st day SA 0/20 (Parry 13, A.J.Richardson 7); 2nd day SA 6/321 (Rymill 101, Alexander 74); 3rd day Vic (2) 0/53
(Woodfull 31, Lansdown 17); 4th day Vic (2) 3/372 (Woodfull 208, Ryder 66); 5th day SA (2) 3/38 (V.Y.Richardson 11,
Alexander 0); 6th day no play; 7th day no play.

Woodfull had an outstanding match, scoring 97 (166 minutes, 4 fours) and a Shield-best 236 (407 minutes, 12 fours). Ryder (95 in 191 minutes, 7 fours), Hendry (59 in 113 minutes, 2 fours) and Ransford (55 in 85 minutes, 8 fours) all scored fifties in Victoria's second-innings 604. Rymill (124 in 191 minutes, 1 six and 8 fours) and Alexander (133 in 190 minutes, 9 fours) established a seventh-wicket partnership of 183 for South Australia, a new State record. V.Y.Richardson scored 56 in 122 minutes with 4 fours. Rain washed out play on the sixth and seventh days and made for a very difficult wicket for South Australian batsmen when they resumed on the eighth day, play lasting less than an hour. F.A.Baring, A.E.V.Hartkopf, A.E.Liddicut, R.E.Mayne, W.H.Ponsford and F.A.Tarrant were all unavailable for Victoria. *Wisden* has incorrect match dates. Sources: *Wisden, C.B.O'Reilly, VCA Report, SACA Report, The Age, The Argus, The Herald, Melbourne Sun.*

VICTORIA

*J.Ryder	c Pritchard b Whitty	16	(5)	b Scott	95
W.M.Woodfull	c Pritchard b Murray	97	(1)	c V.T.Richardson b Whitty	236
H.S.T.L.Hendry	c Whitty b A.J.Richardson	23	(4)	lbw b Whitty	59
†H.S.B.Love	c Pritchard b Whitty	22	(6)	lbw b Scott	14
N.F.Mitchell	c Parry b Scott	26	(3)	b Grimmett	1
V.S.Ransford	c Murray b Scott	15	(7)	c Whitty b A.J.Richardson	55
A.J.W.Lansdown	c Murray b Grimmett	13	(2)	c Pritchard b Grimmett	19
A.O.Thomson	c Murray b A.J.Richardson	5	(9)	b Murray	35
K.J.Millar	c & b Grimmett	1	(8)	run out (Rundell)	33
H.I.Ebeling	c Whitty b A.J.Richardson	6		b Scott	4
D.D.Blackie	not out	0		not out	20
Extras	(b4, lb2, nb2)	8		(b18, lb9, w2, nb4)	33
Total	(67.1 overs, 252 mins)	232		(154.5 overs, 575 mins)	604

SOUTH AUSTRALIA

†C.N.Parry	c Lansdown b Hendry	24		run out (Ransford/Hendry)	10
A.J.Richardson	c & b Blackie	41	(6)	c Ryder b Blackie	10
D.E.Pritchard	lbw b Blackie	2	(8)	c & b Hendry	3
*V.Y.Richardson	c Mitchell b Ryder	56	(3)	c Millar b Hendry	27
P.D.Rundell	b Ebeling	13	(2)	b Hendry	10
J.T.Murray	b Blackie	4	(9)	b Blackie	5
J.W.Rymill	c Love b Hendry	124		c Ebeling b Hendry	0
W.C.Alexander	run out (Thomson/Lansdown)	133	(5)	c Thomson b Hendry	0
C.V.Grimmett	st Love b Hendry	33	(4)	run out (Ransford/Love)	1
J.D.Scott	c Hendry b Ransford	19		st Love b Hendry	5
W.J.Whitty	not out	3		not out	4
Extras	(b6, lb4)	10		(b7, lb5)	12
Total	(106.4 overs, 419 mins)	462		(26.4 overs, 108 mins)	87

SOUTH AUSTRALIA	O	M	R	W	w,nb	O	M	R	W	w,nb
Scott	14	1	51	2	-,1	35	1	152	3	-,4
Whitty	15	0	46	2	-,-	31	6	92	2	1,-
Grimmett	21.1	3	61	2	-,-	52	5	192	2	-,-
A.J.Richardson	11	0	40	3	-,-	27	4	81	1	-,-
Murray	6	1	26	1	-,1	5.5	1	20	1	-,-
Rundell						4	0	34	0	1,-

VICTORIA	O	M	R	W	w,nb	O	M	R	W	w,nb
Ebeling	23	3	85	1	-,-	5	1	13	0	-,-
Blackie	35	2	132	3	-,-	9	2	32	2	-,-
Hendry	21.4	0	84	3	-,-	12.4	3	30	6	-,-
Thomson	6	1	29	0	-,-					
Lansdown	10	1	53	0	-,-					
Ryder	5	0	27	1	-,-					
Millar	3	0	24	0	-,-					
Ransford	3	0	18	1	-,-					

FALL OF WICKETS				
	VIC	SA	VIC	SA
Wkt	1st	1st	2nd	2nd
1st	36	55	64	22
2nd	74	67	78	28
3rd	132	68	209	29
4th	174	111	432	43
5th	204	124	438	61
6th	217	184	469	61
7th	224	367	530	69
8th	225	431	542	74
9th	232	458	554	83
10th	232	462	604	87

NEW SOUTH WALES v SOUTH AUSTRALIA (Shield Match 5)

Played at Sydney Cricket Ground on January 11, 12, 13, 14, 15, 16, 1926. (Timeless match)
Toss : New South Wales.   Result : NEW SOUTH WALES WON BY 541 RUNS.
Debuts: Nil.
12th Men: C.D.Seddon (NSW) and G.W.Harris (SA).
Umpires: A.C.Jones and E.R.Kent.
Attendances: 9431, 9186, 6546, 5941, 5806, 7993.   Total: 44,903.   Receipts: £2905.
Close of Play: 1st day NSW 4/339 (Kelleway 12, Taylor 5); 2nd day SA 1/29 (Rundell 15); 3rd day SA 7/402 (A.J.Richardson 122, Grimmett 4); 4th day NSW (2) 3/294 (Kippax 41, Kelleway 35); 5th day SA (2) 1/27 (Rundell 10, Murray 13).

This match produced 1929 runs, the record aggregate for any first-class match in Australia. Grimmett conceded the record number of runs by a bowler (394) and bowled more balls (848) than any other player in such a match. A high rate of scoring was maintained throughout, the chief run-makers being (for New South Wales): Collins (108 in 183 minutes, 10 fours, chances at 13, 20 and 88), Bardsley (chanceless 159 in 285 minutes, 15 fours), Kelleway (chanceless 111 in 230 minutes, 13 fours), Andrews (98 in 179 minutes, 11 fours) and Punch (47 not out in 80 minutes, 7 fours) in the first innings and Collins (84 in 160 minutes, 4 fours), Macartney (113 in 131 minutes, 12 fours, possible stumping chance off Grimmett at 44), Kippax (71 in 138 minutes, 9 fours), Kelleway (75 in 162 minutes, 4 fours), Taylor (82 in 146 minutes, 10 fours) and Andrews (72 in 146 minutes, 7 fours) in the second innings, and (for South Australia) Vic Richardson (chanceless 107 in 126 minutes, 16 fours), Arthur Richardson (chanceless 153 in 275 minutes, 15 fours) and Alexander (59 in 108 minutes, 7 fours). Arthur Richardson was handicapped during his century innings by an ankle that he had slightly sprained in the field on the previous day. More than 15,000 spectators watched the finish after lunch on the sixth day, the last wicket falling at 3.00pm. It ensured New South Wales of their 17th title in the Sheffield Shield competition (now in its 30th season). J.M.Gregory and H.O.Rock were unavailable for selection and O.P.Asher and A.E.Scanes (also unavailable) were replaced in the New South Wales twelve by Punch and Seddon respectively. Last first-class appearance by W.J.Whitty. *Wisden* and *O'Reilly* incorrectly give NSW (1) Whitty 0/88, A.J.Richardson 2/113. *Wisden* and *NSWCA Report* give incorrect match dates; the game was scheduled to commence on January 8th but was delayed due to the late finish to the Vic v SA match. Sources: *Wisden, C.B.O'Reilly, NSWCA Report, Sydney Morning Herald, Sydney Referee, South Australian Register.*

NEW SOUTH WALES

*H.L.Collins	st Parry b Grimmett	108	b Grimmett		84
W.Bardsley	b A.J.Richardson	159	c V.Y.Richardson b Whitty		13
C.G.Macartney	c Whitty b Scott	20	c Parry b Grimmett		113
A.F.Kippax	c Scott b A.J.Richardson	21	b Whitty		71
C.Kelleway	b Grimmett	111	c Scott b Grimmett		75
J.M.Taylor	c V.Y.Richardson b Scott	5	c & b A.J.Richardson		82
T.J.E.Andrews	run out (Pritchard)	98	b A.J.Richardson		72
A.T.E.Punch	not out	47	c A.J.Richardson b Grimmett		26
†W.A.S.Oldfield	b Grimmett	17	b Grimmett		19
A.A.Mailey	st Parry b Grimmett	6	not out		15
S.C.Everett	b Scott	19	b Grimmett		11
Extras	(b13, lb6, w3, nb9)	31	(b7, lb 4, w1)		12
Total	(154.1 overs, 598 mins)	642	(147.0 overs, 523 mins)		593

SOUTH AUSTRALIA

†C.N.Parry	c Oldfield b Everett	13		b Everett	1
P.D.Rundell	c Everett b Kelleway	25		b Mailey	52
J.W.Rymill	c Collins b Everett	23	(7)	not out	52
V.Y.Richardson	b Kelleway	107		c Everett b Kelleway	27
D.E.Pritchard	c Punch b Macartney	10	(6)	c Macartney b Mailey	27
*A.J.Richardson	c Punch b Macartney	153	(5)	b Macartney	7
W.C.Alexander	c Kelleway b Kippax	59		absent ill	
J.T.Murray	st Oldfield b Andrews	29	(3)	c Oldfield b Everett	31
C.V.Grimmett	c Kelleway b Andrews	32	(8)	c Collins b Mailey	0
J.D.Scott	c Bardsley b Andrews	1	(9)	c Macartney b Mailey	1
W.J.Whitty	not out	12	(10)	run out (Kelleway)	11
Extras	(b1, lb3, nb7)	11		(b2, lb5, nb3)	10
Total	(99.1 overs, 381 mins)	475		(49.1 overs, 187 mins)	219

SOUTH AUSTRALIA	O	M	R	W	w,nb		O	M	R	W	w,nb
Scott	34.1	2	190	3	3,8		30	3	155	0	1,-
Whitty	26	6	89	0	-,-		20	1	99	2	-,-
A.J.Richardson	34	2	112	2	,1	(5)	29	11	35	2	-,-
Grimmett	51	7	192	4	-,-		55	7	202	6	-,-
Murray	8	0	24	0	-,-	(3)	12	0	80	0	-,-
Rundell	1	0	4	0	-,-		1	0	10	0	-,-

NEW SOUTH WALES	O	M	R	W	w,nb	O	M	R	W	w,nb
Everett	19	1	101	2	-,4	10	2	32	2	-,-
Kelleway	20	1	83	2	-,3	10	1	41	1	-,3
Macartney	24	4	83	2	-,-	7.1	1	40	1	-,-
Mailey	23	1	103	0	-,-	22	4	96	4	-,-
Punch	2	0	16	0	-,-					
Kippax	7	0	44	1	-,-					
Andrews	4.1	0	34	3	-,-					

FALL OF WICKETS

Wkt	NSW 1st	SA 1st	NSW 2nd	SA 2nd
1st	203	29	34	4
2nd	254	55	210	52
3rd	322	78	215	120
4th	325	104	354	130
5th	340	219	384	138
6th	534	337	519	164
7th	554	387	522	165
8th	590	461	556	171
9th	612	463	573	219
10th	642	475	593	-

NEW SOUTH WALES v VICTORIA (Shield Match 6)

Played at Sydney Cricket Ground on January 23, 25, 26, 27, 1926. (Timeless match)
Toss : Victoria.   Result : NEW SOUTH WALES WON BY AN INNINGS AND 96 RUNS.
Debuts: Nil.
12th Men: N.E.Phillips (NSW) and P.H.Wallace (Vic).
Umpires: M.Carney and A.P.Williams.
Attendances: 21507, 11648, 20317, 2680.   Total: 56,152.   Receipts: £4134.
Close of Play: 1st day Vic 290 all out; 2nd day NSW 3/372 (Kippax 105, Kelleway 49); 3rd day Vic (2) 2/72 (Ponsford 43, Ellis 2).

Kippax dominated the match with an unbeaten 271, scored in 432 minutes with 30 fours. He shared century stands with Collins (143 in 204 minutes, 14 fours), Kelleway (68 in 126 minutes, 5 fours) and Oldfield for the New South Wales third, fourth and eighth wickets. Ponsford (79 in 156 minutes, 3 fours), Ryder (49 in 75 minutes, 5 fours) and Baring (70 in 131 minutes, 9 fours) batted well on the first day for Victoria. In the second innings Ponsford (138 in 195 minutes, 11 fours) and Woodfull (126 in 168 minutes, 8 fours) combined for a fourth-wicket partnership of 178, but of the others only Love reached double figures. Rayson replaced A.E.V.Hartkopf (unavailable) in the Victorian side while J.M.Taylor was unavailable for New South Wales. *Wisden* incorrectly gives NSW Rock c Hendry b Rayson, Ryder 1/117, Blackie 0/144, Rayson 4/148. Sources: *Wisden, NSWCA Report, VCA Report, The Argus, Sydney Morning Herald, Sydney Referee, Sydney Daily Telegraph.*

VICTORIA

W.M.Woodfull	b Everett	15	(5) b Everett		126
W.H.Ponsford	b Kelleway	79	b Everett		138
H.S.T.L.Hendry	c Oldfield b Everett	9	(6) st Oldfield b Mailey		1
*J.Ryder	run out (Andrews/Oldfield)	49	(1) b Kelleway		5
H.S.B.Love	b Everett	16	(3) lbw b Everett		22
F.A.Baring	b Mailey	70	(7) c Oldfield b Everett		0
V.S.Ransford	b Everett	3	(8) run out (Macartney/Oldfield)		0
A.E.Liddicut	lbw b Macartney	28	(9) st Oldfield b Mailey		6
†J.L.Ellis	b Mailey	9	(4) b Gregory		7
W.J.Rayson	b Macartney	7	not out		3
D.D.Blackie	not out	0	b Everett		8
Extras	(b2, lb2, nb1)	5	(b4, nb2)		6
Total	(82.3 overs, 305 mins)	290	(66.6 overs, 257 mins)		322

NEW SOUTH WALES

*H.L.Collins	c Love b Baring	143
W.Bardsley	c Blackie b Rayson	28
C.G.Macartney	c Ransford b Rayson	36
A.F.Kippax	not out	271
C.Kelleway	c Ellis b Blackie	68
T.J.E.Andrews	b Rayson	22
H.O.Rock	c Hendry b Blackie	39
J.M.Gregory	c Woodfull b Hendry	21
†W.A.S.Oldfield	run out (Love/Ellis)	49
A.A.Mailey	b Hendry	0
S.C.Everett	st Ellis b Hendry	0
Extras	(b26, lb2, w2, nb1)	31
Total	(156.5 overs, 558 mins)	708

NEW SOUTH WALES	O	M	R	W	w,nb		O	M	R	W	w,nb
Gregory	13	0	50	0	-,-		12	0	67	1	-,-
Kelleway	19	5	40	1	-,1		13	1	42	1	-,-
Mailey	21	1	95	2	-,-	(4)	17	1	94	2	-,-
Everett	15	3	57	4	-,-	(3)	16.6	1	91	5	-,2
Macartney	14.3	0	43	2	-,-		8	0	22	0	-,-

VICTORIA	O	M	R	W	w,nb
Ryder	25	1	117	0	-,1
Blackie	34	4	144	2	-,-
Hendry	30.5	1	122	3	-,-
Rayson	30	0	148	3	1,-
Baring	9	0	41	1	-,-
Ransford	6	0	28	0	-,-
Liddicut	22	3	77	0	1,-

	FALL OF WICKETS		
	VIC	NSW	VIC
Wkt	1st	1st	2nd
1st	36	98	9
2nd	68	160	58
3rd	156	260	79
4th	156	420	257
5th	187	465	262
6th	203	533	273
7th	267	560	282
8th	273	708	304
9th	284	708	310
10th	290	708	322

QUEENSLAND v SOUTH AUSTRALIA

Played at Exhibition Ground, Brisbane, on January 23, 25, 26, 1926. (Three-day match)
Toss : South Australia.   Result : SOUTH AUSTRALIA WON BY 44 RUNS.
Debuts: Queensland - E.C.Knowles (f/c); A.D.A.Mayes (Qld only).
12th Men: M.Biggs (Qld). No 12th named for SA.
Umpires: W.H.Carvosso and A.E.Wyeth.
Attendances: 12000, 6000, 6000.   Total: About 24,000.   Receipts: £1586.
Close of Play: 1st day Qld 4/107 (R.K.Oxenham 46, Higgins 19); 2nd day SA (2) 8/160 (Grimmett 4, Scott 4).

J.T.Murray, J.W.Rymill and W.J.Whitty all returned to Adelaide after the match in Sydney. W.Rowe and F.C.Thompson were unavailable for Queensland. In a low-scoring contest A.J.Richardson (71 in 106 minutes, 9 fours) made the equal-highest score on the first day and was supported by McKay (30 not out in 76 minutes, 1 four). O'Connor fell to the fifth ball of Queensland's first innings, R.K.Oxenham (65 in 174 minutes, 4 fours) topscoring. A.J.Richardson took the wickets of Mayes and Noyes with successive balls. Pritchard's second-innings 71 occupied 109 minutes and included 8 fours. R.K.Oxenham (34 in 134 minutes, 1 four), Mayes (36 in 55 minutes, 1 six and 3 fours) and O'Connor (26 in 84 minutes, 2 fours) made the best contributions to Queensland's second innings. Mayes (ex-New South Wales) was playing his first match for his native State. *Cricketer* and *O'Reilly* incorrectly give Qld (1) Higgins c V.Y.Richardson. Sources: *The Cricketer, C.B.O'Reilly, QCA Report, SACA Report, Brisbane Courier, Brisbane Daily Mail, Maryborough Chronicle.*

SOUTH AUSTRALIA

A.J.Richardson	b Hornibrook	13	c O'Connor b R.K.Oxenham	38
G.W.Harris	lbw b Hornibrook	4	c Mayes b Noyes	5
D.E.Pritchard	c Hutcheon b Hornibrook	22	c Sim b Mayes	71
*V.Y.Richardson	lbw b Sim	71	c Sim b Noyes	24
W.C.Alexander	c Hutcheon b R.K.Oxenham	7	b Mayes	0
P.D.Rundell	c O'Connor b R.K.Oxenham	10	c Hornibrook b Noyes	4
D.G.McKay	not out	30	c O'Connor b Noyes	7
C.V.Grimmett	c O'Connor b Sim	7	b Hornibrook	23
†C.N.Parry	lbw b Sim	1	c Hornibrook b Mayes	0
J.D.Scott	b Hornibrook	20	b R.K.Oxenham	21
G.H.Palmer	run out	8	not out	0
Extras	(lb5)	5	(lb7)	7
Total	(53.0 overs, 203 mins)	198	(58.3 overs, 226 mins)	200

QUEENSLAND

*†L.P.D.O'Connor	c McKay b Scott	3	(3) lbw b A.J.Richardson	26
N.C.Beeston	c Scott b A.J.Richardson	7	(6) c & b Grimmett	12
R.K.Oxenham	c Parry b Scott	65	(1) b Grimmett	34
L.E.Oxenham	b Scott	26	b A.J.Richardson	2
E.H.Hutcheon	c Parry b Scott	0	b Scott	10
H.J.R.Higgins	c Pritchard b Grimmett	27	(2) b Scott	6
E.C.Knowles	st Parry b Grimmett	8	b Scott	11
A.D.A.Mayes	c & b A.J.Richardson	2	c Alexander b A.J.Richardson	36
H.D.Noyes	c Pritchard b A.J.Richardson	0	c Parry b Scott	3
P.M.Hornibrook	b Grimmett	30	b A.J.Richardson	16
C.V.Sim	not out	4	not out	0
Extras	(b5, lb4, nb2)	11	(b5, lb6, nb4)	15
Total	(57.6 overs, 212 mins)	183	(61.5 overs, 215 mins)	171

QUEENSLAND	O	M	R	W	w,nb		O	M	R	W	w,nb
Hornibrook	15	0	61	4	-,-		12	0	51	1	-,-
Noyes	6	0	23	0	-,-		19	8	60	4	-,-
Mayes	9	2	33	0	-,-	(4)	13	3	38	3	-,-
R.K.Oxenham	14	2	29	2	-,-	(3)	14.3	4	44	2	-,-
Sim	9	2	47	3	-,-						

SOUTH AUSTRALIA	O	M	R	W	w,nb		O	M	R	W	w,nb
Scott	18	3	54	4	-,1		13	1	44	4	-,3
Palmer	2	0	11	0	-,-	(4)	2	0	3	0	-,-
A.J.Richardson	13	4	30	3	-,1	(2)	20.5	8	32	4	-,1
Grimmett	24.6	2	77	3	-,-	(3)	26	9	77	2	-,-

FALL OF WICKETS

Wkt	SA 1st	QLD 1st	SA 2nd	QLD 2nd
1st	13	4	12	13
2nd	18	33	86	68
3rd	57	84	141	72
4th	76	86	141	80
5th	130	117	141	90
6th	130	135	146	106
7th	144	138	153	108
8th	146	138	156	116
9th	183	151	198	170
10th	198	183	200	171

TASMANIA v AUSTRALIAN XI

Played at N.T.C.A. Ground, Launceston, on February 27, March 1, 2, 1926. (Three-day match)
Toss : Tasmania.   Result : AUSTRALIAN XI WON BY AN INNINGS AND 175 RUNS.
Debuts: Tasmania - C.L.Lee, D.M.S.Wardlaw, R.Wilkins (all f/c).
12th Men: A.O.Burrows (Tas) and S.C.Everett (Aust).
Umpires: G.S.Pennefather and F.C.Tabart.
Attendances: 3500, 2000, 500.   Total: About 6000.   Receipts: £450.
Close of Play: 1st day Aust 3/187 (Macartney 66, Taylor 5); 2nd day Tas (2) 6/159 (Martin 47, Newton 23).

The first of three matches played by the Australians on their way to England. After dismissing Tasmania in under two hours, the Test batsmen piled on runs at nearly eight an over. Woodfull (148 in 100 minutes, 15 fours) scored 88 before lunch on the second day while Macartney (66 in 73 minutes, 9 fours), Ponsford (62 in 44 minutes, 9 fours) and Taylor (66 in 79 minutes, 1 six and 6 fours) all compiled rapid fifties. Gregory however was out first ball. Allan (37 in 66 minutes, 1 four), Martin (52 in 69 minutes, 6 fours) and Newton (36 not out in 56 minutes) stood out in Tasmania's second innings, Mailey completing a ten-wicket haul. Davis, who topscored in the first innings with 37 in 46 minutes (1 six and 3 fours), faced only three balls in the second. Sources: *The Cricketer, Launceston Examiner, Hobart Mercury.*

TASMANIA

*G.H.Allan	st Ellis b Macartney	18	b Gregory		37
R.Wilkins	b Ryder	4	c Gregory b Mailey		16
A.P.Findlay	c Ellis b Gregory	3	b Gregory		10
G.W.Martin	c Gregory b Mailey	7	lbw b Mailey		52
N.W.Davis	c Ellis b Mailey	37	b Gregory		0
H.C.Smith	b Mailey	0	(7) run out (Woodfull/Ellis)		0
A.C.Newton	b Mailey	3	(8) not out		36
C.L.Lee	not out	19	(6) c Ellis b Mailey		14
†P.G.Henty	b Macartney	4	(10) st Ellis b Mailey		6
A.H.Davis	st Ellis b Mailey	4	(9) b Gregory		3
D.M.S.Wardlaw	b Macartney	1	st Ellis b Mailey		4
Extras	(b3, lb1)	4	(b8, lb9, nb1)		18
Total	(31.2 overs, 114 mins)	104	(47.5 overs, 170 mins)		196

AUSTRALIAN XI

*H.L.Collins	c Findlay b Newton	24
A.J.Richardson	c N.W.Davis b Newton	20
C.G.Macartney	c Allan b A.H.Davis	66
W.H.Ponsford	c Lee b Allan	62
J.M.Taylor	c Allan b Wilkins	66
W.M.Woodfull	c Newton b Allan	148
T.J.E.Andrews	c Martin b Wardlaw	48
J.Ryder	b Newton	14
J.M.Gregory	c Lee b Newton	0
†J.L.Ellis	not out	5
A.A.Mailey	st Henty b Wardlaw	2
Extras	(b4, lb9, w4, nb3)	20
Total	(61.4 overs, 230 mins)	475

AUSTRALIAN XI	O	M	R	W	w,nb		O	M	R	W	w,nb
Gregory	6	1	16	1	-,-		17	0	90	4	-,-
Ryder	4	0	6	1	-,-		2	0	10	0	-,1
Mailey	11	1	46	5	-,-		20.5	2	69	5	-,-
Richardson	4	0	16	0	-,-						
Macartney	6.2	3	16	3	-,-	(4)	7	4	3	0	-,-
Andrews						(5)	1	0	6	0	-,-

TASMANIA	O	M	R	W	w,nb
Newton	18	1	96	4	-,-
A.H.Davis	17	0	107	1	-,-
Wardlaw	9.4	0	88	2	-,2
Findlay	7	0	62	0	-,-
Lee	2	0	25	0	-,-
Allan	6	0	51	2	-,-
Wilkins	2	0	26	1	4,1

FALL OF WICKETS

	TAS	AUST	TAS
Wkt	1st	1st	2nd
1st	12	40	61
2nd	15	55	67
3rd	22	168	89
4th	62	188	89
5th	63	330	110
6th	74	430	110
7th	83	460	170
8th	98	460	183
9th	103	466	190
10th	104	475	196

TASMANIA v AUSTRALIAN XI

Played at T.C.A. Ground, Hobart, on March 4, 5, 6, 1926. (Three-day match)
Toss : Tasmania.   Result : AUSTRALIAN XI WON BY AN INNINGS AND 184 RUNS.
Debuts: Tasmania - A.E.Watson (f/c).
12th Men: A.W.Rushforth (Tas) and C.V.Grimmett (Aust).
Umpires: M.Leonard and A.O'Leary.
Attendances: 4000, 3000, 1000.   Total: About 8000.   Receipts: £494.
Close of Play: 1st day Aust 2/128 (Bardsley 62, Woodfull 38); 2nd day Tas (2) 1/15 (Bennett 11).

Bardsley (124 in 199 minutes) added 108 for the third wicket with Woodfull (64 in 69 minutes, 5 fours) and 106 for the sixth wicket with Macartney (163 not out in 186 minutes, 20 fours, chance at 7). Macartney and Everett (2 sixes and 12 fours) shared a tenth-wicket stand of 147 in just 62 minutes. Green topscored for Tasmania with 40 in 112 minutes including 3 fours in the first innings. Martin (35 minutes, 5 fours) and Newton (44 minutes, 6 fours) each scored 33 in the second innings. An exhibition innings occupying 90 minutes was given by Australia after the conclusion of the match. Score: 1/224 (Richardson 100 in 53 minutes, 2 sixes and 12 fours, Woodfull 78*, Andrews 43*. Sources: *The Cricketer, Launceston Examiner, Hobart Mercury.*

TASMANIA

Batsman	Dismissal 1	Score	Dismissal 2	Score
*†R.L.Bennett	run out (Richardson/Ellis)	0	c Everett b Mailey	17
R.Wilkins	b Everett	20	lbw b Richardson	3
D.C.Green	b Macartney	40	st Ellis b Mailey	11
G.W.Martin	b Everett	5	c & b Everett	33
A.P.Findlay	c Ellis b Richardson	14	c Ellis b Everett	8
H.C.Smith	lbw b Richardson	18	st Ellis b Mailey	4
A.C.Newton	c Richardson b Mailey	15	b Andrews	33
A.E.Watson	c Collins b Mailey	28	st Ellis b Andrews	4
A.O.Burrows	run out (Mailey/Ellis)	0	b Richardson	3
A.K.E.Watt	not out	8	not out	0
D.M.S.Wardlaw	st Ellis b Mailey	16	c Macartney b Andrews	0
Extras	(b5, lb3, w1, nb4)	13	(b1, lb1, nb5)	7
Total	(50.2 overs, 184 mins)	187	(32.0 overs, 126 mins)	123

AUSTRALIAN XI

Batsman	Dismissal	Score
*H.L.Collins	c Findlay b Newton	7
W.Bardsley	run out (Wilkins/Bennett)	124
W.H.Ponsford	c Bennett b Watt	17
W.M.Woodfull	c Bennett b Watson	64
J.M.Gregory	lbw b Newton	8
T.J.E.Andrews	b Watson	1
C.G.Macartney	not out	163
A.J.Richardson	c Bennett b Newton	8
†J.L.Ellis	b Watson	6
A.A.Mailey	run out (/Findlay)	5
S.C.Everett	c Martin b Watson	77
Extras	(b6, lb5, nb3)	14
Total	(80.5 overs, 315 mins)	494

AUSTRALIAN XI	O	M	R	W	w,nb		O	M	R	W	w,nb
Gregory	9	1	26	0	-,1	(4)	4	0	16	0	-,-
Everett	9	2	33	2	1,3	(5)	6	4	13	2	-,2
Mailey	18.2	1	62	3	-,-		10	1	43	3	-,-
Richardson	8	1	25	2	-,-	(2)	6	3	8	2	-,-
Macartney	6	2	28	1	-,-						
Collins						(1)	2	0	12	0	-,1
Andrews						(6)	4	0	24	3	-,2

TASMANIA	O	M	R	W	w,nb
Newton	26	3	156	3	-,-
Watson	21.5	1	95	4	-,-
Watt	6	0	61	1	-,-
Burrows	12	0	78	0	-,-
Wardlaw	9	0	44	0	-,3
Findlay	4	0	42	0	-,-
Martin	2	0	4	0	-,-

FALL OF WICKETS

Wkt	TAS 1st	AUST 1st	TAS 2nd
1st	35	16	15
2nd	44	58	23
3rd	57	166	67
4th	76	181	67
5th	105	185	71
6th	128	291	90
7th	153	301	100
8th	156	312	109
9th	170	347	123
10th	187	494	123

WESTERN AUSTRALIA v AUSTRALIAN XI

Played at W.A.C.A. Ground, Perth, on March 12, 13, 15, 1926. (Three-day match)
Toss : Australian XI.   Result : AUSTRALIAN XI WON BY AN INNINGS AND 45 RUNS.
Debuts: Western Australia - H.W.Harrold, A.E.C.Smith (both f/c).
12th Men: R.J.Bryant (WA) and A.A.Mailey (Aust).
Umpires: C.Sinclair and E.Walker.
Attendances: 4000, 11000, 2000.   Total: About 17,000.   Receipts: About £1550 (£894 Net).
Close of Play: 1st day WA 7/220 (Freemantle 76, Evans 9); 2nd day Aust 7/337 (Richardson 13, Everett 8).

Play began at 12.25pm on the first day because the *Great Western* express had arrived 80 minutes late from Kalgoorlie. Freemantle batted 126 minutes and hit 2 sixes and 9 fours in making the highest score for Western Australia in the match. Taylor (160 minutes, 3 sixes and 12 fours) survived two chances to partner Ponsford (140 minutes, 1 six and 2 fours) in a fourth wicket stand of 234. The attendance and takings of £1034 on the second day were a new record for the ground. *Cricketer* incorrectly gives WA (1) Drew c Hendry; Aust 9/424 dec. when in fact all out due to Grimmett (groin strain) being unable to bat. Sources: *The Cricketer, The West Australian, Daily News.*

WESTERN AUSTRALIA

P.F.Quinlan	b Grimmett	12		b Hendry	5
F.H.Taaffe	st Ellis b Richardson	28		c Ellis b Ryder	13
A.D.Drew	lbw b Richardson	34		b Ryder	5
A.E.C.Smith	c Everett b Richardson	14		c Ponsford b Richardson	16
H.J.Herbert	c & b Grimmett	0	(7)	b Ryder	12
*S.H.D.Rowe	b Andrews	24	(5)	b Everett	12
L.F.Freemantle	b Richardson	87	(6)	b Everett	9
M.Inverarity	b Grimmett	10		b Everett	0
W.A.Evans	c Hendry b Richardson	33		c Ponsford b Everett	10
†R.H.Hewson	lbw b Richardson	0		not out	6
H.W.Harrold	not out	21		lbw b Ryder	0
Extras	(b12, lb6, w1)	19		(b8, lb1)	9
Total	(92.3 overs, 297 mins)	282		(42.6 overs, 165 mins)	97

AUSTRALIAN XI

*H.L.Collins	c Freemantle b Harrold	13
J.Ryder	lbw b Harrold	37
W.M.Woodfull	run out (Inverarity/Hewson)	0
J.M.Taylor	lbw b Herbert	149
W.H.Ponsford	c Drew b Inverarity	102
T.J.E.Andrews	c Freemantle b Inverarity	6
H.S.T.L.Hendry	b Herbert	8
A.J.Richardson	st Hewson b Freemantle	49
S.C.Everett	c Freemantle b Inverarity	15
†J.L.Ellis	not out	41
C.V.Grimmett	absent hurt	-
Extras	(b2, lb2)	4
Total	(81.4 overs, 314 mins)	424

AUSTRALIAN XI	O	M	R	W	w,nb		O	M	R	W	w,nb
Everett	9	3	27	0	-,-		12	1	30	4	-,-
Hendry	10	1	21	0	-,-		5	3	7	1	-,-
Richardson	25.3	5	71	6	-,-	(4)	13	4	21	1	-,-
Grimmett	33	6	88	3	-,-						
Collins	4	0	12	0	1,-		3	1	3	0	-,-
Andrews	6	1	35	1	-,-		3	0	13	0	-,-
Ryder	5	0	9	0	-,-	(3)	6.6	2	14	4	-,-

WESTERN AUSTRALIA	O	M	R	W	w,nb
Harrold	21	1	89	2	-,-
Evans	18	3	60	0	-,-
Taaffe	5	0	26	0	-,-
Freemantle	15.4	0	97	1	-,-
Inverarity	17	0	118	3	-,-
Herbert	5	0	30	2	-,-

FALL OF WICKETS

Wkt	WA 1st	AUST 1st	WA 2nd
1st	25	47	13
2nd	50	50	19
3rd	74	50	34
4th	75	284	40
5th	110	303	67
6th	130	313	72
7th	183	319	72
8th	253	350	88
9th	257	424	97
10th	282	-	97

Queensland participated in the Sheffield Shield competition for the first time, ending a 20-year struggle to gain admission. In granting their entry, the Interstate Conference of the Board of Control decreed that Queensland would play New South Wales and Victoria twice, but would meet South Australia only once. Travelling costs were reportedly the reason for the imbalance of fixtures, which lasted for one season only. Queensland's better-than-expected performances led to a full program of matches from 1927-28.

The odd number of matches led the authorities to amend the method of determining the winner of the Sheffield Shield. Points were scrapped, placings being decided instead by percentage of victories from matches played. South Australia won the competition for the first time since 1912-13, ending a long run of mediocre performances since the war. Their batting stalwarts, Arthur and Victor Richardson, received excellent support from Schneider, Alexander and Rymill, but the crucial factor was the improved legspin bowling of Grimmett and Williams, who invariably led the wicket-taking in their matches. The offspinner, Lee, joined them late in the season.

New South Wales and Victoria both won three of their six engagements. Victoria had the opportunity to claim the Shield by winning either of their final two matches but, handicapped by the unavailability of several key players, they lost both by substantial margins. Their total of 1107 against New South Wales at Melbourne - a record in all first-class cricket - was compiled in astonishingly quick time, over the Christmas break. The Victorian batting, led by Ponsford who became the first to score 1000 runs in Shield matches alone, was probably the strongest in the competition, but their bowling hopes rested with Blackie and to a lesser extent Morton.

New South Wales played without the services of former stalwarts Bardsley, Collins, Gregory and Kelleway, but were still a formidable combination. Andrews, Macartney and Kippax continued to score heavily and they were joined by new players, Morgan, Jackson, Steele and Phillips. The 17-year-old Jackson created a great impression with his stylish and effortless strokeplay. McNamee headed the bowling aggregates in his first season.

Queensland enjoyed a creditable first season in the competition, winning two of their five contests. Their inaugural match, against New South Wales at Brisbane, was a memorable affair. Set 400 to win, they failed by only 9 runs to achieve the target when O'Connor, the captain, was run out, having contributed an innings of 196. The veterans O'Connor, Ron Oxenham and Thompson, led the way with bat and ball and were the chief architects in their two victories. O'Connor compiled three centuries in four innings against New South Wales. He was a highly competent wicket-keeper and a sound leader.

A match between the 1926 Australians and The Rest was staged at Sydney as a benefit for C.G.Macartney. The Australian XI remained on top throughout the game and won it comfortably despite centuries from Kippax and O'Connor for The Rest.

The first-class program was rounded off with a match between Victoria and Tasmania at Melbourne and a visit by South Australia to Perth which incorporated two games against Western Australia.

Leading Aggregates

Batsmen	M	I	NO	Runs	HS	Ave.	Bowlers	Runs	Wkts	Ave.
W.H.Ponsford (V)	6	10	0	1229	352	122.90	N.L.Williams (SA)	1121	35	32.02
A.F.Kippax (NSW)	7	13	1	1039	217*	86.58	D.D.Blackie (V)	813	33	24.63
H.S.T.L.Hendry (V)	6	10	0	780	177	78.00	R.L.A.McNamee (NSW)	973	32	30.40
L.P.D.O'Connor (Q)	6	12	1	731	196	66.45	C.V.Grimmett (SA)	1030	30	34.33
V.Y.Richardson (SA)	8	15	1	727	157	51.92	F.L.Morton (V)	800	23	34.78
A.J.Richardson (SA)	7	13	0	662	232	50.92	A.A.Mailey (NSW)	841	20	42.05
K.J.Schneider (SA)	7	13	1	605	146	50.41				
R.K.Oxenham (Q)	5	10	1	514	134*	57.11				
A.Jackson (NSW)	7	13	3	500	104*	50.00				

SHEFFIELD SHIELD TABLE

	P	W	L	D	%	Quotient	Runs Scored	Wkts Lost	Runs Conceded	Wkts Taken
SOUTH AUSTRALIA	5	3	2	-	60%	1.032	3293	87	3519	96
VICTORIA	6	3	3	-	50%	1.368	4158	100	3252	107
NEW SOUTH WALES	6	3	3	-	50%	0.835	3741	105	4477	105
QUEENSLAND	5	2	3	-	40%	0.845	3456	95	3400	79
TOTAL	11	11	11	-	100%	1.000	14648	387	14648	387

QUEENSLAND v NEW SOUTH WALES (Shield Match 1)

Played at Exhibition Ground, Brisbane on November 26, 27, 29, 30, December 1, 1926. (Timeless match)
Toss : New South Wales.   Result : NEW SOUTH WALES WON BY 8 RUNS.
Debuts: New South Wales - G.S.Amos, A.Jackson, R.L.A.McNamee, C.D.Seddon, H.C.Steele (all f/c).
12th Men: N.C.Beeston (Qld) and J.L.Wall (NSW).
Umpires: J.A.Scott and A.E.Wyeth.
Attendances: 3000, 10000, 3000, 4000, 3000.   Total: About 23,000.   Receipts: £1144.
Close of Play: 1st day Qld 3/134 (Thompson 38, Higgins 35); 2nd day NSW (2) 2/157 (Steele 67, Kippax 53); 3rd day Qld (2) 1/13
    (Higgins 4); 4th day Qld (2) 8/378 (O'Connor 191, Mayes 17).

Queensland's first match in the Sheffield Shield competition produced a close finish. P.M.Hornibrook was unavailable for the historic occasion due to dentistry exams. New South Wales were without their Test players, still en route to Australia after touring England. Osborne replaced A.T.Ratcliffe (unavailable) as wicket-keeper. Highlights included a century in each innings by Kippax (127 in 157 minutes, 21 fours and 131 in 234 minutes, 12 fours) in his first match as captain and a century on debut by Steele (130 in 267 minutes, 9 fours, chances at 42, 79, 92 and 95). Jackson, also making his debut aged 17 years 82 days, scored 86 in 190 minutes, including 7 fours. Thompson (134 in 171 minutes, 14 fours) became Queensland's first Shield century-maker and had support in the lower order from R.K.Oxenham (57 in 64 minutes, 10 fours) in the first innings. O'Connor scored a career-highest 196 (356 minutes, 17 fours) and shared a 135-run partnership with R.K.Oxenham (62 in 106 minutes, 5 fours) in the second innings. Campbell (right-arm leg breaks and googlies) claimed his best innings and match analyses in 11 first-class matches. *Wisden* incorrectly gives NSW (1) Seddon b R.K.Oxenham; Qld (1) Brew st Osborne, Campbell 6/120, Morgan 3/85; Qld (2) Mayes c Kippax. Sources: *Wisden, NSWCA Report, QCA Report, Sydney Morning Herald, Brisbane Courier, Brisbane Daily Mail, Maryborough Chronicle.*

NEW SOUTH WALES

N.E.Phillips	c Gough b Mayes	39		c O'Connor b Gough	32
H.C.Steele	c R.K.Oxenham b Mayes	27		c Brew b Bensted	130
J.G.Morgan	c Rowe b Gough	3		lbw b R.K.Oxenham	0
*A.F.Kippax	c Gough b Mayes	127		c R.K.Oxenham b Bensted	131
A.Jackson	c O'Connor b Gough	5	(6)	run out (/O'Connor)	86
C.D.Seddon	lbw b R.K.Oxenham	6	(5)	b R.K.Oxenham	4
A.E.Scanes	b R.K.Oxenham	38		b Mayes	47
J.N.Campbell	b R.K.Oxenham	0		b Bensted	29
G.S.Amos	b R.K.Oxenham	9		b R.K.Oxenham	1
†R.H.Osborne	c Noyes b Mayes	19		run out (Mayes/R.K.Oxenham)	3
R.L.A.McNamee	not out	0		not out	0
Extras	(b1, lb2, w4)	7		(b5, lb4, w1, nb2)	12
Total	(66.1 overs, 199 mins)	280		(135.3 overs, 435 mins)	475

QUEENSLAND

*†L.P.D.O'Connor	c Morgan b McNamee	18	(3)	run out (Amos)	196
L.E.Oxenham	b Campbell	34	(1)	c Steele b Campbell	8
E.C.Bensted	b Morgan	4	(7)	b McNamee	14
F.C.Thompson	b Morgan	134		b Campbell	2
H.J.R.Higgins	c Osborne b Morgan	36	(2)	c Osborne b Campbell	19
W.Rowe	c Phillips b Campbell	17		c Osborne b Phillips	18
R.K.Oxenham	b Campbell	57	(5)	c Jackson b McNamee	62
F.M.Brew	c Osborne b Campbell	17	(9)	b Campbell	14
F.J.Gough	not out	18	(8)	run out	0
A.D.A.Mayes	c Steele b Campbell	2		c McNamee b Phillips	19
H.D.Noyes	lbw b Campbell	7		not out	4
Extras	(b7, lb5)	12		(b17, lb17, w1)	35
Total	(72.3 overs, 253 mins)	356		(108.0 overs, 361 mins)	391

QUEENSLAND	O	M	R	W	w,nb		O	M	R	W	w,nb
Mayes	15.1	3	53	4	4,-		26	3	67	1	-,1
Noyes	12	1	84	0	-,-		15	0	71	0	-,-
Gough	14	1	82	2	-,-		20	0	84	1	-,-
R.K.Oxenham	20	5	54	4	-,-		30	7	78	3	-,-
Rowe							12	3	23	0	-,-
Thompson							9.3	2	41	0	-,-
Brew							4	0	37	0	-,1
Bensted							19	1	62	3	1,-

NEW SOUTH WALES	O	M	R	W	w,nb		O	M	R	W	w,nb
McNamee	20	2	67	1	-,-		35	5	87	2	-,-
Amos	11	1	60	0	-,-	(4)	6	0	19	0	-,-
Campbell	17.3	1	118	6	-,-	(2)	33	1	162	4	1,-
Morgan	22	2	87	3	-,-	(3)	12	2	30	0	-,-
Phillips	2	0	12	0	-,-	(6)	13	3	28	2	-,-
Kippax						(5)	9	1	30	0	-,-

FALL OF WICKETS

Wkt	NSW 1st	QLD 1st	NSW 2nd	QLD 2nd
1st	49	42	59	13
2nd	67	53	60	71
3rd	73	57	292	79
4th	84	136	297	214
5th	119	177	309	279
6th	198	295	403	309
7th	198	321	448	311
8th	228	339	457	337
9th	263	347	467	381
10th	280	356	475	391

SOUTH AUSTRALIA v VICTORIA (Shield Match 2)

Played at Adelaide Oval on December 3, 4, 6, 7, 8, 1926. (Timeless match)
Toss : Victoria.   Result : SOUTH AUSTRALIA WON BY TWO WICKETS.
Debuts: South Australia - K.J.Schneider (SA only).
12th Men: L.T.Gun (SA) and C.A.H.Sindrey (Vic).
Umpires: G.A.Hele and J.J.Quinn.
Attendances: 5000, 12000, 5000, 5500, 3800.   Total: About 31,300.   Receipts: £1352.
Close of Play: 1st day SA 0/25 (Schneider 17, Parry 6); 2nd day SA 6/334 (Rymill 37); 3rd day Vic (2) 1/181 (Woodfull 84, Hendry 40);
    4th day SA (2) 3/135 (V.Y.Richardson 38, Rymill 13).

S.P.King and K.E.Rigg, both unavailable due to university exams, were replaced in the Victorian twelve by Mitchell and Sindrey. H.S.B.Love and J.Ryder were unavailable for selection due to work commitments. Ponsford (214 in 272 minutes, 1 six and 22 fours, chance at 200) dominated the first day, scoring 67.9 per cent of Victoria's 315. Liddicut was out first ball. Rymill (hand injury) was off the field for a short time on the first day, Gun substituting in his place. Schneider (69 in 218 minutes, 3 fours), V.Y.Richardson (137 in 195 minutes, 18 fours, chance at 39) and Rymill (142 in 226 minutes, 13 fours) gave South Australia a substantial first-innings lead. Richardson completed a fine double in the second innings with 92 in 220 minutes including 7 fours and a chance when 74. Woodfull (84 in 175 minutes, 2 fours), Ponsford (54 in 92 minutes, 3 fours) and Hendry (177 in 235 minutes, 1 six and 11 fours) headed the Victorian second innings. Schneider had played in two matches for Victoria before his South Australia debut at age 21. *Wisden* and *O'Reilly* incorrectly give Vic (2) Mitchell 6, Wallace 6; SA (2) Wallace 0/21, Blackie 3/96. *SACA Report* incorrectly gives SA (1) 6/356; Vic (1) 3/91. Sources: *Wisden, C.B.O'Reilly, VCA Report, SACA Report, The Age, Adelaide Advertiser, South Australian Register.*

VICTORIA

*W.M.Woodfull	run out (Grimmett/Parry)	1	run out (Parry/Pritchard)		84
W.H.Ponsford	c Rymill b Williams	214	b Williams		54
H.S.T.L.Hendry	c Alexander b Williams	30	c V.Y.Richardson b Grimmett		177
C.B.Willis	b Williams	3	b Scott		33
A.E.Liddicut	lbw b Williams	0	b Williams		19
N.F.Mitchell	c Parry b Grimmett	32	c Pritchard b Williams		12
K.J.Millar	st Parry b Grimmett	0	b Williams		6
†J.L.Ellis	c sub (L.T.Gun) b Williams	25	b Williams		12
P.H.Wallace	b Williams	0	run out (Alexander)		0
W.J.Rayson	not out	1	c A.J.Richardson b Grimmett		11
D.D.Blackie	c Scott b A.J.Richardson	0	not out		7
Extras	(b5, lb4)	9	(b3, lb8, w1, nb3)		15
Total	(71.7 overs, 272 mins)	315	(98.3 overs, 337 mins)		430

SOUTH AUSTRALIA

K.J.Schneider	c Woodfull b Blackie	69		c Woodfull b Liddicut	28
†C.N.Parry	c Woodfull b Blackie	8	(10)	not out	5
D.E.Pritchard	b Liddicut	32		st Ellis b Blackie	0
*V.Y.Richardson	lbw b Blackie	137		c Willis b Rayson	92
A.J.Richardson	c & b Blackie	15	(2)	c Wallace b Blackie	47
J.W.Rymill	st Ellis b Blackie	142	(5)	c Ponsford b Blackie	38
W.C.Alexander	b Blackie	26	(6)	b Rayson	2
N.L.Williams	b Wallace	6	(7)	c Ellis b Rayson	1
C.V.Grimmett	c & b Blackie	29	(8)	not out	33
J.D.Scott	run out (Ponsford)	1	(9)	c Willis b Rayson	0
G.H.Palmer	not out	1			
Extras	(lb9, nb6)	15		(b10, lb8, w1, nb2)	21
Total	(123.7 overs, 474 mins)	481		(83.2 overs, 307 mins) (8 wkts)	267

SOUTH AUSTRALIA	O	M	R	W	w,nb		O	M	R	W	w,nb		FALL OF WICKETS			
Scott	15	1	41	0	-,-		16	0	76	1	1,-		VIC	SA	VIC	SA
Palmer	5	0	40	0	-,-		7	0	36	0	-,-	Wkt	1st	1st	2nd	2nd
Grimmett	22	0	110	2	-,-	(5)	31.3	2	107	1	-,-	1st	6	28	98	53
A.J.Richardson	9.7	2	27	1	-,-		17	2	39	0	-,-	2nd	86	73	186	82
Williams	20	1	88	6	-,-	(3)	25	1	146	6	-,3	3rd	94	171	242	93
Schneider							2	0	11	0	-,-	4th	94	219	249	180
												5th	191	294	283	203
VICTORIA	O	M	R	W	w,nb		O	M	R	W	w,nb	6th	191	334	313	205
Wallace	21	3	84	1	-,6		5	0	31	0	1,1	7th	304	356	371	237
Hendry	9	1	48	0	-,-							8th	310	423	391	247
Blackie	51.7	12	159	7	-,-	(2)	41	10	86	3	-,1	9th	315	438	423	-
Liddicut	22	3	73	1	-,-	(3)	20	4	55	1	-,-	10th	315	481	430	-
Rayson	16	0	75	0	-,-	(4)	17.2	1	74	4	-,-					
Millar	4	0	27	0	-,-											

NEW SOUTH WALES v QUEENSLAND (Shield Match 3)

Played at Sydney Cricket Ground on December 6 (no play), 7, 8, 9, 10, 11, 1926. (Timeless match)
Toss : New South Wales.   Result : QUEENSLAND WON BY FIVE WICKETS.
Debuts: New South Wales - R.Loder (f/c). Queensland - L.L.Gill (Qld only).
12th Men: C.D.Seddon (NSW) and F.M.Brew (Qld).
Umpires: W.G.French and A.P.Williams.
Attendances: No play, 5782, 4429, 3434, 3500, 7232.   Total: 24,377.   Receipts: £1518.
Close of Play: 1st day no play; 2nd day Qld 2/48 (L.E.Oxenham 16, Gough 16); 3rd day Qld 6/323 (Rowe 35, R.K.Oxenham 24); 4th-day
    NSW (2) 0/152 (Phillips 71, Steele 69); 5th day NSW (2) 7/557 (Jackson 78, Campbell 2).

Queensland won their first match in the Shield competition at their second attempt after rain delayed the start by a day. R.K.Oxenham suffered a leg strain in his 10th over before lunch, fielded no further in match and had to bat with a runner throughout both innings - Bensted in the first while scoring an unbeaten 134 in 285 minutes with 7 fours, and Brew in the second for 52 in 106 minutes with 9 fours. O'Connor became the first to score a century in each innings for Queensland, 103 in 210 minutes (15 fours) and 143 not out in 239 minutes, (13 fours). Macartney (114 in 139 minutes, 11 fours) was hampered by a leg strain during his innings but his absence after the first day was due to a stiff neck and and shoulder muscles caused by a chill; Kippax (182 in 228 minutes, 22 fours) assumed the captaincy for the remainder. Phillips (144 in 277 minutes, 12 fours), Jackson (100 in 158 minutes, 9 fours - maiden century in his second match aged 17 years 97 days) and Steele (78 in 158 minutes, 2 fours) also scored well. A.E.Scanes was unavailable for New South Wales, Seddon and Wall being omitted from the thirteen before the start. Gill returned to first-class cricket after a 14-year hiatus; he had played for Tasmania before the War. *Wisden* incorrectly gives NSW (1) Macartney 144, Andrews 37. *SMH* incorrectly gives NSW (2) Andrews c Gough. Sources: *Wisden, NSWCA Report, QCA Report, Sydney Morning Herald, Sydney Referee, Sydney Daily Telegraph.*

NEW SOUTH WALES

N.E.Phillips	c & b R.K.Oxenham	12	c O'Connor b Thompson	144
H.C.Steele	c Thompson b R.K.Oxenham	12	c Mayes b Gough	78
*C.G.Macartney	c Mayes b Gill	114	absent ill	-
A.F.Kippax	b R.K.Oxenham	4	(3) b Bensted	182
T.J.E.Andrews	c & b Gill	67	(4) c sub (F.M.Brew) b Mayes	33
A.Jackson	b Gill	4	(5) lbw b Bensted	100
†A.T.Ratcliffe	not out	28	(6) c Higgins b Rowe	6
R.Loder	c Gough b Mayes	4	(7) c O'Connor b Rowe	0
J.G.Morgan	lbw b Bensted	27	(8) c Gough b Gill	7
J.N.Campbell	lbw b Bensted	0	(9) b Bensted	11
R.L.A.McNamee	b Bensted	1	(10) not out	0
Extras	(lb10, w1, nb3)	14	(b11, lb11, w3, nb2)	27
Total	(76.3 overs, 263 mins)	287	(141.1 overs, 476 mins)	588

QUEENSLAND

L.E.Oxenham	b Campbell	60	b McNamee	23
E.C.Bensted	c Campbell b McNamee	10	(7) not out	30
N.C.Beeston	b Macartney	4		
F.J.Gough	c Kippax b McNamee	22		
*†L.P.D.O'Connor	lbw b Campbell	103	(3) not out	143
F.C.Thompson	b Morgan	43	(4) c McNamee b Morgan	31
W.Rowe	run out (Andrews)	65	(5) c Morgan b Phillips	3
R.K.Oxenham	not out	134	(6) b Phillips	52
L.L.Gill	lbw b Morgan	54	(2) c Ratcliffe b McNamee	8
H.J.R.Higgins	c & b Morgan	9		
A.D.A.Mayes	c Loder b Morgan	26		
Extras	(b32, lb10, w3, nb2)	47	(b6, lb1, w2, nb1)	10
Total	(179.5 overs, 550 mins)	577	(84.3 overs, 255 mins) (5 wkts)	300

QUEENSLAND	O	M	R	W	w,nb		O	M	R	W	w,nb
Mayes	29	6	85	1	-,3		27	0	122	1	-,2
Gill	22	3	89	3	-,-		20	1	83	1	1,-
R.K.Oxenham	9.4	2	29	3	-,-						
Bensted	5.7	1	26	3	1,-		20.1	2	68	3	-,-
Gough	4	0	29	0	-,-	(6)	14	0	74	1	-,-
Rowe	4	1	13	0	-,-	(5)	31	3	112	2	-,-
Thompson	2	1	2	0	-,-	(3)	21	1	76	1	1,-
Higgins						(7)	6	0	22	0	1,-
L.E.Oxenham						(8)	2	0	4	0	-,-

NEW SOUTH WALES	O	M	R	W	w,nb		O	M	R	W	w,nb
McNamee	53	15	118	2	2,1		23	3	55	2	1,1
Macartney	8	1	20	1	-,1						
Campbell	42	4	176	2	1,-		14	0	75	0	-,-
Morgan	32.5	5	110	4	-,-	(2)	29.3	6	100	1	1,-
Phillips	26	2	58	0	-,-	(4)	16	3	50	2	-,-
Kippax	11	2	42	0	-,-						
Steele	7	4	6	0	-,-	(5)	2	0	10	0	-,-

FALL OF WICKETS				
	NSW	QLD	NSW	QLD
Wkt	1st	1st	2nd	2nd
1st	22	24	186	17
2nd	31	31	324	60
3rd	37	56	401	121
4th	213	156	502	132
5th	223	223	512	234
6th	227	268	516	-
7th	242	401	553	-
8th	285	515	587	-
9th	285	533	588	-
10th	287	577	-	-

VICTORIA v QUEENSLAND (Shield Match 4)

Played at Melbourne Cricket Ground on December 17 (no play), 18, 20, 21, 22, 1926. (Timeless match)
Toss : Queensland.   Result : VICTORIA WON BY AN INNINGS AND 169 RUNS.
Debuts: Victoria - S.P.King, K.E.Rigg (both f/c); F.L.Morton (Vic only).
12th Men: N.F.Mitchell (Vic) and J.K.Farquhar (Qld).
Umpires: F.W.Dixon and P.E.Smith.
Attendances: No play, 14804, 8559, 4369, ? .   Total: About 29,000.   Receipts: £1169.
Close of Play: 1st day no play; 2nd day Vic 0/108 (Woodfull 50, Ponsford 58); 3rd day Vic 7/511 (King 39, Ellis 1); 4th day Qld (2)
    5/123 (Rowe 19, Mayes 16).

King, originally 12th man, replaced H.S.B.Love (business commitments) in the Victorian side. Rain washed out play on the first day.
Ponsford (151 in 233 minutes, 12 fours, chances at 10 and 144) shared partnerships of 115 with Woodfull (56 in 89 minutes, 3 fours) and
217 with Hendry (140 in 156 minutes, 1 six and 8 fours, chance at 27) for the first two wickets. Rigg (62 in 122 minutes, 5 fours) and
King (50 in 103 minutes, 2 fours) also scored fifties for Victoria. Mayes (70 in 135 minutes, 2 fours, chance at 4) topscored for
Queensland in the role of night-watchman. Gill (36 in 119 minutes, no fours) and O'Connor (38 in 91 minutes, 1 four) compiled the next
best. No admission was charged for entry on the last day. Morton's previous five matches were for South Australia. Sources: *Wisden*,
VCA Report, QCA Report, The Age, The Argus, The Herald, Melbourne Sun.

QUEENSLAND

L.E.Oxenham	c Blackie b Hendry	19	(6)	c & b Ryder	6
L.L.Gill	b Morton	36		b Blackie	14
*†L.P.D.O'Connor	b Morton	8		b Hartkopf	38
F.C.Thompson	b Blackie	9		lbw b Blackie	6
W.Rowe	c King b Blackie	23		c Ellis b Morton	20
R.K.Oxenham	c Ellis b Blackie	2	(1)	c Blackie b Morton	10
E.C.Bensted	b Morton	1	(8)	b Morton	2
F.J.Gough	c Rigg b Blackie	15	(10)	b Ryder	21
H.J.R.Higgins	run out (Ryder)	19		b Morton	5
F.M.Brew	c Hendry b Liddicut	0	(11)	not out	8
A.D.A.Mayes	not out	12	(7)	c Ellis b Ryder	70
Extras	(b2, lb1)	3		(b7, lb7, w3)	17
Total	(62.0 overs, 221 mins)	147		(79.9 overs, 280 mins)	217

VICTORIA

*W.M.Woodfull	b R.K.Oxenham	56
W.H.Ponsford	c Gough b Brew	151
H.S.T.L.Hendry	c O'Connor b Mayes	140
K.E.Rigg	c R.K.Oxenham b Bensted	62
J.Ryder	c & b Bensted	37
A.E.V.Hartkopf	b R.K.Oxenham	3
S.P.King	b R.K.Oxenham	50
A.E.Liddicut	c R.K.Oxenham b Gough	16
†J.L.Ellis	b R.K.Oxenham	1
F.L.Morton	b Thompson	3
D.D.Blackie	not out	1
Extras	(b5, lb8)	13
Total	(129.6 overs, 431 mins)	533

VICTORIA	O	M	R	W	w,nb		O	M	R	W	w,nb
Morton	14	0	39	3	-,-		24	3	67	4	-,-
Liddicut	12	3	22	1	-,-		4	1	7	0	-,-
Blackie	23	3	49	4	-,-		24	5	56	2	-,-
Hendry	7	2	6	1	-,-		3	0	7	0	-,-
Hartkopf	6	0	28	0	-,-	(6)	12	1	36	1	3,-
Ryder						(5)	12.7	2	27	3	-,-

QUEENSLAND	O	M	R	W	w,nb
Mayes	26	1	98	1	-,-
Gill	8	0	37	0	-,-
Thompson	16	4	47	1	-,-
Bensted	19	1	70	2	-,-
Gough	6	0	27	1	-,-
Brew	10	0	71	1	-,-
R.K.Oxenham	29.6	3	126	4	-,-
Rowe	15	2	44	0	-,-

FALL OF WICKETS

Wkt	QLD 1st	VIC 1st	QLD 2nd
1st	38	115	16
2nd	60	332	48
3rd	67	358	56
4th	77	426	77
5th	85	435	84
6th	86	475	128
7th	114	510	136
8th	116	516	156
9th	117	525	206
10th	147	533	217

AFCM No. 622/62
SSM No. 180/59

SOUTH AUSTRALIA v NEW SOUTH WALES (Shield Match 5)

Played at Adelaide Oval on December 17, 18, 20, 21, 22, 1926. (Timeless match)
Toss : South Australia.   Result : NEW SOUTH WALES WON BY FOUR WICKETS.
Debuts: New South Wales - J.E.P.Hogg, H.V.McGuirk (both f/c).
12th Men: D.G.McKay (SA) and J.N.Campbell (NSW).
Umpires: G.A.Hele and J.J.Quinn.
Attendances: 6000, 12500, 5000, 5000, ?   Total: No figures published.   Receipts: £1428.
Close of Play: 1st day SA 4/355 (V.Y.Richardson 135, Alexander 50); 2nd day NSW 3/203 (Andrews 66, Ratcliffe 7); 3rd day SA (2)
   5/168 (Alexander 44, Pritchard 27); 4th day NSW (2) 2/174 (Andrews 69, Kippax 37).

In scoring 6-446 New South Wales set a new record for the highest winning fourth-innings total in Australia. Chief scorers in the historic innings were Andrews (126 in 222 minutes, 8 fours) and Morgan (116 in 169 minutes, 12 fours, early chance) assisted by Phillips (52 in 90 minutes, 4 fours) and Jackson (56 not out in 109 minutes, 3 fours). South Australia were given a good start on the first day by Schneider (82 in 195 minutes, 1 four, chance at 10) and A.J.Richardson (64 in 119 minutes, 3 fours) who added 120 for the first wicket. V.Y.Richardson (157 in 222 minutes, 16 fours) and Alexander (55 in 90 minutes, 2 fours) also helped to build a potential match-winning total. Alexander completed a fine match with his second-innings 104 (223 minutes, 4 fours). Phillips (54 in 106 minutes, no fours and 32 singles) and Andrews 86 in 143 minutes, 6 fours) topscored in the first New South Wales innings. H.L.Collins and C.G.Macartney were unavailable for New South Wales. *Wisden* incorrectly gives SA (2) Alexander c & b McGuirk. Sources: *Wisden, C.B.O'Reilly, NSWCA Report, SACA Report, Adelaide Advertiser, South Australian Register.*

SOUTH AUSTRALIA

K.J.Schneider	c & b Morgan	82	b McNamee		8
A.J.Richardson	c Steele b Mailey	64	c Ratcliffe b McNamee		0
L.T.Gun	st Ratcliffe b Mailey	1	lbw b McNamee		20
*V.Y.Richardson	c Mailey b Kippax	157	lbw b Mailey		13
J.W.Rymill	b Phillips	12	c Ratcliffe b Morgan		50
W.C.Alexander	c Phillips b Mailey	55	c Ratcliffe b McGuirk		104
D.E.Pritchard	lbw b Mailey	40	c & b McNamee		27
C.V.Grimmett	c Phillips b Mailey	48	c McNamee b McGuirk		36
N.L.Williams	c & b Mailey	13	b Mailey		4
J.D.Scott	b Kippax	7	not out		2
†C.N.Parry	not out	8	b McGuirk		2
Extras	(b4, lb5, w1, nb3)	13	(b8, lb11, nb1)		20
Total	(133.2 overs, 439 mins)	500	(99.3 overs, 332 mins)		286

NEW SOUTH WALES

N.E.Phillips	c & b Grimmett	54	b Grimmett		52
H.C.Steele	b Williams	28	b A.J.Richardson		11
T.J.E.Andrews	c V.Y.Richardson b Williams	86	st Parry b Williams		126
*A.F.Kippax	lbw b A.J.Richardson	39	run out (Pritchard)		42
†A.T.Ratcliffe	b Williams	46	lbw b Scott		15
A.Jackson	c V.Y.Richardson b Williams	4	(7) not out		56
J.E.P.Hogg	st Parry b Williams	24	(8) not out		9
J.G.Morgan	not out	26	(6) c Williams b Scott		116
A.A.Mailey	c V.Y.Richardson b Grimmett	21			
H.V.McGuirk	b Grimmett	0			
R.L.A.McNamee	b Grimmett	0			
Extras	(b9, lb2, w1, nb1)	13	(b8, lb8, w1, nb2)		19
Total	(87.7 overs, 305 mins)	341	(107.0 overs, 365 mins) (6 wkts)		446

NEW SOUTH WALES	O	M	R	W	w,nb		O	M	R	W	w,nb
McNamee	23	3	60	0	-,3		30	9	63	4	-,1
McGuirk	12	0	57	0	-,-		12.3	2	20	3	-,-
Mailey	51.2	4	191	6	-,-		32	5	90	2	-,-
Morgan	9	0	45	1	-,-		7	0	37	1	-,-
Phillips	21	4	75	1	-,-		13	0	42	0	-,-
Kippax	18	2	59	2	1,-		5	0	14	0	-,-

SOUTH AUSTRALIA	O	M	R	W	w,nb		O	M	R	W	w,nb
Scott	16	3	54	0	1,-		18	1	108	2	1,-
A.J.Richardson	12	5	9	1	-,-		31	9	54	1	-,-
Grimmett	31.7	2	110	4	-,-	(4)	33	2	123	1	-,-
Williams	28	2	155	5	-,1	(3)	24	0	142	1	-,2

FALL OF WICKETS

Wkt	SA 1st	NSW 1st	SA 2nd	NSW 2nd
1st	120	67	1	28
2nd	121	121	8	97
3rd	186	190	41	188
4th	235	234	54	216
5th	364	265	131	301
6th	408	268	169	431
7th	436	312	263	-
8th	460	341	282	-
9th	475	341	282	-
10th	500	341	286	-

VICTORIA v NEW SOUTH WALES (Shield Match 6)

Played at Melbourne Cricket Ground on December 24, 27, 28, 29, 1926. (Timeless match)
Toss : New South Wales.   Result : VICTORIA WON BY AN INNINGS AND 656 RUNS.
Debuts: Nil.
12th Men: K.E.Rigg (Vic) and H.C.Steele (NSW).
Umpires: J.Richards and J.Stafford.
Attendances: 8174, 22893, 22348, 7717.   Total: 61,132.   Receipts: £2920.
Close of Play: 1st day NSW 221 all out; 2nd day Vic 1/573 (Ponsford 334, Hendry 86); 3rd day Vic 1107 all out.

Victoria's batsmen took only two days to compile the highest total in first-class cricket. The score progressed thus: lunch second day Victoria 0/132 (Woodfull 50, Ponsford 75), tea 0/364 (Woodfull 127, Ponsford 227), stumps 1/573 (Ponsford 334, Hendry 86); lunch third day 5/697 (Ryder 63, Hartkopf 15), tea 7/929 Ryder 210, Ellis 2), stumps all out 1107. Woodfull (133 in 223 minutes, 7 fours, chance at 117) and Ponsford (352 in 363 minutes, 36 fours, chance at 265) began the innings with a first-wicket partnership of 375. Hendry (100 in 117 minutes, 7 fours, chance at 6) and Ryder (295 in 245 minutes, 6 sixes and 33 fours, chances at 139 and 274) also scored centuries. Ponsford reached 100 in 125 minutes, 200 in 203 minutes and 300 in 285 minutes while Ryder reached 100 in 115 minutes and 200 in 189 minutes. Hartkopf (61 in 94 minutes, 6 fours) and Ellis (63 in 102 minutes, 5 fours) assisted Ryder in pushing the total past 1000. Mailey conceded the greatest number of runs in an innings in a first-class match. Topscorers in the New South Wales first innings, puny by comparison, were Phillips (52 in 144 minutes, 2 fours), Andrews (42 in 71 minutes, 1 four) and Hogg (40 not out in 97 minutes, 2 fours). Jackson's unbeaten 59 in the second innings occupied 105 minutes, 2 fours. *Wisden* incorrectly gives NSW (1) Morton 0/45.
Sources: *Wisden, NSWCA Report, VCA Report, The Age, The Argus, The Herald, Melbourne Sun, Sydney Morning Herald, The Sporting Globe, The Australasian.*

NEW SOUTH WALES

N.E.Phillips	c Blackie b Liddicut	52	lbw b Hartkopf	36
J.G.Morgan	c Love b Liddicut	13	c King b Liddicut	26
T.J.E.Andrews	st Ellis b Hartkopf	42	b Liddicut	0
*A.F.Kippax	b Liddicut	36	b Hartkopf	26
†A.T.Ratcliffe	c Ryder b Liddicut	2	c Morton b Hartkopf	44
A.Jackson	c Ellis b Blackie	4	not out	59
J.E.P.Hogg	not out	40	c Hendry b Liddicut	13
A.A.Mailey	b Ryder	20	c Morton b Hartkopf	3
J.N.Campbell	lbw b Blackie	0	c Ryder b Hartkopf	8
R.L.A.McNamee	b Ryder	8	b Liddicut	7
H.V.McGuirk	b Ryder	0	b Hartkopf	0
Extras	(b1, lb1, nb2)	4	(b2, lb4, nb2)	8
Total	(81.0 overs, 304 mins)	221	(51.3 overs, 207 mins)	230

VICTORIA

*W.M.Woodfull	c Ratcliffe b Andrews	133
W.H.Ponsford	b Morgan	352
H.S.T.L.Hendry	c Morgan b Mailey	100
J.Ryder	c Kippax b Andrews	295
H.S.B.Love	st Ratcliffe b Mailey	6
S.P.King	st Ratcliffe b Mailey	7
A.E.V.Hartkopf	c McGuirk b Mailey	61
A.E.Liddicut	b McGuirk	36
†J.L.Ellis	run out (Andrews)	63
F.L.Morton	run out	0
D.D.Blackie	not out	27
Extras	(b17, lb8, nb2)	27
Total	(190.7 overs, 633 mins)	1107

VICTORIA	O	M	R	W	w,nb		O	M	R	W	w,nb		FALL OF WICKETS		
													NSW	VIC	NSW
Morton	15	4	43	0	-,2	(2)	11	0	42	0	-,2	Wkt	1st	1st	2nd
Liddicut	21	7	50	4	-,-	(1)	19	2	66	4	-,-	1st	25	375	67
Ryder	9	1	32	3	-,-							2nd	96	594	67
Blackie	16	3	34	2	-,-	(3)	5	1	16	0	-,-	3rd	122	614	77
Hendry	3	2	1	0	-,-							4th	133	631	112
Hartkopf	17	1	57	1	-,-	(4)	16.3	0	98	6	-,-	5th	152	657	164
												6th	152	834	184
NEW SOUTH WALES	O	M	R	W	w,nb							7th	207	915	189
McNamee	24	2	124	0	-,1							8th	208	1043	206
McGuirk	26	1	130	1	-,-							9th	217	1046	229
Mailey	64	0	362	4	-,1							10th	221	1107	230
Campbell	11	0	89	0	-,-										
Phillips	11.7	0	64	0	-,-										
Morgan	26	0	137	1	-,-										
Andrews	21	2	148	2	-,-										
Kippax	7	0	26	0	-,-										

SOUTH AUSTRALIA v QUEENSLAND (Shield Match 7)

Played at Adelaide Oval on December 25, 27, 28, 1926. (Timeless match)
Toss : South Australia.   Result : SOUTH AUSTRALIA WON BY TEN WICKETS.
Debuts: South Australia - R.A.Halcombe, G.B.Inkster (both f/c).
12th Men: D.G.McKay (SA) and N.C.Beeston (Qld).
Umpires: G.A.Hele and J.J.Quinn.
Attendances: 13000, 14000, 3500.   Total: About 30,500.   Receipts: £1512.
Close of Play: 1st day SA 6/432 (Alexander 17, Grimmett 1); 2nd day Qld 251 all out.

A.J.Richardson's 232 in 222 minutes (4 sixes and 22 fours, 4 chances) included 152 runs out of 196 scored in 120 minutes between lunch and tea on Christmas Day. He added 135 for the first wicket with Schneider (54 in 102 minutes, 3 fours) and 199 for the second wicket with Gun (63 in 161 minutes, 1 four). Alexander (88 in 150 minutes, 6 fours) and Williams (56 in 63 minutes, 5 fours) shared a 112-run stand for South Australia's eighth wicket. R.K.Oxenham suffered a recurrence of a strained leg while fielding early in the match and was unable to bowl in either innings. A similar strain restricted Mayes, Beeston and 13th man H.J.R.Higgins being forced to substitute for both at one time. Thompson topscored in each Queensland innings with 91 (108 minutes, 14 fours) and 77 (150 minutes, 4 fours). Rowe (74 in 120 minutes, 8 fours) and Gough (73 in 101 minutes, 6 fours) also scored well, Gough adding 101 runs in 75 minutes with Gill for the ninth wicket to force South Australia to bat a second time. Sources: *Wisden, C.B.O'Reilly, QCA Report, SACA Report, Adelaide Advertiser, South Australian Register, The News.*

SOUTH AUSTRALIA

A.J.Richardson	c Gill b Rowe	232		
K.J.Schneider	c Bensted b Mayes	54	not out	22
L.T.Gun	st Farquhar b Rowe	63		
*V.Y.Richardson	c O'Connor b Thompson	8	(1) not out	28
J.W.Rymill	c O'Connor b Rowe	33		
W.C.Alexander	c L.E.Oxenham b Bensted	88		
D.E.Pritchard	c Rowe b Gill	16		
C.V.Grimmett	c Farquhar b Bensted	11		
N.L.Williams	c Rowe b Brew	56		
†G.B.Inkster	run out (/Farquhar)	8		
R.A.Halcombe	not out	0		
Extras	(b4, lb4, w1, nb1)	10	(b3, lb1)	4
Total	(117.2 overs, 417 mins)	579	(6.3 overs, 23 mins) (0 wkts)	54

QUEENSLAND

L.E.Oxenham	c Inkster b Williams	47	lbw b Grimmett	6
L.L.Gill	b Halcombe	20	(10) b Grimmett	36
*L.P.D.O'Connor	c Rymill b Grimmett	1	b Grimmett	25
F.C.Thompson	c Alexander b Grimmett	91	lbw b A.J.Richardson	77
R.K.Oxenham	st Inkster b Williams	14	c Pritchard b Williams	6
W.Rowe	b Alexander	11	(7) c Inkster b A.J.Richardson	74
A.D.A.Mayes	b Williams	0	(9) c sub (D.G.McKay) b Williams	4
†J.K.Farquhar	b Halcombe	12	(11) not out	9
E.C.Bensted	not out	20	(2) st Inkster b Grimmett	42
F.J.Gough	c A.J.Richardson b Schneider	14	(8) st Inkster b Williams	73
F.M.Brew	b Schneider	6	(6) c & b Grimmett	11
Extras	(b5, lb6, nb4)	15	(b8, lb3, w5)	16
Total	(57.7 overs, 214 mins)	251	(87.5 overs, 304 mins)	379

QUEENSLAND	O	M	R	W	w,nb		O	M	R	W	w,nb		FALL OF WICKETS			
														SA	QLD	QLD	SA
Mayes	15	1	67	1	-,-								Wkt	1st	1st	2nd	2nd
Gill	18	0	78	1	-,-	(1)	3	0	17	0	-,-		1st	135	34	29	
Bensted	25.2	1	121	2	-,-	(2)	2	0	17	0	-,-		2nd	334	36	68	-
Rowe	20	3	82	3	-,-								3rd	350	129	97	-
Thompson	22	1	80	1	-,1	(3)	1	0	7	0	-,-		4th	384	181	110	-
Brew	11	0	96	1	1,-								5th	399	185	131	-
Gough	6	0	45	0	-,-								6th	425	185	234	-
O'Connor						(4)	0.3	0	9	0	-,-		7th	448	209	253	-
													8th	560	213	268	-
SOUTH AUSTRALIA	O	M	R	W	w,nb		O	M	R	W	w,nb		9th	579	245	369	-
Halcombe	12	1	37	2	-,3		14	0	58	0	5,-		10th	579	251	379	-
A.J.Richardson	7	0	25	0	-,-		18	5	46	2	-,-						
Grimmett	16	2	72	2	-,-		24.5	2	107	5	-,-						
Williams	17	1	66	3	-,-		24	0	109	3	-,-						
Alexander	5	1	26	1	-,1	(6)	3	0	20	0	-,-						
Schneider	0.7	0	10	2	-,-	(5)	4	0	23	0	-,-						

VICTORIA v SOUTH AUSTRALIA (Shield Match 8)

Played at Melbourne Cricket Ground on January 1, 3, 4, 5, 6, 1927. (Timeless match)
Toss : Victoria.   Result : VICTORIA WON BY 571 RUNS.
Debuts: Nil.
12th Men: K.E.Rigg (Vic) and D.G.McKay (SA).
Umpires: J.Richards and P.E.Smith.
Attendances: 28063, 30219, 12306, 6501, 5001.   Total: 82,090.   Receipts: £3924.
Close of Play: 1st day SA 1/25 (Schneider 5, Williams 15); 2nd day Vic (2) 3/168 (Hendry 36, Love 0); 3rd day Vic (2) 5/541 (Love 170, Hartkopf 101); 4th day Vic (2) 649 all out.

The South Australians failed to counter the bowling of Morton and Blackie in either innings, only Pritchard (56 in 104 minutes, 7 fours) and Schneider (53 in 127 minutes, 4 fours) reaching 50. A.J.Richardson was dismissed first ball. Ponsford (108 in 183 minutes, 5 fours and 84 in 140 minutes, 7 fours) and Hendry (68 in 79 minutes, 6 fours and 85 in 159 minutes, 6 fours) batted well in each innings for Victoria. Love (188 in 377 minutes, 9 fours) and Hartkopf (126 in 192 minutes, 19 fours) added 217 in 171 minutes for the sixth wicket while Inkster became the first wicket-keeper to complete nine dismissals in an Australian match. Halcombe ran into the fence attempting to save a boundary on the third day and strained his back; he took no further part in the match and J.D.Scott was brought from Adelaide to take his place in the following match in Sydney. J.W.Rymill (business) was unavailable for South Australia. Sources: *Wisden, C.B.O'Reilly, VCA Report, SACA Report, The Age, The Argus, The Herald, Melbourne Sun, The Australasian.*

VICTORIA

Batsman	Dismissal (1st)	Runs	Dismissal (2nd)	Runs
*W.M.Woodfull	c Pritchard b A.J.Richardson	6	st Inkster b Grimmett	34
W.H.Ponsford	c Lee b Halcombe	108	lbw b Grimmett	84
H.S.T.L.Hendry	st Inkster b Grimmett	68	st Inkster b Williams	85
J.Ryder	b Lee	34	c Inkster b Grimmett	5
H.S.B.Love	c V.Y.Richardson b Grimmett	12	c Inkster b Williams	188
S.P.King	st Inkster b Grimmett	12	c Inkster b A.J.Richardson	33
A.E.V.Hartkopf	not out	29	c Grimmett b Williams	126
A.E.Liddicut	c A.J.Richardson b Halcombe	5	b Grimmett	39
†J.L.Ellis	c Pritchard b Lee	3	c Pritchard b Williams	21
D.D.Blackie	lbw b Lee	2	not out	1
F.L.Morton	st Inkster b Grimmett	8	c Inkster b Grimmett	3
Extras	(b12, lb3, w1, nb1)	17	(b26, lb2, nb2)	30
Total	(72.3 overs, 260 mins)	304	(177.4 overs, 590 mins)	649

SOUTH AUSTRALIA

Batsman	Dismissal (1st)	Runs	Dismissal (2nd)	Runs
L.T.Gun	c Ellis b Morton	2	(3) c Ellis b Morton	11
K.J.Schneider	c Ellis b Morton	17	st Ellis b Blackie	53
N.L.Williams	lbw b Blackie	21	(8) c Ponsford b Blackie	14
A.J.Richardson	c Hendry b Blackie	0	(1) b Morton	30
*V.Y.Richardson	b Morton	7	(4) c & b Morton	41
W.C.Alexander	b Blackie	2	b Blackie	10
D.E.Pritchard	run out (Liddicut/Morton)	56	(5) b Morton	22
P.K.Lee	b Morton	1	(7) b Ryder	2
C.V.Grimmett	b Morton	19	not out	21
†G.B.Inkster	c & b Blackie	11	run out (/Ellis)	18
R.A.Halcombe	not out	1	absent hurt	-
Extras	(b4, lb5, nb3)	12	(b10, nb1)	11
Total	(52.3 overs, 189 mins)	149	(74.0 overs, 261 mins)	233

SOUTH AUSTRALIA	O	M	R	W	w,nb		O	M	R	W	w,nb
Halcombe	18	0	60	2	1,-		12	2	50	0	-,-
A.J.Richardson	14	4	36	1	-,1		43	8	115	1	-,1
Williams	9	0	58	0	-,-	(5)	26.4	0	103	4	-,1
Grimmett	21.3	1	101	4	-,-	(3)	53	6	180	5	-,-
Lee	10	1	32	3	-,-	(4)	25	6	92	0	-,-
V.Y.Richardson							9	0	54	0	-,-
Schneider							9	1	25	0	-,-

VICTORIA	O	M	R	W	w,nb		O	M	R	W	w,nb
Morton	24.3	3	70	5	-,3		21	1	70	4	-,1
Liddicut	6	3	8	0	-,-	(3)	8	1	21	0	-,-
Blackie	22	5	59	4	-,-	(2)	30	7	75	3	-,-
Hartkopf							7	0	29	0	-,-
Hendry							3	0	4	0	-,-
Ryder							5	0	23	1	-,-

FALL OF WICKETS

Wkt	VIC 1st	SA 1st	VIC 2nd	SA 2nd
1st	21	3	104	85
2nd	153	36	159	103
3rd	227	36	167	103
4th	229	45	272	132
5th	250	49	361	149
6th	255	58	578	158
7th	267	60	593	177
8th	275	113	643	201
9th	281	143	647	233
10th	304	149	649	-

NEW SOUTH WALES v SOUTH AUSTRALIA (Shield Match 9)

Played at Sydney Cricket Ground on January 8, 10, 11, 12, 1927. (Timeless match)
Toss : South Australia.   Result : SOUTH AUSTRALIA WON BY 340 RUNS.
Debuts: New South Wales - N.H.Fox, E.F.O'Brien (both f/c).
12th Men: C.D.Seddon (NSW) and L.T.Gun (SA).
Umpires: A.C.Jones and A.P.Williams.
Attendances: 12673, 7968, 4706, 3840.   Total: 29,187.   Receipts: £1901.
Close of Play: 1st day SA 5/242 (A.J.Richardson 135, McKay 5); 2nd day SA (2) 0/25 (Schneider 4, A.J.Richardson 20); 3rd day SA (2) 6/347 (Lee 22, Grimmett 0).

W.Bardsley and H.L.Collins, who had both retired, were replaced in the New South Wales twelve by Gwynne and Seddon. T.J.E.Andrews, J.M.Gregory, C.Kelleway, A.A.Mailey and J.M.Taylor were also unavailable. The match began at 2pm due to the arrival of the South Australians in Sydney that morning. A.J.Richardson (189 in 285 minutes, 1 six and 16 fours) and Schneider (146 in 302 minutes, 2 fours) topscored in each innings. New South Wales failed twice with the bat, the only consolation being Jackson's unbeaten hundred (104 in 127 minutes with 11 fours). Gwynne (43 in 91 minutes, 2 fours), Macartney (43 in 42 minutes, 1 six and 4 fours) and Kippax (52 in 118 minutes, 6 fours) were all dismissed when well set. *Wisden* incorrectly gives SA (2) V.Y.Richardson lbw b McNamee. Sources: *Wisden, C.B.O'Reilly, NSWCA Report, SACA Report, Sydney Morning Herald, Sydney Referee.*

SOUTH AUSTRALIA

Player		Runs			Runs
K.J.Schneider	c Morgan b Fox	9		c Kippax b Macartney	146
A.J.Richardson	c O'Brien b Macartney	189		b Fox	30
*V.Y.Richardson	b O'Brien	29		b McNamee	55
D.E.Pritchard	c & b O'Brien	43		lbw b McNamee	7
W.C.Alexander	b Fox	14		b Fox	26
C.V.Grimmett	b McNamee	3	(8)	c Osborne b McNamee	4
D.G.McKay	b O'Brien	17	(6)	run out (sub C.D.Seddon/Osborne)	49
P.K.Lee	b O'Brien	5	(7)	b McNamee	23
N.L.Williams	b O'Brien	14		c sub (C.D.Seddon) b McNamee	21
J.D.Scott	b Macartney	5		not out	7
†G.B.Inkster	not out	4		b Macartney	12
Extras	(b9, lb2, nb2)	13		(b10, lb3, w2, nb4)	19
Total	(87.7 overs, 310 mins)	345		(115.7 overs, 410 mins)	399

NEW SOUTH WALES

Player		Runs			Runs
N.E.Phillips	lbw b A.J.Richardson	15		b Grimmett	4
L.W.Gwynne	c Inkster b McKay	43		c Inkster b Scott	0
*C.G.Macartney	c & b McKay	43	(4)	c & b Grimmett	0
A.F.Kippax	c & b Scott	32	(3)	b Lee	52
A.Jackson	c Inkster b McKay	0	(6)	not out	104
J.E.P.Hogg	st Inkster b Grimmett	20	(7)	lbw b Lee	5
J.G.Morgan	b Grimmett	28	(5)	c V.Y.Richardson b Scott	10
†R.H.Osborne	b Grimmett	7	(9)	c Scott b Lee	8
E.F.O'Brien	b Grimmett	1	(8)	b Lee	7
N.H.Fox	lbw b McKay	2		b Lee	0
R.L.A.McNamee	not out	0		c Schneider b Williams	4
Extras	(b3, lb1, w1, nb2)	7		(b7, w1, nb4)	12
Total	(45.4 overs, 173 mins)	198		(43.2 overs, 180 mins)	206

NEW SOUTH WALES	O	M	R	W	w,nb		O	M	R	W	w,nb
Fox	16	1	79	2	-,-		22	1	99	2	-,1
McNamee	22	4	75	1	-,2		40	6	86	5	2,3
Phillips	6	0	16	0	-,-	(6)	4	0	19	0	-,-
O'Brien	21.7	0	99	5	-,-	(3)	16	0	69	0	-,-
Macartney	22	2	63	2	-,-		16.7	5	28	2	-,-
Morgan						(4)	14	2	70	0	-,-
Kippax							3	0	9	0	-,-

SOUTH AUSTRALIA	O	M	R	W	w,nb		O	M	R	W	w,nb
Scott	10	0	44	1	1,1		9	2	23	2	-,4
A.J.Richardson	7	1	25	1	-,-		2	1	4	0	-,-
Williams	2	0	20	0	-,1	(4)	9.2	0	49	1	-,-
Grimmett	15.4	0	70	4	-,-	(3)	10	0	50	2	-,-
McKay	11	2	32	4	-,-		6	0	32	0	1,-
Lee							7	0	36	5	-,-

FALL OF WICKETS				
Wkt	SA 1st	NSW 1st	SA 2nd	NSW 2nd
1st	11	30	44	1
2nd	64	98	151	9
3rd	182	119	163	9
4th	225	119	211	37
5th	230	156	313	142
6th	301	158	343	156
7th	319	193	356	174
8th	321	195	357	200
9th	331	198	382	201
10th	345	198	399	206

VICTORIA v TASMANIA

Played at Melbourne Cricket Ground on January 25, 26, 27, 1927. (Three-day match)
Toss : Victoria.   Result : VICTORIA WON BY AN INNINGS AND 78 RUNS.
Debuts: Victoria - L.S.Darling, J.C.Makin, C.E.Morgan, J.W.Scaife, F.B.Warne (all f/c). Tasmania - R.C.Townley (f/c); J.A.Atkinson
      (Tas only).
12th Men: F.L.Butler (Tas). No 12th named for Victoria (see below).
Umpires: H.E.Nichols and G.Oakley.
Attendances: 1551, 1278, not known.   Total: About 3500.   Receipts: £80.
Close of Play: 1st day Vic 6/390 (Mitchell 195, Onyons 27); 2nd day Tas 9/203 (Watson 9, Townley 0).

Morgan replaced S.E.Wootton (unavailable) in the Victorian side. Mitchell survived chances at 21, 112 and 153 to compile 220 in 344 minutes with 18 fours. Onyons' 128 (140 minutes, 15 fours) included 101 in the pre-lunch session on the second day. Darling (46 in 94 minutes, 5 fours) and Scaife (46 in 97 minutes, 1 four) were among those making their debuts. Atkinson, playing his first game for Tasmania after four appearances with Victoria, scored 44 (93 minutes, 3 fours) and shared a sound opening partnership with Allan (53 in 150 minutes, 1 four) who was run out attempting a third run. But apart from Rushforth (40 in 79 minutes, 2 fours and 36 in 55 minutes, 2 fours), Watson (47 in 90 minutes, 4 fours) and Newton (78 in 91 minutes, 10 fours) the rest of the visitors failed with the bat. H.E.Brereton, secretary of the Victorian Cricket Association, substituted for Onyons during the last session of the third day's play; the captain had left to prepare for Melbourne Cricket Club's tour to New Zealand and Mitchell was put in charge for the remainder of the match. Admission on the last day was free despite the fact that Tasmania had not yet begun their second innings. Sources: *The Cricketer, VCA Report, The Age, The Argus, Melbourne Sun, The Herald, The Sporting Globe, The Australasian.*

VICTORIA

G.A.Davies	c Henty b Wardlaw	6
C.A.H.Sindrey	c Henty b Wardlaw	11
L.S.Darling	c C.W.B.Martin b Newton	46
N.F.Mitchell	c Henty b Townley	220
W.H.Bailey	st Henty b Townley	27
J.W.Scaife	run out (/C.W.B.Martin)	46
F.B.Warne	c Rushforth b Watson	20
*B.A.Onyons	c Burrows b Wardlaw	128
†C.E.Morgan	c Wardlaw b Burrows	33
H.S.Gamble	c Rushforth b Burrows	1
J.C.Makin	not out	1
Extras	(b10, lb2, w1)	13
Total	(126.6 overs, 455 mins)	552

TASMANIA

J.A.Atkinson	c Morgan b Davies	44		c Sindrey b Warne	19
*G.H.Allan	run out (Sindrey/Morgan)	53		c Mitchell b Davies	4
C.W.B.Martin	b Gamble	21		b Davies	4
A.W.Rushforth	b Warne	40		c & b Makin	36
G.W.Martin	b Gamble	1		b Makin	28
A.O.Burrows	c Mitchell b Gamble	0		b Makin	1
A.C.Newton	c Mitchell b Warne	12		b Davies	78
†P.G.Henty	c Bailey b Makin	3	(9)	c Makin b Warne	10
A.E.Watson	c Onyons b Mitchell	47	(8)	b Mitchell	29
D.M.S.Wardlaw	c Gamble b Warne	6	(11)	not out	0
R.C.Townley	not out	7	(10)	c Morgan b Gamble	0
Extras	(b6, lb5, w1, nb6)	18		(b5, lb6, w2)	13
Total	(91.7 overs, 299 mins)	252		(49.3 overs, 180 mins)	222

TASMANIA	O	M	R	W	w,nb
Wardlaw	29.6	2	155	3	-,-
Newton	27	3	97	1	-,-
Watson	21	4	62	1	-,-
Burrows	16	1	69	2	1,-
Townley	15	1	79	2	-,-
Allan	10	0	38	0	-,-
C.W.B.Martin	8	0	39	0	-,-

VICTORIA	O	M	R	W	w,nb		O	M	R	W	w,nb
Gamble	20	4	51	3	1,6		10	0	50	1	-,-
Makin	23	2	72	1	-,-	(4)	9	2	39	3	-,-
Warne	25	5	57	3	-,-		12	2	48	2	-,-
Davies	9	1	22	1	-,-	(2)	10.3	1	23	3	-,-
Bailey	3	1	4	0	-,-		5	0	25	0	-,-
Mitchell	11.7	0	28	1	-,-		3	0	24	1	2,-

FALL OF WICKETS

Wkt	VIC 1st	TAS 1st	TAS 2nd
1st	18	87	8
2nd	23	119	18
3rd	98	138	43
4th	155	143	92
5th	261	147	95
6th	325	179	96
7th	437	186	188
8th	530	188	217
9th	534	202	222
10th	552	252	222

NEW SOUTH WALES v VICTORIA (Shield Match 10)

Played at Sydney Cricket Ground on January 26, 27, 28, 1927. (Timeless match)
Toss : New South Wales.   Result : NEW SOUTH WALES WON BY AN INNINGS AND 253 RUNS.
Debuts: Victoria - L.C.Salvana (f/c); B.J.J.Davie (Vic only).
12th Men: C.D.Seddon (NSW) and S.P.King (Vic).
Umpires: W.J.R.Bowes and M.Carney.
Attendances: 15209, 1789, 3964.   Total: 20,962.   Receipts: £1404.
Close of Play: 1st day NSW 8/424 (Kippax 187, Fox 0); 2nd day Vic 2/16 (Salvana 5, Liddicut 1).

Morgan, originally named 12th man, and O'Brien replaced A.A.Mailey and the nominated captain H.L.Collins in the New South Wales side. W.M.Woodfull announced himself unavailable for Victoria whose problems were compounded by the withdrawal of A.E.V.Hartkopf, H.S.B.Love, N.F.Mitchell, J.Ryder (captain) and W.H.Ponsford for various reasons. Baring, Davie (playing his only game for Victoria following two matches for Tasmania), King, Millar and Salvana were consequently brought into the side. Kippax's 217 not out occupied 320 minutes and included 24 fours, but of the others only Oldfield (56 in 68 minutes, 7 fours) reached fifty for New South Wales. Rain prevented any play on the second day before 3.00pm and softened the pitch to such an extent that the Victorians lasted only an hour at the crease, McNamee (off breaks) claiming a career-best analysis including a spell of 5-0 in the middle order. Salvana was bowled by the third ball of the second innings and Mullett completed a king pair in the most ignominious fashion. Unspecified injury curtailed O'Brien's ninth over. Sources: *Wisden, NSWCA Report, VCA Report, The Age, Sydney Morning Herald, Sydney Referee.*

NEW SOUTH WALES

N.E.Phillips	c Ellis b Morton	12
J.G.Morgan	lbw b Blackie	29
*C.G.Macartney	lbw b Blackie	41
A.F.Kippax	not out	217
J.M.Taylor	c Salvana b Mullett	28
A.Jackson	b Morton	42
†W.A.S.Oldfield	b Millar	56
S.C.Everett	lbw b Blackie	10
E.F.O'Brien	c Baring b Hendry	5
N.H.Fox	c Ellis b Mullett	8
R.L.A.McNamee	c Ellis b Liddicut	8
Extras	(b7, lb3, w1, nb2)	13
Total	(107.0 overs, 397 mins)	469

VICTORIA

L.C.Salvana	c Morgan b McNamee	6		b Macartney	0
F.A.Baring	c Oldfield b McNamee	0	(4)	c Fox b Everett	35
*H.S.T.L.Hendry	c Morgan b Macartney	7		c Fox b Everett	28
A.E.Liddicut	lbw b Macartney	1	(5)	c Everett b Fox	55
†J.L.Ellis	b McNamee	1	(7)	b McNamee	4
K.E.Rigg	c Everett b McNamee	1		run out (Kippax)	17
K.J.Millar	b McNamee	0	(8)	c Oldfield b McNamee	7
B.J.J.Davie	not out	10	(2)	c Oldfield b Macartney	15
L.T.Mullett	b McNamee	0		b McNamee	0
F.L.Morton	b Macartney	4		b Fox	5
D.D.Blackie	st Oldfield b McNamee	1		not out	0
Extras	(b2, lb2)	4		(b7, lb5, nb3)	15
Total	(18.4 overs, 66 mins)	35		(49.5 overs, 165 mins)	181

VICTORIA	O	M	R	W	w,nb
Morton	24	0	129	2	1,-
Liddicut	21	3	78	1	-,-
Blackie	37	6	126	3	-,1
Mullett	11	0	45	2	-,-
Hendry	7	0	29	1	-,-
Davie	3	0	23	0	-,-
Millar	4	0	26	1	-,1

NEW SOUTH WALES	O	M	R	W	w,nb		O	M	R	W	w,nb
McNamee	8.4	3	21	7	-,-	(2)	16	2	49	3	-,1
Macartney	9	3	10	3	-,-	(1)	9	4	14	2	-,-
Morgan	1	1	0	0	-,-						
O'Brien						(3)	8.3	0	41	0	-,-
Everett						(4)	11	0	45	2	-,2
Fox						(5)	5.2	0	17	2	-,-

FALL OF WICKETS

Wkt	NSW 1st	VIC 1st	VIC 2nd
1st	22	2	0
2nd	70	15	20
3rd	91	16	77
4th	155	17	99
5th	249	18	130
6th	360	18	140
7th	405	19	163
8th	424	19	163
9th	457	30	178
10th	469	35	181

QUEENSLAND v VICTORIA (Shield Match 11)

Played at Exhibition Ground, Brisbane on February 5, 7, 8, 9, 10, 11, 1927. (Timeless match)
Toss : Queensland.   Result : QUEENSLAND WON BY 234 RUNS.
Debuts: Queensland - N.F.Grant (f/c).
12th Men: H.J.R.Higgins (Qld) and L.C.Salvana (Vic).
Umpires: J.Bartlett and J.A.Scott.
Attendances: 12000, 5000, 3500, 5000, 3500, 1000.   Total: About 30,000.   Receipts: £1809.
Close of Play: 1st day Qld 4/261 (Thompson 53, Knowles 14); 2nd day Qld (2) 0/10 (Gill 10, Grant 0); 3rd day Qld (2) 6/261
    (Knowles 58); 4th day Vic (2) 0/223 (Ponsford 114, Hendry 101); 5th day Vic (2) 7/491 (Ellis 27, Blackie 9).

Ponsford, unavailable against New South Wales in Sydney, reinforced the Victorian team. Queensland ended their first season in the Shield competition by recording their second victory in five matches. R.K.Oxenham (104 in 273 minutes, 8 fours), O'Connor (72 in 190 minutes, 4 fours) and Thompson (65 in 138 minutes, 6 fours) topscored in Queensland's first innings which saw 10 catches held. Victoria were bundled out for 86 in benign conditions on the second day. R.K.Oxenham (62) retired at the tea score of 4/230 on the third day with a wrist injury; he resumed next morning at 6/261 and batted 233 minutes in all (2 fours) but was unable to bowl again in the match. Knowles (144 in 252 minutes, 7 fours) hit his sole first-class hundred. Salvana substituted for Blackie (strained leg muscle) on the fourth day. Chasing an impossible 753 to win, Victoria scored 518 with big contributions from Ponsford (116 in 168 minutes, 8 fours), Hendry (137 in 265 minutes, 10 fours) and Baring (73 in 163 minutes, 4 fours). *Wisden* incorrectly gives Qld (2) Gill dismissal, Liddicut 1/21, Millar 1/46. Sources: *Wisden, VCA Report, QCA Report, Brisbane Courier, Brisbane Daily Mail.*

QUEENSLAND

R.K.Oxenham	c Liddicut b Mullett	104	(3)	b Mullett	73
E.C.Bensted	c Hendry b Morton	7	(8)	b Hendry	7
*†L.P.D.O'Connor	c King b Morton	72	(4)	c Liddicut b Blackie	21
F.C.Thompson	c Millar b Blackie	65	(5)	c Rigg b Blackie	19
F.J.Gough	c Hendry b Mullett	0	(9)	c sub (L.C.Salvana) b King	21
E.C.Knowles	c Ellis b Mullett	40		c Hendry b Liddicut	144
L.E.Oxenham	c Ellis b Morton	42		b Hendry	6
A.D.A.Mayes	c Hendry b Morton	3	(10)	not out	37
L.L.Gill	not out	22	(1)	c Baring b Hendry	40
N.F.Grant	c Ponsford b Blackie	26	(2)	run out (Ponsford/Ellis)	36
P.M.Hornibrook	c Hendry b Blackie	5		lbw b Millar	10
Extras	(b7, lb2, nb4)	13		(b20, lb3, nb2)	25
Total	(130.0 overs, 471 mins)	399		(114.6 overs, 413 mins)	439

VICTORIA

W.H.Ponsford	c Thompson b Gill	12		b Mayes	116
K.J.Millar	c Knowles b R.K.Oxenham	34	(4)	b Mayes	64
*H.S.T.L.Hendry	b Mayes	8	(2)	lbw b Hornibrook	137
F.A.Baring	c Hornibrook b Mayes	3	(3)	c Gill b Grant	73
K.E.Rigg	c Hornibrook b Mayes	3		run out (Thompson/Hornibrook)	29
A.E.Liddicut	lbw b R.K.Oxenham	10		b Hornibrook	2
S.P.King	not out	4	(8)	b Grant	12
†J.L.Ellis	c O'Connor b Hornibrook	4	(7)	lbw b Hornibrook	32
L.T.Mullett	c R.K.Oxenham b Hornibrook	1	(11)	not out	0
F.L.Morton	b R.K.Oxenham	1		c Gill b Hornibrook	6
D.D.Blackie	c Knowles b R.K.Oxenham	4	(9)	c & b Gill	22
Extras	(nb2)	2		(b8, lb10, nb7)	25
Total	(34.6 overs, 136 mins)	86		(143.2 overs, 527 mins)	518

VICTORIA	O	M	R	W	w,nb		O	M	R	W	w,nb		FALL OF WICKETS			
Morton	34	0	130	4	-,3		21	1	79	0	-,-		QLD	VIC	QLD	VIC
Liddicut	17	4	33	0	-,-1	(3)	7	1	27	1	-,-	Wkt	1st	1st	2nd	2nd
Blackie	41	1	84	3	-,-	(5)	21	4	69	2	-,2	1st	13	17	60	225
Mullett	15	1	68	3	-,-	(2)	34	7	131	1	-,-	2nd	169	33	80	297
King	3	0	19	0	-,-	(7)	2	0	16	1	-,-	3rd	218	41	116	379
Hendry	15	1	33	0	-,-	(4)	15	1	51	3	-,-	4th	226	57	139	431
Baring	5	0	19	0	-,-							5th	289	66	245	436
Millar						(6)	14.6	2	41	1	-,-	6th	322	71	261	446
												7th	329	77	311	467
QUEENSLAND	O	M	R	W	w,nb		O	M	R	W	w,nb	8th	348	81	369	508
Hornibrook	11	1	28	2	-,-		32.2	6	109	4	-,1	9th	385	82	409	518
Gill	4	0	17	1	-,-		13	2	41	1	-,1	10th	399	86	439	518
Mayes	8	1	21	3	-,2		31	3	95	2	-,2					
R.K.Oxenham	11.6	3	18	4	-,-											
Grant						(4)	26	2	107	2	-,-					
Bensted						(5)	17	2	52	0	-,3					
Thompson						(6)	9	1	38	0	-,-					
Gough						(7)	15	1	51	0	-,-					

AUSTRALIAN XI v THE REST

Played at Sydney Cricket Ground on February 18, 19, 21, 22, 1927. (Four-day match)
Toss : The Rest.   Result : AUSTRALIAN XI WON BY SEVEN WICKETS.
Debuts: The Rest - S.M.Smith (f/c).
12th Men: J.L.Ellis (Aust) and N.E.Phillips (Rest).
Umpires: A.C.Jones and A.P.Williams.
Attendances: 8963, 27684, 1000, 3000.   Total: 40,647.   Receipts: £2634.
Close of Play: 1st day Aust 0/82 (Ponsford 47, Woodfull 31); 2nd day Rest (2) 0/32 (Morgan 20, Richardson 10); 3rd day The Rest (2)
2/146 (Morgan 63, Jackson 12).

The match was staged as a benefit for C.G.Macartney and raised £2598. Morgan (89 in 133 minutes, 9 fours) and Kippax (100 in 134 minutes, 9 fours) shared a second-wicket partnership of 151 in 108 minutes for the Rest on the first day. In reply Ponsford (131 in 149 minutes, 16 fours, chance at 15) and Woodfull (140 in 177 minutes, 2 sixes and 13 fours) added 223 for the Australian first wicket. Andrews scored an unbeaten 115 in 150 minutes with 9 fours. Thompson and Morton for the Rest and Taylor for the Australians all suffered first-ball dismissals. Rain delayed the start of the third day until 4.00pm and resulted in only 95 minutes' play. Morgan (73 in 157 minutes, 7 fours) and O'Connor (101 in 114 minutes, made big contributions in the Rest's second innings, in which all batsmen were caught out. Ryder led the Australian team to victory with an unbeaten '55 in 58 minutes including 2 sixes and 3 fours. Last first-class appearances by W.Bardsley and J.M.Taylor. Only first-class appearance by S.M.Smith. Sources: *Wisden, NSWCA Report, VCA Report, The Age, The Argus, Sydney Morning Herald, Sydney Referee.*

THE REST

J.G.Morgan	c & b Andrews	89		c Woodfull b Gregory	73
†L.P.D.O'Connor	b Mailey	5	(7)	c Ponsford b Mailey	101
A.F.Kippax	c Ryder b Gregory	100		c Woodfull b Everett	51
*V.Y.Richardson	b Macartney	36	(2)	c Gregory b Mailey	16
F.C.Thompson	c Mailey b Gregory	0	(6)	c Everett b Mailey	12
A.Jackson	c Oldfield b Ryder	4	(4)	c & b Mailey	32
W.C.Alexander	st Oldfield b Mailey	22	(5)	c & b Mailey	9
N.L.Williams	c Ryder b Everett	18		c Ponsford b Ryder	0
S.M.Smith	not out	13		c Oldfield b Everett	25
F.L.Morton	b Everett	0	(11)	not out	1
R.L.A.McNamee	b Everett	12	(10)	c Ryder b Mailey	14
Extras	(lb3, w1, nb2)	6		(b2, lb4, w1, nb3)	10
Total	(70.1 overs, 244 mins)	305		(95.6 overs, 323 mins)	344

AUSTRALIAN XI

W.H.Ponsford	c McNamee b Williams	131		b McNamee	7
W.M.Woodfull	c Richardson b McNamee	140	(5)	not out	29
J.M.Taylor	lbw b Williams	0			
T.J.E.Andrews	not out	115	(3)	c Richardson b McNamee	2
C.G.Macartney	st O'Connor b Williams	26	(2)	b McNamee	19
J.Ryder	c Richardson b Williams	14	(4)	not out	55
J.M.Gregory	c Jackson b Williams	44			
*W.Bardsley	c O'Connor b Smith	7			
†W.A.S.Oldfield	c Morgan b Morton	13			
S.C.Everett	c Thompson b McNamee	26			
A.A.Mailey	st O'Connor b Williams	12			
Extras	(b1, lb4)	5		(b4, lb1)	5
Total	(83.4 overs, 304 mins)	533		(20.4 overs, 75 mins) (3 wkts)	117

AUSTRALIAN XI	O	M	R	W	w,nb		O	M	R	W	w,nb
Gregory	10	1	50	2	-,-		15	0	49	1	1,-
Everett	10.1	0	49	3	-,2	(3)	18	1	76	2	-,3
Mailey	22	2	99	2	1,-	(4)	24.6	1	99	6	-,-
Ryder	8	0	50	1	-,-	(2)	13	1	40	1	-,-
Macartney	15	6	25	1	-,-		18	5	36	0	-,-
Andrews	5	0	26	1	-,-		7	1	34	0	-,-

THE REST	O	M	R	W	w,nb		O	M	R	W	w,nb
Morton	18	1	110	1	-,-		4	0	21	0	-,-
McNamee	24	1	122	2	-,-		7	1	46	3	-,-
Williams	20.4	0	174	6	-,-		2.4	0	11	0	-,-
Smith	10	0	62	1	-,-						
Morgan	5	0	23	0	-,-		3	0	21	0	-,-
Kippax	6	0	37	0	-,-						
Thompson						(4)	4	0	13	0	-,-

FALL OF WICKETS

Wkt	REST 1st	AUST 1st	REST 2nd	AUST 2nd
1st	32	223	44	18
2nd	183	223	115	21
3rd	215	283	159	28
4th	215	324	174	-
5th	224	344	197	-
6th	248	427	198	-
7th	271	435	203	-
8th	275	458	300	-
9th	275	519	338	-
10th	305	533	344	-

WESTERN AUSTRALIA v SOUTH AUSTRALIA

Played at W.A.C.A. Ground, Perth on March 19 (no play), 21, 22, 23, 1927. (Three-day match)
Toss : South Australia.   Result : SOUTH AUSTRALIA WON BY 93 RUNS.
Debuts: Western Australia - F.J.Bryant, W.J.Bryant, W.J.Horrocks (all f/c). South Australia - E.A.Johnson, L.R.Lewis, C.P.L.Power,
    H.E.Whitfield (all f/c).
12th Men: A.Rigby (WA) and C.L.B.Starr (SA).
Umpires: A.E.Lawrence and C.Sinclair.
Attendances: 2000, 2000, 2000.   Total: about 6000.   Receipts: No figures published.
Close of Play: 1st day no play; 2nd day WA 2/9 (Quinlan 3, Drew 0); 3rd day SA (2) 105 all out.

C.V.Grimmett, D.E.Pritchard, J.W.Rymill and N.L.Williams all announced their unavailability for selection in South Australia's team to Perth. Rain washed out all of the first day and the match length was extended to make up for the lost time. The wicket played truly throughout, contrary to expectations, and could not be held accountable for the low scoring. Lewis (61 in 105 minutes, 1 six and 5 fours) and Ryan rescued the South Australian first innings with a sixth wicket stand of 95, a figure similar to the match result margin. Whitfield destroyed the home team's first innings, beginning the second day with the wickets of Drew, R.J.Bryant, F.J.Bryant and Inverarity in his first two overs at a cost of a single run only. Quinlan (1 four) carried his bat through the innings. Bowlers of both sides remained on top during the respective second innings. Lewis, topscorer in the game, was out to the first ball he received in the second innings. Sources: *The Cricketer, C.B.O'Reilly, The West Australian, Daily News.*

SOUTH AUSTRALIA

A.J.Richardson	c F.J.Bryant b Inverarity	6	c Drew b Inverarity	8
K.J.Schneider	c Stokes b Inverarity	10	lbw b Evans	0
E.A.Johnson	c W.J.Bryant b Quinlan	28	run out (Inverarity)	9
*V.Y.Richardson	c Quinlan b Evans	37	c Evans b Inverarity	8
P.K.Lee	c & b Evans	0	c R.J.Bryant b Evans	11
L.R.Lewis	b Evans	61	c Stokes b Inverarity	0
A.J.Ryan	b Quinlan	44	b Evans	13
C.P.L.Power	run out	29	c F.J.Bryant b Evans	33
H.E.Whitfield	b Inverarity	8	c Quinlan b Evans	13
†G.B.Inkster	not out	2	c Drew b Quinlan	6
R.A.Halcombe	b Inverarity	0	not out	2
Extras	(b8, lb6)	14	(b2)	2
Total	(76.1 overs, 265 mins)	239	(36.4 overs, 130 mins)	105

WESTERN AUSTRALIA

*P.F.Quinlan	not out	40	c Ryan b Whitfield	3
W.J.Bryant	c Inkster b Halcombe	6	(3) run out (A.J.Richardson)	0
†W.Stokes	b Halcombe	0	(11) st Inkster b Schneider	3
A.D.Drew	c Inkster b Whitfield	0	(2) b Whitfield	0
R.J.Bryant	b Whitfield	0	(4) b A.J.Richardson	15
F.J.Bryant	b Whitfield	0	(5) c Johnson b Lewis	17
M.Inverarity	b Whitfield	0	(6) b Halcombe	16
W.J.Horrocks	c Inkster b Whitfield	10	(7) not out	27
A.E.C.Smith	st Inkster b Schneider	16	(8) b Lewis	15
W.A.Evans	c Halcombe b Whitfield	27	(9) c V.Y.Richardson b A.J.Richardson	9
L.C.Renfrey	st Inkster b Schneider	21	(10) b Lee	11
Extras	(b11)	11	(b2, lb1, nb1)	4
Total	(34.6 overs, 135 mins)	131	(46.4 overs, 185 mins)	120

WESTERN AUSTRALIA	O	M	R	W	w,nb		O	M	R	W	w,nb
Quinlan	15	3	38	2	-,-	(4)	2.4	0	6	1	-,-
Renfrey	15	4	43	0	-,-	(3)	3	0	10	0	-,-
Inverarity	20.1	3	65	4	-,-	(1)	16	2	50	3	-,-
Evans	19	4	56	3	-,-	(2)	15	2	37	5	-,-
Drew	3	1	9	0	-,-						
R.J.Bryant	4	1	14	0	-,-						

SOUTH AUSTRALIA	O	M	R	W	w,nb		O	M	R	W	w,nb
Halcombe	8	2	28	2	-,-		9	0	34	1	-,1
Whitfield	14	2	47	6	-,-		7	1	16	2	-,-
Schneider	8.6	1	33	2	-,-	(5)	4.4	0	20	1	-,-
A.J.Richardson	2	1	5	0	-,-		10	5	14	2	-,-
Lee	2	0	7	0	-,-	(6)	2	0	5	1	-,-
Lewis						(3)	14	5	27	2	-,-

FALL OF WICKETS

Wkt	SA 1st	WA 1st	SA 2nd	WA 2nd
1st	15	9	3	2
2nd	32	9	19	3
3rd	93	10	23	8
4th	93	10	38	31
5th	93	12	38	37
6th	188	12	40	59
7th	208	40	63	79
8th	236	63	96	92
9th	239	100	99	111
10th	239	131	105	120

WESTERN AUSTRALIA v SOUTH AUSTRALIA

Played at W.A.C.A. Ground, Perth on March 26, 28, 29, 1927.   (Three-day match)
Toss : South Australia.　　　　　Result : SOUTH AUSTRALIA WON BY SEVEN WICKETS.
Debuts: Western Australia - R.O.Doig, A.Rigby, R.J.Wilberforce (all f/c). South Australia - C.L.B.Starr (f/c).
12th Men: C.M.B.Jarvis (WA) and P.K.Lee (SA).
Umpires: P.Bastow and C.Sinclair.
Attendances: 2000, no other figures published.　　　Total & Receipts: No figures published.
Close of Play: 1st day SA 8/326 (Whitfield 28, Inkster 14); 2nd day WA (2) 1/29 (Evans 19, Doig 2).

P.F.Quinlan, named as Western Australia's captain, withdrew on the morning of the match due to a knee injury sustained in the game against South Australia earlier in the week. Drew, originally named as 12th man, was brought in to the team and Herbert made captain. Schneider, who according to *"The West Australian"* at the time "must be the shortest man playing first-class cricket in Australia", compiled 107 in 145 minutes. In an incident reported late on the first day, Whitfield was given out lbw to a ball from Inverarity by umpire Bastow, but stayed on. No explanation was offered as to why the batsman was allowed to continue, and the incident remains a mystery. Inkster did not take the field for the third day's play, due to an unspecified injury. Lee fielded in his stead and V.Y.Richardson kept wickets for the remainder of Western Australia's second innings. Sources: *The Cricketer, C.B.O'Reilly, SACA Report, The West Australian, Daily News, Sunday Times, Western Mail.*

SOUTH AUSTRALIA

L.R.Lewis	c R.J.Bryant b Evans	21	(2) not out		24
A.J.Ryan	b Herbert	45			
E.A.Johnson	b Inverarity	19	(5) not out		0
A.J.Richardson	c Stokes b Evans	3	(1) b Evans		38
K.J.Schneider	c Herbert b Evans	107			
*V.Y.Richardson	c Drew b Inverarity	63			
C.L.B.Starr	c Wilberforce b Evans	15			
C.P.L.Power	c F.J.Bryant b Inverarity	9	(4) b Evans		6
H.E.Whitfield	not out	28	(3) lbw b Evans		8
†G.B.Inkster	not out	14			
R.A.Halcombe	did not bat				
Extras	(b1, lb1)	2	(b2, lb5)		7
Total	(83.0 overs) (8 wkts dec)	326	(18.0 overs) (3 wkts)		83

WESTERN AUSTRALIA

A.D.Drew	c & b Power	31	c V.Y.Richardson b Halcombe		7
R.O.Doig	b A.J.Richardson	8	(3) c sub (Lee) b Halcombe		5
F.J.Bryant	b A.J.Richardson	0	(4) c sub (Lee) b Whitfield		39
R.J.Bryant	b A.J.Richardson	3	(8) c V.Y.Richardson b Halcombe		51
W.J.Horrocks	b A.J.Richardson	0	(6) c A.J.Richardson b Whitfield		60
M.Inverarity	b Lewis	15	(7) c V.Y.Richardson b Halcombe		11
R.J.Wilberforce	st Inkster b Power	33	(5) c Johnson b Whitfield		1
A.Rigby	b Power	4	(10) c Ryan b Whitfield		5
*H.J.Herbert	c Starr b Whitfield	10	not out		10
W.A.Evans	c Inkster b Halcombe	33	(2) c Ryan b Power		48
†W.Stokes	not out	5	run out		3
Extras	(b2, lb4, nb2)	8	(b14, w4)		18
Total	(63.4 overs)	150	(52.2 overs)		258

WESTERN AUSTRALIA	O	M	R	W	w,nb		O	M	R	W	w,nb			
Evans	25	4	88	4	-,-		9	1	32	3	-,-			
Inverarity	26	4	114	3	-,-		3	0	21	0	-,-			
Herbert	14	1	51	1	-,-		6	0	23	0	-,-			
Rigby	5	1	17	0	-,-									
Drew	4	0	10	0	-,-									
R.J.Bryant	7	1	29	0	-,-									
Wilberforce	2	1	15	0	-,-									

FALL OF WICKETS				
Wkt	SA 1st	WA 1st	WA 2nd	SA 2nd
1st	35	24	27	57
2nd	68	24	39	69
3rd	71	30	97	79
4th	114	30	103	-
5th	239	57	104	-
6th	275	63	133	-
7th	276	77	225	-
8th	296	94	249	-
9th	-	139	254	-
10th	-	150	258	-

SOUTH AUSTRALIA	O	M	R	W	w,nb		O	M	R	W	w,nb
Halcombe	12	2	33	1	-,2		16.2	4	61	4	-,-
Whitfield	14	3	33	1	-,-		15	0	80	4	3,-
A.J.Richardson	18	5	26	4	-,-		8	1	23	0	-,-
Lewis	8	4	9	1	-,-	(6)	4	0	21	0	-,-
Power	11.4	1	41	3	-,-	(4)	7	1	35	1	1,-
Schneider						(5)	2	0	20	0	-,-

The rules governing the Sheffield Shield competition received a fundamental change prior to the start of the 1927-28 season. The Interstate Conference to the Board of Control decided at their September meeting to impose a time limit on matches for the first time. They would be restricted to four days of play (each of five and a half hours' duration) plus the pre-lunch session of a fifth day (comprising two and a half hours). The decision was directly due to Queensland's entry into the competition the previous season. Owing to the doubling of fixtures, scheduled starting dates now had to be adhered to. Teams were allocated Shield points on the following basis : 4 for an outright win (WO), 3 for a first-innings lead in the event of a drawn match (W1), 2 for a tie or a match in which no result was obtained on the first innings (D), and 1 for a first-innings deficit in the event of a draw (L1). An outright loss earned nothing, any first-innings points being forfeited.

Victoria achieved outright wins in each of their first four engagements - three of them by an innings - and duly took out the trophy. Ponsford again exceeded 1000 runs in the competition - a feat he achieved in December alone with scores of 133, 437 (surpassing his own world record), 202, 38 and 336. He was soundly supported by Woodfull, Hendry and Ryder. The bowling of Blackie, Ironmonger and Morton capitalised on the ruthless batting efforts.

South Australia missed Arthur Richardson, who had taken up a coaching appointment in Perth, and their other former stalwart Vic Richardson was below form. Batting hopes rested with the young players, Schneider and Harris. Grimmett, the leading wicket-taker in the Shield, received strongest support from Scott and the promising Wall.

New South Wales depended on McNamee performing with the ball, as Mailey's wickets were obtained at a heavy cost. The New South Wales batting, as resilient as ever, was headed by Kippax, the veteran Andrews, and the exciting youngsters Jackson and Bradman. Bradman registered a century on debut and promised a bright future, but nobody realised the impact he would make over the next two decades. In fact, Jackson was generally rated higher. Another future giant of the game in O'Reilly made his first appearance this season in first-class cricket.

Queensland, who were granted a return match against South Australia for the first time, were unable to sustain the momentum of their inaugural season despite a sound performance in their opening match, at home to New South Wales. Their veterans, O'Connor, Thompson and Rowe, again batted well but their bowling fell down, incapable of either restricting the opposition batting or breaking through with any regularity. The two best bowlers, Hornibrook and Ron Oxenham, were only available for three games.

A New Zealand team which toured England in 1927 stopped off at Sydney on the way home to play New South Wales. The locals completely outplayed a side that had been at sea for five weeks, and the outcome was never in question. Tasmania contested two matches, against New South Wales and Victoria, and Western Australia played host to Victoria for two matches to bring the season to a close.

Australia sent a team to New Zealand for a short tour commencing mid-February. The team was: V.Y.Richardson (captain), W.C.Alexander, D.D.Blackie, C.V.Grimmett, A.Jackson, A.F.Kippax, R.L.A.McNamee, F.L.Morton, W.A.S.Oldfield, R.K.Oxenham, W.H.Ponsford, K.J.Schneider and W.M.Woodfull.

Leading Aggregates

Batsmen	M	I	NO	Runs	HS	Ave.	Bowlers	Runs	Wkts	Ave.
W.H.Ponsford (V)	6	8	0	1217	437	152.12	C.V.Grimmett (SA)	1151	42	27.40
A.F.Kippax (NSW)	7	12	1	926	315*	84.18	D.D.Blackie (V)	689	31	22.22
W.M.Woodfull (V)	5	7	2	645	191*	129.00	H.Ironmonger (V)	869	31	28.03
H.S.T.L.Hendry (V)	6	7	0	561	168	80.14	F.L.Morton (V)	783	28	27.96
K.J.Schneider (SA)	6	10	0	520	143	52.00	E.L.a'Beckett (V)	597	22	27.13
T.J.E.Andrews (NSW)	6	11	0	509	134	46.27	R.L.A.McNamee (NSW)	761	22	34.59
G.W.Harris (SA)	6	11	1	485	77	48.50	J.D.Scott (SA)	639	21	30.42
W.Rowe (Q)	5	8	1	480	147	68.57				

SHEFFIELD SHIELD TABLE

	P	WO	W1	LO	L1	D	Pts	Quotient	Runs Scored	Wkts Lost	Runs Conceded	Wkts Taken
VICTORIA	6	4	-	-	2	-	18	1.826	3744	66	3323	107
SOUTH AUSTRALIA	6	3	-	3	-	-	12	0.842	3226	101	3676	97
NEW SOUTH WALES	6	1	2	2	1	-	11	0.850	3661	108	3864	97
QUEENSLAND	6	-	2	3	1	-	7	0.789	3330	98	3098	72
TOTAL	12	8	4	8	4	-	48	1.000	13961	373	13961	373

NEW SOUTH WALES v NEW ZEALAND XI

Played at Sydney Cricket Ground on October 28, 29, 31, 1927. (Four-day match)
Toss : New South Wales.   Result : NEW SOUTH WALES WON BY TEN WICKETS.
Debuts: New South Wales - W.J.O'Reilly (f/c).
12th Men: C.J.Oliver (NZ - see below). No 12th named for NSW.
Umpires: E.G.Borwick and E.R.Kent.
Attendances: 5322, 9250, 1789.   Total: 16,361.   Receipts: £780.
Close of Play: 1st day NSW 571 all out; 2nd day NZ (2) 1/10 (Mills 2, Lowry 1).

James, the New Zealand wicket-keeper, fell heavily while attempting to take a wild return in the opening minutes of the match and dislocated his shoulder, forcing him to leave the field and take no further part in the match. Oliver was permitted to take his place as a full member of the team and Lowry donned the pads and gloves to assume the wicket-keeping duties. Gregory (152 in 135 minutes, 2 sixes and 20 fours) scored 103 out of 1/192 in 105 minutes before lunch. Andrews (134 in 148 minutes, 18 fours), Kippax (119 in 133 minutes) and Jackson (104 in 72 minutes, 11 fours) also flogged the bowling as 571 runs were tallied on the first day, all batsmen being particularly merciless on Merritt's leg breaks and googlies. Blunt (63 in 101 minutes and 53 in 80 minutes, 4 fours), Page (51 in 72 minutes, no fours) and Dacre (54 in 42 minutes) scored fifties for New Zealand. *Reese incorrectly gives NSW Oldfield c Lowry; NZ (2) dismissal of Lowry.* Sources: *T.W.Reese, NSWCA Report, VCA Report, Sydney Morning Herald, Sydney Referee, Sydney Daily Telegraph.*

NEW SOUTH WALES

N.E.Phillips	b Henderson	6	not out	0
J.M.Gregory	st Lowry b Merritt	152		
T.J.E.Andrews	b Henderson	134		
*A.F.Kippax	c McGirr b Merritt	119	(2) not out	0
A.Jackson	b McGirr	104		
J.G.Morgan	lbw b McGirr	7		
†W.A.S.Oldfield	st Lowry b McGirr	0		
S.C.Everett	c Blunt b Merritt	10		
A.A.Mailey	st Lowry b Merritt	9		
W.J.O'Reilly	c Henderson b Merritt	4		
R.L.A.McNamee	not out	1		
Extras	(b13, lb4, w8)	25	(b 7, lb1)	8
Total	(78.2 overs, 283 mins)	571	(1.1 overs, 5 mins) (0 wkts)	8

NEW ZEALAND XI

C.S.Dempster	c Gregory b Mailey	32	b Gregory	3
J.E.Mills	hit wkt b Everett	16	c Oldfield b McNamee	12
M.L.Page	c & b Mailey	38	(5) b Gregory	51
R.C.Blunt	c Mailey b McNamee	63	run out (Andrews/Oldfield)	53
*T.C.Lowry	c Oldfield b Everett	44	(3) c & b Andrews	35
C.C.R.Dacre	c Oldfield b Gregory	10	(7) b McNamee	54
C.F.W.Allcott	c Oldfield b Gregory	43	(6) b O'Reilly	11
H.M.McGirr	c Gregory b O'Reilly	9	b Everett	13
C.J.Oliver	b O'Reilly	7	run out (Andrews/Oldfield)	0
W.E.Merritt	not out	6	b Gregory	22
M.Henderson	run out	0	not out	25
†K.C.James	absent hurt	-	absent hurt	-
Extras	(lb5, w5, nb8)	18	(b3, lb7, nb3)	13
Total	(71.6 overs, 270 mins)	286	(60.3 overs, 220 mins)	292

NEW ZEALAND XI	O	M	R	W	w,nb		O	M	R	W	w,nb
McGirr	16	2	87	3	-,-		1	1	0	0	-,-
Henderson	13	1	76	2	8,-						
Merritt	23.2	0	218	5	-,-						
Allcott	8	0	33	0	-,-						
Blunt	12	0	83	0	-,-						
Page	5	0	42	0	-,-						
Dempster	1	0	7	0	-,-						
Mills						(2)	0.1	0	0	0	-,-

NEW SOUTH WALES	O	M	R	W	w,nb		O	M	R	W	w,nb
Gregory	10	1	27	2	1,-		8.3	2	40	3	-,-
McNamee	17	0	54	1	3,6		14	0	62	2	-,2
Everett	14	1	63	2	-,1		7	0	41	1	-,1
Mailey	15	1	64	2	-,-						
Morgan	5	0	23	0	1,-		5	0	29	0	-,-
O'Reilly	10.6	1	37	2	-,1	(4)	16	2	53	1	-,-
Andrews						(6)	9	0	45	1	-,-
Phillips						(7)	1	0	9	0	-,-

FALL OF WICKETS

Wkt	NSW 1st	NZ 1st	NZ 2nd	NSW 2nd
1st	10	36	8	-
2nd	272	72	26	-
3rd	329	116	110	-
4th	505	207	110	-
5th	521	207	127	-
6th	525	240	222	-
7th	553	272	232	-
8th	561	272	249	-
9th	566	286	250	-
10th	571	286	292	-

QUEENSLAND v NEW SOUTH WALES (Shield Match 1)

Played at Exhibition Ground, Brisbane, on November 26, 28 - 29 (no play), 30, December 1, 1927. (Five-day match)
Toss : Queensland.   Result : MATCH DRAWN.
Debuts: Queensland - G.S.Amos, O.E.Nothling (both Qld only). New South Wales - F.S.Jordan, B.F.Watson (both f/c).
12th Men: L.L.Gill (Qld) and R.L.A.McNamee (NSW).
Umpires: J.P.Orr and J.A.Scott.
Attendances: 9500, no play, no play, 4500, 1500.   Total: 15,500.   Receipts: £991.
Close of Play: 1st day Qld 8/354 (Rowe 96, Hornibrook 6); 2nd day no play; 3rd day no play; 4th day NSW 7/131 (Everett 19, Jordan 15).

The first Shield match to be officially restricted by time was ruined by rain. The second and third days were completely lost as well as part of the fourth, and the fifth day, as with all five-day Shield matches, was restricted to two hours. Oxenham (63 in 131 minutes, 7 fours) and Rowe (128 not out in 238 minutes, 11 fours) topscored for Queensland, Rowe sharing partnerships of 91 in 91 minutes for the fifth wicket with Nothling and 100 in 89 minutes for the seventh wicket with Bensted. Rain had affected the pitch by the time New South Wales went to the crease, the absence of T.J.E.Andrews and J.M.Gregory (both unavailable) further weakening the side's chances. Amos and Nothling both represented New South Wales before their Queensland debuts in this match. Sources: *Wisden, NSWCA Report, QCA Report, Sydney Morning Herald, Brisbane Courier, Brisbane Daily Mail.*

QUEENSLAND

R.K.Oxenham	c Mailey b Everett	63
*†L.P.D.O'Connor	c Morgan b Jordan	21
F.J.Gough	c & b Everett	38
F.C.Thompson	c Everett b Mailey	11
W.Rowe	not out	128
O.E.Nothling	c Oldfield b Jordan	46
H.J.R.Higgins	c Oldfield b Morgan	0
E.C.Bensted	c Oldfield b Phillips	44
A.Hurwood	lbw b Phillips	0
P.M.Hornibrook	run out (Kippax/Oldfield)	10
G.S.Amos	c Love b Morgan	23
Extras	(b14, lb10, w4, nb7)	35
Total	(101.5 overs, 362 mins)	419

NEW SOUTH WALES

N.E.Phillips	lbw b Hornibrook	1			
J.G.Morgan	c Amos b Hornibrook	2			
H.S.B.Love	c Amos b Hurwood	6			
*A.F.Kippax	c Nothling b Hurwood	28			
A.Jackson	b Hurwood	2			
B.F.Watson	c Bensted b Hurwood	32			
†W.A.S.Oldfield	c Hornibrook b Oxenham	21			
S.C.Everett	c Amos b Hurwood	19	(3) lbw b Nothling	10
F.S.Jordan	not out	35	(1) lbw b Hurwood	1
A.A.Mailey	b Amos	4			
W.J.O'Reilly	b Oxenham	9	(2) not out	9
Extras	(b6, lb2)	8	(b1, lb1)	2
Total	(71.1 overs, 249 mins)	167	(10.5 overs, 35 mins) (2 wkts)	22

NEW SOUTH WALES	O	M	R	W	w,nb
Everett	21	2	82	2	-,3
Jordan	25	5	77	2	4,-
Mailey	26	1	120	1	-,-
O'Reilly	13	1	43	0	-,4
Morgan	9.5	1	44	2	-,-
Phillips	5	1	11	2	-,-
Kippax	2	0	7	0	-,-

QUEENSLAND	O	M	R	W	w,nb		O	M	R	W	w,nb
Hornibrook	8	1	25	2	-,-						
Hurwood	25	7	50	5	-,-	(1)	4	0	6	1	-,-
Oxenham	19.1	5	64	2	-,-						
Amos	9	4	11	1	-,-	(2)	3	1	3	0	-,-
Nothling	3	2	2	0	-,-	(4)	1.5	0	7	1	-,-
Gough	3	2	2	0	-,-						
Rowe	2	2	0	0	-,-						
Bensted	2	0	5	0	-,-	(3)	2	0	4	0	-,-

FALL OF WICKETS

Wkt	QLD 1st	NSW 1st	NSW 2nd
1st	48	2	2
2nd	118	9	22
3rd	136	11	-
4th	146	17	-
5th	237	62	-
6th	242	93	-
7th	342	107	-
8th	342	131	-
9th	361	147	-
10th	419	167	-

SOUTH AUSTRALIA v VICTORIA (Shield Match 2)

Played at Adelaide Oval on December 2, 3, 5 ,6, 1927. (Five-day match)
Toss : Victoria.   Result : VICTORIA WON BY AN INNINGS AND 310 RUNS.
Debuts: Nil.
12th Men: A.J.Ryan (SA) and C.A.H.Sindrey (Vic).
Umpires: G.A.Hele and J.J.Quinn.
Attendances: 6000, 12470, 5630, 2700.   Total: 26,800.   Receipts: £1155.
Close of Play: 1st day Vic 2/305 (Hendry 95, Ryder 22); 2nd day Vic 8/646 (Hartkopf 111, Morton 1); 3rd day SA (2) 0/54 (Harris 27, Johnson 25).

Flags were flown at half-mast in memory of George Giffen who had died on November 29th. J.W.Rymill was unavailable for South Australia while L.T.Gun, who replaced D.E.Pritchard in the twelve, also withdrew and was replaced by Ryan. Sindrey replaced K.E.Rigg (unavailable) for Victoria. Woodfull (43 in 98 minutes, no fours) and Ponsford (chanceless 133 in 208 minutes, 5 fours) began the match in ideal conditions. After Woodfull's departure Hendry (168 in 285 minutes, 1 six and 12 fours, 2 chances) shared century stands with both Ponsford and Ryder (70 in 124 minutes, 1 six and 7 fours). Hartkopf (111 not out in 179 minutes, 13 fours) and Blackie (55 in 102 minutes, 4 fours) continued by adding 120 for the eighth wicket. South Australia were unfortunate to be caught on a rain-affected pitch in both innings, only Whitfield (48 in 109 minutes, 1 four) and Harris (61 in 142 minutes, 2 fours) offering prolonged resistance to Victoria's bowlers. Harris fell to the seventh ball of the first innings and Williams was out first ball later on. Sources: *Wisden, C.B.O'Reilly, VCA Report, SACA Report, Adelaide Advertiser, South Australian Register.*

VICTORIA

*W.M.Woodfull	c Williams b Grimmett	43
W.H.Ponsford	c Whitfield b Halcombe	133
H.S.T.L.Hendry	c Halcombe b Williams	168
J.Ryder	lbw b Grimmett	70
B.A.Onyons	b Grimmett	2
J.W.Scaife	st Inkster b Whitfield	28
A.E.V.Hartkopf	not out	111
†J.L.Ellis	lbw b Williams	3
D.D.Blackie	c Richardson b Schneider	55
F.L.Morton	not out	1
H.Ironmonger	did not bat	
Extras	(b15, lb10, nb7)	32
Total	(164.0 overs, 566 mins) (8 wkts dec)	646

SOUTH AUSTRALIA

K.J.Schneider	lbw b Ironmonger	21	(5)	run out (Onyons/Blackie)	6
G.W.Harris	c Ryder b Morton	1	(1)	c Ellis b Ironmonger	61
*V.Y.Richardson	c Hendry b Ironmonger	21		st Ellis b Ironmonger	25
W.C.Alexander	c Blackie b Ironmonger	5		c Ponsford b Blackie	4
E.A.Johnson	run out (Woodfull/Blackie)	16	(2)	b Morton	27
H.E.Whitfield	c Ellis b Morton	48		c Hartkopf b Blackie	4
P.K.Lee	c Morton b Ironmonger	12		b Morton	11
C.V.Grimmett	st Ellis b Ironmonger	13		not out	10
N.L.Williams	c Blackie b Morton	0		c Scaife b Morton	2
†G.B.Inkster	b Morton	10		b Blackie	1
R.A.Halcombe	not out	3		b Blackie	0
Extras	(b22, lb3, nb2)	27		(b5, nb3)	8
Total	(66.5 overs, 239 mins)	177		(60.5 overs, 224 mins)	159

SOUTH AUSTRALIA	O	M	R	W	w,nb
Halcombe	26	1	119	1	-,6
Whitfield	26	2	100	1	-,-
Grimmett	56	7	175	3	-,-
Lee	18	3	62	0	-,-
Williams	27	1	119	2	-,1
Alexander	4	0	16	0	-,-
Schneider	7	0	23	1	-,-

VICTORIA	O	M	R	W	w,nb		O	M	R	W	w,nb
Morton	11.5	0	35	4	-,2		14	3	47	3	-,3
Ironmonger	32	11	50	5	-,-	(4)	23	6	52	2	-,-
Blackie	20	7	54	0	-,-		20.5	4	45	4	-,-
Hendry	3	0	11	0	-,-						
Ryder						(2)	3	0	7	0	-,-

FALL OF WICKETS

Wkt	VIC 1st	SA 1st	SA 2nd
1st	97	3	68
2nd	261	45	115
3rd	407	53	122
4th	409	58	122
5th	455	96	132
6th	492	118	135
7th	517	160	156
8th	637	160	158
9th	-	166	159
10th	-	177	159

VICTORIA v QUEENSLAND (Shield Match 3)

Played at Melbourne Cricket Ground on December 16, 17, 19, 20, 21, 1927. (Five-day match)
Toss : Queensland.   Result : VICTORIA WON BY AN INNINGS AND 197 RUNS.
Debuts: Queensland - J.L.Litster (f/c).
12th Men: K.E.Rigg (Vic) and H.J.R.Higgins (Qld).
Umpires: J.Richards and P.E.Smith.
Attendances: 4880, 10977, 5126, 1869, -.   Total: 22,852.   Receipts: £886.
Close of Play: 1st day Vic 2/400 (Ponsford 234, Ryder 4); 2nd day Vic 793 all out; 3rd day Qld (2) 1/32 (Nothling 16, Rowe 9); 4th day
     Qld (2) 7/338 (Gill 22, Litster 13).

Ponsford's 437 in 621 minutes included 42 fours and surpassed his previous world-record score of 429 made five years earlier. His score
moved from 61 at lunch on the first day (Victoria 1/100) to 152 at tea (1/257), 234 at stumps (2/400), 315 at lunch on the second day
(3/562), 381 at tea (5/680) and ended when he was eighth out at 792. He offered difficult chances when 162 and 239 and shared century
partnerships of 314 for the second wicket with Hendry (129 in 221 minutes, 5 fours) and 143 for the third wicket with Ryder (70 in 91
minutes, 9 fours). Morton was dismissed first ball after Ponsford's dismissal and Amos finished the innings by dismissing Blackie in the
same over. Nothling (66 in 124 minutes, 7 fours) topscored in Queensland's first innings against the off-spin of Blackie who strained a
muscle in his side and was replaced in the field over the last two days by A.E.Liddicut, 12th man Rigg being released to play in the
Melbourne-Adelaide inter-varsity match. Ryder was unable to complete his sixth over due to a leg strain, though he remained on the field.
O'Connor (66 in 123 minutes, 6 fours), Thompson (chanceless 118 in 247 minutes, 9 fours), Gough (54 in 125 minutes, 3 fours) and
Litster (43 in 94 minutes, 4 fours) batted well against the depleted attack. No admission was charged for the last day. P.M.Hornibrook,
E.C.Knowles, A.D.A.Mayes and R.K.Oxenham were all unavailable for Queensland's southern tour. Sources: *Wisden, VCA Report, QCA
Report, The Age, The Argus, The Herald, Melbourne Sun.*

VICTORIA

*W.M.Woodfull	run out (Gill/O'Connor)	31
W.H.Ponsford	c & b Amos	437
H.S.T.L.Hendry	b Gough	129
J.Ryder	c Rowe b Nothling	70
J.W.Scaife	b Amos	18
A.E.V.Hartkopf	b Amos	15
C.A.H.Sindrey	c Bensted b Rowe	27
†J.L.Ellis	c Nothling b Thompson	15
D.D.Blackie	b Amos	35
F.L.Morton	c O'Connor b Amos	0
H.Ironmonger	not out	1
Extras	(b6, lb3, w6)	15
Total	(169.0 overs, 625 mins)	793

QUEENSLAND

*†L.P.D.O'Connor	c Ellis b Blackie	11	(5) c sub (A.E.Liddicut) b Ironmonger	66
L.E.Oxenham	lbw b Ryder	19	lbw b Morton	3
F.J.Gough	b Blackie	0	(7) b Ironmonger	54
F.C.Thompson	lbw b Blackie	8	(6) c Ellis b Ironmonger	118
W.Rowe	b Morton	34	(3) b Ryder	9
O.E.Nothling	lbw b Ironmonger	66	(1) b Morton	18
J.L.Litster	c Hendry b Ironmonger	10	(9) b Ironmonger	43
E.C.Bensted	not out	11	(4) run out (Scaife/Ellis)	14
L.L.Gill	b Blackie	0	(8) c Ellis b Ironmonger	27
A.Hurwood	lbw b Blackie	1	b Morton	1
G.S.Amos	st Ellis b Blackie	0	not out	27
Extras	(b15, lb9, w2, nb3)	29	(b16, lb8, nb3)	27
Total	(65.5 overs, 251 mins)	189	(119.4 overs, 435 mins)	407

QUEENSLAND	O	M	R	W	w,nb						
Amos	29	0	148	5	-,-
Hurwood	28	3	133	0	-,-
Gill	19	0	91	0	-,-
Nothling	26	6	101	1	-,-
Bensted	20	0	95	0	1,-
Rowe	13	1	65	1	-,-
Thompson	22	2	74	1	5,-
Gough	10	1	56	1	-,-
Litster	2	0	15	0	-,-

VICTORIA	O	M	R	W	w,nb		O	M	R	W	w,nb
Morton	13	3	34	1	-,2		32	6	103	3	-,1
Ironmonger	17	5	26	2	-,-	(4)	40.6	12	88	5	-,1
Blackie	23.5	5	46	6	-,-		3	2	2	0	-,-
Ryder	5	1	17	1	-,1	(2)	5.6	0	12	1	-,-
Hartkopf	7	0	37	0	2,-		22	1	128	0	-,1
Hendry							16	4	47	0	-,-

FALL OF WICKETS

Wkt	VIC 1st	QLD 1st	QLD 2nd
1st	74	34	9
2nd	388	36	32
3rd	531	43	38
4th	588	49	61
5th	612	128	155
6th	683	167	290
7th	742	180	305
8th	792	183	344
9th	792	189	349
10th	793	189	407

SOUTH AUSTRALIA v NEW SOUTH WALES (Shield Match 4)

Played at Adelaide Oval on December 16, 17, 19, 20, 21, 1927. (Five-day match)
Toss : New South Wales.   Result : SOUTH AUSTRALIA WON BY ONE WICKET.
Debuts: South Australia - A.T.Hack (f/c). New South Wales - D.G.Bradman (f/c).
12th Men: C.L.B.Starr (SA) and A.Jackson (SA).
Umpires: G.A.Hele and J.J.Quinn (J.F.Dodds and A.G.Jenkins deputised).
Attendances: 4794, 7180, 6175, 5035, 4372.   Total: 27,556.   Receipts: £1051.
Close of Play: 1st day NSW 7/400 (Bradman 65); 2nd day SA 1/208 (Schneider 85, Richardson 37); 3rd day NSW (2) 1/26 (Scanes 13, Andrews 0); 4th day (2) 6/121 (Hack 4, Whitfield 1).

Players and umpires suffered in extremely hot conditions on the first two days. Kippax (143 in 177 minutes, 15 fours) twice retired on the first day through heat exhaustion - when 28 at 2/194 (he resumed at 6/306) and again when 81 at 6/393 (he resumed next morning at 7/400) - and umpire Hele was off the field for part of the second day, Jenkins replacing him. Dodds stood for umpire Quinn on the last day. Bradman batted with an injured finger to record a century in his first first-class innings. He had been included in the New South Wales twelve along with Scanes to replace J.M.Gregory and H.S.B.Love, who both withdrew after the team was named, and owed his place in the final side to Jackson (boil on knee) being relegated to 12th man. He cracked two fours in his first over (off Grimmett) and brought up 50 in 67 minutes, before going on to three figures on the second day in 161 minutes with a pull for four off Lee. He gave no chances in scoring 118 in 188 minutes with 8 fours. Phillips (112 in 181 minutes, 8 fours), Andrews (58 in 97 minutes, 4 fours) and Scanes (44 in 44 minutes, 2 fours) also batted well for New South Wales. Harris (77 in 170 minutes, 10 fours), Schneider (108 in 305 minutes, 9 fours), Richardson (80 in 108 minutes, 10 fours), Alexander (42 in 39 minutes, 6 fours), Hack (45 in 118 minutes, 2 fours) and Grimmett (43 not out in 123 minutes, 2 fours) led the scoring for South Australia, while Scott was out to the first ball he faced. Grimmett's 8 for 57 was his best analysis in the Sheffield Shield so far; he dismissed the first ten New South Wales batsmen in either innings (Oldfield in both). Alexander (49 in 88 minutes, 1 four) topscored in the second innings. L.T.Gun, D.E.Pritchard and J.W.Rymill were unavailable for the home side. Hack replaced G.B.Inkster (business) after selection. B.F.Watson had announced his unavailability for New South Wales.
Sources: *Wisden, C.B.O'Reilly, NSWCA Report, SACA Report, Adelaide Advertiser, South Australian Register.*

NEW SOUTH WALES

N.E.Phillips	b Whitfield	112		lbw b Grimmett	11
J.G.Morgan	b Scott	11	(5)	b Grimmett	34
T.J.E.Andrews	c Williams b Grimmett	58		b Scott	20
*A.F.Kippax	c Alexander b Williams	143		c & b Grimmett	0
A.E.Scanes	c Williams b Schneider	44	(2)	c Whitfield b Grimmett	26
†W.A.S.Oldfield	c Hack b Grimmett	12	(9)	c Richardson b Grimmett	4
D.G.Bradman	c Williams b Scott	118	(6)	b Grimmett	33
F.S.Jordan	lbw b Scott	1		lbw b Grimmett	0
S.C.Everett	st Hack b Grimmett	5	(7)	c Harris b Scott	8
A.A.Mailey	b Scott	0		c Schneider b Grimmett	5
R.L.A.McNamee	not out	1		not out	1
Extras	(b2, lb5, w1, nb6)	14		(b1, lb1, w1, nb5)	8
Total	(105.6 overs, 398 mins)	519		(47.7 overs, 177 mins)	150

SOUTH AUSTRALIA

G.W.Harris	c & b Andrews	77	(2)	b McNamee	18
K.J.Schneider	c & b Mailey	108	(1)	lbw b McNamee	11
*V.Y.Richardson	b Jordan	80		b McNamee	0
W.C.Alexander	st Oldfield b Mailey	42		b Andrews	49
E.A.Johnson	st Oldfield b Andrews	0	(7)	b Mailey	0
H.E.Whitfield	b Jordan	15	(8)	run out (Scanes/Oldfield)	17
†A.T.Hack	c Morgan b Everett	45	(6)	b McNamee	6
P.K.Lee	st Oldfield b Mailey	28	(9)	not out	27
C.V.Grimmett	not out	43	(5)	c Oldfield b McNamee	32
J.D.Scott	c Phillips b Everett	0		c Phillips b Mailey	14
N.L.Williams	b Everett	21		not out	0
Extras	(b8, lb12, nb2)	22		(b4, lb11)	15
Total	(147.7 overs, 499 mins)	481		(70.2 overs, 220 mins) (9 wkts)	189

SOUTH AUSTRALIA	O	M	R	W	w,nb		O	M	R	W	w,nb
Scott	19.6	1	99	4	-,6		17	3	46	2	1,5
Whitfield	17	3	43	1	1,-		7	1	26	0	-,-
Grimmett	31	1	160	3	-,-		21.7	5	57	8	-,-
Williams	11	0	70	1	-,-		2	0	13	0	-,-
Lee	17	1	76	0	-,-						
Schneider	6	0	39	1	-,-						
Alexander	3	0	14	0	-,-						
Johnson	1	0	4	0	-,-						

NEW SOUTH WALES	O	M	R	W	w,nb		O	M	R	W	w,nb
Everett	26.7	4	92	3	-,-		3	0	16	0	-,-
McNamee	22	11	34	0	-,1		29.2	12	53	5	-,-
Jordan	21	1	65	2	-,-	(4)	4	0	13	0	-,-
Mailey	50	9	143	3	-,-	(3)	28	2	79	2	-,-
Andrews	18	0	86	2	-,1		6	1	13	1	-,-
Phillips	7	0	22	0	-,-						
Morgan	3	0	17	0	-,-						

FALL OF WICKETS

Wkt	NSW 1st	SA 1st	NSW 2nd	SA 2nd
1st	15	140	25	27
2nd	137	268	59	27
3rd	224	306	59	34
4th	250	315	61	112
5th	298	319	126	116
6th	306	342	135	117
7th	400	373	139	131
8th	511	438	139	158
9th	514	438	149	184
10th	519	481	150	-

VICTORIA v NEW SOUTH WALES (Shield Match 5)

Played at Melbourne Cricket Ground on December 23, 24, 26, 27, 1927. (Five-day match)
Toss : Victoria.   Result : VICTORIA WON BY 222 RUNS.
Debuts: - Nil.
12th Men: K.E.Rigg (Vic) and F.S.Jordan (NSW).
Umpires: D.A.Elder and J.Richards.
Attendances: 8463, 12205, 22146, 24000.   Total: 66,814.   Receipts: £3283.
Close of Play: 1st day Vic 355 all out; 2nd day NSW 7/340 (Oldfield 20, Everett 8); 3rd day Vic (2) 5/357 (Woodfull 178, Scaife 41).

Liddicut replaced J.Ryder (injured leg) in the Victorian side. Both teams wore black armbands in memory of J.V.Saunders who had died on December 21st. Ponsford (202 in 286 minutes, 16 fours) became the first to score consecutive double hundreds in Australia, following his 437 against Queensland seven days previously. As a partner for Woodfull (99 in 175 minutes, 5 fours) he provided Victoria with a great start but the rest of the batting failed in the face of some fine off-break bowling from McNamee. Woodfull (191 not out in 281 minutes, 10 fours, chances at 87, 140 and 174) completed an outstanding match by batting throughout the second innings which also saw fifties from Hendry (59 in 108 minutes, 2 fours, following his second-ball duck in the first innings) and Scaife (54 in 63 minutes, 2 fours). Morgan (93 in 183 minutes, 11 fours) and Andrews (110 in 213 minutes, 9 fours, chance at 45) added 151 for the New South Wales second wicket. Andrews also topscored in the second innings with 53 in 88 minutes, and 3 fours. Sources: *Wisden, NSWCA Report, VCA Report, The Age, The Argus, The Herald, Melbourne Sun.*

VICTORIA

*W.M.Woodfull	c & b McNamee	99		not out	191
W.H.Ponsford	c Bradman b McNamee	202		b McNamee	38
H.S.T.L.Hendry	c Oldfield b McNamee	0		run out (Andrews)	59
A.E.V.Hartkopf	lbw b Mailey	18		c Oldfield b Mailey	7
J.W.Scaife	st Oldfield b Mailey	0	(7)	run out (Mailey/Everett)	54
A.E.Liddicut	b McNamee	10	(5)	b Everett	10
C.A.H.Sindrey	b McNamee	9	(6)	b Everett	17
†J.L.Ellis	b McNamee	1		b Everett	0
D.D.Blackie	b Mailey	4		not out	3
F.L.Morton	not out	0			
H.Ironmonger	c Phillips b McNamee	8			
Extras	(lb2, nb2)	4		(b2, lb4, nb1)	7
Total	(88.5 overs, 311 mins)	355		(89.0 overs, 281 mins) (7 wkts dec)	386

NEW SOUTH WALES

N.E.Phillips	b Ironmonger	26	b Morton	4
J.G.Morgan	lbw b Ironmonger	93	lbw b Morton	4
T.J.E.Andrews	b Ironmonger	110	c Hartkopf b Morton	53
*A.F.Kippax	lbw b Morton	26	lbw b Blackie	35
A.Jackson	c Woodfull b Blackie	6	lbw b Blackie	16
D.G.Bradman	lbw b Hartkopf	31	b Blackie	5
A.E.Scanes	b Ironmonger	3	lbw b Blackie	1
†W.A.S.Oldfield	not out	30	not out	11
S.C.Everett	lbw b Blackie	10	c Hendry b Ironmonger	13
A.A.Mailey	c Woodfull b Ironmonger	8	c & b Blackie	0
R.L.A.McNamee	b Blackie	1	c Hendry b Blackie	0
Extras	(b11, lb7, w1, nb4)	23	(b4, lb4, nb2)	10
Total	(94.2 overs, 358 mins)	367	(33.6 overs, 137 mins)	152

NEW SOUTH WALES	O	M	R	W	w,nb		O	M	R	W	w,nb		FALL OF WICKETS			
														VIC	NSW	VIC	NSW
Everett	11	0	45	0	-,1		13	0	66	3	-,-	Wkt	1st	1st	2nd	2nd
McNamee	23.5	4	77	7	-,1		29	0	118	1	-,1	1st	227	44	71	5
Phillips	9	0	40	0	-,-							2nd	227	195	198	25
Mailey	28	3	117	3	-,-		25	0	122	1	-,-	3rd	300	243	222	100
Morgan	9	0	35	0	-,-	(3)	6	1	29	0	-,-	4th	306	257	252	106
Andrews	5	0	25	0	-,-	(5)	16	2	44	0	-,-	5th	327	279	284	113
Kippax	3	0	12	0	-,-							6th	340	293	381	119
VICTORIA	O	M	R	W	w,nb		O	M	R	W	w,nb	7th	342	318	382	137
Morton	13	1	41	1	-,3		10	0	52	3	-,1	8th	347	345	-	152
Liddicut	8	1	23	0	-,-							9th	347	360	-	152
Blackie	26.2	3	103	3	-,-		11.6	3	32	6	-,-	10th	355	367	-	152
Hendry	3	0	17	0	-,-											
Ironmonger	34	5	108	5	-,1	(2)	12	0	58	1	-,1					
Hartkopf	10	0	52	1	1,-											

SOUTH AUSTRALIA v QUEENSLAND (Shield Match 6)

Played at Adelaide Oval on December 23, 24, 26, 27, 1927. (Five-day match)
Toss : South Australia.   Result : SOUTH AUSTRALIA WON BY EIGHT WICKETS.
Debuts: South Australia - C.B.Sangster (f/c).
12th Men: H.E.Whitfield (SA) and J.L.Litster (Qld).
Umpires: G.A.Hele and A.G.Jenkins.
Attendances: ? , 8600, 8750, ? .   Total: About 24,000.   Receipts: £1232.
Close of Play: 1st day SA 6/296 (Sangster 20, Hack 3); 2nd day Qld 6/167 (Thompson 4, Bensted 0); 3rd day (2) 8/284 (Gill 1, Hurwood 0).

Whitfield was unable to obtain leave from work for the first day's play and his place in the South Australian side went to the nominated reserve, Sangster. Whitfield later acted as 12th man and participated in two dismissals. Harris (44 in 78 minutes, 2 fours), Alexander (84 in 146 minutes, 8 fours), Ryan (86 in 172 minutes, 4 fours), Sangster (54 in 127 minutes, 6 fours) and Hack (65 in 102 minutes, 7 fours) all made contributions in South Australia's first innings. Queensland's run-makers were Oxenham (61 in 134 minutes, 2 fours) in the first innings and Thompson (61 in 82 minutes, 8 fours), Higgins (45 in 57 minutes, 6 fours) and Nothling (67 in 52 minutes, 2 sixes and 8 fours) in the second innings. *Wisden* and *SACA Report* incorrectly give Qld (2) Nothling c Richardson. Sources: *Wisden, C.B.O'Reilly, QCA Report, SACA Report, Adelaide Advertiser, South Australian Register.*

SOUTH AUSTRALIA

K.J.Schneider	c O'Connor b Bensted	25			
G.W.Harris	c & b Bensted	44	(1) not out		42
*V.Y.Richardson	c O'Connor b Bensted	24	c Bensted b Gough		57
C.V.Grimmett	run out (Gill/O'Connor)	2			
W.C.Alexander	c Oxenham b Gill	84	(4) not out		2
A.J.Ryan	b Thompson	86	(2) b Bensted		0
C.B.Sangster	b Thompson	54			
†A.T.Hack	c Rowe b Bensted	65			
P.K.Lee	c Rowe b Hurwood	29			
J.D.Scott	not out	33			
N.L.Williams	c Hurwood b Thompson	17			
Extras	(b4, lb3, w1)	8			-
Total	(132.7 overs, 477 mins)	471	(18.5 overs, 67 mins) (2 wkts)		101

QUEENSLAND

L.E.Oxenham	lbw b Grimmett	61	(2) run out (Ryan/Hack/Williams)		31
H.J.R.Higgins	lbw b Williams	38	(6) b Sangster		45
F.J.Gough	c Hack b Williams	37	st Hack b Schneider		17
W.Rowe	run out (sub H.E.Whitfield/Hack)	11	(5) lbw b Grimmett		17
*†L.P.D.O'Connor	c Alexander b Lee	1	(1) c Hack b Lee		24
F.C.Thompson	not out	36	(4) c Ryan b Grimmett		61
O.E.Nothling	c sub (H.E.Whitfield) b Grimmett	5	c Lee b Grimmett		67
E.C.Bensted	c Lee b Grimmett	7	c Ryan b Grimmett		0
L.L.Gill	lbw b Grimmett	27	not out		21
G.S.Amos	c Hack b Grimmett	0	(11) st Hack b Grimmett		9
A.Hurwood	b Lee	18	(10) b Scott		1
Extras	(b3, lb9, nb3)	15	(b8, lb14)		22
Total	(71.1 overs, 250 mins)	256	(69.4 overs, 237 mins)		315

QUEENSLAND	O	M	R	W	w,nb		O	M	R	W	w,nb		FALL OF WICKETS			
														SA	QLD	QLD	SA
Bensted	27	2	105	4	-,-		5	0	28	1	-,-	Wkt	1st	1st	2nd	2nd
Hurwood	18	3	42	1	-,-	(3)	3	0	15	0	-,-	1st	63	54	61	1
Nothling	25	7	80	0	1,-	(4)	4.5	0	12	0	-,-	2nd	86	130	68	98
Amos	9	0	44	0	-,-	(2)	2	0	15	0	-,-	3rd	103	151	112	-
Rowe	8	1	22	0	-,-							4th	105	158	160	-
Thompson	16.7	4	54	3	-,-							5th	241	158	171	-
Gough	15	2	56	0	-,-	(5)	4	0	31	1	-,-	6th	287	167	272	-
Gill	14	3	60	1	-,-							7th	359	191	283	-
												8th	399	229	284	-
SOUTH AUSTRALIA	O	M	R	W	w,nb		O	M	R	W	w,nb	9th	448	229	286	-
Scott	17	2	60	0	-,1		14	2	57	1	-,-	10th	471	256	315	-
Ryan	2	0	12	0	-,-	(5)	4	1	7	0	-,-					
Grimmett	24	4	85	5	-,-		19.4	2	101	5	-,-					
Williams	11	2	46	2	-,2		8	1	39	0	-,-					
Sangster	7	0	16	0	-,-	(7)	2	0	14	1	-,-					
Lee	10.1	3	22	2	-,-	(2)	20	3	48	1	-,-					
Schneider						(6)	2	0	27	1	-,-					

NEW SOUTH WALES v TASMANIA

Played at Sydney Cricket Ground on December 24, 26, 27, 1927. (Three-day match)
Toss : New South Wales.   Result : NEW SOUTH WALES WON BY 105 RUNS.
Debuts: New South Wales - J.P.Alleyne, F.H.Dupain, W.H.W.Lampe (all f/c), B.C.J.Bettington (NSW only). Tasmania - R.G.Friend (f/c).
12th Men: G.C.H.Hogg (NSW) and C.L.Lee (Tas).
Umpires: H.Parsons and E.J.Shaw.
Attendances: 3382, 2091, 2259.   Total: 7732.   Receipts: £290.
Close of Play: 1st day Tas 7/163 (Newton 50, Findlay 0); 2nd day NSW (2) 8/281 (Nicholls 12, O'Reilly 4).

Lee and Smith replaced G.T.H.James (unavailable) and A.T.E.Punch (ill) in the selected Tasmanian twelve before leaving. The New South Wales first innings ended in confusion. Bettington and Lampe had attempted a run but were stranded and stationary in mid-pitch when Henty removed the bails. Many spectators thought Bettington was out but after consultation the umpires decided that it was Lampe who had been run out. Steele (111 in 174 minutes, 8 fours) and Bettington (69 in 86 minutes, 6 fours) made the top scores of the match in the New South Wales second innings. Newton (9 fours) and Henty (6 fours) hit half-centuries in even time for the visitors. Wardlaw twisted an ankle during his eighth over and was unable to continue. Bettington had played for Oxford University in 1920 and 1922. *The Cricketer* incorrectly gives Tas (1) Dupain 5/44. Sources: *The Cricketer, NSWCA Report, TCA Report, Sydney Morning Herald, Sydney Daily Telegraph, Sydney Referee, Hobart Mercury.*

NEW SOUTH WALES

H.C.Steele	b Burrows	33		b Burrows	111
†H.S.B.Love	c Henty b Newton	37	(6)	st Henty b Burrows	15
*A.T.Ratcliffe	b Burrows	13		c Davis b Watson	27
C.D.Seddon	c Davis b Findlay	10		c Henty b Watson	22
B.F.Watson	b Newton	46	(2)	c Rushforth b Wardlaw	10
J.P.Alleyne	c Henty b Burrows	1	(5)	lbw b Findlay	0
F.H.Dupain	b Burrows	3	(8)	c Henty b Newton	5
C.O.Nicholls	c Watson b Burrows	10	(9)	st Henty b Watson	21
B.C.J.Bettington	not out	29	(7)	c Henty b Newton	69
W.J.O'Reilly	b Newton	18		not out	23
W.H.W.Lampe	run out (/Henty)	0		b Newton	9
Extras	(b8, lb4, w1, nb1)	14		(b5, lb5, w1)	11
Total	(55.4 overs, 200 mins)	214		(69.6 overs, 250 mins)	323

TASMANIA

R.G.Friend	b Lampe	12		c Nicholls b Lampe	19
A.W.Rushforth	lbw b Nicholls	1		c Nicholls b Dupain	15
*A.E.Watson	b Lampe	12		c Watson b Bettington	9
G.W.Martin	b Dupain	43		lbw b Bettington	1
A.O.Burrows	lbw b Dupain	1		b Dupain	13
N.W.Davis	b O'Reilly	34	(7)	b Lampe	29
A.C.Newton	c Love b Nicholls	51	(8)	b Dupain	36
H.C.Smith	c Lampe b O'Reilly	3	(9)	c Love b Dupain	10
A.P.Findlay	b O'Reilly	5	(10)	c Nicholls b Dupain	7
†P.G.Henty	c Nicholls b O'Reilly	51	(6)	b Bettington	9
D.M.S.Wardlaw	not out	42		not out	0
Extras	(b8, lb8, w1)	17		(b7, lb5)	12
Total	(53.6 overs, 200 mins)	272		(44.6 overs, 150 mins)	160

TASMANIA	O	M	R	W	w,nb		O	M	R	W	w,nb			FALL OF WICKETS			
Wardlaw	12	0	36	0	-,1		7.2	0	42	1	-,-			NSW	TAS	NSW	TAS
Newton	17.4	3	58	3	-,-		18.4	1	84	3	-,-	Wkt	1st	1st	2nd	2nd
Burrows	16	2	59	5	1,-		16	1	71	2	-,-	1st	48	2	33	36
Findlay	6	0	38	1	-,-	(5)	5	0	38	1	1,-	2nd	68	18	82	41
Watson	4	0	9	0	-,-	(4)	23	3	77	3	-,-	3rd	81	69	128	42
												4th	145	69	129	61
NEW SOUTH WALES	O	M	R	W	w,nb		O	M	R	W	w,nb	5th	149	84	160	63
Nicholls	13	0	68	2	-,-		7	1	24	0	-,-	6th	149	157	213	76
Lampe	9	0	67	2	-,-	(3)	6	0	24	2	-,-	7th	158	163	228	133
Dupain	17	3	51	2	-,-	(2)	15.6	3	44	5	-,-	8th	175	169	276	147
Bettington	6	0	34	0	1,-		11	2	35	3	-,-	9th	214	182	304	159
O'Reilly	8.6	0	35	4	-,-		5	2	21	0	-,-	10th	214	272	323	160

AFCM No. 641/75
SSM No. 193/62

VICTORIA v SOUTH AUSTRALIA (Shield Match 7)

Played at Melbourne Cricket Ground on December 30, 31, 1927, January 2, 3, 1928. (Five-day match)
Toss : Victoria.   Result : VICTORIA WON BY AN INNINGS AND 35 RUNS.
Debuts: Nil.
12th Men: K.E.Rigg (Vic) and C.B.Sangster (SA).
Umpires: J.Richards and P.E.Smith.
Attendances: 22027, 24387, 18323, 7729.   Total: 72,466.   Receipts: £3445.
Close of Play: 1st day Vic 4/472 (Ponsford 258, Hartkopf 2); 2nd day SA 3/135 (Harris 66, Ryan 16); 3rd day SA (2) 0/119
     (Schneider 53, Harris 65).

Ponsford continued his unprecedented heavy scoring with his fourth century in five innings to complete 1146 runs in the month, average 229.20. He went from 71 at lunch to 155 at tea on the first day and then scored 103 in the last session as Victoria's score mounted to 4/472 in 305 minutes. Ponsford batted 386 minutes in all, hit 33 fours, survived chances at 90 and 200 and shared century stands of 236 for the first wicket with Woodfull (106 in 156 minutes, 2 fours), 140 for the third wicket with Ryder (52 in 74 minutes, 4 fours) and 104 for the sixth wicket with Scaife (33 in 99 minutes, 2 fours) before being sixth out at 582. Grimmett dismissed Ellis with the next ball. Schneider (38 in 76 minutes, 1 four) and Harris (69 in 159 minutes, 4 fours) began well for South Australia in reply and Grimmett (61 not out in 162 minutes, 5 fours) and Lee (66 in 56 minutes, 9 fours) added 93 for the seventh wicket but the visitors had no hope of avoiding the follow-on. Harris (74 in 163 minutes, 7 fours) and Schneider (143 in 314 minutes, 13 fours) again batted well in the second innings in which Richardson suffered a first-ball dismissal. H.E.Whitfield, unable to obtain leave, was unavailable for South Australia. Sources: *Wisden, C.B.O'Reilly, VCA Report, The Age, The Argus, The Herald, Melbourne Sun, The Sporting Globe.*

VICTORIA

*W.M.Woodfull	c Richardson b Wall	106
W.H.Ponsford	st Hack b Grimmett	336
H.S.T.L.Hendry	lbw b Grimmett	35
J.Ryder	c Wall b Ryan	52
C.A.H.Sindrey	b Grimmett	5
A.E.V.Hartkopf	c Scott b Wall	4
J.W.Scaife	c Richardson b Scott	33
†J.L.Ellis	c Lee b Grimmett	0
D.D.Blackie	not out	28
F.L.Morton	st Hack b Grimmett	13
H.Ironmonger	c Hack b Wall	8
Extras	(b10, lb6, nb1)	17
Total	(12.16 overs, 453 mins)	637

SOUTH AUSTRALIA

K.J.Schneider	b Blackie	38		st Ellis b Hendry	143
G.W.Harris	b Morton	69		b Blackie	74
*V.Y.Richardson	c Woodfull b Blackie	5		b Morton	0
W.C.Alexander	c & b Ironmonger	1	(5)	b Ironmonger	8
A.J.Ryan	c Morton b Ironmonger	34	(6)	c Ryder b Morton	11
†A.T.Hack	st Ellis b Blackie	5	(7)	not out	13
C.V.Grimmett	not out	61	(4)	c Hendry b Ironmonger	17
P.K.Lee	c Ryder b Morton	66		b Hendry	7
J.D.Scott	c Hendry b Morton	0		b Ironmonger	1
N.L.Williams	b Morton	1		b Morton	2
T.W.Wall	b Hartkopf	18		run out	2
Extras	(b16, lb3, nb2)	21		(lb3, nb2)	5
Total	(92.0 overs, 335 mins)	319		(93.2 overs, 352 mins)	283

SOUTH AUSTRALIA	O	M	R	W	w,nb						
Scott	28	3	114	1	-,-						
Wall	16.6	0	83	3	-,-						
Grimmett	41	2	170	5	-,-						
Lee	18	0	135	0	-,-						
Williams	9	0	78	0	-,1						
Ryan	8	1	28	1	-,-						
Schneider	1	0	12	0	-,-						

VICTORIA	O	M	R	W	w,nb		O	M	R	W	w,nb
Morton	24	2	111	4	-,1		18.2	2	57	3	-,1
Ironmonger	25	2	68	2	-,-	(4)	27	7	67	3	-,-
Blackie	33	9	68	3	-,1		26	6	59	1	-,1
Hendry	3	0	24	0	-,-	(2)	15	2	50	2	-,-
Hartkopf	7	1	27	1	-,-		7	0	45	0	-,-

FALL OF WICKETS

Wkt	VIC 1st	SA 1st	SA 2nd
1st	236	89	138
2nd	304	97	139
3rd	444	100	191
4th	463	141	199
5th	478	146	251
6th	582	178	261
7th	582	271	273
8th	598	271	274
9th	624	273	280
10th	637	319	283

NEW SOUTH WALES v QUEENSLAND (Shield Match 8)

Played at Sydney Cricket Ground on December 31, 1927, January 2, 3, 4, 5, 1928. (Five-day match)
Toss : New South Wales. Result : MATCH DRAWN.
Debuts: Nil.
12th Men: F.S.Jordan (NSW) and G.S.Amos (Qld).
Umpires: S.Parsons and A.P.Williams.
Attendances: 13220, 15032, 3775, 1897, 1672. Total: 35,596. Receipts: £2290.
Close of Play: 1st day NSW 5/436 (Kippax 170, Morgan 97); 2nd day Qld 5/167 (Litster 51, Nothling 25); 3rd day Qld (2) 4/325
   (Higgins 174, Rowe 30); 4th day NSW (2) 1/4 (Jackson 1, Phillips 3).

A.A.Mailey and W.A.S.Oldfield (both ill) were unavailable for New South Wales. Kippax's chanceless unbeaten 315 - his career-highest score - occupied 384 minutes and included 41 fours. He shared a sixth-wicket stand of 253 with Morgan (121 in 155 minutes, 16 fours), whose score was at the close of the first day was changed from 94 to 97 due to 3 runs having been incorrectly credited as byes. Higgins, out first ball in Queensland's first innings, was sent in to open after the follow on and ran up 179 in 236 minutes with 1 five and 22 fours, his sole first-class century. Litster topped the first innings (82 in 145 minutes, 6 fours) but was bowled by the first ball of Queensland's second innings; he left for Townsville on the fourth day and Amos substituted in the field in his place. Rowe also scored a first-ball duck and a hundred, compiling a career-best 147 in 252 minutes with 13 fours. Gregory was run out from the third ball of the New South Wales second innings, which was played on a rain-affected pitch. Jordan subbed for Ratcliffe (selection meeting for the forthcoming NSW-SA match) on the fourth day and N.F.Grant fielded for Bensted (sore knee) on the fifth. Sources: *Wisden, NSWCA Report, QCA Report, Sydney Morning Herald, Sydney Referee.*

NEW SOUTH WALES

N.E.Phillips	c Hurwood b Bensted	17	(3) lbw b Nothling	29
J.M.Gregory	c & b Nothling	63	(1) run out (Bensted/O'Connor)	0
T.J.E.Andrews	b Hurwood	41	(4) b Nothling	11
*A.F.Kippax	not out	315	(5) c O'Connor b Nothling	9
A.T.Ratcliffe	c O'Connor b Nothling	25	(6) b Nothling	0
A.Jackson	c O'Connor b Bensted	19	(2) c O'Connor b Hurwood	9
J.G.Morgan	c O'Connor b Bensted	121	c Gough b Thompson	12
D.G.Bradman	b Gough	0	c O'Connor b Nothling	13
†H.S.B.Love	b Rowe	26	not out	13
E.F.O'Brien	b Gough	6	not out	0
R.L.A.McNamee	st O'Connor b Gough	1		
Extras	(b2, w1, nb2)	5	(b2, lb1, nb1)	4
Total	(146.5 overs, 475 mins)	639	(50.0 overs, 175 mins) (8 wkts)	100

QUEENSLAND

L.L.Gill	lbw b O'Brien	29	(10) b McNamee	3
L.E.Oxenham	b Gregory	1	(8) st Love b Bradman	50
W.Rowe	b Gregory	0	(6) c O'Brien b Bradman	147
F.C.Thompson	lbw b Phillips	18	c Kippax b Phillips	68
J.L.Litster	st Love b McNamee	82	(1) b Gregory	0
*†L.P.D.O'Connor	run out(Kippax)	37	(7) b Morgan	32
O.E.Nothling	b Phillips	74	(5) c Gregory b Phillips	5
F.J.Gough	c Love b Phillips	17	(9) b McNamee	42
H.J.R.Higgins	c Gregory b Phillips	0	(2) run out (Andrews)	179
E.C.Bensted	c Jackson b O'Brien	6	(3) run out (Andrews)	38
A.Hurwood	not out	1	not out	5
Extras	(b1, lb7, w3)	11	(b7, lb13, w1)	21
Total	(75.3 overs, 258 mins)	276	(128.6 overs, 465 mins)	590

QUEENSLAND	O	M	R	W	w,nb		O	M	R	W	w,nb
Bensted	27	1	126	3	-,1		2	0	4	0	-,-
Hurwood	27	4	118	1	-,-		18	4	40	1	-,-
Nothling	28	3	109	2	-,-		21	7	39	5	-,-
Gill	8	0	57	0	1,-	(7)	1	0	1	0	-,-
Thompson	17	1	68	0	-,-	(4)	4	1	5	1	-,-
Gough	16.5	0	100	3	-,1		2	1	3	0	-,1
Rowe	13	1	56	1	-,-	(5)	2	0	4	0	-,-

NEW SOUTH WALES	O	M	R	W	w,nb		O	M	R	W	w,nb
Gregory	17	1	63	2	1,-		16	0	99	1	-,-
McNamee	19	6	50	1	2,-		33.6	5	110	2	-,-
Phillips	11	3	26	4	-,-		22	2	85	1	-,-
O'Brien	16.3	1	73	2	-,-		15	0	88	0	-,-
Andrews	8	0	45	0	-,-	(6)	4	0	30	0	-,-
Morgan	4	2	8	0	-,-	(5)	22	1	95	2	1,-
Kippax							6	0	21	0	-,-
Bradman							10	0	41	2	-,-

FALL OF WICKETS

Wkt	NSW 1st	QLD 1st	QLD 2nd	NSW 2nd
1st	32	6	0	0
2nd	107	6	92	23
3rd	137	32	237	48
4th	188	73	252	59
5th	214	137	335	59
6th	467	216	411	60
7th	468	267	525	74
8th	557	267	560	99
9th	611	274	580	-
10th	639	276	590	-

TASMANIA v VICTORIA

Played at T.C.A. Ground, Hobart, on December 31, January 2, 3, 1928. (Three-day match)
Toss : Tasmania.   Result : VICTORIA WON BY FIVE WICKETS.
Debuts: Tasmania - C.R.Driscoll, V.R.Driscoll, (both f/c); A.T.E.Punch (Tas only). Victoria - E.L.a'Beckett, T.G.Armstrong,
    A.A.Davidson, R.N.Ellis, W.W.Reddrop (all f/c).
12th Men: V.L.Hooper (Tas) and H.C.Hunt (Vic).
Umpires: M.Leonard and W.M.McHugo.
Attendances: 1000, "moderate", unknown.   Total: No figures published.   Receipts: £60.
Close of Play: 1st day Vic 0/77 (Baring 34, Onyons 39); 2nd day Tas (2) 2/79 (Atkinson 51, C.R.Driscoll 0).

Atkinson, bowled by the first ball of the match (a'Beckett's first ball in first-class cricket) carried his bat in Tasmania's second innings, hitting 1 six and 9 fours. Burrows (69 in 102 minutes, 7 fours) and C.R.Driscoll (48 not out in 58 minutes, 5 fours) saved face for the home side in the first innings. An opening stand of 147 in Victoria's first innings was mounted by Baring (98 in 171 minutes, 11 fours) and Onyons (64 in 135 minutes, 1 six and 8 fours). A spectacular century by Ellis (100 in 88 minutes, 1 six and 14 fours) guided Victoria to a win with four minutes to spare on the last day. N.W.Davis, unavailable, was replaced in the Tasmanian side by V.R.Driscoll (originally 12th man) before the start. Only first-class appearance by T.G.Armstrong aged 38 - younger brother of W.W.Armstrong. Punch, a New South Wales representative for 10 years, played his sole match for Tasmania. *The Cricketer* incorrectly gives Vic (2) Makin 4 instead of Millar. Sources: *The Cricketer, VCA Report, TCA Report, The Age, The Argus, The Sporting Globe, Hobart Mercury.*

TASMANIA

J.A.Atkinson	b a'Beckett	0		not out	144
G.H.Allan	c Baring b Makin	5		b Wilkinson	14
A.T.E.Punch	lbw b a'Beckett	1	(5)	b Wilkinson	47
G.W.Martin	c Baring b a'Beckett	2	(6)	c Onyons b Armstrong	28
A.W.Rushforth	c King b a'Beckett	2	(9)	b Armstrong	5
A.C.Newton	c King b a'Beckett	24	(7)	c Makin b Armstrong	0
*A.E.Watson	c Millar b Makin	1	(10)	c Ellis b Armstrong	0
A.O.Burrows	st King b Armstrong	69		b Makin	5
V.R.Driscoll	c Ellis b Davidson	30	(3)	st King b Armstrong	0
†C.R.Driscoll	not out	48	(4)	lbw b Armstrong	1
D.M.S.Wardlaw	c Makin b Armstrong	15		lbw b Makin	0
Extras	(lb3, nb1)	4		(b18, lb12, nb3)	33
Total	(54.0 overs, 200 mins)	201		(65.5 overs, 244 mins)	277

VICTORIA

*F.A.Baring	c Newton b Allan	98	(5)	c Atkinson b Burrows	5
B.A.Onyons	c Atkinson b Allan	64	(6)	not out	21
R.N.Ellis	c Rushforth b Allan	1	(4)	c Rushforth b Newton	100
W.W.Reddrop	c Punch b Wardlaw	46			
†S.P.King	c Allan b Burrows	19			
A.A.Davidson	lbw b Burrows	0	(3)	lbw b Burrows	6
K.J.Millar	c Rushforth b Burrows	23	(1)	run out (Punch/C.R.Driscoll)	4
T.G.Armstrong	b Burrows	5	(7)	not out	2
W.A.Wilkinson	run out (Newton/C.R.Driscoll)	0			
E.L.a'Beckett	not out	24	(2)	c Watson b Burrows	35
J.C.Makin	b Wardlaw	5			
Extras	(b8, lb2, nb2)	12		(b9)	9
Total	(85.2 overs, 300 mins)	297		(33.3 overs, 131 mins) (5 wkts)	182

VICTORIA	O	M	R	W	w,nb		O	M	R	W	w,nb
a'Beckett	20	4	63	5	-,-		12	2	44	0	-,-
Makin	12	0	48	2	-,-		12.5	0	49	2	-,-
Wilkinson	5	1	13	0	-,-	(5)	14	1	52	2	-,-
Armstrong	10	0	46	2	-,1	(3)	21	4	66	6	-,3
Davidson	7	1	27	1	-,-	(6)	5	0	31	0	-,-
Baring						(4)	1	0	2	0	-,-

TASMANIA	O	M	R	W	w,nb		O	M	R	W	w,nb
Wardlaw	20.2	5	56	2	-,2		8.3	2	37	0	-,-
Newton	18	1	64	0	-,-	(3)	7	1	34	1	-,-
Burrows	16	3	51	4	-,-	(2)	11	1	55	3	-,-
Watson	13	1	45	0	-,-	(5)	2	0	19	0	-,-
Punch	2	0	9	0	-,-						
Allan	15	1	58	3	-,-	(4)	4	0	22	0	-,-
Atkinson	1	0	2	0	-,-	(6)	1	0	6	0	-,-

FALL OF WICKETS

Wkt	TAS 1st	VIC 1st	TAS 2nd	VIC 2nd
1st	0	147	77	4
2nd	4	157	78	22
3rd	8	177	83	99
4th	8	221	171	137
5th	13	221	232	179
6th	20	253	238	-
7th	50	263	257	-
8th	116	263	272	-
9th	171	284	272	-
10th	201	297	277	-

NEW SOUTH WALES v SOUTH AUSTRALIA (Shield Match 9)

Played at Sydney Cricket Ground on January 6, 7, 9, 10, 1928. (Five-day match)
Toss : New South Wales. Result : NEW SOUTH WALES WON BY 118 RUNS.
Debuts: New South Wales - H.L.Davidson (f/c).
12th Men: A.E.Scanes (NSW) and C.B.Sangster (SA).
Umpires: E.G.Borwick and W.J.R.Bowes.
Attendances: 5509, 16126, 6614, 518. Total: 28,767. Receipts: £1747.
Close of Play: 1st day SA 3/62 (Ryan 30, Hack 5); 2nd day NSW (2) 3/208 (Jackson 112, Ratcliffe 22); 3rd day SA (2) 6/189 (McKay 1, Hack 0).

J.M.Gregory, W.A.S.Oldfield and N.E.Phillips were unavailable for New South Wales and Davidson and Steele replaced H.S.B.Love (injured hand) and J.G.Morgan (unavailable) after the selection of the team. Jackson batted stylishly to register a century in each innings, 131 (242 minutes, 1 six and 11 fours) and 122 (178 minutes, 15 fours). Kippax (58 in 80 minutes, 7 fours) and Bradman (73 in 79 minutes, 10 fours) scored half-centuries in the second innings. Schneider was out to the first ball of South Australia's first innings but fifties by Hack (50 in 89 minutes), Grimmett (54 in 92 minutes, 2 fours) and Alexander (58 in 47 minutes, 9 fours) helped restore the position. However the task set in the second innings proved too great, despite the efforts of Schneider (54 in 112 minutes, 4 fours), Richardson (86 in 149 minutes, 10 fours) and McKay (40 in 83 minutes, 4 fours). Sources: *Wisden, C.B.O'Reilly, NSWCA Report, SACA Report, Sydney Referee, Sydney Morning Herald, South Australian Register.*

NEW SOUTH WALES

H.C.Steele	b Scott	14	b Scott		5
A.Jackson	c McKay b Wall	131	b Grimmett		122
T.J.E.Andrews	b Wall	44	lbw b Scott		2
*A.F.Kippax	c Wall b Lee	17	lbw b McKay		58
A.T.Ratcliffe	c Richardson b Grimmett	10	c Hack b Scott		30
D.G.Bradman	c & b McKay	2	st Hack b Grimmett		73
F.S.Jordan	c Alexander b Wall	12	b Grimmett		31
C.O.Nicholls	b Scott	18	st Hack b Grimmett		5
A.A.Mailey	st Hack b Grimmett	1	b Scott		7
†H.L.Davidson	c Hack b Wall	10	b Scott		2
R.L.A.McNamee	not out	0	not out		4
Extras	(b14, lb8, w7, nb3)	32	(b15, lb8, w3, nb3)		29
Total	(63.0 overs, 245 mins)	291	(67.2 overs, 263 mins)		368

SOUTH AUSTRALIA

K.J.Schneider	c Jordan b Nicholls	0	run out (Davidson)		54
G.W.Harris	c Davidson b Nicholls	24	b Mailey		14
*V.Y.Richardson	c Ratcliffe b Nicholls	1	b Nicholls		86
A.J.Ryan	c Davidson b Nicholls	41	b Nicholls		4
†A.T.Hack	c Davidson b Nicholls	50	(8) b Nicholls		22
C.V.Grimmett	c Kippax b Mailey	54	lbw b Mailey		8
W.C.Alexander	c & b McNamee	58	(5) c & b Jordan		13
D.G.McKay	b Jordan	16	(7) c Davidson b Nicholls		40
P.K.Lee	c Nicholls b McNamee	0	c Mailey b Jordan		30
J.D.Scott	run out (Bradman)	1	not out		9
T.W.Wall	not out	0	c Nicholls b Mailey		1
Extras	(lb3)	3	(b4, lb7, w1)		12
Total	(64.2 overs, 223 mins)	248	(89.5 overs, 300 mins)		293

SOUTH AUSTRALIA	O	M	R	W	w,nb	O	M	R	W	w,nb	FALL OF WICKETS				
Scott	13	2	57	2	4,2	22.2	2	108	5	2,3		NSW	SA	NSW	SA
Wall	17	3	51	4	2,-	11	2	51	0	-,-	Wkt	1st	1st	2nd	2nd
Grimmett	24	1	106	2	-,-	26	0	137	4	-,-	1st	28	0	14	36
McKay	7	0	30	1	1,1	5	0	21	1	-,-	2nd	116	4	18	123
Lee	2	0	15	1	-,-	2	0	18	0	1,-	3rd	173	52	150	134
Schneider						1	0	4	0	-,-	4th	190	77	224	167
											5th	193	162	238	185
NEW SOUTH WALES	O	M	R	W	w,nb	O	M	R	W	w,nb	6th	214	196	336	185
Nicholls	21	1	115	5	-,-	25	3	84	4	1,-	7th	250	245	351	253
McNamee	16	1	50	2	-,-	15	2	45	0	-,-	8th	259	245	360	254
Mailey	16	2	56	1	-,-	31	3	113	3	-,-	9th	289	246	364	261
Jordan	8.2	2	13	1	-,-	17.5	6	33	2	-,-	10th	291	248	368	293
Bradman	3	0	11	0	-,-										
Kippax						(5) 1	0	6	0	-,-					

QUEENSLAND v SOUTH AUSTRALIA (Shield Match 10)

Played at Exhibition Ground, Brisbane, on January 14, 16, 17, 18, 1928. (Five-day match)
Toss : Queensland.   Result : SOUTH AUSTRALIA WON BY AN INNINGS AND 11 RUNS.
Debuts: Nil.
12th Men: L.L.Gill (Qld) and A.J.Ryan (SA).
Umpires: J.P.Orr and J.A.Scott.
Attendances: 10000, 4700, 2000, 200.   Total: About 16,900.   Receipts: £1069.
Close of Play: 1st day SA 2/126 (Schneider 55, Hack 9); 2nd day SA 6/438 (Grimmett 48, McKay 3); 3rd day Qld (2) 5/188
    (Thompson 69, O'Connor 54).

E.C.Knowles was unavailable for Queensland while Beeston, Brew and L.E.Oxenham replaced F.J.Gough, J.L.Litster and W.Rowe (all unavailable) after selection. E.C.Bensted (knee injury) was a further withdrawal just before the match began, Amos (originally 12th) taking his place. R.K.Oxenham suffered an attack of pleurisy and took no further part in the match after the first day; Gill took his place in the field. O'Connor was again Queensland's best batsman by far, scoring 46 (110 minutes, 2 fours) and 133 not out (281 minutes, 7 fours). He added 179 for the sixth wicket with Thompson (93 in 206 minutes, 11 fours) in the second innings. In what was destined to be his last first-class match in Australia, Schneider scored 114 in 259 minutes and hit 6 fours. It was the 22-year-old's third century of the season but leukaemia was to claim his life before the start of the next season. Harris (61 in 112 minutes, 5 fours), Hack (77 in 170 minutes, 6 fours), Alexander (62 in 87 minutes, 5 fours), Sangster (62 in 129 minutes, 5 fours) and Grimmett (60 in 135 minutes, 6 fours) all helped South Australia establish a commanding first innings lead. Sources: *Wisden, C.B.O'Reilly, QCA Report, SACA Report, Brisbane Courier, Brisbane Daily Mail*.

QUEENSLAND

R.K.Oxenham	lbw b Grimmett	26		absent ill	-
H.J.R.Higgins	c Hack b Scott	2		c Richardson b Scott	5
*†L.P.D.O'Connor	c Harris b Grimmett	46	(7)	not out	133
F.C.Thompson	c Hack b Wall	2	(4)	c Hack b Scott	93
O.E.Nothling	c Richardson b Scott	3	(6)	run out (Scott)	2
L.E.Oxenham	st Hack b Grimmett	9	(1)	b Scott	20
F.M.Brew	b Wall	8	(5)	b Wall	8
A.D.A.Mayes	c Sangster b Wall	5	(8)	c Alexander b Grimmett	32
N.C.Beeston	not out	18	(3)	c Wall b Grimmett	12
P.M.Hornibrook	b Wall	0	(9)	b Grimmett	4
G.S.Amos	c & b Grimmett	19	(10)	b Scott	15
Extras	(lb2, nb3)	5		(b11, lb5, nb11)	27
Total	(41.7 overs, 172 mins)	143		(97.3 overs, 363 mins)	351

SOUTH AUSTRALIA

K.J.Schneider	b Hornibrook	114
G.W.Harris	run out (Thompson/O'Connor)	61
*V.Y.Richardson	c & b Brew	0
†A.T.Hack	c Nothling b Amos	77
W.C.Alexander	c & b Amos	62
C.B.Sangster	run out (Brew/O'Connor)	62
C.V.Grimmett	b Hornibrook	60
D.G.McKay	not out	36
P.K.Lee	c Mayes b Amos	3
T.W.Wall	c Amos b Nothling	10
J.D.Scott	lbw b Nothling	7
Extras	(b5, lb6, w2)	13
Total	(136.4 overs, 527 mins)	505

SOUTH AUSTRALIA	O	M	R	W	w,nb		O	M	R	W	w,nb		FALL OF WICKETS		
Scott	11	1	27	2	-,3		20.3	4	71	4	-,4			QLD	SA	QLD
Wall	11	1	42	4	-,-		13	0	60	1	-,3	Wkt	1st	1st	2nd
Grimmett	16.7	1	62	4	-,-		32	3	98	3	-,-	1st	5	108	27
McKay	3	0	7	0	-,-	(5)	5	0	24	0	-,-	2nd	51	115	30
Lee						(4)	25	9	53	0	-,-	3rd	58	243	43
Sangster							2	0	18	0	-,4	4th	70	271	52
												5th	92	344	58
QUEENSLAND	O	M	R	W	w,nb							6th	94	419	237
Hornibrook	42	6	123	2	1,-							7th	101	462	287
Amos	31	3	127	3	1,-							8th	106	475	308
R.K.Oxenham	7	3	13	0	-,-							9th	110	497	351
Nothling	17.4	1	59	2	-,-							10th	143	505	-
Brew	11	0	59	1	-,-										
Mayes	16	3	58	0	-,-										
Thompson	12	0	53	0	-,-										

NEW SOUTH WALES v VICTORIA (Shield Match 11)

Played at Sydney Cricket Ground on January 26, 27, 28, 30, 31, 1928. (Five-day match)
Toss : New South Wales.   Result : MATCH DRAWN.
Debuts: Nil.
12th Men: F.S.Jordan (NSW) and A.J.W.Lansdown (Vic).
Umpires: W.G.French and A.C.Jones.
Attendances: 30386, 13378, 15830, 6986, 1036.   Total: 67,616.   Receipts: £4606.
Close of Play: 1st day NSW 7/349 (Oldfield 18, Nicholls 39); 2nd day Vic 1/158 (Woodfull 74, Hendry 73); 3rd day NSW (2) 0/0
  (Phillips 0, Jackson 0); 4th day NSW (2) 8/353 (Bradman 134, Mailey 11).

Eight centuries, a new Australian record, were scored over the five days of the match. The New South Wales first innings was dominated by two partnerships. Kippax (134 in 221 minutes, 15 fours, chances at 107 and 132) and Morgan (110 in 207 minutes, 11 fours) added 245 for the fourth wicket and Oldfield (101 in 178 minutes, 7 fours) and Nicholls (110 in 160 minutes, 13 fours) added 204 to establish the current New South Wales record for the eighth wicket. Bradman's second innings occupied 225 minutes and included 13 fours. Woodfull (94 in 177 minutes, 6 fours) and Hendry (138 in 250 minutes, 12 fours) shared a second-wicket stand of 192 in Victoria's first innings while Ryder scored 106 in 148 minutes with 14 fours. Woodfull (81 not out in 150 minutes, 7 fours) again batted well in the second innings, sharing an unbroken 195-run stand for the second wicket with Rigg (110 not out in 130 minutes, 15 fours). A light appeal ended play on the third day before a ball was bowled in the New South Wales second innings. Sources: *Wisden, NSWCA Report, VCA Report, The Age, The Argus, Sydney Morning Herald, Sydney Referee.*

NEW SOUTH WALES

J.M.Gregory	lbw b Morton	12	(7) c Ryder b a'Beckett	4
A.Jackson	c Hendry b a'Beckett	11	b Blackie	44
T.J.E.Andrews	c & b Morton	4	b Blackie	32
*A.F.Kippax	b a'Beckett	134	b Blackie	42
J.G.Morgan	b Blackie	110	c & b Blackie	0
D.G.Bradman	st Ellis b Blackie	7	not out	134
N.E.Phillips	lbw b a'Beckett	0	(1) b Morton	2
†W.A.S.Oldfield	c sub (A.J.W.Lansdown) b a'Beckett	101	b Blackie	49
C.O.Nicholls	b a'Beckett	110	c Rigg b Blackie	18
A.A.Mailey	b a'Beckett	12	not out	11
R.L.A.McNamee	not out	8		
Extras	(b16, lb1, w1, nb6)	24	(b9, lb4, w2, nb2)	17
Total	(123.6 overs, 476 mins)	533	(87.0 overs, 330 mins) (8 wkts dec)	353

VICTORIA

*W.M.Woodfull	c Nicholls b McNamee	94	not out	81
W.H.Ponsford	b Gregory	6	c Gregory b Nicholls	2
H.S.T.L.Hendry	c Oldfield b Gregory	138		
J.Ryder	lbw b Mailey	106		
K.E.Rigg	c Nicholls b Gregory	1	(3) not out	110
J.W.Scaife	not out	35		
E.L.a'Beckett	b Mailey	14		
†J.L.Ellis	c Oldfield b Nicholls	9		
D.D.Blackie	c Morgan b Nicholls	0		
F.L.Morton	b Mailey	0		
H.Ironmonger	b Gregory	10		
Extras	(lb6, w1, nb2)	9	(b5, lb6, nb1)	12
Total	(105.6 overs, 380 mins)	422	(45.0 overs, 150 mins) (1 wkt)	205

VICTORIA	O	M	R	W	w,nb		O	M	R	W	w,nb
Morton	26	0	175	2	1,6		12	1	55	1	-,1
a'Beckett	32.6	3	119	6	-,-		17	2	63	1	-,-
Blackie	41	10	128	2	-,-	(4)	29	2	101	6	2,1
Ironmonger	19	4	67	0	-,-	(3)	21	2	80	0	-,-
Hendry	5	0	20	0	-,-		5	1	12	0	-,-
Ponsford							3	0	25	0	-,-

NEW SOUTH WALES	O	M	R	W	w,nb		O	M	R	W	w,nb
Gregory	23.6	3	81	4	-,-		4	2	8	0	-,-
Nicholls	21	0	103	2	1,-		6	0	24	1	-,-
Mailey	28	1	128	3	-,-		8	0	37	0	-,-
McNamee	21	4	79	1	-,2		7	0	29	0	-,1
Phillips	12	2	22	0	-,-	(6)	3	0	25	0	-,-
Bradman						(5)	3	0	14	0	-,-
Kippax							3	0	19	0	-,-
Morgan							8	1	24	0	-,-
Jackson							3	0	13	0	-,-

FALL OF WICKETS

Wkt	NSW 1st	VIC 1st	NSW 2nd	VIC 2nd
1st	25	11	8	10
2nd	25	203	77	-
3rd	31	312	86	-
4th	276	315	86	-
5th	290	369	149	-
6th	291	391	158	-
7th	291	400	276	-
8th	495	400	304	-
9th	510	403	-	-
10th	533	422	-	-

QUEENSLAND v VICTORIA (Shield Match 12)

Played at Exhibition Ground, Brisbane, on February 3, 4, 6, 7 (no play), 1928. (Four-day match)
Toss : Victoria.   Result : MATCH DRAWN.
Debuts: Queensland - M.Biggs (f/c).
12th Men: F.M.Brew (Qld) and H.E.Brereton (Vic).
Umpires: J.P.Orr and J.A.Scott.
Attendances: 4500, 10,500, 2523.   Total: 17,523.   Receipts: £1096.
Close of Play: 1st day Vic 8/265 (a'Beckett 23, Morton 13); 2nd day Qld 2/180 (Rowe 36, Thompson 7); 3rd day Qld 9/384 (Biggs 8, Hornibrook 1).

Victorian captain W.M.Woodfull had not recovered from a leg injury sustained in the previous match and was forced to stand down. Ryder assumed the captaincy and Brereton, the Victorian Cricket Association secretary, acted as 12th man. Queensland made a late change due to the unavailability of A.Hurwood, Biggs (originally 12th man) coming into the side. Brew subbed throughout the Victorian innings for Thompson who had suffered a painful blow on the leg at a pre-match warm-up. Ponsford (63 in 130 minutes, 3 fours), Ryder (84 in 126 minutes, 1 six and 7 fours) and a'Beckett (47 in 92 minutes, 7 fours) topscored for Victoria. O'Connor (54 in 124 minutes, 1 four) and Oxenham (65 in 205 minutes, 3 fours) put on 98 for Queensland's first wicket in reply, Rowe following up with a chanceless 134 (315 minutes, 2 fours). No play was possible on the fourth day due to rain and the scheduled fifth day was abandoned because of the departure of Blackie, Oxenham, Morton and Ponsford for the Australian tour of New Zealand. *Wisden* gives incorrect match dates. Sources: *Wisden, VCA Report, QCA Report, Brisbane Courier, Brisbane Daily Mail, Maryborough Chronicle.*

VICTORIA

W.H.Ponsford	st O'Connor b Oxenham	63
H.S.T.L.Hendry	c O'Connor b Oxenham	32
*J.Ryder	b Amos	84
K.E.Rigg	run out (Sub F.M.Brew/Oxenham)	1
J.W.Scaife	c O'Connor b Hornibrook	39
A.J.W.Lansdown	b Oxenham	4
E.L.a'Beckett	c & b Oxenham	47
†J.L.Ellis	b Oxenham	2
D.D.Blackie	c Biggs b Oxenham	1
F.L.Morton	not out	23
H.Ironmonger	b Amos	0
Extras	(b1, lb3)	4
Total	(89.1 overs, 339 mins)	300

QUEENSLAND

*†L.P.D.O'Connor	b Morton	54
R.K.Oxenham	b a'Beckett	65
W.Rowe	c Rigg b Hendry	134
F.C.Thompson	c Ponsford b Morton	27
O.E.Nothling	b Morton	8
H.J.R.Higgins	run out (Ponsford/Ellis)	20
J.L.Litster	st Ellis b Hendry	20
F.J.Gough	run out (/Ellis)	16
M.Biggs	not out	8
G.S.Amos	run out (/Ellis)	2
P.M.Hornibrook	not out	1
Extras	(b13, lb9, w1, nb6)	29
Total	(124.0 overs, 473 mins) (9 wkts)	384

QUEENSLAND	O	M	R	W	w,nb
Hornibrook	16	2	44	1	-,-
Amos	23.1	3	92	2	-,-
Oxenham	28	8	79	6	-,-
Nothling	19	2	66	0	-,-
Gough	2	0	12	0	-,-
Rowe	1	0	3	0	-,-

VICTORIA	O	M	R	W	w,nb
Morton	23	2	73	3	1,5
a'Beckett	37	3	101	1	-,-
Ironmonger	20	3	64	0	-,1
Blackie	27	3	51	0	-,-
Hendry	14	1	51	2	-,-
Lansdown	3	0	12	0	-,-

FALL OF WICKETS

	VIC	QLD
Wkt	1st	1st
1st	82	98
2nd	117	162
3rd	120	229
4th	217	249
5th	223	297
6th	230	341
7th	234	361
8th	238	380
9th	291	382
10th	300	-

WESTERN AUSTRALIA v VICTORIA

Played at W.A.C.A. Ground, Perth, on February 25, 27, 28, 1928. (Three-day match)
Toss : Western Australia.   Result : MATCH DRAWN.
Debuts: Western Australia - W.A.McRae, H.A.Newman (both f/c), A.J.Richardson (WA only). Victoria - H.C.Hunt (f/c).
12th Men: J.R.Jones (WA) and L.E.Nagel (Vic).
Umpires: Believed to be P.Bastow and A.E.Lawrence.
Attendances: 2500, 1500, 600.   Total: 4600.   Receipts: £471.
Close of Play: 1st day WA 174 all out; 2nd day WA (2) 0/23 (Quinlan 7, F.J.Bryant 15).

H.S.T.L.Hendry, K.E.Rigg and J.Ryder all announced their unavailability for Victoria's tour to the West, while D.D.Blackie, F.L.Morton, W.H.Ponsford and W.M.Woodfull were in New Zealand with the Australian XI. Western Australia struggled on the first day, with F.J.Bryant (40 in 108 minutes, no fours) and Richardson (25 in 109 minutes, no fours) concentrating solely on survival. A half-century stand for the seventh wicket was mounted by R.J.Bryant and W.A.Evans. Onyons (63 in 150 minutes) held the Victorian innings together, R.J.Bryant's fielding being the main highlight. Quinlan (50 in 152 minutes) and Taaffe (32 not out in 160 minutes) batted dourly in Western Australia's second innings. Sources: *The Cricketer, VCA Report, WACA Report, The West Australian, Daily News.*

WESTERN AUSTRALIA

P.F.Quinlan	run out (Scaife/Ellis)	12	b a'Beckett		50
F.J.Bryant	b a'Beckett	19	b a'Beckett		19
A.D.Drew	c Liddicut b Ironmonger	4	b a'Beckett		0
F.H.Taaffe	b Ironmonger	2	not out		32
*A.J.Richardson	b a'Beckett	25			
W.A.McRae	c a'Beckett b Liddicut	17	not out		16
R.J.Bryant	c Ellis b Wilkinson	40	(5) b Wilkinson		26
W.A.Evans	c Hunt b a'Beckett	29			
†R.H.Hewson	b Ironmonger	10			
H.A.Newman	b a'Beckett	1			
L.C.Renfrey	not out	2			
Extras	(b5, lb5, w3)	13	(b2, lb2, w1)		5
Total	(77.4 overs, 277 mins)	174	(69.0 overs, 234 mins) (4 wkts dec)		148

VICTORIA

B.A.Onyons	c Evans b Richardson	63			
E.T.Austen	c Taaffe b Renfrey	12	(1) not out		36
C.A.H.Sindrey	b Evans	4			
J.W.Scaife	lbw b Renfrey	10			
H.C.Hunt	c Evans b Richardson	3	(2) not out		36
A.E.Liddicut	run out (R.J.Bryant/Hewson)	18			
W.A.Wilkinson	b Evans	0			
*V.S.Ransford	run out (R.J.Bryant/Hewson)	12			
E.L.a'Beckett	run out (R.J.Bryant/Hewson)	8			
†J.L.Ellis	b Richardson	11			
H.Ironmonger	not out	4			
Extras	(b5, lb1)	6	(b1, w1)		2
Total	(65.1 overs, 234 mins)	151	(24.0 overs, 75 mins) (0 wkts)		74

VICTORIA	O	M	R	W	w,nb		O	M	R	W	w,nb		FALL OF WICKETS			
													WA	VIC	WA	VIC
a'Beckett	24.4	4	67	4	3,-		20	3	40	3	-,-	Wkt	1st	1st	2nd	2nd
Wilkinson	12	5	19	1	-,-		15	4	31	1	1,-					
Ironmonger	28	10	42	3	-,-	(4)	20	3	39	0	-,-	1st	33	39	38	-
Liddicut	13	2	33	1	-,-	(3)	12	2	27	0	-,-	2nd	40	48	42	-
Hunt							1	1	0	0	-,-	3rd	42	81	89	-
Sindrey							1	0	6	0	-,-	4th	49	90	123	-
												5th	86	102	-	-
												6th	95	109	-	-
WESTERN AUSTRALIA	O	M	R	W	w,nb		O	M	R	W	w,nb	7th	149	116	-	-
Newman	10	1	26	0	-,-		2	0	11	0	-,-	8th	171	131	-	-
Renfrey	17	5	34	2	-,-							9th	172	136	-	-
Evans	21	1	52	2	-,-							10th	174	151	-	-
R.J.Bryant	5	1	15	0	-,-		5	0	14	0	-,-					
Richardson	12.1	3	18	3	-,-	(6)	3	0	4	0	-,-					
Drew						(2)	3	1	5	0	-,-					
Taaffe							4	0	13	0	-,-					
Quinlan						(3)	4	3	9	0	1,-					
McRae						(5)	3	0	16	0	-,-					

WESTERN AUSTRALIA v VICTORIA

Played at W.A.C.A. Ground, Perth, on March 3, 5, 6, 1928. (Three-day match)
Toss : Victoria.   Result : MATCH DRAWN.
Debuts: Victoria - L.E.Nagel (f/c).
12th Men: J.R.Jones (WA) and H.C.Hunt (Vic).
Umpires: A.E.Lawrence and E.A.Walker.
Attendances & Receipts: No figures published, but considered disappointing.
Close of Play: 1st day Vic 7/276 (Wilkinson 14, a'Beckett 4); 2nd day WA 7/134 (Richardson 43, Evans 8).

The Victorians showed improved batting form in comparison with the previous game. Onyons "played a masterful innings" (*West Australian*) to compile 136 in 283 minutes (15 fours) and a'Beckett hit hard on the second morning. Western Australia began badly and never really recovered from there on, only a sound half-century from Richardson adding any respectability to the final total. Following on, the early loss of Horrocks promised a repeat of the first innings but F.J.Bryant (113 not out in 229 minutes, 8 fours) and McRae (119 in 205 minutes, 13 fours) established a new Western Australian second wicket record of 238 to save the match. Neither gave a chance, Bryant scoring by "beautiful placements all round the wicket" and McRae producing several "cannon-like" drives in a forceful display. The match was called off just before the scheduled time for stumps, on the dismissal of Taaffe. Last first-class appearance by V.S.Ransford. Sources: *The Cricketer, VCA Report, WACA Report, The West Australian, Daily News, Sunday Times, Western Mail.*

VICTORIA

E.T.Austen	run out (Stokes)	23
B.A.Onyons	lbw b Richardson	136
J.W.Scaife	c F.J.Bryant b Renfrey	14
C.A.H.Sindrey	c Stokes b Quinlan	31
A.E.Liddicut	c R.J.Bryant b McRae	9
L.E.Nagel	run out (R.J.Bryant)	6
*V.S.Ransford	c Taaffe b Evans	33
W.A.Wilkinson	b Renfrey	21
E.L.a'Beckett	c F.J.Bryant b R.J.Bryant	48
†J.L.Ellis	not out	25
H.Ironmonger	c Horrocks b R.J.Bryant	7
Extras	(b7, lb3)	10
Total	(111.2 overs, 440 mins)	363

WESTERN AUSTRALIA

P.F.Quinlan	b Ironmonger	16			
F.J.Bryant	st Ellis b Wilkinson	4		not out	113
F.H.Taaffe	st Ellis b Ironmonger	25	(4)	b Liddicut	0
W.A.McRae	b Ironmonger	0	(3)	b Liddicut	119
W.J.Horrocks	run out	5	(1)	b a'Beckett	0
R.J.Bryant	b Nagel	11			
*A.J.Richardson	c Ellis b Nagel	56			
R.J.Wilberforce	b a'Beckett	18			
W.A.Evans	b Wilkinson	23			
†W.Stokes	b Wilkinson	2			
L.C.Renfrey	not out	1			
Extras	(b3, lb4, w1)	8		(b10, lb4, w1)	15
Total	(70.0 overs, 243 mins)	169		(61.6 overs, 229 mins) (3 wkts)	247

WESTERN AUSTRALIA	O	M	R	W	w,nb
Evans	21	3	55	1	-,-
Renfrey	23	3	67	2	-,-
Richardson	29	4	73	1	-,-
McRae	13	1	53	1	-,-
Taaffe	9	2	19	0	-,-
Quinlan	10	1	55	1	-,-
R.J.Bryant	5.2	0	25	2	-,-
Wilberforce	1	0	6	0	-,-

VICTORIA	O	M	R	W	w,nb		O	M	R	W	w,nb
Nagel	20	3	54	2	1,-	(7)	4	0	20	0	-,-
Wilkinson	17	5	37	3	-,-	(4)	5	0	27	0	-,-
a'Beckett	13	3	33	1	-,-	(1)	14	1	64	1	1,-
Ironmonger	14	6	25	3	-,-	(3)	11	1	35	0	-,-
Liddicut	6	2	12	0	-,-	(2)	20.6	5	58	2	-,-
Onyons							3	0	8	0	-,-
Sindrey						(5)	4	0	20	0	-,-

FALL OF WICKETS

	VIC	WA	WA
Wkt	1st	1st	2nd
1st	55	6	9
2nd	73	38	247
3rd	136	38	247
4th	158	49	-
5th	164	65	-
6th	220	65	-
7th	270	112	-
8th	294	153	-
9th	355	162	-
10th	363	169	-

A.P.F.Chapman's MCC Touring team to Australia in 1928-29 was one of the strongest to ever visit the country. They retained The Ashes and took the Test series 4-1, the loss in the Fifth Test being in fact the only defeat they suffered on the tour. They played 24 matches in all, 17 of which were first-class. Their batting was extremely strong; Hammond, Jardine and Hendren each hit over 1000 runs in the first-class games alone while Hobbs, Sutcliffe and Leyland also scored consistently. Hammond's aggregate of 905 runs in the Test matches established a record for any series on Australian soil. His first-class aggregate of 1553 runs was similarly a record for any visiting overseas player. Tate, Larwood, White, Geary and Freeman combined with the ball to form a purposeful English attack. S.J.Staples (illness) was forced to return home without playing a match.

The Australians generally batted capably in the Tests. Ryder, Woodfull and Hendry, seasoned players by now, all did well. So too did Bradman and Jackson (who hit a sparkling century on debut at Adelaide) and Kippax, batsmen whose styles heartened the nation. Grimmett and Blackie toiled manfully with the ball but received little support. Gregory (injured) and Kelleway (ill) broke down in the First Test and several new bowlers were tried in the remaining Tests. Of these, Wall appeared the most promising.

New South Wales, with a fine blend of youth and experience, won the Sheffield Shield. Bradman gave the first insight into his prolific scoring abilities with consecutive innings of 131, 133*, 87, 132*, 1 and 71* for the State. He also scored an unbeaten 340 against Victoria and his season's tally of 1690 runs created a record for any batsman in an Australian first-class season. Kippax and Jackson also enjoyed superb domestic seasons, while Fairfax put in several good allround performances. Hooker led the bowling and at one stage captured four wickets with consecutive balls. The New South Wales campaign was highlighted by a remarkable tenth-wicket partnership of 307 - a world record - between Kippax and Hooker in the match against Victoria at Melbourne.

Victoria began well with two outright wins in their first three Shield matches but thereafter failed to win another game. Woodfull, Ponsford, Hendry and Ryder were unavailable for much of the season, through either injury or Test duty, and their talents were missed. Ironmonger was the most consistent Victorian bowler.

Queensland fared little better than the previous year, achieving a sole outright win over South Australia in their six matches. They lost to New South Wales at Brisbane after leading on the first innings. The experienced O'Connor and Thompson again led the batting, although performances from Levy, Nothling and McCoombe gave hope for the future. Ron Oxenham, again Queensland's leading bowler, was supported by Nothling and Thurlow.

South Australia finished with a similar record to Queensland, their sole success coming at the expense of that State. They relied on Vic Richardson and Harris for runs and Grimmett and Wall to bowl sides out.

It should be noted that prior to this season the Interstate Conference amended the points awarded for an outright win in the Shield from 4 to 5.

Tasmania played matches against New South Wales and Victoria, in addition to their fixtures against the MCC team. Western Australia had to be content with a sole fixture against the tourists.

The total of 32 first-class matches represented a new record for a season in Australia.

Leading Aggregates

Batsmen	M	I	NO	Runs	HS	Ave.	Bowlers	Runs	Wkts	Ave.
D.G.Bradman (NSW)	13	24	6	1690	340*	93.88	C.V.Grimmett (SA)	2432	71	34.25
W.R.Hammond (MCC)	13	18	1	1553	251	91.35	J.C.White (MCC)	1471	65	22.63
D.R.Jardine (MCC)	12	19	1	1168	214	64.88	M.W.Tate (MCC)	1329	44	30.20
A.F.Kippax (NSW)	11	19	2	1079	260*	63.47	H.Larwood (MCC)	1254	40	31.35
J.Ryder (V)	10	17	2	1045	175	69.66	G.Geary (MCC)	956	37	25.83
E.H.Hendren (MCC)	12	17	1	1033	169	64.56	T.W.Wall (SA)	1149	37	31.05
A.Jackson (NSW)	12	21	1	992	164	49.60	A.P.Freeman (MCC)	1136	35	32.45
J.B.Hobbs (MCC)	11	18	1	962	142	56.58	H.Ironmonger (V)	1203	32	37.59
G.W.Harris (SA)	10	19	1	941	183	52.27	J.E.H.Hooker (NSW)	877	30	29.23

SHEFFIELD SHIELD TABLE

	P	WO	W1	LO	L1	D	Pts	Quotient	Runs Scored	Wkts Lost	Runs Conceded	Wkts Taken
NEW SOUTH WALES	6	3	3	-	-	-	24	1.275	4139	88	4167	113
VICTORIA	6	2	-	-	4	-	14	1.011	4164	101	3627	89
QUEENSLAND	6	1	1	3	1	-	9	0.855	3729	119	3701	101
SOUTH AUSTRALIA	6	1	1	4	-	-	8	0.908	3537	107	4074	112
TOTAL	12	7	5	7	5	-	55	1.000	15569	415	15569	415

WESTERN AUSTRALIA v M.C.C.

Played at W.A.C.A Ground, Perth, on October 18, 19, 20, 1928. (Three-day match)
Toss : M.C.C.   Result : MATCH DRAWN.
Debuts: Western Australia - R.A.Halcombe (WA only).
12th Men: R.J.Wilberforce (WA) and G.Duckworth (MCC).
Umpires: J.Hart and W.L.Menkens.
Attendances: 5000, 4000, 8000.   Total: About 17,000.   Receipts: £1246.
Close of Play: 1st day MCC 6/306 (Hendren 55, Ames 3); 2nd day WA 4/181 (F.J.Bryant 53, Horrocks 24).

Mead was a last minute replacement for A.P.Freeman (stiff neck) in the selected M.C.C. team. Tyldesley (66 in 166 minutes, 6 fours), Jardine (109 in 147 minutes, 11 fours) and Hendren (90 in 120 minutes, 2 sixes and 7 fours) demonstrated that they had adapted well to Australian conditions. Halcombe "gathered considerable pace and made the ball kick awkwardly at times" (*West Australian*) but was handicapped by a nose bleed soon after lunch on the first day. Geary felt the full force of this hostility in the brief second innings when he sustained "a terrific blow full in the face" from a sharply rising delivery at 0/24. He had to be carried from the field on a makeshift stretcher, his broken nose keeping him out for over a month. Richardson (44 in 66 minutes, 6 fours), F.J.Bryant (61 in 191 minutes, 7 fours) and Horrocks (75 not out in 174 minutes, 8 fours) batted well for the home team. Sources: *Wisden, WACA Report, The West Australian, Daily News.*

M.C.C.

H.Sutcliffe	lbw b Halcombe	28			
M.Leyland	c Halcombe b Evans	15	(1) not out		6
G.E.Tyldesley	b Halcombe	66			
W.R.Hammond	b Evans	14			
C.P.Mead	lbw b Inverarity	1	(3) not out		1
D.R.Jardine	c Richardson b Halcombe	109			
E.H.Hendren	c Taaffe b Richardson	90			
†L.E.G.Ames	c Stokes b Richardson	36			
*A.P.F.Chapman	c Richardson b Evans	26			
G.Geary	run out (Taaffe/Stokes/Richardson)	1	(2) retired hurt		15
J.C.White	not out	1			
Extras	(b7, lb9, nb3,)	19	(b2, lb2,)		4
Total	(94.2 overs, 364 mins)	406	(9.0 overs, 50 mins) (0 wkts)		26

WESTERN AUSTRALIA

*A.J.Richardson	c Chapman b White	44
P.F.Quinlan	c Chapman b White	14
F.J.Bryant	run out (Chapman/Ames)	61
F.H.Taaffe	c Hammond b White	0
W.A.McRae	c Ames b Jardine	34
W.J.Horrocks	not out	75
R.J.Bryant	c Sutcliffe b Leyland	2
M.Inverarity	b Hammond	2
W.A.Evans	c Ames b Geary	2
†W.Stokes	c Leyland b Hammond	5
R.A.Halcombe	b Hammond	0
Extras	(b13, lb4, w1)	18
Total	(107.6 overs, 333 mins)	257

WESTERN AUSTRALIA	O	M	R	W	w,nb		O	M	R	W	w,nb
Halcombe	21	0	114	3	-,3		4	1	10	0	-,-
Evans	24	3	82	3	-,-		3	2	5	0	-,-
Richardson	19.2	4	58	2	-,-						
Inverarity	23	1	92	1	-,-	(3)	2	0	7	0	-,-
R.J.Bryant	3	0	25	0	-,-						
Taaffe	1	0	7	0	-,-						
Quinlan	3	0	9	0	-,-						

M.C.C.	O	M	R	W	w,nb
Hammond	33.6	12	67	3	1,-
Leyland	13	3	47	1	-,-
Geary	24	4	55	1	-,-
White	34	8	59	3	-,-
Mead	1	0	11	0	-,-
Jardine	2	2	0	1	-,-

FALL OF WICKETS

Wkt	MCC 1st	WA 1st	MCC 2nd
1st	34	59	-
2nd	74	64	-
3rd	96	68	-
4th	105	134	-
5th	189	197	-
6th	297	205	-
7th	357	214	-
8th	398	228	-
9th	404	257	-
10th	406	257	-

AUSTRALIAN XI v THE REST

Played at Melbourne Cricket Ground on October 19, 20, 22, 1928. (Four-day match)
Toss : The Rest.   Result : AUSTRALIAN XI WON BY AN INNINGS AND 43 RUNS.
Debuts: Nil.
12th Men: C.B.Willis (both teams).
Umpires: J.Richards and P.E.Smith.
Attendances: 7487, 9962, 2293.   Total: 19,742.   Receipts: £794.
Close of Play: 1st day Aust 1/90 (Ponsford 44, Andrews 1); 2nd day Rest (2) 0/3 (Harris 3, Jackson 0).

Played for the benefit of the "Distressed Cricketers Fund" this match was a trial for Australian prospects for the forthcoming series against England. J.G.Morgan (injured knee) was replaced as 12th man by Scaife who in turn replaced J.Ryder (ill) in the Australian side. O'Connor (31 in 140 minutes, 2 fours) was the only batsman to survive for any length of time in the first innings against the Australian attack. Ponsford (79 in 134 minutes, 7 fours, chance at 1), Hendry (45 in 74 minutes, 4 fours), Andrews (44 in 111 minutes, 5 fours), Grimmett (43 in 49 minutes, 5 fours) and Oldfield (58 in 85 minutes, 4 fours) all contributed towards Australia's 398, the last two named sharing a ninth-wicket stand of 86. Woodfull batted down the order due to a heavy cold. The Rest again folded to the bowling of Oxenham and Grimmett despite the efforts of Harris (51 in 85 minutes, 4 fours) and some strong hitting from Nothling (62 not out in 61 minutes, 1 six and 7 fours) and Nicholls (47 in 29 minutes, 1 six and 5 fours). E.L.a'Beckett (university exams) and J.M.Taylor announced their unavailability for selection in the match.   Sources: *Wisden, NSWCA Report, VCA Report, The Age, The Argus, The Herald, The Australasian.*

THE REST

G.W.Harris	c Oxenham b Gregory	6	st Oldfield b Grimmett		51
†L.P.D.O'Connor	b Oxenham	31	(7) b Oxenham		0
A.Jackson	c Oldfield b Oxenham	18	(2) c & b Grimmett		27
C.Kelleway	run out (Hendry)	15	lbw b Oxenham		26
*V.Y.Richardson	c Hendry b Gregory	5	b Oxenham		0
D.G.Bradman	c Oldfield b Grimmett	14	b Oxenham		5
F.C.Thompson	st Oldfield b Grimmett	5	(3) c Oldfield b Grimmett		20
O.E.Nothling	lbw b Grimmett	8	not out		62
C.O.Nicholls	lbw b Oxenham	0	st Oldfield b Grimmett		47
J.D.Scott	b Oxenham	0	b Oxenham		1
H.Ironmonger	not out	2	b Oxenham		4
Extras	(b1, lb5, nb1)	7	(lb1)		1
Total	(56.2 overs, 183 mins)	111	(56.2 overs, 182 mins)		244

AUSTRALIAN XI

W.H.Ponsford	c Jackson b Nicholls	79
H.S.T.L.Hendry	c Kelleway b Scott	45
T.J.E.Andrews	c O'Connor b Nothling	44
A.F.Kippax	c & b Kelleway	34
R.K.Oxenham	c O'Connor b Scott	1
J.W.Scaife	b Kelleway	2
*W.M.Woodfull	lbw b Nothling	21
J.M.Gregory	st O'Connor b Bradman	38
C.V.Grimmett	c Nicholls b Kelleway	43
†W.A.S.Oldfield	c O'Connor b Nicholls	58
D.D.Blackie	not out	18
Extras	(b7, lb7, nb1)	15
Total	(93.1 overs, 380 mins)	398

AUSTRALIAN XI	O	M	R	W	w,nb	O	M	R	W	w,nb
Gregory	11	2	26	2	-,-	9	1	34	0	-,-
Blackie	17	8	21	0	-,1	9	0	22	0	-,-
Oxenham	17.2	9	28	4	-,-	19.2	2	62	6	-,-
Grimmett	11	3	29	3	-,-	19	1	125	4	-,-

THE REST	O	M	R	W	w,nb
Scott	19	3	76	2	-,-
Ironmonger	22	4	76	0	-,-
Kelleway	18	2	72	3	-,1
Nicholls	15.1	0	72	2	-,-
Nothling	14	2	51	2	-,-
Bradman	5	0	36	1	-,-

FALL OF WICKETS

	REST	AUST	REST
Wkt	1st	1st	2nd
1st	12	87	60
2nd	31	143	85
3rd	66	192	116
4th	79	206	124
5th	86	206	124
6th	100	211	124
7th	108	273	133
8th	109	275	199
9th	109	361	200
10th	111	398	244

SOUTH AUSTRALIA v M.C.C.

Played at Adelaide Oval on October 26, 27, 29, 30, 1928. (Four-day match)
Toss : M.C.C.　　　　　　　　　Result : MATCH DRAWN.
Debuts: Nil.
12th Men: E.A.Johnson (SA) and L.E.G.Ames (MCC).
Umpires: G.A.Hele and A.G.Jenkins.
Attendances: 12994, 25000, 15994, 5654.　　　Total: 59,642.　　　Receipts: £3693.
Close of Play: 1st day MCC 4/292 (Hammond 116, Leyland 3); 2nd day SA 1/155 (Richardson 84, Pritchard 29); 3rd day SA 9/496
　　　(Wall 4, Scott 0).

With the sole exception of Tyldesley, the English batsmen took advantage of ideal batting conditions to score heavily in both innings. Sutcliffe (76 in 144 minutes, 1 six and 4 fours), Hammond (145 in 237 minutes, 1 six and 11 fours), Chapman (145 in 133 minutes, 1 six and 19 fours), Mead (58) and even Larwood (46) did well in the first innings. Hobbs (64 in 76 minutes, 5 fours), Sutcliffe (70 in 91 minutes, 11 fours) and Leyland (114 in 146 minutes, 13 fours) topscored in the second innings, Mead making another 58. South Australia's innings was dominated by a second-wicket partnership of 255 between Richardson (career-highest 231 in 307 minutes, 1 six and 27 fours) and Pritchard (119 in 176 minutes, 11 fours). Other contributions came from Harris (41 in 73 minutes, 1 four) and Hack (43 in 112 minutes, 1 five and 4 fours). Sources: *Wisden, VCA Report, SACA Report, Adelaide Advertiser, South Australian Register.*

M.C.C.

J.B.Hobbs	b Scott	26		c Pritchard b Williams	64
H.Sutcliffe	b Whitfield	76		c Pritchard b Williams	70
G.E.Tyldesley	c Hack b Grimmett	8		st Hack b Grimmett	21
W.R.Hammond	c Alexander b Whitfield	145			
C.P.Mead	c & b Grimmett	58		not out	58
M.Leyland	c Scott b Whitfield	5	(4)	c Richardson b Williams	114
*A.P.F.Chapman	c Whitfield b Grimmett	145			
H.Larwood	c Scott b Grimmett	46			
J.C.White	c Richardson b Grimmett	0	(6)	not out	0
A.P.Freeman	not out	11			
†G.Duckworth	c Pellew b Grimmett	0			
Extras	(b4, lb2, nb2)	8		(b2, lb10, nb2)	14
Total	(113.3 overs, 428 mins)	528		(65.0 overs, 250 mins) (4 wkts)	341

SOUTH AUSTRALIA

G.W.Harris	lbw b Freeman	41
*V.Y.Richardson	c Sutcliffe b White	231
D.E.Pritchard	c Freeman b White	119
†A.T.Hack	c Sutcliffe b Freeman	43
C.E.Pellew	st Duckworth b Freeman	14
W.C.Alexander	lbw b Freeman	3
C.V.Grimmett	b Freeman	23
H.E.Whitfield	c Chapman b Leyland	12
N.L.Williams	c White b Leyland	0
T.W.Wall	c Tyldesley b White	5
J.D.Scott	not out	27
Extras	(b2, lb4)	6
Total	(135.1 overs, 445 mins)	524

SOUTH AUSTRALIA	O	M	R	W	w,nb	O	M	R	W	w,nb
Scott	20	1	102	1	-,2	10	1	43	0	-,-
Whitfield	27	1	134	3	-,-	12	2	35	0	-,-
Wall	21	2	65	0	-,-	9	0	60	0	-,2
Williams	7	0	55	0	-,-	20	0	127	3	-,-
Grimmett	27.3	4	109	6	-,-	6	0	22	1	-,-
Pellew	11	1	55	0	-,-	5	0	32	0	-,-
Alexander						2	0	5	0	-,-
Harris						1	0	3	0	-,-

M.C.C.	O	M	R	W	w,nb
Larwood	20	0	116	0	-,-
Hammond	19	0	82	0	-,-
Freeman	44	6	180	5	-,-
White	35.1	4	103	3	-,-
Leyland	17	5	37	2	-,-

FALL OF WICKETS

		MCC	SA	MCC
Wkt		1st	1st	2nd
1st		78	83	131
2nd		93	338	146
3rd		129	410	199
4th		283	450	336
5th		299	454	-
6th		386	455	-
7th		489	486	-
8th		489	486	-
9th		528	496	-
10th		528	524	-

QUEENSLAND v NEW SOUTH WALES (Shield Match 1)

Played at Exhibition Ground, Brisbane, on October 27, 29, 30, 31, November 1, 1928. (Five-day match)
Toss : Queensland.   Result : NEW SOUTH WALES WON BY SIX WICKETS.
Debuts: Queensland - H.M.Thurlow (f/c). New South Wales - W.J.S.Carter (f/c).
12th Men: C.A.McCoombe (Qld) and A.G.Fairfax (NSW).
Umpires: J.P.Orr and J.A.Scott.
Attendances: 1st day 6000, other days not published.   Total: About 11,500.   Receipts: £578.
Close of Play: 1st day Qld 7/293 (Higgins 47, Bensted 19); 2nd day Qld (2) 0/0 (Bensted 0, Hornibrook 0); 3rd day Qld (2) 322 all out;
    4th day NSW (2) 3/319 (Bradman 88, Morgan 6).

New South Wales were set 399 runs to win and achieved the target easily, establishing the highest fourth-innings total in matches between these teams in the process. Bradman made a century in each innings for the first time, scoring 131 (212 minutes, 14 fours) and an unbeaten 133 (264 minutes, 11 fours) and earned himself serious consideration for a spot in the Test team. Other contributions for New South Wales came from Jackson (50 in 96 minutes, 5 fours and 71 in 125 minutes, 5 fours), Loder (49 in 123 minutes, 2 fours) and Kippax (47 in 83 minutes, 5 fours and 96 in 151 minutes, 10 fours), who shared a 185-run stand with Bradman for the third wicket, and with the ball Hooker, who took his only ten-wicket-match haul (10 for 118) at first-class level. A collapse claimed the last 6 for 2 in the first innings (Oxenham 3 for 0), Thurlow on debut taking his best-ever figures of 6 for 59. Queensland's topscorers were O'Connor (72 in 130 minutes, 1 six and 7 fours), Gough (67 in 115 minutes, 1 six and and 7 fours) and Higgins (58 in 147 minutes, 4 fours) in the first innings and Gough (39 in 74 minutes, 7 fours) and Thompson (158 not out in 246 minutes, 19 fours) in the second. Nicholls kept wicket for the final hour on the first day in place of Love (ill). J.L.Litster (Queensland), T.J.E.Andrews, J.M.Gregory, C.Kelleway and W.A.S.Oldfield (New South Wales) were unavailable for selection and Fairfax replaced F.S.Jordan after the New South Wales team had been named. McCoombe and G.S.Amos were omitted from the Queensland thirteen. *Wisden* incorrectly gives Qld (1) Oxenham c Love. Sources: *Wisden, NSWCA Report, QCA Report, Sydney Morning Herald, Brisbane Courier, Brisbane Daily Mail.*

QUEENSLAND

*†L.P.D.O'Connor	c Love b Hooker	72	(3)	b Hooker	2
R.K.Oxenham	c Nicholls b McNamee	1	(4)	b Morgan	7
F.J.Gough	b Hooker	67	(5)	c & b Carter	39
F.C.Thompson	lbw b Hooker	29	(6)	not out	158
W.Rowe	c Nicholls b Morgan	15	(8)	b Nicholls	22
H.J.R.Higgins	c Morgan b Hooker	58	(10)	b McNamee	33
O.E.Nothling	b Morgan	18	(9)	c Nicholls b Hooker	3
E.C.Knowles	c Love b Morgan	2	(7)	b Campbell	30
E.C.Bensted	not out	36	(1)	b McNamee	0
P.M.Hornibrook	c Love b Hooker	0	(2)	c Nicholls b Hooker	16
H.M.Thurlow	b Hooker	1		c Morgan b Hooker	1
Extras	(b11, lb10, nb4)	25		(lb7, nb4)	11
Total	(97.3 overs, 335 mins)	324		(89.6 overs, 311 mins)	322

NEW SOUTH WALES

A.Jackson	c Hornibrook b Nothling	50	(2)	c Nothling b Rowe	71
R.Loder	b Thurlow	1	(1)	run out (Nothling/O'Connor)	49
D.G.Bradman	c O'Connor b Thurlow	131		not out	133
*A.F.Kippax	b Thurlow	47		c Hornibrook b Rowe	96
J.G.Morgan	lbw b Thurlow	4		b Thurlow	6
†H.S.B.Love	c O'Connor b Thurlow	5		not out	31
C.O.Nicholls	b Thurlow	2			
J.E.H.Hooker	b Oxenham	0			
W.J.S.Carter	lbw b Oxenham	0			
J.N.Campbell	b Oxenham	0			
R.L.A.McNamee	not out	0			
Extras	(lb4, nb4)	8		(b11, lb3, nb1)	15
Total	(65.2 overs, 238 mins)	248		(111.4 overs, 388 mins) (4 wkts)	401

NEW SOUTH WALES	O	M	R	W	w,nb		O	M	R	W	w,nb		FALL OF WICKETS				
														QLD	NSW	QLD	NSW
Nicholls	17	1	64	0	-,-		9	2	50	1	-,-		Wkt	1st	1st	2nd	2nd
Hooker	24.3	9	46	6	-,1	(3)	31.6	5	72	4	-,1		1st	21	7	1	121
McNamee	29	7	85	1	-,3	(2)	27	5	93	2	-,3		2nd	150	120	10	121
Carter	11	0	47	0	-,-	(6)	7	1	31	1	-,-		3rd	155	213	19	306
Morgan	11	1	36	3	-,-	(4)	9	3	28	1	-,-		4th	176	227	43	322
Campbell	5	0	21	0	-,-	(5)	6	0	37	1	-,-		5th	230	246	82	-
													6th	254	247	157	-
QUEENSLAND	O	M	R	W	w,nb		O	M	R	W	w,nb		7th	258	248	206	-
Hornibrook	12	2	52	0	-,-		20.4	3	62	0	-,-		8th	320	248	215	-
Thurlow	15	3	59	6	-,2		21	2	94	1	-,1		9th	320	248	295	-
Oxenham	18.2	3	56	3	-,-	(4)	29	2	77	0	-,-		10th	324	248	322	-
Nothling	8	1	22	1	-,-	(5)	13	0	52	0	-,-						
Rowe	5	0	15	0	-,-	(6)	11	3	45	2	-,-						
Bensted	6	0	30	0	-,2	(3)	9	0	35	0	-,-						
Thompson	1	0	6	0	-,-		8	3	21	0	-,-						

VICTORIA v M.C.C.

Played at Melbourne Cricket Ground on November 1, 2, 3, 5 (no play), 1928. (Four-day match)
Toss : Victoria.   Result : MATCH DRAWN.
Debuts: Nil.
12th Men: A.J.W.Lansdown (Vic) and L.E.G.Ames (MCC).
Umpires: F.W.Dixon and H.E.Nichols.
Attendances: 11535, 16187, 22959, 3429.   Total: 54,110.   Receipts: £3240.
Close of Play: 1st day Vic 9/163 (Woodfull 66, Ironmonger 16); 2nd day MCC 3/248 (Hendren 50, White 2); 3rd day Vic (2) 0/135
    (Hendry 74, Ponsford 60).

Ebeling replaced E.L.a'Beckett (exams) in the Victorian team. Larwood's analysis on a rain-interrupted first day included the wickets of Hartkopf and Scaife in succession and Ellis two balls later. Woodfull carried his bat through the innings, hitting 3 fours. Jardine (104 in 258 minutes, 6 fours) and Hendren (100 in 131 minutes, 11 fours) continued their good form with centuries for M.C.C. while Hobbs (51 in 126 minutes, 3 fours), Chapman (71 in 68 minutes, 1 six and 6 fours) and Larwood (79 in 93 minutes, 1 six and 6 fours) all exceeded fifty. Leyland however was out first ball. Hendry was dropped by Mead from the first ball of Victoria's second innings but offered no further chances as he and Ponsford scored quickly against an attack handicapped by drizzling rain. The elements intensified to prevent any further play on the last day. Last first-class appearance by A.E.V.Hartkopf. Sources: *Wisden, NSWCA Report, VCA Report, The Age, The Argus, The Herald, Melbourne Sun.*

VICTORIA

*W.M.Woodfull	not out	67			
W.H.Ponsford	b Larwood	14		not out	60
H.S.T.L.Hendry	b Larwood	8	(1)	not out	74
J.Ryder	b Larwood	25			
A.E.V.Hartkopf	b Larwood	13			
J.W.Scaife	c White b Larwood	0			
†J.L.Ellis	c Chapman b Larwood	0			
D.D.Blackie	c Chapman b Larwood	3			
H.I.Ebeling	st Duckworth b White	4			
F.L.Morton	c Duckworth b Tate	14			
H.Ironmonger	c Hendren b White	16			
Extras		-		(nb1)	1
Total	(54.0 overs, 194 mins)	164		(26.0 overs, 96 mins) (0 wkts)	135

M.C.C.

J.B.Hobbs	st Ellis b Hartkopf	51
D.R.Jardine	c & b Morton	104
C.P.Mead	lbw b Hartkopf	37
E.H.Hendren	run out (Scaife)	100
J.C.White	b Ironmonger	20
M.Leyland	b Ironmonger	0
*A.P.F.Chapman	c sub (A.J.W.Lansdown) b Ebeling	71
M.W.Tate	lbw b Blackie	1
H.Larwood	run out (Ponsford/Ellis)	79
A.P.Freeman	c Blackie b Ebeling	6
†G.Duckworth	not out	4
Extras	(b5, lb7, w1)	13
Total	(115.0 overs, 445 mins)	486

M.C.C.	O	M	R	W	w,nb		O	M	R	W	w,nb
Larwood	13	2	51	7	-,-	(2)	3	0	16	0	-,1
Tate	19	6	45	1	-,-	(1)	4	0	30	0	-,-
Freeman	7	0	25	0	-,-						
White	15	1	43	2	-,-	(3)	10	0	35	0	-,-
Leyland						(4)	6	0	37	0	-,-
Jardine						(5)	3	0	16	0	-,-

VICTORIA	O	M	R	W	w,nb
Morton	14	2	51	1	-,-
Ebeling	20	1	89	2	-,-
Ironmonger	36	10	116	2	-,-
Blackie	29	2	120	1	-,-
Hartkopf	11	1	76	2	1,-
Ryder	5	1	21	0	-,-

FALL OF WICKETS

Wkt	VIC 1st	MCC 1st	VIC 2nd
1st	19	93	-
2nd	27	164	-
3rd	63	232	-
4th	85	317	-
5th	85	317	-
6th	85	331	-
7th	101	342	-
8th	112	435	-
9th	141	449	-
10th	164	486	-

NEW SOUTH WALES v M.C.C.

Played at Sydney Cricket Ground on November 9, 10, 12, 13, 1928. (Four-day match)
Toss : M.C.C.   Result : MATCH DRAWN.
Debuts: Nil.
12th Men: C.D.Seddon (NSW) and G.Geary (MCC).
Umpires: W.J.R.Bowes and A.C.Jones.
Attendances: 20230, 42757, 14601, 7115.   Total: 84,703.   Receipts: £7728.
Close of Play: 1st day MCC 3/372 (Hammond 96, Hendren 57); 2nd day NSW 3/52 (Kippax 26, Bradman 6); 3rd day NSW (2) 0/28
    (Morgan 17, Jackson 8).

Marylebone Cricket Club raised its highest-ever total in first-class matches over the first two days in front of a huge crowd. Sutcliffe (67 in 131 minutes, 5 fours) and Jardine (140 in 220 minutes, 16 fours) combined for a first-wicket stand of 148 to pave the way for Hammond (225 in 324 minutes, 1 six and 30 fours) and Hendren (167 in 229 minutes, 3 sixes and 19 fours) to add 333 for the fourth wicket. Hammond, whose innings included 20 runs off an over from Campbell, followed up by dismissing Morgan with his first ball. Kippax (64 in 110 minutes, 7 fours), Bradman (87 in 131 minutes, 8 fours) and Kelleway (93 not out in 190 minutes, 8 fours) batted well in the New South Wales first innings but could not prevent the follow-on. An unbroken 249-run partnership in the second innings, again involving Kippax (136 not out in 207 minutes, 14 fours) and Bradman (132 not out in 156 minutes, 14 fours), saved the match. Seddon replaced F.S.Jordan as New South Wales 12th man after the team was named. Sources: *Wisden, NSWCA Report, VCA Report, The Age, The Argus, Sydney Morning Herald, Sydney Referee.*

M.C.C

H.Sutcliffe	b Kelleway	67
D.R.Jardine	b Hooker	140
G.E.Tyldesley	c Oldfield b Kelleway	1
W.R.Hammond	run out (Bradman/Oldfield)	225
E.H.Hendren	c Campbell b Bradman	167
M.Leyland	not out	47
†L.E.G.Ames	b Morgan	25
*A.P.F.Chapman	c Gregory b Morgan	16
M.W.Tate	not out	21
H.Larwood	) did not bat	
A.P.Freeman	)	
Extras	(b12, lb5, w2, nb6)	25
Total	(145.0 overs, 538 mins) (7 wkts dec)	734

NEW SOUTH WALES

J.G.Morgan	b Hammond	1	c Ames b Larwood	18	
A.Jackson	b Tate	4	run out (Jardine/Freeman)	40	
T.J.E.Andrews	c Chapman b Tate	14	b Tate	19	
*A.F.Kippax	lbw b Hammond	64	not out	136	
D.G.Bradman	b Freeman	87	not out	132	
C.Kelleway	not out	93			
J.M.Gregory	st Ames b Tate	7			
†W.A.S.Oldfield	c Ames b Freeman	33			
C.O.Nicholls	c Jardine b Freeman	26			
J.E.H.Hooker	c Hammond b Freeman	14			
J.N.Campbell	c Chapman b Freeman	0			
Extras	(b3, lb3)	6	(b14, lb5)	19	
Total	(98.2 overs, 300 mins)	349	(95.0 overs, 295 mins) (3 wkts)	364	

NEW SOUTH WALES	O	M	R	W	w,nb
Gregory	29	2	130	0	-,-
Kelleway	37	6	140	2	-,3
Nicholls	12	0	38	0	1,-
Hooker	34	3	150	1	-,3
Campbell	14	0	119	0	-,-
Morgan	14	1	47	2	1,-
Bradman	5	0	55	1	-,-

M.C.C.	O	M	R	W	w,nb		O	M	R	W	w,nb
Tate	28	3	98	3	-,-		15	2	36	1	-,-
Hammond	17	3	64	2	-,-		15	0	73	0	-,-
Freeman	37.2	3	136	5	-,-		25	3	81	0	-,-
Larwood	4	1	10	0	-,-	(5)	16	5	33	1	-,-
Leyland	12	1	35	0	-,-	(4)	12	1	61	0	-,-
Jardine							3	0	22	0	-,-
Hendren							5	0	21	0	-,-
Sutcliffe							4	1	18	0	-,-

FALL OF WICKETS

Wkt	MCC 1st	NSW 1st	NSW 2nd
1st	148	5	42
2nd	158	7	72
3rd	263	38	115
4th	596	128	-
5th	622	196	-
6th	675	205	-
7th	697	268	-
8th	-	328	-
9th	-	347	-
10th	-	349	-

VICTORIA v SOUTH AUSTRALIA (Shield Match 2)

Played at Melbourne Cricket Ground on November 9, 10, 12, 13, 1928. (Five-day match)
Toss : Victoria.   Result : VICTORIA WON BY 310 RUNS.
Debuts: Nil.
12th Men: R.N.Ellis (Vic) and E.A.Johnson (SA).
Umpires: A.N.Barlow and P.E.Smith.
Attendances: 5869, 14044, 4223, 2289.   Total: 26,425.   Receipts: £898.
Close of Play: 1st day SA 1/24 (Richardson 8, Wall 0); 2nd day Vic (2) 1/69 (Ponsford 38, Ryder 26); 3rd day SA (2) 0/11 (Harris 10, Richardson 1).

Ebeling and Rigg replaced E.L.a'Beckett (exams) and W.M.Woodfull (ill) in the Victorian team. Enterprising batting by Ryder (138 in 125 minutes, 1 six and 16 fours) with support from Rigg (58 in 112 minutes, 5 fours) added 192 for the third wicket on the first day. Ponsford's 275 not out in 339 minutes included 1 six and 30 fours; his only blemish was a hard chance to Grimmett at mid-on from the bowling of Lee when 151. He scored 113 (85 to 198) between lunch and tea on the third day, sharing partnerships of 91 for the second wicket with Ryder (50 in 84 minutes, 6 fours), 249 for the third wicket with Rigg (90 in 177 minutes, 6 fours) and 113 for the fourth wicket with Scaife. Grimmett (44 not out in 103 minutes, 3 fours) in the first innings and Pellew (76 in 124 minutes, 9 fours) and Scott (86 not out in 102 minutes, 1 five and 11 fours) in the second innings were the only South Australian batsmen to show out. Due to the onset of influenza, Grimmett was unable to bat in the second innings. Sources: *Wisden, VCA Report, SACA Report, The Age, The Argus, The Herald, Melbourne Sun.*

VICTORIA

W.H.Ponsford	b Grimmett	7	not out	275
H.S.T.L.Hendry	b Scott	7	c Pritchard b Scott	4
*J.Ryder	c Lee b Grimmett	138	c Wall b Grimmett	50
K.E.Rigg	st Hack b Williams	58	c Hack b Scott	90
J.W.Scaife	c Hack b Grimmett	23	c & b Pellew	27
A.J.W.Lansdown	c Wall b Scott	17		
†J.L.Ellis	b Williams	38		
D.D.Blackie	c Whitfield b Wall	21		
F.L.Morton	b Williams	1		
H.I.Ebeling	lbw b Williams	1		
H.Ironmonger	not out	1		
Extras	(b1, lb1, w3)	5	(b8, lb6, w1, nb3)	18
Total	(67.6 overs, 271 mins)	317	(91.7 overs, 339 mins) (4 wkts dec)	464

SOUTH AUSTRALIA

G.W.Harris	c Ellis b Blackie	16		c Lansdown b Blackie	22
*V.Y.Richardson	st Ellis b Ironmonger	13		c Lansdown b Morton	1
T.W.Wall	b Ironmonger	9	(10)	c Ellis b Morton	27
D.E.Pritchard	b Ironmonger	12	(3)	c Morton b Ironmonger	15
†A.T.Hack	b Ironmonger	23	(4)	b Blackie	0
C.E.Pellew	c Rigg b Blackie	15	(7)	c & b Ebeling	76
C.V.Grimmett	not out	44		absent ill	-
P.K.Lee	b Blackie	0	(5)	b Blackie	7
H.E.Whitfield	c Ponsford b Lansdown	24	(6)	c Ebeling b Blackie	32
N.L.Williams	lbw b Blackie	7	(9)	run out (Rigg/Ellis)	3
J.D.Scott	st Ellis b Ironmonger	7	(8)	not out	86
Extras	(lb5, nb1)	6		(b17, lb9)	26
Total	(73.4 overs, 264 mins)	176		(61.7 overs, 258 mins)	295

SOUTH AUSTRALIA	O	M	R	W	w,nb		O	M	R	W	w,nb
Scott	17	0	100	2	3,-		18	3	56	2	1,2
Grimmett	23	3	99	3	-,-		23	3	109	1	-,-
Wall	10	0	44	1	-,-		13	1	45	0	-,-
Whitfield	6	1	24	0	-,-	(5)	12	0	57	0	-,1
Williams	7.6	1	30	4	-,-	(4)	15	0	120	0	-,-
Lee	4	1	15	0	-,-		7	0	37	0	-,-
Pellew							3.7	0	22	1	-,-

VICTORIA	O	M	R	W	w,nb		O	M	R	W	w,nb
Morton	7	0	29	0	-,-	(4)	8.7	0	39	2	-,-
Ebeling	8	0	26	0	-,-		9	1	39	1	-,-
Blackie	23.4	5	45	4	-,-		20	2	89	4	-,-
Ironmonger	30	9	45	5	-,1	(1)	19	5	62	1	-,-
Lansdown	5	0	25	1	-,-		5	0	40	0	-,-

FALL OF WICKETS

Wkt	VIC 1st	SA 1st	VIC 2nd	SA 2nd
1st	16	21	11	16
2nd	16	41	102	40
3rd	208	44	351	44
4th	216	63	464	44
5th	241	90	-	59
6th	268	94	-	139
7th	311	95	-	222
8th	314	133	-	227
9th	316	155	-	295
10th	317	176	-	-

AUSTRALIAN XI v M.C.C.

Played at Sydney Cricket Ground on November 16, 17, 19, 20, 1928. (Four-day match)
Toss : Australian XI.　　　　　　Result : M.C.C. WON BY EIGHT WICKETS.
Debuts: Nil.
12th Men: J.W.Scaife (Aust) and W.R.Hammond (MCC).
Umpires: W.G.French and S.Parsons.
Attendances: 11194, 27020, 5281, 6462.　　　Total: 49,957.　　　Receipts: £4063.
Close of Play: 1st day MCC 0/20 (Hobbs 2, Sutcliffe 17); 2nd day MCC 8/319 (Tate 40, Geary 18); 3rd day Aust (2) 3/128 (Jackson 22, Bradman 0).

The Australian XI was representative in name only; apart from the Queenslander Nothling, the players were all drawn from New South Wales and South Australia. D.D.Blackie, A.E.V.Hartkopf, W.H.Ponsford and W.M.Woodfull (all Victorians) withdrew from the original twelve and H.S.T.L.Hendry, K.E.Rigg, J.Ryder and N.L.Williams declined invitations as replacements. The Victorians considered expenses of £1 per day to be inadequate. Bradman (58 not out in 198 minutes, 4 fours) in the first innings and Harris (56 in 139 minutes, 5 fours) and Jackson (61 in 141 minutes, 7 fours) in the second innings made the biggest impressions with the bat on the national selectors. Sutcliffe and Hobbs (58 in 100 minutes and 67 not out in 106 minutes, 4 fours) gave M.C.C. a solid start in each innings. Mead and Tyldesley also scored fifties and Tate (59 in 81 minutes, 1 six and 5 fours) added 76 for the eighth wicket with Geary. Sources: *Wisden, NSWCA Report, VCA Report, The Age, The Argus, Sydney Morning Herald, Sydney Referee.*

AUSTRALIAN XI

*V.Y.Richardson	b White	24	c Geary b Larwood	21
G.W.Harris	b Larwood	19	b White	56
T.J.E.Andrews	b White	39	c Hobbs b Geary	25
A.Jackson	c Geary b Larwood	14	c Duckworth b Tate	61
D.G.Bradman	not out	58	lbw b Tate	18
J.G.Morgan	c Duckworth b Tate	15	b Geary	9
O.E.Nothling	c Sutcliffe b White	11	not out	29
R.H.B.Bettington	c Hendren b Geary	34	b Larwood	8
†W.A.S.Oldfield	c Hendren b Tate	9	run out (Sutcliffe/Duckworth)	7
J.D.Scott	c Hendren b Larwood	5	b Tate	0
J.E.H.Hooker	c Larwood b Tate	2	c Hendren b Geary	1
Extras	(w1)	1	(b3, lb4, w1)	8
Total	(75.7 overs, 266 mins)	231	(74.1 overs, 269 mins)	243

M.C.C.

J.B.Hobbs	lbw b Scott	58	not out	67
H.Sutcliffe	c Oldfield b Nothling	42	b Hooker	31
D.R.Jardine	b Bettington	6	lbw b Bettington	13
C.P.Mead	lbw b Hooker	58	not out	5
G.E.Tyldesley	lbw b Nothling	69		
E.H.Hendren	b Hooker	4		
H.Larwood	c Scott b Nothling	10		
M.W.Tate	lbw b Bettington	59		
*J.C.White	b Bettington	0		
G.Geary	c Bettington b Scott	33		
†G.Duckworth	not out	4		
Extras	(b1, lb7, nb6)	14	(lb1, nb1)	2
Total	(96.1 overs, 342 mins)	357	(30.4 overs, 106 mins) (2 wkts)	118

M.C.C.	O	M	R	W	w,nb	O	M	R	W	w,nb			FALL OF WICKETS		
													AUST	MCC	AUST	MCC
Larwood	18	1	80	3	-,-	19	0	81	2	-,-	Wkt	1st	1st	2nd	2nd
Tate	16.7	4	38	3	-,-	22	2	65	3	1,-	1st	26	93	41	80
Geary	13	1	65	1	1,-	14.1	4	42	3	-,-	2nd	66	104	86	107
White	28	8	47	3	-,-	19	5	47	1	-,-	3rd	91	112	128	-
											4th	101	234	171	-
AUSTRALIAN XI	O	M	R	W	w,nb	O	M	R	W	w,nb	5th	127	243	189	-
Scott	21.1	3	61	2	-,4	8	1	38	0	-,-	6th	142	257	205	-
Hooker	25	5	84	2	-,2	14.4	2	42	1	-,1	7th	192	276	216	-
Nothling	19	7	61	3	-,-						8th	219	277	241	-
Bettington	23	1	98	3	-,-	6	0	25	1	-,-	9th	224	353	242	-
Morgan	5	2	16	0	-,-	(3) 2	0	11	0	-,-	10th	231	357	243	-
Andrews	3	0	23	0	-,-										

QUEENSLAND v M.C.C.

Played at Exhibition Ground, Brisbane, on November 24, 26, 27, 1928. (Four-day match)
Toss : Queensland.   Result : M.C.C. WON BY AN INNINGS AND 17 RUNS.
Debuts: Nil.
12th Men: E.C.Bensted (Qld) and M.W.Tate (MCC).
Umpires: J.P.Orr and J.A.Scott.
Attendances: 12000, 5116, 3000.   Total: About 20,000.   Receipts: £979.
Close of Play: 1st day MCC 6/112 (Ames 4, Leyland 0); 2nd day Qld (2) 3/39 (Knowles 17, Rowe 8).

Oxenham requested that he be rested from this match on the grounds that he had been included in the twelve for the First Test, but the Australian selectors insisted that he play. Bensted and F.M.Brew were omitted from the squad of thirteen. Queensland batted on a rain-affected wicket on the first day, Thompson topscoring with 41 not out in 131 minutes with 3 fours. An eighth-wicket partnership of 137 between Leyland (114 in 192 minutes, 11 fours, 4 chances) and Geary put M.C.C. in a winning position. Gough was dismissed by the fourth ball of Queensland's second innings, Litster making 59 in 97 minutes with 9 fours. Sources: *Wisden, NSWCA Report, QCA Report, Sydney Morning Herald, Brisbane Courier, Brisbane Daily Mail.*

QUEENSLAND

Batsman	1st innings	Runs		2nd innings	Runs
*†L.P.D.O'Connor	c Hobbs b White	25	(7)	b White	31
F.J.Gough	c Mead b Freeman	9	(1)	lbw b Geary	0
O.E.Nothling	st Ames b Freeman	8	(8)	c sub (E.H.Hendren) b White	10
F.C.Thompson	not out	41		c sub (E.H.Hendren) b Geary	9
W.Rowe	c Leyland b Freeman	1		b Geary	8
R.K.Oxenham	c Hammond b White	0		b Geary	4
J.L.Litster	st Ames b Freeman	11	(9)	st Ames b Freeman	59
H.J.R.Higgins	run out (Hobbs/Ames)	0	(2)	b Geary	0
E.C.Knowles	c Leyland b White	3	(3)	run out (sub E.H.Hendren)	29
P.M.Hornibrook	c Hammond b White	2		not out	0
H.M.Thurlow	st Ames b Freeman	9		lbw b Freeman	0
Extras	(b3, lb4)	7		(b6, lb2, w2)	10
Total	(54.6 overs, 170 mins)	116		(68.5 overs, 215 mins)	160

M.C.C.

Batsman		Runs
J.B.Hobbs	c Rowe b Hornibrook	30
H.Sutcliffe	c Thompson b Nothling	34
C.P.Mead	run out (O'Connor)	1
W.R.Hammond	c Litster b Nothling	0
G.E.Tyldesley	c Hornibrook b Nothling	8
*A.P.F.Chapman	c O'Connor b Nothling	35
†L.E.G.Ames	c Oxenham b Nothling	10
M.Leyland	c Gough b Rowe	114
G.Geary	not out	32
A.P.Freeman	c Hornibrook b Rowe	17
J.C.White	c O'Connor b Rowe	1
Extras	(b4, lb6, nb1)	11
Total	(88.7 overs, 325 mins)	293

M.C.C.	O	M	R	W	w,nb		O	M	R	W	w,nb
Hammond	8	1	23	0	-,-						
Geary	5	1	9	0	-,-	(1)	23	5	47	5	2,-
Freeman	23.6	8	51	5	-,-		14.5	2	47	2	-,-
White	18	8	26	4	-,-	(2)	26	9	45	2	-,-
Leyland						(4)	5	1	11	0	-,-

QUEENSLAND	O	M	R	W	w,nb
Hornibrook	17	2	57	1	-,-
Thurlow	16	1	62	0	-,-
Nothling	28	4	78	5	-,-
Oxenham	15	3	52	0	-,-
Thompson	2	0	10	0	-,1
Rowe	10.7	5	23	3	-,-

FALL OF WICKETS

Wkt	QLD 1st	MCC 1st	QLD 2nd
1st	17	62	0
2nd	31	64	3
3rd	79	64	17
4th	80	65	39
5th	80	91	49
6th	97	112	59
7th	97	135	75
8th	103	272	160
9th	107	291	160
10th	116	293	160

AUSTRALIA v ENGLAND (1st Test)

Played at Exhibition Ground, Brisbane, on November 30, December 1, 3, 4, 5, 1928. (Timeless match)
Toss : England.   Result : ENGLAND WON BY 675 RUNS.
Debuts: Australia - D.G.Bradman, H.Ironmonger (both Test).
12th Men: R.K.Oxenham (Aust) and M.Leyland (Eng).
Umpires: D.A.Elder and G.A.Hele.
Attendances: 21696, 24422, 12885, 9503, 5116.   Total: 73,622.   Receipts: £7503.
Close of Play: 1st day Eng 5/272 (Hendren 52, Chapman 39); 2nd day Aust 4/44 (Hendry 14, Ryder 4); 3rd day Eng (2) 2/103 (Mead 40, Hammond 19); 4th day Aust (2) 1/17 (Woodfull 4, Kippax 6).

The first Test match to be staged at Brisbane (one of only two at this particular venue) resulted in the biggest victory yet by a runs margin in a first-class match in Australia. Chapman, who declined to enforce the follow-on after leading by 399 runs, became the first captain to declare a Test innings in this country. Hendren (chanceless 169 in 308 minutes, 16 fours) and Larwood (70 in 118 minutes, 1 six and 7 fours) added 124 to establish a new eighth-wicket record for England against Australia. Hobbs (49 in 95 minutes, 6 fours) and Chapman (50 in 57 minutes, 8 fours) also batted well in the first innings. Gregory suffered a recurrence of a severe knee injury when he fell to the ground attempting to catch Larwood off his own bowling on the second day. He retired from the match and never played cricket again. Australia also lost the services of Kelleway (also playing his last Test) with food poisoning after the second day. Oxenham and F.C.Thompson substituted and O.E.Nothling was summoned to act as 14th man. Off the fourth ball of Australia's first innings Woodfull fell to an outstanding gully catch by Chapman. Hendry (30 in 64 minutes, 4 fours) and Ryder (33 in 83 minutes, 2 fours) were the only batsmen to survive the wholehearted bowling of Larwood (Test-best figures of 6 for 32) and Tate for any time on a still-perfect batting strip. Mead (73 in 212 minutes, 7 fours), Jardine (65 not out in 188 minutes, 4 fours), Hendren (45 in 56 minutes, 2 sixes and 5 fours) and Larwood again (37 in 32 minutes, 6 fours) led the scoring in England's second innings against a much-reduced Australian attack. Woodfull (30 not out in 82 minutes 1 four) batted through Australia's second innings after overnight rain had made batting tricky on a wet fifth-day pitch. He was the second batsman and first Australian to carry his bat through a completed Test innings (although two men were absent) in this country. Bradman completed an inauspicious debut by being out to the second ball he faced in the last innings, White finishing the match with the wickets of Grimmett and Ironmonger with consecutive balls. Ironmonger, at 46 years 237 days, was for a fortnight the oldest Australian to make his Test debut. Sources: *Wisden, QCA Report, The Herald, Sydney Morning Herald, Brisbane Courier, Brisbane Mail, The Australasian.*

ENGLAND

J.B.Hobbs	run out (Bradman/Oldfield)	49	lbw b Grimmett		11
H.Sutcliffe	c Ponsford b Gregory	38	c sub (R.K.Oxenham) b Ironmonger		32
C.P.Mead	lbw b Grimmett	8	lbw b Grimmett		73
W.R.Hammond	c Woodfull b Gregory	44	c sub (F.C.Thompson) b Ironmonger		28
D.R.Jardine	c Woodfull b Ironmonger	35	not out		65
E.H.Hendren	c Ponsford b Ironmonger	169	c Ponsford b Grimmett		45
*A.P.F.Chapman	c Kelleway b Gregory	50	c Oldfield b Grimmett		27
M.W.Tate	c Ryder b Grimmett	26	c Bradman b Grimmett		20
H.Larwood	lbw b Hendry	70	c Ponsford b Grimmett		37
J.C.White	lbw b Grimmett	14			
†G.Duckworth	not out	5			
Extras	(lb10, nb3)	13	(lb3, nb1)		4
Total	(175.3 overs, 510 mins)	521	(135.1 overs, 359 mins) (8 wkts dec)		342

AUSTRALIA

W.M.Woodfull	c Chapman b Larwood	0	(2) not out		30
W.H.Ponsford	b Larwood	2	(1) c Duckworth b Larwood		6
A.F.Kippax	c & b Tate	16	c & b Larwood		15
H.S.T.L.Hendry	lbw b Larwood	30	c Larwood b White		6
C.Kelleway	b Larwood	8	absent ill		-
*J.Ryder	c Jardine b Larwood	33	(5) c Larwood b Tate		1
D.G.Bradman	lbw b Tate	18	(6) c Chapman b White		1
†W.A.S.Oldfield	lbw b Tate	2	(7) c Larwood b Tate		5
C.V.Grimmett	not out	7	(8) c Chapman b White		1
H.Ironmonger	b Larwood	4	(9) c Chapman b White		0
J.M.Gregory	absent hurt	-	absent hurt		-
Extras	(b1, lb1)	2	(nb1)		1
Total	(50.4 overs, 146 mins)	122	(25.3 overs, 82 mins)		66

AUSTRALIA	O	M	R	W	w,nb		O	M	R	W	w,nb
Gregory	41	3	142	3	-,-						
Kelleway	34	9	77	0	-,3						
Grimmett	40	2	167	3	-,-	(2)	44.1	9	131	6	-,-
Ironmonger	44.3	18	79	2	-,-	(3)	50	20	85	2	-,-
Ryder	6	2	23	0	-,-	(4)	14	3	43	0	-,1
Hendry	10	1	20	1	-,-	(1)	27	6	79	0	-,-

ENGLAND	O	M	R	W	w,nb		O	M	R	W	w,nb
Larwood	14.4	4	32	6	-,-		7	0	30	2	-,1
Tate	21	6	50	3	-,-		11,	3	26	2	-,-
Hammond	15	5	38	0	-,-		1	0	2	0	-,-
White							6.3	2	7	4	-,-

FALL OF WICKETS

Wkt	ENG 1st	AUST 1st	ENG 2nd	AUST 2nd
1st	85	0	25	6
2nd	95	7	69	33
3rd	108	24	117	46
4th	161	40	165	47
5th	217	71	228	49
6th	291	101	263	62
7th	319	105	285	66
8th	443	116	342	66
9th	495	122	-	-
10th	521	-	-	-

SOUTH AUSTRALIA v VICTORIA (Shield Match 3)

Played at Adelaide Oval on November 30, December 1, 3, 4, 5, 1928. (Five-day match)
Toss : South Australia.   Result : MATCH DRAWN.
Debuts: South Australia - B.W.Hone (f/c).
12th Men: E.A.Johnson (SA) and D.D.Blackie (Vic).
Umpires: T.W.Cook and C.L.Cornish.
Attendances: 3770, 7557, 2107, 1524, 492.   Total: 15,450.   Receipts: £713.
Close of Play: 1st day SA 4/386 (Hone 103, McKay 20); 2nd day Vic 3/123 (Onyons 53, Scaife 33); 3rd day Vic (2) 0/51 (Sandford 31, R.N.Ellis 17); 4th day Vic (2) 7/380 (J.L.Ellis 83, Ebeling 71).

Blackie was made 12th man when a hand injury sustained the previous week did not heal as expected. A century on debut by Hone (137 in 209 minutes, 15 fours) combined with innings by Harris (155 in 292 minutes, 10 fours, chance at 154), Pellew (64 in 115 minutes, 6 fours), Whitfield (66 in 130 minutes, 1 five and 5 fours) and Parry (48 not out in 76 minutes, 4 fours) led the way for South Australia. Onyons (116 in 271 minutes, 7 fours), Scaife (69 in 155 minutes, 6 fours) and Willis (47 in 81 minutes, 1 four) made the highest scores in Victoria's first innings. Lansdown suffered a first-ball dismissal. Scott strained a groin muscle while bowling on the second day and took no further part in the match; Johnson substituted in the field for the remainder. Following-on, Victoria looked certain to be defeated despite innings from Scaife (62 in 126 minutes, 4 fours) and Baring (87 in 153 minutes, 10 fours) but an eighth-wicket stand of 167 between Ellis (a career-highest 119 in 216 minutes, 1 five and 9 fours) and Ebeling (76 in 160 minutes, 5 fours) saved the day. Sources: *Wisden, VCA Report, SACA Report, Adelaide Advertiser, South Australian Register.*

SOUTH AUSTRALIA

G.W.Harris	c R.N.Ellis b Mullett	155	c J.L.Ellis b Morton		8
*V.Y.Richardson	c Lansdown b Morton	27	not out		57
A.J.Ryan	b Mullett	5	b Ebeling		2
C.E.Pellew	b Ebeling	64	not out		13
B.W.Hone	b Morton	137			
D.G.McKay	c R.N.Ellis b Mullett	22			
H.E.Whitfield	c R.N.Ellis b Ebeling	66			
J.D.Scott	c J.L.Ellis b Mullett	20			
†C.N.Parry	not out	48			
N.L.Williams	c Mullett b Lansdown	13			
T.W.Wall	c Scaife b Lansdown	4			
Extras	(b6, lb6, w2, nb7)	21	(b1, w1)		2
Total	(125.7 overs, 500 mins)	582	(20.0 overs, 77 mins) (2 wkts)		82

VICTORIA

B.A.Onyons	run out (Parry/Whitfield)	116	(4) c Whitfield b Williams		3
H.C.A.Sandford	c Wall b Williams	30	(1) b Williams		31
R.N.Ellis	run out (Whitfield)	4	(2) c Whitfield b Wall		19
A.J.W.Lansdown	b Williams	0	(7) c Parry b Wall		2
J.W.Scaife	c & b Williams	69	(3) st Parry b Williams		62
*F.A.Baring	c Pellew b Williams	38	(5) lbw b Wall		87
C.B.Willis	st Parry b Williams	47	(6) c Richardson b Pellew		8
†J.L.Ellis	lbw b Williams	10	b Williams		119
H.I.Ebeling	c Richardson b Wall	13	st Parry b Williams		76
F.L.Morton	c Parry b Wall	0	b Wall		1
L.T.Mullett	not out	4	not out		5
Extras	(b7, lb2, w1, nb3)	13	(b2, lb10, w1, nb2)		15
Total	(101.7 overs, 371 mins)	344	(114.2 overs, 422 mins)		428

VICTORIA	O	M	R	W	w,nb		O	M	R	W	w,nb
Morton	31	0	139	2	-,4	(2)	5	0	25	1	-,-
Ebeling	34	3	130	2	-,-	(1)	7	3	18	1	-,-
Mullett	36	1	174	4	2,3		3	1	11	0	-,-
Lansdown	7.7	0	43	2	-,-		3	1	14	0	-,-
R.N.Ellis	16	2	72	0	-,-						
Willis	1	0	3	0	-,-	(5)	2	0	12	0	1,-

SOUTH AUSTRALIA	O	M	R	W	w,nb		O	M	R	W	w,nb
Scott	3	0	12	0	-,1						
Whitfield	21	2	59	0	-,-		6	0	30	0	-,-
Wall	23.7	3	82	2	-,-	(1)	30	2	83	4	1,1
Williams	34	1	134	6	1,-	(3)	44.2	2	192	5	-,1
McKay	11	2	18	0	-,2	(4)	11	0	39	0	-,-
Pellew	4	2	9	0	-,-	(5)	9	2	29	1	-,-
Ryan	5	0	17	0	-,-	(6)	11	0	23	0	-,-
Richardson						(7)	3	0	17	0	-,-

FALL OF WICKETS

Wkt	SA 1st	VIC 1st	VIC 2nd	SA 2nd
1st	48	47	51	21
2nd	60	58	57	34
3rd	179	58	62	-
4th	344	200	183	-
5th	395	249	199	-
6th	447	280	201	-
7th	492	304	226	-
8th	546	333	393	-
9th	570	337	400	-
10th	582	344	428	-

AUSTRALIA v ENGLAND (2nd Test)

Played at Sydney Cricket Ground on December 14, 15, 17, 18, 19, 20, 1928. (Timeless match)
Toss : Australia.   Result : ENGLAND WON BY EIGHT WICKETS.
Debuts: Australia - D.D.Blackie, O.E.Nothling (both Test).
12th Men: D.G.Bradman (Aust) and M.Leyland (Eng).
Umpires: D.A.Elder and G.A.Hele.
Attendances: 40723, 58446, 32428, 17358, 14053, 7101.   Total: 170,109.   Receipts: £17,188.
Close of Play: 1st day Aust 8/251 (Oldfield 40, Ironmonger 0); 2nd day Eng 2/113 (Hammond 33, Jardine 23); 3rd day Eng 5/420
     (Hammond 201, Larwood 37); 4th day Aust (2) 1/39 (Woodfull 17, Hendry 21); 5th day Aust (2) 4/339 (Ryder 77, Nothling 20).

The selectors dropped Bradman from the Australian side following his unsuccessful Test debut in Brisbane. However, he fielded throughout both England innings for Ponsford, who suffered a broken hand just after lunch on the first day when he was struck by a ball from Larwood with the score at 2/7. Hammond (251 in 461 minutes, 30 fours) led England to the highest Test total yet made in Australia. His only chance was a hard caught-and-bowled to Ryder on 148. He was well supported by Hendren (74 in 122 minutes, 8 fours) and Geary (66 in 162 minutes, 8 fours). Woodfull (111 in 258 minutes, 6 fours) and Hendry (112 in 239 minutes, 7 fours) gave no chances in their 215-run stand, although Woodfull did play a ball from Tate which rolled into his stumps without dislodging the bails when he was 10. Ryder (79 in 86 minutes, 1 six and 7 fours) reached 50 after only 36 minutes out of 56 added; he put on 101 in all with Nothling (44 in 98 minutes, 6 fours) for the fifth wicket. In the first innings Woodfull (68 in 175 minutes, 4 fours) and Oldfield (41 not out in 103 minutes) were the highest scorers. Some controversy surrounded the dismissal of Kippax on the opening day. The ball deflected from his left pad into the stumps as he attempted to leg-glance the last delivery of a Geary over, and the umpires were moving into position for the next over while Duckworth was motioning that the ball had not come off his pads. It was then confirmed by the square-leg umpire that Kippax was bowled. "There seems to be no doubt that he was out, but the wrong umpire gave the decision," concluded the *SMH* correspondent. "The incident was responsible for a demonstration by the crowd, which did not seem to realise what happened". The second-day crowd (58,446) was a record for Sydney and Don Blackie (46 years 253 days) became the oldest Australian to make his Test debut. Sources: *Wisden, NSWCA Report, VCA Report, The Age, Sydney Morning Herald, Sydney Referee*.

AUSTRALIA

W.M.Woodfull	lbw b Geary	68		run out (Tate/Duckworth)	111
V.Y.Richardson	b Larwood	27		c Hendren b Tate	0
A.F.Kippax	b Geary	9	(4)	lbw b Tate	10
W.H.Ponsford	retired hurt	5		absent hurt	-
H.S.T.L.Hendry	b Geary	37	(3)	lbw b Tate	112
*J.Ryder	lbw b Geary	25	(5)	c Chapman b Larwood	79
O.E.Nothling	b Larwood	8	(6)	run out (Hendren/Duckworth)	44
†W.A.S.Oldfield	not out	41	(7)	lbw b Tate	0
C.V.Grimmett	run out (Tate)	9	(8)	c Chapman b Geary	18
D.D.Blackie	b Geary	8	(9)	not out	11
H.Ironmonger	c Duckworth b Larwood	1	(10)	b Geary	0
Extras	(b4, lb9, w2)	15		(b5, lb6, w1)	12
Total	(108.2 overs, 302 mins)	253		(151.4 overs, 415 mins)	397

ENGLAND

J.B.Hobbs	c Oldfield b Grimmett	40			
H.Sutcliffe	c Hendry b Ironmonger	11			
W.R.Hammond	b Ironmonger	251			
D.R.Jardine	run out (Blackie)	28			
E.H.Hendren	c Richardson b Blackie	74			
*A.P.F.Chapman	c Ryder b Blackie	20			
H.Larwood	c Ryder b Grimmett	43			
G.Geary	lbw b Blackie	66	(1)	b Hendry	8
M.W.Tate	lbw b Blackie	25	(2)	c sub (D.G.Bradman) b Hendry	4
†G.Duckworth	not out	39	(3)	not out	2
J.C.White	st Oldfield b Hendry	29	(4)	not out	2
Extras	(b2, lb3, w4, nb1)	10			-
Total	(272.1 overs, 662 mins)	636		(7.0 overs, 20 mins) (2 wkts)	16

ENGLAND	O	M	R	W	w,nb		O	M	R	W	w,nb
Larwood	26.2	4	77	3	-,-		35	5	105	1	-,-
Tate	21	9	29	0	-,-		46	14	99	4	-,-
White	38	10	79	0	-,-	(4)	30	5	83	0	-,-
Geary	18	5	35	5	2,-	(3)	31.4	11	55	2	-,-
Hammond	5	0	18	0	-,-		9	0	43	0	1,-

AUSTRALIA	O	M	R	W	w,nb		O	M	R	W	w,nb
Nothling	42	15	60	0	-,-		4	0	12	0	-,-
Grimmett	64	14	191	2	-,-						
Ironmonger	68	21	142	2	-,1						
Blackie	59	10	148	4	-,-						
Hendry	23.1	4	52	1	4,-	(2)	3	2	4	2	-,-
Ryder	11	3	22	0	-,-						
Kippax	5	3	11	0	-,-						

FALL OF WICKETS

	AUST	ENG	AUST	ENG
Wkt	1st	1st	2nd	2nd
1st	51	37	0	8
2nd	65	65	215	13
3rd	152	148	234	-
4th	153	293	246	-
5th	171	341	347	-
6th	192	432	348	-
7th	222	496	370	-
8th	251	523	397	-
9th	253	592	397	-
10th	-	636	-	-

VICTORIA v QUEENSLAND (Shield Match 4)

Played at Melbourne Cricket Ground on December 14, 15, 17, 18, 19, 1928. (Five-day match)
Toss : Victoria.   Result : VICTORIA WON BY 50 RUNS.
Debuts: Victoria - F.D.Chapman (f/c). Queensland - C.A.McCoombe (f/c).
12th Men: A.J.W.Lansdown (Vic) and M.Biggs (Qld).
Umpires: A.N.Barlow and W.J.Moore.
Attendances: 3425, 8843, 2257, 1560, 1000.   Total: 17,085.   Receipts: £480.
Close of Play: 1st day Vic 4/203 (Scaife 38, R.N.Ellis 18); 2nd day Vic (2) 2/90 (Rigg 16, Scaife 11); 3rd day Qld (2) 0/88
   (O'Connor 28, McCoombe 45); 4th day Qld (2) 4/376 (Thompson 107, Gough 0).

Biggs, the visitors' 12th man, did not arrive from Queensland until the second day; he was sent for when O.E.Nothling, one of the original twelve, was called up for his only Test. R.N.Ellis was a late replacement for A.E.V.Hartkopf (unavailable) in the Victorian side. Rain restricted play on the first day to 206 minutes. Rigg (59 in 157 minutes, 4 fours) and Baring (50 in 88 minutes, 3 fours) scored first-innings fifties for Victoria while R.N.Ellis (107 not out in 220 minutes, 5 fours) and Wilkinson (56 in 83 minutes, 7 fours) added 108 for the seventh wicket in the second innings. Ebeling dismissed seven batsmen for ducks including five in the first innings. In his seventh over Ebeling dismissed Thompson with his second ball and then Gough, Bensted and Brew with his fifth, sixth and seventh balls to record a hat-trick. He finished off the innings by dismissing Litster, Amos and Thurlow with the second, fifth and sixth balls of his 11th over and in the second innings continued the pattern by dismissing Thompson and Higgins in succession. O'Connor (44 in 78 minutes, 3 fours and 160 in 363 minutes, 5 fours) topscored in each Queensland innings and was given support in the second innings by McCoombe (61 in 103 minutes, 5 fours) and Thompson (115 in 235 minutes, 9 fours). Spectators were admitted free of charge on the last day. Sources: *Wisden, VCA Report, QCA Report, The Age, The Argus, The Herald, Melbourne Sun.*

VICTORIA

B.A.Onyons	c O'Connor b Rowe	20	c Amos b Bensted	19
H.C.A.Sandford	b Thurlow	10	c Bensted b Rowe	41
K.E.Rigg	c Brew b Thurlow	59	c O'Connor b Thurlow	38
*F.A.Baring	c Rowe b Bensted	50	(6) c Bensted b Thurlow	28
J.W.Scaife	c O'Connor b Thurlow	39	(4) lbw b Amos	36
R.N.Ellis	hit wkt b Rowe	18	(5) not out	107
F.D.Chapman	c O'Connor b Rowe	2	b Thurlow	5
W.A.Wilkinson	c Higgins b Thurlow	2	c & b Amos	56
†J.L.Ellis	c O'Connor b Thurlow	0	not out	3
E.L.a'Beckett	c O'Connor b Bensted	32		
H.I.Ebeling	not out	17		
Extras	(lb3, nb7)	10	(b2, lb4, w1, nb4)	11
Total	(75.2 overs, 270 mins)	259	(90.0 overs, 327 mins) (7 wkts dec)	344

QUEENSLAND

*†L.P.D.O'Connor	c J.L.Ellis b a'Beckett	44	lbw b a'Beckett	160
C.A.McCoombe	lbw b a'Beckett	8	lbw b R.N.Ellis	61
W.Rowe	b a'Beckett	6	b Wilkinson	13
F.C.Thompson	lbw b Ebeling	9	c a'Beckett b Ebeling	115
J.L.Litster	b Ebeling	16	lbw b Ebeling	0
F.J.Gough	b Ebeling	0	lbw b a'Beckett	8
E.C.Bensted	b Ebeling	0	(8) run out (Scaife)	17
F.M.Brew	b Ebeling	0	(9) not out	35
H.J.R.Higgins	not out	8	(7) b Ebeling	0
G.S.Amos	b Ebeling	0	c J.L.Ellis b a'Beckett	8
H.M.Thurlow	b Ebeling	0	b R.N.Ellis	0
Extras	(b4, lb2)	6	(b28, lb11)	39
Total	(34.6 overs, 133 mins)	97	(129.6 overs, 462 mins)	456

QUEENSLAND	O	M	R	W	w,nb		O	M	R	W	w,nb	FALL OF WICKETS				
													VIC	QLD	VIC	QLD
Thurlow	26	3	88	5	-,1		24	0	102	3	-,-	Wkt	1st	1st	2nd	2nd
Amos	9	1	47	0	-,-		15	2	89	2	1,-	1st	14	22	61	126
Rowe	25	5	48	3	-,-	(4)	20	3	47	1	-,-	2nd	46	50	64	165
Bensted	8.2	0	24	2	-,6	(3)	18	1	44	1	-,4	3rd	135	65	117	362
Brew	7	0	42	0	-,-		6	1	31	0	-,-	4th	158	76	150	363
Thompson							7	1	20	0	-,-	5th	203	76	202	392
												6th	205	76	218	392
VICTORIA	O	M	R	W	w,nb		O	M	R	W	w,nb	7th	209	76	326	394
Ebeling	10.6	1	33	7	-,-		28	0	118	3	-,-	8th	209	97	-	434
a'Beckett	14	2	29	3	-,-		47	8	123	3	-,-	9th	210	97	-	455
Wilkinson	9	1	24	0	-,-		29	2	93	1	-,-	10th	259	97	-	456
Chapman	1	0	5	0	-,-	(5)	4	0	11	0	-,-					
R.N.Ellis						(4)	13.6	2	44	2	-,-					
Baring							7	2	19	0	-,-					
Sandford							1	0	9	0	-,-					

VICTORIA v NEW SOUTH WALES (Shield Match 5)

Played at Melbourne Cricket Ground on December 22, 24, 25, 26, 27, 1928. (Five-day match)
Toss : Victoria.   Result : MATCH DRAWN.
Debuts: New South Wales - A.G.Fairfax (f/c).
12th Men: W.A.Wilkinson (Vic) and F.S.Jordan (NSW).
Umpires: J.Richards and P.E.Smith.
Attendances: 10647, 15887, 14887, 10323, 2141.   Total: 53,885.   Receipts: £2184.
Close of Play: 1st day Vic 5/162 (Ryder 95, a'Beckett 17); 2nd day NSW 7/58 (Kippax 1); 3rd day NSW 9/367 (Kippax 221, Hooker 51);
    4th day Vic (2) 6/251 (Hendry 69, Rayson 4).

The remarkable world record tenth-wicket partnership of 307 between Kippax (260 not out in 387 minutes, 30 fours) and Hooker (62 in 304 minutes, 3 fours) for New South Wales overshadowed all other events in the match. Coming together early on Christmas Day with Kippax's score a mere 20 and the team in diabolical trouble, the pair made it through to lunch (9/170, Kippax 60, Hooker 18) and then tea (9/270, Kippax 145, Hooker 32) and were still together when stumps were drawn with New South Wales 9/367. The great stand, in which neither batsman offered a chance, finally came to an end after 45 minutes on the fourth day when Hooker drove a ball from a'Beckett straight to Ryder at mid-off. Earlier, Fairfax was dismissed by the fifth ball of the innings. Bradman's unbeaten 71 occupied 103 minutes and included 4 fours. Rain restricted play on the first day to 194 minutes. Ryder (175 in 289 minutes, 13 fours, chance at 120) and a'Beckett (113 in 213 minutes, 1 six and 13 fours) dominated the scoring in Victoria's first innings, a'Beckett again getting in on the act in the second innings (95 in 171 minutes, 12 fours). Hendry scored an unbeaten 69 in 97 minutes and hit 5 fours. D.D.Blackie (business), W.H.Ponsford (injured) and W.M.Woodfull (ill) were all unavailable for Victoria. Sources: *Wisden, NSWCA Report, VCA Report, The Age, The Argus, The Herald, Melbourne Sun.*

VICTORIA

F.A.Baring	c Love b Hooker	12		lbw b Fairfax	30
H.S.T.L.Hendry	c Kelleway b Nicholls	8	(7)	not out	69
*J.Ryder	c & b Andrews	175			
K.E.Rigg	c Hooker b Nicholls	3	(3)	b Nicholls	0
R.N.Ellis	c Love b Kelleway	20	(2)	c Love b Fairfax	4
J.W.Scaife	b Hooker	0	(4)	b Fairfax	6
E.L.a'Beckett	c Jackson b Andrews	113	(5)	c Kippax b Hooker	95
†J.L.Ellis	not out	19	(6)	c & b Andrews	23
H.I.Ebeling	lbw b Fairfax	1			
W.J.Rayson	b Everett	10	(8)	not out	4
H.Ironmonger	c Jackson b Hooker	3			
Extras	(b7, lb2, nb3)	12		(b1, lb7, w1, nb11)	20
Total	(108.7 overs, 405 mins)	376		(68.0 overs, 252 mins) (6 wkts dec)	251

NEW SOUTH WALES

A.G.Fairfax	c Ironmonger b a'Beckett	2	(2)	b R.N.Ellis	30
A.Jackson	c J.L.Ellis b Ironmonger	19			
T.J.E.Andrews	b Hendry	33			
*A.F.Kippax	not out	260			
D.G.Bradman	b Hendry	1	(3)	not out	71
C.Kelleway	b Hendry	0	(1)	c a'Beckett b Ironmonger	13
C.D.Seddon	lbw b Ironmonger	0	(4)	not out	38
†H.S.B.Love	lbw b Ebeling	0			
C.O.Nicholls	b Ebeling	10			
S.C.Everett	lbw b Ironmonger	20			
J.E.H.Hooker	c Ryder b a'Beckett	62			
Extras	(b5, lb6, nb2)	13		(lb3, w1)	4
Total	(127.1 overs, 452 mins)	420		(40.0 overs, 150 mins) (2 wkts)	156

NEW SOUTH WALES	O	M	R	W	w,nb		O	M	R	W	w,nb					
Everett	26	2	91	1	-,1		8	0	28	0	-,-					
Kelleway	24	5	53	1	-,1		14	3	39	0	-,8					
Nicholls	17	2	41	2	-,-		12	2	35	1	-,-					
Hooker	23.7	5	100	3	-,1	(5)	8	0	38	1	-,2					
Andrews	10	1	49	2	-,-	(6)	8	0	46	1	-,-					
Fairfax	8	0	30	1	-,-	(4)	18	6	45	3	1,1					

FALL OF WICKETS

Wkt	VIC 1st	NSW 1st	VIC 2nd	NSW 2nd
1st	21	2	33	17
2nd	21	46	36	75
3rd	29	54	40	-
4th	112	55	45	-
5th	117	55	125	-
6th	293	57	227	-
7th	348	58	-	-
8th	349	74	-	-
9th	371	113	-	-
10th	376	420	-	-

VICTORIA	O	M	R	W	w,nb		O	M	R	W	w,nb
a'Beckett	29.1	2	92	2	-,-	(3)	10	3	19	0	-,-
Ebeling	25	1	81	2	-,-	(1)	4	1	10	0	-,-
Ironmonger	33	4	95	3	-,2	(2)	8	2	12	1	-,-
Hendry	18	5	58	3	-,-						
Rayson	7	0	42	0	-,-	(4)	5	0	41	0	-,-
R.N.Ellis	10	1	31	0	-,-	(5)	6	1	29	1	-,-
Baring	5	1	8	0	-,-	(6)	5	0	22	0	-,-
Rigg						(7)	2	0	19	0	1,-

SOUTH AUSTRALIA v QUEENSLAND (Shield Match 6)

Played at Adelaide Oval on December 22, 24, 25, 26, 1928. (Five-day match)
Toss : South Australia.　　　　　Result : SOUTH AUSTRALIA WON BY FOUR WICKETS.
Debuts: Nil.
12th Men: W.C.Alexander (SA) and G.S.Amos (Qld).
Umpires: T.W.Cook and A.G.Jenkins.
Attendances: 8219, 4968, 6750, 2687.　　　　Total: 22,624.　　　Receipts: £1097.
Close of Play: 1st day SA 4/380 (Hack 61, Wall 7); 2nd day Qld 6/200 (Gough 43, Higgins 7); 3rd day Qld (2) 4/262 (Nothling 7, Litster 2).

An opening stand of 201 between Harris (career-best 183 in 296 minutes, 9 fours) and Richardson (115 in 160 minutes, 10 fours) set the match up for South Australia. Pellew had been appointed captain but he gave the job to Richardson who had aspirations to the Test captaincy. Hack (100 in 232 minutes, 7 fours) lost his wicket to the next ball after reaching his century. McKay (87 in 117 minutes, 7 fours) and Whitfield (55 not out in 78 minutes, 4 fours) added 116 for South Australia's ninth wicket. Queensland's first innings included contributions from McCoombe (51 in 83 minutes, 5 fours) and Gough (95 in 128 minutes, 1 six and 11 fours). Brew (35) was struck on the jaw by a ball from Wall and retired hurt at 6/185. He had knocked the bails off as he fell but "Richardson instructed the team not to appeal" (*Register*). He was able to resume at 7/250 next morning. Thurlow was thrown out by the bowler when he failed to regain his crease after playing a forward stroke. Following on, O'Connor (61 in 103 minutes, 5 fours) and McCoombe (112 in 187 minutes, 11 fours) added 123 for the first wicket, Rowe (52 in 96 minutes, 4 fours), Nothling (46 in 77 minutes, 4 fours) and Litster (45 in 65 minutes, 5 fours) chipping in with support. Thurlow dismissed Harris with the fourth ball of South Australia's second innings in which Pellew (53 in 80 minutes, 6 fours) guided his team to victory. Sources: *Wisden, QCA Report, SACA Report, Adelaide Advertiser, South Australian Register*.

SOUTH AUSTRALIA

G.W.Harris	st O'Connor b Brew	183		lbw b Thurlow	0
*V.Y.Richardson	c Bensted b Thompson	115			
†A.T.Hack	b Nothling	100	(7)	not out	12
C.E.Pellew	c Gough b Thompson	6	(3)	c McCoombe b Bensted	53
P.K.Lee	c Gough b Thompson	2	(6)	lbw b Nothling	1
T.W.Wall	c Gough b Thurlow	15			
B.W.Hone	b Thurlow	0	(2)	c Thompson b Bensted	17
E.A.Johnson	c O'Connor b Thurlow	3	(4)	c Thompson b Bensted	20
D.G.McKay	c Brew b Bensted	87	(5)	b Bensted	1
H.E.Whitfield	not out	55	(8)	not out	19
N.L.Williams	b Brew	2			
Extras	(b8, lb4, nb2)	14		(b8, nb1)	9
Total	(132.3 overs, 479 mins)	582		(36.4 overs, 143 mins) (6 wkts)	132

QUEENSLAND

*†L.P.D.O'Connor	c McKay b Wall	10		c Hone b Williams	61
C.A.McCoombe	c Whitfield b Wall	51		c Wall b Pellew	112
W.Rowe	b Wall	0		run out (Pellew)	52
F.C.Thompson	c Whitfield b Wall	18	(7)	not out	39
O.E.Nothling	c Wall b Williams	10		b Lee	46
J.L.Litster	c Hack b Wall	16		c McKay b Williams	45
F.M.Brew	b Williams	39	(9)	b Wall	8
F.J.Gough	b McKay	95		c Wall b Lee	7
H.J.R.Higgins	c Whitfield b Williams	25	(10)	b Wall	3
E.C.Bensted	not out	19	(4)	c Whitfield b Williams	15
H.M.Thurlow	run out (Lee)	1		b Williams	13
Extras	(b4, lb7, nb1)	12		(b4, lb11)	15
Total	(60.0 overs, 227 mins)	296		(93.5 overs, 355 mins)	416

QUEENSLAND	O	M	R	W	w,nb		O	M	R	W	w,nb
Thurlow	22	2	116	3	-,-		10	1	42	1	-,-
Nothling	23	4	69	1	-,-		12	2	30	1	-,-
Bensted	24	1	121	1	-,-		9	0	28	4	-,-
Rowe	12	1	45	0	-,-	(5)	1.4	0	5	0	-,-
Thompson	19	2	71	3	-,2	(4)	4	0	18	0	-,1
Brew	20.3	1	104	2	-,-						
Gough	12	0	42	0	-,-						

SOUTH AUSTRALIA	O	M	R	W	w,nb		O	M	R	W	w,nb
Wall	23	3	82	5	-,1		19	0	82	2	-,-
Whitfield	10	0	41	0	-,-		16	4	44	0	-,-
Williams	17	0	121	3	-,-		24.5	1	145	4	-,-
Lee	8	2	21	0	-,-		24	3	85	2	-,-
McKay	2	0	9	1	-,-		3	0	16	0	-,-
Pellew							7	0	29	1	-,-

FALL OF WICKETS

Wkt	SA 1st	QLD 1st	QLD 2nd	SA 2nd
1st	201	24	123	0
2nd	361	24	227	32
3rd	368	52	252	90
4th	371	79	253	98
5th	393	104	335	101
6th	393	115	353	101
7th	413	250	369	-
8th	456	256	378	-
9th	572	294	390	-
10th	582	296	416	-

AUSTRALIA v ENGLAND (3rd Test)

Played at Melbourne Cricket Ground on December 29, 31, 1928, January 1, 2, 3, 4, 5, 1929. (Timeless match)
Toss : Australia.   Result : ENGLAND WON BY THREE WICKETS.
Debuts: Australia - E.L.a'Beckett, R.K.Oxenham (both f/c).
12th Men: T.J.E.Andrews (Aust) and M.Leyland (Eng).
Umpires: D.A.Elder and G.A.Hele.
Attendances: 63247, 62259, 31455, 28345, 33664, 25391, 18106.   Total: 262,467.   Receipts: £22,561.
Close of Play: 1st day Aust 4/276 (Ryder 111, Bradman 26); 2nd day Eng 1/47 (Sutcliffe 15, Hammond 12); 3rd day Eng 4/312
     (Hammond 169, Jardine 21); 4th day Aust (2) 2/118 (Woodfull 64, Kippax 34); 5th day Aust (2) 8/347 (Oxenham 39, Grimmett 0)
     6th day Eng (2) 1/171 (Sutcliffe 83, Jardine 18).

This Test produced six centuries, all of them chanceless. Hammond (200 in 398 minutes, 17 fours) was the first batsman to score consecutive double-hundreds at the highest level. He shared century partnerships with Sutcliffe (58 in 195 minutes, 3 fours) and Jardine (62 in 192 minutes, 6 fours). In his second Test match Bradman scored 79 (194 minutes, 9 fours) and 112 (247 minutes, 7 fours) while Kippax (100 in 217 minutes, 9 fours), Ryder (112 in 224 minutes, 1 six and 6 fours plus 51 singles) and Woodfull (107 in 271 minutes, 7 fours) also enjoyed the perfect conditions under which Australia batted. Hobbs (49 in 138 minutes, 1 four) and Sutcliffe (135 in 385 minutes, 9 fours) set England up for victory with a superb opening stand in the second innings on a most difficult wicket. Hobbs was missed on 3 but Sutcliffe batted flawlessly to complete his fourth hundred in five successive Test innings at Melbourne. Heavy overnight rain had delayed the start of the sixth day's play until 1.22pm and the afternoon sun produced a spiteful and unpredictable wicket that only the great skills of the England openers were able to negate. The worst of the conditions was past before the dismissal of Hobbs and, despite the loss of four late wickets, the tourists coasted to victory. The Ashes were thus retained. Sources: *Wisden, VCA Report, The Age, The Argus, The Herald, The Australasian.*

AUSTRALIA

W.M.Woodfull	c Jardine b Tate	7	c Duckworth b Tate		107
V.Y.Richardson	c Duckworth b Larwood	3	b Larwood		5
H.S.T.L.Hendry	c Jardine b Larwood	23	st Duckworth b White		12
A.F.Kippax	c Jardine b Larwood	100	b Tate		41
*J.Ryder	c Hendren b Tate	112	b Geary		5
D.G.Bradman	b Hammond	79	c Duckworth b Geary		112
†W.A.S.Oldfield	b Geary	3	b White		7
E.L.a'Beckett	c Duckworth b White	41	b White		6
R.K.Oxenham	b Geary	15	b White		39
C.V.Grimmett	c Duckworth b Geary	5	not out		4
D.D.Blackie	not out	2	b White		0
Extras	(b4, lb3)	7	(b6, lb7)		13
Total	(180.5 overs, 497 mins)	397	(165.5 overs, 459 mins)		351

ENGLAND

J.B.Hobbs	c Oldfield b a'Beckett	20	lbw b Blackie		49
H.Sutcliffe	b Blackie	58	lbw b Grimmett		135
W.R.Hammond	c a'Beckett b Blackie	200	(4) run out (Oldfield)		32
*A.P.F.Chapman	b Blackie	24	(6) c Woodfull b Ryder		5
E.H.Hendren	c a'Beckett b Hendry	19	b Oxenham		45
D.R.Jardine	c & b Blackie	62	(3) b Grimmett		33
H.Larwood	c & b Blackie	0			
G.Geary	lbw b Grimmett	1	not out		4
M.W.Tate	c Kippax b Grimmett	21	(7) run out (Bradman)		0
†G.Duckworth	b Blackie	3	(9) not out		0
J.C.White	not out	8			
Extras	(b1)	1	(b15, lb14)		29
Total	(195.0 overs, 504 mins)	417	(159.5 overs, 409 mins) (7 wkts)		332

ENGLAND	O	M	R	W	w,nb		O	M	R	W	w,nb
Larwood	37	3	127	3	-,-		16	3	37	1	-,-
Tate	46	17	87	2	-,-		47	15	70	2	-,-
Geary	31.5	4	83	3	-,-	(4)	30	4	94	2	-,-
Hammond	8	4	19	1	-,-	(5)	16	6	30	0	-,-
White	57	30	64	1	-,-	(3)	56.5	20	107	5	-,-
Jardine	1	0	10	0	-,-						

AUSTRALIA	O	M	R	W	w,nb		O	M	R	W	w,nb
a'Beckett	37	7	92	1	-,-		22	5	39	0	-,-
Hendry	20	8	35	1	-,-		23	5	33	0	-,-
Grimmett	55	14	114	2	-,-	(5)	42	12	96	2	-,-
Oxenham	35	11	67	0	-,-		28	10	44	1	-,-
Blackie	44	13	94	6	-,-	(3)	39	11	75	1	-,-
Ryder	4	0	14	0	-,-		5.5	1	16	1	-,-

FALL OF WICKETS

Wkt	AUST 1st	ENG 1st	AUST 2nd	ENG 2nd
1st	5	28	7	105
2nd	15	161	60	199
3rd	57	201	138	257
4th	218	238	143	318
5th	282	364	201	326
6th	287	364	226	328
7th	373	381	252	328
8th	383	385	345	-
9th	394	391	351	-
10th	397	417	351	-

NEW SOUTH WALES v QUEENSLAND (Shield Match 7)

Played at Sydney Cricket Ground on December 31, 1928, January 1, 2, 3, 4, 1929. (Five-day match)
Toss : Queensland.   Result : MATCH DRAWN.
Debuts: New South Wales - W.C.Andrews, S.J.McCabe, N.O.Morris (all f/c).
12th Men: A.E.Marks (NSW) and M.Biggs (Qld).
Umpires: M.Carney and E.J.Shaw.
Attendances: 4461, 5503, 1439, 1109, 464.   Total: 12,976.   Receipts: £711.
Close of Play: 1st day NSW 0/33 (Fairfax 19, Jackson 10); 2nd day NSW 7/379 (Ratcliffe 29, Jordan 13); 3rd day Qld (2) 5/228
    (Thompson 76, Nothling 37); 4th day NSW (2) 4/201 (McCabe 28, Jordan 0).

S.C.Everett, J.E.H.Hooker and H.S.B.Love were unavailable for New South Wales in addition to Test players D.G.Bradman, A.F.Kippax and W.A.S.Oldfield. C.Kelleway, the nominated captain, withdrew and his replacement J.G.Morgan also announced his unavailability; Ratcliffe, one of the selectors was brought in. McCoombe (62 in 101 minutes, 4 fours) and Bensted (93 not out in 98 minutes, 13 fours) contributed most for Queensland towards the 468 runs scored on the first day. After O'Connor was dismissed in the first over of the second innings, McCoombe (56 in 88 minutes, 4 fours), Thompson (76 in 173 minutes, 6 fours) and Nothling, his only first-class hundred, (121 in 145 minutes, 15 fours) made the highest scores. Fairfax (58 in 121 minutes, 8 fours), Seddon (80 in 157 minutes, 4 fours), Punch (72 in 137 minutes, 10 fours) and McCabe (60 in 107 minutes, 5 fours) registered fifties in the New South Wales first innings while Punch (90 in 183 minutes, 11 fours) and Seddon (59 in 74 minutes, 6 fours) again did so in the second innings, Nicholls being dismissed first ball. Jackson's unbeaten 53 occupied 135 minutes and included 3 fours. Sources: *Wisden, NSWCA Report, QCA Report, The Herald, Sydney Morning Herald, Sydney Referee, Sydney Telegraph.*

QUEENSLAND

*†L.P.D.O'Connor	c McCabe b Nicholls	17		c McCabe b Nicholls	1
C.A.McCoombe	lbw b Punch	62		b Nicholls	56
W.Rowe	st Davidson b Jordan	4	(5)	b Jordan	39
F.C.Thompson	c Davidson b Fairfax	143		c Ratcliffe b Nicholls	76
O.E.Nothling	run out (Seddon/Davidson)	0	(7)	b Nicholls	121
J.L.Litster	lbw b Nicholls	13	(8)	b Fairfax	10
F.J.Gough	c Davidson b Nicholls	34	(6)	c Fairfax b Jordan	1
F.M.Brew	run out (Davidson/Nicholls)	8	(9)	c Morris b Fairfax	4
E.C.Bensted	not out	93	(3)	b Jordan	9
G.S.Amos	c Andrews b Nicholls	39		run out (Marks/Davidson)	16
H.M.Thurlow	c Fairfax b Nicholls	4		not out	12
Extras	(b8, lb5, w3, nb2)	18		(b3, lb5, w10, nb1)	19
Total	(74.5 overs, 287 mins)	435		(83.5 overs, 320 mins)	364

NEW SOUTH WALES

A.G.Fairfax	b Brew	58		lbw b Nothling	9
A.Jackson	b Thurlow	17	(8)	not out	53
C.D.Seddon	b Amos	80		run out (Amos/O'Connor)	59
W.C.Andrews	st O'Connor b Brew	26		lbw b Nothling	9
A.T.E.Punch	c Thurlow b Thompson	72	(2)	c Nothling b Thompson	90
S.J.McCabe	c Nothling b Thompson	60	(5)	b Thompson	34
*A.T.Ratcliffe	b Brew	37	(9)	not out	0
C.O.Nicholls	c Bensted b Thompson	7	(7)	c O'Connor b Thompson	0
F.S.Jordan	st O'Connor b Rowe	39	(6)	b Nothling	41
†H.L.Davidson	st O'Connor b Rowe	38			
N.O.Morris	not out	1			
Extras	(b12, lb8, w5, nb1)	26		(b2, lb5, w2)	9
Total	(122.3 overs, 427 mins)	457		(96.0 overs, 339 mins) (7 wkts)	304

NEW SOUTH WALES	O	M	R	W	w,nb		O	M	R	W	w,nb		FALL OF WICKETS			
Nicholls	23.5	2	97	5	2,-		21.5	1	111	4	1,1			QLD	NSW	QLD	NSW
Fairfax	16	1	69	1	1,2		17	4	66	2	4,-	Wkt	1st	1st	2nd	2nd
Jordan	15	0	105	1	-,-		19	3	65	3	2,-	1st	36	45	2	19
Morris	11	0	78	0	-,-		9	0	51	0	-,-	2nd	48	120	51	128
Punch	9	1	68	1	-,-							3rd	142	172	84	158
McCabe						(5)	17	2	52	0	3,-	4th	143	213	170	201
												5th	165	316	172	210
QUEENSLAND	O	M	R	W	w,nb		O	M	R	W	w,nb	6th	262	329	236	210
Thurlow	29	1	130	1	-,-		16	5	40	0	2,-	7th	280	341	269	300
Bensted	12	2	45	0	1,1		4	0	13	0	-,-	8th	321	393	284	-
Amos	12	2	45	1	-,-	(4)	2	0	15	0	-,-	9th	420	454	338	-
Rowe	16.3	4	40	2	-,-	(6)	13	2	48	0	-,-	10th	435	457	364	-
Brew	26	2	114	3	-,-		14	0	67	0	-,-					
Nothling	16	5	34	0	-,-	(3)	23	4	64	3	-,-					
Gough	1	0	2	0	-,-											
Thompson	10	2	21	3	4,-	(7)	24	7	48	3	-,-					

SOUTH AUSTRALIA v NEW SOUTH WALES (Shield Match 8)

Played at Adelaide Oval on January 11, 12, 14, 15, 16, 1929. (Five-day match)
Toss : New South Wales.   Result : NEW SOUTH WALES WON BY 60 RUNS.
Debuts: South Australia - T.A.Carlton (SA only). New South Wales - B.A.Cooper (f/c).
12th Men: M.P.Hutton (SA) and A.E.Marks (NSW).
Umpires: G.A.Hele and A.G.Jenkins.
Attendances: 7177, 11281, 5201, ? , ? .   Total: No figures published.   Receipts: £1301.
Close of Play: 1st day NSW 5/343 (Fairfax 19, W.C.Andrews 1); 2nd day SA 8/225 (Grimmett 31, Wall 10); 3rd day NSW (2) 6/205
    (W.C.Andrews 40, Oldfield 31); 4th day SA (2) 7/250 (McKay 10).

Two fine innings by Jackson, 162 (292 minutes, 15 fours) and 90 (159 minutes, 7 fours), earned him a spot in the Test side. Kippax (107 in 179 minutes, 1 six and 9 fours). W.C.Andrews (87 in 198 minutes, 4 fours) and Oldfield (48 in 100 minutes, 5 fours) also scored well for New South Wales. Grimmett's unbeaten 71 (132 minutes, 4 fours) remained his career-highest score; with Wall (43 in 105 minutes, 2 fours) he shared a ninth-wicket stand of 93. Alexander (79 in 92 minutes, 10 fours) and McKay (74 in 142 minutes, 6 fours) topscored in South Australia's second innings. Bradman failed in the match as an opening bat, falling to the sixth ball of the New South Wales second innings. Carlton, formerly of Canterbury, Victoria and Otago, replaced H.E.Whitfield (business) in the South Australian side while New South Wales included Cooper for F.S.Jordan (unavailable) Last first-class appearance by C.E.Pellew. *Wisden* and *O'Reilly* incorrectly give SA (1) Alexander c T.J.E.Andrews. Sources: *Wisden, NSWCA Report, SACA Report, Adelaide Advertiser, South Australian Register, C.B.O'Reilly.*

NEW SOUTH WALES

Batsman	Dismissal	Runs		Dismissal	Runs
A.Jackson	b Grimmett	162	(2)	c Grimmett b Carlton	90
D.G.Bradman	c Grimmett b Wall	5	(1)	b Wall	2
T.J.E.Andrews	b Wall	32		c Richardson b Wall	7
*A.F.Kippax	lbw b McKay	107		b Wall	7
A.G.Fairfax	c Hone b Grimmett	36		c & b Grimmett	20
C.D.Seddon	c Alexander v Carlton	8		b Grimmett	0
W.C.Andrews	lbw b Grimmett	1		c Pellew b Wall	87
†W.A.S.Oldfield	c Pellew b Carlton	26		c & b Grimmett	48
C.O.Nicholls	b Carlton	5		c Wall b Williams	29
B.A.Cooper	b Carlton	9		c Wall b Williams	12
N.O.Morris	not out	2		not out	0
Extras	(b4, lb3, nb2)	9		(b5, lb6)	11
Total	(109.0 overs, 381 mins)	402		(92.2 overs, 311 mins)	313

SOUTH AUSTRALIA

Batsman	Dismissal	Runs	Dismissal	Runs
G.W.Harris	lbw b Nicholls	11	st Oldfield b Morris	42
*V.Y.Richardson	c Kippax b Nicholls	27	b Fairfax	19
†A.T.Hack	run out (Bradman/Oldfield)	34	b Fairfax	29
C.E.Pellew	c Oldfield b Nicholls	0	c Nicholls b Morris	13
W.C.Alexander	c W.C.Andrews b Fairfax	18	c Morris b Nicholls	79
B.W.Hone	b Fairfax	35	b T.J.E.Andrews	24
D.G.McKay	c Oldfield b Cooper	24	c T.J.E.Andrews b Kippax	74
C.V.Grimmett	not out	71	lbw b Kippax	5
N.L.Williams	run out (Jackson/T.J.E.Andrews)	8	not out	2
T.W.Wall	c Cooper b Fairfax	43	run out (Seddon/Oldfield)	29
T.A.Carlton	c Cooper b Fairfax	4	b Fairfax	1
Extras	(b11, lb1, w1, nb5)	18	(b14, lb20)	34
Total	(93.7 overs, 337 mins)	304	(96.3 overs, 327 mins)	351

SOUTH AUSTRALIA	O	M	R	W	w,nb		O	M	R	W	w,nb
Wall	22	2	92	2	-,1		24	1	78	4	-,-
Carlton	34	6	95	4	-,-		21	3	51	1	-,-
Grimmett	37	4	128	3	-,-		32	2	105	3	-,-
Williams	8	0	43	0	-,-		11.2	0	52	2	-,-
Pellew	3	1	15	0	-,-						
McKay	5	0	20	1	-,1	(5)	4	0	16	0	-,-

NEW SOUTH WALES	O	M	R	W	w,nb		O	M	R	W	w,nb
Nicholls	25	6	63	3	-,-		16	2	52	1	-,-
Cooper	11	1	36	1	1,-	(3)	3	0	24	0	-,-
Fairfax	21.7	3	54	4	-,5	(2)	30.3	8	82	3	-,-
Morris	31	5	115	0	-,-		21	1	75	2	-,-
T.J.E.Andrews	5	0	18	0	-,-		14	2	43	1	-,-
Bradman							5	0	22	0	-,-
Kippax							7	1	19	2	-,-

FALL OF WICKETS

Wkt	NSW 1st	SA 1st	NSW 2nd	SA 2nd
1st	7	54	2	25
2nd	60	55	12	93
3rd	281	55	20	112
4th	325	80	77	115
5th	342	146	83	192
6th	343	146	142	237
7th	386	191	241	250
8th	386	205	288	346
9th	395	298	313	348
10th	402	304	313	351

TASMANIA v M.C.C.

Played at N.T.C.A. Ground, Launceston, on January 12, 14, 15, 1929. (Three-day match)
Toss : Tasmania.   Result : M.C.C. WON BY AN INNINGS AND 116 RUNS.
Debuts: Tasmania - A.S.Horton, S.L.Wellington (both f/c).
12th Men: C.C.Wood (Tas) and G.Geary (MCC).
Umpires: E.C.Knight and E.V.Knight (see below).
Attendances: 4500, 4000, unknown.   Total: About 9000.   Receipts: £650.
Close of Play: 1st day MCC 2/75 (Jardine 36, Hammond 31); 2nd day Tas (2) 1/40 (Atkinson 16, C.W.B.Martin 16).

E.H.Hendren, J.B.Hobbs and H.Sutcliffe remained on the mainland and did not make the trip to Tasmania with the M.C.C. party. This match provided the first instance of brothers umpiring together at first-class level in Australia, though E.V.Knight was "unable to attend" on the last day and former Tasmanian player G.S.Pennefather deputised. Jardine (214 in 248 minutes, 26 fours, chances at 7, 103 and 136) took his score from 103 to 213 in the lunch-tea session on the second day and shared a 224-run partnership with Mead (106 in 124 minutes, 13 fours) for the fourth wicket. G.W.Martin (92 in 134 minutes, 10 fours) played a fine knock on the first day for Tasmania. Atkinson (47 in 92 minutes, 6 fours) and C.W.B.Martin (42 in 61 minutes, 5 fours) batted well in the second innings. A.W.Rushforth was unavailable for Tasmania due to a leg injury. *NSWCA Report* incorrectly gives MCC Horton 0/67, Atkinson 0/46. Sources: *Wisden, NSWCA Report, VCA Report, Hobart Mercury, Launceston Examiner.*

TASMANIA

*J.A.Atkinson	run out (Ames)	17	lbw b Freeman	47
R.G.Friend	b White	19	st Ames b White	8
C.W.B.Martin	c & b White	14	c Ames b Tate	42
N.W.Davis	b Freeman	6	b Tate	0
S.L.Wellington	c Leyland b Freeman	24	st Ames b Tate	3
G.W.Martin	b Larwood	92	b Freeman	13
A.C.Newton	c Hammond b Freeman	7	c Chapman b Tate	0
A.O.Burrows	c Hammond b White	24	b Freeman	0
A.S.Horton	c Hammond b Larwood	0	b Freeman	17
D.M.S.Wardlaw	st Ames b Freeman	8	c Larwood b Tate	0
†P.G.Henty	not out	1	not out	4
Extras	(b3, lb14)	17	(b2, lb1)	3
Total	(78.3 overs, 202 mins)	229	(46.3 overs, 132 mins)	137

M.C.C.

M.Leyland	b Wardlaw	4
D.R.Jardine	c Newton b Burrows	214
G.E.Tyldesley	st Henty b Newton	1
W.R.Hammond	c G.W.Martin b Burrows	43
C.P.Mead	c Friend b C.W.B.Martin	106
†L.E.G.Ames	c G.W.Martin b C.W.B.Martin	34
J.C.White	c Atkinson b C.W.B.Martin	30
M.W.Tate	b Burrows	10
*A.P.F.Chapman	not out	27
H.Larwood	) did not bat	
A.P.Freeman	)	
Extras	(b7, lb3, nb3)	13
Total	(101.4 overs, 279 mins) (8 wkts dec)	482

M.C.C.	O	M	R	W	w,nb		O	M	R	W	w,nb
Tate	20	6	45	0	-,-	(3)	14.3	2	35	5	-,-
Hammond	7	3	21	0	-,-						
White	26	5	58	3	-,-	(2)	12	2	27	1	-,-
Freeman	16.3	1	56	4	-,-		11	2	45	4	-,-
Leyland	6	0	26	0	-,-						
Larwood	3	1	6	2	-,-	(1)	9	0	27	0	-,-

TASMANIA	O	M	R	W	w,nb
Wardlaw	24	3	104	1	-,3
Newton	22	2	98	1	-,-
Burrows	20	0	77	3	-,-
Horton	15	0	68	0	-,-
C.W.B.Martin	11.4	0	77	3	-,-
Atkinson	9	0	45	0	-,-

FALL OF WICKETS

Wkt	TAS 1st	MCC 1st	TAS 2nd
1st	30	14	14
2nd	50	15	91
3rd	59	104	97
4th	61	328	101
5th	104	409	103
6th	113	425	103
7th	205	450	108
8th	214	482	132
9th	217	-	133
10th	229	-	137

TASMANIA v M.C.C.

Played at T.C.A. Ground, Hobart, on January 18, 19, 1929. (Three-day match)
Toss : M.C.C.   Result : M.C.C. WON BY AN INNINGS AND 64 RUNS.
Debuts: Tasmania - V.L.Hooper, G.T.H.James, L.W.Richardson (all f/c).
12th Men: G.G.Gibson (Tas) and G.Duckworth (MCC).
Umpires: M.Leonard and W.T.Lonergan.
Attendances: 5000, 5500.   Total: About 10,500.   Receipts: £786.
Close of Play: 1st day MCC 5/118 (Ames 36, White 1).

After being sent in on a rain-affected pitch, Atkinson (20 in 40 minutes, 3 fours) and Rushforth (18 in 94 minutes, 4 fours) started well for Tasmania before the side crumbled in just over two hours. Tyldesley (39 in 115 minutes, 2 fours) topscored for M.C.C. on the first day while Ames went on to an unbeaten hundred (142 minutes, 10 fours) on the second day in easier batting conditions. Wardlaw tore ankle ligaments during his 13th over late on the first day and took no further part in the match. Tasmania used two substitutes in the field on the second day, Gibson for Wardlaw and the Hobart-based R.G.Friend for Rushforth who had a recurrence of a leg injury sustained in the North-South match over Christmas. Atkinson (30 in 55 minutes, 4 fours) again topscored for Tasmania in the second innings. Larwood bowled Rushforth and C.W.B.Martin with consecutive deliveries while G.W.Martin and Burrows each survived at the crease for an hour. Townley replaced N.W.Davis (unavailable) in the Tasmanian side prior to the match. Sources: *Wisden, NSWCA Report, VCA Report, TCA Report, Hobart Mercury, Launceston Examiner.*

TASMANIA

*J.A.Atkinson	run out (Leyland)	20		c & b Geary	30
A.W.Rushforth	c Chapman b White	18		b Larwood	1
C.W.B.Martin	c Hammond b Tate	0		b Larwood	0
G.W.Martin	lbw b Tate	1		c Chapman b Tate	20
A.O.Burrows	run out (Freeman/Ames)	3		st Ames b Freeman	12
L.W.Richardson	c White b Geary	12		b Tate	0
G.T.H.James	c Hammond b White	0	(8)	b Freeman	6
†A.Limb	c Tate b White	0	(7)	c Tyldesley b Tate	13
R.C.Townley	c Ames b Geary	0		b Geary	2
V.L.Hooper	not out	0		not out	0
D.M.S.Wardlaw	lbw b Geary	6		absent hurt	-
Extras	(b5, nb1)	6		(b4, lb5)	9
Total	(44.5 overs, 123 mins)	66		(46.1 overs, 142 mins)	93

M.C.C.

M.W.Tate	c James b Wardlaw	13
M.Leyland	run out (Burrows/Limb)	3
G.E.Tyldesley	b Townley	39
C.P.Mead	c G.W.Martin b Wardlaw	11
W.R.Hammond	lbw b James	7
†L.E.G.Ames	not out	100
J.C.White	c Atkinson b Hooper	3
*A.P.F.Chapman	c Hooper b Burrows	15
H.Larwood	c James b Hooper	23
G.Geary	c G.W.Martin b Hooper	0
A.P.Freeman	b James	1
Extras	(b3, lb5)	8
Total	(73.1 overs, 210 mins)	223

M.C.C.	O	M	R	W	w,nb		O	M	R	W	w,nb
Tate	14	8	19	2	-,-	(2)	15	5	37	3	-,-
White	22	14	12	3	-,1	(3)	10	6	11	0	-,-
Freeman	6	0	23	0	-,-	(4)	6.1	1	15	2	-,-
Geary	2.5	1	6	3	-,-	(5)	12	3	20	2	-,-
Larwood						(1)	3	2	1	2	-,-

TASMANIA	O	M	R	W	w,nb
Wardlaw	12.1	0	38	2	-,-
James	27	4	61	2	-,-
Hooper	17	2	54	3	-,-
Atkinson	5	1	12	0	-,-
Burrows	5	1	22	1	-,-
Townley	7	1	28	1	-,-

FALL OF WICKETS

Wkt	TAS 1st	MCC 1st	TAS 2nd
1st	32	4	17
2nd	32	22	17
3rd	38	47	53
4th	45	56	59
5th	52	109	59
6th	56	122	75
7th	60	160	90
8th	60	202	93
9th	60	202	93
10th	66	223	-

NEW SOUTH WALES v VICTORIA (Shield Match 9)

Played at Sydney Cricket Ground on January 24, 25, 26, 28, 29, 1929. (Five-day match)
Toss : New South Wales.   Result : MATCH DRAWN.
Debuts: New South Wales - J.H.W.Fingleton, A.E.Marks (both f/c); R.H.B.Bettington (NSW only). Victoria - T.R.Bird (f/c).
12th Men: G.C.H.Hogg (NSW) and W.A.Wilkinson (Vic).
Umpires: W.H.Bayfield and A.C.Jones.
Attendances: 5175, 5030, 8048, 1582, 250.   Total: 20,085.   Receipts: £1108.
Close of Play: 1st day NSW 3/358 (Bradman 129, McCabe 43); 2nd day Vic 0/27 (Onyons 10, Austen 16); 3rd day Vic 7/260 (Ellis 16, Ebeling 2); 4th day Vic (2) 3/342 (Darling 83, Ebeling 0).

Bradman's chanceless 340 not out (488 minutes, 38 fours) set a new record individual score for the ground. He reached 100 in 189 minutes and 300 in 450 minutes (details for 200 unknown), progressing from 196 at lunch to 301 at tea on the second day. He suffered a groin strain while batting but did not need a runner, however, he fielded for only the first 45 minutes of Victoria's first innings, Hogg subbing for the remainder of the match. Jackson (41 in 86 minutes, 2 fours), Fairfax (104 in 231 minutes, 8 fours), McCabe (60 in 73 minutes, 9 fours), Marks (56 in 60 minutes, 1 five and 5 fours) and Bettington (40 in 78 minutes, 6 fours) also contributed to the huge total. Marks scored 17 from Austen's over and Bradman (21) and Bettington (1) took 22 from one over from Onyons. Hooker finished off the Victorian first innings with a hat-trick (Ebeling, Gamble, Ironmonger) and followed with the wicket of Austen with his first ball in the second, becoming the first to take four wickets in four balls in the Sheffield Shield. Victoria's chief scorers were Onyons (61 in 235 minutes, 4 fours and 131 in 275 minutes, 9 fours), Scaife (91 in 159 minutes, 8 fours), Darling (96 in 169 minutes, 4 fours) and Bird (63 in 65 minutes, 9 fours). New South Wales rested A.F.Kippax and W.A.S.Oldfield and were without W.C.Andrews and F.S.Jordan (business). Victoria also rested their Fourth Test players and had to replace K.E.Rigg and H.C.A.Sandford. NSW sources incorrectly give Vic player A.Lansdown. Bettington (ex-Middlesex and Oxford University) made his Australian debut. Sources: *Wisden, NSWCA Report, VCA Report, The Age, The Argus, Sydney Morning Herald, Sydney Referee*.

NEW SOUTH WALES

A.Jackson	b Ironmonger	41			
A.G.Fairfax	b Gamble	104			
D.G.Bradman	not out	340			
*T.J.E.Andrews	lbw b Ironmonger	19			
S.J.McCabe	b Gamble	60			
A.E.Marks	c Lansdown b Darling	56			
R.H.B.Bettington	c Austen b Darling	40			
J.H.W.Fingleton	not out	25			
†H.L.Davidson	)				
C.O.Nicholls	) did not bat				
J.E.H.Hooker	)				
Extras	(b11, lb15, nb2)	28			
Total	(146.0 overs, 576 mins) (6 wkts dec)	713			

VICTORIA

B.A.Onyons	st Davidson b Bettington	61	(2) c Fingleton b Hooker	131
E.T.Austen	b Hooker	19	(1) b Hooker	5
J.W.Scaife	c Fingleton b Bettington	42	run out (McCabe/Davidson)	91
L.S.Darling	c Davidson b Hooker	37	c McCabe b Fairfax	96
W.W.Reddrop	b Hooker	33	(6) b McCabe	14
H.C.Lansdown	b Bettington	4	(7) not out	48
T.R.Bird	c & b Nicholls	22	(8) c Fingleton b Marks	63
*†J.L.Ellis	not out	19	(9) not out	7
H.I.Ebeling	b Hooker	4	(5) b Fairfax	14
H.S.Gamble	b Hooker	0		
H.Ironmonger	c & b Hooker	0		
Extras	(b14, lb2, nb8)	24	(b27, lb7, w1, nb6)	41
Total	(103.0 overs, 354 mins)	265	(128.0 overs, 438 mins) (7 wkts)	510

VICTORIA	O	M	R	W	w,nb
Gamble	29	1	193	2	-,2
Ebeling	39	3	142	0	-,-
Darling	18	1	77	2	-,-
Ironmonger	56	7	220	2	-,-
Scaife	2	0	14	0	-,-
Austen	1	0	17	0	-,-
Onyons	1	0	22	0	-,-

NEW SOUTH WALES	O	M	R	W	w,nb		O	M	R	W	w,nb
Nicholls	23	7	52	1	-,-		18	3	88	0	-,-
Hooker	28	11	42	6	-,3		27	3	94	2	-,2
Bettington	27	3	92	3	-,-	(4)	25	3	96	0	-,-
Fairfax	19	4	35	0	-,5	(3)	19	4	54	2	1,4
McCabe	5	3	10	0	-,-	(6)	16	2	44	1	-,-
Andrews	1	0	10	0	-,-	(7)	6	0	33	0	-,-
Marks						(5)	15	4	59	1	-,-
Fingleton							2	1	1	0	-,-

FALL OF WICKETS

	NSW	VIC	VIC
Wkt	1st	1st	2nd
1st	76	35	5
2nd	237	108	192
3rd	283	156	335
4th	401	177	365
5th	482	185	390
6th	602	224	392
7th	-	241	475
8th	-	265	-
9th	-	265	-
10th	-	265	-

SOUTH AUSTRALIA v M.C.C.

Played at Adelaide Oval on January 25, 26, 28, 29, 1929. (Four-day match)
Toss : M.C.C.   Result : MATCH DRAWN.
Debuts: Nil.
12th Men: M.P.Hutton (SA). No 12th named for MCC.
Umpires: T.W.Cook and C.L.Cornish.
Attendances: 8000, 14000, 6000, 2000.   Total: 29783.   Receipts: £990.
Close of Play: 1st day MCC 5/313 (Hendren 54, Leyland 5); 2nd day SA 9/163 (Hone 17, Carlton 11); 3rd day MCC (2) 5/307 (Ames 51).
Scott replaced T.W.Wall (family bereavement) in the South Australian side. Hobbs (75 in 144 minutes, 7 fours) and Sutcliffe (122 in 233 minutes, 9 fours) gave M.C.C. a fine start with a 155-run partnership but only Hendren (90 in 110 minutes, 1 five and 10 fours) took advantage in the middle order. Richardson (82 in 144 minutes, 5 fours) topscored for South Australia against the bowling of White who operated through the innings to take 7 for 66. Hobbs (101 in 177 minutes, 8 fours) and Jardine (114 in 185 minutes, 10 fours) scored second-innings centuries. South Australia lost Richardson cheaply on the last day but Harris (44 not out in 90 minutes, 2 fours) and Hack (27 not out in 75 minutes, 3 fours) held on until the rain came. Sources: *Wisden, NSWCA Report, VCA Report, SACA Report, Adelaide Advertiser, South Australian Register.*

M.C.C.

J.B.Hobbs	c McKay b Carlton	75		b McKay	101
H.Sutcliffe	c Whitfield b Grimmett	122		c Grimmett b Scott	27
G.E.Tyldesley	lbw b Grimmett	22		c Whitfield b Scott	4
*A.P.F.Chapman	c Hone b Grimmett	23			
E.H.Hendren	c Whitfield b Carlton	90	(4)	c Hone b Harris	114
D.R.Jardine	c Hack b Scott	8	(6)	c McKay b Harris	5
M.Leyland	c & b Carlton	9	(5)	not out	51
†L.E.G.Ames	c Pritchard b Carlton	17			
G.Geary	c Pritchard b Grimmett	12			
J.C.White	c Whitfield b Carlton	8			
A.P.Freeman	not out	0			
Extras	(b5, lb1)	6		(b2, w1, nb2)	5
Total	(109.6 overs, 377 mins)	392		(71.2 overs, 240 mins) (5 wkts dec)	307

SOUTH AUSTRALIA

G.W.Harris	c Ames b Geary	4		not out	44
*V.Y.Richardson	run out (Chapman)	82		lbw b White	3
†A.T.Hack	c & b White	1		not out	27
D.E.Pritchard	run out (Hobbs/White)	5			
W.C.Alexander	c Chapman b White	11			
H.E.Whitfield	c Leyland b White	16			
C.V.Grimmett	c Chapman b White	4			
D.G.McKay	b White	2			
B.W.Hone	not out	27			
J.D.Scott	c Chapman b White	0			
T A Carlton	b White	15			
Extras	(b7, lb1, w3)	11		(w1)	1
Total	(62.5 overs, 199 mins)	178		(29.0 overs, 90 mins) (1 wkt)	75

SOUTH AUSTRALIA	O	M	R	W	w,nb	O	M	R	W	w,nb		FALL OF WICKETS			
												MCC	SA	MCC	SA
Scott	19	2	81	1	-,-	14	1	74	2	1,2	Wkt	1st	1st	2nd	2nd
Whitfield	13	2	32	0	-,-	10	2	24	0	-,-	1st	155	11	44	5
Carlton	31	10	64	5	-,-	12	3	42	0	-,-	2nd	201	18	52	-
Grimmett	38.6	5	174	4	-,-	21	2	88	0	-,-	3rd	243	23	201	-
McKay	8	1	35	0	,	7	0	27	1	-,-	4th	243	50	302	-
Alexander						2	0	14	0	-,-	5th	284	80	307	-
Pritchard						2	0	21	0	-,-	6th	326	93	-	-
Harris						1.2	0	8	2	-,-	7th	369	117	-	-
Hone						1	0	1	0	-,-	8th	378	140	-	-
Richardson						1	0	3	0	-,-	9th	392	140	-	-
											10th	392	178	-	-
M.C.C.	O	M	R	W	w,nb	O	M	R	W	w,nb					
White	31.5	5	66	7	-,-	14	5	25	1	-,-					
Geary	12	4	26	1	3,-	13	1	41	0	1,-					
Freeman	19	0	75	0	-,-	1	0	5	0	-,-					
Leyland						1	0	3	0	-,-					

QUEENSLAND v VICTORIA (Shield Match 10)

Played at Exhibition Ground, Brisbane, on February 1, 2, 4, 5, 6, 1929. (Five-day match)
Toss : Queensland.   Result : MATCH DRAWN.
Debuts: Queensland - R.M.Levy, M.Peachey (both f/c).
12th Men: N.C.Beeston (Qld) and W.W.Reddrop (Vic).
Umpires: J.Bartlett and J.A.Scott.
Attendances: No daily figures published except 5530 for 2nd day.   Total: About 9500.   Receipts: £467.
Close of Play: 1st day Qld 6/329 (Levy 96, Peachey 0); 2nd day Vic 2/185 (Onyons 102, Darling 37); 3rd day Qld (2) 4/96 (Thompson 9, Nothling 9); 4th day Vic (2) 2/183 (Onyons 109, Darling 2).

Queensland used two wicket-keepers, Levy in the first innings and O'Connor in the second. Levy was never again chosen to keep wickets though he kept his place as a batsman and later captained the State. His century on debut (129 in 240 minutes, 1 five and 14 fours) included 4 chances. O'Connor (76 in 193 minutes, 4 fours), Nothling (56 in 78 minutes, 7 fours) and Thompson (90 in 242 minutes, 1 six and 7 fours) scored fifties for Queensland. Onyons became the sixth to record a century in each innings for Victoria, scoring 105 (236 minutes, 15 fours) and 127 (211 minutes, 13 fours). An outright result was possible for either side at the start of the final day's play but the loss of 35 minutes of the possible 2 hours through rain left the match unfinished, with Victoria 45 runs short of victory with three wickets to fall. W.Rowe (unavailable) was replaced by Peachey in the Queensland team. Sources: *Wisden, VCA Report, QCA Report, The Herald, Sydney Morning Herald, Brisbane Courier.*

QUEENSLAND

L.P.D.O'Connor	lbw b Darling	76		c Ellis b Gamble	43
C.A.McCoombe	c Wilkinson b Ebeling	27		b Gamble	5
F.J.Gough	lbw b Wilkinson	9		c Austen b Ironmonger	6
F.C.Thompson	c Ellis b Ironmonger	24	(5)	c Bird b Ironmonger	90
†R.M.Levy	c Ellis b Scaife	129	(4)	c Ellis b Ebeling	16
*O.E.Nothling	c Ellis b Gamble	56		lbw b Ironmonger	12
E.C.Bensted	c Ellis b Ironmonger	21		run out (Darling)	0
M.Peachey	c & b Ironmonger	30		c Ellis b Gamble	5
F.M.Brew	b Ironmonger	12		c Wilkinson b Gamble	25
P.M.Hornibrook	not out	19		c Wilkinson b Ironmonger	0
H.M.Thurlow	b Ebeling	0		not out	2
Extras	(b18, lb3, nb2)	23		(b6, lb7, nb7)	20
Total	(97.1 overs, 411 mins)	426		(78.5 overs, 320 mins)	224

VICTORIA

B.A.Onyons	c Nothling b Thurlow	105		c & b Bensted	127
E.T.Austen	c & b Hornibrook	40		c Nothling b Thompson	15
J.W.Scaife	b Thompson	1		c Nothling b Thompson	45
L.S.Darling	c McCoombe b Thurlow	60		c Hornibrook b Nothling	2
T.R.Bird	c Levy b Nothling	20		c Gough b Bensted	12
H.C.Lansdown	c Brew b Nothling	44		c Brew b Bensted	16
*†J.L.Ellis	lbw b Thompson	17	(8)	not out	15
W.A.Wilkinson	not out	10	(7)	c O'Connor b Hornibrook	6
H.I.Ebeling	c Levy b Hornibrook	10		not out	10
H.S.Gamble	c Bensted b Thurlow	12			
H.Ironmonger	b Hornibrook	0			
Extras	(b4, lb12, nb1)	17		(b12, lb5, w1, nb4)	22
Total	(93.4 overs, 365 mins)	336		(67.0 overs, 265 mins) (7 wkts)	270

VICTORIA	O	M	R	W	w,nb		O	M	R	W	w,nb
Ebeling	26.1	3	112	2	-,-		17	4	41	1	-,-
Ironmonger	24	4	71	4	-,-	(3)	32.5	9	60	4	-,1
Gamble	15	1	106	1	-,1	(2)	17	2	66	4	-,6
Wilkinson	14	2	39	1	-,1	(6)	4	1	8	0	-,-
Scaife	3	0	16	1	-,-	(4)	4	0	23	0	-,-
Darling	15	0	59	1	-,-	(5)	4	1	6	0	-,-

QUEENSLAND	O	M	R	W	w,nb		O	M	R	W	w,nb
Hornibrook	25.4	7	57	3	-,-		18	1	73	1	-,-
Thurlow	18	3	54	3	-,-	(4)	8	0	40	0	-,2
Nothling	15	2	65	2	-,-	(6)	17	3	44	1	-,-
Brew	10	0	70	0	-,-	(5)	1	0	14	0	-,-
Bensted	10	1	39	0	-,1	(2)	10	1	28	3	-,1
Thompson	15	2	34	2	-,-	(3)	13	2	49	2	1,1

FALL OF WICKETS

Wkt	QLD 1st	VIC 1st	QLD 2nd	VIC 2nd
1st	59	87	6	36
2nd	78	88	19	170
3rd	114	201	51	183
4th	158	212	81	208
5th	266	269	103	223
6th	314	296	103	233
7th	394	304	135	247
8th	394	315	192	-
9th	423	336	193	-
10th	426	336	224	-

AUSTRALIA v ENGLAND (4th Test)

Played at Adelaide Oval on February 1, 2, 4, 5, 6, 7, 8, 1929. (Timeless match)
Toss : England.   Result : ENGLAND WON BY 12 RUNS.
Debuts: Australia - A.Jackson (Test).
12th Men: T.J.E.Andrews (Aust) and M.Leyland (Eng).
Umpires: D.A.Elder and G.A.Hele.
Attendances: 21380, 37700, 23800, 15250, 10250, 16914, 13700.   Total: 138,994.   Receipts: £12,435.
Close of Play: 1st day Eng 5/246 (Hammond 47, Duckworth 0); 2nd day Aust 3/131 (Jackson 70, Ryder 54); 3rd day Aust 9/365
     (Oldfield 31); 4th day Eng (2) 2/206 (Hammond 105, Jardine 73); 5th day Aust (2) 0/24 (Woodfull 7, Jackson 16); 6th day Aust (2)
     6/260 (Bradman 16, Oxenham 2).

Hammond scored a chanceless century in each innings, 119 not out (263 minutes, 9 fours) and 177 (440 minutes, 17 fours), to become the second batsman after H.Sutcliffe (1924-25) to score four centuries in a single Test series. His partnership of 262 with Jardine (98 in 347 minutes, 10 fours) was a third-wicket record for England against Australia. Hobbs (74 in 164 minutes, 2 fours), Sutcliffe (64 in 166 minutes, 6 fours) and Tate (47 in 50 minutes, 7 fours) also batted well for the tourists. Jackson's debut masterpiece (a chanceless 164 in 318 minutes, 15 fours) ranks amongst the most famous of Test innings. At 19 years 152 days of age, he was the youngest batsman to score a hundred in matches between these teams. Ryder (63 in 149 minutes, 3 fours and 87 in 152 minutes, 5 fours), Kippax (51 in 140 minutes, 7 fours) and Bradman (58 in 138 minutes, 4 fours) scored half-centuries for Australia. At 7/320 on the seventh day the odds favoured the home side, however Bradman was then run out (for the only time in his Test career) after Oldfield tapped the ball to cover and called him through for a suicidal single, and the tail was exposed *Wisden* incorrectly gives Aust (1) a'Beckett b White. Sources: *Wisden, VCA Report, SACA Report, The Age, The Argus, Adelaide Advertiser.*

ENGLAND

J.B.Hobbs	c Ryder b Hendry	74		c Oldfield b Hendry	1
H.Sutcliffe	st Oldfield b Grimmett	64		c Oldfield b a'Beckett	17
W.R.Hammond	not out	119		c & b Ryder	177
D.R.Jardine	lbw b Grimmett	1		c Woodfull b Oxenham	98
E.H.Hendren	b Blackie	13		c Bradman b Blackie	11
*A.P.F.Chapman	c a'Beckett b Ryder	39		c Woodfull b Blackie	0
†G.Duckworth	c Ryder b Grimmett	5	(11)	lbw b Oxenham	1
H.Larwood	b Hendry	3	(7)	lbw b Oxenham	5
G.Geary	run out (Bradman/Oldfield)	3	(8)	c & b Grimmett	6
M.W.Tate	b Grimmett	2	(9)	lbw b Oxenham	47
J.C.White	c Ryder b Grimmett	0	(10)	not out	4
Extras	(b3, lb7, w1)	11		(b6, lb10)	16
Total	(183.1 overs, 427 mins)	334		(200.4 overs, 506 mins)	383

AUSTRALIA

W.M.Woodfull	c Duckworth b Tate	1	c Geary b White	30
A.Jackson	lbw b White	164	c Duckworth b Geary	36
H.S.T.L.Hendry	c Duckworth b Larwood	2	c Tate b White	5
A.F.Kippax	b White	3	c Hendren b White	51
*J.Ryder	lbw b White	63	c & b White	87
D.G.Bradman	c Larwood b Tate	40	run out (Hobbs/Duckworth)	58
E.L.a'Beckett	hit wkt b White	36	c Hammond b White	21
R.K.Oxenham	c Chapman b White	15	c Chapman b White	12
†W.A.S.Oldfield	b Tate	32	not out	15
C.V.Grimmett	b Tate	4	c Tate b White	9
D.D.Blackie	not out	3	c Larwood b White	0
Extras	(lb5, w1)	6	(b9, lb3)	12
Total	(160.0 overs, 457 mins)	369	(151.5 overs, 439 mins)	336

AUSTRALIA	O	M	R	W	w,nb		O	M	R	W	w,nb
a'Beckett	31	8	44	0	1,-		27	9	41	1	-,-
Hendry	31	14	49	2	-,-		28	11	56	1	-,-
Grimmett	52.1	12	102	5	-,-	(5)	52	15	117	1	-,-
Oxenham	35	14	51	0	-,-	(3)	47.4	21	67	4	-,-
Blackie	29	6	57	1	-,-	(4)	39	11	70	2	-,-
Ryder	5	1	20	1	-,-		5	1	13	1	-,-
Kippax							2	0	3	0	-,-

ENGLAND	O	M	R	W	w,nb		O	M	R	W	w,nb
Larwood	37	6	92	1	-,-		20	4	60	0	-,-
Tate	42	10	77	4	1,-		37	9	75	0	-,-
White	60	16	130	5	-,-		64.5	21	126	8	-,-
Geary	12	3	32	0	-,-	(5)	16	2	42	1	-,-
Hammond	9	1	32	0	-,-	(4)	14	3	21	0	-,-

FALL OF WICKETS

	ENG	AUST	ENG	AUST
Wkt	1st	1st	2nd	2nd
1st	143	1	1	65
2nd	143	6	21	71
3rd	149	19	283	74
4th	179	145	296	211
5th	246	227	297	224
6th	263	287	302	258
7th	270	323	327	308
8th	308	336	337	320
9th	312	365	381	336
10th	334	369	383	336

TASMANIA v NEW SOUTH WALES

Played at T.C.A. Ground, Hobart, on February 8, 10, 11, 1929. (Three-day match)
Toss : New South Wales.   Result : NEW SOUTH WALES WON BY AN INNINGS AND 182 RUNS.
Debuts: Tasmania - G.G.Gibson, L.R.Phelps, C.C.Wood (all f/c). New South Wales - S.J.W.Burt, H.R.Eaton, F.Henderson, G.C.H.Hogg (all f/c).
12th Men: L.W.Richardson (Tas) and A.G.Chipperfield (NSW).
Umpires: W.T.Lonergan and W.M.McHugo.
Attendances: No daily figures published.   Total: About 1000.   Receipts: £42.
Close of Play: 1st day NSW 443 all out; 2nd day Tas (2) 6/69 (Townley 13, Wood 15).

Despite losing Fingleton to the fourth ball of the match, New South Wales scored 443 on the first day, their batsmen hitting 1 six and 61 fours. Seddon (134 in 155 minutes, 18 fours, chances at 22 and 124), Henderson (40 in 38 minutes, 6 fours), Kelleway (54 in 96 minutes, 6 fours), Davidson (109 in 88 minutes, 18 fours) and Burt (42 not out in 57 minutes, 1 six and 5 fours) scored most of the runs, Davidson hitting 95 after tea and combining with Burt for a ninth-wicket stand of 106. Atkinson scored Tasmania's only innings of note, 60 in 126 minutes with 7 fours. Wood was out first ball on debut. Only 42 minutes were needed on the last day to complete the match. Phelps, Townley and Wood replaced G.T.H.James and W.H.McDonald (both unavailable) and D.M.S.Wardlaw (injured leg) in the Tasmanian side. Last first-class appearance by C.Kelleway. *NSWCA Report* incorrectly gives umpire Lonergan as Donergan. Sources: *The Cricketer, NSWCA Report, TCA Report, Hobart Mercury, Launceston Examiner.*

NEW SOUTH WALES

J.H.W.Fingleton	c Atkinson b Hooper	0
G.C.H.Hogg	c Limb b Hooper	26
C.D.Seddon	c G.W.Martin b Townley	134
F.Henderson	lbw b Burrows	40
*C.Kelleway	c Limb b Burrows	54
J.N.Campbell	lbw b Burrows	16
F.S.Jordan	lbw b Townley	0
E.A.Dwyer	b Townley	2
†H.L.Davidson	lbw b Atkinson	109
S.J.W.Burt	not out	42
H.R.Eaton	b C.W.B.Martin	7
Extras	(b7, lb2, w2, nb2)	13
Total	(71.4 overs, 273 mins)	443

TASMANIA

*J.A.Atkinson	c Davidson b Jordan	60	(6) c Kelleway b Jordan		0
A.W.Rushforth	c Fingleton b Kelleway	0	(1) c Fingleton b Kelleway		6
C.W.B.Martin	c & b Jordan	2	(2) c Jordan b Eaton		2
C.C.Wood	b Jordan	0	(8) b Eaton		18
G.W.Martin	b Eaton	14	(7) c & b Campbell		1
G.G.Gibson	c Davidson b Eaton	4	(5) c Davidson b Jordan		0
A.O.Burrows	c Eaton b Burt	23	(3) lbw b Kelleway		27
†A.Limb	c Campbell b Jordan	2	(9) c Fingleton b Jordan		15
R.C.Townley	not out	24	(4) b Kelleway		13
V.L.Hooper	c Davidson b Eaton	7	not out		3
L.R.Phelps	b Eaton	1	b Jordan		0
Extras	(b7, lb8, nb6)	21	(b7, lb6, nb5)		18
Total	(51.3 overs, 189 mins)	158	(26.7 overs, 117 mins)		103

TASMANIA	O	M	R	W	w,nb
Hooper	17	0	101	2	-,2
Burrows	16	2	67	3	1,-
Townley	13	0	108	3	-,-
Atkinson	5	0	49	1	1,-
Wood	10	2	41	0	-,-
Phelps	7	2	36	0	-,-
C.W.B.Martin	3.4	0	28	1	-,-

NEW SOUTH WALES	O	M	R	W	w,nb		O	M	R	W	w,nb
Eaton	10.3	1	39	4	-,4		8	0	30	2	-,3
Kelleway	2	0	10	1	-,2		8	4	15	3	-,2
Burt	12	5	22	1	-,-						
Jordan	10	3	18	4	-,-	(3)	7.7	0	25	4	-,-
Campbell	16	2	47	0	-,-	(4)	3	0	15	1	-,-
Fingleton	1	0	1	0	-,-						

FALL OF WICKETS

Wkt	NSW 1st	TAS 1st	TAS 2nd
1st	0	3	3
2nd	38	29	14
3rd	114	29	37
4th	254	51	38
5th	259	55	42
6th	260	110	43
7th	262	114	72
8th	325	122	84
9th	431	144	103
10th	443	158	103

NEW SOUTH WALES v M.C.C.

Played at Sydney Cricket Ground on February 15 (no play), 16, 18, 19 (no play), 1929. (Four-day match)
Toss : M.C.C.   Result : MATCH DRAWN.
Debuts: Nil.
12th Men: J.E.P.Hogg (NSW) and E.H.Hendren (MCC).
Umpires: W.H.Bayfield and A.C.Jones.
Attendances: No play, 15506, 7321, no play.   Total: 22,827.   Receipts: £1415.
Close of Play: 1st day no play; 2nd day NSW 8/126 (Oldfield 3, Morris 4); 3rd day MCC 4/144 (Tyldesley 68, Ames 22).

Rain prevented any play on the scheduled first and last days and delayed the start of the match on the second day. Only Chapman, Geary and White of the M.C.C. team were present at 2.30pm when the umpires wished the game to get underway. The rest had to rush from their hotel where they had stayed in anticipation of a 3.45pm start. The first ball was delayed until 3.00pm with Freeman keeping wickets for the opening two overs until the arrival of Ames. Fairfax (40 in 157 minutes, 0 fours) topscored as New South Wales collapsed in three hours. White dismissed Morris and McNamee with successive balls to wrap up the innings. Rain and bad light restricted play to 2.15pm - 5.40pm on the third day, Tyldesley (68 not out in 143 minutes, 3 fours) topscoring for M.C.C. in their unfinished innings. Sutcliffe strained a shoulder while fielding and would have been unable to bat had the innings continued; the injury ruled him out of the last Test.
Sources: *Wisden, NSWCA Report, VCA Report, The Age, Sydney Morning Herald, Sydney Referee.*

NEW SOUTH WALES

A.Jackson	lbw b Tate	5
A.G.Fairfax	c Tyldesley b Tate	40
T.J.E.Andrews	c & b White	2
*A.F.Kippax	c Tate b Geary	17
D.G.Bradman	c Tyldesley b White	15
A.E.Marks	b Freeman	17
S.J.McCabe	b Freeman	11
†W.A.S.Oldfield	not out	3
J.E.H.Hooker	lbw b White	3
N.O.Morris	c sub (E.H.Hendren) b White	4
R.L.A.McNamee	c Mead b White	0
Extras	(b9, lb2)	11
Total	(55.5 overs, 189 mins)	128

M.C.C.

J.B.Hobbs	b Fairfax	39
M.Leyland	c Hooker b Fairfax	5
G.E.Tyldesley	not out	68
C.P.Mead	c Fairfax b Hooker	2
*A.P.F.Chapman	c Bradman b Fairfax	8
†L.E.G.Ames	not out	22
G.Geary	)	
M.W.Tate	)	
J.C.White	) did not bat	
H.Sutcliffe	)	
A.P.Freeman	)	
Extras		-
Total	(51.0 overs, 180 mins) (4 wkts)	144

M.C.C.	O	M	R	W	w,nb
Tate	10	2	21	2	-,-
White	23.5	8	48	5	-,-
Geary	9	3	16	1	-,-
Freeman	13	3	32	2	-,-

NEW SOUTH WALES	O	M	R	W	w,nb
Fairfax	15	4	36	3	-,-
Hooker	18	0	66	1	-,-
McNamee	8	1	21	0	-,-
Marks	3	0	9	0	-,-
McCabe	3	0	5	0	-,-
Morris	2	0	6	0	-,-
Andrews	2	1	1	0	-,-

FALL OF WICKETS

Wkt	NSW 1st	MCC 1st
1st	8	15
2nd	18	64
3rd	45	71
4th	66	80
5th	92	-
6th	110	-
7th	112	-
8th	118	-
9th	128	-
10th	128	-

VICTORIA v TASMANIA

Played at Melbourne Cricket Ground on February 19, 20, 21, 1929. (Four-day match)
Toss : Victoria.   Result : TASMANIA WON BY NINE WICKETS.
Debuts: Victoria - H.H.Alexander, G.K.Bennetts, H.P.Gibaud, H.F.Guthrie, J.R.Wootton (all f/c). Tasmania - E.A.Pickett (f/c)
   W.H.McDonald (Tas only).
12th Men: J.H.Edwards (Vic) and G.G.Gibson (Tas).
Umpires: F.W.Dixon and W.J.Moore.
Attendances: 578, 642, 50.   Total: 1270.   Receipts: £37.
Close of Play: 1st day Tas 2/43 (Atkinson 22, Burrows 2); 2nd day Vic (2) 6/93 (Warne 2).

Heavy rain on the night prior to the match penetrated the covers at one end and damaged the pitch. The batsmen's problems were compounded by the humid conditions throughout the game. Cosgrave was bowled by the fourth ball and only Darling (23 in 40 minutes, 3 fours) and Gibaud (26 in 57 minutes, 2 fours) exceeded 20 in Victoria's first innings. Atkinson (54 in 141 minutes, 3 fours), Davis (45 in 73 minutes, 4 fours) and Richardson (67 in 113 minutes, 7 fours) gave Tasmania a match-winning lead, a sixth-wicket stand of 87 proving crucial to the outcome. Six of Atkinson's catches were taken close in on the leg-side, the other, that of Davidson, was held at silly point. Bird (36 in 52 minutes, 4 fours) and Warne (33 in 72 minutes, 1 six and 2 fours) headed Victoria's scoring in the second innings. Had the fourth day been required, the times of play would have been 10.30am - 2.30pm only. Edwards and Gibson replaced A.W.Dummett and R.C.Townley (both unavailable) respectively in the twelves. McDonald, aged 44, playing his only match for Tasmania, had formerly represented Victoria and Queensland. Sources: *The Cricketer, VCA Report, The Age, The Argus, The Herald, Melbourne Sun.*

VICTORIA

F.B.Warne	c Atkinson b James	1	(7)	not out	33
B.Cosgrave	b Hooper	0	(1)	c & b McDonald	12
L.S.Darling	c Martin b Burrows	23		c James b McDonald	27
†T.R.Bird	c & b Burrows	11		st Pickett b McDonald	36
H.F.Guthrie	c Hooper b James	3		c Atkinson b Hooper	0
*H.P.Gibaud	run out (James/Pickett)	26		c Pickett b James	9
A.A.Davidson	c Burrows b Burrows	2	(8)	c Burrows b Hooper	1
J.R.Wootton	c Atkinson b McDonald	14	(2)	c Martin b James	3
G.K.Bennetts	c Atkinson b McDonald	8	(10)	c Atkinson b McDonald	3
J.C.Makin	c Atkinson b McDonald	6	(9)	b Burrows	14
H.H.Alexander	not out	14		c McDonald b James	7
Extras	(lb2, nb1)	3		(b3, lb3)	6
Total	(37.7 overs, 140 mins)	111		(46.4 overs, 167 mins)	151

TASMANIA

*J.A.Atkinson	c Wootton b Alexander	54	not out	3
A.W.Rushforth	c Bennetts b Makin	12	c Gibaud b Makin	7
W.H.McDonald	c Davidson b Makin	7	not out	3
A.O.Burrows	lbw b Makin	10		
C.C.Wood	c & b Warne	22		
G.W.Martin	b Alexander	6		
N.W.Davis	st Bird b Bennetts	45		
L.W.Richardson	b Davidson	67		
†E.A.Pickett	b Alexander	3		
G.T.H.James	b Bennetts	1		
V.L.Hooper	not out	12		
Extras	(b2, lb9)	11		–
Total	(80.0 overs, 277 mins)	250	(3.3 overs, 10 mins) (1 wkt)	13

TASMANIA	O	M	R	W	w,nb	O	M	R	W	w,nb			FALL OF WICKETS		
Hooper	10	0	29	1	-,1	11	1	37	2	-,-		VIC	TAS	VIC	TAS
James	13	5	38	2	-,-	14.4	4	38	3	-,-	Wkt	1st	1st	2nd	2nd
Burrows	8	0	20	3	-,-	10	1	25	1	-,-	1st	2	24	8	10
McDonald	6.7	0	21	3	-,-	11	3	45	4	-,-	2nd	2	40	33	-
											3rd	32	69	52	-
VICTORIA	O	M	R	W	w,nb	O	M	R	W	w,nb	4th	39	100	58	-
Alexander	22	2	69	3	-,-	2	0	8	0	-,-	5th	39	109	83	-
Davidson	9	0	29	1	-,-						6th	44	119	93	-
Makin	15	2	39	3	-,-	(2) 1.3	0	5	1	-,-	7th	77	206	95	-
Darling	7	1	25	0	-,-						8th	86	211	119	-
Gibaud	4	1	9	0	-,-						9th	94	216	130	-
Bennetts	11	2	28	2	-,-						10th	111	250	151	-
Warne	12	1	40	1	-,-										

QUEENSLAND v SOUTH AUSTRALIA (Shield Match 11)

Played at Exhibition Ground, Brisbane, on February 22, 23, 25, 26, 1929. (Five-day match)
Toss : South Australia.　　　　　Result : QUEENSLAND WON BY ONE WICKET.
Debuts: South Australia - M.P.Hutton (f/c).
12th Men: G.S.Amos (Qld) and C.W.Walker (SA).
Umpires: J.Bartlett and J.P.Orr.
Attendances: 1600, 4000, 600, 300.　　　Total: About 6500.　　　Receipts: £307.
Close of Play: 1st day Qld 0/0 (O'Connor 0, McCoombe 0); 2nd day SA (2) 2/29 (Richardson 17, Whitfield 0); 3rd day Qld (2) 4/80
　　(Levy 22, Bensted 12).

Had Grimmett held a difficult catch to dismiss Levy with the scores level, this match would have provided the Sheffield Shield with its first tie. Instead the batsmen scrambled the winning run to give Queensland their first victory over South Australia at their eighth meeting, the first seven matches between the teams having been decisively won by the latter. A hat-trick by Grimmett (Oxenham, Rowe, Gough) late in the match - the first by a South Australian in the Shield competition - had thrown the game open after Queensland needed only 21 runs with five wickets in hand. Play on the first day was interrupted by rain and later bad light, which ended proceedings before a ball could be bowled at the Queenslanders. Conditions favoured the bowlers throughout and the four team totals fell within a range of just seven runs. Half-centuries were scored by Harris (61 in 180 minutes, 2 fours), Alexander (66 in 147 minutes, 1 four) and Whitfield (65 with 2 fours) for South Australia and Nothling (50 in 97 minutes, 1 four and Levy (85 not out) for Queensland. Sources: *Wisden, QCA Report, SACA Report, The Age, Sydney Morning Herald, Brisbane Courier, South Australian Register, Maryborough Chronicle.*

SOUTH AUSTRALIA

Batsman	Dismissal 1	Score		Dismissal 2	Score
G.W.Harris	b Rowe	61	(2)	lbw b Oxenham	10
*V.Y.Richardson	c O'Connor b Thurlow	15	(1)	b Hornibrook	25
†A.T.Hack	lbw b Thurlow	1		lbw b Oxenham	0
H.E.Whitfield	b Nothling	5		lbw b Oxenham	65
W.C.Alexander	b Oxenham	66		c O'Connor b Hornibrook	0
D.G.McKay	run out (Rowe/O'Connor)	4		c Levy b Hornibrook	40
M.P.Hutton	b Oxenham	4		c O'Connor b Nothling	7
C.V.Grimmett	b Hornibrook	1		b Oxenham	4
T.W.Wall	c Nothling b Hornibrook	3		c Rowe b Hornibrook	13
J.D.Scott	c Gough b Oxenham	4		st O'Connor b Hornibrook	2
T.A.Carlton	not out	7		not out	10
Extras	(b12, lb1, nb1)	14		(b2, lb4, nb1)	7
Total	(65.1 overs, 259 mins)	185		(76.3 overs, 290 mins)	183

QUEENSLAND

Batsman	Dismissal 1	Score		Dismissal 2	Score
†L.P.D.O'Connor	b Wall	2		b Wall	19
C.A.McCoombe	c Richardson b Wall	1		c Whitfield b Wall	17
R.K.Oxenham	c Hack b Wall	2	(7)	b Grimmett	17
R.M.Levy	c Harris b Wall	4	(3)	not out	85
F.C.Thompson	run out (　　　/Hack)	37	(4)	b Wall	5
W.Rowe	c McKay b Whitfield	2	(8)	lbw b Grimmett	0
*O.E.Nothling	c Wall b Grimmett	50	(5)	lbw b Grimmett	1
F.J.Gough	c Hack b Grimmett	21	(9)	st Hack b Grimmett	0
E.C.Bensted	c Wall b Whitfield	40	(6)	c Carlton b Grimmett	20
P.M.Hornibrook	b Whitfield	14		b Carlton	8
H.M.Thurlow	not out	0		not out	0
Extras	(b8, lb5, w1, nb1)	15		(b2, lb6, nb1)	9
Total	(59.1 overs, 255 mins)	188		(52.4 overs, 200 mins) (9 wkts)	181

QUEENSLAND	O	M	R	W	w,nb		O	M	R	W	w,nb
Hornibrook	18	3	48	2	-,-		27.3	7	60	5	-,-
Thurlow	12	1	40	2	-,1		10	0	40	0	-,1
Nothling	7	1	21	1	-,-	(7)	8	1	12	1	-,-
Oxenham	19.1	5	30	3	-,-	(3)	21	5	43	4	-,-
Bensted	5	0	26	0	-,-		3	1	5	0	-,-
Rowe	4	0	6	1	-,-	(4)	4	0	10	0	-,-
Thompson						(6)	3	1	6	0	-,-

SOUTH AUSTRALIA	O	M	R	W	w,nb		O	M	R	W	w,nb
Wall	17	0	57	4	1,1		13.4	2	57	3	-,-
Whitfield	10.1	3	31	3	-,-		6	0	33	0	-,1
Scott	9	2	22	0	-,-	(4)	6	0	25	0	-,-
Carlton	8	2	14	0	-,-	(5)	10	4	8	1	-,-
Grimmett	15	3	49	2	-,-	(3)	17	4	49	5	-,-

FALL OF WICKETS

Wkt	SA 1st	QLD 1st	SA 2nd	QLD 2nd
1st	20	8	29	33
2nd	23	9	29	42
3rd	36	13	41	48
4th	130	15	41	55
5th	148	21	130	96
6th	166	95	154	160
7th	167	116	158	160
8th	169	148	158	160
9th	177	179	160	178
10th	185	188	183	-

VICTORIA v M.C.C.

Played at Melbourne Cricket Ground on March 1, 2, 4, 5, 1929. (Four-day match)
Toss : Victoria.   Result : MATCH DRAWN.
Debuts: Nil.
12th Men: T.R.Bird (Vic) and C.P.Mead (MCC).
Umpires: J.Richards and P.E.Smith.
Attendances: 6461, 12696, 6347, 3607.   Total: 29,111.   Receipts: £1511.
Close of Play: 1st day Vic 4/346 (Woodfull 158, a'Beckett 14); 2nd day MCC 2/83 (Hammond 46, Tyldesley 13); 3rd day MCC (2) 0/51 (Jardine 23, Leyland 28).

Ames, in taking a ball from Larwood in the first over, fractured the little finger of his right hand and retired from the field just before lunch on the first day. He took no further part in the tour, Hammond and Jardine sharing the role of wicket-keeper for the remainder of this match. Woodfull (275 not out in 459 minutes, 1 five and 21 fours) batted throughout the Victorian innings and was on the field for the duration of the match. He shared stands with Ryder (60 in 72 minutes, 1 six and 6 fours), Darling (87 in 116 minutes, 8 fours), a'Beckett (38 in 47 minutes, 4 fours) and Makin (44 in 65 minutes, 1 six and 5 fours). The top scorers for M.C.C. were Hammond (114 in 192 minutes, 5 fours), Tyldesley (81 in 187 minutes, 3 fours) and Hendren (46 in 73 minutes, 3 fours) in the first innings and Jardine (115 in 253 minutes, 11 fours), Leyland (54 in 83 minutes, 1 six and 6 fours) and again Tyldesley (68 not out in 130 minutes, 6 fours) in the second innings. Sources: *Wisden, NSWCA Report, VCA Report, The Age, The Argus, Sydney Morning Herald.*

VICTORIA

W.M.Woodfull	not out	275	
B.A.Onyons	c Ames b Larwood	1	
H.S.T.L.Hendry	st Ames b Freeman	19	
*J.Ryder	c sub (C.P.Mead) b Freeman	60	
L.S.Darling	b Tate	87	
E.L.a'Beckett	b Larwood	38	
J.W.Scaife	st Hammond b Freeman	18	
†J.L.Ellis	c Chapman b Larwood	15	
J.C.Makin	c Chapman b Jardine	44	
H.H.Alexander	c Leyland b Freeman	2	
H.Ironmonger	not out	4	
Extras	(b6, lb3)	9	
Total	(164.3 overs, 459 mins) (9 wkts dec)	572	

M.C.C.

D.R.Jardine	c Ryder b Hendry	4	c Darling b Alexander	115
M.Leyland	lbw b Makin	16	c Darling b Ironmonger	54
W.R.Hammond	b Alexander	114	c Scaife b Alexander	20
G.E.Tyldesley	lbw b Ironmonger	81	not out	68
E.H.Hendren	b Ironmonger	46	not out	31
H.Larwood	b Alexander	21		
G.Geary	c Darling b Alexander	5		
M.W.Tate	c Makin b Alexander	0		
*A.P.F.Chapman	b Ironmonger	2		
A.P.Freeman	not out	1		
†L.E.G.Ames	absent hurt	-		
Extras	(b8, lb5)	13	(b14, lb6)	20
Total	(108.2 overs, 300 mins)	303	(116.0 overs, 315 mins) (3 wkts)	308

M.C.C.	O	M	R	W	w,nb
Larwood	24.3	4	61	3	-,-
Tate	38	9	97	1	-,-
Freeman	55	3	245	4	-,-
Geary	31	7	95	0	-,-
Leyland	6	0	39	0	-,-
Hammond	3	1	7	0	-,-
Jardine	7	1	19	1	-,-

VICTORIA	O	M	R	W	w,nb		O	M	R	W	w,nb
Alexander	27.2	1	98	4	-,-		26	0	110	2	-,-
Hendry	19	4	39	1	-,-		6	3	14	0	-,-
Ironmonger	33	6	84	3	-,-	(5)	30	11	56	1	-,-
Makin	19	2	48	1	-,-	(3)	16	4	40	0	-,-
Darling	10	3	21	0	-,-	(7)	11	6	13	0	-,-
Ryder						(4)	10	1	24	0	-,-
a'Beckett						(6)	17	6	31	0	-,-

FALL OF WICKETS

	VIC	MCC	MCC
Wkt	1st	1st	2nd
1st	7	15	98
2nd	41	49	168
3rd	135	200	247
4th	316	252	-
5th	381	295	-
6th	424	295	-
7th	457	296	-
8th	557	301	-
9th	560	303	-
10th	-	-	-

NEW SOUTH WALES v SOUTH AUSTRALIA (Shield Match 12)

Played at Sydney Cricket Ground on March 1, 2, 4, 5, 6, 1929. (Five-day match)
Toss : New South Wales.   Result : NEW SOUTH WALES WON BY 60 RUNS.
Debuts: South Australia - C.W.Walker (f/c).
12th Men: J.H.W.Fingleton (NSW). No 12th for SA.
Umpires: A.H.Farrow and A.C.Jones.
Attendances: 4265, 7564, 3272, 2078, 351.   Total: 17,530.   Receipts: £982.
Close of Play: 1st day SA 0/0 (Richardson 0, Harris 0); 2nd day SA 7/197 (Grimmett 2, Wall 0); 3rd day NSW (2) 4/262 (Bradman 125, Marks 2); 4th day SA (2) 3/218 (Richardson 30, Whitfield 4).

Lampe replaced C.D.Seddon (unavailable) in the New South Wales side. D.G.McKay (appendicitis) was unable to act as South Australia's 12th man. Marks (92 in 130 minutes, 7 fours), Jordan (65 in 135 minutes, 1 six, 1 five and 4 fours) and Hooker (62 in 76 minutes, 7 fours) rescued New South Wales with fifties on the first day. The umpires upheld a light appeal by Richardson before a ball was bowled in South Australia's first innings several minutes before the scheduled time for stumps. Harris (107 in 290 minutes, 6 fours) topscored on the second day while Grimmett's 43 occupied 121 minutes and included 2 fours. Bradman (175 in 210 minutes, 14 fours) enabled New South Wales to declare with a lead of 445 runs. Subsequent fifties by South Australians Harris (94 in 174 minutes), Hack (79 in 112 minutes), Richardson (56 in 76 minutes, 6 fours) and Whitfield (91 in 152 minutes, 6 fours) made for a close finish but the loss of 4 for 23 in the middle order put the task beyond the visitors. Both wicket-keepers - Walker was on debut - were acclaimed after the match as fine prospects. Sources: *Wisden, NSWCA Report, SACA Report, Sydney Morning Herald, Sydney Referee, Sydney Daily Telegraph, C.B.O'Reilly.*

NEW SOUTH WALES

A.G.Fairfax	lbw b Grimmett	17	st Walker b Grimmett		41
A.Jackson	c Walker b Scott	6	st Walker b Grimmett		38
D.G.Bradman	c Walker b Grimmett	35	c Walker b Carlton		175
*T.J.E.Andrews	c Carlton b Whitfield	0	b Wall		23
S.J.McCabe	c Grimmett b Wall	5	c Scott b Alexander		27
A.E.Marks	run out (Wall)	92	lbw b Grimmett		26
†H.L.Davidson	run out (Alexander/Walker)	16	b Grimmett		13
F.S.Jordan	st Walker b Grimmett	65	not out		19
J.E.H.Hooker	st Walker b Grimmett	62	st Walker b Grimmett		6
W.H.W.Lampe	c Richardson b Whitfield	3	run out (Walker/Whitfield)		17
N.O.Morris	not out	8			
Extras	(b7, lb7, w1, nb2)	17	(b5, lb3, w1, nb5)		14
Total	(76.0 overs, 298 mins)	326	(90.4 overs, 324 mins) (9 wkts dec)		399

SOUTH AUSTRALIA

*V.Y.Richardson	c Davidson b Hooker	6	(4) b Fairfax		56
G.W.Harris	c Davidson b Morris	107	(1) c Davidson b Marks		94
A.T.Hack	c Jackson b Hooker	29	c Hooker b Morris		79
H.E.Whitfield	b Lampe	8	(5) c Marks b Fairfax		91
†C.W.Walker	b Morris	26	(2) c Jackson b Fairfax		3
W.C.Alexander	c Fairfax b Hooker	5	c Davidson b Fairfax		0
M.P.Hutton	st Davidson b Andrews	4	c Davidson b Jordan		5
C.V.Grimmett	st Davidson b Andrews	43	run out (McCabe/Marks)		2
T.W.Wall	c & b Andrews	15	c Davidson b Bradman		28
J.D.Scott	not out	23	run out (Hooker/Davidson)		8
T.A.Carlton	st Davidson b Andrews	0	not out		6
Extras	(b6, lb4, w3, nb1)	14	(b6, lb4, w1, nb2)		13
Total	(119.0 overs, 392 mins)	280	(96.4 overs, 327 mins)		385

SOUTH AUSTRALIA	O	M	R	W	w,nb		O	M	R	W	w,nb
Wall	17	1	64	1	-,1		17	0	59	1	-,1
Scott	10	1	62	1	1,1		11	2	61	0	-,2
Whitfield	16	3	47	2	-,-		13	2	69	0	-,1
Grimmett	27	1	112	4	-,-		26.4	1	116	5	-,-
Carlton	6	0	24	0	-,-	(7)	18	2	47	1	-,-
Hack						(5)	4	0	23	0	1,1
Alexander						(6)	1	0	10	1	-,-

NEW SOUTH WALES	O	M	R	W	w,nb		O	M	R	W	w,nb
Fairfax	22	4	47	0	1,1		19.4	2	55	4	1,1
Hooker	32	7	73	3	1,-		16	4	70	0	-,1
Morris	11	1	27	2	1,-		18	0	78	1	-,-
Jordan	19	6	32	0	-,-		12	1	27	1	-,-
Lampe	21	8	44	1	-,-		11	2	50	0	-,-
Andrews	9	0	34	4	-,-		8	0	47	0	-,-
Marks	5	1	9	0	-,-		8	1	19	1	-,-
Bradman							4	0	26	1	-,-

FALL OF WICKETS

Wkt	NSW 1st	SA 1st	NSW 2nd	SA 2nd
1st	12	14	65	14
2nd	60	84	90	153
3rd	61	99	148	207
4th	69	104	257	251
5th	79	172	340	251
6th	117	195	348	268
7th	221	197	359	274
8th	287	225	367	360
9th	296	280	399	373
10th	326	280	-	385

AUSTRALIA v ENGLAND (5th Test)

Played at Melbourne Cricket Ground on March 8, 9, 11, 12, 13, 14, 15, 16, 1929. (Timeless match)
Toss : England.   Result : AUSTRALIA WON BY FIVE WICKETS.
Debuts: Australia - A.G.Fairfax, P.M.Hornibrook, T.W.Wall (all Test).
12th Men: E.L.a'Beckett (Aust) and A.P.F.Chapman (Eng).
Umpires: G.A.Hele and A.C.Jones.
Attendances: 21425, 49809, 31864, 20796, 15132, 20511, 34884, 19373.   Total: 213,794.   Receipts: £15,745.
Close of Play: 1st day Eng 4/240 (Duckworth 3); 2nd day Eng 9/485 (Leyland 110, White 2); 3rd day Aust 2/152 (Woodfull 78, Ryder 4);
    4th day Aust 4/367 (Bradman 109, Fairfax 50); 5th day Eng (2) 1/18 (Hobbs 3, Larwood 11); 6th day Aust (2) 0/7 (Oldfield 6,
    Hornibrook 1); 7th day Aust (2) 4/173 (Kippax 12, Ryder 8).

This was the longest first-class match to be played in Australia, both in days of play (eight) and actual playing time (33 hours 17 minutes).
England were unable to consider L.E.G.Ames (broken finger, A.P.F.Chapman (flu) and H.Sutcliffe (shoulder strain). Hobbs (142 in 278
minutes, 11 fours, chance at 77) scored his last Test century and, at the age of 46 years 82 days, became the oldest player to score a first-
class hundred in this country. Hendren (95 in 191 minutes, 1 eight - an all-run four plus four overthrows - and 10 fours) and Leyland (137
in 301 minutes, 18 fours, chance at 13) added 140 for England's sixth wicket. A careful and chanceless innings by Woodfull (102 in 325
minutes, 3 fours) preceded a fifth-wicket stand of 183 between Bradman (123 in 217 minutes, 8 fours, chance at 46) and Fairfax (65 in 232
minutes, 2 fours) which kept Australia within reach. Half-centuries were scored in the respective second innings by Hobbs (65 in 116
minutes, 6 fours), Leyland (53 not out in 140 minutes, 6 fours), Tate (54 in 55 minutes, 8 fours) and Ryder (57 not out in 169 minutes, 4
fours). Hammond's 905 runs, average 113.12, established a Test record aggregate for a series in Australia. *Wisden* incorrectly gives Aust
(2) Larwood 0/85, Tate 0/72. Sources: *Wisden, VCA Report, The Age, The Argus, The Herald, The Australasian.*

ENGLAND

J.B.Hobbs	lbw b Ryder	142	c Fairfax b Grimmett		65
D.R.Jardine	c Oldfield b Wall	19	c Oldfield b Wall		0
W.R.Hammond	c Fairfax b Wall	38	(4) c Ryder b Fairfax		16
G.E.Tyldesley	c Hornibrook b Ryder	31	(5) c Oldfield b Wall		21
†G.Duckworth	c Fairfax b Hornibrook	12	(11) lbw b Oxenham		9
E.H.Hendren	c Hornibrook b Fairfax	95	b Grimmett		1
M.Leyland	c Fairfax b Oxenham	137	not out		53
H.Larwood	b Wall	4	(3) b Wall		11
G.Geary	b Hornibrook	4	b Wall		3
M.W.Tate	c sub (E.L.a'Beckett) b Hornibrook	15	(8) c Fairfax b Hornibrook		54
*J.C.White	not out	9	(10) c Oxenham b Wall		4
Extras	(b4, lb6, w1, nb2)	13	(b19, lb1)		20
Total	(215.1 overs, 615 mins)	519	(86.3 overs, 265 mins)		257

AUSTRALIA

W.M.Woodfull	c Geary b Larwood	102	(3) b Hammond		35
A.Jackson	run out (Larwood/Geary)	30	(4) b Geary		46
A.F.Kippax	c Duckworth b White	38	(5) run out (Larwood/Tate)		28
*J.Ryder	c Tate b Hammond	30	(6) not out		57
D.G.Bradman	c Tate b Geary	123	(7) not out		37
A.G.Fairfax	lbw b Geary	65			
R.K.Oxenham	c Duckworth b Geary	7			
†W.A.S.Oldfield	c & b Geary	6	(1) b Hammond		48
C.V.Grimmett	not out	38			
T.W.Wall	c Duckworth b Geary	9			
P.M.Hornibrook	lbw b White	26	(2) b Hammond		18
Extras	(b6, lb9, w2)	17	(b12, lb6)		18
Total	(271.3 overs, 732 mins)	491	(134.1 overs, 385 mins) (5 wkts)		287

AUSTRALIA	O	M	R	W	w,nb		O	M	R	W	w,nb			FALL OF WICKETS		
Wall	49	8	123	3	1,1		26	5	66	5	-,-			ENG	AUST	ENG	AUST
Hornibrook	48	8	142	3	-,-		19	5	51	1	-,-		Wkt	1st	1st	2nd	2nd
Oxenham	45.1	15	86	1	-,-	(5)	10.3	1	34	1	-,-		1st	64	54	1	51
Grimmett	25	11	40	0	-,-		24	7	66	2	-,-		2nd	146	143	19	80
Fairfax	27	4	84	1	-,1	(3)	7	0	20	1	-,-		3rd	235	203	75	129
Ryder	18	5	29	2	-,-								4th	240	203	119	158
Kippax	3	1	2	0	-,-								5th	261	386	123	204
													6th	401	399	131	-
ENGLAND	O	M	R	W	w,nb		O	M	R	W	w,nb		7th	409	409	212	-
Larwood	34	7	83	1	-,-		32.1	5	81	0	-,-		8th	428	420	217	-
Tate	62	26	108	0	-,-		38	13	76	0	-,-		9th	470	432	231	-
Geary	81	36	105	5	2,-	(4)	20	5	31	1	-,-		10th	519	491	257	-
White	75.3	22	136	2	-,-	(3)	18	8	28	0	-,-						
Hammond	16	3	31	1	-,-		26	8	53	3	-,-						
Leyland	3	0	11	0	-,-												

AUSTRALIAN XI v M.C.C.

Played at W.A.C.A. Ground, Perth, on March 21, 22, 23, 1929. (Three-day match)
Toss : Australian XI.   Result : MATCH DRAWN.
Debuts: Nil.
12th Men: F.J.Bryant (both teams - only 11 players available for MCC).
Umpires: F.R.Buttsworth and W.L.Menkens.
Attendances: 6500, 6300, 9000.   Total: About 21,800.   Receipts: £1821.
Close of Play: 1st day Aust XI 5/269 (Richardson 84, Rowe 65); 2nd day MCC 3/156 (Mead 33, Hendren 9).

H.I.Ebeling, W.H.Ponsford and W.M.Woodfull were invited by the Western Australian Cricket Association to play, but all declined. Ryder agreed to play but refused the captaincy. Hammond kept wickets for M.C.C. on the second and third days instead of Duckworth (influenza). Richardson batted 256 minutes with 8 fours, while Rowe's innings lasted 113 minutes with 11 fours. Tate was hit on the knee by Halcombe in the first over of the M.C.C. innings and retired hurt when 0 at 0/1, resuming the next day at 6/214. Hammond (80 in 136 minutes, 1 six and 4 fours) topscored for M.C.C. In the second innings Ryder (140 minutes, 3 sixes and 4 fours) and Horrocks (86 minutes, 6 fours) combined for the biggest partnership of the match. White raised the ire of the crowd before tea on the last day by bringing Duckworth on to bowl. The paying crowd hooted and then "counted him out", regarding it as an insult to see a wicket-keeper being brought on to bowl (who had only the day before been laid-up with 'flu, too ill to take the field). The match takings of £1821 set a new record for the ground. *NSWCA Report* and *VCA Report* give Aust bowling Halcombe 2/49, Evans 3/37, Darling 0/6. Sources: *Wisden, NSWCA Report, VCA Report, Sydney Morning Herald, The West Australian, Daily News.*

AUSTRALIAN XI

J.Ryder	lbw b Geary	24		not out	81
A.D.Drew	b White	37		b Leyland	0
W.J.Horrocks	st Duckworth b Hammond	31		c Duckworth b Tate	76
A.J.Richardson	not out	101			
W.A.McRae	b Tate	18		not out	15
L.S.Darling	c Geary b Tate	0	(4)	c Leyland b Freeman	9
*S.H.D.Rowe	run out (sub F.J.Bryant/Hammond)	73			
C.V.Grimmett	b Larwood	0			
W.A.Evans	c Tate b Larwood	0			
†J.L.Ellis	st Hammond b Freeman	14			
R.A.Halcombe	st Hammond b White	1			
Extras	(b5, lb4, w1, nb1)	11		(b1, lb4)	5
Total	(95.2 overs, 350 mins)	310		(43.0 overs, 140 mins) (3 wkts)	186

M.C.C.

M.Leyland	c Ellis b Halcombe	27
M.W.Tate	c Darling b Halcombe	4
G.E.Tyldesley	c Horrocks b Evans	1
†W.R.Hammond	lbw b Evans	80
C.P.Mead	b Grimmett	41
E.H.Hendren	st Ellis b Richardson	33
H.Larwood	c Ryder b Evans	15
G.Geary	c Ryder b Grimmett	22
*J.C.White	not out	4
†G.Duckworth	c Ryder b Grimmett	0
A.P.Freeman	b Grimmett	6
Extras	(b2, lb5, w1)	8
Total	(76.5 overs, 310 mins)	241

M.C.C.	O	M	R	W	w,nb		O	M	R	W	w,nb
Larwood	18	4	40	2	-,1	(6)	2	0	8	0	-,-
Tate	21	3	55	2	1,-	(7)	3	0	11	1	-,-
Geary	14	0	57	1	-,-						
White	20.2	0	52	2	-,-	(5)	2	1	7	0	-,-
Freeman	14	0	58	1	-,-	(3)	11	0	62	1	-,-
Hammond	8	0	37	1	-,-						
Hendren						(1)	10	2	36	0	-,-
Leyland						(2)	14	1	50	1	-,-
Duckworth						(4)	1	0	7	0	-,-

AUSTRALIAN XI	O	M	R	W	w,nb
Halcombe	16	1	50	2	1,-
Evans	17	6	38	3	-,-
Richardson	15	4	39	1	-,-
Grimmett	21.5	3	94	4	-,-
Ryder	6	2	8	0	-,-
Darling	1	0	4	0	-,-

FALL OF WICKETS

Wkt	AUST 1st	MCC 1st	AUST 2nd
1st	40	2	2
2nd	90	81	130
3rd	118	134	140
4th	158	188	-
5th	160	192	-
6th	277	214	-
7th	277	231	-
8th	277	231	-
9th	309	231	-
10th	310	241	-

The individual performances of Bradman and Grimmett dominated the season. Bradman's first-class aggregate of 1586 runs (average 113.28) included an innings of 452 not out against Queensland - the highest to date in Australian first-class cricket. It remained a world first-class record for nearly 30 years. Grimmett's tally of 82 wickets, which included two seven-wicket analyses, stood third to C.T.B.Turner (106 wickets in 1887-88) and George Giffen (93 in 1894-95) as a record for an Australian season.

An MCC team played five matches in Australia (all first-class) early in the season, on the way to New Zealand for an inaugural Test series. The team was not fully representative owing to a simultaneous England tour of the West Indies. Nevertheless, they recorded victories over Western Australia and South Australia before unsuccessful encounters with the three easternmost States.

Victoria battled with New South Wales to establish Sheffield Shield supremacy. New South Wales led Victoria on the first innings of a drawn match at Melbourne but the reverse occurred in the drawn game at Sydney. A loss to South Australia at Adelaide proved to be New South Wales's undoing, and Victoria took the Shield. The bowling of Blackie and Ironmonger stood out for the winners. Ponsford, Ryder, a'Beckett, Hendry, Rigg, Scaife and Ellis also played their part, and Woodfull's absence through injury was barely felt.

New South Wales, though failing to keep the Shield, still owned the best batting lineup. In addition to Bradman they had McCabe, Kippax, Allsopp and Jackson all performing well. But their bowling, with the notable exception of Fairfax, was unable to make the same impact.

South Australia relied extraordinarily on Grimmett but also extracted some value from Richardson, Hone, Pritchard and the allrounder Whitfield.

The bowling of Hurwood and allround form of Oxenham were the only encouraging aspects of Queensland's season. They lost five Shield matches outright, and the other on the first innings. Their sole first-class success came with a win over the England side.

Western Australia's fourth tour east, following previous ventures in 1892-93, 1912-13 and 1925-26, included an inaugural meeting against Tasmania at Hobart. During the tour, the WACA sought support for the introduction of a 'minor States' competition, comprising teams from Western Australia and Tasmania plus second XIs from the Sheffield Shield States. The proposal was not put to the Board of Control until 1931.

As usual, intense public interest surrounded the selection of an Australian team to tour England the following winter. The 17th Australians comprised W.M.Woodfull (captain), E.L.a'Beckett, D.G.Bradman, A.G.Fairfax, C.V.Grimmett, P.M.Hornibrook, A.Hurwood, A.Jackson, A.F.Kippax, S.J.McCabe, W.A.S.Oldfield, W.H.Ponsford, V.Y.Richardson, C.W.Walker and T.W.Wall. The omission of J.Ryder was surprising and was strongly criticised. Oxenham was also considered unlucky to miss out.

In addition to the 29 first-class matches staged this season, the Victorian Cricket Association proposed that a match involving the Australian team to England be played at Melbourne on March 4, 5 and 6 as a testimonial for Ryder. But the Board of Control ruled it out owing to the team's departure on March 7.

Leading Aggregates

Batsmen	M	I	NO	Runs	HS	Ave.	Bowlers	Runs	Wkts	Ave.
D.G.Bradman (NSW)	11	16	2	1586	452*	113.28	C.V.Grimmett (SA)	1943	82	23.69
S.J.McCabe (NSW)	11	16	1	844	103	56.26	A.Hurwood (Q)	913	46	19.84
A.F.Kippax (NSW)	10	13	1	744	170	62.00	A.G.Fairfax (NSW)	950	42	22.61
W.H.Ponsford (V)	10	16	0	729	166	45.56	H.Ironmonger (V)	763	38	20.07
V.Y.Richardson (SA)	11	17	0	728	126	42.82	D.D.Blackie (V)	786	36	21.83
A.H.Allsopp (NSW)	8	12	1	645	136	58.63	P.M.Hornibrook (Q)	770	35	22.00
D.E.Pritchard (SA)	8	15	0	637	148	42.46	H.E.Whitfield (SA)	881	29	30.37
A.Jackson (NSW)	6	10	1	630	182	70.00	E.L.a'Beckett (V)	411	27	15.22
B.W.Hone (SA)	7	14	2	620	126	51.66	R.K.Oxenham (Q)	464	24	19.33
J.Ryder (V)	8	14	3	552	168	50.18	T.W.Wall (SA)	854	23	37.13

SHEFFIELD SHIELD TABLE

	P	WO	W1	LO	L1	D	Pts	Quotient	Runs Scored	Wkts Lost	Runs Conceded	Wkts Taken
VICTORIA	6	4	-	-	1	1	23	1.374	2482	80	2303	102
NEW SOUTH WALES	6	3	1	1	-	1	20	1.492	3727	90	2720	98
SOUTH AUSTRALIA	6	2	1	3	-	-	13	0.817	3102	114	3428	103
QUEENSLAND	6	-	-	5	1	-	1	0.623	2456	120	3316	101
TOTAL	12	9	2	9	2	1	57	1.000	11767	404	11767	404

WESTERN AUSTRALIA v M.C.C.

Played at W.A.C.A. Ground, Perth, on October 31, November 1, 2, 1929. (Three-day match)
Toss : Western Australia.   Result : M.C.C. WON BY SEVEN WICKETS.
Debuts: Western Australia - A.M.C.Webster (f/c).
12th Men: E.T.Benson (MCC). No 12th named for WA.
Umpires: F.R.Buttsworth and W.L.Menkens.
Attendances: 2500, 2600, 4500.   Total: 9600.   Receipts: £685.
Close of Play: 1st day MCC 0/25 (Dawson 7, Turnbull 17); 2nd day WA (2) 1/59 (Taaffe 23, Horrocks 22).

F.Barratt was unavailable for MCC selection due to a boil on his bowling arm. Rain interrupted play several times on the first day. Horrocks (77 minutes, 5 fours) and R.J.Bryant (74 minutes, 4 fours) batted well for Western Australia. Bowley was struck on the wrist by the first ball of the MCC innings and retired hurt soon after at 0/1. He resumed next day at 5/54 and batted in all for 138 minutes, with 1 six and 11 fours. He was bowled by the first ball of the second innings, completing an unusual first-ball double. Earle hit two sixes in his brief stay. Horrocks (81 minutes, 6 fours) again did well in the WA second innings. Duleepsinhji batted 115 minutes and hit 6 fours to guide MCC to victory at 4.40pm. Rowe, the WA captain, then suggested that MCC continue their innings to give the crowd an exhibition of cricket; Gilligan replied that, although he was quite willing to do so, he did not know whether MCC or the Australian Board of Control would approve and therefore he could not "introduce an innovation that might be regarded as a precedent". Last first-class appearance in Australia by A.J.Richardson - he played one further match in England in 1933. Sources: *Wisden, NSWCA Report, VCA Report, The West Australian, Daily News.*

WESTERN AUSTRALIA

A.J.Richardson	c Cornford b Allom	3	(4) c Allom b Woolley	0
F.H.Taaffe	b Nichols	3	(1) st Cornford b Woolley	30
F.J.Bryant	b Worthington	20	(2) c Cornford b Worthington	7
W.J.Horrocks	c Allom b Nichols	51	(3) c Earle b Woolley	39
R.J.Bryant	c Cornford b Nichols	34	st Cornford b Bowley	2
*S.H.D.Rowe	b Worthington	2	(7) st Cornford b Woolley	0
M.Inverarity	c Cornford b Allom	24	(6) c Turnbull b Bowley	18
W.A.Evans	c & b Woolley	24	(10) c Nichols b Bowley	15
†R.H.Hewson	run out	1	(8) c Nichols b Bowley	4
A.M.C.Webster	not out	4	(9) c Woolley b Bowley	1
R.A.Halcombe	b Nichols	4	not out	0
Extras	(b9, lb6)	15	(b7, lb2, w2)	11
Total	(50.4 overs, 201 mins)	185	(36.7 overs, 148 mins)	127

M.C.C.

E.H.Bowley	not out	79	b Halcombe	0
E.W.Dawson	c Inverarity b Webster	7	c Inverarity b Webster	8
M.J.L.Turnbull	c Richardson b Webster	20	(5) not out	27
K.S.Duleepsinhji	b Richardson	1	(3) not out	64
F.E.Woolley	lbw b Evans	13	(4) lbw b Halcombe	16
T.S.Worthington	c Horrocks b Richardson	8		
*A.H.H.Gilligan	lbw b Richardson	2		
M.S.Nichols	c Hewson b Halcombe	23		
G.F.Earle	c Taaffe b Halcombe	14		
†W.L.Cornford	c Hewson b Evans	10		
M.J.C.Allom	b Halcombe	7		
Extras	(lb7)	7	(b5, lb3)	8
Total	(51.4 overs, 225 mins)	191	(28.3 overs, 116 mins) (3 wkts)	123

M.C.C.	O	M	R	W	w,nb		O	M	R	W	w,nb		FALL OF WICKETS			
														WA	MCC	WA	MCC
Nichols	14.4	0	57	4	-,-		10	0	33	0	-,-		Wkt	1st	1st	2nd	2nd
Allom	16	3	50	2	-,-		4	0	12	0	1,-		1st	7	26	20	0
Worthington	12	2	46	2	-,-		4	1	7	1	-,-		2nd	21	33	84	8
Bowley	4	0	17	0	-,-	(5)	6.7	1	30	5	-,-		3rd	48	33	84	65
Woolley	4	4	0	1	-,-	(4)	12	4	34	4	1,-		4th	113	54	87	-
													5th	118	54	90	-
WESTERN AUSTRALIA	O	M	R	W	w,nb		O	M	R	W	w,nb		6th	122	58	91	-
Halcombe	9.4	2	35	3	-,-		10	2	30	2	-,-		7th	170	107	98	-
Evans	11	1	46	2	-,-		4	1	9	0	-,-		8th	171	123	100	-
Webster	14	3	36	2	-,-		5.3	1	34	1	-,-		9th	178	158	123	-
Richardson	17	4	67	3	-,-		7	1	21	0	-,-		10th	185	191	127	-
Inverarity							2	0	21	0	-,-						

QUEENSLAND v NEW SOUTH WALES (Shield Match 1)

Played at Exhibition Ground, Brisbane, on November 8, 9, 11, 12, 1929. (Five-day match)
Toss : New South Wales.   Result : NEW SOUTH WALES WON BY 23 RUNS.
Debuts: Queensland - V.H.V.Goodwin (f/c).
12th Men: A.Hurwood (Qld) and A.G.Chipperfield (NSW).
Umpires: J.P.Orr and J.A.Scott.
Attendances: 2000, 6596, 2264, 1500.   Total: 12,360.   Receipts: £642.
Close of Play: 1st day NSW 6/340 (McCabe 65, Oldfield 0); 2nd day NSW (2) 0/11 (Andrews 10, Bettington 0); 3rd day Qld (2) 0/7
    (Higgins 4, Hornibrook 3).

W.Rowe and H.M.Thurlow were unavailable for Queensland and Brew, originally named 12th man, was a late replacement for
F.C.Thompson (injured shoulder). Jackson (80 in 207 minutes, 8 fours) and McCabe (77 in 143 minutes, 8 fours) in the first innings and
Bradman (66 in 195 minutes, 1 four) and Marks (51 in 96 minutes, 8 fours) in the second innings scored half-centuries for New South
Wales. Oxenham for Queensland had a fine match, scoring 49 (88 minutes, 6 fours) and 117 (210 minutes, 5 fours) and taking 6-113 with
his right-arm medium pacers. Gough's 69 occupied 80 minutes and included 1 five and 8 fours. Last first-class appearance by
O.E.Nothling. Sources: *Wisden, NSWCA Report, QCA Report, Sydney Morning Herald, Brisbane Courier.*

NEW SOUTH WALES

A.G.Fairfax	lbw b Oxenham	49	(5)	lbw b Oxenham	21
A.Jackson	c O'Connor b Oxenham	80	(3)	c Amos b Hornibrook	7
D.G.Bradman	run out (Oxenham/Brew)	48	(4)	c O'Connor b Brew	66
W.C.Andrews	lbw b Amos	40	(1)	lbw b Amos	12
S.J.McCabe	c Brew b Oxenham	77	(6)	b Hornibrook	3
R.H.B.Bettington	c O'Connor b Oxenham	9	(2)	c Nothling b Hornibrook	8
A.E.Marks	c Brew b Amos	46		c O'Connor b Hornibrook	51
*†W.A.S.Oldfield	run out (Gough/O'Connor/Oxenham)	3		lbw b Brew	7
J.E.H.Hooker	c O'Connor b Amos	2		not out	6
A.A.Mailey	not out	4		c & b Brew	0
F.H.Dupain	c Levy b Oxenham	10		b Brew	6
Extras	(b2, lb3)	5		(b4, lb7)	11
Total	(96.6 overs, 363 mins)	373		(81.3 overs, 309 mins)	198

QUEENSLAND

†L.P.D.O'Connor	c Dupain b Hooker	35	(4)	b Mailey	27
R.M.Levy	c Oldfield b Fairfax	12	(3)	b McCabe	17
H.J.R.Higgins	st Oldfield b Mailey	14	(1)	b Mailey	27
R.K.Oxenham	c Mailey b Fairfax	49	(5)	c Mailey b McCabe	117
V.H.V.Goodwin	c Oldfield b Mailey	23	(7)	c Bettington b Fairfax	23
*O.E.Nothling	c Mailey b Fairfax	5	(9)	b Dupain	16
F.J.Gough	b Mailey	69	(8)	c Dupain b Fairfax	10
F.M.Brew	c & b Hooker	19	(10)	st Oldfield b McCabe	4
E.C.Bensted	b Hooker	26	(6)	b Dupain	10
G.S.Amos	st Oldfield b Bettington	9	(11)	not out	1
P.M.Hornibrook	not out	0	(2)	c Oldfield b Fairfax	13
Extras	(b4, nb8)	12		(b5, lb3, nb2)	10
Total	(65.2 overs, 240 mins)	273		(87.0 overs, 314 mins)	275

QUEENSLAND	O	M	R	W	w,nb		O	M	R	W	w,nb
Hornibrook	17	4	51	0	-,-		19	6	43	4	-,-
Amos	20	2	98	3	-,-		11	1	45	1	-,-
Brew	13	0	88	0	-,-	(5)	14.3	2	31	4	-,-
Oxenham	25.6	3	72	5	-,-		28	12	41	1	-,-
Nothling	16	4	42	0	-,-	(3)	9	1	27	0	-,-
Bensted	5	0	17	0	-,-						

NEW SOUTH WALES	O	M	R	W	w,nb		O	M	R	W	w,nb
Dupain	9	1	38	0	-,-	(3)	10	5	16	2	-,-
Fairfax	18	1	47	3	-,7	(1)	21	7	47	3	-,2
Bettington	8.2	0	35	1	-,-	(6)	5	0	30	0	-,-
Hooker	14	2	38	3	-,1	(2)	15	3	52	0	-,-
Mailey	16	0	103	3	-,-	(4)	24	1	79	2	-,-
McCabe						(5)	12	2	41	3	-,-

FALL OF WICKETS

Wkt	NSW 1st	QLD 1st	NSW 2nd	QLD 2nd
1st	72	29	15	45
2nd	148	59	21	49
3rd	202	83	37	71
4th	235	131	66	115
5th	264	146	73	156
6th	338	166	166	208
7th	345	212	185	226
8th	351	253	188	255
9th	359	269	188	274
10th	373	273	198	275

SOUTH AUSTRALIA v M.C.C.

Played at Adelaide Oval on November 8, 9, 11, 12, 1929. (Four-day match)
Toss : M.C.C.   Result : M.C.C. WON BY 239 RUNS.
Debuts: South Australia - A.R.Lonergan, H.K.Sincock (both f/c).
12th Men: A.J.Ryan (SA) and E.T.Benson (MCC).
Umpires: G.A.Hele and A.G.Jenkins.
Attendances: 6580, ? , ? , ? .   Total: 23,478.   Receipts: £961.
Close of Play: 1st day SA 4/90 (Pritchard 24, Whitfield 10); 2nd day MCC (2) 2/107 (Duleepsinhji 38, Woolley 35); 3rd day SA (2) 5/40 (Richardson 1).

E.H.Bowley (lumbago) was unavailable for M.C.C. whose highest scores came from Nichols (46 in 55 minutes, 2 sixes and 4 fours and 82 in 134 minutes, 6 fours), Duleepsinhji (54 in 90 minutes, 2 fours) and Woolley (146 in 218 minutes, 1 six and 15 fours). Earle's 43 included 22 runs with 3 sixes off an over from Grimmett. Lonergan was out first ball on debut for South Australia. Hone alone reached fifty for the home side, batting 193 minutes and hitting 6 fours in the first innings. Overnight rain saturated the wicket for the final day in favour of the bowlers, the start being delayed until 1.00pm. *Wisden* incorrectly gives MCC (2) Dawson 13, extras 13, Sincock 2/33.
Sources: *Wisden, VCA Report, SACA Report, Sydney Morning Herald, C.B.O'Reilly, South Australian Register.*

M.C.C.

E.W.Dawson	c Harris b Grimmett	23	c Carlton b Wall	14
*A.H.H.Gilligan	c Walker b Whitfield	9	c Richardson b Wall	19
K.S.Duleepsinhji	c Walker b Whitfield	31	st Walker b Grimmett	54
F.E.Woolley	st Walker b Grimmett	0	c Pritchard b Whitfield	146
M.J.L.Turnbull	st Walker b Grimmett	26	st Walker b Grimmett	6
T.S.Worthington	lbw b Sincock	10	c Richardson b Grimmett	10
M.S.Nichols	c Whitfield b Grimmett	46	c Pritchard b Sincock	82
G.F.Earle	c Hone b Grimmett	1	run out (Richardson/Walker)	43
F.Barratt	c Harris b Grimmett	6	c Richardson b Sincock	17
†W.L.Cornford	c Whitfield b Sincock	0	c Walker b Carlton	1
M.J.C.Allom	not out	10	not out	12
Extras	(b3, lb1, nb2)	6	(b6, lb6)	12
Total	(43.5 overs, 175 mins)	168	(73.1 overs, 298 mins)	416

SOUTH AUSTRALIA

G.W.Harris	lbw b Barratt	22		c Turnbull b Allom	16
†C.W.Walker	c Duleepsinhji b Barratt	4	(8)	c Allom b Barratt	3
D.E.Pritchard	c & b Barratt	27		c Nichols b Allom	0
*V.Y.Richardson	c Woolley b Nichols	18		c Woolley b Allom	17
A.R.Lonergan	lbw b Nichols	0	(6)	b Allom	2
H.E.Whitfield	b Allom	35	(5)	c Cornford b Barratt	5
B.W.Hone	not out	70	(2)	b Barratt	12
C.V.Grimmett	b Nichols	19	(7)	c Woolley b Barratt	0
H.K.Sincock	c Nichols b Worthington	31		c Nichols b Barratt	7
T.W.Wall	b Allom	8		not out	6
T.A.Carlton	c Worthington b Barratt	3		c Worthington b Allom	5
Extras	(b6, lb12, nb4)	22		(b6, lb4, nb3)	13
Total	(81.7 overs, 317 mins)	259		(28.3 overs, 105 mins)	86

SOUTH AUSTRALIA	O	M	R	W	w,nb		O	M	R	W	w,nb
Wall	9	0	26	0	-,2		16	0	91	2	-,-
Whitfield	11	1	22	2	-,-		15	0	81	1	-,-
Carlton	6	3	14	0	-,-	(4)	13.1	2	62	1	-,-
Grimmett	12.5	0	61	6	-,-	(3)	25	1	136	3	-,-
Sincock	5	0	39	2	-,-		4	0	34	2	-,-

M.C.C.	O	M	R	W	w,nb		O	M	R	W	w,nb
Nichols	19	2	66	3	-,2	(3)	3	0	15	0	-,-
Allom	20	1	56	2	-,2		11.3	2	26	5	-,3
Barratt	25.7	3	61	4	-,-	(1)	14	4	32	5	-,-
Woolley	9	3	23	0	-,-						
Worthington	8	0	31	1	-,-						

FALL OF WICKETS

Wkt	MCC 1st	SA 1st	MCC 2nd	SA 2nd
1st	14	25	25	28
2nd	55	34	44	28
3rd	62	72	134	28
4th	72	72	158	37
5th	98	94	178	40
6th	106	127	314	43
7th	117	162	382	63
8th	124	219	402	71
9th	124	238	402	74
10th	168	259	416	86

VICTORIA v M.C.C.

Played at Melbourne Cricket Ground on November 15, 16, 18, 19, 1929. (Four-day match)
Toss : M.C.C.   Result : VICTORIA WON BY SEVEN WICKETS.
Debuts: Nil.
12th Men: H.C.Hunt (Vic) and E.T.Benson (MCC).
Umpires: A.N.Barlow and R.M.Crockett.
Attendances: 7446, 14827, 6218, ? .   Total: 28,491.   Receipts: £1397.
Close of Play: 1st day Vic 4/30 (Ryder 12); 2nd day MCC (2) 2/26 (Dawson 9); 3rd day Vic (2) 3/179 (Woodfull 93, Rigg 39).

Barlow and W.J.Moore were appointed to umpire but Gilligan asked that Crockett be included. The V.C.A. agreed to his request and both Barlow and Moore volunteered to stand aside, whereupon Barlow won a draw of names from a hat to decide who would partner Crockett. Rigg replaced E.L.a'Beckett (university exams) for Victoria. Worthington (influenza) was too ill to participate on the first two days; Ryder offered M.C.C. an opportunity to choose a replacement but the offer was turned down. Cornford retired at 8/112 when he was hit above the eye by a ball from Ironmonger on the third day, Duleepsinhji keeping wickets in the second innings while Benson substituted in the field. Gilligan (53 in 94 minutes, 7 fours) and Ryder (50 in 126 minutes, 0 fours) scored half-centuries for their respective teams. Woodfull, dismissed in the first over of Victoria's first innings, returned to score an unbeaten hundred in 164 minutes with 6 fours in the second innings. Rigg, his partner on the last day, refused scoring chances for himself to enable Woodfull to reach his century with the winning hit. Gilligan had refused to continue past 6pm on the third day even though Victoria needed a mere 7 runs for victory; 15 minutes were sufficient to decide the issue on the last day. Sources: *Wisden, NSWCA Report, VCA Report, The Age, The Argus, The Herald, Melbourne Sun.*

M.C.C.

E.W.Dawson	c Woodfull b Blackie	44	c Ironmonger b Blackie		19
*A.H.H.Gilligan	c Hendry b Ironmonger	53	c Hendry b Blackie		11
K.S.Duleepsinhji	c Alexander b Blackie	37	c Ryder b Blackie		0
F.E.Woolley	st Ellis b Blackie	5	c Rigg b Alexander		26
M.J.L.Turnbull	c Ironmonger b Blackie	11	lbw b Ironmonger		9
M.S.Nichols	c Ellis b Blackie	13	c Hendry b Blackie		24
G.F.Earle	c Ellis b Ironmonger	21	b Blackie		3
F.Barratt	c Scaife b Ironmonger	32	c Darling b Blackie		0
†W.L.Cornford	not out	15	retired hurt		6
M.J.C.Allom	b Darling	0	not out	(11)	2
T.S.Worthington	absent ill	-	c Ironmonger b Blackie	(10)	6
Extras	(b4, w2, nb1)	7	(b3, lb3, w2)		8
Total	(67.6 overs, 248 mins)	238	(50.0 overs, 188 mins)		114

VICTORIA

W.M.Woodfull	c Cornford b Nichols	0	not out		100
W.H.Ponsford	c Cornford b Barratt	5	c Woolley b Barratt		0
H.S.T.L.Hendry	c Duleepsinhji b Barratt	2	c Nichols b Barratt		9
*J.Ryder	c Dawson b Allom	50	c Earle b Nichols		35
L.S.Darling	c Woolley b Barratt	6			
K.E.Rigg	lbw b Nichols	20	not out	(5)	39
J.W.Scaife	b Nichols	27			
†J.L.Ellis	b Allom	6			
D.D.Blackie	st Cornford b Barratt	1			
H.H.Alexander	b Barratt	15			
H.Ironmonger	not out	17			
Extras	(b13, lb3, nb2)	18	(b1, lb1, w1, nb1)		4
Total	(49.1 overs, 197 mins)	167	(45.4 overs, 164 mins) (3 wkts)		187

VICTORIA	O	M	R	W	w,nb		O	M	R	W	w,nb
Alexander	16	1	51	0	2,1		10	0	43	1	2,-
Blackie	25	6	82	5	-,-	(4)	19	8	25	7	-,-
Ironmonger	18	4	81	3	-,-		15	6	23	1	-,-
Hendry	7	2	10	0	-,-	(2)	4	1	8	0	-,-
Darling	1.6	0	7	1	-,-		2	0	7	0	-,-

M.C.C.	O	M	R	W	w,nb		O	M	R	W	w,nb
Nichols	16	1	62	3	-,1		10	0	49	1	-,-
Barratt	19	1	45	5	-,-		14.4	1	60	2	-,-
Allom	10.1	4	23	2	-,-		10	0	40	0	1,-
Woolley	4	0	19	0	-,1		9	1	33	0	-,-
Worthington							2	1	1	0	-,1

FALL OF WICKETS

Wkt	MCC 1st	VIC 1st	MCC 2nd	VIC 2nd
1st	85	1	26	2
2nd	117	4	26	26
3rd	127	16	61	100
4th	149	30	63	-
5th	158	59	85	-
6th	187	121	92	-
7th	191	124	92	-
8th	237	125	104	-
9th	238	141	114	-
10th	-	167	-	-

NEW SOUTH WALES v M.C.C.

Played at Sydney Cricket Ground on November 22, 23, 25, 26, 1929. (Four-day match)
Toss : New South Wales.   Result : MATCH DRAWN.
Debuts: - New South Wales - A.H.Allsopp (f/c).
12th Men: O.W.Bill (NSW) and W.L.Cornford (MCC).
Umpires: W.H.Bayfield and M.Carney.
Attendances: 11375, 22404, 6273, 2753.   Total: 42,805.   Receipts: £3535.
Close of Play: 1st day NSW 5/453 (Allsopp 47, McCabe 16); 2nd day MCC 3/171 (Woolley 61, Turnbull 28); 3rd day NSW (2) 0/46
    (Fairfax 16, Jackson 28).

Batsmen dominated the game, 1607 runs being scored at 73.04 per wicket. M.C.C. were unable to select M.S.Nichols (ill), W.L.Cornford and G.F.Earle (both injured) and were further handicapped by injuries to Bowley (recurrence of leg strain), Barratt (strained arm while bowling) and Gilligan (bruised hand fielding a hot drive) during the match. For a time on the fourth day they fielded four substitutes - the less-than-well Nichols, Cornford and Earle as well as Bill - with Dawson acting as captain. Woolley (219 in 244 minutes, 24 fours) and Turnbull (100 in 203 minutes, 9 fours) added 265 for the fourth wicket. Fairfax dismissed Woolley and Benson with consecutive balls. Bradman (157 in 175 minutes, 16 fours - 50 up in 45 minutes, 100 in 103 minutes), Kippax (108 in 173 minutes, 10 fours), Allsopp on debut (117 in 147 minutes, 12 fours and 63 not out in 73 minutes), McCabe (90 in 114 minutes, 7 fours) and Jackson (168 not out in 200 minutes, 17 fours, stumping chance at 76) scored highest for New South Wales. Allsopp survived an appeal for hit wicket when 19 off Bowley during his debut hundred, fieldsmen noting that a bail was on the ground after the batsman had hit a four through the covers off the back foot. Oldfield injured a finger while keeping wicket on the second day and Allsopp replaced him behind the stumps for the last two days. Sources: *Wisden, NSWCA Report, VCA Report, The Age, Sydney Morning Herald, Sydney Referee.*

NEW SOUTH WALES

A.G.Fairfax	lbw b Allom	14		lbw b Worthington	19
A.Jackson	c Benson b Allom	49		not out	168
D.G.Bradman	b Worthington	157			
*A.F.Kippax	c Dawson b Bowley	108			
A.E.Marks	c & b Bowley	38	(4)	lbw b Woolley	26
A.H.Allsopp	c Turnbull b Allom	117	(5)	not out	63
S.J.McCabe	b Worthington	90			
W.C.Andrews	not out	11	(3)	c & b Woolley	17
†W.A.S.Oldfield	c Duleepsinhji b Worthington	3			
J.E.H.Hooker	not out	6			
F.H.Dupain	did not bat				
Extras	(b20, lb13, nb3)	36		(b8, lb1, nb3)	12
Total	(114.3 overs, 425 mins) (8 wkts dec)	629		(51.0 overs, 200 mins) (3 wkts dec)	305

M.C.C.

E.W.Dawson	c Hooker b Fairfax	3		not out	83
*A.H.H.Gilligan	lbw b Hooker	45		b Hooker	15
K.S.Duleepsinhji	b Dupain	34		st Allsopp b Marks	47
F.E.Woolley	b Fairfax	219			
M.J.L.Turnbull	c & b Bradman	100			
T.S.Worthington	c & b Hooker	7			
G.B.Legge	c Andrews b Dupain	42	(4)	not out	47
†E.T.Benson	b Fairfax	0			
F.Barratt	not out	12			
M.J.C.Allom	b Fairfax	2			
E.H.Bowley	absent hurt	-			
Extras	(lb3, w2)	5		(b7, lb5)	12
Total	(100.3 overs, 373 mins)	469		(38.0 overs, 130 mins) (2 wkts)	204

M.C.C.	O	M	R	W	w,nb		O	M	R	W	w,nb		FALL OF WICKETS			
														NSW	MCC	NSW	MCC
Barratt	30	1	130	0	-,-									1st	1st	2nd	2nd
Allom	27	1	127	3	-,-	(1)	19	0	92	0	-,2	Wkt					
Worthington	24	1	151	3	-,1	(2)	13	1	63	1	-,1	1st	26	11	58	22
Bowley	13.3	0	80	2	-,-							2nd	143	82	94	88
Woolley	16	0	77	0	-,2	(3)	12	0	84	2	-,-	3rd	292	96	166	-
Duleepsinhji	4	0	28	0	-,-	(4)	4	0	24	0	-,-	4th	372	361	-	-
Dawson						(5)	3	0	30	0	-,-	5th	417	386	-	-
												6th	602	446		
NEW SOUTH WALES	O	M	R	W	w,nb		O	M	R	W	w,nb	7th	613	446	-	-
Fairfax	27.3	2	102	4	1,-		5	1	7	0	-,-	8th	618	454	-	-
Dupain	25	2	117	2	1,-	(3)	6	1	23	0	-,-	9th	-	469	-	-
Hooker	23	0	102	2	-,-	(2)	9	1	33	1	-,-	10th	-	-	-	-
Bradman	12	0	83	1	-,-		3	0	34	0	-,-					
McCabe	12	1	56	0	-,-	(7)	3	0	21	0	-,-					
Marks	1	0	4	0	-,-	(5)	5	0	28	1	-,-					
Jackson						(6)	4	0	28	0	-,-					
Andrews							2	0	10	0	-,-					
Kippax							1	0	8	0	-,-					

QUEENSLAND v M.C.C.

Played at Brisbane Cricket Ground (Woolloongabba) on November 29, 30, December 2, 1929. (Three-day match)
Toss : M.C.C.   Result : QUEENSLAND WON BY FIVE WICKETS.
Debuts: - Queensland - E.F.Hubbard, H.S.Weir (both f/c).
12th Men: C.B.P.McFarlane (both sides). No 12th available for MCC.
Umpires: J.A.Scott and B.L.Turner.
Attendances: No figures published.   Total: No figures published.   Receipts: £623.
Close of Play: 1st day Qld 6/187 (Hubbard 7, Brew 3); 2nd day MCC (2) 6/165 (Worthington 12, Legge 16).

This was Queensland's first win against an English team in their eight first-class meetings to date, and was achieved with only 3 minutes to spare; it was not until 1982-83 that Queensland won their next match in the series. M.C.C. were beset by injuries and selected in their side Ducat, a Surrey professional who was in Australia to coach the Queensland team. Gilligan had requested that the match be cancelled because of the injury problem, with E.H.Bowley (leg strain), G.F.Earle (back), W.L.Cornford (cut over eye in Melbourne) and F.E.Woolley all out, but this was refused. Queensland also had selection problems with O.E.Nothling being unavailable and E.C.Bensted, V.H.V.Goodwin, H.J.R.Higgins, J.L.Litster, F.C.Thompson and H.M.Thurlow all withdrawing from the team named for the match. Gilligan (53 in 80 minutes, 6 fours and 58 in 105 minutes, 7 fours) and Duleepsinhji (68 in 61 minutes, 9 fours) topscored for the Englishmen, while Levy (86 in 85 minutes, 13 fours), Gough (52 in 95 minutes, 6 fours and 104 in 163 minutes, 11 fours) and Rowe (53 in 135 minutes) did so for the Queenslanders. Benson was struck in the face by a bouncer from Nichols early in the second innings. Duleepsinhji kept wickets in his stead while McFarlane fielded as substitute. *Wisden* incorrectly gives Qld (2) Gough lbw b Nichols. Sources: *Wisden, NSWCA Report, VCA Report, QCA Report, The Age, Sydney Morning Herald, Brisbane Courier-Mail, The Sporting Globe.*

M.C.C.

E.W.Dawson	c Brew b Hornibrook	7		c Hurwood b Amos	26
*A.H.H.Gilligan	b Rowe	53		c Amos b Brew	58
K.S.Duleepsinhji	c Brew b Hurwood	68		b Oxenham	13
A.Ducat	lbw b Oxenham	13		c & b Hurwood	10
M.J.L.Turnbull	c O'Connor b Hurwood	3		b Hornibrook	14
T.S.Worthington	lbw b Oxenham	4	(7)	c Brew b Hornibrook	66
M.S.Nichols	lbw b Oxenham	0	(6)	lbw b Oxenham	9
G.B.Legge	b Oxenham	4		c Amos b Hornibrook	22
F.Barratt	c Hubbard b Hurwood	11		c Levy b Hornibrook	0
†E.T.Benson	c O'Connor b Hurwood	4		c Hornibrook b Amos	14
M.J.C.Allom	not out	0		not out	18
Extras	(b4)	4		(b3, lb6)	9
Total	(39.4 overs, 150 mins)	171		(87.4 overs, 317 mins)	259

QUEENSLAND

*†L.P.D.O'Connor	b Nichols	4		c Nichols b Barratt	3
R.M.Levy	c Duleepsinhji b Nichols	86		c Duleepsinhji b Nichols	5
F.J.Gough	b Nichols	52		c Legge b Nichols	104
W.Rowe	b Nichols	0		c Duleepsinhji b Allom	53
R.K.Oxenham	b Duleepsinhji	26	(6)	not out	2
H.S.Weir	b Nichols	3			
E.F.Hubbard	lbw b Nichols	22			
F.M.Brew	b Nichols	8	(7)	not out	1
A.Hurwood	lbw b Nichols	6			
P.M.Hornibrook	c & b Allom	24			
G.S.Amos	not out	4	(5)	b Allom	5
Extras	(b5, lb5, nb3)	13		(b1, lb7, nb2)	10
Total	(49.3 overs, 220 mins)	248		(40.6 overs, 177 mins) (5 wkts)	183

QUEENSLAND	O	M	R	W	w,nb		O	M	R	W	w,nb
Hornibrook	9	2	26	1	-,-	(3)	22.4	4	75	4	-,-
Hurwood	14.4	3	48	4	-,-		14	4	38	1	-,-
Amos	2	0	21	0	-,-	(1)	18	2	66	2	-,-
Oxenham	9	2	37	4	-,-		26	11	44	2	-,-
Brew	3	0	25	0	-,-	(6)	3	0	15	1	-,-
Rowe	2	1	10	1	-,-	(5)	4	0	12	0	-,-

M.C.C.	O	M	R	W	w,nb		O	M	R	W	w,nb
Nichols	15	1	65	8	-,2		13.6	1	60	2	-,1
Barratt	17	1	70	0	-,-		16	2	57	1	-,-
Allom	11.3	1	67	1	-,1		9	1	39	2	-,-
Worthington	4	0	25	0	-,-		2	0	17	0	-,1
Duleepsinhji	2	0	8	1	-,-						

FALL OF WICKETS

Wkt	MCC 1st	QLD 1st	MCC 2nd	QLD 2nd
1st	22	4	87	5
2nd	131	142	91	13
3rd	133	142	108	171
4th	141	153	118	179
5th	146	157	131	181
6th	146	184	135	-
7th	150	197	196	-
8th	163	203	196	-
9th	171	244	223	-
10th	171	248	259	-

J.RYDER'S XI v W.M.WOODFULL'S XI

Played at Sydney Cricket Ground on December 6, 7, 9, 10, 11, 1929. (Five-day match)
Toss : Ryder's XI.   Result : RYDER'S XI WON BY ONE WICKET.
Debuts: Nil.
12th Men: G.W.Harris (R) and L.S.Darling (W).
Umpires: M.Carney and A.C.Jones.
Attendances: 6747, 12938, 4944, 3706, ? .   Total: 28,335.   Receipts: £1761.
Close of Play: 1st day Ryder 4/433 (Marks 64, Horrocks 8); 2nd day Woodfull 4/184 (Bradman 54, Rigg 35); 3rd day Woodfull (2) 2/341
    (Bradman 205, Kippax 58); 4th day Ryder (2) 8/152 (Ponsford 8, Ryder 9).

Teams of near-equal strength were chosen to aid selection for the forthcoming tour of England. All states including Tasmania and Western
Australia were asked to nominate players for consideration. Burrows and Ellis replacing E.L.a'Beckett (exams) and W.A.S.Oldfield (injured
finger) in Woodfull's side. Jackson (182 in 187 minutes, 1 six and 27 fours) and Ponsford (131 in 242 minutes, 1 six and 10 fours) began
brilliantly, Marks (83 in 163 minutes, 10 fours), Whitfield (68 in 94 minutes, 8 fours) and Oxenham (84 not out in 143 minutes, 7 fours)
also scoring well. Alexander began Woodfull's XI's first innings with three successive wides. Bradman (124 in 166 minutes, 16 fours and
225 in 252 minutes, 1 five and 28 fours) scored 275 runs in 325 minutes on the third day, including 120 between tea and stumps after
opening the second innings. Bradman's twin centuries overshadowed Rigg (73 in 99 minutes, 1 six and 7 fours) and even Kippax (170 in
268 minutes, 21 fours). *Wisden* incorrectly gives Woodfull (1) Marks 0/39, McCabe 0/26. Sources: *Wisden, NSWCA Report, VCA
Report, The Age, Sydney Morning Herald, Sydney Referee.*

RYDER'S XI

A.Jackson	c Kippax b Hornibrook	182	(7)	c Ellis b Hornibrook	15
W.H.Ponsford	c Rigg b Blackie	131	(9)	c Fairfax b Hornibrook	25
A.E.Marks	c Kippax b Blackie	83	(2)	run out (Wall/Blackie)	14
*J.Ryder	c Rigg b Hornibrook	6	(10)	not out	18
S.J.McCabe	c Kippax b Burrows	35	(1)	c Fairfax b Blackie	46
W.J.Horrocks	lbw b Blackie	25	(3)	c Burrows b Blackie	5
H.E.Whitfield	c Bradman b Hornibrook	68	(4)	lbw b Blackie	20
R.K.Oxenham	not out	84	(6)	c & b Hornibrook	4
†C.W.Walker	c Wall b Bradman	12	(5)	run out (Rigg)	9
C.V.Grimmett	c Blackie b Wall	13	(11)	not out	7
H.H.Alexander	c Allsopp b Wall	6	(8)	b Hornibrook	8
Extras	(b8, lb8, w1, nb1)	18		(b8, lb12)	20
Total	(130.7 overs, 510 mins)	663		(49.0 overs, 170 mins) (9 wkts)	191

WOODFULL'S XI

*W.M.Woodfull	st Walker b Oxenham	36		c & b Grimmett	43
A.G.Fairfax	c & Alexander	27	(3)	st Walker b Grimmett	26
A.F.Kippax	st Walker b Grimmett	17	(4)	c Walker b Oxenham	170
D.G.Bradman	c Jackson b Oxenham	124	(2)	lbw b Grimmett	225
A.H.Allsopp	b Oxenham	4		c McCabe b Grimmett	5
K.E.Rigg	b Whitfield	73		c Ponsford b McCabe	9
A.O.Burrows	b Oxenham	7		c & b Grimmett	0
†J.L.Ellis	lbw b Oxenham	4		b Oxenham	24
D.D.Blackie	c McCabe b Grimmett	0		b Grimmett	11
P.M.Hornibrook	st Walker b Grimmett	2		c Alexander b Grimmett	1
T.W.Wall	not out	0		not out	2
Extras	(b2, lb9, w3, nb1)	15		(b14, lb7, w3, nb1)	25
Total	(60.6 overs, 235 mins)	309		(106.5 overs, 387 mins)	541

WOODFULL'S XI	O	M	R	W	w,nb		O	M	R	W	w,nb
Wall	27.7	0	131	2	-,1		5	0	20	0	-,-
Hornibrook	22	4	102	3	-,-	(3)	22	4	67	4	-,-
Fairfax	27	0	116	0	-,-	(2)	2	0	19	0	-,-
Blackie	29	0	163	3	-,-		20	3	65	3	-,-
Burrows	14	1	77	1	1,-						
Bradman	11	0	56	1	-,-						

RYDER'S XI	O	M	R	W	w,nb		O	M	R	W	w,nb
Alexander	11	1	73	1	3,1		11	0	73	0	1,1
Whitfield	12	2	46	1	-,-		14	0	71	0	2,-
Oxenham	14.6	2	42	5	-,-		30.5	7	97	2	-,-
Grimmett	15	2	68	3	-,-		33	3	173	7	-,-
Marks	3	0	26	0	-,-	(6)	6	0	45	0	-,-
McCabe	5	0	39	0	-,-	(5)	7	1	42	1	-,-
Ryder							5	0	15	0	-,-

FALL OF WICKETS

Wkt	1st	1st	2nd	2nd
	R	W	W	R
1st	278	50	94	55
2nd	347	85	160	65
3rd	364	93	378	76
4th	424	98	394	97
5th	472	269	417	104
6th	482	286	418	115
7th	594	298	495	131
8th	624	299	524	138
9th	651	301	530	183
10th	663	309	541	-

VICTORIA v QUEENSLAND (Shield Match 2)

Played at Melbourne Cricket Ground on December 18, 19, 20, 1929. (Five-day match)
Toss : Queensland.   Result : VICTORIA WON BY FIVE WICKETS.
Debuts: Nil.
12th Men: L.S.Darling (Vic) and H.F.Leeson (Qld).
Umpires: F.W.Dixon and B.Heathcote.
Attendances: 3971, 4074, 2583.   Total: 10,628   Receipts: £296.
Close of Play: 1st day Vic 4/52 (Rigg 2); 2nd day Vic (2) 1/10 (Ryder 4, Ellis 3).

Levy (50 in 91 minutes, 1 six and 5 fours) and Gough (68 in 155 minutes, 9 fours) for Queensland and Rigg (79 not out in 121 minutes, 5 fours) and a'Beckett (56 in 99 minutes, 4 fours) for Victoria were the only batsmen to surpass 30 in what was a low-scoring affair; the last two named shared a fifth-wicket stand of 125 to clinch the game for the home team after victory seemed unlikely at 4/30. Woodfull retired at 0/2 early in the first innings when he was struck on the left hand by Thurlow's third ball, sustaining several broken bones which ruled him out for the rest of the season. a'Beckett fell on his wicket when he recoiled after being struck by his first ball, the bowler again being Thurlow. Although rain in the days leading up to the match softened the wicket surrounds and slowed the pace of the outfield, the covered pitch was unaffected and was not held responsible for the low scoring. *Wisden* incorrectly gives Vic (1) a'Beckett b Thurlow. *NSWCA Report* incorrectly gives Woodfull as Vic captain. Sources: *Wisden, NSWCA Report, VCA Report, QCA Report, The Age, The Argus, The Herald, Melbourne Sun.*

QUEENSLAND

*†L.P.D.O'Connor	b Ironmonger	27	run out (a'Beckett/Ellis)		4
R.M.Levy	c Rigg b Blackie	50	b Blackie		14
F.J.Gough	c & b Ironmonger	0	b Blackie		68
F.C.Thompson	lbw b Blackie	7	lbw b Blackie		1
W.Rowe	not out	18	b Ironmonger		12
E.C.Bensted	c Ellis b Ironmonger	3	(7) lbw b Blackie		3
V.H.V.Goodwin	lbw b a'Beckett	4	(6) c Scaife b Blackie		17
F.M.Brew	b a'Beckett	0	run out (Scaife/Ellis)		2
A.Hurwood	b a'Beckett	2	b Ironmonger		1
G.S.Amos	lbw b Ironmonger	0	b Ryder		21
H.M.Thurlow	b a'Beckett	0	not out		3
Extras	(lb2, nb1)	3	(b9, lb1, nb2)		12
Total	(53.4 overs, 204 mins)	114	(59.1 overs, 215 mins)		158

VICTORIA

W.M.Woodfull	retired hurt	2			
W.H.Ponsford	c Goodwin b Thurlow	28	c Amos b Hurwood		3
H.S.T.L.Hendry	b Hurwood	6	(4) c Hurwood b Thurlow		12
*J.Ryder	b Bensted	7	(1) lbw b Hurwood		4
K.E.Rigg	c Hurwood b Thurlow	25	not out		79
E.L.a'Beckett	hit wkt b Thurlow	0	lbw b Amos		56
J.W.Scaife	c Levy b Thurlow	13	not out		6
H.I.Ebeling	c O'Connor b Hurwood	14			
†J.L.Ellis	b Thurlow	0	(3) c Levy b Thurlow		5
D.D.Blackie	b Thurlow	2			
H.Ironmonger	not out	0			
Extras	(b5, lb4, nb1)	10	(b1, lb1, nb1)		3
Total	(24.5 overs, 108 mins)	107	(37.3 overs, 149 mins) (5 wkts)		168

VICTORIA	O	M	R	W	w,nb	O	M	R	W	w,nb		FALL OF WICKETS			
a'Beckett	7.4	1	25	4	-,-	10	3	19	0	-,-	Wkt	QLD 1st	VIC 1st	QLD 2nd	VIC 2nd
Ebeling	10	1	26	0	-,-	8	1	22	0	-,-	1st	70	24	8	6
Blackie	20	5	40	2	-,1	15	6	28	5	-,-	2nd	73	46	32	11
Ironmonger	16	6	20	4	-,-	24	8	54	2	-,2	3rd	79	52	34	15
Ryder						2.1	0	23	1	-,-	4th	89	52	82	30
											5th	92	78	122	155
QUEENSLAND	O	M	R	W	w,nb	O	M	R	W	w,nb	6th	100	91	128	-
Thurlow	11.5	0	60	6	-,1	14	2	77	2	-,-	7th	100	91	133	-
Hurwood	11	1	33	2	-,-	15	1	42	2	-,-	8th	104	107	134	-
Amos	1	0	2	0	-,-	3	0	20	1	-,1	9th	109	107	134	-
Bensted	1	0	2	1	-,-						10th	114	-	158	-
Rowe						(4) 3	1	14	0	-,-					
Brew						(5) 2.3	0	12	0	-,-					

SOUTH AUSTRALIA v NEW SOUTH WALES (Shield Match 3)

Played at Adelaide Oval on December 19, 20, 21, 23, 24, 1929. (Five-day match)
Toss : New South Wales.   Result : SOUTH AUSTRALIA WON BY FIVE WICKETS.
Debuts: South Australia - H.C.Nitschke (f/c).
12th Men: H.K.Sincock (SA) and W.C.Andrews (NSW).
Umpires: T.W.Cook and G.A.Hele.
Attendances: 4892, 6176, 10475, 5277, 2381.   Total: 29,201.   Receipts: £1185.
Close of Play: 1st day SA 0/21 (Harris 14, Hone 6); 2nd day SA 2/364 (Pritchard 142, Richardson 37); 3rd day NSW (2) 2/178 (Marks 2, Davidson 1); 4th day SA (2) 1/76 (Hone 44, Pritchard 14).

Fifties were scored in each innings for New South Wales by McCabe (69 in 76 minutes, 8 fours and 70 in 81 minutes, 6 fours) and Allsopp (77 in 103 minutes, 1 six and 9 fours and 73 in 113 minutes, 5 fours). Davidson (52 in 70 minutes, 5 fours) contributed in the late order while Jackson (82 in 145 minutes, 1 six and 4 fours) and Bradman (84 in 142 minutes, 5 fours) added 172 for the first wicket in the second innings. Campbell, who split a finger on his bowling hand while fielding a drive from Hone before lunch on the second day, left the field and was unable to bowl or field again in the match. Century partnerships were scored for South Australia's first three wickets, Hone (126 in 275 minutes, 5 fours, chance at 107) and Pritchard (148 in 250 minutes, 12 fours) getting hundreds. Each also scored a second-innings fifty, Hone, 61 (135 minutes, 4 fours) and Pritchard 75 (141 minutes, 2 fives, and 7 fours), victory coming with half an hour to spare. Diagnosed with tuberculosis, Jackson was confined to an Adelaide hospital bed for several days after the match. Sources: *Wisden, NSWCA Report, SACA Report, Adelaide Advertiser, The News, C.B.O'Reilly, South Australian Register.*

NEW SOUTH WALES

A.G.Fairfax	c Wall b Whitfield	39	(9)	c Hone b Grimmett	46
A.Jackson	c Walker b Grimmett	19	(1)	c Pritchard b Grimmett	82
D.G.Bradman	run out (Lonergan/Walker)	2	(2)	lbw b Grimmett	84
*A.F.Kippax	c Palmer b Wall	26	(5)	b Palmer	6
A.E.Marks	c & b Wall	1	(3)	c Pritchard b Whitfield	23
S.J.McCabe	b Wall	69		lbw b Grimmett	70
A.H.Allsopp	c Walker b Grimmett	77		c & b Grimmett	73
S.C.Everett	lbw b Whitfield	1		b Whitfield	10
†H.L.Davidson	c Richardson b Grimmett	52	(4)	c & b Grimmett	7
J.E.H.Hooker	not out	13		c Pritchard b Grimmett	9
J.N.Campbell	c Pritchard b Whitfield	7		not out	4
Extras	(lb3, nb5)	8		(b13, lb5, nb2)	20
Total	(76.1 overs, 292 mins)	314		(107.1 overs, 376 mins)	434

SOUTH AUSTRALIA

G.W.Harris	st Davidson b Campbell	46	c Davidson b Hooker	10
B.W.Hone	b Hooker	126	run out (sub W.C.Andrews/Davidson)	61
D.E.Pritchard	c McCabe b Hooker	148	c & b McCabe	75
*V.Y.Richardson	b Fairfax	64	c Marks b Hooker	44
H.C.Nitschke	lbw b Fairfax	12	b Fairfax	10
H.E.Whitfield	c Allsopp b Bradman	45	not out	7
A.R.Lonergan	c Davidson b Fairfax	0	not out	21
C.V.Grimmett	run out (Marks/Everett)	35		
†C.W.Walker	b Everett	2		
T.W.Wall	c Everett b Bradman	3		
G.H.Palmer	not out	4		
Extras	(b7, lb9, nb7)	23	(b2, lb8, nb6)	16
Total	(139.4 overs, 504 mins)	508	(58.6 overs, 214 mins) (5 wkts)	244

SOUTH AUSTRALIA	O	M	R	W	w,nb		O	M	R	W	w,nb
Wall	17	1	74	3	-,4		5	0	25	0	-,1
Whitfield	15.1	1	67	3	-,1		25	2	104	2	-,1
Grimmett	31	9	91	3	-,-		44.1	5	136	7	-,-
Palmer	13	2	74	0	-,-		26	3	121	1	-,-
Richardson							7	0	28	0	-,-

NEW SOUTH WALES	O	M	R	W	w,nb		O	M	R	W	w,nb
Everett	33	6	117	1	-,1		11	2	30	0	-,2
Fairfax	29	5	80	3	-,6		17	0	39	1	-,3
Campbell	9.5	0	42	1	-,-						
Hooker	29	4	100	2	-,-	(3)	19.6	2	89	2	-,1
Bradman	21.7	0	93	2	-,-		1	0	8	0	-,-
McCabe	13	3	46	0	-,-	(4)	7	0	39	1	-,-
Kippax	4	2	7	0	-,-	(6)	3	0	23	0	-,-

FALL OF WICKETS

Wkt	NSW 1st	SA 1st	NSW 2nd	SA 2nd
1st	34	100	172	28
2nd	40	275	175	124
3rd	82	378	185	194
4th	85	403	202	212
5th	104	412	237	219
6th	199	412	321	-
7th	209	498	351	-
8th	262	499	387	-
9th	303	502	407	-
10th	314	508	434	-

SOUTH AUSTRALIA v QUEENSLAND (Shield Match 4)

Played at Adelaide Oval on December 25, 26, 27 (no play), 28, 30, 1929. (Five-day match)
Toss : Queensland.   Result : MATCH DRAWN.
Debuts: Nil.
12th Men: G.H.Palmer (SA) and H.F.Leeson (Qld).
Umpires: A.G.Jenkins and E.B.Selth.
Attendances: 5390, 6098, no play, 7362, 5746.   Total: 24,596.   Receipts: £1099.
Close of Play: 1st day Qld 380 all out; 2nd day SA 6/363 (Hack 18, Grimmett 15); 3rd day no play; 4th day Qld (2) 209 all out.

Chasing 209 for victory on the last morning, South Australia collapsed to lose 7 for 36 and it was left to tail-enders Grimmett and Carlton to survive four overs, somewhat shakily, to salvage a draw for the home side. Carlton's brief innings included a chance to Brew off Hurwood, while Grimmett offered a possible chance in the slips in the last scheduled over, again off Hurwood's bowling. Rowe (17) the non-striker, was forced to retire at 3/80 on the opening day of the match when a straight drive by Thompson struck him hard in the kidneys "dropping him like a log". He resumed at 4/220 but did not add to his score. Thompson (74 in 158 minutes, 7 fours) and Bensted (82 in 108 minutes, 1 five and 10 fours) added 140 for the fourth wicket and Goodwin (93 in 95 minutes, 1 five and 9 fours) and Hurwood (51 in 88 minutes) added a new Queensland record of 140 for the eighth wicket. Levy (40 in 40 minutes, 3 fours) topscored in the second innings. South Australia gained the slimmest of first innings leads through contributions from Harris (78 in 115 minutes, 6 fours), Pritchard (62 in 91 minutes, 6 fours) and Richardson (126 in 147 minutes, 15 fours), after rain had prevented any play on the third day. Sincock, originally named as 12th man, replaced N.L.Williams (work commitments) in the South Australian team. *Wisden* incorrectly gives Qld (2) Bensted c Harris b Carlton. Hurwood c Carlton b Whitfield; SA (1) Whitfield 10, Grimmett 24; SA (2) Harris 16, Whitfield 2. Sources: *Wisden, QCA Report, SACA Report, Adelaide Advertiser, The News, South Australian Register, C.B.O'Reilly.*

QUEENSLAND

*†L.P.D.O'Connor	c Pritchard b Grimmett	13	c Whitfield b Carlton		27
R.M.Levy	b Whitfield	14	c Harris b Whitfield		40
F.J.Gough	c & b Grimmett	18	c Harris b Carlton		15
F.C.Thompson	c Walker b Grimmett	74	(5) c Pritchard b Grimmett		29
W.Rowe	b Grimmett	17	(6) c Hack b Carlton		36
E.C.Bensted	c & b Carlton	82	(4) c Harris b Whitfield		19
V.H.V.Goodwin	c Walker b Grimmett	93	(9) c Richardson b Whitfield		10
F.M.Brew	st Walker b Grimmett	5	(10) c Carlton b Whitfield		6
A.Hurwood	c Sincock b Whitfield	51	(7) c Whitfield b Carlton		23
G.S.Amos	c Carlton b Whitfield	0	(8) st Walker b Grimmett		0
H.M.Thurlow	not out	2	not out		1
Extras	(b5, lb5, nb1)	11	(b1, lb2)		3
Total	(95.1 overs, 316 mins)	380	(51.1 overs, 170 mins)		209

SOUTH AUSTRALIA

G.W.Harris	c O'Connor b Hurwood	78	st O'Connor b Hurwood		15
B.W.Hone	c O'Connor b Brew	24	c Hurwood b Amos		35
D.E.Pritchard	run out (Rowe/Thompson)	62	c Gough b Thurlow		43
*V.Y.Richardson	c Thurlow b Bensted	126	st O'Connor b Hurwood		42
H.E.Whitfield	b Rowe	19	(6) run out (Goodwin)		3
H.C.Nitschke	c Gough b Amos	10	(5) c Gough b Hurwood		2
A.T.Hack	c Amos b Hurwood	24	(8) b Thurlow		2
C.V.Grimmett	c Brew b Hurwood	15	(9) not out		12
H.K.Sincock	c Goodwin b Hurwood	11	(7) c Thompson b Hurwood		17
†C.W.Walker	run out (Goodwin/O'Connor)	1	b Hurwood		0
T.A.Carlton	not out	0	not out		0
Extras	(b4, lb6, w1)	11	(b3, lb3)		6
Total	(91.1 overs, 337 mins)	381	(38.0 overs, 150 mins) (9 wkts)		177

SOUTH AUSTRALIA	O	M	R	W	w,nb		O	M	R	W	w,nb
Whitfield	17.1	3	51	3	-,-	(2)	15.1	2	53	4	-,-
Carlton	23	3	83	1	-,-	(1)	21	4	85	4	-,-
Grimmett	34	2	146	6	-,-		15	1	68	2	-,-
Sincock	10	0	53	0	-,1						
Richardson	8	1	21	0	-,-						
Hack	3	0	15	0	-,-						

QUEENSLAND	O	M	R	W	w,nb		O	M	R	W	w,nb
Thurlow	16	2	60	0	-,-		15	1	72	2	-,-
Hurwood	27.1	6	81	4	-,-		16	4	62	5	-,-
Amos	8	0	51	1	1,-	(4)	3	0	13	1	-,-
Brew	12	1	70	1	-,-						
Thompson	12	1	40	0	-,-		1	0	5	0	-,-
Rowe	11	2	56	1	-,-						
Bensted	5	1	12	1	-,-	(3)	3	0	19	0	-,-

FALL OF WICKETS

	QLD 1st	SA 1st	QLD 2nd	SA 2nd
Wkt				
1st	21	64	58	23
2nd	48	156	75	66
3rd	51	192	82	134
4th	220	255	129	142
5th	225	270	132	145
6th	230	340	179	146
7th	236	363	180	156
8th	376	376	201	170
9th	377	381	201	170
10th	380	381	209	-

VICTORIA v NEW SOUTH WALES (Shield Match 5)

Played at Melbourne Cricket Ground on December 26, 27, 28, 30, 31 1929. (Five-day match)
Toss : Victoria.   Result : MATCH DRAWN.
Debuts: New South Wales - H.C.Chilvers (all f/c).
12th Men: L.S.Darling (Vic) and W.C.Andrews (NSW).
Umpires: W.J.Moore and J.Richards.
Attendances: 12645, 15984, 5274, 10714, 4153.   Total: 48,770.   Receipts: £1654.
Close of Play: 1st day NSW 0/8 (Phillips 6, Fairfax 2); 2nd day NSW 7/358 (Davidson 0, Everett 2); 3rd day Vic (2) 2/33 (Hendry 3, J.L.Ellis 11); 4th day Vic (2) 7/341 (Scaife 60, Blackie 37).

Chilvers and Phillips replaced J.N.Campbell (injured) and A.Jackson (ill) in the New South Wales side prior to the start. Rain and bad light caused several interruptions on the first day and restricted play on the third day to 17 minutes before lunch plus the tea to stumps session. Everett dismissed Ryder with the last ball of the first over of the match and took three wickets in four balls - Scaife, ball, Alexander, Ironmonger - to finish off Victoria's first innings in which Ponsford (65 in 100 minutes, 2 fours), Hendry (43 in 70 minutes, 2 fours) and Rigg (44 in 66 minutes, 3 fours) were the topscorers. Bradman (89 in 100 minutes, 12 fours), Kippax (80 in 142 minutes, 9 fours), Marks (68 in 124 minutes, 8 fours) and McCabe (70 in 100 minutes, 9 fours) combined to give New South Wales a lead of 173 on the first innings. Hendry (103 in 253 minutes, 3 fours), a'Beckett (50 in 121 minutes, 4 fours) and Scaife (60 not out in 98 minutes, 3 fours) topscored in Victoria's second innings to set New South Wales 171 for victory in two hours. Phillips (45 in 100 minutes, 3 fours) and McCabe (50 not out in 58 minutes, 5 fours) batted well until time ran out. *NSWCA Report* incorrectly gives Vic (2) Ironmonger b Hooker. Sources: *Wisden, NSWCA Report, VCA Report, The Age, The Argus, The Herald, Melbourne Sun.*

VICTORIA

*J.Ryder	c Davidson b Everett	0	(5) c & b McCabe		1
W.H.Ponsford	c Davidson b Hooker	65	c Allsopp b Fairfax		12
R.N.Ellis	b Everett	25	(1) c Davidson b Fairfax		4
H.S.T.L.Hendry	run out (Everett)	43	(3) run out (Marks/Everett)		103
K.E.Rigg	lbw b Hooker	44	(6) b Fairfax		24
E.L.a'Beckett	c & b McCabe	7	(7) c Chilvers b Everett		50
J.W.Scaife	c Fairfax b Everett	17	(8) not out		60
†J.L.Ellis	lbw b Hooker	6	(4) b Chilvers		40
D.D.Blackie	not out	15	lbw b Fairfax		37
H.H.Alexander	c Davidson b Everett	0	b Fairfax		0
H.Ironmonger	b Everett	0	c Davidson b Hooker		1
Extras	(lb5, nb2)	7	(lb4, nb7)		11
Total	(53.4 overs, 213 mins)	229	(110.2 overs, 372 mins)		343

NEW SOUTH WALES

N.E.Phillips	c Blackie b Alexander	10	st J.L.Ellis b Ryder		45
A.G.Fairfax	c Blackie b a'Beckett	2	c & b Blackie		15
D.G.Bradman	b Alexander	89	(4) not out		26
*A.F.Kippax	lbw b Blackie	80			
A.E.Marks	b Alexander	68			
S.J.McCabe	c J.L.Ellis b Ironmonger	70	(3) not out		50
A.H.Allsopp	c Ironmonger b a'Beckett	26			
†H.L.Davidson	c J.L.Ellis b Blackie	24			
S.C.Everett	lbw b Blackie	17			
J.E.H.Hooker	c Ponsford b Ironmonger	3			
H.C.Chilvers	not out	0			
Extras	(b6, lb6, nb1)	13	(b8, nb1)		9
Total	(92.7 overs, 349 mins)	402	(34.0 overs, 123 mins) (2 wkts)		145

NEW SOUTH WALES	O	M	R	W	w,nb		O	M	R	W	w,nb					
Everett	12.4	2	57	5	-,1		22	4	61	1	-,1					
Fairfax	16	2	54	0	-,-		32	2	104	5	-,5					
Phillips	3	0	24	0	-,-											
Hooker	13	0	48	3	-,1	(3)	16.2	4	49	1	-,1					
McCabe	9	1	39	1	-,-		11	0	34	1	-,-					
Chilvers						(4)	29	2	84	1	-,-					

FALL OF WICKETS				
	VIC	NSW	VIC	NSW
Wkt	1st	1st	2nd	2nd
1st	1	8	18	53
2nd	68	24	19	103
3rd	107	151	85	-
4th	167	223	86	-
5th	185	311	126	-
6th	187	356	240	-
7th	197	356	244	-
8th	229	393	341	-
9th	229	402	341	-
10th	229	402	343	-

VICTORIA	O	M	R	W	w,nb		O	M	R	W	w,nb
Alexander	16	1	115	3	-,1		4	1	8	0	-,-
a'Beckett	19	2	48	2	-,-		7	2	12	0	-,-
Hendry	4	0	27	0	-,-	(7)	1	0	2	0	-,-
Ironmonger	28.7	5	89	2	-,-	(3)	8	0	33	0	-,-
Blackie	20	4	71	3	-,-	(4)	6	0	31	1	-,-
R.N.Ellis	4	0	33	0	-,-		4	0	27	0	-,-
Ryder	1	0	6	0	-,-	(5)	4	0	23	1	-,1

TASMANIA v VICTORIA

Played at T.C.A. Ground, Hobart, on December 26, 27, 28 (no play), 1929. (Three-day match)
Toss : Tasmania.   Result : MATCH DRAWN.
Debuts: Victoria - H.T.Baring, B.A.Barnett, A.P.Chivers, E.L.McCormick, L.P.J.O'Brien, J.O.Perraton, J.Thomas (all f/c).
12th Men: A.W.Rushforth (Tas 1st day), D.K.Brain (Tas 2nd day) and E.T.Austen (Vic).
Umpires: M.Leonard and W.T.Lonergan.
Attendances: No figures published.   Total: About 1200.   Receipts: £60.
Close of Play: 1st day Tas 2/10 (Townley 4, Wood 4); 2nd day Tas (2) 0/25 (Atkinson 19, Townley 5).

Austen replaced R.N.Ellis (transferred to Shield match against New South Wales) in the selected Victorian team. Sent in after rain delayed the start until 12.45pm, the visitors struggled on a damp wicket, Tolhurst (51 in 98 minutes, 4 fours) and Liddicut (39 in 57 minutes, 5 fours) making the topscores. Liddicut then bowled unchanged to return career-best figures of 7 for 40. O'Brien on debut scored 87 in 76 minutes with 12 fours in the second innings. Barnett, another of seven debutants, continued in first-class cricket until 1961, when he played in England aged 53. Heavy rain prevented play on the scheduled last day. Late on the second day controversy arose when umpire Leonard signalled a wide for a ball which slipped from McCormick's hand in the delivery stride and rolled about halfway down the wicket, the batsmen decided to run one without hitting the ball. It is believed the scorers incorrectly gave two wides to the Tasmanian total (newspapers and *TCA Report* give Tas (2) extras 2, total 0/26) over the incident. *VCA Report* gives 0/24 - overruling the umpire's decision as well as the scorer's mistake - but the score given here is in accordance with the umpire's decision (although incorrect) followed by correct scoring procedure. No evidence has been found of Leonard's decision being subsequently revoked in favour of the correct "dead ball - no run". Sources: *VCA Report, TCA Report, The Age, The Argus, Hobart Mercury.*

VICTORIA

L.P.J.O'Brien	b Burrows	15		c Pickett b Burrows	87
A.J.W.Lansdown	c Atkinson b Hooper	0	(4)	b James	25
H.T.Baring	c Atkinson b Burrows	11	(2)	c Wood b James	9
†B.A.Barnett	c Richardson b Newton	4	(3)	c Wood b Hooper	26
F.D.Chapman	b Newton	3	(8)	b Townley	8
E.K.Tolhurst	b Burrows	51	(7)	c James b Hooper	4
J.O.Perraton	c & b Hooper	13	(5)	lbw b Burrows	0
*A.E.Liddicut	c Richardson b Burrows	39	(9)	c Wood b Hooper	3
J.Thomas	b Newton	2	(6)	lbw b James	8
E.L.McCormick	c Newton b Burrows	3	(11)	b Hooper	4
A.P.Chivers	not out	7	(10)	not out	5
Extras	(b5, lb2, nb1)	8		(b10, lb2, nb1)	13
Total	(59.1 overs, 213 mins)	156		(38.1 overs, 143 mins)	192

TASMANIA

R.C.Townley	c McCormick b Liddicut	8	(2)	not out	5
†E.A.Pickett	c Baring b Liddicut	0			
V.L.Hooper	c Chivers b Liddicut	0			
C.C.Wood	c Lansdown b McCormick	5			
*J.A.Atkinson	b Chivers	14	(1)	not out	19
D.C.Green	c Chivers b Liddicut	3			
V.R.Driscoll	lbw b Liddicut	0			
A.O.Burrows	not out	18			
L.W.Richardson	c Barnett b Chivers	6			
A.C.Newton	c Chivers b Liddicut	6			
G.T.H.James	c Perraton b Liddicut	12			
Extras	(b3, lb1, nb1)	5		(w1)	1
Total	(26.7 overs, 109 mins)	77		(5.0 overs, 19 mins) (0 wkts)	25

TASMANIA	O	M	R	W	w,nb		O	M	R	W	w,nb		FALL OF WICKETS			
												Wkt	VIC	TAS	VIC	TAS
Burrows	23.1	5	38	5	-,-		10	1	42	2	-,-			1st	1st	2nd	2nd
Hooper	12	2	23	2	-,1	(3)	9.1	1	50	4	-,1		1st	2	4	26	-
Newton	15	0	62	3	-,-	(5)	1	0	3	0	-,-		2nd	21	4	93	-
James	7	2	14	0	-,-	(2)	13	3	49	3	-,-		3rd	26	11	138	-
Atkinson	2	0	11	0	-,-								4th	30	15	138	-
Townley						(4)	5	0	35	1	-,-		5th	34	33	159	-
													6th	88	35	166	-
VICTORIA	O	M	R	W	w,nb		O	M	R	W	w,nb		7th	115	35	168	-
Liddicut	13.7	2	40	7	-,-		3	0	13	0	-,-		8th	136	44	182	-
McCormick	7	3	11	1	-,1		2	0	11	0	1,-		9th	148	63	188	-
Chapman	1	0	4	0	-,-								10th	156	77	192	-
Chivers	5	1	17	2	-,-												

TASMANIA v VICTORIA

Played at N.T.C.A. Ground, Launceston, on December 31, 1929, January 1, 2, 1930. (Three-day match)
Toss : Victoria.　　　　　　　　　Result : VICTORIA WON BY AN INNINGS AND 80 RUNS.
Debuts: Tasmania - L.J.Nash (f/c).
12th Men: T.D.Room (Tas) and J.Thomas.
Umpires: E.C.Knight and F.C.Tabart.
Attendances & Receipts: No figures published.
Close of Play: 1st day Vic 6/355 (Perraton 4, Liddicut 16); 2nd day Tas (2) 0/40 (Atkinson 23, Wood 14).

D.C.Green (injured) was unavailable for Tasmania. Driscoll tore a ligament while fielding on the first day and took no further part. Austen, his only century, last first-class innings, (122 in 224 minutes, 10 fours) and Barnett, his second match and maiden hundred, (131 in 165 minutes, 9 fours) added 178 for the Victorian fourth wicket while Liddicut's unbeaten 75 occupied 90 minutes and included 6 fours. Atkinson, who survived a difficult chance at the wicket before he had scored from the third ball, carried his bat for Tasmania and hit 8 fours. Of the rest only Burrows (18 in 57 minutes) and Hooper (10 in 29 minutes) reached double figures. Following on, Atkinson (41 in 75 minutes, 2 fours), Wood (20 in 84 minutes), Burrows (35 in 75 minutes, 2 fours) and Nash (48 in 74 minutes, 3 fours) each batted more than one hour. Sources: *VCA Report, The Age, The Argus, Launceston Examiner, Hobart Mercury.*

VICTORIA

E.T.Austen	c Martin b James	122
L.P.J.O'Brien	c Pickett b Nash	10
E.K.Tolhurst	b James	18
H.T.Baring	b Nash	13
†B.A.Barnett	c Atkinson b Hooper	131
A.J.W.Lansdown	b Hooper	32
J.O.Perraton	run out (　　　　/James)	5
*A.E.Liddicut	not out	75
F.D.Chapman	b Burrows	29
E.L.McCormick	b Newton	0
A.P.Chivers	lbw b James	11
Extras	(b3, lb4, nb3)	10
Total	(95.5 overs, 362 mins)	456

TASMANIA

*J.A.Atkinson	not out	104	c Barnett b Lansdown		41
C.C.Wood	c Barnett b McCormick	6	lbw b Lansdown		20
L.W.Richardson	c Baring b Chapman	2	c Perraton b Lansdown		2
A.O.Burrows	b Lansdown	18	b Chivers		35
G.W.Martin	b McCormick	0	c Barnett b Chivers		16
L.J.Nash	b Lansdown	1	b Perraton		48
A.C.Newton	b McCormick	4	c Barnett b Chivers		4
†E.A.Pickett	b McCormick	9	not out		16
V.L.Hooper	b Chivers	10	b Perraton		0
G.T.H.James	b Chapman	3	b McCormick		3
V.R.Driscoll	absent hurt	-	absent hurt		-
Extras	(b7, lb6, nb3)	16	(b10, lb7, nb1)		18
Total	(39.3 overs, 155 mins)	173	(52.2 overs, 202 mins)		203

TASMANIA	O	M	R	W	w,nb
Nash	23	3	97	2	-,-
Burrows	22	1	86	1	-,-
Hooper	12	0	74	2	-,3
James	21.5	3	101	3	-,-
Newton	11	1	45	1	-,-
Atkinson	2	0	19	0	-,-
Wood	4	0	24	0	-,-

VICTORIA	O	M	R	W	w,nb		O	M	R	W	w,nb
McCormick	12	1	52	4	-,1	(4)	9.2	1	21	1	-,-
Chapman	11.3	2	36	2	-,1		11	1	48	0	-,1
Chivers	7	2	19	1	-,1	(5)	11	2	32	3	-,-
Lansdown	8	0	48	2	-,-	(3)	13	1	65	3	-,-
Perraton	1	0	2	0	-,-	(1)	8	2	19	2	-,-

FALL OF WICKETS

Wkt	VIC 1st	TAS 1st	TAS 2nd
1st	19	9	66
2nd	38	20	70
3rd	78	72	70
4th	256	73	99
5th	334	80	150
6th	335	93	160
7th	356	109	186
8th	419	154	186
9th	420	173	203
10th	456	-	-

VICTORIA v SOUTH AUSTRALIA (Shield Match 6)

Played at Melbourne Cricket Ground on January 1, 2, 3, 4, 6, 1930. (Five-day match)
Toss : South Australia.   Result : VICTORIA WON BY SEVEN WICKETS.
Debuts: Nil.
12th Men: L.S.Darling (Vic) and G.H.Palmer (SA).
Umpires: A.N.Barlow and D.A.Elder.
Attendances: 15476, 15713, 10156, 19299, ? .   Total: 60,644.   Receipts: £2389.
Close of Play: 1st day SA 8/226 (Grimmett 12); 2nd day Vic 7/297 (Scaife 51, Blackie 21); 3rd day SA (2) 4/235 (Hone 104, Walker 0);
    4th day Vic (2) 2/200 (Ponsford 107, Ryder 23).

Hone (46 in 103 minutes, 3 fours), Pritchard (36 in 103 minutes, 2 fours), Nitschke (53 in 140 minutes, 5 fours) and Hack (44 in 158 minutes, 3 fours) all batted doggedly for South Australia on a slow-scoring first day. Ponsford (47 in 64 minutes, 4 fours), Ryder (77 in 149 minutes, 7 fours) and Scaife (69 in 137 minutes, 8 fours) led Victoria's reply. Hone did not field on the second day due to a back strain sustained while batting. However, aided by missed chances at 17 and 90, he went on to score 106 in 275 minutes with 8 fours in South Australia's second innings, support coming from Harris (40 in 65 minutes, 3 fours) and Pritchard (35 in 89 minutes, 2 fours). Ponsford (110 in 182 minutes, 9 fours) guided his team to victory. Spectators were admitted free on the final day to see 13 runs scored. Sources: *Wisden, VCA Report, SACA Report, The Age, The Argus, C.B.O'Reilly.*

SOUTH AUSTRALIA

G.W.Harris	b a'Beckett	2	b Ironmonger		40
B.W.Hone	b a'Beckett	46	c J.L.Ellis b a'Beckett		106
D.E.Pritchard	lbw b a'Beckett	36	lbw b a'Beckett		35
*V.Y.Richardson	run out (Ponsford/J.L.Ellis)	4	lbw b Ironmonger		29
H.E.Whitfield	lbw b Blackie	15	b Ironmonger		11
H.C.Nitschke	c Ryder b Blackie	53	(7) c a'Beckett b Ironmonger		17
A.T.Hack	b Alexander	44	(8) b a'Beckett		24
C.V.Grimmett	c Hendry b Ironmonger	15	(9) c J.L.Ellis b a'Beckett		9
†C.W.Walker	run out (Scaife)	3	(6) b Alexander		1
T.W.Wall	lbw b Blackie	2	lbw b a'Beckett		1
T.A.Carlton	not out	12	not out		0
Extras	(lb8, w1, nb3)	12	(b10, lb12, nb2)		24
Total	(97.2 overs, 347 mins)	244	(112.0 overs, 392 mins)		297

VICTORIA

R.N.Ellis	run out (sub G.H.Palmer/Walker/Grimmett)	27	(2) c Walker b Wall		26
W.H.Ponsford	c sub (G.H.Palmer) b Wall	47	(1) b Grimmett		110
H.S.T.L.Hendry	b Whitfield	24	c & b Grimmett		36
*J.Ryder	b Wall	77	not out		29
K.E.Rigg	c Richardson b Grimmett	23			
E.L.a'Beckett	b Carlton	1			
J.W.Scaife	run out (Richardson/Walker)	69			
†J.L.Ellis	lbw b Carlton	18			
D.D.Blackie	c Richardson b Wall	21			
H.H.Alexander	c Hone b Wall	4	(5) not out		4
H.Ironmonger	not out	10			
Extras	(b5, lb2, nb3)	10	(lb6, w1, nb1)		8
Total	(87.7 overs, 314 mins)	331	(55.7 overs, 186 mins) (3 wkts)		213

VICTORIA	O	M	R	W	w,nb		O	M	R	W	w,nb
Alexander	11	1	35	1	1,3		12	0	48	1	-,2
a'Beckett	20	4	40	3	-,-		31	6	63	5	-,-
Blackie	34	6	87	3	-,-	(4)	24	6	63	0	-,-
Ironmonger	28.2	8	64	1	-,-	(3)	39	11	88	4	-,-
R.N.Ellis	2	0	3	0	-,-						
Hendry	2	0	3	0	-,-						
Ryder						(5)	6	1	11	0	-,-

SOUTH AUSTRALIA	O	M	R	W	w,nb		O	M	R	W	w,nb
Wall	19	3	67	4	-,3		9	1	38	1	-,1
Whitfield	17.7	1	75	1	-,-		9	0	43	0	1,-
Grimmett	29	3	135	1	-,-		24.7	6	80	2	-,-
Carlton	22	5	44	2	-,-		13	1	44	0	-,-

FALL OF WICKETS

Wkt	SA 1st	VIC 1st	SA 2nd	VIC 2nd
1st	10	57	69	37
2nd	84	79	142	144
3rd	88	126	205	209
4th	94	160	235	-
5th	114	170	237	-
6th	184	219	243	-
7th	220	265	269	-
8th	226	297	294	-
9th	230	305	296	-
10th	244	331	297	-

NEW SOUTH WALES v QUEENSLAND (Shield Match 7)

Played at Sydney Cricket Ground on January 3, 4, 6, 7, 1930. (Five-day match)
Toss : New South Wales.   Result : NEW SOUTH WALES WON BY 685 RUNS.
Debuts: Queensland - H.F.Leeson (f/c).
12th Men: O.W.Bill (NSW) and G.S.Amos (Qld).
Umpires: E.G.Borwick and E.J.Shaw.
Attendances: 7972, 12102, 7848, 153.   Total: 28,075.   Receipts: £1728.
Close of Play: 1st day Qld 6/126 (Goodwin 18); 2nd day NSW (2) 3/368 (Bradman 205, McCabe 19); 3rd day Qld (2) 7/72 (Hurwood 6, Brew 16).

Bradman's monumental 452 not out, the highest innings in first-class cricket in Australia to date, occupied only 415 minutes and was technically chanceless. His only mistakes were at 264, when mid-on failed to move in quickly enough for a ball put up from Rowe's bowling, and at 345 when the keeper obstructed first slip in trying for a snick off Thurlow. He reached 100 in 104, 200 in 185, 300 in 288 and 400 in 377 minutes, passing Ponsford's previous world-record score of 437 with a pull for four off Thurlow. Starting soon after lunch on the second day, he had 85 by tea and 205 by stumps, and resumed after a day's rest to reach 310 by lunch and was still at the wicket when Kippax closed at tea-time on the third day, Goodwin having just dismissed Davidson with his first first-class delivery. Along the way Bradman added 272 with Kippax (115 in 145 minutes, 12 fours), 156 with McCabe (60 in 81 minutes, 10 fours) and 180 with Allsopp (66 in 90 minutes, 4 fours). Other fifties in the match came from Andrews (56 in 90 minutes, 7 fours), Bensted (51 in 114 minutes) and Goodwin (67 in 119 minutes, 6 fours). Only 21 balls were required on the fourth day to finish off the shell-shocked Queenslanders; the final runs margin remains the biggest in all first-class cricket. A.Jackson (ill) and W.A.S.Oldfield were unavailable for New South Wales, Andrews and Burt replacing J.E.H.Hooker (injured) and N.E.Phillips (work) in the selected side. Amos (carbuncle removed from arm) carried the drinks. Sources: *Wisden, NSWCA Report, QCA Report, Sydney Morning Herald, Sydney Referee.*

NEW SOUTH WALES

D.G.Bradman	c Leeson b Hurwood	3	(3) not out		452
W.C.Andrews	st Leeson b Hurwood	56	(1) c Levy b Hurwood		16
A.E.Marks	c Hurwood b Thurlow	40	(6) c Bensted b Hurwood		5
*A.F.Kippax	lbw b Thurlow	15	lbw b Rowe		115
S.J.McCabe	c Leeson b Thurlow	15	c Leeson b Hurwood		60
A.H.Allsopp	c & b Hurwood	9	(7) b Hurwood		66
A.G.Fairfax	b Brew	20	(2) st Leeson b Hurwood		10
S.C.Everett	c Bensted b Brew	41	c Goodwin b Hurwood		4
†H.L.Davidson	lbw b Hurwood	14	c & b Goodwin		22
S.J.W.Burt	b Thurlow	10			
H.C.Chilvers	not out	6			
Extras	(b3, lb3)	6	(b6, lb1, w2, nb2)		11
Total	(54.1 overs, 197 mins)	235	(117.1 overs, 433 mins) (8 wkts dec)		761

QUEENSLAND

*L.P.D.O'Connor	c Andrews b Fairfax	21	(2) b McCabe		17
R.M.Levy	c Everett b Fairfax	6	(1) b Everett		0
E.C.Bensted	c Davidson b McCabe	51	b Everett		3
F.C.Thompson	lbw b Chilvers	1	(5) lbw b Everett		0
W.Rowe	b McCabe	11	(6) c Bradman b Chilvers		1
F.J.Gough	c Marks b McCabe	14	(7) c Allsopp b Chilvers		20
V.H.V.Goodwin	c Marks b Fairfax	67	(4) run out (Andrews/Davidson)		4
A.Hurwood	b Chilvers	4	b Everett		6
F.M.Brew	b McCabe	20	c Davidson b Everett		26
†H.F.Leeson	c Davidson b McCabe	14	not out		2
H.M.Thurlow	not out	3	b Everett		0
Extras	(b9, lb3, nb3)	15	(b1, lb1, w1, nb2)		5
Total	(68.1 overs, 228 mins)	227	(30.5 overs, 114 mins)		84

QUEENSLAND	O	M	R	W	w,nb		O	M	R	W	w,nb		FALL OF WICKETS			
														NSW	QLD	NSW	QLD
Thurlow	18.1	0	83	4	-,-		25	0	147	0	-,-		Wkt	1st	1st	2nd	2nd
Hurwood	22	6	57	4	-,-		34	1	179	6	1,1		1st	3	18	22	0
Bensted	6	0	39	0	-,-		12	0	70	0	-,1		2nd	102	40	33	6
Brew	8	0	50	2	-,-		6	0	61	0	-,-		3rd	106	42	305	19
Rowe							19	0	143	1	-,-		4th	133	63	461	19
Thompson							15	0	90	0	1,-		5th	144	100	469	23
Gough							4	0	40	0	-,-		6th	144	126	649	42
Levy							2	0	20	0	-,-		7th	192	137	669	51
Goodwin							0.1	0	0	1	-,-		8th	211	185	761	75
													9th	227	214	-	84
NEW SOUTH WALES	O	M	R	W	w,nb		O	M	R	W	w,nb		10th	235	227	-	84
Everett	10	1	46	0	-,-		8.5	1	23	6	-,1						
Fairfax	15	1	53	3	-,2		7	3	12	0	-,-						
Chilvers	20	5	52	2	-,1		8	0	22	2	1,1						
McCabe	15.1	5	36	5	-,-		5	3	15	1	-,-						
Burt	8	1	25	0	-,-		2	0	7	0	-,-						

NEW SOUTH WALES v SOUTH AUSTRALIA (Shield Match 8)

Played at Sydney Cricket Ground on January 9, 10, 11, 13, 1930. (Five-day match)
Toss : New South Wales.   Result : NEW SOUTH WALES WON BY AN INNINGS AND 220 RUNS.
Debuts: Nil.
12th Men: O.W.Bill (NSW) and H.K.Sincock (SA).
Umpires: E.G.Borwick and A.C.Jones
Attendances: 7955, 8410, 3324, 4607.   Total: 24,296.   Receipts: £1355.
Close of Play: 1st day NSW 7/403 (Allsopp 123, Everett 37); 2nd day SA 9/183 (Grimmett 26, Wall 19); 3rd day SA 9/212
   (Grimmett 40, Wall 32).

Bradman (0) was struck on the head by a return from Grimmett at cover while regaining his crease. He retired hurt at 1/27 and resumed at 5/163, batting in all for 89 minutes with 5 fours. He did not field until the last day, Bill taking his place. Sincock, South Australia's reserve, also took the field due to the absence of Everett with a muscle strain sustained after bowling three overs. Allsopp (136 in 131 minutes, 22 fours) scored 111 runs after tea on the first day and shared an eighth-wicket partnership of 133 with Everett (62 in 110 minutes, 6 fours). Contributions from McCabe (81 in 136 minutes, 8 fours), Hooker (39 not out in 80 minutes, 3 fours) and Chilvers (52 in 49 minutes, 6 fours) helped the side reach 535. Hone (140 minutes, 2 fours) and Grimmett (147 minutes) each scored 42 for South Australia. Rain permitted only an hour of play on the third day and made batting difficult for the remainder. Hack took 65 minutes to score his first run on the last day and batted 125 minutes for his 12 runs. Fairfax dismissed Nitschke and Walker with successive deliveries in the second innings. Sources: *Wisden, NSWCA Report, SACA Report, Sydney Morning Herald, Sydney Referee, C.B.O'Reilly.*

NEW SOUTH WALES

W.C.Andrews	b Wall	9
†H.S.B.Love	st Walker b Whitfield	38
D.G.Bradman	c Richardson b Whitfield	47
*A.F.Kippax	b Whitfield	14
S.J.McCabe	c Nitschke b Grimmett	81
A.E.Marks	lbw b Grimmett	11
A.G.Fairfax	lbw b Whitfield	29
A.H.Allsopp	c Richardson b Grimmett	136
S.C.Everett	b Whitfield	62
J.E.H.Hooker	not out	39
H.C.Chilvers	c Harris b Grimmett	52
Extras	(b6, lb6, nb5)	17
Total	(105.7 overs, 415 mins)	535

SOUTH AUSTRALIA

G.W.Harris	c Love b Everett	1	(8)	b Chilvers	16
B.W.Hone	b McCabe	42	(10)	not out	7
D.E.Pritchard	c Love b Chilvers	23	(9)	b Chilvers	4
*V.Y.Richardson	lbw b Chilvers	14	(7)	b Chilvers	7
H.C.Nitschke	c Hooker b Fairfax	1	(3)	c Love b Fairfax	5
H.E.Whitfield	c Love b Chilvers	23	(11)	b Hooker	19
A.T.Hack	b Chilvers	16	(5)	lbw b Chilvers	12
C.V.Grimmett	c Marks b Fairfax	42	(1)	c Bradman b Fairfax	2
†C.W.Walker	b Fairfax	0	(4)	c sub (O.W.Bill) b Fairfax	7
T.A.Carlton	b McCabe	4	(6)	c Chilvers b Fairfax	10
T.W.Wall	not out	33	(2)	c Chilvers b Hooker	3
Extras	(b7, lb6, nb3)	16		(lb6, nb2)	8
Total	(81.5 overs, 274 mins)	215		(48.3 overs, 170 mins)	100

SOUTH AUSTRALIA	O	M	R	W	w,nb
Wall	26	2	145	1	-,4
Whitfield	26	2	106	5	-,-
Grimmett	33.7	3	163	4	-,-
Carlton	18	2	99	0	-,1
Richardson	2	1	5	0	-,-

NEW SOUTH WALES	O	M	R	W	w,nb		O	M	R	W	w,nb
Everett	3	0	17	1	-,-						
Hooker	14	1	35	0	-,-		15.3	6	35	2	-,2
Fairfax	18.5	2	43	3	-,2	(1)	16	7	19	4	-,-
Chilvers	25	6	57	4	-,1		16	5	38	4	-,-
McCabe	17	5	35	2	-,-	(3)	1	1	0	0	-,-
Marks	4	0	12	0	-,-						

FALL OF WICKETS

Wkt	NSW 1st	SA 1st	SA 2nd
1st	27	2	3
2nd	56	52	7
3rd	71	74	22
4th	84	75	22
5th	163	111	32
6th	198	113	45
7th	285	133	68
8th	418	134	72
9th	457	146	77
10th	535	215	100

QUEENSLAND v SOUTH AUSTRALIA (Shield Match 9)

Played at Exhibition Ground, Brisbane, on January 17, 18, 20, 21, 1930. (Five-day match)
Toss : Queensland.   Result : SOUTH AUSTRALIA WON BY 147 RUNS.
Debuts: Queensland - G.H.Cooper, K.L.M.Mossop (both f/c).
12th Men: N.C.Beeston (Qld) and G.H.Palmer (SA).
Umpires: J.Bartlett and B.L.Turner.
Attendances: ? , 5000, ? , ? .   Total: About 12,000.   Receipts: £665.
Close of Play: 1st day SA 6/295 (Hack 25, Grimmett 13); 2nd day Qld 7/171 (Higgins 45, Hurwood 7); 3rd day SA (2) 8/216 (Walker 20).

H.F.Leeson, R.M.Levy, O.E.Nothling and F.C.Thompson were all unavailable for Queensland while Mossop replaced V.H.V.Goodwin who withdrew from the named side. Lapses in the field coupled with a generous decision by O'Connor, who was making his last first-class appearance, to insert the visitors aided Richardson's 112 (169 minutes, 1 six and 14 fours, chance at 76) and 96 (130 minutes, 13 fours, chances at 80 and 84) for South Australia. Grimmett hit 53 in 125 minutes. Hurwood's 6 for 80 (right-arm medium pace and off breaks) remained his best first-class analysis. Higgins (5) was struck on the leg by a ball from Wall in the first over of Queensland's first innings and retired at 0/6, resuming at 5/111. After failing in his first innings, Mossop was missed behind the stumps before he had scored in his second, but went on to make 66 in 92 minutes with 6 fours. Gough's 50 occupied 65 minutes and included 1 six and 5 fours. Sources: *Wisden, QCA Report, SACA Report, Sydney Morning Herald, Brisbane Courier, C.B.O'Reilly.*

SOUTH AUSTRALIA

G.W.Harris	lbw b Thurlow	42	c O'Connor b Thurlow	2
B.W.Hone	c Oxenham b Thurlow	6	c Hornibrook b Hurwood	15
D.E.Pritchard	b Hornibrook	33	b Hurwood	22
*V.Y.Richardson	c O'Connor b Hornibrook	112	st O'Connor b Hurwood	96
H.E.Whitfield	c O'Connor b Bensted	32	c Hornibrook b Oxenham	3
H.C.Nitschke	lbw b Oxenham	26	c Hornibrook b Hurwood	0
A.T.Hack	c Hurwood b Oxenham	43	c O'Connor b Thurlow	1
C.V.Grimmett	b Hurwood	16	c Hornibrook b Hurwood	53
†C.W.Walker	not out	33	not out	30
T.W.Wall	c Gough b Oxenham	1	lbw b Hurwood	0
T.A.Carlton	c Hurwood b Hornibrook	14	b Hurwood	12
Extras	(b4, lb3)	7	(b2, lb2)	4
Total	(119.3 overs, 447 mins)	365	(77.7 overs, 286 mins)	238

QUEENSLAND

H.J.R.Higgins	c Richardson b Wall	45	(3) c Richardson b Wall	16
E.F.Hubbard	c Walker b Grimmett	41	(5) c Hack b Wall	23
F.J.Gough	c Walker b Wall	8	(4) c Harris b Grimmett	50
E.C.Bensted	c Whitfield b Grimmett	28	(6) c Carlton b Grimmett	18
R.K.Oxenham	c Walker b Wall	3	(2) c Carlton b Whitfield	13
*†L.P.D.O'Connor	b Whitfield	24	(1) c Pritchard b Grimmett	20
K.L.M.Mossop	c Hack b Whitfield	1	(8) lbw b Carlton	66
G.H.Cooper	c Whitfield b Grimmett	5	(7) c Pritchard b Grimmett	15
A.Hurwood	c Pritchard b Grimmett	18	c Carlton b Wall	16
P.M.Hornibrook	not out	13	not out	9
H.M.Thurlow	c Pritchard b Whitfield	1	b Carlton	0
Extras	(lb5, nb4)	9	(lb8, w1, nb5)	14
Total	(60.3 overs, 239 mins)	196	(62.5 overs, 250 mins)	260

QUEENSLAND	O	M	R	W	w,nb		O	M	R	W	w,nb
Hornibrook	32.3	5	79	3	-,-	(4)	10	3	34	0	-,-
Hurwood	25	6	65	1	-,-		28.7	4	80	6	-,-
Thurlow	27	3	125	2	-,-	(1)	16	1	61	2	-,-
Oxenham	30	8	76	3	-,-	(3)	16	2	41	2	-,-
Bensted	4	0	11	1	-,-		2	0	11	0	-,-
Cooper	1	0	2	0	-,-						
Gough						(6)	5	1	7	0	-,-

SOUTH AUSTRALIA	O	M	R	W	w,nb		O	M	R	W	w,nb
Wall	14	2	37	3	-,4		16	1	75	3	1,4
Whitfield	18.3	4	49	3	-,-		15	1	49	1	-,-
Carlton	6	2	18	0	,		9.5	3	24	2	-,1
Grimmett	22	0	83	4	-,-		22	2	98	4	-,-

FALL OF WICKETS

Wkt	SA 1st	QLD 1st	SA 2nd	QLD 2nd
1st	20	15	2	26
2nd	81	57	33	45
3rd	81	63	68	64
4th	192	110	75	121
5th	242	111	79	150
6th	260	125	115	152
7th	299	136	153	180
8th	331	171	216	207
9th	343	195	216	260
10th	365	196	238	260

VICTORIA v WESTERN AUSTRALIA

Played at Melbourne Cricket Ground on January 17, 18, 20, 21, 1930. (Four-day match)
Toss : Western Australia.   Result : VICTORIA WON BY FOUR WICKETS.
Debuts: Victoria - R.J.Hassett, L.J.Junor, W.F.Muir, W.B.Wedgwood (all f/c). Western Australia - K.H.Baird, E.H.Bromley (both f/c).
12th Men: H.H.Oakley (Vic) and H.A.Newman (WA).
Umpires: A.N.Barlow and W.J.Moore.
Attendances: 2536, 2733, 1453, 500.   Total: 7222.   Receipts: £135.
Close of Play: 1st day Vic 2/57 (Muir 23, Hunt 15); 2nd day WA (2) 3/154 (Wilberforce 58, Drew 0); 3rd day Vic (2) 3/159 (Muir 60, Hunt 20).

Leonard John Junor, aged 15 years 265 days on debut, became the youngest to play first-class cricket in Australia. Halcombe opened the bowling for Western Australia with three very fast deliveries and was then no-balled for throwing six times in succession by umpire Barlow at square leg and did not bowl again. O'Brien edged one of the no-balls to the boundary but was hit on the hand by another and retired hurt at 0/12. He resumed at 3/70 but was caught at the wicket from his first ball. Inverarity (61 in 127 minutes, 5 fours), Wilberforce (56 in 174 minutes, 4 fours and 59 in 147 minutes, 4 fours), Bromley (56 in 95 minutes, 7 fours) and R.J.Bryant (86 in 117 minutes, 9 fours) for Western Australia and Hassett (58 in 89 minutes, 7 fours), Muir (61 in 141 minutes, 3 fours) and Hunt (93 in 165 minutes, 7 fours) for Victoria all surpassed fifty. Due to bronchitis, F.J.Bryant was unable to bat in the second innings. Perraton replaced the unavailable W.A.Scott in the Victorian side. Sources: *VCA Report, WACA Report, The Age, The Argus, The Herald, Melbourne Sun.*

WESTERN AUSTRALIA

A.D.Drew	b McCormick	4	(5)	b Wedgwood	0
F.J.Bryant	run out (O'Brien/Barnett)	18		absent ill	-
W.J.Horrocks	b McCormick	4		c Barnett b Chivers	16
M.Inverarity	c Barnett b Wedgwood	61	(1)	b McCormick	13
*R.J.Bryant	c Barnett b Chivers	1	(6)	b Wedgwood	86
E.H.Bromley	c Muir b Wedgwood	5	(4)	c Perraton b O'Brien	56
R.J.Wilberforce	c Junor b Hassett	56	(2)	b McCormick	59
W.A.Evans	b Chivers	21	(7)	c Barnett b Hassett	15
†R.H.Hewson	c McCormick b Hassett	1	(8)	c McCormick b Chivers	35
K.H.Baird	c Junor b Hassett	0	(9)	run out (Perraton)	0
R.A.Halcombe	not out	3	(10)	not out	10
Extras	(b6, lb3, w1, nb3)	13		(b12, lb6, w2, nb1)	21
Total	(65.3 overs, 249 mins)	187		(80.5 overs, 309 mins)	311

VICTORIA

*C.A.H.Sindrey	b Bromley	4		st Hewson b Inverarity	32
L.P.J.O'Brien	c Hewson b Bromley	4		b Evans	7
W.F.Muir	c Drew b Wilberforce	41		c Horrocks b Bromley	61
†B.A.Barnett	run out (R.J.Bryant/Hewson)	6		lbw b R.J.Bryant	37
H.C.Hunt	c Drew b Bromley	25		run out (Drew/Hewson)	93
L.J.Junor	b Evans	41		st Hewson b Wilberforce	6
J.O.Perraton	lbw b Evans	7		not out	43
R.J.Hassett	c Drew b Inverarity	58		not out	4
E.L.McCormick	c & b Bromley	3		
W.B.Wedgwood	lbw b Inverarity	8		
A.P.Chivers	not out	5		
Extras	(b1, lb1, nb5)	7		(b6, lb2)	8
Total	(64.4 overs, 240 mins)	209		(82.3 overs, 293 mins) (6 wkts)	291

VICTORIA	O	M	R	W	w,nb		O	M	R	W	w,nb					
McCormick	16	4	33	2	1,3		24	5	72	2	1,1					
Chivers	15	1	34	2	-,-	(4)	13.5	2	43	2	-,-					
Hassett	17.3	2	59	3	-,-	(5)	16	1	67	1	-,-					
Wedgwood	12	3	30	2	-,-	(6)	16	2	56	2	-,-					
Perraton	4	0	13	0	-,-	(2)	2	0	13	0	-,-					
O'Brien	1	0	5	0	-,-	(7)	2	1	3	1	-,-					
Hunt						(3)	6	1	25	0	1,-					
Muir							1	0	11	0	-,-					

FALL OF WICKETS

Wkt	WA 1st	VIC 1st	WA 2nd	VIC 2nd
1st	20	15	17	16
2nd	29	30	39	50
3rd	31	70	154	122
4th	33	70	156	165
5th	46	92	158	186
6th	131	112	214	286
7th	170	147	280	-
8th	173	170	280	-
9th	173	199	311	-
10th	187	209	-	-

WESTERN AUSTRALIA	O	M	R	W	w,nb		O	M	R	W	w,nb
Halcombe	1	0	7	0	-,5						
Evans	25	7	58	2	-,-	(1)	28	6	60	1	-,-
Bromley	18	2	64	4	-,-	(2)	20.3	5	75	1	-,-
Baird	6	0	34	0	-,-	(7)	10	1	36	0	-,-
R.J.Bryant	1	1	0	0	-,-		3	0	15	1	-,-
Inverarity	8.4	1	27	2	-,-	(4)	8	0	44	1	-,-
Wilberforce	5	0	12	1	-,-	(3)	9	0	33	1	-,-
Drew						(6)	2	0	13	0	-,-
Horrocks						(8)	2	1	7	0	-,-

NEW SOUTH WALES v VICTORIA (Shield Match 10)

Played at Sydney Cricket Ground on January 24 (no play), 25 (no play), 27 (no play), 28, 29, 1930. (Five-day match)
Toss : Victoria.   Result : MATCH DRAWN.
Debuts: New South Wales - H.J.T.Theak (f/c).
12th Men: A.E.Marks (NSW) and L.S.Darling (Vic).
Umpires: E.G.Borwick and A.C.Jones.
Attendances: no play, no play, no play, 8015, 3340.   Total: 11,355.   Receipts: £589.
Close of Play: 1st day no play; 2nd day no play; 3rd day no play; 4th day Vic 2/45 (Hendry 21, Ryder 10).

After the first three days were completely lost to the elements, Bradman (77 in 103 minutes, 8 fours), Allsopp (65 in 63 minutes, 1 six and 8 fours) and Fairfax (64 in 133 minutes, 1 six and 3 fours) got the match under way with fifties on a drying pitch. Hendry (95 in 173 minutes, 9 fours) and Ryder (100 not out in 172 minutes, 9 fours) added 177 for Victoria's third wicket in reply but time prevented a first-innings result for the first time in the history of the competition. S.C.Everett was unavailable for New South Wales due to injury.
Sources: *Wisden, NSWCA Report, VCA Report, The Age, Sydney Morning Herald, Sydney Referee.*

NEW SOUTH WALES

A.Jackson	b a'Beckett	5
W.C.Andrews	b Alexander	12
D.G.Bradman	c R.N.Ellis b Ironmonger	77
*A.F.Kippax	b Ironmonger	9
S.J.McCabe	c Blackie b a'Beckett	29
A.H.Allsopp	lbw b Blackie	65
A.G.Fairfax	c J.L.Ellis b Hendry	64
H.C.Chilvers	c J.L.Ellis b Ironmonger	0
†H.L.Davidson	b Hendry	22
J.E.H.Hooker	c Hendry b Ryder	30
H.J.T.Theak	not out	2
Extras	(b6, lb7, nb2)	15
Total	(69.1 overs, 266 mins)	330

VICTORIA

W.H.Ponsford	c Davidson b Theak	13
R.N.Ellis	b Fairfax	0
H.S.T.L.Hendry	c Theak b Fairfax	95
*J.Ryder	not out	100
E.L.a'Beckett	not out	7
K.E.Rigg	)	
J.W.Scaife	)	
†J.L.Ellis	) did not bat	
D.D.Blackie	)	
H.H.Alexander	)	
H.Ironmonger	)	
Extras	(b3, lb1, nb3)	7
Total	(56.0 overs, 190 mins) (3 wkts)	222

VICTORIA	O	M	R	W	w,nb
Alexander	14	0	79	1	-,2
a'Beckett	21	2	57	2	-,-
Ironmonger	20	0	100	3	-,-
Blackie	11	0	69	1	-,-
Hendry	2.1	0	4	2	-,-
Ryder	1	0	6	1	-,-

NEW SOUTH WALES	O	M	R	W	w,nb
Fairfax	9	0	44	2	-,2
Theak	16	1	59	1	-,-
Chilvers	13	1	38	0	-,-
Hooker	12	2	47	0	-,1
McCabe	5	0	21	0	-,-
Allsopp	1	0	6	0	-,-

FALL OF WICKETS

Wkt	NSW 1st	VIC 1st
1st	14	4
2nd	40	26
3rd	54	203
4th	129	-
5th	149	-
6th	228	-
7th	231	-
8th	266	-
9th	324	-
10th	330	-

TASMANIA v WESTERN AUSTRALIA

Played at T.C.A. Ground, Hobart, on January 24, 25, 27, 1930. (Three-day match)
Toss : Western Australia.   Result : MATCH DRAWN.
Debuts: Tasmania - G.J.Lethborg (f/c).
12th Men: V.L.Hooper (Tas) and H.A.Newman (WA).
Umpires: A.J.Buttsworth and W.T.Lonergan.
Attendances: No daily figures published.   Total: About 1600.   Receipts: £83.
Close of Play: 1st day Tas 0/61 (Rushforth 16, Atkinson 34); 2nd day WA (2) 1/14 (Drew 5, Wilberforce 1).

Despite the closeness of the first encounter between the non-Sheffield Shield teams, this match was destined to be their sole meeting until Tasmania gained admittance to the national competition 47 years later. V.R.Driscoll (injured) was unavailable for Tasmania and Lethborg replaced T.D.Room (committed to work) after the teams were chosen. Halcombe was twice no-balled for throwing by Buttsworth at square leg on the first day, and bowling from the opposite end on the following day he was called 10 times in succession in his first over (his fourth of the innings) by Lonergan at square leg. Horrocks scored 65 (72 minutes, 10 fours) and an unbeaten 148 (195 minutes, 12 fours) for Western Australia, sharing a second-wicket stand of 88 in 72 minutes in the first innings with F.J.Bryant (69 in 155 minutes, 1 five and 6 fours). R.J.Bryant scored 40 in 45 minutes with 6 fours and 38 in 53 minutes. Evans suffered a shoulder strain on the second day and was unable to take any further part, Newman replacing him for the remainder. Atkinson (42 in 82 minutes, 4 fours) and Green (46 in 120 minutes, 3 fours) topscored for Tasmania. Sources: *TCA Report, WACA Report, The Cricketer, Hobart Mercury.*

WESTERN AUSTRALIA

Batsman	Dismissal	Runs		2nd innings	Runs
R.J.Wilberforce	c Rushforth b Burrows	14	(3)	run out (Atkinson)	17
F.J.Bryant	b Burrows	69	(1)	c Burrows b James	8
W.J.Horrocks	c Atkinson b Nash	65	(4)	not out	148
M.Inverarity	c James b Nash	2	(5)	b Townley	10
A.D.Drew	c Pickett b Newton	4	(2)	b Burrows	35
E.H.Bromley	b Newton	2		b Townley	14
*R.J.Bryant	c & b James	40		c Lethborg b Burrows	38
W.A.Evans	c Rushforth b James	6		lbw b Burrows	2
†R.H.Hewson	not out	22		not out	27
A.M.C.Webster	st Pickett b Townley	8			
R.A.Halcombe	run out (/Pickett)	3			
Extras	(b10, lb2, nb1)	13		(b3, w1)	4
Total	(60.0 overs, 229 mins)	248		(70.0 overs, 265 mins) (7 wkts dec)	303

TASMANIA

Batsman	Dismissal	Runs		2nd innings	Runs
A.W.Rushforth	b Evans	36		run out (R.J.Bryant/Hewson)	18
*J.A.Atkinson	b Inverarity	42		not out	18
D.C.Green	c Horrocks b Halcombe	46		not out	1
A.O.Burrows	b Inverarity	39			
C.C.Wood	c Bromley b Inverarity	22			
G.J.Lethborg	lbw b Halcombe	10			
L.J.Nash	st Hewson b Wilberforce	8			
A.C.Newton	b Webster	23			
R.C.Townley	c & b Halcombe	15			
†E.A.Pickett	b Bromley	0			
G.T.H.James	not out	11			
Extras	(b21, lb6, nb11)	38		(b4, nb1)	5
Total	(71.1 overs, 283 mins)	290		(13.0 overs, 45 mins) (1 wkt)	42

TASMANIA	O	M	R	W	w,nb		O	M	R	W	w,nb
Nash	19	5	85	2	-,-		12	1	40	0	-,-
Burrows	17	3	47	2	-,1	(3)	16	3	71	3	1,-
James	10	1	27	2	-,-	(2)	14	1	54	1	-,-
Townley	4	0	32	1	-,-	(6)	9	0	65	2	-,-
Newton	10	1	44	2	-,-	(4)	13	1	45	0	-,-
Atkinson						(5)	3	0	16	0	-,-
Wood							3	0	8	0	-,-

WESTERN AUSTRALIA	O	M	R	W	w,nb		O	M	R	W	w,nb
Halcombe	20	6	61	3	-,11		2	1	2	0	-,-
Webster	8.1	1	26	1	-,-		4	1	8	0	-,1
Bromley	14	3	59	1	-,-	(5)	2	0	5	0	-,-
Evans	13	1	42	1	-,-						
Inverarity	14	1	57	3	-,-	(3)	3	1	18	0	-,-
Wilberforce	2	0	7	1	-,-						
Drew						(4)	2	0	4	0	-,-

FALL OF WICKETS

Wkt	WA 1st	TAS 1st	WA 2nd	TAS 2nd
1st	38	86	13	39
2nd	126	122	43	-
3rd	138	193	92	-
4th	155	212	107	-
5th	161	231	143	-
6th	166	240	215	-
7th	196	242	217	-
8th	216	270	-	-
9th	232	271	-	-
10th	248	290	-	-

SOUTH AUSTRALIA v WESTERN AUSTRALIA

Played at Adelaide Oval on January 31, February 1, 3, 1930. (Three-day match)
Toss : Western Australia.   Result : SOUTH AUSTRALIA WON BY AN INNINGS AND 234 RUNS.
Debuts: South Australia - L.G.Holton (f/c).
12th Men: W.E.Catchlove (SA) and K.H.Baird (WA).
Umpires: T.W.Cook and G.A.Hele.
Attendances: 2649, ? , ? .   Total: 3799.   Receipts: £264.
Close of Play: 1st day SA 0/65 (Johnson 19, Nitschke 45); 2nd day SA 8/614 (Parry 2, Holton 7).

South Australia's total, their highest to date, was put together in rapid fashion, 100 being reached in 74 minutes, 200 in 125 minutes, 300 in 195 minutes, 400 in 248 minutes, 500 in 308 minutes and 600 in 350 minutes. The second day saw 549 runs scored in 304 minutes (73 eight-ball overs) with innings from Nitschke (chanceless 172 in 213 minutes, 1 five and 19 fours), Pritchard (80 in 76 minutes, 7 fours), Lonergan (86 in 108 minutes, 8 fours), Richardson (58 in 49 minutes, 1 six and 7 fours), Starr (72 in 109 minutes, 5 fours) and Lee (100 in 73 minutes, 3 sixes and 10 fours, 5 chances). Nitschke's 172, his maiden first-class hundred, remained his career-best score while Lee's hundred in a session (he began after tea at 5/434 and was out at 6/593) included the last 50 in just 17 minutes. Horrocks (58 in 73 minutes, 8 fours) and R.J.Bryant (54 in 88 minutes, 8 fours) exceeded 50 for Western Australia. Catchlove, Holton, Parry and Starr replaced A.T.Hack, G.W.Harris, C.W.Walker and T.W.Wall who were all unavailable for South Australia. Johnson replaced B.W.Hone (also unavailable) at the last moment. Sources: *SACA Report, WACA Report, Adelaide Advertiser, South Australian Register, C.B.O'Reilly.*

WESTERN AUSTRALIA

F.J.Bryant	c Carlton b Lee	18		c & b Grimmett	21
A.D.Drew	c Pritchard b Holton	24		st Parry b Grimmett	31
W.J.Horrocks	run out (Lonergan/Parry)	58		c & b Lee	2
R.J.Wilberforce	c & b Lee	25		lbw b Grimmett	9
M.Inverarity	c Parry b Pritchard	34		c Parry b Lee	7
E.H.Bromley	c Starr b Carlton	16	(7)	b Lee	6
*R.J.Bryant	c Richardson b Lee	54	(6)	c Nitschke b Grimmett	13
†R.H.Hewson	b Carlton	16		not out	16
H.A.Newman	b Lee	15		b Lee	4
A.M.C.Webster	not out	0		c Richardson b Grimmett	0
R.A.Halcombe	b Lee	0		c Starr b Grimmett	0
Extras	(lb2, w1, nb3)	6		(b2, lb1, nb2)	5
Total	(72.7 overs, 260 mins)	266		(31.7 overs, 116 mins)	114

SOUTH AUSTRALIA

E.A.Johnson	c Hewson b Halcombe	19
H.C.Nitschke	b Inverarity	172
D.E.Pritchard	c Inverarity b Bromley	80
A.R.Lonergan	c Inverarity b Bromley	86
*V.Y.Richardson	b Inverarity	58
C.L.B.Starr	b Wilberforce	72
P.K.Lee	c Wilberforce b Inverarity	100
C.V.Grimmett	b Wilberforce	10
†C.N.Parry	not out	2
L.G.Holton	not out	7
T.A.Carlton	did not bat	
Extras	(b2, lb4, nb2)	8
Total	(84.0 overs, 361 mins) (8 wkts dec)	614

SOUTH AUSTRALIA	O	M	R	W	w,nb	O	M	R	W	w,nb
Holton	15	0	58	1	-,3	4	0	14	0	-,-
Carlton	15	4	36	2	-,-	6	2	8	0	-,1
Lee	18.7	3	68	5	-,-	12	1	37	4	-,1
Grimmett	15	0	67	0	-,-	9.7	1	50	6	-,-
Pritchard	4	0	14	1	1,-					
Starr	5	1	17	0	-,-					

WESTERN AUSTRALIA	O	M	R	W	w,nb
Halcombe	13	1	100	1	-,-
Newman	18	0	126	0	-,-
Inverarity	19	0	189	3	-,1
Webster	14	0	77	0	-,1
Bromley	14	0	79	2	-,-
R.J.Bryant	3	0	21	0	-,-
F.J.Bryant	1	0	10	0	-,-
Wilberforce	2	0	4	2	-,-

FALL OF WICKETS

	WA	SA	WA
Wkt	1st	1st	2nd
1st	29	65	53
2nd	86	201	56
3rd	113	330	58
4th	138	388	68
5th	162	434	82
6th	194	593	91
7th	232	597	91
8th	259	605	111
9th	266	-	114
10th	266	-	114

QUEENSLAND v VICTORIA (Shield Match 11)

Played at Exhibition Ground, Brisbane, on February 1, 3, 4, 1930. (Five-day match)
Toss : Victoria. Result : VICTORIA WON BY AN INNINGS AND 33 RUNS.
Debuts: Queensland - H.Fewin, A.N.Marshall (both f/c).
12th Men: A.H.F.Rofe (Qld) and R.N.Ellis (Vic).
Umpires: J.P.Orr and J.A.Scott.
Attendances: ? , 2500, ? . Total: No figures published. Receipts: £496.
Close of Play: 1st day Vic 3/82 (Ryder 35, Darling 0); 2nd day Qld (2) 2/74 (Bensted 53, Hubbard 5).

Sent in on a rain-affected pitch, Queensland collapsed to the unchanged combination of a'Beckett (3 for 44) and Ironmonger (7 for 35). Bensted (79 in 135 minutes, 10 fours) and Hubbard (65 in 179 minutes, 7 fours) added 97 for the third wicket in the second innings. The Victorians also failed with the bat, except Ryder whose 168 runs occupied 295 minutes and included 1 six and 8 fours. He gave a difficult chance to Mossop off Bensted when 15 and shared a seventh-wicket stand of 88 in 84 minutes with Ellis before being eighth out at 305. All 10 wickets in the innings fell to catches. Queensland were weakened by the absence of L.P.D.O'Connor who declined to play due to a dispute with the Q.C.A. over his role in the team. Marshall replaced H.F.Leeson (unavailable) as the side's wicket-keeper. *Wisden* incorrectly gives Qld (1) Marshall hit wkt b Ironmonger; Qld (2) w5 instead of nb5. Sources: *Wisden, VCA Report, QCA Report, The Age, The Argus, Brisbane Courier.*

QUEENSLAND

F.J.Gough	st Ellis b Ironmonger	6	c Hendry b Alexander		1
*R.K.Oxenham	c & b Ironmonger	21	b Alexander		6
E.C.Bensted	c & b a'Beckett	15	lbw b Blackie		79
E.F.Hubbard	c Scaife b Ironmonger	0	b Blackie		65
V.H.V.Goodwin	c Rigg b Ironmonger	5	st Ellis b a'Beckett		9
H.Fewin	c Rigg b Ironmonger	7	Hendry b Ironmonger		11
K.L.M.Mossop	c & b Ironmonger	0	st Ellis b Ironmonger		0
A.Hurwood	c Blackie b a'Beckett	0	b Blackie	(10)	2
P.M.Hornibrook	c Hendry b a'Beckett	18	run out (Ryder)		3
†A.N.Marshall	b Ironmonger	7	not out	(8)	0
H.M.Thurlow	not out	0	c a'Beckett b Ironmonger		1
Extras	(w1)	1	(b9, lb9, nb5)		23
Total	(25.3 overs, 101 mins)	80	(60.1 overs, 237 mins)		200

VICTORIA

W.H.Ponsford	c & b Hurwood	15
H.S.T.L.Hendry	c Mossop b Hurwood	6
*J.Ryder	c Hubbard b Hornibrook	168
K.E.Rigg	c Bensted b Hornibrook	13
L.S.Darling	c Goodwin b Hurwood	10
J.W.Scaife	c Mossop b Bensted	16
E.L.a'Beckett	c Marshall b Thurlow	8
†J.L.Ellis	c Marshall b Thurlow	32
D.D.Blackie	c Mossop b Hurwood	9
H.H.Alexander	not out	2
H.Ironmonger	c Goodwin b Hornibrook	6
Extras	(b20, lb6, w2)	28
Total	(82.4 overs, 319 mins)	313

VICTORIA	O	M	R	W	w,nb		O	M	R	W	w,nb
a'Beckett	13	3	44	3	1,-	(3)	10	0	23	1	-,-
Ironmonger	12.3	5	35	7	-,-		19.1	4	51	3	-,-
Alexander						(1)	15	3	41	2	-,4
Blackie							16	1	62	3	-,1

QUEENSLAND	O	M	R	W	w,nb
Hurwood	29	4	88	4	-,-
Oxenham	5	1	14	0	-,-
Hornibrook	25.4	2	87	3	1,-
Fewin	2	0	11	0	-,-
Thurlow	11	0	50	2	-,-
Bensted	10	1	35	1	1,-

FALL OF WICKETS

Wkt	QLD 1st	VIC 1st	QLD 2nd
1st	20	13	9
2nd	33	38	22
3rd	39	80	119
4th	47	97	146
5th	54	133	194
6th	54	170	194
7th	54	258	194
8th	56	305	197
9th	77	305	199
10th	80	313	200

SOUTH AUSTRALIA v VICTORIA (Shield Match 12)

Played at Adelaide Oval on February 14, 15, 17, 1930. (Five-day match)
Toss : Victoria. Result : VICTORIA WON BY 223 RUNS.
Debuts: Victoria - H.H.Oakley (f/c).
12th Men: A.R.Lonergan (SA) and L.P.J.O'Brien (Vic).
Umpires: T.W.Cook and G.A.Hele.
Attendances: 6277, 10358, 4323. Total: 20,958. Receipts: £914.
Close of Play: 1st day SA 7/109 (Grimmett 0, Walker 0); 2nd day Vic (2) 8/396 (Ellis 45, Alexander 0).

Needing only to lead on the first innings and not lose the match outright to overtake New South Wales and win the Sheffield Shield, Victoria won the game with two days to spare and thus won the competition for the 12th time. D.D.Blackie, R.N.Ellis and K.E.Rigg were unavailable for the trip to Adelaide and O'Brien was made 12th man after he was injured in a fall from a horse the day before the match got under way. South Australia gained a quick breakthrough when Wall bowled Hendry with the second ball of the first over, but batsmen from both sides struggled on the opening day on the fast pitch. Davidson dismissed Grimmett and Carlton with successive deliveries as South Australia collapsed, losing 7 for 15 (including 5 for 1) to fall unexpectedly short of Victoria's 118. Ponsford scored 54 (71 minutes, 9 fours) in the second innings, but a'Beckett secured the Shield for Victoria virtually single-handed with his career-best 152 (172 minutes, 3 sixes and 17 fours). He scored his last 103 runs in the tea-stumps session on the second day (last 52 in 26 minutes) and added 77 for the seventh wicket with Oakley (43 in 48 minutes, 5 fours) and 136 for the eighth wicket with Ellis (68 in 111 minutes, 6 fours). Hone (47 in 99 minutes, 5 fours) made the topscore in South Australia's second innings. *Wisden* incorrectly gives SA (2) Harris 32, Carlton 25.
Sources: *Wisden, VCA Report, SACA Report, Adelaide Advertiser, The News, South Australian Register, C.B.O'Reilly.*

VICTORIA

Batsman	Dismissal	Runs		Dismissal	Runs
W.H.Ponsford	c Pritchard b Grimmett	19	(2)	lbw b Grimmett	54
H.S.T.L.Hendry	b Wall	0	(1)	st Walker b Grimmett	29
*J.Ryder	st Walker b Grimmett	37		lbw b Carlton	20
L.S.Darling	c Pritchard b Whitfield	14		c Walker b Whitfield	21
J.W.Scaife	c Pritchard b Grimmett	8		c Hone b Grimmett	1
E.L.a'Beckett	c Pritchard b Wall	4	(7)	c Richardson b Grimmett	152
H.H.Oakley	c Walker b Grimmett	0	(8)	st Walker b Grimmett	43
A.A.Davidson	c Richardson b Lee	31	(6)	b Carlton	26
†J.L.Ellis	c Carlton b Grimmett	2		b Wall	68
H.H.Alexander	c & b Lee	1		c Richardson b Whitfield	17
H.Ironmonger	not out	0		not out	0
Extras	(lb1, nb1)	2		(b1, lb4, nb2)	7
Total	(37.5 overs, 155 mins)	118		(90.1 overs, 338 mins)	438

SOUTH AUSTRALIA

Batsman	Dismissal	Runs	Dismissal	Runs
G.W.Harris	c Ellis b Alexander	26	c Ryder b Ironmonger	31
B.W.Hone	lbw b Alexander	23	lbw b Ironmonger	47
D.E.Pritchard	st Ellis b Davidson	19	c & b a'Beckett	30
*V.Y.Richardson	st Ellis b Ironmonger	1	lbw b a'Beckett	18
H.C.Nitschke	c Ryder b Davidson	27	c Ryder b Ironmonger	5
H.E.Whitfield	run out (a'Beckett/Ellis)	3	b a'Beckett	0
P.K.Lee	c Ellis b Ironmonger	7	b Ironmonger	37
C.V.Grimmett	c Ponsford b Davidson	1	c Darling b Ironmonger	0
†C.W.Walker	lbw b Ironmonger	0	c Hendry b Davidson	15
T.A.Carlton	b Davidson	0	lbw b Hendry	26
T.W.Wall	not out	0	not out	2
Extras	(lb3)	3	(b5, lb6, w1)	12
Total	(40.7 overs, 162 mins)	110	(57.0 overs, 217 mins)	223

SOUTH AUSTRALIA	O	M	R	W	w,nb	O	M	R	W	w,nb
Wall	8	1	24	2	,1	16	2	54	1	-,1
Whitfield	10	1	24	1	-,-	12.1	3	40	2	-,-
Grimmett	15	1	55	5	-,-	31	0	155	5	-,-
Lee	4.5	0	13	2	-,-	9	1	82	0	-,-
Carlton						19	2	82	2	-,1
Pritchard						3	0	18	0	-,-

VICTORIA	O	M	R	W	w,nb	O	M	R	W	w,nb
Alexander	10	0	43	2	-,-	7	0	32	0	1,-
a'Beckett	8	0	21	0	-,-	13	6	20	3	-,-
Ironmonger	15.7	1	37	3	-,-	25	3	88	5	-,-
Davidson	7	4	6	4	-,-	10	1	61	1	-,-
Hendry						2	0	10	1	-,-

FALL OF WICKETS				
Wkt	VIC 1st	SA 1st	VIC 2nd	SA 2nd
1st	1	42	43	64
2nd	45	57	104	103
3rd	64	58	104	129
4th	74	95	108	136
5th	82	102	142	136
6th	82	109	182	138
7th	93	109	259	142
8th	106	110	395	179
9th	118	110	438	197
10th	118	110	438	223

VICTORIA v TASMANIA

Played at Melbourne Cricket Ground on February 17, 18, 19, 1930. (Three-day match)
Toss : Victoria. Result : VICTORIA WON BY AN INNINGS AND 95 RUNS.
Debuts: Victoria - J.R.Barnes, R.G.Nettleton, H.C.Schrader, W.A.Scott (all f/c). Tasmania - C.L.Badcock, A.G.Cuff (both f/c).
12th Men: F.E.Fontaine (Vic) and V.L.Hooper (Tas).
Umpires: P.Maxwell and G.Strickland.
Attendances: 978, 601, -. Total: 1579. Receipts: £32.
Close of Play: 1st day Vic 451 all out; 2nd day Tas (2) 8/173 (Nash 49, Cuff 6).

Victoria totalled 451 runs on the first day due to early fifties from Tolhurst (chanceless 95 in 151 minutes, 11 fours), King (55 in 97 minutes, 6 fours), Barnes (51 in 59 minutes, 5 fours) and Wootton (57 in 66 minutes, 5 fours). Nettleton (68 not out in 95 minutes, 3 fours) and Schrader added 89 in 46 minutes for the tenth wicket late in the day. Tasmania missed several chances, including Wootton when 17, though Scott, King and Guthrie were all victims of notable catches. Newton (95 in 145 minutes, 9 fours) dominated the batting for Tasmania, also scoring 48 (50 minutes, 8 fours) in the second innings with support coming from Nash (55 in 91 minutes, 7 fours). Admission for the 15 minutes required on the last day was free. Badcock made his debut in first-class cricket at 15 years 313 days.
Sources: *NSWCA Report, VCA Report, The Age, The Argus, The Herald, Melbourne Sun, The Sporting Globe, The Cricketer.*

VICTORIA

*E.K.Tolhurst	c Rushforth b Burrows	95	
W.A.Scott	c Newton b Nash	21	
†S.P.King	c Burrows b Nash	55	
H.F.Guthrie	c Burrows b Newton	36	
J.R.Barnes	c Rushforth b Townley	51	
J.R.Wootton	c Lethborg b Townley	57	
R.G.Nettleton	not out	68	
R.J.Hassett	lbw b Newton	2	
J.C.Makin	c & b Townley	1	
E.L.McCormick	b Nash	8	
H.C.Schrader	c Badcock b Newton	42	
Extras	(b5, lb9, w1)	15	
Total	(94.2 overs, 345 mins)	451	

TASMANIA

*A.W.Rushforth	c Guthrie b Schrader	12		b McCormick	18
G.J.Lethborg	c Scott b McCormick	9	(3)	b Schrader	5
A.O.Burrows	c Tolhurst b Nettleton	5	(4)	b Hassett	2
A.C.Newton	run out (Wootton/King)	95	(7)	b Wootton	48
C.L.Badcock	st King b Hassett	18		st King b Hassett	10
G.G.Gibson	b Hassett	0		b Makin	11
L.J.Nash	st King b Hassett	4	(8)	b McCormick	55
R.C.Townley	c & Makin	11	(9)	c Nettleton b Hassett	9
A.G.Cuff	b Schrader	5	(10)	b Hassett	8
G.T.H.James	not out	6	(2)	b McCormick	4
†E.A.Pickett	b Wootton	0		not out	0
Extras	(b1, lb3, nb2)	6		(b15)	15
Total	(55.2 overs, 208 mins)	171		(42.2 overs, 166 mins)	185

TASMANIA	O	M	R	W	w,nb
Nash	19	2	70	3	-,-
Burrows	14	1	74	1	-,-
Newton	20.2	3	67	3	-,-
James	19	1	102	0	1,-
Townley	18	0	94	3	-,-
Lethborg	4	0	29	0	-,-

VICTORIA	O	M	R	W	w,nb		O	M	R	W	w,nb
McCormick	14	0	53	1	-,2		11.2	2	41	3	-,-
Schrader	12	1	31	2	-,-		8	0	29	1	-,-
Nettleton	5	1	15	1	-,-	(5)	2	0	23	0	-,-
Makin	9	2	23	1	-,-		4	2	11	1	-,-
Wootton	3.2	0	16	1	-,-	(6)	4	1	16	1	-,-
Hassett	12	2	27	3	-,-	(3)	13	2	50	4	-,-

FALL OF WICKETS

Wkt	VIC 1st	TAS 1st	TAS 2nd
1st	69	24	15
2nd	155	24	26
3rd	211	40	32
4th	215	83	34
5th	298	87	51
6th	331	99	57
7th	335	158	124
8th	341	161	145
9th	362	171	181
10th	451	171	185

NEW SOUTH WALES v TASMANIA

Played at Sydney Cricket Ground on February 22, 24, 1930. (Three-day match)
Toss : New South Wales.   Result : NEW SOUTH WALES WON BY AN INNINGS AND 262 RUNS.
Debuts: New South Wales - O.W.Bill, J.L.Donnelly, W.A.Hunt, L.R.Leabeater (all f/c).
12th Men: A.G.Chipperfield (NSW) and A.G.Cuff (Tas).
Umpires: H.J.Armstrong and A.H.Farrow.
Attendances: 2215, 881.   Total: 3096.   Receipts: £108.
Close of Play: 1st day NSW 477 all out.

After losing three early wickets, New South Wales completely recovered to reach 477 on the first day, Bill (115 in 180 minutes, 9 fours, chances at 53, 61, and 115) and Leabeater (128 in 146 minutes, 13 fours) scoring centuries on debut. Leabeater went from 8 to 108 between lunch and tea while Hogg (57 in 51 minutes, 6 fours) and Henderson (101 in 131 minutes, 12 fours in his second and last first-class match) also scored freely. Tasmania, handicapped by the absence of leading batsmen J.A.Atkinson, N.W.Davis and D.C.Green who were all unavailable for the trip to Melbourne and Sydney, were bowled out twice on the second day, Nash (33 in 48 minutes, 4 fours) and Burrows (43 in 108 minutes, 5 fours) making the highest scores. Chilvers took the wickets of Badcock and Nash in one over and dismissed James and Pickett with successive balls to finish the match. Cummins, originally 12th man, and Leabeater replaced W.C.Andrews and A.E.Marks in the New South Wales side. Sources: *NSWCA Report, VCA Report, Sydney Morning Herald, Sydney Referee, Hobart Mercury.*

NEW SOUTH WALES

O.W.Bill	b Nash	115
J.L.Donnelly	c Lethborg b Nash	5
F.S.Cummins	b James	5
†A.H.Allsopp	c Newton b Hooper	4
*J.E.P.Hogg	c & b Townley	57
L.R.Leabeater	c Rushforth b Nash	128
F.Henderson	b James	101
H.C.Chilvers	c Newton b Hooper	5
W.A.Hunt	c Rushforth b James	28
B.A.Cooper	not out	14
H.J.T.Theak	c & b James	0
Extras	(b10, lb4, w1)	15
Total	(76.2 overs, 315 mins)	477

TASMANIA

*A.W.Rushforth	b Theak	19	lbw b Cooper	2
R.C.Townley	c Hogg b Hunt	0	b Theak	8
A.O.Burrows	b Theak	11	c Hogg b Chilvers	43
A.C.Newton	c & b Theak	9	b Theak	14
C.L.Badcock	c Cummins b Hunt	3	st Allsopp b Chilvers	0
L.J.Nash	b Chilvers	33	c Theak b Chilvers	0
G.G.Gibson	b Hunt	4	c Allsopp b Theak	14
G.J.Lethborg	b Theak	12	b Theak	8
G.T.H.James	b Chilvers	12	c Hogg b Chilvers	4
V.L.Hooper	b Theak	2	not out	0
†E.A.Pickett	not out	1	b Chilvers	0
Extras	(b10, lb2, nb1)	13	(b2, lb1)	3
Total	(32.2 overs, 131 mins)	119	(33.7 overs, 119 mins)	96

TASMANIA	O	M	R	W	w,nb
Nash	15	1	75	3	1,-
James	14.2	0	67	4	-,-
Hooper	12	1	81	2	-,-
Newton	6	0	43	0	-,-
Burrows	18	1	105	0	-,-
Townley	11	0	91	1	-,-

NEW SOUTH WALES	O	M	R	W	w,nb		O	M	R	W	w,nb
Theak	11	1	41	5	-,-	(3)	10	0	50	4	-,-
Hunt	10	4	20	3	-,-		5	3	7	0	-,-
Cummins	1	0	4	0	-,-	(5)	2	0	4	0	-,-
Cooper	5	0	19	0	-,1	(1)	5	1	9	1	-,-
Chilvers	5.2	0	22	2	-,-	(4)	11.7	4	23	5	-,-

FALL OF WICKETS

Wkt	NSW 1st	TAS 1st	TAS 2nd
1st	8	6	2
2nd	21	32	17
3rd	28	42	35
4th	111	47	36
5th	252	47	36
6th	393	57	75
7th	411	103	83
8th	452	103	94
9th	477	113	96
10th	477	119	96

TASMANIA v AUSTRALIAN XI

Played at N.T.C.A. Ground, Launceston, on March 8, 10, 11, 1930. (Three-day match)
Toss : Tasmania.　　　　　　　　　　Result : AUSTRALIAN XI WON BY TEN WICKETS.
Debuts: Nil.
12th Men: G.J.Lethborg (Tas) and C.W.Walker (Aust XI).
Umpires: P.G.Henty and G.S.Pennefather.
Attendances: 3000, 2500, 500.　　　　Total: About 6000.　　　Receipts: About £540.
Close of Play: 1st day Aust 1/140 (McCabe 93, Kippax 8); 2nd day Tas (2) 6/109 (Badcock 2, James 0).

Woodfull played for the first time since his hand injury in mid-December. McCabe (103 in 95 minutes, 15 fours) reached his maiden first-class century in 84 minutes and shared an opening stand of 120 in 57 minutes with Ponsford. Woodfull's unbeaten 50 occupied 71 minutes and included 7 fours. Atkinson (84 minutes, 6 fours) scored Tasmania's only fifty but was out to the sixth ball of the second innings. Nash contributed with scores of 31 (48 minutes, 3 fours) and 49 (94 minutes, 4 fours) but the rest of the local batting failed. Oldfield, while keeping up to Fairfax early on the last day, sustained a blow to the head from a full toss and left the field, Richardson taking the gloves for the remainder of the innings. *NSWCA Report* incorrectly gives Tas (2) reversed dismissals of Hooper and Townley. Sources: *NSWCA Report, VCA Report, The Age, Hobart Mercury, Launceston Examiner.*

TASMANIA

*J.A.Atkinson	c Oldfield b Fairfax	50		c Hornibrook b Wall	2
D.C.Green	b Fairfax	7		b Hornibrook	18
N.W.Davis	c Hornibrook b Fairfax	2	(4)	c Hornibrook b Fairfax	4
G.W.Martin	b Hornibrook	5	(5)	lbw b Fairfax	29
L.J.Nash	c Fairfax b Hurwood	31	(3)	c Oldfield b Fairfax	49
A.C.Newton	b Fairfax	6		run out (Oldfield/Hurwood)	0
C.L.Badcock	c Oldfield b McCabe	9		c Hornibrook b Fairfax	5
G.T.H.James	b Hornibrook	21		b Hornibrook	4
V.L.Hooper	lbw b Hurwood	1		c Ponsford b Hornibrook	20
R.C.Townley	not out	11		c Ponsford b Hurwood	16
†E.A.Pickett	c McCabe b Hornibrook	9		not out	0
Extras	(lb2, w1, nb2)	5		(b6, lb3, nb2)	11
Total	(53.2 overs, 192 mins)	157		(49.7 overs, 181 mins)	158

AUSTRALIAN XI

W.H.Ponsford	lbw b James	36			
S.J.McCabe	b Hooper	103			
A.F.Kippax	lbw b James	17			
V.Y.Richardson	c Martin b Townley	33			
D.G.Bradman	lbw b Nash	20			
A.G.Fairfax	c Pickett b James	18			
*W.M.Woodfull	not out	50			
†W.A.S.Oldfield	run out (Newton/James)	4			
A.Hurwood	b James	1	(1)	not out	2
P.M.Hornibrook	b James	12			
T.W.Wall	c Atkinson b Townley	4	(2)	not out	4
Extras	(b3, lb4, nb6)	13			-
Total	(56.0 overs, 216 mins)	311		(2.5 overs, 10 mins) (0 wkts)	6

AUSTRALIAN XI	O	M	R	W	w,nb	O	M	R	W	w,nb
Wall	7	1	19	0	-,-	8	2	28	1	-,-
Hurwood	12	2	41	2	-,-	6.7	2	13	1	-,-
Fairfax	13	3	36	4	1,2	17	4	43	4	-,2
Hornibrook	14.2	3	38	3	-,-	15	2	51	3	-,-
McCabe	7	2	18	1	-,-	3	0	12	0	-,-

TASMANIA	O	M	R	W	w,nb	O	M	R	W	w,nb
Nash	13	0	82	1	-,-					
James	22	1	97	5	-,-					
Hooper	13	0	69	1	-,6					
Newton	5	0	34	0	-,-					
Townley	3	0	16	2	-,-					
Atkinson						(1)	1	0	2	0	-,-
Martin						(2)	1	0	2	0	-,-
Green						(3)	0.5	0	2	0	-,-

FALL OF WICKETS

Wkt	TAS 1st	AUST 1st	TAS 2nd	AUST 2nd
1st	50	120	2	-
2nd	57	163	52	-
3rd	68	163	57	-
4th	68	199	106	-
5th	78	228	106	-
6th	115	249	107	-
7th	121	268	114	-
8th	130	273	118	-
9th	143	293	141	-
10th	157	311	158	-

TASMANIA v AUSTRALIAN XI

Played at T.C.A. Ground, Hobart, on March 13 (no play), 14, 15, 1930. (Three-day match)
Toss : Tasmania.   Result : MATCH DRAWN.
Debuts: Tasmania - D.M.Vautin (f/c).
12th Men: A.J.Trebilcock (Tas) and A.Jackson (Aust XI).
Umpires: M.Leonard and W.T.Lonergan.
Attendances: No play, 3000, 3062.   Total: 6062.   Receipts: £570.
Close of Play: 1st day no play; 2nd day Aust 1/178 (Ponsford 83, Bradman 70).

Ponsford (166 in 176 minutes, 13 fours) and Bradman (139 in 152 minutes, 16 fours) shared a second-wicket partnership of 296 for the Australians, neither offering a chance. Kippax's unbeaten 53 occupied 51 minutes and included 9 fours. Only Atkinson (25 in 44 minutes, 4 fours), Rushforth (25 in 88 minutes, 0 fours) and Green (47 in 126 minutes, 5 fours) reached double figures in Tasmania's first innings. The declaration left Tasmania two and a half hours to survive; Nash (15 fours) remained at the crease for precisely two hours to thwart the visitors, atoning for his second-ball dismissal in the first innings. N.W.Davis, A.S.Horton, G.J.Lethborg and E.A.Pickett were all unavailable for Tasmania. Sources: *NSWCA Report, VCA Report, TCA Report, The Age, Hobart Mercury*.

TASMANIA

Batsman	Dismissal 1	R	Dismissal 2	R
*J.A.Atkinson	b Hornibrook	25	c Walker b Fairfax	19
A.W.Rushforth	c Hornibrook b Grimmett	25	lbw b Grimmett	11
L.J.Nash	b Hornibrook	0	c Hornibrook b Hurwood	93
D.C.Green	c & b Hurwood	47	b McCabe	18
A.O.Burrows	b Hornibrook	0	c Walker b Hornibrook	0
G.W.Martin	lbw b Hurwood	9	not out	20
A.C.Newton	c Kippax b Grimmett	6	not out	11
C.L.Badcock	st Walker b Grimmett	1		
†D.M.Vautin	st Walker b Grimmett	0		
G.T.H.James	st Walker b Grimmett	2		
R.C.Townley	not out	0		
Extras	(b12, lb3, nb1)	16	(lb2)	2
Total	(54.4 overs, 177 mins)	131	(46.0 overs, 155 mins) (5 wkts)	174

AUSTRALIAN XI

Batsman	Dismissal	R
W.H.Ponsford	run out (Burrows/Vautin)	166
S.J.McCabe	c Rushforth b James	18
D.G.Bradman	c Rushforth b Atkinson	139
A.F.Kippax	not out	53
A.G.Fairfax	c Martin b Atkinson	33
V.Y.Richardson	)	
*W.M.Woodfull	)	
C.V.Grimmett	) did not bat	
†C.W.Walker	)	
A.Hurwood	)	
P.M.Hornibrook	)	
Extras	(b4, lb6)	10
Total	(64.2 overs, 229 mins) (4 wkts dec)	419

AUSTRALIAN XI	O	M	R	W	w,nb		O	M	R	W	w,nb
Fairfax	5	0	19	0	-,1		8	1	27	1	-,-
Hurwood	13.4	4	24	2	-,-		10	1	40	1	-,-
Hornibrook	14	1	42	3	-,-	(4)	9	4	17	1	-,-
Grimmett	22	6	30	5	-,-	(3)	7	2	20	1	-,-
McCabe							6	1	30	1	-,-
Bradman							4	0	21	0	-,-
Richardson							2	0	17	0	-,-

TASMANIA	O	M	R	W	w,nb
Burrows	19	0	113	0	-,-
James	18	0	109	1	-,-
Nash	10	0	78	0	-,-
Newton	9	0	38	0	-,-
Townley	5	0	36	0	-,-
Atkinson	3.2	0	35	2	-,-

FALL OF WICKETS			
	TAS	AUST	TAS
Wkt	1st	1st	2nd
1st	40	36	22
2nd	40	332	46
3rd	80	332	88
4th	81	419	89
5th	105	-	154
6th	112	-	-
7th	115	-	-
8th	121	-	-
9th	125	-	-
10th	131	-	-

WESTERN AUSTRALIA v AUSTRALIAN XI

Played at W.A.C.A. Ground, Perth, on March 21, 22, 24, 1930. (Three-day match)
Toss : Australian XI.　　　　　　Result : AUSTRALIAN XI WON BY AN INNINGS AND 25 RUNS.
Debuts: Western Australia - H.K.Lang, W.J.Truscott (both f/c).
12th Men: P.W.E.Curtin (WA) and T.W.Wall (Aust).
Umpires: F.R.Buttsworth and W.L.Menkens.
Attendances: 4600, 10000, 800.　　　Total: About 15,400.　　　Receipts: £1151.
Close of Play: 1st day Aust 1/59 (Jackson 23, Bradman 4); 2nd day WA (2) 4/67 (Wilberforce 9, R.J.Bryant 20).

Truscott replaced R.H.Hewson (unavailable) in the selected Western Australian team. The home batsmen were unable to find an effective counter to the variations of Grimmett on the opening day, although some late-order aggression from Fidock (35 in 18 minutes, 1 six and 6 fours) mounted a brief challenge. Kippax (114 in 155 minutes, 1 six and 16 fours) captivated the Saturday crowd with his artistry while Richardson (45 in 42 minutes, 8 fours) and Grimmett (40 in 51 minutes, 1 six and 4 fours) hit out. The Western Australians offered little resistance in their second innings, a'Beckett and Grimmett accounting for the last 6 wickets in the pre-lunch session of the final day.
Sources: *NSWCA Report, VCA Report, The Age, The West Australian, Daily News.*

WESTERN AUSTRALIA

F.J.Bryant	st Walker b Grimmett	18	(2) lbw b a'Beckett	4
H.K.Lang	c Hornibrook b Grimmett	29	(1) b Hornibrook	5
W.J.Horrocks	c Richardson b Grimmett	7	c Walker b Fairfax	15
R.J.Wilberforce	c Hornibrook b Hurwood	22	st Walker b Grimmett	25
E.H.Bromley	st Walker b Grimmett	0	run out (Bradman/Walker)	12
*R.J.Bryant	c Walker b Fairfax	17	run out (Hurwood)	21
M.Inverarity	c Hurwood b Hornibrook	25	c & b Grimmett	30
W.A.Evans	st Walker b Grimmett	8	c Walker b a'Beckett	2
H.E.Fidock	c Walker b Grimmett	35	b a'Beckett	0
†W.J.Truscott	c Richardson b Hornibrook	0	lbw b a'Beckett	2
R.A.Halcombe	not out	0	not out	14
Extras	(b4, lb2)	6	(b1, lb1)	2
Total	(53.2 overs, 175 mins)	167	(49.2 overs, 178 mins)	132

AUSTRALIAN XI

S.J.McCabe	st Truscott b Inverarity	28
A.Jackson	lbw b Evans	23
D.G.Bradman	c R.J.Bryant b Evans	27
A.F.Kippax	c Bromley b Wilberforce	114
*V.Y.Richardson	c & b Bromley	45
A.G.Fairfax	lbw b Bromley	11
E.L.a'Beckett	c & b Evans	24
C.V.Grimmett	c F.J.Bryant b Inverarity	40
A.Hurwood	lbw b Fidock	1
†C.W.Walker	not out	3
P.M.Hornibrook	lbw b Fidock	0
Extras	(b4, lb4)	8
Total	(57.6 overs, 250 mins)	324

AUSTRALIAN XI	O	M	R	W	w,nb		O	M	R	W	w,nb
a'Beckett	10	3	13	0	-,-		10	2	26	4	-,-
Hurwood	11	4	20	1	-,-	(5)	3	1	2	0	-,-
Hornibrook	9	2	24	2	-,-	(2)	12	0	34	1	-,-
Fairfax	9	1	29	1	-,-		5	1	10	1	-,-
Grimmett	14.2	1	75	6	-,-	(3)	18.2	4	53	2	-,-
Bradman							1	0	5	0	-,-

WESTERN AUSTRALIA	O	M	R	W	w,nb
Halcombe	9	0	47	0	-,-
Evans	19	2	71	3	-,-
Fidock	11.6	0	54	2	-,-
Inverarity	10	0	84	2	-,-
Bromley	7	1	43	2	-,-
Wilberforce	1	0	17	1	-,-

FALL OF WICKETS

Wkt	WA 1st	AUST 1st	WA 2nd
1st	33	52	9
2nd	56	60	9
3rd	69	83	29
4th	69	154	44
5th	95	174	69
6th	105	215	101
7th	119	312	108
8th	167	318	108
9th	167	324	112
10th	167	324	132

1930-31 SEASON (30 MATCHES)

A team from the West Indies toured Australia for the first time in 1930-31, playing 16 matches. They recorded three wins and eight losses from their 14 first-class matches and went down 4-1 in the Tests. Headley and Constantine encountered great personal success, but the inexperience of the visitors told. Bradman, Ponsford and Kippax all hit centuries against them in the Test series. Bradman began slowly but slipped into gear with innings of 223 and 152 in the Third and Fourth Tests. The spin bowling of Grimmett and Ironmonger puzzled the tourists and remained unmastered.

Sheffield Shield matches were restricted to four days for the first time. Victoria retained the Shield narrowly ahead of New South Wales, the bowling of Blackie and Ironmonger again playing a crucial role. Queensland showed a vast improvement in competitiveness at home, where they pressed the other States strongly. Thompson's innings of 275 not out against New South Wales was the highlight of the season. South Australia finished last in the Shield race despite Lonergan, Lee and Nitschke performing well, in addition to Grimmett.

The season was marked by a bitter three-way dispute between the Queensland Cricket Association selectors, players and the new State captain, Gough. It centred on the responsibility for the final selection of Queensland XIs on tour. Traditionally a team 'executive' comprising the captain and two senior players had been entrusted with the job. This year, however, the QCA appointed Gough captain and figurehead tour 'selector' and instructed him on the specific makeup of the final XI. Gough himself was unhappy with the arrangement and, once Queensland's southern tour began, he attempted to leave Gilbert, the new Aboriginal fast bowler, out of the side for the match at Sydney - contrary to the selectors' wishes. He had voiced his opposition to the selection of Gilbert in the touring party in the first place and had even threatened to withdraw himself if Gilbert was selected - a threat he was forced to rescind. The situation became complicated with knowledge that Gough's appointment as captain had not been well received by senior players. At a team meeting before the Sydney match, the players overruled Gough and included Gilbert in the XI. But the team, with Bourne and Hurwood omitted, was still contrary to Gough's original instructions from the QCA selectors, and the players were told to front the QCA on their return to Brisbane. They did not all attend, Bourne (to Goomeri), Gilbert (to Barambah), Leeson (to Rockhampton) and Biggs and Thompson (to Ipswich) all travelling directly to their country homes after the game at Adelaide. Those present were asked 'to express regret at their actions' (*Brisbane Courier*) but only Oxenham did so. The rest were suspended, apart from Thompson, Gilbert and Bourne, which left the QCA needing a near-new lineup for the final match against Victoria at Brisbane.

This last match never began, owing to heavy rain during the scheduled days (January 31, February 2, 3 and 4) which led to it being abandoned without a ball bowled. The Victorian twelve was: J.Ryder (captain), H.H.Alexander, B.A.Barnett, D.D.Blackie, L.S.Darling, A.A.Davidson, H.S.T.L.Hendry, H.Ironmonger, G.H.Newstead, H.H.Oakley, L.P.J.O'Brien and K.E.Rigg. Queensland went through numerous changes before their side was finally settled, O.E.Nothling (medical duties) declining the captaincy and 10 others knocking back invitations to play for various reasons. The final twelve was: L.L.Gill (captain), J.W.Adams, H.V.Burns, C.P.Christ, G.G.Cook, K.L.M.Mossop, F.W.Sides, A.W.Flugge, A.G.Harding, J.C.A.Pizzey, A.H.F.Rofe and H.N.M.Yeates. The last five were destined never to make a first-class appearance. The appointed umpires were J.P.Orr and J.A.Scott. No toss was made.

Leading Aggregates

Batsmen	M	I	NO	Runs	HS	Ave.	Bowlers	Runs	Wkts	Ave.
D.G.Bradman (NSW)	12	18	0	1422	258	79.00	C.V.Grimmett (SA)	1417	74	19.14
G.A.Headley (WI)	13	25	1	1066	131	44.41	H.Ironmonger (V)	972	68	14.29
A.F.Kippax (NSW)	13	18	0	902	158	50.11	L.N.Constantine (WI)	950	47	20.21
H.C.Nitschke (SA)	9	16	1	830	142	55.33	O.C.Scott (WI)	1325	40	33.12
W.H.Ponsford (V)	9	13	2	816	187	74.18	R.K.Oxenham (Q)	602	33	18.24
G.C.Grant (WI)	14	24	4	739	102	36.95	W.A.Hunt (NSW)	712	32	22.25
L.N.Constantine (WI)	13	23	0	708	100	30.78	P.K.Lee (SA)	859	32	26.84
S.J.McCabe (NSW)	12	18	1	704	161	41.41	T.A.Carlton (SA)	663	31	21.38
C.A.Roach (WI)	14	26	0	637	104	24.50	H.C.Griffith (WI)	1107	31	35.70
F.R.Martin (WI)	13	24	2	606	123*	27.54	H.C.Chilvers (NSW)	986	30	32.86

SHEFFIELD SHIELD TABLE

	P	WO	W1	LO	L1	D	Pts	Quotient	Runs Scored	Wkts Lost	Runs Conceded	Wkts Taken
VICTORIA	5*	1	2	-	1	1	16	1.231	2150	67	2163	83
NEW SOUTH WALES	6	2	-	-	3	1	15	1.276	3024	80	2814	95
QUEENSLAND	5*	1	2	2	-	-	13	0.755	2072	81	2235	66
SOUTH AUSTRALIA	6	1	1	3	1	-	9	0.841	2789	108	2823	92
TOTAL	11	5	5	5	5	1	53	1.000	10035	336	10035	336

* The match between Queensland and Victoria at Brisbane was abandoned without a ball bowled. Each team received 2 points.

QUEENSLAND v SOUTH AUSTRALIA (Shield Match 1)

Played at Exhibition Ground, Brisbane, on October 31, November 1, 3, 1930. (Four-day match)
Toss : Queensland.   Result : QUEENSLAND WON BY SEVEN WICKETS.
Debuts: Queensland - H.V.Burns, E.Gilbert, F.W.Sides (all f/c). South Australia - C.S.Deverson, B.J.Tobin, M.G.Waite, L.S.Walsh
   (all f/c).
12th Men: K.L.M.Mossop (Qld) and G.H.Palmer (SA).
Umpires: J.Bartlett and B.L.Turner.
Attendances: 5000, 12000, 1500.   Total: About 18,500.   Receipts: £520.
Close of Play: 1st day Qld 7/271 (Cooper 18, Burns 2); 2nd day SA (2) 3/180 (Tobin 14, Lonergan 25).

Biggs (108 in 143 minutes, 14 fours) added 165 runs for the Queensland third wicket with Thompson (78 in 184 minutes, 4 fours). Overnight rain following the first day was responsible for South Australia's poor first-innings total of 72, completed on a drying wicket. Put in again, Nitschke (54 in 95 minutes, 5 fours), Lee (57 not out in 70 minutes, 2 sixes and 5 fours) and Pritchard (52 in 101 minutes, 4 fours) registered half-centuries but none of the batsmen went on after getting a start. With a Queensland victory imminent, the umpires dispensed with the tea adjournment on the third day, though Biggs (47 in 72 minutes, 6 fours) was run out attempting the winning run. *NSWCA Report* incorrectly gives SA (1) Bensted 1/13. Sources: *Wisden, NSWCA Report, VCA Report, Brisbane Courier, Brisbane Daily Mail, Sydney Morning Herald, Maryborough Chronicle.*

QUEENSLAND

Batsman	Dismissal	Runs	2nd innings	Runs
R.K.Oxenham	c Parry b Deverson	7		
W.Rowe	c Tobin b Carlton	3	(1) run out (Waite/Parry)	8
M.Biggs	c Lonergan b Lee	108	(2) run out (Waite)	47
F.C.Thompson	c Parry b Lee	78	(5) not out	1
*F.J.Gough	c Walsh b Carlton	7	(4) not out	13
F.W.Sides	c Deverson b Carlton	3	(3) b Lee	18
E.C.Bensted	c Parry b Lee	37		
G.H.Cooper	b Lee	25		
†H.V.Burns	b Carlton	2		
E.Gilbert	run out	6		
H.M.Thurlow	not out	0		
Extras	(b4, lb2, nb7)	13	(nb1)	1
Total	(66.5 overs, 285 mins)	289	(19.0 overs, 75 mins) (3 wkts)	88

SOUTH AUSTRALIA

Batsman	Dismissal	Runs	2nd innings	Runs
G.W.Harris	c Bensted b Thurlow	8	lbw b Oxenham	29
H.C.Nitschke	lbw b Thurlow	4	c Thurlow b Gilbert	54
*D.E.Pritchard	c Cooper b Bensted	11	c & b Oxenham	52
A.R.Lonergan	b Thurlow	10	c & b Bensted	29
B.J.Tobin	b Gilbert	6	b Thurlow	25
L.S.Walsh	b Gilbert	0	b Rowe	23
P.K.Lee	c Biggs b Thurlow	3	not out	57
M.G.Waite	c & b Thurlow	3	run out (Sides/Oxenham)	0
†C.N.Parry	run out (/Oxenham)	8	c Gough b Gilbert	0
T.A.Carlton	c Rowe b Oxenham	17	run out (Oxenham/Burns)	5
C.S.Deverson	not out	0	b Oxenham	18
Extras	(lb1, nb1)	2	(b5, lb6, nb1)	12
Total	(29.0 overs, 123 mins)	72	(76.3 overs, 298 mins)	304

SOUTH AUSTRALIA	O	M	R	W	w,nb		O	M	R	W	w,nb
Deverson	14	0	53	1	-,-		4	0	20	0	-,1
Carlton	26	8	67	4	-,3		4	0	20	0	-,-
Tobin	5	1	22	0	-,2						
Lee	17.5	0	98	4	-,2	(3)	6	1	19	1	-,-
Waite	4	0	36	0	-,-	(4)	5	1	28	0	-,-

QUEENSLAND	O	M	R	W	w,nb		O	M	R	W	w,nb
Gilbert	11	4	22	2	-,-		19	2	76	2	-,-
Thurlow	9	2	25	5	-,1		16	0	63	1	-,-
Bensted	5	0	16	1	-,-		11	1	44	1	-,1
Oxenham	4	1	7	1	-,-		22.3	5	60	3	-,-
Rowe							7	1	46	1	-,-
Gough							1	0	3	0	-,-

FALL OF WICKETS

Wkt	QLD 1st	SA 1st	SA 2nd	QLD 2nd
1st	11	11	50	17
2nd	13	16	115	48
3rd	178	27	156	87
4th	185	35	188	-
5th	190	36	214	-
6th	240	43	254	-
7th	267	47	256	-
8th	271	47	258	-
9th	289	72	271	-
10th	289	72	304	-

NEW SOUTH WALES v SOUTH AUSTRALIA (Shield Match 2)

Played at Sydney Cricket Ground on November 7, 8, 10, 11, 1930. (Four-day match)
Toss : New South Wales.   Result : NEW SOUTH WALES WON BY 213 RUNS.
Debuts: New South Wales - G.L.Stewart (f/c).
12th Men: J.H.W.Fingleton (NSW) and G.H.Palmer (SA).
Umpires: W.H.Bayfield and M.Carney.
Attendances: 8146, 12731, 2436, 109.   Total: 23,422.   Receipts: £969.
Close of Play: 1st day SA 5/74 (Nitschke 29, Lee 25); 2nd day NSW (2) 5/317 (Allsopp 52, Davidson 19); 3rd day SA (2) 8/243
     (Nitschke 124, Carlton 4).

Despite the presence of Bradman, Fairfax and Kippax in the home side, both teams were below full strength. The remainder of the 1930 tourists eligible, A.Jackson, S.J.McCabe and W.A.S.Oldfield for New South Wales and C.V.Grimmett, V.Y.Richardson, C.W.Walker and T.W.Wall for South Australia had not returned from England in time for the match. Bradman (61 in 108 minutes, 7 fours), Fairfax (62 in 96 minutes, 6 fours) and Hooker (54 in 50 minutes, 7 fours) scored first-innings fifties for New South Wales. Hooker suffered a split finger while fielding on the second day and took no further part. Stewart dismissed Harris with the third ball of South Australia's first innings and repeated the dismissal in the third over of the second innings. A third-wicket stand of 219 between Bradman (121 in 142 minutes, 13 fours) and Kippax (104 in 158 minutes, 11 fours) plus 93 from Allsopp (103 minutes, 10 fours) gave New South Wales a lead of 500 runs. Despite Nitschke's 141 (266 minutes, 15 fours, chances at 33 and 115) South Australia finished well short. *Wisden* incorrectly gives NSW (2) Andrews c Parry. Sources: *Wisden, NSWCA Report, SACA Report, Sydney Morning Herald, Sydney Referee, The Herald.*

NEW SOUTH WALES

Batsman	Dismissal	Runs		2nd innings	Runs
W.C.Andrews	b Deverson	6		lbw b Carlton	0
O.W.Bill	c Parry b Carlton	2		run out (Waite/Parry)	5
D.G.Bradman	c Pritchard b Deverson	61		c Waite b Deverson	121
*A.F.Kippax	lbw b Tobin	19		b Deverson	104
A.H.Allsopp	b Tobin	9		b Carlton	93
A.G.Fairfax	b Carlton	62		b Deverson	6
†H.L.Davidson	c Walsh b Deverson	2		c Tobin b Deverson	19
J.E.H.Hooker	b Deverson	54		absent hurt	-
H.C.Chilvers	b Carlton	3	(8) c Lonergan b Lee	29
W.A.Hunt	st Parry b Carlton	2	(9) not out	7
G.L.Stewart	not out	4	(10) run out (Waite/Parry)	2
Extras	(w1, nb3)	4		(b4, lb1, w1, nb4)	10
Total	(47.1 overs, 200 mins)	228		(68.3 overs, 285 mins)	396

SOUTH AUSTRALIA

Batsman	Dismissal	Runs		2nd innings	Runs
G.W.Harris	b Stewart	0		b Stewart	0
H.C.Nitschke	b Stewart	31		c Fairfax b Hunt	141
*D.E.Pritchard	b Stewart	8		b Fairfax	30
A.R.Lonergan	lbw b Hooker	0	(5) c Davidson b Chilvers	9
B.J.Tobin	run out (Hunt/Davidson)	3	(6) lbw b Fairfax	6
L.S.Walsh	lbw b Hooker	0	(7) c Allsopp b Fairfax	18
P.K.Lee	b Hooker	40	(4) run out (Fingleton/Davidson)	36
M.G.Waite	not out	17		lbw b Hunt	8
†C.N.Parry	c Davidson b Hooker	8		b Hunt	0
T.A.Carlton	c Hunt b Hooker	2		c Hunt b Fairfax	22
C.S.Deverson	c Andrews b Hunt	6		not out	4
Extras	(b6, lb3)	9		(b4, lb8, nb1)	13
Total	(52.3 overs, 193 mins)	124		(79.1 overs, 283 mins)	287

SOUTH AUSTRALIA	O	M	R	W	w,nb		O	M	R	W	w,nb
Deverson	15	1	60	4	-,-		19	1	86	4	-,-
Carlton	9.1	1	28	4	-,1		15.3	1	61	2	1,2
Lee	5	0	21	0	-,-		15	0	107	1	-,-
Tobin	9	0	75	2	-,2		3	0	25	0	-,2
Waite	9	0	40	0	1,-		16	1	107	0	-,-

NEW SOUTH WALES	O	M	R	W	w,nb		O	M	R	W	w,nb
Stewart	15	4	25	3	-,-		18	3	72	1	-,1
Hooker	11	1	28	5	-,-						
Fairfax	10	3	12	0	-,-	(2)	18.1	4	54	4	-,-
Chilvers	13	2	35	0	-,-	(3)	19	0	67	1	-,-
Hunt	3.3	0	15	1	-,-	(4)	14	4	37	3	-,-
Bradman						(5)	7	0	41	0	-,-
Kippax						(6)	3	0	3	0	-,-

FALL OF WICKETS

Wkt	NSW 1st	SA 1st	NSW 2nd	SA 2nd
1st	8	0	7	2
2nd	8	14	9	57
3rd	52	15	228	137
4th	75	18	249	150
5th	126	25	268	157
6th	130	82	324	210
7th	213	99	383	238
8th	219	111	391	238
9th	223	115	396	271
10th	228	124	-	287

AUSTRALIAN XI v THE REST

Played at Melbourne Cricket Ground on November 14, 15, 17 (no play), 18, 1930. (Four-day match)
Toss : The Rest.　　　　　　Result : MATCH DRAWN.
Debuts: Nil.
12th Men: V.Y.Richardson (Aust) and L.S.Darling (Rest).
Umpires: A.N.Barlow and D.A.Elder.
Attendances: 12519, 44434, no play, 8337.　　　Total: 65,290.　　　Receipts: £2892.
Close of Play: 1st day Rest 6/267 (Ellis 3, Blackie 0); 2nd day Aust 6/298 (Woodfull 53, a'Beckett 10); 3rd day no play.

Staged for the benefit of Ryder who was subsequently presented with a cheque for £2463, the match was handicapped by rain which caused several delays on the first day and washed out all of the third day. The Australian side comprised members of the 1930 team to England. Harris (108 in 207 minutes, 7 fours), Hendry (45 in 69 minutes, 3 fours), Rigg (74 in 135 minutes, 3 fours) and Ryder (38 in 73 minutes, 3 fours and 65 not out in 84 minutes, 1 five and 5 fours) made the highest scores for the Rest. Alexander was out first ball. Bradman (73 in 128 minutes, 4 fours), Kippax (70 in 164 minutes, 3 fours) and Woodfull (53 in 86 minutes, 2 fours) scored fifties for Australia. Last first-class appearance by T.J.E.Andrews and A.A.Mailey. Sources: *Wisden, VCA Report, NSWCA Report, The Age, The Argus, The Herald, Melbourne Sun.*

THE REST

G.W.Harris	lbw b Grimmett	108	(5)	not out	13
H.S.T.L.Hendry	c Fairfax b Grimmett	45	(2)	c Grimmett b McCabe	74
K.E.Rigg	b Wall	29		not out	65
*J.Ryder	b Grimmett	38	(1)	b a'Beckett	15
A.H.Allsopp	lbw b Fairfax	20	(3)	lbw b Fairfax	17
T.J.E.Andrews	lbw b Grimmett	17			
†J.L.Ellis	not out	21			
D.D.Blackie	run out (Ponsford/Oldfield/Jackson)	5			
H.H.Alexander	b a'Beckett	0			
A.A.Mailey	run out (Grimmett/a'Beckett)	2			
H.Ironmonger	c Oldfield b Grimmett	0			
Extras	(b5, lb3)	8		(b4, lb2, nb1)	7
Total	(77.1 overs, 280 mins)	293		(47.0 overs, 155 mins) (3 wkts dec)	191

AUSTRALIAN XI

W.H.Ponsford	lbw b Alexander	14	(3)	lbw b Ironmonger	0
A.Jackson	c Ellis b Alexander	4		b Alexander	5
D.G.Bradman	b Mailey	73	(1)	c & b Mailey	29
A.F.Kippax	lbw b Blackie	70		b Blackie	17
S.J.McCabe	c Alexander b Ironmonger	27		b Blackie	20
*W.M.Woodfull	b Ironmonger	53		not out	13
A.G.Fairfax	c Alexander b Ironmonger	39			
E.L.a'Beckett	c Andrews b Mailey	30			
†W.A.S.Oldfield	run out (Harris/Ellis)	18			
C.V.Grimmett	b Mailey	28			
T.W.Wall	not out	2			
Extras	(b4, lb5)	9		(b8, lb2, w1, nb1)	12
Total	(94.3 overs, 330 mins)	367		(20.5 overs, 85 mins) (5 wkts)	96

AUSTRALIAN XI	O	M	R	W	w,nb		O	M	R	W	w,nb
Wall	15	0	75	1	-,-						
Fairfax	15	1	52	1	-,-	(1)	10	1	24	1	-,1
Grimmett	29.1	3	89	5	-,-		10	0	32	0	-,-
McCabe	7	0	40	0	-,-		8	0	42	1	-,-
a'Beckett	11	2	29	1	-,-	(2)	13	1	42	1	-,-
Bradman						(5)	4	0	27	0	-,-
Kippax						(6)	2	0	17	0	-,-

THE REST	O	M	R	W	w,nb		O	M	R	W	w,nb
Alexander	15	1	64	2	-,-		5	1	24	1	1,1
Hendry	7	0	27	0	-,-						
Blackie	17	2	45	1	-,-		5.5	0	15	2	-,-
Ironmonger	28	3	76	3	-,-	(2)	6	0	17	1	-,-
Mailey	23.3	2	126	3	-,-	(4)	4	0	28	1	-,-
Ryder	2	0	11	0	-,-						
Andrews	2	0	9	0	-,-						

FALL OF WICKETS

	REST	AUST	REST	AUST
Wkt	1st	1st	2nd	2nd
1st	82	9	25	20
2nd	139	24	63	25
3rd	224	129	162	61
4th	231	186	-	65
5th	259	191	-	96
6th	267	276	-	-
7th	278	298	-	-
8th	278	332	-	-
9th	293	343	-	-
10th	293	367	-	-

NEW SOUTH WALES v WEST INDIES XI

Played at Sydney Cricket Ground on November 21, 22, 24, 25, 1930. (Four-day match)
Toss : West Indies XI.   Result : NEW SOUTH WALES WON BY FOUR WICKETS.
Debuts: Nil.
12th Men: W.C.Andrews (NSW) and O.S.Wight (WI).
Umpires: E.G.Borwick and W.G.French.
Attendances: 17830, 28809, 7077, 2738.   Total: 56,454.   Receipts: £3488.
Close of Play: 1st day NSW 2/71 (Bradman 39, Kippax 6); 2nd day WI (2) 3/61 (Headley 29, Grant 0); 3rd day NSW (2) 5/134 (Fairfax 2, Hunt 0).

West Indies' inaugural first-class match in Australia. J.E.H.Hooker (injured hand) was unavailable for New South Wales. Roach (43 in 101 minutes, 6 fours), Headley 82 in 159 minutes, 5 fours), Grant (44 in 113 minutes, 3 fours) and Constantine (59 in 35 minutes, 4 sixes and 4 fours) each surpassed 40 for the visitors. Bradman (73 in 85 minutes, 10 fours) and Jackson (62 in 86 minutes, 4 fours) top-scored for New South Wales. Kippax was absent on the third day due to illness but was present on the fourth day to bat if needed; the captaincy was handled by Oldfield in the meantime. *Wisden* incorrectly gives NSW (2) Stewart batting instead of Hunt, Francis 0/37, Scott 0/28. Due to a scoreboard error in NSW (1) which recorded Fairfax 10, total 207, all sources except *SMH* give incorrect falls of wickets. Sources: *Wisden, NSWCA Report, VCA Report, Sydney Morning Herald, Sydney Referee, The Herald.*

WEST INDIES XI

C.A.Roach	b Fairfax	43		b McCabe	20
F.R.Martin	c Oldfield b Fairfax	21		st Oldfield b Chilvers	4
G.A.Headley	st Oldfield b Chilvers	25		c Bradman b Chilvers	82
E.L.Bartlett	b Fairfax	0	(6)	c Bradman b Hunt	9
*G.C.Grant	c Oldfield b Chilvers	30		run out (Jackson/Oldfield)	44
L.S.Birkett	st Oldfield b Chilvers	31	(4)	c Oldfield b Chilvers	7
L.N.Constantine	c Bill b McCabe	18		c & b Chilvers	59
G.N.Francis	c Oldfield b McCabe	8	(10)	run out	2
†I.Barrow	st Oldfield b Chilvers	2	(8)	st Oldfield b Chilvers	2
E.L.St Hill	c Hunt b McCabe	1	(11)	not out	4
O.C.Scott	not out	4	(9)	c Bradman b Fairfax	1
Extras	(b2, lb2, nb1)	5		(b4, lb2, nb1)	7
Total	(63.2 overs, 221 mins)	188		(68.0 overs, 228 mins)	241

NEW SOUTH WALES

A.G.Fairfax	b Constantine	9	(5)	not out	32
O.W.Bill	c Constantine b St Hill	13		lbw b Martin	34
D.G.Bradman	c Barrow b Francis	73		c Headley b Martin	22
*A.F.Kippax	b Constantine	6			
S.J.McCabe	b Constantine	18	(8)	not out	37
A.Jackson	lbw b Constantine	13	(1)	b Martin	62
A.H.Allsopp	run out (Grant)	32	(4)	b Constantine	3
†W.A.S.Oldfield	st Barrow b Scott	21	(6)	lbw b Constantine	0
H.C.Chilvers	b Francis	8			
W.A.Hunt	b Francis	5	(7)	c Roach b St Hill	20
G.L.Stewart	not out	1			
Extras	(lb1, nb6)	7		(b3, lb4, nb7)	14
Total	(43.0 overs, 174 mins)	206		(45.1 overs, 179 mins) (6 wkts)	224

NEW SOUTH WALES	O	M	R	W	w,nb		O	M	R	W	w,nb			WI	NSW	WI	NSW
Stewart	8	1	25	0	-,-		11	1	38	0	-,-		Wkt	1st	1st	2nd	2nd
Fairfax	14	3	42	3	-,1		18	1	57	1	-,1		1st	64	21	21	97
Chilvers	23	2	84	4	-,-	(4)	22	2	73	5	-,-		2nd	83	49	46	120
McCabe	14.2	6	23	3	-,-	(3)	8	0	31	1	-,-		3rd	83	71	60	123
Hunt	4	0	9	0	-,-		9	2	35	1	-,-		4th	95	105	159	131
													5th	151	135	159	131
WEST INDIES XI	O	M	R	W	w,nb		O	M	R	W	w,nb		6th	165	157	187	168
Constantine	11	1	43	4	-,-		11.1	2	53	2	-,-		7th	181	186	212	-
Francis	11	2	38	3	-,6		8	0	43	0	-,7		8th	182	200	235	-
St Hill	10	2	46	1	-,-		14	1	57	1	-,-		9th	184	205	235	-
Scott	8	0	50	1	-,-		4	0	22	0	-,-		10th	188	206	241	-
Martin	3	0	22	0	-,-		8	0	35	3	-,-						

VICTORIA v WEST INDIES XI

Played at Melbourne Cricket Ground on November 28, 29, December 1, 1930. (Four-day match)
Toss : West Indies XI.   Result : VICTORIA WON BY AN INNINGS AND 254 RUNS.
Debuts: Nil.
12th Men: L.P.J.O'Brien (Vic) and J.E.D.Sealy (WI).
Umpires: H.E.Nichols and R.Shaw.
Attendances: 11233, 25083, 10265.   Total: 46,581.   Receipts: £1706.
Close of Play: 1st day Vic 2/137 (Ponsford 53, Ryder 38); 2nd day Vic 5/562 (Darling 65, Barnett 58).

Hassett replaced D.D.Blackie (influenza) in the Victorian side before the start. Headley (131 in 141 minutes, 14 fours) compiled 61.8 per cent of the West Indies' first-innings total as he became their first batsman to score a hundred in Australia. Griffith was given out 'lbw' even though the ball continued into the stumps after striking his leg. After Constantine bowled Woodfull with the third ball of Victoria's innings, Ponsford (187 in 286 minutes, 13 fours) shared century partnerships with Ryder (65 in 95 minutes, 4 fours) and Rigg (126 in 179 minutes, 2 fives, 10 fours, chance at 125) for the third and fourth wickets. Hendry (44 in 48 minutes, 3 fours), Darling (83 in 152 minutes, 5 fours) and Barnett (58 in 71 minutes, 5 fours) also contributed. Headley (34 in 54 minutes, 3 fours) again top-scored for West Indies, Ironmonger capturing career-best figures of 8 for 31. *Wisden* incorrectly gives WI (1) dismissal of Griffith and gives incomplete WI bowling. Sources: *Wisden, NSWCA Report, VCA Report, The Age, The Argus, The Herald, Melbourne Sun.*

WEST INDIES XI

C.A.Roach	c Rigg b Ironmonger	10		lbw b Alexander	3
F.R.Martin	lbw b a'Beckett	3	(4)	c Barnett b Ironmonger	13
G.A.Headley	c Darling b a'Beckett	131		lbw b Ironmonger	34
F.I.de Caires	lbw b Ironmonger	0	(6)	lbw b Ironmonger	0
*G.C.Grant	c Rigg b Ironmonger	0		c Hendry b Hassett	26
L.S.Birkett	c Hendry b Ironmonger	0	(8)	c a'Beckett b Ironmonger	7
L.N.Constantine	c a'Beckett b Ironmonger	34		c Darling b Ironmonger	1
O.S.Wight	c Barnett b Alexander	7	(9)	b Ironmonger	7
†E.A.C.Hunte	not out	19	(2)	c Alexander b Ironmonger	12
O.C.Scott	b a'Beckett	5		c Hendry b Ironmonger	7
H.C.Griffith	lbw b a'Beckett	0		not out	9
Extras	(lb2, nb1)	3		(b6, nb3)	9
Total	(44.5 overs, 183 mins)	212		(40.3 overs, 155 mins)	128

VICTORIA

*W.M.Woodfull	b Constantine	0
W.H.Ponsford	c Grant b Scott	187
H.S.T.L.Hendry	c Birkett b Martin	44
J.Ryder	c Roach b Scott	65
K.E.Rigg	c & b Birkett	126
L.S.Darling	b Constantine	83
†B.A.Barnett	c de Caires b Constantine	58
R.J.Hassett	b Constantine	0
E.L.a'Beckett	not out	13
H.H.Alexander	b Constantine	0
H.Ironmonger	c Constantine b Griffith	0
Extras	(b14, lb2, nb2)	18
Total	(126.2 overs, 446 mins)	594

VICTORIA	O	M	R	W	w,nb		O	M	R	W	w,nb
Alexander	9	1	33	1	-,-		6	0	25	1	-,3
a'Beckett	15.5	2	51	4	-,-		10	3	15	0	-,-
Ironmonger	14	1	87	5	-,1		14.3	3	31	8	-,-
Hassett	6	0	38	0	-,-		10	1	48	1	-,-

WEST INDIES XI	O	M	R	W	w,nb
Constantine	15	1	64	5	-,-
Griffith	28.2	3	104	1	-,2
Martin	28	2	109	1	-,-
Scott	28	0	153	2	-,-
Roach	8	1	45	0	-,-
Birkett	19	1	101	1	-,-

	FALL OF WICKETS		
Wkt	WI 1st	VIC 1st	VIC 2nd
1st	6	0	10
2nd	24	69	55
3rd	26	192	60
4th	26	392	75
5th	36	448	75
6th	102	562	83
7th	127	562	92
8th	204	593	110
9th	212	593	114
10th	212	594	128

QUEENSLAND v NEW SOUTH WALES (Shield Match 3)

Played at Exhibition Ground, Brisbane, on November 28, 29, December 1, 2, 1930. (Four-day match)
Toss : New South Wales. Result : MATCH DRAWN.
Debuts: Nil.
12th Men: G.S.Amos (Qld) and W.C.Andrews (NSW).
Umpires: W.R.Fraser and J.P.Orr.
Attendances: ? , 2000, ? , 5000. Total: About 16,000. Receipts: £911.
Close of Play: 1st day NSW 5/414 (McCabe 42, Love 23); 2nd day Qld 2/166 (Gough 93, Thompson 37); 3rd day Qld 4/490
  (Thompson 186, Bensted 47).

Queensland marked the last Shield match at the Exhibition Ground by compiling their highest first-class total to date. Gough (137 in 308 minutes, 16 fours) and Thompson (275 not out in 628 minutes, 25 fours, chance at 133) made their career-highest scores. Thompson shared successive century partnerships with Gough, Oxenham (67 in 112 minutes, 7 fours) and Bensted (52 in 125 minutes, 6 fours). Hurwood's 47 took 31 minutes and included 7 fours. Three individual performances accounted for nearly all of New South Wales's 566: Bill (career-best 153 in 284 minutes, 20 fours), Kippax (158 in 202 minutes, 1 five and 20 fours) and McCabe (161 in 155 minutes, 24 fours) were the only batsmen to exceed the twenties. Allsopp's pair included a first-ball duck in the second innings. D.G.Bradman was unavailable for New South Wales and Love replaced W.A.S.Oldfield (work commitments) after selection. *Wisden* incorrectly gives Qld Hurwood st Allsopp. Sources: *Wisden, NSWCA Report, QCA Report, Brisbane Courier, Sydney Morning Herald, The Herald.*

NEW SOUTH WALES

A.Jackson	b Hurwood	23		c Leeson b Oxenham	53
O.W.Bill	c & b Gilbert	153		b Thurlow	2
A.G.Fairfax	lbw b Hurwood	3	(5)	not out	18
*A.F.Kippax	c Thurlow b Thompson	158			
S.J.McCabe	b Gilbert	161	(3)	b Oxenham	53
A.H.Allsopp	c Oxenham b Hurwood	0	(4)	c Leeson b Oxenham	0
†H.S.B.Love	b Gilbert	24	(6)	b Oxenham	12
J.E.H.Hooker	b Oxenham	6	(7)	not out	5
H.C.Chilvers	c Gough b Oxenham	24			
W.A.Hunt	b Gilbert	0			
G.L.Stewart	not out	1			
Extras	(b4, lb9)	13		(b12, lb4)	16
Total	(122.0 overs, 433 mins)	566		(37.0 overs, 125 mins) (5 wkts)	159

QUEENSLAND

*F.J.Gough	lbw b Chilvers	137
K.L.M.Mossop	b Chilvers	12
M.Biggs	c Love b McCabe	16
F.C.Thompson	not out	275
R.K.Oxenham	c Love b Hunt	67
E.C.Bensted	b Stewart	52
†H.F.Leeson	lbw b Stewart	0
P.M.Hornibrook	lbw b Hunt	27
A.Hurwood	st Love b Hooker	47
E.Gilbert	b Hunt	4
H.M.Thurlow	b Hunt	17
Extras	(b13, lb17, w1, nb2)	33
Total	(211.3 overs, 703 mins)	687

QUEENSLAND	O	M	R	W	w,nb		O	M	R	W	w,nb
Gilbert	25	2	118	4	-,-		8	0	31	0	-,-
Thurlow	19	2	83	0	-,-		6	0	30	1	-,-
Oxenham	29	2	109	2	-,-	(5)	9	3	19	4	-,-
Bensted	4	0	13	0	-,-						
Hurwood	26	2	108	3	-,-	(3)	8	0	35	0	-,-
Hornibrook	10	2	51	0	-,-	(4)	6	1	28	0	-,-
Gough	2	0	29	0	-,-						
Thompson	7	1	42	1	-,-						

NEW SOUTH WALES	O	M	R	W	w,nb
Stewart	19	1	72	2	1,-
Fairfax	36	9	76	0	-,1
Hooker	33	11	61	1	-,1
Chilvers	45	3	219	2	-,-
McCabe	28	8	65	1	-,-
Hunt	33.3	1	128	4	-,-
Kippax	17	9	33	0	-,-

FALL OF WICKETS

	NSW	QLD	NSW
Wkt	1st	1st	2nd
1st	39	45	14
2nd	55	72	121
3rd	335	256	121
4th	359	386	124
5th	362	499	148
6th	431	499	-
7th	457	580	-
8th	558	651	-
9th	558	660	-
10th	566	687	-

SOUTH AUSTRALIA v WEST INDIES

Played at Adelaide Oval on December 5, 6, 8, 1930. (Four-day match)
Toss : West Indies XI.   Result : SOUTH AUSTRALIA WON BY TEN WICKETS.
Debuts: Nil.
12th Men: B.J.Tobin (SA) and O.S.Wight (WI).
Umpires: G.A.Hele and A.J.Jenkins.
Attendances: 8088, 10861, 1125.   Total: 20,074.   Receipts: £800.
Close of Play: 1st day SA 4/117 (Lee 38, Grimmett 26); 2nd day WA (2) 7/122 (Bartlett 22).

Waite, South Australia's nominated 12th man, replaced H.E.Whitfield (unavailable). Roach (64 in 85 minutes, 1 six and 7 fours) was the only West Indian to register fifty. After losing their first four batsmen for 53 in return, South Australia recovered through Lee (55 in 114 minutes, 5 fours) and Grimmett (50 in 124 minutes, 2 fours) with a 97-run stand for the fifth wicket. Walker (45 in 66 minutes, 1 four) and Wall (53 in 83 minutes, 3 fours) later added 93 runs for the tenth wicket to establish a match-winning lead. Francis bowled Nitschke with his no-ball in the first innings. Grimmett dismissed Roach and Birkett with successive deliveries in the second innings, in which Bartlett (33 in 54 minutes, 3 fours) top-scored. *Wisden* incorrectly gives WI (1) Sealy b Grimmett. Sources: *Wisden, SACA Report, Adelaide Advertiser, South Australian Register, The News.*

WEST INDIES XI

C.A.Roach	c Lee b Carlton	64		c Wall b Grimmett	23
L.S.Birkett	c Wall b Lee	14		st Walker b Grimmett	26
G.A.Headley	run out (Waite/Walker)	27		c & b Waite	16
F.R.Martin	c Walker b Wall	1		lbw b Waite	22
E.L.Bartlett	b Grimmett	5	(6)	c Nitschke b Wall	33
*G.C.Grant	c Carlton b Grimmett	0	(5)	c & b Grimmett	1
L.N.Constantine	hit wkt b Carlton	18	(9)	c Walker b Grimmett	3
†E.A.C.Hunte	c Walker b Grimmett	12	(7)	c Nitschke b Waite	2
J.E.D.Sealy	c & b Grimmett	13	(8)	c Richardson b Grimmett	6
G.N.Francis	not out	11		not out	12
H.C.Griffith	c Walker b Carlton	2		c Walker b Lee	7
Extras	(b3, lb1)	4		(b4, lb5, nb2)	11
Total	(37.5 overs, 155 mins)	171		(40.1 overs, 152 mins)	162

SOUTH AUSTRALIA

G.W.Harris	run out (Constantine/Martin)	21		not out	4
H.C.Nitschke	b Francis	22		not out	0
D.E.Pritchard	run out (Roach/Hunte)	5			
*V.Y.Richardson	lbw b Constantine	2			
P.K.Lee	c Hunte b Constantine	55			
C.V.Grimmett	lbw b Martin	50			
A.R.Lonergan	c Roach b Martin	19			
M.G.Waite	c Roach b Griffith	39			
T.A.Carlton	c Grant b Griffith	11			
†C.W.Walker	c Grant b Griffith	45			
T.W.Wall	not out	53			
Extras	(b5, lb2, nb1)	8			–
Total	(84.5 overs, 318 mins)	330		(2.1 overs, 8 mins) (0 wkts)	4

SOUTH AUSTRALIA	O	M	R	W	w,nb		O	M	R	W	w,nb	
Wall	10	3	31	1	-,-		9	1	43	1	-,-	
Carlton	8.5	0	42	3	-,-		7	2	19	0	-,2	
Grimmett	14	0	71	4	-,-		14	0	43	5	-,-	
Lee	5	0	23	1	-,-	(5)	0.1	0	0	1	-,-	
Waite						(4)	10	0	46	3	-,-	

WEST INDIES XI	O	M	R	W	w,nb		O	M	R	W	w,nb
Francis	16	0	77	1	-,1						
Constantine	19	0	86	2	-,-	(1)	1.1	0	4	0	-,-
Griffith	23.5	4	75	3	-,-	(2)	1	1	0	0	-,-
Martin	20	3	60	2	-,-						
Birkett	4	0	12	0	-,-						
Headley	2	0	12	0	-,-						

FALL OF WICKETS

Wkt	WI 1st	SA 1st	WI 2nd	SA 2nd
1st	31	40	51	-
2nd	103	49	51	-
3rd	106	49	79	-
4th	112	53	82	-
5th	112	150	101	-
6th	112	174	105	-
7th	130	184	122	-
8th	152	220	136	-
9th	166	237	140	-
10th	171	330	162	-

NEW SOUTH WALES v QUEENSLAND (Shield Match 4)

Played at Sydney Cricket Ground on December 11, 12, 14, 15 (no play), 1930. (Four-day match)
Toss : Queensland.　　　　　　　Result : MATCH DRAWN.
Debuts: Nil.
12th Men: W.C.Andrews (NSW) and G.A.Bourne (Qld).
Umpires: H.J.Armstrong and A.H.Farrow.
Attendances: 4334, 3630, 6339, 173.　　　Total: 14,476.　　　Receipts: £500.
Close of Play: 1st day NSW 6/104 (Fingleton 55, Chilvers 4); 2nd day Qld (2) 5/301 (Goodwin 45, Amos 10); 3rd day NSW (2) 1/212
　　(Bill 93, Love 32).

After suffering a first-ball dismissal, Litster sustained a severe strain in the field and took no further part, returning to Brisbane on the first evening.　Oxenham (53 in 151 minutes, 2 fours) and Goodwin (62 in 101 minutes, 6 fours) for Queensland and Fingleton (56 in 121 minutes, 4 fours) for New South Wales scored first-innings fifties. Hooker dismissed Biggs in his first over in the first innings. Gough (58 in 101 minutes, 8 fours), Bensted (92 in 173 minutes, 6 fours, chance at 83) and Goodwin (64 in 113 minutes, 6 fours) helped to set New South Wales 393 to win and the match was interestingly poised when rain washed out the last day. Fingleton (71 in 156 minutes, 7 fours) and Bill (93 not out in 242 minutes) had added 154 for the first wicket. Stewart replaced S.C.Everett (work) in the New South Wales team. Sources: *Wisden, NSWCA Report, QCA Report, Sydney Morning Herald, Sydney Referee, Brisbane Courier*.

QUEENSLAND

*F.J.Gough	lbw b Stewart	2	b Cummins	58
M.Biggs	b Hooker	0	b Stewart	4
E.C.Bensted	b Hooker	7	c & b Stewart	92
F.C.Thompson	c & b Hunt	15	lbw b Hooker	37
R.K.Oxenham	b Campbell	53	b Hunt	32
J.L.Litster	b Hunt	0	absent hurt	-
V.H.V.Goodwin	c Stewart b Hunt	62	(6) b Hooker	64
†H.F.Leeson	run out (Chilvers/Love)	1	lbw b Hooker	1
G.S.Amos	st Love b Hunt	9	(7) b Hooker	20
H.M.Thurlow	b Hunt	10	(9) not out	10
E.Gilbert	not out	1	(10) b Hunt	24
Extras	(b1, lb3, nb2)	6	(b7, lb14, nb6)	27
Total	(63.4 overs, 210 mins)	166	(94.3 overs, 333 mins)	369

NEW SOUTH WALES

J.H.W.Fingleton	lbw b Oxenham	56	c Leeson b Thompson	71
O.W.Bill	c Leeson b Amos	10	not out	93
A.E.Marks	st Leeson b Goodwin	16		
F.S.Cummins	c Thurlow b Gilbert	1		
J.E.H.Hooker	b Gilbert	0		
A.H.Allsopp	b Oxenham	1		
J.N.Campbell	b Gilbert	0		
H.C.Chilvers	c Amos b Thompson	19		
*†H.S.B.Love	c Leeson b Thurlow	9	(3) not out	32
W.A.Hunt	not out	13		
G.L.Stewart	b Gilbert	0		
Extras	(b9, lb8, w1)	18	(b12, lb1, nb3)	16
Total	(43.6 overs, 165 mins)	143	(72.0 overs, 242 mins) (1 wkt)	212

NEW SOUTH WALES	O	M	R	W	w,nb	O	M	R	W	w,nb
Stewart	11	3	25	1	-,-	14	1	57	2	-,2
Hooker	13	2	31	2	-,1	27	4	63	4	-,2
Hunt	20.4	7	37	5	-,1	21.3	3	51	2	-,1
Chilvers	11	0	32	0	-,-	13	0	73	0	-,1
Campbell	8	2	35	1	-,-	6	0	41	0	-,-
Cummins						11	2	49	1	-,-
Marks						2	0	8	0	-,-

QUEENSLAND	O	M	R	W	w,nb	O	M	R	W	w,nb
Gilbert	14.6	0	44	4	-,-	16	3	51	0	-,1
Thurlow	8	1	15	1	-,-	13	4	23	0	-,-
Oxenham	13	5	21	2	-,-	21	14	22	0	-,1
Amos	5	0	26	1	1,-	6	0	35	0	-,-
Goodwin	2	0	17	1	-,-	1	0	12	0	-,-
Thompson	1	0	2	1	-,-	13	3	45	1	-,1
Bensted						2	0	8	0	-,-

FALL OF WICKETS

Wkt	QLD 1st	NSW 1st	QLD 2nd	NSW 2nd
1st	0	23	10	154
2nd	6	80	119	-
3rd	18	91	199	-
4th	36	91	220	-
5th	36	94	262	-
6th	129	99	322	-
7th	138	105	332	-
8th	151	126	338	-
9th	155	136	369	-
10th	166	143	-	-

AUSTRALIA v WEST INDIES (1st Test)

Played at Adelaide Oval on December 12, 13, 15, 16, 1930. (Timeless match)
Toss : West Indies.   Result : AUSTRALIA WON BY TEN WICKETS.
Debuts: Australia - A.Hurwood (Test). West Indies - L.S.Birkett, G.C.Grant (both Test).
12th Men: K.E.Rigg (Aust) and J.E.D.Sealy (WI).
Umpires: G.A.Hele and A.G.Jenkins.
Attendances: 8069, 13762, 5272, 2924.   Total: 30,027.   Receipts: £1813.
Close of Play: 1st day WI 7/286 (Grant 49, Francis 3); 2nd day Aust 5/297 (Kippax 118, Fairfax 7); 3rd day WI (2) 7/203 (Grant 50).

The first-ever Test between these countries began 46 years to the day after the inaugural Test match at Adelaide. Despite Headley sustaining a first-ball dismissal, West Indies performed well on the first day. Innings by Roach (56 in 132 minutes, 1 six and 2 fours) and Martin (39 in 88 minutes, 6 fours) preceded a sixth-wicket partnership of 114 between Grant (53 not out in 188 minutes) and Bartlett (84 in 119 minutes, 7 fours). Grimmett took his best figures in a Test in Australia. Kippax (146 in 229 minutes, 18 fours, chance at 9) shared stands of 182 for the fourth wicket with McCabe (90 in 132 minutes, 9 fours) and 72 for the sixth wicket with Fairfax (41 not out in 108 minutes, 1 six and 3 fours). Birkett (64 in 104 minutes, 5 fours) and Grant (71 not out in 160 minutes, 6 fours) hit half-centuries in West Indies' second innings. Ponsford (92 not out with 5 fours) and Jackson (70 not out with 3 fours) encountered little trouble in making the winning runs. Sources: *Wisden, SACA Report, Adelaide Advertiser, South Australian Register, The Herald, The News.*

WEST INDIES

C.A.Roach	st Oldfield b Hurwood	56	b Hurwood	9
L.S.Birkett	c & b Grimmett	27	st Oldfield b Grimmett	64
G.A.Headley	c Wall b Grimmett	0	st Oldfield b Grimmett	11
F.R.Martin	b Grimmett	39	run out (Bradman/Oldfield)	3
L.N.Constantine	c Wall b Grimmett	1	b Grimmett	14
*G.C.Grant	not out	53	not out	71
E.L.Bartlett	lbw b Grimmett	84	c Grimmett b Hurwood	11
†I.Barrow	c Bradman b Grimmett	12	lbw b Bradman	27
G.N.Francis	lbw b Hurwood	5	b Hurwood	3
O.C.Scott	c Fairfax b Grimmett	3	c Kippax b Hurwood	8
H.C.Griffith	b Hurwood	1	st Oldfield b Grimmett	10
Extras	(b6, lb8, nb1)	15	(b16, lb2)	18
Total	(127.1 overs, 318 mins)	296	(98.0 overs, 229 mins)	249

AUSTRALIA

W.H.Ponsford	c Birkett b Francis	24	not out	92
A.Jackson	c Barrow b Francis	31	not out	70
D.G.Bradman	c Grant b Griffith	4		
A.F.Kippax	c Barrow b Griffith	146		
S.J.McCabe	c & b Constantine	90		
*W.M.Woodfull	run out (Constantine/Barrow/Griffith)	6		
A.G.Fairfax	not out	41		
†W.A.S.Oldfield	c Francis b Scott	15		
C.V.Grimmett	c Barrow b Scott	0		
A.Hurwood	c Martin b Scott	0		
T.W.Wall	lbw b Scott	0		
Extras	(b2, lb10, nb7)	19	(b8, w1, nb1)	10
Total	(117.5 overs, 351 mins)	376	(55.3 overs, 148 mins) (0 wkts)	172

AUSTRALIA	O	M	R	W	w,nb		O	M	R	W	w,nb
Wall	16	0	64	0	-,1		10	1	20	0	-,-
Fairfax	11	1	36	0	-,-	(6)	3	2	6	0	-,-
Grimmett	48	19	87	7	-,-		38	7	96	4	-,-
Hurwood	36.1	14	55	3	-,-	(2)	34	11	86	4	-,-
McCabe	12	3	32	0	-,-	(4)	8	2	15	0	-,-
Bradman	4	0	7	0	-,-	(5)	5	1	8	1	-,-

WEST INDIES	O	M	R	W	w,nb		O	M	R	W	w,nb
Francis	18	7	43	2	-,2		10	1	30	0	-,-
Constantine	22	0	89	1	-,-	(4)	9.3	3	27	0	-,-
Griffith	28	4	69	2	-,5	(2)	10	1	20	0	1,-
Martin	29	3	73	0	-,-	(3)	11	0	28	0	-,-
Scott	20.5	2	83	4	-,-		13	0	55	0	-,1
Birkett							2	0	2	0	-,-

FALL OF WICKETS

	WI	AUST	WI	AUST
Wkt	1st	1st	2nd	2nd
1st	58	56	15	-
2nd	58	59	47	-
3rd	118	64	52	-
4th	123	246	74	-
5th	131	269	115	-
6th	245	341	138	-
7th	269	374	203	-
8th	290	374	208	-
9th	295	374	220	-
10th	296	376	249	-

VICTORIA v QUEENSLAND (Shield Match 5)

Played at Melbourne Cricket Ground on December 18, 19, 20, 1930. (Four-day match)
Toss : Queensland.   Result : VICTORIA WON BY AN INNINGS AND 242 RUNS.
Debuts: Queensland - G.A.Bourne (f/c).
12th Men: H.H.Oakley (Vic) and G.S.Amos (Qld).
Umpires: E.C.Ramsden and W.R.Wetenhall.
Attendances: 4767, 5764, 3918.   Total: 14,449.   Receipts: £365.
Close of Play: 1st day Vic 5/303 (O'Brien 11, a'Beckett 9); 2nd day Qld (2) 0/5 (Gough 1, Leeson 3).

O'Brien and Tolhurst replaced W.H.Ponsford and W.M.Woodfull (both unavailable) in the Victorian team. Gough finalised his side contrary to directions from the State selection committee and a subsequent dispute between players and the Q.C.A. officials raged until the end of the season. Put in, Victoria managed 474 due to partnerships of 219 for the third wicket between Rigg (124 in 265 minutes, 10 fours) and Ryder (114 in 199 minutes, 6 fours) and 139 for the sixth wicket between O'Brien (65 in 180 minutes, 4 fours) and a'Beckett (92 in 192 minutes, 9 fours). Oxenham dismissed a'Beckett and Ironmonger with successive balls to finish the innings. Queensland lost Biggs to the first ball of the second over and then collapsed to the spin of Ironmonger (11 for 70) and Blackie (7 for 94) in both innings. Bensted top-scored with 40 in 68 minutes with 6 fours. *Wisden* incorrectly gives Qld (1) Thompson st Love. Sources: *Wisden, VCA Report, QCA Report, The Age, The Argus, The Herald, Melbourne Sun.*

VICTORIA

H.S.T.L.Hendry	b Oxenham	15
E.K.Tolhurst	b Oxenham	22
K.E.Rigg	c Oxenham b Bensted	124
*J.Ryder	c Bensted b Hurwood	114
L.S.Darling	c Leeson b Gilbert	0
L.P.J.O'Brien	lbw b Oxenham	65
E.L.a'Beckett	c & b Oxenham	92
†B.A.Barnett	b Oxenham	7
D.D.Blackie	c Leeson b Hurwood	15
H.H.Alexander	not out	0
H.Ironmonger	b Oxenham	0
Extras	(b12, lb6, nb2)	20
Total	(145.4 overs, 495 mins)	474

QUEENSLAND

*F.J.Gough	b Alexander	19		c & b Blackie	27
M.Biggs	lbw b a'Beckett	0	(7)	c Rigg b Ironmonger	6
E.C.Bensted	lbw b Blackie	20		c Rigg b Blackie	40
F.C.Thompson	st Barnett b Ironmonger	13		c Hendry b Ironmonger	6
V.H.V.Goodwin	c Rigg b Ironmonger	5	(6)	c Barnett b Ironmonger	4
R.K.Oxenham	lbw b Ironmonger	18	(5)	c Alexander b Blackie	1
G.A.Bourne	c O'Brien b Blackie	4	(8)	not out	6
A.Hurwood	lbw b Ironmonger	3	(9)	b Ironmonger	6
†H.F.Leeson	not out	10	(2)	lbw b Blackie	14
E.Gilbert	c Ryder b Blackie	5		c a'Beckett b Ironmonger	0
H.M.Thurlow	b Ironmonger	0		b Ironmonger	11
Extras	(b4, lb2)	6		(b4, lb4)	8
Total	(32.6 overs, 129 mins)	103		(35.2 overs, 136 mins)	129

QUEENSLAND	O	M	R	W	w,nb
Gilbert	25	4	78	1	-,-
Thurlow	18	2	70	0	-,1
Oxenham	43.4	15	92	6	-,-
Hurwood	33	4	115	2	-,-
Thompson	14	3	38	0	-,1
Bensted	10	0	48	1	-,-
Goodwin	2	0	13	0	-,-

VICTORIA	O	M	R	W	w,nb		O	M	R	W	w,nb
Alexander	6	1	17	1	-,-		4	1	10	0	-,-
a'Beckett	3	0	14	1	-,-	(3)	3	0	13	0	-,-
Ironmonger	10.6	4	29	5	-,-	(2)	14.2	3	41	6	-,-
Blackie	13	1	37	3	-,-		14	1	57	4	-,-

FALL OF WICKETS

Wkt	VIC 1st	QLD 1st	QLD 2nd
1st	30	0	42
2nd	49	33	61
3rd	268	47	80
4th	268	61	89
5th	291	68	100
6th	430	75	100
7th	444	84	108
8th	467	87	117
9th	474	102	117
10th	474	103	129

SOUTH AUSTRALIA v NEW SOUTH WALES (Shield Match 6)

Played at Adelaide Oval on December 18, 19, 20, 22, 1930. (Four-day match)
Toss : New South Wales.　　　　Result : NEW SOUTH WALES WON BY AN INNINGS AND 134 RUNS.
Debuts: Nil.
12th Men: B.J.Tobin (SA) and G.L.Stewart (NSW).
Umpires: G.A.Hele and A.G.Jenkins.
Attendances: 4265, 4373, 3722, 392.　　　Total: 12,752　　　Receipts: £399.
Close of Play: 1st day NSW 3/455 (Kippax 20, McCabe 1); 2nd day SA 6/140 (Lee 5, Carlton 1); 3rd day SA (2) 8/246 (Grimmett 20, Wall 3).

A second-wicket partnership of 334 in 223 minutes on the first day between Jackson (166 in 259 minutes, 15 fours) and Bradman (258 in 282 minutes, 37 fours) dominated the game. Neither gave any semblance of a chance, Bradman reaching 100 in 128 minutes and 200 in 234 minutes and taking his score from 142 at tea to 258 in the final session of play. Bill sustained a first-ball dismissal on the second day. Nitschke, the only South Australian to exceed fifty, top-scored in each innings with 69 (138 minutes, 3 fours) and 102 (212 minutes, 6 fours). Grimmett and Walker were both out to the first ball they faced. Hunt (left-arm medium) captured a career-best 5 for 36 in the first innings. Wall scored an unbeaten 45 in 57 minutes with 2 fours. Sources: *Wisden, NSWCA Report, VCA Report, Adelaide Advertiser, South Australian Register, The News.*

NEW SOUTH WALES

A.Jackson	c Richardson b Waite	166
J.H.W.Fingleton	st Walker b Grimmett	6
D.G.Bradman	b Richardson	258
*A.F.Kippax	b Grimmett	42
S.J.McCabe	lbw b Carlton	7
A.G.Fairfax	b Grimmett	38
O.W.Bill	lbw b Grimmett	0
†H.S.B.Love	lbw b Grimmett	4
J.E.H.Hooker	b Carlton	45
H.C.Chilvers	run out (Richardson)	23
W.A.Hunt	not out	15
Extras	(b4, lb2)	6
Total	(144.2 overs, 484 mins)	610

SOUTH AUSTRALIA

G.W.Harris	b Hunt	11		c Kippax b Bradman	25
H.C.Nitschke	c Hooker b Chilvers	69		c Fingleton b Hunt	102
D.E.Pritchard	b Chilvers	18	(5)	b Hunt	1
*V.Y.Richardson	c McCabe b Chilvers	25		b Hunt	17
A.T.Hack	lbw b Hunt	4	(3)	b Hunt	25
P.K.Lee	not out	13		b Bradman	25
M.G.Waite	b Hunt	0		lbw b Chilvers	0
T.A.Carlton	c Love b Chilvers	2	(9)	st Love b Bradman	15
C.V.Grimmett	c & b Chilvers	0	(8)	b Chilvers	26
T.W.Wall	lbw b Hunt	14		not out	45
†C.W.Walker	b Hunt	0		b Hooker	16
Extras	(b6, lb4)	10		(b11, lb2)	13
Total	(57.7 overs, 192 mins)	166		(105.6 overs, 330 mins)	310

SOUTH AUSTRALIA	O	M	R	W	w,nb
Wall	23	0	89	0	-,-
Carlton	20.2	0	99	2	-,-
Lee	38	4	144	0	-,-
Grimmett	48	5	180	5	-,-
Waite	7	0	54	1	-,-
Richardson	8	0	38	1	-,-

NEW SOUTH WALES	O	M	R	W	w,nb		O	M	R	W	w,nb
Hunt	17.7	4	36	5	-,-	(2)	38	8	105	4	-,-
Fairfax	6	1	23	0	-,-	(4)	2	0	7	0	-,-
Hooker	13	2	29	0	-,-	(1)	9.6	0	20	1	-,-
Chilvers	21	3	68	5	-,-	(3)	32	8	81	2	-,-
Bradman							12	2	54	3	-,-
McCabe							8	2	20	0	-,-
Kippax							4	2	10	0	-,-

FALL OF WICKETS

Wkt	NSW 1st	SA 1st	SA 2nd
1st	24	39	47
2nd	358	70	105
3rd	448	128	159
4th	465	133	167
5th	500	133	192
6th	500	134	193
7th	506	141	209
8th	549	141	235
9th	589	166	267
10th	610	166	310

TASMANIA v WEST INDIES XI

Played at N.T.C.A. Ground, Launceston, on December 20, 22, 23, 1930. (Three-day match)
Toss : Tasmania.   Result : WEST INDIES XI WON BY AN INNINGS AND 50 RUNS.
Debuts: Tasmania - D.M.Brain, J.H.Brain, S.G.Taylor (all f/c).
12th Men: E.H.Smith (Tas) and O.S.Wight (WI).
Umpires: E.C.Knight and B.Parker (see below).
Attendances & Receipts: No figures published.
Close of Play: 1st day WI 4/88 (Hunte 20, Grant 6); 2nd day Tas (2) 5/89 (Green 44, D.M.Brain 4).

J.A.Atkinson and S.W.L.Putman both had business commitments and were replaced by D.M.Brain and J.H.Brain. Tasmania lost J.H.Brain to the first ball of the second over of the match. Burrows (46 in 62 minutes, 1 five and 8 fours) and Nash (41 in 63 minutes, 1 six and 5 fours) added 81 but the side then lost 9 for 100. Green (45 in 78 minutes, 5 fours) top-scored in the second innings. Constantine (100 in 52 minutes, 1 six, 1 five and 10 fours) raced to 50 in 20 minutes and 100 in 52 minutes and was out next ball. He had offered a chance to D.M.Brain off James when 48. Grant (65 in 137 minutes, 3 fours) and Sealy (42 not out in 53 minutes, 4 fours) also batted well for West Indies. *NSWCA Report* gives umpires E.C.Knight and J.Pennefather, *Hobart Mercury* as shown, other sources no names. *Wisden* and *Hobart Mercury* give Tas (2) James c Headley, all other sources as shown. *NSWCA Report* incorrectly gives Green as Tasmania's captain.
Sources: *The Cricketer, Wisden, TCA Report, NSWCA Report, VCA Report, Hobart Mercury, Launceston Examiner.*

TASMANIA

J.H.Brain	c Birkett b Griffith	3	c Grant b Griffith		4
A.O.Burrows	c Sealy b Constantine	46	c Constantine b Scott		19
L.J.Nash	c Griffith b Constantine	41	c Sealy b Griffith		0
D.C.Green	st Hunte b Scott	28	c Grant b Griffith		45
*G.W.Martin	c Birkett b St Hill	31	b St Hill		1
N.W.Davis	c Sealy b St Hill	0	c Constantine b Sealy		15
D.M.Brain	c Sealy b St Hill	11	b Scott		16
†E.A.Pickett	run out (/Hunte)	12	lbw b Scott		7
G.T.H.James	c Constantine b Scott	10	c Sealy b Scott		10
S.G.Taylor	b St Hill	0	not out		0
V.L.Hooper	not out	0	c Headley b Scott		0
Extras	(lb1, nb1)	2	(lb2)		2
Total	(43.5 overs, 161 mins)	184	(38.7 overs, 141 mins)		119

WEST INDIES

C.A.Roach	c Green b Hooper	12
L.S.Birkett	c Burrows b Hooper	31
G.A.Headley	c D.M.Brain b James	3
†E.A.C.Hunte	c J.H.Brain b Burrows	29
E.L.Bartlett	b Nash	10
*G.C.Grant	c & b Burrows	65
L.N.Constantine	b Nash	100
J.E.D.Sealy	not out	42
E.L.St Hill	lbw b James	1
O.C.Scott	c Green b Burrows	23
H.C.Griffith	run out (Taylor)	17
Extras	(b19, lb1)	20
Total	(73.5 overs, 273 mins)	353

WEST INDIES XI	O	M	R	W	w,nb		O	M	R	W	w,nb		FALL OF WICKETS		
													TAS	WI	TAS
Constantine	9	1	35	2	-,-							Wkt	1st	1st	2nd
Griffith	11	1	45	1	-,1	(1)	12	2	20	3	-,-	1st	3	40	12
St Hill	13	1	57	4	-,-	(2)	10	2	30	1	-,-	2nd	84	47	12
Scott	10.5	0	45	2	-,-	(3)	13.7	2	63	5	-,-	3rd	98	47	40
Sealy						(4)	3	1	4	1	-,-	4th	137	76	43
												5th	137	131	65
TASMANIA	O	M	R	W	w,nb							6th	149	259	90
Nash	19	2	87	2	-,-							7th	170	267	105
Burrows	13	1	67	3	-,-							8th	175	272	116
James	17	2	53	2	-,-							9th	180	327	119
Hooper	12	2	61	2	-,-							10th	184	353	119
Taylor	12.5	2	65	0	-,-										

TASMANIA v WEST INDIES XI

Played at T.C.A. Ground, Hobart, on December 24, 25, 26, 1930. (Three-day match)
Toss : Tasmania.   Result : MATCH DRAWN.
Debuts: Tasmania - N.E.Murray, S.W.L.Putman, E.H.Smith (all f/c).
12th Men: G.G.Gibson (Tas) and E.L.Bartlett (WI).
Umpires: M.Leonard and W.T.Lonergan.
Attendances: 1000, 2500, 500.   Total: About 4000.   Receipts: £187.
Close of Play: 1st day Tas 5/216 (Burrows 44, Smith 5); 2nd day WI 2/139 (Birkett 74, Martin 36).
G.W.Martin was unavailable for Tasmania and Murray and Smith replaced N.W.Davis and E.A.Pickett (unavailable) in the side. Rain interrupted proceedings several times on the first day and permitted only 75 minutes play on the last day. Brain (30 in 98 minutes, 4 fours), Green (33 in 85 minutes, 1 four), Nash (53 in 70 minutes, 5 fours), Burrows (54 in 121 minutes, 5 fours) and Putman (34 in 44 minutes, 4 fours) shared the runs for Tasmania. Birkett (128 not out in 210 minutes, 9 fours, chance at 43) and Martin (79 not out in 146 minutes, 9 fours, chance at 0) added an unbroken 173 for the West Indies third wicket. All sources except *Hobart Mercury* incorrectly give E.A.C.Hunte instead of Barrow in West Indies' team. Sources: *Wisden, TCA Report, NSWCA Report, VCA Report, The Cricketer, Hobart Mercury.*

TASMANIA

*J.A.Atkinson	c Griffith b Scott	11
J.H.Brain	c Constantine b Scott	30
D.C.Green	c Birkett b Francis	33
L.J.Nash	c & b Sealy	53
A.O.Burrows	b Constantine	54
S.W.L.Putman	c Barrow b Constantine	34
E.H.Smith	c Griffith b Constantine	10
G.T.H.James	b Constantine	17
V.L.Hooper	not out	16
S.G.Taylor	b Constantine	12
†N.E.Murray	c Barrow b Constantine	0
Extras	(b1, lb6, nb3)	10
Total	(67.0 overs, 294 mins)	280

WEST INDIES XI

C.A.Roach	c Murray b James	23
L.S.Birkett	not out	128
F.I.de Caires	run out (James/Murray)	5
F.R.Martin	not out	79
L.N.Constantine	)	
*G.C.Grant	)	
†I.Barrow	)	
J.E.D.Sealy	) did not bat	
G.N.Francis	)	
O.C.Scott	)	
H.C.Griffith	)	
Extras	(b5, lb2)	7
Total	(59.0 overs, 210 mins) (2 wkts)	242

WEST INDIES XI	O	M	R	W	w,nb
Francis	7	3	46	1	-,1
Griffith	14	3	66	0	-,1
Scott	20	1	69	2	-,-
Martin	10	3	18	0	-,-
Sealy	6	0	41	1	-,1
Constantine	8	0	25	6	-,-
Birkett	2	0	5	0	-,-

TASMANIA	O	M	R	W	w,nb
Nash	13	0	42	0	-,-
Burrows	10	0	43	0	-,-
James	21	5	62	1	-,-
Hooper	8	0	48	0	-,-
Taylor	4	0	25	0	-,-
Atkinson	1	0	7	0	-,-
Putman	2	0	8	0	-,-

FALL OF WICKETS

Wkt	TAS 1st	WI 1st
1st	30	48
2nd	65	69
3rd	93	-
4th	142	-
5th	199	-
6th	230	-
7th	233	-
8th	260	-
9th	280	-
10th	280	-

VICTORIA v NEW SOUTH WALES (Shield Match 7)

Played at Melbourne Cricket Ground on December 24, 26 (no play), 27 (no play), 29, 1930. (Four-day match)
Toss : Victoria.   Result : MATCH DRAWN.
Debuts: Nil.
12th Men: L.P.J.O'Brien (Vic) and O.W.Bill (NSW).
Umpires: A.N.Barlow and J.Richards.
Attendances: 3965, no play, no play, 13065.   Total: 17,030.   Receipts: £569.
Close of Play: 1st day Vic 3/30 (Ponsford 22, Rigg 2); 2nd day no play; 3rd day no play.

Rain completely ruined the game, allowing only 38 minutes play on the first day and none at all on the second and third days. Ponsford carried his bat for Victoria, hitting 4 fours in his unbeaten 109, and giving his only chance at 107. He shared a ninth-wicket stand of 66 in 67 minutes with Alexander (4 fours). Jackson played a similar role for New South Wales, hitting 2 fours in his unbeaten 52. *NSWCA Report* and *VCA Report* incorrectly give Kippax b Blackie. Sources: *Wisden, NSWCA Report, VCA Report, The Age, The Argus. The Herald, Melbourne Sun.*

VICTORIA

*W.M.Woodfull	c Hooker b Fairfax	3
W.H.Ponsford	not out	109
H.S.T.L.Hendry	b Stewart	0
J.Ryder	c Stewart b Fairfax	1
K.E.Rigg	b Fairfax	2
E.L.a'Beckett	b Stewart	1
L.S.Darling	c McCabe b Hunt	16
†B.A.Barnett	b Fairfax	9
D.D.Blackie	run out (Jackson/Oldfield)	0
H.H.Alexander	c Stewart b Chilvers	21
H.Ironmonger	run out (Fingleton/Chilvers)	4
Extras	(b8, lb5, nb6)	19
Total	(60.3 overs, 215 mins)	185

NEW SOUTH WALES

A.Jackson	not out	52
J.H.W.Fingleton	run out (Woodfull/Barnett)	9
D.G.Bradman	c Hendry b a'Beckett	2
S.J.McCabe	b Blackie	10
*A.F.Kippax	hit wkt b Blackie	4
A.G.Fairfax	st Barnett b Ironmonger	3
†W.A.S.Oldfield	c Rigg b Ironmonger	8
J.E.H.Hooker	not out	2
W.A.Hunt	)	
H.C.Chilvers	) did not bat	
G.L.Stewart	)	
Extras	(lb3, nb4)	7
Total	(39.0 overs, 144 minutes) (6 wkts)	97

NEW SOUTH WALES	O	M	R	W	w,nb
Stewart	16	1	65	2	-,3
Fairfax	21	1	41	4	-,2
Hunt	10	1	31	1	-,-
Hooker	9	0	20	0	-,1
McCabe	3	1	3	0	-,-
Chilvers	1.3	0	6	1	-,-

VICTORIA	O	M	R	W	w,nb
Alexander	6	1	21	0	-,2
a'Beckett	10	2	26	1	-,-
Ironmonger	15	5	26	2	-,2
Blackie	7	2	16	2	-,-
Darling	1	0	1	0	-,-

FALL OF WICKETS

Wkt	VIC 1st	NSW 1st
1st	16	29
2nd	19	33
3rd	26	56
4th	43	62
5th	48	65
6th	79	83
7th	105	-
8th	111	-
9th	177	-
10th	185	-

SOUTH AUSTRALIA v QUEENSLAND (Shield Match 8)

Played at Adelaide Oval on December 25, 26, 1930. (Four-day match)
Toss : South Australia.   Result : SOUTH AUSTRALIA WON BY AN INNINGS AND 64 RUNS.
Debuts: Nil.
12th Men: A.R.Lonergan (SA) and G.A.Bourne (Qld).
Umpires: G.A.Hele and A.G.Jenkins.
Attendances: 5422, 5236.   Total: 10,658.   Receipts: £478.
Close of Play: 1st day SA 7/286 (Tobin 36, Waite 3).

Nitschke (142 in 278 minutes, 15 fours) reached his third century of the season in 242 minutes and was out at 250. Overnight rain softened the wicket to Queensland's disadvantage and the second day saw 22 wickets fall and an early conclusion to the match. Thompson (50 in 80 minutes, 5 fours) was struck on the back of the head by a return from Waite as he completed a run. Play was held up for several minutes while he regained his composure, however he was unable to bat later in the day when Queensland followed on. Grimmett returned match figures of 9 for 54 and when he dismissed Biggs in the second innings he surpassed the previous record of 209 Shield wickets held by E.Jones. *VCA Report* incorrectly gives Qld (2) 7/89. Sources: *Wisden, SACA Report, VCA Report, Adelaide Advertiser, South Australian Register, Australian Cricketer, The News.*

SOUTH AUSTRALIA

G.W.Harris	b Thurlow	6
H.C.Nitschke	c & b Oxenham	142
A.T.Hack	b Oxenham	8
*V.Y.Richardson	b Oxenham	19
P.K.Lee	c Leeson b Gilbert	39
H.E.Whitfield	run out (Gough/Leeson)	12
B.J.Tobin	c Amos b Oxenham	40
C.V.Grimmett	c Amos b Oxenham	7
M.G.Waite	b Gilbert	11
C.S.Deverson	not out	1
†C.W.Walker	c Amos b Oxenham	6
Extras	(b8, lb6)	14
Total	(83.7 overs, 329 mins)	305

QUEENSLAND

*F.J.Gough	c Deverson b Whitfield	2		c Richardson b Grimmett	36
†H.F.Leeson	c Richardson b Whitfield	6	(7)	c Lee b Grimmett	3
E.C.Bensted	lbw b Deverson	4		st Walker b Lee	14
F.C.Thompson	b Grimmett	50		absent hurt	-
R.K.Oxenham	run out (Waite/Walker)	2	(4)	run out (Richardson/Walker)	9
V.H.V.Goodwin	b Grimmett	21	(5)	not out	27
M.Biggs	c Deverson b Lee	4	(6)	st Walker b Grimmett	1
F.M.Brew	not out	24	(2)	b Tobin	11
G.S.Amos	c Waite b Lee	0	(8)	c Nitschke b Grimmett	8
H.M.Thurlow	b Grimmett	4		lbw b Grimmett	0
E.Gilbert	st Walker b Grimmett	0	(9)	c Deverson b Waite	5
Extras	(b2, lb5)	7		(lb2, nb1)	3
Total	(27.4 overs, 116 mins)	124		(34.3 overs, 125 mins)	117

QLD	O	M	R	W	w,nb
Gilbert	23	1	82	2	-,-
Thurlow	11	0	49	1	-,-
Brew	9	1	41	0	-,-
Amos	6	1	20	0	-,-
Oxenham	24.7	12	51	6	-,-
Goodwin	1	0	2	0	-,-
Thompson	3	0	14	0	-,-
Bensted	6	0	32	0	-,-

SOUTH AUSTRALIA	O	M	R	W	w,nb		O	M	R	W	w,nb
Deverson	5	0	24	1	-,-		3	0	12	0	-,-
Whitfield	7	1	39	2	-,-		4	0	16	0	-,-
Grimmett	7.4	2	23	4	-,-	(5)	10.3	1	31	5	-,-
Lee	8	2	31	2	-,-		10	2	36	1	-,1
Tobin						(3)	4	0	11	1	-,-
Waite							3	0	8	1	-,-

FALL OF WICKETS

Wkt	SA 1st	QLD 1st	QLD 2nd
1st	11	8	31
2nd	45	9	54
3rd	77	13	70
4th	145	22	82
5th	191	82	83
6th	250	93	89
7th	264	93	99
8th	298	102	117
9th	298	124	117
10th	305	124	-

AUSTRALIA v WEST INDIES (2nd Test)

Played at Sydney Cricket Ground on January 1, 2 (no play), 3, 5, 1931. (Timeless match)
Toss : Australia.   Result : AUSTRALIA WON BY AN INNINGS AND 172 RUNS.
Debuts: Nil.
12th Men: K.E.Rigg (Aust) and J.E.D.Sealy (WI).
Umpires: E.G.Borwick and W.G.French.
Attendances: 22058, no play, 18052, 735.   Total: 40,845.   Receipts: £3302.
Close of Play: 1st day Aust 4/323 (Ponsford 174, Woodfull 58); 2nd day no play; 3rd day WI (2) 5/67 (Grant 10, Barrow 10).

Ponsford (183 in 348 minutes, 11 fours) gave his only chance when 113, a caught-and-bowled opportunity to Birkett. With Woodfull he added 183 in 139 minutes for Australia's fifth wicket. Overnight rain prevented any play on the second day and produced favourable bowling conditions when the game resumed, the ball being inclined to kick from the part of the pitch which had not been covered. Woodfull, the first of 20 wickets to fall on the third day was caught at the wicket off the third ball without addition to the overnight score. Only 24 minutes were needed on the fourth day to conclude the match. Bartlett fractured a finger in catching Kippax just after lunch on the opening day. Bradman brought his Test aggregate since June 14th 1930 to 1003 runs in 201 days - the quickest sequence of 1000 runs by a batsman yet at the highest level. *Wisden* gives incorrect WI bowling order. Sources: *Wisden, NSWCA Report, Sydney Morning Herald, Sydney Referee, Brisbane Courier, The Herald.*

AUSTRALIA

W.H.Ponsford	b Scott	183
A.Jackson	c Francis b Griffith	8
D.G.Bradman	c Barrow b Francis	25
A.F.Kippax	c Bartlett b Griffith	10
S.J.McCabe	lbw b Scott	31
*W.M.Woodfull	c Barrow b Constantine	58
A.G.Fairfax	c Constantine b Francis	15
†W.A.S.Oldfield	run out (Headley)	0
C.V.Grimmett	b Scott	12
A.Hurwood	c Martin b Scott	5
H.Ironmonger	not out	3
Extras	(b6, lb5, w5, nb3)	19
Total	(116.4 overs, 358 mins)	369

WEST INDIES

C.A.Roach	run out (Hurwood/Oldfield)	7	c Kippax b McCabe	25
L.S.Birkett	c Hurwood b Fairfax	3	c McCabe b Hurwood	8
G.A.Headley	b Fairfax	14	c Jackson b Hurwood	2
F.R.Martin	lbw b Grimmett	10	c McCabe b Hurwood	0
*G.C.Grant	c Hurwood b Ironmonger	6	not out	15
L.N.Constantine	c Bradman b Grimmett	12	b Hurwood	8
†I.Barrow	c Jackson b Fairfax	17	c McCabe b Ironmonger	10
G.N.Francis	b Grimmett	8	c Oldfield b Ironmonger	0
O.C.Scott	not out	15	c Woodfull b Ironmonger	17
H.C.Griffith	c Kippax b Grimmett	8	lbw b Grimmett	0
E.L.Bartlett	absent hurt	-	absent hurt	-
Extras	(b6, nb1)	7	(b1, lb2, w1, nb1)	5
Total	(50.1 overs, 133 mins)	107	(30.3 overs, 89 mins)	90

WEST INDIES	O	M	R	W	w,nb
Francis	27	3	70	2	-,1
Constantine	18	2	56	1	-,-
Griffith	28	4	57	2	3,2
Martin	18	1	60	0	-,-
Scott	15.4	0	66	4	-,-
Birkett	10	1	41	0	2,-

AUSTRALIA	O	M	R	W	w,nb		O	M	R	W	w,nb
Fairfax	13	4	19	3	-,1		5	1	21	0	-,-
Hurwood	5	1	7	0	-,-		11	2	22	4	1,-
Grimmett	19.1	3	54	4	-,-	(5)	3.3	1	9	1	-,-
Ironmonger	13	3	20	1	-,-		4	1	13	3	-,1
McCabe						(3)	7	0	20	1	-,-

FALL OF WICKETS

	AUST	WI	WI
Wkt	1st	1st	2nd
1st	12	3	26
2nd	52	26	32
3rd	69	36	32
4th	140	36	42
5th	323	57	53
6th	341	63	67
7th	344	80	67
8th	361	88	90
9th	364	107	90
10th	369	-	-

VICTORIA v SOUTH AUSTRALIA (Shield Match 9)

Played at Melbourne Cricket Ground on January 1, 2, 3, 5, 1931. (Four-day match)
Toss : South Australia. Result : MATCH DRAWN.
Debuts: Victoria - L.O.Cordner (f/c).
12th Men: G.H.Newstead (Vic) and C.S.Deverson (SA).
Umpires: W.J.Moore and J.Richards.
Attendances: 13373, 10714, 13256, 5360. Total: 42,703. Receipts: £1398.
Close of Play: 1st day SA 275 all out; 2nd day Vic 6/243 (Oakley 41, Barnett 1); 3rd day SA (2) 2/110 (Hack 31, Richardson 29).

South Australia nearly brought about an improbable victory on the last afternoon, Richardson declaring once Lonergan had reached his hundred and the side then capturing seven cheap Victorian wickets inside two hours. Oakley, who strained a leg during the course of his maiden hundred earlier in the match, had not bothered to turn up on the last day and had to rush to the ground when he became aware of his team's deteriorating position from a radio broadcast. Nitschke's 22 for South Australia included a five scored when a return from the field struck his partner Hack's bat and was deflected to the boundary, umpire Richards instructing the scorers to add four runs to Nitschke's single contrary to a request from Hack. South Australia's top scorers were Nitschke (43 in 84 minutes, 4 fours), Richardson (64 in 154 minutes, 2 fours) and Waite (44 in 92 minutes, 3 fours) in the first innings and Hack (87 in 203 minutes, 5 fours), Lonergan (100 not out in 172 minutes, 6 fours) and Waite again (59 in 79 minutes, 2 fours) in the second, the last two adding 125 for the seventh wicket to put the visitors safe from defeat. Victoria's best with the bat were O'Brien (75 in 154 minutes, 8 fours), Ryder (49 in 127 minutes, 3 fours) and Oakley (108 in 214 minutes, 8 fours), and in the second innings Hendry (32 in 52 minutes, 1 four). H.E.Whitfield was unavailable to play for South Australia. *Wisden* incorrectly gives SA (2) reversed dismissals of Richardson and Lee; Vic (2) Alexander batting instead of Cordner. Sources: *Wisden, VCA Report, SACA Report, The Age, The Argus, The Herald, Melbourne Sun.*

SOUTH AUSTRALIA

G.W.Harris	b a'Beckett	2	run out (Ryder/Barnett)		20
H.C.Nitschke	c Ryder b Blackie	43	c Barnett b Blackie		22
A.T.Hack	c Barnett b Blackie	37	b a'Beckett		87
*V.Y.Richardson	b Alexander	64	b Alexander		29
P.K.Lee	c Ryder b Blackie	27	c Darling b Blackie		12
B.J.Tobin	lbw b Cordner	2	lbw b Alexander		0
A.R.Lonergan	c a'Beckett b Blackie	6	not out		100
M.G.Waite	c O'Brien b Blackie	44	b Ryder		59
T.W.Wall	b a'Beckett	8	b Ryder		0
T.A.Carlton	b Blackie	23	not out		7
†C.W.Walker	not out	7			
Extras	(b7, lb5)	12	(b14, lb1, nb2)		17
Total	(86.0 overs, 306 mins)	275	(109.0 overs, 368 mins) (8 wkts dec)		353

VICTORIA

E.K.Tolhurst	lbw b Lee	25	(2) lbw b Carlton		0
L.P.J.O'Brien	c Harris b Lee	75	(4) c Wall b Lee		0
*J.Ryder	c Carlton b Lee	49	(7) not out		9
H.S.T.L.Hendry	c Tobin b Carlton	2	(1) b Carlton		32
L.S.Darling	c Walker b Carlton	31	(3) lbw b Carlton		15
H.H.Oakley	c & b Carlton	108			
E.L.a'Beckett	c Tobin b Wall	13	(6) c Lonergan b Lee		5
†B.A.Barnett	c Richardson b Lee	54	(5) lbw b Waite		10
L.O.Cordner	not out	4	(8) b Waite		0
D.D.Blackie	st Walker b Lee	10	(9) not out		2
H.H.Alexander	b Carlton	0			
Extras	(b8, lb2, nb5)	15	(b11, lb1)		12
Total	(116.0 overs, 442 mins)	386	(29.0 overs, 110 mins) (7 wkts)		85

VICTORIA	O	M	R	W	w,nb		O	M	R	W	w,nb
Alexander	19	3	58	1	-,-		17	4	75	2	-,1
a'Beckett	23	4	71	2	-,-		24	6	44	1	-,-
Blackie	31	7	70	6	-,-		37	9	84	2	-,-
Cordner	10	0	47	1	-,-		20	2	78	0	-,-
Darling	3	0	17	0	-,-		8	1	46	0	-,-
Ryder							3	0	9	2	-,1

SOUTH AUSTRALIA	O	M	R	W	w,nb		O	M	R	W	w,nb
Wall	24	4	79	1	-,1		6	0	18	0	-,-
Tobin	10	0	48	0	-,-						
Carlton	38	7	91	4	-,3	(2)	9	2	28	3	-,-
Lee	34	5	106	5	-,1	(3)	10	3	18	2	-,-
Waite	8	0	39	0	-,-	(4)	4	0	9	2	-,-
Richardson	2	0	8	0	-,-						

FALL OF WICKETS

Wkt	SA 1st	VIC 1st	SA 2nd	VIC 2nd
1st	2	42	38	12
2nd	77	135	76	57
3rd	100	140	114	58
4th	144	156	137	58
5th	154	215	137	66
6th	165	241	211	77
7th	214	371	336	77
8th	231	373	336	-
9th	256	385	-	-
10th	275	386	-	-

QUEENSLAND v WEST INDIES XI

Played at Brisbane Cricket Ground (Woolloongabba) on January 10, 12, 13, 14, 1931. (Four-day match)
Toss : West Indies XI.   Result : WEST INDIES XI WON BY 219 RUNS.
Debuts: Queensland - J.W.Adams, W.Duncan (both f/c).
12th Men: A.G.Harding (Qld) and F.I.de Caires (WI).
Umpires: W.R.Fraser and J.A.Scott.
Attendances: 4800, 2120, 1200, 100.   Total: 8220.   Receipts: £717.
Close of Play: 1st day WI 309 all out; 2nd day WI (2) 5/80 (Sealy 17); 3rd day Qld (2) 5/149 (Goodwin 51, Mossop 35).

Goodwin, who came into the Queensland team as a late replacement for F.C.Thompson (unavailable), topped the batting in each innings with 60 (141 minutes, 3 fours) and 54 (131 minutes). McFarlane in the first innings and Duncan in the second innings suffered first-ball dismissals. Constantine again did spectacularly well for the visitors, scoring 75 (59 minutes, 1 six and 8 fours) and 97 (93 minutes, 13 fours), capturing 7 for 56 and holding 3 catches. Roach fell to the second ball of the West Indies' second innings. Sealy was hit on the head by a ball from Thurlow at 5/101 and retired to take no further part in the match. Sources: *Wisden, QCA Report, NSWCA Report, Brisbane Courier, Australian Cricketer.*

WEST INDIES XI

C.A.Roach	c Gough b Bensted	42		c Oxenham b Gilbert	0
F.R.Martin	c Duncan b Gilbert	38		c Duncan b Thurlow	11
G.A.Headley	b Thurlow	19		lbw b Oxenham	17
L.S.Birkett	c Thurlow b Gilbert	49	(9)	c Gilbert b Bensted	41
*G.C.Grant	c Oxenham b Gilbert	28	(7)	b Gilbert	26
L.N.Constantine	b Brew	75	(8)	c Brew b Bensted	97
J.E.D.Sealy	c Adams b Gilbert	13	(6)	retired hurt	25
O.S.Wight	c Duncan b Bensted	5	(4)	lbw b Oxenham	0
†E.A.C.Hunte	not out	14	(5)	c Brew b Thurlow	28
O.C.Scott	b Gilbert	0		not out	3
G.N.Francis	c Duncan b Brew	1		b Bensted	5
Extras	(b21, lb3, w1)	25		(b8, lb4)	12
Total	(79.2 overs, 295 mins)	309		(59.7 overs, 245 mins)	265

QUEENSLAND

*F.J.Gough	c Francis b Constantine	1		c Headley b Constantine	9
E.C.Bensted	b Constantine	3	(5)	st Hunte b Scott	0
J.W.Adams	c Hunte b Francis	16	(2)	c Hunte b Martin	9
R.K.Oxenham	c Hunte b Constantine	5	(6)	b Martin	9
V.H.V.Goodwin	c Roach b Martin	60	(4)	c Hunte b Francis	54
K.L.M.Mossop	c Sealy b Francis	24	(7)	c Hunte b Francis	37
C.B.P.McFarlane	b Constantine	0	(8)	b Constantine	5
F.M.Brew	c Constantine b Scott	30	(3)	c Headley b Scott	25
E.Gilbert	lbw b Scott	5		not out	14
†W.Duncan	c Constantine b Scott	3		b Constantine	0
H.M.Thurlow	not out	0		c Constantine b Scott	12
Extras	(b13, lb6, nb1)	20		(b7, lb5, nb2)	14
Total	(48.2 overs, 200 mins)	167		(53.6 overs, 192 mins)	188

QUEENSLAND	O	M	R	W	w,nb		O	M	R	W	w,nb		FALL OF WICKETS			
Gilbert	19	1	65	5	1,-		7	1	26	2	-,-			WI	QLD	WI	QLD
Oxenham	23	11	32	0	-,-	(3)	15	7	34	2	-,-	Wkt	1st	1st	2nd	2nd
Thurlow	9	0	54	1	-,-	(2)	18	0	88	2	-,-	1st	75	1	0	12
Brew	11.2	2	60	2	-,-	(5)	3	0	17	0	-,-	2nd	109	21	26	32
Bensted	12	1	34	2	-,-	(4)	12.7	2	57	3	-,-	3rd	119	21	36	52
Goodwin	3	0	21	0	-,-		4	0	31	0	-,-	4th	181	28	36	52
Mossop	2	0	18	0	-,-							5th	214	89	80	65
												6th	281	90	130	153
WEST INDIES XI	O	M	R	W	w,nb		O	M	R	W	w,nb	7th	287	109	257	158
Francis	9	2	38	2	-,1		10	2	21	2	-,2	8th	305	159	260	175
Constantine	12	3	33	4	-,-		5	0	23	3	-,-	9th	306	167	265	175
Martin	12	2	21	1	-,-		11	3	20	2	-,-	10th	309	167	-	188
Scott	12.2	1	46	3	-,-		19.6	2	79	3	-,-					
Sealy	2	1	3	0	-,-											
Birkett	1	0	6	0	-,-	(7)	4	0	10	0	-,-					
Headley						(5)	1	0	3	0	-,-					
Roach						(6)	3	0	18	0	-,-					

AUSTRALIA v WEST INDIES (3rd Test)

Played at Exhibition Ground, Brisbane, on January 16, 17, 19, 20, 1931. Timeless match)
Toss : Australia.   Result : AUSTRALIA WON BY AN INNINGS AND 217 RUNS.
Debuts: Nil.
12th Men: K.E.Rigg (Aust) and O.S.Wight (WI).
Umpires: J.P.Orr and A.E.Wyeth.
Attendances: 10500, 19700, 6500, 200.   Total: About 36,900.   Receipts: £2921.
Close of Play: 1st day Aust 3/428 (Bradman 223, McCabe 1); 2nd day WI 3/51 (Headley 21, Grant 2); 3rd day WI (2) 8/115 (Sealy 2, Francis 2).

Jackson was out to the third ball of the match (his first). Bradman (223 in 297 minutes, 24 fours) was put down in the slips by Birkett when only 4. He gave no further chances and went on to surpass V.T.Trumper's 214 not out in 1910-11 as the highest innings by an Australian in a home Test so far, reaching his 100 in 142 minutes and 200 in 251 minutes. He scored his last 94 runs in the tea-stumps session of the first day, in which Australia compiled 428 runs in just 294 minutes. With Ponsford (109 in 165 minutes, 12 fours, chance after reaching three figures) Bradman put on 229 for the 2nd wicket - the second-highest stand yet for any Australian Test wicket at home - and he added a further 193 with Kippax (84 in 118 minutes, 7 fours) for the third wicket. Oxenham (48 in 80 minutes, 6 fours) and Oldfield took Australia past 500. Headley (102 not out in 247 minutes, 10 fours) scored the first Test hundred for West Indies in Australia. On the third day Rigg fielded for Ponsford who was unwell, and when Jackson (ill - ostensibly suffering from flu) left the ground later in the day Australia had only ten men in the field for one over. Wight then fielded. Sources: *Wisden, QCA Report, Brisbane Courier, Sydney Morning Herald, The Australasian*.

AUSTRALIA

W.H.Ponsford	c Birkett b Francis	109
A.Jackson	lbw b Francis	0
D.G.Bradman	c Grant b Constantine	223
A.F.Kippax	b Birkett	84
S.J.McCabe	c Constantine b Griffith	8
*W.M.Woodfull	c Barrow b Griffith	17
A.G.Fairfax	c Sealy b Scott	9
R.K.Oxenham	lbw b Griffith	48
†W.A.S.Oldfield	not out	38
C.V.Grimmett	c Constantine b Francis	4
H.Ironmonger	c Roach b Griffith	2
Extras	(b2, lb7, nb7)	16
Total	(147.0 overs, 457 mins)	558

WEST INDIES

C.A.Roach	lbw b Oxenham	4	b McCabe	1
F.R.Martin	lbw b Grimmett	21	lbw b Oxenham	11
G.A.Headley	not out	102	c Oldfield b b Ironmonger	28
J.E.D.Sealy	c McCabe b Ironmonger	3	(9) not out	16
*G.C.Grant	c McCabe b Grimmett	8	(4) run out (Fairfax)	10
L.N.Constantine	c Fairfax b Ironmonger	9	(5) lbw b Oxenham	7
L.S.Birkett	lbw b Oxenham	8	(6) b Grimmett	13
†I.Barrow	st Oldfield b Grimmett	19	(7) st Oldfield b Grimmett	17
O.C.Scott	b Oxenham	0	(8) lbw b Grimmett	15
G.N.Francis	b Oxenham	8	c Oldfield b Grimmett	7
H.C.Griffith	lbw b Grimmett	8	c Bradman b Grimmett	12
Extras	(b1, lb2)	3	(b5, lb4, nb2)	11
Total	(104.3 overs, 265 mins)	193	(60.3 overs, 165 mins)	148

WEST INDIES	O	M	R	W	w,nb
Francis	26	4	76	3	-,4
Constantine	26	2	74	1	-,-
Griffith	33	4	133	4	-,2
Scott	24	0	125	1	-,-
Martin	27	3	85	0	-,-
Sealy	3	0	32	0	-,1
Birkett	7	0	16	1	-,-
Grant	1	0	1	0	-,-

AUSTRALIA	O	M	R	W	w,nb		O	M	R	W	w,nb
Fairfax	7	2	13	0	-,-		6	2	6	0	-,2
Oxenham	30	15	39	4	-,-	(3)	18	5	37	2	-,-
Ironmonger	26	15	43	2	-,-	(4)	15	8	29	1	-,-
Grimmett	41.3	9	95	4	-,-	(5)	14.3	4	49	5	-,-
McCabe						(2)	7	1	16	1	-,-

FALL OF WICKETS

Wkt	AUST 1st	WI 1st	WI 2nd
1st	1	5	13
2nd	230	36	29
3rd	423	41	47
4th	431	60	58
5th	441	94	72
6th	462	116	82
7th	468	159	94
8th	543	162	112
9th	551	182	128
10th	558	193	148

TASMANIA v VICTORIA

Played at T.C.A. Ground, Hobart, on January 21, 22, 23, 1931. (Three-day match)
Toss : Victoria.   Result : MATCH DRAWN.
Debuts: Tasmania - T.H.Matthews, R.E.Ward (both f/c). Victoria - G.M.Eaton, P.A.Ellis, F.E.Fontaine, E.F.Healy R.J.Lawson, S.O.Quin (all f/c).
12th Men: R.O.G.Morrisby (Tas) and J.O.Perraton (Vic).
Umpires: A.J.Buttsworth and W.T.Lonergan.
Attendances: No figures published.   Total: About 600.   Receipts: £30.
Close of Play: 1st day Tas 0/17 (Atkinson 13, Matthews 4); 2nd day Tas 6/209 (Newton 12, Ward 12).

Cyclonic winds made play difficult on the second day which was ended by heavy rain at 4pm. Lawson, on his first-class debut (he played only once more at that level), fell to the second ball of the match before returning in the second innings to score 119 in 168 minutes with 6 fours. Fontaine - another debutant for Victoria - survived chances at 25, 65 and 104 in his maiden innings of 118 which occupied 177 minutes and included 15 fours. Hassett (114 not out in 150 minutes, 14 fours) added 101 in 66 minutes for the eighth wicket with Wilkinson, and Ellis in the second innings scored 59 in 70 minutes with 7 fours. Atkinson (65 in 85 minutes, 8 fours), Matthews (78 in 165 minutes, 9 fours) and Newton (66 not out in 98 minutes, 8 fours) each scored a fifty for Tasmania. Matthews and Ward had replaced N.W.Davis and A.W.Rushforth (both unavailable) in the local line-up and G.G.Gibson (12th man) withdrew to be replaced by Morrisby.
Sources: *The Cricketer, TCA Report, VCA Report, Hobart Mercury.*

VICTORIA

Batsman	Dismissal	Score		Dismissal	Score
R.J.Lawson	c Martin b Nash	0	(3)	lbw b Putman	119
F.E.Fontaine	c Martin b Nash	118	(1)	c Atkinson b Nash	2
P.A.Ellis	b Hooper	15	(2)	c James b Newton	59
G.M.Eaton	b Newton	15		b James	22
S.P.King	b Newton	0	(6)	not out	19
R.G.Nettleton	b Nash	13	(5)	b Hooper	3
†S.O.Quin	run out (Atkinson/Murray)	3		not out	14
R.J.Hassett	not out	114			
W.A.Wilkinson	c Atkinson b Putman	38			
E.F.Healy	run out (Nash/Murray)	2			
*F.L.Morton	c Martin b Putman	11			
Extras	(b10, lb3)	13		(b4, lb4)	8
Total	(71.6 overs, 270 mins)	342		(58.0 overs, 195 mins) (5 wkts)	246

TASMANIA

Batsman	Dismissal	Score
*J.A.Atkinson	b Hassett	65
T.H.Matthews	run out (Fontaine)	78
D.C.Green	b Morton	24
L.J.Nash	b Morton	8
G.W.Martin	b Healy	1
S.W.L.Putman	c Ellis b Morton	0
A.C.Newton	not out	66
R.E.Ward	c Quin b Fontaine	16
V.L.Hooper	c & b Morton	6
G.T.H.James	b Morton	7
†N.E.Murray	b Hassett	7
Extras	(b9, lb2, nb1)	12
Total	(82.6 overs, 258 mins)	290

TASMANIA	O	M	R	W	w,nb		O	M	R	W	w,nb
Nash	16	0	84	3	-,-		6	0	31	1	-,-
James	21	3	52	0	-,-	(3)	15	3	67	1	-,-
Hooper	12	0	67	1	-,-	(2)	10	0	45	1	-,-
Newton	13	1	31	2	-,-		9	0	25	1	-,-
Putman	7.6	0	75	2	-,-		12	0	50	1	-,-
Ward	2	0	20	0	-,-		2	0	7	0	-,-
Martin							3	0	11	0	-,-
Green							1	0	2	0	-,-

VICTORIA	O	M	R	W	w,nb
Wilkinson	19	2	56	0	-,-
Morton	29	3	111	5	-,-
Healy	21	4	51	1	-,1
Hassett	11.6	0	58	2	-,-
Fontaine	2	1	2	1	-,-

FALL OF WICKETS

Wkt	VIC 1st	TAS 1st	VIC 2nd
1st	0	95	5
2nd	32	159	101
3rd	65	179	173
4th	67	180	188
5th	86	185	219
6th	98	185	-
7th	210	222	-
8th	311	243	-
9th	320	251	-
10th	342	290	-

NEW SOUTH WALES v VICTORIA (Shield Match 10)

Played at Sydney Cricket Ground on January 24, 26, 27, 28, 1931. (Four-day match)
Toss : New South Wales.　　　　Result : MATCH DRAWN.
Debuts: Nil.
12th Men: W.C.Andrews (NSW) and G.H.Newstead (Vic).
Umpires: H.J.Armstrong and W.G.French.
Attendances: 8715, 13399, 7784, 5485.　　　Total: 35,383.　　　Receipts: £1490.
Close of Play: 1st day Vic 0/23 (Hendry 11, O'Brien 8); 2nd day Vic 9/306 (Alexander 0); 3rd day NSW (2) 4/382 (Bradman 208, Bill 100).

A.Jackson (ill), W.H.Ponsford and W.M.Woodfull were unavailable for their respective sides. O'Brien (119 in 269 minutes, 1 six and 10 fours) completed his first Shield century to give Victoria a first-innings lead of 122. Bradman (220 in 308 minutes, 13 fours) reached 100 in 174 minutes and 200 in 282 minutes, giving a chance when 166 and sharing a fifth-wicket partnership of 234 with Bill (100 in 140 minutes) to save New South Wales. It was Bradman's third double century of the season. Rigg (98 in 280 minutes) was dismissed in trying to reach his hundred in the last over of the match. *Wisden* incorrectly gives Vic (1) Alexander 7, Ironmonger 4*. Sources: *Wisden, NSWCA Report, VCA Report, Sydney Morning Herald, Sydney Referee, The Age, The Argus.*

NEW SOUTH WALES

A.G.Fairfax	c a'Beckett b Blackie	46	(5) c O'Brien b Blackie	12
J.H.W.Fingleton	b Alexander	6	(8) st Barnett b Blackie	4
D.G.Bradman	c Barnett b Alexander	33	(2) c Rigg b Ironmonger	220
*A.F.Kippax	b Alexander	6	(3) c & b Blackie	26
S.J.McCabe	c Barnett b Ironmonger	29	(1) b Alexander	20
A.E.Marks	b Blackie	9	(4) b Ironmonger	9
O.W.Bill	c a'Beckett b Blackie	39	(6) b Blackie	100
†W.A.S.Oldfield	c Barnett b a'Beckett	9	(9) c Darling b Ironmonger	1
J.E.H.Hooker	c Barnett b a'Beckett	0	(10) not out	0
W.A.Hunt	st Barnett b Blackie	15	(7) c Rigg b Blackie	16
H.C.Chilvers	not out	1		
Extras	(b1, lb1, w1)	3	(b3, lb4, w2)	9
Total	(57.3 overs, 221 mins)	196	(82.4 overs, 316 mins) (9 wkts dec)	417

VICTORIA

H.S.T.L.Hendry	c Oldfield b McCabe	39	c Oldfield b Hunt	4
L.P.J.O'Brien	c Oldfield b Fairfax	119	c Hunt b McCabe	14
K.E.Rigg	c Bill b McCabe	24	c Hunt b Chilvers	98
*J.Ryder	b Fairfax	31	lbw b Hunt	36
H.H.Oakley	b Hooker	18	c Oldfield b Hunt	29
L.S.Darling	c Oldfield b McCabe	4	c Kippax b Chilvers	0
E.L.a'Beckett	lbw b McCabe	4		
†B.A.Barnett	b Chilvers	23	(7) not out	11
D.D.Blackie	st Oldfield b Hooker	28		
H.H.Alexander	not out	4		
H.Ironmonger	c McCabe b Chilvers	7		
Extras	(b14, lb2, nb1)	17	(b2, lb1, w2, nb5)	10
Total	(116.2 overs, 365 mins)	318	(97.4 overs, 286 mins) (6 wkts)	202

VICTORIA	O	M	R	W	w,nb		O	M	R	W	w,nb
Alexander	13	0	43	3	1,-		15	1	89	1	-,-
a'Beckett	14	2	41	2	-,-		13	0	58	0	-,-
Ironmonger	16	5	56	1	-,-		22.4	0	91	3	1,-
Hendry	2	0	8	0	-,-	(5)	3	0	20	0	-,-
Blackie	12.3	0	45	4	-,-	(4)	23	2	101	5	-,-
Ryder							4	0	39	0	-,-
Darling							2	0	10	0	1,-

NEW SOUTH WALES	O	M	R	W	w,nb		O	M	R	W	w,nb
Fairfax	20	2	68	2	-,1		9	4	14	0	2,3
Hunt	22	6	38	0	-,-		23	9	38	3	-,-
Hooker	27	7	45	2	-,-	(5)	13	4	26	0	-,2
Chilvers	19.2	1	73	2	-,-		30.4	7	66	2	-,-
McCabe	22	7	46	4	-,-	(3)	10	2	25	1	-,-
Bradman	6	0	31	0	-,-		8	1	16	0	-,-
Marks							3	1	4	0	-,-
Fingleton							1	0	3	0	-,-

FALL OF WICKETS

	NSW	VIC	NSW	VIC
Wkt	1st	1st	2nd	2nd
1st	14	86	26	14
2nd	68	142	103	35
3rd	78	226	126	92
4th	108	241	157	148
5th	126	247	391	149
6th	130	253	412	202
7th	147	264	415	-
8th	147	304	417	-
9th	183	306	417	-
10th	196	318	-	-

TASMANIA v VICTORIA

Played at N.T.C.A. Ground, Launceston, on January 24, 26, 27, 1931. (Three-day match)
Toss : Tasmania.   Result : MATCH DRAWN.
Debuts: Nil.
12th Men: F.A.Davis (Tas) and R.G.Nettleton (Vic)
Umpires: E.C.Knight and B.Parker.
Attendances & Receipts: No figures published.
Close of Play: 1st day Tas 6/362 (Davis 17, Ward 9); 2nd day Vic 3/245 (Eaton 111, King 72).

J.A.Atkinson was unavailable for Tasmania and Findlay replaced D.M.Brain (unavailable) after the team was named. Nash (110 in 175 minutes, 1 six and 9 fours, chance at 44) and Green (147 in 249 minutes, 1 five and 10 fours, chance at 128) added 197 for the Tasmanian second wicket to set the pattern for the game. Martin (57 in 87 minutes, 8 fours), Davis (42 in 89 minutes, 6 fours), Ward (47 not out in 83 minutes, 3 fours) and then James in the second innings (50 not out in 30 minutes, 1 six, 6 fours) also contributed. Martin, who sustained a hand injury while fielding on the second day, and N.W.Davis (business) were absent on the last day and both 12th men substituted in the field. Victoria's leading scorers were Eaton (184 in 319 minutes, 18 fours, chances at 27 and 165), King (73 in 152 minutes, 7 fours) and Hassett (102 in 157 minutes, 9 fours). Nash (right-arm fast) was once no-balled "for what was an obvious throw" (umpire not named) during the final session of the second day, possibly due to frustration at lack of success. He went on to claim 5 for 76 to complement his century. *Cricketer* incorrectly gives bowling figures for Findlay and Ward. *VCA Report* incorrectly gives Tas (1) Findlay c & b. Sources: *TCA Report, VCA Report, Hobart Mercury, Launceston Examiner.*

TASMANIA

L.J.Nash	c & b Morton	110			
†E.A.Pickett	b Wilkinson	5	b Fontaine		1
*D.C.Green	run out (Perraton/Quin)	147			
G.W.Martin	b Healy	57			
N.W.Davis	c Hassett b Morton	42			
E.H.Smith	b Healy	6	(5) not out		27
S.W.L.Putman	c Lawson b Hassett	1	(4) st Quin b Healy		18
R.E.Ward	not out	47	(3) lbw b Perraton		0
A.P.Findlay	c Hassett b Wilkinson	1			
V.L.Hooper	b Morton	0	(1) b Healy		32
G.T.H.James	c Quin b Wilkinson	17	(6) not out		50
Extras	(b5, lb5, nb3)	13	(lb5, nb2)		7
Total	(103.0 overs, 372 mins)	446	(26.0 overs, 90 mins) (4 wkts)		135

VICTORIA

R.J.Lawson	b Nash	8
F.E.Fontaine	b James	14
P.A.Ellis	c Martin b Putman	28
G.M.Eaton	c Nash b Findlay	184
S.P.King	lbw b Nash	73
R.J.Hassett	c Smith b Nash	102
J.O.Perraton	lbw b Nash	16
†S.O.Quin	c sub (F.A.Davis) b Nash	16
W.A.Wilkinson	c Ward b Putman	35
E.F.Healy	not out	12
*F.L.Morton	st Pickett b Putman	16
Extras	(b10, lb8, w1, nb1)	20
Total	(116.4 overs, 553 mins)	524

VICTORIA	O	M	R	W	w,nb		O	M	R	W	w,nb
Morton	18	1	117	3	-,-	(4)	4	0	14	0	-,1
Perraton	9	0	54	0	-,1	(1)	3	0	12	1	-,1
Wilkinson	23	2	80	3	-,-		4	0	15	0	-,-
Healy	28	4	74	2	-,2	(5)	5	1	20	2	-,-
Hassett	24	0	106	1	-,-	(6)	4	0	22	0	-,-
Fontaine	1	0	2	0	-,-	(2)	2	0	4	1	-,-
King							2	0	18	0	-,-
Lawson							2	0	23	0	-,-

TASMANIA	O	M	R	W	w,nb
Nash	26	3	76	5	1,1
Hooper	25	1	110	0	-,-
James	32	5	126	1	-,-
Putman	14.4	0	97	3	-,-
Findlay	11	0	55	1	-,-
Ward	7	0	29	0	-,-
Martin	1	0	11	0	-,-

FALL OF WICKETS

Wkt		TAS	VIC	TAS
		1st	1st	2nd
1st		15	17	4
2nd		212	25	5
3rd		325	78	54
4th		325	254	61
5th		337	404	-
6th		340	430	-
7th		409	455	-
8th		410	457	-
9th		417	504	-
10th		446	524	-

VICTORIA v WEST INDIES XI

Played at Melbourne Cricket Ground on January 31, February 2, 3, 4, 1931. (Four-day match)
Toss : West Indies XI.   Result : MATCH DRAWN.
Debuts: Victoria - J.Rush (f/c).
12th Men: R.G.Nettleton (Vic) and O.S.Wight (WI).
Umpires: W.J.Moore and E.C.Ramsden.
Attendances: 7728, 3832, 2633, 1234.   Total: 15,427.   Receipts: £475.
Close of Play: 1st day WI 4/347 (de Caires 71, Grant 23); 2nd day Vic 3/210 (Fontaine 69, Rush 22); 3rd day WI (2) 3/186 (de Caires 32, Birkett 3).

Because of a clash in fixtures - Victoria were due to play a Shield match in Brisbane on the same dates, though that match was eventually abandoned without a ball being bowled due to rain - the Victorian selectors were forced to field a Second Eleven for the return match against the West Indies. Cordner and Healy held out for 20 minutes on the last afternoon to save the game, adding an unbroken 30 for the last Victorian wicket. Healy was missed in the slips when 3 by substitute fieldsman Wight from the bowling of St Hill. West Indies' 495 included innings from Roach (104 in 181 minutes, 10 fours, stumping chance at 92), Martin (44 in 108 minutes, 1 four), Headley (77 in 100 minutes, 6 fours), de Caires (76 in 117 minutes, 8 fours), Grant (84 in 138 minutes, 6 fours) and Sealy (41 in 47 minutes, 2 fours). In the second innings, Headley (113 in 128 minutes, 11 fours) and de Caires (64 in 71 minutes, 1 six and 6 fours) added 120 for the second wicket, the innings being characterised by an unusual absence of extras. Ellis was out to the second ball of the Victorian first innings, Eaton (43 in 68 minutes, 5 fours), Fontaine (76 in 134 minutes, 3 fours), Sandford (70 in 68 minutes, 10 fours), and Rush (42 in 70 minutes, 7 fours) making the top scores. Ellis (47 in 80 minutes, 4 fours), Quin (43 in 75 minutes, 4 fours) and Tolhurst (63 in 106 minutes, 4 fours) top-scored in the second innings. *Wisden* incorrectly gives Vic (1) Sandford 76, Quin 31; V.G. instead of L.E.Nagel. Sources: *Wisden, VCA Report, NSWCA Report, Australian Cricketer, The Age, The Argus, The Herald.*

WEST INDIES XI

C.A.Roach	st Quin b Cordner	104	c Quin b Nagel		1
F.R.Martin	run out (Sandford/Quin)	44			
G.A.Headley	lbw b Cordner	77	c Nagel b Wilkinson		113
F.I.de Caires	c Eaton b Nagel	76	b Wilkinson		64
L.S.Birkett	c Fontaine b Cordner	20	c Rush b Cordner		9
*G.C.Grant	run out (Eaton/Nagel)	84			
J.E.D.Sealy	c Rush b Nagel	41	(6) not out		14
†I.Barrow	c Fontaine b Nagel	8	(2) c & b Cordner		37
G.N.Francis	not out	16			
H.C.Griffith	b Nagel	10			
E.L.St Hill	run out (Eaton/Quin)	0			
Extras	(b12, lb2, w1)	15			-
Total	(118.4 overs, 396 mins)	495	(51.4 overs, 170 mins) (5 wkts dec)		238

VICTORIA

P.A.Ellis	c Grant b Francis	0	run out (Barrow)		47
G.M.Eaton	c Francis b St Hill	43	b St Hill		8
F.E.Fontaine	c Grant b Francis	76	b Martin		32
H.C.A.Sandford	c St Hill b Griffith	70	c Headley b St Hill		4
J.Rush	b Griffith	42	b Martin		10
*E.K.Tolhurst	c Birkett b St Hill	15	(7) b Martin		63
†S.O.Quin	lbw b Francis	37	(6) c sub (O.S.Wight) b de Caires		43
L.E.Nagel	c Barrow b Francis	4	(9) lbw b St Hill		0
W.A.Wilkinson	not out	11	(8) c Barrow b Francis		25
L.O.Cordner	b Martin	5	not out		30
E.F.Healy	c Francis b St Hill	0	not out		9
Extras	(b11, lb5, w1, nb5)	22	(b2, lb6, w1)		9
Total	(78.3 overs, 313 mins)	325	(73.0 overs, 240 mins) (9 wkts)		280

VICTORIA	O	M	R	W	w,nb	O	M	R	W	w,nb			FALL OF WICKETS		
												WI	VIC	WI	VIC
Nagel	32	4	111	4	-,-	14	1	50	1	-,-	Wkt	1st	1st	2nd	2nd
Wilkinson	33	7	112	0	-,-	12.4	0	60	2	-,-	1st	89	0	2	36
Healy	25.4	4	75	0	-,-	8	0	27	0	-,-	2nd	205	79	122	86
Cordner	24	0	154	3	-,-	17	0	101	2	-,-	3rd	242	178	172	93
Fontaine	3	1	15	0	1,-						4th	280	226	197	95
Sandford	1	0	13	0	-,-						5th	355	245	238	114
											6th	435	274	-	184
WEST INDIES XI	O	M	R	W	w,nb	O	M	R	W	w,nb	7th	451	290	-	223
Francis	20	0	80	4	-,1	12	2	46	1	-,-	8th	479	311	-	224
Griffith	26	4	106	2	1,4	8	0	40	0	1,-	9th	494	324	-	250
St Hill	17.3	1	81	3	-,-	21	2	76	3	-,-	10th	495	325	-	-
Martin	15	3	34	1	-,-	24	3	65	3	-,-					
Headley						4	0	24	0	-,-					
de Caires						4	0	20	1	-,-					

SOUTH AUSTRALIA v WEST INDIES XI

Played at Adelaide Oval on February 7, 9, 10, 11, 1931. (Four-day match)
Toss : West Indies XI.   Result : SOUTH AUSTRALIA WON BY ONE WICKET.
Debuts: Nil.
12th Men: R.C.Teagle (SA) and J.E.D.Sealy (WI).
Umpires: L.G.Bickle and G.A.Hele.
Attendances: No daily figures published.   Total: 10,935.   Receipts: £435.
Close of Play: 1st day WI 6/303 (Grant 50, Hunte 9); 2nd day SA 8/244 (Grimmett 40, Carlton 2); 3rd day SA (2) 0/48 (Richardson 34, Nitschke 7).

Carlton and Walker added 22 for the last wicket to take South Australia to their second victory against West Indies with six minutes remaining in the game. Lee (106 in 131 minutes, 11 fours), Grimmett (54 in 79 minutes), Richardson (52 in 65 minutes), Lonergan (68 in 79 minutes, 4 fours) and Waite (82 in 109 minutes, 1 six and 7 fours) made batting contributions along the way, Lee and Grimmett also taking their share of wickets. West Indies' first innings featured notable scores from Headley (75 in 158 minutes, 5 fours), Grant (102 in 159 minutes, 1 six and 8 fours) and Constantine (63 in 51 minutes, 10 fours). *Wisden* incorrectly gives WI (2) St Hill c Waite b Lee.
Sources: *Wisden, SACA Report, Australian Cricketer, South Australian Register, Adelaide Advertiser, The News.*

WEST INDIES XI

C.A.Roach	run out (Hack/Walker)	26	lbw b Whitfield		8
F.R.Martin	c Waite b Grimmett	22	c Richardson b Grimmett		30
G.A.Headley	c Whitfield b Grimmett	75	lbw b Carlton		39
F.I.de Caires	st Walker b Grimmett	14	c Walker b Grimmett		6
E.L.Bartlett	b Carlton	34	st Walker b Grimmett		7
*G.C.Grant	c Carlton b Grimmett	102	c Whitfield b Lee		42
L.N.Constantine	c & b Lee	63	c sub (R.C.Teagle) b Lee		34
†E.A.C.Hunte	hit wkt b b Grimmett	19	c & b Lee		0
O.C.Scott	c Nitschke b Carlton	5	c Lonergan b Lee		30
E.L.St Hill	b Carlton	9	c Lonergan b Lee		1
H.C.Griffith	not out	0	not out		3
Extras	(b8, lb6)	14	(b3, lb5)		8
Total	(113.1 overs, 370 mins)	383	(60.5 overs, 210 mins)		208

SOUTH AUSTRALIA

H.C.Nitschke	c de Caires b St Hill	28	(2) c Constantine b Scott		14
B.J.Tobin	b Constantine	4	(7) b Griffith		9
A.T.Hack	b Constantine	0	(8) run out (Constantine/Hunte)		19
*V.Y.Richardson	c Griffith b Constantine	3	(1) c Constantine b Scott		52
A.R.Lonergan	c Roach b Constantine	36	(4) c Constantine b St Hill		68
H.E.Whitfield	lbw b Griffith	0	(5) c St Hill b Scott		3
P.K.Lee	b Scott	106	(3) lbw b Scott		7
M.G.Waite	lbw b St Hill	10	(6) b Griffith		82
C.V.Grimmett	c Roach b Scott	54	c Grant b Scott		12
T.A.Carlton	lbw b Scott	4	not out		10
†C.W.Walker	not out	17	not out		9
Extras	(b12, lb4)	16	(b19, lb8, nb2)		29
Total	(63.1 overs, 239 mins)	278	(65.4 overs, 259 mins) (9 wkts)		314

SOUTH AUSTRALIA	O	M	R	W	w,nb	O	M	R	W	w,nb
Tobin	7	0	33	0	-,-	3	1	10	0	-,-
Whitfield	11	2	63	0	-,-	4	0	14	1	-,-
Carlton	29.1	8	65	3	-,-	12	4	18	1	-,-
Grimmett	42	6	144	5	-,-	25	2	93	3	-,-
Lee	21	4	39	1	,	15.5	2	57	5	-,-
Waite	3	0	25	0	-,-	1	0	8	0	-,-

WEST INDIES XI	O	M	R	W	w,nb	O	M	R	W	w,nb
Constantine	17	2	73	4	-,-	4	0	20	0	-,-
Griffith	11	1	59	1	-,-	13	1	48	2	-,1
St Hill	11	1	45	2	-,-	17	0	85	1	-,-
Scott	14.1	0	69	3	-,-	19.4	0	100	5	-,1
Martin	10	5	16	0	-,-	12	3	32	0	-,-

FALL OF WICKETS

Wkt	WI 1st	SA 1st	WI 2nd	SA 2nd
1st	39	21	9	73
2nd	64	21	68	78
3rd	89	33	78	87
4th	176	45	86	105
5th	182	46	96	201
6th	279	123	152	224
7th	348	153	152	268
8th	363	225	185	292
9th	383	247	189	292
10th	383	278	208	-

AUSTRALIA v WEST INDIES (4th Test)

Played at Melbourne Cricket Ground on February 13, 14, 1931. (Timeless match)
Toss : West Indies.   Result : AUSTRALIA WON BY AN INNINGS AND 122 RUNS.
Debuts: Nil.
12th Men: K.E.Rigg (Aust) and J.E.D.Sealy (WI).
Umpires: A.N.Barlow and J.Richards.
Attendances: 3969, 9896.   Total: 13,865   Receipts: £693.
Close of Play: 1st day Aust 1/197 (Woodfull 75, Bradman 92).

West Indies failed to capitalise after opting to bat on a perfect pitch, losing their last seven wickets for 18 runs on the opening day. Woodfull (83 in 142 minutes, 7 fours) and Bradman (152 in 154 minutes, 2 fives and 13 fours, chance at 92) shared a fine second-wicket partnership for Australia which realised 147 runs in 78 minutes. Heavy overnight rain made the wicket sticky next morning and Bradman gave his only chance without adding to his overnight score, Headley missing him at silly point off Martin. Woodfull was run out when Bradman, uncharacteristically, did not respond to his call for an easy run. Bradman reached his century in 102 minutes and was later involved in another run out, both he and McCabe finishing at the same end. (Bradman actually headed off the field, thinking he was out). Woodfull's declaration enabled his bowlers to make use of a wicket which was still providing awkward bounce. Ironmonger's match figures of 11 for 79 remained the best for Australia against West Indies until M.G.Hughes took 13 for 217 at Perth in 1988-89. *Wisden* incorrectly gives WI bowling, Birkett 3 overs. Sources: *Wisden, VCA Report, NSWCA Report, The Age, The Argus, The Australasian, The Herald.*

WEST INDIES

C.A.Roach	c Kippax b Grimmett	20		lbw b Fairfax	7
F.R.Martin	lbw b Ironmonger	17	(6)	c Oldfield b Fairfax	10
G.A.Headley	c Jackson b Ironmonger	33		c Fairfax b Ironmonger	11
L.S.Birkett	c McCabe b Ironmonger	0		c Jackson b Ironmonger	13
E.L.Bartlett	st Oldfield b Ironmonger	9	(7)	b Fairfax	6
*G.C.Grant	c Oldfield b Ironmonger	0	(5)	c McCabe b Ironmonger	3
L.N.Constantine	c Jackson b Grimmett	7	(2)	c Kippax b Fairfax	10
†I.Barrow	c Fairfax b Ironmonger	0		c Oxenham b Ironmonger	13
O.C.Scott	run out (Grimmett/Oldfield)	11		not out	20
G.N.Francis	not out	0	(11)	c Jackson b Grimmett	0
H.C.Griffith	c Fairfax b Ironmonger	0	(10)	b Grimmett	4
Extras	(nb2)	2		(b3, lb6, nb1)	10
Total	(50.0 overs, 141 mins)	99		(35.4 overs, 115 mins)	107

AUSTRALIA

*W.M.Woodfull	run out (Headley/Francis)	83
W.H.Ponsford	st Barrow b Constantine	24
D.G.Bradman	c Roach b Martin	152
A.Jackson	c Birkett b Constantine	15
S.J.McCabe	run out (Roach/Constantine)	2
A.G.Fairfax	c Birkett b Martin	16
A.F.Kippax	b Martin	24
R.K.Oxenham	c Constantine b Griffith	0
†W.A.S.Oldfield	not out	1
C.V.Grimmett	) did not bat	
H.Ironmonger	)	
Extras	(b 7, lb3, nb1)	11
Total	(89.2 overs, 249 minutes) (8 wkts dec)	328

AUSTRALIA	O	M	R	W	w,nb		O	M	R	W	w,nb		FALL OF WICKETS		
Fairfax	5	0	14	0	-,-		14	2	31	4	-,1		WI	AUST	WI
Oxenham	6	1	14	0	-,-							Wkt	1st	1st	2nd
Ironmonger	20	7	23	7	-,2	(2)	17	4	56	4	-,-	1st	32	50	8
Grimmett	19	7	46	2	-,-	(3)	4.4	0	10	2	-,-	2nd	51	206	32
												3rd	53	265	36
WEST INDIES	O	M	R	W	w,nb							4th	81	275	49
Francis	13	0	51	0	-,-							5th	81	286	60
Griffith	8	1	33	1	-,1							6th	88	325	60
Scott	11	0	47	0	-,-							7th	88	326	67
Constantine	25	4	83	2	-,-							8th	88	328	92
Martin	30.2	3	91	3	-,-							9th	99	-	97
Birkett	2	0	12	0	-,-							10th	99	-	107

SOUTH AUSTRALIA v VICTORIA (Shield Match 11)

Played at Adelaide Oval on February 20, 21, 23, 24, 1931. (Four-day match)
Toss : South Australia. Result : MATCH DRAWN.
Debuts: South Australia - R.C.Teagle (f/c).
12th Men: C.L.B.Starr (SA) and R.J.Hassett (Vic).
Umpires: G.A.Hele and A.G.Jenkins.
Attendances: 3994, 6680, 4328, 2169. Total: 17,171. Receipts: £607.
Close of Play: 1st day SA 7/330 (Lonergan 151, Grimmett 12); 2nd day Vic 3/152 (Woodfull 83); 3rd day SA (2) 4/32 (Nitschke 12).

Teagle (originally 12th man) and Tobin replaced G.W.Harris and T.W.Wall (both unavailable) in the South Australian line-up. E.L.a'Beckett and D.D.Blackie were unavailable for Victoria, who went into the match needing only to avoid defeat to retain the Sheffield Shield. Lonergan (159 in 295 minutes, 17 fours) made his career-best score and shared a 151-run partnership for South Australia's sixth wicket with Waite (74 in 116 minutes, 7 fours). Ironmonger, approaching his 49th birthday, captured match figures of 12 for 195. Walker's unbeaten 44 at No. 11 occupied 55 minutes and included 1 five and 5 fours. Woodfull (177 in 437 minutes, 5 fours and 85 singles) reached his century in 253 minutes for Victoria. Rigg (50 in 152 minutes, 1 four), Oakley (73 in 108 minutes, 12 fours) and later Ryder (48 not out in 104 minutes, 3 fours) also batted in keeping with the team's requirements. *Wisden* incorrectly gives Vic (1) Oakley 72, Barnett 26; Vic (2) O'Brien 19, Woodfull 17*. Sources: *Wisden, VCA Report, SACA Report, Adelaide Advertiser, The News.*

SOUTH AUSTRALIA

*V.Y.Richardson	run out (Oakley/Barnett)	36		b Alexander	8
H.C.Nitschke	c Barnett b Ironmonger	13		c Woodfull b Ironmonger	25
A.R.Lonergan	b Ironmonger	159		c Hendry b Ironmonger	7
P.K.Lee	b Ironmonger	2		run out (Woodfull/Barnett)	0
R.C.Teagle	b Ironmonger	20		st Barnett b Ironmonger	0
B.J.Tobin	c Barnett b Ryder	11	(7)	c O'Brien b Ironmonger	16
M.G.Waite	c Barnett b Davidson	74	(8)	not out	38
H.E.Whitfield	b Ironmonger	2	(9)	lbw b Ironmonger	13
C.V.Grimmett	c Ryder b Ironmonger	32	(6)	c & b Alexander	6
T.A.Carlton	lbw b Ironmonger	34		b Davidson	4
†C.W.Walker	not out	44		c & b Davidson	14
Extras	(b3, lb9)	12		(b9, lb13, nb1)	23
Total	(127.4 overs, 429 mins)	439		(72.5 overs, 249 mins)	154

VICTORIA

*W.M.Woodfull	b Grimmett	177	(6)	not out	27
W.H.Ponsford	b Tobin	16	(1)	b Tobin	23
K.E.Rigg	c Walker b Waite	50		c Carlton b Tobin	4
A.A.Davidson	c & b Lee	0			
H.S.T.L.Hendry	lbw b Grimmett	8	(4)	lbw b Grimmett	2
J.Ryder	b Grimmett	2	(5)	not out	48
L.P.J.O'Brien	lbw b Tobin	9	(2)	b Tobin	9
H.H.Oakley	c Tobin b Lee	73			
†B.A.Barnett	st Walker b Lee	25			
H H Alexander	b Grimmett	0			
H.Ironmonger	not out	0			
Extras	(b5, lb4)	9		(b10, lb6, w1, nb1)	18
Total	(144.6 overs, 444 mins)	369		(44.0 overs, 140 mins) (4 wkts)	131

VICTORIA	O	M	R	W	w,nb		O	M	R	W	w,nb
Alexander	23	3	102	0	-,-		22	8	38	2	-,-
Hendry	19	4	70	0	-,-						
Ironmonger	48.4	13	135	7	-,-	(2)	35	14	60	5	-,1
Davidson	31	3	118	1	-,-	(3)	15.5	7	33	2	-,-
Ryder	6	4	2	1	-,-						

SOUTH AUSTRALIA	O	M	R	W	w,nb		O	M	R	W	w,nb
Whitfield	11	4	14	0	-,-						
Grimmett	48	13	105	4	-,-	(3)	13	7	13	1	-,-
Tobin	21	2	65	2	-,-	(1)	7	1	26	3	-,-
Carlton	26	14	47	0	-,-	(2)	4	1	16	0	-,-
Lee	26.6	4	67	3	-,-	(4)	7	4	3	0	-,-
Waite	12	0	62	1	-,-	(5)	4	0	13	0	-,-
Lonergan						(6)	2	0	12	0	-,-
Teagle						(7)	4	1	12	0	-,1
Nitschke						(8)	3	0	18	0	1,-

FALL OF WICKETS

Wkt	SA 1st	VIC 1st	SA 2nd	VIC 2nd
1st	25	33	14	33
2nd	82	149	32	38
3rd	90	152	32	41
4th	142	168	32	45
5th	161	176	47	-
6th	312	207	69	-
7th	315	322	80	-
8th	351	369	112	-
9th	371	369	125	-
10th	439	369	154	-

NEW SOUTH WALES v WEST INDIES XI

Played at Sydney Cricket Ground on February 21, 23, 24, 25, 1931. (Four-day match)
Toss : West Indies XI.   Result : WEST INDIES XI WON BY 86 RUNS.
Debuts: New South Wales - A.Bennett, L.D.McGuirk (both f/c).
12th Men: J.E.H.Hooker (NSW) and E.L.Bartlett(WI).
Umpires: A.C.Jones and E.J.Shaw.
Attendances: 9297, 6779, 3770, 3410.   Total: 23,256   Receipts: £1146.
Close of Play: 1st day NSW 0/0 (Davidson 0, Bill 0); 2nd day WI (2) 3/98 (Martin 46, Sealy 36); 3rd day NSW (2) 2/124 (Bradman 63, Kippax 21).

A.G.Fairfax, A.Jackson and W.A.S.Oldfield were all unavailable for New South Wales. Sealy, at 18 years 5 months the youngest member of West Indies' touring party, played a major role in his team's victory, scoring 58 in 77 minutes with 5 fours and 92 in 116 minutes with 11 fours. Other fifties came from Roach (55 in 66 minutes, 7 fours), Headley (70 in 104 minutes, 6 fours), Martin (56 in 132 minutes, 6 fours) and Scott (67 not out in 65 minutes, 11 fours), while Constantine scored 41 (36 minutes, 1 five and 6 fours) and 93 (103 minutes, 8 fours) and captured seven wickets. Bill (41 in 85 minutes, 3 fours) successfully appealed against the light before a ball was bowled in the New South Wales first innings and was run out in an unusual fashion on the second day. Involved in a mix-up with Kippax, Bill made no attempt to regain his crease and walked off though Griffith had removed the bails with a hand not holding the ball. Grant subsequently ran in and pulled out a stump with ball in hand to complete the dismissal. Bennett, in his sole match in Australia, was dismissed first ball by Griffith. Bradman (73 in 78 minutes, 9 fours), Kippax (141 in 222 minutes, 11 fours and 2 chances), McCabe (100 in 122 minutes, 9 fours) and Chilvers (43 not out in 48 minutes, 8 fours) led the chase to score 553 for victory, helping New South Wales become the first team to exceed 450 in the fourth innings on three separate occasions. *Wisden* incorrectly gives WI (1) Francis c Davidson; WI (2) Scott run out, NSW (2) McCabe c Barrow. Sources: *Wisden, NSWCA Report, NSWCA Scorebook, Sydney Morning Herald, Sydney Referee, The Age.*

WEST INDIES XI

C.A.Roach	c Hunt b Theak	55	lbw b Theak	9	
F.R.Martin	b McGuirk	8	lbw b Chilvers	56	
G.A.Headley	run out (Kippax)	70	lbw b Hunt	2	
*G.C.Grant	c Davidson b Hunt	36	c Davidson b Hunt	0	
J.E.D.Sealy	b McCabe	58	b McGuirk	92	
L.N.Constantine	b McCabe	41	run out (Davidson)	93	
O.S.Wight	run out	4	c Kippax b Chilvers	22	
†I.Barrow	c Kippax b Chilvers	29	run out (Kippax/Hunt)	45	
O.C.Scott	c Hunt b Chilvers	17	not out	67	
G.N.Francis	st Davidson b Chilvers	6	st Davidson b Chilvers	0	
H.C.Griffith	not out	1			
Extras	(b5, lb6, nb3)	14	(b11, lb6)	17	
Total	(69.5 overs, 250 mins)	339	(88.3 overs, 304 mins) (9 wkts dec)	403	

NEW SOUTH WALES

†H.L.Davidson	b Constantine	16	(8) b Francis	32	
O.W.Bill	run out (Scott/Griffith/Grant)	41	lbw b Francis	11	
D.G.Bradman	b Constantine	10	lbw b Griffith	73	
*A.F.Kippax	lbw b Griffith	32	c Sealy b Griffith	141	
S.J.McCabe	b Constantine	26	c Francis b Martin	100	
A.Bennett	b Griffith	0	c Barrow b Scott	16	
J.H.W.Fingleton	not out	32	(1) lbw b Constantine	26	
W.A.Hunt	b Constantine	2	(7) c Sealy b Scott	6	
H.J.T.Theak	b Constantine	0	(10) b Francis	2	
H.C.Chilvers	c Headley b Scott	6	(9) not out	43	
L.D.McGuirk	b Constantine	15	b Francis	2	
Extras	(b6, lb3, nb1)	10	(b9, lb5)	14	
Total	(44.3 overs, 170 mins)	190	(96.6 overs, 361 mins)	466	

NEW SOUTH WALES	O	M	R	W	w,nb		O	M	R	W	w,nb
Theak	16	1	95	1	-,1		8	1	28	1	-,-
McGuirk	12	1	44	1	-,2		22	3	72	1	-,-
Hunt	14	1	53	1	-,-		19	0	99	2	-,-
Chilvers	12.5	2	56	3	-,-	(5)	15.3	5	53	3	-,-
McCabe	13	0	62	2	-,-	(4)	15	0	77	0	-,-
Bennett	2	0	15	0	-,-		4	0	26	0	-,-
Kippax							5	1	31	0	-,-

WEST INDIES XI	O	M	R	W	w,nb		O	M	R	W	w,nb
Francis	8	0	25	0	-,-		20.6	4	76	4	-,-
Griffith	9	2	36	2	-,1		19	0	115	2	-,-
Scott	18	0	74	1	-,-		19	0	107	2	-,-
Constantine	9.3	0	45	6	-,-		8	0	39	1	-,-
Martin							19	2	68	1	-,-
Sealy							11	0	47	0	-,-

FALL OF WICKETS

Wkt	WI 1st	NSW 1st	WI 2nd	NSW 2nd
1st	38	36	16	33
2nd	94	48	37	60
3rd	154	101	37	140
4th	203	105	123	314
5th	265	105	203	374
6th	277	143	276	376
7th	299	149	294	383
8th	324	149	399	452
9th	336	168	403	464
10th	339	190	-	466

VICTORIA v TASMANIA

Played at Melbourne Cricket Ground on February 23, 24, 25, 1931. (Three-day match)
Toss : Victoria   Result : MATCH DRAWN.
Debuts: Victoria - A.R.McInnes, G.H.Newstead (both f/c).
12th Men: J.O.Perraton (Vic) and R.E.Ward (Tas).
Umpires: H.E.Nichols and W.R.Wetenhall.
Attendances: 1025, 1259, 200.   Total: 2484   Receipts: £55.
Close of Play: 1st day Vic 3/30 (Fontaine 22, Darling 6); 2nd day Tas (2) 4/119 (Green 22, Newton 2).

Rush (originally 12th man) and Chapman replaced L.O.Cordner and A.L.Hassett (both unavailable) in the Victorian side. Tasmania's highest scorers were Atkinson (39 in 65 minutes, 1 four) and Nash (59 in 161 minutes, 6 fours) in the first innings and Matthews (51 in 83 minutes, 5 fours), Brain (93 in 162 minutes, 7 fours) and James (38 in 32 minutes, 2 fours) in the second. Nash took catches of his own bowling from the third and seventh balls of his opening over to dismiss Eaton and Newstead when Victoria batted. Fontaine (40 in 98 minutes, 2 fours), Darling (88 in 132 minutes, 1 six and 7 fours), Chapman (33 in 68 minutes, 5 fours) and Rush (51 in 64 minutes, 6 fours) then rescuing the innings. Darling (70 in 86 minutes, 6 fours) again top-scored in the second innings, the game being drawn upon his dismissal. *VCA Report* gives Tas (2) Matthews c Eaton. *Cricketer* incorrectly gives Tas (2) Schrader 0/66, Darling 0/32. Sources: *The Cricketer, Australian Cricketer, VCA Report, TCA Report, The Age, The Argus, The Herald, Melbourne Sun, Hobart Mercury.*

TASMANIA

Batsman	Dismissal (1st)	Score	Dismissal (2nd)	Score
*J.A.Atkinson	c Schrader b Healy	39	c Schrader b Morton	21
†T.H.Matthews	b Chapman	16	c Newstead b Chapman	51
D.C.Green	c Darling b Healy	1	b Healy	27
L.J.Nash	b Schrader	59	c Scaife b Chapman	22
G.W.Martin	run out (Darling/McInnes)	22	c Rush b Chapman	0
A.C.Newton	c Newstead b Schrader	31	lbw b Morton	4
D.M.Brain	lbw b Morton	21	b Healy	93
G.G.Gibson	run out (Scaife/McInnes)	6	c Darling b Chapman	24
G.T.H.James	c & b Morton	6	run out (Scaife/Darling)	38
V.L.Hooper	not out	12	b Healy	22
R.C.Townley	b Morton	8	not out	2
Extras	(b20, lb2, nb3)	25	(b15, lb12, nb2)	19
Total	(82.3 overs, 260 mins)	246	(92.6 overs, 306 mins)	323

VICTORIA

Batsman	Dismissal (1st)	Score	Dismissal (2nd)	Score
G.M.Eaton	c & b Nash	0	b Newton	23
F.E.Fontaine	run out (/Matthews)	40	run out (/Matthews)	10
G.H.Newstead	c & b Nash	0	c Martin b Hooper	20
J.W.Scaife	c Atkinson b Nash	1	b Newton	10
L.S.Darling	c Matthews b Nash	88	(6) c Newton b Townley	70
J.Rush	c Nash b Hooper	51	(5) c Matthews b Newton	13
F.D.Chapman	lbw b Newton	33	b James	14
†A.R.McInnes	c Martin b Newton	1	c Townley b Newton	17
E.F.Healy	not out	12	not out	9
H.C.Schrader	run out	2		
*F.L.Morton	b Nash	3		
Extras	(b5, lb3, w1)	9	(b8, lb1)	9
Total	(59.3 overs, 231 mins)	240	(35.5 overs, 145 mins) (8 wkts)	195

VICTORIA	O	M	R	W	w,nb		O	M	R	W	w,nb
Morton	17.3	2	64	3	-,3		17	1	71	2	-,1
Schrader	19	4	65	2	-,-		15	1	67	0	-,-
Darling	10	1	29	0	-,-	(4)	14	2	31	0	-,-
Healy	18	4	32	2	-,-	(3)	22.6	6	66	3	-,1
Chapman	16	9	23	1	-,-		24	5	69	4	-,-
Scaife	2	0	8	0	-,-						

TASMANIA	O	M	R	W	w,nb		O	M	R	W	w,nb
Nash	16.3	2	65	5	-,-		6	0	29	0	-,-
James	16	0	64	0	-,-		8	0	50	1	-,-
Hooper	6	1	16	1	-,-		8	0	47	1	-,-
Newton	18	4	62	2	1,-		10	0	36	4	-,-
Townley	3	0	24	0	-,-		3.5	0	24	1	-,-

FALL OF WICKETS

Wkt	TAS 1st	VIC 1st	TAS 2nd	VIC 2nd
1st	75	0	30	12
2nd	75	0	84	50
3rd	79	4	113	54
4th	111	94	113	72
5th	163	174	127	81
6th	198	188	127	122
7th	216	189	202	175
8th	220	232	264	195
9th	231	237	308	-
10th	246	240	323	-

AFCM No. 738/5
Test No. 203/5
TM No. 16/14

AUSTRALIA v WEST INDIES (5th Test)

Played at Sydney Cricket Ground on February 27, 28, March 2, 3 (no play), 4, 1931. (Timeless match)
Toss : West Indies.   Result : WEST INDIES WON BY 30 RUNS.
Debuts: Australia - K.E.Rigg (Test).
12th Men: A.Jackson (Aust) and L.S.Birkett (WI).
Umpires: H.J.Armstrong and W.G.French.
Attendances: 7516, 11678, 8856, no play, 7218.   Total: 35,268.   Receipts: £1958.
Close of Play: 1st day WI 2/299 (Martin 100, Grant 48); 2nd day Aust 5/89 (McCabe 0, Fairfax 0); 3rd day WI (2) 5/124 (Grant 27, Bartlett 0); 4th day no play.

Timely declarations by Grant twice caught the home batsmen on a drying pitch, enabling the West Indies to achieve their first Test victory over Australia. Martin (123 not out in 347 minutes, 11 fours) and Headley (105 in 146 minutes, 13 fours) scored chanceless centuries in ideal conditions on the opening day. Grant (62 in 99 minutes, 8 fours) also batted well. Rain in the morning delayed the start of the second day until 2.25 pm and West Indies lost 4 for 51 in an hour before the closure, when tea was taken. With the ball still kicking awkwardly from a patch at the southern end, Australia lost 5 for 89 in the evening session and, although the pitch had flattened out by the third day, the damage to the top order had been done. There was no play on the fourth day and the match resumed punctually on the fifth, but throughout the morning the hot sun had been drying the pitch after the previous day's rain and Grant declared immediately to allow his bowlers maximum assistance from the "sticky". Bradman was dismissed for his first Test duck and Oldfield, who was sent in at No. 5 to hold out until lunch, went first ball. The *SMH* correspondent wrote of the pitch that "the fast bowlers did not appear to cut it up, but the ball bumped and kicked at either end". Fairfax made the top score in each innings for Australia with 54 (116 minutes, 5 fours) and 60 not out (147 minutes, 3 fours); he was off the field for most of West Indies' second innings with a bruised heel and used Jackson as his runner on the last day. It was the last time Jackson appeared on the field in a first-class match. Bradman (43 in 51 minutes, 3 fours) and McCabe (44 in 64 minutes, 3 fours) made other scores. Sources: *NSWCA Scorebook, Wisden, NSWCA Report, Sydney Morning Herald, Sydney Referee, The Australasian, The Herald.*

WEST INDIES

F.R.Martin	not out	123	(2) c McCabe b Grimmett	20
C.A.Roach	lbw b Grimmett	31	(1) c Oldfield b Ironmonger	34
G.A.Headley	lbw b McCabe	105	b Oxenham	30
*G.C.Grant	c McCabe b Ironmonger	62	not out	27
J.E.D.Sealy	c Kippax b Grimmett	4	run out (McCabe)	7
L.N.Constantine	c McCabe b Ironmonger	0	c Bradman b Ironmonger	4
E.L.Bartlett	b Grimmett	0	not out	0
†I.Barrow	not out	7		
O.C.Scott	)			
G.N.Francis	) did not bat			
H.C.Griffith	)			
Extras	(b6, lb5, w1, nb6)	18	(b1, lb1)	2
Total	(135.0 overs, 347 minutes) (6 wkts dec)	350	(51.0 overs, 130 mins) (5 wkts dec)	124

AUSTRALIA

*W.M.Woodfull	c Constantine b Martin	22	c Constantine b Griffith	18
W.H.Ponsford	c Bartlett b Francis	7	c Constantine b Martin	28
D.G.Bradman	c Francis b Martin	43	b Griffith	0
A.F.Kippax	c Sealy b Constantine	3	c Roach b Constantine	10
K.E.Rigg	c Barrow b Francis	14	(6) c Barrow b Constantine	16
S.J.McCabe	c Headley b Francis	21	(8) c Grant b Martin	44
A.G.Fairfax	st Barrow b Scott	54	not out	60
R.K.Oxenham	c Barrow b Francis	0	(9) lbw b Scott	14
†W.A.S.Oldfield	run out (Francis/Barrow)	36	(5) lbw b Griffith	0
C.V.Grimmett	not out	15	c Constantine b Griffith	12
H.Ironmonger	b Griffith	1	run out (Martin/Grant)	4
Extras	(b1, nb7)	8	(b3, lb7, w2, nb2)	14
Total	(79.2 overs, 232 mins)	224	(75.3 overs, 229 mins)	220

AUSTRALIA	O	M	R	W	w,nb		O	M	R	W	w,nb			FALL OF WICKETS			
														WI	AUST	WI	AUST
Fairfax	21	2	60	0	-,5								Wkt	1st	1st	2nd	2nd
Oxenham	24	10	51	0	1,-		10	4	14	1	-,-						
Ironmonger	42	16	95	2	-,1	(4)	16	7	44	2	-,-		1st	70	7	46	49
Grimmett	33	7	100	3	-,-	(3)	18	4	47	1	-,-		2nd	222	66	66	49
McCabe	15	5	26	1	-,-	(1)	7	2	17	0	-,-		3rd	332	69	103	53
													4th	337	89	113	53
WEST INDIES	O	M	R	W	w,nb		O	M	R	W	w,nb		5th	338	89	124	65
Francis	19	6	48	4	-,-		16	2	32	0	-,-		6th	341	130	-	76
Griffith	13.2	3	31	1	-,-	(4)	13.3	3	50	4	-,-		7th	-	134	-	155
Martin	27	3	67	2	-,-		18	4	44	2	1,-		8th	-	196	-	180
Constantine	10	2	28	1	-,-	(2)	17	2	50	2	1,-		9th	-	215	-	214
Scott	10	1	42	1	-,-		11	0	30	1	-,2		10th	-	224	-	220

SOUTH AUSTRALIA v TASMANIA

Played at Adelaide Oval on February 28, March 2, 3, 1931. (Three-day match)
Toss : Tasmania.   Result : SOUTH AUSTRALIA WON BY SIX WICKETS.
Debuts: South Australia - M.D.Hutton (f/c).
12th Men: D.V.Kingsley (SA) and G.G.Gibson (Tas).
Umpires: G.A.Hele and L.G.Wallace.
Attendances: No daily figures published.   Total: 4705.   Receipts: £132.
Close of Play: 1st day SA 1/82 (Nitschke 24); 2nd day Tas (2) 0/34 (Atkinson 20, Matthews 10).

This match was Tasmania's first in South Australia since the 1877-78 season, ending a break of more than 53 years. Kingsley was a late replacement for C.S.Deverson as the South Australian reserve. Atkinson was out to the second ball of the match. Tasmania's best innings came from Green (90 in 179 minutes, 8 fours and 47 in 144 minutes, 2 fours), Martin (52 in 69 minutes, 8 fours) and James (51 not out in 54 minutes, 5 fours and 55 in 57 minutes). Carlton took three wickets in four balls - Nash, ball, Martin, Newton - in one over in the second innings to deal the knock out blow against the visitors. South Australia had gained an imposing start with innings from Richardson (58 in 71 minutes, 4 fours), Nitschke (120 in 240 minutes, 9 fours, chance at 103) and Lonergan (98 in 131 minutes, 7 fours), though only Lee (57 in 66 minutes, 6 fours) made any score of note after them. Hutton, in his only match, was out first ball. *Cricketer* incorrectly gives Tas (1) Tobin 3/93; Tas (2) Tobin 2/59; SA (1) Newton 1/66, Hooper 0/56, Atkinson 0/23. Sources: *The Cricketer, SACA Report, TCA Report, Adelaide Advertiser, Hobart Mercury, The News.*

TASMANIA

*J.A.Atkinson	c Teagle b Tobin	0	b Tobin	20
†T.H.Matthews	c Teagle b Tobin	7	b Tobin	12
D.C.Green	b Lee	90	lbw b Carlton	47
L.J.Nash	c Walker b Carlton	8	b Carlton	28
G.W.Martin	b Waite	52	b Carlton	0
A.C.Newton	lbw b Waite	6	c Starr b Carlton	0
D.M.Brain	b Lee	15	c Teagle b Lee	0
R.E.Ward	c Carlton b Tobin	20	c Walker b Tobin	23
G.T.H.James	not out	51	c Teagle b Lee	55
V.L.Hooper	b Waite	6	c Richardson b Lee	0
R.C.Townley	lbw b Waite	0	not out	5
Extras	(b3, lb5, nb1)	9	(b7, lb6, w1, nb1)	15
Total	(67.5 overs, 238 mins)	264	(59.7 overs, 217 mins)	205

SOUTH AUSTRALIA

*V.Y.Richardson	hit wkt b Townley	58		
H.C.Nitschke	c Nash b James	120		
A.R.Lonergan	c Nash b James	98		
C.L.B.Starr	c Green b Ward	6	(1) lbw b James	5
M.D.Hutton	b Ward	0	(2) not out	20
P.K.Lee	c sub (G.G.Gibson) b Nash	57		
M.G.Waite	lbw b Newton	18	(6) not out	2
B.J.Tobin	run out	0	(5) c Atkinson b James	12
R.C.Teagle	b Nash	11	(3) b Nash	1
T.A.Carlton	not out	14		
†C.W.Walker	b Nash	2	(4) b James	4
Extras	(b35, lb5)	40	(b5)	5
Total	(92.0 overs, 329 mins)	424	(17.5 overs, 50 mins) (4 wkts)	49

SOUTH AUSTRALIA	O	M	R	W	w,nb		O	M	R	W	w,nb	FALL OF WICKETS				
														TAS	SA	TAS	SA
Tobin	18	1	94	3	-,1		15	1	59	3	1,1	Wkt	1st	1st	2nd	2nd
Carlton	14	4	40	1	-,-		15	8	22	4	-,-	1st	0	82	36	7
Lee	12	2	41	2	-,-	(4)	14.7	2	49	3	-,-	2nd	11	270	39	12
Waite	19.5	5	61	4	-,-	(3)	9	2	36	0	-,-	3rd	20	305	69	19
Starr	4	0	19	0	-,-							4th	106	305	69	35
Hutton	.					(5)	6	0	24	0	-,-	5th	130	311	69	-
												6th	161	370	70	-
TASMANIA	O	M	R	W	w,nb		O	M	R	W	w,nb	7th	183	372	116	-
Nash	18	1	67	3	-,-		5	0	11	1	-,-	8th	248	396	189	-
Newton	19	2	56	1	-,-	(3)	4	1	8	0	-,-	9th	264	422	192	-
Hooper	11	0	66	0	-,-							10th	264	424	205	-
James	16	0	64	2	-,-	(2)	8.5	2	25	3	-,-					
Townley	13	0	67	1	-,-											
Atkinson	9	2	33	0	-,-											
Ward	6	0	31	2	-,-											

1931-32 SEASON (31 MATCHES)

H.B.Cameron led the second South African team to visit Australia and the first since 1910-11. The players travelled on to New Zealand at the conclusion of the Fifth Test against Australia and played their final match, against Western Australia at Perth, on their way home. They contested 18 matches in all on Australian soil, 16 of which were first-class. Their failure to adjust properly to local conditions made them no match for the home side in the Tests, and they were comprehensively defeated in all five encounters. Mitchell and Taylor batted the most impressively on the tour and Christy played some good innings away from the major internationals. Bell and Quinn formed a hard-working opening attack that impressed the Australians but McMillan, who began the tour well, proved expensive in the big games.

Bradman was especially severe on the tourists' attack. In his matches against South Africa and Australia, he scored 1190 runs (average 170.00) comprising consecutive innings of 30, 135, 226, 219, 112, 2, 167 and 299*. Woodfull also enjoyed facing their bowling - though to a saner extent - and others to do well included McCabe, Rigg, Kippax and Ponsford. Grimmett and Ironmonger repeated their success of the previous summer by combining to capture 64 wickets in the five Tests.

New South Wales won the Sheffield Shield ahead of South Australia by virtue of superior batting and bowling averages. Results were achieved in all 12 games for the first time. McCabe, who scored 438 Shield runs for once out, led the New South Wales batting along with Bradman. They were well supported by Fingleton, Bill, Nutt and Hird. Kippax (injured) was unavailable for much of the season. A most significant factor for New South Wales came with the reappearance in first-class cricket of O'Reilly, the aggressive legspin bowler. Since making his debut four years previously, he had been unavailable for the State through teaching duties in outback New South Wales. He quickly made up for lost time, and by season's end was in the Test side.

South Australia enjoyed their best Shield season for several years. Vic Richardson returned to his best form and Nitschke and Lonergan also scored consistently. Grimmett, despite turning 40 years old before the New Year, continued to be the most prolific wicket-taker in the country and he had good support from Lee, Wall and Carlton.

Injury forced Blackie from the Victorian side and his presence was badly missed, not least by his spin-bowling partner Ironmonger, who paid a higher price for his State wickets than he did his Test scalps. Queensland, who defeated Victoria twice, successfully introduced young players in Cook, Mossop, Andrews and Hogg (both from New South Wales). It was their veteran Oxenham, however, who performed most consistently with bat and ball. Gilbert caused a sensation with some very fast bowling in Queensland's opening match against New South Wales at Brisbane and he became a key member of the attack.

The Western Australian Cricket Association's campaign for a Second XI competition continued when their proposal went before the Interstate Conference on September 11, 1931. No decision was taken and the matter was deferred.

Leading Aggregates

Batsmen	M	I	NO	Runs	HS	Ave.	Bowlers	Runs	Wkts	Ave.
D.G.Bradman (NSW)	10	13	1	1403	299*	116.91	C.V.Grimmett (SA)	1535	77	19.93
J.A.J.Christy (SAf)	14	24	1	909	119	39.52	H.Ironmonger (V)	1168	63	18.53
V.Y.Richardson (SA)	8	16	0	873	138	54.56	A.J.Bell (SAf)	1273	51	24.96
W.M.Woodfull (V)	9	15	2	849	161	65.30	Q.McMillan (SAf)	1469	51	28.80
H.W.Taylor (SAf)	13	24	1	813	124	35.34	N.A.Quinn (SAf)	1003	42	23.88
S.J.McCabe (NSW)	10	12	3	783	229*	87.00	L.O.Fleetwood-Smith (V)	602	37	16.27
A.R.Lonergan (SA)	8	16	0	778	137	48.62	C.L.Vincent (SAf)	1186	33	35.93
B.Mitchell (SAf)	15	26	0	715	125	27.50	W.J.O'Reilly (NSW)	697	32	21.78
H.B.Cameron (SAf)	15	24	3	642	74	30.57	P.K.Lee (SA)	727	30	24.23
S.H.Curnow (SAf)	13	23	2	599	81*	28.52	T.W.Wall (SA)	787	30	26.23

SHEFFIELD SHIELD TABLE

	P	WO	W1	LO	L1	D	Pts	Quotient	Runs Scored	Wkts Lost	Runs Conceded	Wkts Taken
NEW SOUTH WALES	6	4	-	2	-	-	20	1.399	3229	101	2581	113
SOUTH AUSTRALIA	6	4	-	2	-	-	20	1.044	3260	117	2882	108
VICTORIA	6	2	-	4	-	-	10	0.932	2940	106	3271	110
QUEENSLAND	6	2	-	4	-	-	10	0.749	2763	113	3458	106
TOTAL	12	12	-	12	-	-	60	1.000	12192	437	12192	437

WESTERN AUSTRALIA v SOUTH AFRICAN XI

Played at W.A.C.A. Ground, Perth, on October 22, 23, 24, 1931. (Three-day match)
Toss : South African XI.   Result : MATCH DRAWN.
Debuts: Western Australia - P.W.E.Curtin, E.N.McKenzie (both f/c).
12th Men: A.E.Read (WA) and X.C.Balaskas (SAF).
Umpires: F.R.Buttsworth and N.Goode.
Attendances: 2500, 2000, 3000.   Total: About 7500.   Receipts: £483.
Close of Play: 1st day SAF 6/273 (Dalton 22); 2nd day WA 205 all out.

B.Mitchell (ill) was replaced in the South African 12 by Balaskas. Christy (102 in 202 minutes, 11 fours) and Curnow (58 in 190 minutes, 6 fours) added 160 for the first wicket. In an unfortunate incident during their partnership, a quick single was attempted and Hewson threw the ball at the stumps, hitting Curnow on the head. The batsman collapsed but after a brief delay was able to continue his innings. Dalton (53 in 104 minutes, 3 fours and 53 not out in 67 minutes) hit a half-century in each innings. Bromley scored quickly for Western Australia, making 48 (33 minutes, 7 fours, 1 six) and 78 (69 minutes, 7 fours, 2 sixes). South Africa were unable to enforce the follow-on, as matches in Australia at the time required a mandatory 200 run lead, despite being scheduled for three days only. *The West Australian* noted before the match: "Motor cars can be parked inside the ground at a fee of one shilling." Sources: *Wisden, NSWCA Report, VCA Report, Australian Cricketer, The West Australian, Daily News.*

SOUTH AFRICAN XI

J.A.J.Christy	b Newman	102		run out (Inverarity/Hewson)	36
S.H.Curnow	lbw b Bryant	58	(3)	b Bryant	20
K.G.Viljoen	b Bryant	35	(4)	not out	37
H.W.Taylor	lbw b Bryant	6	(2)	b Doig	1
*†H.B.Cameron	lbw b Curtin	12			
E.L.Dalton	run out (Curtin)	53	(5)	not out	53
D.P.B.Morkel	b Bryant	29			
Q.McMillan	not out	38			
C.L.Vincent	not out	20			
L.S.Brown	) did not bat				
A.J.Bell	)				
Extras	(b7, w1, nb1)	9		(b1, lb1, w1, nb1)	4
Total	(107.0 overs, 392 mins) (7 wkts dec)	362		(44.0 overs, 153 mins) (3 wkts dec)	151

WESTERN AUSTRALIA

F.H.Taaffe	b Bell	6		lbw b Bell	5
H.K.Lang	b Bell	0		c Taylor b Bell	8
E.N.McKenzie	b Brown	26		c Vincent b McMillan	17
R.O.Doig	b Vincent	16		b Bell	0
E.H.Bromley	b Bell	48		c Curnow b McMillan	78
P.W.E.Curtin	c Christy b McMillan	35	(9)	not out	3
*R.J.Bryant	b McMillan	16		st Cameron b McMillan	0
M.Inverarity	b Brown	14	(6)	b McMillan	11
W.A.Evans	c & b Christy	15	(8)	not out	24
H.A.Newman	not out	17			
†R.H.Hewson	c Vincent b McMillan	2			
Extras	(lb2, w8)	10		(b13)	13
Total	(53.4 overs, 193 mins)	205		(37.0 overs, 137 mins) (7 wkts)	159

WESTERN AUSTRALIA	O	M	R	W	w,nb		O	M	R	W	w,nb		FALL OF WICKETS			
Newman	22	5	81	1	-,-		8	1	21	0	1,1			SAF	WA	SAF	WA
Evans	26	5	54	0	-,-	(6)	9	1	17	0	-,-	Wkt	1st	1st	2nd	2nd
Curtin	19	2	67	1	1,1		7	2	20	0	-,-	1st	160	0	6	12
Inverarity	15	1	60	0	-,-		6	0	31	0	-,-	2nd	176	27	51	13
Bromley	4	0	27	0	-,-							3rd	185	57	67	13
Bryant	17	3	48	4	-,-	(5)	6	1	21	1	-,-	4th	208	57	-	87
Doig	4	0	16	0	-,-	(2)	8	2	37	1	-,-	5th	225	114	-	128
												6th	273	133	-	128
SOUTH AFRICAN XI	O	M	R	W	w,nb		O	M	R	W	w,nb	7th	317	163	-	139
Morkel	4	1	7	0	8,-	(4)	2	0	10	0	-,-	8th	-	179	-	-
Bell	10	1	48	3	-,-	(1)	10	2	29	3	-,-	9th	-	191	-	-
Brown	15	3	60	2	-,-	(2)	12	3	38	0	-,-	10th	-	205	-	-
Vincent	11	2	28	1	-,-	(3)	3	1	11	0	-,-					
McMillan	9.4	0	35	3	-,-		10	1	58	4	-,-					
Christy	4	0	17	1	-,-											

SOUTH AUSTRALIA v SOUTH AFRICAN XI

Played at Adelaide Oval on October 30, 31, November 2, 3, 1931. (Four-day match)
Toss : South African XI.   Result : SOUTH AFRICAN XI WON BY 192 RUNS.
Debuts: Nil.
12th Men: A.F.Richter (SA) and S.H.Curnow (SAF).
Umpires: G.A.Hele and A.G.Jenkins.
Attendances: 7800, ? , ? , ? .   Total: 26,060.   Receipts: £986.
Close of Play: 1st day SA 1/19 (Nitschke 10); 2nd day SAF (2) 1/86 (Christy 55, Viljoen 17); 3rd day SA (2) 0/9 (Richardson 8, Nitschke 0).

Starr replaced G.W.Harris (work) in the South Australian side. McMillan's leg-breaks and googlies captured 9 for 53 in the second innings, the best analysis to date by a touring bowler in Australia. A low-scoring match, only Christy (63 in 210 minutes, 1 four and 59 in 93 minutes, 6 fours) and Balaskas (61 in 155 minutes, 6 fours following his first-ball dismissal) surpassed fifty for the visitors. Cameron (41 in 91 minutes, 6 fours), McMillan (44 in 164 minutes, 4 fours) and Vincent (43 in 91 minutes, 4 fours) weighed in with second-innings contributions. South Australia's topscorers were Waite (45 in 119 minutes, 2 fours) and Richardson (36 in 54 minutes, 6 fours). Sources: *Wisden, SACA Report, Australian Cricketer, Adelaide Advertiser, The News.*

SOUTH AFRICAN XI

Batsman	Dismissal 1	R	Dismissal 2	R
J.A.J.Christy	lbw b Grimmett	63	c & b Grimmett	59
B.Mitchell	lbw b Grimmett	14	b Lee	13
K.G.Viljoen	st Walker b Grimmett	7	b Wall	17
H.W.Taylor	b Grimmett	10	b Wall	3
E.L.Dalton	b Wall	15	c Carlton b Grimmett	0
*†H.B.Cameron	run out (Lee/Walker)	25	b Lee	41
X.C.Balaskas	b Tobin	0	lbw b Carlton	61
Q.McMillan	c Richardson b Lee	10	c & b Starr	44
C.L.Vincent	c Waite b Grimmett	13	c Lonergan b Carlton	43
N.A.Quinn	c Wall b Grimmett	3	b Starr	0
A.J.Bell	not out	2	not out	1
Extras	(b1, lb12)	13	(b6, lb4, nb1)	11
Total	(72.5 overs, 245 mins)	175	(118.7 overs, 384 mins)	293

SOUTH AUSTRALIA

Batsman	Dismissal 1	R	Dismissal 2	R
H.C.Nitschke	lbw b Bell	14	(2) lbw b McMillan	30
C.L.B.Starr	c Balaskas b Bell	6	(4) lbw b McMillan	2
A.R.Lonergan	lbw b McMillan	33	b McMillan	17
*V.Y.Richardson	b Vincent	33	(1) c Mitchell b McMillan	36
P.K.Lee	lbw b Vincent	1	c Dalton b McMillan	6
B.J.Tobin	st Cameron b McMillan	1	(7) b Vincent	1
M.G.Waite	b Bell	45	(6) b McMillan	0
C.V.Grimmett	lbw b Quinn	8	c sub (S.H.Curnow) b McMillan	2
†C.W.Walker	b Quinn	20	c & b McMillan	1
T.A.Carlton	b Bell	3	not out	5
T.W.Wall	not out	0	c Dalton b McMillan	1
Extras	(b4, lb2)	6	(b1, lb4)	5
Total	(69.5 overs, 232 mins)	170	(33.1 overs, 121 mins)	106

SOUTH AUSTRALIA

Bowler	O	M	R	W	w,nb		O	M	R	W	w,nb
Wall	11	1	33	1	-,-		18	2	46	2	-,-
Tobin	9	1	32	1	-,-		7	0	29	0	-,-
Carlton	8	2	15	0	-,-	(5)	19	10	25	2	-,-
Grimmett	22.5	7	50	6	-,-	(3)	37	14	82	2	-,-
Lee	19	8	29	1	-,-	(4)	29	5	67	2	-,-
Waite	3	1	3	0	-,-		7	1	30	0	-,1
Starr							1.7	0	3	2	-,-

SOUTH AFRICAN XI

Bowler	O	M	R	W	w,nb		O	M	R	W	w,nb
Bell	16.5	7	37	4	-,-		7	2	29	0	-,-
Quinn	16	4	31	2	-,-		5	1	8	0	-,-
Christy	4	3	6	0	-,-						
Vincent	17	5	34	2	-,-		7	4	5	1	-,-
McMillan	16	0	56	2	-,-	(3)	13.1	2	53	9	-,-
Balaskas						(5)	1	0	6	0	-,-

FALL OF WICKETS

Wkt	SAF 1st	SA 1st	SAF 2nd	SA 2nd
1st	37	19	45	71
2nd	45	24	89	72
3rd	63	72	93	82
4th	86	76	93	90
5th	127	79	93	91
6th	127	97	162	94
7th	151	123	225	99
8th	163	158	292	99
9th	171	161	292	100
10th	175	170	293	106

VICTORIA v SOUTH AFRICAN XI

Played at Melbourne Cricket Ground on November 6, 7, 9, 1931. (Four-day match)
Toss : Victoria. Result : VICTORIA WON BY 87 RUNS.
Debuts: Nil.
12th Men: J.W.Scaife (Vic) and X.C.Balaskas (SAF).
Umpires: A.N.Barlow and J.Richards.
Attendances: 7841, 13670, 5153. Total: 26,664. Receipts: £927.
Close of Play: 1st day SAF 0/7 (Christy 3, Curnow 3); 2nd day SAF 6/212 (Morkel 2, McMillan 0).

Nagel replaced E.L.a'Beckett (university exams) in the Victorian team. Struck on the hand while batting on the first day, Blackie sustained a broken finger and took no further part after losing his wicket, Scaife substituting in the field in both innings. Rain, which shortened play on the second day and delayed the start of the third, made for a spiteful pitch and resulted in the rapid fall of 23 wickets and an early end to the match. Woodfull, missed on 97, reached his hundred in 229 minutes and scored 121 in 270 minutes, hitting 8 fours. An opening stand of 181 between Christy (119 in 200 minutes, 15 fours) and Curnow (50 in 193 minutes, 2 fours) accounted for 77.0 per cent of South Africa's first-innings total of 235. Ironmonger led the bowling with 10 for 108 for the match. Sources: *Wisden, VCA Report, Australian Cricketer, The Age, The Argus, The Herald, Melbourne Sun.*

VICTORIA

*W.M.Woodfull	st Cameron b McMillan	121		c Vincent b Quinn	0
W.H.Ponsford	st Cameron b Vincent	37		c Viljoen b Bell	4
K.E.Rigg	b Vincent	14		b Bell	14
J.Ryder	b Quinn	2		c Vincent b Quinn	0
L.P.J.O'Brien	b Quinn	33		not out	37
H.H.Oakley	c Cameron b Morkel	28		b Vincent	4
†B.A.Barnett	b Bell	12		b Bell	11
L.E.Nagel	lbw b Bell	9		c Cameron Vincent	1
D.D.Blackie	c Vincent b Quinn	21		absent hurt	-
E.L.McCormick	c Vincent b Quinn	2	(9)	c Christy b Quinn	0
H.Ironmonger	not out	1	(10)	b Morkel	1
Extras	(b3, nb1)	4		(b13, lb4, nb2)	19
Total	(76.7 overs, 276 mins)	284		(26.3 overs, 113 mins)	91

SOUTH AFRICAN XI

J.A.J.Christy	b Ironmonger	119	(6)	c Rigg b Ironmonger	9
S.H.Curnow	b Ironmonger	50	(7)	lbw b Nagel	0
B.Mitchell	lbw b McCormick	15	(4)	hit wkt b McCormick	3
H.W.Taylor	c Rigg b Ironmonger	0	(2)	b Ironmonger	2
K.G.Viljoen	lbw b McCormick	3	(8)	b Nagel	10
*†H.B.Cameron	c Barnett b McCormick	6	(1)	c Ryder b Ironmonger	11
D.P.B.Morkel	c & b McCormick	3	(9)	b Ironmonger	5
Q.McMillan	c Ryder b McCormick	4	(5)	st Barnett b Ironmonger	1
C.L.Vincent	c O'Brien b Ironmonger	10	(3)	c sub (J.W.Scaife) b McCormick	0
N.A.Quinn	c Nagel b Ironmonger	1		b Nagel	1
A.J.Bell	not out	1		not out	0
Extras	(b11, lb2, nb10)	23		(b11)	11
Total	(72.0 overs, 282 mins)	235		(24.4 overs, 107 mins)	53

SOUTH AFRICAN XI	O	M	R	W	w,nb		O	M	R	W	w,nb
Bell	22	4	62	2	-,1		11	5	19	3	-,2
Quinn	18.7	3	36	4	-,-		9	3	27	3	-,-
Morkel	6	0	30	1	-,-	(4)	1.3	0	3	1	-,-
Vincent	22	3	82	2	-,-	(3)	5	0	23	2	-,-
McMillan	7	0	61	1	-,-						
Mitchell	1	0	9	0	-,-						

VICTORIA	O	M	R	W	w,nb		O	M	R	W	w,nb
McCormick	23	3	65	5	-,9		9	4	13	2	-,-
Nagel	11	1	37	0	-,1	(3)	3.4	2	8	3	-,-
Ironmonger	30	10	87	5	-,-	(2)	12	4	21	5	-,-
Ryder	8	1	23	0	-,-						

FALL OF WICKETS

Wkt	VIC 1st	SAF 1st	VIC 2nd	SAF 2nd
1st	67	181	10	2
2nd	95	186	10	9
3rd	102	186	12	17
4th	166	197	30	19
5th	209	205	45	20
6th	232	212	62	29
7th	242	221	80	33
8th	276	224	82	45
9th	282	234	91	46
10th	284	235	-	53

QUEENSLAND v NEW SOUTH WALES (Shield Match 1)

Played at Brisbane Cricket Ground (Woolloongabba) on November 6, 7, 9 (no play), 10, 1931. (Four-day match)
Toss : Queensland.　　　　　　Result : NEW SOUTH WALES WON BY AN INNINGS AND 238 RUNS.
Debuts: Queensland - C.D.Hansen, B.V.Suche, L.W.Waterman (all f/c). New South Wales - S.F.Hird (f/c).
12th Men: J.W.Adams (Qld) and A.Jackson (NSW).
Umpires: J.Bartlett and J.A.Scott.
Attendances: 4000, 7400, no play, 837.　　　　Total: 12,237.　　　Receipts: £721.
Close of Play: 1st day NSW 3/52 (Fingleton 13, McCabe 11); 2nd day Qld (2) 0/2 (Suche 2, Waterman 0); 3rd day no play.

Hansen, Queensland's nominated 12th man, replaced F.C.Thompson. A.Jackson (influenza) withdrew from the New South Wales team on the morning of the match. Mossop (44 not out in 129 minutes, 3 fours) topscored for Queensland. Amos (right-arm fast-medium) taking a career-best 5 for 22 against his team-mates of the previous season. After a maiden from Thurlow, Gilbert dismissed Bill and Bradman from the first and sixth balls of his opening over in a spell rated by Bradman in his retirement as the fastest he had ever faced. Though not called, Gilbert was accused after the match by New South Wales manager A.L.Rose of consistently throwing. Kippax, hit in the face by a ball from Thurlow, retired at 2/26 and was taken to hospital to receive six stitches. McCabe (229 not out in 339 minutes, 1 six and 30 fours, chance at 103) compiled his highest score for New South Wales and shared partnerships of 195 for the fourth wicket with Fingleton (93 in 261 minutes, 5 fours, chance at 17) and 157 for the sixth wicket with Oldfield. Gilbert brilliantly ran out Hunt after intercepting a McCabe drive off his own bowling and throwing down the stumps at the non-striker's end before Hunt, backing up, could regain his ground. Rain prevented play on the third day and assisted the visitors in bowling out Queensland cheaply next morning. Oxenham and Thurlow registered pairs - ten ducks were scored in the match. All sources except *Courier* give NSW fall of 10 wickets. Sources: *Wisden, QCA Report, NSWCA Report, Australian Cricketer, Brisbane Courier.*

QUEENSLAND

*F.J.Gough	b Fairfax	14	(3) lbw b Fairfax		0
H.R.J.Higgins	b Amos	3	(4) lbw b McCabe		8
K.L.M.Mossop	not out	44	(5) c McCabe b Hunt		2
F.W.Sides	c Oldfield b Amos	1	(8) not out		22
R.K.Oxenham	b Amos	0	(7) c Bradman b Hunt		0
C.D.Hansen	c Oldfield b Amos	20	c Hird b Hunt		0
A.Hurwood	lbw b Amos	0	(9) c Oldfield b Campbell		9
†L.W.Waterman	c Oldfield b McCabe	18	(2) c Campbell b Fairfax		20
B.V.Suche	c Bradman b Campbell	6	(1) c & b Hunt		12
H.M.Thurlow	b Campbell	0	c Bill b Campbell		0
E.Gilbert	b McCabe	0	lbw b Campbell		5
Extras	(b2, w1)	3	(b4, lb3)		7
Total	(44.5 overs, 153 mins)	109	(28.5 overs, 108 mins)		85

NEW SOUTH WALES

J.H.W.Fingleton	b Oxenham	93
O.W.Bill	c Waterman b Gilbert	0
D.G.Bradman	c Waterman b Gilbert	0
*A.F.Kippax	retired hurt	16
A.G.Fairfax	b Gilbert	5
S.J.McCabe	not out	229
S.F.Hird	lbw b Oxenham	3
†W.A.S.Oldfield	b Hurwood	46
J.N.Campbell	c Oxenham b Hurwood	4
G.S.Amos	lbw b Gilbert	2
W.A.Hunt	run out (Gilbert)	3
Extras	(b17, lb9, nb5)	31
Total	(113.7 overs, 400 mins)	432

NEW SOUTH WALES	O	M	R	W	w,nb	O	M	R	W	w,nb
Amos	13	5	22	5	1,-	6	1	12	0	-,-
Fairfax	9	2	21	1	-,-	6	1	24	2	-,-
McCabe	9.5	1	23	2	-,-	5	1	4	1	-,-
Hunt	8	1	22	0	-,-	8	1	25	4	-,-
Campbell	5	0	18	2	-,-	3.5	1	13	3	-,-

QUEENSLAND	O	M	R	W	w,nb
Thurlow	22	4	69	0	-,3
Gilbert	20.7	2	74	4	-,-
Hurwood	25	5	95	2	-,-
Oxenham	27	7	79	2	-,2
Suche	14	1	50	0	-,-
Gough	5	0	34	0	-,-

FALL OF WICKETS

Wkt	QLD 1st	NSW 1st	QLD 2nd
1st	15	0	28
2nd	19	0	28
3rd	20	31	45
4th	20	226	47
5th	61	232	47
6th	61	389	47
7th	92	399	54
8th	101	414	76
9th	106	432	76
10th	109	-	85

NEW SOUTH WALES v SOUTH AFRICAN XI

Played at Sydney Cricket Ground on November 13, 14, 16, 17, 1931. (Four-day match)
Toss : South African XI.   Result : MATCH DRAWN.
Debuts: Nil.
12th Men: C.M.Solomon (NSW) and L.S.Brown (SAF).
Umpires: E.G.Borwick and W.G.French.
Attendances: 15543, 33100, 8564, 9001.   Total: 66,208.   Receipts: £3596.
Close of Play: 1st day SAF 7/384 (Taylor 116); 2nd day SAF (2) 0/11 (Mitchell 2, Curnow 7); 3rd day SAF (2) 3/190 (Curnow 79).

Set a near-impossible 448 to win in five hours on the last day, New South Wales fell only 18 short of their target when time ran out. All five batsmen called on played their part in the chase: Fingleton (117 in 233 minutes, 9 fours), Bill (47 in 94 minutes, 5 fours), Bradman (135 in 128 minutes, 15 fours), McCabe (79 not out in 71 minutes, 12 fours) and Marks (36 not out in 62 minutes, 2 fours). Bradman, who had gone to the crease in the first over after lunch, reached 50 in 37 minutes and 100 in 100 minutes and was well caught by Bell at backward point just before tea. The New South Wales first innings in contrast had been a failure, with Bill falling to the second ball (his second successive "golden duck") and the side conceded a 257-run deficit. South Africa's highest scorers in their first innings were Cameron (74 in 86 minutes, 11 fours), Taylor (124 in 196 minutes, 10 fours) and Dalton (87 in 121 minutes, 8 fours) and in their second innings Curnow (79 not out in 205 minutes, 6 fours) and Cameron (49 in 62 minutes, 2 sixes and 4 fours). A.Jackson (ill) and A.F.Kippax (injured) were unavailable for New South Wales. All sources except *NSWCA Scorebook* and *SMH* incorrectly give SAF (2) Taylor 0*.
Sources: *Wisden, NSWCA Report, NSWCA Scorebook, Australian Cricketer, Sydney Morning Herald, Sydney Referee.*

SOUTH AFRICAN XI

J.A.J.Christy	b Amos	8			
S.H.Curnow	lbw b Bettington	39		not out	79
B.Mitchell	lbw b Hunt	16	(1)	b Hunt	42
*†H.B.Cameron	c Fingleton b McCabe	74		b Hunt	49
H.W.Taylor	lbw b Hunt	124			
E.L.Dalton	st Oldfield b McCabe	87			
D.P.B.Morkel	b Bettington	30	(3)	lbw b Hunt	14
X.C.Balaskas	b Hunt	3			
Q.McMillan	c Oldfield b McCabe	9			
C.L.Vincent	c Oldfield b Hunt	17			
A.J.Bell	not out	1			
Extras	(b8, lb6, nb3)	17		(b1, lb4, nb1)	6
Total	(109.0 overs, 352 mins)	425		(61.7 overs, 205 mins) (3 wkts dec)	190

NEW SOUTH WALES

J.H.W.Fingleton	b Bell	30		c McMillan b Morkel	117
O.W.Bill	b Bell	0		b Morkel	47
D.G.Bradman	c & b McMillan	30		c Bell b Morkel	135
S.J.McCabe	st Cameron b McMillan	37		not out	79
A.E.Marks	b Vincent	16		not out	36
A.G.Fairfax	c Dalton b Vincent	3			
S.F.Hird	c Mitchell b McMillan	18			
*†W.A.S.Oldfield	c Vincent b McMillan	10			
R.H.B.Bettington	b Bell	7			
W.A.Hunt	st Cameron b Bell	3			
G.S.Amos	not out	3			
Extras	(b8, lb2, w1)	11		(b13, lb3)	16
Total	(52.6 overs, 193 mins)	168		(84.0 overs, 296 mins) (3 wkts)	430

NEW SOUTH WALES	O	M	R	W	w,nb		O	M	R	W	w,nb			FALL OF WICKETS		
Amos	10	0	36	1	-,-		16	6	34	0	-,1			SAF	NSW	SAF	NSW
Fairfax	15	0	62	0	-,3		3	1	5	0	-,-	Wkt	1st	1st	2nd	2nd
McCabe	30	6	89	3	-,-	(4)	12	3	19	0	-,-	1st	11	1	77	81
Hunt	28	8	84	4	-,-	(3)	20.7	3	62	3	-,-	2nd	46	53	110	297
Bettington	20	0	78	2	-,-	(6)	3	0	29	0	-,-	3rd	106	98	190	316
Hird	3	0	24	0	-,-	(5)	7	0	35	0	-,-	4th	169	109	-	-
Bradman	3	0	35	0	-,-							5th	339	120	-	-
												6th	379	130	-	-
SOUTH AFRICAN XI	O	M	R	W	w,nb		O	M	R	W	w,nb	7th	384	151	-	-
Bell	14.6	2	36	4	-,-		27	2	110	0	-,-	8th	393	158	-	-
Morkel	5	0	23	0	1,-		18	1	80	3	-,-	9th	423	163	-	-
Vincent	20	7	46	2	-,-		27	4	125	0	-,-	10th	425	168	-	-
McMillan	13	1	52	4	-,-	(5)	8	0	72	0	-,-					
Balaskas						(4)	4	1	27	0	-,-					

SOUTH AUSTRALIA v VICTORIA (Shield Match 2)

Played at Adelaide Oval on November 13, 14, 16, 17, 1931. (Four-day match)
Toss : South Australia.   Result : SOUTH AUSTRALIA WON BY 21 RUNS.
Debuts: Nil.
12th Men: C.L.B.Starr (SA) and J.W.Scaife (Vic).
Umpires: G.A.Hele and A.G.Jenkins.
Attendances: 3663, 6671, 3451, 2105.   Total: 15,890.   Receipts: £502.
Close of Play: 1st day SA 7/285 (Grimmett 28, Walker 13); 2nd day Vic 5/286 (O'Brien 13, Darling 0); 3rd day Vic (2) 2/18
    (Woodfull 9, McCormick 8).

Hack and Pritchard replaced G.W.Harris and H.E.Whitfield (both unavailable) in the local team. Victoria omitted Scaife and L.O.Cordner from their thirteen. Nitschke batted stylishly for South Australia, scoring 57 (72 minutes, 1 six and 6 fours) and 62 (75 minutes, 2 sixes and 6 fours), while Lonergan (43 in 87 minutes, 5 fours), Hack (36 in 165 minutes, 1 four), Waite (63 in 91 minutes, 7 fours and 38 in 66 minutes, 5 fours) and Grimmett (40 not out in 105 minutes, 3 fours) made other contributions. Ironmonger dismissed Nitschke and Richardson with successive deliveries in the second innings. Nagel (right-arm fast-medium) captured his best analysis for Victoria. Ponsford (134 in 257 minutes, 12 fours) and Ryder (64 in 100 minutes, 3 fours) in the first innings and Ryder (32 in 69 minutes, 1 six and 1 four) and Oakley (44 in 77 minutes, 6 fours) in the second innings made Victoria's leading scores. Sources: *Wisden, SACA Report, VCA Report, Australian Cricketer, Adelaide Advertiser, The News.*

SOUTH AUSTRALIA

H.C.Nitschke	c Nagel b Ironmonger	57		c O'Brien b Ironmonger	62
*V.Y.Richardson	lbw b McCormick	24		c & b Ironmonger	26
A.R.Lonergan	c Nagel b Ironmonger	43		b McCormick	10
D.E.Pritchard	c Barnett b McCormick	6		c Oakley b Nagel	0
A.T.Hack	run out (Oakley/Barnett)	36	(8)	b Nagel	0
P.K.Lee	b Nagel	0	(7)	lbw b Nagel	7
M.G.Waite	c Darling b McCormick	63	(5)	lbw b Ironmonger	38
C.V.Grimmett	not out	40	(6)	b Nagel	4
†C.W.Walker	st Barnett b Ironmonger	19		b Nagel	0
T.A.Carlton	lbw b McCormick	3		c Barnett b Nagel	0
T.W.Wall	b McCormick	7		not out	0
Extras	(b9, lb4, w1, nb5)	19		(b20, lb2, w1)	23
Total	(84.6 overs, 342 mins)	317		(44.1 overs, 184 mins)	170

VICTORIA

*W.M.Woodfull	c Carlton b Grimmett	32		c Waite b Carlton	9
W.H.Ponsford	lbw b Lee	134		b Wall	0
K.E.Rigg	c & b Carlton	34		lbw b Carlton	1
J.Ryder	b Wall	64	(5)	b Lee	32
L.P.J.O'Brien	c Richardson b Grimmett	25	(7)	c Nitschke b Lee	9
L.E.Nagel	c Carlton b Grimmett	1	(8)	lbw b Grimmett	14
L.S.Darling	run out (Lonergan)	0	(9)	not out	13
H.H.Oakley	c Lee b Carlton	15	(6)	c sub (C.L.B.Starr) b Grimmett	44
†B.A.Barnett	lbw b Grimmett	1	(10)	run out (Nitschke)	0
E.L.McCormick	not out	0	(4)	c Carlton b Wall	9
H.Ironmonger	c Waite b Grimmett	0		c Grimmett b Lee	0
Extras	(b3, lb5, nb1)	9		(b13, lb7)	20
Total	(98.6 overs, 337 mins)	315		(49.5 overs, 188 mins)	151

VICTORIA	O	M	R	W	w,nb	O	M	R	W	w,nb
McCormick	26.6	2	103	5	-,5	11	1	50	1	1,-
Darling	6	1	17	0	-,-					
Nagel	15	2	53	1	-,-	17.1	4	35	6	-,-
Ironmonger	32	9	110	3	1,-	(2) 16	5	62	3	-,-
Ryder	5	1	15	0	-,-					

SOUTH AUSTRALIA	O	M	R	W	w,nb	O	M	R	W	w,nb
Wall	14	0	64	1	-,-	11	1	28	2	-,-
Carlton	22	3	83	2	-,-	12	1	49	2	-,-
Grimmett	31.6	3	93	5	-,-	11	2	32	2	-,-
Lee	30	8	54	1	-,1	15.5	7	22	3	-,-
Waite	1	0	12	0	-,-					

FALL OF WICKETS

Wkt	SA 1st	VIC 1st	SA 2nd	VIC 2nd
1st	60	66	96	5
2nd	96	126	96	6
3rd	116	252	97	19
4th	146	283	135	21
5th	147	286	162	99
6th	235	286	162	105
7th	259	310	167	133
8th	302	314	167	149
9th	309	315	167	151
10th	317	315	170	151

QUEENSLAND v SOUTH AFRICAN XI

Played at Brisbane Cricket Ground (Woolloongabba) on November 20 (no play), 21, 23, 24, 1931. (Four-day match)
Toss : Queensland.   Result : MATCH DRAWN.
Debuts: Queensland - G.G.Cook (f/c).
12th Men: P.M.Hornibrook (Qld) and A.J.Bell (SAF).
Umpires: J,Bartlett and J.P.Orr.
Attendances: no play, 8032, 4238, 2726.   Total: 14,996.   Receipts: £843.
Close of Play: 1st day no play; 2nd day SAF 2/38 (Curnow 23, Viljoen 6); 3rd day Qld (2) 4/78 (Gough 33, Hansen 34).

When play finally got under way after rain washed out the opening day, Mossop was bowled by Morkel's first ball and Queensland collapsed to 7/66 before Cook (29 in 89 minutes, 1 four) and Hurwood (career-best 89 in 123 minutes, 11 fours) chipped in with a 68-run stand to help establish a reasonable score. In their second innings Gough (61 in 200 minutes, 1 five and 3 fours) and Hansen (65 in 190 minutes, 1 five and 4 fours) shared a fifth-wicket partnership of 133 which accounted for all but 23 of the Queensland total. Needing 164 for victory, the South Africans concentrated on survival. Taylor's first-innings 48 took just 47 minutes and included 1 six and 6 fours. Hornibrook reacted to being named 12th man by announcing his retirement from first-class cricket. *Wisden* and *Australian Cricketer* give Qld (2) Hansen hit wkt b Mitchell. Sources: *Wisden, NSWCA Report, QCA Report, Australian Cricketer, Brisbane Courier.*

QUEENSLAND

H.R.J.Higgins	run out (Quinn)	25		lbw b Morkel	0
K.L.M.Mossop	b Morkel	0	(3)	b Quinn	3
R.K.Oxenham	c Mitchell b Quinn	11	(8)	not out	9
F.W.Sides	c Vincent b Quinn	0		c Mitchell b Quinn	2
*F.J.Gough	c van der Merwe b Vincent	17		c Dalton b Brown	61
C.D.Hansen	c van der Merwe b Vincent	3		b Mitchell	65
G.G.Cook	c van der Merwe b Quinn	29	(2)	b Quinn	1
†H.V.Burns	c Dalton b Vincent	3	(9)	c van der Merwe b Brown	0
A.Hurwood	b Vincent	89	(7)	lbw b Brown	1
E.Gilbert	st van der Merwe b Vincent	16		c & b Mitchell	0
H.M.Thurlow	not out	0		b Brown	3
Extras	(b7, lb2)	9		(b5, lb4, nb2)	11
Total	(71.5 overs, 225 mins)	202		(76.2 overs, 254 mins)	156

SOUTH AFRICAN XI

B.Mitchell	c Burns b Thurlow	8		b Gilbert	5
S.H.Curnow	lbw b Oxenham	36		c Burns b Gilbert	32
E.L.Dalton	b Thurlow	0	(4)	b Gilbert	0
K.G.Viljoen	lbw b Oxenham	26	(3)	c Burns b Gilbert	48
H.W.Taylor	c Oxenham b Hurwood	48		b Oxenham	0
*D.P.B.Morkel	c Mossop b Thurlow	26		b Oxenham	8
Q.McMillan	c Sides b Hurwood	18		not out	29
C.L.Vincent	lbw b Hurwood	8		not out	10
†E.A.van der Merwe	run out (Oxenham)	5			
L.S.Brown	not out	10			
N.A.Quinn	b Gilbert	0			
Extras	(b6, lb2, nb2)	10		(lb1, nb2)	3
Total	(66.1 overs, 220 mins)	195		(45.0 overs, 178 mins) (6 wkts)	135

SOUTH AFRICAN XI	O	M	R	W	w,nb		O	M	R	W	w,nb
Quinn	26	6	51	3	-,-	(2)	20	8	30	3	-,-
Morkel	7	2	21	1	-,-	(1)	10	4	14	1	-,2
Brown	11	4	22	0	-,-	(5)	14.2	4	26	4	-,-
McMillan	6	0	40	0	-,-		14	2	43	0	-,-
Vincent	21.5	7	59	5	-,-	(3)	13	7	17	0	-,-
Mitchell							5	0	15	2	-,-

QUEENSLAND	O	M	R	W	w,nb		O	M	R	W	w,nb
Gilbert	11.1	1	32	1	-,-	(3)	11	4	42	4	-,1
Hurwood	18	3	79	3	-,-		8	0	29	0	-,-
Thurlow	13	2	26	3	-,2	(1)	9	0	33	0	-,1
Oxenham	21	10	31	2	-,-		16	9	27	2	-,-
Gough	3	0	17	0	-,-						
Cook						(5)	1	0	1	0	-,-

FALL OF WICKETS

Wkt	QLD 1st	SAF 1st	QLD 2nd	SAF 2nd
1st	2	20	1	21
2nd	21	20	1	63
3rd	21	71	6	63
4th	34	76	9	64
5th	60	142	142	85
6th	60	159	143	111
7th	66	175	148	-
8th	134	180	150	-
9th	197	195	151	-
10th	202	195	156	-

AUSTRALIA v SOUTH AFRICA (1st Test)

Played at Brisbane Cricket Ground (Woolloongabba) on November 27, 28, 30 (no play), December 1 (no play), 2, 3, 1931. (Timeless match)

Toss : Australia. Result : AUSTRALIA WON BY AN INNINGS AND 163 RUNS.

Debuts: Australia - H.C.Nitschke (Test).

12th Men: K.E.Rigg (Aust) and K.G.Viljoen (SAF).

Umpires: E.G.Borwick and G.A.Hele.

Attendances: 10069, 19500, no play, no play, 300, 1500. Total: 31,369. Receipts: £3074.

Close of Play: 1st day Aust 6/341 (Bradman 200, Oldfield 3); 2nd day SAF 3/126 (Mitchell 45, Taylor 38); 3rd day no play; 4th day no play; 5th day SAF 6/152 (Mitchell 53, Morkel 3).

The first Test match to be staged at the Brisbane Cricket Ground was dominated by Bradman, who survived slips chances when 10 (to Vincent off Quinn) and 15 (to Mitchell off Quinn) before going on to break his own record for the highest innings by an Australian batsman in a home Test. He reached 100 in 144 minutes and 200 in 252 minutes and took his score from 108 to 200 in the last session of the first day's play, in all compiling 226 in 277 minutes with 22 fours. Woodfull (76 in 178 minutes, 8 fours) and Oldfield (56 not out in 117 minutes, 1 six and 5 fours) supported him with half-centuries. Following rain, which washed out play on the third and fourth days, the fifth did not start until 4.00pm; Mitchell (58 in 291 minutes, 6 fours) did not add to his overnight score of 45 until 5.30pm - a 90-minute wait. Taylor batted well in both innings for the tourists, contributing 41 (100 minutes, 5 fours) and 47 (83 minutes, 7 fours), but the rest failed in difficult conditions. McMillan and Quinn both suffered first-ball dismissals in the second innings. Rigg fielded in place of Kippax, who was suffering from bouts of dizziness following the injury he had sustained in the NSW v Qld match earlier in the month; he returned to Sydney. In addition, A.H.F.Rofe substituted for Bradman (ill) on the fifth day. Sources: *Wisden, QCA Report, Brisbane Courier, The Herald.*

AUSTRALIA

*W.M.Woodfull	lbw b Vincent	76
W.H.Ponsford	c Mitchell b Bell	19
D.G.Bradman	lbw b Vincent	226
A.F.Kippax	c Cameron b Vincent	1
S.J.McCabe	c Vincent b Morkel	27
H.C.Nitschke	c Cameron b Bell	6
R.K.Oxenham	b Bell	1
†W.A.S.Oldfield	not out	56
C.V.Grimmett	b Bell	14
T.W.Wall	lbw b Quinn	14
H.Ironmonger	b Quinn	2
Extras	(b5, lb1, w1,nb1)	8
Total	(137.3 overs, 391 mins)	450

SOUTH AFRICA

J.A.J.Christy	b Wall	24		c McCabe b Ironmonger	15
S.H.Curnow	b Ironmonger	11		b Grimmett	8
B.Mitchell	run out (Bradman/Oldfield)	58		b Wall	0
*†H.B.Cameron	st Oldfield b Grimmett	4		b Ironmonger	21
H.W.Taylor	b Wall	41		c Oxenham b Ironmonger	47
E.L.Dalton	c & b Ironmonger	11		b Wall	6
Q.McMillan	c Oxenham b Ironmonger	0	(8)	c Nitschke b Wall	0
D.P.B.Morkel	c McCabe b Ironmonger	3	(7)	b Wall	5
C.L.Vincent	c Nitschke b Grimmett	10		c sub (K.E.Rigg) b Wall	1
N.A.Quinn	c sub (K.E.Rigg) b Ironmonger	1		c McCabe b Ironmonger	0
A.J.Bell	not out	1		not out	0
Extras	(b2, lb4)	6		(b6, lb5, nb3)	14
Total	(138.1 overs, 366 mins)	170		(60.1 overs, 165 mins)	117

SOUTH AFRICA	O	M	R	W	w,nb						
Bell	42	5	120	4	-,-						
Morkel	13	1	57	1	1,-						
Quinn	38.3	6	113	2	-,1						
Vincent	34	0	100	3	-,-						
McMillan	10	0	52	0	-,-						

AUSTRALIA	O	M	R	W	w,nb		O	M	R	W	w,nb
Wall	28	14	39	2	-,-		15.1	7	14	5	-,1
McCabe	11	4	16	0	-,-						
Grimmett	41.1	21	49	2	-,-		15	3	45	1	-,-
Ironmonger	47	29	42	5	-,-	(2)	30	16	44	4	-,2
Oxenham	11	5	18	0	-,-						

FALL OF WICKETS

	AUST	SAF	SAF
Wkt	1st	1st	2nd
1st	32	25	16
2nd	195	44	19
3rd	211	49	34
4th	292	129	78
5th	316	140	97
6th	320	140	111
7th	380	152	111
8th	407	157	117
9th	446	168	117
10th	450	170	117

NEW SOUTH WALES v SOUTH AFRICAN XI

Played at Sydney Cricket Ground on December 5 (no play), 7, 8, 9 (no play), 1931. (Four-day match)
Toss : New South Wales.   Result : MATCH DRAWN.
Debuts: New South Wales - C.M.Solomon (f/c).
12th Men: L.R.Leabeater (NSW) and S.S.L.Steyn (SAF).
Umpires: E.G.Borwick and W.G.French.
Attendances: no play (1933), 10515, 4284, no play.   Total: 14,799.   Receipts: £703.
Close of Play: 1st day no play; 2nd day NSW 8/446 (Hird 76, Amos 6); 3rd day SAF 1/185 (Curnow 81, Morkel 70).

Bradman (chanceless 219 in 234 minutes, 15 fours) scored his third century in successive innings against the South Africans. He reached 100 in 127 minutes and made 93 runs between lunch and tea (61-154) on the second day. Hird (101 in 133 minutes, 8 fours) compiled his maiden first-class hundred and received support from Hunt (45 in 41 minutes, 1 five and 3 fours) and Amos in the late order. McMillan captured the last six wickets to fall. The tourists began well in reply through Curnow (81 not out in 180 minutes, 4 fours) and Morkel (70 not out in 135 minutes, 3 fours) but rain, which had prevented any play on the first day, returned on the third day and became heavier during the night, making a start on the final day impossible. McCabe tore an ankle ligament while bowling his ninth over. Solomon (originally named as 12th man) was a late replacement for Kippax (the nominated captain), who had still not recovered from his injury in the match against Queensland. A.G.Fairfax had left Australia to fulfill a commitment to play league cricket in England and was consequently also unavailable for New South Wales. *Wisden* incorrectly gives NSW Oldfield 9. Sources: *NSWCA Scorebook, Wisden, NSWCA Report, Australian Cricketer, Sydney Morning Herald.*

NEW SOUTH WALES

O.W.Bill	c Morkel b Bell	10
J.H.W.Fingleton	lbw b Morkel	2
D.G.Bradman	c Curnow b McMillan	219
S.J.McCabe	c Christy b Bell	28
A.E.Marks	c Cameron b Bell	6
C.M.Solomon	st Cameron b McMillan	11
*†W.A.S.Oldfield	c Mitchell b McMillan	29
S.F.Hird	c Cameron b McMillan	101
W.A.Hunt	c Curnow b McMillan	45
G.S.Amos	st Cameron b McMillan	24
H.J.T.Theak	not out	10
Extras	(b13, lb2)	15
Total	(88.4 overs, 340 mins)	500

SOUTH AFRICAN XI

J.A.J.Christy	c Hunt b Theak	27
S.H.Curnow	not out	81
D.P.B.Morkel	not out	70
B.Mitchell	)	
*†H.B.Cameron	)	
K.G.Viljoen	)	
X.C.Balaskas	) did not bat	
Q.McMillan	)	
C.L.Vincent	)	
A.J.Bell	)	
N.A.Quinn	)	
Extras	(b4, lb3)	7
Total	(51.2 overs, 180 mins) (one wkt)	185

SOUTH AFRICAN XI	O	M	R	W	w,nb
Bell	26	2	107	3	-,-
Morkel	8	0	33	1	-,-
Vincent	11	0	51	0	-,-
Quinn	20	1	105	0	-,-
McMillan	23.4	0	189	6	-,-

NEW SOUTH WALES	O	M	R	W	w,nb
Theak	15	3	54	1	-,-
McCabe	8.6	1	27	0	-,-
Amos	8	0	31	0	-,-
Hunt	12.4	3	29	0	-,-
Hird	6	1	30	0	-,-
Bradman	1	0	7	0	-,-

FALL OF WICKETS

Wkt	NSW 1st	SAF 1st
1st	8	48
2nd	14	-
3rd	102	-
4th	116	-
5th	159	-
6th	258	-
7th	348	-
8th	436	-
9th	485	-
10th	500	-

AUSTRALIA v SOUTH AFRICA (2nd Test)

Played at Sydney Cricket Ground on December 18, 19, 21, 1931. (Timeless match)
Toss : South Africa.   Result : AUSTRALIA WON BY AN INNINGS AND 155 RUNS.
Debuts: Australia - P.K.Lee (Test). South Africa - L.S.Brown (Test).
12th Men: J.H.W.Fingleton (Aust) and S.S.L.Steyn (SAF).
Umpires: E.G.Borwick and G.A.Hele.
Attendances: 20928, 27845, 7579.   Total: 56,352.   Receipts: £4310.
Close of Play: 1st day Aust 1/78 (Woodfull 36, Rigg 35); 2nd day Aust 7/444 (Oldfield 4).

South Africa failed to take advantage of first use of a good batting wicket. Viljoen (37 in 90 minutes, 3 fours) and Vincent (31 not out in 84 minutes, 5 fours) did best. Despite the early loss of Ponsford, the Australians ground home the advantage. Woodfull (58 in 152 minutes, 3 fours) and Rigg (127 in 240 minutes, 12 fours, 2 chances) added 137 for the second wicket, Rigg and Bradman (112 in 155 minutes, 10 fours) scored a further 111 for the third wicket, McCabe (79 in 122 minutes, 7 fours) partnered Bradman in a fourth-wicket stand of 93, and Nitschke and McCabe put on another 85 immediately afterwards. Bradman's hundred was his fourth in successive first-class innings - all against the South Africans - and this was a new record for any batsman in first-class cricket in Australia. Christy began the South African second innings in Cavalier fashion. He was first out, having batted for 32 minutes (7 fours). A.F.Kippax who was still suffering from dizziness, was unavailable for Australia. Sources: *Wisden, NSWCA Report, Sydney Morning Herald, Sydney Referee, The Age, The Herald.*

SOUTH AFRICA

J.A.J.Christy	c Nitschke b Grimmett	14	c Woodfull b Ironmonger		41
B.Mitchell	b McCabe	1	c Oldfield b Wall		24
D.P.B.Morkel	st Oldfield b Grimmett	20	lbw b Grimmett		17
*†H.B.Cameron	b Wall	11	b Wall		0
H.W.Taylor	c Lee b Grimmett	7	c Grimmett b Ironmonger		6
K.G.Viljoen	b Ironmonger	37	b Grimmett		0
E.L.Dalton	b Grimmett	21	c Bradman b Ironmonger		14
C.L.Vincent	not out	31	c Ponsford b Grimmett		35
L.S.Brown	b McCabe	2	c Wall b Lee		8
N.A.Quinn	lbw b McCabe	5	st Oldfield b Grimmett		1
A.J.Bell	b McCabe	0	not out		1
Extras	(lb3, w1)	4	(b5, lb 8, nb1)		14
Total	(73.0 overs, 202 mins)	153	(73.3 overs, 204 mins)		161

AUSTRALIA

*W.M.Woodfull	c Mitchell b Vincent	58
W.H.Ponsford	b Quinn	5
K.E.Rigg	b Bell	127
D.G.Bradman	c Viljoen b Morkel	112
S.J.McCabe	c Christy b Vincent	79
H.C.Nitschke	b Bell	47
P.K.Lee	c Cameron b Brown	0
†W.A.S.Oldfield	c Cameron b Bell	8
C.V.Grimmett	not out	9
T.W.Wall	c Morkel b Bell	6
H.Ironmonger	c Cameron b Bell	0
Extras	(b 5, lb12, w1)	18
Total	(154.5 overs, 416 mins)	469

AUSTRALIA	O	M	R	W	w,nb	O	M	R	W	w,nb
Wall	18	4	46	1	1,-	18	5	31	2	-,1
McCabe	12	5	13	4	-,-	3	0	25	0	-,-
Grimmett	24	12	28	4	-,-	20.3	7	44	4	-,-
Ironmonger	12	1	38	1	-,-	19	10	22	3	-,-
Lee	7	1	24	0	-,-	13	4	25	1	-,-

SOUTH AFRICA	O	M	R	W	w,nb
Bell	46.5	6	140	5	-,-
Quinn	42	10	95	1	-,-
Brown	29	3	100	1	1,-
Vincent	24	5	75	2	-,-
Morkel	12	2	33	1	-,-
Mitchell	1	0	8	0	-,-

FALL OF WICKETS

Wkt	SAF 1st	AUST 1st	SAF 2nd
1st	6	6	70
2nd	31	143	89
3rd	36	254	89
4th	54	347	100
5th	62	432	100
6th	91	433	100
7th	136	444	122
8th	143	457	144
9th	153	469	160
10th	153	469	161

VICTORIA v QUEENSLAND (Shield Match 3)

Played at Melbourne Cricket Ground on December 18, 19, 21, 22, 1931. (Four-day match)
Toss : Queensland.   Result : QUEENSLAND WON BY 22 RUNS.
Debuts: Victoria - I.S.Lee, S.A.J.Smith (both f/c). Queensland - J.E.P.Hogg (Qld only).
12th Men: F.E.Fontaine (Vic) and K.L.M.Mossop (Qld).
Umpires: A.N.Barlow and W.J.Moore.
Attendances: 4812, 6679, 2871, 1988.   Total: 16,350.   Receipts: £380.
Close of Play: 1st day Vic 1/25 (Lee 3, McCormick 3); 2nd day Qld (2) 2/108 (Cook 11, Hansen 14); 3rd day Vic (2) 0/1 (Ryder 0, Lee 0).

Queensland won their first Shield match in Melbourne at the sixth attempt. Batsmen from both sides struggled on the fast pitch, Darling (52 in 88 minutes, 6 fours) and Barnett (94 in 129 minutes, 1 six and 8 fours, chances at 0, 8 and 71) on the losing side scoring the only fifties. Barnett had added 99 for the ninth wicket with Smith (47 in 66 minutes, 4 fours) late in the match to nearly bring off an outside victory. Umpire Barlow at square leg no-balled Gilbert for throwing eight times in his two overs late on the first day and five times in his only over the following morning which also included a wide, making 14 balls in the over. McCormick delivered only three balls (wide, ball, wide) in the second innings, pulling a thigh muscle in the act of bowling the second wide. Bensted severely twisted his knee when falling in an attempt to field a drive by Barnett in his ninth over. Hogg played four times for New South Wales prior to his Queensland debut in this match. Sources: *Wisden, VCA Report, QCA Report, Australian Cricketer, The Age, The Argus, The Herald, Melbourne Sun.*

QUEENSLAND

*F.J.Gough	lbw b a'Beckett	3		b a'Beckett	32
J.E.P.Hogg	b Nagel	20		c Barnett b Smith	47
R.K.Oxenham	b Smith	14	(7)	b Smith	25
C.D.Hansen	c Ryder b Nagel	30		c & b Smith	43
E.C.Bensted	c Barnett b McCormick	1		c Lee b Smith	29
G.G.Cook	run out (Oakley/Barnett)	44	(3)	c sub (F.E.Fontaine) b a'Beckett	23
F.W.Sides	lbw b McCormick	24	(6)	run out (Scaife)	5
A.Hurwood	c Barnett b Nagel	22		st Barnett b Smith	6
†H.V.Burns	c Ryder b Nagel	14		not out	22
E.Gilbert	not out	5		run out (Oakley)	5
H.M.Thurlow	b Smith	1		run out (Ryder/Smith)	0
Extras	(b8, lb7, nb7)	22		(b4, lb6, w2, nb2)	14
Total	(75.1 overs, 286 mins)	200		(88.6 overs, 333 mins)	251

VICTORIA

*J.Ryder	c Burns b Gilbert	9		c Burns b Thurlow	4
I.S.Lee	lbw b Hurwood	15		b Thurlow	4
E.L.McCormick	st Burns b Oxenham	12	(11)	not out	0
H.H.Oakley	b Oxenham	7	(3)	b Oxenham	14
L.S.Darling	lbw b Oxenham	52	(4)	lbw b Hurwood	33
J.Thomas	b Bensted	23	(5)	c Hogg b Hurwood	23
E.L.a'Beckett	lbw b Oxenham	0	(6)	b Oxenham	1
J.W.Scaife	b Bensted	8	(7)	lbw b Hurwood	13
†B.A.Barnett	c Burns b Bensted	3	(8)	b Oxenham	94
L.E.Nagel	not out	6	(9)	b Thurlow	13
S.A.J.Smith	c Hansen b Oxenham	0	(10)	st Burns b Oxenham	47
Extras	(b4, lb4, w1, nb12)	21		(b19, lb7, w1)	27
Total	(46.3 overs, 184 mins)	156		(70.2 overs, 278 mins)	273

VICTORIA	O	M	R	W	w,nb		O	M	R	W	w,nb
McCormick	15	0	44	2	-,3		0.1	0	1	0	2,-
a'Beckett	19	4	37	1	-,3		28	6	64	2	-,-
Nagel	20	7	45	4	-,1		22	4	61	0	-,2
Smith	17.1	7	37	2	-,-		32.5	5	96	5	-,-
Darling	4	1	15	0	-,-		6	0	15	0	-,-

QUEENSLAND	O	M	R	W	w,nb		O	M	R	W	w,nb
Gilbert	3	0	10	1	1,11						
Hurwood	12	4	21	1	-,-	(4)	14	1	55	3	-,-
Thurlow	10	0	39	0	-,1	(1)	19	3	69	3	-,-
Oxenham	14.3	3	37	5	-,-	(2)	24.1	6	64	4	-,-
Bensted	7	2	28	3	-,-	(3)	8.1	0	19	0	-,-
Cook						(5)	5	0	39	0	1,-

FALL OF WICKETS

Wkt	QLD 1st	VIC 1st	QLD 2nd	VIC 2nd
1st	17	17	83	8
2nd	39	51	85	11
3rd	57	61	140	34
4th	65	62	176	87
5th	99	129	188	88
6th	153	130	192	90
7th	154	143	217	118
8th	188	146	237	163
9th	197	155	249	262
10th	200	156	251	273

AFCM No. 751/72
SSM No. 237/69

SOUTH AUSTRALIA v NEW SOUTH WALES (Shield Match 4)

Played at Adelaide Oval on December 18, 19, 21, 22, 1931. (Four-day match)
Toss : New South Wales.   Result : NEW SOUTH WALES WON BY 117 RUNS.
Debuts: South Australia - W.E.Catchlove, D.G.Jamieson, H.Laycock (all f/c). New South Wales - R.N.Nutt (f/c).
12th Men: A.F.Richter (SA) and J.L.Donnelly (NSW).
Umpires: A.G.Jenkins and L.G.Wallace.
Attendances: 3304, 4379, 1700, 2175.   Total: 11,558.   Receipts: £361.
Close of Play: 1st day NSW 393 all out; 2nd day SA 8/320 (Laycock 21, Walker 13); 3rd day NSW (2) 7/157 (Hird 34, Theak 0).

Richter replaced G.W.Harris (unavailable) in the South Australian twelve. A.E.Marks and C.M.Solomon withdrew from the New South Wales side before its departure from Sydney and one of the replacements, Nutt (the other was Donnelly), answered his selection with a hundred on debut, 102 in 203 minutes with 7 fours. Salmon fell to the second ball he faced in the opening over of the match after two no-balls and a three to Bill. Hird (60 in 109 minutes, 2 fours), Leabeater (57 in 97 minutes, 5 fours) and Love (69 in 154 minutes, 5 fours) scored fifties for New South Wales. Richardson (122 in 171 minutes, 11 fours) easily topscored for South Australia, the next best being Tobin (47 in 83 minutes, 7 fours), Waite (38 in 85 minutes, 4 fours) and Starr (33 in 109 minutes, 2 fours). Sources: *Wisden, SACA Report, NSWCA Report, Australian Cricketer, Adelaide Advertiser, The News.*

NEW SOUTH WALES

O.W.Bill	lbw b Carlton	44	b Jamieson		3
B.M.Salmon	lbw b Tobin	0	b Tobin		25
†H.S.B.Love	c Walker b Carlton	24	lbw b Carlton		69
R.N.Nutt	b Laycock	102	b Jamieson		6
S.F.Hird	c Laycock b Carlton	60	c Walker b Tobin		34
L.R.Leabeater	b Laycock	57	c Tobin b Carlton		3
*R.H.B.Bettington	c & b Laycock	42	b Jamieson		2
W.A.Hunt	run out (/Walker)	34	c Lonergan b Jamieson		5
H.J.T.Theak	b Tobin	2	b Tobin		3
W.J.O'Reilly	not out	6	not out		31
G.S.Amos	c Laycock b Tobin	1	c Walker b Tobin		14
Extras	(b7, lb11, nb3)	21	(b3, lb7)		10
Total	(96.4 overs, 327 mins)	393	(68.7 overs, 253 mins)		205

SOUTH AUSTRALIA

*V.Y.Richardson	c Leabeater b Hird	122		lbw b Hunt	22
W.E.Catchlove	b Theak	25		lbw b Amos	4
A.R.Lonergan	b Hunt	0		b Theak	17
C.L.B.Starr	run out (sub J.L.Donnelly/Hird)	21	(6)	b Hunt	33
M.G.Waite	lbw b Bettington	14	(4)	c O'Reilly b Theak	38
A.T.Hack	b O'Reilly	29	(7)	lbw b Hunt	9
B.J.Tobin	b Bettington	47	(5)	c Nutt b O'Reilly	4
D.G.Jamieson	c & b Bettington	5		b Amos	0
H.Laycock	lbw b Hunt	21		b Hunt	7
†C.W.Walker	not out	14		c Love b Theak	14
T.A.Carlton	lbw b Theak	0		not out	5
Extras	(b10, lb11, nb2)	23		(b1, lb5, nb1)	7
Total	(102.5 overs, 334 mins)	321		(60.5 overs, 213 mins)	160

SOUTH AUSTRALIA	O	M	R	W	w,nb		O	M	R	W	w,nb
Tobin	17.4	2	78	3	-,3		17.7	3	63	4	-,-
Jamieson	20	1	51	0	-,-		29	6	83	4	-,-
Carlton	24	6	82	3	-,-		18	6	36	2	-,-
Laycock	20	2	92	3	-,-		1	0	2	0	-,-
Waite	4	0	31	0	-,-						
Starr	5	0	21	0	-,-						
Richardson	6	0	17	0	-,-	(5)	3	1	11	0	-,-

NEW SOUTH WALES	O	M	R	W	w,nb		O	M	R	W	w,nb
Amos	8	0	34	0	-,-	(2)	12	0	36	2	-,-
Theak	18.5	1	67	2	-,-	(1)	15.5	3	40	3	-,-
Hunt	27	8	38	2	-,-	(4)	16	3	38	4	-,-
O'Reilly	16	4	61	1	-,2	(3)	11	4	20	1	-,1
Bettington	17	3	56	3	-,-		6	0	19	0	-,-
Hird	16	2	42	1	-,-						

FALL OF WICKETS

Wkt	NSW 1st	SA 1st	NSW 2nd	SA 2nd
1st	5	109	15	10
2nd	60	110	50	37
3rd	89	173	81	51
4th	189	177	133	64
5th	299	201	139	98
6th	304	261	148	115
7th	380	274	154	116
8th	385	289	157	129
9th	391	320	169	144
10th	393	321	205	160

VICTORIA v NEW SOUTH WALES (Shield Match 5)

Played at Melbourne Cricket Ground on December 24, 26, 28, 29, 1931. (Four-day match)
Toss : Victoria.   Result : VICTORIA WON BY THREE WICKETS.
Debuts: Nil.
12th Men: H.H.Oakley (Vic) and G.S.Amos (NSW).
Umpires: A.N.Barlow and J.Richards.
Attendances: 4593, 13503, 12126, 6439.   Total: 36,661.   Receipts: £1156.
Close of Play: 1st day Vic 2/8 (Ponsford 6, Barnett 0); 2nd day NSW (2) 9/248 (O'Reilly 35, Theak 10); 3rd day Vic (2) 5/314
     (Darling 52, a'Beckett 9).

Victoria, at one stage 6 for 26 in their first innings, staged an improbable recovery over the last two days to score 435 runs - the second-highest winning score in the fourth innings of an Australian match. Put in, New South Wales began well through Bill (86 in 126 minutes, 1 six, 1 five and 7 fours) and Love, who added 89 in 77 minutes. Darling (51 in 53 minutes, 3 fours) helped Victoria reach 103 after their disastrous start. Alexander, who had not expected to bat before lunch on the second day, failed to get to the ground in time and forfeited his turn at the crease. O'Reilly (right-arm medium-paced leg-breaks and googlies) captured his first five-wicket analysis. Leabeater (56 in 90 minutes, 6 fours) topscored when New South Wales batted again while Hird (40 in 44 minutes, 4 fours) and O'Reilly (43 in 30 minutes, 3 sixes and 3 fours) scored rapidly. Woodfull (147 in 280 minutes, 6 fours), O'Brien (51 in 106 minutes, 4 fours) and Darling (111 not out in 159 minutes, 9 fours) led their team to victory. Oakley and L.E.Nagel (injured finger) were omitted from the Victorian thirteen. Sources: *Wisden, VCA Report, NSWCA Report, Australian Cricketer, The Age, The Argus, The Herald, Melbourne Sun*.

NEW SOUTH WALES

Batsman	Dismissal	Score	Dismissal (2nd)	Score
O.W.Bill	c Ryder b Ironmonger	86	lbw b Smith	12
†H.S.B.Love	b Smith	37	lbw b a'Beckett	0
R.N.Nutt	c Barnett b a'Beckett	21	c Ponsford b Smith	23
J.L.Donnelly	c Rigg b Alexander	1	c Ponsford b Ironmonger	15
S.F.Hird	c Barnett b Ironmonger	6	c Barnett b Darling	40
B.M.Salmon	c Barnett b Darling	15	lbw b Smith	41
L.R.Leabeater	c & b Alexander	37	lbw b Smith	56
*R.H.B.Bettington	c Barnett b Ironmonger	38	b Ryder	6
W.A.Hunt	c Rigg b a'Beckett	18	c Barnett b Smith	5
W.J.O'Reilly	c & b Ironmonger	5	b Ironmonger	43
H.J.T.Theak	not out	2	not out	14
Extras	(b3, lb6, nb1)	10	(b3, lb2)	5
Total	(71.3 overs, 275 mins)	276	(58.3 overs, 226 mins)	260

VICTORIA

Batsman	Dismissal	Score	Dismissal (2nd)	Score
*W.M.Woodfull	lbw b O'Reilly	2	c & b Salmon	147
W.H.Ponsford	c Love b Theak	6	b Theak	5
S.A.J.Smith	b O'Reilly	0	(9) not out	18
†B.A.Barnett	lbw b O'Reilly	9	(8) b Hird	21
K.E.Rigg	c Hird b Theak	3	(3) lbw b O'Reilly	28
J.Ryder	c Hird b O'Reilly	0	(4) b Bettington	7
L.P.J.O'Brien	b Hunt	20	(5) c Hird b Theak	51
L.S.Darling	b Hunt	51	(6) not out	111
E.L.a'Beckett	c Bill b O'Reilly	3	(7) b O'Reilly	21
H.Ironmonger	not out	6		
H.H.Alexander	absent	-		
Extras	(b1, lb2)	3	(b9, lb9, nb8)	26
Total	(32.1 overs, 124 mins)	103	(117.7 overs, 402 mins) (7 wkts)	435

VICTORIA	O	M	R	W	w,nb		O	M	R	W	w,nb
Alexander	18	1	71	2	-,1		9	0	29	0	-,-
a'Beckett	16	1	45	2	-,-		12	1	30	1	,
Smith	13	0	64	1	-,-	(4)	13	1	86	5	-,-
Ironmonger	22.3	5	75	4	-,-	(3)	15.3	2	58	2	-,-
Darling	2	0	11	1	-,-		4	0	20	1	-,-
Ryder							5	0	32	1	-,-

NEW SOUTH WALES	O	M	R	W	w,nb		O	M	R	W	w,nb
Theak	9	0	35	2	-,-		25	1	94	2	-,-
Hunt	10	3	18	2	-,-		31	1	90	0	-,1
O'Reilly	9.1	1	22	5	-,-		35.7	6	112	2	-,7
Bettington	4	0	25	0	-,-		12	2	46	1	-,-
Hird							11	0	57	1	-,-
Salmon							3	0	10	1	-,-

FALL OF WICKETS

Wkt	NSW 1st	VIC 1st	NSW 2nd	VIC 2nd
1st	89	6	2	19
2nd	146	8	27	111
3rd	148	8	46	125
4th	159	16	51	227
5th	161	17	115	280
6th	212	26	173	345
7th	212	83	186	393
8th	254	96	193	-
9th	269	103	214	-
10th	276	-	260	-

SOUTH AUSTRALIA v QUEENSLAND (Shield Match 6)

Played at Adelaide Oval on December 25, 26, 28, 29, 1931. (Four-day match)
Toss : South Australia.   Result : SOUTH AUSTRALIA WON BY 280 RUNS.
Debuts: Nil.
12th Men: W.E.Catchlove (SA) and J.H.Holdsworth (Qld).
Umpires: G.A.Hele and A.G.Jenkins.
Attendances: 5697, 4389, 2846, 940.   Total: 13,872.   Receipts: £664.
Close of Play: 1st day SA 7/407 (Grimmett 9, Jamieson 6); 2nd day SA (2) 0/58 (Richardson 40, Nitschke 9); 3rd day Qld (2) 2/105
     (Hogg 70, Burns 2).

T.W.Wall (injured) and Catchlove were omitted from South Australia's squad of thirteen. Holdsworth, the Queensland manager, acted as 12th man for the side because E.C.Bensted had not recovered from the knee injury he sustained in Melbourne. Richardson (75 in 112 minutes, 9 fours), Lonergan (137 in 221 minutes, 1 five and 16 fours), Whitfield (82 in 115 minutes, 1 six and 11 fours) and Waite (44 in 68 minutes, 5 fours) topscored in South Australia's first innings of 421. In the second innings Richardson (138 in 192 minutes, 3 sixes and 12 fours) was supported by Lee (54 in 38 minutes, 9 fours), whose off-breaks combined with the leg-spin of Grimmett to dismiss Queensland cheaply. Oxenham (82 in 144 minutes, 8 fours), Sides (74 in 81 minutes, 1 six and 11 fours) and in the second innings Hogg (71 in 107 minutes, 8 fours) scored fifties for the visitors. Sources: *Wisden, SACA Report, QCA Report, Australian Cricketer, Adelaide Advertiser, The News.*

SOUTH AUSTRALIA

*V.Y.Richardson	b Gilbert	75	c Hansen b Cook		138
H.C.Nitschke	run out (Oxenham/Burns)	5	lbw b Thurlow		24
A.R.Lonergan	c Hansen b Hurwood	137	c Burns b Thurlow		22
H.E.Whitfield	c Gough b Gilbert	82	lbw b Hurwood		16
M.G.Waite	b Mossop	44	b Thurlow		33
B.J.Tobin	c Sides b Mossop	27	b Cook		11
P.K.Lee	b Gilbert	9	c Hansen b Hurwood		54
C.V.Grimmett	lbw b Oxenham	21			
D.G.Jamieson	b Oxenham	6	(8) not out		16
†C.W.Walker	b Oxenham	1	(9) not out		2
T.A.Carlton	not out	1			
Extras	(b8, lb4, nb1)	13	(b12, lb6, w1)		19
Total	(89.7 overs, 343 mins)	421	(69.0 overs, 261 mins) (7 wkts dec)		335

QUEENSLAND

J.E.P.Hogg	run out (Waite/Tobin)	13	lbw b Grimmett		71
*F.J.Gough	st Walker b Grimmett	28	(5) lbw b Grimmett		19
G.G.Cook	b Whitfield	10	c & b Lee		32
C.D.Hansen	st Walker b Grimmett	11	(2) b Carlton		0
R.K.Oxenham	lbw b Whitfield	82	(7) c Tobin b Lee		6
F.W.Sides	b Lee	74	b Grimmett		1
K.L.M.Mossop	lbw b Lee	19	(8) not out		25
A.Hurwood	run out (Jamieson)	8	(9) c Jamieson b Lee		6
†H.V.Burns	not out	2	(4) c Tobin b Lee		19
E.Gilbert	c Richardson b Lee	7	c Richardson b Lee		0
H.M.Thurlow	b Lee	0	c Waite b Grimmett		23
Extras	(b1, lb11, nb1)	13	(b3, lb3, nb1)		7
Total	(57.2 overs, 224 mins)	267	(55.1 overs, 204 mins)		209

QUEENSLAND	O	M	R	W	w,nb		O	M	R	W	w,nb
Gilbert	21	0	117	3	-,-		6	0	44	0	1,-
Thurlow	16	1	77	0	-,-	(5)	17	1	141	3	-,-
Hurwood	21	0	96	1	-,-	(2)	21	5	50	2	-,-
Oxenham	23.7	5	73	3	-,-	(6)	15	3	46	0	-,-
Gough	5	0	30	0	-,-						
Mossop	3	0	15	2	-,1	(3)	3	1	8	0	-,-
Hogg						(4)	1	0	2	0	-,-
Cook						(7)	6	0	25	2	-,-

SOUTH AUSTRALIA	O	M	R	W	w,nb		O	M	R	W	w,nb
Tobin	7	0	52	0	-,-		3	0	13	0	-,-
Jamieson	9	1	31	0	-,-	(6)	3	0	17	0	-,-
Whitfield	12	0	56	2	-,-		2	0	14	0	-,-
Carlton	6	0	8	0	-,1	(2)	4	1	18	1	-,-
Lee	12.2	2	39	4	-,-		20	2	70	5	-,1
Grimmett	11	0	68	2	-,-	(4)	23.1	8	70	4	-,-

FALL OF WICKETS

Wkt	SA 1st	QLD 1st	SA 2nd	QLD 2nd
1st	23	15	78	4
2nd	135	36	131	97
3rd	302	60	189	108
4th	316	69	232	132
5th	377	179	259	135
6th	381	247	265	142
7th	395	257	328	155
8th	408	260	-	162
9th	414	267	-	162
10th	421	267	-	209

TASMANIA v VICTORIA

Played at T.C.A. Ground, Hobart, on December 25, 26, 28, 1931. (Three-day match)

Toss : Tasmania.   Result : VICTORIA WON BY AN INNINGS AND 26 RUNS.

Debuts: Tasmania - K.W.J.Cahill, R.O.G.Morrisby (both f/c); C.N.Parry (Tas only). Victoria - L.O.Fleetwood-Smith, J.D.Kinnear (both f/c).

12th Men: G.G.Gibson (Tas) and F.Jinks (Vic).

Umpires: A.J.Buttsworth and W.Crosby.

Attendances: No figures published .   Total: About 2000.   Receipts: £105.

Close of Play: 1st day Vic 0/12 (Fontaine 4, Quin 8); 2nd day Vic 8/375 (Healy 1, Fleetwood-Smith 4).

H.H.Alexander (representing Victoria v New South Wales), S.P.King and V.G.Nagel were unavailable from the eleven players originally selected by Victoria. Hassett, Kinnear, Liddicut and Quin were brought into the twelve. Atkinson fell to the first ball of the match and Nash was also out to the first ball he faced soon after. Fleetwood-Smith claimed 10 for 145 on debut with his left-arm unorthodox deliveries. Green (78 in 127 minutes, 8 fours) and Morrisby (67 in 130 minutes, 4 fours) were Tasmania's best batsmen. Consistent scoring by the visitors (all eleven reached double figures) included highlights from Fontaine (59 in 149 minutes, 3 fours), Cosgrave (100 in 180 minutes, 10 fours, chances at 46 and 82) and Liddicut (56 in 67 minutes). Parry played 10 matches for South Australia before his Tasmanian debut in this match. Sources: *Australian Cricketer, TCA Report, VCA Report, Hobart Mercury*.

TASMANIA

*J.A.Atkinson	lbw b Liddicut	0	lbw b Fleetwood-Smith	22
R.O.G.Morrisby	b Liddicut	3	c Quin b Liddicut	67
D.C.Green	b Fleetwood-Smith	78	lbw b Fleetwood-Smith	0
L.J.Nash	b Liddicut	0	c Quin b Liddicut	34
C.L.Badcock	run out (Quin/Liddicut)	34	run out (Fleetwood-Smith/Quin)	19
A.O.Burrows	b Fleetwood-Smith	34	c Cosgrave b Fleetwood-Smith	21
K.W.J.Cahill	b Fleetwood-Smith	4	st Quin b Liddicut	5
S.W.L.Putman	st Quin b Fleetwood-Smith	0	st Quin b Fleetwood-Smith	1
G.T.H.James	c Quin b Liddicut	3	not out	14
L.W.Richardson	not out	26	lbw b Fleetwood-Smith	0
†C.N.Parry	c Hassett b Fleetwood-Smith	11	st Quin b Liddicut	12
Extras	(b6, lb1)	7	(lb3)	3
Total	(51.2 overs, 185 mins)	200	(60.4 overs, 208 mins)	198

VICTORIA

F.E.Fontaine	c Atkinson b Burrows	59
†S.O.Quin	run out (Cahill/Parry)	39
B.Cosgrave	c Cahill b Nash	100
G.H.Newstead	run out (Morrisby/Richardson)	23
L.J.Junor	b Nash	32
*G.A.Davies	c Parry b Burrows	29
A.E.Liddicut	c James b Atkinson	56
R.J.Hassett	lbw b Richardson	29
E.F.Healy	not out	22
L.O.Fleetwood-Smith	st Parry b Putman	19
J.D.Kinnear	c Nash b Putman	13
Extras	(b2, lb1)	3
Total	(95.7 overs, 358 mins)	424

VICTORIA	O	M	R	W	w,nb		O	M	R	W	w,nb
Liddicut	22	2	79	4	-,-		22.4	4	48	4	-,-
Fleetwood-Smith	15.2	0	69	5	-,-	(3)	17	2	76	5	-,-
Kinnear	7	1	20	0	-,-	(5)	5	2	13	0	-,-
Healy	4	0	7	0	-,-	(6)	5	0	17	0	-,-
Hassett	3	0	18	0	-,-	(4)	8	0	28	0	-,-
Davies						(2)	3	0	13	0	-,-

TASMANIA	O	M	R	W	w,nb
Nash	27	0	103	2	-,-
Burrows	16	1	66	2	-,-
James	27	4	81	0	-,-
Richardson	8	0	41	1	-,-
Putman	13.7	0	104	2	-,-
Cahill	2	0	14	0	-,-
Atkinson	2	0	12	1	-,-

FALL OF WICKETS			
	TAS	VIC	TAS
Wkt	1st	1st	2nd
1st	0	53	55
2nd	9	149	55
3rd	9	203	122
4th	116	253	129
5th	135	256	166
6th	143	299	166
7th	143	369	168
8th	146	369	176
9th	182	406	177
10th	200	424	198

TASMANIA v VICTORIA

Played at N.T.C.A. Ground, Launceston, on December 30, 31, 1931, January 1, 1932. (Three-day match)
Toss : Victoria.　　　　　　　Result : TASMANIA WON BY SIX WICKETS.
Debuts: Victoria - F.Jinks (f/c).
12th Men: J.M.Walsh (Tas) and E.F.Healy (Vic).
Umpires: B.Parker and F.C.Tabart.
Attendances & Receipts: No figures published.
Close of Play: 1st day Tas 1/57 (Morrisby 19, Badcock 32); 2nd day Vic (2) 4/85 (Hassett 16, Junor 11).

D.C.Green was unavailable for Tasmania and Driscoll was a late replacement for the nominated captain, J.A.Atkinson, who had work commitments. Quin (114 not out in 147 minutes, 14 fours) rescued the Victorian first innings after a poor start. Burrows (right-arm fast-medium) claimed his best figures, 5 for 35. Hassett (40 in 98 minutes, 3 fours) and Junor (42 in 88 minutes, 4 fours) topscored in the second innings while Kinnear sustained a first-ball dismissal, Badcock (44 in 94 minutes, 3 fours), Richardson (64 in 80 minutes, 8 fours), Putman (37 in 95 minutes, 3 fours), Nash (84 in 144 minutes, 9 fours) and Rushworth (51 not out in 76 minutes, 7 fours) all contributed to Tasmania's victory. *Cricketer* incorrectly gives Tas (2) Burrows 22. *VCA Report* gives Vic (2) fall 6/146, Tas (2) 3/106. Sources: *The Cricketer, TCA Report, VCA Report, Hobart Mercury, Launceston Examiner.*

VICTORIA

*G.A.Davies	b Burrows	4	(8)	c Burrows b Putman	12
F.E.Fontaine	c Parry b Nash	12		st Parry b Putman	16
B.Cosgrave	c & b James	19		c Morrisby b Nash	14
G.H.Newstead	b James	32		st Parry b Putman	18
L.J.Junor	c Driscoll b Nash	8	(6)	c & b James	42
F.Jinks	c Parry b James	2	(7)	c Burrows b Putman	13
R.J.Hassett	lbw b Burrows	9	(5)	c Nash b Burrows	40
†S.O.Quin	not out	114	(1)	b Nash	4
A.E.Liddicut	c Badcock b Burrows	29		not out	16
L.O.Fleetwood-Smith	st Parry b Burrows	8	(11)	run out (Morrisby/Parry)	6
J.D.Kinnear	b Burrows	4	(10)	lbw b Putman	0
Extras	(b3, lb6, w2)	11		(b7, lb7)	14
Total	(63.7 overs, 250 mins)	252		(58.0 overs, 223 mins)	195

TASMANIA

*A.W.Rushforth	c Newstead b Davies	1	(5)	not out	51
R.O.G.Morrisby	lbw b Fleetwood-Smith	20	(1)	st Quin b Fleetwood-Smith	22
C.L.Badcock	c Quin b Hassett	44	(2)	st Quin b Liddicut	3
L.J.Nash	b Fleetwood-Smith	4	(3)	c Cosgrave b Kinnear	84
A.O.Burrows	b Fleetwood-Smith	12	(4)	run out (　　　/Quin)	24
V.R.Driscoll	st Quin b Hassett	12		not out	7
K.W.J.Cahill	c Fleetwood-Smith b Hassett	25			
G.T.H.James	b Fleetwood-Smith	3			
L.W.Richardson	b Liddicut	64			
S.W.L.Putman	c Fontaine b Fleetwood-Smith	37			
†C.N.Parry	not out	18			
Extras	(b5, lb7, w2)	14		(lb3)	3
Total	(69.4 overs, 250 mins)	254		(47.7 overs, 170 mins) (4 wkts)	194

TASMANIA	O	M	R	W	w,nb		O	M	R	W	w,nb					
Nash	21	2	102	2	-,-		14	2	70	2	-,-					
Burrows	11.7	1	35	5	2,-		11	2	25	1	-,-					
Richardson	11	2	28	0	-,-	(5)	7	1	22	0	-,-					
James	15	1	53	3	-,-	(3)	13	1	28	1	-,-					
Putman	5	0	23	0	-,-	(4)	13	2	36	5	-,-					

FALL OF WICKETS				
	VIC	TAS	VIC	TAS
Wkt	1st	1st	2nd	2nd
1st	7	9	6	3
2nd	20	62	24	45
3rd	70	68	45	102
4th	79	86	56	179
5th	79	91	142	-
6th	83	110	142	-
7th	141	115	171	-
8th	228	141	180	-
9th	238	220	180	-
10th	252	254	195	-

VICTORIA	O	M	R	W	w,nb		O	M	R	W	w,nb
Liddicut	22	8	45	1	-,-		17	3	48	1	-,-
Davies	5	0	13	1	2,-						
Kinnear	9	1	21	0	-,-	(2)	9	0	29	1	-,-
Hassett	13	0	68	3	-,-		10.7	0	60	0	-,-
Fleetwood-Smith	20.4	0	93	5	-,-	(3)	11	0	54	1	-,-

AUSTRALIA v SOUTH AFRICA (3rd Test)

Played at Melbourne Cricket Ground on December 31, 1931, January 1, 2, 4, 5, 6, 1932. (Timeless match)
Toss : Australia.   Result : AUSTRALIA WON BY 169 RUNS.
Debuts: Nil.
12th Men: J.H.W.Fingleton (Aust) and E.L.Dalton (SAF).
Umpires: E.G.Borwick and G.A.Hele.
Attendances: 19146, 20550, 27947, 31786, 8691, 500.   Total: About 108,620.   Receipts: £6477.
Close of Play: 1st day SAF 1/46 (Curnow 22, Christy 3); 2nd day SAF 7/268 (Viljoen 65, McMillan 10); 3rd day Aust (2) 1/206
        (Woodfull 73, Bradman 97); 4th day Aust (2) 9/554 (Grimmett 16, Ironmonger 0); 5th day SAF (2) 7/198 (Vincent 10, McMillan 1).

Australia's batsmen were restricted by Bell and Quinn in the first innings, Kippax (52 in 114 minutes, 1 six and 4 fours) and Rigg (68 in 98 minutes, 5 fours) being the leading scorers. In the second innings, Woodfull (161 in 300 minutes, 5 fours) and Bradman (167 in 183 minutes, 18 fours) shared a stand of 274 in 183 minutes, a new record for Australia's second wicket in all Tests. Bradman began his innings just after tea on the third day and was out before lunch on the fourth. Kippax (67 in 150 minutes, 5 fours) and McCabe (71 in 97 minutes, 1 six and 5 fours) scored half-centuries. Curnow (47 in 144 minutes, 3 fours) and Viljoen (111 in 205 minutes, 9 fours) led an even South African performance in the first innings, all men reaching double figures. Mitchell (46 in 177 minutes, 0 fours), Christy (63 in 112 minutes, 5 fours), Taylor and Vincent (34 in 40 minutes, 1 six and 5 fours) were the only Springboks to survive the varied spin of Grimmett and Ironmonger for any length of time in the second innings. *Australian Cricketer* incorrectly gives SAF (1) Curnow c McCabe b Grimmett; Aust (2) 3/405. Sources: *Wisden, Australian Cricketer, The Australasian, The Age, The Herald.*

AUSTRALIA

*W.M.Woodfull	c Cameron b Bell	7	c Mitchell b McMillan	161
W.H.Ponsford	b Bell	7	c Mitchell b Bell	34
D.G.Bradman	c Cameron b Quinn	2	lbw b Vincent	167
A.F.Kippax	c Bell b Quinn	52	c Curnow b McMillan	67
S.J.McCabe	c Morkel b Bell	22	c Mitchell b McMillan	71
K.E.Rigg	c Mitchell b Bell	68	c Mitchell b Vincent	1
E.L.a'Beckett	c Mitchell b Quinn	6	b Vincent	4
†W.A.S.Oldfield	c Vincent b Quinn	0	lbw b McMillan	0
C.V.Grimmett	c Morkel b Bell	9	not out	16
T.W.Wall	not out	6	b Vincent	12
H.Ironmonger	run out (McMillan/Cameron)	12	b Quinn	0
Extras	(b1, lb4, w1, nb1)	7	(b17, lb3, nb1)	21
Total	(77.1 overs, 215 mins)	198	(164.4 overs, 453 mins)	554

SOUTH AFRICA

B.Mitchell	c McCabe b Wall	17	c & b Grimmett	46
S.H.Curnow	b Grimmett	47	b Grimmett	9
J.A.J.Christy	c McCabe b Ironmonger	16	c Oldfield b Ironmonger	63
H.W.Taylor	lbw b Grimmett	11	b Grimmett	38
D.P.B.Morkel	lbw b Ironmonger	33	b Ironmonger	4
*†H.B.Cameron	st Oldfield b Ironmonger	39	lbw b Ironmonger	13
K.G.Viljoen	c Wall b McCabe	111	b Ironmonger	2
C.L.Vincent	c Oldfield b Wall	16	c Ponsford b Grimmett	34
Q.McMillan	c Oldfield b Wall	29	c Wall b Grimmett	1
N.A.Quinn	b McCabe	11	not out	0
A.J.Bell	not out	10	b Grimmett	0
Extras	(b3, lb13, nb2)	18	(b8, lb6, nb1)	15
Total	(188.3 overs, 496 mins)	358	(115.0 overs, 296 mins)	225

SOUTH AFRICA	O	M	R	W	w,nb		O	M	R	W	w,nb
Bell	26.1	9	69	5	-,1		36	6	101	1	-,1
Quinn	31	13	42	4	-,-		36.4	6	113	1	-,-
Morkel	3	0	12	0	1,-	(5)	4	0	15	0	-,-
Vincent	12	1	32	0	-,-	(3)	55	16	154	4	-,-
McMillan	2	0	22	0	-,-	(4)	33	3	150	4	-,-
Christy	3	0	14	0	-,-						

AUSTRALIA	O	M	R	W	w,nb		O	M	R	W	w,nb
Wall	37	5	98	3	-,-		13	3	35	0	-,-
a'Beckett	18	5	29	0	-,-		3	1	6	0	-,-
Grimmett	63	23	100	2	-,-		46	14	92	6	-,-
Ironmonger	49	26	72	3	-,2		42	18	54	4	-,-
McCabe	21.3	4	41	2	-,-		10	1	21	0	-,1
Bradman							1	0	2	0	-,-

FALL OF WICKETS

Wkt	AUST 1st	SAF 1st	AUST 2nd	SAF 2nd
1st	11	39	54	18
2nd	16	79	328	120
3rd	25	89	408	133
4th	74	108	519	138
5th	135	163	521	178
6th	143	183	521	186
7th	143	225	524	188
8th	173	329	530	208
9th	179	333	550	225
10th	198	358	554	225

NEW SOUTH WALES v QUEENSLAND (Shield Match 7)

Played at Sydney Cricket Ground on January 1, 2, 4, 5, 1932. (Four-day match)
Toss : New South Wales.　　　　　Result : NEW SOUTH WALES WON BY 188 RUNS.
Debuts: Queensland - H.S.Gamble (Qld only).
12th Men: J.L.Donnelly (NSW) and J.H.Holdsworth (Qld).
Umpires: H.J.Armstrong and W.G.French.
Attendances: 7893, 5320, 2478, 139.　　　　Total: 15,830.　　　　Receipts: £604.
Close of Play: 1st day Qld 1/18 (Cook 3, Burns 0); 2nd day NSW (2) 5/173 (Hird 52, Solomon 24); 3rd day Qld (2) 5/189 (Hurwood 0, Gamble 0).

O'Reilly replaced the nominated captain, R.H.B.Bettington (unavailable), in the New South Wales line-up. Gamble a former Victorian player, was brought from Brisbane to reinforce the Queensland team due to the loss of E.C.Bensted and E.Gilbert through injury. Further problems arose when Gough fractured a bone in his ankle while batting in the nets before the match; he fielded until tea on the first day and Oxenham took over the captaincy for the remainder of the game. Early on the second day Hansen was caught after deflecting a ball from Theak into his face; he required four stitches above the left eye and, like Gough, took no further part. Holdsworth, the Queensland manager, substituted for Gough and Donnelly, the New South Wales 12th man, for Hansen. Marks (71 in 141 minutes, 7 fours) and Hird (74 in 147 minutes, 6 fours) each registered a fifty for New South Wales. Cook (79 in 190 minutes, 6 fours) and Oxenham (45 in 89 minutes) topscored for Queensland. Despite leading by 160 runs on the first innings, Love elected not to enforce the follow-on. *Wisden* incorrectly gives NSW (1) O'Reilly c & b Oxenham; Qld (1) Gamble st Leabeater. *NSWCA Report* and *Australian Cricketer* incorrectly give NSW (2) Hunt c Burns b Thurlow. Sources: *Wisden, NSWCA Report, QCA Report, Australian Cricketer, Sydney Morning Herald, Sydney Referee, NSWCA Scorebook.*

NEW SOUTH WALES

O.W.Bill	c Cook b Thurlow	44		c Oxenham b Thurlow	24
*†H.S.B.Love	b Gamble	39		b Thurlow	10
R.N.Nutt	b Oxenham	28		lbw b Oxenham	39
A.E.Marks	c Mossop b Oxenham	71		b Thurlow	2
L.R.Leabeater	c Hogg b Thurlow	17		c Burns b Thurlow	17
S.F.Hird	lbw b Oxenham	39		run out (sub J.L.Donnelly)	74
C.M.Solomon	c Burns b Gamble	7		c Burns b Thurlow	26
W.A.Hunt	not out	27		c Burns b Gamble	31
W.J.O'Reilly	c Cook b Oxenham	11		run out (Sides/Burns)	4
J.E.H.Hooker	b Oxenham	1		not out	8
H.J.T.Theak	run out (Cook/Oxenham)	9		b Gamble	1
Extras	(b5, lb8, nb5)	18		(b14, nb3)	17
Total	(71.0 overs, 279 mins)	308		(60.4 overs, 222 mins)	253

QUEENSLAND

J.E.P.Hogg	c Love b Hooker	10		c Bill b Hunt	26
G.G.Cook	c Theak b Hird	24		c Hunt b Hird	79
†H.V.Burns	lbw b Hooker	1	(8)	c Bill b Hunt	13
C.D.Hansen	c Solomon b Theak	9		absent hurt	-
R.K.Oxenham	b O'Reilly	12	(4)	lbw b Hird	45
F.W.Sides	c Hooker b O'Reilly	0	(5)	b Hird	6
K.L.M.Mossop	c Love b Hunt	25	(3)	lbw b Hird	26
A.Hurwood	run out (Hird)	21	(6)	b Hunt	0
H.S.Gamble	st Love b Hird	17	(7)	run out (Solomon/Love)	16
H.M.Thurlow	not out	12	(9)	not out	5
*F.J.Gough	absent hurt	-		absent hurt	-
Extras	(b11, lb2, w1, nb3)	17		(lb6, nb3)	9
Total	(59.3 overs, 194 mins)	148		(83.0 overs, 263 mins)	225

QUEENSLAND	O	M	R	W	w,nb		O	M	R	W	w,nb
Thurlow	14	0	49	2	-,-		17	1	74	5	-,-
Hurwood	14	1	52	0	-,-	(3)	18	3	61	0	-,-
Oxenham	22	2	78	5	-,-	(4)	11	3	41	1	-,1
Gamble	19	1	88	2	-,5	(2)	14.4	2	60	2	-,2
Cook	2	0	23	0	-,-						

SOUTH AUSTRALIA	O	M	R	W	w,nb		O	M	R	W	w,nb
Theak	13	3	46	1	-,-		11	0	41	0	-,-
Hooker	13	3	30	2	1,2		16	1	46	0	-,2
O'Reilly	16	7	19	2	-,1		18	5	37	0	-,-
Hunt	15	4	31	1	-,-		22	7	45	3	-,1
Hird	2.3	1	5	2	-,-		16	4	47	4	-,-

FALL OF WICKETS

Wkt	NSW 1st	QLD 1st	NSW 2nd	QLD 2nd
1st	80	15	23	60
2nd	105	22	40	104
3rd	148	33	42	168
4th	177	53	74	188
5th	248	53	123	189
6th	257	80	175	189
7th	257	114	234	207
8th	275	116	239	225
9th	282	148	249	-
10th	308	-	253	-

TASMANIA v SOUTH AFRICAN XI

Played at N.T.C.A. Ground, Launceston, on January 8, 9, 11, 1932. (Three-day match)
Toss : South African XI.   Result : MATCH DRAWN.
Debuts: Nil.
12th Men: J.M.Walsh (Tas) and J.A.J.Christy (SAF).
Umpires: B.Parker and C.A.Pickett.
Attendances: 1000, 1500, 750.   Total: 3194   Receipts: £223.
Close of Play: 1st day Tas 1/13 (Atkinson 11); 2nd day Tas 8/228 (Parry 3, Townley 0).

D.C.Green and S.W.L.Putman were unavailable for Tasmania. Dalton (100 in 145 minutes, 1 six and 9 fours) scored his only century of the tour. Promoted in the second innings, McMillan (46 in 84 minutes, 7 fours) and Taylor (49 in 79 minutes, 4 fours) scored forties for the tourists. For Tasmania, Atkinson's chanceless 90 occupied 158 minutes and included 9 fours. Burrows (62 in 135 minutes, 5 fours) also surpassed fifty. Rushworth (44 in 87 minutes, 4 fours) and Cahill held out for a draw with an unbroken fifth-wicket stand of 61 in 33 minutes. *Wisden* and *Hobart Mercury* give SAF (1) Mitchell b Burrows, Curnow b James. Sources: *Wisden, TCA Report, VCA Report, Australian Cricketer, Hobart Mercury, Launceston Examiner.*

SOUTH AFRICAN XI

B.Mitchell	b James	6		lbw b Nash	14
S.H.Curnow	b Burrows	21		lbw b Townley	24
H.W.Taylor	c Nash b James	37	(5)	c James b Nash	49
S.S.L.Steyn	b Nash	18	(6)	not out	19
*H.B.Cameron	c Cahill b Burrows	17			
E.L.Dalton	c Atkinson b Burrows	100	(7)	not out	6
C.L.Vincent	c Rushforth b James	14			
D.P.B.Morkel	c Nash b Townley	15	(4)	hit wkt b Townley	0
Q.McMillan	b James	7	(3)	c Rushforth b Cahill	46
†E.A.van der Merwe	b Townley	35			
L.S.Brown	not out	1			
Extras	(lb6)	6		(b3, lb1)	4
Total	(71.6 overs, 262 mins)	277		(41.0 overs, 155 mins) (5 wkts dec)	162

TASMANIA

*J.A.Atkinson	b Morkel	90		c Cameron b Brown	1
R.O.G.Morrisby	b Morkel	0	(5)	c Mitchell b McMillan	15
C.L.Badcock	b McMillan	9		b McMillan	12
L.J.Nash	c Vincent b Brown	17	(2)	c Brown b Morkel	9
A.W.Rushforth	b McMillan	0	(4)	not out	44
A.O.Burrows	b Morkel	62			
K.W.J.Cahill	c Mitchell b Vincent	21	(6)	not out	35
G.T.H.James	c Brown b Vincent	7			
†C.N.Parry	b Brown	4			
R.C.Townley	c Brown b Morkel	1			
L.W.Richardson	not out	0			
Extras	(b13, lb6)	19		(b3, lb1)	4
Total	(66.1 overs, 232 mins)	230		(31.0 overs, 100 mins) (4 wkts)	120

TASMANIA	O	M	R	W	w,nb		O	M	R	W	w,nb
Nash	16	2	68	1	-,-		12	1	45	2	-,-
Burrows	16	2	59	3	-,-		8	0	36	0	-,-
Richardson	11	1	37	0	-,-						
James	22	4	67	4	-,-	(3)	11	1	21	0	-,-
Townley	6.6	0	40	2	-,-	(4)	7	0	32	2	-,-
Cahill						(5)	3	0	24	1	-,-

SOUTH AFRICAN XI	O	M	R	W	w,nb		O	M	R	W	w,nb
Morkel	15.1	1	53	4	-,-		9	0	31	1	-,-
Brown	17	3	45	2	-,-		11	0	37	1	-,-
McMillan	18	3	68	2	-,-		9	1	44	2	-,-
Steyn	1	0	8	0	-,-						
Vincent	10	2	23	2	-,-						
Mitchell	5	0	14	0	-,-						
Dalton						(4)	1	0	2	0	-,-
Taylor						(5)	1	0	2	0	-,-

FALL OF WICKETS

Wkt	SAF 1st	TAS 1st	SAF 2nd	TAS 2nd
1st	11	13	26	5
2nd	48	20	48	11
3rd	83	75	48	27
4th	89	76	98	59
5th	110	166	151	-
6th	138	207	-	-
7th	168	225	-	-
8th	196	228	-	-
9th	274	230	-	-
10th	277	230	-	-

AFCM No. 759/4
TM No. 13/11

TASMANIA v SOUTH AFRICAN XI

Played at T.C.A. Ground, Hobart, on January 15, 16, 18, 1932. (Three-day match)
Toss : Tasmania.   Result : SOUTH AFRICAN XI WON BY FOUR WICKETS.
Debuts: Nil.
12th Men: G.G.Gibson (Tas) and E.A.van der Merwe (SAF).
Umpires: M.Leonard and W.T.Lonergan.
Attendances: 2200, 3500, 2000.   Total: 7664   Receipts: £395.
Close of Play: 1st day SAF 6/111 (Morkel 52, Cameron 14); 2nd day Tas (2) 5/199 (Richardson 23, Morrisby 17).

A fifth-wicket partnership of 101 in 52 minutes between Christy (108 not out in 159 minutes, 2 sixes and 5 fours, chance at 14) and Morkel (64 in 52 minutes, 2 sixes and 7 fours) enabled the South Africans to win the match on the last afternoon, despite Morkel and McMillan falling to successive deliveries from Richardson late in the piece. Nash's first-innings 7 for 50, his career-best bowling, earned him a place in the Fifth Test team the following month. In his second over he dismissed Mitchell and Christy with consecutive deliveries and then hit Dalton on the jaw with his next ball, forcing his immediate retirement at 2/4. Despite a confirmed fracture, Dalton resumed his innings the following day at 7/119, but took no further part in the match after his dismissal, van der Merwe substituting in the field throughout Tasmania's second innings. Fifties by Morkel (54 in 86 minutes, 1 six and 7 fours) and Cameron (72 not out in 115 minutes, 10 fours) gave the tourists a first-innings lead. Quinn was their outstanding bowler, capturing nine wickets. Atkinson topped both innings for Tasmania, scoring 48 (63 minutes, 8 fours) and 55 (77 minutes, 1 six and 6 fours). *Wisden* incorrectly gives SAF (1) Richardson 0/52, Townley 2/20. Sources: *Wisden, TCA Report, VCA Report, Australian Cricketer, Hobart Mercury.*

TASMANIA

*J.A.Atkinson	c Mitchell b McMillan	48		c Morkel b Quinn	55
C.L.Badcock	st Cameron b McMillan	36		c Cameron b Quinn	4
L.J.Nash	b Bell	0		c Morkel b Quinn	11
D.C.Green	c Morkel b Bell	10		c Christy b McMillan	44
A.W.Rushforth	b Bell	0		c Morkel b Christy	24
A.O.Burrows	b Quinn	20	(8)	st Cameron b McMillan	23
R.O.G.Morrisby	c McMillan b Quinn	5		c Mitchell b McMillan	36
L.W.Richardson	b Quinn	28	(6)	b Quinn	24
G.T.H.James	b Quinn	0		b Morkel	1
†C.N.Parry	not out	2		b Morkel	4
R.C.Townley	c McMillan b Quinn	2		not out	4
Extras	(b6, lb4, nb3)	13		(b23, lb9)	32
Total	(43.4 overs, 154 mins)	164		(67.1 overs, 245 mins)	262

SOUTH AFRICAN XI

B.Mitchell	c Parry b Nash	1		st Parry b Townley	31
S.H.Curnow	b Nash	13		c Parry b Nash	6
J.A.J.Christy	b Nash	0		not out	108
E.L.Dalton	c Rushforth b Nash	28			
S.S.L.Steyn	c Parry b Burrows	1	(4)	b Townley	4
K.G.Viljoen	c Atkinson b Nash	27	(5)	c & b Nash	3
D.P.B.Morkel	b Nash	54	(6)	c Green b Richardson	64
Q.McMillan	c Nash b Townley	1	(7)	b Richardson	0
*†H.B.Cameron	not out	72	(8)	not out	10
N.A.Quinn	st Parry b Townley	2			
A.J.Bell	lbw b Nash	1			
Extras	(lb3)	3			-
Total	(50.7 overs, 213 mins)	203		(40.6 overs, 170 mins) (6 wkts)	226

SOUTH AFRICAN XI	O	M	R	W	w,nb		O	M	R	W	w,nb
Bell	14	2	43	3	-,3		16	0	56	0	-,-
Quinn	13.4	3	36	5	-,-		21	1	52	4	-,-
McMillan	13	1	55	2	-,-	(4)	17.1	1	77	3	-,-
Morkel	3	0	17	0	-,-	(3)	9	2	36	2	-,-
Christy							4	0	9	1	-,-

TASMANIA	O	M	R	W	w,nb		O	M	R	W	w,nb
Nash	16.7	5	50	7	-,-		15.6	0	87	2	-,-
Burrows	12	2	45	1	-,-	(3)	5	0	33	0	-,-
James	10	2	33	0	-,-	(2)	9	1	41	0	-,-
Richardson	4	0	20	0	-,-	(6)	3	0	13	2	-,-
Townley	8	0	52	2	-,-	(4)	6	0	34	2	-,-
Atkinson						(5)	2	0	18	0	-,-

FALL OF WICKETS

Wkt	TAS 1st	SAF 1st	TAS 2nd	SAF 2nd
1st	82	4	20	7
2nd	83	4	40	93
3rd	99	7	90	103
4th	99	25	146	110
5th	118	84	164	211
6th	130	91	204	211
7th	137	119	241	-
8th	137	181	242	-
9th	162	184	246	-
10th	164	203	262	-

NEW SOUTH WALES v VICTORIA (Shield Match 8)

Played at Sydney Cricket Ground on January 22, 23, 25, 26, 1932. (Four-day match)
Toss : New South Wales.   Result : NEW SOUTH WALES WON BY 239 RUNS.
Debuts: Nil.
12th Men: J.L.Donnelly (NSW) and I.S.Lee (Vic).
Umpires: H.J.Armstrong and W.G.French.
Attendances: 6760, 8106, 7111, 3738.   Total: 25,715.   Receipts: £1005.
Close of Play: 1st day NSW 9/347 (O'Reilly 25, Theak 17); 2nd day NSW (2) 0/24 (Fingleton 9, Bill 15); 3rd day Vic (2) 0/21
     (O'Brien 9, Thomas 12).

Two centuries by McCabe, who took his Shield average for the season to 438, separated the teams. He scored 106 in 156 minutes (12 fours) and 103 not out in only 89 minutes (15 fours), Kippax declaring immediately he reached his hundred in the second innings. Bradman, whose 167 in 224 minutes (22 fours) was the only other score above 50 for New South Wales, completed 1000 runs in the season when 86, in his tenth innings. Oakley topscored in each innings for Victoria, making 48 (111 minutes, 3 fours) and an unbeaten 93 (162 minutes, 6 fours). Thomas' 70 in 82 minutes with 10 fours was reckoned to be "the innings of the match" by the *Australian Cricketer*'s correspondent. Sources: *Wisden, NSWCA Scorebook, NSWCA Report, VCA Report, Sydney Morning Herald, Australian Cricketer.*

NEW SOUTH WALES

J.H.W.Fingleton	c a'Beckett b Nagel	40		lbw b Smith	40
O.W.Bill	c Barnett b McCormick	27		lbw b McCormick	15
D.G.Bradman	c Smith b Ironmonger	23		b Nagel	167
S.J.McCabe	c Barnett b Ironmonger	106	(5)	not out	103
R.N.Nutt	c Darling b a'Beckett	15	(6)	not out	8
S.F.Hird	c Barnett b McCormick	23			
*A.F.Kippax	c & b Darling	36	(4)	c Barnett b McCormick	44
†W.A.S.Oldfield	c Oakley b Darling	2			
W.A.Hunt	c Darling b Ironmonger	0			
W.J.O'Reilly	not out	26			
H.J.T.Theak	run out (O'Brien/Barnett)	17			
Extras	(b16, lb11, w5, nb1)	33		(b3, lb3, w4, nb2)	12
Total	(77.4 overs, 324 mins)	348		(77.3 overs, 310 mins) (4 wkts dec)	389

VICTORIA

L.P.J.O'Brien	c Oldfield b Theak	38		c Kippax b Hunt	34
J.Thomas	lbw b McCabe	19		st Oldfield b Hunt	70
L.S.Darling	lbw b Theak	5		lbw b Hird	23
*J.Ryder	b McCabe	20		run out (Kippax/Hird)	13
H.H.Oakley	b O'Reilly	48		not out	93
E.L.a'Beckett	b O'Reilly	3		c Fingleton b Theak	14
†B.A.Barnett	b O'Reilly	4		c & b Theak	3
L.E.Nagel	lbw b McCabe	30		b Hird	10
S.A.I.Smith	c Bradman b Hird	16		c Nutt b O'Reilly	7
E.L.McCormick	c McCabe b Hird	8		c Hird b McCabe	16
H.Ironmonger	not out	3		c McCabe b Bradman	1
Extras	(b6, lb3, nb1)	10		(b2, lb2, w2, nb4)	10
Total	(69.6 overs, 238 mins)	204		(84.5 overs, 280 mins)	294

VICTORIA	O	M	R	W	w,nb		O	M	R	W	w,nb
McCormick	15.4	4	42	2	2,-		13	0	54	2	3,2
a'Beckett	15	3	44	1	-,-		13.3	0	68	0	-,-
Ironmonger	20	2	94	3	-,-		17	4	52	0	-,-
Nagel	14	1	63	1	1,1		12	1	57	1	-,-
Smith	5	0	33	0	-,-		15	1	100	1	-,-
Darling	8	0	39	2	2,-		3	0	34	0	1,-
Ryder							4	0	12	0	-,-

NEW SOUTH WALES	O	M	R	W	w,nb		O	M	R	W	w,nb
Theak	13	1	39	2	-,-		17	2	64	2	1,-
McCabe	18	4	57	3	-,-	(4)	11	3	18	1	-,1
O'Reilly	21	6	52	3	-,1		20	3	73	1	-,3
Hunt	10	3	15	0	-,-	(2)	18	5	67	2	-,-
Hird	6.6	0	25	2	-,-		17	0	58	2	1,-
Bradman	1	0	6	0	-,-		1.5	0	4	1	-,-

FALL OF WICKETS

Wkt	NSW 1st	VIC 1st	NSW 2nd	VIC 2nd
1st	72	28	28	93
2nd	80	37	106	114
3rd	119	82	216	131
4th	174	88	303	149
5th	238	103	-	202
6th	274	113	-	218
7th	291	170	-	239
8th	296	172	-	248
9th	302	200	-	291
10th	348	204	-	294

SOUTH AUSTRALIA v SOUTH AFRICAN XI

Played at Adelaide Oval on January 22, 23, 25, 26, 1932. (Four-day match)
Toss : South Australia.   Result : SOUTH AFRICAN XI WON BY SEVEN WICKETS.
Debuts: Nil.
12th Men: W.E.Catchlove (SA) and S.H.Curnow (SAF).
Umpires: G.A.Hele and A.G.Jenkins.
Attendances: No daily figures published.   Total: 8870.   Receipts: £424.
Close of Play: 1st day SAF 1/178 (Mitchell 49, Taylor 51); 2nd day SAF 512 all out; 3rd day SA (2) 8/380 (Grimmett 38, Wall 14).

Richardson (53 in 57 minutes, 2 sixes and 2 fours) and Nitschke (62 in 95 minutes, 7 fours) gave South Australia a good start before McMillan (6 for 91) restricted the home side to 197. Christy (74 in 70 minutes, 2 sixes and 8 fours), Mitchell (82 in 208 minutes, 8 fours), Taylor (97 in 90 minutes, 12 fours) and Vincent (83 in 134 minutes, 12 fours) topscored for the visitors. Second-innings contributions from Richardson (61 in 112 minutes, 5 fours), Nitschke (44 in 61 minutes, 4 fours), Lonergan (chanceless 119 in 195 minutes, 10 fours) and Grimmett (63 not out in 119 minutes, 1 five and 2 fours) led South Australia to 430. Wall dismissed Christy with his fifth ball when South Africa batted again, Taylor (68 not out in 88 minutes, 9 fours) scoring more than half the runs needed. *Wisden* incorrectly gives SA (2) Lee hit wkt. Sources: *Wisden, SACA Report, VCA Report, Adelaide Advertiser, Australian Cricketer, The News.*

SOUTH AUSTRALIA

*V.Y.Richardson	b McMillan	53	run out (Brown/McMillan)		61
H.C.Nitschke	b McMillan	62	run out (Balaskas/van der Merwe)		44
A.R.Lonergan	st van der Merwe b McMillan	23	c Viljoen b Vincent		119
M.G.Waite	lbw b Brown	5	c Viljoen b Vincent		9
B.J.Tobin	lbw b Brown	2	lbw b Vincent		12
D.G.Jamieson	c van der Merwe b McMillan	6	st van der Merwe b Christy		34
P.K.Lee	lbw b Brown	11	b Vincent		28
C.V.Grimmett	run out	5	not out		63
†C.W.Walker	not out	7	b Vincent		1
T.W.Wall	b McMillan	5	c & b Balaskas		32
T.A.Carlton	c Balaskas b McMillan	10	b Balaskas		4
Extras	(b2, lb6)	8	(b15, lb6, w2)		23
Total	(47.1 overs, 172 mins)	197	(104.5 overs, 356 mins)		430

SOUTH AFRICAN XI

J.A.J.Christy	c Walker b Jamieson	74	b Wall		4
B.Mitchell	b Grimmett	82	c Walker b Carlton		8
H.W.Taylor	b Carlton	97	not out		68
K.G.Viljoen	c Walker b Lee	30			
*H.B.Cameron	hit wkt b Grimmett	37	not out		30
X.C.Balaskas	c Grimmett b Waite	25	(4) lbw b Grimmett		5
C.L.Vincent	st Walker b Grimmett	83			
Q.McMillan	c Wall b Grimmett	39			
†E.A.van der Merwe	b Grimmett	22			
L.S.Brown	b Grimmett	1			
A.J.Bell	not out	7			
Extras	(b10, lb5)	15	(b1, lb1)		2
Total	(113.5 overs, 400 mins)	512	(25.0 overs, 93 mins) (3 wkts)		117

SOUTH AFRICAN XI	O	M	R	W	w,nb		O	M	R	W	w,nb		FALL OF WICKETS			
														SA	SAF	SA	SAF
Bell	5	2	8	0	-,-		2	0	8	0	-,-	Wkt	1st	1st	2nd	2nd
Christy	5	0	31	0	-,-	(8)	7	1	37	1	-,-	1st	75	96	71	4
Vincent	9	2	36	0	-,-		37	11	78	5	-,-	2nd	128	241	129	41
Brown	11	2	23	3	-,-	(2)	23	3	89	0	-,-	3rd	139	280	143	58
McMillan	17.1	0	91	6	-,-	(4)	25	0	146	0	-,-	4th	151	328	165	-
Mitchell						(5)	5	0	22	0	-,-	5th	153	328	247	-
Balaskas						(6)	3.5	0	14	2	-,-	6th	164	378	298	-
Cameron						(7)	2	0	13	0	2,-	7th	171	465	335	-
												8th	177	479	337	-
SOUTH AUSTRALIA	O	M	R	W	w,nb		O	M	R	W	w,nb	9th	183	489	420	-
Wall	18	1	103	0	-,-		4	0	22	1	-,-	10th	197	512	430	-
Carlton	16	4	40	1	-,-		8	2	16	1	-,-					
Jamieson	17	5	38	1	-,-	(4)	3	0	24	0	-,-					
Tobin	7	1	27	0	-,-											
Grimmett	31.5	3	155	6	-,-	(3)	9	2	45	1	-,-					
Lee	17	0	83	1	-,-	(5)	1	0	8	0	-,-					
Waite	7	0	51	1	-,-											

AUSTRALIA v SOUTH AFRICA (4th Test)

Played at Adelaide Oval on January 29, 30, February 1, 2, 1932. (Timeless match)
Toss : South Africa.   Result : AUSTRALIA WON BY TEN WICKETS.
Debuts: Australia - W.A.Hunt, W.J.O'Reilly, H.M.Thurlow (all Test).
12th Men: J.H.W.Fingleton (Aust) and L.S.Brown (SAF).
Umpires: E.G.Borwick and G.A.Hele.
Attendances: 13300, 25100, 17643, 6209.   Total: 62,252.   Receipts: £4181.
Close of Play: 1st day SAF 7/265 (Vincent 18, McMillan 10); 2nd day Aust 4/302 (Bradman 170, Rigg 32), 3rd day SAF (2) 2/124
   (Mitchell 54, Taylor 11).

Bradman (299 not out in 396 minutes, 23 fours) brought his tally of runs in this series to 806, average 201.50. A difficult chance when
185 was his only blemish as he compiled the highest Test innings yet in Australia, surpassing R.E.Foster's 287 in 1903-04. He shared
century partnerships with Woodfull (82 in 140 minutes, 6 fours) for the second wicket and Rigg (35 in 88 minutes) for the fifth wicket.
He went to 50 in 62 minutes, 100 in 133 minutes, 150 in 185 minutes, 200 in 284 minutes and 250 in 346 minutes; by sessions he was
2* (lunch), 84* (tea), 170* (stumps) and 219* (lunch). Mitchell and Taylor shared a century stand for the third wicket in each innings for
South Africa, Mitchell scoring 75 (175 minutes, 7 fours) and 95 (293 minutes) and Taylor 78 (129 minutes, 1 six and 8 fours) and 84 (122
minutes, 1 six and 8 fours). Cameron (52 in 89 minutes, 7 fours), Vincent (48 not out in 126 minutes, 4 fours) and Christy (51 in 78
minutes, 1 five and 4 fours) also batted well for the tourists. Grimmett began his famous association with O'Reilly by capturing a match
analysis of 14 for 199 - the best yet by an Australian in a home Test. *Wisden* incorrectly gives SAF (1) Vincent lbw b O'Reilly, Bell not
out; SAF (2) Mitchell c Thurlow. Sources: *Wisden, SACA Report, Australian Cricketer, Adelaide Advertiser, The Herald, The News*.

SOUTH AFRICA

S.H.Curnow	c Ponsford b Grimmett	20		b McCabe	3
B.Mitchell	c & b McCabe	75		c O'Reilly b Grimmett	95
J.A.J.Christy	b O'Reilly	7		b Grimmett	51
H.W.Taylor	c Rigg b Grimmett	78		b O'Reilly	84
*†H.B.Cameron	lbw b Grimmett	52		b O'Reilly	4
D.P.B.Morkel	c & b Grimmett	0	(8)	b Grimmett	15
K.G.Viljoen	c & b Grimmett	0		b Grimmett	1
C.L.Vincent	not out	48	(6)	b Grimmett	5
Q.McMillan	b Grimmett	19		c Hunt b Grimmett	3
N.A.Quinn	c Ponsford b Grimmett	1		b Grimmett	1
A.J.Bell	lbw O'Reilly	2		not out	0
Extras	(lb2, nb4)	6		(b4, lb3, nb5)	12
Total	(140.4 overs, 346 mins)	308		(123.2 overs, 295 mins)	274

AUSTRALIA

*W.M.Woodfull	c Morkel b Bell	82		not out	37
W.H.Ponsford	b Quinn	5		not out	27
D.G.Bradman	not out	299			
A.F.Kippax	run out (Taylor/Cameron)	0			
S.J.McCabe	c Vincent b Bell	2			
K.E.Rigg	c Taylor b Bell	35			
†W.A.S.Oldfield	lbw b Vincent	23			
C.V.Grimmett	b Bell	21			
W.A.Hunt	c Vincent b Quinn	0			
W.J.O'Reilly	b Bell	23			
H.M.Thurlow	run out (Curnow/Cameron)	0			
Extras	(b 18, lb3, w1, nb1)	23		(b4, lb5)	9
Total	(138.0 overs, 413 mins)	513		(19.2 overs, 45 mins) (0 wkts)	73

AUSTRALIA	O	M	R	W	w,nb		O	M	R	W	w,nb		FALL OF WICKETS			
														SAF	AUST	SAF	AUST
Thurlow	27	6	53	0	-,-		12	1	33	0	-,-			1st	1st	2nd	2nd
McCabe	17	6	34	1	-,-		14	1	51	1	-,-	Wkt				
O'Reilly	39.4	10	74	2	-,4		42	13	81	2	-,5	1st	27	9	22	-
Grimmett	47	11	116	7	-,-		49.2	17	83	7	-,-	2nd	45	185	103	-
Hunt	10	1	25	0	-,-		6	1	14	0	-,-	3rd	165	191	224	-
												4th	202	194	232	-
SOUTH AFRICA	O	M	R	W	w,nb		O	M	R	W	w,nb	5th	204	308	240	-
Bell	40	2	142	5	-,1							6th	204	357	246	-
Quinn	37	5	114	2	-,-	(1)	3	0	5	0	-,-	7th	243	418	262	-
Vincent	34	5	110	1	1,-	(4)	7	0	31	0	-,-	8th	286	421	268	-
McMillan	9	0	53	0	-,-	(3)	7.2	0	23	0	-,-	9th	300	499	274	-
Morkel	18	1	71	0	-,-	(2)	2	0	5	0	-,-	10th	308	513	274	-

AFCM No. 763/21
SSM No. 242/11

QUEENSLAND v VICTORIA (Shield Match 9)

Played at Brisbane Cricket Ground (Woolloongabba) on January 29, 30, February 1, 2, 1932. (Four-day match)
Toss : Queensland.   Result : QUEENSLAND WON BY 139 RUNS.
Debuts: Queensland - W.C.Andrews (Qld only).
12th Men: A.H.F.Rofe (Qld) and I.S.Lee (Vic).
Umpires: J.P.Orr and B.L.Turner (J.S.Redgrave deputised).
Attendances: 2508, 417, ? , ? .   Total: About 10,000.   Receipts: £446.
Close of Play: 1st day Qld 5/330 (Oxenham 98, Bensted 40); 2nd day Vic 6/172 (a'Beckett 35, Barnett 2); 3rd day Qld (2) 6/216 (Sides 56, Mossop 20).

Andrews, the former New South Wales batsman, scored a century on debut for his new State (110 in 212 minutes, 13 fours). Oxenham (career-best 162 in 374 minutes, 1 six and 14 fours) anchored the innings - Queensland's highest yet against Victoria - and shared century partnerships with Andrews and Bensted (83 in 125 minutes, 15 fours). Sides (56 not out in 98 minutes, 6 fours) topscored in the second innings. O'Brien was out to the tenth ball of the opening over in Victoria's first innings after umpire Orr had allowed an extra ball in addition to a wide by Gilbert. Oakley continued his good form from the match against New South Wales the previous week by scoring 38 (83 minutes, 4 fours) and 88 (211 minutes, 1 five and 6 fours) while Darling (48 in 44 minutes, 7 fours), a'Beckett (47 in 102 minutes, 5 fours and 55 in 98 minutes, 1 six, 1 five and 4 fours), Barnett (60 in 140 minutes, 8 fours) and Ryder (71 in 80 minutes, 1 five and 9 fours) also batted well for the visitors. At the conclusion of their first innings Ryder successfully appealed for 4 overthrows for an earlier incident when an incoming throw hit a'Beckett's bat, deflecting the ball to the boundary. (The batsmen had declined to run at the time and no signal was given). The first over of Queensland's second innings yielded 22 runs, including 18 to Hogg. Early on the final day a fierce pull shot by Ryder struck umpire Orr, who was officiating at square-leg, in the head; Redgrave stood for the remainder while Orr went to hospital to get three stitches inserted in the wound. Prior to the match Rofe had replaced F.M.Brew, who was unavailable, as 12th man.
VCA Report gives Vic (2) 7/211, 8/232, 9/253. Sources: *Wisden, VCA Report, QCA Report, Brisbane Courier, Brisbane Daily Mail, Australian Cricketer.*

QUEENSLAND

*J.E.P.Hogg	run out (Darling)	4		c a'Beckett b McCormick	26
G.G.Cook	b a'Beckett	36		b Nagel	17
C.D.Hansen	c Ryder b a'Beckett	1	(4)	c a'Beckett b Ironmonger	13
W.C.Andrews	b a'Beckett	110	(3)	b Nagel	19
R.K.Oxenham	not out	162		c Thomas b a'Beckett	21
F.W.Sides	b Nagel	23		not out	56
E.C.Bensted	c Barnett b McCormick	83		c Darling b Ironmonger	27
K.L.M.Mossop	lbw b a'Beckett	29		not out	20
H.S.Gamble	c McCormick b Smith	17			
†L.W.Waterman	c Oakley b Smith	8			
E.Gilbert	lbw b Smith	1			
Extras	(b15, lb11, nb4)	30		(b6, lb6, w 1, nb4)	17
Total	(121.4 overs, 484 mins)	504		(57.0 overs, 225 mins) (6 wkts dec)	216

VICTORIA

L.P.J.O'Brien	c Waterman b Gilbert	1		b Gilbert	1
J.Thomas	b Bensted	25		st Waterman b Bensted	10
L.S.Darling	c Hansen b Bensted	48		c Mossop b Gilbert	4
H.H.Oakley	c Sides b Gamble	38		c Waterman b Oxenham	88
*J.Ryder	lbw b Oxenham	15		b Gilbert	71
E.L.a'Beckett	b Gamble	47		c Hogg b Cook	55
L.E.Nagel	b Cook	5		b Gilbert	15
†B.A.Barnett	st Waterman b Oxenham	60	(9)	b Gamble	31
S.A.J.Smith	b Gilbert	15	(8)	b Gilbert	7
E.L.McCormick	lbw b Bensted	10		not out	13
H.Ironmonger	not out	4		b Gamble	1
Extras	(b6, lb1, w1, nb1)	9		(b6, lb2)	8
Total	(62.1 overs, 259 mins)	277		(69.1 overs, 279 mins)	304

VICTORIA	O	M	R	W	w,nb		O	M	R	W	w,nb		FALL OF WICKETS			
McCormick	28	2	117	1	-,4		7	0	46	1	1,4			QLD	VIC	QLD	VIC
a'Beckett	29	3	105	4	-,-		11	2	31	1	-,-		Wkt	1st	1st	2nd	2nd
Ironmonger	29	9	93	0	-,-		21	5	72	2	-,-		1st	5	2	32	10
Nagel	24	3	87	1	-,-		13	3	30	2	-,-		2nd	9	72	62	14
Smith	7.4	0	51	3	-,-		5	0	20	0	-,-		3rd	71	85	79	20
Darling	4	0	21	0	-,-								4th	212	116	101	117
													5th	259	144	119	218
QUEENSLAND	O	M	R	W	w,nb		O	M	R	W	w,nb		6th	392	153	157	246
Gilbert	15	0	77	2	1,-		15	0	67	5	-,-		7th	463	215	-	250
Gamble	14	0	83	2	-,-	(3)	11.1	0	49	2	-,-		8th	491	236	-	258
Bensted	17	1	70	3	-,1	(2)	18	0	92	1	-,-		9th	499	257	-	302
Oxenham	12.1	5	23	2	-,-		17	5	36	0	-,-		10th	504	277	-	304
Cook	4	1	15	1	-,-		6	0	40	1	-,-						
Andrews							2	0	12	0	-,-						

VICTORIA v SOUTH AFRICAN XI

Played at Melbourne Cricket Ground on February 6 (no play), 8, 9, 10 (no play), 1932. (Four-day match)

Toss : Victoria.   Result : MATCH DRAWN.

Debuts: Nil.

12th Men: J.Thomas (Vic) and Q.McMillan (SAF).

Umpires: A.N.Barlow and J.Richards.

Attendances: No play, 4518, 2666, no play.   Total: 7184 (days 2 & 3 only).   Receipts: £212.

Close of Play: 1st day no play; 2nd day SAF 2/48 (Christy 20, Taylor 12); Third day Vic (2) 0/158 (Woodfull 73, Ponsford 84).

J.Ryder was unavailable for Victoria and Thomas, L.E.Nagel and S.A.J.Smith were omitted from the fourteen named. A.J.Bell and E.L.Dalton (both injured) were unavailable for South Africa. Rain restricted play to the second and third scheduled days and made a result impossible. Fleetwood-Smith claimed a five-wicket-innings for the fourth time in his three matches to date. Christy (36 in 80 minutes, 1 four), Taylor (54 in 103 minutes, 6 fours), Viljoen (43 in 112 minutes, 3 fours) and Cameron (45 in 73 minutes, 5 fours) topscored for the visitors. Woodfull, 44 in 86 minutes with 1 four in the first innings, hit 4 fours in the second innings as he and Ponsford (7 fours) ran up an unbroken stand of 158 in 83 minutes. Sources: *Wisden, VCA Report, NSWCA Report, Australian Cricketer, The Age, The Argus.*

VICTORIA

*W.M.Woodfull	run out (Balaskas/Cameron)		44	not out	73
W.H.Ponsford	run out (Quinn/Brown)		8	not out	84
K.E.Rigg	b Quinn		0		
L.S.Darling	lbw b Brown		33		
H.H.Oakley	c Steyn b Balaskas		16		
L.P.J.O'Brien	c Mitchell b Quinn		23		
E.L.a'Beckett	c & b Balaskas		23		
†B.A.Barnett	c Viljoen b Morkel		27		
E.L.McCormick	not out		25		
L.O.Fleetwood-Smith	st Cameron b Balaskas		11		
H.Ironmonger	b Morkel		1		
Extras	(b15, lb5)		20	(b1)	1
Total	(65.3 overs, 217 mins)		231	(26.0 overs, 83 mins) (0 wkts)	158

SOUTH AFRICAN XI

B.Mitchell	c Barnett b McCormick	10
S.H.Curnow	run out (O'Brien/Barnett)	4
J.A.J.Christy	c Rigg b Ironmonger	36
H.W.Taylor	lbw b Fleetwood-Smith	54
K.G.Viljoen	lbw b Fleetwood-Smith	43
X.C.Balaskas	b Fleetwood-Smith	0
D.P.B.Morkel	c Oakley b Fleetwood-Smith	11
S.S.L.Steyn	c & b Fleetwood-Smith	6
*†H.B.Cameron	c Darling b Ironmonger	45
L.S.Brown	c Ponsford b Fleetwood-Smith	11
N.A.Quinn	not out	0
Extras	(b8, lb8, nb3)	19
Total	(71.2 overs, 257 mins)	239

SOUTH AFRICAN XI	O	M	R	W	w,nb		O	M	R	W	w,nb
Brown	17	4	41	1	-,-	(3)	8	1	52	0	-,-
Quinn	21	7	50	2	-,-		3	0	7	0	-,-
Morkel	10.3	1	36	2	-,-	(1)	5	0	20	0	-,-
Balaskas	15	0	79	3	-,-		8	0	62	0	-,-
Christy	2	0	5	0	-,-		2	0	16	0	-,-

VICTORIA	O	M	R	W	w,nb
McCormick	20	1	68	1	-,3
a'Beckett	8	0	18	0	-,-
Fleetwood-Smith	23.2	3	80	6	-,-
Ironmonger	20	6	54	2	-,-

FALL OF WICKETS

	VIC	SAF	VIC
Wkt	1st	1st	2nd
1st	35	10	-
2nd	35	21	-
3rd	89	92	-
4th	101	131	-
5th	121	131	-
6th	153	147	-
7th	190	163	-
8th	190	184	-
9th	224	237	-
10th	231	239	-

AUSTRALIA v SOUTH AFRICA (5th Test)

Played at Melbourne Cricket Ground on February 12, 13 (no play), 15, 1932. (Timeless match)
Toss : South Africa.   Result : AUSTRALIA WON BY AN INNINGS AND 72 RUNS.
Debuts: Australia - J.H.W.Fingleton, L.J.Nash (both Tests).
12th Men: L.S.Darling (Aust) and X.C.Balaskas (SAF).
Umpires: E.G.Borwick and G.A.Hele.
Attendances: 9869, no play, 3163.   Total: 13,032.   Receipts: £638.
Close of Play: 1st day SAF (2) 1/5 (Curnow 1, Bell 4); 2nd day no play.

Rigg (originally 12th man) replaced Ponsford (flu) in the selected Australian team prior to the start of the match. Bradman twisted his ankle when his sprigs caught in the coir matting of the dressing room as he was going out to field at the start of the game and was unable to field or bat on the first day. Rain, which had badly interrupted the match between Victoria and the tourists, continued intermittently before and during the Test and Ironmonger (11 for 24) extracted full advantage. The pitch was soft on the first day without ever being spiteful, however, the rain which prevented any play on the second day, followed by the sun on the third day, produced the dreaded Australian "sticky" and the South Africans succumbed cheaply for a second time. McMillan, one of four batsmen to suffer a golden duck on the opening day - Woodfull, McCabe and Christy were the others - became the second batsman after R.Peel in 1894-95 to be dismissed twice for a pair in one Test series in Australia. The highest scorers were Fingleton (40 in 77 minutes, 1 four) and Kippax (42 in 84 minutes, 2 fours) and the match took only 5 hours 53 minutes of playing time to resolve. Sources: *Wisden, VCA Report, Australian Cricketer, The Age, The Argus, The Australasian, Melbourne Sun.*

SOUTH AFRICA

B.Mitchell	c Rigg b McCabe	2	(4)	c Oldfield b Ironmonger	4
S.H.Curnow	c Oldfield b Nash	3		c Fingleton b Ironmonger	16
J.A.J.Christy	c Grimmett b Nash	4	(1)	c & b Nash	0
H.W.Taylor	c Kippax b Nash	0	(6)	c Bradman b Ironmonger	2
K.G.Viljoen	c sub (L.S.Darling) b Ironmonger	1	(8)	c Oldfield b O'Reilly	0
*†H.B.Cameron	c McCabe b Nash	11	(5)	c McCabe b O'Reilly	0
D.P.B.Morkel	c Nash b Ironmonger	1		c Rigg b Ironmonger	0
C.L.Vincent	c Nash b Ironmonger	1	(9)	not out	8
Q.McMillan	st Oldfield b Ironmonger	0	(10)	c Oldfield b Ironmonger	0
N.A.Quinn	not out	5	(11)	c Fingleton b Ironmonger	5
A.J.Bell	st Oldfield b Ironmonger	0	(3)	c McCabe b O'Reilly	6
Extras	(b2, lb3, nb3)	8		(b3, lb1)	4
Total	(23.2 overs, 89 mins)	36		(31.3 overs, 105 mins)	45

AUSTRALIA

*W.M.Woodfull	b Bell	0
J.H.W.Fingleton	c Vincent b Bell	40
K.E.Rigg	c Vincent b Quinn	22
A.F.Kippax	c Curnow b McMillan	42
S.J.McCabe	c Cameron b Bell	0
L.J.Nash	b Quinn	13
†W.A.S.Oldfield	c Curnow b McMillan	11
C.V.Grimmett	c Cameron b Quinn	9
W.J.O'Reilly	c Curnow b McMillan	13
H.Ironmonger	not out	0
D.G.Bradman	absent hurt	-
Extras	(lb3)	3
Total	(54.3 overs, 159 mins)	153

AUSTRALIA	O	M	R	W	w,nb		O	M	R	W	w,nb
Nash	12	6	18	4	-,3		7	4	4	1	-,-
McCabe.	4	1	4	1	-,-						
Ironmonger	7.2	5	6	5	-,-	(2)	15.3	7	18	6	-,-
O'Reilly						(3)	9	5	19	3	-,-

SOUTH AFRICA	O	M	R	W	w,nb
Bell	16	0	52	3	-,-
Quinn	19.3	4	29	3	-,-
Vincent	11	2	40	0	-,-
McMillan	8	0	29	3	-,-

FALL OF WICKETS

Wkt	SAF 1st	AUST 1st	SAF 2nd
1st	7	0	0
2nd	16	51	12
3rd	16	75	25
4th	17	75	30
5th	19	112	30
6th	25	125	30
7th	31	131	32
8th	31	148	32
9th	33	153	33
10th	36	-	45

VICTORIA v SOUTH AUSTRALIA (Shield Match 10)

Played at Melbourne Cricket Ground on March 4, 5, 7 (no play), 8, 1932. (Four-day match)
Toss : South Australia.   Result : VICTORIA WON BY AN INNINGS AND 88 RUNS.
Debuts: Nil.
12th Men: L.J.Junor (Vic) and D.G.Jamieson (SA).
Umpires: A.N.Barlow and W.J.Moore.
Attendances: 3628, 5335, no play, 1525.   Total: 10,488.   Receipts: £258.
Close of Play: 1st day Vic 0/15 (Ponsford 11, O'Brien 3); 2nd day Vic 5/364 (Oakley 104, a'Beckett 28); 3rd day no play.

Alexander, Lee and Newstead came into the Victorian team to replace E.L.McCormick, J.Thomas and W.M.Woodfull, who were all suffering the effects of an influenza epidemic. Richardson (69 in 84 minutes, 10 fours) and Nitschke (54 in 112 minutes, 5 fours) added 111 for the first wicket. Lonergan (72 in 184 minutes, 4 fours) also scored well for South Australia but the rest succumbed to Fleetwood-Smith who, assisted by a damp pitch in the second innings, took his tally of first-class wickets to 33 in his fourth match. Darling (97) ran a three for his hundred only to have 'one short' signalled. He soon scored the single required but was out without further addition, having batted 145 minutes. O'Brien (57 in 144 minutes, 5 fours) and Oakley (115 in 217 minutes, 12 fours, missed when 2) also contributed for Victoria, the latter sharing a fifth-wicket stand of 102 in 108 minutes with Lee. A'Beckett (37 in 47 minutes, 3 fours) dismissed Nitschke in his first over in the second innings but this was to be his final first-class appearance at the age of 24. He sustained a fractured skull in an Australian Rules football match the following winter and thereafter concentrated on his law career. Sources: *Wisden, VCA Report, SACA Report, Australian Cricketer, The Age, The Argus, The Herald.*

SOUTH AUSTRALIA

Batsman	Dismissal	Runs	Dismissal 2	Runs 2
*V.Y.Richardson	c Barnett b Alexander	69	c Ironmonger b Alexander	13
H.C.Nitschke	c Darling b Ironmonger	54	lbw b a'Beckett	0
A.R.Lonergan	c Alexander b Ironmonger	72	c a'Beckett b Alexander	5
W.E.Catchlove	b Fleetwood-Smith	1	b Alexander	11
H.E.Whitfield	lbw b Fleetwood-Smith	5	lbw b Fleetwood-Smith	9
M.G.Waite	c Oakley b Fleetwood-Smith	0	b Fleetwood-Smith	8
P.K.Lee	lbw b Fleetwood-Smith	5	b Fleetwood-Smith	9
C.V.Grimmett	lbw b Fleetwood-Smith	0	c Barnett b Ironmonger	9
†C.W.Walker	b Fleetwood-Smith	35	st Barnett b Fleetwood-Smith	0
T.W.Wall	lbw b Fleetwood-Smith	13	run out (a'Beckett/Barnett)	2
T.A.Carlton	not out	13	not out	0
Extras	(lb4, nb1)	5	(b1, lb1)	2
Total	(74.1 overs, 270 mins)	272	(26.3 overs, 105 mins)	68

VICTORIA

Batsman	Dismissal	Runs
*W.H.Ponsford	c Richardson b Wall	24
L.P.J.O'Brien	c Whitfield b Wall	57
L.S.Darling	c Richardson b Wall	100
H.H.Oakley	st Walker b Lee	115
G.H.Newstead	b Wall	0
I.S.Lee	c Richardson b Grimmett	36
E.L.a'Beckett	b Grimmett	37
†B.A.Barnett	b Lee	10
L.O.Fleetwood-Smith	b Grimmett	29
H.H.Alexander	not out	5
H.Ironmonger	b Lee	0
Extras	(b8, lb3, nb4)	15
Total	(98.6 overs, 390 mins)	428

VICTORIA	O	M	R	W	w,nb		O	M	R	W	w,nb
Alexander	11	1	62	1	-,1		8	2	22	3	-,-
a'Beckett	9	1	19	0	-,-		6	0	16	1	-,-
Ironmonger	30.1	5	85	2	-,-	(4)	5.3	0	9	1	-,-
Fleetwood-Smith	24	1	101	7	-,-	(3)	7	0	19	4	-,-

SOUTH AUSTRALIA	O	M	R	W	w,nb
Wall	23	4	86	4	-,3
Whitfield	10	0	49	0	-,-
Carlton	14	3	56	0	-,-
Grimmett	26	3	118	3	-,-
Lee	24.6	5	99	3	-,1
Waite	1	0	5	0	-,-

FALL OF WICKETS

Wkt	SA 1st	VIC 1st	SA 2nd
1st	111	34	8
2nd	128	162	15
3rd	138	215	20
4th	156	216	35
5th	164	318	45
6th	178	383	55
7th	178	385	60
8th	240	422	64
9th	256	428	68
10th	272	428	68

QUEENSLAND v SOUTH AUSTRALIA (Shield Match 11)

Played at Brisbane Cricket Ground (Woolloongabba) on March 12, 14, 15, 16, 1932. (Four-day match)
Toss : South Australia.   Result : SOUTH AUSTRALIA WON BY 150 RUNS.
Debuts: South Australia - A.G.Shepherd (f/c).
12th Men: K.J.Hickey (Qld) and M.G.Waite (SA).
Umpires: J.Bartlett and J.A.Scott.
Attendances: 3111, 1803, 1640, 1301.   Total: 7855.   Receipts: £290.
Close of Play: 1st day SA 8/383 (Catchlove 90); 2nd day Qld 6/255 (Bensted 56, Mossop 22); 3rd day SA (2) 7/198 (Shepherd 8, Grimmett 7).

Richardson (121 in 152 minutes, 19 fours) and Lonergan (95 in 166 minutes, 1 six and 11 fours) added 191 for the second wicket on the opening day and, followed by Catchlove (103 not out in 196 minutes, 6 fours), established a sound start for South Australia. Bensted (145 in 155 minutes, 1 six and 24 fours) rescued Queensland from 6/199 by mounting another 191-run stand, with Mossop (59 in 128 minutes, 6 fours) for the seventh wicket. Wall strained a knee in the field on the second day, bowling no further; the lameness led to his run out in the second innings. Lonergan (97 in 164 minutes, 12 fours) again missed out on a hundred and Hubbard captured Walker and Jamieson with consecutive balls shortly after his dismissal. Grimmett made the best use of the wearing last-day wicket. Sources: *Wisden, SACA Report, QCA Report, Brisbane Courier, Brisbane Daily Mail, Australian Cricketer, Maryborough Chronicle.*

SOUTH AUSTRALIA

H.C.Nitschke	c Hubbard b Thurlow	7		c Bensted b Gilbert	11
*V.Y.Richardson	c Waterman b Hubbard	121		c Mossop b Bensted	43
A.R.Lonergan	c Thurlow b Gilbert	95		run out (Cook/Waterman)	97
W.E.Catchlove	not out	103		run out (Gilbert/Mossop)	23
A.G.Shepherd	c Waterman b Thurlow	2	(6)	b Bensted	29
P.K.Lee	c Waterman b Thurlow	3	(5)	c Cook b Oxenham	1
D.G.Jamieson	b Gilbert	9	(8)	st Waterman b Hubbard	0
C.V.Grimmett	b Gilbert	0	(9)	b Gilbert	19
†C.W.Walker	b Gilbert	32	(7)	b Hubbard	0
T.W.Wall	c Cook b Thurlow	11		run out (/Waterman)	17
T.A.Carlton	c Cook b Hubbard	2		not out	33
Extras	(b12, lb13)	25		(b12, lb3, w1)	16
Total	(97.1 overs, 350 mins)	410		(76.6 overs, 284 mins)	289

QUEENSLAND

*J.E.P.Hogg	c Lee b Grimmett	39		c Jamieson b Carlton	3
G.G.Cook	b Wall	52		b Grimmett	26
W.C.Andrews	c Shepherd b Lee	22		c Walker b Jamieson	1
C.D.Hansen	b Lee	44		c Lee b Carlton	10
R.K.Oxenham	b Wall	7		c sub (M.G.Waite) b Grimmett	57
E.C.Bensted	c Richardson b Lee	145		c Walker b Lee	3
E.F.Hubbard	c Walker b Grimmett	3		st Walker b Grimmett	9
K.L.M.Mossop	c Walker b Carlton	59		c Nitschke b Grimmett	3
†L.W.Waterman	run out	19		b Carlton	0
H.M.Thurlow	b Grimmett	0		c Walker b Grimmett	4
E.Gilbert	not out	4		not out	5
Extras	(b13, lb9, nb4)	26		(b7, lb1)	8
Total	(99.2 overs, 357 mins)	420		(49.1 overs, 161 mins)	129

QUEENSLAND	O	M	R	W	w,nb		O	M	R	W	w,nb			FALL OF WICKETS		
Gilbert	22	0	98	4	-,-		14.6	1	68	2	-,-			SA	QLD	SA	QLD
Cook	5	1	16	0	-,-	(7)	5	0	18	0	-,-	Wkt	1st	1st	2nd	2nd
Thurlow	22	1	106	4	-,-		14	1	50	0	-,-	1st	19	54	15	11
Oxenham	20	8	36	0	-,-	(5)	17	6	35	1	-,-	2nd	210	79	106	12
Bensted	13	0	67	0	-,-	(6)	8	1	44	2	1,-	3rd	243	160	180	29
Hubbard	11.1	2	42	2	-,-	(2)	17	3	48	2	-,-	4th	255	166	182	64
Hansen	4	0	20	0	-,-	(4)	1	0	10	0	-,-	5th	263	180	188	75
												6th	309	199	188	90
SOUTH AUSTRALIA	O	M	R	W	w,nb		O	M	R	W	w,nb	7th	309	390	188	98
Wall	15	2	55	2	-,2							8th	383	394	231	107
Carlton	22	6	72	1	-,1		15	5	24	3	-,-	9th	404	414	237	116
Jamieson	12	1	49	0	-,-	(1)	6	2	13	1	-,-	10th	410	420	289	129
Grimmett	27.2	1	114	3	-,-		17.1	5	44	5	-,-					
Lee	23	1	104	3	-,1	(3)	11	2	40	1	-,-					

VICTORIA v TASMANIA

Played at South Melbourne Cricket Ground on March 15, 16, 17, 18, 1932. (Four-day match)
Toss : Victoria.   Result : TASMANIA WON BY FIVE WICKETS.
Debuts: Victoria - E.R.Lanigan (f/c).
12th Men: G.H.Newstead (Vic) and D.Jones (Tas).
Umpires: C.Juliff and H.E.Nichols.
Attendances: 294, 513, 1054, 744.   Total: 2605   Receipts: £41.
Close of Play: 1st day Vic 0/28 (O'Brien 9, Thomas 19); 2nd day Vic 5/203 (Oakley 51, Quin 17); 3rd day Tas 8/176 (Newton 25, Putman 4).

E.L.McCormick (ill) and V.G.Nagel were unavailable for Victoria. Lanigan was chosen to replace H.H.Alexander (a late withdrawal) solely on his performance for Sale-Maffra in the Country Week competition. Rain curtailed play to 25 minutes on the first day and 150 minutes on the second. Though scheduled for only three days, the captains agreed to continue the match into a fourth (10.30 am - 1.30 pm only) in view of the time lost. Morton, whose declaration challenged Tasmania to score a modest 92 in 75 minutes, did the hat-trick (Atkinson, Richardson, Parry) in his last first-class appearance as Nash led his team to victory with 18 minutes to spare. Thomas (68 in 81 minutes, 1 six and 7 fours) and Oakley (84 in 142 minutes, 6 fours) for Victoria and Atkinson (58 in 165 minutes, 2 fours) for Tasmania registered fifties. This was the second and last first-class match to be staged at the ground otherwise known as the Lakeside Oval. Sources: *Australian Cricketer, VCA Report, TCA Report, The Age, The Argus, The Herald.*

VICTORIA

L.P.J.O'Brien	c Atkinson b Richardson	10	b Nash	9
J.Thomas	c Putman b Newton	68		
L.S.Darling	c & b Newton	38		
H.H.Oakley	b Richardson	84		
I.S.Lee	c Parry b Burrows	4		
L.J.Junor	c Parry b Newton	8	(3) not out	0
†S.O.Quin	lbw b Burrows	22	(2) lbw b Nash	14
R.J.Hassett	not out	39		
L.O.Fleetwood-Smith	b Putman	4		
E.R.Lanigan	b Richardson	6		
*F.L.Morton	b Putman	7		
Extras	(b5, lb6, w1)	12		–
Total	(58.5 overs, 249 mins)	302	(6.1 overs, 26 mins) (2 wkts dec)	23

TASMANIA

*J.A.Atkinson	b Fleetwood-Smith	58	b Morton	17
C.L.Badcock	run out (Oakley)	3	(7) not out	10
D.C.Green	c Junor b Fleetwood-Smith	27		
L.J.Nash	b Fleetwood-Smith	4	(2) not out	43
A.O.Burrows	c Fleetwood-Smith b Lanigan	2		
R.O.G.Morrisby	c Hassett b Fleetwood-Smith	24		
A.C.Newton	c Fleetwood-Smith b Hassett	41	(6) c Lee b Morton	17
L.W.Richardson	st Quin b Hassett	13	(3) c Fleetwood-Smith b Morton	0
K.W.J.Cahill	st Quin b Hassett	1		
S.W.L.Putman	not out	20	(5) b Morton	4
†C.N.Parry	c Morton b Lanigan	24	(4) b Morton	0
Extras	(b6, lb9, nb2)	17	(b1)	1
Total	(79.1 overs, 271 mins)	234	(13.0 overs, 57 mins) (5 wkts)	92

TASMANIA	O	M	R	W	w,nb	O	M	R	W	w,nb
Nash	18	2	78	0	-,-	3.1	2	8	2	-,-
Burrows	12	0	50	2	1,-	3	0	15	0	-,-
Richardson	10	0	47	3	-,-					
Newton	15	1	84	3	-,-					
Putman	3.5	0	31	2	-,-					

VICTORIA	O	M	R	W	w,nb	O	M	R	W	w,nb
Lanigan	20.1	1	44	2	-,-	2	0	15	0	-,-
Morton	18	9	30	0	-,2	6	0	40	5	-,-
Darling	3	0	11	0	-,-	2	0	14	0	-,-
Fleetwood-Smith	28	3	88	4	-,-	3	0	22	0	-,-
Hassett	10	0	44	3	-,-					

FALL OF WICKETS

	VIC	TAS	VIC	TAS
Wkt	1st	1st	2nd	2nd
1st	30	5	18	33
2nd	108	55	23	33
3rd	128	73	-	33
4th	143	86	-	41
5th	160	129	-	79
6th	225	134	-	-
7th	265	162	-	-
8th	278	164	-	-
9th	287	204	-	-
10th	302	234	-	-

NEW SOUTH WALES v SOUTH AUSTRALIA (Shield Match 12)

Played at Sydney Cricket Ground on March 19, 21, 22, 1932. (Four-day match)
Toss : South Australia.   Result : SOUTH AUSTRALIA WON BY 132 RUNS.
Debuts: Nil.
12th Men: R.C.Rowe (NSW) and D.G.Jamieson (SA).
Umpires: E.G.Borwick and W.G.French.
Attendances: 9985, 7979, 3553.   Total: 21,517.   Receipts: £998.
Close of Play: 1st day NSW 2/9 (Nutt 6, Hird 0); 2nd day SA (2) 2/117 (Nitschke 70, Catchlove 8).

Despite South Australia winning this last match of the Shield season with more than a day to spare, drawing level with New South Wales on 20 points, the side had little prospect of winning the competition due to a significantly inferior batting average and the title consequently went to the home team. Bill and Donnelly (originally 12th man) replaced A.F.Kippax and L.R.Leabeater (both unavailable) in the New South Wales line-up, Oldfield assuming the captaincy in Kippax's absence. Lonergan (68 in 135 minutes, 6 fours), Whitfield (51 in 91 minutes, 4 fours) and in the second innings Nitschke (119 in 213 minutes, 6 fours) made the highest scores for South Australia. O'Reilly ended his first big season by securing five wickets in each innings; in the first over after lunch on the third day he took 3 for 2, dismissing Grimmett, Walker and Wall with his first, third and seventh balls. Donnelly (57 in 75 minutes, 7 fours) and Bill (76 not out in 138 minutes, 5 fours) scored the only fifties for New South Wales, after Wall had bowled Fingleton and Hunt with the fourth and seventh balls of the first innings. McCabe took no further part after straining a hip on the first day; he thus preserved his Shield average of 438 for the season (three hundreds in three innings, once out). *Wisden* incorrectly gives SA (2) Whitfield 20. Sources: *Wisden, Australian Cricketer, NSWCA Report, SACA Report, Sydney Morning Herald, NSWCA Scorebook.*

SOUTH AUSTRALIA

*V.Y.Richardson	lbw b Hunt	23	lbw b Hunt	14
H.C.Nitschke	c Oldfield b Theak	45	run out (Donnelly)	119
A.R.Lonergan	b O'Reilly	68	b O'Reilly	20
W.E.Catchlove	lbw b O'Reilly	9	c & b O'Reilly	11
H.E.Whitfield	c Bill b O'Reilly	51	run out	30
M.G.Waite	c Oldfield b Theak	23	lbw b Theak	15
P.K.Lee	b Theak	8	c O'Reilly b Theak	4
C.V.Grimmett	b O'Reilly	3	c Donnelly b O'Reilly	1
†C.W.Walker	c & b O'Reilly	6	lbw b O'Reilly	2
T.W.Wall	c & b Hird	10	b O'Reilly	0
T.A.Carlton	not out	6	not out	0
Extras	(b6, lb12, nb2)	20	(b7, nb2)	9
Total	(85.6 overs, 299 mins)	272	(69.0 overs, 244 mins)	225

NEW SOUTH WALES

J.H.W.Fingleton	b Wall	0	(6) b Grimmett	24
R.N.Nutt	b Lee	33	b Whitfield	6
W.A.Hunt	b Wall	0	(9) c Richardson b Lee	1
S.F.Hird	lbw b Carlton	2	(5) lbw b Grimmett	5
D.G.Bradman	b Carlton	23	(3) b Wall	0
J.L.Donnelly	c Walker b Wall	57	(1) c Carlton b Grimmett	18
O.W.Bill	not out	76	(4) st Walker b Grimmett	46
*†W.A.S.Oldfield	lbw b Grimmett	31	(7) c Richardson b Lee	6
W.J.O'Reilly	c Richardson b Lee	5	(8) run out	0
H.J.T.Theak	st Walker b Lee	1	not out	4
S.J.McCabe	absent hurt	-	absent hurt	-
Extras	(b8, lb7, w1, nb3)	19	(b3, lb5)	8
Total	(55.1 overs, 229 mins)	247	(46.2 overs, 167 mins)	118

NEW SOUTH WALES	O	M	R	W	w,nb		O	M	R	W	w,nb
Theak	22	2	68	3	-,-		20	3	62	2	-,1
McCabe	5	1	13	0	-,-						
O'Reilly	29	4	68	5	-,2		25	6	59	5	-,-
Hunt	14	1	40	1	-,-	(2)	12	3	44	1	-,1
Hird	15.6	1	63	1	-,-	(4)	12	0	51	0	-,-

SOUTH AUSTRALIA	O	M	R	W	w,nb		O	M	R	W	w,nb
Wall	16	1	63	3	-,3		5	0	24	1	-,-
Whitfield	8	0	31	0	1,-		4	1	8	1	-,-
Carlton	8	1	30	2	-,-		4	1	12	0	-,-
Grimmett	16	1	75	1	-,-		19	9	32	4	-,-
Lee	7.1	2	29	3	-,-		14.2	1	34	2	-,-

FALL OF WICKETS

Wkt	SA 1st	NSW 1st	SA 2nd	NSW 2nd
1st	43	0	41	15
2nd	116	0	92	16
3rd	140	11	123	44
4th	160	55	187	56
5th	234	85	213	97
6th	244	151	218	106
7th	248	227	219	106
8th	248	240	221	113
9th	266	247	221	118
10th	272	-	225	-

WESTERN AUSTRALIA v SOUTH AFRICAN XI

Played at W.A.C.A. Ground, Perth, on March 19, 21, 22, 1932. (Four-day match)
Toss : Western Australia.   Result : SOUTH AFRICAN XI WON BY AN INNINGS AND 242 RUNS.
Debuts: Western Australia - F.J.Alexander, W.Hill-Smith, P.B.Wood (all f/c).
12th Men: A.D.Drew (WA) and L.S.Brown (SAF).
Umpires: F.R.Buttsworth and J.Hart.
Attendances: 3500, 1320, 650.   Total: 5470.   Receipts: £360.
Close of Play: 1st day SAF 1/98 (Mitchell 56, Cameron 6); 2nd day SAF 8/437 (Morkel 109, Quinn 16).

R.J.Bryant (ill) was unavailable for Western Australia. South Africa were without H.W.Taylor, who had left for England, and S.S.L.Steyn and E.A.van der Merwe who had earlier returned to South Africa. Mitchell's 125 occupied 187 minutes (16 fours) with a chance at 86. Morkel made the highest score by a South African on the tour, batting 167 minutes with 16 fours and 3 sixes. He gave only one chance, in the 90's, and dominated a ninth-wicket partnership of 171 in 138 minutes with Quinn. Morkel followed up with a devastating spell of swing bowling. Hill-Smith's first innings (75 minutes, 8 fours) was the only bright spot in a disappointing display of batting by Western Australia. *The West Australian* gives WA (2) extras 6, total 62. Sources: *Wisden, NSWCA Report, VCA Report, Australian Cricketer, The West Australian, Daily News.*

WESTERN AUSTRALIA

F.H.Taaffe	c Cameron b Bell	23	(2) b Bell		0
W.Hill-Smith	c Bell b Balaskas	56	(1) c Bell b Morkel		13
F.J.Alexander	run out (Dalton/Cameron)	6	(5) b Morkel		0
E.H.Bromley	c Cameron b Quinn	5	b Morkel		5
P.W.E.Curtin	run out (Dalton)	12	(3) c Cameron b Bell		14
P.B.Wood	c Cameron b Vincent	6	c Balaskas b Morkel		2
R.O.Doig	c & b Balaskas	12	(8) not out		15
M.Inverarity	b Quinn	28	(7) b Morkel		0
W.A.Evans	lbw b Balaskas	0	c Balaskas b Morkel		1
*†R.H.Hewson	c Cameron b Quinn	16	c Mitchell b Morkel		1
R.A.Halcombe	not out	5	c & b Morkel		5
Extras	(b10, lb4)	14	(lb2, w1, nb4)		7
Total	(60.0 overs, 213 mins)	183	(20.0 overs, 85 mins)		63

SOUTH AFRICAN XI

J.A.J.Christy	c Evans b Inverarity	29
B.Mitchell	c Wood b Inverarity	125
*†H.B.Cameron	c & b Inverarity	58
S.H.Curnow	lbw b Halcombe	19
X.C.Balaskas	c Hill-Smith b Halcombe	38
K.G.Viljoen	lbw b Halcombe	0
E.L.Dalton	c Evans b Inverarity	11
D.P.B.Morkel	not out	150
C.L.Vincent	c Evans b Inverarity	8
N.A.Quinn	run out (sub A.D.Drew)	24
A.J.Bell	not out	1
Extras	(b17, lb6, nb2)	25
Total	(113.0 overs, 430 mins) (9 wkts dec)	488

SOUTH AFRICAN XI	O	M	R	W	w,nb	O	M	R	W	w,nb
Bell	13	1	35	1	-,-	7	2	22	2	1,-
Quinn	17	6	38	3	-,-	5	1	21	0	-,-
Morkel	4	1	17	0	-,-	8	2	13	8	-,4
Balaskas	12	1	48	3	-,-					
Vincent	13	4	26	1	-,-					
Mitchell	1	0	5	0	-,-					

WESTERN AUSTRALIA	O	M	R	W	w,nb
Halcombe	27	3	101	3	-,1
Evans	19	3	59	0	-,-
Curtin	10	2	36	0	-,-
Inverarity	25	0	144	5	-,-
Bromley	18	5	56	0	-,-
Alexander	6	0	25	0	-,1
Doig	4	0	26	0	-,-
Wood	4	0	16	0	-,-

		FALL OF WICKETS		
		WA	SAF	WA
Wkt	1st	1st	2nd	
1st	81	82	4	
2nd	85	219	20	
3rd	90	228	28	
4th	112	264	28	
5th	112	264	36	
6th	121	294	36	
7th	137	298	36	
8th	137	309	45	
9th	178	480	48	
10th	183	-	63	

The tour of the 22nd English team to Australia, under the leadership of D.R.Jardine, was one of the most acrimonious and controversial cricket tours of all time. Jardine's insistence on the use of packed leg-side field placings and fast short-pitched bowling at the upper bodies of the local batsmen - Bodyline, as it became known - was deeply resented by all Australians for its malicious and unsporting nature. Jardine had devised Bodyline to combat Bradman's run-scoring powers, and ti this extent the tactics succeeded, but at cost. Relations between the countries were put under great strain at the highest level and the tour came close to being called off, following an exchange of cables between the Australian Board of Control and MCC during the Third Test. Fortunately, relations were restored in the following years with skilful management and leadership, and no lasting damage was done.

The Englishmen played 22 matches on the tour (17 first-class), winning 10 of these and drawing 10. They tied one match against Victoria and sustained their single loss in the Second Test at Melbourne. They took the Test series 4-1. Sutcliffe, Hammond, Leyland, Wyatt, Jardine, Pataudi and Ames all scored heavily, but the sustained accuracy of Larwood's fast bowling held the key to the success of the team. Larwood was well supported by Voce (left-arm fast), Allen (right-arm fast), Bowes (right-arm fast-medium) and Verity (left-arm spin).

Bradman, although curbed, was still the most successful of the Australian batsmen in the Test matches. He often adopted unorthodox methods in his attempt to combat Bodyline - stepping to leg and hitting through the vacant off side field wherever possible. Richardson and Woodfull showed great courage in their resolute batting and McCabe's innings of 187 not out in the First test is recognised as one of the greatest of all Test Innings. O'Reilly was the outstanding Australian bowler, Ironmonger and Wall toiling hard in support.

New South Wales retained the Sheffield Shield and were clearly the best side in the competition. They possessed the best batsman (Bradman) and best bowler (O'Reilly) in the country, and the secondary players gave them sufficient backup support. Fingleton and Brown forged an opening partnership that would serve both State and country in time, and McCabe and Kippax contributed depth in the middle order.

Woodfull and Ponsford continued their successful partnership for Victoria, whose lineup of talented young players included Darling, Rigg, O'Brien, Oakley and Bromley. Ironmonger and Fleetwood-Smith, left-arm spin bowlers with contrasting styles, led the bowling and received pace support from Alexander. But Victoria failed to capitalise on their promise, and two of their wins were recorded against lowly Queensland.

South Australia experienced similar results with a side which also looked basically sound. Richardson, Nitschke and Lonergan (batting) and Grimmett, Lee and Wall (bowling) provided the nucleus of the team. Wall had the distinction of becoming the first bowler to capture 10 wickets in an innings in the Sheffield Shield competition, in the match against New South Wales at Sydney. Queensland experienced a dismal season, losing all their six matches outright despite the continuing contributions of Oxenham, the allrounder.

As in the 1928-29 season when England last toured, 32 first-class matches were played this summer. This remained the record number for an Australian season until after the Second World War.

Leading Aggregates

Batsmen	M	I	NO	Runs	HS	Ave.	Bowlers	Runs	Wkts	Ave.
H.Sutcliffe (MCC)	13	19	1	1318	194	73.22	W.J.O'Reilly (NSW)	1237	62	19.95
D.G.Bradman (NSW)	11	21	2	1171	238	61.63	C.V.Grimmett (SA)	1577	55	28.67
W.R.Hammond (MCC)	12	18	1	948	203	55.76	L.O.Fleetwood-Smith (V)	1095	50	21.90
V.Y.Richardson (SA)	13	25	1	924	203	38.50	H.Larwood (MCC)	817	49	16.67
R.E.S.Wyatt (MCC)	16	25	2	883	78	38.39	H.Ironmonger (V)	933	47	19.85
M.Leyland (MCC)	13	21	1	880	152*	44.00	H.Verity (MCC)	698	44	15.86
S.J.McCabe (NSW)	12	20	1	872	187*	45.89	G.O.B.Allen (MCC)	899	39	23.05
L.S.Darling (V)	10	16	0	809	185	50.56	P.K.Lee (SA)	787	33	23.84
H.C.Nitschke (SA)	8	15	0	695	105	46.33	W.Voce (MCC)	866	32	27.06
L.P.J.O'Brien (V)	11	19	2	650	145*	38.23	W.E.Bowes (MCC)	838	30	27.93

SHEFFIELD SHIELD TABLE

	P	WO	W1	LO	L1	D	Pts	Quotient	Runs Scored	Wkts Lost	Runs Conceded	Wkts Taken
NEW SOUTH WALES	6	5	1	-	-	-	28	1.627	3065	88	2333	109
VICTORIA	6	3	-	2	1	-	16	1.281	2668	89	2269	97
SOUTH AUSTRALIA	6	3	-	3	-	-	15	1.107	2407	98	2573	116
QUEENSLAND	6	-	-	6	-	-	0	0.390	1783	118	2748	71
TOTAL	12	11	1	11	1	-	59	1.000	9923	393	9923	393

WESTERN AUSTRALIA v M.C.C.

Played at W.A.C.A. Ground, Perth, on October 21, 22 (no play), 24, 1932. (Three-day match)
Toss : M.C.C.   Result : MATCH DRAWN.
Debuts: Western Australia - H.Calder, C.M.B.Jarvis, O.I.Lovelock, E.J.Martin, B.O'Shaughnessy (all f/c).
12th Men: W.A.Evans (WA) and E.Paynter (MCC).
Umpires: F.R.Buttsworth and J.Hart.
Attendances: 4450, 'very few', 3000.   Total: About 7500.   Receipts: £419.
Close of Play: 1st day MCC 8/334 (Larwood 28, Mitchell 3); 2nd day no play.

Pataudi recorded a century in his first innings in Australia. He batted 252 minutes, hit 15 fours and 1 six, and a stumping chance just prior to reaching 50 was his only mistake. Sutcliffe (121 minutes, 4 fours) and Jardine (41 minutes, 3 fours) also found some early form. Rain prevented any play on the second day as the pitch - although covered at each end - was soaked. Larwood bowled Curtin with the sixth ball of the Western Australian innings, during which Bryant (45 minutes, 3 fours, 1 five) was the topscorer. WA saved the follow-on by the smallest possible margin. In the second innings Leyland (85 minutes, 9 fours, 1 six) did well for MCC. Brown was missed five times (four from the bowling of Martin and one from Halcombe) during his 44 minute stay. The first murmurs of the Bodyline crisis were recorded on the third day. 'When Bowes struck Drew on the shoulder with a bumping ball the crowd became caustic,' noted one local paper. *Wisden* has incorrect match dates and records Curtin as 'Curtis'. Sources: *Wisden, NSWCA Report, VCA Report, The West Australian, Daily News, Australian Cricketer.*

M.C.C.

H.Sutcliffe	st Lovelock b Martin	54			
M.Leyland	c O'Shaughnessy b Inverarity	15	c Hill-Smith b Martin	69	
Nawab of Pataudi, sr	c Jarvis b Martin	166			
R.E.S.Wyatt	lbw b Martin	22	(1) b Halcombe	14	
*D.R.Jardine	b Halcombe	38	(6) not out	2	
†L.E.G.Ames	b Halcombe	0	(3) b O'Shaughnessy	19	
F.R.Brown	c Calder b Curtin	2	(4) c Jarvis b Martin	28	
H.Larwood	not out	28			
H.Verity	lbw b Halcombe	1	(5) st Lovelock b Martin	17	
T.B.Mitchell	not out	3			
W.E.Bowes	did not bat				
Extras	(b2, lb1, nb2)	5	(lb1, w1, nb1)	3	
Total	(78.0 overs, 295 mins) (8 wkts dec)	334	(31.6 overs, 110 mins) (5 wkts)	152	

WESTERN AUSTRALIA

P.W.E.Curtin	b Larwood	0
W.Hill-Smith	c Wyatt b Brown	26
A.D.Drew	c Wyatt b Brown	17
H.Calder	b Brown	9
C.M.B.Jarvis	b Larwood	3
*R.J.Bryant	b Verity	35
M.Inverarity	c & b Verity	15
†O.I.Lovelock	not out	14
E.J.Martin	b Mitchell	2
B.O'Shaughnessy	run out (Brown/Ames)	0
R.A.Halcombe	c Brown b Mitchell	1
Extras	(b9, lb3, w1)	13
Total	(45.0 overs, 175 mins)	135

WESTERN AUSTRALIA	O	M	R	W	w,nb		O	M	R	W	w,nb
Halcombe	17	2	48	3	-,1		9	0	38	1	-,-
O'Shaughnessy	13	1	50	0	-,1		5	1	31	1	-,1
Inverarity	14	2	43	1	-,-	(4)	4	1	18	0	-,-
Curtin	11	1	40	1	-,-						
Martin	16	1	115	3	-,-		7.6	0	50	3	1,-
Bryant	4	0	13	0	-,-		3	1	5	0	-,-
Drew	3	1	20	0	-,-	(3)	3	0	7	0	-,-

M.C.C.	O	M	R	W	w,nb
Larwood	6	0	17	2	-,-
Bowes	12	1	33	0	-,-
Mitchell	6	1	19	2	-,-
Brown	10	2	29	3	1,-
Verity	9	2	20	2	-,-
Wyatt	2	1	4	0	-,-

FALL OF WICKETS

	MCC	WA	MCC
Wkt	1st	1st	2nd
1st	25	0	17
2nd	118	36	75
3rd	180	58	122
4th	253	60	144
5th	255	62	152
6th	260	116	-
7th	324	119	-
8th	330	124	-
9th	-	126	-
10th	-	135	-

AUSTRALIAN XI v M.C.C.

Played at W.A.C.A. Ground, Perth, on October 27, 28, 29, 1932. (Three-day match)
Toss : M.C.C.   Result : MATCH DRAWN.
Debuts: Nil.
12th Men: M.Inverarity (Aust) and W.E.Bowes (MCC).
Umpires: F.R.Buttsworth and J.Hart.
Attendances: 10947, 12000, 19970.   Total: 42,917   Receipts: £3343.
Close of Play: 1st day MCC 3/359 (Hammond 37, Ames 15); 2nd day Aust 0/59 (Richardson 21, Fingleton 28).

In a match which aroused tremendous excitement among Western Australians, new attendance records were easily set for a match and a single day's play at the ground. Bryant was forced to leave the field on the first day with a leg strain which he had reportedly carried into the match; Richardson led the Australians in his absence. Sutcliffe (235 minutes, 16 fours, 1 five, 1 six) and Pataudi (268 minutes, 12 fours, 1 six) added 283 for the second wicket for MCC, while Hammond (192 minutes, 6 fours, 1 six) and Jardine (168 minutes, with 11 fours) were partly responsible for one of Bradman's rarer on-field centuries. Overnight precipitation forced the Australians to bat on a rain-affected wicket on the last day. *NSWCA Report* and *VCA Report* incorrectly give Ames 28 runs. Sources: *Wisden, NSWCA Report, VCA Report, The West Australian, Daily News, Australian Cricketer.*

M.C.C

H.Sutcliffe	c sub (M.Inverarity) b Evans	169
M.Leyland	lbw b McCabe	2
Nawab of Pataudi, sr	c Evans b Halcombe	129
W.R.Hammond	b Bryant	77
L.E.G.Ames	b McCabe	23
*D.R.Jardine	c McCabe b Bradman	98
G.O.B.Allen	b Bradman	16
E.Paynter	not out	32
H.Verity	not out	14
†G.Duckworth	) did not bat	
T.B.Mitchell	)	
Extras	(b9, lb12, w1, nb1)	23
Total	(153.0 overs, 520 mins) (7 wkts dec)	583

AUSTRALIAN XI

V.Y.Richardson	c Sutcliffe b Verity	27		b Allen	0
J.H.W.Fingleton	c Duckworth b Verity	29		not out	53
D.G.Bradman	c Hammond b Verity	3		c Pataudi b Allen	10
A.R.Lonergan	c Duckworth b Verity	10		b Paynter	23
S.J.McCabe	b Paynter	43			
W.Hill-Smith	c Jardine b Verity	17	(5)	c Duckworth b Ames	32
*R.J.Bryant	c Mitchell b Verity	0	(6)	not out	12
†O.I.Lovelock	c Hammond b Mitchell	11			
W.A.Evans	c Allen b Verity	0			
E.J.Martin	st Duckworth b Mitchell	1			
R.A.Halcombe	not out	1			
Extras	(b11, lb5, nb1)	17		(lb7, w1, nb1)	9
Total	(46.2 overs, 171 mins)	159		(42.0 overs, 143 mins) (4 wkts)	139

AUSTRALIAN XI	O	M	R	W	w,nb
Halcombe	29	3	81	1	1,1
McCabe	36	7	87	2	-,-
Evans	34	10	89	1	-,-
Martin	16	0	126	0	-,-
Bradman	19	1	106	2	-,-
Richardson	3	0	13	0	-,-
Bryant	16	1	58	1	-,-

M.C.C.	O	M	R	W	w,nb		O	M	R	W	w,nb
Allen	4	0	24	0	-,1		7	2	16	2	1,1
Hammond	9	1	29	0	-,-	(4)	3	1	7	0	-,-
Mitchell	13	2	37	2	-,-						
Verity	18	7	37	7	-,-	(3)	1	0	2	0	-,-
Leyland	2	0	15	0	-,-		8	1	23	0	-,-
Paynter	0.2	0	0	1	-,-	(2)	12	1	31	1	-,-
Ames						(6)	6	0	25	1	-,-
Sutcliffe						(7)	3	0	18	0	-,-
Jardine						(8)	2	1	8	0	-,-

FALL OF WICKETS

Wkt	MCC 1st	AUST 1st	AUST 2nd
1st	4	61	0
2nd	287	67	19
3rd	335	76	53
4th	384	89	113
5th	462	115	-
6th	509	115	-
7th	544	148	-
8th	-	149	-
9th	-	154	-
10th	-	159	-

QUEENSLAND v VICTORIA (Shield Match 1)

Played at Brisbane Cricket Ground (Woolloongabba) on October 28, 29, 31, 1932. (Four-day match)
Toss : Victoria.   Result : VICTORIA WON BY AN INNINGS AND 329 RUNS.
Debuts: Queensland - J.M.Govan (f/c).
12th Men: B.V.Suche (Qld) and J.Thomas (Vic).
Umpires: J.Bartlett and J.A.Scott.
Attendances: 4000, 5403, 500.   Total: 9903.   Receipts: £497.
Close of Play: 1st day Vic 3/382 (O'Brien 105, Darling 116); 2nd day Qld (2) 2/42 (Gough 17, Hansen 7).

Queensland suffered their all-time heaviest defeat by an innings margin and recorded their lowest total in the Sheffield Shield so far, losing all ten first-innings wickets for just 27 runs in faultless conditions to left-arm spinners Fleetwood-Smith and Ironmonger. Gough (34 in 91 minutes, 2 fours) and Hansen (59 in 111 minutes, 8 fours) topscored in the follow-on. Victoria amassed 552 after winning the toss, Woodfull (35 in 82 minutes, 2 fours) and Ponsford (98 in 173 minutes, 4 fours) giving way to O'Brien (145 not out in 370 minutes, 13 fours, 2 late chances) and Darling (chanceless 185 in 226 minutes, 23 fours) who added 301 in partnership, a new State fourth-wicket record. Sides, a regular gloveman in Townsville before he moved to Brisbane, kept wicket serviceably on the second day as a replacement for Waterman, who had sustained a slight hand injury. Oxenham took 3 for 1 as Victoria lost their last 6 for 40. Govan was introduced to first-class cricket at the age of 17 years 302 days. Sources: *Wisden, QCA Report, VCA Report, Brisbane Courier, Australian Cricketer.*

VICTORIA

*W.M.Woodfull	b Govan	35
W.H.Ponsford;	run out (Hansen/Waterman)	98
K.E.Rigg	st Waterman b Govan	13
L.P.J.O'Brien	not out	145
L.S.Darling	st Sides b Govan	185
H.H.Oakley	b Oxenham	27
†B.A.Barnett	b Bensted	18
D.D.Blackie	run out (Gough/Bensted)	3
H.H.Alexander	b Oxenham	0
L.O.Fleetwood-Smith	b Oxenham	0
H.Ironmonger	b Oxenham	1
Extras	(b18, lb3, w1, nb5)	27
Total	(129.1 overs, 482 mins)	552

QUEENSLAND

*F.J.Gough	b Fleetwood-Smith	13		c Woodfull b Ironmonger	34
G.G.Cook	b Ironmonger	13		lbw b Darling	0
W.C.Andrews	lbw b Fleetwood-Smith	6		b Fleetwood-Smith	16
C.D.Hansen	b Fleetwood-Smith	0		b Alexander	59
E.C.Bensted	c Blackie b Ironmonger	5	(6)	run out (Oakley/Barnett)	8
F.W.Sides	b Ironmonger	1	(7)	c Fleetwood-Smith b Blackie	15
R.K.Oxenham	not out	3	(5)	lbw b Fleetwood-Smith	9
†L.W.Waterman	c Ponsford b Ironmonger	6		b Alexander	16
E.Gilbert	b Fleetwood-Smith	0		c Ponsford b Blackie	1
J.M.Govan	b Fleetwood-Smith	1		run out (Darling/Barnett)	2
H.M.Thurlow	b Fleetwood-Smith	0		not out	0
Extras	(b6)	6		(b4, lb5)	9
Total	(30.0 overs, 108 mins)	54		(53.2 overs, 184 mins)	169

QUEENSLAND	O	M	R	W	w,nb
Gilbert	8	0	58	0	1,-
Thurlow	22	2	79	0	-,5
Oxenham	36.1	6	95	4	-,-
Bensted	27	3	86	1	-,-
Govan	31	2	194	3	-,-
Andrews	3	0	9	0	-,-
Cook	2	0	4	0	-,-

VICTORIA	O	M	R	W	w,nb	O	M	R	W	w,nb
Alexander	5	0	12	0	-,-	9	2	21	2	-,-
Darling	3	0	5	0	-,-	2	0	14	1	-,-
Fleetwood-Smith	12	2	22	6	-,-	18	3	77	2	-,-
Ironmonger	10	8	9	4	-,-	17	7	29	1	-,-
Blackie						7.2	1	19	2	-,-

FALL OF WICKETS

Wkt	VIC 1st	QLD 1st	QLD 2nd
1st	76	27	2
2nd	114	33	32
3rd	180	33	82
4th	481	33	113
5th	512	41	133
6th	543	44	133
7th	548	52	155
8th	548	52	160
9th	548	54	168
10th	552	54	169

NEW SOUTH WALES v VICTORIA (Shield Match 2)

Played at Sydney Cricket Ground on November 4, 5, 7, 8, 1932. (Four-day match)
Toss : Victoria.   Result : NEW SOUTH WALES WON BY NINE WICKETS.
Debuts: New South Wales - C.J.Hill (f/c).
12th Men: W.A.Brown (NSW) and H.H.Oakley (Vic).
Umpires: E.G.Borwick and W.G.French.
Attendances: 9694, 24658, 7015, 689.   Total: 42,056   Receipts: £1907.
Close of Play: 1st day Vic 6/306 (Ponsford 163, Blackie 2); 2nd day NSW 4/358 (McCabe 36, Theak 0); 3rd day NSW (2) 0/0
  (Fingleton 0, Bill 0).

Despite Ponsford recording a double century (200 in 377 minutes, 13 fours, chance at 36), the match was dominated by the run-gathering of Bradman who scored a chanceless 238 (200 minutes, 32 fours) and an unbeaten 52 (41 minutes, 8 fours) including the winning boundary early on the last day. Arriving at the crease soon after lunch on the second day, he brought up his first fifty in 30 minutes and reached 100 in 73 minutes, being 126 at the tea break, before going on to 150 in 129 minutes and 200 in 172 minutes, the fastest-ever double century in a Sheffield Shield match. He was dismissed shortly before stumps, having made 238 out of 339 while at the crease. Supporting fifties came from Kippax (52 in 83 minutes, 5 fours) and McCabe (56 in 129 minutes, 2 fours). Alexander (right-arm fast) captured a career-best 7 for 95; his only five-wicket haul for Victoria, this earned him a sole Test berth at the end of the season. Woodfull compiled 74 (141 minutes, 7 fours) and 83 (128 minutes, 4 fours) in a losing cause, Ponsford being unable to partner him in the second innings because of an ankle injury sustained while fielding. Hird (legbreaks and googlies) took his best figures as the visitors lost their last 8 wickets for 53. Blackie replaced L.E.Nagel (unavailable) in the side before it left Melbourne. Sources: *Wisden, NSWCA Report, VCA Report, Sydney Morning Herald, The Age, The Argus.*

VICTORIA

*W.M.Woodfull	run out (Kippax)	74	st Oldfield b Hird		83
W.H.Ponsford	c Kippax b Hird	200	absent hurt		-
L.P.J.O'Brien	st Oldfield b Hird	15	(2) c Theak b McCabe		13
K.E.Rigg	lbw b O'Reilly	0	(3) run out (Bradman/Oldfield)		10
L.S.Darling	c Fingleton b O'Reilly	0	(4) b Hird		2
J.Thomas	b Hird	5	(5) not out		24
†B.A.Barnett	lbw b Bradman	36	(6) c Bradman b Hird		0
D.D.Blackie	c Oldfield b O'Reilly	20	(7) st Oldfield b Hird		1
L.O.Fleetwood-Smith	b O'Reilly	38	(8) c Bill b Hird		5
H.H.Alexander	c Hird b O'Reilly	1	(9) c Theak b Hird		6
H.Ironmonger	not out	3	(10) run out		0
Extras	(b9, lb2, nb1)	12	(lb4, w1, nb1)		6
Total	(125.4 overs, 393 mins)	404	(55.4 overs, 172 mins)		150

NEW SOUTH WALES

J.H.W.Fingleton	lbw b Alexander	6	not out	20
O.W.Bill	b Fleetwood-Smith	19	b Alexander	8
D.G.Bradman	c O'Brien b Fleetwood-Smith	238	not out	52
*A.F.Kippax	c Barnett b Alexander	52		
S.J.McCabe	c Fleetwood-Smith b Alexander	56		
H.J.T.Theak	b Alexander	39		
S.F.Hird	c Barnett b Alexander	6		
F.S.Cummins	b Alexander	13		
W.J.O'Reilly	c Barnett b Alexander	0		
†W.A.S.Oldfield	not out	22		
C.J.Hill	b Ironmonger	10		
Extras	(b8, lb6)	14	(b1, lb1)	2
Total	(93.1 overs, 335 mins)	475	(15.2 overs, 56 mins) (1 wkt)	82

NEW SOUTH WALES	O	M	R	W	w,nb		O	M	R	W	w,nb					
Theak	19	1	64	0	-,1		5	0	24	0	-,-					
McCabe	8	0	44	0	-,-	(5)	3	0	13	1	-,1	Wkt	1st	1st	2nd	2nd
Hill	21	5	48	0	-,-	(2)	10	1	15	0	-,-		VIC	NSW	VIC	NSW
O'Reilly	44.4	17	81	5	-,-	(3)	20	8	36	0	-,-	1st	138	16	71	19
Hird	23	0	115	3	-,-	(4)	17.4	1	56	6	1,-	2nd	185	93	97	-
Cummins	7	0	32	0	-,-							3rd	188	221	105	-
Bradman	3	0	8	1	-,-							4th	188	355	116	-
												5th	205	417	116	-
												6th	304	423	122	-
VICTORIA	O	M	R	W	w,nb		O	M	R	W	w,nb	7th	354	440	130	-
Alexander	22	1	95	7	-,-		3	0	23	1	-,-	8th	378	443	142	-
Darling	7	0	40	0	-,-		1	0	7	0	-,-	9th	383	444	150	-
Fleetwood-Smith	19	0	145	2	-,-		5	0	27	0	-,-	10th	404	475	-	-
Ironmonger	26.1	3	96	1	-,-		5	2	17	0	-,-					
Blackie	19	1	85	0	-,-		1.2	0	6	0	-,-					

FALL OF WICKETS

SOUTH AUSTRALIA v M.C.C.

Played at Adelaide Oval on November 4, 5, 7, 8, 1932. (Four-day match)
Toss : M.C.C.   Result : M.C.C. WON BY AN INNINGS AND 128 RUNS.
Debuts: South Australia - R.S.Whitington (f/c).
12th Men: C.S.Deverson (SA) and E.Paynter (MCC).
Umpires: G.A.Hele and E.H.Kitson.
Attendances: 12414, 23171, 13676, 2054.   Total: 51,315.   Receipts: £2311.
Close of Play: 1st day MCC 5/341 (Jardine 6, Verity 3); 2nd day SA 2/145 (Richardson 72); 3rd day SA (2) 2/106 (Lonergan 20, Catchlove 27).

Deverson and Whitington replaced G.W.Harris (business) and T.W.Wall (ill) in the selected South Australian side. Sutcliffe (154 in 259 minutes, 2 sixes and 13 fours) and Leyland (127 in 196 minutes, 14 fours) put on 223 for the first wicket after Leyland had been missed before he had scored and again when 93. Jardine (108 not out in 213 minutes, 10 fours) added 135 with Wyatt (61 in 108 minutes, 7 fours) and 106 with Larwood (81 in only 42 minutes, 2 sixes and 10 fours), who reached fifty in 27 minutes. Brown's 27 took just 7 minutes (2 sixes and 3 fours). Richardson (134 in 235 minutes, 17 fours) and Nitschke (69 in 85 minutes, 3 sixes and 6 fours) replied promisingly with an opening stand of 134, but after the rest failed, Jardine enforced the follow-on, in which Catchlove (65 in 209 minutes, 3 fours) topscored. Larwood, troubled by a blister on each big toe, was bowled sparingly and Bodyline tactics were not tested. Sources: *Wisden, SACA Report, VCA Report, Adelaide Advertiser, The Age, Sydney Morning Herald.*.

M.C.C.

H.Sutcliffe	c Nitschke b Grimmett	154
M.Leyland	c Nitschke b Grimmett	127
Nawab of Pataudi, sr	run out (Nitschke/Walker)	0
W.R.Hammond	st Walker b Grimmett	27
†L.E.G.Ames	c & b Jamieson	10
*D.R.Jardine	not out	108
H.Verity	lbw b Tobin	15
R.E.S.Wyatt	lbw b Grimmett	61
H.Larwood	c Whitington b Waite	81
F.R.Brown	c Nitschke b Waite	27
W.E.Bowes	not out	3
Extras	(b5, lb14, nb2)	21
Total	(139.0 overs, 486 mins) (9 wkts dec)	634

SOUTH AUSTRALIA

*V.Y.Richardson	c Leyland b Wyatt	134	lbw b Verity	25
H.C.Nitschke	b Verity	69	lbw b Brown	28
A.R.Lonergan	lbw b Brown	3	c Brown b Verity	20
W.E.Catchlove	st Ames b Verity	17	c Pataudi b Verity	65
R.S.Whitington	lbw b Brown	5	(6) run out (Ames)	0
D.G.Jamieson	c Hammond b Verity	1	(7) c & b Verity	7
B.J.Tobin	b Bowes	10	(8) c Hammond b Verity	19
M.G.Waite	c Verity b Bowes	3	(9) b Bowes	1
P.K.Lee	not out	22	(5) lbw b Brown	29
C.V.Grimmett	c Ames b Brown	17	b Bowes	2
†C.W.Walker	b Brown	1	not out	0
Extras	(b3, lb3, nb2)	8	(b8, lb9, nb3)	20
Total	(74.1 overs, 269 mins)	290	(73.6 overs, 269 mins)	216

SOUTH AUSTRALIA	O	M	R	W	w,nb
Tobin	28	5	119	1	-,2
Jamieson	33	3	113	1	-,-
Grimmett	40	5	176	4	-,-
Lee	15	3	46	0	-,-
Waite	18	0	108	2	-,-
Whitington	2	0	20	0	-,-
Richardson	3	0	31	0	-,-

M.C.C.	O	M	R	W	w,nb		O	M	R	W	w,nb
Larwood	5	0	35	0	-,-						
Bowes	13	1	82	2	-,1	(1)	19	3	57	2	-,3
Brown	21.1	5	81	4	-,-	(4)	18	2	66	2	-,-
Verity	26	10	45	3	-,1	(3)	24.6	13	42	5	-,-
Hammond	7	1	24	0	-,-		6	1	17	0	-,-
Wyatt	2	0	15	1	-,-	(2)	6	1	14	0	-,-

FALL OF WICKETS

	MCC	SA	SA
Wkt	1st	1st	2nd
1st	223	134	52
2nd	231	145	56
3rd	310	186	106
4th	327	191	154
5th	333	194	154
6th	358	207	168
7th	493	232	196
8th	599	252	204
9th	628	281	210
10th	-	290	216

VICTORIA v M.C.C.

Played at Melbourne Cricket Ground on November 11, 12, 14, 1932. (Four-day match)
Toss : Victoria.   Result : M.C.C. WON BY AN INNINGS AND 83 RUNS.
Debuts: Victoria - V.G.Nagel (f/c).
12th Men: S.P.King (Vic) and W.E.Bowes (MCC).
Umpires: A.N.Barlow and W.J.Moore.
Attendances: 16407, 33500, 10762.   Total: 60,669.   Receipts: £2567.
Close of Play: 1st day MCC 2/41 (Wyatt 19, Duckworth 0); 2nd day MCC 7/362 (Hammond 169, Paynter 28).

L.E.Nagel strained his right arm while attempting to start his car with a crank handle before the match and was replaced by his brother V.G.Nagel in the Victorian side, giving Australia its second set of first-class twins after L.S.Walsh and N.A.Walsh (South Australia). King replaced W.H.Ponsford (ankle injury). O'Brien (45 in 141 minutes, 3 fours) and Darling (45 in 78 minutes, 4 fours) added 90 for the third wicket but apart from Oakley (83 not out in 120 minutes, 8 fours, chance at 46) the rest of the Victorian batting succumbed to the pace of Voce and Allen on the first day. Hammond (203 in 279 minutes, 1 six and 23 fours, chance at 103) dominated the M.C.C. innings and was particularly severe on the bowling of Fleetwood-Smith. With Paynter he shared an unbroken stand of 121 for the seventh wicket which ended at 6/350 when Paynter (26) took a ball in the mouth from Nagel. He resumed at 7/359 after the run out of Verity and added a further 21 runs with Hammond, this time for the eighth wicket. Wyatt earlier hit 74 in 142 minutes with 9 fours. M.C.C. won with well over a day to spare after Victoria collapsed in their second innings mid-way through the third day. Sources: *Wisden, VCA Report, NSWCA Report, The Age, The Herald, Melbourne Sun.*

VICTORIA

*W.M.Woodfull	c Hammond b Allen	5		b Verity	25
L.P.J.O'Brien	c Verity b Allen	45		lbw b Verity	4
K.E.Rigg	b Allen	1		b Mitchell	7
L.S.Darling	lbw b Voce	45	(6)	c Duckworth b Allen	6
H.H.Oakley	not out	83	(4)	b Hammond	21
J.Thomas	c Duckworth b Allen	1	(5)	c Duckworth b Hammond	6
†B.A.Barnett	c Duckworth b Voce	16		b Allen	4
V.G.Nagel	b Voce	4		run out (Mitchell/Allen)	2
L.O.Fleetwood-Smith	b Verity	0		run out (Paynter/Duckworth)	1
H.H.Alexander	b Voce	3		b Allen	0
H.Ironmonger	run out (Voce)	1		not out	7
Extras	(b7, lb7, nb13)	27		(b3, lb4, w1, nb3)	11
Total	(55.6 overs, 227 mins)	231		(31.5 overs, 133 mins)	94

M.C.C.

R.E.S.Wyatt	c Barnett b Ironmonger	74
G.O.B.Allen	lbw b Nagel	15
Nawab of Pataudi, sr	lbw b Ironmonger	6
†G.Duckworth	lbw b Fleetwood-Smith	15
W.R.Hammond	b Ironmonger	203
*D.R.Jardine	lbw b Darling	19
L.E.G.Ames	c Rigg b Alexander	15
E.Paynter	c Barnett b Fleetwood-Smith	37
H.Verity	run out (Ironmonger/Nagel)	3
W.Voce	not out	3
T.B.Mitchell	did not bat	
Extras	(b7, lb10, nb1)	18
Total	(109.0 overs, 383 mins) (9 wkts dec)	408

M.C.C.	O	M	R	W	w,nb		O	M	R	W	w,nb
Allen	12	0	45	4	-,9		5.5	1	21	3	1,2
Voce	13.6	0	55	4	-,4		11	0	28	0	-,1
Verity	15	3	52	1	-,-		6	2	10	2	-,-
Hammond	6	0	25	0	-,-	(5)	5	2	8	2	-,-
Mitchell	7	2	20	0	-,-	(4)	4	0	16	1	-,-
Wyatt	2	0	7	0	-,-						

VICTORIA	O	M	R	W	w,nb
Alexander	20	0	80	1	-,-
Nagel	19	2	86	1	-,1
Ironmonger	38	19	62	3	-,-
Fleetwood-Smith	25	3	124	2	-,-
Darling	7	0	38	1	-,-

FALL OF WICKETS

Wkt	VIC 1st	MCC 1st	VIC 2nd
1st	8	30	22
2nd	14	39	35
3rd	104	82	59
4th	146	134	67
5th	153	187	76
6th	198	229	84
7th	202	359	85
8th	205	380	86
9th	214	408	87
10th	231	-	94

QUEENSLAND v NEW SOUTH WALES (Shield Match 3)

Played at Brisbane Cricket Ground (Woolloongabba) on November 11, 12, 14, 1932. (Four-day match)
Toss : Queensland.   Result : NEW SOUTH WALES WON BY AN INNINGS AND 274 RUNS.
Debuts: Queensland - G.R.Clem (f/c). New South Wales - W.A.Brown (f/c).
12th Men: J.G.Maddern (Qld) and R.N.Nutt (NSW).
Umpires: J.Bartlett and J.A.Scott.
Attendances: 3036, 3820, 800.   Total: 7656   Receipts: £331.
Close of Play: 1st day NSW 4/440 (Kippax 179, Hird 42); 2nd day Qld 7/145 (Gough 46, Suche 2).

D.G.Bradman (ill) was replaced by Nutt in the New South Wales twelve. Brown on debut was run out from the third ball of the match without facing a delivery. McCabe (91 in 119 minutes, 7 fours), Kippax (chanceless 179 in 241 minutes, 25 fours), Bill (80 in 130 minutes, 9 fours) and Hird (106 in 166 minutes, 1 six and 9 fours) in the middle order all went on, establishing a big total for New South Wales. Kippax was out to the first ball of the second day after sharing successive stands worth 171 and 123 with Bill and Hird for the fourth and fifth wickets. Against an attack headed by the economical O'Reilly (9 for 66 in 40 overs), Queensland's only half-centuries were scored by Gough (52 in 147 minutes, 7 fours) and the ex-New South Welshman Andrews (51 in 94 minutes, 4 fours). Sources: *Wisden, NSWCA Report, VCA Report, Brisbane Courier, Brisbane Daily Mail.*

NEW SOUTH WALES

J.H.W.Fingleton	c Suche b Gamble	31
W.A.Brown	run out (Andrews)	0
S.J.McCabe	run out (Gough)	91
*A.F.Kippax	b Cook	179
O.W.Bill	b Gamble	80
S.F.Hird	b Clem	106
F.S.Cummins	c Cook b Suche	25
†W.A.S.Oldfield	c Andrews b Gamble	46
W.J.O'Reilly	run out (/Marshall)	0
H.J.T.Theak	b Gamble	6
C.J.Hill	not out	17
Extras	(b9, lb5, nb7)	21
Total	(130.3 overs, 468 mins)	602

QUEENSLAND

G.G.Cook	lbw b McCabe	6	(4)	b O'Reilly	16
†A.N.Marshall	b Theak	2		lbw b McCabe	19
W.C.Andrews	lbw b O'Reilly	33		b O'Reilly	51
C.D.Hansen	lbw b McCabe	6	(5)	lbw b O'Reilly	0
*F.J.Gough	c Cummins b Hill	52	(1)	c Fingleton b O'Reilly	17
E.C.Bensted	c & b O'Reilly	2		st Oldfield b Hird	17
K.L.M.Mossop	c Bill b McCabe	32		b O'Reilly	10
H.S.Gamble	c Bill b McCabe	4	(9)	c Kippax b Hird	1
B.V.Suche	c Fingleton b O'Reilly	15	(8)	not out	6
G.R.Clem	not out	7		c Bill b O'Reilly	2
H.M.Thurlow	b Hill	3		c Brown b Hird	5
Extras	(b11, lb2, nb5)	18		(b2, lb1, nb1)	4
Total	(66.0 overs, 193 mins)	180		(51.6 overs, 151 mins)	148

QUEENSLAND	O	M	R	W	w,nb
Thurlow	23	3	70	0	-,3
Suche	26	1	133	1	-,-
Clem	22	2	107	1	-,-
Gamble	25.3	2	91	4	-,2
Bensted	17	1	75	0	-,1
Gough	6	0	55	0	-,1
Cook	10	0	41	1	-,-
Andrews	1	0	9	0	-,-

NEW SOUTH WALES	O	M	R	W	w,nb	O	M	R	W	w,nb
Theak	11	1	26	1	-,3	6	1	25	0	-,-
McCabe	11	0	22	4	-,2	11	1	19	1	-,1
O'Reilly	22	11	30	3	-,-	18	6	36	6	-,-
Hird	7	0	40	0	-,-	9.6	1	40	3	-,-
Hill	15	3	44	2	-,-	5	1	11	0	-,-
Cummins						2	0	13	0	-,-

FALL OF WICKETS

Wkt	NSW 1st	QLD 1st	QLD 2nd
1st	0	8	37
2nd	91	10	37
3rd	146	25	82
4th	317	79	82
5th	440	83	121
6th	483	136	129
7th	555	141	134
8th	555	149	135
9th	579	175	138
10th	602	180	148

AUSTRALIAN XI v M.C.C.

Played at Melbourne Cricket Ground on November 18, 19, 21, 22, 1932. (Four-day match)
Toss : M.C.C.   Result : MATCH DRAWN.
Debuts: Nil.
12th Men: H.H.Oakley (Aust) and T.B.Mitchell (MCC).
Umpires: A.N.Barlow and J.Richards.
Attendances: 23484, 53916, 15286, 16815.   Total: 109,501.   Receipts: £4811.
Close of Play: 1st day MCC 8/238 (Allen 12, Duckworth 3); 2nd day Aust 9/216 (Barnett 19, Ironmonger 4); 3rd day Aust (2) 0/0
    (Woodfull 0, O'Brien 0).

A fast pitch aided the full complement of English fast bowlers, Larwood, Voce and Bowes, in the first serious trial of Bodyline tactics on the tour. Ironically, it was Wyatt and not Jardine (who had gone fishing) who instructed the bowlers before a bumper crowd of 53,916 on the second day. The Australian batsmen, faced by a barrage of very fast balls rising viciously from short of a length at their chests or heads, found that any attempt at a defensive shot was likely to result in giving a catch on the leg side to a well-packed close field. The most serious injury befell Woodfull, who was struck painfully over the heart but was able to continue after a ten-minute delay. Topscorers in the innings were O'Brien (46 in 158 minutes, 1 four, 2 chances). Bradman (36 in 46 minutes, 4 fours) and Lee (28 in 36 minutes, 2 fours). A storm on the third afternoon ended play at 3.04 pm before a ball could be bowled in the Australians' second innings and rain washed out the final day after 34 minutes after Woodfull had fallen to a catch in the first over; Bodyline tactics were not adopted on the last day. Sutcliffe (87 in 234 minutes, 5 fours) scored the only fifty of the match, Leyland (38 in 77 minutes, 4 fours) and Allen (48 in 110 minutes, 7 fours) also batting well for the tourists. The 6ft 6 ins Nagel, bowling unchanged into a stiff breeze on the third day, swung the ball disconcertingly and captured a wicket in all but his fifth and sixth overs, finishing with a career-best 8 for 32 as the Englishmen collapsed for 60. The second-day crowd and total attendance of 109,501 remains first-class records outside of Tests in Australia. A.F.Kippax, S.J.McCabe, W.A.S.Oldfield and W.H.Ponsford all withdrew from the Australian XI before the match and were replaced by Barnett, Nagel, O'Brien and Rigg. Sources: *Wisden, VCA Report, NSWCA Report, The Age, The Herald, Melbourne Sun.*

M.C.C.

*R.E.S.Wyatt	lbw b Oxenham	29	(2) c Barnett b Nagel	3
H.Sutcliffe	c Bradman b Ironmonger	87	(1) b Nagel	10
Nawab of Pataudi, sr	b Nash	23	(4) c O'Brien b Nagel	5
M.Leyland	c Darling b Ironmonger	38	(3) b Nagel	6
G.O.B.Allen	c Barnett b Nash	48	lbw b Nagel	6
E.Paynter	c Barnett b Oxenham	6	b Nagel	12
H.Larwood	c Darling b Oxenham	2	c O'Brien b Nagel	0
F.R.Brown	b Oxenham	27	b Oxenham	10
W.Voce	lbw b Oxenham	0	not out	0
†G.Duckworth	c Rigg b Nash	3	lbw b Nagel	4
W.E.Bowes	not out	2	b Oxenham	0
Extras	(b12, lb5)	17	(lb4)	4
Total	(94.5 overs, 339 mins)	282	(18.2 overs, 91 mins)	60

AUSTRALIAN XI

*W.M.Woodfull	lbw b Bowes	18	c Duckworth b Larwood	0
L.P.J.O'Brien	b Larwood	46	not out	5
D.G.Bradman	lbw b Larwood	36	b Larwood	13
K.E.Rigg	c Brown b Bowes	13	not out	0
L.S.Darling	b Bowes	4		
R.K.Oxenham	c Larwood b Voce	12		
L.J.Nash	b Larwood	0		
P.K.Lee	c Paynter b Brown	28		
†B.A.Barnett	b Voce	20		
L.E.Nagel	lbw b Larwood	15		
H.Ironmonger	not out	5		
Extras	(b11, lb2, nb8)	21	(b1)	1
Total	(51.5 overs, 243 mins)	218	(6.7 overs, 34 mins) (2 wkts)	19

AUSTRALIAN XI	O	M	R	W	w,nb		O	M	R	W	w,nb
Nash	11.5	0	39	3	-,-		4	0	18	0	-,-
Nagel	20	6	37	0	-,-		10	3	32	8	-,-
Ironmonger	27	8	90	2	-,-		2	1	2	0	-,-
Lee	10	1	35	0	-,-						
Oxenham	24	8	53	5	-,-	(4)	4.2	2	4	2	-,-
Darling	2	0	11	0	-,-						

M.C.C.	O	M	R	W	w,nb		O	M	R	W	w,nb
Larwood	14	0	54	4	-,5		3.7	1	5	2	-,-
Bowes	15	2	63	3	-,1						
Voce	15.5	2	55	2	-,2						
Brown	7	0	25	1	-,-						
Allen						(2)	3	1	13	0	-,-

FALL OF WICKETS

Wkt	MCC 1st	AUST 1st	MCC 2nd	AUST 2nd
1st	56	51	4	0
2nd	102	105	19	18
3rd	182	119	22	-
4th	182	131	30	-
5th	188	131	44	-
6th	198	131	44	-
7th	230	175	55	-
8th	230	175	55	-
9th	277	210	59	-
10th	282	218	60	-

NEW SOUTH WALES v M.C.C.

Played at Sydney Cricket Ground on November 25, 26, 28, 29, 1932. (Four-day match)
Toss : New South Wales.   Result : M.C.C. WON BY AN INNINGS AND 44 RUNS.
Debuts: New South Wales - W.H.Howell (f/c).
12th Men: W.A.Brown (NSW) and H.Larwood (MCC).
Umpires: E.G.Borwick and W.G.French.
Attendances: 26384, 36718, 12746, 2107.   Total: 77,955   Receipts: £5080.
Close of Play: 1st day MCC 0/6 (Wyatt 2, Sutcliffe 3); 2nd day MCC 4/339 (Sutcliffe 157); 3rd day NSW (2) 3/68 (Kippax 7, Hird 5).

Oldfield was unable to take the field after the first day because of influenza and Jardine gave permission for H.S.B.Love to act as substitute wicketkeeper, even though he was not in the twelve. Love responded by completing the first stumpings by a substitute in Australian matches, also catching Jardine off the legspin of Hird. Fingleton (13 fours) carried his bat through the first New South Wales innings, sharing a fourth-wicket partnership of 118 with McCabe (67 in 82 minutes, 11 fours). Cummins (71 in 77 minutes, 12 fours) topscored in the second innings in which Oldfield was unable to bat and Bradman (also ill) batted under difficulty. Sutcliffe (182 in 352 minutes, 22 fours) added 140 for the M.C.C. first wicket with Wyatt (72 in 120 minutes, 1 five and 8 fours) and 133 for the third wicket with Pataudi (61 in 96 minutes, 6 fours). Ames (90 in 185 minutes, 7 fours) and Voce (46 in 96 minutes, 5 fours) added 100 for the eighth wicket.
Sources: *Wisden, NSWCA Report, VCA Report, Sydney Referee, Sydney Morning Herald, The Age.*

NEW SOUTH WALES

J.H.W.Fingleton	not out	119		b Brown	18
O.W.Bill	c Jardine b Tate	22		b Voce	1
D.G.Bradman	lbw b Tate	18	(6)	b Voce	23
*A.F.Kippax	c Voce b Tate	3		c Sutcliffe b Voce	24
S.J.McCabe	c Allen b Tate	67	(3)	c Brown b Voce	29
S.F.Hird	c Ames b Allen	9	(5)	c Tate b Voce	15
F.S.Cummins	lbw b Voce	0		c Jardine b Brown	71
†W.A.S.Oldfield	c Sutcliffe b Allen	5		absent ill	-
W.J.O'Reilly	b Allen	0	(8)	b Allen	11
H.J.T.Theak	b Allen	9	(9)	b Allen	4
W.H.Howell	b Allen	7	(10)	not out	0
Extras	(lb8, nb6)	14		(b2, lb6, w1, nb8)	17
Total	(68.2 overs, 276 mins)	273		(44.5 overs, 185 mins)	213

M.C.C.

R.E.S.Wyatt	lbw b O'Reilly	72
H.Sutcliffe	b Hird	182
W.R.Hammond	c Bradman b O'Reilly	20
Nawab of Pataudi, sr	st sub (H.S.B.Love) b Hird	61
F.R.Brown	st sub (H.S.B.Love) b Hird	6
†L.E.G.Ames	c Fingleton b O'Reilly	90
*D.R.Jardine	c sub (H.S.B.Love) b Hird	4
G.O.B.Allen	lbw b Hird	15
W.Voce	b Hird	46
H.Verity	lbw b O'Reilly	2
M.W.Tate	not out	2
Extras	(b16, lb8, nb6)	30
Total	(157.5 overs, 496 mins)	530

M.C.C.	O	M	R	W	w,nb		O	M	R	W	w,nb
Allen	16.2	2	69	5	-,2	(3)	10	1	52	2	-,4
Voce	19	3	53	1	-,4	(1)	15	1	85	5	-,4
Tate	17	2	53	4	-,-	(2)	6	1	21	0	-,-
Brown	5	0	28	0	-,-		5.5	0	19	2	-,-
Hammond	5	0	26	0	-,-	(6)	4	0	12	0	1,-
Verity	6	1	30	0	-,-	(5)	4	1	7	0	-,-

NEW SOUTH WALES	O	M	R	W	w,nb
Theak	18	1	76	0	-,2
McCabe	19	4	53	0	-,-
O'Reilly	45.5	16	86	4	-,4
Howell	22	4	59	0	-,-
Hird	30	1	135	6	-,-
Bradman	11	3	24	0	-,-
Cummins	9	0	57	0	-,-
Kippax	3	0	10	0	-,-

FALL OF WICKETS

Wkt	NSW 1st	MCC 1st	NSW 2nd
1st	43	140	7
2nd	75	194	53
3rd	90	327	60
4th	208	339	90
5th	238	384	98
6th	240	392	161
7th	251	420	206
8th	253	520	211
9th	263	524	213
10th	273	530	-

SOUTH AUSTRALIA v VICTORIA (Shield Match 4)

Played at Adelaide Oval on November 25, 26, 28, 29, 1932. (Four-day match)
Toss : Victoria.   Result : SOUTH AUSTRALIA WON BY THREE WICKETS.
Debuts: Nil.
12th Men: J.R.Davey (SA) and J.Thomas (Vic).
Umpires: G.A.Hele and E.H.Kitson.
Attendances: 5119, 5976, 2458, 1697.   Total: 15,250.   Receipts: £494.
Close of Play: 1st day Vic 4/380 (Rigg 159, King 6); 2nd day SA 3/202 (Richardson 115, Lee 10); 3rd day Vic (2) 92 all out.

H.Ironmonger, L.E.Nagel, W.H.Ponsford and W.M.Woodfull, all named in Australia's thirteen for the First Test, announced their unavailability for Victoria whereas South Australia's national representatives, Grimmett, Richardson and Wall, played. Rigg (166 in 342 minutes, 8 fours, 2 chances) and Darling (150 in 215 minutes, 14 fours, 1 chance) added 281 for the Victorians, a new third-wicket record for the State. O'Brien (42 in 75 minutes, 3 fours) and King (41 in 96 minutes, 4 fours) also batted well. Richardson led his side from the front, topscoring in each innings with 203 (346 minutes, 20 fours) and 55 (104 minutes, 4 fours), with support coming from Nitschke (40 in 117 minutes, 2 fours) and Whitington (47 in 68 minutes, 3 fours) in the first innings. Nagel (strained hip) was unable to bowl on the last day, Lonergan sustaining a first-ball dismissal to McCormick. Victoria's second-innings collapse in ideal conditions was attributed to good bowling by Wall, Tobin and Grimmett. *Wisden* incorrectly gives Vic (2) King b Grimmett. Sources: *Wisden, SACA Report, VCA Report, Adelaide Advertiser, Australian Cricketer, The News.*

VICTORIA

L.P.J.O'Brien	run out (Jamieson/Walker)	42		b Tobin	8
K.E.Rigg	c Richardson b Grimmett	166		c Walker b Tobin	0
*H.S.T.L.Hendry	lbw b Grimmett	2	(5)	b Tobin	1
L.S.Darling	c & b Jamieson	150	(3)	b Wall	15
H.H.Oakley	c & b Jamieson	3	(4)	b Tobin	9
S.P.King	b Grimmett	41		lbw b Grimmett	25
†B.A.Barnett	c Walker b Tobin	5		b Wall	16
V.G.Nagel	lbw b Grimmett	12		c Richardson b Wall	5
E.L.McCormick	b Wall	9		not out	3
L.O.Fleetwood-Smith	not out	0		c Tobin b Wall	0
H.H.Alexander	lbw b Grimmett	5		lbw b Jamieson	2
Extras	(b7, lb9, nb3)	19		(b4, nb4)	8
Total	(117.3 overs, 431 mins)	454		(36.6 overs, 151 mins)	92

SOUTH AUSTRALIA

*V.Y.Richardson	run out (Oakley/Darling)	203		lbw b McCormick	55
H.C.Nitschke	c Hendry b Alexander	40		c O'Brien b McCormick	7
A.R.Lonergan	c Rigg b Nagel	20		lbw b McCormick	0
W.E.Catchlove	lbw b Fleetwood-Smith	8		c Barnett b Alexander	19
P.K.Lee	c Darling b Alexander	19		c Hendry b Alexander	5
R.S.Whitington	lbw b Fleetwood-Smith	47		c Rigg b Fleetwood-Smith	8
B.J.Tobin	lbw b Fleetwood-Smith	19		c Rigg b Fleetwood-Smith	19
D.G.Jamieson	lbw b Darling	7		not out	8
C.V.Grimmett	c Hendry b Alexander	7		not out	5
T.W.Wall	b Alexander	8			
†C.W.Walker	not out	1			
Extras	(b21, lb1, w1, nb1)	24		(b12, lb1, w3, nb2)	18
Total	(92.7 overs, 372 mins)	403		(37.1 overs, 154 mins) (7 wkts)	144

SOUTH AUSTRALIA	O	M	R	W	w,nb		O	M	R	W	w,nb		FALL OF WICKETS			
Wall	22	2	99	1	-,2		10	2	30	4	-,4			VIC	SA	VIC	SA
Tobin	9	1	42	1	-,-		10	0	31	4	-,-	Wkt	1st	1st	2nd	2nd
Jamieson	21	1	56	2	-,1	(5)	0.6	0	0	1	-,-	1st	76	113	6	26
Grimmett	43.3	3	161	5	-,-		13	7	13	1	-,-	2nd	78	147	16	26
Lee	22	4	77	0	-,-	(3)	3	0	10	0	-,-	3rd	359	162	28	83
												4th	363	241	29	95
VICTORIA	O	M	R	W	w,nb		O	M	R	W	w,nb	5th	395	319	38	96
Alexander	20.7	0	101	4	-,-		9	0	32	2	2,-	6th	407	353	73	125
McCormick	15	1	56	0	1,1	(4)	10	2	36	3	1,2	7th	434	385	83	128
Nagel	14	2	50	1	-,-							8th	449	385	88	-
Fleetwood-Smith	35	3	146	3	-,-	(3)	15.1	2	53	2	-,-	9th	449	398	88	-
Darling	5	1	14	1	-,-							10th	454	403	92	-
King	3	0	12	0	-,-											
Hendry						(2)	3	1	5	0	-,-					

AUSTRALIA v ENGLAND (1st Test)

Played at Sydney Cricket Ground on December 2, 3, 5, 6, 7, 1932. (Timeless match)
Toss : Australia.　　　　　　　Result : ENGLAND WON BY TEN WICKETS.
Debuts: Australia - L.E.Nagel (Test). England - Nawab of Pataudi, sr (Test).
12th Men: S.F.Hird (Aust) and E.Paynter (Eng).
Umpires: E.G.Borwick and G.A.Hele.
Attendances: 46709, 58058, 2938, 25488, 100.　　　Total: 158,293　　　Receipts: £14,683.
Close of Play: 1st day Aust 6/290 (McCabe 127, Grimmett 17); 2nd day Eng 1/252 (Sutcliffe 116, Hammond 87); 3rd day Eng 6/479
　　(Pataudi 80); 4th day Aust (2) 9/164 (Nagel 21, O'Reilly 7).

Australia omitted D.G.Bradman (ill) and H.Ironmonger from their selected thirteen.　McCabe countered the menacing, short-pitched deliveries of Larwood and especially Voce with a magnificent innings of 187 not out in 242 minutes (233 balls, 25 balls, 25 fours).　He gave two difficult chances, when 159 and 170, during his dazzling exhibition of hooking, and added 129 in 120 minutes with Richardson (5 fours) for the fifth wicket and 55 (of which he contributed 51 himself) in 33 minutes with Wall for the last wicket.　Sutcliffe (194 in 436 minutes, 496 balls, 13 fours) shared century stands with Wyatt, Hammond (112 in 192 minutes, 242 balls, 16 fours) and Pataudi (102 in 317 minutes, 380 balls, 6 fours) for England's first three wickets after he had played a ball from O'Reilly on to his stumps, without dislodging the bails, when he was 43.　Pataudi was the second batsman after K.S.Ranjitsinhji to score centuries in both his first first-class match in Australia and his first Test in Australia.　Larwood bowled extremely fast to capture ten wickets in the match, Fingleton (40 in 144 minutes, 5 fours) and McCabe (32 in 65 minutes, 1 six and 4 fours) topscoring in the second innings.　Sources: *Wisden, NSWCA Report, Sydney Referee, Sydney Morning Herald, Sydney Daily Telegraph.*

AUSTRALIA

*W.M.Woodfull	c Ames b Voce	7		b Larwood	0
W.H.Ponsford	b Larwood	32		b Voce	2
J.H.W.Fingleton	c Allen b Larwood	26		c Voce b Larwood	40
A.F.Kippax	lbw b Larwood	8	(6)	b Larwood	19
S.J.McCabe	not out	187	(4)	lbw b Hammond	32
V.Y.Richardson	c Hammond b Voce	49	(5)	c Voce b Hammond	0
†W.A.S.Oldfield	c Ames b Larwood	4		c Leyland b Larwood	1
C.V.Grimmett	c Ames b Voce	19		c Allen b Larwood	5
L.E.Nagel	b Larwood	0		not out	21
W.J.O'Reilly	b Voce	4	(11)	b Voce	7
T.W.Wall	c Allen b Hammond	4	(10)	c Ames b Allen	20
Extras	(b12, lb4, nb4)	20		(b12, lb2, w1, nb2)	17
Total	(102.2 overs, 356 mins)	360		(63.3 overs, 214 mins)	164

ENGLAND

H.Sutcliffe	lbw b Wall	194	not out	1
R.E.S.Wyatt	lbw b Grimmett	38	not out	0
W.R.Hammond	c Grimmett b Nagel	112		
Nawab of Pataudi, sr	b Nagel	102		
M.Leyland	c Oldfield b Wall	0		
*D.R.Jardine	c Oldfield b McCabe	27		
H.Verity	lbw b Wall	2		
G.O.B.Allen	c & b O'Reilly	19		
†L.E.G.Ames	c McCabe b O'Reilly	0		
H.Larwood	lbw b O'Reilly	0		
W.Voce	not out	0		
Extras	(b7, lb17, nb6)	30		—
Total	(229.4 overs, 609 mins)	524	(0.1 overs, 1 mins) (0 wkts)	1

ENGLAND	O	M	R	W	w,nb	O	M	R	W	w,nb
Larwood	31	5	96	5	-,1	18	4	28	5	-,-
Voce	29	4	110	4	-,3	17.3	5	54	2	-,1
Allen	15	1	65	0	-,-	9	5	13	1	1,1
Hammond	14.2	0	34	1	-,-	15	6	37	2	-,-
Verity	13	4	35	0	-,-	4	1	15	0	-,-

AUSTRALIA	O	M	R	W	w,nb		O	M	R	W	w,nb
Wall	38	4	104	3	-,3						
Nagel	43.4	9	110	2	-,-						
O'Reilly	67	32	117	3	-,3						
Grimmett	64	22	118	1	-,-						
McCabe	15	2	42	1	-,-	(1)	0.1	0	1	0	-,-
Kippax	2	1	3	0	-,-						

FALL OF WICKETS

Wkt	AUST 1st	ENG 1st	AUST 2nd	ENG 2nd
1st	22	112	2	-
2nd	65	300	10	-
3rd	82	423	61	-
4th	87	423	61	-
5th	216	470	100	-
6th	231	479	104	-
7th	299	518	105	-
8th	300	522	113	-
9th	305	522	151	-
10th	360	524	164	-

TASMANIA v M.C.C.

Played at N.T.C.A. Ground, Launceston, on December 16, 17, 19, 1932. (Three-day match)
Toss : M.C.C.   Result : M.C.C. WON BY AN INNINGS AND 126 RUNS.
Debuts: Tasmania - K.G.Gourlay, J.M.Walsh (both f/c).
12th Men: R.A.Broomby (Tas) and H.Verity (MCC).
Umpires: E.C.Knight and B.Parker.
Attendances: 3300, 4200, 1500.   Total: About 9000.   Receipts: £480.
Close of Play: 1st day MCC 3/395 (Ames 91, Paynter 52); 2nd day Tas 3/137 (Martin 12, Putman 1).

Rushforth severely twisted a tendon in his knee while fielding a ball on the first day and Green led the Tasmanians for the rest of the match in his absence. Sutcliffe (101 in 146 minutes, 2 sixes and 6 fours), Pataudi (109 in 145 minutes, 8 fours), Ames (107 in 169 minutes, 10 fours) and Paynter (102 in 128 minutes, 1 six and 12 fours) all scored hundreds for the tourists, the second instance for M.C.C. in Australia (also against South Australia in 1907-08). Wickets fell steadily on the second day in the quest for quick runs, James taking his best figures in 35 matches for Tasmania spread over 17 years. Badcock (57 in 117 minutes, 4 fours) and Burrows (41 in 86 minutes, 3 fours) added 93 for Tasmania's first wicket but of the rest only Putman 56 not out in 81 minutes, 7 fours) resisted for any length the leg-spin of Mitchell who captured 11 for 144 in the match. Badcock carried his bat through the second innings, hitting 1 four. *VCA Report* gives MCC 1/88. *NSWCA Report* gives Tas (1) 4/151. Sources: *Wisden, TCA Report, VCA Report, Hobart Mercury, Launceston Examiner.*

M.C.C.

H.Sutcliffe	c James b Putman	101
*R.E.S.Wyatt	lbw b Putman	33
Nawab of Pataudi, sr	b James	109
†L.E.G.Ames	c Green b James	107
E.Paynter	c Green b James	102
F.R.Brown	b Putman	1
H.Larwood	c Green b Putman	1
W.Voce	c & b James	20
M.W.Tate	not out	10
W.E.Bowes	b James	3
T.B.Mitchell	st Parry b James	0
Extras	(b9, lb6)	15
Total	(109.0 overs, 365 mins)	502

TASMANIA

C.L.Badcock	b Mitchell	57	not out		43
A.O.Burrows	st Ames b Mitchell	41	c Wyatt b Tate		1
D.C.Green	run out (Paynter/Mitchell)	8	b Mitchell		21
G.W.Martin	lbw b Mitchell	19	lbw b Brown		13
S.W.L.Putman	not out	56	b Mitchell		5
R.O.G.Morrisby	b Bowes	4	c & b Brown		20
K.G.Gourlay	st Ames b Mitchell	1	st Ames b Brown		0
†C.N.Parry	st Ames b Mitchell	0	c Voce b Mitchell		24
G.T.H.James	c Paynter b Mitchell	16	c Brown b Mitchell		10
J.M.Walsh	run out (Voce/Ames)	5	c Wyatt b Mitchell		0
*A.W.Rushforth	absent hurt	-	absent hurt		-
Extras	(b15, lb4, nb3)	22	(b6, lb3, nb1)		10
Total	(51.0 overs, 200 mins)	229	(41.6 overs, 151 mins)		147

TASMANIA	O	M	R	W	w,nb
Burrows	12	1	48	0	-,-
Walsh	20	1	69	0	-,-
James	31	2	96	6	-,-
Putman	24	0	156	4	-,-
Gourlay	21	1	102	0	-,-
Martin	1	0	16	0	-,-

M.C.C.	O	M	R	W	w,nb		O	M	R	W	w,nb
Voce	4	0	12	0	-,2	(3)	4	0	10	0	-,1
Bowes	16	2	70	1	-,-	(1)	6	1	15	0	-,-
Brown	10	2	45	0	-,1	(5)	11	3	28	3	-,-
Tate	4	1	10	0	-,-	(2)	7	2	10	1	-,-
Mitchell	17	0	70	6	-,-	(4)	13.6	6	74	5	-,-

FALL OF WICKETS

Wkt	MCC 1st	TAS 1st	TAS 2nd
1st	86	93	4
2nd	193	117	41
3rd	289	127	60
4th	427	150	69
5th	429	155	98
6th	433	156	98
7th	487	156	129
8th	498	212	147
9th	502	229	147
10th	502	-	-

VICTORIA v QUEENSLAND (Shield Match 5)

Played at Melbourne Cricket Ground on December 16 (no play), 17, 19, 20, 1932. (Four-day match)
Toss : Queensland.   Result : VICTORIA WON BY AN INNINGS AND 139 RUNS.
Debuts: Queensland - J.G.Maddern (f/c).
12th Men: S.P.King (Vic) and F.W.Sides (Qld).
Umpires: A.N.Barlow and W.R.Wetenhall.
Attendances: No play, 9069, 4779, 926.   Total: 14.774.   Receipts: £441.
Close of Play: 1st day no play; 2nd day Vic 1/59 (Woodfull 28, O'Brien 2), 3rd day Qld (2) 1/19 (Cook 11, Bensted 3).

After the first day was lost to rain, Queensland came up against the left-arm spin combination of Fleetwood-Smith and Ironmonger, the latter taking a remarkable 7 for 13 in 13.6 overs to bundle the northerners out for 74 in the second innings. Cook, the only batsman to escape their wiles, topscored in each innings with 33 in 140 minutes and an unbeaten 36 in 121 minutes, becoming only the second Queenslander to carry his bat through an innings. Hansen injured a hand in the field on the third day and was forced to miss the next match against South Australia. Darling's chanceless 128 (182 minutes, 11 fours) was his second hundred in successive matches for Victoria. O'Brien scored 64 in 176 minutes and hit 3 fours. Sources: *Wisden, VCA Report, QCA Report, The Age, The Argus, The Herald.*

QUEENSLAND

†A.N.Marshall	b Fleetwood-Smith	9		lbw b Alexander	2
G.G.Cook	run out (Rigg)	33		not out	36
W.C.Andrews	lbw b Fleetwood-Smith	7	(4)	st Barnett b Ironmonger	5
C.D.Hansen	b Fleetwood-Smith	16		absent hurt	-
R.K.Oxenham	hit wkt b Alexander	5	(6)	c Fleetwood-Smith b Ironmonger	1
K.L.M.Mossop	lbw b Fleetwood-Smith	8	(7)	b Ironmonger	13
*E.C.Bensted	c Barnett b Alexander	1	(3)	lbw b Ironmonger	3
J.G.Maddern	lbw b Fleetwood-Smith	5		c & b Fleetwood-Smith	1
F.M.Brew	c Rigg b Ironmonger	25	(5)	b Ironmonger	0
H.S.Gamble	b Fleetwood-Smith	6	(9)	b Ironmonger	1
H.M.Thurlow	not out	7	(10)	c Alexander b Ironmonger	5
Extras	(lb3, w1)	4		(b5, lb1, w1)	7
Total	(54.4 overs, 196 mins)	126		(33.6 overs, 121 mins)	74

VICTORIA

*W.M.Woodfull	c Gamble b Thurlow	38
W.H.Ponsford	c Bensted b Brew	24
L.P.J.O'Brien	b Thurlow	64
K.E.Rigg	c Bensted b Brew	22
L.S.Darling	c Cook b Oxenham	128
H.H.Oakley	b Bensted	0
†B.A.Barnett	c Andrews b Oxenham	15
E.L.McCormick	c & b Gamble	0
L.O.Fleetwood-Smith	c Maddern b Oxenham	32
H.H.Alexander	b Oxenham	0
H.Ironmonger	not out	1
Extras	(b7, lb2, nb6)	15
Total	(95.6 overs, 365 mins)	339

VICTORIA	O	M	R	W	w,nb		O	M	R	W	w,nb				
Alexander	16	3	41	2	-,-		4	2	5	1	1,-				
McCormick	6	1	12	0	1,-		2	1	9	0	-,-				
Ironmonger	10.4	6	10	1	-,-	(4)	13.6	5	13	7	-,-				
Fleetwood-Smith	22	2	59	6	-,-	(3)	14	1	40	1	-,-				

QUEENSLAND	O	M	R	W	w,nb
Thurlow	24	3	109	2	-,3
Gamble	19	2	57	1	-,2
Oxenham	27.6	10	54	4	-,-
Brew	15	2	71	2	-,-
Bensted	10	2	33	1	-,1

FALL OF WICKETS

Wkt	QLD 1st	VIC 1st	QLD 2nd
1st	22	55	3
2nd	36	77	20
3rd	60	125	30
4th	73	205	30
5th	82	206	34
6th	82	246	64
7th	84	248	65
8th	94	329	68
9th	106	338	74
10th	126	339	-

SOUTH AUSTRALIA v NEW SOUTH WALES (Shield Match 6)

Played at Adelaide Oval on December 16, 17, 19, 20, 1932. (Four-day match)
Toss : South Australia.   Result : NEW SOUTH WALES WON BY THREE WICKETS.
Debuts: Nil.
12th Men: M.G.Waite (SA) and A.E.Marks (NSW).
Umpires: G.A.Hele and E.H.Kitson.
Attendances: 4246, 6127, 2055, 200.   Total: 12,628.   Receipts: £398.
Close of Play: 1st day NSW 0/76 (Fingleton 41, Brown 33); 2nd day SA (2) 1/37 (Nitschke 10); 3rd day NSW (2) 7/75 (Oldfield 8, O'Reilly 4).

Without D.G.Bradman (ill), New South Wales made heavy work of an 86 run target for victory, losing Fingleton first ball and all the established batsmen soon after, Oldfield and O'Reilly finally seeing the side through early on the last day. Whitington in the first innings (73 in 138 minutes, 7 fours) and Tobin in the second (61 in 73 minutes, 1 six and 7 fours) scored the only fifties for South Australia. Fingleton (68 in 135 minutes, 6 fours), McCabe (67 in 114 minutes, 8 fours) and Cummins (78 in 112 minutes, 10 fours) led New South Wales to a substantial lead on the first innings; decisive as it turned out. Sources: *Wisden, NSWCA Report, SACA Report, Adelaide Advertiser, The News*.

SOUTH AUSTRALIA

*V.Y.Richardson	b Howell	28	b Howell		27
H.C.Nitschke	c Fingleton b Stewart	8	c & b O'Reilly		27
A.R.Lonergan	lbw b Howell	10	c McCabe b Howell		19
W.E.Catchlove	b O'Reilly	3	b McCabe		32
P.K.Lee	lbw b O'Reilly	13	c Stewart b O'Reilly		31
B.J.Tobin	lbw b O'Reilly	8	c Kippax b Stewart		61
R.S.Whitington	b Stewart	73	b McCabe		21
D.G.Jamieson	c McCabe b Howell	5	c Oldfield b Stewart		6
C.V.Grimmett	c McCabe b O'Reilly	36	b Stewart		0
T.W.Wall	c McCabe b Stewart	15	b O'Reilly		11
†C.W.Walker	not out	1	not out		0
Extras	(b5, lb5, nb3)	13	(b6, lb2, w4, nb4)		16
Total	(70.7 overs, 231 mins)	213	(62.1 overs, 219 mins)		251

NEW SOUTH WALES

J.H.W.Fingleton	b Tobin	68	c Whitington b Wall		0
W.A.Brown	c & b Grimmett	40	b Wall		4
S.J.McCabe	c sub (M.G.Waite) b Wall	67	lbw b Grimmett		19
*A.F.Kippax	c Walker b Grimmett	9	c Richardson b Wall		6
S.F.IIird	lbw b Grimmett	39	c Walker b Lee		17
O.W.Bill	lbw b Grimmett	15	st Walker b Grimmett		0
F.S.Cummins	b Jamieson	78	c Richardson b Wall		13
†W.A.S.Oldfield	c Nitschke b Lee	40	not out		13
W.J.O'Reilly	c Nitschke b Lee	12	not out		10
W.H.Howell	not out	1			
G.L.Stewart	c Richardson b Lee	0			
Extras	(b3, lb5, nb2)	10	(b1, lb3)		4
Total	(99.0 overs, 368 mins)	379	(33.2 overs, 129 mins) (7 wkts)		86

NEW SOUTH WALES	O	M	R	W	w,nb		O	M	R	W	w,nb
Stewart	8.7	0	45	3	-,-		9	0	59	3	4,-
McCabe	8	0	18	0	-,-	(4)	6.1	1	25	2	-,-
O'Reilly	27	10	47	4	-,2		20	6	55	3	-,3
Howell	22	2	61	3	-,1	(2)	19	4	51	2	-,1
Hird	5	0	29	0	-,-		6	0	37	0	-,-
Cummins							2	0	8	0	-,-

SOUTH AUSTRALIA	O	M	R	W	w,nb		O	M	R	W	w,nb
Wall	22	2	85	1	-,1		11	2	31	4	-,-
Tobin	16	1	66	1	-,1		1	0	5	0	-,-
Jamieson	7	2	32	1	-,-						
Grimmett	39	3	138	4	-,-	(3)	15.2	3	41	2	-,-
Lee	15	5	48	3	-,-	(4)	6	3	5	1	-,-

FALL OF WICKETS				
	SA	NSW	SA	NSW
Wkt	1st	1st	2nd	2nd
1st	15	102	37	0
2nd	49	122	72	23
3rd	52	139	80	23
4th	54	231	125	35
5th	63	232	211	36
6th	84	263	213	56
7th	97	358	226	67
8th	169	373	226	-
9th	206	379	251	-
10th	213	379	251	-

TASMANIA v M.C.C.

Played at T.C.A. Ground, Hobart, on December 23, 24, 26, 1932. (Three-day match)
Toss : Tasmania.   Result : MATCH DRAWN.
Debuts: Tasmania - R.A.Broomby (f/c).
12th Men: G.G.Gibson (Tas) and W.Voce (MCC).
Umpires: M.Leonard and W.T.Lonergan.
Attendances: 1730, 3665, 3000.   Total: 8395.   Receipts: £478.
Close of Play: 1st day Tas 2/13 (Green 9, Burrows 0); 2nd day MCC 0/56 (Wyatt 36, Leyland 18).

Rain prevented any chance of a result and the M.C.C. team did not take the game very seriously. Jardine did not wish play to commence on the second day due to a wet wicket but the umpires decreed otherwise when the weather abated. Jardine's use of non-bowlers, although seen as a form of protest, was a justifiable measure to protect his main-line bowlers in the circumstances. Tasmania lost Atkinson to the second ball of the match, only 48 minutes of play being possible on the first day, and Badcock to the fourth ball of the second innings. Wyatt (51 in 79 minutes, 2 sixes and 4 fours), Leyland (65 in 125 minutes, 8 fours), Ames (52 in 40 minutes, 8 fours) and Verity (54 not out in 75 minutes) scored half-centuries for M.C.C., Ames racing from 17 to 49 in boundaries. G.W.Martin and A.W.Rushforth were unavailable for Tasmania. The T.C.A was able to recoup an additional £200 on the match through rain insurance. *Wisden* incorrectly gives Tas (2) breakdown of extras. Sources: *Wisden, TCA Report, VCA Report, Hobart Mercury, Australian Cricketer.*

TASMANIA

*J.A.Atkinson	c Ames b Allen	0	b Bowes	4
C.L.Badcock	c Ames b Verity	4	c Allen b Bowes	0
D.C.Green	c Jardine b Paynter	18	c Verity b Bowes	7
A.O.Burrows	b Paynter	38	not out	33
S.W.L.Putman	c & b Paynter	20	c Allen b Bowes	29
R.O.G.Morrisby	not out	10	not out	10
R.A.Broomby	not out	10		
K.G.Gourlay	)			
†C.N.Parry	) did not bat			
G.T.H.James	)			
J.M.Walsh	)			
Extras	(b3)	3	(lb3, nb3)	6
Total	(51.0 overs, 196 mins) (5 wkts dec)	103	(26.0 overs, 105 mins) (4 wkts)	89

M.C.C.

R.E.S.Wyatt	c Green b Burrows	51
M.Leyland	c Morrisby b Walsh	65
*D.R.Jardine	lbw b James	13
G.O.B.Allen	c & b Putman	20
F.R.Brown	c & b Putman	35
E.Paynter	st Parry b Putman	5
L.E.G.Ames	c Gourlay b James	52
H.Verity	not out	54
†G.Duckworth	not out	27
W.E.Bowes	) did not bat	
T.B.Mitchell	)	
Extras	(b5, lb2, nb1)	8
Total	(71.0 overs, 250 mins) (7 wkts dec)	330

M.C.C.	O	M	R	W	w,nb		O	M	R	W	w,nb			FALL OF WICKETS		
														TAS	MCC	TAS
Allen	5	3	7	1	-,-	(2)	5	0	17	0	-,1	Wkt	1st	1st	2nd
Bowes	5	2	6	0	-,-	(1)	8	1	18	4	-,-	1st	0	83	1
Verity	1	1	0	1	-,-	(6)	4	1	6	0	-,-	2nd	13	116	12
Jardine	10	2	21	0	-,-							3rd	32	152	19
Paynter	20	6	40	3	-,-							4th	71	167	72
Ames	10	1	26	0	-,-							5th	86	187	-
Mitchell						(3)	5	1	8	0	-,-	6th	-	205	-
Brown						(4)	2	0	24	0	-,2	7th	-	255	-
Wyatt						(5)	1	0	6	0	-,-	8th	-	-	-
Leyland						(7)	1	0	4	0	-,-	9th	-	-	-
												10th	-	-	-

TASMANIA	O	M	R	W	w,nb
Gourlay	6	0	26	0	-,-
Walsh	16	1	60	1	-,1
Burrows	8	0	57	1	-,-
James	20	1	82	2	-,-
Atkinson	6	0	25	0	-,-
Putman	15	1	72	3	-,-

VICTORIA v NEW SOUTH WALES (Shield Match 7)

Played at Melbourne Cricket Ground on December 23 (no play), 24 (no play), 26, 27, 1932. (Four-day match)
Toss : Victoria.   Result : MATCH DRAWN.
Debuts: Victoria - E.H.Bromley (Vic only).
12th Men: K.E.Rigg (Vic) and A.E.Marks (NSW).
Umpires: A.N.Barlow and W.J.Moore.
Attendances: no play, no play, 21187, 15938.   Total: 37,125.   Receipts: £1680.
Close of Play: 1st day no play; 2nd day no play; 3rd day NSW 7/348 (Cummins 3, Howell 2).

W.A.S.Oldfield was granted a rest from the match by the New South Wales selectors for the forthcoming Test. Rain prevented any play on the first two scheduled days. Brown (21) retired at 0/67 after a delivery from Alexander inflicted a cut near his eye; he resumed at 8/365 next morning. Bradman returned from illness with 157 in 199 minutes, including 16 fours. When 130 he reached 10,000 first-class runs in his 126th innings aged 24 years 121 days, the youngest so far. (Javed Miandad, 23 years in 1980, and Graeme Ashley Hick, 22 years 237 days in 1989, inherited this title from him in due course.) Fingleton (85 in 163 minutes, 2 fours) and McCabe (48 in 81 minutes, 2 fours) also batted well for New South Wales. Bromley, who had moved from Western Australia to Victoria to enhance his Test prospects, gave an early chance but thereafter batted soundly to make 84 in 115 minutes with 10 fours. O'Brien (53 in 149 minutes, 3 fours) also registered a fifty. Howell took the last three wickets without addition. *Wisden* incorrectly gives NSW (2) O'Reilly 7* instead of Howell. Sources: *Wisden, VCA Report, NSWCA Report, Australian Cricketer, The Age, The Argus, The Herald.*

NEW SOUTH WALES

J.H.W.Fingleton	lbw b Nagel	85			
W.A.Brown	not out	35			
D.G.Bradman	c Bromley b Ironmonger	157			
S.J.McCabe	lbw b Alexander	48			
*A.F.Kippax	c King b Ironmonger	17			
S.F.Hird	c Barnett b Ironmonger	3			
F.S.Cummins	c Bromley b Ironmonger	15			
†H.S.B.Love	lbw b Alexander	1			
W.J.O'Reilly	c & b Alexander	2			
W.H.Howell	b Alexander	5	(1) not out		7
G.L.Stewart	c Darling b Ironmonger	7	(2) not out		1
Extras	(b6, lb7)	13			-
Total	(98.2 overs, 362 mins)	388	(1.0 overs, 4 mins) (0 wkts)		8

VICTORIA

*W.M.Woodfull	c Love b O'Reilly	19
W.H.Ponsford	b Howell	12
L.P.J.O'Brien	c McCabe b O'Reilly	53
L.S.Darling	b O'Reilly	4
S.P.King	run out (Hird/Love)	30
E.H.Bromley	c Stewart b McCabe	84
†B.A.Barnett	b O'Reilly	39
L.E.Nagel	not out	5
L.O.Fleetwood-Smith	c O'Reilly b Howell	1
H.H.Alexander	b Howell	0
H.Ironmonger	b Howell	0
Extras	(b1, lb4, w1, nb5)	11
Total	(76.0 overs, 253 mins)	258

VICTORIA	O	M	R	W	w,nb		O	M	R	W	w,nb		FALL OF WICKETS			
Alexander	26	3	107	4	-,-									NSW	VIC	NSW
Nagel	24	1	90	1	-,-							Wkt	1st	1st	2nd
Ironmonger	30.2	6	87	5	-,-							1st	145	32	-
Fleetwood-Smith	14	0	73	0	-,-							2nd	248	32	-
Darling	4	0	18	0	-,-							3rd	308	36	-
Bromley							(1)	1	0	8	0	-,-	4th	338	84	-
													5th	340	174	-
NEW SOUTH WALES	O	M	R	W	w,nb								6th	341	235	-
Stewart	13	0	61	0	1,-								7th	345	255	-
McCabe	7	0	34	1	-,-								8th	365	258	-
Howell	25	6	69	4	-,-								9th	369	258	-
O'Reilly	24	9	52	4	-,5								10th	388	258	-
Hird	5	0	23	0	-,-											
Bradman	2	0	8	0	-,-											

SOUTH AUSTRALIA v QUEENSLAND (Shield Match 8)

Played at Adelaide Oval on December 23, 24, 26, 1932. (Four-day match)
Toss : Queensland.   Result : SOUTH AUSTRALIA WON BY TEN WICKETS.
Debuts: Nil.
12th Men: W.E.Catchlove (SA) and E.A.Shaw (Qld).
Umpires: A.G.Jenkins and E.H.Kitson.
Attendances: 2721, 4444, 652.   Total: 7817.   Receipts: £240.
Close of Play: 1st day SA 2/170 (Lonergan 48, Walker 0); 2nd day Qld (2) 6/101 (Mossop 0).

T.W.Wall was rested from the South Australian team for the Second Test. The touring manager Shaw acted as 12th man in the absence of C.D.Hansen, who was injured in the previous match at Melbourne. Queensland struggled from the outset, losing Cook in the third over of the match. Only Mossop (54 in 111 minutes) passed 50 in either innings. Wicketkeeper-batsman Marshall injured a thumb during his 33 (106 minutes, 1 four), badly missed Lonergan at 48 off Thurlow, which cost a further 97 runs, and was struck below the eye by a ball from Tobin in the second innings, forcing his retirement at 0/16. (Sides is thought to have kept wickets for the six balls in Marshall's absence.) Bensted (33 in 49 minutes, 1 six and 3 fours), Andrews (37 in 80 minutes, 3 fours), Sides (31 in 79 minutes, 4 fours) and Oxenham (39 in 73 minutes, 3 fours) scored thirties. Nitschke (94 in 144 minutes, 2 sixes and 9 fours) and Lonergan (145 in 256 minutes, 1 six and 17 fours) dominated the local scoring, Lonergan giving a single chance as mentioned above. Sources: *Wisden, SACA Report, QCA Report, Adelaide Advertiser, Australian Cricketer, The News.*

QUEENSLAND

G.G.Cook	c Richardson b Tobin	1		c & b Tobin	12
†A.N.Marshall	b Tobin	33		retired hurt	5
W.C.Andrews	c Nitschke b Grimmett	12		lbw b Waite	37
R.K.Oxenham	c Walker b Tobin	5	(9)	lbw b Grimmett	39
F.W.Sides	c Walker b Grimmett	18		lbw b Lee	31
*E.C.Bensted	lbw b Grimmett	33		b Waite	1
K.L.M.Mossop	lbw b Grimmett	11	(8)	c Richardson b Lee	54
F.M.Brew	b Grimmett	7	(10)	not out	19
J.G.Maddern	st Walker b Lee	7	(4)	b Waite	8
H.S.Gamble	b Grimmett	1	(7)	b Lee	1
H.M.Thurlow	not out	1		lbw b Lee	0
Extras	(b1, lb4)	5		(b4, lb8)	12
Total	(45.5 overs, 162 mins)	134		(70.6 overs, 231 mins)	219

SOUTH AUSTRALIA

*V.Y.Richardson	b Gamble	26			
H.C.Nitschke	b Oxenham	94			
A.R.Lonergan	b Bensted	145			
†C.W.Walker	c Maddern b Brew	15			
A.G.Shepherd	c Bensted b Gamble	25			
P.K.Lee	b Brew	4			
B.J.Tobin	c Sides b Brew	5			
R.S.Whitington	c Bensted b Oxenham	31			
M.G.Waite	b Bensted	2	(1)	not out	1
D.G.Jamieson	lbw b Oxenham	3	(2)	not out	1
C.V.Grimmett	not out	0			
Extras	(b1, nb1)	2			—
Total	(93.0 overs, 319 mins)	352		(0.6 overs, 2 mins) (0 wkts)	2

SOUTH AUSTRALIA	O	M	R	W	w,nb		O	M	R	W	w,nb
Tobin	13	1	48	3	-,-		10	2	37	1	-,-
Jamieson	7	1	12	0	-,-		13	0	42	0	-,-
Grimmett	19.5	4	55	6	-,-	(5)	9	1	31	1	-,-
Lee	6	2	14	1	-,-		19.6	8	31	4	-,-
Waite						(3)	19	4	66	3	-,-

QUEENSLAND	O	M	R	W	w,nb		O	M	R	W	w,nb
Thurlow	11	0	61	0	-,-						
Gamble	22	1	93	2	-,1	(1)	0.6	0	2	0	-,-
Oxenham	36	16	73	3	-,-						
Brew	22	1	115	3	-,-						
Bensted	2	1	8	2	-,-						

FALL OF WICKETS

Wkt	QLD 1st	SA 1st	QLD 2nd	SA 2nd
1st	2	52	21	-
2nd	23	166	44	-
3rd	40	197	87	-
4th	65	251	91	-
5th	81	261	92	-
6th	110	277	101	-
7th	121	340	185	-
8th	132	346	213	-
9th	133	352	219	-
10th	134	352	-	-

TASMANIA v VICTORIA

Played at N.T.C.A. Ground, Launceston, on December 29, 30, 31, 1932. (Three-day match)
Toss : Tasmania.   Result : MATCH DRAWN.
Debuts: Tasmania - J.Tringrove (f/c). Victoria - J.C.Francis, L.D.Kemp, H.J.Plant, J.G.Stanes, J.L.Stephens (all f/c).
12th Men: R.B.S.Wardlaw (Tas) and E.H.G.Vernon (Vic).
Umpires: E.C.Knight and R.S.Williams.
Attendances & Receipts: No figures published; probably very low.
Close of Play: 1st day Vic 1/56 (Francis 30, Stanes 3); 2nd day Tas (2) 1/29 (Burrows 12, Green 13).

J.A.Atkinson, G.T.H.James, S.WL.Putman and A.W.Rushforth were all unavailable for Tasmania. Lethborg, the original 12th man, replaced R.H.Nash (unavailable) after the side was named. Late Victorian unavailables E.H.Bromley, H.I.Ebeling and J.Thomas were replaced by Millar, Oakley and Plant. Badcock (68 in 183 minutes, 3 fours) and Burrows (41 in 155 minutes, 3 fours) gave Tasmania a sound start but the rest of the batting failed on the first day. Martin, fortunate to survive the first ball he faced as the leg-bail came off in the process of his getting a single to fine leg, was out two balls later. Plant (off-breaks) took his best figures on debut while another debutant, Francis, scored 135 in 193 minutes and hit 13 fours. Oakley (53 in 75 minutes, 5 fours) and Quin (58 in 104 minutes, 4 fours) scored half-centuries, Townley dismissing Quin and McCormick with consecutive balls to wrap up the Victorian innings. Green saved Tasmania from defeat with his highest score, compiled in 344 minutes with 9 fours. *VCA Report* incorrectly gives Tas (2) Townley c & b Smith; Vic 9/430. Sources: *The Cricketer, TCA Report, VCA Report, Launceston Examiner, Hobart Mercury, Australian Cricketer.*

TASMANIA

C.L.Badcock	c McCormick b Plant	68	c Quin b Kemp	3
A.O.Burrows	lbw b Smith	41	b McCormick	37
*D.C.Green	st Quin b Plant	26	not out	150
G.W.Martin	lbw b McCormick	1	c Quin b McCormick	43
R.A.Broomby	c Smith b Plant	2	b Liddicut	25
G.G.Gibson	c Kemp b Plant	11	c & b Stephens	6
G.J.Lethborg	run out (Francis/Quin)	1	st Quin b Stephens	2
†C.N.Parry	run out (Kemp)	1	b Stephens	10
R.C.Townley	lbw b Plant	1	c Liddicut b Smith	18
J.M.Walsh	not out	0	not out	16
J.Tringrove	b Plant	2		
Extras	(b11, lb1, w3, nb2)	17	(b6, lb 9,w1)	16
Total	(71.2 overs, 265 mins)	171	(96.0 overs, 357 mins) (8 wkts)	326

VICTORIA

L.D.Kemp	run out (Green)	15
J.C.Francis	b Walsh	135
J.G.Stanes	c Green b Burrows	35
H.H.Oakley	c Green b Burrows	53
K.J.Millar	b Walsh	33
J.L.Stephens	c Burrows b Townley	41
†S.O.Quin	c Walsh b Townley	58
*A.E.Liddicut	lbw b Townley	31
S.A.J.Smith	lbw b Burrows	14
H.J.Plant	not out	13
E.L.McCormick	st Parry b Townley	0
Extras	(b5, lb6, nb1)	12
Total	(89.3 overs, 346 mins)	440

VICTORIA	O	M	R	W	w,nb		O	M	R	W	w,nb				
McCormick	16	3	39	1	2,1		23	4	61	2	-,-				
Kemp	7	2	17	0	-,-		6	0	21	1	-,-				
Millar	9	1	12	0	-,-	(4)	7	0	29	0	1,-				
Plant	17.2	2	43	6	-,1	(5)	8	0	25	0	-,-				
Smith	14	1	30	1	1,-	(3)	17	1	69	1	-,-				
Liddicut	8	2	13	0	-,-		14	2	40	1	-,-				
Stephens							20	1	59	3	-,-				
Oakley							1	0	6	0	-,-				

		FALL OF WICKETS			
		TAS	VIC	TAS	
Wkt		1st	1st	2nd	
1st		99	34	9	
2nd		128	111	73	
3rd		129	219	135	
4th		139	267	198	
5th		166	286	215	
6th		167	342	219	
7th		168	398	243	
8th		169	419	299	
9th		169	440	-	
10th		171	440	-	

TASMANIA	O	M	R	W	w,nb
Burrows	23	1	128	3	-,-
Walsh	25	3	104	2	-,1
Tringrove	17	2	67	0	-,-
Townley	21.3	0	111	4	-,-
Lethborg	3	0	18	0	-,-

AUSTRALIA v ENGLAND (2nd Test)

Played at Melbourne Cricket Ground on December 30, 31, 1932, January 2, 3, 1933. (Timeless match)
Toss : Australia.   Result : AUSTRALIA WON BY 111 RUNS.
Debuts: Australia - L.P.J.O'Brien (Test).
12th Men: W.H.Ponsford (Aust) and E.Paynter (Eng).
Umpires: E.G.Borwick and G.A.Hele.
Attendances: 63993, 36944, 68238, 31460.   Total: 200,635.   Receipts: £16,158.
Close of Play: 1st day Aust 7/194 (Oldfield 13); 2nd day Eng 9/161 (Allen 26); 3rd day Eng (2) 0/43 (Sutcliffe 33, Leyland 10).

A slow wicket which gave more assistance to the bowlers as the game progressed was responsible for the low scoring throughout. Fingleton (83 in 234 minutes, 277 balls, 3 fours) played a dour and courageous innings on the first day in the face of a most hostile attack. The celebrated first-ball dismissal of Bradman, who bottom-edged a hook into his stumps, provided Bowes with his only Test wicket on Australian soil. Bradman atoned in the second innings with a chanceless unbeaten century (103 not out in 185 minutes, 146 balls, 7 fours). Richardson made contributions of 34 (74 minutes, 5 fours) and 32 (44 minutes, 3 fours). O'Reilly took full advantage of the conditions and his ten wickets, together with Bradman's century, did most to win the match for his team. He was well supported by Wall in the first innings and Ironmonger in the second. Sutcliffe topscored for England on both occasions, batting for 156 minutes (5 fours) in the first innings and for 53 minutes (4 fours) in the second. Allen hit well both times, when he had only the tail for support. For the first time, England had not included a specialist spinner in their Test side. Twice in the match a new world record attendance was set for one day's cricket. Sources: *Wisden, VCA Report, The Age, The Argus, The Australasian, The Herald.*

AUSTRALIA

J.H.W.Fingleton	b Allen	83	c Ames b Allen	1
*W.M.Woodfull	b Allen	10	c Allen b Larwood	26
L.P.J.O'Brien	run out (Pataudi/Ames)	10	b Larwood	11
D.G.Bradman	b Bowes	0	not out	103
S.J.McCabe	c Jardine b Voce	32	b Allen	0
V.Y.Richardson	c Hammond b Voce	34	lbw b Hammond	32
†W.A.S.Oldfield	not out	27	b Voce	6
C.V.Grimmett	c Sutcliffe b Voce	2	b Voce	0
T.W.Wall	run out (Allen)	1	lbw b Hammond	3
W.J.O'Reilly	b Larwood	15	c Ames b Hammond	0
H.Ironmonger	b Larwood	4	run out (Larwood/Ames)	0
Extras	(b5, lb1, w2, nb2)	10	(b3, lb1, w4, nb1)	9
Total	(86.3 overs, 326 mins)	228	(56.5 overs, 216 mins)	191

ENGLAND

H.Sutcliffe	c Richardson b Wall	52	b O'Reilly	33
R.E.S.Wyatt	lbw b O'Reilly	13	(7) lbw b O'Reilly	25
W.R.Hammond	b Wall	8	(4) c O'Brien b O'Reilly	23
Nawab of Pataudi, sr	b O'Reilly	15	(3) c Fingleton b Ironmonger	5
M.Leyland	b O'Reilly	22	(2) b Wall	19
*D.R.Jardine	c Oldfield b Wall	1	(5) c McCabe b Ironmonger	0
†L.E.G.Ames	b Wall	4	(6) c Fingleton b O'Reilly	2
G.O.B.Allen	c Richardson b O'Reilly	30	st Oldfield b O'Reilly	23
H.Larwood	b O'Reilly	9	c Wall b Ironmonger	4
W.Voce	c McCabe b Grimmett	6	c O'Brien b O'Reilly	0
W.E.Bowes	not out	4	not out	0
Extras	(b1, lb2, nb2)	5	(lb4, nb1)	5
Total	(85.3 overs, 251 mins)	169	(55.1 overs, 173 mins)	139

ENGLAND	O	M	R	W	w,nb		O	M	R	W	w,nb
Larwood	20.3	2	52	2	-,2		15	2	50	2	-,-
Voce	20	3	54	3	-,-	(4)	15	2	47	2	-,1
Allen	17	3	41	2	2,-	(2)	12	1	44	2	4,-
Hammond	10	3	21	0	-,-	(5)	10.5	2	21	3	-,-
Bowes	19	2	50	1	-,-	(3)	4	0	20	0	-,-

AUSTRALIA	O	M	R	W	w,nb		O	M	R	W	w,nb
Wall	21	4	52	4	-,2		8	2	23	1	-,1
O'Reilly	34.3	17	63	5	-,-		24	5	66	5	-,-
Grimmett	16	4	21	1	-,-	(4)	4	0	19	0	-,-
Ironmonger	14	4	28	0	-,-	(3)	19.1	8	26	4	-,-

FALL OF WICKETS

Wkt	AUST 1st	ENG 1st	AUST 2nd	ENG 2nd
1st	29	30	1	53
2nd	67	43	27	53
3rd	67	83	78	70
4th	131	98	81	70
5th	156	104	135	77
6th	188	110	150	85
7th	194	122	156	135
8th	200	138	184	137
9th	222	161	186	138
10th	228	169	191	139

NEW SOUTH WALES v QUEENSLAND (Shield Match 9)

Played at Sydney Cricket Ground on December 30, 31, 1932, January 2, 3, 1933. (Four-day match)
Toss : New South Wales.　　　　　Result : NEW SOUTH WALES WON BY 218 RUNS.
Debuts: New South Wales - T.G.Parsonage (f/c).
12th Men: J.Griffin (NSW) and E.A.Shaw (Qld - manager).
Umpires: H.J.Armstrong and W.G.French.
Attendances: 2643, 2936, 1641, 177.　　　　Total: 7397.　　　Receipts: £225.
Close of Play: 1st day NSW 273 all out; 2nd day NSW (2) 7/132 (Hird 4, Hill 13); 3rd day Qld (2) 5/170 (Hansen 35, Leeson 4).

Although depleted by the absence of Test men D.G.Bradman, J.H.W.Fingleton, A.F.Kippax, S.J.McCabe, W.A.S.Oldfield and W.J.O'Reilly plus O.W.Bill (unavailable - replaced by original 12th man Parsonage), New South Wales easily accounted for an out-of-form Queensland side missing A.N.Marshall (injured) and R.K.Oxenham (unavailable). Hill brought in to replace O'Reilly, played the match of his life, returning match figures of 12 for 67 with his slow left-arm spinners in addition to making 108 runs (91 in 108 minutes, 9 fours). Both bat and ball performances remained his best at first-class level. Others to do well for New South Wales were Nutt (58 in 102 minutes, 5 fours), Marks (45 in 55 minutes, 2 fours), Solomon (47 in 46 minutes, 7 fours) and in the second innings Love (51) and Hird (62 in 108 minutes, 5 fours). Leeson, sent from Brisbane to fill in, scored Queensland's only half-century (52 in 93 minutes, 1 six and 6 fours). Cook (49 in 142 minutes, 4 fours) and Andrews (42 in 89 minutes, 6 fours) scored best in the second innings. Sources: *Wisden, NSWCA Report, QCA Report, Sydney Morning Herald, The Herald, Sydney Referee.*

NEW SOUTH WALES

R.N.Nutt	c Gamble b Bensted	58	c sub (E.A.Shaw) b Gamble	12
W.A.Brown	run out (Brew/　　　　)	17	b Gamble	0
*†H.S.B.Love	lbw b Brew	22	c Maddern b Bensted	51
A.E.Marks	c Mossop b Brew	45	b Gamble	26
S.F.Hird	c Bensted b Brew	38	c Bensted Cook	62
F.S.Cummins	c Hansen b Thurlow	2	c Leeson b Gamble	0
C.M.Solomon	c Gamble b Bensted	47	lbw b Bensted	20
T.G.Parsonage	c sub (E.A.Shaw) b Bensted	6	c Leeson b Brew	3
C.J.Hill	b Gamble	17	c sub (E.A.Shaw) b Gamble	91
W.H.Howell	c Brew b Gamble	1	b Gamble	20
G.L.Stewart	not out	7	not out	6
Extras	(b6, lb4, nb3)	13	(b6, lb4, w1, nb1)	12
Total	(66.1 overs, 247 mins)	273	(66.1 overs, 262 mins)	303

QUEENSLAND

G.G.Cook	b Hill	7	(2) b Marks	49
F.M.Brew	c Parsonage b Howell	8	(8) b Hill	0
F.W.Sides	b Hill	17	(4) b Hill	1
†H.F.Leeson	c Parsonage b Stewart	52	(7) not out	14
*E.C.Bensted	lbw b Hill	37	c Howell b Stewart	25
K.L.M.Mossop	b Hill	0	(1) c Marks b Stewart	9
W.C.Andrews	lbw b Hill	3	(3) b Stewart	42
C.D.Hansen	hit wkt b Hill	5	(6) c Cummins b Hill	35
J.G.Maddern	b Cummins	11	c Love b Stewart	7
H.S.Gamble	c Cummins b Hill	1	c Howell b Hill	3
H.M.Thurlow	not out	0	b Hill	14
Extras	(b6, lb2, nb1)	9	(b4, lb1, w3, nb1)	9
Total	(51.0 overs, 174 mins)	150	(63.1 overs, 215 mins)	208

QUEENSLAND	O	M	R	W	w,nb		O	M	R	W	w,nb
Thurlow	13	2	34	1	-,-						
Gamble	21.1	1	82	2	-,2	(1)	27.1	1	115	6	-,1
Bensted	14	1	53	3	-,1	(2)	15	1	58	2	1,-
Brew	18	0	91	3	-,-	(3)	19	2	100	1	-,-
Cook						(4)	5	0	18	1	-,-

NEW SOUTH WALES	O	M	R	W	w,nb		O	M	R	W	w,nb
Howell	10	1	49	1	-,-	(3)	7	1	24	0	-,-
Hill	17	10	18	7	-,-		23.1	9	49	5	-,-
Stewart	10	1	21	1	-,1	(1)	15	3	58	4	2,-
Hird	8	2	36	0	-,-						
Cummins	6	1	17	1	-,-	(4)	8	3	19	0	-,1
Marks						(5)	8	0	34	1	-,-
Parsonage						(6)	2	0	15	0	1,-

FALL OF WICKETS

Wkt	NSW 1st	QLD 1st	NSW 2nd	QLD 2nd
1st	46	8	1	19
2nd	95	36	22	100
3rd	114	37	70	101
4th	177	124	80	113
5th	183	132	105	164
6th	210	133	116	170
7th	246	133	116	170
8th	247	142	274	187
9th	250	148	276	190
10th	273	150	303	208

TASMANIA v VICTORIA

Played at T.C.A. Ground , Hobart, on January 2, 3, 4 (no play), 1933. (Three-day match)
Toss : Tasmania.   Result : MATCH DRAWN.
Debuts: Tasmania - C.L.Jeffrey, A.J.Trebilcock (both f/c). Victoria - E.H.G.Vernon (f/c).
12th Men: S.A.J.Smith (Vic). No 12th for Tasmania.
Umpires: W.T.Lonergan and A.O'Leary.
Attendances: 600, 200, no play.   Total: About 800.   Receipts: £26.
Close of Play: 1st day Vic 5/158 (Stephens 4, Kemp 6); 2nd day Tas (2) 2/78 (Badcock 34, Burrows 17).

Jeffrey, named as Tasmania's 12th man, came into the side as a late replacement for G.T.H.James, who withdrew. Atkinson was dismissed in the opening over of the match and only Burrows (29 in 135 minutes, 1 four) and Hooper (40 not out in 48 minutes, 7 fours) reached double figures in the first innings, Hooper making his runs out of 50 while he was at the crease. Victorians Vernon (67 in 135 minutes, 1 four) and Stanes (41 in 75 minutes) saw their side ahead. An eighth-wicket partnership of 179 in 118 minutes was shared by Kemp (114 in 169 minutes, 9 fours) and Quin (113 in 135 minutes, 12 fours), both being dropped by Putman, Kemp at 50 off Hooper and Quin at 17, a caught-and-bowled chance. Plant's 58 took 50 minutes and included 6 fours. Badcock (34 not out in 110 minutes, 2 fours) began well in the second innings but the intervention of rain prevented any play on the final day. Sources: *Australian Cricketer, TCA Report, VCA Report, Hobart Mercury.*

TASMANIA

*J.A.Atkinson	c Plant b McCormick	2	b Plant	20
C.L.Badcock	b Kemp	1	not out	34
D.C.Green	c McCormick b Kemp	5	c Stanes b Plant	0
A.O.Burrows	c Oakley b McCormick	29	not out	17
S.W.L.Putman	b Millar	4		
A.J.Trebilcock	st Quin b Millar	7		
G.G.Gibson	c Stephens b Millar	5		
C.L.Jeffrey	b McCormick	3		
V.L.Hooper	not out	40		
†C.N.Parry	c & b Stephens	0		
J.Tringrove	b McCormick	1		
Extras	(b7, lb5, nb1)	13	(lb2, nb5)	7
Total	(43.3 overs, 168 mins)	110	(32.0 overs, 110 mins) (2 wkts)	78

VICTORIA

J.C.Francis	c Putman b Burrows	14
E.H.G.Vernon	st Parry b Putman	67
H.H.Oakley	c Burrows b Hooper	13
J.G.Stanes	c Hooper b Putman	41
K.J.Millar	st Parry b Putman	8
J.L.Stephens	b Hooper	20
L.D.Kemp	c Jeffrey b Putman	114
*A.E.Liddicut	c Atkinson b Tringrove	12
†S.O.Quin	c Burrows b Jeffrey	113
H.J.Plant	run out (Parry)	58
E.L.McCormick	not out	7
Extras	(b8, lb1, w1, nb8)	18
Total	(104.2 overs, 359 mins)	485

VICTORIA	O	M	R	W	w,nb		O	M	R	W	w,nb
McCormick	13.3	5	32	4	-,1	(2)	9	1	24	0	-,4
Kemp	8	4	12	2	-,-	(4)	4	1	12	0	-,-
Millar	13	4	24	3	-,-	(1)	6	2	6	0	-,1
Plant	5	2	8	0	-,-	(3)	10	3	26	2	-,-
Stephens	4	0	21	1	-,-						
Liddicut						(5)	3	1	3	0	-,-

TASMANIA	O	M	R	W	w,nb
Hooper	24	4	99	2	-,8
Burrows	16	0	62	1	-,-
Putman	27	0	138	4	-,-
Tringrove	19	4	79	1	-,-
Jeffrey	17	0	83	1	1,-
Atkinson	1.2	0	6	0	-,-

FALL OF WICKETS

Wkt	TAS 1st	VIC 1st	TAS 2nd
1st	2	28	48
2nd	6	47	48
3rd	25	135	-
4th	31	143	-
5th	44	148	-
6th	55	181	-
7th	60	199	-
8th	108	378	-
9th	109	430	-
10th	110	485	-

AUSTRALIA v ENGLAND (3rd Test)

Played at Adelaide Oval on January 13, 14, 16, 17, 18, 19, 1933. (Timeless match)
Toss : England.   Result : ENGLAND WON BY 338 RUNS.
Debuts: Nil.
12th Men: L.P.J.O'Brien (Aust) and F.R.Brown (Eng).
Umpires: E.G.Borwick and G.A.Hele.
Attendances: 37201, 50962, 32527, 19821, 24529, 7321.   Total: 172, 361.   Receipts: £16,236.
Close of Play: 1st day Eng 7/236 (Paynter 25, Verity 5); 2nd day Aust 4/109 (Ponsford 45, Richardson 21); 3rd day Eng (2) 1/85
     (Jardine 24, Wyatt 47); 4th day Eng (2) 6/296 (Ames 18); 5th day Aust (2) 4/120 (Woodfull 36, Richardson 0).

The Bodyline controversy, which had been building up throughout the tour, reached its height when Australia batted. Woodfull was painfully struck over the heart early on, while facing a conventional field setting (Jardine then reverted to Bodyline), but the real crisis came when Oldfield was hit on the head attempting to hook Larwood at 7/218 on the third day. He suffered a fractured skull and took no further part in the match (Richardson kept wicket in the second innings). The crowd - booing, hooting and counting Larwood out - threatened to invade the ground and mounted police were sent in to restore order around the boundary line. Cables debating the fairness of the English bowling tactics were exchanged between the Australian Board of Control and M.C.C. in the ensuing weeks, and for a time it seemed that the tour might be abandoned. (The fact that both Woodfull and Oldfield had accidently sustained their injuries, through little fault of the bowler, made it difficult to fully appreciate the gravity of the situation from afar.) Ponsford (85 in 216 minutes, 8 fours), Woodfull (73 not out in 235 minutes, 2 fours) and Bradman (66 in 73 minutes, 71 balls, 1 six and 10 fours) scored half-centuries for Australia, Woodfull becoming the first batsman to twice carry his bat for the country in Tests. England recovered from 4/30 on the first day thanks to steadfast batting by Leyland (83 in 180 minutes, 13 fours), Wyatt (78 in 164 minutes, 3 sixes and 3 fours), Paynter (77 in 185 minutes, 9 fours) and Verity (45 in 157 minutes, 2 fours). Second innings by Jardine (56 in 254 minutes), Wyatt (49 in 133 minutes, 4 fours), Hammond (85 in 221 minutes, 8 fours) and lastly Ames (69 in 164 minutes, 6 fours) put England in an unassailable position. Paynter, who injured an ankle while fielding, was dropped down the order. The Saturday attendance was a record for Adelaide. Sources: *Wisden, SACA Report, Adelaide Advertiser, The Age, The News.*

ENGLAND

H.Sutcliffe	c Wall b O'Reilly	9		c sub (L.P.J.O'Brien) b Wall	7
*D.R.Jardine	b Wall	3		lbw b Ironmonger	56
W.R.Hammond	c Oldfield b Wall	2	(5)	b Bradman	85
†L.E.G.Ames	b Ironmonger	3	(7)	b O'Reilly	69
M.Leyland	b O'Reilly	83	(6)	c Wall b Ironmonger	42
R.E.S.Wyatt	c Richardson b Grimmett	78	(3)	c Wall b O'Reilly	49
E.Paynter	c Fingleton b Wall	77	(10)	not out	1
G.O.B.Allen	lbw b Grimmett	15	(4)	lbw b Grimmett	15
H.Verity	c Richardson b Wall	45	(8)	lbw b O'Reilly	40
W.Voce	b Wall	8	(11)	b O'Reilly	8
H.Larwood	not out	3	(9)	c Bradman b Ironmonger	8
Extras	(b1, lb7, nb7)	15		(b17, lb11, nb4)	32
Total	(146.1 overs, 437 mins)	341		(191.3 overs, 560 mins)	412

AUSTRALIA

J.H.W.Fingleton	c Ames b Allen	0		b Larwood	0
*W.M.Woodfull	b Allen	22		not out	73
D.G.Bradman	c Allen b Larwood	8	(4)	c & b Verity	66
S.J.McCabe	c Jardine b Larwood	8	(5)	c Leyland b Allen	7
W.H.Ponsford	b Voce	85	(3)	c Jardine b Larwood	3
V.Y.Richardson	b Allen	28		c Allen b Larwood	21
†W.A.S.Oldfield	retired hurt	41		absent hurt	-
C.V.Grimmett	c Voce b Allen	10	(7)	b Allen	6
T.W.Wall	b Hammond	6	(8)	b Allen	0
W.J.O'Reilly	b Larwood	0	(9)	b Larwood	5
H.Ironmonger	not out	0	(10)	b Allen	0
Extras	(b2, lb11, nb1)	14		(b4, lb2, w1, nb5)	12
Total	(95.4 overs, 332 mins)	222		(69.2 overs, 235 mins)	193

AUSTRALIA	O	M	R	W	w,nb		O	M	R	W	w,nb
Wall	34.1	10	72	5	-,3		29	6	75	1	-,2
O'Reilly	50	19	82	2	-,4		50.3	21	79	4	-,1
Ironmonger	20	6	50	1	-,-		57	21	87	3	-,-
Grimmett	28	6	94	2	-,-		35	9	74	1	-,-
McCabe	14	3	28	0	-,-		16	0	42	0	-,1
Bradman							4	0	23	1	-,-

ENGLAND	O	M	R	W	w,nb		O	M	R	W	w,nb
Larwood	25	6	55	3	-,-		19	3	71	4	-,2
Allen	23	4	71	4	-,-		17.2	5	50	4	1,2
Hammond	17.4	4	30	1	-,-	(4)	9	3	27	0	-,-
Voce	14	5	21	1	-,1	(3)	4	1	7	0	-,-
Verity	16	7	31	0	-,-		20	12	26	1	-,1

FALL OF WICKETS

	ENG	AUST	ENG	AUST
Wkt	1st	1st	2nd	2nd
1st	4	1	7	3
2nd	16	18	91	12
3rd	16	34	123	100
4th	30	51	154	116
5th	186	131	245	171
6th	196	194	296	183
7th	228	212	394	183
8th	324	222	395	192
9th	336	222	403	193
10th	341	-	412	-

NEW SOUTH WALES v M.C.C.

Played at Sydney Cricket Ground on January 26, 27, 28, 1933. (Four-day match)
Toss : New South Wales.   Result : M.C.C. WON BY FOUR WICKETS.
Debuts: New South Wales - R.C.Rowe (f/c).
12th Men: L.Bennett (NSW). No 12th named for MCC.
Umpires: E.G.Borwick and W.G.French.
Attendances: 23248, 8329, 15156.   Total: 46,733.   Receipts: £2928.
Close of Play: 1st day NSW 5/169 (Rowe 67, Love 0); 2nd day NSW (2) 1/36 (Brown 18, Bradman 10).

W.A.S.Oldfield (injured), S.F.Hird and S.J.McCabe were all unavailable for New South Wales while Chilvers replaced W.J.O'Reilly who rested after being selected to play. Bennett, from rural Junee, was named 12th man as a result of his performance in the New South Wales Country XI v M.C.C. fixture at Wagga Wagga in December. E.Paynter and W.Voce were both unavailable for M.C.C. with ankle injuries. Rain prevented any play after 4.48 pm on the first day and further rain that night affected the partially-covered wicket. Brown (69 in 163 minutes, 3 fours) and Rowe (70 in 92 minutes, 1 five and 4 fours) added 101 for the fifth wicket after Fingleton had assisted Brown in an opening stand of 58, but the remainder completely failed as New South Wales lost 5 for 4 early on the second day. Brown (25 in 85 minutes, 1 four) held out for a time with Bradman (71 in 123 minutes, 6 fours) in the second innings as the medium pace of Hammond accounted for a further six batsmen. The M.C.C. line-up also struggled on the rain damaged wicket, Wyatt (63 in 120 minutes, 2 fours), Verity (33 in 73 minutes) and Leyland (29 in 33 minutes, 1 six and 4 fours) batting most effectively in the first innings and Leyland (33 in 68 minutes, 5 fours) again performing in the second. Wicketkeeper Love was struck in the face by a ball from Chilvers at 3/53 on the third day and Fingleton kept for the rest as the visitors knocked off the required runs. Sources: *Wisden, NSWCA Report, VCA Report, Sydney Morning Herald, Australian Cricketer, Sydney Referee.*

NEW SOUTH WALES

Batsman	Dismissal (1st)	Score	Dismissal (2nd)	Score
J.H.W.Fingleton	b Mitchell	19	lbw b Tate	7
W.A.Brown	c Ames b Bowes	69	c Duckworth b Hammond	25
D.G.Bradman	b Mitchell	1	c Ames b Hammond	71
*A.F.Kippax	c Mitchell b Bowes	3	c Verity b Hammond	1
F.S.Cummins	b Mitchell	0	c Verity b Hammond	3
R.C.Rowe	c Mitchell b Verity	70	c Bowes b Hammond	11
†H.S.B.Love	c Ames b Hammond	4	b Verity	2
C.J.Hill	c Verity b Hammond	0	c Mitchell b Hammond	0
H.C.Chilvers	lbw b Hammond	4	run out (Brown/Duckworth)	0
W.H.Howell	c Brown b Verity	0	b Verity	6
G.L.Stewart	not out	0	not out	0
Extras	(b7, lb2, nb1)	10	(b1, lb1)	2
Total	(51.5 overs, 195 mins)	180	(38.1 overs, 153 mins)	128

M.C.C.

Batsman	Dismissal (1st)	Score	Dismissal (2nd)	Score
*R.E.S.Wyatt	lbw b Hill	63	run out (Cummins/Love)	3
Nawab of Pataudi, sr	c Chilvers b Howell	2	b Hill	0
W.R.Hammond	c Rowe b Howell	7	(4) st Love b Chilvers	24
H.Verity	c Stewart b Chilvers	33	(6) c Chilvers b Howell	1
L.E.G.Ames	b Chilvers	6	st Fingleton b Chilvers	3
M.Leyland	c Rowe b Chilvers	29	(3) c Stewart b Chilvers	33
F.R.Brown	c Stewart b Hill	29	not out	12
M.W.Tate	c Fingleton b Hill	15	not out	26
†G.Duckworth	not out	6		
W.E.Bowes	st Love b Chilvers	0		
T.B.Mitchell	lbw b Chilvers	0		
Extras	(b6, lb1, w1, nb1)	9	(b5, lb3)	8
Total	(55.3 overs, 165 mins)	199	(29.4 overs, 100 mins) (6 wkts)	110

M.C.C.	O	M	R	W	w,nb	O	M	R	W	w,nb
Bowes	15	2	48	2	-,-	7	1	19	0	-,-
Tate	10	1	42	0	-,-	4	0	10	1	-,-
Mitchell	10	1	32	3	-,-	5	0	28	0	-,-
Hammond	8.5	1	22	3	-,-	13	1	43	6	-,-
Verity	5	1	9	2	-,1	9.1	3	26	2	-,-
Brown	3	0	17	0	-,-					

NEW SOUTH WALES	O	M	R	W	w,nb		O	M	R	W	w,nb
Stewart	6	0	38	0	-,1						
Howell	13	2	40	2	-,-	(1)	12	2	33	1	-,-
Hill	19	6	39	3	-,-	(2)	10	0	40	1	-,-
Chilvers	17.3	2	73	5	1,-	(3)	7.4	0	29	3	-,-

FALL OF WICKETS

Wkt	NSW 1st	MCC 1st	NSW 2nd	MCC 2nd
1st	58	6	11	2
2nd	60	35	74	11
3rd	67	106	78	51
4th	68	118	84	59
5th	169	118	110	70
6th	176	163	116	70
7th	176	189	119	-
8th	176	196	122	-
9th	179	199	128	-
10th	180	199	128	-

QUEENSLAND v SOUTH AUSTRALIA (Shield Match 10)

Played at Brisbane Cricket Ground (Woolloongabba) on January 27, 28, 30, 31, 1933. (Four-day match)
Toss : Queensland.   Result : SOUTH AUSTRALIA WON BY NINE WICKETS.
Debuts: Nil.
12th Men: C.D.Hansen (Qld) and M.G.Waite (SA).
Umpires: J.Bartlett and B.L.Turner.
Attendances: 1801, 3800, 4100, 200.   Total: 9901.   Receipts: £467.
Close of Play: 1st day Qld 1/37 (Cook 21, Andrews 15); 2nd day SA 6/184 (Tobin 36, Lee 6); 3rd day SA (2) 0/24 (Richardson 15, Nitschke 9).

Rain restricted play on the first day to 44 minutes. Grimmett's combined analysis of 13 for 135, aided by five stumpings and a catch by Walker, remained the best in a Brisbane Shield match to the time of writing. Only Levy (68 in 108 minutes, 9 fours) exceeded 35; his was the topscore in a dismal season for the State in which all matches were lost outright. Nitschke (47 in 109 minutes) and Tobin (47 in 73 minutes, 2 sixes and 4 fours) made joint topscore for South Australia. Lonergan was adjudged out when he played a ball on to his wicket, dislodging a bail from its groove without it falling to the ground. Leeson, who injured a hand while keeping, gave way to Levy on the last day. *Wisden* incorrectly gives SA Walker c Lee b Oxenham. Sources: *Wisden, SACA Report, QCA Report, Brisbane Courier, Australian Cricketer.*

QUEENSLAND

G.G.Cook	c Walker b Wall	28	st Walker b Grimmett		23
R.M.Levy	b Tobin	1	b Lee		68
W.C.Andrews	lbw b Grimmett	34	st Walker b Grimmett		22
J.L.Litster	b Wall	2	c Lonergan b Grimmett		8
*F.J.Gough	c Richardson b Wall	0	c Ryan b Grimmett		0
E.C.Bensted	c Ryan b Grimmett	20	b Grimmett		2
R.K.Oxenham	st Walker b Grimmett	3	b Grimmett		15
†H.F.Leeson	b Grimmett	13	lbw b Grimmett		12
F.M.Brew	st Walker b Grimmett	16	c Ryan b Lee		16
H.S.Gamble	st Walker b Grimmett	7	not out		7
E.Gilbert	not out	1	lbw b Lee		10
Extras	(b2, nb2)	4	(b7, lb1, nb1)		9
Total	(36.6 overs, 160 mins)	129	(60.4 overs, 221 mins)		192

SOUTH AUSTRALIA

*V.Y.Richardson	c Cook b Gamble	21	not out		39
H.C.Nitschke	c Gough b Brew	47	b Oxenham		9
A.R.Lonergan	b Gilbert	31	not out		28
A.J.Ryan	c Levy b Brew	7			
R.S.Whitington	lbw b Andrews	29			
B.J.Tobin	b Gilbert	47			
W.E.Catchlove	b Gilbert	3			
P.K.Lee	c Cook b Gilbert	11			
C.V.Grimmett	b Oxenham	31			
T.W.Wall	not out	0			
†C.W.Walker	c Levy b Oxenham	12			
Extras	(b3, lb2, nb5)	10			—
Total	(60.2 overs, 241 mins)	249	(18.1 overs, 72 mins) (1 wkt)		76

SOUTH AUSTRALIA	O	M	R	W	w,nb		O	M	R	W	w,nb
Wall	12	3	25	3	-,2		8	0	24	0	-,1
Tobin	4	0	30	1	-,-		5	2	7	0	-,-
Grimmett	15.6	2	49	6	-,-		24	0	86	7	-,-
Lee	5	0	21	0	-,-		19.4	3	57	3	-,-
Ryan							4	0	9	0	-,-

QUEENSLAND	O	M	R	W	w,nb		O	M	R	W	w,nb
Gilbert	16	1	58	4	-,-		7	1	24	0	-,-
Gamble	13	2	52	1	-,4		3	0	15	0	-,-
Oxenham	14.2	6	30	2	-,-		5	3	12	1	-,-
Bensted	3	0	11	0	-,-						
Brew	12	0	82	2	-,-	(4)	3.1	0	25	0	-,-
Andrews	2	0	6	1	-,1						

FALL OF WICKETS

Wkt	QLD 1st	SA 1st	QLD 2nd	SA 2nd
1st	3	27	98	24
2nd	57	88	98	-
3rd	59	104	110	-
4th	59	113	116	-
5th	81	162	118	-
6th	92	170	147	-
7th	97	201	148	-
8th	107	204	168	-
9th	126	247	180	-
10th	129	249	192	-

NEW SOUTH WALES v SOUTH AUSTRALIA (Shield Match 11)

Played at Sydney Cricket Ground on February 3, 4, 6, 1933. (Four-day match)
Toss : New South Wales.   Result : NEW SOUTH WALES WON BY 98 RUNS.
Debuts: Nil.
12th Men: L.Bennett (NSW) and W.E.Catchlove (SA).
Umpires: E.G.Borwick and W.G.French.
Attendances: 7089, 14051, 5006.   Total: 26,146.   Receipts: £1009.
Close of Play: 1st day SA all out; 2nd day NSW (2) 5/284 (Cummins 9, Love 9).

Slightly aided by a stiff cross-breeze but operating in conditions which otherwise favoured the batsmen, Thomas (Tim) Welbourn Wall became the first bowler in the Sheffield Shield and only the second in Australia to take all ten wickets in a first-class innings. His lunchtime analysis of 1 for 31 on the first day was boosted by a remarkable spell of 9 for 5 from 5.4 overs after the adjournment, which included the wickets of Fingleton, McCabe (first ball), Rowe and Cummins in his ninth over, his second after lunch. Fingleton (43 in 72 minutes, 3 fours) and Bradman (56 in 109 minutes, 5 fours) were the only batsmen to exceed 4 in the innings. Inexplicably, South Australia continued the pattern by being dismissed for 114 before the day ended, McCabe (67 in 95 minutes, 7 fours) and Brown (79 in 210 minutes) preceded a rare Bradman ninety on the second day (97 in 172 minutes, 8 fours) before Cummins and Love added 66 together for the sixth wicket. Nitschke (105 in 132 minutes, 1 six, 2 fives and 12 fours) topscored on the last day and Bradman finished the game with the wicket of the man of the match. Cummins, originally named as 12th man, and Rowe replaced S.F.Hird, who had left for England to play in the Lancashire League, and A.F.Kippax (unavailable), Love taking the captaincy in Kippax's absence. Sources: *Wisden, NSWCA Report, SACA Report, Australian Cricketer, Sydney Morning Herald*.

NEW SOUTH WALES

J.H.W.Fingleton	b Wall	43	(4)	c Tobin b Wall	0
W.A.Brown	c Whitington b Wall	0		c Walker b Wall	79
D.G.Bradman	c Ryan b Wall	56		b Lee	97
S.J.McCabe	c Walker b Wall	0	(1)	lbw b Grimmett	67
R.C.Rowe	b Wall	0		c Tobin b Lee	19
F.S.Cummins	c Walker b Wall	0		b Grimmett	36
*†H.S.B.Love	b Wall	1		lbw b Ryan	31
C.J.Hill	b Wall	0		not out	9
W.H.Howell	b Wall	0		b Ryan	8
W.J.O'Reilly	b Wall	4		c Walker b Lee	5
G.L.Stewart	not out	2		b Lee	0
Extras	(lb1, w1, nb5)	7		(b1, lb2, nb2)	5
Total	(28.4 overs, 134 mins)	113		(87.5 overs, 351 mins)	356

SOUTH AUSTRALIA

*V.Y.Richardson	b McCabe	5		b O'Reilly	35
H.C.Nitschke	c O'Reilly b Howell	12		c Rowe b O'Reilly	105
A.R.Lonergan	lbw b O'Reilly	22		lbw b Hill	20
A.J.Ryan	c Stewart b Howell	4	(5)	c Rowe b Hill	33
R.S.Whitington	c Love b Howell	1	(7)	c sub (L.Bennett) b O'Reilly	2
B.J.Tobin	b Howell	8		b O'Reilly	1
A.G.Shepherd	c Brown b Bradman	32	(4)	c sub (L.Bennett) b O'Reilly	0
P.K.Lee	c Brown b McCabe	8		b Hill	11
C.V.Grimmett	run out (Bradman)	1		b Hill	10
T.W.Wall	c Cummins b Howell	13		st Love b Bradman	19
†C.W.Walker	not out	0		not out	6
Extras	(b5, w1, nb2)	8		(b11, lb1, w1, nb2)	15
Total	(42.2 overs, 145 mins)	114		(67.4 overs, 236 mins)	257

SOUTH AUSTRALIA	O	M	R	W	w,nb		O	M	R	W	w,nb
Wall	12.4	2	36	10	1,5		22	1	91	2	,2
Tobin	5	0	23	0	-,-		12	0	69	0	-,-
Grimmett	11	0	47	0	-,-		20	2	84	2	-,-
Ryan							17	3	38	2	-,-
Lee							16.5	2	69	4	-,-

NEW SOUTH WALES	O	M	R	W	w,nb		O	M	R	W	w,nb
Stewart	3	1	8	0	1,-		6	0	32	0	1,-
McCabe	6	1	18	2	-,-						
Howell	15	5	31	5	-,1		9	1	57	0	-,-
O'Reilly	13	2	34	1	-,1	(2)	25	8	56	5	-,2
Hill	4	2	11	0	-,-	(4)	22	2	61	4	-,-
Bradman	1.2	0	4	1	-,-	(5)	5.4	0	36	1	-,-

FALL OF WICKETS

	NSW	SA	NSW	SA
Wkt	1st	1st	2nd	2nd
1st	12	8	95	76
2nd	87	39	217	143
3rd	87	44	217	152
4th	88	48	262	175
5th	88	49	268	178
6th	99	57	334	185
7th	105	70	338	207
8th	105	77	349	228
9th	106	114	356	239
10th	113	114	356	257

QUEENSLAND v M.C.C.

Played at Brisbane Cricket Ground (Woolloongabba) on February 4, 6, 7, 1933. (Four-day match)
Toss : Queensland.   Result : M.C.C. WON BY AN INNINGS AND 61 RUNS.
Debuts: Nil.
12th Men: C.D.Hansen (Qld) and T.B.Mitchell (MCC).
Umpires: J.Bartlett and J.A.Scott.
Attendances: 9999, 5951, 2443.   Total: 18,393.   Receipts: £1428.
Close of Play: 1st day MCC 0/6 (Jardine 4, Verity 1); 2nd day MCC 8/303 (Ames 44).

F.M.Brew and H.F.Leeson were unavailable for Queensland and Hansen and R.C.Raymond were omitted from the thirteen on the morning of the match. Queensland lost a wicket to the second ball of each innings, Levy in the first and Gough in the second, both caught by Allen off Larwood. Cook (53 in 184 minutes, 1 six and 3 fours), Andrews (45 in 100 minutes, 4 fours) and Litster (67 in 141 minutes, 8 fours) were the only locals to exceed 20 runs. Oxenham in the first innings was given not out to a catch by Allen close in on leg the side from Larwood's bowling. He was bowled shortly after without adding to his score, but not before Larwood had subjected him to a barrage of very fast short-pitched balls in protest at the umpire's decision and the batsman not walking. All M.C.C. batsmen except Leyland got a start, Wyatt (40 in 121 minutes, 4 fours), Allen (66 in 116 minutes, 1 six and 10 fours) and Ames (80 in 76 minutes, 1 six and 11 fours) making the best scores. Sources: *Wisden, NSWCA Report, QCA Report, Australian Cricketer, Brisbane Courier.*

QUEENSLAND

R.M.Levy	c Allen b Larwood	0	(4)	c Ames b Larwood	6
G.G.Cook	c & b Verity	53		c Jardine b Larwood	11
W.C.Andrews	c Allen b Larwood	45		c Jardine b Larwood	5
*F.J.Gough	b Verity	11	(1)	c Allen b Larwood	0
J.L.Litster	b Bowes	67		c Hammond b Verity	5
E.C.Bensted	b Bowes	1		lbw b Verity	9
R.K.Oxenham	b Allen	8		lbw b Verity	17
†L.W.Waterman	run out (Bowes)	0		c Paynter b Verity	0
H.S.Gamble	b Bowes	1		c Verity b Larwood	14
E.Gilbert	st Ames b Leyland	6		b Larwood	1
J.M.Govan	not out	5		not out	10
Extras	(b4)	4		(b2, nb1)	3
Total	(73.5 overs, 278 mins)	201		(21.3 overs, 100 mins)	81

M.C.C.

*D.R.Jardine	b Oxenham	34
H.Verity	b Oxenham	21
H.Sutcliffe	lbw b Oxenham	35
M.Leyland	b Gilbert	2
R.E.S.Wyatt	c Levy b Govan	40
W.R.Hammond	c Levy b Litster	27
G.O.B.Allen	c Gough b Govan	66
E.Paynter	lbw b Gilbert	19
†L.E.G.Ames	st Waterman b Oxenham	80
H.Larwood	c Litster b Govan	1
W.E.Bowes	not out	2
Extras	(b4, lb8, nb4)	16
Total	(92.6 overs, 335 mins)	343

M.C.C.	O	M	R	W	w,nb		O	M	R	W	w,nb
Larwood	9	1	24	2	-,-		8	1	38	6	-,1
Allen	11	3	37	1	-,-	(4)	2	0	5	0	-,-
Bowes	15	1	43	3	-,-		3	0	10	0	-,-
Verity	28	12	49	2	-,-	(5)	6.3	1	20	4	-,-
Hammond	6	3	15	0	-,-	(2)	2	0	5	0	-,-
Wyatt	3	0	16	0	-,-						
Leyland	1.5	0	13	1	-,-						

QUEENSLAND	O	M	R	W	w,nb
Gilbert	25	3	93	2	-,-
Gamble	18	3	58	0	-,4
Oxenham	33.6	11	70	4	-,-
Govan	6	0	59	3	-,-
Litster	4	0	10	1	-,-
Bensted	4	1	19	0	-,-
Andrews	2	0	18	0	-,-

FALL OF WICKETS

	QLD	MCC	QLD
Wkt	1st	1st	2nd
1st	0	28	0
2nd	79	75	15
3rd	94	78	23
4th	131	115	24
5th	134	165	35
6th	154	169	38
7th	175	228	38
8th	184	303	52
9th	195	306	57
10th	201	343	81

AUSTRALIA v ENGLAND (4th Test)

Played at Brisbane Cricket Ground (Woolloongabba) on February 10, 11, 13, 14, 15, 16, 1933. (Timeless match)
Toss : Australia.   Result : ENGLAND WON BY SIX WICKETS
Debuts: Australia - E.H.Bromley, L.S.Darling, H.S.B.Love (all Test). England - T.B.Mitchell (Test).
12th Men: B.J.Tobin (Aust) and F.R.Brown (Eng).
Umpires: E.G.Borwick and G.A.Hele.
Attendances: 22516, 28794, 14177, 16992, 8793, 1591.   Total: 92,863.   Receipts: £10,905.
Close of Play: 1st day Aust 3/251 (Bradman 71, Ponsford 8); 2nd day Eng 0/99 (Jardine 41, Sutcliffe 51); 3rd day Eng 8/271 (Paynter 24,
    Verity 1); 4th day Aust (2) 4/108 (McCabe 14, Darling 8); 5th day Eng (2) 2/107 (Leyland 66, Hammond 8).

Australia were given a fine start by Richardson (83 in 159 minutes, 6 fours), Woodfull (67 in 244 minutes, 7 fours) and Bradman (76 in 156 minutes, 11 fours) but lost their last eight wickets for 107. England also began well, Jardine (46 in 190 minutes, 3 fours) and Sutcliffe (86 in 266 minutes, 10 fours) batting soundly if rather slowly. Rot in the middle order was repaired by Paynter (83 in 238 minutes, 10 fours) who, despite suffering from acute tonsillitis, went straight from hospital to commence his innings on the third afternoon. He returned to care that night before resuming his innings next day, adding a vital 92 runs for England's ninth wicket with Verity. Richardson (32 in 64 minutes, 2 fours) and Darling (39 in 109 minutes, 3 fours) topped Australia's batting in a disappointing second innings. Owing partly to the easy nature of the wicket, Bodyline tactics when deployed, did not arouse much excitement in the crowd, apart from some hooting on occasions. Voce (ankle injury) was also not fit to play, and the hot, stifling weather mitigated against Larwood bowling hostile spells of any duration. Leyland (86 in 222 minutes, 9 fours) ensured England of winning the Ashes with his half-century on the fifth day. Paynter won the match when he lofted a slow McCabe full toss for six. A sad day for Australian cricket, February 16th 1933 also saw Archie Jackson, 23, lose his battle with tuberculosis. Sources: *Wisden, QCA Report, Brisbane Courier, The Age, The Argus, The Herald.*

AUSTRALIA

Batsman	Dismissal	Runs		Dismissal	Runs
V.Y.Richardson	st Ames b Hammond	83		c Jardine b Verity	32
*W.M.Woodfull	b Mitchell	67		c Hammond b Mitchell	19
D.G.Bradman	b Larwood	76		c Mitchell b Larwood	24
S.J.McCabe	c Jardine b Allen	20	(5)	b Verity	22
W.H.Ponsford	b Larwood	19	(4)	c Larwood b Allen	0
L.S.Darling	c Ames b Allen	17		run out (Mitchell)	39
E.H.Bromley	c Verity b Larwood	26		c Hammond b Allen	7
†H.S.B.Love	lbw b Mitchell	5		lbw b Larwood	3
T.W.Wall	not out	6		c Jardine b Allen	2
W.J.O'Reilly	c Hammond b Larwood	6		b Larwood	4
H.Ironmonger	st Ames b Hammond	8		not out	0
Extras	(b5, lb1, nb1)	7		(b13, lb9, nb1)	23
Total	(121.0 overs, 411 mins)	340		(68.3 overs, 244 mins)	175

ENGLAND

Batsman	Dismissal	Runs		Dismissal	Runs
*D.R.Jardine	c Love b O'Reilly	46		lbw b Ironmonger	24
H.Sutcliffe	lbw b O'Reilly	86		c Darling b Wall	2
W.R.Hammond	b McCabe	20	(4)	c Bromley b Ironmonger	14
R.E.S.Wyatt	c Love b Ironmonger	12			
M.Leyland	c Bradman b O'Reilly	12	(3)	c McCabe b O'Reilly	86
†L.E.G.Ames	c Darling b Ironmonger	17	(5)	not out	14
G.O.B.Allen	c Love b Wall	13			
E.Paynter	c Richardson b Ironmonger	83	(6)	not out	14
H.Larwood	b McCabe	23			
H.Verity	not out	23			
T.B.Mitchell	lbw b O'Reilly	0			
Extras	(b6, lb12, nb3)	21		(b2, lb4, nb2)	8
Total	(185.4 overs, 599 mins)	356		(79.4 overs, 247 mins)	162

ENGLAND	O	M	R	W	w,nb		O	M	R	W	w,nb
Larwood	31	7	101	4	-,1		17.3	3	49	3	-,1
Allen	24	4	83	2	-,-		17	3	44	3	-,-
Hammond	23	5	61	2	-,-		10	4	18	0	-,-
Mitchell	16	5	49	2	-,-	(5)	5	0	11	1	-,-
Verity	27	12	39	0	-,-	(4)	19	6	30	2	-,-

AUSTRALIA	O	M	R	W	w,nb		O	M	R	W	w,nb
Wall	33	6	66	1	-,2		7	1	17	1	-,-
O'Reilly	67.4	27	120	4	-,1		30	11	65	1	-,-
Ironmonger	43	19	69	3	-,-		35	13	47	2	-,-
McCabe	23	7	40	2	-,-		7.4	2	25	0	-,2
Bromley	10	4	19	0	-,-						
Bradman	7	1	17	0	-,-						
Darling	2	0	4	0	-,-						

FALL OF WICKETS

Wkt	AUST 1st	ENG 1st	AUST 2nd	ENG 2nd
1st	133	114	46	5
2nd	200	157	79	78
3rd	233	165	81	118
4th	264	188	91	138
5th	267	198	136	-
6th	292	216	163	-
7th	315	225	169	-
8th	317	264	169	-
9th	329	356	171	-
10th	340	356	175	-

VICTORIA v SOUTH AUSTRALIA (Shield Match 12)

Played at Melbourne Cricket Ground on February 10, 11, 13, 1933. (Four-day match)
Toss : Victoria.   Result : VICTORIA WON BY 73 RUNS.
Debuts: Victoria - A.L.Hassett (f/c). South Australia - R.G.Williams (f/c).
12th Men: J.G.Stanes (Vic) and W.E.Catchlove (SA).
Umpires: W.J.Moore and T.A.Wells.
Attendances: 2457, 3609, 970.   Total: 7036.   Receipts: £155.
Close of Play: 1st day Vic 299 all out; 2nd day Vic (2) 6/88 (Kemp 7).

K.E.Rigg was unavailable for Victoria and Plant replaced L.E.Nagel (work) after the selection of the team. O'Brien (44 in 141 minutes, 3 fours), Thomas (53 in 83 minutes, 6 fours), Oakley (103 in 201 minutes, 10 fours) and Plant (43 in 93 minutes, 1 six and 5 fours) batted soundly on the first day against the slow right-arm deliveries of Lee (4 for 80) and Grimmett (6 for 109). After scooping his first ball in first-class cricket to the leg boundary, off Grimmett, Hassett fell two balls later to the same bowler. Nitschke was dropped by Barnett in the first over of the South Australian first innings and went on to topscore with 88 in 186 minutes, hitting 8 fours. Second-innings fifties were achieved by O'Brien for Victoria (52 in 101 minutes, 7 fours) and Lonergan for South Australia (52 in 71 minutes, 5 fours). Sources: *Wisden, VCA Report, SACA Report, Australian Cricketer, The Age, The Argus, The Herald.*

VICTORIA

L.P.J.O'Brien	b Lee	44	b Grimmett	52
J.Thomas	b Lee	53	c Williams b Holton	1
H.H.Oakley	lbw b Grimmett	103	c Holton b Lee	15
*S.P.King	b Grimmett	4	c Whitington b Grimmett	1
A.L.Hassett	lbw b Grimmett	4	c Walker b Lee	9
L.D.Kemp	c Walker b Lee	4	c Ryan b Lee	25
H.J.Plant	c Whitington b Lee	43	lbw b Grimmett	1
†B.A.Barnett	st Walker b Grimmett	5	run out (Waite/Walker/Grimmett)	8
L.O.Fleetwood-Smith	st Walker b Grimmett	0	b Lee	0
E.L.McCormick	c Waite b Grimmett	13	lbw b Lee	0
H.H.Alexander	not out	23	not out	5
Extras	(b1, lb2)	3	(lb2, w1)	3
Total	(81.7 overs, 315 mins)	299	(38.5 overs, 143 mins)	120

SOUTH AUSTRALIA

H.C.Nitschke	c Barnett b Plant	88	b Fleetwood-Smith	36
A.J.Ryan	lbw b Alexander	18	c Oakley b Alexander	7
A.R.Lonergan	st Barnett b Fleetwood-Smith	17	c King b Fleetwood-Smith	52
R.S.Whitington	run out (King/Barnett)	19	c Barnett b McCormick	0
A.G.Shepherd	c Oakley b Plant	20	c Hassett b Fleetwood-Smith	3
M.G.Waite	c Barnett b McCormick	1	lbw b Fleetwood-Smith	8
P.K.Lee	c Barnett b Plant	0	run out (Barnett)	5
*C.V.Grimmett	c Barnett b McCormick	6	not out	17
R.G.Williams	not out	2	c Barnett b Kemp	13
†C.W.Walker	c Plant b Fleetwood-Smith	14	c King b Fleetwood-Smith	0
L.G.Holton	c Thomas b Fleetwood-Smith	0	run out (Hassett/Barnett)	4
Extras	(b1, lb8, w2, nb1)	12	(b4)	4
Total	(49.6 overs, 209 mins)	197	(34.6 overs, 143 mins)	149

SOUTH AUSTRALIA	O	M	R	W	w,nb		O	M	R	W	w,nb
Holton	14	1	50	0	-,-		4	0	23	1	-,-
Williams	5	1	29	0	-,-		4	0	19	0	1,-
Ryan	12	3	28	0	-,-						
Lee	26	7	80	4	-,-	(3)	15.5	8	23	5	-,-
Grimmett	24.7	1	109	6	-,-	(4)	15	1	52	3	-,-

VICTORIA	O	M	R	W	w,nb		O	M	R	W	w,nb
Alexander	15	1	51	1	-,1		8	0	36	1	-,-
McCormick	12	0	31	2	2,-		8	0	39	1	-,-
Kemp	2	0	15	0	-,-	(5)	2.6	1	3	1	-,-
Plant	9	1	31	3	-,-		2	0	13	0	-,-
Fleetwood-Smith	11.6	1	57	3	-,-	(3)	14	2	54	5	-,-

FALL OF WICKETS

Wkt	VIC 1st	SA 1st	VIC 2nd	SA 2nd
1st	81	49	6	15
2nd	124	92	48	57
3rd	141	120	57	58
4th	145	159	76	73
5th	158	162	82	102
6th	244	163	88	111
7th	263	172	103	111
8th	263	182	103	140
9th	268	197	103	141
10th	299	197	120	149

AUSTRALIA v ENGLAND (5th Test)

Played at Sydney Cricket Ground on February 23, 24, 25, 27, 28, 1933. (Timeless match)
Toss : Australia.   Result : ENGLAND WON BY EIGHT WICKETS.
Debuts: Australia - H.H.Alexander (Test).
12th Men: E.H.Bromley (Aust) and T.B.Mitchell (Eng).
Umpires: E.G.Borwick and G.A.Hele.
Attendances: 26143, 25687, 33032, 43380, 8604.   Total: 136,846.   Receipts: £11,804.
Close of Play: 1st day Aust 5/296 (Darling 66, Oldfield 13); 2nd day Eng 2/159 (Hammond 72, Larwood 5); 3rd day Eng 8/418
   (Allen 25); 4th day Eng (2) 0/11 (Jardine 6, Wyatt 5).

T.W.Wall (injured ankle) was unfit for Australian selection and L.E.Nagel (work) announced his unavailability when he was considered as a replacement. Richardson was dismissed by Larwood for a pair, to the fifth and second deliveries of the respective Australian innings. Bradman (48 in 72 minutes, 7 fours), O'Brien (61 in 107 minutes, 7 fours), McCabe (73 in 172 minutes, 11 fours), Darling (85 in 148 minutes, 8 fours), Oldfield (52 in 138 minutes, 4 fours) and Lee (42 in 35 minutes, 7 fours) contributed significantly to Australia's highest total against Bodyline bowling, Jardine enforcing its use despite the fact that the series had been decided. The Australians were abeted by at least seven dropped catches. Larwood (98 in 138 minutes, 148 balls, 1 six, 1 five and 9 fours) batted brilliantly after being sent in as nightwatchman to partner Hammond (101 in 207 minutes, 205 balls, 12 fours, several chances) and he was received, for once, with a great ovation on his return to the pavilion. It was Larwood's last Test; he broke down in the middle of his 11th over in the second innings in great pain - his big toe later proved to be broken - and completed it, under orders, by simply standing at the stumps and swinging his arm over, Woodfull patting the ball back to him. The stand of 115 between Woodfull (67 in 185 minutes, 5 fours) and Bradman (71 in 97 minutes, 9 fours) on the fourth day, a Monday, drew the biggest attendance of the match. Later in the day the crowd loudly barracked Jardine when he protested at Alexander's follow through; the bowler then sent down several short ones - one of which struck Jardine a painful blow on the hip - and cheering rang out across the ground. Sutcliffe (56 in 155 minutes, 4 fours) and Wyatt (51 in 160 minutes, 5 fours and 61 not out in 195 minutes, 4 fours) hit valuable half-centuries for England while Hammond (75 not out in 123 minutes, 2 sixes and 6 fours) ended the match with a straight-driven six. Alexander, in his sole Test, was out to his first ball in the second innings.
Sources: *Wisden, NSWCA Report, Sydney Referee, Sydney Morning Herald, Sydney Daily Telegraph.*

AUSTRALIA

V.Y.Richardson	c Jardine b Larwood	0	c Allen b Larwood	0
*W.M.Woodfull	b Larwood	14	b Allen	67
D.G.Bradman	b Larwood	48	b Verity	71
L.P.J.O'Brien	c Larwood Voce	61	c Verity b Voce	5
S.J.McCabe	c Hammond b Verity	73	c Jardine b Voce	4
L.S.Darling	b Verity	85	c Wyatt b Verity	7
†W.A.S.Oldfield	run out (Paynter)	52	c Wyatt b Verity	5
P.K.Lee	c Jardine b Verity	42	b Allen	15
W.J.O'Reilly	b Allen	19	b Verity	1
H.H.Alexander	not out	17	lbw b Verity	0
H.Ironmonger	b Larwood	1	not out	0
Extras	(b13, lb9, w1)	23	(b4, nb3)	7
Total	(108.2 overs, 410 mins)	435	(54.4 overs, 198 mins)	182

ENGLAND

*D.R.Jardine	c Oldfield b O'Reilly	18	c Richardson b Ironmonger	24
H.Sutcliffe	c Richardson b O'Reilly	56		
W.R.Hammond	lbw b Lee	101	(4) not out	75
H.Larwood	c Ironmonger b Lee	98		
M.Leyland	run out (Darling/Oldfield)	42	(3) b Ironmonger	0
R.E.S.Wyatt	c Ironmonger b O'Reilly	51	(2) not out	61
†L.E.G.Ames	run out (Bradman/Oldfield)	4		
E.Paynter	b Lee	9		
G.O.B.Allen	c Bradman b Lee	48		
H.Verity	c Oldfield b Alexander	4		
W.Voce	not out	7		
Extras	(b7, lb7, nb2)	16	(b6, lb1, nb1)	8
Total	(171.2 overs, 500 mins)	454	(71.2 overs, 195 mins) (2 wkts)	168

ENGLAND	O	M	R	W	w,nb		O	M	R	W	w,nb
Larwood	32.2	10	98	4	-,-		11	0	44	1	-,-
Voce	24	4	80	1	1,-	(4)	10	0	34	2	-,-
Allen	25	1	128	1	-,-	(2)	11.4	2	54	2	-,3
Hammond	8	0	32	0	-,-	(3)	3	0	10	0	-,-
Verity	17	3	62	3	-,-		19	9	33	5	-,-
Wyatt	2	0	12	0	-,-						

AUSTRALIA	O	M	R	W	w,nb		O	M	R	W	w,nb
Alexander	35	1	129	1	-,-		11	2	25	0	-,-
McCabe	12	1	27	0	-,-	(5)	5	2	10	0	-,-
O'Reilly	45	7	100	3	-,2	(2)	15	5	32	0	-,1
Ironmonger	31	13	64	0	-,-	(3)	26	12	34	2	-,-
Lee	40.2	11	111	4	-,-	(4)	12.2	3	52	0	-,-
Darling	7	5	3	0	-,-		2	0	7	0	-,-
Bradman	1	0	4	0	-,-						

FALL OF WICKETS

Wkt	AUST 1st	ENG 1st	AUST 2nd	ENG 2nd
1st	0	31	0	43
2nd	59	153	115	43
3rd	64	245	135	-
4th	163	310	139	-
5th	244	330	148	-
6th	328	349	161	-
7th	385	374	177	-
8th	414	418	178	-
9th	430	434	178	-
10th	435	454	182	-

VICTORIA v M.C.C.

Played at Melbourne Cricket Ground on March 3, 4, 6, 7, 1933. (Four-day match)
Toss : M.C.C.   Result : MATCH TIED.
Debuts: Nil.
12th Men: S.P.King (Vic) and L.E.G.Ames (MCC).
Umpires: A.N.Barlow and W.J.Moore.
Attendances: 10970, 8922, 10086, 6435.   Total: 36,413.   Receipts: £1396.
Close of Play: 1st day Vic 0/9 (O'Brien 6, Rigg 3); 2nd day Vic 1/48 (O'Brien 16, Darling 6); 3rd day MCC (2) 1/29 (Wyatt 13, Hammond 4).

Despite an incomplete fourth innings, this match resulted in the first tie in Australian first-class cricket. (After the 1948-49 season a match was considered tied only if the side batting last had been dismissed.) Victoria required five runs from the last over to win but could only achieve three singles and a leg-bye from the first seven balls before Rigg was caught off the last ball attempting to drive past Mitchell at mid-on. Rain restricted play on the second day to only 45 minutes. Sutcliffe (75 in 121 minutes, 7 fours), Hammond (59 in 49 minutes, 2 sixes and 8 fours) and Tate (94 not out in 116 minutes, 15 fours) registered first-innings half-centuries for the tourists, Hammond again (64 in 156 minutes, 6 fours) and Allen (48 in 95 minutes, 5 fours) topscoring in the second innings. Victoria's chief run-scorers were Darling (103 in 164 minutes, 12 fours), Oakley (50 in 76 minutes, 6 fours), Ebeling (68 not out in 82 minutes, 11 fours); Rigg (88 in 113 minutes, 7 fours) and Bromley (56 not out in 82 minutes, 1 six and 4 fours). L.E.Nagel (work) and W.M.Woodfull (unavailable) withdrew from the selected Victorian team and were replaced by Ebeling and J.Thomas, but Thomas was forced out through illness and Plant (original 12th man) played. Sources: *Wisden, VCA Report, NSWCA Report, Australian Cricketer, The Age, The Argus, The Herald.*

M.C.C.

H.Sutcliffe	b Plant	75	b Ebeling	11
*R.E.S.Wyatt	c O'Brien b Ebeling	8	c & b Fleetwood-Smith	29
W.R.Hammond	c Plant b Fleetwood-Smith	59	c O'Brien b Ironmonger	64
E.Paynter	c Ironmonger b Plant	30	b Ironmonger	2
G.O.B.Allen	c Oakley b Ironmonger	0	lbw b Fleetwood-Smith	48
F.R.Brown	st Barnett b Ironmonger	4	lbw b Ironmonger	5
M.W.Tate	not out	94	c Bromley b Ironmonger	6
W.Voce	b Ebeling	7	not out	2
†G.Duckworth	c Ebeling b Darling	15	c Ebeling b Fleetwood-Smith	2
T.B.Mitchell	c Oakley b Ironmonger	6	c Rigg b Ironmonger	5
W.E.Bowes	run out (Oakley/Barnett)	20		
Extras	(b1, w1, nb1)	3	(b3, lb5, nb1)	9
Total	(67.3 overs, 263 mins)	321	(60.1 overs, 237 mins) (9 wkts dec)	183

VICTORIA

L.P.J.O'Brien	lbw b Voce	20	c Duckworth b Bowes	7
*K.E.Rigg	c sub (H.Verity) b Bowes	21	c Mitchell b Bowes	88
L.S.Darling	c Duckworth b Bowes	103	c Hammond b Tate	19
E.H.Bromley	c Hammond b Brown	19	not out	56
H.H.Oakley	c Wyatt b Bowes	50		
H.J.Plant	lbw b Tate	1		
†B.A.Barnett	st Duckworth b Mitchell	17		
H.I.Ebeling	not out	68		
L.O.Fleetwood-Smith	st Duckworth b Brown	8		
H.H.Alexander	lbw b Brown	0		
H.Ironmonger	b Voce	6		
Extras	(b6, lb6, w2)	14	(b2, lb5)	7
Total	(68.3 overs, 283 mins)	327	(27.0 overs, 113 mins) (3 wkts)	177

VICTORIA	O	M	R	W	w,nb	O	M	R	W	w,nb
Alexander	13	0	49	0	1,1	12	3	33	0	-,1
Ebeling	17	3	56	2	-,-	13	4	44	1	-,-
Ironmonger	19	2	82	3	-,-	18.1	7	31	5	-,-
Fleetwood-Smith	7	0	67	1	-,-	17	1	66	3	-,-
Plant	8	1	55	2	-,-					
Darling	2	0	4	1	-,-					
Bromley	1.3	0	5	0	-,-					

M.C.C.	O	M	R	W	w,nb	O	M	R	W	w,nb
Bowes	19	2	93	3	-,-	8	1	56	2	-,-
Voce	14.3	1	62	2	-,-	3	0	22	0	-,-
Tate	13	4	31	1	-,-	6	0	35	1	-,-
Hammond	2	0	14	0	-,-	7	0	40	0	-,-
Mitchell	8	1	50	1	-,-	2	0	15	0	-,-
Brown	12	1	63	3	2,-	1	0	2	0	-,-

FALL OF WICKETS

Wkt	MCC 1st	VIC 1st	MCC 2nd	VIC 2nd
1st	18	35	21	18
2nd	100	65	75	47
3rd	157	108	86	177
4th	170	219	151	-
5th	175	220	165	-
6th	195	220	165	-
7th	208	272	171	-
8th	242	287	178	-
9th	268	287	183	-
10th	321	327	-	-

SOUTH AUSTRALIA v M.C.C

Played at Adelaide Oval on March 10, 11, 13, 14, 1933. (Four-day match)
Toss : M.C.C. Result : MATCH DRAWN.
Debuts: South Australia - J.S.Palmer (f/c).
12th Men: M.G.Waite (SA) and F.R.Brown (MCC).
Umpires: E.H.Kitson and J.D.Scott.
Attendances: 4989, ? , ? , ? . Total: 19,314. Receipts: £638.
Close of Play: 1st day MCC 4/240 (Jardine 48, Ames 36); 2nd day MCC (2) 0/6 (Paynter 5, Duckworth 1); 3rd day MCC (2) 8/371
 (Leyland 152, Voce 33).

Without G.O.B.Allen and H.Larwood (both injured), the Nawab of Pataudi (returned to England via India) and H.Sutcliffe (in New Zealand), the tourists appeared little interested for most of the match despite holding the upper hand. Paynter (62 in 130 minutes, 1 six and 5 fours), Wyatt (43 in 95 minutes), Leyland (36 in 109 minutes), Jardine (48 in 153 minutes) and Ames (63 in 81 minutes, 7 fours) all received starts before losing their wickets. Bowes dismissed Richardson with the second ball of the South Australian reply, in which Ryan (61 in 93 minutes, 10 fours) topscored. Williams and Tobin subjected M.C.C. to a mild form of Bodyline in the second innings, having four and sometimes five on the leg-side, but neither had the pace or accuracy to cause any great discomfort. Contributions from Paynter (47 in 70 minutes), Leyland (152 not out in 264 minutes, 18 fours, chances at 104 and 127) and Jardine (65 in 138 minutes) enabled an overnight declaration, setting the locals an impossible 479 runs on the last day. Nitschke (87 in 117 minutes, 1 six and 8 fours, 2 chances) again batted well. Tobin (52 not out in 53 minutes, 1 six and 8 fours) was hit in the face by a ball from Voce when 32 and retired at approximately 5/220, resuming at 8/287. Williams replaced T.W.Wall (injured) in the selected South Australian side. Sources: *Wisden, Australian Cricketer, SACA Report, VCA Report, Adelaide Advertiser, The News, The Herald.*

M.C.C.

E.Paynter	c Ryan b Grimmett	62		c Lonergan b Lee	47
H.Verity	c Ryan b Williams	12	(8)	b Lee	13
R.E.S.Wyatt	c Williams b Grimmett	43		c Richardson b Williams	11
M.Leyland	c Nitschke b Lee	36		not out	152
*D.R.Jardine	c Walker b Tobin	48		c Walker b Tobin	65
L.E.G.Ames	c Lonergan b Tobin	63		c Ryan b Williams	23
M.W.Tate	b Tobin	0		b Williams	4
W.Voce	c Walker b Williams	3	(10)	not out	33
†G.Duckworth	not out	13	(2)	run out (Palmer/Walker)	4
W.E.Bowes	run out (Grimmett/Walker)	4			
T.B.Mitchell	c Shepherd b Grimmett	10	(9)	b Lee	4
Extras	(b1, lb3)	4		(lb12, w1, nb2)	15
Total	(94.1 overs, 351 mins)	298		(76.0 overs, 303 mins) (8 wkts dec)	371

SOUTH AUSTRALIA

*V.Y.Richardson	c Verity b Bowes	0		b Voce	20
H.C.Nitschke	c Paynter b Voce	38		lbw b Mitchell	87
A.R.Lonergan	b Bowes	13		c Verity b Bowes	36
A.G.Shepherd	b Voce	17		b Bowes	6
B.J.Tobin	b Verity	18	(6)	not out	52
A.J.Ryan	c Tate b Bowes	61	(5)	c Voce b Bowes	25
J.S.Palmer	c Wyatt b Tate	15	(8)	b Tate	22
P.K.Lee	b Tate	8	(7)	c Verity b Bowes	5
C.V.Grimmett	c Mitchell b Verity	7	(10)	not out	15
R.G.Williams	not out	9	(9)	c Voce b Mitchell	23
†C.W.Walker	c Duckworth b Tate	0			
Extras	(b3, lb1, nb1)	5		(b19, lb3)	22
Total	(49.7 overs, 210 mins)	191		(70.0 overs, 289 mins) (8 wkts)	313

SOUTH AUSTRALIA	O	M	R	W	w,nb		O	M	R	W	w,nb				
Tobin	15	1	65	3	-,-		11	0	65	1	-,2				
Williams	20	3	46	2	-,-		21	2	107	3	1,-				
Lee	24	7	43	1	-,-	(4)	15	3	65	3	-,-				
Grimmett	25.1	2	124	3	-,-	(3)	23	3	85	0	-,-				
Ryan	10	4	16	0	-,-		6	1	34	0	-,-				

M.C.C.	O	M	R	W	w,nb		O	M	R	W	w,nb				
Bowes	10	0	60	3	-,-		15	0	95	4	-,-				
Tate	11.7	3	36	3	-,-		18	2	61	1	-,-				
Voce	9	0	33	2	-,1		13	2	44	1	-,-				
Verity	15	5	28	2	-,-		12	2	44	0	-,-				
Mitchell	4	0	29	0	-,-		11	2	34	2	-,-				
Jardine							1	0	13	0	-,-				

FALL OF WICKETS

Wkt	MCC 1st	SA 1st	MCC 2nd	SA 2nd
1st	23	0	10	57
2nd	117	34	41	135
3rd	121	68	78	151
4th	189	75	220	175
5th	241	107	261	213
6th	241	164	265	240
7th	266	173	314	255
8th	272	176	322	287
9th	277	190	-	-
10th	298	191	-	-

VICTORIA v TASMANIA

Played at Richmond Cricket Ground, Melbourne, on March 14, 15, 1933. (Three-day match)
Toss : Tasmania.   Result : VICTORIA WON BY SIX WICKETS.
Debuts: Victoria - W.J.Cornelius, W.Stalker (both f/c). Tasmania - G.A.Combes, M.J.Combes (both f/c).
12th Men: R.E.Marsh (Vic) and C.L.Jeffrey (Tas).
Umpires: C.Dwyer and T.A.Wells.
Attendances: 1337, 100.   Total: 1437.   Receipts: £40.
Close of Play: 1st day Tas (2) 3/33 (Badcock 15, Rushforth 0).

On a pitch variously described as 'two-paced' and 'inclined to be uncertain', Fleetwood-Smith achieved a personal best of 9 for 36, an analysis bettered only once by a Victorian bowler in the previous 82 years. His match figures, 14 for 85, were the best against Tasmania to date. James (39 in 35 minutes, 6 fours) and M.J.Combes (38 in 42 minutes, 3 fours) made the top scores for the islanders, Badcock (24 in 80 minutes, 3 fours) doing next best after getting a reprieve in the first over of the second innings. Francis (30 in 36 minutes, 4 fours), Stanes (44 in 73 minutes, 3 fours), Bromley (61 in 51 minutes, 8 fours) and King (32 in 74 minutes, 1 four) made notable contributions for Victoria. Cornelius, named 12th man, replaced L.D.Kemp (unavailable) in the Victorian team. This was the sole first-class match staged at the ground close to the M.C.G. also known as the Punt Road Oval; Victoria's sixth first-class venue since 1851-82. In its report after the season, the V.C.A. stated 'it has been the policy of the Association to give other grounds than the Melbourne Cricket Ground an opportunity of receiving an interstate fixture. The appointment at Richmond had nothing whatever to do with the failure of Tasmanian batsmen'. *TCA Report* incorrectly gives Tas (2) Walsh c Quin. *Age* and *Argus* give Vic (2) 1/7, 2/7. Sources: *VCA Report, TCA Report, Australian Cricketer, The Age, The Argus, The Herald, Melbourne Sun.*

TASMANIA

C.L.Badcock	c & b Fleetwood-Smith	10	b Bromley		24
A.O.Burrows	c King b Fleetwood-Smith	15	c Fleetwood-Smith b Stalker		1
D.C.Green	b Fleetwood-Smith	14	lbw b Fleetwood-Smith		9
R.E.Ward	run out (Plant)	5	c Quin b Fleetwood-Smith		4
*A.W.Rushforth	b Fleetwood-Smith	8	lbw b Plant		0
G.T.H.James	c King b Fleetwood-Smith	13	c Francis b Plant		39
R.O.G.Morrisby	c Bromley b Fleetwood-Smith	11	b Fleetwood-Smith		23
M.J.Combes	c Plant b Fleetwood-Smith	0	c Hassett b Fleetwood-Smith		38
†C.N.Parry	hit wkt b Fleetwood-Smith	2	b Fleetwood-Smith		18
J.M.Walsh	st Quin b Fleetwood-Smith	0	st Quin b King		0
G.A.Combes	not out	6	not out		2
Extras	(b2, lb4)	6	(b4)		4
Total	(28.0 overs, 104 mins)	90	(40.6 overs, 138 mins)		162

VICTORIA

J.C.Francis	c & b James	30	c Rushforth b Burrows		7
E.H.G.Vernon	c & b James	18	(6) not out		0
J.G.Stanes	c Parry b James	44			
E.H.Bromley	st Parry b Walsh	61	(5) not out		9
*S.P.King	c Burrows b Walsh	32			
A.L.Hassett	lbw b G.A.Combes	12	(4) c Badcock b Walsh		0
W.J.Cornelius	b Burrows	5	(3) c Ward b Burrows		0
H.J.Plant	lbw b Walsh	12			
†S.O.Quin	st Parry b Burrows	1	(2) c Burrows b Walsh		5
L.O.Fleetwood-Smith	c Ward b Walsh	0			
W.Stalker	not out	0			
Extras	(b11, lb2, w1)	14	(b2, w1)		3
Total	(49.2 overs, 177 mins)	229	(9.6 overs, 39 mins) (4 wkts)		24

VICTORIA	O	M	R	W	w,nb		O	M	R	W	w,nb
Stalker	7	1	17	0	-,-		5	2	9	1	-,-
Bromley	8	0	29	0	-,-		6	1	22	1	-,-
Fleetwood-Smith	10	0	36	9	-,-		12	2	49	5	-,-
Plant	3	2	2	0	-,-		12	3	45	2	-,-
King							5.6	0	33	1	-,-

TASMANIA	O	M	R	W	w,nb		O	M	R	W	w,nb
Walsh	15	2	67	4	-,-		5	2	4	2	1,-
James	12	3	31	3	-,-						
G.A.Combes	11	0	54	1	-,-	(2)	1	0	2	0	-,-
M.J.Combes	3	0	31	0	-,-						
Burrows	8.2	0	32	2	1,-	(3)	3.6	1	15	2	-,-

	FALL OF WICKETS			
Wkt	TAS 1st	VIC 1st	TAS 2nd	VIC 2nd
1st	22	56	5	10
2nd	31	59	22	10
3rd	41	150	26	11
4th	53	171	33	16
5th	70	199	72	-
6th	73	206	86	-
7th	73	225	133	-
8th	79	229	160	-
9th	79	229	160	-
10th	90	229	162	-

1933-34 SEASON (25 MATCHES)

In the absence of any visiting international team for the first time since the 1926-27 season, chief interest again focused on the Sheffield Shield competition. The selection of the forthcoming Australian team to tour England also brought forth much speculation and comment.

Victoria regained the Sheffield Shield narrowly from New South Wales. Both teams won three of their six matches, New South Wales boasting a far superior percentage. However, Victoria's ability to not lose a match outright remained the telling factor.

Bradman, in his final season for New South Wales, again secured an outstanding batting record. He scored in excess of 1100 runs for the sixth successive season, compiling 922 of these in Sheffield Shield matches alone. Other established batsmen, Kippax, Woodfull, Ponsford and Richardson, again came to the fore for their respective States, and the emergence of Darling, Brown, Badcock, Fingleton, Lonergan and Bromley excited followers of the game.

Grimmett, Fleetwood-Smith and O'Reilly, all wrist spinners, held the bowling limelight. Grimmett exceeded 50 wickets for the sixth successive season, an outstanding achievement in an era of mammoth scoring on unresponsive wickets.

The Board of Control amended the no-ball law (Law 48) in response to the events of the previous season. Umpires were empowered to no-ball any delivery directed with intent to injure or intimidate a batsman. The bowler would be advised of the reason for the call and, should he infringe a second time, he would not be permitted to bowl again in that innings. No instance arose during the season of the law coming into use.

Western Australia continued their attempts for a more regular first-class program. The WACA's proposal for a 'Second XI' competition, which had been addressed in September 1932 with the formation of a sub-committee at the Interstate Conference, resulted in a recommendation in September 1933 for matches between Tasmania, Western Australia and Second XIs of the four Sheffield Shield States to be played annually in Melbourne and Sydney, with costs to be equally shared. The recommendation was fully supported by VCA delegates, but there was not enough support from the other States for the Board to adopt the proposal. Spasmodic attempts to revive the concept continued until the cessation of cricket due to the war in 1941.

The 18th Australian team selected to tour England in 1934 was: W.M.Woodfull (captain), D.G.Bradman (vice-captain), B.A.Barnett, E.H.Bromley, W.A.Brown, A.G.Chipperfield, L.S.Darling, H.I.Ebeling, L.O.Fleetwood-Smith, C.V.Grimmett, A.F.Kippax, S.J.McCabe, W.A.S.Oldfield, W.J.O'Reilly, W.H.Ponsford and T.W.Wall. The only real surprise was the selection of Chipperfield after just three first-class matches and the omission of Fingleton - believed to be for allegations that he leaked dressing room comments during the bodyline series.

The Board of Control accepted an invitation from the New Zealand Cricket Council to send a second Australian team for a short tour in March-April 1934. The selected team comprised V.Y.Richardson (captain), K.E.Rigg (vice-captain), W.C.Andrews, C.L.Badcock, H.C.Chilvers, J.R.Davey, J.H.W.Fingleton, C.J.Hill, A.R.Lonergan, E.L.McCormick, L.E.Nagel, H.C.Nitschke and C.W.Walker. However, Richardson, Rigg, Hill, McCormick and Nagel all subsequently withdrew, owing to the meagre allowance put up by the Australian Board, and J.Ryder, J.W.Scaife, H.J.T.Theak, T.J.Trembath and E.R.Wyeth were called on to replace them. The lack of prominent players as drawcards eventually prompted the NZCC to cancel the tour, fearing a heavy financial loss.

Leading Aggregates

Batsmen	M	I	NO	Runs	HS	Ave.	Bowlers	Runs	Wkts	Ave.
D.G.Bradman (NSW)	7	11	2	1192	253	132.44	C.V.Grimmett (SA)	1441	66	21.83
W.A.Brown (NSW)	10	14	1	878	205	67.53	L.O.Fleetwood-Smith (V)	1385	53	26.13
A.F.Kippax (NSW)	11	14	2	863	141	71.91	W.J.O'Reilly (NSW)	860	38	22.63
L.S.Darling (V)	11	17	0	828	188	48.70	T.W.Wall (SA)	951	34	27.97
W.M.Woodfull (V)	10	14	1	818	129	62.92	H.I.Ebeling (V)	938	30	31.26
C.L.Badcock (T)	5	10	1	803	274	89.22	H.C.Chilvers (NSW)	854	27	31.62
J.H.W.Fingleton (NSW)	8	12	1	655	145	59.54	R.K.Oxenham (Q)	541	23	23.52
A.R.Lonergan (SA)	7	13	0	624	115	48.00	S.G.Francis (WA)	484	22	22.00
W.H.Ponsford (V)	8	13	1	606	122	50.50	S.A.J.Smith (V)	358	20	17.90
E.H.Bromley (V)	8	14	3	549	161	49.90				

SHEFFIELD SHIELD TABLE

	P	WO	W1	LO	L1	D	Pts	Quotient	Runs Scored	Wkts Lost	Runs Conceded	Wkts Taken
VICTORIA	6	3	1	-	2	-	20	1.141	3304	89	2894	89
NEW SOUTH WALES	6	3	1	1	1	-	19	1.880	3085	59	2920	105
SOUTH AUSTRALIA	6	2	-	4	-	-	10	0.847	2687	102	2859	92
QUEENSLAND	6	1	1	4	-	-	8	0.557	2519	102	2922	66
TOTAL	12	9	3	9	3	-	57	1.000	11595	352	11595	352

AFCM No. 803/61
SSM No. 258/15

QUEENSLAND v NEW SOUTH WALES (Shield Match 1)

Played at Brisbane Cricket Ground (Woolloongabba) on November 3, 4, 6 (no play), 7, 1933. (Four-day match)
Toss : Queensland.   Result : NEW SOUTH WALES WON BY AN INNINGS AND 171 RUNS.
Debuts: Queensland - T.Allen, R.C.Raymond, E.R.Wyeth, S.F.M.Yeates (all f/c). New South Wales - F.Mair (f/c).
12th Men: G.G.Cook (Qld) and R.C.J.Little (NSW).
Umpires: J.Bartlett and J.A.Scott.
Attendances: 3034, 5000, no play, 1000.   Total: 9034.   Receipts: £597.
Close of Play: 1st day NSW 0/66 (Fingleton 40, Brown 23); 2nd day NSW 4/494 (Kippax 46, Rowe 13); 3rd day no play.

Brown (154 in 302 minutes, 11 fours, chance at 108) and Bradman (200 in 184 minutes, 26 fours, chance at 103) put on 294 in 171 minutes for the New South Wales second wicket, a new record stand in matches between these teams. Bradman reached 50 in 34 minutes and 100 in 92 minutes, scoring 120 runs in the lunch-tea session on the second day before falling in the last over prior to the adjournment, including 23 off a Wyeth over. Fingleton (53 in 129 minutes, 4 fours) and Kippax (46 not out in 81 minutes, 6 fours) also batted well for the visitors. O'Reilly's match figures (13 for 111) were the best by any bowler at this venue. Andrews (59 in 146 minutes, 4 fours) and Bensted (70 in 145 minutes, 2 sixes and 6 fours) scored fifties for Queensland after McCabe had bowled Levy with the second ball of the match. Rain prevented play on the third day. *NSWCA Report* incorrectly gives umpires as R.Warner and S.Johnston. Sources: *Wisden, NSWCA Report, QCA Report, Brisbane Courier-Mail, Sydney Morning Herald, The Age.*

QUEENSLAND

*R.M.Levy	b McCabe	0	(6) lbw b O'Reilly	37
T.Allen	c Hill b O'Reilly	5	(8) st Oldfield b Mair	20
W.C.Andrews	lbw b McCabe	59	(4) b Mair	31
F.C.Thompson	c Oldfield b O'Reilly	12	(5) c Fingleton b O'Reilly	1
E.C.Bensted	c Bradman b Mair	70	(7) c Rowe b Mair	1
R.K.Oxenham	c Fingleton b O'Reilly	6	(9) c Hill b O'Reilly	16
R.C.Raymond	b O'Reilly	0	(2) c Brown b O'Reilly	19
†H.F.Leeson	c & b O'Reilly	0	(1) c Hill b O'Reilly	3
H.S.Gamble	b O'Reilly	9	(10) not out	1
S.F.M.Yeates	not out	13	(3) c McCabe b O'Reilly	0
E.R.Wyeth	b Mair	0	c Oldfield b O'Reilly	0
Extras	(lb5, nb4)	9	(b6, lb3, w1, nb1)	11
Total	(69.4 overs, 214 mins)	183	(59.0 overs, 175 mins)	140

NEW SOUTH WALES

J.H.W.Fingleton	c Leeson b Yeates	53
W.A.Brown	st Leeson b Yeates	154
D.G.Bradman	c Andrews b Levy	200
*A.F.Kippax	not out	46
S.J.McCabe	c Thompson b Oxenham	20
R.C.Rowe	not out	13
†W.A.S.Oldfield	)	
F.Mair	)	
C.J.Hill	) did not bat	
W.J.O'Reilly	)	
W.H.Howell	)	
Extras	(b2, lb1, nb5)	8
Total	(108.0 overs, 384 mins) (4 wkts dec)	494

NEW SOUTH WALES	O	M	R	W	w,nb		O	M	R	W	w,nb
McCabe	13	2	33	2	-,1		13	1	30	0	-,1
Hill	12	6	16	0	-,-		11	6	11	0	-,-
O'Reilly	22	9	58	6	-,3		20	8	53	7	-,-
Howell	10	3	28	0	-,-		4	0	5	0	-,-
Mair	12.4	1	39	2	-,-		11	1	30	3	1,-

QUEENSLAND	O	M	R	W	w,nb
Gamble	24	6	89	0	-,3
Bensted	8	3	33	0	-,2
Oxenham	30	8	81	1	-,-
Raymond	12	0	57	0	-,-
Wyeth	10	3	54	0	-,-
Yeates	22	1	155	2	-,-
Thompson	1	0	11	0	-,-
Levy	1	0	6	1	-,-

FALL OF WICKETS

Wkt	QLD 1st	NSW 1st	QLD 2nd
1st	0	101	23
2nd	17	395	23
3rd	38	426	23
4th	106	467	27
5th	128	-	94
6th	139	-	101
7th	139	-	103
8th	169	-	138
9th	177	-	140
10th	183	-	140

SOUTH AUSTRALIA v VICTORIA (Shield Match 2)

Played at Adelaide Oval on November 3, 4, 6, 7, 1933. (Four-day match)
Toss : Victoria.   Result : VICTORIA WON BY 169 RUNS.
Debuts: South Australia - J.R.Davey (f/c).
12th Men: M.G.Waite (SA) and H.H.Oakley (Vic).
Umpires: E.H.Kitson and J.D.Scott.
Attendances: 3864, 7550, 2876, 1166.   Total: 15,456.   Receipts: £510.
Close of Play: 1st day SA 1/77 (Nitschke 39, Lonergan 5); 2nd day Vic (2) 0/132 (Ponsford 59, Rigg 69); 3rd day SA (2) 1/70
     (Richardson 37, Lonergan 17).

In a match otherwise dominated by slow men Grimmett (7 for 80), Fleetwood-Smith (6 for 61 and 3 for 74) and Ironmonger (6 for 65), Davey (right-arm fast-medium) took a wicket (Ponsford) with his first ball in first-class cricket, the first South Australian to do so. Ponsford's revenge came in the second innings in the form of his 21st and last Shield hundred (122 in 208 minutes, 9 fours); he shared a decisive opening stand of 240 with Rigg (123 in 226 minutes, 10 fours). Woodfull, whose first-innings 52 took 135 minutes with 3 fours, batted down the order in the second innings due to a hand injury, leaving Darling (48 in 70 minutes, 6 fours) and Barnett (65 not out in 62 minutes, 9 fours) to assist in the target-setting. O'Brien scored 49 in 115 minutes and hit 5 fours. Nitschke (55 in 138 minutes, 6 fours) and Richardson (102 in 187 minutes, 12 fours) were South Australia's best batsmen. Sources: *Wisden, SACA Report, VCA Report, Adelaide Advertiser, The News.*

VICTORIA

*W.M.Woodfull	lbw b Grimmett	52	(7) not out		22
W.H.Ponsford	b Davey	1	(1) c Davey b Tobin		122
L.P.J.O'Brien	c Walker b Grimmett	49	(5) c Whitington b Davey		12
L.S.Darling	lbw b Tobin	6	(3) c Richardson b Lee		48
K.E.Rigg	c Ryan b Grimmett	30	(2) c Richardson b Tobin		123
E.H.Bromley	b Grimmett	28	(4) c Tobin b Davey		22
†B.A.Barnett	b Grimmett	17	(6) not out		65
L.E.Nagel	st Walker b Grimmett	1			
H.H.Alexander	not out	12			
L.O.Fleetwood-Smith	b Grimmett	0			
H.Ironmonger	b Lee	0			
Extras	(b1)	1	(b11, lb6)		17
Total	(63.0 overs, 224 mins)	197	(101.0 overs, 344 mins) (5 wkts dec)		431

SOUTH AUSTRALIA

*V.Y.Richardson	c Rigg b Fleetwood-Smith	32	st Barnett b Ironmonger		102
H.C.Nitschke	c Woodfull b Nagel	55	b Ironmonger		11
A.R.Lonergan	b Nagel	22	b Nagel		36
A.J.Ryan	b Fleetwood-Smith	20	c Alexander b Ironmonger		10
A.G.Shepherd	lbw b Fleetwood-Smith	19	c Darling b Ironmonger		20
R.S.Whitington	b Fleetwood-Smith	12	lbw b Fleetwood-Smith		2
B.J.Tobin	c Bromley b Fleetwood-Smith	0	c Bromley b Ironmonger		1
P.K.Lee	lbw b Fleetwood-Smith	22	not out		20
†C.W.Walker	c Barnett b Alexander	10	c Rigg b Ironmonger		1
C.V.Grimmett	c Ponsford b Alexander	22	lbw b Fleetwood-Smith		1
J.R.Davey	not out	1	c Nagel b Fleetwood-Smith		4
Extras	(b5, lb6, nb2)	13	(b14, lb8, nb1)		23
Total	(82.6 overs, 306 mins)	228	(68.5 overs, 240 mins)		231

SOUTH AUSTRALIA	O	M	R	W	w,nb		O	M	R	W	w,nb
Tobin	14	2	42	1	-,-		19	0	94	2	-,-
Davey	8	2	23	1	-,-		23	3	81	2	-,-
Lee	19	4	51	1	-,-	(4)	15	2	94	1	-,-
Grimmett	22	2	80	7	-,-	(3)	32	4	122	0	-,-
Ryan							12	1	23	0	-,-

VICTORIA	O	M	R	W	w,nb		O	M	R	W	w,nb
Alexander	14.6	2	48	2	-,-		4	0	26	0	-,-
Nagel	23	5	46	2	-,2		15	1	41	1	-,1
Ironmonger	23	2	60	0	-,-		29	10	65	6	-,-
Fleetwood-Smith	22	3	61	6	-,-		19.5	2	74	3	-,-
Bromley							1	0	2	0	-,-

FALL OF WICKETS

Wkt	VIC 1st	SA 1st	VIC 2nd	SA 2nd
1st	2	65	240	34
2nd	98	110	265	124
3rd	107	113	319	141
4th	111	149	335	187
5th	163	154	341	196
6th	176	154	-	199
7th	177	167	-	211
8th	186	188	-	216
9th	186	221	-	225
10th	197	228	-	231

V.Y.RICHARDSON'S XI v W.M.WOODFULL'S XI

Played at Melbourne Cricket Ground on November 17 (no play), 18, 20, 21, 22, 1933. (Four-day match)
Toss : Richardson's XI.　　　　Result : MATCH DRAWN.
Debuts: Nil.
12th Men: E.H.Bromley (R) and H.H.Oakley (W).
Umpires: A.N.Barlow and G.A.Hele.
Attendances: No play, 22402, 8373, 9859, 3911.　　　Total: 44,545 (excluding first day).　　　Receipts: £1856.
Close of Play: 1st day no play; 2nd day Richardson 2/160 (Fingleton 63, Rigg 12); 3rd day Richardson 8/491 (Grimmett 16, Nagel 8);
　　4th day Woodfull 4/317 (McCabe 74, Darling 24).

The match was staged for the benefit of Blackie and Ironmonger who received £908 each from the gate receipts. Ironmonger however strained a leg while fielding on the second day of play and took no further part in the game. Rain prevented any play on the scheduled first day and as a result a fifth day was added to the arrangements. Fingleton, missed in the first over of the match, went on to score 105 in 251 minutes; he hit just 3 fours. Bradman (55 in 61 minutes, 6 fours), Rigg (94 in 203 minutes, 7 fours), O'Brien (90 in 202 minutes, 9 fours) and Barnett (60 in 60 minutes, 5 fours) scored fifties for V.Y.Richardson's side. Woodfull scored a chanceless 118 in 220 minutes with 8 fours for his Eleven, Ponsford (42 in 120 minutes, 3 fours) and McCabe (82 in 166 minutes, 6 fours) also contributing. Nagel bowled only five overs due to a ricked neck. Bradman (101 in 166 minutes, 12 fours) hit a century on the final day. L.J.Nash (leg strain) was unavailable for selection in the match. *NSWCA Report* incorrectly gives Ryder (2) Richardson 0 instead of Fingleton. Sources: *Wisden, VCA Report, NSWCA Report, Australian Cricketer, The Age, The Argus, The Sporting Globe.*

RICHARDSON'S XI

*V.Y.Richardson	run out (Kippax/Oldfield)	28			
J.H.W.Fingleton	lbw b McCabe	105	(1)	b Wall	0
D.G.Bradman	c Woodfull b Wall	55		c Darling b Blackie	101
K.E.Rigg	b Blackie	94	(2)	b McCabe	2
L.P.J.O'Brien	c Ponsford b Fleetwood-Smith	90	(4)	run out (Darling/Kippax)	42
P.K.Lee	lbw b Fleetwood-Smith	17			
†B.A.Barnett	st Oldfield b Blackie	60			
H.I.Ebeling	c Wall b Blackie	4			
C.V.Grimmett	not out	16			
L.E.Nagel	not out	8			
W.J.O'Reilly	did not bat		(5)	not out	20
Extras	(b6, lb7, nb1)	14		(lb3, nb1)	4
Total	(131.0 overs, 476 mins) (8 wkts dec)	491		(45.7 overs, 177 mins) (4 wkts)	169

WOODFULL'S XI

*W.M.Woodfull	c Richardson b Grimmett	118
W.H.Ponsford	c & b Ebeling	42
H.C.Nitschke	st Barnett b Lee	12
S.J.McCabe	b Ebeling	82
A.F.Kippax	lbw b Grimmett	34
L.S.Darling	c Richardson b Ebeling	30
†W.A.S.Oldfield	b Ebeling	16
D.D.Blackie	run out (O'Brien)	2
T.W.Wall	not out	0
L.O.Fleetwood-Smith	b Ebeling	0
H.Ironmonger	absent hurt	-
Extras	(b8, lb4, nb2)	14
Total	(105.7 overs, 373 mins)	350

WOODFULL'S XI	O	M	R	W	w,nb		O	M	R	W	w,nb
Wall	25	2	104	1	-,-		10	5	20	1	-,1
McCabe	14	1	51	1	-,1		11	3	25	1	-,-
Fleetwood-Smith	36	3	140	2	-,-	(4)	9	0	49	0	-,-
Ironmonger	26	5	88	0	-,-						
Darling	5	0	25	0	-,-		2	0	16	0	-,-
Blackie	25	5	69	3	-,-	(3)	11.7	2	36	1	-,-
Kippax						(6)	2	0	19	0	-,-

RICHARDSON'S XI	O	M	R	W	w,nb
Ebeling	26.7	5	72	5	-,-
Nagel	5	1	16	0	-,-
Grimmett	30	5	108	2	-,-
O'Reilly	25	2	78	0	-,2
Lee	16	2	44	1	-,-
Bradman	3	0	18	0	-,-

FALL OF WICKETS

Wkt	R 1st	W 1st	R 2nd
1st	52	104	2
2nd	131	135	2
3rd	252	209	120
4th	321	270	169
5th	350	329	-
6th	444	340	-
7th	455	350	-
8th	473	350	-
9th	-	350	-
10th	-	-	-

NEW SOUTH WALES v THE REST

Played at Sydney Cricket Ground on November 24, 25, 27, 28, 1933. (Four-day match)
Toss : New South Wales.   Result : THE REST WON BY TWO WICKETS.
Debuts: Nil.
12th Men: L.R.Leabeater (both sides).
Umpires: E.G.Borwick and W.G.French.
Attendances: 8763, 15934, 10126, 2664.   Total: 37,487.   Receipts: £1699.
Close of Play: 1st day Rest 1/27 (Ponsford 13); 2nd day NSW (2) 0/41 (Fingleton 21, Brown 18); 3rd day NSW (2) 4/390 (Kippax 111, Rowe 66).

Staged as a benefit for T.J.E.Andrews, H.L.Collins and C.Kelleway who each received £500, the match finished thrillingly when The Rest needed 13 runs from the last possible over and got them, Nash hitting 4, 2 and 6 from the first five balls and scrambling the winning run, a bye, from the sixth. Woodfull (129 in 228 minutes, 8 fours), O'Brien (44 in 115 minutes, 3 fours), Darling (77 in 84 minutes, 11 fours), Nitschke (76 in 95 minutes, 10 fours) and Bromley (42 in 71 minutes, 4 fours) all played a hand in making 409 runs on the day. Ponsford (70 in 151 minutes, 3 fours) and Lee (69 in 119 minutes, 9 fours) had topscored in the first innings. New South Wales, the reigning Sheffield Shield champions, recovered from an ordinary start on the first day with a fifth-wicket stand of 145 in 117 minutes between McCabe (110 in 172 minutes, 14 fours) and Rowe (66 in 122 minutes, 6 fours). Fingleton (78 in 155 minutes, 8 fours), Bradman (92 in 157 minutes, 12 fours), Kippax (111 not out in 212 minutes, 16 fours) and Rowe (66 not out in 125 minutes, 6 fours) tamed the bowling on the third day. Ebeling and Lee were brought into The Rest for H.Ironmonger (leg injury) and L.E.Nagel (ricked neck). Sources: *Wisden, NSWCA Report, VCA Report, Sydney Morning Herald, The Age, The Argus.*

NEW SOUTH WALES

J.H.W.Fingleton	b Ebeling	33	c Walker b Ebeling		78
W.A.Brown	b Nash	8	b Chilvers		29
D.G.Bradman	c Walker b Chilvers	22	b Ebeling		92
S.J.McCabe	c Walker b Darling	110	(5) st Walker b Chilvers		8
*A.F.Kippax	c Walker b Chilvers	15	(4) not out		111
R.C.Rowe	c Walker b Ebeling	66	not out		66
†W.A.S.Oldfield	c Bromley b Ebeling	4			
F.Mair	b Ebeling	2			
C.J.Hill	c Walker b Darling	2			
W.J.O'Reilly	c Darling b Ebeling	4			
W.H.Howell	not out	1			
Extras	(b3, lb2, w1)	6	(b5, lb1)		6
Total	(78.1 overs, 281 mins)	273	(103.0 overs, 368 mins) (4 wkts dec)		390

THE REST

*W.M.Woodfull	c O'Reilly b Mair	7	c Brown b Hill		129
W.H.Ponsford	c O'Reilly b Mair	70	c Oldfield b McCabe		9
L.P.J.O'Brien	c Oldfield b O'Reilly	10	c O'Reilly b Hill		44
L.S.Darling	c Oldfield Howell	10	b Bradman		77
H.C.Nitschke	c Oldfield b O'Reilly	20	c Bradman b Rowe		76
E.H.Bromley	c Brown b Mair	7	c Fingleton b Kippax		42
P.K.Lee	c Oldfield b McCabe	69	lbw b Kippax		0
L.J.Nash	b Hill	17	not out		20
H.I.Ebeling	lbw b Hill	0	b Kippax		1
H.C.Chilvers	lbw b O'Reilly	22	not out		0
†C.W.Walker	not out	5			
Extras	(b6, lb8, nb4)	18	(b3, lb4, nb4)		11
Total	(89.0 overs, 286 mins)	255	(101.6 overs, 325 mins) (8 wkts)		409

THE REST	O	M	R	W	w,nb		O	M	R	W	w,nb
Nash	10	0	48	1	1,-	(4)	11	0	57	0	-,-
Ebeling	22.1	3	66	5	-,-	(1)	28	4	87	2	,
Lee	14	2	39	0	-,-	(5)	23	2	67	0	-,-
Chilvers	19	2	69	2	-,-	(3)	26	2	95	2	-,-
Bromley	7	1	31	0	-,-	(6)	7	0	33	0	-,-
Darling	6	1	14	2	-,-	(2)	8	2	45	0	-,-

NEW SOUTH WALES	O	M	R	W	w,nb		O	M	R	W	w,nb
McCabe	15	2	46	1	-,1		15	1	49	1	-,4
Hill	9	2	26	2	-,-		21	2	83	2	-,-
O'Reilly	30	7	59	3	-,3		17	3	53	0	-,-
Mair	23	2	81	3	-,-		19	3	84	0	-,-
Howell	12	5	25	1	-,-		17	3	53	0	-,-
Bradman							3	0	30	1	-,-
Rowe							5.6	0	36	1	-,-
Kippax							4	1	10	3	-,-

FALL OF WICKETS				
	NSW	REST	NSW	REST
Wkt	1st	1st	2nd	2nd
1st	16	27	64	11
2nd	51	49	166	121
3rd	75	85	224	250
4th	106	126	240	278
5th	251	138	-	375
6th	259	138	-	376
7th	265	208	-	390
8th	268	208	-	396
9th	270	247	-	-
10th	273	255	-	-

QUEENSLAND v VICTORIA (Shield Match 3)

Played at Brisbane Cricket Ground (Woolloongabba) on December 1, 2, 4, 5, 1933. (Four-day match)
Toss : Queensland.   Result : VICTORIA WON BY AN INNINGS AND 31 RUNS.
Debuts: Queensland - A.H.Tait, D.Tallon (both f/c).
12th Men: G.G.Cook (Qld) and L.E.Nagel (Vic).
Umpires: J.Bartlett and J.A.Scott.
Attendances: 2279, 4641,   ? ,   ? .   Total: About 8500.   Receipts: £507.
Close of Play: 1st day Qld 9/310 (Tait 32, Wyeth 8); 2nd day Vic 3/214 (Rigg 61, Darling 57); 3rd day Qld (2) 3/10 (Thompson 6, Levy 4).

Queensland suffered their third successive defeat by an innings margin at the hands of the Victorians. Brew, the mainstay of the Queensland first innings with 102 (150 minutes, 15 fours), survived chances before he had scored and again at 98. Tait on debut (61 in 136 minutes, 4 fours) also survived an early chance at 7. The second innings started spectacularly, Brew, Andrews and Allen all falling inside two overs without a run on the board. Bensted's 97 (157 minutes, 8 fours) accounted for 59.9 per cent of the team total. Ponsford (55 in 112 minutes, 8 fours), Rigg (92 in 252 minutes, 7 fours), Darling (188 in 298 minutes, 18 fours, chances at 57 and 83), Scaife (73 in 134 minutes) and Barnett (78 in 108 minutes) scored freely against the local bowlers. Allen, who was originally named 12th man, replaced J.L.Litster (unavailable) in the selected Queensland side. Victoria lost H.H.Oakley (unavailable) and H.Ironmonger (leg injury) before the team left Melbourne and included Ebeling and Scaife as replacements. Sources: *Wisden, VCA Report, QCA Report, Sydney Morning Herald, Brisbane Courier-Mail, The Age, The Herald.*

QUEENSLAND

F.M.Brew	c & b Bromley	102		b Alexander		0
T.Allen	b Fleetwood-Smith	36		c Barnett b Ebeling		0
W.C.Andrews	lbw b Fleetwood-Smith	30		lbw b Alexander		0
F.C.Thompson	run out (Ponsford)	27		b Alexander		6
*R.M.Levy	lbw b Alexander	18		c Barnett b Ebeling		23
E.C.Bensted	b Alexander	6		b Fleetwood-Smith		97
R.K.Oxenham	c Darling b Ebeling	6		st Barnett b Fleetwood-Smith		8
†D.Tallon	b Alexander	17	(9)	b Ebeling		3
A.H.Tait	c Ebeling b Fleetwood-Smith	61	(8)	lbw b Fleetwood-Smith		0
S.F.M.Yeates	c Alexander b Bromley	16		b Ebeling		15
E.R.Wyeth	not out	18		not out		3
Extras	(b6, lb5, nb1)	12		(b3, lb3, nb1)		7
Total	(98.7 overs, 350 mins)	349		(50.0 overs, 195 mins)		162

VICTORIA

*W.M.Woodfull	b Oxenham	16
W.H.Ponsford	c Tallon b Oxenham	55
L.P.J.O'Brien	c Andrews b Oxenham	8
K.E.Rigg	c Tait b Brew	92
L.S.Darling	c Allen b Andrews	188
E.H.Bromley	run out (Levy)	3
J.W.Scaife	lbw b Tait	73
†B.A.Barnett	c Bensted b Andrews	78
H.I.Ebeling	lbw b Oxenham	3
H.H.Alexander	b Brew	2
L.O.Fleetwood-Smith	not out	1
Extras	(b6, lb10, w2, nb5)	23
Total	(137.4 overs, 510 mins)	542

VICTORIA	O	M	R	W	w,nb		O	M	R	W	w,nb
Alexander	25	3	78	3	-,1		13	2	25	3	-,1
Ebeling	32	4	89	1	-,-		19	4	42	4	-,-
Fleetwood-Smith	25.7	3	114	3	-,-		18	0	88	3	-,-
Bromley	12	3	39	2	-,-						
Darling	4	0	17	0	-,-						

QUEENSLAND	O	M	R	W	w,nb
Tait	17	2	74	1	-,-
Bensted	12	0	62	0	-,5
Oxenham	53	14	111	4	-,-
Wyeth	9	1	36	0	-,-
Yeates	18	1	90	0	2,-
Brew	18	1	83	2	-,-
Levy	5	0	26	0	-,-
Andrews	5.4	0	37	2	-,-

FALL OF WICKETS

	QLD	VIC	QLD
Wkt	1st	1st	2nd
1st	118	37	0
2nd	176	51	0
3rd	178	100	0
4th	213	291	14
5th	225	301	49
6th	235	423	89
7th	236	489	89
8th	260	511	92
9th	284	540	132
10th	349	542	162

VICTORIA v QUEENSLAND (Shield Match 4)

Played at Melbourne Cricket Ground on December 15 (no play), 16, 18, 19, 1933. (Four-day match)

Toss : Victoria.   Result : MATCH DRAWN.

Debuts: Nil.

12th Men: J.W.Scaife (Vic) and S.F.M.Yeates (Qld).

Umpires: A.N.Barlow and G.A.Hele.

Attendances: No play, 3210, 3586, 1691.   Total: 8487 (excluding first day).   Receipts: £217.

Close of Play: 1st day no play; 2nd day Vic 3/136 (O'Brien 34, Darling 63); 3rd day Qld 4/89 (Levy 7, Bensted 5).

Little time was left for a result after rain wiped out the first day's play and allowed only seven minutes before lunch on the second. All the Victorian batsmen had difficulty facing Oxenham when the match began, the 42-year-old seamer conceding just 36 runs from 35.3 eight-ball overs. A defensive O'Brien (72 in 297 minutes, 8 fours) added 88 for the fourth wicket with Darling (63 in 108 minutes, 4 fours). Oxenham also helped secure first-innings points for Queensland with the bat, making an unbeaten 33 (126 minutes, 2 fours) and sharing a crucial ninth-wicket stand of 56 with Leeson (34 in 69 minutes, 3 fours). Cook (32 in 164 minutes, 1 four), Andrews (25 in 83 minutes, 2 fours) and Levy (47 in 130 minutes, 4 fours) batted doggedly earlier on. Cook's score was first shown as 34 but was later changed at the direction of the umpires vice extras. Rigg completed a pair when he fell in the first over of Victoria's second innings, Ponsford (54 not out in 125 minutes, 2 fours), Darling (33 in 44 minutes, 4 fours) and Bromley (57 in 56 minutes, 1 six and 6 fours) seeing the match out with varying attitudes. Sources: *Wisden, VCA Report, QCA Report, The Age, The Argus, The Herald, Melbourne Sun.*

VICTORIA

*W.M.Woodfull	c Leeson b Gamble	10			
W.H.Ponsford	c Andrews b Oxenham	23	not out		54
L.P.J.O'Brien	c Levy b Oxenham	72			
K.E.Rigg	c Cook b Bensted	0	(1) c Brew b Bensted		0
L.S.Darling	lbw b Gamble	63	(3) c & b Tait		33
E.H.Bromley	c Levy b Oxenham	11	(4) b Brew		57
†B.A.Barnett	c Leeson b Oxenham	2	(5) b Tait		5
H.I.Ebeling	st Leeson b Brew	1			
H.H.Alexander	c Gamble b Brew	0			
L.O.Fleetwood-Smith	b Brew	11			
H.Ironmonger	not out	2			
Extras	(b3, lb4, nb2)	9	(b1, lb3, w1, nb1)		6
Total	(92.3 overs, 333 mins)	204	(31.5 overs, 125 mins) (4 wkts)		155

QUEENSLAND

F.M.Brew	lbw b Alexander	3
G.G.Cook	st Barnett b Ironmonger	32
W.C.Andrews	lbw b Fleetwood-Smith	25
F.C.Thompson	st Barnett b Ironmonger	13
*R.M.Levy	c Fleetwood-Smith b Ironmonger	47
E.C.Bensted	c Barnett b Ebeling	7
T.Allen	lbw b Fleetwood-Smith	9
R.K.Oxenham	not out	33
A.H.Tait	b Ebeling	8
†H.F.Leeson	b Alexander	34
H.S.Gamble	st Barnett b Fleetwood-Smith	24
Extras	(b5, lb2)	7
Total	(108.5 overs, 390 mins)	242

QUEENSLAND	O	M	R	W	w,nb		O	M	R	W	w,nb
Gamble	28	5	75	2	-,2						
Oxenham	35.3	17	36	4	-,-	(3)	7	0	37	0	-,-
Bensted	13	1	39	1	-,-	(1)	6	0	30	1	-,1
Brew	12	1	32	3	-,-		8	0	44	1	-,-
Tait	4	0	13	0	-,-	(2)	10.5	1	38	2	1,-

VICTORIA	O	M	R	W	w,nb
Alexander	14	1	49	2	-,-
Ebeling	32	7	58	2	-,-
Ironmonger	36	14	65	3	-,-
Fleetwood-Smith	26.5	4	63	3	-,-

FALL OF WICKETS

Wkt	VIC 1st	QLD 1st	VIC 2nd
1st	23	6	0
2nd	47	51	56
3rd	48	74	142
4th	136	77	155
5th	153	90	-
6th	161	131	-
7th	174	141	-
8th	178	153	-
9th	194	209	-
10th	204	242	-

AFCM No. 809/76
SSM No. 262/73

SOUTH AUSTRALIA v NEW SOUTH WALES (Shield Match 5)

Played at Adelaide Oval on December 15, 16, 18, 1933. (Four-day match)
Toss : New South Wales.   Result : SOUTH AUSTRALIA WON BY TEN WICKETS.
Debuts: South Australia - F.H.K.Collins (f/c).
12th Men: M.G.Waite (SA) and A.D.McGilvray (NSW).
Umpires: E.H.Kitson and J.D.Scott.
Attendances: 4953, 8706, 6534.   Total: 20,193.   Receipts: £922.
Close of Play: 1st day SA 2/124 (Nitschke 67, Ryan 3); 2nd day NSW (2) 0/50 (Fingleton 22, Brown 26).

McGilvray replaced S.J.McCabe (appendicitis) in the New South Wales line-up for the trip to Adelaide and Melbourne. The S.A.C.A. determined that the proceeds of the gate, less the average amount from the past three corresponding games in Adelaide, would be directed to assist the benefit fund of the ex-Australian and South Australian bowler E.Jones. Jones received £470 and other contributions took the total to £1000. South Australia twice accounted for the New South Wales batting, all of whom failed in the first innings. Only Fingleton (30 in 98 minutes), Brown (38 in 107 minutes, 1 four), Bradman (76 in 104 minutes, 6 fours) and Kippax (90 in 154 minutes, 9 fours) made any headway in the second innings. Consistent batting from Nitschke (82 in 174 minutes, 6 fours), Lonergan (50 in 117 minutes), Ryan (94 not out in 242 minutes, 7 fours) and Shepherd (43 in 109 minutes, 3 fours) compensated for the loss in the South Australian second over of Richardson, establishing a match-winning lead. Richardson (1 four) and Nitschke (1 six and 5 fours) were untroubled in the bid for victory, winning with a day to spare. Sources: *Wisden, SACA Report, NSWCA Report, Australian Cricketer, Adelaide Advertiser, The News.*

NEW SOUTH WALES

J.H.W.Fingleton	c Walker b Tobin	27	c Walker b Grimmett	30
W.A.Brown	c Ryan b Wall	4	c Walker b Collins	38
D.G.Bradman	b Collins	1	c Wall b Grimmett	76
*A.F.Kippax	b Tobin	9	st Walker b Grimmett	90
R.C.Rowe	c Wall b Tobin	1	b Wall	6
†W.A.S.Oldfield	run out (Grimmett)	0	c Richardson b Grimmett	20
H.C.Chilvers	not out	16	b Grimmett	0
F.Mair	b Grimmett	14	lbw b Lee	2
W.J.O'Reilly	c Richardson b Grimmett	6	not out	2
C.J.Hill	run out (Ryan/Walker)	24	b Lee	1
W.H.Howell	b Lee	1	b Lee	0
Extras	(b1, lb1, nb3)	5	(lb6)	6
Total	(37.1 overs, 159 mins)	108	(79.0 overs, 290 mins)	271

SOUTH AUSTRALIA

*V.Y.Richardson	c O'Reilly b Hill	3	not out	20
H.C.Nitschke	st Oldfield b Chilvers	82	not out	44
A.R.Lonergan	st Oldfield b Hill	50		
A.J.Ryan	not out	94		
A.G.Shepherd	c O'Reilly b Howell	43		
B.J.Tobin	c Oldfield b Mair	0		
F.H.K.Collins	lbw b Mair	8		
P.K.Lee	lbw b Chilvers	23		
†C.W.Walker	b Mair	1		
C.V.Grimmett	c O'Reilly b Mair	7		
T.W.Wall	c Oldfield b Chilvers	0		
Extras	(b4, w1)	5	(b1)	1
Total	(126.3 overs, 378 mins)	316	(14.1 overs, 41 mins) (0 wkts)	65

SOUTH AUSTRALIA	O	M	R	W	w,nb		O	M	R	W	w,nb
Wall	10	3	24	1	-,2		18	1	66	1	-,-
Collins	9	1	30	1	-,-		13	0	43	1	-,-
Tobin	8	1	20	3	-,1	(4)	10	0	49	0	-,-
Lee	4.1	0	12	1	-,-	(5)	5	2	4	3	-,-
Grimmett	6	2	17	2	-,-	(3)	33	3	103	5	-,-

NEW SOUTH WALES	O	M	R	W	w,nb		O	M	R	W	w,nb
Howell	27	6	73	1	-,-						
Hill	22	8	30	2	-,-		7	3	20	0	-,-
O'Reilly	31	6	91	0	-,-	(1)	3	1	18	0	-,-
Chilvers	23.3	2	48	3	1,-	(3)	4.1	0	26	0	-,-
Mair	23	2	69	4	-,-						

FALL OF WICKETS

	NSW	SA	NSW	SA
Wkt	1st	1st	2nd	2nd
1st	17	3	68	-
2nd	18	117	76	-
3rd	38	143	194	-
4th	43	232	217	-
5th	44	237	263	-
6th	44	259	263	-
7th	62	302	268	-
8th	71	307	268	-
9th	107	315	271	-
10th	108	316	271	-

VICTORIA v NEW SOUTH WALES (Shield Match 6)

Played at Melbourne Cricket Ground on December 22, 23, 26, 27, 1933. (Four-day match)
Toss : Victoria.   Result : MATCH DRAWN.
Debuts: New South Wales - A.D.McGilvray (f/c).
12th Men: J.W.Scaife (Vic) and C.J.Hill (NSW).
Umpires: A.N.Barlow and G.A.Hele.
Attendances: 6822, 15148, 20689, 8553.   Total: 51,212.   Receipts: £2119.
Close of Play: 1st day Vic 5/294 (Darling 78, Barnett 0); 2nd day NSW 3/199 (Bradman 68); 3rd day Vic (2) 1/68 (Ponsford 40,
   O'Brien 11).

Compelled by a back strain to take things easy, Bradman reached his hundred on the third day in 178 minutes and batted 294 minutes in all, hitting 13 fours in his unbeaten 187. He opened the innings with Kippax on the last afternoon when New South Wales required 228 to win in under two hours and hit 5 fours in another unbeaten effort. Fingleton (76 in 156 minutes, 7 fours) was the only other New South Wales batsman to exceed 50 in the match, Bradman having scored more than half his side's runs. Fifties were scored for Victoria by Woodfull (60 in 158 minutes, 1 four), O'Brien (86 in 232 minutes, 10 fours) and Darling (91 in 140 minutes, 7 fours) in the first innings and Darling again (53 in 78 minutes, 6 fours) in the second. Mair, who fractured a hip-bone in a fielding mishap on the first day, used a runner when batting. He did not take the field in the second innings, in which O'Reilly captured the best innings figures in matches between these teams; McGilvray on debut spoiling an otherwise perfect spell of bowling by the fiery leg-spinner. Both men went on to play major roles in cricket reporting, O'Reilly as a trenchant supporter in the Press of tradition and McGilvray as an enduring radio commentator for the Australian Broadcasting Commission. *NSWCA Report* incorrectly gives Vic (2) McGilvray 1/57. Sources: *Wisden, VCA Report, NSWCA Report, The Age, The Argus, The Herald, Australian Cricketer*.

VICTORIA

*W.M.Woodfull	c & b Howell	60	lbw b O'Reilly	15
W.H.Ponsford	c Fingleton b O'Reilly	30	b O'Reilly	40
L.P.J.O'Brien	run out (McGilvray)	86	c Rowe b O'Reilly	29
K.E.Rigg	c Oldfield b Chilvers	20	c Howell b O'Reilly	19
L.S.Darling	c O'Reilly b Howell	91	c Oldfield b O'Reilly	53
E.H.Bromley	c O'Reilly b Howell	13	lbw b O'Reilly	0
†B.A.Barnett	c & b Howell	20	b McGilvray	13
L.E.Nagel	not out	17	b O'Reilly	10
H.I.Ebeling	c Oldfield b O'Reilly	32	b O'Reilly	15
L.O.Fleetwood-Smith	c Chilvers b O'Reilly	2	not out	1
H.Ironmonger	c McGilvray b Howell	1	b O'Reilly	0
Extras	(b2, lb2, w2, nb4)	10	(b2, nb3)	5
Total	(141.5 overs, 423 mins)	382	(117.0 overs, 343 mins)	200

NEW SOUTH WALES

J.H.W.Fingleton	lbw b Ebeling	76		
W.A.Brown	lbw b Fleetwood-Smith	23		
D.G.Bradman	not out	187	(1) not out	77
*A.F.Kippax	b Fleetwood-Smith	23	(2) c Barnett b Ebeling	28
A.D.McGilvray	b Fleetwood-Smith	11		
R.C.Rowe	c Barnett b Fleetwood-Smith	5	(3) not out	39
†W.A.S.Oldfield	c Darling b Fleetwood-Smith	2		
H.C.Chilvers	b Ironmonger	5		
W.J.O'Reilly	lbw b Fleetwood-Smith	6		
F.Mair	c Barnett b Ironmonger	3		
W.H.Howell	b Fleetwood-Smith	2		
Extras	(b8, lb2, nb2)	12		–
Total	(118.0 overs, 418 mins)	355	(27.0 overs, 104 mins) (1 wkt)	144

NEW SOUTH WALES	O	M	R	W	w,nb		O	M	R	W	w,nb
McGilvray	21	2	65	0	-,-		23	5	51	1	-,-
Howell	38.5	11	97	5	-,3		33	15	54	0	-,1
O'Reilly	43	9	92	3	-,-		35	14	50	9	-,2
Chilvers	33	7	85	1	-,-		24	11	38	0	-,-
Mair	6	0	33	0	2,1						
Kippax						(5)	2	1	2	0	-,-

VICTORIA	O	M	R	W	w,nb		O	M	R	W	w,nb
Ebeling	29	7	53	1	-,-		10	0	56	1	-,-
Nagel	20	3	70	0	-,2		3	0	28	0	-,-
Ironmonger	30	10	51	2	-,-		9	0	26	0	-,-
Fleetwood-Smith	32	3	138	7	-,-						
Bromley	7	0	31	0	-,-	(4)	3	0	26	0	-,-
Darling						(5)	2	0	8	0	-,-

FALL OF WICKETS

Wkt	VIC 1st	NSW 1st	VIC 2nd	NSW 2nd
1st	45	88	24	54
2nd	134	130	70	-
3rd	170	199	94	-
4th	260	231	144	-
5th	292	251	144	-
6th	325	259	161	-
7th	328	280	178	-
8th	371	299	195	-
9th	375	316	200	-
10th	382	355	200	-

SOUTH AUSTRALIA v QUEENSLAND (Shield Match 7)

Played at Adelaide Oval on December 22, 23, 25, 26, 1933. (Four-day match)
Toss : South Australia.   Result : SOUTH AUSTRALIA WON BY EIGHT WICKETS.
Debuts: Nil.
12th Men: M.G.Waite (SA) and S.F.M.Yeates (Qld).
Umpires: E.H.Kitson and J.D.Scott.
Attendances: 2963, 6038, 2297, 554.   Total: 11,852   Receipts: £422.
Close of Play: 1st day SA 7/335 (Tobin 54); 2nd day Qld (2) 2/35 (Andrews 9, Thompson 0); 3rd day SA (2) 1/35 (Richardson 26, Lonergan 1).

Lonergan (49 in 104 minutes, 4 fours) and Ryan (124 in 228 minutes, 1 five and 14 fours) re-established the South Australian first innings after the loss of openers Richardson and Nitschke. Lee (30 in 48 minutes, 3 fours), Tobin (55 in 120 minutes, 1 five and 6 fours) and Collins (36 in 48 minutes, 5 fours) further bolstered the batting. Queensland lost the wicket of Brew to the first ball of the second over and despite a second-wicket stand worth 68 between Cook and Andrews never really recovered. Following on, Andrews (48 in 83 minutes, 5 fours) again batted well, adding 84 with Thompson (42 in 93 minutes, 3 fours). Levy (career-best 148 in 174 minutes, 1 six, 1 five and 16 fours) played the innings of the match, dominating a seventh-wicket stand of 155 in 120 minutes with Oxenham. Grimmett (11 for 192) was the outstanding bowler. Richardson hit 9 fours as he led his side to its fifth consecutive win against Queensland. Sources: *Wisden, SACA Report, QCA Report, Australian Cricketer, Adelaide Advertiser, The News.*

SOUTH AUSTRALIA

*V.Y.Richardson	b Gamble	22	not out		69
H.C.Nitschke	lbw b Bensted	3	c Allen b Bensted		7
A.R.Lonergan	c & b Brew	49	c Gamble b Tait		9
A.J.Ryan	run out (Levy)	124	not out		9
A.G.Shepherd	c Gamble b Tait	12			
P.K.Lee	c Cook b Brew	30			
B.J.Tobin	c Leeson b Bensted	55			
F.H.K.Collins	b Gamble	36			
C.V.Grimmett	not out	27			
†C.W.Walker	lbw b Andrews	27			
T.W.Wall	b Oxenham	2			
Extras	(b2, lb2, nb2)	6	(nb2)		2
Total	(110.2 overs, 401 mins)	393	(22.2 overs, 83 mins) (2 wkts)		96

QUEENSLAND

F.M.Brew	b Collins	1	(7) b Wall		0
G.G.Cook	b Grimmett	41	b Grimmett		9
W.C.Andrews	c Lee Tobin	34	c Tobin b Grimmett		48
F.C.Thompson	lbw b Grimmett	6	lbw b Grimmett		42
*R.M.Levy	b Wall	26	st Walker b Grimmett		148
E.C.Bensted	b Grimmett	1	c Walker b Grimmett		1
T.Allen	b Grimmett	25	(1) b Tobin		17
R.K.Oxenham	c Walker b Wall	7	lbw b Grimmett		50
A.H.Tait	lbw b Grimmett	2	lbw b Lee		5
†H.F.Leeson	not out	2	not out		13
H.S.Gamble	b Wall	0	c Richardson b Lee		0
Extras	(b1, lb1)	2	(b1, lb3, nb2)		6
Total	(42.3 overs, 162 mins)	147	(80.7 overs, 332 mins)		339

QUEENSLAND	O	M	R	W	w,nb		O	M	R	W	w,nb
Gamble	26	4	103	2	-,-		7	0	39	0	-,1
Bensted	19	3	53	2	-,1		7	1	31	1	-,-
Oxenham	22.2	10	44	1	-,-		4.2	3	12	0	-,-
Brew	28	3	128	2	-,-						
Tait	12	3	46	1	-,1	(4)	4	1	12	1	-,1
Levy	2	0	8	0	-,-						
Andrews	1	0	5	1	-,-						

SOUTH AUSTRALIA	O	M	R	W	w,nb		O	M	R	W	w,nb
Wall	7.3	0	32	3	-,-		20	0	81	1	-,2
Collins	5	1	13	1	-,-		7	0	31	0	-,-
Tobin	7	2	26	1	-,-	(4)	9	3	33	1	-,-
Grimmett	17	3	58	5	-,-	(3)	30	2	134	6	-,-
Lee	6	1	16	0	-,-		14.7	0	54	2	-,-

FALL OF WICKETS

Wkt	SA 1st	QLD 1st	QLD 2nd	SA 2nd
1st	13	5	25	27
2nd	39	73	27	77
3rd	116	82	111	-
4th	136	85	133	-
5th	196	89	159	-
6th	281	121	160	-
7th	335	133	315	-
8th	339	145	321	-
9th	390	146	339	-
10th	393	147	339	-

TASMANIA v VICTORIA

Played at T.C.A. Ground, Hobart, on December 23, 25, 26, 27, 1933. (Four-day match)
Toss : Victoria.   Result : VICTORIA WON BY 122 RUNS.
Debuts: Tasmania - F.A.Davis (f/c). Victoria - P.J.Beames, D.J.A.Fitzmaurice, I.D.Miller, T.J.Trembath (all f/c); A.H.Allsopp (Vic only).
12th Men: J.W.Rothwell (Tas) and G.W.Hawkins (Vic).
Umpires: A.J.Buttsworth and J.Gardner.
Attendances: No figures published.   Total: About 1500.   Receipts: £82.
Close of Play: 1st day Vic 8/245 (Fitzmaurice 15, Smith 11); 2nd day Tas 9/135 (Combes 4); 3rd day Tas (2) 2/51 (Badcock 17, Green 1).
Fitzmaurice and Hawkins replaced E.L.McCormick and H.H.Oakley (both unavailable due to work commitments) in the Victorian team before leaving Melbourne. The Tasmanian captain Green was one of three local players prevented from arriving at the match until it was well underway due to their being required to work on the last shopping morning before Christmas. Atkinson deputised for Green until he turned up while three substitutes fielded. Vernon (42 in 132 minutes, 1 four), Quin (54 in 111 minutes, 1 four), Kemp (46 in 95 minutes, 0 fours) and Smith (43 in 55 minutes, 6 fours) topped the first innings, Smith following up with his best figures of 8 for 44 (leg-breaks and googlies) as Green (46 in 96 minutes, 5 fours) topscored for Tasmania. Allsopp's hundred on debut for Victoria (123 not out in 103 minutes, 17 fours) came up in just 92 minutes; he scored his last 50 runs in 29 minutes. As he had also scored a hundred on his first-class debut for New South Wales in 1929-30, this made Allsopp the first batsman to score a century on debut for two Australian States. Lee's 46 took 66 minutes and included 5 fours. Badcock, aged 19 years 261 days, compiled his maiden first-class century (107 in 270 minutes, 8 fours) and Morrisby (60 in 116 minutes, 4 fours) also batted well but Victoria won with 17 minutes to spare. Sources: *Australian Cricketer, TCA Report, VCA Report, Hobart Mercury.*

VICTORIA

I.D.Miller	b Walsh	39	(2) c Parry b Burrows		5
E.H.G.Vernon	c & b James	42			
I.S.Lee	b Walsh	1	c Walsh b James		46
P.J.Beames	lbw b Burrows	11	b James		0
*B.L.Cohen	lbw b Burrows	7	(1) run out (Atkinson)		39
†S.O.Quin	b Walsh	54	(8) c Atkinson b Putman		8
L.D.Kemp	c Burrows b Combes	46	(6) st Parry b James		2
A.H.Allsopp	c Badcock b Combes	14	(5) not out		123
D.J.A.Fitzmaurice	not out	37	(7) b James		20
S.A.J.Smith	c Parry b Putman	43			
T.J.Trembath	c Badcock b Combes	5			
Extras	(b1, lb5)	6	(b1, lb5)		6
Total	(100.0 overs, 341 mins)	305	(55.3 overs, 195 mins) (7 wkts dec)		249

TASMANIA

C.L.Badcock	b Smith	25	c & b Kemp		107
A.O.Burrows	c Quin b Smith	22	c Quin b Trembath		3
J.A.Atkinson	st Quin b Smith	3	c Allsopp b Vernon		25
*D.C.Green	c & b Smith	46	b Trembath		24
S.W.L.Putman	b Smith	7	c Quin b Beames		6
†C.N.Parry	c Quin b Trembath	1	(9) b Beames		0
F.A.Davis	lbw b Smith	1	c Kemp b Beames		16
R.O.G.Morrisby	b Trembath	1	(6) b Beames		60
G.T.H.James	c Beames b Smith	20	(10) c & b Smith		31
G.A.Combes	not out	5	(8) c Kemp b Beames		0
J.M.Walsh	b Smith	8	not out		1
Extras	(b1, lb5)	6	(b5, lb4, w5)		14
Total	(44.0 overs, 165 mins)	145	(95.4 overs, 325 mins)		287

TASMANIA	O	M	R	W	w,nb		O	M	R	W	w,nb
Walsh	29	3	79	3	-,-		14	2	64	0	-,-
Burrows	17	1	42	2	-,-		9	4	36	1	-,-
Davis	8	1	20	0	-,-						
Combes	16	1	54	3	-,-	(3)	9	1	36	0	-,-
Putman	16	0	69	1	-,-	(4)	10.3	0	61	1	-,-
James	14	1	35	1	-,-	(5)	13	1	46	4	-,-

VICTORIA	O	M	R	W	w,nb		O	M	R	W	w,nb
Trembath	15	1	60	2	-,-	(2)	18	1	65	2	-,-
Kemp	7	2	25	0	-,-	(1)	12	1	32	1	4,-
Smith	17	2	44	8	-,-		27	6	80	1	-,-
Fitzmaurice	5	1	10	0	-,-		10	3	11	0	1,-
Vernon							1	0	2	1	-,-
Beames							19.4	4	52	5	-,-
Allsopp							5	0	19	0	-,-
Cohen							3	1	12	0	-,-

FALL OF WICKETS

Wkt	VIC 1st	TAS 1st	VIC 2nd	TAS 2nd
1st	73	37	24	10
2nd	75	41	82	49
3rd	91	66	86	114
4th	103	80	109	149
5th	106	83	113	209
6th	202	84	187	242
7th	205	93	249	244
8th	226	130	-	244
9th	294	135	-	283
10th	305	145	-	287

VICTORIA v SOUTH AUSTRALIA (Shield Match 8)

Played at Melbourne Cricket Ground on December 29, 30, 1933, January 1, 2, 1934. (Four-day match)
Toss : South Australia.   Result : VICTORIA WON BY FIVE WICKETS.
Debuts: Nil.
12th Men: L.J.Junor (Vic) and M.G.Waite (SA).
Umpires: A.N.Barlow and G.A.Hele.
Attendances: 8869, 15121, 17900, 4764.   Total: 46,654.   Receipts: £1747.
Close of Play: 1st day SA 313 all out; 2nd day Vic 7/291 (Bromley 101, McCormick 3); 3rd day SA (2) 198 all out.

Lonergan became only the third player to score a hundred in each innings for South Australia. He batted 194 minutes in the first innings (9 fours) and 171 minutes in the second (7 fours). Fleetwood-Smith restricted the other batsmen, capturing 12 wickets. Ponsford, who inherited the captaincy of Victoria from Woodfull (neuritis - replaced by nominated 12th man, Scaife) scored 94 in 176 minutes and hit 8 fours. Bromley arriving at 4/127, gave a chance at 12 during his career-best 161. He was last man out after 282 minutes, hitting 13 fours. He was stoutly supported by Barnett (52 minutes), Ebeling (54 minutes), McCormick (4 in 86 minutes) and Ironmonger (46 minutes), Ebeling being run out by the deflection of a Bromley straight drive via the bowler's hand. Sources: *Wisden, VCA Report, SACA Report, Australian Cricketer, The Age, The Argus, The Herald.*

SOUTH AUSTRALIA

*V.Y.Richardson	c sub (L.J.Junor) b Fleetwood-Smith	28	b Ebeling		12
H.C.Nitschke	c Darling b Ironmonger	33	c McCormick b Ebeling		1
A.R.Lonergan	b Ebeling	115	c Bromley b Ironmonger		100
A.J.Ryan	b Fleetwood-Smith	1	b McCormick		5
A.G.Shepherd	b Fleetwood-Smith	14	run out (O'Brien/Barnett)		3
P.K.Lee	c Scaife b Fleetwood-Smith	22	c O'Brien b Fleetwood-Smith		16
B.J.Tobin	b Fleetwood-Smith	17	c Ponsford b Fleetwood-Smith		5
F.H.K.Collins	b Fleetwood-Smith	19	run out (Barnett/McCormick)		16
C.V.Grimmett	b Fleetwood-Smith	30	lbw b Fleetwood-Smith		30
†C.W.Walker	not out	22	not out		1
T.W.Wall	lbw b Fleetwood-Smith	3	b Fleetwood-Smith		5
Extras	(b1, lb8)	9	(lb3, nb1)		4
Total	(83.6 overs, 317 mins)	313	(51.0 overs, 195 mins)		198

SOUTH AUSTRALIA

*W.H.Ponsford	run out (Shepherd/Walker)	94	hit wkt b Tobin		27
K.E.Rigg	c Shepherd b Wall	14	c Nitschke b Grimmett		50
L.P.J.O'Brien	lbw b Wall	24	b Grimmett		11
L.S.Darling	c Nitschke b Wall	4	lbw b Grimmett		17
J.W.Scaife	b Grimmett	3	lbw b Grimmett		16
E.H.Bromley	st Walker b Collins	161	not out		13
†B.A.Barnett	c Walker b Wall	22	not out		4
H.I.Ebeling	run out (Ryan)	17			
E.L.McCormick	b Tobin	4			
L.O.Fleetwood-Smith	b Tobin	4			
H.Ironmonger	not out	5			
Extras	(b6, lb5, w1, nb2)	14	(b1, lb5, w1, nb1)		8
Total	(111.1 overs, 432 mins)	366	(35.7 overs, 136 mins) (5 wkts)		146

VICTORIA	O	M	R	W	w,nb		O	M	R	W	w,nb		FALL OF WICKETS			
McCormick	15	1	56	0	-,-		9	0	55	1	-,1		SA	VIC	SA	VIC
Ebeling	18	6	61	1	-,-		11	1	45	2	-,-	Wkt	1st	1st	2nd	2nd
Ironmonger	22	10	58	1	-,-		16	4	40	1	-,-	1st	53	23	6	53
Fleetwood-Smith	23.6	4	111	8	-,-		14	3	47	4	-,-	2nd	72	108	20	80
Bromley	3	1	9	0	-,-							3rd	74	114	25	103
Darling	2	0	9	0	-,-	(5)	1	0	7	0	-,-	4th	96	127	46	116
												5th	132	156	75	135
SOUTH AUSTRALIA	O	M	R	W	w,nb		O	M	R	W	w,nb	6th	165	208	80	-
Wall	29	4	64	4	-,2		5	0	21	0	1,1	7th	195	257	101	-
Collins	16.1	2	42	1	-,-		3	1	8	0	-,-	8th	275	312	192	-
Tobin	19	4	73	2	1,-	(4)	4	0	23	1	-,-	9th	309	318	192	-
Grimmett	19	2	76	1	-,-	(3)	14.7	3	52	4	-,-	10th	313	366	198	-
Lee	26	3	83	0	-,-		9	2	34	0	-,-					
Ryan	2	0	14	0	-,-											

TASMANIA v VICTORIA

Played at N.T.C.A. Ground, Launceston, on December 29, 30, 1933, January 1, 1934. (Three-day match)
Toss : Tasmania.   Result : MATCH DRAWN.
Debuts: Tasmania - R.A.Ferrall, J.W.Rothwell (both f/c). Victoria - G.W.Hawkins (f/c).
12th Men: R.V.Thomas (Tas) and I.D.Miller (Vic).
Umpires: A.W.Beaumont and F.C.Tabart.
Attendances: No figures published; last day "large".   Total & Receipts: No figures published.
Close of Play: 1st day Tas 8/374 (Badcock 229, Walsh 0); 2nd day Vic 4/220 (Lee 102, Allsopp 36).

The 19-year-old Badcock, who came off his motorbike the day before the match (badly shaken but not hurt), quickly recovered to compile Tasmania's first double century (274 in 374 minutes, 1 six and 35 fours). He remained on the field throughout the match, being last out in the first innings and scoring an unbeaten 71 in the second. Ferrall (67 in 171 minutes, 7 fours), Morrisby (45 in 93 minutes, 4 fours) and Burrows (45 in 81 minutes, 3 fours) were the only other Tasmanians to reach double figures, Putman sustaining a first-ball dismissal. Lee (122 in 207 minutes, 14 fours), Allsopp (48 in 74 minutes), Quin (50 in 84 minutes) and Smith (64 not out in 76 minutes, 1 six and 2 fours) scored well for Victoria. Allsopp kept wicket throughout the second innings, allowing Quin, the regular wicket-keeper, his only first-class cricket bowl. Rain prevented play on the second day until 1.00pm. The match was called off at 5.15pm on the third day to allow the southerners in the Tasmanian team time to catch the train back to Hobart. Ferrall, Newton and Rothwell had earlier replaced J.A.Atkinson (nominated captain), D.C.Green and G.T.H.James (all work commitments) in the selected Tasmanian side. Newton, a left-hander described by *Wisden* as "probably Tasmania's most gifted all-round athlete", made the last of 27 appearances for his State in a career which spanned 22 years. Sources: *TCA Report, VCA Report, Australian Cricketer, Hobart Mercury, Launceston Examiner.*

TASMANIA

C.L.Badcock	lbw b Trembath	274	not out		71
A.O.Burrows	b Trembath	3	c Beames b Quin		45
R.A.Ferrall	b Smith	67	not out		8
S.W.L.Putman	lbw b Smith	0			
R.O.G.Morrisby	st Quin b Vernon	45			
*A.C.Newton	b Beames	9			
J.W.Rothwell	c Trembath b Beames	0			
F.A.Davis	b Smith	8			
†C.N.Parry	lbw b Smith	1			
J.M.Walsh	hit wkt b Smith	6			
G.A.Combes	not out	0			
Extras	(b6, lb8, nb2)	16	(b4, lb1)		5
Total	(102.3 overs, 374 mins)	429	(30.0 overs, 102 mins) (1 wkt)		129

VICTORIA

*B.L.Cohen	c Ferrall b Combes	31
I.S.Lee	c Walsh b Putman	122
E.H.G.Vernon	lbw b Walsh	22
G.W.Hawkins	c Putman b Walsh	16
P.J.Beames	b Putman	8
A.H.Allsopp	b Burrows	48
L.D.Kemp	c Newton b Burrows	44
†S.O.Quin	c Burrows b Walsh	50
D.J.A.Fitzmaurice	c Parry b Walsh	24
S.A.J.Smith	not out	64
T.J.Trembath	b Walsh	5
Extras	(b3, lb3, nb1)	7
Total	(98.1 overs, 363 mins)	441

VICTORIA	O	M	R	W	w,nb		O	M	R	W	w,nb		FALL OF WICKETS			
Kemp	9	0	42	0	-,-	(4)	3	1	4	0	-,-			TAS	VIC	TAS
Trembath	27.3	1	108	2	-,-	(1)	5	1	12	0	-,-	Wkt	1st	1st	2nd
Fitzmaurice	13	2	39	0	-,2	(2)	4	0	6	0	-,-	1st	4	53	97
Beames	21	4	87	2	-,-	(3)	2	0	9	0	-,-	2nd	179	91	-
Smith	23	3	79	5	-,-		3	0	14	0	-,-	3rd	179	117	-
Hawkins	4	0	19	0	-,-		3	0	23	0	-,-	4th	315	133	-
Cohen	3	0	15	0	-,-		2	0	10	0	-,-	5th	346	242	-
Vernon	2	0	24	1	-,-	(9)	3	0	22	0	-,-	6th	346	261	-
Quin						(8)	3	0	16	1	-,-	7th	357	336	-
Lee							2	0	8	0	-,-	8th	367	352	-
												9th	429	435	-
TASMANIA	O	M	R	W	w,nb							10th	429	441	-
Walsh	32.1	2	134	5	-,1											
Burrows	24	0	89	2	-,-											
Putman	18	0	115	2	-,-											
Combes	12	3	48	1	-,-											
Newton	8	0	27	0	-,-											
Davis	4	0	21	0	-,-											

NEW SOUTH WALES v QUEENSLAND (Shield Match 9)

Played at Sydney Cricket Ground on December 30, 1933, January 1, 2, 3, 1934. (Four-day match)
Toss : Queensland.　　　　　　　　Result : NEW SOUTH WALES WON BY AN INNINGS AND 84 RUNS.
Debuts: New South Wales - A.G.Chipperfield, F.A.Easton (both f/c).
12th Men: R.C.J.Little (NSW) and S.F.M.Yeates (Qld).
Umpires: H.J.Armstrong and E.G.Borwick.
Attendances: 9574, 14,953, 9027, 369.　　　Total: 33,923.　　　Receipts: £1576.
Close of Play: 1st day Qld 6/254 (Allen 32, Oxenham 5); 2nd day NSW 2/291 (Bradman 122, Kippax 66); 3rd day Qld (2) 4/70 (Bensted 20, Levy 2).

After an opening stand of 94 by Fingleton (42 in 113 minutes, 4 fours) and Brown (50 in 86 minutes) for New South Wales, Bradman and Kippax decimated the Queensland bowling, adding 363 runs in just 172 minutes, the highest third-wicket partnership yet in Australia. Bradman dominated the stand, scoring 253 in 204 minutes with 4 sixes and 29 fours, completing 1000 runs for a record sixth successive Australian season when 189. He progressed from single figures at tea on the second day to 122 at stumps, and scored a further 131 in 98 minutes before lunch on the third day before throwing his wicket away to end a sequence of 517 runs without dismissal. He reached 100 in 86 minutes and 200 in 185 minutes, going from 200 to 250 in just 16 minutes. In excess of 20 runs were taken from four separate overs, Brew 21 (Bradman 13), Tait 23 (Bradman 18) and 25 and 22 of successive overs from Levy (all to Bradman). Kippax's 125 (172 minutes) included 1 five and 12 fours. Chipperfield, whose 84 in 115 minutes on debut contained 9 fours, was selected (largely on his fielding at slip) for the tour of England after only two more matches, in which he scored 12 and 9. Gamble injured a toe while bowling late on the second day and left the field, returning only to complete his pair at the batting crease. Thompson, playing in his last first-class match (92 in 240 minutes, 13 fours), Allen (86 in 172 minutes, 12 fours) and Oxenham (51 in 106 minutes, 4 fours) scored fifties for Queensland. F.Mair (injured) was unavailable for New South Wales, whose selectors rested W.A.S.Oldfield and W.J.O'Reilly. Sources: *Wisden, NSWCA Report, QCA Report, Sydney Morning Herald, The Age, The Argus, The Herald.*

QUEENSLAND

G.G.Cook	lbw b Chilvers	24	(8) c Chipperfield b Chilvers	2
F.M.Brew	run out (McGilvray/Easton)	14	(1) c Bradman b Howell	23
W.C.Andrews	c Bradman b Chipperfield	38	lbw b Hill	8
F.C.Thompson	st Easton b Chipperfield	92	st Easton b Chilvers	10
*R.M.Levy	b Chilvers	45	(6) c & b Chilvers	16
E.C.Bensted	c Easton b Howell	0	(5) st Easton b Chilvers	29
T.Allen	run out (Chilvers/Easton)	86	(2) c Chipperfield b McGilvray	0
R.K.Oxenham	st Easton b Hill	51	(7) st Easton b Chilvers	24
A.H.Tait	not out	3	c Easton b Chilvers	35
†H.F.Leeson	c Chipperfield b Hill	14	not out	0
H.S.Gamble	c Easton b Hill	0	run out (Chilvers/Easton)	0
Extras	(lb4, w1)	5	(b8, lb1, w2)	11
Total	(166.4 overs, 458 mins)	372	(63.3 overs, 174 mins)	158

NEW SOUTH WALES

J.H.W.Fingleton	c Bensted b Brew	42
W.A.Brown	c Levy b Oxenham	50
D.G.Bradman	b Brew	253
*A.F.Kippax	c sub (S.F.M.Yeates) b Oxenham	125
R.C.Rowe	c Leeson b Oxenham	7
A.G.Chipperfield	c Leeson b Andrews	84
A.D.McGilvray	not out	34
C.J.Hill	not out	2
†F.A.Easton	)	
H.C.Chilvers	) did not bat	
W.H.Howell	)	
Extras	(b8, lb2, w5, nb2)	17
Total	(114.0 overs, 426 mins) (6 wkts dec)	614

NEW SOUTH WALES	O	M	R	W	w,nb		O	M	R	W	w,nb
McGilvray	14	3	36	0	-,-		8	1	18	1	2,-
Hill	30.4	12	51	3	-,-		13	8	13	1	-,-
Chilvers	48	17	95	2	1,-	(4)	22.3	5	62	6	-,-
Howell	43	16	79	1	-,-	(3)	15	3	35	1	-,-
Chipperfield	25	3	88	2	-,-		5	1	19	0	-,-
Kippax	5	0	16	0	-,-						
Bradman	1	0	2	0	-,-						

QUEENSLAND	O	M	R	W	w,nb
Gamble	6	0	17	0	-,1
Bensted	19	2	97	0	1,-
Brew	25	1	176	2	-,-
Oxenham	42	9	116	3	-,-
Tait	10	1	77	0	-,1
Cook	4	0	32	0	4,-
Andrews	3	0	19	1	-,-
Levy	5	0	63	0	-,-

FALL OF WICKETS

	QLD	NSW	QLD
Wkt	1st	1st	2nd
1st	24	94	1
2nd	43	118	14
3rd	109	481	39
4th	183	487	49
5th	192	507	90
6th	238	610	95
7th	353	-	97
8th	356	-	153
9th	372	-	158
10th	372	-	158

NEW SOUTH WALES v SOUTH AUSTRALIA (Shield Match 10)

Played at Sydney Cricket Ground on January 5, 6, 8, 9, 1934. (Four-day match)
Toss : South Australia.   Result : NEW SOUTH WALES WON BY NINE WICKETS.
Debuts: Nil.
12th Men: A.D.McGilvray (NSW) and R.S.Whitington (SA).
Umpires: E.G.Borwick and P.M.Solomon.
Attendances: 8094, 11642, 6251, 1510.   Total: 27,497.   Receipts: £1103.
Close of Play: 1st day NSW 0/33 (Fingleton 6, Brown 22); 2nd day NSW 3/187 (Kippax 79, Rowe 2); 3rd day NSW (2) 0/11
     (Fingleton 4, Brown 6).

S.J.McCabe (appendicitis) was still unavailable for New South Wales and Bill replaced D.G.Bradman (back strain) in the side selected for the match. Howell fractured a bone in his knee on the first day and took no further part. Nitschke scored his fourth century in successive Shield matches in Sydney as he carried his bat for South Australia, hitting 14 fours; he offered his only chance just before the innings closed. Ryan (56 in 113 minutes, 3 fours) and Collins (36 not out in 68 minutes, 3 fours) impressed in the second innings. Kippax, who offered a difficult chance before he had scored, went on to play the key innings for New South Wales, making 128 in 193 minutes with 20 fours. Brown (43 in 59 minutes, 3 fours and 83 in 113 minutes, 1 six and 7 fours) batted well in both innings. Fingleton (58 not out in 120 minutes, 2 fours) adding 142 for the first wicket to ensure victory. Rain shortened the first day's play and restricted the second.
Sources: *Wisden, NSWCA Report, SACA Report, Sydney Morning Herald, The Age, The Argus.*

SOUTH AUSTRALIA

*V.Y.Richardson	c Oldfield b Theak	13		lbw b Chilvers	24
H.C.Nitschke	not out	130		b O'Reilly	6
A.R.Lonergan	lbw b O'Reilly	14		c Bill b Theak	0
A.J.Ryan	c Oldfield b Chilvers	5	(6)	c Kippax b Chilvers	56
P.K.Lee	st Oldfield b Chilvers	0	(4)	run out (Fingleton/Oldfield)	5
B.J.Tobin	c Chipperfield b Chilvers	17	(5)	c Oldfield b Theak	10
M.G.Waite	c Chipperfield b Theak	19		b Chipperfield	22
F.H.K.Collins	c Theak b Howell	9		not out	36
C.V.Grimmett	c Fingleton b O'Reilly	0		b Theak	0
†C.W.Walker	c Oldfield b O'Reilly	5		c & b Chipperfield	12
T.W.Wall	st Oldfield b Chipperfield	26		c Oldfield b Chipperfield	0
Extras	(b4, lb1, nb3)	8		(b2, lb1, nb3)	6
Total	(61.5 overs, 220 mins)	246		(48.7 overs, 179 mins)	177

NEW SOUTH WALES

J.H.W.Fingleton	st Walker b Grimmett	8	not out	58
W.A.Brown	c Collins b Wall	43	st Walker b Waite	83
O.W.Bill	b Wall	41	not out	10
*A.F.Kippax	c Ryan b Tobin	128		
R.C.Rowe	b Collins	14		
A.G.Chipperfield	lbw b Grimmett	12		
†W.A.S.Oldfield	c Richardson b Wall	1		
H.C.Chilvers	hit wkt b Grimmett	0		
H.J.T.Theak	b Wall	4		
W.J.O'Reilly	not out	1		
W.H.Howell	absent hurt	-		
Extras	(b6, lb10, w1, nb4)	21	(b1, lb1, nb1)	3
Total	(64.6 overs, 268 mins)	273	(35.3 overs, 120 mins) (1 wkt)	154

NEW SOUTH WALES	O	M	R	W	w,nb		O	M	R	W	w,nb
Theak	13	1	52	2	-,3		12.7	0	43	3	-,3
Howell	9	0	54	1	-,-						
O'Reilly	20	8	59	3	-,-	(2)	15	1	56	1	-,-
Chilvers	18	1	67	3	-,-	(3)	14	1	43	2	-,-
Chipperfield	1.5	0	6	1	-,-	(4)	7	0	29	3	-,-

SOUTH AUSTRALIA	O	M	R	W	w,nb		O	M	R	W	w,nb
Wall	18.6	3	68	4	1,3		6	1	17	0	-,-
Tobin	10	1	41	1	-,-		5	0	18	0	-,1
Collins	11	1	42	1	-,1		2	0	5	0	-,-
Grimmett	19	5	75	3	-,-		7	0	34	0	-,-
Lee	6	1	26	0	-,-		7	1	24	0	-,-
Waite							8.3	0	53	1	-,-

FALL OF WICKETS

Wkt	SA 1st	NSW 1st	SA 2nd	NSW 2nd
1st	23	40	15	142
2nd	65	56	16	-
3rd	82	169	32	-
4th	88	225	41	-
5th	120	261	67	-
6th	160	267	105	-
7th	182	267	150	-
8th	182	271	176	-
9th	192	273	176	-
10th	246	-	177	-

QUEENSLAND v SOUTH AUSTRALIA (Shield Match 11)

Played at Brisbane Cricket Ground (Woolloongabba) on January 12, 13, 15, 16, 1934. (Four-day match)
Toss : South Australia. Result : QUEENSLAND WON BY EIGHT WICKETS.
Debuts: Queensland - K.J.Boag (f/c).
12th Men: K.L.M.Mossop (Qld) and M.G.Waite (SA).
Umpires: J.Bartlett and J.A.Scott.
Attendances: 3652, 5214, 3139, 100.   Total: 12,105.   Receipts: £780.
Close of Play: 1st day Qld 1/87 (Cook 40, Andrews 14); 2nd day SA (2) 0/15 (Richardson 11, Nitschke 2); 3rd day Qld (2) 1/58 (Allen 21, Andrews 32).

With this win, Queensland ended a sequence of 12 consecutive Shield matches without victory which included 11 outright defeats. The ageing Oxenham, who captured 10 for 104, Queensland's best match figures against South Australia to date, was the chief architect in his side's performance. Only Richardson in both innings with 67 (88 minutes, 10 fours) and 64 (113 minutes, 1 six and 5 fours), and Lonergan in the second (112 in 156 minutes, 12 fours) exceeded 20 for South Australia, the two adding 104 in 81 minutes for the second wicket. Cook was first in and last out for Queensland, hitting 13 fours in his 156 and offering his only chance when 104. With Oxenham (38 in 117 minutes) he added 96 for the sixth wicket. Cook was out to the first ball of the second innings but Andrews (68 not out in 92 minutes, 10 fours) saw Queensland home to a convincing victory. Sources: *Wisden, SACA Report, QCA Report, Brisbane Courier-Mail, The Age, Sydney Morning Herald.*

SOUTH AUSTRALIA

*V.Y.Richardson	b Gamble	67	lbw b Oxenham	64
H.C.Nitschke	c Bensted b Oxenham	2	c Hornibrook b Gamble	6
A.R.Lonergan	lbw b Yeates	14	c Gamble b Hornibrook	112
A.J.Ryan	b Oxenham	20	c Gamble b Yeates	19
R.S.Whitington	lbw b Oxenham	17	lbw b Oxenham	6
B.J.Tobin	c Tallon b Oxenham	18	st Tallon b Oxenham	11
P.K.Lee	c & b Yeates	4	c Levy b Hornibrook	3
F.H.K.Collins	c Gamble b Yeates	11	c Andrews b Hornibrook	3
†C.W.Walker	c & b Oxenham	3	b Oxenham	2
T.W.Wall	b Oxenham	18	c Cook b Hornibrook	8
C.V.Grimmett	not out	3	not out	0
Extras	(b2, lb3, nb2)	7	(b3, lb2, nb1)	6
Total	(55.7 overs, 207 mins)	184	(71.3 overs, 255 mins)	240

QUEENSLAND

G.G.Cook	run out (Tobin/Walker)	156	c Tobin b Wall	0
T.Allen	b Grimmett	32	c Ryan b Grimmett	21
W.C.Andrews	lbw b Grimmett	26	not out	68
K.J.Boag	lbw b Grimmett	8		
*R.M.Levy	b Lee	5	(4) not out	16
E.C.Bensted	c Ryan b Lee	11		
R.K.Oxenham	c Collins b Grimmett	38		
†D.Tallon	c & b Lee	13		
S.F.M.Yeates	lbw b Grimmett	2		
P.M.Hornibrook	c Richardson b Lee	18		
H.S.Gamble	not out	0		
Extras	(b3, lb5)	8	(b4, lb1)	5
Total	(116.7 overs, 396 mins)	317	(26.7 overs, 93 mins) (2 wkts)	110

QUEENSLAND	O	M	R	W	w,nb		O	M	R	W	w,nb
Gamble	5	0	31	1	-,2		12	2	52	1	-,1
Oxenham	23.7	6	48	6	-,-	(3)	26	5	56	4	-,-
Hornibrook	17	4	51	0	-,-	(2)	17.3	4	43	4	-,-
Yeates	10	1	47	3	-,-		11	0	69	1	-,-
Bensted							5	0	14	0	-,-

SOUTH AUSTRALIA	O	M	R	W	w,nb		O	M	R	W	w,nb
Wall	19	2	55	0	-,-		6	1	16	1	-,-
Tobin	15	1	51	0	-,-		2	0	12	0	-,-
Collins	7	3	11	0	-,-	(5)	4	0	13	0	-,-
Grimmett	46	12	132	5	-,-	(3)	10	1	45	1	-,-
Lee	29.7	6	60	4	-,-	(4)	3	0	6	0	-,-
Whitington							1	0	4	0	-,-
Nitschke							0.7	0	9	0	-,-

FALL OF WICKETS

Wkt	SA 1st	QLD 1st	SA 2nd	QLD 2nd
1st	24	56	29	0
2nd	81	118	133	74
3rd	85	132	195	-
4th	125	149	209	-
5th	126	169	213	-
6th	147	265	216	-
7th	151	283	219	-
8th	160	288	227	-
9th	165	317	240	-
10th	184	317	240	-

NEW SOUTH WALES v VICTORIA (Shield Match 12)

Played at Sydney Cricket Ground on January 26, 27, 29, 30, 1934. (Four-day match)
Toss : New South Wales.　　　　Result : MATCH DRAWN.
Debuts: Nil.
12th Men: O.W.Bill (NSW) and I.S.Lee (Vic).
Umpires: H.J.Armstrong and E.G.Borwick.
Attendances: 32587, 16001, 10907, 4800.　　　　Total: 64,295.　　　　Receipts: £3268.
Close of Play: 1st day NSW 2/445 (Brown 187, Rowe 1); 2nd day Vic 1/98 (Woodfull 61, Rigg 21); 3rd day Vic (2) 0/1 (Woodfull 0, O'Brien 0).

Although a record 340 runs were added for the New South Wales first wicket, Fingleton (78) retired at 0/148 after a severe attack of cramp (he resumed at 4/486) and hence two stands, Fingleton/Brown and Brown/Bradman, were involved. Brown (205 in 340 minutes, 1 five and 16 fours) and Bradman (128 in 96 minutes, 4 sixes and 17 fours) put on 192 in only 96 minutes. Playing his last match for New South Wales, Bradman reached his century in 87 minutes and scored his last 118 in 58 minutes, hitting 3 sixes off a Fleetwood-Smith over before being caught in the deep. Quick runs were at a premium because New South Wales needed to win outright to keep the Sheffield Shield. Kippax (44 in 52 minutes, 5 fours), Rowe (42 in 119 minutes, 2 fours) and Chilvers (42 in 84 minutes, 5 fours) made other contributions. Resuming on the second day, Fingleton on 86 was dropped by Ebeling at slip off Ironmonger, whereupon Ebeling picked up the ball and returned it to Barnett, who whipped off the bails with Fingleton (patting down the wicket) out of his crease. Borwick at square-leg gave him out, but amid protests from the gallery, Woodfull recalled him. Fingleton's eventual 145 occupied 244 minutes with 1 six and 15 fours. Kippax (gastric upset) was absent on the third day but resumed on the last, Oldfield leading in his absence. Victorians Woodfull (83 in 158 minutes, 9 fours), Scaife (120 in 209 minutes, 12 fours and 80 in 131 minutes, 9 fours), Bromley (92 in 117 minutes, 12 fours) and Darling (93 in 160 minutes, 7 fours) all helped prevent defeat and thereby win the trophy by a one-point margin. Ironmonger played his last match in Australia at the age of 51 years 298 days, which remains the record for both a Sheffield Shield participant and an Australian first-class cricketer in the 20th Century. *Wisden* incorrectly gives Vic (1) Ebeling b Hill. Sources: *Wisden, NSWCA Report, VCA Report, Australian Cricketer, Sydney Morning Herald, Sydney Referee*.

NEW SOUTH WALES

J.H.W.Fingleton	c Bromley b Ironmonger	145
W.A.Brown	lbw b Fleetwood-Smith	205
D.G.Bradman	c Darling b b Fleetwood-Smith	128
*A.F.Kippax	c Barnett b McCormick	44
R.C.Rowe	run out (Darling/Barnett)	42
A.G.Chipperfield	c Barnett b Ebeling	9
H.C.Chilvers	run out (O'Brien)	42
†W.A.S.Oldfield	run out (Scaife/Barnett)	2
C.J.Hill	not out	32
W.J.O'Reilly	not out	11
H.J.T.Theak	did not bat	
Extras	(b4, lb8)	12
Total	(132.0 overs, 523 mins) (8 wkts dec)	672

VICTORIA

*W.M.Woodfull	c Oldfield b O'Reilly	83	c Fingleton b O'Reilly	11
L.P.J.O'Brien	lbw b O'Reilly	16	b Hill	1
K.E.Rigg	run out (Bradman)	25	c Oldfield b O'Reilly	35
L.S.Darling	b Chilvers	8	lbw b Theak	93
J.W.Scaife	st Oldfield b Chilvers	120	c Chipperfield b Hill	80
E.H.Bromley	st Oldfield b Chipperfield	92	not out	33
†B.A.Barnett	c Oldfield b Chipperfield	25	not out	13
H.I.Ebeling	lbw b Hill	21		
E.L.McCormick	not out	6		
L.O.Fleetwood Smith	b Hill	4		
H.Ironmonger	b Hill	0		
Extras	(b1, lb3, nb3)	7	(b2, lb4, nb2)	8
Total	(113.6 overs, 379 mins)	407	(91.0 overs, 300 mins) (5 wkts)	274

VICTORIA	O	M	R	W	w,nb
McCormick	34	1	148	1	-,-
Ebeling	29	1	154	1	-,-
Fleetwood-Smith	31	0	178	2	-,-
Ironmonger	22	3	86	1	-,-
Bromley	6	0	42	0	-,-
Darling	9	0	52	0	-,-

NEW SOUTH WALES	O	M	R	W	w,nb	O	M	R	W	w,nb
Theak	23	3	68	0	-,2	19	6	47	1	-,2
Hill	20.6	5	40	3	-,-	27	13	54	2	-,-
O'Reilly	30	6	94	2	-,1	15	2	33	2	-,-
Chilvers	26	3	124	2	-,-	8	0	30	0	-,-
Chipperfield	14	0	74	2	-,-	8	0	46	0	-,-
Bradman						3	0	19	0	-,-
Rowe						6	1	25	0	-,-
Kippax						3	1	8	0	-,-
Brown						1	0	4	0	-,-
Fingleton						1	1	0	0	-,-

FALL OF WICKETS

Wkt	NSW 1st	VIC 1st	VIC 2nd
1st	340	37	8
2nd	430	110	22
3rd	475	131	95
4th	486	135	212
5th	542	293	236
6th	609	349	-
7th	615	391	-
8th	639	402	-
9th	-	407	-
10th	-	407	-

VICTORIA v TASMANIA

Played at Melbourne Cricket Ground on February 6, 7, 8, 1934. (Three-day match)
Toss : Victoria.   Result : MATCH DRAWN.
Debuts: Victoria - E.J.Cleary, T.W.Leather, E.C.Gunston (all f/c). Tasmania - R.V.Thomas (f/c).
12th Men: C.A.Gardner (Vic) and A.G.Cuff (Tas).
Umpires: C.Dwyer and H.R.McLean.
Attendances: 1563, 968, 315.   Total: 2846.   Receipts: £64.
Close of Play: 1st day Tas 4/251 (Green 26, Jeffrey 21); 2nd day Vic (2) 3/187 (Lee 102, Quin 46).

After collapsing unaccountably on the first day to register their lowest total against Tasmania in the 20th Century, Victoria conceded a formidable first-innings deficit and appeared headed for defeat until Lee and Quin added 424 in 312 minutes to establish an Australian fourth-wicket record which stood until 1986-87. Coming together at 3/74 soon after tea on the second day, the pair took the total to 3/187 at stumps and then 3/320 at lunch the following day (Lee 181, Quin 100) before eventually parting prior to the tea break at 3.45pm, when the innings was declared. Quin (210 in 309 minutes, 1 six and 24 fours) survived a stumping chance off Rothwell when 16 and a run-out opportunity when 71, while the 19-year-old Lee (258 in 386 minutes, 1 six and 23 fours) offered no chances. Both hit their career-best scores and compiled their stand at the rate of 100 in 102 minutes, 200 in 184 minutes, 300 in 247 minutes and 400 in 289 minutes. Thomas (left-arm medium pace) took 5 for 14 on debut, aged 18 years 138 days, but in the remainder of his 26-match career which lasted until 1950-51 he took only 14 further wickets for 1106 runs. Badcock (104 in 186 minutes, 7 fours) and Ferrall (84 in 142 minutes, 9 fours) added 165 for the Tasmanians' second wicket on the first day. Badcock (40 in 39 minutes, 2 fours) and Morrisby (77 not out in 114 minutes, 8 fours) impressed on the last day, which saw 536 runs scored in 346 minutes (87 overs). A.O.Burrows and S.W.L.Putman (both unavailable) were replaced by Cuff and Jeffrey before the islanders left for Melbourne. Sources: *Australian Cricketer, VCA Report, TCA Report, The Age, The Argus, The Herald, Melbourne Sun.*

VICTORIA

I.D.Miller	c Walsh b Thomas	2	(6) not out		16
E.H.G.Vernon	c Parry b Walsh	3	(1) run out (Green/Thomas)		4
I.S.Lee	c James b Thomas	1	(2) c Thomas b Jeffrey		258
E.C.Gunston	b Thomas	11	c Jeffrey b Walsh		8
L.J.Junor	c Parry b Thomas	2	(3) b Jeffrey		22
*†S.O.Quin	c & b James	21	(5) c Combes b Rothwell		210
H.J.Plant	lbw b James	2	(8) not out		36
E.J.Cleary	c Parry b Walsh	5	(7) b Jeffrey		0
S.A.J.Smith	c Parry b Walsh	19			
T.J.Trembath	b Thomas	1			
T.W.Leather	not out	0			
Extras	(lb1)	1	(b5, lb1)		6
Total	(29.3 overs, 113 mins)	68	(113.0 overs, 419 mins) (6 wkts dec)		560

TASMANIA

C.L.Badcock	c Leather b Trembath	104	c sub (C.A.Gardner) b Cleary		40
R.O.G.Morrisby	c Quin b Leather	5	not out		77
R.A.Ferrall	c Cleary b Leather	84	b Smith		7
R.V.Thomas	st Quin b Cleary	7			
*D.C.Green	c Quin b Leather	39			
C.L.Jeffrey	b Trembath	24	(5) c & b Smith		4
J.W.Rothwell	c Gunston b Smith	43	(4) c Quin b Smith		2
M.J.Combes	lbw b Smith	9			
G.T.H.James	b Trembath	0	(7) c & b Smith		23
†C.N.Parry	b Trembath	46	(6) c sub (C.A.Gardner) b Plant		5
J.M.Walsh	not out	20	(8) not out		4
Extras	(b5, lb2)	7	(b1)		1
Total	(105.0 overs, 389 mins)	388	(28.0 overs, 114 mins) (6 wkts)		163

TASMANIA	O	M	R	W	w,nb		O	M	R	W	w,nb		FALL OF WICKETS			
Walsh	7	3	16	3	-,-		21	2	75	1	-,-			VIC	TAS	VIC	TAS
Thomas	10.3	4	14	5	-,-		29	1	118	0	-,-	Wkt	1st	1st	2nd	2nd
James	8	2	13	2	-,-		22	0	119	0	-,-	1st	5	10	19	63
Rothwell	4	0	24	0	-,-		21	0	136	1	-,-	2nd	5	175	56	78
Jeffrey							17	2	81	3	-,-	3rd	11	200	74	90
Combes							1	0	5	0	-,-	4th	13	202	498	100
Badcock							2	0	20	0	-,-	5th	22	258	509	113
												6th	35	277	509	152
VICTORIA	O	M	R	W	w,nb		O	M	R	W	w,nb	7th	44	320	-	-
Trembath	22	2	77	4	-,-		3	0	20	0	-,-	8th	63	321	-	-
Leather	24	1	96	3	-,-		4	0	19	0	-,-	9th	68	329	-	-
Smith	22	3	86	2	-,-	(4)	9	0	55	4	-,-	10th	68	388	-	-
Cleary	21	4	61	1	-,-	(3)	6	0	34	1	-,-					
Plant	13	1	51	0	-,-		5	0	23	1	-,-					
Vernon	3	0	20	0	-,-											
Junor						(6)	1	0	11	0	-,-					

SOUTH AUSTRALIA v WESTERN AUSTRALIA

Played at Adelaide Oval on February 10, 12, 13, 1934. (Three-day match)
Toss : South Australia.   Result : MATCH DRAWN.
Debuts: South Australia - R.A.Parker, R.R.Wright (both f/c). Western Australia - A.J.Ditchburn, S.G.Francis, J.R.Jones, R.T.Ryan, R.J.Sartori (all f/c).
12th Men: G.Young (SA) and W.A.Roach (WA).
Umpires: A.G.Jenkins and J.D.Scott.
Attendances: 1771, 1329, 1009.   Total: 4109.   Receipts: £132.
Close of Play: 1st day WA 2/32 (Hill-Smith 11, Ryan 14); 2nd day SA (2) 5/92 (Wright 8, Waite 6).

F.H.Taaffe, nominated vice-captain of the Western Australian thirteen to tour the Eastern States, withdrew prior to the team's departure and was replaced by Ditchburn. R.A.Halcombe also announced his unavailability for the trip. Wright was a late inclusion for A.G.Shepherd (work) in the South Australian side. Whitington was dismissed in the first over of the match, Ditchburn's first in first-class cricket, and batsmen struggled over the three days. Lonergan scored 69 (142 minutes, 8 fours) and 34 (64 minutes, 4 fours), establishing the only hundred partnership - 110 for the fourth wicket - with Wright (77 in 161 minutes, 8 fours), who was missed on three occasions. Francis's left-arm medium-pace returned nine wickets on debut. F.J.Bryant was out to the third ball of Western Australia's first innings, Hill-Smith (59 in 177 minutes, 1 six and 2 fours) and R.J.Bryant (44 in 64 minutes) making the top scores for the visitors. Sources: *Australian Cricketer, SACA Report, WACA Report, Adelaide Advertiser, The News.*

SOUTH AUSTRALIA

*V.Y.Richardson	c & b Francis	4		c R.J.Bryant b Francis	8
R.S.Whitington	c Lovelock b Ditchburn	0	(4)	run out (R.J.Bryant/Lovelock)	1
A.R.Lonergan	c Ditchburn b Sartori	69		c Lovelock b R.J.Bryant	34
R.A.Parker	b Ditchburn	2	(5)	c Lovelock b Ditchburn	1
R.R.Wright	c Alexander b Francis	77	(6)	b Francis	12
F.H.K.Collins	lbw b Francis	6	(8)	c Alexander b Jones	20
M.G.Waite	c Ditchburn b Francis	10		c Jones b Francis	18
C.V.Grimmett	b Francis	10	(9)	run out (R.J.Bryant)	26
†C.W.Walker	not out	20	(2)	c Hill-Smith b Francis	30
T.W.Wall	b Jones	2		b Ditchburn	6
J.R.Davey	c Lovelock b Ditchburn	0		not out	0
Extras	(b8)	8		(b8, lb3)	11
Total	(60.2 overs, 233 mins)	208		(61.3 overs, 226 mins)	167

WESTERN AUSTRALIA

F.J.Bryant	c Whitington b Wall	0	lbw b Grimmett	31
W.Hill-Smith	b Collins	59	b Grimmett	8
F.J.Alexander	run out (Wright/Walker)	3	run out (Collins/Walker)	2
R.T.Ryan	b Collins	29	c Walker b Wall	28
†O.I.Lovelock	lbw b Grimmett	1	b Waite	6
M.Inverarity	st Walker b Grimmett	4	b Grimmett	7
*R.J.Bryant	b Grimmett	44	not out	30
S.G.Francis	st Walker b Grimmett	26	b Davey	7
A.J.Ditchburn	c & b Waite	0	b Davey	3
J.R.Jones	c Davey b Waite	5	not out	4
R.J.Sartori	not out	3		
Extras	(b8, lb12)	20	(b3, lb4)	7
Total	(64.0 overs, 216 mins)	194	(50.0 overs, 176 mins) (8 wkts)	133

WESTERN AUSTRALIA	O	M	R	W	w,nb		O	M	R	W	w,nb
Ditchburn	16.2	2	51	3	-,-		14	2	38	2	-,-
Francis	17	2	49	5	-,-		22.3	9	39	4	-,-
Sartori	12	2	38	1	-,-		9	2	33	0	-,-
Jones	11	0	32	1	-,-		8	1	29	1	-,-
Inverarity	4	0	30	0	-,-						
R.J.Bryant						(5)	7	2	11	1	-,-
Alexander						(6)	1	0	6	0	-,-

SOUTH AUSTRALIA	O	M	R	W	w,nb		O	M	R	W	w,nb
Wall	11	2	40	1	-,-		10	2	34	1	-,-
Davey	15	2	37	0	-,-		9	1	28	2	-,-
Collins	14	1	29	2	-,-		10	4	22	0	-,-
Grimmett	17	3	45	4	-,-		19	7	38	3	-,-
Waite	7	0	23	2	-,-		2	0	4	1	-,-

FALL OF WICKETS

Wkt	SA 1st	WA 1st	SA 2nd	WA 2nd
1st	3	0	9	26
2nd	9	7	76	36
3rd	12	53	76	53
4th	122	58	77	79
5th	158	70	78	81
6th	167	140	99	95
7th	182	160	120	110
8th	187	163	137	120
9th	190	181	163	-
10th	208	194	167	-

VICTORIA v WESTERN AUSTRALIA

Played at Melbourne Cricket Ground on February 15, 16, 17, 1934. (Three-day match)
Toss : Western Australia.   Result : VICTORIA WON BY AN INNINGS AND 120 RUNS.
Debuts: Victoria - C.A.Gardner, R.G.Gregory, M.W.Sievers (all f/c).
12th Men: L.S.Darling (Vic) and I.J.Campbell (WA).
Umpires: W.J.Craddock and C.Juliff.
Attendances: 1051, 909, 145.   Total: 2105.   Receipts: £45.
Close of Play: 1st day Vic 0/77 (Lee 36, Vernon 40); 2nd day WA (2) 1/10 (Alexander 7, Hill-Smith 1).

L.D.Kemp (nominated captain), R.J.Hassett and I.D.Miller announced their inability to play for Victoria after being selected and were replaced by Gregory (aged 17 years 353 days), Gunston and Sievers. Only F.J.Bryant (55 in 119 minutes, 8 fours), Alexander (45 in 131 minutes, 4 fours) and Lovelock (31 in 48 minutes, 3 fours) surpassed 30 for Western Australia. Lee (36 in 90 minutes, 1 four) and Vernon (47 in 119 minutes, 5 fours) made a sound start for Victoria, Allsopp (146 in 183 minutes, 1 five and 14 fours) then adding 187 in 123 minutes with Gardner for the third wicket before Gardner retired at 2/289 with a leg strain. Sievers (53 not out in 116 minutes, 4 fours) and Cleary (37 not out in 95 minutes, 2 fours) added an unfinished 89 for the eighth wicket. Sources: *Australian Cricketer, VCA Report, WACA Report, The Age, The Argus, The Herald, Melbourne Sun.*

WESTERN AUSTRALIA

F.J.Bryant	c Quin b Sievers	55		c Plant b Sievers	2
W.Hill-Smith	c Plant b Leather	7	(3)	b Plant	17
F.J.Alexander	c & b Gregory	45	(2)	lbw b Cleary	14
R.T.Ryan	c Quin b Leather	15	(5)	c Sievers b Leather	26
M.Inverarity	b Cleary	7	(4)	c & b Gregory	9
†O.I.Lovelock	b Sievers	31	(7)	c Plant b Sievers	8
*R.J.Bryant	c Vernon b Gregory	4	(6)	b Leather	0
S.G.Francis	not out	10		c Gunston b Plant	21
A.J.Ditchburn	c & b Gregory	2	(11)	not out	20
J.R.Jones	c & b Gregory	7	(9)	c sub (L.S.Darling) b Plant	3
R.J.Sartori	lbw b Leather	0	(10)	lbw b Plant	8
Extras	(lb2)	2		(lb5)	5
Total	(70.2 overs, 249 mins)	185		(59.5 overs, 211 mins)	133

VICTORIA

I.S.Lee	st Lovelock b Francis	36
E.H.G.Vernon	b Francis	47
A.H.Allsopp	b Sartori	146
C.A.Gunston	retired hurt	78
E.C.Gardner	c Ditchburn b Jones	0
*†S.O.Quin	run out (Ditchburn)	10
M.W.Sievers	not out	53
H.J.Plant	lbw b Sartori	11
R.G.Gregory	b Inverarity	5
E.J.Cleary	not out	37
T.W.Leather	did not bat	
Extras	(b11, lb4)	15
Total	(108.0 overs, 401 mins) (7 wkts dec)	438

VICTORIA	O	M	R	W	w,nb	O	M	R	W	w,nb
Leather	18.2	1	50	3	-,-	16	3	36	2	-,-
Sievers	16	6	35	2	-,-	13	3	18	2	-,-
Cleary	15	6	28	1	-,-	10	2	26	1	-,-
Plant	5	1	20	0	-,-	11.5	2	25	4	-,-
Gregory	16	1	50	4	-,-	9	1	23	1	-,-

WESTERN AUSTRALIA	O	M	R	W	w,nb
Ditchburn	20	2	81	0	-,-
Francis	20	6	73	2	-,-
R.J.Bryant	15	4	38	0	-,-
Jones	21	4	81	1	-,-
Sartori	20	1	76	2	-,-
Inverarity	12	1	74	1	-,-

	FALL OF WICKETS		
Wkt	WA 1st	VIC 1st	WA 2nd
1st	13	79	5
2nd	95	102	27
3rd	116	290	41
4th	128	332	67
5th	138	332	71
6th	153	344	71
7th	165	349	90
8th	174	-	108
9th	184	-	114
10th	185	-	133

NEW SOUTH WALES v WESTERN AUSTRALIA

Played at Sydney Cricket Ground on February 23, 24, 26, 1934. (Three-day match)
Toss : Western Australia.   Result : MATCH DRAWN.
Debuts: New South Wales - G.H.Bennett, J.G.Lush (both f/c). Western Australia - I.J.Campbell (f/c).
12th Men: R.C.J.Little (NSW) and F.J.Alexander (WA).
Umpires: A.L.Christie and P.M.Solomon.
Attendances & Receipts: No figures published.
Close of Play: 1st day NSW 1/54 (Brown 17, Marks 6); 2nd day WA 1/33 (F.J.Bryant 17, Hill-Smith 5).

McGilvray captained New South Wales in his third match and promoted himself to open the batting. A severe thunderstorm reduced the first day's play to only 75 minutes. Marks (110 in 219 minutes, 8 fours) was missed twice from Jones's bowling - a stumping chance at 31 and a dropped catch at 103. Bill (47 in 91 minutes, 3 fours) and Rowe (52 in 95 minutes, 4 fours) shared partnerships of 112 and 74 with Marks for the third and fourth wickets for New South Wales. F.J.Bryant (69 in 138 minutes, 5 fours) and Hill-Smith (52 in 138 minutes, 2 fours) added 97 for Western Australia's second wicket but the innings fell away after Bryant was run out attempting a third run.
Sources: *Australian Cricketer, NSWCA Report, WACA Report, Sydney Morning Herald, NSWCA Scorebook.*

NEW SOUTH WALES

W.A.Brown	c Inverarity b Sartori	28	not out	19
*A.D.McGilvray	c Sartori b Francis	29		
A.E.Marks	c R.J.Bryant b Francis	110		
O.W.Bill	lbw b Jones	47		
R.C.Rowe	st Lovelock b Jones	52		
J.G.Lush	c Jones b Francis	8	(3) not out	9
G.H.Bennett	c Ditchburn b Francis	2		
H.C.Chilvers	c Ditchburn b Jones	2		
C.J.Hill	c R.J.Bryant b Francis	14		
H.J.T.Theak	c sub (F.J.Alexander) b Jones	19		
†F.A.Easton	not out	3	(2) c R.J.Bryant b Inverarity	13
Extras	(b13, lb5)	18	(lb1, nb1)	2
Total	(90.0 overs, 343 mins)	332	(12.0 overs, 40 mins) (1 wkt)	43

WESTERN AUSTRALIA

F.J.Bryant	run out (Rowe/Easton)	69
I.J.Campbell	b Bennett	9
W.Hill-Smith	c Hill b Bennett	52
R.T.Ryan	b Chilvers	17
*R.J.Bryant	c Easton b Chilvers	12
M.Inverarity	b Bennett	11
†O.I.Lovelock	c Lush b Hill	21
S.G.Francis	c Hill b Bennett	16
A.J.Ditchburn	b Chilvers	9
J.R.Jones	st Easton b Chilvers	3
R.J.Sartori	not out	0
Extras	(b4, lb8, w1, nb2)	15
Total	(85.1 overs, 282 mins)	234

WESTERN AUSTRALIA	O	M	R	W	w,nb		O	M	R	W	w,nb
Ditchburn	15	2	53	0	-,-		6	2	12	0	-,-
Francis	30	8	94	5	-,-						
Jones	30	2	114	4	-,-						
Sartori	11	1	40	1	-,-						
R.J.Bryant	4	0	13	0	-,-						
Inverarity						(2)	6	0	29	1	-,1

NEW SOUTH WALES	O	M	R	W	w,nb
Theak	13	1	41	0	1,1
Hill	14	3	32	1	-,-
Bennett	26	5	62	4	-,1
Chilvers	26.1	3	72	4	-,-
McGilvray	6	2	12	0	-,-

FALL OF WICKETS			
Wkt	NSW 1st	WA 1st	NSW 2nd
1st	41	24	27
2nd	80	121	-
3rd	192	149	-
4th	266	161	-
5th	290	174	-
6th	292	184	-
7th	293	220	-
8th	296	228	-
9th	322	232	-
10th	332	234	-

VICTORIA v WESTERN AUSTRALIA

Played at Melbourne Cricket Ground on February 27, 28, March 1, 1934. (Three-day match)
Toss : Victoria,   Result : MATCH DRAWN.
Debuts: Western Australia - W.A.Roach (f/c).
12th Men: L.J.Junor (Vic) and R.T.Ryan (WA).
Umpires: J.H.Hughes and T.A.Wells.
Attendances: 408, 432, 241.   Total: 1081.   Receipts: £23.
Close of Play: 1st day Vic 6/174 (Sievers 52, Cleary 19); 2nd day WA 2/245 (F.J.Bryant 111, R.J.Bryant 66).

The start of the match was delayed until 2.20pm because the visitors' train from Sydney was late. Lee was caught by team-mate Gunston, one of several Victorians substituting for Western Australians whose baggage was delayed. F.J.Bryant (115 in 250 minutes, 16 fours) and R.J.Bryant (103 in 150 minutes, 13 fours) - the second pair of brothers after C.Hill and L.R.Hill (SA v NSW at Sydney 1910-11) to score hundreds in the same innings in Australia - added 136 for the third wicket. Alexander (48 in 120 minutes, 4 fours) and Hill-Smith (68 in 143 minutes, 5 fours) also batted proficiently. Allsopp (48 in 63 minutes, 4 fours), Sievers (72 in 186 minutes, 6 fours) and Cleary (58 in 157 minutes, 5 fours) topscored for Victoria, Ditchburn trapping Lee in the first over of the second innings. R.G.Gregory and E.H.G.Vernon were unavailable for Victoria, while Cordner replaced S.A.J.Smith (also unavailable) after the team was selected. Sources: *VCA Report, WACA Report, Australian Cricketer, The Age, The Argus, The Herald, Melbourne Sun.*

VICTORIA

I.D.Miller	c Lovelock b Ditchburn	4	(2)	c Francis b Ditchburn	37
I.S.Lee	c sub (E.C.Gunston) b Francis	6	(1)	lbw b Ditchburn	0
A.H.Allsopp	c F.J.Bryant b Francis	48		c Lovelock b R.J.Bryant	27
C.A.Gardner	c Alexander b R.J.Bryant	13		c & b R.J.Bryant	12
E.C.Gunston	b R.J.Bryant	0		run out (R.J.Bryant/Lovelock)	21
*†S.O.Quin	b Inverarity	28		c Campbell b Jones	15
M.W.Sievers	c & b Jones	72		not out	3
E.J.Cleary	st Lovelock b Jones	58		c Jones Inverarity	8
H.J.Plant	lbw b Jones	6		not out	1
L.O.Cordner	c R.J.Bryant b Jones	4			
T.W.Leather	not out	0			
Extras	(lb4)	4		(b4, lb2)	6
Total	(83.7 overs, 313 mins)	243		(42.0 overs, 160 mins) (7 wkts)	130

WESTERN AUSTRALIA

F.J.Bryant	b Leather	115
F.J.Alexander	c & b Cordner	48
I.J.Campbell	b Leather	7
*R.J.Bryant	b Plant	103
W.Hill-Smith	c Sievers b Plant	68
W.A.Roach	c & b Plant	17
M.Inverarity	lbw b Cleary	20
†O.I.Lovelock	run out (Miller)	1
S.G.Francis	not out	26
A.J.Ditchburn	not out	3
J.R.Jones	did not bat	
Extras	(b10, lb2, w1, nb2)	15
Total	(121.0 overs, 425 mins) (8 wkts dec)	423

WESTERN AUSTRALIA	O	M	R	W	w,nb	O	M	R	W	w,nb
Ditchburn	16	3	48	1	-,-	12	5	22	2	-,-
Francis	28	10	58	2	-,-	9	2	38	0	-,-
R.J.Bryant	15	5	43	2	-,-	9	2	19	2	-,-
Jones	17.7	3	59	4	-,-	10	1	39	1	-,-
Inverarity	7	0	31	1	-,-	2	0	6	1	-,-

VICTORIA	O	M	R	W	w,nb
Leather	26	5	94	2	-,2
Sievers	19	4	58	0	1,-
Plant	30	6	77	3	-,-
Cleary	22	2	77	1	-,-
Cordner	24	1	102	1	-,-

FALL OF WICKETS

Wkt	VIC 1st	WA 1st	VIC 2nd
1st	10	114	0
2nd	10	127	40
3rd	63	263	60
4th	71	299	87
5th	71	323	110
6th	126	366	118
7th	219	368	128
8th	233	411	-
9th	243	-	-
10th	243	-	-

SOUTH AUSTRALIA v WESTERN AUSTRALIA

Played at Adelaide Oval on March 3, 5, 1934. (Two-day match)
Toss : South Australia.   Result : MATCH DRAWN.
Debuts: South Australia - R.N.Hack, E.J.R.Moyle, L.A.Smith (all f/c).
12th Men: R.A.Hamence (SA) and I.J.Campbell (WA).
Umpires: T.W.Cook and J.D.Scott.
Attendances: 639, 463.   Total: 1102.   Receipts: £35.
Close of Play: 1st day SA 7/260 (Walker 23, Grimmett 11).

This was the last first-class match in Australia to be scheduled for two days only. The home selectors rested leading players such as V.Y.Richardson, H.C.Nitschke, P.K.Lee and A.R.Lonergan in order to test Hack, Moyle and Smith at a higher level. Hack and Smith were never chosen again although Smith later became an umpire. Whitington (50 in 119 minutes, 4 fours) scored the sole half-century and lost his wicket when he lifted Jones to the long field and "Alexander after running more than 40 yards brought off a brilliantly-judged catch" (*News*). The batting was staid and unenterprising apart from a 91-run stand in 101 minutes involving Parker and Moyle. Smith was given out when a ball from Francis dislodged a bail from its groove but did not remove it from the top of his wicket. Grimmett's 7 for 57 included a spell of 3 for 1; he dismissed Roach and Inverarity with successive balls shortly after getting Hill-Smith, and he later bowled Ryan and Francis inside three balls (one of his rare wides intervened) to have figures of 7 for 29. Lovelock (33 not out in 77 minutes) and Hill-Smith (30 in 45 minutes) topscored for Western Australia. Wall took three wickets in his first three overs in the follow-on. To compensate for the duration, hours of play were extended, starting at 11.00am instead of noon on both days. Sources: *SACA Report, WACA Report, Adelaide Advertiser, The News, The West Australian.*

SOUTH AUSTRALIA

L.A.Smith	b Francis	9
W.E.Catchlove	b Jones	21
R.S.Whitington	c Alexander b Jones	50
R.R.Wright	c Ryan b Ditchburn	37
R.A.Parker	c Inverarity b Ditchburn	46
E.J.R.Moyle	c Jones b Ditchburn	45
R.N.Hack	c sub (I.J.Campbell) b Francis	5
†C.W.Walker	c & b Jones	37
*C.V.Grimmett	c Ditchburn b Jones	13
T.W.Wall	b Ditchburn	8
J.R.Davey	not out	1
Extras	(b13, lb2)	15
Total	(105.2 overs, 394 mins)	287

WESTERN AUSTRALIA

F.J.Bryant	lbw b Grimmett	10	lbw b Grimmett		21
F.J.Alexander	c & b Grimmett	13	b Wall		2
R.T.Ryan	b Grimmett	26	b Wall		0
*R.J.Bryant	b Wall	16	c & b Wall		4
W.Hill-Smith	c Hack b Grimmett	1	c Whitington b Grimmett		30
W.A.Roach	st Walker b Grimmett	0	(7) not out		14
M.Inverarity	lbw b Grimmett	0			
†O.I.Lovelock	not out	33	(6) not out		18
S.G.Francis	b Grimmett	0			
A.J.Ditchburn	b Hack	6			
J.R.Jones	b Wall	22			
Extras	(b10, lb2, w1)	13	(b2, lb1, nb1)		4
Total	(48.4 overs, 173 mins)	140	(29.0 overs, 108 mins) (5 wkts)		93

WESTERN AUSTRALIA	O	M	R	W	w,nb
Ditchburn	28	8	67	4	-,-
Francis	31	10	55	2	-,-
R.J.Bryant	5	0	19	0	-,-
Jones	32.2	7	81	4	-,-
Inverarity	9	0	50	0	-,-

SOUTH AUSTRALIA	O	M	R	W	w,nb		O	M	R	W	w,nb
Wall	7.4	1	26	2	-,-		6	2	8	3	-,1
Davey	9	2	11	0	-,-		7	1	20	0	-,-
Grimmett	19	3	57	7	1,-	(4)	7	1	33	2	-,-
Hack	13	1	33	1	-,-	(3)	5	1	16	0	-,-
Wright							4	0	12	0	-,-

FALL OF WICKETS

		SA	WA	WA
Wkt		1st	1st	2nd
1st		35	30	3
2nd		51	33	3
3rd		127	56	9
4th		128	69	51
5th		219	71	58
6th		220	71	-
7th		224	78	-
8th		262	79	-
9th		283	92	-
10th		287	140	-

TASMANIA v AUSTRALIAN XI

Played at N.T.C.A. Ground, Launceston, on March 10, 12, 13, 1934. (Three-day match)
Toss : Tasmania.　　　　　　　　　Result : MATCH DRAWN.
Debuts: Tasmania - A.L.Pearsall (f/c).
12th Men: G.J.Lethborg (Tas) and H.I.Ebeling (Aust).
Umpires: E.C.Knight and B.Parker.
Attendances: 6000, 3500, 2000.　　　Total: 11,500.　　　Receipts: £605.
Close of Play: 1st day Tas 9/336 (Parry 11, Walsh 11); 2nd day Aust 4/415 (McCabe 91, Chipperfield 16).

Badcock, not yet 20 years old, scored his fourth hundred in as many matches for Tasmania, 105 in 163 minutes with 11 fours. Morrisby (44 in 50 minutes, 7 fours), Ferrall (47 in 92 minutes, 6 fours) and Thomas (34 in 82 minutes, 4 fours) also impressed in the first innings. Woodfull (126 in 162 minutes, 9 fours) and Brown (96 in 158 minutes, 7 fours) added 220 for the Australian first wicket on the second day, Darling (60 in 73 minutes, 1 six and 5 fours), McCabe (119 in 97 minutes, 17 fours) and Chipperfield (43 in 73 minutes, 2 fours) capitalising on the start. Woodfull's last 76 runs took an uncharacteristic 57 minutes. The Tasmanians held out with innings from Ferrall (39 in 80 minutes, 4 fours), Rushforth (49 in 81 minutes, 3 fours) and Rothwell (62 in 98 minutes, 4 fours) on the last day, Barnett keeping wickets after tea and completing two stumpings. D.C.Green was unavailable for Tasmania while D.G.Bradman, named vice-captain of the Australian side to England and now a resident of South Australia, did not travel to Tasmania and Western Australia for the three pre-tour matches due to a need for rest. He boarded the *R.M.S.Orford* at Adelaide before it travelled on to Perth to pick up the remainder of the team. Sources: *Australian Cricketer, NSWCA Report, VCA Report, Hobart Mercury, Launceston Examiner.*

TASMANIA

C.L.Badcock	c Woodfull b Darling	105	c Chipperfield b Fleetwood-Smith		24
R.O.G.Morrisby	b Darling	44	c Chipperfield b Darling		3
R.A.Ferrall	b Grimmett	47	c Wall b Fleetwood-Smith		39
R.V.Thomas	b Fleetwood-Smith	34	run out (Darling)		6
*A.W.Rushforth	lbw b Grimmett	26	lbw b Fleetwood-Smith		49
J.W.Rothwell	c Woodfull b Fleetwood-Smith	14	c Wall b Kippax		62
A.L.Pearsall	st Oldfield b Fleetwood-Smith	1	st Barnett b Grimmett		1
G.T.H.James	c & b Chipperfield	26	st Barnett b Grimmett		1
C.L.Jeffrey	c Barnett b Fleetwood-Smith	4	not out		14
†C.N.Parry	c & b Fleetwood-Smith	16	not out		10
J.M.Walsh	not out	15			
Extras	(b1, lb10, w1, nb1)	13	(lb4, nb1)		5
Total	(86.6 overs, 297 mins)	345	(60.0 overs, 198 mins) (8 wkts)		214

AUSTRALIAN XI

*W.M.Woodfull	c Rushforth b Rothwell	126
W.A.Brown	b Pearsall	96
L.S.Darling	lbw b Jeffrey	60
A.F.Kippax	c Parry b Walsh	17
S.J.McCabe	c Ferrall b James	119
A.G.Chipperfield	c & b Rothwell	43
B.A.Barnett	c Thomas b Jeffrey	27
†W.A.S.Oldfield	b Jeffrey	5
C.V.Grimmett	not out	23
T.W.Wall	c Morrisby b Rothwell	11
L.O.Fleetwood-Smith	b Jeffrey	0
Extras	(b4, lb3, nb3)	10
Total	(100.3 overs, 343 mins)	537

AUSTRALIAN XI	O	M	R	W	w,nb		O	M	R	W	w,nb
Wall	15	1	52	0	-,1		7	0	32	0	-,1
Darling	10	2	45	2	1,-		6	2	21	1	-,-
Fleetwood-Smith	24.6	1	108	5	-,-	(4)	21	4	64	3	-,-
Grimmett	29	5	96	2	-,-	(3)	16	3	46	2	-,-
Chipperfield	8	0	31	1	-,-		7	0	31	0	-,-
Kippax							2	0	5	1	-,-
Woodfull							1	0	10	0	-,-

TASMANIA	O	M	R	W	w,nb
Walsh	19	0	98	1	-,3
Thomas	17	1	85	0	-,-
James	20	4	82	1	-,-
Rothwell	20	1	110	3	-,-
Jeffrey	12.3	0	70	4	-,-
Pearsall	12	0	82	1	-,-

FALL OF WICKETS

Wkt	TAS 1st	AUST 1st	TAS 2nd
1st	79	220	10
2nd	187	230	54
3rd	214	267	69
4th	262	365	80
5th	264	459	164
6th	266	483	171
7th	295	501	183
8th	309	520	204
9th	310	535	-
10th	345	537	-

TASMANIA v AUSTRALIAN XI

Played at T.C.A. Ground, Hobart, on March 15, 16, 17, 1934. (Three-day match)
Toss : Tasmania.   Result : MATCH DRAWN.
Debuts: Nil.
12th Men: D.Jones (Tas) and W.J.O'Reilly (Aust).
Umpires: J.Gardiner and W.T.Lonergan.
Attendances: 2700, 5000, 4200.   Total: About 11,900.   Receipts: £649.
Close of Play: 1st day Tas 7/230 (Jeffrey 10); 2nd day Aust 4/360 (Kippax 76, Chipperfield 28).

Woodfull (124 in 138 minutes, 1 six and 4 fours) and Brown (98 in 163 minutes, 6 fours) added their second successive 200-run opening stand for the Australians against Tasmania on the second afternoon. Kippax (141 in 145 minutes, 22 fours) took full advantage of the reduced attack as Jeffrey (torn leg muscle) was out of action; he returned late in the match to help stave off defeat and was missed of his first ball with 8 minutes remaining. Badcock (47 in 90 minutes, 5 fours) in his last game for the State, Thomas (53 in 125 minutes, 5 fours), Rothwell (47 in 76 minutes, 6 fours) and the fast-scoring James (career-best 70 in 53 minutes, 8 fours) topscored for Tasmania, whose regular captain A.W.Rushforth was unavailable. Sources: *Australian Cricketer, NSWCA Report, VCA Report, Hobart Mercury.*

TASMANIA

C.L.Badcock	c Chipperfield b Fleetwood-Smith	47		lbw b Wall	6
R.O.G.Morrisby	st Oldfield b Fleetwood-Smith	17		lbw b Fleetwood-Smith	23
R.A.Ferrall	c Ebeling b Wall	16		b Wall	5
R.V.Thomas	c Oldfield b Wall	53		run out (Fleetwood-Smith)	27
*D.C.Green	c Chipperfield b Wall	6		c Oldfield b Wall	23
J.W.Rothwell	c McCabe b Darling	47		not out	15
S.W.L.Putman	b Wall	21		b Wall	0
C.L.Jeffrey	c Oldfield b Wall	13	(10)	not out	6
G.T.H.James	c Oldfield b Ebeling	70	(8)	c McCabe b Fleetwood-Smith	2
†C.N.Parry	not out	30	(9)	b Wall	10
J.M.Walsh	c Darling b Ebeling	0			
Extras	(b8, lb9, nb1)	18		(lb6, nb1)	7
Total	(76.2 overs, 312 mins)	338		(34.0 overs, 147 mins) (8 wkts)	124

AUSTRALIAN XI

*W.M.Woodfull	st Parry b Putman	124
W.A.Brown	c Thomas b Walsh	98
L.S.Darling	lbw b Walsh	0
A.F.Kippax	c sub (D.Jones) b Rothwell	141
S.J.McCabe	c Ferrall b James	27
A.G.Chipperfield	lbw b Thomas	36
B.A.Barnett	b Rothwell	24
†W.A.S.Oldfield	c Walsh b James	19
H.I.Ebeling	not out	9
T.W.Wall	b Rothwell	11
L.O.Fleetwood-Smith	c Walsh b Rothwell	1
Extras	(b5, lb5, w1)	11
Total	(88.7 overs, 321 mins)	501

AUSTRALIAN XI	O	M	R	W	w,nb		O	M	R	W	w,nb
Wall	23	2	112	5	-,1		12	2	47	5	-,1
Ebeling	18.2	1	54	2	-,-		10	4	21	0	-,-
Fleetwood-Smith	20	0	105	2	-,-	(4)	11	0	45	2	-,-
Darling	11	1	27	1	-,-	(3)	1	0	4	0	-,-
Chipperfield	4	0	22	0	-,-						

TASMANIA	O	M	R	W	w,nb
Walsh	24	1	94	2	-,-
Thomas	24	0	135	1	-,-
Jeffrey	2	0	10	0	-,-
Rothwell	11.7	0	92	4	-,-
James	19	2	78	2	1,-
Putman	8	0	81	1	-,-

FALL OF WICKETS

	TAS	AUST	TAS
Wkt	1st	1st	2nd
1st	38	224	16
2nd	79	225	26
3rd	85	236	42
4th	104	294	89
5th	190	383	90
6th	205	448	90
7th	230	480	93
8th	257	480	112
9th	334	499	-
10th	338	501	-

WESTERN AUSTRALIA v AUSTRALIAN XI

Played at W.A.C.A. Ground, Perth, on March 23, 24, 26, 1934. (Three-day match)
Toss : Western Australia.   Result : MATCH DRAWN.
Debuts: Western Australia - A.G.Zimbulis (f/c).
12th Men: R.T.Ryan (WA) and L.O.Fleetwood-Smith (Aust).
Umpires: F.R.Buttsworth and E.T.Tonkinson.
Attendances: 7800, 11113, 1145.   Total: 20,058.   Receipts: £1625.
Close of Play: 1st day WA 4/226 (Taaffe 68, Lovelock 34); 2nd day Aust 3/237 (Bromley 59, Kippax 38).

Only 506 minutes of play took place out of the scheduled 900 minutes. Play on the first day began an hour late due to the late arrival of the visiting team from Kalgoorlie and rain on the final day restricted play to only 42 minutes. F.J.Bryant (70) strained a leg muscle on the first day and retired hurt at 1/89. He resumed the following day at 5/236 and batted in all for 119 minutes (13 fours). Taaffe (244 minutes, 10 fours) and R.J.Bryant (43 minutes, 7 fours) batted in contrasting styles, while the locally-born Bromley (124 minutes, 8 fours) topscored for Australia in their unfinished innings. The decision to abandon play on the last day was made at 2.00pm and the Australians departed for England on the *Orford* at 6.00pm. Sources: *Australian Cricketer, NSWCA Report, VCA Report, The West Australian, Daily News.*

WESTERN AUSTRALIA

F.J.Bryant	b Grimmett	76
F.J.Alexander	lbw b Ebeling	1
F.H.Taaffe	c Kippax b O'Reilly	79
W.Hill-Smith	b Grimmett	7
*R.J.Bryant	lbw b O'Reilly	45
W.A.Roach	b Grimmett	0
†O.I.Lovelock	b Ebeling	42
S.G.Francis	not out	22
A.G.Zimbulis	lbw b Grimmett	12
J.R.Jones	c Wall b Ebeling	6
R.A.Halcombe	c O'Reilly b Grimmett	11
Extras	(b1, lb2, nb1)	4
Total	(87.6 overs, 334 mins)	305

AUSTRALIAN XI

*W.M.Woodfull	b Halcombe	45
W.H.Ponsford	c Roach b Francis	39
L.S.Darling	c Zimbulis b Jones	47
E.H.Bromley	not out	67
A.F.Kippax	b Francis	52
A.G.Chipperfield	c Lovelock b Halcombe	1
†B.A.Barnett	not out	9
H.I.Ebeling	)	
W.J.O'Reilly	) did not bat	
C.V.Grimmett	)	
T.W.Wall	)	
Extras	(b5, lb7, nb2)	14
Total	(50.0 overs, 206 mins) (5 wkts)	274

AUSTRALIAN XI	O	M	R	W	w,nb
Wall	11	1	32	0	-,1
Ebeling	21	4	80	3	-,-
O'Reilly	19	5	66	2	-,-
Grimmett	28.6	2	90	5	-,-
Bromley	4	0	14	0	-,-
Chipperfield	4	1	19	0	-,-

WESTERN AUSTRALIA	O	M	R	W	w,nb
Halcombe	14	1	57	2	-,1
Francis	16	0	78	2	-,1
R.J.Bryant	7	1	37	0	-,-
Jones	9	0	61	1	-,-
Zimbulis	4	0	27	0	-,-

FALL OF WICKETS

Wkt	WA 1st	AUST 1st
1st	8	70
2nd	97	115
3rd	166	162
4th	169	251
5th	236	252
6th	246	-
7th	260	-
8th	277	-
9th	284	-
10th	305	-

1934-35 SEASON (16 MATCHES)

Only 16 matches were played this season, 12 Sheffield Shield games, Victoria v Tasmania, Western Australia v New South Wales (2) and the benefit match between Woodfull's XI and Richardson's XI. The season was notable for the absence of many leading players. Bradman, who had transferred to South Australia, was unavailable for the whole summer because of serious illness, McCabe (injured) and O'Reilly (employment) missed most matches for New South Wales, and Woodfull, Ponsford, Blackie and Ironmonger all went into retirement from Victoria.

Despite the loss of their experienced players, Victoria retained the Sheffield Shield, winning five of their six fixtures outright. Darling, Rigg, O'Brien, Barnett, McCormick and Scaife all responded to the additional responsibility and Fleetwood-Smith and Ebeling carried their bowling form from previous seasons. New South Wales, who again finished second (in fact the four placings were identical to the previous year), twice defeated South Australia early in the campaign but were unable to match the Victorians in either of their encounters. Brown and Fingleton remained a fine opening pair and Chipperfield showed the benefit of his tour to England. South Australia and Queensland did not mount a serious challenge at any stage, although the South Australians overcame Victoria at Adelaide once the title had been decided. Richardson, Grimmett, Badcock (transferred from Tasmania) and Lonergan led the way for South Australia and Oxenham, Andrews, Hansen and Levy performed best for Queensland.

The Board of Control accepted an invitation from South Africa for a full tour in 1935-36. The following team was selected: V.Y.Richardson (captain), S.J.McCabe (vice-captain), B.A.Barnett, W.A.Brown, A.G.Chipperfield, L.S.Darling, H.I.Ebeling, J.H.W.Fingleton, L.O.Fleetwood-Smith, C.V.Grimmett, E.L.McCormick, L.P.J.O'Brien, W.A.S.Oldfield and W.J.O'Reilly. Bradman was unavailable through illness and Ebeling subsequently advised he was unable to obtain leave. M.W.Sievers was brought in as a replacement. It was Australia's first full-length tour of South Africa.

The Board of Control also received a request from former Victorian and Middlesex cricketer F.A.Tarrant to approve an Australian tour of India involving players selected by Tarrant himself. Tarrant was acting on behalf of the Maharaja of Patiala, a benefactor of Indian cricket, who had agreed to finance the tour. Board approval was given reluctantly, after much negotiation and on the proviso that all selections be approved by the Board. The Board did not want the Sheffield Shield competition to suffer through the absence of more leading players, the tour of South Africa having already been approved to coincide with the following Australian summer. Six players selected by Tarrant, W.M.Woodfull, W.H.Ponsford, A.F.Kippax, K.E.Rigg, H.C.Nitschke and H.C.Chilvers, were subsequently vetoed by the Board. The team finally approved was: J.Ryder (captain), C.G.Macartney (vice-captain), H.H.Alexander, A.H.Allsopp, O.W.Bill, F.J.Bryant, J.L.Ellis, H.S.T.L.Hendry, H.Ironmonger, T.W.Leather, H.S.B.Love, F.Mair, R.O.G.Morrisby, L.E.Nagel and R.K.Oxenham.

The VCA staged a testimonial match at the MCG in November 1934 for the benefit of Woodfull and Ponsford, who had announced their retirements. It was a great success in all respects, and proved a fitting conclusion to two outstanding careers.

Leading Aggregates

Batsmen	M	I	NO	Runs	HS	Ave.	Bowlers	Runs	Wkts	Ave.
J.H.W.Fingleton (NSW)	9	15	0	880	134	58.66	L.O.Fleetwood-Smith (V)	1282	63	20.34
W.A.Brown (NSW)	9	15	0	683	116	45.53	C.V.Grimmett (SA)	1215	58	20.94
L.S.Darling (V)	7	12	3	634	159	70.44	H.C.Chilvers (NSW)	857	46	18.63
V.Y.Richardson (SA)	7	13	0	572	185	44.00	H.J.T.Theak (NSW)	799	26	30.73
A.G.Chipperfield (NSW)	8	13	1	531	119	44.25	E.L.McCormick (V)	786	24	32.75
C.L.Badcock (SA)	7	14	1	517	137	39.76	H.I.Ebeling (V)	584	22	26.54
A.R.Lonergan (SA)	6	11	0	514	137	46.72	R.K.Oxenham (Q)	732	22	33.27
W.C.Andrews (Q)	6	11	0	486	253	44.18	E.R.Wyeth (Q)	682	20	34.10
L.P.J.O'Brien (V)	7	11	1	498	173	49.80				

SHEFFIELD SHIELD TABLE

	P	WO	W1	LO	L1	D	Pts	Quotient	Runs Scored	Wkts Lost	Runs Conceded	Wkts Taken
VICTORIA	6	5	-	1	–	-	25	1.550	2927	80	2784	118
NEW SOUTH WALES	6	3	-	2	1	-	16	1.072	3311	103	2998	100
SOUTH AUSTRALIA	6	2	-	4	-	-	10	0.838	3120	106	3405	97
QUEENSLAND	6	1	1	4	-	-	8	0.713	2969	106	3140	80
TOTAL	12	11	1	11	1	-	59	1.000	12327	395	12327	395

V.Y.RICHARDSON'S XI v W.M.WOODFULL'S XI

Played at Melbourne Cricket Ground on November 16, 17, 19, 20, 1934. (Four-day match)
Toss : Richardson's XI.   Result : WOODFULL'S XI WON BY SEVEN WICKETS.
Debuts: Nil.
12th Men: K.E.Rigg (both sides).
Umpires: A.N.Barlow and G.A.Hele (H.E.Brereton deputised).
Attendances: 9930, 22637, 6528, 4783.   Total: 43,878.   Receipts: £1831.
Close of Play: 1st day Woodfull 0/1 (Brown 0, McCabe 0); 2nd day Woodfull 316 all out; 3rd day Woodfull (2) 0/0 (Brown 0, O'Reilly 0).

This match was staged as a benefit for Ponsford and Woodfull, who were both making their final first-class appearance. Each received £1042. Fittingly, they shared a century stand in their last association, 132 for the fourth wicket, Ponsford making 83 (148 minutes, 6 fours) and Woodfull 111 (187 minutes, 4 fours). McCabe retired at 0/6 with a broken bone in his hand when he was struck by a ball from McCormick. Chief scorers in the second innings were Brown (102 in 153 minutes, 7 fours), Ponsford (48 in 90 minutes, 4 fours), Darling (55 not out in 89 minutes, 7 fours) and Kippax (43 not out in 60 minutes, 6 fours). Fingleton (57 in 68 minutes, 4 fours) and Badcock (64 in 177 minutes, 4 fours) in the first innings and Richardson (107 in 123 minutes, 3 sixes and 8 fours), Badcock again (87 in 119 minutes, 7 fours), O'Brien (47 in 74 minutes, 2 fours) and Nagel (44 in 68 minutes, 5 fours) in the second top-scored for Richardson's XI. Barnett suffered a first-ball dismissal. Umpire Hele at square-leg sustained a severe crack on the ankle by a Badcock pull after lunch on the third day and V.C.A. secretary, H.E.Brereton, deputised for an hour until he recovered. Sources: *Wisden, NSWCA Report, VCA Report, The Age, The Argus, The Herald, Melbourne Sun.*

RICHARDSON'S XI

*V.Y.Richardson	c Darling b Wall	10	b Grimmett	107
J.H.W.Fingleton	c McCabe b O'Reilly	57	b Darling	6
C.L.Badcock	c Oldfield b Grimmett	64	c Chipperfield b Darling	87
L.P.J.O'Brien	c McCabe b Grimmett	7	c Grimmett b Darling	47
J.W.Scaife	b O'Reilly	5	lbw b O'Reilly	35
†B.A.Barnett	c McCabe b Chipperfield	27	lbw b O'Reilly	0
H.I.Ebeling	c Wall b Chipperfield	1	lbw b Grimmett	36
L.E.Nagel	b Grimmett	8	st Oldfield b Grimmett	44
C.J.Hill	c McCabe b Grimmett	8	not out	5
E.L.McCormick	not out	6	b Grimmett	0
L.O.Fleetwood-Smith	c Wall b Grimmett	3	c Kippax b Woodfull	21
Extras		-	(b3, lb3, w5)	11
Total	(62.0 overs, 209 minutes)	196	(84.2 overs, 290 mins)	399

WOODFULL'S XI

S.J.McCabe	retired hurt	5		
W.A.Brown	c Ebeling b McCormick	7	(1) c Nagel b Fleetwood-Smith	102
A.G.Chipperfield	b Nagel	6		
A.F.Kippax	c Badcock b Ebeling	21	(5) not out	43
W.H.Ponsford	run out (Barnett)	83	(3) c Hill b McCormick	48
*W.M.Woodfull	c McCormick b Nagel	111		
L.S.Darling	b Ebeling	32	(4) not out	55
†W.A.S.Oldfield	c McCormick b Nagel	18		
C.V.Grimmett	not out	10		
W.J.O'Reilly	c Richardson b Fleetwood-Smith	5	(2) c Barnett b Ebeling	19
T.W.Wall	c Nagel b Fleetwood-Smith	8		
Extras	(b4, lb5, w1)	10	(b9, lb3, w1)	13
Total	(69.3 overs, 295 minutes)	316	(56.2 overs, 215 mins) (3 wkts)	280

WOODFULL'S XI	O	M	R	W	w,nb		O	M	R	W	w,nb
Wall	8	0	37	1	-,-		15	0	86	0	-,-
McCabe	3	0	21	0	-,-						
Grimmett	21	2	64	5	-,-		20	1	108	4	-,-
O'Reilly	21	8	41	2	-,-		22	3	69	2	-,-
Chipperfield	7	0	30	2	-,-		14	2	46	0	-,-
Darling	2	1	3	0	-,-	(2)	11	0	57	3	5,-
Woodfull						(6)	1.2	0	12	1	-,-
Ponsford						(7)	1	0	10	0	-,-

RICHARDSON'S XI	O	M	R	W	w,nb		O	M	R	W	w,nb
McCormick	18	0	77	1	-,-		11	0	53	1	-,-
Ebeling	16	2	56	2	-,-		11	1	48	1	-,-
Nagel	15	0	63	3	-,-	(4)	14	1	45	0	-,-
Fleetwood-Smith	12.3	1	75	2	1,-	(3)	9	0	70	1	-,-
Hill	8	0	35	0	-,-		10	1	44	0	-,-
Fingleton							1	0	3	0	-,-
Badcock							0.2	0	4	0	1,-

FALL OF WICKETS

	R	W	R	W
Wkt	1st	1st	2nd	2nd
1st	12	17	21	54
2nd	80	25	202	157
3rd	97	57	227	189
4th	106	189	284	-
5th	163	249	284	-
6th	165	286	303	-
7th	178	292	371	-
8th	181	301	376	-
9th	192	316	376	-
10th	196	-	399	-

NEW SOUTH WALES v SOUTH AUSTRALIA (Shield Match 1)

Played at Sydney Cricket Ground on November 23, 24, 26, 27, 1934. (Four-day match)
Toss : New South Wales.   Result : NEW SOUTH WALES WON BY AN INNINGS AND 158 RUNS.
Debuts: New South Wales - G.C.Horsfield, A.H.Simmons (both f/c). South Australia - F.R.Edwards, N.H.Hutton (both f/c) C.L.Badcock
     (SA only).
12th Men: R.C.Rowe (NSW) and M.G.Waite (SA).
Umpires: H.J.Armstrong and E.G.Borwick.
Attendances: 4137, 7999, 1377, 172.   Total: 13,685.   Receipts: £596.
Close of Play: 1st day NSW 7/422 (Oldfield 57, Chilvers 11); 2nd day SA (2) 1/66 (Richardson 33, Badcock 9); 3rd day SA (2) 4/139
     (Whitington 25, Tobin 0).

S.J.McCabe and W.J.O'Reilly (both injured) were unavailable for New South Wales. Late withdrawals A.F.Kippax and A.G.Chipperfield
were replaced by Bill (originally 12th man) and Marks. C.W.Walker and T.W.Wall were unable to appear for South Australia for business
reasons and illness prevented D.G.Bradman from playing at all in his first season with his new State. Brown (111 in 178 minutes, 10
fours) and Fingleton (134 in 182 minutes, 14 fours) set New South Wales on the road to victory with an opening stand of 249 on the first
day. Oldfield (88 in 162 minutes, 1 five and 9 fours) also batted well to mark his appointment as captain. Hill was given out on appeal by
Borwick at square leg when he played a ball on to his wicket and a bail was disturbed from its groove without falling to the ground.
Horsfield was out second ball on his debut. Rain severely curtailed play on the third day with only one ball bowled after lunch. Tobin, not
out overnight, was unable to resume his innings on the final day due to influenza. Nitschke alone (63 in 81 minutes, 9 fours) reached 50
for South Australia, Chilvers capturing 11 for 125 with leg-spin. Badcock had moved to South Australia during the winter after 19
matches for Tasmania, the last five of which yielded four centuries. *Wisden* incorrectly gives NSW Horsfield's dismissal; SA (1) Nitschke
c Fingleton; SA (2) Tobin absent ill. Sources: *Wisden, NSWCA Report, SACA Report, The Age, The Argus, Sydney Morning Herald,
NSWCA Scorebook.*

NEW SOUTH WALES

W.A.Brown	c Tobin b Davey	111
J.H.W.Fingleton	c Edwards b Davey	134
A.D.McGilvray	c Lee b Grimmett	35
O.W.Bill	b Lee	13
G.C.Horsfield	lbw b Lee	0
A.E.Marks	c Richardson b Grimmett	3
*†W.A.S.Oldfield	lbw b Grimmett	88
A.H.Simmons	run out (/Edwards)	41
H.C.Chilvers	c Richardson b Grimmett	29
C.J.Hill	b Lee	3
H.J.T.Theak	not out	4
Extras	(b4, lb9, nb5)	18
Total	(104.2 overs, 377 minutes)	479

SOUTH AUSTRALIA

*V.Y.Richardson	st Oldfield b Chilvers	21	lbw b Hill		44
H.C.Nitschke	c Brown b Chilvers	63	lbw b Chilvers		24
C.L.Badcock	st Oldfield b Chilvers	5	c Oldfield b Chilvers		17
A.R.Lonergan	b Hill	12	b Chilvers		27
R.S.Whitington	c Bill b Chilvers	0	b Chilvers		27
B.J.Tobin	run out (Fingleton)	20	retired ill		0
P.K.Lee	lbw b Chilvers	8	c Brown b Chilvers		8
C.V.Grimmett	b Simmons	4	b Hill		4
N.H.Hutton	c Oldfield b Hill	7	lbw b Hill		8
†F.R.Edwards	c & b Chilvers	10	b Hill		4
J.R.Davey	not out	0	not out		1
Extras	(b2, lb1, nb1)	4	(b1, lb1, nb1)		3
Total	(49.3 overs, 175 minutes)	154	(70.5 overs, 225 mins)		167

SOUTH AUSTRALIA	O	M	R	W	w,nb
Hutton	16	1	82	0	-,1
Davey	23	1	121	2	-,-
Tobin	8	0	64	0	-,4
Grimmett	31.2	4	124	4	-,-
Lee	26	7	70	3	-,-

NEW SOUTH WALES	O	M	R	W	w,nb		O	M	R	W	w,nb
Theak	7	0	38	0	-,1		10	2	37	0	-,1
Simmons	8	3	16	1	-,-		12	3	22	0	-,-
Chilvers	17.3	2	67	6	-,-	(4)	25	5	58	5	-,-
McGilvray	4	0	21	0	-,-	(5)	6	1	13	0	-,-
Hill	13	8	8	2	-,-	(3)	16.5	7	33	4	-,-
Horsfield							1	0	1	0	-,-

FALL OF WICKETS

Wkt	NSW 1st	SA 1st	SA 2nd
1st	249	42	46
2nd	254	78	87
3rd	277	103	87
4th	277	103	138
5th	282	109	145
6th	331	122	154
7th	400	128	154
8th	464	140	166
9th	471	154	167
10th	479	154	-

QUEENSLAND v SOUTH AUSTRALIA (Shield Match 2)

Played at Brisbane Cricket Ground (Woolloongabba) on November 30, December 1, 3, 4, 1934. (Four-day match)
Toss : South Australia.　　　　　Result : QUEENSLAND WON BY THREE WICKETS.
Debuts: Queensland - B.R.D.O'Connor (f/c); J.A.J.Christy (Qld only).
12th Men: K.J.Boag (Qld) and B.J.Tobin (SA).
Umpires: V.R.Castles and J.A.Scott.
Attendances: 1200, 5000, 2500, 2000.　　　　Total: About 10,700.　　　Receipts: £605.
Close of Play: 1st day SA 281 all out; 2nd day Qld 7/374 (Oxenham 60); 3rd day SA (2) 7/295 (Whitington 39, Edwards 13).

Included in the Queensland team as a late replacement for the unavailable G.G.Cook, Hansen provided two innings that virtually decided the match. On the second day he scored 147 in 186 minutes with 14 fours, surviving chances at 48 and 125 before falling to the last ball of the day. His unbeaten 64 on the last day (106 minutes, 8 fours) steered his side to victory. With Bensted (59 in 89 minutes, 9 fours) and Oxenham (70 in 144 minutes, 8 fours), he added 98 for the fifth wicket and 151 for the seventh wicket. Christy, a South African tourer in 1931-32, now made his first appearance for Queensland; he coached the northern team for two seasons. South Australia played without Hutton after the second day, who was hospitalised with a severe bout of influenza. Nitschke (86 in 119 minutes, 10 fours) and Waite (51 in 136 minutes, 1 six and 4 fours) in the first innings and Lonergan (69 in 124 minutes, 9 fours), Waite (51 in 136 minutes, 1 six and 8 fours) and Whitington (52 in 131 minutes, 5 fours) in the second scored fifties for the visitors. *Wisden* incorrectly gives SA (2) Whitington c Oxenham. Sources: *Wisden, QCA Report, SACA Report, Sydney Morning Herald, Brisbane Courier-Mail.*

SOUTH AUSTRALIA

*V.Y.Richardson	c Levy b Oxenham	28		c Andrews b O'Connor	28
H.C.Nitschke	c Christy b Oxenham	86		c Thurlow b Oxenham	35
C.L.Badcock	b Wyeth	35		b Wyeth	0
A.R.Lonergan	c Andrews b Oxenham	7		c Bensted b Levy	69
M.G.Waite	c Levy b Wyeth	51	(6)	run out (Wyeth/Leeson)	77
R.S.Whitington	c & b Wyeth	44	(7)	c Hansen b Levy	52
P.K.Lee	c Levy b Wyeth	1	(8)	c Thurlow b Levy	17
C.V.Grimmett	not out	12	(5)	c Leeson b Wyeth	9
N.H.Hutton	c Leeson b Oxenham	1		absent ill	-
†F.R.Edwards	b Wyeth	3	(9)	not out	19
J.R.Davey	st Leeson b Wyeth	4	(10)	b Oxenham	15
Extras	(b4, lb3, nb2)	9		(b3, lb2, w1, nb2)	8
Total	(77.4 overs, 286 minutes)	281		(88.5 overs, 330 mins)	329

QUEENSLAND

J.A.J.Christy	b Lee	31		lbw b Grimmett	12
T.Allen	c Richardson b Grimmett	22		c & b Grimmett	9
W.C.Andrews	c Waite b Grimmett	1		c Lonergan b Grimmett	26
*R.M.Levy	c Hutton b Grimmett	24		c Lonergan b Grimmett	34
E.C.Bensted	c Nitschke b Lee	59		c Whitington b Grimmett	15
C.D.Hansen	c Edwards b Davey	147		not out	64
†H.F.Leeson	c Richardson b Hutton	10		c Grimmett b Lee	9
R.K.Oxenham	lbw b Grimmett	70		b Davey	20
B.R.D.O'Connor	b Grimmett	13		not out	11
E.R.Wyeth	c Edwards b Grimmett	0			
H.M.Thurlow	not out	1			
Extras	(b7, lb10, w1, nb5)	23		(b5, lb5)	10
Total	(102.4 overs, 357 minutes)	401		(55.4 overs, 182 mins) (7 wkts)	210

QUEENSLAND	O	M	R	W	w,nb		O	M	R	W	w,nb
O'Connor	13	1	80	0	-,-	(2)	10	0	51	1	-,-
Thurlow	14	0	71	0	-,2	(1)	9	1	46	0	-,2
Oxenham	27	10	68	4	-,-		28.5	6	76	2	-,-
Wyeth	17.4	7	33	6	-,-		24	5	68	2	-,-
Levy	2	0	6	0	-,-	(6)	9	1	44	3	1,-
Bensted	4	1	14	0	-,-	(5)	8	0	36	0	-,-

SOUTH AUSTRALIA	O	M	R	W	w,nb		O	M	R	W	w,nb
Hutton	15	3	56	1	1,5						
Davey	19	2	60	1	-,-	(1)	14	2	48	1	-,-
Grimmett	34.4	2	138	6	-,-		24.4	2	94	5	-,-
Lee	31	6	92	2	-,-	(2)	17	1	58	1	-,-
Waite	3	0	32	0	-,-						

FALL OF WICKETS

Wkt	SA 1st	QLD 1st	SA 2nd	QLD 2nd
1st	84	54	59	17
2nd	154	60	60	26
3rd	156	64	83	83
4th	170	96	100	92
5th	255	194	190	112
6th	257	223	241	123
7th	261	374	278	193
8th	274	400	310	-
9th	277	400	329	-
10th	281	401	-	-

VICTORIA v QUEENSLAND (Shield Match 3)

Played at Melbourne Cricket Ground on December 14, 15, 17, 1934. (Four-day match)
Toss : Victoria.   Result : VICTORIA WON BY AN INNINGS AND 32 RUNS.
Debuts: Nil.
12th Men: I.S.Lee (Vic) and K.J.Boag (Qld).
Umpires: A.N.Barlow and G.A.Hele.
Attendances: 2729, 3247, 1139.   Total: 7115.   Receipts: £227.
Close of Play: 1st day Vic 8/276 (Barnett 36, McCormick 50); 2nd day Qld (2) 1/4 (Christy 2, Bensted 0).

After Rigg (87 in 194 minutes, 4 fours) and Oakley (44 in 43 minutes, 6 fours) had helped Victoria to 8/199 on the first day with contrasting approaches, McCormick (77 not out in 107 minutes, 11 fours) and the ferret Fleetwood-Smith (63 in 57 minutes, 1 six and 9 fours) lashed their career-best scores, McCormick adding 77 for the ninth wicket with Barnett and 98 for the tenth wicket with Fleetwood-Smith, who also captured nine wickets. Levy (31 in 78 minutes, 2 fours) and Hansen (56 not out in 105 minutes, 6 fours) top-scored in the Queensland first innings. Facing imminent defeat on the third afternoon, last man Wyeth held out for 38 minutes to enable Levy to progress from 58 to 107 - the last of his three first-class centuries. Sources: *Wisden, VCA Report, QCA Report, The Age, The Argus, The Herald, Melbourne Sun.*

VICTORIA

L.P.J.O'Brien	c Andrews b O'Connor	21
K.E.Rigg	b Oxenham	87
L.S.Darling	c Christy b O'Connor	1
J.W.Scaife	hit wkt b Oxenham	9
E.H.Bromley	lbw b Oxenham	0
M.W.Sievers	run out (O'Connor/Leeson)	21
H.H.Oakley	c sub (K.J.Boag) b Oxenham	44
†B.A.Barnett	b Bensted	36
*H.I.Ebeling	lbw b Wyeth	1
E.L.McCormick	not out	77
L.O.Fleetwood-Smith	c Allen b Levy	63
Extras	(b10, lb3, nb1)	14
Total	(94.3 overs, 354 minutes)	374

QUEENSLAND

J.A.J.Christy	c Sievers b Ebeling	4		lbw b McCormick	12
T.Allen	b Ebeling	3		c Ebeling b McCormick	0
W.C.Andrews	c McCormick b Ebeling	5	(5)	c Rigg b McCormick	30
*R.M.Levy	b Fleetwood-Smith	31	(6)	run out (Darling)	107
E.C.Bensted	b Fleetwood-Smith	9	(3)	c Barnett b McCormick	1
C.D.Hansen	not out	56	(4)	c Ebeling b Sievers	12
R.K.Oxenham	lbw b Fleetwood-Smith	0	(8)	b Fleetwood-Smith	8
D.Tallon	c Oakley b Fleetwood-Smith	15	(7)	lbw b Fleetwood-Smith	0
B.R.D.O'Connor	lbw b McCormick	0		b Fleetwood-Smith	4
†H.F.Leeson	lbw b Fleetwood-Smith	6		b Fleetwood-Smith	4
E.R.Wyeth	b Ebeling	20		not out	3
Extras	(b2, lb4)	6		(b1, lb5)	6
Total	(46.2 overs, 190 minutes)	155		(49.7 overs, 223 mins)	187

QUEENSLAND	O	M	R	W	w,nb
Bensted	11	0	50	1	-,1
O'Connor	18	2	72	2	-,-
Oxenham	40	10	135	4	-,-
Wyeth	15	1	62	1	-,-
Levy	10.3	1	41	1	-,-

VICTORIA	O	M	R	W	w,nb	O	M	R	W	w,nb
McCormick	14	1	45	1	-,-	15	2	54	4	-,-
Ebeling	13.2	3	33	4	-,-	10	0	32	0	-,-
Sievers	5	0	14	0	-,-	6.7	1	16	1	-,-
Fleetwood-Smith	14	3	57	5	-,-	18	1	81	4	-,-

FALL OF WICKETS

Wkt	VIC 1st	QLD 1st	QLD 2nd
1st	36	7	1
2nd	44	10	14
3rd	59	15	17
4th	59	43	44
5th	138	64	75
6th	166	64	75
7th	193	94	121
8th	199	101	125
9th	276	108	133
10th	374	155	187

AFCM No. 832/79
SSM No. 273/76

SOUTH AUSTRALIA v NEW SOUTH WALES (Shield Match 4)

Played at Adelaide Oval on December 14, 15, 17, 18, 1934. (Four-day match)
Toss : New South Wales.   Result : NEW SOUTH WALES WON BY 234 RUNS.
Debuts: New South Wales - R.H.Robinson (f/c).
12th Men: W.E.Catchlove (SA) and E.C.S.White (NSW).
Umpires: E.H.Kitson and J.D.Scott.
Attendances: 2909, 6577, 1481, 297.   Total: 11,264.   Receipts: £415.
Close of Play: 1st day NSW 8/336 (Kippax 114, Hill 8); 2nd day NSW (2) 0/8 (Brown 1, Fingleton 5); 3rd day SA (2) 5/110 (Moyle 19, Grimmett 1).

Persistent injury forced S.J.McCabe, the nominated captain, to withdraw from the New South Wales team, White being his replacement in the twelve. South Australia replaced H.C.Nitschke and R.S.Whitington (ill) with Moyle and Shepherd. Brown (81 in 134 minutes, 9 fours) and Fingleton (55 in 96 minutes, 6 fours) opened with another century stand for New South Wales. Kippax (139 in 219 minutes, 12 fours) taking advantage. In the second innings Fingleton (43 in 70 minutes, 5 fours) and Chipperfield (62 in 106 minutes, 5 fours) batted well in the face of fine bowling by Grimmett (7 for 90). Chilvers - like Grimmett - took his second successive 10-wicket match, to bowl his side to victory. Richardson (57 in 79 minutes, 1 six and 6 fours) was the only South Australian to exceed 40 in either innings. *SACA Report* and *Wisden* incorrectly give umpires V.R.Castles and J.A.Scott. Sources: *Wisden, NSWCA Report, SACA Report, NSWCA Scorebook, Adelaide Advertiser.*

NEW SOUTH WALES

W.A.Brown	lbw b Lee	81	c Shepherd b Grimmett	23
J.H.W.Fingleton	c Waite b Wall	55	b Grimmett	43
R.H.Robinson	b Collins	21	b Grimmett	6
A.G.Chipperfield	c Edwards b Waite	11	b Lee	62
A.F.Kippax	c Moyle b Grimmett	139	c Lee b Wall	33
G.C.Horsfield	c Richardson b Grimmett	27	not out	33
*†W.A.S.Oldfield	b Collins	10	b Lee	12
A.H.Simmons	b Grimmett	5	lbw b Grimmett	1
H.C.Chilvers	b Grimmett	0	c Moyle b Grimmett	2
C.J.Hill	c Edwards b Collins	30	c Richardson b Grimmett	7
H.J.T.Theak	not out	9	c Edwards b Grimmett	3
Extras	(b7, lb3, nb2)	12	(b4)	4
Total	(107.5 overs, 377 minutes)	400	(62.3 overs, 213 mins)	229

SOUTH AUSTRALIA

*V.Y.Richardson	b Hill	57	b Theak	5
C.L.Badcock	st Oldfield b Chilvers	15	c Chipperfield b Chilvers	12
A.R.Lonergan	b Chilvers	40	c Robinson b Chilvers	36
M.G.Waite	b Chipperfield	10	c Chipperfield b Chilvers	7
A.G.Shepherd	b Robinson	1	c Brown b Chilvers	25
E.J.R.Moyle	b Chilvers	20	b Chilvers	35
F.H.K.Collins	c Oldfield b Robinson	9	(8) lbw b Theak	5
P.K.Lee	c Oldfield b Chilvers	17	(9) c sub (E.C.S.White) b Theak	4
C.V.Grimmett	c Hill b Theak	35	(7) c Simmons b Theak	8
†F.R.Edwards	not out	22	c Chilvers b Robinson	0
T.W.Wall	c Brown b Chilvers	11	not out	0
Extras	(b6, lb5, w1)	12	(b4, lb5)	9
Total	(69.2 overs, 227 minutes)	249	(46.0 overs, 154 mins)	146

SOUTH AUSTRALIA	O	M	R	W	w,nb		O	M	R	W	w,nb
Wall	19	0	82	1	-,2		9	0	46	1	-,-
Collins	28.5	1	101	3	-,-		7	0	34	0	-,-
Grimmett	34	2	140	4	-,-	(4)	27.3	5	90	7	-,-
Lee	23	6	60	1	-,-	(5)	18	3	50	2	-,-
Waite	3	1	5	1	-,-	(3)	1	0	5	0	-,-

NEW SOUTH WALES	O	M	R	W	w,nb		O	M	R	W	w,nb
Theak	11	0	53	1	1,-		11	2	25	4	-,-
Simmons	6	0	28	0	-,-	(4)	3	0	10	0	-,-
Hill	19	7	41	1	-,-	(2)	5	2	16	0	-,-
Chilvers	19.2	2	58	5	-,-	(3)	16	0	51	5	-,-
Chipperfield	5	1	15	1	-,-		4	1	15	0	-,-
Robinson	9	1	42	2	-,-		7	2	20	1	-,-

FALL OF WICKETS

Wkt	NSW 1st	SA 1st	NSW 2nd	SA 2nd
1st	124	58	64	8
2nd	157	92	71	32
3rd	161	112	76	54
4th	192	121	137	61
5th	280	146	180	108
6th	303	149	192	130
7th	310	177	197	138
8th	312	187	207	143
9th	385	230	215	144
10th	400	249	229	146

VICTORIA v NEW SOUTH WALES (Shield Match 5)

Played at Melbourne Cricket Ground on December 21, 22, 24, 26, 1934. (Four-day match)
Toss : Victoria.   Result : VICTORIA WON BY NINE WICKETS.
Debuts: New South Wales - E.C.S.White (f/c).
12th Men: I.S.Lee (Vic) and A.H.Simmons (NSW).
Umpires: A.N.Barlow and G.A.Hele.
Attendances: 4822, 9292, 6006, 4707.   Total: 24,827.   Receipts: £876.
Close of Play: 1st day Vic 3/364 (Darling 76, Bromley 31); 2nd day NSW 0/121 (Brown 66, Fingleton 53); 3rd day NSW (2) 3/106
    (Chipperfield 49, Kippax 22).

For the third time four Victorians scored hundreds in an innings, O'Brien (chanceless 126 in 253 minutes, 1 five and 10 fours) and Rigg (111 in 237 minutes, 10 fours, chances at 54 and 56, both off Hill) adding 234 for the first wicket and Darling (106 in 114 minutes, 13 fours) and Bromley (102 in 140 minutes, 11 fours) sharing a fourth-wicket stand of 136 in just 76 minutes. Brown (71 in 168 minutes, 6 fours) and Fingleton (65 in 195 minutes, 4 fours) mounted their fifth hundred partnership in as many matches together for the New South Wales first wicket. Chipperfield (84 in 169 minutes, 9 fours) and Kippax (52 in 72 minutes, 8 fours) added 92 and Oldfield (63 in 140 minutes, 7 fours) and White (52 in 145 minutes, 2 fours) 100 in the second innings, but Fleetwood-Smith in his premier season again bowled well to set up an easy win for the home side. Sources: *Wisden, NSWCA Report, VCA Report, The Age, The Argus, The Herald, Melbourne Sun.*

VICTORIA

L.P.J.O'Brien	run out (Brown)	126	c Oldfield b Theak	10
K.E.Rigg	run out (Fingleton/Oldfield)	111	not out	29
L.S.Darling	c & b Theak	106	not out	1
J.W.Scaife	lbw b White	15		
E.H.Bromley	b Chilvers	102		
M.W.Sievers	st Oldfield b Chilvers	9		
H.H.Oakley	st Oldfield b Chilvers	15		
*B.A.Barnett	not out	35		
†H.I.Ebeling	b Theak	3		
E.L.McCormick	c White b Chipperfield	13		
L.O.Fleetwood-Smith	c Robinson b Chipperfield	9		
Extras	(b2, lb12)	14	(lb1)	1
Total	(146.4 overs, 483 minutes)	558	(9.0 overs, 31 mins) (1 wkts)	41

NEW SOUTH WALES

W.A.Brown	c Rigg b McCormick	71	lbw b Sievers	26
J.H.W.Fingleton	b Fleetwood-Smith	65	c Barnett b McCormick	0
R.H.Robinson	b McCormick	34	c Fleetwood-Smith b McCormick	2
A.G.Chipperfield	b Fleetwood-Smith	19	c McCormick b Fleetwood-Smith	84
A.F.Kippax	c McCormick b Sievers	1	lbw b Fleetwood-Smith	52
G.C.Horsfield	b Fleetwood-Smith	14	c Sievers b Ebeling	1
*†W.A.S.Oldfield	c Scaife b McCormick	7	run out (Scaife)	63
E.C.S.White	lbw b Fleetwood-Smith	7	c Scaife b Fleetwood-Smith	52
C.J.Hill	c Barnett b Fleetwood-Smith	31	lbw b Fleetwood-Smith	1
H.C.Chilvers	b Fleetwood-Smith	20	c Scaife b Fleetwood-Smith	0
H.J.T.Theak	not out	2	not out	8
Extras	(b13, lb4, w1)	18	(b9, lb8, w1)	18
Total	(100.2 overs, 367 minutes)	289	(90.4 overs, 338 mins)	307

NEW SOUTH WALES	O	M	R	W	w,nb		O	M	R	W	w,nb
Theak	29	1	122	2	-,-		5	1	23	1	-,-
Hill	32	9	86	0	-,-		4	0	17	0	-,-
White	36	8	93	1	-,-						
Chilvers	25	0	144	3	-,-						
Robinson	6	0	31	0	-,-						
Chipperfield	18.4	2	68	2	-,-						

VICTORIA	O	M	R	W	w,nb		O	M	R	W	w,nb
McCormick	24	2	65	3	-,-		20	1	72	2	1,-
Ebeling	23	7	45	0	-,-		18	6	34	1	-,-
Sievers	17	2	54	1	1,	(4)	17	3	56	1	-,-
Fleetwood-Smith	36.2	3	107	6	-,-	(3)	34.4	5	121	5	-,-
Darling							1	0	6	0	-,-

FALL OF WICKETS

Wkt	VIC 1st	NSW 1st	NSW 2nd	VIC 2nd
1st	234	130	1	30
2nd	259	150	11	-
3rd	290	188	58	-
4th	426	197	150	-
5th	480	212	155	-
6th	483	226	187	-
7th	496	226	287	-
8th	503	239	288	-
9th	548	284	288	-
10th	558	289	307	-

SOUTH AUSTRALIA v QUEENSLAND (Shield Match 6)

Played at Adelaide Oval on December 22, 24, 25, 26, 1934. (Four-day match)
Toss : Queensland.　　　　　　　Result : SOUTH AUSTRALIA WON BY EIGHT WICKETS.
Debuts: Nil.
12th Men: W.E.Catchlove (SA) and K.J.Boag (Qld).
Umpires: A.G.Jenkins and J.D.Scott.
Attendances: 3822, 3135, 6180, 1923.　　　Total: 15,060.　　　Receipts: £630.
Close of Play: 1st day Qld 7/397 (Oxenham 63, O'Connor 17); 2nd day SA 2/337 (Lonergan 26, Badcock 7); 3rd day Qld (2) 0/55
　　(Christy 24, Andrews 30).

South Australia's highest total to date (it remained so for only 14 months) included hundreds from Richardson (185 in 240 minutes, 1 six, 1 five and 20 fours), Nitschke (116 in 202 minutes, 10 fours), Lonergan (137 in 249 minutes, 1 six and 12 fours) and Badcock (137 in 234 minutes, 16 fours) and partnerships of 255 for the first wicket (Richardson/Nitschke) and 238 for the third wicket (Lonergan/Badcock), both of which were records for South Australia in this series of matches. Leeson, the nominated wicket-keeper, reinjured a troublesome finger while taking a ball early in the record innings and Tallon replaced him immediately after lunch on the second day and kept for the rest of the match. Grimmett's 16 for 289, which included the wickets of all eleven batsmen, was the second-best match return in the Sheffield Shield; only G.Giffen (16 for 168, SA v NSW at Adelaide 1894-95) has done better. Queensland's highest scorers were Christy (80 in 161 minutes, 6 fours), Levy (90 in 119 minutes, 9 fours), Oxenham (74 not out in 153 minutes, 5 fours) and Tallon (58 in 68 minutes, 2 sixes and 6 fours) in the first innings and Andrews (68 in 95 minutes, 7 fours) and again Tallon (86 in 81 minutes, 14 fours) in the second. *Wisden* misspells Waite as "Wade" in Qld (2) dismissal of Hansen. Sources: *Wisden, QCA Report, SACA Report, Adelaide Advertiser, The News.*

QUEENSLAND

J.A.J.Christy	lbw b Lee	80		b Grimmett	29
T.Allen	c Moyle b Grimmett	24	(4)	run out (Lonergan)	14
C.D.Hansen	c & b Grimmett	28		c Waite b Grimmett	9
W.C.Andrews	c Moyle b Grimmett	5	(2)	b Lee	68
*R.M.Levy	b Grimmett	90		b Lee	8
E.C.Bensted	lbw b Grimmett	16		c & b Grimmett	4
R.K.Oxenham	not out	74	(8)	b Grimmett	15
D.Tallon	b Grimmett	58	(7)	c Nitschke b Grimmett	86
B.R.D.O'Connor	lbw b Grimmett	18		not out	4
†H.F.Leeson	c Moyle b Grimmett	14		st Edwards b Grimmett	0
E.R.Wyeth	st Edwards b Grimmett	4		lbw b Grimmett	5
Extras	(b13, lb2, nb4)	19		(b3, lb4)	7
Total	(100.2 overs, 362 minutes)	430		(63.3 overs, 217 mins)	249

SOUTH AUSTRALIA

*V.Y.Richardson	b Wyeth	185			
H.C.Nitschke	c Bensted b Wyeth	116			
A.R.Lonergan	c Oxenham b Christy	137			
C.L.Badcock	run out (Allen/Tallon)	137		not out	10
M.G.Waite	b Oxenham	10	(1)	lbw b Wyeth	8
E.J.R.Moyle	c Andrews b Wyeth	0			
P.K.Lee	hit wkt b Oxenham	25			
F.H.K.Collins	not out	28	(2)	b O'Connor	9
†F.R.Edwards	)		(3)	not out	10
C.V.Grimmett	) did not bat				
T.W.Wall	)				
Extras	(b4, nb2)	6			-
Total	(148.0 overs, 520 minutes) (7 wkts dec)	644		(7.3 overs, 25 mins) (2 wkts)	37

SOUTH AUSTRALIA	O	M	R	W	w,nb		O	M	R	W	w,nb
Wall	24	1	85	0	-,4		14	0	59	0	-,-
Collins	22	2	72	0	-,-		10	2	33	0	-,-
Grimmett	33.2	1	180	9	-,-		27.3	3	109	7	-,-
Lee	16	2	49	1	-,-		12	1	41	2	-,-
Waite	5	0	25	0	-,-						

QUEENSLAND	O	M	R	W	w,nb		O	M	R	W	w,nb
Oxenham	40	8	121	2	-,-						
O'Connor	17	0	120	0	-,-	(1)	4	0	17	1	-,-
Bensted	16	0	72	0	-,-						
Wyeth	48	8	169	3	-,-	(2)	3.3	0	20	1	-,-
Levy	16	0	105	0	-,-						
Christy	7	0	22	1	-,2						
Andrews	1	0	4	0	-,-						
Allen	3	0	25	0	-,-						

FALL OF WICKETS

Wkt	QLD 1st	SA 1st	QLD 2nd	SA 2nd
1st	44	255	71	17
2nd	109	323	93	17
3rd	121	561	111	-
4th	188	589	119	-
5th	244	591	135	-
6th	263	591	145	-
7th	371	644	234	-
8th	399	-	241	-
9th	420	-	241	-
10th	430	-	249	-

VICTORIA v SOUTH AUSTRALIA (Shield Match 7)

Played at Melbourne Cricket Ground on December 29, 31, 1934, January 1, 2, 1935. (Four-day match)
Toss : South Australia.　　　　　　Result : VICTORIA WON BY TEN WICKETS.
Debuts: Nil.
12th Men: I.S.Lee (Vic) and W.E.Catchlove (SA).
Umpires: A.N.Barlow and G.A.Hele.
Attendances: 7598, 9435, 11673, 3943.　　　Total: 32,649.　　　Receipts: £1267.
Close of Play: 1st day SA 3/34 (Badcock 4, Shepherd 12); 2nd day Vic 1/21 (Rigg 9, Barnett 0); 3rd day Vic 416 all out.

Catchlove replaced E.J.R.Moyle (leg injury) in the South Australian team before its departure from Adelaide. Grimmett was unable to take any part in the match after the second day due to gastritis, having bowled only one over. Rain limited play on the first day to 59 minutes. An early collapse was halted by Badcock (48 in 125 minutes, 3 fours) and Shepherd (80 in 187 minutes, 5 fours) who added 107 for the fourth wicket, Waite (36 in 68 minutes, 3 fours) also contributing. Darling (a chanceless 159 in 237 minutes, 20 fours) shared hundred-wicket partnerships with Scaife (45 in 79 minutes, 3 fours) and Bromley (59 in 58 minutes, 9 fours) to give Victoria a significant lead. Rigg (49 in 126 minutes, 3 fours) also batted well. Nitschke, playing in his last first-class match (48 in 72 minutes, 6 fours), Lonergan (64 in 83 minutes, 6 fours) and Badcock (39 in 70 minutes, 5 fours) top-scored in South Australia's second innings, but batting one man short the side lost 7 for 59 and Rigg and Darling made light work of the 83-run target. Sources: *Wisden, VCA Report, SACA Report, The Age, The Argus, The Herald, Melbourne Sun.*

SOUTH AUSTRALIA

Batsman	1st innings		2nd innings	
*V.Y.Richardson	c Barnett b McCormick	5	c Oakley b Fleetwood-Smith	21
H.C.Nitschke	run out (Ebeling)	8	c Sievers b Fleetwood-Smith	48
A.R.Lonergan	c Barnett b Ebeling	0	b Sievers	64
C.L.Badcock	lbw b McCormick	48	lbw b Fleetwood-Smith	39
A.G.Shepherd	b Sievers	80	b Ebeling	19
M.G.Waite	b McCormick	36	c Darling b Fleetwood-Smith	6
C.V.Grimmett	c Darling b McCormick	11	absent ill	-
F.H.K.Collins	c McCormick b Fleetwood-Smith	25	(7) b Ebeling	23
P.K.Lee	c Bromley b Fleetwood-Smith	18	(8) b Ebeling	1
†F.R.Edwards	b Sievers	6	(9) not out	4
T.W.Wall	not out	2	(10) run out	1
Extras	(b12, lb11, w2)	25	(b5, lb2, w1)	8
Total	(72.5 overs, 300 minutes)	264	(68.7 overs, 248 mins)	234

VICTORIA

Batsman	1st innings		2nd innings	
L.P.J.O'Brien	c Collins b Wall	11		
K.E.Rigg	c sub (W.E.Catchlove) b Wall	49	(1) not out	38
†B.A.Barnett	c Edwards b Collins	5		
M.W.Sievers	c Richardson b Wall	0		
L.S.Darling	c & b Collins	159	(2) not out	41
J.W.Scaife	lbw b Wall	45		
E.H.Bromley	c Richardson b Lee	59		
H.H.Oakley	b Lee	27		
*H.I.Ebeling	c Richardson b Lee	14		
E.L.McCormick	not out	4		
L.O.Fleetwood-Smith	run out (Badcock/Edwards)	22		
Extras	(b13, lb6, w1, nb1)	21	(lb3, w1)	4
Total	(83.7 overs, 334 minutes)	416	(9.7 overs, 37 mins) (0 wkts)	83

VICTORIA	O	M	R	W	w,nb	O	M	R	W	w,nb
McCormick	27	1	82	4	1,-	5	0	16	0	1,-
Ebeling	19	6	51	1	-,-	18.7	5	52	3	-,-
Sievers	6.5	0	32	2	-,-	11	2	27	1	-,-
Fleetwood-Smith	19	0	74	2	-,-	22	3	96	4	-,-
Darling	1	1	0	0	1,-					
Bromley						(5) 12	4	35	0	-,-

SOUTH AUSTRALIA	O	M	R	W	w,nb	O	M	R	W	w,nb
Wall	25	0	132	4	-,1	5	1	42	0	-,-
Collins	22	2	85	2	-,-	4.7	0	37	0	1,-
Grimmett	1	1	0	0	-,-					
Lee	22.7	1	123	3	-,-					
Waite	13	1	55	0	1,-					

FALL OF WICKETS

Wkt	SA 1st	VIC 1st	SA 2nd	VIC 2nd
1st	12	20	59	-
2nd	14	33	94	-
3rd	16	34	175	-
4th	123	123	178	-
5th	191	227	184	-
6th	191	332	224	-
7th	208	347	226	-
8th	248	389	229	-
9th	259	390	234	-
10th	264	416	-	-

NEW SOUTH WALES v QUEENSLAND (Shield Match 8)

Played at Sydney Cricket Ground on December 31, 1934, January 1, 2, 3, 1935. (Four-day match)
Toss : New South Wales.   Result : MATCH DRAWN.
Debuts: Nil.
12th Men: A.E.Marks (NSW) and H.F.Leeson (Qld).
Umpires: H.J.Armstrong and E.G.Borwick.
Attendances: 5883, 7264, 3010, 1147.   Total: 17,304.   Receipts: £919.
Close of Play: 1st day NSW 9/267 (Chilvers 6, Theak 1); 2nd day Qld 6/299 (Andrews 139, Bensted 91); 3rd day NSW (2) 1/178
     (Fingleton 87, White 0).

Coming together at 6/113 on the second day, Andrews (253 in 417 minutes, 26 fours) and Bensted (155 in 239 minutes, 19 fours) saved Queensland from likely defeat with an extraordinary seventh-wicket partnership of 335 in 239 minutes, the highest stand on record for that wicket in Australian first-class cricket. It remained the Queensland record for any wicket until 1982-83 when K.C.Wessels (249) and R.B.Kerr (132) added 388 for the first wicket against Victoria. Both compiled their career-highest scores and both gave a solitary chance, Andrews at 68 (caught-and-bowled to Chilvers) and Bensted at 141 (difficult caught-and-bowled to McGilvray). An opening stand of 177 between Brown (89 in 152 minutes, 5 fours) and Fingleton (108 in 204 minutes, 7 fours) exactly cleared the first-innings arrears for New South Wales before Fingleton's straight drive was deflected into the non-striker's stump, Brown backing up too far. Chipperfield (119 in 230 minutes, 15 fours) anchored the first innings, Fingleton (40 in 88 minutes, 3 fours), Chilvers (44 in 98 minutes, 6 fours) and Kippax (40 not out in 80 minutes, 5 fours) scoring forties. Rain ended the game at 2.20pm on the final day. O'Connor injured a knee on the first day, did not bowl again, and was unable to field again until late in the match. Theak had replaced L.J.O'Brien (knee injury) in the New South Wales line-up. *Wisden* incorrectly gives Qld Tallon c & b Chipperfield, the batsman falling to the first ball he faced. Sources: *Wisden, NSWCA Report, QCA Report, The Age, Sydney Morning Herald, NSWCA Scorebook, Brisbane Courier-Mail.*

NEW SOUTH WALES

W.A.Brown	c Boag b Wyeth	11		run out (Oxenham)	89
J.H.W.Fingleton	lbw b Wyeth	40		lbw b Oxenham	108
A.D.McGilvray	c Boag b Oxenham	24	(6)	not out	11
A.G.Chipperfield	b Oxenham	119		c O'Connor b Oxenham	14
A.F.Kippax	c Bensted b Oxenham	4		not out	40
R.H.Robinson	c Levy b Wyeth	5			
E.C.S.White	c & b O'Connor	17	(3)	c Tallon b Bensted	14
G.C.Horsfield	lbw b Bensted	19			
*†W.A.S.Oldfield	c Bensted b Wyeth	18			
H.C.Chilvers	c Levy b Oxenham	44			
H.J.T.Theak	not out	14			
Extras	(b1, lb1, nb1)	3		(b5, lb4, w1)	10
Total	(106.1 overs, 370 minutes)	318		(76.1 overs, 277 mins) (4 wkts)	286

QUEENSLAND

J.A.J.Christy	b Theak	16
W.C.Andrews	c Oldfield b Chilvers	253
C.D.Hansen	b Theak	11
T.Allen	c Oldfield b Theak	0
*R.M.Levy	c McGilvray b Chipperfield	28
†D.Tallon	c Kippax b Chipperfield	0
R.K.Oxenham	lbw b White	2
E.C.Bensted	b Chilvers	155
K.J.Boag	c Oldfield b White	12
B.R.D.O'Connor	st Oldfield b Chilvers	0
E.R.Wyeth	not out	1
Extras	(b4, lb9, nb4)	17
Total	(125.7 overs, 421 minutes)	495

QUEENSLAND	O	M	R	W	w,nb		O	M	R	W	w,nb
Bensted	13	1	51	1	-,1		16	1	58	1	-,-
O'Connor	15	0	56	1	-,-						
Oxenham	42.1	10	95	4	-,-	(2)	32.1	5	92	2	-,-
Wyeth	36	8	113	4	-,-	(3)	19	2	61	0	1,-
Boag						(4)	3	0	29	0	-,-
Levy						(5)	5	0	33	0	-,-
Christy						(6)	1	0	3	0	-,-

NEW SOUTH WALES	O	M	R	W	w,nb
Theak	31	3	122	3	-,4
McGilvray	15	2	72	0	-,-
White	27	6	79	2	-,-
Chilvers	27.7	4	91	3	-,-
Chipperfield	13	1	65	2	-,-
Robinson	12	1	49	0	-,-

	FALL OF WICKETS		
	NSW	QLD	NSW
Wkt	1st	1st	2nd
1st	45	27	177
2nd	54	55	207
3rd	86	60	226
4th	95	104	229
5th	106	104	-
6th	154	113	-
7th	204	448	-
8th	252	494	-
9th	266	494	-
10th	318	495	-

QUEENSLAND v VICTORIA (Shield Match 9)

Played at Brisbane Cricket Ground (Woolloongabba) on January 18, 19, 21, 1935. (Four-day match)
Toss : Queensland.   Result : VICTORIA WON BY TEN WICKETS.
Debuts: Nil.
12th Men: R.M.Hubbard (Qld) and I.S.Lee (Vic).
Umpires: J.Bartlett and J.A.Scott.
Attendances: 3240, 6100, 1500.   Total: 10,840.   Receipts: £756.
Close of Play: 1st day Vic 3/129 (Darling 83, Sievers 0); 2nd day Qld (2) 5/111 (Bensted 23, Oxenham 4).

Victoria named a squad of thirteen for their northern tour but E.L.a'Beckett withdrew before departure. R.M.Levy (injured finger) was unavailable for Queensland. Fleetwood-Smith (11 for 129) headed the Victorian attack, only Bensted (61 in 135 minutes, 1 six and 3 fours) registering fifty for the home side. Blurred vision - believed to have resulted from a knock on the head by a delivery from H.J.T.Theak in the match against New South Wales the previous month - prevented Hansen batting a second time and dogged him for years afterwards. Gilbert, who had Rigg caught at the wicket with the fourth ball of the Victorian first innings, twice struck O'Brien, the second a blow to the head which caused his retirement at 1/34. O'Brien spent the next 24 hours in hospital under observation but was not seriously injured. Darling (147 in 197 minutes, 1 six and 16 fours) offered a single chance when 88 and added 110 for the fourth wicket with Sievers (58 in 139 minutes, 1 six and 4 fours). Sources: *Wisden, VCA Report, QCA Report, Sydney Morning Herald, Brisbane Courier-Mail.*

QUEENSLAND

J.A.J.Christy	c Bromley b McCormick	6		b Ebeling	26
W.C.Andrews	c Barnett b Ebeling	0		st Barnett b Fleetwood-Smith	36
T.Allen	lbw b Fleetwood-Smith	11		c & b Fleetwood-Smith	14
F.W.Sides	b Fleetwood-Smith	29		b Ebeling	2
†D.Tallon	c Barnett b Ebeling	17	(8)	c Oakley b Fleetwood-Smith	0
C.D.Hansen	b Fleetwood-Smith	0		absent ill	-
*E.C.Bensted	c Oakley b McCormick	24	(5)	lbw b Fleetwood-Smith	61
J.G.Maddern	lbw b Fleetwood-Smith	0	(6)	lbw b Fleetwood-Smith	0
R.K.Oxenham	c Sievers b Fleetwood-Smith	8	(7)	b Fleetwood-Smith	28
E.Gilbert	b McCormick	6	(9)	b Ebeling	0
E.R.Wyeth	not out	0	(10)	not out	5
Extras	(b7, lb1, w1, nb4)	13		(b4, lb5, nb5)	14
Total	(36.7 overs, 160 minutes)	114		(60.0 overs, 238 mins)	186

VICTORIA

L.P.J.O'Brien	retired hurt	5			
K.E.Rigg	c Tallon b Gilbert	0			
L.S.Darling	b Christy	147			
J.W.Scaife	b Bensted	16			
E.H.Bromley	c Christy b Gilbert	18			
M.W.Sievers	b Oxenham	58	(1)	not out	6
H.H.Oakley	c & b Christy	2			
†B.A.Barnett	b Gilbert	24	(2)	not out	5
*H.I.Ebeling	not out	4			
E.L.McCormick	b Gilbert	0			
L.O.Fleetwood-Smith	b Gilbert	4			
Extras	(b8, lb4)	12			-
Total	(65.7 overs, 260 minutes)	290		(3.0 overs, 10 mins) (0 wkts)	11

VICTORIA	O	M	R	W	w,nb		O	M	R	W	w,nb
McCormick	10.7	1	31	3	1,4		15	2	46	0	-,5
Ebeling	10	1	26	2	-,-		15	5	30	3	-,-
Sievers	3	1	5	0	-,-	(4)	2	0	6	0	-,-
Fleetwood-Smith	13	3	39	5	-,-	(3)	28	2	90	6	-,-

QUEENSLAND	O	M	R	W	w,nb		O	M	R	W	w,nb
Gilbert	19.7	3	77	5	-,-						
Bensted	12	0	46	1	-,-						
Oxenham	14	1	53	1	-,-	(1)	2	1	5	0	-,-
Wyeth	14	1	72	0	-,-						
Christy	6	0	30	2	-,-						
Andrews						(2)	1	0	6	0	-,-

FALL OF WICKETS

Wkt	QLD 1st	VIC 1st	QLD 2nd	VIC 2nd
1st	6	1	66	-
2nd	6	94	66	-
3rd	43	126	70	-
4th	61	236	98	-
5th	63	240	100	-
6th	75	282	158	-
7th	76	286	158	-
8th	99	286	163	-
9th	111	290	186	-
10th	114	-	-	-

NEW SOUTH WALES v VICTORIA (Shield Match 10)

Played at Sydney Cricket Ground on January 25, 26, 28, 29, 1935. (Four-day match)
Toss : Victoria.   Result : VICTORIA WON BY 213 RUNS.
Debuts: Nil.
12th Men: G.C.Horsfield (NSW) and H.H.Oakley (Vic).
Umpires: H.J.Armstrong and E.G.Borwick.
Attendances: 8409, 11486, 9630, 4036.   Total: 33,561.   Receipts: £1852.
Close of Play: 1st day Vic 5/269 (O'Brien 138, Lee 12); 2nd day NSW 5/178 (Robinson 38, Oldfield 7); 3rd day Vic (2) 226 all out.

Fleetwood-Smith (7 for 113 and 8 for 113) became the first Victorian bowler to return 15 wickets in a Sheffield Shield match, a feat he repeated two seasons later against Queensland. McCabe, returning after injury, top-scored in each New South Wales innings with 92 (140 minutes, 10 fours) and 53 (53 minutes, 7 fours). Robinson (57 in 102 minutes, 6 fours) and Fingleton (49 in 115 minutes, 4 fours) performed next best while Oldfield and Theak suffered first-ball dismissals. O'Brien's 176 occupied 406 minutes and included 15 fours. He added 98 with Sievers (44 in 122 minutes, 6 fours) and 101 with Lee (84 in 169 minutes, 10 fours). O'Brien was missed by Chilvers at third slip from the third ball of the second innings before falling to the same bowler, Theak. Scaife (44 in 84 minutes, 4 fours) and Lee (54 in 90 minutes, 4 fours) top-scored in the second innings. Chilvers' nine wickets included Sievers and Barnett with successive balls. Sources: *Wisden, NSWCA Report, VCA Report, The Age, The Argus, The Herald, Sydney Morning Herald, NSWCA Scorebook.*

VICTORIA

L.P.J.O'Brien	st Oldfield b O'Reilly	173	c Oldfield b Theak		12
K.E.Rigg	run out (Kippax)	22	c O'Reilly b Chilvers		33
L.S.Darling	b Chipperfield	17	c Fingleton b White		12
J.W.Scaife	c Chilvers b O'Reilly	12	c & b Theak		44
E.H.Bromley	b White	16	b Chilvers		4
M.W.Sievers	b O'Reilly	44	lbw b Chilvers		29
I.S.Lee	c & b Chilvers	84	c White b Robinson		54
†B.A.Barnett	not out	26	c White b Chilvers		0
*H.I.Ebeling	st Oldfield b Chilvers	7	c & b Chilvers		19
E.L.McCormick	c & b O'Reilly	3	st Oldfield b Chilvers		9
L.O.Fleetwood-Smith	st Oldfield b Chilvers	3	not out		1
Extras	(b4, lb5, nb2)	11	(b2, lb7)		9
Total	(146.7 overs, 474 minutes)	420	(72.7 overs, 238 mins)		226

NEW SOUTH WALES

J.H.W.Fingleton	c Barnett b Ebeling	3	c Sievers b Fleetwood-Smith		49
W.A.Brown	c Barnett b Ebeling	19	c Barnett b McCormick		0
S.J.McCabe	c Sievers b Fleetwood-Smith	92	(4) c Lee b Fleetwood-Smith		53
A.F.Kippax	b McCormick	7	(5) c & b Fleetwood-Smith		17
A.G.Chipperfield	c O'Brien b Fleetwood-Smith	10	(7) b Fleetwood-Smith		1
R.H.Robinson	hit wkt b Fleetwood-Smith	57	not out		28
*†W.A.S.Oldfield	lbw b Fleetwood-Smith	12	(8) c O'Brien b Fleetwood-Smith		0
E.C.S.White	c & b Fleetwood-Smith	8	(3) st Barnett b Fleetwood-Smith		21
W.J.O'Reilly	not out	20	c McCormick b Fleetwood-Smith		1
H.C.Chilvers	st Barnett b Fleetwood-Smith	10	run out (/Barnett)		2
H.J.T.Theak	c Lee b Fleetwood-Smith	4	c Sievers b Fleetwood-Smith		0
Extras	(b12, lb1)	13	(b2, lb3, nb1)		6
Total	(57.6 overs, 235 minutes)	255	(43.6 overs, 177 mins)		178

NEW SOUTH WALES	O	M	R	W	w,nb		O	M	R	W	w,nb
Theak	14	1	43	0	-,1		8	0	32	2	-,-
McCabe	14	3	36	0	-,1		5	2	11	0	-,-
O'Reilly	43	14	85	4	-,-	(4)	21	7	56	0	-,-
Chilvers	38.7	3	120	3	-,-	(5)	23.7	3	76	6	-,-
Chipperfield	15	2	47	1	-,-	(6)	6	0	19	0	-,-
White	16	3	46	1	-,-	(3)	8	2	17	1	-,-
Robinson	3	0	16	0	-,-		1	0	6	1	-,-
Kippax	3	0	16	0	-,-						

VICTORIA	O	M	R	W	w,nb		O	M	R	W	w,nb
McCormick	17	1	73	1	-,-		10	1	33	1	-,1
Ebeling	14	4	43	2	-,-		16	7	26	0	-,-
Sievers	6	1	13	0	-,-						
Fleetwood-Smith	20.6	3	113	7	-,-	(3)	17.6	0	113	8	-,-

FALL OF WICKETS

Wkt	VIC 1st	NSW 1st	VIC 2nd	NSW 2nd
1st	54	8	30	9
2nd	85	45	47	58
3rd	116	62	82	107
4th	142	91	88	139
5th	240	153	136	144
6th	341	191	144	146
7th	398	214	144	146
8th	412	217	193	160
9th	415	251	217	178
10th	420	255	226	178

VICTORIA v TASMANIA

Played at Melbourne Cricket Ground on February 5, 6, 7, 1935. (Three-day match)
Toss : Victoria.   Result : MATCH DRAWN.
Debuts: Victoria - H.J.Britt, R.A.Dempster, J.A.Ledward (all f/c). Tasmania - P.Dulling, C.J.Sankey (both f/c).
12th Men: R.B.Scott (Vic) and A.L.Pearsall (Tas).
Umpires: C.Juliff and H.R.McLean.
Attendances: 780, 597, negligible.   Total: About 1400   Receipts: £32.
Close of Play: 1st day Tas 0/44 (Morrisby 19, Thomas 17); 2nd day Vic (2) 6/240 (Fitzmaurice 5, Smith 3).

R.G.Gregory, I.D.Miller (both unable to obtain leave) and R.B.Scott (hand injury) withdrew from the selected Victorian team and were replaced by Fitzmaurice, Junor (originally 12th man) and Smith. Putman's leg-breaks and googlies returned his best figures of 7 for 102, Victoria slumping to 7/134 before Fitzmaurice (102 in 162 minutes, 8 fours), Smith (92 in 90 minutes, 15 fours) and Britt (37 in 65 minutes, 2 fours) combined to add 140 in 90 minutes for the eighth wicket and 78 for the ninth wicket. Ledward on debut (76 in 102 minutes, 10 fours) and Junor (33 in 38 minutes, 3 fours) earlier added 63, while Quin was out first ball. Tasmania started well through Morrisby (45 in 144 minutes, 2 fours) and Thomas (49 in 141 minutes, 4 fours) but then lost 7/22 before the advent of Putman and James (58 in 75 minutes, 5 fours). After Walsh dismissed Dempster with the first ball of Victoria's second innings, Allsopp (122 in 103 minutes, 1 six and 17 fours) and Junor (57 in 49 minutes, 7 fours) shared a fast stand of 108 for the fourth wicket, Allsopp reaching 50 in 35 minutes and 100 in 78 minutes. The Victorian innings had commenced at 3.55pm after an early tea adjournment, so Allsopp's entire innings was played in the final session of the second day. The loss of two sessions to rain on the final day produced a tame finish.
Sources: *VCA Report, TCA Report, The Argus, The Age, The Herald, Melbourne Sun, The Sporting Globe.*

VICTORIA

Batsman	Dismissal	R		Dismissal	R
R.A.Dempster	lbw b Walsh	8		lbw b Walsh	0
E.H.G.Vernon	c James b Walsh	1		b James	27
J.A.Ledward	c & b Putman	76		b Walsh	9
L.J.Junor	c Ferrall b Putman	33	(5)	c & b Thomas	57
A.H.Allsopp	st Pickett b Putman	1	(4)	lbw b Thomas	122
*†S.O.Quin	b Putman	0		st Pickett b Putman	11
H.J.Plant	lbw b Putman	8	(9)	lbw b Thomas	12
D.J.A.Fitzmaurice	run out (Thomas/Pickett)	102	(7)	not out	17
S.A.J.Smith	c James b Putman	92	(8)	b Thomas	20
H.J.Britt	c & b Putman	37			
T.W.Leather	not out	5			
Extras	(b4, lb1, nb2)	7		(b9, lb1)	10
Total	(71.2 overs, 272 minutes)	370		43.6 overs, 160 mins) (8 wkts dec)	285

TASMANIA

Batsman	Dismissal	R		Dismissal	R
R.O.G.Morrisby	b Plant	45		not out	20
R.V.Thomas	run out (Ledward/Plant)	49		not out	22
*R.A.Ferrall	b Leather	0			
E.H.Smith	lbw b Leather	9			
J.M.Walsh	b Leather	0			
M.J.Combes	b Leather	7			
C.J.Sankey	c Leather b Plant	5			
S.W.L.Putman	c Quin b Britt	35			
G.T.H.James	b Britt	58			
†E.A.Pickett	not out	16			
P.Dulling	c Quin b Fitzmaurice	20			
Extras	(b7, lb1, nb3)	11		(b2, lb3)	5
Total	(72.4 overs, 290 minutes)	255		(14.0 overs, 53 mins) (0 wkts)	47

TASMANIA	O	M	R	W	w,nb		O	M	R	W	w,nb
Walsh	18	3	96	2	-,2		9	0	66	2	-,-
Thomas	9	1	47	0	-,-		14.6	0	64	4	-,-
James	12	1	48	0	-,-	(4)	8	0	61	1	-,-
Putman	20.2	0	102	7	-,-	(3)	12	0	84	1	-,-
Dulling	12	0	70	0	-,-						

VICTORIA	O	M	R	W	w,nb		O	M	R	W	w,nb
Leather	24	4	64	4	-,3		4	0	16	0	-,-
Britt	17	5	58	2	-,-	(4)	2	0	6	0	-,-
Fitzmaurice	7.4	1	24	1	-,-	(2)	3	0	9	0	-,-
Smith	11	1	63	0	-,-						
Plant	13	2	35	2	-,-	(3)	4	1	8	0	-,-
Dempster						(5)	1	0	3	0	-,-

FALL OF WICKETS

Wkt	VIC 1st	TAS 1st	VIC 2nd	TAS 2nd
1st	3	102	0	-
2nd	10	102	18	-
3rd	73	102	107	-
4th	75	103	215	-
5th	75	115	232	-
6th	105	122	234	-
7th	134	124	261	-
8th	274	215	285	-
9th	352	228	-	-
10th	370	255	-	-

AFCM No. 840/64
SSM No. 280/18

QUEENSLAND v NEW SOUTH WALES (Shield Match 11)

Played at Brisbane Cricket Ground (Woolloongabba) on February 15, 16, 18, 19, 1935. (Four-day match)
Toss : New South Wales.　　　　　Result : NEW SOUTH WALES WON BY 28 RUNS.
Debuts: Queensland - A.Fisher (f/c). New South Wales - R.C.J.Little, G.W.Ryan (both f/c).
12th Men: R.M.Hubbard (Qld) and L.J.Fallowfield (NSW).
Umpires: V.R.Castles and D.W.Given.
Attendances: 2647, 6154, 1800, 450.　　　　Total: 11,051.　　　Receipts: £754.
Close of Play: 1st day Qld 3/94 (Sides 33, Levy 27); 2nd day NSW (2) 3/146 (Robinson 52, Marks 57); 3rd day Qld (2) 3/143
　　(Bensted 40, Hansen 22).

New South Wales introduced two new players for this match and both failed spectacularly; Little bagged a king pair at the hands of Gilbert (who returned career-best figures of 6 for 64) and Ryan, in what was to be his sole first-class appearance, broke a finger on the second day, attempting to stop a Tallon cut, and retired from the match altogether. Fingleton (74 in 168 minutes, 6 fours), Marks (56 in 92 minutes, 8 fours) and Chipperfield (63 in 69 minutes, 9 fours) in the first innings and Robinson (67 in 156 minutes, 5 fours) and again Marks (107 in 192 minutes, 13 fours) and Chipperfield (69 in 158 minutes, 9 fours) in the second made the top scores for New South Wales, while Sides (68 in 189 minutes, 6 fours), Hansen (63 in 102 minutes, 7 fours), Tallon (40 in 54 minutes, 5 fours), Andrews (41 in 93 minutes, 2 fours) and Bensted (71 in 93 minutes, 9 fours) batted well for Queensland, who omitted Hubbard and J.Coats from their squad of thirteen. Christy fell to the second ball of the second innings. Gilbert followed his best figures by achieving his highest score (34 not out); he added 42 for the last wicket with Wyeth. *Wisden* incorrectly gives Qld (1) Christy lbw. *NSWCA Report* incorrectly gives Qld (1) Tallon c Chipperfield. Sources: *Wisden, NSWCA Report, QCA Report, NSWCA Scorebook, Brisbane Courier-Mail, Brisbane Telegraph.*

NEW SOUTH WALES

J.H.W.Fingleton	c & b Levy	74	st Tallon b Oxenham		22
W.A.Brown	lbw b Fisher	5	b Gilbert		12
R.C.J.Little	c Fisher b Gilbert	0	b Gilbert		0
R.H.Robinson	c Tallon b Gilbert	0	b Wyeth		67
A.E.Marks	c & b Gilbert	56	lbw b Levy		107
A.G.Chipperfield	b Gilbert	63	st Tallon b Wyeth		69
*†W.A.S.Oldfield	c & b Oxenham	16	c Tallon b Gilbert		6
E.C.S.White	b Gilbert	12	c Levy b Wyeth		23
H.C.Chilvers	lbw b Oxenham	3	lbw b Fisher		17
G.W.Ryan	b Gilbert	1	absent hurt		-
H.J.T.Theak	not out	0	not out	(10)	0
Extras	(lb2, w1)	3	(b6, lb5, w2, nb1)		14
Total	(54.2 overs, 218 minutes)	233	(85.2 overs, 335 mins)		337

QUEENSLAND

J.A.J.Christy	b Theak	7	b Theak		0
W.C.Andrews	b Chilvers	21	c sub (L.J.Fallowfield) b Chilvers		41
F.W.Sides	lbw b White	68	b Chilvers		32
E.C.Bensted	run out (Fingleton/Chilvers)	3	c Brown b Chilvers		71
*R.M.Levy	c Oldfield b Theak	27	b Theak	(6)	35
C.D.Hansen	c Oldfield b Chilvers	63	c Oldfield b Theak	(5)	25
†D.Tallon	c Marks b Chilvers	40	st Oldfield b Chilvers		0
R.K.Oxenham	run out (Fingleton/Oldfield)	13	run out (sub L.J.Fallowfield)		7
A.Fisher	c & b White	13	c Oldfield b Chilvers		10
E.Gilbert	b Chilvers	1	not out		34
E.R.Wyeth	not out	0	st Oldfield b Chilvers		8
Extras	(b1, lb1, nb3)	5	(b6, lb7, w1, nb4)		18
Total	(73.1 overs, 265 minutes)	261	(79.1 overs, 283 mins)		281

QUEENSLAND	O	M	R	W	w,nb		O	M	R	W	w,nb
Gilbert	16	3	64	6	1,-		19	0	114	3	2,-
Fisher	12	1	65	1	-,-		10	1	53	1	-,-
Oxenham	14.2	3	46	2	-,-		27	9	41	1	-,1
Wyeth	10	1	36	0	-,-		18.2	3	48	3	-,-
Levy	2	0	19	1	-,-	(7)	6	0	44	1	-,-
Bensted						(5)	3	0	12	0	-,-
Christy						(6)	2	0	11	0	-,-

NEW SOUTH WALES	O	M	R	W	w,nb		O	M	R	W	w,nb
Theak	19	3	74	2	-,3		17	2	54	3	1,4
Ryan	10	1	31	0	-,-						
White	16	3	33	2	-,-	(2)	24	4	53	0	-,-
Chilvers	14.1	1	68	4	-,-	(3)	30.1	2	124	6	-,-
Chipperfield	9	1	30	0	-,-	(4)	5	0	17	0	-,-
Robinson	5	0	20	0	-,-		2	0	8	0	-,-
Little						(5)	1	0	7	0	-,-

FALL OF WICKETS

Wkt	NSW 1st	QLD 1st	NSW 2nd	QLD 2nd
1st	6	14	27	0
2nd	7	49	27	71
3rd	7	58	44	83
4th	97	94	177	155
5th	192	193	244	182
6th	203	195	258	183
7th	227	241	308	193
8th	230	260	337	206
9th	233	261	337	239
10th	233	261	-	281

SOUTH AUSTRALIA v VICTORIA (Shield Match 12)

Played at Adelaide Oval on February 15, 16, 18, 19, 1935. (Four-day match)
Toss : South Australia.   Result : SOUTH AUSTRALIA WON BY 107 RUNS.
Debuts: Nil.
12th Men: R.A.Parker (SA) and I.D.Miller (Vic).
Umpires: E.H.Kitson and J.D.Scott.
Attendances: 3155, 7256, 4165, 2346.   Total: 16,922.   Receipts: £613.
Close of Play: 1st day Vic 3/61 (O'Brien 15, Scaife 11); 2nd day SA (2) 3/173 (Lonergan 59, Moyle 45); 3rd day Vic (2) 0/51
   (O'Brien 24, Rigg 23).

Despite Fleetwood-Smith taking his season's tally to 60 wickets, a new and long-standing Shield record, Victoria needed 416 in the fourth innings to become the first team to win outright all six matches in a single competition. O'Brien (55 in 158 minutes, 5 fours) and Rigg (50 in 152 minutes, 3 fours) shared an opening stand of 102 and Darling (53 in 76 minutes, 5 fours) and Scaife (56 in 79 minutes, 5 fours) added a further 98 for the third wicket to make it possible, but the loss of 5 for 34 put paid to the attempt. Rain interruptions shortened the first day's play, Badcock (47 in 111 minutes, 3 fours), Lonergan (45 in 78 minutes, 5 fours) and Lee (46 in 47 minutes, 9 fours) registering forties for South Australia. Collins took his only five-wicket haul as Scaife (74 in 145 minutes, 5 fours) guided Victoria to first-innings equality. Richardson (58 in 91 minutes, 1 six and 7 fours), Lonergan (77 in 175 minutes, 4 fours), Moyle (81 in 132 minutes, 1 six, 1 five and 8 fours), Waite (79 in 133 minutes, 9 fours) and Tobin (60 in 131 minutes, 7 fours) top-scored for South Australia in their second innings. Tobin replaced T.W.Wall (unavailable) in the home side while Miller replaced H.H.Oakley (also unavailable) for Victoria. *Wisden* incorrectly gives SA (1) Waite b Fleetwood-Smith. Sources: *Wisden, VCA Report, SACA Report, Adelaide Advertiser, The News.*

SOUTH AUSTRALIA

*V.Y.Richardson	c Lee b McCormick	3	c Bromley b Fleetwood-Smith	58
C.L.Badcock	c Barnett b Sievers	47	b McCormick	1
A.R.Lonergan	c Barnett b Sievers	45	b McCormick	77
A.G.Shepherd	b Fleetwood-Smith	8	c Barnett b Ebeling	5
E.J.R.Moyle	b Fleetwood-Smith	2	c Darling b Fleetwood-Smith	81
M.G.Waite	c O'Brien b Fleetwood-Smith	35	c Rigg b Ebeling	79
B.J.Tobin	st Barnett b Fleetwood-Smith	2	c Sievers b Darling	60
P.K.Lee	lbw b Fleetwood-Smith	46	b Ebeling	3
F.H.K.Collins	run out (Bromley/Fleetwood-Smith)	0	run out (Barnett)	5
C.V.Grimmett	not out	0	lbw b Fleetwood-Smith	22
†C.W.Walker	run out (Rigg)	1	not out	6
Extras	(b8, lb3)	11	(b10, lb6, w2)	18
Total	(46.2 overs, 192 minutes)	200	(105.2 overs, 395 mins)	415

VICTORIA

L.P.J.O'Brien	lbw b Collins	31	c Richardson b Lee	55
K.E.Rigg	c Waite b Collins	12	run out (Lonergan/Waite)	50
L.S.Darling	b Collins	10	lbw b Collins	53
I.S.Lee	b Collins	9	(6) lbw b Grimmett	7
J.W.Scaife	c Collins b Grimmett	74	(4) c Walker b Collins	56
E.H.Bromley	c Waite b Grimmett	5	(5) c & b Tobin	2
M.W.Sievers	b Collins	6	c Richardson b Grimmett	3
†B.A.Barnett	c & b Lee	33	lbw b Lee	36
*H.I.Ebeling	st Walker b Grimmett	9	lbw b Grimmett	35
E.L.McCormick	not out	0	run out (Lonergan)	0
L.O.Fleetwood-Smith	b Grimmett	6	not out	0
Extras	(b2, lb3)	5	(b4, lb6, nb1)	11
Total	(64.0 overs, 209 minutes)	200	(101.4 overs, 331 mins)	308

VICTORIA	O	M	R	W	w,nb		O	M	R	W	w,nb				
McCormick	13.2	0	46	1	-,-		20	1	95	2	2,-				
Ebeling	9	0	45	0	-,-		31	7	63	3	-,-				
Fleetwood-Smith	14	1	60	5	-,-	(4)	33.2	1	186	3	-,-				
Sievers	10	1	38	2	-,-	(3)	16	4	40	0	-,-				
Darling							5	1	13	1	-,-				

SOUTH AUSTRALIA	O	M	R	W	w,nb		O	M	R	W	w,nb				
Tobin	9	2	37	0	-,-		10	1	39	1	-,-				
Collins	25	3	78	5	-,-		32	6	82	2	-,-				
Grimmett	23	3	70	4	-,-		40.4	12	98	3	-,-				
Lee	7	2	10	1	-,-		14	4	54	2	-,-				
Waite							5	0	24	0	-,1				

FALL OF WICKETS

Wkt	SA 1st	VIC 1st	SA 2nd	VIC 2nd
1st	18	16	16	102
2nd	104	28	96	113
3rd	110	45	105	211
4th	114	88	203	224
5th	119	93	251	224
6th	121	112	351	234
7th	199	167	355	245
8th	199	183	367	303
9th	199	194	399	303
10th	200	200	415	308

WESTERN AUSTRALIA v NEW SOUTH WALES

Played at W.A.C.A Ground, Perth, on March 9, 11, 12, 1935. (Three-day match)
Toss : Western Australia.   Result : MATCH DRAWN.
Debuts: Western Australia - D.C.McKenzie, R.Roe (both f/c). New South Wales - N.L.Cush, L.J.Fallowfield (both f/c).
12th Men: C.F.Newman (WA) and R.C.J.Little (NSW).
Umpires: F.R.Buttsworth and E.T.Tonkinson.
Attendances: 4000, 3650, 1000.   Total: 8650.   Receipts: £604.
Close of Play: 1st day WA 233 all out; 2nd day NSW 7/380 (Oldfield 35, Campbell 28).

McKenzie top-scored in each innings of his debut for Western Australia with 59 (113 minutes) and 53 (103 minutes, 8 fours). Fingleton (184 minutes, 3 sixes and 10 fours) and Fallowfield (1 six and 7 fours) added 145 in 129 minutes for the second wicket for New South Wales. Chipperfield scored quickly, making 70 in 79 minutes with 10 fours. The attendances were regarded as most disappointing.
Sources: *NSWCA Report, WACA Report, The West Australian, Daily News.*

WESTERN AUSTRALIA

F.J.Bryant	run out (Fingleton/Oldfield)	12	b Theak	16
F.J.Alexander	b Theak	27	st Oldfield b Cush	10
F.H.Taaffe	st Oldfield b Campbell	6	c & b Campbell	44
R.Roe	run out (White/Campbell)	35	c Campbell b Robinson	29
D.C.McKenzie	c Fallowfield b Robinson	59	hit wkt b Chipperfield	53
†O.I.Lovelock	b Campbell	44	b Fingleton	39
*R.J.Bryant	b Cush	22	not out	19
A.J.Ditchburn	b Theak	0	not out	6
J.R.Jones	not out	14		
A.G.Zimbulis	c Robinson b Theak	1		
R.A.Halcombe	b Theak	3		
Extras	(lb9, nb1)	10	(lb1, w2, nb1)	4
Total	(76.1 overs, 284 minutes)	233	(72.0 overs, 250 mins) (6 wkts)	220

NEW SOUTH WALES

W.A.Brown	lbw b Ditchburn	10
J.H.W.Fingleton	c Jones b Zimbulis	124
L.J.Fallowfield	st Lovelock b Zimbulis	65
R.H.Robinson	c Lovelock b Zimbulis	2
A.E.Marks	run out (Halcombe/Lovelock)	5
A.G.Chipperfield	lbw b R.J.Bryant	70
E.C.S.White	c Roe b Jones	27
*†W.A.S.Oldfield	lbw b Jones	46
J.N.Campbell	b Zimbulis	48
H.J.T.Theak	b Jones	4
N.L.Cush	not out	0
Extras	(b3, lb10, w1, nb1)	15
Total	(87.5 overs, 338 minutes)	416

NEW SOUTH WALES	O	M	R	W	w,nb		O	M	R	W	w,nb
Theak	17.1	1	62	4	-,1		12	0	37	1	-,1
Cush	13	4	24	1	-,-		9	0	26	1	-,-
White	12	4	18	0	-,-		13	5	30	0	-,-
Fallowfield	8	3	14	0	-,-	(6)	5	3	15	0	-,-
Campbell	16	2	68	2	-,-	(4)	12	0	35	1	2,-
Chipperfield	4	0	14	0	-,-	(8)	6	1	19	1	-,-
Robinson	6	0	23	1	-,-	(5)	7	0	36	1	-,-
Marks						(7)	6	1	7	0	-,-
Fingleton							1	0	6	1	-,-
Brown							1	0	5	0	-,-

FALL OF WICKETS			
	WA	NSW	WA
Wkt	1st	1st	2nd
1st	23	13	12
2nd	42	158	41
3rd	70	170	92
4th	110	207	111
5th	176	209	182
6th	201	287	214
7th	202	330	-
8th	220	412	-
9th	229	412	-
10th	233	416	-

WESTERN AUSTRALIA	O	M	R	W	w,nb
Halcombe	17	3	57	0	-,1
Ditchburn	22	3	73	1	1,-
Jones	24.5	1	109	3	-,-
Zimbulis	17	0	143	4	-,-
R.J.Bryant	7	1	19	1	-,-

WESTERN AUSTRALIA v NEW SOUTH WALES

Played at W.A.C.A. Ground, Perth, on March 16, 18, 19, 1935. (Three-day match)
Toss : New South Wales.   Result : MATCH DRAWN.
Debuts: Western Australia - G.A.Gardiner (f/c).
12th Men: S.Briggs(WA) and N.L.Cush (NSW).
Umpires: F.R.Buttsworth and E.T.Tonkinson.
Attendances: 2000, 650, 200.   Total: About 2850.   Receipts: £190.
Close of Play: 1st day NSW 3/333 (Fallowfield 51, Little 25); 2nd day WA 4/188 (Lovelock 9).

Briggs replaced F.J.Alexander (unavailable) as 12th man for Western Australia. Fingleton (100 in 195 minutes, 10 fours) and Brown (116 in 225 minutes, 12 fours) began the match with a partnership of 205 to put New South Wales in a commanding position. Fallowfield (101 not out in 236 minutes, 9 fours) and Little followed up with a stand of 101 for the fourth wicket. Fallowfield (54 not out in 72 minutes, 6 fours) and Robinson (59 not out in 67 minutes, 4 sixes and 2 fours) were involved in an unbeaten partnership of 112 in the second innings. The best performers for Western Australia in the first innings were Taaffe (79 in 178 minutes, 4 fours) and Roe (58 in 106 minutes, 7 fours) who added 112. As in the previous match New South Wales used 10 bowlers. The game ended in a light-hearted spirit with Fingleton turning on an imitation of Bodyline attack. *NSWCA Report* omits c Marks from dismissal of Lovelock in WA (2).
Sources: *NSWCA Report, WACA Report, The West Australian, Daily News.*

NEW SOUTH WALES

Batsman	Dismissal	R	2nd Innings	R
J.H.W.Fingleton	c Jones b Zimbulis	100		
W.A.Brown	c Zimbulis b Ditchburn	116		
L.J.Fallowfield	not out	101	(1) not out	54
R.H.Robinson	c Gardiner b Halcombe	30	(3) not out	59
R.C.J.Little	b Gardiner	53	(2) c Gardiner b Halcombe	3
A.E.Marks	c R.J.Bryant b Jones	13		
A.G.Chipperfield	not out	3		
*†W.A.S.Oldfield	)			
E.C.S.White	) did not bat			
J.N.Campbell	)			
H.J.T.Theak	)			
Extras	(b5, lb6)	11	(b1)	1
Total	(107.0 overs, 432 minutes) (5 wkts dec)	427	(19.0 overs, 72 mins) (1 wkt dec)	117

WESTERN AUSTRALIA

Batsman	Dismissal	R	2nd Innings	R
F.J.Bryant	b Theak	25	c Chipperfield b White	12
F.H.Taaffe	c & b Chipperfield	79	c Oldfield b Theak	3
R.Roe	lbw b Robinson	58	st Oldfield b Campbell	14
D.C.McKenzie	c White c Robinson	5		
†O.I.Lovelock	b Theak	12	(7) c Marks b Brown	0
*R.J.Bryant	c Oldfield b White	17	(4) b Campbell	16
A.J.Ditchburn	not out	27	(6) c Marks b Little	27
G.A.Gardiner	b White	0	(5) b Robinson	28
J.R.Jones	st Oldfield b Campbell	1		
A.G.Zimbulis	c Fingleton b Campbell	20	(8) not out	16
R.A.Halcombe	st Oldfield b Campbell	5		
Extras	(b7, lb11, w1, nb4)	23	(b3)	3
Total	(85.4 overs, 287 minutes)	272	(27.4 overs, 105 mins) (7 wkts)	119

WESTERN AUSTRALIA	O	M	R	W	w,nb		O	M	R	W	w,nb
Halcombe	25	6	68	1	-,-		4	0	13	1	-,-
Ditchburn	23	2	56	1	-,-		4	0	12	0	-,-
Gardiner	15	1	57	1	-,-		4	0	21	0	-,-
R.J.Bryant	6	0	31	0	-,-						
Jones	21	2	83	1	-,-		2	0	25	0	-,-
Zimbulis	17	0	121	1	-,-	(4)	5	0	45	0	-,-

NEW SOUTH WALES	O	M	R	W	w,nb		O	M	R	W	w,nb
Theak	19	5	55	2	-,4		5	0	22	1	-,-
Fallowfield	7	1	14	0	-,-	(4)	4	1	10	0	-,-
White	26	11	39	2	1,-	(2)	7	0	17	1	-,-
Campbell	15.4	1	64	3	-,-	(3)	4	0	17	2	-,-
Chipperfield	8	0	37	1	-,-						
Robinson	10	0	40	2	-,-	(5)	4	0	19	1	-,-
Marks						(6)	1	1	0	0	-,-
Brown						(7)	1	0	8	1	-,-
Fingleton						(8)	1	0	16	0	-,-
Little						(9)	0.4	0	7	1	-,-

FALL OF WICKETS

Wkt	NSW 1st	WA 1st	NSW 2nd	WA 2nd
1st	205	29	5	5
2nd	236	141	-	23
3rd	285	149	-	38
4th	386	188	-	55
5th	413	194	-	86
6th	-	222	-	86
7th	-	222	-	119
8th	-	225	-	-
9th	-	259	-	-
10th	-	272	-	-

The presence of the Australian Test team in South Africa this season somewhat took the polish off domestic affairs. Nevertheless, some exciting cricket was played - especially as Bradman was still available - and an English team stopped off en route to New Zealand early in the summer, adding variety to the interstate program.

England undertook their six-match tour of Australia at the request of the New Zealand Cricket Council, who received 75 percent of the profits to help offset costs of the New Zealand leg of the English tour. Of the six matches played by MCC, three were won and two drawn. A single loss was recorded against New South Wales. J.Hardstaff exhibited stylish strokeplay and J.M.Sims bowled his legbreaks to useful effect, a fact which was borne in mind when England selected their team to tour Australia the following season.

South Australia won the Sheffield Shield for the first time in 10 years, breaking the New South Wales-Victoria domination of that period. Bradman returned to the game, fully recovered from his serious illness, and his presence in the South Australian side for the first time had the desired effect. South Australia won four of their six matches (all by big margins) and were undefeated in the other two. They ended the season with a huge percentage. Badcock, Ward, Waite, Ryan, Walker and Wall all provided excellent support for their new captain.

New South Wales and Victoria missed their Australian representatives badly and struggled to dismiss sides. New players to make their mark from the various States included Robinson, Marks, Easton and White (New South Wales), Scaife and Lee (Victoria) and Tallon (Queensland).

Prior to their departure for South Africa in October, the Australians played Western Australia at Perth. It provided the westerners with their only first-class fixture of the season, and they were no match for the Test players. An Australian team was selected from those who remained in the country to play the visiting MCC team in December but it was far from representative. Bradman was invited to captain the side but was not available for business reasons. The final XI comprised eight players from New South Wales, two from Victoria and one from Queensland. South Australia, the strongest State as it turned out, were not represented. MCC won easily.

Tasmania hosted two matches against Victoria at the New Year and won both, scraping home by one wicket in the second encounter. Encouraged by their success, they travelled to Melbourne for a return match and then on to Adelaide to meet South Australia, only to lose both games by an innings. At Adelaide, Bradman took 369 off the Tasmanian attack in sensationally quick time. It was his second triple-century of the summer, and the third by a South Australian.

Leading Aggregates

Batsmen	M	I	NO	Runs	HS	Ave.	Bowlers	Runs	Wkts	Ave.
D.G.Bradman (SA)	8	9	0	1173	369	130.33	F.A.Ward (SA)	1047	50	20.94
K.E.Rigg (V)	8	15	2	773	128	59.46	E.C.S.White (NSW)	673	33	20.39
C.L.Badcock (SA)	7	9	1	694	325	86.75	J.M.Sims (MCC)	834	33	25.27
R.H.Robinson (NSW)	8	14	1	681	103	52.38	M.G.Waite (SA)	554	27	20.51
J.Hardstaff (MCC)	6	11	2	634	230*	70.44	H.I.Ebeling (V)	687	27	25.44
A.E.Marks (NSW)	8	14	1	580	201	44.61	T.W.Wall (SA)	376	22	17.09
J.W.Scaife (V)	7	12	1	573	100	52.09				
D.Tallon (Q)	6	12	1	569	193	51.72				

SHEFFIELD SHIELD TABLE

	P	WO	W1	LO	L1	D	Pts	Quotient	Runs Scored	Wkts Lost	Runs Conceded	Wkts Taken
SOUTH AUSTRALIA	6	4	1	-	-	1	25	2.041	2814	54	2578	101
NEW SOUTH WALES	6	2	-	2	1	1	13	0.990	3353	104	3027	93
VICTORIA	6	1	2	2	1	-	12	0.875	3267	96	3344	86
QUEENSLAND	6	-	1	3	2	-	5	0.647	3050	104	3535	78
TOTAL	12	7	4	7	4	1	55	1.000	12484	358	12484	358

WESTERN AUSTRALIA v AUSTRALIAN XI

Played at W.A.C.A. Ground, Perth, on October 26, 28, 29, 1935. (Three-day match)
Toss : Western Australia.   Result : AUSTRALIAN XI WON BY AN INNINGS AND 249 RUNS.
Debuts: Nil.
12th Men: A.D.Drew (WA) and M.W.Sievers (Aust).
Umpires: F.R.Buttsworth and E.T.Tonkinson.
Attendances: 3000, 2000, "handful".   Total: About 5025.   Receipts: £262.
Close of Play: 1st day Aust 1/104 (Fingleton 47, McCabe 0); 2nd day WA (2) 0/13 (Taaffe 7, Alexander 4).

The match was played immediately prior to the departure of the Australian team to South Africa. F.J.Bryant and R.Roe were unavailable for Western Australia, while Drew replaced S.Briggs (also unavailable) as 12th man after the side had been named. Fingleton (147 minutes, 5 fours) and Brown (5 fours) put on 104 in 100 minutes for the first wicket. Rain caused the abandonment of the first day's play just as McCabe reached the crease after Brown's dismissal. The chief contributors on the second day were Darling (100 minutes, 5 fours), Chipperfield (92 minutes, 12 fours) and Barnett (88 minutes, 5 fours). The seventh-wicket partnership between Chipperfield and Barnett added 146 runs in 82 minutes. The virtually unplayable bowling of Fleetwood-Smith, who took three wickets for no runs in one over in the second innings (not including the hat-trick), caused *The West Australian* to comment: "From a WA viewpoint the match was an absolute failure." Sources: *NSWCA Report, WACA Report, The Age, The West Australian, Daily News.*

WESTERN AUSTRALIA

F.H.Taaffe	b McCormick	1	c & b McCormick		13
F.J.Alexander	b Fleetwood-Smith	8	b Fleetwood-Smith		14
†O.I.Lovelock	b Fleetwood-Smith	25	c Chipperfield b Fleetwood-Smith		8
D.C.McKenzie	b Fleetwood-Smith	4	b Fleetwood-Smith		5
S.G.Francis	b McCormick	11	lbw b O'Reilly		0
G.A.Gardiner	c McCabe b O'Reilly	20	lbw b Fleetwood-Smith		0
*R.J.Bryant	c Richardson b McCormick	4	b Fleetwood-Smith		0
A.J.Ditchburn	lbw b O'Reilly	7	c Fingleton b O'Reilly		2
A.G.Zimbulis	st Barnett b Fleetwood-Smith	6	st Barnett b Fleetwood-Smith		4
J.R.Jones	not out	10	not out		9
R.A.Halcombe	c & b O'Reilly	0	c Chipperfield b Fleetwood-Smith		6
Extras	(b8, lb10)	18	(nb1)		1
Total	(33.0 overs, 128 mins)	114	(26.0 overs, 99 mins)		62

AUSTRALIAN XI

J.H.W.Fingleton	c Halcombe b Jones	66	
W.A.Brown	b Bryant	55	
S.J.McCabe	c Zimbulis b Jones	24	
L.S.Darling	b Francis	66	
*V.Y.Richardson	run out (Gardiner)	21	
L.P.J.O'Brien	c Bryant b Jones	15	
A.G.Chipperfield	c Ditchburn b Zimbulis	88	
†B.A.Barnett	lbw b Zimbulis	58	
W.J.O'Reilly	c Jones b Ditchburn	14	
E.L.McCormick	not out	2	
L.O.Fleetwood-Smith	run out	4	
Extras	(b1, lb7, w2, nb2)	12	
Total	(88.0 overs, 347 mins)	425	

AUSTRALIAN XI	O	M	R	W	w,nb		O	M	R	W	w,nb
McCormick	8	1	29	3	-,-		8	2	19	1	-,1
McCabe	3	0	6	0	-,-		3	1	3	0	-,-
O'Reilly	14	5	37	3	-,-	(4)	5	1	19	2	-,-
Fleetwood-Smith	8	1	24	4	-,-	(3)	10	3	20	7	-,-

WESTERN AUSTRALIA	O	M	R	W	w,nb
Halcombe	23	3	100	0	-,2
Ditchburn	18	1	67	1	-,-
Francis	14	1	56	1	2,-
Zimbulis	10	0	74	2	-,-
Jones	17	0	85	3	-,-
Bryant	5	1	16	1	-,-
Gardiner	1	0	15	0	-,-

FALL OF WICKETS

Wkt	WA 1st	AUST 1st	WA 2nd
1st	2	104	23
2nd	31	146	34
3rd	37	151	40
4th	46	215	41
5th	65	249	41
6th	77	255	41
7th	92	401	41
8th	99	408	44
9th	107	418	48
10th	114	425	62

WESTERN AUSTRALIA v M.C.C.

Played at W.A.C.A. Ground, Perth, on October, 31, November 1, 2, 1935. (Three-day match)
Toss : M.C.C.   Result : MATCH DRAWN.
Debuts: Western Australia - D.T.Everett, R.W.Kimpton, C.F.Newman (all f/c).
12th Men: J.Elliott (WA) and J.H.Human (MCC).
Umpires: F.R.Buttsworth and E.T.Tonkinson.
Attendances: 900, 1025, 2000.   Total: 3925.   Receipts: £192.
Close of Play: 1st day MCC 7/292 (Langridge 48, Griffith 5); 2nd day WA 6/169 (Bryant 21, Kimpton 1).

D.C.McKenzie was unavailable to play for Western Australia and three changes were made to the team announced for the match; F.J.Alexander (injured), S.Briggs and G.A.Gardiner (both work commitments) being replaced by Elliott, Everett and Newman. For MCC, Smith scored 83 in 116 minutes with 1 six and 7 fours. Taaffe top-scored for Western Australia by compiling 76 in 185 minutes with 5 fours. In MCC's second innings, Mitchell-Innes struck 30 in 13 minutes with 2 sixes and 3 fours; his first scoring shots were 4, 4, 4, 6, 6. Holmes also scored quickly, making 51 in 36 minutes with 3 sixes and 3 fours. Everett twisted an ankle trying to save a four from Parks early in the second innings and was replaced on the field by Elliott. *Wisden* incorrectly gives WA (1) Everett 1, Halcombe 6; MCC bowling (2) Hardstaff 0/4, Mitchell-Innes 0/0, Smith 1/6 and omits c sub from dismissal of Hardstaff and Sims in MCC (2). Sources: *Wisden, WACA Report, Adelaide Advertiser, The West Australian, Daily News, Sunday Times.*

M.C.C.

Batsman	1st innings		2nd innings	
W.Barber	b Ditchburn	9	lbw b Ditchburn	15
J.H.Parks	c Zimbulis b Ditchburn	13	c Jones b Newman	51
D.Smith	c Ditchburn b Zimbulis	83	st Lovelock b Jones	11
J.Hardstaff, jr	b Ditchburn	13	c sub (J.Elliott) b Jones	55
N.S.Mitchell-Innes	c & b Zimbulis	58	lbw b Zimbulis	30
*E.R.T.Holmes	lbw b Bryant	19	c Halcombe b Zimbulis	51
J.Langridge	b Ditchburn	59	(9) not out	28
C.J.Lyttelton	c Ditchburn b Newman	27	(7) c & b Zimbulis	2
†S.C.Griffith	c Halcombe b Newman	17	(10) b Ditchburn	8
J.M.Sims	not out	18	(8) c sub (J.Elliott) b Jones	6
A.D.Baxter	c Kimpton b Zimbulis	9	st Lovelock b Ditchburn	0
Extras	(b5, lb13, nb1)	19	(b8, lb1)	9
Total	(86.0 overs, 316 mins)	344	(43.5 overs, 172 mins)	266

WESTERN AUSTRALIA

Batsman	1st innings		2nd innings	
F.H.Taaffe	c Mitchell-Innes b Langridge	76	not out	13
D.T.Everett	b Baxter	0		
A.J.Ditchburn	c Parks b Sims	15		
W.J.Horrocks	c Smith b Sims	3		
†O.I.Lovelock	c Parks b Sims	18	(2) b Smith	8
C.F.Newman	lbw b Sims	22		
*R.J.Bryant	c & b Sims	22		
R.W.Kimpton	b Sims	8		
J.R.Jones	not out	20		
A.G.Zimbulis	c Mitchell-Innes b Holmes	23		
R.A.Halcombe	c Smith b Sims	7		
Extras	(b9, lb6, w1, nb2)	18	(w2)	2
Total	(84.0 overs, 257 mins)	232	(6.6 overs, 20 mins) (1 wkt)	23

WESTERN AUSTRALIA	O	M	R	W	w,nb		O	M	R	W	w,nb
Halcombe	16	2	64	0	-,1		8	1	26	0	-,-
Bryant	7	3	19	1	-,-	(6)	1	0	17	0	-,-
Ditchburn	25	8	46	4	-,-	(2)	10.5	2	48	3	-,-
Jones	15	2	75	0	-,-		10	0	66	3	-,-
Zimbulis	15	0	83	3	-,-		8	0	56	3	-,-
Newman	8	1	38	2	-,-	(3)	6	0	44	1	-,-

M.C.C.	O	M	R	W	w,nb		O	M	R	W	w,nb
Baxter	25	2	77	1	-,2						
Parks	5	2	4	0	-,-						
Lyttelton	4	1	6	0	1,-	(2)	3	0	11	0	2,-
Sims	30	2	95	7	-,-						
Langridge	16	5	29	1	-,-						
Holmes	4	2	3	1	-,-						
Hardstaff						(1)	2	0	3	0	-,-
Mitchell-Innes						(3)	1	0	2	0	-,-
Smith						(4)	0.6	0	5	1	-,-

FALL OF WICKETS

Wkt	MCC 1st	WA 1st	MCC 2nd	WA 2nd
1st	26	7	36	23
2nd	27	55	66	-
3rd	59	63	84	-
4th	181	113	140	-
5th	193	139	210	-
6th	223	163	219	-
7th	276	176	227	-
8th	311	181	241	-
9th	323	219	266	-
10th	344	232	266	-

QUEENSLAND v NEW SOUTH WALES (Shield Match 1)

Played at Brisbane Cricket Ground (Woolloongabba) on November 8, 9, 11, 12, 1935. (Four-day match)
Toss : New South Wales.   Result : MATCH DRAWN.
Debuts: Queensland - V.G.Honour (f/c). New South Wales - T.C.J.Caldwell, A.F.Cooper, N.K.Miller (all f/c).
12th Men: J.G.Maddern (Qld) and H.Mudge (NSW).
Umpires: V.R.Castles and D.W.Given.
Attendances: 1500, 3632, 1563, 658.   Total: 7353.   Receipts: £440.
Close of Play: 1st day NSW 6/309 (White 59, Easton 67); 2nd day Qld 3/249 (Allen 119, Tallon 53); 3rd day NSW (2) 2/30 (Little 16, Chilvers 5).

Honour, originally named as 12th man, was a late replacement for E.Gilbert (declared unfit for selection by the Department of Aborigines in Queensland). A.F.Kippax was unavailable for New South Wales. Miller, in his sole first-class match, was missed by Bensted off the first ball he faced (the second ball of the match) and eventually fell in identical fashion. McGilvray (68 in 151 minutes, 7 fours), White (63 in 212 minutes, 3 fours) and Easton (83 in 154 minutes, 1 six and 8 fours) all made their highest scores for New South Wales, while Little (78 in 181 minutes, 12 fours) and Robinson (103 in 148 minutes, 15 fours) added 108 for the fifth wicket in the second innings after Fallowfield misjudged a single in the first over. Easton was run out when a straight drive by White was deflected by the bowler into the non-striker's stumps. Queensland reached their highest total so far at the 'Gabba Ground thanks to Allen (146 in 286 minutes, 1 six and 17 fours), Hansen (44 in 54 minutes, 5 fours), Tallon (58 in 98 minutes, 6 fours), Levy (52 in 84 minutes, 8 fours), Bensted (102 in 148 minutes, 1 six and 15 fours) and Cook (48 not out in 144 minutes, 4 fours). Bensted fell to the fourth ball of the second innings, in which Christy's unbeaten 44 occupied 67 minutes. Sources: *Wisden, NSWCA Report, QCA Report, The Age, Sydney Morning Herald, Brisbane Courier-Mail.*

NEW SOUTH WALES

L.J.Fallowfield	b Cook	28		run out (Levy)	0
N.K.Miller	c Bensted b Cook	21		c Bensted b Cook	9
R.C.J.Little	c Tait b Cook	4		c & b Wyeth	78
A.E.Marks	run out (Levy)	29	(5)	b Wyeth	14
*A.D.McGilvray	b Andrews	68	(7)	b Wyeth	6
R.H.Robinson	c Tallon b Wyeth	12		c Allen b Wyeth	103
E.C.S.White	c Allen b Bensted	63	(8)	lbw b Wyeth	6
†F.A.Easton	c Hansen b Cook	83	(9)	run out (Tait)	0
H.C.Chilvers	c Christy b Bensted	13	(4)	b Tait	6
T.C.J.Caldwell	hit wkt b Allen	26		st Tallon b Levy	15
A.F.Cooper	not out	0		not out	0
Extras	(b14, lb1, w2, nb6)	23		(b8, lb7, w1, nb2)	18
Total	(117.2 overs, 415 mins)	370		(88.0 overs, 301 mins)	265

QUEENSLAND

W.C.Andrews	c Easton b McGilvray	19			
T.Allen	c & b Caldwell	146			
V.G.Honour	run out (Little/Easton)	11			
C.D.Hansen	c McGilvray b White	44	(5)	not out	5
†D.Tallon	b Cooper	58	(2)	c Robinson b White	20
J.A.J.Christy	c McGilvray b Chilvers	2	(3)	not out	44
*R.M.Levy	c White b Chilvers	52	(4)	c Robinson b McGilvray	18
E.C.Bensted	st Easton b Chilvers	102	(1)	b McGilvray	0
G.G.Cook	not out	48			
A.H.Tait	c Easton b Caldwell	12			
E.R.Wyeth	c & b Marks	25			
Extras	(b5, lb4)	9		(b1)	1
Total	(151.2 overs, 480 mins)	528		(21.0 overs, 73 mins) (3 wkts)	88

QUEENSLAND	O	M	R	W	w,nb		O	M	R	W	w,nb
Cook	34	8	111	4	2,-		20	7	46	1	-,-
Tait	17	0	63	0	-,5	(4)	18	1	76	1	-,2
Bensted	14.2	2	47	2	-,1	(2)	5	1	14	0	1,-
Wyeth	31	10	56	1	-,-	(3)	31	14	51	5	-,-
Christy	3	0	17	0	-,-	(7)	5	1	17	0	-,-
Levy	11	0	30	0	-,-		7	1	32	1	-,-
Andrews	3	0	10	1	-,-						
Allen	4	1	13	1	-,-	(5)	2	0	11	0	-,-

NEW SOUTH WALES	O	M	R	W	w,nb		O	M	R	W	w,nb
Cooper	25	4	85	1	-,-						
McGilvray	27	5	98	1	-,-	(1)	11	0	58	2	-,-
White	28	8	62	1	-,-	(2)	10	0	29	1	-,-
Chilvers	41	8	142	3	-,-						
Caldwell	17	7	55	2	-,-						
Robinson	9	0	46	0	-,-						
Little	1	0	7	0	-,-						
Fallowfield	2	0	18	0	-,-						
Marks	1.2	0	6	1	-,-						

FALL OF WICKETS

Wkt	NSW 1st	QLD 1st	NSW 2nd	QLD 2nd
1st	50	29	0	0
2nd	60	58	25	44
3rd	69	146	39	79
4th	115	262	71	-
5th	146	273	179	-
6th	199	305	228	-
7th	325	353	234	-
8th	334	474	238	-
9th	370	493	265	-
10th	370	528	265	-

SOUTH AUSTRALIA v M.C.C.

Played at Adelaide Oval on November 8, 9, 11, 12, 1935. (Four-day match)
Toss : M.C.C.   Result : M.C.C. WON BY 36 RUNS.
Debuts: South Australia - H.M.Thompson, F.A.Ward (both f/c); D.G.Bradman (SA only).
12th Men: A.G.Shepherd (SA) and S.C.Griffith (MCC).
Umpires: R.A.Nelson and J.D.Scott.
Attendances: No daily figures published.   Total: 23,453.   Receipts: £894.
Close of Play: 1st day MCC 5/314 (Langridge 11, Sims 1); 2nd day SA 5/200 (Waite 22, Williams 24); 3rd day MCC (2) 5/125
    (Human 26, Sims 1).

T.W.Wall was unavailable for South Australia and the M.C.C. captain, E.R.T.Holmes was unable to play due to a hand injury. Bradman appeared for South Australia for the first time after seven seasons with New South Wales. It was also his first appearance in first-class cricket for more than 12 months because of illness. The lay-off was reflected in his batting: 15 in 23 minutes and 50 in 105 minutes (0 fours and 32 singles). Thompson was given a rude introduction, Park (67 in 151 minutes, 4 fours) hitting three fours in the opening over of Thompson's sole first-class match. Smith (52 in 98 minutes, 3 fours), Hardstaff (90 in 166 minutes, 7 fours) and Human (87 in 122 minutes, 9 fours) also hit fifties for M.C.C. Waite did the hat-trick to finish off the innings, dismissing Lyttelton and Baxter with the seventh and eighth balls of his 13th over and Read with the first ball of his 14th over. Badcock (45 in 107 minutes, 3 fours), Waite (58 in 136 minutes, 5 fours) and Walker (65 not out in 132 minutes, 2 fours) top-scored in the local first innings. Sources: *Wisden, SACA Report, Sydney Morning Herald, Adelaide Advertiser, The News.*

M.C.C

J.H.Parks	c Walker b Waite	67	c Moyle b Ward	21
D.Smith	c Moyle b Ward	52	c Waite b Thompson	10
J.Hardstaff, jr	c Waite b Ward	90	b Ryan	24
N.S.Mitchell-Innes	c & b Waite	0	c Walker b Ward	4
J.H.Human	c Bradman b Ward	87	c Walker b Ward	26
J.Langridge	b Ward	29	lbw b Williams	34
J.M.Sims	run out (Moyle/Walker)	12	lbw b Ryan	7
*C.J.Lyttelton	c Walker b Waite	25	b Ryan	31
†A.G.Powell	not out	3	b Ward	3
A.D.Baxter	b Waite	0	lbw b Ryan	5
H.D.Read	b Waite	0	not out	0
Extras	(lb2, w2, nb2)	6	(b4, lb3, nb2)	9
Total	(106.1 overs, 363 mins)	371	(64.3 overs, 220 mins)	174

SOUTH AUSTRALIA

C.L.Badcock	c Powell b Read	45	c Parks b Baxter	14
R.A.Parker	c & b Sims	30	lbw b Sims	18
*D.G.Bradman	lbw b Sims	15	lbw b Parks	50
E.J.R.Moyle	c & b Langridge	39	b Baxter	2
A.J.Ryan	c Hardstaff b Langridge	13	b Parks	27
M.G.Waite	c Mitchell-Innes b Read	58	b Read	30
R.G.Williams	c Powell b Read	24	b Sims	9
†C.W.Walker	not out	65	c Powell b Sims	5
F.H.K.Collins	b Sims	6	b Read	0
F.A.Ward	lbw b Langridge	7	not out	10
H.M.Thompson	b Sims	7	run out (Human/Powell)	12
Extras	(b5, lb1, nb7)	13	(b5, lb1, nb4)	10
Total	(91.7 overs, 355 mins)	322	(52.5 overs, 202 mins)	187

SOUTH AUSTRALIA	O	M	R	W	w,nb		O	M	R	W	w,nb
Thompson	14	0	70	0	-,-		5	0	34	1	-,2
Williams	19	4	51	0	2,2		9	2	20	1	-,-
Collins	21	5	48	0	-,-	(6)	5	2	6	0	-,-
Ward	28	4	127	4	-,-	(3)	21	3	62	4	-,-
Waite	13.1	4	42	5	-,-		7	1	30	0	-,-
Ryan	11	3	27	0	-,-	(4)	17.3	10	13	4	-,-

M.C.C.	O	M	R	W	w,nb		O	M	R	W	w,nb
Baxter	17	3	53	0	-,-		9	0	35	2	-,2
Read	20	2	81	3	-,5		5	0	14	2	-,2
Parks	3	0	16	0	-,-	(5)	12	1	32	2	-,-
Sims	34.7	3	134	4	-,2	(3)	20	0	76	3	-,-
Langridge	17	4	25	3	-,-	(4)	6.5	0	20	0	-,-

FALL OF WICKETS

	MCC	SA	MCC	SA
Wkt	1st	1st	2nd	2nd
1st	93	64	31	29
2nd	146	90	55	37
3rd	146	101	63	39
4th	283	154	63	101
5th	313	163	122	136
6th	338	200	126	149
7th	368	265	150	165
8th	369	278	164	165
9th	369	303	169	167
10th	371	322	174	187

VICTORIA v M.C.C.

Played at Melbourne Cricket Ground on November 15, 16, 18, 19, 1935. (Four-day match)
Toss : Victoria.   Result : MATCH DRAWN.
Debuts: Nil.
12th Men: E.H.Bromley (Vic) and A.G.Powell (MCC).
Umpires: A.N.Barlow and H.R.McLean.
Attendances: 1754, 8778, 4637, 2147.   Total: 17,316.   Receipts: £607.
Close of Play: 1st day Vic 1/30 (Rigg 17, Vernon 7); 2nd day Vic 6/229 (Plant 4, Quin 9); 3rd day MCC 4/167 (Sims 0).

Play was restricted on the first day to 43 minutes due to rain and a start could not be made on the second day until 2.00pm. Rigg (112 in 193 minutes, 1 five and 8 fours) survived three chances in making the match top score and followed up with a chanceless unbeaten 59 (98 minutes, 2 fours) in the second innings. Scaife (60 in 105 minutes, 1 four), Plant (64 in 112 minutes) and Vernon (42 not out in 74 minutes, 3 fours) also batted well for Victoria. Parks (72 in 194 minutes, 3 fours) alone surpassed 50 for M.C.C. Gregory (leg breaks) took his best figures of 5 for 69 while Mitchell-Innes sustained a first-ball dismissal to another wrist-spinner in Smith. *Wisden* incorrectly gives Vic (1) Lee c Barber; MCC (2) Lee omitted from bowling. Sources: *Wisden, VCA Report, The Age, The Argus, Sydney Morning Herald.*

VICTORIA

Batsman	Dismissal	Score	Dismissal 2	Score 2
K.E.Rigg	c Langridge b Sims	112	not out	59
I.S.Lee	c Smith b Holmes	4	c Mitchell-Innes b Read	16
E.H.G.Vernon	run out (Read/Parks)	27	not out	42
J.W.Scaife	c Smith b Read	60		
R.G.Gregory	lbw b Langridge	1		
I.D.Miller	c Griffith b Read	6		
H.J.Plant	c Barber b Langridge	64		
†S.O.Quin	c Holmes b Sims	19		
S.A.J.Smith	not out	22		
*H.I.Ebeling	b Sims	4		
V.G.Nagel	not out	6		
Extras	(b1, lb3, nb3)	7	(b1, lb1, w1, nb2)	5
Total	(90.0 overs, 347 mins) (9 wkts dec)	332	(28.0 overs, 98 mins) (1 wkt dec)	122

M.C.C.

Batsman	Dismissal	Score	Dismissal 2	Score 2
J.H.Parks	c Scaife b Gregory	72		
W.Barber	c Nagel b Plant	32		
D.Smith	lbw b Gregory	24	(4) not out	20
J.Hardstaff, jr	hit wkt b Smith	34	(5) not out	8
J.M.Sims	c & b Gregory	10		
N.S.Mitchell-Innes	lbw b Smith	0	(2) c Plant b Nagel	12
*E.R.T.Holmes	c Gregory Plant	34	(3) b Ebeling	0
J.Langridge	not out	27		
C.J.Lyttelton	c Nagel b Smith	7	(1) lbw b Ebeling	2
†S.C.Griffith	c Nagel b Gregory	7		
H.D.Read	c Plant b Gregory	0		
Extras	(b2, lb1, nb2)	5	(b1, w1, nb2)	4
Total	(86.7 overs, 301 mins)	252	(14.0 overs, 60 mins) (3 wkts)	46

M.C.C.	O	M	R	W	w,nb		O	M	R	W	w,nb
Read	26	0	95	2	-,2		6	0	32	1	-,2
Holmes	13	1	46	1	-,-		1	0	3	0	-,-
Lyttelton	1	0	6	0	-,1						
Parks	19	4	43	0	-,-	(3)	5	0	21	0	-,-
Sims	21	0	101	3	-,-		7	1	39	0	1,-
Langridge	10	2	34	2	-,-	(4)	8	1	19	0	-,-
Mitchell-Innes						(6)	1	0	3	0	-,-

VICTORIA	O	M	R	W	w,nb		O	M	R	W	w,nb
Ebeling	9	1	22	0	-,-		4	0	9	2	-,1
Nagel	10	1	44	0	-,2		4	0	18	1	-,1
Plant	19	3	51	2	-,-		2	0	3	0	1,-
Gregory	24.7	3	69	5	-,-		2	0	9	0	-,-
Smith	24	3	61	3	-,-						
Scaife						(5)	1	0	3	0	-,-
Lee						(6)	1	1	0	0	-,-

FALL OF WICKETS

Wkt	VIC 1st	MCC 1st	VIC 2nd	MCC 2nd
1st	14	61	31	13
2nd	80	104	-	13
3rd	198	167	-	23
4th	199	167	-	-
5th	213	167	-	-
6th	216	187	-	-
7th	281	222	-	-
8th	309	229	-	-
9th	322	252	-	-
10th	-	252	-	-

NEW SOUTH WALES v M.C.C.

Played at Sydney Cricket Ground on November 22, 23, 25, 1935. (Four-day match)
Toss : M.C.C.   Result : NEW SOUTH WALES WON BY TEN WICKETS.
Debuts: New South Wales - H.Mudge (f/c); A.R.Lonergan (NSW only).
12th Men: R.C.J.Little (NSW) and N.S.Mitchell-Innes (MCC).
Umpires: H.J.Armstrong and E.G.Borwick,
Attendances: 4845, 10661, 3494.   Total: 19,000.   Receipts: £1047.
Close of Play: 1st day NSW 0/29 (Fallowfield 14, Mudge 15); 2nd day NSW 8/373 (Easton 76, Chilvers 12).

T.C.J.Caldwell (fluid on knee) and N.K.Miller (ill) were unavailable for New South Wales. Only Parks (55 in 102 minutes, 5 fours) and Hardstaff (77 in 136 minutes, 9 fours) exceeded 50 for M.C.C., White, left-arm medium pace, taking seven wickets in the match. Fallowfield (49 in 117 minutes, 3 fours) and Mudge (43 in 104 minutes, 1 four) added 86 to give the home side a solid start. Marks (88 in 139 minutes, 6 fours) and McGilvray (66 in 147 minutes, 4 fours) halted a middle-order collapse with a century stand for the sixth wicket and Easton (77 in 81 minutes, 10 fours) hit hard late on the second day. Lonergan played the first of three matches for New South Wales after serving South Australia 39 times. *Wisden* incorrectly gives NSW (1) Read 2/96, Holmes 0/23; MCC (2) Baxter c Cooper. Sources: *Wisden, NSWCA Report, The Age, The Argus, The Herald, Sydney Morning Herald, NSWCA Scorebook.*

M.C.C.

J.H.Parks	b Cooper	55	(8) c McGilvray b Mudge	19
W.Barber	b Cooper	12	st Easton b Chilvers	19
D.Smith	b White	2	(2) b White	16
J.Hardstaff, jr	c & b Chilvers	77	b Cooper	37
J.H.Human	run out (McGilvray/Easton)	12	(3) b White	9
*E.R.T.Holmes	b White	17	(5) c & b Mudge	12
J.Langridge	b McGilvray	31	(6) run out (McGilvray)	9
†A.G.Powell	b White	32	(7) c McGilvray b Mudge	0
J.M.Sims	st Easton b Mudge	4	not out	27
A.D.Baxter	not out	9	c Chilvers b White	5
H.D.Read	b White	4	run out	1
Extras	(lb4, w1)	5	(b6, lb2, nb1)	9
Total	(73.2 overs, 245 mins)	260	(65.0 overs, 212 mins)	163

NEW SOUTH WALES

L.J.Fallowfield	c Read b Sims	49		
H.Mudge	lbw b Sims	43	(1) not out	11
A.R.Lonergan	lbw b Sims	3	(2) not out	27
A.E.Marks	run out (Read)	88		
A.F.Kippax	b Sims	13		
R.H.Robinson	b Read	4		
*A.D.McGilvray	lbw b Read	66		
E.C.S.White	lbw b Sims	0		
†F.A.Easton	lbw b Sims	77		
H.C.Chilvers	not out	23		
A.F.Cooper	run out (/Powell)	0		
Extras	(b8, lb9, nb2)	19	(b1)	1
Total	(91.1 overs, 358 mins)	385	(4.7 overs, 22 mins) (0 wkts)	39

NEW SOUTH WALES	O	M	R	W	w,nb	O	M	R	W	w,nb
Cooper	14	2	55	2	-,-	8	0	36	1	-,1
McGilvray	13	2	38	1	1,-	5	0	15	0	-,-
White	20.2	6	43	4	-,-	25	10	36	3	-,-
Chilvers	18	2	73	1	-,-	16	3	38	1	-,-
Mudge	8	0	46	1	-,-	11	0	29	3	-,-

M.C.C.	O	M	R	W	w,nb	O	M	R	W	w,nb
Read	24.1	0	97	2	-,2	2.7	0	15	0	-,-
Baxter	22	2	84	0	-,-	2	0	23	0	-,-
Parks	5	2	15	0	-,-					
Sims	28	1	125	6	-,-					
Langridge	8	1	23	0	-,-					
Holmes	3	0	22	0	-,-					
Human	1	1	0	0	-,-					

FALL OF WICKETS

Wkt	MCC 1st	NSW 1st	MCC 2nd	NSW 2nd
1st	27	86	35	-
2nd	31	97	39	-
3rd	111	98	68	-
4th	132	126	85	-
5th	174	134	97	-
6th	178	257	98	-
7th	230	259	110	-
8th	245	317	157	-
9th	251	374	162	-
10th	260	385	163	-

QUEENSLAND v M.C.C.

Played at Brisbane Cricket Ground (Woolloongabba) on November 29, 30, December 2, 3, 1935. (Four-day match)
Toss : Queensland.   Result : M.C.C. WON BY AN INNINGS AND 106 RUNS.
Debuts: Queensland - G.W.Hardcastle , J.E.McCarthy (both f/c).
12th Men: V.G.Honour (Qld) and H.D.Read (MCC).
Umpires: D.W.Given and J.A.Scott.
Attendances: 2500, 5799, 1461, 500.   Total: 10,260.   Receipts: £637.
Close of Play: 1st day MCC 0/60 (Barber 23, Smith 35); 2nd day MCC 6/436 (Langridge 15, Lyttelton 11); 3rd day Qld (2) 6/164
    (Christy 20).

McCarthy replaced W.C.Andrews (injured hand) in the Queensland team. Barber (91 in 194 minutes, 12 fours) and Smith (109 in 195 minutes, 9 fours) opened the M.C.C. innings with a 204-run partnership. Human (118 in 145 minutes, 14 fours) and Holmes (80 in 182 minutes, 1 six and 5 fours) added a further 182 for the fifth wicket. Queensland's highest scorers were Bensted (64 in 138 minutes, 4 fours), Tallon (45 in 48 minutes, 4 fours) and McCarthy (38 in 73 minutes, 3 fours) in the first innings, while Levy (76 in 124 minutes, 8 fours) and Christy (66 not out in 151 minutes, 4 fours) hit half-centuries in the second innings. Allen (leg-breaks and googlies) completed his only five-wicket analysis. *Wisden* incorrectly gives MCC: McCarthy 0/47, Levy 1/31. Sources: *Wisden, QCA Report, Brisbane Courier-Mail, Brisbane Telegraph.*

QUEENSLAND

T.Allen	c Griffith b Baxter	0		b Baxter	3
*R.M.Levy	c Langridge b Sims	10		c Hardstaff b Sims	76
E.C.Bensted	b Langridge	64		b Baxter	0
C.D.Hansen	b Baxter	2		b Baxter	24
†D.Tallon	b Baxter	45		c Griffith b Sims	21
J.A.J.Christy	c & b Langridge	21		not out	66
J.E.McCarthy	c Smith b Langridge	38		b Baxter	11
B.R.D.O'Connor	run out (Holmes/Griffith)	13		lbw b Human	20
G.W.Hardcastle	b Sims	1	(11)	b Sims	1
E.Gilbert	not out	1		b Baxter	3
E.R.Wyeth	c Barber b Langridge	3	(9)	c Smith b Holmes	11
Extras	(b3, lb1, nb1)	5		(b7, lb2, nb4)	13
Total	(60.0 overs, 216 mins)	203		(79.4 overs, 276 mins)	249

M.C.C.

W.Barber	c Tallon b Christy	91
D.Smith	st Tallon b Allen	109
J.Hardstaff, jr	c Wyeth b O'Connor	3
N.S.Mitchell-Innes	b Allen	4
J.H.Human	st Tallon b Allen	118
*E.R.T.Holmes	st Tallon b Allen	80
J.Langridge	st Tallon b Allen	36
C.J.Lyttelton	c Allen b Hardcastle	42
J.M.Sims	not out	31
†S.C.Griffith	run out (Hardcastle/Levy)	35
A.D.Baxter	st Tallon b Levy	0
Extras	(b1, lb7, nb1)	9
Total	(141.4 overs, 497 mins)	558

M.C.C.	O	M	R	W	w,nb		O	M	R	W	w,nb
Baxter	16	1	58	3	-,1		23	4	61	5	-,4
Holmes	7	1	11	0	-,-	(5)	9	0	24	1	-,-
Sims	18	1	70	2	-,-	(4)	23.4	1	69	3	-,-
Langridge	16	2	53	4	-,-	(3)	12	2	30	0	-,-
Human	3	0	6	0	-,-	(6)	7	0	26	1	-,-
Lyttelton						(2)	5	0	26	0	-,-

QUEENSLAND	O	M	R	W	w,nb
Gilbert	27	3	111	0	-,-
O'Connor	18	4	54	1	-,-
Bensted	11	2	36	0	-,1
Allen	20	1	108	5	-,-
Wyeth	23	5	72	0	-,-
McCarthy	8	0	41	0	-,-
Levy	8.4	0	37	1	-,-
Hardcastle	13	1	51	1	-,-
Christy	11	1	32	1	-,-
Hansen	2	1	7	0	-,-

	FALL OF WICKETS		
	QLD	MCC	QLD
Wkt	1st	1st	2nd
1st	6	204	14
2nd	22	204	20
3rd	25	208	80
4th	103	219	128
5th	142	401	131
6th	151	418	164
7th	179	487	210
8th	189	491	235
9th	199	557	246
10th	203	558	249

AUSTRALIAN XI v M.C.C.

Played at Sydney Cricket Ground on December 6, 7, 9, 10, 1935. (Four-day match)
Toss : M.C.C.   Result : M.C.C. WON BY 203 RUNS.
Debuts: Nil.
12th Men: A.R.Lonergan (Aust) and N.S.Mitchell-Innes (MCC).
Umpires: E.G.Borwick and A.L.Christie.
Attendances: 4174, 10016, 2029, 1575.   Total: 17,794.   Receipts: £899.
Close of Play: 1st day MCC 6/266 (Hardstaff 150, Lyttelton 5); 2nd day Aust 8/209 (Easton 28, Ebeling 16); 3rd day Aust (2) 2/34 (Mudge 18).

Hardstaff's 230 not out in 368 minutes (1 five and 19 fours) included a solitary chance at 121 to Bensted off McGilvray. He dominated a sixth-wicket partnership of 150 with Langridge (53 in 145 minutes, 2 fours). Lyttelton (35 in 72 minutes, 3 fours) and Sims (35 in 70 minutes, 5 fours) added 91 for the ninth wicket. Hardstaff again impressed in the second innings with 63 (120 minutes, 1 five and 3 fours). Marks topped the scoring for the Australians with 64 in the first innings (99 minutes, 6 fours) and 40 (84 minutes, 4 fours) in the second innings. Robinson (37 in 41 minutes, 4 fours) and Easton (45 not out in 66 minutes, 3 fours) also contributed, while Ebeling took 11 for 159 with the ball. Mudge was out first ball in the first over of the first innings. White injured a thumb while in the field on the third day and was unable to bat on the final day. Last first-class appearance by A.F.Kippax. *Wisden* incorrectly gives MCC (2) Sims b Ebeling. Sources: *Wisden, NSWCA Report, The Age, The Argus, Sydney Morning Herald, NSWCA Scorebook.*

M.C.C.

J.H.Parks	lbw b Chilvers	10	c White b Ebeling		7
D.Smith	b Ebeling	12	b Ebeling		22
W.Barber	st Easton b Chilvers	13	st Easton b Chilvers		35
J.Hardstaff, jr	not out	230	b Ebeling		63
J.H.Human	b Ebeling	13	b McGilvray		26
*E.R.T.Holmes	b Ebeling	2	c McGilvray b Ebeling		24
J.Langridge	c & b Ebeling	53	not out		23
C.J.Lyttelton	lbw b White	35	c White b Chilvers		5
†A.G.Powell	c Easton b Chilvers	0	b Ebeling		1
J.M.Sims	b Ebeling	35	lbw b Ebeling		0
A.D.Baxter	did not bat				
Extras	(b5, lb3)	8	(b1)		1
Total	(120.4 overs, 416 mins) (9 wkts dec)	411	(58.7 overs, 203 mins) (9 wkts dec)		207

AUSTRALIAN XI

K.E.Rigg	lbw b Baxter	7	c Powell b Baxter		11
H.Mudge	lbw b Baxter	0	b Sims		30
R.H.Robinson	b Baxter	37	(4) b Sims		27
A.E.Marks	c Sims b Human	64	(5) c Sims b Parks		40
A.F.Kippax	b Baxter	1	(6) b Sims		18
E.C.Bensted	lbw b Sims	25	(7) b Parks		12
A.D.McGilvray	c Holmes b Parks	22	(8) c Human b Sims		2
†F.A.Easton	not out	45	(9) b Parks		27
E.C.S.White	c Human b Parks	2	absent hurt		-
*H.I.Ebeling	lbw b Parks	16	not out		6
H.C.Chilvers	c Smith b Holmes	1	(3) c Powell b Baxter		1
Extras	(b5, lb1, nb1)	7	(b4, lb9, nb1)		14
Total	(47.6 overs, 187 mins)	227	(54.5 overs, 193 mins)		188

AUSTRALIAN XI	O	M	R	W	w,nb		O	M	R	W	w,nb
Ebeling	30.4	5	101	5	-,-		18.7	1	58	6	-,-
McGilvray	9	2	26	0	-,-		13	0	43	1	-,-
White	29	5	66	1	-,-	(4)	11	0	37	0	-,-
Chilvers	39	2	149	3	-,-	(3)	16	1	68	2	-,-
Mudge	11	1	49	0	-,-						
Robinson	2	0	12	0	-,-						

M.C.C.	O	M	R	W	w,nb		O	M	R	W	w,nb
Baxter	12	0	63	4	-,1		20	4	57	2	-,1
Holmes	5.6	1	26	1	-,-						
Parks	14	0	64	3	-,-	(2)	12.5	2	30	3	-,-
Sims	11	1	44	1	-,-	(3)	21	4	81	4	-,-
Human	3	0	12	1	-,-	(4)	1	0	6	0	-,-
Langridge	2	0	11	0	-,-						

FALL OF WICKETS

Wkt	MCC 1st	AUST 1st	MCC 2nd	AUST 2nd
1st	23	1	30	28
2nd	25	23	35	34
3rd	52	62	113	65
4th	91	66	145	84
5th	95	125	177	134
6th	245	162	180	145
7th	319	164	189	153
8th	320	168	199	188
9th	411	210	207	188
10th	-	227	-	-

VICTORIA v QUEENSLAND (Shield Match 2)

Played at Melbourne Cricket Ground on December 18, 19, 20, 21, 1935. (Four-day match)
Toss : Victoria.   Result : MATCH DRAWN.
Debuts: Nil.
12th Men: A.L.Hassett (Vic) and A.Fisher (Qld).
Umpires: A.N.Barlow and H.R.McLean.
Attendances: 2442, 2414, 1547, 1097.   Total: 7500.   Receipts: £186.
Close of Play: 1st day Vic 6/350 (Gregory 34, Plant 3); 2nd day Qld 2/94 (Andrews 46, Hansen 12); 3rd day Qld (2) 1/105 (Allen 61, Andrews 37).

Fisher came into the Queensland twelve to replace G.R.Clem, who had taken a job offer in Melbourne. Hassett replaced I.D.Miller (unavailable) as Victoria's 12th man. Rain and bad light on the last day helped avert defeat for Queensland, restricting play to 158 minutes from 2.37 pm to 5.15 pm. After Lee fell to the seventh ball of the match Rigg (128 in 253 minutes, 6 fours) and Scaife (100 in 181 minutes, 8 fours) shared a 201-run stand and Bromley (49 in 70 minutes, 6 fours) Gregory (60 in 122 minutes, 4 fours) and Smith (80 not out in 84 minutes, 6 fours) took Victoria to 9/522 at lunch on the second day. Allen's hundred for Queensland (210 minutes, 9 fours) included a sharp chance to Ebeling off Gregory when 86. Andrews scored 46 in 122 minutes (4 fours) and 58 in 166 minutes (3 fours), adding 152 with Allen for the second wicket. Sources: *Wisden, VCA Report, QCA Report, The Age, The Argus, The Herald.*

VICTORIA

K.E.Rigg	c Tallon b Bensted	128
I.S.Lee	b Gilbert	0
E.H.G.Vernon	c Levy b Bensted	8
J.W.Scaife	b Cook	100
E.H.Bromley	lbw b Wyeth	49
R.G.Gregory	st Tallon b Allen	60
†S.O.Quin	st Tallon b Allen	15
H.J.Plant	st Tallon b Wyeth	29
S.A.J.Smith	not out	80
*H.I.Ebeling	c Hansen b Cook	20
H.J.Britt	not out	18
Extras	(b6, lb3, w4, nb2)	15
Total	(127.0 overs, 463 mins) (9 wkts dec)	522

QUEENSLAND

T.Allen	c Quin b Plant	12		b Gregory	100
G.G.Cook	run out (Britt/Quin)	21		b Britt	0
W.C.Andrews	c Scaife b Ebeling	46		c Lee b Gregory	58
C.D.Hansen	lbw b Plant	12	(5)	c Quin b Ebeling	33
†D.Tallon	c Plant b Smith	25	(6)	not out	33
*R.M.Levy	c & b Gregory	17	(7)	not out	0
J.A.J.Christy	not out	28	(4)	lbw b Smith	1
V.G.Honour	b Smith	1			
E.C.Bensted	b Smith	0			
E.Gilbert	c Lee b Gregory	12			
E.R.Wyeth	c Bromley b Gregory	6			
Extras	(b3, lb1)	4		(b1, lb7, w1)	9
Total	(81.5 overs, 275 mins)	184		(80.5 overs, 270 mins) (5 wkts)	234

QUEENSLAND	O	M	R	W	w,nb
Gilbert	25	1	128	1	-,-
Cook	28	1	99	2	-,-
Bensted	20	7	48	2	2,1
Wyeth	23	2	76	2	-,-
Christy	8	1	38	0	-,1
Allen	20	1	82	2	2,-
Levy	3	0	36	0	-,-

VICTORIA	O	M	R	W	w,nb		O	M	R	W	w,nb
Ebeling	15	4	34	1	-,-		8.5	2	18	1	-,-
Britt	11	6	17	0	-,-		13	1	38	1	-,-
Smith	22	2	57	3	-,-	(5)	16	0	49	1	1,-
Plant	20	8	26	2	-,-	(3)	13	3	42	0	-,-
Gregory	13.5	3	46	3	-,-	(4)	26	5	66	2	-,-
Bromley							4	0	12	0	-,-

FALL OF WICKETS

	VIC	QLD	QLD
Wkt	1st	1st	2nd
1st	3	9	0
2nd	23	68	152
3rd	224	94	161
4th	264	94	169
5th	311	123	234
6th	344	151	-
7th	402	154	-
8th	404	156	-
9th	450	171	-
10th	-	184	-

SOUTH AUSTRALIA v NEW SOUTH WALES (Shield Match 3)

Played at Adelaide Oval on December 18, 19, 20, 21, 1935. (Four-day match)
Toss : South Australia. Result : SOUTH AUSTRALIA WON BY AN INNINGS AND 5 RUNS.
Debuts: South Australia - T.R.O'Connell (f/c).
12th Men: R.G.Williams (SA) and L.C.Hynes (NSW).
Umpires: R.A.Nelson and J.D.Scott.
Attendances: 2045, 3669, 1200, 1005. Total: 7919. Receipts: £332.
Close of Play: 1st day SA 3/397 (Moyle 39, Waite 12); 2nd day NSW 1/83 (Fallowfield 37, Little 43); 3rd day NSW 8/324 (White 22, Howell 4).

In his first Shield match for South Australia, Bradman scored a chanceless 117 in 158 minutes with 7 fours, emulating the performance in his first Shield match of all eight years before: on December 17, 1927 in the corresponding match at the same ground he had scored 118 for the other team. He added 202 for the second wicket in 149 minutes with Badcock (150 in 276 minutes, 16 fours) after Parker (74 in 125 minutes, 9 fours) had added 139 with Badcock for the first. Moyle (98 in 186 minutes, 14 fours) compiled his highest score for the State, Mudge dismissing Moyle and Collins with successive balls. Fallowfield (54 in 200 minutes, 5 fours) and Little (76 in 171 minutes, 7 fours) added 129 in a dour second-wicket stand for New South Wales before the promising Robinson (102 in 178 minutes, 14 fours) scored a maiden hundred. Ward, in his second match, took the first of 24 five-wicket analyses in first-class cricket with his leg-breaks and googlies. A.F.Kippax had announced his inability to visit Adelaide and Melbourne with the New South Wales team and Howell replaced H.C.Chilvers (work commitments) after the side was selected. Sources: *Wisden, NSWCA Report, SACA Report, Adelaide Advertiser, The News*.

SOUTH AUSTRALIA

C.L.Badcock	c Lonergan b Robinson	150
R.A.Parker	c White b Cooper	74
*D.G.Bradman	c & b Robinson	117
E.J.R.Moyle	c Easton b Mudge	98
M.G.Waite	c Little b Cooper	22
A.J.Ryan	b Howell	5
T.R.O'Connell	b Cooper	24
†C.W.Walker	run out	28
F.H.K.Collins	c & b Mudge	0
F.A.Ward	b Howell	32
T.W.Wall	not out	10
Extras	(b6, lb4, w1, nb4)	15
Total	(161.4 overs, 530 mins)	575

NEW SOUTH WALES

L.J.Fallowfield	c Walker b Ryan	54		c Collins b Ryan	38
H.Mudge	b Wall	1		lbw b Ryan	17
R.C.J.Little	c Moyle b Ward	76		b Ward	1
A.E.Marks	c Ward b Waite	6		lbw b Ryan	31
A.R.Lonergan	c Ryan b O'Connell	28		c Moyle b Waite	39
R.H.Robinson	c Waite b Ward	102		c Collins b Wall	39
E.C.S.White	c Ryan b Ward	29		lbw b Ryan	1
†F.A.Easton	c Bradman b Ward	16		c O'Connell b Wall	42
*A.D.McGilvray	b Ward	0	(10)	lbw b Wall	2
W.H.Howell	c Parker b Ward	20	(9)	c Wall b O'Connell	1
A.F.Cooper	not out	2		not out	0
Extras	(b9, lb7, w1)	17		(b5, lb3)	8
Total	(143.4 overs, 471 mins)	351		(85.2 overs, 274 mins)	219

NEW SOUTH WALES	O	M	R	W	w,nb
Cooper	27	3	103	3	-,1
McGilvray	14	2	36	0	1,-
White	37	7	97	0	-,-
Mudge	28	3	113	2	-,-
Howell	25.4	5	98	2	-,3
Little	4	0	24	0	-,-
Robinson	9	0	53	2	-,-
Marks	17	3	36	0	-,-

SOUTH AUSTRALIA	O	M	R	W	w,nb		O	M	R	W	w,nb
Wall	23	6	58	1	-,-		9	3	15	3	-,-
O'Connell	12	2	24	1	-,-		6.2	1	11	1	-,-
Ward	45.4	11	127	6	1,-		30	4	117	1	-,-
Collins	16	3	34	0	-,-	(5)	9	3	14	0	-,-
Waite	18	2	60	1	-,-	(6)	8	0	27	1	-,-
Ryan	29	18	31	1	-,-	(4)	23	15	27	4	-,-

FALL OF WICKETS

Wkt	SA 1st	NSW 1st	NSW 2nd
1st	139	5	25
2nd	341	134	26
3rd	349	140	89
4th	415	146	122
5th	438	221	134
6th	499	302	135
7th	505	318	210
8th	505	318	217
9th	550	334	219
10th	575	351	219

VICTORIA v NEW SOUTH WALES (Shield Match 4)

Played at Melbourne Cricket Ground on December 24, 26, 27, 28, 1935. (Four-day match)
Toss : Victoria.   Result : VICTORIA WON BY 88 RUNS.
Debuts: Victoria - C.W.Welch (f/c).
12th Men: J.Thomas (Vic) and L.C.Hynes (NSW).
Umpires: A.N.Barlow and H.R.McLean.
Attendances: 2383, 7906, 4679, 4089.   Total: 19,057.   Receipts: £652.
Close of Play: 1st day Vic 6/253 (Plant 17, Smith 4); 2nd day NSW 5/146 (Robinson 20, McGilvray 8); 3rd day Vic (2) 2/148 (Lee 73, Scaife 35).

Hassett (originally 12th man) and Welch were late replacements for R.G.Gregory and E.H.G.Vernon (both unable to obtain leave) in the Victorian side. Rigg (51 in 148 minutes, 2 fours), Lee (94 in 175 minutes, 8 fours), Bromley (40 in 58 minutes, 5 fours), Plant (76 in 130 minutes, 6 fours) and Ebeling (50 not out in 129 minutes, 2 fours) were the main contributors in the first innings. Lee (75 in 135 minutes, 6 fours) again played the leading role in the second innings in which Victoria lost their last 8 for 62. Needing 308 to win, Fallowfield (72 in 115 minutes, 7 fours) and Easton (61 in 82 minutes, 9 fours) shared a fourth-wicket partnership of 107 but after their separation only Marks (44 in 70 minutes, 5 fours) reached double figures. Mudge (59 in 137 minutes, 3 fours) and Robinson (66 in 118 minutes, 6 fours) scored fifties in the first innings. Cooper (right-arm fast) captured his only five-wicket analysis. Sources: *Wisden, NSWCA Report, VCA Report, The Age, The Argus, The Herald.*

VICTORIA

K.E.Rigg	c McGilvray b White	51	lbw b McGilvray	12
†S.O.Quin	c Robinson b Cooper	11	c sub (L.C.Hynes) b White	24
I.S.Lee	c Easton b Cooper	94	b Cooper	75
J.W.Scaife	c Robinson b Cooper	21	st Easton b Howell	35
E.H.Bromley	c Little b McGilvray	40	c McGilvray b White	36
A.L.Hassett	c Little b McGilvray	12	lbw b White	4
H.J.Plant	lbw b Cooper	76	b Howell	6
S.A.J.Smith	c Little b Cooper	19	c & b McGilvray	7
*H.I.Ebeling	not out	50	c Lonergan b White	0
C.W.Welch	c White b Cooper	10	not out	5
H.J.Britt	b White	5	b McGilvray	1
Extras	(b1, lb2)	3	(b5)	5
Total	(119.2 overs, 418 mins)	392	(71.5 overs, 274 mins)	210

NEW SOUTH WALES

L.J.Fallowfield	hit wkt b Smith	26	b Welch	72
H.Mudge	b Plant	59	(9) c Quin b Plant	4
R.C.J.Little	c Plant b Welch	13	c Ebeling b Britt	18
A.E.Marks	b Welch	13	(6) not out	44
A.R.Lonergan	c Plant b Smith	1	(2) c &b Britt	4
R.H.Robinson	c Scaife b Plant	66	(4) b Ebeling	1
*A.D.McGilvray	lbw b Britt	42	st Quin b Welch	3
†F.A.Easton	c Plant b Ebeling	7	(5) c Lee b Welch	61
E.C.S.White	not out	28	(8) b Ebeling	0
W.H.Howell	c Welch b Smith	15	st Quin b Welch	5
A.F.Cooper	c Plant b Smith	16	run out (Hassett/Quin)	0
Extras	(b2, lb7)	9	(b3, lb2, nb2)	7
Total	(90.5 overs, 322 mins)	295	(49.0 overs, 187 mins)	219

NEW SOUTH WALES	O	M	R	W	w,nb	O	M	R	W	w,nb					
Cooper	30	3	128	6	-,-	14	2	50	1	-,-					
McGilvray	16	2	49	2	-,-	11.5	1	39	3	-,-					
White	30.2	14	51	2	-,-	22	7	51	4	-,-					
Howell	23	3	76	0	-,-	24	4	65	2	-,-					
Mudge	20	2	85	0	-,-										

											FALL OF WICKETS				
										Wkt	VIC	NSW	VIC	NSW
											1st	1st	2nd	2nd
VICTORIA	O	M	R	W	w,nb	O	M	R	W	w,nb	1st	21	54	27	12
Ebeling	21	3	48	1	-,-	18	2	60	2	-,-	2nd	109	87	67	46
Britt	15	4	44	1	-,-	9	1	50	2	-,-	3rd	180	103	148	47
Plant	11	2	31	2	-,-	9	1	34	1	-,-	4th	183	108	150	154
Smith	17.5	3	73	4	-,-	3	0	24	0	-,-	5th	228	126	170	182
Welch	26	5	90	2	-,-	10	1	44	4	-,2	6th	247	222	185	189
											7th	274	235	200	190
											8th	346	245	202	204
											9th	362	270	208	219
											10th	392	295	210	219

SOUTH AUSTRALIA v QUEENSLAND (Shield Match 5)

Played at Adelaide Oval on December 24, 26, 27, 28, 1935. (Four-day match)
Toss : South Australia.   Result : SOUTH AUSTRALIA WON BY AN INNINGS AND 226 RUNS.
Debuts: Nil.
12th Men: R.G.Williams (SA) and E.C.Bensted (Qld).
Umpires: R.A.Nelson and J.D.Scott.
Attendances: 9618, 8156, 2667, 2990.   Total: 23,431.   Receipts: £983.
Close of Play: 1st day SA 5/464 (Waite 19, Ryan 16); 2nd day Qld 8/115 (Christy 16); 3rd day Qld (2) 6/259 (Hansen 76).

Badcock (91 in 169 minutes, 9 fours) and Bradman (233 in 191 minutes, 1 six and 28 fours) added 183 in 135 minutes, Bradman and Walker (71 in 134 minutes, 5 fours) 159 in 90 minutes, and Waite (99 in 206 minutes, 6 fours) and Ryan (72 in 99 minutes, 5 fours) 131 in 99 minutes as South Australia ran up their second total of more than 600 in as many matches against Queensland. Bradman, who took his score from 43 to 200 in the two-hour lunch-tea session (2.00-4.00) on the first day, went from 150 to 200 in 14 minutes and completed 200 in 168 minutes - his third successive double century against Queensland, an unequalled feat against one State by any batsman. His only blemish was a stumping chance off Levy when 219. Allen (54 in 125 minutes, 2 sixes and 7 fours), Hansen (80 in 152 minutes, 5 fours, 3 chances) and Tallon (88 in 118 minutes, 10 fours) scored half-centuries for Queensland, who omitted Bensted from their side due to a leg strain he sustained in the previous match at Melbourne. Levy's pair included a first-ball duck in the first, and possibly second, innings. *Wisden* omits c sub from Qld (2) dismissal of Hansen. Sources: *Wisden, QCA Report, SACA Report, Brisbane Courier-Mail, Adelaide Advertiser.*

SOUTH AUSTRALIA

C.L.Badcock	c Tallon b Gilbert	91
R.A.Parker	c Levy b Fisher	10
*D.G.Bradman	c Tallon b Levy	233
†C.W.Walker	c Andrews b Fisher	71
E.J.R.Moyle	b Levy	13
M.G.Waite	lbw b Cook	99
A.J.Ryan	b Christy	72
T.R.O'Connell	c Honour b Gilbert	41
F.H.K.Collins	not out	0
F.A.Ward	) did not bat	
T.W.Wall	)	
Extras	(b7, lb3, w1, nb1)	12
Total	(134.5 overs, 483 mins) (8 wkts dec)	642

QUEENSLAND

T.Allen	c Ward b Waite	54		st Walker b Ward	30
G.G.Cook	b Wall	2		b Collins	34
W.C.Andrews	c & b Ward	12		b Collins	10
V.G.Honour	b Ward	17	(8)	lbw b Collins	1
C.D.Hansen	b O'Connell	2		c sub (R.G.Williams) b Ward	80
*D.Tallon	c Walker b Waite	2		c Bradman b Wall	88
†R.M.Levy	c Bradman b Waite	0		c Walker b Wall	0
J.A.J.Christy	not out	19	(4)	run out (Wall/Walker)	10
A.Fisher	b Wall	3		lbw b Ward	18
E.Gilbert	b Wall	4		b Collins	0
E.R.Wyeth	c Walker b Collins	4		not out	6
Extras	(b1, lb7)	8		(b4, lb8)	12
Total	(49.4 overs, 175 mins)	127		(93.2 overs, 316 mins)	289

QUEENSLAND	O	M	R	W	w,nb
Gilbert	27.5	1	121	2	-,-
Cook	29	3	108	1	-,-
Fisher	20	2	103	2	1,-
Wyeth	20	2	98	0	-,-
Allen	7	0	52	0	-,1
Levy	19	0	116	2	-,-
Christy	11	2	24	1	-,-
Andrews	1	0	8	0	-,-

SOUTH AUSTRALIA	O	M	R	W	w,nb		O	M	R	W	w,nb
Wall	9	2	13	3	-,-		10	1	24	2	-,-
O'Connell	8	5	7	1	-,-		17	3	44	0	-,-
Ward	13	5	40	2	-,-	(4)	25.2	3	95	3	-,-
Collins	9.4	1	23	1	-,-	(3)	18	5	41	4	-,-
Ryan	5	2	7	0	-,-		10	4	17	0	-,-
Waite	5	0	29	3	-,-		13	2	56	0	-,-

FALL OF WICKETS

Wkt	SA 1st	QLD 1st	QLD 2nd
1st	32	5	57
2nd	215	26	76
3rd	374	72	85
4th	404	93	100
5th	437	95	259
6th	568	95	259
7th	640	100	265
8th	642	115	271
9th	-	120	271
10th	-	127	289

TASMANIA v VICTORIA

Played at N.T.C.A. Ground, Launceston, on December 31, 1935, January 1, 2, 1936. (Three-day match)
Toss : Victoria.   Result : TASMANIA WON BY SIX WICKETS.
Debuts: Victoria - V.K.Brown, R.Gardner, I.W.Johnson, H.J.Kroger, R.B.Scott, F.J.Watmuff, W.Y.Wilson, L.A.Wynne, H.Zachariah (all f/c).
12th Men: R.A.Ferrall (Tas) and A.Jinks(Vic).
Umpires: A.W.Beaumont and W.R.Boscoe.
Attendances: No daily figures published.   Total: About 700.   Receipts: £36.
Close of Play: 1st day Tas 2/119 (Smith 57, Ward 34); 2nd day Vic (2) 3/144 (Ledward 42, Johnson 22).

Newstead, Watmuff and Wilson replaced C.W.Welch (transferred to Shield team), I.D.Miller and J.Thomas (both unavailable) in the visitor's line-up. Nine Victorians consequently were given their first-class debuts in this match. Gardner (45 in 72 minutes, 7 fours), Johnson (34 in 51 minutes, 5 fours) and Kroger (36 in 43 minutes, 3 fours) top-scored for Victoria on the first day. Smith (90 in 191 minutes, 6 fours) scored his best-ever innings for Tasmania, Ward (39 in 75 minutes, 2 fours), Rushforth (36 in 90 minutes, 4 fours) and Jeffery (72 in 125 minutes, 10 fours) helping the side to a lead of 90 runs. Wynne (43 in 85 minutes, 2 fours), Gardner (32 in 45 minutes, 5 fours) and Ledward (44 in 80 minutes, 3 fours) top-scored in the second innings for Victoria. Set 123 for victory in just under three hours, Tasmania won with 45 minutes to spare thanks to Pearsall (56 in 105 minutes, 9 fours) who reached his highest score in seven matches for the State. Sources: *NTCA Report, VCA Report, Hobart Mercury, Launceston Examiner.*

VICTORIA

L.A.Wynne	lbw b Jeffery	28		c Rushforth b Ward	43
R.Gardner	lbw b Jeffery	45		c Rushforth b Putman	32
*G.H.Newstead	lbw b Putman	20		run out (Jeffery)	1
J.A.Ledward	lbw b Walsh	30		c Pickett b Putman	44
V.K.Brown	b Putman	19	(6)	b Walsh	1
W.Y.Wilson	b Putman	10	(7)	c Thomas b Walsh	12
I.W.Johnson	c Sankey b Thomas	34	(5)	c Pickett b Walsh	26
†H.J.Kroger	c Pearsall b James	36		c Ward b Walsh	9
R.B.Scott	c Ward b James	15		lbw b James	12
H.Zachariah	not out	2	(11)	c Rushforth b Putman	4
F.J.Watmuff	run out (Sankey/Pickett)	0	(10)	not out	23
Extras	(lb1)	1		(b3, lb1, nb1)	5
Total	(53.6 overs, 215 mins)	240		(50.5 overs, 206 mins)	212

TASMANIA

A.L.Pearsall	b Wilson	2		b Wilson	56
R.V.Thomas	c Brown b Watmuff	11		lbw b Johnson	14
E.H.Smith	b Watmuff	90		st Kroger b Johnson	1
R.E.Ward	c Zachariah b Johnson	39		b Watmuff	1
S.W.L.Putman	c Zachariah b Wilson	27	(6)	not out	21
*A.W.Rushforth	b Scott	36			
C.L.Jeffery	b Zachariah	72			
†E.A.Pickett	lbw b Johnson	7			
C.J.Sankey	c Wilson b Zachariah	12	(5)	not out	27
G.T.H.James	c Zachariah b Brown	9			
J.M.Walsh	not out	2			
Extras	(b7, lb13, nb3)	23		(b1, lb2)	3
Total	(88.5 overs, 370 mins)	330		(35.0 overs, 132 mins) (4 wkts)	123

TASMANIA	O	M	R	W	w,nb		O	M	R	W	w,nb
Walsh	13	3	50	1	-,-		15	2	47	4	-,1
Thomas	8	1	37	1	-,-		6	0	26	0	-,-
James	12.6	1	52	2	-,-	(5)	8	0	26	1	-,-
Jeffery	10	2	31	2	-,-	(3)	2	0	14	0	-,-
Putman	10	0	69	3	-,-	(4)	15.5	0	80	3	-,-
Ward							4	0	14	1	-,-

VICTORIA	O	M	R	W	w,nb		O	M	R	W	w,nb
Scott	15	4	37	1	-,2		5	1	17	0	-,-
Zachariah	22	5	72	2	-,1		5	1	23	0	-,-
Wilson	17	3	60	2	-,-	(6)	6	1	22	1	-,-
Watmuff	12	0	73	2	-,-	(3)	5	1	20	1	-,-
Johnson	13	2	39	2	-,-	(4)	12	3	24	2	-,-
Ledward	6	2	9	0	-,-	(5)	2	0	14	0	-,-
Brown	3.5	0	17	1	-,-						

FALL OF WICKETS

Wkt	VIC 1st	TAS 1st	VIC 2nd	TAS 2nd
1st	71	15	55	41
2nd	78	33	56	43
3rd	108	127	105	54
4th	142	178	146	84
5th	144	205	149	-
6th	158	244	156	-
7th	222	271	168	-
8th	224	315	175	-
9th	240	326	199	-
10th	240	330	212	-

NEW SOUTH WALES v QUEENSLAND (Shield Match 6)

Played at Sydney Cricket Ground on January 1, 2, 3, 4, 1936. (Four-day match)
Toss : New South Wales.   Result : NEW SOUTH WALES WON BY 182 RUNS.
Debuts: New South Wales - L.C.Hynes (f/c).
12th Men: G.C.Horsfield (NSW) and H.K.Thomsett (Qld).
Umpires: E.G.Borwick and A.L.Christie.
Attendances: 6111, 3138, 2938, 2425.   Total: 14,612.   Receipts: £689.
Close of Play: 1st day NSW 366 all out; 2nd day Qld 8/330 (Christy 43); 3rd day NSW (2) 9/376 (Cooper 0).

Gilbert, no-balled by Borwick on the third day for intimidatory bowling and further warned that he faced debarment if his tactics persisted, caused the retirements of Mudge at approximately 1/40 and Robinson (5) at 2/108, both with hand injuries. Robinson returned at 3/198 but the inability of Mudge to resume on the fourth day ended the innings at the overnight score. Marks (201 in 255 minutes, 2 fives and 24 fours) scored his runs out of 286 while he was at the crease, falling to the last ball of the third day. He had been bowled by a Christy no-ball when 91, attempting a big hit after hearing the umpire's call. Half-centuries for New South Wales were scored by Mudge (94 in 199 minutes, 2 fours), Robinson (67 in 68 minutes, 10 fours) and McGilvray (62 in 98 minutes, 4 fours). Andrews (118 in 205 minutes, 10 fours), Tallon (51 in 52 minutes, 8 fours) and Christy (51 not out in 107 minutes, 3 fours) top-scored for the visitors. Hynes replaced A.R.Lonergan (gastritis) in the New South Wales team. Sources: *Wisden, NSWCA Report, QCA Report, The Age, Sydney Morning Herald, Brisbane Courier-Mail, The Sporting Globe.*

NEW SOUTH WALES

L.J.Fallowfield	run out (Andrews/Tallon)	37	c Tallon b Cook	12
H.Mudge	c Levy b Cook	94	retired hurt	12
R.C.J.Little	b Allen	20	b Gilbert	24
A.E.Marks	c Christy b Wyeth	21	b Levy	201
R.H.Robinson	c Cook b Gilbert	67	c Christy b Gilbert	11
L.C.Hynes	lbw b Cook	2	c Honour b Allen	36
*A.D.McGilvray	c Levy b Gilbert	62	b Gilbert	1
†F.A.Easton	c sub (H.K.Thomsett) b Cook	23	b Levy	40
E.C.S.White	c Gilbert b Wyeth	22	c Christy b Wyeth	23
H.C.Chilvers	not out	1	b Wyeth	3
A.F.Cooper	c Allen b Cook	1	not out	0
Extras	(b8, lb3, w3, nb2)	16	(b4, lb7, w1, nb1)	13
Total	(85.2 overs, 321 mins)	366	(71.5 overs, 294 mins)	376

QUEENSLAND

T.Allen	b White	17	st Easton b Chilvers	28
G.G.Cook	c Little b Chilvers	18	b Hynes	21
W.C.Andrews	c Little b Hynes	118	b Cooper	38
V.G.Honour	c Little b White	30	c Easton b Chilvers	34
C.D.Hansen	b Mudge	1	(7) not out	22
†D.Tallon	c White b Cooper	51	c Easton b Chilvers	9
J.A.J.Christy	not out	51	(5) st Easton b Chilvers	29
*R.M.Levy	c Easton b Hynes	5	c Chilvers b Hynes	14
A.Fisher	b McGilvray	26	b McGilvray	0
E.R.Wyeth	b Cooper	6	(11) b Hynes	0
E.Gilbert	b Cooper	0	(10) lbw b Hynes	7
Extras	(b10, lb10, w1)	21	(b6, lb5, nb3)	14
Total	(104.4 overs, 348 mins)	344	(72.3 overs, 256 mins)	216

QUEENSLAND	O	M	R	W	w,nb		O	M	R	W	w,nb
Gilbert	24	1	98	2	-,-		20	1	113	3	1,-
Cook	27.2	3	101	4	1,2		13	1	56	1	-,-
Fisher	8	0	37	0	1,-		7	0	42	0	-,-
Wyeth	19	1	73	2	-,-		15	1	54	2	-,-
Allen	7	0	41	1	1,-		4	0	37	1	-,-
Christy							5	0	16	0	-,1
Levy							7.5	0	45	2	-,-

NEW SOUTH WALES	O	M	R	W	w,nb		O	M	R	W	w,nb
Cooper	19.4	1	66	3	-,-		14	1	35	1	-,3
McGilvray	23	6	69	1	1,-		7	0	18	1	-,-
White	26	16	28	2	-,-		7	6	3	0	-,-
Chilvers	23	2	104	1	-,-		24	2	78	4	-,-
Mudge	6	0	30	1	-,-						
Hynes	7	0	26	2	-,-	(5)	15.3	1	43	4	-,-
Robinson						(6)	5	0	25	0	-,-

FALL OF WICKETS

Wkt	NSW 1st	QLD 1st	NSW 2nd	QLD 2nd
1st	96	38	21	34
2nd	127	56	90	79
3rd	160	122	198	106
4th	231	133	211	144
5th	252	224	215	161
6th	256	275	311	171
7th	297	287	362	204
8th	355	330	376	205
9th	365	339	376	216
10th	366	344	-	216

VICTORIA v SOUTH AUSTRALIA (Shield Match 7)

Played at Melbourne Cricket Ground on January 1, 2, 3, 4, 1936. (Four-day match)
Toss : South Australia.   Result : MATCH DRAWN.
Debuts: South Australia - A.F.Richter (f/c).
12th Men: A.L.Hassett (Vic) and R.G.Williams (SA).
Umpires: A.N.Barlow and C.Dwyer.
Attendances: 23,456, 16035, 3488, 4450.   Total: 47,429.   Receipts: £2125.
Close of Play: 1st day SA 5/349 (Bradman 229, O'Connell 8); 2nd day Vic 3/124 (Scaife 17, Nagel 0); 3rd day Vic 9/310 (Welch 0, Ebeling 0).

Bradman's fifth treble-century in first-class cricket (357 in 421 minutes, 40 fours) was the highest score ever made against Victoria. It was his third Shield innings for South Australia and followed scores of 117 and 233 in his previous innings. He went from 60 at lunch on the first day to 143 at tea and 229 at stumps, and raced to 338 at lunch on the following day (109 in 105-minute session) before falling shortly afterwards, without offering a chance. His milestones were 50 in 70, 100 in 152, 150 in 222, 200 in 267, 250 in 328, 300 in 399 and 350 in 413 minutes. Parker (63 in 187 minutes, 6 fours) was the only other batsman in the side to exceed 50, the captain's innings forming a remarkable 62.7 per cent of the total. Rigg, dismissed second ball in Victoria's first innings, atoned in the second innings (124 in 230 minutes, 7 fours). Quin (52 in 87 minutes, 6 fours and 47 in 128 minutes, 0 fours), Lee (50 in 148 minutes, 2 fours), Scaife (48 in 146 minutes, 3 fours), Gregory (80 in 193 minutes, 8 fours) and Plant (42 in 90 minutes, 5 fours) made other scores of note. C.L.Badcock (injured hand) was unable to play for South Australia. Victoria were handicapped by the loss of H.I.Ebeling (strained muscle in side) early on the first day. He was unable to field again and Rigg led the side. Sources: *Wisden, VCA Report, SACA Report, The Age, The Argus, The Herald, Sydney Morning Herald.*

SOUTH AUSTRALIA

A.J.Ryan	run out (Bromley/Quin)	7
R.A.Parker	c Rigg b Welch	63
*D.G.Bradman	c Quin b Bromley	357
E.J.R.Moyle	c Quin b Welch	9
M.G.Waite	b Gregory	24
A.F.Richter	c Smith b Welch	7
T.R.O'Connell	c Quin b Plant	22
†C.W.Walker	lbw b Welch	8
F.H.K.Collins	not out	37
F.A.Ward	st Quin b Welch	29
T.W.Wall	lbw b Smith	0
Extras	(lb4, nb2)	6
Total	(128.1 overs, 492 mins)	569

VICTORIA

K.E.Rigg	lbw b Wall	0		c Ryan b O'Connell	124
†S.O.Quin	b Ryan	52		c Bradman b O'Connell	47
I.S.Lee	c & b Waite	50		run out (Bradman/Waite)	14
J.W.Scaife	b Wall	48		c Wall b O'Connell	25
V.G.Nagel	st Walker b Ward	0			
E.H.Bromley	c Waite b Ryan	1	(5)	c Walker b Wall	2
R.G.Gregory	lbw b Ward	80	(6)	not out	18
H.J.Plant	c Ryan b Waite	42	(7)	not out	16
S.A.J.Smith	c Walker b Wall	22			
C.W.Welch	c Ryan b Wall	1			
*H.I.Ebeling	not out	1			
Extras	(b3, lb13)	16		(b1, lb3)	4
Total	(109.2 overs, 398 mins)	313		(84.0 overs, 288 mins) (5 wkts)	250

VICTORIA	O	M	R	W	w,nb
Ebeling	4	1	9	0	-,-
Nagel	25	5	85	0	-,2
Plant	27	2	86	1	-,-
Smith	14.1	2	56	1	-,-
Welch	25	1	155	5	-,-
Gregory	19	1	101	1	-,-
Bromley	14	2	71	1	-,-

SOUTH AUSTRALIA	O	M	R	W	w,nb		O	M	R	W	w,nb
Wall	25.2	4	77	4	-,-		9	0	15	1	-,-
O'Connell	11	1	33	0	-,-		15	2	42	3	-,-
Collins	13	2	24	0	-,-		28	2	66	0	-,-
Waite	14	3	45	2	-,-	(5)	9	1	30	0	-,-
Ward	25	6	77	2	-,-	(7)	5	0	29	0	-,-
Ryan	18	8	26	2	-,-	(4)	4	1	6	0	-,-
Richter	3	0	15	0	-,-	(6)	13	0	58	0	-,-
Bradman							1	1	0	0	-,-

FALL OF WICKETS

Wkt	SA 1st	VIC 1st	VIC 2nd
1st	8	0	111
2nd	186	83	159
3rd	211	123	206
4th	276	125	213
5th	323	126	219
6th	421	180	-
7th	471	269	-
8th	510	306	-
9th	564	310	-
10th	569	313	-

TASMANIA v VICTORIA

Played at T.C.A. Ground, Hobart, on January 3, 4, 6, 1936. (Three-day match)
Toss : Victoria. Result : TASMANIA WON BY ONE WICKET.
Debuts: Tasmania - J.Gardiner (f/c). Victoria - A.Jinks (f/c).
12th Men: V.K.Brown (Vic). None named for Tas.
Umpires: A.J.Buttsworth and M.Hansen.
Attendances: No daily figures published. Total: About 500. Receipts: £27.
Close of Play: 1st day Vic 8/296 (Ledward 114, Scott 9); 2nd day Tas 7/199 (Rushforth 9, Gardiner 11).

This match was scheduled to commence on December 26th, prior to the Launceston game, but a shipping strike forced a rearrangement of the program. Burrows, originally named 12th man, was a late replacement for C.L.Jeffery who withdrew from the Tasmanian team at the last minute. Ledward's best-ever 154 for Victoria (230 minutes, 18 fours) included a chance in the 60s. With Scott (26 in 81 minutes) he shared an important ninth-wicket stand of 101 to bolster the total. Newstead (53 in 90 minutes) and Wilson (33 in 69 minutes) made other scores. For Tasmania, Pearsall (43 in 147 minutes) and M.J.Combes (70 in 130 minutes, 4 fours) established a first-wicket partnership of 123, while Rushforth (57 in 150 minutes, 8 fours) and Gardiner (39 in 90 minutes, 4 fours) added a further 76 for the eighth wicket. Tasmania's victory target was 160 in 110 minutes; with one hour remaining 110 runs were still required. When the last batsman, G.A.Combes, came to the crease 8 runs were needed in 8 minutes. When Zachariah commenced the final over, 5 runs were needed. Four singles were taken from the first six deliveries, Combes then hitting the seventh ball to the square-leg boundary to give Tasmania victory by the slenderest margin with one ball to spare. A long drought set in after this match, Tasmania winning only one further first-class match in the next 41 years, against Victoria in January 1954, until their defeat of an Indian XI in December 1977. Sources: *TCA Report, VCA Report, Hobart Mercury, The Argus.*

VICTORIA

L.A.Wynne	c Putman b Walsh	13	not out	47
*G.H.Newstead	st Gardiner b Putman	53		
R.Gardner	c Putman b Walsh	31	(2) b G.A.Combes	19
J.A.Ledward	c & b G.A.Combes	154	not out	3
I.W.Johnson	c Walsh b G.A.Combes	15		
W.Y.Wilson	c Gardiner b James	33	(3) b G.A.Combes	20
A.Jinks	lbw b Walsh	2		
†H.J.Kroger	b James	19		
F.J.Watmuff	b James	2		
R.B.Scott	c James b G.A.Combes	26		
H.Zachariah	not out	1		
Extras	(b13, lb1)	14	(b4, lb3)	7
Total	(80.0 overs, 292 mins)	363	(23.0 overs, 78 mins) (2 wkts dec)	96

TASMANIA

A.L.Pearsall	c sub (V.K.Brown) b Scott	43	b Zachariah	28
M.J.Combes	run out (Gardner)	70	c Ledward b Johnson	22
E.H.Smith	c Jinks b Zachariah	6	(4) run out (Newstead/Kroger)	21
A.O.Burrows	lbw b Johnson	25	(8) st Kroger b Zachariah	2
S.W.L.Putman	c Watmuff b Johnson	16	(6) run out (Wilson/Kroger)	29
*A.W.Rushforth	c & b Zachariah	57	(7) b Watmuff	12
R.V.Thomas	c & b Zachariah	3	(3) run out (Ledward/Kroger)	0
G.T.H.James	run out (Jinks/Kroger)	3	(5) c Newstead b Watmuff	27
†J.Gardiner	st Kroger b Johnson	39	st Kroger b Wilson	5
J.M.Walsh	st Kroger b Zachariah	14	not out	3
G.A.Combes	not out	1	not out	8
Extras	(b13, lb10)	23	(b5, lb1)	6
Total	(94.0 overs, 351 mins)	300	(27.7 overs, 110 mins) (9 wkts)	163

TASMANIA	O	M	R	W	w,nb	O	M	R	W	w,nb
Walsh	22	0	119	3	-,-	5	0	24	0	-,-
Burrows	3	0	13	0	-,-					
James	21	0	83	3	-,-	(2) 11	0	41	0	-,-
Putman	12	0	56	1	-,-					
Thomas	9	1	36	0	-,-					
G.A.Combes	13	2	42	3	-,-	(3) 7	0	24	2	-,-

VICTORIA	O	M	R	W	w,nb	O	M	R	W	w,nb
Scott	26	5	67	1	-,-	6	0	19	0	-,-
Zachariah	27	3	83	4	-,-	(3) 6.7	0	59	2	-,-
Jinks	9	2	22	0	-,-					
Wilson	14	3	41	0	-,-	(2) 6	0	23	1	-,-
Johnson	14	1	40	3	-,-	(4) 5	0	27	1	-,-
Watmuff	4	0	24	0	-,-	(5) 4	1	29	2	-,-

FALL OF WICKETS

Wkt	VIC 1st	TAS 1st	VIC 2nd	TAS 2nd
1st	24	123	54	40
2nd	82	130	86	40
3rd	118	132	-	73
4th	142	172	-	73
5th	209	174	-	111
6th	212	177	-	137
7th	247	180	-	147
8th	253	256	-	151
9th	354	299	-	152
10th	363	300	-	-

QUEENSLAND v SOUTH AUSTRALIA (Shield Match 8)

Played at Brisbane Cricket Ground (Woolloongabba) on January 10, 11, 13, 14, 1936. (Four-day match)
Toss : South Australia.   Result : SOUTH AUSTRALIA WON BY TEN WICKETS.
Debuts: Queensland - G.D.Gunthorpe, A.H.Muhl, R.E.Rogers, H.K.Thomsett (all f/c).
12th Men: A.Fisher (Qld) and A.F.Richter (SA).
Umpires: J.Bartlett and J.A.Scott.
Attendances: 3892, 15716, 2032, 1016.   Total: 22,656.   Receipts: £1792.
Close of Play: 1st day Qld 4/136 (Hansen 19, Honour 11); 2nd day SA 5/245 (Ryan 119. O'Connell 9); 3rd day Qld (2) 1/24 (Allen 9).

Queensland were inserted on a damp pitch after rain had penetrated the tarpaulin covers and delayed the start until 2.00pm. Rogers on debut (39 in 88 minutes, 2 fours) top-scored for Queensland with support from Andrews (30 in 126 minutes, 3 fours) and Honour (32 in 97 minutes, 3 fours). Gilbert's 22 took 15 minutes and had 4 fours. Ryan (144 in 284 minutes, 1 six and 11 fours) held the South Australian innings together against some very fast bowling from Gilbert (5 for 87), Bradman (31 in 47 minutes, 4 fours), Waite (41 in 73 minutes, 3 fours) and O'Connell (36 in 96 minutes, 5 fours) helping to create a substantial lead. Hansen (35 in 80 minutes, 3 fours) and Gunthorpe (46 in 75 minutes, 6 fours) top-scored when Queensland batted a second time. E.C.Bensted (injured thumb), G.G.Cook and R.M.Levy were unavailable for Queensland, while Gunthorpe was a late replacement for D.Tallon (injured leg). *Wisden* incorrectly gives Qld (2) Allen lbw b Wall, Andrews c Waite b Ward. Sources: *Wisden, QCA Report, SACA Report, Sydney Morning Herald, Brisbane Courier-Mail, Brisbane Telegraph.*

QUEENSLAND

T.Allen	b Wall	2	lbw b Ward	12
R.E.Rogers	b Ward	39	b Williams	14
W.C.Andrews	c Moyle b Ward	30	c Waite b Wall	4
*J.A.J.Christy	c & b Waite	24	c Waite b Ward	15
C.D.Hansen	c Wall b Waite	23	c Moyle b Waite	35
V.G.Honour	st Walker b Ward	32	st Walker b Ward	4
H.K.Thomsett	lbw b Waite	9	c O'Connell b Waite	13
†G.D.Gunthorpe	lbw b Ryan	9	c Moyle b Waite	46
A.H.Muhl	c Walker b Wall	1	run out	16
E.R.Wyeth	b Ward	2	c Walker b Ryan	0
E.Gilbert	not out	22	not out	0
Extras	(b2, lb8, nb2)	12	(b2, nb2)	4
Total	(83.0 overs, 310 mins)	205	(59.1 overs, 220 mins)	163

SOUTH AUSTRALIA

C.L.Badcock	b Thomsett	16	not out	16
R.A.Parker	c Allen b Gilbert	1	not out	12
A.J.Ryan	lbw b Wyeth	144		
*D.G.Bradman	c Wyeth b Gilbert	31		
E.J.R.Moyle	c Hansen b Gilbert	21		
M.G.Waite	c Rogers b Muhl	41		
T.R.O'Connell	c Gunthorpe b Gilbert	36		
†C.W.Walker	b Wyeth	0		
R.G.Williams	c Wyeth b Gilbert	23		
F.A.Ward	lbw b Wyeth	12		
T.W.Wall	not out	7		
Extras	(b5, lb2, nb1)	8	(lb1)	1
Total	(103.2 overs, 345 mins)	340	(9.0 overs, 27 mins) (0 wkts)	29

SOUTH AUSTRALIA	O	M	R	W	w,nb		O	M	R	W	w,nb		FALL OF WICKETS			
														QLD	SA	QLD	SA
Wall	15	6	23	2	-,-		13	2	40	1	-,-	Wkt	1st	1st	2nd	2nd
Williams	17	3	30	0	-,2		8	1	25	1	-,2	1st	8	5	24	-
O'Connell	5	0	10	0	-,-		5	2	9	0	-,-	2nd	61	38	31	-
Ryan	15	6	33	1	-,-	(6)	5	3	5	1	-,-	3rd	91	94	31	-
Waite	17	1	45	3	-,-		13.1	0	44	3	-,-	4th	114	150	58	-
Ward	14	3	52	4	-,-	(4)	15	5	36	3	-,-	5th	147	235	65	-
												6th	161	296	99	-
QUEENSLAND	O	M	R	W	w,nb		O	M	R	W	w,nb	7th	180	296	102	-
Gilbert	29	6	87	5	-,-		3	1	11	0	-,-	8th	180	300	163	-
Andrews	5	0	25	0	-,-		3	0	9	0	-,-	9th	183	321	163	-
Wyeth	31.2	9	101	3	-,-							10th	205	340	163	-
Thomsett	7	0	26	1	-,-											
Christy	6	0	9	0	-,1											
Muhl	15	3	48	1	-,-	(3)	2	0	6	0	-,-					
Allen	10	0	36	0	-,-	(4)	1	0	2	0	-,-					

NEW SOUTH WALES v SOUTH AUSTRALIA (Shield Match 9)

Played at Sydney Cricket Ground on January 17 (no play), 18, 20, 21 (no play), 1936. (Four-day match)
Toss : New South Wales.   Result : MATCH DRAWN.
Debuts: Nil.
12th Men: G.C.Horsfield (NSW) and A.F.Richter (SA).
Umpires: H.J.Armstrong and E.G.Borwick.
Attendances: no play, 11101, 7615, no play.   Total: 18,716.   Receipts: £1074.
Close of Play: 1st day no play; 2nd day NSW 0/14 (Fallowfield 8, Mudge 6); 3rd day NSW 6/286 (Robinson 94, White 27).

A storm on Thursday - the day before the scheduled start - soaked the pitch (despite tarpaulins covering it) and caused the abandonment of the first day's play. Further rain hindered the drying of the wicket which was badly affected at one end, and New South Wales sent the visitors in when the game commenced after lunch on the second day. Parker and Badcock kept the bowling at bay until White was introduced. The left-armer's career-best of 8 for 31 contained a spell of 4 for 0, including the wickets of Ryan and Waite in his first over after tea. Bradman was caught at leg slip from the eighth ball he received. Robinson (94 not out in 177 minutes, 13 fours) was deprived of a likely hundred when the last day's play was called off following news of the death of King George V, Fallowfield (53 in 186 minutes, 4 fours), Little (30 in 75 minutes, 2 fours) and Hynes (41 in 92 minutes, 1 six and 5 fours) also batted well for New South Wales. Both captains achieved run outs by throwing the stumps down. Illogically, each side was awarded two points because New South Wales had not completed their innings. A.R.Lonergan (ill) was unavailable for the locals. Sources: *Wisden, NSWCA Report, SACA Report, The Age, The Herald, Sydney Morning Herald, NSWCA Scorebook.*

SOUTH AUSTRALIA

R.A.Parker	c McGilvray b White	14
C.L.Badcock	c McGilvray b White	24
*D.G.Bradman	c Little b Hynes	0
A.J.Ryan	c Little b White	2
T.R.O'Connell	c Marks b White	13
M.G.Waite	c Marks b White	0
E.J.R.Moyle	b White	5
†C.W.Walker	c Robinson b White	7
R.G.Williams	not out	10
F.A.Ward	c Mudge b White	12
T.W.Wall	run out (McGilvray)	0
Extras	(b2, lb2, w1, nb2)	7
Total	(46.3 overs, 175 mins)	94

NEW SOUTH WALES

L.J.Fallowfield	c Williams b Ward	53
H.Mudge	lbw b Wall	8
R.C.J.Little	c Walker b Ward	30
A.E.Marks	lbw b Ward	25
R.H.Robinson	not out	94
L.C.Hynes	run out (Bradman)	41
†F.A.Easton	c Walker b Williams	1
E.C.S.White	not out	27
*A.D.McGilvray	)	
H.C.Chilvers	) did not bat	
A.F.Cooper	)	
Extras	(lb3, nb4)	7
Total	(96.0 overs, 350 mins) (6 wkts)	286

NEW SOUTH WALES	O	M	R	W	w,nb
Cooper	9	3	11	0	1,2
McGilvray	4	0	11	0	-,-
Hynes	11.3	2	25	1	-,-
White	19	8	31	8	-,-
Chilvers	3	0	9	0	-,-

SOUTH AUSTRALIA	O	M	R	W	w,nb
Wall	15	2	58	1	-,-
Williams	17	5	34	1	-,4
O'Connell	15	1	60	0	-,-
Ward	18	1	57	3	-,-
Ryan	23	12	41	0	-,-
Waite	8	1	29	0	-,-

FALL OF WICKETS

	SA	NSW
Wkt	1st	1st
1st	34	20
2nd	39	79
3rd	39	115
4th	44	124
5th	44	220
6th	60	223
7th	68	-
8th	73	-
9th	92	-
10th	94	-

NEW SOUTH WALES v VICTORIA (Shield Match 10)

Played at Sydney Cricket Ground on January 25, 27, 29, 30, 1936. (Four-day match)
Toss : New South Wales.　　　　Result : NEW SOUTH WALES WON BY 26 RUNS.
Debuts: Nil.
12th Men: N.K.Miller (NSW) and G.H.Newstead (Vic.).
Umpires: E.G.Borwick and A.L.Christie.
Attendances: 7737, 8380, 1250, 1003.　　　Total: 18,370.　　　Receipts: £933.
Close of Play: 1st day NSW 9/323 (Chilvers 36, Cooper 17); 2nd day NSW (2) 0/84 (Fallowfield 45, Mudge 39); 3rd day Vic (2) 0/34 (Rigg 24, Quin 7).

Victoria were able to field only ten fit men on the first day because E.H.Bromley and J.A.Ledward had both contracted tonsillitis, Ledward going to hospital. Hassett and Newstead were sent for as replacements but did not arrive from Melbourne until the second morning. H.E.Withers (Mosman) fielded as substitute and A.Ward (Randwick) acted as 12th man on the first day. Mudge (76 in 143 minutes, 6 fours) and Easton (50 in 111 minutes, 5 fours) in the first innings and Fallowfield (63 in 133 minutes, 4 fours) and Robinson (94 in 112 minutes, 1 six and 9 fours) in the second scored half-centuries for New South Wales. Hynes dismissed Rigg (68 in 166 minutes, 2 fours) and Plant in his second over and Smith and Ebeling in his third to capture 4 for 2; he took 6 for 14 in his last 8 overs. Second-innings fifties from Rigg (54 in 99 minutes, 4 fours), Lee (85 in 147 minutes, 1 five and 8 fours), Scaife (70 in 119 minutes, 8 fours) and Hassett (51 in 100 minutes, 1 five and 1 four) gave Victoria their highest fourth-innings total at Sydney but could not prevent a New South Wales victory with 16 minutes to spare. Rearrangement of the match dates before the start ensured that January 28th, a Tuesday, would not be used as a mark of respect for the funeral of King George V. All sources except *NSWCA Scorebook* and *NSWCA Report* incorrectly give NSW (1) Chilvers 36*, Cooper 19. Sources: *Wisden, NSWCA Report, VCA Report, The Age, The Herald, Sydney Morning Herald, NSWCA Scorebook, The Sporting Globe.*

NEW SOUTH WALES

L.J.Fallowfield	b Ebeling	17	b Plant		63
H.Mudge	c Plant b Welch	76	b Scott		39
R.C.J.Little	c Lee b Ebeling	4	lbw b Plant		36
A.E.Marks	lbw b Ebeling	0	c Gregory b Plant		4
R.H.Robinson	c Quin b Welch	24	c Plant b Scott		94
L.C.Hynes	c & b Welch	23	b Scott		0
*A.D.McGilvray	c Plant b Scott	34	c Quin b Ebeling		14
†F.A.Easton	run out (Rigg/Welch)	50	b Ebeling		23
E.C.S.White	b Plant	27	b Ebeling		4
H.C.Chilvers	not out	38	not out		1
A.F.Cooper	run out (Smith/Rigg)	17			
Extras	(b11, lb3, w1)	15	(b2, lb1)		3
Total	(84.2 overs, 326 mins)	325	(63.1 overs, 247 mins) (9 wkts dec)		281

VICTORIA

K.E.Rigg	c Cooper b Hynes	68	c Fallowfield b White		54
†S.O.Quin	lbw b McGilvray	4	run out (Mudge/Easton)		20
I.S.Lee	b White	9	run out (McGilvray/Easton)		85
J.W.Scaife	c Easton b White	32	c Little b McGilvray		70
R.G.Gregory	c & b White	12	c White b Chilvers		23
A.L.Hassett	c Little b Hynes	21	c McGilvray b White		51
H.J.Plant	b Hynes	0	c Marks b White		44
S.A.J.Smith	c sub (N.K.Miller) b Hynes	7	c Easton b White		16
*H.I.Ebeling	lbw b Hynes	0	run out		5
R.B.Scott	b Hynes	7	not out		4
C.W.Welch	not out	2	run out		6
Extras	(lb2, nb1)	3	(b23, lb12, nb2)		37
Total	(60.6 overs, 220 mins)	165	(94.5 overs, 344 mins)		415

VICTORIA	O	M	R	W	w,nb		O	M	R	W	w,nb
Scott	18.2	3	67	1	-,-		22.1	1	103	3	-,-
Ebeling	17	2	52	3	1,-		18	2	65	3	-,-
Plant	13	2	53	1	-,-	(5)	8	1	49	3	-,-
Welch	23	1	98	3	-,-	(3)	11	2	44	0	-,-
Gregory	5	1	19	0	-,-	(4)	4	0	17	0	-,-
Smith	8	0	21	0	-,-						

NEW SOUTH WALES	O	M	R	W	w,nb		O	M	R	W	w,nb
Cooper	6	0	15	0	-,1		9	3	29	0	-,1
McGilvray	6	2	11	1	-,-		24	3	84	1	-,-
Hynes	12.6	3	25	6	-,-		16.5	1	76	0	-,1
Chilvers	13	1	59	0	-,-		8	0	33	1	-,-
White	17	5	25	3	-,-		30	4	114	4	-,-
Mudge	6	0	27	0	-,-		3	0	19	0	-,-
Robinson							1	0	4	0	-,-
Marks							3	0	19	0	-,-

	FALL OF WICKETS			
	NSW	VIC	NSW	VIC
Wkt	1st	1st	2nd	2nd
1st	43	6	84	58
2nd	47	35	139	84
3rd	51	92	140	233
4th	107	120	153	262
5th	142	137	154	284
6th	165	137	202	379
7th	241	145	249	395
8th	257	145	265	405
9th	283	160	281	405
10th	325	165	-	415

QUEENSLAND v VICTORIA (Shield Match 11)

Played at Brisbane Cricket Ground (Woolloongabba) on February 1, 3, 4, 5, 1936. (Four-day match)
Toss : Queensland.   Result : MATCH DRAWN.
Debuts: Nil.
12th Men: A.Fisher (Qld) and S.A.J.Smith (Vic).
Umpires: J.Bartlett and J.A.Scott.
Attendances: 3535, 1152, 789, 918.   Total: 6394.   Receipts: £356.
Close of Play: 1st day Vic 1/49 (Lee 17, Scaife 22); 2nd day Vic 6/423 (Hassett 48, Plant 62); 3rd day Qld (2) 4/374 (Hansen 55, Cook 14).

Tallon's career-best 193, which took only 187 minutes and included 1 six and 28 fours, rescued Queensland from a precarious position on the third day. Going to the crease shortly before lunch, he raced to 130 at tea-time (scoring about 120 in the session) and added 103 in 60 minutes with Allen (44 in 109 minutes, 4 fours) and 143 in 88 minutes with Hansen (72 in 161 minutes, 8 fours) for the second and fourth wickets. Earlier Tallon had completed five dismissals in the Victorian innings. Cook with 44 (125 minutes, 3 fours) and 56 not out (204 minutes, 3 fours) was Queensland's other batting success. Rigg (3) retired at 0/8 on the first day when he was hit on the left elbow by a ball from Gilbert, playing his last match for Queensland. He resumed at 2/178 the following day, scoring 42 in 128 minutes with 1 four. His unbeaten 78 in the second innings included 5 fours. Lee (95 in 186 minutes, 6 fours and 43 in 72 minutes, 5 fours), Scaife (99 in 129 minutes, 12 fours and 46 not out in 69 minutes, 2 fours), Gregory (59 in 81 minutes, 5 fours), Hassett (49 in 110 minutes, 4 fours) and Plant (67 in 110 minutes, 7 fours) also batted well for Victoria. *Wisden* and *VCA Report* incorrectly give Vic (2) Lee b Wyeth. Sources: *Wisden, VCA Report, QCA Report, The Argus, Sydney Morning Herald, Brisbane Courier-Mail, Brisbane Telegraph.*

QUEENSLAND

Batsman	Dismissal	Score	Dismissal	Score
T.Allen	c Quin b Scott	5	c Ebeling b Gregory	44
R.E.Rogers	lbw b Welch	35	c Rigg b Welch	32
*D.Tallon	c Ebeling b Plant	24	c Scott b Plant	193
†J.A.J.Christy	run out (Newstead/Quin)	36	b Plant	27
C.D.Hansen	c Ebeling b Scott	4	lbw b Welch	72
G.G.Cook	c Gregory b Ebeling	44	not out	56
V.G.Honour	c Lee b Gregory	4	c Scott b Gregory	13
H.K.Thomsett	c Hassett b Plant	25	not out	22
A.H.Muhl	run out	7		
E.Gilbert	c Lee b Plant	3		
E.R.Wyeth	not out	2		
Extras	(b3, nb2)	5	(b9, lb2, nb8)	19
Total	(75.4 overs, 261 mins)	194	(117.7 overs, 442 mins) (6 wkts dec)	478

VICTORIA

Batsman	Dismissal	Score	Dismissal	Score
K.E.Rigg	c Tallon b Muhl	42	not out	78
†S.O.Quin	c Rogers b Gilbert	5	c Rogers b Gilbert	5
I.S.Lee	c Hansen b Gilbert	95	hit wkt b Wyeth	43
J.W.Scaife	st Tallon b Allen	99	not out	46
R.G.Gregory	c Tallon b Gilbert	59		
G.H.Newstead	c Christy b Gilbert	3		
A.L.Hassett	c Tallon b Cook	49		
H.J.Plant	c Allen b Cook	67		
*H.I.Ebeling	c Tallon b Gilbert	9		
R.B.Scott	c Honour b Cook	7		
C.W.Welch	not out	1		
Extras	(b5, lb5)	10	(b5, lb1, w1)	7
Total	(121.7 overs, 410 mins)	446	(44.0 overs, 154 mins) (2 wkts)	179

VICTORIA	O	M	R	W	w,nb		O	M	R	W	w,nb
Scott	15	4	43	2	-,2		24.7	3	92	0	-,8
Ebeling	15	4	24	1	-,-		35	9	90	0	-,-
Plant	15.4	2	41	3	-,-	(4)	17	4	81	2	-,-
Welch	17	3	50	1	-,-	(3)	21	1	116	2	-,-
Gregory	13	3	31	1	-,-		20	3	80	2	-,-

QUEENSLAND	O	M	R	W	w,nb		O	M	R	W	w,nb
Gilbert	32	2	109	5	-,-		9	1	33	1	-,-
Cook	27.7	4	93	3	-,-		9	0	42	0	-,-
Wyeth	33	7	69	0	-,-		12	1	38	1	-,-
Muhl	15	1	93	1	-,-		6	1	23	0	1,-
Allen	9	0	51	1	-,-		7	0	26	0	-,-
Christy	3	1	4	0	-,-						
Thomsett	2	0	17	0	-,-						
Honour						(6)	1	0	10	0	-,-

FALL OF WICKETS

Wkt	QLD 1st	VIC 1st	QLD 2nd	VIC 2nd
1st	13	9	44	15
2nd	57	178	147	93
3rd	75	218	200	-
4th	80	302	343	-
5th	132	312	400	-
6th	139	313	423	-
7th	171	425	-	-
8th	189	432	-	-
9th	190	438	-	-
10th	194	446	-	-

SOUTH AUSTRALIA v VICTORIA (Shield Match 12)

Played at Adelaide Oval on February 21, 22, 24, 25, 1936. (Four-day match)
Toss : Victoria.   Result : SOUTH AUSTRALIA WON BY AN INNINGS AND 190 RUNS.
Debuts: Nil.
12th Men: R.A.Hamence (SA) and W.E.Pearson (Vic).
Umpires: R.A.Nelson and J.D.Scott.
Attendances: 3469, 7977, 4578, 2581.   Total: 18,605.   Receipts: £780.
Close of Play: 1st day Vic 201 all out; 2nd day SA 3/304 (Badcock 155, Ryan 36); 3rd day Vic (2) 0/36 (Rigg 15, Quin 20).

South Australia capped their Shield-winning season with this emphatic victory. Badcock (325 in 587 minutes, 34 fours) became the second team member after D.G.Bradman (357 in Melbourne) to score 300 against Victoria. His chanceless innings, his highest in first-class cricket, was completed at the age of 21 years 320 days and progressed as follows, 50 in 110 minutes, 100 in 183 minutes, 150 in 320 minutes, 200 in 434 minutes, 250 in 509 minutes, 300 in 561 minutes. Badcock remained on the field for the entire match and shared a new State first-wicket record for matches against Victoria with Parker (88 in 203 minutes, 1 six and 9 fours), also adding 198 for the fourth wicket with Ryan (77 in 236 minutes, 3 fours) and 119 for the sixth wicket with Walker before Bradman declared at the loss of his wicket. Hassett (73 in 176 minutes, 7 fours) was the only Victorian to reach 50 against an accurate local attack, Ledward (47 in 140 minutes, 4 fours) making top score in the second innings. Last first-class appearance by T.W.Wall. *VCA Report* incorrectly gives some falls of wickets in Vic (1) and SA (1). Sources: *Wisden, VCA Report, SACA Report, Adelaide Advertiser, The News.*

VICTORIA

K.E.Rigg	st Walker b Ward	6	c Walker b Ward	21
†S.O.Quin	c Ryan b Ward	30	c Collins b Wall	26
I.S.Lee	st Walker b Ward	12	b Ward	0
J.W.Scaife	c Walker b Wall	4	c Waite b Ward	33
R.G.Gregory	b Wall	2	lbw b Williams	4
J.A.Ledward	b Ward	19	st Walker b Waite	47
A.L.Hassett	c Collins b Wall	73	st Walker b Ward	2
H.J.Plant	c Bradman b Ward	26	c Parker b Waite	25
W.Y.Wilson	c Bradman b Waite	13	c Ward b Waite	5
*H.I.Ebeling	st Walker b Waite	5	b Waite	0
R.B.Scott	not out	2	not out	0
Extras	(b3, lb5, w1)	9	(b8, lb3)	11
Total	(86.4 overs, 323 mins)	201	(57.6 overs, 226 mins)	174

SOUTH AUSTRALIA

R.A.Parker	c Scott b Wilson	88
C.L.Badcock	c Rigg b Gregory	325
*D.G.Bradman	c Ledward b Ebeling	1
E.J.R.Moyle	b Ebeling	5
A.J.Ryan	b Wilson	77
M.G.Waite	c Rigg b Wilson	8
†C.W.Walker	not out	33
F.H.K.Collins	)	
R.G.Williams	) did not bat	
F.A.Ward	)	
T.W.Wall	)	
Extras	(b6, lb12, w1, nb9)	28
Total	(159.6 overs, 587 mins) (6 wkts dec)	565

SOUTH AUSTRALIA	O	M	R	W	w,nb		O	M	R	W	w,nb		FALL OF WICKETS		
													VIC	SA	VIC
Wall	14	3	21	3	1,-		9	1	32	1	-,-	Wkt	1st	1st	2nd
Williams	9	2	15	0	-,-		11	4	12	1	-,-	1st	21	210	48
Ward	23	2	74	5	-,-		15	1	72	4	-,-	2nd	51	211	49
Ryan	17	5	31	0	-,-	(6)	4	3	1	0	-,-	3rd	54	219	50
Waite	12.4	4	35	2	-,-		9.6	1	29	4	-,-	4th	57	417	65
Collins	11	4	16	0	-,-	(4)	9	4	17	0	-,-	5th	58	446	91
												6th	78	565	101
VICTORIA	O	M	R	W	w,nb							7th	142	-	160
Scott	30	3	110	0	1,5							8th	194	-	169
Ebeling	41	6	97	2	-,-							9th	194	-	169
Wilson	30	4	122	3	-,4							10th	201	-	174
Gregory	22.6	1	99	1	-,-										
Plant	36	11	109	0	-,-										

VICTORIA v TASMANIA

Played at Melbourne Cricket Ground on February 24, 25, 26, 1936. (Three-day match)
Toss : Victoria.   Result : VICTORIA WON BY AN INNINGS AND 134 RUNS.
Debuts: Victoria - E.A.Baker, F.B.Deveney, J.Frederick, H.H.E.Grangel, W.G.Kinnear, E.A.Williams, W.J.Wilson (all f/c).
12th Men: M.R.Harvey (Vic) and R.V.Thomas (Tas).
Umpires: H.P.Crossley and T.A.Wells.
Attendances: 425, 383, 200.   Total: 1008.   Receipts: £24.
Close of Play: 1st day Vic 7/489 (Frederick 64, Baker 36); 2nd day Tas (2) 2/39 (Smith 20, Jeffery 0).

Grangel (108 in 116 minutes, 1 six, 1 five and 13 fours, stumping chance at 78) became the third and last Australian after N.F.Callaway (NSW v Qld at Sydney 1914-15) and S.E.Wootton (Vic v Tas at Hobart 1923-24) to score a hundred in his only first-class match. Five other Victorians registered fifties in the innings, Vernon (74 in 135 minutes, 8 fours), Williams (78 in 140 minutes, 5 fours), Newstead (86 in 114 minutes, 9 fours), Frederick (69 in 85 minutes, 3 fours) and Baker (59 not out in 88 minutes, 6 fours). Frederick, also on debut, enhanced the first of three first-class appearances by taking nine wickets for 81 runs with his leg-breaks and googlies. Jeffery batted well in both innings for Tasmania, scoring 45 (89 minutes, 4 fours) and 50 (121 minutes, 3 fours). Pearsall (36 in 119 minutes, 2 fours) and Smith (72 in 103 minutes, 5 fours) made other notable scores. Sources: *VCA Report, TCA Report, The Age, The Argus, The Herald, Melbourne Sun.*

VICTORIA

W.G.Kinnear	c G.A.Combes b Pearsall	2
R.Gardner	lbw b Pearsall	19
E.H.G.Vernon	run out (Pearsall/Gardiner)	74
E.A.Williams	c Davis b Townley	78
*G.H.Newstead	c Pearsall b Jeffery	86
H.H.E.Grangel	c James b Townley	108
J.Frederick	c Walsh b Jeffery	69
A.Jinks	lbw b Townley	10
†E.A.Baker	not out	59
F.B.Deveney	lbw b Jeffery	7
W.J.Wilson	not out	6
Extras	(b8, lb4, w1)	13
Total	(101.0 overs, 396 mins) (9 wkts dec)	531

TASMANIA

M.J.Combes	c Jinks b Grangel	7	lbw b Grangel	8
A.L.Pearsall	c Newstead b Wilson	36	c & b Jinks	9
E.H.Smith	lbw b Wilson	0	c Grangel b Wilson	72
C.L.Jeffery	c Grangel b Jinks	45	c Grangel b Wilson	50
N.W.Davis	b Frederick	10	b Wilson	19
*A.W.Rushforth	st Baker b Frederick	2	lbw b Frederick	16
G.T.H.James	st Baker b Frederick	9	lbw b Frederick	5
†J.Gardiner	b Frederick	9	lbw b Frederick	3
J.M.Walsh	not out	30	run out (Frederick/Baker)	18
R.C.Townley	c Deveney b Frederick	2	c Deveney b Frederick	2
G.A.Combes	c Vernon b Wilson	30	not out	0
Extras	(lb2, nb6)	8	(b2, lb4, nb1)	7
Total	(57.4 overs, 235 mins)	188	(69.2 overs, 226 mins)	209

TASMANIA	O	M	R	W	w,nb
Walsh	18	1	91	0	-,-
James	17	2	61	0	-,-
Pearsall	16	2	64	2	1,-
G.A.Combes	13	1	69	0	-,-
Townley	18	0	142	3	-,-
Jeffery	18	1	81	3	-,-
M.J.Combes	1	0	10	0	-,-

VICTORIA	O	M	R	W	w,nb		O	M	R	W	w,nb
Deveney	13	1	36	0	-,5		9	2	26	0	-,1
Grangel	9	2	23	1	-,1		13	1	41	1	-,-
Wilson	16.4	1	58	3	-,-	(5)	18	4	66	3	-,-
Frederick	12	3	39	5	-,-	(3)	19.2	3	42	4	-,-
Jinks	7	0	24	1	-,-	(4)	10	1	27	1	-,-

FALL OF WICKETS

	VIC	TAS	TAS
Wkt	1st	1st	2nd
1st	11	26	18
2nd	30	27	39
3rd	161	81	116
4th	184	94	156
5th	358	100	163
6th	385	108	170
7th	407	113	182
8th	505	126	193
9th	515	130	209
10th	-	188	209

SOUTH AUSTRALIA v TASMANIA

Played at Adelaide Oval on February 29, March 2, 3, 1936. (Three-day match)
Toss : Tasmania.   Result : SOUTH AUSTRALIA WON BY AN INNINGS AND 349 RUNS.
Debuts: South Australia - H.N.J.Cotton, R.A.Hamence, B.H.Leak, H.R.Shepherdson, R.M.Stanford (all f/c).
12th Men: M.J.Doherty (SA) and N.W.Davis (Tas).
Umpires: C.W.James and J.D.Scott.
Attendances: 2618, 1503, 846.   Total: 4967.   Receipts: £208.
Close of Play: 1st day SA 2/222 (Bradman 127, Hamence 60); 2nd day Tas (2) 0/29 (M.J.Combes 10, Thomas 9).

Bradman (369 in just 253 minutes, 4 sixes and 46 fours) batted at his brilliant best to compile the highest innings by a South Australian in first-class cricket. Previously Clem Hill (365 not out, SA v NSW at Adelaide 1900-01) had held the record. South Australia's total was also their highest yet. Bradman, whose 369 - his sixth and last triple-century - included only one chance (at 305), scored over 100 runs in each of the three sessions in which he batted: 127 in 95 minutes before stumps on the first day, 135 in 105 minutes before lunch on the second day and 107 in the lunch-tea session. He gave a deliberate catch to the bowler after breaking Hill's record, shortly before the tea break. It was his second score of 300 or more in the season, equalling a feat by W.H.Ponsford in 1927-28, and further, it was the highest innings made at the Adelaide Oval. He scored at the following rate (in minutes): 50 in 29, 100 in 70, 150 in 126, 200 in 173, 250 in 194, 300 in 213 and 350 in 242. His partnership of 356 in three hours with Hamence (121 in 181 minutes, 11 fours), who scored a century on debut, remains the South Australian record for any wicket until 1986-87. Waite (43 in 81 minutes, 7 fours) and O'Connell (53 in 49 minutes, 7 fours) added 77 after Bradman's departure at 552. Thomas (44 in 255 minutes, 3 fours) defended stubbornly in a hopeless situation in Tasmania's second innings, scoring only 15 in 100 minutes before lunch on the last day. Sources: *TCA Report, SACA Report, Adelaide Advertiser, The News.*

TASMANIA

M.J.Combes	c Ward b Shepherdson	14		c Shepherdson b Cotton	10
R.V.Thomas	c O'Connell b Shepherdson	42		c sub (M.J.Doherty) b Ward	44
E.H.Smith	c Ward b O'Connell	62	(4)	c O'Connell b Ward	0
C.L.Jeffery	b Cotton	0	(5)	c O'Connell b Ward	4
A.L.Pearsall	run out (Leak/Walker)	1	(3)	c O'Connell b Ward	11
*A.W.Rushforth	b Cotton	0		c Walker b Ward	73
J.M.Walsh	st Walker b Ward	8		b Waite	11
G.T.H.James	c & b Ward	3		not out	6
†J.Gardiner	c Waite b Ward	11		b Waite	0
G.A.Combes	c Cotton b O'Connell	8		c Cotton b Ward	0
R.C.Townley	not out	0		b Waite	1
Extras	(b4, lb3, w1, nb1)	9		(b11,lb7, w1, nb2)	21
Total	(47.5 overs, 183 mins)	158		(86.4 overs, 295 mins)	181

SOUTH AUSTRALIA

C.L.Badcock	b Thomas	13
†C.W.Walker	c Thomas b Walsh	11
*D.G.Bradman	c & b Townley	369
R.A.Hamence	c & b Townley	121
B.H.Leak	b Townley	19
R.M.Stanford	run out (/Gardiner)	0
M.G.Waite	c Gardiner b G.A.Combes	43
T.R.O'Connell	c G.A.Combes b Thomas	53
F.A.Ward	c Gardiner b James	6
H.N.J.Cotton	b G.A.Combes	5
H.R.Shepherdson	not out	28
Extras	(b18, nb2)	20
Total	(104.2 overs, 388 mins)	688

SOUTH AUSTRALIA	O	M	R	W	w,nb		O	M	R	W	w,nb		FALL OF WICKETS			
Cotton	11	0	32	2	-,-		17	6	34	1	-,-			TAS	SA	TAS
Shepherdson	10	2	26	2	1,1		13	3	35	0	-,2	Wkt	1st	1st	2nd
O'Connell	10.5	2	31	2	-,-		13	8	16	0	1,-	1st	23	23	29
Waite	8	3	25	0	-,-	(5)	13.4	6	28	3	-,-	2nd	88	31	54
Ward	8	1	35	3	-,-	(4)	30	13	47	6	-,-	3rd	94	387	54
												4th	95	533	58
TASMANIA	O	M	R	W	w,nb							5th	96	550	148
Walsh	16	0	75	1	-,1							6th	126	552	171
Thomas	16	1	91	2	-,-							7th	130	629	177
G.A.Combes	20.2	2	116	2	-,-							8th	146	645	177
James	15	2	92	1	-,-							9th	154	655	180
Townley	20	2	169	3	-,1							10th	158	688	181
Jeffery	6	0	54	0	-,-										
Pearsall	11	0	71	0	-,-										

Extraordinary public interest surrounded the goodwill visit of the 23rd English team to Australia under G.O.B.Allen. More than 950,000 spectators - an alltime record - were drawn to the five England-Australia Test matches. They saw Australia come from 2-0 down to snatch the series 3-2. The Englishmen contested 25 matches in all on the tour, of which 17 were first-class including the five Tests. Of these, they won five, drew seven and lost five.

As was anticipated, the performance of Bradman held the key to the outcome of the Test series. He scored 810 runs - a new record for Australia in any series in this country - 690 of them in the final three matches which Australia won. Rain had a bearing on the results of all but one of the Tests, the fourth, although neither side was favoured in the long run. McCabe, Fingleton and Badcock hit centuries in support of Bradman, and O'Reilly and Fleetwood-Smith headed the Australian bowling aggregates. England were beset by injuries to key players, particularly in the crucial early stages of the tour. Hammond, Leyland, Barnett and Hardstaff each exceeded 1000 runs in all matches and they were the most consistent batsmen in the Tests. Voce headed the Test wicket-taking list, but wickets were distributed evenly when all matches were considered.

On the domestic front, Victoria recaptured the Sheffield Shield which they had surrendered to South Australia the previous season. The title remained in doubt until the final match between these teams, Victoria being successful by virtue of an outstanding bowling display from McCormick (3 for 56 and 9 for 40), backed up by Fleetwood-Smith (6 for 66). The experienced Rigg, Darling and O'Brien received handsome support in the batting department this year from young players such as Hassett, Lee, Gregory and Ledward. Fleetwood-Smith, McCormick, Ebeling and Sievers formed a good bowling attack.

South Australia felt the absence of their Test representatives, Bradman, Badcock and Ward, to a far greater degree than Victoria. Neither New South Wales nor Queensland mounted a serious challenge for the Shield at any stage.

The presence of the English team in the country restricted first-class opportunities for the non-Shield States, Tasmania and Western Australia, to matches against the tourists. The English itinerary also provided for Combined XIs to meet the Englishmen at both Hobart and Perth to cater further for the local players and to provide revenue for the local associations.

The NSWCA staged a testimonial match at Sydney in October 1936 for the benefit of former stalwarts Warren Bardsley and Jack Gregory. Vic Richardson's successful touring team to South Africa was opposed by a Bradman-led XI drawn from the rest of Australia. Aside from helping two former greats, the game provided Test aspirants with an early chance to make a bid for selection in the forth coming series against England.

Leading Aggregates

Batsmen	M	I	NO	Runs	HS	Ave.	Bowlers	Runs	Wkts	Ave.
D.G.Bradman (SA)	12	19	1	1552	270	86.22	L.O.Fleetwood-Smith (V)	1073	53	20.24
C.J.Barnett (MCC)	15	25	0	1375	259	55.00	F.A.Ward (SA)	1506	53	28.41
W.R.Hammond (MCC)	12	20	2	1206	231*	67.00	W.J.O'Reilly (NSW)	1052	51	20.62
S.J.McCabe (NSW)	10	18	0	956	112	53.11	C.V.Grimmett (SA)	1443	48	30.06
M.Leyland (MCC)	12	22	4	902	126	50.11	K.Farnes (MCC)	845	41	20.60
J.Hardstaff (MCC)	16	28	3	850	110	34.00	J.M.Sims (MCC)	945	38	24.86
C.L.Badcock (SA)	13	18	1	831	182	48.88	G.O.B.Allen (MCC)	997	38	26.23
R.G.Gregory (V)	11	17	1	775	128	48.43	W.Voce (MCC)	1052	35	30.05
K.E.Rigg (V)	11	18	2	739	167*	46.18	E.L.McCormick (V)	794	32	24.81

SHEFFIELD SHIELD TABLE

	P	WO	W1	LO	L1	D	Pts	Quotient	Runs Scored	Wkts Lost	Runs Conceded	Wkts Taken
VICTORIA	6	3	3	-	-	-	24	1.556	3304	86	2394	97
SOUTH AUSTRALIA	6	3	-	1	2	-	17	0.996	2369	93	2761	108
NEW SOUTH WALES	6	1	1	2	2	-	10	0.876	2879	106	3283	106
QUEENSLAND	6	1	-	5	-	-	5	0.751	2669	120	2783	94
TOTAL	12	8	4	8	4	-	56	1.000	11221	405	11221	405

D.G.BRADMAN'S XI v V.Y.RICHARDSON'S XI

Played at Sydney Cricket Ground on October 9, 10, 12, 13, 1936. (Four-day match)
Toss : Richardson's XI.   Result : BRADMAN'S XI WON BY SIX WICKETS.
Debuts: Nil.
12th Men: K.C.Gulliver (both teams).
Umpires: E.G.Borwick and A.L.Christie.
Attendances: 7257, 19858, 2691, 500.   Total: 30,306.   Receipts: £1411.
Close of Play: 1st day Richardson 9/345 (Oldfield 66, McCormick 24); 2nd day Bradman 385 all out; 3rd day Bradman (2) 3/92
(Robinson 10, Morrisby 0).

The match was arranged as a benefit for W.Bardsley and J.M.Gregory. Richardson's XI was chosen from the Australian team which toured South Africa the previous summer, excluding L.O.Fleetwood-Smith who was not available because of tendon trouble. Another tourist, O'Brien, played for Bradman's XI, which was otherwise drawn from the remainder of Australia's best players considered to be on trial for the coming Test series. Bardsley and Gregory each received £762 from the testimonial. Brown (111 in 206 minutes, 14 fours) recorded an elegant century for Richardson's XI on the first day while McCabe (76 in 146 minutes, 10 fours) and Oldfield (78 in 112 minutes, 6 fours) exceeded 50. Ward's legspin claimed match figures of 12 for 227. Facing the bowling of O'Reilly for the first time at first-class level, Bradman (212 in 202 minutes, 2 sixes and 26 fours) scored his second successive double hundred, following 369 against Tasmania at the end of 1935-36, the fourth and last time he performed such a double in Australia. After reaching 100 in 130 minutes, he raced to 200 in 191 minutes, offering a chance at 200 in the deep off O'Reilly before being caught at long-on with the score at 7/378, having made his last 116 runs after tea. Bradman shared stands of 177 for the fifth wicket with O'Brien (85 in 190 minutes, 7 fours) and 149 for the sixth wicket with McGilvray. Badcock (43 in 85 minutes, 6 fours) and Robinson (57 in 64 minutes) batted well in the second innings. Sources: *Wisden, NSWCA Report, VCA Report, The Age, The Argus, The Herald, Sydney Morning Herald, NSWCA Scorebook.*

RICHARDSON'S XI

J.H.W.Fingleton	c Tallon b Ebeling	4	b Leather	10
W.A.Brown	hit wkt b Ward	111	lbw b Ebeling	17
S.J.McCabe	c O'Brien b Ebeling	76	c McGilvray b Ward	28
L.S.Darling	c & b Ward	3	c White b Ward	35
A.G.Chipperfield	lbw b Ward	3	lbw b Ward	10
*V.Y.Richardson	c McGilvray b Leather	26	c Tallon b Ebeling	0
M.W.Sievers	c Tallon b Ward	0	not out	43
†W.A.S.Oldfield	c Bradman b Ward	78	run out (Robinson/Tallon)	16
C.V.Grimmett	b Ward	14	b White	0
W.J.O'Reilly	lbw b Ward	7	lbw b Ward	1
E.L.McCormick	not out	30	b Ward	13
Extras	(b7, nb4)	11	(b2, lb4, nb1)	7
Total	(95.3 overs, 339 mins)	363	(49.6 overs, 190 mins)	180

BRADMAN'S XI

L.P.J.O'Brien	lbw b McCormick	85		lbw b O'Reilly	18
C.L.Badcock	c Fingleton b O'Reilly	18		c Darling b Grimmett	43
R.H.Robinson	b O'Reilly	2	(4)	c Fingleton b Grimmett	57
R.O.G.Morrisby	b O'Reilly	4	(5)	not out	19
†D.Tallon	b Sievers	3	(6)	not out	0
*D.G.Bradman	c O'Reilly b Grimmett	212	(3)	c Fingleton b Grimmett	13
A.D.McGilvray	st Oldfield b Grimmett	42			
E.C.S.White	b O'Reilly	2			
F.A.Ward	not out	5			
H.I.Ebeling	lbw b Grimmett	1			
T.W.Leather	st Oldfield b Grimmett	0			
Extras	(b4, lb2, nb5)	11		(b7, lb4)	11
Total	(73.7 overs, 286 mins)	385		(38.6 overs, 138 mins) (4 wkts)	161

BRADMAN'S XI	O	M	R	W	w,nb		O	M	R	W	w,nb					
Leather	16	0	84	1	-,4		7	1	12	1	-,1					
Ebeling	21	4	44	2	-,-		12	4	35	2	-,-	Wkt	1st	1st	2nd	2nd
White	19	3	68	0	-,-		14	3	26	1	-,-	1st	9	38	19	63
Ward	32.3	5	127	7	-,-		16.6	1	100	5	-,-	2nd	178	44	31	76
McGilvray	7	1	29	0	-,-							3rd	181	48	66	92
												4th	191	51	82	157

FALL OF WICKETS

RICHARDSON'S XI	O	M	R	W	w,nb		O	M	R	W	w,nb					
McCormick	13	0	50	1	-,2		6	0	30	0	-,-	5th	210	200	95	-
Sievers	13	1	49	1	-,3		3	0	11	0	-,-	6th	214	377	105	-
O'Reilly	22	0	96	4	-,-	(4)	13.6	4	27	1	-,-	7th	240	378	153	-
Grimmett	20.7	2	146	4	-,-	(3)	16	2	82	3	-,-	8th	282	382	153	-
McCabe	4	1	21	0	-,-							9th	294	385	154	-
Chipperfield	1	0	12	0	-,-							10th	363	385	180	-

WESTERN AUSTRALIA v M.C.C.

Played at W.A.C.A. Ground, Perth, on October 16, 17, 19, 1936. (Three-day match)
Toss : Western Australia. Result : M.C.C. WON BY AN INNINGS AND 180 RUNS.
Debuts: Nil.
12th Men: G.A.Gardiner (WA) and W.H.Copson (MCC).
Umpires: F.R.Buttsworth and E.T.Tonkinson.
Attendances: 2200, 4100, 700. Total: About 7000. Receipts: £599.
Close of Play: 1st day MCC 1/91 (Wyatt 14, Hammond 16); 2nd day MCC 4/469 (Hardstaff 87, Worthington 39).

Gardiner replaced R.W.Kimpton (work) as 12th man after selection. Taaffe, fielding at second slip, sustained a broken finger when he attempted to catch Barnett from Halcombe's bowling late on the first day. He took no further part in the match and was replaced by Gardiner in the field; indeed the injury was so severe that amputation was considered at one stage. Duckworth also suffered a broken finger when he attempted to take a ball from Farnes in the fourth over of Western Australia's second innings. Wyatt took over as wicket-keeper until the lunch break and then handed the gloves to Hardstaff, who kept for the rest of the innings and caught Inverarity in that position. Hammond survived chances at 81 and 129 to compile 141 in 180 minutes with 2 sixes and 14 fours. His second-wicket partnership with Wyatt (106 in 282 minutes, 5 fours, out at 328) was worth 221. Hardstaff (87 not out in 132 minutes, 1 six and 7 fours) and Barnett (54 in 66 minutes, 1 six and 8 fours) hit half-centuries. Sources: *Wisden, VCA Report, WACA Report, The Age, Sydney Morning Herald, The West Australian, Daily News, Sunday Times, Western Mail, WACA Scorebook.*

WESTERN AUSTRALIA

F.J.Bryant	b Allen	4		b Sims	43
F.J.Alexander	b Allen	18		b Robins	32
W.J.Horrocks	c Allen b Farnes	18		b Sims	4
F.H.Taaffe	b Allen	0		absent hurt	-
*†O.I.Lovelock	c Worthington b Farnes	25		b Farnes	5
R.J.Wilberforce	not out	33	(4)	lbw b Sims	1
M.Inverarity	c Farnes b Sims	3	(6)	c Hardstaff b Farnes	5
S.G.Francis	b Farnes	0		c & b Robins	10
C.F.Newman	c Wyatt b Barnett	28	(7)	c Hammond b Sims	17
A.G.Zimbulis	lbw b Robins	2	(9)	c & b Sims	0
R.A.Halcombe	b Sims	4	(10)	not out	0
Extras	(b1, lb6)	7		(b25, lb5)	30
Total	(46.6 overs, 190 mins)	142		(32.3 overs, 133 mins)	147

M.C.C.

R.E.S.Wyatt	c Lovelock b Halcombe	106
C.J.Barnett	c Francis b Zimbulis	54
W.R.Hammond	c sub (Gardiner) b Newman	141
J.Hardstaff, jr	not out	87
L.B.Fishlock	c & b Inverarity	30
T.S.Worthington	not out	39
*G.O.B.Allen	)	
R.W.V.Robins	)	
K.Farnes	) did not bat	
J.M.Sims	)	
†G.Duckworth	)	
Extras	(b6, lb5,w1)	12
Total	(104.0 overs, 387 mins) (4 wkts dec)	469

M.C.C.	O	M	R	W	w,nb		O	M	R	W	w,nb
Farnes	10	0	35	3	-,-		8	1	26	2	-,-
Allen	10	1	32	3	-,-		4	0	21	0	-,-
Hammond	6	2	17	0	-,-		3	0	10	0	-,-
Sims	9.6	1	22	2	-,-	(5)	10	3	37	5	-,-
Robins	8	2	23	1	-,-	(4)	7.3	0	23	2	-,-
Barnett	3	0	6	1	-,-						

WESTERN AUSTRALIA	O	M	R	W	w,nb
Halcombe	25	2	108	1	1,-
Wilberforce	27	1	87	0	-,-
Francis	14	0	52	0	-,-
Zimbulis	20	0	131	1	-,-
Inverarity	6	2	18	1	-,-
Newman	12	1	61	1	-,-

FALL OF WICKETS

Wkt	WA	MCC	WA
	1st	1st	2nd
1st	17	70	96
2nd	26	291	107
3rd	26	328	108
4th	52	387	109
5th	77	-	114
6th	82	-	125
7th	84	-	147
8th	128	-	147
9th	133	-	147
10th	142	-	-

COMBINED XI v M.C.C.

Played at W.A.C.A. Ground, Perth, on October 22, 23, 24, 1936. (Three-day match)
Toss : M.C.C.   Result : MATCH DRAWN.
Debuts: Combined XI - J.A.Shea (f/c).
12th Men: C.F.Newman (Comb XI). T.H.Wade stood as MCC emergency.
Umpires: F.R.Buttsworth and E.T.Tonkinson.
Attendances: 5000, 8300, 12000.   Total: About 25,300.   Receipts: £1851.
Close of Play: 1st day MCC 6/420 (Fishlock 91, Allen 8); 2nd day Comb XI 1/293 (Badcock 149, Horrocks 128).

Ames (stiff back caused by a chill), Duckworth (broken finger) and Robins (broken finger) were all unavailable for MCC. T.H.Wade, an Essex wicket-keeper holidaying in Australia to watch the Englishmen, was asked by Allen to stand by in case of emergency; he left with the team on the midnight train to South Australia following the match. MCC made 420 in 296 minutes on the first day, Hammond batting 108 minutes with 2 sixes and 13 fours. Worthington (141 minutes, 15 fours), Fishlock (133 minutes, 4 sixes and 13 fours) and Allen (83 minutes, 1 six and 5 fours) were other big contributors. Zimbulis's seventh over cost 20 runs but included the wicket of Hammond. After Fingleton was bowled by a shooter early on, Badcock (253 minutes, 13 fours, chances at 13 and 35) and Horrocks (243 minutes, 2 sixes and 14 fours, chance at 109) combined for a second-wicket partnership of 306 in 235 minutes. *Wisden* incorrectly includes R.J.Bryant in the Combined XI instead of his brother, Frank. Sources: *Wisden, VCA Report, WACA Report, The Age, Sydney Morning Herald, The West Australian, Daily News, Sunday Times, WACA Scorebook.*

M.C.C.

R.E.S.Wyatt	lbw b Grimmett	27			
†A.E.Fagg	b Halcombe	35			
W.R.Hammond	c Wilberforce b Zimbulis	107			
T.S.Worthington	c & b McCabe	89	(1)	run out (Halcombe)	25
L.B.Fishlock	c Wilberforce b Halcombe	91		b McCabe	1
J.Hardstaff, jr	c & b Zimbulis	11	(4)	not out	30
C.J.Barnett	c McCabe b Wilberforce	24	(2)	c Fingleton b McCabe	37
*G.O.B.Allen	b Wilberforce	65	(6)	not out	14
H.Verity	lbw b Halcombe	2	(3)	lbw b Grimmett	11
W.Voce	lbw b Halcombe	0			
W.H.Copson	not out	10			
Extras	(b19, lb11, w2, nb4)	36		(lb2)	2
Total	(101.0 overs, 354 mins)	497		(30.0 overs, 105 mins) (4 wkts)	120

COMBINED XI

J.H.W.Fingleton	b Voce	1
C.L.Badcock	c Allen b Copson	167
W.J.Horrocks	b Copson	140
*S.J.McCabe	lbw b Allen	23
F.J.Bryant	b Copson	12
J.A.Shea	b Verity	0
†O.I.Lovelock	c Wyatt b Verity	8
R.J.Wilberforce	b Copson	2
C.V.Grimmett	not out	30
A.G.Zimbulis	c Copson b Hammond	23
R.A.Halcombe	c Voce b Hammond	7
Extras	(b11, lb6, w1, nb5)	23
Total	(107.3 overs, 396 mins)	436

COMBINED XI	O	M	R	W	w,nb		O	M	R	W	w,nb
Halcombe	27	3	124	4	1,3		6	0	39	0	-,-
Wilberforce	22	1	60	2	1,-		5	0	15	0	-,-
Grimmett	29	5	137	1	-,-		7	2	13	1	-,-
Zimbulis	13	0	107	2	-,1	(5)	3	0	28	0	-,-
McCabe	10	1	33	1	-,-	(4)	7	2	15	2	-,-
Shea							2	0	8	0	-,-

M.C.C.	O	M	R	W	w,nb
Voce	26	1	125	1	-,5
Copson	25	4	82	4	1,-
Hammond	13.3	1	38	2	-,-
Allen	12	2	57	1	-,-
Verity	24	4	65	2	-,-
Worthington	4	0	15	0	-,-
Wyatt	3	0	31	0	-,-

FALL OF WICKETS

Wkt	MCC 1st	AUST 1st	MCC 2nd
1st	59	15	48
2nd	82	321	72
3rd	230	326	76
4th	294	360	80
5th	329	361	-
6th	370	363	-
7th	423	371	-
8th	425	371	-
9th	427	420	-
10th	497	436	-

QUEENSLAND v NEW SOUTH WALES (Shield Match 1)

Played at Brisbane Cricket Ground (Woolloongabba) on October 30, 31, November 2, 3, 1936. (Four-day match)
Toss : Queensland.   Result : NEW SOUTH WALES WON BY ONE WICKET.
Debuts: Queensland - P.L.Dixon (f/c); W.A.Brown (Qld only). New South Wales - V.E.Jackson (f/c).
12th Men: G.W.Baker (Qld) and A.G.Cheetham (NSW).
Umpires: A.Adams and J.A.Scott.
Attendances: 2101, 3526, 1527, 851.   Total: 8005.   Receipts: £478.
Close of Play: 1st day NSW 3/109 (Marks 48, Robinson 24); 2nd day Qld (2) 1/56 (Brown 19, Andrews 20); 3rd day Qld (2) 7/368
    (Oxenham 32, Amos 74).

New South Wales completed a one-wicket win with 2 minutes to spare, extending their unbeaten run against Queensland to a new record of 19 matches since December 1926. Tallon reached his hundred (157 minutes, 1 six and 7 fours) in extraordinary circumstances; he was dismissed on 96 but Oldfield pointed out that Tallon had earlier touched a ball signalled as 4 byes, and umpire Adams instructed the scorers at the close of the third day to redistribute the runs accordingly. This kept Oldfield's byeless record for the match (548 runs) intact. The following day, a second most unusual incident occurred. Tallon's view of a fast return from Brown was obscured by Chipperfield as he completed a single with Marks. The ball shot through to the boundary but the batsmen declined the extra runs under the circumstances. However, the runs were claimed by the New South Wales captain McGilvray at the tea interval and added to Marks's score (hence his five) as well as to the total. Their addition proved vital given the closeness of the final result and the time it was achieved. Andrews (85 in 233 minutes, 8 fours), Oxenham (50 not out in 168 minutes, 3 fours) and Amos (career-best 93 in 126 minutes, 5 sixes and 3 fours) scored fifties for Queensland, the last two-named adding 125 for the eighth wicket. Robinson's 163 (245 minutes, 1 six and 22 fours) was the highest of his four hundreds for New South Wales. Marks (57 in 108 minutes, 1 five and 5 fours) and Chipperfield (50 in 115 minutes, 4 fours) topscored in the second innings. Brown (22 matches for New South Wales) made his first appearance for Queensland. Sources: *Wisden, NSWCA Report, QCA Report, The Herald, Sydney Morning Herald, Brisbane Courier-Mail.*

QUEENSLAND

W.A.Brown	c Oldfield b O'Reilly	8	run out (Chipperfield/Oldfield)		31
R.E.Rogers	c Jackson b Hynes	10	c Robinson b Hynes		17
W.C.Andrews	run out (Jackson)	22	b Hynes		85
T.Allen	b Jackson	12	c Robinson b Hynes		10
†D.Tallon	c Marks b Jackson	29	c Oldfield b Hynes		100
E.C.Bensted	b O'Reilly	10	b Jackson		2
G.G.Cook	c Oldfield b Hynes	16	lbw b O'Reilly		8
*R.K.Oxenham	b O'Reilly	7	not out		50
G.S.Amos	b Hynes	9	c White b O'Reilly		93
E.R.Wyeth	c Marks b O'Reilly	3	c Oldfield b White		0
P.L.Dixon	not out	3	b O'Reilly		9
Extras	(lb1, nb2)	3	(lb9, nb2)		11
Total	(49.0 overs, 174 mins)	132	(141.4 overs, 472 mins)		416

NEW SOUTH WALES

L.J.Fallowfield	c Tallon b Dixon	19	b Oxenham		26
H.Mudge	lbw b Oxenham	13	lbw b Oxenham		10
A.E.Marks	run out (Rogers/Tallon)	48	lbw b Wyeth		57
A.G.Chipperfield	b Dixon	2	lbw b Oxenham		50
R.H.Robinson	c Tallon b Amos	163	hit wkt b Wyeth		26
V.E.Jackson	c Tallon b Dixon	30	c Brown b Wyeth		19
*A.D.McGilvray	c Tallon b Dixon	1	lbw b Dixon		6
L.C.Hynes	b Oxenham	14	b Oxenham		12
†W.A.S.Oldfield	c Dixon b Cook	13	run out (Amos)		11
E.C.S.White	c Allen b Cook	1	not out		5
W.J.O'Reilly	not out	8	not out		1
Extras	(b8, w1, nb1)	10	(b2, lb1, nb1)		4
Total	(92.1 overs, 336 mins)	322	(69.0 overs, 254 mins) (9 wkts)		227

NEW SOUTH WALES	O	M	R	W	w,nb		O	M	R	W	w,nb		FALL OF WICKETS			
Hynes	13	1	41	3	-,2		25	1	69	4	-,-			QLD	NSW	QLD	NSW
O'Reilly	20	5	47	4	-,-		48.4	10	154	3	-,2		Wkt	1st	1st	2nd	2nd
White	6	2	8	0	-,-		29	10	37	1	-,-		1st	21	29	25	25
McGilvray	4	1	3	0	-,-								2nd	21	51	102	60
Jackson	6	0	30	2	-,-	(4)	12	3	24	1	-,-		3rd	54	61	124	132
Mudge						(5)	25	4	107	0	-,-		4th	62	119	216	170
Robinson						(6)	2	0	14	0	-,-		5th	85	228	219	180
													6th	106	240	239	196
QUEENSLAND	O	M	R	W	w,nb		O	M	R	W	w,nb		7th	112	274	272	203
Amos	13.1	0	56	1	-,-								8th	122	297	397	221
Dixon	20	2	79	4	-,-	(1)	15	1	63	1	-,-		9th	129	309	407	221
Oxenham	22	9	34	2	1,-		18	7	33	4	-,-		10th	132	322	416	-
Wyeth	18	6	55	0	-,-		18	3	43	3	-,-						
Allen	2	0	11	0	-,-	(6)	7	0	43	0	-,-						
Cook	12	0	55	2	-,1	(2)	8	0	28	0	-,-						
Bensted	5	0	22	0	-,-	(5)	3	0	13	0	-,1						

SOUTH AUSTRALIA v M.C.C.

Played at Adelaide Oval on October 30, 31, November 2, 3, 1936. (Four-day match)
Toss : M.C.C.   Result : M.C.C. WON BY 105 RUNS.
Debuts: Nil.
12th Men: B.H.Leak (SA). No 12th named for M.C.C.
Umpires: A.J.Richardson and J.D.Scott.
Attendances: 11333, 20571, 10171, 770.   Total: 42,845.   Receipts: £2182.
Close of Play: 1st day SA 1/11 (Parker 1, Walker 1); 2nd day MCC (2) 3/100 (Hammond 60, Verity 5); 3rd day SA (2) 5/138
    (Richardson 44, Moyle 6).

M.C.C. were unable to consider L.E.G.Ames (back injury), G.Duckworth (broken finger), M.Leyland (ill), R.W.V.Robins (broken finger) or R.E.S.Wyatt (broken wrist) for selection. In the absence of both wicketkeepers, the tourists co-opted the Essex professional T.H.Wade, who was privately visiting Australia, for this and the next match. D.G.Bradman, chosen to lead South Australia, was a late withdrawal due to the death of his new-born son. Moyle, originally 12th man, came into the side to replace him and Richardson captained the State for the last time. Hammond scored 51.2 per cent of M.C.C.'s runs with innings of 104 (196 minutes, 10 fours) and 136 (219 minutes, 11 fours) to become the first tourist to have twice scored hundreds in each innings in Australia (also Fourth Test at Adelaide 1928-29). Richardson (55 in 118 minutes, 4 fours) was the only other batsman to register fifty in the match. Grimmett and Cotton shared a spirited tenth-wicket stand of 73 in 62 minutes on the second day to save face for South Australia, and Cotton followed up by bowling Fagg with the opening delivery of the M.C.C. second innings. Sources: *Wisden, SACA Report, The Age, The Herald, Sydney Morning Herald, Adelaide Advertiser.*

M.C.C.

A.E.Fagg	b Waite	4		b Cotton	0
C.J.Barnett	c Walker b Cotton	3		c Hamence b Waite	5
W.R.Hammond	lbw b Ward	104		c Moyle b Cotton	136
T.S.Worthington	run out (Cotton/Walker)	25		c & b Ward	29
L.B.Fishlock	st Walker b Grimmett	1	(6)	b Ward	11
J.Hardstaff, jr	c & b Ward	20	(7)	b Cotton	3
*G.O.B.Allen	c Moyle b Ward	12	(8)	not out	13
H.Verity	lbw b Ward	31	(5)	st Walker b Ward	23
J.M.Sims	b Ward	1		c & b Ward	7
†T.H.Wade	b Grimmett	10		b Ward	0
W.Voce	not out	16		c Walker b Cotton	0
Extras	(b2, lb4)	6		(b6, lb3)	9
Total	(78.0 overs, 266 mins)	233		(68.7 overs, 248 mins)	236

SOUTH AUSTRALIA

C.L.Badcock	lbw b Allen	8		b Allen	23
R.A.Parker	c Allen b Voce	14		c Hammond b Verity	24
†C.W.Walker	b Allen	3	(9)	c Worthington b Verity	5
A.J.Ryan	lbw b Hammond	5	(3)	run out (Fishlock/Wade)	24
R.A.Hamence	b Allen	16		b Sims	4
*V.Y.Richardson	b Allen	29	(4)	c Verity b Allen	55
M.G.Waite	b Sims	2	(6)	lbw b Verity	4
E.J.R.Moyle	c Hammond b Allen	5	(7)	c Fishlock b Allen	32
C.V.Grimmett	b Sims	33	(8)	c Allen b Sims	5
F.A.Ward	b Allen	0		b Verity	11
H.N.J.Cotton	not out	37		not out	1
Extras	(b4, lb3, nb3)	10		(b10, nb4)	14
Total	(44.7 overs, 190 mins)	162		(61.3 overs, 232 mins)	202

SOUTH AUSTRALIA	O	M	R	W	w,nb	O	M	R	W	w,nb
Cotton	10	1	32	1	-,-	12.7	1	38	4	-,-
Waite	9	3	32	1	-,-	6	0	19	1	-,-
Ryan	17	4	22	0	-,-	19	2	46	0	-,-
Grimmett	21	2	62	2	-,-	9	0	26	0	-,-
Ward	21	2	79	5	-,-	22	2	98	5	-,-

M.C.C.	O	M	R	W	w,nb	O	M	R	W	w,nb
Allen	15	1	53	6	-,-	12	1	32	3	-,-
Voce	9	0	25	1	-,3	8	0	30	0	-,2
Hammond	6	0	15	1	-,-	2	0	13	0	-,-
Sims	11.7	0	36	2	-,-	22	1	76	2	-,2
Verity	3	0	23	0	-,-	16.3	5	35	4	-,-
Worthington						1	0	2	0	-,-

FALL OF WICKETS

Wkt	MCC 1st	SA 1st	MCC 2nd	SA 2nd
1st	9	8	0	36
2nd	19	20	18	76
3rd	81	28	90	85
4th	84	32	158	104
5th	138	66	182	111
6th	164	71	199	180
7th	176	80	216	181
8th	182	89	231	185
9th	205	89	231	191
10th	233	162	236	202

VICTORIA v M.C.C.

Played at Melbourne Cricket Ground on November 6, 7, 9, 10, 1936. (Four-day match)
Toss : M.C.C.   Result : MATCH DRAWN.
Debuts: Nil.
12th Men: J.A.Ledward (Vic) and H.Verity (MCC).
Umpires: A.N.Barlow and C.Dwyer.
Attendances: 10550, 9772, 12603, 2181.   Total: 35,106.   Receipts: £1600.
Close of Play: 1st day MCC 7/326 (Fishlock 26); 2nd day MCC 344 all out; 3rd day Vic 5/294 (Gregory 109, Barnett 2).

W.H.Copson (sprained leg) was unavailable in addition to L.E.G.Ames, G.Duckworth, R.W.V.Robins and R.E.S.Wyatt (all injured) for M.C.C. who again fielded a depleted side. L.O.Fleetwood-Smith (tendon injury) was unavailable for Victoria. Barnett (131 in 216 minutes, 19 fours) and Hardstaff (85 in 154 minutes, 11 fours) batted well for the tourists on the opening day, adding 143 for the fourth wicket. Weather restricted playing time on the second day to just 28 minutes, Fishlock (42 not out in 104 minutes, 7 fours) running out of partners as the bespectacled Frederick captured the last six wickets with his legbreaks. (Despite having taken 17 wickets in his first two matches, Frederick played only once more for Victoria at first-class level before being discarded). After losing O'Brien and Darling to the fifth and sixth balls of Voce's first over, the Victorians were steered to safety with a fourth-wicket partnership of 262 between Lee (160 in 226 minutes, 9 fours) and the twenty-year-old Gregory (128 in 242 minutes, 11 fours). Further rain severely restricted play on the last day. *Wisden* incorrectly gives MCC (1) Hardstaff c Sievers. Sources: *Wisden, NSWCA Report, VCA Report, The Age, The Argus, The Herald, Melbourne Sun.*

M.C.C

A.E.Fagg	c Barnett b Ebeling	20	(2) lbw b Frederick	11
C.J.Barnett	c Rigg b Ebeling	131		
T.S.Worthington	b McCormick	0	(1) c Plant b Ebeling	5
M.Leyland	run out (Lee)	24	(3) not out	18
J.Hardstaff, jr	c Plant b Frederick	85	(4) lbw b Frederick	0
L.B.Fishlock	not out	42	(5) not out	1
*G.O.B.Allen	st Barnett b Frederick	11		
J.M.Sims	lbw b Frederick	16		
K.Farnes	b Frederick	0		
†T.H.Wade	c Barnett b Frederick	0		
W.Voce	st Barnett b Frederick	2		
Extras	(b5, lb5, nb3)	13	(w1)	1
Total	(82.1 overs, 322 mins)	344	(13.0 overs, 50 mins) (3 wkts)	36

VICTORIA

L.P.J.O'Brien	c Worthington b Voce	1
K.E.Rigg	c Fishlock b Allen	10
L.S.Darling	b Voce	0
I.S.Lee	b Farnes	160
R.G.Gregory	b Farnes	128
M.W.Sievers	lbw b Sims	1
†B.A.Barnett	c Sims b Farnes	18
H.J.Plant	not out	21
J.Frederick	b Allen	0
*H.I.Ebeling	b Allen	15
E.L.McCormick	st Wade b Sims	4
Extras	(b19, lb3, nb4)	26
Total	(84.3 overs, 347 mins)	384

VICTORIA	O	M	R	W	w,nb		O	M	R	W	w,nb
McCormick	16	3	77	1	-,2		3	1	11	0	1,-
Ebeling	16	2	49	2	-,-		2	0	4	1	-,-
Sievers	18	3	61	0	-,1	(4)	2	0	3	0	-,-
Plant	15	1	68	0	-,-						
Frederick	16.1	1	65	6	-,-	(3)	4	0	10	2	-,-
Gregory	1	0	11	0	-,-	(5)	2	0	7	0	-,-

M.C.C.	O	M	R	W	w,nb
Farnes	22	2	56	3	-,-
Voce	11	1	51	2	-,4
Sims	19.3	0	86	2	-,-
Allen	20	0	97	3	-,-
Worthington	8	0	42	0	-,-
Leyland	4	0	26	0	-,-

FALL OF WICKETS

Wkt	MCC 1st	VIC 1st	MCC 2nd
1st	29	1	9
2nd	34	1	29
3rd	96	27	29
4th	239	289	-
5th	290	290	-
6th	306	331	-
7th	326	338	-
8th	334	339	-
9th	342	375	-
10th	344	384	-

NEW SOUTH WALES v M.C.C.

Played at Sydney Cricket Ground on November 13, 14, 16, 17, 1936. (Four-day match)
Toss : New South Wales.   Result : NEW SOUTH WALES WON BY 135 RUNS.
Debuts: Nil.
12th Men: V.E.Jackson (NSW). No 12th named for MCC.
Umpires: E.G.Borwick and A.L.Christie.
Attendances: 13515, 24211, 8760, 4107.   Total: 50,593.   Receipts: £3134.
Close of Play: 1st day MCC 0/1 (Fagg 1, Barnett 0); 2nd day NSW (2) 4/122 (Chipperfield 2, McGilvray 0); 3rd day MCC (2) 2/95
     (Hammond 23, Sims 5).

O'Reilly captured 4 for 4 from 3.6 overs to decide the match in the last possible over, ousting Fagg (5.36pm) at 7/302, Fishlock (5.47pm) at 8/308, Allen (5.51pm) at 9/310 and Hardstaff (5.59pm) to secure victory with two balls to spare. Hardstaff had refused a single from the fourth ball of the last over to keep Copson away from the strike. Hammond (91 in 305 minutes, 11 fours) and Leyland (79 in 177 minutes, 8 fours) had scored half-centuries earlier in the day. Barnett (70 in 143 minutes, 8 fours) and Hammond (39 in 82 minutes, 5 fours) were the top run-makers in the first innings. Mudge's part-time legbreaks returning 6 for 42 for New South Wales. Allen's pair included a first-ball dismissal in the first innings. McCabe (83 in 133 minutes, 10 fours), Robinson (91 in 170 minutes, 11 fours) and in the second innings Chipperfield (97 in 227 minutes, 5 fours) scored fifties for New South Wales. McCabe strained a groin muscle during his 83 and did not field in either M.C.C. innings, McGilvray leading the team instead. (He batted down the order in the second innings with Fingleton to run for him.) R.W.V.Robins (broken finger) and R.E.S.Wyatt (broken wrist) were unavailable for the tourists. Sources: *Wisden, NSWCA Report, VCA Report, The Age, The Herald, Sydney Morning Herald, NSWCA Scorebook, The Sporting Globe.*

NEW SOUTH WALES

J.H.W.Fingleton	lbw b Sims	39		lbw b Hammond	42
H.Mudge	lbw b Copson	2		c Barnett b Allen	34
A.E.Marks	st Ames b Sims	21		b Allen	33
*S.J.McCabe	c Fishlock b Hammond	83	(7)	c Allen b Copson	46
R.H.Robinson	b Allen	91	(4)	run out (Hammond/Ames)	4
A.G.Chipperfield	c Ames b Hammond	14	(5)	not out	97
A.D.McGilvray	lbw b Hammond	1	(6)	b Copson	12
L.C.Hynes	b Allen	3		b Worthington	15
†W.A.S.Oldfield	lbw b Hammond	1	(11)	b Sims	12
E.C.S.White	not out	3	(9)	c Ames b Sims	5
W.J.O'Reilly	c Fagg b Hammond	1	(10)	c Hardstaff b Sims	2
Extras	(b6, lb7, nb1)	14		(b15, lb5, nb4)	24
Total	(71.4 overs, 275 mins)	273		(79.3 overs, 311 mins)	326

M.C.C.

A.E.Fagg	lbw b White	1	(7)	lbw b O'Reilly	17
C.J.Barnett	st Oldfield b Mudge	70		run out (Robinson/Oldfield)	35
W.R.Hammond	st Oldfield b Mudge	39		st Oldfield b White	91
M.Leyland	c sub (V.E.Jackson) b Mudge	0	(5)	b White	79
J.Hardstaff, jr	c Fingleton b O'Reilly	0	(8)	lbw b O'Reilly	20
L.B.Fishlock	b Mudge	1	(9)	lbw b O'Reilly	3
T.S.Worthington	b O'Reilly	1	(1)	b O'Reilly	28
†L.E.G.Ames	c Marks b Mudge	13	(6)	b Mudge	20
*G.O.B.Allen	c McGilvray b Mudge	0	(10)	lbw b O'Reilly	0
J.M.Sims	not out	18	(4)	c Chipperfield b Mudge	9
W.H.Copson	b O'Reilly	8		not out	0
Extras	(lb1, nb1)	2		(b4, lb4, nb1)	9
Total	(47.5 overs, 165 mins)	153		(126.6 overs, 389 mins)	311

M.C.C.	O	M	R	W	w,nb		O	M	R	W	w,nb
Allen	16	0	45	2	-,-	(2)	17	2	69	2	-,3
Copson	15	0	71	1	-,-	(1)	20	2	91	2	-,-
Hammond	17.4	2	39	5	-,-	(4)	15	3	31	1	-,-
Sims	14	0	73	2	-,1	(3)	24.3	2	103	3	-,1
Worthington	9	0	31	0	-,-		3	1	8	1	-,-

NEW SOUTH WALES	O	M	R	W	w,nb		O	M	R	W	w,nb
Hynes	5	0	19	0	-,1		8	1	43	0	-,1
White	9	1	18	1	-,-	(4)	18	9	23	2	-,-
McGilvray	3	0	19	0	-,-	(2)	6	1	14	0	-,-
O'Reilly	18.5	1	53	3	-,-	(5)	38.6	18	67	5	-,-
Mudge	12	3	42	6	-,-	(3)	37	8	86	2	-,-
Chipperfield							7	1	15	0	-,-
Robinson							12	1	54	0	-,-

	FALL OF WICKETS			
	NSW	MCC	NSW	MCC
Wkt	1st	1st	2nd	2nd
1st	20	1	59	41
2nd	63	79	100	86
3rd	74	85	113	106
4th	219	103	115	237
5th	257	104	151	264
6th	259	107	247	274
7th	265	121	282	302
8th	266	121	295	308
9th	270	140	303	310
10th	273	153	326	311

VICTORIA v SOUTH AUSTRALIA (Shield Match 2)

Played at Melbourne Cricket Ground on November 13, 14, 16, 17, 1936. (Four-day match)
Toss : South Australia.   Result : MATCH DRAWN.
Debuts: Nil.
12th Men: J.A.Ledward (Vic) and E.J.R.Moyle (SA).
Umpires: A.N.Barlow and C.Dwyer.
Attendances: 6921, 21254, 1805, 2836.   Total: 32,816.   Receipts: £1204.
Close of Play: 1st day Vic 4/329 (Gregory 80, Sievers 34); 2nd day SA 5/295 (Hamence 9, Walker 0); 3rd day Vic (2) 1/97 (Rigg 52, Darling 40).

Bradman was absent on the first day recovering from an overnight attack of gastro-enteritis. Richardson, the stand-in captain, won the toss and sent Victoria in to bat so that Bradman had time to recover before batting. All the local batsmen got a start on the true wicket with Rigg (97 in 191 minutes, 6 fours), Gregory (85 in 148 minutes, 7 fours) and Sievers (54 in 122 minutes, 3 fours) recording half-centuries. Cotton, whose bowling action was widely considered controversial, was no-balled for throwing on one occasion by umpire Barlow at square-leg late on the first day. Bradman showed few ill effects when he came to the crease on the second afternoon, scoring 192 in 180 minutes with 32 fours and offering chances at 128 (off Frederick) and at 190, the ball prior to his dismissal, to Lee at straight hit. He made 127 runs after the tea adjournment before being caught at long-on at 5.58pm, having scored his last 93 in 47 minutes, the last 42 of them in 16 minutes including 19 off an over from Plant and 27 from two overs from Frederick. He scored 94 of his 108-run partnership for the fifth wicket with Hamence. Rigg (105 in 183 minutes, 8 fours) completed a fine personal double in the second innings, adding 186 in 154 minutes for the second wicket with Darling (102 in 169 minutes, 1 six and 10 fours). Lee (93 in 156 minutes, 9 fours) and Barnett (55 in 106 minutes, 7 fours) added 115 for the sixth wicket. Sources: *Wisden, VCA Report, SACA Report, The Age, The Argus, The Herald, The Sporting Globe*.

VICTORIA

L.P.J.O'Brien	run out (Badcock/Grimmett)	30	c Waite b Cotton	5
K.E.Rigg	lbw b Ward	97	c & b Waite	105
L.S.Darling	st Walker b Ward	39	lbw b Cotton	102
I.S.Lee	c Badcock b Waite	38	c & b Waite	93
R.G.Gregory	c Richardson b Cotton	85	c & b Waite	12
M.W.Sievers	c Waite b Ward	54	lbw b Grimmett	9
†B.A.Barnett	c Cotton b Ward	20	c Badcock b Waite	55
H.J.Plant	lbw b Ward	20	not out	8
J.Frederick	c Walker b Ward	3	not out	5
*H.I.Ebeling	st Walker b Grimmett	0		
E.L.McCormick	not out	2		
Extras	(b1, lb8, w3, nb1)	13	(b5, lb3, w1)	9
Total	(125.1 overs, 417 mins)	401	(112.0 overs, 374 mins) (7 wkts)	403

SOUTH AUSTRALIA

C.L.Badcock	lbw b McCormick	2
R.A.Parker	st Barnett b Sievers	33
A.J.Ryan	lbw b McCormick	9
*D.G.Bradman	c O'Brien b Gregory	192
V.Y.Richardson	lbw b Sievers	38
R.A.Hamence	b Frederick	37
†C.W.Walker	b Ebeling	34
M.G.Waite	c & b Ebeling	11
C.V.Grimmett	c Barnett b Ebeling	8
F.A.Ward	not out	3
H.N.J.Cotton	lbw b Ebeling	0
Extras	(b12, lb1, w2, nb4)	19
Total	(96.2 overs, 374 mins)	386

SOUTH AUSTRALIA	O	M	R	W	w,nb		O	M	R	W	w,nb
Cotton	21	0	82	1	2,1		16	0	83	2	1,-
Waite	13	2	37	1	1,-		21	1	65	4	-,-
Ryan	22	3	50	0	-,-	(5)	21	4	50	0	-,-
Grimmett	37.1	6	112	1	-,-	(3)	30	9	85	1	-,-
Ward	32	3	107	6	-,-	(4)	24	2	111	0	-,-

VICTORIA	O	M	R	W	w,nb
McCormick	15	1	85	2	1,3
Ebeling	26.2	5	74	4	-,-
Sievers	13	3	36	2	-,1
Frederick	15	2	90	1	-,-
Plant	15	6	50	0	-,-
Gregory	10	3	27	1	-,-
Darling	2	0	5	0	1,-

FALL OF WICKETS

Wkt	VIC 1st	SA 1st	VIC 2nd
1st	72	3	24
2nd	153	27	210
3rd	185	104	224
4th	237	187	253
5th	345	295	266
6th	364	336	381
7th	391	372	394
8th	396	377	-
9th	399	386	-
10th	401	386	-

AUSTRALIAN XI v M.C.C.

Played at Sydney Cricket Ground on November 20, 21, 23, 24, 1936. (Four-day match)
Toss : M.C.C.   Result : MATCH DRAWN.
Debuts: Nil.
12th Men: A.E.Marks (Aust). No 12th named for MCC.
Umpires: H.J.Armstrong and E.G.Borwick.
Attendances: 13554, 36534, 9446, 5211.   Total: 64,745.   Receipts: £4299.
Close of Play: 1st day MCC 5/274 (Leyland 79, Robins 44); 2nd day Aust 2/221 (Brown 66, Badcock 20); 3rd day Aust 8/544 (Ryan 40, Waite 11).

Selection of the Australian XI emphasised batsmen on trial for the Test series. Leading bowlers such as L.O.Fleetwood-Smith, E.L.McCormick, W.J.O'Reilly, M.W.Sievers and F.A.Ward were not exposed to the visitors. Leyland (118 not out in 232 minutes, 10 fours) and Voce held out for the final 30 minutes to save the match, though Duckworth - still suffering from his broken finger - was padded up to bat if required. First-innings practice was had by Fagg (49 in 169 minutes, 6 fours), Ames (76 in 113 minutes, 10 fours), Leyland (80 in 156 minutes, 5 fours) and Robins (53 in 91 minutes, 6 fours). Chipperfield's analyses provided him with the only five- and ten-wicket hauls of his career. Fingleton (56 in 99 minutes, 4 fours), Brown (71 in 259 minutes, 3 fours), Bradman (63 in 89 minutes, 8 fours), Badcock (182 in 304 minutes, 24 fours), Chipperfield (39 in 51 minutes, 3 fours), Tallon (31 in 62 minutes, 4 fours) and Ryan (40 not out in 105 minutes, 1 six and 2 fours) shared the runs for the Australians. Gregory replaced S.J.McCabe (leg injury) in the named team. Sources: *Wisden, NSWCA Report, VCA Report, The Age, The Herald, Sydney Morning Herald, NSWCA Scorebook.*

M.C.C.

A.E.Fagg	c Brown b Chipperfield	49	(3)	c Ebeling b Ryan	10
T.S.Worthington	c Robinson b Waite	6		st Tallon b Chipperfield	28
L.E.G.Ames	c Brown b Chipperfield	76	(5)	b Gregory	37
M.Leyland	c & b Chipperfield	80		not out	118
J.Hardstaff, jr	c Tallon b Chipperfield	12	(6)	b Gregory	2
L.B.Fishlock	st Tallon b Chipperfield	0	(1)	b Waite	2
*R.W.V.Robins	b Ebeling	53		c Ryan b Ebeling	33
H.Verity	c Tallon b Chipperfield	0		lbw b Chipperfield	2
W.Voce	c Bradman b Chipperfield	4	(10)	not out	2
†G.Duckworth	not out	0			
K.Farnes	c Brown b Chipperfield	0	(9)	b Ebeling	1
Extras	(lb7, w1)	8		(b4, lb6)	10
Total	(93.1 overs, 323 mins)	288		(87.0 overs, 295 mins) (8 wkts)	245

AUSTRALIAN XI

J.H.W.Fingleton	lbw b Verity	56
W.A.Brown	lbw b Farnes	71
*D.G.Bradman	b Worthington	63
C.L.Badcock	c Farnes b Verity	182
R.H.Robinson	c Worthington b Farnes	0
R.G.Gregory	c Worthington b Verity	14
A.G.Chipperfield	c Duckworth b Voce	39
†D.Tallon	c Hardstaff b Robins	31
A.J.Ryan	not out	40
M.G.Waite	not out	11
H.I.Ebeling	did not bat	
Extras	(b14, lb15, nb8)	37
Total	(141.0 overs, 529 mins) (8 wkts dec)	544

AUSTRALIAN XI	O	M	R	W	w,nb		O	M	R	W	w,nb
Ebeling	25	6	71	1	-,-		18	5	38	2	-,-
Waite	16	4	48	1	1,-		14	1	33	1	-,-
Gregory	13	0	64	0	-,-	(5)	19	3	56	2	-,-
Ryan	16	5	31	0	-,-		5	0	11	1	-,-
Chipperfield	23.1	4	66	8	-,-	(3)	29	7	88	2	-,-
Robinson							2	0	9	0	-,-

M.C.C.	O	M	R	W	w,nb
Farnes	24	4	112	2	-,-
Voce	27	4	89	1	-,8
Robins	13	0	72	1	-,-
Verity	48	5	130	3	-,-
Worthington	25	5	81	1	-,-
Leyland	4	0	23	0	-,-

	FALL OF WICKETS		
	MCC	AUST	MCC
Wkt	1st	1st	2nd
1st	12	103	9
2nd	128	194	38
3rd	147	228	50
4th	174	228	118
5th	178	271	134
6th	284	332	202
7th	284	412	213
8th	285	519	226
9th	288	-	-
10th	288	-	-

QUEENSLAND v M.C.C.

Played at Brisbane Cricket Ground (Woolloongabba) on November 27, 28, 30, December 1, 1936. (Four-day match)
Toss : M.C.C.   Result : MATCH DRAWN.
Debuts: Queensland - G.W.Baker, J.S.D.Cockburn (both f/c).
12th Men: C.D.Hansen (Qld) and W.H.Copson (MCC).
Umpires: J.Bartlett and D.W.Given.
Attendances: 5000, 9782, 2880, 1277.   Total: 18,939.   Receipts: £1735.
Close of Play: 1st day Qld 0/71 (Brown 38, Rogers 32); 2nd day MCC (2) 0/19 (Fagg 9, Barnett 10); 3rd day MCC (2) 3/453
    (Fishlock 41, Ames 25).

The last pair of Wyeth and Dixon held the Englishmen out on the final afternoon after Robins had decided to bat on with a lead of 425 runs. Fagg (112 in 226 minutes, 13 fours) and Barnett (career-best 259 in 273 minutes, 2 sixes and 39 fours) shared a first-wicket stand of 295 for M.C.C. - the highest so far recorded for that wicket in Brisbane. Barnett progressed from 76 at lunch on the third day to 184 at tea and from 100 (150 minutes) to 200 (237 minutes) in less than 90 minutes. Leyland (98 in 159 minutes, 16 fours) and Ames (60 in 84 minutes, 7 fours) scored fifties. Fagg was caught off the third ball of the match, Hardstaff falling to his first ball later in the innings. Brown (74 in 177 minutes, 7 fours) and Rogers (62 in 123 minutes, 7 fours) established the first opening century partnership by Queensland against England but a fine spell by Verity (5 for 50 from 30 8-ball overs) minimised the damage. Tallon was run out attempting a single off his first ball. Baker on debut (63 in 113 minutes, 7 fours) topscored in the second innings; both he and the two bowlers who dismissed him died on active service in the Second World War. *State Annual Reports* give MCC (2) Hammond 3, Voce 5*. *VCA Report* incorrectly gives Qld (1) Rogers c Hammond b Verity. Sources: *Wisden, NSWCA Report, VCA Report, QCA Report, The Herald, Brisbane Courier-Mail*.

M.C.C.

A.E.Fagg	c Andrews b Dixon	0		c Brown b Allen	112
C.J.Barnett	c Baker b Dixon	20		c Brown b Amos	259
W.R.Hammond	c Tallon b Dixon	36	(8)	not out	4
M.Leyland	c Brown b Allen	98	(9)	c Dixon b Wyeth	2
†L.E.G.Ames	c Amos b Allen	41		c Dixon b Wyeth	60
J.Hardstaff, jr	c & b Allen	0	(4)	c & b Allen	12
L.B.Fishlock	run out (Baker/Tallon)	6	(3)	c Cockburn b Dixon	41
*R.W.V.Robins	c Tallon b Oxenham	1	(6)	b Wyeth	17
H.Verity	st Tallon b Allen	0	(7)	c Baker b Amos	8
W.Voce	not out	6		not out	4
K.Farnes	run out (Brown/Tallon)	4			
Extras	(b2, w1)	3		(b6, lb2, w1)	9
Total	(58.0 overs, 220 mins)	215		(113.0 overs, 422 mins) (8 wkts dec)	528

QUEENSLAND

W.A.Brown	c Fishlock b Verity	74	(2)	c Ames b Farnes	5
R.E.Rogers	c Hammond b Farnes	62	(1)	lbw b Robins	11
W.C.Andrews	c & b Verity	24		lbw b Robins	44
T.Allen	b Verity	12		b Robins	4
†D.Tallon	run out (Farnes/Ames)	0		lbw b Verity	18
G.W.Baker	c & b Verity	5		lbw b Farnes	63
J.S.D.Cockburn	c Verity b Leyland	2		c Fishlock b Verity	2
*R.K.Oxenham	b Voce	19		lbw b Robins	12
G.S.Amos	b Verity	3		c Fagg b Farnes	39
E.R.Wyeth	c Verity b Farnes	29		not out	4
P.L.Dixon	not out	5		not out	4
Extras	(b1, lb5, nb2)	8		(b8, lb12, nb1)	21
Total	(81.4 overs, 312 mins)	243		(56.0 overs, 213 mins) (9 wkts)	227

QUEENSLAND	O	M	R	W	w,nb		O	M	R	W	w,nb
Dixon	12	3	50	3	-,-		26	1	126	1	1,-
Cockburn	9	1	46	0	-,-		11	1	49	0	-,-
Oxenham	16	8	34	1	-,-		20	7	56	0	-,-
Amos	4	0	11	0	-,-		20	3	90	2	-,-
Wyeth	10	2	44	0	-,-		22	2	95	3	-,-
Allen	7	1	27	4	1,-		14	0	103	2	-,-

M.C.C.	O	M	R	W	w,nb		O	M	R	W	w,nb
Voce	18	0	51	1	-,2		10	1	37	0	-,-
Farnes	19.4	4	75	2	-,-		9	1	45	3	-,1
Hammond	5	0	17	0	-,-	(6)	1	0	12	0	-,-
Robins	3	0	23	0	-,-	(3)	17	1	63	4	-,-
Verity	30	9	50	5	-,-	(4)	15	5	31	2	-,-
Leyland	6	0	19	1	-,-	(5)	4	0	18	0	-,-

FALL OF WICKETS

	MCC	QLD	MCC	QLD
Wkt	1st	1st	2nd	2nd
1st	0	117	295	14
2nd	43	145	401	43
3rd	86	166	417	55
4th	193	166	454	91
5th	193	178	483	93
6th	203	183	512	105
7th	205	187	519	132
8th	205	193	522	209
9th	205	237	-	218
10th	215	243	-	-

AUSTRALIA v ENGLAND (1st Test)

Played at Brisbane Cricket Ground (Woolloongabba) on December 4, 5, 7, 8, 9, 1936. (Timeless match)
Toss : England.   Result : ENGLAND WON BY 322 RUNS.
Debuts: Australia - C.L.Badcock, R.H.Robinson, M.W.Sievers, F.A.Ward (all Test).
12th Men: W.A.Brown (Aust) and J.M.Sims (Eng).
Umpires: E.G.Borwick and J.D.Scott.
Attendances: 14303, 30598, 12600, 7917, 7400.   Total: 72,818.   Receipts: £10,336.
Close of Play: 1st day Eng 6/263 (Hardstaff 27, Robins 6); 2nd day Aust 2/151 (Fingleton 61, McCabe 37); 3rd day Eng (2) 2/75
     (Fagg 24, Hammond 12); 4th day Aust (2) 1/3 (Badcock 0, Sievers 2).

McCormick, bowling at great pace with lift, took the wicket of Worthington with the first ball of the game and later dismissed Fagg and Hammond with successive balls. Due to an attack of lumbago, he bowled only three further overs in the innings and was forced from the field before the first day was out, Brown (named 12th man because of an injured thumb) fielding in his place for the remainder. Barnett (69 in 125 minutes, 1 six and 9 fours) and Leyland (126 in 251 minutes, 11 fours, chances at 19 and 71) and in the second innings Allen (68 in 194 minutes, 8 fours) led the scoring for the Englishmen. Fingleton (100 in 297 minutes, 6 fours) became the first batsman to score four Test centuries in a row (112, 108 and 118 in his three previous innings, in South Africa). McCabe (51 in 116 minutes, 6 fours) also batted well. Fingleton was out to the first ball of Australia's second innings and overnight rain turned the worn pitch into a nightmare for the batsmen on the fifth day. England took 8/55 in 10.5 overs to wrap up the match. The omission from the Australian side of C.V.Grimmett, who had performed outstandingly in South Africa, taking 44 wickets in five Tests (average 14.59), coincided with the introduction of Bradman to the selection committee and the national captaincy. Sources: *Wisden, QCA Report, The Age, The Herald, Sydney Morning Herald, Brisbane Courier-Mail.*

ENGLAND

T.S.Worthington	c Oldfield b McCormick	0	st Oldfield b McCabe	8
C.J.Barnett	c Oldfield b O'Reilly	69	c Badcock b Ward	26
A.E.Fagg	c Oldfield b McCormick	4	st Oldfield b Ward	27
W.R.Hammond	c Robinson b McCormick	0	hit wkt b Ward	25
M.Leyland	b Ward	126	c Bradman b Ward	33
†L.E.G.Ames	c Chipperfield b Ward	24	b Sievers	9
J.Hardstaff, jr	c McCabe b O'Reilly	43	(8) st Oldfield b Ward	20
R.W.V.Robins	c sub (W.A.Brown) b O'Reilly	38	(9) c Chipperfield b Ward	0
*G.O.B.Allen	c McCabe b O'Reilly	35	(7) c Fingleton b Sievers	68
H.Verity	c Sievers b O'Reilly	7	lbw b Sievers	19
W.Voce	not out	4	not out	2
Extras	(b1, lb3, nb4)	8	(b14, lb4, nb1)	19
Total	(113.6 overs, 401 mins)	358	(116.6 overs, 391 mins)	256

AUSTRALIA

J.H.W.Fingleton	b Verity	100	b Voce	0
C.L.Badcock	b Allen	8	c Fagg b Allen	0
*D.G.Bradman	c Worthington b Voce	38	(5) c Fagg b Allen	0
S.J.McCabe	c Barnett b Voce	51	(6) c Leyland b Allen	7
R.H.Robinson	c Hammond b Voce	2	(7) c Hammond b Voce	3
A.G.Chipperfield	c Ames b Voce	7	(8) not out	26
M.W.Sievers	b Allen	8	(3) c Voce b Allen	5
†W.A.S.Oldfield	c Ames b Voce	6	(4) b Voce	10
W.J.O'Reilly	c Leyland b Voce	3	b Allen	0
F.A.Ward	c Hardstaff b Allen	0	b Voce	1
E.L.McCormick	not out	1	absent ill	-
Extras	(b4, lb1, nb5)	10	(nb6)	6
Total	(85.6 overs, 348 mins)	234	(12.3 overs, 71 mins)	58

AUSTRALIA	O	M	R	W	w,nb		O	M	R	W	w,nb		FALL OF WICKETS			
														ENG	AUST	ENG	AUST
McCormick	8	1	26	3	-,1							Wkt	1st	1st	2nd	2nd
Sievers	16	5	42	0	-,2	(1)	19.6	9	29	3	-,-	1st	0	13	17	0
O'Reilly	40.6	13	102	5	-,1	(4)	35	15	59	0	-,-	2nd	20	89	50	3
Ward	36	2	138	2	-,-	(3)	46	16	102	6	-,-	3rd	20	166	82	7
Chipperfield	11	3	32	0	-,-		10	2	33	0	-,-	4th	119	176	105	7
McCabe	2	0	10	0	-,-	(2)	6	1	14	1	-,1	5th	162	202	122	16
												6th	252	220	144	20
ENGLAND	O	M	R	W	w,nb		O	M	R	W	w,nb	7th	311	229	205	35
Allen	16	2	71	3	-,-	(2)	6	0	36	5	-,1	8th	311	231	205	41
Voce	20.6	5	41	6	-,5	(1)	6.3	0	16	4	-,5	9th	343	231	247	58
Hammond	4	0	12	0	-,-							10th	358	234	256	-
Verity	28	11	52	1	-,-											
Robins	17	0	48	0	-,-											

AUSTRALIA v ENGLAND (2nd Test)

Played at Sydney Cricket Ground on December 18, 19, 21, 22, 1936. (Timeless match)
Toss : England.   Result : ENGLAND WON BY AN INNINGS AND 22 RUNS.
Debuts: Nil.
12th Men: R.H.Robinson (Aust) and L.B.Fishlock (Eng).
Umpires: E.G.Borwick and J.D.Scott.
Attendances: 35107, 43326, 24894, 23620.   Total: 126,947.   Receipts: £12,038.
Close of Play: 1st day Eng 3/307 (Hammond 167, Ames 14); 2nd day Eng 6/426 (Hammond 231, Verity 0); 3rd day Aust (2) 1/145
 (Fingleton 67, Bradman 57).

W.A.Brown (injured thumb) was still unavailable for Australia. Badcock (gastro-enteritis) was unable to take the field on the second day. Hammond (231 not out in 458 minutes, 27 fours) offered his one chance when 215, a caught-and-bowled to Ward. Barnett (57 in 107 minutes, 5 fours) and Leyland (42 in 154 minutes, 3 fours) gave him solid support. Rain prevented play after 4.30pm on the second day and a storm the next morning saturated the wicket, prompting Allen to declare. Voce captured the wickets of O'Brien and Bradman with the last two balls of his opening over (Bradman sustaining his second Test duck in a row) and dismissed McCabe with the second ball of his next over, giving him three in four balls. O'Reilly (37 not out in 44 minutes, 3 sixes and 2 fours) hit out. Fingleton (73 in 196 minutes, 4 fours), Bradman (82 in 171 minutes, 6 fours) and McCabe (93 in 174 minutes, 10 fours) batted well in the follow-on in improved conditions, but the deficit was too great. Sources: *Wisden, NSWCA Report, The Herald, Sydney Morning Herald, The Australasian, Sydney Referee*.

ENGLAND

A.E.Fagg	c Sievers b McCormick	11	
C.J.Barnett	b Ward	57	
W.R.Hammond	not out	231	
M.Leyland	lbw b McCabe	42	
†L.E.G.Ames	c sub (R.H.Robinson) b Ward	29	
*G.O.B.Allen	lbw b O'Reilly	9	
J.Hardstaff, jr	b McCormick	26	
H.Verity	not out	0	
R.W.V.Robins	)		
J.M.Sims	) did not bat		
W.Voce	)		
Extras	(b8, lb2, w1, nb4)	21	
Total	(141.2 overs, 489 mins) (6 wkts dec)	426	

AUSTRALIA

J.H.W.Fingleton	c Verity b Voce	12	(2)	b Sims	73
L.P.J.O'Brien	c Sims b Voce	0	(1)	c Allen b Hammond	17
*D.G.Bradman	c Allen b Voce	0		b Verity	82
S.J.McCabe	c Sims b Voce	0		lbw b Voce	93
A.G.Chipperfield	c Sims b Allen	13		b Voce	21
M.W.Sievers	c Voce b Verity	4	(7)	run out (Barnett/Ames)	24
†W.A.S.Oldfield	b Verity	1	(8)	c Ames b Voce	1
W.J.O'Reilly	not out	37	(9)	b Hammond	3
E.L.McCormick	b Allen	10	(10)	lbw b Hammond	0
F.A.Ward	b Allen	0	(11)	not out	1
C.L.Badcock	absent ill	-	(6)	lbw b Allen	2
Extras	(b1, lb1, nb1)	3		(lb3, nb4)	7
Total	(23.7 overs, 107 mins)	80		(96.7 overs, 390 mins)	324

AUSTRALIA	O	M	R	W	w,nb
McCormick	20	1	79	2	1,4
Sievers	16.2	4	30	0	-,-
Ward	42	8	132	2	-,-
O'Reilly	41	17	86	1	-,-
Chipperfield	13	2	47	0	-,-
McCabe	9	1	31	1	-,-

ENGLAND	O	M	R	W	w,nb		O	M	R	W	w,nb
Voce	8	1	10	4	-,-		19	4	66	3	-,1
Allen	5.7	1	19	3	-,1		19	4	61	1	-,3
Verity	3	0	17	2	-,-	(5)	19	7	55	1	-,-
Hammond	4	0	6	0	-,-	(3)	15.7	3	29	3	-,-
Sims	2	0	20	0	-,-	(4)	17	0	80	1	-,-
Robins	1	0	5	0	-,-		7	0	26	0	-,-

FALL OF WICKETS

	ENG	AUST	AUST
Wkt	1st	1st	2nd
1st	27	1	38
2nd	118	1	162
3rd	247	1	186
4th	351	16	220
5th	368	28	226
6th	424	30	318
7th	-	37	319
8th	-	80	323
9th	-	80	323
10th	-	-	324

VICTORIA v QUEENSLAND (Shield Match 3)

Played at Melbourne Cricket Ground on December 18, 19, 21, 1936. (Four-day match)
Toss : Victoria.   Result : VICTORIA WON BY AN INNINGS AND 85 RUNS.
Debuts: Victoria - W.E.Pearson (f/c).
12th Men: R.A.Dempster (Vic) and G.D.Gunthorpe (Qld).
Umpires: A.N.Barlow and C.Dwyer.
Attendances: 2180, 3575, 329.   Total: 6084.   Receipts: £160.
Close of Play: 1st day Vic 2/143 (Darling 81, Gregory 36); 2nd day Qld (2) 5/105(Allen 58).

Inserted after an hour's delay due to inclement weather on a wicket which, although found to be a little soft after the tarpaulin had been removed, was not considered bad, Queensland recorded their second-lowest total to date in first-class cricket. Allen fell to the sixth ball of the opening over and no boundaries were struck in the meagre total of 49. Fleetwood-Smith captured all his wickets (7 for 17) in his last 5 overs, beginning with that of Rogers in his sixth. His career-best match analysis of 15 for 96 was the best by a Victorian, the best by a bowler at Melbourne and the third best in the Sheffield Shield so far. Allen's second-innings 101 (212 minutes, 9 fours) was the only score over 18 for Queensland; he was last man out. Darling (111 in 168 minutes, 8 fours) who scored his runs out of 171, shared a third-wicket stand of 137 with Gregory (46 in 116 minutes, 3 fours). Ledward (57 in 91 minutes, 6 fours) and Pearson (36 in 82 minutes, 2 fours) also batted well for Victoria, adding 93 together. *Wisden* incorrectly gives Qld (2) total as 157. Sources: *Wisden, VCA Report, QCA Report, The Age, The Argus, The Herald, The Sporting Globe.*

QUEENSLAND

R.E.Rogers	b Fleetwood-Smith	14		c Barnett b Pearson	7
T.Allen	c Plant b Ebeling	0		c Plant b Fleetwood-Smith	101
W.C.Andrews	lbw b Fleetwood-Smith	16		lbw b Fleetwood-Smith	1
†D.Tallon	c Barnett b Fleetwood-Smith	3		c Ledward b Fleetwood-Smith	11
G.W.Baker	lbw b Fleetwood-Smith	0	(6)	lbw b Pearson	18
C.D.Hansen	c Rigg b Fleetwood-Smith	0	(7)	c Lee b Fleetwood-Smith	2
G.G.Cook	not out	8	(5)	lbw b Fleetwood-Smith	7
*R.K.Oxenham	c Ebeling b Pearson	1		lbw b Fleetwood-Smith	15
G.S.Amos	c Hassett b Fleetwood-Smith	1		b Fleetwood-Smith	4
E.R.Wyeth	lbw b Fleetwood-Smith	3		lbw b Fleetwood-Smith	4
P.L.Dixon	c Darling b Pearson	1		not out	0
Extras	(b2)	2		(b2, lb2, w1)	5
Total	(32.6 overs, 116 mins)	49		(59.1 overs, 212 mins)	175

VICTORIA

K.E.Rigg	c Tallon b Dixon	11
I.S.Lee	c Wyeth b Amos	13
L.S.Darling	b Cook	111
R.G.Gregory	c Hansen b Amos	46
A.L.Hassett	c Wyeth b Amos	5
J.A.Ledward	c Rogers b Dixon	57
W.E.Pearson	b Dixon	36
†R.A.Barnett	not out	9
H.J.Plant	lbw b Cook	10
*H.I.Ebeling	lbw b Cook	6
L.O.Fleetwood-Smith	c sub (G.D.Gunthorpe) b Cook	0
Extras	(b1, lb1, w1, nb2)	5
Total	(79.7 overs, 319 mins)	309

VICTORIA	O	M	R	W	w,nb	O	M	R	W	w,nb
Ebeling	13	2	21	1	-,-	11	1	24	0	-,-
Pearson	9.6	3	9	2	-,-	12	2	25	2	-,-
Fleetwood-Smith	10	2	17	7	-,-	23.1	3	79	8	1,-
Gregory						10	0	36	0	-,-
Plant						3	0	6	0	-,-

QUEENSLAND	O	M	R	W	w,nb
Dixon	21	3	87	3	-,2
Amos	16	3	67	3	1,-
Oxenham	12	3	28	0	-,-
Cook	15.7	1	60	4	-,-
Wyeth	10	2	30	0	-,-
Allen	5	0	32	0	-,-

FALL OF WICKETS

Wkt	QLD 1st	VIC 1st	QLD 2nd
1st	1	14	11
2nd	19	38	23
3rd	25	175	35
4th	27	185	57
5th	31	191	105
6th	38	284	114
7th	39	284	140
8th	40	299	148
9th	44	309	170
10th	49	309	175

AFCM No. 880/82
SSM No. 297/79

SOUTH AUSTRALIA v NEW SOUTH WALES (Shield Match 4)

Played at Adelaide Oval on December 18, 19, 21, 22, 1936. (Four-day match)
Toss : South Australia.   Result : SOUTH AUSTRALIA WON BY 109 RUNS.
Debuts: South Australia - N.H.Oswald, B.Schultz (both f/c). New South Wales - A.G.Cheetham, K.C.Gulliver, M.J.Ward (all f/c).
12th Men: M.J.Doherty (SA) and J.G.Lush (NSW).
Umpires: A.G.Jenkins and A.J.Richardson.
Attendances: 784, 1773, 401, 80.   Total: 3038.   Receipts: £185.
Close of Play: 1st day NSW 2/43 (Ward 16, Jackson 6); 2nd day SA (2) 5/144 (Schultz 13); 3rd day NSW (2) 5/118 (Marks 24, Mudge 3).

Both Sides were weakened by Test call-ups, New South Wales (six men) and South Australia (three) providing 75 per cent of the Test twelve at Sydney. Only four scores of more than 50 were compiled, Whitington (57 in 162 minutes, 3 fours), Ryan (67 in 108 minutes, 3 fours) and Waite (77 in 176 minutes, 4 fours) for South Australia and Marks (74 in 191 minutes, 4 fours) for New South Wales. Cheetham (47 not out in 129 minutes, 5 fours) ran out of partners in the first innings. Schultz, who dismissed Mudge in his first over, and Oswald, who dismissed Gulliver in his second, claimed early wickets in their first-class careers. White was out to the last ball of the first over in the second innings. Sources: *Wisden, NSWCA Report, SACA Report, The Herald, Sydney Morning Herald, NSWCA Scorebook, Adelaide Advertiser, The News.*

SOUTH AUSTRALIA

A.J.Ryan	c Marks b Cheetham	33		c Gulliver b Mudge	67
R.A.Parker	c Gulliver b Hynes	1		lbw b Mudge	25
R.S.Whitington	lbw b Mudge	57		c McGilvray b Cheetham	17
R.A.Hamence	b White	7		c Jackson b Hynes	19
B.H.Leak	st Easton b Cheetham	15		c & b Gulliver	0
M.G.Waite	c Cheetham b White	14	(7)	c Caldwell b Hynes	77
B.Schultz	b Hynes	30	(6)	c Caldwell b Mudge	28
N.H.Oswald	b White	0	(10)	c & b Mudge	12
R.G.Williams	c Gulliver b Hynes	5	(11)	not out	3
*†C.W.Walker	c Caldwell b Hynes	1	(9)	st Easton b Mudge	37
C.V.Grimmett	not out	0	(8)	c sub (J.G.Lush) b Mudge	6
Extras	(b9, lb7, nb2)	18		(b8, nb2)	10
Total	(70.7 overs, 249 mins)	181		(99.3 overs, 343 mins)	301

NEW SOUTH WALES

M.J.Ward	lbw b Grimmett	27		c Whitington b Waite	2
H.Mudge	lbw b Schultz	11	(7)	c & b Oswald	17
A.E.Marks	b Grimmett	9	(6)	b Williams	74
V.E.Jackson	st Walker b Grimmett	6	(5)	c Leak b Oswald	39
*A.D.McGilvray	c Walker b Schultz	22	(3)	c Leak b Ryan	34
A.G.Cheetham	not out	47	(4)	lbw b Grimmett	12
K.C.Gulliver	lbw b Oswald	5	(8)	b Williams	18
†F.A.Easton	c Ryan b Grimmett	2	(10)	not out	2
L.C.Hynes	st Walker b Oswald	17		c & b Williams	12
E.C.S.White	c Walker b Grimmett	1	(2)	c Walker b Williams	1
T.C.J.Caldwell	lbw b Grimmett	0		b Grimmett	5
Extras	(lb2)	2		(b2, lb4, nb2)	8
Total	(58.4 overs, 219 mins)	149		(89.2 overs, 312 mins)	224

NEW SOUTH WALES	O	M	R	W	w,nb		O	M	R	W	w,nb
Hynes	14.7	3	35	4	-,2		19	4	63	2	,2
McGilvray	6	0	28	0	-,-		5	0	17	0	-,-
Cheetham	9	0	44	2	-,-	(7)	6	2	9	1	-,-
White	20	11	23	3	-,-		15	6	21	0	-,-
Mudge	18	4	30	1	-,-		29.3	3	97	6	-,-
Gulliver	3	2	3	0	-,-	(8)	11	0	46	1	-,-
Caldwell						(6)	10	1	30	0	-,-
Jackson						(3)	4	1	8	0	-,-

SOUTH AUSTRALIA	O	M	R	W	w,nb		O	M	R	W	w,nb
Williams	7	0	19	0	-,-		13	2	44	4	-,2
Waite	4	0	15	0	-,-		9	3	13	1	-,-
Schultz	8	1	29	2	-,-	(4)	2	0	16	0	-,-
Grimmett	22.4	6	64	6	-,-	(3)	35.2	7	81	2	-,-
Ryan	14	5	15	0	-,-		21	5	32	1	-,-
Oswald	3	1	5	2	-,-		9	1	30	2	-,-

FALL OF WICKETS				
Wkt	SA 1st	NSW 1st	SA 2nd	NSW 2nd
1st	3	27	72	3
2nd	59	36	99	10
3rd	70	44	117	29
4th	110	61	118	65
5th	136	95	144	108
6th	142	104	172	166
7th	144	120	180	202
8th	154	148	267	212
9th	168	149	291	217
10th	181	149	301	224

VICTORIA v NEW SOUTH WALES (Shield Match 5)

Played at Melbourne Cricket Ground on December 24, 26, 28, 29, 1936. (Four-day match)
Toss : Victoria.   Result : MATCH DRAWN.
Debuts: Nil.
12th Men: G.H.Newstead (Vic) and K.C.Gulliver (NSW).
Umpires: A.N.Barlow and C.Dwyer.
Attendances: 3596, 15667, 8738, 4699.   Total: 32,700.   Receipts: £1235.
Close of Play: 1st day Vic 7/315 (Barnett 45, Plant 0); 2nd day Vic (2) 0/16 (Rigg 6, Lee 6); 3rd day Vic (2) 3/277 (Rigg 151, Hassett 56).

After narrowly missing a hundred in each innings against South Australia at the same ground the previous month, Rigg achieved the feat (the seventh to do so for Victoria) with 100 (198 minutes, 3 fours) and an unbeaten 167 (295 minutes, 9 fours). Lee was out to the fourth ball of the match, the first he faced. Hassett with 83 (171 minutes, 5 fours) and 71 not out (135 minutes, 5 fours) and Ledward with 60 (110 minutes, 6 fours) scored fifties for the side. Mudge (46 in 105 minutes, 4 fours) and Jackson (46 in 84 minutes, 5 fours) in the first innings and Ward (68 in 156 minutes, 6 fours) and Jackson again (88 in 154 minutes, 9 fours) in the second topscored for New South Wales. Rain and bad light caused the abandonment of the match at 5.18pm on the final day. Both teams were weakened by the loss of players participating in the Second Test. *Wisden* omits Vic (1) Barnett & Ebeling c sub. Sources: *Wisden, NSWCA Report, VCA Report, The Age, The Argus, The Herald, NSWCA Scorebook, The Sporting Globe.*

VICTORIA

K.E.Rigg	c & b White	100	not out	167
I.S.Lee	b Lush	0	c Easton b Hynes	12
L.S.Darling	c Marks b Lush	3	lbw b Lush	17
R.G.Gregory	b Lush	5	c Caldwell b Mudge	28
A.L.Hassett	c & b McGilvray	82	not out	71
J.A.Ledward	c Lush b Caldwell	60		
W.E.Pearson	c & b McGilvray	7		
†B.A.Barnett	c sub (K.C.Gulliver) b McGilvray	45		
H.J.Plant	not out	1		
*H.I.Ebeling	c sub (K.C.Gulliver) b Lush	1		
L.O.Fleetwood-Smith	c & b Lush	1		
Extras	(b4, lb6, nb2)	12	(b7, lb1, w1, nb4)	13
Total	(90.2 overs, 329 mins)	318	(85.7 overs, 295 mins) (3 wkts dec)	308

NEW SOUTH WALES

M.J.Ward	lbw b Fleetwood-Smith	17	c Hassett b Fleetwood-Smith	68
H.Mudge	c Barnett b Fleetwood-Smith	46	b Pearson	3
A.G.Cheetham	c Pearson b Fleetwood-Smith	20	c Plant b Pearson	4
A.E.Marks	b Pearson	11	lbw b Fleetwood-Smith	11
V.E.Jackson	c Plant b Gregory	46	st Barnett b Gregory	88
*A.D.McGilvray	lbw b Gregory	24	not out	16
J.G.Lush	c Hassett b Fleetwood-Smith	21	not out	12
L.C.Hynes	c Barnett b Fleetwood-Smith	39		
†F.A.Easton	b Ebeling	7		
E.C.S.White	not out	9		
T.C.J.Caldwell	c Barnett b Ebeling	2		
Extras	(lb8, w2)	10	(b5, lb6)	11
Total	(72.7 overs, 260 mins)	252	(67.4 overs, 231 mins) (5 wkts)	213

NEW SOUTH WALES	O	M	R	W	w,nb		O	M	R	W	w,nb
Lush	15.2	1	74	5	-,1		10	0	50	1	1,2
Hynes	12	2	41	0	-,1		7	0	25	1	-,2
White	23	7	45	1	-,-	(4)	32	5	74	0	-,-
Mudge	13	1	38	0	-,-	(5)	17	2	65	1	-,-
Cheetham	7	1	27	0	-,-						
Caldwell	11	1	46	1	-,-		7.7	0	31	0	-,-
McGilvray	9	1	35	3	-,-	(3)	12	3	50	0	-,-

VICTORIA	O	M	R	W	w,nb		O	M	R	W	w,nb
Ebeling	14.7	1	41	2	-,-		10	4	23	0	-,-
Pearson	17	3	48	1	-,-		10	0	35	2	-,-
Fleetwood-Smith	27	3	110	5	2,-		22.4	3	70	2	-,-
Gregory	11	0	41	2	-,-		18	5	60	1	-,-
Plant	3	1	2	0	-,-		7	3	14	0	-,-

FALL OF WICKETS

Wkt	VIC 1st	NSW 1st	VIC 2nd	NSW 2nd
1st	1	39	27	4
2nd	12	77	73	10
3rd	23	89	153	34
4th	192	105	-	157
5th	198	153	-	189
6th	206	178	-	-
7th	315	194	-	-
8th	315	213	-	-
9th	316	249	-	-
10th	318	252	-	-

SOUTH AUSTRALIA v QUEENSLAND (Shield Match 6)

Played at Adelaide Oval on December 25, 26, 28, 29, 1936. (Four-day match)
Toss : South Australia.   Result : SOUTH AUSTRALIA WON BY 112 RUNS.
Debuts: Nil.
12th Men: B.H.Leak (SA) and G.D.Gunthorpe (Qld).
Umpires: A.G.Jenkins and A.J.Richardson.
Attendances: 4865, 3748, 2430, 803.   Total: 11,846.   Receipts: £567.
Close of Play: 1st day SA 8/285 (Grimmett 33, Williams 2); 2nd day SA (2) 2/46 (Whitington 22, Hamence 12); 3rd day Qld (2) 4/66 (Rogers 33, Wyeth 8).

Going into the match without Test men C.L.Badcock, G.D.Bradman and F.A.Ward, South Australia lost Ryan to the first ball but recovered with maiden Shield hundreds from Hamence (104 in 207 minutes, 10 fours) in the first innings and Whitington (125 in 275 minutes, 14 fours) in the second. Allen was out in the first over (fifth ball) of a Queensland innings for the second consecutive match (a second-innings century at Melbourne splitting his ducks). Tallon (101 in 149 minutes, 14 fours) and Rogers (113 in 160 minutes, 10 fours) scored the bulk of Queensland's run after Rogers and Andrews had fallen to successive balls from Williams in the second over of the first innings. Oxenham made 43 not out (89 minutes) and 48 (61 minutes, 2 fours). Amos (5 for 83) and Dixon (5 for 66) returned their best innings bowling figures for Queensland. Sources: *Wisden, NSWCA Report, QCA Report, SACA Report, Adelaide Advertiser, The News.*

SOUTH AUSTRALIA

A.J.Ryan	c Cook b Dixon	0	lbw b Dixon		8
R.A.Parker	st Tallon b Allen	27	b Dixon		1
R.S.Whitington	c Dixon b Amos	35	c Tallon b Dixon		125
R.A.Hamence	c Baker b Amos	104	b Baker		52
M.G.Waite	run out (Amos/Tallon)	13	b Dixon		20
B.Schultz	c Allen b Amos	41	c Amos b Allen		33
*†C.W.Walker	c Wyeth b Oxenham	11	b Dixon		11
C.V.Grimmett	c Baker b Amos	33	c Tallon b Cook		1
N.H.Oswald	b Amos	13	(10) not out		1
R.G.Williams	not out	10	(9) c Tallon b Cook		8
H.N.J.Cotton	b Oxenham	1	run out		0
Extras	(b4, lb1, nb1)	6	(b6, lb1)		7
Total	(94.7 overs, 351 mins)	294	(88.5 overs, 313 mins)		267

QUEENSLAND

R.E.Rogers	c Waite b Williams	2	c Williams b Ryan		113
T.Allen	c Walker b Cotton	0	(4) lbw b Williams		2
W.C.Andrews	c Walker b Williams	2	(2) b Cotton		11
G.G.Cook	lbw b Grimmett	22	(3) b Cotton		0
†D.Tallon	c Whitington b Williams	101	run out (Schultz)		6
G.W.Baker	c & b Grimmett	1	(7) b Cotton		0
C.D.Hansen	c Ryan b Grimmett	8	(8) lbw b Cotton		7
*R.K.Oxenham	not out	43	(9) c Cotton b Grimmett		48
G.S.Amos	b Williams	2	(10) b Williams		34
E.R.Wyeth	lbw b Williams	2	(6) st Walker b Grimmett		8
P.L.Dixon	b Cotton	11	not out		5
Extras	(b3, lb8)	11	(b5, lb5)		10
Total	(52.5 overs, 220 mins)	205	(41.1 overs, 184 mins)		244

QUEENSLAND	O	M	R	W	w,nb		O	M	R	W	w,nb
Dixon	17	4	48	1	-,-		19.5	4	66	5	-,-
Cook	17	5	50	0	-,1	(3)	6	2	19	2	-,-
Amos	22	2	83	5	-,-	(2)	12	3	38	0	-,-
Oxenham	25.7	6	53	2	-,-		23	8	26	0	-,-
Allen	6	0	36	1	-,-		9	0	47	1	-,-
Wyeth	7	0	18	0	-,-		13	0	47	0	-,-
Baker							5	2	13	1	-,-
Andrews							1	0	4	0	-,-

SOUTH AUSTRALIA	O	M	R	W	w,nb		O	M	R	W	w,nb
Cotton	12.5	1	35	2	-,-		14	1	61	4	-,-
Williams	11	1	29	5	-,-		7.1	0	49	2	-,-
Waite	1	0	10	0	-,-						
Grimmett	18	0	89	3	-,-	(3)	13	1	71	2	-,-
Oswald	5	0	26	0	-,-		3	0	34	0	-,-
Ryan	5	2	5	0	-,-		2	1	5	1	-,-
Schultz						(4)	2	0	14	0	-,-

FALL OF WICKETS

Wkt	SA 1st	QLD 1st	SA 2nd	QLD
1st	0	1	3	13
2nd	58	5	20	13
3rd	64	5	112	33
4th	96	94	144	54
5th	168	106	224	66
6th	197	124	255	67
7th	246	153	258	91
8th	270	157	262	204
9th	287	165	266	206
10th	294	205	267	244

AUSTRALIA v ENGLAND (3rd Test)

Played at Melbourne Cricket Ground on January 1, 2, 4, 5, 6, 7, 1937. (Timeless match)
Toss : Australia.   Result : AUSTRALIA WON BY 365 RUNS.
Debuts: Nil.
12th Men: C.L.Badcock (Aust) and L.B.Fishlock (Eng).
Umpires: E.G.Borwick and J.D.Scott.
Attendances: 79630, 65235, 87798, 64826, 45528, 7517.   Total: 350,534.   Receipts: £29,169.
Close of Play: 1st day Aust 6/181 (McCabe 63, Oldfield 21); 2nd day Aust (2) 1/3 (Fleetwood-Smith 0, Ward 1); 3rd day Aust (2) 5/194
    (Fingleton 39, Bradman 56); 4th day Aust (2) 6/500 (Bradman 248, McCabe 14); 5th day Eng (2) 6/236 (Leyland 69, Robins 27).

This rain-affected Test, a memorable match in its own right, attracted a crowd of 350,534 - a record for any first-class match in Australia. E.L.McCormick (lumbago) and L.P.J.O'Brien (muscle strain) were unavailable for the home side. McCabe (63 in 144 minutes, 6 fours) hit a half-century on the opening day prior to rain, which prevented play between 4.52 pm and 5.45pm. Overnight showers delayed the start of the second day until 2.15pm and, on a very wet and difficult pitch, the Australian innings was quickly terminated. Under the influence of a hot sun, the pitch worsened further for England's reply. Worthington fell to the third ball. A highly-skilled innings by Hammond (32 in 81 minutes, 4 fours) in the conditions was ended by one of two unforgettable catches by Darling at short leg; he also disposed of Leyland in spectacular fashion. Sievers, after having 1 for 10 from his first ten overs, captured 4 for 6 (Hammond, Sims, Robins, Ames) in 7 balls during his second spell but was then instructed by his captain not to get any further wickets that day so that the pitch would be given time to improve for Australia's second innings. By opening with his tailenders Bradman thwarted Allen's delayed declaration; although O'Reilly fell first ball, the plan enabled Fingleton (136 in 386 minutes, 6 fours, chance at 56) and Bradman himself (a chanceless 270 in 458 minutes, 375 balls, 22 fours) to add 346 together, the highest sixth-wicket stand in Australian first-class cricket. Rigg (47 in 122 minutes, 3 fours) had earlier batted well on an improving wicket. Hammond (51 in 78 minutes, 7 fours), Leyland (111 not out in 194 minutes, 11 fours) and Robins (61 in 65 minutes, 7 fours) made big contributions for England, who were chasing 689 to secure the Ashes. Sources: *Wisden, VCA Report, The Age, The Argus, The Herald, Melbourne Sun, The Australasian.*

AUSTRALIA

Batsman	1st innings			2nd innings	
J.H.W.Fingleton	c Sims b Robins	38	(6)	c Ames b Sims	136
W.A.Brown	c Ames b Voce	1	(5)	c Barnett b Voce	20
*D.G.Bradman	c Robins b Verity	13	(7)	c Allen b Verity	270
K.E.Rigg	c Verity b Allen	16		lbw b Sims	47
S.J.McCabe	c Worthington b Voce	63	(8)	lbw b Allen	22
L.S.Darling	c Allen b Verity	20	(9)	b Allen	0
M.W.Sievers	st Ames b Robins	1	(10)	not out	25
†W.A.S.Oldfield	not out	27	(11)	lbw b Verity	7
W.J.O'Reilly	c Sims b Hammond	4	(1)	c & b Voce	0
F.A.Ward	st Ames b Hammond	7	(3)	c Hardstaff b Verity	18
L.O.Fleetwood-Smith	did not bat		(2)	c Verity b Voce	0
Extras	(b2, lb6, nb2)	10		(b6, lb2, w1, nb10)	19
Total	(65.3 overs, 283 mins) (9 wkts dec)	200		(149.7 overs, 622 mins)	564

ENGLAND

Batsman	1st innings			2nd innings	
T.S.Worthington	c Bradman b McCabe	0		c Sievers b Ward	16
C.J.Barnett	c Darling b Sievers	11		lbw b O'Reilly	23
W.R.Hammond	c Darling b Sievers	32		b Sievers	51
M.Leyland	c Darling b O'Reilly	17		not out	111
J.M.Sims	c Brown b Sievers	3	(10)	lbw b Fleetwood-Smith	0
†L.E.G.Ames	b Sievers	3	(5)	b Fleetwood-Smith	19
R.W.V.Robins	c O'Reilly b Sievers	0	(8)	b O'Reilly	61
J.Hardstaff, jr	b O'Reilly	3	(6)	c Ward b Fleetwood-Smith	17
*G.O.B.Allen	not out	0	(7)	c Sievers b Fleetwood-Smith	11
H.Verity	c Brown b O'Reilly	0	(9)	c McCabe b O'Reilly	11
W.Voce	not out	0		c Bradman b Fleetwood-Smith	0
Extras	(b5, lb1, nb1)	7		(lb3)	3
Total	(28.2 overs, 114 mins) (9 wkts dec)	76		(78.6 overs, 278 mins)	323

ENGLAND	O	M	R	W	w,nb		O	M	R	W	w,nb
Voce	18	3	49	2	-,-		29	2	120	3	-,6
Allen	12	2	35	1	-,2	(3)	23	2	84	2	1,1
Sims	9	1	35	0	-,-	(6)	23	1	109	2	-,3
Verity	14	4	24	2	-,-		37.7	9	79	3	-,-
Robins	7	0	31	2	-,-		11	2	46	0	-,-
Hammond	5.3	0	16	2	-,-	(2)	22	3	89	0	-,-
Worthington							4	0	18	0	-,-

AUSTRALIA	O	M	R	W	w,nb		O	M	R	W	w,nb
McCabe	2	1	7	1	-,-	(2)	8	0	32	0	-,-
Sievers	11.2	5	21	5	-,1	(1)	12	2	39	1	-,-
O'Reilly	12	5	28	3	-,-		21	6	65	3	-,-
Fleetwood-Smith	3	1	13	0	-,-		25.6	2	124	5	-,-
Ward							12	1	60	1	-,-

FALL OF WICKETS

Wkt	AUST 1st	ENG 1st	AUST 2nd	ENG 2nd
1st	7	0	0	29
2nd	33	14	3	65
3rd	69	56	38	117
4th	79	68	74	155
5th	122	71	97	179
6th	130	71	443	195
7th	183	76	511	306
8th	190	76	511	322
9th	200	76	549	323
10th	-	-	564	323

NEW SOUTH WALES v QUEENSLAND (Shield Match 7)

Played at Sydney Cricket Ground on January 1, 2, 4, 5, 1937. (Four-day match)
Toss : Queensland.   Result : QUEENSLAND WON BY 87 RUNS.
Debuts: New South Wales - R.G.Beatty (f/c).
12th Men: K.C.Gulliver (NSW) and C.D.Hansen (Qld).
Umpires: A.L.Christie and F.W.Lyons.
Attendances: 4585, 3882, 1146, 594.   Total: 10,207.   Receipts: £484.
Close of Play: 1st day Qld 4/224 (Cook 23, Baker 22); 2nd day NSW 119 all out; 3rd day NSW (2) 3/154 (Robinson 67, Marks 31).

With this win Queensland ended a 10-year sequence of 19 matches without victory against New South Wales, who were weakened by the absence of Test men J.H.W.Fingleton, S.J.McCabe, W.A.S.Oldfield and W.J.O'Reilly. Queensland, who by comparison missed only W.A.Brown, had fifties from Andrews (70 in 122 minutes, 8 fours), Allen (54 in 118 minutes, 5 fours) and Cook (72 in 189 minutes, 3 fours and 70 in 154 minutes, 7 fours). Rain prevented play on the first day after 4.28pm. Oxenham, hit in the ribs by a ball from Lush on the second day, fielded only briefly at the start of the New South Wales innings and though he batted a second time, he did not return to the field until the final day. Allen led the side meanwhile. Andrews injured a finger attempting to field a ball during the first innings and batted down the order in the second innings. Gulliver and Hansen acted as the Queensland substitutes. Robinson (143 in 187 minutes, 1 five and 14 fours) and Marks (59 in 140 minutes, 4 fours) shared a fourth-wicket partnership of 180 for New South Wales over the last two days. Queensland had elected not to enforce the follow-on. Sources: *Wisden, NSWCA Report, QCA Report, The Herald, Sydney Morning Herald, NSWCA Scorebook, Brisbane Courier-Mail.*

QUEENSLAND

W.C.Andrews	b Hynes	70	(6)	b Chipperfield	11
R.E.Rogers	c Chipperfield b White	35	(1)	lbw b Lush	3
T.Allen	lbw b Jackson	54	(2)	c Easton b Lush	10
†D.Tallon	b Hynes	11		c & b Lush	5
G.G.Cook	c Chipperfield b Hynes	72	(3)	c Easton b Hynes	70
G.W.Baker	b Lush	30	(7)	lbw b Hynes	19
*R.K.Oxenham	c Chipperfield b White	18	(10)	not out	15
G.D.Gunthorpe	c Easton b White	0	(5)	b Chipperfield	14
G.S.Amos	c Easton b Hynes	30	(8)	c White b Chipperfield	7
E.R.Wyeth	not out	17	(9)	c Lush b Chipperfield	16
P.L.Dixon	c Easton b White	18		lbw b White	4
Extras	(b4, lb5, nb1)	10		(b2, lb3, nb4)	9
Total	(100.1 overs, 381 mins)	365		(51.2 overs, 193 mins)	183

NEW SOUTH WALES

R.G.Beatty	lbw b Cook	3		lbw b Amos	30
*A.D.McGilvray	c Gunthorpe b Cook	4		c Tallon b Cook	11
A.G.Cheetham	b Dixon	28		c sub (C.D.Hansen) b Cook	10
R.H.Robinson	b Cook	0		c sub (C.D.Hansen) b Amos	143
A.E.Marks	c Tallon b Dixon	8		c Tallon b Dixon	59
A.G.Chipperfield	c Baker b Amos	32		lbw b Amos	10
V.E.Jackson	c Cook b Amos	5		b Oxenham	8
J.G.Lush	b Baker	18		c Amos b Wyeth	30
L.C.Hynes	b Dixon	0		b Oxenham	23
†F.A.Easton	not out	17		c Oxenham b Wyeth	9
E.C.S.White	c Tallon b Cook	1		not out	0
Extras	(lb2, nb1)	3		(b6, lb3)	9
Total	(35.1 overs, 144 mins)	119		(85.1 overs, 327 mins)	342

NEW SOUTH WALES	O	M	R	W	w,nb		O	M	R	W	w,nb
Lush	15	1	48	1	-,-		11	0	50	3	-,2
Hynes	29	3	88	4	-,-		16	0	40	2	-,2
Chipperfield	22	0	113	0	-,-	(5)	16	1	72	4	-,-
White	18.1	3	51	4	-,-		5.2	3	4	1	-,-
Cheetham	3	0	13	0	-,-						
Jackson	9	2	28	1	-,1	(3)	3	1	8	0	-,-
McGilvray	3	1	5	0	-,-						
Robinson	1	0	9	0	-,-						

QUEENSLAND	O	M	R	W	w,nb		O	M	R	W	w,nb
Dixon	9	0	32	3	-,-		16	1	77	1	-,-
Cook	12.1	3	45	4	-,1		14	1	61	2	-,-
Oxenham	1	1	0	0	-,-	(7)	15	7	27	2	-,-
Wyeth	5	2	10	0	-,-		13.1	3	39	2	-,-
Amos	7	0	28	2	-,-	(3)	18	0	90	3	-,-
Baker	1	0	1	1	-,-	(5)	4	0	24	0	-,-
Allen						(6)	2	0	15	0	-,-

FALL OF WICKETS

Wkt	QLD 1st	NSW 1st	QLD 2nd	NSW 2nd
1st	65	6	4	22
2nd	126	7	22	56
3rd	152	11	30	56
4th	186	30	63	236
5th	241	72	87	261
6th	287	78	126	276
7th	287	88	137	282
8th	322	88	153	316
9th	331	118	170	342
10th	365	119	183	342

TASMANIA v M.C.C.

Played at N.T.C.A. Ground, Launceston, on January 9, 11, 1937. (Three-day match)
Toss : Tasmania.   Result : M.C.C. WON BY AN INNINGS AND 4 RUNS.
Debuts: Tasmania - J.N.W.Nicolson, D.H.Thollar, R.B.S.Wardlaw (all f/c).
12th Men: C.J.Sankey (Tas) and C.J.Barnett (MCC).
Umpires: W.R.Boscoe and E.C.Knight.
Attendances: 6000, 2900.   Total: About 8900.   Receipts: £596.
Close of Play: 1st day MCC 7/283 (Ames 85).

G.O.B.Allen, W.R.Hammond, M.Leyland, H.Verity and W.Voce remained in Melbourne after the Third Test and did not accompany the rest of the team to Tasmania. Gourlay (original 12th man) replaced J.M.Walsh (neck strain) in the Tasmanian team. Thomas was caught from the third ball of the match and the home side struggled from then on, Putman topscoring in each innings with 28 (44 minutes, 1 four) and 77 (134 minutes, 6 fours). Wardlaw, after failing to score in his first innings on debut, hit 34 in just 18 minutes with 1 six and 4 fours in the second innings. M.C.C. also lost a wicket in their first over, Fishlock to the fifth ball, but Fagg (60 in 84 minutes, 7 fours) and Worthington (50 in 67 minutes, 6 fours) rallied with a second-wicket stand worth 102. Ames (109 in 130 minutes, 2 sixes and 11 fours) began his innings immediately after the tea break on the first day and was 85 by stumps, having added 115 for the fifth wicket with Hardstaff (55 in 68 minutes, 2 sixes and 4 fours). Putman's success with legspin (5 for 87) continued a pattern established against the Englishmen early in the tour. *Wisden* incorrectly gives umpire Boscoe as Briscoe. Sources: *Wisden, VCA Report, TCA Report, The Herald, Hobart Mercury, The Sporting Globe.*

TASMANIA

R.O.G.Morrisby	c Duckworth b Copson	14	c Duckworth b Robins	25
R.V.Thomas	c Copson b Farnes	0	c Farnes b Copson	20
D.C.Green	b Farnes	17	b Farnes	8
S.W.L.Putman	b Robins	28	st Duckworth b Sims	77
C.L.Jeffery	b Sims	9	c Duckworth Wyatt	8
R.B.S.Wardlaw	b Sims	0	c Duckworth b Sims	34
*A.W.Rushforth	lbw b Sims	8	b Sims	24
J.N.W.Nicolson	c Duckworth b Copson	8	c Farnes b Sims	9
K.G.Gourlay	b Sims	0	st Duckworth b Ames	1
†J.Gardiner	lbw b Copson	14	not out	0
D.H.Thollar	not out	1	lbw b Sims	0
Extras	(b4, nb1)	5	(lb3)	3
Total	(22.3 overs, 95 mins)	104	(51.6 overs, 204 mins)	209

M.C.C.

A.E.Fagg	lbw b Putman	60
L.B.Fishlock	lbw b Gourlay	4
T.S.Worthington	b Putman	50
R.E.S.Wyatt	c & b Thollar	1
L.E.G.Ames	c Jeffery b Thollar	109
J.Hardstaff, jr	c Gardiner b Thomas	55
*R.W.V.Robins	c Jeffery b Gourlay	24
J.M.Sims	st Gardiner b Putman	0
†G.Duckworth	lbw b Putman	9
K.Farnes	b Putman	0
W.H.Copson	not out	1
Extras	(b1, lb2, nb1)	4
Total	(57.7 overs, 220 mins)	317

M.C.C.	O	M	R	W	w,nb		O	M	R	W	w,nb
Farnes	5	0	27	2	-,-		10	1	30	1	-,-
Copson	5.3	0	17	3	-,-		8	0	33	1	-,-
Sims	7	1	20	4	-,1	(5)	10.6	0	39	5	-,-
Robins	4	0	22	1	-,-	(3)	14	2	40	1	-,-
Ames	1	0	13	0	-,-	(7)	1	0	1	1	-,-
Wyatt						(4)	6	0	40	1	-,-
Hardstaff						(6)	2	0	23	0	-,-

TASMANIA	O	M	R	W	w,nb
Gourlay	15	1	83	2	-,-
Thomas	7	0	34	1	-,-
Jeffery	10	1	38	0	-,1
Putman	15.7	0	87	5	-,-
Thollar	10	0	71	2	-,-

FALL OF WICKETS

	TAS	MCC	TAS
Wkt	1st	1st	2nd
1st	1	7	36
2nd	27	109	50
3rd	39	112	56
4th	54	118	83
5th	65	233	122
6th	79	264	179
7th	81	283	206
8th	81	314	207
9th	103	316	209
10th	104	317	209

COMBINED XI v M.C.C.

Played at T.C.A. Ground, Hobart, on January 15, 16, 18 (no play), 1937. (Three-day match)
Toss : M.C.C.   Result : MATCH DRAWN.
Debuts: Nil.
12th Men: G.T.H.James (Comb XI) and T.S.Worthington (MCC).
Umpires: M.Hansen and W.T.Lonergan.
Attendances: 7800, 11000, no play.   Total: About 18,800.   Receipts: £1366.
Close of Play: 1st day MCC 8/392 (Hardstaff 94, Farnes 2); 2nd day MCC (2) 1/111 (Wyatt 68, Fagg 10).

Following similar contests as Brisbane and Perth on recent M.C.C. tours, this match was conceived by the T.C.A. during the 1935-36 season and put to the Australian Board of Control. Four players from outside the island - Badcock, Grimmett, Oldfield and Ward - were invited to participate by the Board. Allen rejoined the M.C.C. party from the mainland to take the captaincy, Ames being rested, while James was a last-minute replacement for C.L.Jeffery as 12th man for the Combined XI. Barnett (129 in 177 minutes, 3 sixes and 14 fours) and Hardstaff (110 in 153 minutes, 3 sixes and 12 fours).hit centuries, Hardstaff sharing a 124-run stand for the sixth wicket with Allen (55 in 71 minutes, 6 fours). Oldfield's unbeaten 60 for the Combined Team occupied 97 minutes and included 7 fours. Allen's decision not to enforce the follow-on enabled Wyatt (68 not out in 68 minutes, 10 fours) to find form after his 2-1/2-month layoff. Despite a torrential downpour, which prevented any play on the last day, new attendance records (second day and match) were set for cricket in Tasmania. *Wisden* incorrectly gives M.J.Combes instead of G.A.Combes in Combined XI. Sources: *Wisden, VCA Report, TCA Report, The Herald, The Sporting Globe, Hobart Mercury.*

M.C.C.

C.J.Barnett	lbw b Grimmett	129			
L.B.Fishlock	lbw b Walsh	13	c Badcock b Grimmett		31
A.E.Fagg	c Burrows b Walsh	28	not out		10
R.E.S.Wyatt	c Rushforth b Combes	30	(1) not out		68
J.Hardstaff, jr	c Badcock b Ward	110			
R.W.V.Robins	b Grimmett	10			
*G.O.B.Allen	c Putman b Ward	55			
J.M.Sims	run out (Combes/Oldfield)	7			
†G.Duckworth	c & b Putman	6			
K.Farnes	not out	8			
W.H.Copson	st Oldfield b Ward	4			
Extras	(b12, lb4, w1, nb1)	18	(b1, lb1)		2
Total	(93.3 overs, 320 mins)	418	(20.0 overs, 68 mins) (1 wkt)		111

COMBINED XI

R.V.Thomas	c Fishlock b Copson	20
A.O.Burrows	c Fagg b Farnes	4
R.O.G.Morrisby	b Copson	0
C.L.Badcock	c Sims b Copson	0
S.W.L.Putman	c Copson b Farnes	17
A.W.Rushforth	c Allen b Farnes	1
*†W.A.S.Oldfield	not out	60
C.V.Grimmett	c Fagg b Farnes	0
J.M.Walsh	b Allen	8
F.A.Ward	b Sims	16
G.A.Combes	b Copson	1
Extras	(b3, lb2, nb2)	7
Total	(35.1 overs, 152 mins)	134

COMBINED XI	O	M	R	W	w,nb		O	M	R	W	w,nb		FALL OF WICKETS		
Walsh	15	2	46	2	1,-		2	0	20	0	-,-		MCC	COMB	MCC
Burrows	8	0	32	0	-,1		3	0	15	0	-,-	Wkt	1st	1st	2nd
Thomas	3	0	18	0	-,-							1st	38	9	80
Grimmett	19	0	114	2	-,-		7	0	31	1	-,-	2nd	112	11	-
Ward	23.3	1	125	3	-,-		3	0	17	0	-,-	3rd	190	11	-
Combes	22	8	50	1	-,-	(3)	5	0	26	0	-,-	4th	212	40	-
Putman	3	0	15	1	-,-							5th	222	43	-
												6th	346	48	-
M.C.C.	O	M	R	W	w,nb							7th	354	51	-
Farnes	12	3	31	4	-,-							8th	379	77	-
Copson	10.1	2	32	4	-,2							9th	409	123	-
Sims	7	0	32	1	-,-							10th	418	134	-
Allen	3	0	21	1	-,-										
Robins	3	0	11	0	-,-										

QUEENSLAND v VICTORIA (Shield Match 8)

Played at Brisbane Cricket Ground (Woolloongabba) on January 15, 16, 18, 19, 1937. (Four-day match)
Toss : Victoria. Result : VICTORIA WON BY FIVE WICKETS.
Debuts: Queensland - M.S.Guttormsen, R.F.K.Rushbrook (all f/c).
12th Men: G.D.Gunthorpe (Qld) and M.W.Sievers (Vic).
Umpires: J.Bartlett and J.A.Scott.
Attendances: 2886, 4495, 1292, 1008. Total: 9681. Receipts: £579.
Close of Play: 1st day Vic 5/286 (Hassett 93, Ledward 24); 2nd day Qld 6/109 (Cook 13, Cockburn 2); 3rd day Qld (2) 3/304 (Allen 56, Tallon 93).

Guttormsen and Rushbrook replaced W.C.Andrews (injured thumb) and P.L.Dixon (leg injury) in the Queensland team. Victoria relegated Sievers, under the influenza, to 12th man. Amos bowled O'Brien with the third ball of the match, but Gregory (75 in 159 minutes, 5 fours), Hassett (93 in 173 minutes, 1 five and 10 fours), Ledward (115 in 243 minutes, 14 fours) and Pearson (91 in 148 minutes, 11 fours) combined in the middle order to give Victoria 497. Brown (50 in 88 minutes, 3 fours) made top score for Queensland who, 320 runs behind, were asked to follow on. Fifties from Brown again (91 in 153 minutes, 12 fours), Cook (51 in 117 minutes, 7 fours), Allen (66 in 151 minutes, 10 fours), Tallon (96 in 134 minutes, 11 fours) and Baker (66 in 89 minutes, 10 fours) in the second innings were not enough to save the side, Hassett (56 not out in 85 minutes, 6 fours) taking Victoria to victory on the final day. Rushbrook registered a pair on debut; these were his only innings. *VCA Report* incorrectly gives Vic (1) Gregory lbw b Rushbrook. Sources: *Wisden, VCA Report, QCA Report, The Herald, Brisbane Courier-Mail, The Sporting Globe, Brisbane Telegraph.*

VICTORIA

L.P.J.O'Brien	b Amos	0	(2)	c Tallon b Rushbrook	3
K.E.Rigg	c Amos b Cockburn	36	(1)	b Cook	5
L.S.Darling	c Cook b Rushbrook	21		lbw b Rushbrook	17
I.S.Lee	lbw b Rushbrook	33		b Cook	6
R.G.Gregory	b Rushbrook	75		lbw b Oxenham	20
A.L.Hassett	c Tallon b Oxenham	93		not out	56
J.A.Ledward	c Brown b Cook	115		not out	16
W.E.Pearson	c Baker b Cook	91			
†B.A.Barnett	not out	13			
*H.I.Ebeling	run out (Amos)	13			
L.O.Fleetwood-Smith	b Oxenham	0			
Extras	(lb6, nb1)	7		(b4, nb2)	6
Total	(135.0 overs, 523 mins)	497		(38.4 overs, 149 mins) (5 wkts)	129

QUEENSLAND

W.A.Brown	lbw b Fleetwood-Smith	50		c Lee b Fleetwood-Smith	91
R.E.Rogers	c Rigg b Pearson	3	(3)	lbw b Pearson	5
T.Allen	c Pearson b Fleetwood-Smith	9	(4)	b Ebeling	66
†D.Tallon	run out (Ledward/Barnett)	21	(5)	b Ebeling	96
G.G.Cook	not out	32	(2)	run out (Fleetwood-Smith)	51
G.W.Baker	c & b Gregory	0		run out (/Barnett)	66
M.S.Guttormsen	c Rigg b Gregory	8		c Barnett b Ebeling	0
J.S.D.Cockburn	lbw b Fleetwood-Smith	4		b Gregory	35
*R.K.Oxenham	st Barnett b Gregory	15		not out	11
G.S.Amos	c Darling b Fleetwood-Smith	32		b Pearson	13
R.F.K.Rushbrook	b Fleetwood-Smith	0		c Gregory b Pearson	0
Extras	(lb3)	3		(b5, lb8)	13
Total	(53.0 overs, 181 mins)	177		(105.7 overs, 397 mins)	447

QUEENSLAND	O	M	R	W	w,nb		O	M	R	W	w,nb			FALL OF WICKETS			
															VIC	QLD	QLD	VIC
Amos	22	1	88	1	-,-	(5)	2	0	11	0	-,-	Wkt	1st	1st	2nd	2nd
Cook	36	6	109	2	-,-		13	1	40	2	-,2	1st	0	4	127	7
Rushbrook	28	3	109	3	-,1	(1)	11	1	35	2	-,-	2nd	49	43	136	28
Cockburn	12	1	47	1	-,-		3	0	6	0	-,-	3rd	61	84	159	31
Oxenham	27	5	75	2	-,-	(3)	9	1	24	1	-,-	4th	125	87	317	45
Allen	7	0	53	0	-,-							5th	226	88	326	77
Baker	3	0	9	0	-,-							6th	286	102	342	-
Brown						(6)	0.4	0	7	0	-,-	7th	452	111	419	-
												8th	471	132	419	-
VICTORIA	O	M	R	W	w,nb		O	M	R	W	w,nb	9th	497	177	447	-
Ebeling	7	1	19	0	-,-		26	7	50	3	-,-	10th	497	177	447	-
Pearson	5	1	15	1	-,-		16.7	3	55	3	-,-					
Fleetwood-Smith	22	1	75	5	-,-		33	2	167	1	-,-					
Darling	5	0	20	0	-,-	(6)	3	0	24	0	-,-					
Gregory	14	2	45	3	-,-	(4)	21	2	83	1	-,-					
O'Brien						(5)	6	0	55	0	-,-					

NEW SOUTH WALES v VICTORIA (Shield Match 9)

Played at Sydney Cricket Ground on January 22, 23, 25, 26, 1937. (Four-day match)
Toss : Victoria.   Result : MATCH DRAWN.
Debuts: Nil.
12th Men: S.G.Barnes (NSW) and I.S.Lee (Vic).
Umpires: H.J.Armstrong and E.G.Borwick.
Attendances: 3712, 5516, 1966, 943.   Total: 12,137.   Receipts: £494.
Close of Play: 1st day Vic 7/295 (Barnett 57, Ebeling 21); 2nd day NSW 5/209 (McGilvray 25, Hynes 32); 3rd day Vic (2) 4/148
    (Hassett 15, Ledward 10).

Attempting to field a ball on the first day, Lush received a nasty blow on the kneecap and was unable to bowl or field again in the match. Robinson (eye) and White (foot) also suffered minor ailments while fielding on the first day and G.V.Guest, a long-serving first-grade player with the Waverley club, was called up to help Barnes fill the gaps. Gregory (65 in 98 minutes, 7 fours), Hassett (58 in 137 minutes, 2 fours) and Barnett (59 in 87 minutes, 1 six and 4 fours) for Victoria and Beatty (60 in 100 minutes, 5 fours) and Hynes (54 in 106 minutes, 3 fours) for New South Wales scored first-innings fifties. Cheetham had to be assisted from the field after he slipped and strained a leg in an unsuccessful attempt to regain his crease; he returned later to score 62 (82 minutes, 5 fours) as the game dwindled to a draw. Darling (62 in 110 minutes, 6 fours), Hassett (68 in 189 minutes, 9 fours) and Sievers (76 in 164 minutes, 8 fours) made other scores. Only Beatty and the wicketkeepers did not bowl at some stage. Sources: *Wisden, NSWCA Report, VCA Report, The Age, The Herald, Sydney Morning Herald, NSWCA Scorebook, Sydney Referee.*

VICTORIA

K.E.Rigg	run out (Hynes/Easton)	12	b Hynes		6
L.P.J.O'Brien	c Hynes b Cheetham	17	c Easton b Cheetham		18
L.S.Darling	c Hynes b Lush	24	c Jackson b White		62
R.G.Gregory	c McGilvray b Robinson	65	b Hynes		33
A.L.Hassett	lbw b Hynes	58	c Easton b White		68
J.A.Ledward	c Easton b Jackson	20	c Robinson b Cheetham		20
M.W.Sievers	b Jackson	1	run out (Gulliver)		76
†B.A.Barnett	c Beatty b Jackson	59	c Marks b Cheetham		14
*H.I.Ebeling	not out	43	not out		22
E.L.McCormick	c Beatty b McGilvray	12	b Robinson		0
L.O.Fleetwood-Smith	run out (sub G.V.Guest/Easton)	4	c & b Gulliver		5
Extras	(b16, lb3, nb3)	22	(b7, lb6, nb3)		16
Total	(107.6 overs, 388 mins)	337	(114.4 overs, 404 mins)		340

NEW SOUTH WALES

R.G.Beatty	b Sievers	60	c Barnett b O'Brien		35
A.G.Cheetham	run out (McCormick/Barnett)	49	c Hassett b Gregory		62
A.E.Marks	b Sievers	0			
R.H.Robinson	c Sievers b McCormick	21			
V.E.Jackson	c Barnett b McCormick	8			
*A.D.McGilvray	b Sievers	45			
L.C.Hynes	c Gregory b Ebeling	54			
J.G.Lush	lbw b Gregory	15			
K.C.Gulliver	lbw b Sievers	17			
†F.A.Easton	not out	14	(3) not out		8
E.C.S.White	c Barnett b Sievers	0	(4) not out		22
Extras	(b16, lb3, w2, nb1)	22	(nb2)		2
Total	(81.4 overs, 330 mins)	305	(30.0 overs, 105 mins) (2 wkts)		129

NEW SOUTH WALES	O	M	R	W	w,nb		O	M	R	W	w,nb		
Lush	9	0	45	1	-,1								
Hynes	20	1	61	1	-,2	(1)	22	3	80	2	-,3		
Cheetham	7	1	14	1	-,-		14	2	43	3	-,-		
Jackson	23	9	44	3	-,-	(2)	23	8	49	0	-,-		
Gulliver	8	0	36	0	-,-	(8)	1.4	0	4	1	-,-		
White	25.6	8	58	0	-,-	(4)	31	11	58	2	-,-		
McGilvray	9	0	28	1	-,-	(5)	7	0	24	0	-,-		
Robinson	6	1	29	1	-,-	(6)	9	1	37	1	-,-		
Marks						(7)	7	1	29	0	-,-		

	FALL OF WICKETS			
	VIC	NSW	VIC	NSW
Wkt	1st	1st	2nd	2nd
1st	22	107	10	93
2nd	66	107	55	99
3rd	71	129	110	-
4th	174	146	125	-
5th	205	148	178	-
6th	210	244	259	-
7th	231	258	283	-
8th	297	291	333	-
9th	327	295	335	-
10th	337	305	340	-

VICTORIA	O	M	R	W	w,nb		O	M	R	W	w,nb
McCormick	16	0	75	2	2,-		3	1	6	0	-,1
Ebeling	23	5	62	1	-,-		4	2	8	0	-,-
Gregory	19	3	83	1	-,-	(7)	3	0	19	1	-,-
Sievers	21.4	4	57	5	-,1	(3)	3	0	16	0	-,1
Darling	2	0	7	0	-,-		4	0	22	0	-,-
Fleetwood-Smith						(4)	4	0	2	0	-,-
O'Brien						(6)	5	1	20	1	-,-
Hassett							2	0	4	0	-,-
Rigg							1	0	11	0	-,-
Ledward							1	0	1	0	-,-

SOUTH AUSTRALIA v M.C.C.

Played at Adelaide Oval on January 22, 23, 25 (no play), 26 (no play), 1937. (Four-day match)
Toss : M.C.C. Result : MATCH DRAWN.
Debuts: Nil.
12th Men: R.G.Williams (SA) and A.E.Fagg (MCC).
Umpires: A.J.Richardson and J.D.Scott.
Attendances: 10600, 19682, 352, -. Total: 30,634. Receipts: £1603.
Close of Play: 1st day MCC 6/239 (Wyatt 52, Allen 16); 2nd day SA 4/194 (Whitington 33, Hamence 3); 3rd day no play.

Steady rain over the last two days saturated the pitch and outfield, ending the match prematurely. Barnett (78 in 176 minutes, 6 fours) and Fishlock (40 in 126 minutes, 1 four) had given the tourists a solid start on the first day with an opening stand of 96. After Fishlock's innings it was found that a bone in his hand had been broken by a rising ball from Cotton, and he was unable to play again until after the Fifth Test. Later contributions from Wyatt (53 in 176 minutes, 6 fours), Ames (36 in 61 minutes, 4 fours) and Allen (60 in 117 minutes, 4 fours) enabled M.C.C. to reach 300. Ryan (71 in 121 minutes, 8 fours) batted brightly when South Australia went to the crease. Bradman, handicapped by a leg strain for much of his innings, batted with the aid of a runner. Sources: *Wisden, NSWCA Report, VCA Report, SACA Report, The Argus, Adelaide Advertiser, The Sporting Globe.*

M.C.C.

C.J.Barnett	c Bradman b Grimmett	78
L.B.Fishlock	lbw b Ward	40
W.R.Hammond	c Ward b Cotton	10
M.Leyland	b Grimmett	1
R.E.S.Wyatt	lbw b Cotton	53
†L.E.G.Ames	b Grimmett	36
R.W.V.Robins	c Walker b Cotton	2
*G.O.B.Allen	c Richardson b Grimmett	60
H.Verity	run out (Bradman/Walker)	11
W.Voce	b Ward	5
K.Farnes	not out	0
Extras	(b2, lb2, nb1)	5
Total	(105.4 overs, 375 mins)	301

SOUTH AUSTRALIA

A.J.Ryan	c sub (A.E.Fagg) b Verity	71
†C.W.Walker	c Verity b Farnes	29
C.L.Badcock	c Ames b Voce	13
*D.G.Bradman	c Ames b Barnett	38
R.S.Whitington	not out	33
R.A.Hamence	not out	3
V.Y.Richardson	)	
M.G.Waite	)	
C.V.Grimmett	) did not bat	
F.A.Ward	)	
H.N.J.Cotton	)	
Extras	(lb6, nb1)	7
Total	(50.0 overs, 200 mins)	194

SOUTH AUSTRALIA	O	M	R	W	w,nb
Cotton	22	3	76	3	-,-
Waite	15	2	37	0	-,1
Ryan	20	5	36	0	-,-
Grimmett	28	7	77	4	-,-
Ward	20.4	4	70	2	-,-

M.C.C.	O	M	R	W	w,nb
Voce	8	0	32	1	-,1
Allen	9	1	44	0	-,-
Farnes	10	1	28	1	-,-
Hammond	2	0	11	0	-,-
Robins	7	0	36	0	-,-
Verity	12	2	33	1	-,-
Barnett	2	0	3	1	-,-

FALL OF WICKETS

Wkt	MCC 1st	SA 1st
1st	96	65
2nd	121	109
3rd	122	131
4th	139	167
5th	197	-
6th	204	-
7th	247	-
8th	290	-
9th	297	-
10th	301	-

AFCM No. 890/76
Test No. 258/138
TM No. 18/14

AUSTRALIA v ENGLAND (4th Test)

Played at Adelaide Oval on January 29, 30, February 1, 2, 3, 4, 1937. (Timeless match)
Toss : Australia.   Result : AUSTRALIA WON BY 148 RUNS.
Debuts: Australia - R.G.Gregory (Test).
12th Men: C.L.Badcock (Aust) and J.M.Sims (Eng).
Umpires: E.G.Borwick and J.D.Scott.
Attendances: 35643, 33526, 28975, 38334, 21982, 12675.   Total: 171,135.   Receipts: £17,504.
Close of Play: 1st day Aust 7/267 (Chipperfield 45, O'Reilly 3); 2nd day Eng 2/174 (Barnett 92, Leyland 35); 3rd day Aust (2) 1/63
    (Brown 23, Bradman 26); 4th day Aust (2) 4/341 (Bradman 174, Gregory 36); 5th day Eng (2) 3/148 (Hammond 39, Leyland 17).

Australia were restricted by good bowling and fielding to a small score despite the efforts of Brown (42 in 91 minutes, 1 four), McCabe (88 in 134 minutes, 9 fours) and Chipperfield (57 not out in 103 minutes, 4 fours). Barnett (129 in 341 minutes, 1 six and 13 fours) anchored the English reply and with the help of Leyland (45 in 98 minutes, 4 fours) and Ames (52 in 119 minutes, 8 fours) took the tourists to a lead on the first innings. Bradman (212 in 437 minutes, 14 fours) shared century stands with McCabe (55 in 92 minutes, 7 fours) and 20-year-old Gregory (50 in 175 minutes, 1 four) to turn the match around. During his innings Bradman passed the previous record number of first-class runs scored by a batsman in Australia (11,137 by Clem Hill); he also established a new Test landmark by scoring a record 17th Test century. Set 392 to win, England began promisingly until Fleetwood-Smith captured the key wicket of Hammond (39 in 124 minutes, 3 fours) with an outstanding delivery early on the last morning. He returned the best innings and match figures of his Test career. Wyatt (50 in 101 minutes, 5 fours) and Hardstaff (43 in 92 minutes, 2 fours) fought hard. Sources: *Wisden, SACA Report, The Australasian, The Herald, Adelaide Advertiser.*

AUSTRALIA

J.H.W.Fingleton	run out (Voce)	10		lbw b Hammond	12
W.A.Brown	c Allen b Farnes	42		c Ames b Voce	32
K.E.Rigg	c Ames b Farnes	20	(5)	c Hammond b Farnes	7
*D.G.Bradman	b Allen	26	(3)	c & b Hammond	212
S.J.McCabe	c Allen b Robins	88	(4)	c Wyatt b Robins	55
R.G.Gregory	lbw b Hammond	23		run out (Barnett)	50
A.G.Chipperfield	not out	57		c Ames b Hammond	31
†W.A.S.Oldfield	run out (Leyland)	5		c Ames b Hammond	1
W.J.O'Reilly	c Leyland b Allen	7		c Hammond b Farnes	1
E.L.McCormick	c Ames b Hammond	4		b Hammond	1
L.O.Fleetwood-Smith	b Farnes	1		not out	4
Extras	(lb2, nb3)	5		(b10, lb15, w1, nb1)	27
Total	(77.6 overs, 335 mins)	288		(123.2 overs, 519 mins)	433

ENGLAND

C.J.Barnett	lbw b Fleetwood-Smith	129	(2)	c Chipperfield b Fleetwood-Smith	21
H.Verity	c Bradman b O'Reilly	19	(1)	b Fleetwood-Smith	17
W.R.Hammond	c McCormick b O'Reilly	20	(4)	b Fleetwood-Smith	39
M.Leyland	c Chipperfield b Fleetwood-Smith	45	(5)	c Chipperfield b Fleetwood-Smith	32
R.E.S.Wyatt	c Fingleton b O'Reilly	3	(6)	c Oldfield b McCabe	50
†L.E.G.Ames	b McCormick	52	(7)	lbw b Fleetwood-Smith	0
J.Hardstaff, jr	c & b McCormick	20	(3)	b O'Reilly	43
*G.O.B.Allen	lbw b Fleetwood-Smith	11		c Gregory b McCormick	9
R.W.V.Robins	c Oldfield b b O'Reilly	10		b McCormick	4
W.Voce	c Rigg b Fleetwood-Smith	8		b Fleetwood-Smith	1
K.Farnes	not out	0		not out	7
Extras	(b6, lb2, w1, nb4)	13		(b12, lb2, nb6)	20
Total	(113.4 overs, 435 mins)	330		(74.0 overs, 294 mins)	243

ENGLAND	O	M	R	W	w,nb		O	M	R	W	w,nb
Voce	12	0	49	0	-,1	(4)	20	2	86	1	-,1
Allen	16	0	60	2	-,1	(3)	14	1	61	0	-,-
Farnes	20.6	1	71	3	-,1	(1)	24	2	89	2	-,-
Hammond	6	0	30	2	-,-	(2)	15.2	1	57	5	-,-
Verity	16	4	47	0	-,-		37	17	54	0	-,-
Robins	7	1	26	1	-,-		6	0	38	1	-,-
Barnett							5	1	15	0	1,-
Leyland							2	0	6	0	-,-

AUSTRALIA	O	M	R	W	w,nb		O	M	R	W	w,nb
McCormick	21	2	81	2	1,3		13	1	43	2	-,6
McCabe	9	2	18	0	-,-		5	0	15	1	-,-
Fleetwood-Smith	41.4	10	129	4	-,-		30	1	110	6	-,-
O'Reilly	30	12	51	4	-,1		26	8	55	1	-,-
Chipperfield	9	1	24	0	-,-						
Gregory	3	0	14	0	-,-						

FALL OF WICKETS

Wkt	AUST 1st	ENG 1st	AUST 2nd	ENG 2nd
1st	26	53	21	45
2nd	72	108	88	50
3rd	73	190	197	120
4th	136	195	237	149
5th	206	259	372	190
6th	226	299	422	190
7th	249	304	426	225
8th	271	318	427	231
9th	283	322	429	235
10th	288	330	433	243

QUEENSLAND v SOUTH AUSTRALIA (Shield Match 10)

Played at Brisbane Cricket Ground (Woolloongabba) on February 12, 13, 15, 1937. (Four-day match)
Toss : South Australia.   Result : SOUTH AUSTRALIA WON BY TEN WICKETS.
Debuts: Nil.
12th Men: G.D.Gunthorpe (Qld) and R.S.Whitington (SA).
Umpires: J.Bartlett and J.A.Scott.
Attendances: 2426, 7177, 50.   Total: 9653.   Receipts: £621.
Close of Play: 1st day SA 3/138 (Badcock 50, Bradman 45); 2nd day SA (2) 0/7 (Williams 3, Waite 3).

W.C.Andrew (injured thumb) was unavailable for Queensland. Rain leading up to the match led to uncertainty on the state of the pitch and Bradman sent Queensland in on winning the toss. Allen (68 in 102 minutes, 3 sixes and 4 fours) and Baker (39 in 83 minutes, 1 six and 4 fours) added 101 for the fifth wicket which amounted to 73.7 per cent of the Queensland total. Bradman (123 in 165 minutes, 1 six and 10 fours) added 109 with Badcock (56 in 129 minutes, 4 fours) and 67 with Hamence to establish a lead for South Australia. Grimmett, backing up, was run out when a straight drive by Hamence was deflected by the bowler into the non-striker's stumps. Rogers (46 in 62 minutes, 6 fours) and Tallon (48 in 71 minutes, 6 fours) topscored in Queensland's second innings. South Australia's inability to score 20 runs before 6pm on the second day meant they had to stay another two days to knock off the runs early on Monday. Oxenham, aged 45 years 202 days on the last day of the game, made his final first-class appearance. He died only two years later from injuries received in a car crash. *Wisden* incorrectly gives Qld (2) Brown 5, Amos 1. Sources: *Wisden, VCA Report, QCA Report, SACA Report, The Herald, Brisbane Courier-Mail, The Sporting Globe, Brisbane Telegraph.*

QUEENSLAND

W.A.Brown	c Hamence b Williams	1	c Grimmett b Williams		3
G.G.Cook	c Richardson b Williams	4	lbw b Cotton		12
R.E.Rogers	c Ryan b Cotton	10	b Cotton		46
T.Allen	c Cotton b Grimmett	68	c Walker b Williams		2
†D.Tallon	c Walker b Cotton	3	c Grimmett b Cotton		48
G.W.Baker	c Walker b Cotton	39	lbw b Grimmett		14
J.G.Maddern	st Walker b Grimmett	5	st Walker b Ward		7
*R.K.Oxenham	c Richardson b Grimmett	2	st Walker b Ward		1
G.S.Amos	run out (Richardson/Walker)	1	st Walker b Ward		3
E.R.Wyeth	b Grimmett	0	b Ward		0
P.L.Dixon	not out	1	not out		1
Extras	(lb2, w1)	3	(lb2)		2
Total	(33.0 overs, 154 mins)	137	(36.7 overs, 156 mins)		139

SOUTH AUSTRALIA

A.J.Ryan	b Wyeth	15			
†C.W.Walker	c Maddern b Cook	13			
V.Y.Richardson	b Wyeth	8			
C.L.Badcock	c Amos b Dixon	56			
*D.G.Bradman	st Tallon b Wyeth	123			
R.A.Hamence	b Wyeth	28			
M.G.Waite	lbw b Dixon	0	(2) not out		6
R.G.Williams	lbw b Dixon	2	(1) not out		13
F.A.Ward	c Baker b Dixon	1			
C.V.Grimmett	run out (Wyeth)	2			
H.N.J.Cotton	not out	0			
Extras	(b7, lb2)	9	(w1)		1
Total	(72.7 overs, 275 mins)	257	(6.7 overs, 25 mins) (0 wkts)		20

SOUTH AUSTRALIA	O	M	R	W	w,nb		O	M	R	W	w,nb
Cotton	10	1	27	3	-,-		9	1	50	3	-,-
Williams	8	0	38	2	1,-		8	1	39	2	-,-
Ward	5	0	40	0	-,-	(5)	3.7	1	3	4	-,-
Waite	4	1	11	0	-,-		3	1	10	0	-,-
Grimmett	6	1	18	4	-,-	(3)	13	3	35	1	-,-

QUEENSLAND	O	M	R	W	w,nb		O	M	R	W	w,nb
Dixon	19.7	4	70	4	-,-		3	0	7	0	1,-
Cook	12	1	56	1	-,-						
Oxenham	10	2	16	0	-,-						
Wyeth	23	4	52	4	-,-	(3)	2.7	1	9	0	-,-
Amos	8	0	54	0	-,-	(2)	1	0	3	0	-,-

		FALL OF WICKETS			
	Wkt	QLD 1st	SA 1st	QLD 2nd	SA 2nd
	1st	2	22	5	-
	2nd	13	34	21	-
	3rd	23	59	38	-
	4th	27	168	86	-
	5th	128	235	127	-
	6th	128	235	127	-
	7th	135	237	129	-
	8th	136	245	136	-
	9th	136	257	136	-
	10th	137	257	139	-

NEW SOUTH WALES v M.C.C.

Played at Sydney Cricket Ground on February 13, 15, 16, 17, 1937. (Four-day match)
Toss : New South Wales.   Result : NEW SOUTH WALES WON BY BY 105 RUNS.
Debuts: Nil.
12th Men: S.G.Barnes (NSW). No 12th named for MCC.
Umpires: E.G.Borwick and F.W.Lyons.
Attendances: 14354, 6276, 4904, 200.   Total: 25,734.   Receipts: £1448.
Close of Play: 1st day MCC 2/24 (Leyland 9, Duckworth 1); 2nd day NSW (2) 6/205 (Lush 5, Oldfield 1); 3rd day MCC (2) 7/280
    (Ames 44, Duckworth 10).

Chipperfield fell on his wicket in the first innings when he was struck on the jaw by a rising delivery from Farnes. An X-ray revealed a fractured jaw and Chipperfield took no further part in the match or the remainder of the season. His replacement at the crease, Lush, a part-time batsman and right-arm fast bowler, topped the innings (49 in 96 minutes, 4 fours) and went on to capture 13 for 115, his only 10-wicket match. Lush finished the game early on the last day with three wickets in four balls: Ames, Farnes, ball, Copson. Fingleton (60 in 130 minutes, 1 four) and McCabe (93 in 142 minutes, 9 fours) added 135 for the third wicket in the New South Wales second innings after the loss of Beatty and Hynes in the same over. Barnett (117 in 173 minutes, 2 sixes and 13 fours), Hardstaff (64 in 129 minutes, 4 fours) and Ames (60 in 90 minutes, 7 fours) were the only Englishmen to surpass 20, their first innings being ruined by Lush and Chilvers, who conceded two singles while capturing four wickets in seven overs. *Wisden* incorrectly gives MCC (2) Ames b Lush. *NSWCA Report* incorrectly gives NSW (2) Chilvers b Farnes. Sources: *Wisden, NSWCA Report, Sydney Morning Herald, NSWCA Scorebook, Sydney Referee, The Sporting Globe.*

NEW SOUTH WALES

J.H.W.Fingleton	c Duckworth b Farnes	8		c Duckworth b Worthington	60
R.G.Beatty	b Farnes	8		c Robins b Farnes	5
*S.J.McCabe	c Farnes b Worthington	9	(4)	c Barnett b Sims	93
R.H.Robinson	run out (Farnes/Duckworth)	2	(5)	c Ames b Copson	25
A.G.Chipperfield	hit wkt b Farnes	37		absent hurt	-
V.E.Jackson	c Ames b Robins	42		c Worthington b Copson	10
J.G.Lush	c Duckworth b Sims	49		c Sims b Farnes	5
L.C.Hynes	c & b Sims	35	(3)	c Duckworth b Farnes	0
†W.A.S.Oldfield	b Sims	2	(8)	not out	30
H.C.Chilvers	not out	18	(9)	c Duckworth b Farnes	8
E.C.S.White	c Robins b Sims	3	(10)	b Copson	0
Extras	(b13, lb5)	18		(b1, lb8, nb1)	10
Total	(56.6 overs, 219 mins)	231		(59.3 overs, 234 mins)	246

M.C.C.

T.S.Worthington	c sub (S.G.Barnes) b Lush	4	(2)	c & b Lush	6
C.J.Barnett	c Beatty b Lush	6	(1)	b Hynes	117
M.Leyland	b Lush	16	(5)	c McCabe b Lush	1
†G.Duckworth	c Oldfield b Lush	1	(9)	not out	15
J.Hardstaff, jr	c Robinson b Chilvers	9	(3)	c White b Lush	64
R.E.S.Wyatt	b Lush	12	(4)	c Robinson b Lush	11
L.E.G.Ames	b Lush	0	(6)	c Hynes b Lush	60
*R.W.V.Robins	st Oldfield b Chilvers	4	(7)	b Hynes	7
J.M.Sims	st Oldfield b Chilvers	1	(8)	lbw b Hynes	8
K.Farnes	c Hynes b Chilvers	0		b Lush	0
W.H.Copson	not out	9		b Lush	0
Extras	(b8, lb2, nb1)	11		(b3, lb4, w2, nb1)	10
Total	(24.5 overs, 114 mins)	73		(66.5 overs, 264 mins)	299

M.C.C.	O	M	R	W	w,nb	O	M	R	W	w,nb
Farnes	13	1	65	3	-,-	15	0	59	4	-,-
Copson	12	2	35	0	-,-	17.3	5	42	3	-,-
Worthington	11	1	28	1	-,-	8	0	48	1	-,1
Sims	12.6	1	46	4	-,-	13	1	55	1	-,-
Robins	8	0	39	1	-,-	6	0	32	0	-,-

NEW SOUTH WALES	O	M	R	W	w,nb	O	M	R	W	w,nb
Lush	12.5	2	43	6	-,1	15.5	2	72	7	2,-
Hynes	5	1	17	0	-,-	13	1	76	3	-,1
Chilvers	7	5	2	4	-,-	17	2	95	0	-,-
White						15	4	33	0	-,-
Jackson						6	3	13	0	-,-

FALL OF WICKETS

Wkt	NSW 1st	MCC 1st	NSW 2nd	MCC 2nd
1st	11	8	11	7
2nd	26	19	11	172
3rd	26	26	146	200
4th	32	43	182	202
5th	76	43	194	202
6th	152	43	199	220
7th	188	48	210	245
8th	192	50	241	299
9th	215	50	246	299
10th	231	73	-	299

VICTORIA v M.C.C

Played at Melbourne Cricket Ground on February 19, 20, 22 (no play), 23, 1937. (Four-day match)
Toss : M.C.C.　　　　　　　Result : MATCH DRAWN.
Debuts: Victoria - L.J.Nash (Vic only).
12th Men: L.P.J.O'Brien (Vic) and T.S.Worthington (MCC).
Umpires: A.N.Barlow and C.Dwyer.
Attendances: 6824, 12358, no play, 3426.　　　Total: 22,608.　　　Receipts: £975.
Close of Play: 1st day MCC 8/169 (Ames 59, Voce 8); 2nd day Vic 2/144 (Gregory 53, Hassett 28); 3rd day no play.

After an absence of more than three years from the first-class scene, Nash, a renowned Australian Rules footballer and former Tasmanian cricketer, returned to play his only match for Victoria. His aggressive fast bowling captured 4 for 37 and earned him an immediate recall to the Australian side for the Fifth Test at the expense of the favoured J.G.Lush of New South Wales. Overnight rain delayed the match until 2.30pm because of a sodden outfield. Inclement weather continued on the second day with no play until 3.45pm, and not a ball was bowled on the third. Ames (64 in 121 minutes, 7 fours), Hardstaff (60 not out in 102 minutes, 6 fours) and Hammond (56 in 67 minutes, 9 fours) for M.C.C. and Gregory (86 in 191 minutes, 2 fours) and Hassett (54 in 112 minutes, 4 fours) for Victoria scored fifties. Makeshift opener Verity was out to the second ball of M.C.C.'s second innings. G.O.B.Allen (leg strain), A.E.Fagg (ill) and Fishlock (broken hand) were unavailable for the visitors, while L.O.Fleetwood-Smith was rested by the Victorian Selectors in order to be fresh for the Fifth Test.
Sources: *Wisden, VCA Report, The Age, The Argus, The Herald, Sydney Morning Herald, The Sporting Globe.*

M.C.C.

H.Verity	c Pearson b Nash	1	c Sievers b Nash	0
C.J.Barnett	c Pearson b McCormick	1	c Lee b Nash	11
J.Hardstaff, jr	c Pearson b Nash	14	not out	60
W.R.Hammond	b Ebeling	14	c Lee b Ledward	56
M.Leyland	c Ledward b Sievers	19	not out	5
R.E.S.Wyatt	c Barnett b McCormick	1		
†L.E.G.Ames	b McCormick	64		
*R.W.V.Robins	c Nash b Pearson	33		
J.M.Sims	c Ledward b Ebeling	16		
W.Voce	b Sievers	15		
W.H.Copson	not out	2		
Extras	(b5, lb2)	7		—
Total	(45.1 overs, 212 mins)	187	(26.0 overs, 105 mins) (3 wkts)	132

VICTORIA

K.E.Rigg	lbw b Sims	18
I.S.Lee	run out (Hammond/Ames)	40
R.G.Gregory	c Ames b Copson	86
A.L.Hassett	c Ames b Voce	54
J.A.Ledward	c Barnett b Copson	7
W.E.Pearson	c Ames b Voce	15
M.W.Sievers	b Verity	6
†B.A.Barnett	lbw b Robins	7
L.J.Nash	c Barnett b Leyland	29
*H.I.Ebeling	lbw b Sims	6
E.L.McCormick	not out	10
Extras	(b7, lb6, nb1)	14
Total	(85.3 overs, 332 mins)	292

VICTORIA	O	M	R	W	w,nb		O	M	R	W	w,nb
McCormick	11	2	35	3	-,-	(2)	2	0	14	0	-,-
Nash	9	3	21	2	,	(1)	3	0	16	2	-,-
Ebeling	8	1	20	2	-,-	(6)	2	0	7	0	-,-
Sievers	7.1	0	36	2	-,-	(3)	4	0	15	0	-,-
Gregory	6	0	28	0	-,-		3	0	22	0	-,-
Pearson	4	0	40	1	-,-	(4)	7	1	47	0	-,-
Ledward							2	1	1	1	-,-
Hassett							2	0	6	0	-,-
Lee							1	0	4	0	-,-

M.C.C.	O	M	R	W	w,nb
Copson	19	0	64	2	-,-
Hammond	5	1	12	0	-,-
Voce	16	1	52	2	-,1
Sims	16	0	76	2	-,-
Verity	21	7	39	1	-,-
Robins	8	0	34	1	-,-
Leyland	0.3	0	1	1	-,-

FALL OF WICKETS

	MCC	VIC	MCC
Wkt	1st	1st	2nd
1st	3	37	0
2nd	3	101	27
3rd	29	203	121
4th	37	209	-
5th	40	222	-
6th	66	230	-
7th	122	242	-
8th	155	246	-
9th	177	259	-
10th	187	292	-

NEW SOUTH WALES v SOUTH AUSTRALIA (Shield Match 11)

Played at Sydney Cricket Ground on February 19, 20, 22, 23, 1937. (Four-day match)
Toss : New South Wales.   Result : MATCH DRAWN.
Debuts: New South Wales - S.G.Barnes (f/c).
12th Men: J.H.Fitzpatrick (NSW) and M.G.Waite (SA).
Umpires: E.G.Borwick and F.W.Lyons.
Attendances: 7550, 18493, 3558, 3152.   Total: 32,753.   Receipts: £1714.
Close of Play: 1st day NSW 8/317 (Oldfield 58, White 78); 2nd day SA 8/208 (Badcock 93, Grimmett 6); 3rd day SA (2) 1/39 (Ryan 24, Ward 0).

Rain, which allowed only 108 minutes' play on the last day, killed an impending close finish, South Australia needing a further 196 in the 220 minutes remaining, Bradman and Badcock both well set. Oldfield (63 in 151 minutes, 2 fours) and No. 10 batsman White (career-best 108 not out in 156 minutes, 10 fours) rescued the New South Wales first innings with a ninth-wicket stand of 164. McCabe (68 in 101 minutes, 1 six and 7 fours) batted well in the second innings. Ryan fell to the sixth ball of South Australia's first innings, in which Badcock (136 in 224 minutes, 16 fours) easily made top score. Barnes, originally named 12th man, replaced H.C.Chilvers (work) at the last moment in the New South Wales side. *Wisden* and *NSWCA Report* incorrectly give reversed bowling analyses in NSW (1) and (2). *SACA Report* incorrectly gives NSW (2) White c Walker b Grimmett. Sources: *Wisden, NSWCA Report, SACA Report, The Herald, Sydney Morning Herald, NSWCA Scorebook, The Sporting Globe.*

NEW SOUTH WALES

J.H.W.Fingleton	c Hamence b Williams	1		c Badcock b Grimmett	12
R.G.Beatty	b Grimmett	24		lbw b Williams	5
R.H.Robinson	c & b Cotton	47		b Grimmett	7
*S.J.McCabe	st Walker b Ward	39		b Ryan	68
V.E.Jackson	c Ryan b Cotton	18		c Walker b Williams	32
S.G.Barnes	lbw b Ward	31		lbw b Ward	44
J.G.Lush	c Ryan b Grimmett	4		c Whitington b Cotton	40
L.C.Hynes	lbw b Grimmett	12	(9)	c Walker b Grimmett	2
†W.A.S.Oldfield	c Whitington b Ward	63	(10)	c Ryan b Cotton	18
E.C.S.White	not out	108	(8)	b Grimmett	3
W.J.O'Reilly	lbw b Ward	2		not out	4
Extras	(lb4, nb2)	6		(b1, lb5, nb1)	7
Total	(91.1 overs, 357 mins)	355		(50.1 overs, 205 mins)	242

SOUTH AUSTRALIA

A.J.Ryan	c Hynes b Lush	0		b O'Reilly	41
†C.W.Walker	c Fingleton b O'Reilly	4		b O'Reilly	11
R.S.Whitington	c Beatty b Lush	29			
*D.G.Bradman	lbw b O'Reilly	24		not out	38
C.L.Badcock	c White b Jackson	136		not out	27
R.A.Hamence	c Oldfield b Robinson	27			
V.Y.Richardson	st Oldfield b Robinson	9			
R.G.Williams	lbw b O'Reilly	2			
F.A.Ward	b O'Reilly	0	(3)	c Oldfield b White	8
C.V.Grimmett	b Lush	12			
H.N.J.Cotton	not out	12			
Extras	(b4, lb1, nb10)	15		(b4, lb1, nb2)	7
Total	(78.0 overs, 304 mins)	270		(41.0 overs, 156 mins) (3 wkts)	132

SOUTH AUSTRALIA	O	M	R	W	w,nb		O	M	R	W	w,nb
Cotton	20	3	72	2	-,-		13.1	1	45	2	-,-
Williams	16	2	75	1	-,2		10	0	62	2	-,1
Grimmett	27	4	77	3	-,-		15	0	71	4	-,-
Ryan	9	1	36	0	-,-	(5)	3	1	13	1	-,-
Ward	19.1	1	89	4	-,-	(4)	9	0	44	1	-,-

NEW SOUTH WALES	O	M	R	W	w,nb		O	M	R	W	w,nb
Lush	16	2	77	3	-,3		5	0	24	0	-,1
Hynes	18	1	76	0	-,7		8	0	38	0	-,1
O'Reilly	20	8	40	4	-,-	(4)	10	3	13	2	-,-
Jackson	5	2	9	1	-,-	(3)	6	2	14	0	-,-
White	10	1	16	0	-,-		12	2	36	1	-,-
Robinson	9	0	37	2	-,-						

FALL OF WICKETS

Wkt	NSW 1st	SA 1st	NSW 2nd	SA 2nd
1st	3	0	12	39
2nd	53	23	25	62
3rd	85	45	28	84
4th	115	94	99	-
5th	143	173	150	-
6th	157	187	182	-
7th	171	192	185	-
8th	177	192	191	-
9th	341	236	235	-
10th	355	270	242	-

AUSTRALIA v ENGLAND (5th Test)

Played at Melbourne Cricket Ground on February 26, 27, March 1, 2, 3, 1937. (Timeless match)
Toss : Australia.   Result : AUSTRALIA WON BY AN INNINGS AND 200 RUNS.
Debuts: Nil.
12th Men: W.A.Brown (Aust) and L.B.Fishlock (Eng).
Umpires: E.G.Borwick and J.D.Scott.
Attendances: 52342, 77181, 63340, 31253, 12000.   Total: 236,116.   Receipts: £18,271.
Close of Play: 1st day Aust 3/342 (Bradman 165, Badcock 12); 2nd day Aust 9/593 (McCormick 9, Fleetwood-Smith 11); 3rd day Eng
    4/184 (Hardstaff 73, Wyatt 20); 4th day Eng (2) 8/165 (Verity 2, Voce 1).

Having lost the first two Tests in the rubber, Australia ensured the retention of The Ashes by winning the last three. Bradman (chanceless 169 in 223 minutes, 15 fours) and McCabe (112 in 163 minutes, 16 fours, chances at 11 and 86) added 249 in 163 minutes, the highest third-wicket stand yet for Australia in a home Test. Badcock, included as a replacement for A.G.Chipperfield, who had fractured his jaw in the NSW v MCC match, responded with his sole Test century (a chanceless and highly-acclaimed 118 in 205 minutes, 15 fours) and put on 161 with Gregory (80 in 195 minutes, 5 fours), whose second Test was destined to be his last. Rain, which had played a big part in the outcome of the first three Tests, fell after the third day and badly affected the wicket to England's disadvantage. Worthington (44 in 98 minutes, 7 fours) and Hardstaff (83 in 240 minutes, 8 fours) led the scoring before the downpour. Barnett (41 in 61 minutes, 4 fours) and Hammond (56 in 95 minutes, 9 fours) hit out in the follow-on. Fleetwood-Smith finished the match with the wickets of Voce and Farnes with the only two balls required on the fifth morning before an estimated 12,000 people, admitted free. This outstanding five-match series, which had attracted an unprecedented total attendance of 954,290, brought to an end the era of timeless first-class matches in Australia.
Sources: *Wisden, VCA Report, The Age, The Argus, The Herald, Melbourne Sun, The Australasian.*

AUSTRALIA

J.H.W.Fingleton	c Voce b Farnes	17
K.E.Rigg	c Ames b Farnes	28
*D.G.Bradman	b Farnes	169
S.J.McCabe	c Farnes b Verity	112
C.L.Badcock	c Worthington b Voce	118
R.G.Gregory	c Verity b Farnes	80
†W.A.S.Oldfield	c Ames b Voce	21
L.J.Nash	c Ames b Farnes	17
W.J.O'Reilly	b Voce	1
E.L.McCormick	not out	17
L.O.Fleetwood-Smith	b Farnes	13
Extras	(b1, lb5, w1, nb4)	11
Total	(140.5 overs, 606 mins)	604

ENGLAND

C.J.Barnett	c Oldfield b Nash	18	lbw b O'Reilly	41
T.S.Worthington	hit wkt b Fleetwood-Smith	44	c Bradman b McCormick	6
J.Hardstaff, jr	c McCormick b O'Reilly	83	b Nash	1
W.R.Hammond	c Nash b O'Reilly	14	c Bradman b O'Reilly	56
M.Leyland	b O'Reilly	7	c McCormick b Fleetwood-Smith	28
R.E.S.Wyatt	c Bradman b O'Reilly	38	run out (Rigg/Oldfield)	9
†L.E.G.Ames	b Nash	19	c McCabe b McCormick	11
*G.O.B.Allen	c Oldfield b Nash	0	c Nash b O'Reilly	7
H.Verity	c Rigg b Nash	0	not out	2
W.Voce	st Oldfield b O'Reilly	3	c Badcock b Fleetwood-Smith	1
K.Farnes	not out	0	c Nash b Fleetwood-Smith	0
Extras	(lb12, nb1)	13	(lb3)	3
Total	(71.5 overs, 324 mins)	239	(49.2 overs, 208 mins)	165

ENGLAND	O	M	R	W	w,nb
Allen	17	0	99	0	1,3
Farnes	28.5	5	96	6	-,-
Voce	29	3	123	3	-,1
Hammond	16	1	62	0	-,-
Verity	41	5	127	1	-,-
Worthington	6	0	60	0	-,-
Leyland	3	0	26	0	-,-

AUSTRALIA	O	M	R	W	w,nb		O	M	R	W	w,nb
McCormick	13	1	54	0	-,1		9	0	33	2	-,-
Nash	17.5	1	70	4	-,-		7	1	34	1	-,-
O'Reilly	23	7	51	5	-,-		19	6	58	3	-,-
Fleetwood-Smith	18	3	51	1	-,-	(5)	13.2	3	36	3	-,-
McCabe						(4)	1	0	1	0	-,-

FALL OF WICKETS

	AUST	ENG	ENG
Wkt	1st	1st	2nd
1st	42	33	9
2nd	54	96	10
3rd	303	130	70
4th	346	140	121
5th	507	202	142
6th	544	236	142
7th	563	236	153
8th	571	236	162
9th	576	239	165
10th	604	239	165

SOUTH AUSTRALIA v VICTORIA (Shield Match 12)

Played at Adelaide Oval on March 12, 13, 15, 1937. (Four-day match)
Toss : South Australia.   Result : VICTORIA WON BY NINE WICKETS.
Debuts: Nil.
12th Men: B.H.Leak (SA) and F.W.Sides (Vic).
Umpires: A.J.Richardson and J.D.Scott.
Attendances: 2672, ? , ? .   Total: 9279.   Receipts: £317.
Close of Play: 1st day Vic 2/97 (Lee 42, Hassett 9); 2nd day Vic (2) 0/22 (Rigg 10, Lee 12).

Played between the top teams, the last match of the season decided the winner of the 41st Sheffield Shield. Batsmen struggled throughout despite ideal weather and a perfect batting strip, South Australia incurring their first outright defeat in the competition for more than two years in a contest which barely lasted two days. McCormick (right-arm fast) returned the best innings and match analyses of his career, capturing the first nine wickets in the second innings and bowling unchanged, Sievers spoiling a perfect ten by bowling Williams. McCormick began by bowling Ryan with the fourth ball of the match and later dismissed Badcock and Waite with consecutive balls. In the second innings he dismissed Walker with the last ball of his opening over and then Bradman and Badcock, again with consecutive balls, in his fifth over to have South Australia reeling at 4 for 37, from which they could not recover. Lee (109 not out in 270 minutes, 9 fours) carried his bat through Victoria's first innings and was the only batsman to exceed 35 in the match. Sources: *Wisden, VCA Report, SACA Report, The Age, The Argus, Adelaide Advertiser, The News, The Sporting Globe.*

SOUTH AUSTRALIA

Batsman	Dismissal 1	Runs 1	Dismissal 2	Runs 2
A.J.Ryan	b McCormick	0	c Hassett b McCormick	19
†C.W.Walker	lbw b Fleetwood-Smith	7	c Sievers b McCormick	0
R.S.Whitington	c Pearson b Sievers	30	c Hassett b McCormick	13
*D.G.Bradman	c Ebeling b Fleetwood-Smith	31	c Hassett b McCormick	8
C.L.Badcock	c Hassett b McCormick	28	b McCormick	0
R.A.Hamence	lbw b Fleetwood-Smith	35	c Lee b McCormick	4
M.G.Waite	c Sievers b McCormick	0	hit wkt b McCormick	7
C.V.Grimmett	b Fleetwood-Smith	7	b McCormick	0
R.G.Williams	b Fleetwood-Smith	7	b Sievers	9
F.A.Ward	c Barnett b Fleetwood-Smith	25	c Sievers b McCormick	11
H.N.J.Cotton	not out	4	not out	0
Extras	(b1, lb4, w1, nb2)	8	(b1, lb3, w1, nb3)	8
Total	(50.4 overs, 210 mins)	182	(21.6 overs, 119 mins)	79

VICTORIA

Batsman	Dismissal 1	Runs 1	Dismissal 2	Runs 2
K.E.Rigg	c Walker b Williams	33	not out	21
I.S.Lee	not out	109	c Walker b Waite	15
R.G.Gregory	lbw b Waite	12	not out	13
A.L.Hassett	c Walker b Cotton	15		
J.A.Ledward	lbw b Williams	6		
W.E.Pearson	st Walker b Waite	6		
†B.A.Barnett	b Waite	3		
M.W.Sievers	c Ward b Waite	8		
*H.I.Ebeling	st Walker b Grimmett	12		
E.L.McCormick	b Grimmett	0		
L.O.Fleetwood-Smith	st Walker b Grimmett	4		
Extras	(lb5)	5		—
Total	(72.0 overs, 270 mins)	213	(13.7 overs, 52 mins) (1 wkt)	49

VICTORIA	O	M	R	W	w,nb		O	M	R	W	w,nb
McCormick	14	1	56	3	1,2		11	1	40	9	1,3
Ebeling	6	1	16	0	-,-		8	0	21	0	-,-
Sievers	10	0	36	1	-,-	(4)	0.6	0	4	1	-,-
Fleetwood-Smith	20.4	3	66	6	-,-	(3)	2	1	6	0	-,-

SOUTH AUSTRALIA	O	M	R	W	w,nb		O	M	R	W	w,nb
Cotton	11	1	35	1	-,-		3	0	8	0	-,-
Williams	10	1	46	2	-,-		3	0	14	0	-,-
Grimmett	15	3	52	3	-,-						
Waite	18	5	35	4	-,-	(3)	4	3	3	1	-,-
Ward	18	4	40	0	-,-	(4)	3.7	0	24	0	-,-

FALL OF WICKETS

Wkt	SA 1st	VIC 1st	SA 2nd	VIC 2nd
1st	0	48	7	25
2nd	27	80	27	-
3rd	71	108	37	-
4th	73	116	37	-
5th	119	132	48	-
6th	119	136	57	-
7th	134	164	57	-
8th	142	209	58	-
9th	177	209	75	-
10th	182	213	79	-

1937-38 SEASON (24 MATCHES)

The 1937 New Zealanders stopped off to play three matches in Australia on the way home from their tour of England. It was their fifth first-class visit to Australia. The Board of Control agreed to the games at the request of the New Zealand Cricket Council, who wanted some income to help offset losses from the England tour. However, the team's poor showing in Australia - all three matches were lost by comfortable margins - limited the attendances and the public interest in the visit. As a result, the three State associations (New South Wales, South Australia and Victoria) generously agreed to hand over the total net receipts to the NZCC, instead of the previously agreed figure of 75 percent.

New South Wales won the Sheffield Shield for the first time since 1932-33. McCabe, Fingleton and Barnes all batted brightly, but the bowling of O'Reilly held the key to the success of the team. He captured 14 wickets in the match against South Australia, including Bradman in both innings, and was never mastered at any stage.

Bradman scored as heavily as had come to be expected but, apart from Badcock, South Australia did not get much value from the other batsmen. The Victorian batting was led by Lee, Rigg and Hassett. Wrist spin remained by far the most effective bowling method in the country. Grimmett and Ward (South Australia) and Fleetwood-Smith (Victoria) led their attacks to provide competition for O'Reilly. Rogers and Brown hit centuries for Queensland but the northerners again struggled to dismiss the opposition and finished last for the sixth successive season. They failed to win a match.

Western Australia travelled to the Eastern States for a series of matches. They met Victoria (twice), New South Wales and South Australia. The games against Victoria and South Australia were considered first-class by the respective associations, but the NSWCA designated their team a 'Second XI' and refused to recognise the match as first-class. Attempts by cricket followers to upgrade the match to first-class status continued for years, but the NSWCA steadfastly refused to change their ruling and their verdict has been accepted here. The Western Australians failed to extend Victoria and South Australia and were comfortably defeated in all their matches.

Western Australia, with the support of Victoria, revived their proposal for an 'All States Competition' but the continuing doubts of the other State associations delayed any further consideration. The WACA envisaged the competition beginning in the 1939-40 season.

Competition for places in the 19th Australian team to tour England in 1938 was unusually open, particularly in the middle order batting and pace bowling departments. The team selected was: D.G.Bradman (captain), S.J.McCabe (vice-captain), C.L.Badcock, S.G.Barnes, B.A.Barnett, W.A.Brown, A.G.Chipperfield, J.H.W.Fingleton, L.O.Fleetwood-Smith, A.L.Hassett, E.L.McCormick, W.J.O'Reilly, M.G.Waite, C.W.Walker, F.A.Ward and E.C.S.White. The omission of Grimmett was received with widespread disappointment. D.Tallon was also considered unfortunate by many to have missed out.

Leading Aggregates

Batsmen	M	I	NO	Runs	HS	Ave.	Bowlers	Runs	Wkts	Ave.
D.G.Bradman (SA)	12	18	2	1437	246	89.81	W.J.O'Reilly (NSW)	784	64	12.25
C.L.Badcock (SA)	11	19	2	872	159	51.29	L.O.Fleetwood-Smith (V)	1436	64	22.43
J.H.W.Fingleton (NSW)	11	18	1	862	160	50.70	F.A.Ward (SA)	1100	51	21.56
S.G.Barnes (NSW)	10	17	1	809	110	50.56	C.V.Grimmett (SA)	845	41	20.60
S.J.McCabe (NSW)	11	16	0	720	122	45.00	M.G.Waite (SA)	505	25	20.20
A.L.Hassett (V)	11	15	2	693	127*	53.30	R.G.Williams (SA)	581	24	24.20
I.S.Lee (V)	9	14	0	604	122	43.14	E.C.S.White (NSW)	383	23	16.65
K.E.Rigg (V)	9	14	1	478	118	36.76	M.W.Sievers (V)	605	23	26.30
M.G.Waite (SA)	11	18	3	470	58	31.33	E.L.McCormick (V)	685	23	29.78

SHEFFIELD SHIELD TABLE

	P	WO	W1	LO	L1	D	Pts	Quotient	Runs Scored	Wkts Lost	Runs Conceded	Wkts Taken
NEW SOUTH WALES	6	3	1	-	1	1	21	1.216	2587	91	2033	87
SOUTH AUSTRALIA	6	2	1	2	1	-	14	1.215	3293	107	2709	107
VICTORIA	6	1	2	1	1	1	14	1.169	2465	76	2717	98
QUEENSLAND	6	-	-	3	1	2	5	0524	1775	84	2661	66
TOTAL	12	6	4	6	4	2	54	1.000	10120	358	10120	358

AFCM No. 897/69
SSM No. 306/23

QUEENSLAND v NEW SOUTH WALES (Shield Match 1)

Played at Brisbane Cricket Ground (Woolloongabba) on November 5, 6, 8, 9 (no play), 1937. (Four-day match)
Toss : Queensland.   Result : MATCH DRAWN.
Debuts: Queensland - C.P.Christ, H.J.H.Mahoney (both f/c).
12th Men: J.G.Maddern (Qld) and R.G.Beatty (NSW).
Umpires: K.E.Fagg and J.A.Scott.
Attendances: 930, 1177, 854, no play.   Total: 2961 (excluding last day).   Receipts: £126.
Close of Play: 1st day NSW 3/42 (McCabe 23, Barnes 0); 2nd day NSW 3/103 (McCabe 70, Barnes 13); 3rd day Qld 2/39 (Cook 16, Tallon 9).

Consistent rain in the week preceding the match severely hampered preparation of the pitch and doubts about its quality prompted Brown to insert the New South Welshmen on winning the toss. Further rain restricted play to little more than an hour in the pre-lunch session on each of the first two days. New South Wales lost several early wickets on the soft pitch until a fourth-wicket stand of 147 between McCabe (119 in 149 minutes, 14 fours) and Barnes (68 in 169 minutes, 4 fours) restored the balance. Oldfield was run out without facing a ball. Queensland had also lost early wickets when light rain and bad light ended the third day's play at 4.55pm. Further rain overnight and the following day caused the abandonment of the match without a further ball bowled. *NSWCA Report* incorrectly includes no-balls in the bowling analyses. Sources: *Wisden, NSWCA Report, QCA Report, The Age, The Herald, Sydney Morning Herald, Brisbane Courier-Mail.*

NEW SOUTH WALES

J.H.W.Fingleton	b Dixon	10
A.G.Cheetham	c Cook b Dixon	5
*S.J.McCabe	st Tallon b Govan	119
V.E.Jackson	c Dixon b Cook	0
S.G.Barnes	c Brown b Christ	68
A.G.Chipperfield	c Rogers b Govan	9
L.C.Hynes	st Tallon b Govan	0
J.G.Lush	c Dixon b Christ	13
E.C.S.White	not out	12
†W.A.S.Oldfield	run out (Brown/Tallon)	0
W.J.O'Reilly	c Rogers b Cook	16
Extras	(lb3, nb2)	5
Total	(61.3 overs, 233 mins)	257

QUEENSLAND

*W.A.Brown	lbw b O'Reilly	6
G.G.Cook	not out	16
R.E.Rogers	c Oldfield b Lush	4
†D.Tallon	not out	9
T.Allen	)	
G.W.Baker	)	
H.J.H.Mahoney	)	
J.M.Govan	) did not bat	
E.R.Wyeth	)	
C.P.Christ	)	
P.L.Dixon	)	
Extras	(nb4)	4
Total	(14.0 overs, 56 mins)	39

QUEENSLAND	O	M	R	W	w,nb
Dixon	12	2	41	2	-,2
Cook	20.3	1	76	2	-,-
Wyeth	8	1	31	0	-,-
Christ	11	0	45	2	-,-
Govan	10	0	59	3	-,-

NEW SOUTH WALES	O	M	R	W	w,nb
Lush	5	0	23	1	-,-
O'Reilly	7	5	3	1	-,4
Jackson	2	0	9	0	-,-

FALL OF WICKETS

Wkt	NSW 1st	QLD 1st
1st	11	8
2nd	32	18
3rd	33	-
4th	180	-
5th	194	-
6th	194	-
7th	209	-
8th	239	-
9th	239	-
10th	257	-

SOUTH AUSTRALIA v NEW ZEALAND XI

Played at Adelaide Oval on November 5, 6, 8, 1937. (Four-day match)
Toss : New Zealand XI.   Result : SOUTH AUSTRALIA WON BY TEN WICKETS.
Debuts: South Australia - R.H.Robinson (SA only).
12th Men: J.W.Scaife (SA) and W.N.Carson (NZ).
Umpires: A.G.Jenkins and J.D.Scott.
Attendances: 1890, 4257, 415.   Total: 6562.   Receipts: £310.
Close of Play: 1st day SA 2/64 (Badcock 34, Bradman 11); 2nd day SA 8/299 (Ward 20, Grimmett 6).

Parsloe joined the New Zealanders returning from their tour of England as a replacement for J.A.Dunning who had returned home directly. The visitors were unable to come to terms with the leg-spin of Grimmett and Ward on the first day and were all out soon after tea. Cowie had Bradman caught at the wicket from the first ball he received on the second day. New Zealand continued to restrict the scoring with tight bowling but Badcock (114 in 257 minutes, 6 fours), Hamence (56 in 148 minutes, 2 fours), Waite (45 in 102 minutes, 1 six and 1 four) and Ward (41 not out in 124 minutes, 1 four) gave South Australia a lead of 180 on the first innings. Grimmett suffered a ricked knee while batting and took no further part in the match after he was dismissed. Vivian hit 18 runs including 4 fours from the first over of the second innings and scored 64 in 61 minutes with 10 fours. Wallace (37 in 55 minutes, 3 fours) did next best for New Zealand but Ward swept through the batting to secure his best figures for South Australia. Robinson played the first of seven matches for the croweaters before returning to his native New South Wales the following year. Sources:*VCA Report, SACA Report, The Herald, Sydney Morning Herald, Adelaide Advertiser, The News.*

NEW ZEALAND XI

H.G.Vivian	c Walker b Cotton	11	c sub (J.W.Scaife) b Cotton	64
J.L.Kerr	c Cotton b Grimmett	10	c Cotton b Ward	15
W.M.Wallace	c & b Grimmett	17	(4) lbw b Williams	37
D.A.R.Moloney	c Richardson b Williams	25	(3) b Cotton	2
M.P.Donnelly	lbw b Grimmett	0	(7) c Robinson b Ward	24
G.L.Weir	c Hamence b Ward	38	(5) c Robinson b Ward	1
*M.L.Page	not out	21	(6) c & b Ward	20
A.W.Roberts	c Hamence b Ward	6	c sub (J.W.Scaife) b Ward	9
C.K.Parsloe	c & b Ward	0	c Williams b Ward	3
†E.W.T.Tindill	lbw b Ward	5	not out	0
J.Cowie	b Waite	11	c Bradman b Ward	4
Extras	(b2, nb5)	7	(lb5, nb2)	7
Total	(52.3 overs, 197 mins)	151	(45.2 overs, 170 mins)	186

SOUTH AUSTRALIA

C.L.Badcock	c Tindill b Vivian	114	not out	5
†C.W.Walker	lbw b Parsloe	9	not out	1
V.Y.Richardson	b Vivian	9		
*D.G.Bradman	c Tindill b Cowie	11		
R.H.Robinson	b Vivian	16		
R.A.Hamence	c Page b Parsloe	56		
M.G.Waite	run out (/Tindill)	45		
R.G.Williams	b Cowie	3		
F.A.Ward	not out	41		
C.V.Grimmett	b Cowie	9		
H.N.J.Cotton	lbw b Moloney	6		
Extras	(b6, lb2, w2, nb2)	12	(b1)	1
Total	(113.3 overs, 430 mins)	331	(3.3 overs, 10 mins) (0 wkts)	7

SOUTH AUSTRALIA	O	M	R	W	w,nb	O	M	R	W	w,nb
Cotton	10	2	18	1	-,2	9	0	59	2	-,1
Williams	11	1	32	1	-,3	9	0	38	1	-,1
Grimmett	10	4	21	3	-,-					
Waite	9.3	2	14	1	-,-	8	2	10	0	-,-
Ward	12	2	59	4	-,-	17.2	1	62	7	-,-
Robinson						2	0	10	0	-,-

NEW ZEALAND XI	O	M	R	W	w,nb		O	M	R	W	w,nb
Cowie	33	4	72	3	1,-						
Parsloe	19	2	86	2	1,2	(1)	2	0	4	0	-,-
Roberts	23	8	45	0	-,-						
Vivian	30	9	84	3	-,-						
Moloney	4.3	0	12	1	-,-						
Weir	2	0	13	0	-,-	(2)	1.3	0	2	0	-,-
Donnelly	2	0	7	0	-,-						

FALL OF WICKETS

Wkt	NZ 1st	SA 1st	NZ 2nd	SA 2nd
1st	18	23	58	-
2nd	42	38	72	-
3rd	45	65	91	-
4th	45	108	94	-
5th	92	208	130	-
6th	113	238	161	-
7th	123	246	176	-
8th	126	285	181	-
9th	134	308	182	-
10th	151	331	186	-

VICTORIA v NEW ZEALAND XI

Played at Melbourne Cricket Ground on November 12, 13, 15, 16, 1937. (Four-day match)
Toss : New Zealand XI.   Result : VICTORIA WON BY FIVE WICKETS.
Debuts: Nil.
12th Men: W.E.Pearson (Vic) and W.N.Carson (NZ).
Umpires: A.N.Barlow and W.J.Moore.
Attendances: 2295, 3899, 1028, 623.   Total: 7845.   Receipts: £263.
Close of Play: 1st day NZ 4/124 (Wallace 32, Donnelly 0); 2nd day NZ (2) 1/18 (Vivian 4, Parsloe 4); 3rd day Vic (2) 0/35 (Rigg 24, Lee 11).

M.L.Page (thigh injury) was unable to lead New Zealand and J.Cowie (slight strain) was rested. The match began in perfect conditions but bad light and rain arrived later to end the first day's play at 3.05pm. Kerr (41 in 139 minutes, 2 fours), Wallace (39 in 68 minutes, 4 fours) and Hadlee (51 in 66 minutes, 2 sixes and 6 fours) topscored in New Zealand's first innings, while Vivian (66 in 121 minutes, 2 sixes and 3 fours) and Wallace (63 in 112 minutes, 3 sixes and 5 fours) scored fifties in the second. Parsloe reduced the Victorian first innings to 141 with some fine swing bowling, Hassett (36 in 104 minutes, 1 four) and Ledward (49 not out in 79 minutes, 3 fours) resisting most successfully. Hassett (127 not out in 220 minutes, 1 six and 8 fours) saw Victoria home on the final day, adding 112 for the third wicket with Lee (72 in 183 minutes, 4 fours) and an unbroken 99 for the sixth wicket with Barnett (47 not out in 86 minutes, 3 fours). *NSWCA Report* and *VCA Report* incorrectly name Vivian as NZ captain. Sources: *NSWCA Report, VCA Report, The Age, The Argus, The Herald, Melbourne Sun, The Sporting Globe.*

NEW ZEALAND XI

H.G.Vivian	c Barnett b McCormick	30		c Hassett b Gregory	66
J.L.Kerr	b Ebeling	41		b McCormick	9
D.A.R.Moloney	lbw b Fleetwood-Smith	11	(5)	c Barnett b Bromley	1
W.M.Wallace	c Sievers b McCormick	39		c Hassett b Gregory	63
G.L.Weir	lbw b Ebeling	0	(7)	c McCormick b Gregory	26
M.P.Donnelly	b McCormick	14	(8)	lbw b Gregory	2
W.A.Hadlee	run out (Ledward/Ebeling)	51	(6)	c & b Bromley	0
A.W.Roberts	c Rigg b Fleetwood-Smith	0	(11)	c Barnett b Bromley	4
J.R.Lamason	c McCormick b Sievers	2		lbw b Bromley	29
*†T.C.Lowry	lbw b Sievers	0		not out	8
C.K.Parsloe	not out	9	(3)	c Sievers b Ebeling	9
Extras	(lb6, nb7)	13		(lb5, nb1)	6
Total	(51.7 overs, 233 mins)	210		(54.0 overs, 214 mins)	223

VICTORIA

K.E.Rigg	c Roberts b Parsloe	27		lbw b Vivian	24
I.S.Lee	b Parsloe	7		run out (Wallace/Lamason)	72
M.W.Sievers	c Weir b Parsloe	1			
R.G.Gregory	hit wkt b Moloney	10	(3)	c Lowry b Vivian	12
A.L.Hassett	c Weir b Parsloe	36	(4)	not out	127
E.H.Bromley	b Vivian	3	(5)	c Parsloe b Donnelly	9
J.A.Ledward	not out	49	(6)	c & b Vivian	0
†B.A.Barnett	c Roberts b Vivian	2	(7)	not out	47
*H.I.Ebeling	c Donnelly b Vivian	4			
E.L.McCormick	c Lowry b Parsloe	0			
L.O.Fleetwood-Smith	c Donnelly b Vivian	0			
Extras	(lb2)	2		(b2)	2
Total	(49.3 overs, 191 mins)	141		(88.3 overs, 311 mins) (5 wkts)	293

VICTORIA	O	M	R	W	w,nb		O	M	R	W	w,nb			FALL OF WICKETS		
McCormick	14	1	38	3	-,7		8	1	30	1	-,1			NZ	VIC	NZ	VIC
Ebeling	9.7	2	22	2	-,-		7	0	13	1	-,-	Wkt	1st	1st	2nd	2nd
Sievers	11	0	45	2	-,-		6	0	22	0	-,-	1st	49	11	14	35
Fleetwood-Smith	17	0	92	2	-,-		5	0	52	0	-,-	2nd	78	17	27	62
Bromley						(6)	15	4	50	4	-,-	3rd	112	34	141	174
Gregory						(7)	13	1	50	4	-,-	4th	122	58	142	192
												5th	131	69	142	194
NEW ZEALAND XI	O	M	R	W	w,nb		O	M	R	W	w,nb	6th	146	111	178	-
Parsloe	15	2	47	5	-,-		14	1	43	0	-,-	7th	159	126	181	-
Weir	1	0	6	0	-,-							8th	168	138	184	-
Moloney	8	2	28	1	-,-	(4)	12	1	49	0	-,-	9th	168	140	217	-
Vivian	15.3	7	33	4	-,-	(3)	32	7	89	3	-,-	10th	210	141	223	-
Roberts	9	1	22	0	-,-	(2)	9	0	40	0	-,-					
Donnelly	1	0	3	0	-,-	(7)	16.3	1	56	1	-,-					
Wallace						(5)	2	0	7	0	-,-					
Lamason						(6)	3	1	7	0	-,-					

VICTORIA v WESTERN AUSTRALIA

Played at Melbourne Cricket Ground on November 17, 18, 19, 1937. (Three-day match)
Toss : Western Australia.   Result : VICTORIA WON BY 125 RUNS.
Debuts: Victoria - M.W.Rayson (f/c), F.W.Sides (Vic only). Western Australia - G.C.Arthur, G.N.Evans, G.Eyres, J.A.Jeffreys, R.L.Mills, W.T.Rowlands (all f/c).
12th Men: R.A.Dempster (Vic) and W.F.Buttsworth (WA).
Umpires: G.A.Browne and W.J.Craddock.
Attendances: No daily figures published.   Total: 1139.   Receipts: £36.
Close of Play: 1st day Vic 316 all out; 2nd day Vic (2) 0/29 (O'Brien 7, Lee 17).

The Victorian selectors rested a number of leading team members in order to blood several fringe players. Deveney was a late inclusion for R.B.Scott (leg strain). Flags were flown at half-mast in memory of former Victorian and Australian player and critic J.Worrall, who died on November 17th. Ebeling was absent on the second afternoon as team representative at the funeral and Barnett captained Victoria in his absence. O'Brien recorded a century (102 in 201 minutes, 8 fours) and unbeaten half-century (65 not out in 143 minutes, 6 fours) on his final first-class appearance. Bromley (114 in 147 minutes, 1 six and 14 fours) also notched three figures for the home team. Lovelock (94 not out in 201 minutes, 11 fours) became the third left-hander to succeed with the bat in the match, Arthur keeping wickets in Victoria's second innings to give Lovelock a rest in the outfield. Rayson (leg-breaks and googlies) captured eight wickets in the first of three matches for Victoria, three of them - Gardiner, Evans and Wilberforce - in one over in the second innings, Evans completing a pair on debut. Deveney finished the game by dismissing Eyres and Mills with successive balls. Sides had previously played for Queensland. Sources: *VCA Report, The Age, The Argus, The Herald, Melbourne Sun, The Sporting Globe.*

VICTORIA

L.P.J.O'Brien	c Zimbulis b Wilberforce	102	not out	65
I.S.Lee	c Mills b Eyres	17	c Arthur b Gardiner	26
J.A.Ledward	lbw b Eyres	28	not out	41
F.W.Sides	c Lovelock b Eyres	3		
E.H.Bromley	b Gardiner	114		
W.E.Pearson	c Lovelock b Gardiner	13		
J.G.Stanes	lbw b Gardiner	11		
†B.A.Barnett	c Eyres b Gardiner	8		
*H.I.Ebeling	st Lovelock b Wilberforce	1		
F.B.Deveney	not out	4		
M.W.Rayson	lbw b Gardiner	1		
Extras	(b6, lb7, nb1)	14	(b 9, lb1)	10
Total	(78.4 overs, 319 mins)	316	(38.0 overs, 143 mins) (1 wkt dec)	142

WESTERN AUSTRALIA

J.A.Jeffreys	b Ebeling	10		c Stanes b Ebeling	14
F.J.Alexander	c Ebeling b Deveney	6		c Barnett b Ebeling	19
*W.T.Rowlands	b Ebeling	13		c & b Rayson	49
G.C.Arthur	c Rayson b Pearson	3		b Rayson	27
†O.I.Lovelock	not out	94	(8)	not out	10
R.J.Wilberforce	c & b Rayson	7	(7)	lbw b Rayson	0
G.A.Gardiner	c & b Rayson	11	(5)	c Lee b Rayson	4
G.N.Evans	b Bromley	0	(6)	b Rayson	0
A.G.Zimbulis	c Barnett b Bromley	23		b Deveney	11
G.Eyres	c Lee b Bromley	6		b Deveney	0
R.L.Mills	st Barnett b Rayson	14		lbw b Deveney	0
Extras	(lb3, nb4)	7		(lb1, nb4)	5
Total	(70.2 overs, 276 mins)	194		(49.1 overs, 185 mins)	139

WESTERN AUSTRALIA	O	M	R	W	w,nb		O	M	R	W	w,nb			
Mills	14	0	54	0	-,1		8	0	25	0	-,-			
Eyres	24	0	98	3	-,-		7	2	17	0	-,-			
Rowlands	10	0	31	0	-,-	(5)	2	0	8	0	-,-			
Wilberforce	15	0	58	2	-,-	(3)	9	3	17	0	-,-			
Zimbulis	6	0	40	0	-,-	(6)	5	0	33	0	-,-			
Gardiner	9.4	1	21	5	-,-	(4)	7	0	32	1	-,-			

FALL OF WICKETS

Wkt	VIC 1st	WA 1st	VIC 2nd	WA 2nd
1st	39	18	50	35
2nd	99	26	-	46
3rd	111	33	-	113
4th	206	37	-	114
5th	251	75	-	114
6th	298	105	-	114
7th	301	120	-	121
8th	306	157	-	139
9th	314	164	-	139
10th	316	194	-	139

VICTORIA	O	M	R	W	w,nb		O	M	R	W	w,nb
Deveney	19	3	44	1	-,4		7.1	0	24	3	-,4
Ebeling	11	5	7	2	-,-		9	3	11	2	-,-
Pearson	5	1	17	1	-,-		7	0	24	0	-,-
Rayson	18.2	1	75	3	-,-		15	2	56	5	-,-
Bromley	17	4	44	3	-,-		11	6	19	0	-,-

NEW SOUTH WALES v NEW ZEALAND XI

Played at Sydney Cricket Ground on November 19, 20, 22, 1937 . (Four-day match)
Toss : New Zealand XI.   Result : NEW SOUTH WALES WON BY EIGHT WICKETS.
Debuts: Nil.
12th Men: J.H.Fitzpatrick (NSW) and M.P.Donnelly(NZ).
Umpires: E.G.Borwick and F.W.Lyons.
Attendances: 3368, 7662, 748.   Total: 11,778.   Receipts: £448.
Close of Play: 1st day NSW 4/126 (Barnes 43, Jackson 62); 2nd day NZ (2) 8/180 (Hadlee 21, Tindill 5).

M.L.Page was again unable to lead New Zealand because of his injured thigh. R.G.Beatty withdrew from the New South Wales twelve named for the match and was replaced by Fitzpatrick. O'Reilly (9 for 118) troubled the visitors in both innings. Wallace attempted to hit him out of the attack on the first day with 2 sixes and 4 fours but was caught by McCabe on the fence attempting a third six. Carson (40 not out in 117 minutes, 5 fours) batted solidly. Barnes (97 in 192 minutes, 11 fours) and Jackson (68 in 95 minutes, 6 fours) rescued New South Wales after early wickets fell to Cowie and Parsloe by adding 113 for the fifth wicket. Moloney (42 in 53 minutes, 4 fours), Wallace (58 in 82 minutes, 7 fours) and Hadlee (46 in 75 minutes, 7 fours) carried the New Zealand second innings. Fingleton (61 not out in 119 minutes, 5 fours) and Chipperfield (67 not out in 105 minutes, 8 fours) shared an unfinished stand of 131 to finalise New Zealand's third defeat on tour in as many matches; their second with more than a day in hand. Sources: *NSWCA Report, VCA Report, The Age, The Herald, Sydney Morning Herald, NSWCA Scorebook, Sydney Referee, Sydney Daily Telegraph.*

NEW ZEALAND XI

*H.G.Vivian	lbw b Lush	17	b Lush	16
J.L.Kerr	c Chipperfield b Jackson	28	c Oldfield b Hynes	2
D.A.R.Moloney	lbw b O'Reilly	11	c & b O'Reilly	42
W.M.Wallace	c McCabe b O'Reilly	32	c Oldfield b O'Reilly	58
G.L.Weir	b O'Reilly	11	c Fingleton b O'Reilly	2
W.N.Carson	not out	40	lbw b White	27
J.R.Lamason	lbw b O'Reilly	0	c Oldfield b White	3
W.A.Hadlee	c McCabe b Jackson	7	c Oldfield b White	46
C.K.Parsloe	b White	15	c & b Hynes	0
†E.W.T.Tindill	run out	25	lbw b O'Reilly	11
J.Cowie	c Cheetham b O'Reilly	3	not out	0
Extras	(b1, lb4, nb1)	6	(b1, lb5, nb1)	7
Total	(54.1 overs, 199 mins)	195	(53.1 overs, 207 mins)	214

NEW SOUTH WALES

J.H.W.Fingleton	c Tindill b Parsloe	0	not out	61
A.G.Cheetham	b Parsloe	4	lbw b Cowie	1
*S.J.McCabe	b Cowie	12	b Cowie	0
A.G.Chipperfield	b Cowie	1	not out	67
S.G.Barnes	c Lamason b Carson	97		
V.E.Jackson	c Vivian b Moloney	68		
L.C.Hynes	c Moloney b Cowie	3		
J.G.Lush	c Tindill b Carson	21		
E.C.S.White	not out	29		
†W.A.S.Oldfield	b Cowie	17		
W.J.O'Reilly	c Vivian b Moloney	14		
Extras	(b1, lb7)	8	(b5, lb2)	7
Total	(67.4 overs, 260 mins)	274	(35.6 overs, 119 mins) (2 wkts)	136

NEW SOUTH WALES	O	M	R	W	w,nb		O	M	R	W	w,nb		FALL OF WICKETS			
														NZ	NSW	NZ	NSW
Lush	5	0	32	1	-,-		5	1	26	1	-,-	Wkt	1st	1st	2nd	2nd
Hynes	8	0	32	0	-,-		9	1	37	2	-,1	1st	32	1	18	5
Jackson	14	3	46	2	-,-	(4)	7	1	43	0	-,-	2nd	54	16	18	5
O'Reilly	18.1	4	57	5	-,1	(3)	17.1	3	61	4	-,-	3rd	70	16	92	-
White	5	3	6	1	-,-	(6)	7	2	19	3	-,-	4th	98	20	106	-
Chipperfield	4	0	16	0	-,-							5th	120	133	125	-
Cheetham						(5)	8	1	21	0	-,-	6th	120	136	144	-
												7th	127	188	162	-
NEW ZEALAND XI	O	M	R	W	w,nb		O	M	R	W	w,nb	8th	144	217	163	-
Cowie	22	4	76	4	-,-		6	0	27	2	-,-	9th	187	255	214	-
Parsloe	12	0	56	2	-,-	(5)	1	0	7	0	-,-	10th	195	274	214	-
Vivian	12	5	40	0	-,-	(4)	8	3	17	0	-,-					
Moloney	15.4	2	77	2	-,-	(3)	9	1	28	0	-,-					
Carson	6	1	17	2	-,-	(2)	5	0	16	0	-,-					
Lamason							3	0	14	0	-,-					
Hadlee							2	0	10	0	-,-					
Kerr							1.6	0	10	0	-,-					

D.G.BRADMAN'S XI v V.Y.RICHARDSON'S XI

Played at Adelaide Oval on November 26, 27, 29 (no play), 30 (no play), 1937. (Four-day match)
Toss : Bradman's XI.   Result : MATCH DRAWN.
Debuts: Nil.
12th Men: M.G.Waite (both sides).
Umpires: A.G.Jenkins and J.D.Scott.
Attendances: 4853, 10305, no play, no play.   Total: 15,158 (excluding last two days).   Receipts: £619.
Close of Play: 1st day Richardson 1/53 (Badcock 34, Sievers 2); 2nd day Richardson 9/380 (Robinson 37); 3rd day no play.

The game was arranged for the benefit of Richardson, aged 43, who was playing his last first-class match, and Grimmett, aged nearly 46, who continued playing for South Australia a further four seasons. In addition, the S.A.C.A. opened a fund with £200 and staged non-first-class matches at Clare, Nuriootpa and Unley Oval to raise further monies. Despite the loss of the third and fourth days in the main match through rain and Bradman's dismissal before lunch on the first day, greatly reducing potential gate receipts, a payment of £1028 was made to each beneficiary. A suggestion to extend the match to December 1st was abandoned when further rain fell. W.H.Ponsford, chosen by the South Australian selectors to return from retirement and represent Richardson's side, withdrew on the grounds of depriving a younger player an opportunity and was replaced by Rigg. Fingleton (32 in 89 minutes, 2 fours) and Brown (42 in 150 minutes, 4 fours) gave Bradman's XI a sound start but the remainder struggled against the high bounce of Sievers and accurate spin of Grimmett. Badcock (102 in 173 minutes, 11 fours), Chipperfield (41 in 65 minutes, 4 fours), McCabe (72 in 104 minutes, 8 fours) and Richardson (42 in 67 minutes, 2 fours) made significant contributions on the second day. Sources: *Wisden, NSWCA Report, VCA Report, SACA Report, The Age, The Herald, Sydney Morning Herald, Adelaide Advertiser, The News.*

BRADMAN'S XI

J.H.W.Fingleton	c Oldfield b McCormick	32
W.A.Brown	b Sievers	42
*D.G.Bradman	b Grimmett	17
A.L.Hassett	c Oldfield b Grimmett	13
R.G.Gregory	c Oldfield b Grimmett	1
V.E.Jackson	b Sievers	0
L.C.Hynes	b McCabe	6
J.G.Lush	b Sievers	28
†C.W.Walker	b O'Reilly	29
F.A.Ward	not out	7
L.O.Fleetwood-Smith	b Sievers	4
Extras	(b3, nb2)	5
Total	(62.4 overs, 238 mins)	184

RICHARDSON'S XI

C.L.Badcock	b Ward	102
K.E.Rigg	c Bradman b Hynes	12
M.W.Sievers	c Brown b Jackson	32
A.G.Chipperfield	b Ward	41
S.J.McCabe	b Hynes	72
*V.Y.Richardson	b Ward	42
R.H.Robinson	not out	37
C.V.Grimmett	b Ward	1
†W.A.S.Oldfield	c Fingleton b Jackson	20
W.J.O'Reilly	st Walker b Fleetwood-Smith	7
E.L.McCormick	did not bat	
Extras	(b4, lb3, nb7)	14
Total	(87.0 overs, 322 mins) (9 wkts)	380

RICHARDSON'S XI	O	M	R	W	w,nb
McCormick	9	0	34	1	-,2
Sievers	9.4	0	27	4	-,-
O'Reilly	14	6	21	1	-,-
Grimmett	18	3	39	3	-,-
Chipperfield	3	0	22	0	-,-
McCabe	5	2	10	1	-,-
Robinson	4	0	26	0	-,-

BRADMAN'S XI	O	M	R	W	w,nb
Lush	16	0	101	0	-,5
Hynes	14	0	82	2	-,2
Ward	18	1	71	4	-,-
Fleetwood-Smith	23	2	81	1	-,-
Jackson	16	5	31	2	-,-

FALL OF WICKETS

Wkt	1st B	1st R
1st	64	48
2nd	87	112
3rd	101	186
4th	106	209
5th	107	291
6th	107	323
7th	123	324
8th	167	369
9th	179	380
10th	184	-

VICTORIA v WESTERN AUSTRALIA

Played at Melbourne Cricket Ground on November 29, 30, December 1, 1937. (Three-day match)
Toss : Western Australia.   Result : VICTORIA WON BY FIVE WICKETS.
Debuts: Victoria - F.L.O.Thorn (f/c). Western Australia - W.F.Buttsworth (f/c); J.A.Shea (WA only).
12th Men: J.B.Lowry (Vic) and J.A.Jeffreys (WA).
Umpires: G.A.Browne and W.J.Craddock.
Attendances & Receipts: No figures published.
Close of Play: 1st day Vic 2/114 (Sides 50, Bromley 8); 2nd day WA (2) 5/212 (Arthur 3, Eyres 0).

Deveney took 3 for 7 in his first five overs of the match. Buttsworth (35 in 112 minutes, 2 fours) topscored for Western Australia who made only 137 on a fast and true first-day pitch. In the second innings Shea (110 in 205 minutes, 12 fours) scored a hundred on debut for Western Australia, his only previous first-class appearance being for a Combined XI V M.C.C. the previous season. He shared an opening stand worth 78 with Alexander (37 in 79 minutes, 2 fours). Sides (75 in 117 minutes, 7 fours and 99 in 137 minutes, 8 fours) batted well in both innings for Victoria, who were undermanned by the absence of L.O.Fleetwood-Smith, R.G.Gregory, A.L.Hassett, E.L.McCormick, K.E.Rigg and M.W.Sievers - all in Adelaide for the Grimmett-Richardson testimonial. Sides added 94 with Pearson (53 not out in 80 minutes, 4 fours) for the fifth wicket to decide the match in Victoria's favour. Stanes was bowled by the second ball (his first) of the second innings. The leg-spin of Zimbulis returned 5 for 80, his best first-class figures. Sources: *VCA Report, The Age, The Argus, The Herald, Melbourne Sun, The Sporting Globe.*

WESTERN AUSTRALIA

F.J.Alexander	c Rayson b Deveney	6		c Quin b Deveney	37
J.A.Shea	c Rayson b Deveney	6		c & b Rayson	110
†G.C.Arthur	c Quin b Deveney	2	(6)	lbw b Pearson	7
O.I.Lovelock	c Pearson b Dempster	5	(5)	lbw b Thorn	12
*W.T.Rowlands	st Quin b Thorn	16	(3)	hit wkt b Rayson	17
W.F.Buttsworth	c Quin b Dempster	35	(4)	lbw b Rayson	25
G.A.Gardiner	c Pearson b Deveney	10	(9)	not out	19
G.N.Evans	c Quin b Rayson	26		c Deveney b Pearson	0
A.G.Zimbulis	c & b Dempster	11	(10)	b Bromley	22
G.Eyres	st Quin b Rayson	6	(7)	b Pearson	1
R.L.Mills	not out	0		run out (Deveney/Quin)	2
Extras	(b5, lb1, w1, nb7)	14		(b11, nb2)	13
Total	(50.7 overs, 204 mins)	137		(76.0 overs, 291 mins)	265

VICTORIA

*†S.O.Quin	c Lovelock b Eyres	24			
R.A.Dempster	c Arthur b Zimbulis	27	(1)	c Arthur b Eyres	12
F.W.Sides	b Zimbulis	75		b Zimbulis	99
E.H.Bromley	b Zimbulis	17		c Zimbulis b Mills	0
W.E.Pearson	b Gardiner	10	(6)	not out	53
L.J.Junor	c Arthur b Zimbulis	2	(7)	not out	4
J.G.Stanes	c Buttsworth b Eyres	9	(2)	b Mills	0
P.J.Beames	not out	29	(5)	b Zimbulis	16
F.B.Deveney	st Arthur b Zimbulis	3			
F.L.O.Thorn	run out (Zimbulis/Arthur)	3			
M.W.Rayson	run out (Rowlands/Arthur)	1			
Extras	(b5, lb1, nb1)	7		(b10, lb3, nb1)	14
Total	(56.6 overs, 222 mins)	207		(37.4 overs, 156 mins) (5 wkts)	198

VICTORIA	O	M	R	W	w,nb		O	M	R	W	w,nb
Deveney	9	2	15	4	-,7		12	4	34	1	-,2
Pearson	10	1	21	0	-,-	(3)	13	1	55	3	-,-
Dempster	9	3	17	3	-,-	(4)	11	2	35	0	-,-
Thorn	11	2	32	1	-,-	(2)	11	0	44	1	-,-
Rayson	11.7	1	38	2	1,-	(6)	11	0	39	3	-,-
Bromley						(5)	18	3	45	1	-,-

WESTERN AUSTRALIA	O	M	R	W	w,nb		O	M	R	W	w,nb
Mills	9	0	37	0	-,1		9	0	42	2	-,-
Eyres	17	3	43	2	-,-		10	1	35	1	-,-
Gardiner	10	1	27	1	-,-		7	0	25	0	-,-
Rowlands	6	0	13	0	-,-		3	0	15	0	-,-
Zimbulis	14.6	0	80	5	-,-		8.4	0	67	2	-,1

FALL OF WICKETS

Wkt	WA 1st	VIC 1st	WA 2nd	VIC 2nd
1st	12	41	78	1
2nd	16	89	118	35
3rd	20	142	177	38
4th	31	151	200	81
5th	45	161	208	175
6th	60	161	215	-
7th	116	185	217	-
8th	122	196	218	-
9th	135	203	256	-
10th	137	207	265	-

SOUTH AUSTRALIA v WESTERN AUSTRALIA

Played at Adelaide Oval on December 3, 4, 6, 1937. (Three-day match)
Toss : Western Australia.   Result : SOUTH AUSTRALIA WON BY TEN WICKETS.
Debuts: South Australia - M.E.C.Mueller, P.L.Ridings, W.M.Roberts, J.A.Scott (all f/c).
12th Men: M.J.Doherty (SA) and G.N.Evans (WA).
Umpires: R.B.Ridings and J.D.Scott.
Attendances: 1210, 3262, 500.   Total: About 5000.   Receipts: £120.
Close of Play: 1st day SA 3/90 (Mueller 44, Waite 1); 2nd day WA (2) 0/60 (Alexander 33, Jeffreys 23).

Poor batting by the visitors gave them little chance in the game. Alexander (44 in 124 minutes, 0 fours) survived for two hours in the second innings but had little support. Mueller (56 in 152 minutes) showed a well-organised defence but played few strokes in his debut match for South Australia. Bradman (101 in 160 minutes, 3 fours) was the dominant batsman. Ridings scored 20 in his first first-class innings after his father turned down an lbw appeal when he was 3. Eyres sent down an impressive spell of accurate, fast-medium swing bowling for Western Australia. Both wicket-keepers suffered facial injuries while performing their duties. Lovelock - who became the fifth keeper and the first Western Australian to complete six dismissals in a first-class innings in Australia - was struck in the mouth by a ball from Zimbulis on the second day and suffered a split lip. Arthur took over for a time before lunch until he recovered. Walker was hit above the right eye by a ball from Oswald in the second over of the final day's play and took no further part and Doherty, who had never kept in senior cricket, took the gloves and performed creditably. He achieved the third stumping by a substitute in Australian first-class cricket and held two catches, but was never to be chosen in a first-class eleven. *SACA Report* incorrectly gives WA (2) Shea c sub.
Sources: *SACA Report, The Herald, Adelaide Advertiser, The News, The Sporting Globe.*

WESTERN AUSTRALIA

F.J.Alexander	run out (Hamence/Walker)	11	c Ridings b Oswald		44
J.A.Jeffreys	b Waite	2	lbw b Ridings		27
J.A.Shea	b Ridings	19	st sub (M.J.Doherty) b Oswald		26
*W.T.Rowlands	c Walker b Scott	1	(7) c & b Roberts		24
†O.I.Lovelock	lbw b Ridings	16	c Badcock b Waite		1
W.F.Buttsworth	c Ridings b Oswald	2	c sub (M.J.Doherty) b Waite		0
R.J.Wilberforce	c Bradman b Oswald	1	(4) b Oswald		3
G.C.Arthur	b Roberts	10	(9) c sub (M.J.Doherty) b Roberts		4
G.A.Gardiner	c Bradman b Scott	28	(8) not out		28
A.G.Zimbulis	run out (Bradman)	1	lbw b Roberts		11
G.Eyres	not out	3	b Roberts		2
Extras	(b3, nb3)	6	(b9, lb4, w1, nb1)		15
Total	(50.5 overs, 169 mins)	100	(85.0 overs, 273 mins)		185

SOUTH AUSTRALIA

†C.W.Walker	c Lovelock b Wilberforce	30		
M.E.C.Mueller	st Lovelock b Zimbulis	56		
R.A.Hamence	c Lovelock b Eyres	13		
B.H.Leak	st Lovelock b Zimbulis	1	(2) not out	13
M.G.Waite	b Zimbulis	21		
*D.G.Bradman	c Wilberforce b Eyres	101		
C.L.Badcock	c Shea b Wilberforce	12	(1) not out	8
P.L.Ridings	st Lovelock b Eyres	20		
W.M.Roberts	lbw b Eyres	0		
N.H.Oswald	c Lovelock b Eyres	6		
J.A.Scott	not out	1		
Extras	(b1, lb1, nb1)	3	(b1)	1
Total	(94.3 overs, 321 mins)	264	(8.2 overs, 25 mins) (0 wkts)	22

SOUTH AUSTRALIA	O	M	R	W	w,nb		O	M	R	W	w,nb
Ridings	9	2	22	2	-,3		10	1	16	1	1,1
Waite	5	1	5	1	-,-		18	9	12	2	-,-
Scott	16.5	9	19	2	-,-		12	6	18	0	-,-
Roberts	14	3	42	1	-,-	(5)	15	1	35	4	-,-
Oswald	6	3	6	2	-,-	(4)	30	4	89	3	-,-

WESTERN AUSTRALIA	O	M	R	W	w,nb		O	M	R	W	w,nb
Eyres	24.3	6	58	5	-,-		4.2	1	11	0	-,-
Gardiner	6	0	22	0	-,1						
Rowlands	7	0	22	0	-,-						
Wilberforce	25	6	60	2	-,-	(2)	4	0	10	0	-,-
Zimbulis	31	1	98	3	-,-						
Alexander	1	0	1	0	-,-						

FALL OF WICKETS

Wkt	WA 1st	SA 1st	WA 2nd	SA 2nd
1st	8	57	73	-
2nd	18	86	79	-
3rd	20	89	87	-
4th	46	116	92	-
5th	49	137	92	-
6th	52	152	121	-
7th	55	233	149	-
8th	89	233	157	-
9th	93	259	183	-
10th	100	264	185	-

VICTORIA v QUEENSLAND (Shield Match 2)

Played at Melbourne Cricket Ground on December 17, 18, 20, 21, 1937. (Four-day match)
Toss : Victoria.   Result : VICTORIA WON BY AN INNINGS AND 99 RUNS.
Debuts: Queensland - J.Coats (f/c); C.C.Loxton (Qld only).
12th Men: E.H.Bromley (both sides).
Umpires: A.N.Barlow and W.J.Moore.
Attendances: 1458, 3412, 2126, 1007.   Total: 8003.   Receipts: £201.
Close of Play: 1st day Vic 0/40 (Rigg 18, Lee 20); 2nd day Vic 4/302 (Hassett 63, Sides 0); 3rd day Qld 150 all out.

Queensland were unable to choose G.G.Cook due to an infected finger and therefore had no reserve. Bromley acted as 12th man for both teams by agreement. Baker received news of his mother's death in Townsville on the evening of the first day, but because of the length of time required for a return journey he remained with the team. His two innings, 47 in 72 minutes with 7 fours, and 43 in 77 minutes with 4 fours, were full of merit under the circumstances. Victoria won the game emphatically despite rain restricting play on the first day to 62 minutes (2.45pm to the tea break). Lee (122 in 295 minutes, 9 fours), Gregory (71 in 140 minutes, 4 fours), Hassett (90 in 171 minutes, 6 fours) all made contributions as Victoria batted well into the third day. Coats on debut (46 in 67 minutes, 5 fours) performed well in the second innings for the visitors. Loxton, another playing his first match for Queensland, after a sole appearance for Cambridge University in 1935, scored a stubborn 25 in 133 minutes with 2 fours. Sources: *Wisden, VCA Report, QCA Report, The Age, The Argus, The Herald, Melbourne Sun, The Sporting Globe.*

VICTORIA

*K.E.Rigg	c Rogers b Wyeth	18
I.S.Lee	c Brown b Wyeth	122
R.G.Gregory	st Tallon b Govan	71
A.L.Hassett	c Tallon b Loxton	90
J.A.Ledward	c Brown b Govan	18
F.W.Sides	run out (Govan/Baker/Loxton)	61
W.E.Pearson	not out	63
M.W.Sievers	not out	5
†B.A.Barnett	)	
E.L.McCormick	) did not bat	
L.O.Fleetwood-Smith	)	
Extras	(b7, lb3, w1, nb2)	13
Total	(114.4 overs, 455 mins) (6 wkts dec)	461

QUEENSLAND

*W.A.Brown	lbw b Fleetwood-Smith	19	b Sievers		12
C.C.Loxton	b McCormick	2	run out (McCormick/Barnett)		25
J.Coats	c Sievers b Fleetwood-Smith	21	b Fleetwood-Smith		46
R.E.Rogers	lbw b Fleetwood-Smith	3	c McCormick b Fleetwood-Smith		2
†D.Tallon	c Sievers b McCormick	12	run out (Pearson/Fleetwood-Smith)		31
T.Allen	b McCormick	6	b Sievers		7
G.W.Baker	lbw b Pearson	47	c Sievers b Gregory		43
H.J.H.Mahoney	lbw b Sievers	8	lbw b Fleetwood-Smith		4
E.R.Wyeth	not out	20	b Sievers		0
J.M.Govan	st Barnett b Fleetwood-Smith	1	not out		24
P.L.Dixon	b Fleetwood-Smith	0	lbw b McCormick		7
Extras	(b3, lb4, nb4)	11	(b3, lb3, w1, nb4)		11
Total	(49.1 overs, 190 mins)	150	(61.4 overs, 238 mins)		212

QUEENSLAND	O	M	R	W	w,nb
Dixon	30.4	2	125	0	-,2
Loxton	17	0	73	1	1,-
Wyeth	43	8	121	2	-,-
Govan	18	1	92	2	-,-
Baker	5	0	33	0	-,-
Allen	1	0	4	0	-,-

VICTORIA	O	M	R	W	w,nb		O	M	R	W	w,nb
McCormick	7	1	19	3	-,2		11.4	1	40	1	-,1
Sievers	12	1	24	1	-,2		18	4	40	3	-,3
Pearson	6	1	10	1	-,-	(5)	1	0	1	0	-,-
Fleetwood-Smith	17.1	1	60	5	-,-		25	1	101	3	-,-
Gregory	7	1	26	0	-,-	(3)	6	1	19	1	1,-

FALL OF WICKETS

Wkt	VIC 1st	QLD 1st	QLD 2nd
1st	40	9	18
2nd	167	31	90
3rd	255	37	92
4th	299	54	113
5th	380	69	128
6th	418	72	132
7th	-	93	140
8th	-	140	150
9th	-	150	194
10th	-	150	212

SOUTH AUSTRALIA v NEW SOUTH WALES (Shield Match 3)

Played at Adelaide Oval on December 17, 18, 20, 21, 1937. (Four-day match)
Toss : New South Wales.   Result : NEW SOUTH WALES WON BY 33 RUNS.
Debuts: New South Wales - L.J.O'Brien (f/c).
12th Men: B.H.Leak (SA) and E.E.Crossan (SA).
Umpires: A.G.Jenkins and J.D.Scott.
Attendances: 4710, 6000, other days not published.   Total: 18,252.   Receipts: £521.
Close of Play: 1st day NSW 6/292 (Barnes 62, Oldfield 0); 2nd day SA 6/163 (Hamence 5, Ward 2); 3rd day SA (2) 3/34 (Badcock 19, Bradman 2).

A superb exhibition of hostile, accurate leg-spin bowling by O'Reilly dominated this high-class contest. His first-innings analysis of 9 for 41 was the best by a New South Wales bowler in first-class cricket to date, bettering his own 9 for 50 against Victoria in 1933-34. It included a spell of 5 for 1 in six overs. Although Whitington (54 in 192 minutes, 4 fours) and Bradman (91 in 212 minutes, 4 fours) surpassed 50, *The Advertiser* noted that, throughout his innings, Bradman "was pinned to the crease by O'Reilly, and it was a magnificent tribute to the New South Wales bowler that the greatest batsman in the world, eager for opportunities to score, was restricted to a desperate defence". Badcock (77 in 153 minutes, 12 fours) and Bradman (62 in 112 minutes, 6 fours) scored half-centuries in the second innings after the loss of three night-watchmen on the third day, on which 17 wickets fell. New South Wales's highest scorers were Fingleton (81 in 208 minutes, 6 fours), McCabe (chanceless 106 in 146 minutes, 10 fours) and Barnes (79 in 187 minutes, 7 fours). O'Brien in his first over in first-class cricket, bowled two no-balls, conceded a two to Badcock and dismissed the batsman with his next ball. Sources: *Wisden, NSWCA Report, SACA Report, The Age, The Herald, NSWCA Scorebook, Adelaide Advertiser, The News.*

NEW SOUTH WALES

Batsman	Dismissal	Runs		Dismissal (2nd)	Runs
J.H.W.Fingleton	c Badcock b Ward	81		b Cotton	10
A.G.Cheetham	c & b Grimmett	4		run out (Waite)	18
*S.J.McCabe	c Grimmett b Waite	106		c Badcock b Grimmett	10
S.G.Barnes	lbw b Grimmett	79		lbw b Cotton	5
A.G.Chipperfield	run out (Hamence/Walker)	21		c Waite b Cotton	20
V.E.Jackson	c Hamence b Grimmett	4		c Badcock b Grimmett	2
L.C.Hynes	lbw b Ward	7	(9) not out	11
†W.A.S.Oldfield	b Grimmett	15		c Whitington b Grimmett	0
E.C.S.White	not out	7	(7) b Waite	5
W.J.O'Reilly	lbw b Grimmett	2		b Grimmett	0
L.J.O'Brien	b Williams	4		b Ward	21
Extras	(lb4, w1, nb2)	7		(b1, lb1)	2
Total	(110.4 overs, 396 mins)	337		(48.0 overs, 177 mins)	104

SOUTH AUSTRALIA

Batsman	Dismissal	Runs		Dismissal (2nd)	Runs
C.L.Badcock	lbw b O'Brien	2		b O'Brien	77
R.S.Whitington	c Fingleton b O'Reilly	54	(6) lbw b O'Brien	1
*D.G.Bradman	c O'Brien b O'Reilly	91	(5) c Chipperfield b O'Reilly	62
R.H.Robinson	b O'Reilly	0	(8) c O'Brien b O'Reilly	16
R.A.Hamence	c Oldfield b O'Reilly	17	(7) b O'Brien	4
M.G.Waite	c Oldfield b O'Reilly	3	(9) c Oldfield b McCabe	7
†C.W.Walker	b O'Reilly	1	(2) lbw b O'Reilly	9
F.A.Ward	c Chipperfield b O'Reilly	23	(3) run out (O'Brien/White)	0
R.G.Williams	c Chipperfield b O'Reilly	6	(10) c & b O'Reilly	0
C.V.Grimmett	lbw b O'Reilly	4	(4) c Fingleton b O'Reilly	3
H.N.J.Cotton	not out	10		not out	10
Extras	(lb2, nb4)	6		(lb1, nb1)	2
Total	(88.6 overs, 332 mins)	217		(54.1 overs, 214 mins)	191

SOUTH AUSTRALIA	O	M	R	W	w,nb	O	M	R	W	w,nb
Cotton	20	1	60	0	1,-	12	5	22	3	-,-
Williams	23.4	6	46	1	-,2	8	3	14	0	-,-
Grimmett	32	5	103	5	-,-	19	5	51	4	-,-
Waite	18	5	35	1	-,-	8	3	15	1	-,-
Ward	17	2	86	2	-,-	1	1	0	1	-,-

NEW SOUTH WALES	O	M	R	W	w,nb	O	M	R	W	w,nb
O'Brien	19	1	67	1	-,3	12	0	58	3	-,-
Hynes	11	1	34	0	-,1	6	0	24	0	-,1
O'Reilly	33.6	12	41	9	-,-	20	8	57	5	-,-
Jackson	8	3	14	0	-,-	5	2	7	0	-,-
Cheetham	6	1	20	0	-,-	2	0	17	0	-,-
White	11	3	35	0	-,-	7	0	17	0	-,-
McCabe						2.1	0	9	1	-,-

FALL OF WICKETS

Wkt	NSW 1st	SA 1st	NSW 2nd	SA 2nd
1st	19	4	18	24
2nd	182	145	29	24
3rd	206	145	41	32
4th	261	152	43	153
5th	270	155	46	153
6th	291	157	65	158
7th	319	191	70	159
8th	328	198	70	177
9th	330	206	70	181
10th	337	217	104	191

VICTORIA v NEW SOUTH WALES (Shield Match 4)

Played at Melbourne Cricket Ground on December 24, 27, 28, 29, 1937. (Four-day match)
Toss : Victoria.   Result : MATCH DRAWN.
Debuts: New South Wales - E.E.Crossan (f/c).
12th Men: E.H.Bromley (Vic) and L.C.Hynes (NSW).
Umpires: A.N.Barlow and W.J.Moore.
Attendances: 6290, 18016, 8513, 2163.   Total: 34,982.   Receipts: £1419.
Close of Play: 1st day Vic 3/301 (Hassett 33, Sievers 0); 2nd day NSW 2/74 (Fingleton 34, Barnes 14); 3rd day NSW (2) 4/100
    (Barnes 28, Fingleton 22).

Cautious batting from Rigg (91 in 223 minutes, 8 fours), Lee (83 in 134 minutes, 11 fours), Gregory (84 in 188 minutes, 7 fours) and Hassett (81 in 302 minutes, 4 fours) over the first two days set the pattern though Victoria lost their last seven wickets for 95 runs. Fleetwood-Smith (6 for 94) reduced New South Wales first innings to 184 on the third day, Fingleton (59 in 245 minutes, 2 fours) holding out for more than four hours. Jackson was unable to bat due to a leg strain sustained in the field on the first day. Following on, Fingleton (160 in 314 minutes, 9 fours) again fought a dour rearguard action, adding 162 for the fifth wicket with Barnes (97 in 191 minutes, 5 fours) to avert an outright defeat. Sources: *Wisden, NSWCA Report, VCA Report, The Age, The Argus, The Herald, The Sporting Globe.*

VICTORIA

*K.E.Rigg	run out (O'Brien/Oldfield)	91		
I.S.Lee	lbw b O'Reilly	83		
R.G.Gregory	c Oldfield b Cheetham	84		
A.L.Hassett	c & b O'Brien	81		
M.W.Sievers	c Oldfield b White	14		
J.A.Ledward	lbw b O'Reilly	0	(2) not out	26
F.W.Sides	b White	2	(1) c Fingleton b O'Brien	5
W.E.Pearson	c Crossan b White	31		
†B.A.Barnett	lbw b McCabe	7	(3) not out	16
E.L.McCormick	lbw b O'Brien	9		
L.O.Fleetwood-Smith	not out	1		
Extras	(b3, lb7, w2)	12		-
Total	(149.0 overs, 525 mins)	415	(11.0 overs, 39 mins) (1 wkt)	47

NEW SOUTH WALES

J.H.W.Fingleton	c Barnett b Fleetwood-Smith	59	(6) c Hassett b Gregory	160
A.G.Cheetham	c Sievers b Fleetwood-Smith	9	c Fleetwood-Smith b Sievers	1
*S.J.McCabe	run out (Sides/Fleetwood-Smith)	16	c & b Pearson	5
S.G.Barnes	lbw b Fleetwood-Smith	14	c Hassett b McCormick	97
A.G.Chipperfield	c Barnett b Pearson	36	lbw b Fleetwood-Smith	22
E.E.Crossan	not out	35	(1) c Barnett b Sievers	14
E.C.S.White	c Pearson b Fleetwood-Smith	4	lbw b Fleetwood-Smith	21
†W.A.S.Oldfield	run out (Hassett/Barnett)	1	c & b Gregory	11
W.J.O'Reilly	st Barnett b Fleetwood-Smith	3	run out (Fleetwood-Smith/Barnett)	1
L.J.O'Brien	c Hassett b Fleetwood-Smith	3	(11) not out	0
V.E.Jackson	absent hurt	-	(10) c Pearson b Gregory	11
Extras	(lb3, nb1)	4	(b6, lb5, w5, nb1)	17
Total	(80.2 overs, 292 mins)	184	(101.3 overs, 381 mins)	360

NEW SOUTH WALES	O	M	R	W	w,nb		O	M	R	W	w,nb		FALL OF WICKETS			
O'Brien	22	0	88	2	-,-		3	0	8	1	-,-			VIC	NSW	NSW	VIC
Cheetham	12	4	17	1	-,-							Wkt	1st	1st	2nd	2nd
O'Reilly	47	11	136	2	-,-							1st	144	27	6	12
Jackson	4	0	19	0	-,-							2nd	199	46	18	-
White	39	16	67	3	-,-							3rd	301	74	32	-
Crossan	11	0	28	0	-,-	(2)	3	0	8	0	-,-	4th	320	124	64	-
McCabe	13	0	41	1	2,-	(4)	2	0	18	0	-,-	5th	329	143	226	-
Barnes	1	0	7	0	-,-	(3)	3	0	13	0	-,-	6th	336	153	276	-
												7th	382	157	322	-
VICTORIA	O	M	R	W	w,nb		O	M	R	W	w,nb	8th	395	168	323	-
McCormick	10	3	14	0	-,1		12	3	30	1	4,-	9th	414	184	347	-
Sievers	22	7	40	0	-,-		25	3	64	2	-,1	10th	415	-	360	-
Pearson	12	4	25	1	-,-		16	1	65	1	-,-					
Fleetwood-Smith	31.2	4	94	6	-,-		28	2	95	2	-,-					
Gregory	5	3	7	0	-,-	(6)	13.3	0	62	3	-,-					
Ledward						(5)	7	2	27	0	1,-					

SOUTH AUSTRALIA v QUEENSLAND (Shield Match 5)

Played at Adelaide Oval on December 25, 27, 28, 29, 1937. (Four-day match)
Toss : Queensland.   Result : SOUTH AUSTRALIA WON BY EIGHT WICKETS.
Debuts: Nil.
12th Men: B.H.Leak (SA) and H.J.H.Mahoney (Qld).
Umpires: A.G.Jenkins and J.D.Scott.
Attendances: 10436, other days not published.   Total: 25,410.   Receipts: £726.
Close of Play: 1st day SA 3/61 (Bradman 28, Williams 8); 2nd day SA 8/429 (Waite 52, Grimmett 5); 3rd day Qld (2) 6/330 (Rogers 117, Coats 7).

Mainly due to a spell of fine swing bowling by Williams, who captured a career-best 6 for 21 in ideally humid weather, Queensland collapsed to be 93 all out in 150 minutes on the first day. Bradman (246 in 364 minutes, 20 fours) rescued the South Australian innings after some early setbacks and relentlessly batted his side into an unassailable position. He went from 98 to 102 when Baker at mid-off had a shot at the non-striker's end to run out Robinson, the ball missing the wicket and flying to the fence for four overthrows. With Waite (52 in 127 minutes, 4 fours) he added 161 in 120 minutes to establish a new South Australian eighth-wicket record in Sheffield Shield matches. Brown (132 in 293 minutes, 9 fours) and Rogers (career-best 181 in 231 minutes, 23 fours) hit Queensland's only hundreds of the season, Rogers's last 100 taking just 97 minutes. *Wisden* incorrectly gives Qld (2) Loxton 1; SA (2) Baker 0/9 instead of Allen.
Sources: *Wisden, QCA Report, SACA Report, The Age, The Herald, Adelaide Advertiser, The News*.

QUEENSLAND

*W.A.Brown	c Walker b Williams	10		c Williams b Grimmett	132
G.G.Cook	b Williams	0		b Ward	11
J.Coats	st Walker b Ward	21	(8)	lbw b Waite	13
C.C.Loxton	c Robinson b Ward	2	(3)	st Walker b Ward	0
R.E.Rogers	b Williams	19	(7)	c Walker b Williams	181
†D.Tallon	c Walker b Williams	3	(5)	st Walker b Waite	24
T.Allen	c Cotton b Grimmett	6	(6)	run out	26
G.W.Baker	c & b Williams	13	(4)	lbw b Ward	1
E.R.Wyeth	lbw b Grimmett	4		c Badcock b Ward	7
J.M.Govan	not out	7		c Walker b Grimmett	9
P.L.Dixon	c Hamence b Williams	2		not out	5
Extras	(b2, w1, nb3)	6		(b5, lb10, nb2)	17
Total	(34.1 overs, 150 mins)	93		(123.3 overs, 421 mins)	426

SOUTH AUSTRALIA

C.L.Badcock	c Dixon b Cook	10		st Tallon b Govan	45
†C.W.Walker	run out (Loxton)	11		c Loxton b Dixon	0
*D.G.Bradman	c Baker b Williams	246		not out	39
F.A.Ward	c Tallon b Loxton	0			
R.G.Williams	c Baker b Govan	34			
R.H.Robinson	c Loxton b Dixon	49			
R.A.Hamence	c Tallon b Dixon	5	(4)	not out	9
R.S.Whitington	run out (/Tallon)	3			
M.G.Waite	not out	52			
C.V.Grimmett	not out	5			
H.N.J.Cotton	did not bat				
Extras	(b3, lb8, nb3)	2			-
Total	(97.0 overs, 395 mins) (8 wkts dec)	429		(23.2 overs, 90 mins) (2 wkts)	93

SOUTH AUSTRALIA	O	M	R	W	w,nb		O	M	R	W	w,nb
Cotton	8	0	27	0	-,-		20	3	62	0	-,-
Williams	11.1	4	21	6	1,3		16	2	57	1	-,2
Waite	3	0	12	0	-,-		24	10	31	2	-,-
Ward	6	1	16	2	-,-		30	2	152	4	-,-
Grimmett	6	2	11	2	-,-		33.3	3	107	2	-,-

QUEENSLAND	O	M	R	W	w,nb		O	M	R	W	w,nb
Dixon	24	0	130	3	-,2		4	0	22	1	-,-
Cook	23	1	87	1	-,1		10	1	30	0	-,-
Loxton	11	0	41	1	-,-		4	1	11	0	-,-
Govan	12	0	72	1	-,-	(6)	1.2	0	9	1	-,-
Wyeth	24	3	70	0	-,-	(4)	3	0	12	0	-,-
Baker	3	1	15	0	-,-						
Allen						(5)	1	0	9	0	-,-

FALL OF WICKETS	QLD 1st	SA 1st	QLD 2nd	SA 2nd
Wkt				
1st	6	14	22	1
2nd	19	50	22	79
3rd	27	50	24	-
4th	44	107	66	-
5th	55	217	121	-
6th	58	239	273	-
7th	71	253	363	-
8th	76	414	389	-
9th	87	-	415	-
10th	93	-	426	-

VICTORIA v SOUTH AUSTRALIA (Shield Match 6)

Played at Melbourne Cricket Ground on December 31, 1937, January 1, 3, 4, 1938. (Four-day match)
Toss : South Australia.   Result : MATCH DRAWN.
Debuts: Nil.
12th Men: E.H.Bromley (Vic) and B.H.Leak (SA).
Umpires: A.N.Barlow and W.J.Moore.
Attendances: 19343, 15172, 24801, 6332.   Total: 65,648.   Receipts: £2878.
Close of Play: 1st day SA 9/287 (Ward 15, Cotton 2); 2nd day Vic 4/290 (Ledward 21, Sievers 1); 3rd day SA (2) 3/148 (Robinson 45, Hamence 32).

Leak and P.L.Ridings were omitted from the South Australian thirteen named for the match. Badcock (50 in 72 minutes, 6 fours), Whitington (81 in 212 minutes, 5 fours) and Bradman (54 in 82 minutes, 4 fours) scored half-centuries in South Australia's first innings, Fleetwood-Smith returning a nine-wicket analysis for the second time in his career. Rigg (118 in 218 minutes, 1 six and 14 fours) and Lee (67 in 153 minutes, 8 fours) opened Victoria's reply with 157 for the first wicket and Gregory (61 in 134 minutes, 6 fours) and Sides (47 in 75 minutes, 7 fours) took the team to first-innings points. Badcock was out to the third ball of South Australia's second innings but consistent batting from a middle order led by Robinson (62 in 110 minutes, 3 fours), Hamence (64 in 117 minutes, 6 fours) and Waite (51 in 130 minutes) brought a recovery. Ledward (58 not out in 34 minutes, 9 fours) compiled a rapid fifty in the last session of the match.
Sources: *Wisden, VCA Report, SACA Report, The Age, The Argus, The Herald, Melbourne Sun.*

SOUTH AUSTRALIA

Player	Dismissal 1	Runs 1	Dismissal 2	Runs 2
C.L.Badcock	c Pearson b Fleetwood-Smith	50	b McCormick	0
R.S.Whitington	c Rigg b Fleetwood-Smith	81	lbw b Fleetwood-Smith	29
*D.G.Bradman	c Sievers b Gregory	54	c Sievers b Gregory	35
R.H.Robinson	c Rigg b Fleetwood-Smith	12	run out (Pearson)	62
R.A.Hamence	st Barnett b Fleetwood-Smith	8	c Hassett b McCormick	64
M.G.Waite	c Pearson b Fleetwood-Smith	30	c Barnett b Gregory	51
†C.W.Walker	c Pearson b Fleetwood-Smith	13	run out (Hassett/Barnett/Gregory)	25
R.G.Williams	b Fleetwood-Smith	15	st Barnett b Fleetwood-Smith	11
F.A.Ward	not out	26	c Gregory b Fleetwood-Smith	9
C.V.Grimmett	c Pearson b Fleetwood-Smith	4	c Barnett b Sievers	31
H.N.J.Cotton	c Ledward b Fleetwood-Smith	8	not out	18
Extras	(lb1, nb2)	3	(b13, lb3, w1, nb4)	21
Total	(91.3 overs, 346 mins)	304	(95.2 overs, 359 mins)	356

VICTORIA

Player	Dismissal 1	Runs 1	Dismissal 2	Runs 2
*K.E.Rigg	c Walker b Williams	118	c Robinson b Williams	20
I.S.Lee	c & b Grimmett	67	c Bradman b Grimmett	34
R.G.Gregory	st Walker b Grimmett	61	c Hamence b Ward	11
A.L.Hassett	lbw b Grimmett	17		
J.A.Ledward	b Grimmett	29	(4) not out	58
M.W.Sievers	st Walker b Ward	1	not out	0
F.W.Sides	c Whitington b Grimmett	47		
W.E.Pearson	c & b Grimmett	13		
†B.A.Barnett	not out	3	(5) lbw b Ward	17
E.L.McCormick	lbw b Waite	0		
L.O.Fleetwood-Smith	run out (Ward/Walker)	0		
Extras	(b1, lb3, w2, nb2)	8	(b4)	4
Total	(100.6 overs, 384 mins)	364	(33.0 overs, 125 mins) (4 wkts)	144

VICTORIA	O	M	R	W	w,nb	O	M	R	W	w,nb
McCormick	16	1	60	0	-,1	20	1	91	2	-,3
Sievers	17	5	39	0	-,-	18.2	4	45	1	-,1
Pearson	17	3	41	0	-,1	3	0	13	0	-,-
Fleetwood-Smith	31.3	1	135	9	-,-	37	3	137	3	1,-
Gregory	10	1	26	1	-,-	16	1	46	2	-,-
Ledward						1	0	3	0	-,-

SOUTH AUSTRALIA	O	M	R	W	w,nb		O	M	R	W	w,nb
Cotton	15	1	76	0	2,2		6	0	21	0	-,-
Williams	18	2	49	1	-,-		6	0	17	1	-,-
Grimmett	30.6	4	95	6	-,-	(4)	11	1	62	1	-,-
Waite	18	5	38	1	-,-						
Ward	19	4	98	1	-,-	(3)	10	1	40	2	-,-

FALL OF WICKETS

Wkt	SA 1st	VIC 1st	SA 2nd	VIC 2nd
1st	69	157	0	33
2nd	149	213	63	61
3rd	179	245	67	73
4th	204	288	194	139
5th	213	290	201	-
6th	241	312	242	-
7th	258	360	254	-
8th	271	361	278	-
9th	279	364	321	-
10th	304	364	356	-

NEW SOUTH WALES v QUEENSLAND (Shield Match 7)

Played at Sydney Cricket Ground on January 1, 3, 4, 1938. (Four-day match)
Toss : Queensland.   Result : NEW SOUTH WALES WON BY EIGHT WICKETS.
Debuts: New South Wales - B.V.McCauley (f/c).
12th Men: J.H.Fitzpatrick (NSW) and H.J.H.Mahoney (Qld).
Umpires: E.G.Borwick and F.W.Lyons,
Attendances: 8430, 9012, 2043.   Total: 19,485.   Receipts: £1043.
Close of Play: 1st day NSW 1/33 (Fingleton 15, Oldfield 3); 2nd day Qld (2) 7/105 (Cook 15, Govan 0).

Humid conditions prevailed throughout and kept the scoring in check. Cook's medium-paced outswingers claimed 6 for 94 for Queensland, his best first-class figures. Fingleton (65 in 178 minutes, 5 fours) and Barnes (50 in 78 minutes, 6 fours) scored fifties for New South Wales, who gained a first innings lead through a last-wicket stand of 41 in 22 minutes between O'Reilly and O'Brien. McCauley (49 not out in 76 minutes, 3 fours) and Oldfield (42 not out in 45 minutes, 7 fours) scored the winning runs. Rogers (41 in 56 minutes, 6 fours) and Baker (75 in 123 minutes, 9 fours) topscored in Queensland's first innings, Cook's 17 occupying 131 minutes. Tallon (41 in 64 minutes, 5 fours) batted well in the second innings. Sources: *Wisden, NSWCA Report, QCA Report, The Herald, Sydney Morning Herald, NSWCA Scorebook, Brisbane Courier-Mail, The Sporting Globe.*

QUEENSLAND

*W.A.Brown	b White	23		lbw b McCabe	1
G.G.Cook	c McCabe b O'Brien	17	(8)	c Oldfield b White	28
J.Coats	b O'Reilly	8	(7)	st Oldfield b Mair	18
T.Allen	c McCabe b O'Reilly	2	(2)	c Oldfield b McCabe	6
†D.Tallon	b O'Brien	5	(4)	b O'Reilly	41
R.E.Rogers	st Oldfield b O'Reilly	41	(5)	c Oldfield b O'Brien	19
G.W.Baker	b Mair	75	(6)	b O'Reilly	0
C.C.Loxton	c Fingleton b White	0	(3)	c Oldfield b O'Brien	4
E.R.Wyeth	c O'Brien b Mair	2	(10)	c White b O'Reilly	0
J.M.Govan	run out (/Oldfield)	23	(9)	run out (/Oldfield)	11
P.L.Dixon	not out	0		not out	2
Extras	(b6, lb3, nb1)	10		(lb1)	1
Total	(73.0 overs, 259 mins)	206		(46.7 overs, 172 mins)	131

NEW SOUTH WALES

J.H.W.Fingleton	c Tallon b Cook	65			
E.E.Crossan	lbw b Cook	12	(1)	b Loxton	5
†W.A.S.Oldfield	c Rogers b Cook	12	(4)	not out	42
*S.J.McCabe	c Tallon b Dixon	6			
S.G.Barnes	c Rogers b Cook	50	(3)	b Loxton	0
A.G.Chipperfield	run out (Dixon)	2			
B.V.McCauley	c Rogers b Cook	35	(2)	not out	49
E.C.S.White	c Dixon b Loxton	1			
F.Mair	c Tallon b Dixon	4			
W.J.O'Reilly	not out	17			
L.J.O'Brien	c Dixon b Cook	24			
Extras	(b6, lb4, nb3)	13		(b1, lb2)	3
Total	(57.2 overs, 235 mins)	241		(18.6 overs, 76 mins) (2 wkts)	99

NEW SOUTH WALES	O	M	R	W	w,nb		O	M	R	W	w,nb
O'Brien	13	1	50	2	-,-		8	0	25	1	-,-
Crossan	6	1	11	0	-,-						
O'Reilly	21	6	56	3	-,1		17	3	45	4	-,-
White	18	6	29	2	-,-		12.7	2	31	1	-,-
Mair	12	5	42	2	-,-		4	0	13	1	-,-
McCabe	3	0	8	0	-,-	(2)	5	0	16	2	-,-

QUEENSLAND	O	M	R	W	w,nb		O	M	R	W	w,nb
Dixon	17	4	42	2	-,1		5	0	30	0	-,-
Cook	22.2	1	94	6	-,2		5	0	19	0	-,-
Loxton	7	0	39	1	-,-		6	0	27	2	-,-
Wyeth	5	0	23	0	-,-						
Govan	6	0	30	0	-,-						
Allen						(4)	2	0	14	0	-,-
Brown						(5)	0.6	0	6	0	-,-

FALL OF WICKETS

Wkt	QLD 1st	NSW 1st	QLD 2nd	NSW 2nd
1st	31	20	1	19
2nd	48	44	10	21
3rd	50	53	14	-
4th	56	151	68	-
5th	81	153	72	-
6th	113	162	73	-
7th	116	169	105	-
8th	138	199	122	-
9th	205	200	127	-
10th	206	241	131	-

QUEENSLAND v SOUTH AUSTRALIA (Shield Match 8)

Played at Brisbane Cricket Ground (Woolloongabba) on January 8, 10, 11, 12, 1938. (Four-day match)
Toss : South Australia.   Result : MATCH DRAWN.
Debuts: Queensland - J.V.Hackett (f/c).
12th Men: B.L.Webb (Qld) and B.H.Leak (SA).
Umpires: J.Bartlett and K.E.Fagg.
Attendances: 12329, 4485, 3387, 100.   Total: 20,301.   Receipts: £1547.
Close of Play: 1st day SA 8/381 (Williams 65, Grimmett 41); 2nd day SA (2) 1/37 (Whitington 15, Bradman 20); 3rd day Qld (2) 5/113
  (Cook 12, Govan 0).

South Australia were denied an almost certain victory when rain allowed only 70 minutes of play on the last day. Bradman, who scored a hundred in each innings for the third time in his career (107 in 164 minutes, 9 fours and 113 in 143 minutes, 10 fours, both innings chanceless) and became the first to have twice done so in the Sheffield Shield, had elected not to enforce the follow-on. With his 88th run in the first innings Bradman surpassed C.Hill's aggregate of 6274 to also become the highest run-scorer in Shield history. The Queenslanders were badly handicapped after the first day by the absence of their leader Brown, who tore his left thigh when he turned to make a throw after a fast run in the outfield in the post-tea session. He took no further part in the match and Allen assumed the captaincy for the remainder. Williams (75 not out in 116 minutes, 1 six and 8 fours) and Grimmett (46 in 68 minutes, 4 fours) shared a ninth-wicket stand of 100 for South Australia. Waite (58 in 109 minutes, 4 fours) hit a second-innings fifty, the innings being declared when Walker was struck by a throw from Loxton in the outfield while he completed a run. Tallon (48 in 85 minutes, 4 fours) and Baker (70 not out in 151 minutes, 9 fours) contributed to Queensland's first innings, Allen who was dismissed second ball, scoring a crucial half-century (55 in 127 minutes, 1 six and 6 fours) in the second. Sources: *Wisden, QCA Report, SACA Report, The Age, The Herald, Brisbane Courier-Mail, The Sporting Globe.*

SOUTH AUSTRALIA

C.L.Badcock	c Tallon b Christ	37		b Dixon	1
R.S.Whitington	c Loxton b Christ	28		b Cook	18
*D.G.Bradman	c Tallon b Dixon	107		c Hackett b Allen	113
R.H.Robinson	c Govan b Christ	43		st Tallon b Cook	0
R.A.Hamence	c Rogers b Loxton	16		st Tallon b Christ	11
M.G.Waite	c Rogers b Cook	16		c sub (B.L.Webb) b Cook	58
†C.W.Walker	c Loxton b Cook	11	(9)	not out	25
R.G.Williams	not out	75	(7)	c Rogers b Cook	37
F.A.Ward	lbw b Cook	10	(10)	not out	15
C.V.Grimmett	c Rogers b Dixon	46			
H.N.J.Cotton	lbw b Cook	1	(8)	c Tallon b Dixon	1
Extras	(lb6, nb2)	8		(b2, lb3, nb3)	8
Total	(87.6 overs, 345 mins)	398		(58.5 overs, 240 mins) (8 wkts dec)	287

QUEENSLAND

G.G.Cook	b Cotton	10	(6)	b Ward	21
C.C.Loxton	lbw b Cotton	16	(1)	c Bradman b Ward	12
T.Allen	b Cotton	0	(2)	b Cotton	55
R.E.Rogers	lbw b Waite	14	(3)	c Waite b Ward	27
†D.Tallon	b Cotton	48	(4)	st Walker b Ward	1
G.W.Baker	not out	70	(5)	c Cotton b Ward	2
J.V.Hackett	run out (Bradman)	0	(8)	lbw b Grimmett	10
J.M.Govan	lbw b Grimmett	14	(7)	b Waite	18
C.P.Christ	st Walker b Grimmett	4		not out	5
P.L.Dixon	c Walker b Grimmett	10			
*W.A.Brown	absent hurt	-			
Extras	(b3, lb2, nb1)	6		(lb4)	4
Total	(61.1 overs, 230 mins)	192		(57.3 overs, 188 mins) (8 wkts)	155

QUEENSLAND	O	M	R	W	w,nb		O	M	R	W	w,nb		FALL OF WICKETS			
Dixon	17	1	85	2	-,1		14	1	60	2	-,1			SA	QLD	SA	QLD
Cook	20.6	2	69	4	-,1		22	1	108	4	-,2	Wkt	1st	1st	2nd	2nd
Loxton	5	0	15	1	-,-							1st	61	19	2	29
Govan	17	0	105	0	-,-		3	0	30	0	-,-	2nd	77	19	41	71
Christ	26	2	99	3	-,-	(3)	16.5	2	66	1	-,-	3rd	162	40	57	79
Baker	2	0	17	0	-,-							4th	194	43	74	81
Allen						(5)	3	0	15	1	-,-	5th	234	116	177	113
												6th	264	116	236	137
SOUTH AUSTRALIA	O	M	R	W	w,nb		O	M	R	W	w,nb	7th	268	150	237	145
Cotton	15	3	37	4	-,1		8	3	11	1	-,-	8th	287	158	257	155
Williams	10	1	25	0	-,-		6	0	20	0	-,-	9th	387	192	-	-
Waite	13	1	49	1	-,-	(4)	12	4	26	1	-,-	10th	398	-	-	-
Ward	9	1	33	0	-,-	(3)	21	3	66	5	-,-					
Grimmett	14.1	3	42	3	-,-		10.3	1	28	1	-,-					

QUEENSLAND v VICTORIA (Shield Match 9)

Played at Brisbane Cricket Ground (Woolloongabba) on January 14, 15, 17, 18 (no play), 1938. (Four-day match)
Toss : Queensland.   Result : MATCH DRAWN.
Debuts: Queensland - B.L.Webb (f/c).
12th Men: J.Coats (Qld) and E.H.Bromley (Vic).
Umpires: J.Bartlett and J.A.Scott.
Attendances: 3320, 6650, 500, no play.   Total: 10,470 (excluding last day).   Receipts: £740.
Close of Play: 1st day Vic 6/289 (Sides 67, Barnett 1); 2nd day Qld 4/164 (Tallon 29); 3rd day Qld 5/171 (Cook 3, Baker 3).

Rain permitted just 27 minutes' play in two spells on the third day and prevented any play on the last. W.A.Brown (leg injury) and C.C.Loxton (strained arm) were unavailable for Queensland. Lee (108 in 234 minutes, 13 fours) batted soundly for Victoria on the first day, setting up fifties for Ledward (54 in 147 minutes, 4 fours), Sides (74 in 120 minutes, 1 six and 10 fours) and Barnett (83 not out in 105 minutes, 13 fours). Webb (59 in 208 minutes, 6 fours) for Queensland compiled a half-century in his sole first-class appearance. Allen (42 in 128 minutes, 3 fours) also batted well in his only match as captain (deputising for Brown). Sources: *Wisden, VCA Report, QCA Report, The Age, The Herald, Brisbane Courier-Mail, The Sporting Globe.*

VICTORIA

*K.E.Rigg	c Tallon b Cook	19
I.S.Lee	run out (Webb)	108
R.G.Gregory	run out (Baker/Tallon)	1
A.L.Hassett	c Tallon b Rushbrook	32
J.A.Ledward	run out	54
F.W.Sides	c & b Dixon	74
W.E.Pearson	c Cook b Rogers	4
†B.A.Barnett	not out	83
M.W.Sievers	c Baker b Christ	12
E.L.McCormick	lbw b Rushbrook	4
L.O.Fleetwood-Smith	b Rushbrook	0
Extras	(lb4, w1)	5
Total	(112.0 overs, 425 mins)	396

QUEENSLAND

R.E.Rogers	c & b Sievers	30
H.J.H.Mahoney	c McCormick b Pearson	0
B.L.Webb	c Sievers b McCormick	59
*T.Allen	run out (Lee/Fleetwood-Smith)	42
†D.Tallon	c Barnett b McCormick	30
G.G.Cook	not out	3
G.W.Baker	not out	3
J.V.Hackett	)	
R.F.K.Rushbrook	) did not bat	
C.P.Christ	)	
P.L.Dixon	)	
Extras	(lb1, nb3)	4
Total	(63.3 overs, 248 mins) (5 wkts)	171

QUEENSLAND	O	M	R	W	w,nb
Dixon	19	1	80	1	-,-
Rushbrook	27	3	116	3	1,-
Cook	20	3	60	1	-,-
Christ	31	8	72	1	-,-
Allen	12	2	46	0	-,-
Rogers	3	0	17	1	-,-

VICTORIA	O	M	R	W	w,nb
McCormick	11.3	0	53	2	-,2
Sievers	23	10	32	1	-,1
Pearson	3	1	2	1	-,-
Fleetwood-Smith	16	2	63	0	-,-
Gregory	10	3	17	0	-,-

FALL OF WICKETS

	VIC	QLD
Wkt	1st	1st
1st	26	9
2nd	27	40
3rd	108	127
4th	181	164
5th	260	165
6th	282	-
7th	318	-
8th	350	-
9th	396	-
10th	396	-

NEW SOUTH WALES v SOUTH AUSTRALIA (Shield Match 10)

Played at Sydney Cricket Ground on January 15, 17, 18, 19, 1938. (Four-day match)
Toss : South Australia.　　　　　　Result : NEW SOUTH WALES WON BY FOUR WICKETS.
Debuts: Nil.
12th Men: J.H.Fitzpatrick (NSW) and B.H.Leak (SA).
Umpires: E.G.Borwick and F.W.Lyons.
Attendances: 20106, 7881, 7058, 2441.　　　Total: 37,486.　　　Receipts: £2116.
Close of Play: 1st day NSW 4/147 (Chipperfield 27, Jackson 1); 2nd day SA (2) 0/11 (Badcock 5, Whitington 4); 3rd day SA (2) 8/330
　　(Bradman 101, Cotton 2).

Rain, which dogged most of the season's fixtures, caused four interruptions on the second day. Bradman (44 in 81 minutes, 4 fours) and Hamence (49 in 80 minutes, 7 fours) performed best for the South Australians on the first day. Bradman had collided with mid-on in going for a single early in his innings, as a result of which he was dazed and his lip cut. New South Wales gained a lead of 108 with McCabe (83 in 108 minutes, 12 fours) and Jackson (63 in 149 minutes, 4 fours, several chances) registering fifties. Cotton, who injured his foot while fielding, was unable to bowl in the second innings. Walker broke a finger while keeping wickets on the second day and Bradman, despite a cut thumb which required taping, took the gloves for the rest of the match to achieve his only career stumping (plus three catches), Leak and P.L.Ridings substituting in the field. Badcock (132 in 199 minutes, 18 fours) and Bradman (chanceless 104 not out in 217 minutes, 13 fours) hit centuries in the second innings, their 95-run stand being broken when a throw from McCabe at third man smashed the stumps at the bowler's end with Badcock well out of his crease. When 80, Bradman reached 1000 first-class runs for the ninth successive season in Australia in which he played, a clear record, and he took his score from 86 to 104 with the last man at the wicket. Fingleton (74 in 208 minutes, 6 fours), out at 191, guided New South Wales to victory. Sources: *Wisden, NSWCA Report, SACA Report, The Herald, Sydney Morning Herald, NSWCA Scorebook, Brisbane Courier-Mail, Sydney Telegraph.*

SOUTH AUSTRALIA

C.L.Badcock	c O'Reilly b O'Brien	6		run out (McCabe)	132
R.S.Whitington	b McCabe	4		st Oldfield b O'Reilly	29
*D.G.Bradman	c McCabe b O'Brien	44		not out	104
R.H.Robinson	b Jackson	13		lbw b McCabe	21
R.A.Hamence	c Oldfield b Mair	49		lbw b O'Reilly	13
M.G.Waite	lbw b O'Reilly	21		lbw b O'Brien	7
†C.W.Walker	run out	0		absent hurt	-
R.G.Williams	b O'Reilly	12	(7)	c Oldfield b O'Brien	6
F.A.Ward	not out	11	(8)	c Fingleton b O'Reilly	8
C.V.Grimmett	run out (O'Brien/Oldfield)	1	(9)	c Chipperfield b O'Brien	0
H.N.J.Cotton	run out (　　　/Oldfield)	18	(10)	c Chipperfield b O'Reilly	3
Extras	(b7, lb1)	8		(b8, lb3)	11
Total	(49.6 overs, 189 mins)	187		(95.6 overs, 355 mins)	334

NEW SOUTH WALES

*S.J.McCabe	c Hamence b Ward	82	(2)	c Bradman b Waite	39
J.H.W.Fingleton	c Cotton b Grimmett	20	(1)	c Hamence b Grimmett	74
B.V.McCauley	c Williams b Cotton	7		c Bradman b Williams	8
S.G.Barnes	lbw b Williams	6		lbw b Waite	21
A.G.Chipperfield	c Grimmett b Ward	31		b Waite	30
V.E.Jackson	b Williams	63		c Bradman b Ward	0
E.C.S.White	b Williams	1		not out	36
†W.A.S.Oldfield	b Grimmett	9		not out	13
F.Mair	b Ward	39			
W.J.O'Reilly	st Bradman b Ward	20			
L.J.O'Brien	not out	2			
Extras	(b5, lb6, w1, nb2)	14		(b3, lb2, nb1)	6
Total	(73.7 overs, 288 mins)	295		(72.3 overs, 238 mins) (6 wkts)	227

NEW SOUTH WALES	O	M	R	W	w,nb		O	M	R	W	w,nb					
O'Brien	9	0	42	2	-,-		22		2	90	3	-,-				
McCabe	5	0	12	1			12		1	39	1	-,-				
O'Reilly	16	3	36	2	-,-	(4)	25.6	7	65	4	-,-					
Jackson	6	0	20	1	-,-	(3)	12	4	28	0	-,-					
White	2	0	10	0	-,-	(6)	11	0	38	0	-,-					
Mair	11.6	0	59	1	-,-	(5)	7	1	26	0	-,-					
Chipperfield							6	0	37	0	-,-					

FALL OF WICKETS				
	SA	NSW	SA	NSW
Wkt	1st	1st	2nd	2nd
1st	10	65	106	53
2nd	12	80	201	77
3rd	39	117	239	116
4th	93	143	270	160
5th	133	154	283	161
6th	133	163	295	191
7th	149	178	312	-
8th	156	214	313	-
9th	157	273	334	-
10th	187	295	-	-

SOUTH AUSTRALIA	O	M	R	W	w,nb		O	M	R	W	w,nb
Cotton	10	0	52	1	-,2						
Williams	21.7	1	93	3	1,-	(1)	14	0	57	1	-,1
Waite	12	3	35	0	-,-	(2)	21.3	3	55	3	-,-
Grimmett	12	2	50	2	-,-	(3)	14	3	52	1	-,-
Ward	18	2	51	4	-,-	(4)	23	6	57	1	-,-

NEW SOUTH WALES v VICTORIA (Shield Match 11)

Played at Sydney Cricket Ground on January 21, 22 (no play), 24, 25, 1938. (Four-day match)
Toss : New South Wales.   Result : MATCH DRAWN.
Debuts: New South Wales - J.H.Fiztpatrick (f/c).
12th Men: E.E.Crossan (NSW) and E.H.Bromley (Vic).
Umpires: E.G.Borwick and F.W.Lyons.
Attendances: 2069, no play, 6071, 2797.   Total: 10937 (excluding second day).   Receipts: £488.
Close of Play: 1st day NSW 5/177 (Barnes 54, White 7); 2nd day no play; 3rd day Vic 5/78 (Hassett 30, Pearson 15).

The match did not start until 2.15pm owing to rain, which returned to prevent any play on the second day. First-innings points gave New South Wales the Sheffield Shield for the first time since 1932-33, ending their longest break from the title to date. Barnes (110 in 218 minutes, 12 fours) retired when 93, at 5/252, after a ball from McCormick struck him in the chest and deflected into his jaw as he attempted a pull shot; he resumed at 6/327. White (52 in 178 minutes, 3 fours) and Oldfield (62 in 100 minutes, 1 five and 7 fours) hit fifties. Only Hassett (57 in 172 minutes, 6 fours) made any impression when Victoria batted. With New South Wales holding a lead of 248 runs early on the last day, McCabe elected not to enforce the follow-on. Pearson (51 in 40 minutes, 2 sixes and 6 fours) hit hard in the second innings in which Barnett suffered a first-ball dismissal, one of 14 wickets to fall on the last day. Sources: *Wisden, NSWCA Report, VCA Report, The Herald, Melbourne Sun, Sydney Morning Herald, NSWCA Scorebook, The Sporting Globe.*

NEW SOUTH WALES

J.H.W.Fingleton	b Pearson	15			
J.H.Fitzpatrick	c Sievers b Pearson	31	lbw b Pearson		13
*S.J.McCabe	b McCormick	32			
S.G.Barnes	b Fleetwood-Smith	110	(3) c & b Gregory		42
A.G.Chipperfield	run out (Gregory/Barnett)	5	(4) c Pearson b Gregory		34
V.E.Jackson	c Barnett b Sievers	18	(5) not out		11
E.C.S.White	b Sievers	52	(1) c Barnett b McCormick		3
†W.A.S.Oldfield	lbw b Fleetwood-Smith	62	(6) not out		3
F.Mair	c Sievers b Fleetwood-Smith	0			
W.J.O'Reilly	c Sides b Fleetwood-Smith	16			
L.J.O'Brien	not out	0			
Extras	(b12, lb9, w2, nb7)	30	(b2, lb4)		6
Total	(99.6 overs, 396 mins)	371	(31.0 overs, 120 mins) (4 wkts dec)		112

VICTORIA

*K.E.Rigg	b O'Brien	5	(6) not out		5
I.S.Lee	c Chipperfield b O'Brien	8			
R.G.Gregory	c Oldfield b O'Brien	4			
A.L.Hassett	c McCabe b White	57			
J.A.Ledward	st Oldfield b O'Reilly	1	(2) b Mair		24
F.W.Sides	b White	15	(4) b Barnes		36
W.E.Pearson	b Chipperfield	15	(5) c sub (E.E.Crossan) b McCabe		51
†B.A.Barnett	lbw b O'Reilly	6	(3) c Oldfield b Mair		0
M.W.Sievers	lbw b O'Reilly	2	(1) c Mair b Jackson		23
E.L.McCormick	not out	6			
L.O.Fleetwood-Smith	b White	0			
Extras	(lb4)	4	(b3, nb1)		4
Total	(54.2 overs, 210 mins)	123	(24.1 overs, 96 mins) (5 wkts)		143

VICTORIA	O	M	R	W	w,nb		O	M	R	W	w,nb
McCormick	18	3	52	1	2,6		4	1	15	1	-,-
Sievers	29	3	91	2	-,-		6	1	20	0	-,-
Pearson	16	4	27	2	-,1		9	1	30	1	-,-
Ledward	1	0	3	0	-,-	(6)	1	0	5	0	-,-
Gregory	8	0	50	0	-,-		6	1	12	2	-,-
Fleetwood-Smith	27.6	4	118	4	-,-	(4)	5	0	24	0	-,-

NEW SOUTH WALES	O	M	R	W	w,nb		O	M	R	W	w,nb
O'Brien	12	0	44	3	-,-		5	1	18	0	-,-
McCabe	4	1	5	0	-,-	(6)	1.1	0	4	1	-,-
O'Reilly	18	9	25	3	-,-						
White	12.2	5	25	3	-,-						
Mair	2	0	10	0	-,-	(3)	6	0	47	2	-,1
Chipperfield	6	1	10	1	-,-	(4)	2	0	21	0	-,-
Jackson						(2)	8	0	35	1	-,-
Barnes						(5)	2	0	14	1	-,-

FALL OF WICKETS

	NSW	VIC	NSW	VIC
Wkt	1st	1st	2nd	2nd
1st	45	6	16	48
2nd	58	12	35	48
3rd	95	21	93	48
4th	109	22	100	127
5th	158	43	-	143
6th	327	78	-	-
7th	349	104	-	-
8th	349	116	-	-
9th	371	116	-	-
10th	371	123	-	-

VICTORIA v TASMANIA

Played at Melbourne Cricket Ground on February 1, 2, 3, 1938 . (Three-day match)
Toss : Tasmania.   Result : MATCH DRAWN.
Debuts: Victoria - A.G.Andrew-Street, H.Dowsley, J.B.Lowry, G.S.Meikle, K.R.Miller, H.G.Smith, R.T.Tuttle (all f/c). Tasmania -
   E.W.Dwyer, J.I.Murfett (both f/c).
12th Men: R.Gardner (Vic) and D.H.Thollar (Tas).
Umpires: W.J.Craddock and A.Sharp.
Attendances: No daily figures published.   Total: 864.   Receipts: £17.
Close of Play: 1st day Vic 1/56 (Dowsley 33); 2nd day Tas (2) 0/19 (Morrisby 16, Thomas 3).

Miller, aged 18 years 66 days, scored 181 in 289 minutes with 5 fours on his first-class debut. Others to score well for Victoria were Dowsley (46 in 61 minutes, 5 fours and 72 not out in 105 minutes), Lowry (62 in 113 minutes, 2 fours) and Deveney (47 not out in 61 minutes, 6 fours) Morrisby (50 in 114 minutes, 4 fours), M.J.Combes (84 not out in 205 minutes, 5 fours) and Putman (92 in 78 minutes, 2 sixes and 11 fours, including 21 off an over from Stephens with 2 sixes and 2 fours) compiled first-innings fifties for Tasmania. Batting again, Morrisby, missed in slips from the first ball, went on to make 93 (120 minutes, 8 fours). He shared a new first-wicket record stand of 163 for Tasmania against Victoria with Thomas (125 in 182 minutes, 1 six and 15 fours). *VCA Report* incorrectly gives Vic (1) 4/134. Sources: *VCA Report, The Age, The Argus, The Herald, Melbourne Sun, The Sporting Globe, Hobart Mercury, Launceston Examiner.*

TASMANIA

R.O.G.Morrisby	run out (Dowsley/Meikle/Quin)	50	c Deveney b Dowsley		93
R.V.Thomas	c Andrew-Street b Stephens	33	c Andrew-Street b Meikle		125
J.N.W.Nicolson	lbw b Tuttle	14	b Smith		15
M.J.Combes	not out	84			
E.H.Smith	lbw b Tuttle	24	(4) not out		49
*S.W.L.Putman	c Dowsley b Stephens	92			
C.J.Sankey	run out (Andrew-Street/Quin)	0	(5) not out		43
†J.Gardiner	lbw b Tuttle	26			
J.I.Murfett	lbw b Meikle	8			
E.W.Dwyer	st Quin b Meikle	3			
G.A.Combes	lbw b Meikle	5			
Extras	(b3, lb8, nb3)	14	(b9, lb2, nb1)		12
Total	(77.7 overs, 296 mins)	353	(66.0 overs, 265 mins) (3 wkts dec)		337

VICTORIA

H.Dowsley	c Murfett b Putman	46	not out		72
A.G.Andrew-Street	c Morrisby b Putman	21	c Thomas b Murfett		16
L.J.Junor	lbw b Murfett	30	c Thomas b Putman		8
J.B.Lowry	c Gardiner b Dwyer	62	run out (Murfett/Gardiner)		3
K.R.Miller	c Murfett b Nicolson	181			
*†S.O.Quin	b Dwyer	10			
G.S.Meikle	c Gardiner b Putman	31	(5) c Dwyer b G.A.Combes		31
J.L.Stephens	c Gardiner b Murfett	31	(6) not out		0
H.G.Smith	b Murfett	6			
F.B.Deveney	not out	47			
R.T.Tuttle	lbw b G.A.Combes	1			
Extras	(b3, lb2)	4	(b2)		2
Total	(101.2 overs, 376 mins)	470	(29.0 overs, 105 mins) (4 wkts)		132

VICTORIA	O	M	R	W	w,nb		O	M	R	W	w,nb
Deveney	12	1	61	0	-,2		12	1	59	0	-,-
Smith	12	0	39	0	-,-		13	1	36	1	-,-
Stephens	19	1	84	2	-,-	(4)	3	0	19	0	-,-
Dowsley	4	2	7	0	-,1	(3)	7	2	25	1	-,1
Tuttle	18	2	82	3	-,-		9	0	66	0	-,-
Meikle	12.7	1	66	3	-,-		17	2	76	1	-,-
Lowry							5	0	44	0	-,-

TASMANIA	O	M	R	W	w,nb		O	M	R	W	w,nb
Dwyer	15	0	69	2	-,-		3	0	18	0	-,-
Murfett	22	0	97	3	-,-		5	0	18	1	-,-
Thomas	18	2	84	0	-,-	(5)	2	0	14	0	-,-
Putman	19	0	125	3	-,-		7	0	36	1	-,-
G.A.Combes	24.2	0	75	1	-,-	(3)	11	0	37	1	-,-
Nicolson	3	0	16	1	-,-		1	0	7	0	-,-

FALL OF WICKETS

Wkt	TAS 1st	VIC 1st	TAS 2nd	VIC 2nd
1st	55	56	163	32
2nd	80	81	232	58
3rd	122	112	244	61
4th	169	234	-	125
5th	290	248	-	-
6th	293	321	-	-
7th	332	377	-	-
8th	341	393	-	-
9th	347	468	-	-
10th	353	470	-	-

SOUTH AUSTRALIA v VICTORIA (Shield Match 12)

Played at Adelaide Oval on February 4, 5, 7, 8, 1938. (Four-day match)
Toss : South Australia.   Result : SOUTH AUSTRALIA WON BY 125 RUNS.
Debuts: South Australia - J.A.J.Horsell (f/c).
12th Men: P.L.Ridings (SA) and I.W.Johnson (Vic).
Umpires: A.G.Jenkins and J.D.Scott.
Attendances: No daily figures published.   Total: 11,147.   Receipts: £318.
Close of Play: 1st day SA 6/122 (Waite 29, Horsell 6); 2nd day SA (2) 0/34 (Whitington 17, Mueller 14); 3rd day SA (2) 340 all out.

A thunderstorm and later light rain disrupted the first day, allowing only 136 minutes' play in all. Sievers (right-arm fast-medium) relished bowling in the heavy atmosphere and captured 6 for 43, only Whitington (42 in 114 minutes, 4 fours) and Waite (45 not out in 106 minutes, 2 fours) resisting for any length. Hamence was out to the first ball he received. Waite bowled his medium pacers impressively in both Victorian innings in support of the faster Williams, clinching his place on the forthcoming tour to England. Whitington (86 in 212 minutes, 6 fours) and Bradman (85 in 83 minutes, 9 fours) set up a match-winning lead for the South Australians with a second-wicket partnership of 113. Victoria went into the match missing E.H.Bromley, L.O.Fleetwood-Smith, R.G.Gregory and F.W.Sides, all unavailable for business reasons. Sources: *Wisden, VCA Report, SACA Report, The Age, The Herald, Adelaide Advertiser, The News.*

SOUTH AUSTRALIA

R.S.Whitington	c Rigg b Thorn	42	run out (Beames/Barnett)		86
M.E.C.Mueller	lbw b Sievers	1	c Thorn b Rayson		37
*D.G.Bradman	b McCormick	3	c Ledward b Thorn		85
R.H.Robinson	lbw b Sievers	19	b Pearson		8
R.A.Hamence	c Pearson b Sievers	0	run out (Ledward/Hassett/Barnett)		18
B.H.Leak	b Sievers	9	b Pearson		31
M.G.Waite	not out	45	c Pearson b Sievers		10
†J.A.J.Horsell	c Barnett b McCormick	9	lbw b Pearson		1
R.G.Williams	b Sievers	5	st Barnett b Rayson		29
F.A.Ward	c Barnett b Rayson	1	c Rigg b Thorn		22
C.V.Grimmett	c Pearson b Sievers	2	not out		1
Extras	(b17, lb1, nb3)	21	(b5, lb3, nb4)		12
Total	(42.7 overs, 182 mins)	157	(82.7 overs, 360 mins)		340

VICTORIA

*K.E.Rigg	c Ward b Waite	15	b Waite		6
I.S.Lee	b Grimmett	44	(5) b Williams		11
A.L.Hassett	c Waite b Williams	7	c sub (P.L.Ridings) b Waite		14
J.A.Ledward	c Grimmett b Waite	25	st Horsell b Ward		2
P.J.Beames	c Grimmett b Williams	27	(6) c sub (P.L.Ridings) b Williams		23
W.E.Pearson	c & b Williams	14	(7) c Horsell b Williams		36
†B.A.Barnett	c Bradman b Ward	26	(8) b Williams		41
M.W.Sievers	c Horsell b Ward	19	(2) b Waite		21
M.W.Rayson	not out	6	run out		3
E.L.McCormick	st Horsell b Grimmett	6	not out		8
F.L.O.Thorn	st Horsell b Grimmett	0	c Horsell b Williams		0
Extras	(b2, lb4)	6	(b8, lb4)		12
Total	(47.4 overs, 187 mins)	195	(64.4 overs, 233 mins)		177

VICTORIA	O	M	R	W	w,nb		O	M	R	W	w,nb
McCormick	9	1	27	2	-,2		16	1	54	0	-,3
Sievers	12.7	2	43	6	-,-		25	5	73	1	-,1
Pearson	8	1	22	0	-,-	(4)	17	1	70	3	-,-
Thorn	11	1	37	1	-,1	(3)	13	0	53	2	-,-
Rayson	2	1	7	1	-,-		11.7	0	78	2	-,-

SOUTH AUSTRALIA	O	M	R	W	w,nb		O	M	R	W	w,nb
Williams	14	1	60	3	-,-		18.4	1	52	5	-,-
Waite	11	1	31	2	-,-		18	6	28	3	-,-
Ward	9	0	42	2	-,-		17	3	56	1	-,-
Grimmett	13.4	0	56	3	-,-		11	3	29	0	-,-

FALL OF WICKETS

Wkt	SA 1st	VIC 1st	SA 2nd	VIC 2nd
1st	4	25	95	11
2nd	7	36	208	40
3rd	39	92	218	49
4th	39	96	226	49
5th	59	132	260	83
6th	100	139	284	90
7th	129	179	284	137
8th	149	186	294	159
9th	154	195	332	177
10th	157	195	340	177

S.J.McCABE'S XI v K.E.RIGG'S XI

Played at Sydney Cricket Ground on February 18, 19, 1938. (Four-day match)
Toss : Rigg's XI.   Result : McCABE'S XI WON BY THREE WICKETS.
Debuts: Nil.
12th Men: J.H.Fitzpatrick (both sides).
Umpires: E.G.Borwick and F.W.Lyons.
Attendances: 4588, 8960.   Total: 13,548.   Receipts: £560.
Close of Play: 1st day McCabe 5/143 (Waite 11, Barnett 1).

The match was arranged as part of Australia's 150th Anniversary celebrations at the request of the Federal Government Minister responsible for the program of events. D.G.Bradman was invited to lead one of the teams but declined for business reasons. Barnes and Rogers were swapped between the sides after they had been named so that McCabe's XI was comprised solely of players selected for the England tour. (The teams were referred to as Australia v The Rest in the newspapers.) T.W.Garrett, aged 79 years 207 days - the sole survivor of the first Test match of all and Australia's 1878 tour of England was invited to bowl an opening delivery (unrecorded in the score), which he managed to Rigg. Both captains agreed late on the second day to continue playing until the match was decided; this occurred at 6.10pm. Rigg (58 in 112 minutes, 4 fours and 60 in 74 minutes, 8 fours), Robinson (53 in 51 minutes, 1 six and 6 fours) and White (52 in 48 minutes, 7 fours) for Rigg's XI and Hassett (54 in 101 minutes, 7 fours) and Barnes (55 in 62 minutes, 5 fours) for McCabe's XI scored half-centuries. Fleetwood-Smith (11 for 159) took the bowling honours. Twenty-two wickets fell on the second day. Waite hit 24 runs including a six and 4 fours off an over from Jackson late in the game as his side pressed for victory before nightfall. Last first-class appearance by W.A.S.Oldfield. Sources: *NSWCA Report, VCA Report, The Herald, Melbourne Sun, Sydney Morning Herald, NSWCA Scorebook, The Sporting Globe.*

RIGG'S XI

*K.E.Rigg	st Barnett b Fleetwood-Smith	58		c McCormick b Fleetwood-Smith	60
I.S.Lee	c McCabe b McCormick	4		b Waite	1
R.G.Gregory	c Barnett b Fleetwood-Smith	42		c Ward b McCormick	0
R.H.Robinson	c Hassett b Fleetwood-Smith	53		c McCabe b McCormick	11
R.E.Rogers	c McCormick b Fleetwood-Smith	10		b O'Reilly	40
W.E.Pearson	c & b Ward	1	(7)	st Barnett b Fleetwood-Smith	8
V.E.Jackson	c Fingleton b Fleetwood-Smith	5	(6)	b Fleetwood-Smith	10
E.C.S.White	b Waite	52		c Fingleton b Fleetwood-Smith	1
†W.A.S.Oldfield	c McCormick b Fleetwood-Smith	4		run out (McCabe)	3
C.V.Grimmett	run out (McCabe)	17		b Fleetwood-Smith	7
L.J.O'Brien	not out	0		not out	0
Extras	(b7, lb3, nb1)	11		(b5, nb2)	7
Total	(49.6 overs, 188 mins)	257		(29.4 overs, 124 mins)	148

McCABE'S XI

J.H.W.Fingleton	c Gregory b White	24		st Oldfield b Grimmett	28
*S.J.McCabe	b O'Brien	11	(3)	c White b Grimmett	4
A.L.Hassett	b Gregory	54	(4)	c Oldfield b Jackson	37
S.G.Barnes	c Oldfield b Grimmett	1	(5)	c Rigg b Jackson	55
A.G.Chipperfield	c White b Grimmett	36			
M.G.Waite	c Jackson b White	32	(7)	c Rigg b Gregory	33
†B.A.Barnett	c O'Brien b Grimmett	11	(6)	c Rigg b Gregory	14
F.A.Ward	c & b White	18	(2)	lbw b White	13
W.J.O'Reilly	c Lee b White	4	(8)	not out	17
E.L.McCormick	not out	2	(9)	not out	1
L.O.Fleetwood-Smith	b White	0			
Extras	(b4, lb1)	5		(b2, lb4)	6
Total	(49.4 overs, 186 mins)	198		(37.3 overs, 138 mins) (7 wkts)	208

McCABE'S XI	O	M	R	W	w,nb		O	M	R	W	w,nb	FALL OF WICKETS			
McCormick	7	0	44	1	-,1		6	0	48	2	-,2		R	M	R	M
Waite	5.6	0	15	1	-,-		4	1	6	1	-,-	Wkt	1st	1st	2nd	2nd
O'Reilly	5	0	24	0	-,-	(4)	7	3	30	1	-,-	1st	9	31	4	41
Fleetwood-Smith	19	0	106	6	-,-	(3)	10.4	0	53	5	-,-	2nd	90	42	5	50
Ward	12	1	48	1	-,-		2	0	4	0	-,-	3rd	142	43	32	52
Chipperfield	1	0	9	0	-,-							4th	177	93	113	117
												5th	177	142	129	154
RIGG'S XI	O	M	R	W	w,nb		O	M	R	W	w,nb	6th	178	154	129	206
O'Brien	11	0	67	1	-,-		4	0	10	0	-,-	7th	190	192	137	208
Pearson	5	0	16	0	-,-		4	0	16	0	-,-	8th	204	192	140	-
Jackson	8	0	41	0	-,-	(5)	6	0	38	2	-,-	9th	257	198	148	-
White	7.4	1	12	5	-,-	(3)	9	0	39	1	-,-	10th	257	198	148	-
Grimmett	17	4	56	3	-,-	(4)	7	0	43	2	-,-					
Gregory	1	0	1	1	-,-		6	0	46	2	-,-					
Robinson							1.3	0	10	0	-,-					

TASMANIA v AUSTRALIAN XI

Played at N.T.C.A. Ground, Launceston, on February 26, 28, March 1, 1938. (Three-day match)
Toss : Australian XI.   Result : AUSTRALIAN XI WON BY 386 RUNS.
Debuts: Nil.
12th Men: K.W.J.Cahill (Tas) and A.G.Chipperfield (Aust).
Umpires: G.T.Godden and E.C.Knight.
Attendances: 7700, 2500, 700.   Total: About 10,900.   Receipts: £995.
Close of Play: 1st day Aust 6/411 (Barnes 25, Waite 14); 2nd day Aust (2) 3/150 (Barnes 80, Hassett 12).

Fingleton (66 in 105 minutes, 2 sixes and 4 fours), Hassett (75 in 92 minutes, 7 fours), Bradman (79 in 84 minutes, 1 six and 5 fours), McCabe (83 in 70 minutes, 1 six and 12 fours) and Barnes (53 not out in 88 minutes, 6 fours) all hit half-centuries for the Australians in their rapidly-compiled first innings. Barnes (89 in 97 minutes, 11 fours) in the second innings was run out when a straight drive by Hassett was deflected by the bowler into the stumps at the non-striker's end with Barnes, backing up, out of his ground. Thollar's wicket-taking leg-breaks had conceded 116 runs in 13 overs in the first innings. Fleetwood-Smith (8 for 78) and Ward (6 for 91) accounted for the local batting. Sources: *NSWCA Report, VCA Report, TCA Report, The Herald, Hobart Mercury, Launceston Examiner.*

AUSTRALIAN XI

J.H.W.Fingleton	st Gardiner b Thollar	66	(4) run out (Thomas/Gardiner)		1
†B.A.Barnett	c Gardiner b Thomas	27			
A.L.Hassett	b James	75	(5) not out		24
*D.G.Bradman	c Sankey b Thomas	79			
S.J.McCabe	st Gardiner b Thollar	83			
C.L.Badcock	c James b Nicolson	36	(1) b Thomas		42
S.G.Barnes	not out	53	(2) run out (Thollar)		89
M.G.Waite	c Morrisby b Thollar	38	(6) not out		1
E.C.S.White	lbw b Thollar	0	(3) c Sankey b Thollar		15
F.A.Ward	c Nicolson b Thollar	9			
L.O.Fleetwood-Smith	run out (/Gardiner)	4			
Extras	(b5, w1, nb1)	7			-
Total	(78.0 overs, 294 mins)	477	(29.0 overs, 103 mins) (4 wkts dec)		172

TASMANIA

*R.O.G.Morrisby	c Badcock b Fleetwood-Smith	29	c Waite b Ward		38
R.V.Thomas	c Barnett b Fleetwood-Smith	30	c McCabe b Fleetwood-Smith		7
E.H.Smith	st Barnett b Fleetwood-Smith	1	st Barnett b Fleetwood-Smith		1
M.J.Combes	b White	9	b Ward		37
C.J.Sankey	run out (Fingleton)	2	c McCabe b Ward		6
C.L.Jeffery	c McCabe b Ward	2	(7) lbw b Fleetwood-Smith		11
J.N.W.Nicolson	c Fingleton b Fleetwood-Smith	0	(8) b White		4
†J.Gardiner	run out (Bradman/Barnett)	0	(9) b Waite		4
G.T.H.James	not out	19	(6) c McCabe b Fleetwood-Smith		24
J.I.Murfett	c & b Ward	15	c Ward b Waite		7
D.H.Thollar	st Barnett b Ward	0	not out		10
Extras	(b3, lb2)	5	(lb2)		2
Total	(39.0 overs, 134 mins)	112	(43.2 overs, 142 mins)		151

TASMANIA	O	M	R	W	w,nb		O	M	R	W	w,nb
Murfett	15	0	84	0	-,-		4	0	25	0	-,-
James	27	3	129	1	1,-		4	0	35	0	-,-
Thomas	12	0	63	2	-,-	(4)	9	1	57	1	-,-
Jeffery	9	0	55	0	-,1	(3)	4	0	12	0	-,-
Thollar	13	0	116	5	-,-		7	0	37	1	-,-
Nicolson	2	0	23	1	-,-		1	0	6	0	-,-

AUSTRALIAN XI	O	M	R	W	w,nb		O	M	R	W	w,nb
Waite	8	1	25	0	-,-		7.2	2	14	2	-,-
McCabe	4	1	17	0	-,-		4	1	6	0	-,-
Fleetwood-Smith	11	2	22	4	-,-		15	2	56	4	-,-
White	11	5	17	1	-,-	(5)	4	2	8	1	-,-
Ward	5	1	26	3	-,-	(4)	13	1	65	3	-,-

FALL OF WICKETS

Wkt	AUST 1st	TAS 1st	AUST 2nd	TAS 2nd
1st	38	45	88	13
2nd	138	51	121	25
3rd	189	70	126	76
4th	302	73	170	89
5th	340	73	-	90
6th	392	75	-	120
7th	457	75	-	125
8th	458	80	-	132
9th	472	112	-	134
10th	477	112	-	151

TASMANIA v AUSTRALIAN XI

Played at T.C.A. Ground, Hobart, on March 3, 4, 5, 1938. (Three-day match)
Toss : Australian XI.　　　　　Result : AUSTRALIAN XI WON BY 485 RUNS.
Debuts: Tasmania - C.J.G.Oakes (f/c).
12th Men: J.W.Rothwell (Tas) and A.L.Hassett (Aust).
Umpires: S.J.Alford and D.G.Hickman.
Attendances: 4889, 3235, 6239.　　　　Total: 14,363.　　　Receipts: £1076.
Close of Play: 1st day Aust 8/516 (White 27); 2nd day Aust (2) 0/72 (Fingleton 39, Brown 33).

The Australians were dismissed for 520 in the opening over of the second day, having maintained a scoring rate of almost 2 runs per minute. A sound start by Fingleton (47 in 82 minutes, 5 fours) and Brown (46 in 57 minutes, 5 fours) was followed by a third-wicket stand of 241 in just 98 minutes between Badcock (159 in 186 minutes, 19 fours) and Bradman (144 in 98 minutes, 3 sixes and 19 fours). Badcock gave a chance when 111 and Bradman one when 50, a caught-and-bowled to Oakes, before offering another shortly before his dismissal. Bradman hit his 3 sixes off consecutive balls from Putman (16 overs for 155 runs) and took a further 24 (6 fours) runs off an over from James. Chipperfield's 42 in 22 minutes included 1 six and 6 fours. Barnes (22) retired hurt at 3/407 when hit on the body by a rising ball from Murfett. He resumed at the start of the second day at 8/516, replacing O'Reilly who had fallen the previous evening, but did not add to his score. Putman (40 with 1 six and 4 fours) topscored for Tasmania, O'Reilly capturing match figures of 11 for 50. In the second innings Brown (108 in 137 minutes, 1 five and 12 fours) shared his third opening stand of more than 200 in as many matches for Australian sides against Tasmania, this time with Fingleton (109 in 132 minutes, 2 sixes, 1 five and 8 fours); Woodfull had been his partner in the previous instances in 1934. Sources: *NSWCA Report, TCA Report, The Herald, Melbourne Sun, Sydney Daily Telegraph, Hobart Mercury, Launceston Examiner.*

AUSTRALIAN XI

J.H.W.Fingleton	c Gardiner b Putman	47	c Jeffery b Thomas	109
W.A.Brown	c Gardiner b Putman	46	c James b Jeffery	108
C.L.Badcock	c & b Oakes	159		
*D.G.Bradman	b Jeffery	144		
S.G.Barnes	c & b James	22		
A.G.Chipperfield	c James b Oakes	42	(4) not out	9
M.G.Waite	lbw b James	0		
†B.A.Barnett	c Murfett b Putman	15		
E.C.S.White	not out	27		
W.J.O'Reilly	c Smith b Putman	3	(3) c Murfett b Thomas	14
L.O.Fleetwood-Smith	c Gardiner b James	4		
Extras	(b4, lb3, w4)	11		-
Total	(70.5 overs, 271 mins)	520	(40.2 overs, 151 mins) (3 wkts dec)	240

TASMANIA

*R.O.G.Morrisby	st Barnett b Fleetwood-Smith	17	b White	5
R.V.Thomas	lbw b O'Reilly	14	c Chipperfield b White	15
M.J.Combes	c Fingleton b Fleetwood-Smith	17	c Bradman b O'Reilly	1
S.W.L.Putman	b Fleetwood-Smith	40	c Bradman b O'Reilly	3
E.H.Smith	c Brown b O'Reilly	37	lbw b Fleetwood-Smith	5
G.T.H.James	c Chipperfield b Waite	24	lbw b O'Reilly	0
C.J.Sankey	b Waite	3	(8) lbw b Fleetwood-Smith	13
C.L.Jeffery	not out	15	(7) b O'Reilly	19
†J.Gardiner	b O'Reilly	0	c Fingleton b O'Reilly	7
J.I.Murfett	lbw b O'Reilly	6	c Badcock b O'Reilly	0
C.J.G.Oakes	b O'Reilly	3	not out	1
Extras	(b16, lb2)	18	(b10, lb2)	12
Total	(58.3 overs, 199 mins)	194	(20.6 overs, 87 mins)	81

TASMANIA	O	M	R	W	w,nb	O	M	R	W	w,nb		FALL OF WICKETS			
Oakes	16	0	98	2	4,-	12	0	61	0	-,-		AUST	TAS	AUST	TAS
James	15.5	1	86	3	-,-	14	1	61	0	-,-	Wkt	1st	1st	2nd	2nd
Putman	16	0	155	4	-,-	4	0	48	0	-,-	1st	74	27	214	24
Murfett	10	0	60	0	-,-	5	0	31	0	-,-	2nd	111	39	217	25
Thomas	4	0	47	0	-,-	3.2	0	25	2	-,-	3rd	352	97	240	27
Jeffery	9	1	63	1	-,-	2	0	14	1	-,-	4th	469	100	-	41
											5th	471	145	-	41
AUSTRALIAN XI	O	M	R	W	w,nb	O	M	R	W	w,nb	6th	473	153	-	42
Waite	15	4	38	2	-,-	4	1	11	0	-,-	7th	506	166	-	73
White	8	4	16	0	-,-	6	0	14	2	-,-	8th	516	166	-	73
O'Reilly	14.3	3	34	5	-,-	6.6	2	16	6	-,-	9th	516	188	-	80
Fleetwood-Smith	18	1	70	3	-,-	4	1	28	2	-,-	10th	520	194	-	81
Chipperfield	3	0	18	0	-,-										

WESTERN AUSTRALIA v AUSTRALIAN XI

Played at W.A.C.A. Ground, Perth, on March 18, 19, 21, 1938. (Three-day match)
Toss : Western Australia.   Result : AUSTRALIAN XI WON BY AN INNINGS AND 126 RUNS.
Debuts: Western Australia - M.O.Bessen, K.S.Jeffreys (both f/c).
12th Men: L.H.Bandy (WA) and M.G.Waite (Aust).
Umpires: F.R.Buttsworth and E.T.Tonkinson.
Attendances: 10200, 15000, very few.   Total: About 25,500.   Receipts: £1630.
Close of Play: 1st day Aust 2/120 (Bradman 68, McCabe 14); 2nd day WA (2) 6/60 (Alexander 18, Zimbulis 0).

Jeffreys made his debut for Western Australia at the age of 17 years 59 days. Eyres hit 24 (46064400) in one over from Ward; he batted 17 minutes in all with 5 fours and 2 sixes, adding 36 in 11 minutes with Halcombe for the tenth wicket. Bradman (122 minutes, 10 fours) and McCabe (140 minutes, 2 sixes and 15 fours) were involved in a partnership of 121 in 72 minutes. Heavy rain early on the last day raised prospects of an abandonment, but play began at 12.54pm. and in 17 minutes the match was concluded. The Australians departed on the *Orontes* at 7.30pm. Sources: *NSWCA Report, The West Australian, Daily News, WACA Scorebook*.

WESTERN AUSTRALIA

J.A.Jeffreys	lbw b O'Reilly	12		b Ward	14
F.J.Alexander	b Fleetwood-Smith	7	(3)	c Badcock b Fleetwood-Smith	18
J.A.Shea	lbw b O'Reilly	0	(2)	lbw b O'Reilly	17
*W.T.Rowlands	c O'Reilly b McCormick	22		lbw b O'Reilly	2
K.S.Jeffreys	c Ward b Fleetwood-Smith	14		st Walker b Ward	0
†O.I.Lovelock	c Bradman b McCormick	9		b O'Reilly	1
M.O.Bessen	b O'Reilly	39		c Walker b Fleetwood-Smith	1
A.G.Zimbulis	st Walker b Ward	33		c Brown b O'Reilly	1
G.A.Gardiner	b O'Reilly	0		not out	9
G.Eyres	b Ward	41		c Ward b O'Reilly	0
R.A.Halcombe	not out	2		c Chipperfield b Fleetwood-Smith	0
Extras	(b6, lb2, w1, nb4)	13		(b2, lb7, nb1)	10
Total	(44.6 overs, 182 mins)	192		(25.1 overs, 99 mins)	73

AUSTRALIAN XI

W.A.Brown	c Rowlands b Eyres	1
C.L.Badcock	b Zimbulis	34
*D.G.Bradman	st Lovelock b Zimbulis	102
S.J.McCabe	c Rowlands b Halcombe	122
A.L.Hassett	c J.A.Jeffreys b Zimbulis	29
A.G.Chipperfield	c Rowlands b Halcombe	42
†C.W.Walker	run out (Gardiner/Lovelock)	22
F.A.Ward	b Halcombe	11
W.J.O'Reilly	not out	3
E.L.McCormick	c Rowlands b Gardiner	0
L.O.Fleetwood-Smith	st Lovelock b Gardiner	4
Extras	(b10, lb10, nb1)	21
Total	(68.0 overs, 267 mins)	391

AUSTRALIAN XI	O	M	R	W	w,nb		O	M	R	W	w,nb
McCormick	8	0	22	2	-,3		4	0	14	0	-,1
McCabe	3	1	3	0	-,-		3	1	9	0	-,-
Fleetwood-Smith	13	2	44	2	1,-	(5)	2.1	0	5	3	-,-
O'Reilly	14	2	65	4	-,1		9	4	12	5	-,-
Ward	6.6	0	45	2	-,-	(3)	7	0	23	2	-,-

WESTERN AUSTRALIA	O	M	R	W	w,nb
Eyres	21	3	87	1	-,-
Gardiner	9	0	51	2	-,-
Zimbulis	22	0	160	3	-,-
Halcombe	10	0	43	3	-,1
Rowlands	3	0	15	0	-,-
K.S.Jeffreys	3	0	14	0	-,-

FALL OF WICKETS

Wkt	WA 1st	AUST 1st	WA 2nd
1st	24	2	38
2nd	24	68	38
3rd	24	189	41
4th	57	296	46
5th	76	307	47
6th	76	342	60
7th	142	379	61
8th	147	386	65
9th	156	387	69
10th	192	391	73

1938-39 SEASON (17 MATCHES)

Don Bradman's feat of scoring six centuries in successive innings in first-class matches transcended all else this season. The sequence began from South Australia's opening game and included scores of 118, 143, 225, 107, 186 and 135*, each in a separate match. Almost 18,000 people attended the Adelaide Oval on the second day of South Australia's clash with Victoria in February in the expectation of a seventh century, but Bradman was dismissed for 5. The sequence in Australia actually extended to eight centuries, as Bradman had scored 144 and 102 in his final two innings of 1937-38 prior to departing for England.

Bradman's performance in scoring 801 runs (average 160.20) in South Australia's six games naturally had a huge impact on the success of the side. South Australia won the Sheffield Shield, albeit by a single point from Victoria. The outcome hung in the balance until the last match between the teams, rain washing out the final two days and dashing Victoria's hopes. Victoria had removed Bradman cheaply and were heading for victory when the skies opened. Whitington, K.L.Ridings, Hamence and especially Badcock batted well in support of Bradman while Grimmett and Ward again bowled soundly throughout South Australia's campaign.

Victoria's batting lineup of Hassett, Gregory, Lee, Rigg, Sides and Barnett took on a formidable look this year, and they rarely failed. But the side relied too heavily on Fleetwood-Smith and McCormick to do the damage with the ball.

Queensland climbed off the bottom of the Shield table thanks to some improved performances and the failure of New South Wales to win a single match - for the first time in the history of the competition. Brown (990 runs) experienced a sensational Shield season for Queensland and Baker, Cook, Allen, Rogers and Don Tallon all chipped in to support him. New South Wales were severely handicapped by the loss for most of the season of McCabe (ill) and O'Reilly and Fingleton, who both took a temporary break. It was left to Barnes and Chipperfield to carry the batting. The bowling was devoid of penetration and this was the only season between 1907-08 and 1968-69 in which New South Wales finished on the bottom of the ladder.

Melbourne Cricket Club arranged a match between teams led by D.G.Bradman and K.E.Rigg to mark the centenary of the club's foundation. The Board of Control gave the match first-class status, despite the fact that it was arranged outside their jurisdiction.

Victorian sides visited Tasmania and Western Australia this season to provide them with their only opportunity for first-class matches. Western Australia more than held their own and achieved two creditable draws. Tasmania, however, were no match for Victoria.

Leading Aggregates

Batsmen	M	I	NO	Runs	HS	Ave.	Bowlers	Runs	Wkts	Ave.
W.A.Brown (Q)	7	11	1	1057	215	105.70	L.O.Fleetwood-Smith (V)	1192	30	39.73
A.L.Hassett (V)	9	15	2	967	211*	74.38	C.V.Grimmett (SA)	563	27	20.85
D.G.Bradman (SA)	7	7	1	919	225	153.16	F.A.Ward (SA)	845	24	35.20
S.G.Barnes (NSW)	7	14	0	650	121	46.42	E.L.McCormick (V)	857	24	35.70
K.E.Rigg (V)	9	14	0	549	84	39.21	R.B.Scott (V)	515	23	22.39
C.L.Badcock (SA)	7	8	3	540	271*	108.00	J.A.Ellis (Q)	591	21	28.14
R.G.Gregory (V)	7	13	0	538	77	41.38	C.P.Christ (Q)	777	20	38.85

SHEFFIELD SHIELD TABLE

	P	WO	W1	LO	L1	D	Pts	Quotient	Runs Scored	Wkts Lost	Runs Conceded	Wkts Taken
SOUTH AUSTRALIA	6	3	1	-	1	1	21	1.874	2727	48	3061	101
VICTORIA	6	3	1	1	-	1	20	0.969	3386	91	3033	79
QUEENSLAND	6	2	1	3	-	-	13	1.137	3260	83	3247	94
NEW SOUTH WALES	6	-	-	4	2	-	2	0.537	2918	114	2950	62
TOTAL	12	8	3	8	3	1	56	1.000	12291	336	12291	336

QUEENSLAND v NEW SOUTH WALES (Shield Match 1)

Played at Brisbane Cricket Ground (Woolloongabba) on November 25, 26, 28, 29. 1938. (Four-day match)
Toss : Queensland.   Result : MATCH DRAWN.
Debuts: Queensland - L.W.T.Tallon (f/c). New South Wales - R.V.James, V.W.McCaffrey, E.J.Minter, J.J.Murphy, C.G.Pepper (all f/c).
12th Men: C.G.R.Stibe (Qld) and D.K.Carmody (NSW).
Umpires: K.E.Fagg and J.A.Scott.
Attendances: 3200, 3468, 2552, 500.   Total: 9720.   Receipts: £611.
Close of Play: 1st day Qld 4/288 (Cook 31, Baker 41); 2nd day Qld 8/495 (L.W.T.Tallon 0, Hansen 21); 3rd day NSW (2) 4/122
    (Barnes 75, O'Brien 3).

The last pair of Pepper and Murphy held out for 23 minutes to save the match after the loss of Fitzpatrick and McCabe to the third and fifth balls of the opening over of New South Wales's second innings. Barnes (121 in 214 minutes, 1 six and 11 fours) topscored. In the first innings Fitzpatrick (61 in 188 minutes, 3 fours), McCabe (35 in 42 minutes, 3 fours) and Barnes (38 in 53 minutes, 3 fours) were the only batsmen to get started, Christ (left-arm orthodox) taking a career-best 5 for 47 in the middle order. Brown (84 in 205 minutes, 8 fours) was run out at the non-striker's end when a D.Tallon straight drive was deflected by the bowler into the stumps; Rogers (55 in 108 minutes, 5 fours) had added 100 with him for the Queensland first wicket. Cook (82 in 243 minutes, 5 fours) and Baker (157 in 274 minutes, 18 fours) shared a stand of 210 runs, a new Queensland fifth-wicket record. Don Tallon completed eight dismissals and did even better in the next match between the teams with 12. Sources: *Wisden, NSWCA Report, QCA Report, The Herald, Sydney Morning Herald, NSWCA Scorebook, Brisbane Courier-Mail, The Sporting Globe.*

QUEENSLAND

*W.A.Brown	run out (White)	84
R.E.Rogers	c Minter b James	55
T.Allen	c Barnes b McCabe	31
†D.Tallon	c Easton b Murphy	36
G.G.Cook	c James b Murphy	82
G.W.Baker	b Barnes	157
M.S.Guttormsen	b Barnes	6
C.D.Hansen	c Easton b O'Brien	24
P.L.Dixon	c Easton b Barnes	5
L.W.T.Tallon	not out	3
C.P.Christ	c McCabe b Murphy	0
Extras	(b11, lb4, nb3)	18
Total	(141.3 overs, 521 mins)	501

NEW SOUTH WALES

J.H.Fitzpatrick	c D.Tallon b Cook	61	(2) c Cook b Dixon	0
*S.J.McCabe	c Christ b Dixon	35	(1) c Rogers b Dixon	1
V.W.McCaffrey	c Guttormsen b Cook	4	c Rogers b L.W.T.Tallon	27
S.G.Barnes	c Baker b Christ	38	c D.Tallon b Cook	121
E.J.Minter	c D.Tallon b Christ	0	(7) c Guttormsen b Cook	33
R.V.James	st D.Tallon b Christ	8	(8) c Brown b Christ	31
†F.A.Easton	c D.Tallon b Christ	0	(9) c Rogers b L.W.T.Tallon	16
C.G.Pepper	st D.Tallon b Christ	3	(10) not out	26
E.C.S.White	run out	12	(5) st D.Tallon b L.W.T.Tallon	13
L.J.O'Brien	st D.Tallon b L.W.T.Tallon	3	(6) b Christ	19
J.J.Murphy	not out	2	not out	8
Extras	(lb4, nb1)	5	(b4, lb2, nb2)	8
Total	(50.2 overs, 191 mins)	171	(84.2 overs, 307 mins) (9 wkts)	303

NEW SOUTH WALES	O	M	R	W	w,nb
O'Brien	24	1	81	1	-,3
Murphy	34.3	2	143	3	-,-
White	31	6	67	0	-,-
Pepper	14	0	72	0	-,-
James	16	3	65	1	-,-
McCabe	12	1	26	1	-,-
Barnes	10	2	29	3	-,-

QUEENSLAND	O	M	R	W	w,nb	O	M	R	W	w,nb
Dixon	12	1	48	1	-,-	20.2	2	80	2	-,2
Cook	11	1	37	2	-,1	17	2	63	2	-,-
Christ	17	3	47	5	-,-	24	6	56	2	-,-
L.W.T.Tallon	10.2	2	34	1	-,-	18	1	84	3	-,-
Baker						3	0	5	0	-,-
Rogers						2	0	7	0	-,-

FALL OF WICKETS

Wkt	QLD 1st	NSW 1st	NSW 2nd
1st	100	54	1
2nd	176	63	2
3rd	189	123	93
4th	228	123	119
5th	438	133	161
6th	456	133	207
7th	473	143	224
8th	495	165	261
9th	501	169	277
10th	501	171	-

D.G.BRADMAN'S XI v K.E.RIGG'S XI

Played at Melbourne Cricket Ground on December 9, 10, 12, 13, 1938. (Four-day match)
Toss : Rigg's XI.　　　　　　　　　Result : MATCH DRAWN.
Debuts: Nil.
12th Men: W.E.Pearson (both sides).
Umpires: A.N.Barlow and G.A.Browne.
Attendances: 5608, 15023, 4090, 1199.　　　Total: 25,920.　　　Receipts: £1218.
Close of Play: 1st day Rigg 4/151 (Barnes 51, Bromley 3); 2nd day Bradman 2/220 (Bradman 83, McCabe 39); 3rd day Rigg 0/23 (Rigg 12, Lee 10).

Arranged to mark Melbourne Cricket Club's Centenary and referred to in the newspapers as Australia v The Rest, this match was played between a team of tourists to England led by Bradman and a Victorian-based side which included New South Welshman Barnes (who had also toured England), Queenslanders Christ and Tallon, and Eyres from Western Australia. Bradman (118 in 218 minutes, 12 fours) and McCabe (105 in 140 minutes, 11 fours) shared a stand of 163 for the third wicket, with Brown (67 in 149 minutes, 7 fours) and Badcock (51 not out in 99 minutes, 5 fours) scoring half-centuries for Bradman's XI. Rigg (48 in 100 minutes, 6 fours and 71 in 129 minutes, 7 fours), Barnes (63 in 118 minutes, 7 fours), Ledward (85 in 107 minutes, 9 fours) and Sievers (44 not out in 28 minutes, 9 fours) scored freely for Rigg's XI. *Wisden* incorrectly gives Rigg (1) Fleetwood-Smith 2/79; Rigg (2) Bradman 1 over. Sources: *Wisden, VCA Report, The Age, The Argus, The Herald, Melbourne Sun, The Sporting Globe.*

RIGG'S XI

*K.E.Rigg	lbw b Fleetwood-Smith	48		c Hassett b O'Reilly	71
I.S.Lee	run out (Brown)	12		st Barnett b Fleetwood-Smith	27
R.G.Gregory	lbw b Fleetwood-Smith	14		lbw b Fleetwood-Smith	32
J.A.Ledward	lbw b O'Reilly	11	(5)	c sub (W.E.Pearson) b Fingleton	85
S.G.Barnes	lbw b O'Reilly	63	(4)	lbw b Waite	4
E.H.Bromley	c Brown b Fleetwood-Smith	34		b O'Reilly	17
†D.Tallon	c McCabe b O'Reilly	7		b Hassett	23
M.W.Sievers	lbw b O'Reilly	0		not out	44
L.E.Nagel	b Fleetwood-Smith	6		b Bradman	11
G.Eyres	c & b O'Reilly	1			
C.P.Christ	not out	6			
Extras	(b6, lb2, w4, nb1)	13		(b3, lb4, nb3)	10
Total	(56.5 overs, 235 mins)	215		(71.1 overs, 260 mins) (8 wkts)	324

BRADMAN'S XI

J.H.W.Fingleton	c Sievers b Eyres	23
W.A.Brown	c & b Christ	67
*D.G.Bradman	b Nagel	118
S.J.McCabe	c Lee b Nagel	105
A.L.Hassett	run out (Bromley/Tallon)	12
C.L.Badcock	not out	51
M.G.Waite	b Sievers	28
†B.A.Barnett	lbw b Sievers	0
W.J.O'Reilly	c Christ b Bromley	0
L.O.Fleetwood-Smith	b Sievers	2
E.L.McCormick	c Gregory b Bromley	3
Extras	(b11, lb6)	17
Total	(108.7 overs, 392 mins)	426

BRADMAN'S XI	O	M	R	W	w,nb	O	M	R	W	w,nb
McCormick	10	0	39	0	-,1	14	0	58	0	-,3
Waite	7	2	9	0	-,-	13	2	47	1	-,-
O'Reilly	18.5	2	75	5	4,-	18	2	54	2	-,-
Fleetwood-Smith	21	2	79	4	-,-	19	2	93	2	-,-
Hassett						3	0	26	1	-,-
Fingleton						2	0	18	1	-,-
Brown						1	0	8	0	-,-
Badcock						1	0	10	0	-,-
Bradman						0.1	0	0	1	-,-

RIGG'S XI	O	M	R	W	w,nb
Eyres	23	2	81	1	-,-
Sievers	15	3	53	3	-,-
Nagel	26	4	93	2	-,-
Christ	29	4	104	1	-,-
Bromley	11.7	0	53	2	-,-
Barnes	1	1	0	0	-,-
Gregory	3	0	25	0	-,-

FALL OF WICKETS

Wkt	R 1st	B 1st	R 2nd
1st	35	48	74
2nd	63	138	116
3rd	79	301	123
4th	112	332	178
5th	177	353	207
6th	201	409	257
7th	201	409	305
8th	203	412	324
9th	209	419	-
10th	215	426	-

VICTORIA v QUEENSLAND (Shield Match 2)

Played at Melbourne Cricket Ground on December 16, 17, 19, 20, 1938. (Four-day match)
Toss : Queensland.   Result : VICTORIA WON BY THREE WICKETS.
Debuts: Queensland - J.A.Ellis (f/c).
12th Men: W.E.Pearson (Vic) and C.D.Hansen (Qld).
Umpires: A.N.Barlow and G.A.Browne.
Attendances: 2813, 5583, 2069, 1981.   Total: 12,446.   Receipts: £391.
Close of Play: 1st day Vic 1/55 (Rigg 29, Gregory 19); 2nd day Qld (2) 0/35 (Brown 10, Rogers 22); 3rd day Qld (2) 3/405 (Allen 121, Cook 43).

Victoria accepted a challenge to score 319 in four hours on the last day and secured victory with 11 minutes to spare, Barnett hitting the winning boundary. Rigg (49 in 47 minutes, 6 fours), Lee (34 in 71 minutes, 3 fours), Gregory (77 in 128 minutes, 2 fours), Hassett (73 in 199 minutes, 7 fours) and Ledward (44 in 47 minutes, 5 fours) had all played a part in the chase. On the first day Brown (61 in 125 minutes, 6 fours) and Rogers (41 in 61 minutes, 5 fours) had opened the game with a 70-run partnership. Victoria took a first-innings lead through Gregory (53 in 128 minutes, 2 fours), Hassett (104 in 199 minutes, 7 fours) and Sides (42 in 81 minutes, 1 six and 2 fours), magnified by a last-wicket stand of 95 between Sievers (67 not out in 72 minutes, 10 fours) and McCormick. Brown (99 in 223 minutes, 8 fours) and Rogers (104 in 167 minutes, 10 fours) added 181 for the first wicket in Queensland's second innings, Allen (136 in 204 minutes, 18 fours) and Cook (58 in 142 minutes, 5 fours) adding a further 142 for the fourth wicket. Baker (51 not out in 56 minutes, 7 fours) also contributed. Sources: *Wisden, VCA Report, QCA Report, The Age, The Argus, The Herald, Melbourne Sun, The Sporting Globe.*

QUEENSLAND

*W.A.Brown	lbw b Fleetwood-Smith	61	c sub (W.E.Pearson) b McCormick		99
R.E.Rogers	c Sievers b Fleetwood-Smith	41	lbw b Bromley		104
T.Allen	b Fleetwood-Smith	2	c Barnett b McCormick		136
†D.Tallon	b McCormick	7	b Fleetwood-Smith		19
G.G.Cook	b Bromley	12	c Hassett b McCormick		58
G.W.Baker	b Fleetwood-Smith	7	not out		51
M.S.Guttormsen	lbw b Fleetwood-Smith	4	not out		23
P.L.Dixon	c Barnett b Fleetwood-Smith	0			
L.W.T.Tallon	b McCormick	36			
J.A.Ellis	b Sievers	4			
C.P.Christ	not out	4			
Extras	(b2, lb3, nb1)	6	(b14, lb3, w1, nb2)		20
Total	(54.4 overs, 224 mins)	184	(110.0 overs, 431 mins) (5 wkts dec)		510

VICTORIA

*K.E.Rigg	b Ellis	36	lbw b Dixon		49
I.S.Lee	run out (Dixon/Christ)	7	b Dixon		34
R.G.Gregory	c D.Tallon b Ellis	53	lbw b Ellis		77
A.L.Hassett	c Dixon b Ellis	104	c & b Dixon		73
J.A.Ledward	c D.Tallon b Ellis	8	(7) c Guttormsen b Christ		44
F.W.Sides	lbw b Cook	42	(5) b Dixon		5
E.H.Bromley	b Cook	0	(6) run out (Baker/Ellis)		4
†B.A.Barnett	c & b Cook	21	not out		24
M.W.Sievers	not out	67	not out		0
L.O.Fleetwood-Smith	c Brown b Ellis	0			
E.L.McCormick	b Christ	29			
Extras	(b6, lb2, nb1)	9	(b5, lb4, w3)		12
Total	(98.7 overs, 374 mins)	376	(56.3 overs, 230 mins) (7 wkts)		322

VICTORIA	O	M	R	W	w,nb		O	M	R	W	w,nb
McCormick	11.4	1	47	2	-,1		22	0	125	3	1,2
Sievers	15	2	44	1	-,-		28	2	92	0	-,-
Fleetwood-Smith	20	3	58	6	-,-		20	1	73	1	-,-
Bromley	8	2	29	1	-,-	(5)	24	4	114	1	-,-
Ledward						(4)	10	1	49	0	-,-
Gregory							6	0	37	0	-,-

QUEENSLAND	O	M	R	W	w,nb		O	M	R	W	w,nb
Ellis	25	2	104	5	-,-		14	0	101	1	-,-
Cook	16	2	67	3	-,-		7	1	26	0	1,-
Dixon	10	1	53	0	-,1	(4)	11.3	0	67	4	-,-
Christ	29.7	12	47	1	-,-	(3)	19	1	90	1	-,-
L.W.T.Tallon	18	0	96	0	-,-						
Rogers						(5)	5	0	26	0	2,-

FALL OF WICKETS

Wkt	QLD 1st	VIC 1st	QLD 2nd	VIC 2nd
1st	70	28	181	77
2nd	88	64	250	90
3rd	105	130	281	219
4th	118	142	423	233
5th	126	236	454	242
6th	134	236	-	264
7th	138	278	-	318
8th	156	281	-	-
9th	161	281	-	-
10th	184	376	-	-

AFCM No. 924/86
SSM No. 320/83

SOUTH AUSTRALIA v NEW SOUTH WALES (Shield Match 3)

Played at Adelaide Oval on December 16, 17, 19, 20, 1938. (Four-day match)
Toss : South Australia.   Result : SOUTH AUSTRALIA WON BY AN INNINGS AND 55 RUNS.
Debuts: South Australia - K.L.Ridings (f/c).
12th Men: P.L.Ridings (SA) and V.W.McCaffrey (NSW).
Umpires: A.G.Jenkins and J.D.Scott.
Attendances: No daily figures published.   Total: 9310.   Receipts: £398.
Close of Play: 1st day SA 3/353 (Badcock 130, Hamence 47); 2nd day NSW 0/40 (Fitzpatrick 22, Cheetham 16); 3rd day NSW 6/346
    (Chipperfield 149, Easton 16).

S.J.McCabe was unable to lead New South Wales because of illness: he had contracted gastric influenza in Melbourne during the Bradman-Rigg M.C.C. Centenary match and was restricted to club cricket for the rest of the season. Murphy dismissed Whitington with the first ball of the match but a recovery led by Bradman (143 in 230 minutes, 11 fours and 91 singles), Badcock (271 not out in 495 minutes, 2 sixes and 17 fours) and Hamence (90 in 214 minutes, 8 fours) gave South Australia their first 600 total against New South Wales. Bradman scored 98 runs (39* to 137*) in the lunch-tea session on the first day when the temperature reached 103° F (39.5°C). Barnes (117 in 215 minutes, 11 fours) and Chipperfield (154 in 286 minutes, 19 fours) added 185 in 184 minutes for the New South Wales fifth wicket. *Wisden* and *NSWCA Report* incorrectly give NSW (1) extras 4, total 389. Sources: *Wisden, NSWCA Report, SACA Report, The Herald, NSWCA Scorebook, Adelaide Advertiser, The News.*

SOUTH AUSTRALIA

R.S.Whitington	c James b Murphy	0
K.L.Ridings	b O'Reilly	31
*D.G.Bradman	b Murphy	143
C.L.Badcock	not out	271
R.A.Hamence	c Barnes b Fitzpatrick	90
†C.W.Walker	lbw b O'Reilly	0
M.G.Waite	run out (Solomon/White)	21
F.A.Ward	b Barnes	0
C.V.Grimmett	run out (Barnes/Fingleton)	35
J.A.Scott	) did not bat	
H.N.J.Cotton	)	
Extras	(b3, lb4, nb2)	9
Total	(151.5 overs, 590 mins) (8 wkts dec)	600

NEW SOUTH WALES

J.H.Fitzpatrick	b Grimmett	23		b Cotton	5
A.G.Cheetham	st Walker b Grimmett	27		c Cotton b Scott	9
C.M.Solomon	c Walker b Grimmett	1		c & b Grimmett	13
S.G.Barnes	b Cotton	117		c Whitington b Ward	28
*J.H.W.Fingleton	c Walker b Scott	0	(6)	c Ward b Grimmett	3
A.G.Chipperfield	c Walker b Cotton	154	(5)	lbw b Ward	13
R.V.James	lbw b Grimmett	9	(8)	lbw b Grimmett	42
†F.A.Easton	c Walker b Grimmett	17	(10)	not out	7
E.C.S.White	lbw b Grimmett	14	(7)	c & b Ward	21
W.J.O'Reilly	lbw b Grimmett	20	(9)	c Bradman b Ward	7
J.J.Murphy	not out	3		c Badcock b Grimmett	4
Extras	(b1, lb1, nb3)	5		(b1, lb2)	3
Total	(123.6 overs, 399 mins)	390		(44.7 overs, 159 mins)	155

NEW SOUTH WALES	O	M	R	W	w,nb
Murphy	32	1	126	2	-,-
Cheetham	20	1	85	0	-,-
O'Reilly	36	9	99	2	-,2
White	28	1	103	0	-,-
Chipperfield	8	0	60	0	-,-
Barnes	15	2	62	1	-,-
James	1	0	13	0	-,-
Fitzpatrick	11	0	40	1	-,-
Fingleton	0.5	0	3	0	-,-

SOUTH AUSTRALIA	O	M	R	W	w,nb		O	M	R	W	w,nb
Cotton	23	1	76	2	-,2		6	0	24	1	-,-
Waite	15	3	37	0	-,1		5	0	17	0	-,-
Ward	20	2	81	0	-,-	(5)	14	3	40	4	-,-
Scott	29	10	75	1	-,-	(3)	5	1	12	1	-,-
Grimmett	36.6	11	116	7	-,-	(4)	14.7	1	59	4	-,-

FALL OF WICKETS

		SA	NSW	NSW
Wkt		1st	1st	2nd
1st		0	43	8
2nd		67	45	21
3rd		242	66	49
4th		445	67	59
5th		446	252	74
6th		512	288	76
7th		514	350	120
8th		600	356	134
9th		-	379	149
10th		-	390	155

VICTORIA v NEW SOUTH WALES (Shield Match 4)

Played at Melbourne Cricket Ground on December 23, 24, 26, 27, 1938. (Four-day match)
Toss : New South Wales.   Result : VICTORIA WON BY FOUR WICKETS.
Debuts: Victoria - D.T.Ring (f/c).
12th Men: E.H.Bromley (Vic) and R.V.James (NSW).
Umpires: A.N.Barlow and G.A.Browne.
Attendances: 3891, 9232, 8197, 7268.   Total: 28,588.   Receipts: £1003.
Close of Play: 1st day Vic 0/9 (Rigg 8, Lee 0); 2nd day Vic 3/348 (Hassett 40, Ledward 13); 3rd day NSW (2) 3/215 (Chipperfield 72, Solomon 17).

Fleetwood-Smith (10 for 244) and O'Reilly (10 for 212) dominated the wicket-taking. Fingleton (45 in 132 minutes, 4 fours), Cheetham (42 in 131 minutes, 5 fours), Chipperfield (66 in 82 minutes, 7 fours) and O'Reilly (47 in 42 minutes, 5 fours) topscored in the first innings and Barnes (98 in 109 minutes, 10 fours), Chipperfield again (73 in 127 minutes, 4 fours) and Solomon (99 in 102 minutes, 15 fours) did so in the second innings for New South Wales. Rigg (84 in 171 minutes, 8 fours) and Lee (121 in 255 minutes, 15 fours) gave Victoria an opening stand of 171, Gregory (71 in 122 minutes, 3 fours), Hassett (56 in 108 minutes, 5 fours) and Sides (53 not out in 115 minutes, 5 fours) capitalising with fifties. The winning runs came with 26 minutes to spare on the last afternoon, Sievers (48 in 81 minutes, 5 fours) and Sides (43 in 53 minutes, 5 fours) the chief run-getters. Hassett was out to the first ball he faced. Sources: *Wisden, NSWCA Report, VCA Report, The Age, The Argus, The Herald, Melbourne Sun.*

NEW SOUTH WALES

*J.H.W.Fingleton	c Ledward b Fleetwood-Smith	45	(6)	b McCormick	10
J.H.Fitzpatrick	c Ledward b McCormick	5	(1)	c Sides b Ring	16
A.G.Cheetham	b Fleetwood-Smith	42	(2)	b Fleetwood-Smith	8
S.G.Barnes	c Sides b Ring	16	(3)	c McCormick b Fleetwood-Smith	98
A.G.Chipperfield	c & b McCormick	66	(4)	lbw b Fleetwood-Smith	73
C.M.Solomon	c Hassett b McCormick	30	(5)	st Barnett b Ring	99
V.W.McCaffrey	b McCormick	5		c Ring b Fleetwood-Smith	18
†F.A.Easton	b McCormick	7		c Ledward b Fleetwood-Smith	2
E.C.S.White	not out	14		not out	38
W.J.O'Reilly	c Sievers b Fleetwood-Smith	47		b Fleetwood-Smith	0
J.J.Murphy	st Barnett b Ring	8		c Hassett b Fleetwood-Smith	10
Extras	(b4, lb3, nb2)	9		(b10, lb4, nb2)	16
Total	(72.4 overs, 304 mins)	294		(76.4 overs, 309 mins)	388

VICTORIA

*K.E.Rigg	b O'Reilly	84			
I.S.Lee	c Barnes b Cheetham	121	(1)	c Easton b O'Reilly	37
R.G.Gregory	lbw b White	71		c White b Barnes	5
A.L.Hassett	c Easton b O'Reilly	56		lbw b O'Reilly	0
J.A.Ledward	c Barnes b Fitzpatrick	37		c White b O'Reilly	27
F.W.Sides	not out	53		c Cheetham b White	43
*B.A.Barnett	c Barnes b Fitzpatrick	7		not out	9
M.W.Sievers	lbw b O'Reilly	33	(2)	c Fitzpatrick b O'Reilly	48
D.T.Ring	c Chipperfield b O'Reilly	15	(8)	not out	4
E.L.McCormick	c & b O'Reilly	5			
L.O.Fleetwood-Smith	b O'Reilly	0			
Extras	(b9, lb10, nb3)	22		(b2, lb3, nb1)	6
Total	(123.2 overs, 482 mins)	504		(35.0 overs, 143 mins) (6 wkts)	179

VICTORIA	O	M	R	W	w,nb		O	M	R	W	w,nb
McCormick	17	0	62	5	-,2		15	0	71	1	-,2
Sievers	18	5	54	0	-,-		14	0	61	0	-,-
Ledward	1	0	4	0	-,-						
Fleetwood-Smith	22	0	100	3	-,-	(3)	26.4	1	144	7	-,-
Ring	14.4	1	65	2	-,-	(4)	21	2	96	2	-,-

NEW SOUTH WALES	O	M	R	W	w,nb		O	M	R	W	w,nb
Murphy	22	1	84	0	-,-		6	1	31	0	-,-
O'Reilly	43.2	7	152	6	-,2	(3)	13	0	60	4	-,1
Cheetham	15	0	89	1	-,1	(2)	6	0	24	0	-,-
Fitzpatrick	10	1	47	2	-,-	(5)	1	0	5	0	-,-
Barnes	17	1	50	0	-,-	(4)	5	0	32	1	-,-
White	15	4	57	1	-,-		4	0	21	1	-,-
Chipperfield	1	0	3	0	-,-						

FALL OF WICKETS

Wkt	NSW 1st	VIC 1st	NSW 2nd	VIC 2nd
1st	9	171	24	86
2nd	93	269	28	95
3rd	112	317	187	95
4th	114	385	221	95
5th	210	391	283	150
6th	212	421	332	175
7th	220	472	333	-
8th	228	498	338	-
9th	285	504	358	-
10th	294	504	388	-

SOUTH AUSTRALIA v QUEENSLAND (Shield Match 5)

Played at Adelaide Oval on December 24, 26, 27, 28, 1938. (Four-day match)
Toss : Queensland.   Result : SOUTH AUSTRALIA WON BY AN INNINGS AND 20 RUNS.
Debuts: Nil.
12th Men: P.L.Ridings (SA) and P.L.Dixon (Qld).
Umpires: A.G.Jenkins and J.D.Scott.
Attendances: 6694, 8000, 1500, ? .   Total: 16,300.   Receipts: £698.
Close of Play: 1st day SA 2/134 (Bradman 83, Badcock 79); 2nd day Qld (2) 0/0 (Brown 0, Rogers 0); 3rd day Qld (2) 4/152 (Brown 91, Cook 16).

Grimmett swept aside the Queensland batting on the first day, taking the last 3 for 0 in seven balls. Bradman (225 in 329 minutes, 15 fours, chance at 146 and 156) and Badcock (chanceless 100 in 151 minutes, 7 fours) added 202 for the third wicket after the early loss of both openers. Badcock was out next ball after reaching his century to end a sequence of 422 runs without dismissal in the season to date. Waite (52 in 148 minutes, 5 fours) added 131 for the fifth wicket with Bradman. Christ (slow left-arm) bowled splendidly, his figures in no way reflecting the value of his performance. Baker captured three wickets in five balls, all clean bowled, to end the innings. A light appeal was upheld before a ball could be bowled in the Queensland second innings and rain prevented play on the following day before 2.30pm. Rogers, having been dismissed in the second over of the first innings, fell in the first over of the second. Brown (chanceless 174 in 351 minutes, 10 fours) survived a close call on 27, when he played a ball onto his wicket without dislodging the bails, and went on to carry his bat. Baker (43 in 96 minutes, 3 fours) and Cook in both innings (34 not out in 103 minutes, 1 four and 35 in 112 minutes, 1 five and 1 four) put up resistance in the middle order. Players of both sides wore black armbands on the first day and flags were flown at half-mast out of respect for Albert Wright, former South Australian player and Adelaide Oval curator, who died the previous day. Sources: *Wisden, QCA Report, SACA Report, The Herald, Adelaide Advertiser, The News, The Sporting Globe.*

QUEENSLAND

*W.A.Brown	c Walker b Scott	12		not out	174
R.E.Rogers	c Walker b Waite	0		c Bradman b Cotton	2
T.Allen	b Grimmett	21		lbw b Ward	16
†D.Tallon	b Grimmett	6	(5)	b Cotton	11
G.G.Cook	not out	34	(6)	b Grimmett	35
G.W.Baker	lbw b Grimmett	22	(7)	st Walker b Ward	43
C.D.Hansen	run out (Waite/Walker)	12	(4)	run out (Cotton/Walker)	11
M.S.Guttormsen	c Ridings b Ward	8		run out (Whitington)	7
L.W.T.Tallon	b Grimmett	6		lbw b Grimmett	0
J.A.Ellis	lbw b Grimmett	0		b Grimmett	0
C.P.Christ	st Walker b Grimmett	0		st Walker b Ward	0
Extras	(b1, lb3, nb6)	10		(b10, lb1, w1)	12
Total	(41.7 overs, 160 mins)	131		(108.4 overs, 351 mins)	311

SOUTH AUSTRALIA

R.S.Whitington	st D.Tallon b Cook	11
K.L.Ridings	c D.Tallon b Ellis	7
*D.G.Bradman	c Baker b Christ	225
C.L.Badcock	c L.W.T.Tallon b Ellis	100
R.A.Hamence	c & b L.W.T.Tallon	17
M.G.Waite	c Guttormsen b Cook	52
†C.W.Walker	b Baker	32
F.A.Ward	run out	9
C.V.Grimmett	not out	0
H.N.J.Cotton	b Baker	0
J.A.Scott	b Baker	0
Extras	(b5, lb3, w1)	9
Total	(120.5 overs, 431 mins)	462

SOUTH AUSTRALIA	O	M	R	W	w,nb		O	M	R	W	w,nb		FALL OF WICKETS		
Cotton	10	1	51	0	-,6		18	2	62	2	1,-			QLD	SA	QLD
Waite	4	0	9	1	-,-		9	1	20	0	-,-	Wkt	1st	1st	2nd
Scott	7	3	11	1	-,-	(5)	9	7	15	0	-,-	1st	4	17	3
Grimmett	14.7	2	33	6	-,-		34	3	96	3	-,-	2nd	28	23	53
Ward	6	0	17	1	-,-	(3)	38.4	8	106	3	-,-	3rd	41	225	73
												4th	46	274	98
QUEENSLAND	O	M	R	W	w,nb							5th	82	405	206
Ellis	26	0	87	2	-,-							6th	105	426	301
Cook	25	2	85	2	-,-							7th	118	456	310
Christ	33	3	102	1	-,-							8th	131	462	310
Baker	8.5	0	36	3	1,-							9th	131	462	310
L.W.T.Tallon	18	1	90	1	-,-							10th	131	462	311
Allen	2	0	11	0	-,-										
Rogers	8	1	42	0	-,-										

TASMANIA v VICTORIA

Played at N.T.C.A. Ground, Launceston, on December 26, 27 (no play), 28, 1938. (Three-day match)
Toss : Victoria.   Result : MATCH DRAWN.
Debuts: Victoria - D.H.Fothergill (f/c).
12th Men: J.N.W.Nicolson (Tas) and R.A.Dempster (Vic).
Umpires: M.Conway and H.Sayer.
Attendances & Receipts: No figures published.
Close of Play: 1st day Vic 9/437 (Beames 226, Scott 13); 2nd day no play.

Beames (career-best 226 not out in 215 minutes, 1 six and 28 fours) was given out lbw when 93 but received a generous recall from the Tasmanian captain Morrisby, who told the umpire that Beames had hit the ball. Taking the attitude that all runs were now a bonus, the batsman hit out and raced from 100 to 200 (193 minutes) in just 60 minutes; he progressed from 39 at lunch on the first day to 122 at tea and scored a further 104 in the final session, adding an unbroken 90 in 40 minutes with Scott, a tenth-wicket record for Victoria in this series. Oakley (60 in 75 minutes, 9 fours) had opened well for his side. Steady rain prevented any play on the second day and Oakley declared before play got under way on the third. Scott bowled Morrisby with the fifth ball of the innings and Jeffrey (46 in 95 minutes), Pearsall (43 in 188 minutes) and Gardiner (65 in 65 minutes, 1 six and 11 fours), though failing to avert the follow-on had Victoria insisted, batted sufficiently long to ensure a draw. *VCA Report* gives Vic (1) 3/94, 4/138; Tas 7/224, 9/255. Sources: *VCA Report, TCA Report, Launceston Examiner, Hobart Mercury.*

VICTORIA

*H.H.Oakley	hit wkt b Putman	60		
H.Dowsley	lbw b Murfett	16		
K.R.Miller	st Gardiner b Putman	4	(1) not out	7
D.H.Fothergill	c Putman b Oakes	39		
P.J.Beames	not out	226		
I.W.Johnson	lbw b Pearsall	23		
D.J.A.Fitzmaurice	c Putman b Murfett	22	(3) not out	8
†E.A.Baker	c Putman b Jeffrey	3	(2) b Oakes	0
G.S.Meikle	lbw b Putman	28		
F.L.O.Thorn	b Oakes	0		
R.B.Scott	not out	13		
Extras	(b1, lb2)	3		–
Total	(66.0 overs, 292 mins) (9 wkts dec)	437	(6.0 overs, 22 mins) (1 wkt)	15

TASMANIA

*R.O.G.Morrisby	b Scott	4
R.V.Thomas	b Scott	15
E.H.Smith	c Scott b Dowsley	7
M.J.Combes	b Johnson	28
S.W.L.Putman	c Miller b Thorn	9
C.L.Jeffrey	lbw b Scott	46
A.L.Pearsall	lbw b Thorn	43
†J.Gardiner	b Fitzmaurice	64
J.I.Murfett	hit wkt b Scott	20
D.H.Thollar	not out	8
C.J.G.Oakes	lbw b Scott	2
Extras	(b8, lb1, nb3)	12
Total	(67.0 overs, 266 mins)	258

TASMANIA	O	M	R	W	w,nb		O	M	R	W	w,nb
Oakes	15	0	102	2	-,-	(2)	2	0	6	1	-,-
Thomas	8	1	62	0	-,-	(1)	3	1	7	0	-,-
Putman	17	0	106	3	-,-						
Murfett	7	0	54	2	-,-	(3)	1	0	2	0	-,-
Thollar	8	0	44	0	-,-						
Pearsall	6	0	34	1	-,-						
Jeffrey	5	0	32	1	-,-						

VICTORIA	O	M	R	W	w,nb
Scott	21	2	62	5	-,2
Dowsley	5	0	26	1	-,1
Thorn	15	2	44	2	-,-
Meikle	12	0	58	0	-,-
Johnson	8	1	21	1	-,-
Fitzmaurice	6	0	35	1	-,-

FALL OF WICKETS

Wkt	VIC 1st	TAS 1st	VIC 2nd
1st	61	5	2
2nd	76	28	-
3rd	99	28	-
4th	139	47	-
5th	188	90	-
6th	260	133	-
7th	265	223	-
8th	342	242	-
9th	347	256	-
10th	-	258	-

AFCM No. 928/96
SSM No. 323/83

VICTORIA v SOUTH AUSTRALIA (Shield Match 6)

Played at Melbourne Cricket Ground on December 30, 31, 1938, January 2, 3, 1939. (Four-day match)
Toss : Victoria.   Result : MATCH DRAWN.
Debuts: Nil.
12th Men: E.H.Bromley (Vic) and E.J.R.Moyle (SA).
Umpires: A.N.Barlow and G.A.Browne.
Attendances: 16706, 28637, 16542, 4843.   Total: 66,728.   Receipts: £2897.
Close of Play: 1st day Vic 7/363 (Hassett 151, Ring 19); 2nd day SA 4/240 (Walker 4, Ward 0); 3rd day Vic (2) 0/16 (Lee 6, Barnett 8).

Both captains, Rigg (groin strain) and Bradman (laryngitis) were absent on the last two days, wicket-keepers Barnett and Walker controlling the match in their absence. As Grimmett was also absent (leg strain sustained while batting) both 12th men fielded in Victoria's second innings, Bromley catching a team-mate. Hassett (211 not out in 355 minutes, 17 fours) led the Victorian batting in the first innings with support coming from Gregory (71 in 111 minutes, 5 fours), Sides (44 in 64 minutes, 1 six and 4 fours), Barnett (50 in 69 minutes, 4 fours), Ring (51 in 62 minutes, 8 fours) and No. 11 Fleetwood-Smith (43 in 43 minutes, 1 six and 6 fours). Sides was run out when a Hassett straight drive was deflected by Ridings into the bowler's stumps, Ridings dislocating a finger in the process and being unable to complete his over. Whitington (100 in 224 minutes, 10 fours), Bradman (107 in 106 minutes, 9 fours, chance at 6), Ward (62 in 155 minutes, 6 fours) and Hamence (84 in 173 minutes, 1 five and 8 fours) all surpassed 50 for South Australia. Bradman's hundred, reached in 91 minutes, was his fourth in consecutive innings and 22nd at first-class level in the calendar year and took his 1938 aggregate to 3838 runs (avge 112.88). Lee (51 in 95 minutes, 5 fours), Hassett (54 in 86 minutes, 8 fours), Sides (61 in 98 minutes, 1 six and 7 fours) and Barnett (54 in 99 minutes, 6 fours) scored fifties for Victoria on the last day with no chance of an outright result. H.N.J.Cotton was unable to represent South Australia due to influenza. Sources: *Wisden, VCA Report, SACA Report, The Age, The Argus, The Herald, Melbourne Sun, The Sporting Globe.*

VICTORIA

*K.E.Rigg	b Waite	7			
I.S.Lee	c Walker b Scott	6	(1)	b Waite	51
R.G.Gregory	st Walker b Ward	71		c sub (E.H.Bromley) b Ward	9
A.L.Hassett	not out	211		st Walker b Ward	54
J.A.Ledward	c Scott b Waite	2		c & b Ward	0
F.W.Sides	run out (P.L.Ridings)	44		c Scott b P.L.Ridings	61
†B.A.Barnett	lbw b Ward	50	(2)	lbw b Ward	54
M.W.Sievers	b Ward	1	(7)	not out	20
D.T.Ring	c Hamence b Waite	51	(8)	st Walker b Ward	19
E.L.McCormick	b P.L.Ridings	0	(9)	not out	1
L.O.Fleetwood-Smith	b Ward	43			
Extras	(lb6, nb7)	13		(b6, lb2, w1, nb5)	14
Total	(118.2 overs, 415 mins)	499		(73.0 overs, 255 mins) (7 wkts dec)	283

SOUTH AUSTRALIA

R.S.Whitington	lbw b Sievers	100		not out	27
K.L.Ridings	c Lee b Sievers	27		not out	18
*D.G.Bradman	c Hassett b Sievers	107			
C.L.Badcock	c & b McCormick	1			
†C.W.Walker	b Sievers	14			
F.A.Ward	c Barnett b Sievers	62			
R.A.Hamence	b Sievers	84			
M.G.Waite	lbw b Ring	0			
P.L.Ridings	c & b Ring	33			
C.V.Grimmett	st Barnett b Ring	34			
J.A.Scott	not out	4			
Extras	(b5, lb15, nb2)	22		(b5)	5
Total	(135.1 overs, 538 mins)	488		(21.0 overs, 75 mins) (0 wkts)	50

SOUTH AUSTRALIA	O	M	R	W	w,nb		O	M	R	W	w,nb
P.L.Ridings	19.2	3	73	1	-,7		9	0	37	1	-,5
Waite	32	5	123	3	-,-		24	6	63	1	-,-
Scott	17	2	67	1	-,-		13	1	43	0	1,-
Grimmett	25	0	98	0	-,-						
Ward	25	1	125	4	-,-	(4)	27	4	126	5	-,-

VICTORIA	O	M	R	W	w,nb		O	M	R	W	w,nb
McCormick	22	4	78	1	-,2		3	1	13	0	-,-
Sievers	43	11	95	6	-,-		3	0	9	0	-,-
Ring	31.1	2	116	3	-,-		6	1	8	0	-,-
Fleetwood-Smith	35	4	152	0	-,-		3	1	2	0	-,-
Gregory	4	0	25	0	-,-		4	3	3	0	-,-
Hassett							2	0	10	0	-,-

FALL OF WICKETS

Wkt	VIC 1st	SA 1st	VIC 2nd	SA 2nd
1st	12	70	108	-
2nd	23	227	112	-
3rd	129	230	135	-
4th	134	238	150	-
5th	219	263	195	-
6th	312	379	255	-
7th	314	380	281	-
8th	426	424	-	-
9th	427	483	-	-
10th	499	488	-	-

TASMANIA v VICTORIA

Played at T.C.A. Ground, Hobart, on December 30, 31, 1938, January 2, 1939. (Three-day match)
Toss : Tasmania.   Result : VICTORIA WON BY TEN WICKETS.
Debuts: Nil.
12th Men: D.Calvert (Tas) and D.J.A.Fitzmaurice (Vic).
Umpires: T.V.Barnes and M.Hansen.
Attendances & Receipts: No figures published.
Close of Play: 1st day Tas 8/308 (Jeffrey 77, Smith 7); 2nd day Vic 4/491 (Beames 169, Johnson 88).

Morrisby (70 in 160 minutes, 6 fours) and Thomas (67 in 151 minutes, 7 fours) began the match with a century opening stand in the face of some fiery pace bowling by Scott. Pearsall (42 in 93 minutes, 2 fours) and Jeffrey (80 not out in 177 minutes, 7 fours) continued the good work but the last four wickets added just 7 runs on the second morning. Nicolson was struck on the head by a fast, rising ball from Scott at 7/312 and took no further part in the match; he was detained in hospital for observation. Oakley (162 in 175 minutes, 15 fours) and Beames (169 not out in 160 minutes, 1 six and 21 fours) continued their brilliant form from the match at Launceston. They were well supported by Dowsley (64 in 115 minutes, 1 five and 4 fours), who added 157 with Oakley, and Johnson (88 not out in 106 minutes, 8 fours), who added an unfinished 209 in just 106 minutes with Beames for the fifth wicket. Thomas (42 in 51 minutes, 6 fours) and Jeffrey (53 in 85 minutes, 4 fours) again batted well in the second innings but Thorn completed his second five-wicket haul for the match and Victoria completed a comfortable victory. Calvert replaced C.G.Richardson (unavailable) as Tasmania's 12th man prior to the start.
Sources: *VCA Report, TCA Report, Melbourne Sun, The Sporting Globe, Launceston Examiner, Hobart Mercury.*

TASMANIA

*R.O.G.Morrisby	c Beames b Scott	70	b Johnson	21
R.V.Thomas	c Fothergill b Scott	67	c Dowsley b Johnson	42
A.L.Pearsall	b Dempster	42	run out (Meikle/Beames)	27
C.L.Jeffrey	not out	80	c Baker b Meikle	53
S.W.L.Putman	b Thorn	28	b Thorn	7
G.T.H.James	b Thorn	6	c Dowsley b Thorn	15
E.H.Smith	b Thorn	9	c Oakley b Thorn	7
†J.Gardiner	c Oakley b Thorn	0	b Thorn	5
J.N.W.Nicolson	retired hurt	0	absent hurt	-
J.I.Murfett	c Oakley b Thorn	1	(9) not out	11
J.Tringrove	c Beames b Scott	1	(10) c Meikle b Thorn	3
Extras	(b3, lb7, nb1)	11	(b3, lb2)	5
Total	(81.1 overs, 340 mins)	315	(50.7 overs, 182 mins)	196

VICTORIA

*H.H.Oakley	c & b Murfett	162		
H.Dowsley	c Murfett b Pearsall	64		
K.R.Miller	lbw b Pearsall	3		
P.J.Beames	not out	169		
D.H.Fothergill	c Gardiner b James	0		
I.W.Johnson	not out	88		
R.A.Dempster	)		(1) not out	12
†E.A.Baker	)		(2) not out	11
G.S.Meikle	) did not bat			
F.L.O.Thorn	)			
R.B.Scott	)			
Extras	(b3, lb2)	5		-
Total	(77.0 overs, 290 mins) (4 wkts dec)	491	(3.4 overs, 13 mins) (0 wkts)	23

VICTORIA	O	M	R	W	w,nb		O	M	R	W	w,nb						
Scott	27.1	4	79	3	-,-		10	0	60	0	-,-						
Dempster	11	2	39	1	,		3	2	10	0	-,-						
Thorn	23	1	111	5	-,-		19.7	1	74	5	-,-						
Meikle	9	0	35	0	-,-	(5)	9	0	24	1	-,-						
Fothergill	4	0	13	0	-,-												
Dowsley	3	0	16	0	-,1												
Johnson	4	1	11	0	-,-	(4)	7	0	14	2	-,-						
Beames						(6)	2	0	9	0	-,-						

FALL OF WICKETS

Wkt	TAS 1st	VIC 1st	TAS 2nd	VIC 2nd
1st	138	157	59	-
2nd	144	168	68	-
3rd	239	281	126	-
4th	285	282	135	-
5th	291	-	169	-
6th	312	-	171	-
7th	312	-	181	-
8th	313	-	182	-
9th	315	-	196	-
10th	-	-	-	-

TASMANIA	O	M	R	W	w,nb		O	M	R	W	w,nb
James	13	2	55	1	-,-	(2)	1.4	0	11	0	-,-
Murfett	17	0	96	1	-,-	(1)	2	0	12	0	-,-
Tringrove	14	0	111	0	-,-						
Putman	11	0	74	0	-,-						
Pearsall	14	1	94	2	-,-						
Thomas	8	0	56	0	-,-						

NEW SOUTH WALES v QUEENSLAND (Shield Match 7)

Played at Sydney Cricket Ground on December 31, 1938, January 2, 3, 4, 1939. (Four-day match)
Toss : New South Wales.   Result : QUEENSLAND WON BY EIGHT WICKETS.
Debuts: Nil.
12th Men: H.V.Stapleton (NSW) and M.S.Guttormsen (Qld).
Umpires: E.G.Borwick and F.W.Lyons.
Attendances: 5886, 7578, 3775, 959.   Total: 18,198.   Receipts: £936.
Close of Play: 1st day Qld 1/18 (Brown 8, Cook 4); 2nd day NSW (2) 2/76 (Barnes 37, Solomon 27); 3rd day Qld (2) 0/112 (Brown 78, Cook 30).

D.Tallon completed 12 dismissals in the match (9 caught, 3 stumped), setting a new Australian record and equalling the world mark for a wicket-keeper established by E.Pooley for Surrey against Sussex at Kennington Oval in 1868. Brown, nearing the peak of his best-ever season, scored 95 (254 minutes, 10 fours) and 168 (253 minutes, 13 fours), founding a new record partnership for the Queensland first wicket with Cook (93 in 251 minutes, 3 fours) to ensure victory. New South Wales were unable to select S.J.McCabe, A.G.Chipperfield, W.J.O'Reilly and J.H.W.Fingleton for a variety of reasons, White (44 in 52 minutes, 8 fours) and Barnes (51 in 99 minutes, 5 fours) topscoring for the weakened side. Fitzpatrick was out to the third ball of their second innings. Sources: *Wisden, NSWCA Report, QCA Report, The Herald, Melbourne Sun, Sydney Morning Herald, NSWCA Scorebook, Sydney Daily Telegraph.*

NEW SOUTH WALES

Batsman	Dismissal	Runs	Dismissal (2nd)	Runs
J.H.Fitzpatrick	st D.Tallon b Christ	26	c D.Tallon b Ellis	0
A.G.Cheetham	c D.Tallon b Dixon	20	c Christ b Ellis	10
S.G.Barnes	c D.Tallon b Christ	21	c sub (M.S.Guttormsen) b Christ	51
C.M.Solomon	b Ellis	4	c Baker b Ellis	31
V.W.McCaffrey	c D.Tallon b Ellis	4	st D.Tallon b L.W.T.Tallon	40
C.G.Pepper	b Dixon	39	c D.Tallon b Dixon	17
*K.C.Gulliver	c D.Tallon b Dixon	31	c D.Tallon b Dixon	40
R.V.James	st D.Tallon b Christ	11	c Christ b L.W.T.Tallon	42
†F.A.Easton	b Dixon	0	(10) c D.Tallon b Ellis	0
E.C.S.White	c & b Ellis	44	(9) c D.Tallon b Ellis	17
J.J.Murphy	not out	3	not out	5
Extras	(b2, lb4, nb5)	11	(lb9, nb2)	11
Total	(57.0 overs, 230 mins)	214	(68.0 overs, 290 mins)	264

QUEENSLAND

Batsman	Dismissal	Runs	Dismissal (2nd)	Runs
*W.A.Brown	c Pepper b Cheetham	95	c Cheetham b Murphy	168
R.E.Rogers	lbw b Cheetham	2		
G.G.Cook	lbw b Barnes	19	(2) run out (McCaffrey/Cheetham)	93
T.Allen	b Cheetham	5	not out	3
C.D.Hansen	c sub (H.V.Stapleton) b Fitzpatrick	7		
†D.Tallon	b Gulliver	28	(3) not out	9
G.W.Baker	c Gulliver b Murphy	0		
L.W.T.Tallon	b Barnes	13		
P.L.Dixon	lbw b Barnes	10		
C.P.Christ	run out (Pepper)	0		
J.A.Ellis	not out	7		
Extras	(b10, lb1, w3)	14	(b3, lb3)	6
Total	(78.2 overs, 283 mins)	200	(73.0 overs, 285 mins)	279

QUEENSLAND	O	M	R	W	w,nb		O	M	R	W	w,nb
Ellis	13	1	42	3	-,-		21	2	67	5	-,-
Cook	9	1	27	0	-,-		9	0	41	0	-,1
Dixon	15	1	61	4	-,5		14	1	59	2	-,1
Christ	18	3	60	3	-,-	(5)	15	1	51	1	-,-
L.W.T.Tallon	2	0	13	0	-,-	(6)	8	1	32	2	-,-
Baker						(4)	1	0	3	0	-,-

NEW SOUTH WALES	O	M	R	W	w,nb		O	M	R	W	w,nb
Murphy	18	5	31	1	-,-		16	2	54	1	-,-
Cheetham	18	1	52	3	3,-		20	4	71	0	-,-
White	12	5	18	0	-,-	(6)	8	3	18	0	-,-
Fitzpatrick	9	2	22	1	-,-	(3)	9	2	18	0	-,-
Pepper	3	0	16	0	-,-		8	0	38	0	-,-
Barnes	10.2	6	20	3	-,-	(4)	8	0	46	0	-,-
Gulliver	8	2	27	1	-,-		2	0	14	0	-,-
James							1	0	5	0	-,-
McCaffrey							1	0	9	0	-,-

FALL OF WICKETS

Wkt	NSW 1st	QLD 1st	NSW 2nd	QLD 2nd
1st	31	5	0	265
2nd	67	74	27	268
3rd	75	83	89	-
4th	79	96	95	-
5th	79	140	114	-
6th	137	145	191	-
7th	154	178	197	-
8th	158	182	229	-
9th	175	184	229	-
10th	214	200	264	-

QUEENSLAND v SOUTH AUSTRALIA (Shield Match 8)

Played at Brisbane Cricket Ground (Woolloongabba) on January 7, 9, 10, 11, 1939. (Four-day match)
Toss : Queensland.   Result : SOUTH AUSTRALIA WON BY TEN WICKETS.
Debuts: Queensland - C.G.R.Stibe (f/c).
12th Men: M.S.Guttormsen (Qld) and P.L.Ridings (SA).
Umpires: J.Bartlett and K.E.Fagg.
Attendances: 15172, 11250, 4278, 800.   Total: 31,500.   Receipts: £2691.
Close of Play: 1st day Qld 7/325 (L.W.T.Tallon 17, Dixon 0); 2nd day SA 1/280 (Ridings 108, Bradman 42); 3rd day Qld (2) 1/73
    (Brown 21, Rogers 41).

Bradman's chanceless 186 (287 minutes, 19 fours) was his fifth successive first-class hundred, a record for an Australian surpassing four in a row by himself in 1931-32 and four by C.G.Macartney in England in 1921. Whitington (125 in 222 minutes, 16 fours) and Ridings (122 in 319 minutes, 10 fours) also registered hundreds in the match for South Australia. D.Tallon for Queensland (115 in 164 minutes, 12 fours) injured a thumb while keeping wickets on the second day. He took no further part in the match, Brown taking over the gloves and dismissing Moyle and Cotton in the position. Stibe on debut (58 in 119 minutes, 7 fours), Baker (78 in 99 minutes, 11 fours) and in the second innings Brown (81 in 180 minutes, 7 fours) hit fifties for Queensland. Waite contracted tonsillitis on the first night and spent the rest of the game in hospital while Grimmett, who strained a leg in South Australia's previous match in Melbourne, could not be chosen. Sources: *Wisden, QCA Report, SACA Report, The Age, The Herald, Brisbane Courier-Mail, The Sporting Globe.*

QUEENSLAND

*W.A.Brown	c Ridings b Waite	1		lbw b Ridings	81
G.G.Cook	b Cotton	22	(6)	b Ridings	2
T.Allen	c Ward b Cotton	5	(2)	b Cotton	5
R.E.Rogers	run out (Whitington)	11	(3)	c Ridings b Ward	45
†D.Tallon	b Cotton	115		absent hurt	-
C.G.R.Stibe	c Walker b Ridings	58	(4)	lbw b Scott	23
G.W.Baker	b Ridings	78	(5)	b Ridings	17
L.W.T.Tallon	c Walker b Ward	23	(7)	not out	40
P.L.Dixon	b Cotton	2	(8)	b Ridings	4
J.A.Ellis	b Cotton	1		c Ridings b Cotton	5
C.P.Christ	not out	2	(9)	run out	1
Extras	(b6, lb9, nb3)	18		(b4, lb2, w1, nb3)	10
Total	(98.0 overs, 350 mins)	336		(62.6 overs, 233 mins)	233

SOUTH AUSTRALIA

R.S.Whitington	c D.Tallon b L.W.T.Tallon	125			
K.L.Ridings	b Ellis	122	(1)	not out	10
*D.G.Bradman	c Christ b L.W.T.Tallon	186			
C.L.Badcock	c Rogers b Christ	1	(2)	not out	4
R.A.Hamence	c Stibe b Christ	13			
E.J.R.Moyle	c Brown b Cook	46			
†C.W.Walker	c & b L.W.T.Tallon	20			
F.A.Ward	b Ellis	18			
H.N.J.Cotton	st Brown b L.W.T.Tallon	2			
J.A.Scott	not out	5			
M.G.Waite	absent ill	-			
Extras	(b3, lb9, w5, nb2)	19			-
Total	(143.7 overs, 539 mins)	557		(2.7 overs, 11 mins) (0 wkts)	14

SOUTH AUSTRALIA	O	M	R	W	w,nb		O	M	R	W	w,nb		FALL OF WICKETS			
Cotton	25	5	49	5	-,3		16.6	4	49	2	-,2			QLD	SA	QLD	SA
Waite	21	2	86	1	-,-							Wkt	1st	1st	2nd	2nd
Scott	23	6	48	0	-,-	(2)	15	1	55	1	-,-	1st	4	197	13	-
Ward	24	1	108	1	-,-	(3)	25	6	93	1	-,1	2nd	11	306	92	-
Ridings	5	1	27	2	-,-	(4)	6	1	26	4	1,-	3rd	28	311	138	-
												4th	163	337	179	-
QUEENSLAND	O	M	R	W	w,nb		O	M	R	W	w,nb	5th	168	469	180	-
Ellis	32.7	1	126	2	-,-							6th	301	530	185	-
Cook	25	0	101	1	5,-							7th	322	541	189	-
Dixon	19	2	93	0	-,2							8th	333	551	204	-
Christ	43	9	110	2	-,-							9th	333	557	233	-
L.W.T.Tallon	20	2	80	4	-,-							10th	336	-	-	-
Allen	1	0	4	0	-,-											
Baker	3	0	24	0	-,-	(1)	1	1	0	0	-,-					
Stibe						(2)	1	0	9	0	-,-					
Rogers						(3)	0.7	0	5	0	-,-					

NEW SOUTH WALES v SOUTH AUSTRALIA (Shield Match 9)

Played at Sydney Cricket Ground on January 14, 16 (no play), 17 (no play), 18, 1939. (Four-day match)
Toss : New South Wales.   Result : MATCH DRAWN.
Debuts: New South Wales - S.G.Sismey (f/c).
12th Men: K.C.Gulliver (NSW) and J.A.Scott (SA).
Umpires: E.G.Borwick and F.W.Lyons.
Attendances: 7717, no play, no play, 4464.   Total: 12,181.   Receipts: £656.
Close of Play: 1st day SA 2/116 (Bradman 22, Ward 4); 2nd day no play; 3rd day no play.

South Australia were without a regular wicket-keeper, Walker having further injured during the previous match in Brisbane the left forefinger he broke on the tour of England. Bradman kept wicket throughout the first innings and Moyle did the job in the second. The New South Wales batting failed on the first day until James (45 in 78 minutes, 5 fours) and Hynes (63 not out in 71 minutes, 1 six and 8 fours) added 77 for the eighth wicket. Bradman's chanceless 135 not out (201 minutes, 7 fours) was his sixth century in succession and equalled the world record established by C.B.Fry in England in 1901. It was also his eighth straight hundred in Australia, a record unlikely to be ever approached. Great publicity had been given in the Press on Bradman's attempt to equal Fry's six-in-a-row and he batted cautiously until he reached three figures; thereafter he "jumped down the wicket and drove all bowlers," scoring his last 35 in 20 minutes. Players had sprinted in from the outfield to congratulate Bradman on his feat amid loud cheers from the crowd. Rain on the second and third days prevented any play with Bradman having already started his innings. Whitington (59 in 86 minutes, 8 fours) and Badcock (98 in 126 minutes, 8 fours) helped the side to first-innings points. McCauley (76 in 135 minutes, 5 fours) batted well for New South Wales on the last afternoon. Sources: *Wisden, NSWCA Report, SACA Report, The Herald, Melbourne Sun, Sydney Morning Herald, NSWCA Scorebook, The Sporting Globe.*

NEW SOUTH WALES

B.V.McCauley	lbw b Grimmett	25	run out (/Moyle)		76
A.G.Cheetham	c Bradman b Grimmett	10	c Moyle b P.L.Ridings		25
S.G.Barnes	b P.L.Ridings	12	c Cotton b Grimmett		33
*A.G.Chipperfield	c Cotton b Waite	15	st Moyle b Waite		12
C.M.Solomon	c P.L.Ridings b Ward	34	c P.L.Ridings b Grimmett		0
C.G.Pepper	c Waite b Grimmett	17	(7) not out		0
V.W.McCaffrey	c P.L.Ridings b Grimmett	6			
R.V.James	b Cotton	45	(6) not out		4
L.C.Hynes	not out	63			
†S.G.Sismey	c P.L.Ridings b Cotton	6			
L.J.O'Brien	b Cotton	0			
Extras	(b8, w1, nb4)	13	(b3, lb3)		6
Total	(52.6 overs, 218 mins)	246	(40.0 overs, 139 mins) (5 wkts)		156

SOUTH AUSTRALIA

R.S.Whitington	lbw b Barnes	59
K.L.Ridings	lbw b Cheetham	28
*†D.G.Bradman	not out	135
F.A.Ward	c O'Brien b Hynes	18
C.L.Badcock	c & b Hynes	98
R.A.Hamence	)	
E.J.R.Moyle	)	
M.G.Waite	) did not bat	
P.L.Ridings	)	
C.V.Grimmett	)	
H.N.J.Cotton	)	
Extras	(b1, lb2, nb8)	11
Total	(69.3 overs, 276 mins) (4 wkts dec)	349

SOUTH AUSTRALIA	O	M	R	W	w,nb		O	M	R	W	w,nb
Cotton	10.6	1	44	3	-,1		3	0	14	0	-,-
Waite	11	1	49	1	1,-		8	1	15	1	-,-
Grimmett	15	3	53	4	-,-	(4)	15	1	51	2	-,-
P.L.Ridings	7	1	37	1	-,3	(3)	5	0	19	1	-,-
Ward	7	0	41	1	-,-		9	0	51	0	-,-
K.L.Ridings	2	0	9	0	-,-						

NEW SOUTH WALES	O	M	R	W	w,nb
O'Brien	15	0	76	0	-,5
Hynes	16.3	0	86	2	-,3
Cheetham	23	1	104	1	-,-
Pepper	7	0	47	0	-,-
Barnes	8	2	25	1	-,-

FALL OF WICKETS

Wkt	NSW 1st	SA 1st	NSW 2nd
1st	32	76	53
2nd	46	94	98
3rd	50	163	133
4th	90	349	134
5th	102	-	156
6th	118	-	-
7th	143	-	-
8th	220	-	-
9th	246	-	-
10th	246	-	-

NEW SOUTH WALES v VICTORIA (Shield Match 10)

Played at Sydney Cricket Ground on January 28, 30, 31, 1939. (Four-day match)
Toss : New South Wales.   Result : VICTORIA WON BY EIGHT WICKETS.
Debuts: New South Wales - F.P.J.Gilmore (f/c).
12th Men: D.James (NSW) and D.T.Ring (Vic).
Umpires: E.G.Borwick and F.W.Lyons.
Attendances: 7796, 8799, 356.   Total: 16,951.   Receipts: £814.
Close of Play: 1st day Vic 2/176 (Gregory 65, Hassett 64); 2nd day NSW (2) 217 all out.

Scott - brought into the Victorian line-up after his performances for the second-strength side against the Tasmanians earlier in the month - bowled with great pace and accuracy on a lively pitch to capture a decisive 12 for 79. The only fifties in a match where batsmen struggled, were raised by Gregory (76 in 172 minutes, 5 fours) and Hassett (82 in 122 minutes, 6 fours) who shared the only hundred partnership, 154 for Victoria's third wicket. Lee scored a useful 30 (53 minutes, 3 fours) and an unbeaten 43 (75 minutes, 5 fours) and hit the winning shot early on the third day. New South Wales's chief scorers were James (34 in 59 minutes, 3 fours), Barnes (48 in 64 minutes, 6 fours) and Solomon (49 in 78 minutes, 5 fours). Hynes (injured in a car crash after the second day) and McCauley (broken finger when caught off the glove in the second innings) were both absent on the final day. Don James (brother of R.V.), who had replaced K.C.Gulliver (unavailable) as 12th man for New South Wales, substituted with Scott and McCormick (alternatively) in their places. Sources: *Wisden, NSWCA Report, VCA Report, The Herald, Melbourne Sun, Sydney Morning Herald, NSWCA Scorebook, Sydney Daily Telegraph.*

NEW SOUTH WALES

A.G.Cheetham	c Fleetwood-Smith b Scott	17	lbw b Fleetwood-Smith		16
B.V.McCauley	c Rigg b McCormick	6	c McCormick b Scott		22
S.G.Barnes	c Hassett b Scott	0	run out (Lee/Barnett)		48
†A.G.Chipperfield	c Sievers b McCormick	27	lbw b Fleetwood-Smith		25
C.M.Solomon	c Gregory b Scott	8	c Hassett b Scott		49
R.V.James	b Scott	34	b Scott		17
V.W.McCaffrey	b Scott	7	(8) c Sievers b Scott		13
C.G.Pepper	run out (Gregory/Barnett)	13	(7) b Fleetwood-Smith		5
L.C.Hynes	c McCormick b Scott	0	c Barnett b Scott		6
†S.G.Sismey	b Scott	0	not out		2
F.P.J.Gilmore	not out	1	run out		1
Extras	(lb2, nb5)	7	(b5, lb4, nb4)		13
Total	(34.7 overs, 163 mins)	120	(47.7 overs, 213 mins)		217

VICTORIA

*K.E.Rigg	b Cheetham	7	c Sismey b Gilmore		5
I.S.Lee	b Hynes	30	not out		43
R.G.Gregory	c Sismey b Gilmore	76	lbw b Pepper		25
A.L.Hassett	lbw b Pepper	82	not out		0
F.W.Sides	lbw b Gilmore	10			
H.H.Oakley	c Sismey b Cheetham	6			
†B.A.Barnett	b Gilmore	7			
M.W.Sievers	c Solomon b Cheetham	17			
R.B.Scott	c Sismey b Hynes	1			
E.L.McCormick	c Gilmore b Hynes	8			
L.O.Fleetwood-Smith	not out	2			
Extras	(b3, lb6, w1, nb3)	13	(b1, lb5)		6
Total	(62.4 overs, 255 mins)	259	(20.2 overs, 75 mins) (2 wkts)		79

VICTORIA	O	M	R	W	w,nb		O	M	R	W	w,nb
McCormick	6	0	26	2	-,2		6	0	37	0	-,2
Sievers	7	3	18	0	-,-		13.7	0	38	0	-,1
Scott	11.7	3	33	7	-,3		13	0	46	5	-,1
Fleetwood-Smith	10	1	36	0	-,-		15	0	83	3	-,-

NEW SOUTH WALES	O	M	R	W	w,nb		O	M	R	W	w,nb
Gilmore	15	0	50	3	1,1		5	0	13	1	-,-
Cheetham	18.4	1	60	3	-,1		6	0	20	0	-,-
Hynes	13	2	57	3	-,1						
Barnes	6	0	14	0	-,-	(3)	3	0	18	0	-,-
Chipperfield	4	0	24	0	-,-						
James	2	0	11	0	-,-						
Pepper	4	0	30	1	-,-	(5)	3	0	13	1	-,-
Solomon						(4)	3.2	0	9	0	-,-

FALL OF WICKETS

Wkt	NSW 1st	VIC 1st	NSW 2nd	VIC 2nd
1st	22	28	41	16
2nd	22	47	62	75
3rd	40	201	104	-
4th	52	214	129	-
5th	75	221	165	-
6th	103	221	178	-
7th	104	233	206	-
8th	105	237	212	-
9th	113	255	215	-
10th	120	259	217	-

QUEENSLAND v VICTORIA (Shield Match 11)

Played at Brisbane Cricket Ground (Woolloongabba) on February 4, 6, 7, 8, 1939. (Four-day match)
Toss : Victoria.　　　　　　　　　Result : QUEENSLAND WON BY AN INNINGS AND 11 RUNS.
Debuts: Nil.
12th Men: M.S.Guttormsen (Qld) and D.T.Ring (Vic).
Umpires: D.W.Given and J.A.Scott.
Attendances: 9193, 4000, 2900, 1000.　　　Total: 17,093.　　　Receipts: £1264.
Close of Play: 1st day Vic 7/289 (Hassett 114); 2nd day Qld 1/168 (Brown 76, Allen 34); 3rd day Qld 7/575 (L.W.T.Tallon 37).

Queensland beat Victoria for the first time since February 1932 to end a sequence of 13 matches without victory against the State. Brown (215 in 521 minutes, 12 fours) compiled his highest score in 50 matches for Queensland, adding 94 for the first wicket with Cook (44 in 153 minutes, 4 fours), 165 for the second wicket with Allen (79 in 181 minutes, 8 fours), 68 for the fourth wicket with D.Tallon (44 in 54 minutes, 1 six and 4 fours) and 95 for the sixth wicket with Baker (97 in 128 minutes, 11 fours). Hassett (139 in 302 minutes, 11 fours) provided the backbone of Victoria's first innings in which D.Tallon recorded the first instance in Australia of seven dismissals in an innings (in the second-last match he had become the first keeper in the country to complete 12 dismissals in a match). Rigg (54 in 149 minutes, 3 fours) and Lee (64 in 166 minutes, 6 fours) scored the majority of the second-innings runs in their opening stand. Sievers strained a leg muscle while fielding and could not bat. *Wisden* omits Vic (2) c sub from dismissal of Hassett. Sources: *Wisden, VCA Report, QCA Report, The Age, The Herald, Brisbane Courier-Mail, The Sporting Globe.*

VICTORIA

*K.E.Rigg	st D.Tallon b Christ	46	c Christ b L.W.T.Tallon		54
I.S.Lee	c D.Tallon b Ellis	9	lbw b L.W.T.Tallon		64
R.G.Gregory	b L.W.T.Tallon	27	b Cook		45
A.L.Hassett	b Christ	139	c sub (M.S.Guttormsen) b L.Tallon		9
F.W.Sides	lbw b Ellis	40	c D.Tallon b L.W.T.Tallon		0
H.H.Oakley	st D.Tallon b Cook	40	st D.Tallon b L.W.T.Tallon		7
†B.A.Barnett	c D.Tallon b Ellis	6	b Cook		22
M.W.Sievers	st D.Tallon b L.W.T.Tallon	1	absent hurt		-
R.B.Scott	c D.Tallon b Dixon	27	lbw b Dixon	(8)	2
E.L.McCormick	not out	3	b Dixon	(9)	0
L.O.Fleetwood-Smith	st D.Tallon b Christ	1	not out	(10)	9
Extras	(lb6, nb3)	9	(b1, lb2, nb1)		4
Total	(103.1 overs, 405 mins)	348	(70.5 overs, 265 mins)		216

QUEENSLAND

*W.A.Brown	lbw b Fleetwood-Smith	215
G.G.Cook	b McCormick	44
T.Allen	lbw b Gregory	79
R.E.Rogers	lbw b McCormick	30
†D.Tallon	c Lee b Gregory	44
C.G.R.Stibe	b Scott	0
G.W.Baker	c Gregory b McCormick	97
L.W.T.Tallon	not out	37
P.L.Dixon	)	
C.P.Christ	) did not bat	
J.A.Ellis	)	
Extras	(b12, lb6, w4, nb7)	29
Total	(132.3 overs, 574 mins) (7 wkts dec)	575

QUEENSLAND	O	M	R	W	w,nb		O	M	R	W	w,nb
Ellis	23	1	64	3	-,-						
Cook	10	0	41	1	-,-		15	4	35	2	-,-
Dixon	19	0	81	1	-,3	(1)	11.5	1	38	2	-,1
Christ	21.1	6	48	3	-,-	(3)	23	3	62	0	-,-
L.W.T.Tallon	25	4	87	2	-,-	(4)	21	1	77	5	-,-
Baker	5	0	18	0	-,-						

VICTORIA	O	M	R	W	w,nb
McCormick	34.3	2	105	3	-,6
Scott	33	1	161	1	3,1
Sievers	10	5	15	0	-,-
Fleetwood-Smith	34	3	146	1	1,-
Gregory	15	0	96	2	-,-
Hassett	6	0	23	0	-,-

FALL OF WICKETS

Wkt	VIC 1st	QLD 1st	VIC 2nd
1st	22	94	117
2nd	61	259	132
3rd	123	326	152
4th	210	394	153
5th	277	396	165
6th	288	491	203
7th	289	575	206
8th	331	-	207
9th	345	-	216
10th	348	-	-

SOUTH AUSTRALIA v VICTORIA (Shield Match 12)

Played at Adelaide Oval on February 24, 25, 27 (no play), 28 (no play), 1939. (Four-day match)
Toss : South Australia.   Result : MATCH DRAWN.
Debuts: Victoria - G.E.Tamblyn (f/c).
12th Men: E.J.R.Moyle (SA) and D.T.Ring (Vic).
Umpires: A.G.Jenkins and J.D.Scott.
Attendances: 8473, 17777, no play, no play.   Total: 26,250.   Receipts: £1124.
Close of Play: 1st day Vic 6/284 (Hassett 84, Scott 1); 2nd day SA 7/207 (Waite 63, Ward 2); 3rd day no play.

Victoria, one point behind South Australia at the start of the season's final Shield match, were denied the trophy when rain prevented play on the last two days. A first-innings victory for which they were poised would have been sufficient. Rigg (78 in 184 minutes, 5 fours), Hassett (102 in 259 minutes, 3 fours) and Barnett (51 in 89 minutes, 5 fours) made significant contributions on the first day for the visitors. Scott became the latest batsman to be accidentally run out while backing up, Hassett's straight drive cannoning into the non-striker's stumps via Cotton's foot. Remarkably, it was the third time in the past 12 months in Australia that Hassett had run out a team-mate in this fashion. Hamence (35 in 145 minutes, 5 fours) and Waite (63 not out in 145 minutes, 5 fours) topscored for South Australia. Adelaide's biggest-ever Shield crowd, 17,777 on the second day, was disappointed at Bradman's inability to score a record seventh consecutive hundred. Sources: *Wisden, VCA Report, SACA Report, The Age, The Herald, Adelaide Advertiser.*

VICTORIA

*K.E.Rigg	c Horsell b P.L.Ridings	78
I.S.Lee	b Cotton	13
R.G.Gregory	b Cotton	33
A.L.Hassett	b Ward	102
F.W.Sides	c Cotton b Ward	10
G.E.Tamblyn	lbw b Ward	0
†B.A.Barnett	run out (Hamence/Waite)	51
R.B.Scott	run out (Cotton)	2
E.L.McCormick	c Cotton b Ward	14
F.L.O.Thorn	c Horsell b Grimmett	3
L.O.Fleetwood-Smith	not out	1
Extras	(b3, lb5, nb6)	14
Total	(103.4 overs, 378 mins)	321

SOUTH AUSTRALIA

R.S.Whitington	b Scott	18
K.L.Ridings	lbw b Thorn	14
*D.G.Bradman	c Fleetwood-Smith b Thorn	5
C.L.Badcock	c Lee b Scott	14
R.A.Hamence	lbw b Fleetwood-Smith	35
M.G.Waite	not out	63
P.L.Ridings	lbw b McCormick	12
†J.A.J.Horsell	lbw b Fleetwood-Smith	29
F.A.Ward	not out	2
C.V.Grimmett	) did not bat	
H.N.J.Cotton	)	
Extras	(b6, lb2, nb7)	15
Total	(63.0 overs, 264 mins) (7 wkts)	207

SOUTH AUSTRALIA	O	M	R	W	w,nb
Cotton	23	3	73	2	-,4
Waite	25	5	65	0	-,-
P.L.Ridings	12	1	55	1	-,2
Grimmett	24	4	57	1	-,-
Ward	19.4	1	57	4	-,-

VICTORIA	O	M	R	W	w,nb
McCormick	16	2	45	1	-,3
Scott	15	1	49	2	-,4
Thorn	16	2	51	2	-,-
Fleetwood-Smith	14	1	34	2	-,-
Gregory	2	0	13	0	-,-

FALL OF WICKETS

Wkt	VIC 1st	SA 1st
1st	32	30
2nd	98	38
3rd	160	42
4th	182	78
5th	182	113
6th	277	135
7th	285	198
8th	304	-
9th	313	-
10th	321	-

WESTERN AUSTRALIA v VICTORIA

Played at W.A.C.A. Ground, Perth, on March 4, 6, 7, 1939. (Three-day match)
Toss : Victoria.   Result : MATCH DRAWN.
Debuts: Western Australia - A.E.O.Barras, C.W.T.MacGill, A.E.Read, A.D.Watt (all f/c).
12th Men: G.N.Evans (WA) and F.W.Sides (Vic).
Umpires: F.R.Buttsworth and J.P.Robbins.
Attendances: 2500, 2000, 750.   Total: 5250.   Receipts: £344.
Close of Play: 1st day WA 0/5 (MacGill 1, Read 2); 2nd day WA 5/276 (Barras 70, Inverarity 35).

B.A.Barnett, R.G.Gregory and M.W.Sievers were all unavailable for Victoria's two-match visit to Western Australia. Tamblyn (100 in 193 minutes, 11 fours) dominated the Victorian first innings. Barras (113 in 207 minutes, 10 fours) scored his first century in any grade of cricket while on debut, combining in partnerships of 112 in 95 minutes with Inverarity and 97 in 61 minutes with Lovelock, who hit 9 fours and 1 five. Scott strained a knee during his tenth over and took no further part in the match. Although Halcombe (bruised heel) was unable to bowl in the second innings after Western Australia declared at lunch, it was understood that he could have batted. Neither Scott nor Halcombe recovered in time for the return match two days later. The last day saw 430 runs made in 280 minutes, with Hassett (103 in 87 minutes, 3 sixes and 12 fours) getting a quick century between lunch and tea. MacGill was no-balled for throwing once in the second innings by umpire Buttsworth at square leg; he had never been called before and little was made of the incident. All sources except *WACA Scorebook* give Barras c Tamblyn but Sides was on the field at the time as substitute for the injured Scott and the scorebook version has been accepted. Sources: *VCA Report, The West Australian, Daily News, WACA Scorebook.*

VICTORIA

*K.E.Rigg	c MacGill b Halcombe	6		c Read b Zimbulis	52
I.S.Lee	b Halcombe	1		b MacGill	1
A.L.Hassett	lbw b Halcombe	14		st Lovelock b Jeffreys	103
†G.E.Tamblyn	b Halcombe	100		b Jeffreys	9
K.R.Miller	c Barras b Zimbulis	38		lbw b Zimbulis	55
E.A.Baker	st Lovelock b Zimbulis	7		c & b Zimbulis	17
D.T.Ring	b MacGill	26		c Zimbulis b MacGill	25
R.B.Scott	lbw b Zimbulis	49		absent hurt	-
E.L.McCormick	b Halcombe	8	(8)	b MacGill	4
F.L.O.Thorn	c Read b Zimbulis	1	(9)	not out	11
L.O.Fleetwood-Smith	not out	0	(10)	c Mills b Zimbulis	23
Extras	(b9, lb3, w1, nb3)	16		(b6, lb3, nb1)	10
Total	(63.6 overs, 285 mins)	266		(47.7 overs, 195 mins)	310

WESTERN AUSTRALIA

C.W.T.MacGill	c Miller b Ring	48
A.E.Read	c Hassett b Ring	13
*W.T.Rowlands	c & b Ring	6
A.D.Watt	c Baker b Ring	54
K.S.Jeffreys	c Baker b McCormick	16
A.E.O.Barras	c sub (F.W.Sides) b Ring	113
M.Inverarity	b Thorn	38
†O.I.Lovelock	not out	71
A.G.Zimbulis	st Baker b Ring	2
R.L.Mills	b Fleetwood-Smith	1
R.A.Halcombe	did not bat	
Extras	(b27, lb5, w2)	34
Total	(88.3 overs, 400 mins) (9 wkts dec)	396

WESTERN AUSTRALIA	O	M	R	W	w,nb		O	M	R	W	w,nb
Halcombe	17	1	40	5	1,3						
Mills	17	3	55	0	-,-	(1)	5	0	33	0	-,-
MacGill	10	2	34	1	-,-	(2)	12	1	77	3	-,1
Zimbulis	19.6	0	121	4	-,-	(3)	12.7	0	108	4	-,-
Jeffreys						(4)	11	0	56	2	-,-
Inverarity						(5)	4	0	18	0	-,-
Rowlands						(6)	3	0	8	0	-,-

VICTORIA	O	M	R	W	w,nb
McCormick	18	1	60	1	1,-
Scott	9.4	0	25	0	-,-
Thorn	19	5	84	1	1,-
Ring	23	0	97	6	-,-
Fleetwood-Smith	18.7	3	96	1	-,-

FALL OF WICKETS

Wkt	VIC 1st	WA 1st	VIC 2nd
1st	5	58	6
2nd	9	78	87
3rd	38	91	137
4th	123	128	172
5th	146	171	210
6th	196	283	268
7th	212	380	269
8th	249	393	279
9th	250	396	310
10th	266	-	-

WESTERN AUSTRALIA v VICTORIA

Played at W.A.C.A. Ground, Perth, on March 9, 10, 11, 1939. (Three-day match)
Toss : Western Australia.　　　　　Result : MATCH DRAWN.
Debuts: Nil.
12th Men: G.N.Evans (WA) and R.B.Scott (Vic).
Umpires: F.R.Buttsworth and J.P.Robbins.
Attendances: 1200, 1000, 2000.　　　Total: 4200.　　　Receipts: £240.
Close of Play: 1st day WA 257 all out; 2nd day WA (2) 0/21 (Read 5, Zimbulis 7).

Scott was named 12th man for Victoria despite having not recovered from his knee injury; no other player was on hand. MacGill fell to the first ball of the match and had to retire hurt in the second innings with the score at 0/10 when he was struck on the hand by a ball from McCormick. Sides (121 in 190 minutes, 17 fours) dominated the Victorian first-innings, reaching 50 in 95 minutes and 100 in 160 minutes. The appropriately named pairing of Thorn and Sides thwarted Western Australia's bid for a substantial first innings lead by adding 78 in 68 minutes for the ninth wicket. Following his fine debut, Barras made a major in 98 minutes contribution again for Western Australia, with 54 (86 minutes, 7 fours) and 95 (116 minutes, 10 fours). Inverarity (68 not out in 140 minutes, 7 fours) and Lovelock (51 in 98 minutes, 6 fours) also batted well. Play on the last day finished at 4.50pm. (no tea interval) to allow the Victorians to catch their train at 5.40pm. Sides hit a six off Watt from the last ball of the match, an unusual finish to a drawn game. Last first-class appearance by K.E.Rigg. Sources: *VCA Report, The West Australian, Daily News, Sunday Times, Western Mail, WACA Scorebook.*

WESTERN AUSTRALIA

Batsman	Dismissal	Runs	2nd innings	Runs
C.W.T.MacGill	lbw b McCormick	0	retired hurt	6
A.E.Read	c Baker b Thorn	41	c Baker b Hassett	24
*W.T.Rowlands	c Baker b McCormick	18		
A.D.Watt	b McCormick	3	b Hassett	19
K.S.Jeffreys	c Miller b McCormick	1	(6) c Fleetwood-Smith b Ring	33
A.E.O.Barras	c Fleetwood-Smith b Thorn	54	(5) st Baker b Thorn	95
M.Inverarity	not out	68		
†O.I.Lovelock	b Ring	51	(7) not out	15
A.G.Zimbulis	lbw b Ring	1	(3) c Miller b McCormick	21
G.Eyres	c Miller b Ring	1		
R.L.Mills	c Baker b Thorn	3		
Extras	(b6, lb4, nb6)	16	(b5, lb1, w2, nb4)	12
Total	(68.0 overs, 295 mins)	257	(51.2 overs, 213 mins) (5 wkts dec)	225

VICTORIA

Batsman	Dismissal	Runs	2nd innings	Runs
*K.E.Rigg	c MacGill b Eyres	6		
I.S.Lee	c Lovelock b MacGill	12		
A.L.Hassett	b Eyres	8		
F.W.Sides	b MacGill	121	(5) not out	13
G.E.Tamblyn	b Eyres	1	(1) b Mills	4
K.R.Miller	lbw b Eyres	1	(4) not out	17
†E.A.Baker	c Barras b Eyres	19	(2) lbw b Barras	24
D.T.Ring	b Jeffreys	1	(3) b Watt	13
E.L.McCormick	b MacGill	13		
F.L.O.Thorn	c & b MacGill	30		
L.O.Fleetwood-Smith	not out	0		
Extras	(b9, lb5)	14	(b7)	7
Total	(55.4 overs, 235 mins)	226	(20.0 overs, 78 mins) (3 wkts)	78

VICTORIA	O	M	R	W	w,nb		O	M	R	W	w,nb
McCormick	15	3	48	4	-,6		12	2	43	1	1,4
Thorn	20	1	68	3	-,-		13.2	2	46	1	1,-
Fleetwood-Smith	14	2	59	0	-,-	(5)	6	0	37	0	-,-
Ring	19	2	66	3	-,-		11	2	45	1	-,-
Hassett						(3)	9	0	42	2	-,-

WESTERN AUSTRALIA	O	M	R	W	w,nb		O	M	R	W	w,nb
Eyres	19	4	47	5	-,-		5	3	14	0	-,-
Mills	7	2	32	0	-,-		4	0	6	1	-,-
MacGill	14.4	2	45	4	-,-						
Zimbulis	9	0	50	0	-,-						
Jeffreys	6	0	38	1	-,-						
Watt						(3)	6	0	29	1	-,-
Barras						(4)	5	1	22	1	-,-

FALL OF WICKETS

Wkt	WA 1st	VIC 1st	WA 2nd	VIC 2nd
1st	0	8	40	9
2nd	30	32	76	31
3rd	36	38	77	61
4th	44	40	174	-
5th	119	42	225	-
6th	136	98	-	-
7th	229	116	-	-
8th	231	137	-	-
9th	241	215	-	-
10th	257	226	-	-

The outbreak of war in Europe in September brought uncertainty to the Australian cricket scene. However, the Government encouraged the cricket authorities to proceed with their plans to assist public morale and help maintain the everyday lifestyle as much as possible. Consequently, competition for the Sheffield Shield continued.

New South Wales rectified their failures of the previous season to win the Shield in convincing fashion. They were pressed by the title-holders, South Australia, but still won four of their six matches outright. The availability of McCabe and O'Reilly had a profound effect on team performance and morale. Both had outstanding seasons, and Barnes, Solomon, Cheetham, Mudge and Pepper provided excellent backup. A win over Victoria at Sydney in the final match of the competition was required for New South Wales to win the Shield and this was achieved despite a century in each innings from Hassett.

Bradman continued to master all bowlers who came before him. His 1475 runs were amassed from only nine matches and, just as importantly, they were scored at a rapid rate. His efforts alone kept South Australia in contention for the Shield right up until the final match. Badcock, Waite and Ridings also rallied with the bat. The ageless Grimmett continued to bowl as well as ever for South Australia. He turned 48 years old during the season, yet still managed to capture 73 wickets. He was easily the most prolific wicket-taker in the land. Ward provided his chief support.

Victoria made the battle for the Shield a three-way contest by also remaining in the hunt until the death. They fielded a well-balanced team but poor returns in their games against South Australia nearly put paid to their chances. Nevertheless, a win in the final match against New South Wales would still have given Victoria the title. Hassett, clearly their best batsman, was one of the few to play the bowling of O'Reilly with confidence this year. Lee, Barnett, Tamblyn, Sievers, Miller and Beames completed a sound batting lineup. Ring made a fine impression with his legspin but the remaining bowlers paid a high price for their wickets.

Queensland's efforts this season led to a solitary victory over South Australia at Brisbane. J.Stackpoole enjoyed a sensational start to the first-class scene with his first-ball dismissal of Bradman in that game. Brown was again the leading batsman for the State, but Rogers, Don Tallon, Baker and Cook also did well. Queensland continued to be stymied by their poor bowling.

A match between the new Shield champions, New South Wales, and an XI selected from the rest of the country was staged at Sydney in March as a fund-raiser for the war effort. South Australia also travelled to Perth for two matches to give Western Australia a taste of the first-class game, but Tasmania missed out and did not appear again in a first-class match until 1945-46.

An Australian team was scheduled to tour New Zealand in February-March 1940 but the war caused the situation to be reassessed. No team was selected.

Leading Aggregates

Batsmen	M	I	NO	Runs	HS	Ave.	Bowlers	Runs	Wkts	Ave.
D.G.Bradman (SA)	9	15	3	1475	267	122.91	C.V.Grimmett (SA)	1654	73	22.65
A.L.Hassett (V)	7	12	0	897	136	74.75	W.J.O'Reilly (NSW)	832	55	15.12
W.A.Brown (Q)	7	14	0	857	156	61.21	D.T.Ring (V)	986	34	29.00
S.J.McCabe (NSW)	7	13	0	699	114	53.76	F.A.Ward (SA)	1144	33	34.66
M.G.Waite (SA)	9	14	2	565	137	47.08	C.G.Pepper (NSW)	1033	31	33.32
R.E.Rogers (Q)	7	14	0	541	74	38.64	R.B.Scott (V)	813	21	38.71
S.G.Barnes (NSW)	7	13	1	530	135*	44.16				

SHEFFIELD SHIELD TABLE

	P	WO	W1	LO	L1	D	Pts	Quotient	Runs Scored	Wkts Lost	Runs Conceded	Wkts Taken
NEW SOUTH WALES	6	4	-	2	-	-	20	1.266	3350	102	2878	111
SOUTH AUSTRALIA	6	3	1	2	-	-	18	1.295	3474	87	3605	117
VICTORIA	6	3	-	2	1	-	16	1.013	3692	102	3677	103
QUEENSLAND	6	1	-	5	-	-	5	0.589	3069	117	3425	77
TOTAL	12	11	1	11	1	-	59	1.000	13585	408	13585	408

QUEENSLAND v NEW SOUTH WALES (Shield Match 1)

Played at Brisbane Cricket Ground (Woolloongabba) on November 17, 18, 20, 21, 1939. (Four-day match)
Toss : Queensland.   Result : NEW SOUTH WALES WON BY THREE WICKETS.
Debuts: New South Wales - D.K.Carmody (f/c).
12th Men: M.S.Guttormsen (Qld) and R.V.James (NSW).
Umpires: K.E.Fagg and J.A.Scott.
Attendances: 2917, 7914, 2545, 100.   Total: 13,476.   Receipts: £923.
Close of Play: 1st day NSW 5/66 (Robinson 9, Cheetham 5); 2nd day Qld (2) 4/156 (Brown 90); 3rd day NSW (2) 7/258 (Pepper 6, O'Reilly 0).

Brown led Queensland from the front, topscoring in each innings with 87 (145 minutes, 7 fours) and 137 (230 minutes, 14 fours). He shared a second-wicket stand of 136 with Allen (77 in 148 minutes, 8 fours) on the opening day. Rogers, Queensland's other successful batsman, scored a pair of 45's in 53 minutes (7 fours) and 60 minutes (7 fours) respectively. Ellis dismissed McCabe with the fourth ball of his opening over but strained his arm soon after and took no further part in the match. Contrasting eighties were made by Cheetham (85 in 192 minutes, 1 six and 10 fours) and Pepper (81 in 61 minutes, 7 sixes and 8 fours) for New South Wales on the second day, Pepper hitting 74 (91.36%) of his runs in boundaries. Chasing 267 to win, McCabe (98 in 127 minutes, 13 fours) and Solomon (89 in 111 minutes, 3 sixes and 8 fours) put on 147 in just 77 minutes for the third wicket. O'Reilly struck two fours in the first over of a last day that needed only 5 minutes' play. Sources: *Wisden, NSWCA Report, The Herald, Sydney Morning Herald, NSWCA Scorebook, Brisbane Courier-Mail, The Sporting Globe*.

QUEENSLAND

*W.A.Brown	c & b Pepper	87	c Sismey b Pepper	137
G.G.Cook	c Sismey b Cheetham	9	b Cheetham	7
T.Allen	c Gilmore b Pepper	77	c Sismey b Pepper	5
†D.Tallon	st Sismey b Barnes	12	(6) b Gilmore	24
R.E.Rogers	c Sismey b Cheetham	45	(4) c McCabe b Barnes	45
G.W.Baker	c Pepper b Cheetham	32	(5) c Sismey b O'Reilly	5
C.G.R.Stibe	lbw b O'Reilly	1	b O'Reilly	5
L.W.T.Tallon	c & b O'Reilly	1	b O'Reilly	1
P.L.Dixon	b Cheetham	13	c Solomon b Pepper	7
C.P.Christ	not out	0	not out	6
J.A.Ellis	b O'Reilly	0	absent hurt	-
Extras	(b3, lb4, nb6)	13	(b9, lb8, nb4)	21
Total	(60.2 overs, 236 mins)	290	(65.5 overs, 248 mins)	263

NEW SOUTH WALES

*S.J.McCabe	c D.Tallon b Ellis	0	c Christ b Dixon	98
J.H.W.Fingleton	c D.Tallon b Cook	0	c D.Tallon b Dixon	5
S.G.Barnes	c Dixon b Christ	10	c Christ b Baker	8
C.M.Solomon	lbw b L.W.T.Tallon	39	c D.Tallon b Dixon	89
D.K.Carmody	b Dixon	0	c L.W.T.Tallon b Dixon	30
R.H.Robinson	c Allen b Christ	30	lbw b Cook	4
A.G.Cheetham	c Rogers b L.W.T.Tallon	85	b Cook	13
C.G.Pepper	lbw b Dixon	81	not out	7
W.J.O'Reilly	b Dixon	0	not out	9
F.P.J.Gilmore	not out	21		
†S.G.Sismey	lbw b Cook	15		
Extras	(b3, nb3)	6	(lb5)	5
Total	(77.5 overs, 281 mins)	287	(51.2 overs, 200 mins) (7 wkts)	268

NEW SOUTH WALES	O	M	R	W	w,nb		O	M	R	W	w,nb
Gilmore	13	0	83	0	-,1		12	1	56	1	-,1
Cheetham	14	1	75	4	-,2		8	0	33	1	-,1
O'Reilly	14.2	6	27	3	-,3		21	5	53	3	-,2
Pepper	15	1	86	2	-,-		18.5	2	75	3	-,-
Robinson	1	1	0	0	-,-						
Barnes	3	0	6	1	-,-	(5)	6	0	25	1	-,-

QUEENSLAND	O	M	R	W	w,nb		O	M	R	W	w,nb
Ellis	3	0	4	1	-,-						
Cook	16.5	1	57	2	-,-		12.2	0	59	2	-,-
Dixon	19	2	44	3	-,3	(1)	17	1	67	4	-,-
Christ	18	7	62	2	-,-		13	1	80	0	-,-
L.W.T.Tallon	17	1	104	2	-,-		2	0	26	0	-,-
Baker	4	0	10	0	-,-	(3)	7	1	31	1	-,-

FALL OF WICKETS

Wkt	QLD 1st	NSW 1st	QLD 2nd	NSW 2nd
1st	34	0	17	19
2nd	170	2	38	35
3rd	189	33	132	182
4th	197	34	156	233
5th	274	57	214	236
6th	275	97	238	241
7th	276	203	246	258
8th	290	203	252	-
9th	290	268	263	-
10th	290	287	-	-

SOUTH AUSTRALIA v VICTORIA (Shield Match 2)

Played at Adelaide Oval on November 17, 18, 20, 21, 1939. (Four-day match)
Toss : Victoria.   Result : SOUTH AUSTRALIA WON BY THREE WICKETS.
Debuts: South Australia - T.E.Klose (f/c).
12th Men: J.Tregoning (SA) and R.A.Dempster (Vic).
Umpires: A.G.Jenkins and J.D.Scott.
Attendances: No daily figures published.   Total: 16,140.   Receipts: £485.
Close of Play: 1st day SA 6/142 (Klose 47); 2nd day Vic (2) 1/104 (Lee 61, Hassett 13); 3rd day SA (2) 1/11 (Whitington 9, Walker 1).

Both sides lost a wicket in their first over; Lee to the fifth ball of the match. Bradman (76 in 121 minutes, 6 fours) was run out for the fourth and last time in 338 first-class innings (the first three were in 1929) by Miller's swift pick-up and throw from cover late on the first day. Klose on debut (80 in 171 minutes, 4 fours) and Waite (67 in 116 minutes, 10 fours) who also scored half-centuries were the only other locals to reach double figures in the first innings. Leading contributors in the winning total on the last day were Bradman (64 in 101 minutes, 6 fours), Hamence (99 in 175 minutes, 8 fours) and Waite (42 not out in 63 minutes, 6 fours). Badcock (lumbago) was unable to field in the second innings. Victoria's best scores came from Tamblyn (67 in 142 minutes, 1 five and 7 fours) and Barnett (51 in 90 minutes, 1 five and 5 fours) in the first innings and Lee (68 in 146 minutes, 9 fours), Hassett (89 in 189 minutes, 8 fours), Johnson (41 in 128 minutes, 3 fours) and Sievers (56 in 102 minutes, 8 fours) in the second. Wrist spinners Grimmett (8 wickets) and Ring (7 wickets) were the leading bowlers. Umpire Scott was struck on the shin by a drive from Sievers on the third day and left the field for several overs, R.B.Pounsett substituting. Sources: *Wisden, SACA Report, The Herald, Adelaide Advertiser, The News, The Sporting Globe.*

VICTORIA

I.S.Lee	c Walker b Cotton	0	c sub (J.Tregoning) b Grimmett	68
G.E.Tamblyn	b Grimmett	67	b Grimmett	29
A.L.Hassett	c Grimmett Waite	5	c Walker b Cotton	89
K.R.Miller	c Whitington b Cotton	4	b Grimmett	7
I.W.Johnson	lbw b Grimmett	33	c Bradman b Grimmett	41
D.H.Fothergill	c Walker b Grimmett	1	lbw b Waite	10
*†B.A.Barnett	lbw b Waite	51	run out	2
M.W.Sievers	st Walker b Ward	23	c Klose b Grimmett	56
D.T.Ring	c Whitington b Cotton	19	lbw b Waite	31
R.B.Scott	b Ward	0	c & b Waite	14
L.O.Fleetwood-Smith	not out	0	not out	4
Extras	(b2, lb1, nb1)	4	(b3, lb7, nb2)	12
Total	(50.2 overs, 189 mins)	207	(116.4 overs, 406 mins)	363

SOUTH AUSTRALIA

R.S.Whitington	c Fleetwood-Smith b Scott	0		b Fleetwood-Smith	27
K.L.Ridings	c Sievers b Scott	6		c Ring b Sievers	1
*D.G.Bradman	run out (Miller/Sievers)	76	(4)	lbw b Ring	64
R.A.Hamence	lbw b Scott	6	(5)	c Sievers b Ring	99
C.L.Badcock	lbw b Fleetwood-Smith	3	(6)	c Barnett b Scott	30
T.E.Klose	c Hassett b Ring	80	(8)	lbw b Ring	0
F.A.Ward	lbw b Fleetwood-Smith	1	(9)	not out	1
M.G.Waite	c Miller b Sievers	67	(7)	not out	42
†C.W.Walker	c & b Ring	4	(3)	b Ring	20
C.V.Grimmett	c Sievers b Ring	9			
H.N.J.Cotton	not out	1			
Extras	(b1, lb1, nb6)	8		(b17, lb6, w2, nb1)	26
Total	(60.4 overs, 255 mins)	261		(74.7 overs, 295 mins) (7 wkts)	310

SOUTH AUSTRALIA	O	M	R	W	w,nb		O	M	R	W	w,nb		FALL OF WICKETS			
Cotton	12.2	1	78	3	-,1		23	1	74	1	-,1			VIC	SA	VIC	SA
Waite	13	1	48	2	-,-		35	8	76	3	-,1	Wkt	1st	1st	2nd	2nd
Grimmett	19	4	67	3	-,-		34.4	7	118	5	-,-	1st	0	0	50	10
Ward	6	0	10	2	-,-		16	0	75	0	-,-	2nd	5	16	120	44
Klose							8	3	8	0	-,-	3rd	18	28	138	70
												4th	66	35	221	182
VICTORIA	O	M	R	W	w,nb		O	M	R	W	w,nb	5th	72	137	253	243
Scott	11	0	55	3	-,5		14	0	50	1	2,-	6th	151	142	253	284
Sievers	17	4	63	1	-,-		14	3	40	1	-,-	7th	167	220	260	290
Fleetwood-Smith	14	0	59	2	-,-	(4)	16	0	78	1	-,-	8th	192	226	320	-
Ring	18.4	1	76	3	-,1	(3)	26	2	104	4	-,1	9th	192	260	353	-
Johnson							4.7	0	12	0	-,-	10th	207	261	363	-

VICTORIA v QUEENSLAND (Shield Match 3)

Played at Melbourne Cricket Ground on December 15, 16, 18, 19, 1939. (Four-day match)
Toss : Queensland.   Result : VICTORIA WON BY SEVEN WICKETS.
Debuts: Queensland - D.Watt (f/c).
12th Men: P.J.Beames (Vic) and C.D.Hansen (Qld).
Umpires: A.N.Barlow and W.J.Craddock.
Attendances: 3932, 7381, 2418, -.   Total: 13,731.   Receipts: £438.
Close of Play: 1st day Vic 0/3 (Lee 3, Tamblyn 0); 2nd day Vic 5/363 (Johnson 41, Barnett 28); 3rd day Qld (2) 9/238 (Watt 56, Ellis 7).

Cook (62 in 187 minutes, 6 fours), Rogers (53 in 76 minutes, 6 fours) and D.Tallon (56 in 89 minutes, 4 fours) hit half-centuries on the opening day in a moderate Queensland total. Tamblyn (107 in 202 minutes, 11 fours) scored his second hundred in five matches for Victoria and shared partnerships of 91 for the first wicket with Lee (52 in 93 minutes, 4 fours) and 126 for the second wicket with Hassett (83 in 150 minutes, 6 fours). Miller (41 in 61 minutes, 4 fours), Johnson (44 in 94 minutes, 4 fours) and Barnett (37 in 71 minutes, 3 fours) took the total beyond 400. Watt's 59 not out on debut occupied 118 minutes and included 5 fours. Miller (47 not out in 76 minutes, 1 five and 6 fours) and Johnson (37 not out in 69 minutes, 2 fours) hit off the required runs on the final day, for which admission was free, after the loss of three early wickets including Tamblyn to the seventh ball of the opening over. Sources: *Wisden, NSWCA Report, QCA Report, The Age, The Argus, The Herald, Melbourne Sun, The Sporting Globe.*

QUEENSLAND

*W.A.Brown	st Barnett b Ring	20	b Sievers		27
G.G.Cook	c Johnson b Ring	62	b Sievers		9
T.Allen	b Sievers	1	run out (Miller/Barnett)		3
R.E.Rogers	c Sievers b Johnson	53	b Fleetwood-Smith		39
G.W.Baker	b Ring	17	lbw b Fleetwood-Smith		25
†D.Tallon	c Johnson b Sievers	56	b Fleetwood-Smith		6
D.Watt	b Fleetwood-Smith	6	not out		59
L.W.T.Tallon	c Barnett b Scott	19	lbw b Fleetwood-Smith		1
P.L.Dixon	b Scott	4	(10) b Sievers		25
C.P.Christ	b Ring	18	(9) lbw b Johnson		32
J.A.Ellis	not out	14	run out (Miller/Barnett)		8
Extras	(b4, lb1, w1, nb3)	9	(b1, lb5, nb2)		8
Total	(77.2 overs, 296 mins)	279	(58.0 overs, 221 mins)		242

VICTORIA

I.S.Lee	lbw b Ellis	52	c Cook b Ellis		4
G.E.Tamblyn	c Cook b Ellis	107	b Ellis		0
A.L.Hassett	c D.Tallon b Dixon	83			
K.R.Miller	c & b Christ	41	not out		47
I.W.Johnson	c D.Tallon b Ellis	44	not out		37
D.H.Fothergill	st D.Tallon b Christ	5	(3) b Ellis		10
*†B.A.Barnett	b Ellis	37			
M.W.Sievers	c Watt b Cook	12			
D.T.Ring	c Baker b Cook	15			
R.B.Scott	not out	11			
L.O.Fleetwood-Smith	c D.Tallon b Ellis	0			
Extras	(b3, lb6, nb2)	11	(lb2, w5)		7
Total	(107.2 overs, 427 mins)	418	(23.2 overs, 93 mins) (3 wkts)		105

VICTORIA	O	M	R	W	w,nb	O	M	R	W	w,nb
Scott	13	0	44	2	1,-	7	0	42	0	-,2
Sievers	18	3	49	2	-,2	13	0	45	3	-,-
Ring	20.2	3	74	4	-,1	14	0	50	0	-,-
Fleetwood-Smith	15	0	71	1	-,-	18	1	77	4	-,-
Johnson	11	1	32	1	-,-	6	0	20	1	-,-

QUEENSLAND	O	M	R	W	w,nb		O	M	R	W	w,nb
Ellis	30.2	2	110	5	-,1		5	0	14	3	-,-
Cook	21	4	69	2	-,1		7	0	36	0	-,-
L.W.T.Tallon	12	0	85	0	-,-						
Dixon	16	5	52	1	-,-	(3)	4	1	10	0	-,-
Christ	23	3	65	2	-,-	(4)	3	0	12	0	4,-
Watt	3	0	24	0	-,-	(5)	2.2	0	16	0	-,-
Baker	2	1	2	0	-,-						
Rogers						(6)	2	0	10	0	1,-

FALL OF WICKETS

Wkt	QLD 1st	VIC 1st	QLD 2nd	VIC 2nd
1st	33	91	37	1
2nd	34	217	38	14
3rd	111	271	52	15
4th	150	297	106	-
5th	167	307	109	-
6th	198	369	116	-
7th	228	382	120	-
8th	243	398	189	-
9th	243	416	224	-
10th	279	418	242	-

SOUTH AUSTRALIA v NEW SOUTH WALES (Shield Match 4)

Played at Adelaide Oval on December 15, 16, 18, 1939. (Four-day match)
Toss : New South Wales.   Result : SOUTH AUSTRALIA WON BY SEVEN WICKETS.
Debuts: South Australia - J.Tregoning (f/c). New South Wales - A.W.Roper, J.E.Walsh (both f/c).
12th Men: P.L.Ridings (SA) and R.H.Robinson (NSW).
Umpires: A.G.Jenkins and J.D.Scott (H.C.Newman deputised).
Attendances: No daily figures published.   Total: 17,456.   Receipts: £525.
Close of Play: 1st day SA 1/68 (Ridings 29, Bradman 27); 2nd day NSW (2) 4/139 (Chipperfield 38).

Tregoning replaced C.L.Badcock (sciatica) in the South Australian side selected for the match. Bradman scored 58.2% of his team's runs with unbeaten innings of 251 (272 minutes, 2 sixes and 38 fours) and 90 (100 minutes, 14 fours). A hard chance on 177 was his only blemish as he raced from 107 to 231 in the lunch-tea session on the second day; he took 23 minutes over his last 51 runs. Hamence (41 in 69 minutes, 7 fours) and Waite (46 in 87 minutes, 4 fours) contributed to the 501 runs scored on the second day. Attacking roles for New South Wales were played by Solomon (131 in 154 minutes, 18 fours), Chipperfield (57 in 61 minutes, 1 six and 5 fours) and Pepper (47 in 38 minutes, 2 sixes and 4 fours). Cotton took no further part after tearing a groin muscle early in the match. Newman replaced umpire Jenkins (ill) after the first day. The game yielded an entertaining 1170 runs for 32 wickets in slightly more than 2-1/2 days. Sources: *Wisden, NSWCA Report, SACA Report, The Herald, Sydney Morning Herald, NSWCA Scorebook, Adelaide Advertiser, The News.*

NEW SOUTH WALES

S.J.McCabe	lbw b Grimmett	40		lbw b Grimmett	47
*J.H.W.Fingleton	c Bradman b Grimmett	29		b Klose	2
S.G.Barnes	b Waite	2	(6)	c Walker b Ward	33
C.M.Solomon	c Tregoning b Klose	131	(3)	c Tregoning b Grimmett	46
A.G.Chipperfield	b Cotton	32	(4)	lbw b Grimmett	57
A.G.Cheetham	c Bradman b Tregoning	32	(7)	b Grimmett	2
C.G.Pepper	lbw b Klose	22	(8)	c Grimmett b Klose	47
A.W.Roper	c Ridings b Grimmett	15	(5)	c & b Ward	0
W.J.O'Reilly	c Walker b Klose	16		c Tregoning b Grimmett	5
†S.G.Sismey	not out	5		c Tregoning b Grimmett	3
J.E.Walsh	b Klose	1		not out	0
Extras	(b2, lb8, w1)	11		(b1, lb5)	6
Total	(64.4 overs, 253 mins)	336		(54.5 overs, 183 mins)	248

SOUTH AUSTRALIA

R.S.Whitington	c Sismey b Roper	6			
K.L.Ridings	c Sismey b Walsh	29	(1)	b Cheetham	20
*D.G.Bradman	not out	251		not out	90
R.A.Hamence	lbw b Pepper	41		lbw b Pepper	12
M.G.Waite	b Cheetham	46		not out	28
T.E.Klose	c & b O'Reilly	4	(2)	b Roper	2
J.Tregoning	b O'Reilly	0			
†C.W.Walker	b O'Reilly	1			
F.A.Ward	b O'Reilly	4			
C.V.Grimmett	b O'Reilly	17			
H.N.J.Cotton	absent hurt	-			
Extras	(b21, lb4, nb6)	31		(b1, lb3)	4
Total	(72.1 overs, 293 mins)	430		(30.2 overs, 112 mins) (3 wkts)	156

SOUTH AUSTRALIA	O	M	R	W	w,nb		O	M	R	W	w,nb
Cotton	12	0	51	1	-,-						
Waite	19	0	98	1	-,-	(1)	12	1	22	0	-,-
Grimmett	20	0	102	3	-,-		20.5	0	122	6	-,-
Ward	5	0	42	0	-,-		15	4	61	2	-,-
Tregoning	3	0	9	1	1,-						
Klose	5.4	1	23	4	-,-	(2)	7	1	37	2	-,-

NEW SOUTH WALES	O	M	R	W	w,nb		O	M	R	W	w,nb
Roper	14	0	83	1	-,3		3	0	26	1	-,-
Cheetham	15	1	80	1	-,2		7	0	33	1	-,-
O'Reilly	22.1	4	108	5	-,1		10	0	29	0	-,-
Pepper	9	0	56	1	-,-		8	0	31	1	-,-
Walsh	12	0	72	1	-,-		2.2	0	33	0	-,-

FALL OF WICKETS

Wkt	NSW 1st	SA 1st	NSW 2nd	SA 2nd
1st	63	17	16	9
2nd	70	69	60	57
3rd	74	161	122	87
4th	130	308	139	-
5th	225	313	171	-
6th	283	313	179	-
7th	298	317	238	-
8th	322	349	244	-
9th	330	430	248	-
10th	336	-	248	-

VICTORIA v NEW SOUTH WALES (Shield Match 5)

Played at Melbourne Cricket Ground on December 22, 23, 26, 1939. (Four-day match)
Toss : Victoria.   Result : VICTORIA WON BY 72 RUNS.
Debuts: Nil.
12th Men: D.H.Fothergill (Vic) and J.E.Walsh (NSW).
Umpires: A.N.Barlow and W.J.Craddock.
Attendances: 3086, 8894, 9810.   Total: 21,790.   Receipts: £844.
Close of Play: 1st day Vic 280 all out; 2nd day Vic (2) 3/99 (Hassett 35, Johnson 13).

Rain and bad light interrupted play several times on the opening day, in which Tamblyn (58 in 113 minutes, 7 fours), Johnson (41 in 121 minutes, 3 fours) and Sievers (53 in 82 minutes, 1 six and 3 fours) batted well for Victoria. Fingleton fell to the fourth ball when New South Wales began their innings on the second day, McCabe (52 in 73 minutes, 4 fours), Solomon (52 in 81 minutes, 5 fours) and Barnes (98 in 109 minutes, 11 fours) scoring fast fifties for the side. Roper strained a leg tendon while fielding early on the first day and was unable to field or bowl again in the match. Though able to bat without a runner, he failed to score in either innings. Hassett (57 in 105 minutes, 5 fours) and Barnett (66 in 110 minutes, 6 fours) hit half-centuries in Victoria's second innings against the leg-spin of O'Reilly and Pepper. Set 202 to win, New South Wales lost Fingleton to the third ball of Siever's first over, and then McCabe, Solomon and Barnes before reaching double figures. Chipperfield (68 in 104 minutes, 10 fours) easily made top score. *NSWCA Report* incorrectly gives NSW (2) Cheetham lbw b Scott. Sources: *Wisden, NSWCA Report, The Age, The Argus, The Herald, Melbourne Sun, NSWCA Scorebook, The Sporting Globe.*

VICTORIA

I.S.Lee	c McCabe b Cheetham	4	lbw b Pepper	18
G.E.Tamblyn	b Pepper	58	lbw b O'Reilly	15
A.L.Hassett	c Chipperfield b Pepper	33	lbw b Pepper	57
K.R.Miller	b Pepper	14	c Sismey b O'Reilly	14
I.W.Johnson	lbw b O'Reilly	41	c Fingleton b O'Reilly	13
P.J.Beames	c Pepper b Cheetham	34	b Pepper	3
*†B.A.Barnett	c Cheetham b Chipperfield	21	c sub (J.E.Walsh) b O'Reilly	66
M.W.Sievers	b O'Reilly	53	c Solomon b Pepper	29
D.T.Ring	b O'Reilly	8	c Sismey b O'Reilly	4
R.B.Scott	c Sismey b O'Reilly	4	not out	13
L.O.Fleetwood-Smith	not out	0	b Pepper	1
Extras	(b4, lb2, w1, nb3)	10	(lb6, nb3)	9
Total	(68.3 overs, 252 mins)	280	(72.0 overs, 241 mins)	242

NEW SOUTH WALES

*S.J.McCabe	c Scott b Fleetwood-Smith	52	(2) c Johnson b Scott	4
J.H.W.Fingleton	b Scott	0	(1) lbw b Sievers	3
C.M.Solomon	lbw b Ring	52	c Barnett b Scott	1
S.G.Barnes	c Fleetwood-Smith b Sievers	98	run out (Lee/Barnett)	1
A.G.Chipperfield	c Tamblyn b Ring	40	lbw b Sievers	68
R.H.Robinson	c Johnson b Scott	16	lbw b Scott	6
A.G.Cheetham	lbw b Ring	16	b Scott	23
C.G.Pepper	st Barnett b Fleetwood-Smith	19	c Barnett b Sievers	1
W.J.O'Reilly	c Miller b Ring	17	c Hassett b Ring	15
A.W.Roper	run out (Hassett)	0	c Sievers b Ring	0
†S.G.Sismey	not out	0	not out	4
Extras	(b6, lb5)	11	(b2, lb1)	3
Total	(50.3 overs, 217 mins)	321	(33.4 overs, 143 mins)	129

NEW SOUTH WALES	O	M	R	W	w,nb		O	M	R	W	w,nb					
Roper	4	0	22	0	1,-											
Cheetham	17	2	72	2	-,2	(1)	9	1	27	0	-,-	Wkt	1st	1st	2nd	2nd
O'Reilly	20.3	6	75	4	-,1	(4)	27	3	72	5	-,3	1st	9	3	33	5
Pepper	20	0	91	3	-,-	(3)	31	6	114	5	-,-	2nd	78	103	37	8
Chipperfield	7	1	10	1	-,-	(2)	4	0	16	0	-,-	3rd	98	121	76	9
Barnes						(5)	1	0	4	0	-,-	4th	123	214	100	9
												5th	162	247	115	30
VICTORIA	O	M	R	W	w,nb		O	M	R	W	w,nb	6th	203	273	126	102
Scott	11	0	71	2	-,-		10	1	35	4	-,-	7th	233	297	205	103
Sievers	14	0	74	1	-,-		8	2	18	3	-,-	8th	253	319	217	110
Ring	14.3	0	85	4	-,-	(4)	8.4	2	33	2	-,-	9th	257	319	234	124
Fleetwood-Smith	9	0	61	2	-,-	(3)	7	0	40	0	-,-	10th	280	321	242	129
Johnson	2	0	19	0	-,-											

FALL OF WICKETS

SOUTH AUSTRALIA v QUEENSLAND (Shield Match 6)

Played at Adelaide Oval on December 22, 23, 25, 26, 1939. (Four-day match)
Toss : South Australia.   Result : SOUTH AUSTRALIA WON BY AN INNINGS AND 222 RUNS.
Debuts: Nil.
12th Men: G.Burton (SA) and L.W.T.Tallon (Qld).
Umpires: H.C.Newman and J.D.Scott.
Attendances: No daily figures published.   Total: 21,420.   Receipts: £644.
Close of Play: 1st day SA 4/553 (Badcock 172, Waite 57); 2nd day Qld 4/177 (Rogers 38, Tallon 53); 3rd day Qld (2) 6/346 (Hansen 13, Christ 11).

South Australia put up their highest total in first-class cricket and created a record for the most runs scored on the opening day of a match in this country, 553 in 328 minutes (80 eight-ball overs). Ken Ridings (chanceless career-best 151 in 238 minutes, 14 fours) and Bradman (chanceless 138 in 115 minutes, 22 fours) added 196 for the second wicket. Bradman made his first 86 runs before lunch and reached his hundred in 80 minutes, it was his 10th hundred in his last 12 innings against Queensland (his fifth in successive innings). Ridings took his score from 50* to 146* in the middle session. Badcock (236 in 249 minutes, 4 sixes and 26 fours) scored 115 after tea and shared with Waite (137 in 204 minutes, 14 fours), a stand of 281 in 180 minutes, a State fifth-wicket record. However, both were dropped, off consecutive balls from Ellis late on the first day. Whitington (67 in 83 minutes, 1 six and 9 fours) and Phil Ridings (44 not out in 59 minutes, 7 fours) added 108 prior to the declaration at 3.15 pm on the second day. Rogers (49 in 70 minutes, 9 fours) and Tallon (70 in 63 minutes, 10 fours) stood out in the Queensland first innings, adding 107 in 54 minutes. Brown (chanceless 156 in 230 minutes, 23 fours) batted in fine style in the follow-on, but apart from Rogers (50 in 97 minutes, 7 fours) and Baker (52 in 93 minutes, 5 fours) he received little support, Grimmett and Ward again sharing the wickets. Only 28 minutes were required on the last day to finish the match. Sources: *Wisden, SACA Report, The Age, The Herald, Adelaide Advertiser, The News, The Sporting Globe.*

SOUTH AUSTRALIA

K.L.Ridings	lbw b Baker	151
T.E.Klose	c Ellis b Cook	13
*D.G.Bradman	c Hansen b Ellis	138
R.A.Hamence	lbw b Cook	6
C.L.Badcock	b Dixon	236
M.G.Waite	c & b Dixon	137
R.S.Whitington	c Rogers b Christ	67
P.L.Ridings	not out	44
†C.W.Walker	)	
C.V.Grimmett	) did not bat	
F.A.Ward	)	
Extras	(b10, lb17, nb2)	29
Total	(127.1 overs, 505 mins) (7 wkts dec)	821

QUEENSLAND

*W.A.Brown	b Grimmett	20		st Walker b Ward	156
G.G.Cook	st Walker b Ward	27		c Waite b Grimmett	15
T.Allen	c Klose b Ward	35		c Waite b Ward	22
R.E.Rogers	c Waite b Grimmett	49		c Klose b Grimmett	50
G.W.Baker	c Walker b Klose	0		lbw b Grimmett	52
†D.Tallon	c Badcock b Ward	70		c Waite b Ward	14
C.D.Hansen	b Grimmett	2		c Walker b Grimmett	15
D.Watt	c Waite b Grimmett	6	(9)	lbw b Grimmett	8
C.P.Christ	c Walker b Ward	1	(8)	b Ward	12
P.L.Dixon	not out	3		c Walker b Grimmett	17
J.A.Ellis	c Badcock b Ward	5		not out	1
Extras	(lb3, nb1)	4		(b8, lb3, w1, nb3)	15
Total	(54.7 overs, 190 mins)	222		(90.4 overs, 303 mins)	377

QUEENSLAND	O	M	R	W	w,nb
Ellis	14	0	95	1	-,-
Cook	22	1	129	2	-,-
Dixon	24	0	142	2	-,2
Christ	27.1	3	144	1	-,-
Baker	22	0	127	1	-,-
Watt	14	1	135	0	-,-
Rogers	4	1	20	0	-,-

SOUTH AUSTRALIA	O	M	R	W	w,nb	O	M	R	W	w,nb
P.L.Ridings	5	0	29	0	-,1	11	1	48	0	1,1
Waite	9	2	40	0	-,-	13	2	21	0	-,2
Grimmett	19	2	71	4	-,-	33.4	5	124	6	-,-
Ward	16.7	2	62	5	-,-	30	3	165	4	-,-
Klose	5	1	16	1	-,-	3	0	4	0	-,-

FALL OF WICKETS

	SA	QLD	QLD
Wkt	1st	1st	2nd
1st	36	41	27
2nd	232	76	84
3rd	268	91	205
4th	404	92	291
5th	685	199	311
6th	713	207	329
7th	821	213	348
8th	-	214	350
9th	-	216	364
10th	-	222	377

NEW SOUTH WALES v QUEENSLAND (Shield Match 7)

Played at Sydney Cricket Ground on December 29, 30, 1939. (Four-day match)
Toss : Queensland.   Result : NEW SOUTH WALES WON BY AN INNINGS AND 130 RUNS.
Debuts: - Nil.
12th Men: R.A.Saggers (NSW) and C.D.Hansen (Qld).
Umpires: E.G.Borwick and R.McGrath.
Attendances: 8161, 8626.   Total: 16,787.   Receipts: £1009.
Close of Play: 1st day NSW 5/240 (Barnes 78, Pepper 7).

In conditions which favoured batting, O'Reilly (14 for 45) captured the best combined bowling figures in matches between these teams to give New South Wales victory inside two days. It remained his career-best match analysis and his eight first-innings wickets were split either side of lunch, 4 for 16 in 8 overs before and 4 for 7 in 3.1 overs after. Baker (51 in 81 minutes, 5 fours) scored Queensland's only half century. In his first State match for three years Mudge (79 in 120 minutes, 8 fours) batted well to partner Barnes (119 in 159 minutes, 13 fours), Lush (54 in 101 minutes, 5 fours) lending support. J.H.W.Fingleton and A.W.Roper were unavailable for New South Wales due to leg injuries. The naming of Saggers, a wicket-keeper, as 12th man to replace D.K.Carmody, was roundly criticised in the Press. Sources: *Wisden, NSWCA Report, QCA Report, The Herald, Sydney Morning Herald, NSWCA Scorebook, Brisbane Courier-Mail, The Sporting Globe.*

QUEENSLAND

*W.A.Brown	c Chipperfield b Lush	24	(4) c Mudge b O'Reilly		14
G.G.Cook	lbw b O'Reilly	15	(3) c Sismey b Pepper		3
T.Allen	b O'Reilly	2	(2) lbw b Pepper		17
R.E.Rogers	c Sismey b O'Reilly	18	(1) b Cheetham		18
G.W.Baker	run out (Lush)	10	c Mudge b O'Reilly		51
†D.Tallon	b O'Reilly	16	c Solomon b O'Reilly		0
D.Watt	b O'Reilly	0	b O'Reilly		6
L.W.T.Tallon	b O'Reilly	3	(9) c Lush b O'Reilly		0
C.P.Christ	not out	5	(8) b Walsh		9
P.L.Dixon	b O'Reilly	2	c Mudge b O'Reilly		7
J.A.Ellis	b O'Reilly	2	not out		4
Extras	(b7, nb1)	8	(b9, lb4, nb2)		15
Total	(34.1 overs, 129 mins)	105	(42.2 overs, 153 mins)		144

NEW SOUTH WALES

*S.J.McCabe	c Brown b Ellis	13
H.Mudge	lbw b Baker	79
C.M.Solomon	b Dixon	24
S.G.Barnes	c Ellis b Baker	119
A.G.Chipperfield	b Cook	10
A.G.Cheetham	st D.Tallon b Christ	21
C.G.Pepper	st D.Tallon b Cook	8
J.G.Lush	b Ellis	54
W.J.O'Reilly	c & b Christ	26
†S.G.Sismey	c & b L.W.T.Tallon	5
J.E.Walsh	not out	10
Extras	(b4, lb5, nb1)	10
Total	(73.3 overs, 293 mins)	379

NEW SOUTH WALES	O	M	R	W	w,nb		O	M	R	W	w,nb
Lush	6	0	27	1	-,-		3	0	18	0	-,-
Cheetham	4	1	10	0	-,1		5	0	18	1	-,2
Pepper	13	2	37	0	-,-	(4)	14	2	45	2	-,-
O'Reilly	11.1	3	23	8	-,-	(3)	15.2	7	22	6	-,-
Walsh							5	0	26	1	-,-

QUEENSLAND	O	M	R	W	w,nb
Ellis	16.3	0	60	2	-,1
Cook	12	0	67	2	-,-
Baker	11	0	65	2	-,-
Dixon	7	2	26	1	-,-
L.W.T.Tallon	11	0	71	1	-,-
Christ	12	0	53	2	-,-
Watt	4	0	27	0	-,-

FALL OF WICKETS			
	QLD	NSW	QLD
Wkt	1st	1st	2nd
1st	37	20	31
2nd	44	84	47
3rd	51	159	48
4th	76	191	104
5th	82	233	104
6th	82	242	116
7th	94	307	125
8th	101	350	125
9th	103	361	140
10th	105	379	144

AFCM No. 945/99
SSM No. 337/86

VICTORIA v SOUTH AUSTRALIA (Shield Match 8)

Played at Melbourne Cricket Ground on December 29, 30, 1939, January 1, 2, 1940. (Four-day match)
Toss : Victoria.   Result : MATCH DRAWN.
Debuts: South Australia - G.Burton (f/c).
12th Men: D.H.Fothergill (Vic) and P.L.Ridings (SA).
Umpires: A.N.Barlow and W.J.Craddock.
Attendances: 12103, 29660, 30587, 4672.   Total: 77,022.   Receipts: £3374.
Close of Play: 1st day Vic 5/289 (Beames 7, Sievers 0); 2nd day SA 2/213 (Bradman 52, Badcock 41); 3rd day Vic (2) 0/10 (Barnett 10, Sievers 0).

Tamblyn (21) was struck by a return from Whitington on the first morning and was forced to retire at 1/64, resuming at 6/313 the next day. On the third day he badly gashed his knee on the boundary fence in trying to save a four and took no further part in the match, E.J.R.Moyle (omitted from the South Australia thirteen along with P.L.Ridings) replacing him in the field before R.G.Gregory was called in to substitute in the afternoon. Fothergill, Victoria's first reserve was substituting for Lee who suffered a gastric attack and consequently batted down the order in the second innings. Bradman's 267 in 340 minutes included 27 fours and was chanceless; he scored 90 and 93 either side of lunch on the third day before falling in the slips at 7/556. He had progressed from 88 to his hundred with three fours in four balls and this gave him 746 runs in four successive innings (251*, 90*, 138, 267). Ridings (56 in 89 minutes, 4 fours), Klose (54 in 101 minutes, 5 fours), Badcock (58 in 110 minutes, 4 fours) and Waite (64 in 119 minutes, 2 sixes and 5 fours) scored supporting fifties. Hassett (92 in 138 minutes, 6 fours), Miller (108 in 169 minutes, 7 fours) and Beames (chanceless 104 in 143 minutes, 8 fours) played major innings for Victoria. Hassett followed up with another half-century (66 in 82 minutes, 7 fours) in the second innings. Burton captured five wickets on debut, his best return in a three-match career. *Wisden* incorrectly gives SA batting first. Sources: *Wisden, SACA Report, The Age, The Argus, The Herald, Melbourne Sun, The Sporting Globe.*

VICTORIA

I.S.Lee	b Klose	36	(7)	c Grimmett b Ward	39
G.E.Tamblyn	c Walker b Ward	38		absent hurt	-
A.L.Hassett	st Walker b Grimmett	92		c & b Ward	66
K.R.Miller	c Bradman b Burton	108		c Bradman b Klose	1
I.W.Johnson	lbw b Waite	14		lbw b Klose	23
P.J.Beames	c & b Burton	104		b Burton	32
*†B.A.Barnett	b Burton	7	(1)	lbw b Klose	46
M.W.Sievers	lbw b Burton	16	(2)	c Badcock b Grimmett	36
D.T.Ring	st Walker b Grimmett	32	(8)	not out	41
R.B.Scott	c Waite b Burton	7	(9)	b Grimmett	17
L.O.Fleetwood-Smith	not out	11	(10)	st Walker b Ward	4
Extras	(b5, lb5)	10		(b5, lb3)	8
Total	(114.2 overs, 389 mins)	475		(73.4 overs, 262 mins)	313

SOUTH AUSTRALIA

K.L.Ridings	c Johnson b Ring	56		not out	29
T.E.Klose	b Scott	54		lbw b Ring	15
*D.G.Bradman	c Johnson b Fleetwood-Smith	267			
C.L.Badcock	lbw b Ring	58			
R.A.Hamence	lbw b Fleetwood-Smith	20	(3)	not out	11
R.S.Whitington	c Ring b Scott	41			
†C.W.Walker	lbw b Scott	1			
M.G.Waite	c Hassett b Ring	64			
F.A.Ward	c & b Ring	26			
C.V.Grimmett	c Sievers b Ring	6			
G.Burton	not out	1			
Extras	(b6, lb9, w1)	16		(b3, lb1, nb1)	5
Total	(119.4 overs, 478 mins)	610		(16.0 overs, 57 mins) (1 wkt)	60

SOUTH AUSTRALIA	O	M	R	W	w,nb		O	M	R	W	w,nb
Burton	20.2	0	99	5	-,-		11	1	44	1	-,-
Waite	21	3	90	1	-,-		10	1	38	0	-,-
Grimmett	33	2	136	2	-,-		21	2	78	2	-,-
Klose	21	3	42	1	-,-		17	4	43	3	-,-
Ward	19	0	98	1	-,-		14.4	2	102	3	-,-

VICTORIA	O	M	R	W	w,nb		O	M	R	W	w,nb
Scott	25	0	135	3	1,-		3	0	9	0	-,-
Sievers	29	1	120	0	-,-		3	0	12	0	-,-
Ring	25.4	1	123	5	-,-	(4)	4	1	13	1	-,1
Fleetwood-Smith	27	0	156	2	-,-						
Johnson	13	0	60	0	-,-	(3)	5	2	14	0	-,-
Hassett						(5)	1	0	7	0	-,-

FALL OF WICKETS

Wkt	VIC 1st	SA 1st	VIC 2nd	SA 2nd
1st	60	108	74	36
2nd	225	122	96	-
3rd	275	259	102	-
4th	277	330	178	-
5th	289	420	178	-
6th	313	430	239	-
7th	353	556	261	-
8th	440	596	298	-
9th	460	609	313	-
10th	475	610	-	-

QUEENSLAND v SOUTH AUSTRALIA (Shield Match 9)

Played at Brisbane Cricket Ground (Woolloongabba) on January 6, 8, 9, 10, 1940. (Four-day match)
Toss : South Australia.   Result : QUEENSLAND WON BY TWO WICKETS.
Debuts: Queensland - W.C.J.Bryce, G.A.Gooma, J.Stackpoole (all f/c).
12th Men: T.Allen (Qld) and P.L.Ridings (SA).
Umpires: D.W.Given and S.Ryan.
Attendances: 6500, 5670, 5800, 2400.   Total: 20,370.   Receipts: £1641.
Close of Play: 1st day SA 6/164 (Walker 10, Moyle 12); 2nd day SA (2) 3/62 (Bradman 29, Walker 0); 3rd day Qld (2) 0/128 (Brown 81, Cook 46).

Stackpoole's bright entry into first-class cricket (9 for 138) included four wickets on a rain-affected first day, including Bradman for a first-ball duck. He began the second innings by dismissing Ridings and Whitington with successive balls in the opening over but played only two further matches for Queensland before being discarded. Bradman (97 in 157 minutes, 10 fours) and Waite (62 in 123 minutes, 8 fours) hit half-centuries for South Australia. Queensland lost their last 6 for 1 in 2 overs in the first innings; debutants Bryce (third ball), Gooma and Stackpoole (both first ball) were among the victims. Grimmett's first wicket in the second innings, that of Bryce, was his 500th in the Sheffield Shield competition. Brown (111 in 213 minutes, 12 fours), Cook (54 in 162 minutes, 3 fours) and Rogers (74 in 94 minutes, 10 fours) led Queensland to their first win against South Australia in 11 matches since December 1934; Watt (59 not out in 90 minutes, 8 fours) saw the side home with an unbroken ninth-wicket stand of 45 in 36 minutes with Dixon. C.L.Badcock (ankle injury) was unavailable for South Australia. Sources: *Wisden, QCA Report, SACA Report, The Age, The Herald, Brisbane Courier-Mail, The Sporting Globe.*

SOUTH AUSTRALIA

K.L.Ridings	c Tallon b Stackpoole	35		b Stackpoole	1
T.E.Klose	c Tallon b Stackpoole	27		st Tallon b Christ	31
*D.G.Bradman	c Dixon b Stackpoole	0	(4)	c Tallon b Cook	97
R.S.Whitington	b Gooma	38	(3)	b Stackpoole	0
R.A.Hamence	c Stackpoole b Christ	26	(6)	c Brown b Christ	2
M.G.Waite	c Christ b Stackpoole	13	(8)	b Dixon	62
†C.W.Walker	b Stackpoole	37	(5)	b Christ	18
E.J.R.Moyle	b Stackpoole	32	(7)	b Dixon	6
F.A.Ward	c Tallon b Dixon	4		c Baker b Stackpoole	15
C.V.Grimmett	b Dixon	12	(11)	not out	5
G.Burton	not out	2	(10)	b Dixon	11
Extras	(lb2, nb2)	4		(b1, lb2, w1)	4
Total	(69.1 overs, 268 mins)	230		(64.3 overs, 250 mins)	252

QUEENSLAND

*W.A.Brown	c Walker b Ward	37		c Ward b Burton	111
G.G.Cook	c Walker b Grimmett	8		lbw b Ward	54
R.E.Rogers	run out (Whitington/Walker)	19		lbw b Waite	74
G.W.Baker	lbw b Burton	20		c Bradman b Klose	28
†D.Tallon	c Walker b Grimmett	41		b Waite	0
D.Watt	b Waite	6		not out	59
W.C.J.Bryce	lbw b Grimmett	0		b Grimmett	1
G.A.Gooma	b Grimmett	0	(9)	c Klose b Grimmett	0
C.P.Christ	not out	0	(8)	c Klose b Grimmett	3
P.L.Dixon	st Walker b Waite	1		not out	14
J.Stackpoole	b Waite	0			
Extras	(lb1)	1		(b4, lb2)	6
Total	(54.3 overs, 180 mins)	133		(107.1 overs, 354 mins) (8 wkts)	350

QUEENSLAND	O	M	R	W	w,nh		O	M	R	W	w,nh	
Stackpoole	18.1	0	72	6	-,-		14	1	66	3	-,-	
Cook	11	1	35	0	-,1		8	1	32	1	-,-	Wkt
Dixon	16	5	33	2	-,1		10.3	2	33	3	1,-	1st
Gooma	6	0	27	1	-,-	(5)	5	0	27	0	-,-	2nd
Christ	16	3	53	1	-,-	(4)	25	2	87	3	-,-	3rd
Baker	2	0	6	0	-,-		2	1	3	0	-,-	4th
												5th
SOUTH AUSTRALIA	O	M	R	W	w,nb		O	M	R	W	w,nb	6th
Burton	11	1	33	1	-,-		12	0	54	1	-,-	7th
Waite	16.3	6	25	3	-,-		25	2	89	2	-,-	8th
Grimmett	20	3	52	4	-,-		38.1	0	116	3	-,-	9th
Ward	4	0	15	1	-,-	(5)	13	0	47	1	-,-	10th
Klose	3	2	7	0	-,-	(4)	19	6	38	1	-,-	

FALL OF WICKETS

Wkt	SA 1st	QLD 1st	SA 2nd	QLD 2nd
1st	53	22	8	143
2nd	53	44	8	214
3rd	68	83	61	255
4th	119	99	107	261
5th	140	132	121	294
6th	145	132	130	295
7th	203	132	173	305
8th	212	132	229	305
9th	228	133	245	-
10th	230	133	252	-

NEW SOUTH WALES v SOUTH AUSTRALIA (Shield Match 10)

Played at Sydney Cricket Ground on January 13, 15, 16, 17, 1940. (Four-day match)
Toss : New South Wales.   Result : NEW SOUTH WALES WON BY 237 RUNS.
Debuts: New South Wales - M.B.Cohen, R.A.Saggers (both f/c).
12th Men: D.K.Carmody (NSW) and P.L.Ridings (SA).
Umpires: E.G.Borwick and R.McGrath.
Attendances: 30400, 24317, 10038, 11010.   Total: 75,765.   Receipts: £4915.
Close of Play: 1st day SA 2/54 (Whitington 23, Bradman 24); 2nd day NSW (2) 0/49 (Cohen 26, Mudge 23); 3rd day SA (2) 3/74
     (Bradman 35, Badcock 14).

C.M.Solomon (appendicitis) was unavailable for New South Wales. South Australia again omitted E.J.R.Moyle and P.L.Ridings from their touring party. Both Cohen (74 in 125 minutes, 4 fours and 70 in 87 minutes, 7 fours) and Saggers (45 in 98 minutes, 3 fours and 57 in 95 minutes, 4 fours) batted well on debut for New South Wales, Grimmett affecting the middle-order in each innings. Selected as a specialist batsman, Saggers had his first taste of wicket-keeping in first-class cricket late in the match when Sismey retired after being struck in the face by a top edge from Walker. Mudge (57 in 125 minutes, 6 fours) and McCabe (59 in 53 minutes, 7 fours and 55 in 77 minutes, 7 fours) also hit fifties for the home side. Two hours were lost on the second day due to rain and just 67 minutes were required on the last day to complete the match, the second on South Australia's eastern tour to attract more than 75,000 people. *SMH* incorrectly gives NSW (2) McCabe st Walker in both commentary and scoreboard. Sources: *Wisden, NSWCA Report, SACA Report, The Herald, Sydney Morning Herald, NSWCA Scorebook, The Sporting Globe*.

NEW SOUTH WALES

M.B.Cohen	c Walker b Klose	74	b Ward	70
H.Mudge	st Walker b Grimmett	14	c Bradman b Ward	57
*S.J.McCabe	st Walker b Grimmett	59	c Walker b Grimmett	55
S.G.Barnes	lbw b Grimmett	34	c Bradman b Grimmett	25
A.G.Chipperfield	lbw b Grimmett	0	st Walker b Grimmett	1
R.A.Saggers	c Walker b Klose	45	b Ward	57
A.G.Cheetham	lbw b Waite	14	b Grimmett	1
C.G.Pepper	lbw b Grimmett	9	c Waite b Burton	26
J.G.Lush	st Walker b Klose	1	st Walker b Grimmett	13
W.J.O'Reilly	st Walker b Grimmett	6	c Bradman b Ward	0
†S.G.Sismey	not out	2	not out	0
Extras	(b6, lb6)	12	(b5, lb1)	6
Total	(61.3 overs, 222 mins)	270	(73.1 overs, 255 mins)	311

SOUTH AUSTRALIA

K.L.Ridings	b Lush	3	b Cheetham	1
T.E.Klose	c Sismey b Lush	0	b Pepper	13
R.S.Whitington	c Barnes b O'Reilly	37	c Chipperfield b Pepper	11
*D.G.Bradman	lbw b O'Reilly	39	c sub (D.K.Carmody) b Pepper	40
C.L.Badcock	c Mudge b O'Reilly	40	c Chipperfield b O'Reilly	20
R.A.Hamence	c Mudge b O'Reilly	43	c Cohen b O'Reilly	0
M.G.Waite	run out (Pepper)	9	c Mudge b Pepper	19
†C.W.Walker	lbw b O'Reilly	1	c McCabe b Pepper	10
F.A.Ward	b Pepper	17	b O'Reilly	1
C.V.Grimmett	not out	7	b O'Reilly	6
G.Burton	c McCabe b O'Reilly	7	not out	11
Extras	(b5, lb2, w1)	8	(nb1)	1
Total	(65.5 overs, 223 mins)	211	(34.7 overs, 125 mins)	133

SOUTH AUSTRALIA	O	M	R	W	w,nb	O	M	R	W	w,nb			FALL OF WICKETS		
Burton	12	1	44	0	-,-	11	0	27	1	-,-			NSW	SA NSW	SA
Waite	13	0	43	1	-,-	7	0	32	0	-,-	Wkt	1st	1st	2nd	2nd
Grimmett	22	0	118	6	-,-	29	2	111	5	-,-	1st	22	1	111	1
Ward	3	0	32	0	-,-	22.1	1	120	4	-,-	2nd	130	8	156	22
Klose	11.3	3	21	3	-,-	4	0	15	0	-,-	3rd	189	77	199	27
											4th	189	103	207	85
NEW SOUTH WALES	O	M	R	W	w,nb	O	M	R	W	w,nb	5th	189	140	212	85
Lush	8	0	26	2	1,-	4	0	13	0	-,-	6th	223	156	222	85
Cohen	5	2	9	0	-,-						7th	238	162	265	112
O'Reilly	24.5	7	77	6	-,-	13.7	2	62	4	-,1	8th	249	187	304	115
Pepper	27	3	85	1	-,-	12	1	49	5	-,-	9th	262	201	305	117
Mudge	1	0	6	0	-,-						10th	270	211	311	133
Cheetham						(2) 5	1	8	1	-,-					

QUEENSLAND v VICTORIA (Shield Match 11)

Played at Brisbane Cricket Ground (Woolloongabba) on January 19, 20, 22, 23, 1940. (Four-day match)
Toss : Queensland.   Result : VICTORIA WON BY NINE WICKETS.
Debuts: Nil.
12th Men: W.C.J.Bryce (Qld) and F.L.O.Thorn (Vic).
Umpires: D.W.Given and R.Weitemeyer.
Attendances: 3200, 8000, 2300, 2160.   Total: 15,660.   Receipts: £1148.
Close of Play: 1st day Vic 0/28 (Lee 12, Barnett 15); 2nd day Vic 9/435 (Sievers 55); 3rd day Qld (2) 5/343 (Tallon 103, Watt 21).

Lee (90 in 111 minutes, 8 fours and 93 in 122 minutes, 14 fours) and Barnett (92 in 180 minutes, 6 fours and 104 not out in 181 minutes, 9 fours) became the first openers to put on 150 in each innings of an Australian match. Beames (55 in 88 minutes, 1 six and 5 fours), Sievers (55 not out in 124 minutes, 7 fours) and Ring (45 in 45 minutes, 7 fours) also batted well for Victoria. Brown (60 in 151 minutes, 3 fours) and Cook (64 in 168 minutes, 3 fours) began the match for Queensland with another hundred stand. In the second innings Rogers (73 in 124 minutes, 6 fours) and Baker (80 in 177 minutes, 4 fours) added 106 for the third wicket before Tallon (154 in 185 minutes, 1 six and 15 fours) arrived to dominate a stand of 115 for the sixth wicket with Watt. Sources: *Wisden, NSWCA Report, QCA Report, The Age, The Herald, Brisbane Courier-Mail, The Sporting Globe.*

QUEENSLAND

*W.A.Brown	c Scott b Ring	60	c & b Fleetwood-Smith	32
G.G.Cook	b Fleetwood-Smith	64	st Barnett b Fleetwood-Smith	24
R.E.Rogers	c Barnett b Ring	16	c Lee b Johnson	73
G.W.Baker	lbw b Johnson	34	lbw b Sievers	80
T.Allen	c Beames b Fleetwood-Smith	42	c Barnett b Johnson	4
†D.Tallon	lbw b Ring	0	c Hassett b Johnson	154
D.Watt	c Sievers b Scott	10	c Miller b Scott	29
C.P.Christ	b Johnson	5	not out	13
G.A.Gooma	c Miller b Johnson	2	b Ring	1
P.L.Dixon	c Hassett b Fleetwood-Smith	0	b Johnson	1
J.Stackpoole	not out	1	c Lee b Ring	0
Extras	(b4, lb5, w1)	10	(b5, lb4)	9
Total	(69.5 overs, 296 mins)	244	(95.5 overs, 391 mins)	420

VICTORIA

I.S.Lee	c Watt b Dixon	90	c & b Stackpoole	93
*†B.A.Barnett	c Christ b Stackpoole	92	not out	104
A.L.Hassett	c Watt b Stackpoole	17		
K.R.Miller	b Cook	37		
I.W.Johnson	c Stackpoole b Cook	7		
P.J.Beames	st Tallon b Christ	55		
D.H.Fothergill	c Baker b Cook	0	(3) not out	26
M.W.Sievers	not out	55		
D.T.Ring	st Tallon b Watt	45		
R.B.Scott	c Brown b Gooma	33		
L.O.Fleetwood-Smith	did not bat			
Extras	(b2, lb2)	4	(b6, w1)	7
Total	(92.7 overs, 351 mins) (9 wkts dec)	435	(47.2 overs, 181 mins) (1 wkt)	230

VICTORIA	O	M	R	W	w,nb	O	M	R	W	w,nb
Scott	13	1	52	1	-,-	15	1	58	1	-,-
Sievers	12	1	18	0	-,-	15	2	53	1	-,-
Ring	19	1	71	3	-,-	19.5	0	108	2	-,-
Fleetwood-Smith	19.5	3	77	3	1,-	23	0	131	2	-,-
Johnson	6	1	16	3	-,-	23	4	61	4	-,-

QUEENSLAND	O	M	R	W	w,nb	O	M	R	W	w,nb
Stackpoole	16	0	91	2	-,-	9.2	1	39	1	-,-
Dixon	17	0	81	1	-,-	6	0	33	0	-,-
Christ	19	2	73	1	-,-	7	0	23	0	-,-
Cook	16	1	55	3	-,-	9	0	36	0	1,-
Gooma	13.7	0	75	1	-,-	6	0	30	0	-,-
Watt	10	1	51	1	-,-	4	0	25	0	-,-
Baker	1	0	5	0	-,-	4	1	29	0	-,-
Allen						2	0	8	0	-,-

FALL OF WICKETS

	QLD	VIC	QLD	VIC
Wkt	1st	1st	2nd	2nd
1st	112	152	50	169
2nd	141	180	71	-
3rd	149	230	177	-
4th	194	243	183	-
5th	197	248	255	-
6th	226	252	370	-
7th	241	325	413	-
8th	243	398	419	-
9th	243	435	420	-
10th	244	-	420	-

NEW SOUTH WALES v VICTORIA (Shield Match 12)

Played at Sydney Cricket Ground on January 26, 27, 29, 30, 1940. (Four-day match)
Toss : New South Wales.   Result : NEW SOUTH WALES WON BY 177 RUNS.
Debuts: Nil.
12th Men: V.E.Jackson (NSW) and F.L.O.Thorn (Vic).
Umpires: E.G.Borwick and R.McGrath.
Attendances: 10134, 18034, 19074, 4887.   Total: 52,129.   Receipts: £3185.
Close of Play: 1st day Vic 1/18 (Lee 10, Sievers 0); 2nd day NSW (2) 1/87 (Mudge 29, McCabe 45); 3rd day Vic (2) 2/89 (Hassett 23, Barnett 0).

This was the final Sheffield Shield match until 1946-47 because of war and the winner took out the trophy for the season. Twin innings of 122 by Hassett, which occupied 173 minutes (16 fours) and 177 minutes (13 fours) respectively, were punctuated by repeated lofted straight drives off the bowling of O'Reilly. Lee (50 in 82 minutes, 7 fours) and Sievers (54 in 66 minutes, 10 fours) each scored a fifty for the visitors. Cohen (73 in 136 minutes, 5 fours), Mudge (82 in 182 minutes, 8 fours), McCabe (49 in 85 minutes, 6 fours) and Cheetham (55 in 59 minutes, 1 six and 7 fours) batted well for New South Wales on the first day. In the second innings Mudge (61 in 147 minutes, 6 fours), McCabe (114 in 139 minutes, 11 fours), Barnes (135 not out in 170 minutes, 16 fours), Saggers (71 in 75 minutes, 10 fours) and finally Cheetham (70 not out in 50 minutes, 2 sixes and 9 fours) combined to set Victoria an unattainable target of 504. *NSWCA Report* omits Vic (2) Cohen 0/14. Sources: *Wisden, NSWCA Report, The Herald, Sydney Morning Herald, NSWCA Scorebook, The Sporting Globe, Sydney Daily Telegraph.*

NEW SOUTH WALES

M.B.Cohen	run out (Scott/Barnett)	73	b Sievers		13
H.Mudge	c Scott b Ring	82	c & b Johnson		61
*S.J.McCabe	b Scott	49	c Beames b Ring		114
S.G.Barnes	c Ring b Sievers	17	not out		135
R.A.Saggers	lbw b Scott	0	c Sievers b Johnson		71
A.G.Chipperfield	c Lee b Johnson	8	lbw b Johnson		15
A.G.Cheetham	b Ring	55	not out		70
C.G.Pepper	c Fothergill b Ring	4			
J.G.Lush	run out (Fothergill)	5			
W.J.O'Reilly	c Barnett b Ring	8			
†S.G.Sismey	not out	1			
Extras	(b1, lb6)	7	(b11, lb2)		13
Total	(71.5 overs, 291 mins)	309	(80.0 overs, 319 mins) (5 wkts dec)		492

VICTORIA

I.S.Lee	run out (Lush/Sismey)	50	c O'Reilly b Cheetham		8
*†B.A.Barnett	c Sismey b Lush	6	(4) c Sismey b Pepper		11
M.W.Sievers	c Chipperfield b Pepper	30	(2) c McCabe b Pepper		54
A.L.Hassett	c Pepper b O'Reilly	122	(3) c Chipperfield b Lush		122
K.R.Miller	lbw b O'Reilly	1	run out (Lush/Sismey)		24
I.W.Johnson	c Barnes b O'Reilly	0	c Chipperfield b Lush		40
P.J.Beames	b O'Reilly	1	b O'Reilly		23
D.H.Fothergill	c Chipperfield b Mudge	32	not out		32
D.T.Ring	c Chipperfield b Cheetham	29	b O'Reilly		3
R.B.Scott	b O'Reilly	9	c Pepper b O'Reilly		0
L.O.Fleetwood-Smith	not out	4	b Pepper		0
Extras	(b8, lb4, nb2)	14	(b4, lb4, nb1)		9
Total	(68.1 overs, 265 mins)	298	(64.4 overs, 237 mins)		326

VICTORIA	O	M	R	W	w,nb		O	M	R	W	w,nb					
Scott	16	0	60	2	-,-		17	0	82	0	-,-					
Sievers	13	1	37	1	-,-		18	1	94	1	-,-					
Johnson	20	0	84	1	-,-		23	0	142	3	-,-					
Fleetwood-Smith	12	0	58	0	-,-	(5)	10	0	77	0	-,-					
Ring	10.5	0	63	4	-,-	(4)	12	0	84	1	-,-					

	FALL OF WICKETS			
Wkt	NSW 1st	VIC 1st	NSW 2nd	VIC 2nd
1st	131	11	25	9
2nd	186	80	171	89
3rd	218	103	217	120
4th	223	106	329	192
5th	228	110	359	259
6th	259	118	-	266
7th	268	185	-	317
8th	293	241	-	325
9th	308	293	-	325
10th	309	298	-	326

NEW SOUTH WALES	O	M	R	W	w,nb		O	M	R	W	w,nb
Lush	12	3	37	1	-,-		10	1	51	2	-,-
Cheetham	9	0	54	1	-,-		8	0	30	1	-,1
O'Reilly	22.1	3	78	5	-,2	(4)	19	2	79	3	-,-
Pepper	18	0	66	1	-,-	(5)	23.4	0	115	3	-,-
Mudge	6	0	45	1	-,-						
Barnes	1	0	4	0	-,-		3	0	28	0	-,-
Cohen						(3)	1	0	14	0	-,-

WESTERN AUSTRALIA v SOUTH AUSTRALIA

Played at W.A.C.A. Ground, Perth, on February 10, 12, 13, 1940. (Three-day match)
Toss : South Australia.   Result : MATCH DRAWN.
Debuts: Western Australia - L.H.Bandy (f/c). South Australia - V.R.Gibson, J.M.Kierse, L.Michael (all f/c).
12th Men: A.E.Read (WA) and F.L.Teisseire (SA).
Umpires: J.P.Robbins and M.J.Troy.
Attendances: 8000, 2770, 3000.   Total: 13,770.   Receipts: £754.
Close of Play: 1st day WA 0/7 (MacGill 4, J.A.Jeffreys 3); 2nd day SA (2) 0/1 (Walker 0, Ward 0).

Bradman batted 65 minutes in the first innings, facing 64 balls with 1 four. In the second innings he reached 50 in 45 minutes, 100 in 99 minutes, 150 in 125 minutes and 200 in 155, batting in all for 161 minutes (1 six and 30 fours). Difficult chances at 161 and 183 were the only blemishes in an otherwise flawless exhibition. His unbroken fourth-wicket stand with Michael raised 171 in 99 minutes, Michael contributing 27. The eighth-wicket partnership for Western Australia between Inverarity and Zimbulis was worth 64 in 58 minutes. MacGill (78 in about 180 minutes, 7 fours) and Watt (52 in 49 minutes, 5 fours) hit half-centuries for the home team. *SACA Report* incorrectly gives WA bowling (1) Eyres 1/49. Sources: *SACA Report, The West Australian, Daily News, Sunday Times, Western Mail, WACA Scorebook.*

SOUTH AUSTRALIA

K.L.Ridings	c Bandy b Halcombe	46			
T.E.Klose	b MacGill	6			
R.A.Hamence	c Lovelock b Eyres	3	(4)	c & b Eyres	14
*D.G.Bradman	c Lovelock b MacGill	42	(3)	not out	209
L.Michael	c Eyres b MacGill	5		not out	27
M.G.Waite	lbw b MacGill	37			
V.R.Gibson	c J.A.Jeffreys b Zimbulis	35			
J.M.Kierse	c J.A.Jeffreys b Watt	23			
F.A.Ward	c K.S.Jeffreys b Halcombe	15	(2)	b Eyres	12
C.V.Grimmett	c Inverarity b Zimbulis	14			
†C.W.Walker	not out	2	(1)	c Inverarity b Zimbulis	34
Extras	(b16, lb2, w1, nb1)	20		(b9, lb1)	10
Total	(67.1 overs, 284 mins)	248		(51.0 overs, 175 mins) (3 wkts dec)	306

WESTERN AUSTRALIA

C.W.T.MacGill	c Ward b Grimmett	78		run out (Waite)	11
J.A.Jeffreys	c Klose b Ward	36		c Bradman b Kierse	8
A.D.Watt	st Walker b Ward	18		b Ridings	52
A.E.O.Barras	lbw b Klose	11			
L.H.Bandy	c Klose b Ward	1	(4)	not out	20
K.S.Jeffreys	st Walker b Ward	7	(5)	not out	27
*M.Inverarity	st Walker b Ward	57			
†O.I.Lovelock	b Grimmett	13			
A.G.Zimbulis	not out	42			
G.Eyres	c Ward b Grimmett	9			
R.A.Halcombe	b Ward	2			
Extras	(b1)	1		(lb3)	3
Total	(92.3 overs, 288 mins)	275		(35.0 overs, 105 mins) (3 wkts)	121

WESTERN AUSTRALIA	O	M	R	W	w,nb		O	M	R	W	w,nb
Eyres	22	2	81	1	-,1		16	2	65	2	-,-
MacGill	18	1	49	4	1,-		15	3	66	0	-,-
Halcombe	13	1	51	2	-,-	(4)	9	0	59	0	-,-
Zimbulis	9.1	0	36	2	-,-	(3)	5	0	50	1	-,-
Watt	3	1	6	1	-,-						
Barras	2	1	5	0	-,-	(5)	4	0	28	0	-,-
K.S.Jeffreys						(6)	2	0	28	0	-,-

SOUTH AUSTRALIA	O	M	R	W	w,nb		O	M	R	W	w,nb
Waite	8	1	26	0	-,-						
Kierse	3	1	6	0	-,-	(1)	7	2	19	1	-,-
Grimmett	33	8	94	3	-,-		4	0	26	0	-,-
Klose	10	2	18	1	-,-	(6)	6	4	8	0	-,-
Gibson	12	3	25	0	-,-	(2)	7	1	21	0	-,-
Ward	26.3	1	105	6	-,-	(4)	7	1	32	0	-,-
Ridings						(5)	4	0	12	1	-,-

FALL OF WICKETS

Wkt	SA 1st	WA 1st	SA 2nd	WA 2nd
1st	21	69	25	15
2nd	28	91	83	26
3rd	97	123	135	91
4th	103	135	-	-
5th	115	151	-	-
6th	155	153	-	-
7th	200	188	-	-
8th	227	252	-	-
9th	227	265	-	-
10th	248	275	-	-

WESTERN AUSTRALIA v SOUTH AUSTRALIA

Played at W.A.C.A. Ground, Perth, on February 16, 17, 19, 1940. (Three-day match)
Toss : Western Australia.   Result : MATCH DRAWN.
Debuts: Western Australia - C.W.Puckett (f/c). South Australia - F.L.Teisseire (f/c).
12th Men: W.A.Roach (WA) and J.M.Kierse (SA).
Umpires: J.P.Robbins and M.J.Troy.
Attendances: 2000, 6000, 800.   Total: About 8800.   Receipts: £590.
Close of Play: 1st day WA 7/256 (Lovelock 40, Zimbulis 24); 2nd day SA 6/363 (Teisseire 25, Gibson 3).

J.A.Jeffreys was unavailable for Western Australia due to business commitments, while Kierse was stood down by South Australia to allow Teisseire to make his debut. On the second day Roach fielded for Watt (ill). Bradman reached 50 in 79 minutes and 100 in 135 minutes, batting in all for 148 minutes with 14 fours. He was saved on 99 when Hamence (63 in 98 minutes, 7 fours) ran through and sacrificed his own wicket after a running mix-up. On Sunday while playing golf at a local course, Bradman received a badly swollen big toe on his right foot which required bandaging when struck by a wayward tee-shot from Ridings only a few feet away; he was however able to field on the third day. Teisseire (56 in 133 minutes, 5 fours) reached the half-century in his debut innings. Due to influenza Jeffreys did not field on the third day but left his sick-bed to bat "when he learnt from a broadcast of his team's slump". He went out purely to keep an end going and batted 74 minutes undefeated. The eighth WA wicket fell at 5.20pm with 7 runs still needed to avoid an innings defeat, but thanks to some big hitting by Eyres (18 minutes, 3 sixes and 2 fours) Western Australia survived until shortly before 6pm when the last wicket fell. Sources: *SACA Report, The West Australian, Daily News, Sunday Times, Western Mail, WACA Scorebook.*

WESTERN AUSTRALIA

C.W.T.MacGill	b Klose	17		c Klose b Gibson	17
A.E.Read	c Teisseire b Grimmett	55		b Grimmett	46
A.D.Watt	c Walker b Grimmett	1	(8)	b Grimmett	10
A.E.O.Barras	run out (Michael/Walker)	6		c Teisseire b Grimmett	23
*M.Inverarity	b Gibson	52		b Ward	3
K.S.Jeffreys	lbw b Grimmett	26	(9)	not out	21
L.H.Bandy	c Klose b Ward	30	(6)	st Walker b Grimmett	4
†O.I.Lovelock	c Walker b Grimmett	45	(7)	c Klose b Ward	29
A.G.Zimbulis	c Michael b Klose	33	(3)	c & b Ward	1
C.W.Puckett	c Walker b Grimmett	4	(11)	lbw b Grimmett	2
G.Eyres	not out	1	(10)	b Grimmett	39
Extras	(b3, lb2)	5		(b7, lb3, w1)	11
Total	(107.6 overs, 325 mins)	275		(62.2 overs, 195 mins)	206

SOUTH AUSTRALIA

K.L.Ridings	c Barras b Zimbulis	34
T.E.Klose	c Zimbulis b Eyres	60
*D.G.Bradman	c Zimbulis b Eyres	135
R.A.Hamence	run out (MacGill)	63
L.Michael	c & b Zimbulis	10
F.L.Teisseire	b MacGill	56
M.G.Waite	c Eyres b Zimbulis	24
V.R.Gibson	c & b Puckett	21
†C.W.Walker	b Puckett	3
F.A.Ward	run out	8
C.V.Grimmett	not out	5
Extras	(b4, lb6)	10
Total	(92.3 overs, 344 mins)	429

SOUTH AUSTRALIA	O	M	R	W	w,nb		O	M	R	W	w,nb			FALL OF WICKETS		
Waite	17	4	43	0	-,-	(2)	6	0	26	0	1,-			WA	SA	WA
Gibson	15	5	39	1	-,-	(1)	9	5	20	1	-,-	Wkt	1st	1st	2nd
Klose	21	12	24	2	-,-	(6)	3	3	0	0	-,-	1st	21	79	42
Grimmett	33.6	6	67	5	-,-		19.2	6	57	6	-,-	2nd	24	113	45
Ward	21	2	97	1	-,-	(3)	21	3	81	3	-,-	3rd	31	263	73
Ridings						(5)	4	1	11	0	-,-	4th	133	303	82
												5th	141	319	93
WESTERN AUSTRALIA	O	M	R	W	w,nb							6th	189	355	94
Eyres	23	3	79	2	-,-							7th	195	400	120
MacGill	22	3	108	1	-,-							8th	270	410	147
Puckett	24.3	4	89	2	-,-							9th	272	424	200
Zimbulis	22	0	131	3	-,-							10th	275	429	206
Bandy	1	0	12	0	-,-										

NEW SOUTH WALES v THE REST

Played at Sydney Cricket Ground on March 8, 9, 11, 1940. (Four-day match)
Toss : The Rest.   Result : NEW SOUTH WALES WON BY TWO WICKETS.
Debuts: New South Wales - C.L.McCool (f/c).
12th Men: J.W.Chegwyn (NSW) and K.L.Ridings (Rest).
Umpires: E.G.Borwick and R.McGrath.
Attendances: 8054, 18175, 4276.   Total: 30,505.   Receipts: £1886.
Close of Play: 1st day NSW 5/137 (McCabe 67, Cheetham 9); 2nd day NSW (2) 0/21 (Cohen 6, Mudge 13).

Arranged for patriotic purposes between the Sheffield Shield-winners and an eleven drawn from the remaining States, the profits of this match were directed to war funds. Soldiers and sailors in uniform were let in at half price. Hassett (chanceless 136 in 132 minutes, 4 sixes and 15 fours) hit a brilliant century on the first day, reaching three figures in 107 minutes, his third hundred in as many innings. He and Grimmett added 100 in only 31 minutes for the ninth wicket including 24 off an O'Reilly over (12 including a six to Hassett and 12 to Grimmett). Hassett was equally fast in the second innings (75 in 60 minutes, 8 fours), Brown (97 in 137 minutes, 9 fours) missing his hundred when thrown out from cover. McCabe (72 in 120 minutes, 8 fours and 96 in 78 minutes, 12 fours) led New South Wales in the tightly-contested match. Cheetham (58 in 103 minutes, 4 fours) lent support in the first innings while Cohen (67 in 161 minutes, 3 fours) and Barnes (46 in 50 minutes, 7 fours) did so in the second. Grimmett (10 for 195) gave a fine display of leg-spin and held five catches, four off his own bowling. Lush, whose length and direction were faulty, was bowled sparingly Sources: *Wisden, NSWCA Report, The Herald, Sydney Morning Herald, NSWCA Scorebook, The Sporting Globe, Sydney Daily Telegraph.*

THE REST

Batsman	Dismissal	R	Dismissal 2	R
W.A.Brown	c Saggers b Pepper	35	run out (Barnes)	97
I.S.Lee	c & b Cheetham	0	c Saggers b Cheetham	14
*D.G.Bradman	c Saggers b O'Reilly	25	c McCool b Cheetham	2
A.L.Hassett	c Mudge b Cheetham	136	b Pepper	75
R.E.Rogers	c O'Reilly b Lush	25	c & b McCool	17
M.G.Waite	c McCabe b O'Reilly	5	c O'Reilly b Cohen	12
I.W.Johnson	b Pepper	12	c McCool b Cheetham	8
†D.Tallon	b Pepper	0	c & b Cohen	8
D.T.Ring	c Mudge b O'Reilly	2	c McCool b Cohen	14
C.V.Grimmett	c McCabe b Cheetham	27	c McCool b Cohen	0
R.B.Scott	not out	13	not out	2
Extras	(b5, lb3, nb1)	9	(lb2, nb1)	3
Total	(51.7 overs, 195 mins)	289	(49.7 overs, 182 mins)	252

NEW SOUTH WALES

Batsman	Dismissal	R	Dismissal 2	R
M.B.Cohen	b Waite	12	run out	67
H.Mudge	c & b Grimmett	21	b Grimmett	21
*S.J.McCabe	c Tallon b Grimmett	72	c Grimmett b Ring	96
S.G.Barnes	c & b Grimmett	2	lbw b Grimmett	46
C.M.Solomon	c Lee b Grimmett	20	b Waite	5
†R.A.Saggers	c Waite b Scott	3	c Johnson b Grimmett	32
A.G.Cheetham	c Bradman b Waite	58	c & b Grimmett	2
C.L.McCool	c & b Grimmett	19	c Johnson b Grimmett	15
C.G.Pepper	b Scott	4	not out	25
J.G.Lush	not out	2	not out	2
W.J.O'Reilly	b Waite	1		
Extras	(b1, lb4)	5	(b2, lb8, w1, nb1)	12
Total	(59.2 overs, 223 mins)	219	(63.1 overs, 241 mins) (8 wkts)	323

NEW SOUTH WALES	O	M	R	W	w,nb		O	M	R	W	w,nb
Lush	6	0	34	1	-,1						
Cheetham	8.7	1	41	3	-,1	(1)	11	0	43	3	-,1
O'Reilly	18	4	78	3	-,-		8	0	49	0	-,-
Pepper	17	1	102	3	-,-		14	0	81	1	-,-
Cohen	2	0	25	0	-,-	(2)	7.7	1	25	4	-,-
McCool						(5)	9	1	51	1	-,-

THE REST	O	M	R	W	w,nb		O	M	R	W	w,nb
Scott	14	0	57	2	-,-		11	0	63	0	1,1
Waite	8.2	2	12	3	-,-		16	1	37	1	-,-
Ring	12	0	54	0	-,-	(4)	8	0	48	1	-,-
Grimmett	21	2	65	5	-,-	(3)	23.1	2	130	5	-,-
Johnson	4	0	26	0	-,-		5	0	33	0	-,-

FALL OF WICKETS

Wkt	REST 1st	NSW 1st	REST 2nd	NSW 2nd
1st	2	17	31	36
2nd	64	62	37	176
3rd	64	64	145	236
4th	108	108	196	245
5th	115	119	210	247
6th	142	157	227	254
7th	142	203	229	294
8th	166	214	247	303
9th	266	216	247	-
10th	289	219	252	-

1940-41 - (11 MATCHES)

Competition for the Sheffield Shield ceased because of the war but 11 matches of first-class status were staged for patriotic purposes. The State Associations decided that 75 percent of the net gate receipts from each match would be donated to the war effort. However, the attendances fell below expectations and the amounts raised were minimal.

S.G.Barnes appeared in eight of the matches and compiled in excess of 1000 runs, including six centuries. He was by far the most outstanding batsman in a season that saw several extraordinary batting performances. C.L.Badcock and R.A.Hamence each scored a century in each innings of South Australia's match against Victoria at Melbourne - the first such instance in Australian first-class cricket. A.R.Morris created another first when he scored a century in each innings of his first-class debut for New South Wales against Queensland at Sydney. Morris went on to build an outstanding post-war career and came to be considered one of the finest left-handers ever produced by Australia.

Bradman was not in the best of health this season but he appeared in two matches, in fact sustaining first-ball dismissals in each, events that received headlines despite world incidents of higher significance.

O'Reilly was again the outstanding bowler in Australia. His bowling displayed hostility, accuracy and variety - all the attributes necessary to destroy the opposition. He captured 55 wickets at a miserly average of 12.43. It was a tragedy that he was unable to make more appearances in Test cricket at the peak of his form and ability.

The enlistment of players in the armed services began to have an impact on cricket at all levels. Residential restrictions for club cricket were relaxed to allow servicemen on leave to participate in games. First-class appearances for some players were limited by the call to arms.

Leading Aggregates

Batsmen	M	I	NO	Runs	HS	Ave.	Bowlers	Runs	Wkts	Ave.
S.G.Barnes (NSW)	8	14	0	1050	185	75.00	W.J.O'Reilly (NSW)	684	55	12.43
C.L.Badcock (SA)	5	9	0	659	172	73.22	C.G.Pepper (NSW)	768	26	29.53
R.A.Hamence (SA)	5	10	1	569	130	63.22	C.V.Grimmett (SA)	668	25	26.72
R.E.Rogers (Q)	5	9	0	488	114	54.22	I.W.Johnson (V)	690	25	27.60
S.J.McCabe (NSW)	6	9	0	432	88	48.00	C.L.McCool (NSW)	564	24	23.50
C.L.McCool (NSW)	6	11	3	416	100	52.00	M.W.Sievers (V)	758	24	31.58
V.E.Jackson (V)	8	15	2	415	70	31.92	J.A.Ellis (Q)	495	21	23.57
R.A.Saggers (NSW)	8	15	1	413	63	29.50				

1941-42 - (1 MATCH)

The Sheffield Shield competition was again cancelled and in its place an 'International Patriotic Competition' was arranged. Eight matches were scheduled, each of three days duration, but only the first match was played. The entry of Japan into the war in December opened the Pacific theatre and the remaining fixtures were cancelled, ending first-class cricket in Australia until the cessation of hostilities in 1945. The full program of matches for this season, with starting dates, was as follows:

November 28	Queensland v New South Wales at Brisbane
December 19	Victoria v Queensland at Melbourne
December 25	Victoria v New South Wales at Melbourne
December 25	South Australia v Queensland at Adelaide
January 1	New South Wales v Queensland at Sydney
January 1	Victoria v South Australia at Melbourne
January 16	Queensland v Victoria at Brisbane
January 23	New South Wales v Victoria at Sydney

QUEENSLAND v NEW SOUTH WALES

Played at Brisbane Cricket Ground (Woolloongabba) on November 15 (no play), 16, 18, 19, 1940. (Four-day match)
Toss: New South Wales.   Result: NEW SOUTH WALES WON BY 27 RUNS.
Debuts: Queensland - V.N.Raymer (f/c). New South Wales - J.W.Chegwyn, B.Cook, V.Trumper jr (all f/c) .
12th Men: J.E.McCarthy (Qld) and K.C.Gulliver (NSW).
Umpires: D.W.Given and R.Weitemeyer.
Attendances: No play, 4721, 1852, 1081.   Total: 7654.   Receipts: £540.
Close of Play: 1st day no play; 2nd day Qld 4/144 (Tallon 55, Baker 33); 3rd day NSW (2) 9/289 (Jackson 36, O'Reilly 6).

Rain prevented any play on the first day but the well-covered pitch remained unaffected and had no bearing on the poor first-innings totals. Trumper (fast-medium) took the wickets of Brown and Cook, both clean bowled, with the fifth and eighth balls of his opening over in first-class cricket. Tallon (55 in 83 minutes, 1 six and 5 fours), Baker (58 in 95 minutes, 7 fours) and on the last day Brown (84 in 120 minutes, 1 five and 12 fours) hit fifties for Queensland. Ellis captured the wickets of Cohen and Barnes with successive balls early in the match. McCabe top-scored in each New South Wales innings with 88 (132 minutes, 10 fours) and 57 (51 minutes, 10 fours); Carmody (47 in 88 minutes, 3 fours), Chegwyn (48 in 91 minutes, 6 fours), Saggers (45 in 85 minutes, 5 fours) and Jackson (55 not out in 82 minutes, 6 fours) also batted well in the second innings. *Wisden* incorrectly gives NSW (2) Cohen b Cook; Qld (2) Ellis c McCabe. Sources: *NSWCA Scorebook, Wisden, NSWCA Report, Brisbane Courier-Mail, Brisbane Telegraph, Sydney Morning Herald.*

NEW SOUTH WALES

M.B.Cohen	b Ellis	7	c Tallon b Cook	11
D.K.Carmody	c Brown c Ellis	2	c & b Raymer	47
S.G.Barnes	c Brown b Ellis	0	lbw b Raymer	15
*S.J.McCabe	c Tallon b Stackpoole	88	b Ellis	57
J.W.Chegwyn	c Stackpoole b Cook	3	c Christ b Ellis	48
†R.A.Saggers	st Tallon b Raymer	22	run out (Allen)	45
B.Cook	b Raymer	15	c Tallon b Ellis	1
V.E.Jackson	lbw b Raymer	19	not out	55
C.L.McCool	c Christ b Ellis	37	b Cook	6
V.Trumper, jr	c Christ b Cook	18	b Raymer	3
W.J.O'Reilly	not out	1	c Allen b Stackpoole	15
Extras		-	(b8, lb6, w1)	15
Total	(50.2 overs, 203 mins)	212	(68.5 overs, 270 mins)	318

QUEENSLAND

*W.A.Brown	b Trumper	1	c Saggers b Barnes	84
G.G.Cook	b Trumper	1	b Jackson	35
T.Allen	run out (Chegwyn/Saggers)	18	c McCabe b McCool	39
R.E.Rogers	st Saggers b McCool	31	lbw b Trumper	43
†D.Tallon	b McCool	55	b Jackson	6
G.W.Baker	st Saggers b McCool	58	st Saggers b McCool	1
D.Watt	b O'Reilly	34	c & b McCool	43
V.N.Raymer	c Jackson b O'Reilly	2	lbw b Trumper	20
J.A.Ellis	not out	13	c McCool b O'Reilly	0
C.P.Christ	lbw b O'Reilly	0	run out	0
J.Stackpoole	c Cook b O'Reilly	0	not out	5
Extras	(b1, lb5)	6	(b5, lb2, nb1)	8
Total	(57.6 overs, 206 mins)	219	(65.3 overs, 238 mins)	284

QUEENSLAND	O	M	R	W	w,nb		O	M	R	W	w,nb
Ellis	14.2	2	62	4	-,-		19	2	73	3	-,-
Cook	8	2	21	2	-,-		18	4	58	2	1,-
Stackpoole	7	0	28	1	-,-		10.5	1	63	1	-,-
Christ	8	1	38	0	-,-	(5)	8	0	42	0	-,-
Raymer	13	0	63	3	-,-	(4)	13	0	67	3	-,-

NEW SOUTH WALES	O	M	R	W	w,nb		O	M	R	W	w,nb
Trumper	10	0	42	2	-,-		11	3	49	2	-,-
Jackson	11	1	37	0	-,-		16	4	65	2	-,-
O'Reilly	15.6	4	42	4	-,-		12	4	36	1	-,1
McCool	20	0	85	3	-,-		20.3	0	106	3	-,-
McCabe	1	0	7	0	-,-						
Barnes						(5)	6	1	20	1	-,-

FALL OF WICKETS

Wkt	NSW 1st	QLD 1st	NSW 2nd	QLD 2nd
1st	7	2	29	115
2nd	7	3	59	121
3rd	20	32	124	186
4th	27	84	150	193
5th	105	144	230	208
6th	135	199	236	220
7th	137	202	236	254
8th	170	207	245	266
9th	204	207	275	267
10th	212	219	318	284

COMBINED QUEENSLAND-VICTORIA v NEW SOUTH WALES

Played at Brisbane Cricket Ground (Woolloongabba) on November 22, 23, 25, 26, 1940. (Four-day match)
Toss: Combined XI.   Result: NEW SOUTH WALES WON BY ONE WICKET.
Debuts: Nil.
12th Men: D.Watt (Comb XI) and B.Cook (NSW).
Umpires: K.E.Fagg and D.W.Given.
Attendances: 1079, 4018, 1100, 100.   Total: 6297.   Receipts: £404.
Close of Play: 1st day NSW 4/184 (Barnes 94, Saggers 0); 2nd day Comb XI (2) 2/126 (Hassett 30, Rogers 27); 3rd day NSW (2) 6/134 (McCabe 20, McCool 7).

The States agreed before the 1940-41 season that 75 per cent of net profits from all matches would go to the war effort, and this match was devised in an attempt to boost gate receipts. Saggers (with some assistance from Gulliver's leg-breaks and googlies) equalled a world wicket-keeping record with seven dismissals in the second innings. Tallon, who was coincidentally the only keeper to have previously achieved this in Australia, batted brilliantly in both innings for the Combined team, scoring 55 (42 minutes, 1 six and 8 fours) and 152 (116 minutes, 1 six and 20 fours). In the first innings he reached his fifty in 40 minutes, and in the second he brought up 50 in 47 minutes and 100 in 84 minutes, scoring his first 109 runs in 90 minutes before lunch on the third day. Hassett (96 in 143 minutes, 6 fours) also batted in fine style; his fourth-wicket stand of 162 with Tallon took 90 minutes. Barnes (144 in 225 minutes, 16 fours) gave a chanceless display after arriving at the crease in the first over for New South Wales. Saggers (58 in 102 minutes, 5 fours), McCool (52 in 76 minutes, 4 fours), Gulliver (66 not out in 108 minutes, 5 fours) and McCabe (53 in 53 minutes, 1 six and 7 fours) hit half-centuries. A small crowd granted free admission on the last day saw McCool and O'Reilly take the visitors to the narrowest of victories. Sources: *NSWCA Scorebook, Wisden, NSWCA Report, QCA Report, Brisbane Courier-Mail, Brisbane Telegraph, Sydney Morning Herald.*

COMBINED XI

*W.A.Brown	c Chegwyn b Trumper	13		c Jackson b O'Reilly	43
G.G.Cook	b Jackson	5		c Saggers b Gulliver	22
R.E.Rogers	c & b O'Reilly	29	(4)	c Saggers b Gulliver	34
†D.Tallon	c Chegwyn b O'Reilly	55	(5)	c Trumper b Cohen	152
A.L.Hassett	c McCool b Trumper	14	(3)	c Saggers b McCool	96
K.R.Miller	c Saggers b McCool	8		c Saggers b Jackson	24
G.W.Baker	c Gulliver b Trumper	22		c Saggers b Gulliver	12
M.W.Sievers	not out	23		c Saggers b Gulliver	25
V.N.Raymer	c Saggers b McCool	15		b Jackson	1
D.T.Ring	st Saggers b McCool	5		c Saggers b Gulliver	0
J.A.Ellis	c Chegwyn b O'Reilly	1		not out	1
Extras	(b7, lb4, nb1)	12		(lb5, w1)	6
Total	(42.4 overs, 162 mins)	202		(80.5 overs, 281 mins)	416

NEW SOUTH WALES

M.B.Cohen	c Tallon b Ellis	0		b Baker	34
D.K.Carmody	b Sievers	7		run out	36
S.G.Barnes	c Tallon b Ring	144		lbw b Baker	3
*S.J.McCabe	c Cook b Ring	43	(6)	c Cook b Ring	53
J.W.Chegwyn	c Tallon b Sievers	37	(4)	c & b Raymer	21
†R.A.Saggers	c Hassett b Raymer	58	(5)	c Tallon b Baker	5
V.E.Jackson	c Rogers b Ring	7		lbw b Raymer	2
C.L.McCool	c Miller b Raymer	52		not out	27
K.C.Gulliver	not out	66		c Brown b Ring	0
V.Trumper, jr	c Baker b Raymer	4		run out (Rogers/Tallon)	0
W.J.O'Reilly	b Cook	4		not out	4
Extras	(b4, lb3)	7		(b2, lb5)	7
Total	(91.3 overs, 360 mins)	429		(49.4 overs, 194 mins) (9 wkts)	192

NEW SOUTH WALES	O	M	R	W	w,nb		O	M	R	W	w,nb
Trumper	9	0	37	3	-,1		10	2	46	0	1,-
Jackson	6	0	18	1	-,-		17.5	2	69	2	-,-
O'Reilly	10.4	0	46	3	-,-	(5)	17	1	85	1	-,-
Gulliver	7	0	44	0	-,-	(3)	16	0	80	5	-,-
Barnes	1	0	6	0	-,-						
McCool	9	0	39	3	-,-		11	0	91	1	-,-
Cohen						(4)	9	2	39	1	-,-

COMBINED XI	O	M	R	W	w,nb		O	M	R	W	w,nb
Ellis	20	5	76	1	-,-		10	3	26	0	-,-
Sievers	17	1	68	2	-,-	(3)	5	1	20	0	-,-
Ring	20	0	143	3	-,-	(4)	9.4	2	50	2	-,-
Cook	12.3	3	29	1	-,-	(2)	7	1	17	0	-,-
Raymer	19	0	85	3	-,-	(6)	9	0	55	2	-,-
Baker	3	0	21	0	-,-	(5)	9	1	17	3	-,-

FALL OF WICKETS

Wkt	COMB 1st	NSW 1st	COMB 2nd	NSW 2nd
1st	14	0	58	69
2nd	30	16	78	74
3rd	108	83	147	85
4th	111	184	309	105
5th	129	278	364	105
6th	146	288	379	118
7th	157	309	397	177
8th	177	388	414	178
9th	187	415	414	182
10th	202	429	416	-

NEW SOUTH WALES v SOUTH AUSTRALIA

Played at Sydney Cricket Ground on December 6, 7, 9, 1940. (Four-day match)
Toss: New South Wales.   Result: NEW SOUTH WALES WON BY 374 RUNS.
Debuts: New South Wales - R.B.Scott (NSW only).
12th Men: J.W.Chegwyn (NSW) and P.L.Ridings (SA).
Umpires: E.G.Borwick and R.McGrath.
Attendances: 2466, 5789, 500.   Total: 8755.   Receipts: £413.
Close of Play: 1st day NSW 402 all out; 2nd day NSW (2) 7/167 (McCool 39).

New South Wales easily accounted for a Bradmanless South Australia, whose captain for the past five seasons was undergoing Army physical training in Victoria. Barnes (108 in 164 minutes, 15 fours) shared a fourth wicket stand of 116 with Saggers (47 in 98 minutes, 6 fours) on the first day, McCool (90 in 112 minutes, 11 fours) later adding 133 in 66 minutes with Pepper (77 in 66 minutes, 2 sixes and 11 fours) for the seventh wicket. South Australia got away to a bad start when Klose received a severe blow over the heart from a lifting delivery, Scott's fourth of the innings, and retired at 0/1. Klose was unable to resume and did not take the field in the New South Wales second innings when McCabe declined to enforce the follow-on. Faced with a victory target of 422, the South Australians folded to be all out 47, their second-lowest total to date and their lowest against New South Wales. Sources: *NSWCA Scorebook, Wisden, NSWCA Report, Sydney Morning Herald, Sydney Daily Telegraph, The Herald, The Sporting Globe.*

NEW SOUTH WALES

M.B.Cohen	c Walker b Klose	20			
D.K.Carmody	c Walker b Waite	7	(1) c Walker b Grimmett		32
S.G.Barnes	c Roberts b Ward	108	st Walker b Ward		3
*S.J.McCabe	c & b Grimmett	18	c sub (P.L.Ridings) b Ward		9
†R.A.Saggers	st Walker b Ward	47	(2) b Roberts		29
V.E.Jackson	lbw b Ward	21	(5) c Cotton b Roberts		11
C.L.McCool	b Cotton	90	(6) not out		39
C.G.Pepper	c Waite b Ward	77	(7) b Cotton		35
W.J.O'Reilly	c Waite b Ward	12	(8) b Ward		3
V.Trumper jr	st Walker b Ward	0			
R.B.Scott	not out	1			
Extras	(b1)	1	(b5, lb1)		6
Total	(84.4 overs, 309 mins)	402	(38.0 overs, 140 mins) (7 wkts dec)		167

SOUTH AUSTRALIA

K.L.Ridings	c Jackson b Trumper	4	c McCabe b Trumper		10
T.E.Klose	retired hurt	0	(8) c Barnes b O'Reilly		1
C.L.Badcock	c Scott b Pepper	38	(4) lbw b O'Reilly		11
R.A.Hamence	c O'Reilly b Scott	41	(5) c McCabe b Trumper		4
M.G.Waite	c Saggers b Scott	0	(6) lbw b O'Reilly		3
B.H.Leak	c Barnes b O'Reilly	8	(7) st Saggers b Pepper		1
W.M.Roberts	c McCool b O'Reilly	1	(9) b O'Reilly		2
*†C.W.Walker	st Saggers b O'Reilly	2	(2) b Scott		0
C.V.Grimmett	c Jackson b McCool	23	(10) c Barnes b O'Reilly		5
F.A.Ward	not out	24	(3) c McCool b Scott		2
H.N.J.Cotton	b McCool	0	not out		1
Extras	(b6, lb1)	7	(nb1)		1
Total	(49.3 overs, 186 mins)	148	(24.4 overs, 111 mins)		47

SOUTH AUSTRALIA	O	M	R	W	w,nb		O	M	R	W	w,nb
Cotton	13.4	0	42	1	-,-		6	0	23	1	-,-
Waite	6	0	46	1	-,-		6	1	13	0	-,-
Klose	15	4	56	1	-,-						
Grimmett	19	4	83	1	-,-	(3)	7	0	32	1	-,-
Ward	20	0	131	6	-,-	(4)	13	0	66	3	-,-
Roberts	11	1	43	0	-,-	(5)	6	1	27	2	-,-

NEW SOUTH WALES	O	M	R	W	w,nb		O	M	R	W	w,nb
Scott	5	0	11	2	-,-		6	0	10	2	-,1
Trumper	5	1	15	1	-,-		6	2	14	2	-,-
Jackson	10	0	34	0	-,-						
O'Reilly	12	1	28	3	-,-	(3)	6.4	2	11	5	-,-
Pepper	15	1	51	1	-,-	(4)	6	2	11	1	-,-
McCool	2.3	1	2	2	-,-						

FALL OF WICKETS

Wkt	NSW 1st	SA 1st	NSW 2nd	SA 2nd
1st	27	5	45	10
2nd	27	78	49	12
3rd	59	78	65	14
4th	175	90	85	20
5th	217	94	94	27
6th	222	94	162	36
7th	355	104	167	37
8th	381	148	-	39
9th	392	148	-	46
10th	402	-	-	47

VICTORIA v SOUTH AUSTRALIA

Played at Melbourne Cricket Ground on December 13, 14, 16, 17, 1940. (Four-day match)
Toss: South Australia. Result: MATCH DRAWN.
Debuts: Victoria - W.J.Dudley (f/c).
12th man: D.H.Fothergill (Vic) and W.M.Roberts (SA).
Umpires: A.N.Barlow and W.J.Craddock.
Attendances: 1820, 5716, 2448, 1034. Total: 11,018. Receipts: £345.
Close of Play: 1st day SA 5/311 (Hamence 60, Leak 20); 2nd day Vic 2/168 (Lee 70, Miller 52); 3rd day SA (2) 2/65 (Badcock 12, Hamence 20).

For the first time in Australia two batsmen from the same side, Badcock (120 in 174 minutes, 9 fours and 102 in 148 minutes, 10 fours) and Hamence (130 in 231 minutes, 12 fours and 103 not out in 130 minutes, 8 fours), scored a hundred in each innings of a match. Cotton, who had been no-balled for throwing by umpire Barlow in the corresponding match four years previously, was again judged to have delivered improperly, Barlow calling him once from square-leg during his fourth over in the first innings. Ridings (69 in 187 minutes, 1 six and 3 fours) and Leak (79 in 159 minutes, 5 fours) for South Australia and Lee (93 in 201 minutes, 8 fours), Miller (63 in 87 minutes, 1 six and 6 fours) and Hassett (67 in 112 minutes, 7 fours) for Victoria hit half-centuries. Miller was granted his first bowl in his twelfth match for the State, three years after his debut as a batsman. For the 127th and last time in his career, Grimmett, aged almost 49, claimed five or more wickets in a first-class innings. *Wisden* incorrectly gives SA (1) Waite b Dempster. Sources: *Wisden, NSWCA Report, The Age, The Argus, The Herald, Melbourne Sun, The Sporting Globe.*

SOUTH AUSTRALIA

Batsman	Dismissal	Runs	2nd innings	Runs
K.L.Ridings	c Baker b Ring	69	lbw b Johnson	22
T.E.Klose	c Ring b Dudley	2		
C.L.Badcock	c Ring b Sievers	120	c Tamblyn b Sievers	102
*†C.W.Walker	c Johnson b Sievers	10		
R.A.Hamence	c Dudley b Sievers	130	(4) not out	103
M.G.Waite	hit wkt b Dempster	15		
B.H.Leak	b Dudley	79		
P.L.Ridings	lbw b Johnson	42		
C.V.Grimmett	st Baker b Johnson	14		
F.A.Ward	c Dempster b Johnson	7	(2) b Ring	10
H.N.J.Cotton	not out	7		
Extras	(b5, lb10, w1, nb4)	20	(b6, lb2)	8
Total	(123.1 overs, 493 mins)	515	(52.5 overs, 199 mins) (3 wkts dec)	245

VICTORIA

Batsman	Dismissal	Runs	2nd innings	Runs
I.S.Lee	b Cotton	91	(3) b Ward	41
G.E.Tamblyn	b Grimmett	32	(1) c & b Ward	29
R.A.Dempster	lbw b Grimmett	10	(2) lbw b Waite	2
K.R.Miller	b Grimmett	63	b Waite	16
*A.L.Hassett	c Waite b Grimmett	67	(6) not out	36
P.J.Beames	st Walker b Grimmett	42	(7) c Cotton b Grimmett	1
I.W.Johnson	c Klose b Grimmett	0	(8) c P.L.Ridings b Ward	9
M.W.Sievers	lbw b Waite	41	(5) b Ward	1
†E.A.Baker	lbw b Grimmett	15	not out	12
D.T.Ring	not out	12		
W.J.Dudley	c Cotton b Waite	4		
Extras	(b1, lb6, nb3)	10	(b12, lb2)	14
Total	(102.1 overs, 370 overs)	389	(43.0 overs, 159 mins) (7 wkts)	161

VICTORIA	O	M	R	W	w,nb		O	M	R	W	w,nb
Dudley	24	0	71	2	1,1		10	0	45	0	-,-
Sievers	30	3	100	3	-,3		9.5	0	49	1	-,-
Johnson	26.1	0	117	3	-,-	(4)	12	0	50	1	-,-
Ring	27	1	139	1	-,-	(3)	14	4	56	1	-,-
Dempster	15	1	65	1	-,-		4	0	16	0	-,-
Miller	1	0	3	0	-,-						
Hassett						(6)	3	0	21	0	-,-

SOUTH AUSTRALIA	O	M	R	W	w,nb		O	M	R	W	w,nb
Cotton	11	2	47	1	-,3		4	0	8	0	-,-
Waite	19.1	0	55	2	-,-		11	3	14	2	-,-
P.L.Ridings	7	0	23	0	-,-		4	1	11	0	-,-
Grimmett	38	6	114	7	-,-	(6)	7	1	36	1	-,-
Klose	14	3	46	0	-,-						
Ward	13	0	94	0	-,-	(4)	13	2	53	4	-,-
Hamence						(5)	4	0	25	0	-,-

FALL OF WICKETS

Wkt	SA 1st	VIC 1st	SA 2nd	VIC 2nd
1st	9	57	30	3
2nd	195	85	44	70
3rd	206	198	245	91
4th	221	214	-	95
5th	264	308	-	95
6th	440	312	-	102
7th	444	317	-	119
8th	493	371	-	-
9th	506	381	-	-
10th	515	389	-	-

SOUTH AUSTRALIA v VICTORIA

Played at Adelaide Oval on December 25, 26, 27, 28, 1940. (Four-day match)
Toss: South Australia.　　　　　　Result: SOUTH AUSTRALIA WON BY 175 RUNS.
Debuts: Nil.
12th Men: T.E.Klose (SA) and M.R.Harvey (Vic).
Umpires: J.D.Scott and L.A.Smith.
Attendances: 6213, 2290, ? , ? .　　　　　　Total: 17,167.　　　　　Receipts: £516.
Close of Play: 1st day Vic 2/7 (Ring 6); 2nd day SA (2) 3/222 (Badcock 133, Leak 0); 3rd day Vic (2) 3/77 (Hassett 41, Fothergill 14).

The match began dramatically when K.L.Ridings was run out off the second ball and Bradman was caught out off the next. Hamence (85 in 135 minutes) scored half his side's runs on the weather-interrupted first day. Victoria began their reply similarly, losing Tamblyn in the first over and Lee in the second, night-watchman Ring (72 in 163 minutes, 1 six, 1 five and 2 fours) making top score. In the second innings Badcock (172 in 217 minutes, 1 six and 21 fours, including 20 off an over from Johnson) added 186 with Hamence for the South Australian third wicket, P.L.Ridings (90 in 120 minutes, 12 fours) also batting well. Hassett (113 in 142 minutes, 1 six and 4 fours) dominated Victoria's chase in vain to score 441. Cotton (leg strain) was off the field on the third day. Sources: *Wisden, SACA Report, NSWCA Report, Adelaide Advertiser, The Herald, The Age, Melbourne Sun, The News.*

SOUTH AUSTRALIA

C.L.Badcock	c Sievers b Dempster	25	c Dudley b Sievers	172
K.L.Ridings	run out (Hassett/Baker)	0	c Hassett b Sievers	17
*D.G.Bradman	c Sievers b Dudley	0	b Sievers	6
R.A.Hamence	c Baker b Dudley	85	c Baker b Dempster	62
B.H.Leak	c Ring b Sievers	12	b Dudley	6
M.G.Waite	lbw b Sievers	2	c Johnson b Dempster	20
P.L.Ridings	lbw b Ring	2	lbw b Ring	90
†C.W.Walker	c Baker b Johnson	40	c Meikle b Ring	4
C.V.Grimmett	run out	2	(10) c & b Johnson	31
F.A.Ward	c Hassett b Sievers	10	(9) c Baker b Dempster	4
H.N.J.Cotton	not out	9	not out	2
Extras	(b1, lb2, nb1)	4	(b1, lb4, nb2)	7
Total	(44.4 overs 179 mins)	191	(81.0 overs, 339 mins)	421

VICTORIA

I.S.Lee	b Waite	0	c Badcock b P.L.Ridings	1
G.E.Tamblyn	c Waite b Cotton	0	st Walker b Grimmett	10
D.T.Ring	c Cotton b Grimmett	72	(9) run out (K.L.Ridings/Walker)	24
R.A.Dempster	lbw b Cotton	3	(3) c Waite b Grimmett	10
*A.L.Hassett	b Cotton	7	(4) b Ward	113
D.H.Fothergill	c Walker b P.L.Ridings	18	(5) b Ward	14
M.W.Sievers	st Walker b Ward	14	(8) c Waite b Ward	31
G.S.Meikle	lbw b Grimmett	12	(6) c Leak b Waite	13
I.W.Johnson	c Walker b Cotton	29	(7) b Grimmett	27
†E.A.Baker	not out	13	not out	14
W.J.Dudley	c Leak b Grimmett	0	b Grimmett	5
Extras	(b1, lb3)	4	(lb2, nb1)	3
Total	(43.7 overs, 172 mins)	172	(76.3 overs, 267 mins)	265

VICTORIA	O	M	R	W	w,nb		O	M	R	W	w,nb
Dudley	7	0	34	2	-,-		11	2	38	1	-,1
Sievers	11.4	1	45	3	-,1		25	1	104	3	-,1
Ring	9	1	32	1	-,-	(5)	11	0	67	2	-,-
Johnson	3	0	8	1	-,-		8	0	66	1	-,-
Dempster	6	0	21	1	,	(3)	15	1	66	3	-,-
Meikle	8	0	47	0	-,-		4	0	26	0	-,-
Fothergill							6	0	40	0	-,-
Hassett							1	0	7	0	-,-

SOUTH AUSTRALIA	O	M	R	W	w,nb		O	M	R	W	w,nb
Cotton	11	0	39	4	-,-	(5)	8	0	30	0	-,-
Waite	7	2	15	1	-,-		14	2	37	1	-,-
Grimmett	12.7	1	54	3	-,-		24.3	3	75	4	-,-
P.L.Ridings	3	1	5	1	-,-	(1)	8	1	34	1	-,1
Ward	10	0	55	1	-,-	(4)	22	3	86	3	-,-

FALL OF WICKETS

Wkt	SA 1st	VIC 1st	SA 2nd	VIC 2nd
1st	1	1	30	5
2nd	1	7	36	22
3rd	61	12	222	23
4th	97	26	240	82
5th	101	56	281	109
6th	106	79	303	189
7th	154	100	314	195
8th	173	152	323	231
9th	175	172	385	253
10th	191	172	421	265

NEW SOUTH WALES v QUEENSLAND

Played at Sydney Cricket Ground on December 26, 27, 28, 30, 1940. (Four-day match)
Toss: New South Wales.   Result: NEW SOUTH WALES WON BY 404 RUNS.
Debuts: New South Wales - A.R.Morris (f/c). Queensland - D.E.Cox (f/c).
12th Men: D.K.Carmody (NSW) and J.Stackpoole (Qld).
Umpires: E.G.Borwick and R.McGrath.
Attendances: 6406, 4336, 4954, not known.   Total: 15,696.   Receipts: about £890.
Close of Play: 1st day NSW 7/489 (Jackson 41, O'Reilly 26); 2nd day NSW (2) 0/32 (Cohen 11, Morris 15); 3rd day Qld (2) 0/50 (Brown 27, Cook 22).

Morris became the first player in world cricket to register a century in each innings on first-class debut. He scored 148 (214 minutes, 18 fours) and 111 (142 minutes, 7 fours), offered only one chance - a catch to Christ when 93 in the first innings - and shared two double-century partnerships, 261 in 176 minutes for the second wicket with Barnes (133 in 176 minutes, 14 fours) and 200 in 142 minutes for the first wicket with Cohen (118 in 192 minutes, 5 fours and 60 singles). McCabe, under the handicap of an old wrist injury, scored 75 in 86 minutes (8 fours) in the first innings, but elected not to aggravate it and opted out of the second, handing the captaincy over to O'Reilly after the second day. Rogers (114 in 143 minutes, 15 fours) and Brown (57 in 89 minutes, 7 fours) top-scored for Queensland. Pepper and O'Reilly wrapped the match up in 90 minutes on the last day. *Wisden* incorrectly gives NSW (2) Morris b Watt, Pepper c Tallon. *NSWCA Report* incorrectly gives Qld (2) Christ c Saggers. Sources: *NSWCA Scorebook, Wisden, NSWCA Report, QCA Report, Sydney Morning Herald, Sydney Daily Telegraph, The Age, The Herald, Melbourne Sun.*

NEW SOUTH WALES

Batsman	Dismissal	R		Dismissal	R
M.B.Cohen	c Christ b Ellis	5		b Cox	118
A.R.Morris	b McCarthy	148		c Ellis b Watt	111
S.G.Barnes	c McCarthy b Cook	133		c Tallon b Cook	5
*S.J.McCabe	c Rogers b Watt	75			
C.L.McCool	lbw b Christ	45	(4)	lbw b Ellis	0
†R.A.Saggers	b Christ	1	(5)	c Tallon b Cox	33
V.E.Jackson	c McCarthy b Ellis	47	(6)	not out	47
C.G.Pepper	c Brown b Watt	7	(7)	st Tallon b Watt	6
W.J.O'Reilly	b Cook	30	(8)	c Baker b Watt	13
V.Trumper, jr	not out	5	(9)	c Ellis b Watt	11
R.B.Scott	run out	4	(10)	c Brown b Cox	2
Extras	(b13, lb3)	16		(b14, lb8, nb1)	23
Total	(82.7 overs, 351 mins)	516		(58.5 overs, 252 mins) (9 wkts dec)	369

QUEENSLAND

Batsman	Dismissal	R		Dismissal	R
*W.A.Brown	c Pepper b Trumper	7		c Scott b Pepper	57
G.G.Cook	b Scott	4		run out	25
R.E.Rogers	c Pepper b Jackson	114		b Pepper	26
†D.Tallon	lbw b O'Reilly	34		c & b Pepper	0
G.W.Baker	b Jackson	48		c Barnes b Pepper	3
D.Watt	b Pepper	13		c Trumper b Pepper	0
V.N.Raymer	not out	41		b Pepper	10
J.E.McCarthy	run out	18		lbw b O'Reilly	4
D.E.Cox	b McCool	16		b O'Reilly	14
J.A.Ellis	st Saggers b McCool	0		not out	1
C.P.Christ	b Jackson	18		st Saggers b O'Reilly	0
Extras	(b10, lb6, w1, nb4)	21		(b6, lb1)	7
Total	(62.6 overs, 238 mins)	334		(40.6 overs, 149 mins)	147

QUEENSLAND	O	M	R	W	w,nb		O	M	R	W	w,nb
Ellis	17	1	82	2	-,-		12	1	54	1	-,-
Cook	13.7	0	67	2	-,-		12	0	66	1	-,1
Cox	10	1	73	0	-,-	(5)	10.5	0	63	3	-,-
Christ	17	0	78	2	-,-		5	0	23	0	-,-
Raymer	5	0	46	0	-,-	(7)	4	0	23	0	-,-
Watt	11	0	110	2	,-		10	0	90	4	-,-
McCarthy	9	1	44	1	-,-	(3)	5	1	27	0	-,-

SOUTH AUSTRALIA	O	M	R	W	w,nb		O	M	R	W	w,nb
Scott	8	1	36	1	1,3		4	0	12	0	-,-
Trumper	7	0	34	1	-,-		3	0	13	0	-,-
Jackson	9.6	1	30	3	-,-		7	2	15	0	-,-
Pepper	16	2	82	1	-,-	(5)	13	1	57	6	-,-
O'Reilly	7	1	34	1	-,1	(4)	13.6	2	43	3	-,-
McCool	12	0	96	2	-,-						
Cohen	3	2	1	0	-,-						

FALL OF WICKETS

Wkt	NSW 1st	QLD 1st	NSW 2nd	QLD 2nd
1st	6	7	200	62
2nd	267	13	215	94
3rd	309	80	216	94
4th	408	211	276	115
5th	409	219	299	115
6th	410	231	316	127
7th	435	272	338	132
8th	497	301	366	146
9th	499	301	369	147
10th	516	334	-	147

D.G.BRADMAN'S XI v S.J.McCABE'S XI

Played at Melbourne Cricket Ground on January 1, 2 (no play), 3, 4, 1941. (Four-day match)
Toss: McCabe's XI.   Result: McCABE'S XI WON BY AN INNINGS AND 103 RUNS.
Debuts: Nil.
12th men: G.E.Tamblyn (both sides).
Umpires: A.N.Barlow and W.J.Craddock.
Attendances: 8690, no play, 6628, 5220.   Total: 20,538.   Receipts: £923.
Close of Play: 1st day McCabe 7/393 (Sievers 30, Grimmett 0); 2nd day no play; 3rd day Bradman 3/111 (Hamence 54).

In determining the fixtures pre-season, the Board of Control set aside the New Year for "a special patriotic match between selected teams at Melbourne". The resulting game was referred to as "an inter-Australian Test" by the Press of the day. C.L.McCool and L.E.Nagel were invited but unavailable and their places went to Jackson and Waite. Badcock (105 in 226, minutes, 9 fours) and Barnes (137 in 204 minutes, 15 fours) added 212 for the second wicket on the first day. Sievers (55 not out in 113 minutes, 5 fours) also batted well - his innings was interrupted by the abandonment of the second day due to rain - but he was struck on the foot by a ball from Scott and the bruising and swelling kept him off the field for the rest of the match, Tamblyn taking his place. Riding (50 in 126 minutes, 0 fours) and Hamence (73 in 119 minutes, 3 fours) scored half-hundreds but Bradman for the second match running was out first ball. McCabe, who turned an ankle while bowling; on the third day, was absent on the last which saw Grimmett and O'Reilly capture 16 of 17 wickets in 179 minutes on a rain-damaged pitch. Miller claimed the other - his first in first-class cricket. O'Reilly led the side in McCabe's absence and Pepper and Ridings alternated as substitute, Ridings catching Jackson. Sources: *Wisden, NSWCA Report, The Age, The Argus, The Herald, Melbourne Sun, The Sporting Globe.*

McCABE'S XI

I.S.Lee	b Waite	14
C.L.Badcock	b Waite	105
S.G.Barnes	c Hamence b Jackson	137
R.E.Rogers	lbw b Waite	16
*S.J.McCabe	lbw b Pepper	7
†D.Tallon	b Pepper	21
K.R.Miller	b Scott	29
M.W.Sievers	not out	55
C.V.Grimmett	b Jackson	5
W.J.O'Reilly	c Saggers b Scott	5
J.A.Ellis	not out	19
Extras	(b19, lb6, w4, nb7)	36
Total	(95.0 overs, 388 mins) (9 wkts dec)	449

BRADMAN'S XI

W.A.Brown	c O'Reilly b Ellis	13	c Barnes b O'Reilly		16
K.L.Ridings	lbw b Ellis	50	c Tallon b Miller		5
*D.G.Bradman	c sub (G.E.Tamblyn) b Ellis	0	b O'Reilly		12
R.A.Hamence	c Lee b O'Reilly	73	st Tallon b Grimmett		35
A.L.Hassett	c Rogers b Grimmett	31	c Ellis b Grimmett		20
†R.A.Saggers	not out	13	lbw b Grimmett		5
M.G.Waite	c Miller b O'Reilly	15	c Barnes b O'Reilly		18
V.E.Jackson	lbw b O'Reilly	0	c sub (K.L.Ridings) b Grimmett		14
C.G.Pepper	c Badcock b O'Reilly	1	lbw b O'Reilly		10
R.B.Scott	st Tallon b Grimmett	1	lbw b O'Reilly		0
V.Trumper, jr	lbw b Grimmett	0	not out		1
Extras	(b3, lb3, nb2)	8	(b2, lb1, w1, nb1)		5
Total	(56.2 overs, 193 mins)	205	(28.0 overs, 112 mins)		141

BRADMAN'S XI

	O	M	R	W	w,nb
Scott	23	1	87	2	1,6
Trumper	14	1	60	0	3,1
Waite	24	2	84	3	-,-
Jackson	22	3	97	2	-,-
Pepper	12	0	85	2	-, -

McCABE'S XI

	O	M	R	W	w,nb		O	M	R	W	w,nb
Ellis	10	2	23	3	-,-		4	0	13	0	1,-
McCabe	5	1	10	0	-,-						
Grimmett	22.2	1	100	3	-,-	(4)	8	0	46	4	-,-
O'Reilly	14	2	41	4	-,2	(3)	10	1	53	5	-,1
Barnes	5	0	23	0	-,-						
Miller						(2)	6	0	24	1	-,-

FALL OF WICKETS

	M	B	B
Wkt	1st	1st	2nd
1st	29	25	10
2nd	241	25	35
3rd	295	118	36
4th	300	169	66
5th	322	173	75
6th	331	195	104
7th	387	196	122
8th	398	200	135
9th	407	205	135
10th	-	205	141

QUEENSLAND v VICTORIA

Played at Brisbane Cricket Ground (Woolloongabba) on January 18, 20, 21, 22, 1941. (Four-day match)
Toss: Queensland. Result: MATCH DRAWN.
Debuts: Queensland - J.F.Barnes, H.F.Bendixen, T.E.Thwaites (all f/c). Victoria - M.R.Harvey, T.K.Sarovich, (both f /c).
12th Men: D.E.Cox (Qld) and D.H.Fothergill (Vic).
Umpires: K.E.Fagg and R.Weitemeyer.
Attendances: 3000, 1619, 1045, 300.   Total: 5964.   Receipts: About £300.
Close of Play: 1st day Qld 0/54 (Rogers 48, Cook 5); 2nd day Vic 1/26 (Tamblyn 1, Harvey 25); 3rd day Vic 7/436 (Sarovich 68, Ring 50).

P.J.Beames, A.L.Hassett and K.R.Miller were unavailable for Victoria's trip north. Further changes were needed when W.F.Cockburn, W.E.Pearson and D.S.T.Williams withdrew after being selected; Dudley, Fothergill and Sarovich were brought in. (Williams never represented the State of his birth but appeared for Western Australia after the War when he received a job transfer). Play on the first day was restricted to 65 minutes after 332 points of rain in an hour turned the oval into a lake. Rogers (92 in 138 minutes, 10 fours) scored the bulk of an opening stand of 117 with Cook, who batted 335 minutes and hit 6 fours. Raymer at No.9 bolstered the lower order with 50 in 63 minutes, including 7 fours. Lee was out to the fourth ball of the Victorian innings, the bowler Ellis claiming a career-best of 7 for 86. Contributions from Tamblyn (136 in 259 minutes, 15 fours), Johnson (85 in 107 minutes, 4 sixes and 6 fours), Sarovich (78 in 194 minutes, 4 fours) and Ring (60 in 60 minutes, 1 six and 9 fours) took Victoria to 460. Rogers completed a fine double in the second innings (103 in 139 minutes, 8 fours), Watt (55 in 97 minutes, 6 fours) making next-best score. Bendixen retired hurt at 6/258 after being struck by a ball from Dudley. *NSWCA Report* incorrectly gives Qld (2) Watt c & b Meikle. Sources: *Wisden, NSWCA Report, QCA Report, Brisbane Courier-Mail, Brisbane Telegraph, The Age, Melbourne Sun.*

QUEENSLAND

R.E.Rogers	c Johnson b Ring	92	c Harvey b Johnson	103
G.G.Cook	b Johnson	117	lbw b Dempster	24
†D.Tallon	c Dudley b Johnson	18	b Johnson	38
G.W.Baker	b Dudley	5	b Sievers	3
*W.A.Brown	c Baker b Dudley	26	c Baker b Dudley	47
D.Watt	c Lee b Sievers	9	c sub (D.H.Fothergill) b Meikle	55
J.F.Barnes	c Dudley b Dempster	8	run out	7
H.E.Bendixen	b Dempster	1	retired hurt	0
V.N.Raymer	c Ring b Johnson	50	not out	23
T.E.Thwaites	b Johnson	0	not out	24
J.A.Ellis	not out	7		
Extras	(b1, lb2)	3	(b10, lb2)	12
Total	(98.0 overs, 353 mins)	336	(66.0 overs, 252 mins) (7 wkts)	336

VICTORIA

*I.S.Lee	c Cook b Ellis	0
G.E.Tamblyn	b Ellis	136
M.R.Harvey	c Tallon b Ellis	25
R.A.Dempster	c & b Watt	15
I.W.Johnson	c Tallon b Ellis	85
M.W.Sievers	lbw b Ellis	5
T.K.Sarovich	b Ellis	78
G.S.Meikle	run out	42
D.T.Ring	b Ellis	60
†E.A.Baker	b Bendixen	4
W.J.Dudley	not out	0
Extras	(b9, lb1)	10
Total	(108.5 overs, 385 mins)	460

SOUTH AUSTRALIA	O	M	R	W	w,nb		O	M	R	W	w,nb
Dudley	16	1	59	2	-,-		13	0	60	1	-,-
Sievers	17	4	42	1	-,-		11	0	54	1	-.-
Dempster	11	1	27	2	-,-	(4)	9	0	25	1	-,-
Ring	32	2	107	1	-,-	(3)	9	0	34	0	-.-
Johnson	17	0	73	4	-,-		13	1	79	2	-.-
Meikle	5	0	25	0	-,-		9	0	46	1	-,-
Lee							2	0	26	0	-,-

SOUTH AUSTRALIA	O	M	R	W	w,nb
Ellis	22.5	2	86	7	-,-
Cook	14	2	25	0	-,-
Bendixen	23	1	75	1	-,-
Watt	16	1	94	1	-,-
Baker	9	2	32	0	-,-
Raymer	9	0	61	0	-,-
Thwaites	12	2	58	0	-,-
Rogers	3	0	19	0	-,-

FALL OF WICKETS

Wkt	QLD 1st	VIC 1st	QLD 2nd
1st	117	0	65
2nd	146	28	145
3rd	152	55	152
4th	210	206	190
5th	229	214	246
6th	240	297	258
7th	246	367	300
8th	309	455	-
9th	309	460	-
10th	336	460	-

NEW SOUTH WALES v VICTORIA

Played at Sydney Cricket Ground on January 25, 27, 28, 29, 1941. (Four-day match)
TOSS: Victoria.   Result: VICTORIA WON BY 24 RUNS.
Debuts: Nil.
12th Men: J.W.Chegwyn (NSW) and W.J.Dudley (Vic).
Umpires: E.G.Borwick and R.McGrath.
Attendances: 3739, 5597, 1074, 250.   Total: 10,660.   Receipts: £428.
Close of Play: 1st day Vic 9/229 (Fothergill 27, Baker 3); 2nd day NSW 8/417 (Gulliver 41, Scott 8); 3rd day Vic (2) 403 all out.
S.J.McCabe (ankle and wrist injuries) and C.L.McCool (military duties) were unavailable for New South Wales. Meikle (46 in 42 minutes, 5 fours) scored rapidly for the visitors on the first day. Barnes (132 in 167 minutes, 1 six and 6 fours) scored his fifth hundred in as many matches. Jackson (54 in 103 minutes, 2 fours) and Pepper (62 in 57 minutes, 10 fours) and in the second innings Barnes again (55 in 91 minutes, 5 fours) scored fifties for New South Wales. Harvey (70 in 60 minutes, 11 fours) and Tamblyn (48 in 100 minutes, 5 fours) gave the Victorian second innings a flying start, mounting 115 runs in an hour, Fothergill (86 in 103 minutes, 9 fours) and Dempster (87 not out in 144 minutes, 7 fours) adding a further 109 for the seventh wicket. O'Reilly (9 for 99) was again the dominant bowler. *Wisden* incorrectly gives NSW (2) Gulliver b Ring, O'Reilly c Lee b Johnson. Sources: *NSWCA Scorebook, Wisden, NSWCA Report, Sydney Morning Herald, Sydney Daily Telegraph, The Age, The Herald, Melbourne Sun.*

VICTORIA

M.R.Harvey	c Barnes b O'Reilly	35		b O'Reilly	70
G.E.Tamblyn	lbw b Pepper	36		b Gulliver	48
T.K.Sarovich	lbw b Pepper	13		c Barnes b Gulliver	4
*I.S.Lee	b O'Reilly	14	(5)	b Pepper	4
I.W.Johnson	c Saggers b O'Reilly	22	(6)	c Cohen b Jackson	40
M.W.Sievers	c Saggers b O'Reilly	24	(4)	b O'Reilly	18
R.A.Dempster	lbw b Pepper	2	(8)	not out	87
D.H.Fothergill	not out	30	(7)	c Trumper b O'Reilly	86
G.S.Meikle	c Saggers b Pepper	46		b Gulliver	2
D.T.Ring	st Saggers b Pepper	0		c Saggers b O'Reilly	31
†E.A.Baker	b Pepper	7		c Barnes b O'Reilly	0
Extras	(b1, lb3, nb3)	7		(b2, lb4, w3, nb4)	13
Total	(68.0 overs, 243 mins)	236		(80.7 overs, 286 mins)	403

NEW SOUTH WALES

M.B.Cohen	b Sievers	5		b Sievers	12
A.R.Morris	c Meikle b Johnson	37		b Sievers	1
S.G.Barnes	c Sarovich b Sievers	132		c Fothergill b Johnson	55
D.K.Carmody	lbw b Johnson	21		c Baker b Sievers	7
†R.A.Saggers	c Ring b Sievers	35		b Johnson	4
V.E.Jackson	c Ring b Meikle	54	(7)	c Baker b Sievers	11
C.G.Pepper	c Tamblyn b Ring	62	(6)	c Dempster b Ring	30
K.C.Gulliver	not out	49		b Johnson	9
*W.J.O'Reilly	c Meikle b Johnson	4		c Lee b Ring	14
R.B.Scott	c Ring b Johnson	9		not out	11
V.Trumper, jr	run out	14		c Fothergill b Ring	13
Extras	(b11, lb6, w1)	18		(b3, lb5)	8
Total	(92.4 overs, 323 mins)	440		(40.7 overs, 156 mins)	175

NEW SOUTH WALES	O	M	R	W	w,nb		O	M	R	W	w,nb			FALL OF WICKETS		
														VIC	NSW	VIC	NSW
Scott	9	2	32	0	-,2		9	0	66	0	1,3	Wkt	1st	1st	2nd	2nd
Trumper	4	0	22	0	-,-		7	0	48	0	1,-	1st	75	15	115	3
Jackson	5	0	25	0	-,-	(6)	9	0	32	1	-,-	2nd	75	70	125	16
O'Reilly	22	8	43	4	-,1		20.7	6	56	5	-,-	3rd	102	126	146	48
Pepper	24	2	85	6	-,-	(3)	18	0	99	1	1,-	4th	104	233	146	57
Gulliver	4	0	22	0	-,-	(5)	15	0	76	3	-,1	5th	143	240	180	92
Barnes							2	0	13	0	-,-	6th	152	339	205	105
												7th	152	388	314	127
VICTORIA	O	M	R	W	w,nb		O	M	R	W	w,nb	8th	218	400	320	140
Sievers	16	1	74	3	-,-		15	1	44	4	-,-	9th	218	419	401	152
Dempster	11	3	31	0	1,-		5	0	16	0	-,-	10th	236	440	403	175
Meikle	7	0	58	1	-,-											
Ring	25	0	118	1	-,-		8.7	0	55	3	-,-					
Johnson	31.4	2	117	4	-,-	(3)	12	1	52	3	-,-					
Fothergill	2	0	24	0	-,-											

VICTORIA v NEW SOUTH WALES

Played at Melbourne Cricket Ground on February 14, 15, 17, 18, 1941. (Four-day match)
TOSS: New South Wales.   Result: NEW SOUTH WALES WON BY 235 RUNS.
Debuts: Nil.
12th Men: I.R.Porter (Vic) and K.C.Gulliver (NSW).
Umpires: A.N.Barlow and W.J.Craddock.
Attendances: 2144, 6486, 2109, 359.   Total: 11,098.   Receipts: £395.
Close of Play: 1st day NSW 416 all out; 2nd day NSW (2) 0/18 (Cohen 7, Morris 11); 3rd day Vic (2) 4/73 (Johnson 10, Baker 1).

Sarovich (originally twelfth man) replaced G.E.Tamblyn (after-effects of Army vaccination) in the Victorian side. Both teams were handicapped by the loss of players, Chegwyn and McCabe suffering leg injuries in the field on the second day and taking no further part, and Lee aggravating an old thigh strain on the third day. O'Reilly again deputised for McCabe, Gulliver and Porter fielding as substitutes in both Victorian innings. Barnes (185 in 233 minutes, 16 fours) continued his prolific form, achieving his sixth hundred in successive matches; his second innings 79 occupied 118 minutes and included 4 fours. McCabe (82 in 76 minutes, 6 fours), Chegwyn (78 in 139 minutes, 5 fours), Jackson (57 in 104 minutes, 4 fours); Lee (67 in 120 minutes, 6 fours), Johnson (60 in 93 minutes, 6 fours) and Fothergill (63 in 91 minutes, 9 fours) exceeded 50. Sources: *NSWCA Scorebook, Wisden, NSWCA Report, The Age, The Argus, The Herald, Melbourne Sun, The Sporting Globe.*

NEW SOUTH WALES

M.B.Cohen	c Lee b Dempster	13		c Dudley b Johnson	19
A.R.Morris	lbw b Ring	25		c Baker b Sievers	31
S.G.Barnes	b Sievers	185		b Dempster	79
*S.J.McCabe	c Sarovich b Meikle	82		absent hurt	-
J.W.Chegwyn	b Dudley	78		absent hurt	-
C.L.McCool	not out	20	(4)	b Johnson	0
†R.A.Saggers	hit wkt b Johnson	6	(5)	c Meikle b Ring	47
V.E.Jackson	c Baker b Johnson	0	(6)	c Sievers b Ring	57
C.G.Pepper	lbw b Dudley	1	(7)	c Baker b Sievers	32
W.J.O'Reilly	c Sievers b Johnson	0	(8)	c Sievers b Johnson	26
V.Trumper, jr	c Baker b Dudley	0	(9)	not out	5
Extras	(b3, nb3)	6		(b4, lb3, nb1)	8
Total	(78.6 overs, 316 mins)	416		(70.4 overs, 266 mins)	304

VICTORIA

*I.S.Lee	c Pepper b Trumper	67		absent hurt	-
M.R.Harvey	b O'Reilly	14	(1)	c sub (K.C.Gulliver) b Pepper	38
T.K.Sarovich	b Pepper	7		b O'Reilly	0
I.W.Johnson	c Morris b Pepper	60		c Morris b O'Reilly	20
R.A.Dempster	lbw b O'Reilly	11	(2)	b O'Reilly	16
D.H.Fothergill	c Barnes b O'Reilly	63	(5)	lbw b Pepper	1
G.S.Meikle	lbw b O'Reilly	31	(8)	c O'Reilly b McCool	4
M.W.Sievers	b Pepper	29	(7)	b McCool	37
D.T.Ring	b O'Reilly	7		lbw b McCool	4
†E.A.Baker	c Saggers b O'Reilly	8	(6)	st Saggers b McCool	20
W.J.Dudley	not out	9	(10)	not out	11
Extras	(b8, lb6, w3, nb3)	20		(b7, lb1)	8
Total	(77.0 overs, 291 mins)	326		(39.5 overs, 143 mins)	159

VICTORIA	O	M	R	W	w,nb		O	M	R	W	w,nb	FALL OF WICKETS				
													NSW	VIC	NSW	VIC
Dudley	12.6	2	46	3	- 2		12	1	49	0	-,-	Wkt	1st	1st	2nd	2nd
Sievers	19	0	94	1	-,-		15	0	64	2	-,1	1st	21	49	49	54
Dempster	14	0	63	1	-,1	(5)	6	0	12	1	-,-	2nd	57	73	53	54
Ring	16	0	112	1	-,-	(3)	18.4	0	92	2	-,-	3rd	195	144	54	60
Johnson	12	0	49	3	-,-	(4)	19	0	79	3	-,-	4th	378	176	169	70
Meikle	5	0	46	1	-,-							5th	393	178	185	94
												6th	402	261	239	128
SOUTH AUSTRALIA	O	M	R	W	w,nb		O	M	R	W	w,nb	7th	402	284	293	140
Trumper	10	0	36	1	2,-		5	1	17	0	-,-	8th	403	307	304	144
Jackson	10	2	51	0	-,-		4	0	32	0	-,-	9th	412	311	-	159
O'Reilly	24	2	60	6	-,3		10	5	17	3	-,-	10th	416	326	-	-
Pepper	23	1	106	3	1,-		14	1	56	2	-,-					
Cohen	3	1	6	0	-,-											
McCool	5	0	39	0	-,-	(5)	6.5	0	29	4	-,-					
Barnes	2	0	8	0	-,-											

SOUTH AUSTRALIA v NEW SOUTH WALES

Played at Adelaide Oval on February 21, 22, 24, 1941. (Four-day match)
Toss: South Australia.   Result: NEW SOUTH WALES WON BY AN INNINGS AND 45 RUNS.
Debuts: South Australia - L.D.Duldig, H.V.Heairfield, R.S.Holman (all f/c). New South Wales - H.V.Stapleton (f/c)
12th Men: F.L.Teisseire (SA) and V.Trumper, jr (NSW).
Umpires: J.D.Scott and L.A.Smith.
Attendances: No daily figures published.   Total: 4711.   Receipts: £141.
Close of Play: 1st day NSW 3/284 (Chegwyn 103, McCool 69); 2nd day SA (2) 3/108 (K.L.Ridings 46, Duldig 15).

B.Dooland (unable to obtain leave) and W.M.Roberts (military duties) had to decline invitations from the South Australian selectors. Duldig, originally named as twelfth man, replaced T.E.Klose (ill) on the morning the match began. New South Wales were without their captain S.J.McCabe, who had returned to Sydney with his injured ankle, and Stapleton was brought from Sydney as his replacement. After O'Reilly accounted for the local batting, Barnes (51 in 51 minutes, 8 fours - whose first run gave him 1000 for the season), Chegwyn (103 in 110 minutes, 13 fours), McCool (100 in 158 minutes, 7 fours), Saggers (63 in 120 minutes, 5 fours) and Jackson (70 in 94 minutes, 10 fours) set up a handsome first-innings lead for the visitors. Chegwyn reached his century in 105 minutes and is reckoned to have scored about 100 runs in the final session on the first day. The South Australians succumbed inside three days despite contributions in the top order from Ridings (62 in 113 minutes, 8 fours) and Badcock (40 in 37 minutes, 6 fours) and later fifties from Waite (94 in 128 minutes, 13 fours) and Grimmett (67 in 100 minutes, 5 fours), who at 49 years 62 days of age was playing his last first-class match. His 668 wickets for South Australia remains a clear record for any State bowler in Australia, as does his 905 first-class wickets in this country. *Advertiser* incorrectly gives SA (l) Waite c McCool. Sources: *NSWCA Scorebook, Wisden, NSWCA Report, Adelaide Advertiser, The Age, The Herald, Melbourne Sun, The Sporting Globe, The News.*

SOUTH AUSTRALIA

K.L.Ridings	b Pepper	11		st Saggers b McCool	62
C.L.Badcock	b O'Reilly	40		b Pepper	40
R.A.Hamence	st Saggers b Gulliver	31		lbw b O'Reilly	5
B.H.Leak	st Saggers b McCool	21		b O'Reilly	1
M.G.Waite	c Morris b Gulliver	3	(7)	b Pepper	94
R.S.Holman	b O'Reilly	1		hit wkt b McCool	3
L.D.Duldig	run out	9	(5)	c Saggers b McCool	23
P.L.Ridings	c Barnes b O'Reilly	4		c Stapleton b Gulliver	21
*C.V.Grimmett	b O'Reilly	9		c O'Reilly b McCool	67
†H.V.Heairfield	b O'Reilly	0		not out	4
H.N.J.Cotton	not out	0		c Stapleton b McCool	8
Extras	(nb3)	3		(b3, w1, nb3)	7
Total	(36.3 overs, 131 mins)	132		(79.7 overs, 268 mins)	335

NEW SOUTH WALES

M.B.Cohen	lbw b Waite	21
A.R.Morris	b Grimmett	33
S.G.Barnes	c K.L.Ridings b P.L.Ridings	51
J.W.Chegwyn	c P.L.Ridings b Cotton	103
C.L.McCool	c Leak b Cotton	100
†R.A.Saggers	c P.L.Ridings b Cotton	63
H.V.Stapleton	lbw b Cotton	1
V.E.Jackson	c Cotton b Waite	70
K.C.Gulliver	b P.L.Ridings	29
C.G.Pepper	not out	25
*W.J.O'Reilly	c Heairfield b P.L.Ridings	1
Extras	(b7, lb3, w1, nb4)	15
Total	(95.6 overs, 383 mins)	512

NEW SOUTH WALES	O	M	R	W	w,nb		O	M	R	W	w,nb
Jackson	7	0	17	0	-,-		11	2	39	0	-,-
Stapleton	4	1	9	0	-,-		6	0	29	0	-,-
Pepper	9	0	47	1	-,1		16	0	89	2	1,-
O'Reilly	9.3	1	28	5	-,2		25	2	61	2	-,2
McCool	2	0	12	1	-,-	(6)	13.7	0	65	5	-,-
Gulliver	5	1	16	2	-,-	(5)	8	1	45	1	-,1

SOUTH AUSTRALIA	O	M	R	W	w,nb
Cotton	15	2	85	4	-,-
Waite	27	4	111	2	- 1
P.L.Ridings	10.6	1	76	3	- 3
Grimmett	24	1	128	1	-,-
K.L.Ridings	19	0	97	0	1,-

	FALL OF WICKETS		
	SA	NSW	SA
Wkt	1st	1st	2nd
1st	42	23	61
2nd	68	102	66
3rd	99	124	72
4th	102	284	134
5th	112	353	135
6th	112	362	138
7th	123	412	183
8th	123	477	313
9th	123	509	327
10th	132	512	335

QUEENSLAND v NEW SOUTH WALES

Played at Brisbane Cricket Ground (Woolloongabba) on November 28, 29, December 1, 1941. (Three-day match)
Toss : Queensland. Result : QUEENSLAND WON BY 19 RUNS.
Debuts: Queensland - E.C.La Frantz, A.H.McGinn (both f/c). New South Wales - V.Collins, D.R.Cristofani, R.R.Lindwall, L.Livingston, G.Powell (all f/c).
12th Men: J.E.McCarthy (Qld) and S.J.Carroll (NSW).
Umpires: C.V.Pengelly and R.Weitemeyer.
Attendances: 1200, 5000, 1800. Total: About 8000. Receipts: £462.
Close of Play: 1st day NSW 3/80 (Chegwyn 25, Horsfield 0); 2nd day Qld (2) 6/169 (Raymer 51, Watt 5).

This was the first of eight matches arranged for "an Interstate Patriotic Competition", the proceeds of which would be directed to the War effort. The entry of Japan into the War, via the raid on Pearl Harbour on December 7th, caused the cancellation of the remaining seven matches. New South Wales were forced to make changes when S.G.Barnes, K.C.Gulliver, A.R.Morris, R.A.Saggers and V.Trumper all withdrew for varying reasons before the team left Sydney, Carroll, Cristofani, James, Lindwall and Livingston replacing them. McGinn took the wickets of Fallowfield and McCabe with the first and last balls of his initial over in first-class cricket. Although 16 batsmen reached 40, none surpassed 77. Fifties were scored for Queensland by Cook (68 in 185 minutes, 5 fours), Brown (56 in 56 minutes, 7 fours and 69 in 89 minutes, 9 fours), Watt (50 in 64 minutes, 5 fours) and Raymer (53 not out in 73 minutes, 1 six and 7 fours and 77 in 120 minutes, 12 fours) and for New South Wales by Chegwyn (61 in 139 minutes, 3 fours). O'Reilly took five wickets in an innings for the fourth successive match. *Wisden* incorrectly gives NSW (2) McCabe c & b Ellis. Sources: *Wisden, QCA Report, Sydney Morning Herald, NSWCA Scorebook, Brisbane Courier-Mail, Brisbane Telegraph.*

QUEENSLAND

R.E.Rogers	b Collins	16		c Lindwall b O'Reilly	20
G.G.Cook	c McCabe b Cristofani	68		b Lindwall	1
E.C.La Frantz	b O'Reilly	6		b Lindwall	7
†D.Tallon	c & b Cristofani	13	(6)	c & b O'Reilly	0
*W.A.Brown	c Horsfield b Powell	56		lbw b O'Reilly	69
G.W.Baker	lbw b O'Reilly	40	(4)	b Lindwall	4
D.Watt	b Cristofani	50	(8)	lbw b O'Reilly	47
V.N.Raymer	not out	53	(7)	c Livingston b Cristofani	77
C.P.Christ	b Collins	3		c Collins b O'Reilly	3
J.A.Ellis	c Horsfield b Cristofani	7		not out	5
A.H.McGinn	b O'Reilly	5		c & b O'Reilly	2
Extras	(b2, lb3, nb12)	17		(b7, lb4, nb3)	14
Total	(72.2 overs, 276 mins)	334		(50.7 overs, 185 mins)	249

NEW SOUTH WALES

†L.Livingston	c Brown b Christ	46		c Tallon b Ellis	7
L.J.Fallowfield	c Ellis b McGinn	0		st Tallon b Watt	42
*S.J.McCabe	c Baker b McGinn	8		b Ellis	41
J.W.Chegwyn	c & b Watt	61		lbw b McGinn	24
G.C.Horsfield	run out (sub J.E.McCarthy/Tallon)	43		run out (Rogers/Tallon)	35
R.V.James	c Tallon b Cook	44		c sub (J.E.McCarthy) b Raymer	46
G.Powell	c Tallon b Watt	47		lbw b Baker	0
V.Collins	not out	29		c Ellis b Cook	20
D.R.Cristofani	b Watt	10		b Cook	10
R.R.Lindwall	b Ellis	1		b Ellis	10
W.J.O'Reilly	c Rogers b Watt	4		not out	7
Extras	(b10, lb7)	17		(b11, lb1)	12
Total	(71.5 overs, 284 mins)	310		(56.1 overs, 221 mins)	254

NEW SOUTH WALES	O	M	R	W	w,nb	O	M	R	W	w,nb
Lindwall	15	0	81	0	-,6	7	0	36	3	-,2
Collins	11	2	33	2	-,-	4	0	16	0	-,-
O'Reilly	16.2	5	35	3	-,6	21.7	2	89	6	-,1
Cristofani	21	2	97	4	-,-	15	1	67	1	-,-
Powell	9	0	71	1	-,-	3	0	27	0	-,-

QUEENSLAND	O	M	R	W	w,nb		O	M	R	W	w,nb
Ellis	20	2	81	1	-,-		16.1	1	61	3	-,-
McGinn	10	1	46	2	-,-		7	0	34	1	-,-
Cook	8	0	41	1	-,-		10	2	38	2	-,-
Christ	6	3	5	1	-,-						
Raymer	12	1	51	0	-,-		7	0	35	1	-,-
Baker	3	0	6	0	-,-	(7)	4	2	6	1	-,-
Watt	8.5	0	40	4	-,-	(4)	10	0	57	1	-,-
La Frantz	4	0	23	0	-,-	(6)	2	0	11	0	-,-

FALL OF WICKETS

Wkt	QLD 1st	NSW 1st	QLD 2nd	NSW 2nd
1st	20	4	3	8
2nd	31	12	13	58
3rd	50	80	20	100
4th	135	153	62	128
5th	204	180	62	202
6th	215	235	143	202
7th	301	284	231	210
8th	307	298	240	235
9th	314	301	247	238
10th	334	310	249	254

INDEX TO PLAYERS

This index shows the full biographical details of every cricketer to appear in an Australian first-class cricket match during the period covered by this volume. In addition to full name, date and place of birth (and death where appropriate), major teams played for, team function, and relationship to other players in the volume are shown. The number after the players particulars is the AFCM (Australian First Class Match) number.

The following standard abbreviations are used throughout the index:

b	Born		d	died
RHB	Right-Hand Batsman		LHB	Left-Hand Batsman
RaB	Right-Arm Bowler		LaB	Left-Arm Bowler
RaB(r)	Right-Arm Round-Arm Bowler		LaB(r)	Left-Arm Round-Arm Bowler
RF	Right-Arm Fast Bowler		LF	Left-Arm Fast Bowler
RF(r)	Right-Arm Fast Round-Arm Bowler		LF(r)	Left-Arm Fast Round-Arm Bowler
RFM	Right-Arm Fast-Medium Bowler		LFM	Left-Arm Fast-Medium Bowler
RFM(r)	Right-Arm Fast-Medium Round-Arm Bowler		LFM(r)	Left-Arm Fast-Medium Round-Arm Bowler
RM	Right-Arm Medium Bowler		LM	Left-Arm Medium Bowler
RM(r)	Right-Arm Medium Round-Arm Bowler		LM(r)	Left-Arm Medium Round-Arm Bowler
LB	Right-Arm Leg-Break Bowler		SLA	Left-Arm Slow Orthodox Bowler
LBG	Right-Arm Leg-Break/Googly Bowler		SLC	Left-Arm Slow 'Chinaman' Bowler
OB	Right-Arm Off-Break Bowler		WK	Wicket-keeper

a'BECKETT, Edward Fitzhayley; *Vic*. Brother of M.a'Beckett. b 16 Apr 1836 (Holborn, London), d 25 Mar 1922 (Upper Beaconsfield, Vic). 2, 5.

a'BECKETT, Edward Lambert; *Vic*. RHB, RFM. b 11 Aug 1907 (East St Kilda, Vic), d 2 Jun 1989 (Terang, Vic). 643, 646, 647, 648, 649, 662, 663, 665, 673, 678, 689, 692, 695, 700, 703, 704, 709, 712, 714, 719, 723, 726, 730, 750, 752, 756, 760, 763, 764, 766.

a'BECKETT, Malwyn; *Vic*. Brother of E.F.a'Beckett. b 26 Sep 1834 (London), d 25 Jun 1906 (Sale, Vic). 2.

ABEL, Robert; *Eng*. RHB/RaB. b 30 Nov 1857 (Rotherhithe, Surrey), d 10 Dec 1936 (Stockwell, London). 105, 106, 108, 112, 113, 118, 121, 123, 143, 144, 145, 147, 150, 151, 152, 153.

§ABELL, William Mutlow; *Qld*. /WK. b 1874 (, NSW), d ( ). 281.

ABSOLOM, Charles Alfred; *Eng*. RHB/RM. b 7 Jun 1846 (Blackheath, Kent), d 30 Jul 1889 (Port of Spain, Trinidad). 38, 39, 40, 41, 42.

ACHURCH, Claude Septimus; *NSW*. RHB. b 16 Aug 1896 (Dubbo, NSW), d 15 Aug 1979 (Nambour, Qld). 533, 534.

ADAMS, Edward William; *NSW*. RHB/RMF. b 10 Jul 1896 (Bathurst, NSW), d 25 May 1977 (Bexley, NSW). 510.

ADAMS, Francis; *NSW*. b 1835 (Ireland), d 10 Feb 1911 (Nth Sydney). 9.

ADAMS, James William; *Qld*. LHB. b 22 Feb 1904 (Brisbane). 727.

ADAMSON, Charles Young; *Qld*. LHB/LaB. b 1875 (Durham, UK), d 17 Sep 1918 (Salonica, Greece). 245.

ADDISON, Alexander Gallan; *Tas*. b 29 Sep 1877 (Adelaide), d 12 Oct 1935 (Double Bay, NSW). 305.

AINSLIE, James; *Vic*. RHB/RFM. b 9 Jun 1880 (Elsternwick, Vic), d 31 Dec 1953 (St Kilda, Vic). 252, 334, 337, 341, 384, 385, 389, 397, 399.

ALEXANDER, Francis James; *West Aust*. RHB/LB. b 15 Apr 1911 (Perth). 770, 820, 821, 823, 824, 827, 842, 844, 868, 900, 903, 904, 920.

ALEXANDER, George; *Vic*. RHB/RF(r). b 22 Apr 1851 (Fitzroy, Vic), d 6 Nov 1930 (Melbourne). 30, 31, 41, 42, 43, 44, 47, 49, 72, 78.

ALEXANDER, Harry Houston; *Vic*. RHB/RF. b 9 Jun 1905 (Ascot Vale, Vic). 676, 678, 685, 688, 692, 695, 700, 703, 704, 712, 714, 719, 723, 726, 730, 735, 752, 766, 773, 774, 776, 780, 783, 786, 798, 799, 800, 804, 807, 808.

ALEXANDER, William Colin; *Sth Aust*. RHB/OB. b 14 Sep 1907 (Gawler, SA). 597, 609, 611, 612, 614, 619, 622, 624, 625, 626, 630, 635, 637, 639, 641, 644, 645, 652, 667, 671, 677, 679.

ALLAN, Francis Erskine; *Vic*. LHB/LFM(r). b 2 Dec 1849 (Allansford, Vic), d 9 Feb 1917 (Melbourne). 18, 20, 22, 24, 30, 31, 38, 41, 43, 44, 46, 48, 52, 53, 63.

ALLAN, George Harold; *Tas*. RHB/RM. Son of H.A.Allan. b 18 Feb 1887 (, NSW), d 2 Nov 1932 (Adelaide). 553, 570, 589, 590, 615, 627, 643.

ALLAN, Henry Alexander; *NSW*. b 6 Jan 1846 ( ) d ( ). 24.

ALLCOTT, Cyril Francis Walter; *NZ*. LHB/SLA. b 7 Oct 1896 (Lower Moutere, NZ), d 19 Nov 1973 (Auckland). 603, 605, 609, 610, 633.

ALLEE, Charles George; *Vic*. RHB/RF(r). b 10 Feb 1848 (Melbourne), d 7 Jun 1896 (East Melbourne). 26, 27, 30, 31, 36, 37.

ALLEN, George Oswald Browning; *Eng*. RHB/RF. Nephew of R.C.Allen. b 31 Jul 1902 (Bellevue Hill, NSW), d 29 Nov 1989 (St Johns Wood, London). 772, 776, 778, 779, 781, 785, 789, 792, 796, 797, 799, 800, 868, 869, 871, 872, 873, 883, 886, 889, 890, 895.

ALLEN, Harold Eric; *Tas*. RHB/RFM. b 13 Oct 1886 (Invercargill, NZ), d 9 Jul 1939 (West Hobart). 469, 484.

ALLEN, Reginald Charles; *NSW*. RHB/RFM. b 2 Jul 1858 (Glebe, NSW), d 2 May 1952 (Sydney). 39, 53, 62, 71, 74, 77, 93, 97, 98, 101, 102, 107, 108, 109, 111, 114, 118.

ALLEN, Thomas; *Qld*. RHB/LBG. b 5 Sep 1912 (Toowoomba, Qld), d 18 Mar 1954 (Cambooya, Qld). 803, 807, 808, 811, 815, 817, 830, 831, 834, 836, 837, 846, 850, 852, 855, 857, 860, 863, 870, 876, 879, 882, 884, 887, 891, 897, 905, 908, 910, 911, 912, 921, 923, 926, 930, 931, 934, 938, 940, 943, 944, 948, 953.

ALLEN, Thorpe; *Qld*. LHB/LM. b 7 Mar 1870 (Oxley, Qld), d 25 Jan 1950 (East Brisbane). 234.

ALLEN, William Miller; *Vic*. RHB/RF. b 7 Jul 1889 (Ballarat, Vic), d 13 Nov 1948 (Ringwood, Vic). 489, 492.

ALLEYNE, John Placid; *NSW*. RHB. b 1 Aug 1908 (Glebe, NSW), d 24 Jun 1980 (Glebe, NSW). 640.

ALLISON, Henry; *Tas*. b 14 Jul 1828 (Campbell Town, Tas), d c1893 ( ). 2, 7.

ALLOM, Maurice James Carrick; *Eng*. RHB/RFM. b 23 Mar 1906 (Northwood, Middlesex). 682, 684, 685, 686, 687.

ALLOO, Arthur William; *NZ*. RHB/OB. b 9 Jan 1892 (Sydney, NSW), d 16 Sep 1950 (Nelson, NZ). 603, 605, 609, 610.

ALLSOPP, Arthur Henry; *NSW & Vic*. RHB/WK. b 1 Mar 1908 (Lithgow, NSW). 686, 688, 690, 692, 696, 697, 700, 706, 711, 712, 713, 715, 717, 812, 814, 821, 823, 839.

ALSOP, Charles James; *Vic*. RHB. b 24 Nov 1868 (Moonee Ponds, Vic), d 17 Sep 1948 (Melbourne). 175.

AMBLER, Albert Mark; *Sth Aust*. RHB/WK. b 27 Sep 1892 (Murray Bridge, SA), d 27 Nov 1970 (Prospect, SA). 511, 512, 523, 531, 534, 536, 537, 557, 561, 564, 566, 567, 569, 574, 575, 578, 580, 586, 596, 597, 600, 606.

AMES, Leslie Ethelbert George; *Eng*. RHB/WK. b 3 Dec 1905 (Elham, Kent), d 26 Feb 1990 (Canterbury, Kent). 650, 655, 658, 668, 669, 671, 675, 678, 771, 772, 775, 776, 779, 781, 782, 785, 789, 792, 793, 796, 797, 799, 801, 873, 875, 876, 877, 878, 883, 885, 889, 890, 892, 893, 895.

AMOS, Gordon Stanley; *NSW & Qld*. RHB/RFM. b 4 Apr 1905 (Newtown, NSW). 618, 634, 636, 639, 645, 647, 662, 666, 683, 687, 689, 691, 717, 724, 743, 744, 748, 751, 870, 876, 879, 882, 884, 887, 891.

AMOS, William; *Sth Aust*. /LB. b 20 Apr 1860 (Glen Osmond, SA), d 14 May 1935 (Nth Adelaide). 137, 160.

ANDERSON, George; *Anderson's XI*. RHB. b 20 Jan 1826 (Aiskew, Yorks), d 27 Nov 1902 (Bedale, Yorks). 15.

ANDERSON, James Clayton; *Qld*. RHB. b 27 Feb 1895 (, Qld), d   (   ). 387, 388, 402, 403.

ANDERSON, John Theodore; *West Aust*. b 10 Aug 1878 (Warrnambool, Vic), d 20 Aug 1926 (Geelong, Vic). 508, 510.

ANDREWS, Thomas James Edwin; *NSW*. RHB/LBG. b 26 Aug 1890 (Newtown, NSW), d 28 Jan 1970 (Croydon, NSW). 456, 472, 474, 475, 477, 479, 481, 482, 486, 487, 488, 490, 491, 494, 496, 498, 500, 501, 503, 505, 507, 510, 514, 518, 520, 523, 525, 528, 532, 535, 537, 538, 539, 546, 548, 549, 551, 552, 555, 558, 559, 561, 563, 567, 568, 571, 577, 580, 586, 587, 591, 593, 594, 595, 604, 606, 607, 612, 613, 615, 616, 617, 620, 622, 623, 630, 633, 637, 638, 642, 644, 646, 651, 655, 657, 663, 667, 670, 675, 679, 712.

ANDREWS, William Charles; *NSW & Qld*. RHB/RM. b 14 Jul 1908 (West Maitland, NSW), d 9 Jun 1962 (Bombay, India). 666, 667, 683, 686, 696, 697, 700, 711, 763, 767, 773, 777, 783, 787, 790, 794, 796, 803, 807, 808, 811, 815, 817, 830, 831, 834, 836, 837, 840, 846, 852, 855, 857, 860, 870, 876, 879, 882, 884.

ANDREW-STREET, Alfred Gordon; *Vic*. RHB. b 8 Apr 1914 (Bondi, NSW), d 13 Dec 1984 (Concord, NSW). 915.

ANTILL, Thomas Wills; *Vic*. b 20 Nov 1830 (Jarvisfield, NSW), d 11 May 1865 (Nelson, NZ). 1.

ARMITAGE, Thomas; *Eng*. RHB/RM. b 25 Apr 1848 (Walkley, Yorks), d 21 Sep 1922 (Chicago, USA). 32, 33, 34.

ARMSTRONG, Edward Killeen; *Qld*. RHB/RaB. Brother of G.G. & W.Armstrong. b 15 Feb 1881 (Milton, Qld), d 29 Apr 1963 (Brisbane). 324, 338, 429.

ARMSTRONG, George Gort; *Qld*. RHB. Brother of E.K. & W.Armstrong. b 29 Dec 1882 (Milton, Qld), d 12 Jan 1956 (Brisbane). 399, 405.

ARMSTRONG, Thomas Goldsmith; *Vic*. LHB/SLA. Brother of W.W.Armstrong. b 31 Oct 1889 (Caulfield, Vic), d 15 Apr 1963 (Bairnsdale, Vic). 643.

ARMSTRONG, William; *Qld*. RHB/RM. Brother of E.K. & G.G.Armstrong. b 2 May 1886 (Milton, Qld), d 29 May 1955 (Brisbane). 359, 390, 405, 409, 452.

ARMSTRONG, Warwick Windridge; *Vic*. RHB/LB. Brother of T.G.Armstrong. b 22 May 1879 (Kyneton, Vic), d 13 Jul 1947 (Darling Point, NSW). 236, 237, 244, 251, 254, 256, 257, 260, 262, 264, 267, 268, 270, 273, 274, 275, 280, 282, 284, 286, 287, 288, 292, 294, 297, 299, 301, 302, 304, 306, 313, 314, 316, 318, 320, 325, 328, 329, 331, 340, 343, 344, 352, 354, 356, 357, 360, 361, 364, 366, 368, 372, 374, 377, 378, 381, 382, 383, 392, 394, 396, 397, 404, 407, 410, 413, 414, 417, 419, 422, 423, 424, 426, 428, 430, 432, 434, 437, 438, 439, 440, 442, 445, 446, 447, 450, 454, 460, 461, 463, 465, 466, 468, 471, 476, 477, 478, 481, 488, 489, 491, 493, 495, 496, 497, 501, 502, 504, 505, 508, 509, 511, 515, 517, 519, 520, 521, 524, 527, 530, 532, 536, 539.

ARNOLD, Edward George; *Eng*. RHB/RFM. b 7 Nov 1876 (Exmouth, Devon), d 25 Oct 1942 (Worcester, UK). 291, 293, 295, 297, 302, 303, 305, 306, 308, 310.

ARNOLD, Weller; *Tas*. RHB. b 23 Sep 1882 (Nth Hobart), d 28 Oct 1957 (Hobart). 492.

ARNOTT, Percival Sinclair; *NSW*. RHB/LBG. b 9 Jul 1889 (Newcastle, NSW), d 23 Dec 1950 (Strathfield, NSW). 452, 455, 456, 458, 459, 460.

ARTHUR, Charles; *Tas*. b 5 Feb 1808 (Plymouth, Devon), d 29 Jul 1884 (Longford, Tas). 1.

ARTHUR, Gerald Charles; *West Aust*. RHB/WK. b 25 Jul 1913 (Yarloop, WA). 900, 903, 904.

ARTHUR, George Henry; *Tas*. RHB/long stop. Son of C.Arthur and brother of J.L.A.Arthur. b 10 Mar 1849 (Longford, Tas), d 13 Nov 1932 (Longford, Tas). 19, 35.

ARTHUR, John Lake Allen; *Tas*. RHB/RaB. Son of C.Arthur and brother of G.H.Arthur. b 7 Apr 1847 (Longford, Tas), d 26 Apr 1877 (Longford, Tas). 19, 22, 25, 27.

ASHBOLT, Frank Lionel; *NZ*. RHB/OB. b 11 Apr 1876 (Christchurch, NZ), d 16 Jul 1940 (Wellington, NZ). 237, 238.

ASHER, Oswald Philip; *NSW*. RHB/LBG. b 21 May 1891 (Paddington, NSW), d 16 Jul 1970 (Waverton, NSW). 499, 510, 522, 533, 534, 546, 547, 548, 608.

ATKINS, Alfred A   ; *Qld & NSW*. RHB. b 22 Apr 1874 (, NSW), d   (   ). 193, 208, 243, 245, 277, 278, 281, 286, 295, 300, 312, 324.

ATKINSON, James Archibald; *Vic & Tas*. RHB/WK/OB. b 4 Apr 1896 (Nth Fitzroy, Vic), d 11 Jun 1956 (Beaconsfield, Tas). 540, 591, 592, 605, 627, 643, 668, 669, 674, 676, 693, 694, 701, 707, 708, 722, 729, 737, 739, 754, 758, 759, 768, 785, 791, 812.

ATTEWELL, William; *Eng*. RHB/RM. b 12 Jun 1861 (Keyworth, Notts), d 11 Jun 1927 (Long Eaton, Derbyshire). 76, 77, 78, 80, 82, 84, 85, 86, 105, 106, 108, 112, 113, 117, 118, 121, 123, 143, 144, 145, 147, 150, 151, 152, 153.

AUSTEN, Ernest Thomas; *Vic*. RHB. b 23 Sep 1900 (Glenferrie, Vic), d 21 Jun 1983 (Melbourne). 648, 649, 670, 672, 694.

AUSTIN, Sydney Walter; *NSW & Qld*. RHB/LB b 16 Nov 1866 (, NSW), d 9 Sep 1932 (Randwick, NSW). 163, 185, 186.

AYRES, Sydney William; *Qld*. RHB/LBG. b 7 Aug 1889 (Enmore, NSW), d 7 Aug 1974 (Castle Hill, NSW). 470, 472, 486, 493, 494, 499, 506, 510, 516, 529, 533, 547, 560, 584.

BACK, William; *West Aust*. b 1856 (Rottnest Island, WA), d 15 Feb 1911 (Perth). 161, 162.

BACKMAN, Charles James; *Sth Aust*. RHB/RM. b 14 Dec 1890 (Bowden, SA), d 25 Apr 1915 (Gallipoli, Turkey). 431.

BADCOCK, Clayvel Lindsay; *Tas & Sth Aust*. RHB. b 10 Apr 1914 (Exton, Tas), d 13 Dec 1982 (Exton, Tas). 705, 706, 707, 708, 754, 755, 758, 759, 768, 782, 785, 788, 791, 802, 812, 814, 819, 825, 826, 828, 829, 830, 832, 834, 835, 841, 847, 853, 855, 860, 861, 864, 866, 867, 869, 871, 874, 875, 877, 878, 886, 889, 891, 894, 895, 896, 898, 902, 904, 906, 908, 909, 911, 913, 918, 919, 920, 922, 924, 926, 928, 931, 932, 935, 939, 943, 945, 947, 955, 956, 957, 959, 963.

BAILEY, Bertram Theodore; *Sth Aust*. RHB/LB. Brother of E.A.Bailey. b 5 Dec 1874 (Adelaide), d 13 Oct 1964 (Payneham, SA). 201, 203, 204, 207, 257, 258, 261, 264.

BAILEY, Ernest Albert; *Sth Aust*. RHB. Brother of B.T.Bailey. b 15 Nov 1881 (Adelaide), d   (   ). 337.

BAILEY, George Herbert; *Tas*. RHB/RFM(r). b 29 Oct 1853 (Colombo, Ceylon), d 10 Oct 1926 (Hobart). 27, 159.

BAILEY, George Keith Brooke; *Tas*. RHB/LM. Son of G.H.Bailey. b 3 Jan 1882 (Hobart), d 17 Jun 1964 (Hobart). 303, 309.

BAILEY, Rowland Herbert; *Vic*. RHB/RFM. b 5 Oct 1876 (Melbourne), d 24 Mar 1950 (Ivanhoe, Vic). 464.

BAILEY, William Henry; *Vic*. RHB/RM. b 20 Jul 1898 (Condoblin, NSW), d 27 Feb 1983 (Geelong, Vic). 553, 556, 627.

BAIRD, Keith Hugh; *West Aust*. RHB/LB. b 27 Dec 1911 (Perth), d 18 Jul 1965 (Peppermint Grove, WA). 699.

BAKER, Charles Michael; *Vic*. RHB. b 18 Jun 1880 (Ballarat East, Vic), d 4 May 1962 (Ballarat, Vic). 294, 306, 309, 321.

BAKER, Everard Audley; *Vic*. LHB/WK. b 28 Jul 1913 (Cohuna, Vic), d 30 Mar 1987 (Melbourne). 865, 927, 929, 936, 937, 956, 957, 960, 961, 962.

BAKER, Frederick; *Vic*. LHB/LF. b 1851 (   ), d c 1925 (   ). 36, 37, 41, 42, 45, 55, 57, 61.

BAKER, Glen William; *Qld*. RHB/RM. b 9 Aug 1915 (Townsville, Qld), d 15 Dec 1943 (Buna, New Guinea). 876, 879, 882, 884, 887, 891, 897, 905, 908, 910, 911, 912, 921, 923, 926, 930, 931, 934, 938, 940, 943, 944, 946, 948, 953, 954, 958, 960, 964.

BAKER, James Clark; *NZ*. RHB. b 13 Nov 1866 (London), d 1 Feb 1939 (Dunedin, NZ). 237, 238.

BALASKAS, Xenophon Constantine; *Sth Afr*. RHB/LBG. b 15 Oct 1910 (Kimberley, Sth Afr). 741, 744, 748, 761, 764, 770.

BALLANS, David Murray; *Sth Aust*. RHB. b 30 Jun 1868 (at sea), d 26 Jun 1957 (Goodwood Park, SA). 136, 161.

BANDY, Lawrence Henry; *West Aust*. RHB/LB. b 3 Sep 1911 (Perth), d 18 Jul 1984 (Scarborough, WA). 950, 951.

BANKS, Albert James; *West Aust*. RHB/RFM. b 10 Dec 1883 (Maryborough, Vic), d 5 Jul 1930 (Toodyay, WA). 386, 532.

BANNERMAN, Alexander Chalmers; *NSW*. RHB/RM(r). Brother of C.Bannerman. b 22 Mar 1854 (Paddington, NSW), d 19 Sep 1924 (Paddington, NSW). 32, 38, 39, 40, 43, 44, 47, 48, 49, 51, 53, 54, 55, 58, 59, 63, 64, 65, 66, 67, 68, 71, 72, 73, 74, 78, 79, 83, 84, 85, 86, 92, 93, 95, 98, 99, 101, 107, 108, 109, 111, 114, 115, 116, 117, 118, 124, 125, 126, 129, 130, 131, 133, 135, 136, 137, 138, 140, 145, 146, 147, 148, 149, 150, 151, 153, 154, 155, 157, 158, 164, 165.

BANNERMAN, Charles; *NSW*. RHB. Brother of A.C.Bannerman. b 23 Jul 1851 (Woolwich, Kent), d 20 Aug 1930 (Surry Hills, NSW). 23, 24, 25, 26, 28, 30, 31, 32, 33, 34, 38, 39, 40, 43, 44, 46, 48, 49, 51, 53, 55, 67, 77, 79, 82, 83, 89, 118.

BARBER, Wilfred; *Eng*. RHB/RFM. b 18 Apr 1901 (Cleckheaton, Yorks), d 10 Sep 1968 (Bradford, Yorks). 845, 848, 849, 850, 851.

BARBOUR, Eric Pitty; *NSW*. RHB/LBG. Brother of R.R.Barbour. b 27 Jan 1891 (Ashfield, NSW), d 7 Dec 1934 (Darlinghurst, NSW). 379, 393, 400, 415, 418, 422, 429, 433, 436, 439, 441, 445, 448, 452, 458, 462, 463, 466, 474, 481, 486, 539, 571.

BARBOUR, Robert Roy; *Qld*. RHB. Brother of E.P.Barbour. b 29 Mar 1899 (Ashfield, NSW). 499, 506.

BARDSLEY, Raymond; *NSW*. RHB. Brother of W.Bardsley. b 19 Jan 1894 (Glebe Point, NSW), d 25 Jun 1983 ( ). 529, 560, 565, 602, 608, 610.

BARDSLEY, Warren; *NSW*. LHB. Brother of R.Bardsley. b 7 Dec 1882 (Nevertire, NSW), d 20 Jan 1954 (Collaroy, NSW). 312, 317, 323, 324, 326, 336, 346, 347, 359, 367, 372, 373, 376, 377, 380, 381, 382, 383, 391, 392, 395, 396, 397, 408, 412, 413, 415, 417, 419, 422, 424, 425, 426, 429, 433, 436, 438, 439, 440, 441, 442, 445, 447, 448, 462, 463, 466, 474, 475, 477, 479, 481, 487, 488, 490, 491, 496, 498, 500, 501, 503, 505, 507, 514, 518, 519, 520, 521, 523, 524, 525, 527, 528, 530, 532, 538, 539, 546, 548, 549, 551, 552, 555, 558, 559, 561, 563, 567, 568, 571, 577, 583, 585, 591, 593, 604, 606, 607, 612, 613, 616, 630.

BARING, Frederick Albert; *Vic*. RHB/OB. Brother of H.T.Baring. b 15 Dec 1890 (Hotham East, Vic), d 10 Dec 1961 (Doncaster, Vic). 446, 454, 460, 461, 463, 465, 468, 476, 477, 481, 483, 488, 489, 491, 495, 496, 497, 501, 504, 511, 515, 520, 607, 613, 628, 629, 643, 660, 662, 663.

BARING, Hugh Thomas; *Vic*. RHB. Brother of F.A.Baring. b 17 Aug 1907 (East Melbourne), d 9 Jul 1968 (Fitzroy, Vic). 693, 694.

BARLOW, Richard Gorton; *Eng*. RHB/LM. b 28 May 1851 (Bolton, Lancs), d 31 Jul 1919 (Blackpool, Lancs). 51, 52, 54, 56, 57, 58, 59, 61, 62, 64, 65, 66, 68, 69, 91, 92, 93, 94, 96, 97, 99, 101, 102, 103, 104.

BARNARD, Francis George Allman; *Vic*. b 26 Dec 1857 (Kew, Vic), d 1 Jun 1932 (Melbourne). 90.

BARNES, James Charles; *NSW*. RHB/LBG. b 16 Oct 1882 (Sydney), d ( ). 323, 324, 326, 336, 346, 347, 359, 364, 367, 372, 373, 376, 377, 380, 381, 382, 383, 391, 392, 395, 400, 416, 418, 456, 458, 459, 460.

BARNES, John Francis; *Qld*. RHB/WK. b 27 Sep 1916 (Rockhampton, Qld). 960.

BARNES, John Robert; *Vic*. RHB. b 20 May 1905 (Williamstown, Vic). 705.

BARNES, Richard Thomas Bygrove; *Tas*. RHB/RFM(r). b 5 Sep 1852 (Hobart), d 30 Apr 1902 (Heidelberg, Vic). 22, 25.

BARNES, Sydney Francis; *Eng*. RHB/RFM. b 19 Apr 1873 (Smethwick, Staffs), d 26 Dec 1967 (Chadsmoor, Staffs). 261, 262, 263, 266, 268, 270, 348, 349, 350, 351, 356, 357, 360, 361, 365, 366, 368, 371, 431, 433, 435, 437, 438, 440, 442, 443, 444, 446, 447, 448, 450.

BARNES, Sidney George; *NSW*. RHB/LB/WK. b 5 Jun 1916 (Charters Towers, Qld), d 16 Dec 1973 (Collaroy, NSW). 894, 897, 901, 906, 907, 910, 913, 914, 917, 918, 919, 921, 922, 924, 925, 930, 932, 933, 938, 941, 942, 944, 947, 949, 952, 953, 954, 955, 958, 959, 961, 962, 963.

BARNES, William; *Eng*. RHB/RFM. b 27 May 1852 (Sutton-in-Ashfield, Notts), d 24 Mar 1899 (Mansfield Woodhouse, Notts). 61, 62, 64, 65, 66, 68, 69, 76, 77, 78, 80, 82, 84, 85, 86, 91, 92, 93, 94, 96, 97, 99, 104.

BARNETT, Benjamin Arthur; *Vic*. LHB/WK. b 23 Mar 1908 (Auburn, Vic), d 29 Jun 1979 (Newcastle, NSW). 693, 694, 699, 714, 719, 723, 726, 730, 735, 742, 745, 750, 752, 760, 763, 764, 766, 773, 774, 776, 778, 780, 783, 786, 798, 800, 804, 805, 807, 808, 810, 813, 818, 825, 826, 827, 828, 831, 833, 835, 837, 838, 841, 844, 872, 874, 879, 881, 887, 888, 893, 896, 899, 900, 905, 907, 909, 912, 914, 917, 918, 919, 922, 923, 925, 928, 933, 934, 935, 939, 940, 942, 945, 948, 949.

BARNETT, Charles John; *Eng*. RHB/RM. b 3 Jul 1910 (Cheltenham, Glos). 868, 869, 871, 872, 873, 876, 877, 878, 883, 886, 889, 890, 892, 893, 895.

BARRAS, Alexander Edward Owen; *West Aust*. LHB/LB. b 26 Jan 1914 (Auburn, Vic). 936, 937, 950, 951.

BARRATT, Fred; *Eng*. RHB/RF. b 12 Apr 1894 (Annesley, Notts), d 29 Jan 1947 (Nottingham). 684, 685, 686, 687.

BARRETT, Edgar Alfred; *Vic*. Brother of J.E.Barrett. b 26 Jun 1869 (Sth Melbourne), d 29 Apr 1959 (Melbourne). 132, 134, 135, 169, 187.

BARRETT, Henry; *Tas*. RHB/RM(r). b 19 Aug 1837 (Launceston), d ( ). 22.

BARRETT, John Edward; *Vic*. LHB/LM. Brother of E.A.Barrett. b 15 Oct 1866 (Sth Melbourne), d 6 Feb 1916 (Peak Hill, WA). 81, 83, 125, 127, 128, 129, 130, 132, 133, 134, 135, 144, 155, 156, 158.

BARROW, Ivan; *WI*. RHB/WK. b 6 Jan 1911 (Kingston, Jamaica), d 2 Apr 1979 (Kingston Jamaica). 713, 718, 722, 725, 728, 732, 734, 736, 738.

BARSTOW, Charles Banks; *Qld*. RHB/RM/LB. b 14 Mar 1883 (Brisbane), d 12 Jul 1935 (Eagle Junction, Qld). 336, 359, 405, 409, 414, 416, 429, 435, 437, 452, 467, 470, 473,486, 493, 494, 499, 547, 562, 564, 565, 603.

BARTLETT, Albert James; *Sth Aust*. RHB. b 23 Apr 1900 (Unley, SA), d 6 Oct 1968 (Woodville Sth, SA). 601.

BARTLETT, Edward Lawson; *WI*. RHB. b 18 Mar 1906 (Barbados), d 21 Dec 1976 (Henrys, Barbados). 713, 716, 718, 721, 725, 733, 734, 738.

BATEMAN, William Augustus; *West Aust*. RHB. b 11 Sep 1866 (Fremantle, WA), d 27 Jul 1935 (Sth Perth). 161, 162.

BATES, Willie; *Eng*. RHB/OB. b 19 Nov 1855 (Huddersfield, Yorks), d 8 Jan 1900 (Lepton, Yorks). 51, 52, 54, 56, 57, 58, 59, 61, 62, 64, 65, 66, 68, 69, 76, 77, 78, 80, 82, 84, 85, 86, 91, 92, 93, 94, 96, 97, 99, 101, 102, 103, 104, 105, 106, 108.

BAXTER, Arthur Douglas; *Eng*. RHB/RFM. b 20 Jan 1910 (Edinburgh), d 28 Jan 1986 (Edenbridge, Kent). 845, 847, 849, 850, 851.

BAYLES, Robert Charles Alfred Vivian; *Tas*. RHB/RM. Brother of W.H.Bayles & cousin of E.S. & F.E.Headlam. b 7 Jul 1892 (Ross, Tas), d 16 May 1959 (Launceston). 485.

BAYLES, William Headlam; *Tas*. LHB/LM. Brother of R.C.A.V.Bayles & cousin of E.S. & F.E.Headlam. b 8 Jan 1896 (Ross, Tas), d 17 Dec 1960 (Launceston). 485.

BAYLY, Henry Vincent; *Tas*. /RF(r). b 19 Nov 1850 (Dulcot, Tas), d 7 Jan 1903 (New Town, Tas). 22, 35.

BEACHAM, George; *Vic*. RHB/LB. b 27 Oct 1867 (, Qld), d 11 Jan 1925 (Sth Fitzroy, Vic). 219.

BEAL, James Charles; *NSW*. b 16 May 1833 (Sydney), d 24 Aug 1904 (Milton, Qld). 4.

BEAMES, Percy James; *Vic*. RHB/RM. b 27 Jul 1911 (Ballarat, Vic). 812, 814, 903, 916, 927, 929, 942, 945, 948, 949, 956.

BEAN, Ernest Edward; *Vic*. RHB/RFM. b 17 Apr 1866 (Nth Melbourne), d 22 Mar 1939 (Hampton, Vic). 119, 160, 162, 169, 183, 285, 287, 334.

BEAN, George; *Eng*. RHB/RM. b 7 Mar 1864 (Sutton-in-Ashfield, Notts), d 16 Mar 1923 (Warsop, Notts). 143, 144, 145, 147, 150, 152, 153.

BEATTY, Reginald George; *NSW*. RHB. b 1913 (Wickham, NSW), d 27 May 1957 (Waratah, NSW). 884, 888, 892, 894.

BEAUMONT, John; *Eng*. RHB/RF. b 16 Sep 1854 (Armitage Bridge, Yorks), d 1 May 1920 (Lambeth, London). 105, 106, 108, 112, 113, 118, 121, 123.

BEESTON, John Lievesley; *NSW*. RHB b 1830 (Lancs), d 1 Jun 1873 (Newcastle, NSW). 6, 9, 11.

BEESTON, Norman Charles; *Qld*. RHB/RM. b 29 Sep 1900 (Brisbane), d 4 Feb 1985 (Sth Brisbane). 584, 602, 603, 608, 614, 620, 645.

BELCHER, Samuel Harborne; *NSW*. b 1834 (Eng), d 22 Aug 1920 (Garroorigang, NSW). 17.

BELL, Alexander John; *Sth Afr*. RHB/RFM. b 15 Apr 1906 (East London, Sth Afr) d 1 Aug 1985 (Mowbray, Cape Town). 740, 741, 742, 744, 747, 748, 749, 756, 759, 761, 762, 765, 770.

BENBOW, Ernest Aldred; *Qld*. RHB. b 14 Mar 1888 (Mt Walker, Qld), d 28 Dec 1940 (Springsure, Qld). 393, 399.

BENDIXEN, Hilton Fewtrell; *Qld*. RHB/LM. b 21 Feb 1910 (Nambour, Qld), d 15 Apr 1962 (Nambour, Qld). 960.

BENNETT, Albert; *NSW*. RHB/LBG. b 21 May 1910 (St Helens, Lancs). 736.

BENNETT, Frank; *West Aust*. b (Vic), d 4 Oct 1898 (Guildford, WA). 161, 162.

BENNETT, George; *Eng*. RHB/RaB(r). b 12 Feb 1829 (Shorne Ridgway, Kent), d 16 Aug 1866 (Shorne Ridgway, Kent). 13.

BENNETT, George Henry; *NSW*. RHB/RFM. b 16 Aug 1906 (Brookvale, NSW). 822.

BENNETT, Joseph; *Vic*. b ( ), d ( ). 18.

BENNETT, Joseph Henry; *NZ*. RHB/RM. b 28 Feb 1881 (Christchurch, NZ), d 29 Aug 1947 (Christchurch, NZ). 473, 475, 480.

BENNETT, Rex Leland; *Sth Aust & Tas*. RHB/WK. b 25 Jun 1896 (Snowtown, SA), d 14 Dec 1963 (Collaroy, NSW). 544, 548, 550, 551, 554, 589, 590, 616.

BENNETT, Thomas; *Sth Aust*. b 11 Oct 1866 (Littlehampton, SA), d 26 Dec 1942 (Northfield, SA). 188.

BENNETTS, Gordon Kissack; *Vic*. RHB/OB. b 26 Mar 1909 (Wellington, NSW), d 4 Apr 1987 (Geelong, Vic). 676.

BENNISON, James Ernest; *Tas*. RHB. b 16 Feb 1854 (Hobart), d 14 Nov 1916 (Hobart). 35.

BENSON, Edward Turk; *Eng*. RHB/WK. b 20 Nov 1907 (Cardiff, Wales), d 11 Sep 1967 (Cape Town, Sth Afr). 686, 687.

BENSTED, Eric Charles; *Qld*. RHB/RFM. b 11 Feb 1901 (Killarney, Qld), d 24 Mar 1980 (Brisbane). 564, 565, 579, 581, 618, 620, 621, 624, 629, 634, 636, 639, 642, 653, 662, 664, 666, 672, 677, 683, 689, 691, 696, 698, 703, 710, 715, 717, 719, 724, 727, 750, 763, 767, 773, 777, 783, 787, 790, 794, 796, 803, 807, 808, 811, 815, 817, 830, 831, 834, 836, 837, 840, 846, 850, 851, 852, 870.

BERRIE, Edward Bruce; *NSW*. /LM. b 8 Apr 1884 (Tomanbil, NSW), d 8 Dec 1963 (Tamworth, NSW). 482.

BERRY, Walter Lyall; *NSW*. RHB. b 9 Apr 1893 (Woolwich, NSW), d 20 Apr 1970 (Ettalong Beach, NSW). 496, 499, 510.

BESSEN, Mervyn Oscar; *West Aust*. LHB. b 29 Aug 1913 (Tambellup, WA). 920.

BEST, Leslie; *NSW*. RHB/RFM. b c 1894 (Seven Hills, NSW), d 27 Aug 1925 (Redfern, NSW). 490.

BETTINGTON, Brindley Cecil John; *NSW*. RHB/LBG. Brother of R.H.B.Bettington. b 2 Sep 1898 (Parramatta, NSW), d 26 Aug 1931 (Merriwa, NSW). 640.

BETTINGTON, Reginald Henshall Brindley; *NSW*. RHB/LBG. Brother of B.C.J.Bettington. b 24 Feb 1900 (Parramatta, NSW), d 24 Jun 1969 (Gisbourne, NZ). 657, 670, 683, 744, 751, 752.

BETTS, Arthur John; *Tas*. RHB/WK. b 26 Feb 1880 (Launceston), d ( ). 285.

BEVAN, John Lawrence; *Sth Aust*. LHB/LFM. b 10 May 1846 (near Swansea, Wales), d 31 Mar 1918 (Portland Estate, SA). 35.

BIGGS, Malcolm; *Qld*. RHB. b 7 Jul 1904 (Caboolture, Qld), d 1 Aug 1972 (Ipswich, Qld). 647, 710, 715, 717, 719, 724.

BILL, Oscar Wendell; *NSW*. RHB. b 8 Apr 1910 (Waverley, NSW), d 10 May 1988 (Sydney). 706, 711, 713, 715, 717, 720, 730, 736, 743, 744, 748, 751, 752, 757, 760, 769, 774, 777, 779, 784, 816, 822, 829.

BINGHAM, John Edmund; *Tas*. LHB/LM. b 15 Jul 1864 (Forcett, Tas), d 23 Jul 1946 (Hobart). 159, 183, 197, 205, 229, 259.

BINNEY, Edgar James; *Vic*. LHB/RFM. b 31 May 1885 (Port Tremayne, SA), d 9 Sep 1978 (Brighton, Vic). 398.

BIRCH, William Thomas; *Tas*. RHB/u-arm. b 26 Oct 1849 (Hobart), d 18 Aug 1897 (Hobart). 19, 35.

BIRD, Thomas Robert; *Vic*. RHB/WK. b 31 Aug 1904 (Collingwood, Vic), d 12 Apr 1979 (Thornbury, Vic). 670, 672, 676.

BIRKETT, Lionel Sydney; *WI*. RHB/RM. b 14 Apr 1904 (Barbados). 713, 714, 716, 718, 721, 722, 725, 727, 728, 732, 734.

BISHOP, Edward George; *West Aust*. /LF. b 4 Aug 1872 ( ), d 16 Feb 1943 (Nedlands, WA). 161, 162, 242.

BISHOP, Henry Symons; *Vic*. b 1850 (Torrington, Devon), d 18 Jul 1891 (Prahran, Vic). 27.

BLACK, A A ; *Vic*. b ( ), d ( ), 7, 8.

BLACK, George Gordon; *NSW*. RHB/RM. b 19 Jan 1885 (Darling Point, NSW), d 6 Dec 1954 (Orange, NSW). 300.

BLACKHAM, John McCarthy; *Vic*. RHB/WK. b 11 May 1854 (Nth Fitzroy, Vic), d 28 Dec 1932 (Melbourne). 28, 29, 30, 33, 34, 38, 41, 42, 43, 44, 47, 49, 52, 53, 54, 55, 56, 57, 58, 59, 63, 64, 65, 66, 67, 68, 69, 70, 71, 72, 73, 74, 78, 79, 85, 87, 88, 89, 90, 94, 95, 96, 97, 98, 99, 106, 111, 113, 115, 117, 120, 121, 122, 124, 126, 129, 130, 131, 132, 133, 134, 135, 138, 139, 140, 142, 144, 146, 147, 149, 150, 153, 158, 165, 168, 173, 175, 177, 182.

BLACKIE, Donald Dearness; *Vic*. LHB/OB. b 5 Apr 1882 (Bendigo, Vic), d 18 Apr 1955 (Sth Melbourne). 588, 598, 600, 604, 607, 611, 613, 619, 621, 623, 625, 628, 629, 635, 636, 638, 641, 646, 647, 651, 654, 656, 661, 665, 673, 685, 688, 689, 692, 695, 700, 703, 712, 719, 723, 726, 730, 742, 773, 774, 805.

BLACKSTOCK, John MacDonald; *Qld*. RHB. b 16 Jan 1871 (Drum, Scotland), d ( ). 208.

BLANCHARD, C O ; "*Surrey v World*". RHB. b c 1842 ( ), d ( ). 13.

BLAXLAND, Marcus Herbert; *NSW & Qld*. LHB/LM. b 29 Apr 1884 (Callan Park, NSW), d 31 Jul 1958 (Clayfield, Qld). 300, 336, 338, 342, 343, 344, 351, 355, 359, 373, 560.

BLIGH, The Hon. Ivo Francis Walter; *Eng*. RHB. b 13 Mar 1859 (London), d 10 Apr 1927 (Puckle Hill, Kent). 64, 65, 66, 68, 69.

BLINMAN, Harry; *Sth Aust*. RHB. b 30 Dec 1861 (Adelaide), d 23 Jul 1950 (Adelaide). 50, 90, 112, 124, 127, 132, 136, 137, 139, 142, 143, 148, 154, 156, 160, 164, 166, 167, 172, 175, 180, 191, 192.

BLOOMFIELD, George Thomas; *Sth Aust*. LHB. b 5 Feb 1882 (Adelaide), d 1 Nov 1958 (Adelaide). 386, 387, 388.

BLUNDELL, George Robert; *West Aust*. RHB/RM. b 19 Apr 1896 (Perth), d 11 Feb 1940 (West Perth). 542, 543, 558, 559, 573.

BLUNDELL, William Walter; *Vic*. RHB/OB. b 30 Dec 1866 (Majorca, Vic), d 28 Feb 1946 (Kensington, Vic). 285.

BLUNT, Roger Charles; *NZ*. RHB/LBG. b 3 Nov 1900 (Durham, Eng), d 22 Jun 1966 (London). 603, 605, 609, 610, 633.

BLYTHE, Colin; *Eng.* RHB/SLA. b 30 May 1879 (Deptford, Kent), d 8 Nov 1917 (Passchendale, Belgium). 261, 262, 266, 268, 270, 273, 274, 275, 348, 349, 351, 353, 354, 356, 362, 363, 365, 367, 370.

B O A G, Kenneth John; *Qld.* RHB/RM. b 6 Sep 1914 (Toowoomba, Qld). 817, 836.

BOARD, John Henry; *Eng.* RHB/WK. b 23 Feb 1867 (Clifton, Glos), d 15 Apr 1924 (at Sea). 221, 224, 226, 227.

BODDAM, Edmond Tudor; *Tas.* RHB/RM. b 23 Nov 1879 (Hobart), d 9 Sep 1959 (New Town, Tas). 421, 444, 451, 469, 484.

BOGLE, James; *NSW.* LHB. b 4 Jan 1893 (Sydney), d 19 Oct 1963 (Southport, Qld). 498, 500, 501, 503, 518, 520, 523.

B O L T O N, John Turner; *Qld.* RHB/WK. b 3 Oct 1888 (, NSW), d   (   ). 435, 452, 458, 467, 486.

BONNOR, George John; *Vic & NSW.* RHB/RM. b 25 Feb 1855 (Bathurst, NSW), d 27 Jun 1912 (East Orange, NSW). 47, 52, 53, 55, 57, 63, 64, 65, 66, 67, 68, 69, 71, 72, 73, 74, 78, 79, 83, 84, 85, 87, 88, 89, 133, 140.

BOSANQUET, Bernard James Tindal; *Eng.* RHB/LBG. b 13 Oct 1877 (Enfield, Middlesex), d 12 Oct 1936 (Ewhurst, Surrey). 288, 289, 290, 291, 292, 293, 295, 297, 302, 303, 306, 307, 308, 310, 311.

BOSLEY, Marcus Williams; *NSW.* LHB/SLA. b 10 Aug 1897 (Liverpool, NSW), d   (   ). 588.

BOTT, Leonidas Cecil; *West Aust.* RHB/RM. b 14 Jul 1889 (Adelaide), d 21 Aug 1968 (Perth). 453, 455, 456, 457, 532, 542, 543, 558, 559, 572, 597, 598, 599, 601.

B O T T E N, Robert Dyas; *Sth Aust.* RHB. b 11 Oct 1853 (Lewisham, Kent), d 26 Apr 1935 (Medindie, SA). 35.

BOULTER, Edward Samuel; *Vic.* RHB/RM. b 23 Mar 1886 (Nth Fitzroy, Vic), d 10 Jun 1968 (Nth Balwyn, Vic). 457.

BOURNE, Gordon Alister; *Qld.* RHB/RM. b 21 Apr 1913 (Tintenbar, NSW). 719.

B O W D E N, Albert John; *NSW.* RHB/LBG. Brother of S.H.Bowden b 28 Sep 1874 (Sydney), d 8 Aug 1943 (Northwood, NSW). 243, 245, 281, 300, 304, 307, 317, 338, 344, 359, 367.

BOWDEN, Montague Parker; *Eng.* RHB/WK. b 1 Nov 1865 (Stockwell, Surrey), d 19 Feb 1892 (Umtali, Mashonaland). 105, 112, 113, 118, 121, 123.

BOWDEN, Samuel Hedskis; *Qld.* Brother of A.J.Bowden b 29 Sep 1867 (Sydney), d 25 Aug 1945 (Manly, NSW). 171.

B O W E S, William Eric; *Eng.* RHB/RFM. b 25 Jul 1908 (Elland, Yorks), d 5 Sep 1987 (Leeds, Yorks). 771, 775, 778, 782, 785, 789, 793, 796, 800, 801.

BOWLEY, Edward Henry; *Eng.* RHB/LB. b 6 Jun 1890 (Leatherhead, Surrey), d 9 Jul 1974 (Winchester, Hampshire). 682, 686.

BOWLEY, Edwin Leonard; *Sth Aust.* RHB/RFM. b 6 Jun 1888 (Sevenhill, SA), d 22 Apr 1963 (Woodville Sth, SA). 557, 561, 564, 566, 567, 569, 574.

BOWMAN, Alcon Ninus Ascot; *Vic.* b 10 May 1862 (Ascot, Vic), d 30 Jun 1938 (Surrey Hills, Vic). 142, 152.

BOX, Henry; *Vic.* Perhaps b c 1838 (   ), d 3 Jun 1916 (   ). 7, 8.

BOXSHALL, Charles, *NZ.* RHB/WK. b 7 Jul 1862 (Brighton, Vic), d 13 Nov 1924 (Balmain, NSW). 237, 238, 473, 475, 478, 480.

BOYCE, Raymond Charles Manning; *NSW.* b 28 Jun 1891 (   ), d 20 Jan 1941 (Northwood, NSW). 533, 534.

BOYLE, Henry Frederick; *Vic.* RHB/RM(r). b 10 Dec 1847 (Sydney), d 21 Nov 1907 (Bendigo, Vic). 24, 25, 26, 28, 29, 30, 38, 41, 42, 43, 44, 47, 49, 50, 52, 53, 54, 55, 56, 57, 58, 59, 63, 67, 68, 69, 70, 71, 72, 73, 74, 78, 88, 91, 104, 106, 110, 111, 115, 119, 121, 122, 125, 131.

BRACHER, Herbert Henry Gladstone; *Vic.* LHB/Lab. b 28 Aug 1886 (Footscray), d 25 Feb 1974 (Hawthorn, Vic). 463, 465, 476, 477, 488, 489, 542.

BRADLEY, William Francis; *Qld.* RHB/WK. b 8 Oct 1867 (Brisbane), d   (   ). 163, 171, 176, 185, 186, 193, 208, 224, 234, 245.

BRADMAN, Donald George; *NSW & Sth Aust.* RHB/LB. b 27 Aug 1908 (Cootamundra, NSW). 637, 638, 642, 644, 646, 651, 653, 655, 657, 659, 663, 665, 667, 670, 673, 675, 679, 680, 683, 686, 688, 690, 692, 696, 697, 700, 707, 708, 709, 711, 712, 713, 718, 720, 723, 725, 728, 730, 734, 736, 738, 743, 744, 747, 748, 749, 756, 760, 762, 765, 769, 772, 774, 778, 779, 786, 789, 792, 793, 795, 797, 799, 803, 805, 806, 809, 810, 815, 818, 847, 853, 855, 858, 860, 861, 864, 866, 867, 874, 875, 877, 878, 883, 889, 890, 891, 894, 895, 896, 898, 902, 904, 906, 908, 909, 911, 913, 916, 918, 919, 920, 922, 924, 926, 928, 931, 932, 935, 939, 941, 943, 945, 946, 947, 950, 951, 952, 957, 959.

BRADRIDGE, John Sidney; *NSW.* b 1 Dec 1831 (Sydney), d 14 Jul 1905 (Dulwich Hill, NSW). 4.

BRAID, Rupert Lee; *Vic.* LHB/SLA. b 3 Mar 1888 (Amherst, Vic), d 11 Nov 1963 (Upper Ferntree Gully, Vic). 449, 451, 454, 464, 540.

BRAIN, Desmond Morrah; *Tas.* RHB. b 16 Dec 1909 (Hobart), d 1 Mar 1990 (Tumut, NSW). 721, 737, 739.

BRAIN, John Heather; *Tas.* RHB. b 9 Feb 1905 (Hobart), d 21 Jun 1961 (Hobart). 721, 722.

B R A I T H W A I T E, Arthur; *Tas.* /LM. b 2 Sep 1880 (Rushworth, Vic), d   (   ). 384, 385.

B R A N D, David Francis; *Eng.* RHB/RM. b 14 Jun 1902 (Welwyn, Herts), d 4 Sep 1975 (Glynde, Sussex). 543, 545, 546, 555, 556, 557.

B R A N N, George; *Eng.* RHB/RF. b 23 Apr 1865 (near Eastbourne, Sussex), d 14 Jun 1954 (Surbiton Hill, Surrey). 107, 110, 114, 116, 122.

BRAUND, Leonard Charles; *Eng.* RHB/LB. b 18 Oct 1875 (Clewer, Berks), d 23 Dec 1955 (Putney, London). 261, 262, 263, 266, 268, 270, 272, 273, 274, 275, 276, 291, 293, 295, 297, 301, 302, 306, 307, 308, 310, 311, 348, 349, 350, 351, 353, 354, 356, 360, 361, 362, 363, 366, 367, 368, 370, 371.

B R A Y B R O O K, Clive; *Sth Aust.* RHB/LB. b 27 Sep 1901 (Goodwood, SA). 534.

BREW, Francis Malcolm; *Qld.* RHB/LB. b 5 Jul 1903 (Petrie Terrace, Qld), d 13 Jan 1974 (Sandgate, Qld). 584, 602, 603, 608, 618, 621, 624, 645, 662, 664, 666, 672, 683, 687, 689, 691, 696, 724, 727, 783, 787, 790, 794, 807, 808, 811, 815.

BREWSTER, Robert Colin; *NSW.* b 17 Aug 1867 (   ), d 8 Nov 1962 (Killara, NSW). 171.

BRIANT, George William; *Tas.* b 1828 (Hackney, London), d 10 May 1914 (Hobart). 8.

BRIDESON, John Holmes; *Sth Aust.* RHB/ b 9 Jul 1856 (Rushworth, Vic), d c 1897/98 (   ). 75.

BRIDGMAN, Hugh Hossick Mackay; *Sth Aust.* LHB/RM. b 1 Feb 1890 (Findon, SA), d 3 Dec 1953 (Torrensville, SA). 459, 461, 462, 476,497,503, 509, 515, 518, 551.

BRIGGS, John; *Eng.* RHB/SLA. b 3 October 1862 (Sutton-in-Ashfield, Notts), d 11 Jan 1902 (Cheadle, Cheshire). 76, 77, 78, 80, 82, 84, 85, 86, 91, 92, 93, 94, 96, 97, 99, 101, 102, 103, 104, 107, 109, 110, 114, 116, 117, 120, 122, 143, 144, 145, 147, 150, 151, 152, 153, 172, 173, 174, 176, 177, 179, 181, 184, 186, 189, 190, 191, 209, 213, 215, 217, 220, 221, 224, 225.

BRITT, Harold James; *Vic.* LHB/LFM. b 6 May 1911 (Doncaster, Vic). 839, 852, 854.

BROCKWELL, William; *Eng.* RHB/RFM. b 21 Jan 1865 (Kingston-on-Thames, Surrey), d 30 Jun 1935 (Richmond, Surrey). 172, 173, 174, 176, 177, 179, 181, 184, 186, 189, 190, 191.

BRODIE, James Chalmers; *Vic.* b 1821 (Perth, Scotland), d 19 Feb 1912 (Balwyn, Vic). 1, 2, 11.

BRODIE, Richard Sinclair; *Vic.* b 1813 (   ), d 18 Jan 1872 (   ). 3.

BROMLEY, Ernest Harvey; *West Aust & Vic.* LHB/SLA. b 2 Sep 1912 (Fremantle, WA), d 1 Feb 1967 (Clayton, Vic). 699, 701, 702, 709, 740, 770, 786, 797, 800, 802, 804, 806, 807, 808, 810, 813, 818, 827, 831, 833, 835, 837, 838, 841, 852, 854, 858, 899, 900, 903, 922, 923.

BROOMBY, Reginald Arthur; *Tas.* LHB. b 6 Jan 1905 (Launceston), d 10 May 1984 (Southport, Qld). 785, 788.

BROWN, Albert Ernest; *Vic*. RHB. b 22 Dec 1890 (Clifton Hill, Vic), d 17 Nov 1954 (Northcote, Vic). 484, 488, 491, 493, 540, 553.

BROWN, Edward; *NSW*. RHB/WK. believed b Jan 1837 (Uppingham, Rutland), d   (   ). 10.

BROWN, Edward K   ; *NSW*. RHB. b c 1899 (Morpeth, NSW), d   (   ). 529.

BROWN, Frederick Richard; *Eng*. RHB/LBG/RM. b 16 Dec 1910 (Lima, Peru), d 24 July 1991 (Ramsbury, Wiltshire). 771, 775, 778, 779, 782, 785, 793, 800.

BROWN, Guy Archibald Loeman; *Qld*. RHB. b 31 Jul 1884 (Ipswich), d   (   ). 336, 338, 353, 373, 375.

BROWN, John Thomas; *Eng*. RHB. b 20 Aug 1869 (Driffield, Yorks), d 4 Nov 1904 (Westminster, London). 172, 173, 174, 176, 177, 179, 181, 184, 186, 189, 190, 191.

BROWN, Lennox Sidney; *Sth Afr*. RHB/RM. b 24 Nov 1910 (Randfontein, Sth Afr), d 1 Sep 1983 (Durban, Sth Afr). 740, 746, 749, 758, 761, 764.

BROWN, Norman Eric; *Vic*. RHB/RM. b 1 Apr 1889 (Nth Fitzroy, Vic), d 7 Jul 1962 (Sandringham, Vic). 430, 432, 434, 439, 445, 446, 454, 460, 461, 465, 492.

BROWN, Vallancey Kennedy; *Vic*. RHB/RM. b 7 Dec 1912 (Ashfield, NSW), d 24 Oct 1987 (Melbourne). 856.

BROWN, William; *Tas*. /u-arm. b 1807 (Eng), d 28 Aug 1858 (Hobart). 8.

BROWN, William Alfred; *NSW & Qld*. RHB. b 31 Jul 1912 (Toowoomba, Qld). 777, 786, 790, 793, 795, 803, 806, 809, 810, 815, 816, 818, 822, 825, 826, 828, 829, 832, 833, 836, 838, 840, 842, 843, 844, 867, 870, 875, 876, 883, 887, 890, 891, 897, 902, 905, 908, 910, 911, 919, 920, 921, 922, 923, 926, 930, 931, 934, 938, 940, 943, 944, 946, 948, 952, 953, 954, 958, 959, 960, 964.

BROWN, Walter Graham Fairfax; *NSW*. RHB. b 1900 (Five Dock, NSW), d 21 May 1931 (Mosman, NSW). 510, 522, 560, 565, 580, 584, 602, 608, 610.

BROWNE, William Creighton; *Qld*. RHB/RFM. b 6 Nov 1898 (Toowoomba, Qld), d 25 Oct 1980 (Southport, Qld). 533.

BROWNING, George Richard; *Vic*. RHB/RaB. b 12 Dec 1858 (Hepburn, Vic), d 9 Oct 1900 (Nth Carlton, Vic). 75, 81, 104.

BRUCE, William; *Vic*. LHB/LM. b 22 May 1864 (Sth Yarra, Vic), d 3 Aug 1925 (St Kilda, Vic). 61, 63, 72, 76, 79, 80, 81, 86, 87, 88, 89, 90, 94, 95, 96, 97, 98, 103, 104, 111, 113, 115, 123, 125, 127, 129, 130, 133, 135, 138, 139, 141, 144, 146, 147, 149, 150, 152, 153, 155, 156, 158, 165, 166, 178, 179, 181, 184, 187, 189, 190, 194, 196, 198, 200, 202, 203, 206, 210, 212, 214, 218, 222, 224, 226, 228, 231, 232, 235, 244, 247, 252, 284, 286, 288, 292, 294, 299, 304.

BRYAN, John Lindsay; *Eng*. LHB. b 26 May 1896 (Beckenham, Kent), d 23 Apr 1985 (Eastbourne, Sussex). 573, 576, 581, 582, 589, 590, 592, 594.

BRYANT, Francis Joseph; *West Aust*. RHB. Brother of R.J. & W.J.Bryant. b 7 Nov 1909 (Perth), d 11 Mar 1984 (Glendalough, WA). 631, 632, 648, 649, 650, 682, 699, 701, 702, 709, 820, 821, 822, 823, 824, 827, 842, 843, 868, 869.

BRYANT, James Mark; *Vic*. RHB/RM(r). b 1826 (Caterham, Surrey), d 10 Dec 1881 (Sale, Vic). 5, 6, 7, 8, 9, 10, 11, 12, 13.

BRYANT, Richard; *NSW*.   /WK. b 1847 (Maitland, NSW), d 27 Oct 1931 (Stockton, NSW). 67, 77.

BRYANT, Richard John; *West Aust*. RHB/RM. Brother of F.J. & W.J.Bryant. b 8 May 1904 (Perth), d 17 August, 1989 (Mt Lawley, WA). 572, 573, 597, 598, 599, 601, 631, 632, 648, 649, 650, 682, 699, 701, 702, 709, 740, 771, 772, 820, 821, 822, 823, 824, 827, 842, 843, 844, 845.

BRYANT, William James; *West Aust*. RHB. Brother of F.J. & R.J.Bryant. b 15 Jan 1906 (Perth). 631.

BRYCE, William Cecil James; *Qld*. RHB. b 18 Aug 1911 (Maryborough, Qld), d 8 Feb 1986 (Spring Hill, Qld). 946.

BUBB, Ernest Reinhard; *NSW*. RHB. Brother of R.A.Bubb. b 6 Dec 1884 (Summer Hill, NSW), d 26 Nov 1946 (Neutral Bay, NSW). 326, 346, 347, 375, 379.

BUBB, Roy Alfred; *NSW*. LHB/RF. Brother of E.R.Bubb. b 23 Jun 1900 (Darlinghurst, NSW), d 4 Apr 1965 (Hamilton, NSW). 579, 584.

BUCKLE, Frank; *NSW*. RHB. b 11 Nov 1891 (Pyrmont, NSW), d 4 Jun 1982 (Sydney). 482.

BULL, Eric Alister; *NSW*. RHB/RM/LB. b 28 Sep 1886 (Bourke, NSW), d 14 May 1954 (Mt Kuring-Gai, NSW). 482, 491, 494, 506.

BULLOUGH, Walter; *Sth Aust*. LHB/Lab. b 21 Oct 1855 (Hunslet, Yorks), d 17 Sep 1888 (Hindmarsh, SA). 45, 50.

BURCHETT, Alfred; *Vic*. RHB. Brother of F.Burchett. b 1831 (London), d 12 Nov 1888 (St Kilda, Vic). 9, 10.

BURCHETT, Frederick; *Vic*. Brother of A.Burchett. b 1824 (London), d 16 Jul 1861 (Melbourne). 7, 8.

BURN, Edwin James Kenneth; *Tas*. RHB/RM. b 17 Sep 1862 (Richmond, Tas), d 20 Jul 1956 (Hobart). 120, 121, 128, 134, 141, 159, 169, 183, 197, 205, 219, 236, 249, 285, 303, 309, 322, 345, 363, 369, 398, 400.

BURN, James Henry; *Tas*. RHB. b 31 Jul 1849 (Hobart), d   (   ). 19.

BURNS, Harold Vincent; *Qld*. RHB/WK. b 20 May 1908 (Ebagoolah, Qld), d 4 Jun 1944 (Cairns, Qld). 710, 746, 750, 753, 757.

BURNUP, Cuthbert James; *Eng*. RHB. b 21 Nov 1875 (Blackheath, Kent), d 4 Apr 1960 (Golders Green, London). 288, 289, 290.

BURROWS, Arthur Owen; *Tas*. RHB/RFM. b 17 Oct 1903 (Hobart), d 4 Jan 1984 (Sandy Bay, Tas). 570, 616, 627, 640, 643, 668, 669, 674, 676, 688, 693, 694, 701, 705, 706, 708, 721, 722, 754, 755, 758, 759, 768, 782, 785, 788, 791, 802, 812, 814, 859, 886.

BURROWS, J   ; *NSW*. RHB. b   (   ), d   (   ). 36.

BURT, Selby John Wright; *NSW*. RHB/OB. b 12 Dec 1903 (Hillgrove, NSW), d 14 Feb 1959 (Camperdown, NSW). 674, 696.

BURTON, Frederick John; *NSW & Vic*. RHB/WK. b 2 Nov 1865 (Collingwood, Vic), d 25 Aug 1929 (Wanganui, NZ). 87, 89, 92, 93, 95, 98, 102, 107, 108, 109, 111, 114, 115, 116, 117, 118, 125, 129.

BURTON, Garth; *Sth Aust*. RHB/RFM. b 21 Jun 1913 (Black Forest, SA). 945, 946, 947.

BUTLER, Charles William; *Tas*. RHB. Brother of E.H.Butler. b 18 Sep 1854 (Battery Point, Tas), d 10 Jun 1937 (Sandy Bay, Tas). 27, 35, 128, 134, 219, 229.

BUTLER, Edward Henry; *Tas & Vic*. RHB/RFM(r). Brother of C.W.Butler. b 15 Mar 1851 (Battery Point, Tas), d 5 Jan 1928 (Lower Sandy Bay, Tas). 22, 27.

BUTLER, Edward Lionel Austin; *Tas*. RHB. Son of E.H.Butler & nephew of C.W.Butler. b 10 Apr 1883 (Hobart), d 23 Aug 1916 (Puchevillers, France). 482, 492.

BUTLER, Frank Leslie; *Tas*. LHB. b 13 Nov 1889 (Brighton, Vic), d   (   ). 540, 553, 570.

BUTLER, Walter John; *West Aust*. RHB. b 30 May 1882 (Port Adelaide, SA), d 12 Mar 1966 (Bruce Rock, WA). 542.

BUTTERWORTH, Benjamin; *Vic*. Long-stop. Brother of T.Butterworth. b 1832 (Rochdale, Lancs), d 6 Jan 1879 (Chiswick, Eng). 5, 6, 12.

BUTTERWORTH, Thomas; *Vic*. Brother of B.Butterworth. b c 1826 (Rochdale, Lancs), d 15 Jul 1877 (Kensington, London). 7, 8.

BUTTSWORTH, Frederick Richard; *West Aust*. RHB/RFM. b 28 Apr 1880 (Wilberforce, NSW), d 26 Feb 1974 (Perth). 532, 542, 543, 558, 559, 598, 601.

BUTTSWORTH, Wallace Francis; *West Aust*. RHB. Son of F.R.Buttsworth. b 21 Jan 1917 (Nth Perth). 903, 904.

BYRNE, Thomas; *Qld*. LHB/LM. b 11 Jul 1866 (Patterson River, NSW), d 19 Dec 1951 (Herston, Qld). 234, 245, 277, 278, 281, 286, 295, 300, 312, 314, 317, 323, 326.

CAESAR, Julius; *Eng*. RHB/RF(r).   b 25 Mar 1830 (Godalming, Surrey), d 6 Mar 1878 (Godalming, Surrey). 15.

CAFFYN, William; *Eng & NSW*. RHB/RM(r). b 2 Feb 1828 (Reigate, Surrey), d 28 Aug 1919 (Reigate, Surrey). 13, 15, 16, 17, 18, 20, 23.

CAHILL, Keyran William Jack; *Tas*. RHB/RM. b 3 Dec 1911 (Hobart), d 7 Mar 1966 (Launceston). 754, 755, 758, 768.

CALDER, Henry; *West Aust.* RHB. b 3 Jul 1906 (Guildford, WA), d 27 Aug 1970 (Sth Perth). 771.

CAIN, William; *Qld.* RHB. b 17 Dec 1899 (Paddington, Qld), d 24 Dec 1981 (Sherwood, Qld). 579, 581, 584.

CALDWELL, Tim Charles John; *NSW.* RHB/OB. b 29 Oct 1913 (Clayfield, Qld). 846, 880, 881.

CALLACHOR, John Joseph Casimir; *NSW.* RHB/WK. b c 1859 (   ), d 20 Feb 1924 (Stanmore, NSW). 62.

CALLAWAY, Norman Frank; *NSW.* RHB. b May 1895 (Hay, NSW), d 3 May 1917 (2nd Battle of Bullecourt, France). 494.

CALLAWAY, Sydney Thomas; *NSW.* RHB/RFM. b 6 Feb 1868 (Sydney), d 25 Nov 1923 (Christchurch, NZ). 126, 131, 137, 145, 146, 147, 148, 149, 150, 151, 154, 155, 157, 158, 163, 164, 165, 167, 168, 171, 174, 178, 180, 181, 182, 185, 186, 188, 199.

CALTHORPE, Frederick Somerset (Gough); *Eng.* RHB/RM. b 27 May 1892 (Kensington, London), d 19 Nov 1935 (Worplesdon, Surrey). 544, 545, 546, 555, 556, 557.

CAMERON, Horace Brackenridge; *Sth Afr.* RHB/WK. b 5 Jul 1905 (Port Elizabeth, Sth Afr), d 2 Nov 1935 (Johannesburg, Sth Afr). 740, 741, 742, 744, 747, 748, 749, 756, 758, 759, 761, 762, 764, 765, 770.

CAMERON, Verney Lovett; *Vic.* RHB/RM(r). b 1842 (Sorrento, Vic), d 27 May 1881 (Richmond, Vic). 14, 15.

CAMPBELL, Colin Mansfield; *Tas.* RHB. b 13 Aug 1872 (Cressy, Tas), d 3 Apr 1907 (Winlaton, Northumberland). 205.

CAMPBELL, Donald; *Vic.* RHB. b 18 Sep 1851 (Loddon Plains, Vic), d 14 Sep 1887 (Sth Yarra, Vic). 19, 21, 41, 42, 43, 44, 45, 46, 47.

CAMPBELL, Francis Bersford; *Tas.* b 20 Apr 1867 (Hobart). 183.

CAMPBELL, Gordon Cathcart; *Sth Aust.* RHB/WK. b 4 Jun 1885 (Myrtle Bank, SA), d 13 Aug 1961 (Woodville Sth, SA). 389, 391, 394, 395, 404, 406, 453, 459, 461, 462, 466, 468, 480, 483, 487, 489, 490, 495.

CAMPBELL, Ivan James; *West Aust.* RHB. b 29 Oct 1908 (Perth), d 22 Jan 1962 (Hollywood, WA). 822, 823.

CAMPBELL, James Norval; *NSW.* RHB/LBG. b 21 Sep 1908 (Chatswood, NSW), d 11 Sep 1977 (St Ives, NSW). 618, 620, 623, 653, 655, 674, 690, 717, 743, 842, 843.

CAMPBELL, Lyle P   ; *NSW.* RHB/LBG. b 14 Oct 1902 (   ). 602, 610.

CAMPBELL, Malcolm MacDonald; *Qld.* RHB/RFM. b 9 Jan 1881 (Ipswich, Qld), d 14 Dec 1967 (Ipswich, Qld). 243.

CAMPBELL, Stoddart William Grylls; *Vic.* RHB. b 19 Sep 1846 (Melbourne), d 2 Sep 1903 (East Melbourne). 17, 18, 19, 21, 23, 24, 25, 26, 28, 29, 30.

CAMPBELL, Thomas; *Sth Afr.* RHB/WK. b 9 Feb 1882 (Edinburgh, Scotland), d 5 Oct 1924 (Milnedale, Sth Afr). 409, 420, 421, 423, 425.

CAMPHIN, William Joseph; *NSW.* RHB. b 13 Nov 1867 (   ), d 11 Sep 1942 (Quirindi, NSW). 163, 178.

CAMPLING, Campbell Roy; *NSW.* RHB/RM. b 3 Apr 1892 (Burwood, NSW), d 21 Apr 1977 (Harrington, NSW). 547, 548, 549.

CANNON, William Henry; *Vic.* RHB/LBG. b 11 Sep 1871 (Eaglehawk, Vic), d 29 Apr 1933 (Nth Fitzroy, Vic). 460, 463, 465, 468, 471, 476, 477.

CANTWELL, Hubert Richard; *West Aust.* LHB. b 24 Oct 1905 (Warbleton, Sussex), d 22 Apr 1956 (Esperance WA). 573.

CAREW, James; *Qld.* RHB. Brother of P.Carew. b 23 Jan 1872 (Pine Mountain, Qld), d 1 Sep 1950 (Kelvin Grove, Qld). 234, 243, 245, 277, 278, 281, 286, 295, 300, 312, 314, 317, 326.

CAREW, Patrick; *Qld.* RHB/RaB. Brother of J.Carew. b 8 Sep 1875 (Pine Mountain, Qld), d 31 Mar 1942 (Queanbeyan, NSW). 243, 277, 278, 281, 286.

CARKEEK, William; *Vic.* LHB/WK. b 17 Oct 1878 (Walhalla, Vic), d 20 Feb 1937 (Prahran, Vic). 306, 309, 316, 318, 320, 325, 328, 329, 337, 340, 341, 343, 350, 352, 358, 364, 369, 381, 382, 392, 394, 396, 397, 399, 401, 402, 403, 404, 407, 410, 414, 415, 422, 423, 428, 430, 432, 434, 439, 445, 446, 460, 461, 463, 465, 468, 471, 476, 477, 478, 481, 483, 488, 489, 491, 493.

CARLSON, Victor Charles; *West Aust.* RHB. b 16 Jul 1893 (Adelaide), d 23 Feb 1974 (Perth). 543, 598, 601.

CARLTON, Alfred Robert; *Vic.* RHB/OB. Brother of J. & W.Carlton. b 13 Nov 1867 (Bacchus Marsh, Vic) d 10 Sep 1941 (Camberwell, Vic). 159, 169, 259.

CARLTON, John; *Vic & Qld.* RHB/RM. Brother of A.R. & W.Carlton. b 6 Jul 1866 (Bacchus Marsh, Vic), d 13 Aug 1945 (Parkville, Vic). 140, 141, 142, 144, 155, 156, 158, 160, 162, 165, 166, 170, 176, 192, 198, 202, 206.

CARLTON, Thomas Andrew; *NZ, Vic & Sth Aust.* LHB/LM. Nephew of A.R., J. & W.Carlton. b 7 Dec 1890 (Footscray, Vic), d 17 Dec 1973 (Moreland, Vic). 475, 478, 504, 505, 508, 554, 556, 562, 568, 667, 671, 677, 679, 684, 691, 695, 697, 698, 702, 704, 710, 711, 716, 720, 726, 733, 735, 739, 741, 745, 751, 753, 761, 766, 767, 769.

CARLTON, William; *Vic.* RHB/RaB. Brother of A.R. & J.Carlton. b 22 May 1876 (Collingwood, Vic), d 23 Dec 1959 (Nth Melbourne). 236, 252, 267, 271, 320, 484, 485.

CARMODY, Douglas Keith; *NSW.* RHB. b 16 Feb 1919 (Mosman, NSW), d 21 Oct 1977 (Concord, NSW). 938, 953, 954, 955, 961.

CARPENTER, Robert Pearson; *Eng.* RHB. b 18 Nov 1830 (Cambridge, Eng), d 14 Jul 1901 (Cambridge, Eng). 15.

CARR, Charles Seymour; *Vic.* b 22 Nov 1849 (Jamaica, WI), d 30 Mar 1921 (East Melbourne). 26.

CARRACHER, Arthur James; *Sth Aust.* /LM. b 7 Jul 1867 (Heywood, Vic), d 15 Oct 1935 (Nth Adelaide). 204, 207.

CARRAGHER, Edward John; *Sth Aust.* RHB/LBG. b 24 May 1891 (Broken Hill, NSW), d 28 Nov 1977 (Broken Hill, NSW). 554, 557.

CARROLL, Edmund Louis; *Vic.* RHB/LBG. Brother of E.V.Carroll. b 22 Oct 1886 (Albert Park, Vic), d 6 Jun 1959 (Ormond, Vic). 457, 463, 465, 468.

CARROLL, Eugene Vincent; *Vic.* RHB. Brother of E.L.Carroll. b 17 Jan 1885 (Sth Melbourne), d 18 Sep 1965 (Elsternwick, Vic). 325, 328, 329, 332, 334, 337, 340, 341, 343, 350, 352, 358, 365, 369, 374, 377, 378, 381, 383, 392, 398, 454, 460, 461, 463, 465, 468, 471, 476, 477, 478, 481, 483, 484, 485, 540, 570.

CARROLL, Thomas Davis; *Tas.* RHB/RFM. b 26 Feb 1884 (Hobart), d 3 Jun 1957 (Hobart). 369, 384, 400, 418, 420, 421, 444, 451, 484, 492, 540.

CARSON, William Nicol; *NZ.* LHB/LFM. b 3 Jul 1916 (Gisborne, NZ), d 8 Oct 1944 (at sea off Italy). 901.

CARTER, Alfred Snowden; *Vic.* LHB. b 1 Mar 1869 (Kew, Vic), d 7 Jun 1920 (Camberwell, Vic). 236, 252.

CARTER, Edmund Sardinson; *Vic.* RHB/RF(r). b 3 Feb 1845 (Malton, Yorks), d 23 May 1923 (Scarborough, Vic). 20.

CARTER, Hanson; *NSW.* RHB/WK. b 15 Mar 1878 (Halifax, Yorks), d 8 Jun 1948 (Bellevue Hill, NSW). 216, 271, 272, 281, 300, 312, 317, 319, 322, 323, 324, 327, 328, 330, 331, 332, 336, 339, 340, 342, 343, 344, 351, 355, 356, 358, 360, 361, 364, 366, 368, 372, 373, 376, 377, 381, 382, 408, 413, 415, 417, 419, 422, 424, 426, 433, 438, 439, 440, 442, 447, 450, 466, 469, 500, 501, 505, 507, 517, 523, 527, 530, 535, 571.

CARTER, Reginald Clarence; *West Aust.* RHB/RM. b 1 Mar 1888 (East Brunswick, Vic), d 16 Jul 1970 (Subiaco, WA). 401, 402, 403.

CARTER, William Jack Sydney; *NSW.* RHB/LBG. b 7 Dec 1907 (Randwick, NSW). 653.

CATCHLOVE, Walter Evered; *Sth Aust.* RHB. b 24 Feb 1907 (Nth Adelaide). 751, 766, 767, 769, 775, 780, 784, 794, 824.

CATERER, Thomas Ainslie; *Sth Aust.* LHB/LFM. b 16 May 1858 (Woodville, SA), d 25 Aug 1924 (Walkerville, SA). 81.

CAVENAGH, George; *Vic.* b 16 Jun 1836 (Sydney), d 23 Nov 1922 (Albert Park, Vic). 3.

CHAMBERLAIN, Cornelius Thomas; *Sth Aust.* RHB. Brother of J.A. & W.L.Chamberlain. b c 1882 (   ), d 14 Nov 1943 (Rose Park, SA). 333, 335, 406.

CHAMBERLAIN, John Aloysius; *West Aust.* Brother of C.T. & W.L.Chamberlain. b (   ), d 1 Apr 1941 (Leabrook, SA). 346.

CHAMBERLAIN, William Leonard; *Sth Aust.* RHB/RM. Brother of C.T. & J.A.Chamberlain. b 15 Jan 1889 (Port Adelaide, SA), d 21 Mar 1956 (Darlinghurst, NSW). 349, 352, 355, 370, 374, 386, 387, 388, 404, 412, 430, 434, 436, 459, 461, 462, 474, 476, 479.

CHANCELLOR, Frederick Edgar; *Tas.* RHB/RFM. b 28 Aug 1878 (Hobart), d 16 Jun 1939 (Hobart). 285, 309, 321, 322, 345, 369, 384, 398, 400, 420, 444.

CHAPMAN, Arthur Percy Frank; *Eng.* LHB/SLA/LM. b 3 Sep 1900 (Reading, Berks), d 16 Sep 1961 (Alton, Hampshire). 543, 544, 545, 546, 555, 556, 557, 572, 573, 575, 577, 581, 582, 583, 585, 587, 589, 590, 593, 594, 650, 652, 654, 655, 658, 659, 661, 665, 668, 669, 671, 673, 675, 678.

CHAPMAN, Frederick Douglas; *Vic.* RHB/RM. b 21 Mar 1901 (Nth Fitzroy, Vic), d 27 Jun 1964 (Northcote, Vic). 662, 693, 694, 737.

CHAPMAN, George Arthur Northcote, *NSW;* RHB. b 21 Apr 1904 (Chatswood, NSW). 584.

CHAPMAN, Henry William; *Qld.* RHB/WK. b 1 Jan 1868 (   ), d   (   ). 193, 277.

CHARLTON, Percie Chater; *NSW.* RHB/RFM. b 9 Apr 1867 (Surry Hills, NSW), d 30 Sep 1954 (Pymble, NSW). 126, 129, 130, 133, 135, 136, 137, 138, 140, 145, 146, 149, 151, 214.

CHARLWOOD, Henry Rupert James; *Eng.* RHB/Lobs b 19 Dec 1846 (Horsham, Sussex), d 6 Jun 1888 (Scarborough, Yorks). 32, 33, 34.

CHEETHAM, Albert George; *NSW.* RHB/RFM. b 7 Dec 1915 (Ryde, NSW). 880, 881, 884, 888, 897, 901, 906, 907, 924, 925, 930, 932, 933, 938, 941, 942, 944, 947, 949, 952.

CHEGWYN, John William; *NSW.* RHB. b 18 Mar 1909 (Botany, NSW). 953, 954, 962, 963, 964.

CHILVERS, Hugh Cecil; *NSW.* RHB/LBG. b 26 Oct 1902 (Sawbridgeworth, Herts). 692, 696, 697, 700, 706, 711, 713, 715, 717, 720, 723, 730, 736, 793, 806, 809, 810, 815, 816, 818, 822, 829, 832, 833, 836, 838, 840, 846, 849, 851, 857, 861, 862, 892.

CHINNER, Hubert George Williams; *Sth Aust.* RHB. b 30 Aug 1870 (Brighton, SA), d 12 Jun 1953 (Unley Park, SA). 228, 230, 246.

CHIPPERFIELD, Arthur Gordon; *NSW.* RHB/LB. b 17 Nov 1905 (Ashfield, NSW), d 29 Jul 1987 (Ryde, NSW). 815, 816, 818, 825, 826, 827, 828, 832, 833, 836, 838, 840, 842, 843, 844, 867, 870, 873, 875, 877, 878, 884, 890, 892, 897, 901, 902, 906, 907, 910, 913, 914, 917, 919, 920, 924, 925, 932, 933, 941, 942, 944, 947, 949.

CHITTLEBOROUGH, Henry Carew; *Sth Aust.* RHB/Lobs. b 14 Apr 1861 (Wallaroo Mines, SA), d 25 Jun 1925 (Malvern, SA). 75, 81.

CHIVERS, Alfred Percy; *Vic.* RHB/RFM. b 15 Aug 1908 (Templestowe, Vic). 693, 694, 699.

CHRIST, Charles Percival; *Qld.* RHB/SLA. b 10 Jun 1911 (Paddington, Qld). 897, 911, 912, 921, 922, 923, 926, 930, 931, 934, 938, 940, 943, 944, 946, 948, 953, 958, 964.

CHRISTIAN, Arthur Hugh; *Vic & West Aust.* LHB/LM/SLA. b 22 Jan 1877 (Richmond, Vic), d 8 Sep 1950 (Claremont, WA). 309, 321, 325, 328, 329, 332, 334, 346, 347, 348, 371, 386, 387, 388, 401, 402, 403, 453, 454, 455, 456, 457, 532, 542.

CHRISTY, Frederick Collier; *"Surrey v World".* b 9 Sep 1822 (   ), d   (   ). 13.

CHRISTY, James Alexander Joseph; *Sth Afr & Qld.* RHB/RM. b 12 Dec 1904 (Pretoria, Sth Afr), d 1 Feb 1971 (Durban, Sth Afr). 740, 741, 742, 744, 747, 748, 749, 756, 759, 761, 762, 764, 765, 770, 830, 831, 834, 836, 837, 840, 846, 850, 852, 855, 857, 860, 863.

CLARK, Harry Judge; *West Aust.* RHB/RM. b 23 Apr 1892 (Sydney), d 8 Feb 1973 (Perth). 558.

CLARK, James Patrick; *Qld.* RHB. b 14 Mar 1871 (, Qld), d 6 Jun 1941 (Coolangatta, Qld). 234, 243.

CLARKE, Alfred Edward; *NSW.* b 6 Apr 1868 (Surry Hills, NSW), d c 1940 (   ). 148, 149, 151.

CLARKE, Alfred; *Eng.* RHB. b 16 Feb 1831 (Nottingham, Eng), d 17 Oct 1878 (Ruddington, Notts). 15.

CLARKE, Gother Robert Carlisle; *NSW.* LHB/LB. b 27 Apr 1875 (   ), d 12 Oct 1917 (Zonnebeke, Belgium). 249, 263, 267, 269, 271, 272, 277.

CLARKE, John; *NSW.* RHB. b   (   ), d   (   )10, 11, 14.

CLAXTON, Norman; *Sth Aust.* RHB/RFM. Half-brother of W.D.H.Claxton. b 2 Nov 1877 (Nth Adelaide), d 5 Dec 1951 (Nth Adelaide). 242, 246, 269, 276, 279, 282, 283, 287, 290, 291, 294, 296, 298, 311, 313, 315, 318, 319, 325, 327, 329, 330, 333, 335, 337, 339, 341, 342, 349, 352, 355, 370, 374, 378, 380, 386, 387, 389, 391.

CLAXTON, William David Hambridge; *Sth Aust.* LHB. Half-brother of N.Claxton. b 2 Jun 1857 (Kensington, SA), d 12 Mar 1937 (Glenelg, SA). 75, 192.

CLAYTON, Nicholas George; *Tas.* b 11 Mar 1826 (Norfolk Plains, Tas), d c 1865 (   ). 7.

CLEARY, Edward Joseph; *Vic.* RHB/LM. b 18 Apr 1913 (Benalla, Vic), d 6 Apr 1985 (Benalla, Vic). 819, 821, 823.

CLEEVE, James Oatley; *NSW.* /LFM. b 14 Feb 1864 (Sydney), d   (   ). 63, 67, 71.

CLEM, Gordon Rex; *Qld.* LHB/LM/SLA. b 5 Jul 1909 (Milora, Qld), d 3 Mar 1970 (Melbourne). 777.

CLUTTERBUCK, Stanley Herwin; *Sth Aust.* /SLA. b 27 May 1888 (Kapunda, SA), d 24 Jan 1972 (Adelaide). 483.

COATES, Joseph; *NSW.* LHB/LM(r). b 13 Nov 1844 (Huddersfield, Yorks), d 9 Sep 1896 (Sydney). 18, 20, 21, 23, 25, 26, 28, 29, 30, 31, 36, 37, 39, 44.

COATS, James; *Qld.* RHB. b 26 Feb 1914 (Annerley, Qld). 905, 908, 910.

COBCROFT, Leslie Thomas; *NZ.* RHB/OB. b 12 Feb 1867 (Muswellbrook, NSW), d 9 Mar 1938 (Wellington, NZ). 237, 238.

COCKBURN, James Sydney David; *Qld.* RHB/RFM. b 20 May 1916 (Maryborough, Qld), d 13 Nov 1990 (Herston). 876, 887.

CODY, Leslie Alwyn; *NSW & Vic.* RHB/LBG. b 11 Oct 1889 (Paddington, NSW), d 10 Aug 1969 (Toorak, Vic). 455, 456, 463, 466, 467, 469, 470, 472, 475, 477, 479, 491, 493, 495, 502, 504, 505, 541, 542.

COHEN, Bertram Louis; *Vic.* RHB. b 25 Sep 1892 (London), d 30 Jun 1955 (Nth Caulfield, Vic). 485, 492, 812, 814.

COHEN, Morton Barnett; *NSW.* RHB/RM. b 19 Sep 1913 (Paddington, NSW), d 14 Jan 1968 (Vaucluse, NSW). 947, 949, 952, 953, 954, 955, 958, 961, 962, 963.

COLLINS, Frederick Bisset; *Vic.* RHB/RFM. b 25 Feb 1881 (   ), d 4 Oct 1917 (in action in Belgium). 244, 247, 248, 254, 262, 264, 271, 274, 280, 282, 284, 286, 287, 288, 292, 294, 306, 313, 314, 316, 318, 320, 325, 328, 332, 334, 337, 341, 345, 357, 358, 364, 369, 372, 374, 384, 385.

COLLINS, Frank Henry Kenneth; *Sth Aust.* RHB/RFM. b 16 Dec 1910 (Queenstown, SA). 809, 811, 813, 816, 817, 820, 832, 834, 835, 841, 847, 853, 855, 858, 864.

COLLINS, Herbert Leslie; *NSW.* RHB/SLA. b 21 Jan 1889 (Darlinghurst, NSW), d 28 May 1959 (Sydney). 391, 392, 405, 412, 415, 425, 448, 455, 456, 458, 459, 460, 462, 463, 466, 467, 469,470, 472, 475, 477, 479, 481, 491, 504, 506, 507, 510, 514, 517, 519, 520, 521, 523, 524, 525, 527, 528, 530, 532, 535, 538, 539, 546, 547, 548, 549, 551, 552, 555, 561, 563, 567, 568, 571, 577, 583, 585, 587, 591, 593, 594, 595, 599, 604, 606, 607, 612, 613, 615, 616, 617.

COLLINS, Vincent; *NSW.* RHB/RM. b c 1920 (   ). 964.

COLLINS, William Anthony; *Tas.* RHB. Step-son of A.Douglas. b 9 Dec 1837 (Launceston), d 12 Jan 1876 (Launceston). 27.

COLREAVY, Bernard Xavier; *NSW.* b 30 Jun 1871 (Dripstone, NSW), d 30 Nov 1946 (Wellington, NSW). 249.

COMBES, Geoffrey Arthur; *Tas.* RHB/SLA. Brother of M.J.Combes. b 19 May 1913 (Longley, Tas). 802, 812, 814, 859, 865, 866, 886, 915.

COMBES, Maxwell James; *Tas.* RHB. Brother of G.A.Combes. b 29 Jul 1911 (Longley, Tas), d 10 Mar 1983 (Longley, Tas). 802, 819, 839, 859, 865, 866, 915, 918, 919, 927.

COMMAILLE, John McIllwain Moore; *Sth Afr*. RHB. b 21 Feb 1883 (Cape Town, Sth Afr), d 27 Jul 1956 (Cape Town, Sth Afr). 407, 408, 420, 421, 425, 427.

CONINGHAM, Arthur; *NSW & Qld*. LHB/LFM. b 14 Jul 1863 (Sth Melbourne), d 13 Jun 1939 (Gladesville, NSW). 155, 158, 167, 168, 171, 176, 179, 185, 186, 193, 199, 200, 201, 202, 204, 206, 208, 211, 223, 231, 239, 240.

CONNELL, Thomas Christopher; *NSW*. /LFM. b 4 Mar 1869 (   ), d 5 Aug 1916 (Mascot). 208.

CONSTANTINE, Learie Nicholas; *WI*. RHB/RF. b 21 Sep 1901 (Petit Valley, Trinidad), d 1 Jul 1971 (Hampstead, London). 713, 714, 716, 718, 721, 722, 725, 727, 728, 733, 734, 736, 738.

CONWAY, John; *Vic*. RHB/RF(r). b 3 Feb 1842 (Fyansford, Vic), d 22 Aug 1909 (Frankston, Vic). 12, 13, 14, 16, 17, 18, 21, 25, 29.

COOK, Bruce; *NSW*. LHB. b 24 Oct 1914 (Orange, NSW), d 2 Jan 1981 (Balgowlah, NSW). 953.

COOK, Bernard William; *Qld*. RHB/RM. b 15 Mar 1879 (Torquay, Devon), d 15 Mar 1944 (Sherwood, Qld). 390, 414, 416, 429, 435, 452, 465.

COOK, Geoffrey Glover; *Qld*. RHB/RFM. Son of B.W.Cook. b 29 Jun 1910 (Chelmer, Qld), d 12 Sep 1982 (Chelmer, Qld). 746, 750, 753, 757, 763, 767, 773, 777, 783, 787, 790, 794, 796, 808, 811, 815, 817, 846, 852, 855, 857, 863, 870, 879, 882, 884, 887, 891, 897, 908, 910, 911, 912, 921, 923, 926, 930, 931, 934, 938, 940, 943, 944, 946, 948, 953, 954, 958, 960, 964.

COOMBE, Ephraim Henry; *Sth Aust*. b 26 Aug 1858 (Gawler Sth, SA), d 5 Apr 1917 (Semaphore, SA). 119.

COOMBE, Percy Howard; *Sth Aust*. RHB/RM/LB. b 7 Jan 1880 (Brompton, SA), d 28 Jul 1947 (Prospect, SA). 311, 313, 315, 318, 325, 333, 335, 495.

COOMBE, Thomas Melrose; *West Aust*. RHB. b 3 Dec 1877 (Melrose, SA), d 22 Jul 1959 (London). 333.

COOPER, Allan Ferguson; *NSW*. RHB/RF. b 18 Mar 1916 (   ), d 7 Sep 1970 (Waverley, NSW). 846, 849, 853, 854, 857, 861, 862.

COOPER, Bryce Arnott; *NSW*. RHB/RFM. b 19 Dec 1905 (Lewisham, NSW). 667, 706.

COOPER, Bransby Beauchamp; *Vic*. RHB/WK. b 15 Mar 1844 (Dacca, India), d 7 Aug 1914 (Geelong, Vic). 22, 23, 24, 25, 26, 28, 29, 30, 31, 33, 36, 37.

COOPER,D   E   ; *Vic*. b (   ), d (   ). 1.

COOPER, George Henry; *Qld*. LHB/RM/LB. b 15 Feb 1907 (Gympie, Qld). 698, 710.

COOPER, William Henry; *Vic*. RHB/LB. b 11 Sep 1849 (Maidstone, Kent), d 5 Apr 1939 (Malvern, Vic). 41, 42, 43, 44, 45, 46, 48, 49, 50, 52, 54, 55, 57, 61, 67, 69, 70, 72, 74, 78, 104.

COOPER, William Osborne; *Sth Aust*. /RFM. b 13 Feb 1891 (Nth Adelaide), d 28 Jun 1930 (Glenelg, SA). 487.

COPSON, William Henry; *Eng*. RHB/RFM. b 27 Apr 1908 (Stonebroom, Derbyshire), d 13 Sep 1971 (Clay Cross, Derbyshire). 869, 873, 885, 886, 892, 893.

CORDNER, Laurence Osmaston; *Vic*. RHB/LBG. b 7 Feb 1911 (Warrnambool, Vic). 726, 732, 823.

CORNELIUS, William John; *Vic*. RHB. b 17 Feb 1915 (Port Melbourne, Vic). 802.

CORNFORD,Walter Latter; *Eng*. RHB/WK. b 25 Dec 1900 (Hurst Green, Sussex), d 6 Feb 1964 (Brighton, Sussex). 682, 684, 685.

COSGRAVE, Bryan; *Vic*. RHB. b 23 Mar 1903 (Clifton Hill, Vic). 605, 676, 754, 755.

COSSART, Charles Edward; *Qld*. RHB. b 2 Sep 1885 (Rosewood, Qld), d 6 Jun 1963 (Boonah, Qld). 473.

COSSTICK, Samuel; *Vic & NSW*. RHB/RM(r). b 1 Jan 1836 (Croydon, Surrey), d 8 Apr 1896 (West Maitland, NSW). 11, 12, 13, 14, 16, 17, 18, 19, 20, 21, 23, 24, 25, 26, 28, 29, 30, 31.

COTTAM, John Thomas; *NSW*. RHB/LB. b 5 Sep 1867 (Strawberry Hills, NSW), d 30 Jan 1897 (Coolgardie, WA). 101, 102.

COTTER, Albert; *NSW*. RHB/RF. b 3 Dec 1884 (Sydney), d 31 Oct 1917 (Beersheba, Palestine). 271, 304, 307, 308, 310, 312, 315, 316, 319, 320, 327, 328, 330, 331, 332, 336, 339, 340, 342, 343, 344, 351, 354, 356, 358, 360, 376, 377, 380, 381, 382, 383, 396, 408, 412, 413, 415, 417, 419, 422, 424, 426, 428, 429, 433, 436, 438, 439, 440, 441, 442, 445, 447, 463, 477, 479.

COTTER, Denis Francis; *Vic*. /WK. b 1862 (Fitzroy, Vic), d 18 Nov 1905 (Nth Fitzroy, Vic). 103, 119, 131.

COTTON, Harold Norman Jack; *Sth Aust*. RHB/RF. b 3 Dec 1914 (Prospect, SA), d 6 Apr 1966 (Malvern, SA). 866, 871, 874, 882, 889, 891, 894, 896, 898, 906, 908, 909, 911, 913, 924, 926, 931, 932, 935, 939, 941, 955, 956, 957, 963.

COULSTOCK, Richard; *Vic*. RHB/RFM(r). b 1823 (Surrey), d 15 Dec 1870 (Sth Melbourne). 4, 5.

COULTHARD, George; *Vic*. RHB/RM. b 1 Aug 1856 (Boroondara, Vic), d 22 Oct 1883 (Carlton, Vic). 45, 46, 48, 50, 53, 56.

COVERDALE, Miles Colquhoun; *Tas*. b 4 Aug 1846 (Richmond, Tas), d 3 Apr 1898 (Hobart). 22.

COWAN, Robert Francis; *Sth Aust*. RHB/RFM. b 3 May 1880 (Angaston, SA), d 11 Nov 1962 (Neutral Bay, NSW). 315, 319, 329, 330.

COWIE, John; *NZ*. RHB/RFM. b 30 Mar 1912 (Auckland, NZ). 898, 901.

COWPER, George; NSW. RHB. b (   ), d (   ). 126.

COX, Douglas Edward; *Qld*. RHB/RF. b 9 Jul 1919 (West End, Qld), d 9 Jan 1982 (Dakabin, Qld). 958.

COX, John; *Tas & Vic*. b 6 Aug 1823 (Norfolk Plains, Tas), d (   ). 2, 3, 7.

COX, Richard; *Tas*. b 21 Apr 1830 (Hobart), d 27 Mar 1865 (Fingal, Tas). 3.

COYNE, Thomas Harold; *West Aust*. LHB/RFM. b 12 Oct 1873 (near Edgerton, Vic), d 8 Apr 1955 (Christchurch, NZ). 333, 371, 386, 387.

CRAIGIE, John Edwin; *Sth Aust*. RHB. b 25 Aug 1866 (Adelaide), d 13 Oct 1948 (Gilberton, SA). 105, 112.

CRANNEY, Harold; *NSW*. RHB/RaB b 23 Oct 1886 (Parramatta, NSW), d 29 Jan 1971 (Sydney). 390, 393, 400, 412, 416, 455, 470, 482, 486, 487, 488, 533, 534, 535, 537.

CRAWFORD, Cyril Gore; *NZ*. RHB. b 13 Mar 1902 (Christchurch, NZ), d 17 Jun 1988 (Christchurch, NZ). 605, 609.

CRAWFORD, John Neville; *Eng & Sth Aust*. RHB/RFM. b 1 Dec 1886 (Cane Hill, Surrey), d 2 May 1963 (Epsom, Surrey). 348, 349, 350, 351, 353, 354, 356, 357, 360, 361, 362, 365, 366, 368, 370, 371, 391, 394, 395, 404, 406, 410, 427, 430, 431, 434, 436, 437, 441, 453, 459, 461, 462, 466, 468, 474, 476, 479, 480, 483.

CRESSWICK, Ernest Albert; *Qld*. b 16 Oct 1867 (Newcastle, NSW), d (   ). 185, 193.

CRESWICK, Henry; *Vic*. b 13 Apr 1824 (Sheffield, Yorks), d 24 Oct 1892 (Hawthorn, Vic). 7, 8.

CRISTOFANI, Desmond Robert; *NSW*. RHB/RM/LBG. b 14 Nov 1920 (Waverley, NSW). 964.

CROSSAN, Ernest Eric; *NSW*. RHB/RM. b 3 Nov 1915 (Footscray, Vic). 907, 910.

CROUCH, Edward Robert; *Qld*. RHB/LB. Brother of G.S.Crouch. b 11 Jan 1873 (London), d 8 Aug 1962 (Sth Brisbane). 163, 243, 245, 277, 278, 281, 286, 295, 323, 334, 338, 359, 373, 375, 379, 390, 393.

CROUCH, George Stanton; *Qld*. RHB. Brother of E.R.Crouch. b 20 Aug 1878 (Beckenham, Kent), d 21 Aug 1952 (Indooroopilly, Qld). 312, 323, 324, 326, 334.

CROWDER, Arthur Beaumont; *Tas*. RHB/WK. b 4 Jul 1892 (Sorell, Tas), d 16 Feb 1964 (Hobart). 451.

CUFF, Alan Gordon; *Tas*. RHB. Son of L.A.Cuff. b 7 Jun 1908 (Launceston). 705.

CUFF, Leonard Albert; *Tas*. RHB. b 28 Mar 1866 (Christchurch, NZ), d 9 Oct 1954 (Launceston). 303, 305, 321.

CUFFE, John Alexander; *NSW*. RHB/SLA. b 26 Jun 1880 (, NSW), d 16 May 1931 (Burton-on-Trent, Staffs). 281.

CULLEN, Daniel Robert; *NSW*. RHB/RF. Brother of W.Cullen. b c 1888 (Sydney), d 21 Jul 1971 (Concord, NSW). 462, 470.

CULLEN, William; *NSW*. RHB/RF. Brother of D.R.Cullen. b c 1887 (Sydney), d 7 May 1945 (Sydney). 494.

CULLINAN, Thomas; *West Aust*. b (SA), d 31 Jul 1907 (Fremantle, WA). 161.

CUMBERLAND, Charles Brownlow; *Vic*. b c1801 ( ), d 27 Nov 1882 (Leamington, Warwicks). 4, 5.

CUMMINS, Frank Septimus; *NSW*. RHB/RM. Cousin of C.G.Macartney, nephew of Moores. b 8 Aug 1906 (West Maitland, NSW), d 27 Apr 1966 (Lane Cove, NSW). 608, 706, 717, 774, 777, 779, 784, 786, 790, 793, 795.

CUNNINGHAM, William Henry Ranger; *NZ*. RHB/RFM. b 23 Jan 1900 (Christchurch, NZ), d 29 Nov 1984 (Christchurch, NZ). 603, 605, 609, 610.

CURNOW, Sydney Harry; *Sth Afr*. RHB. b 16 Dec 1907 (Benoni, Sth Afr), d 28 Jul 1986 (Perth, WA). 740, 742, 744, 746, 747, 748, 756, 758, 759, 762, 764, 765, 770.

CURRIE, Ernest William; *Qld*. RHB/WK. b 9 Apr 1876 ( ), d ( ). 243.

CURTIN, Pearce William Edward; *West Aust*. RHB/RM. b 27 Sep 1907 (Boulder City, WA). 740, 770, 771.

CURTIS, George Thomas; *NSW*. b 17 Aug 1837 (Sydney), d 2 Apr 1885 (Darlinghurst, NSW). 12, 16.

CUSH, Norman Lloyd; *NSW*. RHB/RFM. b 4 Oct 1911 (Glebe Point, NSW), d 22 Jan 1983 (Maroubra, NSW). 842.

CUTHBERT, Daniel Charles; *Tas*. b 2 Feb 1846 (Franklin, Tas), d 6 Jul 1912 (Hobart). 19, 35.

DACRE, Charles Christian Ralph; *NZ*. RHB/LM. b 15 May 1899 (Auckland, NZ), d 2 Nov 1975 (Auckland, NZ). 603, 605, 609, 610, 633.

DALTON, Eric Londesbrough; *Sth Afr*. RHB/LB. b 2 Dec 1906 (Durban, Sth Afr), d 3 Jun 1981 (Durban, Sth Afr). 740, 741, 744, 746, 747, 749, 758, 759, 770.

DALY, Thomas; *Tas*. /RFM(r). b c 1847 ( ), d 23 Sep 1887 (Inveresk, Tas). 19.

D'ARCY, D ; *NSW*. /Long Stop. b ( ), d ( ). 14.

DARKE, William Floyd; *Vic*. RHB/RM(r). b 24 Jul 1846 (Sydney), d 24 Jan 1925 (Elsternwick, Vic). 23.

DARLING, Joseph; *Sth Aust*. LHB. b 21 Nov 1870 (Glen Osmond, SA), d 2 Jan 1946 (Hobart). 164, 166, 167, 170, 172, 175, 177, 179, 180, 181, 184, 187, 188, 189, 191, 192, 195, 198, 199, 200, 201, 203, 204, 207, 209, 212, 213, 215, 216, 217, 220, 222, 223, 225, 227, 230, 232, 233, 234, 239, 240, 241, 244, 246, 248, 250, 253, 266, 268, 270, 313, 315, 318, 319, 325, 327, 329, 330, 331, 337, 349.

DARLING, Leonard Stuart; *Vic*. LHB/RM. b 14 Aug 1909 (Sth Yarra). 627, 670, 672, 676, 678, 681, 685, 703, 704, 714, 719, 723, 726, 730, 737, 745, 750, 752, 760, 763, 764, 766, 768, 773, 774, 776, 778, 780, 783, 786, 797, 799, 800, 804, 805, 806, 807, 808, 810, 813, 818, 825, 826, 827, 828, 831, 833, 835, 837, 838, 841, 844, 867, 872, 874, 879, 881, 883, 887, 888.

DAVEY, John Ryan; *Sth Aust*. RHB/RFM. b 20 Sep 1913 (Broken Hill, NSW). 804, 820, 824, 829, 830.

DAVIDSON, Alan Alexander; *Vic*. LHB/OB. b 14 Jul 1897 (Ballarat), d 1 Aug 1962 (Ringwood, Vic). 643, 676, 704, 735.

DAVIDSON, Hugh Lavery; *NSW*. RHB/WK. b 17 May 1907 ( ), d 22 Apr 1960 (Wamberal, NSW). 644, 666, 670, 674, 679, 690, 692, 696, 700, 711, 736.

DAVIE, Bert Joseph James; *Tas & Vic*. RHB/LBG. b 2 May 1899 (Hobart), d 3 Jun 1979 (Melbourne). 540, 553, 628.

DAVIES, George Arthur; *Vic*. LHB. b 19 Mar 1895 (Kyneton, Vic), d 27 Nov 1957 (Essendon, Vic). 526, 542, 627, 754, 755.

DAVIES, John George; *Tas*. LHB/WK. b 17 Feb 1846 (Melbourne), d 12 Nov 1913 (New Town, Tas). 22, 27, 35.

DAVIS, Arthur Hugh; *Tas*. RHB/RFM. Brother of F.A., N.W. & R.A.Davis. b 6 Nov 1898 (Launceston), d 5 Mar 1943 (Camberwell, Vic). 589, 615.

DAVIS, Frank Alexander; *Tas*. RHB/RM. Brother of A.H., N.W. & R.A.Davis. b 29 May 1904 (Launceston), d 12 Sep 1973 (Launceston). 812, 814.

DAVIS, Horace Hyman; *NSW*. LHB/SLA. b 1 Feb 1889 (Darlinghurst, NSW), d 4 Feb 1960 (Sydney). 452, 469, 470, 472, 474, 475, 482, 486, 487, 488, 565, 579.

DAVIS, Joseph; *NSW*. b 12 May 1859 ( ), d 18 May 1911 (Waverley, NSW). 44, 51, 53, 55, 62, 63, 107, 111.

DAVIS, Neil Wilton; *Tas*. RHB. Brother of A.H., F.A. & R.A.Davis. b 1 Aug 1900 (Launceston), d 25 Apr 1974 (Evans Head, NSW). 570, 589, 590, 615, 640, 668, 676, 707, 721, 731, 865.

DAVIS, Reginald Augur; *Tas*. RHB/RM, Brother of A.H., F.A. & N.W.Davis. b 22 Oct 1892 (Invermay, Tas), d 11 Jul 1957 (Launceston). 464, 484, 485, 492.

DAWSON, Edward William; *Eng*. RHB. b 13 Feb 1904 (London), d 4 Jun 1979 (Idmiston, Wiltshire). 682, 684, 685, 686, 687.

DAY, Herbert John; *Sth Aust*. b 1 Apr 1868 (Hindmarsh, SA), d 14 Oct 1947 (Hindmarsh, SA). 242.

De CAIRES, Francis Ignatius; *WI*. RHB. b 12 May 1909 (Br Guiana), d 2 Feb 1959 ( ). 714, 722, 732, 733.

DE GRUCHY, Henry William; *Vic*. LHB/RM. b 15 May 1898 (Sydney), d 2 May 1952 (Melbourne). 570.

DEAN, Archibald Herbert; *Vic*. RHB. b 3 Oct 1886 (Hawthorn, Vic), d 3 Sep 1939 (Norfolk Island). 508.

DEAN, Oscar Hessel; *NSW*. RHB. b 30 Apr 1886 ( ), d 11 May 1962 (Windsor, NSW). 373.

DEANE, Norman Younger; *NSW*. RHB/RM. b 29 Aug 1875 (Neutral Bay, NSW), d 30 Sep 1950 (Lindfield, NSW). 281, 300, 317, 375.

DEANE, Sidney; *NSW*. RHB/WK. b 1 Mar 1866 ( ), d 20 Mar 1934 (believed in New York). 135, 136.

DEELY, Patrick Joseph; *Vic*. RHB. b 18 Feb 1864 (Nth Melbourne), d 28 Feb 1925 (Brighton, Vic). 75.

DELANEY, William; *Sth Aust*. LHB/RFM. b c 1868 ( ), d 16 Dec 1921 (near Port Augusta, SA). 124, 127, 143, 154, 157, 161.

DELVES, Frederick Thomas; *Vic*. RHB. Cousin of W.F.Delves. b 23 Aug 1876 (Carlton ,Vic), d 28 Jul 1944 (Heidelberg, Vic). 365, 369, 384, 385, 389, 394, 397, 399, 404, 414.

DELVES, Walter Frederick; *Vic*. RHB/WK. Cousin of F.T.Delves. b 17 Feb 1891 (Brunswick, Vic). 457.

DEMPSTER, Charles Stewart; *NZ*. RHB. b 15 Nov 1903 (Wellington, NZ), d 14 Feb 1974 (Wellington ,NZ). 633.

DEMPSTER, Robert Alexander; *Vic*. LHB/RFM. b 11 Mar 1915 (Nth Melbourne), d 2 Apr 1974 (Fitzroy, Vic). 839, 903, 929, 956, 957, 960, 961, 962.

DESMAZEURES, Pitre Cesar; *Vic & Sth Aust*. LHB/LaB. b 17 Aug 1880 (Collingwood, Vic), d 7 Oct 1942 (New Norfolk, Tas). 345, 395.

DEVENEY, Frank Barclay; *Vic*. LHB/RFM. b 16 Aug 1910 (Berwick, Vic). 865, 900, 903, 915.

DEVENISH-MEARES, Frank; *West Aust & NSW*. RHB. b 25 Apr 1873 (Surry Hills, NSW), d 4 Jul 1952 (Sydney). 242, 271, 277.

DEVERSON, Charles Sydney; *Sth Aust*. RHB/RFM. b 2 Nov 1905 (Alberton ,SA), d 2 Feb 1945 (Port Adelaide, SA). 710, 711, 724.

DIAMOND, Austin; *NSW*. RHB. b 10 Jul 1874 (Huddersfield, Yorks), d 5 Aug 1966 (Roseville, NSW). 249, 277, 278, 281, 300, 317, 322, 323, 324, 327, 330, 331, 332, 339, 340, 342, 343, 344, 351, 355, 359, 367, 377, 391, 392, 395, 400, 405, 452, 496.

DICK, Andrew M ; *Vic*. b ( ), d ( ). 3.

DICKSON, George D ; *NSW*. LHB/Long-stop. b ( ), d ( ). 10, 24.

DITCHBURN, Albert James; *West Aust*. RHB/RM. b 24 Aug 1908 (Boulder, WA), d 7 Mar 1964 (Perth). 820, 821, 822, 823, 824, 842, 843, 844, 845.

DIVE, Percy William; *NSW*. RHB/LB. b 10 Jul 1881 (Paddington, NSW), d 17 Sep 1965 (Roseville, NSW). 584.

DIXON, Joseph Black; *Tas*. b 26 Sep 1836 (Hobart), d 6 Mar 1882 (Battery Point, Tas). 7, 8.

DIXON, Patrick Leslie; *Qld.* RHB/RFM. b 13 Jan 1916 (Brisbane). 870, 876, 879, 882, 884, 891, 897, 905, 908, 910, 911, 912, 921, 923, 930, 931, 934, 938, 940, 943, 944, 946, 948.

DOCKER, Albert Robert; *NSW.* RHB/RF. Brother of E.B.Docker. b 3 Jun 1848 (Thornwaite, NSW), d 8 Apr 1929 (Enfield, Middlesex). 24.

DOCKER, Cyril Talbot; *NSW.* RHB/RFM, Brother of K.B. & P.W.Docker, nephew of A.R. & E.B.Docker. b 3 Mar 1884 (Ryde, NSW), d 26 Mar 1975 (Double Bay, NSW). 390, 504, 506, 507.

DOCKER, Ernest Brougham; *NSW.* Brother of A.R.Docker. b 1 Apr 1842 (Thornwaite, NSW), d 12 Aug 1923 (Elizabeth Bay, NSW). 14.

DOCKER, Keith Brougham; *NSW.* RHB. Brother of C.T. & P.W.Docker, nephew of A.R. & E.B.Docker. b 1 Sep 1888 (Ryde, NSW), d 16 May 1977 (Ashfield, NSW). 499, 507.

DOCKER, Ludford Charles; *Eng.* RHB/RFM. b 26 Nov 1860 (Smethwick, Staffs), d 1 Aug 1940 (Alveston, Warwickshire). 107, 109, 110, 114, 116, 120, 122.

DOCKER, Phillip Wybergh; *NSW.* RHB/LM. Brother of C.T. & K.B.Docker, nephew of A.R. & E.B.Docker. b 8 Apr 1886 (Ryde, NSW), d 29 Oct 1978 (Concord, NSW). 416, 418.

DODDS, Norman; *Tas.* RHB/WK. b 30 Aug 1876 (Hobart), d 15 Dec 1916 (Hobart). 236, 252, 259, 303, 305, 309, 321, 322, 345, 362, 363, 369, 383.

DOIG, Ronald Oldham; *West Aust.* RHB/RFM. b 10 Jul 1909 (Fremantle, WA), d 17 Sep 1932 (Beaconsfield, WA). 632, 740, 770.

DOLLING, Charles Edward; *Sth Aust.* RHB. b 4 Sep 1886 (Wokurna, SA), d 11 Jun 1936 (Adelaide). 329, 330, 339, 341, 342, 352, 355, 370, 372, 376, 378, 380, 410, 412, 427, 428, 434, 436, 441, 544, 548, 557.

DOLPHIN, Arthur; *Eng.* RHB/WK. b 24 Dec 1885 (Wilsden, Yorks), d 23 Oct 1942 (Bradford, Yorks). 513, 516, 526, 527, 531.

DONAHOO, Sydney John; *Vic & Qld.* LHB/RM. b 14 Apr 1871 (St Kilda, Vic), d 14 Jan 1946 (St Kilda, Vic). 138, 139, 141, 159, 196, 208, 224.

DONNAN, Henry; *NSW.* RHB/RM. b 12 Nov 1864 (Liverpool, NSW), d 13 Aug 1956 (Bexley, NSW). 111, 114, 115, 116, 126, 129, 130, 131, 133, 135, 136, 137, 138, 140, 145, 146, 147, 148, 149, 151, 153, 154, 155, 157, 158, 164, 168, 171, 174, 178, 180, 182, 185, 188, 193, 194, 195, 196, 199, 200, 201, 202, 204, 206, 211, 214, 216, 218, 221, 223, 229, 230, 231, 233, 235, 239, 243, 245, 246, 247, 250, 251, 255, 256.

DONNELLY, James Louis; *NSW.* LHB. b 24 Jun 1907 ( ), d 2 Mar 1978 (Koorawatha). 706, 752, 769.

DONNELLY, Martin Patterson; *NZ.* LHB/SLA. b 17 Oct 1917 (Ngaruawahia, NZ). 898, 899.

DOUGLAS, Adye; *Tas.* b 31 May 1815 (Thorpe, Norfolk), d 10 Apr 1906 (Hobart). 2.

DOUGLAS, Alfred Jamieson; *Tas.* LHB. Grand-nephew of A.Douglas. b 4 Feb 1872 (Newstead, Tas), d 9 Jun 1938 (Malvern, Vic). 169, 183, 197.

DOUGLAS, John William Henry Tyler; *Eng.* RHB/RFM. b 3 Sep 1882 (Clapton, Middlesex), d 19 Dec 1930 (at sea off Denmark). 431, 432, 433, 435, 437, 438, 440, 442, 446, 447, 448, 450, 512, 513, 514, 516, 517, 519, 521, 524, 526, 527, 528, 530, 531, 572, 573, 575, 576, 577, 582, 585, 592.

DOUGLAS, Osborne Henry; *Tas.* Son of A.Douglas. b 14 Mar 1880 (Launceston), d 24 Apr 1918 (near Deuancourt, France). 229, 285, 303, 305, 309, 321, 322.

DOWN, Granville Stuart; *Sth Aust.* *RHB.* b 24 May 1883 (Bathurst, NSW), d c 1970 ( ). 430, 431, 434, 436.

DOWNES, Alexander Dalziel; *NZ.* RHB/OB. b 2 Feb 1868 (Emerald Hill, Vic), d 10 Feb 1950 (Dunedin, NZ). 237, 238.

DOWNES, Francis; *NSW.* /LM. b 11 Jun 1864 (Sydney), d 20 May 1916 (Little Bay, NSW). 53, 77, 79, 82, 138, 140.

DOWNEY, Donnell Raymond; *Sth Aust.* RHB/WK. b 12 Apr 1907 (Parkside, SA), d 23 Jan 1966 (Adelaide). 601.

DOWNEY, Joseph Aloysius; *Qld.* RHB/LBG. b 4 Feb 1895 (, Qld), d 18 Apr 1934 (Kangaroo Point, Qld). 458, 465, 467, 470, 471, 472, 473, 486, 493.

DOWSLEY, Harcourt; *Vic.* RHB/RFM. b 15 Jul 1919 (Essendon, Vic). 915, 927, 929.

DOWSON, Edward Maurice; *Eng.* RHB/SLA. b 21 Jun 1880 (Weybridge, Surrey), d 22 Jul 1933 (Hele, Devon). 288, 289, 290.

DRAPE, Isaac Selby; *Vic & Qld.* RHB b 13 May 1866 (Hotham, Vic), d 7 Feb 1916 (St Kilda, Vic). 169, 176.

DREW, Albert David; *West Aust.* RHB/SLA. Nephew of J.L.Drew. b 30 Oct 1906 (West Leederville, WA), d 20 Feb 1984 (Shenton Park, WA). 573, 597, 598, 599, 601, 617, 631, 632, 648, 681, 699, 701, 702, 771.

DREW, Charles Francis; *Sth Aust.* RHB. Brother of T.M.Drew. b 24 Apr 1888 (Kooringa, SA), d 19 Feb 1960 (Adelaide). 441.

DREW, James Leggat; *Vic.* RHB/LM b 20 Jan 1872 (Williamstown, Vic), d 22 Jan 1944 (Maryborough, Vic). 252.

DREW, Thomas Mitchell; *Sth Aust.* LHB/LB. Brother of C.F.Drew. b 9 Jun 1875 (Kooringa, SA), d 9 Jan 1928 (Toowoomba, Qld). 209, 216, 222.

DRISCOLL, Clarence Rheuben; *Tas.* RHB/WK. Brother of V.R.Driscoll. b 4 Sep 1895 (Glebe, Tas), d 1 May 1948 (Hobart). 643.

DRISCOLL, Vernon Reginald; *Tas.* RHB. Brother of C.R.Driscoll. b 11 Apr 1891 (Glebe, Tas), d 19 Mar 1967 (Bellerive, Tas). 643, 693, 694, 755.

DRIVER, Richard; *NSW.* b 16 Sep 1829 (Cabramatta, NSW), d 8 Jul 1880 (Moore Park, NSW). 4.

DRUCE, Norman Frank; *Eng.* RHB. b 1 Jan 1875 (Denmark Hill, Surrey), d 27 Oct 1954 (Milford on Sea, Hampshire). 210, 211, 213, 215, 217, 220, 221, 224, 225, 226, 227.

DRUMMOND, George Henry; *Eng.* RHB. b 3 Mar 1883 (London), d 12 Oct 1963 (Braddan, Isle of Man). 305.

DRYSDALE, John; *Vic.* LHB/RM. b 1863 (Vic), d 15 Feb 1923 (Nth Fitzroy, Vic). 125, 127, 128, 129, 132, 133, 135.

DU CROZ, Gervase Bedford; *Tas & Vic.* b 1820 (Eng), d 19 Feb 1855 (Launceston). 1, 3.

DUCAT, Andrew; *Eng.* RHB. b 16 Feb 1886 (Brixton, Surrey), d 23 Jul 1942 (Lords C.G., London). 687.

DUCKWORTH, George; *Eng.* RHB/WK. b 9 May 1901 (Warrington, Lancs), d 5 Jan 1966 (Warrington, Lancs). 652, 654, 657, 659, 661, 665, 673, 680, 681, 772, 776, 778, 785, 793, 800, 801, 868, 875, 885, 886, 892.

DUDLEY, Walter John; *Vic.* RHB/RF. b 29 May 1918 (Fitzroy, Vic), d 5 Apr 1978 (Northcote, Vic). 956, 957, 960, 962.

DUFF, Reginald Alexander; *NSW.* RHB/RM. Brother of W.S.Duff. b 17 Aug 1878 (Sydney), d 13 Dec 1911 (Nth Sydney). 229, 230, 233, 238, 245, 249, 251, 255, 256, 258, 260, 263, 265, 267, 268, 269, 270, 272, 273, 275, 279, 280, 283, 284, 289, 293, 296, 297, 299, 301, 302, 304, 307, 308, 310, 312, 315, 316, 319, 320, 331, 332, 339, 340, 343, 344, 351, 355.

DUFF, Walter Scott; *NSW.* RHB. Brother of R.A.Duff. b 22 Apr 1876 (Sydney), d 11 Nov 1921 (Sydney). 278, 281, 289.

DUFFY, Jack; *Vic.* /LaB. b ( ), d ( ). 119.

DUFFY, William Vincent; *West Aust.* RHB/RFM. b 8 Jul 1866 (Doutta Galla, Selby, Vic), d 13 Jun 1959 (Subiaco, WA). 104, 161, 162.

DULDIG, Lance Desmond; *Sth Aust.* RHB. b 21 Feb 1922 (Eudunda, SA). 963.

DULEEPSINHJI, Kumar Shri; *Eng.* RHB/LB. b 13 Jun 1905 (Sarodar, India), d 5 Dec 1959 (Bombay, India). 682, 684, 685, 686, 687.

DULLING, Philip; *Tas.* RHB/LM. b 5 May 1909 (Launceston), d 1 Sep 1974 (Launceston). 839.

DUMARESQ, Henry Rowland Gascoigne; *Tas.* LHB. b 20 Feb 1839 (Longford, Tas), d 31 Oct 1924 (Ulverstone, Tas). 19.

DUMMETT, Arthur William; *Vic.* RHB/RFM. b 18 Nov 1900 (Fitzroy, Vic), d 4 Jun 1968 (Ivanhoe, Vic). 540.

DUMMETT, William; *NSW.* b 18 Jul 1840 (Sydney), d c 1906 ( ). 32, 36, 37.

DUNCAN, William; *Qld.* RHB/WK. b 19 Oct 1912 ( ). 727.

DUNN, Martin Matthew Francis; *Qld.* RHB. b 10 May 1883 (Maryborough, Qld), d ( ). 334, 336, 353, 359.

DUNSTAN, William John; *West Aust.* RHB/WK. b 4 Dec 1878 (Glen Osmond, SA), d 11 Apr 1955 (Perth). 335.

DUPAIN, Francois Henri; *NSW*. LHB/RFM. b 1 Jun 1887 (Ashfield, NSW), d 29 Sep 1959 (Burradoo, NSW). 640, 683, 686.

DWYER, Edmund Alfred; *NSW*. RHB. b 19 Oct 1894 (Mosman, NSW), d 10 Sep 1975 (Mosman, NSW). 496, 602, 674.

DWYER, Eric William; *Tas*. RHB/RFM. b 15 Jun 1917 (St Helen's Tas). 915.

DWYER, John Christopher; *Vic*. RHB/RM/OB. b ( ), d 2 Feb 1945 (Fitzroy, Vic). 449, 451, 464.

DYER, Robert Henry; *Sth Aust*. LHB. b 1860 (Eng), d 31 Aug 1950 (Nailsworth, SA). 170, 172, 175, 180, 187, 188, 191, 192.

EADY, Charles John; *Tas*. RHB/RF. b 29 Oct 1870 (Hobart), d 20 Dec 1945 (Hobart). 134, 141, 159, 169, 183, 197, 200, 205, 219, 229, 236, 240, 241, 249, 252, 253, 259, 275, 285, 303, 309, 322, 345, 363, 369.

EARLE, Guy Fife; *Eng*. RHB/RF. b 24 Aug 1891 (Newcastle-on-Tyne, Northumberland), d 30 Dec 1966 (Wincanton, Somerset). 682, 684, 685.

EASTON, Frank Alexander; *NSW*. RHB/WK. b 19 Feb 1910 (Waterloo, NSW), d 5 May 1989 (Sydney). 815, 822, 846, 849, 851, 853, 854, 857, 861, 862, 880, 881, 884, 888, 921, 924, 925, 930.

EATON, George Melville; *Vic*. RHB. b 23 Oct 1904 (Durban, Sth Afr), d 28 May 1938 (East Melbourne). 729, 731, 732, 737.

EATON, Harry Ronald; *NSW*. LHB/RFM. b 1909 ( ), d 13 May 1960 (Castelcrag, NSW). 674.

EBELING, Hans Irvine; *Vic*. RHB/RFM. b 1 Jan 1905 (Avoca, Vic), d 12 Jan 1980 (East Bentleigh, Vic). 570, 605, 611, 654, 656, 660, 662, 663, 670, 672, 689, 800, 805, 806, 807, 808, 810, 813, 818, 826, 827, 828, 831, 833, 835, 837, 838, 841, 848, 851, 852, 854, 858, 862, 863, 864, 867, 872, 874, 875, 879, 881, 887, 888, 893, 896, 899, 900.

EBSWORTH, Norman; *NSW*. RHB. b 2 Jan 1878 (Sydney), d 19 Nov 1949 (Kirribilli, NSW). 278, 279, 280.

EDMONDSON, Henry Pudsey Dawson; *West Aust*. RHB/RM.WK. b 25 Nov 1872 (Hobart), d 18 Aug 1946 (Perth). 333, 453, 454, 455, 456, 457.

EDWARDS, Allen Crisp; *Sth Aust*. b 18 Nov 1868 (Brighton, SA), d 1 Jan 1961 (Adelaide). 161.

EDWARDS, Frederick Raymond; *Sth Aust*. RHB/WK. b 28 Feb 1908 (Sydney), d 27 Apr 1982 (St Leonards, NSW). 829, 830, 832, 834, 835.

EDWARDS, John Dunlop; *Vic*. RHB/LB. b 12 Jun 1862 (Prahran, Vic), d 31 Jul 1911 (Hawksburn, Vic). 46, 48, 49, 52, 53, 61, 88, 120, 121, 122, 124, 125, 126, 129, 130, 131, 133.

EGAN, Thomas Charles Wills; *NSW*. RHB/LBG. b 5 Oct 1906 (Warren, NSW), d 29 Nov 1979 (Double Bay, NSW). 579.

EGGLESTONE, John Waterhouse; *Vic*. b 7 Jul 1847 (Hobart), d 17 Oct 1912 (East Malvern, Vic). 19, 20.

ELLIOTT, Edward Hudspith; *Vic*. RHB/WK. b 1851 (Sunderland, Durham), d 19 Mar 1885 (Nth Carlton, Vic). 26, 31, 37, 45, 46, 47, 49, 50.

ELLIOTT, Gideon; *Vic*. RHB/RF(r). b 1828 (Surrey), d 15 Feb 1869 (Richmond, Vic). 4, 5, 6, 7, 8, 9, 10, 11, 13.

ELLIOTT, Thomas Henry; *Tas*. RHB/RM. b 22 Mar 1879 (Hobart), d 21 Oct 1939 (Launceston). 385, 443, 485.

ELLIS, John Albert; *Qld*. RHB/RFM. b 10 Jun 1916 (Brisbane). 923, 926, 930, 931, 934, 938, 940, 943, 944, 953, 954, 958, 959, 960, 964.

ELLIS, John Leslie; *Vic*. RHB/WK. b 9 May 1890 (Malvern, Vic), d 26 Jul 1974 (Glen Iris, Vic). 496, 497, 501, 502, 504, 505, 508, 509, 511, 513, 515, 520, 525, 526, 535, 536, 538, 541, 542, 545, 549, 550, 552, 554, 556, 563, 566, 568, 569, 574, 576, 578, 588, 592, 598, 600, 613, 615, 616, 617, 619, 621, 623, 625, 628, 629, 635, 636, 638, 641, 646, 647, 648, 649, 654, 656, 660, 662, 663, 670, 672, 678, 681, 685, 688, 689, 692, 695, 700, 703, 704, 712.

ELLIS, Mathew; *Vic*. RHB/LB. b 3 Feb 1870 (Melbourne), d 19 Nov 1940 (Fitzroy, Vic). 259, 282, 284, 286, 287, 288, 292, 294, 309, 332, 334, 343, 345.

ELLIS, Percy Arthur; *Vic*. RHB. b 10 May 1906 (Abbotsford, Vic). 729, 731, 732.

ELLIS, Reginald Newnham; *Vic*. RHB. b 22 Feb 1891 (Randwick, NSW), d 26 May 1959 (Cheltenham, Vic). 643, 660, 662, 663, 692, 695, 700.

ELTHAM, William Keith; *Tas*. RHB/RM. b 11 Oct 1886 (Hobart), d 31 Dec 1916 (near Lesboeuts, France). 398, 400, 418, 420, 421, 443, 444, 464, 469, 482, 484.

EMERY, Sidney Hand; *NSW*. RHB/LBG. b 16 Oct 1885 (Sydney), d 7 Jan 1967 (Petersham, NSW). 376, 377, 380, 381, 392, 395, 396, 397, 408, 412, 415, 422, 425, 428, 429, 439, 441, 445, 448, 459, 460.

EMMETT, Thomas; *Eng*. LHB/RF(r). b 3 Sep 1841 (Halifax, Yorks), d 30 Jun 1904 (Leicester, Eng). 32, 33, 34, 38, 39, 40, 41, 42, 51, 52, 54, 56, 57, 58, 59.

EVAN, Laurence William; *Sth Aust*. RHB. b 27 Oct 1864 (Adelaide), d 12 Aug 1894 (Nth Adelaide). 90, 139.

EVANS, Arthur Ernest; *Sth Aust*. LHB/OB. b 12 Jul 1871 (East Adelaide), d 26 Mar 1950 (Bordertown, SA). 195, 201, 203, 204, 207, 209, 212, 216, 222, 223, 227, 228, 230, 276, 290, 291, 294, 311.

EVANS, Charles F ; *Tas*. b ( ), d ( ). 7.

EVANS, Edwin; *NSW*. RHB/RFM. b 6 Mar 1849 (Emu Plains, NSW), d 2 Jul 1921 (Walgett, NSW). 29, 30, 31, 32, 36, 37, 39, 40, 43, 46, 47, 48, 49, 51, 53, 54, 55, 56, 62, 63, 67, 68, 71, 73, 74, 77, 82, 84, 87, 89, 94, 95, 96, 97, 98, 108, 109.

EVANS, George Nicholas; *West Aust*. RHB. b 24 Dec 1915 (Boulder, WA), d 11 Apr 1965 (Hollywood, WA). 900, 903.

EVANS, Henry; *Tas*. Nephew of N.G.Clayton. b 6 Aug 1846 (Launceston), d ( ). 19.

EVANS, Richard; *Sth Aust*. b c 1867 (Hindmarsh, SA), d 1 Nov 1939 (Hindmarsh, SA). 161.

EVANS, Royston Macauley; *West Aust*. RHB/RM. b 13 Jan 1884 (Adelaide), d 12 Mar 1977 (Perth). 346, 347, 348, 371, 386, 387, 388, 402, 403, 532, 573.

EVANS, Walter Allan; *West Aust*. LHB/RM. b 29 Sep 1897 (Gympie, Qld), d 15 Jan 1955 (Hollywood, WA). 542, 543, 558, 572, 597, 598, 599, 601, 617, 631, 632, 648, 649, 650, 681, 682, 699, 701, 709, 740, 770, 772.

EVANS, William Thomas; *Qld*. RHB/WK/RaB. b 9 Apr 1876 (Indooroopilly, Qld), d 19 Jul 1964 (Buranda, Qld). 234, 278, 286, 295, 300, 312, 314, 317, 323, 324, 326, 334, 336, 338, 353, 354, 359, 373, 375, 379, 390, 393, 405, 411, 414, 416, 435, 437, 465, 473.

EVERETT, Dudley Tabor; *West Aust*. RHB. b 9 Mar 1912 (Perth), d 3 May 1943 (Ontario, Canada). 845.

EVERETT, James Seabrook; *West Aust*. RHB/RFM. b 20 Jul 1884 (Toodyay, WA), d 19 Jun 1968 (Nedlands, WA). 401.

EVERETT, Samuel Charles; *NSW*. LHB/RF. b 17 Jun 1901 (Sydney), d 10 Oct 1970 (Wahroonga, NSW). 533, 534, 547, 548, 559, 565, 567, 571, 591, 599, 602, 606, 612, 613, 616, 617, 628, 630, 633, 634, 637, 638, 663, 690, 692, 696, 697.

EVERS, Harold Albert; *NSW & West Aust*. RHB/WK. b 18 Feb 1876 (Newcastle, NSW), d 6 Feb 1937 (Perth). 208, 223, 238, 249, 253, 277, 333, 346, 347, 348, 371, 387, 388, 453, 454, 455, 456, 457, 532.

EYRES, Gordon; *West Aust*. RHB/RFM. b 20 Dec 1912 (Kalgoorlie, WA). 900, 903, 904, 920, 922, 937, 950, 951.

FACY, Ashley Cooper; *Tas & Vic*. RHB/RFM. b 26 Jan 1886 (Bellerive, Tas), d 2 Dec 1954 (Hobart). 384, 385, 396, 398, 407, 449, 451, 454, 553.

FAGG, Arthur Edward; *Eng*. RHB/RM/occ WK. b 18 Jun 1915 (Chartham, Kent), d 13 Sep 1977 (Tunbridge Wells, Kent). 869, 871, 872, 873, 875, 876, 877, 878, 885, 886.

FAIRFAX, Alan George; *NSW*. RHB/RFM. b 16 Jun 1906 (Summer Hill, NSW), d 17 May 1955 (Kensington, London). 663, 666, 667, 670, 675, 679, 680, 683, 686, 688, 690, 692, 696, 697, 700, 707, 708, 709, 711, 712, 713, 715, 718, 720, 723, 725, 728, 730, 734, 738, 743, 744.

FAIRWEATHER, Robert John; *NSW*. RHB. b 24 Jul 1845 (Pyrmont, NSW), d 31 May 1925 (Waverley, NSW). 20.

FAITHFULL, Henry Montague; *NSW*. RHB/RFM(r). b 16 Jun 1847 (Springfield, NSW), d 22 Oct 1908 (Elizabeth Bay, NSW). 23, 29.

FALLOWFIELD, Leslie John; *NSW*. RHB/RM. b 12 Mar 1916 (Nth Sydney). 842, 843, 846, 849, 853, 854, 857, 861, 862, 870, 964.

FANE, Frederick Luther; *Eng*. RHB. b 27 Apr 1875 (Curragh Camp, Ireland), d 27 Nov 1960 (Brentwood, Essex). 288, 289, 290, 348, 349, 351, 353, 354, 356, 357, 360, 361, 362, 363, 365, 367, 368, 370, 371.

FANNING, Edward; *Vic*. b 16 Mar 1848 (Sydney), d 30 Nov 1917 (St Kilda, Vic). 26.

FARNES, Kenneth; *Eng*. RHB/RF. b 8 Jul 1911 (Leytonstone, Essex), d 20 Oct 1941 (Chipping-Warden, Northants). 868, 872, 875, 876, 885, 886, 889, 890, 892, 895.

FARNSWORTH, Andrew William; *NSW*. RHB b 14 Jan 1887 (Newtown, NSW), d 30 Oct 1966 (Sydney). 379.

FARQUHAR, Barclay Wallace; *NSW*. RHB. b 22 Feb 1875 (West Maitland, NSW), d 31 May 1960 (   ). 174, 238, 243, 245, 246, 247, 250, 265, 271, 298, 299.

FARQUHAR, John Kennedy; *Qld*. RHB/WK. b 30 Jan 1887 (Home Hill, Qld), d 31 Jul 1977 (Chermside, Qld). 473, 493, 494, 499, 506, 508, 510, 522, 529, 533, 547, 560, 562, 564, 565, 624.

FARRAR, Frank Martindale; *NSW*. RHB/RM. b 29 Mar 1893 (Rylestone, NSW), d 30 May 1973 (Waverley, NSW). 491, 494.

FAULKNER, George Aubrey; *Sth Afr*. RHB/LBG. b 17 Dec 1881 (Port Elizabeth, Sth Afr), d 10 Sep 1930 (London). 406, 407, 408, 409, 411, 413, 417, 419, 421, 423, 424, 425, 426, 427.

FAUNCE, Thomas Bowman; *Qld*. b 19 Mar 1883 (, Qld), d 27 May 1968 (Greenslopes, Qld). 324, 326, 336, 338.

FENDER, Percy George Herbert; *Eng*. RHB/LBG b 22 Aug 1892 (Balham, Sth London), d 15 Jun 1985 (Exeter, Devon). 513, 514, 517, 524, 526, 527, 528, 530, 531.

FENNELLY, Sidney James; *Qld*. RHB. b 22 Mar 1887 (Sydney), d 25 Aug 1964 (Brighton, Qld). 390, 399, 405, 409, 411, 414, 416, 429, 435, 437, 452, 458, 465, 467, 470, 471, 472, 473, 516, 522, 529.

F E N T O N, Arthur H   ; *Vic*. RHB/OB. b (   ), d (   ). 197.

F E R G U S O N, James Alexander; *Tas*. b 19 Feb 1848 (Launceston), d 10 May 1913 (Brisbane). 22, 35.

FERGUSON, Leslie Drummond; *Vic*. RHB. b 8 Dec 1892 (Nth Brighton, Vic), d 30 Jan 1957 (Auburn, Vic). 502, 504, 526, 570.

FERRALL, Raymond Alfred; *Tas*. RHB. b 27 May 1906 (Launceston). 814, 819, 825, 826, 839.

FERRIS, John James; *NSW & Sth Aust*. LHB/LM. b 21 May 1867 (Sydney), d 21 Nov 1900 (Durban, Sth Afr). 92, 93, 95, 98, 99, 101, 102, 107, 108, 109, 111, 113, 114, 117, 120, 121, 122, 124, 125, 126, 129, 130, 131, 133, 135, 136, 137, 138, 198, 214, 216.

FETT, Frederick; *Qld*. RHB/RF. b 2 May 1886 (Toowoomba, Qld), d 27 Aug 1979 (Buranda, Qld). 390, 435.

FEWIN, Henry; *Qld*. RHB/RM. b 25 Jan 1896 (Townsville, Qld), d 25 Aug 1980 (Bongaree, Bribie Island, Qld). 703.

FIDOCK, Harold Edward; *West Aust*. RHB/RFM. b 24 Aug 1902 (Adelaide), d 9 Feb 1986 (Nedlands, WA). 572, 573, 709.

FIELD, William; *Tas*. b 17 Mar 1816 (Port Dalrymple, Tas), d 22 Jun 1890 (Bishopsbourne, Tas). 1.

FIELDER, Arthur; *Eng*. RHB/RF. b 19 Jul 1877 (Plaxtol, Kent), d 30 Aug 1949 (Lambeth, London). 292, 295, 301, 302, 303, 305, 311, 350, 351, 354, 356, 357, 360, 361, 363, 366, 367.

FINDLAY, Algernon Percy; *Tas*. RHB/LBG. b 17 Mar 1892 (Launceston), d 9 Jan 1956 (Launceston). 485, 540, 589, 615, 616, 640, 731.

FINGLETON, John Henry Webb; *NSW*. RHB. b 28 Apr 1908 (Waverley, NSW), d 22 Nov 1981 (Killara, NSW). 670, 674, 717, 720, 723, 730, 736, 743, 744, 748, 760, 765, 769, 772, 774, 777, 779, 781, 786, 789, 792, 793, 795, 803, 805, 806, 809, 810, 815, 816, 818, 828, 829, 832, 833, 836, 838, 840, 842, 843, 844, 867, 869, 873, 875, 877, 878, 883, 890, 892, 894, 895, 897, 901, 902, 906, 907, 910, 913, 914, 917, 918, 919, 922, 924, 925, 938, 941, 942.

FISHER, Alexander; *Qld*. LHB/RFM. b 14 Mar 1908 (Gatton, NSW), d 6 Oct 1968 (Maryborough, Qld). 840, 855, 857.

FISHER, Arthur Donnelly Wentworth; *NSW*. RHB/RFM. b 14 Dec 1882 (Lavender Bay, NSW), d 9 Jul 1968 (Neutral Bay, NSW). 293, 300, 359.

FISHER, Arthur Hadfield; *NZ*.   /LM. b 11 Feb 1871 (Nelson, NZ), d 23 Mar 1961 (Dunedin, NZ). 238.

FISHER, Harry Medcalf; *Sth Aust*. RHB/RFM. b 28 May 1899 (Nth Adelaide), d 14 Oct 1982 (Sth Launceston). 515, 518, 523, 554, 557, 561, 566, 567.

FISHER, William Thornton; *Qld*. b 31 Aug 1865 (Brisbane), d 1 Jun 1945 (Herston, Qld). 163, 171.

FISHLOCK, Laurence Barnard; *Eng*. LHB/SLA. b 2 Jan 1907 (Battersea, London), d 26 Jun 1986 (London). 868, 869, 871, 872, 873, 875, 876, 885, 886, 889.

FITZGERALD, James Joseph; *Qld*. RHB/RFM. b 19 Feb 1874 (Sydney), d 20 Aug 1950 (Graceville, Qld). 278, 281, 286, 295, 300, 312, 314, 317.

FITZMAURICE, Dudley James Anthony; *Vic*. RHB/RM. b 21 May 1913 (Carlton, Vic). 812, 814, 839, 927.

FITZPATRICK, Jack Herbert; *NSW*. RHB/LB. b 18 Sep 1915 (Bankstown, NSW). 914, 921, 924, 925, 930.

FITZPATRICK, John Milling; *Vic*. RHB/LB. b Oct 1889 (Sydney), d 16 Aug 1952 (Coogee, NSW). 483.

FLEAY, Clarence William Edward James; *West Aust*. RHB/RM. b 27 Dec 1886 (Gilgering, WA), d 6 Aug 1955 (Katanning, WA). 543.

FLEETWOOD-SMITH, Leslie O'Brien; *Vic*. RHB/SLC. b 30 Mar 1908 (Stawell, Vic), d 16 Mar 1971 (Fitzroy, Vic). 754, 755, 764, 766, 768, 773, 774, 776, 780, 783, 786, 798, 800, 802, 804, 805, 807, 808, 810, 813, 818, 825, 826, 828, 831, 833, 835, 837, 838, 841, 844, 879, 881, 883, 887, 888, 890, 895, 896, 899, 902, 905, 907, 909, 912, 914, 917, 918, 919, 920, 922, 923, 925, 928, 933, 934, 935, 936, 937, 939, 940, 942, 945, 948, 949.

FLETCHER, John Henry; *Qld*. RHB/LB. b 27 Oct 1893 (, Qld), d (   ). 508.

FLETCHER, John R   ; *Qld*. RHB. b 25 Jan 1884 (Woollahra, NSW), d 13 Mar 1965 (Sth Brisbane). 390, 393, 399.

FLOWERS, Wilfred; *Eng*. RHB/OB. b 7 Dec 1856 (Calverton, Notts), d 1 Nov 1926 (Nottingham). 76, 77, 78, 80, 82, 84, 85, 86, 91, 92, 93, 94, 96, 97, 99, 101, 102, 103, 104.

FLYNN, John Paul; *NSW*.   /LFM. b 1890 (Darlinghurst, NSW), d 28 May 1952 (Chatswood, NSW). 486, 491.

FOLKARD, Bernard James; *NSW*. RHB/RM. b 1878 (Gladesville, NSW), d 31 Jan 1937 (Leichardt, NSW). 408, 412, 429, 433, 452, 458, 459, 460, 472, 474, 477, 479, 481, 486, 528.

FONTAINE, Frederick Ernest; *Vic*. RHB/RM. b 14 Dec 1912 (Northcote, Vic), d 24 Oct 1982 (Greensborough, Vic). 729, 731, 732, 737, 754, 755.

FOOT, Charles Francis; *Vic*. RHB. b 14 Aug 1855 (Brighton, Vic), d 2 Jul 1926 (Caulfield, Vic). 60.

FOOT, Henry Boorn; *Vic*. b 1806 (Romsey, Hampshire), d 14 May 1857 (Brighton, Vic). 2.

FORD, Francis Gilbertson Justice; *Eng*. LHB/SLA. b 14 Dec 1866 (Paddington, London), d 7 Feb 1940 (Burwash, Sussex). 172, 174, 176, 177, 179, 181, 184, 186, 189, 190, 191.

FORSSBERG, Edward Ernest Brackley; *NSW*. RHB/RFM. b 10 Dec 1895 (Kangaroo Point, Qld), d 23 May 1953 (Bondi, NSW). 522, 525, 533.

FORSTER, William Robert; *Tas*.   /RFM. b Mar 1884 (Gateshead-on-Tyne, Durham), d 7 Feb 1930 (Richmond, Vic). 363.

FOSTER, Frank Rowbotham; *Eng*. RHB/LFM. b 31 Jan 1889 (Deritend, Birmingham), d 3 May 1958 (Northampton, Eng). 431, 432, 433, 435, 437, 438, 440, 442, 443, 444, 447, 448, 450.

FOSTER, Norman Kelk; *Qld*. RHB. b 19 Jan 1878 (Brisbane), d 15 Mar 1960 (Clayfield, Qld). 234, 295, 300, 312, 314, 317, 323, 324, 326.

FOSTER, Reginald Erskine; *Eng*. RHB/RFM. b 16 Apr 1878 (Malvern, Worcs), d 13 May 1914 (Kensington, London). 291, 292, 293, 295, 297, 301, 302, 303, 306, 307, 308, 310, 311.

FOSTER, Thomas Henry; *NSW*. RHB. b 30 Sep 1883 (   ), d 27 Jun 1974 (Randwick, NSW). 300.

FOTHERGILL, Desmond Hugh; *Vic*. RHB/LB. b 15 Jul 1920 (Northcote, Vic). 927, 929, 939, 940, 948, 949, 957, 961, 962.

FOWLER, Edwin; *Vic.* RHB. b 1841 (London), d 31 May 1909 (Armadale, Vic). 16.

FOX, Alfred; *Vic.* LHB. b ( ), d ( ). 236.

FOX, Norman Henry; *NSW.* RHB/RFM. b 29 Jul 1904 (Longueville, NSW), d 7 May 1972 (Castle Cove, NSW). 626, 628.

FRANCIS, George Nathaniel; *WI.* RHB/RF. b 7 Dec 1897 (Bridgetown, Barbados), d 12 Jan 1942 (Barbados). 713, 716, 718, 722, 725, 727, 728, 732, 734, 736, 738.

FRANCIS, John Charles; *Vic.* RHB. b 22 Jun 1908 (Hawthorn, Vic). 788, 791, 802.

FRANCIS, Stanley George; *West Aust.* LHB/LM. b 14 Apr 1906 (Geelong, Vic). 820, 821, 822, 823, 824, 827, 844, 868.

FRANKISH, Frank Stanley; *NZ.* /LFM. b 2 Nov 1872 (Christchurch, NZ), d 30 May 1909 (Wangui, NZ). 237, 238.

FREDERICK, John; *Vic.* RHB/LBG. b 18 Oct 1910 (Toorak, Vic). 865, 872, 874.

FREE, Ernest Peardon; *Tas.* RHB/WK. b 18 Sep 1870 (Rokeby, Tas), d 5 Jul 1946 (Hobart). 400.

FREEMAN, Alfred Percy; *Eng.* RHB/LBG. b 17 May 1888 (Lewisham, Kent), d 28 Jan 1965 (Bearsted, Kent). 543, 544, 545, 546, 555, 556, 557, 573, 576, 581, 582, 583, 587, 590, 594, 596, 652, 654, 655, 658, 668, 669, 671, 675, 678, 681.

FREEMAN, Edward John; *Tas.* RHB. b 7 Nov 1848 (Hobart), d 11 Aug 1905 (Hobart). 27.

FREEMAN, Harry Septimus; *Vic & Qld.* RHB.d. b 11 Jun 1860 (Carlton, Vic), d 7 Nov 1933 (Brunswick, Vic). 110, 125, 127, 128, 171, 176, 185.

FREEMAN, Thomas Daniel; *Tas.* RHB/LB. b 13 Jun 1894 (Hobart), d 19 Jun 1965 (Heidelberg, Vic). 482.

FREEMANTLE, Leslie Francis; *Vic & West Aust.* RHB/LB. b 11 May 1898 (Canterbury, Vic), d 6 Jun 1963 (Kew, Vic). 505, 508, 549, 550, 562, 572, 573, 617.

FRIEND, Raymond Grattan; *Tas.* RHB. b 11 Apr 1898 (Prahran, Vic). 640, 668.

FROST, Albert Edgar; *Tas.* RHB/RM. Brother of S.R.Frost. b 19 Mar 1878 (Launceston, d 25 Oct 1951 (Launceston). 321, 322, 362.

FROST, Sydney Robert; *Tas.* RHB/RM. Brother of A.E.Frost. b 21 Jan 1881 ( ). 418, 421.

FRY, Herbert James; *Vic.* RHB/OB/WK. b 28 Oct 1870 (Morphett Vale, SA), d 19 Jan 1953 (Hawthorn, Vic). 205, 262, 264, 304, 306, 318, 321, 365.

GAGGIN, William Wakeham; *Vic.* RHB. b 23 Nov 1847 (County Cork, Ireland), d 5 Jul 1925 (Elwood, Vic). 19, 25, 26.

GAMBLE, Herbert Spencer; *Vic & Qld.* LHB/RF. b 2 Mar 1903 (Sunbury, Vic), d 15 Jun 1962 (Shorncliffe, Qld). 553, 562, 591, 605, 627, 670, 672, 757, 763, 777, 783, 787, 790, 794, 796, 803, 808, 811, 815, 817.

GARDINER, George Alan; *West Aust.* RHB/RM. b 27 Nov 1914 (Perth). 843, 844, 900, 903, 904, 920.

GARDINER, Jack; *Tas.* RHB/WK. b 20 May 1913 (Hobart), d 11 Sep 1976 (Hobart). 859, 865, 866, 885, 915, 918, 919, 927, 929.

GARDNER, Charles Allan; *Vic.* RHB. b 28 Oct 1908 (Bentleigh, Vic). 821, 823.

GARDNER, Roy; *Vic.* RHB. b 18 Jan 1914 (Nth Melbourne). 856, 859, 865.

GARLAND, John George Morton; *Vic.* RHB/RFM. b 22 Aug 1875 (Nth Melbourne), d 23 Feb 1938 (Hawthorn, Vic). 321.

GARNETT, Harold Gwyer; *Eng.* LHB/WK/SLA. b 19 Nov 1879 (Aigburgh, Liverpool), d 3 Dec 1917 (Marcoing, France). 262, 272, 274, 276.

GARNSEY, George Leonard; *NSW.* RHB/LB. b 10 Feb 1881 (Sydney), d 18 Apr 1951 (Canberra). 316, 319, 320, 322, 323, 324, 327, 328, 330, 331, 332, 336, 338, 339, 340, 342, 343, 344.

GARRETT, Thomas William; *NSW.* RHB/RFM. b 26 Jul 1858 (Wollongong, NSW), d 6 Aug 1943 (Warrawee, NSW). 32, 33, 34, 38, 39, 43, 44, 46, 47, 48, 49, 51, 53, 55, 56, 58, 59, 63, 64, 65, 66, 67, 71, 73, 74, 77, 79, 82, 83, 84, 85, 86, 87, 89, 94, 95, 96, 97, 98, 99, 101, 102, 107, 108, 109, 111, 113, 114, 115, 116, 117, 118, 129, 131, 133, 135, 136, 138, 140, 146, 149, 164, 165, 171, 178, 180, 182, 188, 194, 195, 196, 199, 201, 202, 204, 206, 211, 214, 216, 218.

GATEHOUSE, George Henry; *Tas.* RHB/WK. b 20 Jun 1864 (Sorell, Tas), d 25 Jan 1947 (Toorak, Vic). 128, 134, 141, 159, 169, 183, 219, 229, 236, 249.

GATENBY, Laurence Frank; *Tas.* RHB. b 10 Apr 1889 (Epping Forest, Tas), d 14 Jan 1917 (Armentieres, France). 484, 485.

GAY, Leslie Hewitt; *Eng.* RHB/WK. b 24 Mar 1871 (Brighton, Sussex), d 1 Nov 1949 (Salcombe Regis, Devon). 172, 173, 174, 177, 190, 191.

GEARY, Alfred; *NSW.* RHB/LM. b 8 Aug 1849 ( ), d 14 Oct 1911 (Brisbane). 36, 37, 43, 48, 62.

GEARY, George; *Eng.* RHB/RFM. b 9 Jul 1893 (Barwell, Leics), d 6 Mar 1981 (Leicester, Eng). 650, 657, 658, 661, 665, 669, 671, 673, 675, 678, 680, 681.

GEE, Daniel Albert; *NSW.* RHB. b 30 Dec 1876 ( ), d 16 Jan 1947 (Adelaide). 300, 470.

GEHRS, Donald Raeburn Algernon; *Sth Aust.* RHB/LB/WK. b 29 Nov 1880 (Port Victor, SA), d 25 Jun 1953 (Kings Park, SA). 279, 282, 283, 287, 290, 291, 294, 296, 298, 310, 311, 313, 315, 318, 319, 327, 330, 331, 333, 335, 337, 339, 341, 342, 352, 355, 370, 374, 376, 378, 380, 382, 383, 386, 387, 388, 389, 391, 404, 406, 410, 412, 413, 417, 419, 424, 427, 428, 453, 461, 462, 468, 497, 500, 502, 503, 511, 512.

GIBAUD, Henry Peter; *Vic.* RHB/OB. b 1 May 1892 (Fitzroy, Vic), d 29 Jul 1963 (Northcote, Vic). 676.

GIBBS, Charles H ; *Sth Aust.* RHB/Long-stop. b c 1845 ( ), d ( ). 35.

GIBLIN, Vincent Wanostrocht; *Tas.* b 13 Nov 1817 (Kingston-on-Thames, Eng), d 15 May 1884 (Milsons Point, NSW). 1.

GIBSON, Clement Herbert; *Eng.* RHB/RFM. b 23 Aug 1900 (Entre Rios, Argentine), d 31 Dec 1976 (Buenos Aires, Argentine). 543, 544, 545, 546, 555, 556, 557.

GIBSON, George; *Tas.* b 15 Oct 1827 (Norfolk Plains, Tas), d 8 Oct 1873 (Sandy Bay, Tas). 1, 3, 7.

GIBSON, Gordon Galloway; *Tas.* RHB. b 1 Nov 1908 (Hobart), d 7 Jul 1967 (Melbourne). 674, 705, 706, 737, 788, 791.

GIBSON, George Watson Hogg; *Vic.* RHB/WK. b 1827 (Thakambau, Jamaica), d 5 Sep 1910 (Carlton, Vic). 16, 17, 18, 19, 20, 22, 24, 25, 26.

GIBSON, Vincent Roy; *Sth Aust.* LHB/LM. b 14 May 1916 (Rose Park, SA), d 28 Nov 1983 (Neutral Bay, NSW). 950, 951.

GIFFEN, George; *Sth Aust.* RHB/RM/OB. Brother of W.F.Giffen. b 27 Mar 1859 (Adelaide), d 29 Nov 1927 (Parkside, SA). 35, 45, 50, 54, 58, 59, 64, 65, 66, 68, 70, 72, 74, 78, 81, 85, 86, 90, 100, 105, 112, 119, 124, 127, 132, 136, 137, 139, 142, 143, 147, 148, 150, 153. 154, 156, 157, 160, 164, 166, 167, 170, 172, 175, 177, 179, 180, 181, 184, 187, 188, 189, 191, 192, 195, 198, 199, 200, 201, 203, 204, 207, 212, 216, 228, 230, 232, 233, 234, 239, 240, 241, 244, 246, 248, 250, 254, 255, 257, 258, 261, 269, 276, 279, 287, 290, 291, 298.

GIFFEN, Walter Frank; *Sth Aust.* RHB. Brother of G.Giffen. b 20 Sep 1861 (Adelaide), d 28 Jun 1949 (Nth Unley, SA). 70, 72, 75, 100, 102, 105, 112, 119, 124, 127, 132, 136, 137, 142, 143, 148, 150, 153, 160, 164, 166, 167, 172, 175, 180, 187, 188, 191, 209, 212, 216, 222, 223, 227, 269.

GILBERT, Eddie; *Qld.* LHB/RF. b Aug 1905 (Woodford, Qld), d 9 Jan 1978 (Wacol, Qld). 710, 715, 717, 719, 724, 727, 743, 746, 750, 753, 763, 767, 773, 794, 796, 837, 840, 850, 852, 855, 857, 860, 863.

GILBERT, George Henry Bailey; *NSW*. RHB/RM(r). Cousin of E.M. & W.G.Grace. b 2 Sep 1829 (Cheltenham, Glos), d 16 Jun 1906 (Summer Hill, NSW). 4, 5, 6, 9, 10, 11, 12, 14, 17, 18, 28, 29.

GILL, Lynwood Laurence; *Tas & Qld*. RHB/RM. b 19 Nov 1891 (Macquarie Plains, Tas), d 4 Dec 1986 (Pullenvale, Qld). 443, 449, 464, 620, 621, 624, 629, 636, 639, 642.

GILLER, James Frederick; *Vic*. RHB/RM. b 1 May 1870 (Melbourne), d 13 Jun 1947 (Albert Park, Vic). 205, 207, 210, 212, 214, 218, 222, 224, 226, 228, 231, 232, 235, 239, 240, 241, 299, 304, 320.

GILLESPIE, Hector David; *NZ*. RHB. b 29 May 1901 (Auckland, NZ), d 12 Oct 1954 (Auckland, NZ). 603.

GILLIGAN, Arthur Edward Robert; *Eng*. RHB/RFM. Brother of A.H.H.Gilligan. b 23 Dec 1894 (Denmark Hill, London), d 5 Sep 1976 (Pullborough, Sussex). 572, 573, 575, 576, 577, 581, 583, 585, 587, 589, 590, 593, 594, 595, 596.

GILLIGAN, Alfred Herbert Harold; *Eng*. RHB/LB. Brother of A.E.R.Gilligan. b 29 Jun 1896 (Denmark Hill, London), d 5 May 1978 (Shamley Green, Surrey). 682, 684, 685, 686, 687.

GILMORE, Francis Patrick John; NSW. RHB/RFM. b 1910 (   ), d 26 Apr 1955 (Eastwood, NSW). 933, 938.

GLYNN, William Thomas; *Tas*. RHB/RM(r). b c 1846 (   ), d 18 Jun 1895 (Fitzroy, Vic. 22.

GODDARD, Henry; *NSW*. RHB/LB. b 16 Nov 1885 (   ), d 13 May 1925 (Maroubra, NSW). 326, 375, 379, 390, 393, 418.

GODFREY, Charles George; *Sth Aust*. RHB. b 17 Nov 1860 (Adelaide), d 27 Mar 1940 (Rose Park, SA). 90, 100, 112, 119, 127.

GOLDMAN, Arthur Edward Albert; *Qld*. LHB. b 4 Oct 1868 (Sydney), d (   ). 163.

GOLDSMITH, Louis; *Vic*. RHB. b 14 Sep 1846 (Melbourne), d 15 Sep 1911 (East Melbourne). 19, 20, 22, 23, 24, 27, 28.

GOOD, Robert Norman Scott; *West Aust*. RHB. b 29 Mar 1885 (East Melbourne), d 16 Jun 1962 (Camberwell, Vic). 402, 403.

GOODEN, Henry Alfred; *Sth Aust*. RHB. Brother of J.E.Gooden. b 12 Jan 1858 (Adelaide), d 30 Mar 1904 (Nth Fitzroy, SA). 35, 45, 50.

GOODEN, James Edward; *Sth Aust*. RHB. Brother of H.A.Gooden. b 23 Dec 1845 (Brentford, Middlesex), d 17 Jul 1913 (Norwood, SA). 25, 45, 50, 60, 70, 75, 81, 137, 139, 161.

GOODEN, Norman Leslie; *Sth Aust*. RHB. Son of H.A. & nephew of J.E.Gooden. b 27 Dec 1889 (Norwood, SA), d 5 Jul 1966 (Unley Park, SA). 453, 480.

GOODFELLOW, James Edward; *Sth Aust*. /LM/SLA. b 21 Aug 1850 (Surrey, Eng), d 22 Jul 1924 (Malvern, SA). 45.

GOODRICK, Garnet Gordon; *Tas*. RHB/RM. b 19 Feb 1895 (Franklin, Tas), d 26 Jan 1929 (Sth Melbourne). 553.

GOODWIN, Victor Henry Vallance; *Qld*. RHB. b 26 Oct 1907 (   ), d 22 Sep 1957 (Leichhardt, NSW). 683, 689, 691, 696, 703, 717, 719, 724, 727.

GOOMA, George Arlington; *Qld*. RHB/LBG. b 25 Jun 1918 (Fortitude Valley, Qld), d 1 Oct 1985 (Greenslopes, Qld). 946, 948.

GORDON, Charles Steward; *Vic*. RHB/u-arm. b 8 Sep 1849 (Oakleaze, Glos), d 24 Mar 1930 (Nottington, Dorset). 21.

GORDON, George Birnie; *Vic*. RHB. b 12 Aug 1860 (Sth Melbourne), d c 1946 (   ). 50, 127, 128, 130, 131.

GORDON, George Hollinworth; *NSW*. RHB. b 20 Sep 1846 (New England District, NSW), d 18 May 1923 (Darling Point. NSW). 17, 18.

GORMAN, Frank O   ; NSW. b   (   ), d (   ). 14.

GORRY, Charles Richard; *NSW*. /WK. b 18 Sep 1878 (Auckland, NZ), d 13 Sep 1950 (Petersham, NSW). 367, 372, 375, 379, 380, 382, 383, 391, 392, 395, 396, 397, 405, 412.

GOSS, Edward Alfred; *Vic*. RHB/LBG. b 28 Nov 1875 (Richmond, Vic), d 1 Sep 1955 (Camberwell, Vic). 321, 337, 341, 345.

GOSTELOW, Reginald Edwin; *NSW*. RHB/WK. b 26 Jul 1900 (Darlingurst, NSW). 529, 533, 584.

GOUGH-CALTHORPE - see Calthorpe.

GOUGH, Francis Joseph; *Qld*. RHB/LB. b 26 Jul 1898 (Sandgate, Qld), d 30 Jan 1980 (Sandgate, Qld). 584, 618, 620, 621, 624, 629, 634, 636, 639, 642, 647, 653, 658, 662, 664, 666, 672, 677, 683, 687, 689, 691, 696, 698, 703, 710, 715, 717, 719, 724, 727, 743, 746, 750, 753, 757, 773, 777, 794, 796.

GOULD, Fred Keen; *Sth Aust*. RHB. b 18 Sep 1891 (Hindmarsh, SA), d 15 Feb 1954 (Kingswood, SA). 548, 550, 554, 566, 567, 578, 580.

GOULD, John William; *NSW*. RHB/LB. b 1 Oct 1872 (   ), d 4 Dec 1908 (Lewisham, NSW). 151, 171, 193, 194.

GOULY, Lionel; *West Aust*. LHB. b 12 Feb 1873 (Woolloomooloo, NSW), d 15 Apr 1911 (Perth). 333, 335, 348, 371.

GOURLAY, Kenneth Garrett; *Tas*. LHB/RFM. b 27 Jun 1914 (Hobart). 782, 785, 885.

GOVAN, John Macmillan; *Qld*. RHB/LBG. b 30 Dec 1914 (Coorparoo). 773, 796, 897, 905, 908, 910, 911.

GOW, Frederick Kingswood; *NSW*. RHB. b 18 Dec 1882 (Richmond, NSW), d 11 Oct 1961 (Randwick, NSW). 391, 396, 397, 400, 405, 412, 416.

GRACE, Edward Mills; *Eng*. RHB/RF(r). Brother of W.G.Grace. b 28 Nov 1841 (Downend, Bristol), d 20 May 1911 (Thornbury, Glos). 15.

GRACE, William Gilbert; *Eng*. RHB/RM(r). Brother of E.M.Grace. b 18 Jul 1848 (Downend, Bristol), d 23 Oct 1915 (Mottingham, Kent). 143, 144, 145, 147, 150, 151, 152, 153.

GRAHAM, Henry; *Vic*. RHB/LB. b 22 Nov 1870 (Carlton, Vic), d 7 Feb 1911 (Dunedin, NZ). 155, 156, 158, 160, 165, 168, 173, 175, 178, 182, 184, 189, 192, 194, 196, 198, 200, 202, 203, 206, 210, 212, 214 218, 222, 224, 228, 231, 232, 235, 237, 239, 240, 244, 247, 248, 251, 253, 254, 256, 257, 260, 262, 264, 280, 282, 284, 286, 287, 288.

GRANGEL, Horace Henry Eric; *Vic*. RHB/RM. b 23 Nov 1908 (Burwood, NSW). 865.

GRANT, Bartholomew; *Vic*. RHB. Brother of T.C.Grant. b 13 Aug 1876 (St Kilda, Vic), d (   ). 285, 321.

GRANT, George Copeland; *WI*. RHB/RFM. b 9 May 1907 (Port of Spain, Trinidad), d 26 Oct 1978 (Cambridge, Eng). 713, 714, 716, 718, 721, 722, 725, 727, 728, 732, 733, 734, 736, 738.

GRANT, Norman Frederic; *Qld*. RHB/LB. b 15 Jan 1891 (Sydney), d 17 Sep 1966 (Coorparoo, Qld). 629.

GRANT, Thomas C   ; *Vic*. RHB. Brother of B.Grant. b 20 Dec 1879 (St Kilda, Vic), d (   ). 345.

GRAY, Arthur Thomas; *NSW*. RHB/RM. b 12 Jun 1892 (Glebe, NSW), d 19 Jul 1977 (Glebe, NSW). 549, 551, 558, 559, 560, 567, 579.

GRAY, Cecil Douglas; *Sth Aust*. RHB/LM. b 28 Apr 1902 (Henley Beach, SA), d 1976 (   ). 534, 544, 548.

GREAVES, William Henry; *Vic*. RHB/RM(r). b 1830 (Eng), d 6 Aug 1869 (Warrnambool, Vic). 14, 16, 17, 18.

GREEN, Albert E   ; *Sth Aust*. RHB, RMF. b 28 Jan 1874 (Medindie, NSW) d c 1913 (   ). 187, 209, 212, 223, 227, 232, 233.

GREEN, Douglas Carling; *Tas*. RHB b 19 May 1902 (Hobart), d 28 Nov 1990 (Hobart). 589, 590, 616, 693, 701, 707, 708, 721, 722, 729, 731, 737, 739, 754, 759, 768, 782, 785, 788, 791, 802, 812, 819, 826, 885.

GREENWOOD, Andrew; *Eng*. RHB. b 20 Aug 1847 (Huddersfield, Yorks), d 12 Feb 1889 (Huddersfield, Yorks). 32, 33, 34.

GREGG, Norman McAlister; *NSW*. RHB. b 7 Mar 1892 (Sydney), d 27 Jul 1966 (Woollahra, NSW). 467, 469, 486.

GREGORY, Arthur Herbert; *NSW*. RHB/LB. Brother of C.S., E.J. & D.W.Gregory. b 7 Jul 1861 (Sydney), d 17 Aug 1929 (Chatswood, NSW). 46, 47, 67, 73, 92, 126.

GREGORY, Charles Smith; *NSW*. RHB. Brother of A.H., E.J. & D.W.Gregory. b 5 Jun 1847 (Wollongong, NSW), d 5 Apr 1935 (Chatswood, NSW). 23, 24.

GREGORY, Charles William; *NSW*. RHB. Son of E.J. & brother of S.E.Gregory. b 30 Sep 1878 (Sydney), d 14 Nov 1910 (Darlinghurst, NSW). 238, 249, 255, 263, 265, 267, 269, 271, 272, 277, 278, 279, 280, 283, 284, 293, 296, 298, 299, 304, 307, 315, 324, 327, 328, 331, 336, 338, 339, 344, 359.

GREGORY, David William; *NSW*. RHB/RF(r). Brother of A.H., C.S. & E.J.Gregory. b 15 Apr 1845 (Fairy Meadow, NSW), d 4 Aug 1919 (Turramurra, NSW). 17, 18, 20, 21, 23, 24, 25, 26, 29, 30, 31, 32, 33, 34, 38, 40, 43, 46, 47, 48, 49, 51, 53, 55, 63.

GREGORY, Edward James; *NSW*. RHB/RM(r). Brother of A.H., C.S. & D.W.Gregory. b 29 May 1839 (Waverley, NSW), d 22 Apr 1899 (Randwick, NSW). 14, 16, 17, 18, 21, 23, 24, 25, 26, 28, 29, 30, 31, 33, 36, 37.

GREGORY, Jack Morrison *NSW*. LHB/RF. Son of C.S.Gregory. b 14 Aug 1895 (Nth Sydney), d 7 Aug 1973 (Bega, NSW). 504, 506, 507, 514, 518, 519, 520, 521, 523, 524, 525, 527, 528, 530, 532, 535, 539, 571, 577, 580, 583, 585, 587, 593, 595, 604, 606, 607, 613, 615, 616, 630, 633, 642, 646, 651, 655, 659.

GREGORY, Ross Gerald; *Vic*. RHB/LB. b 28 Feb 1916 (Murchison, Vic), d 10 Jun 1942 (near Ghafargon, Assam, India). 821, 848, 852, 858, 862, 863, 864, 872, 874, 875, 879, 881, 887, 888, 890, 893, 895, 896, 899, 902, 905, 907, 909, 912, 914, 917, 922, 923, 925, 928, 933, 934, 935.

GREGORY, Sydney Edward; *NSW*. RHB. Son of E.J. & brother of C.W.Gregory. b 14 Apr 1870 (Randwick, NSW), d 1 Aug 1929 (Randwick, NSW). 135, 136, 137, 138, 140, 145, 146, 148, 149, 151, 153, 154, 155, 157, 158, 164, 168, 171, 174, 177, 178, 179, 180, 181, 182, 184, 185, 186, 188, 189, 193, 196, 199, 200, 201, 202, 204, 206, 211, 213, 214, 215, 217, 218, 220, 221, 223, 225, 229, 230, 231, 233, 235, 239, 240, 241, 246, 247, 250, 251, 253, 255, 256, 258, 260, 263, 265, 266, 267, 268, 269, 270, 272, 273, 275, 281, 283, 289, 293, 296, 297, 298, 299, 301, 302, 304, 307, 308, 315, 316, 319, 320, 344, 354, 358, 364, 366, 368, 372, 376, 377, 380, 381, 382, 383, 396, 397, 429, 433, 436, 439, 441, 445, 448, 456.

GREW, Ernest Sadler; *Qld*. b 11 Aug 1867 (Birmingham, Eng), d 4 Sep 1954 (Brisbane). 163.

GRIFFITH, George; *Eng*. LHB/LF(r). b 20 Dec 1833 (Ripley, Surrey), d 3 May 1879 (Stoke-next-Guildford, Surrey). 13.

GRIFFITH, Harold Bickerton; *Qld*. RHB/LB. b 10 Oct 1879 (Manly, NSW), d c 1946 (   ). 278, 286, 295, 300, 323.

GRIFFITH, Herman Clarence; *WI*. RHB/RFM. b 1 Dec 1893 (Port of Spain, Trinidad), d 18 Mar 1980 (Bridgetown, Barbados). 714, 716, 718, 721, 722, 725, 728, 732, 733, 734, 736, 738.

GRIFFITH, Stewart Cathie; *Eng*. RHB/WK. b 16 Jun 1914 (Wandsworth, Surrey). 845, 848, 850.

GRIFFITHS, Charles; *Qld*. LHB/LFM. b 28 May 1889 (Townsville, Qld), d 12 May 1928 (Rockhampton, Qld). 473, 560, 562, 564.

GRIGG, Henry Tattersall; *West Aust*. RHB. b 24 May 1906 (Fremantle, WA), d 9 Jul 1991 (Inglewood, WA). 597, 599, 601.

GRIMMETT, Clarence Victor; *Vic & Sth Aust*. RHB/LBG. b 25 Dec 1891 (Caversham, NZ), d 2 May 1980 (Kensington Park, SA). 498, 526, 540, 545, 569, 571, 574, 575, 578, 580, 582, 586, 595, 596, 597, 600, 601, 604, 606, 609, 611, 612, 614, 617, 619, 622, 624, 625, 626, 635, 637, 639, 641, 644, 645, 651, 652, 656, 659, 661, 665, 667, 671, 673, 677, 679, 680, 681, 684, 688, 690, 691, 695, 697, 698, 702, 704, 708, 709, 712, 716, 718, 720, 724, 725, 728, 733, 734, 735, 738, 741, 745, 747, 749, 753, 756, 761, 762, 765, 766, 767, 769, 775, 780, 781, 784, 787, 789, 792, 794, 795, 798, 801, 804, 805, 809, 811, 813, 816, 817, 820, 824, 825, 827, 828, 829, 830, 832, 834, 835, 841, 867, 869, 871, 874, 880, 882, 886, 889, 891, 894, 896, 898, 902, 906, 908, 909, 911, 913, 916, 917, 924, 926, 928, 932, 935, 939, 941, 943, 945, 946, 947, 950, 951, 952, 955, 956, 957, 959, 963.

GRINDROD, Barton; *Vic*. b 25 Apr 1834 (Liverpool, Eng), d 23 May 1895 (Great Crosby, Lancs). 9.

GROUBE, Thomas Underwood; *Vic*. RHB. b 2 Sep 1857 (Taranaki, NZ), d 5 Aug 1927 (Glenferrie, Vic). 41, 47, 49, 52.

GROUNDS, William Thomas; *NSW*. LHB/RFM. b 1878 (, NSW), d 21 Jul 1950 (Mortlake, NSW). 312, 328.

GULLIVER, Kenneth Charles; *NSW*. LHB/LBG. b 14 Aug 1913 (East Maitland, WA). 880, 888, 930, 954, 961, 963.

GUN, Lancelot Townsend; *Sth Aust*. LHB/RFM. b 13 Apr 1903 (Port Adelaide, SA), d 25 May 1958 (Nth Adelaide). 586, 596, 597, 600, 606, 622, 624, 625.

GUNN, George; *Eng*. RHB. Brother of J.R.Gunn & nephew of W.Gunn. b 13 Jun 1879 (Hucknall Torkard, Notts), d 29 Jun 1958 (Tylers Green, Sussex). 356, 357, 360, 361, 362, 363, 365, 366, 368, 370, 371, 431, 433, 438, 440, 442, 446, 447, 448, 450.

GUNN, John Richmond; *Eng*. LHB/LM. Brother of G.Gunn & nephew of W.Gunn. b 19 Jul 1876 (Hucknall Torkard, Notts), d 21 Aug 1963 (Basford, Nottingham). 261, 263, 266, 268, 270, 272, 273, 275, 276.

GUNN, William; *Eng*. RHB/RaB. b 4 Dec 1858 (Nottingham), d 29 Jan 1921 (Nottingham). 91, 92, 93, 94, 96, 97, 99, 101, 102, 103, 104.

GUNSTON, Edward Claude; *Vic*. RHB. b 7 May 1913 (Brunswick, Vic), d 28 Feb 1991 (Melbourne). 819, 821, 823.

GUNTHORPE, Gilbert Dudley; *Qld*. RHB/WK. b 9 Aug 1910 (Mt Morgan, Qld). 860, 884.

GURR, Gordon Caleb; *Sth Aust*. b 22 Dec 1881 (Adelaide), d 11 Aug 1960 (Loxton, SA). 335.

GUTHRIE, Herbert France; *Vic*. RHB/WK. b 29 Sep 1902 (   ), d 26 Jan 1951 (Bellevue Hill, NSW). 676, 705.

GUTTORMSEN, Maurice Stewart; *Qld*. RHB. b 29 Jul 1916 (Brisbane). 887, 921, 923, 926.

GWYNNE, Leslie William; *NSW*. RHB/RM. b 26 Jan 1893 (Homebush, NSW), d 25 Oct 1962 (, SA). 571, 579, 586, 591, 626.

HACK, Alfred Thomas; *Sth Aust*. RHB/WK. Son of F.T. & brother of N.R.Hack. b 12 Jun 1905 (Glenelg, SA), d 4 Feb 1933 (Adelaide). 637, 639, 641, 644, 645, 652, 656, 664, 667, 671, 677, 679, 691, 695, 697, 698, 720, 724, 726, 733, 745, 751.

HACK, Frederick Theodore; *Sth Aust*. RHB. b 24 Aug 1877 (Aldinga, SA), d 10 Apr 1939 (Brisbane). 232, 233, 234, 241, 242, 244, 248, 250, 254, 255, 257, 258, 261, 264, 265, 269, 279, 282, 283, 287, 290, 291, 294, 296, 298, 311, 313, 315, 318, 319, 325, 327, 329, 330, 333, 335, 386, 387, 388.

HACK, Norman Reginald; *Sth Aust*. LHB/RM/LB. Son of F.T. & brother of A.T.Hack. b 25 Feb 1907 (Glenelg, SA), d 13 Oct 1971 (Keith, SA). 824.

HACKETT, James Victor; *Qld*. RHB/LB. b 8 Oct 1917 (Perth, WA). 911, 912.

HADDRICK, Alfred Page; *Vic*. RHB/LFM. b 14 Jul 1868 (Adelaide), d c 1935 (Adelaide). 159, 162.

HADLEE, Walter Arnold; *NZ*. RHB. b 4 Jun 1915 (Lincoln, Canterbury, NZ). 899, 901.

HALCOMBE, Ronald Andrewes; *Sth Aust & West Aust*. RHB/RF. b 19 Mar 1906 (Petersburg, SA). 624, 625, 631, 632, 635, 650, 681, 682, 699, 701, 702, 709, 770, 771, 772, 827, 842, 843, 844, 845, 868, 869, 920, 936, 950.

HALDANE, Harry; *Sth Aust*. RHB/Lobs. b 13 Jul 1865 (Adelaide), d c 1940's (Beechworth, Vic). 100, 105, 119, 124, 132, 136, 142, 143, 148, 164, 166.

HALE, Harold; *Tas*. RHB/RM/OB. b 27 Mar 1867 (Perth), d 2 Aug 1947 (Melbourne). 249, 252, 259, 285, 303, 345, 398, 400, 418.

HALL, Melmoth; *Vic*. b 26 Apr 1811 (Horringer, Suffolk), d 4 Oct 1885 (Ashfield, NSW). 1, 3.

HALL, Richard; *NSW*.   /WK. b   (   ), d   (   ). 46, 71.

HAMENCE, Ronald Arthur; *Sth Aust*. RHB/RM. b 25 Nov 1915 (Hindmarsh, SA). 866, 871, 874, 880, 882, 889, 891, 894, 896, 898, 904, 906, 908, 909, 911, 913, 916, 924, 926, 928, 931, 932, 935, 939, 941, 943, 945, 946, 947, 950, 951, 955, 956, 957, 959, 963.

HAMILTON, James; *Tas*. b 16 May 1843 (   ), d 23 Jul 1881 (Launceston). 19.

HAMILTON, Thomas Ferrier; *Vic*. RHB/RF(u). b 1820 (Cairnhill, Scotland), d 7 Aug 1905 (St Kilda). 1, 2, 6.

HAMMERSLEY, William Josiah Sumner; *Vic*. RHB/RM(r). b 25 Sep 1826 (Ash, Surrey), d 15 Nov 1886 (Fitzroy, Vic). 5, 6, 9, 10, 11.

HAMMOND, Charles Pitt; *Tas*. b 31 Aug 1868 (Hobart), d 1955 (Hollywood, USA). 229, 249.

HAMMOND, Walter Reginald; *Eng*. RHB/RFM. b 19 Jun 1903 (Dover, Kent), d 1 Jul 1965 (Durban, Sth Afr). 650, 652, 655, 658, 659, 661, 665, 668, 669, 673, 678, 680, 681, 772, 775, 776, 779, 781, 789, 792, 793, 796, 797, 799, 800, 868, 869, 871, 873, 876, 877, 878, 883, 889, 890, 893, 895.

HAND, Walter Charles; *NSW*. RHB. b c 1850 ( ), d ( ). 24.

HANIFY, Cecil Page; *Qld*. RHB/RFM. b 1 Aug 1887 (Brisbane), d 28 Oct 1964 (Manly, Qld). 467.

HANSEN, Christopher Desmond; *Qld*. LHB. b 20 May 1912 (Childers, Qld). 743, 746, 750, 753, 757, 763, 767, 773, 777, 783, 790, 830, 831, 834, 836, 837, 840, 846, 850, 852, 855, 857, 860, 863, 879, 882, 921, 926, 930, 943.

HANSON, Frederick James; *Tas*. LHB/SLA. b 7 Apr 1872 (Hobart), d 24 Sep 1917 (Moonah, Tas). 345, 363.

HANSON, Leopole Harry; *Sth Aust*. b 27 Sep 1883 (Woodville, SA), d 27 Apr 1952 (Kingscote, SA). 327, 333, 335.

HANTKE, Theodore Charles Muncaster; *West Aust*. RHB/OB. b 1 Aug 1875 (Blinman, SA), d 22 May 1931 (Sth Perth). 388.

HARDCASTLE, Gilbert William; *Qld*. RHB/RFM. b 26 Feb 1910 (Brisbane). 850.

HARDIE, Archibald Edward; *West Aust*. RHB/LBG. b 14 Apr 1892 (Warrnambool, Vic), d 31 Mar 1976 (Nedlands, WA. 558, 559.

HARDSTAFF, Joseph (junior); *Eng*. RHB/RM. Son of J.Hardstaff sr. b 3 Jul 1911 (Nuncargate, Notts), d 1 Jan 1990 (Worksop, Notts). 845, 847, 848, 849, 850, 851, 868, 869, 871, 872, 873, 875, 876, 877, 878, 883, 885, 886, 890, 892, 893, 895.

HARDSTAFF, Joseph (senior); *Eng*. RHB/RFM. b 9 Nov 1882 (Kirkby-in-Ashfield, Notts), d 2 Apr 1947 (Nuncargate, Notts). 348, 349, 350, 351, 354, 356, 357, 360, 361, 362, 363, 365, 366, 367, 368, 370, 371.

HARGREAVE, Sam; *Eng*. LHB/SLA. b 22 Sep 1875 (Rusholme, Lancs), d 1 Jan 1929 (Stratford-on-Avon, Warwickshire). 288, 289, 290.

HARPER, Charles Walter; *West Aust*. RHB/LB. b 27 Jan 1880 (Guildford, WA), d 1 Jul 1956 (Sth Perth). 386, 387, 388.

HARRIS, Hon. George Robert Canning; *Eng*. RHB/RF(r). b 3 Feb 1851 (St Anne's, Trinidad), d 24 Mar 1932 (Belmont, Kent). 38, 39, 40, 41, 42.

HARRIS, Gordon William; *Sth Aust*. RHB/RM. b 11 Dec 1897 (Alberton, SA), d 30 Jun 1974 (Kensington Park, SA). 531, 557, 574, 575, 578, 601, 614, 635, 637, 639, 641, 644, 645, 651, 652, 656, 657, 660, 664, 667, 671, 677, 679, 684, 690, 691, 695, 697, 698, 704, 710, 711, 712, 716, 720, 724, 726.

HARRIS, Henry Vere Poulett; *West Aust*. RHB. b 22 Apr 1865 (Hobart), d 7 Mar 1933 (Perth). 242.

HARRISON, Ernest Weedon; *Tas*. RHB. b 22 Jul 1874 (Campbell Town, Tas), d 14 Nov 1968 (New Norfolk, Tas). 285, 305, 309, 321, 362, 369, 384, 385, 418, 420.

HARROLD, Hubert Walton; *West Aust*. RHB/RF. b 9 Mar 1898 (East Perth), d 14 Apr 1968 (Hollywood, WA). 617.

HARRY, John; *Vic*. RHB/RM/WK. b 1 Aug 1857 (Ballarat, Vic), d 27 Oct 1919 (Canterbury, Vic). 75, 83, 110, 132, 133, 141, 142, 159, 160, 162, 165, 166, 168, 170, 173, 175, 178, 181, 182, 187, 192, 194, 196, 202, 203, 205, 207, 210, 212.

HART, Harold William; *Vic*. LHB/LM. b 4 Jan 1889 (Bulwarra, Vic), d 2 Jan 1953 (Yarraville, Vic). 398, 401, 402, 415, 434, 457, 463, 484, 485, 492.

HARTIGAN, Roger Joseph; *NSW & Qld*. RHB. Brother of T.J.Hartigan. b 12 Dec 1879 (Chatswood, NSW), d 7 Jun 1958 (Brisbane). 312, 324, 334, 336, 338, 344, 353, 354, 359, 361, 368, 373, 375, 379, 393, 399, 409, 411, 435, 437, 458, 486, 493, 508, 510, 516.

HARTIGAN, Thomas Joseph; *NSW*. RHB. Brother of R.J.Hartigan. b 8 Dec 1877 (Chatswood, NSW), d 2 May 1963 (Mosman, NSW). 373.

HARTKOPF, Albert Ernst Victor; *Vic*. RHB/LB. b 28 Dec 1889 (Nth Fitzroy, Vic), d 20 May 1968 (Kew, Vic). 439, 445, 449, 451, 454, 461, 471, 501, 502, 535, 536, 538, 541, 545, 549, 550, 552, 554, 562, 563, 566, 568, 569, 576, 578, 585, 588, 607, 621, 623, 625, 635, 636, 638, 641, 654.

HARTLEY, John Cabourn; *Eng*. RHB/LB. b 15 Nov 1874 (Lincoln, Eng), d 8 Mar 1963 (Woodhall Spa, Lincs). 543, 555, 556, 557.

HARVEY, Ernest; *West Aust*. b 14 Dec 1880 (Redfern, NSW), d 19 Oct 1923 (Perth). 335.

HARVEY, George G ; *NSW*. RHB/WK. b ( ), d ( ). 390, 393, 400, 416, 418, 425, 429.

HARVEY, Mervyn Roye; *Vic*. RHB. b 29 Apr 1918 (Broken Hill, NSW). 960, 961, 962.

HASSETT, Arthur Lindsay; *Vic*. RHB/RM. Brother of R.J.Hassett. b 28 Aug 1913 (Geelong, Vic). 798, 802, 854, 862, 863, 864, 879, 881, 887, 888, 893, 896, 899, 902, 905, 907, 909, 912, 914, 916, 917, 918, 920, 922, 923, 925, 928, 933, 934, 935, 936, 937, 939, 940, 942, 945, 948, 949, 952, 954, 956, 957, 959.

HASSETT, Richard Joseph; *Vic*. RHB/LBG. Brother of A.L.Hassett. b 10 Sep 1908 (Geelong, Vic). 699, 705, 714, 729, 731, 754, 755, 768.

HASTINGS, Edward Percival; *Vic*. RHB. b 1849 (Eng), d 31 May 1905 (McKinnon, Vic). 29, 36.

HASTINGS, Thomas James; *Vic*. RHB/WK. b 16 Jan 1865 (Melbourne), d 14 Jun 1938 (Nth Brighton, Vic). 110, 205, 207, 219, 236, 252, 267, 271, 280, 282, 284, 286, 374, 377, 378.

HATHORN, Christopher Maitland Howard; *Sth Afr*. RHB. b 7 Apr 1878 (Pietermaritzburg, Sth Afr), d 17 May 1920 (Johannesburg, Sth Afr). 409, 419.

HAWKE, Hon. Martin Bladen; *Eng*. RHB. b 16 Aug 1860 (Gainsborough, Lincs), d 10 Oct 1938 (Edinburgh, Scotland). 105, 106, 108.

HAWKINS. George William; *Vic*. RHB. b 7 Dec 1908 (Brunswick, Vic), d 20 Jul 1979 (Chiltern, Vic). 814.

HAWSON, Edgar Stanley; *Tas*. RHB. Brother of R.J.Hawson. b 25 Jul 1878 (Hobart), d 29 Sep 1946 (Hobart). 252, 259, 309, 321, 322.

HAWSON, Reginald James; *Tas*. RHB. Brother of E.S.Hawson. b 2 Sep 1880 (Hobart), d 20 Feb 1928 (Hobart). 236, 249, 252, 259, 285, 303, 305, 309, 321, 345, 362, 363, 369, 384, 385, 398, 400, 418, 421, 443, 444, 449, 451, 464, 469, 482, 484.

HAY, Henry; *Sth Aust*. RHB/RFM. b 30 Mar 1874 (Adelaide), d 16 May 1960 (Adelaide). 290, 291, 294, 296, 298.

HAYES, Ernest George; *Eng*. RHB/LB. b 6 Nov 1876 (Peckham, Surrey), d 2 Dec 1953 (West Dulwich, London). 348, 349, 350, 353, 354, 357, 362, 363, 365, 367, 371.

HAYES, William Bede; *Qld*. RHB/LBG. b 16 Oct 1883 (Surry Hills, NSW), d 5 Nov 1926 (Corinda, Qld). 317, 323, 324, 326, 334, 336, 338, 353, 354, 359, 373, 375, 379, 390, 393, 435, 452.

HAYMES, Frederick George; *Tas*. b 5 Apr 1849 (Launceston), d 12 Mar 1928 (Lakes Entrance, Vic). 22, 27.

HAYWARD, Charles Waterfield; *Sth Aust*. b 6 Jun 1867 (Stepney, SA), d 2 Feb 1934 (Nth Adelaide). 142, 143, 148.

HAYWARD, Thomas; *Eng*. RHB/Rm(r) b 21 Mar 1835 (Chatteris, Cambridgeshire), d 21 Jul 1876 (Cambridge). 15.

HAYWARD, Thomas Walter; *Eng*. RHB/RM. Nephew of T.Hayward. b 29 Mar 1871 (Cambridge, Eng), d 19 Jul 1939 (Cambridge). 209, 210, 211, 213, 215, 217, 220, 221, 224, 225, 226, 227, 261, 262, 263, 266, 268, 270, 272, 273, 274, 275, 276, 291, 292, 293, 297, 301, 302, 305, 306, 307, 308, 310.

HAZLITT, Gervys Rignold; *Vic & NSW*. RHB/RFM. b 4 Sep 1888 (Enfield, NSW), d 30 Oct 1915 (Parramatta, NSW). 329, 340, 341, 343, 344, 350, 352, 356, 358, 360, 365, 377, 378, 381, 382, 383, 389, 392, 404, 407, 410, 436, 439, 441, 445, 448, 450, 466.

HEADLAM, Eustace Slade; *Tas*. LHB/SLA. Brother of F.E.Headlam, cousin of R.C.A.V. & W.H.Bayles. b 20 May 1892 (Bothwell, Tas), d 25 May 1958 (Launceston). 451.

HEADLAM, Felix Emmerson; *Tas*. RHB.Brother of E.S.Headlam, cousin of R.C.A.V. & W.H.Bayles. b 20 Jun 1897 (Bothwell, Tas), d 5 Oct 1965 (Bowral, NSW). 485, 492.

HEADLEY, George Alphonso; *WI*. RHB/OB. b 30 May 1909 (Colon, Panama), d 30 Nov 1983 (Kingston, Jamaica). 713, 714, 716, 718, 721, 725, 727, 728, 732, 733, 734, 736, 738.

HEAIRFIELD, Herbert Venters; *Sth Aust.* RHB/WK. b 28 Feb 1907 (Adelaide). 963.

HEALY, Edwin Francis; *Vic.* RHB/OB. b 26 Sep 1909 (Hawthorn, Vic). 729, 731, 732, 737, 754.

HEALY, Eric Nicholas; *West Aust.* RHB. b 5 Nov 1888 (Elizabeth Bay, NSW), d 9 Oct 1954 (Cottesloe, WA). 532.

HEALY, Gerald Edward James; *Vic.* RHB. Son of J.J.Healy. b 26 Mar 1885 (Prahran, Vic), d 12 Jul 1946 (Armadale, Vic). 365, 398, 422, 449, 451, 495.

HEALY, John Joseph; *Vic.* RHB. b 23 Jun 1851 (Burra, SA), d 17 May 1916 (Melbourne). 48, 88.

HEARNE, John Thomas; *Eng.* RHB/RM. b 3 May 1867 (Chalfont St Giles, Bucks), d 17 Apr 1944 (Chalfont St Giles, Bucks). 209, 210, 211, 213, 215, 217, 220, 221, 224, 225, 226, 227.

HEARNE, John William; *Eng.* RHB/LBG. b 11 Feb 1891 (Hillingdon, Middlesex), d 14 Sep 1965 (West Drayton, Middlesex). 432, 433, 435, 437, 438, 440, 442, 443, 444, 446, 447, 448, 450, 512, 513, 514, 516, 519, 521, 572, 573, 575, 576, 583, 585, 589, 592, 593, 595, 596.

HEARNE, Thomas; *Eng.* RHB/RM(r). b 4 Sep 1826 (Chalfont St Peter, Bucks), d 13 May 1900 (Ealing, Middlesex). 13.

HEATH, Henry Francis Trafford; *Sth Aust.* RHB/LM. b 19 Dec 1885 (Kadina, SA), d 9 Jul 1967 (Edinburgh, Scotland). 561, 569.

HEATHER, Edward Drinkall; *Vic.* b 6 Oct 1848 (Marylebone, London), d 10 Jul 1935 (Sth Melbourne). 23.

HEATHER, Percival Jackson; *Vic.* RHB. Son of E.D.Heather. b 6 Oct 1882 (Emerald Hill, Vic), d 29 Jun 1956 (Melbourne). 478.

HEFFERAN, Francis Urban; *Qld.* RHB. b 25 May 1901 (Bowen, Qld), d 21 Sep 1974 (Tweed Heads, NSW). 579, 581.

HEINDRICKS, Adolphos Heinrich Julius Carl; *West Aust.* RHB. b 28 Apr 1883 (Germany), d 24 Jun 1967 (Adelaide). 543, 558.

HEMUS, Lancelot Gerald; *NZ.* RHB. b 13 Nov 1881 (Auckland, NZ), d 27 Oct 1933 (Auckland, NZ),. 473, 475, 478, 480.

HENDERSON, Frank; *NSW.* RHB. b 1 Jun 1908 (Tighes Hill, NSW), d 6 Dec 1954 (Heidelberg, Vic). 674, 706.

HENDERSON, Matthew; *NZ.* LHB/LFM. b 2 Aug 1895 (Auckland, NZ), d 17 Jun 1970 (Wellington, NZ). 633.

HENDREN, Elias Henry; *Eng.* RHB/RaB. b 5 Feb 1889 (Turnham Green, Middlesex), d 4 Oct 1962 (Tooting Bec, London). 512, 513, 514, 516, 517, 519, 521, 524, 526, 527, 528, 530, 575, 576, 577, 581, 582, 583, 585, 587, 589, 590, 593, 594, 595, 596, 650, 654, 655, 657, 659, 661, 665, 671, 673, 678, 680, 681.

HENDRIE, Charles Richard; *Vic.* RHB/LBG. b 5 Jul 1886 (Richmond), d (   ). 457.

HENDRY, Hunter Scott Thomas Laurie; *NSW & Vic.* RHB/RFM. b 24 May 1895 (Double Bay, NSW), d 16 Dec 1988 (Rose Bay, NSW). 496, 498, 499, 500, 501, 503, 505, 507, 510, 514, 518, 520, 523, 525, 528, 535, 537, 538, 546, 547, 548, 549, 551, 552, 555, 558, 559, 560, 561, 563, 567, 568, 574, 576, 578, 582, 583, 588, 592, 598, 600, 604, 605, 607, 611, 613, 617, 619, 621, 623, 625, 628, 629, 635, 636, 638, 641, 646, 647, 651, 654, 656, 659, 661, 663, 665, 673, 678, 685, 689, 692, 695, 700, 703, 704, 712, 714, 719, 723, 726, 730, 735, 780.

HENNAH, Walter Henry; *West Aust.* RHB/RM. b 16 Mar 1880 (Ballarat, Vic), d 13 Aug 1946 (Perth). 401.

HENRI, Harry James Tepapa; *Tas.* RHB. b 27 Jul 1865 (Tauranga, NZ), d 5 Feb 1947 (Lindisfarne, Tas). 362.

HENRY, Albert; *Qld.* /RF. b 1880 (Lowood, Qld), d 13 Mar 1909 (Yarrabah, Qld). 277, 278, 281, 286, 295, 300, 323.

HENRY, Donald McKenzie; *Sth Aust.* RHB. b 24 Jun 1885 (Parkside, SA), d 31 Jul 1973 (Felixstow, SA). 512, 518, 523.

HENTY, Philip Guy; *Tas.* RHB/WK. b 4 Feb 1883 (Berwick, Vic), d 21 Oct 1949 (Hobart). 553, 570, 589, 615, 627, 640, 668.

HENTY, William; *Tas.* /u-arm. b 23 Sep 1808 (West Tarring, Sussex), d 11 Jul 1881 (Hove, Sussex). 1, 2.

HEPBURN, Thomas Robert; *Vic.* b 20 Dec 1839 (Collingwood, Vic), d 22 Apr 1921 (Ripponlea, Vic). 25, 27.

HERBERT, Henry James; *West Aust.* RHB/RFM. b 24 Apr 1895 (Fremantle, WA), d 21 Nov 1957 (Claremont, WA). 558, 559, 572, 617, 632.

HERRING, Llewellyn Lloyd; *West Aust.* b 3 Apr 1871 (Clunes, Vic), d 5 Aug 1922 (Fremantle, WA). 242.

HERRING, Robert Wolseley; *Vic.* RHB. Nephew of L.L.Herring. b 8 Jun 1898 (Maryborough, Vic), d 8 Oct 1964 (Melbourne). 553, 570.

HERVEY, Matthew; *Vic.* /Long-stop. b 1820 (Glasgow), d 1 Dec 1874 (Turnbull Plains, Vic). 1, 2.

HETHERINGTON, Henry Francisco; *Vic.* RHB. b 3 Sep 1874 (West Melbourne), d 11 Jul 1950 (Malvern, Vic). 236.

HEWER, William Albert; *Sth Aust.* RHB/LB. b 7 May 1877 (Unley, SA), d 2 Jun 1948 (Wayville, SA). 242, 282, 370, 374, 389, 404, 412.

HEWITT, Albert Hedley Vickers; *Qld.* LHB/OB. b 21 Jan 1866 (Nowra, NSW), d (   ). 224, 245.

HEWITT, Richard Child; *NSW.* RHB/WK. b 13 Feb 1844 (Beverley, Yorks), d c 1920 (   ). 16, 17, 18, 20, 21, 23, 25, 26.

HEWSON, Robert Henry; *West Aust.* RHB/WK. b 4 Aug 1893 (Carlton, Vic), d 21 Oct 1972 (Toorak, Vic). 572, 573, 598, 599, 601, 617, 648, 682, 699, 701, 702, 740, 770.

HICKMOTT, Robert George; *NZ.* RHB. b 19 Mar 1894 (Christchurch, NZ), d 16 Sep 1916 (in action in France). 473, 475, 478, 480.

HICKSON, Robert Newburgh; *NSW.* RHB. b 2 May 1884 (Newcastle, NSW), d 21 Jun 1963 (Armidale, NSW). 281, 283, 284, 289, 293, 296, 300, 317, 322, 336, 338, 340, 342, 358.

HIDDLESTON, Hugh Charles S   ; *NSW.* RHB. b c 1855 (   ), d 14 May 1934 (Coolgardie, WA). 46, 51, 53, 55, 62, 63, 77, 79, 82, 107, 108, 109, 114, 118, 126.

HIDE, Jesse Bollard; *Sth Aust.* RHB/RFM. b 12 Mar 1857 (Eastbourne, Sussex), d 19 Mar 1924 (Edinburgh, Scotland). 45, 50, 60, 70.

HIGGINS, Henry James Roy; *Qld.* RHB. Son of J.Higgins. b 27 Jan 1900 (Rosalie, Qld), d 24 Feb 1990 (Chermside, Qld). 602, 603, 608, 614, 618, 620, 621, 634, 639, 642, 645, 647, 653, 658, 662, 664, 683, 698, 743, 746.

HIGGINS, James; *Qld.* RHB/RFM. b 14 Nov 1874 (Ormiston, Qld), d 24 Nov 1957 (Sandgate, Qld). 234.

HILL, Allen; *Eng.* RHB/RF(r). b 14 Nov 1843 (Huddersfield, Yorks), d 29 Aug 1910 (Leyland, Lancs). 32, 33, 34.

HILL, Arthur; *Sth Aust.* RHB. Brother of C., H.J., L.R., P. & S.Hill. b 28 May 1871 (Adelaide), d 22 Jun 1936 (Glenelg, SA). 136, 137, 154, 160, 167.

HILL, Clement; *Sth Aust.* LHB/WK/LB. Brother of A., H.J., L.R., P. & S.Hill. b 18 Mar 1877 (Adelaide), d 5 Sep 1945 (Melbourne). 161, 172, 175, 180, 187, 188, 191, 192, 195, 198, 199, 200, 201, 203, 204, 207, 209, 212, 213, 215, 216, 217, 220, 222, 223, 225, 227, 228, 230, 232, 233, 234, 239, 240, 241, 244, 246, 248, 250, 253, 254, 255, 257, 258, 261, 264, 265, 266, 268, 269, 270, 273, 275, 276, 279, 282, 283, 287, 290, 291, 294, 296, 297, 298, 301, 302, 308, 310, 311, 313, 315, 318, 319, 325, 327, 331, 337, 339, 344, 349, 355, 356, 360, 361, 366, 368, 370, 372, 374, 376, 378, 380, 389, 391, 394, 404, 406, 410, 412, 413, 417, 419, 424, 426, 427, 428, 430, 431, 434, 436, 438, 440, 441, 442, 447, 450, 453, 459, 461, 462, 466, 468, 479, 480, 483, 497, 554, 571.

HILL, Clement John; *NSW.* LHB/SLA. b 2 Jul 1904 (Gulgong, NSW). 774, 777, 790, 793, 795, 803, 806, 809, 815, 818, 822, 828, 829, 832, 833.

HILL, Henry John; *Sth Aust.* RHB/RaB. Brother of A., C., L.R., P. & S.Hill. b 7 Jul 1878 (Adelaide), d 30 Oct 1906 (Kensington Park, SA). 311.

HILL, Leslie Roy; *Sth Aust.* RHB/RFM. Brother of A., C., H.J., P. & S.Hill. b 27 Apr 1884 (Adelaide), d 15 Dec 1952 (Nth Adelaide). 325, 327, 337, 341, 342, 349, 352, 355, 370, 374, 376, 378, 380, 389, 391, 410, 412, 427.

HILL, Percival; *Sth Aust.* RHB. Brother of A., C., H.J., L.R., & S.Hill. b 4 Jul 1868 (Kent Town, SA), d 24 Jul 1950 (Adelaide). 161.

HILL, Roland James; *Sth Aust.* RHB/WK. b 18 Oct 1868 (Parkside, SA), d 10 Jan 1929 (Glenelg, SA). 170.

HILL, Stanley; *Sth Aust & NSW.* RHB. Brother of A., C., H.J., L.R. & P. Hill. b 22 Aug 1885 (Adelaide), d 10 May 1970 (Englefield Green, Surrey). 389, 391, 394, 395, 404, 406, 410, 412, 430, 431, 434, 455.

HILL-SMITH, Wyndham; *West Aust.* LHB. b 16 Feb 1909 (Angaston, SA), d 25 Oct 1990 (Angaston, SA). 770, 771, 772, 820, 821, 822, 823, 824, 827.

HILL-WOOD, Wilfred William; *Eng.* RHB/RaB. b 8 Sep 1901 (Chelsea, London), d 10 Oct 1980 (Kensington, London). 543, 544, 555, 556, 557.

HILLIARD, Henry; *NSW.* RHB/RF(u-arm). b 7 Nov 1826 (Sydney), d 19 Mar 1914 (Willoughby, NSW). 4, 5, 6, 9, 10.

HIRD, Sydney Francis; *NSW.* RHB/LBG. b 7 Jan 1910 (Balmain, NSW), d 20 Dec 1980 (Bloemfontein, Sth Afr). 743, 744, 748, 751, 752, 757, 760, 769, 774, 777, 779, 784, 786, 790.

HIRST, George Herbert; *Eng.* RHB/LMF. b 7 Sep 1871 (Kirkheaton, Yorks), d 10 May 1954 (Lindley, Yorks). 209, 210, 211, 213, 215, 217, 221, 224, 225, 226, 227, 291, 292, 293, 297, 301, 302, 305, 306, 307, 308, 310, 311.

HISCOCK, Ernest John; *Sth Aust.* RHB. b 9 Apr 1868 (Penrice, SA), d 16 Dec 1895 (Alberton, SA). 139, 156, 157, 170.

HITCH, John William; *Eng.* RHB/RF. b 7 May 1886 (Radcliffe, Lancs), d 7 Jul 1965 (Rumney, Cardiff). 432, 433, 440, 442, 443, 444, 446, 450, 517, 519, 526.

HITCHCOCK, Oswould Charles; *Qld.* RHB/WK. b 9 Sep 1859 (, NSW), d (   ). 176.

HOARE, William; *Qld.* RHB/OB. b 23 Oct 1868 (Brisbane). 163, 171, 176, 193, 208, 224, 277, 278, 281.

HOBBS, John Berry; *Eng.* RHB/RM. b 16 Dec 1882 (Cambridge, Eng) b 21 Dec 1963 (Hove, Sussex). 350, 353, 357, 360, 361, 362, 363, 365, 366, 367, 368, 370, 371, 431, 432, 433, 435, 438, 440, 442, 446, 447, 448, 450, 512, 513, 514, 517, 519, 521, 524, 526, 527, 528, 530, 531, 573, 575, 576, 577, 581, 583, 585, 587, 593, 595, 652, 654, 657, 658, 659, 661, 665, 671, 673, 675, 680.

HODGES, Jack; *Vic.* LHB/LFM(r). b (   ), d (   ). 33, 34, 36, 37.

HODGKINSON, John Ernest; *NSW.* RHB. b 1873 (, NSW), d 19 Nov 1939 (Burwood, NSW). 375, 390, 393.

HOGG, Geoffrey Charles Huxtable; *NSW.* RHB. Brother of J.E.P.Hogg. b 28 Sep 1909 (Goulburn, NSW), d 14 Aug 1959 (Coorparoo, Qld). 674.

HOGG, Thomas; *Combined XIII.* RHB/RFM(r). b 12 Mar 1845 (Hobart), d 13 Jul 1890 (Trevallyn, Tas). 25.

HOGG, James Edgar Phipps; *NSW & Qld.* RHB. Brother of G.C.H.Hogg. b 16 Oct 1906 (Goulburn, NSW), d 2 Dec 1975 (West Ryde, NSW). 622, 623, 626, 706, 750, 753, 757, 763, 767.

HOGUE, Thomas Herbert; *NSW & West Aust.* RHB/SLA. Brother of W.W.Hogue. b 5 Oct 1877 (Wickham, NSW), d 6 May 1956 (Nedlands, WA). 277, 278, 346, 347, 348, 371, 386, 387, 388, 401, 402, 403, 453, 454, 455, 456, 457.

HOGUE, Wallace White; *West Aust.* LHB/RFM. Brother of T.H.Hogue. b 1880 (Newcastle, NSW). 348, 371, 401, 453, 454, 455, 456, 457.

HOLMAN, Raymond Sidney; *Sth Aust.* RHB/LBG. b 17 Sep 1919 (Largs Bay, SA), d 19 Sep 1989 (Woodville Sth, SA). 963.

HOLMES, Errol Reginald Thorold; *Eng.* RHB/RFM. b 21 Aug 1905 (Calcutta, India), d 16 Aug 1960 (Marylebone, London). 845, 848, 849, 850, 851.

HOLTON, Leslie George; *Sth Aust.* RHB/RFM. b 13 Mar 1903 (Hindmarsh, SA), d c 1949 (   ). 702, 798.

HOMBURG, Robert Otto; *Sth Aust.* RHB/RFM. b 31 Jan 1876 (Norwood, SA), d 21 Oct 1948 (Medindie, SA). 203, 242.

HONE, Brian William; *Sth Aust.* RHB. Brother of G.M.Hone. b 1 Jul 1907 (Semaphore, SA), d 28 May 1978 (Paris, France). 660, 664, 667, 671, 684, 690, 691, 695, 697, 698, 704.

HONE, Garton Maxwell; *Sth Aust.* RHB/LBG. Brother of B.W.Hone. b 21 Feb 1901 (Morphett Vale, SA), d 28 May 1991 (Myrtle Bank, SA). 509.

HONE, Leland; *Eng.* RHB/WK. b 30 Jan 1853 (Dublin), d 31 Dec 1896 (Dublin). 38, 39, 40, 41, 42.

HONEYBONE, George Alfred; *Vic.* RHB/WK. b 2 Apr 1875 (London), d 1 Nov 1956 (Glen Iris, Vic). 237.

HONOUR, Victor Gerald; *Qld.* RHB. b 25 Oct 1910 (Aylesbury, Bucks). 846, 852, 855, 857, 860, 863.

HOOKER, John Edward Halford; *NSW.* RHB/RFM. b 6 Mar 1898 (Summer Hill, NSW), d 12 Feb 1982 (Winmalee, NSW). 584, 591, 594, 653, 655, 657, 663, 670, 675, 679, 683, 686, 690, 692, 697, 700, 711, 715, 717, 720, 723, 730, 757.

HOOPER, Victor Leonard; *Tas.* RHB/RM. b 23 Apr 1905 (Mt Stuart, Tas), d 3 Sep 1990 (New Town, Tas). 669, 674, 676, 693, 694, 706, 707, 721, 722, 729, 731, 737, 739, 791.

HOPE, Adam; *Vic.* b 1834 (Eng), d 9 Oct 1916 (East Melbourne). 14, 15.

HOPE, Raymond William; *NZ.* RHB/RFM. b 19 Jan 1904 (Wanganui, NZ), d 24 Jun 1978 (Christchurch, NZ). 605, 609.

HOPKINS, Albert John Young; *NSW.* RHB/RFM. b 3 May 1874 (Sydney), d 25 Apr 1931 (Nth Sydney). 208, 243, 245, 246, 247, 250, 251, 253, 255, 256, 258, 260, 263, 265, 267, 269, 271, 272, 273, 275, 279, 280, 283, 284, 289. 293, 296, 297, 298, 299, 301, 302, 304, 307, 308, 310, 312, 315, 316, 319, 320, 338, 339, 340, 342, 343, 344, 346, 347, 351, 355, 358, 364, 367, 372, 376, 377, 381, 382, 383, 395, 405, 486.

HOPKINS, Isaac; *Vic.* RHB/WK. b 9 Nov 1870 (Collingwood, Vic), d 25 Oct 1913 (Richmond, Vic). 285.

HOPKINSON, Samuel; *Vic.* /Long-stop. b 1825 (Yorks), d 26 Jun 1887 (Sth Melbourne). 11, 14.

HORAN, James Francis; *Vic.* RHB. Son of T.P. & brother of T.I.B.Horan. b 8 Jun 1880 (Fitzroy, Vic), d 1 Nov 1945 (Malvern, Vic). 259, 285, 292, 294, 309, 321, 325, 328, 329, 332, 334, 357, 358, 369, 384, 385, 389, 401, 402, 403.

HORAN, Thomas Ignatius Bernard; *Vic.* RHB. Son of T.P. & brother of J.F.Horan. b 7 Apr 1886 (Fitzroy, Vic), d 26 May 1952 (East Camberwell, Vic). 341, 343, 345, 364, 381.

HORAN, Thomas Patrick; *Vic.* RHB/RFM(r). b 8 Mar 1854 (Middleton, Ireland), d 16 Apr 1916 (Malvern, Vic). 28, 29, 30, 31, 33, 38, 41, 42, 43, 44, 45, 46, 47, 48, 49, 52, 53, 54, 55, 56, 57, 58, 59, 63, 64, 65, 66, 67, 68, 69, 70, 71, 72, 73, 76, 79, 80, 83, 84, 85, 86, 87, 88, 89, 91, 95, 98, 103, 106, 110, 111, 113, 115, 121, 123, 127, 128, 129, 130, 138, 140, 146.

HORDERN, Herbert Vivian; *NSW.* RHB/LBG. b 10 Feb 1884 (Nth Sydney), d 17 Jun 1938 (Darlinghurst, NSW). 326, 405, 408, 411, 416, 418, 422, 424, 426, 433, 438, 440, 442, 447, 450, 463, 466, 469.

HORNBY, Albert Neilson; *Eng.* RHB. b 10 Feb 1847 (Blackburn, Lancs), d 17 Dec 1925 (Nantwich, Cheshire). 38, 39, 40, 41, 42.

HORNIBROOK, Percival Mitchell; *Qld.* LHB/LM/SLA. b 27 Jul 1899 (Obi Obi, Qld), d 25 Aug 1976 (Spring Hill, Qld). 508, 510, 516, 517, 522, 533, 539, 547, 560, 562, 564, 565, 571, 579, 581, 582, 602, 604, 614, 629, 634, 645, 647, 653, 658, 672, 677, 680, 683, 687, 688, 698, 703, 707, 708, 709, 715, 817.

HORROCKS, William John; *West Aust.* RHB. b 18 Jun 1905 (Warrington, Lancs), d 15 Nov 1985 (Melbourne). 631, 632, 649, 650, 681, 682, 688, 699, 701, 702, 709, 845, 868, 869.

HORSELL, Jack Aymat James; *Sth Aust.* RHB/WK. b 12 Jul 1914 (Stepney, SA), d 20 Apr 1985 (Sydney). 916, 935.

HORSFIELD, Gordon Cameron; *NSW.* LHB/RM. b 24 Mar 1913 (Balmain, NSW), d 25 Aug 1982 (Mosman, NSW). 829, 832, 833, 836, 964.

HORTON, Arnell Stanley; *Tas.* LHB/RM. b 21 Sep 1892 (Burnie, Tas), d 15 Sep 1987 (Newstead, Tas). 668.

HOSIE, Robert; *Vic.* RHB/RM. b 8 Sep 1858 (Collingwood, Vic), d 29 Sep 1932 (Richmond, Vic). 75.

HOSKINGS, Arthur W   ; *West Aust.* RHB. b (   ), d (   ). 242.

HOTCHIN, Mortimer Douglas; *Vic.* RHB. b 20 May 1889 (Windsor, Vic), d 21 Jun 1958 (East Melbourne). 457, 468, 488, 492.

HOTHAM, Augustus Thomas; *Vic.* RHB. b 25 Jan 1817 (Suffolk, Eng), d 24 Dec 1896 (Tunbridge Wells, Kent). 4.

HOUSTON, Richard Shinnock; *Vic.* /WK. b 30 Jun 1863 (Brighton, Vic), d 27 Nov 1921 (Williamstown, Vic). 81, 88, 89, 90, 91, 95, 98, 100, 103, 104, 106, 115, 131, 139, 140, 141, 144, 149, 152, 155, 159, 169, 219.

HOWARD, Harry Cecil; *West Aust.* LHB. b 30 Jun 1885 (Adelaide), d 18 Sep 1960 (Perth). 333, 335, 347, 371, 386, 387, 388, 401, 402, 403, 453, 454, 455, 456, 457, 532, 542, 543, 559, 572.

HOWARD, Leonard Easther; *Sth Aust.* /RF. b 18 Apr 1886 (Adelaide), d 14 Aug 1945 (Prospect, SA). 386, 387, 388, 389, 453, 480.

HOWARD, Thomas Harris; *NSW.* RHB/OB. b 2 May 1877 ( ), d 6 Oct 1965 (Randwick, NSW). 243, 245, 258, 260, 277, 278, 281.

HOWE, John Sidney; *Tas.* LHB. b 27 Dec 1868 (Kotree, India), d 29 Jul 1939 (Neutral Bay, NSW). 183.

HOWELL, George; *NSW.* RHB/Long-stop. b 9 Jun 1822 (Sydney), d 18 Nov 1890 (Sydney). 4, 5, 6, 9.

HOWELL, Henry; *Eng.* RHB/RF. b 29 Nov 1890 (Birmingham, Eng), d 9 Jul 1932 (Birmingham). 512, 513, 514, 516, 521, 524, 527, 531, 573, 582, 589, 590, 592, 594, 596.

HOWELL, William Hunter; *NSW.* LHB/OB. Son of W.P.Howell. b 12 Jan 1902 (Penrith, NSW). 779, 784, 786, 790, 793, 795, 803, 806, 809, 810, 815, 816, 853, 854.

HOWELL, William Peter; *NSW.* LHB/RM. Nephew of E.Evans. b 29 Dec 1869 (Penrith, NSW), d 14 Jul 1940 (Castlereagh, NSW). 174, 178, 180, 182, 185, 188, 193, 194, 195, 196, 200, 201, 202, 204, 206, 208, 211, 216, 217, 220, 221, 225, 229, 230, 231, 233, 235, 238, 239, 240, 241, 246, 247, 250, 251, 255, 256, 263, 265, 266, 267, 268, 269, 270, 273, 279, 280, 283, 284, 289, 293, 296, 297, 298, 299, 301, 302, 307, 315, 316, 319, 320, 331.

HOWLETT, John Thomas; *Vic.* b 8 Apr 1868 (Nth Melbourne), d 15 Jun 1931 (East Melbourne). 309.

HOWSON, Herbert; *Vic.* b 11 Aug 1872 (Newstead, Vic), d 8 May 1948 (Murrumbeena, Vic). 285.

HUBBARD, Edward Francis; *Qld.* RHB/RM, b 27 Jun 1906 (Brisbane), d 1 Oct 1969 (Herston, Qld). 687, 698, 703, 767.

HUDDLESTONE, John; *Vic.* RHB/RM(r). b c 1838 ( ), d 1904 (Brunswick, Vic). 10, 11, 12, 13, 14.

HUDSON, John Lambert; *Tas.* RHB/SLA. b 23 Jul 1882 (Launceston), d 16 Mar 1961 (Hobart). 345, 384, 400, 418, 421, 444.

HUGHES, Walter Cecil; *West Aust.* LHB/LF. b 13 Aug 1882 (Adelaide), d 16 Aug 1917 (Perth). 453, 454, 455, 456, 457.

HUGO, Victor; *Sth Aust.* LHB/RM. b 25 Nov 1877 (Adelaide), d 8 Apr 1930 (Malvern, SA). 222, 223, 227, 228, 230, 232, 234, 242, 250.

HUMAN, John Hanbury; *Eng.* RHB/LB. b 13 Jan 1912 (Castle Ward, Northumberland), d 22 Jul 1991 (Sydney). 847, 849, 850, 851.

HUMPHREYS, John; *NSW.* /LM. b ( ), d ( ). 31.

HUMPHREYS, Walter Alexander; *Eng.* RHB/Lobs. b 28 Oct 1849 (Southsea, Hampshire), d 23 Mar 1924 (Brighton, Sussex). 172, 173, 174, 186.

HUMPHRIES, Joseph; *Eng*; RHB/WK. b 19 May 1876 (Stonebroom, Derbyshire), d 7 May 1946 (Chesterfield, Derbyshire). 348, 349, 351, 353, 354, 357, 360, 361, 365, 366.

HUNT, Horace Charles; *Vic.* RHB/RM. b 15 Jul 1907 (Stawell, Vic), d 15 Oct 1984 (Melbourne). 648, 699.

HUNT, William Alfred; *NSW.* LHB/SLA. b 26 Aug 1908 (Balmain, NSW), d 30 Dec 1983 (Balmain, NSW). 706, 711, 713, 715, 717, 720, 723, 730, 736, 743, 744, 748, 751, 752, 757, 760, 762, 769.

HUNTE, Errol Ashton Clarimore; *WI.* RHB/WK. b 3 Oct 1905 (Port of Spain, Trinidad), d 26 Jun 1967 (Port of Spain, Trinidad). 714, 716, 721, 727, 733.

HUNTER, Joseph; *Eng.* RHB/WK. b 3 Aug 1855 (Scarborough, Yorks), d 4 Jan 1891 (Rotheram, Yorks). 76, 77, 78, 80, 82, 84, 85, 86.

HURWOOD, Alexander; *Qld.* RHB/RM/OB. b 17 Jun 1902 (Brisbane), d 26 Sep 1982 (Coffs Harbour, NSW). 608, 634, 636, 639, 642, 687, 689, 691, 696, 698, 703, 707, 708, 709, 715, 718, 719, 725, 743, 746, 750, 753, 757.

HUSSEY, Percival Leitch; *West Aust.* b 23 Jun 1869 (Perth), d 13 May 1944 (Adelaide). 161, 162.

HUTCHEON, Ernest Henry; *Qld.* RHB. Brother of J.S.Hutcheon. b 17 Jun 1889 (Toowoomba, Qld), d 9 Jun 1937 (Brisbane). 510, 533, 547, 602, 603, 608, 614.

HUTCHEON, John Silvester; *Qld.* RHB/RFM. Brother of E.H.Hutcheon. b 5 Apr 1882 (Warwick, Qld), d 18 Jun 1957 (Albion Heights, Qld). 324, 353, 373, 375, 379, 393, 396, 399, 405, 409, 414, 416.

HUTCHINGS, Kenneth Lotherington; *Eng.* RHB/RF. b 7 Dec 1882 (Southborough, Kent), d 3 Sep 1916 (Ginchy, France). 349, 350, 351, 353, 354, 356, 357, 360, 361, 362, 363, 365, 366, 367, 368, 370, 371.

HUTTON, Ernest Hamilton; *Vic & Qld.* RHB. b 29 Mar 1867 (Mt Rouse, Vic), d 12 Jul 1929 (Ascot, Qld). 149, 171.

HUTTON, Henry George; *Sth Aust.* /RFM. b 26 Aug 1878 (Masterton, NZ), d 13 Aug 1968 (Norwood, SA). 329.

HUTTON, Mervyn Douglas; *Sth Aust.* RHB/LB. Cousin of M.P. and Nephew of W.F.P.Hutton, b 24 Aug 1911 (Port Augusta, SA). 739.

HUTTON, Maurice Percy; *Sth Aust.* LHB. Son of W.F.P.Hutton, brother of N.H.Hutton. b 21 Mar 1903 (Parkside, SA), d 20 Feb 1940 (Mitcham, SA). 677, 679.

HUTTON, Norman Harvey; *Sth Aust.* LHB/RFM. Son of W.F.P.Hutton, brother of M.P.Hutton. b 10 Aug 1911 (Unley, SA), d 27 Aug 1965 (Fullarton, SA). 829, 830.

HUTTON, William Frederick Percy; *Sth Aust.* /WK. b 2 Oct 1876 (Mintaro, SA), d 1 Oct 1951 (Millswood, SA). 327.

HYETT, Francis William; *Vic.* RHB/WK. b 9 Feb 1882 (Brunswick, Vic), d 25 Apr 1919 (Fitzroy, Vic). 492, 495, 498.

HYNES, Lincoln Carruthers; *NSW.* RHB/LFM. b 12 Apr 1912 (Balmain, NSW), d 7 Aug 1977 (Killara, NSW). 857, 861, 862, 870, 873, 880, 881, 884, 888, 892, 894, 897, 901, 902, 906, 932, 933.

ICETON, Thomas Henry; *NSW.* RHB/OB(r). b 12 Dec 1849 (Sydney), d 19 May 1908 (Ashfield, NSW). 36.

IDDISON, Roger; *Eng.* RHB/RF(r). b 15 Sep 1834 (Bedale, Yorks), d 19 Mar 1890 (York, Yorks). 13.

INGLETON, Walter George; *Vic.* LHB. b 16 Feb 1867 (Fitzroy, Vic), d 4 Jan 1923 (Brighton, Vic). 134, 169, 183, 197, 205.

INKSTER, Gordon Bradford; *Sth Aust.* RHB/WK. b 30 Jun 1893 (Portland Estate, SA), d 22 Mar 1957 (Darlinghurst, NSW). 624, 625, 626, 631, 632, 635.

INVERARITY, Mervyn; *West Aust.* RHB/LB/RM. b 25 Oct 1907 (Claremont, WA), d 17 Mar 1979 (Cottesloe, WA). 597, 598, 599, 601, 617, 631, 632, 650, 682, 699, 701, 702, 709, 740, 770, 771, 820, 821, 822, 823, 824, 868, 936, 937, 950, 951.

IREDALE, Francis Adams; *NSW.* RHB. Nephew of F.Adams. b 19 Jun 1867 (Surry Hills, NSW), d 15 Apr 1926 (Nth Sydney). 126, 135, 137, 138, 140, 145, 146, 148, 154, 155, 157, 158, 164, 165, 167, 168, 174, 177, 178, 179, 180, 181, 182, 184, 185, 186, 188, 189, 193, 194, 195, 196, 199, 200, 201, 202, 204, 206, 208, 211, 213, 214, 215, 216, 217, 218, 220, 221, 229, 230, 231, 233, 235, 238, 239, 240, 241, 245, 246, 247, 250, 251, 253, 255, 256, 258, 260, 263, 265, 267, 269.

IREMONGER, James; *Eng.* RHB/RM. b 5 Mar 1876. (Norton, Yorks), d 25 Mar 1956 (West Bridgford, Notts). 432, 435, 437, 443, 444, 446.

IRONMONGER, Herbert; *Qld & Vic.* LHB/LM/SLA. b 7 Apr 1882 (Pine Mountain, Qld), d 31 May 1971 (St Kilda, Vic). 399, 405, 471, 472, 473, 484, 485, 488, 489, 491, 493, 495, 496, 498, 501, 511, 520, 525, 591, 592, 598, 600, 635, 636, 638, 641, 646, 647, 648, 649, 651, 654, 656, 659, 661, 663, 670, 672, 678, 685, 689, 692, 695, 700, 703, 704, 712, 714, 719, 723, 725, 728, 730, 734, 735, 738, 742, 745, 747, 749, 752, 756, 760, 763, 764, 765, 766, 773, 774, 776, 778, 783, 786, 789, 792, 797, 799, 800, 804, 805, 808, 810, 813, 818.

IVES, William Francis; *NSW*. RHB/RFM. b 14 Nov 1896 (Glebe, NSW), d 23 Mar 1975 (Newport Beach, NSW). 499, 500, 501, 503, 522, 529, 537.

IVORY, Wilfred Charles; *Rest of Australia*. /WK. b 12 Sep 1888 (Sth Yarra, Vic), d 13 Oct 1975 (Nth Brighton, Vic). 428.

JACKSON, Archibald; *NSW*. RHB. b 5 Sep 1909 (Rutherglen, Scotland), d 16 Feb 1933 (Clayfield, Qld). 618, 620, 622, 623, 626, 628, 630, 633, 634, 638, 642, 644, 646, 651, 653, 655, 657, 663, 666, 667, 670, 673, 675, 679, 680, 683, 686, 688, 690, 700, 709, 712, 713, 715, 718, 720, 723, 725, 728, 734.

JACKSON, Arthur Enderby; *West Aust*. RHB. b 6 Jan 1872 (Kapunda, SA), d 29 Jun 1935 (Cottesloe, WA). 242.

JACKSON, John; *Eng*. RHB/RF(r). b 21 May 1833 (Bungay, Suffolk), d 4 Nov 1901 (Liverpool, Eng). 15.

JACKSON, Victor Edward; *NSW*. RHB/OB. b 25 Oct 1916 (Sydney), d 30 Jan 1965 (near Manildra, NSW). 870, 880, 881, 884, 888, 892, 894, 897, 901, 902, 906, 907, 913, 914, 917, 953, 954, 955, 958, 959, 961, 962, 963.

JACOMB, John Newton; *Vic*. LHB. b 1843 (   ), d 5 Nov 1891 (Walhalla, Vic). 11.

JAKINS, James Albert; *Tas*. RHB/RM. b 1 Oct 1886 (Hawthorn, Vic), d 12 Dec 1948 (Wivenhoe, Tas). 485.

JAMES, Alec Pearce; *Sth Aust*. /RFM. b May 1889 (Neath, Wales), d 1961 (Newton Abbot, Devon). 487, 489, 490, 495.

JAMES, Eric Lisle; *Tas*. b 21 Oct 1881 (Low Head, Tas), d   (   ). 305.

JAMES, Gerald Thomas Henry; *Tas*. RHB/RFM. b 22 Mar 1908 (New Norfolk, Tas), d 24 Dec 1967 (Hobart). 669, 676, 693, 694, 701, 705, 706, 707, 708, 721, 722, 729, 731, 737, 739, 754, 755, 758, 759, 782, 785, 802, 812, 819, 825, 826, 839, 856, 859, 865, 866, 918, 919, 929.

JAMES, Kenneth Cecil; *NZ*. RHB/WK. b 12 Mar 1904 (Wellington, NZ), d 21 Aug 1976 (Palmertson Nth, NZ). 610, 633.

JAMES, Ronald Victor; *NSW*. RHB/LM. b 23 May 1920 (Paddington, NSW), d 28 Apr 1983 (Auburn, NSW). 921, 924, 930, 932, 933, 964.

JAMES, Sidney Victor Albert; *Tas*. RHB/RFM. b 26 Oct 1895 (Adelaide), d 3 Aug 1966 (Canterbury, Vic). 590.

JAMIESON, Dudley Garfield; *Sth Aust*. RHB/RM. b 4 Jul 1912 (Redruth, SA), d 14 Jan 1979 (Burnside, SA). 751, 753, 761, 767, 775, 780, 784, 787.

JAMIESON, Walter Angus Bethune; *Tas*. RHB/RM(r). b 21 Jul 1828 (Plenty, Tas), d 28 Dec 1881 (Plenty, Tas). 7, 8.

JANSAN, Ernest William; *NSW*. RHB. b 26 August 1874 (Gulgong, NSW), d 31 May 1945 (Leichhardt, NSW). 243, 249, 312.

JARDINE, Douglas Robert; *Eng*. RHB/LB. b 23 Oct 1900 (Bombay, India), d 18 Jun 1958 (Montreux, Switzerland). 650, 654, 655, 657, 659, 661, 665, 668, 671, 673, 678, 680, 771, 772, 775, 776, 779, 781, 785, 789, 792, 796, 797, 799, 801.

JARVIS, Alfred; *Sth Aust*. RHB/RFM. Brother of A.H.Jarvis. b 15 Feb 1868 (Hindmarsh, SA), d 12 Aug 1938 (Semaphore, SA). 132, 136, 137, 139, 142, 143, 148, 154, 156, 157, 160, 161, 164, 166, 167, 170, 172, 175, 180, 187, 188, 191, 192, 195, 198, 199, 201, 209, 212, 216, 222, 223, 227, 228, 230, 232, 233, 234, 241, 242, 244, 246, 248, 250, 253, 255, 257, 258, 261, 264, 265, 269, 276, 287, 333, 335.

JARVIS, Arthur Harwood; *Sth Aust*. RHB/WK. Brother of A.Jarvis. b 19 Oct 1860 (Hindmarsh, SA), d 15 Nov 1933 (Hindmarsh, SA). 35, 49, 50, 60, 70, 72, 75, 80, 84, 86, 88, 90, 94, 96, 97, 100, 105, 112, 119, 120, 124, 125, 126, 132, 137, 139, 142, 143, 148, 154, 156, 157, 160, 164, 166, 167, 172, 179, 180, 181, 184, 187, 189, 191, 192, 195, 201, 203, 232, 233, 234, 241, 242, 246, 248, 250, 254, 255, 257, 258.

JARVIS, Carlisle Melrose Byron; *West Aust*. RHB. b 10 Dec 1906 (East Fremantle), d 6 Nov 1979 (Mt Lawley, WA). 771.

JARVIS, Harwood Samuel Coombe; *Sth Aust*. RHB/WK. Son of A.H.Jarvis. b 30 Aug 1884 (Brompton, SA), d 10 Oct 1936 (Port Pirie, SA). 329, 330.

JEFFREY, Clifton Linley; *Tas*. RHB/RM. b 10 Jan 1913 (Hobart), d 11 Feb 1987 (Launceston). 791, 819, 825, 826, 856, 865, 866, 885, 918, 919, 927, 929.

JEFFREYS, Arthur Frederick; *NSW*. RHB. b 7 Apr 1848 (London), d 4 Feb 1906 (Lasham, Hampshire). 26.

JEFFREYS, John Alan; *West Aust*. RHB. Brother of K.S.Jeffreys. b 17 Apr 1913 (Fremantle, WA), d 3 Nov 1943 (Shipham, Somerset). 900, 904, 920, 950.

JEFFREYS, Keith Stanley; *West Aust*. RHB. Brother of J.A.Jeffreys. b 18 Jan 1921 (Bridgetown, WA). 920, 936, 937, 950, 951.

JENNINGS, Claude Burrows; *Sth Aust & Qld*. RHB/WK. b 5 Jun 1884 (East St Kilda, Vic), d 20 Jun 1950 (Adelaide). 283, 287, 290, 291, 294, 296, 298, 311, 313, 315, 318, 319, 325, 327, 337, 341, 342, 349, 352, 355, 370, 405, 409, 411, 429, 435, 437, 452.

JENNINGS, Henry John; *Vic*. LHB. b 9 Apr 1849 (Launceston), d 6 Jun 1925 (St Kilda, Vic). 27.

JESSOP, Gilbert Laird; *Eng*. RHB/RF. b 19 May 1874 (Cheltenham, Glos), d 11 May 1955 (Fordington, Dorset). 261, 262, 263, 266, 268, 270, 272, 273, 275, 276.

JINKS, Allan; *Vic*. RHB/OB. Brother of F.Jinks. b 29 Dec 1913 (Carlton, Vic). 859, 865.

JINKS, Frederick; *Vic*. RHB. Brother of A.Jinks. b 6 May 1909 (Eaglehawk, Vic). 755.

JOHNS, Alfred Edward; *Vic*. LHB/WK. b 22 Jan 1868 (Hawthorn, Vic), d 13 Feb 1934 (Melbourne). 190, 196, 198, 200, 202, 203, 206, 210, 212, 214, 218, 222, 226, 228, 231, 232, 235, 239, 240.

JOHNSON, Eric Alfred; *Sth Aust*. RHB. b 11 Jul 1902 (Nth Norwood, SA), d 10 Jan 1976 (Adelaide). 631, 632, 635, 637, 664, 702.

JOHNSON, Francis Barry; *NSW*. RHB/LB. b 21 May 1880 (   ), d 28 May 1951 (Longueville, NSW). 296, 298, 312, 315, 319, 320, 322, 331, 346, 347, 351, 355, 358, 364, 375, 379.

JOHNSON, Ian William; *Vic*. RHB/OB. Son of W.J.Johnson. b 8 Dec 1918 (Nth Melbourne). 856, 859, 927, 929, 939, 940, 942, 945, 948, 949, 952, 956, 957, 960, 961, 962.

JOHNSON, Peter Randall; *Eng*. RHB/RF. b 5 Aug 1880 (Wellington, NZ), d 1 Jul 1959 (Sidmouth, Devon). 288, 289, 290.

JOHNSON, William James; *Vic*. RHB/OB. b 22 Sep 1884 (Footscray, Vic), d 14 Aug 1941 (Middle Park, Vic). 570.

JOHNSTON, Aubrey Edmund; *NSW*. RHB. b 7 Sep 1883 (   ), d 16 Jun 1960 (Manly, NSW). 316, 317, 322.

JOHNSTONE, Richard Gordon; *Vic*. b 9 Feb 1885 (Malvern, Vic), d 9 Nov 1961 (Geelong, Vic). 402, 403, 464.

JONES, Arthur Harold; *Qld*. RHB/LB. b 17 Dec 1874 (, Qld), d   (in camp, Salisbury Plains, UK). 208, 414, 416.

JONES, Arthur Owen; *Eng*. RHB/LB. b 16 Aug 1872 (Shelton, Notts), d 21 Dec 1914 (Dunstable, Bedfordshire). 261, 262, 263, 266, 268, 270, 272, 273, 274, 275, 276, 348, 349, 350, 351, 353, 365, 366, 367, 368, 370, 371.

JONES, Charles Frederick; *Vic*. /WK. b 9 Feb 1870 (Williamstown, Vic), d 25 Mar 1957 (Williamstown, Vic). 332.

JONES, Ernest; *Sth Aust & West Aust*. RHB/RF. b 30 Sep 1869 (Auburn, SA), d 23 Nov 1943 (Adelaide). 154, 156, 157, 160, 161, 164, 166, 167, 170, 172, 175, 177, 180, 187, 188, 191, 192, 195, 198, 199, 200, 201, 203, 204, 207, 209, 212, 213, 215, 216, 217, 220, 222, 223, 225, 227, 228, 230, 232, 233, 234, 239, 240, 241, 244, 246, 248, 250, 253, 254, 261, 264, 265, 266, 268, 269, 276, 279, 282, 283, 346, 347, 348.

JONES, John Raymond; *West Aust*. LHB/OB. b 10 May 1899 (Clunes, Vic), d 14 Mar 1991 (Hamilton Hill, WA). 820, 821, 822, 823, 824, 827, 842, 843, 844, 845.

JONES, Sydney; *NSW*. RHB. b   (   ), d   (   ). 14, 16, 21.

JONES, Samuel Percy; *NSW & Qld*. RHB/RFM. b 1 Aug 1861 (Sydney), d 14 Jul 1951 (Auckland, NZ). 46, 48, 51, 55, 56, 58, 63, 67, 71, 72, 73, 74, 77, 79, 80, 82, 83, 84, 85, 86, 87, 89, 94, 95, 96, 97, 98, 99, 101, 108, 114, 115, 116, 117, 118, 120, 121, 122, 124, 125, 126, 129, 130, 131, 135, 136, 145, 148, 151, 154, 155, 185, 186, 208, 224, 243, 245.

JONES, Victor Clarence; *West Aust*. b 11 May 1881 (Bairnsdale, Vic), d 20 Jul 1923 (Mt Lawley, WA). 335.

JONES, William George; *Sth Aust*. /LFM. b 13 May 1864 (Hindmarsh, SA), d 16 Jul 1924 (Adelaide). 60, 75.

JORDAN, Frank Slater; *NSW*. RHB/RFM. b 19 Sep 1905 (Darlington, NSW). 634, 637, 644, 666, 674, 679.

JOSE, Gilbert Edgar; *Sth Aust*. RHB. b 1 Nov 1898 (Taichow, China), d 27 Mar 1942 (Singapore). 497, 531.

JUNOR, Leonard John; *Vic*. RHB. b 27 Apr 1914 (Thornbury, Vic). 699, 754, 755, 768, 819, 839, 903, 915.

JUNOR, Robert Johnston; *Vic*. RHB/LBG. b 10 Jan 1888 (Marcus Hill, Vic), d 26 Jul 1957 (Heidelberg, Vic). 492.

JUPP, Henry; *Eng*. RHB/RF(r). b 19 Nov 1841 (Dorking, Surrey), d 8 Apr 1889 (Bermondsey, Surrey). 33, 34.

KAY, William Malcolm; *Qld*. RHB/RFM. b 4 May 1893 (Gympie, Qld), d 7 Jul 1973 (Taringa, Qld). 506, 522, 529.

KEATING, James Leslie; *Vic*. RHB/RM. b 1 Oct 1891 (Collingwood, Vic), d 13 Mar 1962 (Richmond, Vic). 497, 498, 501, 502, 504, 505, 508, 525, 526, 541, 542, 545, 552, 569, 578, 591.

KEKWICK, Edwin Huntley; *Sth Aust*. RHB. b 5 Mar 1875 (Port MacDonnell, SA), d 29 Aug 1950 (Adelaide). 248, 250.

KELLEWAY, Charles; *NSW*. RHB/RFM. b 25 Apr 1889 (Lismore, NSW), d 16 Nov 1944 (Lindfield, NSW). 355, 364, 375, 379, 380, 381, 382, 383, 395, 396, 397, 405, 408, 412, 413, 415, 417, 419, 422, 424, 425, 426, 428,437, 438, 439, 440, 441, 442, 445, 447, 448, 462, 463, 466, 470, 472, 474, 475, 477, 479, 481, 487, 488, 490, 491, 500, 501, 503, 505, 514, 518, 519, 520, 521, 523, 524, 527, 530, 538, 539, 546, 552, 555, 561, 563, 571, 583, 585, 587, 591, 593, 594, 595, 604, 606, 607, 612, 613, 651, 655, 659, 663, 674.

KELLICK, Charles Moore; *NSW*. LHB. Brother of J.Kellick. b 21 Nov 1842 (Sydney), d 27 Mar 1918 (Strathfield, NSW). 16, 26.

KELLICK, James; *NSW*. Brother of C.M.Kellick. b 24 Aug 1840 (Sydney), d 8 Aug 1926 (Sydney). 20.

KELLY, James Joseph; *NSW*. RHB/WK. b 10 May 1867 (Port Melbourne, Vic), d 14 Aug 1938 (Bellevue Hill, NSW). 174, 178, 180, 182, 185, 188, 193, 194, 195, 196, 199, 200, 201, 202, 204, 206, 211, 213, 214, 215, 217, 218, 220, 221, 223, 225, 229, 230, 231, 233, 235, 239, 240, 241, 243, 245, 246, 247, 250, 251, 253, 255, 256, 258, 260, 263, 265, 266, 267, 268, 269, 270, 273, 275, 279, 280, 283, 284, 289, 293, 296, 297, 298, 299, 301, 302, 304, 307, 308, 310, 315, 316, 320, 331, 344.

KELLY, Otto Harvey; *West Aust*. RHB/OB. Brother of W.H.Kelly. b 15 May 1880 (Sandridge, Vic), d 30 Jul 1946 (Mt Lawley, WA). 346, 347, 371.

KELLY, Richard Terence Bonynge; *Vic*. Brother of W.L.Kelly. b 21 Mar 1870 (Ballan, Vic), d 27 Dec 1941 (St Kilda, Vic). 205.

KELLY, Thomas Joseph Dart; *Vic*. RHB/RaB. b 3 May 1844 (County Waterford, Ireland), d 20 Jul 1893 (Melbourne). 15, 16, 18, 19, 20, 21, 22, 24, 25, 28, 30, 34, 38, 48, 61, 63.

KELLY, William Harvey; *West Aust*. Brother of O.H.Kelly. b 24 Mar 1883 (St Kilda, Vic), d (Croydon, Vic). 333, 335.

KELLY, William Lucius; *Vic*. Brother of R.T.B.Kelly. b 20 Jan 1875 (Rosedale, Vic), d 27 Dec 1968 (Bulla, Vic). 369.

KEMP, Benjamin Charles Ernest; *Sth Aust & Vic*. LHB/SLA. b 30 Jan 1864 (Plymouth, Devon), d 3 Dec 1940 (Albert Park, Vic). 81, 90, 100, 105, 144, 219.

KEMP, Leonard Denton; *Vic*. RHB/RM. b 6 Jun 1909 (Malvern, Vic). 788, 791, 798, 812, 814.

KENDALL, Thomas Kingston; *Vic & Tas*. LHB/LM/SLA. b 24 Aug 1851 (Bedford, Eng), d 17 Aug 1924 (Hobart). 33, 34, 44, 128.

KENNY, Arthur; *Vic*. RHB/LB. b 9 Aug 1878 (Emerald Hill, Vic), d 2 Aug 1934 (Sth Melbourne). 394, 397, 399, 401, 402, 403, 404, 410, 414, 415, 422, 423.

KEOGH, Eustace Julian; *West Aust*. b c 1867 ( ), d 18 Feb 1925 (Sth Yarra, Vic). 242.

KERMODE, Alexander; *NSW*. RHB/RFM. b 15 May 1876 (Sydney), d 17 Jul 1934 (Balmain, NSW). 271, 272.

KERR, John Lambert; *NZ*. RHB. b 28 Dec 1910 (Dannevirke, NZ). 898, 899, 901.

KETTLE, John Louis; *NSW*. b 3 Dec 1830 (Sydney), d 30 Oct 1891 (Newtown, NSW). 10, 11, 12.

KIERNAN, Christopher; *Vic*. RHB/RM. b 23 Mar 1878 (Fitzroy, Vic), d 2 Dec 1925 (Nth Fitzroy, Vic). 398, 464, 471, 478, 481, 483, 492, 495, 496, 497.

KIERSE, John Michael; *Sth Aust*. RHB/RFM. b 11 Jan 1918 (Nhill, Vic). 950.

KILNER, Roy; *Eng*. LHB/SLA. b 17 Oct 1890 (Wombwell, Yorks), d 5 Apr 1928 (Barnsley, Yorks). 572, 576, 577, 582, 587, 589, 590, 592, 593, 594, 595, 596.

KIMPTON, Robert Webb; *West Aust*. RHB. b 5 Jan 1914 (Essendon, Vic). 845.

KING, James Francis; *Sth Aust*. RHB/RF(r). b 23 May 1851 (Hindmarsh, SA), d 28 Jun 1921 (Hindmarsh, SA). 25, 35, 45, 50, 60, 70, 75, 81.

KING, Percy Macgregor; *NSW*. RHB. b 2 Sep 1889 (Richmond, Vic), d 9 Dec 1967 (Rose Bay, NSW). 510.

KING, Stuart Patrick; *Vic*. RHB/WK. b 22 Apr 1906 (Ararat, Vic), d 28 Feb 1943 (on action, Coral Sea). 621, 623, 625, 629, 643, 705, 729, 731, 780, 786, 798, 802.

KINGTON, Philip Oliphant; *Vic*. /WK. b 17 Dec 1832 (Eng), d 2 Jul 1892 (Eng). 4.

KINLOCH, John; *NSW*. b 1833 ( ), d 9 Apr 1897 (Camperdown, NSW). 9, 11, 12.

KINNEAR, Joseph David; *Vic*. LHB/LM. Brother of W.G.Kinnear. b 12 Feb 1912 (West Brunswick, Vic), d 14 Dec 1981 (Moreland, Vic). 754, 755.

KINNEAR, William George; *Vic*. RHB. Brother of J.D.Kinnear. b 19 Aug 1914 (West Brunswick, Vic), d 7 Dec 1982 (West Brunswick, Vic). 865.

KINNEIR, Septimus; *Eng*. LHB/SLA. b 13 May 1871 (Corsham, Wiltshire), d 16 Oct 1928 (Birmingham, Eng). 432, 437, 438, 443, 444.

KIPPAX, Alan Falconer; *NSW*. RHB/LB. b 25 May 1897 (Paddington, NSW), d 4 Sep 1972 (Bellevue Hill, NSW). 496, 498, 499, 500, 501, 503, 505, 507, 517, 523, 546, 548, 549, 551, 552, 555, 561, 563, 567, 568, 571, 577, 580, 582, 586, 588, 594, 595, 599, 604, 606, 607, 612, 613, 618, 620, 622, 623, 626, 628, 630, 633, 634, 637, 638, 642, 644, 646, 651, 653, 655, 659, 661, 663, 665, 667, 673, 675, 680, 686, 688, 690, 692, 696, 697, 700, 707, 708, 709, 711, 712, 713, 715, 718, 720, 723, 725, 728, 730, 734, 736, 738, 743, 747, 756, 760, 762, 765, 774, 777, 779, 781, 784, 786, 793, 803, 805, 806, 809, 810, 815, 816, 818, 825, 826, 827, 828, 832, 833, 836, 838, 849, 851.

KIRKWOOD, Harold Peter; *Sth Aust*. RHB/LB. b 15 Sep 1882 (Orroroo, SA), d 19 May 1943 (Unley, SA). 264, 265, 269, 276, 279, 282, 283, 287, 430, 431, 474, 476, 479.

KITSON, Eugene Henry; *Sth Aust*. RHB. b 28 Nov 1889 (Adelaide), d 4 Aug 1962 (Heidelberg, Vic). 453.

KLOSE, Tom Elliott; *Sth Aust*. RHB/LM. b 22 Jan 1918 (Nth Adelaide), d 13 Jun 1986 (Nailsworth, SA). 939, 941, 943, 945, 946, 947, 950, 951, 955, 956.

KNIGHT, Albert Ernest; *Eng*. RHB. b 8 Oct 1872 (Leicester, Eng), d 25 Apr 1946 (Edmonton, London). 292, 295, 301, 303, 305, 306, 307, 308, 310, 311.

KNILL, William; *Sth Aust*. RHB/WK. b 28 Jan 1859 (, Vic), d 8 Jul 1940 (Nth Adelaide). 50, 60, 70, 90, 100, 105.

KNOWLES, Eric Charles; *Qld*. RHB/RM. b 9 Mar 1896 (Toowoomba, Qld), d 15 Sep 1978 (Southport, Qld). 614, 629, 653, 658.

KORTLANG, Harry Herbert Lorenz; *Vic*. RHB. b 12 Mar 1880 (Carlton, Vic), d 15 Feb 1961 (Cottesloe, WA). 397, 399, 401, 402, 403, 404, 407, 410, 411, 414, 415, 422, 423, 428, 430, 432, 434, 439, 445.

KROGER, Henry Jack; *Vic*. RHB/WK. b 27 Jun 1906 (Caulfield, Vic), d 16 Jul 1987 (Malvern, Vic). 856, 859.

KYLE, James Henderson; *Vic*. RHB/RFM. b 29 May 1879 (Comaida, Vic), d 11 Jan 1919 (Albert Park, Vic). 369, 384, 385, 392, 399, 401, 402, 403, 415, 422, 423, 428, 430, 432, 434, 439, 445.

LAFRANTZ, Errold Campbell; *Qld*. LHB/LB. b 25 May 1919 (Brisbane). 964.

LAMASON, John Rider; *NZ*. RHB/OB. b 29 Oct 1905 (Wellington, NZ), d 25 Jun 1961 (Wellington, NZ). 899, 901.

LAMPARD, Albert Wallis; *Vic.* RHB/LBG/WK. b 3 Jul 1885 (Richmond, Vic), d 11 Jan 1984 (Armadale, Vic). 385, 398, 401, 402, 403, 449, 451, 478, 481, 504, 506, 507, 509, 511, 513, 515, 520, 525, 535, 536, 538, 539.

LAMPE, William Henry Warwick; *NSW.* RHB/LF. b 29 Aug 1902 (Wagga Wagga, NSW). 640, 679.

LANE, John Bayley; *NSW.* RHB/WK. b 7 Jan 1886 (Petersham, NSW), d 30 Aug 1937 (Manly, NSW). 359, 462, 463.

LANG, Harold King; *West Aust.* RHB. b 23 Aug 1905 (Stawell, Vic), d 23 Apr 1991 (Nedlands, WA). 709, 740.

LANGRIDGE, James; *Eng.* LHB/SLA. b 10 Jul 1906 (Newick, Sussex), d 10 Sep 1966 (Brighton, Sussex). 845, 847, 848, 849, 850, 851.

LANIGAN, Emmet Robert; *Vic.* RHB/RFM. b 6 Sep 1909 (Maffra, Vic). 768.

LANIGAN, Joseph Patrick; *West Aust.* RHB/LB. b 8 Jul 1891 (Mogumber, WA), d 30 Sep 1972 (Glendalough, WA). 542, 543.

LANSDOWN, Albert Joseph Walter; *Vic.* RHB/LB. Brother of H.C.Lansdown. b 10 Mar 1897 (Nth Fitzroy, Vic), d 7 Jan 1979 (Frankston, Vic). 553, 605, 611, 647, 656, 660, 693, 694.

LANSDOWN, Harold Charles; *Vic.* LHB. Brother of A.J.W.Lansdown. b 18 Feb 1900 (Nth Fitzroy, Vic), d 18 Apr 1957 (Ivanhoe, Vic). 570, 670, 672.

LARWOOD, Harold; *Eng.* RHB/RF. b 14 Nov 1904 (Nuncargate, Nottingham). 652, 654, 655, 657, 659, 661, 665, 668, 669, 673, 678, 680, 681, 771, 775, 778, 781, 782, 789, 792, 796, 797, 799.

LAVER, Frank Jonas; *Vic.* RHB/RFM. b 7 Dec 1869 (Castelmaine, Vic), d 24 Sep 1919 (East Melbourne). 142, 156, 159, 160, 165, 166, 168, 170, 173, 175, 178, 182, 187, 190, 192, 194, 196, 198, 202, 203, 206, 207, 212, 226, 228, 231, 232, 235, 237, 239, 240, 241, 247, 248, 251, 253, 254, 256, 257, 260, 262, 264, 266, 267, 271, 274, 280, 282, 284, 286, 287, 288, 292, 294, 297, 299, 304, 306, 313, 314, 316, 318, 320, 328, 329, 331, 332, 334, 337, 340, 365, 369, 372, 374, 377, 378, 381, 392, 394, 396, 404, 407, 410, 415, 422, 430, 432.

LAW, Rupert W   ; *Qld.* RHB/LB. b 24 Feb 1890 (, NSW), d   (   ). 465, 467.

LAWES, Charles Henry Wickham; *NSW.* RHB/OB. b 9 Dec 1899 (Cobar, NSW). 588.

LAWLOR, John; *Vic.* RHB. b Jan 1864 (Ireland), d 29 Jan 1908 (Melbourne). 60, 75, 81.

LAWRENCE, Charles; *Eng & NSW.* RHB/RM(r). b 16 Dec 1828 (Hoxton, Middlesex), d 20 Dec 1916 (Canterbury, Vic). 13, 14, 16, 17, 18, 21.

LAWSON, Robert James; *Vic.* RHB. b 23 Mar 1901 (Sth Melbourne), d 28 Nov 1974 (West Brunswick, Vic). 729, 731.

LAYCOCK, Henry; *Sth Aust.* RHB/LB. b 31 Oct 1901 (Edwardstown, SA), d 6 Aug 1983 (Port Noarlunga). 751.

LEABEATER, Leonard Raymond; *NSW.* RHB. b 10 Jul 1906 (Parramatta, NSW). 706, 751, 752, 757.

LEAK, Brian Hedley; *Sth Aust.* RHB. b 5 May 1917 (Hawthorn, SA). 866, 880, 904, 916, 955, 956, 957, 963.

LEAK, Ernest Howard; *Sth Aust.* RHB. b 28 Oct 1872 (Rapid Bay, SA), d 22 Aug 1945 (Adelaide). 198, 199, 207, 244, 246, 254, 255, 261, 264, 265, 394, 395.

LEAK, Stanley Garfield; *Sth Aust.* RHB. b 21 Mar 1886 (Goodwood, SA), d 10 Jan 1963 (Millswood, SA). 453.

LE COUTER, Philip Ridgeway; *Vic.* RHB/LBG. b 26 Jun 1885 (Kyneton, Vic), d 30 Jun 1958 (Gunnedah, NSW). 496, 497, 498.

§LEARY, John Andrew; *Qld.* b 6 Oct 1867 (Frying Pan, near Bathurst, NSW), d 16 Jan 1940 (Herston, Qld). 234.

LEATHER, Thomas William; *Vic.* RHB/RFM. b 2 Jun 1910 (Rutherglen, Scotland), d 10 May 1991 (Prahran, Vic). 819, 821, 823, 839, 867.

LEDWARD, John Allan; *Vic.* RHB/RM. b 22 Apr 1909 (East Melbourne). 839, 856, 859, 864, 879, 881, 887, 888, 893, 896, 899, 900, 905, 907, 909, 912, 914, 916, 922, 923, 925, 928.

LEE, Clarence Leslie; *Tas.* LHB/SLA. b 28 Dec 1890 (Cressy, Tas), d 5 Feb 1959 (Invermay, Tas). 615.

LEE, Ian Somerville; *Vic.* LHB. b 24 Mar 1914 (Brunswick, Vic), d 14 Apr 1976 (Port Melbourne, Vic). 750, 766, 768, 812, 814, 819, 821, 823, 838, 841, 848, 852, 854, 858, 862, 863, 864, 872, 874, 879, 881, 887, 893, 896, 899, 900, 905, 907, 909, 912, 914, 916, 917, 922, 923, 925, 928, 933, 934, 935, 936, 937, 939, 940, 942, 945, 948, 949, 952, 956, 957, 959, 960, 961, 962.

LEE, Philip Keith; *Sth Aust.* RHB/RM/OB. b 15 Sep 1904 (Gladstone, SA), d 9 Aug 1980 (Adelaide). 609, 625, 626, 631, 635, 637, 639, 641, 644, 645, 656, 664, 702, 704, 710, 711, 716, 720, 724, 726, 733, 735, 739, 741, 745, 749, 753, 761, 766, 767, 769, 775, 778, 780, 784, 787, 794, 795, 798, 799, 801, 804, 805, 806, 809, 811, 813, 816, 817, 829, 830, 832, 834, 835, 841.

LEESON, Henry Foley; *Qld.* RHB/WK. b 20 Jul 1909 (Mt Morgan, Qld), d 25 Jun 1950 (Logan River, Qld). 696, 715, 717, 719, 724, 790, 794, 803, 808, 811, 815, 830, 831, 834.

LEGGE, Geoffrey Bevington; *Eng.* RHB. b 26 Jan 1903 (Bromley, Kent), d 21 Nov 1940 (Brampford Speke, Devon). 686, 687.

LEHMANN, Charles Albert; *West Aust.* RHB/RaB. b   (   ), d   (   ). 453, 454.

LESLIE, Charles Frederick Henry; *Eng.* RHB/RF. b 8 Dec 1861 (London), d 12 Feb 1921 (Westminster, London). 61, 62, 64, 65, 66, 68, 69.

LETCHER, Charles; *Vic.* /LFM. b c 1868 (   ), d Nov 1916 (, WA). 123, 125, 152, 169.

LETHBORG, Gordon John; *Tas.* RHB/OB. b 23 Nov 1907 (Scottsdale, Tas), d 31 Aug 1989 (Launceston). 701, 705, 706, 788.

LETTE, Henry Elms; *Tas.* /LaB(u-arm). b 10 Aug 1829 (Curramore, Tas), d 15 Aug 1892 (Launceston). 2.

LEVY, Roy Mark; *Qld.* LHB/RM/WK. b 20 Apr 1906 (Sydney), d 12 Dec 1965 (Clayfield, Qld). 672, 677, 683, 687, 689, 691, 696, 794, 796, 803, 807, 808, 811, 815, 817, 830, 831, 834, 836, 840, 846, 850, 852, 855, 857.

LEWIS, Arthur; *Vic.* b   (   ), d   (   ). 4.

LEWIS, John William; *Qld.* RHB/RFM. b 21 Nov 1867 (St George, Qld), d Sep 1939 (   ). 185, 193, 277, 312, 314, 317, 323, 334, 393, 399, 405, 414, 416, 429.

LEWIS, Lawrence Robert; *Sth Aust.* RHB. b 24 May 1889 (Cherry Gardens, SA), d 2 Sep 1947 (Prospect, SA). 631, 632.

LEWIS, Oswald Hoddle; *NSW.* RHB/RF(u-arm). Brother of T.H.Lewis. b 28 Feb 1833 (Sydney), d 28 Apr 1895 (Darlinghurst, NSW). 5, 6, 9, 11.

LEWIS, Percy Markham; *Vic.* RHB/WK. b 13 Mar 1864 (Ballarat, Vic), d 24 Nov 1922 (St Kilda, Vic). 71, 72, 73, 74, 76, 81, 83, 88, 90, 91, 100, 104, 119, 123, 125, 127, 128, 129, 132, 156, 158, 160, 162, 166, 169, 170, 178, 183, 187, 192, 194, 197.

LEWIS, Thomas Harvie; *NSW.* Brother of O.H.Lewis. b 1828 (London), d 19 Jun 1901 (Darlinghurst, NSW). 5, 6, 10.

LEYLAND, Morris; *Eng.* LHB/SLA. b 20 Jul 1900 (Harrogate, Yorks), d 1 Jan 1967 (Harrogate, Yorks). 650, 652, 654, 655, 658, 668, 669, 671, 675, 678, 680, 681, 771, 772, 775, 778, 781, 785, 789, 792, 793, 796, 797, 799, 801, 872, 873, 875, 876, 877, 878, 883, 889, 890, 892, 893, 895.

LIDDICUT, Arthur Edward; *Vic.* RHB/RFM. b 17 Oct 1891 (Fitzroy, Vic), d 8 Apr 1983 (Parkdale, Vic). 449, 451, 457, 504, 509, 511, 513, 515, 520, 525, 535, 536, 538, 545, 549, 550, 552, 554, 556, 562, 563, 566, 568, 569, 574, 576, 578, 588, 598, 600, 605, 607, 613, 619, 621, 623, 625, 628, 629, 638, 648, 649, 693, 694, 754, 755, 788, 791.

LILLEY, Arthur Frederick Augustus; *Eng.* RHB/WK/RM. b 28 Nov 1866 (Birmingham, Eng), d 17 Nov 1929 (Bristol, Glos). 261, 262, 263, 266, 268, 270, 272, 273, 274, 275, 276, 291, 293, 295, 297, 301, 302, 303, 305, 307, 308, 310.

LILLYWHITE, James; *Eng.* LHB/LSM. b 23 Feb 1842 (Westhampnett, Sussex), d 25 Oct 1929 (Westerton, Sussex). 32, 33, 34.

LIMB, Allen; *Tas.* LHB/WK. b 29 Sep 1886 (Gawler, SA), d 1 Jul 1975 (Battery Point, Tas). 570, 669, 674.

LINDWALL, Raymond Russell; *NSW.* RHB/RF. b 3 Oct 1921 (Mascot, NSW). 964.

LINNEY, George Frederick; *Tas*. RHB/WK. b 18 Nov 1869 (Guildford, Surrey), d 5 Nov 1927 (Weston-super-Mare, Somerset). 469.

LISTER, Charles; *Vic*. b 7 Nov 1811 (   ), d 18 Aug 1873 (Alderbury, Wiltshire). 1, 2.

LISTON, George Grieve; *Sth Aust*. RHB. b 29 Apr 1860 (Tanunda, SA), d 6 Jun 1929 (Kent Town, SA). 105.

LITSTER, John Lewis; *Qld*. RHB/RM. b 2 Feb 1904 (Townsville, Qld), d 11 Mar 1982 (Railway Estate, Townsville, Qld). 636, 642, 647, 658, 662, 664, 666, 717, 794, 796.

LITTLE, Raymond Cecil James; *NSW*. RHB. b 7 Oct 1915 (Armidale, NSW). 840, 843, 846, 853, 854, 857, 861, 862.

LIVINGSTON, Leonard; *NSW*. LHB/WK. b 3 May 1920 (Sydney). 964.

LLEWELLYN, Charles Bennett; *Sth Afr*. LHB/LSM. b 26 Sep 1876 (Pietermaritzburg, Sth Afr), d 7 Jun 1964 (Chertsey, Surrey). 406, 407, 408, 409, 411, 413, 417, 419, 421, 424, 426, 427.

LOCHNER, Augustus Meyer; *Tas*. b 1825 (Eng), d 20 Feb 1865 (Plumstead Common, Kent). 3.

LOCKWOOD, William Henry; *Eng*. RHB/RF. b 25 Mar 1868 (Old Radford, Notts), d 26 Apr 1932 (Radford, Notts). 172, 174, 176, 177, 179, 181, 184, 189, 190, 191.

LOCKWOOD, William Thomas; *West Aust*. RHB. b 26 Jun 1868 (Geelong, Vic), d 29 Aug 1953 (Tuart Hill, WA). 242.

LOCKYER, Thomas; *Eng*. RHB/RFM(r). b 1 Nov 1826 (Croydon, Surrey), d 22 Dec 1869 (Croydon, Surrey). 15.

LODER, Roy; *NSW*. RHB. b 17 Nov 1898 (   ). 620, 653.

LOGAN, W   ; *Vic*.   /LM. b   (   ), d   (   ). 61, 110.

LOHMANN, George Alfred; *Eng*. RHB/RMF. b 2 Jun 1865 (Kensington, London), d 1 Dec 1901 (Matjesfontein, Sth Afr). 91, 92, 93, 94, 96, 97, 99, 101, 102, 103, 104, 107, 109, 110, 114, 116, 117, 120, 122, 143, 144, 145, 147, 150, 151, 152, 153.

LONERGAN, Albert Roy; *Sth Aust & NSW*. RHB. b 6 Dec 1909 (Maylands, WA), d 22 Oct 1956 (Adelaide). 684, 690, 702, 710, 711, 716, 726, 733, 735, 739, 741, 745, 751, 753, 761, 766, 767, 769, 772, 775, 780, 784, 787, 794, 795, 798, 801, 804, 809, 811, 813, 816, 817, 820, 829, 830, 832, 834, 835, 841, 849, 853, 854.

LONEY, Geoffrey Souter; *Tas*. RHB/OB. b 31 Mar 1894 (Campbelltown, NSW), d 7 Apr 1985 (Hobart). 553.

LONG, Edmund James; *NSW*. RHB/WK. b 28 Mar 1880 (Darlinghurst, NSW), d 8 Dec 1947 (Leichhardt, NSW). 436.

LONG, Thomas Tasman Thompson; *Qld*.   /LaB. b 11 Sep 1875 (at sea), d 20 Oct 1926 (Spring Hill, Qld). 208, 224, 314, 317.

LORD, John Carr; *Tas*. RHB. b 17 Aug 1844 (Hobart), d 25 May 1911 (Antill Ponds, Tas). 27.

LORD, Sidney; *Tas*. RHB/WK. b 20 Oct 1886 (   ), d   (   ). 492.

LOTON, Cecil Vernon; *West Aust*. RHB/WK. b 5 Jan 1906 (Upper Swan, WA). 597, 601.

LOTON, Morris William; *West Aust*. LHB. Cousin of C.V.Loton. b 18 Mar 1905 (Springhill, WA), d 2 Mar 1976 (Northam, WA). 573.

§LOUGH, William D   ; *NSW*. RHB. b 1886 (,NSW), d   (   ). 347.

LOUGHNAN, Austin Robert; *Vic*. RHB/RM. b 15 Jun 1851 (Hobart), d 9 Oct 1926 (Cheltenham, Vic). 22, 23, 26, 27, 29.

LOVE, Hampden Stanley Bray; *NSW & Vic*. RHB/WK. b 10 Aug 1895 (Balmain, NSW), d 22 Jul 1969 (Mosman, NSW). 522, 529, 534, 535, 538, 539, 553, 554, 556, 562, 566, 568, 574, 578, 591, 598, 600, 604, 607, 611, 613, 623, 625, 634, 640, 642, 653, 663, 697, 715, 717, 720, 751, 752, 757, 786, 790, 793, 795, 797.

LOVELOCK, Oswald Ifould; *West Aust*. LHB/WK. b 28 Aug 1911 (Highgate, WA), d 1 Aug 1981 (Subiaco, WA). 771, 772, 820, 821, 822, 823, 824, 827, 842, 843, 844, 845, 868, 869, 900, 903, 904, 920, 936, 937, 950, 951.

LOVERIDGE, Eustace Alfred; *Sth Aust*. RHB/RM/LB. b 14 Apr 1891 (Yongala, SA), d 29 Jul 1959 (Adelaide). 531, 536, 537, 541, 544.

LOVERIDGE, Walter David; *NSW*. RHB/WK. b 13 Sep 1867 (Sydney), d 6 Jan 1940 (East Brisbane). 278.

LOVETT, Henry Charles; *Tas*. LHB. b 3 Mar 1856 (Battery Point, Tas), d 20 May 1937 (Hobart). 35.

LOWE, Frederick; *Vic*. RHB/RM(r). b 7 Sep 1827 (Nottingham, Eng), d 15 Oct 1887 (Ararat, Vic). 4.

LOWRY, Jack Brown; *Vic*. RHB/LB. b 25 Nov 1916 (Lambton, Vic). 915.

LOWRY, Thomas Coleman; *Eng & NZ*. RHB/WK/OB. 17 Feb 1898 (Fernhill, NZ), d 20 Jul 1976 (Hastings, NZ). 543, 544, 555, 556, 557, 603, 605, 609, 610, 633, 899.

LOXTON, Colin Cameron; *Qld*. RHB/RFM. b 1 Jan 1914 (Brisbane). 905, 908, 910, 911.

LUCAS, Alfred Percy; *Eng*. RHB/RaB(r). b 20 Feb 1857 (Westminster, London), d 12 Oct 1923 (Great Waltham, Essex). 38, 39, 40, 41, 42.

LUCAS, Clyde Edward; *Tas*. RHB/OB. b 11 Aug 1898 (Kingston, Tas), d 12 Jan 1988 (Palm Beach, Qld). 570.

LUCAS, Edward; *Tas*. LHB. b 16 Jun 1848 (Kingston, Tas), d 19 Apr 1916 (Kingston, Tas). 35.

LUCAS, Frank Russell; *Sth Aust*. RHB/RFM. b 9 Nov 1888 (Port Pirie, SA), d 31 Aug 1941 (Adelaide). 500, 502, 503.

LUCAS, Thomas Turland; *Sth Aust*. b 18 Feb 1852 (Norwood, SA), d 13 Mar 1945 (Norwood, SA). 35.

LUGTON, Frank Leslie; *Vic*. RHB/RFM. b 4 Nov 1893 (Northcote, Vic), d 29 Jul 1916 (in action in France). 478, 481, 483, 484, 485.

LUSH, John Grantley; *NSW*. RHB/RF. b 14 Oct 1913 (Prahran, Vic), d 23 Aug 1985 (Sydney). 822, 881, 884, 888, 892, 894, 897, 901, 902, 944, 947, 949, 952.

LUSK, Hugh Butler; *NZ*. RHB. b 12 Jan 1866 (Mangonui, NZ), d 26 Feb 1944 (Napier, NZ). 237, 238.

LYONS, John James; *Sth Aust*. RHB/RM. b 21 May 1863 (Gawler, SA), d 21 Jul 1927 (Adelaide). 81, 90, 100, 102, 105, 112, 113, 119, 120, 121, 122, 124, 125, 126, 131, 132, 136, 137, 139, 142, 143, 147, 148, 150, 153, 154, 156, 157, 160, 164, 166, 167, 170, 172, 175, 177, 179, 180, 187, 188, 189, 191, 192, 195, 199, 200, 201, 203, 204, 207, 209, 212, 213, 216, 222, 223, 227, 228, 230, 232, 233, 234, 241, 244, 246.

LYTTELTON, Hon. Charles John; *Eng*. RHB/RM. b 8 Aug 1909 (London), d 20 Mar 1977 (Marylebone, London). 845, 847, 848, 850, 851.

McALISTER, Peter Alexander; *Vic*. RHB. b 11 Jul 1869 (Williamstown), d 10 May 1938 (Richmond, Vic). 228, 237, 244, 247, 248, 251, 254, 256, 257, 260, 262, 264, 267, 271, 274, 280, 282, 284, 286, 287, 288, 292, 294, 299, 304, 306, 308, 310, 313, 314, 316, 318, 320, 325, 328, 329, 332, 334, 337, 340, 341, 343, 345, 350, 352, 354, 356, 357, 358, 360, 361, 364, 366, 369, 374, 377, 378, 381, 382, 383, 392, 404.

McALLEN, Charles; *Tas*. RHB/WK. b 2 Jul 1860 (Hobart), d 15 Jan 1924 (Hobart). 134, 141, 169, 205, 219, 229, 236, 249, 252, 259.

McANDREW, John William; *Qld*. LHB/LFM. b 4 Nov 1889 (Byron Bay, NSW), d 10 Apr 1960 (Ipswich, Qld). 486, 493, 494, 499, 506, 508, 516, 517, 522, 529, 579.

MACARTNEY, Charles George; *NSW*. RHB/SLA. b 27 Jun 1886 (West Maitland, NSW), d 9 Sep 1958 (Chatswood, NSW). 324, 327, 328, 330, 331, 332, 336, 338, 339, 340, 342, 343, 344, 346, 347, 351, 354, 356, 358, 360, 361, 364, 366, 367, 368, 372, 373, 376, 377, 380, 381, 382, 383, 408, 411, 413, 415, 417, 419, 422, 425, 426, 428, 429, 433, 436, 439, 441, 445, 448, 450, 462, 463, 466, 467, 472, 474, 475, 477, 479, 481, 482, 490, 491, 494, 505, 514, 517, 519, 520, 528, 530, 532, 539, 546, 547, 548, 549, 552, 555, 558, 559, 560, 561, 563, 568, 571, 577, 599, 604, 606, 607, 612, 613, 615, 616, 620, 626, 628, 630.

McBEATH, Arthur; *NSW & Sth Aust*.   /LFM. b 17 Jun 1876 (Sydney), d 17 Mar 1945 (Surry Hills, NSW). 249, 251, 253, 256, 258, 260, 265, 267, 269, 271, 272, 277, 278, 279, 280, 283, 284, 289, 293, 296, 298, 299, 304, 337, 339, 341, 342, 349.

McBEATH, Daniel Jason; *NZ*. LHB/LM. b 8 Apr 1897 (Kimberley, NZ), d 13 Apr 1963 (Timaru, NZ). 603, 610.

McCABE, Stanley Joseph; *NSW*. RHB/RM. b 16 Jul 1910 (Grenfell, NSW), d 25 Aug 1968 (Mosman, NSW). 666, 670, 675, 679, 683, 686, 688, 690, 692, 696, 697, 700, 707, 708, 709, 712, 713, 715, 718, 720, 723, 725, 728, 730, 734, 736, 738, 743, 744, 747, 748, 749, 756, 760, 762, 765, 769, 772, 774, 777, 779, 781, 786, 789, 792, 795, 797, 799, 803, 805, 806, 825, 826, 828, 838, 844, 867, 869, 873, 877, 878, 883, 890, 892, 894, 895, 897, 901, 902, 906, 907, 910, 913, 914, 917, 918, 920, 921, 922, 938, 941, 942, 944, 947, 949, 952, 953, 954, 955, 958, 959, 962, 964.

McCAFFREY, Michael Francis; *Qld*. LHB/LM. b 18 Feb 1878 (, Qld), d c 1948 (   ). 324, 326, 334, 336, 429.

McCAFFREY, Victor William; *NSW*. RHB. b 11 Aug 1918 (Goulburn, NSW). 921, 925, 930, 932, 933.

McCARTHY, John Edward; *Qld*. RHB/RM. b 22 Feb 1917 (Maryborough, Qld). 850, 958.

McCAULEY, Bede Vincent; *NSW*. RHB. b 11 Jun 1909 (Coogee, NSW). 910, 913, 932, 933.

McCLOY, William Stanley Swain; *Qld & NSW*. RHB/LBG. b 10 Nov 1886 (Paddington, NSW), d 10 Nov 1975 (Bateman's Bay, NSW). 405, 409, 414, 416, 498.

McCOOL, Colin Leslie; *NSW*. RHB/LBG. b 9 Dec 1915 (Paddington, NSW), d 5 Apr 1986 (Concord, NSW). 952, 953, 954, 955, 958, 962, 963.

McCOOMBE, Clarence Arthur; *Qld*. RHB/RM. b 23 Feb 1904 (Cooktown, Qld), d 6 Sep 1955 (Sydney). 662, 664, 666, 672, 677.

McCORMACK, William Henry; *Vic*. LHB/SLA. b 5 May 1877 (St Kilda, Vic), d 26 Apr 1946 (Stawell, Vic). 259, 271.

McCORMICK, Ernest Leslie; *Vic*. LHB/RF. b 16 May 1906 (Nth Carlton, Vic), d 28 June 1991 (Tweed Heads, NSW). 693, 694, 699, 705, 742, 745, 750, 760, 763, 764, 780, 783, 788, 791, 798, 813, 818, 828, 831, 833, 835, 837, 838, 841, 844, 867, 872, 874, 877, 878, 888, 890, 893, 895, 896, 899, 902, 905, 907, 909, 912, 914, 916, 917, 920, 922, 923, 925, 928, 933, 934, 935, 936, 937.

McCOY, Bernard Leslie; *NSW*. RHB/LB. b 26 Mar 1896 (Kangaroo Valley, NSW), d 11 Jun 1970 (   ). 529, 565.

McDONALD, Edgar Arthur; *Tas & Vic*. RHB/RF. b 6 Jan 1891 (Launceston), d 22 Jul 1937 (Bolton, Lancs). 398, 420, 445, 446, 449, 451, 478, 491, 493, 495, 496, 497, 498, 501, 502, 504, 513, 515, 520, 524, 525, 526, 527, 530, 532, 535, 536, 538, 539.

MACDONALD, Robert; *Qld*. RHB/LB. b 14 Feb 1870 (Clunes, Vic), d 7 Mar 1946 (Victoria, Canada). 171, 176, 185, 186, 193, 208, 243, 245, 281, 295, 300.

McDONALD, Walter Hugh; *Vic, Qld & Tas*. RHB/LB. b 24 Mar 1884 (Shepparton, Vic), d 22 Mar 1955 (Kew, Vic). 542, 579, 581, 676.

McDONNELL, Percy Stanislaus; *Vic, NSW & Qld*. RHB. b 13 Nov 1858 (Kensington, London), d 24 Sep 1896 (Brisbane). 37, 43, 44, 47, 49, 52, 53, 54, 55, 56, 57, 58, 59, 63, 64, 65, 66, 67, 69, 70, 71, 72, 73, 74, 78, 79, 85, 87, 89, 92, 93, 95, 98, 99, 101, 102, 107, 108, 109, 111, 114, 115, 116, 117, 118, 120, 121, 122, 124, 125, 126, 129, 130, 131, 151, 176, 185, 186, 193, 200.

McDOWALL, Robert Murray; *Tas*.   /u-arm. b   (Sheffield, Yorks), d   (   ). 1, 3.

McELHONE, Frank Eric; *NSW*. RHB. b 27 Jun 1887 (Sydney), d 21 Jul 1981 (Darlinghurst, NSW). 415, 418, 422, 425, 428, 429, 433.

McEVOY, Frederick Aloysius; *Vic*. Brother of W.McEvoy. b 4 Jul 1856 (   ), d 5 Nov 1913 (Brighton, Vic). 36.

McEVOY, William; *Vic*. Brother of F.A.McEvoy. b   (   ), d   (   ). 36.

McEWAN, W   ; *Tas*. b   (   ), d   (   ). 2.

McFARLAND, Robert; *Vic*. RHB. b 9 Jul 1847 (   ), d 1876 (   ). 23.

McFARLANE, Clement Basil Patrick; *Qld*. RHB/OB. b 20 Aug 1900 (Brisbane), d 2 Mar 1946 (Grange, Qld). 579, 581, 727.

McGAHEY, Charles Percy; *Eng*. RHB/LB. b 12 Feb 1871 (Hackney, Middlesex), d 10 Jan 1935 (Whipps Cross, Essex). 262, 263, 272, 273, 274, 275, 276.

McGAN, Bryan; *Vic*. LHB/SLA. b 1848 (Melbourne), d 9 Jul 1894 (Sth Melbourne). 22, 25, 28.

MacGILL, Charles William Terry; *West Aust*. RHB/RFM. b 16 Jun 1916 (Perth). 936, 937, 950, 951.

McGILVRAY, Alan David; *NSW*. LHB/RFM. b 6 Dec 1910 (Paddington, NSW). 810, 815, 822, 829, 836, 846, 849, 851, 853, 854, 857, 861, 862, 867, 870, 873, 880, 881, 884, 888.

McGINN, Albert Howard; *Qld*. RHB/RFM. b 11 Nov 1913 (Brisbane). 964.

McGIRR, Herbert Mendelson; *NZ*. RHB/RM. b 5 Nov 1891 (Wellington, NZ), d 14 Apr 1964 (Nelson, NZ). 633.

McGLINCHEY, William Walter; *NSW & Qld*. RHB/OB. b 31 Jan 1864 (Newcastle, NSW), d 1 Jul 1946 (Sydney). 87, 93, 163, 171, 176, 185, 193, 208, 243, 245.

MacGREGOR, Gregor; *Eng*. RHB/WK. b 31 Aug 1869 (Edinburgh, Scotland), d 20 Aug 1919 (Marylebone, London). 143, 144, 145, 147, 150, 151, 153.

McGUIRK, Harold Vincent; *NSW*. LHB/RM. Brother of L.D.McGuirk. b 17 Oct 1906 (Crookwell, NSW). 622, 623.

McGUIRK, Leo Daniel; *NSW*. RHB/RMF. Brother of H.V.McGuirk. b 3 May 1908 (Crookwell, NSW), d 15 Jun 1974 (Sydney). 736.

McILWRAITH, John; *Vic*. RHB. b 7 Sep 1857 (Collingwood, Vic), d 5 Jul 1938 (Camberwell, Vic). 76, 87, 88, 90, 94, 96, 97, 100, 103, 106, 111, 119, 123, 125, 127, 129, 132.

McINNES, Alan Roderick; *Vic*. RHB/WK. b 29 May 1907 (Kensington, Vic). 737.

McINTYRE, William Robert; *NSW*. RHB/WK. b 10 Apr 1877 (Forbes, NSW), d 9 Dec 1911 (Glebe, NSW). 326, 338, 346, 347.

McKAY, Douglas Gordon; *Sth Aust*. RHB/RFM. b 2 Jul 1904 (Nth Adelaide). 609, 614, 626, 644, 645, 660, 664, 667, 671, 677.

MACKAY, George; *Vic*. RHB. b 6 Jul 1860 (Castlemaine, Vic), d 22 May 1948 (Bendigo, Vic). 45, 46, 47, 48, 60, 75.

McKAY, Henry James; *Sth Aust*. LHB/SLA. b 1 Jan 1883 (Goodwood, SA), d 12 Feb 1926 (Hawthorn, SA). 459, 462, 468.

MACKAY, James Rainey Munro; *NSW*. RHB. b 9 Sep 1881 (Kentucky, NSW), d 13 Jun 1953 (Walcha, NSW). 281, 298, 299, 304, 307, 312, 315, 316, 322, 323, 324, 327, 328, 330, 331, 332.

MACKENZIE, Alexander Cecil Knox; *NSW*. RHB. b 7 Aug 1870 (Sydney), d 11 Apr 1947 (Epping, NSW). 126, 133, 148, 149, 164, 165, 167, 185, 188, 193, 194, 195, 196, 199, 201, 202, 204, 206, 211, 214, 216, 218, 221, 223, 229, 230, 231, 235, 240, 243, 246, 247, 250, 253, 277, 278, 279, 280, 283, 284, 346.

McKENZIE, Colin; *Vic*. RHB. b 12 Dec 1880 (Trawool, Vic), d 31 Aug 1930 (Avenel, Vic). 350, 352, 357, 358, 364, 369, 372, 374, 377, 378, 384, 385, 389, 398, 401, 402, 403, 422, 445, 446, 449, 451, 468.

McKENZIE, Douglas Charles; *West Aust*. RHB. Brother of E.N.McKenzie. b 15 Mar 1906 (Kew, Vic), d 1 Jul 1979 (Perth). 842, 843, 844.

McKENZIE, Eric Norman; *West Aust*. RHB. Brother of D.C.McKenzie. b 9 Dec 1910 (Kalgoorlie, WA). 740.

McKENZIE, John; *Sth Aust*. LHB/WK/RF. b 11 Oct 1862 (Aldinga, SA), d 3 Jun 1944 (Hazelwood Park, SA). 81, 100, 124, 127, 136, 175, 198, 199, 204, 207, 209, 212, 216, 222, 223, 227, 228, 230, 261, 264, 265, 269.

McKENZIE, Matthew Stanley; *Tas*. RHB. b 17 May 1890 (Launceston), d 8 Dec 1915 (Gallipoli, Turkey). 398, 443, 444, 449, 464.

McKEW, Cecil George; *NSW*. RHB/WK. b 12 Aug 1887 (Leichhardt, NSW), d 12 Oct 1974 (Lilli Pilli, NSW). 445, 448, 452, 455, 458, 459, 460, 474, 475, 477, 479, 481.

McKIBBIN, Thomas Robert; *NSW*. LHB/RM/OB. b 10 Dec 1870 (Raglan, NSW), d 15 Dec 1939 (Bathurst, NSW). 174, 182, 185, 186, 188, 189, 193, 194, 195, 196, 199, 200, 201, 202, 204, 206, 211, 213, 214, 215, 216, 218, 221, 223, 229, 230, 231, 233, 235, 238, 239, 240, 241.

MACKINNON, Francis Alexander; *Eng*. RHB. b 9 Apr 1848 (Kensington, London), d 27 Feb 1947 (Drumduan, Scotland). 38, 41, 42.

McKONE, John James; *NSW*. RHB/RM(u-arm). b 3 Oct 1835 (Sydney), d 7 Aug 1882 (Bathurst, NSW). 4, 5, 6.

MacLAREN, Archibald Campbell; *Eng*. RHB/RFM. b 1 Dec 1871 (Manchester, Eng), d 17 Nov 1944 (Bracknell, Berks). 173, 174, 176, 177, 179, 181, 184, 186, 189, 190, 191, 209, 210, 211, 213, 215, 217, 220, 221, 224, 225, 226, 261, 263, 266, 268, 270, 272, 273, 274, 275, 276, 544, 545, 546.

McLAREN, John William; *Qld*. RHB/RF. b 22 Dec 1886 (Toowong, Qld), d 17 Nov 1921 (Highgate Hill, Qld). 338, 353, 359, 373, 375, 379, 390, 393, 399, 409, 411, 414, 416, 429, 435, 437, 450, 471, 486, 493, 494.

McLEAN, Hugh; *Vic*. RHB. b 26 Nov 1864 (Woodford, Vic), d 19 Feb 1915 (Hawthorn, Vic). 141, 142.

MacLEAN, John Francis: *Eng*. RHB/WK. b 1 Mar 1901 (Alnwick, UK), d 9 Mar 1986 (Ross-on-Wye, Herts). 545, 546, 555, 556, 557.

McLEOD, Charles Edward; *Vic*. RHB/RM. Brother of D.H. & R.W.McLeod. b 24 Oct 1869 (Port Melbourne, Vic), d 26 Nov 1918 (Toorak, Vic). 165, 166, 168, 170, 173, 175, 177, 178, 182, 187, 190, 194, 196, 198, 200, 202, 203, 206, 207, 210, 212, 213, 215, 217, 218, 220, 222, 225, 226, 231, 232, 235, 239, 240, 241, 254, 256, 257, 260, 262, 264, 266, 267, 270, 274, 299, 302, 304, 306, 308, 310, 313, 314, 316, 318, 320.

McLEOD, Daniel Hutton; *Vic*. RHB/RM. Brother of C.E. & R.W.McLeod. b 29 Mar 1872 (Port Melbourne, Vic), d 25 Nov 1901 (Port Melbourne, Vic). 159, 183.

McLEOD, Robert William; *Vic*. LHB/RM. Brother of C.E. & D.H.McLeod. b 19 Jan 1868 (Port Melbourne, Vic), d 14 Jun 1907 (Middle Park, Vic). 132, 133, 134, 135, 138, 139, 142, 146, 147, 149, 150, 152, 153, 155, 156, 158, 160, 170, 173, 175, 178, 182, 187, 190, 192, 194, 196, 198, 244.

McMICHAEL, Samuel Albert; *Vic*. RHB. b 18 Jul 1869 (Clifton Hill, Vic), d 21 Apr 1923 (Brighton, Vic). 146, 205, 207, 210, 212, 214, 218, 222, 228, 231, 232, 235, 237, 244, 247, 248, 251, 254, 256, 257, 260, 262, 264, 267, 271, 274, 309.

McMILLAN, Quintin; *Sth Afr*. RHB/LBG. b 23 Jun 1904 (Germiston, Sth Afr), d 3 Jul 1948 (Randfontein, Sth Afr). 740, 741, 742, 744, 746, 747, 748, 756, 758, 759, 761, 762, 765.

McNAMEE, Raymond Leonard Alphonsus; *NSW*. RHB/OB. b 26 Aug 1895 (Waverley, NSW), d 18 Sep 1949 (Little Bay, NSW). 618, 620, 622, 623, 626, 628, 630, 633, 637, 638, 642, 644, 646, 653, 675.

McNAUGHTON, John Leonard; *Vic*. RHB/RFM, b 15 Jan 1884 (Richmond, Vic), d 26 Dec 1970 (Lower Kingswood, Eng). 460, 461, 464, 468, 471, 474, 476, 477, 502.

MACNISH, William George; *NSW*. b 29 Oct 1842 (Paddington, NSW), d ( ). 14.

McPETRIE, William Martin; *Vic*. LHB. b 15 Feb 1880 (Emerald Hill, Vic), d 30 Jun 1951 (Hawthorn, Vic). 321, 325.

MACPHERSON, Herbert James Keele; *NSW*. RHB. b 20 Feb 1869 (Mudgee, NSW), d 12 Nov 1953 (Mudgee, NSW). 167, 168, 178.

McPHERSON, James Philip; *Vic*. b 20 Nov 1842 (Moonee Ponds, Vic), d 23 Aug 1891 (Melbourne). 15, 17.

McPHILLAMY, Keith; *NSW*. RHB/LM. b 20 Jun 1883 (Bathurst, NSW), d 3 May 1937 (Bowral, NSW). 317.

McRAE, Donald; *Sth Aust*. RHB. b 13 Jun 1873 (Aldinga, SA), d 22 Oct 1940 (Prospect, SA). 339, 341, 342.

McRAE, William Alexander; *West Aust*. RHB/LB. b 18 Jun 1904 (Geelong, Vic), d 25 Jul 1973 (Subiaco, WA). 648, 649, 650, 681.

MACROW, William Reginald Fairbairn; *Vic*. RHB/RF. b 7 Jul 1889 (Hawthorn, Vic), d 19 May 1970 (Heidelberg, Vic). 457, 430, 432, 434, 439.

McSHANE, Frederick George; *Vic*. LHB/LM. b 1857 (Keilor, Vic), d 11 Dec 1903 (Kew, Vic). 45, 46, 48, 49, 50, 52, 53, 55, 60, 61, 67, 69, 70, 71, 72, 75, 76, 79, 81, 83, 86, 88, 89, 91, 95, 98, 99, 100, 103, 106, 110, 115, 116, 117, 123, 159.

MACE, Christopher; *Vic*. Brother of J.Mace. b 24 Dec 1830 (Bedale, Yorks), d 23 Nov 1907 (Sydenham, NZ). 12.

MACE, John; *Vic*. RHB/LM(r). Brother of C.Mace. b 28 Dec 1828 (Bedale, Yorks), d Apr 1905 (Te Aroha, NZ). 11.

MACE, John Cruttenden; *Tas*. RHB/LM(r). b 7 May 1839 (Sydney), d 18 Apr 1906 (Hawley, Hampshire). 8.

MADDERN, James Gregory; *Qld*. RHB. b 22 Mar 1914 (Crows Nest, Qld), d 27 Mar 1987 (Nambour, Qld). 783, 787, 790, 837, 891.

MADDOCK, Charles Edward Rokeby; *Qld*. RHB/LB. b 14 Aug 1887 (, Qld), d 14 Feb 1957 (Herston, Qld). 499, 506.

MADDOX, George; *Tas*. b 1811 (Ireland), d 7 Jul 1867 (Melbourne). 1, 2, 3, 7.

MAGAREY, William Ashley; *Sth Aust*. RHB. b 30 Jan 1868 (Nth Adelaide), d 18 Oct 1929 (Nth Adelaide). 137.

MAHONEY, Hector James Henry; *Qld*. RHB. b 8 Sep 1913 (Maryborough, Qld). 897, 905, 912.

MAILER, David; *Vic*. RHB. b 18 Aug 1875 (Moreland, Vic), d 21 Dec 1937 (Shepparton, Vic). 236, 280, 282, 284, 288.

MAILEY, Arthur Alfred; *NSW*. RHB/LBG. b 3 Jan 1886 (Waterloo, NSW), d 31 Dec 1967 (Kirrawee, NSW). 455, 456, 458, 467, 470, 472, 474, 475, 477, 479, 481, 491, 494, 496, 498, 500, 501, 503, 505, 507, 514, 518, 519, 520, 521, 524, 525, 527, 528, 530, 532, 535, 537, 538, 539, 546, 547, 548, 549, 551, 552, 555, 558, 559, 560, 561, 563, 567, 568, 571, 577, 580, 583, 585, 587, 591, 593, 594, 595, 599, 604, 606, 607, 612, 613, 615, 616, 622, 623, 630, 633, 634, 637, 638, 644, 646, 683, 712.

MAIR, Frederick; *NSW*. RHB/RM/LBG. b 15 Apr 1901 (Sydney), d 25 Dec 1959 (Sydney). 803, 806, 809, 810, 910, 913, 914.

MAJOR, Albert George; *Vic*. RHB/RF(r). b 20 Mar 1851 (Langport, Somerset), d 16 Oct 1921 (Caulfield, Vic). 41.

MAKEPEACE, Joseph William Henry; *Eng*. RHB/LB. b 22 Aug 1881 (Middlesbrough, Yorks), d 19 Dec 1952 (Spital, Cheshire). 512, 514, 516, 521, 524, 526, 527, 528, 530.

MAKIN, James Charles; *Vic*. RHB/RM/OB. b 11 Feb 1904 (Collingwood, Vic), d 15 Jan 1973 (Heidelberg, Vic). 627, 643, 676, 678, 705.

MAKIN, William S ; *NSW*. LHB/LFM. b 1889 (, NSW), d 11 Jan 1962 (West Kogarah, NSW). 416, 418.

MAKINSON, Charles; *Vic*. b 1831 (Salford, Lancs), d 12 Jun 1895 (Rugeley, Staffs). 11, 12.

MAPLESTONE, Henry Carman; *Vic*. RHB/RFM. b 11 Jan 1869 (Parkville, Vic), d 10 Dec 1949 (Moonee Ponds, Vic). 159, 166, 219, 236.

MARKS, Alexander Edward; *NSW*. LHB/SLA. b 10 Dec 1910 (Toowong, Qld), d 28 Jul 1983 (Sydney). 670, 675, 679, 683, 686, 688, 690, 692, 696, 697, 717, 730, 744, 748, 757, 790, 822, 829, 840, 842, 843, 846, 849, 851, 853, 854, 857, 861, 862, 870, 873, 880, 881, 884, 888.

MARR, Alfred Percy; *NSW*. RHB/RM. b 28 Mar 1862 (Pyrmont, NSW), d 15 Mar 1940 (Arncliffe, NSW). 62, 71, 73, 74, 79, 80, 82, 83, 87, 89, 92, 93, 95, 137.

MARRIOTT, Arthur John; *Tas*. b c 1821 (, UK), d 31 Mar 1866 (Nice, France). 2.

MARSDEN, Albert John; *Qld*. RHB/LB. b 13 Jun 1887 (Maryborough, Qld), d 17 Dec 1971 (Kallista, Vic). 508, 510, 516, 517, 529.

MARSDEN, Fredrick William; *Vic*. b 1813 ( ), d 23 Nov 1858 (Avenel, Vic). 1, 2.

MARSH, Jack; *NSW*. /RF. b 1874 (Yugilbar, NSW), d 25 May 1916 (Orange, NSW). 255, 256, 258, 260, 277, 278.

MARSHAL, Alan; *Qld*. RHB/RFM. b 12 Jun 1883 (Warwick, Qld), d 23 Jul 1915 (Tintaria, Malta). 312, 314, 317, 405, 409, 411, 414, 416, 435, 452, 458, 473.

MARSHALL, Angus Neil; *Qld*. RHB/WK. b 27 Jan 1906 (British Guiana), d 29 Aug 1969 (Brisbane). 703, 777, 783, 787.

MARSHALL, George; *Tas*. b 12 Sep 1832 (Sorell, Tas), d 13 Jul 1905 (Sorell, Tas). 8.

MARSHALL, George; *Vic*. RHB/WK. b 20 Dec 1829 (Nottingham, Eng), d 6 Mar 1868 (Melbourne). 5, 6, 7, 8, 9, 10, 11, 12, 13, 14, 15.

MARSHALL, Jack (see J.E.Rogers).

MARTIN, Charles; *Qld*. RHB. b 15 May 1867 (Ipswich, Qld), d ( ). 163, 171.

MARSHALL, John; *Tas*. /WK. b c 1796 (U.K.), d 7 Sep 1876 (New Town, Tas). 1, 2, 3.

MARTIN, Charles; *Sth Aust*. b 29 Mar 1859 (Adelaide), d Mar 1955 (Adelaide). 195, 198, 199.

MARTIN, Charles William Beresford; *Tas.* LHB/LM/SLA. Son of W.Martin. b 6 Oct 1888 (Launceston), d 30 Oct 1951 (Camberwell, Vic). 362, 363, 384, 385, 398, 418, 420, 421, 443, 444, 449, 451, 485, 540, 553, 589, 590, 627, 668, 669, 674.

MARTIN, Edmund John; *West Aust.* LHB/LB. b 30 Sep 1902 (Bendigo, Vic). 771, 772.

MARTIN, Frank Reginald; *WI.* LHB/SLA. b 12 Oct 1893 (Jamaica), d 23 Nov 1967 (Kingston Jamaica). 713, 714, 716, 718, 722, 725, 727, 728, 732, 733, 734, 736, 738.

MARTIN, Gordon Francis; *Qld.* RHB. Brother of G.W.Martin & nephew of W.Martin. b 14 Jan 1885 (Clunes, Vic), d 19 Aug 1974 (Canberra). 338, 353, 359, 373.

MARTIN, Geoffrey William; *Tas.* RHB. Brother of G.F.Martin & nephew of W.Martin. b 7 Mar 1896 (Launceston), d 7 Mar 1968 (Launceston). 540, 570, 589, 590, 615, 616, 627, 640, 643, 668, 669, 674, 676, 694, 707, 708, 721, 729, 731, 737, 739, 782, 788.

MARTIN, James Macfie; *Tas.* RHB/Long-stop. b 25 Feb 1851 (Launceston), d 22 Oct 1930 (Launceston). 27.

MARTIN, William; *Tas.* RHB/RM. b 21 Jun 1856 (Westbury, Tas), d 10 Jul 1938 (Launceston). 35.

MASON, John Richard; *Eng.* RHB/RFM. b 26 Mar 1874 (Blackheath, Kent), d 15 Oct 1958 (Cooden, Sussex). 209, 210, 211, 213, 215, 217, 220, 221, 224, 225, 226, 227.

MASSIE, Hugh Hamon; *NSW.* RHB. b 11 Apr 1854 (near Belfast, Vic), d 12 Oct 1938 (Point Piper, NSW). 37, 39, 40, 43, 44, 46, 47, 48, 49, 51, 53, 54, 55, 56, 58, 59, 63, 64, 65, 66, 67, 73, 74, 77, 83, 84, 93, 115.

MASSIE, Robert John Allwright; *NSW.* LHB/RFM. Son of H.H.Massie. b 8 Jul 1890 (Nth Sydney), d 14 Feb 1966 (Mosman, NSW). 425, 455, 456, 458, 459, 460, 462, 463, 466, 467, 469, 474, 477, 479, 481, 482.

MATHER, Adam; *NSW.* RHB. b May 1864 (   ), d 31 Aug 1917 (Singleton, NSW). 87, 89, 92.

MATHER, John Henry; *Vic.* b 19 Nov 1822 (Everton, Lancs), d 4 Aug 1870 (Iquique, Chile). 4.

MATHERS, James; *Vic.* RHB. b 30 Jun 1894 (Minmi, NSW), d 28 Mar 1977 (Eastwood, NSW). 553.

MATSON, George; *Tas.* b 5 Dec 1817 (U.K.), d 22 Jul 1898 (Brighton, Sussex). 3, 8.

MATTHEWS, James George Facey; *Sth Aust.* RHB/RM. b 27 Sep 1876 (Lyndoch, SA), d 8 Oct 1963 (Prospect, SA). 254, 255, 257, 258, 261, 264, 265.

MATTHEWS, Thomas Harold; *Tas.* RHB/WK. b 9 Feb 1905 (Longley, Tas), d 11 May 1990 (Longley, Tas). 729, 737, 739.

MATTHEWS, Thomas James; *Vic.* RHB/LBG. b 3 Apr 1884 (Williamstown, Vic), d 14 Oct 1943 (Caulfield, Vic). 345, 385, 394, 397, 399, 407, 410, 411, 414, 415, 422, 423, 428, 430, 432, 434, 439, 442, 445, 446, 447, 460, 461, 463, 465, 466, 468, 471, 476, 477, 478, 481, 483, 488, 489, 491, 493.

MAXWELL, Eustace; *Tas.* LHB/LM(r). b 20 Jan 1864 (Hobart), d 18 May 1939 (Hobart). 128, 141, 183, 197, 219.

MAYES, Alexander Dunbar Aitken; *NSW & Qld.* RHB/RM. b 24 Jul 1901 (Toowoomba, Qld), d 8 Feb 1983 (Spring Hill, Qld). 579, 586, 588, 614, 618, 620, 621, 624, 629, 645.

MAYNE, Richard Edgar; *Sth Aust & Vic.* RHB. b 2 Jul 1882 (Jamestown, SA), d 26 Oct 1961 (Carrum, Vic). 339, 341, 342, 349, 352, 355, 370, 372, 374, 376, 378, 380, 382, 383, 389, 391, 394, 395, 396, 406, 410, 412, 427, 428, 430, 431, 434, 436, 441, 459, 461, 462, 466, 468, 474, 476, 479, 480, 483, 487, 489, 490, 495, 496, 498, 501, 502, 504, 505, 508, 509, 511, 513, 515, 520, 525, 526, 535, 538, 541, 542, 545, 549, 550, 552, 554, 562, 563, 566, 568, 569, 574, 576, 578, 588, 592, 598, 600, 605, 607.

MEAD, Charles Philip; *Eng.* LHB/SLA. b 9 Mar 1887 (Battersea, London), d 26 Mar 1958 (Boscombe, Hampshire). 431, 432, 433, 435, 437, 438, 440, 442, 443, 444, 446, 447, 448, 650, 652, 654, 657, 658, 659, 668, 669, 675, 681.

MEECH, James Robert; *Tas.* RHB/RM. b 16 Dec 1884 (Hobart), d 31 Oct 1955 (Hobart). 345, 400.

MEEK, Andrew Bonar; *West Aust.* RHB/RFM. b 7 Dec 1889 (Gulgong, NSW), d 13 Feb 1957 (Perth). 532, 543, 559, 597, 599.

MEIKLE, George Stanley; *Vic.* RHB/LBG. b 22 Oct 1916 (Yarraville, Vic), d 25 Jul 1991 (   ). 915, 927, 929, 957, 960, 961, 962.

MERRITT, William Edward; *NZ.* RHB/LBG. b 18 Aug 1908 (Christchurch, NZ), d 9 Jun 1977 (Christchurch). 633.

METCALFE, Evelyn James; *Qld.* RHB/ b 29 Sep 1865 (Kensington, London), d 14 Jun 1951 (Cambridge, Eng). 185, 234.

MICHAEL, Leonard; *Sth Aust.* RHB/WK. b 3 Jun 1921 (Medindie, SA). 950, 951.

MIDDLETON, Frederick Stewart; *NSW.* RHB/RM. b 28 May 1883 (Boorowa, NSW), d 21 Jul 1956 (Auckland, NZ). 326, 390, 393.

MIDDLETON, Roy Foster; *Sth Aust.* RHB. b 18 Sep 1889 (Kent Town, SA), d 19 Mar 1975 (Adelaide). 468, 474, 483, 487, 495.

MIDWINTER, William Evans; *Vic.* RHB/RMF(r). b 19 Jun 1851 (St Briavels, Glos), d 3 Dec 1890 (Kew, Vic). 29, 31, 33, 34, 46, 47, 48, 49, 51, 52, 54, 56, 57, 58, 59, 63, 67, 68, 69, 70, 71, 72, 74, 95, 98, 99, 100, 102, 103.

MILLAR, Keith James; *Vic.* RHB/RFM. b 15 Aug 1906 (Richmond, Vic), d 13 Jul 1971 (Melbourne). 591, 611, 619, 628, 629, 643, 788, 791.

MILLER, David Lawson; *Qld.* LHB/LF. b 30 Jan 1870 (Holytown, Scotland), d 12 Apr 1943 (Clayfield, Qld). 300, 312, 324.

MILLER, Ivan Derness; *Vic.* LHB. b 30 Dec 1913 (Ivanhoe, Vic), d 6 May 1966 (Heidelberg, Vic). 812, 819, 823, 848.

MILLER, Keith Ross; *Vic.* RHB/RF. b 28 Nov 1919 (Sunshine, Vic). 915, 927, 929, 936, 937, 939, 940, 942, 945, 948, 949, 954, 956, 959.

MILLER, Leslie Percy Robert; *Vic.* LHB/LM. b 16 Jun 1880 (St Kilda, Vic), d   (   ). 414.

MILLER, Noel Keith; *NSW.* RHB. b 1 Jul 1913 (Wyong, NSW). 846.

MILLER, William Edward; *West Aust.* RHB/SLA. b 9 Mar 1905 (East Perth), d 24 Jun 1974 (Perth). 572.

MILLS, George; *NZ.* RHB. Brother of I.Mills. b 23 Mar 1867 (Kent), d 13 Mar 1942 (Auckland, NZ). 238.

MILLS, Isaac; *NZ.* RHB. Brother of G.Mills. b 5 Apr 1869 (Kent), d 16 Aug 1956 (Auckland, NZ). 237.

MILLS, John; *NSW.* b 3 Mar 1836 (   ), d 24 Dec 1899 (   ). 6.

MILLS, John Ernest; *NZ.* LHB. Son of G.Mills. b 3 Sep 1905 (Dunedin, NZ), d 11 Dec 1972 (Hamilton, NZ). 633.

MILLS, Rowland Leslie; *West Aust.* RHB/RF, b 14 Jul 1914 (Leederville, WA). 900, 903, 936, 937.

MINCHIN, James Melbourne; *Vic.* RHB/RM. b 15 Aug 1858 (Sth Melbourne), d 13 Feb 1919 (Heatherton, Vic). 57.

MINNETT, Leslie Alma; *NSW.* RHB/RF. Brother of R.B. & R.V.Minnett. b 19 May 1883 (St Leonards, NSW), d 8 Aug 1934 (Collaroy, NSW). 367, 372, 373, 379, 391, 392, 395, 400, 425, 490.

MINNETT, Roy Baldwin; *NSW.* RHB/RFM. Brother of L.A. & R.V.Minnett. b 13 Jun 1888 (St Leonards, NSW), d 21 Oct 1955 (Manly, NSW). 346, 347, 391, 392, 400, 405, 416, 418, 428, 429, 433, 436, 437, 438, 440, 441, 442, 445, 447, 450, 459, 460, 462, 469, 487, 488.

MINNETT, Rupert Villiers; *NSW.* RHB. Brother of L.A. & R.B.Minnett. b 2 Sep 1884 (St Leonards, NSW), d 24 Jun 1974 (Cremorne, NSW). 390, 393, 395, 397, 486.

MINTER, Eric James; *NSW.* RHB. b 13 Sep 1917 (Kempsey, NSW), d 2 Jul 1985 (Vincentia, NSW). 921.

MITCHELL, Bruce; *Sth Afr.* RHB/LBG. b 8 Jan 1909 (Johannesburg). 741, 742, 744, 746, 747, 748, 749, 756, 758, 759, 761, 762, 764, 765, 770.

MITCHELL, Norman Frederick; *Vic.* RHB. b 19 Feb 1900 (Collingwood, Vic), d 8 Mar 1973 (Melbourne). 605, 611, 619, 627.

MITCHELL, Robert; *Vic.* LHB/LM. b 11 Apr 1863 (Campbellfield, Vic), d 17 Sep 1926 (West Preston, Vic). 119, 128, 155, 159, 162, 170, 173, 175, 197, 252, 259, 285.

MITCHELL, Thomas Bignall; *Eng.* RHB/LBG. b 4 Sep 1902 (Creswell, Derbyshire). 771, 772, 776, 782, 785, 793, 797, 800, 801.

MITCHELL-INNES, Norman Stewart; *Eng*. RHB/RFM. b 7 Sep 1914 (Calcutta, India). 845, 847, 848, 850.

MOFFAT, William; *Sth Aust*. RHB. b 22 Jul 1858 (Byethorne, SA), d 30 Jul 1932 (Jamestown, SA). 35.

MOFFATT, Alfred Augustine; *West Aust*. RHB/RM. b 15 Mar 1870 (Perth), d 8 Dec 1956 (Perth). 161, 162.

MOLONEY, Denis Andrew Robert; *NZ*. RHB/LB. b 11 Aug 1910 (Dunedin, NZ), d 15 Jul 1942 (El Alamein, Egypt). 898, 899, 901.

MONFRIES, John Elliott; *Vic*. RHB/WK. b 25 Dec 1873 (Gumeracha, SA), d 2 Sep 1954 (Hobart). 287, 288, 292, 294, 299, 304.

MONOHAN, Vincent Clifford; *Vic*. LHB/RM. b 22 Apr 1896 (Collingwood, Vic), d 9 Jul 1974 (Linden Park, SA). 540.

MOORE, George; *NSW*. RHB/RM(r). Brother of J.Moore. b 8 Apr 1820 (Ampthill, Bedfordshire), d 29 Sep 1916 (West Maitland, NSW). 23, 24, 26.

MOORE, George Stanley; *NSW & Qld*. RHB. b 18 Apr 1886 (Nth Sydney), d 22 Mar 1948 (Bundaberg, Qld). 458, 459, 460, 467, 516, 517, 522, 529.

MOORE, Henry Thomas; *Sth Aust*. RHB/RF. b c 1860 (U.K.), d ( ). 142.

MOORE, James; *NSW*. RHB. Brother of G.Moore. b 1839 (Ampthill, Bedfordshire), d 19 Apr 1890 (West Maitland, NSW). 12, 13.

MOORE, Leon; *NSW*. RHB. Son of J.Moore & brother of W.H.Moore. b 8 Feb 1871 (West Maitland, NSW), d 11 Sep 1934 (Maitland, NSW). 157, 163, 167, 188.

MOORE, William Henry; *NSW & West Aust*. RHB/WK. Son of J.Moore & brother of L.Moore. b 16 Oct 1864 (West Maitland, NSW), d 25 Feb 1956 (Lane Cove, NSW). 164, 165, 167, 168, 242.

MORCOM, Samuel; *Combined XIII*. /WK. b 1847 ( ), d 15 Jan 1888 (Adelaide). 25.

MORGAN, Charles Edward; *Vic*. RHB/WK. b 10 Aug 1900 (Collingwood, Vic), d 8 Dec 1965 (Preston, Vic). 627.

MORGAN, Charles ; *Qld*. RHB. b 10 Jan 1877 ( ), d 15 April 1937? ( ). 243, 277, 278, 286, 314, 317, 326.

MORGAN, George; *NSW*. RHB. b 1843 (Bathurst, NSW), d 17 Jul 1896 (Sydney). 28.

MORGAN, John Gordon; *NSW*. RHB/RM. b 6 Mar 1893 (Camperdown, NSW), d 7 May 1967 (Concord, NSW). 534, 537, 558, 559, 580, 586, 588, 594, 599, 608, 610, 618, 620, 622, 623, 626, 628, 630, 633, 634, 637, 638, 642, 646, 653, 655, 657.

MORGAN, Walter Millard; *Vic*. RHB. b 1 Nov 1871 (Ballarat, Vic), d 10 Jul 1941 (Ballarat, Vic). 252.

MORKEL, Denys Paul Beck; *Sth Afr*. RHB/RFM. b 25 Jan 1906 (Cape Town, Sth Afr), d 6 Oct 1980 (Nottingham, Eng). 740, 742, 744, 746, 747, 748, 749, 756, 758, 759, 762, 764, 765, 770.

MORLEY, Frederick; *Eng*. LHB/LF. b 16 Dec 1850 (Sutton-in-Ashfield, Notts), d 28 Sep 1884 (Sutton-in-Ashfield, Notts). 61, 62, 65, 66, 68.

MORONEY, Robert; *Sth Aust*. LHB/RFM. b 23 Jan 1885 (Upper Sturt, SA), d 4 Aug 1958 (Parkside, SA). 531.

MORRES, Thomas Furley; *Vic*. RHB/RM(r). b 12 Sep 1829 (Berks), d 28 Sep 1884 (East Melbourne). 4, 6, 7, 8, 9, 10.

MORRIS, Arthur Robert; *NSW*. LHB/SLC. b 19 Jan 1922 (Dungog, NSW). 958, 961, 962, 963.

MORRIS, John Humphrey; *NSW*. RHB/Long-stop. b 5 Jun 1831 (Sydney), d 9 Dec 1921 (Glebe Point, NSW). 9.

MORRIS, Maesmore Alfred; *Vic*. b 1868 (Northcote), d 31 Aug 1917 (Ivanhoe, Vic). 125, 127, 128, 130, 131.

MORRIS, Norman O'Neil; *NSW*. RHB/LB. b 9 May 1907 (Camperdown, NSW). 666, 667, 675, 679.

MORRIS, Samuel; *Vic*. RHB/RM. RHB/RM. b 22 Jun 1855 (Hobart), d 20 Sep 1931 (Albert Park, Vic). 60, 75, 76, 80, 81, 83, 91, 95, 100, 103, 111, 132, 133, 135, 138, 139, 140, 144, 159, 162.

MORRISBY, Ronald Orlando George; *Tas*. RHB. b 12 Jan 1915 (Hobart). 754, 755, 758, 759, 768, 782, 785, 802, 812, 814, 819, 825, 826, 839, 867, 885, 886, 915, 918, 919, 927, 929.

MORRISSEY, Charles Vincent; *NSW*. RHB/RFM. b 26 Apr 1903 (Corowa, NSW), d 20 Feb 1938 (Quirindi, NSW). 579, 580, 584, 586, 588, 602.

MORTLOCK, William; *Eng*. RHB/RM/Lobs. b 18 Jul 1832 (Kennington, Surrey), d 23 Jan 1884 (Brixton, Surrey). 13.

MORTON, Francis Lonsdale; *Sth Aust & Vic*. RHB/RFM. b 21 Dec 1901 (Fullarton, SA), d 14 Oct 1971 (Caulfield, Vic). 541, 544, 548, 550, 551, 621, 623, 625, 628, 629, 630, 635, 636, 638, 641, 646, 647, 654, 656, 660, 729, 731, 737, 768.

MORTON, Hugh Gilbert Stuart; *Qld*. RHB. b 14 Oct 1881 (Maryborough, Qld), d 28 Jan 1936 (Herston, Qld). 314, 317, 323, 334.

MOSES, Henry; *NSW*. LHB. b 13 Feb 1858 (Windsor, NSW), d 7 Dec 1938 (Strathfield, NSW). 51, 62, 71, 73, 74, 77, 79, 83, 89, 92, 93, 95, 98, 99, 101, 102, 107, 108, 109, 111, 114, 115, 116, 117, 120, 129, 130, 131, 133, 135, 136, 137, 138, 140, 145, 146, 147, 150, 154, 155, 165, 167, 168, 171, 180, 182, 184, 188.

MOSSOP, Kenneth Leonard Mario; *Qld*. RHB/RM. b 15 Aug 1909 (New Farm, Qld), d 18 Sep 1975 (Surfers Paradise, Qld). 698, 703, 715, 727, 743, 746, 753, 757, 763, 767, 777, 783, 787, 790.

MOULE, William Henry; *Vic*. RHB/RM. b 31 Jan 1858 (Brighton, Vic), d 24 Aug 1939 (St Kilda, Vic). 41, 42, 53, 87.

MOYES, Alban George; *Sth Aust & Vic*. RHB/LB. b 2 Jan 1893 (Gladstone, SA), d 18 Jan 1963 (Chatswood, NSW). 453, 459, 461, 462, 466, 468, 474, 476, 479, 483, 487, 489, 490, 495, 509, 513.

MOYLE, Charles Rule; *Sth Aust*. /WK. b 16 Apr 1884 (Adelaide), d 2 Aug 1952 (Adelaide). 410, 412.

MOYLE, Edward James Ross; *Sth Aust*. RHB/WK. b 15 Oct 1913 (Moonta Mines, SA), d 24 Oct 1942 (Cairo, Egypt). 824, 832, 834, 841, 847, 853, 855, 858, 860, 861, 864, 871, 931, 932, 946.

MOYSEY, George Bickford; *West Aust*. LHB. b 14 May 1874 (Battery Point, Tas), d 18 May 1932 (Canterbury, Vic). 371.

MUDGE, Harold; *NSW*. RHB/LBG. b 14 Feb 1914 (Stanmore, NSW). 849, 851, 853, 854, 857, 861, 862, 870, 873, 880, 881, 944, 947, 949, 952.

MUDIE, William; *Eng*. RHB/RaB(r). b 26 Apr 1836 (Kennington, Surrey), d 25 Jan 1871 (Vauxhall, Surrey). 13.

MUELLER, Mervyn Edgar Christopher Edgar; *Sth Aust*. RHB b 3 Oct 1914 (Yatala Sth, SA). 904, 916.

MUHL, Arthur Henry; *Qld*. LHB/SLA. b 12 Feb 1913 (Sth Brisbane). 860, 863.

MUIR, William Frederick; *Vic*. LHB. b 8 Feb 1907 (Prahran, Vic), d 27 Nov 1964 (Box Hill, Vic). 699.

MULLARKEY, Desmond Antony; *NSW*. LHB. b 19 Sep 1899 ( ), d Sep 1975 ( ). 560, 565.

MULLETT, Leonard Thomas; *Vic*. RHB/LM. b 27 Nov 1894 (Moonee Ponds, Vic), d 22 Apr 1944 (Toorak, Vic). 509, 513, 553, 628, 629, 660.

MUNN, R A ; NSW. /WK. b ( ), d ( ). 456, 472.

MUNRO, Charles; *West Aust*. RHB/LM. b 21 Mar 1871 (Wallan, Vic), d 7 Feb 1969 (Nth Fremantle, WA). 335, 347, 401.

MUNRO, William; *Qld*. RHB/RM. b 1862 (Manchester, Eng), d 18 Feb 1896 (Stanthorpe, Qld). 163.

MURDOCH, William Lloyd; *NSW*. RHB/WK. b 18 Oct 1854 (Sandhurst, Vic), d 18 Feb 1911 (Melbourne). 30, 31, 32, 34, 38, 39, 40, 43, 44, 47, 49, 51, 53, 54, 55, 56, 58, 59, 63, 64, 65, 66, 67, 68, 71, 72, 73, 74, 78, 79, 136, 165, 167, 168.

MURFETT, Julian Ivor; *Tas*. LHB/RFM. b 2 Jul 1915 (Dunorlan, Tas), d 27 Apr 1982 (Hobart). 915, 918, 919, 927, 929.

MURPHY, James Joseph; *NSW*. /RFM. b 29 Sep 1911 ( ), d 7 May 1984 ( ). 921, 924, 925, 930.

MURPHY, Michael Augustus; *Vic*. RHB/OB. b 1854 (Sydney), d 2 Sep 1890 (Richmond, Vic). 28.

MULLAGH, Johnny (Unaarrimin); *Vic*. RHB. b 13 Aug 1841 (near Harrow, Vic), d 14 Aug 1891 (Pine Hills Station, Vic). 42.

MURRAY, Alfred Wynyatt; *Vic*. RHB/LB. b 4 Feb 1868 (Long Gully, Vic), d 27 Jul 1936 (Preston, Vic). 214, 236, 237, 252, 259.

MURRAY, John Tinline; *Sth Aust*. RHB/RM. b 1 Dec 1892 (Norwood, SA), d 19 Sep 1974 (Stirling, SA). 441, 506, 507, 531, 541, 544, 554, 557, 561, 564, 569, 571, 574, 575, 586, 596, 606, 609, 611, 612.

MURRAY, Norman Eric; *Tas*. RHB/WK. b 2 Nov 1908 (Perth, WA), d 21 Aug 1967 (Sydney). 722, 729.

MURRAY, Richard; *NSW*. LHB/LFM(r)/WK. b 1831 (Sydney), d 21 Nov 1861 (Manly, NSW). 4, 5, 6, 10.

MUSGROVE, Henry Alfred; *Vic*. RHB. b 27 Nov 1858 (Surbiton, Surrey), d 2 Nov 1931 (Darlinghurst, NSW). 60, 80, 83, 104, 106.

MUSGROVE, John; *Sth Aust*. LHB/LF. b 28 Jul 1861 (Adelaide) d 9 Jun 1940 (   ). 105, 112, 119.

MYERS, Hubert; *Tas*. RHB/RM. b 2 Jan 1875 (Yeadon, Yorks), d 12 Jun 1944 (Hobart). 482, 484, 492, 590.

NAGEL, Lisle Ernest; *Vic*. RHB/RFM. Twin brother of V.G.Nagel. b 6 Mar 1905 (Bendigo, Vic), d 23 Nov 1971 (Mornington, Vic). 649, 732, 742, 745, 750, 760, 763, 778, 781, 786, 804, 805, 810, 828, 922.

NAGEL, Vernon George; *Vic*. RHB/RFM. Twin brother of L.E.Nagel. b 6 Mar 1905 (Bendigo, Vic), d 27 Apr 1974 (Sandringham, Vic). 776, 780, 848, 858.

NASH, Laurence John; *Tas & Vic*. RHB/RF. b 2 May 1910 (Fitzroy, Vic), d 24 Jul 1986 (Heidelberg, Vic). 694, 701, 705, 706, 707, 708, 721, 722, 729, 731, 737, 739, 754, 755, 758, 759, 765, 768, 778, 806, 893, 895.

NETTLETON, Robert Glanville; *Vic*. RHB/RMF. b 16 Sep 1909 (Williamstown, Vic), d 6 Apr 1972 (Newport, Vic). 705, 729.

NEWCOMBE, Henry Charles Edwin; *NSW*. b 1835 (   ), d 26 Oct 1908 (Randwick, NSW). 11, 12, 14.

NEWELL, Andrew Livingstone; *NSW*. RHB/RM/OB. b 13 Nov 1870 (   ), d 8 Mar 1915 (Heron's Creek, NSW). 145, 154, 163, 164, 165, 167, 168, 171, 174, 178, 180, 193, 195, 208, 218, 221, 223, 233, 235, 249.

NEWHAM, William; *Eng*. RHB. b 12 Dec 1860 (Shrewsbury, Shropshire), d 26 Jun 1944 (Hove, Sussex). 107, 109, 114, 116, 117, 120, 122.

NEWLAND, Philip Mesner; *Sth Aust*. RHB/WK. b 2 Feb 1875 (Kensington, SA), d 11 Aug 1916 (Knightsbridge, SA). 244, 276, 282, 283, 287, 290, 291, 294, 296, 298, 311, 313, 315, 318, 319, 325.

NEWMAN, Charles Frederick; *West Aust*. RHB/OB. Brother of H.A.Newman. b 7 Nov 1909 (Fremantle, WA), d 28 Mar 1977 (Fremantle, WA). 845, 868.

NEWMAN, Henry Albert; *West Aust*. RHB/RFM. Brother of C.F.Newman. b 13 Mar 1907 (Fremantle, WA). 648, 702, 740.

NEWSTEAD, George Holt; *Vic*. LHB. b 11 Aug 1910 (Brighton, Vic). 737, 754, 755, 766, 856, 859, 863, 865.

NEWTON, Alan Colin; *Tas*. LHB/LFM/SLA. b 6 Apr 1894 (Longford, Tas), d 27 Mar 1979 (Narrabeen, NSW). 449, 451, 469, 484, 540, 553, 570, 589, 590, 615, 616, 627, 640, 643, 668, 693, 694, 701, 705, 706, 707, 708, 729, 737, 739, 768, 814.

NEWTON, Arthur Edward; *Eng*. RHB/WK. b 12 Sep 1862 (Barton Grange, Somerset), d 15 Sep 1952 (Dipford, Somerset). 105, 106, 108, 112, 113, 118, 121, 123.

NEWTON, Percy Allen; *NSW*. RHB/OB. b 21 Dec 1880 (   ), d 25 Apr 1946 (Rose Bay, NSW). 359, 367.

NICHOLLS, Arthur Joseph; *NSW*. RHB. b 3 Sep 1881 (   ), d (   ). 375, 379.

NICHOLLS, Charles Omer; *NSW*. RHB/RFM. b 5 Dec 1901 (Freemans Reach, NSW), d 14 Jan 1983 (Freemans Reach, NSW). 608, 610, 640, 644, 646, 651, 653, 655, 663, 666, 667, 670.

NICHOLS, Morris Stanley; *Eng*. LHB/RF. b 6 Oct 1900 (Stondon Massey, Essex), d 26 Jan 1961 (Newark, Notts). 682, 684, 685, 687.

NICOLSON, John Norman Walter; *Tas*. RHB/RM. b 14 Apr 1917 (Campbell Town, Tas). 885, 915, 918, 929.

NITSCHKE, Homesdale Carl; *Sth Aust*. LHB. b 14 Apr 1905 (Adelaide), d 29 Sep 1982 (Nth Adelaide). 690, 691, 695, 697, 698, 702, 704, 710, 711, 716, 720, 724, 726, 733, 735, 739, 741, 745, 747, 749, 753, 761, 766, 767, 769, 775, 780, 784, 787, 794, 795, 798, 801, 804, 805, 806, 809, 811, 813, 816, 817, 829, 830, 834, 835.

NOBLE, Montague Alfred; *NSW*. RHB/RM/OB. b 28 Jan 1873 (Sydney), d 22 Jun 1940 (Randwick, NSW). 182, 201, 202, 204, 206, 211, 214, 215, 216, 217, 218, 220, 221, 223, 225, 229, 230, 231, 233, 235, 238, 239, 240, 241, 243, 245, 246, 247, 250, 251, 253, 255, 256, 258, 260, 263, 265, 266, 267, 268, 269, 270, 272, 273, 275, 279, 280, 283, 284, 289, 293, 296, 297, 298, 299, 301, 302, 304, 307, 308, 310, 312, 315, 316, 319, 320, 327, 328, 330, 331, 332, 339, 340, 342, 343, 344, 351, 355, 356, 358, 360, 361, 364, 366, 368, 372, 376, 377, 380, 381, 382, 383, 396, 428, 466, 496, 498, 499.

NOEL, John; *Sth Aust*. RHB/RaB. b 28 Mar 1856 (Hindmarsh, SA), d 9 Jan 1938 (Largs Bay, SA). 45, 50, 60, 70, 72, 81, 100, 112, 119, 139, 142, 148, 156, 157, 170, 188.

NOONAN, Daniel Francis; *Vic*. b 11 May 1873 (Nth Melbourne), d 1910 (   ). 259, 280, 282, 284, 286.

NORMAN, Rex; *NSW*. LHB/LFM. b c 1892 (   ), d c 1975 (   ). 496, 498, 499, 500, 501, 505, 507.

NORTH, Frederic Dudley; *West Aust*. RHB. b 9 Nov 1866 (Kensington, London), d 22 Aug 1921 (Cottesloe, WA). 161, 162.

NOTHLING, Otto Ernest; *NSW & Qld*. RHB/RFM. b 1 Aug 1900 (Teutoburg, Qld), d 26 Sep 1965 (Chelmer, Qld). 547, 571, 577, 580, 586, 634, 636, 639, 642, 645, 647, 651, 653, 657, 658, 661, 664, 666, 672, 677, 683.

NOURSE, Arthur William; *Sth Afr*. LHB/LM/SLA. b 26 Jan 1879 (Thornton Heath, Surrey), d 8 Jul 1948 (Port Elizabeth, Sth Afr). 406, 407, 408, 409, 411, 413, 417, 419, 420, 421, 423, 424, 425, 426, 427.

NOYES, Alfred William Finch; *Vic*. b 1835 (Torquay, Devon), d 30 Sep 1902 (Deniliquin, NSW). 20.

NOYES, Harold David; *Qld*. RHB/RFM. b 12 Aug 1892 (Warwick, Qld), d 14 Jul 1968 (Brisbane). 584, 602, 603, 608, 614, 618.

NUNN, Thomas; *NSW*. RHB. b 1846 (Sevenoaks, Kent), d 31 May 1889 (Bexley, NSW). 48, 71, 73, 74, 82.

NUTT, Richard Nathaniel; *NSW*. RHB. b 25 Jun 1911 (Balmain, NSW), d 5 Feb 1985 (Gladesville, NSW). 751, 752, 757, 760, 769, 790.

OAKES, Cecil James Grellis; *Tas*. RHB/RM. b 1 Mar 1915 (Hobart). 919, 927.

OAKLEY, Hector Herbert; *Vic*. RHB. b 10 Jan 1909 (Nth Fitzroy, Vic). 704, 726, 730, 735, 742, 745, 750, 760, 763, 764, 766, 768, 773, 776, 780, 783, 788, 791, 798, 800, 831, 833, 835, 837, 927, 929, 933, 934.

OATLEY, James Napoleon; *NSW*. RHB/Long-stop b 12 Aug 1845 (Newtown, NSW), d 17 Dec 1925 (Cremorne, NSW). 16, 20.

O'BRIEN, Ernest Francis; *NSW*. RHB/LBG. b 26 Aug 1900 (Paddington, NSW), d 2 Nov 1935 (Newcastle, NSW). 626, 628, 642.

O'BRIEN, Lelsie John; *NSW*. LHB/RF. b (   ), d 1968 (   ). 906, 907, 910, 913, 914, 917, 921, 932.

O'BRIEN, Leo Patrick Joseph; *Vic*. LHB/RM. b 2 Jul 1907 (West Melbourne). 693, 694, 699, 719, 726, 730, 735, 742, 745, 752, 760, 763, 764, 766, 768, 773, 774, 776, 778, 780, 783, 786, 789, 798, 799, 800, 804, 805, 806, 807, 808, 810, 813, 818, 828, 831, 833, 835, 837, 838, 841, 844, 867, 872, 874, 878, 887, 888, 900.

**O'BRIEN, M   E   **; *Anderson's XI v Parr's XI*. b (   ), d (   )15.

O'BRIEN, Robert; *Qld*. RHB/RM. b 16 Jul 1869 (Redfern, NSW), d Oct 1922 (   ). 163, 185, 193, 208.

O'BRIEN, Timothy Carew; *Eng*. RHB/LaB. b 5 Nov 1861 (Dublin), d 9 Dec 1948 (Ramsey, Isle of Man). 105, 106, 112, 113, 118, 121, 123.

O'CONNELL, Thomas Reginald; *Sth Aust*. LHB/RFM. b 10 Mar 1916 (Parkside, SA). 853, 855, 858, 860, 861, 866.

O'CONNOR, Brian Redmond Devereaux; *Qld*. RHB/RFM. Son of L.P.D.O'Connor. b 5 Jul 1913 (Sth Brisbane), d 20 Dec 1963 (Red Hill, Qld). 830, 831, 834, 836, 850.

O'CONNOR, John A   ; *Vic*.   /LM. b 19 Aug 1868 (   ), d   (   ). 197, 205.

OATLEY, James Napoleon; *NSW*. RHB/Long-stop b 12 Aug 1845 (Newtown, NSW), d 17 Dec 1925 (Cremorne, NSW). 16, 20.

O'CONNOR, John Denis Alphonsus; *NSW & Sth Aust*. LHB/RM. b 9 Sep 1875 (Burrowa, NSW), d 23 Aug 1941 (Lewisham, NSW). 322, 323, 324, 327, 328, 330, 331, 332, 337, 339, 341, 342, 344, 349, 352, 355, 361, 366, 368, 370, 374, 376, 378, 380, 382, 383, 391, 394, 395, 396.

O'CONNOR, Leo Patrick Devereaux; *Qld*. RHB/WK. b 11 Apr 1890 (Murtoa, Vic), d 16 Jan 1985 (Melbourne). 465, 470, 471, 472, 516, 529, 533, 547, 560, 562, 564, 565, 579, 581, 582, 584, 602, 603, 608, 614, 618, 620, 621, 624, 629, 630, 634, 636, 639, 642, 645, 647, 651, 653, 658, 662, 664, 666, 672, 677, 683, 687, 689, 691, 696, 698.

O G I L V Y, David S   ; *N S W*.   RHB/RM. b   (   ), d   (   ). 87, 92.

O'HALLORAN, James Patrick; *Vic*. RHB/RM. b 12 Jan 1872 (Richmond, Vic), d 28 Apr 1943 (East Melbourne). 203, 206, 207.

O'HANLON, William James; *NSW*. RHB/WK. b 10 Mar 1863 (   ), d 23 Jun 1940 (Randwick, NSW). 79, 82, 83, 130.

OHLSTROM, Patrick Andreas Paul; *Sth Aust*. LHB/OB. b 16 Dec 1890 (Warooka, SA), d 10 Jun 1940 (Adelaide). 561.

O'KEEFFE, Francis Aloysius; *NSW & Vic*. RHB/OB. b 11 May 1896 (Waverley, NSW), d 26 Mar 1924 (Hampstead, London). 503, 518, 522, 525, 529, 538, 539, 541, 542.

OLDFIELD, William Albert Stanley; *NSW*. RHB/WK. b 9 Sep 1894 (Alexandria, NSW), d 10 Aug 1976 (Killara, NSW). 504, 506, 507, 510, 514, 518, 519, 520, 521, 524, 528, 532, 538, 539, 546, 547, 548, 549, 551, 552, 555, 558, 559, 560, 561, 563, 567, 568, 577, 580, 583, 585, 587, 591, 593, 595, 602, 604, 606, 607, 612, 613, 628, 630, 633, 634, 637, 638, 646, 651, 655, 657, 659, 661, 665, 667, 673, 675, 680, 683, 686, 707, 712, 713, 718, 723, 725, 728, 730, 734, 738, 743, 744, 747, 748, 749, 756, 760, 762, 765, 769, 774, 777, 779, 781, 784, 789, 792, 799, 803, 805, 806, 809, 810, 816, 818, 825, 826, 828, 829, 832, 833, 836, 838, 840, 842, 843, 867, 870, 873, 878, 883, 886, 890, 892, 894, 895, 897, 901, 902, 906, 907, 910, 913, 914, 917.

OLIVER, Charles Joshua; *NZ*. RHB. b 1 Nov 1905 (Wanganui, NZ), d 25 Sep 1977 (Brisbane). 603, 605, 609, 610, 633.

OLIVER, Charles Nicholson Jewel; *NSW*. RHB. b 24 Apr 1848 (Hobart), d 14 Jun 1920 (Manly, NSW). 16, 21, 26.

O'MULLANE, George Jeremiah Patrick; *Vic*. LHB/WK. b 3 Dec 1842 (Melbourne), d 20 Dec 1866 (East Melbourne). 16.

ONYONS, Basil Austin; *Vic*. RHB. b 14 Mar 1887 (Windsor), d 31 May 1967 (Glen Iris). 498, 627, 635, 643, 648, 649, 660, 662, 670, 672, 678.

O'REILLY, William Joseph; *NSW*. LHB/LBG. b 20 Dec 1905 (White Cliffs, NSW). 633, 634, 640, 751, 752, 757, 760, 762, 765, 769, 774, 777, 779, 781, 784, 786, 789, 792, 795, 797, 799, 803, 805, 806, 809, 810, 816, 818, 827, 828, 838, 844, 867, 870, 873, 877, 878, 883, 890, 894, 895, 897, 901, 902, 906, 907, 910, 913, 914, 917, 919, 920, 922, 924, 925, 938, 941, 942, 944, 947, 949, 952, 953, 954, 955, 958, 959, 961, 962, 963, 964.

ORR, Herbert Richard; *West Aust*. RHB/RaB. b 3 Feb 1865 (London), d 22 May 1940 (Sevenoaks, Kent). 161, 162.

OSBORNE, Noton Michael; *Vic*. b 1844 (   ), d 10 Dec 1878 (Hobart). 22.

OSBORNE, Robert Henry; *NSW*. RHB/WK. b 4 Feb 1898 (   ), d 21 Feb 1975 (Long Jetty, NSW). 579, 618, 626.

OSBORNE, Robert Moorhead; *Vic*. RHB/LB. b 29 Sep 1881 (St Kilda, Vic), d 19 Nov 1927 (Wesburn, Vic). 309, 314, 316, 318.

O'SHAUGHNESSY, Barney; *West Aust*. RHB/RF. b 28 Feb 1912 (Wiluna, WA). 771.

OSWALD, Norman Hamilton; *Sth Aust*. RHB/LBG. b 31 Oct 1916 (Prospect, SA), d 22 Jun 1970 (Adelaide). 880, 882, 904.

OVER, William; *Vic*. RHB/RFM. b 20 Jan 1862 (Richmond, Vic), d Nov 1910 (Sth Afr). 100, 128, 134, 135.

OXENHAM, Lionel Emmanuel; *Qld*. RHB. Brother of R.K.Oxenham. b 27 Jan 1888 (Nundah, Qld), d 10 Jan 1970 (Clayfield, Qld). 499, 506, 508, 510, 516, 522, 529, 547, 560, 562, 564, 565, 608, 614, 618, 620, 621, 624, 629, 636, 639, 642, 645.

OXENHAM, Ronald Keven; *Qld*. RHB/RM. Brother of L.E.Oxenham. b 28 Jul 1891 (Nundah, Qld), d 16 Aug 1939 (Nundah, Qld). 429, 452, 465, 470, 471, 472, 547, 560, 562, 564, 565, 579, 581, 582, 584, 602, 603, 608, 614, 618, 620, 621, 624, 629, 634, 645, 647, 651, 653, 658, 665, 673, 677, 680, 683, 687, 688, 698, 703, 710, 715, 717, 719, 724, 727, 728, 734, 738, 743, 746, 747, 750, 753, 757, 763, 767, 773, 778, 783, 787, 794, 796, 803, 807, 808, 811, 815, 817, 830, 831, 834, 836, 837, 840, 870, 876, 879, 882, 884, 887, 891.

PACKHAM, Leonard; *West Aust*. RHB/RM, b 15 Sep 1891 (Norwood, SA), d 4 Oct 1958 (Swanbourne, WA). 542.

PAGE, Clive Basil; *Qld*. RHB. b 25 May 1894 (Rockhampton, Qld), d 1 Jul 1967 (Greenslopes, Qld). 533.

PAGE, Milford Laurenson; *NZ*. RHB/RSM. b 8 May 1902 (Littleton, NZ), d 13 Feb 1987 (Christchurch, NZ). 633, 898.

PAGE-HANIFY - see Hanify.

PALMER, George Eugene; *Vic & Tas*. RHB/RM. b 22 Feb 1860 (Mulwala, NSW), d 22 Aug 1910 (Baddaginnie, Vic). 42, 43, 44, 47, 49, 52, 53, 54, 55, 56, 57, 58, 59, 64, 65, 66, 67, 68, 69, 70, 71, 72, 73, 74, 78, 79, 85, 87, 88, 89, 94, 95, 96, 97, 104, 134, 138, 173, 205.

PALMER, George Hamilton; *Sth Aust*. LHB/LFM. b 2 Aug 1903 (Eastwood, SA), d 24 Aug 1986 (Woodville Sth, SA). 578, 580, 586, 596, 600, 609, 614, 619, 690.

PALMER, Jack Stirling; *Sth Aust*. RHB. b 20 Oct 1903 (East Adelaide), d 11 Dec 1979 (Glenelg, SA). 801.

PARK, Alfred Leath; *NSW*. RHB/Long-stop b 15 Apr 1840 (Oatlands, Tas), d 16 Jan 1924 (Liverpool, NSW). 12, 17, 20.

PARK, Roy Lindsay; *Vic*. RHB. b 30 Jul 1892 (Ballarat, NSW), d 23 Jan 1947 (Middle Park, Vic). 457, 476, 477, 481, 483, 484, 485, 489, 491, 493, 495, 501, 502, 505, 508, 509, 511, 513, 515, 520, 521, 525, 526, 535, 536, 545, 549, 550, 552, 556, 563, 566, 569, 574, 576, 591.

PARKER, Ernest Frederick; *West Aust*. RHB. b 5 Nov 1883 (Perth), d 2 May 1918 (in action in France). 333, 335, 346, 347, 348, 382, 383, 386, 387, 388, 401, 402, 403.

PARKER, Ronald Arthur; *Sth Aust*. RHB/LB. b 23 Feb 1916 (Goodwood, SA). 820, 824, 847, 853, 855, 858, 860, 861, 864, 871, 874, 880, 882.

PARKIN, Cecil Harry; *Eng*. RHB/OB/LB. b 18 Feb 1886 (Eaglescliffe, Durham), d 15 Jun 1943 (Manchester, Eng). 512, 513, 516, 519, 521, 524, 526, 527, 528, 530, 531.

PARKIN, George Thomas; *Sth Aust*. RHB/RM/OB. b 11 Oct 1864 (Adelaide), d 6 Aug 1933 (Adelaide). 132, 154, 156, 157, 164, 166, 167.

PARKINSON, Henry; *Tas*. RHB/WK. b   (   ), d   (   ). 384, 398, 418, 421, 444, 484.

PARKS, James Horace; *Eng*. RHB/RSM. b 12 May 1903 (Haywards Heath, Sussex), d 21 Nov 1980 (Cuckfield, Sussex). 845, 847, 848, 849, 851.

PARR, George; *Eng*. RHB/u-arm. b 22 May 1826 (Radcliffe-on-Trent, Notts), d 23 Jun 1891 (Radcliffe-on-Trent, Notts). 15.

PARRY, Cyril Norman; *Sth Aust & Tas*. RHB/WK. b 14 Oct 1900 (Queenstown, SA), d 6 Jul 1984 (Kew, Vic). 609, 611, 612, 614, 619, 622, 660, 702, 710, 711, 754, 755, 758, 759, 768, 782, 785, 788, 791, 802, 812, 814, 819, 825, 826.

PARSLOE, Cyril Keith; *NZ*. LHB/RFM. b 27 Sep 1908 (Wellington, NZ), d 13 Sep 1989 (Wellington, NZ). 898, 899, 901.

PARSONAGE, Thomas Griffith; *NSW*. LHB/RM. b 13 Nov 1910 (Chatswood, NSW), d 3 Feb 1951 (Manly, NSW). 790.

PARSONS, Herbert Fulton; *Vic*. LHB/LB. b 21 May 1875 (Hawthorn, Vic), d 20 Dec 1937 (East Camberwell, Vic). 384, 385, 398, 414, 423.

PATAUDI, Nawab of, Iftikhar Ali Khan; *Eng*. RHB. b 16 Mar 1910 (Pataudi, India), d 5 Jan 1952 (New Delhi, India). 771, 772, 775, 776, 778, 779, 781, 782, 789, 793.

PATEMAN, Robert; *Vic.* RHB. b 28 Aug 1856 (Magpie, Vic), d ( ). 45, 60.

PATFIELD, Alfred Samuel; *West Aust.* RHB/WK. b 6 Sep 1884 (Paterson, NSW), d 9 Nov 1961 (Perth). 386, 402, 403.

PATON, George Douglas; *Tas.* LHB/LM. b 1 Mar 1879 (Hobart), d 5 Oct 1950 (Hobart). 236, 259, 285, 303, 309, 321, 322, 345, 363, 369, 384, 385, 400, 418, 421, 443, 444, 451, 464, 469, 482.

PATRICK, Charles Wright; *NSW & Qld.* RHB. b 13 Jan 1866 (Sydney), d 29 Nov 1919 (Coogee, NSW). 171, 277, 281, 286, 295, 300.

PATRICK, William Robert; *NZ.* RHB/OB. b 17 Jun 1885 (Lyttelton, NZ), d 14 Aug 1946 (Christchurch, NZ). 473, 475, 478, 603, 605, 609, 610.

PATTERSON, Thomas Francis ?; *Tas.* /u-arm. b ( ), d ( ). 8.

PAYNE, Charles Percy; *Tas.* RHB/WK. b 31 Jul 1876 (Hobart), d 28 Jan 1938 (Lower Sandy Bay, Tas). 369, 418, 464, 469.

PAYNTER, Edward; *Eng.* LHB/RM. b 5 Nov 1901 (Oswaldwistle, Lancs), d 5 Feb 1979 (Keighley, Yorks). 772, 776, 778, 782, 785, 792, 796, 797, 799, 800, 801.

PEACHEY, Mark; *Qld.* RHB. b 31 Oct 1900 (Tannymorel, Qld), d 23 Nov 1987 (Ipswich, Qld). 672.

PEARSALL, Alan Louden; *Tas.* RHB/RM. b 24 May 1915 (Hobart), d 8 Mar 1944 (in action over English Channel). 825, 856, 859, 865, 866, 927, 929.

PEARSE, Charles Ormerod Cato; *Sth Afr.* RHB. b 10 Oct 1884 (Pietermaritzburg, Sth Afr), d 7 May 1953 (Durban, Sth Afr). 406, 408, 409, 411, 413, 417, 420, 421, 423, 425, 426.

PEARSON, William Ernest; *Vic.* RHB/RM. b 10 Nov 1912 (Kerang, Vic), d 1989 ( ). 879, 881, 887, 893, 896, 900, 903, 905, 907, 909, 912, 914, 916, 917.

PEATE, Edmund; *Eng.* LHB/SLA. b 2 Mar 1856 (Holbeck, Yorks), d 11 Mar 1900 (Newlay, Yorks). 51, 52, 54, 56, 57, 58, 59.

PEEL, Robert; *Eng.* LHB/SLA. b 12 Feb 1857 (Churwell, Yorks), d 12 Aug 1941 Morley, Yorks). 76, 77, 78, 80, 82, 84, 85, 86, 105, 106, 108, 112, 113, 117, 118, 121, 123, 143, 145, 147, 150, 151, 152, 153, 172, 173, 174, 176, 177, 179, 181, 184, 186, 189, 190, 191.

PEGLER, Sidney James; *Sth Afr.* RHB/LB. b 28 Jul 1888 (Durban, Sth Afr), d 10 Sep 1972 (Cape Town, Sth Afr). 406, 407, 411, 417, 419, 420, 423, 424, 425, 426, 427.

PELLEW, Arthur Howard; *Sth Aust.* Brother of J.H.Pellew. b 20 Jan 1878 (Riverton, SA), d 21 Aug 1948 (Rose Park, SA). 254, 258.

PELLEW, Clarence Everard; *Sth Aust.* RHB/RM. Brother of L.V.Pellew. b 21 Sep 1893 (Port Pirie, SA), d 9 May 1981 (Adelaide). 474, 476, 479, 480, 483, 487, 489, 490, 495, 504, 506, 507, 509, 511, 512, 515, 518, 519, 521, 523, 524, 527, 554, 557, 601, 652, 656, 660, 664, 667.

PELLEW, John Harold; *Sth Aust.* RHB/LB. Brother of A.H.Pellew. b 17 Jul 1882 (Truro, SA), d 17 Oct 1946 (Unley Park, SA). 296, 311, 313, 318, 319, 325, 327, 329, 330, 337, 339, 341, 342, 349, 352, 355, 370, 374, 376, 378, 380.

PELLEW, Lancelot Vivian; *Sth Aust.* RHB. Brother of C.E.Pellew & cousin of A.H. & J.H.Pellew. b 15 Dec 1899 (Port Elliott, SA), d 8 Dec 1970 (Adelaide). 509, 515, 518, 523, 534, 536, 537, 548, 550, 551.

PENMAN, Arthur Percival; *NSW.* RHB/RF. b 23 Jan 1885 (Ultimo, NSW), d 11 Sep 1944 (Wahroonga, NSW). 317, 322, 323, 326, 331.

PENN, Frank; *Eng.* RHB/RaB(r). b 7 Mar 1851 (Lewisham, Kent), d 26 Dec 1916 (Bifrons, Kent). 39, 40.

PENNEFATHER, George Shirley; *Tas.* RHB/OB. b 28 Sep 1864 (Launceston), d 16 Oct 1945 (Launceston). 134, 205.

PENNYCUICK, Rupert James; *Tas.* LHB/LFM. b 11 Apr 1893 (Jericho, Tas), d 17 Jan 1963 (Concord, NSW). 451, 464, 469.

PEPPER, Cecil George; *NSW.* RHB/LBG. b 15 Sep 1918 (Forbes, NSW). 921, 930, 932, 933, 938, 941, 942, 944, 947, 949, 952, 955, 958, 959, 961, 962, 963.

PERRATON, Jack Oldfield; *Vic.* LHB/RM. Son of W.T.C.Perraton. b 26 Feb 1911 (St Kilda, Vic), d 1 Oct 1950 (Kings Cross, NSW). 693, 694, 699, 731.

PERRATON, William Thomas Crooke; *Vic.* RHB. b 27 Aug 1868 (Carlton, Vic), d 23 Sep 1953 (Elsternwick, Vic). 252.

PERRY, Cecil Thomas Henry; *Tas.* RHB. b 3 Mar 1846 (Battery Point, Tas), d 4 Aug 1917 (Timaru, NZ). 19.

PERYMAN, Charles Henry; *Vic.* RHB. b 20 Jan 1872 (Richmond, Vic), d 30 Aug 1950 (St Kilda, Vic). 190, 192, 197.

PETERS, Arthur Ernest; *Sth Aust.* RHB/OB. b 8 Mar 1872 (Adelaide), d 24 Sep 1903 (Henley Beach, SA). 228, 233, 234.

PETTINGER, Aldam Murr; *Sth Aust.* RHB. b 30 Jul 1859 (Kent Town, SA), d 18 Aug 1950 (Lower Mitcham, SA). 45.

PHELPS, Leslie R ; *Tas.* LHB/RFM. b ( ), d ( ). 674.

PHILIPSON, Hylton; *Eng.* RHB/WK. b 8 Jun 1866 (Tynemouth, Northumberland), d 4 Dec 1935 (Westminster, London). 152, 153, 173, 176, 179, 181, 184, 186, 189, 190, 191.

PHILLIPS, Edward George; *Sth Aust.* RHB. b 1 Mar 1851 (Port Adelaide, SA), d 8 Feb 1933 (Nth Adelaide). 35, 90, 112, 124, 127, 132.

PHILLIPS, Edward Lauriston; *Sth Aust.* RHB/RFM. b 2 Sep 1892 (Nth Adelaide), d 8 Jan 1971 (Adelaide). 509, 511, 512.

PHILLIPS, James; *Vic.* RHB/RM. b 1 Sep 1860 (Pleasant Creek, Vic), d 21 Apr 1930 (Vancouver, Canada). 90, 91, 100, 103, 125, 127, 138, 139, 140, 141, 142, 146, 155, 158, 160, 168, 192.

PHILLIPS, Joseph; *Vic.* RHB/WK. b 22 Apr 1840 (Parramatta, NSW), d 7 May 1901 (Heidelberg, Vic). 16, 17, 19, 20, 21, 22.

PHILLIPS, Norbert Eugene; *NSW.* RHB/RM. b 9 Jul 1896 ( ), d 3 Oct 1961 (Sydney). 558, 602, 608, 610, 618, 620, 622, 623, 626, 628, 633, 634, 637, 638, 642, 646, 692.

PHILPOTT, Albert John William; *Vic.* b 14 Mar 1873 (Lauraville, Vic), d 25 Nov 1950 (Kew, Vic). 183.

PHILPOTT, Richard Stamper; *Vic.* Brother of W.Philpott. b 15 May 1827 (Brighton, Sussex), d 7 Sep 1894 (Hammersmith, London). 1.

PHILPOTT, William; *Vic.* /WK. Brother of R.S.Philpott. b c 1819 ( ), d 4 Nov 1891 (Linton, Kent). 1, 4.

PICKERING, George Thomas; *Vic.* LHB. b 1832 (Sydney), d 1 Dec 1858 (Sandridge, Vic). 6.

PICKETT, Alfred William; *Tas.* /RF. b 1871 (Ulverstone, Tas), d 19 Mar 1953 (Ulverstone, Tas). 249, 252.

PICKETT, Edward Arthur; *Tas.* LHB/WK. b 2 Apr 1909 (Ulverstone, Tas). 676, 693, 694, 701, 705, 706, 707, 721, 731, 839, 856.

PICTET, Francis S ; *Tas.* RHB. b c 1866 (Bath, Somerset), d ( ). 219.

PIERCE, Michael; *NSW & Qld.* b 3 Sep 1869 (Paddington, NSW), d 4 Feb 1913 (Sydney). 154, 155, 157, 158, 163, 164, 165, 176.

PILLING, Richard; *Eng* RHB/WK. b 5 Jul 1855 (Bedford, Eng), d 28 Mar 1891 (Old Trafford, Lancs). 51, 52, 54, 56, 57, 58, 59, 107, 109, 110, 114, 116, 117, 120, 122.

PITCHER, Franklyn Joseph; *Vic.* RHB/RM. b 24 Jun 1879 (Collingwood, Vic), d 23 Jan 1921 (Northcote, Vic). 423.

PITE, Walter Edward; *NSW.* RHB/OB. b 24 Sep 1876 ( ), d 7 May 1955 (Waverley, NSW). 271, 494.

PLANT, Hugh Joseph; *Vic.* LHB/OB. b 12 Oct 1911 (Narrandera, NSW). 788, 791, 798, 800, 802, 819, 821, 823, 839, 848, 852, 854, 858, 862, 863, 864, 872, 874, 879, 881.

POCOCK, William Johnstone; *NSW.* RHB/OB. b 1848 (Clifton, Eng), d 27 Sep 1928 (East Brighton, Vic). 26.

POEPPEL, George Augustus; *Qld.* b 6 Nov 1893 (Bundaberg, Qld), d 2 Feb 1917 (German POW camp). 494.

POIDEVIN, Leslie Oswald Sheridan; *NSW.* RHB. b 5 Nov 1876 (Merrila, NSW), d 18 Nov 1931 (Bondi, NSW). 208, 238, 249, 258, 260, 263, 271, 272, 317.

PONSFORD, William Harold; *Vic*. RHB. b 19 Oct 1900 (Nth Fitzroy, Vic), d 6 Apr 1991 (Kyneton, Vic). 526, 540, 553, 554, 556, 562, 563, 566, 568, 569, 574, 576, 578, 582, 583, 585, 587, 591, 593, 595, 598, 600, 604, 607, 613, 615, 616, 617, 619, 621, 623, 625, 629, 630, 635, 636, 638, 641, 646, 647, 651, 654, 656, 659, 661, 685, 688, 689, 692, 695, 700, 703, 704, 707, 708, 712, 714, 718, 723, 725, 728, 734, 735, 738, 742, 745, 747, 749, 752, 756, 762, 764, 766, 773, 774, 781, 783, 786, 792, 797, 804, 805, 806, 807, 808, 810, 813, 827, 828.

POOLEY, Edward; *Eng*. RHB/WK. b 13 Feb 1838 (Richmond, Surrey), d 18 Jul 1907 (Lambeth, London). 32.

POON, Hunter Robert Gordon; *Qld*. RHB/LBG. b 14 May 1894 (Ballina, NSW), d 25 Jan 1980 (Greenslopes, Qld). 562.

POPE, Roland James; *NSW*. RHB. b 18 Feb 1864 (Sydney), d 27 Jul 1952 (Manly, NSW). 79, 80, 82, 83, 131.

POUGHER, Arthur Dick; *Eng*. RHB/RFM. b 19 Apr 1865 (Leicester, Eng), d 20 May 1926 (Leicester, Eng). 107, 109, 110, 114, 120, 122.

POWELL, Adam Gordon; *Eng*. RHB/WK. b 17 Aug 1912 (Boxted, Essex), d 7 Jun 1982 (Sandwich, Kent). 847, 849, 851.

POWELL, George; *NSW*. RHB/LB. b 12 Apr 1918 (Newtown, NSW). 964.

POWELL, Ronald Hartley; *Tas*. RHB/LFM. b 27 Sep 1883 (New Norfolk, Tas), d 1921 (, Qld). 492.

POWELL, Theodore; *NSW*. RHB. b 10 Jul 1852 (Berrima, NSW), d 3 Sep 1913 (Sydney). 26, 28, 29, 30, 31, 32, 36, 37, 40, 44, 48, 62, 73, 74, 82.

POWER, Cornelius Patrick Lewis; *Sth Aust*. RHB/LBG. Brother of L.J.Power. b 10 Oct 1905 (Ovingham, SA). 631, 632.

POWER, Laurence James; *Sth Aust*. RHB. Brother of C.P.L.Power. b 31 Jul 1898 (Ovingham, SA), d 20 Mar 1963 (Glenelg, SA). 531.

POWER, Robert; *Vic*. b 1833 (Galway, Ireland), d 4 Nov 1914 (Toorak, Vic). 7, 8.

POWLETT, Frederick Armand; *Vic*. b 6 Jan 1811 (Dunmow, Essex), d 9 Jun 1865 (Kyneton, Vic). 2, 3.

PRATTEN, Herbert Graham; *NSW*. RHB. b 22 Apr 1892 (Ashfield, NSW), d 11 Sep 1979 (Neutral Bay, NSW). 470, 486, 487, 488, 490.

PRENTICE, Warden Selby; *NSW*. RHB/WK. b 30 Jul 1886 (Homebush, NSW), d 26 Feb 1969 (Rosebery, NSW). 467, 522.

PRESTON, Joseph Merritt; *Eng*. RHB/RF. b 22 Aug 1864 (Yeadon, Yorks), d 26 Nov 1890 (Windhill, Yorks). 107, 109, 110, 114, 116, 120, 122.

PRETTY, Alfred Henry; *Sth Aust*. /LB. b 29 Jan 1874 (Willunga, SA), d 21 Jun 1929 (Mile End, SA). 376.

PRICE, Walter Davies; *Sth Aust*. /RM. b 24 Mar 1886 (Hawthorn, SA), d 29 Jul 1944 (Adelaide). 483.

PRITCHARD, David Edward; *Sth Aust*. LHB. b 5 Jan 1893 (Queenstown, SA), d 4 Jul 1983 (Myrtle Bank, SA). 497, 500, 502, 503, 511, 515, 534, 536, 537, 541, 548, 564, 566, 567, 569, 575, 578, 580, 586, 596, 597, 600, 601, 606, 609, 611, 612, 614, 619, 622, 624, 625, 626, 652, 656, 671, 684, 690, 691, 695, 697, 698, 702, 704, 710, 711, 716, 720, 745.

PROUT, James Alexander; *Qld*. RHB. b 12 Aug 1889 (Flemington, Vic), d 18 Feb 1952 (Double Bay, NSW). 473, 486, 493, 508.

PUCKETT, Charles William; *West Aust*. RHB/RFM. b 21 Feb 1911 (Beddington Corner, Surrey). 951.

PUNCH, Austin Thomas Eugene; *NSW & Tas*. RHB/LB. b 16 Aug 1894 (Nth Sydney), d 25 Aug 1985 (Sydney). 499, 505, 507, 510, 518, 522, 528, 534, 535, 537, 538, 539, 551, 565, 567, 568, 579, 584, 586, 591, 594, 602, 608, 610, 612, 643, 666.

PUTMAN, Sydney William Leslie; *Tas*. LHB/LBG. b 25 Mar 1912 (Hobart), d 20 Sep 1947 (Hobart). 722, 729, 731, 754, 755, 768, 782, 785, 791, 812, 814, 826, 839, 856, 859, 885, 886, 915, 919, 927, 929.

PYE, Leslie Walter; *NSW*. RHB/LB. b 6 Jul 1871 (Parramatta, NSW), d 9 Mar 1949 (Parramatta, NSW). 208, 214, 216, 218, 221, 223, 229, 230, 231, 233, 235, 238, 239, 243, 245, 246, 247, 250, 251, 277, 278, 279, 280, 283, 284, 289, 300, 317, 326.

PYKE, Richard Dimond; *Qld*. RHB/WK. b 15 Aug 1877 (Collingwood, Vic), d 4 Dec 1914 (Gympie, Qld). 312, 399.

QUAIFE, William George; *Eng*. RHB/RM/LB. b 17 Mar 1872 (Newhaven, Sussex), d 13 Oct 1951 (Edgbaston, Birmingham). 261, 262, 263, 266, 268, 270, 272, 273, 274, 275, 276.

QUILTY, John; *Sth Aust*. LHB/LaB b 1860 (Adelaide), d 9 May 1942 (Kent Town, SA). 60, 70.

QUIN, Stanley Oldfield; *Vic*. RHB/WK b 17 Apr 1908 (Caulfield, Vic), d 27 Nov 1967 (Brighton, Vic). 729, 731, 732, 754, 755, 768, 788, 791, 802, 812, 814, 819, 821, 823, 839, 848, 852, 854, 858, 862, 863, 864, 903, 915.

QUINLAN, Patrick Francis; *West Aust*. RHB/RM. b 17 Mar 1891 (Perth), d 15 Aug 1935 (Perth). 597, 598, 599, 617, 631, 648, 649, 650.

QUINN, Neville Anthony; *Sth Afr*. RHB/LMF. b 21 Feb 1908 (Tweefontein, Sth Afr), d 5 Aug 1934 (Kimberley, Sth Afr). 741, 742, 746, 747, 748, 749, 756, 759, 762, 764, 765, 770.

QUIST, Karl Hugo; *NSW, West Aust & Sth Aust*. RHB/LB. b 18 Aug 1875 (Milsons Point, NSW), d 31 Mar 1957 (Plympton, SA). 249, 333, 335, 376, 386, 387, 388, 394, 395, 441.

RADCLIFFE, Octavius Goldney; *Eng*. RHB/OB. b 20 Oct 1859 (Newnton, Wiltshire), d 13 Apr 1940 (Cherhill, Wiltshire). 144, 151.

RAHMANN, Herbert William; *Qld*. RHB/RM. b 23 Aug 1886 (Maryborough, Qld), d 12 Oct 1957 (Nundah, Qld). 584.

RAINEY, Leslie Newburn; *Vic*. RHB/ b 10 Jan 1881 (Sth Yarra, Vic), d 27 Aug 1962 (Melbourne). 285, 321.

RAMSAY, John; *Tas*. b 26 Dec 1872 (Glasgow), d 6 Feb 1944 (Launceston). 219.

RAMSAY, Marmaduke Francis; *Qld*. RHB/RM. b 8 Dec 1860 (Cheltenham, Glos), d 31 Dec 1947 (Lee Priory, Kent). 163, 171, 245.

RANDELL, Alfred Charles; *West Aust*. RHB. b 10 May 1884 (Perth), d 13 Sep 1958 (Sydney). 454, 455, 456, 457, 542.

RANDELL, Ernest Arthur; *West Aust*. LHB/SLA. b 25 Jan 1873 (Perth), d 12 May 1938 (Perth). 161, 162, 242.

RANDELL, James Arthur; *NSW*. RHB/LBG. b 4 Aug 1880 (   ), d 7 Dec 1952 (Balgowlah, NSW). 390, 393, 436, 452, 487, 488, 490, 529, 586.

RANJITSINHJI, Kumar Shri; *Eng*. RHB/RaB. b 10 Sep 1872 (Sarodar, India), d 2 Apr 1933 (Jamnagar, India). 209, 210, 211, 213, 215, 217, 220, 221, 224, 225, 226, 227.

RANSFORD, Vernon Seymour; *Vic*. LHB/SLA. b 20 Mar 1885 (Sth Yarra, Vic), d 19 Mar 1958 (Brighton, Vic). 306, 309, 313, 314, 316, 318, 320, 325, 328, 329, 332, 337, 340, 344, 350, 352, 356, 357, 358, 360, 361, 364, 366, 368, 372, 374, 377, 378, 381, 382, 383, 392, 394, 398, 404, 413, 415, 417, 419, 422, 423, 424, 426, 428, 430, 432, 434, 438, 439, 440, 442, 447, 450, 454, 460, 461, 466, 468, 471, 476, 488, 489, 496, 497, 498, 501, 505, 508, 509, 511, 513, 515, 535, 536, 538, 539, 541, 545, 549, 550, 552, 554, 556, 562, 563, 568, 591, 592, 605, 611, 613, 648, 649.

RATCLIFFE, Andrew Thomas; *NSW*. LHB/WK. b 3 May 1891 (Sydney), d 31 Aug 1974 (Banksia, NSW). 482, 486, 487, 488, 490, 491, 494, 496, 498, 499, 500, 501, 503, 505, 507, 522, 525, 565, 571, 580, 586, 588, 594, 599, 608, 610, 620, 622, 623, 640, 642, 644, 666.

RAWLIN, John Thomas; *Eng*. RHB/RFM. b 10 Nov 1856 (Greasbrough, Yorks), d 19 Jan 1924 (Greasbrough, Yorks). 105, 106, 108, 112, 113, 118, 121, 123.

RAYMOND, Ralph Cossart; *Qld*. RHB/RFM. Nephew of C.E.Cossart. b 28 Nov 1912 (Boonah, Qld), d 11 Oct 1982 (Murgon, Qld). 803.

RAYMER, Vincent Norman; *Qld*. LHB/LM/SLA. b 4 May 1918 (Toowoomba, Qld). 953, 954, 958, 960, 964.

RAYSON, Maxwell William; *Vic*. LHB/LBG. Son of W.J.Rayson. b 26 Aug 1912 (Kew, Vic). 900, 903, 916.

RAYSON, William Jones; *Vic*. RHB/LBG. b 18 Dec 1889 (Malmsbury, Vic), d 8 Sep 1957 (Parkdale, Vic). 591, 592, 598, 613, 619, 663.

READ, Arthur Edwin; *West Aust*. LHB. b 26 May 1908 (Unley, SA). 936, 937, 951.

READ, Holcombe Douglas; *Eng*. RHB/RF. b 28 Jan 1910 (Woodford Green, Essex). 847, 848, 849.

READ, John Maurice; *Eng.* RHB/RFM. b 9 Feb 1859 (Thames Ditton, Surrey), d 17 Feb 1929 (Winchester, Hampshire). 76, 77, 78, 80, 82, 84, 85, 86, 91, 92, 93, 94, 96, 97, 99, 101, 102, 103, 104, 107, 109, 110, 114, 116, 117, 120, 122, 143, 144, 145, 147, 150, 151, 152, 153.

READ, Walter William; *Eng.* RHB/RF(r)/u-arm. b 23 Nov 1855 (Reigate, Surrey), d 6 Jan 1907 (Addiscombe, Surrey). 61, 62, 64, 65, 66, 68, 69, 106, 108, 112, 113, 117, 118, 121, 123.

REDDROP, Walter William; *Vic.* RHB. b 9 Sep 1901 (Kyneton, Vic), d 31 Mar 1983 (Parkville, Vic). 643, 670.

REDFEARN, James; *Vic.* RHB. b 1836 (Yorks), d 10 Mar 1916 (Glenhuntly, Vic). 14.

REDGRAVE, John Sidney; *NSW & Qld.* RHB/RM. b 5 Aug 1878 (Nth Sydney), d 3 Aug 1958 (West End, Qld). 322, 323, 324, 327, 328, 330, 336, 353, 354, 359, 373, 375, 379, 390, 393, 409, 414, 416, 429, 452, 458, 467, 471, 472, 494, 533.

REEDMAN, John Cole; *Sth Aust.* RHB/RM. b 9 Oct 1865 (Gilberton, SA), d 25 Mar 1924 (Gilberton, SA). 119, 124, 127, 132, 136, 137, 139, 142, 143, 148, 154, 156, 157, 160, 164, 166, 167, 170, 172, 175, 177, 180, 187, 188, 191, 192, 195, 198, 199, 201, 203, 204, 207, 209, 212, 216, 222, 223, 227, 228, 230, 232, 233, 234, 239, 240, 241, 244, 246, 248, 250, 253, 254, 255, 257, 258, 261, 264, 265, 269, 276, 279, 282, 283, 287, 290, 291, 294, 296, 298, 315, 318, 319, 325, 329, 330, 333, 335, 386, 387, 388.

REES, John Newman Stace; *Sth Aust.* RHB/WK. Brother of R.B.C.Rees. b 2 Sep 1880 (Hindmarsh, SA), d 17 Jan 1959 (St Peters, SA). 333.

REES, Robert Blackie Colston; *Sth Aust.* RHB/LBG. Brother of J.N.S.Rees. b 15 Apr 1882 (Hindmarsh, SA), d 20 Sep 1966 (Bowmans Green, Herts). 294, 296, 298, 389, 404, 406, 410, 427, 431, 434, 436, 453, 468.

REES, William Gilbert; *NSW.* RHB. Cousin of G.H.B.Gilbert, E.M. & W.G.Grace. b 6 Apr 1827 (Haverford West, Pembrokeshire), d 31 Oct 1898 (Marlborough, NZ). 5.

REES, William Lee; *Vic.* b 16 Dec 1836 (Bristol, Glos), d 13 May 1912 (Gisborne, NZ). 5, 6, 16.

REESE, Daniel; *NZ.* LHB/SLA. b 27 Jan 1879 (Christchurch, NZ), d 12 Jun 1953 (Christchurch, NZ). 237, 238, 473, 475, 478, 480.

REEVES, William Henry; *Vic.* /WK. b ( ), d ( ). 345, 384, 389.

REID, Curtis Alexander; *Vic.* LHB/RaB. b 1838 (Inverary Park, NSW), d 1 Jul 1886 (Hawthorn, Vic). 21, 22, 23.

REID, Douglas C ; *NSW.* RHB. b 23 Sep 1886 ( ), d ( ). 375, 379, 390.

REID, W ; *Sth Aust.* b c 1871 (Nth Adelaide), d ( ). 161.

REID, William; *Tas.* RHB/WK. b ( ), d ( ). 385.

RELF, Albert Edward; *Eng.* RHB/RM. b 26 Jul 1874 (Brightling, Sussex), d 26 Mar 1937 (Wellington College, Berks). 291, 292, 293, 295, 297, 301, 303, 307, 311.

RENFREY, Leslie Cotswold; *West Aust.* RHB/RFM. b 15 Feb 1893 (Wallaroo, SA), d 23 Sep 1958 (Mt Lawley, WA). 559, 572, 573, 597, 598, 599, 601, 631, 648, 649.

RHODES, Wilfred; *Eng.* RHB/SLA. b 29 Oct 1877 (Kirkheaton, Yorks), d 8 Jul 1973 (Branksome, Dorset). 291, 292, 293, 295, 297, 301, 302, 303, 305, 306, 307, 308, 310, 311, 348, 349, 350, 351, 353, 354, 356, 357, 360, 361, 362, 363, 366, 367, 368, 370, 371, 431, 432, 433, 435, 437, 438, 440, 442, 443, 444, 446, 447, 448, 450, 513, 514, 516, 517, 519, 521, 524, 526, 527, 528, 530, 531.

RICHARDS, Frank L ; *Vic.* LHB. b ( ), d ( ). 134.

RICHARDS, Thomas Oliver; *Sth Aust.* RHB/RaB. b 5 Jul 1855 (Norwood,SA), d 14 Dec 1923 (Cottonville, SA). 45, 60, 70, 75

RICHARDSON, Arthur John; *Sth Aust & West Aust.* RHB/OB. b 24 Jul 1888 (Sevenhills, SA), d 23 Dec 1973 (Semaphore, SA). 497, 500, 502, 503, 509, 511, 512, 515, 518, 523, 531, 534, 536, 537, 541, 544, 548, 550, 551, 554, 557, 561, 564, 566, 567, 569, 571, 574, 575, 578, 580, 582, 583, 585, 587, 593, 596, 597, 600, 604, 606, 609, 611, 612, 614, 615, 616, 617, 619, 622, 624, 625, 626, 631, 632, 648, 649, 650, 681, 682.

RICHARDSON, Charles Augustus; *NSW.* RHB. Brother of W.A.Richardson. b 22 Feb 1864 (Sydney), d 17 Aug 1949 (Waipara, NZ). 93, 95, 98, 101, 107, 109, 126, 129, 130, 137, 138, 149, 157, 158, 174.

RICHARDSON, Frederick William; *Tas.* b 29 Mar 1878 (Campbell Town, Tas), d 7 Mar 1955 (Campbell Town, Tas). 285.

RICHARDSON, George Biggs; *NSW.* RHB/OB. b 28 May 1834 (Bathurst, NSW), d 1 May 1911 (Dandaloo, NSW). 10, 11.

RICHARDSON, Howard James; *Vic.* LHB. b 29 Oct 1894 (Narre Warren, Vic), d 21 Dec 1959 (Richmond, Vic). 570.

RICHARDSON, Joseph; *Sth Aust.* /WK. b 28 Feb 1878 (Kooringa, SA), d 13 Jun 1951 (Glenelg, SA). 333, 335.

RICHARDSON, Leslie Lambert; *Tas.* RHB. Brother of W.B.Richardson. b 9 Jan 1887 (Sandford, Tas), d 15 Nov 1962 (Hobart). 540.

RICHARDSON, Leslie Walter; *Tas.* RHB/RM. Son of L.L.Richardson. b 5 Sep 1911 (New Town, Tas), d 1 Nov 1981 (Hobart). 669, 676, 693, 694, 754, 755, 758, 759, 768.

RICHARDSON, Thomas; *Eng.* RHB/RF. b 11 Aug 1870 (Byfleet, Surrey), d 2 Jul 1912 (St Jean d'Arvey, France). 172, 173, 176, 177, 179, 181, 184, 186, 189, 190, 191, 209, 210, 211, 213, 215, 217, 220, 224, 225, 226, 227.

RICHARDSON, Victor York; *Sth Aust.* RHB/RM. b 7 Sep 1894 (Parkside, SA), d 29 Oct 1969 (Fullarton, SA). 497, 500, 502, 503, 509, 512, 515, 518, 523, 534, 536, 537, 539, 544, 548, 550, 551, 554, 557, 564, 566, 567, 571, 574, 575, 578, 580, 583, 585, 586, 587, 596, 597, 600, 604, 606, 609, 611, 612, 614, 619, 622, 624, 625, 626, 630, 631, 632, 635, 637, 639, 641, 644, 645, 651, 652, 656, 657, 660, 661, 664, 665, 667, 671, 677, 679, 684, 690, 691, 695, 697, 698, 702, 704, 707, 708, 709, 716, 720, 724, 726, 733, 735, 739, 741, 745, 751, 753, 761, 766, 767, 769, 772, 775, 780, 781, 784, 787, 789, 792, 794, 795, 797, 799, 801, 804, 805, 809, 811, 813, 816, 817, 820, 828, 829, 830, 832, 834, 835, 841, 844, 867, 871, 874, 889, 891, 894, 898, 902.

RICHARDSON, William Alfred; *NSW.* RHB/RFM. Brother of C.A.Richardson. b 22 Aug 1866 (Sydney), d 3 Jan 1930 (Mosman, NSW). 111, 115, 118, 122, 126, 130, 133, 136, 146, 194, 195, 196.

RICHARDSON, Walter Barrett; *Tas.* RHB/RF. Brother of L.L.Richardson. b 24 Oct 1876 (Sandford, Tas), d 30 May 1962 (Hobart). 229, 362, 363, 451.

RICHTER, Arthur Frederick; *Sth Aust.* RHB/LBG. Nephew of E.Jones. b 1 Sep 1908 (Telowie, SA), d 16 Aug 1936 (Adelaide). 858.

RICKMAN, Wilfred; *Vic.* RHB/RF, b 1849 (Sth Yarra, Vic), d 6 Jun 1911 (Frankston, Vic). 50.

RIDINGS, Kenneth Lovett; *Sth Aust.* RHB/LBG. Brother of P.L.Ridings. b 7 Feb 1920 (Malvern, SA), d 17 May 1943 (in action over Bay of Biscay). 924, 926, 928, 931, 932, 935, 939, 941, 943, 945, 946, 947, 950, 951, 955, 956, 957, 959, 963.

RIDINGS, Phillip Lovett; *Sth Aust.* RHB/RFM. Brother of K.L.Ridings. b 2 Oct 1917 (Malvern, SA). 904, 928, 932, 935, 943, 956, 957, 963.

§RIGAUD, Stephen; *Sth Aust.* /RF. b 25 Nov 1856 (Kenton Valley, Talunga, SA), d ( ). 35.

RIGBY, Albert; *West Aust.* LHB/SLA. b 1901 (Lancs), d 10 Oct 1963 (Hollywood, WA). 632.

RIGG, Keith Edward; *Vic.* RHB. b 21 May 1906 (Malvern, Vic). 621, 628, 629, 646, 647, 656, 662, 663, 685, 688, 689, 692, 695, 700, 703, 712, 714, 719, 723, 730, 735, 738, 742, 745, 749, 752, 756, 762, 764, 765, 773, 774, 776, 778, 780, 783, 800, 804, 805, 807, 808, 810, 813, 818, 831, 833, 835, 837, 838, 841, 848, 851, 852, 854, 858, 862, 863, 864, 872, 874, 879, 881, 883, 887, 888, 890, 893, 895, 896, 899, 902, 905, 907, 909, 912, 914, 916, 917, 922, 923, 925, 928, 933, 934, 935, 936, 937.

RILEY, William Norman; *Sth Aust.* RHB/LFM. b 9 Apr 1894 (Hyde Park, SA), d 2 Oct 1960 (Nth Adelaide). 601.

RIMINGTON, Stanley Garnet; *Vic.* RHB/LBG. b 22 Jan 1892 (Kew, Vic). 540.

RING, Douglas Thomas; *Vic.* RHB/LBG. b 14 Oct 1918 (Hobart). 925, 928, 936, 937, 939, 940, 942, 945, 948, 949, 952, 954, 956, 957, 960, 961, 962.

ROACH, Clifford Archibald; *WI*. RHB. b 13 Mar 1904 (Port of Spain, Trinidad), d 16 Apr 1988 (Trinidad). 713, 714, 716, 718, 721, 722, 725, 727, 728, 732, 733, 734, 736, 738.

ROACH, William Alexander; *West Aust*. LHB. b 12 Dec 1914 (Sth Fremantle, WA), d 8 Jun 1944 (in action over Friesian Island). 823, 824, 827.

ROBERTS, Albert William; *NZ*. RHB/RM. b 20 Aug 1909 (Christchurch, NZ), d 13 May 1978 (Christchurch, NZ). 898, 899.

ROBERTS, William; *NSW*. /WK. b ( ), d ( ). 48.

ROBERTS, William Maurice; *Sth Aust*. RHB/OB. b 26 Aug 1916 (Wallaroo Mines, SA), d 21 Jan 1989 (Adelaide). 904, 955.

ROBERTSON, George Pringle; *Vic*. RHB. b 22 Aug 1842 (Hobart), d 23 Jun 1895 (Colac, Vic). 17, 18, 21, 24.

ROBERTSON, William Roderick; *Vic*. RHB/LB. b 6 Oct 1861 (Deniliquin, NSW), d 24 Jun 1938 (Brighton, Vic). 76, 79, 80, 88, 110, 115, 123.

ROBINS, Robert Walter Vivian; *Eng*. RHB/LB. b 3 Jun 1906 (Stafford, Staffs), d 12 Dec 1968 (Marylebone, London). 868, 875, 876, 877, 878, 883, 885, 886, 889, 890, 892, 893.

ROBINSON, Alexander; *West Aust*. RHB. b 19 Aug 1886 (Brighton, Vic), d 4 Oct 1967 (Perth). 348.

ROBINSON, Charles Henry; *Tas & West Aust*. LHB/RM. b 18 Feb 1879 (Dubbo, NSW), d 23 Sep 1951 (Ashfield, NSW). 464, 469, 482, 484, 532.

ROBINSON, Charles Walter; *NZ*. RHB/RFM. b 28 Mar 1892 (Wellington, NZ), d 22 May 1947 (Lower Hutt, NZ). 473, 475, 478, 480.

ROBINSON, Henry Joseph Wickham; *NSW*. RHB. b 1867 (Sth Head, NSW), d 24 Mar 1931 (Mascot, NSW). 163.

ROBINSON, Rayford Harold; *NSW & Sth Aust*. RHB/LBG. b 26 Mar 1914 (Stockton, NSW), d 10 Aug 1965 (Stockton, NSW). 832, 833, 836, 838, 840, 842, 843, 846, 849, 851, 853, 854, 857, 861, 862, 867, 870, 873, 875, 877, 884, 888, 892, 894, 898, 902, 906, 908, 909, 911, 913, 916, 917, 938, 942.

ROBISON, William Carr; *NSW*. RHB b 14 Dec 1874 ( ), d 5 Jul 1916 (Warrawee, NSW). 171.

ROBSON, Charles; *Eng*. RHB/WK. b 20 Jun 1859 (Twickenham, Middlesex), d 27 Sep 1943 (Abingdon, Berks). 274.

ROCHE, William; *Vic*. RHB/OB. b 20 Jul 1871 (, SA), d 2 Jan 1950 (East Brunswick, Vic). 183, 192, 194, 197, 203, 206, 207, 210, 212, 214, 218, 222, 226.

ROCK, Claude William; *Tas*. RHB/RM(r). Brother of N.V.Rock. b 9 Jun 1863 (Deloraine, Tas), d 27 Jul 1950 (Longford, Tas). 128, 141, 159.

ROCK, Harry Owen; *NSW*. RHB. Son of C.W.Rock. b 18 Oct 1896 (Scone, NSW), d 9 Mar 1978 (Manly, NSW). 580, 588, 599, 604, 607, 613.

ROCK, Norman Vosper; *Tas*. LHB/RFM(r). Brother of C.W.Rock. b 30 Aug 1864 (Deloraine, Tas), d 7 Feb 1945 (Brighton, Vic). 141, 169.

ROCKLIFFE, Thornton Francis Edward; *Tas*. RHB/RF. b 5 Jul 1887 (Sassafras, Tas), d 18 Mar 1961 (East Devonport, Tas). 400.

ROE, Richard; *West Aust*. RHB. b 22 Jan 1913 (Geraldton, WA). 842, 843.

ROGERS, John Edward (played as Jack Marshall); *Vic*. RHB/RFM. b 8 Feb 1858 (Botany Bay, NSW), d 8 Jul 1935 (Sth Melbourne). 141, 142.

ROGERS, Rex Ernest; *Qld*. LHB/RM. b 24 Aug 1916 (Cairns, Qld). 860, 863, 870, 876, 879, 882, 884, 887, 891, 897, 905, 908, 910, 911, 912, 917, 921, 923, 926, 930, 931, 934, 938, 940, 943, 944, 946, 948, 952, 953, 954, 958, 959, 960, 964.

ROPER, Arthur William; *NSW*. RHB/RFM. b 20 Feb 1917 (Petersham, NSW), d 4 Sep 1972 (Woy Woy, NSW). 941, 942.

ROSMAN, Arthur Victor; *Sth Aust*. RHB/LB/OB. b 26 Nov 1870 (Barossa Goldfields, SA), d 10 Jan 1948 (Kent Town, SA). 242.

ROSS, Charles Howard; *Vic*. RHB/RM/WK. b 10 May 1863 (St Kilda, Vic), d 5 Feb 1935 (Sydney). 90, 139, 144, 146, 149, 152, 162, 244, 247, 248, 251, 254, 256, 257, 260.

ROSS, William A ; *Vic*. LHB. b ( ), d ( ). 10.

ROSSER, John; *Vic*. b 22 Apr 1862 (Fremantle, WA), d 25 Dec 1925 (Toowoomba, Qld). 61, 63, 67, 70.

ROTHWELL, John Wilson; *Tas*. RHB/LBG. b 1 Oct 1913 (Hobart). 814, 819, 825, 826.

ROWE, Raymond Curtis; *NSW*. LHB. b 9 Dec 1913 (Harris Park, NSW). 793, 795, 803, 806, 809, 810, 815, 816, 818, 822.

ROWE, Samuel Harold Drew; *West Aust*. RHB. b 5 Nov 1883 (Perth), d 29 Oct 1968 (Perth). 333, 335, 346, 347, 348, 371, 386, 387, 388, 401, 402, 403, 453, 454, 455, 456, 457, 532, 558, 559, 597, 598, 599, 617, 681, 682.

ROWE, William; *Qld*. LHB/SLA. b 10 Jan 1892 (East Brisbane), d 3 Sep 1972 (Sth Brisbane). 458, 465, 467, 470, 471, 472, 473, 486, 493, 494, 499, 506, 510, 516, 522, 529, 533, 547, 560, 562, 564, 565, 579, 581, 584, 602, 603, 618, 620, 621, 624, 634, 636, 639, 642, 647, 653, 658, 662, 664, 666, 677, 687, 689, 691, 696, 710.

ROWLAND, Frank Walter; *NSW*. RHB. b 1 Mar 1892 ( ), d 25 Feb 1957 (Mosman, NSW). 584.

ROWLANDS, Edward Richard; *Vic*. possibly b 1824 ( ), d 1860 ( ). 3.

ROWLANDS, William Trevor; *West Aust*. RHB/RM. b 7 May 1904 (Echuca, Vic), d 18 May 1984 (Subiaco, WA). 900, 903, 904, 920, 936, 937.

ROWLEY, Francis; *NSW*. RHB/Long-stop. b 27 Sep 1835 (Burwood, NSW), d 23 Jun 1862 (Woolloomooloo, NSW). 11, 12.

ROYLE, Vernon Peter Fanshawe Archer; *Eng*. RHB/RaB(r). b 29 Jan 1854 (Brooklands, Cheshire), d 21 May 1929 (Stanmore, Middlesex). 38, 39, 40, 41, 42.

RUNDELL, Joshau Upcott; *Sth Aust*. RHB/RF. b 6 May 1861 (Sandhurst, Vic), d 7 Jan 1922 (Alberton, SA). 75, 81.

RUNDELL, Percy Davies; *Sth Aust*. RHB/RM/LB. Son of J.U.Rundell. b 20 Nov 1890 (Alberton, SA), d 24 Mar 1979 (Nth Adelaide). 459, 468, 474, 476, 480, 489, 490, 497, 500, 502, 503, 509, 511, 512, 515, 518, 531, 534, 536, 537, 541, 550, 551, 569, 586, 596, 606, 611, 612, 614.

RUSH, Edward Reynolds; *Vic*. RHB/WK. Brother of T.R.Rush. b 29 Mar 1868 (Flemington, Vic), d 6 May 1936 (Malvern, Vic). 205, 219, 226.

RUSH, John; *Vic*. RHB. Son of E.R.Rush. b 5 Apr 1910 (Malvern, Vic). 732, 737.

RUSH, Thomas Reynolds; *Vic*. RHB. Brother of E.R.Rush. b 7 Dec 1876 (Collingwood, Vic), d 29 Oct 1926 (Malvern, Vic). 337, 340, 341, 343, 345, 350, 352, 365.

RUSHBROOK, Roy Francis Kerr; *Qld*. RHB/RFM. b 29 Sep 1911 (Spring Hill, Qld), d 31 Mar 1987 (Mackay, Qld). 887, 912.

RUSHFORTH, Alfred William; *Tas*. RHB. b 23 Apr 1898 (Hobart), d 30 Dec 1985 (Taroona, Tas). 553, 570, 627, 640, 643, 669, 674, 676, 701, 705, 706, 708, 755, 758, 759, 782, 802, 825, 856, 859, 865, 866, 885, 886.

RUSSELL, Bernard L ; *NSW*. RHB/RFM. b 1 Aug 1891 (Leichhardt, NSW), d ( ). 529, 533, 534.

RUSSELL, Charles Albert George; *Eng*. RHB/RSM. b 7 Oct 1887 (Leyton, Essex), d 23 Mar 1961 (Whipps Cross, Essex). 512, 513, 514, 516, 517, 519, 521, 524, 530, 531.

RUSSEN, Charles Gordon; *Tas*. RHB. b 9 May 1886 (Launceston), d 16 Dec 1969 (Newstead, Tas). 420.

RYAN, Alfred James; *Sth Aust*. RHB/RM. b 27 Apr 1904 (Adelaide), d 10 Jul 1990 (Semaphore Sth, SA). 601, 631, 632, 639, 641, 644, 660, 794, 795, 798, 801, 809, 811, 813, 816, 817, 853, 855, 858, 860, 861, 864, 874, 875, 880, 882, 889, 891, 894, 896.

RYAN, Gregory William; *NSW*. RHB/RFM. b 13 Mar 1913 (Wallsend, NSW). 840.

RYAN, Roderick Thomas; *West Aust*. LHB. b 15 Nov 1909 (Cannington, WA), d 23 Oct 1979 (Toronto, Canada). 820, 821, 822, 824.

RYAN, Thomas Patrick; *Tas*. /SLA. b 4 May 1865 (Hobart), d 20 Apr 1921 (Hobart). 128, 134.

RYDER, John; *Vic.* RHB/RFM. b 8 Aug 1889 (Collingwood, Vic), d 3 Apr 1977 (Fitzroy, Vic). 454, 457, 460, 461, 463, 465, 466, 471, 476, 477, 481, 483, 488, 489, 491, 493, 495, 496, 497, 498, 501, 502, 504, 505, 508, 509, 511, 513, 515, 519, 520, 521, 524, 525, 526, 527, 530, 532, 535, 536, 538, 539, 549, 550, 552, 556, 563, 566, 568, 574, 576, 587, 591, 592, 593, 595, 600, 604, 607, 611, 613, 615, 617, 621, 623, 625, 630, 635, 636, 641, 646, 647, 654, 656, 659, 661, 663, 665, 673, 678, 680, 681, 685, 688, 689, 692, 695, 700, 703, 704, 712, 714, 719, 723, 726, 730, 735, 742, 745, 750, 752, 760, 763.

RYMILL, Jack Westall; *Sth Aust.* LHB. b 20 Mar 1901 (Nth Adelaide), d 11 Feb 1976 (Adelaide). 541, 544, 550, 551, 557, 561, 564, 566, 567, 580, 586, 596, 597, 600, 604, 606, 609, 611, 612, 619, 622, 624.

SADDLER, Edward; *NSW.* /Long-stop. b ( ), d 28 Oct 1874 ( ). 4, 5, 12.

SAGGERS, Ronald Arthur; *NSW.* RHB/WK. b 15 May 1917 (Sydenham, NSW), d 17 Mar 1987 (Harbord, NSW). 947, 949, 952, 953, 954, 955, 958, 959, 961, 962, 963.

SALMON, Benjamin Melville; *NSW.* LHB/SLA. b 9 Jan 1906 (Footscray, Vic), d 24 Jan 1979 (Mosman, NSW). 579, 584, 588, 751, 752.

SALVANA, Louis Charles; *Vic.* RHB. b 20 Jan 1897 (Camberwell, Vic), d 8 Dec 1974 (Mitcham, Vic). 628.

SAMS, Richard Horace; *Tas.* LHB/LMF. b 1864 (Launceston), d 5 Mar 1933 (Roseville, NSW). 169, 322.

SAMUELS, Edward; NSW. b 25 May 1833 (Sydney), d ( ). 10.

SANDFORD, Horace Charles Augustus; *Vic.* RHB. b 14 Oct 1891 (Sydney), d 16 Aug 1967 (Canterbury, Vic). 457, 525, 526, 535, 536, 538, 553, 660, 662, 732.

SANDHAM, Andrew; *Eng.* RHB. b 6 Jul 1890 (Streatham, Surrey), d 20 Apr 1982 (Westminster, London). 572, 576, 577, 581, 582, 583, 589, 590, 592, 594, 595, 596.

SANDMAN, Donald McKay; *NZ.* RHB/LBG. b 3 Nov 1889 (Christchurch, NZ), d 29 Jan 1973 (Christchurch, NZ). 473, 475, 478, 480.

SANGSTER, Christopher Bagot; *Sth Aust.* RHB/RMF. b 1 May 1908 (Kooringa, SA). 639, 645.

SANKEY, Clarence Joseph; *Tas.* RHB/WK. b 27 Oct 1913 (Northdown, Tas). 839, 856, 915, 918, 919.

SAROVICH, Theodor Keith; *Vic.* RHB. b 20 May 1915 (Port Melbourne, Vic). 960, 961, 962.

SARTORI, Ronald Joseph; *West Aust.* RHB/RFM. b 23 Mar 1915 (Fremantle, WA). 820, 821, 822.

SAUNDERS, John Victor; *Vic.* LHB/LM/SLA. b 3 Feb 1876 (Melbourne), d 21 Dec 1927 (Toorak, Vic). 248, 251, 253, 254, 256, 257, 260, 262, 264, 267, 271, 273, 274, 280, 284, 286, 287, 288, 292, 294, 297, 299, 301, 304, 306, 313, 314, 316, 318, 325, 328, 329, 332, 334, 337, 340, 341, 343, 350, 352, 354, 356, 357, 358, 360, 361, 364, 366, 368, 372, 374, 377, 378, 381, 382, 383, 389, 392, 394, 397, 399, 401, 402, 403.

SAVAGE, Harold; *NSW.* /WK. b ( ), d ( ). 537.

SAVIGNY, John Horatio; *Tas.* RHB/OB/LB. Brother of W.H.Savigny. b 25 Aug 1867 (Bathurst, NSW), d 11 Feb 1923 (Carrick, Tas). 128, 141, 159, 169, 197, 205, 219, 236, 249, 252, 259, 305, 420.

SAVIGNY, William Henry; *Tas.* RHB/RaB. Brother of J.H.Savigny. b 17 Feb 1864 (Sydney), d 6 Aug 1922 (Burwood, NSW). 128, 141, 159, 197.

SCAIFE, John Willie; *Vic.* RHB. b 14 Nov 1909 ( ). 627, 635, 636, 638, 641, 646, 647, 648, 649, 651, 654, 656, 660, 662, 663, 670, 672, 678, 685, 689, 692, 695, 700, 703, 704, 737, 750, 807, 813, 818, 828, 831, 833, 835, 837, 838, 841, 848, 852, 854, 858, 862, 863, 864.

SCANES, Albert Edward; *NSW.* RHB. b 6 Aug 1900 ( ), d Nov 1969 ( ). 533, 546, 547, 599, 602, 608, 610, 618, 637, 638.

SCANLAN, Edmund; *NSW.* RHB. b c 1850 ( ), d 9 Jan 1916 (Newtown, NSW). 36.

SCANNELL, Timothy Francis; *Vic.* RHB/LB. b 1882 (Hotham, Vic), d ( ). 401, 403.

SCHADE, Matias Anderson; *Vic.* RHB/RFM. b 25 Mar 1886 (Bagshot, Vic), d 9 Jun 1957 (Williamstown, Vic). 541.

SCHNEIDER, Karl Joseph; *Vic & Sth Aust.* LHB/LBG. b 15 Aug 1905 (Hawthorn, Vic), d 5 Sep 1928 (Kensington Park, SA). 553, 588, 619, 622, 624, 625, 626, 631, 632, 635, 637, 639, 641, 644, 645.

SCHRADER, Heinrich Christian; *Vic.* RHB/RM. b 5 Dec 1893 (East Prahran, Vic), d 10 Jun 1980 (East Kew, Vic). 705, 737.

SCHREIBER, Sidney Arthur; *Qld.* RHB. b 7 Apr 1873 ( ), d ( ). 234.

SCHULTZ, Bruce; *Sth Aust.* RHB/RFM. Son of J.W.E.Schultz. b 13 Mar 1913 (Royston Park, SA), d 11 Jan 1980 (Modbury, SA). 880, 882.

SCHULTZ, Julius William Eugene; *Sth Aust.* RHB/WK. b 25 Sep 1888 (Summer Town, SA), d 8 Aug 1966 (Berri, SA). 502, 503, 509, 541.

SCHULTZ, Sandford Spence; *Eng.* RHB/RF(r). b 29 Aug 1857 (Birkenhead, Cheshire), d 18 Dec 1937 (Sth Kensington, London). 38, 39, 40, 41, 42.

SCHWARZ, Reginald Oscar; *Sth Afr.* RHB/OB. b 4 May 1875 (Lee, Kent), d 18 Nov 1918 (Etaples, France). 406, 407, 408, 409, 413, 417, 419, 420, 424, 425, 426, 427.

SCOTT, Henry James Herbert; *Vic.* RHB/RM. b 26 Dec 1858 (Toorak, Vic), d 23 Sep 1910 (Scone, NSW). 37, 60, 61, 63, 67, 69, 70, 71, 72, 73, 74, 78, 79, 84, 87, 88, 89.

SCOTT, Jack A ; *Sth Aust.* RHB/LM. b 14 Jan 1910 (Sydney), d 22 May 1980 (Collaroy Beach, NSW). 904, 924, 926, 928, 931.

SCOTT, John Drake; *NSW & Sth Aust.* RHB/RF. b 31 Jan 1888 (Sydney), d 7 Apr 1964 (Springback, SA). 375, 393, 397, 400, 405, 412, 416, 418, 448, 452, 458, 467, 469, 472, 475, 482, 487, 488, 490, 498, 537, 538, 539, 551, 552, 555, 558, 559, 560, 561, 563, 568, 577, 586, 588, 594, 597, 600, 604, 606, 611, 612, 614, 619, 622, 626, 637, 639, 641, 644, 645, 651, 652, 656, 657, 660, 671, 677, 679.

SCOTT, Oscar Charles; *WI.* RHB/LB. b 25 Aug 1893 (Kingston, Jamaica), d 15 Jun 1961 (Kingston, Jamaica). 713, 714, 718, 721, 722, 725, 727, 728, 733, 734, 736, 738.

SCOTT, Robert Barrington; *Vic & NSW.* RHB/RF. b 9 Oct 1916 (Middle Park, Vic), d 6 Apr 1984 (Melbourne). 856, 859, 862, 863, 864, 927, 929, 933, 934, 935, 936, 939, 940, 942, 945, 948, 949, 952, 955, 958, 959, 961.

SCOTT, Walter Aubrey; *Vic.* RHB. b 19 Feb 1907 (Camberwell, Vic). 705.

SCOTT, William John; *Vic.* RHB/RF. b 14 Jun 1882 (West Hotham, Vic), d 30 Sep 1965 (Ferntree Gully, Vic). 306, 309, 313, 314, 316, 318, 320, 389, 394, 397, 399, 407, 410, 414, 415, 446.

SCOTTON, William Henry; *Eng.* LHB/LFM. b 15 Jan 1856 (Nottingham, Eng), d 9 Jul 1893 (St Johns Wood, London). 51, 52, 54, 56, 57, 58, 59, 76, 77, 78, 80, 82, 84, 85, 86, 91, 92, 93, 94, 96, 97, 99, 101, 102, 103, 104.

SCRYMGOUR, Bernard Vincent; *Sth Aust.* b 31 Jul 1864 (Adelaide), d 16 Apr 1943 (Medindie, SA). 139, 143, 170, 195, 204.

SEALE, Joseph; *NSW.* b 18 Apr 1855 (Grafton, NSW), d ( ). 37, 39.

SEALY, James Edward Derek; *WI.* RHB/RM/WK. b 11 Sep 1912 (Barbados), d 3 Jan 1982 (St Patrick, Trinidad). 716, 721, 722, 727, 728, 732, 736, 738.

SEARLE, James; *NSW.* RHB/WK. b 8 Aug 1861 (Surry Hills, NSW), d 28 Dec 1936 (Manly, NSW). 126, 129.

SEDDON, Cecil Dudley; *NSW.* RHB. b 3 Jul 1902 (, NSW), d 18 Apr 1978 (Dulwich Hill, NSW). 618, 640, 663, 666, 667, 674.

SEITZ, John Arnold; *Vic.* RHB. b 19 Sep 1883 (Carlton, Vic), d 1 May 1963 (St Kilda, Vic). 407, 410, 414, 415, 430, 432, 434, 439, 445, 446, 454, 460, 461, 463, 465.

SELBY, John; *Eng.* RHB/RM. b 1 Jul 1849 (Nottingham, Eng), d 11 Mar 1894 (Nottingham, Eng). 32, 33, 34, 51, 52, 54, 56, 57, 58, 59.

SELK, Rudolph Albert; *West Aust.* RHB/RM. b 6 Oct 1871 (Omeo, Vic), d 31 Jan 1940 (Pickering Brook, WA). 242, 333, 335, 346, 347, 348, 386, 387, 388, 402, 403, 453, 454, 455, 456, 457.

SELTH, Victor Poole; *Sth Aust.* RHB/WK. b 1 Jun 1895 (Parkside, SA), d 2 Sep 1967 (Daw Park, SA). 497, 500.

SERJEANT, David Maurice; *Vic.* b 18 Jan 1830 (Ramsey, Huntingdonshire), d 12 Jan 1929 (Camberwell, London). 4, 5.

SEWART, William Isaac; *Qld & Vic.* RHB/RM. b 12 Nov 1881 (Allendale East, SA), d 13 Dec 1928 (Caulfield, Vic). 375, 379, 392, 394, 399, 464, 471, 477, 478, 481, 496, 497, 498.

SEWELL, Thomas; *Eng.* RHB/RF. b 15 Mar 1830 (Mitcham, Surrey), d 13 Jun 1871 (Sevenoaks, Kent). 13.

SHARPE, John William; *Eng.* RHB/RFM. b 9 Dec 1866 (Ruddington, Notts), d 19 Jun 1936 (Ruddington, Notts). 143, 144, 145, 147, 150, 151, 152.

SHAW, Alfred; *Eng.* RHB/RM. b 29 Aug 1842 (Burton Joyce, Nottingham), d 16 Jan 1907 (Gedling, Notts). 32, 33, 34, 51, 52, 54, 56, 57, 58, 59.

SHAWE, P ; *Tas.* /RFM. b ( ), d ( ). 485, 492.

SHEA, John Adrian; *West Aust.* RHB/LB. Nephew of P.A.Shea. b 8 May 1913 (Boulder, WA), d 7 Feb 1986 (Claremont, WA). 869, 903, 904, 920.

SHEA, Patrick Augustus; *Vic.* LHB/RM. b 16 Mar 1886 (Clunes, Vic), d 29 May 1954 (Northbridge, NSW). 464, 505, 508.

SHEPHERD, Alan Gordon; *Sth Aust.* RHB. b 29 Sep 1912 (Kilkenny, SA). 767, 787, 795, 798, 801, 804, 809, 811, 813, 832, 835, 841.

SHEPHERDSON, Hartley Robert; *Sth Aust.* LHB/RFM. b 4 Sep 1913 (Mt Gambier, SA). 866.

SHEPLEY, Herbert Neil; *Sth Aust.* RHB/RFM. b 7 Oct 1899 (Knightsbridge, SA), d 14 Nov 1953 (Tranmere, SA). 601.

SHEPPARD, Benjamin Joseph; *Vic.* RHB/WK. b 23 Jun 1892 (Fitzroy, Vic), d 9 Sep 1931 (Fitzroy, Vic). 484, 485.

SHEPPARD, James Francis; *Qld.* RHB. b 16 Jan 1888 (Brisbane), d 10 Dec 1944 (Hendra, Qld). 458, 465, 467, 470, 471, 472, 486, 493, 494, 499, 506, 508, 510, 522, 529, 533, 560, 562, 564, 565.

SHERIDAN, Edward Orwell; *NSW.* RHB/RM(r). b 3 Jan 1842 (Sydney), d 30 Nov 1923 (West End, Qld). 18, 20, 21, 23, 24, 28, 29, 36, 37, 40.

SHERWELL, Percy William; *Sth Afr.* RHB/WK. b 17 Aug 1880 (Isipingo, Sth Afr), d 17 Apr 1948 (Bulawayo, Rhodesia). 406, 407, 408, 411, 413, 417, 419, 420, 421, 423, 424, 426, 427.

SHERWIN, Mordecai; *Eng.* RHB/WK/RF. b 26 Feb 1851 (Kimberley, Notts), d 3 Jul 1910 (Nottingham, Eng). 91, 92, 93, 94, 96, 97, 99, 101, 102, 103, 104.

SHEWAN, Leslie James; *Qld.* RHB/RFM. b 12 Jun 1892 (Rushworth, Vic), d 25 Sep 1977 (Windsor, Vic). 581.

SHORT, Henry William; *Sth Aust.* b 31 Mar 1874 (Morphett Vale, SA), d 11 May 1916 (Lower Mitcham, SA). 313.

SHORTLAND, Herbert; *NSW.* b 7 Apr 1881 ( ), d 17 Jul 1946 ( ). 452.

SHREWSBURY, Arthur; *Eng.* RHB. b 11 Apr 1856 (New Lenton, Notts), d 19 May 1903 (Gedling, Notts). 51, 52, 54, 56, 57, 58, 59, 76, 77, 78, 80, 82, 84, 85, 86, 91, 92, 93, 94, 96, 97, 99, 101, 102, 103, 104, 107, 109, 110, 114, 116, 117, 120, 122.

SHUGG, Albert William; *Tas.* RHB/RFM. b 5 Jul 1894 (Hawthorn, Vic), d 20 Jul 1941 (Hobart). 589, 590.

SIDEBOTTOM, William Lemuel; *Tas.* LHB/LB. b 24 Sep 1862 (Evandale, Tas), d 11 Apr 1948 (Launceston). 128, 134, 159, 183.

SIDES, Francis William; *Qld & Vic.* LHB. b 15 Dec 1913 (Mackay, Qld), d 25 Aug 1943 (Salamua area, New Guinea). 710, 743, 746, 750, 753, 757, 763, 773, 787, 790, 837, 840, 900, 903, 905, 907, 909, 912, 914, 923, 925, 928, 933, 934, 935, 937.

SIEVERS, Morris William; *Vic.* RHB/RFM. b 13 Apr 1912 (Wonthaggi, Vic), d 10 May 1968 (Brunswick, Vic). 821, 823, 831, 833, 835, 837, 838, 841, 867, 872, 874, 877, 878, 883, 888, 893, 896, 899, 902, 905, 907, 909, 912, 914, 916, 922, 923, 925, 928, 933, 934, 939, 940, 942, 945, 948, 949, 954, 956, 957, 959, 960, 961, 962.

SIM, Charles Vernal; *Qld.* RHB/LB. b 6 Oct 1894 (Capella, Qld), d 7 Jul 1941 (Herston, Qld). 602, 603, 608, 614.

SIMMONDS, W ; *Anderson's XI v Parr's XI.* b ( ), d ( ). 15.

SIMMONS, Arthur Harry; *NSW.* RHB/RFM. b 13 Nov 1909 (Croydon, Vic). 829, 832.

SIMPSON, Charles Edward; *Qld & NSW.* RHB/OB. b 27 Mar 1882 (, NSW), d 26 Jun 1956 (Sydney). 336, 338, 373, 375, 379, 382, 383, 396, 397, 405.

SIMS, Arthur; *NZ.* RHB. b 27 Jul 1877 (Spridlington, Lincs), d 27 Apr 1969 (East Hoathly, Sussex). 237.

SIMS, Alfred Ernest; *Qld.* RHB/WK. b 8 Nov 1875 (, NSW), d ( ). 409, 429.

SIMS, James Morton; *Eng.* RHB/LB. b 13 May 1903 (Leyton, Essex), d 27 Apr 1973 (Canterbury, Kent). 845, 847, 848, 849, 850, 851, 868, 871, 872, 873, 878, 883, 885, 886, 892, 893.

SINCLAIR, Arthur; *NSW.* b ( ), d 29 Nov 1869 (Sydney). 18.

SINCLAIR, James Hugh; *Sth Afr.* RHB/RM. b 16 Oct 1876 (Swellendam, Sth Afr), d 23 Feb 1913 (Johannesburg). 411, 413, 417, 419, 420, 421, 423, 424, 425, 426, 427.

SINCOCK, Harrold Keith; *Sth Aust.* RHB/LB. b 10 Dec 1907 (Eastwood, SA), d 2 Feb 1982 (Plympton, SA). 684, 691.

SINDREY, Clive Alexander Hazell; *Vic.* RHB. b 10 Aug 1903 (Richmond, Vic), d 26 Jun 1981 (Vermont, Vic). 570, 627, 636, 638, 641, 648, 649, 699.

SINGLE, Clive Vallack; *NSW.* RHB/RM. b 17 Sep 1888 (Penrith, NSW), d 10 Jul 1931 (Woollahra, NSW). 455, 456.

SISMEY, Stanley George; *NSW.* RHB/WK. b 15 Jul 1916 (Junee, NSW). 932, 933, 938, 941, 942, 944, 947, 949.

SLADEN, Charles; *Vic.* RHB. b 28 Aug 1816 (near Walmer, Kent), d 22 Feb 1884 (Geelong, Vic). 2.

SLIGHT, Alexander Frank; *Sth Aust.* LHB/WK. Brother of J. & W.Slight. b 13 Apr 1861 (Emerald Hill, Vic), d 5 Jul 1930 (Maylands, SA). 100.

SLIGHT, James; *Vic.* RHB. Brother of A.F. & W.Slight. b 20 Oct 1855 (Geelong, Vic), d 9 Dec 1930 (Elsternwick, Vic). 28, 29, 30, 36, 37, 42, 43, 44, 47, 49, 55, 57, 70, 75, 90, 119.

SLIGHT, William; *Vic & Sth Aust.* RHB/RaB. Brother of A.F. & J.Slight. b 19 Sep 1858 (Emerald Hill, Vic), d 22 Dec 1941 (Toorak Gardens, SA). 36, 45, 50, 60.

SMITH, Andrew; *Sth Aust.* RHB/LBG. b 1 Sep 1889 (Port Adelaide), d 18 May 1983 (Adelaide). 479, 480, 483, 509, 511, 512, 523, 531, 534, 536, 537, 541.

SMITH, Alfred Edward Charles; *West Aust.* b 4 Oct 1908 (Prahran, Vic). 617, 631.

SMITH, Charles Aubrey; *Eng.* RHB/RF. b 21 Jul 1863 (London), d 20 Dec 1948 (Beverley Hills, California). 109, 110, 114, 116, 120, 122.

SMITH, Denis; *Eng.* LHB/RM. b 24 Jan 1907 (Somercotes, Derbyshire), d 12 Sep 1979 (Derby, Eng). 845, 847, 848, 849, 850, 851.

SMITH, David Bertram Miller; *Vic.* RHB. b 14 Sep 1884 (Richmond, Vic), d 29 Jul 1963 (Hawthorn, Vic). 381, 384, 385, 389, 392, 394, 396, 397, 404, 407, 410, 411, 415, 422, 423, 428, 430, 432, 434, 439, 445, 446.

SMITH, Douglas Roy; *Tas.* RHB/RFM. b 9 Oct 1880 (Fingal, Tas), d 27 Feb 1933 (Port Fairy, Vic). 303, 305, 321.

SMITH, Edward Henry; *Tas.* RHB. b 30 Jul 1911 (Nook, Tas). 722, 731, 839, 856, 859, 865, 866, 915, 918, 919, 927, 929.

SMITH, Ernest James; *Eng.* RHB/WK. b 6 Feb 1886 (Birmingham, Eng), d 31 Aug 1979 (Birmingham, Eng). 432, 435, 440, 442, 446, 447, 450.

SMITH, George Elms; *Vic.* /WK. b 22 Jul 1855 (Emerald Hill, Vic), d 7 Apr 1897 (St Kilda, Vic). 36, 76.

SMITH, Horace Clitheroe; *Tas.* RHB. b 31 Oct 1892 (Sandy Bay, Tas), d 6 Apr 1977 (Hobart). 482, 540, 553, 615, 616, 640.

SMITH, Herbert George; *Vic.* RHB/RFM. b 21 Mar 1915 (Collingwood, Vic). 915.

SMITH, Hubert George Selwyn; *Qld.* b 9 Oct 1891 (Beaudesert, Qld), d 7 Jun 1917 (Messines, France). 452, 458, 465.

SMITH, Harry Oxley; *Tas & Vic.* RHB. b 27 Oct 1887 (Launceston), d 24 Aug 1916 (Pinewood, Eng). 362, 420, 421, 464, 492.

SMITH, James; *NSW.* /RFM. b ( ), d ( ). 390, 393.

SMITH, Lavington Albert; *Sth Aust.* RHB. b 9 Oct 1904 (Medindie, SA), d 9 May 1953 (Adelaide). 824.

SMITH, Leonard P ; *Vic.* b ( ), d ( ). 357, 369.

SMITH, Robert Thomas; *Vic.* RHB/RaB. b 1868 (SA), d 21 Aug 1927 (St Albans, Vic). 134.

SMITH, Stanley Arthur John; *Vic.* RHB/LBG. Nephew of D.B.M.Smith. b 8 Jan 1910 (Richmond, Vic), d c 1987 ( ). 750, 752, 760, 763, 788, 812, 814, 819, 839, 848, 852, 854, 858, 862.

SMITH, Struan McKinley; *Rest of Australia.* RHB/LM. b 4 Jun 1906 (Sydney). 630.

SMITH, Thomas Henry; *Qld.* LHB. b 19 Sep 1898 (Talgai, Qld), d 6 Mar 1926 (Warwick, Qld). 533, 547, 565.

SNEDDEN, Andrew Nesbitt Colin; *NZ.* RHB/RM. b 3 Apr 1892 (Auckland, NZ), d 27 Sep 1968 (Auckland, NZ). 473, 475, 478, 480.

SNOOKE, Sibley John; *Sth Africa.* RHB/RFM. b 1 Feb 1881 (St Marks, Sth Afr), d 14 Aug 1966 (Port Elizabeth, Sth Afr). 406, 407, 408, 409, 411, 413, 417, 419, 420, 421, 423, 424, 425, 426, 427.

SOLOMON, Cyril Moss; *NSW.* RHB. b 11 Mar 1911 (Cootamundra, NSW). 748, 757, 790, 924, 925, 930, 932, 933, 938, 941, 942, 944, 952.

SOMERVELL, Robert Cooke; *NZ.* RHB. b 18 May 1892 (Auckland, NZ), d 8 Jun 1967 (Auckland, NZ). 480.

SOUTER, Vernon John; *Vic.* LHB/RM. b 26 Feb 1894 (Uranquinty, NSW), d 17 Jul 1915 (Elsternwick, Vic). 483, 484, 485, 488, 489, 491, 493, 495.

SOUTHERTON, James; *Eng.* RHB/RaB(r). b 16 Nov 1827 (Petworth, Sussex), d 16 Jun 1880 (Mitcham, Surrey). 32, 33, 34.

SPEIRS, Norman Lennox; *Vic.* RHB/RM. b 31 May 1886 (Elsternwick, Vic), d 1 Aug 1960 (Noosa Heads, Qld). 365, 389.

SPENCER, Ernest Lott; *Vic.* RHB. b 1 May 1888 (West Melbourne), d 4 Nov 1953 (Essendon, Vic). 446, 464.

SPOFFORTH, Frederick Robert; *NSW & Vic.* RHB/RFM. b 9 Sep 1853 (Balmain, NSW), d 4 Jun 1926 (Ditton Hill, Surrey). 28, 29, 30, 31, 32, 34, 38, 40, 43, 44, 47, 49, 55, 59, 63, 64, 65, 66, 67, 68, 74, 83, 84, 85, 86, 87, 89, 94, 96, 97, 98, 99, 106, 111.

SPRY, Richard; *Qld.* RHB/RM. b 18 Jul 1862 (Melbourne), d 10 Nov 1920 (Linville, Qld). 163.

ST HILL, Edwin Lloyd; *WI.* RHB/RM. b 9 Mar 1904 (Port of Spain, Trinidad), d 21 May 1957 (Manchester, Eng). 713, 721, 732, 733.

STACK, George Bagot; *NSW.* LHB. b 12 Mar 1846 (West Maitland, NSW), d 7 Oct 1930 (Orange, NSW). 17, 20.

STACK, Walter Jaques; *NSW.* RHB/LBG. Son of G.B.Stack. b 31 Oct 1884 (Croydon, NSW), d 26 Mar 1972 (Bathurst, NSW). 391, 392, 395, 396, 397, 400, 462.

STACKPOOLE, John; *Qld.* RHB/RFM. b 23 Nov 1916 (Jundah, Qld). 946, 948, 953.

STALKER, Walter; *Vic.* RHB/RFM. b 29 Oct 1909 (Mt Doran, Vic), d 13 Jan 1977 (Ballarat, NSW). 802.

STANES, John Gladstone; *Vic.* RHB. b 15 Dec 1910 (Sth Melbourne), d 7 Feb 1983 (Ferntree Gully, Vic). 788, 791, 802, 900, 903.

STANFORD, Ross Milton; *Sth Aust.* RHB. b 25 Sep 1917 (Fulham, SA). 866.

STANNING, John; *Eng.* RHB. b 10 Oct 1877 (Leyland, Lancs), d 19 May 1929 (Nakwin, Kenya). 288, 289, 290.

STEELE, Harry Cornwall; *NSW.* LHB/LB. b 22 Apr 1901 (East Sydney). 618, 620, 622, 640, 644.

STAPLETON, Harold Vincent; *NSW.* LHB/LM. b 7 Jan 1915 (Kyogle, NSW). 963.

STARR, Cecil Leonard Berry; *Sth Aust.* RHB/OB. b 20 Jul 1907 (Quorn, SA). 632, 702, 739, 741, 751.

STEEL, Allan Gibson; *Eng.* RHB/RSM. b 24 Sep 1858 (Liverpool, Eng), d 15 Jun 1914 (Hyde Park, London). 61, 62, 64, 65, 66, 68, 69.

STEELE, Donald Macdonald; *Sth Aust.* RHB. Brother of K.N.Steele. b 17 Aug 1892 (East Adelaide), d 13 Jul 1962 (Adelaide). 441, 459, 461, 462, 474, 476, 479, 480, 487, 489, 490, 495, 500, 502, 503, 511, 515, 518, 523.

STEELE, Kenneth Nagent; *Sth Aust.* RHB/RFM. Brother of D.M.Steele. b 17 Dec 1889 (East Adelaide), d 19 Dec 1956 (Nth Adelaide). 474, 476.

STEPHENS, Jack Lawson; *Vic.* LHB/SLA. b 31 Aug 1913 (Majorca, Vic), d 2 Sep 1967 (Williamstown, Vic). 788, 791, 915.

STEPHENS, Reginald Stanley; *Vic.* LHB/LBG. b 16 Apr 1883 (Creswick, Vic), d 7 Sep 1965 (Malvern, Vic). 484, 485, 493.

STEPHENSON, Edwin; *Eng.* RHB/RF(r)/WK. b 5 Jun 1832 (Sheffield, Yorks), d 5 Jul 1898 (Liverpool, Eng). 13.

STEPHENSON; Heathfield Harman; *Eng.* RHB/RF(r)/WK. b 3 May 1833 (Esher, Surrey), d 17 Dec 1896 (Uppingham, Rutland). 13.

STEVENS, John Whitehall; *Vic.* b ( ), d ( ). 2.

STEWART, Gordon Lionel; *NSW.* RHB/RFM. b 16 Jun 1906 (Petersham, NSW). 711, 713, 715, 717, 723, 784, 786, 790, 793, 795.

STEWART, James C ; *Vic.* b ( ), d ( ). 27.

STEWART, William; *Vic.* /LFM(r). b c 1844 ( ), d ( ). 12.

STEYN, Stephen Sebastian Louis; *Sth Afr.* LHB. b 11 Mar 1905 (Cape Town, Sth Afr). 758, 759, 764.

STIBE, Colin George Reinzi; *Qld.* RHB. b 22 Apr 1916 (Bundaberg, Qld), d 6 Jan 1970 (Sydney). 931, 934, 938.

STILL, Robert Stuart; *Tas.* /RF(r). Brother of W.C.Still. b 15 Mar 1822 (Bathurst, NSW), d 5 Jul 1907 (Launceston). 3, 7.

STILL, William Cathcart; *NSW.* RHB. Brother of R.S.Still. b 1820 (, U.K.), d 5 Jul 1910 (Sydney). 5, 9.

STIRLING, William Stuart; *Sth Aust.* RHB/LM. b 19 Mar 1891 (Jamestown, SA), d 18 Jul 1971 (Adelaide). 387, 388, 427, 430, 431, 434, 436, 441, 453, 487, 489, 490, 495, 504, 507, 512.

STODDART, Andrew Ernest; *Eng.* RHB/RM. b 11 Mar 1863 (Westoe, Durham), d 4 Apr 1915 (St Johns Wood, London). 105, 106, 108, 112, 113, 117, 118, 121, 123, 143, 144, 145, 147, 150, 151, 152, 153, 172, 173, 174, 176, 177, 179, 181, 184, 186, 189, 209, 210, 211, 217, 220, 221, 227.

STOKES, George William; *Vic.* RHB b 11 Dec 1857 (Sth Yarra, Vic), d 16 Aug 1929 (Brighton, Vic). 60.

STOKES, William; *West Aust.* RHB/WK. b 28 Jul 1886 (Geraldton, WA), d 4 Oct 1954 (Perth). 542, 543, 558, 559, 631, 632, 649, 650.

STORER, William; *Eng.* RHB/WK/LB. b 25 Jan 1867 (Butterly, Derbyshire), d 28 Feb 1912 (Derby, Eng). 209, 210, 211, 213, 215, 217, 220, 224, 225, 226, 227.

STRATFORD, H E ; *Vic.* b ( ), d ( ). 3.

STRICKER, Louis Anthony; *Sth Afr.* RHB. b 26 May 1884 (Kimberley, Sth Afr), d 5 Feb 1960 (Cape Town, Sth Afr). 406, 407, 408, 409, 411, 413, 417, 419, 421, 423, 424, 425, 426, 427.

STRUDWICK, Herbert; *Eng.* RHB/WK. b 28 Jan 1880 (Mitcham, Surrey), d 14 Feb 1970 (Shoreham, Sussex). 292, 295, 303, 305, 306, 311, 431, 433, 437, 438, 443, 444, 448, 512, 514, 517, 519, 521, 524, 528, 530, 572, 573, 575, 577, 582, 583, 585, 587, 592, 593, 595.

STUART, William Percy; *Sth Aust.* RHB. b 7 Mar 1871 (Goolwa, SA), d 20 Aug 1956 (Adelaide). 248, 250, 254, 255, 257, 386, 387, 388.

STUCKEY, George; *Vic*. RHB. Brother of J.H.Stuckey. b 6 Jul 1871 (Walhalla, Vic), d 15 Mar 1932 (Nth Melbourne). 183, 219, 285.

STUCKEY, John Henry; *Vic*. LHB. Brother of G.Stuckey. b 3 Jul 1869 (Walhalla, Vic), d 10 Aug 1952 (Cheltenham, Vic). 142, 156, 160, 162, 165, 166, 168, 170, 173, 182, 190, 197, 202, 207, 218, 222, 226, 228, 231, 232, 235, 237, 244, 247, 248, 251, 253, 254, 256, 257, 260, 262, 264, 267, 271, 274, 280, 282, 285, 287, 288, 299, 304, 313, 314, 316, 318, 384, 385, 398, 401, 402, 403.

STUDD, Charles Thomas; *Eng*. RHB/RMF. Brother of G.B.Studd. b 2 Dec 1860 (Spratton, Northants), d 16 Jul 1931 (Ibambi, Belgian Congo). 61, 62, 64, 65, 66, 68, 69.

STUDD, George Brown; *Eng*. RHB. Brother of C.T.Studd. b 20 Oct 1859 (Netheravon, Wiltshire), d 13 Feb 1945 (Pasadena, California). 61, 62, 64, 65, 66, 68, 69.

SUCHE, Bruce Vincent; *Qld*. LHB/RFM. b 1906 (Sydney), d 14 Apr 1933 (Townsville, Qld). 743, 777.

SULLIVAN, Alfred Ernest; *NSW*. LHB/SLA. b 10 Dec 1872 (Balmain, NSW), d 25 Sep 1942 (Balmain, NSW). 323, 346, 347.

SULLIVAN, W   ; *Qld*. RHB/RM. b 19 Aug 1877 (   ), d (   ). 379.

SUTCLIFFE, Herbert; *Eng*. RHB. b 24 Nov 1894 (Harrogate, Yorks), d 22 Jan 1978 (Crosshills, Yorks). 572, 575, 577, 581, 582, 583, 585, 587, 590, 592, 593, 595, 650, 652, 655, 657, 658, 659, 661, 665, 671, 673, 675, 771, 772, 775, 778, 779, 781, 782, 789, 792, 796, 797, 799, 800.

SUTHERLAND, David; *Vic*. RHB. b 4 Jun 1873 (Hawthorn, Vic), d 6 Oct 1971 (Melbourne). 205, 219, 236, 244, 252, 259.

SWAN, Henry Dawes; *Eng*. RHB. b 28 Jul 1879 (Newcastle-on-Tyne, Northumberland), d 21 Dec 1941 (Bournemouth West, Hants). 543.

SWIFT, John Sheddon; *Vic*. RHB/WK. b 3 Feb 1852 (   ), d 28 Feb 1926 (Kew, Vic). 31, 61, 83.

TAAFFE, Frederick Herbert; *West Aust*. RHB/RM. b 7 Jan 1899 (Deolali, India), d 2 Apr 1964 (Ulladulla, NSW). 558, 559, 572, 573, 582, 617, 648, 649, 650, 682, 740, 770, 827, 842, 843, 844, 845, 868.

TABART, John Lewis Benjamin; *Tas*. b 30 Nov 1827 (St Pancras, London), d 9 Sep 1894 (Launceston). 1, 2, 3, 7, 8.

TABART, Thomas Albert; *Tas*. Nephew of J.L.B.Tabart. b 10 Aug 1877 (Campbell Town, Tas), d 29 Aug 1950 (East Melbourne). 205, 219, 229, 285, 309, 322, 362, 363, 369, 384.

TAIT, Alan Houston; *Qld*. LHB/RFM. b 17 Feb 1908 (Toowoomba, Qld), d 27 Jul 1988 (Indooroopilly, Qld). 807, 808, 811, 815, 846.

TAIT, George; *Parr's XI v Anderson's XI*. b 12 Apr 1844 (Parramatta, NSW), d 21 Dec 1934 (East Malvern, Vic). 15.

TALLON, Donald; *Qld*. RHB/WK. Brother of L.W.T.Tallon. b 17 Feb 1916 (Bundaberg, Qld), d 7 Sep 1984 (Bundaberg, Qld). 807, 817, 831, 834, 836, 837, 840, 846, 850, 852, 855, 857, 863, 867, 870, 875, 879, 882, 884, 887, 891, 897, 905, 908, 910, 911, 912, 921, 922, 923, 926, 930, 931, 934, 938, 940, 943, 944, 946, 948, 952, 953, 954, 958, 959, 960, 964.

TALLON, Leslie William Thomas; *Qld*. Brother of D.Tallon. b 9 Jul 1914 (Bundaberg, Qld), d 18 Sep 1972 (Coopers Plains, Qld). 921, 923, 926, 930, 931, 934, 938, 940, 944.

TAMBLYN, Gordon Erle; *Vic*. RHB. b 23 Apr 1918 (Wallaroo Mines, SA). 935, 936, 937, 939, 940, 942, 945, 956, 957, 960, 961.

TARDIF, Joseph Henry; *Sth Aust*. LHB. b 17 May 1860 (Gawler Sth, SA), d 14 Jun 1920 (Prospect, SA). 136, 156, 157, 160.

TARRANT, Francis Alfred; *Vic*. RHB/SLA. Nephew of W.A.Tarrant. b 11 Dec 1880 (Fitzroy, Vic), d 29 Jan 1951 (Upper Hawthorn, Vic). 236, 237, 259, 350, 352, 354, 357, 358, 364, 574, 576, 578, 588, 607.

TARRANT, George Frederick; *Eng*. RHB/RF(r). b 7 Dec 1838 (Cambridge, Eng), d 2 Jul 1870 (Cambridge, Eng). 15.

TARRANT, William Ambrose; *Vic*. RHB. b 22 Sep 1866 (Fitzroy, Vic), d 1 Nov 1938 (Nth Fitzroy, Vic). 134, 140, 146, 149, 152, 160, 162, 169, 219.

TATCHELL, Thomas; *Vic*. RHB. b 13 Jun 1867 (Inglewood, Vic), d 18 Oct 1936 (Melbourne). 169, 183.

TATE, Maurice William; *Eng*. RHB/RFM. b 30 May 1895 (Brighton, Sussex), d 18 May 1956 (Wadhurst, Sussex). 572, 573, 575, 577, 581, 583, 585, 587, 589, 590, 592, 593, 595, 596, 654, 655, 657, 659, 661, 665, 668, 669, 673, 675, 678, 680, 681, 779, 782, 793, 800, 801.

TAYLOR, David; *NSW*. RHB. b 2 May 1881 (Sydney), d   (   ). 373.

TAYLOR, Herbert Wilfred; *Sth Afr*. RHB. b 5 May 1889 (Durban, Sth Afr), d 8 Feb 1973 (Cape Town, Sth Afr). 740, 741, 742, 744, 746, 747, 749, 756, 758, 761, 762, 764, 765.

TAYLOR, John Morris; *NSW*. RHB. b 10 Oct 1895 (Stanmore, NSW), d 12 May 1971 (Turramurra, NSW). 482, 487, 488, 490, 491, 504, 506, 507, 514, 518, 519, 520, 521, 523, 524, 525, 527, 528, 530, 532, 535, 539, 548, 549, 551, 552, 555, 561, 563, 567, 571, 577, 583, 585, 587, 591, 593, 595, 606, 607, 612, 615, 617, 628, 630.

TAYLOR, Joseph Stanley; *NSW*. RHB. b 7 Sep 1886 (   ), d 3 Sep 1954 (Newcastle, NSW). 452, 470.

TAYLOR, Leslie George; *NZ*; RHB. b 26 Jun 1894 (Auckland, NZ), d 17 Jan 1977 (Auckland, NZ). 473, 478, 480.

TAYLOR, Stuart Gifford; *Tas*. RHB/LBG. b 13 Apr 1900 (   ), d   (,WA). 721, 722.

TAYLOR, Tom Launcelot; *Eng*. RHB/WK. b 25 May 1878 (Leeds, Yorks), d 16 Mar 1960 (Leeds, Yorks). 288, 289, 290.

TEAGLE, Reginald Crump; *Sth Aust*. RHB/RFM. b 27 Feb 1909 (Parkside Sth, SA), d 8 Jun 1987 (Adelaide). 735, 739.

TEECE, Richard ; *Combined XIII*. RHB. b 29 Apr 1847 (Paihia, NZ), d 13 Dec 1928 (Point Piper, NSW). 25.

TEISSEIRE, Francis Lawrence; *Sth Aust*. RHB. b 8 Jul 1917 (Rose Park, SA). 951.

TENNENT, John Pattison; *Vic*. b 31 Jul 1846 (Hobart), d 1893 (Clifton Hill, Vic). 37, 43.

TERRY, R   Benjamin; *Vic*. b   (   ), d   (   ). 36, 37, 50.

THAMM, Carl Friedrich Wilhelm; *Sth Aust*. /WK. b 1 Nov 1874 (Nurioopta, SA), d 4 Jul 1944 (Subiaco, WA). 279.

THATCHER, Allen Norman; *NSW*. RHB/LBG. b 17 Apr 1899 (Sydney), d 12 Feb 1932 (Dulwich Hill, NSW). 529, 560, 565.

THEAK, Henry John Thomas; *NSW*. LHB/RF. b 19 Mar 1909 (Pyrmont, NSW), d 14 Sep 1979 (Narwee, NSW). 700, 706, 736, 748, 751, 752, 757, 760, 769, 774, 777, 779, 816, 818, 822, 829, 832, 833, 836, 838, 840, 842, 843.

THOLLAR, Douglas Hugh; *Tas*. RHB/LBG. b 13 Feb 1919 (George Town, Tas). 885, 918, 927.

THOMAS, Arthur Churchill; *Sth Aust*. RHB/WK. b 4 May 1869 (Unley, SA), d 28 Apr 1934 (Unley, SA). 242.

THOMAS, George A   ; *NSW*. RHB. b 30 Apr 1888 (   ). 390, 393.

THOMAS, Josiah; *Vic*. LHB. b 27 Aug 1910 (Golden Square, Vic), d 28 May 1960 (Essendon, Vic). 693, 750, 760, 763, 768, 774, 776, 798.

THOMAS, John Oliver; *Tas*. b 12 Apr 1852 (   ), d   (   ). 22.

THOMAS, Llewellyn; *Tas*. RHB/WK. b 1 Apr 1883 (Fitzroy, Vic), d 2 Nov 1962 (Evandale, Tas). 420, 443, 449, 464, 482, 485, 540.

THOMAS, Ronald Vivian; *Tas*. LHB/LM. b 21 Sep 1915 (Longford, Tas), d 28 May 1987 (Launceston). 819, 825, 826, 839, 856, 859, 866, 885, 886, 915, 918, 919, 927, 929.

THOMLINSON, Arthur; *Tas*. RHB/RM. b c 1887 (   ), d   (   ). 449.

THOMPSON, C   D   ; *NSW*. /Long-stop. b   (   ), d   (   ). 21.

THOMPSON, Francis Cecil; *Qld*. RHB/RM. b 17 Aug 1890 (Stanwell, Qld), d 24 Sep 1963 (Southport, Qld). 458, 467, 470, 471, 472, 494, 499, 506, 508, 510, 516, 522, 547, 560, 562, 564, 565, 571, 579, 581, 582, 584, 602, 603, 608, 618, 620, 621, 624, 629, 630, 634, 636, 639, 642, 645, 647, 651, 653, 658, 662, 664, 666, 672, 677, 689, 691, 696, 710, 715, 717, 719, 724, 803, 807, 808, 811, 815.

THOMPSON, George Joseph; *Eng*. RHB/RFM. b 27 Oct 1877 (Cogenhoe, Northants), d 3 Mar 1943 (Bristol, Glos). 288, 289, 290.

THOMPSON, Horace Malcolm; *Sth Aust.* RHB/RFM. b 29 Oct 1913 (Malvern, SA), d 19 Mar 1936 (Kalgoorlie, WA). 847.

THOMPSON, James Bogne; *Vic.* b 1829 (Yorks), d 18 Jul 1877 (Melbourne). 12.

THOMPSON, Nathaniel; *NSW.* RHB/RM(r)/WK. b 21 Apr 1838 (Birmingham, Eng), d 2 Sep 1896 (Burwood, NSW). 6, 9, 10, 11, 12, 14, 16, 17, 18, 20, 21, 23, 24, 25, 28, 29, 30, 31, 32, 33, 34, 36, 37, 39, 40, 43, 44.

THOMPSON, William James ; *Qld.* RHB. b 2 Jan 1891 (, Qld). 494.

THOMSETT, Harold King; *Qld.* LHB/RM. b 23 Oct 1913 (Yarraman, Qld), d 12 Apr 1991 (Spring Hill, Qld). 860, 863.

§THOMSON, Alan O ; *Vic.* RHB/RF. b 1 Sep 1899 (, NSW), d c 1930 (, Qld). 611.

THOMSON, Alfred Taddy; *Vic.* b 1818 (Dover, Kent), d 12 Oct 1895 (London). 1, 3.

THOMSON, Joseph; *Qld.* LHB/LB. b 27 May 1877 (, Qld), d c 1954 (, Qld). 326, 334, 336, 353, 359, 373, 375, 379, 390, 393, 399, 458, 465, 467, 470, 471, 472, 486, 493, 499, 506, 522.

THORN, Frank Leslie Oliver; *Vic.* RHB/RM. b 16 Aug 1912 (St Arnaud, Vic), d 11 Feb 1942 (Gasmata, New Britain). 903, 916, 927, 929, 935, 936, 937.

THORNTON, John; *Vic.* RHB/Long-stop. b 16 Jan 1835 (Huddersfield, Yorks), d 15 Dec 1919 (Camperdown, Vic). 9, 10.

THORPE, Harry; *Combined XI v Vernon's Team.* /LaB. b ( ), d ( ). 113.

THURGARLAND, Wilfred John; *Sth Aust.* LHB/LFM. b 11 Mar 1892 (Queenstown, SA), d 12 Jul 1974 (Campbelltown, SA). 512.

THURLOW, Hugh Motley; *Qld.* RHB/RFM. b 10 Jan 1903 (Townsville, Qld), d 3 Dec 1975 (Rosalie, Qld). 653, 658, 662, 664, 666, 672, 677, 689, 691, 696, 698, 703, 710, 715, 717, 719, 724, 727, 743, 746, 750, 753, 757, 762, 767, 773, 777, 783, 787, 790, 830.

THWAITES, Thomas Edwin; *Qld.* RHB/LM. b 1 Jul 1910 (Beaudesert, Qld). 960.

TIMBURY, Fredrick Richard Vaughan; *Qld.* RHB/RF. b 12 Jul 1885 (Gladstone, Qld), d 14 Apr 1945 (Sydney). 314, 326, 334, 336, 338, 353.

TINDALL, Edwin; *NSW.* RHB/RM. b 31 Mar 1851 (Liverpool, NSW), d 16 Jan 1926 (Marrickville, NSW). 28, 30, 31, 32, 37, 39, 40, 43, 44, 46, 47.

TINDILL, Eric William Thomas; *NZ.* LHB/WK. b 18 Dec 1910 (Nelson, NZ). 898, 901.

TINLEY, Robert Crispin; *Eng.* RHB/Ru-arm. b 25 Oct 1830 (Southwell, Notts), d 11 Dec 1900 (Burton-on-Trent, Staffs). 15.

TITCHMARSH, Charles Harold; *Eng.* RHB/WK. b 18 Feb 1881 (Royston, Herts), d 23 May 1930 (Royston, Herts). 543, 544, 545, 546, 555, 556, 557.

TOBIN, Bertrandt Joseph; *Sth Aust.* RHB/RFM. b 11 Nov 1910 (Nth Adelaide, SA), d 19 Oct 1969 (Adelaide). 710, 711, 724, 726, 733, 735, 739, 741, 751, 753, 761, 775, 780, 784, 787, 794, 795, 801, 804, 809, 811, 813, 816, 817, 829, 841.

TOBIN, William Andrew; *Vic.* RHB/RF(r). b 7 Jun 1859 (Kensington, Eng), d 17 Jan 1904 (Sth Melbourne). 45, 46, 81.

TOBY, Frederick J ; *Tas.* b 1889 (, NSW), d ( ). 540.

TOLHURST, Edward Keith; *Vic.* RHB. b 29 Oct 1895 (Elsternwick, Vic), d 24 May 1982 (East Prahran, Vic). 540, 542, 693, 694, 705, 719, 726, 732.

TOOHER, John Andrew; *NSW.* RHB. b 18 Nov 1846 ( ), d 23 May 1941 (Neutral Bay, NSW). 30.

TOWNLEY, Reginald Colin; *Tas.* RHB/LB. b 15 Apr 1904 (Hobart), d 3 May 1982 (Hobart). 627, 669, 674, 693, 701, 705, 706, 707, 708, 737, 739, 758, 759, 788, 865, 866.

TOWNSEND, Richard James Bruce; *Sth Aust.* LHB/RM. b 12 Aug 1886 (Mt Torrens, SA), d 17 Jan 1960 (Waikerie, SA). 352, 497, 500, 502, 534, 536, 537, 541, 544, 548, 550, 551, 561, 564, 566, 567, 569.

TOZER, Claude John; *NSW.* RHB. b 27 Sep 1890 (Sydney), d 21 Dec 1920 (Lindfield, NSW). 425, 456, 467, 469, 499, 503, 517.

TRAPP, Vincent Burney; *Vic.* RHB/OB. b 26 Jan 1861 (Prahran, Vic), d 21 Oct 1929 (Toorak, Vic). 50, 60, 73.

TRAVERS, Joseph Patrick Francis; *Sth Aust.* LHB/SLA. b 10 Jan 1871 (Adelaide), d 15 Sep 1942 (Adelaide). 198, 199, 201, 203, 242, 244, 248, 254, 255, 257, 258, 261, 264, 265, 269, 275, 276, 279, 282, 283, 287, 290, 291, 294, 296, 298, 311, 313, 315, 318, 319, 325, 329, 330, 333, 335, 339.

TREBILCOCK, Arthur Joseph; *Tas.* RHB. b 13 Dec 1907 (Zeehan, Tas), d 2 May 1972 (Hobart). 791.

TREGONING, Jack; *Sth Aust.* RHB/RFM. b 13 Jun 1919 (West Adelaide), d 26 Jun 1989 (Nth Adelaide). 941.

TREMBATH, Thomas James; *Vic.* RHB/RFM. b 16 Jan 1912 (Moonta, SA), d 2 Apr 1978 (West Brunswick, Vic). 812, 814, 819.

TRENERRY, Edwin; *NSW.* RHB/RFM. Brother of W.L.Trenerry. b 24 Feb 1897 (Queanbeyan, NSW), d 8 Jul 1983 (Wollahra, NSW). 507, 510, 514, 517, 525.

TRENERRY, William Leo; *NSW.* RHB/LB. Brother of E.Trenerry. b 29 Nov 1892 (Queanbeyan, NSW), d 4 Sep 1975 (Mosman, NSW). 504, 506, 507, 522, 533, 579.

TRINGROVE, James; *Tas.* RHB/OB. b 25 Nov 1907 (Blackmans Bay, Tas), d 11 Sep 1979 (Nth Blackmans Bay, Tas). 788, 791, 929.

TRINNICK, James; *Vic.* RHB. b 13 Dec 1853 (Kingsbridge, Devon), d 12 Jul 1928 (Northcote, Vic). 45, 75, 76, 81, 88, 91.

TROTT, Albert Edwin; *Vic & Eng.* RHB/RFM. Brother of G.H.S.Trott. b 6 Feb 1873 (Abbotsford, Vic), d 30 Jul 1914 (Willesden Green, London). 162, 169, 170, 173, 175, 178, 181, 182, 184, 187, 189, 190, 192, 194, 196, 198, 200, 288, 289, 290.

TROTT, George Henry Stevens; *Vic.* RHB/LB. Brother of A.E.Trott. b 5 Aug 1866 (Collingwood, Vic), d 10 Nov 1917 (Albert Park, Vic). 88, 90, 91, 94, 95, 96, 98, 100, 111, 113, 115, 119, 120, 121, 122, 124, 125, 126, 128, 129, 130, 131, 132, 133, 134, 135, 138, 139, 140, 141, 144, 147, 149, 150, 152, 153, 155, 156, 158, 160, 165, 166, 168, 170, 173, 175, 177, 178, 179, 181, 182, 184, 187, 189, 190, 192, 194, 196, 198, 200, 202, 203, 206, 207, 210, 212, 213, 214, 215, 217, 218, 220, 222, 224, 225, 226, 259, 292, 294, 299, 304, 306, 313, 365.

TRUMAN, Fredrick George; *Vic.* RHB/RFM. b 6 Dec 1886 (Carlton, Vic), d 17 Jun 1955 (Brighton, Vic). 497.

TRUMBLE, Hugh; *Vic.* RHB/OB. Brother of J.W.Trumble. b 12 May 1867 (Abbotsford, Vic), d 14 Aug 1938 (Hawthorn, Vic). 106, 111, 113, 115, 123, 131, 132, 133, 135, 138, 139, 140, 144, 146, 149, 152, 155, 156, 158, 165, 168, 178, 179, 182, 187, 190, 194, 196, 198, 202, 203, 206, 210, 213, 214, 215, 217, 218, 220, 222, 225, 226, 228, 231, 232, 235, 239, 240, 241, 244, 247, 248, 251, 253, 256, 257, 260, 266, 267, 268, 270, 273, 275, 299, 301, 302, 308, 310.

TRUMBLE, John William; *Vic.* RHB/OB. Brother of H.Trumble. b 16 Sep 1863 (Kew, Vic), d 17 Aug 1944 (Brighton, Vic). 73, 76, 79, 80, 83, 84, 85, 86, 87, 88, 89, 90, 94, 95, 96, 97, 98, 103, 106, 110, 111, 113, 123, 125, 127, 130, 133.

TRUMPER, Victor; *NSW.* RHB/RFM. Son of V.T.Trumper. b 7 Oct 1913 (Chatswood, NSW), d 31 Aug 1981 (Sydney). 953, 954, 955, 958, 959, 961, 962.

TRUMPER, Victor Thomas; *NSW.* RHB/RM. b 2 Nov 1877 (Darlinghurst, NSW), d 28 Jun 1915 (Darlinghurst, NSW). 180, 185, 211, 216, 218, 221, 223, 229, 230, 231, 233, 235, 238, 239, 240, 241, 243, 245, 246, 247, 250, 251, 253, 255, 256, 258, 260, 263, 265, 266, 267, 268, 269, 270, 272, 273, 275, 279, 280, 283, 284, 289, 293, 296, 297, 298, 299, 301, 302, 304, 307, 308, 310, 319, 320, 330, 331, 332, 343, 344, 351, 355, 356, 358, 360, 361, 366, 367, 368, 372, 382, 396, 408, 412, 413, 415, 417, 419, 422, 424, 425, 426, 428, 429, 433, 436, 437, 438, 439, 440, 441, 442, 447, 448, 450, 455, 459, 460, 462, 463, 466, 467, 469, 472, 474, 475, 481.

TRUSCOTT, William John; *West Aust.* RHB/WK. b 9 Oct 1886 (Lithgow, NSW), d 20 Jun 1966 (Bayswater, WA). 709.

TUCKWELL, Bertie Joseph; *Vic & NZ.* RHB. b 6 Oct 1882 (Carlton, Vic), d 2 Jan 1943 (Wellington, NZ). 286, 287, 292, 473, 475, 478, 480.

TUMILTY, Leonard Ross; *Tas.* LHB. b 12 Jun 1884 (Launceston), d 27 Mar 1962 (Launceston). 443, 449.

TUNKS, William; *NSW*. b 8 Apr 1816 (Nepean River District, NSW), d 12 Apr 1883 (St Leonards, NSW). 4.
TURNBULL, Maurice Joseph Lawson; *Eng*. RHB. b 16 Mar 1906 (Cardiff, Glamorgan), d 5 Aug 1944 (Montchamp, France). 682, 684, 685, 686, 687.
TURNER, Charles Thomas Biass; *NSW*. RHB/RFM. b 16 Nov 1862 (Bathurst, NSW), d 1 Jan 1944 (Manly, NSW). 62, 77, 87, 89, 92, 93, 95, 98, 99, 101, 102, 107, 108, 109, 111, 114, 115, 116, 117, 118, 120, 121, 122, 124, 125, 126, 129, 130, 131, 133, 135, 140, 145, 146, 147, 148, 149, 150, 151, 153, 157, 158, 165, 167, 168, 174, 177, 178, 179, 180, 182, 184, 185, 186, 196, 199, 200, 201, 202, 204, 206, 396.
TURNER, Edward; *Vic*. RHB/WK. b 8 Aug 1858 (Upper Northcote, Vic), d 26 Jan 1893 (Prahran, Vic). 48, 50, 55, 57, 60, 61, 69, 72, 73.
TURNER, J   B   ; *Vic*. b   (   ), d   (   ). 16, 17.
TURNER, Thomas; *Sth Aust & Vic*.   /LM. b c 1865 (Adelaide), d   (   ). 90, 110, 119, 124, 127.
TUTTLE, Roy Thomas; *Vic*. RHB/SLC. b 11 Sep 1920 (Carlton, Vic). 915.
TWEEDDALE, Ernest Richard; *NSW*. RHB/RF, b 23 Aug 1895 (Newtown, NSW), d 28 May 1956 (Dover Heights, NSW). 599, 608, 610.
TWOPENNY (Murrumgunarriman); *NSW*.   /RF(r). b c 1845 (   ), d 12 Mar 1883 (West Maitland, NSW). 21.
TYLDESLEY, George Ernest; *Eng*. RHB/RSM. Brother of J.T.Tyldesley. b 5 Feb 1889 (Worsley, Lancs), d 5 May 1962 (Rhos-on-Sea, Dendighshire). 650, 652, 655, 657, 658, 668, 669, 671, 675, 678, 680, 681.
TYLDESLEY, Harry; *Eng*. RHB/LB. Brother of R.K.Tyldesley. b 4 Jul 1892 (Bolton, Lancs), d 30 Aug 1935 (Morecambe, Lancs). 543, 544, 545, 546.
TYLDESLEY, John Thomas; *Eng*. RHB. Brother of G.E.Tyldesley. b 22 Nov 1873 (Worsley, Lancs), d 27 Nov 1930 (Monton, Manchester). 261, 262, 263, 266, 268, 270, 272, 273, 274, 275, 276, 291, 292, 293, 297, 301, 302, 303, 305, 306, 307, 308, 310, 311.
TYLDESLEY, Robert Knowles; *Eng*. RHB/LB. Brother of H.Tyldesley. b 11 Mar 1897 (Westhoughton, Lancs), d 17 Sep 1943 (Bolton, Lancs). 572, 575, 577, 581, 582, 585, 589, 592, 594, 596.
TYLECOTE, Edward Ferdinando Sutton; *Eng* RHB/WK. b 23 Jun 1849 (Marston Moretaine, Bedfordshire), d 15 Mar 1938 (New Hunstanton, Norfolk). 61, 62, 64, 65, 66, 68, 69.
ULYETT, George; *Eng*. RHB/RF(r). b 21 Oct 1851 (Sheffield, Yorks), d 18 Jun 1898 (Sheffield, Yorks). 32, 33, 34, 38, 39, 40, 41, 42, 51, 52, 54, 56, 57, 58, 59, 76, 77, 78, 80, 82, 84, 85, 86, 107, 109, 110, 116, 117, 120.
UPHAM, Ernest Frederick; *NZ*. RHB/RM. b 24 Mar 1873 (Wellington, NZ), d 23 Oct 1935 (Paekakariki, NZ). 237, 238.
VAN DER MERWE, Edward Alexander; *Sth Afr*. RHB/WK. b 9 Nov 1904 (Rustenberg, Sth Afr), d 28 Feb 1971 (Johannesburg). 746, 758, 761.
VAUGHAN, Frederick; *Vic*. RHB. b 8 Nov 1876 (   ), d 30 Sep 1926 (Elwood, Vic). 321, 337, 340, 341, 343, 345, 365, 384, 398, 399, 414.
VAUGHAN, Leonard J   ; *NSW*. RHB. b 16 Mar 1908 (   ), d c 1960 (   ). 599, 610.
VAUGHAN, Robert; *NSW*. b c 1834 (   ), d 12 Jul 1865 (at sea between Australia and NZ). 4, 6.
VAUTIN, Charles Edwin; *Tas*. RHB/WK. Brother of G.J.P.Vautin. b 24 Jun 1867 (Orielton, Tas), d 11 Dec 1942 (Moonah, Tas). 128, 197.
VAUTIN, Douglas Maynard; *Tas*. RHB/WK. Son of C.E.Vautin. b 26 Jul 1896 (Hobart), d 11 Jan 1976 (Mt Martha, Vic). 708.
VAUTIN, George James Phillips; *Tas & Vic*. RHB. Brother of C.E.Vautin. b 23 Apr 1869 (Orielton, Tas), d 9 Jan 1949 (West Preston, Vic). 134, 183.

VERITY, Hedley; *Eng*. RHB/SLA. b 18 May 1905 (Leeds, Yorks), d 31 Jul 1943 (Caserta, Italy). 771, 772, 775, 776, 779, 781, 785, 792, 793, 796, 797, 799, 801, 869, 871, 875, 876, 877, 878, 883, 889, 890, 893, 895.
VERNON, Edward Henry George; *Vic*. RHB/LB. b 11 Oct 1911 (Northcote, Vic), d 8 May 1968 (Melbourne). 791, 802, 812, 814, 819, 821, 839, 848, 852, 865.
VERNON, George Frederick; *Eng*. RHB. b 20 Jun 1856 (London), d 10 Aug 1902 (Elmina, Gold Coast). 61, 62, 64, 69, 108, 112, 113, 118, 121, 123.
VERNON, Leslie Phillip; *Vic*. LHB/RFM. b 29 May 1880 (Melbourne), d   (   ). 343, 350, 364, 374, 377, 378, 381.
VILJOEN, Kenneth George; *Sth Afr*; RHB. b 14 May 1910 (Kimberley, Sth Afr). d 21 Jan 1974 (Johannesburg). 740, 741, 742, 746, 748, 749, 756, 759, 761, 762, 764, 765, 770.
VINCENT, Cyril Leverton; *Sth Afr*. RHB/SLA. b 16 Feb 1902 (Johannesburg), d 24 Aug 1968 (Durban, Sth Afr). 740, 741, 742, 744, 746, 747, 748, 749, 756, 758, 761, 762, 765, 770.
VINCENT, Norman Hill; *Tas*. RHB. b 10 Nov 1883 (, UK), d 12 Feb 1958 (Prahran, Vic). 443, 449.
VINE, Joseph; *Eng*. RHB/LB. b 15 May 1875 (Willingdon, Sussex), d 25 Apr 1946 (Hove. Sussex). 431, 435, 437, 443, 444, 447, 448, 450.
VINT, William; *Vic*. RHB/WK. b 1851 or 1852 (Belfast, Northern Ireland), d 28 Mar 1897 (Helens Bay, Ireland). 81.
VIVIAN, Henry Gifford; *NZ*. LHB/SLA. b 4 Nov 1912 (Auckland, NZ), d 12 Aug 1983 (Auckland, NZ). 898, 899, 901.
VOCE, William; *Eng*. RHB/LFM. b 8 Aug 1909 (Annesley Woodhouse, Notts), d 6 Jun 1984 (Nottingham, Eng). 776, 778, 779, 781, 782, 789, 792, 799, 800, 801, 869, 871, 872, 875, 876, 877, 878, 883, 889, 890, 893, 895.
VOGLER, Albert Edward Ernest; *Sth Afr*. RHB/LBG. b 28 Nov 1876 (Swartwater, Sth Afr), d 9 Aug 1946 (Pietermaritzburg, Sth Afr). 406, 407, 408, 409, 411, 413, 420, 421, 423, 424, 425.
WADDINGTON, Abraham; *Eng*. RHB/LFM. b 4 Feb 1893 (Thornton, Yorks), d 28 Oct 1959 (Scarborough, Yorks). 517, 519, 527, 528, 531.
WADDY, Ernest Frederick; *NSW*. RHB. Brother of E.L.Waddy. b 5 Oct 1880 (Morpeth, NSW), d 23 Sep 1958 (Evesham, Worcs). 281, 315, 316, 319, 320, 322, 323, 324, 327, 328, 330, 331, 332, 338, 339, 340, 342, 359, 364, 367, 372, 376, 377, 380, 381, 391, 392, 408, 416.
WADDY, Edgar Lloyd; *NSW*. RHB/RM/WK. Brother of E.F.Waddy. b 3 Dec 1879 (Morpeth, NSW), d 2 Aug 1963 (Collaroy, NSW). 208, 331, 336, 338, 339, 340, 342, 343, 344, 346, 347, 351, 355, 358, 364, 373, 376, 380, 391, 392, 395, 396, 397, 400, 405, 408, 415, 422, 436, 439, 441, 445, 452, 455, 456, 458, 459, 460, 470, 494, 523.
WADE, Thomas Henry; *Eng*. LHB/WK. b 24 Nov 1910 (Maldon, Essex), d 25 Jul 1987 (Colchester, Essex). 871, 872.
WAINWRIGHT, Edward; *Eng*. RHB/RM. b 8 Apr 1865 (Sheffield, Yorks), d 28 Oct 1919 (Sheffield, Yorks). 209, 210, 211, 213, 215, 220, 221, 225, 226, 227.
WAINWRIGHT, Edmund George Chalwin; *Sth Aust*. LHB/LB. b 18 May 1903 (Nth Adelaide). 564, 569, 574, 575, 578, 580, 586, 597, 600.
WAITE, Mervyn George; *Sth Aust*. RHB/RM/OB. b 7 Jan 1911 (Kent Town, SA), d 16 Dec 1985 (Adelaide). 710, 711, 716, 720, 724, 726, 733, 735, 739, 741, 745, 751, 753, 761, 766, 769, 775, 787, 798, 816, 820, 830, 832, 834, 835, 841, 847, 853, 855, 858, 860, 861, 864, 866, 871, 874, 875, 880, 882, 889, 891, 896, 898, 904, 906, 908, 909, 911, 913, 916, 917, 918, 919, 922, 924, 926, 928, 931, 932, 935, 939, 941, 943, 945, 946, 947, 950, 951, 952, 955, 956, 957, 959, 963.
WALDRON, Alfred Edward; *Sth Aust*. LHB. b 26 Feb 1857 (Mornington, Vic), d 7 Jun 1929 (Adelaide). 60, 112.
WALES, Isaac F   ; *NSW*.   /WK. b 31 Jan 1865 (   ), d c 1942 (   ). 101, 133, 137, 138, 140, 145, 146, 148, 149, 151, 154, 155, 157, 158, 163, 171.

WALFORD, Sydney Rundle; *NSW*. RHB. b 19 Nov 1859 (Darlinghurst, NSW), d 2 Jul 1949 (Wollahra, NSW). 163.
WALKER, Charles William; *Sth Aust*. RHB/WK. b 19 Feb 1909 (Brompton Park,SA), d 18 Dec 1942 (Soltau, Russia). 679, 684, 688, 690, 691, 695, 697, 698, 704, 708, 709, 716, 720, 724, 726, 733, 735, 739, 741, 745, 751, 753, 761, 766, 767, 769, 775, 780, 784, 787, 794, 795, 798, 801, 804, 806, 809, 811, 813, 816, 817, 820, 824, 841, 847, 853, 855, 858, 860, 861, 864, 866, 871, 874, 880, 882, 889, 891, 894, 896, 898, 902, 904, 906, 908, 909, 911, 913, 920, 924, 926, 928, 931, 939, 941, 943, 945, 946, 947, 950, 951, 955, 956, 957.
WALKER, William Holden; *Tas*. RHB/Ru-arm/WK. b 16 Dec 1835 (Islington, London), d 14 Jun 1886 (Hobart). 27, 35.
WALKERDEN, Henry Ernest; *West Aust*. RHB/WK. b 20 Nov 1885 (Brunswick, Vic), d   (Coburg, Vic). 401.
§**WALKLEY**, Edwin; *Sth Aust*. RHB/RaB. b 10 May 1876 (Wallaroo, SA), d 18 Apr 1950 (Randwick, NSW). 255, 257, 258, 265.
WALL, John Lyall; *NSW*. LHB/LFM. b 25 Oct 1891 (Birchgrove, NSW), d 9 Jun 1969 (West Pymble, NSW). 494, 533, 534, 535, 537, 538, 558, 559, 565, 568, 584.
WALL, Thomas Welbourn; *Sth Aust*. RHB/RF. b 13 May 1904 (Semaphore, SA), d 26 Mar 1981 (Adelaide). 574, 575, 578, 580, 586, 596, 597, 601, 641, 644, 645, 652, 656, 660, 664, 667, 677, 679, 680, 684, 688, 690, 695, 697, 698, 704, 707, 712, 716, 718, 720, 726, 741, 745, 747, 749, 756, 761, 766, 767, 769, 780, 781, 784, 789, 792, 794, 795, 797, 805, 809, 811, 813, 816, 817, 820, 824, 825, 826, 827, 828, 832, 834, 835, 853, 855, 858, 860, 861, 864.
WALLACE, Percival Henry; *Vic*. RHB/RFM. b 6 Oct 1891 (Bendigo, Vic), d 3 Oct 1959 (Glen Iris, Vic). 540, 541, 542, 545, 549, 550, 552, 554, 556, 563, 566, 568, 569, 574, 576, 578, 582, 588, 592, 619.
WALLACE, Walter Mervyn. *RHB*. b 19 Dec 1916 (Auckland, NZ). 898, 899, 901.
WALSH, John Edward; *NSW*. LHB/SLC. b 4 Dec 1912 (Sydney), d 20 May 1980 (Wallsend, NSW). 941, 944.
WALSH, James Michael; *Tas*. LHB/RFM. b 28 May 1913 (Launceston), d 5 Jul 1986 (Launceston). 782, 785, 788, 802, 812, 814, 819, 825, 826, 839, 856, 859, 865, 866, 886.
WALSH, Laurence Stanley; *Sth Aust*. RHB. Twin Brother of N.A.Walsh. b 8 Feb 1902 (Nth Adelaide), d 12 Jan 1976 (St Georges, SA). 710, 711.
WALSH, Norman Arthur; *Sth Aust*. RHB. Twin Brother of L.S.Walsh. b 8 Feb 1902 (Nth Adelaide), d 7 Dec 1969 (Adelaide). 561, 564, 569, 574, 575, 578, 580, 600, 601.
§**WALSHE**, John Hamilton; *Tas*. b 1841 (, UK) d 17 Apr 1893 (Hobart). 27.
WALTERS, Francis Henry; *Vic & NSW*. RHB/RM. b 9 Feb 1860 (East Melbourne), d 1 Jun 1922 (at sea near Bombay, India). 50, 71, 72, 76, 79, 83, 86, 87, 88, 89, 95, 98, 104, 115, 116, 119, 123, 130, 131, 140, 141, 142, 146, 149, 152, 166, 168, 170, 193, 194, 195, 196, 199.
WARD. Albert; *Eng*. RHB. b 21 Nov 1865 (Leeds, Yorks), d 6 Jan 1939 (Bolton, Lancs). 172, 173, 174, 176, 177, 179, 181, 184, 186, 189, 190, 191.
WARD, Edward Wolstenholme; *NSW*. RHB/LF(r). b 17 Aug 1823 (Calcutta, India), d 5 Feb 1890 (Cannes, France). 5, 9, 11, 12.
WARD, Francis Anthony; *Sth Aust*. RHB/LBG. b 23 Feb 1909 (Sydney), d 25 Mar 1974 (Brooklyn, NSW). 847, 853, 855, 858, 860, 861, 864, 866, 867, 871, 874, 877, 878, 883, 886, 889, 891, 894, 896, 898, 902, 906, 908, 909, 911, 913, 916, 917, 918, 920, 924, 926, 928, 931, 932, 935, 939, 941, 943, 945, 946, 947, 950, 951, 955, 956, 957.
WARD, Leonard Keith; *Tas*. RHB. b 17 Feb 1879 (Sth Kingston, NSW), d 30 Sep 1964 (Heathpool, SA). 362.
WARD, Maxwell John; *NSW*. LHB. b 3 Feb 1907 (Randwick, NSW). 880, 881.
WARD, Ronald Egbert; *Tas*. RHB. b 7 May 1905 (Adelaide). 729, 731, 739, 802, 856.
WARD, William George; *Tas*. RHB/LBG. b 14 Nov 1863 (West Hobart), d 22 Jun 1948 (East Malvern, Vic). 219, 236, 252, 345.

WARDILL, Benjamin Johnson; *Vic*. RHB/WK. Brother of R.W.Wardill. b 15 Oct 1842 (Everton, Lancs), d 15 Oct 1917 (Sandringham, Vic). 17.
WARDILL, Richard Wilson; *Vic*. RHB/RM(r). Brother of B.J.Wardill. b 3 Nov 1840 (Everton, Lancs), d 17 Aug 1873 (Melbourne). 12, 13, 14, 15, 18, 19, 20, 21, 22, 27.
WARDLAW, Douglas McLaren Searl; *Tas*. RHB/RF. Brother of R.B.S.Wardlaw. b 19 Jul 1904 (Hobart), d 20 May 1968 (St Marys, Tas). 615, 616, 627, 640, 643, 668, 669.
WARDLAW, Robert Bruce Searl; *Tas*. LHB. Brother of D.M.S.Wardlaw. b 9 Jan 1914 (Hobart), d 12 Sep 1986 (Launceston). 885.
WARE, Joseph Maitland; *Tas*. b 8 Sep 1822 (, UK), d 23 Sep 1868 (, UK). 3.
WARNE, Frank Belmont; *Vic*. LHB/LBG. Son of T.S.Warne. b 3 Oct 1906 (Nth Carlton, Vic). 627, 676.
WARNE, Tom Summerhayes; *Vic*. RHB/LBG. b 13 Jan 1870 (Nth Melbourne), d 7 Jul 1944 (Carlton, Vic). 183, 190, 197, 205, 214, 231, 232, 235, 247, 248, 251, 271, 274, 280, 282, 285, 309, 320, 325, 328, 329, 332, 334, 340, 350, 352, 357, 358, 364, 372, 374, 377, 378, 389, 397, 404, 407, 410, 423, 428, 449, 451.
WARNER, Pelham Francis; *Eng*. RHB. b 2 Oct 1873 (Port of Spain, Trinidad), d 30 Jan 1963 (West Lavington, Sussex). 288, 289, 290, 291, 292, 293, 295, 297, 301, 302, 303, 305, 306, 307, 308, 310, 311, 431.
WATERMAN, Leonard William; *Qld*. RHB/WK. b 18 Feb 1892 (Brisbane), d 1 Jan 1952 (Kangaroo Point, Qld). 743, 763, 767, 773, 796.
WATERS, Robert William; *Sth Aust*. /RM. b 1874 (Gravesend, Kent), d 20 Feb 1912 (Woodville, SA). 276, 279, 282, 283.
WATLING, Walter Herbert; *Sth Aust*. RHB. b 13 Mar 1864 (Unley, SA), d 19 Dec 1928 (Randfontein, Sth Afr). 75, 81, 119, 124, 127.
WATMUFF, Frederick John; *Vic*. RHB/LBG. b 16 Sep 1915 (Balaclava, Vic), d 10 Aug 1972 (Castlemaine, Vic). 856, 859.
WATSFORD, Goulburn; *Sth Aust & Vic*. RHB/RaB. b 1 Jul 1859 (Goulburn, NSW), d 16 May 1951 (Melbourne). 70, 88.
WATSON, Alfred Edward; *Tas*. RHB/RM/OB. b 31 Aug 1888 (Carlton, Vic), d 6 May 1957 (Sth Melbourne). 616, 627, 640, 643.
WATSON, Bertie Francis; *NSW*. RHB. b 13 Mar 1898 (   ). 634, 640.
WATSON, John Wentworth; *Tas*. b 29 Mar 1828 (Sorell, Tas), d 26 Jun 1920 (Scottsdale, Tas). 2.
WATSON, William; *NSW*. LHB. b 10 Nov 1881 (   ), d 12 Feb 1926 (Nth Sydney). 416, 418.
WATT, Arthur David; *West Aust*. RHB/LB. b 24 Nov 1916 (Edinburgh, Scotland). 936, 937, 950, 951.
WATT, Arthur Kenneth Elwyn; *Tas*. RHB/LBG. Son of J.Watt & brother of J.C.Watt. b 12 Dec 1891 (Hobart), d 8 Oct 1973 (Hobart). 451, 464, 469, 492, 570, 590, 616.
WATT, Donald; *Qld*. RHB/LBG. b 15 Mar 1920 (Southport, Qld). 940, 943, 944, 946, 948, 953, 958, 960, 964.
WATT, John; *Tas*. RHB/LB. b 16 Feb 1858 (Hobart), d 14 Nov 1918 (Glebe, Tas). 169, 183, 197.
WATT, John Charles; *Tas*. RHB/LB. Son of J.Watt & brother of A.K.E.Watt. b 6 Jul 1884 (Hobart), d 4 Aug 1961 (Hobart). 321.
WAYE, Libby Sibly; *Sth Aust*. b 14 Jan 1885 (Willunga, SA), d 12 Jun 1951 (Adelaide). 461.
WEARNE, William Stewart; *NSW*. /LM. b 1857 (   ), d   (   ). 46, 62, 118.
WEBB, Berrowes Littleton; *Qld*. RHB. b 15 Apr 1915 (Brisbane), d 7 Feb 1983 (Greenslopes, Qld). 912.
WEBBE, Alexander Josiah; *Eng*. RHB/RF. b 16 Jan 1855 (London), d 19 Feb 1941 (Abinger Hammer, Surrey). 38, 39, 40, 41, 42.
WEBSTER, Alexander Miles Clifton; *West Aust*. RHB/LF. b 25 Nov 1908 (East Fremantle, WA), d 28 Mar 1964 (Shenton Park, WA). 682, 701, 702.

WEBSTER, Harold Wynne; *Sth Aust.* /WK. b 17 Feb 1889 (Sydney), d 7 Oct 1949 (Randwick, NSW). 427, 430, 431, 434, 436, 441.

WEDGWOOD, Walter Bernard; *Vic.* RHB/SLA. b 23 Oct 1912 (East Malvern, Vic), d 2 Dec 1977 (Mornington, Vic). 699.

WEEKS, Albert Edmund; *Sth Aust.* b 23 Jul 1864 (Adelaide), d 21 Apr 1948 (Hollywood, WA). 105.

WEIR, Gordon Lindsay; *NZ.* RHB/RM. b 2 Jun 1908 (Auckland, NZ). 898, 899, 901.

WEIR, Harold Stanley; *Qld.* LHB/LFM. b 23 Apr 1904 (Croydon Junction, Qld). 687.

WELCH, Charles William; *Vic.* RHB/LB. b 9 Jun 1907 ( ),d 11 Apr 1983 (Melbourne). 854, 858, 862, 863.

WELLINGTON, Clement Wellesley; *West Aust.* RHB. b 12 Aug 1882 (Kadina, SA), d 26 Jul 1956 (Underdale, SA). 346.

WELLINGTON, Stephen Leslie; *Tas.* RHB. b 4 Jul 1899 (Beaconsfield, Tas), d 11 Jun 1974 (Scotts Head, NSW). 668.

WELLS, Arthur Phillip; *NSW.* RHB/RM. b 4 Sep 1900 (Paddington, NSW), d 27 Dec 1964 (Sth Coogee, NSW). 522, 529, 534, 537, 547, 560, 565, 588, 594.

WELLS, George; *Eng.* RHB/RM(r). b 2 Nov 1830 (Whitechapel, Middlesex), d 23 Jan 1891 (Shoreham-by-Sea, Sussex). 13.

WESTBROOK, Keith Raymond; *Tas.* RHB/RaB. Brother of R.A. & nephew of N.R.Westbrook. b 28 May 1887 (Scottsdale, Tas), d 20 Jan 1982 (Burnie, Tas). 398.

WESTBROOK, Norman Russell; *Tas.* RHB. Nephew of T. & W.H.Westbrook. b 25 Jun 1868 (Launceston), d 29 May 1931 (Launceston). 169, 197, 205, 236, 305, 385.

WESTBROOK, Roy Austin; *Tas.* RHB. Brother of K.R. & nephew of N.R.Westbrook. b 3 Jan 1889 (Scottsdale, Tas), d 7 Aug 1961 (Wellington, NZ). 420, 449, 482.

WESTBROOK, Thomas; *Tas.* Brother of W.H.Westbrook. b 18 Sep 1832 (Hobart), d 13 Sep 1911 (Sandy Bay, Tas). 7, 8.

WESTBROOK, Walter Horatio; *Tas.* Brother of T.Westbrook. b 21 Nov 1827 (Hobart), d 3 Jan 1897 (Launceston). 1, 3.

§**WHALLEY**, John; *Qld.* RHB. possibly b 27 Nov 1872 (, Qld), d 13 Jun 1950 ( ). 323.

WHIDDON, Henry; *NSW.* RHB/LB. b 20 Nov 1878 ( ), d 19 Dec 1935 (Manly, NSW). 355, 358, 364.

WHITE, Alfred Becher Stewart; *NSW.* RHB. b 4 Oct 1879 (Mudgee, NSW), d 15 Dec 1962 (Karuah, NSW). 326, 338, 375, 379.

WHITE, Alfred Henry Ebsworth; *NSW.* RHB/RFM. b 18 Oct 1901 (Scone, NSW), d 6 Mar 1964 (Darling Point, NSW). 602.

WHITE, Edward Clive Stewart; *NSW.* RHB/LM. Son of A.B.S.White. b 17 Apr 1913 (Mosman, NSW). 833, 836, 838, 840, 842, 843, 846, 849, 851, 853, 854, 857, 861, 862, 867, 870, 873, 880, 881, 884, 888, 892, 894, 897, 901, 906, 907, 910, 913, 914, 917, 918, 919, 921, 924, 925, 930.

WHITE, John Cornish; *Eng.* RHB/SLA. b 19 Feb 1891 (Holford, Somerset), d 2 May 1961 (Combe-Florey, Somerset). 650, 652, 654, 657, 658, 659, 661, 665, 668, 669, 671, 673, 675, 680, 681.

WHITESIDES, Thomas; *Tas.* RHB/Long-stop. b 7 Sep 1836 (Hobart), d 24 Sep 1919 (Hobart). 8, 19.

WHITFIELD, Henry Edward; *Sth Aust.* RHB/RFM. b 25 Feb 1903 (Kent Town, SA), d 14 Jan 1937 (Royston Park, SA). 631, 632, 635, 637, 652, 656, 660, 664, 671, 677, 679, 684, 688, 690, 691, 695, 697, 698, 704, 724, 733, 735, 753, 766, 769.

WHITING, Albert W H ; *NSW.* RHB. b 1866 ( ), d ( ). 92.

WHITINGTON, Richard Smallpeice; *Sth Aust.* RHB. b 30 Jun 1912 (Unley Park, SA), d 13 Mar 1984 (Sydney). 775, 780, 784, 787, 794, 795, 798, 804, 817, 820, 824, 829, 830, 880, 882, 889, 894, 896, 906, 908, 909, 911, 913, 916, 924, 926, 928, 931, 932, 935, 939, 941, 943, 945, 946, 947.

WHITLOW, Edward Hardmond; *Vic.* /RM(r). b 1832 (Manchester, Eng), d 29 Nov 1870 (Sth Melbourne). 9.

WHITTING, William Charles; *NSW.* RHB/SLA. b 9 Jul 1884 (Drummoyne, NSW), d 26 Oct 1936 (Bellevue Hill, NSW). 326.

WHITTY, William James; *NSW & Sth Aust.* RHB/LFM. b 15 Aug 1886 (Sydney), d 30 Jan 1974 (Tantanoola, SA). 359, 374, 376, 378, 380, 383, 391, 394, 395, 396, 404, 406, 410, 412, 413, 417, 419, 424, 426, 427, 428, 430, 431, 434, 436, 438, 440, 441, 459, 461, 462, 466, 468, 479, 489, 490, 495, 497, 500, 502, 503, 511, 523, 536, 537, 541, 550, 551, 554, 566, 567, 575, 606, 611, 612.

WHYSALL, William Wilfrid; *Eng.* RHB/RM/WK. b 31 Oct 1887 (Woodborough, Notts), d 11 Nov 1930 (Nottingham, Eng). 573, 576, 581, 587, 589, 590, 592, 593, 594, 595, 596.

WIGHT, Oscar Stanley; *WI.* RHB. b c 1906 ( ), d 13 Sep 1986 (Bury St Edmunds, Suffolk). 714, 727, 736.

WIGLEY, Robert Strangways; *Sth Aust.* RHB. b 15 Mar 1864 (Windsor, Vic), d 20 Apr 1926 (Glenelg, SA). 124, 127, 132.

WILBERFORCE, Robert James; *West Aust.* RHB/RM. b 31 Jul 1910 (Subiaco, WA). 632, 649, 699, 701, 702, 709, 868, 869, 900, 904.

WILKIE, Daniel; *Vic.* RHB/Ru-arm. b 1 Dec 1843 (Melbourne), d 11 May 1917 (St Kilda, Vic). 16, 17, 27.

WILKINS, Roy; *Tas.* RHB. b 18 Apr 1892 (Nth Hobart), d 17 Jul 1965 (Hobart). 615, 616.

WILKINSON, Alfred; *Sth Aust.* /RaB. b 2 Jan 1863 (Kooringa, SA), d 22 Jan 1922 (Lower Mitcham, SA). 90, 148, 154, 161.

WILKINSON, Robert B ; *Vic.* b ( ), d ( ). 3.

WILKINSON, William Archer; *Vic.* RHB/LM. b 1 Sep 1899 (Clifton Hill, Vic), d 5 May 1974 (Mildura, Vic). 570, 605, 643, 648, 649, 662, 672, 729, 731, 732.

WILKINSON, William Alexander Camac; *Eng.* RHB. b 6 Dec 1892 (Sydney), d 19 Sep 1983 (Storrington, Sussex). 543, 544, 545, 546.

WILLCOCKS, Robert James; *Qld.* RHB/RFM. b 23 Dec 1891 (Brisbane), d 21 Mar 1965 (Toowoomba, Qld). 470.

WILLIAMS, Edward Alexander; *Vic.* RHB. b 18 Sep 1915 (Nth Fitzroy, Vic). 865.

WILLIAMS, Norman Leonard; *Sth Aust.* RHB/LBG. b 23 Sep 1899 (Semaphore, SA), d 31 May 1947 (Semaphore, SA). 500, 502, 503, 509, 531, 534, 536, 537, 544, 548, 550, 551, 554, 561, 564, 566, 567, 569, 574, 619, 622, 624, 625, 626, 630, 635, 637, 639, 641, 652, 656, 660, 664, 667.

WILLIAMS, Owen Charles; *Vic.* RHB. b 20 Jun 1847 (Impression Bay, Tas), d 18 Nov 1917 (Kandy, Ceylon). 23, 24, 27, 31.

WILLIAMS, Robert Graham; *Sth Aust.* RHB/RFM. b 4 Apr 1911 (St Peters, SA), d 31 Aug 1978 (Adelaide). 798, 801, 847, 860, 861, 864, 880, 882, 891, 894, 896, 898, 906, 908, 909, 911, 913, 916.

WILLIS, Carl Bleackley; *Vic.* RHB. b 23 Mar 1893 (Daylesford, Vic), d 12 May 1930 (Berrigan, NSW). 478, 483, 484, 485, 492, 504, 509, 511, 513, 515, 520, 525, 535, 536, 538, 539, 541, 545, 549, 550, 552, 554, 562, 563, 566, 569, 588, 592, 598, 600, 619, 660.

WILLS, Thomas Wentworth; *Vic.* RHB/RFM(r)/Ru-arm. b 19 Aug 1835 (Molongolo Plains, NSW), d 2 May 1880 (Heidelberg, Vic). 5, 6, 7, 8, 9, 10, 14, 15, 16, 18, 19, 20, 21, 23, 24, 25, 31.

WILLSMORE, Hurtle Binks; *Sth Aust.* RHB/LB. b 26 Dec 1889 (Beverley, SA), d 17 Sep 1985 (Kings Park, SA). 480, 483, 487, 489, 490, 495, 497, 511, 523.

WILSON, Charles Geldart; *Vic.* RHB. b 9 Jan 1869 (Carngham, Vic), d 28 Jun 1952 (Wellington, NZ). 183, 197, 219.

WILSON, Evelyn Rockley; *Eng.* RHB/LB/OB. b 25 Mar 1879 (Bolsterstone, Yorks), d 21 Jul 1957 (Winchester, Hampshire). 512, 516, 517, 526, 528, 530, 531.

WILSON, Geoffrey; *Eng.* RHB. b 21 Aug 1895 (Leeds, Yorks), d 29 Nov 1960 (Southsea, Hampshire). 544, 545, 546, 555, 556, 557.

WILSON, George Lindsay; *Vic.* RHB/RM. b 27 Apr 1868 (Fitzroy, Vic), d 9 Mar 1920 (St Kilda, Vic). 228, 237.

WILSON, Henry; *Tas.* RHB/RM/OB. Brother of J.T.Wilson. b 31 Mar 1865 (Westbury), d 18 Aug 1914 (Sydney). 134, 141, 249, 252, 259, 159.

WILSON, Horace; *West Aust.* LHB/WK. b 16 Jul 1864 (Kadina, SA), d 15 May 1925 (West Perth). 162.

WILSON, John Carandini; *NSW.* LHB/LaB. b 11 Feb 1869 ( ), d 21 May 1915 ( ). 148.

WILSON, John Thomas; *Tas.* Brother of H.Wilson. b 27 Nov 1868 (Westbury), d 24 Jul 1906 (Launceston). 134.

WILSON, Richard; *Qld.* /LB. b 14 Jan 1869 (Sydney), d ( ). 208.

WILSON, William J ; *Vic.* LHB/SLC. b 1912 (Mildura, Vic). 865.

WILSON, William Young; *Vic.* LHB/RFM. b 13 Dec 1909 (Moonee Ponds, Vic), d 30 Sep 1976 (Ascot Vale, Vic). 856, 859, 864.

WINDSOR, Edward Arthur Cartwright; *Tas.* RHB/RFM/OB/LB. b 9 Mar 1869 (Launceston), d 23 Dec 1953 (Launceston). 141, 159, 169, 183, 197, 205, 229, 236, 249, 252, 253, 259, 303, 305, 309, 322, 362, 363, 369, 372, 385, 420, 421, 443, 444, 449.

WINGROVE, Frederick Walter; *Vic.* b 20 Apr 1863 (Eltham, Vic), d 1939 ( ). 88.

WINNING, Charles Samuel; *A.I.F.* LHB/SLA. b 17 Jul 1889 (Paddington, NSW), d 20 Apr 1967 (Newport, NSW). 504, 506, 507.

WINSER, Cyril Legh; *Sth Aust.* RHB/WK. b 27 Nov 1884 (High Legh, Staffs), d 20 Dec 1983 (Barwon Heads, Vic). 474, 476, 479, 515, 518.

WOOD, Cecil Clunas; *Tas.* RHB. b 8 Apr 1896 (Mooreville Road, Tas). 674, 676, 693, 694, 701.

WOOD, John Robert; *NSW.* RHB/RM. b 11 Apr 1865 (Newcastle, NSW), d 14 Feb 1928 (Putney, London). 115, 122.

WOOD, Percival Barnes; *West Aust.* RHB/RM. b 22 Dec 1905 (Wellington, NZ), d 10 Jun 1941 (in action in Syria). 770.

WOOD, Reginald; *Vic & Eng.* LHB/LM. b 7 Mar 1860 (Woodchurch, Cheshire), d 6 Jan 1915 (Manly, NSW). 91, 100, 101, 102, 103.

WOODBURY, William Joseph George; *Vic.* RHB/LBG. b 6 Dec 1892 (Balmain, NSW), d 31 Aug 1983 (Moe, Vic). 492.

WOODFORD, John Robert Herbert; *Vic & Sth Aust.* LHB/WK. b 23 Jun 1881 (Camberwell, Vic), d 1 May 1949 (Nth Fitzroy, Vic). 274, 321, 357, 365, 374, 376, 378, 380, 386, 387, 388, 449, 451, 454, 464.

WOODFULL, William Maldon; *Vic.* RHB. b 22 Aug 1897 (Maldon, Vic), d 11 Aug 1965 (near Tweed Heads, NSW). 541, 542, 545, 549, 550, 552, 554, 556, 562, 563, 566, 568, 569, 574, 576, 578, 588, 592, 598, 600, 604, 607, 611, 613, 615, 616, 617, 619, 621, 623, 625, 630, 635, 636, 638, 641, 646, 651, 654, 659, 661, 665, 673, 678, 680, 685, 688, 689, 707, 708, 712, 714, 718, 723, 725, 728, 734, 735, 738, 742, 745, 747, 749, 752, 756, 762, 764, 765, 773, 774, 776, 778, 781, 783, 786, 789, 792, 797, 799, 804, 805, 806, 807, 808, 810, 818, 825, 826, 827, 828.

WOODS, Julian Augustus; *Tas.* RHB. b 4 Sep 1887 (Oatlands, Tas), d 11 Oct 1975 (Lindisfarne, Tas). 482.

WOODS, William; *NSW.* b ( ), d ( ). 28, 29.

WOOLCOCK, Arthur Henry; *Sth Aust.* LHB. b 10 Jun 1887 (Port Pirie, SA), d 29 Jun 1975 (Adelaide). 389, 394, 395.

WOOLF, Louis Sydney; *Vic.* /Long-stop. b 28 Jul 1855 (Melbourne), d 6 Jul 1942 (Melbourne). 37.

WOOLLEY, Frank Edward; *Eng.* LHB/LM/SLA. b 27 May 1887 (Tonbridge, Kent), d 18 Oct 1978 (Halifax, Canada). 431, 432, 433, 435, 437, 438, 440, 442, 443, 444, 446, 447, 448, 450, 512, 513, 514, 516, 517, 519, 521, 524, 526, 527, 528, 530, 531, 572, 575, 576, 583, 585, 587, 593, 594, 595, 596, 682, 684, 685, 686.

WOOLLEY, H ; *Tas.* b ( ), d ( ). 385.

WOOTTON, John Richard; *Vic.* RHB/RFM. Nephew of S.E.Wootton. b 18 Jan 1906 (Rushworth), d 18 Jul 1986 ( ). 676, 705.

WOOTTON, Stanley Eli; *Vic.* RHB/WK. b 28 Apr 1895 (Sth Yarra, Vic), d 20 Mar 1962 (Heidelberg, Vic). 570.

WORDSWORTH, Charles; *NSW.* /RM. b ( ), d ( ). 373.

WORKER, Rupert Vivian de Renzy; *NZ.* LHB. b 15 Apr 1896 (Auckland, NZ), d 23 Apr 1989 (Napier, NZ). 603, 605, 609, 610.

WORRALL, John; *Vic.* RHB/OB(r). b 12 May 1863 (Maryborough, Vic), d 17 Nov 1937 (Fairfield Park, Vic). 75, 80, 83, 87, 88, 89, 91, 98, 100, 103, 104, 106, 110, 111, 113, 115, 116, 117, 123, 124, 125, 126, 128, 129, 130, 131, 135, 138, 139, 140, 141, 144, 146, 149, 152, 155, 156, 158, 165, 166, 168, 175, 178, 181, 182, 187, 197, 198, 200, 202, 203, 206, 207, 210, 212, 214, 218, 222, 224, 225, 226, 228, 231, 232, 235, 237, 239, 240, 241, 247, 248, 251, 253, 254, 256, 257, 260, 262, 264, 267, 271, 274.

WORTHINGTON, Thomas Stanley; *Eng.* RHB/RFM. b 21 Aug 1905 (Bolsover, Derbyshire), d 31 Aug 1973 (Kings Lynn, Norfolk). 682, 684, 685, 686, 687, 868, 869, 871, 872, 873, 875, 877, 883, 885, 892, 895.

WRAY, Thomas Fawcett; *Vic.* RHB. b 1827 (Yorks), d 6 Sep 1877 (Melbourne). 6, 9, 10.

WRIGHT, Albert William; *Sth Aust.* RHB/LB. b 24 Sep 1875 (Norwood, SA), d 23 Dec 1938 (Nth Adelaide). 327, 329, 330, 337, 339, 341, 342, 344, 349, 352, 355, 378, 380, 386, 388, 391, 394, 395, 404, 406, 410, 412, 427, 430, 436, 487, 489, 490, 515, 518.

WRIGHT, Francis John; *Vic.* LHB/RFM. Brother of H.L.Wright. b 13 Mar 1874 (Ballarat East, Vic), d ( ). 219.

WRIGHT, Harry L ; *Vic.* /WK. Brother of F.J.Wright. b 13 Apr 1872 ( ), d c 1948 ( ). 259, 313, 314.

WRIGHT, Robert Raymond; *Sth Aust.* LHB/SLA. b 11 Nov 1914 (Marryatville, SA), d 20 Jan 1965 (Springfield, SA). 820, 824.

WYATT, Robert Elliott Storey; *Eng.* RHB/RM. b 2 May 1901 (Milford, Surrey). 771, 775, 776, 778, 779, 781, 782, 785, 789, 792, 793, 796, 797, 799, 800, 801, 868, 869, 885, 886, 889, 890, 892, 893, 895.

WYETH, Ezra Robert; *Qld.* RHB/LM. b 13 Mar 1910 (Toowoomba, Qld). 803, 807, 830, 831, 834, 836, 837, 840, 846, 850, 852, 855, 857, 860, 863, 870, 876, 879, 882, 884, 891, 897, 905, 908, 910.

WYNNE, Lester Alan; *Vic.* RHB. b 7 Oct 1908 (Carlton, Vic), d 29 Nov 1980 (Melbourne). 856, 859.

YEATES, Sidney Fergus Macrae; *Qld.* RHB/LBG. b 20 Aug 1912 (Toowoomba, Qld). 803, 807, 817.

YEOMANS, Frederick Caleb; *Vic.* RHB. b 11 Nov 1888 (Northcote, Vic), d 16 Jan 1965 (Brighton, Vic). 492.

YOUILL, George Joseph; *NSW.* RHB. b 2 Oct 1871 (Sydney), d 21 Dec 1936 (Glebe, NSW). 154, 155, 157, 158, 163, 164, 193, 194, 195.

YOUNG, Richard Alfred; *Eng.* RHB/WK. b 16 Sep 1885 (Dharwar, India), d 1 Jul 1968 (Hastings, Sussex). 348, 350, 353, 354, 356, 362, 363, 367, 368, 370.

ZACHARIAH, Harry; *Vic.* RHB/SLA. b 4 Jun 1911 (Stirling, SA). 856, 859.

ZIMBULIS, Anthony George; *West Aust.* RHB/LBG. b 11 Feb 1918 (Perth), d 17 May 1963 (Palm Beach, WA). 827, 842, 843, 844, 845, 868, 869, 900, 903, 904, 920, 936, 937, 950, 951.

ZSCHORN, Paul William; *Sth Aust.* RHB. b 16 Jul 1886 (Nth Unley, SA), d 13 Jun 1953 (Glen Iris, Vic). 404, 406.

ZULCH, John William; *Sth Afr.* RHB. b 2 Jan 1886 (Lydenburg, Sth Afr), d 19 May 1924 (Umkomaas, Sth Afr). 406, 407, 408, 409, 411, 413, 417, 419, 420, 423, 424, 426, 427.

Ray Webster was born in the Melbourne suburb of Moreland, on April 22, 1941. He was educated at Camberwell High School and has lived in Melbourne throughout. His entire working life was spent in the employ of State Bank Victoria and he has recently retired. He, and wife Nancy, have raised a son and two daughters to adulthood. He has been an enthusiastic club cricketer for over 35 years and some 400 games with Box Hill South in Melbourne's Eastern Suburbs Cricket Association. This is his first publication venture but he has had a lifetime interest in cricket's history and statistics.

Allan Miller was born at Whyalla, South Australia, on April 7, 1967. He has lived in Western Australia since 1972. He was educated at Newton Moore Senior High School in Bunbury, and between 1986 and 1989 worked as a journalist for *The West Australian* newspaper in Perth. In 1986 he produced the first edition of *Allan's Australian Cricket Annual* - a new attempt to provide Australia with a reliable source of cricket information.